THE R.S.V. INTERLINEAR
GREEK - ENGLISH
NEW TESTAMENT

THE R.S.V. INTERLINEAR
GREEK - ENGLISH
NEW TESTAMENT

**The Nestle Greek Text
with a Literal English Translation**

by

The Reverend Alfred Marshall D.Litt.

and a Foreword by

The Reverend Prebendary J. B. Phillips M.A.

**also a marginal text of
The Revised Standard Version**

Regency
Reference Library
Zondervan Publishing House
Grand Rapids, Michigan

THE R.S.V. INTERLINEAR GREEK-ENGLISH NEW TESTAMENT
© Literal English Translation
Samuel Bagster and Sons Ltd. 1958

Regency Reference Library is an imprint of Zondervan
Publishing House, 1415 Lake Drive, S.E.,
Grand Rapids, Michigan 49506

© Editorial Interlineation
Samuel Bagster and Sons Ltd. 1958

ISBN 0-310-20410-0

Published by special arrangement with
Samuel Bagster & Sons, Ltd., London

Printed in the United States of America

87   88   89   90 / 22   21   20   19

*F*OREWORD

THE REVEREND PREBENDARY J. B. PHILLIPS M.A.

There is undoubtedly a revived interest in the reading of the New Testament today. The sales of modern versions have, I think, surprised everybody while the demand for the Authorized Version continues as before. It seems that a great many people are turning again to these inspired documents to see for themselves the foundations on which the Christian Faith is built. Naturally, to any Christian these are the most important documents in the world. If we believe with our adult minds that we live on a planet visited by God Himself in human form, the record of His life and teaching and that of the movement which He began are of supreme importance to the entire human race. Anything therefore which makes the significance and relevance of the Personal Visit clearer to the reader is to be welcomed with open arms.

As a modern translator I am delighted to see this new Interlinear Greek-English New Testament. By no means everybody knows of the quiet patient work of the textual critics who, with the utmost care and reverence, compare and revise Greek texts so that we may possess Greek as near as possible to the original documents, none of which, alas, survives. In this book we have the Greek text in its most modern revised form; it is the fruit of many years of diligent scholarship and, to my mind, should be accepted with the respect it deserves. A lot has been learned and a good deal of fresh material has been discovered since the Authorized Version was made in 1611 and indeed since the issue of the Revised Version in 1881. Here, interlined with probably the most accurate Greek that we can arrive at, is a literal English version. Dr. Marshall has obviously done this work of putting the nearest English equivalents to the Greek words with great care and skill and his work should prove of the highest value to any student of the New Testament.

It need hardly be said that this giving of verbal equivalents is not a full translation, but it is an essential stage in that process. The art of translation itself is not only the transferring of words from one language to another but also the accurate transmission of thought, feeling, atmosphere and even of style. But no translator can do his work properly without the transitional stage which Dr. Marshall exhibits so brilliantly in this book. Anyone with even a small knowledge of Greek will be able to see how and why the Authorized Version translators did their work as they did, and will also see how and why a modern translator produces a vastly different verbal result. The intelligent reader cannot fail to find this transitional stage, which is here so clearly shown, both fascinating and revealing. And if, with only a small knowledge of Greek, he should try to make his own translation, so much the better! He will at least be saved from over-familiarity with extremely meaningful words and sayings; and the chances are that the Truth will break over him afresh, as it does over any translator, ancient or modern, professional or amateur.

Although I consider that Dr. Marshall has done his work supremely well, it is a good thing to bear in mind that you cannot always either give an English equivalent for a Greek word or expression, or even always render the same Greek word by the same English one. May I take one word, the Greek verb $EKBA\Lambda\Lambda\Omega$ with its basic meaning of "throwing out". Dr. Marshall renders this word variously: it is "pluck out" (Matthew *ch.* 7, *v.* 5), "cast out" (Matthew *ch.* 8, *v.* 12), "put out" (Matthew *ch.* 9, *v.* 25), "expel" (Matthew *ch.* 12, *v.* 24), "puts forth" (Matthew *ch.* 12, *v.* 35), and "take out" (Luke *ch.* 6, *v.* 42)! And of course there are many other cases where absolute consistency is impossible; for words are not static things but expressions of thought which are inevitably modified by their context. But we must not expect impossibilities and I for one am grateful for an alert and intelligent literal translation wedded to the latest and most reliable Greek

Text. I am glad, for example, to see that Dr. Marshall has not missed the peculiar Greek construction in Matthew *ch*. 16, *v*. 19, where Jesus tells Peter that "what he binds on earth" will be "what has been bound" in Heaven. There is a world of difference between guaranteeing celestial endorsement of the Apostle's actions and promising that his actions guided by the Holy Spirit will be in accordance with the Heavenly pattern! Again, since I know there are many who imagine that the Authorized Version is a particularly literal and accurate translation of the Greek, it is refreshing to turn to Matthew *ch*. 27, *v*. 44 and see that not one single word of the expression "cast the same in his teeth" is in fact in the Greek! It is further made clear that the "bottles" of Matthew *ch*. 9, *v*. 17, were in reality wineskins, and that in Jesus' time people did not "sit at meat" so much as recline! (Luke *ch*. 7, *v*. 36), and naturally there are scores of further examples which are both interesting and important.

It would be unwise to omit reading Dr. Marshall's Introduction; for in it he not only explains some peculiarities of Greek construction, of which the ordinary reader may be quite unaware, but also clearly shows the rules he has set for himself in making this literal translation. Moreover, his Notes on Particular Passages are well worth our attention. In all, I have the greatest pleasure in recommending this book. It is timely because of the great contemporary interest in the New Testament. And it is profoundly interesting because we have here, combined in the most intimate fashion, the results of a great deal of textual research and the interpretation of a scholar thoroughly familiar with New Testament Greek.

*I*NTRODUCTION

THE REVEREND ALFRED MARSHALL D.LITT

THE GREEK TEXT

THE text of the Greek New Testament has come down to us in various manuscripts, printing not being invented until the 15th century (Erasmus published his Greek New Testament in 1516). Some of these manuscripts are more important than others (age is not necessarily determinative of importance). The study of the various manuscript copies, and the assessment of their individual value in attempting to reconstruct the original as nearly as possible, constitutes the science of Textual Criticism. For those who wish to study this seriously there are many books available; it is sufficient to say here that, after Erasmus, a great number of scholars have, over a long period, applied themselves to the task of constructing a reliable text out of the mass of various readings which have arisen from copying and making copies from copies of the old manuscripts: such scholars as Mill, Stephens, Griesbach, Lachmann, Tischendorf, Tregelles, Alford, and many more.

The Revised Standard Version of the New Testament is an authorized revision of the American Standard Version, published in 1901. This was a revision of the King James Version, published in 1611, itself more a revision of older versions than a new translation.

The Greek text used in this book is that of the 21st edition of Eberhard Nestle's *Novum Testamentum Graece*, based on the study and critical research of generations of scholars, except that the passage John 7. 53, 8. 1-11 is not in that text but is relegated to the foot of the page as a critical note. It is here retained in the text. The critical notes of Nestle's work, which enable students to follow the reasons for variations in the text, have been omitted as being outside the scope of this publication. The student who requires these critical notes is referred to the Greek edition published in this country by the British and Foreign Bible Society and in Germany (Stuttgart) by Privilegierte Württembergische Bibelanstalt, by whose permission this recension is used.

In certain places in the Greek text square brackets are found; these indicate only that, according to Nestle, some editors include and others omit the word or words so enclosed. Translation has been made here in the usual way.

Avoiding interpretation, then, we give some details of how we have proceeded in the matter of a literal translation. These should be studied and understood if proper use is to be made of this attempt to promote an intelligent reading of the Greek New Testament.

THE ENGLISH TRANSLATION

The relationship between the Greek text and the interlinear English is as follows: Greek words not required in the translation into English are (a) represented by a short dash, as for example the definite article with proper names. Alternatively (b) italic type is used to show that words or even in some cases letters are not really needed for an idiomatic English rendering. 'Man' is sometimes redundant (see Matthew *ch.* 20, *v.* 1 and Acts *ch.* 2, *v.* 22) and so on. On the other hand, words supplied in English for which there is no Greek equivalent are placed in square brackets [. . .]. Naturally, there will be differences of judgment as to this practice in the passages involved.

In the interlinear translation, a comma has in a number of places been introduced after "Behold". The reason for this is as follows: the Greek ἰδού (or other form), properly an imperative of the defective verb ὁράω, is used as an exclamation, as is its English equivalent; that is to say, it is not then an active verb taking a direct object in the accusative case, but is simply exclamatory and is followed by a noun in the nominative, with its predicate or complement understood.

For example, in John *ch*. 1, *v*. 29, there is not a command to behold the Lamb of God, but, as it might be said (and as in fact a preacher was recently heard to say), "Look! [there goes] . . . " The position is different in such passages as Matthew *ch*. 28, *v*. 6 and Romans *ch*. 11, *v*. 22, where there is a command. Strangely enough, the Authorized Version inserts a comma in I. John *ch*. 3, *v*. 1, where it is not required. There is here a command as in the two passages just cited: "See what manner of love . . . ".

The modern form for the third person singular of verbs (present indicative) has been used (loves) in place of the now obsolete -(e)th (loveth); but the older 'ye' has been retained for the nominative ('you' for the oblique cases) of the second person plural pronoun; and 'thou' (thee), not 'you', for the second person singular. It is a loss that in modern English these differences have disappeared; so unaccustomed are we now to them that even the average reader of the Authorized Version misses the point of Luke *ch*. 22, *v*. 31. The loss is even more to be regretted when God is addressed as 'You'.

The subjunctive mood is dying out in English, and no attempt has been made to represent consistently the Greek mood, except by the use of the analytic form "I may . . . ", with its related optative (of which latter there are only 37 examples in the New Testament, 15 of these being the familiar γένοιτο =may it be). But such words as ἵνα and compounds of ἄν *(ὅταν, ἐάν)*, etc., introducing a subjective or hypothetical element into a verbal idea, require to be followed by the subjunctive mood.

The Greek perfect can generally be taken as represented by an English present: a past action continuing in its effect down to the present, in contrast to an action wholly in the past. But in a literal translation the English perfect has been retained. In John *ch*. 11, *v*. 27, the Authorized Version is idiomatically correct but the Revised Version is literally so (πεπίστευκα =I have believed); *cf*. II. Timothy *ch*. 1, *v*. 12, where the Authorized Version adopts the literal equivalent. So, *e.g.*, τετέλεσται =it has been finished =it is finished. In participles, italics show that the auxiliary verbs may be dispensed with in English.

Where some word other than the strictly literal one seems to be needed in the translation, the former is printed in parentheses immediately after the latter; *e.g.*, Matthew *ch.* 10, *v.* 17, "beware from(of) men."

Occasionally it is not feasible to give a literal rendering without undue explanation; some idiomatic word or phrase has to be used. There are only a few of such passages and they are indicated by the mark †.

There are a number of Greek phrases, other than where † is used, which are not to be taken word for word, but as a whole:

ἐπὶ τὸ αὐτό = on the same = together
διὰ τοῦτο = because-of this = therefore
ἵνα μή = in-order-that not = lest
καθ' ὑπερβολήν = by-way-of excess = excessively

In familiar proper names there will appear some inconsistency, a compromise between the actual spellings preferred by Nestle and the Authorized Version; but this is of no great importance.

Εὐαγγελίζω. This and its cognate noun have been anglicized (evangelize, evangel). But while we can 'evangelize' a city, we do not 'evangelize' a person or a subject; so we must speak of 'preaching (good tidings) to' a person or of 'preaching' a subject. We can of course speak of 'evangelizing' absolutely, as in I. Corinthians *ch.* 1, *v.* 17. Ellicott on I. Thessalonians *ch.* 3, *v.* 6 has some useful information for the student.

There are five idiomatic Greek constructions which, being of frequent occurrence, call for explanation.
a. The *genitive absolute*. This is made up of a participle and a noun or pronoun, both in the genitive case and agreeing otherwise as well, but having no grammatical relation to the context. It is used to indicate time during or at which something takes place, or in some circumstances connected therewith. The close of such a Greek phrase is shown by the superior letter [a]; see Luke *ch.* 3, *v.* 1. There are variations of this. In Luke *ch.* 12, *v.* 36, two participles are used with no noun—it has to be supplied from the context.

So also II. Corinthians *ch.* 7, *v.* 15, and see the note on Romans *ch.* 9, *v.* 11 under "Notes on Particular Passages" below.

b. The *accusative* (or other case) *and infinitive*. Here what is in English the subject of the verb (the doer of the action) is put in the accusative (or other) case and the verb itself in the infinitive. A superior letter ᵇ closes such a phrase; see Luke *ch.* 1, *v.* 21.

c. The *dative of possession*. The possessor is put in the dative case. The idea may be grasped by comparing our English way of saying that a thing 'belongs to so-and-so'. The superior letter ᶜ shows this idiom; see Luke *ch.* 1, *v.* 5, 7, 14.

d. The *genitive of purpose* or *result*. The infinitive of a verb is in the genitive case, as shown by the preceding definite article. The article itself can be ignored. Again the appropriate letter ᵈ shows the existence of the idiom; see Matthew *ch.* 2, *v.* 13. The same idea can be shown without any article; see Matthew *ch.* 4, *v.* 1.

e. The *dative of time*. A point of time 'in' or 'at' which a thing happens is thus shown (ἐν may or may not be used). The letter ᵉ shows this; see Luke *ch.* 2, *v.* 43, and *ch.* 18, *v.* 35.

The constructions b and e can sometimes be combined; see Luke *ch.* 1, *v.* 8.

There is no indefinite article in Greek. The use of it in translation is a matter of individual judgment. The numeral 'one' is sometimes found; whether this means that just one, and no more, is to be understood is again open to argument. See Matthew *ch.* 21, *v.* 19 and *ch.* 26, *v.* 69. We have inserted 'a' or 'an' as a matter of course where it seems called for.

The definite article must sometimes be rendered by a pronoun or a possessive adjective. This is particularly so where parts of the body are indicated; *e.g.,* Matthew *ch.* 8, *v.* 3. Sometimes it is used 'pronominally'—that is, it must be rendered 'he' (or otherwise according to the gender) or 'they'; see Mark *ch.* 10, *v.* 4.

The ending of a Greek verb normally indicates the person (1st, 2nd, or 3rd, sing. or pl.). If the pronoun is separately expressed, this can be clearly seen in the interlinear translation.

μέν ... δέ. These two particles, in contrasted clauses, are not translatable literally, unless "indeed ... but" be used, as we have done in some places. But by adopting the phrases "on one hand ... on the other" the contrast is brought out. These particles are, in fact, somewhat elusive as to their force. See John *ch.* 19, *v.* 24 and 32, where μέν has been left untranslated—an example of the difficulty of rendering it satisfactorily in a literal translation.

It has not been considered necessary always to indicate the order of a noun and its adjective; a knowledge of English is sufficient for this. But where there is any risk of ambiguity small superior figures indicate the order in which the words should be read.

A number of Greek particles are said to be 'post-positive'— that is to say, they cannot stand as the first word in a sentence, but are found in the second, third, or even in the fourth place. Such words must of course be taken first in English; but it has not been thought necessary to show this, as the construction is sufficiently obvious. They include γάρ (for), δέ (and, but, now), οὖν (therefore; "therefore" can be post-positive in English), τις (a certain), μέν (indeed), γε (really—generally too subtle to be reproduced in English).

ὅτι as a conjunction, when meaning "that", is used to introduce spoken words as recorded; it is then known as the 'recitative ὅτι'. In English the original present tense of any verb would in such a construction ('indirect speech') be changed to the past: He said that the man was a liar. But Greek retains the original tense as actually used. What the speaker really said was "The man is a liar". The conjunction thus becomes superfluous and the reported words would in modern usage be put within quotation marks, as above. These, however, are not used in this translation. See Matthew *ch.* 21, *v.* 3.

ἵνα is, strictly, a 'telic' particle—*i.e.*, it denotes purpose (τέλος, an end); hence a full translation is "in order that". But inasmuch as in New Testament times there was a tendency to use it where ὅτι would be expected, it sometimes means no more than the conjunction "that"; see Matthew *ch.* 5, *v.* 29. Sometimes, then, where there may be room for difference of opinion as to its precise force, or even where there is none, "*in order* that" will be found in the literal translation.

A peculiarity of Greek construction is that a neuter plural subject may take a singular verb; but this is by no means invariable, and there appears to be no rule to go by. In translating, the position is sometimes shown by the use of an italic letter for the ending of the verb ([they] commit*s*); at other times the alternative is given in parenthesis (is(are)). But there are places where neither course is possible without taking up too much space, and the matter is left to the intelligence of the reader.

Where there is more than one subject of a verb, Greek will often put the verb in the singular to agree with the nearest subject. This is not in accordance with English grammar, which requires a plural verb if there is more than one subject. In Revelation *ch.* 9, *v.* 2, "sun" and "air" call for the plural "were darkened", as in the Authorized Version. But the Greek verb is in the singular. It is sometimes typographically possible to indicate the difference of grammatical usage, but not always.

In Greek, gender belongs to the word and not necessarily to what is indicated by the word; whereas of course in English we keep the ideas of masculine, feminine, and neuter to men, women, and inanimate things respectively. (English, by the way, is the only great modern language to do so.) Allowance must be made for this in translating: sometimes it is possible to transfer the idea from one language to another, but not always. The note to Revelation *ch.* 13, *v.* 1, may be consulted.

The construction of the demonstrative adjectives is peculiar in Greek. The definite article is used as well as the demonstrative adjective in one of two possible positions: either—

οὖτος ὁ οἶκος
this *the* house

or—

ὁ οἶκος οὖτος
the house this

The definite article is of course not wanted in English, and the proper translation of the phrase is obvious—"this house".

ἐκεῖνος (that) similarly. It is sometimes possible typographically to treat the three-word phrase as a whole, with the idiomatic translation underneath.

Similarly, the definite article is used in Greek with a possessive adjective, as in Matthew *ch.* 18, *v.* 20—

εἰς τὸ ἐμὸν ὄνομα

in *the* my name

or, alternatively again, the construction may be, say—

εἰς τὸ ὄνομα τὸ ἐμόν

in *the* name *the* my

This remark applies only to the first and second persons, singular and plural, but not to the third, where the only possible construction in this respect would be "in the name of him/her/them". This has been followed literally, as the reader can always make the needful English construction for himself. Occasionally such a construction as "in the name of me" will be found, meaning the same thing.

The neuter form of an adjective may be used as an adverb. ἀληθῆ in John *ch.* 19, *v.* 35, is the neuter of ἀληθής (true) and must be rendered "truly". So πρῶτον (firstly), though "first" is quite often used in English as an adverb. Conversely, an adverb may be used as an adjective; *e.g.* νῦν, now=present.

ταῦτα=these things (neuter plural) might be rendered by the singular "this", as in the common phrase μετὰ ταῦτα =after this; but this liberty has not been taken in the present literal translation.

The gender of an adjective may demand 'man', 'woman', or 'thing' to be supplied; *e.g.* Matthew *ch.* 9, *v.* 27—"two blind men".

Greek will often use a preposition in a compound verb and then repeat it (or use one similar) before a noun in the same sentence; in such passages the preposition would not be used twice in English. But in such a phrase as εἰσέρχεσθαι εἰς οἶκον we can say 'to enter into a house' (this has a counterpart in French—*entrer dans une maison*). We can indeed say simply 'to enter a house'. Another exception would be ἀπέρχεσθαι ἀπό =to go away from. But διαφέρειν διὰ τοῦ ἱεροῦ = to carry *through* through the temple (see Mark *ch.* 11, *v.* 16).

As the negatives οὐ(κ) (categorical) and μή (hypothetical) are easily recognizable, it has not been thought necessary always to render them separately, but they are included with any verb with which they may be used. But whereas in English the negative follows the verb, in Greek it precedes; see Matthew *ch.* 3, *v.* 11. If such a phrase happens to be broken at the end of a line this course has not been feasible.

The double negative οὐ μή has been consistently rendered "by no means".

Incidentally, though of importance, these two negative particles, or their compounds, when introducing questions, expect different answers. οὐ appeals to the fact, anticipating 'Yes, it is so'; *e.g.* John *ch.* 11, *v.* 9, "Are there not twelve hours of the day?" The answer would be 'Yes, there are'. μή, on the contrary, denies the suggestion and expects the reply 'No, it is not so'; or, if not so explicit as that, doubts whether it is so; *e.g.* John *ch.* 18, *v.* 35. The form of the question in the Authorized Version and the Revised Version indicates that Pilate was asking for information, whereas he was rejecting the idea with scorn and contempt—'I am not a Jew [am I]?' The answer, if any, would be—'No, certainly not.' This distinction is largely overlooked in the English Versions. To assist to the correct nuance of thought, in such places the latter negative in the interlinear translation is italicized, and the reader must read into the original what is intended; the result is sometimes surprising.

An article in *The Bible Translator* for January, 1953, may be consulted.

While on the subject of negatives, Greek favours the use of two such, one strengthening the other. In such sentences the second negative has to be replaced in English by a positive; *e.g.* Matthew *ch.* 22, *v.* 46.

There is the *genitive of quality*, of which there are many examples in the New Testament. If in English we say "a man of courage" or "an act of kindness", this is equivalent to "a courageous man" or "a kind act" respectively. We have translated literally, with an occasional footnote where this construction is not generally recognized. The Authorized Version itself is not consistent—*cf.* Philippians *ch.* 3, *v.* 21, with Colossians *ch.* 1, *v.* 22, where surely the distinction is between "his glorious body" and "his fleshly body".

Necessity or compulsion is most frequently expressed by the use of an impersonal verb (or a verb used impersonally), with the person concerned in the accusative as the object of the verb: δεῖ με =it behoves me=I must.

As 'first' is used as an adverb as well as 'firstly' it has not been thought necessary always to print 'first*ly*'; the matter is of no great importance.

Finally, but certainly not least in importance, there are the Greek participles, to which we now give special attention.

Greek is "a participle-loving language", said the late A. T. Robertson, and it uses this part of speech much more frequently than we do, and in different ways.

To begin with, it is absolutely essential to grasp the distinction between *continuous, momentary,* and *completed* action. The first is commonly, but wrongly, spoken of as a present participle; the second as an aorist (which does not mean "past"); and the third as a perfect. (There is a rare future participle—continuous in the future.) Now—

1. A participle may be used as an adjective qualifying a noun, just as in English; *e.g.* I. Thessalonians *ch.* 1, *v.* 9—"a living God"; Hebrews *ch.* 7, *v.* 8—"dying men". This is so simple as not to need further remark.

2. A participle may be used, again as in English, as a verb to describe some action; *e.g.* Acts *ch.* 9, *v.* 39—"all the widows stood by . . . weeping and showing . . .".

3. A participle may be used, with the definite article, with, say, "one" understood, where we should use a noun or a relative phrase; *e.g.*, frequently, ὁ πιστεύων=the [one] believing=the believer *or* he who believes. Here the participle is continuous; in Luke *ch.* 1, *v.* 45, it is momentary (and, naturally, feminine in gender as referring to Mary's one act of faith at the Annunciation). If two participles are used with but one definite article, as in John *ch.* 5, *v.* 24, the meaning is that one person is doubly

described, not two persons doing two things. This feature has been preserved in our translation.

4. Very frequently indeed, where in English we use two or more finite verbs to describe associated actions, Greek will use participles and only one finite verb for the main action. But here judgment is necessary to distinguish two (or more) simultaneous actions from consecutive ones; and as we have no aorist participle in English the matter is not always free from difficulty. In Acts *ch.* 10, *v.* 34, "Peter opening his mouth said", the two actions were obviously simultaneous! So in Acts *ch.* 1, *v.* 24—"praying they said". But sometimes one action must be completed before another could begin; *e.g.* Luke *ch.* 22, *v.* 17—"having given thanks, he said . . .". Here the act of giving thanks to God would be complete before Jesus addressed His disciples; therefore the aorist participle must be represented in English by the analytic "having given thanks". That this is not unimportant is shown by Matthew *ch.* 26, *v.* 30—"having sung a hymn they went out". To translate the aorist participle here by "singing a hymn" would certainly convey the idea that the singing occurred as they went out. In Acts *ch.* 21, *v.* 14, it is not easy to see how the keeping silence and the saying could be contemporaneous: "Having said, The will of the Lord be done, we kept silence." These few examples should, we think, suffice to show the principles involved.

NOTES ON PARTICULAR PASSAGES

Mark *ch.* 10, *v.* 11.—An article by Dr. Nigel Turner in *The Bible Translator* for October, 1956, gives good reasons for understanding the verse thus, αὐτήν referring to the last woman mentioned (ἄλλην).

Mark *ch.* 14, *v.* 6.—The use of ἐν here is somewhat puzzling. The parallel in Matthew (*ch.* 26, *v.* 10) has εἰς, which would mean 'to', 'toward', or 'for'; and Mark's ἐν must then be taken as equivalent in meaning to εἰς. This may throw light on I John *ch.* 4, *v.* 16.

Luke *ch.* 7, *v.* 14.—ἐγέρθητι. It does not seem right to insist here on the passive voice; compare with *ch.* 8, *v.* 54, and, in another connection, *ch.* 11, *v.* 8. But our Lord "was raised", as are the dead generally (they do not "rise"). See I. Corinthians *ch.* 15, etc.

John *ch.* 8, *v.* 25.—"The answer of Jesus is one of the most disputed passages in the Gospel" (Godet). Nestle punctuates as a question; hence we have given what appears to be a reasonable rendering interrogatively.

Acts *ch.* 7, *v.* 46.—οἴκῳ is a manuscript variant for θεῷ. There is some uncertainty as to how this reading arose; see the Authorized Version. Has Psalm 24, *v.* 6, text and margin, any bearing on the matter?

Acts *ch.* 18, *v.* 10.—λαὸς πολύς must not be understood as meaning "many persons". λαός is the regular word for the chosen people, Israel (almost without exception). Here in Corinth was to be a new community, taking the place of the Jewish population. Translate—"a great people".

Romans *ch.* 1, *v.* 12.—That is, their faith (=confidence) in one another—Paul and his readers. "Mutual" is correct in A.V., but is generally misunderstood as being equivalent to "common", which it is not.

Romans *ch.* 9, *v.* 11.—There is no noun agreeing with the two participles. But it is nevertheless a 'genitive absolute' construction. The Authorized Version supplies the subject.

II. Corinthians *ch.* 11, *v.* 28.—There is another view of Paul's words here. ἐπίστασις occurs in the New Testament only here and in Acts *ch.* 24, *v.* 12. The related noun ἐπιστάτης (one standing over, superintendent, master) is peculiar to Luke (six times in his gospel). Then there is a variant reading in our verse, μου instead of μοι. So the meaning may be—"my daily superintendence *or* attention". This would bring it into line with the remainder of the verse.

Philippians *ch.* 3, *v.* 16.—This is, according to Burton, the only certain use in the New Testament of the 'imperatival infinitive', Romans *ch.* 12, *v.* 15 being a probable example. Moulton thinks it highly probable in Titus *ch.* 2, *v.* 1-10. The epistolary χαίρειν (Acts *ch.* 15, *v.* 23, *ch.* 23, *v.* 26; James *ch.* 1, *v.* 1) is said to be the same in origin, though a verb of bidding may be assumed, as in fact we do find in II. John *vs.* 10, 11. *Cf.* the French warning in railway carriages—*Ne pas se pencher au dehors.* In English we have such a full expression as "You are 'to do' so and so"; see

II. Thessalonians *ch.* 3, *v.* 14. If Nestle's text is accepted here, it is an additional instance to those given under Philippians *ch.* 3, *v.* 16 above, though with a negative as a prohibition. (Textus Receptus, etc., give a plain imperative.) But perhaps we may insert "so as" —"mark this man, so as not to mix with him."

II. Timothy *ch.* 4, *v.* 3.—The construction of the last three words of this verse is difficult. "Having itching ears" may be a workable paraphrase, but it cannot be said to represent literally the actual Greek. There is no word for "having"; and there is nothing corresponding to "itching" as a participial adjective qualifying "ears". τὴν ἀκοήν is accusative singular, the object of a verb—and the only verb is the participle which precedes. This is masculine plural, agreeing with διδασκάλους, and, while this latter is accusative, whereas the participle is nominative, this must be taken as an example of rational rather than grammatical concord. It is the teachers who "tickle" the ears of those concerned.

Hebrews *ch.* 2, *v.* 10.—That is, it is God who perfected Jesus Christ (the author, or captain, of our salvation) by means of sufferings, whose work it is to lead many sons to glory. This is not what the Authorized Version nor the Revised Version says, but it is demanded by the grammar: ἀγαγόντα (leading) agrees with ἀρχηγόν not with αὐτῷ (=God). Besides, there is a parallel between Joshua and Jesus, as both leaders of their peoples. (The Berkeley version adopts this view, though we were not aware of it until our own order of words had been adopted.) In fine, it is the function of a captain to lead, and Jesus is the leader here.

Hebrews *ch.* 9, *vs.* 16-17.—We are aware of the problem in regard to διαθήκη in this passage; but this translation is no place for purporting to settle a question that has divided commentators. It must suffice to say that we have translated the word consistently as 'covenant'; the idea of a legatee receiving something on the death of a testator by reason of the latter's having made a 'testament' or 'will' is, so far as we can see, quite non-biblical. The covenant victim, then, is 'the one making covenant', unless the person establishing the covenant is to be understood as identifying himself with it; and the covenant is in fact ratified over the dead body or bodies. But other views are taken of the matter.

James *ch.* 2, *v.* 1.—There are other instances of such a construction—two genitives in apposition. Colossians *ch.* 1, *v.* 18: the meaning must be 'of the body (,) *of* the Church'—the body is the Church, as verse 24 says. Colossians *ch.* 2, *v.* 2: 'of God, of Christ'. Romans *ch.* 11, *v.* 17: see note at that place. John *ch.* 8, *v.* 44: 'of the father (,) *of* the devil'—their father was the devil.

Revelation *ch.* 16, *v.* 14: 'Almighty' is not an adjective but another noun in apposition.

NOTE on Mat. 16. 3, 27. 65; Luke 12. 56; Acts 21. 37; I. Thes. 4. 4; I. Tim. 3. 5; Jas. 4. 17; II. Pet. 2. 9.

As in French, so in the Greek of the N.T., we have the idea of "to know (how) to do" a thing as being the same as "to be able to do" it. But while *savoir* only is used in this way, not *connaître*, both γινώσκω and οἶδα are found in the N.T. In fact it is the former in Mat. 16. 3 and the latter in the parallel in Luke (12. 56). So, in French, *Savez-vous nager?* = Know you to swim? = Can you swim? In all the above passages this seems to be the meaning. It may be noted that the A.V. so renders the verbs in some passages, in others giving "know how". The James instance may be arguable. Phil. 4. 12 also may be considered, and Mat. 7. 11 = Luke 11. 13.

THE GREEK ALPHABET

A	α	Alpha	a
B	β	Beta	b
Γ	γ	Gamma	g hard, as in begin[1]
Δ	δ	Delta	d
E	ϵ	Epsilon	e short, as in met
Z	ζ	Zeta	z
H	η	Eta	e long, as in scene
Θ	θ	Theta	th as in thin
I	ι	Iota	i
K	κ	Kappa	k
Λ	λ	Lambda	l
M	μ	Mu	m
N	ν	Nu	n
Ξ	ξ	Xi	x
O	o	Omicron	o short, as in lot
Π	π	Pi	p
P	ρ	Rho	r
Σ	σ, final ς	Sigma	s[2]
T	τ	Tau	t
Y	υ	Upsilon	u
Φ	ϕ	Phi	ph
X	χ	Chi	ch hard, as in loch
Ψ	ψ	Psi	ps
Ω	ω	Omega	o long, as in throne

[1] Except that before κ, χ or another γ it is nasal—ng, as in anchor.
[2] Sharp as in this, but flat before β or μ, as in asbestos, dismal.

THE NAMES AND ORDER OF THE BOOKS
OF THE NEW TESTAMENT

CHAPTER 1

THE book of the genealogy of Jesus Christ, the son of David, the son of Abraham.

2 Abraham was the father of Isaac, and Isaac the father of Jacob, and Jacob the father of Judah and his brothers, ³and Judah the father of Perez and Zerah by Tamar, and Perez the father of Hezron, and Hezron the father of Ram, ⁴and Ram the father of Ammin'adab, and Ammin'adab the father of Nahshon, and Nahshon the father of Salmon, ⁵and Salmon the father of Bo'az by Rahab, and Bo'az the father of Obed by Ruth, and Obed the father of Jesse, ⁶and Jesse the father of David the king.

And David was the father of Solomon by the wife of Uri'ah, ⁷and Solomon the father of Rehobo'am, and Rehobo'am the father of Abi'jah, and Abi'jah the father of Asa, ⁸and Asa the father of Jehosh'-aphat, and Jehosh'aphat the father of Joram, and Joram the father of Uzzi'ah, ⁹and Uzzi'ah the father of Jotham, and Jotham the father of Ahaz, and Ahaz the

1 Βίβλος γενέσεως Ἰησοῦ Χριστοῦ
[The] book of [the] generation of Jesus Christ

υἱοῦ Δαυὶδ υἱοῦ Ἀβραάμ.
son of David son of Abraham.

2 Ἀβραὰμ ἐγέννησεν τὸν Ἰσαάκ, Ἰσαὰκ δὲ
Abraham begat - Isaac, and Isaac

ἐγέννησεν τὸν Ἰακώβ, Ἰακὼβ δὲ ἐγέννησεν τὸν
begat - Jacob, and Jacob begat -

Ἰούδαν καὶ τοὺς ἀδελφοὺς αὐτοῦ, 3 Ἰούδας δὲ
Judas and the brothers of him, and Judas

ἐγέννησεν τὸν Φάρες καὶ τὸν Ζάρα ἐκ τῆς
begat - Phares and - Zara out of -

Θαμάρ, Φάρες δὲ ἐγέννησεν τὸν Ἐσρώμ,
Thamar, and Phares begat - Esrom,

Ἐσρὼμ δὲ ἐγέννησεν τὸν Ἀράμ, 4 Ἀρὰμ δὲ
and Esrom begat - Aram, and Aram

ἐγέννησεν τὸν Ἀμιναδάβ, Ἀμιναδὰβ δὲ
begat - Aminadab, and Aminadab

ἐγέννησεν τὸν Ναασσών, Ναασσὼν δὲ ἐγέννησεν
begat - Naasson, and Naasson begat

τὸν Σαλμών, 5 Σαλμὼν δὲ ἐγέννησεν τὸν Βόες
- Salmon, and Salmon begat - Booz

ἐκ τῆς Ῥαχάβ, Βόες δὲ ἐγέννησεν τὸν Ἰωβὴδ
out of - Rachab, and Booz begat - Obed

ἐκ τῆς Ῥούθ, Ἰωβὴδ δὲ ἐγέννησεν τὸν Ἰεσσαί,
out of - Ruth, and Obed begat - Jesse,

6 Ἰεσσαὶ δὲ ἐγέννησεν τὸν Δαυὶδ τὸν βασιλέα.
and Jesse begat - David the king.

Δαυὶδ δὲ ἐγέννησεν τὸν Σολομῶνα ἐκ τῆς
And David begat - Solomon out of the

τοῦ Οὐρίου, 7 Σολομὼν δὲ ἐγέννησεν
[one who had been the wife]- of Uriah, and Solomon begat

τὸν Ῥοβοάμ, Ῥοβοὰμ δὲ ἐγέννησεν τὸν
- Roboam, and Roboam begat -

Ἀβιά, Ἀβιὰ δὲ ἐγέννησεν τὸν Ἀσάφ, 8 Ἀσὰφ
Abia, and Abia begat - Asaph, and Asaph

δὲ ἐγέννησεν τὸν Ἰωσαφάτ, Ἰωσαφὰτ δὲ
begat - Josaphat, and Josaphat

ἐγέννησεν τὸν Ἰωράμ, Ἰωρὰμ δὲ ἐγέννησεν τὸν
begat - Joram, and Joram begat -

Ὀζίαν, 9 Ὀζίας δὲ ἐγέννησεν τὸν Ἰωαθάμ,
Ozias, and Ozias begat - Joatham,

Ἰωαθὰμ δὲ ἐγέννησεν τὸν Ἀχάζ, Ἀχὰζ δὲ
and Joatham begat - Achaz, and Achaz

father of Hezeki'ah, ¹⁰and Hezeki'ah the father of Manas'seh, and Manas'seh the father of Amos,ᵃ and Amosᵃ the father of Josi'ah, ¹¹and Josi'ah the father of Jechoni'ah and his brothers, at the time of the deportation to Babylon.

12 And after the deportation to Babylon: Jechoni'ah was the father of She-al'ti-el, and She-al'ti-el the father of Zerub'babel, ¹³and Zerub'babel the father of Abi'ud, and Abi'ud the father of Eli'akim, and Eli'akim the father of Azor, ¹⁴and Azor the father of Zadok, and Zadok the father of Achim, and Achim the father of Eli'ud, ¹⁵and Eli'ud the father of Elea'zar, and Elea'zar the father of Matthan, and Matthan the father of Jacob, ¹⁶and Jacob the father of Joseph the husband of Mary, of whom Jesus was born, who is called Christ.ᵇ

17 So all the generations from Abraham to David were fourteen generations, and from David to the deportation to Babylon fourteen generations, and from the deportation to Babylon to the Christ fourteen generations.

18 Now the birth of

ᵃ Other authorities read Amon

ᵇ Other ancient authorities read *Joseph, to whom was betrothed the virgin Mary, was the father of Jesus who is called Christ*

ἐγέννησεν τὸν Ἐζεκίαν, 10 Ἐζεκίας δὲ
begat   -   Hezekias,   and Hezekias

ἐγέννησεν τὸν Μανασσῆ, Μανασσῆς δὲ ἐγέννησεν
begat   -   Manasses,   and Manasses   begat

τὸν Ἀμώς, Ἀμὼς δὲ ἐγέννησεν τὸν Ἰωσίαν,
-   Amos,   and Amos   begat   -   Josias,

11 Ἰωσίας δὲ ἐγέννησεν τὸν Ἰεχονίαν καὶ
and Josias   begat   -   Jechonias   and

τοὺς ἀδελφοὺς αὐτοῦ ἐπὶ τῆς μετοικεσίας
the   brothers   of him   at   the   deportation

Βαβυλῶνος. 12 Μετὰ δὲ τὴν μετοικεσίαν
of Babylon.   And after   the   deportation

Βαβυλῶνος Ἰεχονίας ἐγέννησεν τὸν Σαλαθιήλ,
of Babylon   Jechonias   begat   -   Salathiel,

Σαλαθιὴλ δὲ ἐγέννησεν τὸν Ζοροβαβέλ,
and Salathiel   begat   -   Zorobabel,

13 Ζοροβαβὲλ δὲ ἐγέννησεν τὸν Ἀβιούδ,
and Zorobabel   begat   -   Abiud,

Ἀβιοὺδ δὲ ἐγέννησεν τὸν Ἐλιακίμ, Ἐλιακὶμ δὲ
and Abiud   begat   -   Eliakim,   and Eliakim

ἐγέννησεν τὸν Ἀζώρ, 14 Ἀζὼρ δὲ ἐγέννησεν
begat   -   Azor,   and Azor   begat

τὸν Σαδώκ, Σαδὼκ δὲ ἐγέννησεν τὸν Ἀχίμ,
-   Sadoc,   and Sadoc   begat   -   Achim,

Ἀχὶμ δὲ ἐγέννησεν τὸν Ἐλιούδ, 15 Ἐλιοὺδ δὲ
and Achim   begat   -   Eliud,   and Eliud

ἐγέννησεν τὸν Ἐλεαζάρ, Ἐλεαζὰρ δὲ ἐγέννησεν
begat   -   Eleazar,   and Eleazar   begat

τὸν Ματθάν, Ματθὰν δὲ ἐγέννησεν τὸν Ἰακώβ,
-   Matthan,   and Matthan   begat   -   Jacob,

16 Ἰακὼβ δὲ ἐγέννησεν τὸν Ἰωσὴφ τὸν ἄνδρα
and Jacob   -   Joseph   the husband

Μαρίας, ἐξ ἧς ἐγεννήθη Ἰησοῦς ὁ λεγόμενος
of Mary, of whom   was born   Jesus the [one]   called

Χριστός.
Christ.

17 Πᾶσαι οὖν αἱ γενεαὶ ἀπὸ Ἀβραὰμ
Therefore all   the generations from   Abraham

ἕως Δαυὶδ γενεαὶ δεκατέσσαρες, καὶ ἀπὸ
until   David   generations   fourteen,   and from

Δαυὶδ ἕως τῆς μετοικεσίας Βαβυλῶνος γενεαὶ
David   until   the   deportation   of Babylon   generations

δεκατέσσαρες, καὶ ἀπὸ τῆς μετοικεσίας Βαβυ-
fourteen,   and from   the   deportation   of Baby-

λῶνος ἕως τοῦ Χριστοῦ γενεαὶ δεκατέσσαρες.
lon   until   the   Christ   generations   fourteen.

18 Τοῦ δὲ Ἰησοῦ Χριστοῦ ἡ γένεσις
-   Now   ³of Jesus   ⁴Christ   ¹the   ²birth

Jesus Christ[c] took place in this way. When his mother Mary had been betrothed to Joseph, before they came together she was found to be with child of the Holy Spirit; [19]and her husband Joseph, being a just man and unwilling to put her to shame, resolved to divorce her quietly. [20]But as he considered this, behold, an angel of the Lord appeared to him in a dream, saying, "Joseph, son of David, do not fear to take Mary your wife, for that which is conceived in her is of the Holy Spirit; [21]she will bear a son, and you shall call his name Jesus, for he will save his people from their sins." [22]All this took place to fulfil what the Lord had spoken by the prophet: [23]"Behold, a virgin shall conceive and bear a son,

and his name shall be called Emman'u-el"

(which means, God with us). [24]When Joseph woke from sleep, he did as the angel of the Lord commanded him; he took his

---

οὕτως ἦν. μνηστευθείσης τῆς μητρὸς αὐτοῦ
[1]thus [2]was. Being betrothed the mother of him
= When his mother Mary was betrothed

Μαρίας τῷ Ἰωσήφ, πρὶν ἢ συνελθεῖν αὐτοὺς
Mary[a] - to Joseph, before to come together them[b]
= before they came together

εὑρέθη ἐν γαστρὶ ἔχουσα ἐκ πνεύματος
[1]she was found [3]in [4]womb [2]having of(by)[the] Spirit
= she was pregnant

ἁγίου. 19 Ἰωσὴφ δὲ ὁ ἀνὴρ αὐτῆς,
Holy. Now Joseph the husband of her,

δίκαιος ὢν καὶ μὴ θέλων αὐτὴν δειγμα-
[2]just [1]being and not wishing her to hold up as an

τίσαι, ἐβουλήθη λάθρα ἀπολῦσαι αὐτήν.
example, resolved secretly to dismiss her.

20 ταῦτα δὲ αὐτοῦ ἐνθυμηθέντος, ἰδοὺ
But these things him thinking on,[a] behold
= while he thought on these things,

ἄγγελος κυρίου κατ' ὄναρ ἐφάνη
an angel of [the] Lord by a dream appeared

αὐτῷ λέγων· Ἰωσὴφ υἱὸς Δαυίδ, μὴ
to him saying: Joseph son of David, [2]not

φοβηθῇς παραλαβεῖν Μαρίαν τὴν
[1]fear thou to take Mary the

γυναῖκά σου· τὸ γὰρ ἐν αὐτῇ γεννηθὲν
wife of thee: for the thing in her begotten

ἐκ πνεύματός ἐστιν ἁγίου. 21 τέξεται δὲ
[2]of [3][the] [5]Spirit [1]is [4]Holy. And she will bear

υἱόν, καὶ καλέσεις τὸ ὄνομα αὐτοῦ
a son, and thou shalt call the name of him

Ἰησοῦν· αὐτὸς γὰρ σώσει τὸν λαὸν
Jesus; for he will save the people

αὐτοῦ ἀπὸ τῶν ἁμαρτιῶν αὐτῶν. 22 Τοῦτο δὲ
of him from the sins of them. Now [2]this

ὅλον γέγονεν ἵνα πληρωθῇ τὸ ῥηθὲν
[1]all has occurred in order that might be fulfilled the [thing] spoken

ὑπὸ κυρίου διὰ τοῦ προφήτου λέγοντος·
by [the] Lord through the prophet saying:

23 ἰδοὺ ἡ παρθένος ἐν γαστρὶ ἕξει
Behold the virgin [2]in [3]womb [1]will have

καὶ τέξεται υἱόν, καὶ καλέσουσιν τὸ
and will bear a son, and they will call the

ὄνομα αὐτοῦ Ἐμμανουήλ, ὃ ἐστιν
name of him Emmanuel, which is

μεθερμηνευόμενον μεθ' ἡμῶν ὁ θεός.
being interpreted with us - God.

24 ἐγερθεὶς δὲ [ὁ] Ἰωσὴφ ἀπὸ τοῦ
Then [2]being raised - [1]Joseph from the(his)

ὕπνου ἐποίησεν ὡς προσέταξεν αὐτῷ ὁ
sleep did as bade him the

---

[c] Other ancient authorities read of the Christ

wife, ²⁵ but knew her not until she had borne a son; and he called his name Jesus.

ἄγγελος	κυρίου,	καὶ	παρέλαβεν	τὴν
angel	of [the] Lord,	and	took	the

γυναῖκα	αὐτοῦ·	25 καὶ	οὐκ	ἐγίνωσκεν
wife	of him;	and		knew not

αὐτὴν	ἕως	[οὗ]	ἔτεκεν	υἱόν·	καὶ	ἐκάλεσεν
her	until		she bore	a son;	and	he called

τὸ	ὄνομα	αὐτοῦ	Ἰησοῦν.
the	name	of him	Jesus.

CHAPTER 2

NOW when Jesus was born in Bethlehem of Judea in the days of Herod the king, behold, wise men from the East came to Jerusalem, saying, ² "Where is he who has been born king of the Jews? For we have seen his star in the East, and have come to worship him." ³ When Herod the king heard this, he was troubled, and all Jerusalem with him; ⁴ and assembling all the chief priests and scribes of the people, he inquired of them where the Christ was to be born. ⁵ They told him, "In Bethlehem of Judea; for so it is written by the prophet:
⁶ 'And you, O Bethlehem, in the land of Judah,
are by no means least among the rulers of Judah;
for from you shall come a ruler who will govern my people Israel.' "

2 Τοῦ	δὲ	Ἰησοῦ	γεννηθέντος	ἐν	Βηθλέεμ
-	Now Jesus		having been born ᵃ	in	Bethlehem

ᵃ =when Jesus was born

τῆς	Ἰουδαίας	ἐν	ἡμέραις	Ἡρῴδου	τοῦ
-	of Judæa	in	[the] days	of Herod	the

βασιλέως,	ἰδοὺ	μάγοι	ἀπὸ	ἀνατολῶν
king,	behold	magi	from	[the] east

παρεγένοντο	εἰς	Ἱεροσόλυμα	2 λέγοντες·
arrived	in	Jerusalem	saying:

ποῦ	ἐστιν	ὁ	τεχθεὶς	βασιλεὺς	τῶν
Where	is	the [one]	born	king	of the

Ἰουδαίων;	εἴδομεν	γὰρ	αὐτοῦ	τὸν	ἀστέρα
Jews?	for we saw		of him	the	star

ἐν	τῇ	ἀνατολῇ,	καὶ	ἤλθομεν	προσκυνῆσαι
in	the	east,	and	came	to worship

αὐτῷ.	3 ἀκούσας	δὲ	ὁ	βασιλεὺς	Ἡρῴδης
him.	Now hearing [this] the			king	Herod

ἐταράχθη,	καὶ	πᾶσα	Ἱεροσόλυμα	μετ'
was troubled,	and	all	Jerusalem	with

αὐτοῦ,	4 καὶ	συναγαγὼν	πάντας	τοὺς
him,	and	having assembled	all	the

ἀρχιερεῖς	καὶ	γραμματεῖς	τοῦ	λαοῦ
chief priests	and	scribes	of the	people

ἐπυνθάνετο	παρ'	αὐτῶν	ποῦ	ὁ	χριστὸς
he inquired	from	them	where	the	Christ

γεννᾶται.	5 οἱ	δὲ	εἶπαν	αὐτῷ·	ἐν
is being born.	And they		told	him:	In

Βηθλέεμ	τῆς	Ἰουδαίας·	οὕτως	γὰρ
Bethlehem	-	of Judæa;	for thus	

γέγραπται	διὰ	τοῦ	προφήτου·	6 καὶ
it has been written	through	the	prophet:	And

σὺ	Βηθλέεμ,	γῆ	Ἰούδα,	οὐδαμῶς	ἐλαχίστη
thou	Bethlehem,	land	of Juda,	²not at all	³least

εἶ	ἐν	τοῖς	ἡγεμόσιν	Ἰούδα.	ἐκ	σοῦ	γὰρ
¹art	among the		governors	of Juda.	For out of thee		

ἐξελεύσεται	ἡγούμενος,	ὅστις	ποιμανεῖ
will come forth	a governor,	who	will shepherd

τὸν	λαόν	μου	τὸν	Ἰσραήλ.
the	people	of me	-	Israel.

7 Then Herod summoned the wise men secretly and ascertained from them what time the star appeared; ⁸and he sent them to Bethlehem, saying, "Go and search diligently for the child, and when you have found him bring me word, that I too may come and worship him." ⁹When they had heard the king they went their way; and lo, the star which they had seen in the East went before them, till it came to rest over the place where the child was. ¹⁰When they saw the star, they rejoiced exceedingly with great joy; ¹¹and going into the house they saw the child with Mary his mother, and they fell down and worshiped him. Then, opening their treasures, they offered him gifts, gold and frankincense and myrrh. ¹²And being warned in a dream not to return to Herod, they departed to their own country by another way.

13 Now when they had departed, behold, an angel of the Lord appeared to Joseph in a dream and said, "Rise, take the child and his

7 Τότε   'Ηρῴδης   λάθρα   καλέσας   τοὺς
Then   Herod   secretly calling   the

μάγους   ἠκρίβωσεν   παρ'   αὐτῶν   τὸν
magi   inquired carefully from   them   the

χρόνον   τοῦ   φαινομένου   ἀστέρος,   8 καὶ
time   of the appearing   star,   and

πέμψας   αὐτοὺς   εἰς   Βηθλέεμ   εἶπεν·
sending   them   to   Bethlehem   said:

πορευθέντες   ἐξετάσατε   ἀκριβῶς   περὶ   τοῦ
Going   question ye   carefully concerning the

παιδίου·   ἐπὰν   δὲ   εὕρητε,   ἀπαγγείλατέ
child;   and when   ye find,   report

μοι,   ὅπως   κἀγὼ   ἐλθὼν   προσκυνήσω   αὐτῷ.
to me, so that I also   coming   may worship   him.

9 οἱ   δὲ   ἀκούσαντες   τοῦ   βασιλέως   ἐπορεύθησαν·
So they   hearing   the   king   went;

καὶ   ἰδοὺ   ὁ   ἀστήρ,   ὃν   εἶδον   ἐν   τῇ
and   behold   the   star,   which   they saw   in   the

ἀνατολῇ,   προῆγεν   αὐτοὺς   ἕως   ἐλθὼν
east,   went before   them   until   coming

ἐστάθη   ἐπάνω   οὗ   ἦν   τὸ   παιδίον.   10 ἰδόντες
it stood   over   where was the   child.   ²seeing

δὲ   τὸν   ἀστέρα   ἐχάρησαν   χαρὰν   μεγάλην
¹And the   star   they rejoiced [with] a joy   great

σφόδρα.   11 καὶ   ἐλθόντες   εἰς   τὴν   οἰκίαν
exceedingly.   And   coming   into   the   house

εἶδον   τὸ   παιδίον   μετὰ   Μαρίας   τῆς   μητρὸς
they saw   the   child   with   Mary   the   mother

αὐτοῦ,   καὶ   πεσόντες   προσεκύνησαν   αὐτῷ,
of him,   and   falling   they worshipped   him,

καὶ   ἀνοίξαντες   τοὺς   θησαυροὺς   αὐτῶν
and   opening   the   treasures   of them

προσήνεγκαν   αὐτῷ   δῶρα,   χρυσὸν   καὶ
they offered   to him   gifts,   gold   and

λίβανον   καὶ   σμύρναν.   12 καὶ   χρηματισθέντες
frankincense and   myrrh.   And   having been warned

κατ'   ὄναρ   μὴ   ἀνακάμψαι   πρὸς   'Ηρῴδην,
by   a dream   not   to return   to   Herod,

δι'   ἄλλης   ὁδοῦ   ἀνεχώρησαν   εἰς   τὴν
by   another   way   they departed   to   the

χώραν   αὐτῶν.
country   of them.

13 'Αναχωρησάντων   δὲ   αὐτῶν,   ἰδοὺ
Now having departed   them,ᵃ   behold
= when they had departed,

ἄγγελος   κυρίου   φαίνεται   κατ'   ὄναρ   τῷ
an angel   of [the] Lord appears   by   a dream   -

'Ιωσὴφ   λέγων·   ἐγερθεὶς   παράλαβε   τὸ
to Joseph   saying: Rising   take thou   the

I.G.E.—2

mother, and flee to Egypt, and remain there till I tell you; for Herod is about to search for the child, to destroy him." [14]And he rose and took the child and his mother by night, and departed to Egypt, [15]and remained there until the death of Herod. This was to fulfil what the Lord had spoken by the prophet, "Out of Egypt have I called my son."

16 Then Herod, when he saw that he had been tricked by the wise men, was in a furious rage, and he sent and killed all the male children in Bethlehem and in all that region who were two years old or under, according to the time which he had ascertained from the wise men. [17]Then was fulfilled what was spoken by the prophet Jeremiah:
[18]"And a voice was heard in Ramah,
wailing and loud lamentation,
Rachel weeping for her children;
she refused to be consoled,
because they were no more."

19 But when Herod died, behold, an angel of the Lord appeared in a

παιδίον καὶ τὴν μητέρα αὐτοῦ, καὶ φεῦγε
child and the mother of him, and flee
εἰς Αἴγυπτον, καὶ ἴσθι ἐκεῖ ἕως ἂν εἴπω
into Egypt, and be there until I tell
σοι· μέλλει γὰρ Ἡρῴδης ζητεῖν τὸ παιδίον τοῦ
thee; for [2]is about [1]Herod to seek the child –
ἀπολέσαι αὐτό. **14** ὁ δὲ ἐγερθεὶς παρέλαβεν
to destroy[d] him. So he rising took
τὸ παιδίον καὶ τὴν μητέρα αὐτοῦ
the child and the mother of him
νυκτὸς καὶ ἀνεχώρησεν εἰς Αἴγυπτον,
of(by) night and departed to Egypt,
15 καὶ ἦν ἐκεῖ ἕως τῆς τελευτῆς Ἡρῴδου·
and was there until the death of Herod;
ἵνα πληρωθῇ τὸ ῥηθὲν ὑπὸ κυρίου
in order that might be fulfilled the [thing] spoken by [the] Lord
διὰ τοῦ προφήτου λέγοντος· ἐξ
through the prophet saying: Out of
Αἰγύπτου ἐκάλεσα τὸν υἱόν μου.
Egypt I called the son of me.
16 Τότε Ἡρῴδης ἰδὼν ὅτι ἐνεπαίχθη
Then Herod seeing that he was mocked
ὑπὸ τῶν μάγων ἐθυμώθη λίαν, καὶ
by the magi was angered exceedingly, and
ἀποστείλας ἀνεῖλεν πάντας τοὺς παῖδας
sending killed all the boy-children
τοὺς ἐν Βηθλέεμ καὶ ἐν πᾶσι τοῖς
– in Bethlehem and in all the
ὁρίοις αὐτῆς ἀπὸ διετοῦς καὶ κατωτέρω,
districts of it from two years and under,
κατὰ τὸν χρόνον ὃν ἠκρίβωσεν παρὰ τῶν
according to the time which he strictly inquired from the
μάγων. **17** τότε ἐπληρώθη τὸ ῥηθὲν διὰ
magi. Then was fulfilled the [thing] spoken through
Ἰερεμίου τοῦ προφήτου λέγοντος· **18** φωνὴ
Jeremiah the prophet saying: A voice
ἐν Ῥαμὰ ἠκούσθη, κλαυθμὸς καὶ ὀδυρμὸς
in Rama was heard, weeping and mourning
πολύς· Ῥαχὴλ κλαίουσα τὰ τέκνα αὐτῆς,
much; Rachel weeping for the children of her,
καὶ οὐκ ἤθελεν παρακληθῆναι, ὅτι
and would not to be comforted, because
οὐκ εἰσίν.
they are not.
19 Τελευτήσαντος δὲ τοῦ Ἡρῴδου, ἰδοὺ
But dying – Herod,[a] behold
= Herod having died,
ἄγγελος κυρίου φαίνεται κατ' ὄναρ τῷ
an angel of [the] Lord appears by a dream

dream to Joseph in Egypt, saying, ²⁰"Rise, take the child and his mother, and go to the land of Israel, for those who sought the child's life are dead." ²¹And he rose and took the child and his mother, and went to the land of Israel. ²²But when he heard that Archela'us reigned over Judea in place of his father Herod, he was afraid to go there, and being warned in a dream he withdrew to the district of Galilee. ²³And he went and dwelt in a city called Nazareth, that what was spoken by the prophets might be fulfilled, "He shall be called a Nazarene."

'Ιωσὴφ ἐν Αἰγύπτῳ 20 λέγων· ἐγερθεὶς
to Joseph in Egypt saying: Rising

παράλαβε τὸ παιδίον καὶ τὴν μητέρα
take thou the child and the mother

αὐτοῦ, καὶ πορεύου εἰς γῆν 'Ισραήλ·
of him, and go into [the] land of Israel;

τεθνήκασιν γὰρ οἱ ζητοῦντες τὴν ψυχὴν
for have died the [ones] seeking the life

τοῦ παιδίου. 21 ὁ δὲ ἐγερθεὶς παρέλαβεν
of the child. So he rising took

τὸ παιδίον καὶ τὴν μητέρα αὐτοῦ καὶ
the child and the mother of him and

εἰσῆλθεν εἰς γῆν 'Ισραήλ. 22 ἀκούσας δὲ
entered into [the] land of Israel. But hearing

ὅτι 'Αρχέλαος βασιλεύει τῆς 'Ιουδαίας
that Archelaus reigns over – Judæa

ἀντὶ τοῦ πατρὸς αὐτοῦ 'Ηρῴδου ἐφοβήθη
instead of the father of him Herod he feared

ἐκεῖ ἀπελθεῖν· χρηματισθεὶς δὲ κατ'
there to go; and being warned by

ὄναρ ἀνεχώρησεν εἰς τὰ μέρη τῆς
a dream he departed into the parts –

Γαλιλαίας, 23 καὶ ἐλθὼν κατῴκησεν εἰς
of Galilee, and coming dwelt in

πόλιν λεγομένην Ναζαρέθ· ὅπως πληρωθῇ
a city called Nazareth; so that was fulfilled

τὸ ῥηθὲν διὰ τῶν προφητῶν ὅτι
the [thing] spoken through the prophets[,] –

Ναζωραῖος κληθήσεται.
A Nazarene he shall be called.

CHAPTER 3

IN those days came John the Baptist, preaching in the wilderness of Judea, ²"Repent, for the kingdom of heaven is at hand." ³For this is he who was spoken of by the prophet Isaiah when he said,

"The voice of one crying in the wilderness:
Prepare the way of the Lord,
make his paths straight."

3 'Εν δὲ ταῖς ἡμέραις ἐκείναις παραγίνεται
Now in – days those arrives

'Ιωάννης ὁ βαπτιστὴς κηρύσσων ἐν τῇ
John the Baptist proclaiming in the

ἐρήμῳ τῆς 'Ιουδαίας, 2 λέγων· μετανοεῖτε·
wilderness – of Judæa, saying: Repent ye;

ἤγγικεν γὰρ ἡ βασιλεία τῶν οὐρανῶν.
for has come near the kingdom of the heavens.

3 οὗτος γάρ ἐστιν ὁ ῥηθεὶς διὰ 'Ησαΐου
For this is the [one] spoken [of] through Isaiah

τοῦ προφήτου λέγοντος· φωνὴ βοῶντος
the prophet saying: A voice of [one] crying

ἐν τῇ ἐρήμῳ· ἑτοιμάσατε τὴν ὁδὸν
in the wilderness: Prepare ye the way

κυρίου, εὐθείας ποιεῖτε τὰς τρίβους
of [the] Lord, straight make the paths

⁴Now John wore a garment of camel's hair, and a leather girdle around his waist; and his food was locusts and wild honey. ⁵Then went out to him Jerusalem and all Judea and all the region about the Jordan, ⁶and they were baptized by him in the river Jordan, confessing their sins.

7 But when he saw many of the Pharisees and Sad'ducees coming for baptism, he said to them, "You brood of vipers! Who warned you to flee from the wrath to come? ⁸Bear fruit that befits repentance, ⁹and do not presume to say to yourselves, 'We have Abraham as our father'; for I tell you, God is able from these stones to raise up children to Abraham. ¹⁰Even now the ax is laid to the root of the trees; every tree therefore that does not bear good fruit is cut down and thrown into the fire.

11 "I baptize you with water for repentance, but he who is coming after

αὐτοῦ.	4 Αὐτὸς	δὲ	ὁ	Ἰωάννης	εἶχεν
of him.	Now ²himself	–	¹John		had

τὸ	ἔνδυμα	αὐτοῦ	ἀπὸ	τριχῶν	καμήλου
the	raiment	of him	from	hairs	of a camel

καὶ	ζώνην	δερματίνην	περὶ	τὴν	ὀσφὺν
and	a girdle	leathern	round	the	loin[s]

αὐτοῦ·	ἡ	δὲ	τροφὴ	ἦν	αὐτοῦ	ἀκρίδες
of him;	and the		food	²was	¹of him	locusts

καὶ	μέλι	ἄγριον.	5 Τότε	ἐξεπορεύετο	πρὸς
and	honey	wild.	Then	went out	to

αὐτὸν	Ἱεροσόλυμα	καὶ	πᾶσα	ἡ	Ἰουδαία
him	Jerusalem	and	all	–	Judæa

καὶ	πᾶσα	ἡ	περίχωρος	τοῦ	Ἰορδάνου,
and	all	the	neighbourhood	of the	Jordan,

6 καὶ	ἐβαπτίζοντο	ἐν	τῷ	Ἰορδάνῃ	ποταμῷ
and	were baptized	in	the	Jordan	river

ὑπ'	αὐτοῦ	ἐξομολογούμενοι	τὰς	ἁμαρτίας
by	him	confessing	the	sins

αὐτῶν.	7 Ἰδὼν	δὲ	πολλοὺς	τῶν
of them.	And seeing		many	of the

Φαρισαίων	καὶ	Σαδδουκαίων	ἐρχομένους
Pharisees	and	Sadducees	coming

ἐπὶ	τὸ	βάπτισμα	εἶπεν	αὐτοῖς·	γεννήματα
to	the	baptism	he said	to them:	Offspring

ἐχιδνῶν,	τίς	ὑπέδειξεν	ὑμῖν	φυγεῖν	ἀπὸ
of vipers,	who	warned	you	to flee	from

τῆς	μελλούσης	ὀργῆς;	8 ποιήσατε	οὖν
the	coming	wrath?	Produce	therefore

καρπὸν	ἄξιον	τῆς	μετανοίας·	9 καὶ
fruit	worthy	–	of repentance;	and

μὴ	δόξητε	λέγειν	ἐν	ἑαυτοῖς·	πατέρα
think not	to say	among	[your]selves:	²[as] father

ἔχομεν	τὸν	Ἀβραάμ·	λέγω	γὰρ	ὑμῖν	ὅτι
¹We have	–	¹Abraham;	for I tell		you	that

δύναται	ὁ	θεὸς	ἐκ	τῶν	λίθων	τούτων
²is able		¹God	out of	–	stones	these

ἐγεῖραι	τέκνα	τῷ	Ἀβραάμ.	10 ἤδη	δὲ
to raise	children	–	to Abraham.	And already	

ἡ	ἀξίνη	πρὸς	τὴν	ῥίζαν	τῶν	δένδρων
the	axe	at	the	root	of the	trees

κεῖται·	πᾶν	οὖν	δένδρον	μὴ	ποιοῦν
is laid;	therefore every		tree	not	producing

καρπὸν	καλὸν	ἐκκόπτεται	καὶ	εἰς	πῦρ
fruit	good	is cut down	and	into [the] fire

βάλλεται.	11 ἐγὼ	μὲν	ὑμᾶς	βαπτίζω
is cast.	I	indeed	you	baptize

ἐν	ὕδατι	εἰς	μετάνοιαν·	ὁ	δὲ
in	water	to	repentance;	but the [one]

me is mightier than I, whose sandals I am not worthy to carry; he will baptize you with the Holy Spirit and with fire. [12] His winnowing fork is in his hand, and he will clear his threshing floor and gather his wheat into the granary, but the chaff he will burn with unquenchable fire."

[13] Then Jesus came from Galilee to the Jordan to John, to be baptized by him. [14] John would have prevented him, saying, "I need to be baptized by you, and do you come to me?" [15] But Jesus answered him, "Let it be so now; for thus it is fitting for us to fulfil all righteousness." Then he consented. [16] And when Jesus was baptized, he went up immediately from the water, and behold, the heavens were opened[d] and he saw the Spirit of God descending like a dove, and alighting on him; [17] and lo, a voice from heaven, saying, "This is my beloved Son,[e] with whom I am well pleased."

---

[d] Other ancient authorities add to him
[e] Or my Son, my (or the) Beloved

ὀπίσω μου ἐρχόμενος ἰσχυρότερός μού
after me coming ³stronger ²[than] ⁴I

ἐστιν, οὗ οὐκ εἰμὶ ἱκανὸς τὰ ὑποδήματα
¹is, of whom I am not worthy the sandals

βαστάσαι· αὐτὸς ὑμᾶς βαπτίσει ἐν πνεύματι
to bear; he ²you ¹will baptize in [the] Spirit

ἁγίῳ καὶ πυρί· **12** οὗ τὸ πτύον ἐν τῇ
Holy and fire; of whom the fan [is] in the

χειρὶ αὐτοῦ, καὶ διακαθαριεῖ τὴν ἅλωνα
hand of him, and he will thoroughly cleanse the threshing-floor

αὐτοῦ, καὶ συνάξει τὸν σῖτον αὐτοῦ
of him, and will gather the wheat of him

εἰς τὴν ἀποθήκην, τὸ δὲ ἄχυρον κατα-
into the barn, but the chaff he will

καύσει πυρὶ ἀσβέστῳ.
consume with fire unquenchable.

13 Τότε παραγίνεται ὁ Ἰησοῦς ἀπὸ τῆς
Then arrives - Jesus from -

Γαλιλαίας ἐπὶ τὸν Ἰορδάνην πρὸς τὸν
Galilee at the Jordan to -

Ἰωάννην τοῦ βαπτισθῆναι ὑπ' αὐτοῦ.
John - to be baptized[d] by him.

14 ὁ δὲ διεκώλυεν αὐτὸν λέγων· ἐγὼ
But he forbade him saying: I

χρείαν ἔχω ὑπὸ σοῦ βαπτισθῆναι, καὶ σὺ
²need ¹have ⁴by ³thee ⁵to be baptized, and thou

ἔρχῃ πρὸς μέ; **15** ἀποκριθεὶς δὲ ὁ
comest to me? But answering -

Ἰησοῦς εἶπεν αὐτῷ· ἄφες ἄρτι· οὕτως γὰρ
Jesus said to him: Permit now; for thus

πρέπον ἐστὶν ἡμῖν πληρῶσαι πᾶσαν
²fitting ¹it is to us to fulfil all

δικαιοσύνην. τότε ἀφίησιν αὐτόν.
righteousness. Then he permits him.

16 βαπτισθεὶς δὲ ὁ Ἰησοῦς εὐθὺς ἀνέβη
And having been baptized - Jesus immediately went up

ἀπὸ τοῦ ὕδατος· καὶ ἰδοὺ ἠνεῴχθησαν
from the water; and behold ²were opened

οἱ οὐρανοί, καὶ εἶδεν πνεῦμα θεοῦ
¹the ²heavens, and he saw [the] Spirit of God

καταβαῖνον ὡσεὶ περιστεράν, ἐρχόμενον ἐπ'
coming down as a dove, coming upon

αὐτόν· **17** καὶ ἰδοὺ φωνὴ ἐκ τῶν
him; and behold a voice out of the

οὐρανῶν λέγουσα· οὗτός ἐστιν ὁ υἱός
heavens saying: This is the son

μου ὁ ἀγαπητός, ἐν ᾧ εὐδόκησα.
of me the beloved, in whom I was well pleased.

CHAPTER 4

THEN Jesus was led up by the Spirit into the wilderness to be tempted by the devil. ²And he fasted forty days and forty nights, and afterward he was hungry. ³And the tempter came and said to him, "If you are the Son of God, command these stones to become loaves of bread." ⁴But he answered, "It is written,

'Man shall not live by bread alone,

but by every word that proceeds from the mouth of God.' "

⁵Then the devil took him to the holy city, and set him on the pinnacle of the temple, ⁶and said to him, "If you are the Son of God, throw yourself down; for it is written,

'He will give his angels charge of you,'

and

'On their hands they will bear you up,

lest you strike your foot against a stone.' "

⁷Jesus said to him, "Again it is written, 'You shall not tempt the Lord your God.' "

⁸Again, the devil took him to a very high mountain, and showed him all the kingdoms of the world and the glory of

4 Τότε ὁ 'Ιησοῦς ἀνήχθη εἰς τὴν
Then - Jesus was led up into the

ἔρημον ὑπὸ τοῦ πνεύματος πειρασθῆναι
wilderness by the Spirit to be tempted

ὑπὸ τοῦ διαβόλου. **2** καὶ νηστεύσας ἡμέρας
by the devil. And having fasted days

τεσσεράκοντα καὶ τεσσεράκοντα νύκτας
forty and forty nights

ὕστερον ἐπείνασεν. **3** καὶ προσελθὼν ὁ
afterward he hungered. And approaching the

πειράζων εἶπεν αὐτῷ· εἰ υἱὸς εἶ τοῦ
tempting [one] said to him: If Son thou art -

θεοῦ, εἰπὲ ἵνα οἱ λίθοι οὗτοι ἄρτοι
of God, say in order that - stones these ²loaves

γένωνται. **4** ὁ δὲ ἀποκριθεὶς εἶπεν·
¹may become. But he answering said:

γέγραπται· οὐκ ἐπ' ἄρτῳ μόνῳ ζήσεται
It has been written: Not on bread only shall live

ὁ ἄνθρωπος, ἀλλ' ἐπὶ παντὶ ῥήματι
- man, but on every word

ἐκπορευομένῳ διὰ στόματος θεοῦ. **5** Τότε
proceeding through [the] mouth of God. Then

παραλαμβάνει αὐτὸν ὁ διάβολος εἰς τὴν
takes him the devil into the

ἁγίαν πόλιν, καὶ ἔστησεν αὐτὸν ἐπὶ τὸ
holy city, and stood him on the

πτερύγιον τοῦ ἱεροῦ, **6** καὶ λέγει αὐτῷ·
wing of the temple, and says to him:

εἰ υἱὸς εἶ τοῦ θεοῦ, βάλε σεαυτὸν
If Son thou art - of God, cast thyself

κάτω· γέγραπται γὰρ ὅτι τοῖς ἀγγέλοις
down; for it has been written[,] - To the angels

αὐτοῦ ἐντελεῖται περὶ σοῦ καὶ ἐπὶ χειρῶν
of him he will give command concerning thee and on hands

ἀροῦσίν σε, μήποτε προσκόψῃς πρὸς
they will bear thee, lest thou strike against

λίθον τὸν πόδα σου. **7** ἔφη αὐτῷ ὁ
a stone the foot of thee. Said to him -

'Ιησοῦς· πάλιν γέγραπται· οὐκ ἐκπειράσεις
Jesus: Again it has been written: Not overtempt shalt thou

κύριον τὸν θεόν σου. **8** Πάλιν παρα-
[the] Lord the God of thee. Again

λαμβάνει αὐτὸν ὁ διάβολος εἰς ὄρος
takes him the devil to a mountain

ὑψηλὸν λίαν, καὶ δείκνυσιν αὐτῷ πάσας
high exceedingly, and shows him all

τὰς βασιλείας τοῦ κόσμου καὶ τὴν
the kingdoms of the world and the

them; ⁹and he said to him, "All these I will give you, if you will fall down and worship me." ¹⁰Then Jesus said to him, "Begone, Satan! for it is written,
'You shall worship the Lord your God
and him only shall you serve.' "
¹¹Then the devil left him, and behold, angels came and ministered to him.

12 Now when he heard that John had been arrested, he withdrew into Galilee; ¹³and leaving Nazareth he went and dwelt in Caper′naum by the sea, in the territory of Zeb′ulun and Naph′tali, ¹⁴that what was spoken by the prophet Isaiah might be fulfilled:
¹⁵"The land of Zeb′ulun and the land of Naph′tali,
toward the sea, across the Jordan,
Galilee of the Gentiles—
¹⁶the people who sat in darkness
have seen a great light,
and for those who sat in the region and shadow of death
light has dawned."
¹⁷From that time Jesus began to preach, saying, "Repent, for the kingdom of heaven is at hand."

δόξαν αὐτῶν, 9 καὶ εἶπεν αὐτῷ· ταῦτά
glory of them, and said to him: These things
σοι πάντα δώσω, ἐὰν πεσὼν προσκυνήσῃς
to thee all I will give, if falling thou wilt worship
μοι. 10 τότε λέγει αὐτῷ ὁ Ἰησοῦς·
me. Then says to him – Jesus:
ὕπαγε, σατανᾶ· γέγραπται γάρ· κύριον
Go, Satan; for it has been written: [The] Lord
τὸν θεόν σου προσκυνήσεις καὶ αὐτῷ
the God of thee thou shalt worship and him
μόνῳ λατρεύσεις. 11 Τότε ἀφίησιν αὐτὸν
only thou shalt serve. Then leaves him
ὁ διάβολος, καὶ ἰδοὺ ἄγγελοι προσῆλθον
the devil, and behold angels approached
καὶ διηκόνουν αὐτῷ.
and ministered to him.

12 Ἀκούσας δὲ ὅτι Ἰωάννης παρεδόθη
Now hearing that John was delivered up
ἀνεχώρησεν εἰς τὴν Γαλιλαίαν. 13 καὶ
he departed to – Galilee. And
καταλιπὼν τὴν Ναζαρὰ ἐλθὼν κατῴκησεν
leaving – Nazareth coming he dwelt
εἰς Καφαρναοὺμ τὴν παραθαλασσίαν ἐν
in Capernaum – beside the sea in [the]
ὁρίοις Ζαβουλὼν καὶ Νεφθαλίμ· 14 ἵνα
districts of Zebulon and Naphthali; in order that
πληρωθῇ τὸ ῥηθὲν διὰ Ἡσαΐου
might be fulfilled the [thing] spoken through Isaiah
τοῦ προφήτου λέγοντος· 15 γῆ Ζαβουλὼν
the prophet saying: Land of Zebulon
καὶ γῆ Νεφθαλίμ, ὁδὸν θαλάσσης,
and land of Naphthali, way of [the] sea,
πέραν τοῦ Ἰορδάνου, Γαλιλαία τῶν ἐθνῶν,
beyond the Jordan, Galilee of the nations,
16 ὁ λαὸς ὁ καθήμενος ἐν σκοτίᾳ φῶς
the people – sitting in darkness ²light
εἶδεν μέγα, καὶ τοῖς καθημένοις ἐν
¹saw ²a great, and to the [ones] sitting in
χώρᾳ καὶ σκιᾷ θανάτου, φῶς ἀνέτειλεν
a land and shadow of death, light sprang up
αὐτοῖς.
to them.

17 Ἀπὸ τότε ἤρξατο ὁ Ἰησοῦς κηρύσσειν
From then began – Jesus to proclaim
καὶ λέγειν· μετανοεῖτε· ἤγγικεν γὰρ
and to say: Repent ye; for has drawn near
ἡ βασιλεία τῶν οὐρανῶν.
the kingdom of the heavens.

18 As he walked by the Sea of Galilee, he saw two brothers, Simon who is called Peter and Andrew his brother, casting a net into the sea; for they were fishermen. ¹⁹And he said to them, "Follow me, and I will make you fishers of men." ²⁰Immediately they left their nets and followed him. ²¹And going on from there he saw two other brothers, James the son of Zeb′edee and John his brother, in the boat with Zeb′edee their father, mending their nets, and he called them. ²²Immediately they left the boat and their father, and followed him.

23 And he went about all Galilee, teaching in their synagogues and preaching the gospel of the kingdom and healing every disease and every infirmity among the people. ²⁴So his fame spread throughout all Syria, and they brought him all the sick, those afflicted with various diseases and pains, demoniacs, epileptics, and

---

18 Περιπατῶν δὲ παρὰ τὴν θάλασσαν
    And walking   beside   the   sea

τῆς Γαλιλαίας εἶδεν δύο ἀδελφούς, Σίμωνα
–   of Galilee   he saw   two   brothers,   Simon

τὸν λεγόμενον Πέτρον καὶ 'Ανδρέαν τὸν
–   called   Peter   and   Andrew   the

ἀδελφὸν αὐτοῦ, βάλλοντας ἀμφίβληστρον εἰς
brother   of him,   casting   a net   into

τὴν θάλασσαν· ἦσαν γὰρ ἁλεεῖς. 19 καὶ
the   sea;   for they were   fishers.   And

λέγει αὐτοῖς· δεῦτε ὀπίσω μου, καὶ
he says   to them: Come   after   me,   and

ποιήσω ὑμᾶς ἁλεεῖς ἀνθρώπων. 20 οἱ
I will make   you   fishers   of men.   ²they

δὲ εὐθέως ἀφέντες τὰ δίκτυα ἠκολούθη-
¹And immediately   leaving   the   nets   fol-

σαν αὐτῷ. 21 Καὶ προβὰς ἐκεῖθεν εἶδεν
lowed   him.   And   going on   thence   he saw

ἄλλους δύο ἀδελφούς, 'Ιάκωβον τὸν τοῦ
other   two   brothers,   James   the [son] –

Ζεβεδαίου καὶ 'Ιωάννην τὸν ἀδελφὸν
of Zebedee   and   John   the   brother

αὐτοῦ, ἐν τῷ πλοίῳ μετὰ Ζεβεδαίου τοῦ
of him,   in   the   boat   with   Zebedee   the

πατρὸς αὐτῶν καταρτίζοντας τὰ δίκτυα
father   of them   mending   the   nets

αὐτῶν· καὶ ἐκάλεσεν αὐτούς. 22 οἱ δὲ
of them;   and   he called   them.   And they

εὐθέως ἀφέντες τὸ πλοῖον καὶ τὸν
immediately   leaving   the   boat   and   the

πατέρα αὐτῶν ἠκολούθησαν αὐτῷ.
father   of them   followed   him.

23 Καὶ περιῆγεν ἐν ὅλῃ τῇ Γαλιλαίᾳ,
    And he went about   in   all   –   Galilee,

διδάσκων ἐν ταῖς συναγωγαῖς αὐτῶν
teaching   in   the   synagogues   of them

καὶ κηρύσσων τὸ εὐαγγέλιον τῆς βασιλείας
and   proclaiming   the   gospel   of the   kingdom

καὶ θεραπεύων πᾶσαν νόσον καὶ πᾶσαν
and   healing   every   disease   and   every

μαλακίαν ἐν τῷ λαῷ. 24 καὶ ἀπῆλθεν ἡ
illness   among   the people.   And   went   the

ἀκοὴ αὐτοῦ εἰς ὅλην τὴν Συρίαν· καὶ
report   of him   into   all   –   Syria;   and

προσήνεγκαν αὐτῷ πάντας τοὺς κακῶς
they brought   to him   all   the [ones]   ²ill
                   =those who were ill

ἔχοντας ποικίλαις νόσοις καὶ βασάνοις
¹having   ²various   ³diseases   ⁴and   ⁵tortures

paralytics, and he healed them. ²⁵And great crowds followed him from Galilee and the Decap′olis and Jerusalem and Judea and from beyond the Jordan.

συνεχομένους, δαιμονιζομένους καὶ σεληνιαζ-
¹suffering from,   demon-possessed   and   luna-

ομένους καὶ παραλυτικούς, καὶ ἐθεράπευσεν
tics   and   paralysed,   and   he healed

αὐτούς. 25 καὶ ἠκολούθησαν αὐτῷ ὄχλοι
them.   And   ³followed   ⁴him   ²crowds

πολλοὶ ἀπὸ τῆς Γαλιλαίας καὶ Δεκαπόλεως
¹many   from   –   Galilee   and   Decapolis

καὶ Ἱεροσολύμων καὶ Ἰουδαίας καὶ πέραν
and   Jerusalem   and   Judæa   and   beyond

τοῦ Ἰορδάνου.
the   Jordan.

CHAPTER 5

S EEING the crowds, he went up on the mountain, and when he sat down his disciples came to him. ²And he opened his mouth and taught them, saying:
3 "Blessed are the poor in spirit, for theirs is the kingdom of heaven.
4 "Blessed are those who mourn, for they shall be comforted.
5 "Blessed are the meek, for they shall inherit the earth.
6 "Blessed are those who hunger and thirst for righteousness, for they shall be satisfied.
7 "Blessed are the merciful, for they shall obtain mercy.
8 'Blessed are the pure in heart, for they shall see God.
9 "Blessed are the peacemakers, for they shall be called sons of God.
10 "Blessed are those who are persecuted for righteousness' sake, for

5 Ἰδὼν δὲ τοὺς ὄχλους ἀνέβη εἰς
And seeing   the   crowds   he went up   into

τὸ ὄρος· καὶ καθίσαντος αὐτοῦ προσῆλθαν
the mountain; and   sitting   himᵃ   ⁴approached
=when he sat

αὐτῷ οἱ μαθηταὶ αὐτοῦ· 2 καὶ ἀνοίξας τὸ
⁵to him ¹the ²disciples ³of him;   and   opening   the

στόμα αὐτοῦ ἐδίδασκεν αὐτοὺς λέγων·
mouth   of him   he taught   them   saying:

3 Μακάριοι οἱ πτωχοὶ τῷ πνεύματι,
Blessed [are]   the   poor   –   in spirit,

ὅτι αὐτῶν ἐστιν ἡ βασιλεία τῶν οὐρανῶν.
for   of them   is   the   kingdom   of the   heavens.

4 μακάριοι οἱ πενθοῦντες, ὅτι αὐτοὶ
Blessed [are]   the   mourning [ones],   for   they

παρακληθήσονται. 5 μακάριοι οἱ πραεῖς,
shall be comforted.   Blessed [are]   the   meek,

ὅτι αὐτοὶ κληρονομήσουσιν τὴν γῆν.
for   they   shall inherit   the   earth.

6 μακάριοι οἱ πεινῶντες καὶ διψῶντες
Blessed [are] the   hungering   and   thirsting [ones] [after]

τὴν δικαιοσύνην, ὅτι αὐτοὶ χορτασ-
righteousness,   for   they   shall be

θήσονται. 7 μακάριοι οἱ ἐλεήμονες, ὅτι
satisfied.   Blessed [are]   the   merciful,   for

αὐτοὶ ἐλεηθήσονται. 8 μακάριοι οἱ καθαροὶ
they   shall obtain mercy.   Blessed [are]   the   clean

τῇ καρδίᾳ, ὅτι αὐτοὶ τὸν θεὸν ὄψονται.
–   in heart,   for   they   –   ²God   ¹shall see.

9 μακάριοι οἱ εἰρηνοποιοί, ὅτι [αὐτοὶ]
Blessed [are]   the   peacemakers,   for   they

υἱοὶ θεοῦ κληθήσονται. 10 μακάριοι οἱ
sons of God   shall be called.   Blessed [are] the [ones]

δεδιωγμένοι ἕνεκεν δικαιοσύνης, ὅτι αὐτῶν
having been persecuted for the sake of righteousness, for of them

theirs is the kingdom of heaven.

11 "Blessed are you when men revile you and persecute you and utter all kinds of evil against you falsely on my account. ¹²Rejoice and be glad, for your reward is great in heaven, for so men persecuted the prophets who were before you.

13 "You are the salt of the earth; but if salt has lost its taste, how shall its saltness be restored? It is no longer good for anything except to be thrown out and trodden under foot by men.

14 "You are the light of the world. A city set on a hill cannot be hid. ¹⁵Nor do men light a lamp and put it under a bushel, but on a stand, and it gives light to all in the house. ¹⁶Let your light so shine before men, that they may see your good works and give glory to your Father who is in heaven.

17 "Think not that I have come to abolish the law and the prophets; I have come not to abolish them but to fulfil them.

ἔστιν ἡ βασιλεία τῶν οὐρανῶν. **11** μακάριοί
is the kingdom of the heavens. Blessed

ἐστε ὅταν ὀνειδίσωσιν ὑμᾶς καὶ διώξωσιν
are ye when they reproach you and persecute

καὶ εἴπωσιν πᾶν πονηρὸν καθ' ὑμῶν
and say all evil against you

ψευδόμενοι ἕνεκεν ἐμοῦ. **12** χαίρετε
lying for the sake of me. Rejoice

καὶ ἀγαλλιᾶσθε, ὅτι ὁ μισθὸς ὑμῶν
and be glad, because the reward of you [is]

πολὺς ἐν τοῖς οὐρανοῖς· οὕτως γὰρ
much in the heavens; for thus

ἐδίωξαν τοὺς προφήτας τοὺς πρὸ
they persecuted the prophets - before

ὑμῶν.
you.

13 Ὑμεῖς ἐστε τὸ ἅλας τῆς γῆς· ἐὰν δὲ
Ye are the salt of the earth; but if

τὸ ἅλας μωρανθῇ, ἐν τίνι ἁλισθήσεται;
the salt be tainted, by what shall it be salted?

εἰς οὐδὲν ἰσχύει ἔτι εἰ μὴ βληθὲν ἔξω
for nothing is it strong longer except being cast out

καταπατεῖσθαι ὑπὸ τῶν ἀνθρώπων. **14** Ὑμεῖς
to be trodden down by - men. Ye

ἐστε τὸ φῶς τοῦ κόσμου. οὐ δύναται
are the light of the world. ⁹Not ⁸can

πόλις κρυβῆναι ἐπάνω ὄρους κειμένη·
¹a city ⁷to be hid ³on ⁴a mountain ⁵set;

15 οὐδὲ καίουσιν λύχνον καὶ τιθέασιν
nor do they light a lamp and place

αὐτὸν ὑπὸ τὸν μόδιον, ἀλλ' ἐπὶ τὴν
it under the bushel, but on the

λυχνίαν, καὶ λάμπει πᾶσιν τοῖς ἐν τῇ
lampstand, and it lightens all the [ones] in the

οἰκίᾳ. **16** οὕτως λαμψάτω τὸ φῶς ὑμῶν
house. Thus let shine the light of you

ἔμπροσθεν τῶν ἀνθρώπων, ὅπως ἴδωσιν
before - men, so that they may see

ὑμῶν τὰ καλὰ ἔργα καὶ δοξάσωσιν
of you the good works and may glorify

τὸν πατέρα ὑμῶν τὸν ἐν τοῖς οὐρανοῖς.
the Father of you - in the heavens.

17 Μὴ νομίσητε ὅτι ἦλθον καταλῦσαι
Think not that I came to destroy

τὸν νόμον ἢ τοὺς προφήτας· οὐκ ἦλθον
the law or the prophets; I came not

καταλῦσαι ἀλλὰ πληρῶσαι. **18** ἀμὴν γὰρ
to destroy but to fulfil. For truly

¹⁸ For truly, I say to you, till heaven and earth pass away, not an iota, not a dot, will pass from the law until all is accomplished. ¹⁹ Whoever then relaxes one of the least of these commandments and teaches men so, shall be called least in the kingdom of heaven; but he who does them and teaches them shall be called great in the kingdom of heaven. ²⁰ For I tell you, unless your righteousness exceeds that of the scribes and Pharisees, you will never enter the kingdom of heaven.

21 "You have heard that it was said to the men of old, 'You shall not kill; and whoever kills shall be liable to judgment.' ²² But I say to you that every one who is angry with his brother^f shall be liable to judgment; whoever insults^g his brother shall be liable to the council, and whoever says, 'You fool!' shall be liable to the hell of fire. ²³ So if you are offering your gift at the altar, and there remember that your brother has something against you,

---

λέγω   ὑμῖν,   ἕως   ἂν   παρέλθῃ   ὁ   οὐρανὸς
I say   to you,   until   pass away   the   heaven

καὶ   ἡ   γῆ,   ἰῶτα   ἓν   ἢ   μία   κεραία   οὐ
and   the earth,   iota   one   or   one   point   by no

μὴ   παρέλθῃ   ἀπὸ   τοῦ   νόμου,   ἕως   ἂν
means shall pass away   from   the   law,   until

πάντα   γένηται.   19   ὃς   ἐὰν   οὖν   λύσῃ
all things   come to pass.   ³Whoever   ¹therefore   breaks

μίαν   τῶν   ἐντολῶν   τούτων   τῶν   ἐλαχίστων
one   -   commandments of these   the   least

καὶ   διδάξῃ   οὕτως   τοὺς   ἀνθρώπους,   ἐλάχιστος
and   teaches   thus   -   men,   least

κληθήσεται   ἐν   τῇ   βασιλείᾳ   τῶν   οὐρανῶν·
he shall be called   in   the   kingdom   of the   heavens;

ὃς   δ'   ἂν   ποιήσῃ   καὶ   διδάξῃ,   οὗτος
but whoever   does   and   teaches,   this [one]

μέγας   κληθήσεται   ἐν   τῇ   βασιλεία   τῶν
great   shall be called   in   the   kingdom   of the

οὐρανῶν.   20   λέγω   γὰρ   ὑμῖν   ὅτι   ἐὰν   μὴ
heavens.   For I tell   you   that   except

περισσεύσῃ   ὑμῶν   ἡ   δικαιοσύνη   πλεῖον
shall exceed   of you   the   righteousness   more [than] [that]

τῶν   γραμματέων   καὶ   Φαρισαίων,   οὐ   μὴ
of the   scribes   and   Pharisees,   by no means

εἰσέλθητε   εἰς   τὴν   βασιλείαν   τῶν   οὐρανῶν.
shall ye enter   into   the   kingdom   of the   heavens.

21   Ἠκούσατε   ὅτι   ἐρρέθη   τοῖς   ἀρχαίοις·
Ye heard   that   it was said   to the   ancients:

οὐ   φονεύσεις·   ὃς   δ'   ἂν   φονεύσῃ,
Thou shalt not kill;   and whoever   kills,

ἔνοχος   ἔσται   τῇ   κρίσει.   22   ἐγὼ   δὲ
liable   shall be   to the   judgment.   But I

λέγω   ὑμῖν   ὅτι   πᾶς   ὁ   ὀργιζόμενος   τῷ
tell   you   that   everyone   being angry with   the

ἀδελφῷ   αὐτοῦ   ἔνοχος   ἔσται   τῇ   κρίσει·
brother   of him   liable   shall be   to the judgment;

ὃς   δ'   ἂν   εἴπῃ   τῷ   ἀδελφῷ   αὐτοῦ   ῥακά,
and whoever   says   to the   brother   of him[,]   Raca,

ἔνοχος   ἔσται   τῷ   συνεδρίῳ·   ὃς   δ'   ἂν   εἴπῃ
liable   shall be   to the   council;   and whoever   says[,]

μωρέ,   ἔνοχος   ἔσται   εἰς   τὴν   γέενναν
Fool,   liable   shall be   to   the   gehenna

τοῦ   πυρός.   23   ἐὰν   οὖν   προσφέρῃς   τὸ
-    of fire.   Therefore if   thou bringest   the

δῶρόν   σου   ἐπὶ   τὸ   θυσιαστήριον   κἀκεῖ
gift   of thee   to   the   altar   and there

μνησθῇς   ὅτι   ὁ   ἀδελφός   σου   ἔχει   τι
rememberest that   the   brother   of thee   has   something

---

^f Other ancient authorities insert *without cause*

^g Greek *says Raca* to (an obscure term of abuse)

²⁴leave your gift there before the altar and go; first be reconciled to your brother, and then come and offer your gift. ²⁵Make friends quickly with your accuser, while you are going with him to court, lest your accuser hand you over to the judge, and the judge to the guard, and you be put in prison; ²⁶truly, I say to you, you will never get out till you have paid the last penny.

²⁷"You have heard that it was said, 'You shall not commit adultery.' ²⁸But I say to you that every one who looks at a woman lustfully has already committed adultery with her in his heart. ²⁹If your right eye causes you to sin, pluck it out and throw it away; it is better that you lose one of your members than that your whole body be thrown into hell. ³⁰And if your right hand causes you to sin, cut it off and throw it away; it is better that you lose one of your members than that your whole body go into hell.

κατὰ σοῦ, **24** ἄφες ἐκεῖ τὸ δῶρόν σου
against thee,   leave there the gift of thee

ἔμπροσθεν τοῦ θυσιαστηρίου, καὶ ὕπαγε
before the altar, and go

πρῶτον διαλλάγηθι τῷ ἀδελφῷ σου, καὶ
first be reconciled to the brother of thee, and

τότε ἐλθὼν πρόσφερε τὸ δῶρόν σου.
then coming offer the gift of thee.

25 ἴσθι εὐνοῶν τῷ ἀντιδίκῳ σου
Be well disposed to the opponent of thee

ταχὺ ἕως ὅτου εἶ μετ' αὐτοῦ ἐν τῇ
quickly while thou art with him in the

ὁδῷ· μήποτέ σε παραδῷ ὁ ἀντίδικος τῷ
way; lest ⁴thee ³deliver ¹the ²opponent to the

κριτῇ καὶ ὁ κριτὴς τῷ ὑπηρέτῃ, καὶ
judge and the judge to the attendant, and

εἰς φυλακὴν βληθήσῃ· **26** ἀμὴν λέγω
into prison thou be cast; truly I say

σοι, οὐ μὴ ἐξέλθῃς ἐκεῖθεν ἕως ἂν
to thee, by no means shalt thou come out thence until

ἀποδῷς τὸν ἔσχατον κοδράντην.
thou repayest the last farthing.

27 Ἠκούσατε ὅτι ἐρρέθη· οὐ μοιχεύσεις.
Ye heard that it was said: Thou shalt not commit adultery.

28 ἐγὼ δὲ λέγω ὑμῖν ὅτι πᾶς ὁ βλέπων
But I tell you that everyone seeing

γυναῖκα πρὸς τὸ ἐπιθυμῆσαι [αὐτὴν]
a woman with a view - to desire her

ἤδη ἐμοίχευσεν αὐτὴν ἐν τῇ καρδίᾳ
already committed adultery with her in the heart

αὐτοῦ. **29** εἰ δὲ ὁ ὀφθαλμός σου ὁ δεξιὸς
of him. So if the ²eye ³of thee - ¹right

σκανδαλίζει σε, ἔξελε αὐτὸν καὶ βάλε
⁴causes ⁶to stumble ⁵thee, pluck out it and cast

ἀπὸ σοῦ· συμφέρει γάρ σοι ἵνα ἀπόληται
from thee; for it is expedient for thee that ⁵perish

ἐν τῶν μελῶν σου καὶ μὴ ὅλον τὸ
¹one ²of the ³members ⁴of thee and not all the

σῶμά σου βληθῇ εἰς γέενναν. **30** καὶ
body of thee be cast into gehenna. And

εἰ ἡ δεξιά σου χεὶρ σκανδαλίζει σε, ἔκκοψον
if the ¹right ³of thee ²hand ⁴causes ⁶to stumble ⁵thee, cut out

αὐτὴν καὶ βάλε ἀπὸ σοῦ· συμφέρει γάρ
it and cast from thee; for it is expedient

σοι ἵνα ἀπόληται ἐν τῶν μελῶν σου
for thee that ⁵perish ¹one ²of the ³members ⁴of thee

καὶ μὴ ὅλον τὸ σῶμά σου εἰς γέενναν
and not all the body of thee into gehenna

31 "It was also said, 'Whoever divorces his wife, let him give her a certificate of divorce.' ³²But I say to you that every one who divorces his wife, except on the ground of unchastity, makes her an adulteress; and whoever marries a divorced woman commits adultery.

33 "Again you have heard that it was said to the men of old, 'You shall not swear falsely, but shall perform to the Lord what you have sworn.' ³⁴But I say to you, Do not swear at all, either by heaven, for it is the throne of God, ³⁵or by the earth, for it is his footstool, or by Jerusalem, for it is the city of the great King. ³⁶And do not swear by your head, for you cannot make one hair white or black. ³⁷Let what you say be simply 'Yes' or 'No'; anything more than this comes from evil.

38 "You have heard that it was said, 'An eye for an eye and a tooth for a tooth.' ³⁹But I say to you, Do not resist one who is evil. But if any one strikes you on the right cheek, turn to him

ἀπέλθῃ.   31 Ἐρρέθη δέ· ὃς ἂν ἀπολύσῃ
go away.   And it was said: Whoever   dismisses

τὴν γυναῖκα αὐτοῦ, δότω αὐτῇ ἀποστάσιον.
the   wife   of him, let him give   her   a bill of divorce.

32 ἐγὼ δὲ λέγω ὑμῖν ὅτι πᾶς ὁ ἀπολύων
But I   tell   you   that   everyone   dismissing

τὴν γυναῖκα αὐτοῦ παρεκτὸς λόγου
the   wife   of him   apart from   a matter

πορνείας ποιεῖ αὐτὴν μοιχευθῆναι,
of fornication   makes   her   to commit adultery,

καὶ ὃς ἐὰν ἀπολελυμένην γαμήσῃ,
and   whoever   ¹a dismissed [woman]   ¹marries,

μοιχᾶται.   33 Πάλιν ἠκούσατε ὅτι ἐρρέθη
commits adultery.   Again   ye heard   that   it was said

τοῖς ἀρχαίοις· οὐκ ἐπιορκήσεις, ἀποδώσεις
to the   ancients: Thou shalt not perjure,   ²shalt repay

δὲ τῷ κυρίῳ τοὺς ὅρκους σου.   34 ἐγὼ δὲ
¹but to the Lord   the   oaths   of thee.   But I

λέγω ὑμῖν μὴ ὀμόσαι ὅλως· μήτε ἐν τῷ
tell   you   not   to swear   at all;   neither   by   the

οὐρανῷ, ὅτι θρόνος ἐστὶν τοῦ θεοῦ·
heaven,   because [the] throne   it is   -   of God;

35 μήτε ἐν τῇ γῇ, ὅτι ὑποπόδιόν
nor   by   the   earth,   because   footstool

ἐστιν τῶν ποδῶν αὐτοῦ· μήτε εἰς
it is   of the   feet   of him;   nor   by

Ἱεροσόλυμα, ὅτι πόλις ἐστὶν τοῦ μεγάλου
Jerusalem,   because   city   it is   of the   great

βασιλέως·   36 μήτε ἐν τῇ κεφαλῇ σου
King;   nor   by   the   head   of thee

ὀμόσῃς, ὅτι οὐ δύνασαι μίαν τρίχα
swear,   because   thou canst not   one   hair

λευκὴν ποιῆσαι ἢ μέλαιναν.   37 ἔστω
white   to make   or   black.   ²let ⁶be

δὲ ὁ λόγος ὑμῶν ναὶ ναί, οὒ οὔ·
¹But   ³the   ⁴word   ⁵of you   Yes   yes,   No   no;

τὸ δὲ περισσὸν τούτων ἐκ τοῦ πονηροῦ
for the   excess   of these   of   -   evil

ἐστιν.   38 Ἠκούσατε ὅτι ἐρρέθη· ὀφθαλμὸν
is.   Ye heard   that   it was said: An eye

ἀντὶ ὀφθαλμοῦ καὶ ὀδόντα ἀντὶ ὀδόντος.
instead of   an eye   and   a tooth   instead of   a tooth.

39 ἐγὼ δὲ λέγω ὑμῖν μὴ ἀντιστῆναι
But I   tell   you   not   to oppose

τῷ πονηρῷ· ἀλλ' ὅστις σε ῥαπίζει εἰς
-    evil;   but   who   thee   strikes   on

τὴν δεξιὰν σιαγόνα [σου], στρέψον αὐτῷ
the   right   cheek   of thee,   turn   to him

the other also; ⁴⁰and if any one would sue you and take your coat, let him have your cloak as well; ⁴¹and if any one forces you to go one mile, go with him two miles. ⁴²Give to him who begs from you, and do not refuse him who would borrow from you.

43 "You have heard that it was said, 'You shall love your neighbor and hate your enemy.' ⁴⁴But I say to you, Love your enemies and pray for those who persecute you, ⁴⁵so that you may be sons of your Father who is in heaven; for he makes his sun rise on the evil and on the good, and sends rain on the just and on the unjust. ⁴⁶For if you love those who love you, what reward have you? Do not even the tax collectors do the same? ⁴⁷And if you salute only your brethren, what more are you doing than others? Do not even the Gentiles do the same? ⁴⁸You, therefore, must be perfect, as your heavenly Father is perfect.

καὶ   τὴν   ἄλλην·   **40** καὶ   τῷ   θέλοντί
also   the   other;   and   to the [one]   wishing

σοι   κριθῆναι   καὶ   τὸν   χιτῶνά   σου   λαβεῖν,
thee   to judge   and   the   tunic   of thee   to take,

ἄφες   αὐτῷ   καὶ   τὸ   ἱμάτιον·   **41** καὶ
allow   him   also   the [outer] garment;   and

ὅστις   σε   ἀγγαρεύσει   μίλιον   ἕν,   ὕπαγε
who   ²thee   ¹shall impress   ⁴mile   ³one,   go

μετ'   αὐτοῦ   δύο.   **42** τῷ   αἰτοῦντί
with   him   two.   To the [one]   asking

σε   δός,   καὶ   τὸν   θέλοντα   ἀπὸ   σοῦ
thee   give,   and   the [one]   wishing   from   thee

δανείσασθαι   μὴ   ἀποστραφῇς.   **43** Ἠκούσατε
to borrow   turn not away.   Ye heard

ὅτι   ἐρρέθη·   ἀγαπήσεις   τὸν   πλησίον   σου
that   it was said: Thou shalt love   the   neighbour   of thee

καὶ   μισήσεις   τὸν   ἐχθρόν   σου.   **44** ἐγὼ
and   thou shalt hate   the   enemy   of thee.   ²I

δὲ   λέγω   ὑμῖν·   ἀγαπᾶτε   τοὺς   ἐχθροὺς
¹But   tell   you: Love ye   the   enemies

ὑμῶν   καὶ   προσεύχεσθε   ὑπὲρ   τῶν
of you   and   pray ye   for   the [ones]

διωκόντων   ὑμᾶς·   **45** ὅπως   γένησθε   υἱοὶ
persecuting   you;   so that   ye may become   sons

τοῦ   πατρὸς   ὑμῶν   τοῦ   ἐν   οὐρανοῖς,
of the   Father   of you   —   in   heavens,

ὅτι   τὸν   ἥλιον   αὐτοῦ   ἀνατέλλει   ἐπὶ
because   the   sun   of him   he makes to rise   on

πονηροὺς   καὶ   ἀγαθοὺς   καὶ   βρέχει   ἐπὶ
evil men   and   good   and   rains   on

δικαίους   καὶ   ἀδίκους.   **46** ἐὰν   γὰρ
just men   and   unjust.   For if

ἀγαπήσητε   τοὺς   ἀγαπῶντας   ὑμᾶς,   τίνα
ye love   the [ones]   loving   you,   what

μισθὸν   ἔχετε;   οὐχὶ   καὶ   οἱ   τελῶναι   τὸ
reward   have ye?   ²not   ³even   ⁴the   ⁵tax-collectors   ⁶the

αὐτὸ   ποιοῦσιν;   **47** καὶ   ἐὰν   ἀσπάσησθε
⁷same   ¹do?   and   if   ye greet

τοὺς   ἀδελφοὺς   ὑμῶν   μόνον,   τί   περισσὸν
the   brothers   of you   only,   what   excess

ποιεῖτε;   οὐχὶ   καὶ   οἱ   ἐθνικοὶ   τὸ   αὐτὸ
do ye?   ²not   ³even   ⁴the   ⁵gentiles   ⁶the   ⁷same

ποιοῦσιν;   **48** Ἔσεσθε   οὖν   ὑμεῖς   τέλειοι
¹do?   Be   therefore   ye   perfect

ὡς   ὁ   πατὴρ   ὑμῶν   ὁ   οὐράνιος   τέλειός
as   the   ²Father   ³of you   —   ¹heavenly   perfect

ἐστιν.
is.

CHAPTER 6

"BEWARE of practicing your piety before men in order to be seen by them; for then you will have no reward from your Father who is in heaven.

2 "Thus, when you give alms, sound no trumpet before you, as the hypocrites do in the synagogues and in the streets, that they may be praised by men. Truly, I say to you, they have their reward. ³But when you give alms, do not let your left hand know what your right hand is doing, ⁴so that your alms may be in secret; and your Father who sees in secret will reward you.

5 "And when you pray, you must not be like the hypocrites; for they love to stand and pray in the synagogues and at the street corners, that they may be seen by men. Truly, I say to you, they have their reward. ⁶But when you pray, go into your room and shut the door and pray to your Father who is in secret; and your Father

6 Προσέχετε δὲ τὴν δικαιοσύνην ὑμῶν
And take ye heed   the   righteousness   of you

μὴ ποιεῖν ἔμπροσθεν τῶν ἀνθρώπων πρὸς
not to do   in front of   –   men   with a view to

τὸ θεαθῆναι αὐτοῖς· εἰ δὲ μή γε, μισθὸν
– to be seen by them;   otherwise,   reward

οὐκ ἔχετε παρὰ τῷ πατρὶ ὑμῶν τῷ
ye have not   with   the   Father   of you   –

ἐν τοῖς οὐρανοῖς. **2** Ὅταν οὖν ποιῇς
in   the   heavens.   ²When ¹therefore thou doest

ἐλεημοσύνην, μὴ σαλπίσῃς ἔμπροσθέν σου,
alms,   sound not a trumpet   before   thee,

ὥσπερ οἱ ὑποκριταὶ ποιοῦσιν ἐν ταῖς
as   the   hypocrites   do   in   the

συναγωγαῖς καὶ ἐν ταῖς ῥύμαις, ὅπως
synagogues   and   in   the   streets,   so that

δοξασθῶσιν ὑπὸ τῶν ἀνθρώπων· ἀμὴν
they may be glorified by   –   men;   truly

λέγω ὑμῖν, ἀπέχουσιν τὸν μισθὸν αὐτῶν.
I tell   you,   they have   the   reward   of them.

3 σοῦ δὲ ποιοῦντος ἐλεημοσύνην μὴ
But thee   doing²   alms   not
= when thou doest

γνώτω ἡ ἀριστερά σου τί ποιεῖ ἡ
let know the   left [hand] of thee what does the

δεξιά σου, **4** ὅπως ᾖ σου ἡ ἐλεημοσύνη
right of thee,   so that ⁴may be ⁵of thee ¹the   ²alms

ἐν τῷ κρυπτῷ· καὶ ὁ πατήρ σου
in   –   secret;   and   the   Father   of thee

ὁ βλέπων ἐν τῷ κρυπτῷ ἀποδώσει σοι.
the [one] seeing in   –   secret   will repay   thee.

5 Καὶ ὅταν προσεύχησθε, οὐκ ἔσεσθε
And   when   ye pray,   be not ye

ὡς οἱ ὑποκριταί· ὅτι φιλοῦσιν ἐν ταῖς
as   the hypocrites;   because they love   in   the

συναγωγαῖς καὶ ἐν ταῖς γωνίαις τῶν
synagogues   and   in   the   corners   of the

πλατειῶν ἑστῶτες προσεύχεσθαι, ὅπως
open streets   standing   to pray,   so that

φανῶσιν τοῖς ἀνθρώποις· ἀμὴν λέγω
they may appear   – to men;   truly   I tell

ὑμῖν, ἀπέχουσιν τὸν μισθὸν αὐτῶν. **6** σὺ
you,   they have   the   reward   of them.   ²thou

δὲ ὅταν προσεύχῃ, εἴσελθε εἰς τὸ ταμιεῖόν
¹But ³when ⁴prayest,   enter into the private room

σου καὶ κλείσας τὴν θύραν σου πρόσευξαι
of thee and having shut   the   door   of thee   pray

τῷ πατρί σου τῷ ἐν τῷ κρυπτῷ·
to the Father   of thee the [one] in   –   secret;

who sees in secret will reward you.

7 "And in praying do not heap up empty phrases as the Gentiles do; for they think that they will be heard for their many words. ⁸Do not be like them, for your Father knows what you need before you ask him. ⁹Pray then like this:

Our Father who art in heaven,
Hallowed by thy name.
¹⁰Thy kingdom come,
Thy will be done,
On earth as it is in heaven.
¹¹Give us this day our daily bread;ʰ
¹²And forgive us our debts,
As we also have forgiven our debtors;
¹³And lead us not into temptation,
But deliver us from evil.ⁱ

¹⁴For if you forgive men their trespasses, your heavenly Father also will forgive you; ¹⁵but if you do not forgive men their trespasses, neither will your Father forgive your trespasses.

16 "And when you fast, do not look dismal, like the hypocrites, for

ʰ Or *our bread for the morrow*
ⁱ Or *the evil one.* Other authorities, some ancient, add, in some form, *For thine is the kingdom and the power and the glory, forever. Amen.*

καὶ ὁ πατήρ σου ὁ βλέπων ἐν τῷ
and the Father of thee the [one] seeing in -
κρυπτῷ ἀποδώσει σοι. 7 Προσευχόμενοι δὲ
secret will repay thee. But praying
μὴ βατταλογήσητε ὥσπερ οἱ ἐθνικοί·
do not utter empty words as the gentiles;
δοκοῦσιν γὰρ ὅτι ἐν τῇ πολυλογίᾳ αὐτῶν
for they think that in the much speaking of them
εἰσακουσθήσονται. 8 μὴ οὖν ὁμοιωθῆτε
they will be heard. Not therefore be ye like
αὐτοῖς· οἶδεν γὰρ [ὁ θεός] ὁ πατὴρ
them; for ⁵knows - ¹God ²the ³Father
ὑμῶν ὧν χρείαν ἔχετε πρὸ τοῦ ὑμᾶς
⁴of you of what things ²need ¹ye have before - you
αἰτῆσαι αὐτόν. 9 οὕτως οὖν προσεύχεσθε
to askᵇ him. ²Thus ¹therefore pray
ὑμεῖς· Πάτερ ἡμῶν ὁ ἐν τοῖς οὐρανοῖς·
ye: Father of us the [one] in the heavens:
Ἁγιασθήτω τὸ ὄνομά σου· 10 ἐλθάτω
Let it be hallowed the name of thee; let it come
ἡ βασιλεία σου· γενηθήτω τὸ θέλημά σου,
the kingdom of thee; let it come about the will of thee,
ὡς ἐν οὐρανῷ καὶ ἐπὶ γῆς· 11 Τὸν
as in heaven also on earth; The
ἄρτον ἡμῶν τὸν ἐπιούσιον δὸς ἡμῖν
³bread ²of us - ¹daily give to us
σήμερον· 12 καὶ ἄφες ἡμῖν τὰ ὀφειλή-
to-day; and forgive us the debts
ματα ἡμῶν, ὡς καὶ ἡμεῖς ἀφήκαμεν
of us, as indeed we forgave
τοῖς ὀφειλέταις ἡμῶν· 13 καὶ μὴ εἰσενέγκῃς
the debtors of us; and not bring
ἡμᾶς εἰς πειρασμόν, ἀλλὰ ῥῦσαι ἡμᾶς ἀπὸ
us into temptation, but rescue us from
τοῦ πονηροῦ. 14 Ἐὰν γὰρ ἀφῆτε τοῖς
- evil. For if ye forgive
ἀνθρώποις τὰ παραπτώματα αὐτῶν, ἀφήσει
men the trespasses of them, will forgive
καὶ ὑμῖν ὁ πατὴρ ὑμῶν ὁ οὐράνιος·
also you the ²Father ³of you - ¹heavenly;
15 ἐὰν δὲ μὴ ἀφῆτε τοῖς ἀνθρώποις,
but if ye forgive not - men,
οὐδὲ ὁ πατὴρ ὑμῶν ἀφήσει τὰ παραπτώ-
neither the Father of you will forgive the tres-
ματα ὑμῶν. 16 Ὅταν δὲ νηστεύητε,
passes of you. And when ye fast,
μὴ γίνεσθε ὡς οἱ ὑποκριταὶ σκυθρωποί·
be not as the hypocrites gloomy;

they disfigure their faces that their fasting may be seen by men. Truly, I say to you, they have their reward. [17]But when you fast, anoint your head and wash your face, [18]that your fasting may not be seen by men but by your Father who is in secret; and your Father who sees in secret will reward you.

19 "Do not lay up for yourselves treasures on earth, where moth and rust consume and where thieves break in and steal, [20]but lay up for yourselves treasures in heaven, where neither moth nor rust[j] consumes and where thieves do not break in and steal. [21]For where your treasure is, there will your heart be also.

22 "The eye is the lamp of the body. So, if your eye is sound, your whole body will be full of light; [23]but if your eye is not sound, your whole body will be full of darkness. If then the light in you is darkness, how great is the darkness!

[j] Or worm

ἀφανίζουσιν	γὰρ	τὰ	πρόσωπα	αὐτῶν
for they disfigure		the	faces	of them

ὅπως	φανῶσιν	τοῖς	ἀνθρώποις	νηστεύοντες·
so that	they may appear –		to men	fasting;

ἀμὴν	λέγω	ὑμῖν,	ἀπέχουσιν	τὸν	μισθὸν
truly	I tell	you,	they have	the	reward

αὐτῶν.	17 σὺ	δὲ	νηστεύων	ἄλειψαί	σου
of them.	But thou		fasting	anoint	of thee

τὴν	κεφαλὴν	καὶ	τὸ	πρόσωπόν	σου	νίψαι,
the	head	and	the	face	of thee	wash,

18 ὅπως	μὴ	φανῇς	τοῖς	ἀνθρώποις	νηστεύων
so that thou appearest not	–			to men	fasting

ἀλλὰ	τῷ	πατρί	σου	τῷ	ἐν	τῷ	κρυφαίῳ·
but	to the	Father	of thee	the [one] in	–		secret;

καὶ	ὁ	πατήρ	σου	ὁ	βλέπων	ἐν	τῷ
and	the	Father	of thee	the [one] seeing		in	–

κρυφαίῳ	ἀποδώσει	σοι.
secret	will repay	thee.

19 Μὴ	θησαυρίζετε	ὑμῖν	θησαυροὺς
Do not lay up	*treasure*	for you	treasures

ἐπὶ	τῆς	γῆς,	ὅπου	σὴς	καὶ	βρῶσις
on	the	earth,	where	moth	and	rust

ἀφανίζει,	καὶ	ὅπου	κλέπται	διορύσσουσιν
removes,	and	where	thieves	dig through

καὶ	κλέπτουσιν·	20 θησαυρίζετε	δὲ	ὑμῖν
and	steal;	but lay up *treasure*		for you

θησαυροὺς	ἐν	οὐρανῷ,	ὅπου	οὔτε	σὴς
treasures	in	heaven,	where	neither	moth

οὔτε	βρῶσις	ἀφανίζει,	καὶ	ὅπου	κλέπται
nor	rust	removes,	and	where	thieves

οὐ	διορύσσουσιν	οὐδὲ	κλέπτουσιν·	21 ὅπου
do not dig through		nor	steal;	[2]where

γὰρ	ἐστιν	ὁ	θησαυρός	σου,	ἐκεῖ
[1]for	is	the	treasure	of thee,	there

ἔσται	καὶ	ἡ	καρδία	σου.	22 Ὁ	λύχνος
will be	also	the	heart	of thee.	The	lamp

τοῦ	σώματός	ἐστιν	ὁ	ὀφθαλμός.	ἐὰν	οὖν
of the	body	is	the	eye.	[2]If	[1]therefore

ᾖ	ὁ	ὀφθαλμός	σου	ἁπλοῦς,	ὅλον	τὸ	σῶμά
[4]be	[1]the	[2]eye	[3]of thee	single,	all	the	body

σου	φωτεινὸν	ἔσται·	23 ἐὰν	δὲ	ὁ
of thee	shining	will be;	but if		the

ὀφθαλμός	σου	πονηρὸς	ᾖ,	ὅλον	τὸ	σῶμά
eye	of thee	evil	be,	all	the	body

σου	σκοτεινὸν	ἔσται.	εἰ	οὖν	τὸ	φῶς
of thee	dark	will be.	[2]If	[1]therefore	the	light

τὸ	ἐν	σοὶ	σκότος	ἐστιν,	τὸ	σκότος
–	in	thee	darkness	is,	the	darkness

24 "No one can serve two masters; for either he will hate the one and love the other, or he will be devoted to the one and despise the other. You cannot serve God and mammon.

25 "Therefore I tell you, do not be anxious about your life, what you shall eat or what you shall drink, nor about your body, what you shall put on. Is not life more than food, and the body more than clothing? [26] Look at the birds of the air: they neither sow nor reap nor gather into barns, and yet your heavenly Father feeds them. Are you not of more value than they? [27] And which of you by being anxious can add one cubit to his span of life?[k] [28] And why are you anxious about clothing? Consider the lilies of the field, how they grow; they neither toil nor spin; [29] yet I tell you, even Solomon in all his glory was not arrayed like one of these. [30] But if God so clothes the grass of the field, which today is alive and tomorrow is thrown into the oven,

πόσον. **24** Οὐδεὶς δύναται δυσὶ κυρίοις
how great.   No one   can   two   lords

δουλεύειν· ἢ γὰρ τὸν ἕνα μισήσει καὶ
to serve;   for either   the   one   he will hate   and

τὸν ἕτερον ἀγαπήσει, ἢ ἑνὸς ἀνθέξεται
the   other   he will love,   or   one   he will hold to

καὶ τοῦ ἑτέρου καταφρονήσει. οὐ δύνασθε
and   the   other   he will despise.   Ye cannot

θεῷ δουλεύειν καὶ μαμωνᾷ. **25** Διὰ
God   to serve   and   mammon.   There-

τοῦτο λέγω ὑμῖν· μὴ μεριμνᾶτε τῇ
fore   I say   to you: Be not anxious   for the

ψυχῇ ὑμῶν τί φάγητε [ἢ τί πίητε],
life   of you[,]   what ye may eat   or what ye may drink,

μηδὲ τῷ σώματι ὑμῶν τί ἐνδύσησθε.
nor   for the   body   of you[,]   what ye may put on.

οὐχὶ ἡ ψυχὴ πλεῖόν ἐστιν τῆς τροφῆς καὶ τὸ
²not ³the   ⁴life   ⁵more   ¹Is [than] the   food   and   the

σῶμα τοῦ ἐνδύματος; **26** ἐμβλέψατε εἰς
body [than] the   raiment?   Look ye   at

τὰ πετεινὰ τοῦ οὐρανοῦ, ὅτι οὐ σπείρουσιν
the   birds   —   of heaven,   that   they sow not

οὐδὲ θερίζουσιν οὐδὲ συνάγουσιν εἰς
nor   reap   nor   gather   into

ἀποθήκας, καὶ ὁ πατὴρ ὑμῶν ὁ οὐράνιος
barns,   and the   ¹Father   ²of you   —   ¹heavenly

τρέφει αὐτά· οὐχ ὑμεῖς μᾶλλον διαφέρετε
feeds   them;   do not ye   more   excel

αὐτῶν; **27** τίς δὲ ἐξ ὑμῶν μεριμνῶν
them?   But who   of   you   being anxious

δύναται προσθεῖναι ἐπὶ τὴν ἡλικίαν αὐτοῦ
can   to add   to   the   stature   of him

πῆχυν ἕνα; **28** καὶ περὶ ἐνδύματος τί
cubit   one?   and concerning   clothing   why

μεριμνᾶτε; καταμάθετε τὰ κρίνα τοῦ ἀγροῦ,
be ye anxious?   consider   the   lilies   of the   field,

πῶς αὐξάνουσιν· οὐ κοπιῶσιν οὐδὲ
how   they grow;   they labour not   nor

νήθουσιν· **29** λέγω δὲ ὑμῖν ὅτι οὐδὲ Σολομὼν
spin;   but I tell   you that   not   Solomon

ἐν πάσῃ τῇ δόξῃ αὐτοῦ περιεβάλετο ὡς
in   all   the   glory   of him   was clothed   as

ἓν τούτων. **30** εἰ δὲ τὸν χόρτον τοῦ
one   of these.   But if   the   grass   of the

ἀγροῦ σήμερον ὄντα καὶ αὔριον εἰς
field   to-day   being   and   to-morrow   into

κλίβανον βαλλόμενον ὁ θεὸς οὕτως
an oven   being thrown   —   God   thus

---

[k] Or *to his stature*

will he not much more clothe you, O men of little faith? [31] Therefore do not be anxious, saying, 'What shall we eat?' or 'What shall we drink?' or 'What shall we wear?' [32] For the Gentiles seek all these things; and your heavenly Father knows that you need them all. [33] But seek first his kingdom and his righteousness, and all these things shall be yours as well.

34 "Therefore do not be anxious about tomorrow, for tomorrow will be anxious for itself. Let the day's own trouble be sufficient for the day.

ἀμφιέννυσιν,   οὐ   πολλῷ   μᾶλλον   ὑμᾶς,
clothes,   not   much   more   you,

ὀλιγόπιστοι;   31 μὴ   οὖν   μεριμνήσητε
little-faiths?   Therefore be ye not anxious

λέγοντες·   τί   φάγωμεν;   ἤ·   τί
saying: What   may we eat?   or: What

πίωμεν;   ἤ·   τί   περιβαλώμεθα;   32 πάντα
may we drink? or: What   may we put on?   ²all

γὰρ   ταῦτα   τὰ   ἔθνη   ἐπιζητοῦσιν·   οἶδεν
¹for   these things the   nations   seek after;   ⁶knows

γὰρ   ὁ   πατὴρ   ὑμῶν   ὁ   οὐράνιος   ὅτι
¹for ²the ⁴Father   ⁵of you   -   ³heavenly   that

χρῄζετε   τούτων   ἁπάντων.   33 ζητεῖτε δὲ
ye need   these things   of all.   But seek ye

πρῶτον   τὴν   βασιλείαν   καὶ   τὴν   δικαιοσύνην
first   the   kingdom   and   the   righteousness

αὐτοῦ,   καὶ   ταῦτα   πάντα   προστεθήσεται
of him,   and   these things all   shall be added

ὑμῖν.   34 μὴ   οὖν   μεριμνήσητε   εἰς   τὴν
to you.   Therefore be ye not anxious   for   the

αὔριον,   ἡ   γὰρ   αὔριον   μεριμνήσει
morrow,   for the   morrow   will be anxious

ἑαυτῆς·   ἀρκετὸν   τῇ   ἡμέρᾳ   ἡ   κακία   αὐτῆς.
of itself; sufficient to the day   the   evil   of it.

CHAPTER 7

"JUDGE not, that you be not judged. [2] For with the judgment you pronounce you will be judged, and the measure you give will be the measure you get. [3] Why do you see the speck that is in your brother's eye, but do not notice the log that is in your own eye? [4] Or how can you say to your brother, 'Let me take the speck out of your eye,' when there is the log in your own eye? [5] You hypocrite, first take the log out of your own eye, and then you will

7 Μὴ   κρίνετε,   ἵνα   μὴ   κριθῆτε·   2 ἐν   ᾧ
Judge not,   lest   ye be judged;   ²with ³what

γὰρ   κρίματι   κρίνετε   κριθήσεσθε,   καὶ
¹for judgment   ye judge   ye shall be judged,   and

ἐν   ᾧ   μέτρῳ   μετρεῖτε   μετρηθήσεται   ὑμῖν.
with what measure   ye measure   it shall be measured to you.

3 τί   δὲ   βλέπεις   τὸ   κάρφος   τὸ   ἐν
And why   seest thou   the   chip   -   in

τῷ   ὀφθαλμῷ   τοῦ   ἀδελφοῦ   σου,   τὴν
the   eye   of the   brother   of thee,   ⁵the

δὲ   ἐν   τῷ   σῷ   ὀφθαλμῷ   δοκὸν   οὐ   κατα-
¹but ⁴in   -   ⁵thine   ⁶eye   ³beam   thou consider-

νοεῖς;   4 ἢ   πῶς   ἐρεῖς   τῷ   ἀδελφῷ   σου·
est not?   or   how   wilt thou say   to the   brother   of thee:

ἄφες   ἐκβάλω   τὸ   κάρφος   ἐκ   τοῦ   ὀφθαλμοῦ
Allow [that] I may pluck out   the   chip   out of the   eye

σου,   καὶ   ἰδοὺ   ἡ   δοκὸς   ἐν   τῷ   ὀφθαλμῷ
of thee,   and   behold   the   beam   in   the   eye

σου;   5 ὑποκριτά,   ἔκβαλε   πρῶτον   ἐκ   τοῦ
of thee?   hypocrite,   pluck out   first   out of   the

ὀφθαλμοῦ   σου   τὴν   δοκόν,   καὶ   τότε
eye   of thee   the   beam,   and   then

see clearly to take the speck out of your brother's eye.

6 "Do not give dogs what is holy; and do not throw your pearls before swine, lest they trample them underfoot and turn to attack you.

7 "Ask, and it will be given you; seek, and you will find; knock, and it will be opened to you. ⁸For every one who asks receives, and he who seeks finds, and to him who knocks it will be opened. ⁹Or what man of you, if his son asks him for bread, will give him a stone? ¹⁰Or if he asks for a fish, will give him a serpent? ¹¹If you then, who are evil, know how to give good gifts to your children, how much more will your Father who is in heaven give good things to those who ask him? ¹²So whatever you wish that men would do to you, do so to them; for this is the law and the prophets.

13 "Enter by the narrow gate; for the gate is wide and the way is easy,¹

¹ Other ancient authorities read *for the way is wide and easy*

διαβλέψεις   ἐκβαλεῖν   τὸ   κάρφος   ἐκ
thou wilt see clearly to pluck *out*   the   chip   out of

τοῦ   ὀφθαλμοῦ   τοῦ   ἀδελφοῦ   σου.   6 Μὴ
the   eye   of the   brother   of thee.   not

δῶτε   τὸ   ἅγιον   τοῖς   κυσίν,   μηδὲ   βάλητε
Give   the   holy   to the   dogs,   neither   cast

τοὺς   μαργαρίτας   ὑμῶν   ἔμπροσθεν   τῶν
the   pearls   of you   before   the

χοίρων,   μήποτε   καταπατήσουσιν   αὐτοὺς
pigs,   lest   they will trample   them

ἐν   τοῖς   ποσὶν   αὐτῶν   καὶ   στραφέντες
with   the   feet   of them   and   turning

ῥήξωσιν   ὑμᾶς.   7 Αἰτεῖτε,   καὶ   δοθήσεται
may rend   you.   Ask,   and   it shall be given

ὑμῖν·   ζητεῖτε,   καὶ   εὑρήσετε·   κρούετε,
to you;   seek,   and   ye shall find;   knock,

καὶ   ἀνοιγήσεται   ὑμῖν.   8 πᾶς   γὰρ   ὁ   αἰτῶν
and   it shall be opened   to you.   For every   asking [one]

λαμβάνει,   καὶ   ὁ   ζητῶν   εὑρίσκει,   καὶ
receives,   and   the   seeking [one]   finds,   and

τῷ   κρούοντι   ἀνοιγήσεται.   9 ἢ   τίς   ἐστιν
to the knocking [one] it shall be opened.   Or   ¹what ²is there

ἐξ   ὑμῶν   ἄνθρωπος,   ὃν   αἰτήσει   ὁ   υἱὸς
⁴of   ⁵you   ²man,   whom   ⁴will ask   ¹the   ²son

αὐτοῦ   ἄρτον,   μὴ   λίθον   ἐπιδώσει   αὐτῷ;
³of him   ⁵a loaf,   *not*   a stone   he will give   him?

10 ἢ   καὶ   ἰχθὺν   αἰτήσει,   μὴ   ὄφιν   ἐπιδώσει
or   also   a fish   he will ask,   *not* a serpent he will give

αὐτῷ;   11 εἰ   οὖν   ὑμεῖς   πονηροὶ   ὄντες
him?   If   therefore   ye   ²evil   ¹being

οἴδατε   δόματα   ἀγαθὰ   διδόναι   τοῖς   τέκνοις
know   gifts³   good²   to give¹   to the   children

ὑμῶν,   πόσῳ   μᾶλλον   ὁ   πατὴρ   ὑμῶν   ὁ
of you,   how much   more   the   Father   of you   –

ἐν   τοῖς   οὐρανοῖς   δώσει   ἀγαθὰ   τοῖς
in   the   heavens   will give good things to the [ones]

αἰτοῦσιν   αὐτόν.   12 Πάντα   οὖν   ὅσα   ἐὰν
asking   him.   All things therefore as many soever as

θέλητε   ἵνα   ποιῶσιν   ὑμῖν   οἱ   ἄνθρωποι,
ye wish   that   may do   to you   –   men,

οὕτως   καὶ   ὑμεῖς   ποιεῖτε   αὐτοῖς·   οὗτος
thus   also   ye   do   to them;   ²this

γὰρ   ἐστιν   ὁ   νόμος   καὶ   οἱ   προφῆται.
¹for   is   the   law   and   the   prophets.

13 Εἰσέλθατε   διὰ   τῆς   στενῆς   πύλης·
Enter ye in   through   the   narrow   gate;

ὅτι   πλατεῖα   [ἡ   πύλη]   καὶ   εὐρύχωρ⸴
because wide   the   gate]   and   broad

that leads to destruction, and those who enter by it are many. ¹⁴For the gate is narrow and the way is hard, that leads to life, and those who find it are few.

15 "Beware of false prophets, who come to you in sheep's clothing but inwardly are ravenous wolves. ¹⁶You will know them by their fruits. Are grapes gathered from thorns, or figs from thistles? ¹⁷So, every sound tree bears good fruit, but the bad tree bears evil fruit. ¹⁸A sound tree cannot bear evil fruit, nor can a bad tree bear good fruit. ¹⁹Every tree that does not bear good fruit is cut down and thrown into the fire. ²⁰Thus you will know them by their fruits.

21 "Not every one who says to me, 'Lord, Lord,' shall enter the kingdom of heaven, but he who does the will of my Father who is in heaven. ²²On that day many will say to me, 'Lord, Lord, did we not

ἡ ὁδὸς ἡ ἀπάγουσα εἰς τὴν ἀπώλειαν,
the way – leading away to – destruction,

καὶ πολλοί εἰσιν οἱ εἰσερχόμενοι δι᾽
and many are the [ones] going in through

αὐτῆς· 14 ὅτι στενὴ ἡ πύλη καὶ τεθλιμ-
it; because strait the gate and made

μένη ἡ ὁδὸς ἡ ἀπάγουσα εἰς τὴν ζωήν,
narrow the way – leading away to – life,

καὶ ὀλίγοι εἰσιν οἱ εὑρίσκοντες αὐτήν.
and few are the [ones] finding it.

15 Προσέχετε ἀπὸ τῶν ψευδοπροφητῶν,
Beware from(of) – false prophets,

οἵτινες ἔρχονται πρὸς ὑμᾶς ἐν ἐνδύμασι
who come to you in clothes

προβάτων, ἔσωθεν δέ εἰσιν λύκοι ἅρπαγες.
of sheep, but within are wolves greedy.

16 ἀπὸ τῶν καρπῶν αὐτῶν ἐπιγνώσεσθε
From the fruits of them ye will know

αὐτούς. μήτι συλλέγουσιν ἀπὸ ἀκανθῶν σταφυλὰς
them. They do not gather from thorns grapes

ἢ ἀπὸ τριβόλων σῦκα; 17 οὕτως πᾶν
or from thistles figs? So ¹every

δένδρον ἀγαθὸν καρποὺς καλοὺς ποιεῖ,
³tree ²good ⁶fruits ⁵good ⁴produces,

τὸ δὲ σαπρὸν δένδρον καρποὺς πονηροὺς
but the corrupt tree fruits evil

ποιεῖ. 18 οὐ δύναται δένδρον ἀγαθὸν
produces. ³Cannot ²tree ¹a good

καρποὺς πονηροὺς ἐνεγκεῖν, οὐδὲ δένδρον
⁵fruits ⁶evil ⁴to bear, nor ²tree

σαπρὸν καρποὺς καλοὺς ἐνεγκεῖν. 19 πᾶν
¹a corrupt ⁵fruits ⁴good ³to bear. Every

δένδρον μὴ ποιοῦν καρπὸν καλὸν ἐκκόπτεται
tree not producing fruit good is cut down

καὶ εἰς πῦρ βάλλεται. 20 ἄρα γε ἀπὸ
and into fire is cast. Therefore from

τῶν καρπῶν αὐτῶν ἐπιγνώσεσθε αὐτούς.
the fruits of them ye will know them.

21 Οὐ πᾶς ὁ λέγων μοι κύριε κύριε,
Not everyone saying to me Lord[,] Lord,

εἰσελεύσεται εἰς τὴν βασιλείαν τῶν οὐρανῶν,
will enter into the kingdom of the heavens,

ἀλλ᾽ ὁ ποιῶν τὸ θέλημα τοῦ πατρός
but the [one] doing the will of the Father

μου τοῦ ἐν τοῖς οὐρανοῖς. 22 πολλοὶ
of me – in the heavens. Many

ἐροῦσίν μοι ἐν ἐκείνῃ τῇ ἡμέρᾳ· κύριε
will say to me in that – day· Lord[,]

prophesy in your name, and cast out demons in your name, and do many mighty works in your name?' [23]And then will I declare to them, 'I never knew you; depart from me, you evildoers.'

24 "Every one then who hears these words of mine and does them will be like a wise man who built his house upon the rock; [25]and the rain fell, and the floods came, and the winds blew and beat upon that house, but it did not fall, because it had been founded on the rock. [26]And every one who hears these words of mine and does not do them will be like a foolish man who built his house upon the sand; [27]and the rain fell, and the floods came, and the winds blew and beat against that house, and it fell; and great was the fall of it."

κύριε, οὐ τῷ σῷ ὀνόματι ἐπροφητεύσαμεν,
Lord, not – in thy name we prophesied,

καὶ τῷ σῷ ὀνόματι δαιμόνια ἐξεβάλομεν,
and – in thy name demons we expelled,

καὶ τῷ σῷ ὀνόματι δυνάμεις πολλὰς
and – in thy name mighty works many

ἐποιήσαμεν; 23 καὶ τότε ὁμολογήσω
did? and then I will declare

αὐτοῖς ὅτι οὐδέποτε ἔγνων ὑμᾶς· ἀπο-
to them[,] – Never I knew you; de-

χωρεῖτε ἀπ' ἐμοῦ οἱ ἐργαζόμενοι τὴν
part from me the [ones] working –

ἀνομίαν.
lawlessness.

24 Πᾶς οὖν ὅστις ἀκούει μου τοὺς
Everyone therefore who hears of me

λόγους τούτους καὶ ποιεῖ αὐτούς,
words these and does them,

ὁμοιωθήσεται ἀνδρὶ φρονίμῳ, ὅστις ᾠκοδό-
shall be likened man to a prudent. who built

μησεν αὐτοῦ τὴν οἰκίαν ἐπὶ τὴν πέτραν.
of him the house on the rock.

25 καὶ κατέβη ἡ βροχὴ καὶ ἦλθον οἱ
And came down the rain and came the

ποταμοὶ καὶ ἔπνευσαν οἱ ἄνεμοι καὶ
rivers and blew the winds and

προσέπεσαν τῇ οἰκίᾳ ἐκείνῃ, καὶ οὐκ
fell against – house that, and not

ἔπεσεν· τεθεμελίωτο γὰρ ἐπὶ τὴν
it fell; for it had been founded on the

πέτραν. 26 καὶ πᾶς ὁ ἀκούων μου
rock. And everyone hearing of me

τοὺς λόγους τούτους καὶ μὴ ποιῶν
– words these and not doing

αὐτοὺς ὁμοιωθήσεται ἀνδρὶ μωρῷ, ὅστις
them shall be likened man to a foolish, who

ᾠκοδόμησεν αὐτοῦ τὴν οἰκίαν ἐπὶ τὴν
built of him the house on the

ἄμμον. 27 καὶ κατέβη ἡ βροχὴ καὶ
sand. And came down the rain and

ἦλθον οἱ ποταμοὶ καὶ ἔπνευσαν οἱ
came the rivers and blew the

ἄνεμοι καὶ προσέκοψαν τῇ οἰκίᾳ ἐκείνῃ,
winds and beat against – house that,

καὶ ἔπεσεν, καὶ ἦν ἡ πτῶσις αὐτῆς
and it fell, and was the fall of it

μεγάλη.
great.

28 And when Jesus finished these sayings, the crowds were astonished at his teaching, [29] for he taught them as one who had authority, and not as their scribes.

28 Καὶ ἐγένετο ὅτε ἐτέλεσεν ὁ Ἰησοῦς
And it came to pass when   finished   –   Jesus
τοὺς λόγους τούτους, ἐξεπλήσσοντο οἱ
–   words   these,   were astounded   the
ὄχλοι ἐπὶ τῇ διδαχῇ αὐτοῦ· 29 ἦν γὰρ
crowds   at   the   teaching   of him;   for he was
διδάσκων αὐτοὺς ὡς ἐξουσίαν ἔχων, καὶ
teaching   them   as   authority   having,   and
οὐχ ὡς οἱ γραμματεῖς αὐτῶν.
not   as   the   scribes   of them.

CHAPTER 8

WHEN he came down from the mountain, great crowds followed him; [2] and behold, a leper came to him and knelt before him, saying, "Lord, if you will, you can make me clean." [3] And he stretched out his hand and touched him, saying, "I will; be clean." And immediately his leprosy was cleansed. [4] And Jesus said to him, "See that you say nothing to any one; but go, show yourself to the priest, and offer the gift that Moses commanded, for a proof to the people." [5] As he entered Caper'na-um, a centurion came forward to him, beseeching him [6] and saying, "Lord, my servant is lying paralyzed at home, in terrible distress." [7] And he said to him, "I will come and heal him."

8 Καταβάντος δὲ αὐτοῦ ἀπὸ τοῦ ὄρους
And coming down   him[a]   from   the   mountain
= as he came down
ἠκολούθησαν αὐτῷ ὄχλοι πολλοί. 2 καὶ
followed   him   crowds   many.   And
ἰδοὺ λεπρὸς προσελθὼν προσεκύνει αὐτῷ
behold   a leper   approaching   worshipped   him
λέγων· κύριε, ἐὰν θέλῃς, δύνασαι με
saying: Lord,   if thou art willing,   thou art able   me
καθαρίσαι. 3 καὶ ἐκτείνας τὴν χεῖρα
to cleanse.   And   stretching out   the(his)   hand
ἥψατο αὐτοῦ λέγων· θέλω, καθαρίσθητι.
he touched   him   saying: I am willing,   be thou cleansed.
καὶ εὐθέως ἐκαθαρίσθη αὐτοῦ ἡ λέπρα.
And   immediately   was cleansed   of him   the   leprosy.
4 καὶ λέγει αὐτῷ ὁ Ἰησοῦς· ὅρα μηδενὶ
And   says   to him   –   Jesus: See   *to* no one
εἴπῃς, ἀλλὰ ὕπαγε σεαυτὸν δεῖξον τῷ
thou tellest, but   go   thyself   show   to the
ἱερεῖ καὶ προσένεγκον τὸ δῶρον ὃ
priest   and   offer   the   gift   which
προσέταξεν Μωϋσῆς, εἰς μαρτύριον αὐτοῖς.
commanded   Moses,   for   a testimony   to them.
5 Εἰσελθόντος δὲ αὐτοῦ εἰς Καφαρναοὺμ
And entering   him[a]   into   Capernaum,
= as he entered
προσῆλθεν αὐτῷ ἑκατόνταρχος παρακαλῶν
approached   *to* him   a centurion   beseeching
αὐτὸν 6 καὶ λέγων· κύριε, ὁ παῖς μου
him   and   saying: Lord,   the   boy   of me
βέβληται ἐν τῇ οἰκίᾳ παραλυτικός,
has been laid [aside] in   the   house   a paralytic,
δεινῶς βασανιζόμενος. 7 λέγει αὐτῷ·
terribly   *being* tortured.   He says   to him:
ἐγὼ ἐλθὼν θεραπεύσω αὐτόν. 8 ἀποκριθεὶς
I   coming   will heal   him.   answering

⁸But the centurion answered him, "Lord, I am not worthy to have you come under my roof; but only say the word, and my servant will be healed. ⁹For I am a man under authority, with soldiers under me; and I say to one, 'Go,' and he goes, and to another, 'Come,' and he comes, and to my slave, 'Do this,' and he does it." ¹⁰When Jesus heard him, he marveled, and said to those who followed him, "Truly, I say to you, not even^m in Israel have I found such faith. ¹¹I tell you, many will come from east and west and sit at table with Abraham, Isaac, and Jacob in the kingdom of heaven, ¹²while the sons of the kingdom will be thrown into the outer darkness; there men will weep and gnash their teeth." ¹³And to the centurion Jesus said, "Go; be it done for you as you have believed." And the servant was healed at that very moment.

14 And when Jesus entered Peter's house, he saw his mother-in-law lying sick with a fever;

δὲ ὁ ἑκατόνταρχος ἔφη· κύριε, οὐκ εἰμὶ
But the centurion said: Lord, I am not

ἱκανὸς ἵνα μου ὑπὸ τὴν στέγην εἰσέλθῃς·
worthy that of me under the roof thou mayest enter;

ἀλλὰ μόνον εἰπὲ λόγῳ, καὶ ἰαθήσεται ὁ παῖς
but only say in a word, and will be healed the boy

μου. 9 καὶ γὰρ ἐγὼ ἄνθρωπός εἰμι
of me. ²also ¹For ²I ⁵a man ⁴am

ὑπὸ ἐξουσίαν, ἔχων ὑπ᾽ ἐμαυτὸν στρατιώτας,
under authority, having under myself soldiers,

καὶ λέγω τούτῳ· πορεύθητι, καὶ πορεύεται,
and I say to this: Go, and he goes,

καὶ ἄλλῳ· ἔρχου, καὶ ἔρχεται, καὶ τῷ
and to another: Come, and he comes, and to the

δούλῳ μου· ποίησον τοῦτο, καὶ ποιεῖ.
slave of me: Do this, and he does [it].

10 ἀκούσας δὲ ὁ Ἰησοῦς ἐθαύμασεν
And hearing – Jesus marvelled

καὶ εἶπεν τοῖς ἀκολουθοῦσιν· ἀμὴν λέγω
and said to the [ones] following: Truly I tell

ὑμῖν, παρ᾽ οὐδενὶ τοσαύτην πίστιν ἐν τῷ
you, from no one such faith in –

Ἰσραὴλ εὗρον. 11 λέγω δὲ ὑμῖν ὅτι
Israel I found. And I tell you that

πολλοὶ ἀπὸ ἀνατολῶν καὶ δυσμῶν ἥξουσιν
many from east and west will come

καὶ ἀνακλιθήσονται μετὰ Ἀβραάμ καὶ
and will recline with Abraham and

Ἰσαὰκ καὶ Ἰακὼβ ἐν τῇ βασιλείᾳ τῶν
Isaac and Jacob in the kingdom of the

οὐρανῶν· 12 οἱ δὲ υἱοὶ τῆς βασιλείας
heavens; but the sons of the kingdom

ἐκβληθήσονται εἰς τὸ σκότος τὸ ἐξώτερον·
will be cast out into the darkness – outer;

ἐκεῖ ἔσται ὁ κλαυθμὸς καὶ ὁ βρυγμὸς
there will be the weeping and the gnashing

τῶν ὀδόντων. 13 καὶ εἶπεν ὁ Ἰησοῦς τῷ
of the teeth. And said – Jesus to the

ἑκατοντάρχῃ· ὕπαγε, ὡς ἐπίστευσας γενη-
centurion: Go, as thou believedst let it

θήτω σοι. καὶ ἰάθη ὁ παῖς ἐν τῇ
be to thee. And was healed the boy in –

ὥρᾳ ἐκείνῃ.
hour that.

14 Καὶ ἐλθὼν ὁ Ἰησοῦς εἰς τὴν οἰκίαν
And coming – Jesus into the house

Πέτρου εἶδεν τὴν πενθερὰν αὐτοῦ βεβλη-
of Peter he saw the mother-in-law of him having been

---

^m Other ancient authorities read *with no one*

¹⁵he touched her hand, and the fever left her, and she rose and served him. ¹⁶That evening they brought to him many who were possessed with demons; and he cast out the spirits with a word, and healed all who were sick. ¹⁷This was to fulfil what was spoken by the prophet Isaiah, "He took our infirmities and bore our diseases."

18 Now when Jesus saw great crowds around him, he gave orders to go over to the other side. ¹⁹And a scribe came up and said to him, "Teacher, I will follow you wherever you go." ²⁰And Jesus said to him, "Foxes have holes, and birds of the air have nests; but the Son of man has nowhere to lay his head." ²¹Another of the disciples said to him, "Lord, let me first go and bury my father." ²²But Jesus said to him, "Follow me, and

μένην καὶ πυρέσσουσαν·
laid [aside] and fever-stricken;

15 καὶ ἥψατο
and he touched

τῆς χειρὸς αὐτῆς, καὶ ἀφῆκεν αὐτὴν ὁ
the hand of her, and left her the

πυρετός· καὶ ἠγέρθη, καὶ διηκόνει αὐτῷ.
fever; and she arose, and ministered to him.

16 Ὀψίας δὲ γενομένης προσήνεγκαν
And evening comingª they brought
= when evening came

αὐτῷ δαιμονιζομένους πολλούς· καὶ ἐξέβαλεν
to him being demon-possessed many; and he expelled

τὰ πνεύματα λόγῳ, καὶ πάντας τοὺς
the spirits with a word, and all the [ones]
= those

κακῶς ἔχοντας ἐθεράπευσεν· 17 ὅπως
ill having he healed; so that

πληρωθῇ τὸ ῥηθὲν διὰ Ἡσαΐου τοῦ
was fulfilled the [thing] spoken through Isaiah the

προφήτου λέγοντος· αὐτὸς τὰς ἀσθενείας
prophet saying: He the weaknesses

ἡμῶν ἔλαβεν καὶ τὰς νόσους ἐβάστασεν.
of us took and the diseases he bore.

18 Ἰδὼν δὲ ὁ Ἰησοῦς ὄχλον περὶ
But ²seeing - ¹Jesus a crowd around

αὐτὸν ἐκέλευσεν ἀπελθεῖν εἰς τὸ πέραν.
him commanded to go away to the other side.

19 Καὶ προσελθὼν εἷς γραμματεὺς εἶπεν
And approaching one scribe said

αὐτῷ· διδάςκαλε, ἀκολουθήσω σοι
to him: Teacher, I will follow thee

ὅπου ἐὰν ἀπέρχῃ. 20 καὶ λέγει αὐτῷ
wherever thou mayest go. And says to him

ὁ Ἰησοῦς· αἱ ἀλώπεκες φωλεοὺς ἔχουσιν
- Jesus: The foxes holes have

καὶ τὰ πετεινὰ τοῦ οὐρανοῦ κατα-
and the birds of the heaven nests,

σκηνώσεις, ὁ δὲ υἱὸς τοῦ ἀνθρώπου
but the Son of man

οὐκ ἔχει ποῦ τὴν κεφαλὴν κλίνῃ.
has not where the(his) head he may lay.

21 ἕτερος δὲ τῶν μαθητῶν εἶπεν
And another of the disciples said

αὐτῷ· κύριε, ἐπίτρεψόν μοι πρῶτον
to him: Lord, allow me first

ἀπελθεῖν καὶ θάψαι τὸν πατέρα μου.
to go away and bury the father of me.

22 ὁ δὲ Ἰησοῦς λέγει αὐτῷ· ἀκολούθει
- But Jesus says to him: Follow thou

leave the dead to bury their own dead."
23 And when he got into the boat, his disciples followed him. [24]And behold, there arose a great storm on the sea, so that the boat was being swamped by the waves; but he was asleep. [25]And they went and woke him, saying, "Save, Lord; we are perishing." [26]And he said to them, "Why are you afraid, O men of little faith?" Then he rose and rebuked the winds and the sea; and there was a great calm. [27]And the men marveled, saying, "What sort of man is this, that even winds and sea obey him?"
28 And when he came to the other side, to the country of the Gadarenes,[n] two demoniacs met him, coming out of the tombs, so fierce that no one could pass that way. [29]And behold, they cried out, "What have you to do with us, O Son of God? Have you come here to torment us before the time?" [30]Now a herd

[n] Other ancient authorities read *Gergesenes*; some, *Gerasenes*

μοι, καὶ ἄφες τοὺς νεκροὺς θάψαι τοὺς
me, and leave the dead to bury the

ἑαυτῶν νεκρούς.
of themselves dead.

23 Καὶ ἐμβάντι αὐτῷ εἰς τὸ πλοῖον,
And embarking him[e] in the ship,
= as he embarked

ἠκολούθησαν αὐτῷ οἱ μαθηταὶ αὐτοῦ.
followed him the disciples of him.

24 καὶ ἰδοὺ σεισμὸς μέγας ἐγένετο ἐν
And behold storm a great there was in

τῇ θαλάσσῃ, ὥστε τὸ πλοῖον καλύπτ-
the sea, so as the ship to be en-

εσθαι ὑπὸ τῶν κυμάτων· αὐτὸς δὲ ἐκάθευδεν.
veloped by the waves; but he was sleeping.

25 καὶ προσελθόντες ἤγειραν αὐτὸν λέγοντες·
And approaching they roused him saying:

κύριε, σῶσον, ἀπολλύμεθα. 26 καὶ λέγει
Lord, save, we are perishing. And he says

αὐτοῖς· τί δειλοί ἐστε, ὀλιγόπιστοι;
to them: Why fearful are ye, little-faiths?

τότε ἐγερθεὶς ἐπετίμησεν τοῖς ἀνέμοις καὶ
Then rising he rebuked the winds and

τῇ θαλάσσῃ, καὶ ἐγένετο γαλήνη μεγάλη.
the sea, and there was calm a great.

27 οἱ δὲ ἄνθρωποι ἐθαύμασαν λέγοντες·
And the men marvelled saying:

ποταπός ἐστιν οὗτος, ὅτι καὶ οἱ ἄνεμοι
Of what sort is this [man], that even the winds

καὶ ἡ θάλασσα αὐτῷ ὑπακούουσιν;
and the sea him obey?

28 Καὶ ἐλθόντος αὐτοῦ εἰς τὸ πέραν εἰς
And coming him[a] to the other side into
= when he came

τὴν χώραν τῶν Γαδαρηνῶν ὑπήντησαν
the country of the Gadarenes met

αὐτῷ δύο δαιμονιζόμενοι ἐκ τῶν μνημείων
him two demon-possessed out of the tombs

ἐξερχόμενοι, χαλεποὶ λίαν, ὥστε μὴ
coming out, dangerous exceedingly, so as not

ἰσχύειν τινὰ παρελθεῖν διὰ τῆς ὁδοῦ
to be able anyone[b] to pass through — way

ἐκείνης. 29 καὶ ἰδοὺ ἔκραξαν λέγοντες·
that. And behold they cried out saying:

τί ἡμῖν καὶ σοί, υἱὲ τοῦ θεοῦ; ἦλθες
What to us and to thee, Son — of God? camest thou

ὧδε πρὸ καιροῦ βασανίσαι ἡμᾶς; 30 ἦν
here before [the] time to torture us? there was

of many swine was feeding at some distance from them. ³¹And the demons begged him, "If you cast us out, send us away into the herd of swine." ³²And he said to them, "Go." So they came out and went into the swine; and behold, the whole herd rushed down the steep bank into the sea, and perished in the waters. ³³The herdsmen fled, and going into the city they told everything, and what had happened to the demoniacs. ³⁴And behold, all the city came out to meet Jesus; and when they saw him, they begged him to leave their neighborhood.

δὲ   μακρὰν   ἀπ'   αὐτῶν   ἀγέλη   χοίρων
Now   far off   from   them   a herd   pigs

πολλῶν   βοσκομένη.   31 οἱ   δὲ   δαίμονες
of many   feeding.   And the   demons

παρεκάλουν   αὐτὸν   λέγοντες·   εἰ   ἐκβάλλεις
besought   him   saying: If   thou expellest

ἡμᾶς,   ἀπόστειλον   ἡμᾶς   εἰς   τὴν   ἀγέλην
us,   send   us   into   the   herd

τῶν   χοίρων.   32 καὶ   εἶπεν   αὐτοῖς·
of the   pigs.   And   he said   to them:

ὑπάγετε.   οἱ   δὲ   ἐξελθόντες   ἀπῆλθον   εἰς
Go ye.   So the   coming out [ones]   went away   into

τοὺς   χοίρους·   καὶ   ἰδοὺ   ὥρμησεν   πᾶσα   ἡ
the   pigs;   and behold   rushed   all   the

ἀγέλη   κατὰ   τοῦ   κρημνοῦ   εἰς   τὴν   θάλασσαν,
herd   down   the   precipice   into   the   sea,

καὶ   ἀπέθανον   ἐν   τοῖς   ὕδασιν.   33 οἱ
and   died   in   the   waters.   the

δὲ   βόσκοντες   ἔφυγον,   καὶ   ἀπελθόντες
But   feeding [ones]   fled,   and   going away

εἰς   τὴν   πόλιν   ἀπήγγειλαν   πάντα   καὶ
into   the   city   reported   all things   and

τὰ   τῶν   δαιμονιζομένων.   34 καὶ   ἰδοὺ
the [things] of the   demon-possessed [ones].   And behold

πᾶσα ἡ   πόλις   ἐξῆλθεν   εἰς   ὑπάντησιν
all   the   city   came out   with a view to   a meeting [with]

τῷ   Ἰησοῦ,   καὶ   ἰδόντες   αὐτὸν   παρεκάλεσαν
-   Jesus,   and   seeing   ²him   ¹besought

ὅπως   μεταβῇ   ἀπὸ   τῶν   ὁρίων   αὐτῶν.
so that   he might remove from   the   borders   of them.

CHAPTER 9

AND getting into a boat he crossed over and came to his own city. ²And behold, they brought to him a paralytic, lying on his bed; and when Jesus saw their faith he said to the paralytic, "Take heart, my son; your sins are forgiven." ³And behold, some of the scribes said to themselves, "This man is blaspheming." ⁴But

9 Καὶ   ἐμβὰς   εἰς   πλοῖον   διεπέρασεν,
And   embarking   in   a ship   he crossed over,

καὶ   ἦλθεν   εἰς   τὴν   ἰδίαν   πόλιν.   2 Καὶ
and   came   into   the(his)   own   city.   And

ἰδοὺ   προσέφερον   αὐτῷ   παραλυτικὸν   ἐπὶ
behold   they brought   to him   a paralytic   on

κλίνης   βεβλημένον.   καὶ   ἰδὼν   ὁ   Ἰησοῦς
a mattress   having been laid.   And   ²seeing   -   ¹Jesus

τὴν   πίστιν   αὐτῶν   εἶπεν   τῷ   παραλυτικῷ·
the   faith   of them   said   to the   paralytic:

θάρσει,   τέκνον,   ἀφίενταί   σου   αἱ   ἁμαρτίαι.
Be of good cheer,   child,   are forgiven of thee the   sins.

3 καὶ   ἰδού   τινες   τῶν   γραμματέων   εἶπαν
And   behold   some   of the   scribes   said

ἐν   ἑαυτοῖς·   οὗτος   βλασφημεῖ.   4 καὶ
among themselves: This [man]   blasphemes.   And

Jesus, knowing[o] their thoughts, said, "Why do you think evil in your hearts? [5]For which is easier, to say, 'Your sins are forgiven,' or to say, 'Rise and walk'? [6]But that you may know that the Son of man has authority on earth to forgive sins"—he then said to the paralytic— "Rise, take up your bed and go home." [7]And he rose and went home. [8]When the crowds saw it, they were afraid, and they glorified God, who had given such authority to men.

[9]As Jesus passed on from there, he saw a man called Matthew sitting at the tax office; and he said to him, "Follow me." And he rose and followed him.

[10]And as he sat at table in the house, behold, many tax collectors and sinners came and sat down with Jesus and his disciples. [11]And when the Pharisees saw this, they said to his disciples, "Why does your teacher eat with tax collectors and sinners?" [12]But when

[o] Other ancient authorities read *seeing*

εἰδὼς ὁ Ἰησοῦς τὰς ἐνθυμήσεις αὐτῶν
[2]knowing - [1]Jesus the thoughts of them

εἶπεν· ἱνατί ἐνθυμεῖσθε πονηρὰ ἐν ταῖς
said: Why think ye evil things in the

καρδίαις ὑμῶν; 5 τί γάρ ἐστιν εὐκοπώ-
hearts of you? for which is easier,

τερον, εἰπεῖν· ἀφίενταί σου αἱ ἁμαρτίαι, ἢ
to say: [4]are forgiven [3]of thee [1]The [2]sins, or

εἰπεῖν· ἔγειρε καὶ περιπάτει; 6 ἵνα δὲ
to say: Rise and walk? But in order that

εἰδῆτε ὅτι ἐξουσίαν ἔχει ὁ υἱὸς τοῦ
ye may know that authority has the Son

ἀνθρώπου ἐπὶ τῆς γῆς ἀφιέναι ἁμαρτίας
of man on the earth to forgive sins—

τότε λέγει τῷ παραλυτικῷ· ἔγειρε ἆρόν
then he says to the paralytic: Rise[,] take

σου τὴν κλίνην καὶ ὕπαγε εἰς τὸν οἶκόν
of thee the mattress and go to the house

σου. 7 καὶ ἐγερθεὶς ἀπῆλθεν εἰς τὸν
of thee. And rising he went away to the

οἶκον αὐτοῦ. 8 ἰδόντες δὲ οἱ ὄχλοι
house of him. But seeing the crowds

ἐφοβήθησαν καὶ ἐδόξασαν τὸν θεὸν τὸν
feared and glorified - God the [one]

δόντα ἐξουσίαν τοιαύτην τοῖς ἀνθρώποις.
giving [2]authority [1]such - to men.

9 Καὶ παράγων ὁ Ἰησοῦς ἐκεῖθεν εἶδεν
And [2]passing by - [1]Jesus thence saw

ἄνθρωπον καθήμενον ἐπὶ τὸ τελώνιον,
a man sitting at the custom house,

Μαθθαῖον λεγόμενον, καὶ λέγει αὐτῷ·
Matthew named, and says to him:

ἀκολούθει μοι. καὶ ἀναστὰς ἠκολούθησεν
Follow me. And rising up he followed

αὐτῷ. 10 Καὶ ἐγένετο αὐτοῦ ἀνακει-
him. And it came to pass him reclin-
=as he was reclining

μένου ἐν τῇ οἰκίᾳ, καὶ ἰδοὺ πολλοὶ
ing[a] in the house, and behold many

τελῶναι καὶ ἁμαρτωλοὶ ἐλθόντες συνανέκειντο
tax-collectors and sinners coming reclined at table with

τῷ Ἰησοῦ καὶ τοῖς μαθηταῖς αὐτοῦ.
- Jesus and the disciples of him.

11 καὶ ἰδόντες οἱ Φαρισαῖοι ἔλεγον τοῖς
And [2]seeing [1]the [3]Pharisees said to the

μαθηταῖς αὐτοῦ· διὰ τί μετὰ τῶν τελωλῶν
disciples of him: Why with - tax-collectors

καὶ ἁμαρτωλῶν ἐσθίει ὁ διδάσκαλος ὑμῶν;
and sinners eats the teacher of you?

he heard it, he said, "Those who are well have no need of a physician, but those who are sick. ¹³Go and learn what this means, 'I desire mercy, and not sacrifice.' For I came not to call the righteous, but sinners."

14 Then the disciples of John came to him, saying, "Why do we and the Pharisees fast,ᵖ but your disciples do not fast?" ¹⁵And Jesus said to them, "Can the wedding guests mourn as long as the bridegroom is with them? The days will come, when the bridegroom is taken away from them, and then they will fast. ¹⁶And no one puts a piece of unshrunk cloth on an old garment, for the patch tears away from the garment, and a worse tear is made. ¹⁷Neither is new wine put into old wineskins; if it is, the skins burst, and the wine is spilled, and the skins are destroyed; but

12 ὁ   δὲ   ἀκούσας   εἶπεν·   οὐ   χρείαν
   But he   hearing   said: Not   need

ἔχουσιν   οἱ   ἰσχύοντες   ἰατροῦ   ἀλλ'   οἱ
have   the [ones] being strong of a physician but   the[ones]
                                                    =those

κακῶς   ἔχοντες.   13 πορευθέντες   δὲ   μάθετε
Ill   having.   But going   learn ye
who are ill.

τί   ἐστιν·   ἔλεος   θέλω   καὶ   οὐ   θυσίαν·   οὐ
what it is: Mercy   I desire and   not   sacrifice;   not

γὰρ   ἦλθον   καλέσαι   δικαίους   ἀλλὰ
for   I came   to call   righteous [people]   but

ἁμαρτωλούς.
sinners.

14 Τότε   προσέρχονται   αὐτῷ   οἱ   μαθηταὶ
   Then   approach   to him   the   disciples

Ἰωάννου   λέγοντες·   διὰ τί   ἡμεῖς   καὶ   οἱ
of John   saying: Why   we   and   the

Φαρισαῖοι   νηστεύομεν,   οἱ   δὲ   μαθηταί
Pharisees   fast,   but the   disciples

σου   οὐ   νηστεύουσιν;   15 καὶ   εἶπεν
of thee   fast not?   And   said

αὐτοῖς   ὁ   Ἰησοῦς·   μὴ   δύνανται   οἱ
to them   -   Jesus: not   Can   the

υἱοὶ   τοῦ   νυμφῶνος   πενθεῖν,   ἐφ'   ὅσον
sons   of the bridechamber to mourn,   so long as

μετ'   αὐτῶν   ἐστιν   ὁ   νυμφίος;   ἐλεύσονται
with   them   is   the   bridegroom?   ²will come

δὲ   ἡμέραι   ὅταν   ἀπαρθῇ   ἀπ'   αὐτῶν   ὁ
¹but   ²days   when   is taken away from   them   the

νυμφίος,   καὶ   τότε   νηστεύσουσιν.   16 οὐδεὶς
bridegroom,   and   then   they will fast.   no one

δὲ   ἐπιβάλλει   ἐπίβλημα   ῥάκους   ἀγνάφου
Now   puts on   a patch   cloth   of unfulled

ἐπὶ   ἱματίῳ   παλαιῷ·   αἴρει   γὰρ   τὸ
on   garment   an old;   for takes away   the

πλήρωμα   αὐτοῦ   ἀπὸ   τοῦ   ἱματίου,   καὶ
fullness   of it   from   the   garment,   and

χεῖρον   σχίσμα   γίνεται.   17 οὐδὲ
a worse   rent   becomes.   Neither

βάλλουσιν   οἶνον   νέον   εἰς   ἀσκοὺς
do they put   wine   new   into   wineskins

παλαιούς·   εἰ   δὲ   μή   γε,   ῥήγνυνται
old;   otherwise,   are burst

οἱ   ἀσκοί,   καὶ   ὁ   οἶνος   ἐκχεῖται   καὶ
the   wineskins,   and   the   wine   is poured out   and

οἱ   ἀσκοὶ   ἀπόλλυνται.   ἀλλὰ   βάλλουσιν
the   wineskins   are destroyed.   But   they put

new wine is put into fresh wineskins, and so both are preserved."

18 While he was thus speaking to them, behold, a ruler came in and knelt before him, saying, "My daughter has just died; but come and lay your hand on her, and she will live." ¹⁹And Jesus rose and followed him, with his disciples. ²⁰And behold, a woman who had suffered from a hemorrhage for twelve years came up behind him and touched the fringe of his garment; ²¹for she said to herself, "If I only touch his garment, I shall be made well." ²²Jesus turned, and seeing her he said, "Take heart, daughter; your faith has made you well." And instantly the woman was made well. ²³And when Jesus came to the ruler's house, and saw the flute players, and the crowd making a tumult, ²⁴he said, "Depart; for the girl is not dead but sleeping." And they laughed at him. ²⁵But when the crowd had been put outside, he went in and

οἶνον νέον εἰς ἀσκοὺς καινούς, καὶ
wine new into wineskins fresh, and
ἀμφότεροι συντηροῦνται.
both are preserved.

18 Ταῦτα αὐτοῦ λαλοῦντος αὐτοῖς,
These things him speakingᵃ to them,
=As he was speaking these things
ἰδοὺ ἄρχων [εἷς] προσελθὼν προσ-
behold ruler one approaching wor-
εκύνει αὐτῷ λέγων ὅτι ἡ θυγάτηρ
shipped him saying[,] – The daughter
μου ἄρτι ἐτελεύτησεν· ἀλλὰ ἐλθὼν
of me just now died; but coming
ἐπίθες τὴν χεῖρά σου ἐπ' αὐτήν,
lay on the hand of thee on her,
καὶ ζήσεται. 19 καὶ ἐγερθεὶς ὁ Ἰησοῦς
and she will live. And rising – Jesus
ἠκολούθει αὐτῷ καὶ οἱ μαθηταὶ αὐτοῦ.
followed him[.] also the disciples of him.
20 Καὶ ἰδοὺ γυνὴ αἱμορροοῦσα
And behold a woman suffering from a flow of blood
δώδεκα ἔτη προσελθοῦσα ὄπισθεν ἥψατο
twelve years approaching behind touched
τοῦ κρασπέδου τοῦ ἱματίου αὐτοῦ·
the fringe of the garment of him;
21 ἔλεγεν γὰρ ἐν ἑαυτῇ· ἐὰν μόνον
for she was saying in herself: If only
ἅψωμαι τοῦ ἱματίου αὐτοῦ, σωθήσομαι.
I may touch the garment of him, I shall be healed.
22 ὁ δὲ Ἰησοῦς στραφεὶς καὶ ἰδὼν
– And Jesus turning and seeing
αὐτὴν εἶπεν· θάρσει, θύγατερ· ἡ
her said: Be of good cheer, daughter; the
πίστις σου σέσωκέν σε. καὶ ἐσώθη
faith of thee has healed thee. And was healed
ἡ γυνὴ ἀπὸ τῆς ὥρας ἐκείνης. 23 Καὶ
the woman from – hour that. And
ἐλθὼν ὁ Ἰησοῦς εἰς τὴν οἰκίαν τοῦ ἄρχοντος
coming – Jesus into the house of the ruler
καὶ ἰδὼν τοὺς αὐλητὰς καὶ τὸν ὄχλον
and seeing the flute-players and the crowd
θορυβούμενον 24 ἔλεγεν· ἀναχωρεῖτε· οὐ
terrified he said: Depart ye; not
γὰρ ἀπέθανεν τὸ κοράσιον ἀλλὰ καθεύδει.
for died the girl but sleeps.
καὶ κατεγέλων αὐτοῦ. 25 ὅτε δὲ
And they ridiculed him. But when
ἐξεβλήθη ὁ ὄχλος, εἰσελθὼν ἐκράτησεν
was put out the crowd, entering he took hold of

took her by the hand, and the girl arose. [26]And the report of this went through all that district.

27 And as Jesus passed on from there, two blind men followed him, crying aloud, "Have mercy on us, Son of David." [28]When he entered the house, the blind men came to him; and Jesus said to them, "Do you believe that I am able to do this?" They said to him, "Yes, Lord."[29]Then he touched their eyes, saying, "According to your faith be it done to you." [30]And their eyes were opened. And Jesus sternly charged them, "See that no one knows it." [31]But they went away and spread his fame through all that district.

32 As they were going away, behold, a dumb demoniac was brought to him. [33]And when the demon had been cast out, the dumb man spoke; and the crowds marveled, saying, "Never was anything like this seen in Israel." [34]But the Pharisees said, "He casts out

τῆς   χειρὸς   αὐτῆς,   καὶ ἠγέρθη τὸ κορα-
the   hand   of her,   and was raised the   girl.

σιον.   26 καὶ   ἐξῆλθεν ἡ   φήμη   αὕτη
          And   went out   -   report   this

εἰς ὅλην   τὴν γῆν ἐκείνην.   27 Καὶ
into   all   -   land that.   And

παράγοντι ἐκεῖθεν τῷ   Ἰησοῦ ἠκολούθησαν
passing by   thence   -   Jesus[e]   followed
= as Jesus passed by thence

δύο τυφλοὶ κράζοντες καὶ λέγοντες· ἐλέησον
two blind men crying out   and   saying: Pity

ἡμᾶς,   υἱὸς Δαυίδ.   28 ἐλθόντι δὲ εἰς
us,   son   of David.   And coming[e]   into
                              = when he came

τὴν οἰκίαν προσῆλθον αὐτῷ οἱ τυφλοί,
the   house   approached   to him   the blind men,

καὶ λέγει αὐτοῖς ὁ Ἰησοῦς· πιστεύετε
and   says   to them   -   Jesus: Believe ye

ὅτι δύναμαι τοῦτο ποιῆσαι; λέγουσιν
that   I can   this   to do?   They say

αὐτῷ· ναί, κύριε. 29 τότε ἥψατο τῶν
to him: Yes, Lord.   Then he touched the

ὀφθαλμῶν αὐτῶν λέγων· κατὰ τὴν
eyes   of them   saying: According to the

πίστιν ὑμῶν γενηθήτω ὑμῖν. 30 καὶ
faith   of you   let it be   to you.   And

ἠνεῴχθησαν αὐτῶν οἱ ὀφθαλμοί. καὶ
were opened   of them   the   eyes.   And

ἐνεβριμήθη αὐτοῖς ὁ Ἰησοῦς λέγων·
sternly admonished them   -   Jesus   saying:

ὁρᾶτε μηδεὶς γινωσκέτω. 31 οἱ δὲ
See   [2]no one   [1]let [3]know.   But they

ἐξελθόντες διεφήμισαν αὐτὸν ἐν ὅλη
going out   spread about   him   in   all

τῇ γῇ ἐκείνη. 32 Αὐτῶν δὲ ἐξερχομένων,
-   land that.   And them   going out,[a]
                              = as they were going out,

ἰδοὺ προσήνεγκαν αὐτῷ κωφὸν δαι-
behold   they brought   to him   a dumb man being

μονιζόμενον.   33 καὶ ἐκβληθέντος τοῦ
demon-possessed.   And   being expelled   the
                              = when the demon was expelled

δαιμονίου ἐλάλησεν ὁ κωφός. καὶ ἐθαύμασαν
demon[a]   spoke   the dumb man. And   marvelled

οἱ ὄχλοι λέγοντες· οὐδέποτε ἐφάνη οὕτως
the crowds saying: Never   it appeared thus

ἐν τῷ Ἰσραήλ. 34 οἱ δὲ Φαρισαῖοι
in   -   Israel.   But the   Pharisees

demons by the prince of demons."

35 And Jesus went about all the cities and villages, teaching in their synagogues and preaching the gospel of the kingdom, and healing every disease and every infirmity. ³⁶When he saw the crowds, he had compassion for them, because they were harassed and helpless, like sheep without a shepherd. ³⁷Then he said to his disciples, "The harvest is plentiful, but the laborers are few; ³⁸pray therefore the Lord of the harvest to send out laborers into his harvest."

CHAPTER 10

AND he called to him his twelve disciples and gave them authority over unclean spirits, to cast them out, and to heal every disease and every infirmity. ²The names of the twelve apostles are these: first, Simon, who is called Peter, and Andrew his brother; James the son of Zeb'edee, and John his

ἔλεγον· ἐν τῷ ἄρχοντι τῶν δαιμονίων
said: By the ruler of the demons

ἐκβάλλει τὰ δαιμόνια.
he expels the demons.

35 Καὶ περιῆγεν ὁ Ἰησοῦς τὰς
And went about - Jesus the

πόλεις πάσας καὶ τὰς κώμας, διδάσκων
cities all and the villages, teaching

ἐν ταῖς συναγωγαῖς αὐτῶν καὶ κηρύσσων
in the synagogues of them and proclaiming

τὸ εὐαγγέλιον τῆς βασιλείας καὶ θεραπεύων
the gospel of the kingdom and healing

πᾶσαν νόσον καὶ πᾶσαν μαλακίαν.
every disease and every illness.

36 Ἰδὼν δὲ τοὺς ὄχλους ἐσπλαγχνίσθη
And seeing the crowds he was filled with tenderness

περὶ αὐτῶν, ὅτι ἦσαν ἐσκυλμένοι καὶ
concerning them, because they were distressed and

ἐρριμμένοι ὡσεὶ πρόβατα μὴ ἔχοντα
prostrate as sheep not having

ποιμένα. 37 τότε λέγει τοῖς μαθηταῖς
a shepherd. Then he says to the disciples

αὐτοῦ· ὁ μὲν θερισμὸς πολύς, οἱ δὲ
of him: Indeed the harvest [is] much, but the

ἐργάται ὀλίγοι· 38 δεήθητε οὖν τοῦ κυρίου
workmen few; pray ye therefore the Lord

τοῦ θερισμοῦ ὅπως ἐκβάλῃ
of the harvest so that he may thrust forth

ἐργάτας εἰς τὸν θερισμὸν αὐτοῦ. 10 Καὶ
workmen into the harvest of him. And

προσκαλεσάμενος τοὺς δώδεκα μαθητὰς
calling forward the twelve disciples

αὐτοῦ ἔδωκεν αὐτοῖς ἐξουσίαν πνευμάτων
of him he gave to them authority of(over) spirits

ἀκαθάρτων ὥστε ἐκβάλλειν αὐτά, καὶ
unclean so as to expel them, and

θεραπεύειν πᾶσαν νόσον καὶ πᾶσαν μαλα-
to heal every disease and every ill-

κίαν. 2 Τῶν δὲ δώδεκα ἀποστόλων
ness. Now of the twelve apostles

τὰ ὀνόματά ἐστιν ταῦτα· πρῶτος Σίμων
the names is(are) these: first Simon

ὁ λεγόμενος Πέτρος καὶ Ἀνδρέας ὁ
the [one] named Peter and Andrew the

ἀδελφὸς αὐτοῦ, καὶ Ἰάκωβος ὁ τοῦ
brother of him, and James the [son] -

brother; ³Philip and Bartholomew; Thomas and Matthew the tax collector; James the son of Alphaeus, and Thaddaeus;*q* ⁴Simon the Cananaean, and Judas Iscariot, who betrayed him.

5 These twelve Jesus sent out, charging them, "Go nowhere among the Gentiles, and enter no town of the Samaritans, ⁶but go rather to the lost sheep of the house of Israel. ⁷And preach as you go, saying, 'The kingdom of heaven is at hand.' ⁸Heal the sick, raise the dead, cleanse lepers, cast out demons. You received without pay, give without pay. ⁹Take no gold, nor silver, nor copper in your belts, ¹⁰no bag for your journey, nor two tunics, nor sandals, nor a staff; for the laborer deserves his food. ¹¹And whatever town or village you enter, find out who is worthy in it, and stay with him

Ζεβεδαίου καὶ Ἰωάννης ὁ ἀδελφὸς αὐτοῦ,
of Zebedee and John the brother of him,

3 Φίλιππος καὶ Βαρθολομαῖος, Θωμᾶς
Philip and Bartholomew, Thomas

καὶ Μαθθαῖος ὁ τελώνης, Ἰάκωβος
and Matthew the tax-collector, James

ὁ τοῦ Ἀλφαίου καὶ Θαδδαῖος, 4 Σίμων
the [son] – of Alphæus and Thaddæus, Simon

ὁ Καναναῖος καὶ Ἰούδας ὁ Ἰσκαριώτης
the Cananæan and Judas – Iscariot

ὁ καὶ παραδοὺς αὐτόν. 5 Τούτους
the [one] also betraying him. These

τοὺς δώδεκα ἀπέστειλεν ὁ Ἰησοῦς
– twelve sent forth – Jesus

παραγγείλας αὐτοῖς λέγων·
giving charge to them saying:

Εἰς ὁδὸν ἐθνῶν μὴ ἀπέλθητε, καὶ
Into [the] way of [the] nations go ye not, and

εἰς πόλιν Σαμαριτῶν μὴ εἰσέλθητε·
into a city of Samaritans enter not;

6 πορεύεσθε δὲ μᾶλλον πρὸς τὰ πρόβατα
but go rather unto the sheep

τὰ ἀπολωλότα οἴκου Ἰσραήλ. 7 πορευ-
the lost of [the] house of Israel. And

όμενοι δὲ κηρύσσετε λέγοντες ὅτι ἤγγικεν
going proclaim ye saying[,] – has drawn near

ἡ βασιλεία τῶν οὐρανῶν. 8 ἀσθενοῦντας
The kingdom of the heavens. Ailing [ones]

θεραπεύετε, νεκροὺς ἐγείρετε, λεπροὺς
heal ye, dead [ones] raise, lepers

καθαρίζετε, δαιμόνια ἐκβάλλετε· δωρεὰν
cleanse, demons expel; freely

ἐλάβετε, δωρεὰν δότε. 9 Μὴ κτήσησθε
ye received, freely give. Do not provide

χρυσὸν μηδὲ ἄργυρον μηδὲ χαλκὸν εἰς
gold nor silver nor brass in

τὰς ζώνας ὑμῶν, 10 μὴ πήραν εἰς ὁδὸν
the girdles of you, not a wallet for [the] way

μηδὲ δύο χιτῶνας μηδὲ ὑποδήματα μηδὲ
nor two tunics nor sandals nor

ῥάβδον· ἄξιος γὰρ ὁ ἐργάτης τῆς
a staff; for worthy [is] the workman of the

τροφῆς αὐτοῦ. 11 εἰς ἣν δ' ἂν πόλιν
food of him. And into whatever city

ἢ κώμην εἰσέλθητε, ἐξετάσατε τίς ἐν
or village ye may enter, inquire who in

αὐτῇ ἄξιός ἐστιν· κἀκεῖ μείνατε ἕως ἂν
it worthy is; and there remain until

q Other ancient authorities read *Lebbaeus* or *Lebbaeus called Thaddaeus*

until you depart. [12]As you enter the house, salute it. [13]And if the house is worthy, let your peace come upon it; but if it is not worthy, let your peace return to you. [14]And if any one will not receive you or listen to your words, shake off the dust from your feet as you leave that house or town. [15]Truly, I say to you, it shall be more tolerable on the day of judgment for the land of Sodom and Gomor'rah than for that town.

16 "Behold, I send you out as sheep in the midst of wolves; so be wise as serpents and innocent as doves. [17]Beware of men; for they will deliver you up to councils, and flog you in their synagogues, [18]and you will be dragged before governors and kings for my sake, to bear testimony before them and the Gentiles. [19]When they deliver you up, do not be anxious how you are to speak or what you are to say; for what you are to say will be given to you in that hour; [20]for

ἐξέλθητε.
ye may go out.

12 εἰσερχόμενοι δὲ εἰς τὴν
And entering into the

οἰκίαν ἀσπάσασθε αὐτήν· 13 καὶ ἐὰν μὲν
house greet it; and if indeed

ᾖ ἡ οἰκία ἀξία, ἐλθάτω ἡ εἰρήνη ὑμῶν
be the house worthy, let come the peace of you

ἐπ᾽ αὐτήν· ἐὰν δὲ μὴ ᾖ ἀξία, ἡ εἰρήνη
on it; but if it be not worthy, the peace

ὑμῶν πρὸς ὑμᾶς ἐπιστραφήτω. 14 καὶ
of you unto you let return. And

ὃς ἂν μὴ δέξηται ὑμᾶς μηδὲ ἀκούσῃ
whoever may not receive you nor hear

τοὺς λόγους ὑμῶν, ἐξερχόμενοι ἔξω
the words of you, going out outside

τῆς οἰκίας ἢ τῆς πόλεως ἐκείνης ἐκτινά-
- house or - city that shake

ξατε τὸν κονιορτὸν τῶν ποδῶν ὑμῶν.
off the dust of the feet of you.

15 ἀμὴν λέγω ὑμῖν, ἀνεκτότερον ἔσται
Truly I tell you, more tolerable it will be [for]

γῇ Σοδόμων καὶ Γομόρρων ἐν ἡμέρᾳ κρίσεως
[the] land of Sodom and Gomorra in [the] day of judgment

ἢ τῇ πόλει ἐκείνῃ. 16 Ἰδοὺ ἐγὼ
than [for] - city that. Behold I

ἀποστέλλω ὑμᾶς ὡς πρόβατα ἐν μέσῳ
send forth you as sheep in [the] midst

λύκων· γίνεσθε οὖν φρόνιμοι ὡς οἱ
of wolves; be ye therefore prudent as -

ὄφεις καὶ ἀκέραιοι ὡς αἱ περιστεραί.
serpents and harmless as - doves.

17 Προσέχετε δὲ ἀπὸ τῶν ἀνθρώπων·
And beware from(of) - men;

παραδώσουσιν γὰρ ὑμᾶς εἰς συνέδρια,
for they will deliver up you to councils,

καὶ ἐν ταῖς συναγωγαῖς αὐτῶν μαστιγώ-
and in the synagogues of them they will

σουσιν ὑμᾶς· 18 καὶ ἐπὶ ἡγεμόνας δὲ καὶ
scourge you; and before leaders and also

βασιλεῖς ἀχθήσεσθε ἕνεκεν ἐμοῦ, εἰς
kings ye will be led for the sake of me, for

μαρτύριον αὐτοῖς καὶ τοῖς ἔθνεσιν.
a testimony to them and to the nations.

19 ὅταν δὲ παραδῶσιν ὑμᾶς, μὴ μεριμνή-
But when they deliver up you, do not be

σητε πῶς ἢ τί λαλήσητε· δοθήσεται
anxious how or what ye may say; [2]it will be given

γὰρ ὑμῖν ἐν ἐκείνῃ τῇ ὥρᾳ τί λαλήσητε·
[1]for to you in that - hour what ye may say;

it is not you who speak, but the Spirit of your Father speaking through you. [21] Brother will deliver up brother to death, and the father his child, and children will rise against parents and have them put to death; [22] and you will be hated by all for my name's sake. But he who endures to the end will be saved. [23] When they persecute you in one town, flee to the next; for truly, I say to you, you will not have gone through all the towns of Israel, before the Son of man comes.

24 "A disciple is not above his teacher, nor a servant above his master; [25] it is enough for the disciple to be like his teacher, and the servant like his master. If they have called the master of the house Be-el'zebul, how much more will they malign those of his household.

26 "So have no fear of them; for nothing is covered that will not be revealed, or hidden that will not be known. [27] What I tell you in the dark, utter in the light;

20 οὐ   γὰρ   ὑμεῖς   ἐστε   οἱ   λαλοῦντες,
   for not   ye   are the [ones] speaking,

ἀλλὰ   τὸ   πνεῦμα   τοῦ   πατρὸς   ὑμῶν   τὸ
but   the   Spirit   of the   Father   of you   the [one]

λαλοῦν   ἐν   ὑμῖν.   21 παραδώσει   δὲ
speaking   in   you.   And [2] will deliver up

ἀδελφὸς   ἀδελφὸν   εἰς   θάνατον   καὶ   πατὴρ
[1] brother   brother   to   death   and   father

τέκνον,   καὶ   ἐπαναστήσονται   τέκνα   ἐπὶ
child,   and   will stand up   children   against

γονεῖς   καὶ   θανατώσουσιν   αὐτούς.   22 καὶ
parents   and   put to death   them.   And

ἔσεσθε   μισούμενοι   ὑπὸ   πάντων   διὰ
ye will be   being hated   by   all men   on account of

τὸ   ὄνομά   μου·   ὁ   δὲ   ὑπομείνας   εἰς
the   name   of me; but the [one]   enduring   to

τέλος,   οὗτος   σωθήσεται.   23 ὅταν   δὲ
[the] end,   this   will be saved.   But when

διώκωσιν   ὑμᾶς   ἐν   τῇ   πόλει   ταύτῃ,
they persecute   you   in   -   city   this,

φεύγετε   εἰς   τὴν   ἑτέραν·   ἀμὴν   γὰρ
flee ye   to   -   [an]other;   for truly

λέγω   ὑμῖν,   οὐ   μὴ   τελέσητε   τὰς   πόλεις
I tell   you,   by no means ye will complete   the   cities

[τοῦ]   Ἰσραὴλ   ἕως   ἔλθῃ   ὁ   υἱὸς   τοῦ   ἀν-
  -     of Israel   until   comes   the   Son   -   of

θρώπου.   24 Οὐκ   ἔστιν   μαθητὴς   ὑπὲρ
man.   not   is   A disciple   above

τὸν   διδάσκαλον   οὐδὲ   δοῦλος   ὑπὲρ   τὸν
the   teacher   nor   a slave   above   the

κύριον   αὐτοῦ.   25 ἀρκετὸν   τῷ   μαθητῇ
lord   of him.   Enough   for the   disciple

ἵνα   γένηται   ὡς   ὁ   διδάσκαλος   αὐτοῦ,
that   he be   as   the   teacher   of him,

καὶ   ὁ   δοῦλος   ὡς   ὁ   κύριος   αὐτοῦ.   εἰ
and   the   slave   as   the   lord   of him.   If

τὸν   οἰκοδεσπότην   Βεεζεβοὺλ   ἐπεκάλεσαν,
the   housemaster   Beelzebub   they called,

πόσῳ   μᾶλλον   τοὺς   οἰκιακοὺς   αὐτοῦ.
how much more   the   members of [the] household   of him.

26 μὴ   οὖν   φοβηθῆτε   αὐτούς·   οὐδὲν   γάρ
   Therefore fear ye not   them;   for nothing

ἐστιν   κεκαλυμμένον   ὃ   οὐκ   ἀποκαλυφ-
is   having been veiled   which   will not be un-

θήσεται,   καὶ   κρυπτὸν   ὃ   οὐ   γνωσθήσεται.
veiled,   and   hidden   which   will not be made known.

27 ὃ   λέγω   ὑμῖν   ἐν   τῇ   σκοτίᾳ,   εἴπατε
   What I say   to you   in   the   darkness,   say ye

and what you hear whispered, proclaim upon the housetops. ²⁸And do not fear those who kill the body but cannot kill the soul; rather fear him who can destroy both soul and body in hell. ²⁹Are not two sparrows sold for a penny? And not one of them will fall to the ground without your Father's will. ³⁰But even the hairs of your head are all numbered. ³¹Fear not, therefore; you are of more value than many sparrows. ³²So every one who acknowledges me before men, I also will acknowledge before my Father who is in heaven; ³³but whoever denies me before men, I also will deny before my Father who is in heaven.

34 "Do not think that I have come to bring peace on earth; I have not come to bring peace, but a sword. ³⁵For I have come to set a man against his father, and a daughter against her mother, and a daughter-

ἐν τῷ φωτί· καὶ ὃ εἰς τὸ οὖς ἀκούετε,
in the light; and what in the ear ye hear,

κηρύξατε ἐπὶ τῶν δωμάτων. 28 καὶ
proclaim on the housetops. And

μὴ φοβεῖσθε ἀπὸ τῶν ἀποκτεννόντων
do not fear – the [ones] killing

τὸ σῶμα, τὴν δὲ ψυχὴν μὴ δυναμένων
the body, but the soul not being able

ἀποκτεῖναι· φοβεῖσθε δὲ μᾶλλον τὸν
to kill; but fear ye rather the [one]

δυνάμενον καὶ ψυχὴν καὶ σῶμα ἀπολέσαι
being able both soul and body to destroy

ἐν γεέννῃ. 29 οὐχὶ δύο στρουθία ἀσσα-
in gehenna. Not two sparrows of(for) a

ρίου πωλεῖται; καὶ ἓν ἐξ αὐτῶν οὐ
farthing are sold? and one of them not

πεσεῖται ἐπὶ τὴν γῆν ἄνευ τοῦ πατρὸς
will fall on the earth without the Father

ὑμῶν. 30 ὑμῶν δὲ καὶ αἱ τρίχες τῆς
of you. But of you even the hairs of the

κεφαλῆς πᾶσαι ἠριθμημέναι εἰσίν. 31 μὴ
head all having been numbered are. not

οὖν φοβεῖσθε· πολλῶν στρουθίων διαφέρετε
Therefore fear ye; ³many ⁴sparrows ²excel

ὑμεῖς. 32 Πᾶς οὖν ὅστις ὁμολογήσει
¹ye. Everyone therefore who shall confess

ἐν ἐμοὶ ἔμπροσθεν τῶν ἀνθρώπων,
– me before – men,

ὁμολογήσω κἀγὼ ἐν αὐτῷ ἔμπροσθεν
will confess I also – him before

τοῦ πατρός μου τοῦ ἐν τοῖς οὐρανοῖς·
the Father of me – in the heavens;

33 ὅστις δ' ἂν ἀρνήσηται με ἔμπροσθεν
and whoever denies me before

τῶν ἀνθρώπων, ἀρνήσομαι κἀγὼ αὐτὸν
– men, will deny I also him

ἔμπροσθεν τοῦ πατρός μου τοῦ ἐν
before the Father of me – in

τοῖς οὐρανοῖς. 34 Μὴ νομίσητε ὅτι
the heavens. Do not suppose that

ἦλθον βαλεῖν εἰρήνην ἐπὶ τὴν γῆν· οὐκ ἦλθον
I came to bring peace on the earth; I came not

βαλεῖν εἰρήνην ἀλλὰ μάχαιραν. 35 ἦλθον γὰρ
to bring peace but a sword. For I came

διχάσαι ἄνθρωπον κατὰ τοῦ πατρὸς
to make hostile a man against the father

αὐτοῦ καὶ θυγατέρα κατὰ τῆς μητρὸς
of him and a daughter against the mother

in-law against her mother-in-law; ³⁶and a man's foes will be those of his own household. ³⁷He who loves father or mother more than me is not worthy of me; and he who loves son or daughter more than me is not worthy of me; ³⁸and he who does not take his cross and follow me is not worthy of me. ³⁹He who finds his life will lose it, and he who loses his life for my sake will find it.

40 "He who receives you receives me, and he who receives me receives him who sent me. ⁴¹He who receives a prophet because he is a prophet shall receive a prophet's reward, and he who receives a righteous man because he is a righteous man shall receive a righteous man's reward. ⁴²And whoever gives to one of these little ones even a cup of cold water because he is a disciple, truly, I say to you, he shall not lose his reward."

αὐτῆς καὶ νύμφην κατὰ τῆς πενθερᾶς
of her and a bride against the mother-in-law
αὐτῆς, 36 καὶ ἐχθροὶ τοῦ ἀνθρώπου οἱ
of her, and [the] enemies – of a man the
οἰκιακοὶ αὐτοῦ. 37 Ὁ φιλῶν πατέρα
members of [the] household of him. The [one] loving father
ἢ μητέρα ὑπὲρ ἐμὲ οὐκ ἔστιν μου ἄξιος·
or mother beyond me is not of me worthy;
καὶ ὁ φιλῶν υἱὸν ἢ θυγατέρα ὑπὲρ
and the [one] loving son or daughter beyond
ἐμὲ οὐκ ἔστιν μου ἄξιος· 38 καὶ ὃς
me is not of me worthy; and [he] who
οὐ λαμβάνει τὸν σταυρὸν αὐτοῦ καὶ
takes not the cross of him and
ἀκολουθεῖ ὀπίσω μου, οὐκ ἔστιν μου
follows after me, is not of me
ἄξιος. 39 ὁ εὑρὼν τὴν ψυχὴν αὐτοῦ
worthy. The [one] finding the life of him
ἀπολέσει αὐτήν, καὶ ὁ ἀπολέσας τὴν
will lose it, and the [one] losing the
ψυχὴν αὐτοῦ ἕνεκεν ἐμοῦ εὑρήσει αὐτήν.
life of him for the sake of me will find it.
40 Ὁ δεχόμενος ὑμᾶς ἐμὲ δέχεται, καὶ
The [one] receiving you me receives, and
ὁ ἐμὲ δεχόμενος δέχεται τὸν
the [one] me receiving receives the [one]
ἀποστείλαντά με. 41 ὁ δεχόμενος προ-
having sent me. The [one] receiving a pro-
φήτην εἰς ὄνομα προφήτου μισθὸν
phet in [the] name of a prophet [the] reward
προφήτου λήμψεται, καὶ ὁ δεχόμενος
of a prophet will receive, and the [one] receiving
δίκαιον εἰς ὄνομα δικαίου μισθὸν
a righteous man in [the] name of a righteous man [the] reward
δικαίου λήμψεται. 42 καὶ ὃς ἐὰν ποτίσῃ
of a righteous man will receive. And whoever gives to drink
ἕνα τῶν μικρῶν τούτων ποτήριον ψυχροῦ
one – of these little [ones] a cup of cold water
μόνον εἰς ὄνομα μαθητοῦ, ἀμὴν λέγω ὑμῖν,
only in [the] name of a disciple, truly I tell you,
οὐ μὴ ἀπολέσῃ τὸν μισθὸν αὐτοῦ.
on no account will he lose the reward of him.

CHAPTER 11

AND when Jesus had finished instructing his twelve disciples, he went on from there to teach and preach in their cities.

2 Now when John heard in prison about the deeds of the Christ, he sent word by his disciples ³and said to him, "Are you he who is to come, or shall we look for another?" ⁴And Jesus answered them, "Go and tell John what you hear and see: ⁵the blind receive their sight and the lame walk, lepers are cleansed and the deaf hear, and the dead are raised up, and the poor have good news preached to them. ⁶And blessed is he who takes no offense at me."

7 As they went away, Jesus began to speak to the crowds concerning John: "What did you go out into the wilderness to behold? A reed shaken by the wind? ⁸Why then did you go out? To see a man^r clothed in soft raiment? Behold, those who wear soft raiment are in kings' houses. ⁹Why then did you go out? To see a prophet?^s

^r Or *What then did you go out to see? A man . . .*
^s Other ancient authorities read *What then did you go out to see? A prophet?*

---

11 Καὶ ἐγένετο ὅτε ἐτέλεσεν ὁ
And it came to pass when ended -

ʼΙησοῦς διατάσσων τοῖς δώδεκα μαθηταῖς
Jesus giving charge to the twelve disciples

αὐτοῦ, μετέβη ἐκεῖθεν τοῦ διδάσκειν
of him, he removed thence - to teach^d

καὶ κηρύσσειν ἐν ταῖς πόλεσιν αὐτῶν.
and to proclaim^d in the cities of them.

2 Ὁ δὲ ʼΙωάννης ἀκούσας ἐν τῷ
- But John hearing in the

δεσμωτηρίῳ τὰ ἔργα τοῦ Χριστοῦ,
prison the works of Christ,

πέμψας διὰ τῶν μαθητῶν αὐτοῦ 3 εἶπεν
sending through the disciples of him said

αὐτῷ· σὺ εἶ ὁ ἐρχόμενος, ἢ ἕτερον
to him: Thou art the coming [one], or another

προσδοκῶμεν; 4 καὶ ἀποκριθεὶς ὁ
may we expect? And answering -

ʼΙησοῦς εἶπεν αὐτοῖς· πορευθέντες ἀπαγ-
Jesus said to them: Going report

γείλατε ʼΙωάννῃ ἃ ἀκούετε καὶ βλέπετε·
ye to John [the things] which ye hear and see:

5 τυφλοὶ ἀναβλέπουσιν καὶ χωλοὶ
blind men see again and lame men

περιπατοῦσιν, λεπροὶ καθαρίζονται καὶ κωφοὶ
walk, lepers are cleansed and deaf men

ἀκούουσιν, καὶ νεκροὶ ἐγείρονται καὶ
hear, and dead men are raised and

πτωχοὶ εὐαγγελίζονται· 6 καὶ μακάριός
poor men are evangelized; and blessed

ἐστιν ὃς ἐὰν μὴ σκανδαλισθῇ ἐν ἐμοί.
is whoever is not offended in me.

7 Τούτων δὲ πορευομένων ἤρξατο ὁ
And these going^a began -
= as these were going

ʼΙησοῦς λέγειν τοῖς ὄχλοις περὶ ʼΙωάννου·
Jesus to say to the crowds concerning John:

τί ἐξήλθατε εἰς τὴν ἔρημον θεάσασθαι;
What went ye out into the wilderness to see?

κάλαμον ὑπὸ ἀνέμου σαλευόμενον; 8 ἀλλὰ
a reed by wind being shaken? But

τί ἐξήλθατε ἰδεῖν; ἄνθρωπον ἐν μαλακοῖς
what went ye out to see? a man in soft material

ἠμφιεσμένον; ἰδοὺ οἱ τὰ μαλακὰ
having been clothed? Behold[,] the [ones] - soft material

φοροῦντες ἐν τοῖς οἴκοις τῶν βασιλέων. 9 ἀλλὰ
wearing [are] in the houses - of kings. But

τί ἐξήλθατε; προφήτην ἰδεῖν; ναὶ λέγω
why went ye out? a prophet to see? Yes[,] I tell

Yes, I tell you, and more than a prophet. [10] This is he of whom it is written, 'Behold, I send my messenger before thy face, who shall prepare thy way before thee.' [11] Truly, I say to you, among those born of women there has risen no one greater than John the Baptist; yet he who is least in the kingdom of heaven is greater than he. [12] From the days of John the Baptist until now the kingdom of heaven has suffered violence,[t] and men of violence take it by force. [13] For all the prophets and the law prophesied until John; [14] and if you are willing to accept it, he is Eli'jah who is to come. [15] He who has ears to hear,[u] let him hear.

16 "But to what shall I compare this generation? It is like children sitting in the market places and calling to their playmates,
[17] 'We piped to you, and you did not dance; we wailed, and you did not mourn.'
[18] For John came neither eating nor drinking, and they say, 'He has a demon'; [19] the Son of man came eating and

ὑμῖν, καὶ περισσότερον προφήτου.	you, and more [than] a prophet.
10 οὗτός ἐστιν περὶ οὗ γέγραπται·	10 This is he concerning whom it has been written:
ἰδοὺ ἐγὼ ἀποστέλλω τὸν ἄγγελόν μου	Behold[,] I send forth the messenger of me
πρὸ προσώπου σου, ὃς κατασκευάσει	before [the] face of thee, who will prepare
τὴν ὁδόν σου ἔμπροσθέν σου.	the way of thee before thee.
11 ἀμὴν λέγω ὑμῖν,	11 Truly I tell you,
οὐκ ἐγήγερται ἐν γεννητοῖς γυναικῶν	there has not arisen among [those] born of women
μείζων Ἰωάννου τοῦ βαπτιστοῦ·	a greater [than] John the Baptist;
ὁ δὲ μικρότερος ἐν τῇ βασιλείᾳ τῶν οὐρανῶν	but the lesser in the kingdom of the heavens
μείζων αὐτοῦ ἐστιν.	greater [than] he is.
12 ἀπὸ δὲ τῶν ἡμερῶν Ἰωάννου τοῦ βαπτιστοῦ	12 And from the days of John the Baptist
ἕως ἄρτι ἡ βασιλεία τῶν οὐρανῶν βιάζεται,	until now the kingdom of the heavens is forcibly treated,
καὶ βιασταὶ ἁρπάζουσιν αὐτήν.	and forceful men seize it.
13 πάντες γὰρ οἱ προφῆται καὶ ὁ νόμος	13 For all the prophets and the law
ἕως Ἰωάννου ἐπροφήτευσαν·	until John prophesied;
14 καὶ εἰ θέλετε δέξασθαι,	14 and if ye are willing to receive [it or him],
αὐτός ἐστιν Ἡλίας ὁ μέλλων ἔρχεσθαι.	he is Elias the [one] about to come.
15 ὁ ἔχων ὦτα ἀκουέτω.	15 The [one] having ears let him hear.
16 Τίνι δὲ ὁμοιώσω τὴν γενεὰν ταύτην;	16 But to what shall I liken generation this?
ὁμοία ἐστὶν παιδίοις καθημένοις ἐν ταῖς ἀγοραῖς	Like it is to children sitting in the marketplaces
ἃ προσφωνοῦντα τοῖς ἑτέροις	who calling to the others
17 λέγουσιν· ηὐλήσαμεν ὑμῖν καὶ οὐκ	17 say: We piped to you and not
ὠρχήσασθε· ἐθρηνήσαμεν καὶ οὐκ ἐκόψασθε.	ye did dance; we lamented and ye did not mourn.
18 ἦλθεν γὰρ Ἰωάννης μήτε ἐσθίων μήτε	18 For came John neither eating nor
πίνων, καὶ λέγουσιν· δαιμόνιον ἔχει.	drinking, and they say: a demon He has.
19 ἦλθεν ὁ υἱὸς τοῦ ἀνθρώπου ἐσθίων καὶ	19 Came the Son - of man eating and

---

[t] Or *has been coming violently*
[u] Other ancient authorities omit *to hear*

drinking, and they say, 'Behold, a glutton and a drunkard, a friend of tax collectors and sinners!' Yet wisdom is justified by her deeds."[v]

20 Then he began to upbraid the cities where most of his mighty works had been done, because they did not repent [21]"Woe to you, Chora'zin! woe to you, Bethsa'ida! for if the mighty works done in you had been done in Tyre and Sidon, they would have repented long ago in sackcloth and ashes. [22]But I tell you, it shall be more tolerable on the day of judgment for Tyre and Sidon than for you. [23]And you, Caper'na-um, will you be exalted in heaven? You shall be brought down to Hades. For if the mighty works done in you had been done in Sodom, it would have remained until this day. [24]But I tell you that it shall be more tolerable on the day of judgment for the land of Sodom than for you."

25 At that time Jesus declared, "I thank thee, Father, Lord of heaven and earth, that thou hast hidden these things from the wise and under-

[v] Other ancient authorities read *children* (Luke 7. 35)

πίνων,   καὶ   λέγουσιν·   ἰδοὺ   ἄνθρωπος
drinking,   and   they say: Behold[.]   a man

φάγος καὶ   οἰνοπότης, τελωνῶν φίλος καὶ
gluttonous and a wine-drinker, of tax-collectors a friend and

ἁμαρτωλῶν.   καὶ   ἐδικαιώθη   ἡ   σοφία   ἀπὸ
of sinners.   And   was(is) justified –   wisdom from(by)

τῶν   ἔργων   αὐτῆς.
the   works   of her.

20 Τότε   ἤρξατο   ὀνειδίζειν   τὰς   πόλεις
Then   he began   to reproach   the   cities

ἐν αἷς   ἐγένοντο   αἱ   πλεῖσται   δυνάμεις
in which   happened   the   very many powerful deeds

αὐτοῦ,   ὅτι   οὐ   μετενόησαν·   21 οὐαί   σοι,
of him,   because   they repented not: Woe to thee,

Χοραζίν·   οὐαί   σοι,   Βηθσαϊδά·   ὅτι   εἰ
Chorazin;   woe   to thee,   Bethsaida;   because   if

ἐν Τύρῳ καὶ Σιδῶνι ἐγένοντο αἱ   δυνάμεις
in Tyre   and Sidon   happened the powerful deeds

αἱ   γενόμεναι   ἐν   ὑμῖν,   πάλαι   ἂν
–   having happened   in   you,   long ago

ἐν σάκκῳ καὶ σποδῷ   μετενόησαν.
in sackcloth and ashes they would have repented.

22 πλὴν λέγω ὑμῖν, Τύρῳ καὶ Σιδῶνι
However I tell you, For Tyre and for Sidon

ἀνεκτότερον   ἔσται   ἐν ἡμέρᾳ κρίσεως   ἢ
more tolerable   it will be   in [the] day of judgment than

ὑμῖν.   23 καὶ σύ,   Καφαρναούμ,   μὴ
for you.   And   thou,   Capernaum,   not

ἕως   οὐρανοῦ ὑψωθήσῃ;   ἕως   ᾅδου
as far as heaven wast thou exalted? as far as hades

καταβήσῃ·   ὅτι εἰ ἐν Σοδόμοις ἐγενήθησαν
thou shalt descend; because if in Sodom   happened

αἱ   δυνάμεις   αἱ   γενόμεναι   ἐν   σοί,
the   powerful deeds   –   having happened   in   thee,

ἔμεινεν ἂν   μέχρι τῆς σήμερον.   24 πλὴν
it would have remained until –   to-day.   However

λέγω ὑμῖν ὅτι   γῇ   Σοδόμων ἀνεκτότερον
I tell you that for [the] land of Sodom more tolerable

ἔσται ἐν ἡμέρᾳ κρίσεως ἢ σοί.
it will be in [the] day of judgment than for thee.

25 Ἐν   ἐκείνῳ   τῷ   καιρῷ   ἀποκριθεὶς
At   that   –   time   answering

ὁ Ἰησοῦς εἶπεν·   ἐξομολογοῦμαί   σοι,
–   Jesus   said: I give thanks   to thee,

πάτερ, κύριε τοῦ οὐρανοῦ καὶ τῆς γῆς,
Father, lord of the heaven and of the earth,

ὅτι   ἔκρυψας   ταῦτα ἀπὸ σοφῶν καὶ συνε-
because thou hiddest these things from wise and intel-

standing and revealed them to babes; ²⁶ yea, Father, for such was thy gracious will.ʷ   ²⁷ All things have been delivered to me by my Father; and no one knows the Son except the Father, and no one knows the Father except the Son and any one to whom the Son chooses to reveal him. ²⁸ Come to me, all who labor and are heavy-laden, and I will give you rest. ²⁹ Take my yoke upon you, and learn from me; for I am gentle and lowly in heart, and you will find rest for your souls. ³⁰ For my yoke is easy, and my burden is light.''

τῶν,	καὶ	ἀπεκάλυψας	αὐτὰ	νηπίοις·
ligent men,	and	didst reveal	them	to infants;

26 ναί,	ὁ	πατήρ,	ὅτι	οὕτως	εὐδοκία
yes,	–	Father,	because	thus	good pleasure

ἐγένετο	ἔμπροσθέν	σου.	**27** Πάντα	μοι
it was	before	thee.	All things	to me

παρεδόθη	ὑπὸ	τοῦ	πατρός	μου,	καὶ
were delivered	by	the	Father	of me,	and

οὐδεὶς	ἐπιγινώσκει	τὸν	υἱὸν	εἰ μὴ	ὁ
no one	fully knows	the	Son	except	the

πατήρ,	οὐδὲ	τὸν	πατέρα	τις	ἐπιγινώσκει
Father,	neither	the	Father	anyone	fully knows

εἰ μὴ	ὁ	υἱὸς	καὶ	ᾧ	ἐὰν	βούληται	ὁ
except	the	Son	and [he]	to whom	if	wills	the

υἱὸς	ἀποκαλύψαι.	**28** Δεῦτε	πρός	με
Son	to reveal.	Come	unto	me

πάντες	οἱ	κοπιῶντες	καὶ	πεφορτισμένοι,
all	the [ones]	labouring	and	*having been* burdened,

κἀγὼ	ἀναπαύσω	ὑμᾶς.	**29** ἄρατε	τὸν
and I	will rest	you.	Take	the

ζυγόν	μου	ἐφ᾽	ὑμᾶς	καὶ	μάθετε	ἀπ᾽
yoke	of me	on	you	and	learn	from

ἐμοῦ,	ὅτι	πραῢς	εἰμι	καὶ	ταπεινὸς	τῇ
me,	because	meek	I am	and	lowly	–

καρδίᾳ,	καὶ	εὑρήσετε	ἀνάπαυσιν	ταῖς
in heart,	and	ye will find	rest	to the

ψυχαῖς	ὑμῶν·	**30** ὁ	γὰρ	ζυγός	μου
souls	of you;	for the		yoke	of me

χρηστὸς	καὶ	τὸ	φορτίον	μου	ἐλαφρόν
gentle	and	the	burden	of me	light

ἐστιν.
is.

CHAPTER 12

A T that time Jesus went through the grainfields on the sabbath; his disciples were hungry, and they began to pluck ears of grain and to eat. ² But when the Pharisees saw it, they said to him, ''Look, your disciples are doing what is not lawful to do on the sabbath.'' ³ He said to

ʷ Or *so it was well-pleasing before thee*

12 Ἐν	ἐκείνῳ	τῷ	καιρῷ	ἐπορεύθη	ὁ
At	that	–	time	went	–

Ἰησοῦς	τοῖς	σάββασιν	διὰ	τῶν	σπορίμων·
Jesus	on the	sabbath	through	the	cornfields;

οἱ	δὲ	μαθηταὶ	αὐτοῦ	ἐπείνασαν,	καὶ
and the		disciples	of him	hungered,	and

ἤρξαντο	τίλλειν	στάχυας	καὶ	ἐσθίειν.
began	to pluck	ears [of corn]	and	to eat.

2 οἱ	δὲ	Φαρισαῖοι	ἰδόντες	εἶπαν	αὐτῷ·
But the		Pharisees	seeing	said	to him:

ἰδοὺ	οἱ	μαθηταί	σου	ποιοῦσιν	ὁ	οὐκ
Behold[,] the		disciples	of thee	are doing	what	not

ἔξεστιν	ποιεῖν	ἐν	σαββάτῳ.	**3** ὁ	δὲ
it is lawful	to do	on	a sabbath.		And he

them, "Have you not read what David did, when he was hungry, and those who were with him: ⁴how he entered the house of God and ate the bread of the Presence, which it was not lawful for him to eat nor for those who were with him, but only for the priests? ⁵Or have you not read in the law how on the sabbath the priests in the temple profane the sabbath, and are guiltless? ⁶I tell you, something greater than the temple is here. ⁷And if you had known what this means, 'I desire mercy, and not sacrifice,' you would not have condemned the guiltless. ⁸For the Son of man is lord of the sabbath."

9 And he went on from there, and entered their synagogue. ¹⁰And behold, there was a man with a withered hand. And they asked him, "Is it lawful to heal on the sabbath?" so that they might accuse him.¹¹ He said to them, "What man of you, if he has one sheep and it falls into a pit on the sabbath, will not lay hold of it and lift

εἶπεν αὐτοῖς· οὐκ ἀνέγνωτε τί ἐποίησεν
said to them: Did ye not read what did

Δαυίδ, ὅτε ἐπείνασεν καὶ οἱ μετ᾽
David, when he hungered and the [ones] with

αὐτοῦ; 4 πῶς εἰσῆλθεν εἰς τὸν οἶκον
him? how he entered into the house

τοῦ θεοῦ καὶ τοὺς ἄρτους τῆς προ-
- of God and the loaves of the set-

θέσεως ἔφαγον, ὃ οὐκ ἐξὸν ἦν αὐτῷ
ting forth ate, which not lawful it was for him

φαγεῖν οὐδὲ τοῖς μετ᾽ αὐτοῦ, εἰ μὴ
to eat neither the [ones] with him, except

τοῖς ἱερεῦσιν μόνοις; 5 ἢ οὐκ ἀνέγνωτε
for the priests only? or did ye not read

ἐν τῷ νόμῳ ὅτι τοῖς σάββασιν οἱ
in the law that on the sabbaths the

ἱερεῖς ἐν τῷ ἱερῷ τὸ σάββατον βεβηλοῦ-
priests in the temple the sabbath pro-

σιν καὶ ἀναίτιοί εἰσιν; 6 λέγω δὲ
fane and guiltless are? And I tell

ὑμῖν ὅτι τοῦ ἱεροῦ μεῖζόν ἐστιν ὧδε.
you that [than] the temple a greater [thing] is here.

7 εἰ δὲ ἐγνώκειτε τί ἐστιν· ἔλεος
But if ye had known what it is: Mercy

θέλω καὶ οὐ θυσίαν, οὐκ ἂν κατε-
I desire and not sacrifice, ye would not have

δικάσατε τοὺς ἀναιτίους. 8 κύριος γάρ
condemned the guiltless. For Lord

ἐστιν τοῦ σαββάτου ὁ υἱὸς τοῦ ἀνθρώπου.
is of the sabbath the Son - of man.

9 Καὶ μεταβὰς ἐκεῖθεν ἦλθεν εἰς τὴν
And removing thence he came into the

συναγωγὴν αὐτῶν. 10 καὶ ἰδοὺ ἄνθρωπος
synagogue of them. And behold[,] a man

χεῖρα ἔχων ξηράν· καὶ ἐπηρώτησαν αὐτὸν
¹[this] hand ¹having ²withered; and they questioned him

λέγοντες· εἰ ἔξεστιν τοῖς σάββασιν
saying: If it is lawful on the sabbaths

θεραπεῦσαι; ἵνα κατηγορήσωσιν αὐτοῦ.
to heal? in order that they might accuse him.

11 ὁ δὲ εἶπεν αὐτοῖς· τίς ἔσται ἐξ
So he said to them: ¹What ²will there be ⁴of

ὑμῶν ἄνθρωπος ὃς ἕξει πρόβατον ἕν,
³you ²man who will have sheep one,

καὶ ἐὰν ἐμπέσῃ τοῦτο τοῖς σάββασιν
and if ³fall in ¹this on the sabbaths

εἰς βόθυνον, οὐχὶ κρατήσει αὐτὸ καὶ
into a ditch, will he not lay hold of it and

it out? ¹²Of how much more value is a man than a sheep! So it is lawful to do good on the sabbath." ¹³Then he said to the man, "Stretch out your hand," And the man stretched it out, and it was restored, whole like the other. ¹⁴But the Pharisees went out and took counsel against him, how to destroy him.

15 Jesus, aware of this, withdrew from there. And many followed him, and he healed them all, ¹⁶and ordered them not to make him known. ¹⁷This was to fulfil what was spoken by the prophet Isaiah:

¹⁸"Behold, my servant whom I have chosen,
  my beloved with whom my soul is well pleased.
I will put my Spirit upon him,
  and he shall proclaim justice to the Gentiles.
¹⁹He will not wrangle or cry aloud,
  nor will any one hear his voice in the streets;
²⁰he will not break a bruised reed
  or quench a smoldering wick,
till he brings justice to victory;
²¹ and in his name will the Gentiles hope."

ἐγερεῖ; **12** πόσῳ οὖν διαφέρει ἄνθρωπος
raise?   By how much then   surpasses   a man

προβάτου. ὥστε ἔξεστιν τοῖς σάββασιν
a sheep.   So that   it is lawful   on the   sabbaths

καλῶς ποιεῖν. **13** τότε λέγει τῷ ἀνθρώπῳ·
well   to do.   Then   he says   to the   man:

ἔκτεινόν σου τὴν χεῖρα. καὶ ἐξέτεινεν,
Stretch forth   of thee   the   hand.   And he stretched forth,

καὶ ἀπεκατεστάθη ὑγιὴς ὡς ἡ ἄλλη.
and   it was restored   healthy   as   the   other.

14 ἐξελθόντες δὲ οἱ Φαρισαῖοι συμβούλιον
And going out   the   Pharisees   counsel

ἔλαβον κατ' αὐτοῦ, ὅπως αὐτὸν ἀπολέ-
took   against   him,   so as   him   they might

σωσιν. **15** Ὁ δὲ Ἰησοῦς γνοὺς ἀνε-
destroy.   -   But   Jesus   knowing   de-

χώρησεν ἐκεῖθεν. καὶ ἠκολούθησαν αὐτῷ
parted   thence.   And   followed   him

πολλοί, καὶ ἐθεράπευσεν αὐτοὺς πάντας,
many,   and   he healed   them   all,

16 καὶ ἐπετίμησεν αὐτοῖς ἵνα μὴ φανερὸν
and   warned   them   that ³not   ⁴manifest

αὐτὸν ποιήσωσιν· **17** ἵνα πληρωθῇ τὸ
⁵him ¹they ²should ⁴make;   that might be fulfilled the [thing]

ῥηθὲν διὰ Ἡσαΐου τοῦ προφήτου
spoken   through   Isaiah   the   prophet

λέγοντος· **18** ἰδοὺ ὁ παῖς μου ὃν
saying: Behold[,] the   servant   of me   whom

ᾑρέτισα, ὁ ἀγαπητός μου ὃν εὐδόκησεν
I chose,   the   beloved   of me [with] whom   was well pleased

ἡ ψυχή μου· θήσω τὸ πνεῦμα μου ἐπ'
the   soul   of me;   I will put   the   spirit   of me   on

αὐτόν, καὶ κρίσιν τοῖς ἔθνεσιν ἀπαγγελεῖ.
him,   and   judgment   to the   nations   he will announce.

19 οὐκ ἐρίσει οὐδὲ κραυγάσει, οὐδὲ
He will not strive   nor   will shout,   nor

ἀκούσει τις ἐν ταῖς πλατείαις τὴν
will hear   anyone   in   the   streets   the

φωνὴν αὐτοῦ. **20** κάλαμον συντετριμμένον
voice   of him.   A reed   *having been* bruised

οὐ κατεάξει καὶ λίνον τυφόμενον οὐ
he will not break   and   flax   smoking   not

σβέσει, ἕως ἂν ἐκβάλῃ εἰς νῖκος τὴν
he will quench,   until   he put forth   to   victory   -

κρίσιν. **21** καὶ τῷ ὀνόματι αὐτοῦ ἔθνη
judgment.   And   in the   name   of him   nations

ἐλπιοῦσιν.
will hope.

22 Then a blind and dumb demoniac was brought to him, and he healed him, so that the dumb man spoke and saw. ²³And all the people were amazed, and said, "Can this be the Son of David?" ²⁴But when the Pharisees heard it they said, "It is only by Be-el'zebul, the prince of demons, that this man casts out demons." ²⁵Knowing their thoughts, he said to them, "Every kingdom divided against itself is laid waste, and no city or house divided against itself will stand; ²⁶and if Satan casts out Satan, he is divided against himself; how then will his kingdom stand? ²⁷And if I cast out demons by Be-el'zebul, by whom do your sons cast them out? Therefore they shall be your judges. ²⁸But if it is by the Spirit of God that I cast out demons, then the kingdom of God has come upon you. ²⁹Or how can one enter a strong man's house and plunder his goods, unless

22 Τότε	προσηνέχθη	αὐτῷ	δαιμονιζ-
Then	was brought	to him	a demon-

ὅμενος	τυφλὸς καὶ	κωφός·	καὶ ἐθεράπευσεν
possessed man	blind and	dumb;	and he healed

αὐτόν,	ὥστε	τὸν	κωφὸν	λαλεῖν	καὶ
him,	so as	the	dumb	to speak	and

βλέπειν.	23 καὶ	ἐξίσταντο	πάντες	οἱ
to see^b.	And	were astonished	all	the

ὄχλοι καὶ	ἔλεγον·	μήτι	οὗτός	ἐστιν	ὁ
crowds and	said:	not	This	is	the

υἱὸς Δαυίδ;	24 οἱ δὲ	Φαρισαῖοι	ἀκού-
son of David?	But the	Pharisees	hear-

σαντες	εἶπον·	οὗτος	οὐκ ἐκβάλλει	τὰ
ing	said:	This man	does not expel	the

δαιμόνια	εἰ μὴ	ἐν τῷ	Βεεζεβοὺλ	ἄρχοντι
demons	except	by -	Beelzebub	ruler

τῶν δαιμονίων.	25 εἰδὼς δὲ	τὰς	ἐνθυμήσεις
of the demons.	But knowing	the	thoughts

αὐτῶν	εἶπεν	αὐτοῖς·	πᾶσα	βασιλεία
of them	he said	to them:	Every	kingdom

μερισθεῖσα	καθ'	ἑαυτῆς	ἐρημοῦται,
divided	against	itself	is brought to desolation,

καὶ πᾶσα	πόλις	ἢ	οἰκία	μερισθεῖσα	καθ'
and every	city	or	house	divided	against

ἑαυτῆς	οὐ	σταθήσεται.	26 καὶ	εἰ
itself	will not stand.		And	if

ὁ	σατανᾶς	τὸν	σατανᾶν	ἐκβάλλει,	ἐφ'
-	Satan	-	²Satan	¹expels,	against

ἑαυτὸν	ἐμερίσθη·	πῶς	οὖν	σταθή-
himself	he was(is) divided;	how	therefore	will

σεται	ἡ	βασιλεία	αὐτοῦ;	27 καὶ	εἰ
stand	the	kingdom	of him?	And	if

ἐγὼ	ἐν	Βεεζεβοὺλ	ἐκβάλλω	τὰ	δαιμόνια,
I	by	Beelzebub	expel	the	demons,

οἱ	υἱοὶ	ὑμῶν	ἐν	τίνι	ἐκβάλλουσιν;
the	sons	of you	by	what	do they expel?

διὰ	τοῦτο	αὐτοὶ	κριταὶ	ἔσονται	ὑμῶν.
therefore		they	judges	shall be	of you.

28 εἰ	δὲ	ἐν	πνεύματι	θεοῦ	ἐγὼ
But if		by [the]	Spirit	of God	I

ἐκβάλλω	τὰ	δαιμόνια,	ἄρα	ἔφθασεν
expel	the	demons,	then	came

ἐφ'	ὑμᾶς	ἡ	βασιλεία	τοῦ	θεοῦ.	29 ἢ
upon	you	the	kingdom	-	of God.	Or

πῶς	δύναταί	τις	εἰσελθεῖν	εἰς	τὴν
how	can	anyone	to enter	into	the

οἰκίαν	τοῦ	ἰσχυροῦ	καὶ	τὰ	σκεύη	αὐτοῦ
house	of the	strong man	and	the	vessels	of him

he first binds the strong man? Then indeed he may plunder his house. ³⁰He who is not with me is against me, and he who does not gather with me scatters. ³¹Therefore I tell you, every sin and blasphemy will be forgiven men, but the blasphemy against the Spirit will not be forgiven. ³²And whoever says a word against the Son of man will be forgiven; but whoever speaks against the Holy Spirit will not be forgiven, either in this age or in the age to come.

33 "Either make the tree good, and its fruit good; or make the tree bad, and its fruit bad; for the tree is known by its fruit. ³⁴You brood of vipers! how can you speak good, when you are evil? For out of the abundance of the heart the mouth speaks. ³⁵The good man out of his good treasure brings forth good, and the evil man out of his evil treasure

ἁρπάσαι, ἐὰν μὴ πρῶτον δήσῃ τὸν
to seize, if not first he binds the

ἰσχυρόν; καὶ τότε τὴν οἰκίαν αὐτοῦ
strong man? and then the house of him

διαρπάσει. 30 ὁ μὴ ὢν μετ' ἐμοῦ
he will plunder. The [one] not being with me

κατ' ἐμοῦ ἐστιν, καὶ ὁ μὴ συνάγων μετ'
against me is, and the [one] not gathering with

ἐμοῦ σκορπίζει. 31 Διὰ τοῦτο λέγω
me scatters. Therefore I tell

ὑμῖν, πᾶσα ἁμαρτία καὶ βλασφημία
you, all sin and blasphemy

ἀφεθήσεται τοῖς ἀνθρώποις, ἡ δὲ τοῦ
will be forgiven – to men, but the of the

πνεύματος βλασφημία οὐκ ἀφεθήσεται.
Spirit blasphemy will not be forgiven.

32 καὶ ὃς ἐὰν εἴπῃ λόγον κατὰ τοῦ
And whoever speaks a word against the

υἱοῦ τοῦ ἀνθρώπου, ἀφεθήσεται αὐτῷ·
Son – of man, it will be forgiven to him;

ὃς δ' ἂν εἴπῃ κατὰ τοῦ πνεύματος
but whoever speaks against the Spirit

τοῦ ἁγίου, οὐκ ἀφεθήσεται αὐτῷ
– Holy, it will not be forgiven to him

οὔτε ἐν τούτῳ τῷ αἰῶνι οὔτε ἐν τῷ
neither in this – age nor in the [one]

μέλλοντι. 33 Ἢ ποιήσατε τὸ δένδρον
coming. Either make the tree

καλὸν καὶ τὸν καρπὸν αὐτοῦ καλόν,
good and the fruit of it good,

ἢ ποιήσατε τὸ δένδρον σαπρὸν καὶ τὸν
or make the tree bad and the

καρπὸν αὐτοῦ σαπρόν· ἐκ γὰρ τοῦ
fruit of it bad; for of (by) the

καρποῦ τὸ δένδρον γινώσκεται. 34 γεννή-
fruit the tree is known. Off-

ματα ἐχιδνῶν, πῶς δύνασθε ἀγαθὰ λαλεῖν
spring of vipers, how can ye good things to speak

πονηροὶ ὄντες; ἐκ γὰρ τοῦ περισ-
²evil ¹being? for out of the abund-

σεύματος τῆς καρδίας τὸ στόμα λαλεῖ.
ance of the heart the mouth speaks.

35 ὁ ἀγαθὸς ἄνθρωπος ἐκ τοῦ ἀγαθοῦ
The good man out of the good

θησαυροῦ ἐκβάλλει ἀγαθά, καὶ ὁ πονηρὸς
treasure puts forth good things, and the evil

ἄνθρωπος ἐκ τοῦ πονηροῦ θησαυροῦ
man out of the evil treasure

brings forth evil. ³⁶I tell you, on the day of judgment men will render account for every careless word they utter; ³⁷for by your words you will be justified, and by your words you will be condemned."

38 Then some of the scribes and Pharisees said to him, "Teacher, we wish to see a sign from you." ³⁹But he answered them, "An evil and adulterous generation seeks for a sign; but no sign shall be given to it except the sign of the prophet Jonah. ⁴⁰For as Jonah was three days and three nights in the belly of the whale, so will the Son of man be three days and three nights in the heart of the earth. ⁴¹The men of Nin'eveh will arise at the judgment with this generation and condemn it; for they repented at the preaching of Jonah, and behold, something greater than Jonah is here. ⁴²The queen of the South will arise at the judgment with this generation and condemn it;

ἐκβάλλει πονηρά. **36** λέγω δὲ
puts forth evil things. But I tell

ὑμῖν ὅτι πᾶν ῥῆμα ἀργὸν ὃ λαλήσουσιν
you that every word idle which will speak

οἱ ἄνθρωποι, ἀποδώσουσιν περὶ αὐτοῦ
- men, they will render concerning it

λόγον ἐν ἡμέρᾳ κρίσεως· **37** ἐκ γὰρ
account in [the] day of judgment; for of(by)

τῶν λόγων σου δικαιωθήσῃ, καὶ ἐκ
the words of thee thou wilt be justified, and of(by)

τῶν λόγων σου καταδικασθήσῃ.
the words of thee thou wilt be condemned.

38 Τότε ἀπεκρίθησαν αὐτῷ τινες τῶν
Then answered him some of the

γραμματέων καὶ Φαρισαίων λέγοντες·
scribes and Pharisees saying:

διδάσκαλε, θέλομεν ἀπὸ σοῦ σημεῖον ἰδεῖν.
Teacher, we wish from thee a sign to see.

39 ὁ δὲ ἀποκριθεὶς εἶπεν αὐτοῖς·
But he answering said to them:

γενεὰ πονηρὰ καὶ μοιχαλὶς σημεῖον
generation An evil and adulterous a sign

ἐπιζητεῖ, καὶ σημεῖον οὐ δοθήσεται
seeks, and a sign shall not be given

αὐτῇ εἰ μὴ τὸ σημεῖον Ἰωνᾶ τοῦ
to it except the sign of Jonas the

προφήτου. **40** ὥσπερ γὰρ ἦν Ἰωνᾶς
prophet. For as was Jonas

ἐν τῇ κοιλίᾳ τοῦ κήτους τρεῖς ἡμέρας
in the belly of the sea monster three days

καὶ τρεῖς νύκτας, οὕτως ἔσται ὁ υἱὸς
and three nights, so will be the Son

τοῦ ἀνθρώπου ἐν τῇ καρδίᾳ τῆς γῆς
- of man in the heart of the earth

τρεῖς ἡμέρας καὶ τρεῖς νύκτας. **41** ἄνδρες
three days and three nights. Men

Νινευῖται ἀναστήσονται ἐν τῇ κρίσει
Ninevites will stand up in the judgment

μετὰ τῆς γενεᾶς ταύτης καὶ κατα-
with - generation this and will

κρινοῦσιν αὐτήν· ὅτι μετενόησαν εἰς τὸ
condemn it; because they repented at the

κήρυγμα Ἰωνᾶ, καὶ ἰδοὺ πλεῖον Ἰωνᾶ
proclamation of Jonas, and behold a greater thing [than] Jonas

ὧδε. **42** βασίλισσα νότου ἐγερθήσεται
[is] here. [The] queen of [the] south will be raised

ἐν τῇ κρίσει μετὰ τῆς γενεᾶς ταύτης
in the judgment with - generation this

for she came from the ends of the earth to hear the wisdom of Solomon, and behold, something greater than Solomon is here. 43 "When the unclean spirit has gone out of a man, he passes through waterless places seeking rest, but he finds none. 44 Then he says, 'I will return to my house from which I came.' And when he comes he finds it empty, swept, and put in order. 45 Then he goes and brings with him seven other spirits more evil than himself, and they enter and dwell there; and the last state of that man becomes worse than the first. So shall it be also with this evil generation."

46 While he was still speaking to the people, behold, his mother and his brothers stood outside, asking to speak to him.ˣ 48 But he replied to the man who told him, "Who is my mother, and who are my brothers?"

ˣ Other ancient authorities insert verse 47: *Some one told him, "Your mother and your brothers are standing outside, asking to speak to you"*

καὶ κατακρινεῖ αὐτήν· ὅτι ἦλθεν ἐκ
and will condemn it; because she came out of

τῶν περάτων τῆς γῆς ἀκοῦσαι τὴν σοφίαν
the limits of the earth to hear the wisdom

Σολομῶνος, καὶ ἰδοὺ πλεῖον Σολομῶνος
of Solomon, and behold a greater thing [than] Solomon

ὧδε. 43 Ὅταν δὲ τὸ ἀκάθαρτον πνεῦμα
[is] here. Now when the unclean spirit

ἐξέλθῃ ἀπὸ τοῦ ἀνθρώπου, διέρχεται δι'
goes out from - a man, he goes through

ἀνύδρων τόπων ζητοῦν ἀνάπαυσιν, καὶ
dry places seeking rest, and

οὐχ εὑρίσκει. 44 τότε λέγει· εἰς τὸν
finds not. Then he says: Into the

οἶκόν μου ἐπιστρέψω ὅθεν ἐξῆλθον·
house of me I will return whence I came out;

καὶ ἐλθὸν εὑρίσκει σχολάζοντα [καὶ]
and coming he finds [it] standing empty and

σεσαρωμένον καὶ κεκοσμημένον. 45 τότε
having been swept and *having been* furnished. Then

πορεύεται καὶ παραλαμβάνει μεθ' ἑαυτοῦ
he goes and takes with himself

ἑπτὰ ἕτερα πνεύματα πονηρότερα ἑαυτοῦ,
seven other spirits more evil [than] himself,

καὶ εἰσελθόντα κατοικεῖ ἐκεῖ· καὶ
and entering dwells there; and

γίνεται τὰ ἔσχατα τοῦ ἀνθρώπου ἐκείνου
becomes the last things - man of that

χείρονα τῶν πρώτων. οὕτως ἔσται
worse [than] the first. Thus it will be

καὶ τῇ γενεᾷ ταύτῃ τῇ πονηρᾷ.
also - ³generation ¹to this - ²evil.

46 Ἔτι αὐτοῦ λαλοῦντος τοῖς ὄχλοις,
Yet him speakingª to the crowds,
=While he was still speaking

ἰδοὺ ἡ μήτηρ καὶ οἱ ἀδελφοὶ αὐτοῦ
behold the mother and the brothers of him

εἱστήκεισαν ἔξω ζητοῦντες αὐτῷ λαλῆσαι.
stood outside seeking to him to speak.

47 [εἶπεν δέ τις αὐτῷ· ἰδοὺ ἡ μήτηρ
And said someone to him: Behold[,] the mother

σου καὶ οἱ ἀδελφοί σου ἔξω ἑστήκασιν
of thee and the brothers of thee outside are standing

ζητοῦντές σοι λαλῆσαι.] 48 ὁ δὲ
seeking to thee to speak.] And he

ἀποκριθεὶς εἶπεν τῷ λέγοντι αὐτῷ· τίς
answering said to the [one] saying to him: Who

ἐστιν ἡ μήτηρ μου, καὶ τίνες εἰσὶν οἱ
is the mother of me, and who are the

49And stretching out his hand toward his disciples, he said, "Here are my mother and my brothers! 50For whoever does the will of my Father in heaven is my brother, and sister, and mother."

ἀδελφοί μου;   **49** καὶ ἐκτείνας τὴν
brothers of me?   And stretching forth the

χεῖρα [αὐτοῦ] ἐπὶ τοὺς μαθητὰς αὐτοῦ
hand of him on the disciples of him

εἶπεν· ἰδοὺ ἡ μήτηρ μου καὶ οἱ ἀδελφοί
he said: Behold[,] the mother of me and the brothers

μου.   **50** ὅστις γὰρ ἂν ποιήσῃ τὸ θέλημα
of me.   For whoever does the will

τοῦ πατρός μου τοῦ ἐν οὐρανοῖς, αὐτός
of the Father of me – in heavens, he

μου ἀδελφὸς καὶ ἀδελφὴ καὶ μήτηρ ἐστίν.
of me brother and sister and mother is.

CHAPTER 13

THAT same day Jesus went out of the house and sat beside the sea. 2And great crowds gathered about him, so that he got into a boat and sat there; and the whole crowd stood on the beach. 3And he told them many things in parables, saying: "A sower went out to sow. 4And as he sowed, some seeds fell along the path, and the birds came and devoured them. 5Other seeds fell on rocky ground, where they had not much soil, and immediately they sprang up, since they had no depth of soil, 6but when the sun rose they were scorched; and since they

13 Ἐν τῇ ἡμέρᾳ ἐκείνῃ ἐξελθὼν ὁ
On – day that ²going out of –

Ἰησοῦς τῆς οἰκίας ἐκάθητο παρὰ τὴν
¹Jesus of the house sat beside the

θάλασσαν·   **2** καὶ συνήχθησαν πρὸς αὐτὸν
sea;   and were assembled to him

ὄχλοι πολλοί, ὥστε αὐτὸν εἰς πλοῖον
crowds many, so as him in a ship
=so that embarking in a ship he sat,

ἐμβάντα καθῆσθαι, καὶ πᾶς ὁ ὄχλος
embarking to sit[b], and all the crowd

ἐπὶ τὸν αἰγιαλὸν εἱστήκει.   **3** καὶ ἐλάλησεν
on the beach stood.   And he spoke

αὐτοῖς πολλὰ ἐν παραβολαῖς λέγων·
to them many things in parables saying:

Ἰδοὺ ἐξῆλθεν ὁ σπείρων τοῦ σπείρειν.
Behold went out the [one] sowing – to sow[d].

4 καὶ ἐν τῷ σπείρειν αὐτὸν ἃ μὲν
And in the to sow him[e] some indeed
=as he sowed

ἔπεσεν παρὰ τὴν ὁδόν, καὶ ἐλθόντα τὰ
fell beside the way, and coming the

πετεινὰ κατέφαγεν αὐτά.   **5** ἄλλα δὲ
birds devoured them.   But others

ἔπεσεν ἐπὶ τὰ πετρώδη ὅπου οὐκ
fell on the rocky places where not

εἶχεν γῆν πολλήν, καὶ εὐθέως ἐξανέτειλεν
it had earth much, and immediately it sprang up

διὰ τὸ μὴ ἔχειν βάθος γῆς· **6** ἡλίου
on account of the not to have depth of earth; [the] sun
=because it had not

δὲ ἀνατείλαντος[a] ἐκαυματίσθη, καὶ διὰ
But having risen[a] it was scorched, and on account of
=when the sun rose   =because

had no root they with-
ered away. ⁷Other seeds
fell upon thorns, and the
thorns grew up and
choked them. ⁸Other
seeds fell on good soil
and brought forth grain,
some a hundredfold,
some sixty, some thirty.
⁹He who has ears,ᵛ let
him hear."
10 Then the disciples
came and said to him,
"Why do you speak to
them in parables?" ¹¹And
he answered them, "To
you it has been given to
know the secrets of the
kingdom of heaven, but
to them it has not been
given. ¹²For to him who
has will more be given,
and he will have abun-
dance; but from him who
has not, even what he
has will be taken away.
¹³This is why I speak to
them in parables, be-
cause seeing they do not
see, and hearing they do
not hear, nor do they
understand. ¹⁴With them
indeed is fulfilled the
prophecy of Isaiah which
says:
    'You shall indeed hear
       but never under-
       stand,
    and you shall indeed
       see but never
       perceive.
¹⁵For this people's heart
       has grown dull,
    and their ears are
       heavy of hearing,

ᵛ Other ancient authorities add
here and in verse 43 to hear

τὸ   μὴ   ἔχειν   ῥίζαν   ἐξηράνθη.   7 ἄλλα δὲ
the   not   to have   root   it was dried up.   But others
      it had not

ἔπεσεν   ἐπὶ   τὰς   ἀκάνθας,   καὶ   ἀνέβησαν
fell   on   the   thorns,   and   came up

αἱ   ἄκανθαι   καὶ   ἀπέπνιξαν   αὐτά.   8 ἄλλα δὲ
the   thorns   and   choked   them.   And others

ἔπεσεν   ἐπὶ   τὴν   γῆν   τὴν   καλὴν   καὶ
fell   on   the   earth   -   good   and

ἐδίδου   καρπόν,   ὃ   μὲν   ἑκατόν,   ὃ   δὲ
gave   fruit,   the one   a hundred,   the other

ἑξήκοντα,   ὃ   δὲ   τριάκοντα.   9 ὁ   ἔχων
sixty,   the other   thirty.   The [one] having

ὦτα   ἀκουέτω.   10 Καὶ   προσελθόντες   οἱ
ears   let him hear.   And   approaching   the

μαθηταὶ   εἶπαν   αὐτῷ·   διὰ τί   ἐν   παρα-
disciples   said   to him: Why   in   par-

βολαῖς   λαλεῖς   αὐτοῖς;   11 ὁ   δὲ
ables   speakest thou   to them?   And he

ἀποκριθεὶς   εἶπεν·   ὅτι   ὑμῖν   δέδοται
answering   said: Because   to you it has been given

γνῶναι   τὰ   μυστήρια   τῆς   βασιλείας   τῶν
to know   the   mysteries   of the   kingdom   of the

οὐρανῶν,   ἐκείνοις   δὲ   οὐ   δέδοται.   12 ὅστις
heavens,   but to those   it has not been given.   [he] who

γὰρ   ἔχει,   δοθήσεται   αὐτῷ   καὶ   περισ-
For   has,   it will be given   to him   and   he will

σευθήσεται·   ὅστις   δὲ   οὐκ   ἔχει,   καὶ
have abundance;   but [he] who   has not,   even

ὃ   ἔχει   ἀρθήσεται   ἀπ'   αὐτοῦ.   13 διὰ
what he has   will be taken   from   him.   There-

τοῦτο   ἐν   παραβολαῖς   αὐτοῖς   λαλῶ,   ὅτι
fore   in   parables   to them   I speak,   because

βλέποντες   οὐ   βλέπουσιν   καὶ   ἀκούοντες
seeing   they see not   and   hearing

οὐκ   ἀκούουσιν   οὐδὲ   συνιοῦσιν.   14 καὶ
they hear not   neither   understand.   And

ἀναπληροῦται   αὐτοῖς   ἡ   προφητεία   Ἠσαΐου
is fulfilled   in them   the   prophecy   of Isaiah

ἡ   λέγουσα·   ἀκοῇ   ἀκούσετε   καὶ   οὐ μὴ
-     saying: In hearing   ye will hear   and   by no means

συνῆτε,   καὶ   βλέποντες   βλέψετε
understand,   and   seeing   ye will see

καὶ   οὐ μὴ   ἴδητε.   15 ἐπαχύνθη   γὰρ
and   by no means   perceive.   For waxed gross

ἡ   καρδία   τοῦ   λαοῦ   τούτου,   καὶ   τοῖς
the   heart   -   people   of this,   and   with the

and their eyes they have closed,
lest they should perceive with their eyes, and hear with their ears,
and understand with their heart,
and turn for me to heal them.'

¹⁶ But blessed are your eyes, for they see, and your ears, for they hear. ¹⁷ Truly, I say to you, many prophets and righteous men longed to see what you see, and did not see it, and to hear what you hear, and did not hear it.

18 "Hear then the parable of the sower. ¹⁹ When any one hears the word of the kingdom and does not understand it, the evil one comes and snatches away what is sown in his heart; this is what was sown along the path. ²⁰ As for what was sown on rocky ground, this is he who hears the word and immediately receives it with joy; ²¹ yet he has no root in himself, but endures for a while, and when tribulation or persecution arises on account of the word, immediately he falls away.^z

ὦσὶν βαρέως ἤκουσαν, καὶ τοὺς ὀφθαλμοὺς
ears   heavily   they heard,   and   the   eyes

αὐτῶν ἐκάμμυσαν· μήποτε ἴδωσιν τοῖς
of them   they closed;   lest   they see   with the

ὀφθαλμοῖς καὶ τοῖς ὠσὶν ἀκούσωσιν
eyes   and   with the   ears   hear

καὶ τῇ καρδίᾳ συνῶσιν καὶ ἐπιστρέψωσιν,
and   with the   heart   understand   and   turn back,

καὶ ἰάσομαι αὐτούς.   **16** ὑμῶν δὲ μακάριοι
and   I will heal   them.   But of you   blessed

οἱ ὀφθαλμοὶ ὅτι βλέπουσιν, καὶ τὰ
the   eyes   because   they see,   and   the

ὦτα [ὑμῶν] ὅτι ἀκούουσιν.   **17** ἀμὴν
ears   of you   because   they hear.   truly

γὰρ λέγω ὑμῖν ὅτι πολλοὶ προφῆται καὶ
For   I say   to you   that   many   prophets   and

δίκαιοι ἐπεθύμησαν ἰδεῖν ἃ
righteous men   desired   to see   [the things] which

βλέπετε καὶ οὐκ εἶδαν, καὶ ἀκοῦσαι
ye see   and   did not see,   and   to hear

ἃ ἀκούετε καὶ οὐκ ἤκουσαν.
[the things] which   ye hear   and   did not hear.

18 Ὑμεῖς οὖν ἀκούσατε τὴν παραβολὴν
²Ye   ³therefore   ¹hear   the   parable

τοῦ σπείραντος.   **19** Παντὸς ἀκούοντος^a
of the   sowing [one].   Everyone   hearing^a
                                 = When anyone hears

τὸν λόγον τῆς βασιλείας καὶ μὴ συνιέντος
the   word   of the   kingdom   and   not understanding^a
                                 = does not understand

ἔρχεται ὁ πονηρὸς καὶ ἁρπάζει τὸ
comes   the   evil one   and   seizes the [thing]

ἐσπαρμένον ἐν τῇ καρδίᾳ αὐτοῦ· οὗτός
having been sown   in   the   heart   of him;   this

ἐστιν ὁ παρὰ τὴν ὁδὸν σπαρείς.   **20** ὁ
is   the [word]   by   the   way   sown.   the [word]

δὲ ἐπὶ τὰ πετρώδη σπαρείς, οὗτός ἐστιν
And   on   the   rocky places   sown,   this   is

ὁ τὸν λόγον ἀκούων καὶ εὐθὺς μετὰ
the [one]   ²the   ³word   ¹hearing   and   immediately with

χαρᾶς λαμβάνων αὐτόν·   **21** οὐκ ἔχει δὲ
joy   receiving   it;   but he has not

ῥίζαν ἐν ἑαυτῷ ἀλλὰ πρόσκαιρός ἐστιν,
root   in   himself   but   short-lived   is,

γενομένης δὲ θλίψεως ἢ διωγμοῦ
and occurring   tribulation   or   persecution^a
           = when tribulation or persecution occurs

διὰ τὸν λόγον εὐθὺς σκανδαλίζεται.
on account of the   word   immediately   he is offended.

^z Or *stumbles*

²²As for what was sown among thorns, this is he who hears the word, but the cares of the world and the delight in riches choke the word, and it proves unfruitful. ²³As for what was sown on good soil, this is he who hears the word and understands it; he indeed bears fruit, and yields, in one case a hundredfold, in another sixty, and in another thirty."

24 Another parable he put before them, saying, "The kingdom of heaven may be compared to a man who sowed good seed in his field; ²⁵but while men were sleeping, his enemy came and sowed weeds among the wheat, and went away. ²⁶So when the plants came up and bore grain, then the weeds appeared also. ²⁷And the servants of the householder came and said to him, 'Sir, did you not sow good seed in your field? How then has it weeds?' ²⁸He said to them, 'An enemy has

22 ὁ   δὲ   εἰς   τὰς   ἀκάνθας   σπαρείς,   οὗτός
But the [word] in   the   thorns   sown,   this

ἐστιν   ὁ   τὸν   λόγον   ἀκούων,   καὶ   ἡ
is   the [one] ²the   ³word   ¹hearing,   and   the

μέριμνα   τοῦ   αἰῶνος   καὶ   ἡ   ἀπάτη
anxiety   of the   age   and   the   deceit

τοῦ   πλούτου   συμπνίγει   τὸν   λόγον,   καὶ
-    of riches   chokes   the   word,   and

ἄκαρπος   γίνεται.   23 ὁ   δὲ   ἐπὶ   τὴν
unfruitful   it becomes.   And the [word] on   the

καλὴν   γῆν   σπαρείς,   οὗτός   ἐστιν   ὁ
good   earth   sown,   this   is the [one]

τὸν   λόγον   ἀκούων   καὶ   συνιείς,   ὃς
⁴the   ⁵word   ¹hearing   ²and   ³understanding, who

δὴ   καρποφορεῖ   καὶ   ποιεῖ   ὃ   μὲν   ἑκατόν,
indeed   bears fruit   and   produces one indeed   a hundred,

ὃ   δὲ   ἑξήκοντα,   ὃ   δὲ   τριάκοντα.
the other   sixty,   the other   thirty.

24 Ἄλλην   παραβολὴν   παρέθηκεν   αὐτοῖς
Another   parable   he set before   them

λέγων·   ὡμοιώθη   ἡ   βασιλεία   τῶν
saying: was(is) likened   The   kingdom   of the

οὐρανῶν   ἀνθρώπῳ   σπείραντι   καλὸν   σπέρμα
heavens   to a man   sowing   good   seed

ἐν   τῷ   ἀγρῷ   αὐτοῦ.   25 ἐν   δὲ   τῷ
in   the   field   of him.   But in   the
=while men slept

καθεύδειν   τοὺς   ἀνθρώπους   ἦλθεν   αὐτοῦ
to sleep   -   menᵉ   came   of him

ὁ   ἐχθρὸς   καὶ   ἐπέσπειρεν   ζιζάνια   ἀνὰ μέσον
the   enemy   and   oversowed   tares   in between

τοῦ   σίτου   καὶ   ἀπῆλθεν.   26 ὅτε   δὲ
the   wheat   and   went away.   But when

ἐβλάστησεν   ὁ   χόρτος   καὶ   καρπὸν
sprouted   the   grass   and   fruit

ἐποίησεν,   τότε   ἐφάνη   καὶ   τὰ   ζιζάνια.
produced,   then   appeared   also   the   tares.

27 προσελθόντες   δὲ   οἱ   δοῦλοι   τοῦ   οἰκο-
So approaching   the   slaves   of the   house-

δεσπότου   εἶπον   αὐτῷ·   κύριε,   οὐχὶ   καλὸν
master   said   to him: Lord,   not   good

σπέρμα   ἔσπειρας   ἐν   τῷ   σῷ   ἀγρῷ;
seed   sowedst thou   in   -   thy   field?

πόθεν   οὖν   ἔχει   ζιζάνια;   28 ὁ   δὲ   ἔφη
whence   then   has it   tares?   And he   said

αὐτοῖς·   ἐχθρὸς   ἄνθρωπος   τοῦτο   ἐποίησεν.
to them: An enemy   man   this   did.

done this.' The servants said to him, 'Then do you want to go and gather them?' [29] But he said, 'No; lest in gathering the weeds you root up the wheat along with them. [30] Let both grow together until the harvest; and at harvest time I will tell the reapers, Gather the weeds first and bind them in bundles to be burned, but gather the wheat into my barn.' "

[31] Another parable he put before them, saying, "The kingdom of heaven is like a grain of mustard seed which a man took and sowed in his field; [32] it is the smallest of all seeds, but when it has grown it is the greatest of shrubs and becomes a tree, so that the birds of the air come and make nests in its branches."

[33] He told them another parable. "The kingdom of heaven is like leaven which a woman took and hid in three measures of meal, till it was all leavened."

οἱ δὲ So the	δοῦλοι slaves	αὐτῷ λέγουσιν· to him say:	θέλεις Willest thou
οὖν then	ἀπελθόντες going away	συλλέξωμεν αὐτά; we may collect them?	29 ὁ he
δὲ But	φησιν· says:	οὔ, μήποτε No, lest	συλλέγοντες τὰ collecting the
ζιζάνια tares	ἐκριζώσητε ye should root up	ἅμα αὐτοῖς together with them	τὸν the
σῖτον. wheat.	30 ἄφετε Leave	συναυξάνεσθαι to grow together	ἀμφότερα both
ἕως τοῦ until the	θερισμοῦ· harvest;	καὶ ἐν καιρῷ and in time	τοῦ of the
θερισμοῦ harvest	ἐρῶ τοῖς I will say to the	θερισταῖς· reapers:	συλλέξατε Collect ye
πρῶτον first	τὰ ζιζάνια the tares	καὶ δήσατε and bind	αὐτὰ them
εἰς δέσμας in bundles	πρὸς τὸ – –	κατακαῦσαι to burn	αὐτά, them,
τὸν δὲ but the	σῖτον wheat	συναγάγετε εἰς τὴν gather ye into the	ἀποθήκην barn
μου. of me.	31 Ἄλλην Another	παραβολὴν parable	παρέθηκεν he set before
αὐτοῖς them	λέγων· saying:	ὁμοία ἐστὶν ἡ Like is the	βασιλεία kingdom
τῶν of the	οὐρανῶν heavens	κόκκῳ σινάπεως, to a grain of mustard,	ὃν which
λαβὼν ¹taking	ἄνθρωπος ¹a man	ἔσπειρεν ἐν τῷ sowed in the	ἀγρῷ field
αὐτοῦ· of him;	32 ὃ which	μικρότερον μέν less indeed	ἐστιν is
πάντων [than] all	τῶν the	σπερμάτων, seeds,	ὅταν δὲ but when
αὐξηθῇ, it grows,	μεῖζον τῶν greater [than] the	λαχάνων herbs	ἐστὶν it is
καὶ γίνεται and becomes	δένδρον, a tree,	ὥστε ἐλθεῖν τὰ so as to come the	
πετεινὰ birds	τοῦ of the	οὐρανοῦ καὶ heaven and	κατασκηνοῦν dwell
ἐν τοῖς in the	κλάδοις branches	αὐτοῦ. of it.	33 Ἄλλην Another
παραβολὴν parable	ἐλάλησεν he spoke	αὐτοῖς· to them:	ὁμοία Like
ἐστὶν is	ἡ βασιλεία the kingdom	τῶν οὐρανῶν of the heavens	ζύμῃ, to leaven,
ἣν λαβοῦσα which ²taking	γυνὴ ¹a woman	ἐνέκρυψεν εἰς hid in	ἀλεύρου ³of meal
σάτα ²measures	τρία, ¹three,	ἕως οὗ until	ἐζυμώθη ὅλον. was leavened [the] whole.

34 All this Jesus said to the crowds in parables; indeed he said nothing to them without a parable. [35]This was to fulfil what was spoken by the prophet:[a]
"I will open my mouth in parables,
I will utter what has been hidden since the foundation of the world."
36 Then he left the crowds and went into the house. And his disciples came to him, saying, "Explain to us the parable of the weeds of the field." [37]He answered, "He who sows the good seed is the Son of man; [38]the field is the world, and the good seed means the sons of the kingdom; the weeds are the sons of the evil one, [39]and the enemy who sowed them is the devil; the harvest is the close of the age, and the reapers are angels. [40]Just as the weeds are gathered and burned with fire, so will it be at the close of the age. [41]The Son of man will send his angels, and they will gather out of his kingdom

34 Ταῦτα πάντα ἐλάλησεν ὁ Ἰησοῦς ἐν
These things all spoke – Jesus in

παραβολαῖς τοῖς ὄχλοις, καὶ χωρὶς παραβολῆς
parables to the crowds, and without a parable

οὐδὲν ἐλάλει αὐτοῖς· **35** ὅπως πληρωθῇ
nothing he spoke to them; so that was fulfilled

τὸ ῥηθὲν διὰ τοῦ προφήτου λέγοντος·
the [thing] spoken through the prophet saying:

ἀνοίξω ἐν παραβολαῖς τὸ στόμα μου,
I will open in parables the mouth of me,

ἐρεύξομαι κεκρυμμένα ἀπὸ καταβολῆς.
I will utter things having been hidden from [the] foundation.

36 Τότε ἀφεὶς τοὺς ὄχλους ἦλθεν
Then sending away the crowds he came

εἰς τὴν οἰκίαν. Καὶ προσῆλθον αὐτῷ
into the house. And approached to him

οἱ μαθηταὶ αὐτοῦ λέγοντες· διασάφησον
the disciples of him saying: Explain thou

ἡμῖν τὴν παραβολὴν τῶν ζιζανίων τοῦ
to us the parable of the tares of the

ἀγροῦ. **37** ὁ δὲ ἀποκριθεὶς εἶπεν· ὁ
field. And he answering said: The [one]

σπείρων τὸ καλὸν σπέρμα ἐστὶν ὁ
sowing the good seed is the

υἱὸς τοῦ ἀνθρώπου· **38** ὁ δὲ ἀγρός
Son – of man; and the field

ἐστιν ὁ κόσμος· τὸ δὲ καλὸν σπέρμα,
is the world; and the good seed,

οὗτοί εἰσιν οἱ υἱοὶ τῆς βασιλείας· τὰ δὲ
these are the sons of the kingdom; and the

ζιζάνιά εἰσιν οἱ υἱοὶ τοῦ πονηροῦ, **39** ὁ
tares are the sons of the evil [one], the

δὲ ἐχθρὸς ὁ σπείρας αὐτά ἐστιν ὁ
and enemy the [one] sowing them is the

διάβολος· ὁ δὲ θερισμὸς συντέλεια
devil; and the harvest [the] completion

αἰῶνός ἐστιν, οἱ δὲ θερισταὶ ἄγγελοί
of [the] age is, and the reapers angels

εἰσιν. **40** ὥσπερ οὖν συλλέγεται τὰ
are. As therefore are collected the

ζιζάνια καὶ πυρὶ κατακαίεται, οὕτως
tares and with fire are consumed, thus

ἔσται ἐν τῇ συντελείᾳ τοῦ αἰῶνος·
it will be at the completion of the age;

41 ἀποστελεῖ ὁ υἱὸς τοῦ ἀνθρώπου
will send forth the Son – of man

[a] Other ancient authorities read *the prophet Isaiah*

τοὺς ἀγγέλους αὐτοῦ, καὶ συλλέξουσιν
the angels of him, and they will collect

all causes of sin and all evildoers, ⁴²and throw them into the furnace of fire; there men will weep and gnash their teeth. ⁴³Then the righteous will shine like the sun in the kingdom of their Father. He who has ears, let him hear.

44 "The kingdom of heaven is like treasure hidden in a field, which a man found and covered up; then in his joy he goes and sells all that he has and buys that field.

45 "Again, the kingdom of heaven is like a merchant in search of fine pearls, ⁴⁶who, on finding one pearl of great value, went and sold all that he had and bought it.

47 "Again, the kingdom of heaven is like a net which was thrown into the sea and gathered fish of every kind; ⁴⁸when it was full, men drew it ashore and sat down and sorted the good into vessels but threw away the bad. ⁴⁹So it will be at

ἐκ τῆς βασιλείας αὐτοῦ πάντα
out of the kingdom of him all

τὰ σκάνδαλα καὶ τοὺς ποιοῦντας
the things leading to sin and the [ones] doing

τὴν ἀνομίαν, 42 καὶ βαλοῦσιν αὐτοὺς εἰς
– lawlessness, and will cast them into

τὴν κάμινον τοῦ πυρός· ἐκεῖ ἔσται ὁ
the furnace – of fire; there will be the

κλαυθμὸς καὶ ὁ βρυγμὸς τῶν ὀδόντων.
wailing and the gnashing of the teeth.

43 τότε οἱ δίκαιοι ἐκλάμψουσιν ὡς ὁ
Then the righteous will shine forth as the

ἥλιος ἐν τῇ βασιλείᾳ τοῦ πατρὸς
sun in the kingdom of the Father

αὐτῶν. ὁ ἔχων ὦτα ἀκουέτω.
of them. The [one] having ears let him hear.

44 Ὁμοία ἐστὶν ἡ βασιλεία τῶν
Like is the kingdom of the

οὐρανῶν θησαυρῷ κεκρυμμένῳ ἐν τῷ
heavens to treasure *having been* hidden in the

ἀγρῷ, ὃν εὑρὼν ἄνθρωπος ἔκρυψεν, καὶ
field, which ²finding ¹a man hid, and

ἀπὸ τῆς χαρᾶς αὐτοῦ ὑπάγει καὶ πωλεῖ
from the joy of him goes and sells

ὅσα ἔχει καὶ ἀγοράζει τὸν ἀγρὸν
what things he has and buys – field

ἐκεῖνον. 45 Πάλιν ὁμοία ἐστὶν ἡ
that. Again, like is the

βασιλεία τῶν οὐρανῶν ἐμπόρῳ ζητοῦντι
kingdom of the heavens to a merchant seeking

καλοὺς μαργαρίτας· 46 εὑρὼν δὲ ἕνα πολύτιμον
beautiful pearls; and finding one valuable

μαργαρίτην ἀπελθὼν πέπρακεν πάντα
pearl going away sold all things

ὅσα εἶχεν καὶ ἠγόρασεν αὐτόν.
what he had and bought it.

47 Πάλιν ὁμοία ἐστὶν ἡ βασιλεία τῶν
Again, like is the kingdom of the

οὐρανῶν σαγήνῃ βληθείσῃ εἰς τὴν θάλασσαν
heavens to a net cast into the sea

καὶ ἐκ παντὸς γένους συναγαγούσῃ·
and of every kind gathering;

48 ἣν ὅτε ἐπληρώθη ἀναβιβάσαντες ἐπὶ
which when it was filled bringing up onto

τὸν αἰγιαλὸν καὶ καθίσαντες συνέλεξαν
the shore and sitting collected

τὰ καλὰ εἰς ἄγγη, τὰ δὲ σαπρὰ ἔξω
the good into vessels, but the bad out

the close of the age. The angels will come out and separate the evil from the righteous, ⁵⁰ and throw them into the furnace of fire; there men will weep and gnash their teeth.

51 "Have you understood all this?" They said to him, "Yes." ⁵²And he said to them, "Therefore every scribe who has been trained for the kingdom of heaven is like a householder who brings out of his treasure what is new and what is old."

53 And when Jesus had finished these parables, he went away from there, ⁵⁴ and coming to his own country he taught them in their synagogue, so that they were astonished, and said, "Where did this man get this wisdom and these mighty works? ⁵⁵ Is not this the carpenter's son? Is not his mother called Mary? And are not his brothers James and Joseph and Simon and Judas? ⁵⁶And are not all his sisters with us?

ἔβαλον. **49** οὕτως ἔσται ἐν τῇ συντελείᾳ
cast.   Thus   it will be at   the completion

τοῦ αἰῶνος· ἐξελεύσονται οἱ ἄγγελοι καὶ
of the age: will go forth the angels   and

ἀφοριοῦσιν τοὺς πονηροὺς ἐκ μέσου
will separate the evil men from [the] midst

τῶν δικαίων, **50** καὶ βαλοῦσιν αὐτοὺς
of the righteous,   and will cast   them

εἰς τὴν κάμινον τοῦ πυρός· ἐκεῖ
into the furnace   -   of fire;   there

ἔσται ὁ κλαυθμὸς καὶ ὁ βρυγμὸς τῶν
will be the wailing and the gnashing of the

ὀδόντων. **51** Συνήκατε ταῦτα πάντα;
teeth.   Did ye understand ²these things ¹all?

λέγουσιν αὐτῷ· ναί. **52** ὁ δὲ εἶπεν
They say   to him: Yes.   So he said

αὐτοῖς· διὰ τοῦτο πᾶς γραμματεὺς
to them: Therefore every   scribe

μαθητευθεὶς τῇ βασιλείᾳ τῶν οὐρανῶν
made a disciple to the kingdom of the heavens

ὅμοιός ἐστιν ἀνθρώπῳ οἰκοδεσπότῃ,
like   is   to a man   a housemaster,

ὅστις ἐκβάλλει ἐκ τοῦ θησαυροῦ
who   puts forth out of the treasure

αὐτοῦ καινὰ καὶ παλαιά.
of him new   and old things.

53 Καὶ ἐγένετο ὅτε ἐτέλεσεν ὁ
And it came to pass when ended   -

Ἰησοῦς τὰς παραβολὰς ταύτας, μετῆρεν
Jesus   -   parables   these, he removed

ἐκεῖθεν. **54** καὶ ἐλθὼν εἰς τὴν πατρίδα
thence.   And coming into the native town

αὐτοῦ ἐδίδασκεν αὐτοὺς ἐν τῇ συνα-
of him he taught   them   in the syna-

γωγῇ αὐτῶν, ὥστε ἐκπλήσσεσθαι αὐτοὺς
gogue of them, so as to be astounded   them
                  =so that they were astounded

καὶ λέγειν· πόθεν τούτῳ ἡ σοφία αὕτη
and to say^b: Whence to this man - wisdom this
and said:

καὶ αἱ δυνάμεις; **55** οὐχ οὗτός ἐστιν
and the powerful deeds?   not this man   is

ὁ τοῦ τέκτονος υἱός; οὐχ ἡ μήτηρ
the of the carpenter son? not the mother

αὐτοῦ λέγεται Μαριὰμ καὶ οἱ ἀδελφοὶ
of him called   Mary   and the brothers

αὐτοῦ Ἰάκωβος καὶ Ἰωσὴφ καὶ Σίμων
of him James   and Joseph and Simon

καὶ Ἰούδας; **56** καὶ αἱ ἀδελφαὶ αὐτοῦ
and Judas?   and the sisters of him

Where then did this man get all this?" ⁵⁷And they took offense at him. But Jesus said to them, "A prophet is not without honor except in his own country and in his own house." ⁵⁸And he did not do many mighty works there, because of their unbelief.

οὐχὶ	πᾶσαι	πρὸς	ἡμᾶς	εἰσιν;	πόθεν
not	all	with	us	are?	Whence

οὖν	τούτῳ	ταῦτα	πάντα;	57 καὶ
then	to this man	these things	all?	And

ἐσκανδαλίζοντο	ἐν	αὐτῷ.	ὁ	δὲ	Ἰησοῦς
they were offended	in	him.	-	But	Jesus

εἶπεν	αὐτοῖς·	οὐκ	ἔστιν	προφήτης
said	to them:	²not	²is	¹A prophet

ἄτιμος	εἰ μὴ	ἐν	τῇ	πατρίδι	καὶ
unhonoured	except	in	the(his)	native town	and

ἐν	τῇ	οἰκίᾳ	αὐτοῦ.	58 καὶ	οὐκ	ἐποίησεν	ἐκεῖ
in	the	house	of him.	And	not	he did	there

δυνάμεις	πολλὰς	διὰ	τὴν	ἀπιστίαν	αὐτῶν.
powerful deeds	many	because of	the	unbelief	of them.

CHAPTER 14

AT that time Herod the tetrarch heard about the fame of Jesus; ²and he said to his servants, "This is John the Baptist, he has been raised from the dead; that is why these powers are at work in him." ³For Herod had seized John and bound him and put him in prison, for the sake of Hero'di-as, his brother Philip's wife;ᵇ ⁴because John said to him, "It is not lawful for you to have her." ⁵And though he wanted to put him to death, he feared the people, because they held him to be a prophet. ⁶But when Herod's birthday came, the daughter of Hero'di-as danced before the company, and pleased Herod,

14 Ἐν	ἐκείνῳ	τῷ	καιρῷ	ἤκουσεν
At	that	-	time	heard

Ἡρῴδης	ὁ	τετραάρχης	τὴν	ἀκοὴν	Ἰησοῦ,
Herod	the	tetrarch	the	report	of Jesus,

2 καὶ	εἶπεν	τοῖς	παισὶν	αὐτοῦ·	οὗτός
and	said	to the	servants	of him:	This

ἐστιν	Ἰωάννης	ὁ	βαπτιστής·	αὐτὸς
is	John	the	Baptist;	he

ἠγέρθη	ἀπὸ	τῶν	νεκρῶν,	καὶ	διὰ	τοῦτο
was raised	from	the	dead,	and		therefore

αἱ	δυνάμεις	ἐνεργοῦσιν	ἐν	αὐτῷ.
the	powerful deeds	operate	in	him.

3 Ὁ	γὰρ	Ἡρῴδης	κρατήσας	τὸν	Ἰωάννην
-	For	Herod	seizing	-	John

ἔδησεν	καὶ	ἐν	φυλακῇ	ἀπέθετο	διὰ
bound	and	in	prison	put away	on account of

Ἡρῳδιάδα	τὴν	γυναῖκα	Φιλίππου	τοῦ
Herodias	the	wife	of Philip	the

ἀδελφοῦ	αὐτοῦ·	4 ἔλεγεν	γὰρ	ὁ	Ἰωάννης
brother	of him;	for said	-		John

αὐτῷ·	οὐκ	ἔξεστίν	σοι	ἔχειν	αὐτήν.
to him:	It is not lawful	for thee	to have	her.

5 καὶ	θέλων	αὐτὸν	ἀποκτεῖναι	ἐφοβήθη
And	wishing	him	to kill	he feared

τὸν	ὄχλον,	ὅτι	ὡς	προφήτην	αὐτὸν
the	crowd,	because	as	a prophet	him

εἶχον.	6 γενεσίοις	δὲ	γενομένοις	τοῦ
they had.	Now on the birthday		occurringᵃ	-

Ἡρῴδου	ὠρχήσατο	ἡ	θυγάτηρ	τῆς
of Herod	danced	the	daughter	the

Ἡρῳδιάδος	ἐν	τῷ	μέσῳ	καὶ	ἤρεσεν
of Herodias	in	the	midst	and	pleased

ᵇ Other ancient authorities read his brother's wife

7 so that he promised with an oath to give her whatever she might ask. 8 Prompted by her mother, she said, "Give me the head of John the Baptist here on a platter." 9 And the king was sorry; but because of his oaths and his guests he commanded it to be given; 10 he sent and had John beheaded in the prison, 11 and his head was brought on a platter and given to the girl, and she brought it to her mother. 12 And his disciples came and took the body and buried it; and they went and told Jesus.

13 Now when Jesus heard this, he withdrew from there in a boat to a lonely place apart. But when the crowds heard it, they followed him on foot from the towns. 14 As he went ashore he saw a great throng; and he had compassion on them, and healed their sick. 15 When it was evening, the disciples came to him and said, "This is a lonely place, and the day is now

τῷ 'Ηρῴδη, 7 ὅθεν μεθ' ὅρκου ὡμολόγησεν
- Herod, whence with an oath he promised

αὐτῇ δοῦναι ὃ ἐὰν αἰτήσηται. 8 ἡ δὲ
²her ¹to give whatever she might ask. So she

προβιβασθεῖσα ὑπὸ τῆς μητρὸς αὐτῆς·
being instructed by the mother of her:

δός μοι, φησίν, ὧδε ἐπὶ πίνακι τὴν
Give me, she says, here on a platter the

κεφαλὴν 'Ιωάννου τοῦ βαπτιστοῦ. 9 καὶ
head of John the Baptist. And

λυπηθεὶς ὁ βασιλεὺς διὰ τοὺς
being grieved the king on account of the

ὅρκους καὶ τοὺς συνανακειμένους
oaths and the [ones] reclining at table with [him]

ἐκέλευσεν δοθῆναι, 10 καὶ πέμψας
he commanded to be given, and sending

ἀπεκεφάλισεν 'Ιωάννην ἐν τῇ φυλακῇ.
beheaded John in the prison.

11 καὶ ἠνέχθη ἡ κεφαλὴ αὐτοῦ ἐπὶ
And was brought the head of him on

πίνακι καὶ ἐδόθη τῷ κορασίῳ, καὶ
a platter and was given to the maid, and

ἤνεγκεν τῇ μητρὶ αὐτῆς. 12 καὶ
she brought [it] to the mother of her. And

προσελθόντες οἱ μαθηταὶ αὐτοῦ ἦραν τὸ
⁴approaching ¹the ²disciples ³of him took the

πτῶμα καὶ ἔθαψαν αὐτόν, καὶ ἐλθόντες
corpse and buried him, and coming

ἀπήγγειλαν τῷ 'Ιησοῦ. 13 'Ακούσας δὲ
reported - to Jesus. And ³hearing

ὁ 'Ιησοῦς ἀνεχώρησεν ἐκεῖθεν ἐν
- ¹Jesus departed thence in

πλοίῳ εἰς ἔρημον τόπον κατ' ἰδίαν·
a ship to a desert place privately;

καὶ ἀκούσαντες οἱ ὄχλοι ἠκολούθησαν
and ³hearing ¹the ²crowds followed

αὐτῷ πεζῇ ἀπὸ τῶν πόλεων. 14 Καὶ
him afoot from the cities. And

ἐξελθὼν εἶδεν πολὺν ὄχλον, καὶ
going forth he saw a much crowd, and

ἐσπλαγχνίσθη ἐπ' αὐτοῖς καὶ
was filled with tenderness over them and

ἐθεράπευσεν τοὺς ἀρρώστους αὐτῶν.
healed the sick of them.

15 ὀψίας δὲ γενομένης προσῆλθον αὐτῷ
Now evening coming on ᵃ approached to him
            = when evening came on

οἱ μαθηταὶ λέγοντες· ἔρημός ἐστιν ὁ
the disciples saying: Desert is the

over; send the crowds away to go into the villages and buy food for themselves." [16]Jesus said, "They need not go away; you give them something to eat." [17]They said to him, "We have only five loaves here and two fish." [18]And he said, "Bring them here to me." [19]Then he ordered the crowds to sit down on the grass; and taking the five loaves and the two fish he looked up to heaven, and blessed, and broke and gave the loaves to the disciples, and the disciples gave them to the crowds. [20]And they all ate and were satisfied. And they took up twelve baskets full of the broken pieces left over. [21]And those who ate were about five thousand men, besides women and children.

22 Then he made the disciples get into the boat and go before him to the other side, while he dismissed the crowds. [23]And after he had dismissed the crowds, he went up into the hills by

τόπος　καὶ　ἡ　ὥρα　ἤδη　παρῆλθεν·
place　and　the　hour　already　passed;

ἀπόλυσον　οὖν　τοὺς　ὄχλους,　ἵνα　ἀπελθόντες
dismiss　therefore　the　crowds,　that　going away

εἰς　τὰς　κώμας　ἀγοράσωσιν　ἑαυτοῖς
into　the　villages　they may buy　for themselves

βρώματα.　16 ὁ　δὲ　'Ιησοῦς　εἶπεν　αὐτοῖς·
foods.　- But　Jesus　said　to them:

οὐ　χρείαν　ἔχουσιν　ἀπελθεῖν·　δότε
Not　need　they have　to go away;　give

αὐτοῖς　ὑμεῖς　φαγεῖν.　17 οἱ　δὲ　λέγουσιν
them　ye　to eat.　But they　say

αὐτῷ·　οὐκ　ἔχομεν　ὧδε　εἰ　μὴ　πέντε
to him:　We have not　here　except　five

ἄρτους　καὶ　δύο　ἰχθύας.　18 ὁ　δὲ　εἶπεν·
loaves　and　two　fishes.　And he　said:

φέρετέ　μοι　ὧδε　αὐτούς.　19 καὶ　κελεύσας
Bring　to me　here　them.　And　having commanded

τοὺς　ὄχλους　ἀνακλιθῆναι　ἐπὶ　τοῦ　χόρτου,
the　crowds　to recline　on　the　grass,

λαβὼν　τοὺς　πέντε　ἄρτους　καὶ　τοὺς　δύο
taking　the　five　loaves　and　the　two

ἰχθύας,　ἀναβλέψας　εἰς　τὸν　οὐρανὸν
fishes,　looking up　to　-　heaven

εὐλόγησεν,　καὶ　κλάσας　ἔδωκεν　τοῖς
he blessed,　and　breaking　gave　to the

μαθηταῖς　τοὺς　ἄρτους,　οἱ　δὲ　μαθηταὶ
disciples　the　loaves,　and the　disciples

τοῖς　ὄχλοις.　20 καὶ　ἔφαγον　πάντες　καὶ
to the　crowds,　And　ate　all　and

ἐχορτάσθησαν·　καὶ　ἦραν　τὸ　περισσεῦον
were satisfied;　and　they took　the　excess

τῶν　κλασμάτων,　δώδεκα　κοφίνους　πλήρεις.
of the　fragments,　twelve　baskets　full.

21 οἱ　δὲ　ἐσθίοντες　ἦσαν　ἄνδρες　ὡσεὶ
And the [ones]　eating　were　men　about

πεντακισχίλιοι　χωρὶς　γυναικῶν　καὶ
five thousand　apart from　women　and

παιδίων.　22 Καὶ　[εὐθέως]　ἠνάγκασεν
children.　And　immediately　he constrained

τοὺς　μαθητὰς　ἐμβῆναι　εἰς　τὸ　πλοῖον
the　disciples　to embark　in　the　ship

καὶ　προάγειν　αὐτὸν　εἰς　τὸ　πέραν,
and　to go before　him　to　the　other side,

ἕως　οὗ　ἀπολύσῃ　τοὺς　ὄχλους.　23 Καὶ
until　he should dismiss　the　crowds.　And

ἀπολύσας　τοὺς　ὄχλους　ἀνέβη　εἰς　τὸ
having dismissed　the　crowds　he went up　into　the

himself to pray. When evening came, he was there alone, ²⁴but the boat by this time was many furlongs distant from the land,ᶜ beaten by the waves; for the wind was against them. ²⁵And in the fourth watch of the night he came to them, walking on the sea. ²⁶But when the disciples saw him walking on the sea, they were terrified, saying, "It is a ghost!" And they cried out for fear. ²⁷But immediately he spoke to them, saying, "Take heart, it is I; have no fear."

28 And Peter answered him, "Lord, if it is you, bid me come to you on the water." ²⁹He said, "Come." So Peter got out of the boat and walked on the water and came to Jesus; ³⁰but when he saw the wind,ᵈ he was afraid, and beginning to sink he cried out, "Lord, save me." ³¹Jesus immediately reached out his hand and caught him, saying to him, "O man of little

ὄρος κατ' ἰδίαν προσεύξασθαι. ὀψίας
mountain privately to pray. evening
=And when

δὲ γενομένης μόνος ἦν ἐκεῖ. **24** τὸ δὲ
And coming onᵃ alone he was there. But the
evening came on

πλοῖον ἤδη σταδίους πολλοὺς ἀπὸ τῆς
ship now furlongs many from the

γῆς ἀπεῖχεν, βασανιζόμενον ὑπὸ τῶν
land was away, being distressed by the

κυμάτων, ἦν γὰρ ἐναντίος ὁ ἄνεμος.
waves, ⁴was ¹for ⁵contrary ²the ³wind.

25 τετάρτη δὲ φυλακῇ τῆς νυκτὸς
Now in [the] fourth watch of the night

ἦλθεν πρὸς αὐτοὺς περιπατῶν ἐπὶ τὴν
he came toward them walking on the

θάλασσαν. **26** οἱ δὲ μαθηταὶ ἰδόντες
sea. And the disciples seeing

αὐτὸν ἐπὶ τῆς θαλάσσης περιπατοῦντα
him on the sea walking

ἐταράχθησαν λέγοντες ὅτι φάντασμά
were troubled saying[.] - A phantasm

ἐστιν, καὶ ἀπὸ τοῦ φόβου ἔκραξαν.
it is, and from - fear they cried out.

27 εὐθὺς δὲ ἐλάλησεν [ὁ Ἰησοῦς]
But immediately spoke - Jesus

αὐτοῖς λέγων· θαρσεῖτε, ἐγώ εἰμι·
to them saying: Be of good cheer, I am;

μὴ φοβεῖσθε. **28** ἀποκριθεὶς δὲ αὐτῷ ὁ
do not fear. And answering him -

Πέτρος εἶπεν· κύριε, εἰ σὺ εἶ, κέλευσόν
Peter said: Lord, if thou art, command

με ἐλθεῖν πρὸς σὲ ἐπὶ τὰ ὕδατα. **29** ὁ
me to come to thee on the waters. he

δὲ εἶπεν· ἐλθέ. καὶ καταβὰς ἀπὸ τοῦ
And said: Come. And going down from the

πλοίου Πέτρος περιπάτησεν ἐπὶ τὰ ὕδατα
ship Peter walked on the waters

καὶ ἦλθεν πρὸς τὸν Ἰησοῦν. **30** βλέπων δὲ
and came toward - Jesus. But seeing

τὸν ἄνεμον ἐφοβήθη, καὶ ἀρξάμενος
the wind he was afraid, and beginning

καταποντίζεσθαι ἔκραξεν λέγων·
to sink he cried out saying:

κύριε, σῶσόν με. **31** εὐθέως δὲ ὁ
Lord, save me. And immediately -

Ἰησοῦς ἐκτείνας τὴν χεῖρα ἐπελάβετο
Jesus stretching out the(his) hand took hold

αὐτοῦ, καὶ λέγει αὐτῷ· ὀλιγόπιστε,
of him, and says to him: Little-faith,

faith, why did you doubt?" ³²And when they got into the boat, the wind ceased. ³³And those in the boat worshiped him, saying, "Truly you are the Son of God." 34 And when they had crossed over, they came to land at Gennes'aret. ³⁵And when the men of that place recognized him, they sent round to all that region and brought to him all that were sick, ³⁶and besought him that they might only touch the fringe of his garment; and as many as touched it were made well.

εἰς τί ἐδίστασας;   32 καὶ ἀναβάντων
why   didst thou doubt?   And   going up
                                         =as they went up
αὐτῶν εἰς τὸ πλοῖον ἐκόπασεν ὁ ἄνεμος.
themᵃ into the ship ceased the wind.
33 οἱ δὲ ἐν τῷ πλοίῳ προσεκύνησαν αὐτῷ
And the [ones] in the ship worshipped him
λέγοντες· ἀληθῶς θεοῦ υἱὸς εἶ. 34 Καὶ
saying: Truly of God Son thou art. And
διαπεράσαντες ἦλθον ἐπὶ τὴν γῆν εἰς
crossing over they came onto the land to
Γεννησαρέτ. 35 καὶ ἐπιγνόντες αὐτὸν
Gennesaret. And recognizing him
οἱ ἄνδρες τοῦ τόπου ἐκείνου ἀπέστειλαν
the men – place of that sent
εἰς ὅλην τὴν περίχωρον ἐκείνην, καὶ
into all – neighbourhood that, and
προσήνεγκαν αὐτῷ πάντας τοὺς κακῶς
brought to him all the [ones] ill
                                       =those who were ill,
ἔχοντας, 36 καὶ παρεκάλουν αὐτὸν ἵνα
having, and besought him that
μόνον ἅψωνται τοῦ κρασπέδου τοῦ
only they might touch the fringe of the
ἱματίου αὐτοῦ· καὶ ὅσοι ἥψαντο διεσώθησαν.
garment of him; and as many as touched were completely
                                       healed.

CHAPTER 15

THEN Pharisees and scribes came to Jesus from Jerusalem and said, ²"Why do your disciples transgress the tradition of the elders? For they do not wash their hands when they eat." ³He answered them, "And why do you transgress the commandment of God for the sake of your tradition? ⁴For God commanded, 'Honor your father and your mother,' and, 'He who speaks evil of father or

15 Τότε προσέρχονται τῷ Ἰησοῦ
Then approach – to Jesus
ἀπὸ Ἱεροσολύμων Φαρισαῖοι καὶ γραμματεῖς
from Jerusalem Pharisees and scribes
λέγοντες· 2 διὰ τί οἱ μαθηταί σου
saying: Why the disciples of thee.
παραβαίνουσιν τὴν παράδοσιν τῶν
transgress the tradition of the
πρεσβυτέρων; οὐ γὰρ νίπτονται τὰς χεῖρας
elders? for not they wash the(ir) hands
ὅταν ἄρτον ἐσθίωσιν. 3 ὁ δὲ ἀπο-
whenever bread they eat. And he answer-
κριθεὶς εἶπεν αὐτοῖς· διὰ τί καὶ ὑμεῖς
ing said to them: Why indeed ye
παραβαίνετε τὴν ἐντολὴν τοῦ θεοῦ
transgress the commandment – of God
διὰ τὴν παράδοσιν ὑμῶν; 4 ὁ γὰρ
on account of the tradition of you? For
θεὸς εἶπεν· τίμα τὸν πατέρα καὶ τὴν
God said: Honour the father and the
μητέρα, καί· ὁ κακολογῶν πατέρα
mother, and: The [one] speaking evil of father

mother, let him surely die.' ⁵But you say, 'If any one tells his father or his mother, What you would have gained from me is given to God,ᵉ he need not honor his father.' ⁶So, for the sake of your tradition, you have made void the wordᶠ of God. ⁷You hypocrites! Well did Isaiah prophesy of you, when he said:

⁸'This people honors me with their lips,
but their heart is far from me;
⁹in vain do they worship me,
teaching as doctrines the precepts of men.'"

10 And he called the people to him and said to them, "Hear and understand: ¹¹not what goes into the mouth defiles a man, but what comes out of the mouth, this defiles a man."
¹²Then the disciples came and said to him, "Do you know that the Pharisees were offended when they heard this saying?" ¹³He answered, "Every plant which my heavenly Father has not planted will be rooted up. ¹⁴Let them alone; they are blind guides. And if a

ᵉ Or an offering
ᶠ Other ancient authorities read law

ἢ μητέρα θανάτῳ τελευτάτω. 5 ὑμεῖς δὲ
or mother by death let him die. But ye

λέγετε· ὃς ἂν εἴπῃ τῷ πατρὶ ἢ
say: Whoever says to the(his) father or

τῇ μητρί· δῶρον ὃ ἐὰν ἐξ ἐμοῦ
to the(his) mother: A gift whatever by me

ὠφελήθης, 6 οὐ μὴ τιμήσει τὸν
thou mightest be owed, by no means shall he honour the

πατέρα αὐτοῦ ἢ τὴν μητέρα αὐτοῦ·
father of him or the mother of him;

καὶ ἠκυρώσατε τὸν λόγον τοῦ θεοῦ
and ye annulled the word – of God

διὰ τὴν παράδοσιν ὑμῶν. 7 ὑποκρι-
on account of the tradition of you. Hypocrites,

ταί, καλῶς ἐπροφήτευσεν περὶ ὑμῶν
well prophesied concerning you

Ἠσαΐας λέγων· 8 ὁ λαὸς οὗτος τοῖς
Isaiah saying: This people with the

χείλεσίν με τιμᾷ, ἡ δὲ καρδία αὐτῶν
lips me honours, but the heart of them

πόρρω ἀπέχει ἀπ᾽ ἐμοῦ· 9 μάτην δὲ
far is away from me; and vainly

σέβονται με, διδάσκοντες διδασκαλίας
they worship me, teaching teachings

ἐντάλματα ἀνθρώπων. 10 Καὶ προσκαλε-
ordinances of men. And calling

σάμενος τὸν ὄχλον εἶπεν αὐτοῖς·
forward the crowd he said to them:

ἀκούετε καὶ συνίετε· 11 οὐ τὸ εἰσερχ-
Hear ye and understand: Not the [thing] enter-

όμενον εἰς τὸ στόμα κοινοῖ τὸν ἄνθρωπον,
ing into the mouth defiles the man,

ἀλλὰ τὸ ἐκπορευόμενον ἐκ τοῦ στόματος,
but the [thing] coming forth out of the mouth,

τοῦτο κοινοῖ τὸν ἄνθρωπον. 12 Τότε
this defiles the man. Then

προσελθόντες οἱ μαθηταὶ λέγουσιν αὐτῷ·
approaching the disciples say to him:

οἶδας ὅτι οἱ Φαρισαῖοι ἀκούσαντες τὸν
Dost thou know that the Pharisees hearing the

λόγον ἐσκανδαλίσθησαν; 13 ὁ δὲ ἀπο-
saying were offended? And he answer-

κριθεὶς εἶπεν· πᾶσα φυτεία ἣν οὐκ
ing said: Every plant which not

ἐφύτευσεν ὁ πατήρ μου ὁ οὐράνιος ἐκριζω-
planted the Father of me – heavenly shall be

θήσεται. 14 ἄφετε αὐτούς· τυφλοί εἰσιν
uprooted. Leave them; blind they are

blind man leads a blind man, both will fall into a pit." ¹⁵But Peter said to him, "Explain the parable to us." ¹⁶And he said, "Are you also still without understanding? ¹⁷Do you not see that whatever goes into the mouth passes into the stomach, and so passes on?⁹ ¹⁸But what comes out of the mouth proceeds from the heart, and this defiles a man. ¹⁹For out of the heart come evil thoughts, murder, adultery, fornication, theft, false witness, slander. ²⁰These are what defile a man; but to eat with unwashed hands does not defile a man."

21 And Jesus went away from there and withdrew to the district of Tyre and Sidon. ²²And behold, a Canaanite woman from that region came out and cried, "Have mercy on me, O Lord, Son of David; my daughter is severely possessed by a demon." ²³But he did not answer

⁹ Or is evacuated

ὁδηγοὶ	τυφλῶν·	τυφλὸς	δὲ	τυφλὸν
leaders	of blind;	²a blind man	¹and	²a blind man

ἐὰν	ὁδηγῇ,	ἀμφότεροι	εἰς	βόθυνον	πεσοῦνται.
²if	⁴leads,	both	into	a ditch	will fall.

15 Ἀποκριθεὶς δὲ ὁ Πέτρος εἶπεν αὐτῷ·
And answering – Peter said to him:

φράσον ἡμῖν τὴν παραβολήν. 16 ὁ δὲ
Explain to us the parable. So he

εἶπεν· ἀκμὴν καὶ ὑμεῖς ἀσύνετοί
said: Thus also ye unintelligent

ἐστε; 17 οὐ νοεῖτε ὅτι πᾶν τὸ
are? Do ye not understand that everything

εἰσπορευόμενον εἰς τὸ στόμα εἰς τὴν
entering into the mouth into the

κοιλίαν χωρεῖ καὶ εἰς ἀφεδρῶνα ἐκβάλλεται;
stomach goes and into a drain is cast out?

18 τὰ δὲ ἐκπορευόμενα ἐκ τοῦ
but the things coming forth out of the

στόματος ἐκ τῆς καρδίας ἐξέρχεται,
mouth out of the heart comes forth,

κἀκεῖνα κοινοῖ τὸν ἄνθρωπον. 19 ἐκ
and those defiles the man. out of

γὰρ τῆς καρδίας ἐξέρχονται διαλογισμοὶ
For the heart come forth thoughts

πονηροί, φόνοι, μοιχεῖαι, πορνεῖαι, κλοπαί,
evil, murders, adulteries, fornications, thefts,

ψευδομαρτυρίαι, βλασφημίαι. 20 ταῦτά
false witnessings, blasphemies. These things

ἐστιν τὰ κοινοῦντα τὸν ἄνθρωπον·
is(are) the [ones] defiling the man;

τὸ δὲ ἀνίπτοις χερσὶν φαγεῖν οὐ
– but with unwashed hands to eat not

κοινοῖ τὸν ἄνθρωπον.
defiles the man.

21 Καὶ ἐξελθὼν ἐκεῖθεν ὁ Ἰησοῦς
And going forth thence – Jesus

ἀνεχώρησεν εἰς τὰ μέρη Τύρου καὶ
departed into the parts of Tyre and

Σιδῶνος. 22 καὶ ἰδοὺ γυνὴ Χαναναία
Sidon. And behold woman a Canaanite

ἀπὸ τῶν ὁρίων ἐκείνων ἐξελθοῦσα
from – borders those coming forth

ἔκραζεν λέγουσα· ἐλέησόν με, κύριε
cried out saying: Pity me, Lord[,]

υἱὸς Δαυίδ· ἡ θυγάτηρ μου κακῶς
son of David; the daughter of me badly

δαιμονίζεται. 23 ὁ δὲ οὐκ ἀπεκρίθη
is demon-possessed. But he answered not

her a word. And his disciples came and begged him, saying, "Send her away, for she is crying after us." ²⁴He answered, "I was sent only to the lost sheep of the house of Israel." ²⁵But she came and knelt before him, saying, "Lord, help me." ²⁶And he answered, "It is not fair to take the children's bread and throw it to the dogs." ²⁷She said, "Yes, Lord, yet even the dogs eat the crumbs that fall from their master's table." ²⁸Then Jesus answered her, "O woman, great is your faith! Be it done for you as you desire." And her daughter was healed instantly.

29 And Jesus went on from there and passed along the Sea of Galilee. And he went up into the hills, and sat down there. ³⁰And great crowds came to him, bringing with them the lame, the maimed, the blind, the dumb, and many others, and they put them at his

αὐτῇ λόγον. καὶ προσελθόντες οἱ μαθηταὶ
her a word. And approaching the disciples

αὐτοῦ ἠρώτων αὐτὸν λέγοντες· ἀπόλυσον
of him besought him saying: Dismiss

αὐτήν, ὅτι κράζει ὄπισθεν ἡμῶν. 24 ὁ
her, because she is crying out behind us, he

δὲ ἀποκριθεὶς εἶπεν· οὐκ ἀπεστάλην
But answering said: I was not sent

εἰ μὴ εἰς τὰ πρόβατα τὰ ἀπολωλότα
except to the sheep - lost

οἴκου Ἰσραήλ. 25 ἡ δὲ ἐλθοῦσα
of [the] house of Israel. But she coming

προσεκύνει αὐτῷ λέγουσα· κύριε, βοήθει
worshipped him saying: Lord, help

μοι. 26 ὁ δὲ ἀποκριθεὶς εἶπεν· οὐκ
me. But he answering said: not

ἔστιν καλὸν λαβεῖν τὸν ἄρτον τῶν τέκνων
It is good to take the bread of the children

καὶ βαλεῖν τοῖς κυναρίοις. 27 ἡ δὲ
and to throw to the dogs. And she

εἶπεν· ναί, κύριε· καὶ γὰρ τὰ κυνάρια
said: Yes, Lord; but even the dogs

ἐσθίει ἀπὸ τῶν ψιχίων τῶν πιπτόντων
eats from the crumbs - falling

ἀπὸ τῆς τραπέζης τῶν κυρίων αὐτῶν.
from the table of the masters of them.

28 τότε ἀποκριθεὶς ὁ Ἰησοῦς εἶπεν αὐτῇ·
Then answering - Jesus said to her:

ὦ γύναι, μεγάλη σου ἡ πίστις· γενηθήτω
O woman, great of thee the faith; let it be

σοι ὡς θέλεις. καὶ ἰάθη ἡ
to thee as thou desirest. And was healed the

θυγάτηρ αὐτῆς ἀπὸ τῆς ὥρας ἐκείνης.
daughter of her from - hour that.

29 Καὶ μεταβὰς ἐκεῖθεν ὁ Ἰησοῦς
And removing thence - Jesus

ἦλθεν παρὰ τὴν θάλασσαν τῆς Γαλιλαίας,
came by the sea - of Galilee,

καὶ ἀναβὰς εἰς τὸ ὄρος ἐκάθητο ἐκεῖ.
and going up into the mountain he sat there.

30 καὶ προσῆλθον αὐτῷ ὄχλοι πολλοὶ ἔχοντες
And approached to him crowds many having

μεθ' ἑαυτῶν χωλούς, κυλλούς, τυφλούς,
with themselves lame, maimed, blind,

κωφούς, καὶ ἑτέρους πολλούς, καὶ ἔρριψαν
dumb, and others many, and cast

αὐτοὺς παρὰ τοὺς πόδας αὐτοῦ· καὶ
them at the feet of him; and

feet, and he healed them, [31]so that the throng wondered, when they saw the dumb speaking, the maimed whole, the lame walking, and the blind seeing; and they glorified the God of Israel.

32 Then Jesus called his disciples to him and said, "I have compassion on the crowd, because they have been with me now three days, and have nothing to eat; and I am unwilling to send them away hungry, lest they faint on the way." [33]And the disciples said to him, "Where are we to get bread enough in the desert to feed so great a crowd?" [34]And Jesus said to them, "How many loaves have you?" They said, "Seven, and a few small fish." [35]And commanding the crowd to sit down on the ground, [36]he took the seven loaves and the fish, and having given thanks he broke them and gave them to the disciples, and the disciples gave them to the crowds. [37]And they all ate and were satisfied; and they took up seven baskets full of the broken pieces left over. [38]Those who ate were four

ἐθεράπευσεν αὐτούς·
he healed   them;

31 ὥστε τὸν ὄχλον
so as the   crowd
=so that the crowd marvelled

θαυμάσαι βλέποντας κωφοὺς λαλοῦντας,
to marvel[b] seeing   dumb men   speaking,

κυλλοὺς ὑγιεῖς καὶ χωλοὺς περιπατοῦντας
maimed   whole   and   lame   walking

καὶ τυφλοὺς βλέποντας· καὶ ἐδόξασαν
and blind   seeing;   and they glorified

τὸν θεὸν Ἰσραήλ.   **32** Ὁ δὲ Ἰησοῦς
the God of Israel.   – And   Jesus

προσκαλεσάμενος τοὺς μαθητὰς αὐτοῦ
calling forward   the   disciples   of him

εἶπεν· σπλαγχνίζομαι ἐπὶ τὸν ὄχλον,
said: I am filled with tenderness over the crowd,

ὅτι ἤδη ἡμέραι τρεῖς προσμένουσίν
because now days   three   they remain

μοι καὶ οὐκ ἔχουσιν τί φάγωσιν·
with me and   have not   anything they may eat;

καὶ ἀπολῦσαι αὐτοὺς νήστεις οὐ θέλω,
and to dismiss   them   without food I am not willing,

μήποτε ἐκλυθῶσιν ἐν τῇ ὁδῷ.   **33** καὶ
lest   they fail   in the way.   And

λέγουσιν αὐτῷ οἱ μαθηταί· πόθεν
say   to him the   disciples·   Whence

ἡμῖν ἐν ἐρημίᾳ ἄρτοι τοσοῦτοι ὥστε
to us in a desert   loaves   so many   so as

χορτάσαι ὄχλον τοσοῦτον; **34** καὶ λέγει
to satisfy a crowd so great?   And   says

αὐτοῖς ὁ Ἰησοῦς· πόσους ἄρτους ἔχετε;
to them   –   Jesus: How many loaves   have ye?

οἱ δὲ εἶπαν· ἑπτά, καὶ ὀλίγα ἰχθύδια.
And they   said: Seven, and   a few   fishes.

35 καὶ παραγγείλας τῷ ὄχλῳ ἀναπεσεῖν
And   having enjoined   the   crowd   to recline

ἐπὶ τὴν γῆν **36** ἔλαβεν τοὺς ἑπτὰ
on   the ground   he took   the   seven

ἄρτους καὶ τοὺς ἰχθύας καὶ εὐχαριστήσας
loaves and   the   fishes   and   giving thanks

ἔκλασεν καὶ ἐδίδου τοῖς μαθηταῖς, οἱ δὲ
he broke and   gave   to the   disciples,   and the

μαθηταὶ τοῖς ὄχλοις. **37** καὶ ἔφαγον πάντες
disciples to the crowds.   And   ate   all

καὶ ἐχορτάσθησαν, καὶ τὸ περισσεῦον τῶν
and were satisfied,   and   the   excess   of the

κλασμάτων ἦραν, ἑπτὰ σπυρίδας πλήρεις.
fragments   they took, seven   baskets   full.

38 οἱ δὲ ἐσθίοντες ἦσαν τετρακισχίλιοι
And the [ones] eating   were   four thousand

thousand men, besides women and children. ³⁹And sending away the crowds, he got into the boat and went to the region of Mag'adan.

ἄνδρες χωρὶς γυναικῶν καὶ παιδίων.
men   apart from   women   and   children.
39 Καὶ ἀπολύσας τοὺς ὄχλους ἐνέβη εἰς
And   having dismissed   the   crowds   he embarked   in
τὸ πλοῖον, καὶ ἦλθεν εἰς τὰ ὅρια Μαγαδάν.
the   ship,   and   came   into   the borders of Magadan.

CHAPTER 16

AND the Pharisees and Sad'ducees came, and to test him they asked him to show them a sign from heaven. ²He answered them,ʰ "When it is evening, you say, 'It will be fair weather; for the sky is red.' ³And in the morning, 'It will be stormy today, for the sky is red and threatening.' You know how to interpret the appearance of the sky, but you cannot interpret the signs of the times. ⁴An evil and adulterous generation seeks for a sign, but no sign shall be given to it except the sign of Jonah." So he left them and departed.

5 When the disciples reached the other side, they had forgotten to bring any bread. ⁶Jesus said to them, "Take heed and beware of the leaven of the Pharisees and Sad'ducees." ⁷And they discussed it among themselves, saying, "We brought no bread." ⁸But Jesus, aware of this, said,

16 Καὶ προσελθόντες οἱ Φαρισαῖοι καὶ
And   approaching   the   Pharisees   and
Σαδδουκαῖοι πειράζοντες ἐπηρώτησαν αὐτὸν
Sadducees   tempting   asked   him
σημεῖον ἐκ τοῦ οὐρανοῦ ἐπιδεῖξαι
a sign   out of   *the*   heaven   to show
αὐτοῖς. 2 ὁ δὲ ἀποκριθεὶς εἶπεν αὐτοῖς·
to them.   But he   answering   said   to them:
[ὀψίας γενομένης λέγετε· εὐδία,
Evening   coming onª   ye say: Fair weather,
=When evening comes on
πυρράζει γὰρ ὁ οὐρανός· 3 καὶ πρωΐ·
for is red   the heaven(sky);   and in the morning:
σήμερον χειμών, πυρράζει γὰρ στυγνάζων
To-day   stormy weather,   for is red   being overcast
ὁ οὐρανός. τὸ μὲν πρόσωπον τοῦ
the   heaven(sky).   The   -   face   of the
οὐρανοῦ γινώσκετε διακρίνειν, τὰ δὲ
heaven(sky)   ye know*   to discern,   but the
σημεῖα τῶν καιρῶν οὐ δύνασθε;] 4 γενεὰ
signs   of the   times   can ye not?   A generation
πονηρὰ καὶ μοιχαλὶς σημεῖον ἐπιζητεῖ,
evil   and   adulterous   a sign   seeks,
καὶ σημεῖον οὐ δοθήσεται αὐτῇ εἰ μὴ
and   a sign   shall not be given   to it   except
τὸ σημεῖον Ἰωνᾶ. καὶ καταλιπὼν αὐτοὺς
the   sign   of Jonah.   And   leaving   them
ἀπῆλθεν. 5 Καὶ ἐλθόντες οἱ μαθηταὶ εἰς
he went away.   And   coming   the   disciples   to
τὸ πέραν ἐπελάθοντο ἄρτους λαβεῖν.
the   other side   they forgot   loaves   to take.
ὁ δὲ Ἰησοῦς εἶπεν αὐτοῖς· 6 ὁρᾶτε καὶ
- And   Jesus   said   to them: Beware   and
προσέχετε ἀπὸ τῆς ζύμης τῶν Φαρισαίων
take heed   from   the   leaven   of the   Pharisees
καὶ Σαδδουκαίων. 7 οἱ δὲ διελογίζοντο
and   Sadducees.   But they   reasoned
ἐν ἑαυτοῖς λέγοντες ὅτι ἄρτους οὐκ
among themselves   saying[:]   -   Loaves   not
ἐλάβομεν. 8 γνοὺς δὲ ὁ Ἰησοῦς εἶπεν·
we took.   But knowing   -   Jesus   said:

ʰ Other ancient authorities omit the following words to the end of verse 3

I.G.E.—4

* See note on page xviii. Note the use in the next line of δύνασθε.

"O men of little faith, why do you discuss among yourselves the fact that you have no bread? ⁹Do you not yet perceive? Do you not remember the five loaves of the five thousand, and how many baskets you gathered? ¹⁰Or the seven loaves of the four thousand, and how many baskets you gathered? ¹¹How is it that you fail to perceive that I did not speak about bread? Beware of the leaven of the Pharisees and Sad'ducees." ¹²Then they understood that he did not tell them to beware of the leaven of bread, but of the teaching of the Pharisees and Sad'ducees.

13 Now when Jesus came into the district of Caesare'a Philippi, he asked his disciples, "Who do men say that the Son of man is?" ¹⁴And they said, "Some say John the Baptist, others say Eli'jah, and others Jeremiah or one of the prophets." ¹⁵He said to them, "But who do you say that I am?" ¹⁶Simon Peter replied, "You are the Christ, the Son of the living God." ¹⁷And Jesus answered him, "Blessed

τί διαλογίζεσθε ἐν ἑαυτοῖς, ὀλιγόπιστοι,
Why reason ye among yourselves, little-faiths,

ὅτι ἄρτους οὐκ ἔχετε; 9 οὔπω νοεῖτε,
because loaves ye have not? Do ye not yet understand,

οὐδὲ μνημονεύετε τοὺς πέντε ἄρτους τῶν
neither remember ye the five loaves of the

πεντακισχιλίων καὶ πόσους κοφίνους
five thousand and how many baskets

ἐλάβετε; 10 οὐδὲ τοὺς ἑπτὰ ἄρτους τῶν
ye took? Neither the seven loaves of the

τετρακισχιλίων καὶ πόσας σπυρίδας
four thousand and how many baskets

ἐλάβετε; 11 πῶς οὐ νοεῖτε ὅτι οὐ
ye took? How do ye not understand that not

περὶ ἄρτων εἶπον ὑμῖν; προσέχετε δὲ ἀπὸ
concerning loaves I said to you? But take heed from

τῆς ζύμης τῶν Φαρισαίων καὶ Σαδ-
the leaven of the Pharisees and Sad-

δουκαίων. 12 τότε συνῆκαν ὅτι οὐκ
ducees. Then they understood that not

εἶπεν προσέχειν ἀπὸ τῆς ζύμης [τῶν
he said to take heed from the leaven of the

ἄρτων], ἀλλὰ ἀπὸ τῆς διδαχῆς τῶν
loaves, but from the teaching of the

Φαρισαίων καὶ Σαδδουκαίων.
Pharisees and Sadducees.

13 Ἐλθὼν δὲ ὁ Ἰησοῦς εἰς τὰ μέρη
And coming – Jesus into the parts

Καισαρείας τῆς Φιλίππου ἠρώτα τοὺς
of Caesarea – of Philip he questioned the

μαθητὰς αὐτοῦ λέγων· τίνα λέγουσιν οἱ
disciples of him saying: Whom say –

ἄνθρωποι εἶναι τὸν υἱὸν τοῦ ἀνθρώπου;
men to be the Son of man?

14 οἱ δὲ εἶπαν· οἱ μὲν Ἰωάννην τὸν
And they said: Some indeed John the

βαπτιστήν, ἄλλοι δὲ Ἠλίαν, ἕτεροι δὲ
Baptist, and others Elias, and others

Ἰερεμίαν ἢ ἕνα τῶν προφητῶν. 15 λέγει
Jeremias or one of the prophets. He says

αὐτοῖς· ὑμεῖς δὲ τίνα με λέγετε εἶναι;
to them: But ³ye ¹whom ⁴me ²say to be?

16 ἀποκριθεὶς δὲ Σίμων Πέτρος εἶπεν·
And answering Simon Peter said:

17 σὺ εἶ ὁ χριστὸς ὁ υἱὸς τοῦ θεοῦ
Thou art the Christ the Son – of God

τοῦ ζῶντος. ἀποκριθεὶς δὲ ὁ Ἰησοῦς
of the living. And answering – Jesus

are you, Simon Bar-Jona! For flesh and blood has not revealed this to you, but my Father who is in heaven. ¹⁸And I tell you, you are Peter, and on this rock I will build my church, and the powers of death shall not prevail against it. ¹⁹I will give you the keys of the kingdom of heaven, and whatever you bind on earth shall be bound in heaven, and whatever you loose on earth shall be loosed in heaven." ²⁰Then he strictly charged the disciples to tell no one that he was the Christ.

21 From that time Jesus began to show his disciples that he must go to Jerusalem and suffer many things from the elders and chief priests and scribes, and be killed, and on the third day be raised. ²²And Peter took him and began to rebuke him, saying, "God forbid, Lord! This shall never happen to you." ²³But he turned and said

εἶπεν   αὐτῷ·   μακάριος   εἶ,   Σίμων
said   to him: Blessed   art thou, Simon

Βαριωνά,   ὅτι   σὰρξ   καὶ   αἷμα   οὐκ   ἀπεκά-
Barjonas, because flesh   and   blood   did not

λυψέν   σοι   ἀλλ'   ὁ   πατήρ   μου   ὁ   ἐν
reveal   to thee but the   Father   of me   -   in

τοῖς   οὐρανοῖς.   18 κἀγὼ   δέ   σοι   λέγω
the   heavens.   And I also to thee say[,]

ὅτι   σὺ   εἶ   Πέτρος,   καὶ   ἐπὶ   ταύτῃ   τῇ
-   Thou art   Peter,   and   on   this   -

πέτρᾳ   οἰκοδομήσω   μου   τὴν   ἐκκλησίαν,
rock   I will build   of me the   church,

καὶ   πύλαι   ᾅδου   οὐ   κατισχύσουσιν
and [the] gates of hades   will not prevail against

αὐτῆς.   19 δώσω   σοι   τὰς   κλεῖδας   τῆς
it.   I will give thee the   keys   of the

βασιλείας   τῶν   οὐρανῶν,   καὶ   ὃ   ἐὰν
kingdom   of the   heavens,   and   whatever

δήσῃς   ἐπὶ   τῆς   γῆς   ἔσται   δεδεμένον   ἐν   τοῖς
thou bindest on the   earth shall be having been bound in the

οὐρανοῖς,   καὶ   ὃ   ἐὰν   λύσῃς   ἐπὶ   τῆς
heavens,   and   whatever thou loosest on   the

γῆς   ἔσται   λελυμένον   ἐν   τοῖς   οὐρανοῖς.
earth shall be having been loosed in   the   heavens.

20 τότε   ἐπετίμησεν   τοῖς   μαθηταῖς   ἵνα
Then   he warned   the   disciples   that

μηδενὶ   εἴπωσιν   ὅτι   αὐτός   ἐστιν   ὁ
to no one they should tell that   he   is   the

χριστός.
Christ.

21 Ἀπὸ   τότε   ἤρξατο   Ἰησοῦς   Χριστὸς
From   then   began   Jesus   Christ

δεικνύειν   τοῖς   μαθηταῖς   αὐτοῦ   ὅτι   δεῖ
to show   to the   disciples   of him   that it behoves

αὐτὸν   εἰς   Ἱεροσόλυμα   ἀπελθεῖν   καὶ
him   to   Jerusalem   to go   and

πολλὰ   παθεῖν   ἀπὸ   τῶν   πρεσβυτέρων   καὶ
many things to suffer from the   elders   and

ἀρχιερέων   καὶ   γραμματέων   καὶ   ἀποκτανθῆναι
chief priests and   scribes   and   to be killed

καὶ   τῇ   τρίτῃ   ἡμέρᾳ   ἐγερθῆναι.   22 καὶ
and on the third   day   to be raised.   And

προσλαβόμενος   αὐτὸν   ὁ   Πέτρος   ἤρξατο
taking   him   -   Peter   began

ἐπιτιμᾶν   αὐτῷ   λέγων·   ἵλεώς   σοι,
to rebuke him   saying: Propitious to thee,
                              ▬ May God help thee,

κύριε·   οὐ   μὴ   ἔσται   σοι   τοῦτο.   23 ὁ   δὲ
Lord: by no means shall be to thee this.   But he

to Peter, "Get behind me, Satan! You are a hindrance to me; for you are not on the side of God, but of men."

24 Then Jesus told his disciples, "If any man would come after me, let him deny himself and take up his cross and follow me. 25 For whoever would save his life will lose it, and whoever loses his life for my sake will find it. 26 For what will it profit a man, if he gains the whole world and forfeits his life? Or what shall a man give in return for his life? 27 For the Son of man is to come with his angels in the glory of his Father, and then he will repay every man for what he has done. 28 Truly, I say to you, there are some standing here who will not taste death before they see the Son of man coming in his kingdom."

στραφεὶς εἶπεν τῷ Πέτρῳ· ὕπαγε ὀπίσω
turning said to Peter: Go behind

μου, σατανᾶ· σκάνδαλον εἶ ἐμοῦ,
me, Satan; an offence thou art of me,

ὅτι οὐ φρονεῖς τὰ τοῦ θεοῦ
because thou thinkest not the things – of God

ἀλλὰ τὰ τῶν ἀνθρώπων. 24 Τότε ὁ
but the things – of men. Then –

Ἰησοῦς εἶπεν τοῖς μαθηταῖς αὐτοῦ· εἴ
Jesus said to the disciples of him: If

τις θέλει ὀπίσω μου ἐλθεῖν, ἀπαρνησάσθω
anyone wishes after me to come, let him deny

ἑαυτὸν καὶ ἀράτω τὸν σταυρὸν αὐτοῦ,
himself and let him take the cross of him,

καὶ ἀκολουθείτω μοι. 25 ὃς γὰρ ἐὰν
and let him follow me. For whoever

θέλῃ τὴν ψυχὴν αὐτοῦ σῶσαι, ἀπολέσει
wishes the life of him to save, he will lose

αὐτήν· ὃς δ' ἂν ἀπολέσῃ τὴν ψυχὴν
it; and whoever loses the life

αὐτοῦ ἕνεκεν ἐμοῦ, εὑρήσει αὐτήν. 26 τί
of him for the sake of me, he will find it. what

γὰρ ὠφεληθήσεται ἄνθρωπος, ἐὰν τὸν
For will be benefited a man, if the

κόσμον ὅλον κερδήσῃ, τὴν δὲ ψυχὴν
world whole he should gain, but the soul

αὐτοῦ ζημιωθῇ; ἢ τί δώσει ἄνθρωπος
of him loses? or what will give a man

ἀντάλλαγμα τῆς ψυχῆς αὐτοῦ; 27 μέλλει
an exchange of the soul of him? is about

γὰρ ὁ υἱὸς τοῦ ἀνθρώπου ἔρχεσθαι ἐν τῇ
For the Son of man – to come in the

δόξῃ τοῦ πατρὸς αὐτοῦ μετὰ τῶν ἀγγέλων
glory of the Father of him with the angels

αὐτοῦ, καὶ τότε ἀποδώσει ἑκάστῳ
of him, and then he will reward to each man

κατὰ τὴν πρᾶξιν αὐτοῦ. 28 ἀμὴν λέγω
according to the conduct of him. Truly I say

ὑμῖν ὅτι εἰσίν τινες τῶν ὧδε ἑστώτων
to you[,] – There are some of the [ones] here standing

οἵτινες οὐ μὴ γεύσωνται θανάτου ἕως ἂν
who by no means may taste of death until

ἴδωσιν τὸν υἱὸν τοῦ ἀνθρώπου ἐρχόμενον
they see the Son – of man coming

ἐν τῇ βασιλείᾳ αὐτοῦ.
in the kingdom of him.

CHAPTER 17

AND after six days Jesus took with him Peter and James and John his brother, and led them up a high mountain apart. ²And he was transfigured before them, and his face shone like the sun, and his garments became white as light. ³And behold, there appeared to them Moses and Eli'jah, talking with him. ⁴And Peter said to Jesus, "Lord, it is well that we are here; if you wish, I will make three booths here, one for you and one for Moses and one for Eli'jah." ⁵He was still speaking, when lo, a bright cloud over-shadowed them, and a voice from the cloud said, "This is my beloved Son, with whom I am well pleased; listen to him." ⁶When the disciples heard this, they fell on their faces, and were filled with awe. ⁷But Jesus came and touched them, saying, "Rise, and have no fear." ⁸And when they lifted up their eyes, they saw no one but Jesus only.

17 Καὶ μεθ' ἡμέρας ἓξ παραλαμβάνει ὁ
And after days six takes -

'Ιησοῦς τὸν Πέτρον καὶ 'Ιάκωβον καὶ
Jesus - Peter and James and

'Ιωάννην τὸν ἀδελφὸν αὐτοῦ, καὶ ἀναφέρει
John the brother of him, and leads up

αὐτοὺς εἰς ὄρος ὑψηλὸν κατ' ἰδίαν. 2 καὶ
them to mountain a high privately. And

μετεμορφώθη ἔμπροσθεν αὐτῶν, καὶ
he was transfigured before them, and

ἔλαμψεν τὸ πρόσωπον αὐτοῦ ὡς ὁ ἥλιος,
shone the face of him as the sun,

τὰ δὲ ἱμάτια αὐτοῦ ἐγένετο λευκὰ ὡς
and the garments of him became white as

τὸ φῶς. 3 καὶ ἰδοὺ ὤφθη αὐτοῖς Μωϋσῆς
the light. And behold was seen by them Moses

καὶ 'Ηλίας συλλαλοῦντες μετ' αὐτοῦ.
and Elias conversing with him.

4 ἀποκριθεὶς δὲ ὁ Πέτρος εἶπεν τῷ
And answering - Peter said -

'Ιησοῦ· κύριε, καλόν ἐστιν ἡμᾶς ὧδε
to Jesus: Lord, good it is us here

εἶναι· εἰ θέλεις, ποιήσω ὧδε τρεῖς
to be; if thou willest, I will make here three

σκηνάς, σοὶ μίαν καὶ Μωϋσεῖ
tents, for thee one and for Moses

μίαν καὶ 'Ηλίᾳ μίαν. 5 ἔτι αὐτοῦ
one and for Elias one. Yet him
= While he was yet

λαλοῦντος, ἰδοὺ νεφέλη φωτεινὴ ἐπεσκίασεν
speakingᵃ, behold cloud a bright overshadowed
speaking,

αὐτούς, καὶ ἰδοὺ φωνὴ ἐκ τῆς νεφέλης
them, and behold a voice out of the cloud

λέγουσα· οὗτός ἐστιν ὁ υἱός μου ὁ
saying: This is the son of me the

ἀγαπητός, ἐν ᾧ εὐδόκησα· ἀκούετε
beloved, in whom I was well pleased; hear ye

αὐτοῦ. 6 καὶ ἀκούσαντες οἱ μαθηταὶ
him. And hearing the disciples

ἔπεσαν ἐπὶ πρόσωπον αὐτῶν καὶ
fell on [the] face[s] of them and

ἐφοβήθησαν σφόδρα. 7 καὶ προσῆλθεν ὁ
feared exceedingly. And approached -

'Ιησοῦς καὶ ἁψάμενος αὐτῶν εἶπεν·
Jesus and touching them said:

ἐγέρθητε καὶ μὴ φοβεῖσθε. 8 ἐπάραντες δὲ
Rise and do not fear. And lifting up

τοὺς ὀφθαλμοὺς αὐτῶν οὐδένα εἶδον εἰ
the eyes of them no one they saw ex-

9 And as they were coming down the mountain, Jesus commanded them, "Tell no one the vision, until the Son of man is raised from the dead." 10And the disciples asked him, "Then why do the scribes say that first Eli'jah must come?" 11He replied, "Eli'jah does come, and he is to restore all things; 12but I tell you that Eli'jah has already come, and they did not know him, but did to him whatever they pleased. So also the Son of man will suffer at their hands." 13Then the disciples understood that he was speaking to them of John the Baptist.

14 And when they came to the crowd, a man came up to him and kneeling before him said, 15"Lord, have mercy on my son, for he is an epileptic and he suffers terribly; for often he falls into the fire, and often into the water. 16And I brought him to your disciples, and they could not heal him." 17And

μὴ αὐτὸν Ἰησοῦν μόνον. 9 Καὶ κατα-
cept himself Jesus only.　 And com-
　　　　　　　　　　　　　　　　　　=as
βαινόντων αὐτῶν ἐκ τοῦ ὄρους ἐνετείλατο
ing down　 thema out of the mountain enjoined
they were coming down
αὐτοῖς ὁ Ἰησοῦς λέγων· μηδενὶ εἴπητε
them　 - Jesus saying: To no one tell
τὸ ὅραμα ἕως οὗ ὁ υἱὸς τοῦ ἀνθρώπου
the vision until the Son - of man
ἐκ νεκρῶν ἐγερθῇ. 10 Καὶ ἐπηρώτησαν
out of dead be raised.　 And questioned
αὐτὸν οἱ μαθηταὶ λέγοντες· τί οὖν
him the disciples saying: Why then
οἱ γραμματεῖς λέγουσιν ὅτι Ἠλίαν δεῖ
the scribes say that ²Elias ¹it behoves
ἐλθεῖν πρῶτον; 11 ὁ δὲ ἀποκριθεὶς εἶπεν·
to come first?　 And he answering said:
Ἠλίας μὲν ἔρχεται καὶ ἀποκαταστήσει
Elias indeed is coming and will restore
πάντα· 12 λέγω δὲ ὑμῖν ὅτι Ἠλίας
all things;　 but I tell you that Elias
ἤδη ἦλθεν, καὶ οὐκ ἐπέγνωσαν
already came, and they did not recognize
αὐτόν, ἀλλ' ἐποίησαν ἐν αὐτῷ ὅσα
him, but did by him whatever things
ἠθέλησαν· οὕτως καὶ ὁ υἱὸς τοῦ ἀνθρώπου
they wished; thus also the Son - of man
μέλλει πάσχειν ὑπ' αὐτῶν. 13 τότε
is about to suffer by them.　 Then
συνῆκαν οἱ μαθηταὶ ὅτι περὶ
understood the disciples that concerning
Ἰωάννου τοῦ βαπτιστοῦ εἶπεν αὐτοῖς.
John the Baptist he spoke to them.
14 Καὶ ἐλθόντων πρὸς τὸν ὄχλον προσ-
　 And [they] coming to the crowd ap-
ῆλθεν αὐτῷ ἄνθρωπος γονυπετῶν αὐτὸν
proached to him a man falling on knees to him
15 καὶ λέγων· κύριε, ἐλέησόν μου τὸν
　 and saying: Lord, pity of me the
υἱόν, ὅτι σεληνιάζεται καὶ κακῶς ἔχει·
son, because he is moonstruck and ill has;
　　　　　　　　　　　　　　　　　　　=is ill;
πολλάκις γὰρ πίπτει εἰς τὸ πῦρ καὶ
for often he falls into the fire and
πολλάκις εἰς τὸ ὕδωρ. 16 καὶ προσήνεγκα
often into the water.　 And I brought
αὐτὸν τοῖς μαθηταῖς σου, καὶ οὐκ
him to the disciples of thee, and not
ἠδυνήθησαν αὐτὸν θεραπεῦσαι. 17 ἀπο-
they were able him to heal.　 an-

Jesus answered, "O faithless and perverse generation, how long am I to be with you? How long am I to bear with you? Bring him here to me." [18]And Jesus rebuked him, and the demon came out of him, and the boy was cured instantly. [19]Then the disciples came to Jesus privately and said, "Why could we not cast it out?" [20]He said to them, "Because of your little faith. For truly, I say to you, if you have faith as a grain of mustard seed, you will say to this mountain, 'Move hence to yonder place,' and it will move; and nothing will be impossible to you."[i]

22 As they were gathering[j] in Galilee, Jesus said to them, "The Son of man is to be delivered into the hands of men, [23]and they will kill him, and he will be raised on the third day." And they were greatly distressed.

24 When they came to Caper′na-um, the collectors of the half-shekel

κριθεὶς δὲ ὁ Ἰησοῦς εἶπεν· ὦ γενεὰ
swering And – Jesus said: O generation

ἄπιστος καὶ διεστραμμένη, ἕως πότε
unbelieving and *having been* perverted, until when

μεθ' ὑμῶν ἔσομαι; ἕως πότε
with you shall I be? until when

ἀνέξομαι ὑμῶν; φέρετέ μοι αὐτὸν
shall I endure you? bring to me him

ὧδε. 18 καὶ ἐπετίμησεν αὐτῷ ὁ Ἰησοῦς,
here. And rebuked it – Jesus,

καὶ ἐξῆλθεν ἀπ' αὐτοῦ τὸ δαιμόνιον,
and came out from him the demon,

καὶ ἐθεραπεύθη ὁ παῖς ἀπὸ τῆς ὥρας
and was healed the boy from – hour

ἐκείνης. 19 Τότε προσελθόντες οἱ μαθηταὶ
that. Then *approaching* *the *disciples

τῷ Ἰησοῦ κατ' ἰδίαν εἶπον· διὰ
– to Jesus privately said: Why

τί ἡμεῖς οὐκ ἠδυνήθημεν ἐκβαλεῖν αὐτό;
we were not able to expel it?

20 ὁ δὲ λέγει αὐτοῖς· διὰ τὴν ὀλιγο-
And he says to them: Because of the little

πιστίαν ὑμῶν· ἀμὴν γὰρ λέγω ὑμῖν, ἐὰν
faith of you; for truly I say to you, if

ἔχητε πίστιν ὡς κόκκον σινάπεως,
ye have faith as a grain of mustard,

ἐρεῖτε τῷ ὄρει τούτῳ· μετάβα
ye will say – mountain to this: Remove

ἔνθεν ἐκεῖ, καὶ μεταβήσεται, καὶ οὐδὲν
hence there, and it will be removed, and nothing

ἀδυνατήσει ὑμῖν. ‡
will be impossible to you.

22 Συστρεφομένων δὲ αὐτῶν ἐν τῇ
And strolling them* in –
=as they were strolling

Γαλιλαίᾳ εἶπεν αὐτοῖς ὁ Ἰησοῦς· μέλλει
Galilee said to them – Jesus: is about

ὁ υἱὸς τοῦ ἀνθρώπου παραδίδοσθαι εἰς
The Son – of man to be delivered into

χεῖρας ἀνθρώπων, 23 καὶ ἀποκτενοῦσιν
[the] hands of men, and they will kill

αὐτόν, καὶ τῇ τρίτῃ ἡμέρᾳ ἐγερθήσεται.
him, and on the third day he will be raised.

καὶ ἐλυπήθησαν σφόδρα.
And they were grieved exceedingly.

24 Ἐλθόντων δὲ αὐτῶν εἰς Καφαρναοὺμ
And coming them* to Capernaum
=when they came

προσῆλθον οἱ τὰ δίδραχμα λαμβάνοντες
approached the [ones] the didrachmæ receiving

[i] Other ancient authorities insert verse 21, "*But this kind never comes out except by prayer and fasting*"
[j] Other ancient authorities read *abode*

‡ Verse 21 omitted by Nestle; *cf.* R.V. marg., etc.

tax went up to Peter and
said, "Does not your
teacher pay the tax?"
25 He said, "Yes." And
when he came home,
Jesus spoke to him first,
saying, "What do you
think, Simon? From
whom do kings of the
earth take toll or tribute?
From their sons or from
others?" 26 And when he
said, "From others,"
Jesus said to him, "Then
the sons are free. 27 However, not to give offense
to them, go to the sea
and cast a hook, and take
the first fish that comes
up, and when you open
its mouth you will find a
shekel; take that and
give it to them for me and
for yourself."

τῷ   Πέτρῳ   καὶ   εἶπαν·   ὁ   διδάσκαλος
-       Peter   and   said: The   teacher
ὑμῶν   οὐ   τελεῖ   δίδραχμα;   λέγει·   ναί.
of you   not   pays   drachmae?   He says: Yes.
25 καὶ   ἐλθόντα   εἰς   τὴν   οἰκίαν   προ-
   And   ⁴coming   ⁵into ⁶the   ⁷house   ²pre-
ἔφθασεν   αὐτὸν   ὁ   ᾿Ιησοῦς   λέγων·   τί   σοι
ceded   ³him   -   ¹Jesus   saying: What to thee
δοκεῖ,   Σίμων;   οἱ   βασιλεῖς   τῆς   γῆς
seems it, Simon?   the   kings   of the earth
ἀπὸ   τίνων   λαμβάνουσιν   τέλη   ἢ   κῆνσον;
from   whom   do they take   toll   or   poll-tax?
ἀπὸ   τῶν   υἱῶν   αὐτῶν   ἢ   ἀπὸ   τῶν   ἀλλοτρίων;
from   the   sons   of them   or   from   -   strangers?
26 εἰπόντος   δέ·   ἀπὸ   τῶν   ἀλλο-
   and [he] saying²: From   -   strangers,
   = when he said :
τρίων,   ἔφη   αὐτῷ   ὁ   ᾿Ιησοῦς·   ἄρα   γε
          said   to him   -   Jesus: Then
ἐλεύθεροί   εἰσιν   οἱ   υἱοί.   27 ἵνα   δὲ   μὴ
free   are   the   sons.   But lest
σκανδαλίσωμεν   αὐτούς,   πορευθεὶς   εἰς
we should offend   them,   going   to
θάλασσαν   βάλε   ἄγκιστρον   καὶ   τὸν
[the] sea   cast   a hook   and   the
ἀναβάντα   πρῶτον   ἰχθὺν   ἆρον,   καὶ   ἀνοίξας
²coming up   ³first   ¹fish   take,   and   opening
τὸ   στόμα   αὐτοῦ   εὑρήσεις   στατῆρα·
the   mouth   of it   thou wilt find   a stater;
ἐκεῖνον   λαβὼν   δὸς   αὐτοῖς   ἀντὶ   ἐμοῦ   καὶ
that   taking   give   them   for   me   and
σοῦ.
thee.

CHAPTER 18

AT that time the dis-
ciples came to Jesus,
saying, "Who is the
greatest in the kingdom
of heaven?" 2 And calling
to him a child, he put
him in the midst of them,
3 and said, "Truly, I say
to you, unless you turn
and become like children,
you will never enter the

18 ᾿Εν   ἐκείνῃ   τῇ   ὥρᾳ   προσῆλθον   οἱ
   In   that   -   hour   approached   the
μαθηταὶ   τῷ   ᾿Ιησοῦ   λέγοντες·   τίς   ἄρα
disciples   -   to Jesus   saying: Who   then
μείζων   ἐστὶν   ἐν   τῇ   βασιλείᾳ   τῶν   οὐρανῶν;
greater   is   in   the   kingdom   of the heavens?
2 καὶ   προσκαλεσάμενος   παιδίον   ἔστησεν
   And   calling forward   a child   he set
αὐτὸ   ἐν   μέσῳ   αὐτῶν   3 καὶ   εἶπεν·   ἀμὴν
him   in [the] midst of them   and   said: Truly
λέγω   ὑμῖν,   ἐὰν   μὴ   στραφῆτε   καὶ
I say   to you,   except   ye turn   and
γένησθε   ὡς   τὰ   παιδία,   οὐ   μὴ
become   as   -   children,   by no means

kingdom of heaven.
⁴Whoever humbles himself like this child, he is the greatest in the kingdom of heaven.
5 "Whoever receives one such child in my name receives me; ⁶but whoever causes one of these little ones who believe in me to sin, it would be better for him to have a great millstone fastened round his neck and to be drowned in the depth of the sea.
7 "Woe to the world for temptations to sin! For it is necessary that temptations come, but woe to the man by whom the temptation comes! ⁸And if your hand or your foot causes you to sin, cut it off and throw it from you; it is better for you to enter life maimed or lame than with two hands or two feet to be thrown into the eternal fire. ⁹And if your eye causes you to sin, pluck it out and throw it from you; it is better for you to enter life with one eye than with two eyes to be thrown into the hell of fire.

εἰσέλθητε εἰς τὴν βασιλείαν τῶν
may ye enter into the kingdom of the

οὐρανῶν. 4 ὅστις οὖν ταπεινώσει ἑαυτὸν
heavens. ²[he] who ¹Therefore will humble himself

ὡς τὸ παιδίον τοῦτο, οὗτός ἐστιν ὁ
as – child this, this [one] is the

μείζων ἐν τῇ βασιλείᾳ τῶν οὐρανῶν.
greater in the kingdom of the heavens.

5 καὶ ὃς ἐὰν δέξηται ἓν παιδίον
And whoever receives one child

τοιοῦτο ἐπὶ τῷ ὀνόματί μου, ἐμὲ δέχεται·
such on (in) the name of me, me receives;

6 ὃς δ' ἂν σκανδαλίσῃ ἕνα τῶν
and whoever offends one –

μικρῶν τούτων τῶν πιστευόντων εἰς ἐμέ,
little [ones] of these – believing in me,

συμφέρει αὐτῷ ἵνα κρεμασθῇ μύλος
it is expedient for him that be hanged an upper

ὀνικὸς περὶ τὸν τράχηλον αὐτοῦ καὶ
millstone round the neck of him and

καταποντισθῇ ἐν τῷ πελάγει τῆς θαλάσσης.
he be drowned in the depth of the sea.

7 Οὐαὶ τῷ κόσμῳ ἀπὸ τῶν σκανδάλων·
Woe to the world from – offences;

ἀνάγκη γὰρ ἐλθεῖν τὰ σκάνδαλα, πλὴν
for [it is] a necessity to come – offences, but

οὐαὶ τῷ ἀνθρώπῳ δι' οὗ τὸ σκάνδαλον
woe to the man through whom the offence

ἔρχεται. 8 Εἰ δὲ ἡ χείρ σου ἢ ὁ
comes. Now if the hand of thee or the

πούς σου σκανδαλίζει σε, ἔκκοψον αὐτὸν
foot of thee offends thee, cut off it

καὶ βάλε ἀπὸ σοῦ· καλόν σοί ἐστιν
and cast from thee; good for thee it is

εἰσελθεῖν εἰς τὴν ζωὴν κυλλὸν ἢ χωλόν,
to enter into – life maimed or lame,

ἢ δύο χεῖρας ἢ δύο πόδας ἔχοντα βληθῆναι
than two hands or two feet having to be cast

εἰς τὸ πῦρ τὸ αἰώνιον. 9 καὶ εἰ ὁ
into the fire – eternal. And if the

ὀφθαλμός σου σκανδαλίζει σε, ἔξελε αὐτὸν
eye of thee offends thee, pluck out it

καὶ βάλε ἀπὸ σοῦ· καλόν σοί ἐστιν
and cast from thee; good for thee it is

μονόφθαλμον εἰς τὴν ζωὴν εἰσελθεῖν, ἢ
one-eyed into the life to enter, than

δύο ὀφθαλμοὺς ἔχοντα βληθῆναι εἰς
two eyes having to be cast into

10 "See that you do not despise one of these little ones; for I tell you that in heaven their angels always behold the face of my Father who is in heaven.[k] 12 What do you think? If a man has a hundred sheep, and one of them has gone astray, does he not leave the ninety-nine on the hills and go in search of the one that went astray? 13 And if he finds it, truly, I say to you, he rejoices over it more than over the ninety-nine that never went astray. 14 So it is not the will of my[l] Father who is in heaven that one of these little ones should perish.

15 "If your brother sins against you, go and tell him his fault, between you and him alone. If he listens to you, you have gained your brother. 16 But if he does not listen, take one or two others along with you, that every word may be confirmed by the evidence of two or three witnesses. 17 If he refuses to listen to them, tell it to the church; and if he

[k] Other ancient authorities add verse 11, *For the Son of man came to save the lost*
[l] Other ancient authorities read *your*

τὴν γέενναν τοῦ πυρός.
the gehenna - of fire.

10 Ὁρᾶτε μὴ
See [that] not

καταφρονήσητε ἑνὸς τῶν μικρῶν τούτων·
ye despise one - little [ones] of these;

λέγω γὰρ ὑμῖν ὅτι οἱ ἄγγελοι αὐτῶν
for I tell you that the angels of them

ἐν οὐρανοῖς διὰ παντὸς βλέπουσι τὸ
in heavens always see the

πρόσωπον τοῦ πατρός μου τοῦ ἐν οὐρανοῖς.‡
face of the Father of me - in heavens.

12 Τί ὑμῖν δοκεῖ; ἐὰν γένηταί τινι
What to you seems it? if there be to any
=any man has

ἀνθρώπῳ ἑκατὸν πρόβατα καὶ πλανηθῇ
man a hundred sheep and wanders

ἐν ἐξ αὐτῶν, οὐχὶ ἀφήσει τὰ ἐνενήκοντα
one of them, will he not leave the ninety-

ἐννέα ἐπὶ τὰ ὄρη καὶ πορευθεὶς ζητεῖ τὸ
nine on the mountains and going seeks the

πλανώμενον; 13 καὶ ἐὰν γένηται
wandering [one]? And if he happens

εὑρεῖν αὐτό, ἀμὴν λέγω ὑμῖν ὅτι
to find it, truly I say to you that

χαίρει ἐπ᾽ αὐτῷ μᾶλλον ἢ ἐπὶ τοῖς
he rejoices over it more than over the

ἐνενήκοντα ἐννέα τοῖς μὴ πεπλανημένοις.
ninety-nine - not having wandered.

14 οὕτως οὐκ ἔστιν θέλημα ἔμπροσθεν
So it is not [the] will before

τοῦ πατρὸς ὑμῶν τοῦ ἐν οὐρανοῖς ἵνα
the Father of you - in heavens that

ἀπόληται ἐν τῶν μικρῶν τούτων.
should perish one - little [ones] of these.

15 Ἐὰν δὲ ἁμαρτήσῃ ὁ ἀδελφός σου,
Now if sins the brother of thee,

ὕπαγε ἔλεγξον αὐτὸν μεταξὺ σοῦ καὶ
go reprove him between thee and

αὐτοῦ μόνου. ἐάν σου ἀκούσῃ, ἐκέρδησας
him alone. If thee he hears, thou gainedst

τὸν ἀδελφόν σου· 16 ἐὰν δὲ μὴ
the brother of thee; but if not

ἀκούσῃ, παράλαβε μετὰ σοῦ ἔτι ἕνα ἢ
he hears, take with thee more one or

δύο, ἵνα ἐπὶ στόματος δύο μαρτύρων
two, that on(by) [the] mouth of two witnesses

ἢ τριῶν σταθῇ πᾶν ῥῆμα· 17 ἐὰν δὲ
or three may be established every word; but if

παρακούσῃ αὐτῶν, εἰπὸν τῇ ἐκκλησίᾳ·
he refuses to hear them, tell to the church;

‡ Ver. 11 omitted by Nestle; cf. RSV note.

refuses to listen even to the church, let him be to you as a Gentile and a tax collector. [18]Truly, I say to you, whatever you bind on earth shall be bound in heaven, and whatever you loose on earth shall be loosed in heaven. [19]Again I say to you, if two of you agree on earth about anything they ask, it will be done for them by my Father in heaven. [20]For where two or three are gathered in my name, there am I in the midst of them."

21 Then Peter came up and said to him, "Lord, how often shall my brother sin against me, and I forgive him? As many as seven times?' [22]Jesus said to him, "I do not say to you seven times, but seventy times seven."[m]

23 "Therefore the kingdom of heaven may be compared to a king who wished to settle accounts with his servants. [24]When he began the reckoning, one was brought to him who

[m] Or seventy-seven times

ἐὰν	δὲ	καὶ	τῆς	ἐκκλησίας	παρακούσῃ,
and if		even	the	church	he refuses to hear,

ἔστω	σοι		ὥσπερ	ὁ	ἐθνικὸς	καὶ
let him be	to thee		as	the	gentile	and

ὁ   τελώνης.   18 Ἀμὴν   λέγω   ὑμῖν,
the tax-collector.   Truly   I say   to you,

ὅσα   ἐὰν   δήσητε   ἐπὶ   τῆς   γῆς   ἔσται
whatever things ye bind on the earth shall be

δεδεμένα   ἐν   οὐρανῷ,   καὶ   ὅσα   ἐὰν
having been bound in heaven, and whatever things

λύσητε   ἐπὶ   τῆς   γῆς   ἔσται   λελυμένα
ye loose on the earth shall be *having been* loosed

ἐν   οὐρανῷ.   19 Πάλιν   [ἀμὴν]   λέγω
in heaven.   Again truly I say

ὑμῖν   ὅτι   ἐὰν   δύο   συμφωνήσωσιν   ἐξ
to you that if two agree of

ὑμῶν   ἐπὶ   τῆς   γῆς   περὶ   παντὸς   πράγ-
you on the earth concerning every

ματος   οὗ   ἐὰν   αἰτήσωνται,   γενήσεται
thing whatever they ask, it shall be

αὐτοῖς   παρὰ   τοῦ   πατρός   μου   τοῦ   ἐν
to them from the Father of me – in

οὐρανοῖς.   20 οὗ   γάρ   εἰσιν   δύο   ἢ   τρεῖς
heavens.   For where are two or three

συνηγμένοι   εἰς   τὸ   ἐμὸν   ὄνομα,   ἐκεῖ   εἰμι
having been assembled in my name, there I am

ἐν   μέσῳ   αὐτῶν.
in [the] midst of them.

21 Τότε   προσελθὼν   ὁ   Πέτρος   εἶπεν
Then approaching – Peter said

αὐτῷ·   κύριε,   ποσάκις   ἁμαρτήσει   εἰς
to him: Lord, how often will sin against

ἐμὲ   ὁ   ἀδελφός   μου   καὶ   ἀφήσω   αὐτῷ;
me the brother of me and I will forgive him?

ἕως   ἑπτάκις;   22 λέγει   αὐτῷ   ὁ   Ἰησοῦς·
until seven times? says to him – Jesus:

οὐ   λέγω   σοι   ἕως   ἑπτάκις,   ἀλλὰ
I tell not *to* thee until seven times, but

ἕως   ἑβδομηκοντάκις   ἑπτά.   23 Διὰ   τοῦτο
until seventy times seven. Therefore

ὡμοιώθη   ἡ   βασιλεία   τῶν   οὐρανῶν
was(is) likened the kingdom of the heavens

ἀνθρώπῳ   βασιλεῖ,   ὃς   ἠθέλησεν   συνᾶραι
to *a* man a king, who wished to take

λόγον   μετὰ   τῶν   δούλων   αὐτοῦ.   24 ἀρξα-
account with the slaves of him. And

μένου   δὲ   αὐτοῦ   συναίρειν,   προσήχθη
beginning [a] him to take, [s]was brought forward
= as he began

owed him ten thousand talents; ²⁵ and as he could not pay, his lord ordered him to be sold, with his wife and children and all that he had, and payment to be made. ²⁶ So the servant fell on his knees, imploring him, 'Lord, have patience with me, and I will pay you everything.' ²⁷ And out of pity for him the lord of that servant released him and forgave him the debt. ²⁸ But that same servant, as he went out, came upon one of his fellow servants who owed him a hundred denarii; and seizing him by the throat he said, 'Pay what you owe.' ²⁹ So his fellow servant fell down and besought him, 'Have patience with me, and I will pay you.' ³⁰ He refused and went and put him in prison till he should pay the debt. ³¹ When his fellow servants saw what had taken place, they were greatly distressed, and they went and reported to their lord all that had taken place. ³² Then his lord summoned him and said to

εἷς αὐτῷ ὀφειλέτης μυρίων ταλάντων.
one ᵇto him - ᵃdebtor ³of ten thousand ⁴talents.

25 μὴ ἔχοντος δὲ αὐτοῦ ἀποδοῦναι, ἐκέλευσεν
And not having himᵃ to repay, commanded
= as he had not

αὐτὸν ὁ κύριος πραθῆναι καὶ τὴν
him the lord to be sold and the(his)

γυναῖκα καὶ τὰ τέκνα καὶ πάντα ὅσα
wife and - children and all things whatever

ἔχει, καὶ ἀποδοθῆναι. 26 πεσὼν οὖν ὁ
he has, and to be repaid. Falling therefore the

δοῦλος προσεκύνει αὐτῷ λέγων· μακρο-
slave did obeisance to him saying: Defer

θύμησον ἐπ᾽ ἐμοί, καὶ πάντα ἀποδώσω
anger over me, and all things I will repay

σοι. 27 σπλαγχνισθεὶς δὲ ὁ κύριος τοῦ
thee. And filled with tenderness the lord -

δούλου ἐκείνου ἀπέλυσεν αὐτόν, καὶ τὸ
slave of that released him, and the

δάνειον ἀφῆκεν αὐτῷ. 28 ἐξελθὼν δὲ
loan forgave him. But going out

ὁ δοῦλος ἐκεῖνος εὗρεν ἕνα τῶν
- slave that found one of the

συνδούλων αὐτοῦ, ὃς ὤφειλεν αὐτὸν ἑκατὸν
fellow-slaves of him, who owed him a hundred

δηνάρια, καὶ κρατήσας αὐτὸν ἔπνιγεν
denarii, and seizing him throttled

λέγων· ἀπόδος εἴ τι ὀφείλεις.
saying: Repay if something thou owest.

29 πεσὼν οὖν ὁ σύνδουλος αὐτοῦ παρε-
Falling therefore the fellow-slave of him be-

κάλει αὐτὸν λέγων· μακροθύμησον ἐπ᾽
sought him saying: Defer anger over

ἐμοί, καὶ ἀποδώσω σοι. 30 ὁ δὲ οὐκ
me, and I will repay thee. But he not

ἤθελεν, ἀλλὰ ἀπελθὼν ἔβαλεν αὐτὸν εἰς
wished, but going away threw him into

φυλακὴν ἕως ἀποδῷ τὸ ὀφειλόμενον.
prison until he should repay the thing owing.

31 ἰδόντες οὖν οἱ σύνδουλοι αὐτοῦ τὰ
Seeing therefore the fellow-slaves of him the things

γενόμενα ἐλυπήθησαν σφόδρα, καὶ
having taken place they were grieved exceedingly, and

ἐλθόντες διεσάφησαν τῷ κυρίῳ ἑαυτῶν
coming explained to the lord of themselves

πάντα τὰ γενόμενα. 32 τότε προσ-
all the things having taken place. Then ¹call-

καλεσάμενος αὐτὸν ὁ κύριος αὐτοῦ λέγει
ing ²forward ³him the lord of him says

him, 'You wicked ser-
vant! I forgave you all
that debt because you
besought me; ³³and
should not you have had
mercy on your fellow
servant, as I had mercy
on you?' ³⁴And in anger
his lord delivered him to
the jailers, till he should
pay all his debt. ³⁵So also
my heavenly Father will
do to every one of you,
if you do not forgive
your brother from your
heart."

αὐτῷ·	δοῦλε	πονηρέ,	πᾶσαν	τὴν	ὀφειλὴν
to him:	²Slave	¹wicked,	all	–	debt

ἐκείνην	ἀφῆκά	σοι,	ἐπεὶ	παρεκάλεσάς	με·
that	I forgave	thee,	since	thou besoughtest	me;

33 οὐκ	ἔδει	καὶ	σὲ	ἐλεῆσαι	τὸν
did it not behove	also	thee	to pity	the

σύνδουλόν	σου,	ὡς	κἀγὼ	σὲ	ἠλέησα;
fellow-slave	of thee,	as	I also	thee	pitied?

34 καὶ	ὀργισθεὶς	ὁ	κύριος	αὐτοῦ
And	being angry	the	lord	of him

παρέδωκεν	αὐτὸν	τοῖς	βασανισταῖς	ἕως	οὗ
delivered	him	to the	tormentors	until

ἀποδῷ	πᾶν	τὸ	ὀφειλόμενον	αὐτῷ.
he should repay	all	the thing	owing	to him.

35 Οὕτως	καὶ	ὁ	πατήρ	μου	ὁ	οὐράνιος
Thus	also	the	Father	of me	–	heavenly

ποιήσει	ὑμῖν,	ἐὰν	μὴ	ἀφῆτε	ἕκαστος
will do	to you,	unless		ye forgive	each one

τῷ	ἀδελφῷ	αὐτοῦ	ἀπὸ	τῶν	καρδιῶν
the	brother	of him	from	the	hearts

ὑμῶν.
of you.

CHAPTER 19

NOW when Jesus had
finished these say-
ings, he went away from
Galilee and entered the
region of Judea beyond
the Jordan; ²and large
crowds followed him, and
he healed them there.

3 And Pharisees came
up to him and tested him
by asking, "Is it lawful
to divorce one's wife for
any cause?" ⁴He
answered, "Have you not
read that he who made
them from the beginning
made them male and
female, ⁵and said, 'For

19 Καὶ	ἐγένετο	ὅτε	ἐτέλεσεν	ὁ
And	it came to pass	when	ended	–

Ἰησοῦς	τοὺς	λόγους	τούτους,	μετῆρεν
Jesus	–	words	these,	he removed

ἀπὸ	τῆς	Γαλιλαίας	καὶ	ἦλθεν	εἰς	τὰ
from	–	Galilee	and	came	into	the

ὅρια	τῆς	Ἰουδαίας	πέραν	τοῦ	Ἰορδάνου.
borders	–	of Judæa	across	the	Jordan.

2 καὶ	ἠκολούθησαν	αὐτῷ	ὄχλοι	πολλοί,
And	followed	him	crowds	many,

καὶ	ἐθεράπευσεν	αὐτοὺς	ἐκεῖ.
and	he healed	them	there.

3 Καὶ	προσῆλθον	αὐτῷ	Φαρισαῖοι
And	approached	to him	Pharisees

πειράζοντες	αὐτὸν	καὶ	λέγοντες·	εἰ	ἔξεστιν
tempting	him	and	saying:	If	it is lawful

ἀπολῦσαι	τὴν	γυναῖκα	αὐτοῦ	κατὰ	πᾶσαν
to dismiss	the	wife	of him	for	every

αἰτίαν;	4 ὁ	δὲ	ἀποκριθεὶς	εἶπεν·	οὐκ
cause?	And he		answering	said:	not

ἀνέγνωτε	ὅτι	ὁ	κτίσας	ἀπ'
Did ye read	that	the [one]	creating	from

ἀρχῆς	ἄρσεν	καὶ	θῆλυ	ἐποίησεν	αὐτούς;
[the] beginning	male	and	female	made	them?

this reason a man shall leave his father and mother and be joined to his wife, and the two shall become one'? [6]So they are no longer two but one. What therefore God has joined together, let no man put asunder." [7]They said to him, "Why then did Moses command one to give a certificate of divorce, and to put her away?" [8]He said to them, "For your hardness of heart Moses allowed you to divorce your wives, but from the beginning it was not so. [9]And I say to you: whoever divorces his wife, except for unchastity,[n] and marries another, commits adultery."[o]

10 The disciples said to him, "If such is the case of a man with his wife, it is not expedient to marry." [11]But he said to them, "Not all men can receive this precept, but only those to whom it is given. [12]For there are eunuchs who have been so from birth, and there are eunuchs who have been made eunuchs by men, and there are eunuchs who have made

[n] Other ancient authorities, after *unchastity*, read *makes her commit adultery*
[o] Other ancient authorities insert *and he who marries a divorced woman commits adultery*

5 καὶ εἶπεν· ἕνεκα τούτου καταλείψει
And he said: For the sake of this shall leave

ἄνθρωπος τὸν πατέρα καὶ τὴν μητέρα
a man the(his) father and the(his) mother

καὶ κολληθήσεται τῇ γυναικὶ αὐτοῦ,
and shall cleave to the wife of him,

καὶ ἔσονται οἱ δύο εἰς σάρκα μίαν·
and [2]shall be [1]the [3]two [4]in [5]flesh [6]one;

6 ὥστε οὐκέτι εἰσὶν δύο ἀλλὰ σὰρξ μία.
so as no longer are they two but flesh one.

ὃ οὖν ὁ θεὸς συνέζευξεν, ἄνθρωπος
What therefore - God yoked together, a man

μὴ χωριζέτω. 7 λέγουσιν αὐτῷ· τί οὖν
let not separate. They say to him: Why then

Μωϋσῆς ἐνετείλατο δοῦναι βιβλίον ἀπο-
[2]Moses [1]did [3]enjoin to give a document of

στασίου καὶ ἀπολῦσαι; 8 λέγει αὐτοῖς·
divorce and to dismiss? He says to them:

ὅτι Μωϋσῆς πρὸς τὴν σκληροκαρδίαν
- Moses in view of the obduracy

ὑμῶν ἐπέτρεψεν ὑμῖν ἀπολῦσαι τὰς
of you allowed you to dismiss the

γυναῖκας ὑμῶν· ἀπ' ἀρχῆς δὲ οὐ
wives of you; but from [the] beginning not

γέγονεν οὕτως. 9 λέγω δὲ ὑμῖν ὅτι
it has been so. But I say to you that

ὃς ἂν ἀπολύσῃ τὴν γυναῖκα αὐτοῦ
whoever dismisses the wife of him

μὴ ἐπὶ πορνείᾳ καὶ γαμήσῃ ἄλλην,
not of(for) fornication and marries another,

μοιχᾶται. 10 λέγουσιν αὐτῷ οἱ μαθηταί·
commits adultery. Say to him the disciples:

εἰ οὕτως ἐστὶν ἡ αἰτία τοῦ ἀνθρώπου
If so is the cause of the man

μετὰ τῆς γυναικός, οὐ συμφέρει γαμῆσαι.
with the wife, it is not expedient to marry.

11 ὁ δὲ εἶπεν αὐτοῖς· οὐ πάντες χωροῦσιν
And he said to them: Not all men grasp

τὸν λόγον τοῦτον, ἀλλ' οἷς δέδοται.
- saying this, but [those] to whom it has been given.

12 εἰσὶν γὰρ εὐνοῦχοι οἵτινες ἐκ κοιλίας
For there are eunuchs who from [the] womb

μητρὸς ἐγεννήθησαν οὕτως, καὶ εἰσὶν
of a mother were born so, and there are

εὐνοῦχοι οἵτινες εὐνουχίσθησαν ὑπὸ τῶν
eunuchs who were made eunuchs by -

ἀνθρώπων, καὶ εἰσὶν εὐνοῦχοι οἵτινες
men, and there are eunuchs who

themselves eunuchs for the sake of the kingdom of heaven. He who is able to receive this, let him receive it."

13 Then children were brought to him that he might lay his hands on them and pray. The disciples rebuked the people, ¹⁴but Jesus said, "Let the children come to me, and do not hinder them; for to such belongs the kingdom of heaven." ¹⁵And he laid his hands on them and went away.

16 And behold, one came up to him, saying, "Teacher, what good deed must I do, to have eternal life?" ¹⁷And he said to him, "Why do you ask me about what is good? One there is who is good. If you would enter life, keep the commandments." ¹⁸He said to him, "Which?" And Jesus said, "You shall not kill, You shall not commit adultery, You shall not steal, You shall not bear false witness, ¹⁹Honor your father and mother, and, You shall love your neighbor as yourself." ²⁰The young man said to him, "All these I have observed; what do I still

εὐνούχισαν   ἑαυτοὺς   διὰ   τὴν
made eunuchs   themselves on account of the

βασιλείαν   τῶν   οὐρανῶν.   ὁ   δυνάμενος
kingdom   of the heavens. The [one] being able

χωρεῖν   χωρείτω.
to grasp [it] let him grasp.

13 Τότε   προσηνέχθησαν   αὐτῷ   παιδία,
Then   were brought   to him   children,

ἵνα   τὰς   χεῖρας   ἐπιθῇ   αὐτοῖς   καὶ
that   the(his) hands   he should put on them   and

προσεύξηται·   οἱ   δὲ   μαθηταὶ   ἐπετίμησαν
pray;   but the   disciples   rebuked

αὐτοῖς.   **14** ὁ   δὲ   Ἰησοῦς   εἶπεν·   ἄφετε
them.   – But   Jesus   said·   Permit

τὰ   παιδία   καὶ   μὴ   κωλύετε   αὐτὰ   ἐλθεῖν
the   children   and   do not prevent   them   to come

πρός   με·   τῶν   γὰρ   τοιούτων   ἐστὶν   ἡ
unto   me;   –   for   of such   is   the

βασιλεία   τῶν   οὐρανῶν.   **15** καὶ   ἐπιθεὶς
kingdom   of the heavens.   And   putting on

τὰς   χεῖρας   αὐτοῖς   ἐπορεύθη   ἐκεῖθεν.
the(his) hands on them   he went   thence.

16 Καὶ   ἰδοὺ   εἷς   προσελθὼν   αὐτῷ   εἶπεν·
And   behold   one   approaching   to him   said:

διδάσκαλε,   τί   ἀγαθὸν   ποιήσω   ἵνα
Teacher,   what   good thing may I do   that

σχῶ   ζωὴν   αἰώνιον;   ὁ   δὲ   εἶπεν   αὐτῷ·
I may have life   eternal?   And he   said   to him:

17 τί   με   ἐρωτᾷς   περὶ   τοῦ   ἀγαθοῦ;
Why   me questionest thou concerning the   good?

εἷς   ἐστιν   ὁ   ἀγαθός·   εἰ   δὲ   θέλεις   εἰς
one   is   the   good;   but if   thou wishest into

τὴν   ζωὴν   εἰσελθεῖν,   τήρει   τὰς   ἐντολάς.
–   life   to enter,   keep   the   commandments.

18 λέγει   αὐτῷ·   ποίας;   ὁ   δὲ   Ἰησοῦς
He says   to him: Which?   –   And   Jesus

ἔφη·   τὸ   οὐ   φονεύσεις,   οὐ   μοιχεύσεις,
said: – Thou shalt not kill, Thou shalt not commit adultery,

οὐ   κλέψεις,   οὐ   ψευδομαρτυρήσεις,
Thou shalt not steal,   Thou shalt not bear false witness,

19 τίμα   τὸν   πατέρα   καὶ   τὴν   μητέρα,
Honour   the(thy) father   and   the(thy) mother,

καὶ   ἀγαπήσεις   τὸν   πλησίον   σου   ὡς
and   Thou shalt love the   neighbour   of thee   as

σεαυτόν.   **20** λέγει   αὐτῷ   ὁ   νεανίσκος·
thyself.   Says   to him   the   young man:

ταῦτα   πάντα   ἐφύλαξα·   τί   ἔτι   ὑστερῶ;
³These things ¹all   I kept;   what   yet   do I lack?

lack?" ²¹Jesus said to him, "If you would be perfect, go, sell what you possess and give to the poor, and you will have treasure in heaven; and come, follow me."
²²When the young man heard this he went away sorrowful; for he had great possessions.

23 And Jesus said to his disciples, "Truly, I say to you, it will be hard for a rich man to enter the kingdom of heaven. ²⁴Again I tell you, it is easier for a camel to go through the eye of a needle than for a rich man to enter the kingdom of God." ²⁵When the disciples heard this they were greatly astonished, saying, "Who then can be saved?" ²⁶But Jesus looked at them and said to them, "With men this is impossible, but with God all things are possible." ²⁷Then Peter said in reply, "Lo, we have left everything and followed you. What then shall we have?" ²⁸Jesus said to them, "Truly, I say to you, in the new

21 ἔφη   αὐτῷ   ὁ   'Ιησοῦς·   εἰ   θέλεις τέλειος
   Said   to him   –   Jesus: If thou wishest perfect

εἶναι, ὕπαγε πώλησόν σου   τὰ   ὑπάρχοντα
to be,   go   sell   of thee the   belongings

καὶ   δὸς   πτωχοῖς,   καὶ   ἕξεις
and   give   to [the] poor,   and   thou shalt have

θησαυρὸν ἐν οὐρανοῖς, καὶ   δεῦρο ἀκολούθει
treasure   in   heavens,   and   come   follow

μοι. 22 ἀκούσας   δὲ   ὁ   νεανίσκος   τὸν
me.   But hearing   the   young man   –

λόγον [τοῦτον]   ἀπῆλθεν   λυπούμενος·
word   this   went away   grieving;

ἦν   γὰρ   ἔχων   κτήματα   πολλά.   23 'Ο
for he was   having   possessions   many.   –

δὲ   'Ιησοῦς εἶπεν τοῖς μαθηταῖς αὐτοῦ·
So   Jesus   said   to the   disciples   of him:

ἀμὴν   λέγω   ὑμῖν   ὅτι   πλούσιος   δυσκόλως
Truly   I tell   you   that   a rich man   hardly

εἰσελεύσεται   εἰς   τὴν   βασιλείαν   τῶν
will enter   into   the   kingdom   of the

οὐρανῶν. 24 πάλιν   δὲ   λέγω   ὑμῖν,
heavens.   And again   I tell   you,

εὐκοπώτερόν   ἐστιν   κάμηλον   διὰ   τρήματος
easier   it is   a camel   through   [the] eye

ῥαφίδος   εἰσελθεῖν   ἢ   πλούσιον   εἰς   τὴν
of a needle   to enter   than   a rich man   into   the

βασιλείαν   τοῦ   θεοῦ.   25 ἀκούσαντες   δὲ
kingdom   of God.   And hearing

οἱ   μαθηταὶ   ἐξεπλήσσοντο   σφόδρα
the   disciples   were astounded   exceedingly

λέγοντες·   τίς   ἄρα   δύναται   σωθῆναι;
saying: Who   then   can   to be saved?

26 ἐμβλέψας   δὲ   ὁ   'Ιησοῦς   εἶπεν
   And looking upon   –   Jesus   said

αὐτοῖς·   παρὰ   ἀνθρώποις   τοῦτο   ἀδύνατόν
to them: With   men   this   impossible

ἐστιν,   παρὰ   δὲ   θεῷ   πάντα   δυνατά.
is,   but with   God   all things   [are] possible.

27 Τότε   ἀποκριθεὶς   ὁ   Πέτρος   εἶπεν   αὐτῷ·
   Then   answering   –   Peter   said   to him:

ἰδοὺ   ἡμεῖς   ἀφήκαμεν   πάντα   καὶ
Behold   we   left   all things   and

ἠκολουθήσαμέν   σοι·   τί   ἄρα   ἔσται
   followed   thee;   what   then   shall be
                                      =shall we have?

ἡμῖν;   28 ὁ   δὲ   'Ιησοῦς   εἶπεν   αὐτοῖς·
to us?   –   And   Jesus   said   to them:

ἀμὴν   λέγω   ὑμῖν   ὅτι   ὑμεῖς   οἱ   ἀκολουθή-
Truly   I tell   you   that   ye   the [ones]   having

world, when the Son of man shall sit on his glorious throne, you who have followed me will also sit on twelve thrones, judging the twelve tribes of Israel. 29 And every one who has left houses or brothers or sisters or father or mother or children or lands, for my name's sake, will receive a hundredfold,ᵖ and inherit eternal life. 30 But many that are first will be last, and the last first.

σαντές μοι, ἐν τῇ παλιγγενεσίᾳ, ὅταν
followed me, in the regeneration, when

καθίσῃ ὁ υἱὸς τοῦ ἀνθρώπου ἐπὶ θρόνου
sits the Son - of man on [the] throne

δόξης αὐτοῦ, καθήσεσθε καὶ αὐτοὶ ἐπὶ
of glory of him, ye will sit also [your]selves on

δώδεκα θρόνους κρίνοντες τὰς δώδεκα
twelve thrones judging the twelve

φυλὰς τοῦ Ἰσραήλ. 29 καὶ πᾶς ὅστις
tribes - of Israel. And everyone who

ἀφῆκεν οἰκίας ἢ ἀδελφοὺς ἢ ἀδελφὰς ἢ
left houses or brothers or sisters or

πατέρα ἢ μητέρα ἢ τέκνα ἢ ἀγροὺς
father or mother or children or fields

ἕνεκεν τοῦ ἐμοῦ ὀνόματος, πολλαπλα-
for the sake of - my name, mani-

σίονα λήμψεται καὶ ζωὴν αἰώνιον
fold will receive and life eternal

κληρονομήσει. 30 Πολλοὶ δὲ ἔσονται πρῶτοι
will inherit. But many ²will be ¹first

ἔσχατοι καὶ ἔσχατοι πρῶτοι.
²last and last first.

CHAPTER 20

"FOR the kingdom of heaven is like a householder who went out early in the morning to hire laborers for his vineyard. ²After agreeing with the laborers for a denarius a day, he sent them into his vineyard. ³And going out about the third hour he saw others standing idle in the market place; ⁴and to them he said, 'You go into the vineyard too, and whatever is right I will give you.' So they went. ⁵Going out again

20 Ὁμοία γάρ ἐστιν ἡ βασιλεία τῶν
For like is the kingdom of the

οὐρανῶν ἀνθρώπῳ οἰκοδεσπότῃ, ὅστις
heavens to a man a housemaster, who

ἐξῆλθεν ἅμα πρωὶ μισθώσασθαι
went out early in the morning to hire

ἐργάτας εἰς τὸν ἀμπελῶνα αὐτοῦ. 2 συμ-
workmen in the vineyard of him. And

φωνήσας δὲ μετὰ τῶν ἐργατῶν ἐκ δηναρίου
agreeing with the workmen out of(for) a denarius

τὴν ἡμέραν ἀπέστειλεν αὐτοὺς εἰς τὸν
the day he sent them into the

ἀμπελῶνα αὐτοῦ. 3 καὶ ἐξελθὼν περὶ
vineyard of him. And going out about

τρίτην ὥραν εἶδεν ἄλλους ἑστῶτας
[the] third hour he saw others standing

ἐν τῇ ἀγορᾷ ἀργούς, 4 καὶ ἐκείνοις
in the marketplace idle, and to those

εἶπεν· ὑπάγετε καὶ ὑμεῖς εἰς τὸν
said: Go also ye into the

ἀμπελῶνα, καὶ ὃ ἐὰν ᾖ δίκαιον δώσω
vineyard, and whatever may be just I will give

ὑμῖν. οἱ δὲ ἀπῆλθον. 5 πάλιν [δὲ]
you. And they went. And again

ᵖ Other ancient authorities read *manifold*

about the sixth hour and the ninth hour, he did the same. ⁶And about the eleventh hour he went out and found others standing; and he said to them, 'Why do you stand here idle all day?' ⁷They said to him, 'Because no one has hired us.' He said to them, 'You go into the vineyard too.' ⁸And when evening came, the owner of the vineyard said to his steward, 'Call the laborers and pay them their wages, beginning with the last, up to the first.' ⁹And when those hired about the eleventh hour came, each of them received a denarius. ¹⁰Now when the first came, they thought they would receive more; but each of them also received a denarius. ¹¹And on receiving it they grumbled at the householder, ¹²saying, 'These last worked only one hour, and you have made them equal to us who have borne the burden of the day and the scorching heat.' ¹³But he replied to one of them, 'Friend, I am doing you no wrong; did you not agree with me for a denarius? ¹⁴Take what belongs to

ἐξελθὼν	περὶ	ἕκτην	καὶ	ἐνάτην	ὥραν
going out	about [the] sixth		and [the] ninth		hour

ἐποίησεν	ὡσαύτως.	6 περὶ	δὲ	τὴν
he did	similarly.	And about		the

ἐνδεκάτην	ἐξελθὼν	εὗρεν	ἄλλους	ἑστῶτας,
eleventh	going out	he found	others	standing,

καὶ	λέγει	αὐτοῖς·	τί	ὧδε	ἑστήκατε
and	says	to them:	Why	here	stand ye

ὅλην	τὴν	ἡμέραν	ἀργοί;	7 λέγουσιν	αὐτῷ·
all	the	day	idle?	They say	to him:

ὅτι	οὐδεὶς	ἡμᾶς	ἐμισθώσατο.	λέγει αὐτοῖς·
Because	no one	us	hired.	He says to them:

ὑπάγετε	καὶ	ὑμεῖς	εἰς	τὸν	ἀμπελῶνα.
Go	also	ye	into	the	vineyard.

8 ὀψίας	δὲ	γενομένης	λέγει	ὁ	κύριος
And evening		having comeᵃ = when evening had come	says	the	lord

τοῦ	ἀμπελῶνος	τῷ	ἐπιτρόπῳ	αὐτοῦ·
of the	vineyard	to the	steward	of him:

κάλεσον	τοὺς	ἐργάτας	καὶ	ἀπόδος	τὸν
Call	the	workmen	and	pay	the

μισθόν,	ἀρξάμενος	ἀπὸ	τῶν	ἐσχάτων
wage,	beginning	from	the	last ones

ἕως	τῶν	πρώτων.	9 ἐλθόντες	δὲ	οἱ
until	the	first.	And coming		the [ones]

περὶ	τὴν	ἐνδεκάτην	ὥραν	ἔλαβον	ἀνὰ
about	the	eleventh	hour	received	each

δηνάριον.	10 καὶ	ἐλθόντες	οἱ	πρῶτοι
a denarius.	And	coming	the	first

ἐνόμισαν	ὅτι	πλεῖον	λήμψονται·	καὶ
supposed	that	more	they will receive;	and

ἔλαβον	τὸ	ἀνὰ	δηνάριον	καὶ	αὐτοί.
they received	the	²each	¹denarius	also	[them]selves.

11 λαβόντες	δὲ	ἐγόγγυζον	κατὰ	τοῦ
And receiving		they grumbled	against	the

οἰκοδεσπότου	λέγοντες·	12 οὗτοι	οἱ	ἔσχατοι
housemaster	saying:	These	–	last

μίαν	ὥραν	ἐποίησαν,	καὶ	ἴσους	αὐτοὺς
one	hour	wrought,	and	equal	them

ἡμῖν	ἐποίησας	τοῖς	βαστάσασι	τὸ
to us	thou madest	the [ones]	having borne	the

βάρος	τῆς	ἡμέρας	καὶ	τὸν	καύσωνα.
burden	of the	day	and	the	heat.

13 ὁ	δὲ	ἀποκριθεὶς	ἑνὶ	αὐτῶν	εἶπεν·
But he		answering	one	of them	said:

ἑταῖρε,	οὐκ	ἀδικῶ	σε·	οὐχὶ
Comrade,	I do not injure		thee;	not

δηναρίου	συνεφώνησάς	μοι;	14 ἆρον
of(for) a denarius	thou didst agree with	me?	take

you, and go; I choose to
give to this last as I give
to you. 15 Am I not
allowed to do what I
choose with what belongs
to me? Or do you be-
grudge my generosity?'[q]
16 So the last will be first,
and the first last."
17 And as Jesus was
going up to Jerusalem,
he took the twelve dis-
ciples aside, and on the
way he said to them,
18 "Behold, we are going
up to Jerusalem; and the
Son of man will be
delivered to the chief
priests and scribes, and
they will condemn him to
death, 19 and deliver him
to the Gentiles to be
mocked and scourged
and crucified, and he will
be raised on the third
day."
20 Then the mother of
the sons of Zeb'edee
came up to him, with her
sons, and kneeling before
him she asked him for
something. 21 And he said
to her, "What do you
want?" She said to him,
"Command that these
two sons of mine may
sit, one at your right
hand and one at your left,

[q] Or *is your eye evil because I am good?*

τὸ σὸν καὶ ὕπαγε· θέλω δὲ
the thine and go; but I wish
=that which is thine

τούτῳ τῷ ἐσχάτῳ δοῦναι ὡς καὶ
to this – last man to give as also

σοί· 15 οὐκ ἔξεστίν μοι ὃ θέλω
to thee; is it not lawful to me what I wish

ποιῆσαι ἐν τοῖς ἐμοῖς; ἢ ὁ
to do among *the* my things? or the

ὀφθαλμός σου πονηρός ἐστιν ὅτι ἐγὼ
eye of thee evil is because I

ἀγαθός εἰμι; 16 Οὕτως ἔσονται οἱ ἔσχατοι
good am? Thus will be the last [ones]

πρῶτοι καὶ οἱ πρῶτοι ἔσχατοι.
first and the first last.

17 Μέλλων δὲ ἀναβαίνειν Ἰησοῦς εἰς
And being about to go up Jesus to

Ἱεροσόλυμα παρέλαβεν τοὺς δώδεκα κατ᾽
Jerusalem he took the twelve private-

ἰδίαν, καὶ ἐν τῇ ὁδῷ εἶπεν αὐτοῖς·
ly, and in the way said to them:

18 ἰδοὺ ἀναβαίνομεν εἰς Ἱεροσόλυμα, καὶ
Behold we are going up to Jerusalem, and

ὁ υἱὸς τοῦ ἀνθρώπου παραδοθήσεται τοῖς
the Son – of man will be delivered to the

ἀρχιερεῦσιν καὶ γραμματεῦσιν, καὶ κατα-
chief priests and scribes, and they will

κρινοῦσιν αὐτὸν εἰς θάνατον, 19 καὶ
condemn him to death, and

παραδώσουσιν αὐτὸν τοῖς ἔθνεσιν εἰς
they will deliver him to the nations *for*

τὸ ἐμπαῖξαι καὶ μαστιγῶσαι καὶ
– to mock and to scourge and

σταυρῶσαι, καὶ τῇ τρίτῃ ἡμέρᾳ ἐγερθή-
to crucify, and on the third day he will be

σεται.
raised.

20 Τότε προσῆλθεν αὐτῷ ἡ μήτηρ τῶν
Then approached *to* him the mother of the

υἱῶν Ζεβεδαίου μετὰ τῶν υἱῶν αὐτῆς
sons of Zebedee with the sons of her

προσκυνοῦσα καὶ αἰτοῦσά τι ἀπ᾽ αὐτοῦ.
doing obeisance and asking something from him.

21 ὁ δὲ εἶπεν αὐτῇ· τί θέλεις; λέγει
And he said to her: What wishest thou? She says

αὐτῷ· εἰπὲ ἵνα καθίσωσιν οὗτοι οἱ
to him: Say that may sit these the

δύο υἱοί μου εἷς ἐκ δεξιῶν καὶ εἷς
two sons of me one on [the] right and one

in your kingdom." ²²But Jesus answered, "You do not know what you are asking. Are you able to drink the cup that I am to drink?" They said to him, "We are able." ²³He said to them, "You will drink my cup, but to sit at my right hand and at my left is not mine to grant, but it is for those for whom it has been prepared by my Father." ²⁴And when the ten heard it, they were indignant at the two brothers. ²⁵But Jesus called them to him and said, "You know that the rulers of the Gentiles lord it over them, and their great men exercise authority over them. ²⁶It shall not be so among you; but whoever would be great among you must be your servant, ²⁷and whoever would be first among you must be your slave; ²⁸even as the Son of man came not to be served but to serve, and to give his life as a ransom for many."

29 And as they went out of Jericho, a great

ἐξ εὐωνύμων σου ἐν τῇ βασιλείᾳ	on [the] left of thee in the kingdom
σου. 22 ἀποκριθεὶς δὲ ὁ Ἰησοῦς	of thee. And answering – Jesus
εἶπεν· οὐκ οἴδατε τί αἰτεῖσθε.	said: Ye know not what ye ask.
δύνασθε πιεῖν τὸ ποτήριον ὃ ἐγὼ	Can ye to drink the cup which I
μέλλω πίνειν; λέγουσιν αὐτῷ· δυνάμεθα.	am about to drink? They say to him: We can.
23 λέγει αὐτοῖς· τὸ μὲν ποτήριόν μου	He says to them: Indeed the cup of me
πίεσθε, τὸ δὲ καθίσαι ἐκ δεξιῶν	ye shall drink, – but to sit on [the] right
μου καὶ ἐξ εὐωνύμων οὐκ ἔστιν	of me and on [the] left is not
ἐμὸν τοῦτο δοῦναι, ἀλλ’ οἷς ἡτοί-	mine this to give, but to whom it has
μασται ὑπὸ τοῦ πατρός μου. 24 καὶ	been prepared by the Father of me. And
ἀκούσαντες οἱ δέκα ἠγανάκτησαν περὶ	hearing the ten were incensed about
τῶν δύο ἀδελφῶν. 25 ὁ δὲ Ἰησοῦς	the two brothers. – So Jesus
προσκαλεσάμενος αὐτοῖς εἶπεν· οἴδατε	calling forward them said: Ye know
ὅτι οἱ ἄρχοντες τῶν ἐθνῶν κατακυριεύουσιν	that the rulers of the nations lord it over
αὐτῶν καὶ οἱ μεγάλοι κατεξουσιάζουσιν	them and the great ones have authority over
αὐτῶν. 26 οὐχ οὕτως ἐστὶν ἐν ὑμῖν·	them. Not thus is it among you;
ἀλλ’ ὃς ἐὰν θέλῃ ἐν ὑμῖν μέγας γενέσθαι,	but whoever wishes among you great to become,
ἔσται ὑμῶν διάκονος, 27 καὶ ὃς ἂν	will be of you servant, and whoever
θέλῃ ἐν ὑμῖν εἶναι πρῶτος, ἔσται ὑμῶν	wishes among you to be first, he shall be of you
δοῦλος· 28 ὥσπερ ὁ υἱὸς τοῦ ἀνθρώπου	slave; as the Son – of man
οὐκ ἦλθεν διακονηθῆναι, ἀλλὰ διακο-	came not to be served, but to
νῆσαι καὶ δοῦναι τὴν ψυχὴν αὐτοῦ	serve and to give the life of him
λύτρον ἀντὶ πολλῶν.	a ransom instead of many.
29 Καὶ ἐκπορευομένων αὐτῶνᵃ ἀπὸ Ἰεριχὼ	And going out them from Jericho = as they were going out

crowd followed him.
³⁰And behold, two blind
men sitting by the road-
side, when they heard
that Jesus was passing by,
cried out,ʳ "Have mercy
on us, Son of David!"
³¹The crowd rebuked
them, telling them to be
silent; but they cried out
the more, "Lord, have
mercy on us, Son of
David!" ³²And Jesus
stopped and called them,
saying, "What do you
want me to do for you?"
³³They said to him,
"Lord, let our eyes be
opened." ³⁴And Jesus
in pity touched their
eyes, and immediately
they received their sight
and followed him.

| ἠκολούθησεν | αὐτῷ | ὄχλος | πολύς. | **30** καὶ |
| followed | him | crowd | a much. | And |

ἰδοὺ δύο τυφλοὶ καθήμενοι παρὰ τὴν
behold two blind men sitting beside the

ὁδόν, ἀκούσαντες ὅτι Ἰησοῦς παράγει,
way, hearing that Jesus is passing by,

ἔκραξαν λέγοντες· κύριε, ἐλέησον ἡμᾶς,
cried out saying: Lord, pity us,

υἱὸς Δαυίδ. **31** ὁ δὲ ὄχλος ἐπετίμησεν
son of David. But the crowd rebuked

αὐτοῖς ἵνα σιωπήσωσιν· οἱ δὲ μεῖζον
them that they should be silent; but they more

ἔκραξαν λέγοντες· κύριε, ἐλέησον ἡμᾶς,
cried out saying: Lord, pity us,

υἱὸς Δαυίδ. **32** καὶ στὰς ὁ Ἰησοῦς
son of David. And standing – Jesus

ἐφώνησεν αὐτοὺς καὶ εἶπεν· τί θέλετε
called them and said: What wish ye

ποιήσω ὑμῖν; **33** λέγουσιν αὐτῷ· κύριε,
I may do to you? They say to him: Lord,

ἵνα ἀνοιγῶσιν οἱ ὀφθαλμοὶ ἡμῶν.
that may be opened the eyes of us.

34 σπλαγχνισθεὶς δὲ ὁ Ἰησοῦς ἥψατο
And being filled with tenderness – Jesus touched

τῶν ὀμμάτων αὐτῶν, καὶ εὐθέως ἀνέβλεψαν
the eyes of them, and immediately they saw again

καὶ ἠκολούθησαν αὐτῷ.
and followed him.

CHAPTER 21

AND when they drew
near to Jerusalem
and came to Beth'phage,
to the Mount of Olives,
then Jesus sent two dis-
ciples, ²saying to them,
"Go into the village
opposite you, and im-
mediately you will find
an ass tied, and a colt
with her; untie them and
bring them to me. ³If any
one says anything to you,
you shall say, 'The Lord
has need of them,' and

ʳ Other ancient authorities
insert Lord

21 Καὶ ὅτε ἤγγισαν εἰς Ἰεροσόλυμα
And when they drew near to Jerusalem

καὶ ἦλθον εἰς Βηθφαγὴ εἰς τὸ ὄρος τῶν
and came to Bethphage to the mount of the

ἐλαιῶν, τότε Ἰησοῦς ἀπέστειλεν δύο
olives, then Jesus sent two

μαθητὰς **2** λέγων αὐτοῖς· πορεύεσθε εἰς
disciples telling them: Go ye into

τὴν κώμην τὴν κατέναντι ὑμῶν, καὶ εὐθὺς
the village – opposite you, and at once

εὑρήσετε ὄνον δεδεμένην καὶ πῶλον μετ'
ye will find an ass having been tied and a colt with

αὐτῆς· λύσαντες ἀγάγετέ μοι. **3** καὶ ἐάν
her/it; loosening bring to me. And if

τις ὑμῖν εἴπῃ τι, ἐρεῖτε ὅτι ὁ
anyone to you says anything, ye shall say[,] The

κύριος αὐτῶν χρείαν ἔχει· εὐθὺς δὲ
Lord of them need has; and immediately

he will send them immediately." ⁴This took place to fulfil what was spoken by the prophet, saying,
⁵"Tell the daughter of Zion,
Behold, your king is coming to you,
humble, and mounted on an ass,
and on a colt, the foal of an ass."
⁶The disciples went and did as Jesus had directed them; ⁷they brought the ass and the colt, and put their garments on them, and he sat thereon. ⁸Most of the crowd spread their garments on the road, and others cut branches from the trees and spread them on the road. ⁹And the crowds that went before him and that followed him shouted, "Hosanna to the Son of David! Blessed is he who comes in the name of the Lord! Hosanna in the highest!"
¹⁰And when he entered Jerusalem, all the city was stirred, saying, "Who is this?" ¹¹And the crowds said, "This is the prophet Jesus from Nazareth of Galilee."
12 And Jesus entered the temple of God⁸ and

⁸ Other ancient authorities omit *of God*

ἀποστελεῖ αὐτούς.   4 Τοῦτο δὲ γέγονεν
he will send   them.   Now this   has happened

ἵνα   πληρωθῇ   τὸ   ῥηθὲν   διὰ   τοῦ
that   might be fulfilled the thing spoken   through   the

προφήτου λέγοντος·   5 εἴπατε   τῇ   θυγατρὶ
prophet   saying: Tell ye   the   daughter

Σιών·   ἰδοὺ ὁ βασιλεύς σου ἔρχεταί σοι
of Zion: Behold[,] the king   of thee comes to thee

πραῢς   καὶ   ἐπιβεβηκὼς   ἐπὶ ὄνον   καὶ   ἐπὶ
meek   and   having mounted on an ass   and   on

πῶλον   υἱὸν   ὑποζυγίου.   6 πορευθέντες   δὲ
a colt   son(foal)   of an ass.   And going

οἱ μαθηταὶ καὶ ποιήσαντες καθὼς συνέταξεν
the disciples and   doing   as   directed

αὐτοῖς ὁ Ἰησοῦς   7 ἤγαγον τὴν ὄνον καὶ
them   - Jesus   they brought the ass   and

τὸν   πῶλον,   καὶ   ἐπέθηκαν   ἐπ'   αὐτῶν
the   colt,   and   put on   on   them

τὰ   ἱμάτια,   καὶ   ἐπεκάθισεν ἐπάνω αὐτῶν.
the(ir) garments, and   he sat on   on   them.

8 ὁ δὲ πλεῖστος ὄχλος ἔστρωσαν ἑαυτῶν
And the very large crowd   strewed of themselves

τὰ   ἱμάτια   ἐν τῇ   ὁδῷ,   ἄλλοι δὲ ἔκοπτον
the   garments in the way,   and others   cut

κλάδους   ἀπὸ   τῶν   δένδρων   καὶ   ἐστρών-
branches from   the   trees   and   strewed

νυον   ἐν τῇ   ὁδῷ.   9 οἱ δὲ   ὄχλοι   οἱ
in   the   way.   And the   crowds   the [ones]

προάγοντες αὐτὸν καὶ οἱ ἀκολουθοῦντες
going before   him   and the [ones] following

ἔκραζον λέγοντες·   ὡσαννὰ τῷ υἱῷ Δαυίδ·
cried out   saying: Hosanna to the son of David;

εὐλογημένος   ὁ   ἐρχόμενος   ἐν   ὀνόματι
blessed   the [one] coming   in   [the] name

κυρίου·   ὡσαννὰ ἐν τοῖς ὑψίστοις.   10 καὶ
of [the] Lord; hosanna in   the   highest [places].   And

εἰσελθόντος   αὐτοῦ   εἰς   Ἱεροσόλυμα ἐσείσθη
entering   him⁸   into   Jerusalem   was shaken
= as he entered

πᾶσα ἡ πόλις λέγουσα·   τίς ἐστιν οὗτος;
all   the city saying: Who is   this?

11 οἱ δὲ   ὄχλοι ἔλεγον·   οὗτός ἐστιν ὁ
And the   crowds said: This   is   the

προφήτης Ἰησοῦς ὁ ἀπὸ Ναζαρὲθ τῆς
prophet   Jesus the [one] from   Nazareth   -

Γαλιλαίας.
of Galilee.

12 Καὶ   εἰσῆλθεν   Ἰησοῦς εἰς τὸ ἱερὸν
And   entered   Jesus   into the temple

drove out all who sold and bought in the temple, and he overturned the tables of the money-changers and the seats of those who sold pigeons. [13]He said to them, "It is written, 'My house shall be called a house of prayer'; but you make it a den of robbers."

14 And the blind and the lame came to him in the temple, and he healed them. [15]But when the chief priests and the scribes saw the wonderful things that he did, and the children crying out in the temple, "Hosanna to the Son of David!" they were indignant; [16]and they said to him, "Do you hear what these are saying?" And Jesus said to them, "Yes; have you never read,

'Out of the mouth of babes and sucklings thou hast brought perfect praise'?"

[17]And leaving them, he went out of the city to Bethany and lodged there.

18 In the morning, as he was returning to the city, he was hungry. [19]And seeing a fig tree by the wayside he went to it, and found nothing on it but leaves only. And he said to it, "May no fruit ever come from you

καὶ ἐξέβαλεν πάντας τοὺς πωλοῦντας καὶ
and　cast out　all　the [ones]　selling　and

ἀγοράζοντας ἐν τῷ ἱερῷ, καὶ τὰς τραπέζας
buying　in　the　temple,　and　the　tables

τῶν κολλυβιστῶν κατέστρεψεν καὶ τὰς
of the　money-changers　he overturned　and　the

καθέδρας τῶν πωλούντων τὰς περιστεράς,
seats　of the [ones]　selling　the　doves,

13 καὶ λέγει αὐτοῖς· γέγραπται· ὁ οἶκός
and　says　to them: It has been written: The　house

μου οἶκος προσευχῆς κληθήσεται, ὑμεῖς
of me　a house　of prayer　shall be called,　[2]ye

δὲ αὐτὸν ποιεῖτε σπήλαιον λῃστῶν. 14 Καὶ
[1]but　[4]it　[3]are making　a den　of robbers.　And

προσῆλθον αὐτῷ τυφλοὶ καὶ χωλοὶ ἐν τῷ
approached　to him　blind　and lame [ones]　in　the

ἱερῷ, καὶ ἐθεράπευσεν αὐτούς. 15 ἰδόντες
temple,　and　he healed　them.　[7]seeing

δὲ οἱ ἀρχιερεῖς καὶ οἱ γραμματεῖς τὰ
[1]But　[2]the　[3]chief priests　[4]and　[5]the　[6]scribes　the

θαυμάσια ἃ ἐποίησεν καὶ τοὺς παῖδας
marvels　which　he did　and　the　children

τοὺς κράζοντας ἐν τῷ ἱερῷ καὶ λέγοντας·
-　crying out　in　the　temple　and　saying:

ὡσαννὰ τῷ υἱῷ Δαυίδ, ἠγανάκτησαν, 16 καὶ
Hosanna　to the　son　of David,　they were incensed,　and

εἶπαν αὐτῷ· ἀκούεις τί οὗτοι λέγουσιν;
said　to him:　Hearest thou　what　these　are saying?

ὁ δὲ Ἰησοῦς λέγει αὐτοῖς· ναί· οὐδέποτε
-　And　Jesus　says　to them:　Yes;　never

ἀνέγνωτε ὅτι ἐκ στόματος νηπίων καὶ
did ye read[,]　-　Out of　[the] mouth　of infants　and

θηλαζόντων κατηρτίσω αἶνον; 17 Καὶ
sucking [ones]　thou didst prepare　praise?　And

καταλιπὼν αὐτοὺς ἐξῆλθεν ἔξω τῆς
leaving　them　he went forth　outside　the

πόλεως εἰς Βηθανίαν, καὶ ηὐλίσθη ἐκεῖ.
city　to　Bethany,　and　lodged　there.

18 Πρωῒ δὲ ἐπαναγαγὼν εἰς τὴν πόλιν
Now early　going up　to　the　city

ἐπείνασεν. 19 καὶ ἰδὼν συκῆν μίαν ἐπὶ τῆς
he hungered.　And　seeing　fig-tree　one　on　the

ὁδοῦ ἦλθεν ἐπ' αὐτήν, καὶ οὐδὲν εὗρεν
way　he went　up(to)　it,　and　nothing　found

ἐν αὐτῇ εἰ μὴ φύλλα μόνον, καὶ λέγει
in　it　except　leaves　only,　and　says

αὐτῇ· οὐ μηκέτι ἐκ σοῦ καρπὸς γένηται
to it:　Never　of　thee　fruit　may be

again!" And the fig tree withered at once. ²⁰When the disciples saw it they marveled, saying, "How did the fig tree wither at once?" ²¹And Jesus answered them, "Truly, I say to you, if you have faith and never doubt, you will not only do what has been done to the fig tree, but even if you say to this mountain, 'Be taken up and cast into the sea,' it will be done. ²²And whatever you ask in prayer, you will receive, if you have faith."

23 And when he entered the temple, the chief priests and the elders of the people came up to him as he was teaching, and said, "By what authority are you doing these things, and who gave you this authority?" ²⁴Jesus answered them, "I also will ask you a question; and if you tell me the answer, then I also will tell you by what authority I do these things. ²⁵The baptism of John, whence was it? From heaven or from men?" And they argued with one another, "If we say, 'From heaven,' he will say to us, 'Why then did you not believe him?' ²⁶But if we

εἰς τὸν αἰῶνα.	to the age.
καὶ ἐξηράνθη παραχρῆμα	And was dried up instantly
ἡ συκῆ. **20** καὶ ἰδόντες οἱ μαθηταὶ	the fig-tree. And seeing the disciples
ἐθαύμασαν λέγοντες· πῶς παραχρῆμα	marvelled saying: How instantly
ἐξηράνθη ἡ συκῆ; **21** ἀποκριθεὶς δὲ ὁ	was withered the fig-tree? And answering –
Ἰησοῦς εἶπεν αὐτοῖς· ἀμὴν λέγω ὑμῖν,	Jesus said to them: Truly I say to you,
ἐὰν ἔχητε πίστιν καὶ μὴ διακριθῆτε,	If ye have faith and do not doubt,
οὐ μόνον τὸ τῆς συκῆς ποιήσετε, ἀλλὰ	not only the* of the fig-tree ye will do, but
κἂν τῷ ὄρει τούτῳ εἴπητε· ἄρθητι	also if – mountain to this ye say: Be thou taken
καὶ βλήθητι εἰς τὴν θάλασσαν, γενήσεται·	and cast into the sea, it shall be;
22 καὶ πάντα ὅσα ἂν αἰτήσητε ἐν τῇ	and all things whatever ye may ask in –
προσευχῇ πιστεύοντες λήμψεσθε.	prayer believing ye shall receive.
23 Καὶ ἐλθόντος αὐτοῦ εἰς τὸ ἱερὸν	And coming him* into the temple =as he came
προσῆλθον αὐτῷ διδάσκοντι οἱ ἀρχιερεῖς	approached to him teaching° the chief priests =while he taught
καὶ οἱ πρεσβύτεροι τοῦ λαοῦ λέγοντες·	and the elders of the people saying:
ἐν ποίᾳ ἐξουσίᾳ ταῦτα ποιεῖς; καὶ	By what authority these things doest thou? and
τίς σοι ἔδωκεν τὴν ἐξουσίαν ταύτην;	who thee gave – authority this?
24 ἀποκριθεὶς δὲ ὁ Ἰησοῦς εἶπεν αὐτοῖς·	And answering – Jesus said to them:
ἐρωτήσω ὑμᾶς κἀγὼ λόγον ἕνα, ὃν	will question you I also word one, which
ἐὰν εἴπητέ μοι, κἀγὼ ὑμῖν ἐρῶ ἐν ποίᾳ	if ye tell me, I also you will tell by what
ἐξουσίᾳ ταῦτα ποιῶ· **25** τὸ βάπτισμα	authority these things I do: The baptism
τὸ Ἰωάννου πόθεν ἦν; ἐξ οὐρανοῦ ἢ	– of John whence was it? from heaven or
ἐξ ἀνθρώπων; οἱ δὲ διελογίζοντο ἐν	from men? And they reasoned among
ἑαυτοῖς λέγοντες· ἐὰν εἴπωμεν· ἐξ οὐρανοῦ,	themselves saying: If we say: From heaven,
ἐρεῖ ἡμῖν· διὰ τί οὖν οὐκ ἐπιστεύσατε	he will say to us: Why then believed ye not

* Some such word as 'sign' must be supplied.

say, 'From men,' we are afraid of the multitude; for all hold that John was a prophet." ²⁷So they answered Jesus, "We do not know." And he said to them, "Neither will I tell you by what authority I do these things.
28 "What do you think? A man had two sons; and he went to the first and said, 'Son, go and work in the vineyard today.' ²⁹And he answered, 'I will not'; but afterward he repented and went. ³⁰And he went to the second and said the same; and he answered, 'I go, sir,' but did not go. ³¹Which of the two did the will of his father?" They said, "The first." Jesus said to them, "Truly, I say to you, the tax collectors and the harlots go into the kingdom of God before you. ³²For John came to you in the way of righteousness, and you did not believe him, but the tax collectors and the harlots believed him; and even when you saw it, you did not afterward repent and believe him.
33 "Hear another parable. There was a householder who planted a

αὐτῷ;   26 ἐὰν δὲ εἴπωμεν· ἐξ ἀνθρώπων,
him?   But if   we say: From   men,

φοβούμεθα   τὸν   ὄχλον·   πάντες γὰρ   ὡς
we fear   the   crowd: for all   as

προφήτην   ἔχουσιν   τὸν   Ἰωάννην.   27 καὶ
a prophet   have   –   John.   And

ἀποκριθέντες   τῷ   Ἰησοῦ   εἶπαν·   οὐκ
answering   –   Jesus   they said: We do

οἴδαμεν.   ἔφη   αὐτοῖς   καὶ   αὐτός·   οὐδὲ
not know.   said   to them   also   He: Neither

ἐγὼ   λέγω   ὑμῖν   ἐν   ποίᾳ   ἐξουσίᾳ   ταῦτα
I   tell   you   by   what   authority   these things

ποιῶ.   28 Τί   δὲ   ὑμῖν   δοκεῖ;   ἄνθρωπος
I do.   But what   to you   seems it?   A man

εἶχεν   τέκνα   δύο·   προσελθὼν   τῷ   πρώτῳ
had   children   two: approaching   to the   first

εἶπεν·   τέκνον,   ὕπαγε   σήμερον   ἐργάζου   ἐν
he said: Child,   go   to-day   work   in

τῷ   ἀμπελῶνι.   29 ὁ   δὲ   ἀποκριθεὶς   εἶπεν·
the   vineyard.   But he   answering   said:

ἐγὼ   κύριε,   καὶ   οὐκ   ἀπῆλθεν.   30 προσ-
I [go],   lord,   and   went not.   And

ελθὼν   δὲ   τῷ   δευτέρῳ   εἶπεν   ὡσαύτως.
approaching   to the   second   he said   similarly.

ὁ   δὲ   ἀποκριθεὶς   εἶπεν·   οὐ   θέλω,   ὕστερον
And he   answering   said: I will not,   later

μεταμεληθεὶς   ἀπῆλθεν.   31 τίς ἐκ   τῶν   δύο
repenting   he went.   Which of   the   two

ἐποίησεν   τὸ   θέλημα   τοῦ   πατρός;   λέγουσιν·
did   the   will   of the   father?   They say:

ὁ   ὕστερος.   λέγει   αὐτοῖς   ὁ   Ἰησοῦς·   ἀμὴν
The latter.   Says   to them   –   Jesus: Truly

λέγω   ὑμῖν   ὅτι   οἱ   τελῶναι   καὶ   αἱ   πόρναι
I tell   you[,]   –   The tax-collectors   and   the   harlots

προάγουσιν   ὑμᾶς   εἰς   τὴν   βασιλείαν   τοῦ
are going before   you   into   the   kingdom

θεοῦ.   32 ἦλθεν   γὰρ   Ἰωάννης   πρὸς   ὑμᾶς
of God.   For came   John   to   you

ἐν   ὁδῷ   δικαιοσύνης,   καὶ   οὐκ   ἐπιστεύσατε
in   a way   of righteousness,   and   ye believed not

αὐτῷ·   οἱ   δὲ   τελῶναι   καὶ   αἱ   πόρναι
him;   but the   tax-collectors   and   the   harlots

ἐπίστευσαν   αὐτῷ·   ὑμεῖς   δὲ   ἰδόντες   οὐδὲ
believed   him;   but ye   seeing   not

μετεμελήθητε   ὕστερον   τοῦ   πιστεῦσαι   αὐτῷ.
repented   later   –   to believeᵈ   him.
                                =so as to believe

33 Ἄλλην   παραβολὴν   ἀκούσατε.   Ἄνθρωπος
Another   parable   hear ye.   A man

vineyard, and set a hedge around it, and dug a wine press in it, and built a tower, and let it out to tenants, and went into another country. ³⁴When the season of fruit drew near, he sent his servants to the tenants, to get his fruit; ³⁵and the tenants took his servants and beat one, killed another, and stoned another. ³⁶Again he sent other servants, more than the first; and they did the same to them. ³⁷Afterward he sent his son to them, saying, 'They will respect my son.' ³⁸But when the tenants saw the son, they said to themselves, 'This is the heir; come, let us kill him and have his inheritance.' ³⁹And they took him and cast him out of the vineyard, and killed him. ⁴⁰When therefore the owner of the vineyard comes, what will he do to those tenants?" ⁴¹They said to him, "He will put those wretches to a miserable death, and let out the vineyard to other tenants who will

ἦν οἰκοδεσπότης ὅστις ἐφύτευσεν ἀμπελῶνα,
there was a housemaster who planted a vineyard,

καὶ φραγμὸν αὐτῷ περιέθηκεν καὶ ὤρυξεν
and ⁸a hedge ⁸it ¹put round and dug

ἐν αὐτῷ ληνὸν καὶ ᾠκοδόμησεν πύργον,
in it a winepress and built a tower,

καὶ ἐξέδοτο αὐτὸν γεωργοῖς, καὶ ἀπεδή-
and let it to husbandmen, and departed.

μησεν. 34 ὅτε δὲ ἤγγισεν ὁ καιρὸς τῶν
And when drew near the time of the

καρπῶν, ἀπέστειλεν τοὺς δούλους αὐτοῦ
fruits, he sent the slaves of him

πρὸς τοὺς γεωργοὺς λαβεῖν τοὺς καρποὺς
to the husbandmen to receive the fruits

αὐτοῦ. 35 καὶ λαβόντες οἱ γεωργοὶ
of it. And ²taking ¹the ⁸husbandmen

τοὺς δούλους αὐτοῦ ὃν μὲν ἔδειραν, ὃν
the slaves of him this one they flogged, that

δὲ ἀπέκτειναν, ὃν δὲ ἐλιθοβόλησαν. 36 πάλιν
one they killed, another they stoned. Again

ἀπέστειλεν ἄλλους δούλους πλείονας τῶν
he sent other slaves more [than] the

πρώτων, καὶ ἐποίησαν αὐτοῖς ὡσαύτως.
first [ones], and they did to them similarly.

37 ὕστερον δὲ ἀπέστειλεν πρὸς αὐτοὺς
But later he sent to them

τὸν υἱὸν αὐτοῦ λέγων· ἐντραπήσονται
the son of him saying: They will reverence

τὸν υἱόν μου. 38 οἱ δὲ γεωργοὶ ἰδόντες
the son of me. But the husbandmen seeing

τὸν υἱὸν εἶπον ἐν ἑαυτοῖς· οὗτός ἐστιν
the son said among themselves: This is

ὁ κληρονόμος· δεῦτε ἀποκτείνωμεν αὐτὸν
the heir; come[,] let us kill him

καὶ σχῶμεν τὴν κληρονομίαν αὐτοῦ·
and let us possess the inheritance of him;

39 καὶ λαβόντες αὐτὸν ἐξέβαλον ἔξω τοῦ
and taking ²him ¹they cast out outside the

ἀμπελῶνος καὶ ἀπέκτειναν. 40 ὅταν οὖν
vineyard and killed. When therefore

ἔλθῃ ὁ κύριος τοῦ ἀμπελῶνος, τί ποιήσει
comes the lord of the vineyard, what will he do

τοῖς γεωργοῖς ἐκείνοις; 41 λέγουσιν αὐτῷ·
- husbandmen to those? They say to him:

κακοὺς κακῶς ἀπολέσει αὐτούς, καὶ τὸν
Bad men badly he will destroy them, and the

ἀμπελῶνα ἐκδώσεται ἄλλοις γεωργοῖς,
vineyard he will give out to other husbandmen,

give him the fruits in their seasons."

42 Jesus said to them, "Have you never read in the scriptures:
'The very stone which the builders rejected has become the head of the corner; this was the Lord's doing, and it is marvelous in our eyes'?
43 Therefore I tell you, the kingdom of God will be taken away from you and given to a nation producing the fruits of it."[t]

45 When the chief priests and the Pharisees heard his parables, they perceived that he was speaking about them. 46 But when they tried to arrest him, they feared the multitudes, because they held him to be a prophet.

CHAPTER 22

AND again Jesus spoke to them in parables, saying, 2 "The kingdom of heaven may be compared to a king who gave a marriage feast for his son, 3 and sent his servants to call those who were invited to the

[t] Other ancient authorities add verse 44, "And he who falls on this stone will be broken to pieces; but when it falls on any one, it will crush him"

οἵτινες ἀποδώσουσιν αὐτῷ τοὺς καοπούς
who will render to him the fruits

ἐν τοῖς καιροῖς αὐτῶν. 42 λέγει αὐτοῖς ὁ
in the seasons of them. Says to them -

'Ιησοῦς· οὐδέποτε ἀνέγνωτε ἐν ταῖς
Jesus: Did ye never read in the

γραφαῖς· λίθον ὃν ἀπεδοκίμασαν οἱ
scriptures: A stone which rejected the

οἰκοδομοῦντες, οὗτος ἐγενήθη εἰς κεφαλὴν
building [ones], this became - head

γωνίας· παρὰ κυρίου ἐγένετο αὕτη, καὶ
of [the] corner; from [the] Lord became this, and

ἔστιν θαυμαστὴ ἐν ὀφθαλμοῖς ἡμῶν; 43 διὰ
it is marvellous in [the] eyes of us? There-

τοῦτο λέγω ὑμῖν ὅτι ἀρθήσεται ἀφ' ὑμῶν
fore I tell you[,] - will be taken from you

ἡ βασιλεία τοῦ θεοῦ καὶ δοθήσεται
The kingdom - of God and will be given

ἔθνει ποιοῦντι τοὺς καρποὺς αὐτῆς.
to a nation producing the fruits of it.

44 [καὶ ὁ πεσὼν ἐπὶ τὸν λίθον τοῦτον
And the [one] falling on - stone this

συνθλασθήσεται· ἐφ' ὃν δ' ἂν πέσῃ,
will be broken in pieces; but on whomever it falls,

λικμήσει αὐτόν.] 45 Καὶ ἀκούσαντες οἱ
it will crush to powder him. And hearing the

ἀρχιερεῖς καὶ οἱ Φαρισαῖοι τὰς παραβολὰς
chief priests and the Pharisees the parables

αὐτοῦ ἔγνωσαν ὅτι περὶ αὐτῶν λέγει·
of him they knew that concerning them he tells;

46 καὶ ζητοῦντες αὐτὸν κρατῆσαι ἐφοβήθησαν
and seeking him to seize they feared

τοὺς ὄχλους, ἐπεὶ εἰς προφήτην αὐτὸν εἶχον.
the crowds, since for a prophet him they had.

22 Καὶ ἀποκριθεὶς ὁ 'Ιησοῦς πάλιν
And answering - Jesus again

εἶπεν ἐν παραβολαῖς αὐτοῖς λέγων·
spoke in parables to them saying:

2 ὡμοιώθη ἡ βασιλεία τῶν οὐρανῶν
Was(is) likened the kingdom of the heavens

ἀνθρώπῳ βασιλεῖ, ὅστις ἐποίησεν γάμους
to a man a king, who made a wedding feast

τῷ υἱῷ αὐτοῦ. 3 καὶ ἀπέστειλεν τοὺς
for the son of him. And he sent the

δούλους αὐτοῦ καλέσαι τοὺς κεκλημένους
slaves of him to call the [ones] having been invited

marriage feast; but they would not come. ⁴Again he sent other servants, saying, 'Tell those who are invited, Behold, I have made ready my dinner, my oxen and my fat calves are killed, and everything is ready; come to the marriage feast.' ⁵But they made light of it and went off, one to his farm, another to his business, ⁶while the rest seized his servants, treated them shamefully, and killed them. ⁷The king was angry, and he sent his troops and destroyed those murderers and burned their city. ⁸Then he said to his servants, 'The wedding is ready, but those invited were not worthy. ⁹Go therefore to the thoroughfares, and invite to the marriage feast as many as you find.' ¹⁰And those servants went out into the streets and gathered all whom they found, both bad and good; so the wedding hall was filled with guests.

11 "But when the king came in to look at the guests, he saw there a

εἰς τοὺς γάμους, καὶ οὐκ ἤθελον ἐλθεῖν.
to the feast, and they wished not to come.

4 πάλιν ἀπέστειλεν ἄλλους δούλους λέγων·
Again he sent other slaves saying:

εἴπατε τοῖς κεκλημένοις· ἰδοὺ τὸ
Tell the [ones] having been invited: Behold[,] the

ἄριστόν μου ἡτοίμακα, οἱ ταῦροί μου
supper of me I have prepared, the oxen of me

καὶ τὰ σιτιστὰ τεθυμένα, καὶ πάντα
and the fatted beasts having been killed, and all things

ἕτοιμα· δεῦτε εἰς τοὺς γάμους. 5 οἱ δὲ
[are] ready; come to the feast. But they

ἀμελήσαντες ἀπῆλθον, ὃς μὲν εἰς τὸν
not caring went off, one to the(his)

ἴδιον ἀγρόν, ὃς δὲ ἐπὶ τὴν ἐμπορίαν
own field, another on the trading

αὐτοῦ· 6 οἱ δὲ λοιποὶ κρατήσαντες
of him; and the rest seizing

τοὺς δούλους αὐτοῦ ὕβρισαν καὶ ἀπέκτειναν.
the slaves of him insulted and killed.

7 ὁ δὲ βασιλεὺς ὠργίσθη, καὶ πέμψας
So the king became angry, and sending

τὰ στρατεύματα αὐτοῦ ἀπώλεσεν τοὺς
the armies of him destroyed –

φονεῖς ἐκείνους καὶ τὴν πόλιν αὐτῶν
murderers those and the city of them

ἐνέπρησεν. 8 τότε λέγει τοῖς δούλοις
burned. Then he says to the slaves

αὐτοῦ· ὁ μὲν γάμος ἕτοιμός ἐστιν, οἱ δὲ
of him: Indeed the feast ready is, but the[ones]

κεκλημένοι οὐκ ἦσαν ἄξιοι· 9 πορεύεσθε
having been invited were not worthy; go ye

οὖν ἐπὶ τὰς διεξόδους τῶν ὁδῶν, καὶ
therefore onto the partings of the ways, and

ὅσους ἐὰν εὕρητε καλέσατε εἰς τοὺς
as many as ye find call to the

γάμους. 10 καὶ ἐξελθόντες οἱ δοῦλοι
feast. And going forth – slaves

ἐκεῖνοι εἰς τὰς ὁδοὺς συνήγαγον πάντας
those into the ways assembled all

οὓς εὗρον, πονηρούς τε καὶ ἀγαθούς·
whom they found, both bad and good;

καὶ ἐπλήσθη ὁ νυμφὼν ἀνακειμένων.
and was filled the wedding chamber of(with) reclining [ones].

11 εἰσελθὼν δὲ ὁ βασιλεὺς θεάσασθαι
But entering the king to behold

τοὺς ἀνακειμένους εἶδεν ἐκεῖ
the reclining [ones] he saw there

man who had no wedding garment; ¹²and he said to him, 'Friend, how did you get in here without a wedding garment?' And he was speechless. ¹³Then the king said to the attendants, 'Bind him hand and foot, and cast him into the outer darkness; there men will weep and gnash their teeth.' ¹⁴For many are called, but few are chosen."

15 Then the Pharisees went and took counsel how to entangle him in his talk. ¹⁶And they sent their disciples to him, along with the Hero'di-ans, saying, "Teacher, we know that you are true, and teach the way of God truthfully, and care for no man; for you do not regard the position of men. ¹⁷Tell us, then, what you think. Is it lawful to pay taxes to Caesar, or not?" ¹⁸But Jesus, aware of their malice, said, "Why put me to the test, you hypocrites? ¹⁹Show me the money for the tax."

ἄνθρωπον   οὐκ   ἐνδεδυμένον   ἔνδυμα   γάμου·
a man   not *having been* dressed[in]   a dress   of wedding;

12 καὶ   λέγει   αὐτῷ·   ἑταῖρε,   πῶς
and   he says   to him: Comrade,   how

εἰσῆλθες   ὧδε   μὴ   ἔχων   ἔνδυμα   γάμου;
enteredst thou   here   not   having   a dress   of wedding?

ὁ   δὲ   ἐφιμώθη.   13 τότε   ὁ   βασιλεὺς
And he   was silenced.   Then   the   king

εἶπεν   τοῖς   διακόνοις·   δήσαντες   αὐτοῦ
said   to the   servants: Binding   of him

πόδας   καὶ   χεῖρας   ἐκβάλετε   αὐτὸν
feet   and   hands   throw out   him

εἰς   τὸ   σκότος   τὸ   ἐξώτερον·   ἐκεῖ   ἔσται
into   the   darkness   -   outer;   there   will be

ὁ   κλαυθμὸς   καὶ   ὁ   βρυγμὸς   τῶν
the   wailing   and   the   gnashing   of the

ὀδόντων.   14 Πολλοὶ   γάρ   εἰσιν   κλητοί,
teeth.   For many   are   called,

ὀλίγοι   δὲ   ἐκλεκτοί.
but few   chosen.

15 Τότε   πορευθέντες   οἱ   Φαρισαῖοι   συμ-
Then   going   the   Pharisees   coun-

βούλιον   ἔλαβον   ὅπως   αὐτὸν   παγιδεύσωσιν
sel   took   so as   him   they might ensnare

ἐν   λόγῳ.   16 καὶ   ἀποστέλλουσιν   αὐτῷ
in   a word.   And   they send   to him

τοὺς   μαθητὰς   αὐτῶν   μετὰ   τῶν   Ἡρῳ-
the   disciples   of them   with   the   Hero-

διανῶν   λέγοντας·   διδάσκαλε,   οἴδαμεν
dians   saying: Teacher,   we know

ὅτι   ἀληθὴς   εἶ   καὶ   τὴν   ὁδὸν   τοῦ
that   truthful   thou art   and   the   way   -

θεοῦ   ἐν   ἀληθείᾳ   διδάσκεις,   καὶ   οὐ
of God   in   truth   thou teachest,   and   not

μέλει   σοι   περὶ   οὐδενός,   οὐ   γὰρ
it concerns *to* thee   about   no one(anyone),   ²not   ¹for

βλέπεις   εἰς   πρόσωπον   ἀνθρώπων·
²thou lookest   to   face   of men;

17 εἰπὸν   οὖν   ἡμῖν,   τί   σοι   δοκεῖ;
tell   therefore   us,   what   to thee   seems it?

ἔξεστιν   δοῦναι   κῆνσον   Καίσαρι   ἢ   οὔ;
is it lawful   to give   tribute   to Cæsar   or   no?

18 γνοὺς   δὲ   ὁ   Ἰησοῦς   τὴν   πονηρίαν
But knowing   -   Jesus   the   wickedness

αὐτῶν   εἶπεν·   τί   με   πειράζετε,   ὑποκριταί;
of them   said: Why   me   tempt ye,   hypocrites?

19 ἐπιδείξατέ   μοι   τὸ   νόμισμα   τοῦ   κήνσου.
Show   me   the   money   of the   tribute.

And they brought him a coin. ²⁰And Jesus said to them, "Whose likeness and inscription is this?" ²¹They said, "Caesar's." Then he said to them, "Render therefore to Caesar the things that are Caesar's, and to God the things that are God's." ²²When they heard it, they marveled; and they left him and went away.

23 The same day Sad'ducees came to him, who say that there is no resurrection; and they asked him a question, ²⁴saying, "Teacher, Moses said, 'If a man dies, having no children, his brother must marry the widow, and raise up children for his brother.' ²⁵Now there were seven brothers among us; the first married, and died, and having no children left his wife to his brother. ²⁶So too the second and third, down to the seventh. ²⁷After them all, the woman died. ²⁸In the resurrection, therefore, to which of the seven will she be wife? For they all had her."

29 But Jesus answered them, "You are wrong,

οἱ δὲ προσήνεγκαν αὐτῷ δηνάριον. 20 καὶ
And they brought to him a denarius. And

λέγει αὐτοῖς· τίνος ἡ εἰκὼν αὕτη
he says to them: Of whom - image this

καὶ ἡ ἐπιγραφή; 21 λέγουσιν· Καίσαρος.
and - superscription? They say: Of Cæsar.

τότε λέγει αὐτοῖς· ἀπόδοτε οὖν τὰ
Then he says to them: Render then the things

Καίσαρος Καίσαρι καὶ τὰ τοῦ θεοῦ
of Cæsar to Cæsar and the things - of God

τῷ θεῷ. 22 καὶ ἀκούσαντες ἐθαύμασαν,
- to God. And hearing they marvelled,

καὶ ἀφέντες αὐτὸν ἀπῆλθαν.
and leaving him went away.

23 Ἐν ἐκείνῃ τῇ ἡμέρᾳ προσῆλθον
On that - day approached

αὐτῷ Σαδδουκαῖοι, λέγοντες μὴ εἶναι
to him Sadducees, saying not to be

ἀνάστασιν, καὶ ἐπηρώτησαν αὐτὸν
a resurrection, and questioned him

24 λέγοντες· διδάσκαλε, Μωϋσῆς εἶπεν·
saying: Teacher, Moses said:

ἐάν τις ἀποθάνῃ μὴ ἔχων τέκνα,
If any man dies not having children,

ἐπιγαμβρεύσει ὁ ἀδελφὸς αὐτοῦ τὴν
shall take to wife after the brother of him the

γυναῖκα αὐτοῦ καὶ ἀναστήσει σπέρμα
wife of him and shall raise up seed

τῷ ἀδελφῷ αὐτοῦ. 25 ἦσαν δὲ παρ'
to the brother of him. Now there were with

ἡμῖν ἑπτὰ ἀδελφοί· καὶ ὁ πρῶτος
us seven brothers; and the first

γήμας ἐτελεύτησεν, καὶ μὴ ἔχων
having married died, and not having

σπέρμα ἀφῆκεν τὴν γυναῖκα αὐτοῦ τῷ
seed left the wife of him to the

ἀδελφῷ αὐτοῦ· 26 ὁμοίως καὶ ὁ δεύτερος
brother of him; likewise also the second

καὶ ὁ τρίτος, ἕως τῶν ἑπτά. 27 ὕστερον
and the third, until the seven. last

δὲ πάντων ἀπέθανεν ἡ γυνή. 28 ἐν τῇ
And of all died the woman. In the

ἀναστάσει οὖν τίνος τῶν ἑπτὰ ἔσται
resurrection then of which of the seven will she be

γυνή; πάντες γὰρ ἔσχον αὐτήν. 29 ἀπο-
wife? for all had her. an-

κριθεὶς δὲ ὁ Ἰησοῦς εἶπεν αὐτοῖς·
swering And - Jesus said to them:

because you know neither the scriptures nor the power of God. [30]For in the resurrection they neither marry nor are given in marriage, but are like angels[u] in heaven. [31]And as for the resurrection of the dead, have you not read what was said to you by God, [32]'I am the God of Abraham, and the God of Isaac, and the God of Jacob'? He is not God of the dead, but of the living." [33]And when the crowd heard it, they were astonished at his teaching.

[34]But when the Pharisees heard that he had silenced the Sad'-ducees, they came together. [35]And one of them, a lawyer, asked him a question, to test him. [36]"Teacher, which is the great commandment in the law?" [37]And he said to him, "You shall love the Lord your God with all your heart, and with all your soul, and with all your mind. [38]This is the great and first commandment. [39]And a second is like it, You shall love your neighbor as yourself. [40]On these two commandments depend all the law and the prophets."

[u] Other ancient authorities add of God

πλανᾶσθε μὴ   εἰδότες τὰς γραφὰς μηδὲ
Ye err   not knowing the scriptures nor

τὴν δύναμιν τοῦ θεοῦ. 30 ἐν γὰρ τῇ
the power   -   of God. For in   the

ἀναστάσει οὔτε γαμοῦσιν οὔτε γαμίζονται,
resurrection neither they marry nor are given in marriage,

ἀλλ' ὡς ἄγγελοι ἐν τῷ οὐρανῷ εἰσιν.
but as angels   in the heaven   are.

31 περὶ δὲ τῆς ἀναστάσεως τῶν νεκρῶν
But concerning the resurrection of the dead

οὐκ ἀνέγνωτε τὸ ῥηθὲν ὑμῖν ὑπὸ
did ye not read the thing said to you by

τοῦ θεοῦ λέγοντος· 32 ἐγώ εἰμι ὁ θεὸς
-    God   saying: I   am   the God

Ἀβραὰμ καὶ ὁ θεὸς Ἰσαὰκ καὶ ὁ θεὸς
of Abraham and the God of Isaac and the God

Ἰακώβ; οὐκ ἔστιν [ὁ] θεὸς νεκρῶν
of Jacob? He is not the God of dead men

ἀλλὰ ζώντων. 33 καὶ ἀκούσαντες οἱ ὄχλοι
but of living [ones]. And hearing the crowds

ἐξεπλήσσοντο ἐπὶ τῇ διδαχῇ αὐτοῦ.
were astounded over(at) the teaching of him.

34 Οἱ δὲ Φαρισαῖοι ἀκούσαντες ὅτι
But the   Pharisees hearing that

ἐφίμωσεν τοὺς Σαδδουκαίους, συνήχθησαν
he silenced the Sadducees, were assembled

ἐπὶ τὸ αὐτό, 35 καὶ ἐπηρώτησεν εἷς
together,   and [8]questioned [1]one

ἐξ αὐτῶν νομικὸς πειράζων αὐτόν· 36 δι-
[5]of [3]them [4]a lawyer [6]tempting him: Teach-

δάσκαλε, ποία ἐντολὴ μεγάλη ἐν τῷ
er,   what commandment [is] great in the

νόμῳ; 37 ὁ δὲ ἔφη αὐτῷ· ἀγαπήσεις
law?   And he said to him: Thou shalt love

κύριον τὸν θεόν σου ἐν ὅλῃ τῇ καρδίᾳ
[the] Lord the God of thee with all the heart

σου καὶ ἐν ὅλῃ τῇ ψυχῇ σου καὶ ἐν
of thee and with all the soul of thee and with

ὅλῃ τῇ διανοίᾳ σου. 38 αὕτη ἐστὶν ἡ
all the understanding of thee. This is the

μεγάλη καὶ πρώτη ἐντολή. 39 δευτέρα
great   and first commandment. [The] second

ὁμοία αὐτῇ· ἀγαπήσεις τὸν πλησίον σου
[is] like to it: Thou shalt love the neighbour of thee

ὡς σεαυτόν. 40 ἐν ταύταις ταῖς δυσὶν ἐντολαῖς
as thyself.   In(on) these -   two commandments

ὅλος ὁ νόμος κρέμαται καὶ οἱ προφῆται.
all the law   hangs   and the prophets.

41 Now while the Pharisees were gathered together, Jesus asked them a question, ⁴²saying, "What do you think of the Christ? Whose son is he?" They said to him, "The son of David." ⁴³He said to them, "How is it then that David, inspired by the Spirit,ᵛ calls him Lord, saying, ⁴⁴'The Lord said to my Lord,

Sit at my right hand,
till I put thy enemies
under thy feet'?
⁴⁵If David thus calls him Lord, how is he his son?" ⁴⁶And no one was able to answer him a word, nor from that day did any one dare to ask him any more questions.

---

41 Συνηγμένων δὲ τῶν Φαρισαίων
And having assembled   the   Phariseesᵃ
= when the Pharisees were assembled

ἐπηρώτησεν αὐτοὺς ὁ Ἰησοῦς **42** λέγων· τι
questioned   them   –   Jesus   saying: What

ὑμῖν δοκεῖ περὶ τοῦ χριστοῦ; τίνος
to you   seems it   concerning   the   Christ?   of whom

υἱός ἐστιν; λέγουσιν αὐτῷ· τοῦ Δαυίδ.
son   is he?   They say   to him: –   Of David.

43 λέγει αὐτοῖς· πῶς οὖν Δαυὶδ ἐν
He says   to them: How   then   David   in

πνεύματι καλεῖ αὐτὸν κύριον λέγων·
spirit   calls   him   Lord   saying:

44 εἶπεν κύριος τῷ κυρίῳ μου·
Said   [the] Lord   to the   Lord   of me:

κάθου ἐκ δεξιῶν μου ἕως ἂν θῶ τοὺς
Sit   on [the] right   of me   until   I put   the

ἐχθρούς σου ὑποκάτω τῶν ποδῶν σου;
enemies   of thee   underneath   the   feet   of thee?

45 εἰ οὖν Δαυὶδ καλεῖ αὐτὸν κύριον, πῶς
If   then   David   calls   him   Lord,   how

υἱὸς αὐτοῦ ἐστιν; **46** καὶ οὐδεὶς ἐδύνατο
son   of him   is he?   And   no one   was able

ἀποκριθῆναι αὐτῷ λόγον οὐδὲ ἐτόλμησέν
to answer   him   a word   nor   dared

τις ἀπ' ἐκείνης τῆς ἡμέρας ἐπερωτῆσαι
anyone   from   that   –   day   to question

αὐτὸν οὐκέτι.
him   no(any) more.

CHAPTER 23

THEN said Jesus to the crowds and to his disciples, ²"The scribes and the Pharisees sit on Moses' seat; ³so practice and observe whatever they tell you, but not what they do; for they preach, but do not practice. ⁴They bind heavy burdens, hard to bear,ʷ and lay them on men's shoulders; but

---

23 Τότε ὁ Ἰησοῦς ἐλάλησεν τοῖς ὄχλοις
Then   –   Jesus   spoke   to the   crowds

καὶ τοῖς μαθηταῖς αὐτοῦ **2** λέγων· ἐπὶ
and   to the   disciples   of him   saying: On

τῆς Μωϋσέως καθέδρας ἐκάθισαν οἱ
the   of Moses   seat   sat   the

γραμματεῖς καὶ οἱ Φαρισαῖοι. **3** πάντα
scribes   and   the   Pharisees.   All things

οὖν ὅσα ἐὰν εἴπωσιν ὑμῖν ποιήσατε
therefore   whatever   they may tell   you   do ye

καὶ τηρεῖτε, κατὰ δὲ τὰ ἔργα αὐτῶν
and   keep,   but according to   the   works   of them

μὴ ποιεῖτε· λέγουσιν γὰρ καὶ οὐ ποιοῦσιν.
do ye not;   for they say   and   do not.

4 δεσμεύουσιν δὲ φορτία βαρέα καὶ
And they bind   burdens   heavy   and

ἐπιτιθέασιν ἐπὶ τοὺς ὤμους τῶν ἀνθρώπων,
put on   on   the   shoulders   –   of men,

ᵛ Or *David in the Spirit*

ʷ Other ancient authorities omit *hard to bear*

they themselves will not move them with their finger. ⁵They do all their deeds to be seen by men; for they make their phylacteries broad and their fringes long, ⁶and they love the place of honor at feasts and the best seats in the synagogues, ⁷and salutations in the market places, and being called rabbi by men. ⁸But you are not to be called rabbi, for you have one teacher, and you are all brethren. ⁹And call no man your father on earth, for you have one Father, who is in heaven. ¹⁰Neither be called masters, for you have one master, the Christ. ¹¹He who is greatest among you shall be your servant; ¹²whoever exalts himself will be humbled, and whoever humbles himself will be exalted.

13 "But woe to you, scribes and Pharisees, hypocrites! because you shut the kingdom of heaven against men; for you neither enter yourselves, nor allow those

αὐτοὶ δὲ τῷ δακτύλῳ αὐτῶν οὐ
but they   with the   finger   of them   not

θέλουσιν κινῆσαι αὐτά. 5 πάντα δὲ
are willing   to move   them.   But all

τὰ ἔργα αὐτῶν ποιοῦσιν πρὸς τὸ θεαθῆναι
the works of them   they do   for   -   to be seen

τοῖς ἀνθρώποις· πλατύνουσιν γὰρ τὰ
-      by men;   for they broaden   the

φυλακτήρια αὐτῶν καὶ μεγαλύνουσιν τὰ
phylacteries of them and   enlarge   the

κράσπεδα, 6 φιλοῦσιν δὲ τὴν πρωτο-
fringes,   and they like   the   chief

κλισίαν ἐν τοῖς δείπνοις καὶ τὰς πρωτο-
place   in   the   suppers   and , the   chief

καθεδρίας ἐν ταῖς συναγωγαῖς 7 καὶ τοὺς
seats   in   the   synagogues .   and   the

ἀσπασμοὺς ἐν ταῖς ἀγοραῖς καὶ
greetings   in   the   marketplaces   and

καλεῖσθαι ὑπὸ τῶν ἀνθρώπων ραββί.
to be called   by   -   men   rabbi.

8 ὑμεῖς δὲ μὴ κληθῆτε ραββί· εἷς γάρ
But ye   be not called   rabbi·   for one

ἐστιν ὑμῶν ὁ διδάσκαλος, πάντες δὲ ὑμεῖς
is   of you the   teacher,   and all   ye

ἀδελφοί ἐστε. 9 καὶ πατέρα μὴ καλέσητε
brothers   are.   And   father   call ye not

ὑμῶν ἐπὶ τῆς γῆς· εἷς γάρ ἐστιν
of you on   the   earth;   for one   is

ὑμῶν ὁ πατὴρ ὁ οὐράνιος. 10 μηδὲ
of you the   Father   -   heavenly.   Neither

κληθῆτε καθηγηταί, ὅτι καθηγητὴς
be ye called   leaders,   because   leader

ὑμῶν ἐστιν εἷς ὁ Χριστός. 11 ὁ δὲ
of you   is   one the   Christ.   And the

μείζων ὑμῶν ἔσται ὑμῶν διάκονος.
greater of you shall be of you   servant.

12 Ὅστις δὲ ὑψώσει ἑαυτὸν ταπεινωθήσεται,
And [he] who   will exalt   himself   shall be humbled,

καὶ ὅστις ταπεινώσει ἑαυτὸν ὑψωθήσεται.
and [he] who   will humble   himself   shall be exalted.

13 Οὐαὶ δὲ ὑμῖν, γραμματεῖς καὶ Φαρισαῖοι
But woe   to you,   scribes   and   Pharisees

ὑποκριταί, ὅτι κλείετε τὴν βασιλείαν
hypocrites,   because ye shut   the   kingdom

τῶν οὐρανῶν ἔμπροσθεν τῶν ἀνθρώπων
of the heavens   before   -   men;

ὑμεῖς γὰρ οὐκ εἰσέρχεσθε, οὐδὲ τοὺς
for ye   do not enter,   nor the [ones]

who would enter to go in.[z] [15] Woe to you, scribes and Pharisees, hypocrites! for you traverse sea and land to make a single proselyte, and when he becomes a proselyte, you make him twice as much a child of hell as yourselves.

16 "Woe to you, blind guides, who say, 'If any one swears by the temple, it is nothing; but if any one swears by the gold of the temple, he is bound by his oath.' [17] You blind fools! For which is greater, the gold or the temple that has made the gold sacred? [18] And you say, 'If any one swears by the altar, it is nothing; but if any one swears by the gift that is on the altar, he is bound by his oath.' [19] You blind men! For which is greater, the gift or the altar that makes the gift sacred? [20] So he who swears by the altar, swears by it and by everything on it; [21] and he who swears by the temple, swears by it and by him who dwells in it; [22] and he who swears by heaven, swears by the throne of God and by him who sits upon it.

23 "Woe to you, scribes and Pharisees, hypocrites! for you tithe

εἰσερχομένους ἀφίετε εἰσελθεῖν.‡ 15 Οὐαὶ
entering   do ye allow   to enter.   Woe

ὑμῖν,   γραμματεῖς καὶ   Φαρισαῖοι ὑποκριταί,
to you,   scribes   and   Pharisees   hypocrites,

ὅτι   περιάγετε   τὴν   θάλασσαν   καὶ   τὴν
because ye go about   the   sea   and   the

ξηρὰν   ποιῆσαι   ἕνα   προσήλυτον,   καὶ   ὅταν
dry [land] to make   one   proselyte,   and   when

γένηται,   ποιεῖτε   αὐτὸν   υἱὸν   γεέννης   διπλό-
he becomes, ye make   him   a son   of gehenna   twofold

τερον   ὑμῶν.   16 Οὐαὶ   ὑμῖν,   ὁδηγοὶ   τυφλοὶ
more [than] you.   Woe   to you,   leaders   blind

οἱ   λέγοντες·   ὃς   ἂν   ὀμόσῃ   ἐν   τῷ   ναῷ,
the [ones] saying: Whoever swears   by   the   shrine,

οὐδέν ἐστιν·   ὃς   δ'   ἂν   ὀμόσῃ   ἐν   τῷ   χρυσῷ
nothing   it is;   but whoever swears   by   the   gold

τοῦ   ναοῦ,   ὀφείλει.   17 μωροὶ   καὶ   τυφλοί,
of the shrine, he owes.   Fools   and   blind,

τίς γὰρ   μείζων   ἐστιν,   ὁ   χρυσὸς ἢ ὁ ναὸς
for which   greater   is,   the   gold   or   the shrine

ὁ   ἁγιάσας   τὸν   χρυσόν;   18 καὶ·   ὃς   ἂν
-   sanctifying   the   gold?   And: whoever

ὀμόσῃ   ἐν   τῷ   θυσιαστηρίῳ,   οὐδέν   ἐστιν·
swears   by   the   altar,   nothing   it is;

ὃς   δ'   ἂν   ὀμόσῃ   ἐν   τῷ   δώρῳ   τῷ   ἐπάνω
but whoever swears   by   the   gift   -   upon

αὐτοῦ,   ὀφείλει.   19 τυφλοί,   τί   γὰρ   μεῖζον,
it,   he owes.   Blind,   for which [is] greater,

τὸ   δῶρον   ἢ   τὸ   θυσιαστήριον   τὸ
the   gift   or   the   altar   -

ἁγιάζον   τὸ   δῶρον;   20 ὁ   οὖν   ὀμόσας
sanctifying   the   gift?   Therefore the [one] swearing

ἐν   τῷ   θυσιαστηρίῳ   ὀμνύει   ἐν   αὐτῷ   καὶ
by   the   altar   swears   by   it   and

ἐν   πᾶσι   τοῖς   ἐπάνω   αὐτοῦ·   21 καὶ   ὁ
by   all   the things   upon   it;   and the [one]

ὀμόσας   ἐν   τῷ   ναῷ   ὀμνύει   ἐν   αὐτῷ
swearing   by   the   shrine   swears   by   it

καὶ   ἐν   τῷ   κατοικοῦντι   αὐτόν·   22 καὶ
and   by the [one]   inhabiting   it;   and

ὁ   ὀμόσας   ἐν   τῷ   οὐρανῷ   ὀμνύει   ἐν   τῷ
the [one] swearing   by   the   heaven   swears   by   the

θρόνῳ   τοῦ   θεοῦ   καὶ   ἐν   τῷ   καθημένῳ
throne   -   of God   and   by the [one]   sitting

ἐπάνω   αὐτοῦ.   23 Οὐαὶ   ὑμῖν,   γραμματεῖς
upon   it.   Woe   to you,   scribes

καὶ   Φαρισαῖοι   ὑποκριταί,   ὅτι   ἀποδεκατοῦτε
and   Pharisees   hypocrites,   because   ye tithe

[z] Other authorities add here (or after verse 12) verse 14, *Woe to you, scribes and Pharisees, hypocrites! for you devour widows' houses and for a pretense you make long prayers; therefore you will receive the greater condemnation*

‡ Ver. 14 omitted by Nestle; cf. R.V. marg., etc.

mint and dill and cummin, and have neglected the weightier matters of the law, justice and mercy and faith; these you ought to have done, without neglecting the others. ²⁴ You blind guides, straining out a gnat and swallowing a camel!

25 "Woe to you, scribes and Pharisees, hypocrites! for you cleanse the outside of the cup and of the plate, but inside they are full of extortion and rapacity. ²⁶ You blind Pharisee! first cleanse the inside of the cup and of the plate, that the outside also may be clean.

27 "Woe to you, scribes and Pharisees, hypocrites! for you are like whitewashed tombs, which outwardly appear beautiful, but within they are full of dead men's bones and all uncleanness. ²⁸ So you also outwardly appear righteous to men, but within you are full of hypocrisy and iniquity.

29 "Woe to you, scribes and Pharisees, hypocrites! for you build the tombs of the prophets and adorn the monuments of the righteous, ³⁰ saying, 'If

τὸ ἡδύοσμον καὶ τὸ ἄνηθον καὶ τὸ
the mint and the dill and the

κύμινον, καὶ ἀφήκατε τὰ βαρύτερα
cummin, and ye [have] left the heavier things

τοῦ νόμου, τὴν κρίσιν καὶ τὸ ἔλεος
of the law, – judgment and – mercy

καὶ τὴν πίστιν· ταῦτα δὲ ἔδει ποιῆσαι
and – faith; but these things it behoved to do

κἀκεῖνα μὴ ἀφεῖναι. 24 ὁδηγοὶ τυφλοί,
and those not to leave. Leaders blind,

οἱ διϋλίζοντες τὸν κώνωπα, τὴν δὲ
the [ones] straining the gnat, but ²the

κάμηλον καταπίνοντες. 25 Οὐαὶ ὑμῖν,
²camel ¹swallowing. Woe to you,

γραμματεῖς καὶ Φαρισαῖοι ὑποκριταί, ὅτι
scribes and Pharisees hypocrites, because

καθαρίζετε τὸ ἔξωθεν τοῦ ποτηρίου καὶ
ye cleanse the outside of the cup and

τῆς παροψίδος, ἔσωθεν δὲ γέμουσιν ἐξ
the dish, but within they are full of

ἁρπαγῆς καὶ ἀκρασίας. 26 Φαρισαῖε τυφλέ,
robbery and intemperance. Pharisee blind,

καθάρισον πρῶτον τὸ ἐντὸς τοῦ ποτηρίου
cleanse thou first the inside of the cup

ἵνα γένηται καὶ τὸ ἐκτὸς αὐτοῦ καθαρόν.
that may be also the outside of it clean.

27 Οὐαὶ ὑμῖν, γραμματεῖς καὶ Φαρισαῖοι
Woe to you, scribes and Pharisees

ὑποκριταί, ὅτι παρομοιάζετε τάφοις κεκονια-
hypocrites, because ye resemble graves having been

μένοις, οἵτινες ἔξωθεν μὲν φαίνονται
whitewashed, who(which) outwardly indeed appear

ὡραῖοι, ἔσωθεν δὲ γέμουσιν ὀστέων
beautiful, but within they are full of bones

νεκρῶν καὶ πάσης ἀκαθαρσίας. 28 οὕτως
of dead men and of all uncleanness. Thus

καὶ ὑμεῖς ἔξωθεν μὲν φαίνεσθε τοῖς
also ye outwardly indeed appear –

ἀνθρώποις δίκαιοι, ἔσωθεν δέ ἐστε μεστοὶ
to men righteous, but within ye are full

ὑποκρίσεως καὶ ἀνομίας. 29 Οὐαὶ ὑμῖν,
of hypocrisy and of lawlessness. Woe to you

γραμματεῖς καὶ Φαρισαῖοι ὑποκριταί,
scribes and Pharisees hypocrites,

ὅτι οἰκοδομεῖτε τοὺς τάφους τῶν προφητῶν
because ye build the graves of the prophets

καὶ κοσμεῖτε τὰ μνημεῖα τῶν δικαίων,
and adorn the monuments of the righteous,

we had lived in the days of our fathers, we would not have taken part with them in shedding the blood of the prophets.' ³¹Thus you witness against yourselves, that you are sons of those who murdered the prophets. ³²Fill up, then, the measure of your fathers. ³³You serpents, you brood of vipers, how are you to escape being sentenced to hell? ³⁴Therefore I send you prophets and wise men and scribes, some of whom you will kill and crucify, and some you will scourge in your synagogues and persecute from town to town, ³⁵that upon you may come all the righteous blood shed on earth, from the blood of innocent Abel to the blood of Zechari'ah the son of Barachi'ah, whom you murdered between the sanctuary and the altar. ³⁶Truly, I say to you, all this will come upon this generation.

37 "O Jerusalem, Jerusalem, killing the prophets and stoning those who are sent to you! How often would I have gathered your children together as a

---

30 καὶ λέγετε· εἰ ἤμεθα ἐν ταῖς ἡμέραις
and say: If we were in the days

τῶν πατέρων ἡμῶν, οὐκ ἂν ἤμεθα
of the fathers of us, we would not have been

αὐτῶν κοινωνοὶ ἐν τῷ αἵματι τῶν προ-
of them partakers in the blood of the pro-

φητῶν. 31 ὥστε μαρτυρεῖτε ἑαυτοῖς ὅτι
phets. So ye witness to [your]selves that

υἱοί ἐστε τῶν φονευσάντων τοὺς προφήτας.
sons ye are of the [ones] having killed the prophets.

32 καὶ ὑμεῖς πληρώσατε τὸ μέτρον τῶν
And ²ye ¹fulfil the measure of the

πατέρων ὑμῶν. 33 ὄφεις, γεννήματα ἐχιδνῶν,
fathers of you. Serpents, offspring of vipers,

πῶς φύγητε ἀπὸ τῆς κρίσεως τῆς γεέννης;
how escape ye from the judgment – of gehenna?

34 διὰ τοῦτο ἰδοὺ ἐγὼ ἀποστέλλω πρὸς
Therefore behold I send to

ὑμᾶς προφήτας καὶ σοφοὺς καὶ γραμ-
you prophets and wise men and scribes;

ματεῖς· ἐξ αὐτῶν ἀποκτενεῖτε καὶ
of them ye will kill and

σταυρώσετε, καὶ ἐξ αὐτῶν μαστιγώσετε
will crucify, and of them ye will scourge

ἐν ταῖς συναγωγαῖς ὑμῶν καὶ διώξετε
in the synagogues of you and will persecute

ἀπὸ πόλεως εἰς πόλιν· 35 ὅπως ἔλθῃ
from city to city; so comes

ἐφ' ὑμᾶς πᾶν αἷμα δίκαιον ἐκχυννόμενον
on you all blood righteous being shed

ἐπὶ τῆς γῆς ἀπὸ τοῦ αἵματος ᾽Αβελ τοῦ
on the earth from the blood of Abel the

δικαίου ἕως τοῦ αἵματος Ζαχαρίου υἱοῦ
righteous until the blood of Zacharias son

Βαραχίου, ὃν ἐφονεύσατε μεταξὺ τοῦ ναοῦ
Barachias, whom ye murdered between the shrine

καὶ τοῦ θυσιαστηρίου. 36 ἀμὴν λέγω
and the altar. Truly I tell

ὑμῖν, ἥξει ταῦτα πάντα ἐπὶ τὴν
you, will come all these things on –

γενεὰν ταύτην. 37 ᾽Ιερουσαλὴμ ᾽Ιερουσαλήμ,
generation this. Jerusalem Jerusalem,

ἡ ἀποκτείνουσα τοὺς προφήτας καὶ
the [one] killing the prophets and

λιθοβολοῦσα τοὺς ἀπεσταλμένους πρὸς αὐτήν,
stoning the [ones] sent to her,

ποσάκις ἠθέλησα ἐπισυναγαγεῖν τὰ τέκνα
how often I wished to gather the children

hen gathers her brood under her wings, and you would not! [38]Behold, your house is forsaken and desolate.[y] [39]For I tell you, you will not see me again, until you say, 'Blessed is he who comes in the name of the Lord.' "

σου, ὃν τρόπον ὄρνις ἐπισυνάγει τὰ
of thee, as a bird gathers the

νοσσία [αὐτῆς] ὑπὸ τὰς πτέρυγας, καὶ
young of her under the(her) wings, and

οὐκ ἠθελήσατε. 38 ἰδοὺ ἀφίεται ὑμῖν ὁ
ye wished not. Behold is left to you the

οἶκος ὑμῶν. 39 λέγω γὰρ ὑμῖν, οὐ μή
house of you. For I tell you, by no means

με ἴδητε ἀπ' ἄρτι ἕως ἂν εἴπητε·
me ye see from now until ye say:

εὐλογημένος ὁ ἐρχόμενος ἐν ὀνόματι
Blessed the [one] coming in [the] name

κυρίου.
of [the] Lord.

CHAPTER 24

JESUS left the temple and was going away, when his disciples came to point out to him the buildings of the temple. [2]But he answered them, "You see all these, do you not? Truly, I say to you, there will not be left here one stone upon another, that will not be thrown down."

3 As he sat on the Mount of Olives, the disciples came to him privately, saying, "Tell us, when will this be, and what will be the sign of your coming and of the close of the age?" [4]Jesus answered them, "Take heed that no one leads you astray. [5]For many will come in my name, saying, 'I am the Christ,' and they will lead many astray. [6]And

24 Καὶ ἐξελθὼν ὁ Ἰησοῦς ἀπὸ τοῦ
And going forth - Jesus from the

ἱεροῦ ἐπορεύετο, καὶ προσῆλθον οἱ μαθηταὶ
temple went, and ⁴approached ¹the ²disciples

αὐτοῦ ἐπιδεῖξαι αὐτῷ τὰς οἰκοδομὰς
³of him to show him the buildings

τοῦ ἱεροῦ. 2 ὁ δὲ ἀποκριθεὶς εἶπεν
of the temple. And he answering said

αὐτοῖς· οὐ βλέπετε ταῦτα πάντα; ἀμὴν
to them: See ye not all these things? Truly

λέγω ὑμῖν, οὐ μὴ ἀφεθῇ ὧδε λίθος ἐπὶ
I tell you, by no means will be left here stone on

λίθον ὃς οὐ καταλυθήσεται. 3 Καθημένου
stone which shall not be overthrown. sitting

δὲ αὐτοῦ ἐπὶ τοῦ ὄρους τῶν ἐλαιῶν
and him[a] on the mount of the olives
= And as he sat

προσῆλθον αὐτῷ οἱ μαθηταὶ κατ' ἰδίαν
approached to him the disciples privately

λέγοντες· εἰπὲ ἡμῖν, πότε ταῦτα ἔσται,
saying: Tell us, when these things will be,

καὶ τί τὸ σημεῖον τῆς σῆς παρουσίας
and what the sign - of thy presence

καὶ συντελείας τοῦ αἰῶνος; 4 καὶ ἀπο-
and of [the] completion of the age? And answer-

κριθεὶς ὁ Ἰησοῦς εἶπεν αὐτοῖς· βλέπετε
ing - Jesus said to them: See ye

μή τις ὑμᾶς πλανήσῃ. 5 πολλοὶ γὰρ
not(lest) anyone ²you ¹cause ³to err. For many

ἐλεύσονται ἐπὶ τῷ ὀνόματί μου λέγοντες·
will come on(in) the name of me saying:

ἐγώ εἰμι ὁ χριστός, καὶ πολλοὺς πλανή-
I am the Christ, and ²many ¹will cause

[y] Other ancient authorities omit and desolate

you will hear of wars and rumors of wars; see that you are not alarmed; for this must take place, but the end is not yet. ⁷For nation will rise against nation, and kingdom against kingdom, and there will be famines and earthquakes in various places: ⁸all this is but the beginning of the sufferings.

9 "Then they will deliver you up to tribulation, and put you to death; and you will be hated by all nations for my name's sake. ¹⁰And then many will fall away,ᶻ and betray one another, and hate one another. ¹¹And many false prophets will arise and lead many astray. ¹²And because wickedness is multiplied, most men's love will grow cold. ¹³But he who endures to the end will be saved. ¹⁴And this gospel of the kingdom will be preached throughout the whole world, as a testimony to all nations; and then the end will come.

15 "So when you see the desolating sacrilege spoken of by the prophet

ᶻ Or *stumble*

σουσιν. 6 μελλήσετε δὲ ἀκούειν πολέ-
ᵃto err.   But ye will be about   to hear   [of]

μους καὶ ἀκοὰς πολέμων· ὁρᾶτε μὴ
wars and rumours of wars;   see   not

θροεῖθε· δεῖ γὰρ γενέσθαι, ἀλλ'
ye are disturbed; for it behoves   to happen,   but

οὔπω ἐστὶν τὸ τέλος. 7 ἐγερθήσεται γὰρ
not yet   is   the   end.   For will be raised

ἔθνος ἐπὶ ἔθνος καὶ βασιλεία ἐπὶ βασιλείαν,
nation against nation and kingdom against kingdom,

καὶ ἔσονται λιμοὶ καὶ σεισμοὶ
and   there will be   famines   and   earthquakes

κατὰ τόπους· 8 πάντα δὲ ταῦτα ἀρχὴ
throughout places;   but all these things [are] beginning

ὠδίνων. 9 τότε παραδώσουσιν ὑμᾶς
of birth-pangs.   Then   they will deliver   you

εἰς θλῖψιν καὶ ἀποκτενοῦσιν ὑμᾶς,
to   affliction   and   will kill   you,

καὶ ἔσεσθε μισούμενοι ὑπὸ πάντων
and   ye will be   *being* hated   by   all

τῶν ἐθνῶν διὰ τὸ ὄνομά μου.
the   nations   because of   the   name   of me.

10 καὶ τότε σκανδαλισθήσονται πολλοὶ καὶ
And   then   will be offended   many   and

ἀλλήλους παραδώσουσιν καὶ μισήσουσιν
one another   will deliver   and   they will hate

ἀλλήλους· 11 καὶ πολλοὶ ψευδοπροφῆται
one another;   and   many   false prophets

ἐγερθήσονται καὶ πλανήσουσιν πολλούς·
will be raised   and   will cause to err   many;

12 καὶ διὰ τὸ πληθυνθῆναι τὴν
and   because of   –   to be increased   the

ἀνομίαν ψυγήσεται ἡ ἀγάπη τῶν
lawlessness   will grow cold   the   love   of the

πολλῶν. 13 ὁ δὲ ὑπομείνας εἰς τέλος,
many.   But the [one]   enduring   to   [the] end,

οὗτος σωθήσεται. 14 καὶ κηρυχθήσεται
this   will be saved.   And   will be proclaimed

τοῦτο τὸ εὐαγγέλιον τῆς βασιλείας
this   –   gospel   of the   kingdom

ἐν ὅλη τῇ οἰκουμένῃ εἰς μαρτύριον
in   all   the   inhabited earth   for   a testimony

πᾶσιν τοῖς ἔθνεσιν, καὶ τότε ἥξει τὸ
to all   the   nations,   and   then   will come   the

τέλος. 15 Ὅταν οὖν ἴδητε τὸ
end.   When   therefore   ye see   the

βδέλυγμα τῆς ἐρημώσεως τὸ ῥηθὲν διὰ
abomination   –   of desolation   –   spoken through

Daniel, standing in the holy place (let the reader understand), [16]then let those who are in Judea flee to the mountains; [17]let him who is on the housetop not go down to take what is in his house; [18]and let him who is in the field not turn back to take his mantle. [19]And alas for those who are with child and for those who give suck in those days! [20]Pray that your flight may not be in winter or on a sabbath. [21]For then there will be great tribulation, such as has not been from the beginning of the world until now, no, and never will be. [22]And if those days had not been shortened, no human being would be saved; but for the sake of the elect those days will be shortened. [23]Then if any one says to you, 'Lo, here is the Christ!' or 'There he is!' do not believe it. [24]For false Christs and false prophets will arise and show great signs and wonders, so as to lead astray, if possible, even the elect. [25]Lo, I have told you beforehand. [26]So, if they say to you,

Δανιὴλ τοῦ προφήτου ἑστὸς ἐν τόπῳ
Daniel the prophet stand in place

ἁγίῳ, ὁ ἀναγινώσκων νοείτω,
holy, the [one] reading let him understand,

16 τότε οἱ ἐν τῇ Ἰουδαίᾳ φευγέτωσαν
then the [ones] in - Judæa let them flee

εἰς τὰ ὄρη, **17** ὁ ἐπὶ τοῦ δώματος μὴ
to the mountains, the [one] on the housetop let him

καταβάτω ἆραι τὰ ἐκ τῆς οἰκίας αὐτοῦ,
not come down to take the things out of the house of him,

18 καὶ ὁ ἐν τῷ ἀγρῷ μὴ ἐπιστρεψάτω
and the [one] in the field let him not turn back

ὀπίσω ἆραι τὸ ἱμάτιον αὐτοῦ. **19** οὐαὶ
behind to take the garment of him. woe

δὲ ταῖς ἐν γαστρὶ ἐχούσαις καὶ ταῖς
And to the women in womb having and to the [ones]
= the pregnant women

θηλαζούσαις ἐν ἐκείναις ταῖς ἡμέραις.
giving suck in those - days.

20 προσεύχεσθε δὲ ἵνα μὴ γένηται ἡ
And pray ye lest happen the

φυγὴ ὑμῶν χειμῶνος μηδὲ σαββάτῳ·
flight of you of(in) winter nor on a sabbath;

21 ἔσται γὰρ τότε θλῖψις μεγάλη, οἵα οὐ
for will be then affliction great, such as not

γέγονεν ἀπ’ ἀρχῆς κόσμου ἕως
has happened from [the] beginning of [the] world until

τοῦ νῦν οὐδ’ οὐ μὴ γένηται. **22** καὶ
- now neither by no means may happen. And

εἰ μὴ ἐκολοβώθησαν αἱ ἡμέραι ἐκείναι,
except were cut short - days those,

οὐκ ἂν ἐσώθη πᾶσα σάρξ· διὰ δὲ τοὺς
not was saved all flesh; but on account of the
= no flesh would be saved;

ἐκλεκτοὺς κολοβωθήσονται αἱ ἡμέραι ἐκεῖναι.
chosen will be cut short - days those.

23 τότε ἐάν τις ὑμῖν εἴπῃ· ἰδοὺ ὧδε
Then if anyone to you says: Behold here

ὁ χριστός, ἤ· ὧδε, μὴ πιστεύσητε·
the Christ, or: Here, do not believe;

24 ἐγερθήσονται γὰρ ψευδόχριστοι καὶ
for will be raised false Christs and

ψευδοπροφῆται, καὶ δώσουσιν σημεῖα μεγάλα
false prophets, and they will give signs great

καὶ τέρατα, ὥστε πλανῆσαι, εἰ δυνατόν,
and marvels, so as to cause to err, if possible,

καὶ τοὺς ἐκλεκτούς. **25** ἰδοὺ προείρηκα
even the chosen. Behold I have before told

ὑμῖν. **26** ἐὰν οὖν εἴπωσιν ὑμῖν· ἰδοὺ
you. If therefore they say to you: Behold

'Lo, he is in the wilderness,' do not go out; if they say, 'Lo, he is in the inner rooms,' do not believe it. 27 For as the lightning comes from the east and shines as far as the west, so will be the coming of the Son of man. 28 Wherever the body is, there the eagles[a] will be gathered together.

29 "Immediately after the tribulation of those days the sun will be darkened, and the moon will not give its light, and the stars will fall from heaven, and the powers of the heavens will be shaken; 30 then will appear the sign of the Son of man in heaven, and then all the tribes of the earth will mourn, and they will see the Son of man coming on the clouds of heaven with power and great glory; 31 and he will send out his angels with a loud trumpet call, and they will gather his elect from the four winds, from one end of heaven to the other.

32 "From the fig tree learn its lesson: as soon

ἐν τῇ ἐρήμῳ ἐστίν, μὴ ἐξέλθητε· ἰδοὺ
in the desert he is, go not ye forth; Behold

ἐν τοῖς ταμειίοις, μὴ πιστεύσητε·
in the private rooms, do not ye believe;

27 ὥσπερ γὰρ ἡ ἀστραπὴ ἐξέρχεται ἀπὸ
for as the lightning comes forth from

ἀνατολῶν καὶ φαίνεται ἕως δυσμῶν,
[the] east and shines unto [the] west,

οὕτως ἔσται ἡ παρουσία τοῦ υἱοῦ
so will be the presence of the Son

τοῦ ἀνθρώπου· 28 ὅπου ἐὰν ᾖ τὸ
of man; wherever may be the

πτῶμα, ἐκεῖ συναχθήσονται οἱ ἀετοί.
carcase, there will be assembled the eagles.

29 Εὐθέως δὲ μετὰ τὴν θλῖψιν τῶν
And immediately after the affliction –

ἡμερῶν ἐκείνων ὁ ἥλιος σκοτισθήσεται,
days of those the sun will be darkened,

καὶ ἡ σελήνη οὐ δώσει τὸ φέγγος
and the moon will not give the light

αὐτῆς, καὶ οἱ ἀστέρες πεσοῦνται ἀπὸ τοῦ
of her, and the stars will fall from –

οὐρανοῦ, καὶ αἱ δυνάμεις τῶν οὐρανῶν
heaven, and the powers of the heavens

σαλευθήσονται. 30 καὶ τότε φανήσεται
will be shaken. And then will appear

τὸ σημεῖον τοῦ υἱοῦ τοῦ ἀνθρώπου ἐν
the sign of the Son – of man in

οὐρανῷ, καὶ τότε κόψονται πᾶσαι αἱ
heaven, and then will bewail all the

φυλαὶ τῆς γῆς καὶ ὄψονται τὸν υἱὸν
tribes of the land and they will see the Son

τοῦ ἀνθρώπου ἐρχόμενον ἐπὶ τῶν
– of man coming on the

νεφελῶν τοῦ οὐρανοῦ μετὰ δυνάμεως καὶ
clouds – of heaven with power and

δόξης πολλῆς· 31 καὶ ἀποστελεῖ τοὺς
glory much; and he will send the

ἀγγέλους αὐτοῦ μετὰ σάλπιγγος μεγάλης,
angels of him with trumpet a great,

καὶ ἐπισυνάξουσιν τοὺς ἐκλεκτοὺς αὐτοῦ
and they will assemble the chosen of him

ἐκ τῶν τεσσάρων ἀνέμων ἀπ' ἄκρων
out of the four winds from [the] extremities

οὐρανῶν ἕως [τῶν] ἄκρων αὐτῶν. 32 Ἀπὸ
of [the] heavens unto the extremities of them. from

δὲ τῆς συκῆς μάθετε τὴν παραβολήν·
Now the fig-tree learn ye the parable:

[a] Or vultures

as its branch becomes tender and puts forth its leaves, you know that summer is near. ³³So also, when you see all these things, you know that he is near, at the very gates. ³⁴Truly, I say to you, this generation will not pass away till all these things take place. ³⁵Heaven and earth will pass away, but my words will not pass away.

36 "But of that day and hour no one knows, not even the angels of heaven, nor the Son,ᵇ but the Father only. ³⁷As were the days of Noah, so will be the coming of the Son of man. ³⁸For as in those days before the flood they were eating and drinking, marrying and giving in marriage, until the day when Noah entered the ark, ³⁹and they did not know until the flood came and swept them all away, so will be the coming of the Son of man. ⁴⁰Then two men will be in the field; one is taken and one is left. ⁴¹Two women will be grinding at the mill; one

ὅταν   ἤδη   ὁ   κλάδος   αὐτῆς   γένηται   ἁπαλὸς
When   now   the   branch   of it   becomes   tender

καὶ   τὰ   φύλλα   ἐκφύῃ,   γινώσκετε   ὅτι
and   the   leaves   it puts forth,   ye know   that

ἐγγὺς   τὸ   θέρος·   33 οὕτως   καὶ   ὑμεῖς
near [is]   the   summer;   so   also   ye

ὅταν   ἴδητε   πάντα   ταῦτα,   γινώσκετε   ὅτι
when   ye see   all   these things,   know   that

ἐγγύς   ἐστιν   ἐπὶ   θύραις.   34 ἀμὴν   λέγω
near   it is   on(at) [the] doors.   Truly   I tell

ὑμῖν   ὅτι   οὐ   μὴ   παρέλθῃ   ἡ   γενεὰ
you   that   by no means   passes away   –   generation

αὕτη   ἕως   ἂν   πάντα   ταῦτα   γένηται.
this   until   all   these things   happens.

35 ὁ   οὐρανὸς   καὶ   ἡ   γῆ   παρελεύσεται,   οἱ
The   heaven   and   the earth   will pass away,   ²the

δὲ   λόγοι   μου   οὐ   μὴ   παρέλθωσιν.   36 Περὶ
¹but   words   of me   by no means   may pass away.   concerning

δὲ   τῆς   ἡμέρας   ἐκείνης   καὶ   ὥρας   οὐδεὶς
But   –   day   that   and   hour   no one

οἶδεν,   οὐδὲ   οἱ   ἄγγελοι   τῶν   οὐρανῶν
knows,   neither   the   angels   of the   heavens

οὐδὲ   ὁ   υἱός,   εἰ   μὴ   ὁ   πατὴρ   μόνος.
nor   the   Son,   except   the   Father   only.

37 ὥσπερ   γὰρ   αἱ   ἡμέραι   τοῦ   Νῶε,   οὕτως
For as   the   days   of Noah,   so

ἔσται   ἡ   παρουσία   τοῦ   υἱοῦ   τοῦ   ἀνθρώπου.
will be   the   presence   of the Son   –   of man.

38 ὡς   γὰρ   ἦσαν   ἐν   ταῖς   ἡμέραις
For as   they were   in   –   days

[ἐκείναις]   ταῖς   πρὸ   τοῦ   κατακλυσμοῦ
those   the [ones]   before   the   flood

τρώγοντες   καὶ   πίνοντες,   γαμοῦντες   καὶ
eating   and   drinking,   marrying   and

γαμίζοντες,   ἄχρι   ἧς   ἡμέρας   εἰσῆλθεν
being given in marriage,   until   which   day   entered

Νῶε   εἰς   τὴν   κιβωτόν,   39 καὶ   οὐκ   ἔγνωσαν
Noah   into   the   ark,   and   knew not

ἕως   ἦλθεν   ὁ   κατακλυσμὸς   καὶ   ἦρεν
until   came   the   flood   and   took

ἅπαντας,   οὕτως   ἔσται   καὶ   ἡ   παρουσία
all,   so   will be   also   the   presence

τοῦ   υἱοῦ   τοῦ   ἀνθρώπου   40 τότε   ἔσονται
of the   Son   –   of man.   Then   will be

δύο   ἐν   τῷ   ἀγρῷ,   εἷς   παραλαμβάνεται
two men   in   the   field,   one   is taken

καὶ   εἷς   ἀφίεται·   41 δύο   ἀλήθουσαι
and   one   is left;   two women   grinding

is taken and one is left. [42] Watch therefore, for you do not know on what day your Lord is coming. [43] But know this, that if the householder had known in what part of the night the thief was coming, he would have watched and would not have let his house be broken into. [44] Therefore you also must be ready; for the Son of man is coming at an hour you do not expect.

[45] "Who then is the faithful and wise servant, whom his master has set over his household, to give them their food at the proper time? [46] Blessed is that servant whom his master when he comes will find so doing. [47] Truly, I say to you, he will set him over all his possessions. [48] But if that wicked servant says to himself, 'My master is delayed,' [49] and begins to beat his fellow servants, and eats and drinks with the drunken, [50] the master of that servant will come on a day when he does not expect him and at an hour he does not know, [51] and

ἐν τῷ μύλῳ, μία παραλαμβάνεται καὶ
in(at) the mill, one is taken and

μία ἀφίεται. **42** γρηγορεῖτε οὖν, ὅτι
one is left. Watch ye therefore, because

οὐκ οἴδατε ποίᾳ ἡμέρᾳ ὁ κύριος
ye know not on what day the lord

ὑμῶν ἔρχεται. **43** Ἐκεῖνο δὲ γινώσκετε
of you is coming. And that know ye

ὅτι εἰ ᾔδει ὁ οἰκοδεσπότης ποίᾳ
that if knew the housemaster in what

φυλακῇ ὁ κλέπτης ἔρχεται, ἐγρηγόρησεν
watch the thief is coming, he would have

ἂν καὶ οὐκ ἂν εἴασεν διορυχθῆναι
watched and would not have allowed to be dug through

τὴν οἰκίαν αὐτοῦ. **44** διὰ τοῦτο καὶ
the house of him. Therefore also

ὑμεῖς γίνεσθε ἕτοιμοι, ὅτι ᾗ οὐ δοκεῖτε
ye be ready, because [1]in which [3]ye think not

ὥρᾳ ὁ υἱὸς τοῦ ἀνθρώπου ἔρχεται. **45** Τίς
[2]hour the Son – of man comes. Who

ἄρα ἐστιν ὁ πιστὸς δοῦλος καὶ φρόνιμος
then is the faithful slave and prudent

ὃν κατέστησεν ὁ κύριος ἐπὶ τῆς οἰκετείας
whom appointed the lord over the household

αὐτοῦ τοῦ δοῦναι αὐτοῖς τὴν τροφὴν ἐν
of him – to give[d] to them the food in

καιρῷ; **46** μακάριος ὁ δοῦλος ἐκεῖνος ὃν
season? blessed [is] – slave that whom

ἐλθὼν ὁ κύριος αὐτοῦ εὑρήσει οὕτως
coming the lord of him will find so

ποιοῦντα· **47** ἀμὴν λέγω ὑμῖν ὅτι ἐπὶ
doing; truly I tell you that over

πᾶσιν τοῖς ὑπάρχουσιν αὐτοῦ καταστήσει
all the goods of him he will appoint

αὐτόν. **48** ἐὰν δὲ εἴπῃ ὁ κακὸς δοῦλος
him. But if says – wicked slave

ἐκεῖνος ἐν τῇ καρδίᾳ αὐτοῦ· χρονίζει
that in the heart of him: Delays

μου ὁ κύριος, **49** καὶ ἄρξηται τύπτειν
of me the lord, and begins to strike

τοὺς συνδούλους αὐτοῦ, ἐσθίῃ δὲ καὶ
the fellow-slaves of him, and eats and

πίνῃ μετὰ τῶν μεθυόντων, **50** ἥξει ὁ
drinks with the [ones] being drunk, will come the

κύριος τοῦ δούλου ἐκείνου ἐν ἡμέρᾳ ᾗ
lord – slave of that on a day on which

οὐ προσδοκᾷ καὶ ἐν ὥρᾳ ᾗ οὐ
he does not expect and in an hour in which not

will punish[c] him, and put him with the hypocrites; there men will weep and gnash their teeth.

γινώσκει,	**51** καὶ	διχοτομήσει	αὐτόν,
he knows,	and	will cut asunder	him,
καὶ τὸ		μέρος	αὐτοῦ	μετὰ	τῶν
and the		portion	of him	with	the
ὑποκριτῶν		θήσει·	ἐκεῖ	ἔσται	ὁ
hypocrites		will place;	there	will be	the
κλαυθμὸς	καὶ ὁ	βρυγμὸς	τῶν	ὀδόντων.
wailing	and the	gnashing	of the	teeth.

CHAPTER 25

"THEN the kingdom of heaven shall be compared to ten maidens who took their lamps and went to meet the bridegroom.[d] ²Five of them were foolish, and five were wise. ³For when the foolish took their lamps, they took no oil with them; ⁴but the wise took flasks of oil with their lamps. ⁵As the bridegroom was delayed, they all slumbered and slept. ⁶But at midnight there was a cry, 'Behold, the bridegroom! Come out to meet him.' ⁷Then all those maidens rose and trimmed their lamps. ⁸And the foolish said to the wise, 'Give us some of your oil, for our lamps are going out.' ⁹But the wise replied,

25 Τότε ὁμοιωθήσεται ἡ βασιλεία
Then shall be likened the kingdom
τῶν οὐρανῶν δέκα παρθένοις, αἵτινες
of the heavens to ten virgins, who
λαβοῦσαι τὰς λαμπάδας ἑαυτῶν ἐξῆλθον
taking the lamps of them* went forth
εἰς ὑπάντησιν τοῦ νυμφίου. **2** πέντε δὲ
to a meeting of the bridegroom. Now five
ἐξ αὐτῶν ἦσαν μωραὶ καὶ πέντε φρόνιμοι.
of them were foolish and five prudent.
3 αἱ γὰρ μωραὶ λαβοῦσαι τὰς λαμπάδας
For the foolish [ones] taking the lamps
οὐκ ἔλαβον μεθ' ἑαυτῶν ἔλαιον.
did not take with them oil.
4 αἱ δὲ φρόνιμοι ἔλαβον ἔλαιον ἐν
But the prudent [ones] took oil in
τοῖς ἀγγείοις μετὰ τῶν λαμπάδων ἑαυτῶν.
the vessels with the lamps of them.
5 χρονίζοντος δὲ τοῦ νυμφίου ἐνύσταξαν
But delaying the bridegroom* slumbered
=while the bridegroom delayed
πᾶσαι καὶ ἐκάθευδον. **6** μέσης δὲ
all and slept. And of(in) [the] middle
νυκτὸς κραυγὴ γέγονεν· ἰδοὺ ὁ
of [the] night a cry there has been: Behold[,] the
νυμφίος, ἐξέρχεσθε εἰς ἀπάντησιν. **7** τότε
bridegroom, go ye forth to a meeting. Then
ἠγέρθησαν πᾶσαι αἱ παρθένοι ἐκεῖναι
were raised all – virgins those
καὶ ἐκόσμησαν τὰς λαμπάδας ἑαυτῶν.
and trimmed the lamps of them.
8 αἱ δὲ μωραὶ ταῖς φρονίμοις εἶπαν·
So the foolish [ones] to the prudent said:
δότε ἡμῖν ἐκ τοῦ ἐλαίου ὑμῶν, ὅτι
Give us of the oil of you, because
αἱ λαμπάδες ἡμῶν σβέννυνται. **9** ἀπεκρί-
the lamps of us are being quenched. But

[c] Or *cut him in pieces*

[d] Other ancient authorities add *and the bride*

*Here, and in the three following occurrences, as elsewhere, the strict meaning is emphatic or reflexive—'of themselves'; but this cannot be insisted on.

'Perhaps there will not be enough for us and for you; go rather to the dealers and buy for yourselves.' ¹⁰And while they went to buy, the bridegroom came, and those who were ready went in with him to the marriage feast; and the door was shut. ¹¹Afterward the other maidens came also, saying, 'Lord, lord, open to us.' ¹²But he replied, 'Truly, I say to you, I do not know you.' ¹³Watch therefore, for you know neither the day nor the hour.

14 "For it will be as when a man going on a journey called his servants and entrusted to them his property; ¹⁵to one he gave five talents, to another two, to another one, to each according to his ability. Then he went away. ¹⁶He who had received the five talents went at once and traded with them; and he made five talents more. ¹⁷So also, he who had the two talents made two talents more. ¹⁸But he who had received the

θησαν	δὲ	αἱ	φρόνιμοι	λέγουσαι·	μήποτε
answered	the		prudent	saying:	Lest

οὐ	μὴ	ἀρκέσῃ	ἡμῖν	καὶ	ὑμῖν·
by no means		it suffices	to us	and	to you;

πορεύεσθε	μᾶλλον	πρὸς	τοὺς	πωλοῦντας
go ye	rather	to	the [ones]	selling

καὶ	ἀγοράσατε	ἑαυταῖς.	10 ἀπερχομένων
and	buy	for [your]selves.	And going =as they

δὲ	αὐτῶν	ἀγοράσαι	ἦλθεν	ὁ	νυμφίος,
away	themᵃ were going away	to buy	came	the	bridegroom,

καὶ	αἱ	ἕτοιμοι	εἰσῆλθον	μετ᾽	αὐτοῦ
and	the	ready [ones]	went in	with	him

εἰς	τοὺς	γάμους,	καὶ	ἐκλείσθη	ἡ
to	the	wedding festivities,	and	was shut	the

θύρα.	11 ὕστερον	δὲ	ἔρχονται	καὶ	αἱ
door.	Then later		come	also	the

λοιπαὶ	παρθένοι	λέγουσαι·	κύριε	κύριε,
remaining	virgins	saying:	Lord[,]	Lord,

ἄνοιξον	ἡμῖν.	12 ὁ	δὲ	ἀποκριθεὶς	εἶπεν·
open	to us.	But he		answering	said:

ἀμὴν	λέγω	ὑμῖν,	οὐκ	οἶδα	ὑμᾶς.
Truly	I say	to you,		I know not	you.

13 Γρηγορεῖτε	οὖν,	ὅτι	οὐκ	οἴδατε
Watch ye	therefore,	because		ye know not

τὴν	ἡμέραν	οὐδὲ	τὴν	ὥραν.	14 Ὥσπερ
the	day	nor	the	hour.	as

γὰρ	ἄνθρωπος	ἀποδημῶν	ἐκάλεσεν
For	a man	going from home	called,

τοὺς	ἰδίους	δούλους	καὶ	παρέδωκεν	αὐτοῖς
the(his)	own	slaves	and	delivered	to them

τὰ	ὑπάρχοντα	αὐτοῦ,	15 καὶ	ᾧ	μὲν	ἔδωκεν
the	goods	of him,		and	to one	he gave

πέντε	τάλαντα,	ᾧ	δὲ	δύο,	ᾧ	δὲ
five	talents,	to another		two,		to another

ἕν,	ἑκάστῳ	κατὰ	τὴν	ἰδίαν	δύναμιν,
one,	to each	according to	the(his)	own	ability,

καὶ	ἀπεδήμησεν.	16 εὐθέως	πορευθεὶς
and	went from home.	Immediately	going

ὁ	τὰ	πέντε	τάλαντα	λαβὼν	ἠργάσατο
the [one]	the	five	talents	receiving	traded

ἐν	αὐτοῖς	καὶ	ἐκέρδησεν	ἄλλα
in	them	and	gained	other

πέντε·	17 ὡσαύτως	ὁ	τὰ	δύο	ἐκέρδησεν
five;	similarly	the [one]	the [recciving]	two	gained

ἄλλα	δύο.	18 ὁ	δὲ	τὸ	ἓν	λαβὼν
other	two.	But the [one]		the	one	receiving

one talent, went and dug in the ground and hid his master's money. ¹⁹Now after a long time the master of those servants came and settled accounts with them. ²⁰And he who had received the five talents came forward, bringing five talents more, saying, 'Master, you delivered to me five talents; here I have made five talents more.' ²¹His master said to him, 'Well done, good and faithful servant; you have been faithful over a little, I will set you over much; enter into the joy of your master.' ²²And he also who had the two talents came forward, saying, 'Master, you delivered to me two talents; here I have made two talents more.' ²³His master said to him, 'Well done, good and faithful servant; you have been faithful over a little, I will set you over much; enter into the joy of your master.' ²⁴He also who had received the one talent came forward, saying, 'Master, I knew you to be a hard man,

ἀπελθὼν	ὤρυξεν	γῆν	καὶ	ἔκρυψεν
going away	dug	earth	and	hid

τὸ	ἀργύριον	τοῦ	κυρίου	αὐτοῦ.
the	silver	of the	lord	of him.

19 | μετὰ | δὲ | πολὺν | χρόνον | ἔρχεται | ὁ |
| Then after | much | time | comes | the |

| κύριος | τῶν | δούλων | ἐκείνων | καὶ | συναίρει |
| lord | – | slaves | of those | and | takes |

| λόγον | μετ' | αὐτῶν. | **20** καὶ | προσελθὼν |
| account | with | them. | And | approaching |

| ὁ | τὰ | πέντε | τάλαντα | λαβὼν | προσ- |
| the [one] | the | five | talents | receiving | brought |

| ἤνεγκεν | ἄλλα | πέντε | τάλαντα | λέγων· | κύριε, |
| | other | five | talents | saying: | Lord, |

| πέντε | τάλαντά | μοι | παρέδωκας· | ἴδε | ἄλλα |
| five | talents | to me | thou deliveredst; | behold | other |

| πέντε | τάλαντα | ἐκέρδησα. | **21** ἔφη | αὐτῷ |
| five | talents | I gained. | Said | to him |

| ὁ | κύριος | αὐτοῦ· | εὖ, | δοῦλε | ἀγαθὲ | καὶ |
| the | lord | of him: | Well, | slave | good | and |

| πιστέ, | ἐπὶ | ὀλίγα | ἦς | πιστός, |
| faithful, | over | a few things | thou wast | faithful, |

| ἐπὶ | πολλῶν | σε | καταστήσω· | εἴσελθε |
| over | many | thee | I will set; | enter thou |

| εἰς | τὴν | χαρὰν | τοῦ | κυρίου | σου. | **22** προσ- |
| into | the | joy | of the | lord | of thee. | Ap- |

ελθὼν	καὶ	ὁ	τὰ	δύο	τάλαντα
proaching	also	the [one]	the	two	talents
		[having received]			

| εἶπεν· | κύριε, | δύο | τάλαντά | μοι |
| said: | Lord, | two | talents | to me |

| παρέδωκας· | ἴδε | ἄλλα | δύο | τάλαντα |
| thou deliveredst; | behold | other | two | talents |

| ἐκέρδησα. | **23** ἔφη | αὐτῷ | ὁ | κύριος | αὐτοῦ· |
| I gained. | Said | to him | the | lord | of him: |

| εὖ, | δοῦλε | ἀγαθὲ | καὶ | πιστέ, | ἐπὶ |
| Well, | slave | good | and | faithful, | over |

| ὀλίγα | ἦς | πιστός, | ἐπὶ | πολλῶν |
| a few things | thou wast | faithful, | over | many |

| σε | καταστήσω· | εἴσελθε | εἰς | τὴν |
| thee | I will set; | enter thou | into | the |

| χαρὰν | τοῦ | κυρίου | σου. | **24** προσ- |
| joy | of the | lord | of thee. | ap- |

| ελθὼν | δὲ | καὶ | ὁ | τὸ | ἓν | τάλαντον |
| proaching | And | also | the [one] | the | one | talent |

| εἰληφὼς | εἶπεν· | κύριε, | ἔγνων | σε |
| having received | said: | Lord, | I knew | thee |

| ὅτι | σκληρὸς | εἶ | ἄνθρωπος, | θερίζων |
| that | ²a hard | ¹thou art | ³man, | reaping |

reaping where you did not sow, and gathering where you did not winnow; ²⁵so I was afraid, and I went and hid your talent in the ground. Here you have what is yours.' ²⁶ But his master answered him, 'You wicked and slothful servant! You knew that I reap where I have not sowed, and gather where I have not winnowed? ²⁷ Then you ought to have invested my money with the bankers, and at my coming I should have received what was my own with interest. ²⁸ So take the talent from him, and give it to him who has the ten talents. ²⁹ For to every one who has will more be given, and he will have abundance; but from him who has not, even what he has, will be taken away. ³⁰ And cast the worthless servant into the outer darkness; there men will weep and gnash their teeth.'

31 "When the Son of man comes in his glory, and all the angels with him, then he will sit on his glorious throne. ³² Before him will be gathered all the nations,

ὅπου	οὐκ	ἔσπειρας,	καὶ	συνάγων
where	thou didst not sow,		and	gathering

ὅθεν	οὐ	διεσκόρπισας·	25 καὶ	φοβηθεὶς
whence	thou didst not scatter;		and	fearing

ἀπελθὼν	ἔκρυψα	τὸ	τάλαντόν	σου
going away	I hid	the	talent	of thee

ἐν	τῇ	γῇ·	ἴδε	ἔχεις	τὸ	σόν.
in	the	earth;	behold	thou hast	the	thine.

26 ἀποκριθεὶς δὲ ὁ κύριος αὐτοῦ εἶπεν
And answering the lord of him said

αὐτῷ·	πονηρὲ	δοῦλε	καὶ	ὀκνηρέ,
to him:	Evil	slave	and	slothful,

ᾔδεις	ὅτι	θερίζω	ὅπου	οὐκ	ἔσπειρα,
thou knewest that		I reap	where	I sowed not,	

καὶ	συνάγω	ὅθεν	οὐ	διεσκόρπισα;
and	I gather	whence	I did not scatter?	

27 ἔδει σε οὖν βαλεῖν τὰ ἀργύριά
it behoved thee therefore to put the silver pieces

μου	τοῖς	τραπεζίταις,	καὶ	ἐλθὼν	ἐγὼ
of me	to the	bankers,	and	coming	I

ἐκομισάμην	ἂν	τὸ	ἐμὸν	σὺν	τόκῳ.
would have received		the	mine	with	interest.

28 ἄρατε οὖν ἀπ' αὐτοῦ τὸ τάλαντον
Take therefore from him the talent

καὶ	δότε	τῷ	ἔχοντι	τὰ	δέκα	τάλαντα·
and	give	to the [one] having	the	ten	talents;	

29 τῷ γὰρ ἔχοντι παντὶ δοθήσεται καὶ
for to ²having ¹everyone will be given and

περισσευθήσεται·	τοῦ	δὲ	μὴ	ἔχοντος
he will have abundance;	but from the [one]		not	having

καὶ	ὃ	ἔχει	ἀρθήσεται	ἀπ'	αὐτοῦ.
even	what	he has	will be taken	from	him.

30 καὶ τὸν ἀχρεῖον δοῦλον ἐκβάλετε εἰς
And the useless slave cast ye out into

τὸ	σκότος	τὸ	ἐξώτερον·	ἐκεῖ	ἔσται	ὁ
the	darkness	-	outer;	there	will be the	

κλαυθμὸς	καὶ	ὁ	βρυγμὸς	τῶν	ὀδόντων
wailing	and	the	gnashing	of the	teeth.

31 Ὅταν δὲ ἔλθῃ ὁ υἱὸς τοῦ ἀνθρώπου
And when comes the Son - of man

ἐν	τῇ	δόξῃ	αὐτοῦ	καὶ	πάντες	οἱ	ἄγγελοι
in	the	glory	of him	and	all	the	angels

μετ'	αὐτοῦ,	τότε	καθίσει	ἐπὶ	θρόνου
with	him,	then	he will sit	on	a throne

δόξης	αὐτοῦ·	32 καὶ	συναχθήσονται
of glory	of him;	and	will be assembled

ἔμπροσθεν	αὐτοῦ	πάντα	τὰ	ἔθνη,	καὶ
before	him	all	the	nations,	and

and he will separate them
one from another as a
shepherd separates the
sheep from the goats,
[33] and he will place the
sheep at his right hand,
but the goats at the left.
[34] Then the King will say
to those at his right
hand, 'Come, O blessed
of my Father, inherit the
kingdom prepared for
you from the foundation
of the world; [35] for I was
hungry and you gave me
food, I was thirsty and
you gave me drink, I was
a stranger and you wel-
comed me, [36] I was naked
and you clothed me, I
was sick and you visited
me, I was in prison and
you came to me.' [37] Then
the righteous will answer
him, 'Lord, when did we
see thee hungry and feed
thee, or thirsty and give
thee drink? [38] And when
did we see thee a stranger
and welcome thee, or
naked and clothe thee?
[39] And when did we see
thee sick or in prison and
visit thee?' [40] And the
King will answer them,
'Truly, I say to you, as
you did it to one of the

ἀφορίσει αὐτοὺς ἀπ' ἀλλήλων, ὥσπερ
he will separate them from one another, as

ὁ ποιμὴν ἀφορίζει τὰ πρόβατα ἀπὸ
the shepherd separates the sheep from

τῶν ἐρίφων, 33 καὶ στήσει τὰ μὲν
the goats, and will set the -

πρόβατα ἐκ δεξιῶν αὐτοῦ, τὰ δὲ ἐρίφια
sheep on [the] right of him, but the goats

ἐξ εὐωνύμων. 34 τότε ἐρεῖ ὁ
on [the] left. Then will say the

βασιλεὺς τοῖς ἐκ δεξιῶν αὐτοῦ·
king to the [ones] on [the] right of him:

δεῦτε οἱ εὐλογημένοι τοῦ πατρός μου,
Come the [ones] blessed of the Father of me,

κληρονομήσατε τὴν ἡτοιμασμένην ὑμῖν
inherit ye the ²having been prepared ³for you

βασιλείαν ἀπὸ καταβολῆς κόσμου.
¹kingdom from [the] foundation of [the] world.

35 ἐπείνασα γὰρ καὶ ἐδώκατέ μοι
For I hungered and ye gave me

φαγεῖν, ἐδίψησα , καὶ ἐποτίσατέ με,
to eat, I thirsted and ye gave ²drink ¹me,

ξένος ἤμην καὶ συνηγάγετέ με,
a stranger I was and ye entertained me,

36 γυμνὸς καὶ περιεβάλετέ με, ἠσθένησα
naked and ye clothed me, I ailed

καὶ ἐπεσκέψασθέ με, ἐν φυλακῇ ἤμην
and ye visited me, in prison I was

καὶ ἤλθατε πρός με. 37 τότε ἀποκριθή-
and ye came to me. Then will

σονται αὐτῷ οἱ δίκαιοι λέγοντες· κύριε,
answer him the righteous saying: Lord,

πότε σε εἴδομεν πεινῶντα καὶ ἐθρέψαμεν,
when thee saw we hungering and fed,

ἢ διψῶντα καὶ ἐποτίσαμεν; 38 πότε δέ
or thirsting and gave drink? and when

σε εἴδομεν ξένον καὶ συνηγάγομεν,
thee saw we a stranger and entertained,

ἢ γυμνὸν καὶ περιεβάλομεν; 39 πότε δέ
or naked and clothed? and when

σε εἴδομεν ἀσθενοῦντα ἢ ἐν φυλακῇ καὶ
thee saw we ailing or in prison and

ἤλθομεν πρὸς σέ; 40 καὶ ἀποκριθεὶς ὁ
came to thee? And answering the

βασιλεὺς ἐρεῖ αὐτοῖς· ἀμὴν λέγω
king will say to them: Truly I tell

ὑμῖν, ἐφ' ὅσον ἐποιήσατε ἑνὶ τούτων
you, inasmuch as ye did to one of these

least of these my brethren, you did it to me.' ⁴¹Then he will say to those at his left hand, 'Depart from me, you cursed, into the eternal fire prepared for the devil and his angels; ⁴²for I was hungry and you gave me no food, I was thirsty and you gave me no drink, ⁴³I was a stranger and you did not welcome me, naked and you did not clothe me, sick and in prison and you did not visit me.' ⁴⁴Then they also will answer, 'Lord, when did we see thee hungry or thirsty or a stranger or naked or sick or in prison, and did not minister to thee?' ⁴⁵Then he will answer them, 'Truly, I say to you, as you did it not to one of the least of these, you did not to me.' ⁴⁶And they will go away into eternal punishment, but the righteous into eternal life."

τῶν ἀδελφῶν μου τῶν ἐλαχίστων, ἐμοὶ
– brothers of me the least, to me

ἐποιήσατε. 41 τότε ἐρεῖ καὶ τοῖς ἐξ
ye did. Then he will say also to the [ones] on

εὐωνύμων· πορεύεσθε ἀπ' ἐμοῦ κατ-
[the] left: Go from me having been

ηραμένοι εἰς τὸ πῦρ τὸ αἰώνιον
cursed [ones] into the fire – eternal

τὸ ἡτοιμασμένον τῷ διαβόλῳ καὶ τοῖς
– having been prepared for the devil and the

ἀγγέλοις αὐτοῦ. 42 ἐπείνασα γὰρ καὶ
angels of him. For I hungered and

οὐκ ἐδώκατέ μοι φαγεῖν, ἐδίψησα
ye gave not me to eat, I thirsted

καὶ οὐκ ἐποτίσατέ με, 43 ξένος
and ye ¹gave ²not ⁴drink ³me, a stranger

ἤμην καὶ οὐ συνηγάγετέ με, γυμνὸς
I was and ye entertained not me, naked

καὶ οὐ περιεβάλετέ με, ἀσθενὴς καὶ ἐν
and ye clothed not me, ill and in

φυλακῇ καὶ οὐκ ἐπεσκέψασθέ με. 44 τότε
prison and ye visited not me. Then

ἀποκριθήσονται καὶ αὐτοὶ λέγοντες· κύριε,
will answer also they saying: Lord,

πότε σε εἴδομεν πεινῶντα ἢ διψῶντα ἢ
when thee saw we hungering or thirsting or

ξένον ἢ γυμνὸν ἢ ἀσθενῆ ἢ ἐν φυλακῇ
a stranger or naked or ill or in prison

καὶ οὐ διηκονήσαμέν σοι; 45 τότε
and did not minister to thee? Then

ἀποκριθήσεται αὐτοῖς λέγων· ἀμὴν λέγω
he will answer them saying: Truly I tell

ὑμῖν, ἐφ' ὅσον οὐκ ἐποιήσατε ἑνὶ
you, inasmuch as ye did not to one

τούτων τῶν ἐλαχίστων, οὐδὲ ἐμοὶ
of these – least [ones], neither to me

ἐποιήσατε. 46 καὶ ἀπελεύσονται οὗτοι εἰς
ye did. And will go away these into

κόλασιν αἰώνιον, οἱ δὲ δίκαιοι εἰς
punishment eternal, but the righteous into

ζωὴν αἰώνιον.
life eternal.

CHAPTER 26

WHEN Jesus had finished all these sayings, he said to his disciples, 2 "You know that after two days the Passover is coming, and the Son of man will be delivered up to be crucified."
3 Then the chief priests and the elders of the people gathered in the palace of the high priest, who was called Ca′ia-phas, 4 and took counsel together in order to arrest Jesus by stealth and kill him. 5 But they said, "Not during the feast, lest there be a tumult among the people."
6 Now when Jesus was at Bethany in the house of Simon the leper, 7 a woman came up to him with an alabaster jar of very expensive ointment, and she poured it on his head, as he sat at table. 8 But when the disciples saw it, they were indignant, saying, "Why this waste? 9 For this ointment might have been sold for a large sum, and given to the poor." 10 But Jesus, aware of this, said to them, "Why do you trouble the woman? For she has done a beautiful

26 Καὶ ἐγένετο ὅτε ἐτέλεσεν ὁ
And it came to pass when ended -
'Ιησοῦς πάντας τοὺς λόγους τούτους,
Jesus all - words these,
εἶπεν τοῖς μαθηταῖς αὐτοῦ· **2** οἴδατε
he said to the disciples of him: Ye know
ὅτι μετὰ δύο ἡμέρας τὸ πάσχα γίνεται,
that after two days the passover occurs,
καὶ ὁ υἱὸς τοῦ ἀνθρώπου παραδίδοται εἰς
and the Son - of man is delivered -
τὸ σταυρωθῆναι. **3** Τότε συνήχθησαν οἱ
- to be crucified. Then were assembled the
ἀρχιερεῖς καὶ οἱ πρεσβύτεροι τοῦ λαοῦ
chief priests and the elders of the people
εἰς τὴν αὐλὴν τοῦ ἀρχιερέως τοῦ
in the court of the high priest -
λεγομένον Καϊαφᾶ, **4** καὶ συνεβουλεύ-
named Caiaphas, and con-
σαντο ἵνα τὸν 'Ιησοῦν δόλῳ κρατή-
sulted that - Jesus by guile they might
σωσιν καὶ ἀποκτείνωσιν· **5** ἔλεγον δέ·
seize and might kill; but they said:
μὴ ἐν τῇ ἑορτῇ, ἵνα μὴ θόρυβος
Not at the feast, lest a disturbance
γένηται ἐν τῷ λαῷ.
occurs among the people.
6 Τοῦ δὲ 'Ιησοῦ γενομένου ἐν Βηθανίᾳ
- And Jesus being= in Bethany
=when Jesus was
ἐν οἰκίᾳ Σίμωνος τοῦ λεπροῦ,
in [the] house of Simon the leper,
7 προσῆλθεν αὐτῷ γυνὴ ἔχουσα ἀλάβαστρον
approached to him a woman having an alabaster phial
μύρου βαρυτίμου καὶ κατέχεεν ἐπὶ
of ointment very expensive and poured [it] on
τῆς κεφαλῆς αὐτοῦ ἀνακειμένου. **8** ἰδόντες
the head of him reclining. And see-
δὲ οἱ μαθηταὶ ἠγανάκτησαν λέγοντες·
ing the disciples were angry saying:
εἰς τί ἡ ἀπώλεια αὕτη; **9** ἐδύνατο γὰρ
To what - waste this? for could
τοῦτο πραθῆναι πολλοῦ καὶ δοθῆναι
this to be sold of(for) much and to be given
πτωχοῖς. **10** γνοὺς δὲ ὁ 'Ιησοῦς εἶπεν
to poor. And knowing - Jesus said
αὐτοῖς· τί κόπους παρέχετε τῇ γυναικί;
to them: Why trouble ye the woman?
ἔργον γὰρ καλὸν ἠργάσατο εἰς ἐμέ·
for work a good she wrought to me;

thing to me. [11] For you always have the poor with you, but you will not always have me. [12] In pouring this ointment on my body she has done it to prepare me for burial. [13] Truly, I say to you, wherever this gospel is preached in the whole world, what she has done will be told in memory of her."

14 Then one of the twelve, who was called Judas Iscariot, went to the chief priests [15] and said, "What will you give me if I deliver him to you?" And they paid him thirty pieces of silver. [16] And from that moment he sought an opportunity to betray him.

17 Now on the first day of Unleavened Bread the disciples came to Jesus, saying, "Where will you have us prepare for you to eat the passover?" [18] He said, "Go into the city to such a one, and say to him, 'The Teacher says, My time is at hand; I will keep the passover at your house with my disciples.' " [19] And the

11 πάντοτε γὰρ τοὺς πτωχοὺς ἔχετε μεθ᾽
for always the poor ye have with

ἑαυτῶν, ἐμὲ δὲ οὐ πάντοτε ἔχετε·
yourselves, but me not always ye have;

12 βαλοῦσα γὰρ αὕτη τὸ μύρον τοῦτο
for ²putting ¹this woman - ⁴ointment ³this

ἐπὶ τοῦ σώματός μου πρὸς τὸ ἐνταφιάσαι
on the body of me for - to bury

με ἐποίησεν. 13 ἀμὴν λέγω ὑμῖν, ὅπου
me she did. Truly I tell you, wher-

ἐὰν κηρυχθῇ τὸ εὐαγγέλιον τοῦτο ἐν
ever is proclaimed - gospel this in

ὅλῳ τῷ κόσμῳ, λαληθήσεται καὶ ὃ
all the world, will be spoken also what

ἐποίησεν αὕτη εἰς μνημόσυνον αὐτῆς.
did this woman for a memorial of her.

14 Τότε πορευθεὶς εἷς τῶν δώδεκα, ὁ
Then going one of the twelve, the [one]

λεγόμενος Ἰούδας Ἰσκαριώτης, πρὸς
named Judas Iscariot, to

τοὺς ἀρχιερεῖς 15 εἶπεν· τί θέλετέ μοι
the chief priests he said: What are ye willing me

δοῦναι, κἀγὼ ὑμῖν παραδώσω αὐτόν;
to give, and I to you will deliver him?

οἱ δὲ ἔστησαν αὐτῷ τριάκοντα ἀργύρια.
And they weighed him thirty pieces of silver.

16 καὶ ἀπὸ τότε ἐζήτει εὐκαιρίαν ἵνα
And from then he sought opportunity that

αὐτὸν παραδῷ.
him he might deliver.

17 Τῇ δὲ πρώτῃ τῶν ἀζύμων
Now on the first [day] - of unleavened bread

προσῆλθον οἱ μαθηταὶ τῷ Ἰησοῦ
approached the disciples - to Jesus

λέγοντες· ποῦ θέλεις ἑτοιμάσωμέν
saying: Where willest thou we may prepare

σοι φαγεῖν τὸ πάσχα; 18 ὁ δὲ
for thee to eat the passover? So he

εἶπεν· ὑπάγετε εἰς τὴν πόλιν πρὸς
said: Go ye into the city to

τὸν δεῖνα καὶ εἴπατε αὐτῷ· ὁ
such a one and say to him: The

διδάσκαλος λέγει· ὁ καιρός μου
teacher says: The time of me

ἐγγύς ἐστιν· πρὸς σὲ ποιῶ τὸ πάσχα
near is; with thee I make the passover

μετὰ τῶν μαθητῶν μου. 19 καὶ ἐποίησαν
with the disciples of me. And did

disciples did as Jesus had directed them, and they prepared the passover.

20 When it was evening, he sat at table with the twelve disciples;[e] [21] and as they were eating, he said, "Truly, I say to you, one of you will betray me." [22] And they were very sorrowful, and began to say to him one after another, "Is it I, Lord?" [23] He answered, "He who has dipped his hand in the dish with me will betray me. [24] The Son of man goes as it is written of him, but woe to that man by whom the Son of man is betrayed! It would have been better for that man if he had not been born." [25] Judas, who betrayed him, said, "Is it I, Master?"[f] He said to him, "You have said so."

26 Now as they were eating, Jesus took bread, and blessed, and broke it, and gave it to the disciples and said, "Take, eat; this is my body." [27] And he took a cup, and when he had given thanks

οἱ   μαθηταὶ   ὡς   συνέταξεν   αὐτοῖς   ὁ
the   disciples   as   enjoined   them   -
'Ιησοῦς, καὶ ἡτοίμασαν τὸ πάσχα.   20 'Οψίας
Jesus,   and   prepared   the passover.   evening
δὲ   γενομένης   ἀνέκειτο   μετὰ   τῶν   δώδεκα
And   coming[a]   he reclined   with   the   twelve
= when evening came
[μαθητῶν].   21 καὶ   ἐσθιόντων   αὐτῶν   εἶπεν·
disciples.   And   eating   them[a]   he said:
= as they were eating
ἀμὴν   λέγω   ὑμῖν   ὅτι   εἷς   ἐξ   ὑμῶν   παρα-
Truly   I tell   you   that   one   of   you   will
δώσει   με.   22 καὶ   λυπούμενοι   σφόδρα
betray   me.   And   grieving   exceedingly
ἤρξαντο   λέγειν   αὐτῷ   εἷς   ἕκαστος·
they began   to say   to him   [a]one   [1]each:
μήτι   ἐγώ   εἰμι,   κύριε;   23 ὁ   δὲ   ἀποκριθεὶς
Not   I   am,   Lord?   And he   answering
= It is not I,
εἶπεν·   ὁ   ἐμβάψας   μετ'   ἐμοῦ   τὴν
said: The [one]   dipping   with   me   the(his)
χεῖρα   ἐν   τῷ   τρυβλίῳ,   οὗτός   με   παρα-
hand   in   the   dish,   this man   me   will
δώσει.   24 ὁ   μὲν   υἱὸς   τοῦ   ἀνθρώπου
betray.   Indeed the   Son   -   of man
ὑπάγει   καθὼς   γέγραπται   περὶ   αὐτοῦ,
goes   as   it has been written   concerning   him,
οὐαὶ   δὲ   τῷ   ἀνθρώπῳ   ἐκείνῳ   δι'
but woe   -   man   to that   through
οὗ   ὁ   υἱὸς   τοῦ   ἀνθρώπου   παραδίδοται·
whom the   Son   -   of man   is betrayed;
καλὸν   ἦν   αὐτῷ   εἰ   οὐκ   ἐγεννήθη
good   were it   for him   if   was not born
ὁ   ἄνθρωπος   ἐκεῖνος.   25 ἀποκριθεὶς   δὲ
-    man   that.   And answering
'Ιούδας   ὁ   παραδιδοὺς   αὐτὸν   εἶπεν·
Judas   the [one]   betraying   him   said:
μήτι   ἐγώ   εἰμι,   ῥαββί;   λέγει   αὐτῷ·
Not   I   am,   rabbi?   He says   to him:
= It is not I,
σὺ   εἶπας.   26 'Εσθιόντων   δὲ   αὐτῶν
Thou   saidst.   And eating   them[a]
= as they were eating
λαβὼν   ὁ   'Ιησοῦς   ἄρτον   καὶ   εὐλογήσας
taking   -   Jesus   a loaf   and   blessing
ἔκλασεν   καὶ   δοὺς   τοῖς   μαθηταῖς   εἶπεν·
he broke   and   giving   to the   disciples   said:
λάβετε   φάγετε·   τοῦτό   ἐστιν   τὸ   σῶμά
Take ye[,]   eat ye;   this   is   the   body
μου.   27 καὶ   λαβὼν   ποτήριον   καὶ   εὐχαρι-
of me.   And   taking   a cup   and   giving

[e] Other   authorities   omit
disciples
[f] Or *Rabbi*

he gave it to them, saying, "Drink of it, all of you; [28] for this is my blood of the[g] covenant, which is poured out for many for the forgiveness of sins. [29] I tell you I shall not drink again of this fruit of the vine until that day when I drink it new with you in my Father's kingdom."

30 And when they had sung a hymn, they went out to the Mount of Olives. [31] Then Jesus said to them, "You will all fall away because of me this night; for it is written, 'I will strike the shepherd, and the sheep of the flock will be scattered.' [32] But after I am raised up, I will go before you to Galilee." [33] Peter declared to him, "Though they all fall away because of you, I will never fall away." [34] Jesus said to him, "Truly, I say to you, this very night, before the cock crows, you will deny me three times." [35] Peter said to him, "Even if I must die with you, I will not

[g] Other ancient authorities insert *new*

στήσας ἔδωκεν αὐτοῖς λέγων· πίετε ἐξ
thanks he gave to them saying: Drink ye of
αὐτοῦ πάντες· 28 τοῦτο γάρ ἐστιν τὸ
it all; for this is the
αἷμά μου τῆς διαθήκης τὸ περὶ πολλῶν
blood of me of the covenant the [blood] concerning many
ἐκχυννόμενον εἰς ἄφεσιν ἁμαρτιῶν. 29 λέγω
being shed for forgiveness of sins. I tell
δὲ ὑμῖν, οὐ μὴ πίω ἀπ' ἄρτι ἐκ
And you, by no means will I drink from now of
τούτου τοῦ γενήματος τῆς ἀμπέλου ἕως
this – fruit of the vine until
τῆς ἡμέρας ἐκείνης ὅταν αὐτὸ πίνω μεθ'
– day that when it I drink with
ὑμῶν καινὸν ἐν τῇ βασιλείᾳ τοῦ πατρός
you new in the kingdom of the Father
μου.
of me.

30 Καὶ ὑμνήσαντες ἐξῆλθον εἰς τὸ
And having sung a hymn they went forth to the
ὄρος τῶν ἐλαιῶν. 31 Τότε λέγει αὐτοῖς ὁ
mount of the olives. Then says to them –
Ἰησοῦς· πάντες ὑμεῖς σκανδαλισθήσεσθε
Jesus: All ye will be offended
ἐν ἐμοὶ ἐν τῇ νυκτὶ ταύτῃ· γέγραπται
in me to-night; it has been written
γάρ· πατάξω τὸν ποιμένα, καὶ δια-
for: I will strike the shepherd, and will
σκορπισθήσονται τὰ πρόβατα τῆς ποίμνης·
be scattered the sheep of the flock;
32 μετὰ δὲ τὸ ἐγερθῆναί με προάξω
but after the to be raised me[b] I will go before
= I am raised
ὑμᾶς εἰς τὴν Γαλιλαίαν. 33 ἀποκριθεὶς
you to – Galilee. answering
δὲ ὁ Πέτρος εἶπεν αὐτῷ· εἰ πάντες
And – Peter said to him: If all men
σκανδαλισθήσονται ἐν σοί, ἐγὼ οὐδέποτε
shall be offended in thee, I never
σκανδαλισθήσομαι. 34 ἔφη αὐτῷ ὁ Ἰησοῦς·
will be offended. Said to him – Jesus:
ἀμὴν λέγω σοι ὅτι ἐν ταύτῃ τῇ νυκτὶ
Truly I tell thee that to-night
πρὶν ἀλέκτορα φωνῆσαι τρὶς ἀπαρνήσῃ
before a cock to crow[b] three times thou wilt deny
με. 35 λέγει αὐτῷ ὁ Πέτρος· κἂν
me. Says to him – Peter: Even if
δέῃ με σὺν σοὶ ἀποθανεῖν, οὐ μή σε
it behoves me with thee to die, by no means thee
= I must die with thee,

deny you." And so said all the disciples.

36 Then Jesus went with them to a place called Gethsem′ane, and he said to his disciples, "Sit here, while I go yonder and pray." ³⁷And taking with him Peter and the two sons of Zeb′edee, he began to be sorrowful and troubled. ³⁸Then he said to them, "My soul is very sorrowful, even to death; remain here, and watch[h] with me." ³⁹And going a little farther he fell on his face and prayed, "My Father, if it be possible, let this cup pass from me; nevertheless, not as I will, but as thou wilt." ⁴⁰And he came to the disciples and found them sleeping; and he said to Peter, "So, could you not watch[h] with me one hour? ⁴¹Watch[h] and pray that you may not enter into temptation; the spirit indeed is willing, but the flesh is weak." ⁴²Again, for the second time, he went away and prayed, "My Father, if

---

ἀπαρνήσομαι.   ὁμοίως   καὶ   πάντες   οἱ
I will deny.   Likewise   also   all   the

μαθηταὶ εἶπαν.
disciples   said.

36 Τότε   ἔρχεται   μετ'   αὐτῶν   ὁ   Ἰησοῦς
Then   comes   with   them   –   Jesus

εἰς χωρίον   λεγόμενον   Γεθσημανί,   καὶ   λέγει
to a piece of land   called   Gethsemane,   and   says

τοῖς   μαθηταῖς·   καθίσατε   αὐτοῦ   ἕως   οὗ
to the   disciples: Sit ye   here   until

ἀπελθὼν   ἐκεῖ   προσεύξωμαι.   37 καὶ   παρα-
going away   there   I may pray.   And   tak-

λαβὼν   τὸν   Πέτρον   καὶ   τοὺς   δύο   υἱοὺς
ing   –   Peter   and   the   two   sons

Ζεβεδαίου   ἤρξατο   λυπεῖσθαι   καὶ   ἀδημονεῖν.
of Zebedee   he began   to grieve   and to be distressed.

38 τότε   λέγει   αὐτοῖς·   περίλυπός   ἐστιν
Then   he says   to them: Deeply grieved   is

ἡ   ψυχή   μου   ἕως   θανάτου·   μείνατε
the   soul   of me   unto   death;   remain ye

ὧδε   καὶ   γρηγορεῖτε   μετ'   ἐμοῦ.   39 καὶ
here   and   watch ye   with   me.   And

προελθὼν   μικρὸν   ἔπεσεν   ἐπὶ   πρόσωπον
going forward   a little   he fell   on   [the] face

αὐτοῦ   προσευχόμενος   καὶ   λέγων·   πάτερ
of him   praying   and   saying: Father

μου,   εἰ   δυνατόν   ἐστιν,   παρελθάτω   ἀπ'
of me,   if   possible   it is,   let pass   from

ἐμοῦ   τὸ   ποτήριον   τοῦτο·   πλὴν   οὐχ
me   –   cup   this;   yet   not

ὡς   ἐγὼ   θέλω   ἀλλ'   ὡς   σύ.   40 καὶ
as   I   will   but   as   thou.   And

ἔρχεται   πρὸς   τοὺς   μαθητὰς   καὶ   εὑρίσκει
he comes   to   the   disciples   and   finds

αὐτοὺς   καθεύδοντας,   καὶ   λέγει   τῷ   Πέτρῳ·
them   sleeping,   and   says   –   to Peter:

οὕτως   οὐκ   ἰσχύσατε   μίαν   ὥραν
So   were ye not able   one   hour

γρηγορῆσαι   μετ'   ἐμοῦ;   41 γρηγορεῖτε   καὶ
to watch   with   me?   Watch ye   and

προσεύχεσθε,   ἵνα   μὴ   εἰσέλθητε   εἰς
pray,   lest   ye enter   into

πειρασμόν·   τὸ   μὲν   πνεῦμα   πρόθυμον,
temptation;   indeed the   spirit   [is] eager,

ἡ   δὲ   σὰρξ   ἀσθενής.   42 πάλιν   ἐκ
but the   flesh   weak.   Again   –

δευτέρου   ἀπελθὼν   προσηύξατο   λέγων·
second [time]   going away   he prayed   saying:

---

[h] Or keep awake

this cannot pass unless I drink it, thy will be done." ⁴³And again he came and found them sleeping, for their eyes were heavy. ⁴⁴So, leaving them again, he went away and prayed for the third time, saying the same words. ⁴⁵Then he came to the disciples and said to them, "Are you still sleeping and taking your rest? Behold, the hour is at hand, and the Son of man is betrayed into the hands of sinners. ⁴⁶Rise, let us be going; see, my betrayer is at hand."

47 While he was still speaking, Judas came, one of the twelve, and with him a great crowd with swords and clubs, from the chief priests and the elders of the people. ⁴⁸Now the betrayer had given them a sign, saying, "The one I shall kiss is the man; seize him." ⁴⁹And he came up to Jesus at once and said, "Hail Master!"ⁱ And he kissed him. ⁵⁰Jesus said to him, "Friend, why are you here?"ʲ Then they

ⁱ Or *Rabbi*
ʲ Or *do that for which you have come*

πάτερ μου, εἰ οὐ δύναται τοῦτο παρελθεῖν
Father of me, if cannot this *to* pass away

ἐὰν μὴ αὐτὸ πίω, γενηθήτω τὸ θέλημά
except it I drink, let be done the will

σου. 43 καὶ ἐλθὼν πάλιν εὗρεν αὐτοὺς
of thee. And coming again he found them

καθεύδοντας, ἦσαν γὰρ αὐτῶν οἱ ὀφθαλμοὶ
sleeping, for were of them the eyes

βεβαρημένοι. 44 καὶ ἀφεὶς αὐτοὺς πάλιν
having been burdened. And leaving them again

ἀπελθὼν προσηύξατο ἐκ τρίτου, τὸν
going away he prayed a third [time], the

αὐτὸν λόγον εἰπὼν πάλιν. 45 τότε ἔρχεται
same word saying again. Then he comes

πρὸς τοὺς μαθητὰς καὶ λέγει αὐτοῖς·
to the disciples and says to them:

καθεύδετε λοιπὸν καὶ ἀναπαύεσθε·
Sleep ye now and rest;

ἰδοὺ ἤγγικεν ἡ ὥρα καὶ ὁ υἱὸς τοῦ
behold has drawn near the hour and the Son —

ἀνθρώπου παραδίδοται εἰς χεῖρας
of man is betrayed into [the] hands

ἁμαρτωλῶν. 46 ἐγείρεσθε, ἄγωμεν· ἰδοὺ
of sinners. Rise ye, let us be going; behold

ἤγγικεν ὁ παραδιδούς με.
has drawn near the [one] betraying me.

47 Καὶ ἔτι αὐτοῦ λαλοῦντος, ἰδοὺ
And still him speaking,ᵃ behold
= while he was still speaking,

Ἰούδας εἷς τῶν δώδεκα ἦλθεν, καὶ μετ'
Judas one of the twelve came, and with

αὐτοῦ ὄχλος πολὺς μετὰ μαχαιρῶν καὶ
him crowd a much with swords and

ξύλων ἀπὸ τῶν ἀρχιερέων καὶ πρεσβυτέρων
clubs from the chief priests and elders

τοῦ λαοῦ. 48 ὁ δὲ παραδιδοὺς αὐτὸν ἔδωκεν
of the people. Now the [one] betraying him gave

αὐτοῖς σημεῖον λέγων· ὃν ἂν φιλήσω
them a sign saying: Whomever I may kiss

αὐτός ἐστιν· κρατήσατε αὐτόν. 49 καὶ
he it is; seize ye him. And

εὐθέως προσελθὼν τῷ Ἰησοῦ εἶπεν· χαῖρε,
immediately approaching – *to* Jesus he said: Hail,

ῥαββί, καὶ κατεφίλησεν αὐτόν. 50 ὁ
rabbi, and affectionately kissed him. –

δὲ Ἰησοῦς εἶπεν αὐτῷ· ἑταῖρε,
But Jesus said to him: Comrade, [do that]

ἐφ' ὃ πάρει. τότε προσελθόντες ἐπέβαλον
on what thou art here. Then approaching they laid on

came up and laid hands on Jesus and seized him. ⁵¹And behold, one of those who were with Jesus stretched out his hand and drew his sword, and struck the slave of the high priest, and cut off his ear. ⁵²Then Jesus said to him, "Put your sword back into its place; for all who take the sword will perish by the sword. ⁵³Do you think that I cannot appeal to my Father, and he will at once send me more than twelve legions of angels? ⁵⁴But how then should the scriptures be fulfilled, that it must be so?" ⁵⁵At that hour Jesus said to the crowds, "Have you come out as against a robber, with swords and clubs to capture me? Day after day I sat in the temple teaching, and you did not seize me. ⁵⁶But all this has taken place, that the scriptures of the prophets might be fulfilled." Then all the disciples forsook him and fled.

57 Then those who had seized Jesus led him to Ca'iaphas the high

τὰς χεῖρας ἐπὶ τὸν Ἰησοῦν καὶ ἐκράτησαν
the(ir) hands on - Jesus and seized
αὐτόν. 51 καὶ ἰδοὺ εἷς τῶν μετὰ
him. And behold one of the [ones] with
Ἰησοῦ ἐκτείνας τὴν χεῖρα ἀπέσπασεν
Jesus stretching out the(his) hand drew
τὴν μάχαιραν αὐτοῦ, καὶ πατάξας τὸν
the sword of him, and striking the
δοῦλος τοῦ ἀρχιερέως ἀφεῖλεν αὐτοῦ τὸ
slave of the high priest cut off of him the
ὠτίον. 52 τότε λέγει αὐτῷ ὁ Ἰησοῦς·
ear. Then says to him - Jesus:
ἀπόστρεψον τὴν μάχαιράν σου εἰς τὸν
Put back the sword of thee into the
τόπον αὐτῆς· πάντες γὰρ οἱ λαβόντες
place of it; for all the [ones] taking
μάχαιραν ἐν μαχαίρῃ ἀπολοῦνται. 53 ἢ
a sword by a sword will perish. Or
δοκεῖς ὅτι οὐ δύναμαι παρακαλέσαι
thinkest thou that I cannot to ask
τὸν πατέρα μου, καὶ παραστήσει μοι
the Father of me, and he will provide me
ἄρτι πλείω δώδεκα λεγιῶνας ἀγγέλων;
now more [than] twelve legions of angels?
54 πῶς οὖν πληρωθῶσιν αἱ γραφαὶ ὅτι
how then may be fulfilled the scriptures that
οὕτως δεῖ γενέσθαι; 55 Ἐν ἐκείνῃ τῇ ὥρᾳ
thus it must be? In that - hour
εἶπεν ὁ Ἰησοῦς τοῖς ὄχλοις· ὡς ἐπὶ
said - Jesus to the crowds: As against
λῃστὴν ἐξήλθατε μετὰ μαχαιρῶν καὶ
a robber came ye forth with swords and
ξύλων συλλαβεῖν με; καθ' ἡμέραν ἐν
clubs to take me? daily in
τῷ ἱερῷ ἐκαθεζόμην διδάσκων, καὶ οὐκ
the temple I sat teaching, and not
ἐκρατήσατέ με. 56 τοῦτο δὲ ὅλον
ye seized me. But this all
γέγονεν ἵνα πληρωθῶσιν αἱ γραφαὶ
has come to pass that may be fulfilled the scriptures
τῶν προφητῶν. Τότε οἱ μαθηταὶ πάντες
of the prophets. Then the disciples all
ἀφέντες αὐτὸν ἔφυγον.
leaving him fled.
57 Οἱ δὲ κρατήσαντες τὸν Ἰησοῦν
But the [ones] having seized - Jesus
ἀπήγαγον πρὸς Καϊάφαν τὸν ἀρχιερέα,
led [him] away to Caiaphas the high priest,

priest, where the scribes and the elders had gathered. [58] But Peter followed him at a distance, as far as the courtyard of the high priest, and going inside he sat with the guards to see the end. [59] Now the chief priests and the whole council sought false testimony against Jesus that they might put him to death, [60] but they found none, though many false witnesses came forward. At last two came forward [61] and said, "This fellow said, 'I am able to destroy the temple of God, and to build it in three days.'" [62] And the high priest stood up and said, "Have you no answer to make? What is it that these men testify against you?" [63] But Jesus was silent. And the high priest said to him, "I adjure you by the living God, tell us if you are the Christ, the Son of God." [64] Jesus said to him, "You have said so. But I tell you, hereafter you will see the Son of man seated at the right hand of Power, and coming on the clouds of heaven." [65] Then the high

ὅπου οἱ γραμματεῖς καὶ οἱ πρεσβύτεροι
where the scribes and the elders

συνήχθησαν. 58 ὁ δὲ Πέτρος ἠκολούθει
were assembled. - And Peter followed

αὐτῷ [ἀπὸ] μακρόθεν ἕως τῆς αὐλῆς
him from afar up to the court

τοῦ ἀρχιερέως, καὶ εἰσελθὼν ἔσω ἐκάθητο
of the high priest, and entering within sat

μετὰ τῶν ὑπηρετῶν ἰδεῖν τὸ τέλος.
with the attendants to see the end.

59 Οἱ δὲ ἀρχιερεῖς καὶ τὸ συνέδριον
And the chief priests and the council

ὅλον ἐζήτουν ψευδομαρτυρίαν κατὰ τοῦ
whole sought false witness against -

Ἰησου ὅπως αὐτὸν θανατώσωσιν, 60 καὶ
Jesus so as him they might put to death, and

οὐχ εὗρον πολλῶν προσελθόντων
did not find[,] many approaching
=when many false witnesses approached.

ψευδομαρτύρων. ὕστερον δὲ προσελθόντες
false witnesses[a]. But later approaching

δύο 61 εἶπαν· οὗτος ἔφη· δύναμαι κατα-
two said: This man said: I can to de-

λῦσαι τὸν ναὸν τοῦ θεοῦ καὶ διὰ τριῶν
stroy the shrine - of God and through(after) three

ἡμερῶν οἰκοδομῆσαι. 62 καὶ ἀναστὰς
days to build. And standing up

ὁ ἀρχιερεὺς εἶπεν αὐτῷ· οὐδὲν
the high priest said to him: Nothing

ἀποκρίνῃ, τί οὗτοί σου κατα-
answerest thou, what these men thee give

μαρτυροῦσιν; 63 ὁ δὲ Ἰησοῦς ἐσιώπα.
evidence against? - But Jesus remained silent.

καὶ ὁ ἀρχιερεὺς εἶπεν αὐτῷ· ἐξορκίζω
And the high priest said to him: I adjure

σε κατὰ τοῦ θεοῦ τοῦ ζῶντος ἵνα ἡμῖν
thee by - God the living that us

εἴπῃς εἰ σὺ εἶ ὁ χριστὸς ὁ υἱὸς τοῦ
thou tell if thou art the Christ the Son -

θεοῦ. 64 λέγει αὐτῷ ὁ Ἰησοῦς· σὺ εἶπας·
of God. Says to him - Jesus: Thou saidst;

πλὴν λέγω ὑμῖν, ἀπ' ἄρτι ὄψεσθε τὸν
yet I tell you, from now ye will see the

υἱὸν τοῦ ἀνθρώπου καθήμενον ἐκ
Son - of man sitting on [the]

δεξιῶν τῆς δυνάμεως καὶ ἐρχόμενον
right [hand] of the power and coming

ἐπὶ τῶν νεφελῶν τοῦ οὐρανοῦ. 65 τότε
on the clouds - of heaven. Then

priest tore his robes, and said, "He has uttered blasphemy. Why do we still need witnesses? You have now heard his blasphemy. ⁶⁶What is your judgment?" They answered, "He deserves death." ⁶⁷Then they spat in his face, and struck him; and some slapped him, ⁶⁸saying, "Prophesy to us, you Christ! Who is it that struck you?"

69 Now Peter was sitting outside in the courtyard. And a maid came up to him, and said, "You also were with Jesus the Galilean." ⁷⁰But he denied it before them all, saying, "I do not know what you mean." ⁷¹And when he went out to the porch, another maid saw him, and she said to the bystanders, "This man was with Jesus of Nazareth." ⁷²And again he denied it with an oath, "I do not know the man." ⁷³After a little while the bystanders came up and said to Peter, "Certainly you are also one of them, for your accent betrays you." ⁷⁴Then he began to invoke a curse on himself and to swear, "I do not

ὁ   ἀρχιερεὺς   διέρρηξεν   τὰ   ἱμάτια   αὐτοῦ
the   high priest   rent   the   garments   of him

λέγων·   ἐβλασφήμησεν·   τί   ἔτι   χρείαν   ἔχομεν
saying: He blasphemed;   what   yet   need   have we

μαρτύρων;   ἴδε   νῦν   ἠκούσατε   τὴν   βλασφη-
of witnesses?   behold   now   ye heard   the   blas-

μίαν·   66 τί   ὑμῖν   δοκεῖ;   οἱ   δὲ   ἀπο-
phemy;   what   to you   seems it?   And they   answer-

κριθέντες   εἶπαν·   ἔνοχος   θανάτου   ἐστίν.
ing   said: Liable   of(to) death   he is.

67 Τότε   ἐνέπτυσαν   εἰς   τὸ   πρόσωπον   αὐτοῦ
Then   they spat   in   the   face   of him

καὶ   ἐκολάφισαν   αὐτόν,   οἱ   δὲ
and   violently maltreated   him,   and they

ἐρράπισαν   68 λέγοντες·   προφήτευσον   ἡμῖν,
slapped [him]   saying: Prophesy thou   to us,

χριστέ,   τίς   ἐστιν   ὁ   παίσας   σε;
Christ,   who   is it   the [one] having struck   thee?

69 Ὁ   δὲ   Πέτρος   ἐκάθητο   ἔξω   ἐν
–   And   Peter   sat   outside   in

τῇ   αὐλῇ·   καὶ   προσῆλθεν   αὐτῷ   μία
the   court;   and   approached   to him   one

παιδίσκη   λέγουσα·   καὶ   σὺ   ἦσθα   μετὰ
maidservant   saying: Also   thou   wast   with

Ἰησοῦ   τοῦ   Γαλιλαίου.   70 ὁ   δὲ   ἠρνήσατο
Jesus   the   Galilæan.   But he   denied

ἔμπροσθεν   πάντων   λέγων·   οὐκ   οἶδα
before   all   saying: I know not

τί   λέγεις.   71 ἐξελθόντα   δὲ   εἰς   τὸν
what thou sayest.   And ⁴going out   ⁵into   ⁶the

πυλῶνα   εἶδεν   αὐτὸν   ἄλλη   καὶ   λέγει
⁷porch   ²saw   ³him   ¹another   and   says

τοῖς   ἐκεῖ·   οὗτος   ἦν   μετὰ   Ἰησοῦ   τοῦ
to the [ones]   there: This man   was   with   Jesus   the

Ναζωραίου.   72 καὶ   πάλιν   ἠρνήσατο
Nazarene.   And   again   he denied

μετὰ   ὅρκου   ὅτι   οὐκ   οἶδα   τὸν   ἄνθρωπον.
with   an oath[,]   –   I know not   the   man.

73 μετὰ   μικρὸν   δὲ   προσελθόντες   οἱ
And after a little   approaching   the [ones]

ἑστῶτες   εἶπον   τῷ   Πέτρῳ·   ἀληθῶς   καὶ
standing   said   –   to Peter: Truly   also

σὺ   ἐξ   αὐτῶν   εἶ,   καὶ   γὰρ   ἡ   λαλιά   σου
thou   of   them   art,   for indeed   the   speech   of thee

δῆλόν   σε   ποιεῖ.   74 τότε   ἤρξατο   καταθε-
manifest   thee   makes.   Then   he began   to

ματίζειν   καὶ   ὀμνύειν   ὅτι   οὐκ   οἶδα   τὸν
curse   and   to swear[,]   –   I know not   the

know the man." And
immediately the cock
crowed. ⁷⁵And Peter re-
membered the saying of
Jesus, "Before the cock
crows, you will deny me
three times." And he
went out and wept
bitterly.

ἄνθρωπον.   καὶ   εὐθὺς   ἀλέκτωρ   ἐφώνησεν
man.   And   immediately   a cock   crowed.

75 καὶ   ἐμνήσθη   ὁ   Πέτρος   τοῦ   ῥήματος
   And   remembered   –   Peter   the   word

'Ιησοῦ   εἰρηκότος   ὅτι   πρὶν   ἀλέκτορα
of Jesus   having said[,]   –   Before   a cock

φωνῆσαι   τρὶς   ἀπαρνήσῃ   με·   καὶ
to crow[b]   three times   thou wilt deny   me;   and

ἐξελθὼν   ἔξω   ἔκλαυσεν   πικρῶς.
going forth   outside   he wept   bitterly.

CHAPTER 27

WHEN morning
came, all the chief
priests and the elders of
the people took counsel
against Jesus to put him
to death; ²and they
bound him and led him
away and delivered him
to Pilate the governor.
3 When Judas, his
betrayer, saw that he was
condemned, he repented
and brought back the
thirty pieces of silver to
the chief priests and the
elders, ⁴saying, "I have
sinned in betraying in-
nocent blood." They said,
"What is that to us?
See to it yourself." ⁵And
throwing down the pieces
of silver in the temple, he
departed; and he went
and hanged himself. ⁶But
the chief priests, taking
the pieces of silver, said,
"It is not lawful to put
them into the treasury,
since they are blood
money." ⁷So they took
counsel, and bought with

27 Πρωΐας   δὲ   γενομένης   συμβούλιον
   And early morning   coming[a]   counsel
               = when early morning came

ἔλαβον   πάντες   οἱ   ἀρχιερεῖς   καὶ   οἱ
took   all   the   chief priests   and   the

πρεσβύτεροι   τοῦ   λαοῦ   κατὰ   τοῦ
elders   of the   people   against   –

'Ιησοῦ   ὥστε   θανατῶσαι   αὐτόν·   2 καὶ
Jesus   so as   to put to death   him;   and

δήσαντες   αὐτὸν   ἀπήγαγον   καὶ   παρ-
having bound   him   they led away   and   de-

ἔδωκαν   Πιλάτῳ   τῷ   ἡγεμόνι.   3 Τότε
livered   to Pilate   the   governor.   Then

ἰδὼν   'Ιούδας   ὁ   παραδοὺς   αὐτὸν
[b]seeing   ¹Judas   ²the [one]   ³having betrayed   ⁴him

ὅτι   κατεκρίθη,   μεταμεληθεὶς   ἔστρεψεν   τὰ
that   he was condemned,   repenting   returned   the

τριάκοντα   ἀργύρια   τοῖς   ἀρχιερεῦσιν
thirty   pieces of silver   to the   chief priests

καὶ   πρεσβυτέροις   4 λέγων·   ἥμαρτον
and   elders   saying: I sinned

παραδοὺς   αἷμα   ἀθῷον.   οἱ   δὲ   εἶπαν·
betraying   blood   innocent.   But they   said:

τί   πρὸς   ἡμᾶς;   σὺ   ὄψῃ.   5 καὶ   ῥίψας
What   to   us?   thou shalt see [to it].   And   tossing

τὰ   ἀργύρια   εἰς   τὸν   ναὸν   ἀν-
the   pieces of silver   into   the   shrine   he

ἐχώρησεν,   καὶ   ἀπελθὼν   ἀπήγξατο.   6 οἱ
departed,   and   going away   hanged himself.   the

δὲ   ἀρχιερεῖς   λαβόντες   τὰ   ἀργύρια   εἶπαν·
But   chief priests   taking   the   pieces of silver   said:

οὐκ   ἔξεστιν   βαλεῖν   αὐτὰ   εἰς   τὸν
It is not lawful   to put   them   into   the

κορβανᾶν,   ἐπεὶ   τιμὴ   αἵματός   ἐστιν.
treasury,   since   price   of blood   it is.

7 συμβούλιον   δὲ   λαβόντες   ἠγόρασαν   ἐξ
  So counsel   taking   they bought   of(with)

them the potter's field, to bury strangers in. ⁸Therefore that field has been called the Field of Blood to this day. ⁹Then was fulfilled what had been spoken by the prophet Jeremiah, saying, "And they took the thirty pieces of silver, the price of him on whom a price had been set by some of the sons of Israel, ¹⁰and they gave them for the potter's field, as the Lord directed me."

11 Now Jesus stood before the governor; and the governor asked him, "Are you the King of the Jews?" Jesus said to him, "You have said so." ¹²But when he was accused by the chief priests and elders, he made no answer. ¹³Then Pilate said to him, "Do you not hear how many things they testify against you?" ¹⁴But he gave him no answer, not even to a single charge; so that the governor wondered greatly.

15 Now at the feast the governor was accustomed to release for the crowd any one prisoner whom they wanted. ¹⁶And they had then a notorious prisoner, called Barab′bas.ᵏ ¹⁷So when

---

αὐτῶν τὸν ἀγρὸν τοῦ κεραμέως εἰς ταφὴν
them the field of the potter for burial

τοῖς ξένοις. 8 διὸ ἐκλήθη ὁ ἀγρὸς
for the strangers. Wherefore was called － field

ἐκεῖνος ἀγρὸς αἵματος ἕως τῆς σήμερον.
that Field of blood until － to-day.

9 τότε ἐπληρώθη τὸ ῥηθὲν διὰ
Then was fulfilled the [thing] spoken through

Ἰερεμίου τοῦ προφήτου λέγοντος· καὶ
Jeremiah the prophet saying: And

ἔλαβον τὰ τριάκοντα ἀργύρια, τὴν
they took the thirty pieces of silver, the

τιμὴν τοῦ τετιμημένου ὃν ἐτιμήσαντο
price of the [one] *having been* priced whom they priced

ἀπὸ υἱῶν Ἰσραήλ, 10 καὶ ἔδωκαν
from [the] sons of Israel, and gave

αὐτὰ εἰς τὸν ἀγρὸν τοῦ κεραμέως, καθὰ
them for the field of the potter, as

συνέταξέν μοι κύριος. 11 Ὁ δὲ
directed me [the] Lord. － And

Ἰησοῦς ἐστάθη ἔμπροσθεν τοῦ ἡγεμόνος·
Jesus stood before the governor;

καὶ ἐπηρώτησεν αὐτὸν ὁ ἡγεμὼν λέγων·
and questioned him the governor saying:

σὺ εἶ ὁ βασιλεὺς τῶν Ἰουδαίων; ὁ δὲ
Thou art the king of the Jews? － And

Ἰησοῦς ἔφη· σὺ λέγεις. 12 καὶ ἐν
Jesus said: Thou sayest. And in

τῷ κατηγορεῖσθαι αὐτὸν ὑπὸ τῶν
the to be accused himᵉ by the
　　=as he was accused

ἀρχιερέων καὶ πρεσβυτέρων οὐδὲν
chief priests and elders nothing

ἀπεκρίνατο. 13 τότε λέγει αὐτῷ ὁ Πιλᾶτος·
he answered. Then says to him － Pilate:

οὐκ ἀκούεις πόσα σου κατα-
Hearest thou not what things ³thee ¹they

μαρτυροῦσιν; 14 καὶ οὐκ ἀπεκρίθη αὐτῷ
²give evidence against? And he answered not him

πρὸς οὐδὲ ἓν ῥῆμα, ὥστε θαυμάζειν
to not one word, so as to marvel
　　　　=so that the governor marvelled

τὸν ἡγεμόνα λίαν. 15 Κατὰ δὲ ἑορτὴν
the governorᵇ exceedingly. Now at a feast

εἰώθει ὁ ἡγεμὼν ἀπολύειν ἕνα τῷ ὄχλῳ
was accustomed the governor to release ³one ¹to the ²crowd

δέσμιον ὃν ἤθελον. 16 εἶχον δὲ τότε
⁴prisoner whom they wished. And they had then

δέσμιον ἐπίσημον λεγόμενον Βαραββᾶν
prisoner a notable named Barabbas.

ᵏ Other ancient authorities read *Jesus Barabbas*

they had gathered, Pilate said to them, "Whom do you want me to release for you, Barab'bas[k] or Jesus who is called Christ?" [18] For he knew that it was out of envy that they had delivered him up. [19] Besides, while he was sitting on the judgment seat, his wife sent word to him, "Have nothing to do with that righteous man, for I have suffered much over him today in a dream." [20] Now the chief priests and the elders persuaded the people to ask for Barab'bas and destroy Jesus. [21] The governor again said to them, "Which of the two do you want me to release for you?" And they said, "Barab'bas." [22] Pilate said to them, "Then what shall I do with Jesus who is called Christ?" They all said, "Let him be crucified." [23] And he said, "Why, what evil has he done?" But they shouted all the more, "Let him be crucified."

24 So when Pilate saw that he was gaining nothing, but rather that a riot was beginning, he took water and washed his hands before the

[k] Other ancient authorities read *Jesus Barabbas*

17 συνηγμένων οὖν αὐτῶν εἶπεν αὐτοῖς
Therefore having assembled them[a] said to them
=when they were assembled

ὁ Πιλᾶτος· τίνα θέλετε ἀπολύσω
- Pilate: Whom do ye wish I may release

ὑμῖν, [τὸν] Βαραββᾶν ἢ Ἰησοῦν τὸν
to you, - Barabbas or Jesus -

λεγόμενον χριστόν; 18 ᾔδει γὰρ ὅτι
called Christ? for he knew that

διὰ φθόνον παρέδωκαν αὐτόν. 19 Καθη-
because of envy they delivered him. sit-

μένου δὲ αὐτοῦ ἐπὶ τοῦ βήματος
ting Now him[a] on the tribunal
=Now as he sat

ἀπέστειλεν πρὸς αὐτὸν ἡ γυνὴ αὐτοῦ
sent to him the wife of him

λέγουσα· μηδὲν σοὶ καὶ τῷ δικαίῳ
saying: Nothing to thee and - just man

ἐκείνῳ· πολλὰ γὰρ ἔπαθον σήμερον κατ'
to that; for many things I suffered to-day by

ὄναρ δι' αὐτόν. 20 Οἱ δὲ ἀρχιερεῖς
a dream because of him. But the chief priests

καὶ οἱ πρεσβύτεροι ἔπεισαν τοὺς
and the elders persuaded the

ὄχλους ἵνα αἰτήσωνται τὸν Βαραββᾶν,
crowds that they should ask - Barabbas,

τὸν δὲ Ἰησοῦν ἀπολέσωσιν. 21 ἀπο-
- and Jesus should destroy. So

κριθεὶς δὲ ὁ ἡγεμὼν εἶπεν αὐτοῖς·
answering the governor said to them:

τίνα θέλετε ἀπὸ τῶν δύο ἀπολύσω
Which do ye wish from the two I may release

ὑμῖν; οἱ δὲ εἶπαν· τὸν Βαραββᾶν.
to you? And they said: - Barabbas.

22 λέγει αὐτοῖς ὁ Πιλᾶτος· τί οὖν
Says to them - Pilate: What then

ποιήσω Ἰησοῦν τὸν λεγόμενον χριστόν;
may I do [to] Jesus - called Christ?

λέγουσιν πάντες· σταυρωθήτω. 23 ὁ δὲ
They say all: Let him be crucified. But he

ἔφη· τί γὰρ κακὸν ἐποίησεν; οἱ δὲ
said: Why what evil did he? But they

περισσῶς ἔκραζον λέγοντες· σταυρω-
more cried out saying: Let him be

θήτω. 24 ἰδὼν δὲ ὁ Πιλᾶτος ὅτι οὐδὲν
crucified. And seeing - Pilate that nothing

ὠφελεῖ ἀλλὰ μᾶλλον θόρυβος γίνεται,
is gained but rather an uproar occurs,

λαβὼν ὕδωρ ἀπενίψατο τὰς χεῖρας
taking water he washed the(his) hands

crowd, saying, "I am innocent of this man's blood;[1] see to it yourselves." [25]And all the people answered, "His blood be on us and on our children!" [26]Then he released for them Barab'bas, and having scourged Jesus, delivered him to be crucified.

27 Then the soldiers of the governor took Jesus into the praetorium, and they gathered the whole battalion before him.[28]And they stripped him and put a scarlet robe upon him, [29]and plaiting a crown of thorns they put it on his head, and put a reed in his right hand. And kneeling before him they mocked him, saying, "Hail, King of the Jews!" [30]And they spat upon him, and took the reed and struck him on the head. [31]And when they had mocked him, they stripped him of the robe, and put his own clothes on him, and led him away to crucify him.

32 As they were marching out, they came upon a man of Cyre'ne,

[1] Other authorities read *this righteous blood* or *this righteous man's blood*

κατέναντι	in front of
τοῦ	the
ὄχλου	crowd
λέγων·	saying:
ἀθῷός	Innocent
εἰμι	I am
ἀπὸ	from
τοῦ	the
αἵματος	blood
τούτου·	of this man;
ὑμεῖς	ye
ὄψεσθε.	will see [to it].

25 καὶ ἀποκριθεὶς πᾶς ὁ λαὸς
And answering all the people

εἶπεν· τὸ αἷμα αὐτοῦ ἐφ' ἡμᾶς καὶ
said: The blood of him on us and

ἐπὶ τὰ τέκνα ἡμῶν. **26** τότε ἀπέλυσεν
on the children of us. Then he released

αὐτοῖς τὸν Βαραββᾶν, τὸν δὲ Ἰησοῦν
to them - Barabbas, - but Jesus

φραγελλώσας παρέδωκεν ἵνα σταυρωθῇ.
having scourged he delivered that he might be crucified.

27 Τότε οἱ στρατιῶται τοῦ ἡγεμόνος
Then the soldiers of the governor

παραλαβόντες τὸν Ἰησοῦν εἰς τὸ πραιτώ-
having taken - Jesus into the præ-

ριον συνήγαγον ἐπ' αὐτὸν ὅλην τὴν
torium assembled against him all the

σπεῖραν. **28** καὶ ἐκδύσαντες αὐτὸν χλαμύδα
band. And stripping him cloak

κοκκίνην περιέθηκαν αὐτῷ, **29** καὶ
a purple they placed round him, and

πλέξαντες στέφανον ἐξ ἀκανθῶν ἐπέθηκαν
having plaited a crown of thorns they placed [it] on

ἐπὶ τῆς κεφαλῆς αὐτοῦ καὶ κάλαμον
on the head of him and a reed

ἐν τῇ δεξιᾷ αὐτοῦ, καὶ γονυπετή-
in the right [hand] of him, and bowing

σαντες ἔμπροσθεν αὐτοῦ ἐνέπαιξαν αὐτῷ
the knee in front of him mocked at him

λέγοντες· χαῖρε, βασιλεῦ τῶν Ἰουδαίων,
saying: Hail, king of the Jews,

30 καὶ ἐμπτύσαντες εἰς αὐτὸν ἔλαβον
and spitting at him took

τὸν κάλαμον καὶ ἔτυπτον εἰς τὴν κεφαλὴν
the reed and struck at the head

αὐτοῦ. **31** καὶ ὅτε ἐνέπαιξαν αὐτῷ,
of him. And when they mocked at him,

ἐξέδυσαν αὐτὸν τὴν χλαμύδα καὶ ἐνέδυσαν
they took off him the cloak and put on

αὐτὸν τὰ ἱμάτια αὐτοῦ, καὶ ἀπήγαγον
him the garments of him, and led away

αὐτὸν εἰς τὸ σταυρῶσαι. **32** Ἐξερχόμενοι
him - - to crucify. going forth

δὲ εὗρον ἄνθρωπον Κυρηναῖον, ὀνό-
And they found a man a Cyrenian, by

Simon by name; this man they compelled to carry his cross. ³³And when they came to a place called Gol'gotha (which means the place of a skull), ³⁴they offered him wine to drink, mingled with gall; but when he tasted it, he would not drink it. ³⁵And when they had crucified him, they divided his garments among them by casting lots; ³⁶then they sat down and kept watch over him there. ³⁷And over his head they put the charge against him, which read, "This is Jesus the King of the Jews." ³⁸Then two robbers were crucified with him, one on the right and one on the left. ³⁹And those who passed by derided him, wagging their heads ⁴⁰and saying, "You who would destroy the temple and build it in three days, save yourself! If you are the Son of God, come down from the cross." ⁴¹So also the chief priests, with the scribes and elders, mocked him, saying, ⁴²"He saved others; he cannot save himself. He

ματι	Σίμωνα·	τοῦτον	ἠγγάρευσαν ἵνα
name	Simon;	this man	they impressed that

ἄρῃ	τὸν	σταυρὸν	αὐτοῦ. 33 Καὶ
he should bear	the	cross	of him. And

ἐλθόντες	εἰς	τόπον	λεγόμενον Γολγοθά,
coming	to	a place	called Golgotha,

ὅ	ἐστιν	κρανίου	τόπος λεγόμενος,
which	is	³of a skull	²A place ¹called,

34 ἔδωκαν αὐτῷ πιεῖν οἶνον μετὰ
they gave him to drink wine with

χολῆς μεμιγμένον· καὶ γευσάμενος οὐκ
gall having been mixed; and tasting not

ἠθέλησεν πιεῖν. **35** σταυρώσαντες δὲ
he would to drink. And having crucified

αὐτὸν διεμερίσαντο τὰ ἱμάτια αὐτοῦ
him they divided the garments of him

βάλλοντες κλῆρον, **36** καὶ καθήμενοι ἐτήρουν
casting a lot, and sitting they guarded

αὐτὸν ἐκεῖ. **37** καὶ ἐπέθηκαν ἐπάνω
him there. And they placed on above

τῆς κεφαλῆς αὐτοῦ τὴν αἰτίαν αὐτοῦ
the head of him the charge of him

γεγραμμένην· ΟΥΤΟΣ ΕΣΤΙΝ ΙΗΣΟΥΣ
having been written: THIS IS JESUS

Ο ΒΑΣΙΛΕΥΣ ΤΩΝ ΙΟΥΔΑΙΩΝ. **38** Τότε
THE KING OF THE JEWS. Then

σταυροῦνται σὺν αὐτῷ δύο λῃσταί,
are crucified with him two robbers,

εἷς ἐκ δεξιῶν καὶ εἷς ἐξ εὐωνύμων.
one on [the] right and one on [the] left.

39 Οἱ δὲ παραπορευόμενοι ἐβλασφήμουν
And the [ones] passing by blasphemed

αὐτὸν κινοῦντες τὰς κεφαλὰς αὐτῶν
him wagging the heads of them

40 καὶ λέγοντες· ὁ καταλύων τὸν ναὸν
and saying: The [one] destroying the shrine

καὶ ἐν τρισὶν ἡμέραις οἰκοδομῶν,
and in three days building [it],

σῶσον σεαυτόν, εἰ υἱὸς εἶ τοῦ θεοῦ,
save thyself, if Son thou art - of God,

καὶ κατάβηθι ἀπὸ τοῦ σταυροῦ. **41** ὁμοίως
and come down from the cross. Likewise

[καὶ] οἱ ἀρχιερεῖς ἐμπαίζοντες μετὰ
also the chief priests mocking with

τῶν γραμματέων καὶ πρεσβυτέρων ἔλεγον
the scribes and elders said:

42 ἄλλους ἔσωσεν, ἑαυτὸν οὐ δύναται
Others he saved, himself he cannot

is the King of Israel; let him come down now from the cross, and we will believe in him. ⁴³He trusts in God; let God deliver him now, if he desires him; for he said, 'I am the Son of God.'" ⁴⁴And the robbers who were crucified with him also reviled him in the same way.

45 Now from the sixth hour there was darkness over all the land[m] until the ninth hour. ⁴⁶And about the ninth hour Jesus cried with a loud voice, "Eli, Eli, la'ma sabach-tha'-ni?" that is, "My God, my God, why hast thou forsaken me?" ⁴⁷And some of the bystanders hearing it said, "This man is calling Eli'jah." ⁴⁸And one of them at once ran and took a sponge, filled it with vinegar, and put it on a reed, and gave it to him to drink. ⁴⁹But the others said, "Wait, let us see whether Eli'jah will come to save him."[n] ⁵⁰And Jesus cried again with a loud voice and yielded up his spirit.

51 And behold, the curtain of the temple was torn in two, from top to bottom; and the earth

[m] Or earth
[n] Other ancient authorities insert And another took a spear and pierced his side, and out came water and blood

σῶσαι· βασιλεὺς Ἰσραὴλ ἐστιν,
to save; King of Israel he is,

καταβάτω νῦν ἀπὸ τοῦ σταυροῦ καὶ
let him come down now from the cross and

πιστεύσομεν ἐπ' αὐτόν. 43 πέποιθεν
we will believe on him. He has trusted

ἐπὶ τὸν θεόν, ῥυσάσθω νῦν εἰ θέλει
on - God, let him rescue now if he wants

αὐτόν· εἶπεν γὰρ ὅτι θεοῦ εἰμι υἱός.
him; for he said[,] - of God I am Son.

44 τό δ' αὐτὸ καὶ οἱ λῃσταὶ οἱ συσταυρω-
And the same also the robbers - crucified

θέντες σὺν αὐτῷ ὠνείδιζον αὐτόν. 45 Ἀπὸ
with with him reproached him. from

δὲ ἕκτης ὥρας σκότος ἐγένετο ἐπὶ
Now [the] sixth hour darkness occurred over

πᾶσαν τὴν γῆν ἕως ὥρας ἐνάτης.
all the land until hour [the] ninth.

46 περὶ δὲ τὴν ἐνάτην ὥραν ἀνεβόησεν ὁ
And about the ninth hour cried out -

Ἰησοῦς φωνῇ μεγάλῃ λέγων· ἠλὶ ἠλὶ
Jesus voice with a great saying: Eli Eli

λεμὰ σαβαχθάνι; τοῦτ' ἔστιν· θεέ μου
lema sabachthani? this is: God of me[,]

θεέ μου, ἱνατί με ἐγκατέλιπες; 47 τινὲς
God of me, why me didst thou forsake? some

δὲ τῶν ἐκεῖ ἑστηκότων ἀκούσαντες
And of the [ones] there standing hearing

ἔλεγον ὅτι Ἠλίαν φωνεῖ οὗτος.
said[,] - ³Elias ²calls ¹this man.

48 καὶ εὐθέως δραμὼν εἷς ἐξ αὐτῶν καὶ
And immediately running one of them and

λαβὼν σπόγγον πλήσας τε ὄξους καὶ
taking a sponge and filling of(with) vinegar and

περιθεὶς καλάμῳ ἐπότιζεν αὐτόν.
putting [it] round a reed gave to drink him.

49 οἱ δὲ λοιποὶ εἶπαν· ἄφες ἴδωμεν
But the rest said· Leave[,] let us see

εἰ ἔρχεται Ἠλίας σώσων αὐτόν. 50 ὁ
if comes Elias saving him. -

δὲ Ἰησοῦς πάλιν κράξας φωνῇ
And Jesus again crying out voice

μεγάλῃ ἀφῆκεν τὸ πνεῦμα. 51 Καὶ
with a great released the(his) spirit. And

ἰδοὺ τὸ καταπέτασμα τοῦ ναοῦ ἐσχίσθη
behold the veil of the shrine was rent

[ἀπ'] ἄνωθεν ἕως κάτω εἰς δύο, καὶ ἡ
from above to below in two, and the

shook, and the rocks were split; [52]the tombs also were opened, and many bodies of the saints who had fallen asleep were raised, [53]and coming out of the tombs after his resurrection they went into the holy city and appeared to many. [54]When the centurion and those who were with him, keeping watch over Jesus, saw the earthquake and what took place, they were filled with awe, and said, "Truly this was the Son[nn] of God!"

[55]There were also many women there, looking on from afar, who had followed Jesus from Galilee, ministering to him; [56]among whom were Mary Mag'dalene, and Mary the mother of James and Joseph, and the mother of the sons of Zeb'edee.

[57]When it was evening, there came a rich man from Arimathe'a, named Joseph, who also was a disciple of Jesus. [58]He went to Pilate and asked for the body of Jesus. Then Pilate ordered it to be given to him. [59]And Joseph took

[nn] Or *a son*

γῆ ἐσείσθη, καὶ αἱ πέτραι ἐσχίσ-
earth was shaken, and the rocks were

θησαν, 52 καὶ τὰ μνημεῖα ἀνεῴχθησαν
rent, and the tombs were opened

καὶ πολλὰ σώματα τῶν κεκοιμημένων
and many bodies of the having fallen asleep

ἁγίων ἠγέρθησαν· 53 καὶ ἐξελθόντες
saints were raised; and coming forth

ἐκ τῶν μνημείων μετὰ τὴν ἔγερσιν
out of the tombs after the rising

αὐτοῦ εἰσῆλθον εἰς τὴν ἁγίαν πόλιν καὶ
of him entered into the holy city and

ἐνεφανίσθησαν πολλοῖς. 54 Ὁ δὲ ἑκατόν-
appeared to many. And the centu-

ταρχος καὶ οἱ μετ' αὐτοῦ τηροῦντες
rion and the[ones] with him guarding

τὸν Ἰησοῦν ἰδόντες τὸν σεισμὸν καὶ
- Jesus seeing the earthquake and

τὰ γινόμενα ἐφοβήθησαν σφόδρα,
the things happening feared exceedingly,

λέγοντες· ἀληθῶς θεοῦ υἱὸς ἦν οὗτος.
saying: Truly [4]of God [3]Son [2]was [1]this man.

55 Ἦσαν δὲ ἐκεῖ γυναῖκες πολλαὶ
Now there were there women many

ἀπὸ μακρόθεν θεωροῦσαι, αἵτινες ἠκολού-
from afar beholding, who followed

θησαν τῷ Ἰησοῦ ἀπὸ τῆς Γαλιλαίας
- Jesus from - Galilee

διακονοῦσαι αὐτῷ· 56 ἐν αἷς ἦν
ministering to him; among whom was

Μαρία ἡ Μαγδαληνή, καὶ Μαρία ἡ
Mary the Magdalene, and Mary the

τοῦ Ἰακώβου καὶ Ἰωσὴφ μήτηρ, καὶ ἡ
- of James and of Joseph mother, and the

μήτηρ τῶν υἱῶν Ζεβεδαίου.
mother of the sons of Zebedee.

57 Ὀψίας δὲ γενομένης ἦλθεν ἄνθρωπος
Now evening having come[a] came man
= when evening had come

πλούσιος ἀπὸ Ἀριμαθαίας, τοὔνομα Ἰωσήφ,
a rich from Arimathæa, the name Joseph,

ὃς καὶ αὐτὸς ἐμαθητεύθη τῷ Ἰησοῦ·
who also himself was discipled - to Jesus;

58 οὗτος προσελθὼν τῷ Πιλάτῳ ᾐτήσατο
this man approaching - to Pilate asked

τὸ σῶμα τοῦ Ἰησοῦ. τότε ὁ Πιλᾶτος
the body - of Jesus. Then - Pilate

ἐκέλευσεν ἀποδοθῆναι. 59 καὶ λαβὼν
commanded [it] to be given [him]. And taking

the body, and wrapped it in a clean linen shroud, ⁶⁰and laid it in his own new tomb, which he had hewn in the rock; and he rolled a great stone to the door of the tomb, and departed. ⁶¹Mary Mag'-dalene and the other Mary were there, sitting opposite the sepulchre.

62 Next day, that is, after the day of Preparation, the chief priests and the Pharisees gathered before Pilate ⁶³and said, "Sir, we remember how that impostor said, while he was still alive, 'After three days I will rise again.' ⁶⁴Therefore order the sepulchre to be made secure until the third day, lest his disciples go and steal him away, and tell the people, 'He has risen from the dead,' and the last fraud will be worse than the first." ⁶⁵Pilate said to them, "You have a guard^o of soldiers; go, make it as secure as you can." ⁶⁶So they went and made the sepulchre secure by sealing the stone and setting a guard.

τὸ σῶμα ὁ Ἰωσὴφ ἐνετύλιξεν αὐτὸ [ἐν]
the body – Joseph wrapped it in

σινδόνι καθαρᾷ, 60 καὶ ἔθηκεν αὐτὸ ἐν
sheet a clean, and placed it in

τῷ καινῷ αὐτοῦ μνημείῳ ὃ ἐλατό-
the new of him tomb which he

μησεν ἐν τῇ πέτρᾳ, καὶ προσκυλίσας
hewed in the rock, and having rolled to

λίθον μέγαν τῇ θύρᾳ τοῦ μνημείου
stone a great to the door of the tomb

ἀπῆλθεν. 61 Ἦν δὲ ἐκεῖ Μαριὰμ
went away. And there was there Mary

ἡ Μαγδαληνὴ καὶ ἡ ἄλλη Μαρία,
the Magdalene and the other Mary,

καθήμεναι ἀπέναντι τοῦ τάφου. 62 Τῇ
sitting opposite the grave. on the

δὲ ἐπαύριον, ἥτις ἐστὶν μετὰ τὴν παρα-
And morrow, which is after the prepara-

σκευήν, συνήχθησαν οἱ ἀρχιερεῖς
tion, were assembled the chief priests

καὶ οἱ Φαρισαῖοι πρὸς Πιλᾶτον 63 λέ-
and the Pharisees to Pilate say-

γοντες· κύριε, ἐμνήσθημεν ὅτι ἐκεῖνος
ing: Sir, we remembered that that

ὁ πλάνος εἶπεν ἔτι ζῶν· μετὰ τρεῖς
– deceiver said yet living: After three

ἡμέρας ἐγείρομαι. 64 κέλευσον οὖν
days I am raised. Command therefore

ἀσφαλισθῆναι τὸν τάφον ἕως τῆς
to be made fast the grave until the

τρίτης ἡμέρας, μήποτε ἐλθόντες οἱ μαθηταὶ
third day, lest coming the disciples

κλέψωσιν αὐτὸν καὶ εἴπωσιν τῷ λαῷ·
may steal him and may say to the people:

ἠγέρθη ἀπὸ τῶν νεκρῶν, καὶ ἔσται
He was raised from the dead, and will be

ἡ ἐσχάτη πλάνη χείρων τῆς πρώτης.
the last deceit worse [than] the first.

65 ἔφη αὐτοῖς ὁ Πιλᾶτος· ἔχετε κου-
Said to them – Pilate: Ye have a

στωδίαν· ὑπάγετε ἀσφαλίσασθε ὡς οἴδατε.
guard; go ye make fast as ye know*.

66 οἱ δὲ πορευθέντες ἠσφαλίσαντο τὸν
And they going made fast the

τάφον σφραγίσαντες τὸν λίθον μετὰ τῆς
grave sealing the stone with the

κουστωδίας.
guard.

^o Or *Take a guard*

* can. See note on page xviii.

CHAPTER 28

NOW after the sabbath, toward the dawn of the first day of the week, Mary Mag'-dalene and the other Mary went to see the sepulchre. ²And behold, there was a great earthquake; for an angel of the Lord descended from heaven and came and rolled back the stone, and sat upon it. ³His appearance was like lightning, and his raiment white as snow. ⁴And for fear of him the guards trembled and became like dead men. ⁵But the angel said to the women, "Do not be afraid; for I know that you seek Jesus who was crucified. ⁶He is not here; for he has risen, as he said. Come, see the place where he[p] lay. ⁷Then go quickly and tell his disciples that he has risen from the dead, and behold, he is going before you to Galilee; there you will see him. Lo, I have told you." ⁸So they departed quickly from the tomb with fear and great joy, and ran to tell his disciples. ⁹And behold,

[p] Other ancient authorities read *the Lord*

28 Ὀψὲ δὲ σαββάτων, τῇ ἐπιφωσκούσῃ
But late of [the] sabbaths, at the drawing on

εἰς μίαν σαββάτων, ἦλθεν Μαριὰμ ἡ
toward one of [the] sabbaths, came Mary the
=the first day of the week,

Μαγδαληνὴ καὶ ἡ ἄλλη Μαρία θεωρῆσαι
Magdalene and the other Mary to view

τὸν τάφον. **2** καὶ ἰδοὺ σεισμὸς ἐγένετο
the grave. And behold earthquake occurred

μέγας· ἄγγελος γὰρ κυρίου καταβὰς
a great; for an angel of [the] Lord descending

ἐξ οὐρανοῦ καὶ προσελθὼν ἀπεκύλισεν
out of heaven and approaching rolled away

τὸν λίθον καὶ ἐκάθητο ἐπάνω αὐτοῦ.
the stone and sat upon it.

3 ἦν δὲ ἡ εἰδέα αὐτοῦ ὡς ἀστραπή,
And was the appearance of him as lightning,

καὶ τὸ ἔνδυμα αὐτοῦ λευκὸν ὡς χιών,
and the dress of him white as snow.

4 ἀπὸ δὲ τοῦ φόβου αὐτοῦ ἐσείσθησαν
And from the fear of him were shaken

οἱ τηροῦντες καὶ ἐγενήθησαν ὡς
the [ones] guarding and they became as

νεκροί. **5** ἀποκριθεὶς δὲ ὁ ἄγγελος
dead. And answering the angel

εἶπεν ταῖς γυναιξίν· μὴ φοβεῖσθε ὑμεῖς·
said to the women: Fear not ye;

οἶδα γὰρ ὅτι Ἰησοῦν τὸν ἐσταυρω-
for I know that Jesus the [one] having been

μένον ζητεῖτε· **6** οὐκ ἔστιν ὧδε·
crucified ye seek; he is not here;

ἠγέρθη γὰρ καθὼς εἶπεν· δεῦτε ἴδετε τὸν
for he was raised as he said; come see ye the

τόπον ὅπου ἔκειτο. **7** καὶ ταχὺ πορευθεῖσαι
place where he lay. And quickly going

εἴπατε τοῖς μαθηταῖς αὐτοῦ ὅτι ἠγέρθη
tell the disciples of him that he was raised

ἀπὸ τῶν νεκρῶν, καὶ ἰδοὺ προάγει ὑμᾶς
from the dead, and behold he goes before you

εἰς τὴν Γαλιλαίαν, ἐκεῖ αὐτὸν ὄψεσθε.
to – Galilee, there him ye will see.

ἰδοὺ εἶπον ὑμῖν. **8** καὶ ἀπελθοῦσαι ταχὺ
Behold I told you. And going away quickly

ἀπὸ τοῦ μνημείου μετὰ φόβου καὶ χαρᾶς
from the tomb with fear and joy

μεγάλης ἔδραμον ἀπαγγεῖλαι τοῖς
great they ran to announce to the

μαθηταῖς αὐτοῦ. **9** καὶ ἰδοὺ Ἰησοῦς
disciples of him. And behold Jesus

Jesus met them and said, "Hail!" And they came up and took hold of his feet and worshiped him. ¹⁰Then Jesus said to them, "Do not be afraid; go and tell my brethren to go to Galilee, and there they will see me."

11 While they were going, behold, some of the guard went into the city and told the chief priests all that had taken place. ¹²And when they had assembled with the elders and taken counsel, they gave a sum of money to the soldiers ¹³and said, "Tell people, 'His disciples came by night and stole him away while we were asleep.' ¹⁴And if this comes to the governor's ears, we will satisfy him and keep you out of trouble." ¹⁵So they took the money and did as they were directed; and this story has been spread among the Jews to this day.

16 Now the eleven disciples went to Galilee, to the mountain to which Jesus had directed them. ¹⁷And when they saw him

ὑπήντησεν	αὐταῖς	λέγων·	χαίρετε.	αἱ δὲ
met	them	saying:	Hail.	And they

προσελθοῦσαι	ἐκράτησαν	αὐτοῦ	τοὺς	πόδας
approaching	held	of him	the	feet

καὶ	προσεκύνησαν	αὐτῷ.	10 τότε	λέγει
and	worshipped	him.	Then	says

αὐταῖς	ὁ Ἰησοῦς·	μὴ φοβεῖσθε·	ὑπάγετε
to them	Jesus:	Fear ye not;	go ye

ἀπαγγείλατε	τοῖς	ἀδελφοῖς	μου	ἵνα
announce	to the	brothers	of me	that

ἀπέλθωσιν	εἰς	τὴν	Γαλιλαίαν,	κἀκεῖ
they may go away	into	-	Galilee,	and there

με	ὄψονται.	11 Πορευομένων	δὲ	αὐτῶν
me	they will see.	And going		them^a =as they were going

ἰδού	τινες	τῆς	κουστωδίας	ἐλθόντες	εἰς
behold	some	of the	guard	coming	into

τὴν	πόλιν	ἀπήγγειλαν	τοῖς	ἀρχιερεῦσιν
the	city	announced	to the	chief priests

ἅπαντα	τὰ	γενόμενα.	12 καὶ	συν-
all the things		having happened.	And	being

αχθέντες	μετὰ	τῶν	πρεσβυτέρων	συμβούλιόν
assembled	with	the	elders	²counsel

τε	λαβόντες	ἀργύρια	ἱκανὰ	ἔδωκαν	τοῖς
¹and	²taking	silver	enough	gave	to the

στρατιώταις,	13 λέγοντες·	εἴπατε	ὅτι	οἱ
soldiers,	saying:	Say ye	that	the

μαθηταὶ	αὐτοῦ	νυκτὸς	ἐλθόντες	ἔκλεψαν
disciples	of him	of(by) night	coming	stole

αὐτὸν	ἡμῶν	κοιμωμένων.	14 καὶ	ἐὰν
him	we	sleeping.^a =while we slept.	And	if

ἀκουσθῇ	τοῦτο	ἐπὶ	τοῦ	ἡγεμόνος,
be heard	this	before	the	governor,

ἡμεῖς	πείσομεν	καὶ	ὑμᾶς	ἀμερίμνους
we	will persuade	and	you	free from anxiety

ποιήσομεν.	15 οἱ	δὲ	λαβόντες	ἀργύρια
we will make.	And they		taking	silver

ἐποίησαν	ὡς	ἐδιδάχθησαν.	Καὶ	διεφη-
did	as	they were taught.	And	was spread

μίσθη	ὁ	λόγος	οὗτος	παρὰ	Ἰουδαίοις
about	-	saying	this	by	Jews

μέχρι	τῆς	σήμερον	[ἡμέρας].	16 Οἱ	δὲ
until		to-day.		So the	

ἔνδεκα	μαθηταὶ	ἐπορεύθησαν	εἰς	τὴν
eleven	disciples	went	to	-

Γαλιλαίαν,	εἰς	τὸ	ὄρος	οὗ	ἐτάξατο
Galilee,	to	the	mountain	where	appointed

αὐτοῖς	ὁ Ἰησοῦς,	17 καὶ	ἰδόντες	αὐτὸν
them	- Jesus,	and	seeing	him

they worshiped him; but some doubted. [18] And Jesus came and said to them, "All authority in heaven and on earth has been given to me. [19] Go therefore and make disciples of all nations, baptizing them in the name of the Father and of the Son and of the Holy Spirit, [20] teaching them to observe all that I have commanded you; and lo, I am with you always, to the close of the age."

προσεκύνησαν, οἱ δὲ ἐδίστασαν. **18** καὶ
they worshipped, but some doubted. And

προσελθὼν ὁ Ἰησοῦς ἐλάλησεν αὐτοῖς
approaching - Jesus talked with them

λέγων· ἐδόθη μοι πᾶσα ἐξουσία ἐν
saying: was given to me All authority in

οὐρανῷ καὶ ἐπὶ [τῆς] γῆς. **19** πορευθέντες
heaven and on the earth. Going

οὖν μαθητεύσατε πάντα τὰ ἔθνη, βαπτίζ-
therefore disciple ye all the nations, baptiz-

οντες αὐτοὺς εἰς τὸ ὄνομα τοῦ πατρὸς
ing them in the name of the Father

καὶ τοῦ υἱοῦ καὶ τοῦ ἁγίου πνεύματος,
and of the Son and of the Holy Spirit,

20 διδάσκοντες αὐτοὺς τηρεῖν πάντα
teaching them to observe all things

ὅσα ἐνετειλάμην ὑμῖν· καὶ ἰδοὺ ἐγὼ
whatever I gave command to you; and behold I

μεθ’ ὑμῶν εἰμι πάσας τὰς ἡμέρας ἕως
with you am all the days until

τῆς συντελείας τοῦ αἰῶνος.
the completion of the age.

CHAPTER 1

THE beginning of the gospel of Jesus Christ, the Son of God.[a]
2 As it is written in Isaiah the prophet,[b]
"Behold, I send my messenger before thy face,
who shall prepare thy way;
[3]the voice of one crying in the wilderness:
Prepare the way of the Lord,
make his paths straight—"
[4]John the baptizer appeared[c] in the wilderness, preaching a baptism of repentance for the forgiveness of sins. [5]And there went out to him all the country of Judea, and all the people of Jerusalem; and they were baptized by him in the river Jordan, confessing their sins. [6]Now John was clothed with camel's hair, and had a leather girdle around his waist, and ate locusts and wild honey. [7]And he preached, saying, "After me comes he who is mightier than I, the thong of whose sandals I am not worthy to stoop down and untie. [8]I have baptized you with water; but he will baptize you with the Holy Spirit."

9 In those days Jesus came from Nazareth of

[a] Other ancient authorities omit *the Son of God*
[b] Other ancient authorities read *in the prophets*
[c] Other ancient authorities read *John was baptizing*

1 Ἀρχὴ τοῦ εὐαγγελίου Ἰησοῦ Χριστοῦ.
[The] beginning of the   gospel   of Jesus   Christ.
2 Καθὼς γέγραπται ἐν τῷ Ἠσαΐᾳ τῷ
As   it has been written in –   Isaiah   the
προφήτῃ· ἰδοὺ ἀποστέλλω τὸν ἄγγελόν μου
prophet: Behold[,] I send   the   messenger of me
πρὸ προσώπου σου, ὃς κατασκευάσει τὴν ὁδόν
before [the] face of thee, who will prepare   the way
σου· 3 φωνὴ βοῶντος ἐν τῇ ἐρήμῳ· ἑτοιμάσατε
of thee: a voice of [one] crying in the desert: Prepare ye
τὴν ὁδὸν κυρίου, εὐθείας ποιεῖτε τὰς τρίβους
the way of [the] Lord, straight make   the   paths
αὐτοῦ, 4 ἐγένετο Ἰωάννης ὁ βαπτίζων ἐν τῇ
of him,   came   John   the [one] baptizing in the
ἐρήμῳ κηρύσσων βάπτισμα μετανοίας εἰς
desert proclaiming a baptism of repentance for
ἄφεσιν ἁμαρτιῶν. 5 καὶ ἐξεπορεύετο πρὸς
forgiveness of sins.   And   went out   to
αὐτὸν πᾶσα ἡ Ἰουδαία χώρα καὶ οἱ Ἱεροσο-
him   all the Judæan country and the Jerusa-
λυμῖται πάντες, καὶ ἐβαπτίζοντο ὑπ' αὐτοῦ
lemites all,   and   were baptized   by   him
ἐν τῷ Ἰορδάνῃ ποταμῷ ἐξομολογούμενοι τὰς
in the Jordan   river   confessing   the
ἁμαρτίας αὐτῶν. 6 καὶ ἦν ὁ Ἰωάννης
sins   of them.   And was –   John
ἐνδεδυμένος τρίχας καμήλου καὶ ζώνην
having been clothed [in] hairs of a camel and   girdle
δερματίνην περὶ τὴν ὀσφὺν αὐτοῦ, καὶ ἔσθων
a leathern   round the loin[s] of him, and eating
ἀκρίδας καὶ μέλι ἄγριον. 7 καὶ ἐκήρυσσεν
locusts   and honey   wild.   And he proclaimed
λέγων· ἔρχεται ὁ ἰσχυρότερός μου ὀπίσω
saying: Comes the [one] stronger   of me   after
                                              =than I
[μου], οὗ οὐκ εἰμὶ ἱκανὸς κύψας λῦσαι
me, of whom I am not   competent stooping to loosen
τὸν ἱμάντα τῶν ὑποδημάτων αὐτοῦ. 8 ἐγὼ
the thong of the   sandals   of him.   I
ἐβάπτισα ὑμᾶς ὕδατι, αὐτὸς δὲ βαπτίσει ὑμᾶς
baptized you in water, but he   will baptize   you
πνεύματι ἁγίῳ.
Spirit in [the] Holy.
9 Καὶ ἐγένετο ἐν ἐκείναις ταῖς ἡμέραις
And it came to pass in   those   –   days
ἦλθεν Ἰησοῦς ἀπὸ Ναζαρὲθ τῆς Γαλιλαίας
came   Jesus   from Nazareth –   of Galilee

Galilee and was baptized by John in the Jordan. ¹⁰And when he came up out of the water, immediately he saw the heavens opened and the Spirit descending upon him like a dove; ¹¹and a voice came from heaven, "Thou art my beloved Son;[d] with thee I am well pleased."

12 The Spirit immediately drove him out into the wilderness. ¹³And he was in the wilderness forty days, tempted by Satan; and he was with the wild beasts; and the angels ministered to him.

14 Now after John was arrested, Jesus came into Galilee, preaching the gospel of God, ¹⁵and saying, "The time is fulfilled, and the kingdom of God is at hand; repent and believe in the gospel."

16 And passing along by the Sea of Galilee, he saw Simon and Andrew the brother of Simon casting a net in the sea; for they were fishermen. ¹⁷And Jesus said to them, "Follow me and I will make you become fishers of men." ¹⁸And immed-

[d] Or my Son, my (or the) Beloved

καὶ ἐβαπτίσθη εἰς τὸν Ἰορδάνην ὑπὸ
and was baptized in the Jordan by

Ἰωάννου. 10 καὶ εὐθὺς ἀναβαίνων ἐκ τοῦ
John. And immediately going up out of the

ὕδατος εἶδεν σχιζομένους τοὺς οὐρανοὺς
water he saw being rent the heavens

καὶ τὸ πνεῦμα ὡς περιστερὰν καταβαῖνον
and the Spirit as a dove coming down

εἰς αὐτόν· 11 καὶ φωνὴ [ἐγένετο] ἐκ τῶν
to him; and a voice there was out of the

οὐρανῶν· σὺ εἶ ὁ υἱός μου ὁ ἀγαπητός,
heavens: Thou art the Son of me the beloved,

ἐν σοὶ εὐδόκησα. 12 Καὶ εὐθὺς τὸ
in thee I was well pleased. And immediately the

πνεῦμα αὐτὸν ἐκβάλλει εἰς τὴν ἔρημον.
Spirit him thrusts forth into the desert.

13 καὶ ἦν ἐν τῇ ἐρήμῳ τεσσεράκοντα
And he was in the desert forty

ἡμέρας πειραζόμενος ὑπὸ τοῦ σατανᾶ, καὶ
days being tempted by - Satan, and

ἦν μετὰ τῶν θηρίων, καὶ οἱ ἄγγελοι
was with the wild beasts, and the angels

διηκόνουν αὐτῷ.
ministered to him.

14 Καὶ μετὰ τὸ παραδοθῆναι τὸν
And after the to be delivered -
= after John was delivered

Ἰωάννην[b] ἦλθεν ὁ Ἰησοῦς εἰς τὴν Γαλιλαίαν
John came - Jesus into - Galilee

κηρύσσων τὸ εὐαγγέλιον τοῦ θεοῦ 15 [καὶ
proclaiming the gospel - of God and

λέγων], ὅτι πεπλήρωται ὁ καιρὸς καὶ
saying, - Has been fulfilled the time and

ἤγγικεν ἡ βασιλεία τοῦ θεοῦ· μετανοεῖτε
has drawn near the kingdom - of God; repent ye

καὶ πιστεύετε ἐν τῷ εὐαγγελίῳ. 16 Καὶ
and believe in the gospel. And

παράγων παρὰ τὴν θάλασσαν τῆς Γαλιλαίας
passing along beside the sea - of Galilee

εἶδεν Σίμωνα καὶ Ἀνδρέαν τὸν ἀδελφὸν
he saw Simon and Andrew the brother

Σίμωνος ἀμφιβάλλοντας ἐν τῇ θαλάσσῃ·
of Simon casting [a net] in the sea;

ἦσαν γὰρ ἁλεεῖς. 17 καὶ εἶπεν αὐτοῖς
for they were fishers. And said to them

ὁ Ἰησοῦς· δεῦτε ὀπίσω μου, καὶ ποιήσω
- Jesus: Come after me, and I will make

ὑμᾶς γενέσθαι ἁλεεῖς ἀνθρώπων. 18 καὶ
you to become fishers of men. And

iately they left their nets and followed him. ¹⁹And going on a little farther, he saw James the son of Zeb'edee and John his brother, who were in their boat mending the nets. ²⁰And immediately he called them; and they left their father Zeb'edee in the boat with the hired servants, and followed him.

21 And they went into Caper'na-um; and immediately on the sabbath he entered the synagogue and taught. ²²And they were astonished at his teaching, for he taught them as one who had authority, and not as the scribes. ²³And immediately there was in their synagogue a man with an unclean spirit; ²⁴and he cried out, "What have you to do with us, Jesus of Nazareth? Have you come to destroy us? I know who you are, the Holy One of God." ²⁵But Jesus rebuked him, saying, "Be silent, and come out of him!" ²⁶And the unclean spirit, convulsing him and crying with a loud voice, came out of him. ²⁷And they were all amazed, so that

εὐθὺς	ἀφέντες	τὰ	δίκτυα	ἠκολούθησαν
immediately	leaving	the	nets	they followed

αὐτῷ. **19** Καὶ προβὰς ὀλίγον εἶδεν
him. And going forward a little he saw

Ἰάκωβον τὸν τοῦ Ζεβεδαίου καὶ Ἰωάννην
James the [son] – of Zebedee and John

τὸν ἀδελφὸν αὐτοῦ καὶ αὐτοὺς ἐν τῷ
the brother of him even them in the

πλοίῳ καταρτίζοντας τὰ δίκτυα. **20** καὶ
ship mending the nets. And

εὐθὺς ἐκάλεσεν αὐτούς· καὶ ἀφέντες τὸν
immediately he called them; and leaving the

πατέρα αὐτῶν Ζεβεδαῖον ἐν τῷ πλοίῳ
father of them Zebedee in the ship

μετὰ τῶν μισθωτῶν ἀπῆλθον ὀπίσω αὐτοῦ.
with the hired servants they went after him.

21 Καὶ εἰσπορεύονται εἰς Καφαρναούμ·
And they enter into Capernaum;

καὶ εὐθὺς τοῖς σάββασιν εἰσελθὼν
and immediately on the sabbaths entering

εἰς τὴν συναγωγὴν ἐδίδασκεν. **22** καὶ
into the synagogue he taught. And

ἐξεπλήσσοντο ἐπὶ τῇ διδαχῇ αὐτοῦ· ἦν
they were astounded on(at) the teaching of him; ¹he was

γὰρ διδάσκων αὐτοὺς ὡς ἐξουσίαν ἔχων,
¹for teaching them as authority having,

καὶ οὐχ ὡς οἱ γραμματεῖς. **23** Καὶ εὐθὺς
and not as the scribes. And immediately

ἦν ἐν τῇ συναγωγῇ αὐτῶν ἄνθρωπος
there was in the synagogue of them a man

ἐν πνεύματι ἀκαθάρτῳ, καὶ ἀνέκραξεν
in spirit an unclean, and he cried out

24 λέγων· τί ἡμῖν καὶ σοί, Ἰησοῦ
saying: What to us and to thee, Jesus

Ναζαρηνέ; ἦλθες ἀπολέσαι ἡμᾶς; οἶδά
Nazarene? camest thou to destroy us? I know

σε τίς εἶ, ὁ ἅγιος τοῦ θεοῦ. **25** καὶ
thee who thou art, the holy [one] – of God. And

ἐπετίμησεν αὐτῷ ὁ Ἰησοῦς [λέγων]·
rebuked him – Jesus saying:

φιμώθητι καὶ ἔξελθε [ἐξ αὐτοῦ]. **26** καὶ
Be quiet and come out out of him. And

σπαράξαν αὐτὸν τὸ πνεῦμα τὸ ἀκάθαρτον
throwing him the spirit – unclean

καὶ φωνῆσαν φωνῇ μεγάλῃ ἐξῆλθεν ἐξ
and shouting voice with a great he came out out of

αὐτοῦ. **27** καὶ ἐθαμβήθησαν ἅπαντες, ὥστε
him. And were astounded all, so as
= so that

they questioned among themselves, saying, "What is this? A new teaching! With authority he commands even the unclean spirits, and they obey him." ²⁸And at once his fame spread everywhere throughout all the surrounding region of Galilee.

29 And immediately heᵉ left the synagogue, and entered the house of Simon and Andrew, with James and John. ³⁰Now Simon's mother-in-law lay sick with a fever, and immediately they told him of her. ³¹And he came and took her by the hand and lifted her up, and the fever left her; and she served them.

32 That evening, at sundown, they brought to him all who were sick or possessed with demons. ³³And the whole city was gathered together about the door. ³⁴And he healed many who were sick with various diseases, and cast out many demons; and he would not permit the demons to speak, because they knew him.

35 And in the morning, a great while before day, he rose and went out

ᵉ Other ancient authorities read *they*

συζητεῖν αὐτοὺς λέγοντας· τί ἐστιν τοῦτο;
to debate themᵇ saying: What is this?
they debated

διδαχὴ καινὴ κατ᾽ ἐξουσίαν· καὶ τοῖς
teaching a new by authority; and the

πνεύμασι τοῖς ἀκαθάρτοις ἐπιτάσσει, καὶ
spirits - unclean he commands, and

ὑπακούουσιν αὐτῷ. 28 καὶ ἐξῆλθεν ἡ
they obey him. And went forth the

ἀκοὴ αὐτοῦ εὐθὺς πανταχοῦ εἰς ὅλην
report of him immediately everywhere into all

τὴν περίχωρον τῆς Γαλιλαίας. 29 Καὶ
the neighbourhood - of Galilee. And

εὐθὺς ἐκ τῆς συναγωγῆς ἐξελθόντες ἦλθον
immediately out of the synagogue going forth they came

εἰς τὴν οἰκίαν Σίμωνος καὶ Ἀνδρέου
into the house of Simon and Andrew

μετὰ Ἰακώβου καὶ Ἰωάννου. 30 ἡ δὲ
with James and John. Now the

πενθερὰ Σίμωνος κατέκειτο πυρέσσουσα,
mother-in-law of Simon was laid [aside] fever-stricken,

καὶ εὐθὺς λέγουσιν αὐτῷ περὶ αὐτῆς.
and immediately they tell him about her.

31 καὶ προσελθὼν ἤγειρεν αὐτὴν κρατήσας
And approaching he raised her holding

τῆς χειρός· καὶ ἀφῆκεν αὐτὴν ὁ πυρετός,
the(her) hand; and left her the fever,

καὶ διηκόνει αὐτοῖς. 32 Ὀψίας δὲ γενο-
and she served them. And evening com-
= when evening

μένης, ὅτε ἔδυσεν ὁ ἥλιος, ἔφερον πρὸς
ing,ᵃ when set the sun, they brought to
came,

αὐτὸν πάντας τοὺς κακῶς ἔχοντας καὶ
him all the [ones] ill having and
= those who were ill

τοὺς δαιμονιζομένους· 33 καὶ ἦν ὅλη ἡ
the being demon-possessed; and was all the

πόλις ἐπισυνηγμένη πρὸς τὴν θύραν.
city *having been* assembled at the door.

34 καὶ ἐθεράπευσεν πολλοὺς κακῶς ἔχοντας
And he healed many ill having
= who were ill

ποικίλαις νόσοις, καὶ δαιμόνια πολλὰ
with various diseases, and demons many

ἐξέβαλεν, καὶ οὐκ ἤφιεν λαλεῖν τὰ δαιμόνια,
he expelled, and did not allow to speak the demons,

ὅτι ᾔδεισαν αὐτόν. 35 Καὶ πρωῒ ἔννυχα
because they knew him. And ³early ⁴in the night

λίαν ἀναστὰς ἐξῆλθεν καὶ ἀπῆλθεν εἰς
ᵃvery ¹rising up he went out and went away to

to a lonely place, and there he prayed. ³⁶And Simon and those who were with him followed him, ³⁷and they found him and said to him, "Every one is searching for you." ³⁸And he said to them, "Let us go on to the next towns, that I may preach there also; for that is why I came out." ³⁹And he went throughout all Galilee, preaching in their synagogues and casting out demons.

40 And a leper came to him beseeching him, and kneeling said to him, "If you will, you can make me clean."

⁴¹Moved with pity, he stretched out his hand and touched him, and said to him, "I will; be clean." ⁴²And immediately the leprosy left him, and he was made clean. ⁴³And he sternly charged him, and sent him away at once, ⁴⁴and said to him, "See that you say nothing to any one; but go, show yourself to the priest, and offer for your cleansing what Moses commanded, for a proof to the people." ⁴⁵But he went out and began to talk freely about it, and to spread the news, so that

ἔρημον τόπον, κἀκεῖ προσηύχετο. 36 καὶ
a desert place, and there prayed. And

κατεδίωξεν αὐτὸν Σίμων καὶ οἱ μετ'
hunted down him Simon and the[ones] with

αὐτοῦ, καὶ εὗρον αὐτὸν καὶ λέγουσιν
him, and found him and say

αὐτῷ 37 ὅτι πάντες ζητοῦσίν σε. 38 καὶ
to him[,] – All are seeking thee. And

λέγει αὐτοῖς· ἄγωμεν ἀλλαχοῦ εἰς τὰς
he says to them: Let us go elsewhere into the

ἐχομένας κωμοπόλεις, ἵνα καὶ ἐκεῖ
neighbouring towns, that also there

κηρύξω· εἰς τοῦτο γὰρ ἐξῆλθον. 39 καὶ
I may proclaim; for for this [purpose] I came forth. And

ἦλθεν κηρύσσων εἰς τὰς συναγωγὰς αὐτῶν
he came proclaiming in the synagogues of them

εἰς ὅλην τὴν Γαλιλαίαν καὶ τὰ δαιμόνια
in all – Galilee and the demons

ἐκβάλλων.
expelling.

40 Καὶ ἔρχεται πρὸς αὐτὸν λεπρὸς
And comes to him a leper

παρακαλῶν αὐτὸν καὶ γονυπετῶν λέγων
beseeching him and falling on [his] knees saying

αὐτῷ ὅτι ἐὰν θέλῃς δύνασαί με καθαρίσαι.
to him[,] – If thou art willing thou art able me to cleanse.

41 καὶ σπλαγχνισθεὶς ἐκτείνας τὴν
And being filled with tenderness stretching forth the(his)

χεῖρα αὐτοῦ ἥψατο καὶ λέγει αὐτῷ· θέλω,
hand ²him ¹he touched and says to him: I am willing,

καθαρίσθητι. 42 καὶ εὐθὺς ἀπῆλθεν ἀπ'
be thou cleansed. And immediately departed from

αὐτοῦ ἡ λέπρα, καὶ ἐκαθαρίσθη. 43 καὶ
him the leprosy, and he was cleansed. And

ἐμβριμησάμενος αὐτῷ εὐθὺς ἐξέβαλεν αὐτόν,
sternly admonishing him immediately he put out him,

44 καὶ λέγει αὐτῷ· ὅρα μηδενὶ μηδὲν
and says to him: See no one no(any)thing

εἴπῃς, ἀλλὰ ὕπαγε σεαυτὸν δεῖξον τῷ
thou tellest, but go thyself show to the

ἱερεῖ καὶ προσένεγκε περὶ τοῦ καθαρισμοῦ σου
priest and offer concerning the cleansing of thee

ἃ προσέταξεν Μωϋσῆς, εἰς μαρτύριον
[the things] which commanded Moses, for a testimony

αὐτοῖς. 45 ὁ δὲ ἐξελθὼν ἤρξατο κηρύσσειν
to them. But he going out began to proclaim

πολλὰ καὶ διαφημίζειν τὸν λόγον, ὥστε
many things and to spread about the matter, so as
                                          = so that

Jesus could no longer openly enter a town, but was out in the country; and people came to him from every quarter.

μηκέτι αὐτὸν δύνασθαι φανερῶς εἰς πόλιν
no longer him to be able[b] openly into a city
he was no longer able

εἰσελθεῖν, ἀλλ' ἔξω ἐπ' ἐρήμοις τόποις
to enter, but outside on(in) desert places

ἦν· καὶ ἤρχοντο πρὸς αὐτὸν πάντοθεν.
he was; and they came to him from all directions.

CHAPTER 2

AND when he returned to Caper'-na-um after some days, it was reported that he was at home. ²And many were gathered together, so that there was no longer room for them, not even about the door; and he was preaching the word to them. ³And they came, bringing to him a paralytic carried by four men. ⁴And when they could not get near him because of the crowd, they removed the roof above him; and when they had made an opening, they let down the pallet on which the paralytic lay. ⁵And when Jesus saw their faith, he said to the paralytic, "My son, your sins are forgiven." ⁶Now some of the scribes were sitting there, questioning in their hearts, ⁷"Why does this man speak thus? It is blasphemy! Who can forgive sins but God alone?" ⁸And immediately Jesus, perceiving in his spirit that they thus questioned within themselves, said to them,

2 Καὶ εἰσελθὼν πάλιν εἰς Καφαρναοὺμ
And entering again into Capernaum

δι' ἡμερῶν ἠκούσθη ὅτι ἐν οἴκῳ ἐστίν.
through days it was heard that at home he is(was).
= after [some] days

2 καὶ συνήχθησαν πολλοί, ὥστε μηκέτι
And were assembled many, so as no longer

χωρεῖν μηδὲ τὰ πρὸς τὴν θύραν, καὶ
to have room not - at the door, and

ἐλάλει αὐτοῖς τὸν λόγον. 3 καὶ ἔρχονται
he spoke to them the word. And they come

φέροντες πρὸς αὐτὸν παραλυτικὸν αἰρόμενον
carrying to him a paralytic being borne

ὑπὸ τεσσάρων. 4 καὶ μὴ δυνάμενοι
by four [men]. And not being able

προσενέγκαι αὐτῷ διὰ τὸν ὄχλον
to bring to him because of the crowd

ἀπεστέγασαν τὴν στέγην ὅπου ἦν, καὶ
they unroofed the roof where he was, and

ἐξορύξαντες χαλῶσι τὸν κράβατον ὅπου ὁ
having opened up they lower the mattress where the

παραλυτικὸς κατέκειτο. 5 καὶ ἰδὼν ὁ
paralytic was lying. And seeing -

Ἰησοῦς τὴν πίστιν αὐτῶν λέγει τῷ
Jesus the faith of them he says to the

παραλυτικῷ· τέκνον, ἀφίενταί σου αἱ
paralytic: Child, are forgiven of thee the

ἁμαρτίαι. 6 ἦσαν δέ τινες τῶν γραμματέων
sins. Now there were some of the scribes

ἐκεῖ καθήμενοι καὶ διαλογιζόμενοι ἐν ταῖς
there sitting and reasoning in the

καρδίαις αὐτῶν· 7 τί οὗτος οὕτως λαλεῖ;
hearts of them: Why this [man] thus speaks?

βλασφημεῖ· τίς δύναται ἀφιέναι ἁμαρτίας
he blasphemes; who can to forgive sins

εἰ μὴ εἷς ὁ θεός; 8 καὶ εὐθὺς ἐπιγνοὺς
except one[,] - God? And immediately knowing

ὁ Ἰησοῦς τῷ πνεύματι αὐτοῦ ὅτι οὕτως
- Jesus in the spirit of him that thus

διαλογίζονται ἐν ἑαυτοῖς, λέγει αὐτοῖς·
they reason among themselves, he says to them:

"Why do you question thus in your hearts? [9]Which is easier, to say to the paralytic, 'Your sins are forgiven,' or to say, 'Rise, take up your pallet and walk'? [10]But that you may know that the Son of man has authority on earth to forgive sins"—he said to the paralytic—[11]"I say to you, rise, take up your pallet and go home." [12]And he rose, and immediately took up the pallet and went out before them all; so that they were all amazed and glorified God, saying, "We never saw anything like this!"

13 He went out again beside the sea; and all the crowd gathered about him, and he taught them. [14]And as he passed on, he saw Levi the son of Alphaeus sitting at the tax office, and he said to him, "Follow me." And he rose and followed him

15 And as he sat at table in his house, many tax collectors and sinners were sitting with Jesus

τί ταῦτα διαλογίζεσθε ἐν ταῖς καρδίαις
Why these things reason ye in the hearts

ὑμῶν; 9 τί ἐστιν εὐκοπώτερον, εἰπεῖν
of you? What is easier, to say

τῷ παραλυτικῷ· ἀφίενταί σου αἱ ἁμαρτίαι,
to the paralytic: are forgiven of thee the sins,

ἢ εἰπεῖν· ἔγειρε καὶ ἆρον τὸν κράβατόν
or to say: Rise and take the mattress

σου καὶ περιπάτει; 10 ἵνα δὲ εἰδῆτε
of thee and walk? But that ye may know

ὅτι ἐξουσίαν ἔχει ὁ υἱὸς τοῦ ἀνθρώπου
that authority has the Son - of man

ἀφιέναι ἁμαρτίας ἐπὶ τῆς γῆς,—λέγει τῷ
to forgive sins on the earth,—he says to the

παραλυτικῷ· 11 σοὶ λέγω, ἔγειρε ἆρον
paralytic: To thee I say, rise[,] take

τὸν κράβατόν σου καὶ ὕπαγε εἰς τὸν
the mattress of thee and go to the

οἶκόν σου. 12 καὶ ἠγέρθη καὶ εὐθὺς
house of thee. And he arose and immediately

ἄρας τὸν κράβατον ἐξῆλθεν ἔμπροσθεν
taking the mattress he went forth before

πάντων, ὥστε ἐξίστασθαι πάντας καὶ
all, so as to be astonished all and
= so that they were all astonished and glorified

δοξάζειν τὸν θεὸν λέγοντας ὅτι οὕτως
to glorify[b] - God saying[,] - Thus

οὐδέποτε εἴδαμεν.
never we saw.

13 Καὶ ἐξῆλθεν πάλιν παρὰ τὴν θάλασσαν·
And he went forth again by the sea;

καὶ πᾶς ὁ ὄχλος ἤρχετο πρὸς αὐτόν,
and all the crowd came to him,

καὶ ἐδίδασκεν αὐτούς. 14 Καὶ παράγων
and he taught them. And passing along

εἶδεν Λευὶν τὸν τοῦ Ἀλφαίου καθήμενον
he saw Levi the [son] - Alphæus sitting

ἐπὶ τὸ τελώνιον, καὶ λέγει αὐτῷ· ἀκολούθει
on(in or at)the custom house, and says to him: Follow

μοι. καὶ ἀναστὰς ἠκολούθησεν αὐτῷ.
me. And rising up he followed him.

15 Καὶ γίνεται κατακεῖσθαι αὐτὸν ἐν τῇ
And it comes to pass to recline him[b] in the
= he reclines

οἰκίᾳ αὐτοῦ, καὶ πολλοὶ τελῶναι καὶ
house of him, and many tax-collectors and

ἁμαρτωλοὶ συνανέκειντο τῷ Ἰησοῦ καὶ
sinners reclined with - Jesus and

and his disciples; for there were many who followed him. ¹⁶And the scribes ofᶠ the Pharisees, when they saw that he was eating with sinners and tax collectors, said to his disciples, "Why does he eatᵍ with tax collectors and sinners?" ¹⁷And when Jesus heard it, he said to them, "Those who are well have no need of a physician, but those who are sick; I came not to call the righteous, but sinners."

18 Now John's disciples and the Pharisees were fasting; and people came and said to him, "Why do John's disciples and the disciples of the Pharisees fast, but your disciples do not fast?" ¹⁹And Jesus said to them, "Can the wedding guests fast while the bridegroom is with them? As long as they have the bridegroom with them, they cannot fast. ²⁰The days will come, when the bridegroom is taken away from them, and then they will fast in that day. ²¹No one sews a piece of unshrunk cloth on an old garment; if he does, the

τοῖς   μαθηταῖς   αὐτοῦ·   ἦσαν   γὰρ   πολλοί,
the   disciples   of him;   for there were   many,

καὶ   ἠκολούθουν   αὐτῷ.   16 καὶ   οἱ   γραμματεῖς
and   they followed   him.   And the   scribes

τῶν   Φαρισαίων   ἰδόντες   ὅτι   ἐσθίει
of the   Pharisees   seeing   that   he eats(ate)

μετὰ   τῶν   ἁμαρτωλῶν   καὶ   τελωνῶν   ἔλεγον
with   -   sinners   and   tax-collectors   said

τοῖς   μαθηταῖς   αὐτοῦ·   ὅτι   μετὰ   τῶν
to the   disciples   of him: -   With   -

τελωνῶν   καὶ   ἁμαρτωλῶν   ἐσθίει;   17 καὶ
tax-collectors   and   sinners   does he eat?   And

ἀκούσας   ὁ   Ἰησοῦς   λέγει   αὐτοῖς   [ὅτι]   οὐ
hearing   -   Jesus   says   to them[,]   -   Not

χρείαν   ἔχουσιν   οἱ   ἰσχύοντες   ἰατροῦ   ἀλλ'
need   have   the [ones] being strong   of a physician   but

οἱ   κακῶς   ἔχοντες·   οὐκ   ἦλθον   καλέσαι
the [ones] ill   having;   I came not   to call
= those who are ill;

δικαίους   ἀλλὰ   ἁμαρτωλούς.   18 Καὶ   ἦσαν
righteous men   but   sinners.   And   ⁷were

οἱ   μαθηταὶ   Ἰωάννου   καὶ   οἱ   Φαρισαῖοι
¹the   ²disciples   ³of John   ⁴and   ⁵the   ⁶Pharisees

νηστεύοντες.   καὶ   ἔρχονται   καὶ   λέγουσιν
⁸fasting.   And   they come   and   say

αὐτῷ·   διὰ   τί   οἱ   μαθηταὶ   Ἰωάννου   καὶ
to him: Why   the   disciples   of John   and

οἱ   μαθηταὶ   τῶν   Φαρισαίων   νηστεύουσιν,
the   disciples   of the   Pharisees   fast,

οἱ   δὲ   σοὶ   μαθηταὶ   οὐ   νηστεύουσιν;   19 καὶ
-    but   thy   disciples   do not fast?   And

εἶπεν   αὐτοῖς   ὁ   Ἰησοῦς·   μὴ   δύνανται   οἱ
said   to them   -   Jesus: not   can   the

υἱοὶ   τοῦ   νυμφῶνος,   ἐν   ᾧ   ὁ   νυμφίος
sons   of the   bridechamber,   in   which†   the   bridegroom

μετ'   αὐτῶν   ἐστιν,   νηστεύειν;   ὅσον   χρόνον
with   them   is,   to fast?   what   time

ἔχουσιν   τὸν   νυμφίον   μετ'   αὐτῶν,   οὐ
they have   the   bridegroom   with   them,   not

δύνανται   νηστεύειν.   20 ἐλεύσονται   δὲ   ἡμέραι
they can   to fast.   But will come   days

ὅταν   ἀπαρθῇ   ἀπ'   αὐτῶν   ὁ   νυμφίος,   καὶ
when   taken away   from   them   the   bridegroom,   and

τότε   νηστεύσουσιν   ἐν   ἐκείνῃ   τῇ   ἡμέρᾳ.
then   they will fast   in   that   -   day.

21 Οὐδεὶς   ἐπίβλημα   ῥάκους   ἀγνάφου   ἐπιράπτει
No one   a patch   cloth   of unfulled   sews

ἐπὶ   ἱμάτιον   παλαιόν·   εἰ   δὲ   μή,   αἴρει
on   garment   an old;   otherwise,   ²takes

ᶠ Other ancient authorities read *and*
ᵍ Other ancient authorities add *and drink*

patch tears away from it, the new from the old, and a worse tear is made. 22And no one puts new wine into old wineskins; if he does, the wine will burst the skins, and the wine is lost, and so are the skins; but new wine is for fresh skins."[h]

23 One sabbath he was going through the grainfields; and as they made their way his disciples began to pluck ears of grain. 24And the Pharisees said to him, "Look, why are they doing what is not lawful on the sab ith?" 25And he said to hem, "Have you neve read what David di., when he was in need and was hungry, he and those who were with him: 26how he entered the house of God, when Abi'athar was high priest, and ate the bread of the Presence, which it is not lawful for any but the priests to eat, and also gave it to those who were with him?" 27And he said to them, "The sabbath was made for man, not man for the sabbath; 28so the Son of man is lord even of the sabbath."

[h] Other ancient authorities omit *but new wine is for fresh skins*

τὸ πλήρωμα ἀπ' αὐτοῦ τὸ καινὸν τοῦ
⁴the ⁵fulness ⁶from ⁹itself ¹the ²new ⁷the
παλαιοῦ, καὶ χεῖρον σχίσμα γίνεται. 22 καὶ
⁸old, and a worse rent occurs. And
οὐδεὶς βάλλει οἶνον νέον εἰς ἀσκοὺς παλαιούς·
no one puts wine new into wineskins old;
εἰ δὲ μή, ῥήξει ὁ οἶνος τοὺς ἀσκούς,
otherwise, ²will burst ¹the ²wine the wineskins,
καὶ ὁ οἶνος ἀπόλλυται καὶ οἱ ἀσκοί.
and the wine perishes and the wineskins.
[ἀλλὰ οἶνον νέον εἰς ἀσκοὺς καινούς.]
But wine new into wineskins fresh.
23 Καὶ ἐγένετο αὐτὸν ἐν τοῖς σάββασιν
And it came to pass him on the sabbath*s*
= as he passed on the sabbath
παραπορεύεσθαι διὰ τῶν σπορίμων, καὶ
to pass[b] through the cornfields, and
οἱ μαθηταὶ αὐτοῦ ἤρξαντο ὁδὸν ποιεῖν
the disciples of him began way to make
τίλλοντες τοὺς στάχυας. 24 καὶ οἱ Φαρισαῖοι
plucking the ears of corn. And the Pharisees
ἔλεγον αὐτῷ· ἴδε τί ποιοῦσιν τοῖς σάββασιν
said to him: Behold[,] why do on the sabbath*s*
ὃ οὐκ ἔξεστιν; 25 καὶ λέγει αὐτοῖς·
what is not lawful? And he says to them:
οὐδέποτε ἀνέγνωτε τί ἐποίησεν Δαυίδ,
never read ye what did David,
ὅτε χρείαν ἔσχεν καὶ ἐπείνασεν αὐτὸς
when need he had and hungered he
καὶ οἱ μετ' αὐτοῦ; 26 [πῶς] εἰσῆλθεν
and the [ones] with him? how he entered
εἰς τὸν οἶκον τοῦ θεοῦ ἐπὶ 'Αβιαθὰρ
into the house – of God on(in the days of) Abiathar
ἀρχιερέως καὶ τοὺς ἄρτους τῆς προθέσεως
high priest and the loaves of the setting forth
ἔφαγεν, οὓς οὐκ ἔξεστιν φαγεῖν εἰ μὴ
ate, which it is not lawful to eat except
τοὺς ἱερεῖς, καὶ ἔδωκεν καὶ τοῖς σὺν
the priests, and gave also to the [ones] with
αὐτῷ οὖσιν; 27 καὶ ἔλεγεν αὐτοῖς·
him being? And he said to them:
τὸ σάββατον διὰ τὸν ἄνθρωπον ἐγένετο,
The sabbath on account of – man was,
καὶ οὐχ ὁ ἄνθρωπος διὰ τὸ σάββατον·
and not – man on account of the sabbath;
28 ὥστε κύριός ἐστιν ὁ υἱὸς τοῦ ἀνθρώπου
so as Lord is the Son – of man
καὶ τοῦ σαββάτου.
also of the sabbath.

CHAPTER 3

AGAIN he entered the synagogue, and a man was there who had a withered hand. ²And they watched him, to see whether he would heal him on the sabbath, so that they might accuse him. ³And he said to the man who had the withered hand, "Come here." ⁴And he said to them, "Is it lawful on the sabbath to do good or to do harm, to save life or to kill?" But they were silent. ⁵And he looked around at them with anger, grieved at their hardness of heart, and said to the man, "Stretch out your hand." He stretched it out, and his hand was restored. ⁶The Pharisees went out, and immediately held counsel with the Hero′di-ans against him, how to destroy him.

7 Jesus withdrew with his disciples to the sea, and a great multitude from Galilee followed; also from Judea ⁸and Jerusalem and Idume′a and from beyond the Jordan and from about Tyre and Sidon a great multitude, hearing all

3 Καὶ εἰσῆλθεν πάλιν εἰς συναγωγήν.
And he entered again into a synagogue.

καὶ ἦν ἐκεῖ ἄνθρωπος ἐξηραμμένην ἔχων
And there was there a man ⁴having been withered ¹having

τὴν χεῖρα· 2 καὶ παρετήρουν αὐτὸν εἰ
²the ³hand; and they watched carefully him if

τοῖς σάββασιν θεραπεύσει αὐτόν, ἵνα
on the sabbaths he will heal him, that

κατηγορήσωσιν αὐτοῦ. 3 καὶ λέγει τῷ
they might accuse him. And he says to the

ἀνθρώπῳ τῷ τὴν χεῖρα ἔχοντι ξηράν·
man – the hand having dry:

ἔγειρε εἰς τὸ μέσον. 4 καὶ λέγει αὐτοῖς·
Rise into the midst. And he says to them:

ἔξεστιν τοῖς σάββασιν ἀγαθὸν ποιῆσαι
Lawful on the sabbaths good to do

ἢ κακοποιῆσαι, ψυχὴν σῶσαι ἢ ἀποκτεῖναι;
or to do evil, life to save or to kill?

οἱ δὲ ἐσιώπων. 5 καὶ περιβλεψάμενος
But they were silent. And looking round

αὐτοὺς μετ᾽ ὀργῆς, συλλυπούμενος ἐπὶ
[on] them with anger, being greatly grieved on(at)

τῇ πωρώσει τῆς καρδίας αὐτῶν, λέγει
the hardness of the heart of them, he says

τῷ ἀνθρώπῳ· ἔκτεινον τὴν χεῖρα. καὶ
to the man: Stretch forth the hand. And

ἐξέτεινεν, καὶ ἀπεκατεστάθη ἡ χεὶρ αὐτοῦ.
he stretched forth, and was restored the hand of him.

6 καὶ ἐξελθόντες οἱ Φαρισαῖοι εὐθὺς μετὰ
And going forth the Pharisees immediately with

τῶν Ἡρωδιανῶν συμβούλιον ἐδίδουν κατ᾽
the Herodians counsel gave against

αὐτοῦ, ὅπως αὐτὸν ἀπολέσωσιν.
him, that him they might destroy.

7 Καὶ ὁ Ἰησοῦς μετὰ τῶν μαθητῶν
And – Jesus with the disciples

αὐτοῦ ἀνεχώρησεν πρὸς τὴν θάλασσαν·
of him departed to the sea;

καὶ πολὺ πλῆθος ἀπὸ τῆς Γαλιλαίας
and a much(great) multitude from – Galilee

ἠκολούθησεν· καὶ ἀπὸ τῆς Ἰουδαίας 8 καὶ
followed; and from – Judæa and

ἀπὸ Ἰεροσολύμων καὶ ἀπὸ τῆς Ἰδουμαίας
from Jerusalem and from – Idumæa

καὶ πέραν τοῦ Ἰορδάνου καὶ περὶ Τύρον
and beyond the Jordan and round Tyre

καὶ Σιδῶνα, πλῆθος πολύ, ἀκούοντες ὅσα
and Sidon, multitude a much(great), hearing what things

that he did, came to him. ⁹And he told his disciples to have a boat ready for him because of the crowd, lest they should crush him; ¹⁰for he had healed many, so that all who had diseases pressed upon him to touch him ¹¹And whenever the unclean spirits beheld him, they fell down before him and cried out, "You are the Son of God." ¹²And he strictly ordered them not to make him known.

13 And he went up into the hills, and called to him those whom he desired; and they came to him. ¹⁴And he appointed twelve,ⁱ to be with him, and to be sent out to preach ¹⁵and have authority to cast out demons: ¹⁶Simon whom he surnamed Peter; ¹⁷James the son of Zeb'edee and John the brother of James, whom he surnamed Bo-aner'ges, that is, sons of thunder; ¹⁸Andrew, and Philip, and Bartholomew, and Matthew, and Thomas, and James the son of Alphaeus, and Thaddaeus, and Simon the

ⁱ Other ancient authorities add *whom also he named apostles*

ποιεῖ, ἦλθον πρὸς αὐτόν. 9 καὶ εἶπεν
he does, came to him. And he told

τοῖς μαθηταῖς αὐτοῦ ἵνα πλοιάριον προσκαρτέρῃ
the disciples of him that a boat should remain near

αὐτῷ διὰ τὸν ὄχλον, ἵνα μὴ θλίβωσιν
him because of the crowd, lest they should press upon

αὐτόν· 10 πολλοὺς γὰρ ἐθεράπευσεν, ὥστε
him; for many he healed, so as

ἐπιπίπτειν αὐτῷ ἵνα αὐτοῦ ἅψωνται
to fall upon him that him they might touch

ὅσοι εἶχον μάστιγας. 11 καὶ τὰ πνεύματα
as many as had plagues. And the spirits

τὰ ἀκάθαρτα, ὅταν αὐτὸν ἐθεώρουν, προσέπιπτον
- unclean, when him they saw, fell before

αὐτῷ καὶ ἔκραζον λέγοντα ὅτι σὺ εἶ ὁ
him and cried out saying[,] - Thou art the

υἱὸς τοῦ θεοῦ. 12 καὶ πολλὰ ἐπετίμα
Son - of God. And much he warned

αὐτοῖς ἵνα μὴ αὐτὸν φανερὸν ποιήσωσιν.
them that not him manifest they should make.

13 Καὶ ἀναβαίνει εἰς τὸ ὄρος, καὶ
And he goes up into the mountain, and

προσκαλεῖται οὓς ἤθελεν αὐτός, καὶ
calls to [him] [those] whom wished he, and

ἀπῆλθον πρὸς αὐτόν. 14 καὶ ἐποίησεν δώδεκα
they went to him. And he made twelve

ἵνα ὦσιν μετ' αὐτοῦ, καὶ ἵνα ἀποστέλλῃ
that they might be with him, and that he might send

αὐτοὺς κηρύσσειν 15 καὶ ἔχειν ἐξουσίαν
them to proclaim and to have authority

ἐκβάλλειν τὰ δαιμόνια· 16 καὶ ἐποίησεν
to expel the demons; and he made

τοὺς δώδεκα, καὶ ἐπέθηκεν ὄνομα τῷ
the twelve, and he added a name -

Σίμωνι Πέτρον· 17 καὶ Ἰάκωβον τὸν τοῦ
to Simon[,] Peter; and James the [son] -

Ζεβεδαίου καὶ Ἰωάννην τὸν ἀδελφὸν τοῦ
of Zebedee and John the brother -

Ἰακώβου, καὶ ἐπέθηκεν αὐτοῖς ὄνομα
of James, and he added to them a name[,]

Βοανηργές, ὃ ἐστιν υἱοὶ βροντῆς· 18 καὶ
Boanerges, which is sons of thunder; and

Ἀνδρέαν καὶ Φίλιππον καὶ Βαρθολομαῖον
Andrew and Philip and Bartholomew

καὶ Μαθθαῖον καὶ Θωμᾶν καὶ Ἰάκωβον
and Matthew and Thomas and James

τὸν τοῦ Ἀλφαίου καὶ Θαδδαῖον καὶ
the [son] - of Alphæus and Thaddæus and

Cananaean, ¹⁹and Judas Iscariot, who betrayed him.

Then he went home; ²⁰and the crowd came together again, so that they could not even eat. ²¹And when his friends heard it, they went out to seize him, for they said, "He is beside himself." ²²And the scribes who came down from Jerusalem said, "He is possessed by Be-el'zebul, and by the prince of demons he casts out the demons." ²³And he called them to him, and said to them in parables, "How can Satan cast out Satan? ²⁴If a kingdom is divided against itself, that kingdom cannot stand. ²⁵And if a house is divided against itself, that house will not be able to stand. ²⁶And if Satan has risen up against himself and is divided, he cannot stand, but is coming to an end. ²⁷But no one can enter a strong man's house and plunder his goods, unless he first binds the strong man; then indeed he may plunder his house. 28 "Truly, I say to you, all sins will be

Σίμωνα   τὸν   Καναναῖον   19 καὶ   Ἰούδαν
Simon   the   Cananæan   and   Judas

Ἰσκαριώθ,   ὃς   καὶ   παρέδωκεν   αὐτόν.
Iscariot,   who   indeed   betrayed   him.

20 Καὶ   ἔρχεται   εἰς   οἶκον·   καὶ   συνέρχεται
And   he comes   into   a house;   and   comes together

πάλιν   [ὁ]   ὄχλος,   ὥστε   μὴ   δύνασθαι
again   the   crowd,   so as   not   to be able
                                    = so that they were not able

αὐτοὺς   μηδὲ   ἄρτον   φαγεῖν.   21 καὶ   ἀκούσαντες
themᵇ   not   bread   to eat.   And   hearing

οἱ   παρ’   αὐτοῦ   ἐξῆλθον   κρατῆσαι   αὐτόν·
the[ones] with   him   went forth   to seize   him;
= his relations

ἔλεγον   γὰρ   ὅτι   ἐξέστη.   22 καὶ   οἱ
for they said[,]   – He is beside himself.   And   the

γραμματεῖς   οἱ   ἀπὸ   Ἱεροσολύμων   καταβάντες
scribes   –   from   Jerusalem   coming down

ἔλεγον   ὅτι   Βεεζεβοὺλ   ἔχει,   καὶ   ὅτι   ἐν
said[,]   Beelzebub   he has,   and[,]   –   By

τῷ   ἄρχοντι   τῶν   δαιμονίων   ἐκβάλλει   τὰ
the   ruler   of the   demons   he expels   the

δαιμόνια.   23 καὶ   προσκαλεσάμενος   αὐτοὺς
demons.   And   calling to [him]   them

ἐν   παραβολαῖς   ἔλεγεν   αὐτοῖς·   πῶς   δύναται
in   parables   he said   to them: How   can

σατανᾶς   σατανᾶν   ἐκβάλλειν;   24 καὶ   ἐὰν
Satan   ²Satan   ¹to expel ?   and   if

βασιλεία   ἐφ’   ἑαυτὴν   μερισθῇ,   οὐ   δύναται
a kingdom   against   itself   be divided,   not   cannot

σταθῆναι   ἡ   βασιλεία   ἐκείνη·   25 καὶ   ἐὰν
stand   –   kingdom   that;   and   if

οἰκία   ἐφ’   ἑαυτὴν   μερισθῇ,   οὐ   δυνήσεται
a house   against   itself   be divided,   will not be able

ἡ   οἰκία   ἐκείνη   στῆναι.   26 καὶ   εἰ   ὁ
–   house   that   to stand.   And   if   –

σατανᾶς   ἀνέστη   ἐφ’   ἑαυτὸν   καὶ   ἐμερίσθη,
Satan   stood up   against   himself   and   was divided,

οὐ   δύναται   στῆναι   ἀλλὰ   τέλος   ἔχει.
he cannot   to stand   but   an end   has.

27 ἀλλ’   οὐ   δύναται   οὐδεὶς   εἰς   τὴν   οἰκίαν
But   cannot   no(any)one   into   the   house

τοῦ   ἰσχυροῦ   εἰσελθὼν   τὰ   σκεύη   αὐτοῦ
of the   strong man   entering   the   goods   of him

διαρπάσαι,   ἐὰν   μὴ   πρῶτον   τὸν   ἰσχυρὸν
to plunder,   unless   first   the   strong man

δήσῃ,   καὶ   τότε   τὴν   οἰκίαν   αὐτοῦ   διαρπάσει.
he bind,   and   then   the   house   of him   he will plunder.

28 Ἀμὴν   λέγω   ὑμῖν   ὅτι   πάντα   ἀφεθήσεται
Truly   I tell   you   that   all   will be forgiven

forgiven the sons of men, and whatever blasphemies they utter; [29]but whoever blasphemes against the Holy Spirit never has forgiveness, but is guilty of an eternal sin"—[30]for they had said, "He has an unclean spirit."

31 And his mother and his brothers came; and standing outside they sent to him and called him. [32]And a crowd was sitting about him; and they said to him, "Your mother and your brothers[j] are outside, asking for you." [33]And he replied, "Who are my mother and my brothers?" [34]And looking around on those who sat about him, he said, "Here are my mother and my brothers! [35]Whoever does the will of God is my brother, and sister, and mother."

τοῖς   υἱοῖς   τῶν   ἀνθρώπων   τὰ   ἁμαρτήματα
to the sons   -   of men   the   sins
καὶ   αἱ   βλασφημίαι,   ὅσα   ἐὰν   βλασφημήσωσιν·
and   the   blasphemies,   whatever   they may blaspheme;
29 ὃς   δ'   ἂν   βλασφημήσῃ   εἰς   τὸ   πνεῦμα
but whoever   blasphemes   against the   Spirit
τὸ   ἅγιον,   οὐκ   ἔχει   ἄφεσιν   εἰς   τὸν   αἰῶνα,
-    Holy,   has not   forgiveness   unto the   age,
ἀλλὰ   ἔνοχός   ἐστιν   αἰωνίου   ἁμαρτήματος.
but   liable   is   of an eternal   sin.
30 ὅτι   ἔλεγον·   πνεῦμα   ἀκάθαρτον   ἔχει.
Because   they said: spirit   an unclean   he has.
31 Καὶ   ἔρχονται   ἡ   μήτηρ   αὐτοῦ   καὶ   οἱ
And   come   the   mother   of him   and   the
ἀδελφοὶ   αὐτοῦ,   καὶ   ἔξω   στήκοντες   ἀπέστειλαν
brothers   of him,   and   outside   standing   sent
πρὸς   αὐτὸν   καλοῦντες   αὐτόν.   32 καὶ
to   him   calling   him.   And
ἐκάθητο   περὶ   αὐτὸν   ὄχλος,   καὶ   λέγουσιν
sat   round   him   a crowd,   and   they say
αὐτῷ·   ἰδοὺ   ἡ   μήτηρ   σου   καὶ   οἱ   ἀδελφοί
to him: Behold[,]   the   mother   of thee   and   the   brothers
σου   καὶ   αἱ   ἀδελφαί   σου   ἔξω   ζητοῦσίν   σε.
of thee   and   the   sisters   of thee   outside   seek   thee.
33 καὶ   ἀποκριθεὶς   αὐτοῖς   λέγει·   τίς   ἐστιν
And   answering   them   he says: Who   is
ἡ   μήτηρ   μου   καὶ   οἱ   ἀδελφοί;   34 καὶ
the   mother   of me   and   the   brothers?   And
περιβλεψάμενος   τοὺς   περὶ   αὐτὸν   κύκλῳ
looking round   [at] the [ones]   round   him   in a circle
καθημένους   λέγει·   ἴδε   ἡ   μήτηρ   μου
sitting   he says: Behold[,]   the   mother   of me
καὶ   οἱ   ἀδελφοί   μου.   35 ὃς   ἂν   ποιήσῃ   τὸ
and   the   brothers   of me.   Whoever   does   the
θέλημα   τοῦ   θεοῦ,   οὗτος   ἀδελφός   μου
will   -   of God,   this one   brother   of me
καὶ   ἀδελφὴ   καὶ   μήτηρ   ἐστίν.
and   sister   and   mother   is.

CHAPTER 4

AGAIN he began to teach beside the sea. And a very large crowd gathered about him, so that he got into a boat and sat in it on the sea;

4 Καὶ   πάλιν   ἤρξατο   διδάσκειν   παρὰ   τὴν
And   again   he began   to teach   by   the
θάλασσαν·   καὶ   συνάγεται   πρὸς   αὐτὸν   ὄχλος
sea;   and   is assembled   to   him   crowd
πλεῖστος,   ὥστε   αὐτὸν   εἰς   πλοῖον   ἐμβάντα
a very large,   so as   him   in   a ship   embarking
= so that embarking in a ship he sat
καθῆσθαι   ἐν   τῇ   θαλάσσῃ,   καὶ   πᾶς   ὁ
to sit[b]   in   the   sea,   and   all   the

[j] Other early authorities add and your sisters

and the whole crowd was beside the sea on the land. ²And he taught them many things in parables, and in his teaching he said to them: ³"Listen! A sower went out to sow. ⁴And as he sowed, some seed fell along the path, and the birds came and devoured it. ⁵Other seed fell on rocky ground, where it had not much soil, and immediately it sprang up, since it had no depth of soil; ⁶and when the sun rose it was scorched, and since it had no root it withered away. ⁷Other seed fell among thorns and the thorns grew up and choked it, and it yielded no grain. ⁸And other seeds fell into good soil and brought forth grain, growing up and increasing and yielding thirtyfold and sixtyfold and a hundredfold." ⁹And he said, "He who has ears to hear, let him hear."

10 And when he was alone, those who were about him with the twelve asked him concerning the parables. ¹¹And he said to them, "To you has been given the secret of the kingdom

ὄχλος	πρὸς	τὴν	θάλασσαν	ἐπὶ	τῆς	γῆς
crowd	toward	the	sea	on	the	land

ἦσαν. **2** καὶ ἐδίδασκεν αὐτοὺς ἐν παραβολαῖς
were.   And he taught   them   in   parables

πολλά, καὶ ἔλεγεν αὐτοῖς ἐν τῇ διδαχῇ
many things, and   said   to them   in   the   teaching

αὐτοῦ· **3** ἀκούετε. ἰδοὺ ἐξῆλθεν ὁ σπείρων
of him: Hear ye. Behold[,] went out the [one] sowing

σπεῖραι. **4** καὶ ἐγένετο ἐν τῷ σπείρειν
to sow.   And it came to pass in   the   to sowᵉ
                               = as he sowed

ὃ μὲν ἔπεσεν παρὰ τὴν ὁδόν, καὶ ἦλθεν
some   fell   by   the   way,   and   came

τὰ πετεινὰ καὶ κατέφαγεν αὐτό. **5** καὶ
the   birds   and   devoured   it.   And

ἄλλο ἔπεσεν ἐπὶ τὸ πετρῶδες ὅπου οὐκ
other   fell   on   the   rocky place   where   not

εἶχεν γῆν πολλήν, καὶ εὐθὺς ἐξανέτειλεν
it had   earth   much,   and immediately it sprang up

διὰ τὸ μὴ ἔχειν βάθος γῆς·
on account of the   not   to have   depth   of earth;
= because it had no depth of earth;

6 καὶ ὅτε ἀνέτειλεν ὁ ἥλιος ἐκαυματίσθη, καὶ
and when   rose   the sun   it was scorched,   and

διὰ τὸ μὴ ἔχειν ῥίζαν ἐξηράνθη. **7** καὶ
on account of the   not to have   root it was withered.   And
= because it had no root

ἄλλο ἔπεσεν εἰς τὰς ἀκάνθας, καὶ ἀνέβησαν
other   fell   among the   thorns,   and   came up

αἱ ἄκανθαι καὶ συνέπνιξαν αὐτό, καὶ
the   thorns   and   choked   it,   and

καρπὸν οὐκ ἔδωκεν. **8** καὶ ἄλλα ἔπεσεν
fruit   it gave not.   And   others   fell

εἰς τὴν γῆν τὴν καλὴν καὶ ἐδίδου καρπὸν
into the   earth   –   good   and gave   fruit

ἀναβαίνοντα καὶ αὐξανόμενα καὶ ἔφερεν
coming up   and   growing   and   bore

εἰς τριάκοντα καὶ ἐν ἑξήκοντα καὶ ἐν
in   thirty   and in   sixty   and in

ἑκατόν. **9** καὶ ἔλεγεν· ὃς ἔχει ὦτα
a hundred.   And   he said: Who has   ears

ἀκούειν ἀκουέτω. **10** Καὶ ὅτε ἐγένετο
to hear   let him hear.   And   when   he was

κατὰ μόνας, ἠρώτων αὐτὸν οἱ περὶ
alone,†   asked   him the [ones] round

αὐτὸν σὺν τοῖς δώδεκα τὰς παραβολάς.
him   with   the   twelve   the   parables.

11 καὶ ἔλεγεν αὐτοῖς· ὑμῖν τὸ μυστήριον
And   he said   to them: To you   the   mystery

of God, but for those outside everything is in parables; ¹²so that they may indeed see but not perceive, and may indeed hear but not understand; lest they should turn again, and be forgiven." ¹³And he said to them, "Do you not understand this parable? How then will you understand all the parables? ¹⁴The sower sows the word. ¹⁵And these are the ones along the path, where the word is sown; when they hear, Satan immediately comes and takes away the word which is sown in them. ¹⁶And these in like manner are the ones sown upon rocky ground, who, when they hear the word, immediately receive it with joy; ¹⁷and they have no root in themselves, but endure for a while; then, when tribulation or persecution arises on account of the word, immediately they fall away.ᵏ ¹⁸And others are the ones sown among thorns; they are those who hear the word, ¹⁹but the cares of the world, and the delight in riches, and the desire for other things, enter in and

ᵏ Or *stumble*

δέδοται   τῆς βασιλείας τοῦ θεοῦ· ἐκείνοις δὲ
has been given of the kingdom   – of God; but to those
τοῖς   ἔξω   ἐν   παραβολαῖς τὰ   πάντα
the [ones] outside in   parables   –   all things
γίνεται, 12 ἵνα βλέποντες βλέπωσιν καὶ
is(are),   that seeing   they may see and
μὴ   ἴδωσιν, καὶ ἀκούοντες ἀκούωσιν καὶ
not perceive, and hearing   they may hear and
μὴ   συνιῶσιν, μήποτε ἐπιστρέψωσιν καὶ
not understand, lest   they should turn and
ἀφεθῇ   αὐτοῖς. 13 καὶ λέγει αὐτοῖς·
it should be forgiven them.   And he says to them:
οὐκ οἴδατε τὴν παραβολὴν ταύτην, καὶ πῶς
Know ye not   –   parable   this,   and how
πάσας τὰς παραβολὰς γνώσεσθε; 14   ὁ
all   the parables   will ye know?   The [one]
σπείρων τὸν λόγον σπείρει. 15 οὗτοι δέ εἰσιν
sowing ²the ³word ¹sows.   And these are
οἱ   παρὰ τὴν ὁδόν, ὅπου σπείρεται ὁ
the [ones] by   the   way, where is sown the
λόγος, καὶ ὅταν ἀκούσωσιν, εὐθὺς ἔρχεται
word, and when they hear, immediately comes
ὁ σατανᾶς καὶ αἴρει τὸν λόγον τὸν
–   Satan   and takes the word   –
ἐσπαρμένον εἰς αὐτούς. 16 καὶ οὗτοί εἰσιν
having been sown in them.   And these are
ὁμοίως οἱ ἐπὶ τὰ πετρώδη σπειρόμενοι,
likewise the [ones] on the rocky places being sown,
οἳ ὅταν ἀκούσωσιν τὸν λόγον εὐθὺς
who when they hear   the word   immediately
μετὰ χαρᾶς λαμβάνουσιν αὐτόν, 17 καὶ
with   joy   receive   it,   and
οὐκ ἔχουσιν ῥίζαν ἐν ἑαυτοῖς ἀλλὰ
have not root   in themselves but
πρόσκαιροί εἰσιν, εἶτα γενομένης θλίψεως
shortlived are,   then happening affliction
            = when affliction or persecution happens
ἢ διωγμοῦ διὰ τὸν λόγον εὐθὺς
or persecutionª on account of the   word immediately
σκανδαλίζονται. 18 καὶ ἄλλοι εἰσὶν οἱ εἰς
they are offended.   And others are the [ones] among
τὰς ἀκάνθας σπειρόμενοι· οὗτοί εἰσιν οἱ
the thorns   being sown;   these are the [ones]
τὸν λόγον ἀκούσαντες, 19 καὶ αἱ μέριμναι
the   word hearing,   and the cares
τοῦ αἰῶνος καὶ ἡ ἀπάτη τοῦ πλούτου
of the age   and the deceitfulness – of riches
καὶ αἱ περὶ τὰ λοιπὰ ἐπιθυμίαι
and ¹the ³about ⁴the ⁵other things ²desires

choke the word, and it proves unfruitful. [20]But those that were sown upon the good soil are the ones who hear the word and accept it and bear fruit, thirtyfold and sixtyfold and a hundredfold."

21 And he said to them, "Is a lamp brought in to be put under a bushel, or under a bed, and not on a stand? [22]For there is nothing hid, except to be made manifest; nor is anything secret, except to come to light. [23]If any man has ears to hear, let him hear." [24]And he said to them, "Take heed what you hear; the measure you give will be the measure you get, and still more will be given you. [25]For to him who has will more be given; and from him who has not, even what he has will be taken away."

26 And he said, "The kingdom of God is as if a man should scatter seed upon the ground, [27]and should sleep and rise night and day, and the seed should sprout and grow, he knows not how. [28]The earth produces of itself, first the blade, then

εἰσπορευόμεναι συμπνίγουσιν τὸν λόγον, καὶ
coming in   choke   the   word,   and

ἄκαρπος γίνεται. 20 καὶ ἐκεῖνοί εἰσιν
unfruitful   it becomes.   And   those   are

οἱ ἐπὶ τὴν γῆν τὴν καλὴν σπαρέντες,
the[ones] on   the   earth   -   good   sown,

οἵτινες ἀκούουσιν τὸν λόγον καὶ παραδέχονται
who   hear   the   word   and   welcome [it]

καὶ καρποφοροῦσιν ἐν τριάκοντα καὶ ἐν
and   bear fruit   in   thirty   and   in

ἑξήκοντα καὶ ἐν ἑκατόν. 21 Καὶ ἔλεγεν
sixty   and   in   a hundred.   And   he said

αὐτοῖς ὅτι μήτι ἔρχεται ὁ λύχνος ἵνα
to them[,]   -   not   Comes   the   lamp   that

ὑπὸ τὸν μόδιον τεθῇ ἢ ὑπὸ τὴν
under   the   bushel   it may be placed   or   under   the

κλίνην; οὐχ ἵνα ἐπὶ τὴν λυχνίαν
couch?   not   that   on   the   lampstand

τεθῇ; 22 οὐ γάρ ἐστίν τι κρυπτόν,
it may be placed?   For there is not   anything   hidden,

ἐὰν μὴ ἵνα φανερωθῇ· οὐδὲ ἐγένετο
except   that it may be manifested;   nor   became

ἀπόκρυφον, ἀλλ' ἵνα ἔλθῃ εἰς φανερόν.
covered,   but   that it may come into [the] open.

23 εἴ τις ἔχει ὦτα ἀκούειν ἀκουέτω.
If   anyone   has   ears   to hear   let him hear.

24 Καὶ ἔλεγεν αὐτοῖς· βλέπετε τί
And   he said   to them: Take heed   what

ἀκούετε. ἐν ᾧ μέτρῳ μετρεῖτε
ye hear.   With   what   measure   ye measure

μετρηθήσεται ὑμῖν, καὶ προστεθήσεται ὑμῖν.
it will be measured   to you,   and   it will be added   to you.

25 ὃς γὰρ ἔχει, δοθήσεται αὐτῷ· καὶ ὃς
For [he] who   has,   it will be given   to him;   and   who

οὐκ ἔχει, καὶ ὃ ἔχει ἀρθήσεται ἀπ'
has not,   even   what he has   will be taken   from

αὐτοῦ. 26 Καὶ ἔλεγεν· οὕτως ἐστὶν ἡ
him.   And   he said: Thus   is   the

βασιλεία τοῦ θεοῦ, ὡς ἄνθρωπος βάλῃ
kingdom   -   of God,   as   a man   might cast

τὸν σπόρον ἐπὶ τῆς γῆς, 27 καὶ καθεύδῃ
the   seed   on   the   earth,   and   might sleep

καὶ ἐγείρηται νύκτα καὶ ἡμέραν, καὶ ὁ
and   rise   night   and   day,   and   the

σπόρος βλαστᾷ καὶ μηκύνηται ὡς οὐκ
seed   sprouts   and   lengthens   as   not

οἶδεν αὐτός. 28 αὐτομάτη ἡ γῆ καρποφορεῖ,
knows   he.   Of its own accord   the earth   bears fruit,

the ear, then the full grain in the ear. ²⁹But when the grain is ripe, at once he puts in the sickle, because the harvest has come."

30 And he said, "With what can we compare the kingdom of God, or what parable shall we use for it? ³¹It is like a grain of mustard seed, which, when sown upon the ground, is the smallest of all the seeds on earth; ³²yet when it is sown it grows up and becomes the greatest of all shrubs, and puts forth large branches, so that the birds of the air can make nests in its shade."

33 With many such parables he spoke the word to them, as they were able to hear it; ³⁴he did not speak to them without a parable, but privately to his own disciples he explained everything.

35 On that day, when evening had come, he said to them, "Let us go across to the other side." ³⁶And leaving the crowd, they took him with them, just as he was, in the boat. And other boats were with him. ³⁷And a great storm of wind

---

πρῶτον χόρτον, εἶτεν στάχυν, εἶτεν πλήρης
first   grass,   then an ear, then   full

σῖτος ἐν τῷ στάχυϊ. 29 ὅταν δὲ παραδοῖ
corn in the ear.   But when permits

ὁ καρπός, εὐθὺς ἀποστέλλει τὸ δρέπανον,
the fruit, immediately he sends(puts)forth the sickle,

ὅτι παρέστηκεν ὁ θερισμός. 30 Καὶ ἔλεγεν·
because has come the harvest.   And he said:

πῶς ὁμοιώσωμεν τὴν βασιλείαν τοῦ θεοῦ,
How may we liken the kingdom - of God,

ἢ ἐν τίνι αὐτὴν παραβολῇ θῶμεν; 31 ὡς
or by ¹what ⁴it ²parable ³may we place?   As

κόκκῳ σινάπεως, ὃς ὅταν σπαρῇ ἐπὶ τῆς
a grain of mustard, which when it is sown on the

γῆς, μικρότερον ὂν πάντων τῶν σπερμάτων
earth, smaller being [than] all the   seeds

τῶν ἐπὶ τῆς γῆς, 32 καὶ ὅταν σπαρῇ,
-   on the earth,   and when it is sown,

ἀναβαίνει καὶ γίνεται μεῖζον πάντων τῶν
comes up and becomes greater [than] all the

λαχάνων, καὶ ποιεῖ κλάδους μεγάλους,
herbs, and makes branches great,

ὥστε δύνασθαι ὑπὸ τὴν σκιὰν αὐτοῦ τὰ
so as to be able under the shade of it the
= so that the birds of heaven are able to dwell under its shade.

πετεινὰ τοῦ οὐρανοῦ κατασκηνοῦν. 33 Καὶ
birds   - of heaven to dwell.ᵇ   And

τοιαύταις παραβολαῖς πολλαῖς ἐλάλει αὐτοῖς
³such   ²parables ¹in many he spoke to them

τὸν λόγον, καθὼς ἠδύναντο ἀκούειν·
the word,   as   they were able to hear;

34 χωρὶς δὲ παραβολῆς οὐκ ἐλάλει αὐτοῖς,
and without a parable he spoke not to them,

κατ' ἰδίαν δὲ τοῖς ἰδίοις μαθηταῖς ἐπέλυεν
but privately to the(his) own disciples he explained

πάντα.
all things.

35 Καὶ λέγει αὐτοῖς ἐν ἐκείνῃ τῇ
And he says to them on that -

ἡμέρα ὀψίας γενομένης· διέλθωμεν εἰς τὸ
day evening having comeᵃ: Let us pass over to the
= when evening had come:

πέραν. 36 καὶ ἀφέντες τὸν ὄχλον
other side. And leaving the crowd

παραλαμβάνουσιν αὐτὸν ὡς ἦν ἐν τῷ
they take   him   as he was in the

πλοίῳ, καὶ ἄλλα πλοῖα ἦν μετ' αὐτοῦ.
ship, and other ships were with him.

37 καὶ γίνεται λαῖλαψ μεγάλη ἀνέμου,
And occurs storm a great of wind,

arose, and the waves beat into the boat, so that the boat was already filling. ³⁸ But he was in the stern, asleep on the cushion; and they woke him and said to him, "Teacher, do you not care if we perish?" ³⁹ And he awoke and rebuked the wind, and said to the sea, "Peace! Be still!" And the wind ceased, and there was a great calm. ⁴⁰ He said to them, "Why are you afraid? Have you no faith?" ⁴¹ And they were filled with awe, and said to one another, "Who then is this, that even wind and sea obey him?"

καὶ τὰ κύματα ἐπέβαλλεν εἰς τὸ πλοῖον,
and the waves struck into the ship,

ὥστε ἤδη γεμίζεσθαι τὸ πλοῖον. 38 καὶ
so as now to be filled the ship.ᵇ And

αὐτὸς ἦν ἐν τῇ πρύμνῃ ἐπὶ τὸ
he was in the stern on the

προσκεφάλαιον καθεύδων. καὶ ἐγείρουσιν
pillow sleeping. And they rouse

αὐτὸν καὶ λέγουσιν αὐτῷ· διδάσκαλε, οὐ μέλει
him and say to him: Teacher, matters it not

σοι ὅτι ἀπολλύμεθα; 39 καὶ διεγερθεὶς
to thee that we are perishing? And being roused

ἐπετίμησεν τῷ ἀνέμῳ καὶ εἶπεν τῇ
he rebuked the wind and said to the

θαλάσσῃ· σιώπα, πεφίμωσο. καὶ ἐκόπασεν
sea: Be quiet, be muzzled. And dropped

ὁ ἄνεμος, καὶ ἐγένετο γαλήνη μεγάλη.
the wind, and there was calm a great.

40 καὶ εἶπεν αὐτοῖς· τί δειλοί ἐστε
And he said to them: Why fearful are ye

οὕτως; πῶς οὐκ ἔχετε πίστιν; 41 καὶ
thus? how have ye not faith? And

ἐφοβήθησαν φόβον μέγαν, καὶ ἔλεγον πρὸς
they feared fear a great, and said to

ἀλλήλους· τίς ἄρα οὗτός ἐστιν, ὅτι καὶ
one another: Who then this man is, that both

ὁ ἄνεμος καὶ ἡ θάλασσα ὑπακούει αὐτῷ;
the wind and the sea obeys him?

CHAPTER 5

THEY came to the other side of the sea, to the country of the Ger'asenes. ¹ ² And when he had come out of the boat, there met him out of the tombs a man with an unclean spirit, ³ who lived among the tombs; and no one could bind him any more, even with a chain; ⁴ for he had often been bound with fetters and chains, but

5 Καὶ ἦλθον εἰς τὸ πέραν τῆς θαλάσσης
And they came to the other side of the sea

εἰς τὴν χώραν τῶν Γερασηνῶν. 2 καὶ
into the country of the Gerasenes. And

ἐξελθόντος αὐτοῦ ἐκ τοῦ πλοίου, [εὐθὺς]
coming out himᵃ out of the ship, immediately
= as he came out

ὑπήντησεν αὐτῷ ἐκ τῶν μνημείων ἄνθρωπος
met him out of the tombs a man

ἐν πνεύματι ἀκαθάρτῳ, 3 ὃς τὴν κατοίκησιν
in(with) spirit an unclean, who the(his) dwelling

εἶχεν ἐν τοῖς μνήμασιν, καὶ οὐδὲ ἁλύσει
had among the tombs, and not with a chain
=no one any more

οὐκέτι οὐδεὶς ἐδύνατο αὐτὸν δῆσαι, 4 διὰ
no longer no one was able him to bind, on account of
was able to bind him with a chain, = because

τὸ αὐτὸν πολλάκις πέδαις καὶ ἁλύσεσιν
the him often with fetters and chains
he had often been bound with fetters and chains, and . . .

the chains he wrenched apart, and the fetters he broke in pieces; and no one had the strength to subdue him. ⁵Night and day among the tombs and on the mountains he was always crying out, and bruising himself with stones. ⁶And when he saw Jesus from afar, he ran and worshiped him; ⁷and crying out with a loud voice, he said, "What have you to do with me, Jesus, Son of the Most High God? I adjure you by God, do not torment me." ⁸For he had said to him, "Come out of the man, you unclean spirit!" ⁹And Jesus asked him, "What is your name?" He replied, "My name is Legion; for we are many." ¹⁰And he begged him eagerly not to send them out of the country. ¹¹Now a great herd of swine was feeding there on the hillside; ¹²and they begged him, "Send us to the swine, let us enter them." ¹³So he gave them leave. And the unclean spirits came out, and entered the swine; and the herd, numbering about two thousand, rushed down the steep

δεδέσθαι,   καὶ διεσπάσθαι ὑπ' αὐτοῦ τὰς
to have been bound, and to be burst by   him   the

ἀλύσεις καὶ τὰς πέδας συντετρῖφθαι, καὶ
chains   and the fetters to have been broken, and

οὐδεὶς ἴσχυεν αὐτὸν δαμάσαι· 5 καὶ
no one was able him   to subdue;   and

διὰ παντὸς νυκτὸς καὶ ἡμέρας ἐν τοῖς μνήμασιν
always of(by) night and day among the   tombs

καὶ ἐν τοῖς ὄρεσιν ἦν κράζων καὶ
and in the mountains he was crying out and

κατακόπτων ἑαυτὸν λίθοις. 6 καὶ ἰδὼν
cutting   himself with stones.   And seeing

τὸν Ἰησοῦν ἀπὸ μακρόθεν ἔδραμεν καὶ
–   Jesus   from   afar   he ran   and

προσεκύνησεν αὐτόν, 7 καὶ κράξας φωνῇ
worshipped   him,   and crying out with a voice

μεγάλῃ λέγει· τί ἐμοὶ καὶ σοί, Ἰησοῦ
great(loud) he says: What to me and to thee, Jesus

υἱὲ τοῦ θεοῦ τοῦ ὑψίστου; ὁρκίζω σε
Son – of God the most high ? I adjure thee

τὸν θεόν, μή με βασανίσῃς. 8 ἔλεγεν
– by God, not me thou mayest torment. he said

γὰρ αὐτῷ· ἔξελθε τὸ πνεῦμα τὸ ἀκάθαρτον
For to him: Come out the spirit – unclean

ἐκ τοῦ ἀνθρώπου. 9 καὶ ἐπηρώτα αὐτόν·
out of the   man.   And he questioned him:

τί ὄνομά σοι; καὶ λέγει αὐτῷ· λεγιών·
What name to thee?ᵉ And he says to him: Legion
= What name hast thou ?   = My

ὄνομά μοι, ὅτι πολλοί ἐσμεν. 10 καὶ
name to me,ᵉ because many we are.   And
name is Legion,

παρεκάλει αὐτὸν πολλὰ ἵνα μὴ αὐτὰ
he besought him   much   that not them

ἀποστείλῃ ἔξω τῆς χώρας. 11 ἦν δὲ
he would send outside the country.   Now there was

ἐκεῖ πρὸς τῷ ὄρει ἀγέλη χοίρων μεγάλη
there near the mountain herd of pigs a great

βοσκομένη· 12 καὶ παρεκάλεσαν αὐτὸν
feeding;   and   they besought   him

λέγοντες· πέμψον ἡμᾶς εἰς τοὺς χοίρους,
saying: Send   us   into the   pigs,

ἵνα εἰς αὐτοὺς εἰσέλθωμεν. 13 καὶ ἐπέτρεψεν
that into them   we may enter.   And he allowed

αὐτοῖς. καὶ ἐξελθόντα τὰ πνεύματα τὰ
them.   And coming out the spirits –

ἀκάθαρτα εἰσῆλθον εἰς τοὺς χοίρους, καὶ
unclean   entered   into the   pigs,   and

ὥρμησεν ἡ ἀγέλη κατὰ τοῦ κρημνοῦ εἰς
rushed   the herd down the precipice into

bank into the sea, and were drowned in the sea.

14 The herdsmen fled, and told it in the city and in the country. And people came to see what it was that had happened. [15]And they came to Jesus, and saw the demoniac sitting there, clothed and in his right mind, the man who had had the legion; and they were afraid. [16]And those who had seen it told what had happened to the demoniac and to the swine. [17]And they began to beg Jesus to depart from their neighborhood. [18]And as he was getting into the boat, the man who had been possessed with demons begged him that he might be with him. [19]But he refused, and said to him, "Go home to your friends, and tell them how much the Lord has done for you, and how he has had mercy on you." [20]And he went away and began to proclaim in the Decap'olis how much Jesus had done for him; and all men marveled.

21 And when Jesus had crossed again in the boat to the other side, a great crowd gathered

τὴν θάλασσαν, ὡς δισχίλιοι, καὶ ἐπνίγοντο
the   sea,   about two thousand, and   were choked

ἐν τῇ θαλάσσῃ. **14** καὶ οἱ βόσκοντες
in   the   sea.   And the [ones]   feeding

αὐτοὺς ἔφυγον καὶ ἀπήγγειλαν εἰς τὴν
them   fled   and   reported   in   the

πόλιν καὶ εἰς τοὺς ἀγρούς· καὶ ἦλθον
city   and   in   the   fields;   and they came

ἰδεῖν τί ἐστιν τὸ γεγονός. **15** καὶ
to see   what   is   the thing   having happened.   And

ἔρχονται πρὸς τὸν Ἰησοῦν, καὶ θεωροῦσιν τὸν
they come   to   -   Jesus,   and   see   the

δαιμονιζόμενον καθήμενον ἱματισμένον καὶ
demon-possessed man   sitting   *having been* clothed   and

σωφρονοῦντα, τὸν ἐσχηκότα τὸν λεγιῶνα,
being in his senses, the man   having had   the   legion,

καὶ ἐφοβήθησαν. **16** καὶ διηγήσαντο αὐτοῖς οἱ
and they were afraid.   And   related   to them the [ones]

ἰδόντες πῶς ἐγένετο τῷ δαιμονιζομένῳ
seeing   how   it happened   to the demon-possessed man

καὶ περὶ τῶν χοίρων. **17** καὶ ἤρξαντο
and   about   the   pigs.   And   they began

παρακαλεῖν αὐτὸν ἀπελθεῖν ἀπὸ τῶν ὁρίων
to beseech   him   to depart   from   the   territory

αὐτῶν. **18** καὶ ἐμβαίνοντος αὐτοῦ εἰς τὸ
of them.   And   embarking   him[a]   in   the
                  = as he embarked

πλοῖον παρεκάλει αὐτὸν ὁ δαιμονισθεὶς
ship   besought   him the [one] demon-possessed

ἵνα μετ᾽ αὐτοῦ ᾖ. **19** καὶ οὐκ ἀφῆκεν
that with   him he might be.   And   he permitted not

αὐτόν, ἀλλὰ λέγει αὐτῷ· ὕπαγε εἰς τὸν
him,   but   says   to him: Go   to   the

οἶκόν σου πρὸς τοὺς σούς, καὶ ἀπάγγειλον
house of thee   to   the   thine,   and   report
                = thy people,

αὐτοῖς ὅσα ὁ κύριός σοι πεποίηκεν καὶ
to them what things the   Lord   to thee   has done   and

ἠλέησέν σε. **20** καὶ ἀπῆλθεν καὶ ἤρξατο
pitied   thee.   And   he departed   and   began

κηρύσσειν ἐν τῇ Δεκαπόλει ὅσα ἐποίησεν
to proclaim   in   the   Decapolis   what things   did

αὐτῷ . ὁ Ἰησοῦς, καὶ πάντες ἐθαύμαζον.
to him   -   Jesus,   and   all men   marvelled.

21 Καὶ διαπεράσαντος τοῦ Ἰησοῦ ἐν τῷ
And   crossing over   -   Jesus[a]   in   the
       = when Jesus had crossed over

πλοίῳ πάλιν εἰς τὸ πέραν συνήχθη ὄχλος
ship   again   to   the   other side   was assembled   crowd

about him; and he was
beside the sea. ²²Then
came one of the rulers of
the synagogue, Ja'irus by
name; and seeing him, he
fell at his feet, ²³and
besought him, saying,
"My little daughter is at
the point of death. Come
and lay your hands on
her, so that she may be
made well, and live."
²⁴And he went with him.

And a great crowd
followed him and
thronged about him.
²⁵And there was a woman
who had had a flow of
blood for twelve years,
²⁶and who had suffered
much under many physi-
cians, and had spent all
that she had, and was no
better but rather grew
worse. ²⁷She had heard
the reports about Jesus,
and came up behind him
in the crowd and touched
his garment. ²⁸For she
said, "If I touch even his
garments, I shall be made
well." ²⁹And immediately
the hemorrhage ceased;
and she felt in her body
that she was healed of
her disease. ³⁰And Jesus,
perceiving in himself that
power had gone forth
from him, immediately
turned about in the
crowd, and said, "Who
touched my garments?"
³¹And his disciples said

πολὺς   ἐπ' αὐτόν, καὶ   ἦν   παρὰ τὴν θάλασσαν.
a much(great) to   him,   and he was by   the   sea.

22 Καὶ   ἔρχεται   εἷς   τῶν   ἀρχισυναγώγων,
And   comes   one   of the   synagogue chiefs,

ὀνόματι   'Ιάϊρος,   καὶ   ἰδὼν   αὐτὸν   πίπτει
by name   Jairus,   and   seeing   him   falls

πρὸς   τοὺς   πόδας   αὐτοῦ,   23 καὶ   παρακαλεῖ
at   the   feet   of him,   and   beseeches

αὐτὸν   πολλὰ   λέγων   ὅτι   τὸ   θυγάτριόν μου
him   much   saying[,] –   The   daughter   of me

ἐσχάτως   ἔχει,   ἵνα   ἐλθὼν   ἐπιθῇς
is at the point of death,†   that   coming   thou mayest lay on

τὰς   χεῖρας   αὐτῇ,   ἵνα   σωθῇ   καὶ   ζήσῃ.
the(thy) hands   on her,   that she may be healed and   may live.

24 καὶ   ἀπῆλθεν μετ'   αὐτοῦ. καὶ   ἠκολούθει αὐτῷ
And   he went   with   him.   And   followed   him

ὄχλος   πολύς,   καὶ   συνέθλιβον αὐτόν. 25 Καὶ
crowd a much(great), and   pressed upon   him.   And

γυνὴ   οὖσα   ἐν   ῥύσει   αἵματος   δώδεκα
a woman being   in   a flow   of blood   twelve
                = having

ἔτη,   26 καὶ   πολλὰ   παθοῦσα   ὑπὸ   πολλῶν
years,   and   many things   suffering   by   many

ἰατρῶν   καὶ   δαπανήσασα   τὰ   παρ'   αὐτῆς
physicians   and   having spent   the   with   her

πάντα,   καὶ   μηδὲν   ὠφεληθεῖσα ἀλλὰ   μᾶλλον
all things,   and   nothing having been profited but   rather

εἰς   τὸ   χεῖρον   ἐλθοῦσα,   27 ἀκούσασα   τὰ
to   the   worse   having come,   hearing   the things

περὶ   τοῦ   'Ιησοῦ,   ἐλθοῦσα ἐν   τῷ   ὄχλῳ
about   –   Jesus,   coming   in   the   crowd

ὄπισθεν   ἥψατο   τοῦ   ἱματίου   αὐτοῦ·   28 ἔλεγεν
behind   touched   the   garment   of him;   she said[,]

γὰρ   ὅτι   ἐὰν   ἅψωμαι   κἂν   τῶν   ἱματίων
for   –   If   I may touch   even   the   garments

αὐτοῦ,   σωθήσομαι.   29 καὶ   εὐθὺς   ἐξηράνθη
of him,   I shall be healed.   And immediately   was dried up

ἡ   πηγὴ   τοῦ   αἵματος   αὐτῆς,   καὶ   ἔγνω
the fountain   of the   blood   of her,   and   she knew

τῷ   σώματι   ὅτι   ἴαται   ἀπὸ   τῆς
in the(her) body   that   she is(was) cured from   the

μάστιγος.   30 καὶ   εὐθὺς   ὁ 'Ιησοῦς ἐπιγνοὺς ἐν
plague.   And immediately – Jesus   knowing in

ἑαυτῷ   τὴν   ἐξ   αὐτοῦ   δύναμιν   ἐξελθοῦσαν,
himself   ¹the   ⁴out of   ⁵him   ²power   ³going forth,

ἐπιστραφεὶς ἐν τῷ ὄχλῳ ἔλεγεν· τίς μου ἥψατο τῶν
turning   in the crowd   said: Who of me touched the

ἱματίων;   31 καὶ   ἔλεγον   αὐτῷ   οἱ   μαθηταὶ
garments?   And   said   to him   the   disciples

to him, "You see the crowd pressing around you, and yet you say, 'Who touched me?'" [32]And he looked around to see who had done it. [33]But the woman, knowing what had been done to her, came in fear and trembling and fell down before him, and told him the whole truth. [34]And he said to her, "Daughter, your faith has made you well; go in peace, and be healed of your disease."

35 While he was still speaking, there came from the ruler's house some who said, "Your daughter is dead. Why trouble the Teacher any further?"[36]But ignoring[m] what they said, Jesus said to the ruler of the synagogue, "Do not fear, only believe." [37]And he allowed no one to follow him except Peter and James and John the brother of James. [38]When they came to the house of the ruler of the synagogue, he saw a tumult, and people weeping and wailing loudly. [39]And when he had entered, he said to them, "Why do you make a tumult and weep? The child is not dead but sleeping." [40]And they laughed at him. But he put them all outside, and

[m] Or *overhearing.* Other ancient authorities read *hearing*

αὐτοῦ· βλέπεις τὸν ὄχλον συνθλίβοντά σε,
of him: Thou seest the crowd pressing upon thee,

καὶ λέγεις· τίς μου ἥψατο; 32 καὶ
and thou sayest: Who me touched? And

περιεβλέπετο ἰδεῖν τὴν τοῦτο ποιήσασαν.
he looked round to see the [one] this having done.

33 ἡ δὲ γυνὴ φοβηθεῖσα καὶ τρέμουσα,
And the woman fearing and trembling,

εἰδυῖα ὃ γέγονεν αὐτῇ, ἦλθεν καὶ προσέ-
knowing what has happened to her, came and fell

πεσεν αὐτῷ καὶ εἶπεν αὐτῷ πᾶσαν τὴν ἀλήθειαν.
before him and told him all the truth.

34 ὁ δὲ εἶπεν αὐτῇ· θυγάτηρ, ἡ πίστις
And he said to her: Daughter, the faith

σου σέσωκέν σε· ὕπαγε εἰς εἰρήνην, καὶ
of thee has healed thee; go in peace, and

ἴσθι ὑγιὴς ἀπὸ τῆς μάστιγός σου. 35 Ἔτι
be whole from the plague of thee. Still
                                                    = While

αὐτοῦ λαλοῦντος[a] ἔρχονται ἀπὸ τοῦ
him speaking they come from the
he was still speaking

ἀρχισυναγώγου λέγοντες ὅτι ἡ θυγάτηρ
synagogue chief saying[,] – The daughter

σου ἀπέθανεν· τί ἔτι σκύλλεις τὸν διδάσκαλον;
of thee died; why still troublest thou the teacher?

36 ὁ δὲ Ἰησοῦς παρακούσας τὸν λόγον
– But Jesus overhearing the word

λαλούμενον λέγει τῷ ἀρχισυναγώγῳ· μὴ
being spoken says to the synagogue chief: not

φοβοῦ, μόνον πίστευε. 37 καὶ οὐκ ἀφῆκεν
Fear, only believe. And he allowed not

οὐδένα μετ' αὐτοῦ συνακολουθῆσαι εἰ μὴ
no(any)one with him to accompany except

τὸν Πέτρον καὶ Ἰάκωβον καὶ Ἰωάννην
– Peter and James and John

τὸν ἀδελφὸν Ἰακώβου. 38 καὶ ἔρχονται
the brother of James. And they come

εἰς τὸν οἶκον τοῦ ἀρχισυναγώγου, καὶ
into the house of the synagogue chief, and

θεωρεῖ θόρυβον, καὶ κλαίοντάς καὶ
he sees an uproar, and [men] weeping and

ἀλαλάζοντας πολλά, 39 καὶ εἰσελθὼν λέγει
crying aloud much, and entering he says

αὐτοῖς· τί θορυβεῖσθε καὶ κλαίετε; τὸ
to them: Why make ye an uproar and weep? the

παιδίον οὐκ ἀπέθανεν ἀλλὰ καθεύδει.
child did not die but sleeps.

40 καὶ κατεγέλων αὐτοῦ. αὐτὸς δὲ ἐκβαλὼν
And they ridiculed him. But he putting out

took the child's father and mother and those who were with him, and went in where the child was. ⁴¹Taking her by the hand he said to her, "Tal'itha cu'mi"; which means, "Little girl, I say to you, arise." ⁴²And immediately the girl got up and walked; for she was twelve years old. And immediately they were overcome with amazement. ⁴³And he strictly charged them that no one should know this, and told them to give her something to eat.

πάντας παραλαμβάνει τὸν πατέρα τοῦ
all　takes　the　father　of the
παιδίου καὶ τὴν μητέρα καὶ τοὺς μετ'
child and the mother and the [ones] with
αὐτοῦ, καὶ εἰσπορεύεται ὅπου ἦν τὸ
him, and goes in where was the
παιδίον. 41 καὶ κρατήσας τῆς χειρὸς
child. And taking hold of the hand
τοῦ παιδίου λέγει αὐτῇ· ταλιθὰ κοῦμ, ὅ
of the child he says to her: Talitha koum, which
ἐστιν μεθερμηνευόμενον· τὸ κοράσιον, σοὶ
is being interpreted: - Maid, to thee
λέγω, ἔγειρε. 42 καὶ εὐθὺς ἀνέστη τὸ
I say, arise. And immediately rose up the
κοράσιον καὶ περιεπάτει· ἦν γὰρ
maid and walked; for she was
ἐτῶν δώδεκα. καὶ ἐξέστησαν εὐθὺς
[of the age] twelve. And they were astonished immediately
of years =immediately they were exceedingly astonished.
ἐκστάσει μεγάλῃ. 43 καὶ διεστείλατο
astonishment with a great. And he ordered
αὐτοῖς πολλὰ ἵνα μηδεὶς γνοῖ τοῦτο, καὶ
them much that no one should know this, and
εἶπεν δοθῆναι αὐτῇ φαγεῖν.
told to be given to her to eat.
=[them] to give her [something] to eat.

CHAPTER 6

HE went away from there and came to his own country; and his disciples followed him. ²And on the sabbath he began to teach in the synagogue; and many who heard him were astonished, saying, "Where did this man get all this? What is the wisdom given to him? What mighty works are wrought by his hands! ³Is not this the carpenter, the son of Mary and brother of James and

6 Καὶ ἐξῆλθεν ἐκεῖθεν, καὶ ἔρχεται εἰς
And he went forth thence, and comes into
τὴν πατρίδα αὐτοῦ, καὶ ἀκολουθοῦσιν
the native place of him, and follow
αὐτῷ οἱ μαθηταὶ αὐτοῦ. 2 καὶ γενομένου
him the disciples of him. And coming
= when
σαββάτου ἤρξατο διδάσκειν ἐν τῇ συναγωγῇ·
a sabbathª he began to teach in the synagogue;
a sabbath came
καὶ οἱ πολλοὶ ἀκούοντες ἐξεπλήσσοντο
and the many hearing were astonished
λέγοντες· πόθεν τούτῳ ταῦτα, καὶ τίς ἡ
saying: Whence to this man these things, and what the
σοφία ἡ δοθεῖσα τούτῳ; καὶ αἱ δυνάμεις
wisdom - given to this(him)? And the powerful deeds
τοιαῦται διὰ τῶν χειρῶν αὐτοῦ γινόμεναι;
such through the hands of him coming about?
3 οὐχ οὗτός ἐστιν ὁ τέκτων, ὁ υἱὸς
¹Not ³this man ¹is the carpenter, the son
τῆς Μαρίας καὶ ἀδελφὸς Ἰακώβου καὶ
- of Mary and brother of James and

Joses and Judas and Simon, and are not his sisters here with us?" And they took offense[n] at him. [4]And Jesus said to them, "A prophet is not without honor, except in his own country, and among his own kin, and in his own house." [5]And he could do no mighty work there, except that he laid his hands upon a few sick people and healed them. [6]And he marveled because of their unbelief.

And he went about among the villages teaching.

7 And he called to him the twelve, and began to send them out two by two, and gave them authority over the unclean spirits. [8]He charged them to take nothing for their journey except a staff; no bread, no bag, no money in their belts; [9]but to wear sandals and not put on two tunics. [10]And he said to them, "Where you enter a house, stay there until you leave the place. [11]And if any place will not receive you and they refuse to hear you, when

Ἰωσῆτος καὶ Ἰούδα καὶ Σίμωνος; καὶ
Joses and Judas and Simon? and

οὐκ εἰσὶν αἱ ἀδελφαὶ αὐτοῦ ὧδε πρὸς
[2]not [1]are the sisters of him here with

ἡμᾶς; καὶ ἐσκανδαλίζοντο ἐν αὐτῷ. 4 καὶ
us? And they were offended in(at) him. And

ἔλεγεν αὐτοῖς ὁ Ἰησοῦς ὅτι οὐκ ἔστιν
said to them - Jesus[,] - [2]not [1]is

προφήτης ἄτιμος εἰ μὴ ἐν τῇ πατρίδι
[1]A prophet unhonoured except in the native place

αὐτοῦ καὶ ἐν τοῖς συγγενεῦσιν αὐτοῦ
of him and among the relatives of him

καὶ ἐν τῇ οἰκίᾳ αὐτοῦ. 5 καὶ οὐκ
and in the house of him. And not

ἐδύνατο ἐκεῖ ποιῆσαι οὐδεμίαν δύναμιν,
he could there _to_ do no(any) powerful deed,

εἰ μὴ ὀλίγοις ἀρρώστοις ἐπιθεὶς τὰς
except _on_ a few sick [ones] laying on the(his)

χεῖρας ἐθεράπευσεν. 6 καὶ ἐθαύμασεν διὰ
hands he healed. And he marvelled because of

τὴν ἀπιστίαν αὐτῶν.
the unbelief of them.

Καὶ περιῆγεν τὰς κώμας κύκλῳ
And he went round the villages in circuit

διδάσκων. 7 Καὶ προσκαλεῖται τοὺς δώδεκα,
teaching. And he calls to [him] the twelve,

καὶ ἤρξατο αὐτοὺς ἀποστέλλειν δύο δύο,
and began them to send forth two [by] two,

καὶ ἐδίδου αὐτοῖς ἐξουσίαν τῶν πνευμάτων
and gave them authority the spirits

τῶν ἀκαθάρτων, 8 καὶ παρήγγειλεν αὐτοῖς
- of(over) unclean, and charged them

ἵνα μηδὲν αἴρωσιν εἰς ὁδὸν εἰ μὴ ῥάβδον
that nothing they should take in [the] way except a staff

μόνον, μὴ ἄρτον, μὴ πήραν, μὴ εἰς τὴν
only, not bread, not a wallet, not in the

ζώνην χαλκόν, 9 ἀλλὰ ὑποδεδεμένους σανδάλια,
girdle copper [money], but having had tied on sandals,

καὶ μὴ ἐνδύσησθε δύο χιτῶνας. 10 καὶ
and do not put on two tunics. And

ἔλεγεν αὐτοῖς· ὅπου ἐὰν εἰσέλθητε εἰς
he said to them: Wherever ye enter into

οἰκίαν, ἐκεῖ μένετε ἕως ἂν ἐξέλθητε
a house, there remain until ye go out

ἐκεῖθεν. 11 καὶ ὃς ἂν τόπος μὴ δέξηται
thence. And whatever place receives not

ὑμᾶς μηδὲ ἀκούσωσιν ὑμῶν, ἐκπορευόμενοι
you nor they hear you, going out

---

[n] Or *stumbled*

you leave, shake off the dust that is on your feet for a testimony against them." ¹²So they went out and preached that men should repent. ¹³And they cast out many demons, and anointed with oil many that were sick and healed them. 14 King Herod heard of it; for Jesus' name had become known. Some° said, "John the baptizer has been raised from the dead; that is why these powers are at work in him." ¹⁵But others said, "It is Eli′jah." And others said, "It is a prophet, like one of the prophets of old." ¹⁶But when Herod heard of it he said, "John, whom I beheaded, has been raised." ¹⁷For Herod had sent and seized John, and bound him in prison for the sake of Hero′di-as, his brother Philip's wife; because he had married her. ¹⁸For John said to Herod, "It is not lawful for you to have your brother's wife." ¹⁹And Hero′di-as had a grudge against him, and wanted to kill him. But she could not, ²⁰for Herod feared John, knowing that he

° Other ancient authorities read *he*

ἐκεῖθεν ἐκτινάξατε τὸν χοῦν τὸν ὑποκάτω
thence   shake off   the   dust   –   under

τῶν ποδῶν ὑμῶν εἰς μαρτύριον αὐτοῖς.
the   feet   of you   for   a testimony   to them.

12 Καὶ ἐξελθόντες ἐκήρυξαν ἵνα μετανοῶσιν,
And going forth they proclaimed that men should repent,

13 καὶ δαιμόνια πολλὰ ἐξέβαλλον, καὶ
and   demons   many   they expelled,   and

ἤλειφον ἐλαίῳ πολλοὺς ἀρρώστους καὶ
anointed   with oil   many   sick [ones]   and

ἐθεράπευον.
healed.

14 Καὶ ἤκουσεν ὁ βασιλεὺς Ἡρῴδης,
And   heard   the   king   Herod,

φανερὸν γὰρ ἐγένετο τὸ ὄνομα αὐτοῦ, καὶ
for manifest   became   the   name   of him,   and

ἔλεγον ὅτι Ἰωάννης ὁ βαπτίζων ἐγήγερται
they said[,] –   John   the baptizing [one] has been raised

ἐκ νεκρῶν, καὶ διὰ τοῦτο ἐνεργοῦσιν αἱ
from [the] dead,   and   therefore   operate   the

δυνάμεις ἐν αὐτῷ. 15 ἄλλοι δὲ ἔλεγον
powerful deeds in   him.   But others   said[,]

ὅτι Ἠλίας ἐστίν· ἄλλοι δὲ ἔλεγον ὅτι
–   Elias   it/he is;   and [yet] others   said[,]   ὅτι

προφήτης ὡς εἷς τῶν προφητῶν. 16 ἀκούσας δὲ
A prophet   as one of the   prophets.   But hearing

ὁ Ἡρῴδης ἔλεγεν· ὃν ἐγὼ ἀπεκεφάλισα
–   Herod   said: ²whom   ³I   ⁴beheaded

Ἰωάννην, οὗτος ἠγέρθη. 17 Αὐτὸς γὰρ ὁ
¹John,   this   was raised.   For ²himself   –

Ἡρῴδης ἀποστείλας ἐκράτησεν τὸν Ἰωάννην
¹Herod   sending   seized   –   John

καὶ ἔδησεν αὐτὸν ἐν φυλακῇ διὰ Ἡρῳδιάδα
and   bound   him   in   prison because of   Herodias

τὴν γυναῖκα Φιλίππου τοῦ ἀδελφοῦ αὐτοῦ,
the   wife   of Philip   the   brother   of him,

ὅτι αὐτὴν ἐγάμησεν· 18 ἔλεγεν γὰρ ὁ
because her   he married;   for said   –

Ἰωάννης τῷ Ἡρῴδῃ ὅτι οὐκ ἔξεστίν
John   –   to Herod[,]   –   It is not lawful

σοι ἔχειν τὴν γυναῖκα τοῦ ἀδελφοῦ σου.
for thee to have   the   wife   of the   brother of thee.

19 ἡ δὲ Ἡρῳδιὰς ἐνεῖχεν αὐτῷ καὶ
–   Now   Herodias had a grudge against him   and

ἤθελεν αὐτὸν ἀποκτεῖναι, καὶ οὐκ ἠδύνατο·
wished   ²him   ¹to kill,   and   could not;

20 ὁ γὰρ Ἡρῴδης ἐφοβεῖτο τὸν Ἰωάννην,
–   for   Herod   feared   –   John,

was a righteous and holy man, and kept him safe. When he heard him, he was much perplexed; and yet he heard him gladly. ²¹ But an opportunity came when Herod on his birthday gave a banquet for his courtiers and officers and the leading men of Galilee. ²² For when Hero'di-as' daughter came in and danced, she pleased Herod and his guests; and the king said to the girl, "Ask me for whatever you wish, and I will grant it." ²³ And he vowed to her, "Whatever you ask me, I will give you, even half of my kingdom." ²⁴ And she went out, and said to her mother, "What shall I ask?" And she said, "The head of John the baptizer." ²⁵ And she came in immediately with haste to the king, and asked, saying, "I want you to give me at once the head of John the Baptist on a platter." ²⁶ And the king was exceedingly sorry; but because of his oaths and his guests he did not want to break his word to her.

εἰδὼς αὐτὸν ἄνδρα δίκαιον καὶ ἅγιον, καὶ
knowing   him   a man   just   and   holy,   and

συνετήρει αὐτόν, καὶ ἀκούσας αὐτοῦ πολλὰ
kept safe   him,   and   hearing   him   much
= was

ἠπόρει, καὶ ἡδέως αὐτοῦ ἤκουεν. **21** καὶ
was in difficulties, and gladly   him   heard.   And
in great difficulties,

γενομένης ἡμέρας εὐκαίρου ὅτε Ἡρώδης
coming   day   a suitable^a   when   Herod
= when a suitable day came

τοῖς γενεσίοις αὐτοῦ δεῖπνον ἐποίησεν τοῖς
on the birthday festivities of him   a supper   made   for the

μεγιστᾶσιν αὐτοῦ καὶ τοῖς χιλιάρχοις καὶ
courtiers   of him   and   the   chiliarchs   and

τοῖς πρώτοις τῆς Γαλιλαίας, **22** καὶ
the   chief men   -   of Galilee,   and

εἰσελθούσης τῆς θυγατρὸς αὐτῆς τῆς
entering   the   daughter   ²of herself   -
= when the daughter of Herodias herself entered and danced,

Ἡρωδιάδος καὶ ὀρχησαμένης, ἤρεσεν τῷ
¹of Herodias   and   dancing,^a   she pleased   -

Ἡρώδῃ καὶ τοῖς συνανακειμένοις. ὁ δὲ
Herod   and the [ones] reclining with [him].   And the

βασιλεὺς εἶπεν τῷ κορασίῳ· αἴτησόν με
king   said to the   girl: Ask   me

ὃ ἐὰν θέλῃς, καὶ δώσω σοι· **23** καὶ
whatever thou wishest, and   I will give   thee;   and

ὤμοσεν αὐτῇ ὅτι ὃ ἐὰν αἰτήσῃς δώσω
he swore   to her[,]   -   Whatever thou askest I will give

σοι ἕως ἡμίσους τῆς βασιλείας μου.
thee   up to   half   of the   kingdom   of me.

24 καὶ ἐξελθοῦσα εἶπεν τῇ μητρὶ αὐτῆς·
And   going out   said   to the   mother   of her:

τί αἰτήσωμαι; ἡ δὲ εἶπεν· τὴν κεφαλὴν
What may I ask? And she   said: The   head

Ἰωάννου τοῦ βαπτίζοντος. **25** καὶ
of John   the [one]   baptizing.   And

εἰσελθοῦσα εὐθὺς μετὰ σπουδῆς πρὸς τὸν
entering   immediately with   haste   to   the

βασιλέα ᾐτήσατο λέγουσα· θέλω ἵνα ἐξαυτῆς
king   she asked   saying: I wish   that   at once

δῷς μοι ἐπὶ πίνακι τὴν κεφαλὴν Ἰωάννου
thou mayest give me on   a dish   the   head   of John

τοῦ βαπτιστοῦ. **26** καὶ περίλυπος γενόμενος
the   Baptist.   And   deeply grieved   becoming

ὁ βασιλεὺς διὰ τοὺς ὅρκους καὶ τοὺς
the   king   because of the   oaths   and the [ones]

ἀνακειμένους οὐκ ἠθέλησεν ἀθετῆσαι αὐτήν.
reclining   did not wish   to reject   her.

²⁷And immediately the king sent a soldier of the guard and gave orders to bring his head. He went and beheaded him in the prison, ²⁸and brought his head on a platter, and gave it to the girl; and the girl gave it to her mother. ²⁹When his disciples heard of it, they came and took his body, and laid it in a tomb.

30 The apostles returned to Jesus, and told him all that they had done and taught. ³¹And he said to them, "Come away by yourselves to a lonely place, and rest a while." For many were coming and going, and they had no leisure even to eat. ³²And they went away in the boat to a lonely place by themselves. ³³Now many saw them going, and knew them, and they ran there on foot from all the towns, and got there ahead of them. ³⁴As he landed he saw a great throng, and he had compassion on them, because they were like sheep without a shepherd; and he began to teach them

27 καὶ   εὐθὺς   ἀποστείλας   ὁ   βασιλεὺς
And   immediately   ²sending   ¹the   ³king

σπεκουλάτορα   ἐπέταξεν   ἐνέγκαι   τὴν   κεφαλὴν
an executioner   gave order   to bring   the   head

αὐτοῦ.   καὶ   ἀπελθὼν   ἀπεκεφάλισεν   αὐτὸν
of him.   And   going   he beheaded   him

ἐν   τῇ   φυλακῇ,   28 καὶ   ἤνεγκεν   τὴν   κεφαλὴν
in   the   prison,   and   brought   the   head

αὐτοῦ   ἐπὶ   πίνακι   καὶ   ἔδωκεν   αὐτὴν   τῷ
of him   on   a dish   and   gave   it   to the

κορασίῳ,   καὶ   τὸ   κοράσιον   ἔδωκεν   αὐτὴν
girl,   and   the   girl   gave   it

τῇ   μητρὶ   αὐτῆς.   29 καὶ   ἀκούσαντες   οἱ
to the mother   of her.   And   hearing   the

μαθηταὶ   αὐτοῦ   ἦλθαν   καὶ   ἦραν   τὸ   πτῶμα
disciples   of him   went   and   took   the   corpse

αὐτοῦ   καὶ   ἔθηκαν   αὐτὸ   ἐν   μνημείῳ.
of him   and   put   it   in   a tomb.

30 Καὶ   συνάγονται   οἱ   ἀπόστολοι   πρὸς
And   assemble   the   apostles   to

τὸν   Ἰησοῦν,   καὶ   ἀπήγγειλαν   αὐτῷ   πάντα
-   Jesus,   and   reported   to him   all things

ὅσα   ἐποίησαν   καὶ   ὅσα   ἐδίδαξαν.   31 καὶ
which   they did   and   which   they taught.   And

λέγει   αὐτοῖς·   δεῦτε   ὑμεῖς   αὐτοὶ   κατ'
he says   to them: Come   ye   [your]selves   pri-

ἰδίαν   εἰς   ἔρημον   τόπον   καὶ   ἀναπαύσασθε   ὀλίγον.
vately to.   a desert   place   and   rest   a little.

ἦσαν   γὰρ   οἱ   ἐρχόμενοι   καὶ   οἱ
For ²were   ³the [ones]   ⁴coming   ⁵and   ⁶the [ones]

ὑπάγοντες   πολλοί,   καὶ   οὐδὲ   φαγεῖν
⁷going   ¹many,   and   not   to eat

εὐκαίρουν.   32 καὶ   ἀπῆλθον   ἐν   τῷ   πλοίῳ
they had opportunity.   And   they went away   in   the   ship

εἰς   ἔρημον   τόπον   κατ'   ἰδίαν.   33 καὶ
to   a desert   place   privately.   And

εἶδον   αὐτοὺς   ὑπάγοντας   καὶ   ἐπέγνωσαν
²saw   ³them   ⁴going   ⁵and   ⁶knew

πολλοί,   καὶ   πεζῇ   ἀπὸ   πασῶν   τῶν   πόλεων
¹many,   and   on foot   from   all   the   cities

συνέδραμον   ἐκεῖ   καὶ   προῆλθον   αὐτούς.
ran together   there   and   came before   them.

34 Καὶ   ἐξελθὼν   εἶδεν   πολὺν   ὄχλον,   καὶ
And   going forth   he saw   a much(great)   crowd,   and

ἐσπλαγχνίσθη   ἐπ'   αὐτοὺς   ὅτι   ἦσαν   ὡς
had compassion   on   them   because they were   as

πρόβατα   μὴ   ἔχοντα   ποιμένα,   καὶ   ἤρξατο
sheep   not   having   a shepherd,   and   he began

many things. ³⁵And when it grew late, his disciples came to him and said, "This is a lonely place, and the hour is now late; ³⁶send them away, to go into the country and villages round about and buy themselves something to eat." ³⁷But he answered them, "You give them something to eat." And they said to him, "Shall we go and buy two hundred denarii worth of bread, and give it to them to eat?" ³⁸And he said to them, "How many loaves have you? Go and see." And when they had found out, they said, "Five, and two fish." ³⁹Then he commanded them all to sit down by companies upon the green grass. ⁴⁰So they sat down in groups, by hundreds and by fifties. ⁴¹And taking the five loaves and the two fish he looked up to heaven, and blessed, and broke the loaves, and gave them to the disciples to set before the people; and he divided the two fish among them all. ⁴²And

διδάσκειν	αὐτοὺς	πολλά.	**35** Καὶ	ἤδη	ὤρας
to teach	them	many things.	And	now	an hour = it being

πολλῆς	γενομένης	προσελθόντες	αὐτῷ	οἱ
much late	coming^a	approaching	to him	the

μαθηταὶ	αὐτοῦ	ἔλεγον	ὅτι	ἔρημός	ἐστιν
disciples	of him	said[,]	–	Desert	is

ὁ τόπος	καὶ	ἤδη	ὤρα	πολλή·	**36** ἀπόλυσον
the place	and	now	hour	a much; = it is late;	dismiss

αὐτούς,	ἵνα	ἀπελθόντες	εἰς	τοὺς	κύκλῳ
them,	that	going away	to	the	round about

ἀγροὺς	καὶ	κώμας	ἀγοράσωσιν	ἑαυτοῖς	τί
fields	and	villages	they may buy	for themselves	what

φάγωσιν.	**37** ὁ δὲ	ἀποκριθεὶς	εἶπεν	αὐτοῖς·
they may eat.	But he	answering	said	to them:

δότε	αὐτοῖς	ὑμεῖς	φαγεῖν.	καὶ	λέγουσιν
Give	them	ye	to eat.	And	they say

αὐτῷ·	ἀπελθόντες	ἀγοράσωμεν	δηναρίων
to him:	Going away	may we buy	²of(for) ⁴denarii

διακοσίων	ἄρτους,	καὶ	δώσομεν	αὐτοῖς
³two hundred	¹loaves,	and	shall we give	them

φαγεῖν;	**38** ὁ δὲ	λέγει	αὐτοῖς·	πόσους
to eat ?	And he	says	to them:	How many

ἔχετε	ἄρτους;	ὑπάγετε	ἴδετε.	καὶ	γνόντες
have ye	loaves ?	Go	see.	And	knowing

λέγουσιν·	πέντε,	καὶ	δύο	ἰχθύας.	**39** καὶ
they say:	Five,	and	two	fishes.	And

ἐπέταξεν	αὐτοῖς	ἀνακλιθῆναι	πάντας	συμπόσια
he instructed	them	to recline	all	companies

συμπόσια	ἐπὶ	τῷ	χλωρῷ	χόρτῳ.	**40** καὶ
companies	on	the	green	grass.	And

ἀνέπεσαν	πρασιαὶ	πρασιαὶ	κατὰ	ἑκατὸν
they reclined	groups	groups	by	a hundred

καὶ	κατὰ	πεντήκοντα.	**41** καὶ	λαβὼν	τοὺς
and	by	fifty.	And	taking	the

πέντε	ἄρτους	καὶ	τοὺς	δύο	ἰχθύας,
five	loaves	and	the	two	fishes,

ἀναβλέψας	εἰς	τὸν	οὐρανὸν	εὐλόγησεν	καὶ
looking up	to	–	heaven	he blessed	and

κατέκλασεν	τοὺς	ἄρτους	καὶ	ἐδίδου	τοῖς
broke	the	loaves	and	gave	to the

μαθηταῖς	ἵνα	παρατιθῶσιν	αὐτοῖς,	καὶ
disciples	that	they might set before	them,	and

τοὺς	δύο	ἰχθύας	ἐμέρισεν	πᾶσιν.	**42** καὶ
the	two	fishes	he divided	to all.	And

they all ate and were satisfied. ⁴³And they took up twelve baskets full of broken pieces and of the fish. ⁴⁴And those who ate the loaves were five thousand men.

45 Immediately he made his disciples get into the boat and go before him to the other side, to Beth-sa′ida, while he dismissed the crowd. ⁴⁶And after he had taken leave of them, he went into the hills to pray. ⁴⁷And when evening came, the boat was out on the sea, and he was alone on the land. ⁴⁸And he saw that they were distressed in rowing, for the wind was against them. And about the fourth watch of the night he came to them, walking on the sea. He meant to pass by them, ⁴⁹but when they saw him walking on the sea they thought it was a ghost, and cried out; ⁵⁰for they all saw him, and were terrified. But immediately he spoke to them and said, "Take heart, it is I; have no fear." ⁵¹And he got into the boat with them and the wind ceased. And they were utterly astounded,

ἔφαγον πάντες καὶ ἐχορτάσθησαν, 43 καὶ
they ate   all   and   were satisfied,   and

ἦραν κλάσματα δώδεκα κοφίνων πληρώματα
they took fragments   twelve   ²of baskets   ¹fullnesses

καὶ ἀπὸ τῶν ἰχθύων 44 καὶ ἦσαν οἱ
and   from   the   fishes.   And   were   the

φαγόντες τοὺς ἄρτους πεντακισχίλιοι ἄνδρες.
[ones] eating   the   loaves   five thousand   males.

45 Καὶ εὐθὺς ἠνάγκασεν τοὺς μαθητὰς
And   immediately   he constrained   the   disciples

αὐτοῦ ἐμβῆναι εἰς τὸ πλοῖον καὶ προάγειν
of him   to embark   in   the   ship   and to go before

εἰς τὸ πέραν πρὸς Βηθσαϊδάν, ἕως αὐτὸς
to   the other side   to   Bethsaida,   until   he

ἀπολύει τὸν ὄχλον. 46 καὶ ἀποταξάμενος
dismisses   the   crowd.   And   having said farewell

αὐτοῖς ἀπῆλθεν εἰς τὸ ὄρος προσεύξασθαι.
to them   he went away   into   the   mountain   to pray.

47 καὶ ὀψίας γενομένης ἦν τὸ πλοῖον ἐν
And   evening   coming onᵃ   was   the   ship   in
= when evening came on

μέσῳ τῆς θαλάσσης, καὶ αὐτὸς μόνος ἐπὶ
[the] midst of the   sea,   and   he   alone   on

τῆς γῆς. 48 καὶ ἰδὼν αὐτοὺς βασανιζομένους
the   land.   And   seeing   them   being distressed

ἐν τῷ ἐλαύνειν, ἦν γὰρ ὁ ἄνεμος ἐναντίος
in   the   to row,   ⁴was   ¹for   ²the   ³wind   contrary
= rowing,

αὐτοῖς, περὶ τετάρτην φυλακὴν τῆς νυκτὸς
to them,   about   [the] fourth   watch   of the   night

ἔρχεται πρὸς αὐτοὺς περιπατῶν ἐπὶ τῆς
he comes   toward   them   walking   on   the

θαλάσσης· καὶ ἤθελεν παρελθεῖν αὐτούς.
sea;   and   wished   to go by   them.

49 οἱ δὲ ἰδόντες αὐτὸν ἐπὶ τῆς θαλάσσης
But they   seeing   him   on   the   sea

περιπατοῦντα ἔδοξαν ὅτι φάντασμά ἐστιν,
walking   thought   that   a phantasm   it is(was),

καὶ ἀνέκραξαν· 50 πάντες γὰρ αὐτὸν εἶδαν
and   cried out;   for all   him   saw

καὶ ἐταράχθησαν. ὁ δὲ εὐθὺς ἐλάλησεν
and   were troubled.   But he   immediately   talked

μετ' αὐτῶν, καὶ λέγει αὐτοῖς· θαρσεῖτε,
with   them,   and   says   to them: Be of good cheer,

ἐγώ εἰμι· μὴ φοβεῖσθε. 51 καὶ ἀνέβη
I   am;   be ye not afraid.   And   he went up

πρὸς αὐτοὺς εἰς τὸ πλοῖον, καὶ ἐκόπασεν
to   them   into the   ship,   and   ceased

ὁ ἄνεμος· καὶ λίαν ἐκ περισσοῦ ἐν ἑαυτοῖς
the   wind;   and very much   exceedingly   in themselves

⁵²for they did not under-
stand about the loaves,
but their hearts were
hardened.
53 And when they had
crossed over, they came
to land at Gennes'aret,
and moored to the shore.
⁵⁴And when they got out
of the boat, immediately
the people recognized
him, ⁵⁵and ran about the
whole neighborhood and
began to bring sick
people on their pallets to
any place where they
heard he was. ⁵⁶And
wherever he came, in
villages, cities, or
country, they laid the sick
in the market places, and
besought him that they
might touch even the
fringe of his garment;
and as many as touched
it were made well.

ἐξίσταντο· 52 οὐ γὰρ συνῆκαν ἐπὶ
they were astonished ; for they did not understand concerning
τοῖς ἄρτοις ἀλλ' ἦν αὐτῶν ἡ καρδία
the loaves, but was of them the heart
πεπωρωμένη. 53 Καὶ διαπεράσαντες ἐπὶ
having been hardened. And crossing over ²onto
τὴν γῆν ἦλθον εἰς Γεννησαρὲτ καὶ
³the ¹land ¹they came to Gennesaret and
προσωρμίσθησαν. 54 καὶ ἐξελθόντων αὐτῶν
anchored. And coming out themª
　　　　　　　　　　= as they came
ἐκ τοῦ πλοίου εὐθὺς ἐπιγνόντες αὐτὸν
out of the ship immediately knowing him
55 περιέδραμον ὅλην τὴν χώραν ἐκείνην
they ran round all - country that
καὶ ἤρξαντο ἐπὶ τοῖς κραβάτοις τοὺς
and began on the pallets the [ones]
　　　　　　　　　　　　　　= those
κακῶς ἔχοντας περιφέρειν, ὅπου ἤκουον
ill having to carry round, where they heard
who were ill
ὅτι ἐστίν. 56 καὶ ὅπου ἂν εἰσεπορεύετο
that he is(was). And wherever he entered
εἰς κώμας ἢ εἰς πόλεις ἢ εἰς ἀγρούς,
into villages or into cities or into country,
ἐν ταῖς ἀγοραῖς ἐτίθεσαν τοὺς ἀσθενοῦντας,
in the marketplaces they put the ailing [ones],
καὶ παρεκάλουν αὐτὸν ἵνα κἂν τοῦ
and besought him that if even the
κρασπέδου τοῦ ἱματίου αὐτοῦ ἅψωνται·
fringe of the garment of him they might touch;
καὶ ὅσοι ἂν ἥψαντο αὐτοῦ ἐσῴζοντο.
and as many as touched him were healed.

CHAPTER 7

NOW when the Phari-
sees gathered to-
gether to him, with some
of the scribes, who had
come from Jerusalem,
²they saw that some of
his disciples ate with
hands defiled, that is,
unwashed. ³(For the
Pharisees, and all the
Jews, do not eat unless
they wash their hands,ᴾ

ᴾ One Greek word is of uncertain meaning and is not
translated

7 Καὶ συνάγονται πρὸς αὐτὸν οἱ Φαρισαῖοι
And assemble to him the Pharisees
καὶ τινες τῶν γραμματέων ἐλθόντες ἀπὸ
and some of the scribes coming from
Ἱεροσολύμων. 2 καὶ ἰδόντες τινὰς τῶν
Jerusalem. And seeing some of the
μαθητῶν αὐτοῦ ὅτι κοιναῖς χερσίν, τοῦτ'
disciples of him that with unclean hands, this
ἔστιν ἀνίπτοις, ἐσθίουσιν τοὺς ἄρτους,
is unwashed, they eat bread,
3 — οἱ γὰρ Φαρισαῖοι καὶ πάντες οἱ
— for the Pharisees and all the
Ἰουδαῖοι ἐὰν μὴ πυγμῇ νίψωνται τὰς
Jews unless with [the] fist they wash the
　　　　　　　　= ? carefully

observing the tradition of the elders; ⁴and when they come from he market place, they do not eat unless they purify⁴ themselves; and there are many other traditions which they observe, the washing of cups and pots and vessels of bronze.ʳ) ⁵And the Pharisees and the scribes asked him, "Why do your disciples not live according to the tradition of the elders, but eat with hands defiled?" ⁶And he said to them, "Well did Isaiah prophesy of you hypocrites, as it is written,

'This people honors me with their lips, but their heart is far from me; ⁷in vain do they worship me, teaching as doctrines the precepts of men.'

⁸You leave the commandment of God, and hold fast the tradition of men."

9 And he said to them, "You have a fine way of rejecting the commandment of God, in order to keep your tradition! ¹⁰For Moses said, 'Honor your father and your mother'; and, 'He who speaks evil of father or mother, let him surely die'; ¹¹but you say, 'If a man tells his father or his

χεῖρας οὐκ ἐσθίουσιν, κρατοῦντες τὴν
hands   eat not,   holding   the

παράδοσιν τῶν πρεσβυτέρων, 4 καὶ ἀπ'
tradition   of the   elders,   and   from

ἀγορᾶς ἐὰν μὴ ῥαντίσωνται οὐκ ἐσθίουσιν, καὶ
marketplaces unless   they sprinkle   they eat not,   and

ἄλλα πολλά ἐστιν ἃ παρέλαβον κρατεῖν,
other things many there are which they received to hold,

βαπτισμοὺς ποτηρίων καὶ ξεστῶν καὶ
washings   of cups   and   of utensils   and

χαλκίων, — 5 καὶ ἐπερωτῶσιν αὐτὸν οἱ
of bronze vessels, —   and   questioned   him   the

Φαρισαῖοι καὶ οἱ γραμματεῖς· διὰ τί
Pharisees   and the   scribes: Why

οὐ περιπατοῦσιν οἱ μαθηταί σου κατὰ τὴν
walk not   the disciples of thee according to the

παράδοσιν τῶν πρεσβυτέρων, ἀλλὰ κοιναῖς
tradition   of the   elders,   but with unclean

χερσὶν ἐσθίουσιν τὸν ἄρτον; 6 ὁ δὲ εἶπεν
hands   eat   –   bread ?   And he   said

αὐτοῖς· καλῶς ἐπροφήτευσεν Ἡσαΐας περὶ
to them: Well   prophesied   Esaias concerning

ὑμῶν τῶν ὑποκριτῶν, ὡς γέγραπται ὅτι
you   the   hypocrites, as it has been written[:] –

οὗτος ὁ λαὸς τοῖς χείλεσίν με τιμᾶ,
This – people with the   lips   me honours,

ἡ δὲ καρδία αὐτῶν πόρρω ἀπέχει ἀπ'
but the heart   of them   ²far   ¹is ³away from

ἐμοῦ· 7 μάτην δὲ σέβονταί με, διδάσκοντες
me;   and in vain they worship me,   teaching

διδασκαλίας ἐντάλματα ἀνθρώπων. 8 ἀφέντες
teachings [which are] commands   of men.   Leaving

τὴν ἐντολὴν τοῦ θεοῦ κρατεῖτε τὴν
the commandment – of God ye hold   the

παράδοσιν τῶν ἀνθρώπων. 9 καὶ ἔλεγεν
tradition   –   of men.   And he said

αὐτοῖς· καλῶς ἀθετεῖτε τὴν ἐντολὴν τοῦ
to them: Well ye set aside the commandment –

θεοῦ, ἵνα τὴν παράδοσιν ὑμῶν τηρήσητε.
of God, that the tradition   of you ye may keep.

10 Μωϋσῆς γὰρ εἶπεν· τίμα τὸν πατέρα σου
For Moses   said: Honour the father of thee

καὶ τὴν μητέρα σου, καὶ· ὁ κακολογῶν
and the mother of thee, and: The [one] speaking evil of

πατέρα ἢ μητέρα θανάτω τελευτάτω. 11 ὑμεῖς
father or mother by death let him end(die).   ye

δὲ λέγετε· ἐὰν εἴπη ἄνθρωπος τῷ πατρὶ
But say: If   says   a man   to the(his) father

mother, What you
would have gained from
me is Corban' (that is,
given to God)*—¹²then
you no longer permit him
to do anything for his
father or mother, ¹³thus
making void the word of
God through your
tradition which you hand
on. And many such
things you do."
14 And he called the
people to him again, and
said to them, "Hear me,
all of you, and under-
stand: ¹⁵there is nothing
outside a man which by
going into him can defile
him; but the things which
come out of a man are
what defile him."ᵗ ¹⁷And
when he had entered the
house, and left the
people, his disciples asked
him about the parable.
¹⁸And he said to them,
"Then are you also with-
out understanding? Do
you not see that whatever
goes into a man from
outside cannot defile him,
¹⁹since it enters, not his
heart but his stomach,
and so passes on?"ᵘ
(Thus he declared all
foods clean.) ²⁰And he
said, "What comes out
of a man is what defiles a
man. ²¹For from within,

ἢ τῇ μητρί· κορβᾶν, ὅ ἐστιν δῶρον,
or to the mother: Korban, which is a gift,

ὃ ἐὰν ἐξ ἐμοῦ ὠφεληθῇς, 12 οὐκέτι ἀφίετε
whatever by me thou mightest profit, no longer ye allow

αὐτὸν οὐδὲν ποιῆσαι τῷ πατρὶ ἢ τῇ
him no(any)thing to do for the father or the

μητρί, 13 ἀκυροῦντες τὸν λόγον τοῦ θεοῦ
mother, annulling the word – of God

τῇ παραδόσει ὑμῶν ᾗ παρεδώκατε· καὶ
by the tradition of you which ye received; and

παρόμοια τοιαῦτα πολλὰ ποιεῖτε. 14 Καὶ
²similar things ²such ¹many ye do. And

προσκαλεσάμενος πάλιν τὸν ὄχλον ἔλεγεν
calling to [him] again the crowd he said

αὐτοῖς· ἀκούσατέ μου πάντες καὶ σύνετε.
to them: Hear ye me all and understand.

15 οὐδέν ἐστιν ἔξωθεν τοῦ ἀνθρώπου
Nothing there is from without – a man

εἰσπορευόμενον εἰς αὐτὸν ὃ δύναται κοινῶσαι
entering into him which can to defile

αὐτόν· ἀλλὰ τὰ ἐκ τοῦ ἀνθρώπου ἐκπο-
him; but the things out of – a man coming

ρευόμενά ἐστιν τὰ κοινοῦντα τὸν ἄνθρωπον. ‡
forth are the [ones] defiling – a man.

17 Καὶ ὅτε εἰσῆλθεν εἰς οἶκον ἀπὸ τοῦ
And when he entered into a house from the

ὄχλου, ἐπηρώτων αὐτὸν οἱ μαθηταὶ αὐτοῦ
crowd, questioned him the disciples of him

τὴν παραβολήν. 18 καὶ λέγει αὐτοῖς·
the parable. And he says to them:

οὕτως καὶ ὑμεῖς ἀσύνετοί ἐστε; οὐ
Thus also ye undiscerning are? do ye not

νοεῖτε ὅτι πᾶν τὸ ἔξωθεν εἰσπορευόμενον
understand that everything from without entering

εἰς τὸν ἄνθρωπον οὐ δύναται αὐτὸν
into – a man cannot him

κοινῶσαι, 19 ὅτι οὐκ εἰσπορεύεται αὐτοῦ
to defile, because it enters not of him

εἰς τὴν καρδίαν ἀλλ' εἰς τὴν κοιλίαν,
into the heart but into the belly,

καὶ εἰς τὸν ἀφεδρῶνα ἐκπορεύεται, καθα-
and into the drain goes out, purg-

ρίζων πάντα τὰ βρώματα; 20 ἔλεγεν δὲ
ing all – foods? And he said[,]

ὅτι τὸ ἐκ τοῦ ἀνθρώπου ἐκπορευόμενον,
– The thing out of – a man coming forth,

ἐκεῖνο κοινοῖ τὸν ἄνθρωπον. 21 ἔσωθεν
that defiles – a man. from within

---

* Or an offering
ᵗ Other ancient authorities add
verse 16, "If any man has ears
to hear, let him hear"
ᵘ Or is evacuated

‡ Verse 16 omitted by Nestle; cf. RSV footnote.

out of the heart of man, come evil thoughts, fornication, theft, murder, adultery, 22coveting, wickedness, deceit, licentiousness, envy, slander, pride, foolishness. 23All these evil things come from within, and they defile a man."

24 And from there he arose and went away to the region of Tyre and Sidon.[v] And he entered a house, and would not have any one know it; yet he could not be hid. 25But immediately a woman, whose little daughter was possessed by an unclean spirit, heard of him, and came and fell down at his feet. 26Now the woman was a Greek, a Syrophoeni′cian by birth. And she begged him to cast the demon out of her daughter. 27And he said to her, "Let the children first be fed, for it is not right to take the children's bread and throw it to the dogs." 28But she answered him, "Yes, Lord; yet even the dogs under the table eat the children's crumbs." 29And he said to her, "For this saying you may

γὰρ ἐκ τῆς καρδίας τῶν ἀνθρώπων
For out of the heart – of men
οἱ διαλογισμοὶ οἱ κακοὶ ἐκπορεύονται,
– thoughts – evil come forth,
πορνεῖαι, κλοπαί, φόνοι, 22 μοιχεῖαι,
fornications, thefts, murders, 22 adulteries,
πλεονεξίαι, πονηρίαι, δόλος, ἀσέλγεια, ὀφθαλμὸς
greedinesses, iniquities, deceit, lewdness, eye
πονηρός, βλασφημία, ὑπερηφανία, ἀφροσύνη·
an evil, blasphemy, arrogance, foolishness;
23 πάντα ταῦτα τὰ πονηρὰ ἔσωθεν ἐκπορεύεται
all these – evil things from within comes forth
καὶ κοινοῖ τὸν ἄνθρωπον.
and defile – a man.

24 Ἐκεῖθεν δὲ ἀναστὰς ἀπῆλθεν εἰς τὰ ὅρια
And thence rising up he went away into the district
Τύρου. Καὶ εἰσελθὼν εἰς οἰκίαν οὐδένα ἤθελεν
of Tyre. And entering into a house no one he wished
γνῶναι, καὶ οὐκ ἠδυνάσθη λαθεῖν· 25 ἀλλ'
to know, and could not to be hidden; 25 but
εὐθὺς ἀκούσασα γυνὴ περὶ αὐτοῦ, ἧς
immediately ²hearing ¹a woman about him, of whom = whose
εἶχεν τὸ θυγάτριον αὐτῆς πνεῦμα ἀκάθαρτον,
had the daughter of her spirit an unclean,
daughter had
ἐλθοῦσα προσέπεσεν πρὸς τοὺς πόδας αὐτοῦ·
coming fell at the feet of him;
26 ἡ δὲ γυνὴ ἦν Ἑλληνίς, Συροφοινίκισσα
and the woman was a Greek, a Syrophenician
τῷ γένει· καὶ ἠρώτα αὐτὸν ἵνα τὸ
– by race; and she asked him that the
δαιμόνιον ἐκβάλῃ ἐκ τῆς θυγατρὸς αὐτῆς.
demon he would expel out of the daughter of her.
27 καὶ ἔλεγεν αὐτῇ· ἄφες πρῶτον
And he said to her: Permit first
χορτασθῆναι τὰ τέκνα· οὐ γάρ ἐστιν καλὸν
to be satisfied the children; for it is not good
λαβεῖν τὸν ἄρτον τῶν τέκνων καὶ τοῖς
to take the bread of the children and to the
κυναρίοις βαλεῖν. 28 ἡ δὲ ἀπεκρίθη καὶ
dogs to throw [it]. 28 And she answered and
λέγει αὐτῷ· ναί, κύριε· καὶ τὰ κυνάρια
says to him: Yes, Lord; and yet the dogs
ὑποκάτω τῆς τραπέζης ἐσθίουσιν ἀπὸ τῶν
under the table eat from the
ψιχίων τῶν παιδίων. 29 καὶ εἶπεν αὐτῇ·
crumbs of the children. And he said to her:
διὰ τοῦτον τὸν λόγον ὕπαγε, ἐξελήλυθεν
Because of this – word go, has gone forth

[v] Other ancient authorities omit and Sidon

go your way; the demon has left your daughter." ³⁰And she went home, and found the child lying in bed, and the demon gone. 31 Then he returned from the region of Tyre, and went through Sidon to the Sea of Galilee, through the region of the Decap′olis. ³²And they brought to him a man who was deaf and had an impediment in his speech; and they besought him to lay his hand upon him. ³³And taking him aside from the multitude privately, he put his fingers into his ears, and he spat and touched his tongue; ³⁴and looking up to heaven, he sighed, and said to him, "Eph′-phatha," that is, "Be opened." ³⁵And his ears were opened, his tongue was released, and he spoke plainly. ³⁶And he charged them to tell no one; but the more he charged them, the more zealously they proclaimed it. ³⁷And they were astonished beyond measure, saying, "He has done all things well; he even makes the deaf hear and the dumb speak."

ἐκ τῆς θυγατρός σου τὸ δαιμόνιον. 30 καὶ
out of the   daughter   of thee   the   demon.   And

ἀπελθοῦσα   εἰς   τὸν   οἶκον   αὐτῆς   εὗρεν   τὸ
going away   to   the   house   of her   she found   the

παιδίον   βεβλημένον   ἐπὶ   τὴν   κλίνην   καὶ   τὸ
child   having been laid   on   the   couch   and   the

δαιμόνιον   ἐξεληλυθός.   31 Καὶ   πάλιν   ἐξελθὼν
demon   having gone forth.   And   again   going forth

ἐκ   τῶν   ὁρίων   Τύρου   ἦλθεν   διὰ   Σιδῶνος
out of the   district   of Tyre   he came   through   Sidon

εἰς   τὴν   θάλασσαν   τῆς   Γαλιλαίας   ἀνὰ
to   the   sea   –   of Galilee   in the

μέσον   τῶν   ὁρίων   Δεκαπόλεως.   32 Καὶ
midst   of the   district   of Decapolis.   And

φέρουσιν αὐτῷ κωφὸν καὶ   μογιλάλον,   καὶ
they bring to him a man deaf and speaking with difficulty, and

παρακαλοῦσιν αὐτὸν ἵνα   ἐπιθῇ   αὐτῷ   τὴν
they beseech   him   that he would put on on him the(his)

χεῖρα.   33 καὶ   ἀπολαβόμενος   αὐτὸν   ἀπὸ
hand.   And   taking away   him   from

τοῦ   ὄχλου   κατ᾽   ἰδίαν   ἔβαλεν   τοὺς   δακτύλους
the   crowd   privately   he put   the   fingers

αὐτοῦ   εἰς   τὰ   ὦτα   αὐτοῦ   καὶ   πτύσας
of him   into   the   ears   of him   and   spitting

ἥψατο   τῆς   γλώσσης   αὐτοῦ,   34 καὶ
he touched   the   tongue   of him,   and

ἀναβλέψας   εἰς   τὸν   οὐρανὸν   ἐστέναξεν,
looking up   to   –   heaven   he groaned,

καὶ λέγει αὐτῷ· ἐφφαθά, ὃ ἐστιν διανοίχθ;τι.
and   says   to him: Ephphatha, which   is Be thou opened.

35 καὶ   ἠνοίγησαν   αὐτοῦ   αἱ   ἀκοαί,   καὶ
And   were opened   of him   the   ears,   and

εὐθὺς   ἐλύθη   ὁ   δεσμὸς τῆς γλώσσης αὐτοῦ,
immediately was loosened the   bond   of the tongue   of him,

καὶ   ἐλάλει   ὀρθῶς.   36 καὶ   διεστείλατο
and   he spoke   correctly.   And   he ordered

αὐτοῖς   ἵνα   μηδενὶ   λέγωσιν·   ὅσον   δὲ
them   that   no one they should tell; but as much as

αὐτοῖς διεστέλλετο, αὐτοὶ μᾶλλον περισσότερον
them   he ordered,   they   more   exceedingly

ἐκήρυσσον.   37 καὶ ὑπερπερισσῶς ἐξεπλήσσοντο
proclaimed.   And most exceedingly they were astounded

λέγοντες·   καλῶς   πάντα   πεποίηκεν,   καὶ
saying: Well   all things   he has done,   both

τοὺς   κωφοὺς   ποιεῖ   ἀκούειν   καὶ   ἀλάλους
the   deaf   he makes   to hear   and   dumb

λαλεῖν.
to speak.

CHAPTER 8

IN those days, when again a great crowd had gathered and they had nothing to eat, he called his disciples to him and said to them,² "I have compassion on the crowd, because they have been with me now three days, and have nothing to eat; ³and if I send them away hungry to their homes, they will faint on the way; and some of them have come a long way." ⁴And his disciples answered him, "How can one feed these men with bread here in the desert?" ⁵And he asked them, "How many loaves have you?" They said, "Seven." ⁶And he commanded the crowd to sit down on the ground; and he took the seven loaves, and having given thanks he broke them and gave them to his disciples to set before the people; and they set them before the crowd. ⁷And they had a few small fish; and having blessed them, he commanded that these also should be set before them. ⁸And they ate, and were satisfied; and they took up the broken pieces left over, seven baskets full. ⁹And there were about four thousand people. ¹⁰And he sent them away; and immediately he got into the boat with his disciples,

8 Ἐν ἐκείναις ταῖς ἡμέραις πάλιν πολλοῦ
In those   –   days   again a much(great)
                                = there being

ὄχλου ὄντος καὶ μὴ ἐχόντων τί φάγωσιν,
crowd being[a] and not having[a] anything they might eat,
a great crowd

προσκαλεσάμενος τοὺς μαθητὰς λέγει αὐτοῖς·
calling to [him] the disciples he says to them:

2 σπλαγχνίζομαι ἐπὶ τὸν ὄχλον, ὅτι ἤδη
I have compassion on the crowd, because now

ἡμέραι τρεῖς προσμένουσίν μοι καὶ οὐκ
days three they remain with me and not

ἔχουσιν τί φάγωσιν· 3 καὶ ἐὰν ἀπολύσω
they have anything they may eat; and if I dismiss

αὐτοὺς νήστεις εἰς οἶκον αὐτῶν, ἐκλυθήσονται
them fasting to house of them, they will faint

ἐν τῇ ὁδῷ· καί τινες αὐτῶν ἀπὸ μακρόθεν
in the way; and some of them from afar

εἰσίν. 4 καὶ ἀπεκρίθησαν αὐτῷ οἱ μαθηταὶ
are. And answered him the disciples

αὐτοῦ ὅτι πόθεν τούτους δυνήσεταί τις
of him[,] ¹Whence ⁶these people ²will ⁴be able ²anyone

ὧδε χορτάσαι ἄρτων ἐπ᾽ ἐρημίας; 5 καὶ
⁵here ⁵to satisfy ⁷of(with) loaves ⁸on(in) ¹⁰a desert? And

ἠρώτα αὐτούς· πόσους ἔχετε ἄρτους;
he asked them: How many have ye loaves?

οἱ δὲ εἶπαν· ἑπτά. 6 καὶ παραγγέλλει τῷ
And they said: Seven. And he commands the

ὄχλῳ ἀναπεσεῖν ἐπὶ τῆς γῆς· καὶ λαβὼν
crowd to recline on the ground; and taking

τοὺς ἑπτὰ ἄρτους εὐχαριστήσας ἔκλασεν
the seven loaves giving thanks he broke

καὶ ἐδίδου τοῖς μαθηταῖς αὐτοῦ ἵνα
and gave to the disciples of him that

παρατιθῶσιν, καὶ παρέθηκαν τῷ ὄχλῳ.
they might serve, and they served the crowd.

7 καὶ εἶχον ἰχθύδια ὀλίγα· καὶ εὐλογήσας
And they had fishes a few; and blessing

αὐτὰ εἶπεν καὶ ταῦτα παρατιθέναι. 8 καὶ
them he told also these to be served. And

ἔφαγον καὶ ἐχορτάσθησαν, καὶ ἦραν
they ate and were satisfied, and took

περισσεύματα κλασμάτων, ἑπτὰ σπυρίδας.
excesses of fragments, seven baskets.

9 ἦσαν δὲ ὡς τετρακισχίλιοι. καὶ ἀπέλυσεν
Now they were about four thousand. And he dismissed

αὐτούς. 10 Καὶ εὐθὺς ἐμβὰς εἰς τὸ
them. And immediately embarking in the

πλοῖον μετὰ τῶν μαθητῶν αὐτοῦ
ship with the disciples of him

and went to the district of Dalmanu'tha.[w]

11 The Pharisees came and began to argue with him, seeking from him a sign from heaven, to test him. [12]And he sighed deeply in his spirit, and said, "Why does this generation seek a sign? Truly, I say to you, no sign shall be given to this generation." [13]And he left them, and getting into the boat again he departed to the other side.

14 Now they had forgotten to bring bread; and they had only one loaf with them in the boat. [15]And he cautioned them, saying, "Take heed, beware of the leaven of the Pharisees and the leaven of Herod."[x] [16]And they discussed it with one another, saying, "We have no bread." [17]And being aware of it, Jesus said to them, "Why do you discuss the fact that you have no bread? Do you not yet perceive or understand? Are your hearts hardened? [18]Having eyes do you not see, and having ears do you not hear? And do you not remember? [19]When I broke the five loaves for the five thousand, how many baskets full of broken pieces did you take up?" They said to

[w] Other ancient authorities read *Magadan* or *Magdala*
[x] Other ancient authorities read *the Herodians*

ἦλθεν εἰς τὰ μέρη Δαλμανουθά.
he came into the region of Dalmanutha.

11 Καὶ ἐξῆλθον οἱ Φαρισαῖοι καὶ ἤρξαντο
And came forth the Pharisees and began

συζητεῖν αὐτῷ, ζητοῦντες παρ' αὐτοῦ
to debate with him, seeking from him

σημεῖον ἀπὸ τοῦ οὐρανοῦ, πειράζοντες
a sign from – heaven, tempting

αὐτόν. 12 καὶ ἀναστενάξας τῷ πνεύματι
him. And groaning in the spirit

αὐτοῦ λέγει· τί ἡ γενεὰ αὕτη ζητεῖ
of him he says: Why – generation this does seek

σημεῖον; ἀμὴν λέγω ὑμῖν, εἰ δοθήσεται
a sign? Truly I tell you, if will be given

τῇ γενεᾷ ταύτῃ σημεῖον. 13 καὶ ἀφεὶς
– generation to this a sign. And leaving

αὐτοὺς πάλιν ἐμβὰς ἀπῆλθεν εἰς τὸ
them again embarking he went away to the

πέραν. 14 Καὶ ἐπελάθοντο λαβεῖν ἄρτους,
other side. And they forgot to take loaves,

καὶ εἰ μὴ ἕνα ἄρτον οὐκ εἶχον μεθ'
and except one loaf they had not with

ἑαυτῶν ἐν τῷ πλοίῳ. 15 καὶ διεστέλλετο
themselves in the ship. And he charged

αὐτοῖς λέγων· ὁρᾶτε, βλέπετε ἀπὸ τῆς
them saying: See, look ye from the =Beware of

ζύμης τῶν Φαρισαίων καὶ τῆς ζύμης
leaven of the Pharisees and of the leaven

Ἡρῴδου. 16 καὶ διελογίζοντο πρὸς ἀλλήλους
of Herod. And they reasoned with one another

ὅτι ἄρτους οὐκ ἔχουσιν. 17 καὶ γνοὺς
because loaves they have(had) not. And knowing

λέγει αὐτοῖς· τί διαλογίζεσθε ὅτι ἄρτους
he says to them: Why reason ye because loaves

οὐκ ἔχετε; οὔπω νοεῖτε οὐδὲ συνίετε;
ye have not? not yet understand ye nor realize?

πεπωρωμένην ἔχετε τὴν καρδίαν ὑμῶν;
having been hardened have ye the heart of you?

18 ὀφθαλμοὺς ἔχοντες οὐ βλέπετε, καὶ
eyes having see ye not, and

ὦτα ἔχοντες οὐκ ἀκούετε; καὶ
ears having hear ye not? and

οὐ μνημονεύετε, 19 ὅτε τοὺς πέντε ἄρτους
do ye not remember, when the five loaves

ἔκλασα εἰς τοὺς πεντακισχιλίους, πόσους
I broke to the five thousand, how many

κοφίνους κλασμάτων πλήρεις ἤρατε; λέγουσιν
baskets of fragments full ye took? They say

him, "Twelve." ²⁰"And
the seven for the four
thousand, how many
baskets full of broken
pieces did you take up?"
And they said to him,
"Seven." ²¹And he said
to them, "Do you not
yet understand?"

22 And they came to
Beth-sa'ida. And some
people brought to him a
blind man, and begged
him to touch him. ²³And
he took the blind man by
the hand, and led him
out of the village; and
when he had spit on his
eyes and laid his hands
upon him, he asked him,
"Do you see anything?"
²⁴And he looked up and
said, "I see men; but
they look like trees,
walking." ²⁵Then again
he laid his hands upon
his eyes; and he looked
intently and was restored,
and saw everything
clearly. ²⁶And he sent
him away to his home,
saying, "Do not even
enter the village."

27 And Jesus went on
with his disciples, to the
villages of Caesare'a
Philippi; and on the way
he asked his disciples,
"Who do men say that I
am?" ²⁸And they told
him, "John the Baptist;

αὐτῷ·   δώδεκα.   20 ὅτε   τοὺς   ἑπτὰ   εἰς
to him: Twelve.   When   the   seven   to

τοὺς   τετρακισχιλίους,   πόσων   σπυρίδων
the   four thousand,   ²of how many   ³baskets

πληρώματα   κλασμάτων   ἤρατε;   καὶ   λέγουσιν·
¹fullnesses   ⁴of fragments   ye took?   And   they say:

ἑπτά.   21 καὶ   ἔλεγεν   αὐτοῖς·   οὔπω   συνίετε;
Seven.   And   he said   to them: Not yet do ye realize?

22 Καὶ   ἔρχονται   εἰς   Βηθσαϊδάν.   Καὶ
And   they come   to   Bethsaida.   And

φέρουσιν   αὐτῷ   τυφλόν,   καὶ   παρακαλοῦσιν
they bring   to him   a blind man, and   beseech

αὐτὸν ἵνα αὐτοῦ   ἅψηται.   23 καὶ ἐπιλαβόμενος
him   that him   he would touch.   And   laying hold of

τῆς   χειρὸς   τοῦ   τυφλοῦ   ἐξήνεγκεν   αὐτὸν
the   hand   of the   blind man   he led forth   him

ἔξω   τῆς   κώμης,   καὶ   πτύσας   εἰς   τὰ
outside   the   village,   and   spitting   in   the

ὄμματα   αὐτοῦ,   ἐπιθεὶς   τὰς   χεῖρας   αὐτῷ,
eyes   of him,   putting on   the   hands   on him,

ἐπηρώτα   αὐτόν·   εἴ   τι   βλέπεις;   24 καὶ
questioned   him: If   anything   thou seest?   And

ἀναβλέψας   ἔλεγεν·   βλέπω   τοὺς   ἀνθρώπους,
looking up   he said: I see   -   men,

ὅτι   ὡς   δένδρα   ὁρῶ   περιπατοῦντας.
that   as   trees   I behold   walking.

25 εἶτα   πάλιν   ἐπέθηκεν   τὰς   χεῖρας   ἐπὶ
Then   again   he put on   the   hands   on

τοὺς ὀφθαλμοὺς αὐτοῦ,   καὶ   διέβλεψεν   καὶ
the   eyes   of him,   and   he looked steadily   and

ἀπεκατέστη,   καὶ   ἐνέβλεπεν   τηλαυγῶς   ἅπαντα.
was restored,   and   saw   clearly   all things.

26 καὶ   ἀπέστειλεν   αὐτὸν   εἰς   οἶκον   αὐτοῦ
And   he sent   him   to   house   of him

λέγων·   μηδὲ   εἰς   τὴν   κώμην   εἰσέλθῃς.
saying: Not   into   the   village   thou mayest enter.

27 Καὶ   ἐξῆλθεν   ὁ   Ἰησοῦς   καὶ   οἱ   μαθηταὶ
And   went forth   -   Jesus   and   the   disciples

αὐτοῦ   εἰς   τὰς   κώμας   Καισαρείας   τῆς
of him   to   the   villages   of Caesarea   -

Φιλίππου·   καὶ   ἐν   τῇ   ὁδῷ   ἐπηρώτα   τοὺς
of Philip;   and   in   the   way   he questioned   the

μαθητὰς   αὐτοῦ   λέγων   αὐτοῖς·   τίνα   με
disciples   of him   saying   to them: Whom   me

λέγουσιν   οἱ   ἄνθρωποι   εἶναι;   28 οἱ   δὲ
say   -   men   to be?   And they

εἶπαν   αὐτῷ   λέγοντες   ὅτι   Ἰωάννην   τὸν
told   him   saying[,]   -   John   the

and others say, Eli'jah; and others one of the prophets." ²⁹And he asked them, "But who do you say that I am?" Peter answered him, "You are the Christ." ³⁰And he charged them to tell no one about him.

31 And he began to teach them that the Son of man must suffer many things, and be rejected by the elders and the chief priests and the scribes, and be killed, and after three days rise again. ³²And he said this plainly. And Peter took him, and began to rebuke him. ³³But turning and seeing his disciples, he rebuked Peter, and said, "Get behind me, Satan! For you are not on the side of God, but of men."

34 And he called to him the multitude with his disciples, and said to them, "If any man would come after me, let him deny himself and take up his cross and follow me. ³⁵For whoever would save his life will lose it; and whoever loses

βαπτιστήν, καὶ ἄλλοι 'Ηλίαν, ἄλλοι δὲ
Baptist,   and   others   Elias,   but others[,]

ὅτι εἷς τῶν προφητῶν. 29 καὶ αὐτὸς
–   one of the   prophets.   And   he

ἐπηρώτα αὐτούς· ὑμεῖς δὲ τίνα με λέγετε
questioned   them: But ye   whom me say ye

εἶναι; ἀποκριθεὶς ὁ Πέτρος λέγει αὐτῷ·
to be?   Answering   –   Peter   says   to him:

σὺ εἶ ὁ χριστός. 30 καὶ ἐπετίμησεν
Thou art the   Christ.   And   he warned

αὐτοῖς ἵνα μηδενὶ λέγωσιν περὶ αὐτοῦ.
them   that   no one they might tell about   him.

31 Καὶ ἤρξατο διδάσκειν αὐτοὺς ὅτι δεῖ
And   he began   to teach   them   that it behoves

τὸν υἱὸν τοῦ ἀνθρώπου πολλὰ παθεῖν,
the Son   –   of man   many things to suffer,

καὶ ἀποδοκιμασθῆναι ὑπὸ τῶν πρεσβυτέρων
and   to be rejected   by   the   elders

καὶ τῶν ἀρχιερέων καὶ τῶν γραμματέων
and   the   chief priests   and   the   scribes

καὶ ἀποκτανθῆναι καὶ μετὰ τρεῖς ἡμέρας
and   to be killed   and   after   three   days

ἀναστῆναι· 32 καὶ παρρησίᾳ τὸν λόγον
to rise again;   and   openly   the   word

ἐλάλει. καὶ προσλαβόμενος ὁ Πέτρος
he spoke.   And   ²taking ⁴aside   –   ¹Peter

αὐτὸν ἤρξατο ἐπιτιμᾶν αὐτῷ. 33 ὁ δὲ
³him   began   to rebuke   him.   But he

ἐπιστραφεὶς καὶ ἰδὼν τοὺς μαθητὰς αὐτοῦ
turning round   and   seeing   the   disciples   of him

ἐπετίμησεν Πέτρῳ καὶ λέγει· ὕπαγε ὀπίσω
rebuked   Peter   and   says: Go   behind

μου, σατανᾶ, ὅτι οὐ φρονεῖς τὰ τοῦ
me,   Satan,   because thou mindest not the things   –

θεοῦ ἀλλὰ τὰ τῶν ἀνθρώπων. 34 Καὶ
of God   but the things   –   of men.   And

προσκαλεσάμενος τὸν ὄχλον σὺν τοῖς μαθηταῖς
calling to [him]   the   crowd   with   the   disciples

αὐτοῦ εἶπεν αὐτοῖς· εἴ τις θέλει ὀπίσω
of him   he said   to them: If anyone wishes   after

μου ἐλθεῖν, ἀπαρνησάσθω ἑαυτὸν καὶ ἀράτω
me   to come,   let him deny   himself   and   take

τὸν σταυρὸν αὐτοῦ, καὶ ἀκολουθείτω μοι.
the   cross   of him,   and   let him follow   me.

35 ὃς γὰρ ἐὰν θέλῃ τὴν ψυχὴν αὐτοῦ σῶ-
For whoever   wishes   the   life   of him   to

σαι, ἀπολέσει αὐτήν· ὃς δ' ἂν ἀπολέσει
save,   will lose   it;   but whoever   will lose

his life for my sake and the gospel's will save it. ³⁶For what does it profit a man, to gain the whole world and forfeit his life? ³⁷For what can a man give in return for his life? ³⁸For whoever is ashamed of me and of my words in this adulterous and sinful generation, of him will the Son of man also be ashamed, when he comes in the glory of his Father with the holy angels."

τὴν ψυχὴν αὐτοῦ ἕνεκεν ἐμοῦ καὶ τοῦ
the life of him for the sake of me and the

εὐαγγελίου, σώσει αὐτήν. 36 τί γὰρ ὠφελεῖ
gospel, will save it. For what profits

ἄνθρωπον κερδῆσαι τὸν κόσμον ὅλον καὶ
a man to gain the world whole and

ζημιωθῆναι τὴν ψυχὴν αὐτοῦ; 37 τί γὰρ
to be fined the soul of him? For what

δοῖ ἄνθρωπος ἀντάλλαγμα τῆς ψυχῆς αὐτοῦ;
might give a man an exchange of the soul of him?

38 ὃς γὰρ ἐὰν ἐπαισχυνθῇ με καὶ
For whoever is ashamed of me and

τοὺς ἐμοὺς λόγους ἐν τῇ γενεᾷ ταύτῃ
my words in – generation this

τῇ μοιχαλίδι καὶ ἁμαρτωλῷ, καὶ ὁ
– adulterous and sinful, also the

υἱὸς τοῦ ἀνθρώπου ἐπαισχυνθήσεται αὐτόν,
Son – of man will be ashamed of him,

ὅτι ἔλθῃ ἐν τῇ δόξῃ τοῦ πατρὸς
when he comes in the glory of the Father

αὐτοῦ μετὰ τῶν ἀγγέλων τῶν ἁγίων.
of him with the angels – holy.

CHAPTER 9

AND he said to them, "Truly, I say to you, there are some standing here who will not taste death before they see the kingdom of God come with power."
2 And after six days Jesus took with him Peter and James and John, and led them up a high mountain apart by themselves; and he was transfigured before them, ³and his garments became glistening, intensely white, as no fuller on earth could bleach them.

9 καὶ ἔλεγεν αὐτοῖς· ἀμὴν λέγω ὑμῖν
And he said to them: Truly I tell you

ὅτι εἰσίν τινες ὧδε τῶν ἑστηκότων
that there are some here of the [ones] standing

οἵτινες οὐ μὴ γεύσωνται θανάτου ἕως ἂν
who by no means may taste of death until

ἴδωσιν τὴν βασιλείαν τοῦ θεοῦ ἐληλυθυῖαν
they see the kingdom – of God having come

ἐν δυνάμει.
in power.

2 Καὶ μετὰ ἡμέρας ἓξ παραλαμβάνει
And after days six takes

ὁ Ἰησοῦς τὸν Πέτρον καὶ τὸν Ἰάκωβον
Jesus – Peter and – James

καὶ Ἰωάννην, καὶ ἀναφέρει αὐτοὺς εἰς
and John, and leads up them into

ὄρος ὑψηλὸν κατ' ἰδίαν μόνους. καὶ
mountain a high privately alone. And

μετεμορφώθη ἔμπροσθεν αὐτῶν, 3 καὶ τὰ
he was transfigured before them, and the

ἱμάτια αὐτοῦ ἐγένετο στίλβοντα λευκὰ λίαν,
garments of him became gleaming white exceedingly,

οἷα γναφεὺς ἐπὶ τῆς γῆς οὐ δύναται
such as fuller on the earth cannot

4And there appeared to them Eli'jah with Moses; and they were talking to Jesus. 5And Peter said to Jesus, "Master, it is well that we are here; let us make three booths, one for you and one for Moses and one for Eli'jah." 6For he did not know what to say, for they were exceedingly afraid. 7And a cloud overshadowed them, and a voice came out of the cloud, "This is my beloved Son;*ʸ* listen to him." 8And suddenly looking around they no longer saw any one with them but Jesus only.

9 And as they were coming down the mountain, he charged them to tell no one what they had seen, until the Son of man should have risen from the dead. 10So they kept the matter to themselves, questioning what the rising from the dead meant. 11And they asked him, "Why do the scribes say that first Eli'jah must come?" 12And he said to them, "Eli'jah does come first to restore all things; and how is it written of the Son of man, that he should suffer many

---

οὕτως λευκᾶναι. 4 καὶ ὤφθη αὐτοῖς Ἡλίας
so   to whiten.   And appeared to them   Elias

σὺν Μωϋσεῖ, καὶ ἦσαν συλλαλοῦντες τῷ
with   Moses,   and they were   conversing with   -

Ἰησοῦ. 5 καὶ ἀποκριθεὶς ὁ Πέτρος λέγει
Jesus.   And   answering   -   Peter   says

τῷ Ἰησοῦ· ῥαββί, καλόν ἐστιν ἡμᾶς ὧδε
- to Jesus: Rabbi, good   it is   us   here

εἶναι, καὶ ποιήσωμεν τρεῖς σκηνάς, σοὶ
to be,   and   let us make   three   tents, for thee

μίαν καὶ Μωϋσεῖ μίαν καὶ Ἠλίᾳ μίαν.
one and for Moses   one and for Elias one.

6 οὐ γὰρ ᾔδει τί ἀποκριθῇ· ἔκφοβοι γὰρ
For he knew not what he answered; for exceedingly afraid

ἐγένοντο. 7 καὶ ἐγένετο νεφέλη ἐπισκιάζουσα
they became.   And there came a cloud   overshadowing

αὐτοῖς, καὶ ἐγένετο φωνὴ ἐκ τῆς νεφέλης·
them,   and there came a voice out of the   cloud:

οὗτός ἐστιν ὁ υἱός μου ὁ ἀγαπητός,
This   is   the Son of me the   beloved,

ἀκούετε αὐτοῦ. 8 καὶ ἐξάπινα περιβλεψάμενοι
hear ye   him.   And   suddenly   looking round

οὐκέτι οὐδένα εἶδον εἰ μὴ τὸν Ἰησοῦν
no longer no(any)one they saw except   -   Jesus

μόνον μεθ᾽ ἑαυτῶν. 9 Καὶ καταβαινόντων
only   with themselves.   And   coming down
                                      = as they came down

αὐτῶν ἐκ τοῦ ὄρους διεστείλατο αὐτοῖς
themᵃ out of the   mountain   he ordered   them

ἵνα μηδενὶ ἃ εἶδον διηγήσωνται,
that to no one [the] things which they saw they should relate,

εἰ μὴ ὅταν ὁ υἱὸς τοῦ ἀνθρώπου ἐκ νεκρῶν
except when the Son   -   of man out of [the] dead

ἀναστῇ. 10 καὶ τὸν λόγον ἐκράτησαν πρὸς
should rise.   And the   word   they held   to

ἑαυτοὺς συζητοῦντες τί ἐστιν τὸ ἐκ
themselves   debating   what   is   the "out of

νεκρῶν ἀναστῆναι. 11 Καὶ ἐπηρώτων αὐτὸν
[the] dead   to rise."   And they questioned him

λέγοντες· ὅτι λέγουσιν οἱ γραμματεῖς ὅτι
saying: Why say   the   scribes   that

Ἠλίαν δεῖ ἐλθεῖν πρῶτον; 12 ὁ δὲ ἔφη
Elias it behoves to come   first ?   And he   said

αὐτοῖς· Ἠλίας μὲν ἐλθὼν πρῶτον
to them: Elias indeed coming   first

ἀποκαθιστάνει πάντα· καὶ πῶς γέγραπται
will restore all things; and how has it been written

ἐπὶ τὸν υἱὸν τοῦ ἀνθρώπου, ἵνα πολλὰ
on(concerning) the Son   -   of man,   that many things

things and be treated with contempt? ¹³But I tell you that Eli′jah has come, and they did to him whatever they pleased, as it is written of him."

14 And when they came to the disciples, they saw a great crowd about them, and scribes arguing with them. ¹⁵And immediately all the crowd, when they saw him, were greatly amazed, and ran up to him and greeted him. ¹⁶And he asked them, "What are you discussing with them?" ¹⁷And one of the crowd answered him, "Teacher, I brought my son to you, for he has a dumb spirit; ¹⁸and wherever it seizes him, it dashes him down; and he foams and grinds his teeth and becomes rigid; and I asked your disciples to cast it out, and they were not able." ¹⁹And he answered them, "O faithless generation, how long am I to be with you? How long am I to bear with you? Bring him to me." ²⁰And they brought the boy to him; and when the spirit saw him, immediately it convulsed the boy, and he fell on the ground and rolled about, foaming at

πάθη καὶ ἐξουδενηθῇ; 13 ἀλλὰ λέγω ὑμῖν
he should suffer and be set at naught? But I tell you

ὅτι καὶ 'Ηλίας ἐλήλυθεν, καὶ ἐποίησαν
that indeed Elias has come, and they did

αὐτῷ ὅσα ἤθελον, καθὼς γέγραπται
to him what they wished, as it has been written

ἐπ' αὐτόν.
on(concerning) him.

14 Καὶ ἐλθόντες πρὸς τοὺς μαθητὰς
And coming to the disciples

εἶδον ὄχλον πολὺν περὶ αὐτοὺς καὶ
they saw crowd a much(great) around them and

γραμματεῖς συζητοῦντας πρὸς αὐτούς.
scribes debating with them.

15 καὶ εὐθὺς πᾶς ὁ ὄχλος ἰδόντες αὐτὸν
And immediately all the crowd seeing him

ἐξεθαμβήθησαν, καὶ προστρέχοντες ἠσπάζοντο
were greatly astonished, and running up to greeted

αὐτόν. 16 καὶ ἐπηρώτησεν αὐτούς· τί
him. And he questioned them: What

συζητεῖτε πρὸς αὐτούς; 17 καὶ ἀπεκρίθη
are ye debating with them? And answered

αὐτῷ εἷς ἐκ τοῦ ὄχλου· διδάσκαλε,
him one of the crowd: Teacher,

ἤνεγκα τὸν υἱόν μου πρὸς σέ, ἔχοντα
I brought the son of me to thee, having

πνεῦμα ἄλαλον· 18 καὶ ὅπου ἐὰν αὐτὸν
spirit a dumb; and wherever him

καταλάβῃ, ῥήσσει αὐτόν, καὶ ἀφρίζει καὶ
it seizes, it tears him, and he foams and

τρίζει τοὺς ὀδόντας καὶ ξηραίνεται· καὶ
grinds the(his) teeth and he wastes away; and

εἶπα τοῖς μαθηταῖς σου ἵνα αὐτὸ
I told the disciples of thee that it

ἐκβάλωσιν, καὶ οὐκ ἴσχυσαν. 19 ὁ δὲ
they might expel, and they were not able. And he

ἀποκριθεὶς αὐτοῖς λέγει· ὦ γενεὰ ἄπιστος,
answering them says: O generation unbelieving,

ἕως πότε πρὸς ὑμᾶς ἔσομαι; ἕως πότε
until when with you shall I be? how long
= how long

ἀνέξομαι ὑμῶν; φέρετε αὐτὸν πρός με.
shall I endure you? bring him to me.

20 καὶ ἤνεγκαν αὐτὸν πρὸς αὐτόν. καὶ
And they brought him to him. And

ἰδὼν αὐτὸν τὸ πνεῦμα εὐθὺς συνεσπάραξεν
seeing him the spirit immediately violently threw

αὐτόν, καὶ πεσὼν ἐπὶ τῆς γῆς ἐκυλίετο
him, and falling on the earth he wallowed

the mouth. ²¹And Jesus asked his father, "How long has he had this?" And he said, "From childhood. ²²And it has often cast him into the fire and into the water, to destroy him; but if you can do anything, have pity on us and help us." ²³And Jesus said to him, "If you can! All things are possible to him who believes." ²⁴Immediately the father of the child cried out² and said, "I believe; help my unbelief!" ²⁵And when Jesus saw that a crowd came running together, he rebuked the unclean spirit, saying to it, "You dumb and deaf spirit, I command you, come out of him, and never enter him again." ²⁶And after crying out and convulsing him terribly, it came out, and the boy was like a corpse; so that most of them said, "He is dead." ²⁷But Jesus took him by the hand and lifted him up, and he arose. ²⁸And when he had entered the house, his disciples asked him privately, "Why could we not cast it out?" ²⁹And he said to them, "This kind cannot be

² Other ancient authorities add with tears

ἀφρίζων.
foaming.

21 καὶ ἐπηρώτησεν τὸν πατέρα
And he questioned the father

αὐτοῦ· πόσος χρόνος ἐστὶν ὡς τοῦτο
of him: What time is it while this

γέγονεν αὐτῷ; ὁ δὲ εἶπεν· ἐκ παιδιόθεν·
has happened to him? And he said: From childhood;

22 καὶ πολλάκις καὶ εἰς πῦρ αὐτὸν
and often both into fire him

ἔβαλεν καὶ εἰς ὕδατα ἵνα ἀπολέσῃ αὐτόν· ἀλλ'
it threw and into waters that it may destroy him; but

εἴ τι δύνῃ, βοήθησον ἡμῖν σπλαγχνισθεὶς
if anything thou canst, help us having compassion

ἐφ' ἡμᾶς. **23** ὁ δὲ Ἰησοῦς εἶπεν αὐτῷ· τὸ εἰ
on us. – And Jesus said to him: The "if

δύνῃ, πάντα δυνατὰ τῷ πιστεύοντι.
thou canst," all things possible to the [one] believing.

24 εὐθὺς κράξας ὁ πατὴρ τοῦ παιδίου
Immediately crying out the father of the child

ἔλεγεν· πιστεύω· βοήθει μου τῇ ἀπιστίᾳ.
said: I believe; help thou of me the unbelief.

25 ἰδὼν δὲ ὁ Ἰησοῦς ὅτι ἐπισυντρέχει
And ²seeing – ¹Jesus that is(was) running together

ὄχλος, ἐπετίμησεν τῷ πνεύματι τῷ ἀκαθάρτῳ
a crowd, rebuked the spirit – unclean

λέγων αὐτῷ· τὸ ἄλαλον καὶ κωφὸν
saying to it: – Dumb and deaf

πνεῦμα, ἐγὼ ἐπιτάσσω σοι, ἔξελθε ἐξ
spirit, I command thee, come forth out of

αὐτοῦ καὶ μηκέτι εἰσέλθῃς εἰς αὐτόν.
him and no more mayest thou enter into him.

26 καὶ κράξας καὶ πολλὰ σπαράξας
And crying out and much convulsing [him]

ἐξῆλθεν· καὶ ἐγένετο ὡσεὶ νεκρός, ὥστε
it came out; and he was as dead, so as

τοὺς πολλοὺς λέγειν ὅτι ἀπέθανεν. **27** ὁ
– many to sayᵇ that he died. –
= many said

δὲ Ἰησοῦς κρατήσας τῆς χειρὸς αὐτοῦ
But Jesus taking hold of the hand of him

ἤγειρεν αὐτόν, καὶ ἀνέστη. **28** καὶ
raised him, and he stood up. And

εἰσελθόντος αὐτοῦ εἰς οἶκον οἱ μαθηταὶ
entering himᵃ into a house the disciples
=when he entered

αὐτοῦ κατ' ἰδίαν ἐπηρώτων αὐτόν· ὅτι
of him privately questioned him: Why

ἡμεῖς οὐκ ἠδυνήθημεν ἐκβαλεῖν αὐτό;
we were not able to expel it?

29 καὶ εἶπεν αὐτοῖς· τοῦτο τὸ γένος ἐν
And he told them: This – kind by

driven out by anything but prayer."[a]

30 They went on from there and passed through Galilee. And he would not have any one know it; [31]for he was teaching his disciples, saying to them, "The Son of man will be delivered into the hands of men, and they will kill him; and when he is killed, after three days he will rise." [32]But they did not understand the saying, and they were afraid to ask him.

33 And they came to Caper'na-um; and when he was in the house he asked them, "What were you discussing on the way?" [34]But they were silent; for on the way they had discussed with one another who was the greatest. [35]And he sat down and called the twelve; and he said to them, "If any one would be first, he must be last of all and servant of all." [36]And he took a child, and put him in the midst of them; and taking him in his arms, he said to them, [37]"Whoever receives one such child in my name receives me; and whoever receives me, receives not me but him who sent me."

38 John said to him,

οὐδενὶ δύναται ἐξελθεῖν εἰ μὴ ἐν προσευχῇ.
nothing can to come out except by prayer.

30 Κἀκεῖθεν ἐξελθόντες παρεπορεύοντο διὰ
And thence going forth they passed through

τῆς Γαλιλαίας, καὶ οὐκ ἤθελεν ἵνα
- Galilee, and he wished not that

τις γνοῖ· 31 ἐδίδασκεν γὰρ τοὺς μαθητὰς
anyone should know; for he was teaching the disciples

αὐτοῦ, καὶ ἔλεγεν αὐτοῖς ὅτι ὁ υἱὸς τοῦ
of him, and told them[,] - The Son -

ἀνθρώπου παραδίδοται εἰς χεῖρας ἀνθρώπων,
of man is betrayed into [the] hands of men,

καὶ ἀποκτενοῦσιν αὐτόν, καὶ ἀποκτανθεὶς
and they will kill him, and being killed

μετὰ τρεῖς ἡμέρας ἀναστήσεται. 32 οἱ
after three days he will rise up. they

δὲ ἠγνόουν τὸ ῥῆμα, καὶ ἐφοβοῦντο
But did not know the word, and feared

αὐτὸν ἐπερωτῆσαι.
him to question.

33 Καὶ ἦλθον εἰς Καφαρναούμ. Καὶ
And they came to Capernaum. And

ἐν τῇ οἰκίᾳ γενόμενος ἐπηρώτα αὐτούς·
in the house being he questioned them:

τί ἐν τῇ ὁδῷ διελογίζεσθε; 34 οἱ δὲ
What in the way were ye debating? And

ἐσιώπων· πρὸς ἀλλήλους γὰρ διελέχθησαν
were silent; ²with ³one another ¹for they debated

ἐν τῇ ὁδῷ τίς μείζων. 35 καὶ καθίσας
in the way who [was] greater. And sitting

ἐφώνησεν τοὺς δώδεκα καὶ λέγει αὐτοῖς·
he called the twelve and says to them:

εἴ τις θέλει πρῶτος εἶναι, ἔσται πάντων
If anyone wishes first to be, he shall be of all

ἔσχατος καὶ πάντων διάκονος. 36 καὶ
last and of all servant. And

λαβὼν παιδίον ἔστησεν αὐτὸ ἐν μέσῳ
taking a child he set it(him) in [the] midst

αὐτῶν, καὶ ἐναγκαλισάμενος αὐτὸ εἶπεν
of them, and folding in [his] arms it he said

αὐτοῖς· 37 ὃς ἂν ἓν τῶν τοιούτων παιδίων
to them: Whoever one - of such children

δέξηται ἐπὶ τῷ ὀνόματί μου, ἐμὲ δέχεται·
receives on(in) the name of me, me receives;

καὶ ὃς ἂν ἐμὲ δέχηται, οὐχ ἐμὲ δέχεται
and whoever me receives, not me receives

ἀλλὰ τὸν ἀποστείλαντά με. 38 Ἔφη αὐτῷ
but the [one] having sent me. Said to him

---

[a] Other ancient authorities add and fasting

"Teacher, we saw a man casting out demons in your name,[b] and we forbade him, because he was not following us." [39] But Jesus said, "Do not forbid him; for no one who does a mighty work in my name will be able soon after to speak evil of me. [40] For he that is not against us is for us. [41] For truly, I say to you, whoever gives you a cup of water to drink because you bear the name of Christ, will by no means lose his reward.

[42] "Whoever causes one of these little ones who believe in me to sin, it would be better for him if a great millstone were hung round his neck and he were thrown into the sea. [43] And if your hand causes you to sin, cut it off; it is better for you to enter life maimed than with two hands to go to hell, to the unquenchable fire.[c] [45] And if your foot causes you to sin, cut it off; it is better for you to enter life lame than with two feet to be thrown into

[b] Other ancient authorities add *who does not follow us*

[c] Verses 44 and 46 (which are identical with verse 48) are omitted by the best ancient authorities

ὁ Ἰωάννης· διδάσκαλε, εἴδομέν τινα ἐν
– John: Teacher, we saw someone in

τῷ ὀνόματί σου ἐκβάλλοντα δαιμόνια, ὃς
the name of thee expelling demons, who

οὐκ ἀκολουθεῖ ἡμῖν, καὶ ἐκωλύομεν αὐτόν,
does not follow us, and we forbade him,

ὅτι οὐκ ἠκολούθει ἡμῖν. 39 ὁ δὲ Ἰησοῦς
because he was not following us. – But Jesus

εἶπεν· μὴ κωλύετε αὐτόν· οὐδεὶς γάρ
said: Do not forbid him: for no one

ἐστιν ὃς ποιήσει δύναμιν ἐπὶ τῷ ὀνόματί
there is who shall do a mighty work on(in) the name

μου καὶ δυνήσεται ταχὺ κακολογῆσαί με·
of me and will be able quickly to speak evil of me;

40 ὃς γὰρ οὐκ ἔστιν καθ᾽ ἡμῶν, ὑπὲρ
for who is not against us, for

ἡμῶν ἐστιν. 41 Ὃς γὰρ ἂν ποτίσῃ
us is. For whoever [1]gives [3]drink

ὑμᾶς ποτήριον ὕδατος ἐν ὀνόματι, ὅτι
[2]you a cup of water in [the] name, because

Χριστοῦ ἐστε, ἀμὴν λέγω ὑμῖν ὅτι
of Christ ye are, truly I tell you that

οὐ μὴ ἀπολέσῃ τὸν μισθὸν αὐτοῦ. 42 Καὶ
by no means he will lose the reward of him. And

ὃς ἂν σκανδαλίσῃ ἕνα τῶν μικρῶν τούτων
whoever offends one – [3]little [ones] [1]of these

τῶν πιστευόντων, καλόν ἐστιν αὐτῷ μᾶλλον
– [2]believing, good is it for him rather

εἰ περίκειται μύλος ὀνικὸς περὶ τὸν
if be laid *round* a [heavy] millstone round the

τράχηλον αὐτοῦ καὶ βέβληται εἰς τὴν
neck of him and he be thrown into the

θάλασσαν. 43 Καὶ ἐὰν σκανδαλίσῃ σε ἡ
sea. And if offends thee the

χείρ σου, ἀπόκοψον αὐτήν· καλόν ἐστίν
hand of thee, cut off it; good is it

σε κυλλὸν εἰσελθεῖν εἰς τὴν ζωήν, ἢ τὰς
thee maimed to enter into – life, than the

δύο χεῖρας ἔχοντα ἀπελθεῖν εἰς τὴν
two hands having to go away into –

γέενναν, εἰς τὸ πῦρ τὸ ἄσβεστον.‡ 45 καὶ
gehenna, into the fire *the* unquenchable. And

ἐὰν ὁ πούς σου σκανδαλίζῃ σε, ἀπόκοψον
if the foot of thee offends thee, cut off

αὐτόν· καλόν ἐστίν σε εἰσελθεῖν εἰς τὴν
it; good is it thee to enter into –

ζωὴν χωλόν, ἢ τοὺς δύο πόδας ἔχοντα
life lame, than the two feet having

‡ Verse 44 omitted by Nestle; *cf.* RSV footnote.

hell.*e* ⁴⁷And if your eye causes you to sin, pluck it out; it is better for you to enter the kingdom of God with one eye than with two eyes to be thrown into hell, ⁴⁸where their worm does not die, and the fire is not quenched. ⁴⁹For every one will be salted with fire.*d* ⁵⁰Salt is good; but if the salt has lost its saltness, how will you season it? Have salt in yourselves, and be at peace with one another."

βληθῆναι εἰς τὴν γέενναν.‡ 47 καὶ ἐὰν ὁ
to be cast into – gehenna.   And if the

ὀφθαλμός σου σκανδαλίζῃ σε, ἔκβαλε αὐτόν·
eye of thee offends thee, cast out it;

καλόν σέ ἐστιν μονόφθαλμον εἰσελθεῖν εἰς
good thee is it one-eyed to enter into

τὴν βασιλείαν τοῦ θεοῦ, ἢ δύο ὀφθαλμούς
the kingdom – of God, than two eyes

ἔχοντα βληθῆναι εἰς τὴν γέενναν, 48 ὅπου
having to be cast into – gehenna, where

ὁ σκώληξ αὐτῶν οὐ τελευτᾷ καὶ τὸ
the worm of them dies not and the

πῦρ οὐ σβέννυται. 49 Πᾶς γὰρ πυρὶ
fire is not quenched. For everyone with fire

ἁλισθήσεται. 50 καλὸν τὸ ἅλας· ἐὰν δὲ
shall be salted. Good [is] – salt; but if

τὸ ἅλας ἄναλον γένηται, ἐν τίνι αὐτὸ
– salt saltless becomes, by what it

ἀρτύσετε; ἔχετε ἐν ἑαυτοῖς ἅλα καὶ
will ye season? Have in yourselves salt and

εἰρηνεύετε ἐν ἀλλήλοις.
be at peace among one another.

CHAPTER 10

A ND he left there and went to the region of Judea and beyond the Jordan, and crowds gathered to him again; and again, as his custom was, he taught them.

2 And Pharisees came up and in order to test him asked, "Is it lawful for a man to divorce his wife?" ³He answered them, "What did Moses command you?" ⁴They said, "Moses allowed a man to write a certificate of divorce, and to put her away." ⁵But Jesus said to them, "For your hardness of heart he

10 Καὶ ἐκεῖθεν ἀναστὰς ἔρχεται εἰς τὰ
    And thence rising up he comes into the

ὅρια τῆς Ἰουδαίας καὶ πέραν τοῦ
territory – of Judæa and beyond the

Ἰορδάνου, καὶ συμπορεύονται πάλιν ὄχλοι
Jordan, and ³go with ¹again ²crowds

πρὸς αὐτόν, καὶ ὡς εἰώθει πάλιν ἐδίδασκεν
⁴with ⁵him, and as he was wont again he taught

αὐτούς. 2 Καὶ προσελθόντες Φαρισαῖοι
them. And ²approaching ¹Pharisees

ἐπηρώτων αὐτὸν εἰ ἔξεστιν ἀνδρὶ γυναῖκα
questioned him if it is(was) lawful for a man a wife

ἀπολῦσαι, πειράζοντες αὐτόν. 3 ὁ δὲ
to dismiss, testing him. And he

ἀποκριθεὶς εἶπεν αὐτοῖς· 4 τί ὑμῖν ἐνετείλατο
answering said to them: What you ordered

Μωϋσῆς; οἱ δὲ εἶπαν· ἐπέτρεψεν Μωϋσῆς
Moses? And they said: permitted Moses

βιβλίον ἀποστασίου γράψαι καὶ ἀπολῦσαι.
a roll of divorce to write and to dismiss.

5 ὁ δὲ Ἰησοῦς εἶπεν αὐτοῖς· πρὸς τὴν
– And Jesus said to them: For the

σκληροκαρδίαν ὑμῶν ἔγραψεν ὑμῖν τὴν
hardheartedness of you he wrote to you –

e Verses 44 and 46 (which are identical with verse 48) are omitted by the best ancient authorities
d Other ancient authorities add *and every sacrifice will be salted with salt*

‡ Verse 46 omitted by Nestle; *cf.* RSV footnote.

wrote you this commandment. ⁶But from the beginning of creation, 'God made them male and female.' ⁷'For this reason a man shall leave his father and mother and be joined to his wife,ᵉ ⁸and the two shall become one.' So they are no longer two but one. ⁹What therefore God has joined together, let not man put asunder."

10 And in the house the disciples asked him again about this matter. ¹¹And he said to them, "Whoever divorces his wife and marries another, commits adultery against her; ¹²and if she divorces her husband and marries another, she commits adultery."

13 And they were bringing children to him, that he might touch them; and the disciples rebuked them. ¹⁴But when Jesus saw it he was indignant, and said to them, "Let the children come to me, do not hinder them; for to such belongs the kingdom of God. ¹⁵Truly, I say to you, whoever does not receive the kingdom of God like a child shall not enter it." ¹⁶And he took them in his arms and blessed them, laying his hands upon them.

ᵉ Other ancient authorities omit *and be joined to his wife*

ἐντολὴν ταύτην. 6 ἀπὸ δὲ ἀρχῆς κτίσεως
this commandment. But from [the] beginning of creation

ἄρσεν καὶ θῆλυ ἐποίησεν αὐτούς· 7 ἕνεκεν
male and female he made them; for the sake of

τούτου καταλείψει ἄνθρωπος τὸν πατέρα
this shall leave a man the father

αὐτοῦ καὶ τὴν μητέρα, 8 καὶ ἔσονται
of him and the mother, and shall be

οἱ δύο εἰς σάρκα μίαν· ὥστε οὐκέτι
the two – flesh one; so as no longer

εἰσὶν δύο ἀλλὰ μία σάρξ. 9 ὃ οὖν ὁ
are they two but one flesh. What then –

θεὸς συνέζευξεν, ἄνθρωπος μὴ χωριζέτω.
God yoked together, ³man ²not ¹let ⁴separate.

10 καὶ εἰς τὴν οἰκίαν πάλιν οἱ μαθηταὶ
And in the house again the disciples

περὶ τούτου ἐπηρώτων αὐτόν. 11 καὶ
about this questioned him. And

λέγει αὐτοῖς· ὃς ἂν ἀπολύσῃ τὴν γυναῖκα
he says to them: Whoever dismisses the wife

αὐτοῦ καὶ γαμήσῃ ἄλλην, μοιχᾶται ἐπ'
of him and marries another, commits adultery with

αὐτήν· 12 καὶ ἐὰν αὐτὴ ἀπολύσασα τὸν
her; and if she having dismissed the

ἄνδρα αὐτῆς γαμήσῃ ἄλλον, μοιχᾶται.
husband of her marries another, she commits adultery.

13 Καὶ προσέφερον αὐτῷ παιδία ἵνα
And they brought to him children that

αὐτῶν ἅψηται· οἱ δὲ μαθηταὶ ἐπετίμησαν
them he might touch; but the disciples rebuked

αὐτοῖς. 14 ἰδὼν δὲ ὁ Ἰησοῦς ἠγανάκτησεν
them. But ²seeing – ¹Jesus was angry

καὶ εἶπεν αὐτοῖς· ἄφετε τὰ παιδία
and said to them: Allow the children

ἔρχεσθαι πρός με, μὴ κωλύετε αὐτά·
to come to me, do not prevent them;

τῶν γὰρ τοιούτων ἐστὶν ἡ βασιλεία τοῦ
– for of such is the kingdom –

θεοῦ. 15 ἀμὴν λέγω ὑμῖν, ὃς ἂν
of God. Truly I tell you, whoever

μὴ δέξηται τὴν βασιλείαν τοῦ θεοῦ ὡς
receives not the kingdom – of God as

παιδίον, οὐ μὴ εἰσέλθῃ εἰς αὐτήν. 16 καὶ
a child, by no means may enter into it. And

ἐναγκαλισάμενος αὐτὰ κατευλόγει τιθεὶς τὰς
folding in [his] arms them he blesses putting the(his)

χεῖρας ἐπ' αὐτά.
hands on them.

17 And as he was setting out on his journey, a man ran up and knelt before him, and asked him, "Good Teacher, what must I do to inherit eternal life?" 18And Jesus said to him, "Why do you call me good? No one is good but God alone. 19You know the commandments: 'Do not kill, Do not commit adultery, Do not steal, Do not bear false witness, Do not defraud, Honor your father and mother.'" 20And he said to him, "Teacher, all these I have observed from my youth." 21And Jesus looking upon him loved him, and said to him, "You lack one thing; go, sell what you have, and give to the poor, and you will have treasure in heaven; and come, follow me." 22At that saying his countenance fell, and he went away sorrowful; for he had great possessions. 23 And Jesus looked around and said to his disciples, "How hard it will be for those who have riches to enter the kingdom of God!" 24And the disciples were amazed at his words. But Jesus said to them again,

17 Καὶ ἐκπορευομένου αὐτοῦ εἰς ὁδὸν
And   going forth   him^a   into [the] way
                = as he went forth

προσδραμὼν εἷς καὶ γονυπετήσας αὐτὸν
running to   one   and   kneeling to   him

ἐπηρώτα αὐτόν· διδάσκαλε ἀγαθέ, τί ποιήσω
questioned him: Teacher   good, what may I do

ἵνα ζωὴν αἰώνιον κληρονομήσω; 18 ὁ δὲ
that life   eternal   I may inherit ?   – And

Ἰησοῦς εἶπεν αὐτῷ· τί με λέγεις ἀγαθόν;
Jesus   said   to him: Why me callest thou good?

οὐδεὶς ἀγαθὸς εἰ μὴ εἷς ὁ θεός. 19 τὰς ἐντολὰς
no one   good except one – God.   The commandments

οἶδας·   μὴ   φονεύσῃς,   μὴ   μοιχεύσῃς,
thou knowest: Do not kill,   Do not commit adultery,

μὴ κλέψῃς,   μὴ ψευδομαρτυρήσῃς,   μὴ
Do not steal,   Do not bear false witness,   Do

ἀποστερήσῃς, τίμα τὸν πατέρα σου καὶ
not defraud,   Honour the   father   of thee and

τὴν μητέρα. 20 ὁ δὲ ἔφη αὐτῷ· διδάσκαλε,
the   mother.   And he said   to him: Teacher,

ταῦτα πάντα ἐφυλαξάμην ἐκ νεότητός μου.
all these things I observed   from   youth of me.

21 ὁ δὲ Ἰησοῦς ἐμβλέψας αὐτῷ ἠγάπησεν
 – But Jesus   looking at   him   loved

αὐτὸν καὶ εἶπεν αὐτῷ· ἓν σε ὑστερεῖ·
him   and said   to him: One thing thee is wanting:

ὕπαγε,   ὅσα   ἔχεις πώλησον καὶ δὸς [τοῖς]
go,   what things thou hast   sell   and give to the

πτωχοῖς, καὶ ἕξεις θησαυρὸν ἐν οὐρανῷ,
poor,   and thou wilt have treasure   in   heaven,

καὶ δεῦρο ἀκολούθει μοι. 22 ὁ δὲ στυγνάσας
and come   follow   me.   But he being sad

ἐπὶ τῷ λόγῳ ἀπῆλθεν λυπούμενος, ἦν
at   the   word   went away grieving,   ^bhe was

γὰρ ἔχων κτήματα πολλά. 23 Καὶ
^1for having possessions many.   And

περιβλεψάμενος ὁ Ἰησοῦς λέγει τοῖς
looking round   –   Jesus   says   to the

μαθηταῖς αὐτοῦ· πῶς δυσκόλως οἱ τὰ
disciples   of him: How   hardly   the [ones] the

χρήματα ἔχοντες εἰς τὴν βασιλείαν τοῦ
riches   having into   the   kingdom   –

θεοῦ εἰσελεύσονται. 24 οἱ δὲ μαθηταὶ
of God shall enter.   And the   disciples

ἐθαμβοῦντο ἐπὶ τοῖς λόγοις αὐτοῦ. ὁ δὲ
were amazed at   the   words   of him. – And

Ἰησοῦς πάλιν ἀποκριθεὶς λέγει αὐτοῖς·
Jesus   again   answering   says   to them:

"Children, how hard it is[f] to enter the kingdom of God! ²⁵It is easier for a camel to go through the eye of a needle than for a rich man to enter the kingdom of God." ²⁶And they were exceedingly astonished, and said to him,[g] "Then who can be saved?" ²⁷Jesus looked at them and said, "With men it is impossible, but not with God; for all things are possible with God." ²⁸Peter began to say to him, "Lo, we have left everything and followed you." ²⁹Jesus said, "Truly, I say to you, there is no one who has left house or brothers or sisters or mother or father or children or lands, for my sake and for the gospel, ³⁰who will not receive a hundredfold now in this time, houses and brothers and sisters and mothers and children and lands, with persecutions, and in the age to come eternal life. ³¹But many that are first will be last, and the last first."

32 And they were on the road, going up to

[f] Other ancient authorities add *for those who trust in riches*
[g] Other ancient authorities read *to one another*

τέκνα, πῶς δύσκολόν ἐστιν εἰς τὴν
Children, how hard it is into the

βασιλείαν τοῦ θεοῦ εἰσελθεῖν· 25 εὐκοπώτερόν
kingdom – of God to enter; easier

ἐστιν κάμηλον διὰ τῆς τρυμαλιᾶς τῆς
it is a camel through the eye –

ραφίδος διελθεῖν ἢ πλούσιον εἰς τὴν
of a needle to go *through* than a rich man into the

βασιλείαν τοῦ θεοῦ εἰσελθεῖν. 26 οἱ δὲ
kingdom – of God to enter. But they

περισσῶς ἐξεπλήσσοντο λέγοντες πρὸς
exceedingly were astonished saying to

ἑαυτούς· καὶ τίς δύναται σωθῆναι;
themselves: And who can *to* be saved?

27 ἐμβλέψας αὐτοῖς ὁ Ἰησοῦς λέγει· παρὰ
Looking at them – Jesus says: With

ἀνθρώποις ἀδύνατον, ἀλλ' οὐ παρὰ θεῷ·
men [it is] impossible, but not with God;

πάντα γὰρ δυνατὰ παρὰ τῷ θεῷ. 28 Ἤρξατο
for all things [are] possible with – God. Began

λέγειν ὁ Πέτρος αὐτῷ· ἰδοὺ ἡμεῖς ἀφήκαμεν
to say – Peter to him: Behold [,] we left

πάντα καὶ ἠκολουθήκαμέν σοι. 29 ἔφη ὁ
all things and have followed thee. Said –

Ἰησοῦς· ἀμὴν λέγω ὑμῖν, οὐδείς ἐστιν
Jesus: Truly I tell you, no one there is

ὃς ἀφῆκεν οἰκίαν ἢ ἀδελφοὺς ἢ ἀδελφὰς
who left house or brothers or sisters

ἢ μητέρα ἢ πατέρα ἢ τέκνα ἢ ἀγροὺς
or mother or father or children or fields

ἕνεκεν ἐμοῦ καὶ ἕνεκεν τοῦ εὐαγγελίου,
for the sake of me and for the sake of the gospel,

30 ἐὰν μὴ λάβῃ ἑκατονταπλασίονα νῦν
but he receives a hundredfold now

ἐν τῷ καιρῷ τούτῳ οἰκίας καὶ ἀδελφοὺς
in – time this houses and brothers

καὶ ἀδελφὰς καὶ μητέρας καὶ τέκνα καὶ
and sisters and mothers and children and

ἀγροὺς μετὰ διωγμῶν, καὶ ἐν τῷ αἰῶνι
fields with persecutions, and in the age

τῷ ἐρχομένῳ ζωὴν αἰώνιον. 31 πολλοὶ δὲ
– coming life eternal. And ¹many

ἔσονται πρῶτοι ἔσχατοι καὶ οἱ ἔσχατοι
²will be ³first ⁴last and the last

πρῶτοι.
first.

32 Ἦσαν δὲ ἐν τῇ ὁδῷ ἀναβαίνοντες
Now they were in the way going up

Jerusalem, and Jesus was walking ahead of them; and they were amazed, and those who followed were afraid. And taking the twelve again, he began to tell them what was to happen to him, ³³saying, "Behold, we are going up to Jerusalem; and the Son of man will be delivered to the chief priests and the scribes, and they will condemn him to death, and deliver him to the Gentiles; ³⁴and they will mock him, and spit upon him, and scourge him, and kill him; and after three days he will rise."

35 And James and John, the sons of Zeb'-edee, came forward to him, and said to him, "Teacher, we want you to do for us whatever we ask of you." ³⁶And he said to them, "What do you want me to do for you?" ³⁷And they said to him, "Grant us to sit, one at your right hand and one at your left, in your glory." ³⁸But Jesus said to them, "You do not know what you are asking. Are you able to drink the cup that I drink, or to be baptized with the baptism with

εἰς Ἱεροσόλυμα, καὶ ἦν προάγων αὐτοὺς
to Jerusalem, and was going before them

ὁ Ἰησοῦς, καὶ ἐθαμβοῦντο, οἱ δὲ
- Jesus, and they were astonished, and the

ἀκολουθοῦντες ἐφοβοῦντο. καὶ παραλαβὼν
[ones] following were afraid. And taking

πάλιν τοὺς δώδεκα ἤρξατο αὐτοῖς λέγειν
again the twelve he began them to tell

τὰ μέλλοντα αὐτῷ συμβαίνειν, 33 ὅτι ἰδοὺ
the things about to him to happen, - Behold

ἀναβαίνομεν εἰς Ἱεροσόλυμα, καὶ ὁ υἱὸς
we are going up to Jerusalem, and the Son

τοῦ ἀνθρώπου παραδοθήσεται τοῖς
- of man will be betrayed to the

ἀρχιερεῦσιν καὶ τοῖς γραμματεῦσιν, καὶ
chief priests and to the scribes, and

κατακρινοῦσιν αὐτὸν θανάτῳ καὶ παραδώσουσιν
they will condemn him to death and will deliver

αὐτὸν τοῖς ἔθνεσιν 34 καὶ ἐμπαίξουσιν
him to the nations 34 and they will mock

αὐτῷ καὶ ἐμπτύσουσιν αὐτῷ καὶ μαστι-
him and will spit at him and will

γώσουσιν αὐτὸν καὶ ἀποκτενοῦσιν, καὶ
scourge him and will kill, and

μετὰ τρεῖς ἡμέρας ἀναστήσεται.
after three days he will rise again.

35 Καὶ προσπορεύονται αὐτῷ Ἰάκωβος
And approach to him James

καὶ Ἰωάννης οἱ [δύο] υἱοὶ Ζεβεδαίου
and John the two sons of Zebedee

λέγοντες αὐτῷ· διδάσκαλε, θέλομεν ἵνα ὃ ἐὰν
saying to him: Teacher, we wish that whatever

αἰτήσωμέν σε ποιήσῃς ἡμῖν. 36 ὁ
we may ask thee thou mayest do for us. he

δὲ εἶπεν αὐτοῖς· τί θέλετέ με ποιήσω
And said to them: What wish ye me I may do

ὑμῖν; 37 οἱ δὲ εἶπαν αὐτῷ· δὸς ἡμῖν
for you? And they said to him: Give us

ἵνα εἷς σου ἐκ δεξιῶν καὶ εἷς ἐξ
that one of thee out of(on) [the] right and one on
= on thy right

ἀριστερῶν καθίσωμεν ἐν τῇ δόξῃ σου.
[thy] left we may sit in the glory of thee.

38 ὁ δὲ Ἰησοῦς εἶπεν αὐτοῖς· οὐκ οἴδατε
- And Jesus said to them: Ye know not

τί αἰτεῖσθε. δύνασθε πιεῖν τὸ ποτήριον
what ye ask. Can ye to drink the cup

ὃ ἐγὼ πίνω, ἢ τὸ βάπτισμα ὃ ἐγὼ
which I drink, or the baptism which I

which I am baptized?"
³⁹And they said to him,
"We are able." And
Jesus said to them, "The
cup that I drink you will
drink; and with the
baptism with which I am
baptized, you will be
baptized; ⁴⁰but to sit at
my right hand or at my
left is not mine to grant,
but it is for those for
whom it has been pre-
pared." ⁴¹And when the
ten heard it, they began
to be indignant at James
and John. ⁴²And Jesus
called them to him and
said to them, "You know
that those who are sup-
posed to rule over the
Gentiles lord it over
them, and their great
men exercise authority
over them. ⁴³But it shall
not be so among you;
but whoever would be
great among you must
be your servant, ⁴⁴and
whoever would be first
among you must be slave
of all. ⁴⁵For the Son of
man also came not to be
served but to serve, and
to give his life as a
ransom for many."
46 And they came to
Jericho; and as he was
leaving Jericho with his
disciples and a great
multitude, Bartimae′us, a

βαπτίζομαι   βαπτισθῆναι;   39 οἱ   δὲ   εἶπαν
am baptized   to be baptized [with]?   And they   said

αὐτῷ·   δυνάμεθα.   ὁ   δὲ   ᾿Ιησοῦς   εἶπεν
to him: We can.   -   And   Jesus   said

αὐτοῖς·   τὸ   ποτήριον   ὃ   ἐγὼ   πίνω   πίεσθε,
to them: The   cup   which   I   drink   shall ye drink,

καὶ   τὸ   βάπτισμα   ὃ   ἐγὼ   βαπτίζομαι
and   the   baptism   which   I   am baptized [with]

βαπτισθήσεσθε·   40 τὸ   δὲ   καθίσαι   ἐκ   δεξιῶν
ye shall be baptized;   -   but   to sit   on   right

μου   ἢ   ἐξ   εὐωνύμων   οὐκ   ἔστιν   ἐμὸν
of me or   on   [my] left   is not   mine

δοῦναι,   ἀλλ'   οἷς   ἡτοίμασται.   41 Καὶ
to give,   but   for whom it has been prepared.   And

ἀκούσαντες   οἱ   δέκα   ἤρξαντο   ἀγανακτεῖν
³hearing   ¹the   ²ten   began   to be incensed

περὶ   ᾿Ιακώβου   καὶ   ᾿Ιωάννου.   42 καὶ
about   James   and   John.   And

προσκαλεσάμενος   αὐτοὺς   ὁ   ᾿Ιησοῦς   λέγει
¹calling ³to ⁴[him]   ²them   -   Jesus   says

αὐτοῖς·   οἴδατε   ὅτι   οἱ   δοκοῦντες   ἄρχειν
to them: Ye know that the   [ones] thinking   to rule

τῶν   ἐθνῶν   κατακυριεύουσιν   αὐτῶν   καὶ
the   nations   lord it over   them   and

οἱ   μεγάλοι   αὐτῶν   κατεξουσιάζουσιν   αὐτῶν.
the   great [ones]   of them   exercise authority over   them.

43 οὐχ   οὕτως   δέ   ἐστιν   ἐν   ὑμῖν·   ἀλλ'
²not   ³so   ¹But   is it   among   you;   but

ὃς   ἂν   θέλῃ   μέγας   γενέσθαι   ἐν   ὑμῖν,
whoever wishes   great   to become   among   you,

ἔσται   ὑμῶν   διάκονος,   44 καὶ   ὃς   ἂν
shall be of you   servant,   and   whoever

θέλῃ   ἐν   ὑμῖν   εἶναι   πρῶτος,   ἔσται   πάντων
wishes among you   to be   first,   shall be   of all

δοῦλος·   45 καὶ   γὰρ   ὁ   υἱὸς   τοῦ   ἀνθρώπου
slave;   for even   the   Son   -   of man

οὐκ   ἦλθεν   διακονηθῆναι   ἀλλὰ   διακονῆσαι
did not come   to be served   but   to serve

καὶ   δοῦναι   τὴν   ψυχὴν   αὐτοῦ   λύτρον   ἀντὶ
and   to give   the   life   of him   a ransom   instead of

πολλῶν.
many.

46 Καὶ   ἔρχονται   εἰς   ᾿Ιεριχώ.   Καὶ
And   they come   to   Jericho.   And

ἐκπορευομένου   αὐτοῦ   ἀπὸ   ᾿Ιεριχὼ   καὶ   τῶν
going out   himᵃ   from   Jericho   and   the
= as he was going out

μαθητῶν   αὐτοῦ   καὶ   ὄχλου   ἱκανοῦ   ὁ   υἱὸς
disciplesᵃ   of him   and   crowd a considerableᵃ the   son

blind beggar, the son of Timae'us, was sitting by the roadside. ⁴⁷And when he heard that it was Jesus of Nazareth, he began to cry out and say, "Jesus, Son of David, have mercy on me!" ⁴⁸And many rebuked him, telling him to be silent; but he cried out all the more, "Son of David, have mercy on me!" ⁴⁹And Jesus stopped and said, "Call him." And they called the blind man, saying to him, "Take heart; rise, he is calling you." ⁵⁰And throwing off his mantle he sprang up and came to Jesus. ⁵¹And Jesus said to him, "What do you want me to do for you?" And the blind man said to him, "Master, let me receive my sight." ⁵²And Jesus said to him, "Go your way; your faith has made you well." And immediately he received his sight and followed him on the way.

Τιμαίου	Βαρτιμαῖος,	τυφλὸς	προσαίτης,
of Timæus	Bartimæus,	a blind	beggar,

ἐκάθητο παρὰ τὴν ὁδόν. 47 καὶ ἀκούσας
sat   by   the   way.   And   hearing

ὅτι 'Ιησοῦς ὁ Ναζαρηνός ἐστιν ἤρξατο
that   Jesus   the   Nazarene   it is(was)   he began

κράζειν καὶ λέγειν· υἱὲ Δαυὶδ 'Ιησοῦ,
to cry out   and   to say: Son   of David   Jesus,

ἐλέησόν με. 48 καὶ ἐπετίμων αὐτῷ πολλοὶ
pity   me.   And   rebuked   him   many

ἵνα σιωπήσῃ. ὁ δὲ πολλῷ μᾶλλον ἔκραζεν·
that he should be quiet. But he   much   more   cried out:

υἱὲ Δαυίδ, ἐλέησόν με. 49 καὶ στὰς
Son   of David,   pity   me.   And   standing

ὁ 'Ιησοῦς εἶπεν· φωνήσατε αὐτόν. καὶ
–   Jesus   said: Call   him.   And

φωνοῦσιν τὸν τυφλὸν λέγοντες αὐτῷ·
they call   the   blind man   saying   to him:

θάρσει, ἔγειρε, φωνεῖ σε. 50 ὁ δὲ
Be of good courage, rise,   he calls   thee.   So he

ἀποβαλὼν τὸ ἱμάτιον αὐτοῦ ἀναπηδήσας ἦλθεν
throwing away the   garment   of him   leaping up   came

πρὸς τὸν 'Ιησοῦν. 51 καὶ ἀποκριθεὶς αὐτῷ ὁ
to –   Jesus.   And   answering   him –

'Ιησοῦς εἶπεν· τί σοι θέλεις ποιήσω;
Jesus   said: What for thee wishest thou   I may do?

ὁ δὲ τυφλὸς εἶπεν αὐτῷ· ῥαββουνί, ἵνα
And the   blind man   said   to him: Rabboni,   that

ἀναβλέψω. 52 καὶ ὁ 'Ιησοῦς εἶπεν αὐτῷ·
I may see again.   And   –   Jesus   said   to him:

ὕπαγε, ἡ πίστις σου σέσωκέν σε. καὶ
Go,   the   faith   of thee   has healed   thee.   And

εὐθὺς ἀνέβλεψεν, καὶ ἠκολούθει αὐτῷ ἐν
immediately he saw again,   and   followed   him   in

τῇ ὁδῷ.
the   way.

CHAPTER 11

AND when they drew near to Jerusalem, to Beth'phage and Bethany, at the Mount of Olives, he sent two of his disciples, ²and said to them, "Go into the village opposite you, and

11 Καὶ ὅτε ἐγγίζουσιν εἰς 'Ιεροσόλυμα
And   when   they draw near   to   Jerusalem

εἰς Βηθφαγὴ καὶ Βηθανίαν πρὸς τὸ
to   Bethphage   and   Bethany   at   the

ὄρος τῶν ἐλαιῶν, ἀποστέλλει δύο τῶν
mount   of the   olives,   he sends   two   of the

μαθητῶν αὐτοῦ 2 καὶ λέγει αὐτοῖς· ὑπάγετε
disciples   of him   and   tells   them: Go ye

εἰς τὴν κώμην τὴν κατέναντι ὑμῶν, καὶ
into   the   village   –   opposite   you,   and

immediately as you enter it you will find a colt tied, on which no one has ever sat; untie it and bring it. ³If any one says to you, 'Why are you doing this?' say, 'The Lord has need of it and will send it back here immediately.' " ⁴And they went away, and found a colt tied at the door out in the open street; and they untied it. ⁵And those who stood there said to them," What are you doing, untying the colt?" ⁶And they told them what Jesus had said; and they let them go. ⁷And they brought the colt to Jesus, and threw their garments on it; and he sat upon it. ⁸And many spread their garments on the road, and others spread leafy branches which they had cut from the fields.⁹ And those who went before and those who followed cried out, "Hosanna! Blessed is he who comes in the name of the Lord! ¹⁰Blessed is the kingdom of our father David that is coming! Hosanna in the highest!"

11 And he entered Jerusalem, and went into the temple; and when he had looked round at

εὐθὺς	εἰσπορευόμενοι	εἰς	αὐτὴν	εὑρήσετε
immediately	entering	into	it	ye will find

πῶλον δεδεμένον ἐφ' ὃν οὐδεὶς οὔπω
a colt having been tied on which ¹no one ²not yet

ἀνθρώπων ἐκάθισεν· λύσατε αὐτὸν καὶ
²of men ⁴sat; loosen it and

φέρετε. 3 καὶ ἐάν τις ὑμῖν εἴπῃ· τί
bring. And if anyone to you says: Why

ποιεῖτε τοῦτο; εἴπατε· ὁ κύριος αὐτοῦ
do ye this? say: The Lord of it

χρείαν ἔχει, καὶ εὐθὺς αὐτὸν ἀποστέλλει
need has, and immediately it he sends

πάλιν ὧδε. 4 καὶ ἀπῆλθον καὶ εὗρον
again here. And they went and found

πῶλον δεδεμένον πρὸς θύραν ἔξω ἐπὶ
a colt having been tied at a door outside on

τοῦ ἀμφόδου, καὶ λύουσιν αὐτόν. 5 καὶ
the open street, and they loosen it. And

τινες τῶν ἐκεῖ ἑστηκότων ἔλεγον αὐτοῖς·
some of the [ones] there standing said to them:

τί ποιεῖτε λύοντες τὸν πῶλον; 6 οἱ δὲ
What do ye loosening the colt? And they

εἶπαν αὐτοῖς καθὼς εἶπεν ὁ Ἰησοῦς·
said to them as said - Jesus;

καὶ ἀφῆκαν αὐτούς. 7 καὶ φέρουσιν τὸν
and they let go them. And they bring the

πῶλον πρὸς τὸν Ἰησοῦν, καὶ ἐπιβάλλουσιν
colt to - Jesus, and they throw on

αὐτῷ τὰ ἱμάτια αὐτῶν, καὶ ἐκάθισεν
it the garments of them, and he sat

ἐπ' αὐτόν. 8 καὶ πολλοὶ τὰ ἱμάτια αὐτῶν
on it. And many the garments of them

ἔστρωσαν εἰς τὴν ὁδόν, ἄλλοι δὲ στιβάδας,
strewed in the way, and others wisps of twigs,

κόψαντες ἐκ τῶν ἀγρῶν. 9 καὶ οἱ
cutting out of the fields. And the [ones]

προάγοντες καὶ οἱ ἀκολουθοῦντες ἔκραζον·
going before and the [ones] following cried out:

ὡσαννά· εὐλογημένος ὁ ἐρχόμενος ἐν
Hosanna; blessed the [one] coming in

ὀνόματι κυρίου· 10 εὐλογημένη ἡ ἐρχομένη
[the] name of [the] Lord; blessed the coming

βασιλεία τοῦ πατρὸς ἡμῶν Δαυίδ· ὡσαννὰ
kingdom of the father of us David; Hosanna

ἐν τοῖς ὑψίστοις. 11 Καὶ εἰσῆλθεν εἰς
in the highest [places]. And he entered into

Ἰεροσόλυμα εἰς τὸ ἱερόν· καὶ περιβλεψάμενος
Jerusalem into the temple; and looking round at

everything, as it was already late, he went out to Bethany with the twelve.
12 On the following day, when they came from Bethany, he was hungry. ¹³And seeing in the distance a fig tree in leaf, he went to see if he could find anything on it. When he came to it, he found nothing but leaves, for it was not the season for figs. ¹⁴And he said to it, "May no one ever eat fruit from you again." And his disciples heard it.
15 And they came to Jerusalem. And he entered the temple and began to drive out those who sold and those who bought in the temple, and he overturned the tables of the money-changers and the seats of those who sold pigeons; ¹⁶and he would not allow any one to carry anything through the temple. ¹⁷And he taught, and said to them, "Is it not written, 'My house shall be called a house of prayer for all the nations'? But you have made it a den of robbers." ¹⁸And the chief priests and the scribes heard it and sought a way to destroy him; for they

πάντα, ὀψὲ ἤδη οὔσης τῆς ὥρας, ἐξῆλθεν
all things, ⁵late ⁴now ³being ¹the ²hour,ᵃ he went forth
εἰς Βηθανίαν μετὰ τῶν δώδεκα.
to Bethany with the twelve.
12 Καὶ τῇ ἐπαύριον ἐξελθόντων αὐτῶν
And on the morrow going forth themᵃ
= as they went forth
ἀπὸ Βηθανίας ἐπείνασεν. 13 καὶ ἰδὼν
from Bethany he hungered. And seeing
συκῆν ἀπὸ μακρόθεν ἔχουσαν φύλλα ἦλθεν
a fig-tree from afar having leaves he came
εἰ ἄρα τι εὑρήσει ἐν αὐτῇ, καὶ ἐλθὼν
if perhaps something he will find in it, and coming
ἐπ' αὐτὴν οὐδὲν εὗρεν εἰ μὴ φύλλα·
upon it nothing he found except leaves;
ὁ γὰρ καιρὸς οὐκ ἦν σύκων. 14 καὶ
for the time was not of figs. And
ἀποκριθεὶς εἶπεν αὐτῇ· μηκέτι εἰς τὸν
answering he said to it: No more to the
αἰῶνα ἐκ σοῦ μηδεὶς καρπὸν φάγοι.
age of thee no one fruit may eat.
= May no one eat fruit of thee for ever.
καὶ ἤκουον οἱ μαθηταὶ αὐτοῦ. 15 Καὶ
And ⁴heard ¹the ²disciples ³of him. And
ἔρχονται εἰς Ἱεροσόλυμα. Καὶ εἰσελθὼν
they come to Jerusalem. And entering
εἰς τὸ ἱερὸν ἤρξατο ἐκβάλλειν τοὺς
into the temple he began to cast out the [ones]
πωλοῦντας καὶ τοὺς ἀγοράζοντας ἐν τῷ
selling and the [ones] buying in the
ἱερῷ, καὶ τὰς τραπέζας τῶν κολλυβιστῶν
temple, and the tables of the moneychangers
καὶ τὰς καθέδρας τῶν πωλούντων τὰς
and the seats of the [ones] selling the
περιστερὰς κατέστρεψεν, 16 καὶ οὐκ ἤφιεν
doves he overturned, and did not permit
ἵνα τις διενέγκῃ σκεῦος διὰ τοῦ
that anyone should carry through a vessel through the
ἱεροῦ, 17 καὶ ἐδίδασκεν καὶ ἔλεγεν αὐτοῖς· οὐ
temple, and taught and said to them: Not
γέγραπται ὅτι ὁ οἶκός μου οἶκος προσευχῆς
has it been written that the house of me a house of prayer
κληθήσεται πᾶσιν τοῖς ἔθνεσιν; ὑμεῖς δὲ
shall be called for all the nations? but ye
πεποιήκατε αὐτὸν σπήλαιον λῃστῶν. 18 καὶ
have made it a den of robbers. And
ἤκουσαν οἱ ἀρχιερεῖς καὶ οἱ γραμματεῖς,
⁵heard ¹the ²chief priests ³and ⁴the ⁵scribes,
καὶ ἐζήτουν πῶς αὐτὸν ἀπολέσωσιν·
and they sought how him they might destroy;

feared him, because all the multitude was astonished at his teaching. ¹⁹And when evening came they^h went out of the city.

20 As they passed by in the morning, they saw the fig tree withered away to its roots. ²¹And Peter remembered and said to him, "Master, look! The fig tree which you cursed has withered.' ²²And Jesus answered them, "Have faith in God. ²³Truly, I say to you, whoever says to this mountain, 'Be taken up and cast into the sea,' and does not doubt in his heart, but believes that what he says will come to pass, it will be done for him. ²⁴Therefore I tell you, whatever you ask in prayer, believe that you receive it, and you will. ²⁵And whenever you stand praying, forgive, if you have anything against any one; so that your Father also who is in heaven may forgive you your trespasses."ⁱ

27 And they came again to Jerusalem. And as he was walking in the temple, the chief priests and the scribes and the elders came to him,

^h Other ancient authorities read he

ⁱ Other ancient authorities add verse 26, "But if you do not forgive, neither will your Father who is in heaven forgive your trespasses"

ἐφοβοῦντο γὰρ αὐτόν, πᾶς γὰρ ὁ ὄχλος
for they feared   him,   for all   the   crowd
ἐξεπλήσσετο ἐπὶ τῇ διδαχῇ αὐτοῦ. 19 Καὶ
was astounded   at the teaching of him.   And
ὅταν ὀψὲ ἐγένετο, ἐξεπορεύοντο ἔξω τῆς
when late it became,   they went forth outside the
πόλεως. 20 Καὶ παραπορευόμενοι πρωΐ
city.   And   passing along   early
εἶδον τὴν συκῆν ἐξηραμμένην ἐκ ῥιζῶν.
they saw the fig-tree having been withered from [the] roots.
21 καὶ ἀναμνησθεὶς ὁ Πέτρος λέγει αὐτῷ·
And   ²remembering   - ¹Peter says to him:
ῥαββί, ἴδε ἡ συκῆ ἦν κατηράσω
Rabbi, behold[,] the fig-tree which thou cursedst
ἐξήρανται. 22 καὶ ἀποκριθεὶς ὁ Ἰησοῦς λέγει
has been withered.   And answering   -   Jesus   says
αὐτοῖς· ἔχετε πίστιν θεοῦ. 23 ἀμὴν λέγω ὑμῖν
to them: Have [the] faith of God. Truly I tell you
ὅτι ὃς ἂν εἴπῃ τῷ ὄρει τούτῳ· ἄρθητι
that whoever says - mountain to this: Be thou taken
καὶ βλήθητι εἰς τὴν θάλασσαν, καὶ μὴ
and be thou cast into the   sea,   and   not
διακριθῇ ἐν τῇ καρδίᾳ αὐτοῦ ἀλλὰ πιστεύῃ
doubts in the   heart   of him but believes
ὅτι ὃ λαλεῖ γίνεται, ἔσται αὐτῷ. 24 διὰ
that what he says happens, it will be to him.^c   There-
                                              = he will have it.
τοῦτο λέγω ὑμῖν, πάντα ὅσα προσεύχεσθε
fore I tell you, all things which   ye pray
καὶ αἰτεῖσθε, πιστεύετε ὅτι ἐλάβετε, καὶ
and   ask,   believe   that ye received, and
ἔσται ὑμῖν, 25 καὶ ὅταν στήκετε
it will be to you.^c   And when ye stand
= ye will have it.
προσευχόμενοι, ἀφίετε εἴ τι ἔχετε κατά
praying,   forgive if anything ye have against
τινος, ἵνα καὶ ὁ πατὴρ ὑμῶν ὁ ἐν τοῖς
anyone, that also the Father of you - in the
οὐρανοῖς ἀφῇ ὑμῖν τὰ παραπτώματα ὑμῶν.‡
heavens may forgive you the   trespasses   of you.
27 Καὶ ἔρχονται πάλιν εἰς Ἱεροσόλυμα.
And they come again   to Jerusalem.
καὶ ἐν τῷ ἱερῷ περιπατοῦντος αὐτοῦ
And in the temple   walking   him^a
                                      =as he walked
ἔρχονται πρὸς αὐτὸν οἱ ἀρχιερεῖς καὶ οἱ
come   to   him the chief priests and the
γραμματεῖς καὶ οἱ πρεσβύτεροι, 28 καὶ
scribes   and the   elders,   and

‡ Verse 26 omitted by Nestle; cf. RSV footnote.

28and they said to him, "By what authority are you doing these things, or who gave you this authority to do them?" 29Jesus said to them, "I will ask you a question; answer me, and I will tell you by what authority I do these things. 30Was the baptism of John from heaven or from men? Answer me." 31And they argued with one another, "If we say, 'From heaven,' he will say, 'Why then did you not believe him?' 32But shall we say, 'From men'?"—they were afraid of the people, for all held that John was a real prophet. 33So they answered Jesus, "We do not know." And Jesus said to them, "Neither will I tell you by what authority I do these things."

CHAPTER 12

AND he began to speak to them in parables. "A man planted a vineyard, and set a hedge around it, and dug a pit for the wine press, and built a tower, and let it out to tenants, and went into another country. 2When the time came, he sent a servant to the tenants, to get from them some of the fruit of the vineyard.

ἔλεγον αὐτῷ· ἐν ποίᾳ ἐξουσίᾳ ταῦτα
said to him: By what authority these things

ποιεῖς; ἢ τίς σοι ἔδωκεν τὴν ἐξουσίαν
doest thou? or who thee gave - authority

ταύτην ἵνα ταῦτα ποιῇς; 29 ὁ δὲ Ἰησοῦς
this that these things thou mayest do? - And Jesus

εἶπεν αὐτοῖς· ἐπερωτήσω ὑμᾶς ἕνα λόγον,
said to them: I will question you one word,

καὶ ἀποκρίθητέ μοι, καὶ ἐρῶ ὑμῖν ἐν
and answer ye me, and I will tell you by

ποίᾳ ἐξουσίᾳ ταῦτα ποιῶ. 30 τὸ βάπτισμα
what authority these things I do. The baptism

τὸ Ἰωάννου ἐξ οὐρανοῦ ἦν ἢ ἐξ ἀνθρώπων;
- of John of heaven was it or of men?

ἀποκρίθητέ μοι. 31 καὶ διελογίζοντο πρὸς
answer ye me. And they debated with

ἑαυτοὺς λέγοντες· ἐὰν εἴπωμεν· ἐξ οὐρανοῦ,
themselves saying: If we say: Of heaven,

ἐρεῖ· διὰ τί οὖν οὐκ ἐπιστεύσατε αὐτῷ;
he will say: Why then did ye not believe him?

32 ἀλλὰ εἴπωμεν· ἐξ ἀνθρώπων;—ἐφοβοῦντο
But may we say: Of men? — they feared

τὸν ὄχλον· ἅπαντες γὰρ εἶχον τὸν Ἰωάννην
the crowd; for all men held - John

ὄντως ὅτι προφήτης ἦν. 33 καὶ
³really ¹that ²a prophet ³he was. And

ἀποκριθέντες τῷ Ἰησοῦ λέγουσιν· οὐκ
answering - Jesus they say: not

οἴδαμεν. καὶ ὁ Ἰησοῦς λέγει αὐτοῖς·
We know. And - Jesus says to them:

οὐδὲ ἐγὼ λέγω ὑμῖν ἐν ποίᾳ ἐξουσίᾳ
Neither I tell you by what authority

ταῦτα ποιῶ. 12 Καὶ ἤρξατο αὐτοῖς ἐν
these things I do. And he began to them in

παραβολαῖς λαλεῖν. ἀμπελῶνα ἄνθρωπος
parables to speak. ³a vineyard ¹A man

ἐφύτευσεν, καὶ περιέθηκεν φραγμὸν καὶ ὤρυξεν
²planted, and put round [it] a hedge and dug

ὑπολήνιον καὶ ᾠκοδόμησεν πύργον, καὶ
a winepress and built a tower, and

ἐξέδοτο αὐτὸν γεωργοῖς, καὶ ἀπεδήμησεν.
let out it to husbandmen, and went away.

2 καὶ ἀπέστειλεν πρὸς τοὺς γεωργοὺς τῷ
And he sent to the husbandmen at the

καιρῷ δοῦλον, ἵνα παρὰ τῶν γεωργῶν
time a slave, that from the husbandmen

λάβῃ ἀπὸ τῶν καρπῶν τοῦ ἀμπελῶνος·
he might from(of) the fruits of the vineyard;
receive

³And they took him and beat him, and sent him away empty-handed. ⁴Again he sent to them another servant, and they wounded him in the head, and treated him shamefully. ⁵And he sent another, and him they killed; and so with many others, some they beat and some they killed. ⁶He had still one other, a beloved son; finally he sent him to them, saying, 'They will respect my son.' ⁷But those tenants said to one another, 'This is the heir; come, let us kill him, and the inheritance will be ours.' ⁸And they took him and killed him, and cast him out of the vineyard. ⁹What will the owner of the vineyard do? He will come and destroy the tenants, and give the vineyard to others. ¹⁰Have you not read this scripture:

'The very stone which the builders rejected
has become the head of the corner;
¹¹this was the Lord's doing,
and it is marvelous in our eyes'?"

12 And they tried to arrest him, but feared the multitude, for they perceived that he had told the parable against them;

3 καὶ λαβόντες αὐτὸν ἔδειραν καὶ ἀπέστειλαν
And taking him they beat and sent away

κενόν. 4 καὶ πάλιν ἀπέστειλεν πρὸς αὐτοὺς
empty. And again he sent to them

ἄλλον δοῦλον· κἀκεῖνον ἐκεφαλαίωσαν καὶ
another slave; and that one they wounded in the head and

ἠτίμασαν. 5 καὶ ἄλλον ἀπέστειλεν· κἀκεῖνον
insulted. And another he sent; and that one

ἀπέκτειναν, καὶ πολλοὺς ἄλλους, οὓς μὲν
they killed, and many others, ²some

δέροντες, οὓς δὲ ἀποκτέννοντες. 6 ἔτι ἕνα
¹beating, ²others ¹killing. Still one

εἶχεν, υἱὸν ἀγαπητόν· ἀπέστειλεν αὐτὸν
he had, a son beloved; he sent him

ἔσχατον πρὸς αὐτοὺς λέγων ὅτι ἐντραπήσονται
last to them saying[,] – They will reverence

τὸν υἱόν μου. 7 ἐκεῖνοι δὲ οἱ γεωργοὶ
the son of me. But those – husbandmen

πρὸς ἑαυτοὺς εἶπαν ὅτι οὗτός ἐστιν ὁ
to themselves said[,] – This is the

κληρονόμος· δεῦτε ἀποκτείνωμεν αὐτόν, καὶ
heir; come[,] let us kill him, and

ἡμῶν ἔσται ἡ κληρονομία. 8 καὶ λαβόντες
of us will be the inheritance. And taking

ἀπέκτειναν αὐτόν, καὶ ἐξέβαλον αὐτὸν
they killed him, and cast out him

ἔξω τοῦ ἀμπελῶνος. 9 τί ποιήσει ὁ
outside the vineyard. What will do the

κύριος τοῦ ἀμπελῶνος; ἐλεύσεται καὶ
lord of the vineyard? he will come and

ἀπολέσει τοὺς γεωργούς, καὶ δώσει τὸν
will destroy the husbandmen, and will give the

ἀμπελῶνα ἄλλοις. 10 οὐδὲ τὴν γραφὴν
vineyard to others. ²not – ⁴scripture

ταύτην ἀνέγνωτε· λίθον ὃν ἀπεδοκίμασαν
³this ¹Read ye: A stone which ³rejected

οἱ οἰκοδομοῦντες, οὗτος ἐγενήθη εἰς κεφαλὴν
¹the [ones] ²building, this became for head

γωνίας· 11 παρὰ κυρίου ἐγένετο αὕτη,
of corner; from [the] Lord was this,

καὶ ἔστιν θαυμαστὴ ἐν ὀφθαλμοῖς ἡμῶν;
and it is marvellous in eyes of us ?

12 Καὶ ἐζήτουν αὐτὸν κρατῆσαι, καὶ
And they sought him to seize, and

ἐφοβήθησαν τὸν ὄχλον· ἔγνωσαν γὰρ
feared the crowd; for they knew

ὅτι πρὸς αὐτοὺς τὴν παραβολὴν
that to them the parable

so they left him and went away.

13 And they sent to him some of the Pharisees and some of the Herodians, to entrap him in his talk. ¹⁴And they came and said to him, "Teacher, we know that you are true, and care for no man; for you do not regard the position of men, but truly teach the way of God. Is it lawful to pay taxes to Caesar, or not? ¹⁵Should we pay them, or should we not?" But knowing their hypocrisy, he said to them, "Why put me to the test? Bring me a coin, and let me look at it." ¹⁶And they brought one. And he said to them, "Whose likeness and inscription is this?" They said to him, "Caesar's." ¹⁷Jesus said to them, "Render to Caesar the things that are Caesar's, and to God the things that are God's." And they were amazed at him.

18 And Sad'ducees came to him, who say that there is no resurrection; and they asked him a question, saying, ¹⁹"Teacher, Moses wrote for us that if a man's brother dies and leaves a wife, but leaves no child, the man must take the

εἶπεν.   καὶ   ἀφέντες   αὐτὸν   ἀπῆλθον.
he told.   And   leaving   him   they went away.

13 Καὶ ἀποστέλλουσιν πρὸς αὐτόν τινας τῶν
And   they send   to   him   some of the

Φαρισαίων καὶ τῶν 'Ηρῳδιανῶν ἵνα αὐτὸν
Pharisees   and   of the   Herodians   that   him

ἀγρεύσωσιν   λόγῳ.   14 καὶ   ἐλθόντες
they might catch   in a word.   And   coming

λέγουσιν   αὐτῷ·   διδάσκαλε,   οἴδαμεν   ὅτι
they say   to him: Teacher,   we know   that

ἀληθὴς   εἶ   καὶ   οὐ   μέλει   σοι   περὶ
true   thou art   and   it matters not   to thee   about

οὐδενός·   οὐ   γὰρ   βλέπεις   εἰς   πρόσωπον
no(any)one;   for thou lookest not   at   [the] face

ἀνθρώπων,   ἀλλ᾽   ἐπ᾽   ἀληθείας   τὴν   ὁδὸν
of men,   but   on(in)   truth   the   way

τοῦ   θεοῦ   διδάσκεις·   ἔξεστιν   δοῦναι   κῆνσον
–   of God   teachest;   is it lawful   to give   tribute

Καίσαρι   ἢ   οὔ;   δῶμεν   ἢ   μὴ   δῶμεν;
to Caesar   or   no?   may we give or   may we not give?

15 ὁ   δὲ   εἰδὼς   αὐτῶν   τὴν   ὑπόκρισιν   εἶπεν
But he   knowing   of them   the   hypocrisy   said

αὐτοῖς·   τί   με   πειράζετε;   φέρετέ   μοι
to them: Why   me   tempt ye?   bring   me

δηνάριον   ἵνα   ἴδω.   16 οἱ   δὲ   ἤνεγκαν.   καὶ
a denarius   that I may see.   And they   brought.   And

λέγει   αὐτοῖς·   τίνος   ἡ   εἰκὼν   αὕτη   καὶ   ἡ
he says   to them: Of whom   –   image   this   and   –

ἐπιγραφή;   οἱ   δὲ   εἶπαν   αὐτῷ·   Καίσαρος.
superscription?   And they   tell   him: Of Caesar.

17 ὁ   δὲ   'Ιησοῦς   εἶπεν   αὐτοῖς·   τὰ   Καίσαρος
–   So   Jesus   said   to them: The things   of Caesar

ἀπόδοτε   Καίσαρι   καὶ   τὰ   τοῦ   θεοῦ   τῷ
render   to Caesar   and the things   –   of God   –

θεῷ.   καὶ   ἐξεθαύμαζον   ἐπ᾽   αὐτῷ.
to God.   And   they marvelled   at   him.

18 Καὶ   ἔρχονται   Σαδδουκαῖοι   πρὸς   αὐτόν,
And   come   Sadducees   to   him,

οἵτινες   λέγουσιν   ἀνάστασιν   μὴ   εἶναι,   καὶ
who   say   resurrection   not   to be,   and
= that there is no resurrection,

ἐπηρώτων   αὐτὸν   λέγοντες·   19 διδάσκαλε,
questioned   him   saying: Teacher,

Μωϋσῆς   ἔγραψεν   ἡμῖν   ὅτι   ἐάν   τινος
Moses   wrote   to us   that   if   of anyone

ἀδελφὸς   ἀποθάνῃ   καὶ   καταλίπῃ   γυναῖκα
a brother   should die   and   leave behind   a wife

καὶ   μὴ   ἀφῇ   τέκνον,   ἵνα   λάβῃ   ὁ   ἀδελφὸς
and   leave not   a child,   – ⁴may take ¹the   ²brother

wife, and raise up children for his brother. ²⁰There were seven brothers; the first took a wife, and when he died left no children; ²¹and the second took her, and died, leaving no children; and the third likewise; ²²and the seven left no children. Last of all the woman also died. ²³In the resurrection whose wife will she be? For the seven had her as wife."

24 Jesus said to them, "Is not this why you are wrong, that you know neither the scriptures nor the power of God? ²⁵For when they rise from the dead, they neither marry nor are given in marriage, but are like angels in heaven. ²⁶And as for the dead being raised, have you not read in the book of Moses, in the passage about the bush, how God said to him, 'I am the God of Abraham, and the God of Isaac, and the God of Jacob'? ²⁷He is not God of the dead, but of the living; you are quite wrong."

28 And one of the scribes came up and heard them disputing with one another, and

αὐτοῦ τὴν γυναῖκα καὶ ἐξαναστήσῃ σπέρμα
of him the wife and may raise up seed

τῷ ἀδελφῷ αὐτοῦ. 20 ἑπτὰ ἀδελφοὶ ἦσαν·
to the brother of him. Seven brothers there were;

καὶ ὁ πρῶτος ἔλαβεν γυναῖκα, καὶ
and the first took a wife, and

ἀποθνῇσκων οὐκ ἀφῆκεν σπέρμα· 21 καὶ
dying left not seed; and

ὁ δεύτερος ἔλαβεν αὐτήν, καὶ ἀπέθανεν μὴ
the second took her, and died not

καταλιπὼν σπέρμα· καὶ ὁ τρίτος ὡσαύτως·
leaving behind seed; and the third similarly;

22 καὶ οἱ ἑπτὰ οὐκ ἀφῆκαν σπέρμα.
and the seven left not seed.

ἔσχατον πάντων καὶ ἡ γυνὴ ἀπέθανεν.
Last of all also the wife died.

23 ἐν τῇ ἀναστάσει, ὅταν ἀναστῶσιν,
In the resurrection, when they rise again,

τίνος αὐτῶν ἔσται γυνή; οἱ γὰρ ἑπτὰ
of which of them will she be wife? for the seven

ἔσχον αὐτὴν γυναῖκα. 24 ἔφη αὐτοῖς ὁ
had her [as] wife. Said to them –

Ἰησοῦς· οὐ διὰ τοῦτο πλανᾶσθε μὴ
Jesus: ³not ⁴therefore ¹Do ²ye ⁵err not

εἰδότες τὰς γραφὰς μηδὲ τὴν δύναμιν
knowing the scriptures nor the power

τοῦ θεοῦ; 25 ὅταν γὰρ ἐκ νεκρῶν
– of God? for when out of [the] dead

ἀναστῶσιν, οὔτε γαμοῦσιν οὔτε γαμίζονται,
they rise again, they neither marry nor are given in marriage,

ἀλλ' εἰσὶν ὡς ἄγγελοι ἐν τοῖς οὐρανοῖς.
but are as angels in the heavens.

26 περὶ δὲ τῶν νεκρῶν ὅτι ἐγείρονται,
But concerning the dead that they are raised,

οὐκ ἀνέγνωτε ἐν τῇ βίβλῳ Μωϋσέως ἐπὶ
did ye not read in the roll of Moses at

τοῦ βάτου πῶς εἶπεν αὐτῷ ὁ θεὸς λέγων·
the bush how said to him – God saying:

ἐγὼ ὁ θεὸς Ἀβραὰμ καὶ θεὸς Ἰσαὰκ
I [am] the God of Abraham and God of Isaac

καὶ θεὸς Ἰακώβ; 27 οὐκ ἔστιν θεὸς
and God of Jacob? he is not God

νεκρῶν ἀλλὰ ζώντων. πολὺ πλανᾶσθε.
of dead [persons] but of living [ones]. Much ye err.

28 Καὶ προσελθὼν εἷς τῶν γραμματέων,
And ⁴approaching ¹one ²of the ³scribes,

ἀκούσας αὐτῶν συζητούντων, εἰδὼς ὅτι
hearing them debating, knowing that

seeing that he answered them well, asked him, "Which commandment is the first of all?" [29]Jesus answered, "The first is, 'Hear, O Israel: The Lord our God, the Lord is one; [30]and you shall love the Lord your God with all your heart, and with all your soul, and with all your mind, and with all your strength.' [31]The second is this, 'You shall love your neighbor as yourself.' There is no other commandment greater than these." [32]And the scribe said to him, "You are right, Teacher; you have truly said that he is one, and there is no other but he; [33]and to love him with all the heart, and with all the understanding, and with all the strength, and to love one's neighbor as oneself, is much more than all whole burnt offerings and sacrifices." [34]And when Jesus saw that he answered wisely, he said to him, "You are not far from the kingdom of God." And after that no one dared to ask him any question.

35 And as Jesus taught

καλῶς ἀπεκρίθη αὐτοῖς, ἐπηρώτησεν αὐτόν·
well he answered them, questioned him:
ποία ἐστὶν ἐντολὴ πρώτη πάντων;
What is [the] commandment first of all?
29 ἀπεκρίθη ὁ Ἰησοῦς ὅτι πρώτη ἐστίν·
Answered – Jesus[,] – [The] first is:
ἄκουε, Ἰσραήλ, κύριος ὁ θεὸς ἡμῶν κύριος
Hear, Israel, Lord the God of us Lord
= The Lord our God is one Lord,
εἷς ἐστιν, 30 καὶ ἀγαπήσεις κύριον τὸν
one is, and thou shalt love Lord the
θεόν σου ἐξ ὅλης τῆς καρδίας σου καὶ
God of thee from(with) all the heart of thee and
ἐξ ὅλης τῆς ψυχῆς σου καὶ ἐξ ὅλης
with all the soul of thee and with all
τῆς διανοίας σου καὶ ἐξ ὅλης τῆς ἰσχύος
the mind of thee and with all the strength
σου. 31 δευτέρα αὕτη· ἀγαπήσεις τὸν
of thee. [The] second [is] this: Thou shalt love the
πλησίον σου ὡς σεαυτόν. μείζων τούτων
neighbour of thee as thyself. Greater [than] these
ἄλλη ἐντολὴ οὐκ ἔστιν. 32 καὶ εἶπεν
other commandment there is not. And said
αὐτῷ ὁ γραμματεύς· καλῶς, διδάσκαλε, ἐπ'
to him the scribe: Well, teacher, on(in)
ἀληθείας εἶπες ὅτι εἷς ἐστιν καὶ οὐκ
truth thou sayest that one there is and not
ἔστιν ἄλλος πλὴν αὐτοῦ· 33 καὶ τὸ
there is another besides him; and –
ἀγαπᾶν αὐτὸν ἐξ ὅλης τῆς καρδίας καὶ ἐξ
to love him with all the heart and with
ὅλης τῆς συνέσεως καὶ ἐξ ὅλης τῆς
all the understanding and with all the
ἰσχύος, καὶ τὸ ἀγαπᾶν τὸν πλησίον ὡς
strength, and – to love the(one's) neighbour as
ἑαυτὸν περισσότερόν ἐστιν πάντων τῶν
himself more is [than] all the
ὁλοκαυτωμάτων καὶ θυσιῶν. 34 καὶ ὁ
burnt offerings and sacrifices. And –
Ἰησοῦς, ἰδὼν αὐτὸν ὅτι νουνεχῶς ἀπεκρίθη,
Jesus, seeing him that sensibly he answered,
εἶπεν αὐτῷ· οὐ μακρὰν εἶ ἀπὸ τῆς
said to him: Not far thou art from the
βασιλείας τοῦ θεοῦ. καὶ οὐδεὶς οὐκέτι
kingdom – of God. And no one no(any) more
ἐτόλμα αὐτὸν ἐπερωτῆσαι.
dared him to question.
35 Καὶ ἀποκριθεὶς ὁ Ἰησοῦς ἔλεγεν
And answering – Jesus said

in the temple, he said, "How can the scribes say that the Christ is the son of David? ³⁶ David himself, inspired by[j] the Holy Spirit, declared,

'The Lord said to my Lord,
Sit at my right hand,
till I put thy enemies under thy feet.'

³⁷ David himself calls him Lord; so how is he his son?" And the great throng heard him gladly.

38 And in his teaching he said, "Beware of the scribes, who like to go about in long robes, and to have salutations in the market places ³⁹ and the best seats in the synagogues and the places of honor at feasts,⁴⁰ who devour widows' houses and for a pretense make long prayers. They will receive the greater condemnation."

41 And he sat down opposite the treasury, and watched the multitude putting money into the treasury. Many rich people put in large sums. ⁴²And a poor widow came, and put in two copper coins, which make a penny. ⁴³And he called his disciples to him, and

---

διδάσκων ἐν τῷ ἱερῷ· πῶς λέγουσιν οἱ
teaching   in   the   temple: How   say   the

γραμματεῖς ὅτι ὁ χριστὸς υἱός Δαυίδ
scribes   that the Christ   son of David

ἐστιν; 36 αὐτὸς Δαυὶδ εἶπεν ἐν τῷ πνεύματι
is?   himself David   said by the Spirit

τῷ ἁγίῳ· εἶπεν κύριος τῷ κυρίῳ μου·
–   Holy: said [the] LORD to the Lord of me:

κάθου ἐκ δεξιῶν μου ἕως ἂν θῶ τοὺς
Sit at [the] right [hand] of me until I put the

ἐχθρούς σου ὑποκάτω τῶν ποδῶν σου.
enemies of thee under   the   feet   of thee.

37 αὐτὸς Δαυὶδ λέγει αὐτὸν κύριον, καὶ
   himself David says(calls) him Lord,   and

πόθεν αὐτοῦ ἐστιν υἱός;
whence of him is he   son?

Καὶ ὁ πολὺς ὄχλος ἤκουεν αὐτοῦ
And the much crowd heard   him

ἡδέως. 38 Καὶ ἐν τῇ διδαχῇ αὐτοῦ
gladly.   And in the teaching of him

ἔλεγεν· βλέπετε ἀπὸ τῶν γραμματέων
he said: Beware from(of) the   scribes

τῶν θελόντων ἐν στολαῖς περιπατεῖν καὶ
the [ones] wishing in robes to walk about and

ἀσπασμοὺς ἐν ταῖς ἀγοραῖς 39 καὶ
greetings   in the marketplaces   and

πρωτοκαθεδρίας ἐν ταῖς συναγωγαῖς καὶ
chief seats   in the synagogues   and

πρωτοκλισίας ἐν τοῖς δείπνοις· 40 οἱ
chief places in the dinners;   the [ones]

κατέσθοντες τὰς οἰκίας τῶν χηρῶν καὶ
devouring   the houses of the widows and

προφάσει μακρὰ προσευχόμενοι, οὗτοι
under pretence long   praying,   these

λήμψονται περισσότερον κρίμα. 41 Καὶ
will receive greater condemnation.

καθίσας κατέναντι τοῦ γαζοφυλακείου ἐθεώρει
sitting   opposite the treasury   he beheld

πῶς ὁ ὄχλος βάλλει χαλκὸν εἰς τὸ
how the crowd puts copper money into the

γαζοφυλακεῖον· καὶ πολλοὶ πλούσιοι ἔβαλλον
treasury;   and many rich men   put

πολλά· 42 καὶ ἐλθοῦσα μία χήρα πτωχὴ
much;   and coming   one widow poor

ἔβαλεν λεπτὰ δύο, ὅ ἐστιν κοδράντης.
put   lepta two, which is   a quadrans.

43 καὶ προσκαλεσάμενος τοὺς μαθητὰς αὐτοῦ
And   calling to [him]   the disciples of him

---

[j] Or himself, in

said to them, "Truly, I say to you, this poor widow has put in more than all those who are contributing to the treasury. ⁴⁴For they all contributed out of their abundance; but she out of her poverty has put in everything she had, her whole living."

εἶπεν αὐτοῖς· ἀμὴν λέγω ὑμῖν ὅτι
he said to them: Truly I tell you that
ἡ χήρα αὕτη ἡ πτωχὴ πλεῖον πάντων
– ²widow ¹this – ²poor ⁵more [than] ⁶all
ἔβαλεν τῶν βαλλόντων εἰς τὸ γαζοφυλακεῖον·
⁴put the [ones] putting into the treasury;
44 πάντες γὰρ ἐκ τοῦ περισσεύοντος αὐτοῖς
for all out of the abounding to them
= their abundance
ἔβαλον, αὕτη δὲ ἐκ τῆς ὑστερήσεως αὐτῆς
put, but this woman out of the want of her
πάντα ὅσα εἶχεν ἔβαλεν, ὅλον τὸν βίον
²all things ³how many ⁴she had ¹put, all the living
αὐτῆς.
of her.

CHAPTER 13

AND as he came out of the temple, one of his disciples said to him, "Look, Teacher, what wonderful stones and what wonderful buildings!" ²And Jesus said to him, "Do you see these great buildings? There will not be left here one stone upon another, that will not be thrown down."

3 And as he sat on the Mount of Olives opposite the temple, Peter and James and John and Andrew asked him privately, ⁴"Tell us, when will this be, and what will be the sign when these things are all to be accomplished?" ⁵And Jesus began to say to them, "Take heed that no one leads you astray. ⁶Many will come in my name, saying, 'I

13 Καὶ ἐκπορευομένου αὐτοῦ ἐκ τοῦ
And going forth himᵃ out of the
= as he went forth
ἱεροῦ λέγει αὐτῷ εἷς τῶν μαθητῶν αὐτοῦ·
temple says to him one of the disciples of him:
διδάσκαλε, ἴδε ποταποὶ λίθοι καὶ ποταπαὶ
Teacher, behold[,] what great stones and what great
οἰκοδομαί. 2 καὶ ὁ Ἰησοῦς εἶπεν αὐτῷ·
buildings. And – Jesus said to him:
βλέπεις ταύτας τὰς μεγάλας οἰκοδομάς;
Seest thou these – great buildings?
οὐ μὴ ἀφεθῇ λίθος ἐπὶ λίθον ὃς οὐ
by no means be left stone on stone which by no
= there shall by no means be left stone on stone which will not
μὴ καταλυθῇ. 3 Καὶ καθημένου αὐτοῦ
means be overthrown. And sitting himᵃ
be overthrown. = as he sat
εἰς τὸ ὄρος τῶν ἐλαιῶν κατέναντι τοῦ
in(on) the mount of the olives opposite the
ἱεροῦ, ἐπηρώτα αὐτὸν κατ' ἰδίαν Πέτρος
temple, questioned him privately Peter
καὶ Ἰάκωβος καὶ Ἰωάννης καὶ Ἀνδρέας·
and James and John and Andrew:
4 εἰπὸν ἡμῖν, πότε ταῦτα ἔσται, καὶ τί
Tell us, when these things will be, and what
τὸ σημεῖον ὅταν μέλλῃ ταῦτα συντελεῖσθαι
the sign when ³are about ²these things ⁴to be completed
πάντα; 5 ὁ δὲ Ἰησοῦς ἤρξατο λέγειν
¹all? – And Jesus began to say
αὐτοῖς· βλέπετε μή τις ὑμᾶς πλανήσῃ.
to them: See lest anyone you lead astray.
6 πολλοὶ ἐλεύσονται ἐπὶ τῷ ὀνόματί μου
Many will come on(in) the name of me

am he!' and they will lead many astray. ⁷And when you hear of wars and rumors of wars, do not be alarmed; this must take place, but the end is not yet. ⁸For nation will rise against nation, and kingdom against kingdom; there will be earthquakes in various places, there will be famines; this is but the beginning of the sufferings.

9 "But take heed to yourselves; for they will deliver you up to councils; and you will be beaten in synagogues; and you will stand before governors and kings for my sake, to bear testimony before them. ¹⁰And the gospel must first be preached to all nations. ¹¹And when they bring you to trial and deliver you up, do not be anxious beforehand what you are to say; but say whatever is given you in that hour, for it is not you who speak, but the Holy Spirit. ¹²And brother will deliver up brother to death, and the father his child, and children will rise against parents and have them put to death; ¹³and you will be hated by all for my name's sake. But he who endures to the end will be saved.

14 "But when you see the desolating sacrilege

λέγοντες ὅτι ἐγώ εἰμι, καὶ πολλοὺς
saying[,] - I am, and many

πλανήσουσιν. 7 ὅταν δὲ ἀκούσητε πολέμους
they will lead astray. But when ye hear [of] wars

καὶ ἀκοὰς πολέμων, μὴ θροεῖσθε· δεῖ
and rumours of wars, be not disturbed; it behoves

γενέσθαι, ἀλλ᾽ οὔπω τὸ τέλος. 8 ἐγερθήσεται
to happen, but not yet the end. will be raised

γὰρ ἔθνος ἐπ᾽ ἔθνος καὶ βασιλεία ἐπὶ
For nation against nation and kingdom against

βασιλείαν. ἔσονται σεισμοὶ κατὰ τόπους,
kingdom. There will be earthquakes in places,

ἔσονται λιμοί· ἀρχὴ ὠδίνων ταῦτα.
there will be famines; beginning of birth-pangs these things [are].

9 Βλέπετε δὲ ὑμεῖς ἑαυτούς· παραδώσουσιν
But see ye yourselves; they will deliver

ὑμᾶς εἰς συνέδρια καὶ εἰς συναγωγὰς
you to councils and in synagogues

δαρήσεσθε καὶ ἐπὶ ἡγεμόνων καὶ βασιλέων
ye will be beaten and before rulers and kings

σταθήσεσθε ἕνεκεν ἐμοῦ, εἰς μαρτύριον
ye will stand for the sake of me, for a testimony

αὐτοῖς. 10 καὶ εἰς πάντα τὰ ἔθνη πρῶτον
to them. And to all the nations first

δεῖ κηρυχθῆναι τὸ εὐαγγέλιον. 11 καὶ ὅταν
it behoves to be proclaimed the gospel. And when
= the gospel must be proclaimed.

ἄγωσιν ὑμᾶς παραδιδόντες, μὴ προμεριμνᾶτε
they lead you delivering, be not anxious beforehand

τί λαλήσητε, ἀλλ᾽ ὁ ἐὰν δοθῇ ὑμῖν ἐν
what ye speak, but whatever is given you in

ἐκείνῃ τῇ ὥρᾳ, τοῦτο λαλεῖτε· οὐ γάρ
that - hour. this speak ye; for not

ἐστε ὑμεῖς οἱ λαλοῦντες ἀλλὰ τὸ πνεῦμα
are ye the [ones] speaking but the Spirit

τὸ ἅγιον. 12 καὶ παραδώσει ἀδελφὸς
- Holy. And ²will deliver ¹a brother

ἀδελφὸν εἰς θάνατον καὶ πατὴρ τέκνον, καὶ
a brother to death and a father a child, and

ἐπαναστήσονται τέκνα ἐπὶ γονεῖς καὶ
²will rise against ¹children against parents and

θανατώσουσιν αὐτούς· 13 καὶ ἔσεσθε
will put to death them; and ye will be

μισούμενοι ὑπὸ πάντων διὰ τὸ ὄνομά
being hated by all men on account of the name

μου· ὁ δὲ ὑπομείνας εἰς τέλος, οὗτος
of me; but the [one] enduring to [the] end, this

σωθήσεται. 14 Ὅταν δὲ ἴδητε τὸ βδέλυγμα
will be saved. But when ye see the abomination

set up where it ought not to be (let the reader understand), then let those who are in Judea flee to the mountains; ¹⁵let him who is on the housetop not go down, nor enter his house, to take anything away; ¹⁶and let him who is in the field not turn back to take his mantle. ¹⁷And alas for those who are with child and for those who give suck in those days! ¹⁸Pray that it may not happen in winter. ¹⁹For in those days there will be such tribulation as has not been from the beginning of the creation which God created until now, and never will be. ²⁰And if the Lord had not shortened the days, no human being would be saved; but for the sake of the elect, whom he chose, he shortened the days. ²¹And then if any one says to you, 'Look, here is the Christ!' or 'Look, there he is!' do not believe it. ²²False Christs and false prophets will arise and show signs and wonders, to lead astray, if possible, the elect. ²³But take heed; I have told you all things beforehand.

24 "But in those days,

τῆς ἐρημώσεως ἑστηκότα ὅπου οὐ δεῖ, ὁ
– of desolation   stand   where it behoves not, the
ἀναγινώσκων νοείτω, τότε οἱ ἐν τῇ
[one] reading let him understand, then the [ones] in –
Ἰουδαίᾳ φευγέτωσαν εἰς τὰ ὄρη, 15 ὁ ἐπὶ
Judæa   let them flee to the mountains, the [one] on
τοῦ δώματος μὴ καταβάτω μηδὲ εἰσελθάτω
the   roof   let him not come down nor   let him enter
τι ἆραι ἐκ τῆς οἰκίας αὐτοῦ, 16 καὶ ὁ
anything to take out of the house of him,   and the [one]
εἰς τὸν ἀγρὸν μὴ ἐπιστρεψάτω εἰς τὰ
in   the   field   let him not return   to the things
ὀπίσω ἆραι τὸ ἱμάτιον αὐτοῦ. 17 οὐαὶ
behind   to take the   garment   of him.   woe
δὲ ταῖς ἐν γαστρὶ ἐχούσαις καὶ ταῖς
But to the women   pregnant†   and to the
θηλαζούσαις ἐν ἐκείναις ταῖς ἡμέραις.
[ones] giving suck in   those   –   days.
18 προσεύχεσθε δὲ ἵνα μὴ γένηται χειμῶνος·
But pray ye   that it may not happen of(in) winter;
19 ἔσονται γὰρ αἱ ἡμέραι ἐκεῖναι θλῖψις, οἷα
for ³will be – ²days ¹those ⁴affliction, of such a kind
οὐ γέγονεν τοιαύτη ἀπ' ἀρχῆς κτίσεως
²has not happened ¹as from [the] beginning of [the] creation
ἣν ἔκτισεν ὁ θεὸς ἕως τοῦ νῦν καὶ οὐ
which created – God until – now and by
μὴ γένηται. 20 καὶ εἰ μὴ ἐκολόβωσεν
no means may be.   And unless   ²shortened
κύριος τὰς ἡμέρας, οὐκ ἂν ἐσώθη πᾶσα
¹[the] Lord the   days,   would not be saved   all
= no flesh would be saved;
σάρξ· ἀλλὰ διὰ τοὺς ἐκλεκτοὺς οὓς
flesh;   but on account of the   chosen   whom
ἐξελέξατο ἐκολόβωσεν τὰς ἡμέρας. 21 καὶ
he chose   he shortened   the   days.   And
τότε ἐάν τις ὑμῖν εἴπῃ· ἴδε ὧδε ὁ
then   if anyone ²you   ¹tells: Behold here [is] the
χριστός, ἴδε ἐκεῖ, μὴ πιστεύετε· 22 ἐγερθή-
Christ, behold there,   believe ye not;   ⁵will be
σονται δὲ ψευδόχριστοι καὶ ψευδοπροφῆται
raised   ¹and   ²false Christs   ³and   ⁴false prophets
καὶ ποιήσουσιν σημεῖα καὶ τέρατα πρὸς
and   they will do   signs   and   wonders   for
τὸ ἀποπλανᾶν, εἰ δυνατόν, τοὺς ἐκλεκτούς.
– to lead astray, if   possible,   the   chosen.
23 ὑμεῖς δὲ βλέπετε· προείρηκα ὑμῖν πάντα.
But ²ye   ¹see;   ¹I have told ⁴before ²you ³all things.
24 Ἀλλὰ ἐν ἐκείναις ταῖς ἡμέραις μετὰ
But   in   those   –   days   after

after that tribulation, the sun will be darkened, and the moon will not give its light, ²⁵and the stars will be falling from heaven, and the powers in the heavens will be shaken. ²⁶And then they will see the Son of man coming in clouds with great power and glory. ²⁷And then he will send out the angels, and gather his elect from the four winds, from the ends of the earth to the ends of heaven.

28 "From the fig tree learn its lesson: as soon as its branch becomes tender and puts forth its leaves, you know that summer is near. ²⁹So also, when you see these things taking place, you know that he is near, at the very gates. ³⁰Truly, I say to you, this generation will not pass away before all these things take place. ³¹Heaven and earth will pass away, but my words will not pass away.

32 "But of that day or that hour no one knows, not even the angels in heaven, nor the Son, but only the Father. ³³Take heed, watch;ᵏ for you do not

---

τὴν θλῖψιν ἐκείνην ὁ ἥλιος σκοτισθήσεται,
– affliction that the sun will be darkened,

καὶ ἡ σελήνη οὐ δώσει τὸ φέγγος αὐτῆς,
and the moon, will not give the light of her,

25 καὶ οἱ ἀστέρες ἔσονται ἐκ τοῦ οὐρανοῦ
and the stars ¹will be ²out of – ⁴heaven

πίπτοντες, καὶ αἱ δυνάμεις αἱ ἐν τοῖς
²falling, and the powers – in the

οὐρανοῖς σαλευθήσονται. 26 καὶ τότε ὄψονται
heavens will be shaken. And then they will see

τὸν υἱὸν τοῦ ἀνθρώπου ἐρχόμενον ἐν
the Son – of man coming in

νεφέλαις μετὰ δυνάμεως πολλῆς καὶ δόξης.
clouds with power much and glory.

27 καὶ τότε ἀποστελεῖ τοὺς ἀγγέλους καὶ
And then he will send the angels and

ἐπισυνάξει τοὺς ἐκλεκτοὺς [αὐτοῦ] ἐκ τῶν
they will assemble the chosen of him out of the

τεσσάρων ἀνέμων ἀπ᾽ ἄκρου γῆς ἕως
four winds from [the] extremity of earth to

ἄκρου οὐρανοῦ. 28 Ἀπὸ δὲ τῆς συκῆς
[the] extremity of heaven. Now from the fig-tree

μάθετε τὴν παραβολήν· ὅταν ἤδη ὁ
learn the parable; when now the

κλάδος αὐτῆς ἁπαλὸς γένηται καὶ ἐκφύῃ
branch of it tender becomes and puts forth

τὰ φύλλα, γινώσκετε ὅτι ἐγγὺς τὸ θέρος
the leaves, ye know that near the summer

ἐστίν· 29 οὕτως καὶ ὑμεῖς, ὅταν ἴδητε
is; so also ye, when ye see

ταῦτα γινόμενα, γινώσκετε ὅτι ἐγγύς ἐστιν
these things happening, know that near he/it is

ἐπὶ θύραις. 30 ἀμὴν λέγω ὑμῖν ὅτι οὐ
at [the] doors. Truly I tell you that by no

μὴ παρέλθῃ ἡ γενεὰ αὕτη μέχρις οὗ
means passes – generation this until

ταῦτα πάντα γένηται. 31 ὁ οὐρανὸς καὶ
these things all happen. The heaven and

ἡ γῆ παρελεύσονται, οἱ δὲ λόγοι μου
the earth will pass away, but the words of me

οὐ παρελεύσονται. 32 Περὶ δὲ τῆς ἡμέρας
will not pass away. But concerning – day

ἐκείνης ἢ τῆς ὥρας οὐδεὶς οἶδεν, οὐδὲ
that or – hour no one knows, not

οἱ ἄγγελοι ἐν οὐρανῷ οὐδὲ ὁ υἱός, εἰ
the angels in heaven neither the Son, ex-

μὴ ὁ πατήρ. 33 Βλέπετε, ἀγρυπνεῖτε·
cept the Father. Look, be wakeful;

ᵏ Other ancient authorities add *and pray*

know when the time will come. ³⁴It is like a man going on a journey, when he leaves home and puts his servants in charge, each with his work, and commands the door-keeper to be on the watch. ³⁵Watch therefore—for you do not know when the master of the house will come, in the evening, or at midnight, or at cockcrow, or in the morning—³⁶lest he come suddenly and find you asleep. ³⁷And what I say to you I say to all: Watch.''

οὐκ οἴδατε γὰρ πότε ὁ καιρός ἐστιν.
for ye know not when the time is.

34 ὡς ἄνθρωπος ἀπόδημος ἀφεὶς τὴν οἰκίαν
As a man away from home leaving the house

αὐτοῦ καὶ δοὺς τοῖς δούλοις αὐτοῦ τὴν
of him and giving to the slaves of him —

ἐξουσίαν, ἑκάστῳ τὸ ἔργον αὐτοῦ, καὶ
authority, to each the work of him, and

τῷ θυρωρῷ ἐνετείλατο ἵνα γρηγορῇ.
the doorkeeper he commanded that he should watch.

35 γρηγορεῖτε οὖν· οὐκ οἴδατε γὰρ πότε
Watch ye therefore; for ye know not when

ὁ κύριος τῆς οἰκίας ἔρχεται, ἢ ὀψὲ ἢ
the lord of the house comes, either late or

μεσονύκτιον ἢ ἀλεκτοροφωνίας ἢ πρωΐ·
at midnight or at cock-crowing or early;

36 μὴ ἐλθὼν ἐξαίφνης εὕρῃ ὑμᾶς καθεύδ-
lest coming suddenly he find you sleep-

οντας. 37 ὃ δὲ ὑμῖν λέγω, πᾶσιν λέγω,
ing. And what to you I say, to all I say,

γρηγορεῖτε.
watch ye.

CHAPTER 14

IT was now two days before the Passover and the feast of Un-leavened Bread. And the chief priests and the scribes were seeking how to arrest him by stealth, and kill him; ²for they said, ''Not during the feast, lest there be a tumult of the people.''

3 And while he was at Bethany in the house of Simon the leper, as he sat at table, a woman came with an alabaster jar of ointment of pure nard, very costly, and she broke the jar and poured

14 Ἦν δὲ τὸ πάσχα καὶ τὰ ἄζυμα
Now it was the Passover and [the feast of] the
unleavened bread†

μετὰ δύο ἡμέρας. καὶ ἐζήτουν οἱ ἀρχιερεῖς
after two days. And sought the chief priests

καὶ οἱ γραμματεῖς πῶς αὐτὸν ἐν δόλῳ
and the scribes how ²him ³by ⁴guile

κρατήσαντες ἀποκτείνωσιν. 2 ἔλεγον γάρ·
¹seizing they might kill. For they said:

μὴ ἐν τῇ ἑορτῇ, μήποτε ἔσται θόρυβος
Not at the feast, lest there will be a disturbance

τοῦ λαοῦ.
of the people.

3 Καὶ ὄντος αὐτοῦ ἐν Βηθανίᾳ ἐν τῇ
And being himᵃ in Bethany in the
= when he was

οἰκίᾳ Σίμωνος τοῦ λεπροῦ, κατακειμένου
house of Simon the leper, reclining
= as he reclined

αὐτοῦ ἦλθεν γυνὴ ἔχουσα ἀλάβαστρον
himᵃ came a woman having an alabaster phial

μύρου νάρδου πιστικῆς πολυτελοῦς·
of ointment ³nard ¹of pure ²costly;

συντρίψασα τὴν ἀλάβαστρον κατέχεεν αὐτοῦ
breaking the alabaster phial she poured over of him

it over his head. ⁴But there were some who said to themselves indignantly, "Why was the ointment thus wasted? ⁵For this ointment might have been sold for more than three hundred denarii, and given to the poor." And they reproached her. ⁶But Jesus said, "Let her alone; why do you trouble her? She has done a beautiful thing to me. ⁷For you always have the poor with you, and whenever you will, you can do good to them; but you will not always have me. ⁸She has done what she could; she has anointed my body beforehand for burying. ⁹And truly, I say to you, wherever the gospel is preached in the whole world, what she has done will be told in memory of her."

10 Then Judas Iscariot, who was one of the twelve, went to the chief priests in order to betray him to them. ¹¹And when they heard it they were glad, and promised to give him money. And he sought an opportunity to betray him.

12 And on the first day of Unleavened Bread, when they sacrificed the passover lamb, his disciples said to him,

---

τῆς κεφαλῆς. 4 ἦσαν δέ τινες ἀγανακτοῦντες
the head.   Now there were some   being angry

πρὸς ἑαυτούς· εἰς τί ἡ ἀπώλεια αὕτη
with themselves: Why   –   waste   this

τοῦ μύρου γέγονεν; 5 ἠδύνατο γὰρ τοῦτο
of the ointment has occurred?   for ³could   ¹this

τὸ μύρον πραθῆναι ἐπάνω δηναρίων
–   ²ointment   to be sold   [for] over   denarii

τριακοσίων καὶ δοθῆναι τοῖς πτωχοῖς·
three hundred   and   to be given   to the   poor;

καὶ ἐνεβριμῶντο αὐτῇ. 6 ὁ δὲ Ἰησοῦς
and they were indignant with her.   –   But   Jesus

εἶπεν· ἄφετε αὐτήν· τί αὐτῇ κόπους
said: Leave   her;   why   ³to her   ²troubles

παρέχετε; καλὸν ἔργον ἠργάσατο ἐν ἐμοί.
¹cause ye?   a good   work   she wrought   in   me.

7 πάντοτε γὰρ τοὺς πτωχοὺς ἔχετε μεθ'
For always   the   poor   ye have   with

ἑαυτῶν, καὶ ὅταν θέλητε δύνασθε αὐτοῖς
yourselves,   and   whenever ye wish   ye can   to them

εὖ ποιῆσαι, ἐμὲ δὲ οὐ πάντοτε ἔχετε.
well   to do,   but me   not   always   ye have.

8 ὃ ἔσχεν ἐποίησεν· προέλαβεν μυρίσαι τὸ
What she had   she did;   she was beforehand to anoint   the

σῶμά μου εἰς τὸν ἐνταφιασμόν. 9 ἀμὴν
body   of me   for   the   burial.   truly

δὲ λέγω ὑμῖν, ὅπου ἐὰν κηρυχθῇ τὸ
And   I tell   you,   wherever   is proclaimed   the

εὐαγγέλιον εἰς ὅλον τὸν κόσμον, καὶ ὃ
gospel   in   all   the   world,   also what

ἐποίησεν αὕτη λαληθήσεται εἰς μνημόσυνον
did   this woman   will be spoken   for   a memorial

αὐτῆς. 10 Καὶ Ἰούδας Ἰσκαριώθ, ὁ εἷς
of her.   And   Judas   Iscariot,   the one

τῶν δώδεκα, ἀπῆλθεν πρὸς τοὺς ἀρχιερεῖς
of the twelve,   went   to   the   chief priests

ἵνα αὐτὸν παραδοῖ αὐτοῖς. 11 οἱ δὲ
that   him   he might betray   to them.   And they

ἀκούσαντες ἐχάρησαν καὶ ἐπηγγείλαντο αὐτῷ
hearing   rejoiced   and   promised   him

ἀργύριον δοῦναι. καὶ ἐζήτει πῶς αὐτὸν
silver   to give.   And he sought   how   him

εὐκαίρως παραδοῖ.
opportunely he might betray.

12 Καὶ τῇ πρώτῃ ἡμέρᾳ τῶν ἀζύμων,
And on the   first   day   of unleavened bread,†

ὅτε τὸ πάσχα ἔθυον, λέγουσιν αὐτῷ οἱ
when the   passover they sacrificed,   say   to him   the

"Where will you have us go and prepare for you to eat the passover?" [13]And he sent two of his disciples, and said to them, "Go into the city, and a man carrying a jar of water will meet you; follow him, [14]and wherever he enters, say to the householder, 'The Teacher says, Where is my guest room, where I am to eat the passover with my disciples?' [15]And he will show you a large upper room furnished and ready; there prepare for us." [16]And the disciples set out and went to the city, and found it as he had told them; and they prepared the passover.

17 And when it was evening he came with the twelve. [18]And as they were at table eating, Jesus said, "Truly, I say to you, one of you will betray me, one who is eating with me." [19]They began to be sorrowful, and to say to him one after another, "Is it I?" [20]He said to them, "It is one of the twelve, one who is dipping bread in the same dish with me. [21]For the Son of man goes as it is written of

μαθηταὶ αὐτοῦ· ποῦ θέλεις ἀπελθόντες
disciples of him: Where wishest thou , going
ἐτοιμάσωμεν ἵνα φάγῃς τὸ πάσχα; 13 καὶ
we may prepare that thou eatest the passover? And
ἀποστέλλει δύο τῶν μαθητῶν αὐτοῦ καὶ
he sends two of the disciples of him and
λέγει αὐτοῖς· ὑπάγετε εἰς τὴν πόλιν, καὶ
tells them: Go ye into the city, and
ἀπαντήσει ὑμῖν ἄνθρωπος κεράμιον ὕδατος
will meet you a man a pitcher of water
βαστάζων· ἀκολουθήσατε αὐτῷ, 14 καὶ ὅπου
carrying; follow him, and wher-
ἐὰν εἰσέλθῃ εἴπατε τῷ οἰκοδεσπότῃ ὅτι ὁ
ever he enters tell the housemaster[,] – The
διδάσκαλος λέγει· ποῦ ἐστιν τὸ κατάλυμά
teacher says: Where is the guest room
μου, ὅπου τὸ πάσχα μετὰ τῶν μαθητῶν
of me, where the passover with the disciples
μου φάγω; 15 καὶ αὐτὸς ὑμῖν δείξει
of me I may eat? And he you will show
ἀνάγαιον μέγα ἐστρωμένον ἕτοιμον· καὶ
upper room a large having been spread ready; and
ἐκεῖ ἐτοιμάσατε ἡμῖν. 16 καὶ ἐξῆλθον οἱ
there prepare ye for us. And went forth the
μαθηταὶ καὶ ἦλθον εἰς τὴν πόλιν καὶ
disciples and came into the city and
εὗρον καθὼς εἶπεν αὐτοῖς, καὶ ἡτοίμασαν
found as he told them, and they prepared
τὸ πάσχα. 17 Καὶ ὀψίας γενομένης ἔρχεται
the passover. And evening coming[a] he comes
= when evening came
μετὰ τῶν δώδεκα. 18 καὶ ἀνακειμένων
with the twelve. And reclining
= as they reclined and ate
αὐτῶν καὶ ἐσθιόντων ὁ Ἰησοῦς εἶπεν·
them and eating[a] – Jesus said:
ἀμὴν λέγω ὑμῖν ὅτι εἷς ἐξ ὑμῶν παραδώσει
Truly I tell you that one of you will betray
με, ὁ ἐσθίων μετ' ἐμοῦ. 19 ἤρξαντο
me, the [one] eating with me. They began
λυπεῖσθαι καὶ λέγειν αὐτῷ εἷς κατὰ εἷς·
to grieve and to say to him one by one:
μήτι ἐγώ; 20 ὁ δὲ εἶπεν αὐτοῖς· εἷς τῶν
Not I? And he said to them: One of the
δώδεκα, ὁ ἐμβαπτόμενος μετ' ἐμοῦ εἰς
twelve, the [one] dipping with me in
τὸ [ἓν] τρύβλιον. 21 ὅτι ὁ μὲν υἱὸς τοῦ
the one dish. Because indeed the Son –
ἀνθρώπου ὑπάγει καθὼς γέγραπται περὶ
of man is going as it has been written concerning

him, but woe to that man by whom the Son of man is betrayed! It would have been better for that man if he had not been born."

22 And as they were eating, he took bread, and blessed, and broke it, and gave it to them, and said, "Take; this is my body." 23 And he took a cup, and when he had given thanks he gave it to them, and they all drank of it. 24 And he said to them, "This is my blood of the[1] covenant, which is poured out for many. 25 Truly, I say to you, I shall not drink again of the fruit of the vine until that day when I drink it new in the kingdom of God."

26 And when they had sung a hymn, they went out to the Mount of Olives. 27 And Jesus said to them, "You will all fall away; for it is written, 'I will strike the shepherd, and the sheep will be scattered.' 28 But after I am raised up, I will go before you to Galilee." 29 Peter said to him, "Even though they all fall away, I will not." 30 And Jesus said to him,

---

αὐτοῦ· οὐαὶ δὲ τῷ ἀνθρώπῳ ἐκείνῳ δι'
him; but woe - man to that through

οὗ ὁ υἱὸς τοῦ ἀνθρώπου παραδίδοται·
whom the Son - of man is betrayed;

καλὸν αὐτῷ εἰ οὐκ ἐγεννήθη ὁ ἄνθρωπος
good for him if was not born - man

ἐκεῖνος. 22 Καὶ ἐσθιόντων αὐτῶν λαβὼν
that. And eating them[a] taking
= as they were eating

ἄρτον εὐλογήσας ἔκλασεν καὶ ἔδωκεν αὐτοῖς
a loaf blessing he broke and gave to them

καὶ εἶπεν· λάβετε· τοῦτό ἐστιν τὸ σῶμά
and said: Take ye; this is the body

μου. 23 καὶ λαβὼν ποτήριον εὐχαριστήσας
of me. And taking a cup giving thanks

ἔδωκεν αὐτοῖς, καὶ ἔπιον ἐξ αὐτοῦ πάντες.
he gave to them, and drank of it all.

24 καὶ εἶπεν αὐτοῖς· τοῦτό ἐστιν τὸ αἷμά
And he said to them: This is the blood

μου τῆς διαθήκης τὸ ἐκχυννόμενον ὑπὲρ
of me of the covenant - being shed for

πολλῶν. 25 ἀμὴν λέγω ὑμῖν ὅτι οὐκέτι
many. Truly I tell you[,] - No more

οὐ μὴ πίω ἐκ τοῦ γενήματος τῆς ἀμπέλου
by no(any) will I drink of the fruit of the vine
means

ἕως τῆς ἡμέρας ἐκείνης ὅταν αὐτὸ πίνω
until - day that when it I drink

καινὸν ἐν τῇ βασιλείᾳ τοῦ θεοῦ.
new in the kingdom - of God.

26 Καὶ ὑμνήσαντες ἐξῆλθον εἰς τὸ
And having sung a hymn they went forth to the

ὄρος τῶν ἐλαιῶν. 27 Καὶ λέγει αὐτοῖς ὁ
mount of the olives. And says to them -

Ἰησοῦς ὅτι πάντες σκανδαλισθήσεσθε, ὅτι
Jesus[,] - [3]All [1]ye [2]will [4]be offended, because

γέγραπται· πατάξω τὸν ποιμένα, καὶ τὰ
it has been written: I will strike the shepherd, and the

πρόβατα διασκορπισθήσονται. 28 ἀλλὰ μετὰ
sheep will be scattered. But after

τὸ ἐγερθῆναί με προάξω ὑμᾶς εἰς τὴν
the to be raised me[b] I will go before you to -
= I am raised

Γαλιλαίαν. 29 ὁ δὲ Πέτρος ἔφη αὐτῷ·
Galilee. - And Peter said to him:

εἰ καὶ πάντες σκανδαλισθήσονται, ἀλλ'
If even all men shall be offended, yet

οὐκ ἐγώ. 30 καὶ λέγει αὐτῷ ὁ Ἰησοῦς·
not I. And says to him - Jesus:

---

[1] Other ancient authorities insert *new*

"Truly, I say to you, this very night, before the cock crows twice, you will deny me three times." ³¹But he said vehemently, "If I must die with you, I will not deny you." And they all said the same.

32 And they went to a place which was called Gethsem'ane; and he said to his disciples, "Sit here, while I pray." ³³And he took with him Peter and James and John, and began to be greatly distressed and troubled. ³⁴And he said to them, "My soul is very sorrowful, even to death; remain here, and watch."ᵐ ³⁵And going a little farther, he fell on the ground and prayed that, if it were possible, the hour might pass from him. ³⁶And he said, "Abba, Father, all things are possible to thee; remove this cup from me; yet not what I will, but what thou wilt." ³⁷And he came and found them sleeping, and he said to Peter, "Simon, are you asleep? Could you not watchᵐ one hour? ³⁸Watchᵐ and pray

ᵐ Or keep awake

ἀμὴν λέγω σοι ὅτι σὺ σήμερον ταύτῃ τῇ
Truly I tell thee[,] – Thou to-day in this –
νυκτὶ πρὶν ἢ δὶς ἀλέκτορα φωνῆσαι τρίς
night before twice a cock to soundᵇ thrice
με ἀπαρνήσῃ. 31 ὁ δὲ ἐκπερισσῶς ἐλάλει·
me thou wilt deny. But he more exceedingly said:
ἐὰν δέῃ με συναποθανεῖν σοι, οὐ μή
If it should behove me to die with thee, by no means
= I must
σε ἀπαρνήσομαι. ὡσαύτως [δὲ] καὶ πάντες
thee will I deny. And similarly also all
ἔλεγον.
said.

32 Καὶ ἔρχονται εἰς χωρίον οὗ τὸ
And they come to a piece of land of which the
ὄνομα Γεθσημανί, καὶ λέγει τοῖς μαθηταῖς
name [was] Gethsemane, and he says to the disciples
αὐτοῦ· καθίσατε ὧδε ἕως προσεύξωμαι.
of him: Sit ye here while I pray.
33 καὶ παραλαμβάνει τὸν Πέτρον καὶ τὸν
And he takes – Peter and –
Ἰάκωβον καὶ τὸν Ἰωάννην μετ' αὐτοῦ,
James and – John with him,
καὶ ἤρξατο ἐκθαμβεῖσθαι καὶ ἀδημονεῖν,
and began to be greatly astonished and to be distressed,
34 καὶ λέγει αὐτοῖς· περίλυπός ἐστιν ἡ
and says to them: Deeply grieved is the
ψυχή μου ἕως θανάτου· μείνατε ὧδε καὶ
soul of me unto death; remain ye here and
γρηγορεῖτε. 35 καὶ προελθὼν μικρὸν ἔπιπτεν
watch. And going forward a little he fell
ἐπὶ τῆς γῆς, καὶ προσηύχετο ἵνα εἰ
on the ground, and prayed that if
δυνατόν ἐστιν παρέλθῃ ἀπ' αὐτοῦ ἡ ὥρα,
possible it is might pass away from him the hour,
36 καὶ ἔλεγεν· ἀββὰ ὁ πατήρ, πάντα
and said: Abba – Father, all things
δυνατά σοι· παρένεγκε τὸ ποτήριον τοῦτο
[are] possible to thee; remove – cup this
ἀπ' ἐμοῦ· ἀλλ' οὐ τί ἐγὼ θέλω ἀλλὰ
from me; but not what I wish but
τί σύ. 37 καὶ ἔρχεται καὶ εὑρίσκει
what thou. And he comes and finds
αὐτοὺς καθεύδοντας, καὶ λέγει τῷ Πέτρῳ·
them sleeping, and says – to Peter:
Σίμων, καθεύδεις; οὐκ ἴσχυσας μίαν ὥραν
Simon, sleepest thou? couldest thou not one hour
γρηγορῆσαι; 38 γρηγορεῖτε καὶ προσεύχεσθε,
to watch? Watch ye and pray.

that you may not enter into temptation; the spirit indeed is willing, but the flesh is weak." [39]And again he went away and prayed, saying the same words. [40]And again he came and found them sleeping, for their eyes were very heavy; and they did not know what to answer him. [41]And he came the third time, and said to them, "Are you still sleeping and taking your rest? It is enough; the hour has come; the Son of man is betrayed into the hands of sinners. [42]Rise, let us be going; see, my betrayer is at hand."

43 And immediately, while he was still speaking, Judas came, one of the twelve, and with him a crowd with swords and clubs, from the chief priests and the scribes and the elders. [44]Now the betrayer had given them a sign, saying, "The one I shall kiss is the man; seize him and lead him away safely." [45]And when he came, he went up to him at once, and said, "Master!" And he kissed him. [46]And they laid hands on him and seized him. [47]But one of

ἵνα μὴ ἔλθητε εἰς πειρασμόν· τὸ μὲν	lest ye come into temptation; indeed the
πνεῦμα πρόθυμον, ἡ δὲ σὰρξ ἀσθενής.	spirit [is] eager, but the flesh weak.
39 καὶ πάλιν ἀπελθὼν προσηύξατο τὸν	And again going away he prayed [2]the
αὐτὸν λόγον εἰπών. **40** καὶ πάλιν ἐλθὼν	[3]same [4]word [1]saying. And again coming
εὗρεν αὐτοὺς καθεύδοντας, ἦσαν γὰρ αὐτῶν	he found them sleeping, for were of them
οἱ ὀφθαλμοὶ καταβαρυνόμενοι, καὶ οὐκ	the eyes becoming heavy, and not
ᾔδεισαν τί ἀποκριθῶσιν αὐτῷ. **41** καὶ	they knew what they might answer him. And
ἔρχεται τὸ τρίτον καὶ λέγει αὐτοῖς·	he comes the third [time] and says to them:
καθεύδετε τὸ λοιπὸν καὶ ἀναπαύεσθε·	Sleep ye now† and rest;
ἀπέχει· ἦλθεν ἡ ὥρα, ἰδοὺ παραδίδοται ὁ	it is enough; came the hour, behold is betrayed the
υἱὸς τοῦ ἀνθρώπου εἰς τὰς χεῖρας τῶν	Son – man into the hands –
ἁμαρτωλῶν. **42** ἐγείρεσθε, ἄγωμεν· ἰδοὺ ὁ	of sinners. Rise ye, let us go; behold the
παραδιδούς με ἤγγικεν. **43** Καὶ εὐθὺς ἔτι	[one] betraying me has drawn near. And immediately yet
αὐτοῦ λαλοῦντος παραγίνεται [ὁ] Ἰούδας	him speaking[a] arrives – Judas = while he was still speaking
εἷς τῶν δώδεκα, καὶ μετ' αὐτοῦ ὄχλος	one of the twelve, and with him a crowd
μετὰ μαχαιρῶν καὶ ξύλων παρὰ τῶν	with swords and clubs from the
ἀρχιερέων καὶ τῶν γραμματέων καὶ τῶν	chief priests and the scribes and the
πρεσβυτέρων. **44** δεδώκει δὲ ὁ παραδιδοὺς	elders. [1]Now [2]had given [the one] [3]betraying
αὐτὸν σύσσημον αὐτοῖς λέγων· ὃν ἂν	[4]him [7]a signal [6]them saying: Whomever
φιλήσω αὐτός ἐστιν· κρατήσατε αὐτὸν καὶ	I may kiss he is; seize ye him and
ἀπάγετε ἀσφαλῶς. **45** καὶ ἐλθὼν εὐθὺς	lead away securely. And coming immediately
προσελθὼν αὐτῷ λέγει· ῥαββί, καὶ	approaching to him he says: Rabbi, and
κατεφίλησεν αὐτόν· **46** οἱ δὲ ἐπέβαλαν τὰς	fervently kissed him; and they [1]laid [4]on [2]the(their)
χεῖρας αὐτῷ καὶ ἐκράτησαν αὐτόν. **47** εἷς	[3]hands him and seized him. [8]one

those who stood by drew his sword, and struck the slave of the high priest and cut off his ear. ⁴⁸And Jesus said to them, "Have you come out as against a robber, with swords and clubs to capture me? ⁴⁹Day after day I was with you in the temple teaching, and you did not seize me. But let the scriptures be fulfilled." ⁵⁰And they all forsook him, and fled.

51 And a young man followed him, with nothing but a linen cloth about his body; and they seized him, ⁵²but he left the linen cloth and ran away naked.

53 And they led Jesus to the high priest; and all the chief priests and the elders and the scribes were assembled. ⁵⁴And Peter had followed him at a distance, right into the courtyard of the high priest; and he was sitting with the guards, and warming himself at the fire. ⁵⁵Now the chief priests and the whole council sought testimony against Jesus to put him to death; but they found none. ⁵⁶For many bore false witness against him,

δέ τις τῶν παρεστηκότων σπασάμενος
¹But ²a certain of the [ones] standing by   drawing

τὴν μάχαιραν ἔπαισεν τὸν δοῦλον τοῦ ἀρχιερέως
the   sword   struck   the slave of the high priest

καὶ ἀφεῖλεν αὐτοῦ τὸ ὠτάριον.   48 καὶ
and   cut off   of him   the   ear.   And

ἀποκριθεὶς ὁ Ἰησοῦς εἶπεν αὐτοῖς· ὡς
answering   -   Jesus said to them: As

ἐπὶ λῃστὴν ἐξήλθατε μετὰ μαχαιρῶν καὶ
against a robber came ye forth with   swords   and

ξύλων συλλαβεῖν με; 49 καθ' ἡμέραν ἤμην
clubs   to arrest   me?   Daily   I was

πρὸς ὑμᾶς ἐν τῷ ἱερῷ διδάσκων, καὶ οὐκ
with you in the temple teaching, and not

ἐκρατήσατέ με· ἀλλ' ἵνα πληρωθῶσιν αἱ
ye did seize me; but that may be fulfilled the

γραφαί.   50 καὶ ἀφέντες αὐτὸν ἔφυγον
scriptures.   And leaving   him   they fled

πάντες.   51 Καὶ νεανίσκος τις συνηκολούθει
all.   And a certain young man   accompanied

αὐτῷ περιβεβλημένος σινδόνα ἐπὶ γυμνοῦ,
him   having been clothed [in] a nightgown over [his] naked
                                              [body],

καὶ κρατοῦσιν αὐτόν· 52 ὁ δὲ καταλιπὼν
and they seize   him;   and he   leaving

τὴν σινδόνα γυμνὸς ἔφυγεν.
the nightgown naked   fled.

53 Καὶ ἀπήγαγον τὸν Ἰησοῦν πρὸς τὸν
    And they led away -   Jesus to the

ἀρχιερέα, καὶ συνέρχονται πάντες οἱ
high priest, and come together   all   the

ἀρχιερεῖς καὶ οἱ πρεσβύτεροι καὶ οἱ
chief priests and the   elders   and the

γραμματεῖς. 54 καὶ ὁ Πέτρος ἀπὸ μακρόθεν
scribes.   And - Peter from   afar

ἠκολούθησεν αὐτῷ ἕως ἔσω εἰς τὴν αὐλὴν
followed   him until within in the   court

τοῦ ἀρχιερέως, καὶ ἦν συγκαθήμενος μετὰ
of the high priest, and was   sitting with   with

τῶν ὑπηρετῶν καὶ θερμαινόμενος πρὸς τὸ
the attendants and warming himself by the

φῶς. 55 Οἱ δὲ ἀρχιερεῖς καὶ ὅλον τὸ
bright fire. Now the chief priests and all the

συνέδριον ἐζήτουν κατὰ τοῦ Ἰησοῦ
council   sought against - Jesus

μαρτυρίαν εἰς τὸ θανατῶσαι αὐτόν, καὶ
witness   for the to put to death   him,   and
        = so as

οὐχ ηὕρισκον· 56 πολλοὶ γὰρ ἐψευδομαρτύρουν
found not;   for many   falsely witnessed

and their witness did not agree. ⁵⁷And some stood up and bore false witness against him, saying, ⁵⁸"We heard him say, 'I will destroy this temple that is made with hands, and in three days I will build another, not made with hands.' " ⁵⁹Yet not even so did their testimony agree. ⁶⁰And the high priest stood up in the midst, and asked Jesus, "Have you no answer to make? What is it that these men testify against you?" ⁶¹But he was silent and made no answer. Again the high priest asked him, "Are you the Christ, the Son of the Blessed?" ⁶²And Jesus said, "I am; and you will see the Son of man sitting at the right hand of Power, and coming with the clouds of heaven." ⁶³And the high priest tore his mantle, and said, "Why do we still need witnesses? ⁶⁴You have heard his blasphemy. What is your decision?" And they all condemned him as deserving death. ⁶⁵And some began to spit on him, and to cover his face, and to strike

κατ' αὐτοῦ, καὶ ἴσαι αἱ μαρτυρίαι οὐκ
against him, and ²identical ¹the ²testimonies ⁴not

ἦσαν. 57 καί τινες ἀναστάντες ἐψευδομαρτύρουν
²were. And some standing up falsely witnessed

κατ' αὐτοῦ λέγοντες 58 ὅτι ἡμεῖς ἠκούσαμεν
against him saying[,] – We heard

αὐτοῦ λέγοντος ὅτι ἐγὼ καταλύσω τὸν
him saying[,] – I will overthrow –

ναὸν τοῦτον τὸν χειροποίητον καὶ διὰ
²shrine ⁴this – ²handmade and through(after)

τριῶν ἡμερῶν ἄλλον ἀχειροποίητον οἰκο-
three days another not handmade I will

δομήσω. 59 καὶ οὐδὲ οὕτως ἴση ἦν ἡ
build. And not so identical was the

μαρτυρία αὐτῶν. 60 καὶ ἀναστὰς ὁ
witness of them. And standing up the

ἀρχιερεὺς εἰς μέσον ἐπηρώτησεν τὸν Ἰησοῦν
high priest in [the] midst questioned – Jesus

λέγων· οὐκ ἀποκρίνῃ οὐδὲν τί οὗτοί σου
saying: Answerest thou not no(any)thing what these men ²thee

καταμαρτυροῦσιν; 61 ὁ δὲ ἐσιώπα καὶ
¹testify against? But he was silent and

οὐκ ἀπεκρίνατο οὐδέν. πάλιν ὁ ἀρχιερεὺς
answered not no(any)thing. Again the high priest

ἐπηρώτα αὐτὸν καὶ λέγει αὐτῷ· σὺ εἶ ὁ
questioned him and says to him: Thou art the

χριστὸς ὁ υἱὸς τοῦ εὐλογητοῦ; 62 ὁ δὲ
Christ the Son of the Blessed [one]? – And

Ἰησοῦς εἶπεν· ἐγώ εἰμι, καὶ ὄψεσθε
Jesus said: I am, and ye will see

τὸν υἱὸν τοῦ ἀνθρώπου ἐκ δεξιῶν καθήμενον
the Son – of man ²at [the] right [hand] ¹sitting

τῆς δυνάμεως καὶ ἐρχόμενον μετὰ τῶν
of the Power and coming with the

νεφελῶν τοῦ οὐρανοῦ. 63 ὁ δὲ ἀρχιερεὺς
clouds – of heaven. And the high priest

διαρήξας τοὺς χιτῶνας αὐτοῦ λέγει· τί
rending the tunics of him says: What

ἔτι χρείαν ἔχομεν μαρτύρων; 64 ἠκούσατε
more need have we of witnesses? ye heard

τῆς βλασφημίας· τί ὑμῖν φαίνεται; οἱ δὲ
the blasphemy; what to you appears it? And they

πάντες κατέκριναν αὐτὸν ἔνοχον εἶναι
all condemned him liable to be

θανάτου. 65 Καὶ ἤρξαντό τινες ἐμπτύειν
of(to) death. And began some to spit at

αὐτῷ καὶ περικαλύπτειν αὐτοῦ τὸ πρόσωπον
him and to cover of him the face

him, saying to him, "Prophesy!" And the guards received him with blows.

66 And as Peter was below in the courtyard, one of the maids of the high priest came; [67] and seeing Peter warming himself, she looked at him, and said, "You also were with the Nazarene, Jesus." [68] But he denied it, saying, "I neither know nor understand what you mean." And he went out into the gateway.[n] [69] And the maid saw him, and began again to say to the bystanders, "This man is one of them." [70] But again he denied it. And after a little while again the bystanders said to Peter, "Certainly you are one of them; for you are a Galilean." [71] But he began to invoke a curse on himself and to swear, "I do not know this man of whom you speak." [72] And immediately the cock crowed a second time. And Peter remembered how Jesus had said to him, "Before the cock crows twice, you will deny me three times." And he broke down and wept.

καὶ κολαφίζειν αὐτὸν καὶ λέγειν αὐτῷ·
and to maltreat him and to say to him:

προφήτευσον, καὶ οἱ ὑπηρέται ῥαπίσμασιν
Prophesy, and the attendants with slaps

αὐτὸν ἔλαβον. 66 Καὶ ὄντος τοῦ Πέτρου
²him ¹took. And being Peter^
= as Peter was

κάτω ἐν τῇ αὐλῇ ἔρχεται μία τῶν
below in the court comes one of the

παιδισκῶν τοῦ ἀρχιερέως, 67 καὶ ἰδοῦσα
maidservants of the high priest, and seeing

τὸν Πέτρον θερμαινόμενον ἐμβλέψασα αὐτῷ
– Peter warming himself looking at him

λέγει· καὶ σὺ μετὰ τοῦ Ναζαρηνοῦ ἦσθα
says: And ¹thou ³with ⁴the ⁵Nazarene ²wast

τοῦ Ἰησοῦ. 68 ὁ δὲ ἠρνήσατο λέγων· οὔτε
– ⁶Jesus. But he denied saying: ³neither

οἶδα οὔτε ἐπίσταμαι σὺ τί λέγεις. καὶ
¹I ³know ⁴nor ⁵understand ⁷thou ⁶what ⁸sayest. And

ἐξῆλθεν ἔξω εἰς τὸ προαύλιον· 69 καὶ ἡ
he went forth outside into the forecourt; and the

παιδίσκη ἰδοῦσα αὐτὸν ἤρξατο πάλιν λέγειν
maidservant seeing him began again to say

τοῖς παρεστῶσιν ὅτι οὗτος ἐξ αὐτῶν ἐστιν.
to the [ones] standing by[,] – This man of them is.

70 ὁ δὲ πάλιν ἠρνεῖτο. καὶ μετὰ μικρὸν
But he again denied. And after a little

πάλιν οἱ παρεστῶτες ἔλεγον τῷ Πέτρῳ·
again the [ones] standing by said – to Peter:

ἀληθῶς ἐξ αὐτῶν εἶ· καὶ γὰρ Γαλιλαῖος
Truly of them thou art; ²indeed ¹for ⁴a Galilæan

εἶ. 71 ὁ δὲ ἤρξατο ἀναθεματίζειν καὶ
³thou art. And he began to curse and

ὀμνύναι ὅτι οὐκ οἶδα τὸν ἄνθρωπον
to swear[,] – I know not – man

τοῦτον ὃν λέγετε. 72 καὶ εὐθὺς ἐκ
this whom ye say. And immediately a

δευτέρου ἀλέκτωρ ἐφώνησεν. καὶ ἀνεμνήσθη
second time a cock crew. And remembered

ὁ Πέτρος τὸ ῥῆμα ὡς εἶπεν αὐτῷ ὁ
– Peter the word as said to him –

Ἰησοῦς ὅτι πρὶν ἀλέκτορα δὶς φωνῆσαι
Jesus[,] – Before a cock twice to crow^b

τρίς με ἀπαρνήσῃ· καὶ ἐπιβαλὼν ἔκλαιεν.
thrice me thou wilt deny; and thinking thereon he wept.

[n] Or *fore-court*. Other ancient authorities add *and the cock crowed*

CHAPTER 15

AND as soon as it was morning the chief priests, with the elders and scribes, and the whole council held a consultation; and they bound Jesus and led him away and delivered him to Pilate. ²And Pilate asked him, "Are you the King of the Jews?" And he answered him, "You have said so." ³And the chief priests accused him of many things. ⁴And Pilate again asked him, "Have you no answer to make? See how many charges they bring against you." ⁵But Jesus made no further answer, so that Pilate wondered.

6 Now at the feast he used to release for them any one prisoner whom they asked. ⁷And among the rebels in prison, who had committed murder in the insurrection, there was a man called Barab′bas. ⁸And the crowd came up and began to ask Pilate to do as he was wont to do for them. ⁹And he answered them, "Do you want me to release for you the King of the Jews?" ¹⁰For he perceived that it was out of envy that the chief priests had delivered him up. ¹¹But the chief priests stirred up the crowd to have him release for them Barab′bas instead.

15 Καὶ εὐθὺς πρωὶ συμβούλιον ἑτοιμάσαντες
And immediately early ²a council ¹preparing
οἱ ἀρχιερεῖς μετὰ τῶν πρεσβυτέρων καὶ
the chief priests with the elders and
γραμματέων καὶ ὅλον τὸ συνέδριον, δήσαντες
scribes and all the council, having bound
τὸν Ἰησοῦν ἀπήνεγκαν καὶ παρέδωκαν
- Jesus led [him] away and delivered [him]
Πιλάτῳ. **2** καὶ ἐπηρώτησεν αὐτὸν ὁ
to Pilate. And questioned him -
Πιλᾶτος· σὺ εἶ ὁ βασιλεὺς τῶν Ἰουδαίων;
Pilate: Thou art the king of the Jews?
ὁ δὲ ἀποκριθεὶς αὐτῷ λέγει· σὺ λέγεις.
And he answering him says: Thou sayest.
3 καὶ κατηγόρουν αὐτοῦ οἱ ἀρχιερεῖς πολλά.
And accused him the chief priests many things.
4 ὁ δὲ Πιλᾶτος πάλιν ἐπηρώτα αὐτόν [λέγων]·
- But Pilate again questioned him saying:
οὐκ ἀποκρίνῃ οὐδέν; ἴδε πόσα
Answerest thou not no(any)thing? Behold how many things
σου κατηγοροῦσιν. **5** ὁ δὲ Ἰησοῦς οὐκ-
thee they accuse. - But Jesus no(any)
ἔτι οὐδὲν ἀπεκρίθη, ὥστε θαυμάζειν
more nothing answered, so as to marvel
= so that Pilate marvelled.
τὸν Πιλᾶτον. **6** Κατὰ δὲ ἑορτὴν ἀπέλυεν
- Pilate. Now at a feast he released
αὐτοῖς ἕνα δέσμιον ὃν παρῃτοῦντο. **7** ἦν δὲ
to them one prisoner whom they begged. Now there was
ὁ λεγόμενος Βαραββᾶς μετὰ τῶν
the [one] named Barabbas with the
στασιαστῶν δεδεμένος, οἵτινες ἐν τῇ στάσει
rebels having been bound, who* in the rebellion
φόνον πεποιήκεισαν. **8** καὶ ἀναβὰς ὁ ὄχλος
murder had done. And going up the crowd
ἤρξατο αἰτεῖσθαι καθὼς ἐποίει αὐτοῖς.
began to ask as he used to do for them.
9 ὁ δὲ Πιλᾶτος ἀπεκρίθη αὐτοῖς λέγων·
- But Pilate answered them saying:
θέλετε ἀπολύσω ὑμῖν τὸν βασιλέα τῶν
Do ye wish I may release to you the king of the
Ἰουδαίων; **10** ἐγίνωσκεν γὰρ ὅτι διὰ φθόνον
Jews? For he knew that on account of envy
παραδεδώκεισαν αὐτὸν οἱ ἀρχιερεῖς. **11** οἱ
had delivered him the chief priests. the
δὲ ἀρχιερεῖς ἀνέσεισαν τὸν ὄχλον ἵνα
But chief priests stirred up the crowd that
μᾶλλον τὸν Βαραββᾶν ἀπολύσῃ αὐτοῖς.
rather - Barabbas he should release to them.

* Note the plural.

¹²And Pilate again said to them, "Then what shall I do with the man whom you call the King of the Jews?" ¹³And they cried out again, "Crucify him." ¹⁴And Pilate said to them, "Why, what evil has he done?" But they shouted all the more, "Crucify him." ¹⁵So Pilate, wishing to satisfy the crowd, released for them Barab′bas; and having scourged Jesus, he delivered him to be crucified.

16 And the soldiers led him away inside the palace (that is, the praetorium); and they called together the whole battalion. ¹⁷And they clothed him in a purple cloak, and plaiting a crown of thorns put it on him. ¹⁸And they began to salute him, "Hail, King of the Jews!" ¹⁹And they struck his head with a reed, and spat upon him, and they knelt down in homage to him. ²⁰And when they had mocked him, they stripped him of the purple cloak, and put his own clothes on him. And they led him out to crucify him.

21 And they compelled a passer-by, Simon of Cyre′ne, who was

12 ὁ δὲ Πιλᾶτος πάλιν ἀποκριθεὶς ἔλεγεν
- So Pilate again answering said
αὐτοῖς· τί οὖν ποιήσω [ὃν] λέγετε τὸν
to them: What then may I do [to him] whom ye call the
βασιλέα τῶν Ἰουδαίων; 13 οἱ δὲ πάλιν
king of the Jews? And they again
ἔκραξαν· σταύρωσον αὐτόν. 14 ὁ δὲ
cried out: Crucify him. - But
Πιλᾶτος ἔλεγεν αὐτοῖς· τί γὰρ ἐποίησεν
Pilate said to them: Indeed what ²did he
κακόν; οἱ δὲ περισσῶς ἔκραξαν· σταύρωσον
¹evil? and they more cried out: Crucify
αὐτόν. 15 ὁ δὲ Πιλᾶτος βουλόμενος τῷ
him. - And Pilate resolving the
ὄχλῳ τὸ ἱκανὸν ποιῆσαι ἀπέλυσεν αὐτοῖς
crowd to satisfy† released to them
τὸν Βαραββᾶν, καὶ παρέδωκεν τὸν Ἰησοῦν
- Barabbas, and delivered - Jesus
φραγελλώσας ἵνα σταυρωθῇ.
having scourged [him] that he might be crucified.

16 Οἱ δὲ στρατιῶται ἀπήγαγον αὐτὸν
Then the soldiers led away him
ἔσω τῆς αὐλῆς, ὅ ἐστιν πραιτώριον, καὶ
inside the court, which is prætorium, and
συγκαλοῦσιν ὅλην τὴν σπεῖραν. 17 καὶ
they call together all the cohort. And
ἐνδιδύσκουσιν αὐτὸν πορφύραν καὶ περιτιθέασιν
they put on him a purple [robe] and place round
αὐτῷ πλέξαντες ἀκάνθινον στέφανον· 18 καὶ
him plaiting a thorny crown; and
ἤρξαντο ἀσπάζεσθαι αὐτόν· χαῖρε, βασιλεῦ
they began to salute him: Hail, king
τῶν Ἰουδαίων· 19 καὶ ἔτυπτον αὐτοῦ τὴν
of the Jews; and they struck of him the
κεφαλὴν καλάμῳ καὶ ἐνέπτυον αὐτῷ, καὶ
head with a reed and spat at him, and
τιθέντες τὰ γόνατα προσεκύνουν αὐτῷ.
placing(bending) the(their) knees worshipped him.
20 καὶ ὅτε ἐνέπαιξαν αὐτῷ, ἐξέδυσαν
And when they mocked him, they took off
αὐτὸν τὴν πορφύραν καὶ ἐνέδυσαν αὐτὸν
him the purple [robe] and put on him
τὰ ἱμάτια αὐτοῦ. Καὶ ἐξάγουσιν αὐτὸν
the garments of him. And they lead forth him
ἵνα σταυρώσωσιν αὐτόν. 21 καὶ ἀγγαρεύουσιν
that they might crucify him. And they impress
παράγοντά τινα Σίμωνα Κυρηναῖον ἐρχόμενον
passing by a certain Simon a Cyrenian coming

coming in from the country, the father of Alexander and Rufus, to carry his cross. ²²And they brought him to the place called Gol'gotha (which means the place of a skull). ²³And they offered him wine mingled with myrrh; but he did not take it. ²⁴And they crucified him, and divided his garments among them, casting lots for them, to decide what each should take. ²⁵And it was the third hour, when they crucified him. ²⁶And the inscription of the charge against him read, "The King of the Jews." ²⁷And with him they crucified two robbers, one on his right and one on his left.⁰ ²⁹And those who passed by derided him, wagging their heads, and saying, "Aha! You who would destroy the temple and build it in three days, ³⁰ save yourself, and come down from the cross!" ³¹So also the chief priests mocked him to one another with the scribes, saying, "He saved others; he cannot save himself. ³²Let the Christ, the King of Israel, come down now from the cross, that we may see and believe." Those who

⁰ Other ancient authorities insert verse 28, *And the scripture was fulfilled which says, "He was reckoned with the transgressors."*

ἀπ' ἀγροῦ, τὸν πατέρα 'Αλεξάνδρου καὶ
from [the] country, the father of Alexander and
'Ρούφου, ἵνα ἄρῃ τὸν σταυρὸν αὐτοῦ.
of Rufus, that he might bear the cross of him.
22 καὶ φέρουσιν αὐτὸν ἐπὶ τὸν Γολγοθὰν
And they bring him to the Golgotha
τόπον, ὅ ἐστιν μεθερμηνευόμενος κρανίου
place, which is being interpreted of a skull
τόπος. 23 καὶ ἐδίδουν αὐτῷ ἐσμυρνισμένον
place. And they gave him ¹*having been* spiced
with myrrh
οἶνον· ὃς δὲ οὐκ ἔλαβεν. 24 καὶ σταυροῦσιν
¹wine; but who(he) received not. And they crucify
αὐτόν, καὶ διαμερίζονται τὰ ἱμάτια αὐτοῦ,
him, and divide the garments of him,
βάλλοντες κλῆρον ἐπ' αὐτὰ τίς τί ἄρῃ.
casting a lot on them ²one ¹what might take.
25 ἦν δὲ ὥρα τρίτη καὶ ἐσταύρωσαν
Now it was hour third and they crucified
αὐτόν. 26 καὶ ἦν ἡ ἐπιγραφὴ τῆς αἰτίας
him. And was the superscription of the accusation
αὐτοῦ ἐπιγεγραμμένη· Ο ΒΑΣΙΛΕΥΣ ΤΩΝ
of him *having been* written over: THE KING OF THE
ΙΟΥΔΑΙΩΝ. 27 Καὶ σὺν αὐτῷ σταυροῦσιν
JEWS. And with him they crucify
δύο λῃστάς, ἕνα ἐκ δεξιῶν καὶ ἕνα ἐξ
two robbers, one on [the] right and one on
εὐωνύμων αὐτοῦ. ‡ 29 Καὶ οἱ παραπορευόμενοι
[the] left of him. And the [ones] passing by
ἐβλασφήμουν αὐτὸν κινοῦντες τὰς κεφαλὰς
blasphemed him wagging the heads
αὐτῶν καὶ λέγοντες· οὐὰ ὁ καταλύων
of them and saying: Ah the [one] overthrowing
τὸν ναὸν καὶ οἰκοδομῶν [ἐν] τρισὶν
the shrine and building in three
ἡμέραις, 30 σῶσον σεαυτὸν καταβὰς ἀπὸ
days, save thyself coming down from
τοῦ σταυροῦ. 31 ὁμοίως καὶ οἱ ἀρχιερεῖς
the cross. Likewise also the chief priests
ἐμπαίζοντες πρὸς ἀλλήλους μετὰ τῶν
mocking to one another with the
γραμματέων ἔλεγον· ἄλλους ἔσωσεν, ἑαυτὸν
scribes said: Others he saved, himself
οὐ δύναται σῶσαι· 32 ὁ χριστὸς ὁ βασιλεὺς
he cannot *to* save; the Christ the king
'Ισραὴλ καταβάτω νῦν ἀπὸ τοῦ σταυροῦ,
of Israel let come down now from the cross,
ἵνα ἴδωμεν καὶ πιστεύσωμεν. καὶ οἱ
that we may see and believe. And the
‡ Verse 28 omitted by Nestle; *cf.* RSV footnote.

were crucified with him
also reviled him.

33 And when the sixth
hour had come, there was
darkness over the whole
land[p] until the ninth
hour. [34]And at the ninth
hour Jesus cried with a
loud voice, "E'lo-i,
E'lo-i, la'ma sabach-
tha'ni?" which means,
"My God, my God, why
hast thou forsaken me?"
[35]And some of the by-
standers hearing it said,
"Behold, he is calling
Eli'jah." [36]And one ran
and, filling a sponge full
of vinegar, put it on a
reed and gave it to him to
drink, saying, "Wait, let
us see whether Eli'jah will
come to take him down."
[37]And Jesus uttered a
loud cry, and breathed
his last. [38]And the curtain
of the temple was torn in
two, from top to bottom.
[39]And when the cen-
turion, who stood facing
him, saw that he thus[q]
breathed his last, he said,
"Truly this man was the
son[qq] of God!"

40 There were also
women looking on from
afar, among whom were
Mary Mag'dalene, and
Mary the mother of
James the younger and
of Joses, and Salo'me,
[41]who, when he was in
Galilee, followed him,
and ministered to him;

[p] Or earth
[q] Other ancient authorities
insert cried out and
[qq] Or a son

συνεσταυρωμένοι σὺν αὐτῷ ὠνείδιζον αὐτόν.
[ones] crucified with   with him reproached him.

33 Καὶ γενομένης ὥρας ἔκτης σκότος
And becoming   hour sixth[a] darkness
= when it was the sixth hour

ἐγένετο ἐφ' ὅλην τὴν γῆν ἕως ὥρας
came   over all the land until [the] hour

ἐνάτης. 34 καὶ τῇ ἐνάτῃ ὥρᾳ ἐβόησεν ὁ
ninth.   And at the ninth hour cried   -

Ἰησοῦς φωνῇ μεγάλῃ· ἐλωῒ ἐλωῒ λαμὰ
Jesus with a voice great(loud): Eloi[,] Eloi[,] lama

σαβαχθάνι; ὅ ἐστιν μεθερμηνευόμενον· The
sabachthani? which is   being interpreted: The

θεός μου ὁ θεός μου, εἰς τί ἐγκατέλιπές
God of me[,] the God of me, why didst thou forsake

με; 35 καί τινες τῶν παρεστηκότων
me?   And some of the [ones] standing by

ἀκούσαντες ἔλεγον· ἴδε Ἠλίαν φωνεῖ.
hearing   said: Behold Elias he calls.

36 δραμὼν δέ τις γεμίσας σπόγγον ὄξους
And running one having filled a sponge of(with) vinegar

περιθεὶς καλάμῳ ἐπότιζεν αὐτόν, λέγων·
placing it round a reed [1]gave [2]to drink [3]him, saying:

ἄφετε ἴδωμεν εἰ ἔρχεται Ἠλίας καθελεῖν
Leave[,] let us see if comes Elias [1]to take [3]down

αὐτόν. 37 ὁ δὲ Ἰησοῦς ἀφεὶς φωνὴν
[2]him.   - But Jesus letting go voice

μεγάλην ἐξέπνευσεν. 38 Καὶ τὸ καταπέτασμα
a great(loud) expired.   And the veil

τοῦ ναοῦ ἐσχίσθη εἰς δύο ἀπ' ἄνωθεν
of the shrine was rent in two from top

ἕως κάτω. 39 Ἰδὼν δὲ ὁ κεντυρίων ὁ
to bottom.   And [6]seeing [1]the [2]centurion -

παρεστηκὼς ἐξ ἐναντίας αὐτοῦ ὅτι οὕτως
[3]standing by [4]opposite [5]him that thus

ἐξέπνευσεν, εἶπεν· ἀληθῶς οὗτος ὁ ἄνθρωπος
he expired,   said: Truly this - man

υἱὸς θεοῦ ἦν. 40 Ἦσαν δὲ καὶ γυναῖκες
son of God was. Now there were also women

ἀπὸ μακρόθεν θεωροῦσαι, ἐν αἷς καὶ
from afar   beholding, among whom both

Μαρία ἡ Μαγδαληνὴ καὶ Μαρία ἡ
Mary the Magdalene and Mary [1]the

Ἰακώβου τοῦ μικροῦ καὶ Ἰωσῆτος μήτηρ
[3]of James [4]the [5]little [6]and [7]of Joses [2]mother

καὶ Σαλώμη, 41 αἱ ὅτε ἦν ἐν τῇ Γαλιλαίᾳ
and Salome,   who when he was in - Galilee

ἠκολούθουν αὐτῷ καὶ διηκόνουν αὐτῷ, καὶ
followed   him and served   him,   and

and also many other
women who came up
with him to Jerusalem.
42 And when evening
had come, since it was
the day of Preparation,
that is, the day before the
sabbath, ⁴³Joseph of
Arimathe'a, a respected
member of the council,
who was also himself
looking for the kingdom
of God, took courage
and went to Pilate, and
asked for the body of
Jesus. ⁴⁴And Pilate
wondered it he were
already dead; and sum-
moning the centurion,
he asked him whether he
was already dead.ʳ ⁴⁵And
when he learned from the
centurion that he was
dead, he granted the
body to Joseph. ⁴⁶And
he bought a linen shroud,
and taking him down,
wrapped him in the linen
shroud, and laid him in a
tomb which had been
hewn out of the rock;
and he rolled a stone
against the door of the
tomb. ⁴⁷Mary Mag'-
dalene and Mary the
mother of Joses saw
where he was laid.

CHAPTER 16

AND when the sabbath
was past, Mary
Mag'dalene, Mary the

ʳ Other ancient authorities
read *whether he had been some
time dead*

ἄλλαι   πολλαὶ   αἱ   συναναβᾶσαι   αὐτῷ   εἰς
others   many   -   having come up with him   to
Ἱεροσόλυμα.
Jerusalem.

42 Καὶ   ἤδη   ὀψίας   γενομένης,   ἐπεὶ   ἦν
   And   now   evening   coming,ᵃ   since   it was
                           = when it was evening,
παρασκευή,   ὅ   ἐστιν   προσάββατον,   43 ἐλθὼν
[the] preparation, which is the day before the sabbath, coming
Ἰωσὴφ   ὁ   ἀπὸ   Ἀριμαθαίας,   εὐσχήμων
Joseph the [one] from   Arimathæa,   an honourable
βουλευτής,   ὃς   καὶ   αὐτὸς   ἦν   προσδεχόμενος
councillor,   who   also   [him]self   was   expecting
τὴν   βασιλείαν   τοῦ   θεοῦ,   τολμήσας   εἰσῆλθεν
the   kingdom   -   of God, taking courage   went in
πρὸς   τὸν   Πιλᾶτον   καὶ   ἠτήσατο   τὸ   σῶμα
to   -   Pilate   and   asked   the   body
τοῦ   Ἰησοῦ.   44 ὁ   δὲ   Πιλᾶτος   ἐθαύμασεν
 -    of Jesus.   -   And   Pilate   marvelled
εἰ   ἤδη   τέθνηκεν,   καὶ   προσκαλεσάμενος   τὸν
if   already he has died,   and   calling to [him]   the
κεντυρίωνα   ἐπηρώτησεν   αὐτὸν   εἰ   πάλαι
centurion   questioned   him   ᵗf   long ago
ἀπέθανεν·   45 καὶ   γνοὺς   ἀπὸ   τοῦ   κεντυρίωνος
he died;   and   knowing   from   the   centurion
ἐδωρήσατο   τὸ   πτῶμα   τῷ   Ἰωσήφ.   46 καὶ
he granted   the   corpse   -   to Joseph.   And
ἀγοράσας   σινδόνα   καθελὼν   αὐτὸν   ἐνείλησεν
having bought a piece of   taking down   him   he wrapped
           unused linen
τῇ   σινδόνι   καὶ   κατέθηκεν   αὐτὸν   ἐν   μνήματι
with the linen   and   deposited   him   in   a tomb
ὃ   ἦν   λελατομημένον   ἐκ   πέτρας,   καὶ
which was   *having been* hewn   out of   rock,   and
προσεκύλισεν   λίθον   ἐπὶ   τὴν   θύραν   τοῦ
rolled   a stone   against   the   door   of the
μνημείου.   47 ἡ   δὲ   Μαρία   ἡ   Μαγδαληνὴ
tomb.   - And   Mary   the   Magdalene
καὶ   Μαρία   ἡ   Ἰωσῆτος   ἐθεώρουν   ποῦ
and   Mary   the [mother]   of Joses   beheld   where
τέθειται.
he has been laid.

16 Καὶ   διαγενομένου   τοῦ   σαββάτου   [ἡ]
   And   passing   the   sabbathᵃ   -
               = when the sabbath was past
Μαρία   ἡ   Μαγδαληνὴ   καὶ   Μαρία   ἡ   [τοῦ]
Mary   the   Magdalene   and   Mary   the [mother]   -

mother of James, and Salo′me bought spices, so that they might go and anoint him. ²And very early on the first day of the week they went to the tomb when the sun had risen. ³And they were saying to one another, "Who will roll away the stone for us from the door of the tomb?" ⁴And looking up, they saw that the stone was rolled back; for it was very large. ⁵And entering the tomb, they saw a young man sitting on the right side, dressed in a white robe; and they were amazed. ⁶And he said to them, "Do not be amazed; you seek Jesus of Nazareth, who was crucified. He has risen, he is not here; see the place where they laid him. ⁷But go, tell his disciples and Peter that he is going before you to Galilee; there you will see him, as he told you." ⁸And they went out and fled from the tomb; for trembling and astonishment had come upon them; and they said nothing to any one, for they were afraid.*

---

* Other texts and versions add as 16. 9–20 the following passage:

9 Now when he rose early on the first day of the week, he appeared first to Mary Magdalene, from whom he had cast out seven demons. ¹⁰ She went

---

'Ιακώβου καὶ Σαλώμη ἠγόρασαν ἀρώματα
of James and Salome bought spices

ἵνα ἐλθοῦσαι ἀλείψωσιν αὐτόν. 2 καὶ λίαν
that coming they might anoint him. And very

πρωῒ [τῇ] μιᾷ τῶν σαββάτων ἔρχονται
early on the first day of the week† they come

ἐπὶ τὸ μνῆμα, ἀνατείλαντος τοῦ ἡλίου.
upon the tomb, rising the sun.ᵃ
= as the sun rose.

3 καὶ ἔλεγον πρὸς ἑαυτάς· τίς ἀποκυλίσει
And they said to themselves: Who will roll away

ἡμῖν τὸν λίθον ἐκ τῆς θύρας τοῦ μνημείου;
for us the stone out of the door of the tomb?

4 καὶ ἀναβλέψασαι θεωροῦσιν ὅτι ἀνακεκύλισται
And looking up they behold that has been rolled back

ὁ λίθος· ἦν γὰρ μέγας σφόδρα. 5 καὶ
the stone: for it was great exceedingly. And

εἰσελθοῦσαι εἰς τὸ μνημεῖον εἶδον νεανίσκον
entering into the tomb they saw a young man

καθήμενον ἐν τοῖς δεξιοῖς περιβεβλημένον
sitting on the right having been clothed

στολὴν λευκήν, καὶ ἐξεθαμβήθησαν. 6 ὁ δὲ
robe [in] a white, and they were greatly astonished. But he

λέγει αὐταῖς· μὴ ἐκθαμβεῖσθε· 'Ιησοῦν
says to them: Be not greatly astonished; Jesus

ζητεῖτε τὸν Ναζαρηνὸν τὸν ἐσταυρωμένον·
ye seek the Nazarene – having been crucified;

ἠγέρθη, οὐκ ἔστιν ὧδε· ἴδε ὁ τόπος
he was raised, he is not here; behold[,] the place

ὅπου ἔθηκαν αὐτόν. 7 ἀλλὰ ὑπάγετε εἴπατε
where they put him. But go ye tell

τοῖς μαθηταῖς αὐτοῦ καὶ τῷ Πέτρῳ ὅτι
the disciples of him and – Peter that

προάγει ὑμᾶς εἰς τὴν Γαλιλαίαν· ἐκεῖ
he goes before you to – Galilee; there

αὐτὸν ὄψεσθε, καθὼς εἶπεν ὑμῖν. 8 καὶ
him ye will see, as he told you. And

ἐξελθοῦσαι ἔφυγον ἀπὸ τοῦ μνημείου, εἶχεν
going forth they fled from the tomb, ᵇhad

γὰρ αὐτὰς τρόμος καὶ ἔκστασις· καὶ
¹for ⁶them ²trembling ³and ⁴bewilderment; and

οὐδενὶ οὐδὲν εἶπαν· ἐφοβοῦντο γάρ.
no one no(any)thing they told; for they were afraid.

9 'Αναστὰς δὲ πρωῒ πρώτῃ σαββάτου
And rising early on the first day of the week†

ἐφάνη πρῶτον Μαρίᾳ τῇ Μαγδαληνῇ, παρ'
he appeared first to Mary the Magdalene, from

ἧς ἐκβεβλήκει ἑπτὰ δαιμόνια. 10 ἐκείνη
whom he had expelled seven demons. That [one]
= She

πορευθεῖσα   ἀπήγγειλεν   τοῖς   μετ᾽   αὐτοῦ
going   reported   to the [ones]   with   him
                          = those who had been with him

γενομένοις πενθοῦσι καὶ κλαίουσιν· 11 κἀκεῖνοι
having been   mourning and   weeping;   and those

ἀκούσαντες   ὅτι   ζῇ   καὶ   ἐθεάθη   ὑπ᾽   αὐτῆς
hearing   that he lives and   was seen   by   her

ἠπίστησαν.   12 Μετὰ   δὲ   ταῦτα   δυσὶν   ἐξ
disbelieved.   And after   these things to two   of

αὐτῶν   περιπατοῦσιν   ἐφανερώθη   ἐν   ἑτέρᾳ
them   walking   he was manifested in   a different

μορφῇ   πορευομένοις   εἰς   ἀγρόν· 13 κἀκεῖνοι
form   going   into [the] country;   and those

ἀπελθόντες   ἀπήγγειλαν   τοῖς   λοιποῖς·   οὐδὲ
going   reported   to the   rest;   neither

ἐκείνοις   ἐπίστευσαν.   14 Ὕστερον   [δὲ]
those   they believed.   And later

ἀνακειμένοις   αὐτοῖς   τοῖς   ἕνδεκα   ἐφανερώθη,
to the reclining   them   the   eleven   he was manifested,
= to the eleven as they reclined

καὶ   ὠνείδισεν   τὴν   ἀπιστίαν   αὐτῶν   καὶ
and   reproached   the   disbelief   of them   and

σκληροκαρδίαν   ὅτι   τοῖς   θεασαμένοις   αὐτὸν
hardness of heart   because the [ones]   beholding   him

ἐγηγερμένον   οὐκ   ἐπίστευσαν.   15 καὶ   εἶπεν
having been raised   they did not believe.   And   he said

αὐτοῖς·   πορευθέντες   εἰς   τὸν   κόσμον   ἅπαντα
to them: Going   into   ²the   ³world   ¹all

κηρύξατε   τὸ   εὐαγγέλιον   πάσῃ   τῇ   κτίσει.
proclaim ye   the   gospel   to all   the   creation.

16 ὁ   πιστεύσας καὶ βαπτισθεὶς σωθήσεται,
    The [one] believing   and being baptized   will be saved,

ὁ   δὲ   ἀπιστήσας κατακριθήσεται. 17 σημεῖα
but the [one] disbelieving   will be condemned.   ²signs

δὲ   τοῖς   πιστεύσασιν ταῦτα παρακολουθήσει·
¹And ⁵the [ones] ⁶believing   ³these   ⁴will follow:

ἐν   τῷ   ὀνόματί   μου   δαιμόνια   ἐκβαλοῦσιν,
in   the   name   of me   demons   they will expel,

γλώσσαις   λαλήσουσιν   καιναῖς, 18 ὄφεις
³tongues   ¹they will speak   ²with new,   serpents

ἀροῦσιν   κἂν   θανάσιμόν   τι   πίωσιν
they will take   and if   ³deadly   ²anything ¹they drink

οὐ   μὴ   αὐτοὺς   βλάψῃ,   ἐπὶ   ἀρρώστους   χεῖρας
by no means   them   it will hurt,   on   sick [ones]   hands

ἐπιθήσουσιν καὶ καλῶς ἕξουσιν. 19 Ὁ   μὲν
they will place on and   well   they will have.   ¹The ⁴there-
= they will recover.

οὖν   κύριος   [Ἰησοῦς]   μετὰ   τὸ   λαλῆσαι
fore   ²Lord   ³Jesus   after   the   to speak
= speaking

and told those who had been with him, as they mourned and wept. ¹¹But when they heard that he was alive and had been seen by her, they would not believe it.

12 After this he appeared in another form to two of them, as they were walking into the country. ¹³And they went back and told the rest, but they did not believe them.

14 Afterward he appeared to the eleven themselves as they sat at table; and he upbraided them for their unbelief and hardness of heart, because they had not believed those who saw him after he had risen. ¹⁵And he said to them, "Go into all the world and preach the gospel to the whole creation. ¹⁶He who believes and is baptized will be saved; but he who does not believe will be condemned. ¹⁷And these signs will accompany those who believe: in my name they will cast out demons; they will speak in new tongues; ¹⁸they will pick up serpents, and if they drink any deadly thing, it will not hurt them; they will lay their hands on the sick; and they will recover."

19 So then the Lord Jesus, after he had spoken to them, was

αὐτοῖς ἀνελήμφθη εἰς τὸν οὐρανὸν καὶ
to them   was taken up   into   –   heaven   and

ἐκάθισεν ἐκ δεξιῶν τοῦ θεοῦ. **20** ἐκεῖνοι
sat   at [the] right [hand]   –   of God.   those

δὲ ἐξελθόντες ἐκήρυξαν πανταχοῦ, τοῦ
But   going forth   proclaimed   everywhere,   the

κυρίου συνεργοῦντος καὶ τὸν λόγον
Lord   working with   and   the   word
= while the Lord worked with [them] and confirmed the word

βεβαιοῦντος διὰ τῶν ἐπακολουθούντων
confirming[a]   through   the   accompanying

σημείων.
signs.

taken up into heaven, and sat down at the right hand of God. [20]And they went forth and preached everywhere, while the Lord worked with them and confirmed the message by the signs that attended it. Amen.
Other ancient authorities add after verse 8 the following: *But they reported briefly to Peter and those with him all that they had been told. And after this, Jesus himself sent out by means of them, from east to west, the sacred and imperishable proclamation of eternal salvation.*

CHAPTER 1

INASMUCH as many have undertaken to compile a narrative of the things which have been accomplished among us ²just as they were delivered to us by those who from the beginning were eye witnesses and ministers of the word, ³it seemed good to me also, having followed all things closely*a* for some time past, to write an orderly account for you, most excellent The-oph'ilus, ⁴that you may know the truth concerning the things of which you have been informed.

5 In the days of Herod, king of Judea, there was a priest named Zechari'ah, of the division of Abi'jah; and he had a wife of the daughters of Aaron, and her name was Elizabeth. ⁶And they were both righteous before God, walking in all the commandments and ordinances of the Lord blameless. ⁷But they had no child, because Elizabeth was barren, and both were advanced in years.

8 Now while he was serving as priest before God when his division

a Or *accurately*

1 **'Επειδήπερ** **πολλοὶ** **ἐπεχείρησαν** **ἀνατάξασθαι**
Since   many   took in hand   to draw up

διήγησιν **περὶ** **τῶν** **πεπληροφορημένων**
a narrative concerning ¹the ³having been fully carried out

ἐν **ἡμῖν** **πραγμάτων,** 2 **καθὼς** **παρέδοσαν** **ἡμῖν**
⁴among ⁵us ²matters, as delivered to us

οἱ **ἀπ'** **ἀρχῆς** **αὐτόπται** **καὶ** **ὑπηρέται**
the [ones] from [the] beginning eyewitnesses and attendants

γενόμενοι **τοῦ** **λόγου,** 3 **ἔδοξε** **κἀμοὶ**
becoming of the Word, it seemed good to me also

παρηκολουθηκότι **ἄνωθεν** **πᾶσιν** **ἀκριβῶς**
having investigated from their source all things accurately

καθεξῆς **σοι** **γράψαι,** **κράτιστε** **Θεόφιλε,**
³in order ²to thee ¹to write, most excellent Theophilus,

4 **ἵνα** **ἐπιγνῷς** **περὶ** **ὧν**
that thou mightest know ⁴concerning ⁵which

κατηχήθης **λόγων** **τὴν** **ἀσφάλειαν.**
⁶thou wast instructed ³of [the] things ¹the ²reliability.

5 **'Εγένετο** **ἐν** **ταῖς** **ἡμέραις**
There was in the days

'Ηρῴδου **βασιλέως** **τῆς** **'Ιουδαίας** **ἱερεύς**
of Herod king – of Judæa ³priest

τις **ὀνόματι** **Ζαχαρίας** **ἐξ** **ἐφημερίας** **'Αβιά,**
¹a certain by name Zacharias of [the] course of Abia,

καὶ **γυνὴ** **αὐτῷ** **ἐκ** **τῶν** **θυγατέρων** **'Ααρών,**
and wife to him*c* of the daughters of Aaron,
=his wife

καὶ **τὸ** **ὄνομα** **αὐτῆς** **'Ελισάβετ.** 6 **ἦσαν** **δὲ**
and the name of her Elisabeth. And they were

δίκαιοι **ἀμφότεροι** **ἐναντίον** **τοῦ** **θεοῦ,**
righteous both before – God,

πορευόμενοι **ἐν** **πάσαις** **ταῖς** **ἐντολαῖς** **καὶ**
going in all the commandments and

δικαιώμασιν **τοῦ** **κυρίου** **ἄμεμπτοι.** 7 **καὶ**
ordinances of the Lord blameless. And

οὐκ **ἦν** **αὐτοῖς** **τέκνον,** **καθότι** **ἦν** **ἡ**
there was not to them a child,*e* because ²was ³

=they had no child,

'Ελισάβετ **στεῖρα,** **καὶ** **ἀμφότεροι** **προβεβηκότες**
¹Elisabeth barren, and both *having* advanced

ἐν **ταῖς** **ἡμέραις** **αὐτῶν** **ἦσαν.** 8 **'Εγένετο**
in the days of them were. it came to pass

δὲ **ἐν** **τῷ** **ἱερατεύειν** **αὐτὸν** **ἐν** **τῇ** **τάξει**
Now in the to serve as priest him*be* in the order
=while he served as priest

LUKE 1

was on duty, ⁹according to the custom of the priesthood, it fell to him by lot to enter the temple of the Lord and burn incense. ¹⁰And the whole multitude of the people were praying outside at the hour of incense. ¹¹And there appeared to him an angel of the Lord standing on the right side of the altar of incense. ¹²And Zechari′ah was troubled when he saw him, and fear fell upon him. ¹³But the angel said to him, "Do not be afraid, Zechari′ah, for your prayer is heard, and your wife Elizabeth will bear you a son, and you shall call his name John.

¹⁴And you will have joy and gladness, and many will rejoice at his birth;
¹⁵for he will be great before the Lord, and he shall drink no wine nor strong drink, and he will be filled with the Holy Spirit, even from his mother's womb.
¹⁶And he will turn many of the sons of Israel to the Lord their God,
¹⁷and he will go before him in the spirit and power of Eli′jah, to turn the hearts of the fathers to the children, and the disobedient to the wisdom of

τῆς ἐφημερίας αὐτοῦ ἔναντι τοῦ θεοῦ,
of the course of him before - God,
9 κατὰ τὸ ἔθος τῆς ἱερατείας ἔλαχε τοῦ
according to the custom of the priesthood his lot was -
θυμιᾶσαι εἰσελθὼν εἰς τὸν ναὸν τοῦ κυρίου,
to burn incenseᵈ entering into the shrine of the Lord,
10 καὶ πᾶν τὸ πλῆθος ἦν τοῦ λαοῦ
and all ¹the ²multitude ⁵was ³of the ⁴people
προσευχόμενον ἔξω τῇ ὥρᾳ τοῦ θυμιάματος.
praying outside at the hour - of incense.
11 ὤφθη δὲ αὐτῷ ἄγγελος κυρίου ἑστὼς
And there appeared to him an angel of [the] Lord standing
ἐκ δεξιῶν τοῦ θυσιαστηρίου τοῦ θυμιάματος.
on [the] right of the altar - of incense.
12 καὶ ἐταράχθη Ζαχαρίας ἰδών, καὶ φόβος
And was troubled Zacharias seeing, and fear
ἐπέπεσεν ἐπ᾽ αὐτόν. 13 εἶπεν δὲ πρὸς
fell on upon him. But said to
αὐτὸν ὁ ἄγγελος· μὴ φοβοῦ, Ζαχαρία,
him the angel: Fear not, Zacharias,
διότι εἰσηκούσθη ἡ δέησίς σου, καὶ ἡ
because was heard the request of thee, and the
γυνή σου Ἐλισάβετ γεννήσει υἱόν σοι,
wife of thee Elisabeth will bear a son to thee,
καὶ καλέσεις τὸ ὄνομα αὐτοῦ Ἰωάννην·
and thou shalt call the name of him John;
14 καὶ ἔσται χαρά σοι καὶ ἀγαλλίασις,ᵉ
and there shall be joy to thee and gladness,
=thou shalt have joy and gladness,
καὶ πολλοὶ ἐπὶ τῇ γενέσει αὐτοῦ χαρή-
and many over the birth of him will
σονται. 15 ἔσται γὰρ μέγας ἐνώπιον
rejoice. For he will be great in the eyes of
κυρίου, καὶ οἶνον καὶ σίκερα οὐ μὴ
[the] Lord, and wine and strong drink by no means
πίῃ, καὶ πνεύματος ἁγίου πλησθήσεται
may he drink, and of(with) Spirit [the] Holy he will be filled
ἔτι ἐκ κοιλίας μητρὸς αὐτοῦ, 16 καὶ
even from [the] womb of [the] mother of him, and
πολλοὺς τῶν υἱῶν Ἰσραὴλ ἐπιστρέψει ἐπὶ κύριον
many of the sons of Israel he will turn to [the] Lord
τὸν θεὸν αὐτῶν· 17 καὶ αὐτὸς προελεύσεται
the God of them; and he will go before
ἐνώπιον αὐτοῦ ἐν πνεύματι καὶ δυνάμει
before him in [the] spirit and power
Ἠλίου, ἐπιστρέψαι καρδίας πατέρων ἐπὶ
of Elias, to turn [the] hearts of fathers to
τέκνα καὶ ἀπειθεῖς ἐν φρονήσει
children and disobedient [ones] to [the] understanding

the just,
to make ready for the
Lord a people
prepared."
18And Zechari'ah said to
the angel, "How shall I
know this? For I am an
old man, and my wife is
advanced in years."
19And the angel answered
him, "I am Gabriel, who
stand in the presence of
God; and I was sent to
speak to you, and to
bring you this good
news. 20And behold, you
will be silent and unable
to speak until the day
that these things come to
pass, because you did
not believe my words,
which will be fulfilled in
their time." 21And the
people were waiting for
Zechari'ah, and they
wondered at his delay in
the temple. 22And when
he came out, he could not
speak to them, and they
perceived that he had
seen a vision in the
temple; and he made
signs to them and re-
mained dumb. 23And
when his time of service
was ended, he went to his
home.
24 After these days his
wife Elizabeth con-
ceived, and for five
months she hid herself,

δικαίων, ἐτοιμάσαι κυρίῳ λαὸν κατεσκευασ-
of [the] just, to prepare for [the] Lord a people   *having been*
μένον. 18 καὶ εἶπεν Ζαχαρίας πρὸς τὸν ἄγγελον·
prepared.   And said Zacharias to the angel :
κατὰ τί γνώσομαι τοῦτο; ἐγὼ γάρ εἰμι
By what shall I know this ? for I am
πρεσβύτης καὶ ἡ γυνή μου προβεβηκυῖα
old and the wife of me *having* advanced
ἐν ταῖς ἡμέραις αὐτῆς. 19 καὶ ἀποκριθεὶς
in the days of her.   And answering
ὁ ἄγγελος εἶπεν αὐτῷ· ἐγώ εἰμι Γαβριὴλ
the angel said to him : I am Gabriel
ὁ παρεστηκὼς ἐνώπιον τοῦ θεοῦ, καὶ
the [one] standing before – God, and
ἀπεστάλην λαλῆσαι πρὸς σὲ καὶ εὐαγ-
I was sent to speak to thee and to
γελίσασθαί σοι ταῦτα· 20 καὶ ἰδοὺ
announce to thee these things; and behold
ἔσῃ σιωπῶν καὶ μὴ δυνάμενος λαλῆσαι
thou shalt be being silent and not being able to speak
ἄχρι ἧς ἡμέρας γένηται ταῦτα, ἀνθ' ὧν οὐκ
until which day happens these things, because not
     =the day when these things happen,
ἐπίστευσας τοῖς λόγοις μου, οἵτινες πληρω-
thou believedst the words of me, which will be
θήσονται εἰς τὸν καιρὸν αὐτῶν. 21 καὶ ἦν
fulfilled in the time of them.   And was
ὁ λαὸς προσδοκῶν τὸν Ζαχαρίαν, καὶ
the people expecting – Zacharias, and
ἐθαύμαζον ἐν τῷ χρονίζειν ἐν τῷ ναῷ
they marvelled in(at) the to delay in the shrine
     =when he delayed in the shrine.
αὐτόν. 22 ἐξελθὼν δὲ οὐκ ἐδύνατο λαλῆσαι
him.be   And going out he was not able to speak
αὐτοῖς καὶ ἐπέγνωσαν ὅτι ὀπτασίαν ἑώρακεν
to them, and they knew that a vision he has(had) seen
ἐν τῷ ναῷ· καὶ αὐτὸς ἦν διανεύων
in the shrine; and he was beckoning
αὐτοῖς, καὶ διέμενεν κωφός. 23 καὶ
to them, and remained dumb.   And
ἐγένετο ὡς ἐπλήσθησαν αἱ ἡμέραι τῆς
it came to pass when were fulfilled the days of the
λειτουργίας αὐτοῦ, ἀπῆλθεν εἰς τὸν οἶκον
service of him, he went away to the house
αὐτοῦ. 24 Μετὰ δὲ ταύτας τὰς ἡμέρας
of him.   And after these days
συνέλαβεν Ἐλισάβετ ἡ γυνὴ αὐτοῦ, καὶ
conceived Elisabet the wife of him, and
περιέκρυβεν ἑαυτὴν μῆνας πέντε, λέγουσα
hid herself months five, saying[.]

saying, ²⁵"Thus the Lord has done to me in the days when he looked on me, to take away my reproach among men."

26 In the sixth month the angel Gabriel was sent from God to a city of Galilee named Nazareth, ²⁷to a virgin betrothed to a man whose name was Joseph, of the house of David; and the virgin's name was Mary. ²⁸And he came to her and said, "Hail, O favored one, the Lord is with you!"ᵇ ²⁹But she was greatly troubled at the saying, and considered in her mind what sort of greeting this might be. ³⁰And the angel said to her, "Do not be afraid, Mary, for you have found favor with God. ³¹And behold, you will conceive in your womb and bear a son, and you shall call his name Jesus.

³²He will be great, and will be called the Son of the Most High;
and the Lord God will give to him the throne of his father David,
³³and he will reign over the house of Jacob for ever;
and of his kingdom there will be no end."
³⁴And Mary said to the angel, "How can this be,

ᵇ Other ancient authorities add "Blessed are you among women³"

25 ὅτι   οὕτως   μοι   πεποίηκεν   κύριος   ἐν
— Thus   to me   has done   [the] Lord   in
ἡμέραις   αἷς   ἐπεῖδεν   ἀφελεῖν   ὄνειδός
days   in which   he looked upon   to take away   reproach
μου   ἐν   ἀνθρώποις.
of me   among   men.

26 Ἐν   δὲ   τῷ   μηνὶ   τῷ   ἕκτῳ   ἀπεστάλη
Now in   —   the   month   —   sixth   was sent
ὁ   ἄγγελος   Γαβριὴλ   ἀπὸ   τοῦ   θεοῦ   εἰς
the   angel   Gabriel   from   —   God   to
πόλιν   τῆς   Γαλιλαίας   ᾗ   ὄνομα   Ναζαρέθ,
a city   —   of Galilee   to which   name°   Nazareth,
= the name of which [was]

27 πρὸς   παρθένον   ἐμνηστευμένην   ἀνδρὶ   ᾧ   ὄνομα
to   a virgin   having been   to a man   to whom   name°
betrothed

Ἰωσήφ,   ἐξ   οἴκου   Δαυίδ,   καὶ   τὸ   ὄνομα
Joseph,   of [the]   house   of David,   and   the   name
τῆς   παρθένου   Μαριάμ.   28 καὶ   εἰσελθὼν
of the   virgin   [was] Mary.   And   entering
πρὸς   αὐτὴν   εἶπεν·   χαῖρε,   κεχαριτωμένη,   ὁ
to   her   he said :   Hail,   having been favoured [one],   the
κύριος   μετὰ   σοῦ.   29 ἡ   δὲ   ἐπὶ   τῷ   λόγῳ
Lord [is]   with   thee.   And she   at   the   saying
διεταράχθη,   καὶ   διελογίζετο   ποταπὸς   εἴη
was greatly disturbed,   and   considered   of what sort   ²might be
ὁ   ἀσπασμὸς   οὗτος.   30 καὶ   εἶπεν   ὁ   ἄγγελος
—   ²greeting   ¹this.   And   said   the   angel
αὐτῇ·   μὴ   φοβοῦ,   Μαριάμ·   εὗρες   γὰρ
to her :   Fear not,   Mary :   for thou didst find
χάριν   παρὰ   τῷ   θεῷ.   31 καὶ   ἰδοὺ   συλλήμψῃ
favour   with   —   God.   And behold   thou wilt conceive
ἐν   γαστρὶ   καὶ   τέξῃ   υἱόν,   καὶ   καλέσεις   τὸ
in   womb   and   bear   a son,   and   thou shalt call the
ὄνομα   αὐτοῦ   Ἰησοῦν.   32 οὗτος   ἔσται   μέγας
name   of him   Jesus.   This   will be   great
καὶ   υἱὸς   ὑψίστου   κληθήσεται,   καὶ   δώσει
and   Son   of [the] Most High   will be called,   and   will give
αὐτῷ   κύριος   ὁ   θεὸς   τὸν   θρόνον   Δαυὶδ
him   [the] Lord   —   God   the   throne   of David
τοῦ   πατρὸς   αὐτοῦ,   33 καὶ   βασιλεύσει   ἐπὶ
the   father   of him,   and   he will reign   over
τὸν   οἶκον   Ἰακὼβ   εἰς   τοὺς   αἰῶνας,   καὶ
the   house   of Jacob   unto   the   ages,   and
= for ever,
τῆς   βασιλείας   αὐτοῦ   οὐκ   ἔσται   τέλος.
of the   kingdom   of him   there will not be   an end.
34 εἶπεν   δὲ   Μαριὰμ   πρὸς   τὸν   ἄγγελον·
And said   Mary   to   the   angel :

since I have no husband?" ³⁵And the angel said to her,
"The Holy Spirit will come upon you,
and the power of the Most High will overshadow you;
therefore the child to be born^c will be called holy,
the Son of God.
³⁶And behold, your kinswoman Elizabeth in her old age has also conceived a son; and this is the sixth month with her who was called barren. ³⁷For with God nothing will be impossible." ³⁸And Mary said, "Behold I am the handmaid of the Lord; let it be to me according to your word." And the angel departed from her.

39 In those days Mary arose and went with haste into the hill country, to a city of Judah, ⁴⁰and she entered the house of Zechari'ah and greeted Elizabeth. ⁴¹And when Elizabeth heard the greeting of Mary, the babe leaped in her womb; and Elizabeth was filled with the Holy Spirit ⁴²and she exclaimed with a loud cry, "Blessed are you among women, and blessed is the fruit of your womb! ⁴³And why is this granted me, that the mother of my Lord

^c Other ancient authorities add *of you*

πῶς ἔσται τοῦτο, ἐπεὶ ἄνδρα οὐ γινώσκω;
How will be this, since a man I know not?

35 καὶ ἀποκριθεὶς ὁ ἄγγελος εἶπεν αὐτῇ·
And answering the angel said to her :

πνεῦμα ἅγιον ἐπελεύσεται ἐπὶ σέ, καὶ
¹[The] ²Spirit ³Holy will come *upon* upon thee, and

δύναμις ὑψίστου ἐπισκιάσει σοι· διὸ
[the] power of [the] Most High will overshadow thee; wherefore

καὶ τὸ γεννώμενον ἅγιον κληθήσεται υἱὸς θεοῦ.
also the thing being born holy will be called[,] Son of God.

36 καὶ ἰδοὺ Ἐλισάβετ ἡ συγγενίς σου καὶ
And behold Elisabeth the relative of thee also

αὐτὴ συνείληφεν υἱὸν ἐν γήρει αὐτῆς, καὶ
she conceived a son in old age of her, and

οὗτος μὴν ἔκτος ἐστὶν αὐτῇ τῇ καλουμένῃ
this month sixth is with her the [one] *being* called

στείρᾳ· 37 ὅτι οὐκ ἀδυνατήσει παρὰ τοῦ
barren; because will not be impossible with –

θεοῦ πᾶν ῥῆμα. 38 εἶπεν δὲ Μαριάμ· ἰδοὺ ἡ
God every word. And said Mary: Behold[,] the

δούλη κυρίου· γένοιτό μοι κατὰ
handmaid of [the] Lord; may it be to me according to

τὸ ῥῆμά σου. καὶ ἀπῆλθεν ἀπ’ αὐτῆς
the word of thee. And went away from her

ὁ ἄγγελος. 39 Ἀναστᾶσα δὲ Μαριὰμ ἐν
the angel. And rising up Mary in

ταῖς ἡμέραις ταύταις ἐπορεύθη εἰς τὴν
– days these she went to the

ὀρεινὴν μετὰ σπουδῆς εἰς πόλιν Ἰούδα,
mountain country with haste to a city of Juda,

40 καὶ εἰσῆλθεν εἰς τὸν οἶκον Ζαχαρίου
and entered into the house of Zacharias

καὶ ἠσπάσατο τὴν Ἐλισάβετ. 41 καὶ
and greeted – Elisabeth. And

ἐγένετο ὡς ἤκουσεν τὸν ἀσπασμὸν τῆς
it came to pass when ²heard ³the ⁴greeting –

Μαρίας ἡ Ἐλισάβετ, ἐσκίρτησεν τὸ βρέφος
⁵of Mary – ¹Elisabeth, leaped the babe

ἐν τῇ κοιλίᾳ αὐτῆς, καὶ ἐπλήσθη πνεύματος
in the womb of her, and ²was filled ³of(with) ⁵Spirit

ἁγίου ἡ Ἐλισάβετ, 42 καὶ ἀνεφώνησεν
⁴[the] Holy – ¹Elisabeth, and she called out

κραυγῇ μεγάλῃ καὶ εἶπεν· εὐλογημένη
cry with a great and said : Blessed [art]

σὺ ἐν γυναιξίν, καὶ εὐλογημένος ὁ καρπὸς
thou among women, and blessed [is] the fruit

τῆς κοιλίας σου. 43 καὶ πόθεν μοι τοῦτο
of the womb of thee. And whence to me this

should come to me? ⁴⁴For behold, when the voice of your greeting came to my ears, the babe in my womb leaped for joy. ⁴⁵And blessed is she who believed that there would be*ᵈ* a fulfilment of what was spoken to her from the Lord." ⁴⁶And Mary said,

"My soul magnifies the Lord,
⁴⁷and my spirit rejoices in God my Savior,
⁴⁸for he has regarded the low estate of his handmaiden.

For behold, henceforth all generations will call me blessed;
⁴⁹for he who is mighty has done great things for me,
and holy is his name.
⁵⁰And his mercy is on those who fear him from generation to generation.
⁵¹He has shown strength with his arm,
he has scattered the proud in the imagination of their hearts,
⁵²he has put down the mighty from their thrones,
and exalted those of low degree;
⁵³he has filled the hungry with good things,
and the rich he has sent empty away.
⁵⁴He has helped his servant Israel,
in remembrance of his mercy,
⁵⁵as he spoke to our fathers,

ᵈ Or believed, for there will be

ἵνα   ἔλθη   ἡ   μήτηρ   τοῦ   κυρίου   μου   πρὸς
that   comes the mother   of the Lord   of me to

ἐμέ;   44 ἰδοὺ γὰρ ὡς ἐγένετο ἡ φωνὴ τοῦ
me?   For behold when came the sound of the

ἀσπασμοῦ σου εἰς τὰ ὦτά μου, ἐσκίρτησεν
greeting   of thee in the ears of me, leaped

ἐν   ἀγαλλιάσει   τὸ   βρέφος   ἐν   τῇ   κοιλίᾳ
in   gladness   the   babe   in   the   womb

μου.   45 καὶ   μακαρία   ἡ   πιστεύσασα   ὅτι
of me.   And   blessed the [one] believing because

ἔσται   τελείωσις   τοῖς   λελαλημένοις   αὐτῇ
there shall be a completion to the things having been to her
                                            spoken

παρὰ   κυρίου.   46 Καὶ   εἶπεν   Μαριάμ·
from   [the] Lord.   And   said   Mary:

Μεγαλύνει ἡ ψυχή μου τὸν κύριον, 47 καὶ
Magnifies the soul of me the Lord,   and

ἠγαλλίασεν   τὸ πνεῦμά μου ἐπὶ τῷ θεῷ
exulted   the spirit of me in - God

τῷ σωτῆρί μου· 48 ὅτι ἐπέβλεψεν ἐπὶ τὴν
the saviour of me; because he looked on upon the

ταπείνωσιν τῆς δούλης αὐτοῦ. ἰδοὺ γὰρ
humiliation of the handmaid of him. For behold

ἀπὸ τοῦ νῦν μακαριοῦσίν με πᾶσαι αἱ
from - now ⁴will ⁵deem ⁷blessed ⁶me ¹all ²the

γενεαί· 49 ὅτι ἐποίησέν μοι μεγάλα ὁ
³generations; because he did to me great things the

δυνατός. καὶ ἅγιον τὸ ὄνομα αὐτοῦ,
Mighty [one]. And holy the name of him,

50 καὶ τὸ ἔλεος αὐτοῦ εἰς γενεὰς καὶ
and the mercy of him to generations and

γενεὰς τοῖς φοβουμένοις αὐτόν. 51 Ἐποίησεν
generations to the [ones] fearing him. He did

κράτος ἐν βραχίονι αὐτοῦ, διεσκόρπισεν
might with [the] arm of him, he scattered

ὑπερηφάνους διανοίᾳ καρδίας αὐτῶν·
haughty [ones] in [the] understanding of [the] heart of them;

52 καθεῖλεν δυνάστας ἀπὸ θρόνων καὶ ὕψω-
he pulled down potentates from thrones and exalt-

σεν ταπεινούς, 53 πεινῶντας ἐνέπλησεν
ed humble [ones], hungering [ones] he filled

ἀγαθῶν καὶ πλουτοῦντας ἐξαπέστειλεν
of(with) good things and rich [ones] he sent away

κενούς. 54 ἀντελάβετο Ἰσραὴλ παιδὸς αὐτοῦ,
empty. He succoured Israel servant of him,

μνησθῆναι ἐλέους, 55 καθὼς ἐλάλησεν
to remember mercy, as he spoke

πρὸς τοὺς πατέρας ἡμῶν, τῷ Ἀβραὰμ
to the fathers of us, - to Abraham

to Abraham and to his posterity for ever."

⁵⁶And Mary remained with her about three months, and returned to her home.

57 Now the time came for Elizabeth to be delivered, and she gave birth to a son. ⁵⁸And her neighbors and kinsfolk heard that the Lord had shown great mercy to her, and they rejoiced with her. ⁵⁹And on the eighth day they came to circumcise the child; and they would have named him Zechari′ah after his father, ⁶⁰but his mother said, "Not so; he shall be called John." ⁶¹And they said to her, "None of your kindred is called by this name." ⁶²And they made signs to his father, inquiring what he would have him called. ⁶³And he asked for a writing tablet, and wrote, "His name is John." And they all marveled. ⁶⁴And immediately his mouth was opened and his tongue loosed, and he spoke, blessing God. ⁶⁵And fear came on all their neighbors. And all these things were talked about through all the hill

καὶ   τῷ   σπέρματι   αὐτοῦ   εἰς   τὸν   αἰῶνα.
and   to the   seed   of him   unto   the   age.
=for ever.

56 "Ἔμεινεν   δὲ   Μαριὰμ   σὺν   αὐτῇ   ὡς
And remained   Mary   with   her   about

μῆνας   τρεῖς,   καὶ   ὑπέστρεψεν   εἰς   τὸν
months   three,   and   returned   to   the

οἶκον   αὐτῆς.
house   of her.

57 Τῇ   δὲ   'Ελισάβετ   ἐπλήσθη   ὁ   χρόνος
-    Now   ⁴to Elisabeth   ³was fulfilled   ¹the   ⁵time

τοῦ   τεκεῖν   αὐτήν,   καὶ   ἐγέννησεν   υἱόν.
-    to bear   her,ᵇᵈ   and she brought forth   a son.
=that she should bear,

58 καὶ   ἤκουσαν   οἱ   περίοικοι   καὶ   οἱ
And   heard   the   neighbours   and   the

συγγενεῖς   αὐτῆς   ὅτι   ἐμεγάλυνεν   κύριος   τὸ
relatives   of her   that   magnified   [the] Lord   the

ἔλεος   αὐτοῦ   μετ'   αὐτῆς,   καὶ   συνέχαιρον
mercy   of him   with   her,   and   they rejoiced with

αὐτῇ.   59 Καὶ   ἐγένετο   ἐν   τῇ   ἡμέρᾳ   τῇ
her.   And   it came to pass   on   the   day   -

ὀγδόῃ   ἦλθον   περιτεμεῖν   τὸ   παιδίον,   καὶ
eighth   they came   to circumcise   the   child,   and

ἐκάλουν   αὐτὸ   ἐπὶ   τῷ   ὀνόματι   τοῦ   πατρὸς
were calling   it(him)   by   the   name   of the   father

αὐτοῦ   Ζαχαρίαν.   60 καὶ   ἀποκριθεῖσα   ἡ
of him   Zacharias.   And   answering   the

μήτηρ   αὐτοῦ   εἶπεν·   οὐχί,   ἀλλὰ   κληθήσεται
mother   of him   said :   No,   but   he shall be called

'Ιωάννης.   61 καὶ   εἶπαν   πρὸς   αὐτὴν   ὅτι
John.   And   they said   to   her[.]

οὐδείς   ἐστιν   ἐκ   τῆς   συγγενείας   σου   ὃς
No one   there is   of   the   kindred   of thee   who

καλεῖται   τῷ   ὀνόματι   τούτῳ.   62 ἐνένευον
is called   -   name   by this.   they nodded

δὲ   τῷ   πατρὶ   αὐτοῦ   τὸ   τί   ἂν   θέλοι
And   to the   father   of him   -   what   he might wish

καλεῖσθαι   αὐτό.   63 καὶ   αἰτήσας   πινακίδιον
²to be called   ¹him.   And   asking for   a tablet

ἔγραψεν   λέγων·   'Ιωάννης   ἐστὶν   ὄνομα
he wrote   saying :   John   is   name

αὐτοῦ.   καὶ   ἐθαύμασαν   πάντες.   64 ἀνεῴχθη   δὲ
of him.   And   they marvelled   all.   And was opened

τὸ   στόμα   αὐτοῦ   παραχρῆμα   καὶ   ἡ
the   mouth   of him   instantly   and   the

γλῶσσα   αὐτοῦ,   καὶ   ἐλάλει   εὐλογῶν   τὸν
tongue   of him,   and   he spoke   blessing   -

θεόν.   65 Καὶ   ἐγένετο   ἐπὶ   πάντας   φόβος
God.   And   ²came   ³on   ⁴all   ¹fear

country of Judea; ⁶⁶and all who heard them laid them up in their hearts, saying, "What then will this child be?" For the hand of the Lord was with him.

⁶⁷And his father Zechar'iah was filled with the Holy Spirit, and prophesied, saying,
⁶⁸"Blessed be the Lord God of Israel,
  for he has visited and redeemed his people,
⁶⁹and has raised up a horn of salvation for us
  in the house of his servant David.
⁷⁰as he spoke by the mouth of his holy prophets from of old,
⁷¹that we should be saved from our enemies,
  and from the hand of all who hate us;
⁷²to perform the mercy promised to our fathers,
  and to remember his holy covenant,
⁷³the oath which he swore to our father Abraham, ⁷⁴to grant us
  that we, being delivered from the hand of our enemies,
  might serve him without fear,
⁷⁵in holiness and righteousness before him all the days of our life.
⁷⁶And you, child, will be called the prophet of the Most High;
  for you will go before

τοὺς περιοικοῦντας αὐτούς, καὶ ἐν ὅλῃ τῇ
the [ones] dwelling round them, and in all the
ὀρεινῇ τῆς Ἰουδαίας διελαλεῖτο πάντα
mountain country - of Judæa ⁴were talked over ¹all
τὰ ῥήματα ταῦτα, 66 καὶ ἔθεντο πάντες
- ³facts ²these, and ⁴put ¹all
οἱ ἀκούσαντες ἐν τῇ καρδίᾳ αὐτῶν,
²the [ones] ³hearing in the heart of them,
λέγοντες· τί ἄρα τὸ παιδίον τοῦτο ἔσται;
saying : What then - child this will be ?
καὶ γὰρ χεὶρ κυρίου ἦν μετ' αὐτοῦ.
for indeed [the] hand of [the] Lord was with him.
67 Καὶ Ζαχαρίας ὁ πατὴρ αὐτοῦ ἐπλήσθη
And Zacharias the father of him was filled
πνεύματος ἁγίου καὶ ἐπροφήτευσεν λέγων·
of(with) Spirit [the] Holy and prophesied saying :
68 Εὐλογητὸς κύριος ὁ θεὸς τοῦ Ἰσραήλ,
Blessed [be] [the] Lord the God - of Israel,
ὅτι ἐπεσκέψατο καὶ ἐποίησεν λύτρωσιν τῷ
because he visited and wrought redemption for the
λαῷ αὐτοῦ, 69 καὶ ἤγειρεν κέρας σωτηρίας
people of him, and raised a horn of salvation
ἡμῖν ἐν οἴκῳ Δαυὶδ παιδὸς αὐτοῦ, 70 καθὼς
for us in [the] house of David servant of him, as
ἐλάλησεν διὰ στόματος τῶν ἁγίων ἀπ'
he spoke through [the] mouth of the ¹holy ⁴from
αἰῶνος προφητῶν αὐτοῦ, 71 σωτηρίαν ἐξ
⁵[the] age ²prophets ³of him, salvation out of
ἐχθρῶν ἡμῶν καὶ ἐκ χειρὸς πάντων τῶν
[the]enemies of us and out of [the] hand of all the[ones]
μισούντων ἡμᾶς, 72 ποιῆσαι ἔλεος μετὰ
hating us, to perform mercy with
τῶν πατέρων ἡμῶν καὶ μνησθῆναι διαθήκης
the fathers of us and to remember [the]covenant
ἁγίας αὐτοῦ, 73 ὅρκον ὃν ὤμοσεν πρὸς Ἀβραὰμ
holy of him, [the]oath which he swore to Abraham
τὸν πατέρα ἡμῶν, τοῦ δοῦναι ἡμῖν
the father of us, - to giveᵈ us
74 ἀφόβως ἐκ χειρὸς ἐχθρῶν ῥυσθέντας
⁵fearlessly ²out of ³[the]hand ⁴of[our]enemies ¹having been delivered
λατρεύειν αὐτῷ 75 ἐν ὁσιότητι καὶ δικαιοσύνῃ
⁶to serve him in holiness and righteousness
ἐνώπιον αὐτοῦ πάσαις ταῖς ἡμέραις ἡμῶν.
before him all the daysᵉ of us.
76 Καὶ σὺ δέ, παιδίον, προφήτης ὑψίστου
And thou also, child, a prophet of[the] Most High
κληθήσῃ· προπορεύσῃ γὰρ ἐνώπιον κυρίου
wilt be called; for thou wilt go before before [the] Lord

the Lord to prepare his ways,
77 to give knowledge of salvation to his people in the forgiveness of their sins,
78 through the tender mercy of our God, when the day shall dawn upon[e] us from on high
79 to give light to those who sit in darkness and in the shadow of death, to guide our feet into the way of peace."
80 And the child grew and became strong in spirit, and he was in the wilderness till the day of his manifestation to Israel.

ἐτοιμάσαι ὁδοὺς αὐτοῦ, 77 τοῦ δοῦναι
to prepare [the] ways of him, – to give[d]
γνῶσιν σωτηρίας τῷ λαῷ αὐτοῦ ἐν
a knowledge of salvation to the people of him by
ἀφέσει ἁμαρτιῶν αὐτῶν, 78 διὰ σπλάγχνα ·
forgiveness of sins of them, because of [the] bowels
ἐλέους θεοῦ ἡμῶν, ἐν οἷς ἐπισκέψεται
of mercy of God of us, whereby will visit
ἡμᾶς ἀνατολὴ ἐξ ὕψους, 79 ἐπιφᾶναι τοῖς
us a [sun]rising from [the] height, to appear [to] the [ones]
ἐν σκότει καὶ σκιᾷ θανάτου καθημένοις,
[s]in [d]darkness [s]and [s]in a shadow [s]of death [s]sitting,
τοῦ κατευθῦναι τοὺς πόδας ἡμῶν εἰς ὁδὸν
– to guide[d] the feet of us into a way
εἰρήνης.
of peace.
80 Τὸ δὲ παιδίον ηὔξανεν καὶ ἐκραταιοῦτο
And the child grew and became strong
πνεύματι, καὶ ἦν ἐν ταῖς ἐρήμοις ἕως
in spirit, and was in the deserts until
ἡμέρας ἀναδείξεως αὐτοῦ πρὸς τὸν Ἰσραήλ.
[the] days of showing of him to – Israel.

CHAPTER 2

IN those days a decree went out from Caesar Augustus that all the world should be enrolled. 2 This was the first enrollment, when Quirin'ius was governor of Syria. 3 And all went to be enrolled, each to his own city. 4 And Joseph also went up from Galilee, from the city of Nazareth, to Judea, to the city of David, which is called Bethlehem, because he was of the house and lineage of David, 5 to be enrolled with Mary, his betrothed, who was with child. 6 And while

2 Ἐγένετο δὲ ἐν ταῖς ἡμέραις ἐκείναις
Now it came to pass in – days those
ἐξῆλθεν δόγμα παρὰ Καίσαρος Αὐγούστου
went out a decree from Cæsar Augustus
ἀπογράφεσθαι πᾶσαν τὴν οἰκουμένην. 2 αὕτη
to be enrolled all the inhabited earth. This
ἀπογραφὴ πρώτη ἐγένετο ἡγεμονεύοντος τῆς
[2]enrolment [1]first was governing –
                                              = when Cyrenius governed Syria.
Συρίας Κυρηνίου. 3 καὶ ἐπορεύοντο πάντες
Syria Cyrenius.[a] And went all
ἀπογράφεσθαι, ἕκαστος εἰς τὴν ἑαυτοῦ
to be enrolled, each man to the of himself
πόλιν. 4 Ἀνέβη δὲ καὶ Ἰωσὴφ ἀπὸ τῆς
city. So went up also Joseph from –
Γαλιλαίας ἐκ πόλεως Ναζαρὲθ εἰς τὴν
Galilee out of a city Nazareth to –
Ἰουδαίαν εἰς πόλιν Δαυὶδ ἥτις καλεῖται Βηθλέεμ,
Judæa to a city of David which is called Bethlehem,
διὰ τὸ εἶναι αὐτὸν ἐξ οἴκου καὶ
because of the to be him[b] out of [the] house and
=because he was
πατριᾶς Δαυίδ, 5 ἀπογράψασθαι σὺν Μαριὰμ
family of David, to be enrolled with Mary
τῇ ἐμνηστευμένῃ αὐτῷ, οὔσῃ ἐγκύῳ.
the[one] having been betrothed to him, being pregnant.

---

[e] Or whereby the dayspring will visit. Other ancient authorities read since the dayspring has visited

they were there, the time came for her to be delivered. ⁷And she gave birth to her first-born son and wrapped him in swaddling cloths, and laid him in a manger, because there was no place for them in the inn. 8 And in that region there were shepherds out in the field, keeping watch over their flock by night. ⁹And an angel of the Lord appeared to them, and the glory of the Lord shone around them, and they were filled with fear. ¹⁰And the angel said to them, "Be not afraid; for behold, I bring you good news of a great joy which will come to all the people; ¹¹for to you is born this day in the city of David a Savior, who is Christ the Lord. ¹²And this will be a sign for you: you will find a babe wrapped in swaddling cloths and lying in a manger." ¹³And suddenly there was with the angel a multitude of the heavenly host praising God and saying, ¹⁴"Glory to God in the highest,
and on earth peace among men with whom he is pleased!"ʲ
15 When the angels went away from them

ʲ Other ancient authorities read *peace, goodwill among men*

6 Ἐγένετο δὲ ἐν τῷ εἶναι αὐτοὺς ἐκεῖ
And it came to pass in the to be them^{be} there
=while they were

ἐπλήσθησαν αἱ ἡμέραι τοῦ τεκεῖν αὐτήν,
were fulfilled the days – to bear her,^{bd}
=for her to bear,

7 καὶ ἔτεκεν τὸν υἱὸν αὐτῆς τὸν πρωτότοκον,
and she bore the son of her the firstborn,

καὶ ἐσπαργάνωσεν αὐτὸν καὶ ἀνέκλινεν
and she swathed him and laid

αὐτὸν ἐν φάτνῃ, διότι οὐκ ἦν αὐτοῖς
him in a manger, because there was not for them

τόπος ἐν τῷ καταλύματι. 8 Καὶ ποιμένες
place in the inn. And shepherds

ἦσαν ἐν τῇ χώρᾳ τῇ αὐτῇ ἀγραυλοῦντες
there were in the country – same living in the fields

καὶ φυλάσσοντες φυλακὰς τῆς νυκτὸς ἐπὶ
and keeping guard of(in) the night over

τὴν ποίμνην αὐτῶν. 9 καὶ ἄγγελος κυρίου
the flock of them. And an angel of [the] Lord

ἐπέστη αὐτοῖς καὶ δόξα κυρίου περιέλαμψεν
came upon them and [the] glory of [the]Lord shone around

αὐτούς, καὶ ἐφοβήθησαν φόβον μέγαν.
them, and they feared fear a great.
=exceedingly.

10 καὶ εἶπεν αὐτοῖς ὁ ἄγγελος· μὴ
And said to them the angel : not

φοβεῖσθε· ἰδοὺ γὰρ εὐαγγελίζομαι ὑμῖν
Fear ye; for behold I announce to you

χαρὰν μεγάλην, ἥτις ἔσται παντὶ τῷ λαῷ,
joy a great, which will be to all the people,

11 ὅτι ἐτέχθη ὑμῖν σήμερον σωτήρ, ὅς
because was born to you to-day a Saviour, who

ἐστιν χριστὸς κύριος, ἐν πόλει Δαυίδ.
is Christ [the] Lord, in a city of David.

12 καὶ τοῦτο ὑμῖν σημεῖον, εὑρήσετε βρέφος
And this to you a sign, ye will find a babe

ἐσπαργανωμένον καὶ κείμενον ἐν φάτνῃ.
having been swathed and lying in a manger.

13 καὶ ἐξαίφνης ἐγένετο σὺν τῷ ἀγγέλῳ
And suddenly there was with the angel

πλῆθος στρατιᾶς οὐρανίου αἰνούντων τὸν
a multitude army of a heavenly praising –

θεὸν καὶ λεγόντων· 14 δόξα ἐν ὑψίστοις
God and saying : Glory in highest [places]

θεῷ καὶ ἐπὶ γῆς εἰρήνη ἐν ἀνθρώποις
to God and on earth peace among men

εὐδοκίας. 15 Καὶ ἐγένετο ὡς ἀπῆλθον
of goodwill. And it came to pass when went away

into heaven, the shepherds said to one another, "Let us go over to Bethlehem and see this thing that has happened, which the Lord has made known to us." [16]And they went with haste, and found Mary and Joseph, and the babe lying in a manger. [17]And when they saw it they made known the saying which had been told them concerning this child; [18]and all who heard it wondered at what the shepherds told them. [19]But Mary kept all these things, pondering them in her heart. [20]And the shepherds returned, glorifying and praising God for all they had heard and seen, as it had been told them.

21 And at the end of eight days, when he was circumcised, he was called Jesus, the name given by the angel before he was conceived in the womb.

22 And when the time came for their purification according to the

ἀπ' αὐτῶν εἰς τὸν οὐρανὸν οἱ ἄγγελοι,
from them to - heaven the angels,

οἱ ποιμένες ἐλάλουν πρὸς ἀλλήλους·
the shepherds said to one another :

διέλθωμεν δὴ ἕως Βηθλέεμ καὶ ἴδωμεν
Let us go then unto Bethlehem and let us see

τὸ ῥῆμα τοῦτο τὸ γεγονὸς ὃ ὁ κύριος
- thing this - having happened which the Lord

ἐγνώρισεν ἡμῖν. 16 καὶ ἦλθαν σπεύσαντες,
made known to us. And they came hastening,

καὶ ἀνεῦραν τήν τε Μαριὰμ καὶ τὸν
and found - both Mary and -

Ἰωσὴφ καὶ τὸ βρέφος κείμενον ἐν τῇ
Joseph and the babe lying in the

φάτνῃ· 17 ἰδόντες δὲ ἐγνώρισαν περὶ τοῦ
manger; and seeing they made known concerning the

ῥήματος τοῦ λαληθέντος αὐτοῖς περὶ τοῦ
word - spoken to them concerning -

παιδίου τούτου. 18 καὶ πάντες οἱ ἀκούσαντες
child this. And all the [ones] hearing

ἐθαύμασαν περὶ τῶν λαληθέντων ὑπὸ τῶν
marvelled concerning the things spoken by the

ποιμένων πρὸς αὐτούς· 19 ἡ δὲ Μαρία
shepherds to them; - but Mary

πάντα συνετήρει τὰ ῥήματα ταῦτα συμβάλλουσα
²all ¹kept - ⁴things ³these pondering

ἐν τῇ καρδίᾳ αὐτῆς. 20 καὶ ὑπέστρεψαν
in the heart of her. And returned

οἱ ποιμένες δοξάζοντες καὶ αἰνοῦντες τὸν
the shepherds glorifying and praising -

θεὸν ἐπὶ πᾶσιν οἷς ἤκουσαν καὶ εἶδον
God at all things which they heard and saw

καθὼς ἐλαλήθη πρὸς αὐτούς.
as was spoken to them.

21 Καὶ ὅτε ἐπλήσθησαν ἡμέραι ὀκτὼ
And when were completed days eight

τοῦ περιτεμεῖν αὐτόν, καὶ ἐκλήθη τὸ
- to circumcise himᵈ, and was called the

ὄνομα αὐτοῦ Ἰησοῦς, τὸ κληθὲν ὑπὸ τοῦ
name of him Jesus, the [name] called by the

ἀγγέλου πρὸ τοῦ συλλημφθῆναι αὐτὸν ἐν
angel before the to be conceived himᵇ in
                  =he was conceived

τῇ κοιλίᾳ.
the womb.

22 Καὶ ὅτε ἐπλήσθησαν αἱ ἡμέραι τοῦ
And when were completed the days of the

καθαρισμοῦ αὐτῶν κατὰ τὸν νόμον
cleansing of them according to the law

law of Moses, they brought him up to Jerusalem to present him to the Lord ²³(as it is written in the law of the Lord, "Every male that opens the womb shall be called holy to the Lord") ²⁴and to offer a sacrifice according to what is said in the law of the Lord, "a pair of turtledoves, or two young pigeons." ²⁵Now there was a man in Jerusalem, whose name was Simeon, and this man was righteous and devout, looking for the consolation of Israel, and the Holy Spirit was upon him. ²⁶And it had been revealed to him by the Holy Spirit that he should not see death before he had seen the Lord's Christ. ²⁷And in-spired by the Spirit⁹ he came into the temple; and when the parents brought in the child Jesus, to do for him according to the custom of the law, ²⁸he took him up in his arms and blessed God and said, ²⁹"Lord, now lettest thou thy servant depart in peace, according to thy word; ³⁰for mine eyes have seen thy salvation

Μωϋσέως, ἀνήγαγον αὐτὸν εἰς Ἰεροσόλυμα
of Moses, they took up him to Jerusalem
παραστῆσαι τῷ κυρίῳ, 23 καθὼς γέγραπται
to present to the Lord, as it has been written
ἐν νόμῳ κυρίου ὅτι πᾶν ἄρσεν διανοῖγον
in [the] law of the Lord[,] - Every male opening
μήτραν ἅγιον τῷ κυρίῳ κληθήσεται, 24 καὶ
a womb holy to the Lord shall be called, and
τοῦ δοῦναι θυσίαν κατὰ τὸ εἰρημένον ἐν
- to giveᵈ a sacrifice according to the thing said in
τῷ νόμῳ κυρίου, ζεῦγος τρυγόνων ἢ δύο
the law of [the] Lord, a pair of turtledoves or two
νοσσοὺς περιστερῶν. 25 Καὶ ἰδοὺ ἄνθρωπος
nestlings of doves. And behold[,] a man
ἦν ἐν Ἰερουσαλὴμ ᾧ ὄνομα Συμεών, καὶ
was in Jerusalem to whom nameᶜ Simeon, and
=whose name was
ὁ ἄνθρωπος οὗτος δίκαιος καὶ εὐλαβής,
- man this [was] just and devout,
προσδεχόμενος παράκλησιν τοῦ Ἰσραήλ, καὶ
expecting [the] consolation - of Israel, and
πνεῦμα ἦν ἅγιον ἐπ' αὐτόν· 26 καὶ ἦν
¹[the] ³Spirit ²was ²Holy upon him; and it was
αὐτῷ κεχρηματισμένον ὑπὸ τοῦ πνεύματος
to him having been communicated by the Spirit
τοῦ ἁγίου μὴ ἰδεῖν θάνατον πρὶν ἢ ἂν
- Holy not to see death before
ἴδη τὸν χριστὸν κυρίου. 27 καὶ ἦλθεν
he should see the Christ of [the] Lord. And he came
ἐν τῷ πνεύματι εἰς τὸ ἱερόν· καὶ ἐν τῷ
by the Spirit into the temple; and in the
=as the(his) parents brought in
εἰσαγαγεῖν τοὺς γονεῖς τὸ παιδίον Ἰησοῦν
to bring in the parentsᵇᵉ the child Jesus
τοῦ ποιῆσαι αὐτοὺς κατὰ τὸ εἰθισμένον
- to do themᵇᵈ according to the custom
=for them to do
τοῦ νόμου περὶ αὐτοῦ, 28 καὶ αὐτὸς
of the law concerning him, and he
ἐδέξατο αὐτὸ εἰς τὰς ἀγκάλας καὶ
received him in the(his) arms and
εὐλόγησεν τὸν θεὸν καὶ εἶπεν· 29 νῦν
blessed - God and said: Now
ἀπολύεις τὸν δοῦλόν σου, δέσποτα, κατὰ
thou releasest the slave of thee, Master, according to
τὸ ῥῆμά σου ἐν εἰρήνῃ· 30 ὅτι εἶδον οἱ
the word of thee in peace; because saw the
ὀφθαλμοί μου τὸ σωτήριόν σου, 31 ὃ
eyes of me the salvation of thee, which

⁹ Or in the Spirit

I.G.E.—9

³¹which thou hast pre-
pared in the
presence of all
peoples,
³²a light for revelation
to the Gentiles,
and for glory to thy
people Israel."
33 And his father and
his mother marveled at
what was said about
him; ³⁴and Simeon
blessed them and said to
Mary his mother,
"Behold, this child is
set for the fall and
rising of many in
Israel,
and for a sign that is
spoken against
³⁵(and a sword will
pierce through
your own soul
also),
that thoughts out of
many hearts may
be revealed."
36 And there was a
prophetess, Anna, the
daughter of Phan'u-el, of
the tribe of Asher; she
was of a great age, having
lived with her husband
seven years from her
virginity, ³⁷and as a
widow till she was
eighty-four. She did not
depart from the temple,
worshiping with fasting
and prayer night and
day. ³⁸And coming up
at that very hour she
gave thanks to God, and
spoke of him to all who
were looking for the
redemption of Jerusalem.

ἡτοίμασας   κατὰ   πρόσωπον   πάντων   τῶν
thou didst prepare before [the] face of all   the
λαῶν, 32 φῶς   εἰς   ἀποκάλυψιν   ἐθνῶν   καὶ
peoples, a light for a revelation of [the] nations and
δόξαν   λαοῦ   σου   'Ισραήλ. 33 καὶ   ἦν
a glory of [the] people of thee Israel.   And ⁷was(were)
ὁ   πατὴρ   αὐτοῦ   καὶ   ἡ   μήτηρ   θαυμάζοντες
¹the ²father ³of him ⁴and ⁵the ⁶mother ⁸marvelling
ἐπὶ   τοῖς   λαλουμένοις περὶ   αὐτοῦ.   34 καὶ
at the things being said concerning him.   And
εὐλόγησεν   αὐτοὺς Συμεὼν   καὶ   εἶπεν   πρὸς
blessed   them   Simeon   and   said   to
Μαριὰμ   τὴν   μητέρα   αὐτοῦ· ἰδοὺ   οὗτος
Mary   the   mother   of him : Behold[,] this
κεῖται   εἰς   πτῶσιν   καὶ   ἀνάστασιν   πολλῶν
is set   for   fall   and   rising again of many
ἐν   τῷ   'Ισραὴλ   καὶ   εἰς   σημεῖον   ἀντιλεγ-
in   -   Israel   and   for   a sign   spoken
όμενον — 35 καὶ   σοῦ   δὲ   αὐτῆς   τὴν   ψυχὴν
against   and ⁵of thee ⁷also ⁶[thy]self ³the   ⁴soul
διελεύσεται ῥομφαία—, ὅπως   ἂν ἀποκαλυφθῶσιν
²will go through ¹a sword , so as -   may be revealed
ἐκ   πολλῶν   καρδιῶν   διαλογισμοί.   36 Καὶ
of   many   hearts   [the] thoughts.   And
ἦν   "Αννα προφῆτις, θυγάτηρ Φανουήλ, ἐκ
there was Anna a prophetess, a daughter of Phanuel, of
φυλῆς   'Ασήρ· αὕτη προβεβηκυῖα ἐν ἡμέραις
[the] tribe of Asher; this having advanced in days
πολλαῖς, ζήσασα   μετὰ   ἀνδρὸς   ἔτη   ἑπτὰ
many,   having lived with a husband years seven
ἀπὸ   τῆς   παρθενίας   αὐτῆς,   37 καὶ   αὐτὴ
from   the   virginity   of her,   and she [was]
χήρα   ἕως   ἐτῶν   ὀγδοήκοντα τεσσάρων, ἣ
a widow until years   eighty-four,   who
οὐκ   ἀφίστατο   τοῦ   ἱεροῦ   νηστείαις   καὶ
withdrew not from the   temple   with fastings and
δεήσεσιν   λατρεύουσα   νύκτα   καὶ   ἡμέραν.
petitionings serving   night   and   day.
38 καὶ   αὐτῇ   τῇ   ὥρᾳ   ἐπιστᾶσα   ἀνθωμολογεῖτο
   And at the very hour* coming upon she gave thanks
τῷ   θεῷ   καὶ   ἐλάλει   περὶ   αὐτοῦ πᾶσιν τοῖς
 - to God and   spoke   about   him   to all the [ones]
προσδεχομένοις   λύτρωσιν   'Ιερουσαλήμ.   39 Καὶ
expecting   redemption   in Jerusalem.   And

* Strictly, this construction should mean " the hour itself "; but
the context demands " the same hour ". See 10. 7, 21; 12. 12;
13. 1, 31; 20. 19; 23. 12; 24. 13. " Luke seems to be the only
N.T. writer who affects the construction " (C. F. D. Moule). See
also Acts 16. 18; 22. 13. Of course there is not a great difference
between " the hour itself ", " the very hour ", and " the same hour ".

39 And when they had performed everything according to the law of the Lord, they returned into Galilee, to their own city, Nazareth. ⁴⁰And the child grew and became strong, filled with wisdom; and the favor of God was upon him.
41 Now his parents went to Jerusalem every year at the feast of the Passover. ⁴²And when he was twelve years old, they went up according to custom; ⁴³and when the feast was ended, as they were returning, the boy Jesus stayed behind in Jerusalem. His parents did not know it, ⁴⁴but supposing him to be in the company they went a day's journey, and they sought him among their kinsfolk and acquaintances; ⁴⁵and when they did not find him, they returned to Jerusalem, seeking him. ⁴⁶After three days they found him in the temple, sitting among the teachers, listening to them and asking them questions; ⁴⁷and all who heard him were amazed at his understanding and his answers. ⁴⁸And when

ὡς ἐτέλεσαν πάντα τὰ κατὰ τὸν νόμον
when they finished all things – according to the law
κυρίου, ἐπέστρεψαν εἰς τὴν Γαλιλαίαν εἰς
of [the] Lord, they returned to – Galilee to
πόλιν ἑαυτῶν Ναζαρέθ.
a city of themselves Nazareth.

40 Τὸ δὲ παιδίον ηὔξανεν καὶ ἐκραταιοῦτο
And the child grew and became strong
πληρούμενον σοφίᾳ, καὶ χάρις θεοῦ ἦν ἐπ'
being filled with wisdom, and [the] grace of God was upon
αὐτό.
him.

41 Καὶ ἐπορεύοντο οἱ γονεῖς αὐτοῦ κατ'
And went the parents of him year
ἔτος εἰς Ἰερουσαλὴμ τῇ ἑορτῇ τοῦ πάσχα.
by year† to Jerusalem at the feast of the Passover.
42 Καὶ ὅτε ἐγένετο ἐτῶν δώδεκα, ἀναβαινόντων
And when he became of years twelve, going up
= as they went up
αὐτῶν κατὰ τὸ ἔθος τῆς ἑορτῆς, **43** καὶ
themᵃ according to the custom of the feast, and
τελειωσάντων τὰς ἡμέρας, ἐν τῷ ὑποστρέφειν
fulfillingᵃ the days, in the to return
= when they returned
αὐτοὺς ὑπέμεινεν Ἰησοῦς ὁ παῖς ἐν
themᵇᵉ ⁴remained ²Jesus ¹the ³boy in
Ἰερουσαλήμ, καὶ οὐκ ἔγνωσαν οἱ γονεῖς
Jerusalem, and ⁴knew not ¹the ²parents
αὐτοῦ. **44** νομίσαντες δὲ αὐτὸν εἶναι ἐν
³of him. But supposing him to be in
τῇ συνοδίᾳ ἦλθον ἡμέρας ὁδὸν καὶ ἀνεζήτουν
the company they went of a day a journey and sought
αὐτὸν ἐν τοῖς συγγενεῦσιν καὶ τοῖς
him among the(ir) relatives and the(ir)
γνωστοῖς, **45** καὶ μὴ εὑρόντες ὑπέστρεψαν
acquaintances, and not finding returned
εἰς Ἰερουσαλὴμ ἀναζητοῦντες αὐτόν. **46** καὶ
to Jerusalem seeking him. And
ἐγένετο μετὰ ἡμέρας τρεῖς εὗρον αὐτὸν
it came to pass after days three they found him
ἐν τῷ ἱερῷ καθεζόμενον ἐν μέσῳ τῶν
in the temple sitting in [the] midst of the
διδασκάλων καὶ ἀκούοντα αὐτῶν καὶ
teachers both hearing them and
ἐπερωτῶντα αὐτούς· **47** ἐξίσταντο δὲ πάντες
questioning them; and were astonished all
οἱ ἀκούοντες αὐτοῦ ἐπὶ τῇ συνέσει καὶ
the [ones] hearing him at the intelligence and
ταῖς ἀποκρίσεσιν αὐτοῦ. **48** καὶ ἰδόντες
the answers of him. And seeing

they saw him they were
astonished; and his
mother said to him,
"Son, why have you
treated us so? Behold,
your father and I have
been looking for you
anxiously." ⁴⁹And he said
to them, "How is it that
you sought me? Did you
not know that I must be
in my Father's house?"
⁵⁰And they did not
understand the saying
which he spoke to them.
⁵¹And he went down with
them and came to
Nazareth, and was obed-
ient to them; and his
mother kept all these
things in her heart.
52 And Jesus in-
creased in wisdom and
in stature,ʰ and in favor
with God and man.

αὐτὸν ἐξεπλάγησαν, καὶ εἶπεν πρὸς αὐτὸν
him   they were astounded, and   said   to   him
ἡ μήτηρ αὐτοῦ· τέκνον, τί ἐποίησας ἡμῖν
the mother of him :   Child,   why   didst thou   to us
οὕτως; ἰδοὺ ὁ πατήρ σου κἀγὼ ὀδυνώμενοι
thus?   behold[,] the father of thee and I greatly distressed
ζητοῦμέν σε.   49 καὶ εἶπεν πρὸς αὐτούς·
are seeking thee.   And   he said   to   them :
τί ὅτι ἐζητεῖτέ με; οὐκ ἤδειτε ὅτι ἐν
Why [is it] that ye sought   me?   did ye not know   that   in
                                                        =I
τοῖς   τοῦ πατρός   μου δεῖ εἶναί με;
the [affairs] of the Father of me it behoves to be   me?
must be about my Father's business?
50 καὶ αὐτοὶ οὐ συνῆκαν τὸ ῥῆμα ὃ
   And   they did not understand the   word which
ἐλάλησεν αὐτοῖς.   51 καὶ κατέβη μετ᾽
he spoke   to them.   And he went down with
αὐτῶν καὶ ἦλθεν εἰς Ναζαρέθ, καὶ ἦν
them   and   came   to   Nazareth,   and   was
ὑποτασσόμενος αὐτοῖς.   καὶ ἡ μήτηρ
being subject   to them.   And   the   mother
αὐτοῦ διετήρει πάντα τὰ ῥήματα ἐν τῇ
of him carefully kept   all   the   matters   in   the
καρδίᾳ αὐτῆς.   52 Καὶ Ἰησοῦς προέκοπτεν
heart   of her.   And   Jesus   progressed
ἐν τῇ σοφίᾳ καὶ ἡλικίᾳ καὶ χάριτι παρὰ
in   -   wisdom and   age   and favour before
θεῷ καὶ ἀνθρώποις.
God   and   men.

CHAPTER 3

IN the fifteenth year of
the reign of Tibe′ri-us
Caesar, Pontius Pilate
being governor of Judea,
and Herod being tetrarch
of Galilee, and his
brother Philip tetrarch of
the region of Iturae′a and
Trachoni′tis, and Lysa′-
ni-as tetrarch of Abile′ne,
²in the high-priesthood
of Annas and Ca′iaphas,

3 Ἐν ἔτει δὲ πεντεκαιδεκάτῳ τῆς
Now in [the] year   fifteenth   of the
ἡγεμονίας Τιβερίου Καίσαρος, ἡγεμονεύοντος
government   of Tiberius   Cæsar,   governing
                                     =while Pontius Pilate
Ποντίου   Πιλάτου τῆς Ἰουδαίας, καὶ
Pontius   Pilateª   -   of Judæa,   and
was governing
τετρααρχοῦντος τῆς Γαλιλαίας Ἡρώδου,
ruling as tetrarch   -   of Galilee   Herod,ª
=while Herod was ruling as tetrarch of Galilee,
Φιλίππου δὲ τοῦ ἀδελφοῦ αὐτοῦ τετρα-
and Philip   the   brother   of him   ruling
αρχοῦντος τῆς Ἰτουραίας καὶ Τραχωνίτιδος
as tetrarchª ¹of the ³of Ituræa ⁴and ⁵of Trachonitis
χώρας, καὶ Λυσανίου της Ἀβιληνῆς
²country, and Lysanias   -   of Abilene
τετρααρχοῦντος,   2 ἐπὶ ἀρχιερέως Ἅννα
ruling as tetrarchª,   in the time of [the] high priest Anna

ʰ Or years

the word of God came
to John the son of
Zechari'ah in the wilder-
ness; ³and he went into
all the region about the
Jordan, preaching a bap-
tism of repentance for
the forgiveness of sins.
⁴As it is written in the
book of the words of
Isaiah the prophet,
"The voice of one
    crying in the
    wilderness:
Prepare the way of
    the Lord,
make his paths
    straight.
⁵Every valley shall be
    filled,
and every mountain
    and hill shall be
    brought low,
and the crooked shall
    be made straight,
and the rough ways
    shall be made
    smooth;
⁶and all flesh shall see
    the salvation of
    God."

7 He said therefore to
the multitudes that came
out to be baptized by
him, "You brood of
vipers! Who warned you
to flee from the wrath to
come? ⁸Bear fruits that
befit repentance, and do
not begin to say to your-
selves, 'We have Abra-
ham as our father'; for I
tell you, God is able
from these stones to raise
up children to Abraham.
⁹Even now the ax is laid
to the root of the trees;
every tree therefore that
does not bear good fruit

καὶ Καϊάφα, ἐγένετο ῥῆμα θεοῦ ἐπὶ Ἰωάννην
and Caiaphas, came a word of God to John
τὸν Ζαχαρίου υἱὸν ἐν τῇ ἐρήμῳ. 3 καὶ
the of Zacharias son in the desert. And
ἦλθεν εἰς πᾶσαν τὴν περίχωρον τοῦ
he came into all the neighbourhood of the
Ἰορδάνου κηρύσσων βάπτισμα μετανοίας
Jordan proclaiming a baptism of repentance
εἰς ἄφεσιν ἁμαρτιῶν, 4 ὡς γέγραπται ἐν
for forgiveness of sins, as it has been written in
βίβλῳ λόγων Ἡσαΐου τοῦ προφήτου·
[the] roll of [the] words of Esaias the prophet :
φωνὴ βοῶντος ἐν τῇ ἐρήμῳ· ἑτοιμάσατε
Voice of [one] crying in the desert : Prepare ye
τὴν ὁδὸν κυρίου, εὐθείας ποιεῖτε τὰς
the way of [the] Lord, straight make the
τρίβους αὐτοῦ· 5 πᾶσα φάραγξ πληρωθήσεται
paths of him; every valley shall be filled up
καὶ πᾶν ὄρος καὶ βουνὸς ταπεινωθήσεται,
and every mountain and hill shall be laid low,
καὶ ἔσται τὰ σκολιὰ εἰς εὐθείας καὶ αἱ
and shall be the crooked [places] into straight [ones] and the
τραχεῖαι εἰς ὁδοὺς λείας· 6 καὶ ὄψεται
rough [places] into ways smooth; and ³shall see
πᾶσα σὰρξ τὸ σωτήριον τοῦ θεοῦ.
¹all ²flesh the salvation – of God.
7 Ἔλεγεν οὖν τοῖς ἐκπορευομένοις ὄχλοις
He said therefore to the ²going out ¹crowds
βαπτισθῆναι ὑπ' αὐτοῦ· γεννήματα ἐχιδνῶν,
to be baptized by him : Offspring of vipers,
τίς ὑπέδειξεν ὑμῖν φυγεῖν ἀπὸ τῆς
who warned you to flee from the
μελλούσης ὀργῆς; 8 ποιήσατε οὖν καρποὺς
coming wrath? Produce therefore fruits
ἀξίους τῆς μετανοίας· καὶ μὴ ἄρξησθε
worthy of repentance; and do not begin
λέγειν ἐν ἑαυτοῖς· πατέρα ἔχομεν τὸν
to say among yourselves : Father we have –
Ἀβραάμ· λέγω γὰρ ὑμῖν ὅτι δύναται ὁ
Abraham; for I tell you that ²can –
θεὸς ἐκ τῶν λίθων τούτων ἐγεῖραι τέκνα
¹God out of – stones these to raise children
τῷ Ἀβραάμ. 9 ἤδη δὲ καὶ ἡ ἀξίνη πρὸς
– to Abraham. And ²already ¹even the axe at
τὴν ῥίζαν τῶν δένδρων κεῖται· πᾶν οὖν
the root of the trees is laid; ²every ¹therefore
δένδρον μὴ ποιοῦν καρπὸν καλὸν
tree not producing fruit good

is cut down and thrown into the fire."

10 And the multitudes asked him, "What then shall we do?" [11]And he answered them, "He who has two coats, let him share with him who has none; and he who has food, let him do likewise." [12]Tax collectors also came to be baptized, and said to him, "Teacher, what shall we do?" [13]And he said to them, "Collect no more than is appointed you." [14]Soldiers also asked him, "And we, what shall we do?" And he said to them, "Rob no one by violence or by false accusation, and be content with your wages."

15 As the people were in expectation, and all men questioned in their hearts concerning John, whether perhaps he were the Christ, [16]John answered them all, "I baptize you with water; but he who is mightier than I is coming, the thong of whose sandals I am not worthy to untie; he will baptize you with the Holy Spirit and with fire. [17]His winnowing fork is in his hand, to clear his threshing floor,

ἐκκόπτεται καὶ εἰς πῦρ βάλλεται. 10 Καὶ
is being cut down and into fire is being cast. And
ἐπηρώτων αὐτὸν οἱ ὄχλοι λέγοντες· τί
asked him the crowds saying : What
οὖν ποιήσωμεν; 11 ἀποκριθεὶς δὲ ἔλεγεν
then may we do? And answering he told
αὐτοῖς· ὁ ἔχων δύο χιτῶνας μεταδότω
them : The [one] having two tunics let him impart
τῷ μὴ ἔχοντι, καὶ ὁ ἔχων βρώματα
to the [one] not having, and the [one] having foods
ὁμοίως ποιείτω. 12 ἦλθον δὲ καὶ τελῶναι
likewise let him do. And there came also tax-collectors
βαπτισθῆναι καὶ εἶπαν πρὸς αὐτόν·
to be baptized and they said to him :
διδάσκαλε, τί ποιήσωμεν; 13 ὁ δὲ εἶπεν
Teacher, what may we do? And he said
πρὸς αὐτούς· μηδὲν πλέον παρὰ τὸ
to them : Nothing more besides the [thing]
διατεταγμένον ὑμῖν πράσσετε. 14 ἐπηρώτων δὲ
having been commanded you do ye. And asked
αὐτὸν καὶ στρατευόμενοι λέγοντες· τί
him also men serving in the army saying : What
ποιήσωμεν καὶ ἡμεῖς; καὶ εἶπεν αὐτοῖς·
may do also we? And he told them :
μηδένα διασείσητε μηδὲ συκοφαντήσητε,
No one intimidate nor accuse falsely,
καὶ ἀρκεῖσθε τοῖς ὀψωνίοις ὑμῶν.
and be satisfied with the pay of you.
15 Προσδοκῶντος δὲ τοῦ λαοῦ καὶ
Now expecting the people[a] and
= while the people were expecting and all were debating
διαλογιζομένων πάντων ἐν ταῖς καρδίαις
debating all[a] in the hearts
αὐτῶν περὶ τοῦ Ἰωάννου, μήποτε αὐτὸς
of them concerning - John, perhaps he
εἴη ὁ χριστός, 16 ἀπεκρίνατο λέγων πᾶσιν
might be the Christ, \ [2]answered [3]saying [4]to all
ὁ Ἰωάννης· ἐγὼ μὲν ὕδατι βαπτίζω ὑμᾶς·
- [1]John : I indeed with water baptize you;
ἔρχεται δὲ ὁ ἰσχυρότερός μου, οὗ οὐκ
but there comes the [one] stronger of me, of whom not
= than I,
εἰμὶ ἱκανὸς λῦσαι τὸν ἱμάντα τῶν ὑποδημά-
I am competent to loosen the thong of the san-
των αὐτοῦ· αὐτὸς ὑμᾶς βαπτίσει ἐν
dals of him; he you will baptize with
πνεύματι ἁγίῳ καὶ πυρί· 17 οὗ τὸ πτύον
Spirit [the] Holy and fire; of whom the fan [is]
ἐν τῇ χειρὶ αὐτοῦ διακαθᾶραι τὴν ἅλωνα
in the hand of him thoroughly to cleanse the threshing-floor

and to gather the wheat into his granary, but the chaff he will burn with unquenchable fire." 18 So, with many other exhortations, he preached good news to the people. ¹⁹But Herod the tetrarch, who had been reproved by him for Hero'di-as, his brother's wife, and for all the evil things that Herod had done, ²⁰added this to them all, that he shut up John in prison.

21 Now when all the people were baptized, and when Jesus also had been baptized and was praying, the heaven was opened, ²²and the Holy Spirit descended upon him in bodily form, as a dove, and a voice came from heaven, "Thou art my beloved Son;ⁱ with thee I am well pleased."ʲ

23 Jesus, when he began his ministry, was about thirty years of age, being the son (as was supposed) of Joseph, the son of Heli, ²⁴the son of Matthat, the son of Levi, the son of Melchi, the son of Jan'na-i, the son of Joseph, ²⁵the son of Mattathi'as, the son of Amos, the son of Nahum, the son of Esli, the son of Nag'ga-i, ²⁶the son of Ma'ath, the son of Mattathi'as, the son of Sem'e-in, the son of Josech, the son of Joda,

---

ⁱ Or my Son, my (or the) Beloved
ʲ Other ancient authorities read today I have begotten thee

αὐτοῦ καὶ συναγαγεῖν τὸν σῖτον εἰς τὴν
of him and to gather the wheat into the
ἀποθήκην αὐτοῦ, τὸ δὲ ἄχυρον κατακαύσει
barn of him, but the chaff he will burn up
πυρὶ ἀσβέστῳ. 18 Πολλὰ μὲν οὖν καὶ
with fire unquenchable. Many things indeed therefore and
ἕτερα παρακαλῶν εὐηγγελίζετο τὸν λαόν·
different exhorting he evangelized the people;
19 ὁ δὲ Ἡρῴδης ὁ τετραάρχης, ἐλεγχόμενος
– but Herod the tetrarch, being reproved
ὑπ᾽ αὐτοῦ περὶ Ἡρῳδιάδος τῆς γυναικὸς
by him concerning Herodias the wife
τοῦ ἀδελφοῦ αὐτοῦ καὶ περὶ πάντων ὧν
of the brother of him and concerning ¹all ³things ⁴which
ἐποίησεν πονηρῶν ὁ Ἡρῴδης, 20 προσέθηκεν
⁶did ²evil – ⁵Herod, added
καὶ τοῦτο ἐπὶ πᾶσιν, κατέκλεισεν τὸν
also this above all, he shut up
Ἰωάννην ἐν φυλακῇ.
John in prison.
21 Ἐγένετο δὲ ἐν τῷ βαπτισθῆναι ἅπαντα
Now it came to pass in the to be baptized all
=when all the people were baptized
τὸν λαὸν καὶ Ἰησοῦ βαπτισθέντος καὶ
the peopleᵇᵉ and Jesus being baptized and
=as Jesus had been baptized and was praying
προσευχομένου ἀνεῳχθῆναι τὸν οὐρανὸν 22 καὶ
prayingᵃ to be opened the heaven and
=the heaven was opened and the Holy Spirit came down
καταβῆναι τὸ πνεῦμα τὸ ἅγιον σωματικῷ
to come down the Spirit – Holyᵇ in a bodily
εἴδει ὡς περιστερὰν ἐπ᾽ αὐτόν, καὶ φωνὴν
form as a dove upon him, and a voice
ἐξ οὐρανοῦ γενέσθαι· σὺ εἶ ὁ υἱός μου
out of heaven to comeᵇ: Thou art the Son of me
ὁ ἀγαπητός, ἐν σοὶ εὐδόκησα. 23 Καὶ
– beloved, in thee I was well pleased. And
αὐτὸς ἦν Ἰησοῦς ἀρχόμενος ὡσεὶ ἐτῶν
³himself ²was ¹Jesus ⁴beginning about years
τριάκοντα, ὢν υἱός, ὡς ἐνομίζετο, Ἰωσήφ,
thirty, being son, as was supposed, of Joseph,
τοῦ Ἡλὶ 24 τοῦ Ματθὰτ τοῦ Λευὶ τοῦ
– of Eli – of Matthat – of Levi –
Μελχὶ τοῦ Ἰανναὶ τοῦ Ἰωσὴφ 25 τοῦ
of Melchi – of Jannai – of Joseph –
Ματταθίου τοῦ Ἀμὼς τοῦ Ναοὺμ τοῦ
of Mattathias – of Amos – of Naum –
Ἐσλὶ τοῦ Ναγγαὶ 26 τοῦ Μάαθ τοῦ
of Hesli – of Naggai – of Maath –

²⁷the son of Jo-an'an, the son of Rhesa, the son of Zerub'babel, the son of She-al'ti-el, the son of Neri, ²⁸the son of Melchi, the son of Addi, the son of Cosam, the son of Elma'dam, the son of Er, ²⁹the son of Joshua, the son of Elie'zer, the son of Jorim, the son of Matthat, the son of Levi, ³⁰the son of Simeon, the son of Judah, the son of Joseph, the son of Jonam, the son of Eli'akim, ³¹the son of Me'le-a, the son of Menna, the son of Mat'-tatha, the son of Nathan, the son of David, ³²the son of Jesse, the son of Obed, the son of Bo'az, the son of Sala, the son of Nahshon, ³³the son of Ammin'adab, the son of Admin, the son of Arni, the son of Hezron, the son of Perez, the son of Judah, ³⁴the son of Jacob, the son of Isaac, the son of Abraham, the son of Terah, the son of Nahor, ³⁵the son of Serug, the son of Re'u, the son of Peleg, the son of Eber, the son of Shelah, ³⁶the son of Ca-i'nan, the son of Arpha'xad, the son of Shem, the son of Noah, the son of Lamech, ³⁷the son of Methuselah, the son of Enoch, the son of Jared, the son of Maha'lale-el, the son of Ca-i'nan, ³⁸the son of Enos, the son of Seth, the son of Adam, the son of God.

Ματταθίου	τοῦ	Σεμεῒν	τοῦ	Ἰωσὴχ	τοῦ		
of Mattathias	–	of Semein	–	of Josech	–		
Ἰωδὰ	**27** τοῦ	Ἰωανὰν	τοῦ	Ῥησὰ	τοῦ		
of Jodah	–	of Joanan	–	of Rhesa	–		
Ζοροβαβὲλ	τοῦ	Σαλαθιὴλ	τοῦ	Νηρὶ	**28** τοῦ		
of Zorobabel	–	of Salathiel	–	of Neri	–		
Μελχὶ	τοῦ	Ἀδδὶ	τοῦ	Κωσὰμ	τοῦ		
of Melchi	–	of Addi	–	of Kosam	–		
Ἐλμαδὰμ	τοῦ	Ἢρ	**29** τοῦ	Ἰησοῦ	τοῦ		
of Elmadam	–	of Er	–	of Jesus	–		
Ἐλιέζερ	τοῦ	Ἰωρὶμ	τοῦ	Μαθθὰτ	τοῦ		
of Eliezer	–	of Jorim	–	of Matthat	–		
Λευὶ	**30** τοῦ	Συμεὼν	τοῦ	Ἰούδα	τοῦ		
of Levi	–	of Simeon	–	of Juda	–		
Ἰωσὴφ	τοῦ	Ἰωνὰμ	τοῦ	Ἐλιακὶμ	**31** τοῦ		
of Joseph	–	of Jonam	–	of Eliakim	–		
Μελεὰ	τοῦ	Μεννὰ	τοῦ	Ματταθὰ	τοῦ		
of Melea	–	of Menna	–	of Mattatha	–		
Ναθὰμ	τοῦ	Δαυὶδ	**32** τοῦ	Ἰεσσαὶ	τοῦ		
of Natham	–	of David	–	of Jesse	–		
Ἰωβὴδ	τοῦ	Βόος	τοῦ	Σάλα	τοῦ	Ναασσὼν	
of Jobed	–	of Boos	–	of Sala	–	of Naasson	
33 τοῦ	Ἀμιναδὰβ	τοῦ	Ἀδμὶν	τοῦ	Ἀρνὶ		
–	of Aminadab	–	of Admin	–	of Arni		
τοῦ	Ἐσρὼμ	τοῦ	Φάρες	τοῦ	Ἰούδα		
–	of Hesrom	–	of Phares	–	of Juda		
34 τοῦ	Ἰακὼβ	τοῦ	Ἰσαὰκ	τοῦ	Ἀβραὰμ		
–	of Jacob	–	of Isaac	–	of Abraham		
τοῦ	Θάρα	τοῦ	Ναχὼρ	**35** τοῦ	Σερούχ		
–	of Thara	–	of Nachor	–	of Seruch		
τοῦ	Ῥαγαὺ	τοῦ	Φάλεκ	τοῦ	Ἔβερ	τοῦ	
–	of Rhagau	–	of Phalek	–	of Eber	–	
Σάλα	**36** τοῦ	Καϊνὰμ	τοῦ	Ἀρφαξὰδ	τοῦ		
of Sala	–	of Cainam	–	of Arphaxad	–		
Σὴμ	τοῦ Νῶε	τοῦ Λάμεχ	**37** τοῦ	Μαθουσάλα			
of Sem	– of Noe	– of Lamech	–	of Mathusala			
τοῦ	Ἐνὼχ	τοῦ	Ἰάρετ	τοῦ	Μαλελεὴλ		
–	of Henoch	–	of Jaret	–	of Maleleel		
τοῦ	Καϊνὰμ	**38** τοῦ	Ἐνὼς	τοῦ	Σὴθ	τοῦ	
–	of Cainam	–	of Enos	–	of Seth	–	
Ἀδὰμ	τοῦ	θεοῦ.					
of Adam	–	of God.					

4 Ἰησοῦς	δὲ	πλήρης	πνεύματος	ἁγίου	
And Jesus		full	of ¹[the] ²Spirit	³Holy	
ὑπέστρεψεν	ἀπὸ	τοῦ	Ἰορδάνου,	καὶ	ἤγετο
returned	from	the	Jordan,	and	was led

CHAPTER 4

A ND Jesus, full of the
Holy Spirit, re-
turned from the Jordan,
and was led by the
Spirit ²for forty days in
the wilderness, tempted
by the devil. And he ate
nothing in those days;
and when they were
ended, he was hungry.
³The devil said to him,
"If you are the Son of
God, command this stone
to become bread." ⁴And
Jesus answered him, "It
is written, 'Man shall not
live by bread alone.'"
⁵And the devil took him
up, and showed him all
the kingdoms of the
world in a moment of
time, ⁶and said to him,
"To you I will give all
this authority and their
glory; for it has been
delivered to me, and I
give it to whom I will.
⁷If you, then, will wor-
ship me, it shall all be
yours." ⁸And Jesus
answered him, "It is
written,
'You shall worship the
Lord your God,
and him only shall you
serve.'"
⁹And he took him to
Jerusalem, and set him
on the pinnacle of the
temple, and said to him,
"If you are the Son of
God, throw yourself
down from here; ¹⁰for it
is written,
'He will give his angels
charge of you, to

ἐν τῷ πνεύματι ἐν τῇ ἐρήμῳ 2 ἡμέρας
by the Spirit in the desert days
τεσσεράκοντα πειραζόμενος ὑπὸ τοῦ διαβόλου.
forty being tempted by the devil.
Καὶ οὐκ ἔφαγεν οὐδὲν ἐν ταῖς ἡμέραις
And he ate not no(any)thing in - days
ἐκείναις, καὶ συντελεσθεισῶν αὐτῶν ἐπεί-
those, and being ended themᵃ he
=when they were ended
νασεν. 3 εἶπεν δὲ αὐτῷ ὁ διάβολος·
hungered. And said to him the devil :
εἰ υἱὸς εἶ τοῦ θεοῦ, εἰπὲ τῷ λίθῳ
If Son thou art - of God, tell - stone
τούτῳ ἵνα γένηται ἄρτος. 4 καὶ ἀπεκρίθη
this that it become a loaf. And made answer
πρὸς αὐτὸν ὁ Ἰησοῦς· γέγραπται ὅτι
to him - Jesus : It has been written[,] -
οὐκ ἐπ' ἄρτῳ μόνῳ ζήσεται ὁ ἄνθρωπος.
Not on bread only shall live - man.
5 Καὶ ἀναγαγὼν αὐτὸν ἔδειξεν αὐτῷ πάσας
And leading up him he showed him all
τὰς βασιλείας τῆς οἰκουμένης ἐν στιγμῇ
the kingdoms of the inhabited earth in a moment
χρόνου. 6 καὶ εἶπεν αὐτῷ ὁ διάβολος·
of time. And said to him the devil :
σοὶ δώσω τὴν ἐξουσίαν ταύτην ἅπασαν καὶ
To thee I will give - authority this all and
τὴν δόξαν αὐτῶν, ὅτι ἐμοὶ παραδέδοται
the glory of them, because to me it has been delivered
καὶ ᾧ ἐὰν θέλω δίδωμι αὐτήν· 7 σὺ οὖν
and to whomever I wish I give it; ᵃthou ¹therefore
ἐὰν προσκυνήσῃς ἐνώπιον ἐμοῦ, ἔσται σοῦ
²if worship before me, will be of thee
πᾶσα. 8 καὶ ἀποκριθεὶς ὁ Ἰησοῦς εἶπεν
all. And answering - Jesus said
αὐτῷ· γέγραπται· προσκυνήσεις κύριον τὸν
to him : It has been written: Thou shalt worship [the] Lord the
θεόν σου καὶ αὐτῷ μόνῳ λατρεύσεις.
God of thee and him only shalt thou serve.
9 Ἤγαγεν δὲ αὐτὸν εἰς Ἰερουσαλὴμ καὶ
And he led him to Jerusalem and
ἔστησεν ἐπὶ τὸ πτερύγιον τοῦ ἱεροῦ, καὶ
set on the gable of the temple, and
εἶπεν αὐτῷ· εἰ υἱὸς εἶ τοῦ θεοῦ, βάλε
said to him : If Son thou art - of God, throw
σεαυτὸν ἐντεῦθεν κάτω· 10 γέγραπται γὰρ ὅτι
thyself hence down; for it has been written[,] -
τοῖς ἀγγέλοις αὐτοῦ ἐντελεῖται περὶ
The angels of him he will command concerning

guard you,'
¹¹and
'On their hands they
will bear you up,
lest you strike your
foot against a
stone.' "
¹²And Jesus answered
him, "It is said, 'You
shall not tempt the Lord
your God.' " ¹³And when
the devil had ended every
temptation, he departed
from him until an
opportune time.
14 And Jesus returned
in the power of the
Spirit into Galilee, and a
report concerning him
went out through all the
surrounding country.
¹⁵And he taught in their
synagogues, being glori-
fied by all.
16 And he came to
Nazareth, where he had
been brought up; and he
went to the synagogue,
as his custom was, on the
sabbath day. And he
stood up to read; ¹⁷and
there was given to him
the book of the prophet
Isaiah. He opened the
book and found the
place where it was
written,
¹⁸"The Spirit of the Lord
is upon me,
because he has
anointed me to
preach good news
to the poor.
He has sent me to
proclaim release to
the captives
and recovering of
sight to the blind,
to set at liberty those
who are oppressed,

σοῦ   τοῦ   διαφυλάξαι   σε,   11 καὶ   ὅτι   ἐπὶ
thee   -   to preserveᵈ thee,   and   that   on

χειρῶν   ἀροῦσίν   σε,   μήποτε   προσκόψῃς
[their] hands they will bear thee,   lest   thou dash

πρὸς   λίθον   τὸν   πόδα   σου.   12 καὶ
against   a stone   the   foot   of thee.   And

ἀποκριθεὶς   εἶπεν   αὐτῷ   ὁ   Ἰησοῦς   ὅτι
answering   said   to him   -   Jesus[,]   -

εἴρηται·   οὐκ   ἐκπειράσεις   κύριον   τὸν
It has been said :   Thou shalt not overtempt [the] Lord   the

θεόν   σου.   13 Καὶ   συντελέσας   πάντα   πειρασμὸν
God of thee.   And having finished   every   temptation

ὁ   διάβολος   ἀπέστη   ἀπ'   αὐτοῦ   ἄχρι   καιροῦ.
the   devil   went away from   him   until   a season.

14 Καὶ   ὑπέστρεψεν   ὁ   Ἰησοῦς   ἐν   τῇ
    And   returned   -   Jesus   in   the

δυνάμει   τοῦ   πνεύματος   εἰς   τὴν   Γαλιλαίαν·
power   of the   Spirit   to   -   Galilee;

καὶ   φήμη   ἐξῆλθεν   καθ'   ὅλης   τῆς   περιχώρου
and a rumour went forth throughout all   the   neighbourhood

περὶ   αὐτοῦ.   15 καὶ   αὐτὸς   ἐδίδασκεν   ἐν
concerning him.   And   he   taught   in

ταῖς   συναγωγαῖς   αὐτῶν,   δοξαζόμενος   ὑπὸ
the   synagogues   of them,   being glorified   by

πάντων.
all.

16 Καὶ   ἦλθεν   εἰς   Ναζαρά,   οὗ   ἦν
    And   he came   to   Nazareth,   where he was

τεθραμμένος,   καὶ   εἰσῆλθεν   κατὰ   τὸ   εἰωθὸς
having been   and   entered   accord- the   custom
brought up,   ing to   =his custom

αὐτῷ   ἐν   τῇ   ἡμέρᾳ   τῶν   σαββάτων   εἰς   τὴν
to himᶜ on the   day   of the   sabbaths   into   the

συναγωγήν,   καὶ   ἀνέστη   ἀναγνῶναι.   17 καὶ
synagogue,   and   stood up   to read.   And

ἐπεδόθη   αὐτῷ   βιβλίον   τοῦ   προφήτου
was handed   to him   a roll   of the   prophet

Ἡσαΐου,   καὶ   ἀνοίξας   τὸ   βιβλίον   εὗρεν
Esaias,   and having opened the   roll   he found

[τὸν]   τόπον   οὗ   ἦν   γεγραμμένον· 18 πνεῦμα
the   place where it was having been written : [The] Spirit

κυρίου   ἐπ'   ἐμέ,   οὗ   εἵνεκεν   ἔχρισέν   με
of [the] Lord [is] upon me, wherefore   he anointed   me

εὐαγγελίσασθαι   πτωχοῖς,   ἀπέσταλκέν   με
to evangelize   [the] poor,   he has sent   me

κηρῦξαι   αἰχμαλώτοις   ἄφεσιν   καὶ   τυφλοῖς
to proclaim   to captives   release   and to blind [ones]

ἀνάβλεψιν,   ἀποστεῖλαι   τεθραυσμένους   ἐν
sight,   to send away   having been crushed [ones]   in

¹⁹to proclaim the acceptable year of the Lord."
²⁰And he closed the book, and gave it back to the attendant, and sat down; and the eyes of all in the synagogue were fixed on him. ²¹And he began to say to them, "Today this scripture has been fulfilled in your hearing." ²²And all spoke well of him, and wondered at the gracious words which proceeded out of his mouth; and they said, "Is not this Joseph's son?" ²³And he said to them, "Doubtless you will quote to me this proverb, 'Physician, heal yourself; what we have heard you did at Caper′na-um, do here also in your own country.'" ²⁴And he said, "Truly, I say to you, no prophet is acceptable in his own country. ²⁵But in truth, I tell you, there were many widows in Israel in the days of Eli′jah, when the heaven was shut up three years and six months, when there came a great famine over all the land; ²⁶and Eli′jah was sent to none of them but only to Zar′ephath, in the land of Sidon, to a woman who was a widow. ²⁷And

ἀφέσει, 19 κηρῦξαι ἐνιαυτὸν κυρίου δεκτόν.
release,   to proclaim   a year   of [the] Lord   acceptable.

20 καὶ πτύξας τὸ βιβλίον ἀποδοὺς τῷ
And having closed the   roll   returning [it]   to the

ὑπηρέτῃ ἐκάθισεν· καὶ πάντων οἱ ὀφθαλμοὶ
attendant   he sat;   and   of all   the   eyes

ἐν τῇ συναγωγῇ ἦσαν ἀτενίζοντες αὐτῷ.
in   the   synagogue   were   gazing   at him.

21 ἤρξατο δὲ λέγειν πρὸς αὐτοὺς ὅτι
And he began   to say   to   them[,]   -

σήμερον πεπλήρωται ἡ γραφὴ αὕτη ἐν
To-day   has been fulfilled   -   scripture   this   in

τοῖς ὠσὶν ὑμῶν. 22 καὶ πάντες ἐμαρτύρουν
the   ears   of you.   And   all   bore witness

αὐτῷ καὶ ἐθαύμαζον ἐπὶ τοῖς λόγοις τῆς
to him   and   marvelled   at   the   words   -

χάριτος τοῖς ἐκπορευομένοις ἐκ τοῦ στόματος
of grace   -   proceeding   out of the   mouth

αὐτοῦ, καὶ ἔλεγον· οὐχὶ υἱός ἐστιν Ἰωσὴφ
of him,   and   they said :   ²not   ⁴son   ¹Is   ⁵of Joseph

οὗτος; 23 καὶ εἶπεν πρὸς αὐτούς· πάντως
³this man?   And   he said   to   them :   To be sure

ἐρεῖτέ μοι τὴν παραβολὴν ταύτην· ἰατρέ,
ye will say to me   -   parable   this :   Physician,

θεράπευσον σεαυτόν· ὅσα ἠκούσαμεν γεν-
heal   thyself;   what things   we heard   hap-

όμενα εἰς τὴν Καφαρναούμ, ποίησον καὶ
pening   in   -   Capernaum,   do   also

ὧδε ἐν τῇ πατρίδι σου. 24 εἶπεν δέ·
here   in   the   native place   of thee.   And he said :

ἀμὴν λέγω ὑμῖν ὅτι οὐδεὶς προφήτης
Truly   I tell   you   that   no   prophet

δεκτός ἐστιν ἐν τῇ πατρίδι αὐτοῦ. 25 ἐπ'
acceptable   is   in   the   native place   of him.   ²on(in)

ἀληθείας δὲ λέγω ὑμῖν, πολλαὶ χῆραι ἦσαν
³truth   ¹But I tell   you,   many   widows   were

ἐν ταῖς ἡμέραις Ἠλίου ἐν τῷ Ἰσραήλ,
in   the   days   of Elias   in   -   Israel,

ὅτε ἐκλείσθη ὁ οὐρανὸς ἐπὶ ἔτη τρία καὶ
when   was shut up   the   heaven   over   years   three   and

μῆνας ἕξ, ὡς ἐγένετο λιμὸς μέγας ἐπὶ
months   six,   when   came   famine   a great   over

πᾶσαν τὴν γῆν, 26 καὶ πρὸς οὐδεμίαν
all   the   land,   and   to   not one

αὐτῶν ἐπέμφθη Ἠλίας εἰ μὴ εἰς Σάρεπτα
of them   was sent   Elias   except   to   Sarepta

τῆς Σιδωνίας πρὸς γυναῖκα χήραν. 27 καὶ
-   of Sidon   to   a woman   a widow.   And

there were many lepers in Israel in the time of the prophet Eli'sha; and none of them was cleansed, but only Na'aman the Syrian." 28 When they heard this, all in the synagogue were filled with wrath. 29 And they rose up and put him out of the city, and led him to the brow of the hill on which their city was built, that they might throw him down headlong. 30 But passing through the midst of them he went away.

31 And he went down to Caper'na-um, a city of Galilee. And he was teaching them on the sabbath; 32 and they were astonished at his teaching, for his word was with authority. 33 And in the synagogue there was a man who had the spirit of an unclean demon; and he cried out with a loud voice, 34 "Ah!ᵏ What have you to do with us, Jesus of Nazareth? Have you come to destroy us? I know who you are, the Holy One of God." 35 But Jesus rebuked him, saying, "Be silent, and come out of him!" And when the demon had thrown him down in the midst, he came out of him, having done him no harm. 36 And they were all

ᵏ Or *Let us alone*

πολλοὶ λεπροὶ ἦσαν ἐν τῷ Ἰσραὴλ ἐπὶ
many   lepers   were   in   –   Israel   during

Ἐλισαίου τοῦ προφήτου, καὶ οὐδεὶς αὐτῶν
Elisæus   the   prophet,   and   not one   of them

ἐκαθαρίσθη εἰ μὴ Ναιμὰν ὁ Σύρος.
was cleansed   except   Naaman   the   Syrian.

28 καὶ ἐπλήσθησαν πάντες θυμοῦ ἐν τῇ
And   ²were filled   ¹all   of(with) anger   in   the

συναγωγῇ ἀκούοντες ταῦτα, 29 καὶ ἀναστάντες
synagogue   hearing   these things,   and   rising up

ἐξέβαλον αὐτὸν ἔξω τῆς πόλεως, καὶ
they cast out   him   outside   the   city,   and

ἤγαγον αὐτὸν ἕως ὀφρύος τοῦ ὄρους ἐφ'
led   him   to   a brow   of the   hill   on

οὗ ἡ πόλις ᾠκοδόμητο αὐτῶν, ὥστε
which the   city   was built   of them,   so as

κατακρημνίσαι αὐτόν· 30 αὐτὸς δὲ διελθὼν
to throw down   him;   but he   passing *through*

διὰ μέσου αὐτῶν ἐπορεύετο.
through [the] midst   of them   went.

31 Καὶ κατῆλθεν εἰς Καφαρναούμ πόλιν
And   he went down   to   Capernaum   a city

τῆς Γαλιλαίας. καὶ ἦν διδάσκων αὐτοὺς
–   of Galilee.   And he was   teaching   them

ἐν τοῖς σάββασιν· 32 καὶ ἐξεπλήσσοντο
on   the   sabbaths;   and   they were astounded

ἐπὶ τῇ διδαχῇ αὐτοῦ, ὅτι ἐν ἐξουσίᾳ
at   the   teaching   of him,   because   with   authority

ἦν ὁ λόγος αὐτοῦ. 33 καὶ ἐν τῇ συναγωγῇ
was the word   of him.   And in   the   synagogue

ἦν ἄνθρωπος ἔχων πνεῦμα δαιμονίου
there was   a man   having   a spirit   ²demon

ἀκαθάρτου, καὶ ἀνέκραξεν φωνῇ μεγάλῃ·
¹of an unclean,   and   he shouted   voice   with a great :

34 ἔα, τί ἡμῖν καὶ σοί, Ἰησοῦ Ναζαρηνέ;
Ah,   what to us   and   to thee,   Jesus   Nazarene?

ἦλθες ἀπολέσαι ἡμᾶς; οἶδά σε τίς εἶ,
Camest thou to destroy   us?   I know   thee   who thou art,

ὁ ἅγιος τοῦ θεοῦ. 35 καὶ ἐπετίμησεν αὐτῷ
the holy one   –   of God.   And   rebuked   him

ὁ Ἰησοῦς λέγων· φιμώθητι καὶ ἔξελθε
–   Jesus   saying :   Be muzzled   and   come out

ἀπ' αὐτοῦ. καὶ ῥῖψαν αὐτὸν τὸ δαιμόνιον
from   him.   And   ³throwing   ⁴him   ¹the   ²demon

εἰς τὸ μέσον ἐξῆλθεν ἀπ' αὐτοῦ μηδὲν
in   the   midst   came out   from   him   nothing

βλάψαν αὐτόν. 36 καὶ ἐγένετο θάμβος
injuring   him.   And   came   astonishment

amazed and said to one another, "What is this word? For with authority and power he commands the unclean spirits, and they come out." ³⁷And reports of him went out into every place in the surrounding region.

38 And he arose and left the synagogue, and entered Simon's house. Now Simon's mother-in-law was ill with a high fever, and they besought him for her. ³⁹And he stood over her and rebuked the fever, and it left her; and immediately she rose and served them.

40 Now when the sun was setting, all those who had any that were sick with various diseases brought them to him; and he laid his hands on every one of them and healed them. ⁴¹And demons also came out of many, crying, "You are the Son of God!" But he rebuked them, and would not allow them to speak, because they knew that he was the Christ.

42 And when it was day he departed and went into a lonely place. And the people sought

ἐπὶ πάντας, καὶ συνελάλουν πρὸς ἀλλήλους
on all, and they spoke to one another

λέγοντες· τίς ὁ λόγος οὗτος, ὅτι ἐν
saying : What [is] – word this, because with

ἐξουσίᾳ καὶ δυνάμει ἐπιτάσσει τοῖς
authority and power he commands the

ἀκαθάρτοις πνεύμασιν καὶ ἐξέρχονται; 37 καὶ
unclean spirits and they come out? And

ἐξεπορεύετο ἦχος περὶ αὐτοῦ εἰς πάντα
went forth a rumour concerning him into every

τόπον τῆς περιχώρου. 38 Ἀναστὰς δὲ
place of the neighbourhood. And rising up

ἀπὸ τῆς συναγωγῆς εἰσῆλθεν εἰς τὴν
from the synagogue he entered into the

οἰκίαν Σίμωνος. πενθερὰ δὲ τοῦ Σίμωνος
house of Simon. And [the] mother-in-law – of Simon

ἦν συνεχομένη πυρετῷ μεγάλῳ, καὶ
was being seized fever with a great, and

ἠρώτησαν αὐτὸν περὶ αὐτῆς. 39 καὶ
they ask ,him about her. And

ἐπιστὰς ἐπάνω αὐτῆς ἐπετίμησεν τῷ πυρετῷ,
standing over her he rebuked the fever,

καὶ ἀφῆκεν αὐτήν· παραχρῆμα δὲ ἀναστᾶσα
and it left her; and at once rising up

διηκόνει αὐτοῖς. 40 Δύνοντος δὲ τοῦ
she served them. And setting the
= as the sun was setting

ἡλίου ἅπαντες ὅσοι εἶχον ἀσθενοῦντας
sunᵃ all as many as had ailing [ones]

νόσοις ποικίλαις ἤγαγον αὐτοὺς πρὸς αὐτόν·
diseases with various brought them to him;

ὁ δὲ ἑνὶ ἑκάστῳ αὐτῶν τὰς χεῖρας
and he ⁵one ⁴on each ⁶of them ³the(his) ³hands

ἐπιτιθεὶς ἐθεράπευεν αὐτούς. 41 ἐξήρχετο
¹putting on healed them. came out

δὲ καὶ δαιμόνια ἀπὸ πολλῶν, κραυγάζοντα
And also demons from many, crying out

καὶ λέγοντα ὅτι σὺ εἶ ὁ υἱὸς τοῦ θεοῦ.
and saying[,] – Thou art the Son – of God.

καὶ ἐπιτιμῶν οὐκ εἴα αὐτὰ λαλεῖν, ὅτι
And rebuking he allowed not them to speak, because

ᾔδεισαν τὸν χριστὸν αὐτὸν εἶναι. 42 Γενομένης
they knew ³the ⁴Christ ¹him ²to be. coming
= And when

δὲ ἡμέρας ἐξελθὼν ἐπορεύθη εἰς ἔρημον
And dayᵃ going forth he went to a desert
day came

τόπον· καὶ οἱ ὄχλοι ἐπεζήτουν αὐτόν, καὶ
place; and the crowds sought him, and

him and came to him, and would have kept him from leaving them; [43] but he said to them, "I must preach the good news of the kingdom of God to the other cities also; for I was sent for this purpose." [44] And he was preaching in the synagogues of Judea.[1]

ἦλθον ἔως αὐτοῦ, καὶ κατεῖχον αὐτὸν
came   up to   him,   and   detained   him
τοῦ μὴ πορεύεσθαι ἀπ' αὐτῶν. 43 ὁ δὲ
–   not   to go[d]   from   them.   And he
=so that he should not go
εἶπεν πρὸς αὐτοὺς ὅτι καὶ ταῖς ἑτέραις
said   to   them[,]   –   Also to the   other
πόλεσιν εὐαγγελίσασθαί με δεῖ τὴν
cities   ³to preach   ²me ¹it behoves   the
βασιλείαν τοῦ θεοῦ, ὅτι ἐπὶ τοῦτο ἀπεστάλην.
kingdom   – of God, because on   this   I was sent.
44 καὶ ἦν κηρύσσων εἰς τὰς συναγωγὰς
     And   he was   proclaiming   in   the   synagogues
τῆς Ἰουδαίας.
–   of Judæa.

CHAPTER 5

WHILE the people pressed upon him to hear the word of God, he was standing by the lake of Gennes'aret. [2]And he saw two boats by the lake; but the fishermen had gone out of them and were washing their nets. [3]Getting into one of the boats, which was Simon's, he asked him to put out a little from the land. And he sat down and taught the people from the boat. [4]And when he had ceased speaking, he said to Simon, "Put out into the deep and let down your nets for a catch." [5]And Simon answered, "Master, we toiled all night and took nothing! But at your word I will let down the nets." [6]And

5 Ἐγένετο δὲ ἐν τῷ τὸν ὄχλον ἐπικεῖσθαι
Now it came to pass   in the   the   crowd   to press upon
=as the crowd pressed upon him and heard
αὐτῷ καὶ ἀκούειν τὸν λόγον τοῦ θεοῦ,
him   and   to hear[be]   the   word   –   of God,
καὶ αὐτὸς ἦν ἑστὼς παρὰ τὴν λίμνην
and   he   was   standing   by   the   lake
Γεννησαρέτ, 2 καὶ εἶδεν δύο πλοιάρια
Gennesaret,   and   saw   two   boats
ἑστῶτα παρὰ τὴν λίμνην· οἱ δὲ ἁλεεῖς
standing   by   the   lake;   but the   fishermen
ἀπ' αὐτῶν ἀποβάντες ἔπλυνον τὰ δίκτυα.
from   them   having gone away   were washing the   nets.
3 ἐμβὰς δὲ εἰς ἓν τῶν πλοίων, ὃ ἦν
   And embarking   in   one   of the   boats,   which was
Σίμωνος, ἠρώτησεν αὐτὸν ἀπὸ τῆς γῆς
of Simon,   he asked   him   from   the   land
ἐπαναγαγεῖν ὀλίγον· καθίσας δὲ ἐκ τοῦ
to put out   a little;   and sitting   ⁴out of   ⁵the
πλοίου ἐδίδασκεν τοὺς ὄχλους. 4 ὡς δὲ
⁶boat   ¹he taught   ²the   ³crowds.   And when
ἐπαύσατο λαλῶν, εἶπεν πρὸς τὸν Σίμωνα·
he ceased   speaking,   he said   to   –   Simon :
ἐπανάγαγε εἰς τὸ βάθος, καὶ χαλάσατε
Put out   into   the   deep,   and   let down
τὰ δίκτυα ὑμῶν εἰς ἄγραν. 5 καὶ
the   nets   of you   for   a draught.   And
ἀποκριθεὶς Σίμων εἶπεν· ἐπιστάτα, δι'
answering   Simon   said :   Master,   through
ὅλης νυκτὸς κοπιάσαντες οὐδὲν ἐλάβομεν·
[the] whole night   labouring   nothing   we took;
ἐπὶ δὲ τῷ ῥήματί σου χαλάσω τὰ δίκτυα.
but at   the   word   of thee I will let down the   nets.

[1] Other ancient authorities read Galilee

when they had done this,
they enclosed a great
shoal of fish; and as their
nets were breaking, ⁷they
beckoned to their
partners in the other boat
to come and help them.
And they came and filled
both the boats, so that
they began to sink. ⁸But
when Simon Peter saw it,
he fell down at Jesus'
knees, saying, "Depart
from me, for I am a
sinful man, O Lord."
⁹For he was astonished,
and all that were with
him, at the catch of fish
which they had taken;
¹⁰and so also were James
and John, sons of Zeb′-
edee, who were partners
with Simon. And Jesus
said to Simon, "Do not
be afraid; henceforth you
will be catching men."
¹¹And when they had
brought their boats to
land, they left everything
and followed him.

12 While he was in
one of the cities, there
came a man full of
leprosy; and when he
saw Jesus, he fell on his
face and besought him,
"Lord, if you will, you
can make me clean."

6 καὶ τοῦτο ποιήσαντες συνέκλεισαν πλῆθος
And this doing they enclosed multitude
ἰχθύων πολύ· διερρήσσετο δὲ τὰ δίκτυα
of fishes a much; and were being torn the nets
αὐτῶν. **7** καὶ κατένευσαν τοῖς μετόχοις
of them. And they nodded to the(ir) partners
ἐν τῷ ἑτέρῳ πλοίῳ τοῦ ἐλθόντας
in the other boat — coming
=that they should come
συλλαβέσθαι αὐτοῖς· καὶ ἦλθαν, καὶ ἔπλησαν
to help[d] them; and they came, and filled
ἀμφότερα τὰ πλοῖα ὥστε βυθίζεσθαι αὐτά.
both the boats so as to be sinking them.[b]
=so that they were sinking.

8 ἰδὼν δὲ Σίμων Πέτρος προσέπεσεν τοῖς
And seeing Simon Peter fell at the
γόνασιν Ἰησοῦ λέγων· ἔξελθε ἀπ' ἐμοῦ,
knees of Jesus saying: Depart from me,
ὅτι ἀνὴρ ἁμαρτωλός εἰμι, κύριε. **9** θάμβος
because man a sinful I am, Lord. astonishment
γὰρ περιέσχεν αὐτὸν καὶ πάντας τοὺς
For seized him and all the [ones]
σὺν αὐτῷ ἐπὶ τῇ ἄγρᾳ τῶν ἰχθύων ᾗ
with him at the draught of the fishes which
συνέλαβον, **10** ὁμοίως δὲ καὶ Ἰάκωβον καὶ
they took, and likewise both James and
Ἰωάννην υἱοὺς Ζεβεδαίου, οἳ ἦσαν κοινωνοὶ
John sons of Zebedee, who were sharers
τῷ Σίμωνι. καὶ εἶπεν πρὸς τὸν Σίμωνα
— with Simon. And said to — Simon
ὁ Ἰησοῦς· μὴ φοβοῦ· ἀπὸ τοῦ νῦν
— Jesus: Fear thou not; from — now
ἀνθρώπους ἔσῃ ζωγρῶν. **11** καὶ καταγαγόντες
men thou wilt be taking alive. And bringing down
τὰ πλοῖα ἐπὶ τὴν γῆν, ἀφέντες πάντα
the boats onto the land, leaving all things
ἠκολούθησαν αὐτῷ.
they followed him.

12 Καὶ ἐγένετο ἐν τῷ εἶναι αὐτὸν ἐν
And it came to pass in the to be him[be] in
=as he was
μιᾷ τῶν πόλεων καὶ ἰδοὺ ἀνὴρ πλήρης
one of the cities and behold[,] a man full
λέπρας· ἰδὼν δὲ τὸν Ἰησοῦν, πεσὼν ἐπὶ
of leprosy; and seeing — Jesus, falling on
πρόσωπον ἐδεήθη αὐτοῦ λέγων· κύριε,
[his] face he begged him saying: Lord,
ἐὰν θέλῃς, δύνασαί με καθαρίσαι. **13** καὶ
if thou willest, thou canst me to cleanse. And

¹³And he stretched out his hand, and touched him, saying, "I will; be clean." And immediately the leprosy left him. ¹⁴And he charged him to tell no one; but "go and show yourself to the priest, and make an offering for your cleansing, as Moses commanded, for a proof to the people." ¹⁵But so much the more the report went abroad concerning him; and great multitudes gathered to hear and to be healed of their infirmities. ¹⁶But he withdrew to the wilderness and prayed.

17 On one of those days, as he was teaching, there were Pharisees and teachers of the law sitting by, who had come from every village of Galilee and Judea and from Jerusalem; and the power of the Lord was with him to heal.ᵐ ¹⁸And behold, men were bringing on a bed a man who was paralyzed, and they sought to bring him in and lay him before Jesus; ¹⁹but finding no way to bring him in, because of the crowd, they went up on the roof and let him down with

ᵐ Other ancient authorities read *was present to heal them*

ἐκτείνας τὴν χεῖρα ἥψατο αὐτοῦ λέγων·
stretching out the(his) hand he touched him saying:
θέλω, καθαρίσθητι· καὶ εὐθέως ἡ λέπ|ρα
I am willing, be thou cleansed; and immediately the leprosy
ἀπῆλθεν ἀπ' αὐτοῦ. 14 καὶ αὐτὸς παρήγγειλεν
departed from him. And he · charged
αὐτῷ μηδενὶ εἰπεῖν, ἀλλὰ ἀπελθὼν δεῖξον
him no one to tell, but going away show
σεαυτὸν τῷ ἱερεῖ, καὶ προσένεγκε περὶ
thyself to the priest, and offer concerning
τοῦ καθαρισμοῦ σου καθὼς προσέταξεν
the cleansing of thee as commanded
Μωϋσῆς, εἰς μαρτύριον αὐτοῖς. 15 διήρχετο
Moses, for a testimony to them. went
δὲ μᾶλλον ὁ λόγος περὶ αὐτοῦ, καὶ
But rather the word concerning him, and
συνήρχοντο ὄχλοι πολλοὶ ἀκούειν καὶ
³accompanied ²crowds ¹many to hear and
θεραπεύεσθαι ἀπὸ τῶν ἀσθενειῶν αὐτῶν·
to be healed from the infirmities of them;
16 αὐτὸς δὲ ἦν ὑποχωρῶν ἐν ταῖς ἐρήμοις
but he was withdrawing in the deserts
καὶ προσευχόμενος.
and praying.
17 Καὶ ἐγένετο ἐν μιᾷ τῶν ἡμερῶν καὶ
And it came to pass on one of the days and
αὐτὸς ἦν διδάσκων, καὶ ἦσαν καθήμενοι
he was teaching, and were sitting
Φαρισαῖοι καὶ νομοδιδάσκαλοι οἳ ἦσαν
Pharisees and law-teachers who were
ἐληλυθότες ἐκ πάσης κώμης τῆς Γαλιλαίας
having come out of every village - of Galilee
καὶ Ἰουδαίας καὶ Ἰερουσαλήμ· καὶ δύναμις
and Judæa and Jerusalem; and [the] power
κυρίου ἦν εἰς τὸ ἰᾶσθαι αὐτόν. 18 καὶ
of [the] Lord was ¹in - ³to cure ²him. And
ἰδοὺ ἄνδρες φέροντες ἐπὶ κλίνης ἄνθρωπον
behold[,] men bearing on a couch a man
ὃς ἦν παραλελυμένος, καὶ ἐζήτουν αὐτὸν
who was *having been* paralysed, and they sought ²him
εἰσενεγκεῖν καὶ θεῖναι [αὐτὸν] ἐνώπιον
¹to carry in and to lay him before
αὐτοῦ. 19 καὶ μὴ εὑρόντες ποίας εἰσ-
him. And not finding how† they
ἐνέγκωσιν αὐτὸν διὰ τὸν ὄχλον, ἀναβάντες
might carry in him because of the crowd, going up
ἐπὶ τὸ δῶμα διὰ τῶν κεράμων καθῆκαν
onto the roof through the tiles they let down

his bed through the tiles into the midst before Jesus. ²⁰And when he saw their faith he said, "Man, your sins are forgiven you." ²¹And the scribes and the Pharisees began to question, saying, "Who is this that speaks blasphemies? Who can forgive sins but God only?" ²²When Jesus perceived their questionings, he answered them, "Why do you question in your hearts? ²³Which is easier, to say, 'Your sins are forgiven you,' or to say, 'Rise and walk'? ²⁴But that you may know that the Son of man has authority on earth to forgive sins"— he said to the man who was paralyzed—"I say to you, rise, take up your bed and go home." ²⁵And immediately he rose before them, and took up that on which he lay, and went home, glorifying God. ²⁶And amazement seized them all, and they glorified God and were filled with awe, saying, "We have seen strange things today."

27 After this he went out, and saw a tax

αὐτὸν σὺν τῷ κλινιδίῳ εἰς τὸ μέσον
him   with the couch   into the midst

ἔμπροσθεν τοῦ Ἰησοῦ. 20 καὶ ἰδὼν τὴν
in front of -   Jesus.   And seeing the

πίστιν αὐτῶν εἶπεν· ἄνθρωπε, ἀφέωνταί
faith   of them he said : Man, have been forgiven

σοι αἱ ἁμαρτίαι σου. 21 καὶ ἤρξαντο
thee the sins   of thee.   And began

διαλογίζεσθαι οἱ γραμματεῖς καὶ οἱ Φαρισαῖοι
to reason   the   scribes   and the Pharisees

λέγοντες· τίς ἐστιν οὗτος ὃς λαλεῖ
saying : Who is   this man who speaks

βλασφημίας; τίς δύναται ἁμαρτίας ἀφεῖναι
blasphemies? Who can   sins   to forgive

εἰ μὴ μόνος ὁ θεός; 22 ἐπιγνοὺς δὲ ὁ
except only - God?   But knowing -

Ἰησοῦς τοὺς διαλογισμοὺς αὐτῶν, ἀποκριθεὶς
Jesus   the   reasonings   of them, answering

εἶπεν πρὸς αὐτούς· τί διαλογίζεσθε ἐν
said   to   them : Why   reason ye   in

ταῖς καρδίαις ὑμῶν; 23 τί ἐστιν εὐκοπώτερον,
the   hearts of you? What is   easier,

εἰπεῖν· ἀφέωνταί σοι αἱ ἁμαρτίαι σου, ἢ
to say : Have been forgiven thee the sins of thee, or

εἰπεῖν· ἔγειρε καὶ περιπάτει; 24 ἵνα δὲ
to say : Rise   and   walk ?   but that

εἰδῆτε ὅτι ὁ υἱὸς τοῦ ἀνθρώπου ἐξουσίαν
ye may know that the Son   -   of man   authority

ἔχει ἐπὶ τῆς γῆς ἀφιέναι ἁμαρτίας, —
has on the earth to forgive sins, —

εἶπεν τῷ παραλελυμένῳ· σοὶ λέγω, ἔγειρε
he said to the paralysed [one] : To thee I say, rise

καὶ ἄρας τὸ κλινίδιόν σου πορεύου εἰς
and taking the pallet of thee go   to

τὸν οἶκόν σου. 25 καὶ παραχρῆμα ἀναστὰς
the house of thee. And   at once   rising up

ἐνώπιον αὐτῶν, ἄρας ἐφ᾽ ὃ κατέκειτο,
before   them, taking [that] on which he was lying,

ἀπῆλθεν εἰς τὸν οἶκον αὐτοῦ δοξάζων τὸν
he went away to the house of him glorifying -

θεόν. 26 καὶ ἔκστασις ἔλαβεν ἅπαντας, καὶ
God.   And bewilderment took   all,   and

ἐδόξαζον τὸν θεόν, καὶ ἐπλήσθησαν φόβου
they glorified - God, and were filled of(with) fear

λέγοντες ὅτι εἴδομεν παράδοξα σήμερον.
saying[,] - We saw wonderful things to-day.

27 Καὶ μετὰ ταῦτα ἐξῆλθεν, καὶ ἐθεάσατο
And after these things he went forth, and saw

collector, named Levi, sitting at the tax office; and he said to him, "Follow me." ²⁸And he left everything, and rose and followed him.

29 And Levi made him a great feast in his house; and there was a large company of tax collectors and others sitting at table with them. ³⁰And the Pharisees and their scribes murmured against his disciples, saying, "Why do you eat and drink with tax collectors and sinners?" ³¹And Jesus answered them, "Those who are well have no need of a physician, but those who are sick; ³²I have not come to call the righteous, but sinners to repentance."

33 And they said to him, "The disciples of John fast often and offer prayers, and so do the disciples of the Pharisees, but yours eat and drink." ³⁴And Jesus said to them, "Can you make wedding guests fast while the bridegroom is with them. ³⁵The days will come, when the bridegroom is taken away from them, and then they will fast

τελώνην ὀνόματι Λευὶν καθήμενον ἐπὶ τὸ
a tax-collector by name Levi sitting on(in) the
τελώνιον, καὶ εἶπεν αὐτῷ· ἀκολούθει μοι.
custom house, and said to him : Follow me.
28 καὶ καταλιπὼν πάντα ἀναστὰς ἠκολούθει
And abandoning all things rising up he followed
αὐτῷ. 29 Καὶ ἐποίησεν δοχὴν μεγάλην
him. And ²made ⁴feast ³a great
Λευὶς αὐτῷ ἐν τῇ οἰκίᾳ αὐτοῦ· καὶ ἦν
¹Levi for him in the house of him; and there was
ὄχλος πολὺς τελωνῶν καὶ ἄλλων οἳ ἦσαν
crowd a much of tax-collectors and of others who were
μετ' αὐτῶν κατακείμενοι. 30 καὶ ἐγόγγυζον
²with ³them ¹reclining. And grumbled
οἱ Φαρισαῖοι καὶ οἱ γραμματεῖς αὐτῶν
the Pharisees and the scribes of them
πρὸς τοὺς μαθητὰς αὐτοῦ λέγοντες· διὰ
at the disciples of him saying : Why
τί μετὰ τῶν τελωνῶν καὶ ἁμαρτωλῶν
with the tax-collectors and sinners
ἐσθίετε καὶ πίνετε; 31 καὶ ἀποκριθεὶς ὁ
eat ye and drink ye? And answering –
Ἰησοῦς εἶπεν πρὸς αὐτούς· οὐ χρείαν
Jesus said to them : not need
ἔχουσιν οἱ ὑγιαίνοντες ἰατροῦ ἀλλὰ οἱ
have the [ones] being healthy of a physician but the
        =those who are ill;
κακῶς ἔχοντες· 32 οὐκ ἐλήλυθα καλέσαι
[ones] ill having; I have not come to call
δικαίους ἀλλὰ ἁμαρτωλοὺς εἰς μετάνοιαν.
righteous persons but sinners to repentance.
33 Οἱ δὲ εἶπαν πρὸς αὐτόν· οἱ μαθηταὶ
And they said to him : The disciples
Ἰωάννου νηστεύουσιν πυκνὰ καὶ δεήσεις
of John fast often and prayers
ποιοῦνται, ὁμοίως καὶ οἱ τῶν Φαρισαίων,
make, likewise also those of the Pharisees,
οἱ δὲ σοὶ ἐσθίουσιν καὶ πίνουσιν. 34 ὁ
but those to thee° eat and drink. –
=but thine
δὲ Ἰησοῦς εἶπεν πρὸς αὐτούς· μὴ δύνασθε
And Jesus said to them : not ¹Can ye
τοὺς υἱοὺς τοῦ νυμφῶνος, ἐν ᾧ ὁ νυμφίος
³the ⁴sons ⁵of the ⁶bride-chamber, ⁸while ⁹the ¹⁰bridegroom
μετ' αὐτῶν ἐστιν, ποιῆσαι νηστεῦσαι;
¹²with ¹³them ¹¹is, ²to make ⁷to fast?
35 ἐλεύσονται δὲ ἡμέραι, καὶ ὅταν ἀπαρθῇ
but will come days, and when is taken away
ἀπ' αὐτῶν ὁ νυμφίος, τότε νηστεύσουσιν
from them the bridegroom, then they will fast

in those days." ³⁶He told them a parable also: "No one tears a piece from a new garment and puts it upon an old garment; if he does, he will tear the new, and the piece from the new will not match the old. ³⁷And no one puts new wine into old wineskins; if he does, the new wine will burst the skins and it will be spilled, and the skins will be destroyed. ³⁸But new wine must be put into fresh wineskins. ³⁹And no one after drinking old wine desires new; for he says, 'The old is good.' "ⁿ

ἐν ἐκείναις ταῖς ἡμέραις.   36 Ἔλεγεν δὲ
in   those   -   days.   And he told

καὶ παραβολὴν πρὸς αὐτοὺς ὅτι οὐδεὶς
also a parable   to   them[:]   -   No one

ἐπίβλημα ἀπὸ ἱματίου καινοῦ σχίσας
²a patch ³from ⁵garment ⁴a new ¹tearing

ἐπιβάλλει ἐπὶ ἱμάτιον παλαιόν· εἰ δὲ μή γε,
⁶puts [it] ⁷on ⁹a garment ⁸an old;   otherwise,

καὶ τὸ καινὸν σχίσει καὶ τῷ παλαιῷ
both the   new   will tear and ⁷with the ⁸old

οὐ συμφωνήσει τὸ ἐπίβλημα τὸ ἀπὸ τοῦ
⁶will not agree ¹the ²patch - ³from ⁴the

καινοῦ.   37 καὶ οὐδεὶς βάλλει οἶνον νέον
⁵new.   And no one puts wine new

εἰς ἀσκοὺς παλαιούς· εἰ δὲ μή γε, ῥήξει
into wineskins   old;   otherwise,   ⁴will burst

ὁ οἶνος ὁ νέος τοὺς ἀσκούς, καὶ αὐτὸς
¹the ³wine ²-²new ⁵the ⁶wineskins, and it

ἐκχυθήσεται καὶ οἱ ἀσκοὶ ἀπολοῦνται.
will be poured out and the wineskins will perish.

38 ἀλλὰ οἶνον νέον εἰς ἀσκοὺς καινοὺς
    But   wine   new into wineskins   new

βλητέον.   39 καὶ οὐδεὶς πιὼν παλαιὸν
one must put.   And no one having drunk   old

θέλει νέον· λέγει γάρ· ὁ παλαιὸς χρηστός
desires new;   for he says : The   old   good

ἐστιν.
is.

CHAPTER 6

ON a sabbath,ᵒ while he was going through the grainfields, his disciples plucked and ate some ears of grain, rubbing them in their hands. ²But some of the Pharisees said, "Why are you doing what is not lawful to do on the sabbath?" ³And Jesus answered, "Have you not read what David did when he was hungry, he and those who were with him: ⁴how he entered the

6 Ἐγένετο δὲ ἐν σαββάτῳ διαπορεύεσθαι
  And it came to pass on a sabbath   to go through
                                              =he went through

αὐτὸν διὰ σπορίμων, καὶ ἔτιλλον οἱ
himᵇ   through cornfields,   and ⁴plucked ¹the

μαθηταὶ αὐτοῦ καὶ ἤσθιον τοὺς στάχυας
²disciples ³of him and   ate   the   ears

ψώχοντες ταῖς χερσίν. 2 τινὲς δὲ τῶν
rubbing with the(ir) hands.   And some of the

Φαρισαίων εἶπαν· τί ποιεῖτε ὃ οὐκ ἔξεστιν
Pharisees   said : Why do ye what is not lawful

τοῖς σάββασιν; 3 καὶ ἀποκριθεὶς πρὸς
on the sabbaths?   And replying   to

αὐτοὺς εἶπεν ὁ Ἰησοῦς· οὐδὲ τοῦτο ἀνέγνωτε
them   said - Jesus: ²not ³this ¹read ye

ὃ ἐποίησεν Δαυίδ, ὁπότε ἐπείνασεν αὐτὸς
which did   David,   when   hungered   he

καὶ οἱ μετ' αὐτοῦ ὄντες; 4 ὡς εἰσῆλθεν
and the [ones] with him being?   how he entered

ⁿ Other ancient authorities read better
ᵒ Other ancient authorities read On the second first sabbath (on the second sabbath after the first)

house of God, and took and ate the bread of the Presence, which it is not lawful for any but the priests to eat, and also gave it to those with him?" [5]And he said to them, "The Son of man is lord of the sabbath."

6 On another sabbath, when he entered the synagogue and taught, a man was there whose right hand was withered. [7]And the scribes and the Pharisees watched him, to see whether he would heal on the sabbath, so that they might find an accusation against him. [8]But he knew their thoughts, and he said to the man who had the withered hand, "Come and stand here." And he rose and stood there. [9]And Jesus said to them, "I ask you, is it lawful on the sabbath to do good or to do harm, to save life or to destroy it?" [10]And he looked around on them all, and said to him, "Stretch out your hand." And he did so, and his hand was restored. [11]But they were filled with fury and discussed with one another what they might do to Jesus.

εἰς τὸν οἶκον τοῦ θεοῦ καὶ τοὺς ἄρτους
into the house - of God and the loaves

τῆς προθέσεως λαβὼν ἔφαγεν καὶ ἔδωκεν
of the setting forth taking he ate and gave

τοῖς μετ' αὐτοῦ, οὓς οὐκ ἔξεστιν φαγεῖν
to the [ones] with him, which it is not lawful to eat

εἰ μὴ μόνους τοὺς ἱερεῖς; 5 καὶ ἔλεγεν
except only the priests? And he said

αὐτοῖς· κύριός ἐστιν τοῦ σαββάτου ὁ
to them : Lord is of the sabbath the

υἱὸς τοῦ ἀνθρώπου. 6 Ἐγένετο δὲ ἐν
Son - of man. And it came to pass on

ἑτέρῳ σαββάτῳ εἰσελθεῖν αὐτὸν εἰς τὴν
another sabbath to enter him into the
=he entered into the synagogue and

συναγωγὴν καὶ διδάσκειν· καὶ ἦν ἄνθρωπος
synagogue and to teach[b]; and there was a man
taught;

ἐκεῖ καὶ ἡ χεὶρ αὐτοῦ ἡ δεξιὰ ἦν ξηρά·
there and the [a]hand [a]of him - [1]right was withered;

7 παρετηροῦντο δὲ αὐτὸν οἱ γραμματεῖς
and carefully watched him the scribes

καὶ οἱ Φαρισαῖοι εἰ ἐν τῷ σαββάτῳ
and the Pharisees if on the sabbath

θεραπεύει, ἵνα εὕρωσιν κατηγορεῖν αὐτοῦ.
he heals, that they might find to accuse him.

8 αὐτὸς δὲ ᾔδει τοὺς διαλογισμοὺς αὐτῶν,
But he knew the reasonings of them,

εἶπεν δὲ τῷ ἀνδρὶ τῷ ξηρὰν ἔχοντι τὴν
and said to the man - [3]withered [1]having [2]the

χεῖρα· ἔγειρε καὶ στῆθι εἰς τὸ μέσον·
[4]hand : Rise and stand in the midst;

καὶ ἀναστὰς ἔστη. 9 εἶπεν δὲ ὁ Ἰησοῦς
and rising up he stood. And said - Jesus

πρὸς αὐτούς· ἐπερωτῶ ὑμᾶς εἰ ἔξεστιν
to them: I ask you if it is lawful

τῷ σαββάτῳ ἀγαθοποιῆσαι ἢ κακοποιῆσαι,
on the sabbath to do good or to do evil,

ψυχὴν σῶσαι ἢ ἀπολέσαι; 10 καὶ περι-
life to save or to destroy? And looking

βλεψάμενος πάντας αὐτοὺς εἶπεν αὐτῷ·
round at all them he said to him :

ἔκτεινον τὴν χεῖρά σου. ὁ δὲ ἐποίησεν,
Stretch out the hand of thee. And he did,

καὶ ἀπεκατεστάθη ἡ χεὶρ αὐτοῦ. 11 αὐτοὶ
and was restored the hand of him. they

δὲ ἐπλήσθησαν ἀνοίας, καὶ διελάλουν πρὸς
But were filled of(with) madness, and talked to

ἀλλήλους τί ἂν ποιήσαιεν τῷ Ἰησοῦ.
one another what they might do - to Jesus.

12 In these days he went out into the hills to pray; and all night he continued in prayer to God. ¹³And when it was day, he called his disciples, and chose from them twelve, whom he named apostles; ¹⁴Simon, whom he named Peter, and Andrew his brother, and James and John, and Philip, and Bartholomew, ¹⁵and Matthew, and Thomas, and James the son of Alphaeus, and Simon who was called the Zealot, ¹⁶and Judas the son of James, and Judas Iscariot, who became a traitor.

17 And he came down with them and stood on a level place, with a great crowd of his disciples and a great multitude of people from all Judea and Jerusalem and the seacoast of Tyre and Sidon, who came to hear him and to be healed of their diseases; ¹⁸and those who were troubled with unclean spirits were cured. ¹⁹And all the crowd sought to touch him, for power came forth from him and healed them all.

20 And he lifted up

12 Ἐγένετο δὲ ἐν ταῖς ἡμέραις ταύταις
Now it came to pass in   -   days   these

ἐξελθεῖν αὐτὸν εἰς τὸ ὄρος προσεύξασθαι,
to go forth himᵇ to the mountain to pray,
=he went forth

καὶ ἦν διανυκτερεύων ἐν τῇ προσευχῇ τοῦ
and was spending the whole in the prayer   -
night

θεοῦ. 13 καὶ ὅτε ἐγένετο ἡμέρα, προσεφώνησεν
of God.   And when it became day, he called to [him]

τοὺς μαθητὰς αὐτοῦ, καὶ ἐκλεξάμενος ἀπ'
the disciples of him, and choosing from

αὐτῶν δώδεκα, οὓς καὶ ἀποστόλους ὠνόμασεν
them twelve, whom also apostles he named,

14 Σίμωνα, ὃν καὶ ὠνόμασεν Πέτρον, καὶ
Simon, whom also he named Peter, and

Ἀνδρέαν τὸν ἀδελφὸν αὐτοῦ, καὶ Ἰάκωβον
Andrew the brother of him, and James

καὶ Ἰωάννην, καὶ Φίλιππον καὶ Βαρθο-
and John, and Philip and Bartho-

λομαῖον, 15 καὶ Μαθθαῖον καὶ Θωμᾶν,
lomew, and Matthew and Thomas,

[καὶ] Ἰάκωβον Ἁλφαίου καὶ Σίμωνα τὸν
and James [son] of Alphæus and Simon the [one]

καλούμενον ζηλωτήν, καὶ Ἰούδαν Ἰακώβου,
being called a Zealot, and Judas of James,

16 καὶ Ἰούδαν Ἰσκαριώθ, ὃς ἐγένετο προδότης,
and Judas Iscariot, who became betrayer,

17 καὶ καταβὰς μετ' αὐτῶν ἔστη ἐπὶ
and coming down with them he stood on

τόπου πεδινοῦ, καὶ ὄχλος πολὺς μαθητῶν
place a level, and crowd a much of disciples

αὐτοῦ, καὶ πλῆθος πολὺ τοῦ λαοῦ ἀπὸ
of him, and multitude a much of the people from

πάσης τῆς Ἰουδαίας καὶ Ἰερουσαλὴμ καὶ
all   -   Judæa and Jerusalem and

τῆς παραλίου Τύρου καὶ Σιδῶνος, 18 οἳ
the coast country of Tyre and Sidon, who

ἦλθον ἀκοῦσαι αὐτοῦ καὶ ἰαθῆναι ἀπὸ
came to hear him and to be cured from

τῶν νόσων αὐτῶν, καὶ οἱ ἐνοχλούμενοι
the diseases of them, and the [ones] being tormented

ἀπὸ πνευμάτων ἀκαθάρτων ἐθεραπεύοντο.
from spirits unclean were healed.

19 καὶ πᾶς ὁ ὄχλος ἐζήτουν ἅπτεσθαι
And all the crowd sought to touch

αὐτοῦ, ὅτι δύναμις παρ' αὐτοῦ ἐξήρχετο
him, because power from him went forth

καὶ ἰᾶτο πάντας. 20 Καὶ αὐτὸς ἐπάρας
and cured all.   And he lifting up

his eyes on his disciples, and said:

"Blessed are you poor, for yours is the kingdom of God.

21 "Blessed are you that hunger now, for you shall be satisfied.

"Blessed are you that weep now, for you shall laugh.

22 "Blessed are you when men hate you, and when they exclude you and revile you, and cast out your name as evil, on account of the Son of man! 23 Rejoice in that day, and leap for joy, for behold, your reward is great in heaven; for so their fathers did to the prophets.

24 "But woe to you that are rich, for you have received your consolation.

25 "Woe to you that are full now, for you shall hunger.

"Woe to you that laugh now, for you shall mourn and weep.

26 "Woe to you, when all men speak well of you, for so their fathers did to the false prophets.

27 "But I say to you that hear, Love your enemies, do good to those who hate you,

τοὺς ὀφθαλμοὺς αὐτοῦ εἰς τοὺς μαθητὰς
the eyes of him to the disciples
αὐτοῦ ἔλεγεν·
of him said:
Μακάριοι οἱ πτωχοί, ὅτι ὑμετέρα ἐστὶν
Blessed [are] the poor, because yours is
ἡ βασιλεία τοῦ θεοῦ. 21 μακάριοι οἱ
the kingdom – of God. Blessed [are] the [ones]
πεινῶντες νῦν, ὅτι χορτασθήσεσθε. μακάριοι
hungering now, because ye will be satisfied. Blessed [are]
οἱ κλαίοντες νῦν, ὅτι γελάσετε. 22 μακάριοί
the [ones] weeping now, because ye will laugh. Blessed
ἐστε ὅταν μισήσωσιν ὑμᾶς οἱ ἄνθρωποι,
are ye when ²hate ³you – ¹men,
καὶ ὅταν ἀφορίσωσιν ὑμᾶς καὶ ὀνειδίσωσιν
and when they separate you and reproach
καὶ ἐκβάλωσιν τὸ ὄνομα ὑμῶν ὡς πονηρὸν
and cast out the name of you as evil
ἕνεκα τοῦ υἱοῦ τοῦ ἀνθρώπου. 23 χάρητε
for the sake of the Son – of man. Rejoice
ἐν ἐκείνῃ τῇ ἡμέρᾳ καὶ σκιρτήσατε·
in that – day and leap for joy;
ἰδοὺ γὰρ ὁ μισθὸς ὑμῶν πολὺς ἐν τῷ
for behold[,] the reward of you much in –
οὐρανῷ· κατὰ τὰ αὐτὰ γὰρ ἐποίουν τοῖς
heaven; for according to the same things ⁴did ⁵to the
= in the same way
προφήταις οἱ πατέρες αὐτῶν.
⁶prophets ¹the ²fathers ³of them.
24 Πλὴν οὐαὶ ὑμῖν τοῖς πλουσίοις, ὅτι
But woe to you the rich [ones], because
ἀπέχετε τὴν παράκλησιν ὑμῶν. οὐαὶ ὑμῖν,
ye have the consolation of you. Woe to you,
οἱ ἐμπεπλησμένοι νῦν, ὅτι πεινάσετε.
the [ones] having been filled up now, because ye will hunger.
25 οὐαί, οἱ γελῶντες νῦν, ὅτι πενθήσετε
Woe, the [ones] laughing now, because ye will mourn
καὶ κλαύσετε. 26 οὐαὶ ὅταν καλῶς ὑμᾶς
and lament. Woe when well [of] you
εἴπωσιν πάντες οἱ ἄνθρωποι· κατὰ τὰ
say all – men; for according to
= in the same way
αὐτὰ γὰρ ἐποίουν τοῖς ψευδοπροφήταις οἱ
the same things did to the false prophets the
πατέρες αὐτῶν. 27 Ἀλλὰ ὑμῖν λέγω
fathers of them. But you I tell
τοῖς ἀκούουσιν· ἀγαπᾶτε τοὺς ἐχθροὺς
the [ones] hearing: Love ye the enemies
ὑμῶν, καλῶς ποιεῖτε τοῖς μισοῦσιν ὑμᾶς,
of you, ²well ¹do to the [ones] hating you,

28 bless those who curse
you, pray for those who
abuse you. 29 To him
who strikes you on the
cheek, offer the other
also; and from him who
takes away your cloak
do not withhold your
coat as well. 30 Give to
every one who begs from
you; and of him who
takes away your goods
do not ask them again.
31 And as you wish that
men would do to you,
do so to them.

32 "If you love those
who love you, what
credit is that to you? For
even sinners love those
who love them. 33 And if
you do good to those
who do good to you,
what credit is that to
you? For even sinners do
the same. 34 And if you
lend to those from whom
you hope to receive, what
credit is that to you?
Even sinners lend to
sinners, to receive as
much again. 35 But love
your enemies, and do
good, and lend, expect-
ing nothing in return;[q]
and your reward will be
great, and you will be
sons of the Most High;
for he is kind to the

[q] Other ancient authorities read *despairing of no man*

28 εὐλογεῖτε τοὺς καταρωμένους ὑμᾶς,
bless the [ones] cursing you,

προσεύχεσθε περὶ τῶν ἐπηρεαζόντων ὑμᾶς.
pray about the [ones] insulting you.

29 τῷ τύπτοντί σε ἐπὶ τὴν σιαγόνα
To the [one] striking thee on the cheek

πάρεχε καὶ τὴν ἄλλην, καὶ ἀπὸ τοῦ
turn also the other, and from the [one]

αἴροντός σου τὸ ἱμάτιον καὶ τὸν χιτῶνα
taking of thee the garment also the tunic

μὴ κωλύσῃς. 30 παντὶ αἰτοῦντί σε δίδου,
do not prevent. To everyone asking thee give,

καὶ ἀπὸ τοῦ αἴροντος τὰ σὰ μὴ ἀπαίτει.
and from the [one] taking thy things do not ask back.

31 καὶ καθὼς θέλετε ἵνα ποιῶσιν ὑμῖν
And as ye wish that may do to you

οἱ ἄνθρωποι, ποιεῖτε αὐτοῖς ὁμοίως. 32 καὶ
– men, do ye to them likewise. And

εἰ ἀγαπᾶτε τοὺς ἀγαπῶντας ὑμᾶς, ποία
if ye love the [ones] loving you, what

ὑμῖν χάρις ἐστίν; καὶ γὰρ οἱ ἁμαρτωλοὶ
to you thanks is there?[c] for even – sinners
=thanks have ye?

τοὺς ἀγαπῶντας αὐτοὺς ἀγαπῶσιν. 33 καὶ
[2]the [ones] [3]loving [4]them [1]love. even

γὰρ ἐὰν ἀγαθοποιῆτε τοὺς ἀγαθοποιοῦντας
For if ye do good to the [ones] doing good to

ὑμᾶς, ποία ὑμῖν χάρις ἐστίν; καὶ οἱ
you, what to you thanks is there?[c] even –
=thanks have ye?

ἁμαρτωλοὶ τὸ αὐτὸ ποιοῦσιν. 34 καὶ ἐὰν
sinners the same thing do. And if

δανείσητε παρ' ὧν ἐλπίζετε λαβεῖν, ποία
ye lend from whom ye hope to receive, what

ὑμῖν χάρις [ἐστίν]; καὶ ἁμαρτωλοὶ
to you thanks is there?[c] even sinners
=thanks have ye?

ἁμαρτωλοῖς δανείζουσιν ἵνα ἀπολάβωσιν τὰ
to sinners lend that they may receive back the

ἴσα. 35 πλὴν ἀγαπᾶτε τοὺς ἐχθροὺς ὑμῶν
equal things. But love ye the enemies of you

καὶ ἀγαθοποιεῖτε καὶ δανείζετε μηδὲν
and do good and lend nothing

ἀπελπίζοντες· καὶ ἔσται ὁ μισθὸς ὑμῶν
despairing; and will be the reward of you
=despairing not at all;

πολύς, καὶ ἔσεσθε υἱοὶ ὑψίστου, ὅτι
much, and ye will be sons of [the] Most High, because

αὐτὸς χρηστός ἐστιν ἐπὶ τοὺς ἀχαρίστους
he kind is to the unthankful

ungrateful and the selfish. ³⁶ Be merciful, even as your Father is merciful.

37 "Judge not, and you will not be judged; condemn not, and you will not be condemned; forgive, and you will be forgiven; ³⁸ give, and it will be given to you; good measure, pressed down, shaken together, running over, will be put into your lap. For the measure you give will be the measure you get back."

39 He also told them a parable: "Can a blind man lead a blind man? Will they not both fall into a pit? ⁴⁰A disciple is not above his teacher, but every one when he is fully taught will be like his teacher. ⁴¹Why do you see the speck that is in your brother's eye, but do not notice the log that is in your own eye? ⁴²Or how can you say to your brother, 'Brother, let me take out the speck that is in your eye,' when you yourself do not see the log that is in your own eye? You hypocrite, first take the log out of your own eye, and then you will see clearly to

καὶ πονηρούς.
and evil.

36 Γίνεσθε οἰκτίρμονες,
Be ye compassionate,

καθὼς ὁ πατὴρ ὑμῶν οἰκτίρμων ἐστίν.
as the Father of you compassionate is.

37 καὶ μὴ κρίνετε, καὶ οὐ μὴ κριθῆτε· καὶ
And do not judge, and by no means ye may be and judged;

μὴ καταδικάζετε, καὶ οὐ μὴ καταδικασθῆτε.
do not condemn, and by no means ye may be condemned.

ἀπολύετε, καὶ ἀπολυθήσεσθε· **38** δίδοτε, καὶ
Forgive, and ye will be forgiven; give, and

δοθήσεται ὑμῖν· μέτρον καλὸν πεπιεσμένον
it will be given to you; measure good *having been* pressed down

σεσαλευμένον ὑπερεκχυννόμενον δώσουσιν εἰς
having been shaken running over they will give into

τὸν κόλπον ὑμῶν· ᾧ γὰρ μέτρῳ μετρεῖτε
the bosom of you; for in what measure ye measure

ἀντιμετρηθήσεται ὑμῖν. **39** Εἶπεν δὲ καὶ
it will be measured in return to you. And he told also

παραβολὴν αὐτοῖς· μήτι δύναται τυφλὸς
a parable to them: Not can a blind man

τυφλὸν ὁδηγεῖν; οὐχὶ ἀμφότεροι εἰς βόθυνον
²a blind man ¹guide? not both into a ditch

ἐμπεσοῦνται; **40** οὐκ ἔστιν μαθητὴς ὑπὲρ
will fall *in*? ³not ²is ¹A disciple above

τὸν διδάσκαλον· κατηρτισμένος δὲ πᾶς
the teacher; ¹but ⁴*having been* perfected ²everyone

ἔσται ὡς ὁ διδάσκαλος αὐτοῦ. **41** Τί δὲ
³will be as the teacher of him. And why

βλέπεις τὸ κάρφος τὸ ἐν τῷ ὀφθαλμῷ
seest thou the mote – in the eye

τοῦ ἀδελφοῦ σου, τὴν δὲ δοκὸν τὴν ἐν
of the brother of thee, but the beam – in

τῷ ἰδίῳ ὀφθαλμῷ οὐ κατανοεῖς; **42** πῶς
thine own eye thou considerest not? how

δύνασαι λέγειν τῷ ἀδελφῷ σου· ἀδελφέ,
canst thou *to* say to the brother of thee: Brother,

ἄφες ἐκβάλω τὸ κάρφος τὸ ἐν τῷ
allow I may take out the mote – in the
=allow me to take out

ὀφθαλμῷ σου, αὐτὸς τὴν ἐν τῷ ὀφθαλμῷ
eye of thee, ¹[thy]self ⁴the ⁶in ⁷the ⁸eye

σου δοκὸν οὐ βλέπων; ὑποκριτά, ἔκβαλε
⁹of thee ⁵beam ²not ³seeing? hypocrite, take *out*

πρῶτον τὴν δοκὸν ἐκ τοῦ ὀφθαλμοῦ σου,
first the beam out of the eye of thee,

καὶ τότε διαβλέψεις τὸ κάρφος τὸ ἐν τῷ
and then thou wilt see clearly the mote – in the

take out the speck that is in your brother's eye.

43 "For no good tree bears bad fruit, nor again does a bad tree bear good fruit; [44]for each tree is known by its own fruit. For figs are not gathered from thorns, nor are grapes picked from a bramble bush. [45]The good man out of the good treasure of his heart produces good, and the evil man out of his evil treasure produces evil; for out of the abundance of the heart his mouth speaks.

46 "Why do you call me 'Lord, Lord,' and not do what I tell you? [47]Every one who comes to me and hears my words and does them, I will show you what he is like: [48]he is like a man building a house, who dug deep, and laid the foundation upon rock; and when a flood arose, the stream broke against that house, and could not shake it, because it had been well built.[r] [49]But he who hears and does not do them is like

[r] Other ancient authorities read *founded upon the rock*

ὀφθαλμῷ   τοῦ   ἀδελφοῦ   σου   ἐκβαλεῖν.   43 Οὐ
eye   of the   brother   of thee   to take out.   [3]no

γάρ   ἐστιν   δένδρον   καλὸν   ποιοῦν   καρπὸν
[1]For   [2]there is   [5]tree   [4]good   producing   fruit

σαπρόν,   οὐδὲ   πάλιν   δένδρον   σαπρὸν   ποιοῦν
bad,   nor   again   tree   a bad   producing

καρπὸν   καλόν.   44 ἕκαστον   γὰρ   δένδρον
fruit   good.   For each   tree

ἐκ   τοῦ   ἰδίου   καρποῦ   γινώσκεται·   οὐ   γὰρ
by   the(its)   own   fruit   is known;   for not

ἐξ   ἀκανθῶν   συλλέγουσιν   σῦκα,   οὐδὲ   ἐκ
of   thorns   do they gather   figs,   nor   of

βάτου   σταφυλὴν   τρυγῶσιν.   45 ὁ   ἀγαθὸς
a thorn bush   a grape   do they pick.   The   good

ἄνθρωπος   ἐκ   τοῦ   ἀγαθοῦ   θησαυροῦ   τῆς
man   out of   the   good   treasure   of the(his)

καρδίας   προφέρει   τὸ   ἀγαθόν,   καὶ   ὁ
heart   brings forth   the   good,   and   the
= that which is good,

πονηρὸς   ἐκ   τοῦ   πονηροῦ   προφέρει   τὸ
evil man   out of   the   evil   brings forth   the

πονηρόν·   ἐκ   γὰρ   περισσεύματος   καρδίας
evil;   for out of   [the] abundance   of [his] heart
= that which is evil;

λαλεῖ   τὸ   στόμα   αὐτοῦ.   46 Τί   δέ   με   καλεῖτε·
speaks   the   mouth   of him.   And why   me   call ye :

κύριε   κύριε,   καὶ   οὐ   ποιεῖτε   ἃ
Lord[,]   Lord,   and   do not [the things] which

λέγω;   47 Πᾶς   ὁ   ἐρχόμενος   πρός   με   καὶ
I say?   Everyone   coming   to   me   and

ἀκούων   μου   τῶν   λόγων   καὶ   ποιῶν   αὐτούς,
hearing   of me   the   words   and   doing   them,

ὑποδείξω   ὑμῖν   τίνι   ἐστὶν   ὅμοιος.   48 ὅμοιός
I will show   you   to whom   he is   like.   Like

ἐστιν   ἀνθρώπῳ   οἰκοδομοῦντι   οἰκίαν,   ὃς
he is   to a man   building   a house,   who

ἔσκαψεν   καὶ   ἐβάθυνεν   καὶ   ἔθηκεν   θεμέλιον
dug   and   deepened   and   laid   a foundation

ἐπὶ   τὴν   πέτραν·   πλημμύρης   δὲ   γενομένης
on   the   rock;   and a flood   occurring[a]
= when a flood occurred

προσέρρηξεν   ὁ   ποταμὸς   τῇ   οἰκίᾳ   ἐκείνῃ,
[3]dashed against   [1]the   [2]river   –   house   that,

καὶ   οὐκ   ἴσχυσεν   σαλεῦσαι   αὐτὴν   διὰ
and   was not able   to shake   it   because of

τὸ   καλῶς   οἰκοδομῆσθαι   αὐτήν.   49 ὁ   δὲ
the   well   to be built   it.[b]   But the
= because it was well built.   [one]

ἀκούσας   καὶ   μὴ   ποιήσας   ὅμοιός   ἐστιν
hearing   and   not   doing   [2]like   [1]is

a man who built a house on the ground without a foundation; against which the stream broke, and immediately it fell, and the ruin of that house was great."

ἀνθρώπῳ οἰκοδομήσαντι οἰκίαν ἐπὶ τὴν
a man   having built   a house   on   the
γῆν χωρὶς θεμελίου, ᾗ προσέρρηξεν ὁ
earth without a foundation, ³which ⁵dashed ¹against ²the
ποταμός, καὶ εὐθὺς συνέπεσεν, καὶ ἐγένετο
⁴river,   and immediately it collapsed,   and   ⁵was
τὸ ῥῆγμα τῆς οἰκίας ἐκείνης μέγα.
¹the ²ruin   –   ⁴house ³of that ⁶great.

CHAPTER 7

AFTER he had ended all his sayings in the hearing of the people he entered Caper′na-um. ²Now a centurion had a slave who was dear′ to him, who was sick and at the point of death. ³When he heard of Jesus, he sent to him elders of the Jews, asking him to come and heal his slave. ⁴And when they came to Jesus, they besought him earnestly, saying, "He is worthy to have you do this for him, ⁵for he loves our nation, and he built us our synagogue." ⁶And Jesus went with them. When he was not far from the house, the centurion sent friends to him, saying to him, "Lord, do not trouble yourself, for I am not worthy to have you come under my roof; ⁷therefore I did not presume to come to you. But say the

7 Ἐπειδὴ ἐπλήρωσεν πάντα τὰ ῥήματα
   When   he completed   all   the   words
αὐτοῦ εἰς τὰς ἀκοὰς τοῦ λαοῦ, εἰσῆλθεν
of him in   the   ears of the people, he entered
εἰς Καφαρναούμ. 2 Ἑκατοντάρχου δέ
into Capernaum.   Now ²of ²a ⁶centurion
τινος δοῦλος κακῶς ἔχων ἤμελλεν τελευτᾶν,
⁴certain ¹a slave ⁷ill ⁶having(being) ¹¹was about ¹³to die,
ὃς ἦν αὐτῷ ἔντιμος. 3 ἀκούσας δὲ περὶ
⁸who ⁹was ¹¹to him ¹⁰dear.   And hearing   about
τοῦ Ἰησοῦ ἀπέστειλεν πρὸς αὐτὸν πρε-
 –   Jesus   he sent   to   him   eld-
σβυτέρους τῶν Ἰουδαίων, ἐρωτῶν αὐτὸν
ers   of the   Jews,   asking   him
ὅπως ἐλθὼν διασώσῃ τὸν δοῦλον αὐτοῦ.
that coming he might recover the   slave   of him.
4 οἱ δὲ παραγενόμενοι πρὸς τὸν Ἰησοῦν
And they   coming   to   –   Jesus
παρεκάλουν αὐτὸν σπουδαίως, λέγοντες ὅτι ἄξιός
 besought   him   earnestly,   saying[,] – Worthy
ἐστιν ᾧ παρέξῃ τοῦτο· 5 ἀγαπᾷ γὰρ
he is for whom thou shouldest grant this;   for he loves
τὸ ἔθνος ἡμῶν καὶ τὴν συναγωγὴν
the nation of us   and , the   synagogue
αὐτὸς ᾠκοδόμησεν ἡμῖν. 6 ὁ δὲ Ἰησοῦς
he   built   for us.   – And Jesus
ἐπορεύετο σὺν αὐτοῖς. ἤδη δὲ αὐτοῦ οὐ
 went   with them. And yet   him   not
                                  =while he was yet
μακρὰν ἀπέχοντος ἀπὸ τῆς οἰκίας, ἔπεμψεν
far   being awayᵃ from the   house,   sent
not far away
φίλους ὁ ἑκατοντάρχης λέγων αὐτῷ· κύριε,
friends the centurion   saying to him : Lord,
μὴ σκύλλου· οὐ γὰρ ἱκανός εἰμι ἵνα ὑπὸ
do not trouble; for not worthy am I that under
τὴν στέγην μ̣ου εἰσέλθῃς· 7 διὸ οὐδὲ
the roof of me thou shouldest enter; wherefore not
ἐμαυτὸν ἠξίωσα πρὸς σὲ ἐλθεῖν· ἀλλὰ εἰπὲ
myself I accounted worthy to thee to come; but   say

ᵃ Or valuable

word, and let my servant be healed. ⁸For I am a man set under authority, with soldiers under me: and I say to one, 'Go,' and he goes; and to another, 'Come,' and he comes; and to my slave, 'Do this,' and he does it." ⁹When Jesus heard this he marveled at him, and turned and said to the multitude that followed him, "I tell you, not even in Israel have I found such faith." ¹⁰And when those who had been sent returned to the house, they found the slave well.

11 Soon afterward[t] he went to a city called Na'in, and his disciples and a great crowd went with him. ¹²As he drew near to the gate of the city, behold, a man who had died was being carried out, the only son of his mother, and she was a widow; and a large crowd from the city was with her. ¹³And when the Lord saw her, he had compassion on her and said to her, "Do not weep." ¹⁴And he came and touched the bier, and the bearers stood still. And he said, "Young man, I say to you, arise." ¹⁵And the

[t] Other ancient authorities read *Next day*

λόγῳ,   καὶ   ἰαθήτω   ὁ   παῖς   μου.   8 καὶ
in a word, and   let be cured the servant of me.   ⁸also

γὰρ   ἐγὼ   ἄνθρωπός   εἰμι   ὑπὸ   ἐξουσίαν
¹For   ²I   ⁵a man   ⁴am   ⁷under ⁸authority

τασσόμενος,   ἔχων   ὑπ'   ἐμαυτὸν   στρατιώτας,
⁶being set,   having under   myself   soldiers,

καὶ   λέγω   τούτῳ·   πορεύθητι,   καὶ   πορεύεται,
and   I tell   this one :   Go,   and   he goes,

καὶ   ἄλλῳ·   ἔρχου,   καὶ   ἔρχεται,   καὶ   τῷ
and another : Come,   and   he comes,   and   the

δούλῳ   μου·   ποίησον   τοῦτο,   καὶ   ποιεῖ.
slave   of me :   Do   this,   and   he does.

9 ἀκούσας   δὲ   ταῦτα   ὁ   Ἰησοῦς   ἐθαύμασεν
And hearing   these [words] –   Jesus   marvelled at

αὐτόν,   καὶ   στραφεὶς   τῷ   ἀκολουθοῦντι   αὐτῷ
him,   and   turning   to the   ²following   ³him

ὄχλῳ   εἶπεν·   λέγω   ὑμῖν,   οὐδὲ   ἐν   τῷ
¹crowd   said :   I tell   you,   not   in   –

Ἰσραὴλ   τοσαύτην   πίστιν   εὗρον.   10 καὶ
Israel   such   faith   I found.   And

ὑποστρέψαντες   εἰς   τὸν   οἶκον   οἱ   πεμφθέντες
returning   to   the   house   the [ones] sent

εὗρον   τὸν   δοῦλον   ὑγιαίνοντα.   11 Καὶ
found   the   slave   well.   And

ἐγένετο   ἐν   τῷ   ἑξῆς   ἐπορεύθη   εἰς   πόλιν
it came to pass on the   next day   he went   into   a city

καλουμένην   Ναΐν,   καὶ   συνεπορεύοντο   αὐτῷ
being called   Nain,   and   went with   him

οἱ   μαθηταὶ   αὐτοῦ   καὶ   ὄχλος   πολύς.
the disciples   of him   and   crowd   a much.

12 ὡς   δὲ   ἤγγισεν   τῇ   πύλῃ   τῆς   πόλεως,   καὶ
And as   he drew near to the gate   of the   city,   and

ἰδοὺ   ἐξεκομίζετο   τεθνηκὼς   μονογενὴς
behold   was being carried out   having died   an only born
             [for burial]

υἱὸς   τῇ   μητρὶ   αὐτοῦ,   καὶ   αὕτη   ἦν   χήρα,
son to the   mother   of him,   and   this   was a widow,

καὶ   ὄχλος   τῆς   πόλεως   ἱκανὸς   ἦν   σὺν
and   a ²crowd   ³of the   ⁴city   ¹considerable was   with

αὐτῇ.   13 καὶ   ἰδὼν   αὐτὴν   ὁ   κύριος
her.   And   seeing   her   the   Lord

ἐσπλαγχνίσθη   ἐπ'   αὐτῇ   καὶ   εἶπεν   αὐτῇ·
felt compassion   over   her   and   said   to her :

μὴ   κλαῖε.   14 καὶ   προσελθὼν   ἥψατο   τῆς
Do not weep.   And   approaching   he touched   the

σοροῦ,   οἱ   δὲ   βαστάζοντες   ἔστησαν,   καὶ
bier,   and the [ones] bearing   stood,   and

εἶπεν·   νεανίσκε,   σοὶ   λέγω,   ἐγέρθητι.   15 καὶ
he said :   Young man, to thee I say,   Arise.   And

dead man sat up, and began to speak. And he gave him to his mother. [16]Fear seized them all; and they glorified God, saying, "A great prophet has arisen among us!" and "God has visited his people!" [17]And this report concerning him spread through the whole of Judea and all the surrounding country.

18 The disciples of John told him of all these things. [19]And John, calling to him two of his disciples, sent them to the Lord, saying, "Are you he who is to come, or shall we look for another?" [20]And when the men had come to him, they said, "John the Baptist has sent us to you, saying, 'Are you he who is to come, or shall we look for another?'" [21]In that hour he cured many of diseases and plagues and evil spirits, and on many that were blind he bestowed sight. [22]And he answered them, "Go and tell John what you have seen and heard: the blind receive their sight, the lame walk, lepers are cleansed, and the deaf hear, the dead

ἀνεκάθισεν ὁ νεκρὸς καὶ ἤρξατο λαλεῖν,
sat up   the dead man and   began   to speak,

καὶ ἔδωκεν αὐτὸν τῇ μητρὶ αὐτοῦ.
and he gave   him   to the mother of him.

16 ἔλαβεν δὲ φόβος πάντας, καὶ ἐδόξαζον
And ²took   ¹fear ³all,   and they glorified

τὸν θεὸν λέγοντες ὅτι προφήτης μέγας
 - God   saying[,]   -   prophet   A great

ἠγέρθη ἐν ἡμῖν, καὶ ὅτι ἐπεσκέψατο ὁ
was raised among us,   and[,] - ²visited   -

θεὸς τὸν λαὸν αὐτοῦ. 17 καὶ ἐξῆλθεν ὁ
¹God the people of him.   And went forth -

λόγος οὗτος ἐν ὅλῃ τῇ Ἰουδαίᾳ περὶ
word this in all the Judæa ⁵concerning

αὐτοῦ καὶ πάσῃ τῇ περιχώρῳ.
⁶him ¹and ²all ³the ⁴neighbourhood.

18 Καὶ ἀπήγγειλαν Ἰωάννῃ οἱ μαθηταὶ
And   reported   to John the disciples

αὐτοῦ περὶ πάντων τούτων. καὶ
of him about   all   these things. And

προσκαλεσάμενος δύο τινὰς τῶν μαθητῶν
calling to [him] ²two ¹a certain of the disciples

αὐτοῦ ὁ Ἰωάννης 19 ἔπεμψεν πρὸς τὸν
of him - John   sent   to   the

κύριον λέγων· σὺ εἶ ὁ ἐρχόμενος, ἢ ἄλλον
Lord saying : Thou art the coming [one], or another

προσδοκῶμεν; 20 παραγενόμενοι δὲ πρὸς
may we expect?   And coming   to

αὐτὸν οἱ ἄνδρες εἶπαν· Ἰωάννης ὁ βαπτιστὴς
him the men said : John the Baptist

ἀπέστειλεν ἡμᾶς πρὸς σὲ λέγων· σὺ εἶ ὁ
sent   us   to thee saying : Thou art the

ἐρχόμενος, ἢ ἄλλον προσδοκῶμεν; 21 ἐν
coming [one], or another may we expect?   In

ἐκείνῃ τῇ ὥρᾳ ἐθεράπευσεν πολλοὺς ἀπὸ
that - hour he healed   many from(of)

νόσων καὶ μαστίγων καὶ πνευμάτων πονηρῶν,
diseases and plagues and spirits   evil,

καὶ τυφλοῖς πολλοῖς ἐχαρίσατο βλέπειν.
and blind persons to many he gave   to see.

22 καὶ ἀποκριθεὶς εἶπεν αὐτοῖς· πορευθέντες
And answering he said to them : Going

ἀπαγγείλατε Ἰωάννῃ ἃ εἴδετε καὶ
report   to John [the things] which ye saw and

ἠκούσατε· τυφλοὶ ἀναβλέπουσιν, χωλοὶ
heard: blind men see again,   lame men

περιπατοῦσιν, λεπροὶ καθαρίζονται, καὶ κωφοὶ
walk,   lepers are being cleansed, and deaf men

are raised up, the poor have good news preached to them. [23]And blessed is he who takes no offense at me."

24 When the messengers of John had gone, he began to speak to the crowds concerning John: "What did you go out into the wilderness to behold? A reed shaken by the wind? [25]What then did you go out to see? A man clothed in soft raiment? Behold, those who are gorgeously appareled and live in luxury are in kings' courts. [26]What then did you go out to see? A prophet? Yes, I tell you, and more than a prophet. [27]This is he of whom it is written,

'Behold, I send my messenger before thy face, who shall prepare thy way before thee.'

[28]I tell you, among those born of women none is greater than John; yet he who is least in the kingdom of God is greater than he." [29](When they heard this all the people and the tax collectors justified God, having been baptized with the baptism of John; [30]but the Pharisees and the lawyers rejected the purpose of God for

ἀκούουσιν, νεκροὶ ἐγείρονται, πτωχοὶ
hear, dead men are raised, poor people

εὐαγγελίζονται· 23 καὶ μακάριός ἐστιν ὃς ἐὰν
are evangelized; and blessed is whoever

μὴ σκανδαλισθῇ ἐν ἐμοί. 24 Ἀπελθόντων δὲ
is not offended in me. And going away
=as the

τῶν ἀγγέλων Ἰωάννου ἤρξατο λέγειν πρὸς
the messengers of John[a] he began to say to
messengers of John went away

τοὺς ὄχλους περὶ Ἰωάννου· τί ἐξήλθατε
the crowds concerning John : What went ye forth

εἰς τὴν ἔρημον θεάσασθαι; κάλαμον ὑπὸ
into the desert to see? a reed by

ἀνέμου σαλευόμενον; 25 ἀλλὰ τί ἐξήλθατε
wind being shaken? But what went ye forth

ἰδεῖν; ἄνθρωπον ἐν μαλακοῖς ἱματίοις
to see? a man in soft garments

ἠμφιεσμένον; ἰδοὺ οἱ ἐν ἱματισμῷ ἐνδόξῳ
having been behold[,] the [1]in [2]raiment [3]splendid
clothed? [ones]

καὶ τρυφῇ ὑπάρχοντες ἐν τοῖς βασιλείοις
[4]and [6]in luxury [5]being [3]in - [9]royal palaces

εἰσίν. 26 ἀλλὰ τί ἐξήλθατε ἰδεῖν; προφήτην;
[7]are. But what went ye forth to see? a prophet?

ναὶ λέγω ὑμῖν, καὶ περισσότερον προφήτου.
yes I tell you, and more [than] a prophet.

27 οὗτός ἐστιν περὶ οὗ γέγραπται· ἰδοὺ
This is he concerning whom it has been written : Behold

ἀποστέλλω τὸν ἄγγελόν μου πρὸ προσώπου
I send the messenger of me before [the] face

σου, ὃς κατασκευάσει τὴν ὁδόν σου
of thee, who will prepare the way of thee

ἔμπροσθέν σου. 28 λέγω ὑμῖν, μείζων
before thee. I tell you, [6]greater

ἐν γεννητοῖς γυναικῶν Ἰωάννου οὐδείς
[1]among [2][those] born [3]of women [7][than] [8]John [4]no one

ἐστιν· ὁ δὲ μικρότερος ἐν τῇ βασιλείᾳ τοῦ
[5]is; but the less in the kingdom -

θεοῦ μείζων αὐτοῦ ἐστιν. 29 καὶ πᾶς ὁ
of God greater [than] he is. And all the

λαὸς ἀκούσας καὶ οἱ τελῶναι ἐδικαίωσαν
people hearing and the tax-collectors justified

τὸν θεόν, βαπτισθέντες τὸ βάπτισμα
- God, being baptized [with] the baptism

Ἰωάννου· 30 οἱ δὲ Φαρισαῖοι καὶ οἱ
of John; but the Pharisees and the

νομικοὶ τὴν βουλὴν τοῦ θεοῦ ἠθέτησαν εἰς
lawyers [4]the [5]counsel - [6]of God [1]rejected [3]for

themselves, not having been baptized by him.)

31 "To what then shall I compare the men of this generation, and what are they like? [32] They are like children sitting in the market place and calling to one another,

'We piped to you, and you did not dance; we wailed, and you did not weep.

[33] For John the Baptist has come eating no bread and drinking no wine; and you say, 'He has a demon.' [34] The Son of man has come eating and drinking; and you say, 'Behold, a glutton and a drunkard, a friend of tax collectors and sinners!' [35] Yet wisdom is justified by all her children."

36 One of the Pharisees asked him to eat with him, and he went into the Pharisee's house, and sat at table. [37] And behold, a woman of the city, who was a sinner, when she learned that he was sitting at table in the Pharisee's house, brought an alabaster flask of ointment, [38] and standing behind him at his feet, weeping, she began to wet his feet with her tears, and wiped them with the hair of her head,

ἑαυτούς, μὴ βαπτισθέντες ὑπ' αὐτοῦ. 31 Τίνι
[3]themselves, not being baptized by him. To what

οὖν ὁμοιώσω τοὺς ἀνθρώπους τῆς γενεᾶς
then may I liken the men - generation

ταύτης, καὶ τίνι εἰσὶν ὅμοιοι; 32 ὅμοιοί εἰσιν
of this, and to what are they like? Like are they

παιδίοις τοῖς ἐν ἀγορᾷ καθημένοις καὶ
to children - in a marketplace sitting and

προσφωνοῦσιν ἀλλήλοις ἃ λέγει· ηὐλήσαμεν
calling to one another who says: We piped

ὑμῖν καὶ οὐκ ὠρχήσασθε· ἐθρηνήσαμεν καὶ
to you and ye did not dance; we mourned and

οὐκ ἐκλαύσατε. 33 ἐλήλυθεν γὰρ Ἰωάννης
ye did not weep. For has come John

ὁ βαπτιστὴς μὴ ἐσθίων ἄρτον μήτε πίνων
the Baptist not eating bread nor drinking

οἶνον, καὶ λέγετε· δαιμόνιον ἔχει.
wine, and ye say: A demon he has.

34 ἐλήλυθεν ὁ υἱὸς τοῦ ἀνθρώπου ἐσθίων
Has come the Son - of man eating

καὶ πίνων, καὶ λέγετε· ἰδοὺ ἄνθρωπος
and drinking, and ye say: Behold[,] a man

φάγος καὶ οἰνοπότης, φίλος τελωνῶν καὶ
a glutton and a winebibber, a friend of tax-collectors and

ἁμαρτωλῶν. 35 καὶ ἐδικαιώθη ἡ σοφία
of sinners. And was(is) justified - wisdom

ἀπὸ πάντων τῶν τέκνων αὐτῆς.
from(by) all the children of her.

36 Ἠρώτα δέ τις αὐτὸν τῶν Φαρισαίων
And [4]asked [1]a certain one [5]him [2]of the [3]Pharisees

ἵνα φάγῃ μετ' αὐτοῦ· καὶ εἰσελθὼν εἰς
that he would eat with him; and entering into

τὸν οἶκον τοῦ Φαρισαίου κατεκλίθη. 37 καὶ
the house of the Pharisee he reclined. And[,]

ἰδοὺ γυνὴ ἥτις ἦν ἐν τῇ πόλει ἁμαρτωλός,
behold[,] a woman who was in the city a sinner,

καὶ ἐπιγνοῦσα ὅτι κατάκειται ἐν τῇ
and knowing that he reclines in the

οἰκίᾳ τοῦ Φαρισαίου, κομίσασα ἀλάβαστρον
house of the Pharisee, bringing an alabaster box

μύρου 38 καὶ στᾶσα ὀπίσω παρὰ τοὺς
of ointment and standing behind at the

πόδας αὐτοῦ κλαίουσα, τοῖς δάκρυσιν
feet of him weeping, with the(her) tears

ἤρξατο βρέχειν τοὺς πόδας αὐτοῦ, καὶ
began to wet the feet of him, and

ταῖς θριξὶν τῆς κεφαλῆς αὐτῆς ἐξέμασσεν,
with the hairs of the head of her wiped off,

and kissed his feet, and
anointed them with the
ointment. [39]Now when
the Pharisee who had
invited him saw it, he
said to himself, "If this
man were a prophet, he
would have known who
and what sort of woman
this is who is touching
him, for she is a sinner."
[40]And Jesus answering
said to him, "Simon, I
have something to say to
you." And he answered,
"What is it, Teacher?"
[41]"A certain creditor had
two debtors; one owed
five hundred denarii, and
the other fifty. [42]When
they could not pay, he
forgave them both. Now
which of them will love
him more?" [43]Simon
answered, "The one, I
suppose, to whom he
forgave more." And he
said to him, "You have
judged rightly." [44]Then
turning toward the
woman he said to Simon,
"Do you see this woman?
I entered your house,
you gave me no water for
my feet, but she has wet
my feet with her tears
and wiped them with
her hair. [45]You gave me
no kiss, but from the
time I came in she has
not ceased to kiss my

καὶ κατεφίλει τοὺς πόδας αὐτοῦ καὶ
and fervently kissed the feet of him and

ἤλειφεν τῷ μύρῳ. 39 ἰδὼν δὲ ὁ Φαρισαῖος
anointed with the ointment.   But ⁶seeing ¹the ²Pharisee

ὁ καλέσας αὐτὸν εἶπεν ἐν ἑαυτῷ λέγων·
- ³having invited ⁴him spoke within himself saying :

οὗτος εἰ ἦν [ὁ] προφήτης, ἐγίνωσκεν ἂν
This man if he was the prophet, would have known

τίς καὶ ποταπὴ ἡ γυνὴ ἥτις ἅπτεται
who and what sort the woman who is touching

αὐτοῦ, ὅτι ἁμαρτωλός ἐστιν. 40 καὶ
him, because a sinner she is.   And

ἀποκριθεὶς ὁ Ἰησοῦς εἶπεν πρὸς αὐτόν·
answering - Jesus said to him :

Σίμων, ἔχω σοί τι εἰπεῖν. ὁ δέ· διδάσκαλε,
Simon, I have to thee something to say. And he : Teacher,

εἰπέ, φησίν. 41 δύο χρεοφειλέται ἦσαν
say, says.   Two debtors were
=A certain creditor had two debtors;

δανειστῇ τινι· ὁ εἷς ὤφειλεν δηνάρια
creditor to a certain;ᵉ the one owed denarii

πεντακόσια, ὁ δὲ ἕτερος πεντήκοντα. 42 μὴ
five hundred, and the other fifty.   Not
=As they had no[thing]

ἐχόντων αὐτῶν ἀποδοῦναι ἀμφοτέροις
having themᵃ to repay ᵇboth

ἐχαρίσατο. τίς οὖν αὐτῶν πλεῖον ἀγαπήσει
¹he freely forgave. Who then of them more will love

αὐτόν; 43 ἀποκριθεὶς Σίμων εἶπεν·
him? Answering Simon said :

ὑπολαμβάνω ὅτι ᾧ τὸ πλεῖον ἐχαρίσατο.
I suppose[,] - to whom the more he freely forgave.

ὁ δὲ εἶπεν αὐτῷ· ὀρθῶς ἔκρινας. 44 καὶ
And he said to him : Rightly thou didst judge.   And

στραφεὶς πρὸς τὴν γυναῖκα τῷ Σίμωνι
turning to the woman - to Simon

ἔφη· βλέπεις ταύτην τὴν γυναῖκα; εἰσῆλθόν
he said : Seest thou this - woman? I entered

σου εἰς τὴν οἰκίαν, ὕδωρ μοι ἐπὶ πόδας
of thee into the house, water to me on(for) [my] feet

οὐκ ἔδωκας· αὕτη δὲ τοῖς δάκρυσιν
thou gavest not; but this woman with the(her) tears

ἔβρεξέν μου τοὺς πόδας καὶ ταῖς θριξὶν
wet of me the feet and with the hairs

αὐτῆς ἐξέμαξεν. 45 φίλημά μοι οὐκ ἔδωκας·
of her wiped off.   A kiss to me thou gavest not;

αὕτη δὲ ἀφ᾽ ἧς εἰσῆλθον οὐ διέλειπεν
but this woman from [the time] I entered ceased not
which

feet. ⁴⁶You did not anoint my head with oil, but she has anointed my feet with ointment. ⁴⁷Therefore I tell you, her sins, which are many, are forgiven, for she loved much; but he who is forgiven little, loves little." ⁴⁸And he said to her, "Your sins are forgiven." ⁴⁹Then those who were at table with him began to say among themselves, "Who is this, who even forgives sins?" ⁵⁰And he said to the woman, "Your faith has saved you; go in peace."

καταφιλοῦσά μου τοὺς πόδας. **46** ἐλαίῳ
fervently kissing of me the feet.　　With oil

τὴν κεφαλήν μου οὐκ ἤλειψας· αὔτη δὲ
the head of me thou didst not anoint; but this woman

μύρῳ ἤλειψεν τοὺς πόδας μου. **47** οὗ
with ointment anointed the feet of me.　　Of which
　　　　　　　　　　　　　　　　　= Wherefore

χάριν λέγω σοι, ἀφέωνται αἱ ἁμαρτίαι
for the sake of I tell thee, ⁵have been forgiven ¹the ²sins

αὐτῆς αἱ πολλαί, ὅτι ἠγάπησεν πολύ·
⁴of her － ²many, because she loved much;

ᾧ δὲ ὀλίγον ἀφίεται, ὀλίγον ἀγαπᾷ.
but to whom little is forgiven, little he loves.

48 εἶπεν δὲ αὐτῇ· ἀφέωνταί σου αἱ
And he said to her : Have been forgiven of thee the

ἁμαρτίαι. **49** καὶ ἤρξαντο οἱ συνανακείμενοι
sins.　　And began the [ones] reclining with [him]

λέγειν ἐν ἑαυτοῖς· τίς οὗτός ἐστιν, ὃς καὶ
to say among themselves : Who this is, who even

ἁμαρτίας ἀφίησιν; **50** εἶπεν δὲ πρὸς τὴν
sins forgives?　　But he said to the

γυναῖκα· ἡ πίστις σου σέσωκέν σε·
woman : The faith of thee has saved thee;

πορεύου εἰς εἰρήνην.
go in peace.

CHAPTER 8

SOON afterward he went on through cities and villages, preaching and bringing the good news of the kingdom of God. And the twelve were with him, ²and also some women who had been healed of evil spirits and infirmities: Mary, called Mag'dalene, from whom seven demons had gone out, ³and Jo-an'na, the wife of Chu'za, Herod's steward, and Susanna, and many others, who provided for themᵘ out of their means.

ᵘ Other ancient authorities read *him*

8 Καὶ ἐγένετο ἐν τῷ καθεξῆς καὶ αὐτὸς
And it came to pass afterwards *and* he

διώδευεν κατὰ πόλιν καὶ κώμην κηρύσσων
journeyed through every† city and village proclaiming

καὶ εὐαγγελιζόμενος τὴν βασιλείαν τοῦ
and preaching the kingdom －

θεοῦ, καὶ οἱ δώδεκα σὺν αὐτῷ, **2** καὶ
of God, and the twelve with him, and

γυναῖκές τινες αἳ ἦσαν τεθεραπευμέναι ἀπὸ
women certain who were having been healed from

πνευμάτων πονηρῶν καὶ ἀσθενειῶν, Μαρία
spirits evil and infirmities, Mary

ἡ καλουμένη Μαγδαληνή, ἀφ' ἧς δαιμόνια
－ being called Magdalene, from whom demons

ἑπτὰ ἐξεληλύθει, **3** καὶ Ἰωάννα γυνὴ Χουζᾶ
seven had gone out, and Joanna wife of Chuza

ἐπιτρόπου Ἡρῴδου καὶ Σουσάννα καὶ
steward of Herod and Susanna and

ἕτεραι πολλαί, αἵτινες διηκόνουν αὐτοῖς
others many, who ministered to them

ἐκ τῶν ὑπαρχόντων αὐταῖς.
out of the possessions to them.º

4 And when a great crowd came together and people from town after town came to him, he said in a parable: 5 "A sower went out to sow his seed; and as he sowed, some fell along the path, and was trodden under foot, and the birds of the air devoured it. 6 And some fell on the rock; and as it grew up, it withered away, because it had no moisture. 7 And some fell among thorns; and the thorns grew with it and choked it. 8 And some fell into good soil and grew, and yielded a hundredfold." As he said this, he called out, "He who has ears to hear, let him hear."

9 And when his disciples asked him what this parable meant, 10 he said, "To you it has been given to know the secrets of the kingdom of God; but for others they are in parables, so that seeing they may not see, and hearing they may not understand. 11 Now the parable is this: The seed is the word of God. 12 The ones

4 Συνιόντος δὲ ὄχλου πολλοῦ καὶ τῶν
And coming together crowd a much and the [ones]
= when a great crowd came together and people in each city

κατὰ πόλιν ἐπιπορευομένων πρὸς αὐτὸν
in each city† resorting* to him
resorted

εἶπεν διὰ παραβολῆς· 5 ἐξῆλθεν ὁ σπείρων
he said by a parable : Went forth the [one] sowing

τοῦ σπεῖραι τὸν σπόρον αὐτοῦ. καὶ ἐν τῷ
- to sow^d the seed of him. And in the

σπείρειν αὐτὸν ὃ μὲν ἔπεσεν παρὰ τὴν
to sow him^be this fell by the
= as he sowed

ὁδὸν καὶ κατεπατήθη, καὶ τὰ πετεινὰ τοῦ
way and was trodden down, and the birds of the

οὐρανοῦ κατέφαγεν αὐτό. 6 καὶ ἕτερον
heaven(air) devoured it. And other [seed]

κατέπεσεν ἐπὶ τὴν πέτραν, καὶ φυὲν
fell on the rock, and grown

ἐξηράνθη διὰ τὸ μὴ ἔχειν ἰκμάδα.
it was withered because of the not to have moisture.
= because it had no moisture.

7 καὶ ἕτερον ἔπεσεν ἐν μέσῳ τῶν ἀκανθῶν, καὶ
And other fell in [the] of the thorns, and
midst

συμφυεῖσαι αἱ ἄκανθαι ἀπέπνιξαν αὐτό.
growing up with [it] the thorns choked it.

8 καὶ ἕτερον ἔπεσεν εἰς τὴν γῆν τὴν
And other fell in the soil -

ἀγαθὴν καὶ φυὲν ἐποίησεν καρπὸν
good and grown it produced fruit

ἑκατονταπλασίονα. ταῦτα λέγων ἐφώνει· ὁ
a hundredfold. These things saying he called: The [one]

ἔχων ὦτα ἀκούειν ἀκουέτω. 9 Ἐπηρώτων δὲ
having ears to hear let him hear. And questioned

αὐτὸν οἱ μαθηταὶ αὐτοῦ τίς αὕτη εἴη ἡ
him the disciples of him what ¹this ²might be -

παραβολή. 10 ὁ δὲ εἶπεν· ὑμῖν δέδοται
³parable. And he said : To you it has been given

γνῶναι τὰ μυστήρια τῆς βασιλείας τοῦ
to know the mysteries of the kingdom -

θεοῦ, τοῖς δὲ λοιποῖς ἐν παραβολαῖς, ἵνα
of God, but to the rest in parables, that

βλέποντες μὴ βλέπωσιν καὶ ἀκούοντες μὴ
seeing they may not see and hearing not

συνιῶσιν. 11 ἔστιν δὲ αὕτη ἡ παραβολή.
they may understand. ⁴is ¹Now ²this - ³parable.

ὁ σπόρος ἐστὶν ὁ λόγος τοῦ θεοῦ.
The seed is the word - of God.

I.G.E.—10

along the path are those who have heard; then the devil comes and takes away the word from their hearts, that they may not believe and be saved. ¹³And the ones on the rock are those who, when they hear the word, receive it with joy; but these have no root, they believe for a while and in time of temptation fall away. ¹⁴And as for what fell among the thorns, they are those who hear, but as they go on their way they are choked by the cares and riches and pleasures of life, and their fruit does not mature. ¹⁵And as for that in the good soil, they are those who, hearing the word, hold it fast in an honest and good heart, and bring forth fruit with patience.

16 "No one after lighting a lamp covers it with a vessel, or puts it under a bed, but puts it on a stand, that those who enter may see the light. ¹⁷For nothing is hid that shall not be made manifest, nor anything secret that shall not be known and come to light. ¹⁸Take heed then how you hear; for to him who has will more be given, and from him who

12 οἱ δὲ παρὰ τὴν ὁδόν εἰσιν οἱ ἀκούσαντες,
And the [ones] by the way are the [ones] hearing,

εἶτα ἔρχεται ὁ διάβολος καὶ αἴρει τὸν
then comes the devil and takes the

λόγον ἀπὸ τῆς καρδίας αὐτῶν, ἵνα μὴ
word from the heart of them, lest

πιστεύσαντες σωθῶσιν. 13 οἱ δὲ ἐπὶ τῆς
believing they may be saved. And the [ones] on the

πέτρας οἵ ὅταν ἀκούσωσιν μετὰ χαρᾶς
rock who when they hear with joy

δέχονται τὸν λόγον· καὶ οὗτοι ῥίζαν
receive the word; and these root

οὐκ ἔχουσιν, οἳ πρὸς καιρὸν πιστεύουσιν
have not, who for a time believe

καὶ ἐν καιρῷ πειρασμοῦ ἀφίστανται. 14 τὸ
and in time of trial withdraw. the [one]

δὲ εἰς τὰς ἀκάνθας πεσόν, οὗτοί εἰσιν
And in the thorns falling, these are

οἱ ἀκούσαντες, καὶ ὑπὸ μεριμνῶν καὶ
the [ones] hearing, ¹and ⁴by ⁵cares ⁶and

πλούτου καὶ ἡδονῶν τοῦ βίου πορευόμενοι
⁷riches ⁸and ⁹pleasures – ¹⁰of life ²going

συμπνίγονται καὶ οὐ τελεσφοροῦσιν. 15 τὸ
³are choked and do not bear [fruit] to maturity. the [one]

δὲ ἐν τῇ καλῇ γῇ, οὗτοί εἰσιν οἵτινες ἐν
And in the good soil, these are [those] who in

καρδίᾳ καλῇ καὶ ἀγαθῇ ἀκούσαντες τὸν
heart a worthy and good hearing the

λόγον κατέχουσιν καὶ καρποφοροῦσιν ἐν
word hold fast and bear fruit in

ὑπομονῇ. 16 Οὐδεὶς δὲ λύχνον ἅψας
patience. Now no one a lamp having lit

καλύπτει αὐτὸν σκεύει ἢ ὑποκάτω κλίνης
hides it with a vessel or underneath a couch

τίθησιν, ἀλλ' ἐπὶ λυχνίας τίθησιν, ἵνα οἱ
puts, but on a lampstand puts, that the

εἰσπορευόμενοι βλέπωσιν τὸ φῶς. 17 οὐ
[ones] coming in may see the light. not

γάρ ἐστιν κρυπτὸν ὃ οὐ φανερὸν
For [anything] is hidden which ²not ⁴manifest

γενήσεται, οὐδὲ ἀπόκρυφον ὃ οὐ μὴ
¹will ³become, nor secret which by no means

γνωσθῇ καὶ εἰς φανερὸν ἔλθῃ. 18 βλέπετε
will be known and to [be] manifest come. See

οὖν πῶς ἀκούετε· ὃς ἂν γὰρ ἔχῃ,
therefore how ye hear; for whoever has,

δοθήσεται αὐτῷ· καὶ ὃς ἂν μὴ ἔχῃ,
it will be given to him; and whoever has not,

has not, even what he thinks that he has will be taken away."

19 Then his mother and his brothers came to him, but they could not reach him for the crowd. ²⁰And he was told, "Your mother and your brothers are standing outside, desiring to see you." ²¹But he said to them, "My mother and my brothers are those who hear the word of God and do it."

22 One day he got into a boat with his disciples, and he said to them, "Let us go across to the other side of the lake." So they set out, ²³and as they sailed he fell asleep. And a storm of wind came down on the lake, and they were filling with water, and were in danger. ²⁴And they went and woke him, saying, "Master, Master, we are perishing!" And he awoke and rebuked the wind and the raging waves; and they ceased, and there was a calm. ²⁵He said to them, "Where is your faith?" And they were afraid, and they marveled, saying to one another, "Who then is this, that he commands even wind and water, and they obey him?"

καὶ ὃ δοκεῖ ἔχειν ἀρθήσεται ἀπ' αὐτοῦ.
even what he seems to have will be taken from him.

19 Παρεγένετο δὲ πρὸς αὐτὸν ἡ μήτηρ
And came to him the mother

καὶ οἱ ἀδελφοὶ αὐτοῦ, καὶ οὐκ ἠδύναντο
and the brothers of him, and were not able

συντυχεῖν αὐτῷ διὰ τὸν ὄχλον. 20 ἀπηγγέλη δὲ
to come up with him be- the crowd. And it was reported
cause of

αὐτῷ· ἡ μήτηρ σου καὶ οἱ ἀδελφοί σου
to him : The mother of thee and the brothers of thee

ἑστήκασιν ἔξω ἰδεῖν θέλοντές σε. 21 ὁ δὲ
are standing outside ²to see ¹wishing thee. But he

ἀποκριθεὶς εἶπεν πρὸς αὐτούς· μήτηρ μου
answering said to them : Mother of me

καὶ ἀδελφοί μου οὗτοί εἰσιν οἱ τὸν λόγον
and brothers of me ²these ¹are ³the [ones] ⁷the ⁸word

τοῦ θεοῦ ἀκούοντες καὶ ποιοῦντες.
– ⁹of God ⁴hearing ⁵and ⁶doing.

22 Ἐγένετο δὲ ἐν μιᾷ τῶν ἡμερῶν καὶ
And it came to pass on one of the days and

αὐτὸς ἐνέβη εἰς πλοῖον καὶ οἱ μαθηταὶ
he embarked in a boat and the disciples

αὐτοῦ, καὶ εἶπεν πρὸς αὐτούς· διέλθωμεν
of him, and he said to them; Let us go over

εἰς τὸ πέραν τῆς λίμνης· καὶ ἀνήχθησαν.
to the other side of the lake; and they put to sea.

23 πλεόντων δὲ αὐτῶνª ἀφύπνωσεν. καὶ
And sailing them he fell asleep. And
=as they sailed

κατέβη λαῖλαψ ἀνέμου εἰς τὴν λίμνην, καὶ
came down a storm of wind to the lake, and

συνεπληροῦντο καὶ ἐκινδύνευον. 24 προσ-
they were filling up and were in danger. ap-

ελθόντες δὲ διήγειραν αὐτὸν λέγοντες·
proaching And they awaken him saying :

ἐπιστάτα ἐπιστάτα, ἀπολλύμεθα. ὁ δὲ
Master, Master, we are perishing. But he

διεγερθεὶς ἐπετίμησεν τῷ ἀνέμῳ καὶ τῷ
being awakened rebuked the wind and the

κλύδωνι τοῦ ὕδατος· καὶ ἐπαύσαντο, καὶ ἐγένετο
roughness of the water; and they ceased, and there was

γαλήνη. 25 εἶπεν δὲ αὐτοῖς· ποῦ ἡ πίστις ὑμῶν;
a calm. Then he said to them: Where the faith of you?

φοβηθέντες δὲ ἐθαύμασαν, λέγοντες πρὸς
And fearing they marvelled, saying to

ἀλλήλους· τίς ἄρα οὗτός ἐστιν, ὅτι καὶ
one another : Who then ²this man ¹is, that ²even

τοῖς ἀνέμοις ἐπιτάσσει καὶ τῷ ὕδατι, καὶ
³the ⁴winds ¹he commands and the water, and

26 Then they arrived at the country of the Ger'asenes,ᵛ which is opposite Galilee. ²⁷And as he stepped out on land, there met him a man from the city who had demons; for a long time he had worn no clothes, and he lived not in a house but among the tombs. ²⁸When he saw Jesus, he cried out and fell down before him, and said with a loud voice, "What have you to do with me, Jesus, Son of the Most High God? I beseech you, do not torment me." ²⁹For he had commanded the unclean spirit to come out of the man. (For many a time it had seized him; he was kept under guard, and bound with chains and fetters, but he broke the bonds and was driven by the demon into the desert.) ³⁰Jesus then asked him, "What is your name?" And he said, "Legion"; for many demons had entered him. ³¹And they begged him not to command them to depart into the abyss. ³²Now a large herd of swine was feeding there on the hillside; and they begged him to let them enter these. So he gave

ὑπακούουσιν αὐτῷ;
they obey him?

26 Καὶ κατέπλευσαν εἰς
And they sailed down to

τὴν χώραν τῶν Γερασηνῶν, ἥτις ἐστὶν
the country of the Gerasenes, which is

ἀντιπέρα τῆς Γαλιλαίας.
opposite - Galilee.

27 ἐξελθόντι δὲ
And going out
=as he went out

αὐτῷ ἐπὶ τὴν γῆν ὑπήντησεν ἀνήρ τις
himᵉ onto the land met [him] man a certain

ἐκ τῆς πόλεως ἔχων δαιμόνια, καὶ χρόνῳ
out of the city having demons, and ²time

ἱκανῷ οὐκ ἐνεδύσατο ἱμάτιον, καὶ ἐν οἰκίᾳ
¹for a con- put not on a garment, and in a house
siderable

οὐκ ἔμενεν ἀλλ᾽ ἐν τοῖς μνήμασιν.
remained not but among the tombs.

28 ἰδὼν
seeing

δὲ τὸν Ἰησοῦν ἀνακράξας προσέπεσεν αὐτῷ
And - Jesus crying out he fell prostrate before him

καὶ φωνῇ μεγάλῃ εἶπεν· τί ἐμοὶ καὶ σοί,
and voice in a great(loud) said : What to me and to thee,

Ἰησοῦ υἱὲ τοῦ θεοῦ τοῦ ὑψίστου; δέομαί
Jesus Son - of God - most high? I beg

σου, μή με βασανίσῃς.
of thee, do not me torment.

29 παρήγγελλεν
he charged

γὰρ τῷ πνεύματι τῷ ἀκαθάρτῳ ἐξελθεῖν
For the spirit - unclean to come out

ἀπὸ τοῦ ἀνθρώπου. πολλοῖς γὰρ χρόνοις
from the man. For many times

συνηρπάκει αὐτόν, καὶ ἐδεσμεύετο ἁλύσεσιν
it had seized him, and he was bound with chains

καὶ πέδαις φυλασσόμενος, καὶ διαρήσσων
and fetters being guarded, and tearing asunder

τὰ δεσμὰ ἠλαύνετο ἀπὸ τοῦ δαιμονίου εἰς
the bonds he was driven from(by) the demon into

τὰς ἐρήμους.
the deserts.

30 ἐπηρώτησεν δὲ αὐτὸν ὁ
And questioned him -

Ἰησοῦς· τί σοι ὄνομά ἐστιν; ὁ δὲ εἶπεν·
Jesus : What to thee name is?ᵉ And he said :

λεγιών, ὅτι εἰσῆλθεν δαιμόνια πολλὰ εἰς
Legion, because ³entered ²demons ¹many into

αὐτόν.
him.

31 καὶ παρεκάλουν αὐτὸν ἵνα μὴ
And they besought him that not

ἐπιτάξῃ αὐτοῖς εἰς τὴν ἄβυσσον ἀπελθεῖν.
he would order them into the abyss to go away.

32 ἦν δὲ ἐκεῖ ἀγέλη χοίρων ἱκανῶν
Now there was there a herd pigs of many

βοσκομένη ἐν τῷ ὄρει· καὶ παρεκάλεσαν
feeding in the mountain; and they besought

αὐτὸν ἵνα ἐπιτρέψῃ αὐτοῖς εἰς ἐκείνους
him that he would allow them into those

ᵛ Other ancient authorities read Gadarenes, others Gergesenes

them leave. ³³Then the demons came out of the man and entered the swine, and the herd rushed down the steep bank into the lake and were drowned.

34 When the herdsmen saw what had happened, they fled, and told it in the city and in the country. ³⁵Then people went out to see what had happened, and they came to Jesus, and found the man from whom the demons had gone, sitting at the feet of Jesus, clothed and in his right mind; and they were afraid. ³⁶And those who had seen it told them how he who had been possessed with demons was healed. ³⁷Then all the people of the surrounding country of the Ger′asenes[v] asked him to depart from them; for they were seized with great fear; so he got into the boat and returned. ³⁸The man from whom the demons had gone begged that he might be with him; but he sent him away, saying, ³⁹"Return to your home, and declare how much God has done for you."

[v] Other ancient authorities read *Gadarenes*, others *Gergesenes*

εἰσελθεῖν· καὶ ἐπέτρεψεν αὐτοῖς. 33 ἐξελθόντα
to enter;   and   he allowed   them.   ⁴coming out

δὲ τὰ δαιμόνια ἀπὸ τοῦ ἀνθρώπου εἰσῆλθον
¹So ²the ³demons from the   man   entered

εἰς τοὺς χοίρους, καὶ ὥρμησεν ἡ ἀγέλη
into the   pigs,   and rushed the herd

κατὰ τοῦ κρημνοῦ εἰς τὴν λίμνην καὶ
down the precipice into the   lake   and

ἀπεπνίγη.   34 ἰδόντες δὲ οἱ βόσκοντες
was choked.   And ³seeing ¹the [ones] ²feeding

τὸ   γεγονὸς   ἔφυγον καὶ ἀπήγγειλαν εἰς
⁴the thing ⁵having   fled   and   reported   in
          happened
=what had happened

τὴν πόλιν καὶ εἰς τοὺς ἀγρούς. 35 ἐξῆλθον
the city   and in   the   farms.   they went out

δὲ ἰδεῖν τὸ γεγονός, καὶ ἦλθον πρὸς τὸν
And to see the thing having and   came   to   -
          happened,
=what had happened,

Ἰησοῦν, καὶ εὗρον καθήμενον τὸν ἄνθρωπον
Jesus,   and found   sitting   the   man

ἀφ' οὗ τὰ δαιμόνια ἐξῆλθεν ἱματισμένον
from whom the demons   went out *having been* clothed

καὶ σωφρονοῦντα παρὰ τοὺς πόδας τοῦ
and being in his senses by   the   feet   -

Ἰησοῦ, καὶ ἐφοβήθησαν. 36 ἀπήγγειλαν δὲ
of Jesus, and they were afraid.   And ³reported

αὐτοῖς οἱ ἰδόντες πῶς ἐσώθη ὁ δαιμο-
⁴to them ¹the [ones] ²seeing ⁵how ⁶was healed ⁶the ⁷demon-

νισθείς.   37 καὶ ἠρώτησεν αὐτὸν ἅπαν τὸ
possessed.   And   asked   him   all   the

πλῆθος τῆς περιχώρου τῶν Γερασηνῶν
multitude of the neighbourhood of the   Gerasenes

ἀπελθεῖν ἀπ' αὐτῶν, ὅτι φόβῳ μεγάλῳ
to go away from   them, because fear with a great

συνείχοντο· αὐτὸς δὲ ἐμβὰς εἰς πλοῖον
they were seized;   so he   embarking in   a boat

ὑπέστρεψεν. 38 ἐδεῖτο δὲ αὐτοῦ ὁ ἀνὴρ
returned.   And begged of him the man

ἀφ' οὗ ἐξεληλύθει τὰ δαιμόνια εἶναι σὺν
from whom had gone out the demons to be with

αὐτῷ· ἀπέλυσεν δὲ αὐτὸν λέγων· 39 ὑπόστρεφε
him; but he dismissed him   saying :   Return

εἰς τὸν οἶκόν σου, καὶ διηγοῦ ὅσα σοι
to the house of thee, and relate what ²to thee
                                   things

ἐποίησεν ὁ θεός. καὶ ἀπῆλθεν καθ' ὅλην
²did   - ¹God. And he went away throughout all

And he went away, proclaiming throughout the whole city how much Jesus had done for him. 40 Now when Jesus returned, the crowd welcomed him, for they were all waiting for him. 41And there came a man named Ja'irus, who was a ruler of the synagogue; and falling at Jesus' feet he besought him to come to his house, 42for he had an only daughter, about twelve years of age, and she was dying.

As he went, the people pressed round him. 43And a woman who had had a flow of blood for twelve years[w] and could not be healed by any one 44came up behind him, and touched the fringe of his garment; and immediately her flow of blood ceased. 45And Jesus said, "Who was it that touched me?" When all denied it, Peter[x] said, "Master, the multitudes surround you and press upon you!" 46But Jesus said, "Some one touched me; for I perceive that power has gone forth from me."

τὴν πόλιν κηρύσσων ὅσα ἐποίησεν αὐτῷ
the city proclaiming what things ²did ³to him
ὁ Ἰησοῦς.
– ¹Jesus.

40 Ἐν δὲ τῷ ὑποστρέφειν τὸν Ἰησοῦν
Now in the to return – Jesus[be]
=when Jesus returned
ἀπεδέξατο αὐτὸν ὁ ὄχλος· ἦσαν γὰρ
welcomed him the crowd; for they were
πάντες προσδοκῶντες αὐτόν. 41 καὶ ἰδοὺ
all expecting him. And behold
ἦλθεν ἀνὴρ ᾧ ὄνομα Ἰάϊρος, καὶ οὗτος
came a man to whom name Jairus,[c] and this man
ἄρχων τῆς συναγωγῆς ὑπῆρχεν· καὶ πεσὼν
a ruler of the synagogue was; and falling
παρὰ τοὺς πόδας Ἰησοῦ παρεκάλει αὐτὸν
at the feet of Jesus he besought him
εἰσελθεῖν εἰς τὸν οἶκον αὐτοῦ, 42 ὅτι
to enter into the house of him, because
θυγάτηρ μονογενὴς ἦν αὐτῷ ὡς ἐτῶν
daughter an only born was to him[c] about of years
=he had an only daughter
δώδεκα καὶ αὕτη ἀπέθνῃσκεν. Ἐν δὲ τῷ
twelve and this(she) was dying. Now in the
=as he went
ὑπάγειν αὐτὸν οἱ ὄχλοι συνέπνιγον αὐτόν.
to go him[be] the crowds pressed upon him.
43 καὶ γυνὴ οὖσα ἐν ῥύσει αἵματος ἀπὸ
And a woman being in a flow of blood from
=having
ἐτῶν δώδεκα, ἥτις οὐκ ἴσχυσεν ἀπ'
years twelve, who was not able from
οὐδενὸς θεραπευθῆναι, 44 προσελθοῦσα ὄπισθεν
no(any)one to be healed, approaching behind
ἥψατο τοῦ κρασπέδου τοῦ ἱματίου αὐτοῦ,
touched the fringe of the garment of him,
καὶ παραχρῆμα ἔστη ἡ ῥύσις τοῦ αἵματος
and at once stood the flow of the blood
αὐτῆς. 45 καὶ εἶπεν ὁ Ἰησοῦς· τίς ὁ
of her. And said – Jesus : Who the
ἁψάμενός μου; ἀρνουμένων δὲ πάντων
[one] touching me? And denying all[a]
=when all denied
εἶπεν ὁ Πέτρος· ἐπιστάτα, οἱ ὄχλοι
said – Peter : Master, the crowds
συνέχουσίν σε καὶ ἀποθλίβουσιν. 46 ὁ δὲ
press upon thee and jostle. – But
Ἰησοῦς εἶπεν· ἥψατό μού τις· ἐγὼ γὰρ
Jesus said : Touched me someone; for I
ἔγνων δύναμιν ἐξεληλυθυῖαν ἀπ' ἐμοῦ.
knew power having gone forth from me.

[w] Other ancient authorities add *and had spent all her living upon physicians*

[x] Other ancient authorities add *and those who were with him*

47And when the woman saw that she was not hidden, she came trembling, and falling down before him declared in the presence of all the people why she had touched him, and how she had been immediately healed. 48And he said to her, "Daughter, your faith has made you well; go in peace."

49 While he was still speaking, a man from the ruler's house came and said, "Your daughter is dead; do not trouble the Teacher any more." 50But Jesus on hearing this answered him, "Do not fear; only believe, and she shall be well." 51And when he came to the house, he permitted no one to enter with him, except Peter and John and James, and the father and mother of the child. 52And all were weeping and bewailing her; but he said, "Do not weep; for she is not dead but sleeping." 53And they laughed at him, knowing that she was dead. 54But taking her by the hand he called, saying, "Child, arise." 55And her spirit returned, and she got up at once; and he directed that something should be given her to eat. 56And her parents were

47 ἰδοῦσα δὲ ἡ γυνὴ ὅτι οὐκ ἔλαθεν,
And ³seeing ¹the ²woman that she was not hidden,

τρέμουσα ἦλθεν καὶ προσπεσοῦσα αὐτῷ δι᾽
trembling came and prostrating before him ⁶for

ἣν αἰτίαν ἥψατο αὐτοῦ ἀπήγγειλεν ἐνώπιον
⁷what ⁸cause ⁹she touched ¹⁰him ¹declared ²before

παντὸς τοῦ λαοῦ, καὶ ὡς ἰάθη παραχρῆμα.
³all ⁴the ⁵people, and how she was cured at once.

48 ὁ δὲ εἶπεν αὐτῇ· θυγάτηρ, ἡ πίστις
And he said to her: Daughter, the faith

σου σέσωκέν σε· πορεύου εἰς εἰρήνην.
of thee has healed thee; go in peace.

49 Ἔτι αὐτοῦ λαλοῦντος ἔρχεταί τις παρὰ
Yet him speaking³ comes someone from
=While he was yet speaking

τοῦ ἀρχισυναγώγου λέγων ὅτι τέθνηκεν
the synagogue ruler saying[,] – Has died

ἡ θυγάτηρ σου· μηκέτι σκύλλε τὸν
the daughter of thee; no more trouble the

διδάσκαλον. 50 ὁ δὲ Ἰησοῦς ἀκούσας
teacher. – But Jesus hearing

ἀπεκρίθη αὐτῷ· μὴ φοβοῦ· μόνον πίστευσον,
answered him: Fear thou not; only believe,

καὶ σωθήσεται. 51 ἐλθὼν δὲ εἰς τὴν
and she will be healed. And coming into the

οἰκίαν οὐκ ἀφῆκεν εἰσελθεῖν τινα σὺν
house he allowed not to enter anyone with

αὐτῷ εἰ μὴ Πέτρον καὶ Ἰωάννην καὶ
him except Peter and John and

Ἰάκωβον καὶ τὸν πατέρα τῆς παιδὸς καὶ
James and the father of the maid and

τὴν μητέρα. 52 ἔκλαιον δὲ πάντες καὶ
the mother. And were weeping all and

ἐκόπτοντο αὐτήν. ὁ δὲ εἶπεν· μὴ κλαίετε·
bewailing her. But he said: Weep ye not;

οὐκ ἀπέθανεν ἀλλὰ καθεύδει. 53 καὶ
she did not die but sleeps. And

κατεγέλων αὐτοῦ, εἰδότες ὅτι ἀπέθανεν.
they ridiculed him, knowing that she died.

54 αὐτὸς δὲ κρατήσας τῆς χειρὸς αὐτῆς
But he holding the hand of her

ἐφώνησεν λέγων· ἡ παῖς, ἔγειρε. 55 καὶ
called saying: – Maid, arise. And

ἐπέστρεψεν τὸ πνεῦμα αὐτῆς, καὶ ἀνέστη
returned the spirit of her, and she rose up

παραχρῆμα, καὶ διέταξεν αὐτῇ δοθῆναι
at once, and he commanded ²to her ¹to be given

φαγεῖν. 56 καὶ ἐξέστησαν οἱ γονεῖς
to eat. And were amazed the parents

amazed; but he charged them to tell no one what had happened.

αὐτῆς· ὁ δὲ παρήγγειλεν αὐτοῖς μηδενὶ
of her; but he enjoined them ¹no one

εἰπεῖν τὸ γεγονός.
¹to tell the thing having happened.
=what had happened.

CHAPTER 9

AND he called the twelve together and gave them power and authority over all demons and to cure diseases, ²and he sent them out to preach the kingdom of God and to heal. ³And he said to them, "Take nothing for your journey, no staff, nor bag, nor bread, nor money; and do not have two tunics. ⁴And whatever house you enter, stay there, and from there depart. ⁵And wherever they do not receive you, when you leave that town shake off the dust from your feet as a testimony against them." ⁶And they departed and went through the villages, preaching the gospel and healing everywhere.

7 Now Herod the tetrarch heard of all that was done, and he was perplexed, because it was said by some that John had been raised from the dead, ⁸by some that Eli'jah had appeared, and by others that one

9 Συγκαλεσάμενος δὲ τοὺς δώδεκα ἔδωκεν
And having called together the twelve he gave

αὐτοῖς δύναμιν καὶ ἐξουσίαν ἐπὶ πάντα τὰ
them power and authority over all the

δαιμόνια καὶ νόσους θεραπεύειν· 2 καὶ
demons and diseases to heal; and

ἀπέστειλεν αὐτοὺς κηρύσσειν τὴν βασιλείαν
sent them to proclaim the kingdom

τοῦ θεοῦ καὶ ἰᾶσθαι, 3 καὶ εἶπεν πρὸς
- of God and to cure, and said to

αὐτούς· μηδὲν αἴρετε εἰς τὴν ὁδόν, μήτε
them: Nothing take ye for the way, neither

ῥάβδον μήτε πήραν μήτε ἄρτον μήτε
staff nor wallet nor bread nor

ἀργύριον μήτε ἀνὰ δύο χιτῶνας ἔχειν.
silver nor each two tunics to have.

4 καὶ εἰς ἣν ἂν οἰκίαν εἰσέλθητε, ἐκεῖ
And into whatever house ye may enter, there

μένετε καὶ ἐκεῖθεν ἐξέρχεσθε. 5 καὶ
remain and thence go forth. And

ὅσοι ἂν μὴ δέχωνται ὑμᾶς, ἐξερχόμενοι
as many as may not receive you, going forth

ἀπὸ τῆς πόλεως ἐκείνης τὸν κονιορτὸν
from - city that the dust

ἀπὸ τῶν ποδῶν ὑμῶν ἀποτινάσσετε εἰς
from the feet of you shake off for

μαρτύριον ἐπ᾽ αὐτούς. 6 ἐξερχόμενοι δὲ
a testimony against them. And going forth

διήρχοντο κατὰ τὰς κώμας εὐαγγελιζόμενοι
they went throughout the villages evangelizing
through

καὶ θεραπεύοντες πανταχοῦ. 7 Ἤκουσεν
and healing everywhere. ⁵heard

δὲ Ἡρῴδης ὁ τετραάρχης τὰ γινόμενα
¹And ²Herod ³the ⁴tetrarch the things happening

πάντα, καὶ διηπόρει διὰ τὸ λέγεσθαι
all, and was in perplexity because of the to be said
=because it was said

ὑπό τινων ὅτι Ἰωάννης ἠγέρθη ἐκ νεκρῶν,
by some that John was raised from [the] dead,

8 ὑπό τινων δὲ ὅτι Ἡλίας ἐφάνη, ἄλλων
and by some that Elias appeared, ²others

of the old prophets had risen. ⁹Herod said, "John I beheaded; but who is this about whom I hear such things?" And he sought to see him.

10 On their return the apostles told him what they had done. And he took them and withdrew apart to a city called Bethsa'ida. ¹¹When the crowds learned it, they followed him; and he welcomed them and spoke to them of the kingdom of God, and cured those who had need of healing. ¹²Now the day began to wear away; and the twelve came and said to him, "Send the crowd away, to go into the villages and country round about, to lodge and get provisions; for we are here in a lonely place." ¹³But he said to them, "You give them something to eat." They said, "We have no more than five loaves and two fish—unless we are to go and buy food for all these people." ¹⁴For there were about five thousand men. And he said to his disciples, "Make them

δὲ ὅτι προφήτης τις τῶν ἀρχαίων ἀνέστη.
¹but that prophet a certain of the ancients rose again.

9 εἶπεν δὲ [ὁ] Ἡρῴδης· Ἰωάννην ἐγὼ
But said – Herod : John I

ἀπεκεφάλισα· τίς δέ ἐστιν οὗτος περὶ οὗ
beheaded; but who is this about whom

ἀκούω τοιαῦτα; καὶ ἐζήτει ἰδεῖν αὐτόν.
I hear such things? And he sought to see him.

10 Καὶ ὑποστρέψαντες οἱ ἀπόστολοι
And having returned the apostles

διηγήσαντο αὐτῷ ὅσα ἐποίησαν. Καὶ
narrated to him what things they did. And

παραλαβὼν αὐτοὺς ὑπεχώρησεν κατ' ἰδίαν
taking them he departed privately

εἰς πόλιν καλουμένην Βηθσαϊδά. 11 οἱ δὲ
to a city being called Bethsaida. But the

ὄχλοι γνόντες ἠκολούθησαν αὐτῷ· καὶ
crowds knowing followed him; and

ἀποδεξάμενος αὐτοὺς ἐλάλει αὐτοῖς περὶ
welcoming them he spoke to them about

τῆς βασιλείας τοῦ θεοῦ, καὶ τοὺς χρείαν
the kingdom - of God, and the [ones] ²need

ἔχοντας θεραπείας ἰᾶτο. 12 Ἡ δὲ ἡμέρα
¹having of healing he cured. But the day

ἤρξατο κλίνειν· προσελθόντες δὲ οἱ δώδεκα
began to decline; and approaching the twelve

εἶπαν αὐτῷ· ἀπόλυσον τὸν ὄχλον, ἵνα
said to him : Dismiss the crowd, that

πορευθέντες εἰς τὰς κύκλῳ κώμας καὶ
going to ¹the ⁵around ²villages ³and

ἀγροὺς καταλύσωσιν καὶ εὕρωσιν ἐπισιτισμόν,
⁴farms they may lodge and may find provisions,

ὅτι ὧδε ἐν ἐρήμῳ τόπῳ ἐσμέν. 13 εἶπεν
because here in a desert place we are. he said

δὲ πρὸς αὐτούς· δότε αὐτοῖς φαγεῖν
And to them : ¹Give ³them ⁴to eat

ὑμεῖς. οἱ δὲ εἶπαν· οὐκ εἰσὶν ἡμῖν
²ye. But they said : There are not to usᵉ
=We have not

πλεῖον ἢ ἄρτοι πέντε καὶ ἰχθύες δύο, εἰ
more than loaves five and fishes two, un-

μήτι πορευθέντες ἡμεῖς ἀγοράσωμεν εἰς
less going we may buy for

πάντα τὸν λαὸν τοῦτον βρώματα. 14 ἦσαν
all - people this foods. there were

γὰρ ὡσεὶ ἄνδρες πεντακισχίλιοι. εἶπεν δὲ
For about men five thousand. And he said

πρὸς τοὺς μαθητὰς αὐτοῦ· κατακλίνατε
to the disciples of him : ¹Make ²to recline

sit down in companies, about fifty each." ¹⁵And they did so, and made them all sit down. ¹⁶And taking the five loaves and the two fish he looked up to heaven, and blessed and broke them, and gave them to the disciples to set before the crowd. ¹⁷And all ate and were satisfied. And they took up what was left over, twelve baskets of broken pieces.

18 Now it happened that as he was praying alone the disciples were with him; and he asked them, "Who do the people say that I am?" ¹⁹And they answered, "John the Baptist; but others say, Eli'jah; and others, that one of the old prophets has risen." ²⁰And he said to them, "But who do you say that I am?" And Peter answered, "The Christ of God." ²¹But he charged and commanded them to tell this to no one, ²²saying, "The Son of man must suffer many things, and be rejected by the elders and chief priests and scribes, and

αὐτοὺς κλισίας ὡσεὶ ἀνὰ πεντήκοντα.
²them [in] groups ¹about ²each ²fifty.

15 καὶ ἐποίησαν οὕτως καὶ κατέκλιναν
And they did so and made to recline

ἅπαντας. 16 λαβὼν δὲ τοὺς πέντε ἄρτους
all. And taking the five loaves

καὶ τοὺς δύο ἰχθύας, ἀναβλέψας εἰς τὸν
and the two fishes, looking up to –

οὐρανὸν εὐλόγησεν αὐτοὺς καὶ κατέκλασεν,
heaven he blessed them and broke,

καὶ ἐδίδου τοῖς μαθηταῖς παραθεῖναι τῷ
and gave to the disciples to set before the

ὄχλῳ. 17 καὶ ἔφαγον καὶ ἐχορτάσθησαν
crowd. And they ate and were satisfied

πάντες· καὶ ἤρθη τὸ περισσεῦσαν αὐτοῖς
all; and were taken the excess to them

κλασμάτων κόφινοι δώδεκα.
of fragments baskets twelve.

18 Καὶ ἐγένετο ἐν τῷ εἶναι αὐτὸν
And it came to pass in the to be him ᵇᵉ
=as he was

προσευχόμενον κατὰ μόνας συνῆσαν αὐτῷ
praying alone were with him

οἱ μαθηταί, καὶ ἐπηρώτησεν αὐτοὺς λέγων·
the disciples, and he questioned them saying :

τίνα με οἱ ὄχλοι λέγουσιν εἶναι; 19 οἱ δὲ
Whom me the crowds say to be? And they
=Whom do the crowds say that I am?

ἀποκριθέντες εἶπαν· Ἰωάννην τὸν βαπτιστήν,
answering said : John the Baptist,

ἄλλοι δὲ Ἡλίαν, ἄλλοι δὲ ὅτι προφήτης
but others Elias, and others that prophet

τις τῶν ἀρχαίων ἀνέστη. 20 εἶπεν δὲ
a certain of the ancients rose again. And he said

αὐτοῖς· ὑμεῖς δὲ τίνα με λέγετε εἶναι;
to them : But ye whom me say to be?
=whom say ye that I am?

Πέτρος δὲ ἀποκριθεὶς εἶπεν· τὸν χριστὸν
And Peter answering said: The Christ

τοῦ θεοῦ. 21 ὁ δὲ ἐπιτιμήσας αὐτοῖς
– of God. But he warning ²them

παρήγγειλεν μηδενὶ λέγειν τοῦτο, 22 εἰπὼν
¹charged ⁴no one ³to tell ⁵this, saying

ὅτι δεῖ τὸν υἱὸν τοῦ ἀνθρώπου πολλὰ
that it behoves the Son – of man many things

παθεῖν καὶ ἀποδοκιμασθῆναι ἀπὸ τῶν
to suffer and to be rejected from(by) the

πρεσβυτέρων καὶ ἀρχιερέων καὶ γραμματέων
elders and chief priests and scribes

be killed, and on the third day be raised."

23 And he said to all, "If any man would come after me, let him deny himself and take up his cross daily and follow me. 24 For whoever would save his life will lose it; and whoever loses his life for my sake, he will save it. 25 For what does it profit a man if he gains the whole world and loses or forfeits himself? 26 For whoever is ashamed of me and of my words, of him will the Son of man be ashamed when he comes in his glory and the glory of the Father and of the holy angels. 27 But I tell you truly, there are some standing here who will not taste of death before they see the kingdom of God."

28 Now about eight days after these sayings he took with him Peter and John and James, and went up on the mountain to pray. 29 And as he was praying, the appearance of his countenance was

καὶ   ἀποκτανθῆναι   καὶ   τῇ   τρίτῃ   ἡμέρᾳ
and   to be killed   and   on the   third   day
ἐγερθῆναι.   23 Ἔλεγεν   δὲ   πρὸς   πάντας·
to be raised.   And he said   to   all:
εἴ   τις   θέλει   ὀπίσω   μου   ἔρχεσθαι,   ἀρνησάσθω
If anyone   wishes   after   me   to come,   let him deny
ἑαυτὸν   καὶ   ἀράτω   τὸν   σταυρὸν
himself   and   take   the   cross
αὐτοῦ   καθ'   ἡμέραν,   καὶ   ἀκολουθείτω   μοι.
of him   daily,   and   let him follow   me.
24 ὃς   γὰρ   ἐὰν   θέλῃ   τὴν   ψυχὴν   αὐτοῦ
For whoever   wishes   the   life   of him
σῶσαι,   ἀπολέσει   αὐτήν·   ὃς   δ'   ἂν   ἀπολέσῃ
to save,   he will lose   it;   but whoever   loses
τὴν   ψυχὴν   αὐτοῦ   ἕνεκεν   ἐμοῦ,   οὗτος
the   life   of him   for the sake of   me,   this [one]
σώσει   αὐτήν.   25 τί   γὰρ   ὠφελεῖται
will save   it.   For what   is profited
ἄνθρωπος   κερδήσας   τὸν   κόσμον   ὅλον   ἑαυτὸν
a man   gaining   the   world   whole   ³himself
δὲ   ἀπολέσας   ἢ   ζημιωθείς;   26 ὃς   γὰρ   ἂν
¹but   ²losing   or   suffering loss?   For whoever
ἐπαισχυνθῇ   με   καὶ   τοὺς   ἐμοὺς   λόγους,
is ashamed of   me   and   –   my   words,
τοῦτον   ὁ   υἱὸς   τοῦ   ἀνθρώπου   ἐπαι-
this [one]   the   Son   –   of man   will be
σχυνθήσεται,   ὅταν   ἔλθῃ   ἐν   τῇ   δόξῃ
ashamed of,   when   he comes   in   the   glory
αὐτοῦ   καὶ   τοῦ   πατρὸς   καὶ   τῶν   ἁγίων
of him   and   of the   Father   and   of the   holy
ἀγγέλων.   27 λέγω   δὲ   ὑμῖν   ἀληθῶς,
angels.   But I tell   you   truly,
εἰσίν   τινες   τῶν   αὐτοῦ   ἑστηκότων   οἳ
there are   some   of the [ones]   here   standing   who
οὐ   μὴ   γεύσωνται   θανάτου   ἕως   ἂν   ἴδωσιν
by no means   may taste   of death   until   they see
τὴν   βασιλείαν   τοῦ   θεοῦ.
the   kingdom   –   of God.
28 Ἐγένετο   δὲ   μετὰ   τοὺς   λόγους   τούτους
And it came to pass   ⁴after   –   ⁵sayings   ⁶these
ὡσεὶ   ἡμέραι   ὀκτώ,   καὶ   παραλαβὼν   Πέτρον
¹about   ³days   ²eight,   and   taking   Peter
καὶ   Ἰωάννην   καὶ   Ἰάκωβον   ἀνέβη   εἰς   τὸ
and   John   and   James   he went up   into   the
ὄρος   προσεύξασθαι.   29 καὶ   ἐγένετο   ἐν   τῷ
mountain   to pray.   And   ⁵became   in   the
—¹as   ²he   ³prayed
προσεύχεσθαι   αὐτὸν   τὸ   εἶδος   τοῦ   προσώπου
to pray   himbe   ⁴the   ⁵appearance   ⁶of the   ⁷face

altered, and his raiment became dazzling white. [30]And behold, two men talked with him, Moses and Eli'jah, [31]who appeared in glory and spoke of his departure, which he was to accomplish at Jerusalem. [32]Now Peter and those who were with him were heavy with sleep but kept awake, and they saw his glory and the two men who stood with him. [33]And as the men were parting from him, Peter said to Jesus, "Master, it is well that we are here; let us make three booths, one for you and one for Moses and one for Eli'jah"—not knowing what he said. [34]As he said this, a cloud came and overshadowed them; and they were afraid as they entered the cloud. [35]And a voice came out of the cloud, saying, "This is my Son, my Chosen;[y] listen to him!" [36]And when the voice had spoken, Jesus was found alone. And they kept silence and told no one

αὐτοῦ ἕτερον καὶ ὁ ἱματισμὸς αὐτοῦ
[6]of him [16]different and the raiment of him

λευκὸς ἐξαστράπτων. 30 καὶ ἰδοὺ ἄνδρες
[1]white [1]gleaming. And[,] behold[,] men

δύο συνελάλουν αὐτῷ, οἵτινες ἦσαν Μωϋσῆς
two conversed with him, who were Moses

καὶ Ἠλίας, 31 οἳ ὀφθέντες ἐν δόξῃ ἔλεγον
and Elias, who appearing in glory spoke of

τὴν ἔξοδον αὐτοῦ, ἣν ἤμελλεν πληροῦν
the exodus of him, which he was about to accomplish

ἐν Ἰερουσαλήμ. 32 ὁ δὲ Πέτρος καὶ οἱ
in Jerusalem. – But Peter and the [ones]

σὺν αὐτῷ ἦσαν βεβαρημένοι ὕπνῳ· δια-
with him were having been burdened with sleep; [1]wak-

γρηγορήσαντες δὲ εἶδαν τὴν δόξαν αὐτοῦ
ing thoroughly [1]but they saw the glory of him

καὶ τοὺς δύο ἄνδρας τοὺς συνεστῶτας
and the two men – standing with

αὐτῷ. 33 καὶ ἐγένετο ἐν τῷ διαχωρίζεσθαι
him. And it came to pass in the to part
=when they parted

αὐτοὺς ἀπ' αὐτοῦ εἶπεν ὁ Πέτρος πρὸς
them[be] from him said – Peter to

τὸν Ἰησοῦν· ἐπιστάτα, καλόν ἐστιν ἡμᾶς
– Jesus : Master, good it is [for] us

ὧδε εἶναι, καὶ ποιήσωμεν σκηνὰς τρεῖς,
here to be, and let us make tents three,

μίαν σοὶ καὶ μίαν Μωϋσεῖ καὶ μίαν
one for thee and one for Moses and one

Ἠλίᾳ, μὴ εἰδὼς ὃ λέγει. 34 ταῦτα δὲ
for Elias, not knowing what he says. And these things

αὐτοῦ λέγοντος ἐγένετο νεφέλη καὶ
him saying[a] came a cloud and
=while he said these things

ἐπεσκίαζεν αὐτούς· ἐφοβήθησαν δὲ ἐν τῷ
overshadowed them; and they feared in the
=as they entered

εἰσελθεῖν αὐτοὺς εἰς τὴν νεφέλην. 35 καὶ
to enter them[be] into the cloud. And

φωνὴ ἐγένετο ἐκ τῆς νεφέλης λέγουσα·
a voice came out of the cloud saying :

οὗτός ἐστιν ὁ υἱός μου ὁ ἐκλελεγμένος,
This is the Son of me – having been chosen,

αὐτοῦ ἀκούετε, 36 καὶ ἐν τῷ γενέσθαι
him hear ye, and in the to become
=when the voice came

τὴν φωνὴν εὑρέθη Ἰησοῦς μόνος. καὶ
the voice[be] was found Jesus alone. And

αὐτοὶ ἐσίγησαν καὶ οὐδενὶ ἀπήγγειλαν ἐν ἐκείναις
they were silent and to no one reported in those

[y] Other ancient authorities read my Beloved

in those days anything of what they had seen.

37 On the next day, when they had come down from the mountain, a great crowd met him. ³⁸And behold, a man from the crowd cried, "Teacher, I beg you to look upon my son, for he is my only child; ³⁹and behold, a spirit seizes him, and he suddenly cries out; it convulses him till he foams, and shatters him, and will hardly leave him. ⁴⁰And I begged your disciples to cast it out, but they could not." ⁴¹Jesus answered, "O faithless and perverse generation, how long am I to be with you and bear with you? Bring your son here." ⁴²While he was coming, the demon tore him and convulsed him. But Jesus rebuked the unclean spirit, and healed the boy, and gave him back to his father. ⁴³And all were astonished at the majesty of God.

But while they were all marveling at everything

ταῖς ἡμέραις οὐδὲν ὧν ἑώρακαν.
— days no(any) of [the things] they have
thing which (had) seen.

37 Ἐγένετο δὲ τῇ ἐξῆς ἡμέρᾳ κατελ-
And it came to pass on the following day coming

θόντων αὐτῶν ἀπὸ τοῦ ὄρους συνήντησεν
down themª from the mountain met
=as they came down

αὐτῷ ὄχλος πολύς. 38 καὶ ἰδοὺ ἀνὴρ
him crowd a much. And[,] behold[,] a man

ἀπὸ τοῦ ὄχλου ἐβόησεν λέγων· διδάσκαλε,
from the crowd called aloud saying : Teacher,

δέομαί σου ἐπιβλέψαι ἐπὶ τὸν υἱόν μου,
I beg of thee to look at at the son of me,

ὅτι μονογενής μοί ἐστιν, 39 καὶ ἰδοὺ
because only born to me he is, and[,] behold[,]

πνεῦμα λαμβάνει αὐτόν, καὶ ἐξαίφνης
a spirit takes him, and suddenly

κράζει καὶ σπαράσσει αὐτὸν μετὰ ἀφροῦ,
cries out and throws him with foam,

καὶ μόλις ἀποχωρεῖ ἀπ' αὐτοῦ συντρῖβον
and scarcely departs from him bruising

αὐτόν· 40 καὶ ἐδεήθην τῶν μαθητῶν σου
him; and I begged of the disciples of thee

ἵνα ἐκβάλωσιν αὐτό, καὶ οὐκ ἠδυνήθησαν.
that they would expel it, and they were not able.

41 ἀποκριθεὶς δὲ ὁ Ἰησοῦς εἶπεν· ὦ
And answering — Jesus said : O

γενεὰ ἄπιστος καὶ διεστραμμένη, ἕως πότε
generation unbelieving and having been perverted, until when

ἔσομαι πρὸς ὑμᾶς καὶ ἀνέξομαι ὑμῶν;
shall I be with you and endure you?

προσάγαγε ὧδε τὸν υἱόν σου. 42 ἔτι
Bring here the son of thee. yet

δὲ προσερχομένου αὐτοῦ ἔρρηξεν αὐτὸν τὸ
But approaching himª tore him the
=But while he was yet approaching

δαιμόνιον καὶ συνεσπάραξεν· ἐπετίμησεν δὲ
demon and threw violently; but ²rebuked

ὁ Ἰησοῦς τῷ πνεύματι τῷ ἀκαθάρτῳ, καὶ
— ¹Jesus ³the ⁵spirit — ⁴unclean, and

ἰάσατο τὸν παῖδα καὶ ἀπέδωκεν αὐτὸν τῷ
cured the boy and restored him to the

πατρὶ αὐτοῦ. 43 ἐξεπλήσσοντο δὲ πάντες
father of him. And were astounded all

ἐπὶ τῇ μεγαλειότητι τοῦ θεοῦ.
at the majesty — of God.

Πάντων δὲ θαυμαζόντων ἐπὶ πᾶσιν οἷς
And all marvellingª at all things which
=while all marvelled

he did, he said to his disciples, ⁴⁴"Let these words sink into your ears; for the Son of man is to be delivered into the hands of men." ⁴⁵But they did not understand this saying, and it was concealed from them, that they should not perceive it; and they were afraid to ask him about this saying.

46 And an argument arose among them as to which of them was the greatest. ⁴⁷But when Jesus perceived the thought of their hearts, he took a child and put him by his side, ⁴⁸and said to them, "Whoever receives this child in my name receives me, and whoever receives me receives him who sent me; for he who is least among you all is the one who is great."

49 John answered, "Master, we saw a man casting out demons in your name, and we forbade him, because he does not follow with us." ⁵⁰But Jesus said to him, "Do not forbid him; for he that is not against you is for you."

51 When the days drew near for him to be

ἐποίει εἶπεν πρὸς τοὺς μαθητὰς αὐτοῦ·
he did　he said　to　the　disciples　of him :

44 θέσθε ὑμεῖς εἰς τὰ ὦτα ὑμῶν τοὺς
Lay　ye　in　the　ears　of you　–

λόγους τούτους· ὁ γὰρ υἱὸς τοῦ ἀνθρώπου
sayings　these;　for the　Son　–　of man

μέλλει παραδίδοσθαι εἰς χεῖρας ἀνθρώπων.
is about　to be betrayed　into [the] hands　of men.

45 οἱ δὲ ἠγνόουν τὸ ῥῆμα τοῦτο, καὶ ἦν
But they　knew not　–　word　this,　and it was

παρακεκαλυμμένον ἀπ’ αὐτῶν ἵνα μὴ
having been veiled　from　them　lest

αἴσθωνται αὐτό, καὶ ἐφοβοῦντο ἐρωτῆσαι
they should perceive it,　and　they feared　to ask

αὐτὸν περὶ τοῦ ῥήματος τούτου. 46 Εἰσῆλθεν
him about　–　word　this.　entered

δὲ διαλογισμὸς ἐν αὐτοῖς, τὸ τίς ἂν εἴη
And　a debate　among　them,　–　who　might be
=a debate arose

μείζων αὐτῶν. 47 ὁ δὲ Ἰησοῦς εἰδὼς τὸν
greater(est) of them.　–　And Jesus　knowing　the

διαλογισμὸν τῆς καρδίας αὐτῶν, ἐπιλαβόμενος
debate　of the　heart　of them,　taking

παιδίον ἔστησεν αὐτὸ παρ’ ἑαυτῷ, 48 καὶ
a child　stood　it(him)　beside　himself,　and

εἶπεν αὐτοῖς· ὃς ἐὰν δέξηται τοῦτο τὸ
said　to them :　Whoever　receives　this　–

παιδίον ἐπὶ τῷ ὀνόματί μου, ἐμὲ δέχεται·
child　on(in) the　name　of me,　me　receives;

καὶ ὃς ἂν ἐμὲ δέξηται, δέχεται τὸν [one]
and　whoever　me　receives,　receives the [one]

ἀποστείλαντά με· ὁ γὰρ μικρότερος ἐν
having sent　me;　for ¹the [one]　³lesser　⁴among

πᾶσιν ὑμῖν ὑπάρχων, οὗτός ἐστιν μέγας.
⁶all　⁵you　²being,　this [one]　is　great.

49 Ἀποκριθεὶς δὲ ὁ Ἰωάννης εἶπεν· ἐπιστάτα,
And answering　–　John　said :　Master,

εἴδομέν τινα ἐν τῷ ὀνόματί σου ἐκβάλλοντα
we saw　someone in　the　name　of thee　expelling

δαιμόνια, καὶ ἐκωλύομεν αὐτόν, ὅτι
demons,　and　we prevented　him,　because

οὐκ ἀκολουθεῖ μεθ’ ἡμῶν. 50 εἶπεν δὲ πρὸς
he does not follow　with　us.　And said　to

αὐτὸν Ἰησοῦς· μὴ κωλύετε· ὃς γὰρ οὐκ
him　Jesus:　Do not prevent;　for [he] who　not

ἔστιν καθ’ ὑμῶν, ὑπὲρ ὑμῶν ἐστιν.
is　against　you,　for　you　is.

51 Ἐγένετο δὲ ἐν τῷ συμπληροῦσθαι
And it came to pass　in　the　to be fulfilled

received up, he set his face to go to Jerusalem. And he sent messengers ahead of him, ⁵²who went and entered a village of the Samaritans, to make ready for him; ⁵³but the people would not receive him, because his face was set toward Jerusalem. ⁵⁴And when his disciples James and John saw it, they said, "Lord, do you want us to bid fire come down from heaven and consume them?"ᶻ ⁵⁵But he turned and rebuked them.ᵃ ⁵⁶And they went on to another village.

57 As they were going along the road, a man said to him, "I will follow you wherever you go." ⁵⁸And Jesus said to him, "Foxes have holes, and birds of the air have nests; but the Son of man has nowhere to lay his head." ⁵⁹To another he said, "Follow me." But he said, "Lord, let me first go and bury my father." ⁶⁰But he said to him, "Leave the dead to

τὰς ἡμέρας τῆς ἀναλήμψεως αὐτοῦ καὶ
the   days   of the   assumption   of himᵇᵉ   and
=as the days of his assumption were fulfilled

αὐτὸς τὸ πρόσωπον ἐστήρισεν τοῦ
he the(his)   face   set   -

πορεύεσθαι εἰς Ἰερουσαλήμ, 52 καὶ ἀπέστειλεν
to goᵈ   to   Jerusalem,   and   sent

ἀγγέλους πρὸ προσώπου αὐτοῦ. καὶ
messengers   before   face   of him.   And

πορευθέντες εἰσῆλθον εἰς κώμην Σαμαριτῶν,
going   they entered   into   a village   of Samaritans,

ὥστε ἑτοιμάσαι αὐτῷ· 53 καὶ οὐκ ἐδέξαντο
so as   to prepare   for him;   and   they did not receive

αὐτόν, ὅτι τὸ πρόσωπον αὐτοῦ ἦν
him,   because   the   face   of him   was

πορευόμενον εἰς Ἰερουσαλήμ. 54 ἰδόντες
going   to   Jerusalem.   ⁸seeing

δὲ οἱ μαθηταὶ Ἰάκωβος καὶ Ἰωάννης
And   ¹the   ²disciples   ³James   ⁴and   ⁵John

εἶπαν· κύριε, θέλεις εἴπωμεν πῦρ κατα-
⁷said :   Lord,   wilt thou   we may tell   fire   to come

βῆναι ἀπὸ τοῦ οὐρανοῦ καὶ ἀναλῶσαι
down   from   heaven   and   to destroy

αὐτούς; 55 στραφεὶς δὲ ἐπετίμησεν αὐτοῖς.
them?   But turning   he rebuked   them.

56 καὶ ἐπορεύθησαν εἰς ἑτέραν κώμην.
And   they went   to   another   village.

57 Καὶ πορευομένων αὐτῶν ἐν τῇ ὁδῷ
And   going   themᵃ   in   the   way
=as they went

εἶπέν τις πρὸς αὐτόν· ἀκολουθήσω σοι
said   one   to   him :   I will follow   thee

ὅπου ἐὰν ἀπέρχῃ. 58 καὶ εἶπεν αὐτῷ ὁ
wherever   thou goest.   And   said   to him   -

Ἰησοῦς· αἱ ἀλώπεκες φωλεοὺς ἔχουσιν καὶ
Jesus :   The   foxes   holes   have   and

τὰ πετεινὰ τοῦ οὐρανοῦ κατασκηνώσεις, ὁ
the   birds   -   of heaven   nests,   ²the

δὲ υἱὸς τοῦ ἀνθρώπου οὐκ ἔχει ποῦ τὴν
¹but   Son   -   of man   has not   where the(his)

κεφαλὴν κλίνῃ. 59 Εἶπεν δὲ πρὸς ἕτερον·
head   he may lay.   And he said   to   another :

ἀκολούθει μοι. ὁ δὲ εἶπεν· ἐπίτρεψόν μοι
Follow   me.   But he   said :   Allow   me

πρῶτον ἀπελθόντι θάψαι τὸν πατέρα μου.
first   going   to bury   the   father   of me.

60 εἶπεν δὲ αὐτῷ· ἄφες τοὺς νεκροὺς
But he said   to him :   Leave   the   dead

ᶻ Other ancient authorities add as Elijah did

ᵃ Other ancient authorities add and he said, "You do not know what manner of spirit you are of; for the Son of man came not to destroy men's lives but to save them"

bury their own dead; but as for you, go and proclaim the kingdom of God." 61Another said, "I will follow you, Lord; but let me first say farewell to those at my home." 62Jesus said to him, "No one who puts his hand to the plow and looks back is fit for the kingdom of God."

θάψαι τοὺς ἑαυτῶν νεκρούς, σὺ δὲ ἀπελθὼν
to bury the of themselves dead, but thou going
=their own dead,
διάγγελλε τὴν βασιλείαν τοῦ θεοῦ. 61 Εἶπεν
announce the kingdom - of God. said
δὲ καὶ ἕτερος· ἀκολουθήσω σοι, κύριε·
And also another: I will follow thee, Lord;
πρῶτον δὲ ἐπίτρεψόν μοι ἀποτάξασθαι τοῖς
but first allow me to say farewell to the [ones]
εἰς τὸν οἶκόν μου. 62 εἶπεν δὲ [πρὸς
in the house of me. But said to
αὐτὸν] ὁ Ἰησοῦς· οὐδεὶς ἐπιβαλὼν τὴν
him - Jesus: No one putting on the(his)
χεῖρα ἐπ᾽ ἄροτρον καὶ βλέπων εἰς τὰ
hand on a plough and looking at the things
ὀπίσω εὔθετός ἐστιν τῇ βασιλείᾳ τοῦ θεοῦ.
behind fit is for the kingdom - of God.

CHAPTER 10

AFTER this the Lord appointed seventy[b] others, and sent them on ahead of him, two by two, into every town and place where he himself was about to come. 2And he said to them, "The harvest is plentiful, but the laborers are few; pray therefore the LORD of the harvest to send out laborers into his harvest. 3Go your way; behold, I send you out as lambs in the midst of wolves. 4Carry no purse, no bag, no sandals; and salute no one on the road. 5Whatever house you enter, first say, 'Peace be to this house!' 6And if a son of peace is there, your peace shall rest upon him; but if not,

10 Μετὰ δὲ ταῦτα ἀνέδειξεν ὁ κύριος
Now after these things appointed the Lord
ἑτέρους ἑβδομήκοντα [δύο], καὶ ἀπέστειλεν
others seventy-two, and sent
αὐτοὺς ἀνὰ δύο πρὸ προσώπου αὐτοῦ εἰς
them two by two† before face of him into
πᾶσαν πόλιν καὶ τόπον οὗ ἤμελλεν αὐτὸς
every city and place where ²was about ¹he
ἔρχεσθαι. 2 ἔλεγεν δὲ πρὸς αὐτούς· ὁ
to come. And he said to them: the
μὲν θερισμὸς πολύς, οἱ δὲ ἐργάται ὀλίγοι·
Indeed harvest much, but the workmen few;
δεήθητε οὖν τοῦ κυρίου τοῦ θερισμοῦ
beg ye therefore of the Lord of the harvest
ὅπως ἐργάτας ἐκβάλῃ εἰς τὸν θερισμὸν
that workmen he would thrust forth into the harvest
αὐτοῦ. 3 ὑπάγετε· ἰδοὺ ἀποστέλλω ὑμᾶς
of him. Go ye; behold I send you
ὡς ἄρνας ἐν μέσῳ λύκων. 4 μὴ βαστάζετε
as lambs in [the] midst of wolves. Do not carry
βαλλάντιον, μὴ πήραν, μὴ ὑποδήματα· καὶ
a purse, nor a wallet, nor sandals; and
μηδένα κατὰ τὴν ὁδὸν ἀσπάσησθε. 5 εἰς
no one by the way greet. ²into
ἣν δ᾽ ἂν εἰσέλθητε οἰκίαν, πρῶτον λέγετε·
¹And ³whatever ⁵ye enter ⁴house, first say:
εἰρήνη τῷ οἴκῳ τούτῳ. 6 καὶ ἐὰν ἐκεῖ
Peace - house to this. And if there
ᾖ υἱὸς εἰρήνης, ἐπαναπαήσεται ἐπ᾽ αὐτὸν
there is a son of peace, shall rest on it(?him)

[b] Other ancient authorities read seventy-two

it shall return to you. ⁷And remain in the same house, eating and drinking what they provide, for the laborer deserves his wages; do not go from house to house. ⁸Whenever you enter a town and they receive you, eat what is set before you; ⁹heal the sick in it and say to them, 'The kingdom of God has come near to you.' ¹⁰But whenever you enter a town and they do not receive you, go into its streets and say, ¹¹'Even the dust of your town that clings to our feet, we wipe off against you; nevertheless know this, that the kingdom of God has come near.' ¹²I tell you, it shall be more tolerable on that day for Sodom than for that town.

13 "Woe to you, Chora'zin! woe to you, Beth-sa'ida! for if the mighty works done in you had been done in Tyre and Sidon, they would have repented long ago, sitting in sackcloth and ashes. ¹⁴But it shall

---

ἡ εἰρήνη ὑμῶν· εἰ δὲ μή γε, ἐφ᾽ ὑμᾶς
the peace of you; otherwise, on you

ἀνακάμψει. 7 ἐν αὐτῇ δὲ τῇ οἰκίᾳ μένετε,
it shall return. ²in ⁴same ¹And ³the house* remain,

ἔσθοντες καὶ πίνοντες τὰ παρ᾽ αὐτῶν·
eating and drinking the things with them;

ἄξιος γὰρ ὁ ἐργάτης τοῦ μισθοῦ αὐτοῦ.
for worthy [is] the workman of the pay of him.

μὴ μεταβαίνετε ἐξ οἰκίας εἰς οἰκίαν.
Do not remove from house to house.

8 καὶ εἰς ἣν ἂν πόλιν εἰσέρχησθε καὶ
And into whatever city ye enter and

δέχωνται ὑμᾶς, ἐσθίετε τὰ παρατιθέμενα
they receive you, eat the things being set before

ὑμῖν, 9 καὶ θεραπεύετε τοὺς ἐν αὐτῇ
you, and heal the ²in ³it

ἀσθενεῖς, καὶ λέγετε αὐτοῖς· ἤγγικεν ἐφ᾽
¹sick, and tell them : Has drawn near on(to)

ὑμᾶς ἡ βασιλεία τοῦ θεοῦ. 10 εἰς ἣν δ᾽
you the kingdom – of God. And into what-

ἂν πόλιν εἰσέλθητε καὶ μὴ δέχωνται ὑμᾶς,
ever city ye enter and they do not receive you,

ἐξελθόντες εἰς τὰς πλατείας αὐτῆς εἴπατε·
going forth into the streets of it say :

11 καὶ τὸν κονιορτὸν τὸν κολληθέντα ἡμῖν
Even the dust – adhering to us
=the dust of your city adhering to us, on our feet,

ἐκ τῆς πόλεως ὑμῶν εἰς τοὺς πόδας
of the city of you on the(our) feet

ἀπομασσόμεθα ὑμῖν· πλὴν τοῦτο γινώσκετε,
we shake off to you; nevertheless this know ye,

ὅτι ἤγγικεν ἡ βασιλεία τοῦ θεοῦ. 12 λέγω
that has drawn near the kingdom – of God. I tell

ὑμῖν ὅτι Σοδόμοις ἐν τῇ ἡμέρᾳ ἐκείνῃ
you that for Sodom in – day that

ἀνεκτότερον ἔσται ἢ τῇ πόλει ἐκείνῃ.
more endurable it will be than – city for that.

13 Οὐαί σοι, Χοραζίν, οὐαί σοι, Βηθσαϊδά·
Woe to thee, Chorazin, woe to thee, Bethsaida;

ὅτι εἰ ἐν Τύρῳ καὶ Σιδῶνι ἐγενήθησαν αἱ
because if in Tyre and Sidon happened the

δυνάμεις αἱ γενόμεναι ἐν ὑμῖν, πάλαι ἂν ἐν
powerful deeds – happening in you, long ago - in

σάκκῳ καὶ σποδῷ καθήμενοι μετενόησαν.
sackcloth and ashes sitting they would have repented.

---

* Luke here, and in 2. 38; 10. 21; 12. 12; 13. 31; 24. 13, as well as in Acts 16. 18; 22. 13, ignores the strict idiomatic construction of αὐτός when in apposition. The words here should mean "in the house itself" but obviously do mean "in the same house". So elsewhere. See note on Luke 2. 38.

be more tolerable in the judgment for Tyre and Sidon than for you. [15]And you, Caper'na-um, will you be exalted to heaven? You shall be brought down to Hades. 16 "He who hears you hears me, and he who rejects you rejects me, and he who rejects me rejects him who sent me."

17 The seventy[b] returned with joy, saying, "Lord, even the demons are subject to us in your name!" [18]And he said to them, "I saw Satan fall like lightning from heaven. [19]Behold, I have given you authority to tread upon serpents and scorpions, and over all the power of the enemy; and nothing shall hurt you. [20]Nevertheless do not rejoice in this, that the spirits are subject to you; but rejoice that your names are written in heaven."

21 In that same hour he rejoiced in the Holy Spirit and said, "I thank thee, Father, Lord of heaven and earth, that thou hast hidden these things from the wise and understanding and revealed them to babes; yea, Father, for such was

[b]Other ancient authorities read seventy-two

14 πλὴν Τύρῳ καὶ Σιδῶνι ἀνεκτότερον
Nevertheless for Tyre and Sidon more endurable
ἔσται ἐν τῇ κρίσει ἢ ὑμῖν. 15 καὶ σύ,
it will be in the judgment than for you. And thou,
Καφαρναούμ, μὴ ἕως οὐρανοῦ ὑψωθήσῃ;
Capernaum, not to heaven wast thou lifted?
ἕως τοῦ ᾅδου καταβήσῃ. 16 Ὁ ἀκούων
to - hades thou shalt come down. The [one] hearing
ὑμῶν ἐμοῦ ἀκούει, καὶ ὁ ἀθετῶν ὑμᾶς
you me hears, and the [one] rejecting you
ἐμὲ ἀθετεῖ· ὁ δὲ ἐμὲ ἀθετῶν ἀθετεῖ τὸν
me rejects; and the [one] me rejecting rejects the [one]
ἀποστείλαντά με. 17 Ὑπέστρεψαν δὲ οἱ
having sent me. And returned the
ἑβδομήκοντα [δύο] μετὰ χαρᾶς λέγοντες·
seventy-two with joy saying:
κύριε, καὶ τὰ δαιμόνια ὑποτάσσεται ἡμῖν
Lord, even the demons submits to us
ἐν τῷ ὀνόματί σου. 18 εἶπεν δὲ αὐτοῖς·
in the name of thee. And he said to them:
ἐθεώρουν τὸν σατανᾶν ὡς ἀστραπὴν ἐκ
I beheld Satan as lightning out of
τοῦ οὐρανοῦ πεσόντα. 19 ἰδοὺ δέδωκα
- heaven fall. Behold I have given
ὑμῖν τὴν ἐξουσίαν τοῦ πατεῖν ἐπάνω
you the authority - to tread[d] on
ὄφεων καὶ σκορπίων, καὶ ἐπὶ πᾶσαν τὴν
serpents and scorpions, and on all the
δύναμιν τοῦ ἐχθροῦ, καὶ οὐδὲν ὑμᾶς οὐ μὴ
power of the enemy, and nothing you by no(any)
means
ἀδικήσει. 20 πλὴν ἐν τούτῳ μὴ χαίρετε
shall hurt. Nevertheless in this rejoice not
ὅτι τὰ πνεύματα ὑμῖν ὑποτάσσεται, χαίρετε
that the spirits to you submits, [2]rejoice
δὲ ὅτι τὰ ὀνόματα ὑμῶν ἐγγέγραπται ἐν
[1]but that the names of you have been enrolled in
τοῖς οὐρανοῖς. 21 Ἐν αὐτῇ τῇ ὥρᾳ
the heavens. In [2]same [1]the hour
ἠγαλλιάσατο τῷ πνεύματι τῷ ἁγίῳ καὶ
he exulted in(?by) the Spirit - Holy and
εἶπεν· ἐξομολογοῦμαί σοι, πάτερ, κύριε
said: I praise thee, Father, Lord
τοῦ οὐρανοῦ καὶ τῆς γῆς, ὅτι ἀπέκρυψας
- of heaven and - of earth, because thou didst hide
ταῦτα ἀπὸ σοφῶν καὶ συνετῶν, καὶ
these things from wise and intelligent [ones], and
ἀπεκάλυψας αὐτὰ νηπίοις· ναί, ὁ πατήρ,
didst reveal them to infants; yes, - Father,

thy gracious will.ᶜ ²²All things have been delivered to me by my Father; and no one knows who the Son is except the Father, or who the Father is except the Son and any one to whom the Son chooses to reveal him."
23 Then turning to the disciples he said privately, "Blessed are the eyes which see what you see! ²⁴For I tell you that many prophets and kings desired to see what you see, and did not see it, and to hear what you hear, and did not hear it."
25 And behold, a lawyer stood up to put him to the test, saying, "Teacher, what shall I do to inherit eternal life?" ²⁶He said to him, "What is written in the law? How do you read?" ²⁷And he answered, "You shall love the Lord your God with all your heart, and with all your soul, and with all your strength, and with all your mind; and your neighbor as yourself." ²⁸And he said to him, "You have answered right; do this, and you will live." 29 But he, desiring to justify himself, said to

ὅτι οὕτως εὐδοκία ἐγένετο ἔμπροσθέν σου.
because thus good pleasure it was before thee.

22 πάντα μοι παρεδόθη ὑπὸ τοῦ πατρός
All things to me were delivered by the Father

μου, καὶ οὐδεὶς γινώσκει τίς ἐστιν ὁ
of me, and no one knows who is the

υἱὸς εἰ μὴ ὁ πατήρ, καὶ τίς ἐστιν ὁ πατὴρ
Son except the Father, and who is the Father

εἰ μὴ ὁ υἱὸς καὶ ᾧ ἐὰν βούληται
except the Son and [he] to whomever wills

ὁ υἱὸς ἀποκαλύψαι. 23 Καὶ στραφεὶς
the Son to reveal [him]. And turning

πρὸς τοὺς μαθητὰς κατ' ἰδίαν εἶπεν·
to the disciples privately he said :

μακάριοι οἱ ὀφθαλμοὶ οἱ βλέποντες ἃ
Blessed the eyes – seeing the things which

βλέπετε. 24 λέγω γὰρ ὑμῖν ὅτι πολλοὶ
ye see. For I tell you that many

προφῆται καὶ βασιλεῖς ἠθέλησαν ἰδεῖν ἃ
prophets and kings desired to see the things which

ὑμεῖς βλέπετε καὶ οὐκ εἶδαν, καὶ ἀκοῦσαι
ye see and did not see, and to hear

ἃ ἀκούετε καὶ οὐκ ἤκουσαν.
the things which ye hear and did not hear.

25 Καὶ ἰδοὺ νομικός τις ἀνέστη
And[,] behold[,] lawyer a certain stood up

ἐκπειράζων αὐτὸν λέγων· διδάσκαλε, τί
tempting him saying : Teacher, what

ποιήσας ζωὴν αἰώνιον κληρονομήσω; 26 ὁ
doing ⁵life ⁴eternal ²I ¹may ³inherit? he

δὲ εἶπεν πρὸς αὐτόν· ἐν τῷ νόμῳ τί
And said to him : In the law what

γέγραπται; πῶς ἀναγινώσκεις; 27 ὁ δὲ
has been written? how readest thou? And he

ἀποκριθεὶς εἶπεν· ἀγαπήσεις κύριον τὸν
answering said : Thou shalt love [the] Lord the

θεόν σου ἐξ ὅλης τῆς καρδίας σου καὶ
God of thee from all the heart of thee and

ἐν ὅλῃ τῇ ψυχῇ σου καὶ ἐν ὅλῃ τῇ
with all the soul of thee and with all the

ἰσχύϊ σου καὶ ἐν ὅλῃ τῇ διανοίᾳ σου,
strength of thee and with all the mind of thee,

καὶ τὸν πλησίον σου ὡς σεαυτόν. 28 εἶπεν
and the neighbour of thee as thyself. he said

δὲ αὐτῷ· ὀρθῶς ἀπεκρίθης· τοῦτο ποίει
And to him : Rightly thou didst answer; this do

καὶ ζήσῃ. 29 ὁ δὲ θέλων δικαιῶσαι ἑαυτὸν
and thou shalt live. But he wishing to justify himself

ᶜ Or *so it was well-pleasing before thee*

Jesus, "And who is my neighbor?" ³⁰Jesus replied, "A man was going down from Jerusalem to Jericho, and he fell among robbers, who stripped him and beat him, and departed, leaving him half-dead. ³¹Now by chance a priest was going down that road; and when he saw him he passed by on the other side. ³²So likewise a Levite, when he came to to the place and saw him, passed by on the other side. ³³But a Samaritan, as he journeyed, came to where he was; and when he saw him, he had compassion, ³⁴and went to him and bound up his wounds, pouring on oil and wine; then he set him on his own beast and brought him to an inn, and took care of him. ³⁵And the next day he took out two denarii and gave them to the innkeeper, saying, 'Take care of him; and whatever more you spend, I will repay you when I come back.' ³⁶Which of these three, do you think, proved neighbor to the man who fell among the robbers?" ³⁷He said, "The one who showed mercy on him." And Jesus said to him, "Go

εἶπεν πρὸς τὸν Ἰησοῦν· καὶ τίς ἐστίν
said to   -   Jesus :   And who is

μου πλησίον; 30 ὑπολαβὼν ὁ Ἰησοῦς
of me neighbour?   Taking [him] up - Jesus

εἶπεν· ἄνθρωπός τις κατέβαινεν ἀπὸ
said : A certain man   was going down from

Ἰερουσαλὴμ εἰς Ἰεριχώ, καὶ λῃσταῖς
Jerusalem   to Jericho, and ²robbers

περιέπεσεν, οἳ καὶ ἐκδύσαντες αὐτὸν καὶ
¹fell in with, who both stripping   him and

πληγὰς ἐπιθέντες ἀπῆλθον ἀφέντες ἡμιθανῆ.
²blows ¹laying ³on ⁴[him] went away leaving [him] half dead.

31 κατὰ συγκυρίαν δὲ ἱερεύς τις κατέβαινεν
   And by a coincidence a certain priest was going down

ἐν τῇ ὁδῷ ἐκείνῃ, καὶ ἰδὼν αὐτὸν
in - way   that, and seeing him

ἀντιπαρῆλθεν. 32 ὁμοίως δὲ καὶ Λευίτης
passed by opposite.   And likewise also a Levite

κατὰ τὸν τόπον ἐλθὼν καὶ ἰδὼν
upon the place coming and seeing

ἀντιπαρῆλθεν. 33 Σαμαρίτης δέ τις ὁδεύων
passed by opposite. And a certain Samaritan journeying

ἦλθεν κατ᾽ αὐτὸν καὶ ἰδὼν ἐσπλαγχνίσθη,
came upon him and seeing was filled with pity,

34 καὶ προσελθὼν κατέδησεν τὰ τραύματα
   and approaching bound up the wounds

αὐτοῦ ἐπιχέων ἔλαιον καὶ οἶνον, ἐπιβιβάσας
of him pouring on oil and wine, ²placing

δὲ αὐτὸν ἐπὶ τὸ ἴδιον κτῆνος ἤγαγεν
¹and him on the(his) own beast brought

αὐτὸν εἰς πανδοχεῖον καὶ ἐπεμελήθη αὐτοῦ.
him to an inn and cared for him.

35 καὶ ἐπὶ τὴν αὔριον ἐκβαλὼν δύο
   And on the morrow taking out two

δηνάρια ἔδωκεν τῷ πανδοχεῖ καὶ εἶπεν·
denarii he gave to the innkeeper and said:

ἐπιμελήθητι αὐτοῦ, καὶ ὅ τι ἂν προσδα-
Care thou for him, and whatever thou spendest

πανήσῃς ἐγὼ ἐν τῷ ἐπανέρχεσθαί με
in addition I in the to return me
                      =when I return

ἀποδώσω σοι. 36 τίς τούτων τῶν τριῶν πλησίον
will repay thee. Who of these - three ⁴neighbour

δοκεῖ σοι γεγονέναι τοῦ ἐμπεσόντος
¹seems it ²to thee ³to have become of the [one] falling into

εἰς τοὺς λῃστάς; 37 ὁ δὲ εἶπεν· ὁ ποιήσας
among the robbers?   And he said : The [one] doing

τὸ ἔλεος μετ᾽ αὐτοῦ. εἶπεν δὲ αὐτῷ ὁ
the mercy with him.   And said to him

and do likewise."

38 Now as they went on their way, he entered a village; and a woman named Martha received him into her house. ³⁹And she had a sister called Mary, who sat at the Lord's feet and listened to his teaching. ⁴⁰But Martha was distracted with much serving; and she went to him and said, "Lord, do you not care that my sister has left me to serve alone? Tell her then to help me." ⁴¹But the Lord answered her, "Martha, Martha, you are anxious and troubled about many things; ⁴²one thing is needful.ᵈ Mary has chosen the good portion, which shall not be taken away from her."

Ἰησοῦς· πορεύου καὶ σὺ ποίει ὁμοίως.
Jesus : Go and thou do likewise.

38 Ἐν δὲ τῷ πορεύεσθαι αὐτοὺς αὐτὸς
And in the to go themᵇᵉ he
=as they went

εἰσῆλθεν εἰς κώμην τινά· γυνὴ δέ τις
entered into a certain village; and a certain woman

ὀνόματι Μάρθα ὑπεδέξατο αὐτὸν εἰς τὴν
by name Martha received him into the

οἰκίαν. 39 καὶ τῇδε ἦν ἀδελφὴ καλουμένη
house. And to this was a sisterᵒ being called
=she had a sister

Μαριάμ, ἣ καὶ παρακαθεσθεῖσα πρὸς τοὺς
Mary, who also sitting beside at the

πόδας τοῦ κυρίου ἤκουεν τὸν λόγον αὐτοῦ.
feet of the Lord heard the word of him.

40 ἡ δὲ Μάρθα περιεσπᾶτο περὶ πολλὴν
- But Martha was distracted about much

διακονίαν· ἐπιστᾶσα δὲ εἶπεν· κύριε, οὐ
serving; and coming upon [him] she said : Lord, not

μέλει σοι ὅτι ἡ ἀδελφή μου μόνην με
matters it to thee that the sister of me ²alone ²me

κατέλειπεν διακονεῖν; εἰπὸν οὖν αὐτῇ ἵνα
¹left to serve? tell therefore her that

μοι συναντιλάβηται. 41 ἀποκριθεὶς δὲ εἶπεν
²me ¹she may help. And answering said

αὐτῇ ὁ κύριος· Μάρθα Μάρθα, μεριμνᾷς
to her the Lord : Martha[,] Martha, thou art anxious

καὶ θορυβάζῃ περὶ πολλά, 42 ὀλίγων δὲ
and disturbed about many things, but of few things

ἐστιν χρεία ἢ ἑνός· Μαριὰμ γὰρ τὴν
there is need or of one; for Mary the

ἀγαθὴν μερίδα ἐξελέξατο, ἥτις οὐκ
good part chose, which not

ἀφαιρεθήσεται αὐτῆς.
shall be taken from her.

CHAPTER 11

HE was praying in a certain place, and when he ceased, one of his disciples said to him, "Lord, teach us to pray, as John taught his dis-

ᵈ Other ancient authorities read *few things are needful, or only one*

11 Καὶ ἐγένετο ἐν τῷ εἶναι αὐτὸν ἐν
And it came to pass in the to be himᵇᵉ in
=when he was

τόπῳ τινὶ προσευχόμενον, ὡς ἐπαύσατο,
a certain place praying, as he ceased,

εἰπέν τις τῶν μαθητῶν αὐτοῦ πρὸς
said a certain one of the disciples of him to

αὐτόν· κύριε, δίδαξον ἡμᾶς προσεύχεσθαι,
him : Lord, teach us to pray,

καθὼς καὶ Ἰωάννης ἐδίδαξεν τοὺς μαθητὰς
even as also John taught the disciples

ciples." ²And he said to them, "When you pray, say:
"Father, hallowed be thy name. Thy kingdom come. ³Give us each day our daily bread;ᵉ ⁴and forgive us our sins, for we ourselves forgive every one who is indebted to us; and lead us not into temptation."

5 And he said to them, "Which of you who has a friend will go to him at midnight and say to him, 'Friend, lend me three loaves; ⁶for a friend of mine has arrived on a journey, and I have nothing to set before him'; ⁷and he will answer from within, 'Do not bother me; the door is now shut, and my children are with me in bed; I cannot get up and give you anything'? ⁸I tell you, though he will not get up and give him anything because he is his friend, yet because of his importunity he will rise and give him whatever he needs. ⁹And I tell you, Ask, and it will be given you; seek, and you will find; knock, and it will be opened to you. ¹⁰For every one who asks receives, and he who

ᵉ Or *our bread for the morrow*

αὐτοῦ.   2 εἶπεν   δὲ   αὐτοῖς·   ὅταν
of him.   And he said   to them :   When

προσεύχησθε, λέγετε· Πάτερ, ἁγιασθήτω τὸ
ye pray,   say :   Father,   let be hallowed   the

ὄνομά   σου·   ἐλθάτω   ἡ   βασιλεία   σου·
name   of thee;   let come   the   kingdom   of thee;

3 τὸν   ἄρτον   ἡμῶν   τὸν   ἐπιούσιον   δίδου
the   bread   of us   –   belonging to the morrow   give

ἡμῖν   τὸ καθ'   ἡμέραν·   4 καὶ ἄφες ἡμῖν τὰς
us   each day†;   and forgive   us   the

ἁμαρτίας   ἡμῶν,   καὶ   γὰρ   αὐτοὶ   ἀφίομεν
sins   of us,   for indeed   [our]selves   we forgive

παντὶ   ὀφείλοντι   ἡμῖν·   καὶ   μὴ   εἰσενέγκῃς
everyone   owing   to us;   and   lead not

ἡμᾶς   εἰς   πειρασμόν.   5 Καὶ   εἶπεν   πρὸς
us   into   temptation.   And   he said   to

αὐτούς·   τίς   ἐξ   ὑμῶν   ἕξει   φίλον,   καὶ
them :   Who of   you   shall have   a friend,   and

πορεύσεται   πρὸς   αὐτὸν   μεσονυκτίου   καὶ
will come   to   him   at midnight   and

εἴπῃ   αὐτῷ·   φίλε,   χρῆσόν   μοι   τρεῖς   ἄρτους,
say   to him :   Friend,   lend   me   three   loaves,

6 ἐπειδὴ   φίλος   μου   παρεγένετο   ἐξ   ὁδοῦ
since   a friend   of me   arrived   off   a journey

πρός   με   καὶ   οὐκ   ἔχω   ὃ   παραθήσω   αὐτῷ·
to   me   and   I have not   what   I may set before   him;

7 κἀκεῖνος   ἔσωθεν   ἀποκριθεὶς   εἴπῃ·   μή
and that one   within   answering   may say :   Not

μοι   κόπους   πάρεχε·   ἤδη   ἡ   θύρα   κέκλεισται,
me   troubles   cause;   now   the   door   has been shut,

καὶ   τὰ   παιδία   μου   μετ'   ἐμοῦ   εἰς   τὴν
and   the   children   of me   with   me   in   the

κοίτην   εἰσίν·   οὐ   δύναμαι   ἀναστὰς   δοῦναί
bed   are;   I cannot   rising up   to give

σοι.   8 λέγω   ὑμῖν,   εἰ   καὶ   οὐ   δώσει
thee.   I tell   you,   if   even   he will not give

αὐτῷ   ἀναστὰς   διὰ   τὸ   εἶναι   φίλον   αὐτοῦ,
him   rising up   on account of the   to be   friend   of him,
=because he is his friend,

διά   γε   τὴν   ἀναίδειαν   αὐτοῦ   ἐγερθεὶς
yet on account of   the   importunity   of him   rising

δώσει   αὐτῷ   ὅσων   χρῄζει.   9 Κἀγὼ   ὑμῖν
he will give   him   as many as   he needs.   And I   ¹you

λέγω,   αἰτεῖτε,   καὶ   δοθήσεται   ὑμῖν·   ζητεῖτε,
¹tell,   ask,   and   it will be given   you;   seek,

καὶ   εὑρήσετε·   κρούετε,   καὶ   ἀνοιγήσεται
and   ye will find;   knock,   and   it will be opened

ὑμῖν.   10 πᾶς   γὰρ   ὁ   αἰτῶν   λαμβάνει,   καὶ
to you.   For everyone   asking   receives,   and

seeks finds, and to him who knocks it will be opened. ¹¹What father among you, if his son asks for a fish, will instead of a fish give him a serpent; ¹²or if he asks for an egg, will give him a scorpion? ¹³If you then, who are evil, know how to give good gifts to your children, how much more will the heavenly Father give the Holy Spirit to those who ask him?"

14 Now he was casting out a demon that was dumb; when the demon had gone out, the dumb man spoke, and the people marveled. ¹⁵But some of them said, "He casts out demons by Be-el′zebul, the prince of demons"; ¹⁶while others, to test him, sought from him a sign from heaven. ¹⁷But he, knowing their thoughts, said to them, "Every kingdom divided against itself is laid waste, and house falls upon house. ¹⁸And if Satan also is divided against himself, how will his kingdom stand? For you say that I cast out demons by Be-el′zebul. ¹⁹And if I cast out

---

ὁ   ζητῶν   εὑρίσκει,   καὶ   τῷ   κρούοντι
the [one] seeking   finds,   and   to the [one] knocking

ἀνοιγήσεται.   11 τίνα   δὲ   ἐξ   ὑμῶν   τὸν
it will be opened.   And ¹what   ⁴of   ⁵you   –

πατέρα   αἰτήσει   ὁ   υἱὸς   ἰχθύν,   μὴ
²father ³[is there] ⁶[of whom]   ⁹will ask   ⁷the ⁸son   ¹⁰a fish,   not

ἀντὶ   ἰχθύος   ὄφιν   αὐτῷ   ἐπιδώσει;   12 ἤ
instead of   a fish   ³a serpent   ²to him   ¹will hand?   or

καὶ   αἰτήσει   ᾠόν,   ἐπιδώσει   αὐτῷ   σκορπίον;
even he will ask   an egg,   will hand   to him   a scorpion?

13 εἰ   οὖν   ὑμεῖς   πονηροὶ   ὑπάρχοντες   οἴδατε   δόματα
If therefore ye   ²evil   ¹being   know   gifts

ἀγαθὰ   διδόναι   τοῖς   τέκνοις   ὑμῶν,   πόσῳ
good   to give   to the   children   of you,   how much

μᾶλλον   ὁ   πατὴρ   ὁ   ἐξ   οὐρανοῦ   δώσει
more   the   Father   –   of   heaven   will give

πνεῦμα   ἅγιον   τοῖς   αἰτοῦσιν   αὐτόν.
Spirit   [the] Holy   to the [ones]   asking   him.

14 Καὶ   ἦν   ἐκβάλλων   δαιμόνιον,   καὶ   αὐτὸ
And he was   expelling   a demon,   and   it

ἦν   κωφόν·   ἐγένετο   δὲ   τοῦ   δαιμονίου
was   dumb;   and it came to pass   the   demon
   =as the demon went out

ἐξελθόντος   ἐλάλησεν   ὁ   κωφός·   καὶ
going outᵃ   spoke   the   dumb man;   and

ἐθαύμασαν   οἱ   ὄχλοι·   15 τινὲς   δὲ   ἐξ
marvelled   the   crowds;   but some   of

αὐτῶν   εἶπαν·   ἐν   Βεεζεβοὺλ   τῷ   ἄρχοντι
them   said :   By   Beelzebub   the   chief

τῶν   δαιμονίων   ἐκβάλλει   τὰ   δαιμόνια·
of the   demons   he expels   the   demons;

16 ἕτεροι   δὲ   πειράζοντες   σημεῖον   ἐξ   οὐρανοῦ
and others   tempting   a sign   out of heaven

ἐζήτουν   παρ᾽   αὐτοῦ.   17 αὐτὸς   δὲ   εἰδὼς
sought   from   him.   But he   knowing

αὐτῶν   τὰ   διανοήματα   εἶπεν   αὐτοῖς·   πᾶσα
of them   the   thoughts   said   to them :   Every

βασιλεία   ἐφ᾽   ἑαυτὴν   διαμερισθεῖσα   ἐρημοῦται,
kingdom   against   itself   divided   is made desolate,

καὶ   οἶκος   ἐπὶ   οἶκον   πίπτει.   18 εἰ   δὲ
and   a house   against   a house   falls.   And if

καὶ   ὁ   σατανᾶς   ἐφ᾽   ἑαυτὸν   διεμερίσθη,
also   –   Satan   against   himself   was divided,

πῶς   σταθήσεται   ἡ   βασιλεία   αὐτοῦ;   ὅτι
how   will stand   the   kingdom   of him?   because

λέγετε   ἐν   Βεεζεβοὺλ   ἐκβάλλειν   με   τὰ
ye say   by   Beelzebub   to expel   meᵇ   the
   =[that] by Beelzebub I expel

δαιμόνια.   19 εἰ   δὲ   ἐγὼ   ἐν   Βεεζεβοὺλ
demons.   But if   I   by   Beelzebub

ᶠ Other ancient authorities insert *a loaf, will give him a stone; or if he asks for*

demons by Be-el'zebul, by whom do your sons cast them out? Therefore they shall be your judges. ²⁰But if it is by the finger of God that I cast out demons, then the kingdom of God has come upon you. ²¹When a strong man, fully armed, guards his own palace, his goods are in peace; ²²but when one stronger than he assails him and overcomes him, he takes away his armor in which he trusted, and divides his spoil. ²³He who is not with me is against me, and he who does not gather with me scatters.

24 "When the unclean spirit has gone out of a man, he passes through waterless places seeking rest; and finding none he says, 'I will return to my house from which I came.' ²⁵And when he comes he finds it swept and put in order. ²⁶Then he goes and brings seven other spirits more evil than himself, and they enter and dwell there; and the last state of that man becomes worse than the first."

27 As he said this, a woman in the crowd raised her voice and said

ἐκβάλλω	τὰ	δαιμόνια,	οἱ	υἱοὶ	ὑμῶν	ἐν
expel	the	demons,	the	sons	of you	by

τίνι	ἐκβάλλουσιν;	διὰ	τοῦτο	αὐτοὶ	ὑμῶν
what	do they expel?	therefore		they	of you

κριταὶ	ἔσονται.	20	εἰ	δὲ	ἐν	δακτύλῳ
judges	shall be.		But if		by	[the] finger

θεοῦ	[ἐγὼ]	ἐκβάλλω	τὰ	δαιμόνια,	ἄρα
of God	I	expel	the	demons,	then

ἔφθασεν	ἐφ'	ὑμᾶς	ἡ	βασιλεία	τοῦ	θεοῦ.
came	upon	you	the	kingdom	-	of God.

21 ὅταν ὁ ἰσχυρὸς καθωπλισμένος φυλάσσῃ
When the strong man *having been* well armed guards

τὴν	ἑαυτοῦ	αὐλήν,	ἐν	εἰρήνῃ	ἐστὶν	τὰ
the	of him*self*	palace,	in	peace	is(are)	the

ὑπάρχοντα	αὐτοῦ·	22	ἐπὰν	δὲ	ἰσχυρότερος
goods	of him;		but when		a stronger

αὐτοῦ	ἐπελθὼν	νικήσῃ	αὐτόν,	τὴν	πανοπλίαν
[than] him	coming upon	overcomes	him,	the	armour

αὐτοῦ	αἴρει,	ἐφ'	ᾗ	ἐπεποίθει,	καὶ	τὰ
of him	he takes,	on	which	he had relied,	and	the

σκῦλα	αὐτοῦ	διαδίδωσιν.	23	Ὁ	μὴ	ὢν
arms	of him	distributes.		The [one]	not	being

μετ'	ἐμοῦ	κατ'	ἐμοῦ	ἐστιν,	καὶ	ὁ	μὴ
with	me	against	me	is,	and	the [one]	not

συνάγων	μετ'	ἐμοῦ	σκορπίζει.	24	Ὅταν
gathering	with	me	scatters.		When

τὸ	ἀκάθαρτον	πνεῦμα	ἐξέλθῃ	ἀπὸ	τοῦ
the	unclean	spirit	goes out	from	the

ἀνθρώπου,	διέρχεται	δι'	ἀνύδρων	τόπων
man,	he goes *through* through		dry	places

ζητοῦν	ἀνάπαυσιν,	καὶ	μὴ	εὑρίσκον	λέγει·
seeking	rest,	and	not	finding	says :

ὑποστρέψω	εἰς	τὸν	οἶκόν	μου	ὅθεν	ἐξῆλθον·
I will return	to	the	house	of me	whence	I came out;

25	καὶ	ἐλθὸν	εὑρίσκει	σεσαρωμένον	καὶ
	and	coming	he finds [it]	*having been* swept	and

κεκοσμημένον.	26	τότε	πορεύεται	καὶ
having been furnished.		Then	he goes	and

παραλαμβάνει	ἕτερα	πνεύματα	πονηρότερα
takes	other	spirits	more wicked

ἑαυτοῦ	ἑπτά,	καὶ	εἰσελθόντα	κατοικεῖ
[than] himself	seven,	and	entering	he dwells

ἐκεῖ·	καὶ	γίνεται	τὰ	ἔσχατα	τοῦ	ἀνθρώπου
there;	and	becomes	the	last things	-	man

ἐκείνου	χείρονα	τῶν	πρώτων.	27	Ἐγένετο
of that	worse [than] the		first.		it came to pass

δὲ	ἐν	τῷ	λέγειν	αὐτὸν	ταῦτα	ἐπάρασά	τις
And in	the		to say	him*be*	these things	*b*lifting up *¹a certain*	
=as he said							

to him, "Blessed is the womb that bore you, and the breasts that you sucked!" ²⁸But he said, "Blessed rather are those who hear the word of God and keep it!"

29 When the crowds were increasing, he began to say, "This generation is an evil generation; it seeks a sign, but no sign shall be given to it except the sign of Jonah. ³⁰For as Jonah became a sign to the men of Nin'eveh, so will the Son of man be to this generation. ³¹The queen of the South will arise at the judgment with the men of this generation and condemn them; for she came from the ends of the earth to hear the wisdom of Solomon, and behold, something greater than Solomon is here. ³²The men of Nin'eveh will arise at the judgment with this generation and condemn it; for they repented at the preaching of Jonah, and behold, something greater than Jonah is here.

33 "No one after lighting a lamp puts it in a cellar or under a bushel, but on a stand, that those who enter may see the light. ³⁴Your eye

---

φωνὴν   γυνὴ   ἐκ   τοῦ   ὄχλου   εἶπεν   αὐτῷ·
⁷[her] ⁶voice ³woman ⁵of ⁴the ⁵crowd said   to him :

μακαρία   ἡ   κοιλία   ἡ   βαστάσασά   σε   καὶ
Blessed   the womb   –   having borne thee and

μαστοὶ   οὓς   ἐθήλασας.   28 αὐτὸς   δὲ   εἶπεν·
[the] breasts which thou didst suck. But he   said :

μενοῦν   μακάριοι   οἱ   ἀκούοντες   τὸν   λόγον
Nay rather blessed the [ones] hearing the   word

τοῦ   θεοῦ   καὶ   φυλάσσοντες.
–   of God   and   keeping.

29 Τῶν   δὲ   ὄχλων   ἐπαθροιζομένων   ἤρξατο
And the   crowds   pressing upon²   he began
=as the crowds pressed upon [him]

λέγειν·   ἡ   γενεὰ   αὕτη   γενεὰ   πονηρά   ἐστιν·
to say : – ²generation ¹This ⁵generation ⁴an evil ³is;

σημεῖον   ζητεῖ,   καὶ   σημεῖον   οὐ   δοθήσεται
a sign   it seeks,   and   a sign   will not be given

αὐτῇ   εἰ   μὴ   τὸ   σημεῖον   Ἰωνᾶ.   30 καθὼς
to it   except   the   sign   of Jonas.   even as

γὰρ   ἐγένετο   [ὁ]   Ἰωνᾶς   τοῖς   Νινευίταις
For   ²became   [¹]Jonas   ⁴to the   ⁵Ninevites

σημεῖον,   οὕτως   ἔσται   καὶ   ὁ   υἱὸς   τοῦ
³a sign,   so   will be   also   the   Son   –

ἀνθρώπου   τῇ   γενεᾷ   ταύτῃ.   31 βασίλισσα
of man   –   generation   to this.   [The] queen

νότου   ἐγερθήσεται   ἐν   τῇ   κρίσει   μετὰ   τῶν
of [the] south will be raised in the judgment with   the

ἀνδρῶν   τῆς   γενεᾶς   ταύτης   καὶ   κατακρινεῖ
men   –   generation   of this   and   will condemn

αὐτούς·   ὅτι   ἦλθεν   ἐκ   τῶν   περάτων   τῆς
them;   because she came   from   the   extremities of the

γῆς   ἀκοῦσαι   τὴν   σοφίαν   Σολομῶνος,   καὶ
earth   to hear   the   wisdom   of Solomon,   and

ἰδοὺ   πλεῖον   Σολομῶνος   ὧδε.   32 ἄνδρες
behold   a greater [than] Solomon [is]   here.   Men

Νινευῖται   ἀναστήσονται   ἐν   τῇ   κρίσει   μετὰ
Ninevites   will rise up   in   the   judgment   with

τῆς   γενεᾶς   ταύτης   καὶ   κατακρινοῦσιν   αὐτήν·
–   generation   this   and   will condemn   it;

ὅτι   μετενόησαν   εἰς   τὸ   κήρυγμα   Ἰωνᾶ,   καὶ
because they repented at   the proclamation of Jonas,   and

ἰδοὺ   πλεῖον   Ἰωνᾶ   ὧδε.   33 Οὐδεὶς   λύχνον
behold a greater [than] Jonas [is] here.   No one   ²a lamp

ἅψας   εἰς   κρύπτην   τίθησιν   οὐδὲ   ὑπὸ   τὸν
¹having lit ⁴in   ⁵secret   ³places [it]   nor   under   the

μόδιον,   ἀλλ'   ἐπὶ   τὴν   λυχνίαν,   ἵνα   οἱ
bushel,   but   on   the   lampstand,   that   the

εἰσπορευόμενοι   τὸ   φέγγος   βλέπωσιν.   34 ὁ
ones] entering   the   light   may see.   The

is the lamp of your body; when your eye is sound, your whole body is full of light; but when it is not. sound, your body is full of darkness. 35 Therefore be careful lest the light in you be darkness. 36 If then your whole body is full of light, having no part dark, it will be wholly bright, as when a lamp with its rays gives you light."

37 While he was speaking, a Pharisee asked him to dine with him; so he went in and sat at table. 38 The Pharisee was astonished to see that he did not first wash before dinner. 39 And the Lord said to him, "Now you Pharisees cleanse the outside of the cup and of the dish, but inside you are full of extortion and wickedness. 40 You fools! Did not he who made the outside make the inside also? 41 But give for alms those things which are within; and behold, everything is clean for you.

42 "But woe to you Pharisees! for you tithe mint and rue and every herb, and neglect justice

λύχνος τοῦ σώματός ἐστιν ὁ ὀφθαλμός σου.
lamp of the body is the eye of thee.

ὅταν ὁ ὀφθαλμός σου ἁπλοῦς ᾖ, καὶ
When the eye of thee single is, also

ὅλον τὸ σῶμά σου φωτεινόν ἐστιν· ἐπὰν
all the body of thee bright is; ²when

δὲ πονηρὸς ᾖ, καὶ τὸ σῶμά σου σκοτεινόν.
¹but evil it is, also the body of thee [is] dark.

35 σκόπει οὖν μὴ τὸ φῶς τὸ ἐν σοὶ
Watch therefore lest the light – in thee

σκότος ἐστίν. 36 εἰ οὖν τὸ σῶμά σου
darkness is. If therefore ¹the ³body ⁴of thee

ὅλον φωτεινόν, μὴ ἔχον μέρος τι σκοτεινόν,
²whole [is] bright, not having ²part ¹any dark,

ἔσται φωτεινὸν ὅλον ὡς ὅταν ὁ λύχνος
²will be ³bright ¹all as when the lamp

τῇ ἀστραπῇ φωτίζῃ σε.
with the(its) shining enlightens thee.

37 Ἐν δὲ τῷ λαλῆσαι ἐρωτᾷ αὐτὸν
Now in the to speakᵉ asks him
=as [he] spoke

Φαρισαῖος ὅπως ἀριστήσῃ παρ’ αὐτῷ·
a Pharisee that he would dine with him;

εἰσελθὼν δὲ ἀνέπεσεν. 38 ὁ δὲ Φαρισαῖος
and entering he reclined. But the Pharisee

ἰδὼν ἐθαύμασεν ὅτι οὐ πρῶτον ἐβαπτίσθη
seeing marvelled that not first he washed

πρὸ τοῦ ἀρίστου. 39 εἶπεν δὲ ὁ κύριος
before the dinner. But said the Lord

πρὸς αὐτόν· νῦν ὑμεῖς οἱ Φαρισαῖοι τὸ
to him: Now ye – Pharisees the

ἔξωθεν τοῦ ποτηρίου καὶ τοῦ πίνακος
outside of the cup and of the dish

καθαρίζετε, τὸ δὲ ἔσωθεν ὑμῶν γέμει
cleanse, but the inside of you is full

ἁρπαγῆς καὶ πονηρίας. 40 ἄφρονες, οὐχ
of robbery and wickedness. Foolish men, not

ὁ ποιήσας τὸ ἔξωθεν καὶ τὸ ἔσωθεν
the [one] making the outside also the inside

ἐποίησεν; 41 πλὴν τὰ ἐνόντα δότε
made? Nevertheless the things being within give

ἐλεημοσύνην, καὶ ἰδοὺ πάντα καθαρὰ ὑμῖν
alms, and behold all things clean to you

ἐστιν. 42 ἀλλὰ οὐαὶ ὑμῖν τοῖς Φαρισαίοις,
is(are). But woe to you – Pharisees,

ὅτι ἀποδεκατοῦτε τὸ ἡδύοσμον καὶ τὸ
because ye tithe the mint and the

πήγανον καὶ πᾶν λάχανον, καὶ παρέρχεσθε
rue and every herb, and pass by

and the love of God; these you ought to have done, without neglecting the others. ⁴³Woe to you Pharisees! for you love the best seat in the synagogues and salutations in the market places. ⁴⁴Woe to you! for you are like graves which are not seen, and men walk over them without knowing it."

45 One of the lawyers answered him, "Teacher, in saying this you reproach us also." ⁴⁶And he said, "Woe to you lawyers also! for you load men with burdens hard to bear, and you yourselves do not touch the burdens with one of your fingers. ⁴⁷Woe to you! for you build the tombs of the prophets whom your fathers killed. ⁴⁸So you are witnesses and consent to the deeds of your fathers; for they killed them, and you build their tombs. ⁴⁹Therefore also the Wisdom of God said, 'I will send them prophets and apostles, some of whom they will kill and persecute,' ⁵⁰that the blood of all the prophets,

τὴν κρίσιν καὶ τὴν ἀγάπην τοῦ θεοῦ·
the judgment and the love – of God;
ταῦτα δὲ ἔδει ποιῆσαι κἀκεῖνα μὴ
but these things it behoved to do and those not
παρεῖναι. 43 οὐαὶ ὑμῖν τοῖς Φαρισαίοις,
to pass by. Woe to you – Pharisees,
ὅτι ἀγαπᾶτε τὴν πρωτοκαθεδρίαν ἐν ταῖς
because ye love the chief seat in the
συναγωγαῖς καὶ τοὺς ἀσπασμοὺς ἐν ταῖς
synagogues and the greetings in the
ἀγοραῖς. 44 οὐαὶ ὑμῖν, ὅτι ἐστὲ ὡς τὰ
marketplaces. Woe to you, because ye are as the
μνημεῖα τὰ ἄδηλα, καὶ οἱ ἄνθρωποι οἱ
tombs – unseen, and the men
περιπατοῦντες ἐπάνω οὐκ οἴδασιν.
walking over do not know.
45 Ἀποκριθεὶς δέ τις τῶν νομικῶν λέγει
And answering one of the lawyers says
αὐτῷ· διδάσκαλε, ταῦτα λέγων καὶ ἡμᾶς
to him : Teacher, these things saying also us
ὑβρίζεις. 46 ὁ δὲ εἶπεν· καὶ ὑμῖν τοῖς
thou insultest. And he said : Also to you –
νομικοῖς οὐαί, ὅτι φορτίζετε τοὺς ἀνθρώπους
lawyers woe, because ye burden – men
φορτία δυσβάστακτα, καὶ αὐτοὶ ἑνὶ τῶν
[with] burdens difficult to carry, and [your]selves with one of the
δακτύλων ὑμῶν οὐ προσψαύετε τοῖς φορτίοις.
fingers of you ye do not touch the burdens.
47 οὐαὶ ὑμῖν, ὅτι οἰκοδομεῖτε τὰ μνημεῖα
Woe to you, because ye build the tombs
τῶν προφητῶν, οἱ δὲ πατέρες ὑμῶν
of the prophets, and the fathers of you
ἀπέκτειναν αὐτούς. 48 ἄρα μάρτυρές ἐστε
killed them. Therefore witnesses ye are
καὶ συνευδοκεῖτε τοῖς ἔργοις τῶν πατέρων
and ye entirely approve the works of the fathers
ὑμῶν, ὅτι αὐτοὶ μὲν ἀπέκτειναν αὐτούς,
of you, because they on one hand killed them,
ὑμεῖς δὲ οἰκοδομεῖτε. 49 διὰ τοῦτο καὶ
ye on the other hand build. Therefore also
ἡ σοφία τοῦ θεοῦ εἶπεν· ἀποστελῶ εἰς
the Wisdom – of God said : I will send to
αὐτοὺς προφήτας καὶ ἀποστόλους, καὶ ἐξ
them prophets and apostles, and of
αὐτῶν ἀποκτενοῦσιν καὶ διώξουσιν, 50 ἵνα
them they will kill and persecute, that
ἐκζητηθῇ τὸ αἷμα πάντων τῶν προφητῶν
¹¹may be required ¹the ²blood ³of all ⁴the ⁵prophets

shed from the foundation of the world, may be required of this generation, ⁵¹ from the blood of Abel to the blood of Zechari'ah, who perished between the altar and the sanctuary. Yes, I tell you, it shall be required of this generation. ⁵² Woe to you lawyers! for you have taken away the key of knowledge; you did not enter yourselves, and you hindered those who were entering."

53 As he went away from there, the scribes and the Pharisees began to press him hard, and to provoke him to speak of many things, ⁵⁴ lying in wait for him, to catch at something he might say.

τὸ ἐκκεχυμένον ἀπὸ καταβολῆς κόσμου
- ⁶having been shed ⁷from ⁸[the] ⁹foundation ¹⁰of [the] world

ἀπὸ τῆς γενεᾶς ταύτης, 51 ἀπὸ αἵματος
¹²from - generation this, from [the] blood

Ἀβελ ἕως αἵματος Ζαχαρίου τοῦ
of Abel to [the] blood of Zacharias -

ἀπολομένου μεταξὺ τοῦ θυσιαστηρίου καὶ
destroyed between the altar and

τοῦ οἴκου· ναὶ λέγω ὑμῖν, ἐκζητηθήσεται
the house; yes I tell you, it will be required

ἀπὸ τῆς γενεᾶς ταύτης. 52 οὐαὶ ὑμῖν τοῖς
from - generation this. Woe to you

νομικοῖς, ὅτι ἤρατε τὴν κλεῖδα τῆς
lawyers, because ye took the key -

γνώσεως· αὐτοὶ οὐκ εἰσήλθατε καὶ τοὺς
of knowledge; [your]selves ye did not enter and the

εἰσερχομένους ἐκωλύσατε. 53 Κἀκεῖθεν ἐξελ-
[ones] entering ye prevented. And thence going
　　　　　　　　　　　　　　　　　　　=as he went forth thence

θόντος αὐτοῦ ἤρξαντο οἱ γραμματεῖς καὶ
forth himᵃ began the scribes and

οἱ Φαρισαῖοι δεινῶς ἐνέχειν καὶ ἀποστοματίζειν
the Pharisees ²terribly ¹to be ³angry and to ¹draw ²out

αὐτὸν περὶ πλειόνων, 54 ἐνεδρεύοντες
²him concerning a great number of things, lying in wait for

αὐτὸν θηρεῦσαί τι ἐκ τοῦ στόματος αὐτοῦ.
him to catch something out of the mouth of him.

CHAPTER 12

IN the meantime, when so many thousands of the multitude had gathered together that they trod upon one another, he began to say to his disciples first, "Beware of the leaven of the Pharisees, which is hypocrisy. ² Nothing is covered up that will not be revealed, or hidden that will not be known. ³ Whatever you have said in the dark shall be heard in the light, and what you have whispered in

12 Ἐν οἷς ἐπισυναχθεισῶν τῶν μυριάδων
In which things being assembled the thousands
=Meanwhile as the thousands of the crowd were assembled,

τοῦ ὄχλου, ὥστε καταπατεῖν ἀλλήλους,
of the crowd,ᵃ so as to tread on one another,

ἤρξατο λέγειν πρὸς τοὺς μαθητὰς αὐτοῦ
he began to say to the disciples of him

πρῶτον· προσέχετε ἑαυτοῖς ἀπὸ τῆς ζύμης,
first : Take heed to yourselves from the leaven,

ἥτις ἐστὶν ὑπόκρισις, τῶν Φαρισαίων.
which is hypocrisy, of the Pharisees.

2 οὐδὲν δὲ συγκεκαλυμμένον ἐστὶν ὃ οὐκ
And ²nothing ³having been ¹there is which not
　　　　　　completely covered

ἀποκαλυφθήσεται, καὶ κρυπτὸν ὃ οὐ γνωσθήσεται.
will be uncovered, and hidden which will not be known.

3 ἀνθ' ὧν ὅσα ἐν τῇ σκοτίᾳ εἴπατε ἐν
Therefore what things in the darkness ye said in

τῷ φωτὶ ἀκουσθήσεται, καὶ ὃ πρὸς τὸ
the light will be heard, and what to the

private rooms shall be proclaimed upon the housetops.

4 "I tell you, my friends, do not fear those who kill the body, and after that have no more that they can do. 5 But I will warn you whom to fear: fear him who, after he has killed, has power to cast into hell; yes, I tell you, fear him! 6 Are not five sparrows sold for two pennies? And not one of them is forgotten before God. 7 Why, even the hairs of your head are all numbered. Fear not; you are of more value than many sparrows.

8 "And I tell you, every one who acknowledges me before men, the Son of man also will acknowledge before the angels of God; 9 but he who denies me before men will be denied before the angels of God. 10 And every one who speaks a word against the Son of man will be forgiven; but he who blasphemes against the Holy Spirit will not be forgiven. 11 And when they bring

οὓς ἐλαλήσατε ἐν τοῖς ταμείοις κηρυχθήσεται
ear ye spoke in the private rooms will be proclaimed

ἐπὶ τῶν δωμάτων. 4 Λέγω δὲ ὑμῖν τοῖς
on the roofs. And I say to you the

φίλοις μου, μὴ φοβηθῆτε ἀπὸ τῶν
friends of me, do not be afraid from(of) the [ones]

ἀποκτεννόντων τὸ σῶμα καὶ μετὰ ταῦτα
killing the body and after these things

μὴ ἐχόντων περισσότερόν τι ποιῆσαι.
not having anything more to do.

5 ὑποδείξω δὲ ὑμῖν τίνα φοβηθῆτε·
But I will warn you whom ye may fear :

φοβήθητε τὸν μετὰ τὸ ἀποκτεῖναι ἔχοντα
¹fear ²the [one] ⁵after the ⁶to kill(killing) ³having

ἐξουσίαν ἐμβαλεῖν εἰς τὴν γέενναν. ναὶ
⁴authority ⁷to cast in into – gehenna. Yes[,]

λέγω ὑμῖν, τοῦτον φοβήθητε. 6 οὐχὶ
I say to you, this one fear ye. Not

πέντε στρουθία πωλοῦνται ἀσσαρίων δύο;
five sparrows are sold of(for) farthings two?

καὶ ἓν ἐξ αὐτῶν οὐκ ἔστιν ἐπιλελησμένον
and one of them is not having been forgotten

ἐνώπιον τοῦ θεοῦ. 7 ἀλλὰ καὶ αἱ τρίχες
before – God. But even the hairs

τῆς κεφαλῆς ὑμῶν πᾶσαι ἠρίθμηνται.
of the head of you all have been numbered.

μὴ φοβεῖσθε· πολλῶν στρουθίων διαφέρετε.
Fear ye not; from many sparrows ye differ.

8 λέγω δὲ ὑμῖν, πᾶς ὃς ἂν ὁμολογήσῃ
But I tell you, everyone whoever confesses

ἐν ἐμοὶ ἔμπροσθεν τῶν ἀνθρώπων, καὶ ὁ
– me before – men, also the

υἱὸς τοῦ ἀνθρώπου ὁμολογήσει ἐν αὐτῷ
Son – of man will confess – him

ἔμπροσθεν τῶν ἀγγέλων τοῦ θεοῦ· 9 ὁ δὲ
before the angels – of God; and the

ἀρνησάμενός με ἐνώπιον τῶν ἀνθρώπων
[one] denying me before – men

ἀπαρνηθήσεται ἐνώπιον τῶν ἀγγέλων τοῦ
will be denied before the angels –

θεοῦ. 10 καὶ πᾶς ὃς ἐρεῖ λόγον εἰς τὸν
of God. And everyone who shall say a word against the

υἱὸν τοῦ ἀνθρώπου, ἀφεθήσεται αὐτῷ· τῷ
Son – of man, it will be forgiven him; ²the [one]

δὲ εἰς τὸ ἅγιον πνεῦμα βλασφημήσαντι
¹but against the Holy Spirit blaspheming

οὐκ ἀφεθήσεται. 11 ὅταν δὲ εἰσφέρωσιν
will not be forgiven. And when they bring in

you before the synagogues and the rulers and the authorities, do not be anxious how or what you are to answer or what you are to say; [12]for the Holy Spirit will teach you in that very hour what you ought to say."

13 One of the multitude said to him, "Teacher, bid my brother divide the inheritance with me." [14]But he said to him, "Man, who made me a judge or divider over you?" [15]And he said to them, "Take heed, and beware of all covetousness; for a man's life does not consist in the abundance of his possessions." [16]And he told them a parable, saying, "The land of a rich man brought forth plentifully; [17]and he thought to himself, 'What shall I do, for I have nowhere to store my crops?' [18]And he said, 'I will do this: I will pull down my barns, and build larger ones; and there I will store all my grain and my goods. [19]And I will say to my soul, Soul, you have ample goods laid up for many years; take your ease, eat, drink, be merry.' [20]But God said

ὑμᾶς ἐπὶ τὰς συναγωγὰς καὶ τὰς ἀρχὰς
you before - synagogues and - rulers
καὶ τὰς ἐξουσίας, μὴ μεριμνήσητε πῶς ἢ
and - authorities, do not be anxious how or
τί ἀπολογήσησθε ἢ τί εἴπητε· 12 τὸ γὰρ
what ye may answer or what ye may say; for the
ἅγιον πνεῦμα διδάξει ὑμᾶς ἐν αὐτῇ τῇ
Holy Spirit will teach you in ²same ¹the
ὥρᾳ ἃ δεῖ εἰπεῖν. 13 Εἶπεν δέ τις
hour what things it behoves [you] to say. And said someone
ἐκ τοῦ ὄχλου αὐτῷ· διδάσκαλε, εἰπὲ τῷ
out of the crowd to him : Teacher, tell the
ἀδελφῷ μου μερίσασθαι μετ' ἐμοῦ τὴν
brother of me to divide with me the
κληρονομίαν. 14 ὁ δὲ εἶπεν αὐτῷ· ἄνθρωπε,
inheritance. But he said to him : Man,
τίς με κατέστησεν κριτὴν ἢ μεριστὴν ἐφ'
who me appointed a judge or a divider over
ὑμᾶς; 15 εἶπεν δὲ πρὸς αὐτούς· ὁρᾶτε
you? And he said to them : Beware
καὶ φυλάσσεσθε ἀπὸ πάσης πλεονεξίας,
and guard from(against) all covetousness,
ὅτι οὐκ ἐν τῷ περισσεύειν τινὶ ἡ ζωὴ
because ⁶not ⁵in ⁷the ⁸to abound ⁹to anyone ¹the ²life
αὐτοῦ ἐστιν ἐκ τῶν ὑπαρχόντων αὐτῷ.
³of him ⁴is ¹⁰of the things existing to him.ᶜ
=¹¹his ¹²possessions.
16 Εἶπεν δὲ παραβολὴν πρὸς αὐτοὺς λέγων·
And he told a parable to them saying :
ἀνθρώπου τινὸς πλουσίου εὐφόρησεν ἡ
³of a certain ⁵man ⁴rich ⁶bore well ¹The
χώρα. 17 καὶ διελογίζετο ἐν ἑαυτῷ λέγων·
²land. And he reasoned in himself saying :
τί ποιήσω, ὅτι οὐκ ἔχω ποῦ συνάξω τοὺς
What may I do, because I have not where I may gather the
καρπούς μου; 18 καὶ εἶπεν· τοῦτο ποιήσω·
fruits of me? And he said : This will I do :
καθελῶ μου τὰς ἀποθήκας καὶ μείζονας
I will pull down of me the barns and larger ones
οἰκοδομήσω, καὶ συνάξω ἐκεῖ πάντα τὸν
I will build, and I will gather there all the
σῖτον καὶ τὰ ἀγαθά μου, 19 καὶ ἐρῶ τῇ
wheat and the goods of me, and I will say to the
ψυχῇ μου· ψυχή, ἔχεις πολλὰ ἀγαθὰ
soul of me : Soul, thou hast many goods
κείμενα εἰς ἔτη πολλά· ἀναπαύου, φάγε,
laid [up] for years many; take rest, eat,
πίε, εὐφραίνου. 20 εἶπεν δὲ αὐτῷ ὁ
drink, be glad. But said to him -

to him, 'Fool! This night your soul is required of you; and the things you have prepared, whose will they be?' ²¹So is he who lays up treasure for himself, and is not rich toward God."

22 And he said to his disciples, "Therefore I tell you, do not be anxious about your life, what you shall eat, nor about your body, what you shall put on. ²³For life is more than food, and the body more than clothing. ²⁴Consider the ravens: they neither sow nor reap, they have neither storehouse nor barn, and yet God feeds them. Of how much more value are you than the birds! ²⁵And which of you by being anxious can add a cubit to his span of life?ᵍ ²⁶If then you are not able to do as small a thing as that, why are you anxious about the rest? ²⁷Consider the lilies, how they grow; they neither toil nor spin;ʰ yet I tell you, even Solomon in all his glory was not arrayed like one of these. ²⁸But if God so clothes the grass which is alive in the field today and tomorrow is thrown into the oven, how much more will he clothe you, O men of little faith? ²⁹And do not

ᵍ Or *to his stature*
ʰ Other ancient authorities read *Consider the lilies; they neither spin nor weave*

θεός· ἄφρων, ταύτῃ τῇ νυκτὶ τὴν ψυχήν
God : Foolish man, in this — night the soul
σου ἀπαιτοῦσιν ἀπὸ σοῦ· ἃ δὲ
of thee they demand from thee; then [the] things which
ἡτοίμασας, τίνι ἔσται; 21 οὕτως ὁ
thou preparedst, to whom will they be?ᶜ So the [one]
    =whose will they be?
θησαυρίζων αὐτῷ καὶ μὴ εἰς θεὸν πλουτῶν.
treasuring to himself and not toward God being rich.
22 Εἶπεν δὲ πρὸς τοὺς μαθητὰς [αὐτοῦ]·διὰ τοῦτο
And he said to the disciples of him : Therefore
λέγω ὑμῖν· μὴ μεριμνᾶτε τῇ ψυχῇ τί
I tell you: Do not be anxious for the life what
φάγητε, μηδὲ τῷ σώματι [ὑμῶν] τί
ye may eat, nor for the body of you what
ἐνδύσησθε. 23 ἡ γὰρ ψυχὴ πλεῖόν ἐστιν
ye may put on. For the life more is
τῆς τροφῆς καὶ τὸ σῶμα τοῦ ἐνδύματος.
[than] the food and the body [than] the clothing.
24 κατανοήσατε τοὺς κόρακας, ὅτι οὔτε
Consider ye the ravens, that neither
σπείρουσιν οὔτε θερίζουσιν, οἷς οὐκ ἔστιν°
they sow nor reap, to which is notᶜ
    =which have not
ταμιεῖον οὐδὲ ἀποθήκη, καὶ ὁ θεὸς τρέφει
storehouse nor barn, and — God feeds
αὐτούς· πόσῳ μᾶλλον ὑμεῖς διαφέρετε τῶν
them; by how much rather ye differ from the
πετεινῶν. 25 τίς δὲ ἐξ ὑμῶν μεριμνῶν
birds. And who of you being anxious
δύναται ἐπὶ τὴν ἡλικίαν αὐτοῦ προσθεῖναι
can on the stature of him *to* add
πῆχυν; 26 εἰ οὖν οὐδὲ ἐλάχιστον δύνασθε,
a cubit? If therefore not [the] least ye can,
τί περὶ τῶν λοιπῶν μεριμνᾶτε; 27 κατα-
why concerning the other things are ye anxious? Con-
νοήσατε τὰ κρίνα, πῶς οὔτε νήθει οὔτε
sider ye the lilies, how neither they spin nor
ὑφαίνει· λέγω δὲ ὑμῖν, οὐδὲ Σολομὼν ἐν
weave; but I tell you, not Solomon in
πάσῃ τῇ δόξῃ αὐτοῦ περιεβάλετο ὡς ἓν
all the glory of him was arrayed as one
τούτων. 28 εἰ δὲ ἐν ἀγρῷ τὸν χόρτον
of these. ¹And ²if ⁹in ¹⁰a field ⁶the ⁷grass
ὄντα σήμερον καὶ αὔριον εἰς κλίβανον
⁸being ¹¹to-day ¹²and ¹³tomorrow ¹⁵into ¹⁶an oven
βαλλόμενον ὁ θεὸς οὕτως ἀμφιάζει, πόσῳ
¹⁴being thrown — ³God ⁴so ⁵clothes, by how much
μᾶλλον ὑμᾶς, ὀλιγόπιστοι. 29 καὶ ὑμεῖς
rather you, little-faiths. And ye

seek what you are to eat and what you are to drink, nor be of anxious mind. ³⁰For all the nations of the world seek these things; and your Father knows that you need them. ³¹Instead, seek his[i] kingdom, and these things shall be yours as well.

32 "Fear not, little flock, for it is your Father's good pleasure to give you the kingdom. ³³Sell your possessions, and give alms; provide yourselves with purses that do not grow old, with a treasure in the heavens that does not fail, where no thief approaches and no moth destroys. ³⁴For where your treasure is, there will your heart be also.

35 "Let your loins be girded and your lamps burning, ³⁶and be like men who are waiting for their master to come home from the marriage feast, so that they may open to him at once when he comes and knocks. ³⁷Blessed are those servants whom the master finds awake when he comes; truly, I say to you, he will gird himself and have them sit at table, and he will come and serve them. ³⁸If he

[i] Other ancient authorities read God's

μὴ ζητεῖτε τί φάγητε καὶ τί πίητε, καὶ
do not seek what ye may eat and what ye may drink, and

μὴ μετεωρίζεσθε· 30 ταῦτα γὰρ πάντα τὰ
do not be in suspense; for these things all the

ἔθνη τοῦ κόσμου ἐπιζητοῦσιν· ὑμῶν δὲ
nations of the world seek after; but of you

ὁ πατὴρ οἶδεν ὅτι χρήζετε τούτων·
the Father knows that ye have need of them;

31 πλὴν ζητεῖτε τὴν βασιλείαν αὐτοῦ, καὶ
but seek ye the kingdom of him, and

ταῦτα προστεθήσεται ὑμῖν. 32 Μὴ φοβοῦ,
these things will be added to you. Fear not,

τὸ μικρὸν ποίμνιον· ὅτι εὐδόκησεν ὁ
- little flock; because was well pleased the

πατὴρ ὑμῶν δοῦναι ὑμῖν τὴν βασιλείαν.
Father of you to give you the kingdom.

33 Πωλήσατε τὰ ὑπάρχοντα ὑμῶν καὶ
Sell the possessions of you and

δότε ἐλεημοσύνην· ποιήσατε ἑαυτοῖς βαλ-
give alms; make for yourselves

λάντια μὴ παλαιούμενα, θησαυρὸν ἀνέκλειπτον
purses not becoming old, a treasure unfailing

ἐν τοῖς οὐρανοῖς, ὅπου κλέπτης οὐκ
in the heavens, where a thief not

ἐγγίζει οὐδὲ σὴς διαφθείρει· 34 ὅπου γάρ
comes near nor moth corrupts; for where

ἐστιν ὁ θησαυρὸς ὑμῶν, ἐκεῖ καὶ ἡ
is the treasure of you, there also the

καρδία ὑμῶν ἔσται. 35 Ἔστωσαν ὑμῶν αἱ
heart of you will be. Let be of you the

ὀσφύες περιεζωσμέναι καὶ οἱ λύχνοι
loins having been girded and the lamps

καιόμενοι· 36 καὶ ὑμεῖς ὅμοιοι ἀνθρώποις
burning; and ye like men

προσδεχομένοις τὸν κύριον ἑαυτῶν, πότε
awaiting the lord of themselves, when

ἀναλύσῃ ἐκ τῶν γάμων, ἵνα ἐλθόντος
he returns from the wedding festivities, that coming[a]

καὶ κρούσαντος εὐθέως ἀνοίξωσιν αὐτῷ.
and knocking[a] immediately they may open to him.

37 μακάριοι οἱ δοῦλοι ἐκεῖνοι, οὓς ἐλθὼν
Blessed - slaves those, whom coming

ὁ κύριος εὑρήσει γρηγοροῦντας· ἀμὴν λέγω
the lord will find watching; truly I tell

ὑμῖν ὅτι περιζώσεται καὶ ἀνακλινεῖ αὐτοὺς
you that he will gird himself and ¹make ²to recline ²them

καὶ παρελθὼν διακονήσει αὐτοῖς. 38 κἂν
and coming up to will serve them. And if

comes in the second watch, or in the third, and finds them so, blessed are those servants! ³⁹But know this, that if the householder had known at what hour the thief was coming, he would have been awake and[j] would not have left his house to be broken into. ⁴⁰You also must be ready; for the Son of man is coming at an hour you do not expect."

41 Peter said, "Lord, are you telling this parable for us or for all?" ⁴²And the Lord said, "Who then is the faithful and wise steward, whom his master will set over his household, to give them their portion of food at the proper time? ⁴³Blessed is that servant whom his master when he comes will find so doing. ⁴⁴Truly I tell you, he will set him over all his possessions. ⁴⁵But if that servant says to himself, 'My master is delayed in coming,' and begins to beat the menservants and the maidservants, and to eat and drink and get drunk, ⁴⁶the master of that servant will come on a day when he does not expect him and at an

ἐν τῇ δευτέρᾳ κἂν ἐν τῇ τρίτῃ φυλακῇ
in the second and if in the third watch
ἔλθῃ καὶ εὕρῃ οὕτως, μακάριοί εἰσιν
he comes and finds so, blessed are
ἐκεῖνοι. 39 τοῦτο δὲ γινώσκετε, ὅτι εἰ
those [slaves]. But this know ye, that if
ᾔδει ὁ οἰκοδεσπότης ποίᾳ ὥρᾳ ὁ κλέπτης
knew the house-master in what hour the thief
ἔρχεται, οὐκ ἂν ἀφῆκεν διορυχθῆναι τὸν
comes, he would not have allowed to be dug through the
οἶκον αὐτοῦ. 40 καὶ ὑμεῖς γίνεσθε ἕτοιμοι,
house of him. And ²ye ¹be prepared.
ὅτι ᾗ ὥρᾳ οὐ δοκεῖτε ὁ υἱὸς τοῦ
because in what hour ye think not the Son -
ἀνθρώπου ἔρχεται. 41 Εἶπεν δὲ ὁ Πέτρος·
of man comes. And said - Peter :
κύριε, πρὸς ἡμᾶς τὴν παραβολὴν ταύτην
Lord, to us - parable this
λέγεις ἢ καὶ πρὸς πάντας; 42 καὶ εἶπεν
sayest thou or also to all? And said
ὁ κύριος· τίς ἄρα ἐστὶν ὁ πιστὸς
the Lord : Who then is the faithful
οἰκονόμος ὁ φρόνιμος, ὃν καταστήσει ὁ
steward the prudent, whom will appoint the
κύριος ἐπὶ τῆς θεραπείας αὐτοῦ τοῦ
lord over the household attendants of him -
διδόναι ἐν καιρῷ [τὸ] σιτομέτριον;
to give[d] in season the portion of food?
43 μακάριος ὁ δοῦλος ἐκεῖνος, ὃν ἐλθὼν
Blessed - slave that, whom coming
ὁ κύριος αὐτοῦ εὑρήσει ποιοῦντα οὕτως.
the lord of him will find doing so.
44 ἀληθῶς λέγω ὑμῖν ὅτι ἐπὶ πᾶσιν τοῖς
Truly I tell you that over all the
ὑπάρχουσιν αὐτοῦ καταστήσει αὐτόν. 45 ἐὰν
possessions of him he will appoint him. if
δὲ εἴπῃ ὁ δοῦλος ἐκεῖνος ἐν τῇ καρδίᾳ
But says - slave that in the heart
αὐτοῦ· χρονίζει ὁ κύριός μου ἔρχεσθαι,
of him : Delays the lord of me to come,
καὶ ἄρξηται τύπτειν τοὺς παῖδας καὶ τὰς
and begins to strike the menservants and the
παιδίσκας, ἐσθίειν τε καὶ πίνειν καὶ
maidservants, ²to eat ¹both and to drink and
μεθύσκεσθαι, 46 ἥξει ὁ κύριος τοῦ δούλου
to become drunk, will come the lord - slave
ἐκείνου ἐν ἡμέρᾳ ᾗ οὐ προσδοκᾷ καὶ ἐν
of that in a day in which he does not expect and in

[j] Other ancient authorities omit *would have been awake and*

hour he does not know, and will punish[k] him, and put him with the unfaithful. [47]And that servant who knew his master's will, but did not make ready or act according to his will, shall receive a severe beating. [48]But he who did not know, and did what deserved a beating, shall receive a light beating. Every one to whom much is given, of him will much be required; and of him to whom men commit much they will demand the more.

49 "I came to cast fire upon the earth; and would that it were already kindled! [50]I have a baptism to be baptized with; and how I am constrained until it is accomplished! [51]Do you think that I have come to give peace on earth? No, I tell you, but rather division; [52]for henceforth in one house there will be five divided, three against two and two against three; [53]they will be divided, father against son and son against father, mother against daughter and daughter against her mother, mother-in-law against her daughter-in-law and daughter-in-law against her mother-in-law."

54 He also said to the multitudes, "When you see a cloud rising in the

[k] Or cut him in pieces

ὥρα ᾗ οὐ γινώσκει, καὶ διχοτομήσει
an hour in which he knows not, and will cut asunder

αὐτόν, καὶ τὸ μέρος αὐτοῦ μετὰ τῶν
him, and the portion of him with the

ἀπίστων θήσει. 47 ἐκεῖνος δὲ ὁ δοῦλος
unbelievers will place. But that – slave

ὁ γνοὺς τὸ θέλημα τοῦ κυρίου αὐτοῦ
– having known the will of the lord of him

καὶ μὴ ἑτοιμάσας ἢ ποιήσας πρὸς τὸ θέλημα
and not having prepared or done according to the will

αὐτοῦ δαρήσεται πολλάς· 48 ὁ δὲ
of him will be beaten [with] many [stripes]; but the [one]

μὴ γνούς, ποιήσας δὲ ἄξια πληγῶν,
not having known, but having done things worthy of stripes,

δαρήσεται ὀλίγας. παντὶ δὲ ᾧ
will be beaten [with] few [stripes]. But to everyone to whom

ἐδόθη πολύ, πολὺ ζητηθήσεται παρ' αὐτοῦ, καὶ
was given much, much will be demanded from him, and

ᾧ παρέθεντο πολύ, περισσότερον αἰτήσουσιν
with whom was deposited much, more exceedingly they will ask

αὐτόν. 49 Πῦρ ἦλθον βαλεῖν ἐπὶ τὴν γῆν,
him. Fire I came to cast on the earth,

καὶ τί θέλω εἰ ἤδη ἀνήφθη. 50 βάπτισμα
and what will I if already it was kindled. a baptism

δὲ ἔχω βαπτισθῆναι, καὶ πῶς συνέχομαι
And I have to be baptized [with], and how am I pressed

ἕως ὅτου τελεσθῇ. 51 δοκεῖτε ὅτι εἰρήνην
until it is accomplished. Think ye that peace

παρεγενόμην δοῦναι ἐν τῇ γῇ; οὐχί, λέγω
I came to give in the earth? No, I tell

ὑμῖν, ἀλλ' ἢ διαμερισμόν. 52 ἔσονται γὰρ
you, but rather division. For there will be

ἀπὸ τοῦ νῦν πέντε ἐν ἑνὶ οἴκῳ διαμεμε-
from – now five in one house having been

ρισμένοι, τρεῖς ἐπὶ δυσὶν καὶ δύο ἐπὶ
divided, three against two and two against

τρισὶν 53 διαμερισθήσονται, πατὴρ ἐπὶ υἱῷ
three will be divided, father against son

καὶ υἱὸς ἐπὶ πατρί, μήτηρ ἐπὶ θυγατέρα
and son against father, mother against daughter

καὶ θυγάτηρ ἐπὶ τὴν μητέρα, πενθερὰ
and daughter against the mother, mother-in-law

ἐπὶ τὴν νύμφην αὐτῆς καὶ νύμφη ἐπὶ
against the daughter-in-law of her and daughter-in-law against

τὴν πενθεράν. 54 Ἔλεγεν δὲ καὶ τοῖς
the mother-in-law. And he said also to the

ὄχλοις· ὅταν ἴδητε νεφέλην ἀνατέλλουσαν
crowds : When ye see a cloud rising

west, you say at once, 'A shower is coming'; and so it happens. ⁵⁵And when you see the south wind blowing, you say, 'There will be scorching heat'; and it happens. ⁵⁶You hypocrites! You know how to interpret the appearance of earth and sky; but why do you not know how to interpret the present time?

57 "And why do you not judge for yourselves what is right? ⁵⁸As you go with your accuser before the magistrate, make an effort to settle with him on the way, lest he drag you to the judge, and the judge hand you over to the officer, and the officer put you in prison. ⁵⁹I tell you, you will never get out till you have paid the very last copper."

ἐπὶ δυσμῶν, εὐθέως λέγετε ὅτι ὄμβρος
over [the] west, immediately ye say that a storm
ἔρχεται, καὶ γίνεται οὕτως· 55 καὶ ὅταν
is coming, and it becomes so; and when
νότον πνέοντα, λέγετε ὅτι καύσων ἔσται,
a south wind blowing, ye say that heat there will be,
καὶ γίνεται. 56 ὑποκριταί, τὸ πρόσωπον
and it becomes. Hypocrites, the face
τῆς γῆς καὶ τοῦ οὐρανοῦ οἴδατε δοκιμάζειν,
of the earth and of the heaven ye know* to discern,
τὸν καιρὸν δὲ τοῦτον πῶς οὐ δοκιμάζετε;
– ³time ¹but ²this how do ye not discern?
57 Τί δὲ καὶ ἀφ' ἑαυτῶν οὐ κρίνετε
And why even from yourselves do ye not judge
τὸ δίκαιον; 58 ὡς γὰρ ὑπάγεις μετὰ τοῦ
the righteous thing? For as thou goest with the
ἀντιδίκου σου ἐπ' ἄρχοντα, ἐν τῇ ὁδῷ
adversary of thee to a ruler, in the way
δὸς ἐργασίαν ἀπηλλάχθαι ἀπ' αὐτοῦ, μήποτε
give(take) pains to be rid from(of) him, lest
κατασύρῃ σε πρὸς τὸν κριτήν, καὶ ὁ
he drag thee to the judge, and the
κριτής σε παραδώσει τῷ πράκτορι, καὶ ὁ
judge thee will deliver to the usher, and the
πράκτωρ σε βαλεῖ εἰς φυλακήν. 59 λέγω
usher thee will cast into prison. I tell
σοι, οὐ μὴ ἐξέλθῃς ἐκεῖθεν ἕως
thee, by no means mayest thou come out thence until
καὶ τὸ ἔσχατον λεπτὸν ἀποδῷς.
even the last lepton thou payest.

CHAPTER 13

THERE were some present at that very time who told him of the Galileans whose blood Pilate had mingled with their sacrifices. ²And he answered them, "Do you think that these Galileans were worse sinners than all the other Galileans, because they suffered thus? ³I tell you, No; but unless you repent

13 Παρῆσαν δέ τινες ἐν αὐτῷ τῷ
And there were present some at ²same ¹the
καιρῷ ἀπαγγέλλοντες αὐτῷ περὶ τῶν
time reporting to him about the
Γαλιλαίων ὧν τὸ αἷμα Πιλᾶτος ἔμιξεν
Galilæans of whom the blood Pilate mixed
μετὰ τῶν θυσιῶν αὐτῶν. 2 καὶ ἀποκριθεὶς
with the sacrifices of them. And answering
εἶπεν αὐτοῖς· δοκεῖτε ὅτι οἱ Γαλιλαῖοι
he said to them: Think ye that – Galilæans
οὗτοι ἁμαρτωλοὶ παρὰ πάντας τοὺς Γαλι-
these sinners above all the Gali-
λαίους ἐγένοντο, ὅτι ταῦτα πεπόνθασιν;
læans were, because these things they have suffered?
3 οὐχί, λέγω ὑμῖν, ἀλλ' ἐὰν μὴ μετανοῆτε,
No, I tell you, but unless ye repent,

* can, as Mat. 16. 3. See note on page xviii.

you will all likewise perish. ⁴Or those eighteen upon whom the tower in Silo'am fell and killed them, do you think that they were worse offenders than all the others who dwelt in Jerusalem? ⁵I tell you, No; but unless you repent you will all likewise perish."

6 And he told this parable: "A man had a fig tree planted in his vineyard; and he came seeking fruit on it and found none. ⁷And he said to the vinedresser, 'Lo, these three years I have come seeking fruit on this fig tree, and I find none. Cut it down; why should it use up the ground?' ⁸And he answered him, 'Let it alone, sir, this year also, till I dig about it and put on manure. ⁹And if it bears fruit next year, well and good; but if not, you can cut it down.' "

10 Now he was teaching in one of the synagogues on the sabbath. ¹¹And there was a woman who had had a spirit of infirmity for eighteen years; she was bent over and could not

πάντες ὁμοίως ἀπολεῖσθε. 4 ἢ ἐκεῖνοι οἱ
all   likewise ye will perish.   Or those   -

δεκαοκτὼ ἐφ᾽ οὓς ἔπεσεν ὁ πύργος ἐν
eighteen on whom fell the tower in

τῷ Σιλωὰμ καὶ ἀπέκτεινεν αὐτούς, δοκεῖτε
- Siloam and   killed   them,   think ye

ὅτι αὐτοὶ ὀφειλέται ἐγένοντο παρὰ πάντας
that they debtors   were   above   all

τοὺς ἀνθρώπους τοὺς κατοικοῦντας Ἰερου-
the   men   -   dwelling in   Jeru-

σαλήμ; 5 οὐχί, λέγω ὑμῖν, ἀλλ᾽ ἐὰν μὴ
salem?   No, I tell you,   but   unless

μετανοήσητε, πάντες ὡσαύτως ἀπολεῖσθε.
ye repent,   all   similarly ye will perish.

6 Ἔλεγεν δὲ ταύτην τὴν παραβολήν. συκῆν
And he told this   -   parable.   ²A fig-tree

εἶχέν τις πεφυτευμένην ἐν τῷ ἀμπελῶνι
²had ¹a certain man having been planted in the vineyard

αὐτοῦ, καὶ ἦλθεν ζητῶν καρπὸν ἐν αὐτῇ
of him, and came seeking fruit   in   it

καὶ οὐχ εὗρεν. 7 εἶπεν δὲ πρὸς τὸν
and found not.   And he said to   the

ἀμπελουργόν· ἰδοὺ τρία ἔτη ἀφ᾽ οὗ
vinedresser : Behold[,] three years [it is] since

ἔρχομαι ζητῶν καρπὸν ἐν τῇ συκῇ ταύτῃ
I come seeking fruit in   -   fig-tree this

καὶ οὐχ εὑρίσκω· ἔκκοψον αὐτήν· ἱνατί
and   find not;   cut down   it;   why

καὶ τὴν γῆν καταργεῖ; 8 ὁ δὲ ἀποκριθεὶς
even the ground it spoils?   But he   answering

λέγει αὐτῷ· κύριε, ἄφες αὐτὴν καὶ τοῦτο
says to him : Lord, leave it   also   this

τὸ ἔτος, ἕως ὅτου σκάψω περὶ αὐτὴν καὶ
- year, until   I may dig round it   and

βάλω κόπρια, 9 κἂν μὲν ποιήσῃ καρπὸν
may throw dung, and if indeed it makes   fruit

εἰς τὸ μέλλον· εἰ δὲ μή γε, ἐκκόψεις
in the future;   otherwise,   thou shalt cut down

αὐτήν.
it.

10 Ἦν δὲ διδάσκων ἐν μιᾷ τῶν συναγωγῶν
And he was teaching in one of the synagogues

ἐν τοῖς σάββασιν. 11 καὶ ἰδοὺ γυνὴ
on the sabbaths.   And[,] behold[,] a woman

πνεῦμα ἔχουσα ἀσθενείας ἔτη δεκαοκτώ,
²a spirit ¹having of infirmity years eighteen,

καὶ ἦν συγκύπτουσα καὶ μὴ δυναμένη
and was bending double   and not being able

fully straighten herself.
¹²And when Jesus saw her, he called her and said to her, "Woman, you are freed from your infirmity." ¹³And he laid his hands upon her, and immediately she was made straight, and she praised God. ¹⁴But the ruler of the synagogue, indignant because Jesus had healed on the sabbath, said to the people, "There are six days on which work ought to be done; come on those days and be healed, and not on the sabbath day." ¹⁵Then the Lord answered him, "You hypocrites! Does not each of you on the sabbath untie his ox or his ass from the manger, and lead it away to water it? ¹⁶And ought not this woman, a daughter of Abraham whom Satan bound for eighteen years, be loosed from this bond on the sabbath day?" ¹⁷As he said this, all his adversaries were put to shame; and all the people rejoiced at all the glorious things that were done by him.

18 He said therefore, "What is the kingdom of God like? And to what shall I compare it? ¹⁹It

ἀνακύψαι εἰς τὸ παντελές. 12 ἰδὼν δὲ
to become erect   entirely.†   And seeing

αὐτὴν ὁ Ἰησοῦς προσεφώνησεν καὶ εἶπεν
her   –   Jesus   called to [him]   and   said

αὐτῇ· γύναι, ἀπολέλυσαι τῆς ἀσθενείας
to her : Woman, thou hast been loosed from the infirmity

σου, 13 καὶ ἐπέθηκεν αὐτῇ τὰς χεῖρας·
of thee,   and   he put on   her   the(his)   hands;

καὶ παραχρῆμα ἀνωρθώθη, καὶ ἐδόξαζεν
and   at once   she was straightened, and   glorified

τὸν θεόν. 14 ἀποκριθεὶς δὲ ὁ ἀρχι-
–   God.   But answering   the   syn-

συνάγωγος, ἀγανακτῶν ὅτι τῷ σαββάτῳ
agogue ruler,   being angry   that ³on the ⁴sabbath

ἐθεράπευσεν ὁ Ἰησοῦς, ἔλεγεν τῷ ὄχλῳ
²healed   –   ¹Jesus,   said   to the crowd[,]

ὅτι ἓξ ἡμέραι εἰσὶν ἐν αἷς δεῖ ἐργάζεσθαι·
–   six   days   there are on which it behoves   to work;

ἐν αὐταῖς οὖν ἐρχόμενοι θεραπεύεσθε καὶ
on   them   therefore   coming   be ye healed   and

μὴ τῇ ἡμέρᾳ τοῦ σαββάτου. 15 ἀπεκρίθη δὲ
not on the   day   of the   sabbath.   But answered

αὐτῷ ὁ κύριος καὶ εἶπεν· ὑποκριταί,
him   the Lord   and   said :   Hypocrites,

ἕκαστος ὑμῶν τῷ σαββάτῳ οὐ λύει τὸν
each one   of you   on the   sabbath   does he not loosen the

βοῦν αὐτοῦ ἢ τὸν ὄνον ἀπὸ τῆς φάτνης
ox   of him   or   the   ass   from   the   manger

καὶ ἀπαγαγὼν ποτίζει; 16 ταύτην δὲ
and   leading [it] away   give drink?   And this woman

θυγατέρα Ἀβραὰμ οὖσαν, ἣν ἔδησεν ὁ
a daughter   of Abraham   being,   whom   bound   the

σατανᾶς ἰδοὺ δέκα καὶ ὀκτὼ ἔτη, οὐκ ἔδει
Satan   behold   ten   and   eight   years, behoved it not

λυθῆναι ἀπὸ τοῦ δεσμοῦ τούτου τῇ
to be loosened from   –   bond   this   on the

ἡμέρᾳ τοῦ σαββάτου; 17 καὶ ταῦτα λέγοντος
day   of the   sabbath?   And these things saying
                                    =when he said these things

αὐτοῦ κατῃσχύνοντο πάντες οἱ ἀντικείμενοι
himᵃ   were put to shame   all   the [ones]   opposing

αὐτῷ, καὶ πᾶς ὁ ὄχλος ἔχαιρεν ἐπὶ
him,   and   all   the   crowd   rejoiced   over

πᾶσιν τοῖς ἐνδόξοις τοῖς γινομένοις ὑπ'
all   the   glorious things   –   happening   by

αὐτοῦ. 18 Ἔλεγεν οὖν· τίνι ὁμοία ἐστὶν ἡ
him.   He said therefore: To what   like   is   the

βασιλεία τοῦ θεοῦ, καὶ τίνι ὁμοιώσω
kingdom   –   of God,   and   to what   may I liken

is like a grain of mustard seed which a man took and sowed in his garden; and it grew and became a tree, and the birds of the air made nests in its branches."

20 And again he said, "To what shall I compare the kingdom of God? 21 It is like leaven which a woman took and hid in three measures of meal, till it was all leavened."

22 He went on his way through towns and villages, teaching, and journeying toward Jerusalem.

23 And some one said to him, "Lord, will those who are saved be few?" And he said to them, 24 "Strive to enter by the narrow door; for many, I tell you, will seek to enter and will not be able. 25 When once the householder has risen up and shut the door, you will begin to stand outside and to knock at the door, saying, 'Lord, open to us.' He will answer you,'I do not know where you come from.' 26 Then you will begin to say, 'We ate and drank in your presence, and you taught in our streets.' 27 But he will say, 'I tell

αὐτήν; 19 ὁμοία ἐστὶν κόκκῳ σινάπεως, ὃν
it?   Like   it is   to a grain   of mustard, which
λαβὼν ἄνθρωπος ἔβαλεν εἰς κῆπον ἑαυτοῦ,
²taking   ¹a man   cast   into   a garden   of himself,
καὶ ηὔξησεν καὶ ἐγένετο εἰς δένδρον, καὶ
and   it grew   and   became   into   a tree,   and
τὰ πετεινὰ τοῦ οὐρανοῦ κατεσκήνωσεν
the   birds   of the   heaven(air)   lodged
ἐν τοῖς κλάδοις αὐτοῦ. 20 Καὶ πάλιν
in   the   branches   of it.   And   again
εἶπεν· τίνι ὁμοιώσω τὴν βασιλείαν τοῦ
he said :   To what   may I liken   the   kingdom   of
θεοῦ; 21 ὁμοία ἐστὶν ζύμῃ, ἣν λαβοῦσα
God?   Like   it is   to leaven,   which   ²taking
γυνὴ ἔκρυψεν εἰς ἀλεύρου σάτα τρία,
¹a woman   hid   in   of meal   measures   three,
ἕως οὗ ἐζυμώθη ὅλον.
until   was leavened   all.

22 Καὶ διεπορεύετο κατὰ πόλεις καὶ
And   he journeyed through   throughout   cities   and
κώμας διδάσκων καὶ πορείαν ποιούμενος
villages   teaching   and   journey   making
εἰς Ἱεροσόλυμα. 23 Εἶπεν δέ τις αὐτῷ·
to   Jerusalem.   And said   someone to him :
κύριε, εἰ ὀλίγοι οἱ σωζόμενοι; ὁ δὲ εἶπεν
Lord,   if   few   the [ones] being saved;   And he   said
πρὸς αὐτούς· 24 ἀγωνίζεσθε εἰσελθεῖν διὰ
to   them :   Struggle   to enter   through
τῆς στενῆς θύρας, ὅτι πολλοί, λέγω ὑμῖν,
the   strait   door,   because   many,   I tell   you,
ζητήσουσιν εἰσελθεῖν καὶ οὐκ ἰσχύσουσιν.
will seek   to enter   and   will not be able.
25 ἀφ' οὗ ἂν ἐγερθῇ ὁ οἰκοδεσπότης καὶ
From [the time] when   is risen   the   house-master   and
ἀποκλείσῃ τὴν θύραν, καὶ ἄρξησθε ἔξω
he shuts   the   door,   and   ye begin   outside
ἑστάναι καὶ κρούειν τὴν θύραν λέγοντες·
to stand   and   to knock   the   door   saying :
κύριε, ἄνοιξον ἡμῖν, καὶ ἀποκριθεὶς ἐρεῖ
Lord,   open   to us,   and   answering   he will say
ὑμῖν· οὐκ οἶδα ὑμᾶς πόθεν ἐστέ. 26 τότε
to you :   I know not   you   whence   ye are.   Then
ἄρξεσθε λέγειν· ἐφάγομεν ἐνώπιόν σου καὶ
ye will begin   to say :   We ate   before   thee   and
ἐπίομεν, καὶ ἐν ταῖς πλατείαις ἡμῶν
drank,   and   in   the   streets   of us
ἐδίδαξας· 27 καὶ ἐρεῖ λέγων ὑμῖν· οὐκ
thou didst teach;   and   he will say   telling   you :   not

you, I do not know where you come from; depart from me, all you workers of iniquity!' ²⁸There you will weep and gnash your teeth, when you see Abraham and Isaac and Jacob and all the prophets in the kingdom of God and you yourselves thrust out. ²⁹And men will come from east and west, and from north and south, and sit at table in the kingdom of God. ³⁰And behold, some are last who will be first, and some are first who will be last."

31 At that very hour some Pharisees came, and said to him, "Get away from here, for Herod wants to kill you." ³²And he said to them, "Go and tell that fox, 'Behold, I cast out demons and perform cures today and tomorrow, and the third day I finish my course. ³³Nevertheless I must go on my way today and tomorrow and the day following; for it cannot be that a prophet should perish away from Jerusalem.' ³⁴O Jerusalem, Jerusalem, killing the prophets and stoning those who are sent to you! How often would I have gathered your

οἶδα πόθεν ἐστέ· ἀπόστητε ἀπ' ἐμοῦ
I know whence ye are; stand away from me

πάντες ἐργάται ἀδικίας. 28 ἐκεῖ ἔσται ὁ
all workers of unrighteousness. There will be the

κλαυθμὸς καὶ ὁ βρυγμὸς τῶν ὀδόντων,
weeping and the gnashing of the teeth,

ὅταν ὄψησθε 'Αβραὰμ καὶ 'Ισαὰκ καὶ
when ye see Abraham and Isaac and

'Ιακὼβ καὶ πάντας τοὺς προφήτας ἐν τῇ
Jacob and all the prophets in the

βασιλείᾳ τοῦ θεοῦ, ὑμᾶς δὲ ἐκβαλλομένους
kingdom - of God, but you being thrust out

ἔξω. 29 καὶ ἥξουσιν ἀπὸ ἀνατολῶν καὶ
outside. And they will come from east and

δυσμῶν καὶ ἀπὸ βορρᾶ καὶ νότου, καὶ
west and from north and south, and

ἀνακλιθήσονται ἐν τῇ βασιλείᾳ τοῦ θεοῦ.
will recline in the kingdom - of God.

30 καὶ ἰδοὺ εἰσὶν ἔσχατοι οἳ ἔσονται
And behold there are last [ones] who will be

πρῶτοι, καὶ εἰσὶν πρῶτοι οἳ ἔσονται
first, and there are first [ones] who will be

ἔσχατοι. 31 'Εν αὐτῇ τῇ ὥρᾳ προσῆλθάν
last. In ²same ¹the hour approached

τινες Φαρισαῖοι λέγοντες αὐτῷ· ἔξελθε καὶ
some Pharisees saying to him : Depart and

πορεύου ἐντεῦθεν, ὅτι 'Ηρώδης θέλει σε
go hence, because Herod wishes thee

ἀποκτεῖναι. 32 καὶ εἶπεν αὐτοῖς· πορευθέντες
to kill. And he said to them : Going

εἴπατε τῇ ἀλώπεκι ταύτῃ· ἰδοὺ ἐκβάλλω
tell - fox this : Behold I expel

δαιμόνια καὶ ἰάσεις ἀποτελῶ σήμερον καὶ
demons and ²cures ¹accomplish to-day and

αὔριον, καὶ τῇ τρίτῃ τελειοῦμαι. 33 πλὴν
to-morrow, and on the third [day] I am perfected. Nevertheless

δεῖ με σήμερον καὶ αὔριον καὶ τῇ ἐχομένῃ
it be- me to-day and to- and on the following
hoves   morrow   [day]

πορεύεσθαι, ὅτι οὐκ ἐνδέχεται προφήτην
to journey, because it is not possible a prophet

ἀπολέσθαι ἔξω 'Ιερουσαλήμ. 34 'Ιερουσαλὴμ
to perish outside Jerusalem. Jerusalem[,]

'Ιερουσαλήμ, ἡ ἀποκτείνουσα τοὺς προφήτας
Jerusalem, the [one] killing the prophets

καὶ λιθοβολοῦσα τοὺς ἀπεσταλμένους πρὸς
and stoning the [ones] having been sent to

αὐτήν, ποσάκις ἠθέλησα ἐπισυνάξαι τὰ
her, how often I wished to gather the

children together as a
hen gathers her brood
under her wings, and
you would not! [35] Behold,
your house is forsaken.
And I tell you, you will
not see me until you
say, 'Blessed is he who
comes in the name of the
Lord!' "

τέκνα   σου   ὃν   τρόπον   ὄρνις   τὴν   ἑαυτῆς
children of thee   as †   a bird   the   of herself
νοσσιὰν   ὑπὸ   τὰς   πτέρυγας,   καὶ   οὐκ
brood   under   the(her)   wings,   and   not
ἠθελήσατε.   35 ἰδοὺ   ἀφίεται   ὑμῖν   ὁ   οἶκος
ye wished.   Behold   is left   to you   the   house
ὑμῶν.   λέγω   [δὲ]   ὑμῖν,   οὐ   μὴ   ἴδητέ   με
of you.   And I tell   you,   by no means ye may see   me
ἕως   ἥξει   ὅτε   εἴπητε·   εὐλογημένος   ὁ
until   shall come   [the   ye say :   Blessed   the
            time] when
ἐρχόμενος   ἐν   ὀνόματι   κυρίου.
[one] coming   in   [the] name of [the] Lord.

CHAPTER 14

ONE sabbath when
he went to dine at
the house of a ruler who
belonged to the Pharisees,
they were watching him.
[2] And behold, there was
a man before him who
had dropsy. [3] And Jesus
spoke to the lawyers and
Pharisees, saying, "Is it
lawful to heal on the
sabbath, or not?" [4] But
they were silent. Then he
took him and healed
him, and let him go.
[5] And he said to them,
"Which of you, having
an ass[l] or an ox that has
fallen into a well, will
not immediately pull him
out on a sabbath day?"
[6] And they could not
reply to this.

7 Now he told a
parable to those who
were invited, when he
marked how they chose
the places of honor, say-
ing to them, [8] "When you
are invited by any one to

14 Καὶ   ἐγένετο   ἐν   τῷ   ἐλθεῖν   αὐτὸν   εἰς
And it came to pass in the   to go   him[be]   into
                         =as he went
οἰκόν   τινος   τῶν   ἀρχόντων   τῶν   Φαρισαίων
a house   of one   of the   leaders   of the   Pharisees
σαββάτῳ   φαγεῖν   ἄρτον,   καὶ   αὐτοὶ   ἦσαν
on a sabbath   to eat   bread,   and   they   were
παρατηρούμενοι   αὐτόν.   2 καὶ   ἰδοὺ   ἄνθρωπός
carefully watching   him.   And[,] behold[,]   man
τις   ἦν   ὑδρωπικὸς   ἔμπροσθεν   αὐτοῦ.   3 καὶ
a certain was   dropsical   before   him.   And
ἀποκριθεὶς   ὁ   Ἰησοῦς   εἶπεν   πρὸς   τοὺς
answering   –   Jesus   spoke   to   the
νομικοὺς   καὶ   Φαρισαίους   λέγων·   ἔξεστιν
lawyers   and   Pharisees   saying :   Is it lawful
τῷ   σαββάτῳ   θεραπεῦσαι   ἢ   οὔ;   4 οἱ   δὲ
on the   sabbath   to heal   or   not?   And they
ἡσύχασαν.   καὶ   ἐπιλαβόμενος   ἰάσατο   αὐτὸν
were silent.   And   taking   he cured   him
καὶ   ἀπέλυσεν.   5 καὶ   πρὸς   αὐτοὺς   εἶπεν·
and   dismissed.   And   to   them   he said:
τίνος   ὑμῶν   υἱὸς   ἢ   βοῦς   εἰς   φρέαρ   πεσεῖται,
Of whom   of you a son   or an ox into   a pit   shall fall,
καὶ   οὐκ   εὐθέως   ἀνασπάσει   αὐτὸν   ἐν
and   not   immediately   he will pull up   it   on
ἡμέρα   τοῦ   σαββάτου;   6 καὶ   οὐκ   ἴσχυσαν
a day   of the   sabbath?   And   they were not able
ἀνταποκριθῆναι   πρὸς   ταῦτα.   7 Ἔλεγεν   δὲ
to reply   against these things.   And he said
πρὸς   τοὺς   κεκλημένους   παραβολήν,   ἐπέχων
to the [ones] *having been* invited   a parable,   noting
πῶς   τὰς   πρωτοκλισίας   ἐξελέγοντο,   λέγων
how   ²the   ³chief seats   ¹they were choosing,   saying
πρὸς   αὐτούς·   8 ὅταν   κληθῇς   ὑπό   τινος   εἰς
to   them :   When thou art invited by   anyone   to

---

[l] Other ancient authorities
read *a son*

a marriage feast, do not sit down in a place of honor, lest a more eminent man than you be invited by him; ⁹and he who invited you both will come and say to you, 'Give place to this man,' and then you will begin with shame to take the lowest place. ¹⁰But when you are invited, go and sit in the lowest place, so that when your host comes he may say to you, 'Friend, go up higher'; then you will be honored in the presence of all who sit at table with you. ¹¹For every one who exalts himself will be humbled, and he who humbles himself will be exalted."

12 He said also to the man who had invited him, "When you give a dinner or a banquet, do not invite your friends or your brothers or your kinsmen or rich neighbors, lest they also invite you in return, and you be repaid. ¹³But when you give a feast, invite the poor, the maimed, the lame, the blind, ¹⁴and you will be blessed, because they cannot repay you. You will be repaid at the resurrection of the just."

15 When one of those who sat at table with him heard this, he said to

γάμους,　μὴ κατακλιθῇς εἰς τὴν πρωτοκλισίαν,
wedding festivities, do not recline　in the　chief seat,

μήποτε　ἐντιμότερός　σου　ᾖ κεκλημένος ὑπ'
lest　a more honour-　thou　be *having been* invited　by
　　　　able [than]

αὐτοῦ, 9 καὶ ἐλθὼν　ὁ σὲ καὶ αὐτὸν καλέσας
him,　and coming ¹the [one] ³thee ⁴and ⁵him　²inviting

ἐρεῖ　σοι· δὸς　τούτῳ　τόπον,　καὶ　τότε
will say to thee : Give　this man　place,　and　then

ἄρξῃ　μετὰ αἰσχύνης τὸν ἔσχατον τόπον
thou wilt begin with　shame　the　last　place

κατέχειν.　10 ἀλλ'　ὅταν　κληθῇς,　πορευθεὶς
to take.　But　when thou art invited,　going

ἀνάπεσε εἰς τὸν ἔσχατον τόπον, ἵνα ὅταν ἔλθῃ
recline　in the　last　place,　that when ⁴comes

ὁ　κεκληκώς σε　ἐρεῖ　σοι· φίλε,
¹the [one] ²having invited ³thee he will say to thee : Friend,

προσανάβηθι ἀνώτερον· τότε　ἔσται　σοι δόξα
go up　higher;　then there will be to thee° glory

ἐνώπιον πάντων τῶν συνανακειμένων σοι.
before　all　the [ones]　reclining with　thee.

11 ὅτι　πᾶς ὁ ὑψῶν ἑαυτὸν ταπεινωθήσεται,
Because everyone exalting himself　will be humbled,

καὶ　ὁ　ταπεινῶν　ἑαυτὸν　ὑψωθήσεται.
and　the [one] humbling　himself　will be exalted.

12 Ἔλεγεν δὲ καὶ τῷ κεκληκότι αὐτόν·
And he said　also to the [one] having invited　him :

ὅταν ποιῇς　ἄριστον ἢ δεῖπνον, μὴ φώνει
When thou makest a dinner or　a supper,　do not call

τοὺς　φίλους　σου　μηδὲ　τοὺς　ἀδελφούς
the　friends　of thee　nor　the　brothers

σου　μηδὲ　τοὺς　συγγενεῖς　σου　μηδὲ
of thee　nor　the　relatives　of thee　nor

γείτονας　πλουσίους,　μήποτε　καὶ　αὐτοὶ
neighbours　rich,　lest　also　they

ἀντικαλέσωσίν σε καὶ γένηται ἀνταπόδομά
¹invite ²in ⁴return　²thee and　it becomes　a recompence

σοι.　13 ἀλλ'　ὅταν　δοχὴν ποιῇς,　κάλει
to thee.　But　when　a party thou makest,　invite

πτωχούς,　ἀναπήρους,　χωλούς,　τυφλούς·
poor [persons],　maimed,　lame,　blind;

14 καὶ　μακάριος　ἔσῃ,　ὅτι οὐκ ἔχουσιν
and　blessed thou shalt be,　because　they have not

ἀνταποδοῦναί σοι· ἀνταποδοθήσεται γάρ σοι
to recompense　thee;　for it will be recompensed　to thee

ἐν τῇ ἀναστάσει τῶν δικαίων. 15 Ἀκούσας
in　the　resurrection of the　just.　²hearing

δέ	τις	τῶν	συνανακειμένων ταῦτα εἶπεν
¹And ⁴one ⁵of the [ones]　⁶reclining with　³these things　said

him, "Blessed is he who shall eat bread in the kingdom of God!" ¹⁶But he said to him, "A man once gave a great banquet, and invited many; ¹⁷and at the time for the banquet he sent his servant to say to those who had been invited, 'Come; for all is now ready.' ¹⁸But they all alike began to make excuses. The first said to him, 'I have bought a field, and I must go out and see it; I pray you, have me excused.' ¹⁹And another said, 'I have bought five yoke of oxen, and I go to examine them; I pray you, have me excused.' ²⁰And another said, 'I have married a wife, and therefore I cannot come.' ²¹So the servant came and reported this to his master. Then the householder in anger said to his servant, 'Go out quickly to the streets and lanes of the city, and bring in the poor and maimed and blind and lame.' ²²And the servant said, 'Sir, what you commanded has been done, and still there is room.' ²³And the master said to the servant, 'Go

αὐτῷ· μακάριος ὅστις φάγεται ἄρτον ἐν
to him : Blessed [is he] who eats bread in

τῇ βασιλείᾳ τοῦ θεοῦ. 16 ὁ δὲ εἶπεν
the kingdom – of God. And he said

αὐτῷ· ἄνθρωπός τις ἐποίει δεῖπνον μέγα,
to him : A certain man made supper a great,

καὶ ἐκάλεσεν πολλούς, 17 καὶ ἀπέστειλεν
and invited many, and sent

τὸν δοῦλον αὐτοῦ τῇ ὥρᾳ τοῦ δείπνου
the slave of him at the hour of the supper

εἰπεῖν τοῖς κεκλημένοις· ἔρχεσθε, ὅτι ἤδη
to say to the [ones] having been invited : Come, because ²now

ἕτοιμά ἐστιν. 18 καὶ ἤρξαντο ἀπὸ μιᾶς
³prepared ¹it is. And they began from one [mind]

πάντες παραιτεῖσθαι. ὁ πρῶτος εἶπεν
all to beg off. The first said

αὐτῷ· ἀγρὸν ἠγόρασα, καὶ ἔχω ἀνάγκην
to him : ²A farm ¹I bought, and I am obliged†

ἐξελθὼν ἰδεῖν αὐτόν· ἐρωτῶ σε, ἔχε με
going out to see it; I ask thee, have me

παρῃτημένον. 19 καὶ ἕτερος εἶπεν· ζεύγη
begged off. And another said : ²Yoke

βοῶν ἠγόρασα πέντε, καὶ πορεύομαι
⁴of oxen ¹I bought ²five, and I am going

δοκιμάσαι αὐτά· ἐρωτῶ σε, ἔχε με
to prove them; I ask thee, have me

παρῃτημένον. 20 καὶ ἕτερος εἶπεν· γυναῖκα
begged off. And another said : ²A wife

ἔγημα, καὶ διὰ τοῦτο οὐ δύναμαι ἐλθεῖν.
¹I married, and therefore I cannot to come.

21 καὶ παραγενόμενος ὁ δοῦλος ἀπήγγειλεν
And coming up the slave reported

τῷ κυρίῳ αὐτοῦ ταῦτα. τότε ὀργισθεὶς ὁ
to the lord of him these things. Then being angry the

οἰκοδεσπότης εἶπεν τῷ δούλῳ αὐτοῦ· ἔξελθε
house-master told the slave of him : Go out

ταχέως εἰς τὰς πλατείας καὶ ῥύμας τῆς
quickly into the streets and lanes of the

πόλεως, καὶ τοὺς πτωχοὺς καὶ ἀναπήρους
city, and the poor and maimed

καὶ τυφλοὺς καὶ χωλοὺς εἰσάγαγε ὧδε.
and blind and lame bring in here.

22 καὶ εἶπεν ὁ δοῦλος· κύριε, γέγονεν ὃ
And said the slave : Lord, has happened what

ἐπέταξας, καὶ ἔτι τόπος ἐστίν. 23 καὶ
thou didst command, and yet room there is. And

εἶπεν ὁ κύριος πρὸς τὸν δοῦλον· ἔξελθε εἰς
said the lord to the slave : Go out into

out to the highways and hedges, and compel people to come in, that my house may be filled. [24] For I tell you, none of those men who were invited shall taste my banquet.' " 25 Now great multitudes accompanied him; and he turned and said to them, [26] "If any one comes to me and does not hate his own father and mother and wife and children and brothers and sisters, yes, and even his own life, he cannot be my disciple. [27] Whoever does not bear his own cross and come after me, cannot be my disciple. [28] For which of you, desiring to build a tower, does not first sit down and count the cost, whether he has enough to complete it? [29] Otherwise, when he has laid a foundation, and is not able to finish, all who see it begin to mock him, [30] saying, 'This man began to build, and was not able to finish.' [31] Or what king, going to encounter another king in war, will not sit down

τὰς ὁδοὺς καὶ φραγμοὺς καὶ ἀνάγκασον
the　ways　and　hedges　and　compel

εἰσελθεῖν, ἵνα γεμισθῇ μου ὁ οἶκος·
to come in,　that　may be filled　of me　the　house;

24 λέγω γὰρ ὑμῖν ὅτι οὐδεὶς τῶν ἀνδρῶν
　for I tell　you　that　not one　–　men

ἐκείνων τῶν κεκλημένων γεύσεταί μου
of those　–　having been invited　shall taste　of me

τοῦ δείπνου.
the　supper.

25 Συνεπορεύοντο δὲ αὐτῷ ὄχλοι πολλοί,
　And came together　to him　crowds　many,

καὶ στραφεὶς εἶπεν πρὸς αὐτούς· 26 εἴ τις
and　turning　he said　to　them :　If anyone

ἔρχεται πρός με καὶ οὐ μισεῖ τὸν πατέρα
comes　to　me　and　hates not　the　father

αὐτοῦ καὶ τὴν μητέρα καὶ τὴν γυναῖκα
of him　and　the　mother　and　the　wife

καὶ τὰ τέκνα καὶ τοὺς ἀδελφοὺς καὶ τὰς
and　the　children　and　the　brothers　and　the

ἀδελφάς, ἔτι τε καὶ τὴν ψυχὴν ἑαυτοῦ,
sisters,　and besides also　the　life　of himself,

οὐ δύναται εἶναί μου μαθητής. 27 ὅστις
he cannot　to be　of me　a disciple.　Who

οὐ βαστάζει τὸν σταυρὸν ἑαυτοῦ καὶ
bears not　the　cross　of himself　and

ἔρχεται ὀπίσω μου, οὐ δύναται εἶναί μου
comes　after　me,　he cannot　to be　of me

μαθητής. 28 Τίς γὰρ ἐξ ὑμῶν θέλων
a disciple.　For who　of　you　wishing

πύργον οἰκοδομῆσαι οὐχὶ πρῶτον καθίσας
a tower　to build　not　first　sitting

ψηφίζει τὴν δαπάνην, εἰ ἔχει εἰς ἀπαρ-
counts　the　cost,　if　he has　for　com-

τισμόν; 29 ἵνα μή ποτε θέντος αὐτοῦ
pletion?　Lest　when　laying　him[a]
　　　　　　　　　　　　　　　=he has laid

θεμέλιον καὶ μὴ ἰσχύοντος ἐκτελέσαι πάντες
a foundation　and　not　being able[a]　to finish　all

οἱ θεωροῦντες ἄρξωνται αὐτῷ ἐμπαίζειν
the [ones]　seeing　begin　him　to mock

30 λέγοντες ὅτι οὗτος ὁ ἄνθρωπος ἤρξατο
　saying[,]　–　This　–　man　began

οἰκοδομεῖν καὶ οὐκ ἴσχυσεν ἐκτελέσαι.
to build　and　was not able　to finish.

31 Ἢ τίς βασιλεὺς πορευόμενος ἑτέρῳ βασιλεῖ
　Or what　king　[1]going　[2]another　[3]king

συμβαλεῖν εἰς πόλεμον οὐχὶ καθίσας πρῶτον
[2]to attack　[3]in　[4]war　not　sitting　first

first and take counsel whether he is able with ten thousand to meet him who comes against him with twenty thousand? ³²And if not, while the other is yet a great way off, he sends an embassy and asks terms of peace. ³³So therefore, whoever of you does not renounce all that he has cannot be my disciple. 34 "Salt is good; but if salt has lost its taste, how shall its saltness be restored? ³⁵It is fit neither for the land nor for the dunghill; men throw it away. He who has ears to hear, let him hear."

βουλεύσεται	εἰ	δυνατός	ἐστιν	ἐν	δέκα
will deliberate	if	able	he is	with	ten

χιλιάσιν	ὑπαντῆσαι	τῷ	μετὰ	εἴκοσι	χιλιάδων
thousands	to meet	¹the [one]	⁵with	⁶twenty	⁷thousands

ἐρχομένῳ	ἐπ᾽	αὐτόν;	32 εἰ	δὲ μή	γε, ἔτι
²coming	³upon	⁴him?	Otherwise,		yet = while

αὐτοῦ	πόρρω	ὄντος	πρεσβείαν	ἀποστείλας
him he is yet at a distance	afar	being⁸	a delegation	sending

ἐρωτᾷ	τὰ πρὸς	εἰρήνην.	33 οὕτως	οὖν
he asks the things for		peace.	So	therefore

πᾶς	ἐξ ὑμῶν	ὃς οὐκ	ἀποτάσσεται	πᾶσιν
everyone of you		who does not say farewell		to all

τοῖς	ἑαυτοῦ	ὑπάρχουσιν	οὐ δύναται	εἶναί
¹the	³of himself	²possessions	cannot	to be

μου	μαθητής.	34 Καλὸν	οὖν τὸ	ἅλας·
of me	a disciple.	Good	therefore the	salt;

ἐὰν	δὲ καὶ	τὸ	ἅλας μωρανθῇ,	ἐν τίνι
but if	even	the	salt becomes useless,	with what

ἀρτυθήσεται;	35 οὔτε	εἰς	γῆν οὔτε	εἰς
will it be seasoned?	neither	for	soil nor	for

κοπρίαν	εὔθετόν	ἐστιν·	ἔξω	βάλλουσιν
manure	suitable	is it;	outside	they cast

αὐτό.	ὁ ἔχων	ὦτα	ἀκούειν	ἀκουέτω.
it.	The [one] having	ears	to hear	let him hear.

CHAPTER 15

NOW the tax collectors and sinners were all drawing near to hear him. ²And the Pharisees and the scribes murmured, saying, "This man receives sinners and eats with them."
3 So he told them this parable: ⁴"What man of you, having a hundred sheep, if he has lost one of them, does not leave the ninety-nine in the wilderness, and go after the one which is lost, until he finds it? ⁵And

15 Ἦσαν	δὲ	αὐτῷ ἐγγίζοντες	πάντες
Now there were		to him drawing near	all

οἱ τελῶναι	καὶ	οἱ ἁμαρτωλοὶ	ἀκούειν
the tax-collectors	and	the sinners	to hear

αὐτοῦ.	2 καὶ διεγόγγυζον	οἵ τε	Φαρισαῖοι
him.	And greatly murmured	both the	Pharisees

καὶ	οἱ γραμματεῖς	λέγοντες ὅτι	οὗτος
and	the scribes	saying[,]	– This man

ἁμαρτωλοὺς	προσδέχεται	καὶ συνεσθίει	αὐ-
sinners	receives	and eats with	them.

τοῖς.	3 εἶπεν δὲ	πρὸς αὐτοὺς	τὴν παρα-
	And he spoke	to them	– para-

βολὴν	ταύτην	λέγων· 4 τίς	ἄνθρωπος ἐξ
ble	this	saying : What	man of

ὑμῶν	ἔχων ἑκατὸν	πρόβατα καὶ	ἀπολέσας
you	having a hundred	sheep and	losing

ἐξ	αὐτῶν ἓν	οὐ καταλείπει	τὰ ἐνενήκοντα
of	them one	does not leave	the ninety-

ἐννέα	ἐν τῇ	ἐρήμῳ καὶ	πορεύεται ἐπὶ
nine	in the	desert and	goes after

τὸ	ἀπολωλὸς	ἕως εὕρη	αὐτό; 5 καὶ
the [one]	having been lost	until he finds	it? and

when he has found it, he lays it on his shoulders, rejoicing. ⁶And when he comes home, he calls together his friends and his neighbors, saying to them, 'Rejoice with me, for I have found my sheep which was lost.' ⁷Just so, I tell you, there will be more joy in heaven over one sinner who repents than over ninety-nine righteous persons who need no repentance.

8 "Or what woman, having ten silver coins, if she loses one coin, does not light a lamp and sweep the house and seek diligently until she finds it? ⁹And when she has found it, she calls together her friends and neighbors, saying, 'Rejoice with me, for I have found the coin which I had lost.' ¹⁰Just so, I tell you, there is joy before the angels of God over one sinner who repents."

11 And he said, "There was a man who had two sons; ¹²and the younger of them said to his father, 'Father, give me the share of property that falls to me.' And he divided his living between them. ¹³Not many days later, the younger son gathered all he had and took his journey into a far country, and there

εὑρὼν ἐπιτίθησιν ἐπὶ τοὺς ὤμους αὐτοῦ
finding places on [it] on the shoulders of him

χαίρων, 6 καὶ ἐλθὼν εἰς τὸν οἶκον
rejoicing, and coming into the house

συγκαλεῖ τοὺς φίλους καὶ τοὺς γείτονας,
he calls together the friends and the neighbours,

λέγων αὐτοῖς· συγχάρητέ μοι, ὅτι εὗρον
saying to them: Rejoice with me, because I found

τὸ πρόβατόν μου τὸ ἀπολωλός. 7 λέγω
the sheep of me - having been lost. I tell

ὑμῖν ὅτι οὕτως χαρὰ ἐν τῷ οὐρανῷ
you that thus joy in - heaven

ἔσται ἐπὶ ἑνὶ ἁμαρτωλῷ μετανοοῦντι ἤ
will be over one sinner repenting than

ἐπὶ ἐνενήκοντα ἐννέα δικαίοις οἵτινες οὐ
over ninety-nine just men who no

χρείαν ἔχουσιν μετανοίας. 8 Ἢ τίς γυνὴ
need have of repentance. Or what woman

δραχμὰς ἔχουσα δέκα, ἐὰν ἀπολέσῃ
²drachmae ¹having ²ten, if she loses

δραχμὴν μίαν, οὐχὶ ἅπτει λύχνον καὶ
drachma one, does not light a lamp and

σαροῖ τὴν οἰκίαν καὶ ζητεῖ ἐπιμελῶς
sweep the house and seek carefully

ἕως οὗ εὕρῃ; 9 καὶ εὑροῦσα συγκαλεῖ
until she finds? and finding she calls together

τὰς φίλας καὶ γείτονας λέγουσα· συγχάρητέ
the friends and neighbours saying: Rejoice with

μοι, ὅτι εὗρον τὴν δραχμὴν ἣν ἀπώλεσα.
me, because I found the drachma which I lost.

10 οὕτως, λέγω ὑμῖν, γίνεται χαρὰ ἐνώπιον
So, I tell you, there is joy before

τῶν ἀγγέλων τοῦ θεοῦ ἐπὶ ἑνὶ ἁμαρτωλῷ
the angels of God over one sinner

μετανοοῦντι. 11 Εἶπεν δέ· ἄνθρωπός τις
repenting. And he said: A certain man

εἶχεν δύο υἱούς. 12 καὶ εἶπεν ὁ νεώτερος
had two sons. And said the younger

αὐτῶν τῷ πατρί· πάτερ, δός μοι τὸ
of them to the father: Father, give me the

ἐπιβάλλον μέρος τῆς οὐσίας. ὁ δὲ διεῖλες
falling upon share of the property. And he divided
=share of the property falling to [me].

αὐτοῖς τὸν βίον. 13 καὶ μετ᾽ οὐ πολλὰς
to them the living. And after not many

ἡμέρας συναγαγὼν πάντα ὁ νεώτερος υἱὸς
days having gathered all things the younger son

ἀπεδήμησεν εἰς χώραν μακράν, καὶ ἐκεῖ
departed to country a far, and there

he squandered his
property in loose living.
[14]And when he had spent
everything, a great
famine arose in that
country, and he began to
be in want. [15]So he went
and joined himself to one
of the citizens of that
country, who sent him
into his fields to feed
swine. [16]And he would
gladly have fed on[m] the
pods that the swine ate;
and no one gave him
anything. [17]But when he
came to himself he said,
'How many of my
father's hired servants
have bread enough and
to spare, but I perish
here with hunger! [18]I will
arise and go to my
father, and I will say to
him, "Father, I have
sinned against heaven
and before you; [19]I am
no longer worthy to be
called your son; treat me
as one of your hired
servants." ' [20]And he
arose and came to his
father. But while he was
yet at a distance, his
father saw him and had
compassion, and ran and
embraced him and kissed
him. [21]And the son said
to him, 'Father, I have
sinned against heaven

[m] Other ancient authorities
read *filled his belly with*

διεσκόρπισεν τὴν οὐσίαν αὐτοῦ ζῶν ἀσώτως.
scattered   the   property   of him   living   prodigally.

14 δαπανήσαντος δὲ αὐτοῦ πάντα ἐγένετο
But having spent   him[a]   all things   there came
=when he had spent

λιμὸς ἰσχυρὰ κατὰ τὴν χώραν ἐκείνην,
famine   a severe   throughout   –   country   that,

καὶ αὐτὸς ἤρξατο ὑστερεῖσθαι. 15 καὶ
and   he   began   to be in want.   And

πορευθεὶς ἐκολλήθη ἑνὶ τῶν πολιτῶν τῆς
going   he was joined to one of the   citizens   –

χώρας ἐκείνης, καὶ ἔπεμψεν αὐτὸν εἰς
country   of that,   and   he sent   him   into

τοὺς ἀγροὺς αὐτοῦ βόσκειν χοίρους· 16 καὶ
the   fields   of him   to feed   pigs;   and

ἐπεθύμει γεμίσαι τὴν κοιλίαν αὐτοῦ ἐκ
he longed   to fill   the   stomach   of him   out of(with)

τῶν κερατίων ὧν ἤσθιον οἱ χοῖροι, καὶ
the   husks   which   [2]ate   [1]the   [2]pigs,   and

οὐδεὶς ἐδίδου αὐτῷ. 17 εἰς ἑαυτὸν δὲ
no one   gave   to him.   [3]to   [4]himself   [1]But

ἐλθὼν ἔφη· πόσοι μίσθιοι τοῦ πατρός μου
[2]coming he said: How many hired servants of the father of me

περισσεύονται ἄρτων, ἐγὼ δὲ λιμῷ ὧδε
abound   of loaves,   but I   with famine here
=have abundance of bread,

ἀπόλλυμαι. 18 ἀναστὰς πορεύσομαι πρὸς
am perishing.   Rising up   I will go   to

τὸν πατέρα μου καὶ ἐρῶ αὐτῷ· πάτερ,
the   father   of me   and I will say to him :   Father,

ἥμαρτον εἰς τὸν οὐρανὸν καὶ ἐνώπιόν σου,
I sinned against   –   heaven   and   before   thee,

19 οὐκέτι εἰμὶ ἄξιος κληθῆναι υἱός σου·
no longer am I   worthy   to be called   a son   of thee;

ποίησόν με ὡς ἕνα τῶν μισθίων σου.
make   me   as   one   of the hired servants of thee.

20 καὶ ἀναστὰς ἦλθεν πρὸς τὸν πατέρα
And   rising up   he came   to   the   father

ἑαυτοῦ. ἔτι δὲ αὐτοῦ μακρὰν ἀπέχοντος
of himself.   But yet   him   afar   being away[a]
=while he was yet far away

εἶδεν αὐτὸν ὁ πατὴρ αὐτοῦ καὶ ἐσπλαγχνίσθη,
saw   him   the father   of him   and was moved with pity,

καὶ δραμὼν ἐπέπεσεν ἐπὶ τὸν τράχηλον
and   running   fell *on*   on   the   neck

αὐτοῦ καὶ κατεφίλησεν αὐτόν. 21 εἶπεν δὲ
of him   and   fervently kissed   him.   And said

ὁ υἱὸς αὐτῷ· πάτερ, ἥμαρτον εἰς τὸν
the   son   to him :   Father,   I sinned   against   –

and before you; I am no longer worthy to be called your son.'ⁿ ²²But the father said to his servants, 'Bring quickly the best robe, and put it on him; and put a ring on his hand, and shoes on his feet; ²³and bring the fatted calf and kill it, and let us eat and make merry; ²⁴for this my son was dead, and is alive again; he was lost, and is found.' And they began to make merry.

25 "Now his elder son was in the field; and as he came and drew near to the house, he heard music and dancing. ²⁶And he called one of the servants and asked what this meant. ²⁷And he said to him, 'Your brother has come, and your father has killed the fatted calf, because he has received him safe and sound.' ²⁸But he was angry and refused to go in. His father came out and entreated him, ²⁹but he answered his father, 'Lo, these many years I have served you, and I never disobeyed your command; yet you never gave me a kid, that I

οὐρανὸν	καὶ	ἐνώπιόν	σου,	οὐκέτι	εἰμὶ
heaven	and	before	thee,	no longer	am I

ἄξιος	κληθῆναι	υἱός	σου.	22 εἶπεν	δὲ
worthy	to be called	a son	of thee.	22	But said

ὁ πατὴρ	πρὸς	τοὺς	δούλους	αὐτοῦ·	ταχὺ
the father	to	the	slaves	of him :	Quickly

ἐξενέγκατε	στολὴν	τὴν	πρώτην	καὶ	ἐνδύσατε
bring ye out	a robe	the	first	and	clothe

αὐτόν,	καὶ	δότε	δακτύλιον	εἰς	τὴν	χεῖρα
him,	and	give(put)	a ring	to	the	hand

αὐτοῦ	καὶ	ὑποδήματα	εἰς	τοὺς	πόδας,
of him	and	sandals	to	the	feet,

23 καὶ	φέρετε	τὸν	μόσχον	τὸν	σιτευτόν,
23 and	bring	the	calf	-	fattened,

θύσατε,	καὶ	φαγόντες	εὐφρανθῶμεν,	24 ὅτι
kill,	and	eating	let us be merry,	24 because

οὗτος	ὁ	υἱός	μου	νεκρὸς	ἦν	καὶ	ἀνέζησεν,
this	-	son	of me	dead	was	and	lived again,

ἦν	ἀπολωλὼς	καὶ	εὑρέθη.	καὶ	ἤρξαντο
was	*having been* lost	and	was found.	And	they began

εὐφραίνεσθαι.	25 ἦν	δὲ	ὁ	υἱὸς	αὐτοῦ
to be merry.	25 But was		the	son	of him

ὁ	πρεσβύτερος	ἐν	ἀγρῷ·	καὶ	ὡς	ἐρχόμενος
-	older	in	a field;	and	as	coming

ἤγγισεν	τῇ	οἰκίᾳ,	ἤκουσεν	συμφωνίας	καὶ
he drew near to	the house,		he heard	music	and

χορῶν,	26 καὶ	προσκαλεσάμενος	ἕνα	τῶν
dances,	26 and	calling to [him]	one	of the

παίδων	ἐπυνθάνετο	τί	ἂν	εἴη	ταῦτα.
lads	he inquired	what		might be	these things.

27 ὁ	δὲ	εἶπεν	αὐτῷ	ὅτι	ὁ	ἀδελφός	σου
27 And he		said	to him[,]	-	The	brother	of thee

ἥκει,	καὶ	ἔθυσεν	ὁ	πατήρ	σου	τὸν	μόσχον	τὸν
has come,	and	⁴killed	¹the	²father	³of thee	⁵the	⁷calf	-

σιτευτόν,	ὅτι	ὑγιαίνοντα	αὐτὸν	ἀπέλαβεν.
⁶fattened,	because	⁵being in health	³him	¹he	²received ⁴back.

28 ὠργίσθη	δὲ	καὶ	οὐκ	ἤθελεν	εἰσελθεῖν·
28 But he was angry		and	did not wish		to enter;

ὁ	δὲ	πατὴρ	αὐτοῦ	ἐξελθὼν	παρεκάλει
so the		father	of him	coming out	besought

αὐτόν.	29 ὁ	δὲ	ἀποκριθεὶς	εἶπεν	τῷ
him.	29	But he	answering	said	to the

πατρί·	ἰδοὺ	τοσαῦτα	ἔτη	δουλεύω	σοι	καὶ
father :	Behold[,]	so many	years	I serve	thee	and

οὐδέποτε	ἐντολήν	σου	παρῆλθον,	καὶ	ἐμοὶ
never	a command	of thee	I transgressed,	and	to me

οὐδέποτε	ἔδωκας	ἔριφον	ἵνα	μετὰ	τῶν
never	thou gavest	a goat	that	with	the

might make merry with my friends. ³⁰But when this son of yours came, who has devoured your living with harlots, you killed for him the fatted calf!' ³¹And he said to him, 'Son, you are always with me, and all that is mine is yours. ³²It was fitting to make merry and be glad, for this your brother was dead, and is alive; he was lost, and is found.' "

φίλων   μου   εὐφρανθῶ·   **30** ὅτε   δὲ   ὁ   υἱός
friends   of me   I might be merry;   but when   -   ²son

σου   οὗτος   ὁ   καταφαγών   σου   τὸν   βίον
²of thee   ¹this   -   having devoured   of thee   the   living

μετὰ   πορνῶν   ἦλθεν,   ἔθυσας   αὐτῷ   τὸν
with   harlots   came,   thou killedst   for him   the

σιτευτὸν   μόσχον.   **31** ὁ   δὲ   εἶπεν   αὐτῷ·
fattened   calf.   And he   said   to him :

τέκνον,   σὺ   πάντοτε   μετ'   ἐμοῦ   εἶ,   καὶ
Child,   thou   always   with   me   art,   and

πάντα   τὰ   ἐμὰ   σά   ἐστιν·   **32** εὐφρανθῆναι
¹all ³things   -   ²my   ⁵thine   ⁴is(are);   ³to be merry

δὲ   καὶ   χαρῆναι   ἔδει,   ὅτι   ὁ   ἀδελφός
¹And   ⁴and   ⁵to rejoice   ²it be-   because   -   ²brother
           hoved [us],

σου   οὗτος   νεκρὸς   ἦν   καὶ   ἔζησεν,   καὶ   ἀπο-
²of thee   ¹this   ⁵dead   ⁴was   and came to life,   and   having

λωλὼς   καὶ   εὑρέθη.
been lost   also   was found.

CHAPTER 16

HE also said to the disciples, "There was a rich man who had a steward, and charges were brought to him that this man was wasting his goods. ²And he called him and said to him, 'What is this that I hear about you? Turn in the account of your stewardship, for you can no longer be steward. ³And the steward said to himself, 'What shall I do, since my master is taking the stewardship away from me? I am not strong enough to dig, and I am ashamed to beg. ⁴I have decided what to do, so that people may receive me into their houses when I am put out of the stewardship.' ⁵So, summoning his master's debtors one by one, he

16 Ἔλεγεν   δὲ   καὶ   πρὸς   τοὺς   μαθητάς·
    And he said   also   to   the   disciples :

ἄνθρωπός   τις   ἦν   πλούσιος   ὃς   εἶχεν
²A certain ⁴man   ¹there was   ³rich   who   had

οἰκονόμον,   καὶ   οὗτος   διεβλήθη   αὐτῷ   ὡς
a steward,   and   this   was complained of   to him   as

διασκορπίζων   τὰ   ὑπάρχοντα   αὐτοῦ.   **2** καὶ
wasting   the   possessions   of him.   And

φωνήσας   αὐτὸν   εἶπεν   αὐτῷ·   τί   τοῦτο
calling   him   he said   to him :   What [is]   this

ἀκούω   περὶ   σοῦ;   ἀπόδος   τὸν   λόγον   τῆς
I hear   about   thee?   render   the   account   of the

οἰκονομίας   σου·   οὐ   γὰρ   δύνῃ   ἔτι   οἰκονομεῖν.
stewardship of thee;   for thou canst not longer   to be steward.

3 εἶπεν   δὲ   ἐν   ἑαυτῷ   ὁ   οἰκονόμος·   τί
    And said   in   himself   the   steward :   What

ποιήσω,   ὅτι   ὁ   κύριός   μου   ἀφαιρεῖται   τὴν
may I do,   because   the   lord   of me   takes away   the

οἰκονομίαν   ἀπ'   ἐμοῦ;   σκάπτειν   οὐκ   ἰσχύω,
stewardship   from   me?   to dig   I am not able,

ἐπαιτεῖν   αἰσχύνομαι.   **4** ἔγνων   τί   ποιήσω,
to beg   I am ashamed.   I knew(know) what   I may do,

ἵνα   ὅταν   μετασταθῶ   ἐκ   τῆς   οἰκονομίας
that   when   I am removed   out of   the   stewardship

δέξωνταί   με   εἰς   τοὺς   οἴκους   ἑαυτῶν.
they may receive me   into   the   houses   of themselves.

5 καὶ   προσκαλεσάμενος   ἕνα   ἕκαστον   τῶν
    And   calling to [him]   ²one   ¹each   of the

said to the first, 'How much do you owe my master?' ⁶He said, 'A hundred measures of oil.' And he said to him, 'Take your bill, and sit down quickly and write fifty.' ⁷Then he said to another, 'And how much do you owe?' He said, 'A hundred measures of wheat.' He said to him, 'Take your bill, and write eighty.' ⁸The master commended the dishonest steward for his prudence; for the sons of this world are wiser in their own generation than the sons of light. ⁹And I tell you, make friends for yourselves by means of unrighteous mammon, so that when it fails they may receive you into the eternal habitations. 10 "He who is faithful in a very little is faithful also in much; and he who is dishonest in a very little is dishonest also in much. ¹¹If then you have not been faithful in the unrighteous mammon, who will entrust to you the true riches? ¹²And if you have not been faithful in that which is another's, who will give you that which is your own? ¹³No servant can serve two

---

χρεοφειλετῶν τοῦ κυρίου ἑαυτοῦ ἔλεγεν τῷ
debtors   of the   lord   of him*self*   he said   to the

πρώτῳ· πόσον ὀφείλεις τῷ κυρίῳ μου;
first :   How much   owest thou   to the   lord   of me?

6 ὁ δὲ εἶπεν· ἑκατὸν βάτους ἐλαίου. ὁ δὲ
And he   said :   A hundred   baths   of oil.   And he

εἶπεν αὐτῷ· δέξαι σου τὰ γράμματα καὶ
told   him :   Take   of thee   the   letters(bill)   and

καθίσας ταχέως γράψον πεντήκοντα. 7 ἔπειτα
sitting   quickly   write   fifty.   Then

ἑτέρῳ εἶπεν· σὺ δὲ πόσον ὀφείλεις; ὁ δὲ
to another he said :   ⁴thou ¹And   ²how much   ³owest?   And he

εἶπεν· ἑκατὸν κόρους σίτου. λέγει αὐτῷ·
said :   A hundred   cors   of wheat.   He tells   him :

δέξαι σου τὰ γράμματα καὶ γράψον
Take   of thee   the   bill   and   write

ὀγδοήκοντα. 8 καὶ ἐπήνεσεν ὁ κύριος τὸν
eighty.   And   ³praised   ¹the   ²lord   the

οἰκονόμον τῆς ἀδικίας ὅτι φρονίμως
steward   – of unrighteousness   because   prudently

ἐποίησεν· ὅτι οἱ υἱοὶ τοῦ αἰῶνος τούτου
he acted;   because   the sons   –   age   of this

φρονιμώτεροι ὑπὲρ τοὺς υἱοὺς τοῦ φωτὸς
more prudent   than   the   sons   of the   light

εἰς τὴν γενεὰν τὴν ἑαυτῶν εἰσιν. 9 Καὶ
in   the   generation   – of them*selves* are.   And

ἐγὼ ὑμῖν λέγω, ἑαυτοῖς ποιήσατε φίλους
I   ²you   ¹tell, To yourselves   make   friends

ἐκ τοῦ μαμωνᾶ τῆς ἀδικίας, ἵνα ὅταν
by   the   mammon   – of unrighteousness, that   when

ἐκλίπῃ δέξωνται ὑμᾶς εἰς τὰς αἰωνίους
it fails   they may receive   you   into   the   eternal

σκηνάς. 10 ὁ πιστὸς ἐν ἐλαχίστῳ καὶ ἐν
tabernacles.   The man faithful   in   least   also in

πολλῷ πιστός ἐστιν, καὶ ὁ ἐν ἐλαχίστῳ
much   faithful   is,   and the man in   least

ἄδικος καὶ ἐν πολλῷ ἄδικός ἐστιν. 11 εἰ
unrighteous also in   much   unrighteous   is.   If

οὖν ἐν τῷ ἀδίκῳ μαμωνᾷ πιστοὶ οὐκ
therefore in   the   unrighteous   mammon   faithful   not

ἐγένεσθε, τὸ ἀληθινὸν τίς ὑμῖν πιστεύσει;
ye were,   the   true   who   to you   will entrust ?

12 καὶ εἰ ἐν τῷ ἀλλοτρίῳ πιστοὶ οὐκ
And if   in the thing   belonging to another faithful   not

ἐγένεσθε, τὸ ἡμέτερον τίς δώσει ὑμῖν;
ye were,   the   ours   who   will give   you?
  =that which is ours

13 Οὐδεὶς οἰκέτης δύναται δυσὶ κυρίοις
No   household slave   can   two   lords

masters; for either he will hate the one and love the other, or he will be devoted to the one and despise the other. You cannot serve God and mammon."

14 The Pharisees, who were lovers of money, heard all this, and they scoffed at him. ¹⁵But he said to them, "You are those who justify yourselves before men, but God knows your hearts; for what is exalted among men is an abomination in the sight of God.

16 "The law and the prophets were until John; since then the good news of the kingdom of God is preached, and every one enters it violently. ¹⁷But it is easier for heaven and earth to pass away, than for one dot of the law to become void.

18 "Every one who divorces his wife and marries another commits adultery, and he who marries a woman divorced from her husband commits adultery.

19 "There was a rich man, who was clothed in purple and fine linen and who feasted sumptuously every day. ²⁰And at his gate lay a poor man named Laz'arus, full of

δουλεύειν· ἢ γὰρ τὸν ἕνα μισήσει καὶ τὸν
to serve;   for either the   one   he will hate and   the

ἕτερον ἀγαπήσει, ἢ ἑνὸς ἀνθέξεται καὶ
other   he will love, or   one   he will hold fast to and

τοῦ ἑτέρου καταφρονήσει.   οὐ δύνασθε
the other   he will despise.   Ye cannot

θεῷ δουλεύειν καὶ μαμωνᾷ. 14 Ἤκουον
God to serve   and   mammon.   ⁶heard

δὲ ταῦτα πάντα οἱ Φαρισαῖοι φιλάργυροι
¹Now ⁸these things ⁷all ²the ³Pharisees ⁵moneylovers

ὑπάρχοντες, καὶ ἐξεμυκτήριζον αὐτόν. 15 καὶ
⁴being,   and   they scoffed at   him.   And

εἶπεν αὐτοῖς· ὑμεῖς ἐστε οἱ δικαιοῦντες
he said to them :   Ye   are the [ones] justifying

ἑαυτοὺς ἐνώπιον τῶν ἀνθρώπων, ὁ δὲ
yourselves before   -   men,   -   but

θεὸς γινώσκει τὰς καρδίας ὑμῶν· ὅτι τὸ
God   knows   the hearts   of you; because the thing

ἐν ἀνθρώποις ὑψηλὸν βδέλυγμα ἐνώπιον
²among ³men   ¹lofty [is] an abomination before

τοῦ θεοῦ. 16 Ὁ νόμος καὶ οἱ προφῆται
- God.   The law   and the prophets

μέχρι Ἰωάννου· ἀπὸ τότε ἡ βασιλεία τοῦ
[were] until John; from then the kingdom   -

θεοῦ εὐαγγελίζεται καὶ πᾶς εἰς αὐτὴν
of God is being preached and everyone into   it

βιάζεται. 17 εὐκοπώτερον δέ ἐστιν τὸν οὐρανὸν
is pressing.   But easier   it is the heaven

καὶ τὴν γῆν παρελθεῖν ἢ τοῦ νόμου μίαν
and the earth to pass away than of the law   one

κεραίαν πεσεῖν. 18 Πᾶς ὁ ἀπολύων τὴν
little horn* to fall.   Everyone dismissing the

γυναῖκα αὐτοῦ καὶ γαμῶν ἑτέραν μοιχεύει,
wife   of him and marrying another commits adultery,

καὶ ὁ ἀπολελυμένην ἀπὸ
and ¹the [one] ³a woman having been dismissed ⁴from

ἀνδρὸς γαμῶν μοιχεύει. 19 Ἄνθρωπος δέ
⁵a husband ²marrying ⁶commits adultery.   Now a certain

τις ἦν πλούσιος, καὶ ἐνεδιδύσκετο πορφύραν
man was rich,   and used to put on a purple robe

καὶ βύσσον εὐφραινόμενος καθ᾽ ἡμέραν
and fine linen being merry   every day†

λαμπρῶς. 20 πτωχὸς δέ τις ὀνόματι
splendidly.   And a certain poor man by name

Λάζαρος ἐβέβλητο πρὸς τὸν πυλῶνα αὐτοῦ
Lazarus had been placed at the gate of him

* The little projection which distinguishes some Hebrew letters from those otherwise similar.

sores, ²¹who desired to be fed with what fell from the rich man's table; moreover the dogs came and licked his sores. ²²The poor man died and was carried by the angels to Abraham's bosom. The rich man also died and was buried; ²³and in Hades, being in torment, he lifted up his eyes, and saw Abraham far off and Laz'arus in his bosom. ²⁴And he called out, 'Father Abraham, have mercy upon me, and send Laz'arus to dip the end of his finger in water and cool my tongue; for I am in anguish in this flame.' ²⁵But Abraham said, 'Son, remember that you in your lifetime received your good things, and Laz'arus in like manner evil things; but now he is comforted here, and you are in anguish. ²⁶And besides all this, between us and you a great chasm has been fixed, in order that those who would pass from here to you may not be able, and none may cross from there to us.' ²⁷And he said, 'Then I beg you,

εἰλκωμένος 21 καὶ ἐπιθυμῶν χορτασθῆναι
being covered with sores and desiring to be satisfied

ἀπὸ τῶν πιπτόντων ἀπὸ τῆς τραπέζης
from the things falling from the table

τοῦ πλουσίου· ἀλλὰ καὶ οἱ κύνες ἐρχόμενοι
of the rich man; but even the dogs coming

ἐπέλειχον τὰ ἕλκη αὐτοῦ. 22 ἐγένετο δὲ
licked the sores of him. And it came to pass

ἀποθανεῖν τὸν πτωχὸν καὶ ἀπενεχθῆναι
to die the poor man and to be carried away
=that the poor man died and he was carried away

αὐτὸν ὑπὸ τῶν ἀγγέλων εἰς τὸν κόλπον
himᵇ by the angels into the bosom

Ἀβραάμ· ἀπέθανεν δὲ καὶ ὁ πλούσιος καὶ
of Abraham; and died also the rich man and

ἐτάφη. 23 καὶ ἐν τῷ ᾅδῃ ἐπάρας τοὺς
was buried. And in - hades lifting up the

ὀφθαλμοὺς αὐτοῦ, ὑπάρχων ἐν βασάνοις,
eyes of him, being in torments,

ὁρᾷ Ἀβραὰμ ἀπὸ μακρόθεν καὶ Λάζαρον
he sees Abraham from afar and Lazarus

ἐν τοῖς κόλποις αὐτοῦ. 24 καὶ αὐτὸς
in the bosoms of him. And he

φωνήσας εἶπεν· πάτερ Ἀβραάμ, ἐλέησόν
calling said : Father Abraham, pity

με καὶ πέμψον Λάζαρον ἵνα βάψῃ τὸ
me and send Lazarus that he may dip the

ἄκρον τοῦ δακτύλου αὐτοῦ ὕδατος καὶ
tip of the finger of him of(in) water and

καταψύξῃ τὴν γλῶσσάν μου, ὅτι ὀδυνῶμαι
may cool the tongue of me, because I am suffering

ἐν τῇ φλογὶ ταύτῃ. 25 εἶπεν δὲ Ἀβραάμ·
in - flame this. But said Abraham :

τέκνον, μνήσθητι ὅτι ἀπέλαβες τὰ ἀγαθά
Child, remember that thou didst receive the good things

σου ἐν τῇ ζωῇ σου, καὶ Λάζαρος ὁμοίως
of thee in the life of thee, and Lazarus likewise

τὰ κακά· νῦν δὲ ὧδε παρακαλεῖται, σὺ δὲ
the bad; but now here he is comforted, but thou

ὀδυνᾶσαι. 26 καὶ ἐν πᾶσι τούτοις μεταξὺ
art suffering. And among all these things between

ἡμῶν καὶ ὑμῶν χάσμα μέγα ἐστήρικται,
us and you chasm a great has been firmly fixed,

ὅπως οἱ θέλοντες διαβῆναι ἔνθεν πρὸς
so that the [ones] wishing to pass hence to

ὑμᾶς μὴ δύνωνται, μηδὲ ἐκεῖθεν πρὸς
you cannot, neither thence to

ἡμᾶς διαπερῶσιν. 27 εἶπεν δέ· ἐρωτῶ
us may they cross over. And he said : I ask

father, to send him to
my father's house, ²⁸for
I have five brothers, so
that he may warn them,
lest they also come into
this place of torment.'
²⁹But Abraham said,
'They have Moses and
the prophets; let them
hear them.' ³⁰And he
said, 'No, father Abra-
ham; but if some one
goes to them from the
dead, they will repent.'
³¹He said to them, 'If
they do not hear Moses
and the prophets, neither
will they be convinced if
some one should rise
from the dead.' "

σε   οὖν,   πάτερ,   ἵνα   πέμψῃς   αὐτὸν   εἰς
thee therefore,   father,   that thou mayest send   him   to

τὸν   οἶκον   τοῦ   πατρός   μου·   28 ἔχω   γὰρ
the   house   of the   father   of me;   for I have

πέντε   ἀδελφούς·   ὅπως   διαμαρτύρηται   αὐτοῖς,
five   brothers;   so that   he may witness   to them,

ἵνα   μὴ   καὶ   αὐτοὶ   ἔλθωσιν   εἰς   τὸν   τόπον
lest   also   they   come   to   -   place

τοῦτον   τῆς   βασάνου.   29 λέγει   δὲ   ᾿Αβραάμ·
this   -   of torment.   But says   Abraham :

ἔχουσι   Μωϋσέα   καὶ   τοὺς   προφήτας·
They have   Moses   and   the   prophets;

ἀκουσάτωσαν   αὐτῶν.   30 ὁ   δὲ   εἶπεν·
let them hear   them.   But he   said :

οὐχί,   πάτερ   ᾿Αβραάμ,   ἀλλ᾿   ἐάν   τις   ἀπὸ
No,   father   Abraham,   but   if   someone from

νεκρῶν   πορευθῇ   πρὸς   αὐτούς,   μετανοήσουσιν.
[the] dead   should go   to   them,   they will repent.

31 εἶπεν   δὲ   αὐτῷ·   εἰ   Μωϋσέως   καὶ   τῶν
But he said   to him :   If   Moses   and   the

προφητῶν   οὐκ   ἀκούουσιν,   οὐδὲ   ἐάν   τις
prophets   they do not hear,   neither   if someone

ἐκ   νεκρῶν   ἀναστῇ   πεισθήσονται.
out of   [the] dead   should rise again   will they be persuaded.

CHAPTER 17

AND he said to his
disciples, "Tempta-
tions to sin are sure to
come; but woe to him by
whom they come! ²It
would be better for him
if a millstone were hung
round his neck and he
were cast into the sea,
than that he should
cause one of these little
ones to sin. ³Take heed
to yourselves; if your
brother sins, rebuke him,
and if he repents, forgive
him; ⁴and if he sins
against you seven times
in the day, and turns to
you seven times, and

17 Εἶπεν   δὲ   πρὸς   τοὺς   μαθητὰς   αὐτοῦ·
And he said   to   the   disciples   of him :

ἀνένδεκτόν   ἐστιν   τοῦ   τὰ   σκάνδαλα   μὴ   ἐλθεῖν,ᵈ
Impossible   it is   -   the   offences   not to come,ᵈ

οὐαὶ   δὲ   δι᾿   οὗ   ἔρχεται·   2 λυσιτελεῖ
but woe [to him] through whom they come;   it profits

αὐτῷ   εἰ   λίθος   μυλικὸς   περίκειται   περὶ
him   if   a millstone   is put round   round

τὸν   τράχηλον   αὐτοῦ   καὶ   ἔρριπται   εἰς   τὴν
the   neck   of him   and   he has been thrown into   the

θάλασσαν,   ἢ   ἵνα   σκανδαλίσῃ   τῶν   μικρῶν
sea,   than   that   he should offend   -   ³little ones

τούτων   ἕνα.   3 προσέχετε   ἑαυτοῖς.   ἐὰν
²of these   ¹one.   Take heed   to yourselves.   If

ἁμάρτῃ   ὁ   ἀδελφός   σου,   ἐπιτίμησον   αὐτῷ,
sins   the   brother   of thee,   rebuke   him,

καὶ   ἐὰν   μετανοήσῃ,   ἄφες   αὐτῷ.   4 καὶ
and   if   he repents,   forgive   him.   And

ἐὰν   ἑπτάκις   τῆς   ἡμέρας   ἁμαρτήσῃ   εἰς   σὲ
if   seven times of(in) the   day   he sins   against thee

καὶ   ἑπτάκις   ἐπιστρέψῃ   πρὸς   σὲ   λέγων·
and   seven times   turns   to   thee   saying :

says, 'I repent,' you must forgive him."

5 The apostles said to the Lord, "Increase our faith!" ⁶And the Lord said, "If you had faith as a grain of mustard seed, you could say to this sycamine tree, 'Be rooted up, and be planted in the sea,' and it would obey you.

7 "Will any one of you, who has a servant plowing or keeping sheep, say to him when he has come in from the field, 'Come at once and sit down at table'? ⁸Will he not rather say to him, 'Prepare supper for me, and gird yourself and serve me, till I eat and drink; and afterward you shall eat and drink'? ⁹Does he thank the servant because he did what was commanded? ¹⁰So you also, when you have done all that is commanded you, say, 'We are unworthy servants; we have only done what was our duty.' "

11 On the way to Jerusalem he was passing along between Samar'ia and Galilee. ¹²And as he entered a village, he was met by ten lepers, who stood at a distance ¹³and

μετανοῶ, ἀφήσεις αὐτῷ.
I repent, thou shalt forgive him.

5 Καὶ εἶπαν οἱ
And said the

ἀπόστολοι τῷ κυρίῳ· πρόσθες ἡμῖν πίστιν.
apostles to the Lord: Add to us faith.

6 εἶπεν δὲ ὁ κύριος· εἰ ἔχετε πίστιν ὡς
And said the Lord: If ye have faith as

κόκκον σινάπεως, ἐλέγετε ἂν τῇ συκαμίνῳ
a grain of mustard, ye would have said - sycamine-tree

ταύτῃ· ἐκριζώθητι καὶ φυτεύθητι ἐν τῇ
to this: Be thou uprooted and be thou planted in the

θαλάσσῃ· καὶ ὑπήκουσεν ἂν ὑμῖν. 7 Τίς
sea; and it would have obeyed you. who

δὲ ἐξ ὑμῶν δοῦλον ἔχων ἀροτριῶντα ἢ
But of you ²a slave ¹having ploughing or

ποιμαίνοντα, ὃς εἰσελθόντι ἐκ τοῦ ἀγροῦ
herding, who on [his] coming inᵉ out of the farm

ἐρεῖ αὐτῷ· εὐθέως παρελθὼν ἀνάπεσε,
will say to him: Immediately coming up recline,

8 ἀλλ᾽ οὐχὶ ἐρεῖ αὐτῷ· ἑτοίμασον τί
but will not say to him: Prepare something

δειπνήσω, καὶ περιζωσάμενος διακόνει μοι
I may dine, and having girded thyself serve me

ἕως φάγω καὶ πίω, καὶ μετὰ ταῦτα
until I eat and drink, and after these things

φάγεσαι καὶ πίεσαι σύ; 9 μὴ ἔχει χάριν
eat and drink thou? Not he has thanks

τῷ δούλῳ ὅτι ἐποίησεν τὰ διαταχθέντα;
to the slave because he did the things commanded?

10 οὕτως καὶ ὑμεῖς, ὅταν ποιήσητε πάντα
So also ye, when ye do all

τὰ διαταχθέντα ὑμῖν, λέγετε ὅτι δοῦλοι
the things commanded you, say[,] - Slaves

ἀχρεῖοί ἐσμεν, ὃ ὠφείλομεν ποιῆσαι
unprofitable we are, what we ought to do

πεποιήκαμεν.
we have done.

11 Καὶ ἐγένετο ἐν τῷ πορεύεσθαι εἰς
And it came to pass in the to goᵉ to
                              =as [he] went

Ἰερουσαλήμ, καὶ αὐτὸς διήρχετο διὰ μέσον
Jerusalem, and he passed through [the]
                              through midst

Σαμαρείας καὶ Γαλιλαίας. 12 καὶ εἰσερχομένου
of Samaria and Galilee. And entering
                              =as he entered

αὐτοῦ εἰς τινα κώμην ἀπήντησαν δέκα
himᵃ into a certain village met [him] ten

λεπροὶ ἄνδρες, οἳ ἔστησαν πόρρωθεν, 13 καὶ
leprous men, who stood afar off, and

lifted up their voices and said, "Jesus, Master, have mercy on us." ¹⁴When he saw them he said to them, "Go and show yourselves to the priests." And as they went they were cleansed. ¹⁵Then one of them, when he saw that he was healed, turned back, praising God with a loud voice; ¹⁶and he fell on his face at Jesus' feet, giving him thanks. Now he was a Samaritan. ¹⁷Then said Jesus, "Were not ten cleansed? Where are the nine? ¹⁸Was no one found to return and give praise to God except this foreigner?" ¹⁹And he said to him, "Rise and go your way; your faith has made you well."

20 Being asked by the Pharisees when the kingdom of God was coming, he answered them, "The kingdom of God is not coming with signs to be observed; ²¹nor will they say, 'Lo, here it is!' or 'There!' for behold, the kingdom of God is in the midst of you."⁰

22 And he said to the disciples, "The days are coming when you will desire to see one of the days of the Son of man,

⁰ Or within you

αὐτοὶ	ἦραν	φωνὴν	λέγοντες·	Ἰησοῦ
they	lifted	voice	saying :	Jesus

ἐπιστάτα,	ἐλέησον	ἡμᾶς.	14 καὶ ἰδὼν εἶπεν
Master,	pity	us.	And seeing he said

αὐτοῖς·	πορευθέντες	ἐπιδείξατε	ἑαυτοὺς	τοῖς
to them :	Going	show	yourselves	to the

ἱερεῦσιν.	καὶ	ἐγένετο	ἐν	τῷ	ὑπάγειν
priests.	And	it came to pass	in	the	to go
		= as they went			

αὐτοὺς	ἐκαθαρίσθησαν.	15 εἷς	δὲ	ἐξ
them	they were cleansed.	But one		of

αὐτῶν,	ἰδὼν ὅτι ἰάθη,	ὑπέστρεψεν	μετὰ
them,	seeing that he was cured,	returned	with

φωνῆς	μεγάλης	δοξάζων	τὸν	θεόν,	16 καὶ
voice	a great	glorifying	–	God,	and

ἔπεσεν	ἐπὶ	πρόσωπον	παρὰ	τοὺς	πόδας
fell	on	[his] face	at	the	feet

αὐτοῦ	εὐχαριστῶν	αὐτῷ·	καὶ	αὐτὸς	ἦν
of him	thanking	him;	and	he	was

Σαμαρίτης.	17 ἀποκριθεὶς	δὲ	ὁ	Ἰησοῦς
a Samaritan.	And answering		–	Jesus

εἶπεν·	οὐχ	οἱ	δέκα	ἐκαθαρίσθησαν;	οἱ	[δὲ]
said :	Not	the	ten	were cleansed?		but the

ἐννέα	ποῦ;	18 οὐχ	εὑρέθησαν	ὑποστρέψαντες
nine	where?	were there not found	returning

δοῦναι	δόξαν	τῷ	θεῷ	εἰ μὴ	ὁ	ἀλλογενὴς
to give	glory	–	to God	only	–	stranger

οὗτος;	19 καὶ	εἶπεν	αὐτῷ·	ἀναστὰς	πορεύου·
this ?	And	he said	to him :	Rising up	go;

ἡ	πίστις	σου	σέσωκέν	σε.
the	faith	of thee	has healed	thee.

20 Ἐπερωτηθεὶς	δὲ	ὑπὸ	τῶν	Φαρισαίων
And being questioned		by	the	Pharisees

πότε	ἔρχεται	ἡ	βασιλεία	τοῦ	θεοῦ,
when	comes	the	kingdom	–	of God,

ἀπεκρίθη	αὐτοῖς	καὶ	εἶπεν·	οὐκ	ἔρχεται
he answered	them	and	said :	Comes not

ἡ	βασιλεία	τοῦ	θεοῦ	μετὰ	παρατηρήσεως,
the	kingdom	–	of God	with	observation,

21 οὐδὲ	ἐροῦσιν·	ἰδοὺ	ὧδε	ἤ·	ἐκεῖ·	ἰδοὺ
nor	will they say : Behold[,]	here	or:	there;	²behold

γὰρ	ἡ	βασιλεία	τοῦ	θεοῦ	ἐντὸς	ὑμῶν
¹for	the	kingdom	–	of God	within	you

ἐστιν.	22 Εἶπεν	δὲ	πρὸς	τοὺς	μαθητάς·
is.	And he said		to	the	disciples :

ἐλεύσονται	ἡμέραι	ὅτε	ἐπιθυμήσετε	μίαν
Will come	days	when	ye will long	one

τῶν	ἡμερῶν	τοῦ	υἱοῦ	τοῦ	ἀνθρώπου	ἰδεῖν
of the	days	of the	Son	–	of man	to see

and you will not see it.
²³And they will say to you, 'Lo, there!' or 'Lo, here!' Do not go, do not follow them. ²⁴For as the lightning flashes and lights up the sky from one side to the other, so will the Son of man be in his day.ᵖ ²⁵But first he must suffer many things and be rejected by this generation. ²⁶As it was in the days of Noah, so will it be in the days of the Son of man. ²⁷They ate, they drank, they married, they were given in marriage, until the day when Noah entered the ark, and the flood came and destroyed them all. ²⁸Likewise as it was in the days of Lot—they ate, they drank, they bought, they sold, they planted, they built, ²⁹but on the day when Lot went out from Sodom fire and brimstone rained from heaven and destroyed them all—³⁰so will it be on the day when the Son of man is revealed. ³¹On that day, let him who is on the housetop, with his goods in the house, not come down to take them away; and likewise let him who is in the field not turn

ᵖ Other ancient authorities omit *in his day*

καὶ οὐκ ὄψεσθε. 23 καὶ ἐροῦσιν ὑμῖν·
and will not see. And they will say to you :

ἰδοὺ ἐκεῖ, ἰδοὺ ὧδε· μὴ ἀπέλθητε μηδὲ
Behold there, behold here; do not go away nor

διώξητε. 24 ὥσπερ γὰρ ἡ ἀστραπὴ
follow. For as the lightning

ἀστράπτουσα ἐκ τῆς ὑπὸ τὸν οὐρανὸν
flashing out of the [one part] under – heaven

εἰς τὴν ὑπ᾽ οὐρανὸν λάμπει, οὕτως ἔσται
to the [other part] under heaven shines, so will be

ὁ υἱὸς τοῦ ἀνθρώπου ἐν τῇ ἡμέρᾳ αὐτοῦ.
the Son – of man in the day of him.

25 πρῶτον δὲ δεῖ αὐτὸν πολλὰ παθεῖν καὶ
But first it behoves him many things to suffer and

ἀποδοκιμασθῆναι ἀπὸ τῆς γενεᾶς ταύτης.
to be rejected from – generation this.

26 καὶ καθὼς ἐγένετο ἐν ταῖς ἡμέραις
And as it was in the days

Νῶε, οὕτως ἔσται καὶ ἐν ταῖς ἡμέραις
of Noah, so it will be also in the days

τοῦ υἱοῦ τοῦ ἀνθρώπου· 27 ἤσθιον, ἔπινον,
of the Son – of man; they were eating, drinking,

ἐγάμουν, ἐγαμίζοντο, ἄχρι ἧς ἡμέρας
marrying, giving in marriage, until which day
= the day when

εἰσῆλθεν Νῶε εἰς τὴν κιβωτόν, καὶ
entered Noah into the ark, and

ἦλθεν ὁ κατακλυσμὸς καὶ ἀπώλεσεν πάντας.
came the flood and destroyed all.

28 ὁμοίως καθὼς ἐγένετο ἐν ταῖς ἡμέραις
Likewise as it was in the days

Λώτ· ἤσθιον, ἔπινον, ἠγόραζον, ἐπώλουν,
of Lot; they were eating, drinking, buying, selling,

ἐφύτευον, ᾠκοδόμουν· 29 ᾗ δὲ ἡμέρᾳ ἐξῆλθεν
planting, building; but on which day went forth

Λώτ ἀπὸ Σοδόμων, ἔβρεξεν πῦρ καὶ
Lot from Sodom, it rained fire and

θεῖον ἀπ᾽ οὐρανοῦ καὶ ἀπώλεσεν πάντας.
brimstone from heaven and destroyed all.

30 κατὰ τὰ αὐτὰ ἔσται ᾗ ἡμέρᾳ ὁ υἱὸς
According to the same things it will be on which day the Son
= In the same way = on the day when

τοῦ ἀνθρώπου ἀποκαλύπτεται. 31 ἐν ἐκείνῃ
– of man is revealed. In that

τῇ ἡμέρᾳ ὃς ἔσται ἐπὶ τοῦ δώματος καὶ
– day who will be on the roof and

τὰ σκεύη αὐτοῦ ἐν τῇ οἰκίᾳ, μὴ καταβάτω
the goods of him in the house, let him not come down

ἆραι αὐτά, καὶ ὁ ἐν ἀγρῷ ὁμοίως μὴ
to take them, and the [one] in a field likewise not

back. 32 Remember Lot's wife. 33 Whoever seeks to gain his life will lose it, but whoever loses his life will preserve it. 34 I tell you, in that night there will be two men in one bed; one will be taken and the other left. 35 There will be two women grinding together; one will be taken and the other left."[q] 37 And they said to him, "Where, Lord?" He said to them, "Where the body is, there the eagles[r] will be gathered together."

ἐπιστρεψάτω εἰς τὰ ὀπίσω. 32 μνημονεύετε
let him turn back to the things behind. Remember

τῆς γυναικὸς Λώτ. 33 ὃς ἐὰν ζητήσῃ
the wife of Lot. Whoever seeks

τὴν ψυχὴν αὐτοῦ περιποιήσασθαι, ἀπολέσει
the life of him to preserve, he will lose

αὐτήν, καὶ ὃς ἂν ἀπολέσει, ζῳογονήσει
it, and whoever will lose, will preserve

αὐτήν. 34 λέγω ὑμῖν, ταύτῃ τῇ νυκτὶ
it. I tell you, in this – night

ἔσονται δύο ἐπὶ κλίνης μιᾶς, ὁ εἷς
there will be two men on couch one, the one

παραλημφθήσεται καὶ ὁ ἕτερος ἀφεθήσεται·
will be taken and the other will be left;

35 ἔσονται δύο ἀλήθουσαι ἐπὶ τὸ αὐτό, ἡ
there will be two women grinding together,† the

μία παραλημφθήσεται ἡ δὲ ἑτέρα ἀφεθήσεται.‡
one will be taken but the other will be left.

37 καὶ ἀποκριθέντες λέγουσιν αὐτῷ· ποῦ,
And answering they say to him: Where,

κύριε; ὁ δὲ εἶπεν αὐτοῖς· ὅπου τὸ σῶμα,
Lord? And he said to them: Where the body,

ἐκεῖ καὶ οἱ ἀετοὶ ἐπισυναχθήσονται.
there also the eagles will be gathered together.

CHAPTER 18

AND he told them a parable, to the effect that they ought always to pray and not lose heart. 2 He said, "In a certain city there was a judge who neither feared God nor regarded man; 3 and there was a widow in that city who kept coming to him and saying, 'Vindicate me against my adversary.' 4 For a while he refused; but afterward he said to himself, 'Though I neither fear God nor regard man, 5 yet because

18 Ἔλεγεν δὲ παραβολὴν αὐτοῖς πρὸς
And he told [2]a parable [1]them to =that

τὸ δεῖν πάντοτε προσεύχεσθαι αὐτοὺς καὶ
the [1]to behove [3]always [4]to pray [2]them and
they must always pray and not faint,

μὴ ἐγκακεῖν, 2 λέγων· κριτής τις ἦν ἐν
not to faint, saying: [3]judge [2]a certain [1]There was [4]in

τινι πόλει τὸν θεὸν μὴ φοβούμενος καὶ
[5]a certain [6]city – [3]God [1]not [2]fearing and

ἄνθρωπον μὴ ἐντρεπόμενος. 3 χήρα δὲ ἦν
[3]man [1]not [2]regarding. And [2]a widow [1]there was

ἐν τῇ πόλει ἐκείνῃ, καὶ ἤρχετο πρὸς
in – city that, and she came to

αὐτὸν λέγουσα· ἐκδίκησόν με ἀπὸ τοῦ
him saying: Vindicate me from the

ἀντιδίκου μου. 4 καὶ οὐκ ἤθελεν ἐπὶ
opponent of me. And he would not for

χρόνον· μετὰ ταῦτα δὲ εἶπεν ἐν ἑαυτῷ·
a time; but after these things he said in himself:

εἰ καὶ τὸν θεὸν οὐ φοβοῦμαι οὐδὲ ἄνθρωπον
If indeed – God I fear not nor man

[q] Other ancient authorities add verse 36, "*Two men will be in the field; one will be taken and the other left*"

[r] Or *vultures*

‡ Verse 36 omitted by Nestle; *cf.* RSV footnote.

this widow bothers me, I will vindicate her, or she will wear me out by her continual coming.'"
⁶And the Lord said, "Hear what the unrighteous judge says. ⁷And will not God vindicate his elect, who cry to him day and night? Will he delay long over them? ⁸I tell you, he will vindicate them speedily. Nevertheless, when the Son of man comes, will he find faith on earth?"
9 He also told this parable to some who trusted in themselves that they were righteous and despised others: ¹⁰"Two men went up into the temple to pray, one a Pharisee and the other a tax collector. ¹¹The Pharisee stood and prayed thus with himself, 'God, I thank thee that I am not like other men, extortioners, unjust, adulters, or even like this tax collector. ¹²I give twice a week, I give tithes of all that I get.' ¹³But the tax collector, standing far off, would not even lift up his eyes

ἐντρέπομαι,   5 διά   γε   τὸ   παρέχειν
regard,   at least because of –   to cause
                   =because this widow causes me trouble
μοι κόπον τὴν χήραν ταύτην ἐκδικήσω αὐτήν,
me trouble   –   widow   thisᵇ I will vindicate her,
ἵνα μὴ εἰς τέλος ἐρχομένη ὑπωπιάζῃ με.
lest   in [the] end   coming   she exhausts me.
6 Εἶπεν δὲ ὁ κύριος· ἀκούσατε τί ὁ κριτὴς
And said the Lord: Hear ye what the judge
τῆς ἀδικίας λέγει· 7 ὁ δὲ θεὸς οὐ μὴ
– of unrighteousness says; – and God by no means
ποιήσῃ   τὴν   ἐκδίκησιν   τῶν   ἐκλεκτῶν
will he make the   vindication   of the   chosen [ones]
αὐτοῦ   τῶν   βοώντων   αὐτῷ   ἡμέρας   καὶ
of him   –   crying   to him   day   and
νυκτός, καὶ μακροθυμεῖ ἐπ' αὐτοῖς; 8 λέγω
night,   and be patient over   them?   I tell
ὑμῖν ὅτι ποιήσει τὴν ἐκδίκησιν αὐτῶν
you   that he will make the   vindication   of them
ἐν τάχει. πλὴν ὁ υἱὸς τοῦ ἀνθρώπου ἐλθὼν
quickly. Nevertheless the Son   –   of man   coming
ἆρα εὑρήσει τὴν πίστιν ἐπὶ τῆς γῆς;
then will he find the   faith   on   the   earth?
9 Εἶπεν   δὲ   καὶ   πρός   τινας   τοὺς
And he said also   to   some the [ones]
πεποιθότας   ἐφ'   ἑαυτοῖς   ὅτι   εἰσὶν
relying   on   themselves that   they are
δίκαιοι καὶ ἐξουθενοῦντας τοὺς λοιποὺς
righteous and   despising   the   rest
τὴν παραβολὴν ταύτην.   10 Ἄνθρωποι δύο
–   parable   this.   Men   two
ἀνέβησαν εἰς τὸ ἱερὸν προσεύξασθαι, ὁ εἷς
went up   to the temple to pray,   the one
Φαρισαῖος καὶ ὁ ἕτερος τελώνης. 11 ὁ
a Pharisee and the other a tax-collector.   The
Φαρισαῖος σταθεὶς ταῦτα πρὸς ἑαυτὸν
Pharisee standing these things to   himself
προσηύχετο· ὁ θεός, εὐχαριστῶ σοι ὅτι
prayed :   God,   I thank   thee that
οὐκ εἰμὶ ὥσπερ οἱ λοιποὶ τῶν ἀνθρώπων,
I am not as   the rest   –   of men,
ἅρπαγες, ἄδικοι, μοιχοί, ἢ καὶ ὡς οὗτος
rapacious, unjust, adulterers, or even as this
ὁ τελώνης· 12 νηστεύω δὶς τοῦ σαββάτου,
– tax-collector;   I fast twice of(in) the week,
ἀποδεκατεύω πάντα ὅσα κτῶμαι. 13 ὁ δὲ
I tithe   all things how many I get. But the
τελώνης μακρόθεν ἑστὼς οὐκ ἤθελεν οὐδὲ
tax-collector far off standing would not not even

to heaven, but beat his breast, saying, 'God, be merciful to me a sinner!' ¹⁴I tell you, this man went down to his house justified rather than the other; for every one who exalts himself will be humbled, but he who humbles himself will be exalted."

15 Now they were bringing even infants to him that he might touch them; and when the disciples saw it, they rebuked them. ¹⁶But Jesus called them to him, saying, "Let the children come to me, and do not hinder them; for to such belongs the kingdom of God. ¹⁷Truly, I say to you, whoever does not receive the kingdom of God like a child shall not enter it."

18 And a ruler asked him, "Good Teacher, what shall I do to inherit eternal life?" ¹⁹And Jesus said to him, "Why do you call me good? No one is good but God alone. ²⁰You know the commandments: 'Do not commit adultery, Do not kill, Do not steal, Do not bear false witness, Honor your father and mother.' " ²¹And he said,

τοὺς ὀφθαλμοὺς ἐπᾶραι εἰς τὸν οὐρανόν,
the(his) eyes *to* lift up to – heaven,
ἀλλ' ἔτυπτεν τὸ στῆθος αὐτοῦ λέγων· ὁ
but smote the breast of him saying : –
θεός, ἱλάσθητί μοι τῷ ἁμαρτωλῷ. 14 λέγω
God, be propitious to me the sinner. I tell
ὑμῖν, κατέβη οὗτος δεδικαιωμένος εἰς τὸν
you, went down this man having been justified to the
οἶκον αὐτοῦ παρ' ἐκεῖνον· ὅτι πᾶς ὁ
house of him [rather] than that one; because everyone
ὑψῶν ἑαυτὸν ταπεινωθήσεται, ὁ δὲ ταπεινῶν
exalting himself will be humbled, and the [one] humbling
ἑαυτὸν ὑψωθήσεται.
himself will be exalted.

15 Προσέφερον δὲ αὐτῷ καὶ τὰ βρέφη
And they brought to him also the babes
ἵνα αὐτῶν ἅπτηται· ἰδόντες δὲ οἱ μαθηταὶ
that them he might touch; but ³seeing ¹the ²disciples
ἐπετίμων αὐτοῖς. 16 ὁ δὲ Ἰησοῦς
rebuked them. – But Jesus
προσεκαλέσατο αὐτὰ λέγων· ἄφετε τὰ
called to [him] them* saying : Allow the
παιδία ἔρχεσθαι πρός με καὶ μὴ κωλύετε
children to come to me and do not prevent
αὐτά· τῶν γὰρ τοιούτων ἐστὶν ἡ βασιλεία
them; – for of such is the kingdom
τοῦ θεοῦ. 17 ἀμὴν λέγω ὑμῖν, ὃς ἂν
– of God. Truly I tell you, whoever
μὴ δέξηται τὴν βασιλείαν τοῦ θεοῦ ὡς
does not receive the kingdom – of God as
παιδίον, οὐ μὴ εἰσέλθῃ εἰς αὐτήν.
a child, by no means enters into it.

18 Καὶ ἐπηρώτησέν τις αὐτὸν ἄρχων
And ³questioned ¹a certain ⁴him ²ruler
λέγων· διδάσκαλε ἀγαθέ, τί ποιήσας ζωὴν
saying : Teacher good, what doing life
αἰώνιον κληρονομήσω; 19 εἶπεν δὲ αὐτῷ
eternal may I inherit? And said to him
ὁ Ἰησοῦς· τί με λέγεις ἀγαθόν; οὐδεὶς
– Jesus : Why me sayest thou good? no one
ἀγαθὸς εἰ μὴ εἷς [ὁ] θεός. 20 τὰς ἐντολὰς
[is] good except one[,] – God. The commandments
οἶδας· μὴ μοιχεύσῃς, μὴ φονεύσῃς,
thou knowest : Do not commit adultery, Do not kill,
μὴ κλέψῃς, μὴ ψευδομαρτυρήσῃς, τίμα
Do not steal, Do not bear false witness, Honour
τὸν πατέρα σου καὶ τὴν μητέρα. 21 ὁ δὲ
the father of thee and the mother. And he

---

* That is, "the babes" (τὰ βρέφη in ver. 15).

"All these I have observed from my youth."
²²And when Jesus heard it, he said to him, "One thing you still lack. Sell all that you have and distribute to the poor, and you will have treasure in heaven; and come, follow me." ²³But when he heard this he became sad, for he was very rich. ²⁴Jesus looking at him said, "How hard it is for those who have riches to enter the kingdom of God! ²⁵For it is easier for a camel to go through the eye of a needle than for a rich man to enter the kingdom of God." ²⁶Those who heard it said, "Then who can be saved?" ²⁷But he said, "What is impossible with men is possible with God." ²⁸And Peter said, "Lo, we have left our homes and followed you." ²⁹And he said to them, "Truly, I say to you, there is no man who has left house or wife or brothers or parents or children, for the sake of the kingdom of God, ³⁰who will not receive manifold more in this time, and in the age to come eternal life."

εἶπεν· ταῦτα πάντα ἐφύλαξα ἐκ νεότητος.
said : All these things I kept from youth.

22 ἀκούσας δὲ ὁ Ἰησοῦς εἶπεν αὐτῷ· ἔτι
But hearing – Jesus said to him : Yet

ἕν σοι λείπει· πάντα ὅσα ἔχεις
one thing to thee is lacking; all things how many thou hast

πώλησον καὶ διάδος πτωχοῖς, καὶ ἕξεις
sell and distribute to poor people, and thou wilt have

θησαυρὸν ἐν [τοῖς] οὐρανοῖς, καὶ δεῦρο
treasure in – heavens, and come

ἀκολούθει μοι. 23 ὁ δὲ ἀκούσας ταῦτα
follow me. But he hearing these things

περίλυπος ἐγενήθη, ἦν γὰρ πλούσιος σφόδρα.
very grieved became, for he was rich exceedingly.

24 ἰδὼν δὲ αὐτὸν ὁ Ἰησοῦς εἶπεν· πῶς
And seeing him – Jesus said : How

δυσκόλως οἱ τὰ χρήματα ἔχοντες εἰς τὴν
hardly ¹the [ones] – ²property ³having into the

βασιλείαν τοῦ θεοῦ εἰσπορεύονται· 25 εὐκο-
kingdom – of God go in; ²easi-

πώτερον γάρ ἐστιν κάμηλον διὰ τρήματος
er ¹for it is [for] a camel through [the] eye

βελόνης εἰσελθεῖν ἢ πλούσιον εἰς τὴν
of a needle to enter than a rich man into the

βασιλείαν τοῦ θεοῦ εἰσελθεῖν. 26 εἶπαν
kingdom – of God to enter. said

δὲ οἱ ἀκούσαντες· καὶ τίς δύναται
And the [ones] hearing : And who can

σωθῆναι; 27 ὁ δὲ εἶπεν· τὰ ἀδύνατα παρὰ
to be saved? And he said : The things impossible with

ἀνθρώποις δυνατὰ παρὰ τῷ θεῷ ἐστιν.
men possible with – God is(are).

28 Εἶπεν δὲ ὁ Πέτρος· ἰδοὺ ἡμεῖς ἀφέντες
And said – Peter : Behold[,] we leaving

τὰ ἴδια ἠκολουθήσαμέν σοι. 29 ὁ δὲ
our own things followed thee. And he

εἶπεν αὐτοῖς· ἀμὴν λέγω ὑμῖν ὅτι οὐδείς
said to them : Truly I tell you that no one

ἐστιν ὃς ἀφῆκεν οἰκίαν ἢ γυναῖκα ἢ
there is who left house or wife or

ἀδελφοὺς ἢ γονεῖς ἢ τέκνα εἵνεκεν τῆς
brothers or parents or children for the sake of the

βασιλείας τοῦ θεοῦ, 30 ὃς οὐχὶ μὴ λάβῃ
kingdom – of God, who by no means receives

πολλαπλασίονα ἐν τῷ καιρῷ τούτῳ καὶ ἐν
many times over in – time this and in

τῷ αἰῶνι τῷ ἐρχομένῳ ζωὴν αἰώνιον.
the age – coming life eternal.

31 And taking the twelve, he said to them, "Behold, we are going up to Jerusalem, and everything that is written of the Son of man by the prophets will be accomplished. ³²For he will be delivered to the Gentiles, and will be mocked and shamefully treated and spit upon; ³³they will scourge him and kill him, and on the third day he will rise." ³⁴But they understood none of these things; this saying was hid from them, and they did not grasp what was said.

35 As he drew near to Jericho, a blind man was sitting by the roadside begging; ³⁶and hearing a multitude going by, he inquired what this meant. ³⁷They told him, "Jesus of Nazareth is passing by." ³⁸And he cried, "Jesus, Son of David, have mercy on me!" ³⁹And those who were in front rebuked him, telling him to be silent; but he cried out all the more, "Son of David, have mercy on me!" ⁴⁰And Jesus stopped, and commanded him to be brought to him; and when he came near, he

31 Παραλαβὼν δὲ τοὺς δώδεκα εἶπεν πρὸς
And taking   the   twelve   he said   to

αὐτούς· ἰδοὺ ἀναβαίνομεν εἰς Ἰερουσαλήμ,
them :   Behold   we are going up   to   Jerusalem,

καὶ τελεσθήσεται πάντα τὰ γεγραμ-
and   will be accomplished   all things   –   having been

μένα διὰ τῶν προφητῶν τῷ υἱῷ τοῦ
written through   the   prophets   to the   Son   –

ἀνθρώπου· 32 παραδοθήσεται γὰρ τοῖς ἔθνεσιν
of man;   for he will be delivered   to the   nations

καὶ ἐμπαιχθήσεται καὶ ὑβρισθήσεται καὶ
and   will be mocked   and   will be insulted   and

ἐμπτυσθήσεται, 33 καὶ μαστιγώσαντες
will be spit at,   and   having scourged

ἀποκτενοῦσιν αὐτόν, καὶ τῇ ἡμέρᾳ τῇ
they will kill   him,   and   on the   day   –

τρίτῃ ἀναστήσεται. 34 καὶ αὐτοὶ οὐδὲν
third   he will rise again.   And   they   none

τούτων συνῆκαν, καὶ ἦν τὸ ῥῆμα τοῦτο
of these things understood,   and   ³was – ²utterance ¹this

κεκρυμμένον ἀπ' αὐτῶν, καὶ οὐκ ἐγίνωσκον
⁴having been hidden from   them,   and   they knew not

τὰ λεγόμενα.
the things   being said.

35 Ἐγένετο δὲ ἐν τῷ ἐγγίζειν αὐτὸν εἰς
And it came to pass in   the   to draw near   him^be   to
                      =as he drew near

Ἰεριχὼ τυφλός τις ἐκάθητο παρὰ τὴν ὁδὸν
Jericho   a certain blind man   sat   by   the   way

ἐπαιτῶν. 36 ἀκούσας δὲ ὄχλου διαπορευομένου
begging.   And hearing   a crowd   passing through

ἐπυνθάνετο τί εἴη τοῦτο. 37 ἀπήγγειλαν
he inquired   what ²might be ¹this.   And they re-

δὲ αὐτῷ ὅτι Ἰησοῦς ὁ Ναζωραῖος
ported to him[,]   –   Jesus   the   Nazarene

παρέρχεται. 38 καὶ ἐβόησεν λέγων· Ἰησοῦ
is passing by.   And   he cried   saying: Jesus

υἱὲ Δαυίδ, ἐλέησόν με. 39 καὶ οἱ
son   of David,   pity   me.   And the [ones]

προάγοντες ἐπετίμων αὐτῷ ἵνα σιγήσῃ·
going before   rebuked   him   that he should be quiet;

αὐτὸς δὲ πολλῷ μᾶλλον ἔκραζεν· υἱὲ
but he   by much   more   cried out :   Son

Δαυίδ, ἐλέησόν με. 40 σταθεὶς δὲ ὁ
of David,   pity   me.   And standing   –

Ἰησοῦς ἐκέλευσεν αὐτὸν ἀχθῆναι πρὸς
Jesus   commanded   him   to be brought   to

αὐτόν. ἐγγίσαντος δὲ αὐτοῦ ἐπηρώτησεν
him.   And drawing near   him^a   he questioned
         =as he drew near

asked him, ⁴¹"What do you want me to do for you?" He said, "Lord, let me receive my sight." ⁴²And Jesus said to him, "Receive your sight; your faith has made you well." ⁴³And immediately he received his sight and followed him, glorifying God; and all the people, when they saw it, gave praise to God.

αὐτόν·   **41** τί σοι θέλεις ποιήσω; ὁ δὲ
him :   What for thee wishest thou I may do? And he

εἶπεν· κύριε, ἵνα ἀναβλέψω. **42** καὶ ὁ Ἰησοῦς
said :   Lord, that I may see again.   And -   Jesus

εἶπεν αὐτῷ· ἀνάβλεψον· ἡ πίστις σου
said   to him :   See again;   the   faith   of thee

σέσωκέν σε. **43** καὶ παραχρῆμα ἀνέβλεψεν,
has healed thee.   And   at once   he saw again,

καὶ ἠκολούθει αὐτῷ δοξάζων τὸν θεόν.
and   followed   him   glorifying   -   God.

καὶ πᾶς ὁ λαὸς ἰδὼν ἔδωκεν αἶνον τῷ
And   all   the people   seeing   gave   praise   -

θεῷ.
to God.

CHAPTER 19

HE entered Jericho and was passing through. ²And there was a man named Zacchae'-us; he was a chief tax collector, and rich. ³And he sought to see who Jesus was, but could not, on account of the crowd, because he was small of stature. ⁴So he ran on ahead and climbed up into a sycamore tree to see him, for he was to pass that way. ⁵And when Jesus came to the place, he looked up and said to him, "Zacchae'us, make haste and come down; for I must stay at your house today." ⁶So he made haste and came down, and received him joyfully. ⁷And when they saw it they all murmured, "He has gone in to be the guest of a man who is a sinner."

19 Καὶ εἰσελθὼν διήρχετο τὴν Ἰεριχώ.
And having entered he passed through -   Jericho.

2 Καὶ ἰδοὺ ἀνὴρ ὀνόματι καλούμενος
And   behold[,]   a man   by name   being called

Ζακχαῖος, καὶ αὐτὸς ἦν ἀρχιτελώνης, καὶ
Zacchæus,   and   he   was a chief tax-collector,   and

αὐτὸς πλούσιος· **3** καὶ ἐζήτει ἰδεῖν τὸν
he [was] rich;   and   he sought   to see   -

Ἰησοῦν τίς ἐστιν, καὶ οὐκ ἠδύνατο ἀπὸ
Jesus   who he is(was), and   was not able   from

τοῦ ὄχλου, ὅτι τῇ ἡλικίᾳ μικρὸς ἦν.
the   crowd,   because   -   ³in stature   ²little   ¹he was.

4 καὶ προδραμὼν εἰς τὸ ἔμπροσθεν ἀνέβη
And having run forward to   the   front   he went up

ἐπὶ συκομορέαν, ἵνα ἴδῃ αὐτόν, ὅτι
onto   a sycamore-tree,   that he might see   him,   because

ἐκείνης ἤμελλεν διέρχεσθαι. **5** καὶ ὡς
²that [way] ¹he was about   ²to pass along.   And   as

ἦλθεν ἐπὶ τὸν τόπον, ἀναβλέψας ὁ Ἰησοῦς
he came upon the   place,   looking up   -   Jesus

εἶπεν πρὸς αὐτόν· Ζακχαῖε, σπεύσας
said   to   him :   Zacchæus,   making haste

κατάβηθι· σήμερον γὰρ ἐν τῷ οἴκῳ σου
come down;   for to-day   in   the   house of thee

δεῖ με μεῖναι. **6** καὶ σπεύσας κατέβη,
it behoves me to remain.   And making haste he came down,

καὶ ὑπεδέξατο αὐτὸν χαίρων. **7** καὶ
and   welcomed   him   rejoicing.   And

ἰδόντες πάντες διεγόγγυζον λέγοντες ὅτι
seeing   all   murmured   saying[,]   -

παρὰ ἁμαρτωλῷ ἀνδρὶ εἰσῆλθεν καταλῦσαι.
With   a sinful   man   he entered   to lodge.

[8] And Zacchae'us stood and said to the Lord, "Behold, Lord, the half of my goods I give to the poor; and if I have defrauded any one of anything, I restore it fourfold." [9] And Jesus said to him, "Today salvation has come to this house, since he also is a son of Abraham. [10] For the Son of man came to seek and to save the lost."

[11] As they heard these things, he proceeded to tell a parable, because he was near to Jerusalem, and because they supposed that the kingdom of God was to appear immediately. [12] He said therefore, "A nobleman went into a far country to receive kingly power and return. [13] Calling ten of his servants, he gave them ten pounds, and said to them, 'Trade with these till I come.' [14] But his citizens hated him and sent an embassy after him, saying, 'We do not want this man to reign over us.' [15] When

8 σταθεὶς δὲ Ζακχαῖος εἶπεν πρὸς τὸν
  And standing   Zacchæus   said   to   the

κύριον· ἰδοὺ τὰ ἡμίση μου τῶν ὑπαρχόντων,
Lord : Behold[,] the   half   of me of the   possessions,

κύριε, τοῖς πτωχοῖς δίδωμι, καὶ εἴ τινός
Lord,   to the   poor   I give,   and   if   anyone

τι ἐσυκοφάντησα, ἀποδίδωμι τετραπλοῦν.
anything   I accused falsely,   I restore   fourfold.

9 εἶπεν δὲ πρὸς αὐτὸν ὁ Ἰησοῦς ὅτι
  And said   to   him   -   Jesus[,]   -

σήμερον σωτηρία τῷ οἴκῳ τούτῳ ἐγένετο,
To-day   salvation   -   house   to this   came,

καθότι καὶ αὐτὸς υἱὸς Ἀβραάμ [ἐστιν]·
because   even   he   a son of Abraham   is;

10 ἦλθεν γὰρ ὁ υἱὸς τοῦ ἀνθρώπου ζητῆσαι
   for came   the   Son   -   of man   to seek

καὶ σῶσαι τὸ ἀπολωλός.
and   to save the thing having been lost.

11 Ἀκουόντων δὲ αὐτῶν ταῦτα προσθεὶς
   And hearing   them[a] these things   adding
   = as they heard

εἶπεν παραβολήν, διὰ τὸ ἐγγὺς εἶναι
he told   a parable,   because of the   near   to be
   = because he was near to Jerusalem and they thought

Ἰερουσαλὴμ αὐτὸν καὶ δοκεῖν αὐτοὺς ὅτι
Jerusalem   him   and   to think   them[b]   that

παραχρῆμα μέλλει ἡ βασιλεία τοῦ θεοῦ
at once   is(was) about the   kingdom   -   of God

ἀναφαίνεσθαι· **12** εἶπεν οὖν· ἄνθρωπός τις
to appear;   he said therefore :   A certain man

εὐγενὴς ἐπορεύθη εἰς χώραν μακρὰν λαβεῖν
well born   went   to   country   a far   to receive

ἑαυτῷ βασιλείαν καὶ ὑποστρέψαι. **13** καλέσας
for himself   a kingdom   and   to return.   having called

δὲ δέκα δούλους ἑαυτοῦ ἔδωκεν αὐτοῖς
And   ten   slaves   of himself   he gave   them

δέκα μνᾶς, καὶ εἶπεν πρὸς αὐτούς·
ten   minas,   and   said   to   them :

πραγματεύσασθε ἐν ᾧ ἔρχομαι. **14** οἱ δὲ
   Trade ye   while   I am coming.*   But the

πολῖται αὐτοῦ ἐμίσουν αὐτόν, καὶ ἀπέστειλαν
citizens   of him   hated   him,   and   sent

πρεσβείαν ὀπίσω αὐτοῦ λέγοντες· οὐ θέλομεν
a delegation   after   him   saying :   We do not wish

τοῦτον βασιλεῦσαι ἐφ' ἡμᾶς. **15** καὶ
this man   to reign   over   us.   And

* That is, " again." The present of this verb often has a futurist significance; cf. John 14. 3.

he returned, having received the kingly power, he commanded these servants, to whom he had given the money, to be called to him, that he might know what they had gained by trading. ¹⁶The first came before him, saying, 'Lord, your pound has made ten pounds more.' ¹⁷And he said to him, 'Well done, good servant! Because you have been faithful in a very little, you shall have authority over ten cities.' ¹⁸And the second came, saying, 'Lord, your pound has made five pounds.' ¹⁹And he said to him, 'And you are to be over five cities.' ²⁰Then another came, saying, 'Lord, here is your pound, which I kept laid away in a napkin; ²¹for I was afraid of you, because you are a severe man; you take up what you did not lay down, and reap what you did not sow.' ²²He said to him, 'I will condemn you out of your own mouth, you wicked servant! You knew that I was a severe man, taking up what I did not lay down and reaping what I did not sow? ²³Why then did you not put my money into the bank, and at my coming I should have collected it with interest?' ²⁴And he said to those who stood by, 'Take the

ἐγένετο ἐν τῷ ἐπανελθεῖν αὐτὸν λαβόντα
it came to pass in the to return himᵇᵉ having received
=when he returned

τὴν βασιλείαν καὶ εἶπεν φωνηθῆναι αὐτῷ
the kingdom *and* he said to be called to him

τοὺς δούλους τούτους οἷς δεδώκει τὸ
- slaves these to whom he had given the

ἀργύριον, ἵνα γνοῖ τίς τί
money, that he might know ²anyone ¹what

διεπραγματεύσατο. 16 παρεγένετο δὲ ὁ πρῶτος
gained by trading. And came the first

λέγων· κύριε, ἡ μνᾶ σου δέκα προσηργάσατο
saying: Lord, the mina of thee ²ten ¹gained

μνᾶς. 17 καὶ εἶπεν αὐτῷ· εὖ γε, ἀγαθὲ δοῦλε,
³minas. And he said to him: Well, good slave,

ὅτι ἐν ἐλαχίστῳ πιστὸς ἐγένου, ἴσθι
because in a least thing faithful thou wast, be thou

ἐξουσίαν ἔχων ἐπάνω δέκα πόλεων. 18 καὶ
²authority ¹having over ten cities. And

ἦλθεν ὁ δεύτερος λέγων· ἡ μνᾶ σου,
came the second saying: The mina of thee,

κύριε, ἐποίησεν πέντε μνᾶς. 19 εἶπεν δὲ
lord, made five minas. And he said

καὶ τούτῳ· καὶ σὺ ἐπάνω γίνου πέντε
also to this one: And ²thou ³over ¹be five

πόλεων. 20 καὶ ὁ ἕτερος ἦλθεν λέγων·
cities. And the other came saying:

κύριε, ἰδοὺ ἡ μνᾶ σου, ἣν εἶχον
Lord, behold[,] the mina of thee, which I had

ἀποκειμένην ἐν σουδαρίῳ· 21 ἐφοβούμην γάρ
being put away in a napkin; for I feared

σε, ὅτι ἄνθρωπος αὐστηρὸς εἶ, αἴρεις ὃ
thee, because man an exacting thou art, thou takest what

οὐκ ἔθηκας, καὶ θερίζεις ὃ οὐκ ἔσπειρας.
thou didst not lay, and thou reapest what thou didst not sow.

22 λέγει αὐτῷ· ἐκ τοῦ στόματός σου
He says to him: Out of the mouth of thee

κρινῶ σε, πονηρὲ δοῦλε. ᾔδεις ὅτι ἐγὼ
I will judge thee, wicked slave. Knewest thou that I

ἄνθρωπος αὐστηρός εἰμι, αἴρων ὃ οὐκ
man an exacting am, taking what not

ἔθηκα, καὶ θερίζων ὃ οὐκ ἔσπειρα; 23 καὶ
I laid, and reaping what I sowed not? And

διὰ τί οὐκ ἔδωκάς μου τὸ ἀργύριον ἐπὶ
why didst thou not give of me the money on

τράπεζαν; κἀγὼ ἐλθὼν σὺν τόκῳ ἂν
a table?* And I coming with interest -

αὐτὸ ἔπραξα. 24 καὶ τοῖς παρεστῶσιν
it would have exacted. And to the [ones] standing by

* That is, a moneychanger's or banker's table.

pound from him, and give it to him who has the ten pounds.' ²⁵(And they said to him, 'Lord, he has ten pounds!') ²⁶'I tell you, that to every one who has will more be given; but from him who has not, even what he has, will be taken away. ²⁷But as for these enemies of mine, who did not want me to reign over them, bring them here and slay them before me.' "

28 And when he had said this, he went on ahead, going up to Jerusalem. ²⁹When he drew near to Beth'phage and Bethany, at the mount that is called Olivet, he sent two of the disciples, ³⁰saying, "Go into the village opposite, where on entering you will find a colt tied, on which no one has ever yet sat; untie it and bring it here. ³¹If any one asks you, 'Why are you untying it?' you shall say this, 'The Lord has need of it.' " ³²So those who were sent went away and found it as he had told them. ³³And as they were untying the colt, its owners said to them, "Why are you untying the colt?" ³⁴And they

εἶπεν· ἄρατε ἀπ' αὐτοῦ τὴν μνᾶν καὶ
he said :   Take   from   him   the   mina   and

δότε τῷ τὰς δέκα μνᾶς ἔχοντι. 25 καὶ
give ¹to the [one] ³the ⁴ten ⁵minas ²having.   And

εἶπαν αὐτῷ· κύριε, ἔχει δέκα μνᾶς.
they said to him :   Lord,   he has   ten   minas.

26 λέγω ὑμῖν ὅτι παντὶ τῷ ἔχοντι
I tell   you   that   to everyone   having

δοθήσεται, ἀπὸ δὲ τοῦ μὴ ἔχοντος καὶ
it will be given,   and from   the [one]   not   having   even

ὃ ἔχει ἀρθήσεται. 27 πλὴν τοὺς ἐχθρούς
what he has   will be taken.   Nevertheless –   enemies

μου τούτους τοὺς μὴ θελήσαντάς με
of me   these   the [ones]   not   wishing   me

βασιλεῦσαι ἐπ' αὐτοὺς ἀγάγετε ὧδε καὶ
to reign   over   them   bring ye   here   and

κατασφάξατε αὐτοὺς ἔμπροσθέν μου.
slay   them   before   me.

28 Καὶ εἰπὼν ταῦτα ἐπορεύετο ἔμπροσθεν
And having said these things   he went   in front

ἀναβαίνων εἰς Ἱεροσόλυμα. 29 Καὶ ἐγένετο
going up   to   Jerusalem.   And it came to pass

ὡς ἤγγισεν εἰς Βηθφαγὴ καὶ Βηθανίαν
as   he drew near   to   Bethphage   and   Bethany

πρὸς τὸ ὄρος τὸ καλούμενον ἐλαιών,
toward   the   mount   the   being called   of olives,

ἀπέστειλεν δύο τῶν μαθητῶν λέγων·
he sent   two   of the   disciples   saying :

30 ὑπάγετε εἰς τὴν κατέναντι κώμην, ἐν ᾗ
Go ye   into   the   opposite   village,   in which

εἰσπορευόμενοι εὑρήσετε πῶλον δεδεμένον,
entering   ye will find   a colt   having been tied,

ἐφ' ὃν οὐδεὶς πώποτε ἀνθρώπων ἐκάθισεν,
on which   no one   ever yet   of men   sat,

καὶ λύσαντες αὐτὸν ἀγάγετε. 31 καὶ ἐάν
and   loosening   it   bring.   And   if

τις ὑμᾶς ἐρωτᾷ· διὰ τί λύετε; οὕτως
anyone you   asks :   Why   loosen ye?   thus

ἐρεῖτε· ὅτι ὁ κύριος αὐτοῦ χρείαν ἔχει.
shall ye say : Because the Lord   of it   need   has.

32 ἀπελθόντες δὲ οἱ ἀπεσταλμένοι εὗρον
And going   the [ones]   having been sent   found

καθὼς εἶπεν αὐτοῖς. 33 λυόντων δὲ
as   he told   them.   And loosening
                                        =as they were

αὐτῶν τὸν πῶλον εἶπαν οἱ κύριοι αὐτοῦ
them*   the   colt   said   the   owners   of it
loosening

πρὸς αὐτούς· τί λύετε τὸν πῶλον; 34 οἱ
to   them :   Why loosen ye   the   colt?   ³they

said, "The Lord has need of it." ³⁵And they brought it to Jesus, and throwing their garments on the colt they set Jesus upon it. ³⁶And as he rode along, they spread their garments on the road. ³⁷As he was now drawing near, at the descent of the Mount of Olives, the whole multitude of the disciples began to rejoice and praise God with a loud voice for all the mighty works that they had seen, ³⁸saying, 'Blessed is the King who comes in the name of the Lord! Peace in heaven and glory in the highest!'" ³⁹And some of the Pharisees in the multitude said to him, "Teacher, rebuke your disciples." ⁴⁰He answered, "I tell you, if these were silent, the very stones would cry out."

41 And when he drew near and saw the city he wept over it, ⁴²saying, "Would that even today you knew the things that make for peace! But now they are hid from your eyes. ⁴³For the days shall come upon you, when your enemies will

δὲ εἶπαν· ὅτι ὁ κύριος αὐτοῦ χρείαν ἔχει.
¹And said: Because the Lord of it need has.

35 καὶ ἤγαγον αὐτὸν πρὸς τὸν Ἰησοῦν,
And they led it to - Jesus,

καὶ ἐπιρίψαντες αὐτῶν τὰ ἱμάτια ἐπὶ τὸν
and throwing on of them the garments on the

πῶλον ἐπεβίβασαν τὸν Ἰησοῦν. 36 πορευ-
colt they put on [it] - Jesus. And going

ομένου δὲ αὐτοῦ ὑπεστρώννυον τὰ ἱμάτια
going himᵃ they strewed the garments
=as he went

ἑαυτῶν ἐν τῇ ὁδῷ. 37 ἐγγίζοντος δὲ
of themselves in the way. And drawing near
=as he drew near

αὐτοῦ ἤδη πρὸς τῇ καταβάσει τοῦ ὄρους
himᵃ now to the descent of the mount

τῶν ἐλαιῶν ἤρξαντο ἄπαν τὸ πλῆθος τῶν
of the olives began all the multitude of the

μαθητῶν χαίροντες αἰνεῖν τὸν θεὸν φωνῇ
disciples rejoicing to praise - God voice

μεγάλῃ περὶ πασῶν ὧν εἶδον δυνάμεων,
with a about ¹all ³which ⁴they saw ²[the] powerful
great deeds,

38 λέγοντες· εὐλογημένος ὁ ἐρχόμενος, ὁ
saying: Blessed the coming [one], the

βασιλεὺς ἐν ὀνόματι κυρίου· ἐν οὐρανῷ
king in [the] name of [the] Lord; in heaven

εἰρήνη καὶ δόξα ἐν ὑψίστοις. 39 καὶ
peace and glory in highest places. And

τινες τῶν Φαρισαίων ἀπὸ τοῦ ὄχλου
some of the Pharisees from the crowd

εἶπαν πρὸς αὐτόν· διδάσκαλε, ἐπιτίμησον
said to him: Teacher, rebuke

τοῖς μαθηταῖς σου. 40 καὶ ἀποκριθεὶς
the disciples of thee. And answering

εἶπεν· λέγω ὑμῖν, ἐὰν οὗτοι σιωπήσουσιν,
he said: I tell you, if these shall(should) be silent,

οἱ λίθοι κράξουσιν. 41 Καὶ ὡς ἤγγισεν,
the stones will cry out. And as he drew near,

ἰδὼν τὴν πόλιν ἔκλαυσεν ἐπ’ αὐτήν,
seeing the city he wept over it,

42 λέγων ὅτι εἰ ἔγνως ἐν τῇ ἡμέρᾳ
saying[,] - If thou knewest in - day

ταύτῃ καὶ σὺ τὰ πρὸς εἰρήνην· νῦν δὲ
this even thou the things for peace; but now

ἐκρύβη ἀπὸ ὀφθαλμῶν σου. 43 ὅτι ἥξουσιν
they were hidden from eyes of thee. Because will come

ἡμέραι ἐπὶ σὲ καὶ παρεμβαλοῦσιν οἱ
days upon thee and ⁴will raise up ¹the

cast up a bank about you and surround you, and hem you in on every side, [44]and dash you to the ground, you and your children within you, and they will not leave one stone upon another in you; because you did not know the time of your visitation."

45 And he entered the temple and began to drive out those who sold, [46]saying to them, "It is written, 'My house shall be a house of prayer'; but you have made it a den of robbers."

47 And he was teaching daily in the temple. The chief priests and the scribes and the principal men of the people sought to destroy him; [48]but they did not find anything they could do, for all the people hung upon his words.

ἐχθροί σου χάρακά σοι καὶ περικυκλώσουσίν
'enemies 'of thee 'a rampart to thee and   will surround

σε καὶ συνέξουσίν σε πάντοθεν, 44 καὶ
thee and   will press   thee   on all sides,   and

ἐδαφιοῦσίν σε καὶ τὰ τέκνα σου ἐν σοί,
dash to the ground thee and   the   children of thee   in   thee,

καὶ οὐκ ἀφήσουσιν λίθον ἐπὶ λίθον ἐν σοί,
and   will not leave   stone   upon   stone   in   thee,

ἀνθ᾽ ὧν οὐκ ἔγνως τὸν καιρὸν τῆς
because†   thou knewest not   the   time   of the

ἐπισκοπῆς σου. 45 Καὶ εἰσελθὼν εἰς τὸ
visitation   of thee.   And   entering   into the

ἱερὸν ἤρξατο ἐκβάλλειν τοὺς πωλοῦντας,
temple   he began   to expel   the [ones]   selling,

46 λέγων αὐτοῖς· γέγραπται· καὶ ἔσται ὁ
telling   them :   It has been written :   And   shall be the

οἶκός μου οἶκος προσευχῆς· ὑμεῖς δὲ
house   of me   a house   of prayer;   but ye

αὐτὸν ἐποιήσατε σπήλαιον λῃστῶν.
it   made   a den   of robbers.

47 Καὶ ἦν διδάσκων τὸ καθ᾽ ἡμέραν ἐν
And   he was   teaching   daily†   in

τῷ ἱερῷ· οἱ δὲ ἀρχιερεῖς καὶ οἱ
the   temple;   but the   chief priests   and   the

γραμματεῖς ἐζήτουν αὐτὸν ἀπολέσαι καὶ οἱ
scribes   'sought   'him   'to destroy   'and 'the

πρῶτοι τοῦ λαοῦ, 48 καὶ οὐχ εὕρισκον
'chief men 'of the 'people,   and   did not find

τὸ τί ποιήσωσιν· ὁ λαὸς γὰρ ἅπας
-    what   they might do;   'the 'people   'for   'all

ἐξεκρέματο αὐτοῦ ἀκούων.
hung upon   him   hearing.

CHAPTER 20

ONE day, as he was teaching the people in the temple and preaching the gospel, the chief priests and the scribes with the elders came up [2]and said to him, "Tell us by what authority you do these things, or who it is that gave you this authority." [3]He

20 Καὶ ἐγένετο ἐν μιᾷ τῶν ἡμερῶν
And   it came to pass on   one   of the   days

διδάσκοντος αὐτοῦ τὸν λαὸν ἐν τῷ ἱερῷ
teaching   himᵃ   the   people   in   the   temple
=as he was teaching

καὶ εὐαγγελιζομένου ἐπέστησαν οἱ ἀρχιερεῖς
and   preaching good newsᵃ   came upon [him] the   chief priests

καὶ οἱ γραμματεῖς σὺν τοῖς πρεσβυτέροις,
and   the   scribes   with   the   elders,

2 καὶ εἶπαν λέγοντες πρὸς αὐτόν· εἰπὸν
and   spoke   saying   to   him :   Tell

ἡμῖν ἐν ποίᾳ ἐξουσίᾳ ταῦτα ποιεῖς, ἢ τίς
us   by   what   authority these things thou doest, or who

ἐστιν ὁ δούς σοι τὴν ἐξουσίαν ταύτην;
is   the [one] having given thee   -   authority   this?

answered them, "I also will ask you a question; now tell me, ⁴Was the baptism of John from heaven or from men?" ⁵And they discussed it with one another, saying, "If we say, 'From heaven,' he will say, 'Why did you not believe him?' ⁶But if we say, 'From men,' all the people will stone us; for they are convinced that John was a prophet." ⁷So they answered that they did not know whence it was. ⁸And Jesus said to them, "Neither will I tell you by what authority I do these things."

9 And he began to tell the people this parable: "A man planted a vineyard, and let it out to tenants, and went into another country for a long while. ¹⁰When the time came, he sent a servant to the tenants, that they should give him some of the fruit of the vineyard; but the tenants beat him, and sent him away empty-handed. ¹¹And he sent another servant; him also they beat and treated shamefully, and sent him away empty-handed. ¹²And he sent yet a

3 ἀποκριθεὶς δὲ εἶπεν πρὸς αὐτούς·
And answering he said to them:
ἐρωτήσω ὑμᾶς κἀγὼ λόγον, καὶ εἴπατέ
Will ask you I also a word, and tell ye
μοι· 4 τὸ βάπτισμα Ἰωάννου ἐξ οὐρανοῦ
me: The baptism of John from heaven
ἦν ἢ ἐξ ἀνθρώπων; 5 οἱ δὲ συνελογίσαντο
was it or from men? And they debated
πρὸς ἑαυτοὺς λέγοντες ὅτι ἐὰν εἴπωμεν·
with themselves saying[,] – If we say:
ἐξ οὐρανοῦ, ἐρεῖ· διὰ τί οὐκ ἐπιστεύσατε
From heaven, he will say: Why did ye not believe
αὐτῷ; 6 ἐὰν δὲ εἴπωμεν· ἐξ ἀνθρώπων, ὁ
him? And if we say: From men, the
λαὸς ἅπας καταλιθάσει ἡμᾶς· πεπεισμένος
people all will stone us; for having been per-
γάρ ἐστιν Ἰωάννην προφήτην εἶναι. 7 καὶ
suaded it is* John a prophet to be. And
ἀπεκρίθησαν μὴ εἰδέναι πόθεν. 8 καὶ ὁ
they answered not to know whence. And –
Ἰησοῦς εἶπεν αὐτοῖς· οὐδὲ ἐγὼ λέγω
Jesus said to them: Neither I tell
ὑμῖν ἐν ποίᾳ ἐξουσίᾳ ταῦτα ποιῶ. 9 Ἤρξατο
you by what authority these things I do. he began
δὲ πρὸς τὸν λαὸν λέγειν τὴν παραβολὴν
And to the people to tell – parable
ταύτην. ἄνθρωπος ἐφύτευσεν ἀμπελῶνα,
this. A man planted a vineyard,
καὶ ἐξέδοτο αὐτὸν γεωργοῖς, καὶ ἀπεδή-
and let out it to husbandmen, and went
μησεν χρόνους ἱκανούς. 10 καὶ καιρῷ
away periods for considerable. And in time
=a long time.
ἀπέστειλεν πρὸς τοὺς γεωργοὺς δοῦλον,
he sent to the husbandmen a slave,
ἵνα ἀπὸ τοῦ καρποῦ τοῦ ἀμπελῶνος
that from the fruit of the vineyard
δώσουσιν αὐτῷ· οἱ δὲ γεωργοὶ ἐξαπέστειλαν
they will give him; but the husbandmen ²sent ⁴away out
αὐτὸν δείραντες κενόν. 11 καὶ προσέθετο
³him ¹beating ⁵empty. And he added
ἕτερον πέμψαι δοῦλον· οἱ δὲ κἀκεῖνον
²another ¹to send slave; but they that one also
=he sent another slave in addition;
δείραντες καὶ ἀτιμάσαντες ἐξαπέστειλαν
beating and insulting sent away out
κενόν. 12 καὶ προσέθετο τρίτον πέμψαι·
empty. And he added a third to send;

* That is, the people (a collective singular) have been (=are) persuaded.

third; this one they wounded and cast out. ¹³Then the owner of the vineyard said, 'What shall I do? I will send my beloved son; it may be they will respect him.' ¹⁴But when the tenants saw him, they said to themselves, 'This is the heir; let us kill him, that the inheritance may be ours.' ¹⁵And they cast him out of the vineyard and killed him. What then will the owner of the vineyard do to them? ¹⁶He will come and destroy those tenants, and give the vineyard to others." When they heard this, they said, "God forbid!" ¹⁷But he looked at them and said, "What then is this that is written:

'The very stone which the builders rejected has become the head of the corner?'

¹⁸Every one who falls on that stone will be broken to pieces; but when it falls on any one it will crush him."

19 The scribes and the chief priests tried to lay hands on him at that very hour, but they feared the people; for they perceived that he had told this parable against them. ²⁰So they watched him, and sent

οἱ δὲ καὶ τοῦτον τραυματίσαντες ἐξέβαλον.
but they also this one wounding threw out.

13 εἶπεν δὲ ὁ κύριος τοῦ ἀμπελῶνος· τί
And said the owner of the vineyard: What

ποιήσω; πέμψω τὸν υἱόν μου τὸν ἀγαπητόν·
may I do? I will send the son of me - beloved;

ἴσως τοῦτον ἐντραπήσονται. 14 ἰδόντες δὲ
perhaps this one they will regard. But seeing

αὐτὸν οἱ γεωργοὶ διελογίζοντο πρὸς
him the husbandmen debated with

ἀλλήλους λέγοντες· οὗτός ἐστιν ὁ κληρονόμος·
one another saying: This is the heir;

ἀποκτείνωμεν αὐτόν, ἵνα ἡμῶν γένηται
let us kill him, that of us may become

ἡ κληρονομία. 15 καὶ ἐκβαλόντες αὐτὸν
the inheritance. And throwing out him

ἔξω τοῦ ἀμπελῶνος ἀπέκτειναν. τί οὖν
outside the vineyard they killed. What therefore

ποιήσει αὐτοῖς ὁ κύριος τοῦ ἀμπελῶνος;
will do to them the owner of the vineyard?

16 ἐλεύσεται καὶ ἀπολέσει τοὺς γεωργοὺς
he will come and will destroy - husbandmen

τούτους, καὶ δώσει τὸν ἀμπελῶνα ἄλλοις.
these, and will give the vineyard to others.

ἀκούσαντες δὲ εἶπαν· μὴ γένοιτο. 17 ὁ δὲ
And hearing they said: May it not be. And he

ἐμβλέψας αὐτοῖς εἶπεν· τί οὖν ἐστιν τὸ
looking at them said: What therefore is -

γεγραμμένον τοῦτο· λίθον ὃν ἀπεδοκίμασαν
having been written this: [The] stone which ²rejected

οἱ οἰκοδομοῦντες, οὗτος ἐγενήθη εἰς κεφαλὴν
¹the [ones] ²building, this came to be for [the] head

γωνίας; 18 πᾶς ὁ πεσὼν ἐπ᾽ ἐκεῖνον τὸν
of [the] corner? Everyone falling on that

λίθον συνθλασθήσεται· ἐφ᾽ ὃν δ᾽ ἂν πέσῃ,
stone will be broken in pieces; but on whomever it falls,

λικμήσει αὐτόν. 19 Καὶ ἐζήτησαν οἱ
it will crush to powder him. And sought the

γραμματεῖς καὶ οἱ ἀρχιερεῖς ἐπιβαλεῖν ἐπ᾽
scribes and the chief priests to lay on on

αὐτὸν τὰς χεῖρας ἐν αὐτῇ τῇ ὥρᾳ, καὶ
him the(ir) hands in ²same ¹the hour, and

ἐφοβήθησαν τὸν λαόν· ἔγνωσαν γὰρ ὅτι
feared the people; for they knew that

πρὸς αὐτοὺς εἶπεν τὴν παραβολὴν ταύτην.
at them he told - parable this.

20 Καὶ παρατηρήσαντες ἀπέστειλαν ἐγκαθέτους
And watching carefully they sent spies

spies, who pretended to be sincere, that they might take hold of what he said, so as to deliver him up to the authority and jurisdiction of the governor. ²¹They asked him, "Teacher, we know that you speak and teach rightly, and show no partiality, but truly teach the way of God. ²²Is it lawful for us to give tribute to Caesar, or not?" ²³But he perceived their craftiness, and said to them, ²⁴"Show me a coin. Whose likeness and inscription has it?" They said, "Caesar's." ²⁵He said to them, "Then render to Caesar the things that are Caesar's, and to God the things that are God's." ²⁶And they were not able in the presence of the people to catch him by what he said; but marveling at his answer they were silent.

27 There came to him some Sad'ducees, those who say that there is no resurrection, ²⁸and they asked him a question, saying, "Teacher, Moses wrote for us that if a man's brother dies, having a wife but no children, the man must

ὑποκρινομένους ἑαυτοὺς δικαίους εἶναι, ἵνα
pretending　themselves　righteous　to be,　that

ἐπιλάβωνται αὐτοῦ λόγου, ὥστε παραδοῦναι
they might seize　of him　a word,　so as　to deliver

αὐτὸν τῇ ἀρχῇ καὶ τῇ ἐξουσίᾳ τοῦ
him　to the　rule　and　to the　authority　of the

ἡγεμόνος. 21 καὶ ἐπηρώτησαν αὐτὸν
governor.　　And　they questioned　him

λέγοντες· διδάσκαλε, οἴδαμεν ὅτι ὀρθῶς
saying :　Teacher,　we know　that　¹rightly

λέγεις καὶ διδάσκεις καὶ οὐ λαμβάνεις
¹thou speakest ²and ³teachest　and　receivest not
　　　　　　　　　　　　　　=regardest not persons,

πρόσωπον, ἀλλ᾽ ἐπ᾽ ἀληθείας τὴν ὁδὸν τοῦ
a face,　but on [the basis of]　truth　the　way –

θεοῦ διδάσκεις· 22 ἔξεστιν ἡμᾶς Καίσαρι
of God　teachest;　is it lawful　for us　to Cæsar

φόρον δοῦναι ἢ οὔ; 23 κατανοήσας δὲ
tribute　to give　or　not?　And perceiving

αὐτῶν τὴν πανουργίαν εἶπεν πρὸς αὐτούς·
of them　the　cleverness　he said　to　them :

24 δείξατέ μοι δηνάριον· τίνος ἔχει εἰκόνα
Show　me　a denarius;　of whom　has it　an image

καὶ ἐπιγραφήν; οἱ δὲ εἶπαν· Καίσαρος.
and　superscription?　And they　said :　Of Cæsar.

25 ὁ δὲ εἶπεν πρὸς αὐτούς· τοίνυν ἀπόδοτε
And he　said　to　them :　So　render

τὰ Καίσαρος Καίσαρι καὶ τὰ τοῦ θεοῦ
the things of Cæsar　to Cæsar　and the things – of God

τῷ θεῷ. 26 καὶ οὐκ ἴσχυσαν ἐπιλαβέσθαι
– to God.　And　they were not able　to seize

αὐτοῦ ῥήματος ἐναντίον τοῦ λαοῦ, καὶ
of him　a word　in the presence of　the　people,　and

θαυμάσαντες ἐπὶ τῇ ἀποκρίσει αὐτοῦ
marvelling　at　the　answer　of him

ἐσίγησαν.
they were silent.

27 Προσελθόντες δέ τινες τῶν Σαδ-
　　And ⁴approaching　¹some　²of the　³Sad-

δουκαίων, οἱ ἀντιλέγοντες ἀνάστασιν μὴ
ducees,　the [ones] saying in opposition* a resurrection　not

εἶναι, ἐπηρώτησαν αὐτὸν 28 λέγοντες·
to be,　they questioned　him　　　saying :

διδάσκαλε, Μωϋσῆς ἔγραψεν ἡμῖν, ἐάν
Teacher,　Moses　wrote　to us,　If

τινος ἀδελφὸς ἀποθάνῃ ἔχων γυναῖκα, καὶ
of anyone　a brother　dies　having　a wife,　and

οὗτος ἄτεκνος ᾖ, ἵνα λάβῃ ὁ ἀδελφὸς
this man　childless　is,　that ⁴should take ¹the ²brother

*That is, to the Pharisees and to the generally held opinion.

take the wife and raise up children for his brother. ²⁹Now there were seven brothers; the first took a wife, and died without children; ³⁰and the second ³¹and the third took her, and likewise all seven left no children and died. ³²Afterward the woman also died. ³³In the resurrection, therefore, whose wife will the woman be? For the seven had her as wife."

34 And Jesus said to them, "The sons of this age marry and are given in marriage; ³⁵but those who are accounted worthy to attain to that age and to the resurrection from the dead neither marry nor are given in marriage, ³⁶for they cannot die any more, because they are equal to angels and are sons of God, being sons of the resurrection. ³⁷But that the dead are raised, even Moses showed, in the passage about the bush, where he calls the Lord the God of Abraham and the God of Isaac and the God of Jacob. ³⁸Now he is not God of the dead, but of the living; for all live to him." ³⁹And some of the scribes answered, "Teacher, you have

αὐτοῦ τὴν γυναῖκα καὶ ἐξαναστήσῃ σπέρμα
²of him ⁵the ⁶wife and raise up seed

τῷ ἀδελφῷ αὐτοῦ. 29 ἑπτὰ οὖν ἀδελφοὶ
to the brother of him. Seven therefore brothers

ἦσαν· καὶ ὁ πρῶτος λαβὼν γυναῖκα
there were; and the first having taken a wife

ἀπέθανεν ἄτεκνος· 30 καὶ ὁ δεύτερος 31 καὶ
died childless; and the second and

ὁ τρίτος ἔλαβεν αὐτήν, ὡσαύτως δὲ καὶ
the third took her, and similarly also

οἱ ἑπτὰ οὐ κατέλιπον τέκνα καὶ ἀπέθανον.
the seven did not leave children and died.

32 ὕστερον καὶ ἡ γυνὴ ἀπέθανεν. 33 ἡ
Lastly also the woman died. The

γυνὴ οὖν ἐν τῇ ἀναστάσει τίνος αὐτῶν
woman therefore in the resurrection of which of them

γίνεται γυνή; οἱ γὰρ ἑπτὰ ἔσχον αὐτὴν
becomes she wife? for the seven had her

γυναῖκα. 34 καὶ εἶπεν αὐτοῖς ὁ Ἰησοῦς·
[as] wife. And said to them - Jesus:

οἱ υἱοὶ τοῦ αἰῶνος τούτου γαμοῦσιν καὶ
The sons - age of this marry and

γαμίσκονται, 35 οἱ δὲ καταξιωθέντες τοῦ
are given in marriage, but the [ones] counted worthy -

αἰῶνος ἐκείνου τυχεῖν καὶ τῆς ἀναστάσεως
²age ³of that ¹to obtain and of the resurrection

τῆς ἐκ νεκρῶν οὔτε γαμοῦσιν οὔτε
- out of [the] dead neither marry nor

γαμίζονται· 36 οὐδὲ γὰρ ἀποθανεῖν ἔτι
are given in marriage; for not even to die more

δύνανται, ἰσάγγελοι γάρ εἰσιν, καὶ υἱοί
can they, for equal to angels they are, and ²sons

εἰσιν θεοῦ τῆς ἀναστάσεως υἱοὶ ὄντες.
¹they are ³of God ⁵of the ⁷resurrection ⁵sons ⁶being.

37 ὅτι δὲ ἐγείρονται οἱ νεκροί, καὶ
But that are raised the dead, even

Μωϋσῆς ἐμήνυσεν ἐπι τῆς βάτου, ὡς
Moses pointed out at the bush, as

λέγει κύριον τὸν θεὸν Ἀβραὰμ καὶ θεὸν
he calls [the] Lord the God of Abraham and God

Ἰσαὰκ καὶ θεὸν Ἰακώβ· 38 θεὸς δὲ οὐκ
of Isaac and God of Jacob; but God not

ἔστιν νεκρῶν ἀλλὰ ζώντων· πάντες γὰρ
he is of dead persons but of living; for all

αὐτῷ ζῶσιν. 39 ἀποκριθέντες δέ τινες
to him live. And answering some

τῶν γραμματέων εἶπαν· διδάσκαλε, κελῶς
of the scribes said: Teacher, well

spoken well." ⁴⁰For they no longer dared to ask him any question.
41 But he said to them, "How can they say that the Christ is David's son? ⁴²For David himself says in the Book of Psalms,
'The Lord said to my Lord,
Sit at my right hand,
⁴³till I make thy enemies a stool for thy feet.'
⁴⁴David thus calls him Lord; so how is he his son?"
45 And in the hearing of all the people he said to his disciples, ⁴⁶"Beware of the scribes, who like to go about in long robes, and love salutations in the market places and the best seats in the synagogues and the places of honor at feasts, ⁴⁷who devour widows' houses and for a pretense make long prayers. They will receive the greater condemnation."

εἶπας. 40 οὐκέτι γὰρ ἐτόλμων ἐπερωτᾶν
thou sayest.   For no more   dared they   to question
αὐτὸν οὐδέν.
him   no(any)thing.

41 Εἶπεν δὲ πρὸς αὐτούς· πῶς λέγουσιν
And he said   to   them: How   say they
τὸν χριστὸν εἶναι Δαυὶδ υἱόν; 42 αὐτὸς
the   Christ   to be   of David   son?   himself
γὰρ Δαυὶδ λέγει ἐν βίβλῳ ψαλμῶν·
For   David   says   in   [the] roll   of psalms:
εἶπεν κύριος τῷ κυρίῳ μου· κάθου ἐκ
Said   [the] LORD   to the   Lord   of me: Sit thou   at
δεξιῶν μου 43 ἕως ἂν θῶ τοὺς ἐχθρούς σου
[the] right of me   until   I put   the   enemies of thee
ὑποπόδιον τῶν ποδῶν σου. 44 Δαυὶδ
a footstool   of the   feet   of thee.   David
οὖν αὐτὸν κύριον καλεῖ, καὶ πῶς αὐτοῦ
therefore him   Lord   calls,   and   how   of him
υἱός ἐστιν;
son   is he?

45 Ἀκούοντος δὲ παντὸς τοῦ λαοῦ εἶπεν
And hearing   all   the   people[a]   he said
=as all the people heard
τοῖς μαθηταῖς· 46 προσέχετε ἀπὸ τῶν
to the   disciples: Beware   from(of)   the
γραμματέων τῶν θελόντων περιπατεῖν ἐν
scribes   -   wishing   to walk about   in
στολαῖς καὶ φιλούντων ἀσπασμοὺς ἐν ταῖς
robes   and   liking   greetings   in   the
ἀγοραῖς καὶ πρωτοκαθεδρίας ἐν ταῖς
marketplaces   and   chief seats   in   the
συναγωγαῖς καὶ πρωτοκλισίας ἐν τοῖς
synagogues   and   chief couches   in   the
δείπνοις, 47 οἳ κατεσθίουσιν τὰς οἰκίας
suppers,   who   devour   the   houses
τῶν χηρῶν καὶ προφάσει μακρὰ προσεύχονται·
of the widows and under pretence long   pray;
οὗτοι λήμψονται περισσότερον κρίμα.
these   will receive   severer   judgment.

CHAPTER 21

HE looked up and saw the rich putting their gifts into the treasury; ²and he saw a poor widow put in two copper coins. ³And he

21 Ἀναβλέψας δὲ εἶδεν τοὺς βάλλοντας
And looking up   he saw   ¹the   ²putting
εἰς τὸ γαζοφυλακεῖον τὰ δῶρα αὐτῶν
⁴into ⁵the   ⁶treasury   ⁷the   ⁸gifts   ⁹of them
πλουσίους. 2 εἶδεν δέ τινα χήραν πενιχρὰν
³rich [ones].   And he saw a certain   widow   poor
βάλλουσαν ἐκεῖ λεπτὰ δύο, 3 καὶ εἶπεν·
putting   there   lepta   two,   and   he said:

said, "Truly I tell you, this poor widow has put in more than all of them; ⁴for they all contributed out of their abundance, but she out of her poverty put in all the living that she had."

5 And as some spoke of the temple, how it was adorned with noble stones and offerings, he said, ⁶"As for these things which you see, the days will come when there shall not be left here one stone upon another that will not be thrown down." ⁷And they asked him, "Teacher, when will this be, and what will be the sign when this is about to take place?" ⁸And he said, "Take heed that you are not led astray; for many will come in my name, saying, 'I am he!' and, 'The time is at hand!' Do not go after them. ⁹And when you hear of wars and tumults, do not be terrified; for this must first take place, but the end will not be at once."

10 Then he said to them, "Nation will rise against nation, and kingdom against kingdom; ¹¹there will be great earthquakes, and in

ἀληθῶς λέγω ὑμῖν ὅτι ἡ χήρα αὕτη ἡ
Truly I tell you that – ²widow ¹this –

πτωχὴ πλεῖον πάντων ἔβαλεν· 4 πάντες
²poor more [than] all put; ²all

γὰρ οὗτοι ἐκ τοῦ περισσεύοντος αὐτοῖς
¹for these out of the abounding to them°
=their abundance

ἔβαλον εἰς τὰ δῶρα, αὕτη δὲ ἐκ τοῦ
put into the gifts, but this woman out of the

ὑστερήματος αὐτῆς πάντα τὸν βίον ὃν
want of her ²all ²the ⁴living ⁵which

εἶχεν ἔβαλεν.
⁶she had ¹put.

5 Καί τινων λεγόντων περὶ τοῦ ἱεροῦ, ὅτι
And some speaking° about the temple, that
=as some spoke

λίθοις καλοῖς καὶ ἀναθήμασιν κεκόσμηται,
stones with beautiful and gifts it has(had)
been adorned,

εἶπεν· 6 ταῦτα ἃ θεωρεῖτε, ἐλεύσονται
he said : These things which ye behold, will come

ἡμέραι ἐν αἷς οὐκ ἀφεθήσεται λίθος ἐπὶ
days in which there will not be left stone on

λίθῳ ὃς οὐ καταλυθήσεται. 7 ἐπηρώτησαν δὲ
stone which will not be overthrown. And they questioned

αὐτὸν λέγοντες· διδάσκαλε, πότε οὖν
him saying : Teacher, when therefore

ταῦτα ἔσται; καὶ τί τὸ σημεῖον ὅταν
these things will be? And what [will be] the sign when

μέλλῃ ταῦτα γίνεσθαι; 8 ὁ δὲ εἶπεν·
²are about ¹these things ³to happen? And he said :

βλέπετε μὴ πλανηθῆτε· πολλοὶ γὰρ
Beware lest ye be led astray; for many

ἐλεύσονται ἐπὶ τῷ ὀνόματί μου λέγοντες·
will come on(in) the name of me saying :

ἐγώ εἰμι, καί· ὁ καιρὸς ἤγγικεν· μὴ
I am, and : The time has drawn near; not

πορευθῆτε ὀπίσω αὐτῶν. 9 ὅταν δὲ
go ye after them. And when

ἀκούσητε πολέμους καὶ ἀκαταστασίας, μὴ
ye hear [of] wars and commotions, not

πτοηθῆτε· δεῖ γὰρ ταῦτα γενέσθαι
be ye scared; for it behoves these things to happen

πρῶτον, ἀλλ᾿ οὐκ εὐθέως τὸ τέλος. 10 Τότε
first, but not immediately the end. Then

ἔλεγεν αὐτοῖς· ἐγερθήσεται ἔθνος ἐπ᾿ ἔθνος
he said to them : Will be raised nation against nation

καὶ βασιλεία ἐπὶ βασιλείαν, 11 σεισμοί τε
and kingdom against kingdom, and earthquakes

various places famines and pestilences; and there will be terrors and great signs from heaven. [12] But before all this they will lay their hands on you and persecute you, delivering you up to the synagogues and prisons, and you will be brought before kings and governors for my name's sake. [13] This will be a time for you to bear testimony. [14] Settle it therefore in your minds, not to meditate beforehand how to answer; [15] for I will give you a mouth and wisdom, which none of your adversaries will be able to withstand or contradict. [16] You will be delivered up even by parents and brothers and kinsmen and friends, and some of you they will put to death; [17] you will be hated by all for my name's sake. [18] But not a hair of your head will perish. [19] By your endurance you will gain your lives.

20 "But when you see Jerusalem surrounded by armies, then know that its desolation has come near. [21] Then let those who are in Judea flee to the mountains, and let those who are inside the city depart, and let not

μεγάλοι καὶ κατὰ τόπους λοιμοὶ καὶ λιμοὶ
great and from place to place† pestilences and famines

ἔσονται, φόβητρά τε καὶ ἀπ' οὐρανοῦ
there will be, and terrors and ³from ⁴heaven

σημεῖα μεγάλα ἔσται. 12 πρὸ δὲ τούτων
²signs ¹great there will be. But before these things

πάντων ἐπιβαλοῦσιν ἐφ' ὑμᾶς τὰς χεῖρας
all they will lay on on you the hands

αὐτῶν καὶ διώξουσιν, παραδιδόντες εἰς τὰς
of them and will persecute, delivering to the

συναγωγὰς καὶ φυλακάς, ἀπαγομένους ἐπὶ
synagogues and prisons, being led away on(before)

βασιλεῖς καὶ ἡγεμόνας ἕνεκεν τοῦ ὀνόματός
kings and governors for the sake of the name

μου· 13 ἀποβήσεται ὑμῖν εἰς μαρτύριον.
of me; it will turn out to you for a testimony.

14 θέτε οὖν ἐν ταῖς καρδίαις ὑμῶν μὴ
Put therefore in the hearts of you not

προμελετᾶν ἀπολογηθῆναι· 15 ἐγὼ γὰρ
to practise beforehand to defend [yourselves]; for I

δώσω ὑμῖν στόμα καὶ σοφίαν, ᾗ οὐ
will give you a mouth and wisdom, which not

δυνήσονται ἀντιστῆναι ἢ ἀντειπεῖν ἅπαντες οἱ
will be able to withstand or to contradict all the

ἀντικείμενοι ὑμῖν. 16 παραδοθήσεσθε δὲ καὶ
[ones] opposing you. And ye will be betrayed also

ὑπὸ γονέων καὶ ἀδελφῶν καὶ συγγενῶν
by parents and brothers and relatives

καὶ φίλων, καὶ θανατώσουσιν ἐξ ὑμῶν,
and friends, and they will put to death [some] of you,

17 καὶ ἔσεσθε μισούμενοι ὑπὸ πάντων διὰ
and ye will be being hated by all men because of

τὸ ὄνομά μου. 18 καὶ θρὶξ ἐκ τῆς
the name of me. And a hair of the

κεφαλῆς ὑμῶν οὐ μὴ ἀπόληται· 19 ἐν τῇ
head of you by no means will perish; in the

ὑπομονῇ ὑμῶν κτήσεσθε τὰς ψυχὰς ὑμῶν.
endurance of you ye will gain the souls of you.

20 Ὅταν δὲ ἴδητε κυκλουμένην ὑπὸ
But when ye see ²being surrounded ³by

στρατοπέδων Ἰερουσαλήμ, τότε γνῶτε ὅτι
⁴camps ¹Jerusalem, then know ye that

ἤγγικεν ἡ ἐρήμωσις αὐτῆς. 21 τότε οἱ ἐν
has drawn near the desolation of it. Then the [ones] in

τῇ Ἰουδαίᾳ φευγέτωσαν εἰς τὰ ὄρη, καὶ
- Judæa let them flee to the mountains, and

οἱ ἐν μέσῳ αὐτῆς ἐκχωρείτωσαν, καὶ
the [ones] in [the] midst of it let them depart out, and

those who are out in the country enter it; ²²for these are days of vengeance, to fulfil all that is written. ²³Alas for those who are with child and for those who give suck in those days! For great distress shall be upon the earth and wrath upon this people; ²⁴they will fall by the edge of the sword, and be led captive among all nations; and Jerusalem will be trodden down by the Gentiles, until the times of the Gentiles are fulfilled.

25 "And there will be signs in sun and moon and stars, and upon the earth distress of nations in perplexity at the roaring of the sea and the waves, ²⁶men fainting with fear and with foreboding of what is coming on the world; for the powers of the heavens will be shaken. ²⁷And then they will see the Son of man coming in a cloud with power and great glory. ²⁸Now when these things begin to take place, look up and raise your heads, because your redemption is drawing near."

29 And he told them a parable: "Look at the fig tree, and all the trees; ³⁰as soon as they come out in leaf, you see for

---

οἱ ἐν ταῖς χώραις μὴ εἰσερχέσθωσαν εἰς
the [ones] in the districts let them not enter into

αὐτήν, 22 ὅτι ἡμέραι ἐκδικήσεως αὗταί
it, because days of vengeance these

εἰσιν τοῦ πλησθῆναι πάντα τὰ γεγραμμένα.
are – to be fulfilled^d all the things having been written.

23 οὐαὶ ταῖς ἐν γαστρὶ ἐχούσαις καὶ ταῖς
Woe to the pregnant women† and to the

θηλαζούσαις ἐν ἐκείναις ταῖς ἡμέραις·
[ones] giving suck in those – days;

ἔσται γὰρ ἀνάγκη μεγάλη ἐπὶ τῆς γῆς
for there will be distress great on the land

καὶ ὀργὴ τῷ λαῷ τούτῳ, 24 καὶ πεσοῦνται
and wrath – people to this, and they will fall

στόματι μαχαίρης καὶ αἰχμαλωτισθή-
by [the] mouth(edge) of [the] sword and will be led

σονται εἰς τὰ ἔθνη πάντα, καὶ Ἰερουσαλὴμ
captive to the nations all, and Jerusalem

ἔσται πατουμένη ὑπὸ ἐθνῶν, ἄχρι οὗ
will be being trodden down by nations, until

πληρωθῶσιν καιροὶ ἐθνῶν. 25 Καὶ ἔσονται
are accomplished [the] times of [the] nations. And there will be

σημεῖα ἐν ἡλίῳ καὶ σελήνῃ καὶ ἄστροις,
signs in sun and moon and stars,

καὶ ἐπὶ τῆς γῆς συνοχὴ ἐθνῶν ἐν ἀπορίᾳ
and on the earth anxiety of nations in perplexity

ἤχους θαλάσσης καὶ σάλου, 26 ἀποψυχόντων
of [the] sound of [the] sea and surf, fainting
=while men faint

ἀνθρώπων ἀπὸ φόβου καὶ προσδοκίας τῶν
men^a from fear and expectation of the

ἐπερχομένων τῇ οἰκουμένῃ· αἱ γὰρ δυνάμεις
things coming on the inhabited earth; for the powers

τῶν οὐρανῶν σαλευθήσονται. 27 καὶ τότε
of the heavens will be shaken. And then

ὄψονται τὸν υἱὸν τοῦ ἀνθρώπου ἐρχόμενον
they will see the Son – of man coming

ἐν νεφέλῃ μετὰ δυνάμεως καὶ δόξης
in a cloud with power and glory

πολλῆς. 28 ἀρχομένων δὲ τούτων γίνεσθαι
much(great). And beginning these things^a to happen
=when these things begin

ἀνακύψατε καὶ ἐπάρατε τὰς κεφαλὰς ὑμῶν,
stand erect and lift up the heads of you,

διότι ἐγγίζει ἡ ἀπολύτρωσις ὑμῶν. 29 Καὶ
because draws near the redemption of you. And

εἶπεν παραβολὴν αὐτοῖς· ἴδετε τὴν συκῆν
he told ²a parable ¹them: Ye see the fig-tree

καὶ πάντα τὰ δένδρα· 30 ὅταν προβάλωσιν
and all the trees; when ²they burst into leaf

yourselves and know that the summer is already near. ³¹ So also, when you see these things taking place, you know that the kingdom of God is near. ³²Truly, I say to you, this generation will not pass away till all has taken place. ³³ Heaven and earth will pass away, but my words will not pass away.

34 "But take heed to yourselves lest your hearts be weighed down with dissipation and drunkenness and cares of this life, and that day come upon you suddenly like a snare; ³⁵ for it will come upon all who dwell upon the face of the whole earth. ³⁶ But watch at all times, praying that you may have strength to escape all these things that will take place, and to stand before the Son of man."

37 And every day he was teaching in the temple, but at night he went out and lodged on the mount called Olivet. ³⁸And early in the morning all the people came to him in the temple to hear him.

ἤδη, βλέποντες ἀφ' ἑαυτῶν γινώσκετε ὅτι
now, seeing from(of) yourselves ye know that

ἤδη ἐγγὺς τὸ θέρος ἐστίν· 31 οὕτως καὶ
now near the summer is; so also

ὑμεῖς, ὅταν ἴδητε ταῦτα γινόμενα,
ye, when ye see these things happening,

γινώσκετε ὅτι ἐγγύς ἐστιν ἡ βασιλεία
know that near is the kingdom

τοῦ θεοῦ. 32 ἀμὴν λέγω ὑμῖν ὅτι οὐ μὴ
– of God. Truly I tell you that by no means

παρέλθῃ ἡ γενεὰ αὕτη ἕως ἂν πάντα
will pass away – generation this until all things

γένηται. 33 ὁ οὐρανὸς καὶ ἡ γῆ παρ-
happens. The heaven and the earth will

ελεύσονται, οἱ δὲ λόγοι μου οὐ μὴ παρελεύ-
pass away, but the words of me by no means will pass

σονται. 34 Προσέχετε δὲ ἑαυτοῖς μήποτε
away. And take heed to yourselves lest

βαρηθῶσιν ὑμῶν αἱ καρδίαι ἐν κραιπάλῃ
become burdened of you the hearts with surfeiting

καὶ μέθῃ καὶ μερίμναις βιωτικαῖς, καὶ
and deep drinking and anxieties of life,† and

ἐπιστῇ ἐφ' ὑμᾶς αἰφνίδιος ἡ ἡμέρα ἐκείνη
come on on you suddenly – day that

35 ὡς παγίς· ἐπεισελεύσεται γὰρ ἐπὶ πάντας
as a snare; for it will come in on on all

τοὺς καθημένους ἐπὶ πρόσωπον πάσης τῆς
the [ones] sitting on [the] face of all the

γῆς. 36 ἀγρυπνεῖτε δὲ ἐν παντὶ καιρῷ
earth. But be ye watchful at every time

δεόμενοι ἵνα κατισχύσητε ἐκφυγεῖν ταῦτα
begging that ye may be able to escape these things

πάντα τὰ μέλλοντα γίνεσθαι, καὶ σταθῆναι
all – being about to happen, and to stand

ἔμπροσθεν τοῦ υἱοῦ τοῦ ἀνθρώπου.
before the Son – of man.

37 Ἦν δὲ τὰς ἡμέρας ἐν τῷ ἱερῷ
Now he was [in] the days in the temple

διδάσκων, τὰς δὲ νύκτας ἐξερχόμενος
teaching, and [in] the nights going forth

ηὐλίζετο εἰς τὸ ὄρος τὸ καλούμενον
he lodged in the mountain – being called

ἐλαιών. 38 καὶ πᾶς ὁ λαὸς ὤρθριζεν
of olives. And all the people came in the morning

πρὸς αὐτὸν ἐν τῷ ἱερῷ ἀκούειν αὐτοῦ.
to him in the temple to hear him.

CHAPTER 22

N OW the feast of Unleavened Bread drew near, which is called the Passover. ²And the chief priests and the scribes were seeking how to put him to death; for they feared the people.

3 Then Satan entered into Judas called Iscariot, who was of the number of the twelve; ⁴he went away and conferred with the chief priests and captains how he might betray him to them. ⁵And they were glad, and engaged to give him money. ⁶So he agreed, and sought an opportunity to betray him to them in the absence of the multitude.

7 Then came the day of Unleavened Bread, on which the passover lamb had to be sacrificed. ⁸So Jesus sent Peter and John, saying, "Go and prepare the passover for us, that we may eat it." ⁹They said to him, "Where will you have us prepare it?" ¹⁰He said to them, "Behold, when you have entered the city, a man carrying a jar of water will meet you; follow him into the house which he enters, ¹¹and tell the householder, 'The Teacher says to you, Where is the guest room, where I am to eat the passover with

22 Ἤγγιζεν δὲ ἡ ἑορτὴ τῶν ἀζύμων ἡ
Now drew near the feast of unleavened bread –
λεγομένη πάσχα. 2 καὶ ἐζήτουν οἱ ἀρχιερεῖς
being called Passover. And ⁶sought ¹the ²chief priests
καὶ οἱ γραμματεῖς τὸ πῶς ἀνέλωσιν
³and ⁴the ⁵scribes – how they might destroy
αὐτόν· ἐφοβοῦντο γὰρ τὸν λαόν. 3 Εἰσῆλθεν δὲ
him; for they feared the people. And entered
σατανᾶς εἰς Ἰούδαν τὸν καλούμενον
Satan into Judas – being called
Ἰσκαριώτην, ὄντα ἐκ τοῦ ἀριθμοῦ τῶν
Iscariot, being of the number of the
δώδεκα· 4 καὶ ἀπελθὼν συνελάλησεν τοῖς
twelve; and going he conversed with the
ἀρχιερεῦσιν καὶ στρατηγοῖς τὸ πῶς αὐτοῖς
chief priests and captains – how to them
παραδῷ αὐτόν. 5 καὶ ἐχάρησαν, καὶ
he might betray him. And they rejoiced, and
συνέθεντο αὐτῷ ἀργύριον δοῦναι. 6 καὶ
they agreed ²him ³money ¹to give. And
ἐξωμολόγησεν, καὶ ἐζήτει εὐκαιρίαν τοῦ
he fully consented, and sought opportunity –
παραδοῦναι αὐτὸν ἄτερ ὄχλου αὐτοῖς.
to betray[d] him apart from a crowd to them.
7 Ἦλθεν δὲ ἡ ἡμέρα τῶν ἀζύμων, ᾗ
And came the day of unleavened bread, on which
ἔδει θύεσθαι τὸ πάσχα· 8 καὶ ἀπέστειλεν
it behoved to kill the passover [lamb]; and he sent
Πέτρον καὶ Ἰωάννην εἰπών· πορευθέντες
Peter and John saying : Going
ἑτοιμάσατε ἡμῖν τὸ πάσχα, ἵνα φάγωμεν. 9 οἱ
prepare ye for us the passover, that we may eat. they
δὲ εἶπαν αὐτῷ· ποῦ θέλεις ἑτοιμάσωμεν;
And said to him : Where wishest thou [that] we may prepare?
10 ὁ δὲ εἶπεν αὐτοῖς· ἰδοὺ εἰσελθόντων
And he told them : Behold[,] entering
=as ye enter
ὑμῶν[a] εἰς τὴν πόλιν συναντήσει ὑμῖν
you into the city will meet you
ἄνθρωπος κεράμιον ὕδατος βαστάζων·
a man a pitcher of water bearing;
ἀκολουθήσατε αὐτῷ εἰς τὴν οἰκίαν εἰς ἣν
follow him into the house into which
εἰσπορεύεται· 11 καὶ ἐρεῖτε τῷ οἰκοδεσπότῃ
he enters; and ye will say to the house-master
τῆς οἰκίας· λέγει σοι ὁ διδάσκαλος·
of the house : Says to thee the teacher :
ποῦ ἐστιν τὸ κατάλυμα ὅπου τὸ πάσχα
Where is the guest room where the passover

my disciples?' ¹²And he will show you a large upper room furnished; there make ready." ¹³And they went, and found it as he had told them; and they prepared the passover.

14 And when the hour came, he sat at table, and the apostles with him. ¹⁵And he said to them, "I have earnestly desired to eat this passover with you before I suffer; ¹⁶for I tell you I shall not eat it* until it is fulfilled in the kingdom of God." ¹⁷And he took a cup, and when he had given thanks he said, "Take this, and divide it among yourselves; ¹⁸for I tell you that from now on I shall not drink of the fruit of the vine until the kingdom of God comes." ¹⁹And he took bread, and when he had given thanks he broke it and gave it to them, saying, "This is my body.ᵗ ²¹But

μετὰ	τῶν	μαθητῶν	μου	φάγω;	12 κἀκεῖνος
with	the	disciples	of me	I may eat ?	And that man

ὑμῖν	δείξει	ἀνάγαιον	μέγα	ἐστρωμένον·
you	will show	upper room	a large	having been spread;*

ἐκεῖ	ἑτοιμάσατε.	13 ἀπελθόντες	δὲ	εὗρον
there	prepare ye.	And going		they found

καθὼς	εἰρήκει	αὐτοῖς,	καὶ	ἡτοίμασαν	τὸ
as	he had told	them,	and	they prepared	the

πάσχα.	14 Καὶ	ὅτε	ἐγένετο	ἡ	ὥρα,
passover.	And	when	came	the	hour,

ἀνέπεσεν,	καὶ	οἱ	ἀπόστολοι	σὺν	αὐτῷ.
he reclined,	and	the	apostles	with	him.

15 καὶ	εἶπεν	πρὸς	αὐτούς·	ἐπιθυμίᾳ
And	he said	to	them·	With desire

ἐπεθύμησα	τοῦτο	τὸ	πάσχα	φαγεῖν	μεθ'
I desired	this	-	passover	to eat	with

ὑμῶν	πρὸ	τοῦ	με	παθεῖν·	16 λέγω	γὰρ
you	before	the	me	to suffer;ᵇ =I suffer ;	for I tell	

ὑμῖν	ὅτι	οὐκέτι	οὐ	μὴ	φάγω	αὐτὸ
you	that	no more	by no(any) means		I eat	it

ἕως	ὅτου	πληρωθῇ	ἐν	τῇ	βασιλείᾳ	τοῦ	θεοῦ.
until		it is fulfilled	in	the	kingdom	-	of God.

17 καὶ	δεξάμενος	ποτήριον	εὐχαριστήσας
And	taking	a cup	having given thanks

εἶπεν·	λάβετε	τοῦτο	καὶ	διαμερίσατε	εἰς
he said :	Take	this	and	divide	among

ἑαυτούς·	18 λέγω	γὰρ	ὑμῖν,	οὐ	μὴ	πίω
yourselves;	for I tell		you,	by no means		I drink

ἀπὸ	τοῦ	νῦν	ἀπὸ	τοῦ	γενήματος	τῆς
from	-	now [on]	from	the	produce	of the

ἀμπέλου	ἕως	οὗ	ἡ	βασιλεία	τοῦ	θεοῦ
vine	until		the	kingdom	-	of God

ἔλθῃ.	19 καὶ	λαβὼν	ἄρτον	εὐχαριστήσας
comes.	And	taking	a loaf	having given thanks

ἔκλασεν	καὶ	ἔδωκεν	αὐτοῖς	λέγων·	τοῦτό
he broke	and	gave	to them	saying :	This

ἐστιν	τὸ	σῶμά	μου	[τὸ	ὑπὲρ	ὑμῶν
is	the	body	of me	-	for	you

διδόμενον·	τοῦτο	ποιεῖτε	εἰς	τὴν	ἐμὴν
being given;	this	do ye	for	-	my

ἀνάμνησιν.	20 καὶ	τὸ	ποτήριον	ὡσαύτως
memorial.	And	the	cup	similarly

μετὰ	τὸ	δειπνῆσαι,	λέγων·	τοῦτο	τὸ
after	the	to sup,	saying :	This	-

ποτήριον	ἡ	καινὴ	διαθήκη	ἐν	τῷ	αἵματί
cup [is]	the	new	covenant	in	the	blood

* Other ancient authorities read *never eat it again*
ᵗ Other ancient authorities add *which is given for you. Do this in remembrance of me.* ²⁰*And likewise the cup after supper, saying, "This cup which is poured out for you is the new covenant in my blood"*

* That is, with carpets, and the dining couches supplied with cushions.

behold the hand of him who betrays me is with me on the table. ²²For the Son of man goes as it has been determined; but woe to that man by whom he is betrayed!" ²³And they began to question one another, which of them it was that would do this.

24 A dispute also arose among them, which of them was to be regarded as the greatest. ²⁵And he said to them, "The kings of the Gentiles exercise lordship over them; and those in authority over them are called benefactors. ²⁶But not so with you; rather let the greatest among you become as the youngest, and the leader as one who serves. ²⁷For which is the greater, one who sits at table, or one who serves? Is it not the one who sits at table? But I am among you as one who serves.

28 "You are those who have continued with me in my trials; ²⁹as my Father appointed a kingdom for me, so do I appoint for you ³⁰that you may eat and drink at my table in my kingdom, and sit on thrones

μου, τὸ ὑπὲρ ὑμῶν ἐκχυννόμενον.] 21 πλὴν
of me,   -   for   you   being shed.   However

ἰδοὺ ἡ χεὶρ τοῦ παραδιδόντος με μετ'
behold[,] the hand of the [one] betraying   me   with

ἐμοῦ ἐπὶ τῆς τραπέζης. 22 ὅτι ὁ υἱὸς μὲν
me   on   the   table.   Because ³the ³Son ¹indeed

τοῦ ἀνθρώπου κατὰ τὸ ὡρισμένον
-   of man   according to the [thing]   having been
                                      determined

πορεύεται, πλὴν οὐαὶ τῷ ἀνθρώπῳ ἐκείνῳ
goes,   nevertheless woe   to the   man   to that

δι' οὗ παραδίδοται. 23 καὶ αὐτοὶ ἤρξαντο
through whom   he is betrayed.   And   they   began

συζητεῖν πρὸς ἑαυτοὺς τὸ τίς ἄρα εἴη
to debate   with   themselves   -   who   then it might be

ἐξ αὐτῶν ὁ τοῦτο μέλλων πράσσειν.
of   them the [one] ²this   ¹being about   ²to do.

24 Ἐγένετο δὲ καὶ φιλονεικία ἐν αὐτοῖς,
And there was   also   a rivalry   among   them,

τὸ τίς αὐτῶν δοκεῖ εἶναι μείζων. 25 ὁ δὲ
- who of them seems   to be   greater.   So he

εἶπεν αὐτοῖς· οἱ βασιλεῖς τῶν ἐθνῶν
said   to them :   The   kings   of the   nations

κυριεύουσιν αὐτῶν, καὶ οἱ ἐξουσιάζοντες
lord it over   them,   and the [ones] having authority over

αὐτῶν εὐεργέται καλοῦνται. 26 ὑμεῖς δὲ
them   benefactors   are called.   But ye

οὐχ οὕτως, ἀλλ' ὁ μείζων ἐν ὑμῖν
not   so,   but   the   greater   among   you

γινέσθω ὡς ὁ νεώτερος, καὶ ὁ ἡγούμενος
let him become as the   younger,   and the [one] governing

ὡς ὁ διακονῶν. 27 τίς γὰρ μείζων, ὁ
as the [one] serving.   For who [is] greater,   the

ἀνακείμενος ἢ ὁ διακονῶν; οὐχὶ ὁ
[one] reclining   or   the [one] serving?   not   the

ἀνακείμενος; ἐγὼ δὲ ἐν μέσῳ ὑμῶν εἰμι
[one] reclining?   But I   in [the] midst   of you   am

ὡς ὁ διακονῶν. 28 ὑμεῖς δέ ἐστε οἱ
as the [one] serving.   But ye   are the [ones]

διαμεμενηκότες μετ' ἐμοῦ ἐν τοῖς πειρα-
having remained throughout with   me   in the   tempta-

σμοῖς μου· 29 κἀγὼ διατίθεμαι ὑμῖν καθὼς
tions   of me;   and I   appoint   to you   as

διέθετό μοι ὁ πατήρ μου βασιλείαν,
appointed   to me   the   Father   of me   a kingdom,

30 ἵνα ἔσθητε καὶ πίνητε ἐπὶ τῆς -ραπέζης
that ye may eat and   drink   at   the   table

μου ἐν τῇ βασιλείᾳ μου, καὶ καθήσεσθε
of me in   the   kingdom   of me,   and   ye will sit

judging the twelve tribes of Israel. 31 "Simon, Simon, behold, Satan demanded to have you,ᵘ that he might sift youᵘ like wheat, ³²but I have prayed for you that your faith may not fail; and when you have turned again, strengthen your brethren." ³³And he said to him, "Lord, I am ready to go with you to prison and to death." ³⁴He said, "I tell you, Peter, the cock will not crow this day, until you three times deny that you know me."

35 And he said to them, "When I sent you out with no purse or bag or sandals, did you lack anything?" They said, "Nothing." ³⁶He said to them, "But now, let him who has a purse take it, and likewise a bag. And let him who has no sword sell his mantle and buy one. ³⁷For I tell you that this scripture must be fulfilled in me, 'And he was reckoned with transgressors'; for what is written about me has its fulfilment." ³⁸And they said, "Look, Lord, here are two swords." And he said to them, "It is enough."

39 And he came out, and went, as was his

ᵘ The Greek word for *you* here is plural; in verse 32 it is singular

ἐπὶ θρόνων τὰς δώδεκα φυλὰς κρίνοντες
on thrones ²the ²twelve ⁴tribes ¹judging
τοῦ Ἰσραήλ. 31 Σίμων Σίμων, ἰδοὺ ὁ
- of Israel. Simon[,] Simon, behold[,] -
σατανᾶς ἐξητήσατο ὑμᾶς τοῦ σινιάσαι ὡς
Satan begged earnestly for you - to siftᵈ as
τὸν σῖτον· 32 ἐγὼ δὲ ἐδεήθην περὶ σοῦ
the wheat; but I requested concerning thee
ἵνα μὴ ἐκλίπῃ ἡ πίστις σου· καὶ σύ
that might not fail the faith of thee; and thou
ποτε ἐπιστρέψας στήρισον τοὺς ἀδελφούς
when having turned support the brothers
σου. 33 ὁ δὲ εἶπεν αὐτῷ· κύριε, μετὰ
of thee. And he said to him : Lord, with
σοῦ ἕτοιμός εἰμι καὶ εἰς φυλακὴν καὶ εἰς
thee prepared I am both to prison and to
θάνατον πορεύεσθαι. 34 ὁ δὲ εἶπεν· λέγω
death to go. But he said : I tell
σοι, Πέτρε, οὐ φωνήσει σήμερον ἀλέκτωρ
thee, Peter, will not sound to-day a cock
ἕως τρίς με ἀπαρνήσῃ μὴ εἰδέναι. 35 Καὶ
until thrice me thou wilt deny not to know. And
εἶπεν αὐτοῖς· ὅτε ἀπέστειλα ὑμᾶς ἄτερ
he said to them : When I sent you without
βαλλαντίου καὶ πήρας καὶ ὑποδημάτων, μή
a purse and a wallet and sandals, not
τινος ὑστερήσατε; οἱ δὲ εἶπαν· οὐθενός.
of anything were ye short? And they said : Of nothing.
36 εἶπεν δὲ αὐτοῖς· ἀλλὰ νῦν ὁ ἔχων
And he said to them : But now the[one] having
βαλλάντιον ἀράτω, ὁμοίως καὶ πήραν, καὶ
a purse let him take [it], likewise also a wallet, and
ὁ μὴ ἔχων πωλησάτω τὸ ἱμάτιον αὐτοῦ
the[one] not having let him sell the garment of him
καὶ ἀγορασάτω μάχαιραν. 37 λέγω γὰρ
and let him buy a sword. For I tell
ὑμῖν ὅτι τοῦτο τὸ γεγραμμένον δεῖ
you that this - having been written it behoves
τελεσθῆναι ἐν ἐμοί, τό· καὶ μετὰ ἀνόμων
to be finished in me, - And with lawless men
ἐλογίσθη· καὶ γὰρ τὸ περὶ ἐμοῦ τέλος
he was reckoned; for indeed the thing concerning me an end
ἔχει. 38 οἱ δὲ εἶπαν· κύριε, ἰδοὺ μάχαιραι
has. And they said : Lord, behold[,] swords
ὧδε δύο. ὁ δὲ εἶπεν αὐτοῖς· ἱκανόν ἐστιν.
here two. And he said to them : Enough it is.
39 Καὶ ἐξελθὼν ἐπορεύθη κατὰ τὸ ἔθος
And going forth he went according to the(his) habit

custom, to the Mount of Olives; and the disciples followed him. ⁴⁰And when he came to the place he said to them, "Pray that you may not enter into temptation." ⁴¹And he withdrew from them about a stone's throw, and knelt down and prayed, ⁴²"Father, if thou art willing, remove this cup from me; nevertheless not my will, but thine, be done." ⁴³And there appeared to him an angel from heaven, strengthening him. ⁴⁴And being in an agony he prayed more earnestly; and his sweat became like great drops of blood falling down upon the ground.ᵛ ⁴⁵And when he rose from prayer, he came to the disciples and found them sleeping for sorrow, ⁴⁶and he said to them, "Why do you sleep? Rise and pray that you may not enter into temptation."

47 While he was still speaking, there came a crowd, and the man called Judas, one of the twelve, was leading them. He drew near to Jesus to kiss him; ⁴⁸but Jesus said to him, "Judas, would you betray the Son of man with a kiss?" ⁴⁹And when those who

ᵛ Other ancient authorities omit verses 43 and 44

εἰς τὸ ὄρος τῶν ἐλαιῶν· ἠκολούθησαν δὲ
to   the mountain of the   olives;   and ⁴followed

αὐτῷ καὶ οἱ μαθηταί. 40 γενόμενος δὲ
⁵him   ³also ¹the ²disciples.   And coming

ἐπὶ τοῦ τόπου εἶπεν αὐτοῖς· προσεύχεσθε
upon the   place   he said   to them :   Pray ye

μὴ εἰσελθεῖν εἰς πειρασμόν. 41 καὶ αὐτὸς
not to enter   into   temptation.   And   he

ἀπεσπάσθη ἀπ' αὐτῶν ὡσεὶ λίθου βολήν,
was withdrawn from   them   about of a stone   a throw,

καὶ θεὶς τὰ γόνατα προσηύχετο 42 λέγων·
and placing the   knees   he prayed   saying :

πάτερ, εἰ βούλει παρένεγκε τοῦτο τὸ
Father,   if   thou wilt   take away   this   –

ποτήριον ἀπ' ἐμοῦ· πλὴν μὴ τὸ θέλημά
cup   from   me;   nevertheless not the   will

μου ἀλλὰ τὸ σὸν γινέσθω. 43 [ὤφθη δὲ
of me   but   –   thine   let be.   And appeared

αὐτῷ ἄγγελος ἀπ' οὐρανοῦ ἐνισχύων αὐτόν.
to him   an angel   from   heaven   strengthening   him.

44 καὶ γενόμενος ἐν ἀγωνίᾳ ἐκτενέστερον
And   becoming   in   an agony   more earnestly

προσηύχετο· καὶ ἐγένετο ὁ ἱδρὼς αὐτοῦ
he prayed;   and   became   the   sweat   of him

ὡσεὶ θρόμβοι αἵματος καταβαίνοντες ἐπὶ
as   drops   of blood   falling down   onto

τὴν γῆν.] 45 καὶ ἀναστὰς ἀπὸ τῆς
the   earth.   And   rising up   from   the

προσευχῆς, ἐλθὼν πρὸς τοὺς μαθητὰς
prayer,   coming   to   the   disciples

εὗρεν κοιμωμένους αὐτοὺς ἀπὸ τῆς λύπης,
he found ²sleeping   ¹them   from   the   grief,

46 καὶ εἶπεν αὐτοῖς· τί καθεύδετε;
and   said   to them :   Why   sleep ye?

ἀναστάντες προσεύχεσθε, ἵνα μὴ εἰσέλθητε
rising up   pray ye,   lest   ye enter

εἰς πειρασμόν. 47 Ἔτι αὐτοῦ λαλοῦντος
into   temptation.   Yet   him   speakingᵃ
     =While he was yet speaking

ἰδοὺ ὄχλος, καὶ ὁ λεγόμενος Ἰούδας εἷς
behold[,] a crowd, and the [one] being named Judas   one

τῶν δώδεκα προήρχετο αὐτούς, καὶ ἤγγισεν
of the   twelve   came before   them,   and drew near

τῷ Ἰησοῦ φιλῆσαι αὐτόν. 48 Ἰησοῦς δὲ
–   to Jesus   to kiss   him.   But Jesus

εἶπεν αὐτῷ· Ἰούδα, φιλήματι τὸν υἱὸν
said   to him :   Judas,   with a kiss   the   Son

τοῦ ἀνθρώπου παραδίδως; 49 ἰδόντες δὲ
–   of man   betrayest thou?   And ⁴seeing

were about him saw what would follow, they said, "Lord, shall we strike with the sword?" [50]And one of them struck the slave of the high priest and cut off his right ear. [51]But Jesus said, "No more of this!" And he touched his ear and healed him. [52]Then Jesus said to the chief priests and captains of the temple and elders, who had come out against him, "Have you come out as against a robber, with swords and clubs? [53]When I was with you day after day in the temple, you did not lay hands on me. But this is your hour, and the power of darkness."

[54] Then they seized him and led him away, bringing him into the high priest's house. Peter followed at a distance; [55]and when they had kindled a fire in the middle of the courtyard and sat down together, Peter sat among them. [56]Then a maid, seeing him as he sat in the light and gazing at him, said, "This man also was with him." [57]But he denied it, saying, "Woman, I do not know

---

οἱ   περὶ αὐτὸν   τὸ   ἐσόμενον εἶπαν· κύριε,
[1]the [ones] [2]round [3]him   the thing   going to be   said :   Lord,

εἰ   πατάξομεν   ἐν   μαχαίρῃ;   50 καὶ ἐπάταξεν·
if   we shall strike   with   a sword?   And   [4]struck

εἷς   τις   ἐξ   αὐτῶν   τοῦ   ἀρχιερέως   τὸν
[1]a certain one [2]of [3]them [7]of the [8]high priest [5]the

δοῦλον   καὶ   ἀφεῖλεν   τὸ   οὖς   αὐτοῦ   τὸ
[6]slave   and   cut off   [1]the   [2]ear   [4]of him   –

δεξιόν.   51 ἀποκριθεὶς   δὲ   ὁ   Ἰησοῦς   εἶπεν·
[3]right.   And answering   –   Jesus   said :

ἐᾶτε   ἕως   τούτου·   καὶ   ἁψάμενος   τοῦ
Permit ye   until   this;   and   touching   the

ὠτίου   ἰάσατο   αὐτόν.   52 Εἶπεν   δὲ   Ἰησοῦς
ear   he cured   him.   And said   Jesus

πρὸς   τοὺς   παραγενομένους   ἐπ᾿   αὐτὸν
to   [1]the   [9]coming   [10]upon   [11]him

ἀρχιερεῖς   καὶ   στρατηγοὺς   τοῦ   ἱεροῦ   καὶ
[2]chief priests [3]and [4]captains [5]of the [6]temple [7]and

πρεσβυτέρους·   ὡς   ἐπὶ   λῃστὴν   ἐξήλθατε
[8]elders :   As   against   a robber   came ye out

μετὰ   μαχαιρῶν   καὶ   ξύλων;   53 καθ᾿ ἡμέραν
with   swords   and   clubs?   daily

ὄντος   μου   μεθ᾿   ὑμῶν   ἐν   τῷ   ἱερῷ   οὐκ
being me[a]   with   you   in   the   temple   not
=while I was

ἐξετείνατε   τὰς   χεῖρας   ἐπ᾿   ἐμέ·   ἀλλ᾿ αὕτη
ye stretched out the(your) hands   against me;   but   this

ἐστὶν   ὑμῶν   ἡ   ὥρα   καὶ   ἡ   ἐξουσία   τοῦ
is   of you   the   hour   and   the   authority   of the

σκότους.
darkness.

54 Συλλαβόντες   δὲ   αὐτὸν   ἤγαγον   καὶ
   And having arrested   him   they led   and

εἰσήγαγον   εἰς   τὴν   οἰκίαν   τοῦ   ἀρχιερέως·
brought in   into   the   house   of the   high priest;

ὁ   δὲ   Πέτρος   ἠκολούθει   μακρόθεν.   55 περι-
–   and   Peter   followed   afar off.   light-

αψάντων   δὲ   πῦρ   ἐν   μέσῳ   τῆς   αὐλῆς   καὶ
ing   And a fire   in [the] centre   of the   court   and
=when they had lit a fire . . . and had sat down together

συγκαθισάντων   ἐκάθητο   ὁ   Πέτρος   μέσος
sitting down together[a]   sat   –   Peter   among

αὐτῶν.   56 ἰδοῦσα   δὲ   αὐτὸν   παιδίσκη   τις
them.   And [2]seeing   [3]him [1]a certain maidservant

καθήμενον   πρὸς   τὸ   φῶς   καὶ   ἀτενίσασα
sitting   near   the   light   and   gazing at

αὐτῷ   εἶπεν·   καὶ   οὗτος   σὺν   αὐτῷ   ἦν.   57 ὁ
him   said :   And this man   with   him   was.   he

δὲ   ἠρνήσατο   λέγων·   οὐκ   οἶδα   αὐτόν,
But   denied   saying :   I know not   him,

him." ⁵⁸And a little later some one else saw him and said, "You also are one of them." But Peter said, "Man, I am not." ⁵⁹And after an interval of about an hour still another insisted, saying, "Certainly this man alsc was with him; for he is a Galilean." ⁶⁰But Peter said, "Man, I do not know what you are saying." And immediately, while he was still speaking, the cock crowed. ⁶¹And the Lord turned and looked at Peter. And Peter remembered the word of the Lord, how he had said to him, "Before the cock crows today, you will deny me three times." ⁶²And he went out and wept bitterly.

63 Now the men who were holding Jesus mocked him and beat him; ⁶⁴they also blindfolded him and asked him, "Prophesy! Who is it that struck you?" ⁶⁵And they spoke many other words against him, reviling him.

66 When day came, the assembly of the elders of the people gathered together, both chief priests and scribes; and they led him away to their council, and they said, ⁶⁷"If you are the Christ,

γύναι. 58 καὶ μετὰ βραχὺ ἕτερος ἰδὼν
woman. And after a short while another seeing

αὐτὸν ἔφη· καὶ σὺ ἐξ αὐτῶν εἶ. ὁ
him said: And thou of them art. -

δὲ Πέτρος ἔφη· ἄνθρωπε, οὐκ εἰμί.
But Peter said: Man, I am not.

59 καὶ διαστάσης ὡσεὶ ὥρας μιᾶς ἄλλος
And intervening about hour one[a] [b]other man
=when about an hour had intervened

τις διϊσχυρίζετο λέγων· ἐπ᾽ ἀληθείας καὶ
[1]a cer- emphatically saying: Of a truth also
tain asserted

οὗτος μετ᾽ αὐτοῦ ἦν, καὶ γὰρ Γαλιλαῖός
this man with him was, for indeed a Galilæan

ἐστιν. 60 εἶπεν δὲ ὁ Πέτρος· ἄνθρωπε,
he is. But said - Peter: Man,

οὐκ οἶδα ὃ λέγεις. καὶ παραχρῆμα ἔτι
I know not what thou sayest. And at once yet

λαλοῦντος αὐτοῦ ἐφώνησεν ἀλέκτωρ. 61 καὶ
speaking him[a] sounded a cock. And
=while he was yet speaking

στραφεὶς ὁ κύριος ἐνέβλεψεν τῷ Πέτρῳ,
turning the Lord looked at - Peter,

καὶ ὑπεμνήσθη ὁ Πέτρος τοῦ λόγου τοῦ
and remembered - Peter the word of the

κυρίου, ὡς εἶπεν αὐτῷ ὅτι πρὶν ἀλέκτορα
Lord, as he told him that before a cock

φωνῆσαι σήμερον ἀπαρνήσῃ με τρίς. 62 καὶ
to sound[b] to-day thou wilt deny me thrice. And

ἐξελθὼν ἔξω ἔκλαυσεν πικρῶς. 63 Καὶ οἱ
going out outside he wept bitterly. And the

ἄνδρες οἱ συνέχοντες αὐτὸν ἐνέπαιζον αὐτῷ
men - having in charge him* mocked him

δέροντες, 64 καὶ περικαλύψαντες αὐτὸν
beating, and covering over him

ἐπηρώτων λέγοντες· προφήτευσον, τίς ἐστιν
questioned saying: Prophesy, who is

ὁ παίσας σε; 65 καὶ ἕτερα πολλὰ
the [one] playing thee? And other things many

βλασφημοῦντες ἔλεγον εἰς αὐτόν.
blaspheming they said against him.

66 Καὶ ὡς ἐγένετο ἡμέρα, συνήχθη τὸ
And when came day, was assembled the

πρεσβυτέριον τοῦ λαοῦ, ἀρχιερεῖς τε καὶ
body of elders of the people, both chief priests and

γραμματεῖς, καὶ ἀπήγαγον αὐτὸν εἰς τὸ
scribes, and led away him to the

συνέδριον αὐτῶν· 67 λέγοντες· εἰ σὺ εἶ ὁ
council of them, saying: If thou art the

* That is, Jesus (as some texts have it).

tell us." But he said to them, "If I tell you, you will not believe; [68] and if I ask you, you will not answer. [69] But from now on the Son of man shall be seated at the right hand of the power of God." [70] And they all said, "Are you the Son of God, then?" And he said to them, "You say that I am." [71] And they said, "What further testimony do we need? We have heard it ourselves from his own lips."

χριστός, εἰπὸν ἡμῖν. εἶπεν δὲ αὐτοῖς·
Christ, tell us. And he said to them:

ἐὰν ὑμῖν εἴπω, οὐ μὴ πιστεύσητε· **68** ἐὰν
If you I tell, by no means will ye believe; ²if

δὲ ἐρωτήσω, οὐ μὴ ἀποκριθῆτε. **69** ἀπὸ
¹and I question, by no means will ye answer. ¹from

τοῦ νῦν δὲ ἔσται ὁ υἱὸς τοῦ ἀνθρώπου
- ²now ¹But ⁷will be ⁴the ⁵Son - ⁶of man

καθήμενος ἐκ δεξιῶν τῆς δυνάμεως τοῦ
⁸sitting at [the] right of the power -

θεοῦ. **70** εἶπαν δὲ πάντες· σὺ οὖν εἶ ὁ
of God. And they said all : Thou therefore art the

υἱὸς τοῦ θεοῦ; ὁ δὲ πρὸς αὐτοὺς ἔφη·
Son - of God? And he to them said :

ὑμεῖς λέγετε ὅτι ἐγώ εἰμι. **71** οἱ δὲ
Ye say that I am. And they

εἶπαν· τί ἔτι ἔχομεν μαρτυρίας χρείαν;
said : Why yet have we of witness need ?

αὐτοὶ γὰρ ἠκούσαμεν ἀπὸ τοῦ στόματος
for [our]selves we heard from the mouth

αὐτοῦ.
of him.

CHAPTER 23

THEN the whole company of them arose, and brought him before Pilate. ²And they began to accuse him, saying, "We found this man perverting our nation, and forbidding us to give tribute to Caesar, and saying that he himself is Christ a king." ³And Pilate asked him, "Are you the King of the Jews?" And he answered him, "You have said so." ⁴And Pilate said to the chief priests and the multitudes. "I find no crime in this man."

23 Καὶ ἀναστὰν ἅπαν τὸ πλῆθος αὐτῶν
And rising up all the multitude of them

ἤγαγον αὐτὸν ἐπὶ τὸν Πιλᾶτον. **2** ἤρξαντο
led him before - Pilate. they began

δὲ κατηγορεῖν αὐτοῦ λέγοντες· τοῦτον
And to accuse him saying : This man

εὕραμεν διαστρέφοντα τὸ ἔθνος ἡμῶν καὶ
we found perverting the nation of us and

κωλύοντα φόρους Καίσαρι διδόναι, καὶ
forbidding tribute to Caesar to give, and

λέγοντα ἑαυτὸν χριστὸν βασιλέα εἶναι.
saying himself Christ a king to be.

3 ὁ δὲ Πιλᾶτος ἠρώτησεν αὐτὸν λέγων·
- And Pilate questioned him saying :

σὺ εἶ ὁ βασιλεὺς τῶν Ἰουδαίων; ὁ δὲ
Thou art the king of the Jews? And he

ἀποκριθεὶς αὐτῷ ἔφη· σὺ λέγεις. **4** ὁ δὲ
answering him said : Thou sayest. - And

Πιλᾶτος εἶπεν πρὸς τοὺς ἀρχιερεῖς καὶ
Pilate said to the chief priests and

τοὺς ὄχλους· οὐδὲν εὑρίσκω αἴτιον ἐν
the crowds : ²No ¹I find ²crime in

⁵But they were urgent, saying, "He stirs up the people, teaching throughout all Judea, from Galilee even to this place."

6 When Pilate heard this, he asked whether the man was a Galilean. ⁷And when he learned that he belonged to Herod's jurisdiction, he sent him over to Herod, who was himself in Jerusalem at that time. ⁸When Herod saw Jesus, he was very glad, for he had long desired to see him, because he had heard about him, and he was hoping to see some sign done by him. ⁹So he questioned him at some length; but he made no answer. ¹⁰The chief priests and the scribes stood by, vehemently accusing him. ¹¹And Herod with his soldiers treated him with contempt and mocked him; then, arraying him in gorgeous apparel, he sent him back to Pilate. ¹²And Herod and Pilate became friends with each other that very day, for before this they had been at enmity with each other.

13 Pilate then called

τῷ ἀνθρώπῳ τούτῳ.
 -    man   this.

5 οἱ δὲ ἐπίσχυον λέγοντες
But they   insisted   saying[,]

ὅτι ἀνασείει τὸν λαόν, διδάσκων καθ'
 - He excites   the   people,   teaching throughout

ὅλης τῆς Ἰουδαίας, καὶ ἀρξάμενος ἀπὸ
all   -   Judæa,   even   beginning   from

τῆς Γαλιλαίας ἕως ὧδε. 6 Πιλᾶτος δὲ
 -   Galilee   to   here.   And Pilate

ἀκούσας ἐπηρώτησεν εἰ ὁ ἄνθρωπος
hearing   questioned   if   the   man

Γαλιλαῖός ἐστιν, 7 καὶ ἐπιγνοὺς ὅτι ἐκ
a Galilæan   is(was),   and   perceiving   that   of

τῆς ἐξουσίας Ἡρῴδου ἐστίν, ἀνέπεμψεν
the   authority   of Herod   he is(was),   he sent up

αὐτὸν πρὸς Ἡρῴδην, ὄντα καὶ αὐτὸν ἐν
him   to   Herod,   being   also   him(he)   in

Ἱεροσολύμοις ἐν ταύταις ταῖς ἡμέραις.
Jerusalem   in   these   -   days.

8 ὁ δὲ Ἡρῴδης ἰδὼν τὸν Ἰησοῦν ἐχάρη
 - And   Herod   seeing -   Jesus   rejoiced

λίαν· ἦν γὰρ ἐξ ἱκανῶν χρόνων θέλων
greatly;   for he was   of   a long   times   wishing

ἰδεῖν αὐτὸν διὰ τὸ ἀκούειν περὶ αὐτοῦ,
to see   him   because of the   to hearᵇ   about   him,
              =because he had heard

καὶ ἤλπιζέν τι σημεῖον ἰδεῖν ὑπ' αὐτοῦ
and   he hoped some   sign   to see   by   him

γινόμενον. 9 ἐπηρώτα δὲ αὐτὸν ἐν λόγοις
brought about.   And he questioned   him   in   words

ἱκανοῖς· αὐτὸς δὲ οὐδὲν ἀπεκρίνατο αὐτῷ.
many;   but he   nothing   answered   him.

10 εἱστήκεισαν δὲ οἱ ἀρχιερεῖς καὶ οἱ
And stood   the   chief priests   and   the

γραμματεῖς εὐτόνως κατηγοροῦντες αὐτοῦ.
scribes   vehemently   accusing   him.

11 ἐξουθενήσας δὲ αὐτὸν ὁ Ἡρῴδης σὺν
And despising   him -   Herod   with

τοῖς στρατεύμασιν αὐτοῦ καὶ ἐμπαίξας,
the   soldiery   of him   and   mocking,

περιβαλὼν ἐσθῆτα λαμπρὰν ἀνέπεμψεν αὐτὸν
throwing round clothing   splendid   sent back   him

τῷ Πιλάτῳ. 12 ἐγένοντο δὲ φίλοι ὅ τε
 - to Pilate.   And became   friends - both

Ἡρῴδης καὶ ὁ Πιλᾶτος ἐν αὐτῇ τῇ
Herod   and   the   Pilate   on ²same ¹the

ἡμέρᾳ μετ' ἀλλήλων· προϋπῆρχον γὰρ ἐν
day   with   each other;   for they were previously   in

ἔχθρᾳ ὄντες πρὸς αὐτούς. 13 Πιλᾶτος δὲ
enmity   being   with   themselves.   And Pilate

together the chief priests and the rulers and the people, ¹⁴and said to them, "You brought me this man as one who was perverting the people; and after examining him before you, behold, I did not find this man guilty of any of your charges against him; ¹⁵neither did Herod, for he sent him back to us. Behold, nothing deserving death has been done by him; ¹⁶I will therefore chastise him and release him."ʷ

18 But they all cried out together, "Away with this man, and release to us Barab'bas"—¹⁹a man who had been thrown into prison for an insurrection started in the city, and for murder. ²⁰Pilate addressed them once more, desiring to release Jesus; ²¹but they shouted out, "Crucify, crucify him!" ²²A third time he said to them, "Why, what evil has he done? I have found in him no crime deserving death; I will therefore chastise him and release him." ²³But they were urgent, demanding with loud cries that he should be crucified. And their

συγκαλεσάμενος τοὺς ἀρχιερεῖς καὶ τοὺς
calling together the chief priests and the
ἄρχοντας καὶ τὸν λαὸν 14 εἶπεν πρὸς
leaders and the people said to
αὐτούς· προσηνέγκατέ μοι τὸν ἄνθρωπον
them : Ye brought to me – man
τοῦτον ὡς ἀποστρέφοντα τὸν λαόν, καὶ
this as perverting the people, and
ἰδοὺ ἐγὼ ἐνώπιον ὑμῶν ἀνακρίνας οὐδὲν
behold I ²before ³you ¹examining ⁵nothing
εὗρον ἐν τῷ ἀνθρώπῳ τούτῳ αἴτιον ὧν
⁴found ⁷in – ⁹man ⁸this ⁶crime of the
[things]
which
κατηγορεῖτε κατ' αὐτοῦ. 15 ἀλλ' οὐδὲ
ye bring accusation against him. And neither
'Ηρῴδης· ἀνέπεμψεν γὰρ αὐτὸν πρὸς ἡμᾶς·
Herod; for he sent back him to us;
καὶ ἰδοὺ οὐδὲν ἄξιον θανάτου ἐστὶν
and behold nothing worthy of death is
πεπραγμένον αὐτῷ· 16 παιδεύσας οὖν αὐτὸν
having been done by him; chastising therefore him
ἀπολύσω.‡ 18 ἀνέκραγον δὲ παμπληθεὶ
I will release. But they shouted with the whole
multitude
λέγοντες· αἶρε τοῦτον, ἀπόλυσον δὲ ἡμῖν
saying : Take this man, and release to us
τὸν Βαραββᾶν· 19 ὅστις ἦν διὰ στάσιν
– Barabbas; who was because ²insurrec-
of tion
τινὰ γενομένην ἐν τῇ πόλει καὶ φύνον
¹some happening in the city and murder
βληθεὶς ἐν τῇ φυλακῇ. 20 πάλιν δὲ
thrown in the prison. But again
ὁ Πιλᾶτος προσεφώνησεν αὐτοῖς, θέλων
– Pilate called to them, wishing
ἀπολῦσαι τὸν Ἰησοῦν. 21 οἱ δὲ ἐπεφώνουν
to release – Jesus. But they shouted
λέγοντες· σταύρου σταύρου αὐτόν. 22 ὁ δὲ
saying : Crucify[,] crucify thou him. But he
τρίτον εἶπεν πρὸς αὐτούς· τί γὰρ κακὸν
a third time said to them : But what evil
ἐποίησεν οὗτος; οὐδὲν αἴτιον θανάτου
did this man? nothing cause of death
εὗρον ἐν αὐτῷ· παιδεύσας οὖν αὐτὸν
I found in him; chastising therefore o him
ἀπολύσω. 23 οἱ δὲ ἐπέκειντο φωναῖς
I will release. But they insisted voices
μεγάλαις αἰτούμενοι αὐτὸν σταυρωθῆναι,
with great asking him to be crucified,

ʷ Here, or after verse 19, other ancient authorities add verse 17, *Now he was obliged to release one man to them at the festival*

‡ Ver. 17 omitted by Nestle; *cf.* RSV footnote.

voices prevailed. ²⁴So Pilate gave sentence that their demand should be granted. ²⁵He released the man who had been thrown into prison for insurrection and murder, whom they asked for; but Jesus he delivered up to their will.

26 And as they led him away, they seized one Simon of Cyre'ne, who was coming in from the country, and laid on him the cross, to carry it behind Jesus. ²⁷And there followed him a great multitude of the people, and of women who bewailed and lamented him. ²⁸But Jesus turning to them said, "Daughters of Jerusalem, do not weep for me, but weep for yourselves and for your children. ²⁹For behold, the days are coming when they will say, 'Blessed are the barren, and the wombs that never bore, and the breasts that never gave suck!' ³⁰Then they will begin to say to the mountains, 'Fall on us'; and to the hills, 'Cover us.' ³¹For if they do this when the wood is green, what will happen when it is dry?" 32 Two others also,

καὶ κατίσχυον αἱ φωναὶ αὐτῶν. 24 καὶ
and prevailed the voices of them. And

Πιλᾶτος ἐπέκρινεν γενέσθαι τὸ αἴτημα
Pilate decided to be [carried out] the request

αὐτῶν· 25 ἀπέλυσεν δὲ τὸν διὰ στάσιν
of them; and he released the [one] because of insurrection

καὶ φόνον βεβλημένον εἰς φυλακήν, ὃν
and murder having been thrown into prison, whom

ᾐτοῦντο, τὸν δὲ Ἰησοῦν παρέδωκεν τῷ
they asked, – but Jesus he delivered to the

θελήματι αὐτῶν.
will of them.

26 Καὶ ὡς ἀπήγαγον αὐτόν, ἐπιλαβόμενοι
And as they led away him, seizing

Σίμωνά τινα Κυρηναῖον ἐρχόμενον ἀπ᾽
Simon a certain Cyrenian coming from

ἀγροῦ ἐπέθηκαν αὐτῷ τὸν σταυρὸν φέρειν
[the] country they placed on him the cross to carry

ὄπισθεν τοῦ Ἰησοῦ. 27 Ἠκολούθει δὲ
behind – Jesus. And followed

αὐτῷ πολὺ πλῆθος τοῦ λαοῦ καὶ γυναικῶν
him a much multitude of the people and of women

αἳ ἐκόπτοντο καὶ ἐθρήνουν αὐτόν. 28 στρα-
who mourned and lamented him. turn

φεὶς δὲ πρὸς αὐτὰς Ἰησοῦς εἶπεν·
ing And to them Jesus said :

θυγατέρες Ἰερουσαλήμ, μὴ κλαίετε ἐπ᾽
Daughters of Jerusalem, do not weep over

ἐμέ· πλὴν ἐφ᾽ ἑαυτὰς κλαίετε καὶ ἐπὶ
me; but over yourselves weep and over

τὰ τέκνα ὑμῶν, 29 ὅτι ἰδοὺ ἔρχονται
the children of you, because behold come

ἡμέραι ἐν αἷς ἐροῦσιν· μακάριαι αἱ
days in which they will say : Blessed the

στεῖραι, καὶ αἱ κοιλίαι αἱ οὐκ ἐγέννησαν,
barren, and the wombs which bare not,

καὶ μαστοὶ οἳ οὐκ ἔθρεψαν. 30 τότε
and breasts which gave not suck. Then

ἄρξονται λέγειν τοῖς ὄρεσιν· πέσατε ἐφ᾽
they will begin to say to the mountains : Fall on

ἡμᾶς, καὶ τοῖς βουνοῖς· καλύψατε ἡμᾶς·
us, and to the hills : Cover us;

31 ὅτι εἰ ἐν ὑγρῷ ξύλῳ ταῦτα ποιοῦσιν,
because if in ²full of sap ¹a tree these things they do,

ἐν τῷ ξηρῷ τί γένηται; 32 Ἤγοντο δὲ
in the dry what may happen? And were led

who were criminals, were led away to be put to death with him. ³³And when they came to the place which is called The Skull, there they crucified him, and the criminals, one on the right and one on the left. ³⁴And Jesus said, "Father, forgive them; for they know not what they do."ˣ And they cast lots to divide his garments. ³⁵And the people stood by, watching; but the rulers scoffed at him, saying, "He saved others; let him save himself, if he is the Christ of God, his Chosen One!" ³⁶The soldiers also mocked him, coming up and offering him vinegar, ³⁷and saying, "If you are the King of the Jews, save yourself!" ³⁸There was also an inscription over him,ʸ "This is the King of the Jews."

39 One of the criminals who were hanged railed at him, saying, "Are you not the Christ? Save yourself and us!" ⁴⁰But the other rebuked him, saying, "Do you not fear God, since you are under the same sentence of condemnation?

ˣ Other ancient authorities omit the sentence *And Jesus . . . what they do*
ʸ Other ancient authorities add *in letters of Greek and Latin and Hebrew*

καὶ ἕτεροι κακοῦργοι δύο σὺν αὐτῷ
also others* criminals two with him
ἀναιρεθῆναι. 33 Καὶ ὅτε ἦλθον ἐπὶ τὸν
to be killed. And when they came upon the
τόπον τὸν καλούμενον Κρανίον, ἐκεῖ ἐσταύ-
place - being called Skull, there they
ρωσαν αὐτὸν καὶ τοὺς κακούργους, ὃν μὲν
crucified him and the criminals, one†
ἐκ δεξιῶν ὃν δὲ ἐξ ἀριστερῶν. 34 [ὁ δὲ
on [the] right and one† on [the] left. - And
Ἰησοῦς ἔλεγεν· πάτερ, ἄφες αὐτοῖς· οὐ
Jesus said : Father, forgive them; ²not
γὰρ οἴδασιν τί ποιοῦσιν.] διαμεριζόμενοι
¹for ²they know what they are doing.] dividing
δὲ τὰ ἱμάτια αὐτοῦ ἔβαλον κλήρους.
And the garments of him they cast lots.
35 καὶ εἱστήκει ὁ λαὸς θεωρῶν. ἐξεμυκ-
And stood the people beholding. scoff-
τήριζον δὲ καὶ οἱ ἄρχοντες λέγοντες·
ed And also the rulers saying :
ἄλλους ἔσωσεν, σωσάτω ἑαυτόν, εἰ οὗτός
Others he saved, let him save himself, if this man
ἐστιν ὁ χριστὸς τοῦ θεοῦ ὁ ἐκλεκτός.
is the Christ - of God the chosen [one].
36 ἐνέπαιξαν δὲ αὐτῷ καὶ οἱ στρατιῶται
And mocked him also the soldiers
προσερχόμενοι, ὄξος προσφέροντες αὐτῷ
approaching, vinegar offering to him
37 καὶ λέγοντες· εἰ σὺ εἶ ὁ βασιλεὺς
and saying : If thou art the king
τῶν Ἰουδαίων, σῶσον σεαυτόν. 38 ἦν δὲ
of the Jews, save thyself. And there was
καὶ ἐπιγραφὴ ἐπ' αὐτῷ· Ο ΒΑΣΙΛΕΥΣ
also a superscription over him : THE KING
ΤΩΝ ΙΟΥΔΑΙΩΝ ΟΥΤΟΣ. 39 Εἷς δὲ
OF THE JEWS THIS. And one
τῶν κρεμασθέντων κακούργων ἐβλασφήμει
of the hanged criminals blasphemed
αὐτόν· οὐχὶ σὺ εἶ ὁ χριστός; σῶσον
him : Not thou art the Christ? save
σεαυτὸν καὶ ἡμᾶς 40 ἀποκριθεὶς δὲ ὁ
thyself and us. But answering the
ἕτερος ἐπιτιμῶν αὐτῷ ἔφη· οὐδὲ φοβῇ σὺ
other rebuking him said : Not fearest thou
τὸν θεόν, ὅτι ἐν τῷ αὐτῷ κρίματι εἶ;
- God, because in the same judgment thou art?

* Luke uses ἕτεροι here with strict accuracy = "different." Jesus was not himself a criminal. Note punctuation of A.V. *Cf.* Acts 28. 1.

⁴¹And we indeed justly; for we are receiving the due reward of our deeds; but this man has done nothing wrong." ⁴²And he said, "Jesus, remember me when you come in your kingly power." ⁴³And he said to him, "Truly, I say to you, today you will be with me in Paradise."

44 It was now about the sixth hour, and there was darkness over the whole land[z] until the ninth hour, ⁴⁵while the sun's light failed;[a] and the curtain of the temple was torn in two. ⁴⁶Then Jesus, crying with a loud voice, said, "Father, into thy hands I commit my spirit!" And having said this he breathed his last. ⁴⁷Now when the centurion saw what had taken place, he praised God, and said, "Certainly this man was innocent!" ⁴⁸And all the multitudes who assembled to see the sight, when they saw what had taken place, returned home beating their breasts. ⁴⁹And all his acquaintances and the women who had followed him from Galilee stood at a distance and saw these things.

50 Now there was a man named Joseph from

[z] Or earth
[a] Or the sun was eclipsed. Other ancient authorities read the sun was darkened

---

41 καὶ ἡμεῖς μὲν δικαίως, ἄξια γὰρ ὧν
And we indeed justly, for things worthy of what

ἐπράξαμεν ἀπολαμβάνομεν· οὗτος δὲ οὐδὲν
we did we receive back; but this man nothing

ἄτοπον ἔπραξεν. 42 καὶ ἔλεγεν Ἰησοῦ,
amiss did. And he said : Jesus,

μνήσθητί μου ὅταν ἔλθῃς εἰς τὴν βασιλείαν
remember me when thou comest into the kingdom

σου. 43 καὶ εἶπεν αὐτῷ· ἀμήν σοι λέγω,
of thee. And he said to him. Truly thee I tell,

σήμερον μετ' ἐμοῦ ἔσῃ ἐν τῷ παραδείσῳ.
to-day with me thou wilt be in the paradise.

44 Καὶ ἦν ἤδη ὡσεὶ ὥρα ἕκτη καὶ
And it was now about hour sixth and

σκότος ἐγένετο ἐφ᾽ ὅλην τὴν γῆν ἕως
darkness came over all the land until

ὥρας ἐνάτης 45 τοῦ ἡλίου ἐκλιπόντος·
hour ninth the sun =as the sun failed; failing;[a]

ἐσχίσθη δὲ τὸ καταπέτασμα τοῦ ναοῦ
and was torn the veil of the shrine

μέσον. 46 καὶ φωνήσας φωνῇ μεγάλῃ ὁ
in the middle. And crying voice with a great –

Ἰησοῦς εἶπεν· πάτερ, εἰς χεῖράς σου
Jesus said : Father, into hands of thee

παρατίθεμαι τὸ πνεῦμά μου. τοῦτο δὲ
I commit the spirit of me. And this

εἰπὼν ἐξέπνευσεν. 47 ἰδὼν δὲ ὁ ἑκατον-
saying he expired. And [2]seeing [1]the [2]cen-

τάρχης τὸ γενόμενον ἐδόξαζεν τὸν θεὸν
turion the thing happening glorified – God

λέγων· ὄντως ὁ ἄνθρωπος οὗτος δίκαιος
saying : Really – man this righteous

ἦν. 48 καὶ πάντες οἱ συμπαραγενόμενοι
was. And all [1]the [2]arriving together

ὄχλοι ἐπὶ τὴν θεωρίαν ταύτην, θεωρήσαντες τὰ
[2]crowds at – sight this, beholding the things

γενόμενα, τύπτοντες τὰ στήθη ὑπέστρεφον.
happening, smiting the(ir) breasts returned.

49 εἱστήκεισαν δὲ πάντες οἱ γνωστοὶ αὐτῷ
And [6]stood [1]all [2]the [ones] [3]known [4]to him

ἀπὸ μακρόθεν, καὶ γυναῖκες αἱ συνακο-
[6]afar off, and women the [ones] accom-

λουθοῦσαι αὐτῷ ἀπὸ τῆς Γαλιλαίας, ὁρῶσαι
panying him from – Galilee, seeing

ταῦτα.
these things.

50 Καὶ ἰδοὺ ἀνὴρ ὀνόματι Ἰωσὴφ
And behold[,] a man by name Joseph

the Jewish town of
Arimathe'a. He was a
member of the council, a
good and righteous man,
[51] who had not con-
sented to their purpose
and deed, and he was
looking for the kingdom
of God. [52] This man went
to Pilate and asked for
the body of Jesus. [53] Then
he took it down and
wrapped it in a linen
shroud, and laid him in
a rock-hewn tomb, where
no one had ever yet been
laid. [54] It was the day of
Preparation, and the
sabbath was beginning.
[55] The women who had
come with him from
Galilee followed, and
saw the tomb, and how
his body was laid; [56] then
they returned, and pre-
pared spices and
ointments.
On the sabbath they
rested according to the
commandment.

CHAPTER 24

BUT on the first day
of the week, at early
dawn, they went to the
tomb, taking the spices
which they had prepared.
[2] And they found the
stone rolled away from
the tomb, [3] but when they
went in they did not find
the body.[b] [4] While they
were perplexed about
this, behold, two men

[b] Other ancient authorities add
of the Lord Jesus

βουλευτὴς   ὑπάρχων,   ἀνὴρ   ἀγαθὸς   καὶ
a councillor   being,   a man   good   and

δίκαιος, —   51 οὗτος οὐκ ἦν συγκατατεθειμένος
righteous, —   this man was not   agreeing with

τῇ   βουλῇ   καὶ   τῇ   πράξει   αὐτῶν, — ἀπὸ
the   counsel   and   the   action   of them, — from

Ἀριμαθαίας   πόλεως   τῶν   Ἰουδαίων,   ὃς
Arimathæa   a city   of the   Jews,   who

προσεδέχετο   τὴν   βασιλείαν   τοῦ   θεοῦ,
was awaiting   the   kingdom   -   of God,

52 οὗτος   προσελθὼν   τῷ   Πιλάτῳ   ᾐτήσατο
this man   approaching   -   to Pilate   asked

τὸ   σῶμα   τοῦ   Ἰησοῦ,   53 καὶ   καθελὼν
the   body   -   of Jesus,   and   taking down

ἐνετύλιξεν   αὐτὸ   σινδόνι,   καὶ   ἔθηκεν   αὐτὸν
wrapped   it   in linen,   and   placed   him

ἐν   μνήματι   λαξευτῷ,   οὗ   οὐκ   ἦν   οὐδεὶς
in   tomb   a hewn,   where   was not   no(any)one

οὔπω   κείμενος.   54 καὶ   ἡμέρα   ἦν   παρασκευῆς,
not yet   laid.   And   day   it was   of preparation,

καὶ   σάββατον   ἐπέφωσκεν.   55 Κατακολουθήσασαι
and   a sabbath   was coming on.   [4] following after

δὲ   αἱ   γυναῖκες,   αἵτινες   ἦσαν   συνεληλυθυῖαι
[1] And [2] the   [3] women,   who   were   [1] having come with

ἐκ   τῆς   Γαλιλαίας   αὐτῷ,   ἐθεάσαντο   τὸ
[2] out of -   [4] Galilee   [3] with him,   beheld   the

μνημεῖον   καὶ   ὡς   ἐτέθη   τὸ   σῶμα   αὐτοῦ,
tomb   and   how   was placed the   body   of him,

56 ὑποστρέψασαι   δὲ   ἡτοίμασαν   ἀρώματα   καὶ
and returning   prepared   spices   and

μύρα.
ointment.

Καὶ   τὸ   μὲν   σάββατον   ἡσύχασαν   κατὰ
And [on] the   [2] indeed   [1] sabbath   they rested according to

τὴν   ἐντολήν.   24 τῇ   δὲ   μιᾷ   τῶν   σαββάτων
the commandment.   But on the   one   of the   week

ὄρθρου   βαθέως   ἐπὶ   τὸ   μνῆμα   ἦλθον   φέρουσαι
while still   very early†   upon the   tomb   they came   carrying

ἃ   ἡτοίμασαν   ἀρώματα.   2 εὗρον   δὲ   τὸν
[2] which [3] they prepared   [1] spices.   And they found   the

λίθον   ἀποκεκυλισμένον   ἀπὸ   τοῦ   μνημείου,
stone   having been rolled away   from   the   tomb,

3 εἰσελθοῦσαι   δὲ   οὐχ   εὗρον   τὸ   σῶμα
and entering   they found not   the   body

τοῦ   κυρίου   Ἰησοῦ.   4 καὶ   ἐγένετο   ἐν   τῷ
of the   Lord   Jesus.   And   it was   in   the
= as they were perplexed

ἀπορεῖσθαι   αὐτὰς   περὶ   τούτου   καὶ   ἰδοὺ
to be perplexed   them[be]   about   this   and behold[,]

stood by them in dazzling apparel; ⁵and as they were frightened and bowed their faces to the ground, the men said to them, "Why do you seek the living among the dead?ᶜ ⁶Remember how he told you, while he was still in Galilee, ⁷that the Son of man must be delivered into the hands of sinful men, and be crucified, and on the third day rise." ⁸And they remembered his words, ⁹and returning from the tomb they told all this to the eleven and to all the rest. ¹⁰Now it was Mary Mag'dalene and Jo-an'na and Mary the mother of James and the other women with them who told this to the apostles; ¹¹but these words seemed to them an idle tale, and they did not believe them.ᵈ

13 That very day two of them were going to a village named Emma'us, about seven milesᵈᵈ from Jerusalem, ¹⁴and talking

ἄνδρες δύο ἐπέστησαν αὐταῖς ἐν ἐσθῆτι
men   two stood by   them   in clothing

ἀστραπτούσῃ· 5 ἐμφόβων   δὲ   γενομένων
shining;   and terrified   becoming
            =as they became terrified and bent their faces

αὐτῶν καὶ κλινουσῶν τὰ πρόσωπα εἰς τὴν
them   and bending the(ir) facesᵃ to the

γῆν, εἶπαν πρὸς αὐτάς· τί ζητεῖτε τὸν
earth, they said to   them : Why seek ye the

ζῶντα μετὰ τῶν νεκρῶν; 6 [οὐκ ἔστιν
living [one] with the dead [ones]?   He is not

ὧδε, ἀλλὰ ἠγέρθη.] μνήσθητε ὡς ἐλάλησεν
here, but was raised. Remember how he spoke

ὑμῖν ἔτι ὢν ἐν τῇ Γαλιλαίᾳ, 7 λέγων
to you yet being in -   Galilee,   saying[,]

τὸν υἱὸν τοῦ ἀνθρώπου ὅτι δεῖ παραδο-
The Son   -   of man   - it behoves to be de-

θῆναι εἰς χεῖρας ἀνθρώπων ἁμαρτωλῶν καὶ
livered into hands   men   of sinful   and

σταυρωθῆναι καὶ τῇ τρίτῃ ἡμέρᾳ ἀναστῆναι.
to be crucified and on the third day   to rise again.

8 καὶ ἐμνήσθησαν   τῶν   ῥημάτων αὐτοῦ,
And   they remembered the   words   of him,

9 καὶ ὑποστρέψασαι ἀπὸ τοῦ μνημείου
and   returning   from the   tomb

ἀπήγγειλαν ταῦτα πάντα τοῖς ἕνδεκα καὶ
reported these things all to the eleven and

πᾶσιν τοῖς λοιποῖς. 10 ἦσαν δὲ ἡ
to all the   rest.   Now they were the

Μαγδαληνὴ Μαρία καὶ Ἰωάννα καὶ Μαρία
Magdalene   Mary and Joanna and Mary

ἡ Ἰακώβου· καὶ αἱ λοιπαί* σὺν αὐταῖς*
the [mother] of James; and the rest   with   them

ἔλεγον πρὸς τοὺς ἀποστόλους ταῦτα. 11 καὶ
told   to   the   apostles   these things. And

ἐφάνησαν ἐνώπιον αὐτῶν ὡσεὶ λῆρος
seemed   before   them   as   folly

τὰ ῥήματα ταῦτα, καὶ ἠπίστουν αὐταῖς.* ‡
- words   these, and they disbelieved them.

13 Καὶ ἰδοὺ δύο ἐξ αὐτῶν ἐν αὐτῇ τῇ
And behold[,] two of them on same the

ἡμέρᾳ ἦσαν πορευόμενοι εἰς κώμην ἀπέχουσαν
day   were journeying   to a village being distant

σταδίους ἑξήκοντα ἀπὸ Ἰερουσαλήμ, ᾗ
furlongs sixty   from Jerusalem, to which

ὄνομα Ἐμμαοῦς, 14 καὶ αὐτοὶ ὡμίλουν
name Emmaus,   and they   talked
                * Note the feminines.
        ‡ Verse 12 omitted by Nestle; cf. RSV footnote.

ᶜ Other ancient authorities add
He is not here, but has risen

ᵈ Other ancient authorities add verse 12, *But Peter rose and ran to the tomb; stooping and looking in, he saw the linen cloths by themselves; and he went home wondering at what had happened*

ᵈᵈ *Sixty stadia*; some ancient authorities read *a hundred and sixty stadia*

with each other about all these things that had happened. [15]While they were talking and discussing together, Jesus himself drew near and went with them. [16]But their eyes were kept from recognizing him. [17]And he said to them, "What is this conversation which you are holding with each other as you walk?" And they stood still, looking sad. [18]Then one of them, named Cle'opas, answered him, "Are you the only visitor to Jerusalem who does not know the things that have happened there in these days?" [19]And he said to them, "What things?" And they said to him, "Concerning Jesus of Nazareth, who was a prophet mighty in deed and word before God and all the people, [20]and how our chief priests and rulers delivered him up to be condemned to death, and crucified him. [21]But we had hoped that he was the one to redeem Israel. Yes, and besides all this, it is now the third day since this happened. [22]Moreover, some women of our company

πρὸς ἀλλήλους περὶ πάντων τῶν συμβεβηκότων
to   each other about   all   -   [2]having occurred

τούτων. 15 καὶ ἐγένετο ἐν τῷ ὁμιλεῖν
[1]these things.   And it came to pass in the to talk

αὐτοὺς καὶ συζητεῖν, καὶ αὐτὸς Ἰησοῦς
them   and to discuss[be], and [him]self Jesus
= as they talked and discussed,

ἐγγίσας συνεπορεύετο αὐτοῖς· 16 οἱ δὲ
drawing near journeyed with   them;   but the[1]

ὀφθαλμοὶ αὐτῶν ἐκρατοῦντο τοῦ μὴ
eyes   of them   were held   -   not

ἐπιγνῶναι αὐτόν. 17 εἶπεν δὲ πρὸς αὐτούς·
to recognize[d] him.   And he said to   them :

τίνες οἱ λόγοι οὗτοι οὓς ἀντιβάλλετε
What   -   words these which ye exchange

πρὸς ἀλλήλους περιπατοῦντες; καὶ ἐστάθησαν
with   each other   walking?   And   they stood

σκυθρωποί. 18 ἀποκριθεὶς δὲ εἷς ὀνόματι
sad-faced.   And answering   one by name

Κλεοπᾶς εἶπεν πρὸς αὐτόν· σὺ μόνος
Cleopas   said   to   him :   Thou   only

παροικεῖς Ἰερουσαλὴμ καὶ οὐκ ἔγνως τὰ
a stranger   in Jerusalem   and knewest not the things

γενόμενα ἐν αὐτῇ ἐν ταῖς ἡμέραις ταύταις;
happening in it   in -   days   these ?

19 καὶ εἶπεν αὐτοῖς· ποῖα; οἱ δὲ εἶπαν
  And he said to them : What things? And they said

αὐτῷ· τὰ περὶ Ἰησοῦ τοῦ Ναζαρηνοῦ, ὃς
to him : The things about Jesus   the   Nazarene,   who

ἐγένετο ἀνὴρ προφήτης δυνατὸς ἐν ἔργῳ
was   a man   prophet   powerful in work

καὶ λόγῳ ἐναντίον τοῦ θεοῦ καὶ παντὸς
and word   before   -   God   and   all

τοῦ λαοῦ, 20 ὅπως τε παρέδωκαν αὐτὸν οἱ
the people,   how both [7]delivered   [8]him [1]the

ἀρχιερεῖς καὶ οἱ ἄρχοντες ἡμῶν εἰς
[2]chief priests [3]and [4]the [5]rulers   [6]of us   to

κρίμα θανάτου καὶ ἐσταύρωσαν αὐτόν.
[the] judgment of death and   crucified   him.

21 ἡμεῖς δὲ ἠλπίζομεν ὅτι αὐτός ἐστιν
   But we   were hoping   that   he   it is(was)

ὁ μέλλων λυτροῦσθαι τὸν Ἰσραήλ· ἀλλά
the [one] being about to redeem   -   Israel;   but

γε καὶ σὺν πᾶσιν τούτοις τρίτην ταύτην
- also with   all   these things third   this
                                    = this is the third day

ἡμέραν ἄγει ἀφ' οὗ ταῦτα ἐγένετο.
day   it leads since these things happened.

22 ἀλλὰ καὶ γυναῖκές τινες ἐξ ἡμῶν
   But   also [2]women   [1]some of   us

amazed us. They were at the tomb early in the morning ²³and did not find his body; and they came back saying that they had even seen a vision of angels, who said that he was alive. ²⁴Some of those who were with us went to the tomb, and found it just as the women had said; but him they did not see." ²⁵And he said to them, "O foolish men, and slow of heart to believe all that the prophets have spoken! ²⁶Was it not necessary that the Christ should suffer these things and enter into his glory?" ²⁷And beginning with Moses and all the prophets, he interpreted to them in all the scriptures the things concerning himself.

28 So they drew near to the village to which they were going. He appeared to be going further, ²⁹but they constrained him, saying, "Stay with us, for it is toward evening and the day is now far spent." So he went in to stay with them. ³⁰When he was at table with them, he took the bread and blessed, and broke it, and gave

ἐξέστησαν ἡμᾶς, γενόμεναι ὀρθριναὶ ἐπὶ τὸ
astonished us, being early at the
μνημεῖον, 23 καὶ μὴ εὑροῦσαι τὸ σῶμα
tomb, and not finding the body
αὐτοῦ ἦλθον λέγουσαι καὶ ὀπτασίαν ἀγγέλων
of him came saying also a vision of angels
ἑωρακέναι, οἳ λέγουσιν αὐτὸν ζῆν. 24 καὶ
to have seen, who say him to live. And
=that he lives.
ἀπῆλθόν τινες τῶν σὺν ἡμῖν ἐπὶ τὸ
⁵went ¹some ²of the [ones] ³with ⁴us to the
μνημεῖον, καὶ εὗρον οὕτως καθὼς καὶ αἱ
tomb, and found so as indeed the
γυναῖκες εἶπον, αὐτὸν δὲ οὐκ εἶδον.
women said, but him they saw not.
25 καὶ αὐτὸς εἶπεν πρὸς αὐτούς· ὦ
And he said to them : O
ἀνόητοι καὶ βραδεῖς τῇ καρδίᾳ τοῦ πιστεύειν
foolish [ones] and slow - in heart - to believeᵈ
ἐπὶ πᾶσιν οἷς ἐλάλησαν οἱ προφῆται·
on(in) all things which spoke the prophets :
26 οὐχὶ ταῦτα ἔδει παθεῖν τὸν χριστὸν καὶ
²not ⁶these things ¹behoved it ⁵to suffer ³the ⁴Christ and
εἰσελθεῖν εἰς τὴν δόξαν αὐτοῦ; 27 καὶ
to enter into the glory of him? And
ἀρξάμενος ἀπὸ Μωϋσέως καὶ ἀπὸ πάντων
beginning from Moses and from all
τῶν προφητῶν διηρμήνευσεν αὐτοῖς ἐν
the prophets he explained to them in
πάσαις ταῖς γραφαῖς τὰ περὶ ἑαυτοῦ.
all the scriptures the things concerning himself.
28 Καὶ ἤγγισαν εἰς τὴν κώμην οὗ
And they drew near to the village whither
ἐπορεύοντο, καὶ αὐτὸς προσεποιήσατο
they were journeying, and he pretended
πορρώτερον πορεύεσθαι. 29 καὶ παρε-
farther to journey. And they
βιάσαντο αὐτὸν λέγοντες· μεῖνον μεθ᾽
urged him saying : Remain with
ἡμῶν, ὅτι πρὸς ἑσπέραν ἐστὶν καὶ κέκλικεν
us, because toward evening it is and has declined
ἤδη ἡ ἡμέρα. καὶ εἰσῆλθεν τοῦ μεῖναι
now the day. And he went in - to remainᵈ
σὺν αὐτοῖς. 30 καὶ ἐγένετο ἐν τῷ
with them. And it came to pass in the
=as he reclined
κατακλιθῆναι αὐτὸν μετ᾽ αὐτῶν λαβὼν τὸν
to recline himᵇᵉ with them taking the
ἄρτον εὐλόγησεν καὶ κλάσας ἐπεδίδου
loaf he blessed and having broken he handed

it to them. ³¹And their eyes were opened and they recognized him; and he vanished out of their sight. ³²They said to each other, "Did not our hearts burn within us while he talked to us on the road, while he opened to us the scriptures?" ³³And they rose that same hour and returned to Jerusalem; and they found the eleven gathered together and those who were with them, ³⁴who said, "The Lord has risen indeed, and has appeared to Simon!" ³⁵Then they told what had happened on the road, and how he was known to them in the breaking of the bread.

36 As they were saying this, Jesus himself stood among them.ᵉ ³⁷But they were startled and frightened, and supposed that they saw a spirit. ³⁸And he said to them, "Why are you troubled, and why do questionings arise in your hearts? ³⁹See my hands and my feet, that it is I myself; handle me, and see; for a spirit has not flesh and bones as you see that I have."ᶠ ⁴¹And while they still disbelieved for joy, and wondered, he said to

ᵉ Other ancient authorities add *and said to them, "Peace to you!"*
ᶠ Other ancient authorities add verse 40, *And when he had said this, he showed them his hands and his feet*

αὐτοῖς· 31 αὐτῶν δὲ διηνοίχθησαν οἱ
to them;   and of them   were opened up   the

ὀφθαλμοί, καὶ ἐπέγνωσαν αὐτόν· καὶ αὐτὸς
eyes,   and they recognized him;   and   he

ἄφαντος ἐγένετο ἀπ' αὐτῶν. 32 καὶ
invisible became from them.   And

εἶπαν πρὸς ἀλλήλους· οὐχὶ ἡ καρδία
they said to   each other :   Not   the heart

ἡμῶν καιομένη ἦν ἐν ἡμῖν, ὡς ἐλάλει
of us burning was in us,   as he spoke

ἡμῖν ἐν τῇ ὁδῷ, ὡς διήνοιγεν ἡμῖν τὰς
to us in the way,   as he opened up to us the

γραφάς; 33 Καὶ ἀναστάντες αὐτῇ τῇ ὥρᾳ
scriptures? And rising up   ᶻsame ¹in the hour

ὑπέστρεψαν εἰς Ἰερουσαλήμ, καὶ εὗρον
they returned to   Jerusalem,   and found

ἠθροισμένους τοὺς ἕνδεκα καὶ τοὺς σὺν
having been collected the   eleven and the [ones] with

αὐτοῖς, 34 λέγοντας ὅτι ὄντως ἠγέρθη ὁ
them,   saying[,]   —   Really was raised the

κύριος καὶ ὤφθη Σίμωνι. 35 καὶ αὐτοὶ ἐξηγοῦντο
Lord and appeared to Simon.   And they   related

τὰ ἐν τῇ ὁδῷ καὶ ὡς ἐγνώσθη
the things in the way and how he was known

αὐτοῖς ἐν τῇ κλάσει τοῦ ἄρτου. 36 Ταῦτα
by them in the breaking of the loaf.   these things

δὲ αὐτῶν λαλούντων αὐτὸς ἔστη ἐν
And them   sayingᵃ   he   stood in
    =as they said these things

μέσῳ αὐτῶν. 37 πτοηθέντες δὲ καὶ
[the] midst of them.   But scared   and

ἔμφοβοι γενόμενοι ἐδόκουν πνεῦμα θεωρεῖν.
terrified becoming they thought a spirit to behold.

38 καὶ εἶπεν αὐτοῖς· τί τεταραγμένοι ἐστέ,
And he said to them : Why having been troubled are ye,

καὶ διὰ τί διαλογισμοὶ ἀναβαίνουσιν ἐν
and why   thoughts   come up   in

τῇ καρδίᾳ ὑμῶν; 39 ἴδετε τὰς χεῖράς
the heart   of you?   See   the   hands

μου καὶ τοὺς πόδας μου, ὅτι ἐγώ εἰμι
of me and the   feet of me, that I   am

αὐτός· ψηλαφήσατέ με καὶ ἴδετε, ὅτι
[my]self; feel   me and   see, because

πνεῦμα σάρκα καὶ ὀστέα οὐκ ἔχει καθὼς
a spirit flesh and bones has not   as

ἐμὲ θεωρεῖτε ἔχοντα. ‡ 41 ἔτι δὲ ἀπιστούντων
me ye behold having.   And yet   disbelieving
                              =while they yet disbelieved

αὐτῶν ἀπὸ τῆς χαρᾶς καὶ θαυμαζόντων,
themᵃ from the   joy   and   marvellingᵃ,

‡ Verse 40 omitted by Nestle; *cf.* RSV footnote.

them, "Have you anything here to eat?" [42]They gave him a piece of broiled fish, [43]and he took it and ate before them.

44 Then he said to them, "These are my words which I spoke to you, while I was still with you, that everything written about me in the law of Moses and the prophets and the psalms must be fulfilled." [45]Then he opened their minds to understand the scriptures, [46]and said to them, "Thus it is written, that the Christ should suffer and on the third day rise from the dead, [47]and that repentance and forgiveness of sins should be preached in his name to all nations,[g] beginning from Jerusalem. [48]You are witnesses of these things. [49]And behold, I send the promise of my Father upon you; but stay in the city, until you are clothed with power from on high."

50 Then he led them out as far as Bethany, and lifting up his hands he blessed them. [51]While he blessed them, he parted from them.[h] [52]And

[g] Or nations. Beginning from Jerusalem you are witnesses

[h] Other ancient authorities add and was carried up into heaven

εἶπεν αὐτοῖς· ἔχετέ τι βρώσιμον ἐνθάδε;
he said to them : Have ye any food here?

42 οἱ δὲ ἐπέδωκαν αὐτῷ ἰχθύος ὀπτοῦ
And they handed to him [3]fish [2]of a broiled

μέρος· 43 καὶ λαβὼν ἐνώπιον αὐτῶν ἔφαγεν.
[1]part; and taking before them he ate.

44 Εἶπεν δὲ πρὸς αὐτούς· οὗτοι οἱ λόγοι
And he said to them : These - words

μου οὓς ἐλάλησα πρὸς ὑμᾶς ἔτι ὢν σὺν
of me which I spoke to you yet being with

ὑμῖν, ὅτι δεῖ πληρωθῆναι πάντα τὰ
you, that it behoves to be fulfilled all the things

γεγραμμένα ἐν τῷ νόμῳ Μωϋσέως καὶ
having been written in the law of Moses and

τοῖς προφήταις καὶ ψαλμοῖς περὶ ἐμοῦ.
the prophets and psalms concerning me.

45 τότε διήνοιξεν αὐτῶν τὸν νοῦν τοῦ
Then he opened up of them the mind -

συνιέναι τὰς γραφάς· 46 καὶ εἶπεν αὐτοῖς
to understand[d] the scriptures; and said to them[,]

ὅτι οὕτως γέγραπται παθεῖν τὸν χριστὸν
- Thus it has been written [2]to suffer [1]the [3]Christ

καὶ ἀναστῆναι ἐκ νεκρῶν τῇ τρίτῃ ἡμέρᾳ,
and to rise again out of [the] dead on the third day,

47 καὶ κηρυχθῆναι ἐπὶ τῷ ὀνόματι αὐτοῦ
and to be proclaimed on(in) the name of him

μετάνοιαν εἰς ἄφεσιν ἁμαρτιῶν εἰς πάντα
repentance unto forgiveness of sins to all

τὰ ἔθνη, – ἀρξάμενοι ἀπὸ Ἰερουσαλήμ.
the nations, — beginning from Jerusalem.

48 ὑμεῖς μάρτυρες τούτων. 49 καὶ ἰδοὺ
Ye [are] witnesses of these things. And behold

ἐγὼ ἐξαποστέλλω τὴν ἐπαγγελίαν τοῦ
I send forth the promise of the

πατρός μου ἐφ᾽ ὑμᾶς· ὑμεῖς δὲ καθίσατε
Father of me on you; but ye sit

ἐν τῇ πόλει ἕως οὗ ἐνδύσησθε ἐξ ὕψους
in the city until [1]ye are clothed[with][2]out of [4]height

δύναμιν.
[3]power.

50 Ἐξήγαγεν δὲ αὐτοὺς ἕως πρὸς
And he led out them until toward

Βηθανίαν, καὶ ἐπάρας τὰς χεῖρας αὐτοῦ
Bethany, and lifting up the hands of him

εὐλόγησεν αὐτούς. 51 καὶ ἐγένετο ἐν τῷ
he blessed them. And it came to pass in the

εὐλογεῖν αὐτὸν αὐτοὺς διέστη ἀπ᾽ αὐτῶν.
to bless him[be] them he withdrew from them.
=while he blessed

they⁴ returned to Jerusalem with great joy, ⁵³ and were continually in the temple blessing God.

52 καὶ αὐτοὶ ὑπέστρεψαν εἰς Ἰερουσαλὴμ
And they returned to Jerusalem

μετὰ χαρᾶς μεγάλης, **53** καὶ ἦσαν διὰ παντὸς
with joy great, and were continually

ἐν τῷ ἱερῷ εὐλογοῦντες τὸν θεόν.
in the temple blessing – God.

---

⁴ Other ancient authorities add
worshipped him, and

CHAPTER 1

IN the beginning was the Word, and the Word was with God, and the Word was God. ²He was in the beginning with God; ³all things were made through him, and without him was not anything made that was made. ⁴In him was life,ᵃ and the life was the light of men. ⁵The light shines in the darkness, and the darkness has not overcome it.

6 There was a man sent from God, whose name was John. ⁷He came for testimony, to bear witness to the light, that all might believe through him. ⁸He was not the light, but came to bear witness to the light.

9 The true light that enlightens every man was coming into the world. ¹⁰He was in the world, and the world was made through him, yet the world knew him not. ¹¹He came to his own home, and his own people received him not. ¹²But to all who received him, who believed in his name, he gave power to become children of God; ¹³who

1 Ἐν ἀρχῇ ἦν ὁ λόγος, καὶ ὁ λόγος
In [the] beginning was the Word, and the Word

ἦν πρὸς τὸν θεόν, καὶ θεὸς ἦν ὁ λόγος.*
was with – God, and God was the Word.*

2 οὗτος ἦν ἐν ἀρχῇ πρὸς τὸν θεόν.
This one was in [the] beginning with – God.

3 πάντα δι᾽ αὐτοῦ ἐγένετο, καὶ χωρὶς
All things through him became, and without

αὐτοῦ ἐγένετο οὐδὲ ἕν ὃ γέγονεν. 4 ἐν
him became not one thing which has become. In

αὐτῷ ζωὴ ἦν, καὶ ἡ ζωὴ ἦν τὸ φῶς
him life was, and the life was the light

τῶν ἀνθρώπων· 5 καὶ τὸ φῶς ἐν τῇ
– of men; and the light in the

σκοτίᾳ φαίνει, καὶ ἡ σκοτία αὐτὸ οὐ
darkness shines, and the darkness it not

κατέλαβεν. 6 Ἐγένετο ἄνθρωπος, ἀπεσταλμένος
overtook. There was a man, *having been* sent

παρὰ θεοῦ, ὄνομα αὐτῷ Ἰωάννης· 7 οὗτος
from God, name to himᶜ John; this man

ἦλθεν εἰς μαρτυρίαν, ἵνα μαρτυρήσῃ περὶ
came for witness, that he might witness concerning

τοῦ φωτός, ἵνα πάντες πιστεύσωσιν δι᾽
the light, that all men might believe through

αὐτοῦ. 8 οὐκ ἦν ἐκεῖνος τὸ φῶς, ἀλλ᾽ ἵνα
him. He was not that – light, but that

μαρτυρήσῃ περὶ τοῦ φωτός. 9 Ἦν τὸ φῶς
he might witness concerning the light. It was the light

τὸ ἀληθινόν, ὃ φωτίζει πάντα ἄνθρωπον,
– true, which enlightens every man,

ἐρχόμενον εἰς τὸν κόσμον. 10 ἐν τῷ
coming into the world. In the

κόσμῳ ἦν, καὶ ὁ κόσμος δι᾽ αὐτοῦ
world he was, and the world through him

ἐγένετο, καὶ ὁ κόσμος αὐτὸν οὐκ ἔγνω.
became, and the world him knew not.

11 εἰς τὰ ἴδια ἦλθεν, καὶ οἱ ἴδιοι αὐτὸν
To his own things he came, and his own people him

οὐ παρέλαβον. 12 ὅσοι δὲ ἔλαβον αὐτόν,
received not. But as many as received him,

ἔδωκεν αὐτοῖς ἐξουσίαν τέκνα θεοῦ γεν-
he gave to them right children of God to be-

ᵃ Or *was not anything made. That which has been made was life in him*

* But note that the subject has the article and the predicate has it not; hence translate—" the Word was God ."

were born, not of blood nor of the will of the flesh nor of the will of man, but of God.

14 And the Word became flesh and dwelt among us, full of grace and truth; we have beheld his glory, glory as of the only Son from the Father. ¹⁵(John bore witness to him, and cried, "This was he of whom I said, 'He who comes after me ranks before me, for he was before me.' ") ¹⁶And from his fulness have we all received, grace upon grace. ¹⁷For the law was given through Moses; grace and truth came through Jesus Christ. ¹⁸No one has ever seen God; the only Son,ᵇ who is in the bosom of the Father, he has made him known.

19 And this is the testimony of John, when the Jews sent priests and Levites from Jerusalem to ask him, "Who are you?" ²⁰He confessed, he did not deny, but confessed, "I am not the Christ." ²¹And they

ᵇ Other ancient authorities read God

I.G.E.—13

ἔσθαι,   τοῖς πιστεύουσιν εἰς τὸ ὄνομα αὐτοῦ,
come,   to the [ones] believing   in   the   name   of him,

13 οἳ   οὐκ ἐξ   αἱμάτων   οὐδὲ ἐκ   θελήματος
who   not of   bloods   nor   of   [the] will

σαρκὸς   οὐδὲ ἐκ   θελήματος   ἀνδρὸς   ἀλλ'
of [the] flesh   nor   of   [the] will   of a man   but

ἐκ   θεοῦ   ἐγεννήθησαν.   14 Καὶ   ὁ   λόγος
of   God   were born.   And   the   Word

σὰρξ   ἐγένετο   καὶ   ἐσκήνωσεν   ἐν   ἡμῖν,
flesh   became   and   tabernacled   among   us,

καὶ   ἐθεασάμεθα   τὴν   δόξαν   αὐτοῦ,   δόξαν
and   we beheld   the   glory   of him,   glory

ὡς   μονογενοῦς   παρὰ   πατρός,   πλήρης   χάριτος
as   of an only begotten   from   a father,   full   of grace

καὶ   ἀληθείας.   15 Ἰωάννης   μαρτυρεῖ   περὶ
and   of truth.   John   witnesses   concerning

αὐτοῦ   καὶ   κέκραγεν   λέγων·   οὗτος   ἦν   ὃν
him   and   has cried out   saying :   This man   was he   whom

εἶπον·   ὁ   ὀπίσω   μου   ἐρχόμενος   ἔμπροσθέν
I said :   The [one]   after   me   coming   before

μου   γέγονεν,   ὅτι   πρῶτός   μου   ἦν.   16 ὅτι
me   has become,   because   first   of me   he was.   Because

ἐκ   τοῦ   πληρώματος   αὐτοῦ   ἡμεῖς   πάντες
of   the   fulness   of him   we   all

ἐλάβομεν,   καὶ   χάριν   ἀντὶ   χάριτος·   17 ὅτι
received,   and   grace   instead of   grace;   because

ὁ   νόμος   διὰ   Μωϋσέως   ἐδόθη,   ἡ   χάρις   καὶ
the   law   through   Moses   was given,   the   grace   and

ἡ   ἀλήθεια   διὰ   Ἰησοῦ   Χριστοῦ   ἐγένετο.
the   truth   through   Jesus   Christ   became.

18 Θεὸν   οὐδεὶς   ἑώρακεν   πώποτε·   μονογενὴς
God   no man   has seen   never;   [the] only begotten

θεὸς   ὁ   ὢν   εἰς   τὸν   κόλπον   τοῦ   πατρός,
God   the [one] being   in   the   bosom   of the   Father,

ἐκεῖνος   ἐξηγήσατο.
that one   declared [?him].

19 Καὶ   αὕτη   ἐστὶν   ἡ   μαρτυρία   τοῦ
And   this   is   the   witness   –

Ἰωάννου,   ὅτε   ἀπέστειλαν   πρὸς   αὐτὸν   οἱ
of John,   when   ³sent   ⁴to   ⁵him   ¹the

Ἰουδαῖοι   ἐξ   Ἱεροσολύμων   ἱερεῖς   καὶ   Λευίτας
²Jews   ⁹from   ¹⁰Jerusalem   ⁶priests   ⁷and   ⁸Levites

ἵνα   ἐρωτήσωσιν   αὐτόν·   σὺ   τίς   εἶ;   20 καὶ
that   they might ask   him :   Thou   who   art?   And

ὡμολόγησεν   καὶ   οὐκ   ἠρνήσατο,   καὶ
he confessed   and   denied not,   and

ὡμολόγησεν   ὅτι   ἐγὼ   οὐκ   εἰμὶ   ὁ   χριστός.
he confessed[,]   –   I   am not   the   Christ.

asked him, "What then? Are you Eli′jah?" He said, "I am not." "Are you the prophet?" And he answered "No." ²²They said to him then, "Who are you? Let us have an answer for those who sent us. What do you say about yourself?" ²³He said, "I am the voice of one crying in the wilderness, 'Make straight the way of the Lord,' as the prophet Isaiah said."

24 Now they had been sent from the Pharisees. ²⁵They asked him, "Then why are you baptizing, if you are neither the Christ, nor Eli′jah, nor the prophet?" ²⁶John answered them, "I baptize with water; but among you stands one whom you do not know, ²⁷even he who comes after me, the thong of whose sandal I am not worthy to untie." ²⁸This took place in Bethany beyond the Jordan, where John was baptizing.

29 The next day he saw Jesus coming toward him, and said, "Behold, the Lamb of God, who takes away the sin of the world! ³⁰This is he of whom I said, 'After me comes a man who ranks before

21 καὶ ἠρώτησαν αὐτόν· τί οὖν; Ἡλίας εἶ
And they asked him: What then? Elias art

σύ; καὶ λέγει· οὐκ εἰμί. ὁ προφήτης εἶ σύ;
thou? And he says : I am not. The prophet art thou?

καὶ ἀπεκρίθη· οὔ. 22 εἶπαν οὖν αὐτῷ·
And he answered : No. They said therefore to him :

τίς εἶ; ἵνα ἀπόκρισιν δῶμεν τοῖς
Who art thou? that an answer we may give to the [ones]

πέμψασιν ἡμᾶς· τί λέγεις περὶ σεαυτοῦ;
having sent us; What sayest thou concerning thyself?

23 ἔφη· ἐγὼ φωνὴ βοῶντος ἐν τῇ ἐρήμῳ·
He said : I [am] a voice of [one] crying in the desert :

εὐθύνατε τὴν ὁδὸν κυρίου, καθὼς εἶπεν
Make straight the way of [the] Lord, as said

Ἡσαΐας ὁ προφήτης. 24 Καὶ ἀπεσταλμένοι
Esaias the prophet. And [the ones] having been sent

ἦσαν ἐκ τῶν Φαρισαίων. 25 καὶ ἠρώτησαν
were of the Pharisees. And they asked

αὐτὸν καὶ εἶπαν αὐτῷ· τι οὖν βαπτίζεις
him and said to him: Why then baptizest thou

εἰ σὺ οὐκ εἶ ὁ χριστὸς οὐδὲ Ἡλίας
if thou art not the Christ nor Elias

οὐδὲ ὁ προφήτης; 26 ἀπεκρίθη αὐτοῖς ὁ
nor the prophet? Answered them –

Ἰωάννης λέγων· ἐγὼ βαπτίζω ἐν ὕδατι·
John saying : I baptize in water;

μέσος ὑμῶν στήκει ὃν ὑμεῖς οὐκ οἴδατε,
among you stands [one] whom ye know not,

27 ὁ ὀπίσω μου ἐρχόμενος, οὗ οὐκ εἰμὶ
the [one] after me coming, of whom am not

ἐγὼ ἄξιος ἵνα λύσω αὐτοῦ τὸν ἱμάντα
I worthy that I should loosen of him the thong

τοῦ ὑποδήματος. 28 Ταῦτα ἐν Βηθανίᾳ
of the sandal. These things in Bethany

ἐγένετο πέραν τοῦ Ἰορδάνου, ὅπου ἦν ὁ
happened beyond the Jordan, where was –

Ἰωάννης βαπτίζων. 29 Τῇ ἐπαύριον βλέπει
John baptizing. On the morrow he sees

τὸν Ἰησοῦν ἐρχόμενον πρὸς αὐτόν, καὶ
– Jesus coming toward him, and

λέγει· ἴδε ὁ ἀμνὸς τοῦ θεοῦ ὁ αἴρων
says : Behold[,] the Lamb – of God – taking

τὴν ἁμαρτίαν τοῦ κόσμου. 30 οὗτός ἐστιν
the sin of the world. This is he

ὑπὲρ οὗ ἐγὼ εἶπον· ὀπίσω μου ἔρχεται
as to whom I said : After me comes

ἀνὴρ ὃς ἔμπροσθέν μου γέγονεν, ὅτι
a man who before me has become, because

me, for he was before me.' ³¹I myself did not know him; but for this I came baptizing with water, that he might be revealed to Israel." ³²And John bore witness, "I saw the Spirit descend as a dove from heaven, and it remained on him. ³³I myself did not know him; but he who sent me to baptize with water said to me, 'He on whom you see the Spirit descend and remain, this is he who baptizes with the Holy Spirit.' ³⁴And I have seen and have borne witness that this is the Son of God."

35 The next day again John was standing with two of his disciples; ³⁶and he looked at Jesus as he walked, and said, "Behold, the Lamb of God!" ³⁷The two disciples heard him say this, and they followed Jesus. ³⁸Jesus turned, and saw them following, and said to them, "What do you seek?" And they said to him, "Rabbi (which means Teacher), where are you staying?" ³⁹He said to them, "Come and see." They came and saw where he

πρῶτός μου ἦν. 31 κἀγὼ οὐκ ᾔδειν
first of me he was. And I knew not

αὐτόν, ἀλλ' ἵνα φανερωθῇ τῷ 'Ισραήλ,
him, but that he might be manifested - to Israel,

διὰ τοῦτο ἦλθον ἐγὼ ἐν ὕδατι βαπτίζων.
therefore came I in water baptizing.

32 Καὶ ἐμαρτύρησεν 'Ιωάννης λέγων ὅτι
And witnessed John saying[,] -

τεθέαμαι τὸ πνεῦμα καταβαῖνον ὡς
I have beheld the Spirit coming down as

περιστερὰν ἐξ οὐρανοῦ, καὶ ἔμεινεν ἐπ'
a dove out of heaven, and he remained on

αὐτόν. 33 κἀγὼ οὐκ ᾔδειν αὐτόν, ἀλλ'
him. And I knew not him, but

ὁ πέμψας με βαπτίζειν ἐν ὕδατι, ἐκεῖνός
the [one] having sent me to baptize in water, that [one]

μοι εἶπεν· ἐφ' ὃν ἂν ἴδῃς τὸ πνεῦμα
to me said: On whomever thou seest the Spirit

καταβαῖνον καὶ μένον ἐπ' αὐτόν, οὗτός
coming down and remaining on him, this

ἐστιν ὁ βαπτίζων ἐν πνεύματι ἁγίῳ.
is the [one] baptizing in Spirit Holy.

34 κἀγὼ ἑώρακα, καὶ μεμαρτύρηκα ὅτι
And I have seen, and have witnessed that

οὗτός ἐστιν ὁ υἱὸς τοῦ θεοῦ.
this [one] is the Son - of God.

35 Τῇ ἐπαύριον πάλιν εἱστήκει ὁ 'Ιωάννης
On the morrow again stood - John

καὶ ἐκ τῶν μαθητῶν αὐτοῦ δύο, 36 καὶ
and of the disciples of him two, and

ἐμβλέψας τῷ 'Ιησοῦ περιπατοῦντι λέγει·
looking at - Jesus walking he says:

ἴδε ὁ ἀμνὸς τοῦ θεοῦ. 37 καὶ ἤκουσαν
Behold[,] the Lamb - of God. And ⁴heard

οἱ δύο μαθηταὶ αὐτοῦ λαλοῦντος καὶ
¹the ²two ³disciples ⁵him ⁶speaking and

ἠκολούθησαν τῷ 'Ιησοῦ. 38 στραφεὶς δὲ
they followed - Jesus. And ²turning

ὁ 'Ιησοῦς καὶ θεασάμενος αὐτοὺς ἀκολουθοῦντας
- ¹Jesus and beholding them following

λέγει αὐτοῖς· τί ζητεῖτε; οἱ δὲ εἶπαν
says to them : What seek ye? And they said

αὐτῷ· ῥαββί (ὃ λέγεται μεθερμηνευόμενον
to him : Rabbi (which is called being translated

διδάσκαλε), ποῦ μένεις; 39 λέγει αὐτοῖς·
Teacher), where remainest thou? He says to them :

ἔρχεσθε καὶ ὄψεσθε. ἦλθαν οὖν καὶ εἶδαν
Come and ye will see. They went therefore and saw

was staying; and they stayed with him that day, for it was about the tenth hour. ⁴⁰One of the two who heard John speak, and followed him, was Andrew, Simon Peter's brother. ⁴¹He first found his brother Simon, and said to him, "We have found the Messiah" (which means Christ). ⁴²He brought him to Jesus. Jesus looked at him, and said, "So you are Simon the son of John? You shall be called Cephas" (which means Peter^c).

43 The next day Jesus decided to go to Galilee. And he found Philip and said to him, "Follow me." ⁴⁴Now Philip was from Beth-sa′ida, the city of Andrew and Peter. ⁴⁵Philip found Nathan′-a-el, and said to him, "We have found him of whom Moses in the law and also the prophets wrote, Jesus of Nazareth, the son of Joseph." ⁴⁶Nathan′a-el said to him, "Can anything good come out of Nazareth?" Philip said to him, "Come and see." ⁴⁷Jesus saw Nathan′a-el

^c From the word for *rock* in Aramaic and Greek, respectively

ποῦ   μένει,   καὶ   παρ'   αὐτῷ   ἔμειναν   τὴν
where he remains(ed), and with   him   remained   –
ἡμέραν   ἐκείνην·   ὥρα   ἦν   ὡς   δεκάτη.
day   that;   hour   was   about   tenth.
40 ᾽Ην   ᾽Ανδρέας   ὁ   ἀδελφὸς   Σίμωνος   Πέτρου
It was   Andrew   the   brother   of Simon   Peter
εἷς   ἐκ   τῶν   δύο   τῶν   ἀκουσάντων   παρὰ
one   of   the   two   the   hearing   from
᾽Ιωάννου   καὶ   ἀκολουθησάντων   αὐτῷ·
John   and   following   him;
41 εὑρίσκει   οὗτος   πρῶτον   τὸν   ἀδελφὸν   τὸν
   ³finds   ¹this one ²first   ⁴the(his)   ⁵brother   –
ἴδιον   Σίμωνα   καὶ   λέγει   αὐτῷ·   εὑρήκαμεν
⁶own   Simon   and   tells   him :   We have found
τὸν   Μεσσίαν   (ὅ   ἐστιν   μεθερμηνευόμενον
the   Messiah   (which   is   being translated
χριστός).   42 ἤγαγεν   αὐτὸν   πρὸς   τὸν
Christ).   He led   him   to   –
᾽Ιησοῦν.   ἐμβλέψας   αὐτῷ   ὁ   ᾽Ιησοῦς   εἶπεν·
Jesus.   Looking at   him   –   Jesus   said :
σὺ   εἶ   Σίμων   ὁ   υἱὸς   ᾽Ιωάννου,   σὺ   κληθήσῃ
Thou art   Simon   the   son   of John,   thou shalt be called
Κηφᾶς   (ὃ   ἑρμηνεύεται   Πέτρος).   43 Τῇ
Cephas   (which   is translated   Peter).   On the
ἐπαύριον   ἠθέλησεν   ἐξελθεῖν   εἰς   τὴν   Γαλιλαίαν,
morrow   he wished   to go forth   into   –   Galilee,
καὶ   εὑρίσκει   Φίλιππον.   καὶ   λέγει   αὐτῷ   ὁ
and   finds   Philip.   And   says   to him   –
᾽Ιησοῦς·   ἀκολούθει   μοι.   44 ἦν   δὲ   ὁ
Jesus :   Follow   me.   Now was   –
Φίλιππος   ἀπὸ   Βηθσαϊδά,   ἐκ   τῆς   πόλεως
Philip   from   Bethsaida,   of   the   city
᾽Ανδρέου   καὶ   Πέτρου.   45 εὑρίσκει   Φίλιππος
of Andrew   and   of Peter.   ²Finds   ¹Philip
τὸν   Ναθαναὴλ   καὶ   λέγει   αὐτῷ·   ὃν   ἔγραψεν
–   ³Nathanael   and   tells   him :   [He] whom   wrote
Μωϋσῆς   ἐν   τῷ   νόμῳ   καὶ   οἱ   προφῆται
Moses   in   the   law   and   the   prophets
εὑρήκαμεν,   ᾽Ιησοῦν   υἱὸν   τοῦ   ᾽Ιωσὴφ   τὸν
we have found,   Jesus   son   –   of Joseph   –
ἀπὸ   Ναζαρέθ.   46 καὶ   εἶπεν   αὐτῷ
from   Nazareth.   And   said   to him
Ναθαναήλ·   ἐκ   Ναζαρὲθ   δύναταί   τι   ἀγαθὸν
Nathanael :   Out of   Nazareth   can   anything   good
εἶναι;   λέγει   αὐτῷ   ὁ   Φίλιππος·   ἔρχου   καὶ
to be?   Says   to him   –   Philip :   Come   and
ἴδε.   47 εἶδεν   ᾽Ιησοῦς   τὸν   Ναθαναὴλ
see.   ¹Saw   ¹Jesus   –   ³Nathanael

coming to him, and said of him, "Behold, an Israelite indeed, in whom is no guile!" ⁴⁸Nathan'-a-el said to him, "How do you know me?" Jesus answered him, "Before Philip called you, when you were under the fig tree, I saw you." ⁴⁹Nathan'a-el answered him, "Rabbi, you are the Son of God! You are the King of Israel!" ⁵⁰Jesus answered him, "Because I said to you, I saw you under the fig tree, do you believe? You shall see greater things than these." ⁵¹And he said to him, "Truly, truly, I say to you, you will see heaven opened, and the angels of God ascending and descending upon the Son of man."

ἐρχόμενον πρὸς αὐτὸν καὶ λέγει περὶ
coming toward him and says concerning
αὐτοῦ· ἴδε ἀληθῶς Ἰσραηλίτης, ἐν ᾧ
him: Behold[,] truly an Israelite, in whom
δόλος οὐκ ἔστιν. 48 λέγει αὐτῷ Ναθαναήλ·
guile is not. Says to him Nathanael:
πόθεν με γινώσκεις; ἀπεκρίθη Ἰησοῦς καὶ
Whence me knowest thou? Answered Jesus and
εἶπεν αὐτῷ· πρὸ τοῦ σε Φίλιππον φωνῆσαι
said to him: Before the thee Philip to call
=Philip called thee
ὄντα ὑπὸ τὴν συκῆν εἶδόν σε. 49 ἀπεκρίθη
being under the fig-tree I saw thee. Answered
αὐτῷ Ναθαναήλ· ῥαββί, σὺ εἶ ὁ υἱὸς τοῦ
him Nathanael: Rabbi, thou art the Son
θεοῦ, σὺ βασιλεὺς εἶ τοῦ Ἰσραήλ.
of God, thou king art — of Israel.
50 ἀπεκρίθη Ἰησοῦς καὶ εἶπεν αὐτῷ·
Answered Jesus and said to him:
ὅτι εἶπόν σοι ὅτι εἶδόν σε ὑποκάτω τῆς
Because I told thee that I saw thee underneath the
συκῆς, πιστεύεις; μείζω τούτων ὄψῃ.
fig-tree, believest thou? greater [than] these things thou shalt see.
51 καὶ λέγει αὐτῷ· ἀμὴν ἀμὴν λέγω
And he says to him: Truly truly I tell
ὑμῖν, ὄψεσθε τὸν οὐρανὸν ἀνεῳγότα καὶ
you, ye shall see the heaven having been opened and
τοὺς ἀγγέλους τοῦ θεοῦ ἀναβαίνοντας καὶ
the angels — of God going up and
καταβαίνοντας ἐπὶ τὸν υἱὸν τοῦ ἀνθρώπου.
coming down on the Son — of man.

CHAPTER 2

ON the third day there was a marriage at Cana in Galilee, and the mother of Jesus was there; ²Jesus also was invited to the marriage, with his disciples. ³When the wine failed, the mother of Jesus said to him, "They have no wine." ⁴And Jesus said to her, "O woman, what have you to do with me? My hour has not yet

2 Καὶ τῇ ἡμέρᾳ τῇ τρίτῃ γάμος ἐγένετο
And on the day — third a wedding there was
ἐν Κανὰ τῆς Γαλιλαίας, καὶ ἦν ἡ μήτηρ
in Cana — of Galilee, and was the mother
τοῦ Ἰησοῦ ἐκεῖ· 2 ἐκλήθη δὲ καὶ ὁ
— of Jesus there; and was invited both —
Ἰησοῦς καὶ οἱ μαθηταὶ αὐτοῦ εἰς τὸν
Jesus and the disciples of him to the
γάμον. 3 καὶ ὑστερήσαντος οἴνου λέγει ἡ
wedding. And lacking wine says the
=when wine was lacking
μήτηρ τοῦ Ἰησοῦ πρὸς αὐτόν· οἶνον
mother of Jesus to him: Wine
οὐκ ἔχουσιν. 4 καὶ λέγει αὐτῇ ὁ Ἰησοῦς·
they have not. And says to her — Jesus:
τί ἐμοὶ καὶ σοί, γύναι; οὔπω ἥκει ἡ
What to me and to thee, woman? not yet is come the

come." ⁵His mother said to the servants, "Do whatever he tells you." ⁶Now six stone jars were standing there, for the Jewish rites of purification, each holding twenty or thirty gallons. ⁷Jesus said to them, "Fill the jars with water." And they filled them up to the brim. ⁸He said to them, "Now draw some out, and take it to the steward of the feast." So they took it. ⁹When the steward of the feast tasted the water now become wine, and did not know where it came from (though the servants who had drawn the water knew), the steward of the feast called the bridegroom ¹⁰and said to him, "Every man serves the good wine first; and when men have drunk freely, then the poor wine; but you have kept the good wine until now." ¹¹This, the first of his signs, Jesus did at Cana in Galilee, and manifested his glory; and his disciples believed in him. 12 After this he went down to Caper′na-um, with his mother and his brothers and his disciples; and there they

ὥρα μου. 5 λέγει ἡ μήτηρ αὐτοῦ τοῖς
hour of me. Says the mother of him to the

διακόνοις· ὅ τι ἂν λέγῃ ὑμῖν, ποιήσατε.
servants: Whatever he tells you, do ye.

6 ἦσαν δὲ ἐκεῖ λίθιναι ὑδρίαι ἓξ κατὰ
Now there were there stone water-pots six according to

τὸν καθαρισμὸν τῶν Ἰουδαίων κείμεναι,
the purifying of the Jews lying,

χωροῦσαι ἀνὰ μετρητὰς δύο ἢ τρεῖς.
containing each† measures two or three.

7 λέγει αὐτοῖς ὁ Ἰησοῦς· γεμίσατε τὰς
Tells them – Jesus : Fill ye the

ὑδρίας ὕδατος. καὶ ἐγέμισαν αὐτὰς ἕως
water-pots of(with) water. And they filled them up to

ἄνω. 8 καὶ λέγει αὐτοῖς· ἀντλήσατε νῦν
[the] top. And he tells them : Draw now

καὶ φέρετε τῷ ἀρχιτρικλίνῳ. οἱ δὲ
and carry to the master of the feast. And they

ἤνεγκαν. 9 ὡς δὲ ἐγεύσατο ὁ ἀρχιτρίκλινος
carried. But when tasted the master of the feast

τὸ ὕδωρ οἶνον γεγενημένον, καὶ οὐκ ᾔδει
the water ²wine ¹having become, and did not know

πόθεν ἐστίν, οἱ δὲ διάκονοι ᾔδεισαν οἱ
whence it is(was), but the servants knew the [ones]

ἠντληκότες τὸ ὕδωρ, φωνεῖ τὸν νυμφίον
having drawn the water, ³calls ⁴the ⁵bridegroom

ὁ ἀρχιτρίκλινος 10 καὶ λέγει αὐτῷ· πᾶς
¹the ²master of the feast and says to him : Every

ἄνθρωπος πρῶτον τὸν καλὸν οἶνον τίθησιν,
man first the good wine sets forth,

καὶ ὅταν μεθυσθῶσιν τὸν ἐλάσσω· σὺ
and when they become drunk the worse; thou

τετήρηκας τὸν καλὸν οἶνον ἕως ἄρτι.
hast kept the good wine until now.

11 Ταύτην ἐποίησεν ἀρχὴν τῶν σημείων ὁ
¹This ⁵did ⁶beginning ⁷of the ⁴signs

Ἰησοῦς ἐν Κανὰ τῆς Γαλιλαίας καὶ
Jesus in Cana – of Galilee and

ἐφανέρωσεν τὴν δόξαν αὐτοῦ, καὶ ἐπίστευσαν
manifested the glory of him, and believed

εἰς αὐτὸν οἱ μαθηταὶ αὐτοῦ.
in him the disciples of him.

12 Μετὰ τοῦτο κατέβη εἰς Καφαρναοὺμ
After this went down to Capernaum

αὐτὸς καὶ ἡ μήτηρ αὐτοῦ καὶ
he and the mother of him and

οἱ ἀδελφοὶ καὶ οἱ μαθηταὶ αὐτοῦ, καὶ
the brothers and the disciples of him, and

stayed for a few days. 13 The Passover of the Jews was at hand, and Jesus went up to Jerusalem. ¹⁴In the temple he found those who were selling oxen and sheep and pigeons, and the money-changers at their business. ¹⁵And making a whip of cords, he drove them all, with the sheep and oxen, out of the temple; and he poured out the coins of the money-changers and overturned their tables. ¹⁶And he told those who sold the pigeons, "Take these things away; you shall not make my Father's house a house of trade." ¹⁷His disciples remembered that it was written, "Zeal for thy house will consume me." ¹⁸The Jews then said to him, "What sign have you to show us for doing this?" ¹⁹Jesus answered them, "Destroy this temple, and in three days I will raise it up." ²⁰The Jews then said, "It has taken forty-six years to build this temple, and will you raise it up in three days?" ²¹But he spoke of the temple of

ἐκεῖ ἔμειναν οὐ πολλὰς ἡμέρας.
there remained not many days.

13 Καὶ ἐγγὺς ἦν τὸ πάσχα τῶν Ἰουδαίων,
And near was the Passover of the Jews,

καὶ ἀνέβη εἰς Ἱεροσόλυμα ὁ Ἰησοῦς.
and went up to Jerusalem – Jesus.

14 καὶ εὗρεν ἐν τῷ ἱερῷ τοὺς πωλοῦντας
And he found in the temple the [ones] selling

βόας καὶ πρόβατα καὶ περιστερὰς καὶ τοὺς
oxen and sheep and doves and the

κερματιστὰς καθημένους, 15 καὶ ποιήσας
coindealers sitting, and having made

φραγέλλιον ἐκ σχοινίων πάντας ἐξέβαλεν
a lash out of ropes ²all ¹he expelled

ἐκ τοῦ ἱεροῦ, τά τε πρόβατα καὶ τοὺς
out of the temple, both the sheep and the

βόας, καὶ τῶν κολλυβιστῶν ἐξέχεεν τὰ
oxen, and ⁴of the ³moneychangers ¹poured out ²the

κέρματα καὶ τὰς τραπέζας ἀνέτρεψεν,
²coins ⁶and ⁵the ⁹tables ⁷overturned,

16 καὶ τοῖς τὰς περιστερὰς πωλοῦσιν
and ²to the [ones] ⁴the ⁵doves ³selling

εἶπεν· ἄρατε ταῦτα ἐντεῦθεν, μὴ ποιεῖτε
¹said : Take these things hence, do not make

τὸν οἶκον τοῦ πατρός μου οἶκον ἐμπορίου.
the house of the Father of me a house of merchandise.

17 ἐμνήσθησαν οἱ μαθηταὶ αὐτοῦ ὅτι
Remembered the disciples of him that

γεγραμμένον ἐστίν· ὁ ζῆλος τοῦ οἴκου
having been written it is : The zeal of the house

σου καταφάγεταί με. 18 ἀπεκρίθησαν οὖν
of thee will consume me. Answered therefore

οἱ Ἰουδαῖοι καὶ εἶπαν αὐτῷ· τί σημεῖον
the Jews and said to him: What sign

δεικνύεις ἡμῖν, ὅτι ταῦτα ποιεῖς;
showest thou to us, because these things thou doest?

19 ἀπεκρίθη Ἰησοῦς καὶ εἶπεν αὐτοῖς· λύσατε τὸν
Answered Jesus and said to them: Destroy –

ναὸν τοῦτον, καὶ ἐν τρισὶν ἡμέραις ἐγερῶ αὐτόν.
shrine this, and in three days I will raise it.

20 εἶπαν οὖν οἱ Ἰουδαῖοι· τεσσεράκοντα
Said therefore the Jews : In forty

καὶ ἒξ ἔτεσιν οἰκοδομήθη ὁ ναὸς οὗτος,
and six years was built – shrine this,

καὶ σὺ ἐν τρισὶν ἡμέραις ἐγερεῖς αὐτόν;
and thou in three days wilt raise it?

21 ἐκεῖνος δὲ ἔλεγεν περὶ τοῦ ναοῦ τοῦ
But that [one]* spoke about the shrine of the

* John repeatedly uses the demonstrative adjective ἐκεῖνος in the sense of " he," referring to Christ.

his body. ²²When therefore he was raised from the dead, his disciples remembered that he had said this; and they believed the scripture and the word which Jesus had spoken.

23 Now when he was in Jerusalem at the Passover feast, many believed in his name when they saw the signs which he did; ²⁴but Jesus did not trust himself to them, ²⁵because he knew all men and needed no one to bear witness of man; for he himself knew what was in man.

CHAPTER 3

NOW there was a man of the Pharisees, named Nicode'mus, a ruler of the Jews. ²This man came to Jesus by night and said to him, "Rabbi, we know that you are a teacher come from God; for no one can do these signs that you do, unless God is with him." ³Jesus answered him, "Truly, truly, I say to you, unless one is born anew,[d] he cannot see the kingdom of God." ⁴Nicode'mus said to him, "How can a man be born when he is

[d] Or from above

σώματος αὐτοῦ. 22 ὅτε οὖν ἠγέρθη ἐκ
body   of him.   When therefore he was raised from

νεκρῶν,   ἐμνήσθησαν   οἱ   μαθηταὶ   αὐτοῦ
[the] dead, remembered   the   disciples   of him

ὅτι   τοῦτο   ἔλεγεν,   καὶ   ἐπίστευσαν   τῇ
that   this   he said,   and   they believed   the

γραφῇ   καὶ   τῷ   λόγῳ   ὃν   εἶπεν   ὁ   Ἰησοῦς.
scripture and   the   word   which said   -   Jesus.

23 Ὡς   δὲ   ἦν   ἐν   τοῖς   Ἱεροσολύμοις   ἐν
And when he was in   -   Jerusalem   at

τῷ   πάσχα   ἐν   τῇ   ἑορτῇ,   πολλοὶ   ἐπίστευσαν
the Passover at   the feast,   many   believed

εἰς   τὸ   ὄνομα   αὐτοῦ,   θεωροῦντες   αὐτοῦ   τὰ
in   the   name   of him,   beholding   of him   the

σημεῖα   ἃ   ἐποίει·   24 αὐτὸς   δὲ   Ἰησοῦς
signs   which he was doing; [1]but [3][him]self, [2]Jesus

οὐκ   ἐπίστευεν   αὐτὸν   αὐτοῖς   διὰ   τὸ   αὐτὸν
did not commit   himself   to them because of the   him
                                              =because he knew

γινώσκειν   πάντας,   25 καὶ   ὅτι   οὐ   χρείαν   εἶχεν
to know[b]   all men,   and because no   need   he had

ἵνα   τις   μαρτυρήσῃ   περὶ   τοῦ   ἀνθρώπου·
that anyone should witness concerning -   man;

αὐτὸς   γὰρ   ἐγίνωσκεν   τί   ἦν   ἐν   τῷ   ἀνθρώπῳ.
for he   knew   what was in   -   man.

3 Ἦν   δὲ   ἄνθρωπος   ἐκ   τῶν   Φαρισαίων,
Now there was a man   of   the   Pharisees,

Νικόδημος   ὄνομα   αὐτῷ,   ἄρχων   τῶν
Nicodemus   name   to him[c], a ruler   of the
                    =his name,

Ἰουδαίων·   2 οὗτος   ἦλθεν   πρὸς   αὐτὸν   νυκτὸς
Jews;   this man   came   to   him of(by) night

καὶ   εἶπεν   αὐτῷ·   ῥαββί,   οἴδαμεν   ὅτι   ἀπὸ
and   said   to him : Rabbi,   we know   that   from

θεοῦ   ἐλήλυθας   διδάσκαλος·   οὐδεὶς   γὰρ
God   thou hast come a teacher;   for no one

δύναται   ταῦτα   τὰ   σημεῖα   ποιεῖν   ἃ   σὺ
can   these   -   signs   to do   which thou

ποιεῖς,   ἐὰν   μὴ   ᾖ   ὁ   θεὸς   μετ'   αὐτοῦ.
doest,   except [2]is   -   [1]God   with   him.

3 ἀπεκρίθη   Ἰησοῦς   καὶ   εἶπεν   αὐτῷ·   ἀμὴν
, Answered   Jesus   and   said   to him : Truly

ἀμὴν   λέγω   σοι,   ἐὰν   μή   τις   γεννηθῇ
truly   I tell thee,   except anyone   is born

ἄνωθεν,   οὐ   δύναται   ἰδεῖν   τὴν   βασιλείαν
from above, he cannot   to see   the   kingdom

τοῦ   θεοῦ.   4 λέγει   πρὸς   αὐτὸν   ὁ   Νικόδημος·
-   of God.   Says   to   him   -   Nicodemus :

πῶς   δύναται   ἄνθρωπος   γεννηθῆναι   γέρων   ὤν;
How   can   a man   to be born   old   being?

old? Can he enter a
second time into his
mother's womb and be
born?" ⁵Jesus answered,
"Truly, truly, I say to
you, unless one is born
of water and the Spirit,
he cannot enter the
kingdom of God. ⁶That
which is born of the flesh
is flesh, and that which is
born of the Spirit is
spirit. ⁷Do not marvel
that I said to you, 'You
must be born anew.'ᵈ
⁸The windᵉ blows where
it wills, and you hear the
sound of it, but you do
not know whence it
comes or whither it goes;
so it is with every one
who is born of the
Spirit." ⁹Nicodeʹmus
said to him, "How can
this be?" ¹⁰Jesus answer-
ed him, "Are you a
teacher of Israel, and yet
you do not understand
this? ¹¹Truly, truly, I say
to you, we speak of what
we know, and bear wit-
ness to what we have
seen; but you do not
receive our testimony.
¹²If I have told you
earthly things and you
do not believe, how can
you believe if I tell you
heavenly things? ¹³No
one has ascended into

μὴ   δύναται   εἰς   τὴν   κοιλίαν   τῆς   μητρὸς
not   can he   into   the   womb   of the   mother
αὐτοῦ   δεύτερον   εἰσελθεῖν   καὶ   γεννηθῆναι;
of him   secondly   to enter   and   to be born?
5 ἀπεκρίθη   Ἰησοῦς·   ἀμὴν   ἀμὴν   λέγω   σοι,
Answered   Jesus :   Truly   truly   I tell   thee,
ἐὰν   μή   τις   γεννηθῇ   ἐξ   ὕδατος   καὶ
except   anyone   is born   of   water   and
πνεύματος,   οὐ   δύναται   εἰσελθεῖν   εἰς   τὴν
spirit,   he cannot   to enter   into   the
βασιλείαν   τοῦ   θεοῦ. 6 τὸ   γεγεννημένον   ἐκ
kingdom   —   of God. The thing having been born   of
τῆς   σαρκὸς   σάρξ   ἐστιν,   καὶ   τὸ   γεγεννημένον
the   flesh   flesh   is,   and the thing having been born
ἐκ   τοῦ   πνεύματος   πνεῦμά   ἐστιν. 7 μὴ
of   the   Spirit   spirit   is.   not
θαυμάσῃς   ὅτι   εἶπόν   σοι·   δεῖ   ὑμᾶς
Marvel   because   I told   thee : It behoves   you
γεννηθῆναι   ἄνωθεν. 8 τὸ   πνεῦμα   ὅπου   θέλει
to be born   from above.   The spirit(?wind) where it wishes
πνεῖ,   καὶ   τὴν   φωνὴν   αὐτοῦ   ἀκούεις,   ἀλλ'
blows,   and   the   sound   of it   thou hearest,   but
οὐκ   οἶδας   πόθεν   ἔρχεται   καὶ   ποῦ   ὑπάγει·
thou knowest not whence   it comes   and   whither   it goes;
οὕτως   ἐστὶν   πᾶς   ὁ   γεγεννημένος   ἐκ   τοῦ
so   is   everyone having been born   of   the
πνεύματος. 9 ἀπεκρίθη   Νικόδημος   καὶ
Spirit.   Answered   Nicodemus   and
εἶπεν   αὐτῷ·   πῶς   δύναται   ταῦτα   γενέσθαι;
said   to him : How   can   these things to come about?
10 ἀπεκρίθη   Ἰησοῦς   καὶ   εἶπεν   αὐτῷ·   σὺ
Answered   Jesus   and   said   to him : Thou
εἶ   ὁ   διδάσκαλος   τοῦ   Ἰσραὴλ   καὶ   ταῦτα
art the   teacher   —   of Israel   and these things
οὐ   γινώσκεις; 11 ἀμὴν   ἀμὴν   λέγω   σοι   ὅτι
knowest not?   Truly   truly   I tell   thee[,]   —
ὃ   οἴδαμεν   λαλοῦμεν   καὶ   ὃ   ἑωράκαμεν
What we know   we speak   and   what   we have seen
μαρτυροῦμεν,   καὶ   τὴν   μαρτυρίαν   ἡμῶν
we witness,   and   the   witness   of us
οὐ   λαμβάνετε. 12 εἰ   τὰ   ἐπίγεια   εἶπον
ye receive not.   If   the   earthly things   I told
ὑμῖν   καὶ   οὐ   πιστεύετε,   πῶς   ἐὰν   εἴπω
you   and   ye believe not,   how   if   I tell
ὑμῖν   τὰ   ἐπουράνια   πιστεύσετε; 13 καὶ
you   the   heavenly things   will ye believe?   And

ᵈ Or from above
ᵉ The same Greek word means
both wind and spirit

οὐδεὶς   ἀναβέβηκεν   εἰς   τὸν   οὐρανὸν   εἰ   μὴ
no man   has gone up   into   —   heaven   except

heaven but he who descended from heaven, the Son of man.*ᶠ* ¹⁴And as Moses lifted up the serpent in the wilderness, so must the Son of man be lifted up, ¹⁵that whoever believes in him may have eternal life."*ᵍ*

16 For God so loved the world that he gave his only Son, that whoever believes in him should not perish but have eternal life. ¹⁷For God sent the Son into the world, not to condemn the world, but that the world might be saved through him. ¹⁸He who believes in him is not condemned; he who does not believe is condemned already, because he has not believed in the name of the only Son of God. ¹⁹And this is the judgment, that the light has come into the world, and men loved darkness rather than light, because their deeds were evil. ²⁰For every one who does evil hates the light, and does not come to the light, lest his deeds should be exposed. ²¹But he who does what is true comes to the light, that it may be clearly

ᶠ Other ancient authorities add *who is in heaven*

ᵍ Some interpreters hold that the quotation continues through verse 21

ὁ   ἐκ   τοῦ   οὐρανοῦ   καταβάς,   ὁ   υἱὸς
the[one] out of -   heaven   having come down, the Son

τοῦ ἀνθρώπου. 14 Καὶ καθὼς Μωϋσῆς ὕψωσεν
- of man.   And   as   Moses   lifted up

τὸν ὄφιν ἐν τῇ ἐρήμῳ, οὕτως ὑψωθῆναι
the serpent in the desert,   so   to be lifted up

δεῖ   τὸν υἱὸν τοῦ ἀνθρώπου, 15 ἵνα πᾶς ὁ
it behoves the Son   -   of man,   that everyone

πιστεύων ἐν αὐτῷ ἔχῃ ζωὴν αἰώνιον.
believing in   him may have life   eternal.

16 οὕτως γὰρ ἠγάπησεν ὁ   θεὸς τὸν
For thus   ²loved   -   ¹God   the

κόσμον, ὥστε τὸν υἱὸν τὸν μονογενῆ
world,   so as the Son   the only begotten

ἔδωκεν, ἵνα πᾶς ὁ πιστεύων εἰς αὐτὸν
he gave, that everyone believing in   him

μὴ ἀπόληται ἀλλ' ἔχῃ ζωὴν αἰώνιον.
may not perish but may have life eternal.

17 οὐ γὰρ ἀπέστειλεν ὁ θεὸς τὸν υἱὸν
For ²not   ²sent   - ¹God the Son

εἰς τὸν κόσμον ἵνα κρίνῃ τὸν κόσμον,
into the world that he might judge the world,

ἀλλ' ἵνα σωθῇ ὁ κόσμος δι' αὐτοῦ.
but   that ³might be saved ¹the ²world through him.

18 ὁ   πιστεύων εἰς αὐτὸν οὐ κρίνεται·
The [one] believing in   him   is not judged;

ὁ μὴ πιστεύων ἤδη κέκριται, ὅτι
the[one]not believing already has been judged, because

μὴ πεπίστευκεν εἰς τὸ ὄνομα τοῦ μονογενοῦς
he has not believed in the name of the only begotten

υἱοῦ τοῦ θεοῦ. 19 αὕτη δέ ἐστιν ἡ
Son   - of God.   And this is   the

κρίσις, ὅτι τὸ φῶς ἐλήλυθεν εἰς τὸν
judgment, that the light has come into the

κόσμον καὶ ἠγάπησαν οἱ ἄνθρωποι μᾶλλον
world   and ²loved   -   ¹men   ⁵rather

τὸ σκότος ἢ τὸ φῶς· ἦν γὰρ αὐτῶν
³the ⁴darkness ⁶than the light; for was(were) of them

πονηρὰ τὰ ἔργα. 20 πᾶς γὰρ ὁ φαῦλα
evil   the works.   For everyone evil things

πράσσων μισεῖ τὸ φῶς καὶ οὐκ ἔρχεται
doing   hates the light and does not come

πρὸς τὸ φῶς, ἵνα μὴ ἐλεγχθῇ τὰ ἔργα
to   the light, lest is(are) reproved the works

αὐτοῦ· 21 ὁ δὲ ποιῶν τὴν ἀλήθειαν ἔρχεται
of him;   but the [one] doing the truth   comes

πρὸς τὸ φῶς, ἵνα φανερωθῇ αὐτοῦ τὰ
to   the light, that may be manifested of him the

seen that his deeds have been wrought in God. 22 After this Jesus and his disciples went into the land of Judea; there he remained with them and baptized. 23John also was baptizing at Ae'non near Salim, because there was much water there; and people came and were baptized. 24 For John had not yet been put in prison.

25 Now a discussion arose between John's disciples and a Jew over purifying. 26And they came to John, and said to him, "Rabbi, he who was with you beyond the Jordan, to whom you bore witness, here he is, baptizing, and all are going to him." 27John answered, "No one can receive anything except what is given him from heaven. 28You yourselves bear me witness, that I said, I am not the Christ, but I have been sent before him. 29He who has the bride is the bridegroom; the friend of the bridegroom, who stands and hears him, rejoices greatly at the bridegroom's voice;

ἔργα ὅτι ἐν θεῷ ἐστιν εἰργασμένα.
works that in God they are having been wrought.

22 Μετὰ ταῦτα ἦλθεν ὁ Ἰησοῦς καὶ οἱ
After these things came – Jesus and the
μαθηταὶ αὐτοῦ εἰς τὴν Ἰουδαίαν γῆν, καὶ
disciples of him into the Judæan land, and
ἐκεῖ διέτριβεν μετ᾽ αὐτῶν καὶ ἐβάπτιζεν.
there continued with them and baptized.

23 ἦν δὲ καὶ Ἰωάννης βαπτίζων ἐν
And was also John baptizing in
Αἰνὼν ἐγγὺς τοῦ Σαλίμ, ὅτι ὕδατα
Ainon near – Salim, because waters
πολλὰ ἦν ἐκεῖ, καὶ παρεγίνοντο καὶ
many was(were) there, and they came and
ἐβαπτίζοντο· 24 οὔπω γὰρ ἦν βεβλημένος
were baptized; for ³not yet ²was ⁴having been cast
εἰς τὴν φυλακὴν Ἰωάννης. 25 Ἐγένετο
⁵into ⁶the ⁷prison ¹John. There was
οὖν ζήτησις ἐκ τῶν μαθητῶν Ἰωάννου
therefore a questioning of the disciples of John
μετὰ Ἰουδαίου περὶ καθαρισμοῦ. 26 καὶ
with a Jew about purifying. And
ἦλθον πρὸς τὸν Ἰωάννην καὶ εἶπαν αὐτῷ·
they came to – John and said to him:
ῥαββί, ὃς ἦν μετὰ σοῦ πέραν τοῦ
Rabbi, [he] who was with thee beyond the
Ἰορδάνου, ᾧ σὺ μεμαρτύρηκας, ἴδε
Jordan, to whom thou hast borne witness, behold[,]
οὗτος βαπτίζει καὶ πάντες ἔρχονται πρὸς
this man baptizes and all men are coming to
αὐτόν. 27 ἀπεκρίθη Ἰωάννης καὶ εἶπεν·
him. Answered John and said:
οὐ δύναται ἄνθρωπος λαμβάνειν οὐδὲν ἐὰν μὴ
Cannot a man to receive no(any)thing unless
ᾖ δεδομένον αὐτῷ ἐκ τοῦ οὐρανοῦ.
it is having been given to him out of – heaven.

28 αὐτοὶ ὑμεῖς μοι μαρτυρεῖτε ὅτι εἶπον·
[Your]selves ye to me bear witness that I said:
οὐκ εἰμὶ ἐγὼ ὁ χριστός, ἀλλ᾽ ὅτι
³not ²am ¹I the Christ, but that
ἀπεσταλμένος εἰμὶ ἔμπροσθεν ἐκείνου. 29 ὁ
having been sent I am before that one.* The [one]
ἔχων τὴν νύμφην νυμφίος ἐστίν· ὁ δὲ
having the bride a bridegroom is; but the
φίλος τοῦ νυμφίου, ὁ ἑστηκὼς καὶ ἀκούων
friend of the bridegroom, – standing and hearing
αὐτοῦ, χαρᾷ χαίρει διὰ τὴν φωνὴν τοῦ
him, with joy rejoices because of the voice of the

* See note to 2. 21.

therefore this joy of mine is now full. ³⁰He must increase, but I must decrease."ʰ 31 He who comes from above is above all; he who is of the earth belongs to the earth, and of the earth he speaks; he who comes from heaven is above all. ³²He bears witness to what he has seen and heard, yet no one receives his testimony; ³³he who receives his testimony sets his seal to this, that God is true. ³⁴For he whom God has sent utters the words of God, for it is not by measure that he gives the Spirit; ³⁵the Father loves the Son, and has given all things into his hand. ³⁶He who believes in the Son has eternal life; he who does not obey the Son shall not see life, but the wrath of God rests upon him.

CHAPTER 4

NOW when the Lord knew that the Pharisees had heard that Jesus was making and baptizing more disciples than John ²(although Jesus himself did not baptize, but only his disciples), ³he left Judea

ʰ Some interpreters hold that the quotation continues through verse 36

νυμφίου. αὕτη οὖν ἡ χαρὰ ἡ ἐμὴ
bridegroom. ²This ¹therefore - ⁴joy - ²my
πεπλήρωται. 30 ἐκεῖνον δεῖ αὐξάνειν, ἐμὲ
has been fulfilled. That one it behoves to increase, ²me
δὲ ἐλαττοῦσθαι. 31 Ὁ ἄνωθεν ἐρχόμενος
¹but to decrease. The [one] from above coming
ἐπάνω πάντων ἐστίν· ὁ ὢν ἐκ τῆς γῆς
over all is; the [one] being of the earth
ἐκ τῆς γῆς ἐστιν καὶ ἐκ τῆς γῆς λαλεῖ.
of the earth is and of the earth speaks.
ὁ ἐκ τοῦ οὐρανοῦ ἐρχόμενος ἐπάνω
The [one] of - heaven coming over
πάντων ἐστίν· 32 ὃ ἑώρακεν καὶ ἤκουσεν,
all is; what he has seen and heard,
τοῦτο μαρτυρεῖ, καὶ τὴν μαρτυρίαν αὐτοῦ
this he witnesses [to], and the witness of him
οὐδεὶς λαμβάνει. 33 ὁ λαβὼν αὐτοῦ τὴν
no man receives. The [one] receiving of him the
μαρτυρίαν ἐσφράγισεν ὅτι ὁ θεὸς ἀληθής
witness sealed that - God true
ἐστιν. 34 ὃν γὰρ ἀπέστειλεν ὁ θεὸς τὰ
is. For [he] whom ²sent - ¹God the
ῥήματα τοῦ θεοῦ λαλεῖ· οὐ γὰρ ἐκ
words - of God speaks; for not by
μέτρου δίδωσιν τὸ πνεῦμα. 35 ὁ πατὴρ
measure he gives the Spirit. The Father
ἀγαπᾷ τὸν υἱόν, καὶ πάντα δέδωκεν ἐν
loves the Son, and all things has given in[to]
τῇ χειρὶ αὐτοῦ. 36 ὁ πιστεύων εἰς τὸν
the hand of him. The [one] believing in the
υἱὸν ἔχει ζωὴν αἰώνιον· ὁ δὲ ἀπειθῶν
Son has life eternal; but the [one] disobeying
τῷ υἱῷ οὐκ ὄψεται ζωήν, ἀλλ' ἡ ὀργὴ
the Son will not see life, but the wrath
τοῦ θεοῦ μένει ἐπ' αὐτόν.
- of God remains on him.

4 Ὡς οὖν ἔγνω ὁ κύριος ὅτι ἤκουσαν
²When ¹therefore ⁵knew ³the ⁴Lord ⁶that ⁹heard
οἱ Φαρισαῖοι ὅτι Ἰησοῦς πλείονας μαθητὰς
⁷the ⁸Pharisees that Jesus more disciples
ποιεῖ καὶ βαπτίζει ἢ Ἰωάννης, — 2 καίτοι γε
makes and baptizes than John, — though
Ἰησοῦς αὐτὸς οὐκ ἐβάπτιζεν ἀλλ' οἱ
Jesus [him]self baptized not but the
μαθηταὶ αὐτοῦ, — 3 ἀφῆκεν τὴν Ἰουδαίαν
disciples of him, — he left - Judæa

and departed again to Galilee. ⁴He had to pass through Samar'ia. ⁵So he came to a city of Samar'ia, called Sy'char, near the field that Jacob gave to his son Joseph. ⁶Jacob's well was there, and so Jesus, wearied as he was with his journey, sat down beside the well. It was about the sixth hour.

7 There came a woman of Samar'ia to draw water. Jesus said to her, "Give me a drink." ⁸For his disciples had gone away into the city to buy food. ⁹The Samaritan woman said to him, "How is it that you, a Jew, ask a drink of me, a woman of Samar'ia?" For Jews have no dealings with Samaritans. ¹⁰Jesus answered her, "If you knew the gift of God, and who it is that is saying to you, 'Give me a drink,' you would have asked him, and he would have given you living water." ¹¹The woman said to him, "Sir, you have nothing to draw with, and the well is deep; where do you get that living water? ¹²Are you

καὶ   ἀπῆλθεν   πάλιν   εἰς   τὴν   Γαλιλαίαν.
and   went away   again   into   –   Galilee.

4 ῎Εδει   δὲ   αὐτὸν   διέρχεσθαι   διὰ   τῆς
And it behoved   him   to pass through   through   –

Σαμαρείας.   5 ἔρχεται   οὖν   εἰς   πόλιν   τῆς
Samaria.   He comes   therefore to   a city   –

Σαμαρείας   λεγομένην   Σύχαρ,   πλησίον   τοῦ
of Samaria   being called   Sychar,   near   the

χωρίου   ὃ   ἔδωκεν   ᾽Ιακὼβ   [τῷ]   ᾽Ιωσὴφ
piece of land   which   ²gave   ¹Jacob   –   to Joseph

τῷ   υἱῷ   αὐτοῦ·   6 ἦν   δὲ   ἐκεῖ   πηγὴ   τοῦ
the   son   of him;   and was   there   a fountain   –

᾽Ιακώβ.   ὁ   οὖν   ᾽Ιησοῦς   κεκοπιακὼς   ἐκ
of Jacob.   –   Therefore   Jesus   having become wearied from

τῆς   ὁδοιπορίας   ἐκαθέζετο   οὕτως   ἐπὶ   τῇ
the   journey   sat   thus   at   the

πηγῇ·   ὥρα   ἦν   ὡς   ἕκτη.   7 ἔρχεται   γυνὴ
fountain;   [the] hour   was   about   sixth.   Comes   a woman

ἐκ   τῆς   Σαμαρείας   ἀντλῆσαι   ὕδωρ.   λέγει
of   –   Samaria   to draw   water.   Says

αὐτῇ   ὁ   ᾽Ιησοῦς·   δός   μοι   πεῖν.   8 οἱ   γὰρ
to her   –   Jesus :   Give   me   to drink.   For the

μαθηταὶ   αὐτοῦ   ἀπεληλύθεισαν   εἰς   τὴν
disciples   of him   had gone away   into   the

πόλιν,   ἵνα   τροφὰς   ἀγοράσωσιν.   9 λέγει
city,   that   foods   they might buy.   Says

οὖν   αὐτῷ   ἡ   γυνὴ   ἡ   Σαμαρῖτις·   πῶς
therefore to him   the   woman   –   Samaritan :   How

σὺ   ᾽Ιουδαῖος   ὢν   παρ᾽   ἐμοῦ   πεῖν
thou   ²a Jew   ¹being   ⁵from   ⁶me   ⁴to drink

αἰτεῖς   γυναικὸς   Σαμαρίτιδος   οὔσης;
³askest   ⁹woman   ⁸a Samaritan   ⁷being?

[οὐ   γὰρ   συγχρῶνται   ᾽Ιουδαῖοι   Σαμαρίταις.]
¹For   ⁴not   ³associate   ²Jews   ⁵with Samaritans.

10 ἀπεκρίθη   ᾽Ιησοῦς   καὶ   εἶπεν   αὐτῇ·   εἰ   ᾔδεις
Answered   Jesus   and   said   to her :   If thou knewest

τὴν   δωρεὰν   τοῦ   θεοῦ,   καὶ   τίς   ἐστιν   ὁ
the   gift   –   of God,   and   who   is the [one]

λέγων   σοι·   δός   μοι   πεῖν,   σὺ   ἂν   ᾔτησας
saying   to thee :   Give   me   to drink, thou   wouldest have asked

αὐτὸν   καὶ   ἔδωκεν   ἄν   σοι   ὕδωρ   ζῶν.
him   and   he would have given   thee   water   living.

11 λέγει   αὐτῷ·   κύριε,   οὔτε   ἄντλημα   ἔχεις
She says   to him :   Sir,   no   pail   thou hast

καὶ   τὸ   φρέαρ   ἐστὶν   βαθύ·   πόθεν   οὖν
and   the   well   is   deep;   whence   then

ἔχεις   τὸ   ὕδωρ   τὸ   ζῶν;   12 μὴ   σὺ   μείζων
hast thou   the   water   –   living?   not   thou   greater

greater than our father Jacob, who gave us the well, and drank from it himself, and his sons, and his cattle?" [13]Jesus said to her, "Every one who drinks of this water will thirst again, [14]but whoever drinks of the water that I shall give him will never thirst; the water that I shall give him will become in him a spring of water welling up to eternal life." [15]The woman said to him, "Sir, give me this water, that I may not thirst, nor come here to draw."

16 Jesus said to her, "Go, call your husband, and come here." [17]The woman answered him, "I have no husband." Jesus said to her, "You are right in saying, 'I have no husband'; [18]for you have had five husbands, and he whom you now have is not your husband; this you said truly." [19]The woman said to him, "Sir, I perceive that you are a prophet. [20]Our fathers worshiped on this mountain; and you say that in Jerusalem is the place where men ought to worship."

εἰ τοῦ πατρὸς ἡμῶν Ἰακώβ, ὃς ἔδωκεν
art [than] the father of us Jacob, who gave

ἡμῖν τὸ φρέαρ, καὶ αὐτὸς ἐξ αὐτοῦ
us the well, and [him]self of it

ἔπιεν καὶ οἱ υἱοὶ αὐτοῦ καὶ τὰ θρέμματα
drank and the sons of him and the cattle

αὐτοῦ; 13 ἀπεκρίθη Ἰησοῦς καὶ εἶπεν αὐτῇ·
of him? Answered Jesus and said to her:

πᾶς ὁ πίνων ἐκ τοῦ ὕδατος τούτου
Everyone drinking of – water this

διψήσει πάλιν· 14 ὃς δ᾽ ἂν πίῃ ἐκ τοῦ
will thirst again; but whoever drinks of the

ὕδατος οὗ ἐγὼ δώσω αὐτῷ, οὐ μὴ
water which I will give him, by no means

διψήσει εἰς τὸν αἰῶνα, ἀλλὰ τὸ ὕδωρ ὃ
will thirst unto the age, but the water which

δώσω αὐτῷ γενήσεται ἐν αὐτῷ πηγὴ
I will give him will become in him a fountain

ὕδατος ἁλλομένου εἰς ζωὴν αἰώνιον. 15 λέγει
of water springing to life eternal. Says

πρὸς αὐτὸν ἡ γυνή· κύριε, δός μοι
to him the woman : Sir, give me

τοῦτο τὸ ὕδωρ, ἵνα μὴ διψῶ μηδὲ
this – water, that I thirst not nor

διέρχωμαι ἐνθάδε ἀντλεῖν. 16 λέγει αὐτῇ·
come through hither to draw. He says to her :

ὕπαγε φώνησον τὸν ἄνδρα σου καὶ ἐλθὲ
Go call the husband of thee and come

ἐνθάδε. 17 ἀπεκρίθη ἡ γυνὴ καὶ εἶπεν·
hither. Answered the woman and said :

οὐκ ἔχω ἄνδρα. λέγει αὐτῇ ὁ Ἰησοῦς·
I have not a husband. Says to her – Jesus :

καλῶς εἶπες ὅτι ἄνδρα οὐκ ἔχω· 18 πέντε
Well sayest thou[,] – A husband I have not; ²five

γὰρ ἄνδρας ἔσχες, καὶ νῦν ὃν ἔχεις
¹for husbands thou hadst, and now [he] whom thou hast

οὐκ ἔστιν σου ἀνήρ· τοῦτο ἀληθὲς εἴρηκας.
is not of thee husband; this truly thou hast said.

19 λέγει αὐτῷ ἡ γυνή· κύριε, θεωρῶ
Says to him the woman : Sir, I perceive

ὅτι προφήτης εἶ σύ. 20 οἱ πατέρες
that a prophet art thou. The fathers

ἡμῶν ἐν τῷ ὄρει τούτῳ προσεκύνησαν·
of us in – mountain this worshipped;

καὶ ὑμεῖς λέγετε ὅτι ἐν Ἱεροσολύμοις
and ye say that in Jerusalem

ἐστὶν ὁ τόπος ὅπου προσκυνεῖν δεῖ.
is the place where to worship it behoves.

²¹Jesus said to her, "Woman, believe me, the hour is coming when neither on this mountain nor in Jerusalem will you worship the Father. ²²You worship what you do not know; we worship what we know, for salvation is from the Jews. ²³But the hour is coming, and now is, when the true worshipers will worship the Father in spirit and truth, for such the Father seeks to worship him. ²⁴God is spirit, and those who worship him must worship in spirit and truth." ²⁵The woman said to him, "I know that Messiah is coming (he who is called Christ); when he comes, he will show us all things." ²⁶Jesus said to her, "I who speak to you am he."

27 Just then his disciples came. They marveled that he was talking with a woman, but none said, "What do you wish?" or, "Why are you talking with her?" ²⁸So the woman left her water jar, and went away into the city, and said to the people,

21 λέγει αὐτῇ ὁ Ἰησοῦς· πίστευέ μοι,
Says to her - Jesus : Believe me,
γύναι, ὅτι ἔρχεται ὥρα ὅτε οὔτε ἐν
woman, that is coming an hour when neither in
τῷ ὄρει τούτῳ οὔτε ἐν Ἰεροσολύμοις
- mountain this nor in Jerusalem
προσκυνήσετε τῷ πατρί. 22 ὑμεῖς προσκυ-
will ye worship the Father. Ye wor-
νεῖτε ὃ οὐκ οἴδατε, ἡμεῖς προσκυνοῦμεν ὃ
ship what ye know not, we worship what
οἴδαμεν, ὅτι ἡ σωτηρία ἐκ τῶν Ἰουδαίων
we know, because - salvation of the Jews
ἐστίν· 23 ἀλλὰ ἔρχεται ὥρα καὶ νῦν
is; but is coming an hour and now
ἐστιν, ὅτε οἱ ἀληθινοὶ προσκυνηταὶ προσκυνή-
is, when the true worshippers will
σουσιν τῷ πατρὶ ἐν πνεύματι καὶ ἀληθείᾳ·
worship the Father in spirit and truth;
καὶ γὰρ ὁ πατὴρ τοιούτους ²ζητεῖ τοὺς
for indeed the Father ²such ¹seeks the [ones]
προσκυνοῦντας αὐτόν· 24 πνεῦμα ὁ θεός,
worshipping him; God [is] spirit,*
καὶ τοὺς προσκυνοῦντας ἐν πνεύματι καὶ
and ²the [ones] ³worshipping ²in ⁷spirit ⁷and
ἀληθείᾳ δεῖ προσκυνεῖν. 25 λέγει αὐτῷ
⁸truth ¹it behoves ⁴to worship. Says to him
ἡ γυνή· οἶδα ὅτι Μεσσίας ἔρχεται, ὁ
the woman : I know that Messiah is coming, the [one]
λεγόμενος χριστός· ὅταν ἔλθῃ ἐκεῖνος,
being called Christ; when comes that one,
ἀναγγελεῖ ἡμῖν ἅπαντα. 26 λέγει αὐτῇ
he will announce to us all things. Says to her
ὁ Ἰησοῦς· ἐγώ εἰμι, ὁ λαλῶν σοι.
- Jesus : I am, the [one] speaking to thee.
27 Καὶ ἐπὶ τούτῳ ἦλθαν οἱ μαθηταὶ
And on this came the disciples
αὐτοῦ, καὶ ἐθαύμαζον ὅτι μετὰ γυναικὸς
of him, and marvelled that with a woman
ἐλάλει· οὐδεὶς μέντοι εἶπεν· τί ζητεῖς
he was speaking; no one however said : What seekest thou
ἢ τί λαλεῖς μετ᾽ αὐτῆς; 28 ἀφῆκεν οὖν
or why speakest thou with her? ⁴Left ³therefore
τὴν ὑδρίαν αὐτῆς ἡ γυνὴ καὶ ἀπῆλθεν
⁵the ⁶waterpot ⁷of her ¹the ²woman and went away
εἰς τὴν πόλιν, καὶ λέγει τοῖς ἀνθρώποις·
into the city, and says to the men :

* See note on 1. 1.

29 "Come, see a man who told me all that I ever did. Can this be the Christ?" 30 They went out of the city and were coming to him.

31 Meanwhile the disciples besought him, saying, "Rabbi, eat." 32 But he said to them, "I have food to eat of which you do not know." 33 So the disciples said to one another, "Has any one brought him food?" 34 Jesus said to them, "My food is to do the will of him who sent me, and to accomplish his work. 35 Do you not say, 'There are yet four months, then comes the harvest'? I tell you, lift up your eyes, and see how the fields are already white for harvest. 36 He who reaps receives wages, and gathers fruit for eternal life, so that sower and reaper may rejoice together. 37 For here the saying holds true, 'One sows and another reaps.' 38 I sent you to reap that for which you did not labor; others have labored, and you have entered into their labor."

29 δεῦτε   ἴδετε   ἄνθρωπον   ὃς   εἶπέν   μοι
   Come   see   a man   who   told   me
πάντα   ἃ   ἐποίησα·   μήτι   οὗτός   ἐστιν   ὁ
all things which   I did;   not   this   is   the
χριστός;   30 ἐξῆλθον   ἐκ   τῆς   πόλεως   καὶ
Christ?   They went forth out of   the   city   and
ἤρχοντο   πρὸς   αὐτόν.   31 Ἐν   τῷ   μεταξὺ
came   to   him.   In   the   meantime
ἠρώτων   αὐτὸν   οἱ   μαθηταὶ   λέγοντες·   ῥαββί,
asked   him   the   disciples   saying :   Rabbi,
φάγε.   32 ὁ   δὲ   εἶπεν   αὐτοῖς·   ἐγὼ   βρῶσιν
eat.   But he   said   to them :   I   food
ἔχω   φαγεῖν   ἣν   ὑμεῖς   οὐκ   οἴδατε.   33 ἔλεγον
have   to eat   which   ye   do not know.   Said
οὖν   οἱ   μαθηταὶ   πρὸς   ἀλλήλους·   μή   τις
therefore the disciples   to   one another :   Not   anyone
ἤνεγκεν   αὐτῷ   φαγεῖν;   34 λέγει   αὐτοῖς   ὁ
brought   him   to eat?   Says   to them   –
Ἰησοῦς·   ἐμὸν   βρῶμά   ἐστιν   ἵνα   ποιῶ   τὸ
Jesus :   My   food   is   that I may do the
θέλημα   τοῦ   πέμψαντός   με   καὶ   τελειώσω
will   of the [one]   having sent   me   and   may finish
αὐτοῦ   τὸ   ἔργον.   35 οὐχ   ὑμεῖς   λέγετε   ὅτι
of him   the   work.   ³Not   ²ye   ¹say   that
ἔτι   τετράμηνός   ἐστιν   καὶ   ὁ   θερισμὸς
yet   four months   it is   and   the   harvest
ἔρχεται;   ἰδοὺ   λέγω   ὑμῖν,   ἐπάρατε   τοὺς
comes?   Behold   I tell   you,   lift up   the
ὀφθαλμοὺς   ὑμῶν   καὶ   θεάσασθε   τὰς   χώρας,
eyes   of you   and   behold   the   fields,
ὅτι   λευκαί   εἰσιν   πρὸς   θερισμόν.   ἤδη
because white   they are   to   harvest.   Already
36 ὁ   θερίζων   μισθὸν   λαμβάνει   καὶ   συνάγει
the [one] reaping   wages   receives   and   gathers
καρπὸν   εἰς   ζωὴν   αἰώνιον,   ἵνα   ὁ   σπείρων
fruit   to   life   eternal,   that ¹the [one] ²sowing
ὁμοῦ   χαίρῃ   καὶ   ὁ   θερίζων.   37 ἐν   γὰρ
⁷together ⁶may rejoice ³and ⁴the [one] ⁵reaping.   For in
τούτῳ   ὁ   λόγος   ἐστὶν   ἀληθινὸς   ὅτι   ἄλλος
this   the   word   is   true   that another(one)
ἐστὶν   ὁ   σπείρων   καὶ   ἄλλος   ὁ   θερίζων.
is   the [one] sowing   and   another the [one] reaping.
38 ἐγὼ   ἀπέστειλα   ὑμᾶς   θερίζειν   ὃ   οὐχ
I   sent   you   to reap   what   not
ὑμεῖς   κεκοπιάκατε·   ἄλλοι   κεκοπιάκασιν,   καὶ
ye   have laboured;   others   have laboured,   and
ὑμεῖς   εἰς   τὸν   κόπον   αὐῶν   εἰσεληλύθατε.
ye   into   the   labour   of them   have entered.

39 Many Samaritans from that city believed in him because of the woman's testimony, "He told me all that I ever did." ⁴⁰So when the Samaritans came to him, they asked him to stay with them; and he stayed there two days. ⁴¹And many more believed because of his word. ⁴²They said to the woman, "It is no longer because of your words that we believe, for we have heard for ourselves, and we know that this is indeed the Savior of the world."

43 After the two days he departed to Galilee. ⁴⁴For Jesus himself testified that a prophet has no honor in his own country. ⁴⁵So when he came to Galilee, the Galileans welcomed him, having seen all that he had done in Jerusalem at the feast, for they too had gone to the feast.

46 So he came again to Cana in Galilee, where he had made the water wine. And at Caper'naum there was an official whose son was ill. ⁴⁷When

---

39 Ἐκ δὲ τῆς πόλεως ἐκείνης πολλοὶ
And out of – city   that   many

ἐπίστευσαν εἰς αὐτὸν τῶν Σαμαριτῶν διὰ
believed   in   him   of the   Samaritans   because of

τὸν λόγον τῆς γυναικὸς μαρτυρούσης ὅτι
the   word   of the   woman   witnessing[,]   –

εἶπέν μοι πάντα ἃ ἐποίησα. **40** ὡς
He told   me   all things   which   I did.   When

οὖν ἦλθον πρὸς αὐτὸν οἱ Σαμαρῖται,
therefore   came   to   him   the   Samaritans,

ἠρώτων αὐτὸν μεῖναι παρ' αὐτοῖς· καὶ
they asked   him   to remain   with   them;   and

ἔμεινεν ἐκεῖ δύο ἡμέρας. **41** καὶ πολλῷ
he remained   there   two   days.   And   ²more

πλείους ἐπίστευσαν διὰ τὸν λόγον αὐτοῦ,
¹many   believed   because of   the   word   of him,

42 τῇ τε γυναικὶ ἔλεγον ὅτι οὐκέτι. διὰ
and to the   woman   they said[,]   –   No longer   because of

τὴν σὴν λαλιὰν πιστεύομεν· αὐτοὶ γὰρ
–   thy   talk   we believe;   for [our]selves

ἀκηκόαμεν, καὶ οἴδαμεν ὅτι οὗτός ἐστιν
we have heard,   and   we know   that   this man   is

ἀληθῶς ὁ σωτὴρ τοῦ κόσμου.
truly   the   Saviour   of the   world.

43 Μετὰ δὲ τὰς δύο ἡμέρας ἐξῆλθεν
And after   the   two   days   he went forth

ἐκεῖθεν εἰς τὴν Γαλιλαίαν. **44** αὐτὸς γὰρ
thence   into   –   Galilee.   For   ²[him]self

Ἰησοῦς ἐμαρτύρησεν ὅτι προφήτης ἐν
¹Jesus   witnessed   that   a prophet   in

τῇ ἰδίᾳ πατρίδι τιμὴν οὐκ ἔχει. **45** ὅτε
the(his) own   native place   honour   has not.   When

οὖν ἦλθεν εἰς τὴν Γαλιλαίαν, ἐδέξαντο
therefore he came   into   –   Galilee,   received

αὐτὸν οἱ Γαλιλαῖοι, πάντα ἑωρακότες
him   the   Galilæans,   all things   having seen

ὅσα ἐποίησεν ἐν Ἱεροσολύμοις ἐν τῇ
which   he did   in   Jerusalem   at   the

ἑορτῇ· καὶ αὐτοὶ γὰρ ἦλθον εἰς τὴν
feast;   ²also   ²they   ¹for   went   to   the

ἑορτήν. **46** Ἦλθεν οὖν πάλιν εἰς τὴν
feast.   He came   therefore   again   to   –

Κανὰ τῆς Γαλιλαίας, ὅπου ἐποίησεν τὸ
Cana   –   of Galilee,   where   he made   the

ὕδωρ οἶνον. καὶ ἦν τις βασιλικὸς
water   wine.   And   there was   a certain   courtier

οὗ ὁ υἱὸς ἠσθένει ἐν Καφαρναούμ· **47** οὗτος
of whom the son   ailed   in   Capernaum;   this man

he heard that Jesus had come from Judea to Galilee, he went and begged him to come down and heal his son, for he was at the point of death. ⁴⁸Jesus therefore said to him, "Unless you see signs and wonders you will not believe." ⁴⁹The official said to him, "Sir, come down before my child dies." ⁵⁰Jesus said to him, "Go; your son will live." The man believed the word that Jesus spoke to him and went his way. ⁵¹As he was going down, his servants met him and told him that his son was living. ⁵²So he asked them the hour when he began to mend, and they said to him, "Yesterday at the seventh hour the fever left him." ⁵³The father knew that was the hour when Jesus had said to him, "Your son will live"; and he himself believed, and all his household. ⁵⁴This was now the second sign that Jesus did when he had come from Judea to Galilee.

ἀκούσας ὅτι Ἰησοῦς ἥκει ἐκ τῆς Ἰουδαίας
hearing that Jesus comes(came) out of – Judæa

εἰς τὴν Γαλιλαίαν, ἀπῆλθεν πρὸς αὐτὸν καὶ
into – Galilee, went to him and

ἠρώτα ἵνα καταβῇ καὶ ἰάσηται αὐτοῦ
asked that he would come down and would cure of him

τὸν υἱόν· ἤμελλεν γὰρ ἀποθνῄσκειν. 48 εἶπεν
the son; for he was about to die. Said

οὖν ὁ Ἰησοῦς πρὸς αὐτόν· ἐὰν μὴ σημεῖα
therefore – Jesus to him : Except signs

καὶ τέρατα ἴδητε, οὐ μὴ πιστεύσητε.
and prodigies ye see, by no means ye believe.

49 λέγει πρὸς αὐτὸν ὁ βασιλικός· κύριε,
Says to him the courtier : Sir,

κατάβηθι πρὶν ἀποθανεῖν τὸ παιδίον[ᵇ] μου.
come down before to die the child of me.

50 λέγει αὐτῷ ὁ Ἰησοῦς· πορεύου, ὁ
Tells him – Jesus : Go, the

υἱός σου ζῇ. ἐπίστευσεν ὁ ἄνθρωπος τῷ
son of thee lives. ³Believed ¹the ²man ⁴the

λόγῳ ὃν εἶπεν αὐτῷ ὁ Ἰησοῦς, καὶ
⁵word ⁶which ⁸said ⁹to him – ⁷Jesus, and

ἐπορεύετο. 51 ἤδη δὲ αὐτοῦ καταβαίνοντος
went. And already him going down*
=while he was going down

οἱ δοῦλοι ὑπήντησαν αὐτῷ λέγοντες ὅτι
the slaves met him saying that

ὁ παῖς αὐτοῦ ζῇ. 52 ἐπύθετο οὖν τὴν
the boy of him lives. He inquired therefore the

ὥραν παρ' αὐτῶν ἐν ᾗ κομψότερον ἔσχεν·
hour from them in which better he had;
=he got better:

εἶπαν οὖν αὐτῷ ὅτι ἐχθὲς ὥραν ἑβδόμην
they said therefore to him[,] – Yesterday [at] hour seventh

ἀφῆκεν αὐτὸν ὁ πυρετός. 53 ἔγνω οὖν
left him the fever. Knew therefore

ὁ πατὴρ ὅτι ἐκείνῃ τῇ ὥρᾳ ἐν ᾗ εἶπεν
the father that in that – hour in which told

αὐτῷ ὁ Ἰησοῦς· ὁ υἱός σου ζῇ· καὶ
him – Jesus : The son of thee lives; and

ἐπίστευσεν αὐτὸς καὶ ἡ οἰκία αὐτοῦ ὅλη.
believed he and the household of him whole.

54 Τοῦτο [δὲ] πάλιν δεύτερον σημεῖον
And this again a second sign

ἐποίησεν ὁ Ἰησοῦς ἐλθὼν ἐκ τῆς Ἰουδαίας
did – Jesus having come out of – Judæa

εἰς τὴν Γαλιλαίαν.
into – Galilee.

CHAPTER 5

AFTER this there was a feast of the Jews, and Jesus went up to Jerusalem.

2 Now there is in Jerusalem by the Sheep gate a pool, in Hebrew called Beth-za'tha,[i] which has five porticoes. ³ In these lay a multitude of invalids, blind, lame, paralyzed.[j] ⁵ One man was there, who had been ill for thirty-eight years. ⁶ When Jesus saw him and knew that he had been lying there a long time, he said to him, "Do you want to be healed?" ⁷ The sick man answered him, "Sir, I have no man to put me into the pool when the water is troubled, and while I am going another steps down before me." ⁸ Jesus said to him, "Rise, take up your pallet, and walk." ⁹ And at once the man was healed, and he took up his pallet and walked.

Now that day was the sabbath. ¹⁰ So the Jews said to the man who was cured, "It is the sabbath, it is not lawful for you to carry your pallet." ¹¹ But

---

[i] Other ancient authorities read *Bethesda*, others *Beth-saida*

[j] Other ancient authorities insert, wholly or in part, *waiting for the moving of the water;* 'for an angel of the Lord went down at certain seasons into the pool, and troubled the water: whoever stepped in first after the troubling of the water was healed of whatever disease he had

---

5 Μετὰ ταῦτα ἦν ἑορτὴ τῶν Ἰουδαίων,
After these things there was a feast of the Jews,

καὶ ἀνέβη Ἰησοῦς εἰς Ἱεροσόλυμα. 2 ἔστιν
and went up Jesus to Jerusalem. there is

δὲ ἐν τοῖς Ἱεροσολύμοις ἐπὶ τῇ προβατικῇ
Now in – Jerusalem at the sheepgate

κολυμβήθρα, ἡ ἐπιλεγομένη Ἑβραϊστὶ
a pool, the [one] being called in Hebrew

Βηθζαθά, πέντε στοὰς ἔχουσα. 3 ἐν
Bethzatha, five porches having. In

ταύταις κατέκειτο πλῆθος τῶν ἀσθενούντων,
these lay a multitude of the ailing [ones],

τυφλῶν, χωλῶν, ξηρῶν. ‡ 5 ἦν δέ τις
blind, lame, withered. And there was a

ἄνθρωπος ἐκεῖ τριάκοντα καὶ ὀκτὼ ἔτη
certain man there thirty-eight years

ἔχων ἐν τῇ ἀσθενείᾳ αὐτοῦ· 6 τοῦτον
having in the ailment of him; ³this man

ἰδὼν ὁ Ἰησοῦς κατακείμενον, καὶ γνοὺς
²seeing – ¹Jesus ⁴lying, and knowing

ὅτι πολὺν ἤδη χρόνον ἔχει, λέγει αὐτῷ·
that ³much ²already ⁴time ¹he has, says to him :

θέλεις ὑγιὴς γενέσθαι; 7 ἀπεκρίθη αὐτῷ
Wishest thou whole to become? Answered him

ὁ ἀσθενῶν· κύριε, ἄνθρωπον οὐκ ἔχω,
the ailing [one] : Sir, a man I have not,

ἵνα ὅταν ταραχθῇ τὸ ὕδωρ βάλῃ με εἰς
that when is troubled the water he may put me into

τὴν κολυμβήθραν· ἐν ᾧ δὲ ἔρχομαι ἐγώ,
the pool; but while am coming I,

ἄλλος πρὸ ἐμοῦ καταβαίνει. 8 λέγει αὐτῷ
another before me goes down. Says to him

ὁ Ἰησοῦς· ἔγειρε ἆρον τὸν κράβατόν
– Jesus : Rise[,] take the mattress

σου καὶ περιπάτει. 9 καὶ εὐθέως ἐγένετο
of thee and walk. And immediately became

ὑγιὴς ὁ ἄνθρωπος, καὶ ἦρεν τὸν κράβατον
whole the man, and took the mattress

αὐτοῦ καὶ περιεπάτει. Ἦν δὲ σάββατον
of him and walked. And it was a sabbath

ἐν ἐκείνῃ τῇ ἡμέρᾳ. 10 ἔλεγον οὖν οἱ
on that – day. Said therefore the

Ἰουδαῖοι τῷ τεθεραπευμένῳ· σάββατόν ἐστιν,
Jews to the [one] having been healed : A sabbath it is,

καὶ οὐκ ἔξεστίν σοι ἆραι τὸν κράβατον.
and it is not lawful for thee to take the mattress.

‡ End of ver. 3 and ver. 4 omitted by Nestle; *cf.* RSV footnote.

he answered them, "The man who healed me said to me, 'Take up your pallet, and walk.' "
¹²They asked him, "Who is the man who said to you, 'Take up your pallet, and walk'?"
¹³Now the man who had been healed did not know who it was, for Jesus had withdrawn, as there was a crowd in the place. ¹⁴Afterward, Jesus found him in the temple, and said to him, "See, you are well! Sin no more, that nothing worse befall you." ¹⁵The man went away and told the Jews that it was Jesus who had healed him. ¹⁶And this was why the Jews persecuted Jesus, because he did this on the sabbath. ¹⁷But Jesus answered them, "My Father is working still, and I am working." ¹⁸This was why the Jews sought all the more to kill him, because he not only broke the sabbath but also called God his Father, making himself equal with God.
19 Jesus said to them, "Truly, truly, I say to you, the Son can do nothing of his own

11 ὅς δὲ ἀπεκρίθη αὐτοῖς· ὁ ποιήσας
But who(he) answered them: The [one] making

με ὑγιῆ, ἐκεῖνός μοι εἶπεν· ἆρον τὸν
me whole, that one me told: Take the

κράβατόν σου καὶ περιπάτει. 12 ἠρώτησαν
mattress of thee and walk.   They asked

αὐτόν· τίς ἐστιν ὁ ἄνθρωπος ὁ εἰπών
him: Who is the man - telling

σοι· ἆρον καὶ περιπάτει; 13 ὁ δὲ ἰαθεὶς
thee: Take and walk?   But the [one] cured

οὐκ ᾔδει τίς ἐστιν· ὁ γὰρ Ἰησοῦς
did not know who it is(was); - for Jesus

ἐξένευσεν ὄχλου ὄντος ἐν τῷ τόπῳ.
withdrew a crowd being* in the place.
                    =as there was a crowd

14 μετὰ ταῦτα εὑρίσκει αὐτὸν ὁ Ἰησοῦς
After these things finds him - Jesus

ἐν τῷ ἱερῷ καὶ εἶπεν αὐτῷ· ἴδε ὑγιὴς
in the temple and said to him: Behold[,] whole

γέγονας· μηκέτι ἁμάρτανε, ἵνα μὴ χεῖρόν
thou hast become; no longer sin, lest ²worse

σοί τι γένηται. 15 ἀπῆλθεν ὁ ἄνθρωπος
⁴to thee ¹something ³happens. Went away the man

καὶ εἶπεν τοῖς Ἰουδαίοις ὅτι Ἰησοῦς
and told the Jews that Jesus

ἐστιν ὁ ποιήσας αὐτὸν ὑγιῆ. 16 καὶ διὰ
it is(was) the [one] having made him whole. And there-

τοῦτο ἐδίωκον οἱ Ἰουδαῖοι τὸν Ἰησοῦν,
fore ³persecuted ¹the ²Jews - ⁴Jesus,

ὅτι ταῦτα ἐποίει ἐν σαββάτῳ. 17 ὁ δὲ
because these things he did on a sabbath. But he

ἀπεκρίνατο αὐτοῖς· ὁ πατήρ μου ἕως
answered them: The Father of me until

ἄρτι ἐργάζεται, κἀγὼ ἐργάζομαι· 18 διὰ
now works, and I work; because of

τοῦτο οὖν μᾶλλον ἐζήτουν αὐτὸν οἱ
this therefore ⁴the more ³sought ⁶him ¹the

Ἰουδαῖοι ἀποκτεῖναι, ὅτι οὐ μόνον ἔλυεν
²Jews ⁵to kill, because not only he broke

τὸ σάββατον, ἀλλὰ καὶ πατέρα ἴδιον
the sabbath, but also Father [his] own

ἔλεγεν τὸν θεόν, ἴσον ἑαυτὸν ποιῶν τῷ
said - God [to be], equal himself making -

θεῷ. 19 Ἀπεκρίνατο οὖν ὁ Ἰησοῦς καὶ
to God. Answered therefore - Jesus and

ἔλεγεν αὐτοῖς· ἀμὴν ἀμὴν λέγω ὑμῖν,
said to them: Truly truly I say to you,

οὐ δύναται ὁ υἱὸς ποιεῖν ἀφ' ἑαυτοῦ
cannot the Son to do from himself

accord, but only what he sees the Father doing; for whatever he does, that the Son does likewise. ²⁰ For the Father loves the Son, and shows him all that he himself is doing; and greater works than these will he show him, that you may marvel. ²¹ For as the Father raises the dead and gives them life, so also the Son gives life to whom he will. ²² The Father judges no one, but has given all judgment to the Son, ²³ that all may honor the Son, even as they honor the Father. He who does not honor the Son does not honor the Father who sent him. ²⁴ Truly, truly, I say to you, he who hears my word and believes him who sent me has eternal life; he does not come into judgment, but has passed from death to life.

25 "Truly, truly, I say to you, the hour is coming, and now is, when the dead will hear the voice of the Son of God, and those who hear will live. ²⁶ For as the Father has life in himself, so he has granted the Son also to have life in himself,

οὐδέν,	ἂν	μή	τι	βλέπῃ	τὸν	πατέρα
no(any)thing,	except		what	he sees	the	Father

ποιοῦντα·	ἃ	γὰρ	ἂν	ἐκεῖνος	ποιῇ,	ταῦτα
doing;	for whatever things			that one	does,	these

καὶ	ὁ	υἱὸς	ὁμοίως	ποιεῖ.	20 ὁ	γὰρ
also	the	Son	likewise	does.		For the

πατὴρ	φιλεῖ	τὸν	υἱὸν	καὶ	πάντα	δείκνυσιν
Father	loves	the	Son	and	all things	shows

αὐτῷ	ἃ	αὐτὸς	ποιεῖ,	καὶ	μείζονα	τούτων
him	which	he	does,	and	¹greater	³[than] ⁴these

δείξει	αὐτῷ	ἔργα,	ἵνα	ὑμεῖς	θαυμάζητε.
⁵he will show	⁶him	²works,	that	ye	may marvel.

21 ὥσπερ	γὰρ	ὁ	πατὴρ	ἐγείρει	τοὺς
For as		the	Father	raises	the

νεκροὺς	καὶ	ζωοποιεῖ,	οὕτως	καὶ	ὁ	υἱὸς
dead	and	quickens,	so	also	the	Son

οὓς	θέλει	ζωοποιεῖ.	22 οὐδὲ	γὰρ	ὁ
whom	he wills	quickens.		For not	the

πατὴρ	κρίνει	οὐδένα,	ἀλλὰ	τὴν	κρίσιν
Father	judges	no(any) one,	but	-	judgment

πᾶσαν	δέδωκεν	τῷ	υἱῷ,	23 ἵνα	πάντες
all	he has given	to the	Son,	that	all men

τιμῶσι	τὸν	υἱὸν	καθὼς	τιμῶσι	τὸν	πατέρα.
may honour	the	Son	as	they honour	the	Father.

ὁ	μὴ	τιμῶν	τὸν	υἱὸν	οὐ	τιμᾷ	τὸν	πατέρα
The [one]	not	honouring	the	Son	honours not		the	Father

τὸν	πέμψαντα	αὐτόν.	24 Ἀμὴν	ἀμὴν
-	having sent	him.	Truly	truly

λέγω	ὑμῖν	ὅτι	ὁ	τὸν	λόγον	μου	ἀκούων
I say	to you[,]	-	The [one]	the	word	of me	hearing

καὶ	πιστεύων	τῷ	πέμψαντί	με	ἔχει
and	believing	the [one]	having sent	me	has

ζωὴν	αἰώνιον,	καὶ	εἰς	κρίσιν	οὐκ	ἔρχεται
life	eternal,	and	into	judgment		comes not

ἀλλὰ	μεταβέβηκεν	ἐκ	τοῦ	θανάτου	εἰς
but	has passed over	out of	-	death	into

τὴν	ζωήν.	25 ἀμὴν	ἀμὴν	λέγω	ὑμῖν	ὅτι
-	life.	Truly	truly	I say	to you[,]	-

ἔρχεται	ὥρα	καὶ	νῦν	ἐστιν	ὅτε	οἱ	νεκροὶ
Comes	an hour	and	now	is	when	the	dead

ἀκούσουσιν	τῆς	φωνῆς	τοῦ	υἱοῦ	τοῦ
will hear	the	voice	of the	Son	-

θεοῦ	καὶ	οἱ	ἀκούσαντες	ζήσουσιν.	26 ὥσπερ
of God	and	the [ones] hearing		will live.	as

γὰρ	ὁ	πατὴρ	ἔχει	ζωὴν	ἐν	ἑαυτῷ,	οὕτως
For the		Father	has	life	in	himself,	so

καὶ	τῷ	υἱῷ	ἔδωκεν	ζωὴν	ἔχειν	ἐν	ἑαυτῷ.
also	to the Son		he gave	life	to have	in	himself.

27and has given him authority to execute judgment, because he is the Son of man. 28 Do not marvel at this; for the hour is coming when all who are in the tombs will hear his voice 29and come forth, those who have done good, to the resurrection of life, and those who have done evil, to the resurrection of judgment. 30 "I can do nothing on my own authority; as I hear, I judge; and my judgment is just, because I seek not my own will but the will of him who sent me. 31If I bear witness to myself, my testimony is not true; 32there is another who bears witness to me, and I know that the testimony which he bears to me is true. 33You sent to John, and he has borne witness to the truth. 34Not that the testimony which I receive is from man; but I say this that you may be saved. 35He was a burning and shining lamp, and you were willing to rejoice for a while in his

27 καὶ ἐξουσίαν ἔδωκεν αὐτῷ κρίσιν ποιεῖν,
And authority he gave him judgment to do,
ὅτι υἱὸς ἀνθρώπου ἐστίν. 28 μὴ θαυμάζετε
because son of man* he is. Marvel not [at]
τοῦτο, ὅτι ἔρχεται ὥρα ἐν ᾗ πάντες οἱ
this, because comes an hour in which all the [ones]
ἐν τοῖς μνημείοις ἀκούσουσιν τῆς φωνῆς
in the tombs will hear the voice
αὐτοῦ 29 καὶ ἐκπορεύσονται οἱ τὰ ἀγαθὰ
of him and will come forth the [ones] the good things
ποιήσαντες εἰς ἀνάστασιν ζωῆς, οἱ τὰ
having done to a resurrection of life, the [ones] the
φαῦλα πράξαντες εἰς ἀνάστασιν κρίσεως.
evil things having done to a resurrection of judgment.
30 Οὐ δύναμαι ἐγὼ ποιεῖν ἀπ᾽ ἐμαυτοῦ
Cannot I to do from myself
οὐδέν· καθὼς ἀκούω κρίνω, καὶ ἡ κρίσις
no(any)thing; as I hear I judge, and - judgment
ἡ ἐμὴ δικαία ἐστίν, ὅτι οὐ ζητῶ τὸ
- my just is, because I seek not -
θέλημα τὸ ἐμὸν ἀλλὰ τὸ θέλημα τοῦ
will - my but the will of the [one]
πέμψαντός με. 31 Ἐὰν ἐγὼ μαρτυρῶ
having sent me. If I witness
περὶ ἐμαυτοῦ, ἡ μαρτυρία μου οὐκ ἔστιν
concerning myself, the witness of me is not
ἀληθής· 32 ἄλλος ἐστὶν ὁ μαρτυρῶν περὶ
true; another there is the [one] witnessing concerning
ἐμοῦ, καὶ οἶδα ὅτι ἀληθής ἐστιν ἡ
me, and I know that true is the
μαρτυρία ἣν μαρτυρεῖ περὶ ἐμοῦ. 33 ὑμεῖς
witness which he witnesses concerning me. Ye
ἀπεστάλκατε πρὸς Ἰωάννην, καὶ μεμαρ-
have sent to John, and he has
τύρηκεν τῇ ἀληθείᾳ· 34 ἐγὼ δὲ οὐ παρὰ
witnessed to the truth; but I not from
ἀνθρώπου τὴν μαρτυρίαν λαμβάνω, ἀλλὰ
man the witness receive, but
ταῦτα λέγω ἵνα ὑμεῖς σωθῆτε. 35 ἐκεῖνος
these things I say that ye may be saved. That man
ἦν ὁ λύχνος ὁ καιόμενος καὶ φαίνων,
was the lamp - burning and shining,
ὑμεῖς δὲ ἠθελήσατε ἀγαλλιαθῆναι πρὸς
and ye were willing to exult for
ὥραν ἐν τῷ φωτὶ αὐτοῦ. 36 Ἐγὼ δὲ
an hour in the light of him. But I

* Note the absence of the definite article here. See also Rev. 1. 13 and 14. 14.

light. ³⁶But the testimony which I have is greater than that of John; for the works which the Father has granted me to accomplish, these very works which I am doing, bear me witness that the Father has sent me. ³⁷And the Father who sent me has himself borne witness to me. His voice you have never heard, his form you have never seen; ³⁸and you do not have his word abiding in you, for you do not believe him whom he has sent. ³⁹You search the scriptures, because you think that in them you have eternal life; and it is they that bear witness to me; ⁴⁰yet you refuse to come to me that you may have life. ⁴¹I do not receive glory from men. ⁴²But I know that you have not the love of God within you. ⁴³I have come in my Father's name, and you do not receive me; if another comes in his own name, him you will receive. ⁴⁴How can you believe, who receive glory from one another and do not seek the glory that comes from the only God? ⁴⁵Do not think that I shall accuse you

ἔχω τὴν μαρτυρίαν μείζω τοῦ Ἰωάννου·
have the witness greater [than] – of John;

τὰ γὰρ ἔργα ἃ δέδωκέν μοι ὁ πατὴρ ἵνα
for the works which has given me the Father that

τελειώσω αὐτά, αὐτὰ τὰ ἔργα ἃ ποιῶ,
I may finish them, ³[them]selves ¹the ²works which I do,

μαρτυρεῖ περὶ ἐμοῦ ὅτι ὁ πατήρ με
witnesses concerning me that the Father me

ἀπέσταλκεν. 37 καὶ ὁ πέμψας με πατήρ,
has sent. And ¹the ³having sent ⁴me ²Father,

ἐκεῖνος μεμαρτύρηκεν περὶ ἐμοῦ. οὔτε
that [one] has witnessed concerning me. Neither

φωνὴν αὐτοῦ πώποτε ἀκηκόατε οὔτε εἶδος
voice of him never ye have heard nor form

αὐτοῦ ἑωράκατε, 38 καὶ τὸν λόγον αὐτοῦ
of him ye have seen, and the word of him

οὐκ ἔχετε ἐν ὑμῖν μένοντα, ὅτι ὃν
ye have not in you remaining, because [he] whom

ἀπέστειλεν ἐκεῖνος, τούτῳ ὑμεῖς οὐ πιστεύετε.
²sent ¹that [one], this [one] ye do not believe.

39 ἐρευνᾶτε τὰς γραφάς, ὅτι ὑμεῖς δοκεῖτε
Ye search the scriptures, because ye think

ἐν αὐταῖς ζωὴν αἰώνιον ἔχειν· καὶ ἐκεῖναί
in them life eternal to have; and those

εἰσιν αἱ μαρτυροῦσαι περὶ ἐμοῦ· 40 καὶ
are the [ones] witnessing concerning me; and

οὐ θέλετε ἐλθεῖν πρός με ἵνα ζωὴν
ye wish not to come to me that life

ἔχητε. 41 Δόξαν παρὰ ἀνθρώπων οὐ
ye may have. Glory from men not

λαμβάνω, 42 ἀλλὰ ἔγνωκα ὑμᾶς ὅτι τὴν
I receive, but I have known you that the

ἀγάπην τοῦ θεοῦ οὐκ ἔχετε ἐν ἑαυτοῖς.
love – of God ye have not in yourselves.

43 ἐγὼ ἐλήλυθα ἐν τῷ ὀνόματι τοῦ πατρός
I have come in the name of the Father

μου, καὶ οὐ λαμβάνετέ με· ἐὰν ἄλλος
of me, and ye receive not me; if another

ἔλθῃ ἐν τῷ ὀνόματι τῷ ἰδίῳ, ἐκεῖνον
comes in – name the(his) own, that [one]

λήμψεσθε. 44 πῶς δύνασθε ὑμεῖς πιστεῦσαι,
ye will receive. How can ye to believe,

δόξαν παρὰ ἀλλήλων λαμβάνοντες, καὶ
glory from one another receiving, and

τὴν δόξαν τὴν παρὰ τοῦ μόνου θεοῦ
the glory – from the only God

οὐ ζητεῖτε; 45 μὴ δοκεῖτε ὅτι ἐγὼ κατηγορήσω
ye seek not? Do not think that I will accuse

to the Father; it is Moses who accuses you, on whom you set your hope. ⁴⁶If you believed Moses, you would believe me, for he wrote of me. ⁴⁷But if you do not believe his writings, how will you believe my words?"

ὑμῶν πρὸς τὸν πατέρα· ἐστιν ὁ κατηγορῶν
you   to   the   Father;   there is   the [one] accusing

ὑμῶν Μωϋσῆς, εἰς ὃν ὑμεῖς ἠλπίκατε.   46 εἰ
you[,]   Moses,   in   whom ye   have hoped.   if

γὰρ ἐπιστεύετε Μωϋσεῖ, ἐπιστεύετε ἂν
For   ye believed   Moses,   ye would have believed

ἐμοί· περὶ γὰρ ἐμοῦ ἐκεῖνος ἔγραψεν.
me;   for concerning   me   that [one]   wrote.

47 εἰ δὲ τοῖς ἐκείνου γράμμασιν οὐ
But ¹if   ⁴the   ⁵of that [one]   ⁵letters   ³not

πιστεύετε, πῶς τοῖς ἐμοῖς ῥήμασιν
²ye believe,   how   –   my   words

πιστεύσετε;
will ye believe?

CHAPTER 6

AFTER this Jesus went to the other side of the Sea of Galilee, which is the Sea of Tibe′ri-as. ²And a multitude followed him, because they saw the signs which he did on those who were diseased. ³Jesus went up into the hills, and there sat down with his disciples. ⁴Now the Passover, the feast of the Jews, was at hand. ⁵Lifting up his eyes, then, and seeing that a multitude was coming to him, Jesus said to Philip, "How are we to buy bread, so that these people may eat?" ⁶This he said to test him, for he himself knew what he would do. ⁷Philip answered him, "Two hundred denarii would not buy enough bread for each of them to get a

6 Μετὰ ταῦτα ἀπῆλθεν ὁ Ἰησοῦς πέραν
After these things went away   –   Jesus   across

τῆς θαλάσσης τῆς Γαλιλαίας τῆς Τιβεριάδος.
the   sea   –   of Galilee[,]   –   of Tiberias.

2 ἠκολούθει δὲ αὐτῷ ὄχλος πολύς, ὅτι
And followed   him   crowd   a much, because

ἑώρων τὰ σημεῖα ἃ ἐποίει ἐπὶ τῶν
they saw   the   signs   which   he did   on   the

ἀσθενούντων. 3 ἀνῆλθεν δὲ εἰς τὸ ὄρος
ailing [ones].   And went up   to   the mountain

Ἰησοῦς, καὶ ἐκεῖ ἐκάθητο μετὰ τῶν
Jesus,   and   there   sat   with   the

μαθητῶν αὐτοῦ. 4 ἦν δὲ ἐγγὺς τὸ πάσχα,
disciples   of him.   And was   near   the Passover,

ἡ ἑορτὴ τῶν Ἰουδαίων. 5 ἐπάρας οὖν
the   feast   of the   Jews.   Lifting up therefore

τοὺς ὀφθαλμοὺς ὁ Ἰησοῦς καὶ θεασάμενος
the(his)   eyes   –   Jesus   and   beholding

ὅτι πολὺς ὄχλος ἔρχεται πρὸς αὐτόν,
that   a much   crowd   is(was) coming   toward   him,

λέγει πρὸς Φίλιππον· πόθεν ἀγοράσωμεν
he says   to   Philip :   Whence   may we buy

ἄρτους ἵνα φάγωσιν οὗτοι; 6 τοῦτο δὲ
loaves   that   may eat   these?   And this

ἔλεγεν πειράζων αὐτόν· αὐτὸς γὰρ ᾔδει
he said   testing   him;   for he   knew

τί ἔμελλεν ποιεῖν. 7 ἀπεκρίθη αὐτῷ ὁ
what he was about   to do.   Answered   him   –

Φίλιππος· διακοσίων δηναρίων ἄρτοι οὐκ
Philip :   ²Of two hundred   ³denarii   ¹loaves   not

ἀρκοῦσιν αὐτοῖς, ἵνα ἕκαστος βραχύ τι
are enough   for them,   that   each   a little

little." ⁸One of his disciples, Andrew, Simon Peter's brother, said to him, ⁹"There is a lad here who has five barley loaves and two fish; but what are they among so many?" ¹⁰Jesus said, "Make the people sit down." Now there was much grass in the place; so the men sat down, in number about five thousand. ¹¹Jesus then took the loaves, and when he had given thanks, he distributed them to those who were seated; so also the fish, as much as they wanted. ¹²And when they had eaten their fill, he told his disciples, "Gather up the fragments left over, that nothing may be lost." ¹³So they gathered them up and filled twelve baskets with fragments from the five barley loaves, left by those who had eaten. ¹⁴When the people saw the sign which he had done, they said, "This is indeed the prophet who is to come into the world!" 15 Perceiving then that they were about to come and take him by force to make him king, Jesus

λάβῃ.	8 λέγει	αὐτῷ	εἷς	ἐκ τῶν	μαθητῶν
may take.	Says	to him	one	of the	disciples

αὐτοῦ,	'Ανδρέας	ὁ	ἀδελφὸς	Σίμωνος
of him,	Andrew	the	brother	of Simon

Πέτρου·	9 ἔστιν	παιδάριον	ὧδε	ὃς	ἔχει
Peter :	There is	a lad	here	who	has

πέντε	ἄρτους	κριθίνους	καὶ	δύο	ὀψάρια·
five	loaves	barley	and	two	fishes;

ἀλλὰ	ταῦτα	τί	ἐστιν	εἰς	τοσούτους;
but	³these	¹what	²is(are)	among	so many?

10 εἶπεν	ὁ	'Ιησοῦς·	ποιήσατε	τοὺς	ἀνθρώπους
Said	-	Jesus :	Make	the	men*

ἀναπεσεῖν.	ἦν	δὲ	χόρτος	πολὺς	ἐν	τῷ
to recline.	Now there was	grass	much	in	the

τόπῳ.	ἀνέπεσαν	οὖν	οἱ	ἄνδρες	τὸν	ἀριθμὸν
place.	Reclined	therefore	the	men	the	number

ὡς	πεντακισχίλιοι.	11 ἔλαβεν	οὖν	τοὺς
about	five thousand.	Took	therefore	the

ἄρτους	ὁ	'Ιησοῦς	καὶ	εὐχαριστήσας
loaves	-	Jesus	and	having given thanks

διέδωκεν	τοῖς	ἀνακειμένοις,	ὁμοίως	καὶ
distributed	to the [ones]	lying down,	likewise	also

ἐκ	τῶν	ὀψαρίων	ὅσον	ἤθελον.	12 ὡς	δὲ
of	the	fishes	as much as	they wished.	Now when

ἐνεπλήσθησαν,	λέγει	τοῖς	μαθηταῖς	αὐτοῦ·
they were filled,	he tells	the	disciples	of him:

συναγάγετε	τὰ	περισσεύσαντα	κλάσματα,	ἵνα
Gather ye	the	left over	fragments,	that

μή	τι	ἀπόληται.	13 συνήγαγον	οὖν,	καὶ
not anything	is lost.	They gathered therefore,	and

ἐγέμισαν	δώδεκα	κοφίνους	κλασμάτων	ἐκ
filled	twelve	baskets	of fragments	of

τῶν	πέντε	ἄρτων	τῶν	κριθίνων	ἃ	ἐπερίσσευσαν
the	five	loaves	-	barley	which	were left over

τοῖς	βεβρωκόσιν.	14 Οἱ	οὖν	ἄνθρωποι
to the [ones] having eaten.	Therefore the	men*

ἰδόντες	ὃ	ἐποίησεν	σημεῖον	ἔλεγον	ὅτι
seeing	¹what	³he did	²sign	said[,]	-

οὗτός	ἐστιν	ἀληθῶς	ὁ	προφήτης	ὁ
This	is	truly	the	prophet	-

ἐρχόμενος	εἰς	τὸν	κόσμον.	15 'Ιησοῦς
coming	into	the	world.	Jesus

οὖν	γνοὺς	ὅτι	μέλλουσιν	ἔρχεσθαι	καὶ
therefore	knowing that	they are(were) about	to come	and

ἁρπάζειν	αὐτὸν	ἵνα	ποιήσωσιν	βασιλέα,
seize	him	that	they might make	a king,

* That is, people. Compare ἄνδρες in ver. 10.

withdrew again to the
hills by himself.
16 When evening
came, his disciples went
down to the sea, [17] got
into a boat, and started
across the sea to
Caper'na-um. It was now
dark, and Jesus had not
yet come to them. [18] The
sea rose because a strong
wind was blowing.
[19] When they had rowed
about three or four miles,
they saw Jesus walking
on the sea and drawing
near to the boat. They
were frightened, [20] but he
said to them, "It is I; do
not be afraid." [21] Then
they were glad to take
him into the boat, and
immediately the boat was
at the land to which they
were going.
22 On the next day
the people who re-
mained on the other side
of the sea saw that there
had been only one boat
there, and that Jesus
had not entered the boat
with his disciples, but
that his disciples had
gone away alone. [23] However, boats from
Tibe'ri-as came near the
place where they ate the
bread after the Lord had

ἀνεχώρησεν	πάλιν	εἰς	τὸ	ὄρος	αὐτὸς
departed	again	to	the	mountain	[him]self

μόνος. **16** Ὡς δὲ ὀψία ἐγένετο, κατέβησαν
alone.   And when evening came,   went down

οἱ μαθηταὶ αὐτοῦ ἐπὶ τὴν θάλασσαν,
the disciples of him to the sea,

17 καὶ ἐμβάντες εἰς πλοῖον ἤρχοντο πέραν
and embarking in a boat came across

τῆς θαλάσσης εἰς Καφαρναούμ. καὶ
the sea to Capernaum. And

σκοτία ἤδη ἐγεγόνει καὶ οὔπω ἐληλύθει
darkness now had come and not yet had come

πρὸς αὐτοὺς ὁ Ἰησοῦς, **18** ἥ τε θάλασσα
to them – Jesus, and the sea

ἀνέμου μεγάλου πνέοντος διηγείρετο.
wind a great blowing[a] was roused.
=as a great wind blew

19 ἐληλακότες οὖν ὡς σταδίους εἴκοσι
Having rowed therefore about furlongs twenty-

πέντε ἢ τριάκοντα θεωροῦσιν τὸν Ἰησοῦν
five or thirty they behold – Jesus

περιπατοῦντα ἐπὶ τῆς θαλάσσης καὶ ἐγγὺς
walking on the sea and near

τοῦ πλοίου γινόμενον, καὶ ἐφοβήθησαν.
the boat becoming, and they feared.

20 ὁ δὲ λέγει αὐτοῖς· ἐγώ εἰμι· μὴ
But he says to them : I am; not

φοβεῖσθε. **21** ἤθελον οὖν λαβεῖν αὐτὸν εἰς
fear ye. They wished therefore to take him into

τὸ πλοῖον, καὶ εὐθέως ἐγένετο τὸ πλοῖον
the boat, and immediately was the boat

ἐπὶ τῆς γῆς εἰς ἣν ὑπῆγον.
at the land to which they were going.

22 Τῇ ἐπαύριον ὁ ὄχλος ὁ ἑστηκὼς
On the morrow the crowd – standing

πέραν τῆς θαλάσσης εἶδον ὅτι πλοιάριον
across the sea saw that boat

ἄλλο οὐκ ἦν ἐκεῖ εἰ μὴ ἕν, καὶ ὅτι
other was not there except one, and that

οὐ συνεισῆλθεν τοῖς μαθηταῖς αὐτοῦ ὁ
[2]did not come in with [3]the [4]disciples [5]of him –

Ἰησοῦς εἰς τὸ πλοῖον ἀλλὰ μόνοι οἱ
[1]Jesus in the boat but alone the

μαθηταὶ αὐτοῦ ἀπῆλθον· **23** ἄλλα ἦλθεν
disciples of him went away; [1]other [2]came

πλοιάρια ἐκ Τιβεριάδος ἐγγὺς τοῦ τόπου
[2]boats from Tiberias near the place

ὅπου ἔφαγον τὸν ἄρτον εὐχαριστήσαντος
where they ate the bread having given thanks

given thanks. [24]So when the people saw that Jesus was not there, nor his disciples, they themselves got into the boats and went to Caper′naum, seeking Jesus.

25 When they found him on the other side of the sea, they said to him, "Rabbi, when did you come here?" [26]Jesus answered them, "Truly, truly, I say to you, you seek me, not because you saw signs, but because you ate your fill of the loaves. [27]Do not labor for the food which perishes, but for the food which endures to eternal life, which the Son of man will give to you; for on him has God the Father set his seal." [28]Then they said to him, "What must we do, to be doing the works of God?" [29]Jesus answered them, "This is the work of God, that you believe in him whom he has sent." [30]So they said to him, "Then what sign do you do, that we may see, and believe you? What work do you perform? [31]Our fathers ate the manna in the wilderness; as it is written, 'He gave them

τοῦ κυρίου. 24 ὅτε οὖν εἶδεν ὁ ὄχλος
the Lord.[a] When therefore saw the crowd
=when the Lord had given thanks.

ὅτι Ἰησοῦς οὐκ ἔστιν ἐκεῖ οὐδὲ οἱ
that Jesus is(was) not there nor the

μαθηταὶ αὐτοῦ, ἐνέβησαν αὐτοὶ εἰς τὰ
disciples of him, embarked they in the

πλοιάρια καὶ ἦλθον εἰς Καφαρναοὺμ
boats and came to Capernaum

ζητοῦντες τὸν Ἰησοῦν. 25 καὶ εὑρόντες
seeking the Jesus. And finding

αὐτὸν πέραν τῆς θαλάσσης εἶπον αὐτῷ·
him across the sea they said to him:

ῥαββί, πότε ὧδε γέγονας; 26 ἀπεκρίθη
Rabbi, when here hast thou come? Answered

αὐτοῖς ὁ Ἰησοῦς καὶ εἶπεν· ἀμὴν ἀμὴν
them - Jesus and said: Truly truly

λέγω ὑμῖν, ζητεῖτέ με οὐχ ὅτι εἴδετε
I say to you, ye seek me not because ye saw

σημεῖα, ἀλλ᾽ ὅτι ἐφάγετε ἐκ τῶν ἄρτων
signs, but because ye ate of the loaves

καὶ ἐχορτάσθητε. 27 ἐργάζεσθε μὴ τὴν
and were satisfied. Work not [for] the

βρῶσιν τὴν ἀπολλυμένην, ἀλλὰ τὴν βρῶσιν
food perishing, but [for] the food

τὴν μένουσαν εἰς ζωὴν αἰώνιον, ἣν ὁ
- remaining to life eternal, which the

υἱὸς τοῦ ἀνθρώπου ὑμῖν δώσει· τοῦτον γὰρ
Son - of man you will give; for this [one]

ὁ πατὴρ ἐσφράγισεν ὁ θεός. 28 εἶπον
[2]the [3]Father [4]sealed - [1]God. They said

οὖν πρὸς αὐτόν· τί ποιῶμεν ἵνα ἐργαζ-
therefore to him: What may we do that we may

ώμεθα τὰ ἔργα τοῦ θεοῦ; 29 ἀπεκρίθη
work the works - of God? Answered

Ἰησοῦς καὶ εἶπεν αὐτοῖς· τοῦτό ἐστιν τὸ
Jesus and said to them: This is the

ἔργον τοῦ θεοῦ, ἵνα πιστεύητε εἰς ὃν
work - of God, that ye believe in [him] whom

ἀπέστειλεν ἐκεῖνος. 30 εἶπον οὖν αὐτῷ·
sent that [one]. They said therefore to him:

τί οὖν ποιεῖς σὺ σημεῖον, ἵνα ἴδωμεν
[1]What [2]then [3]doest [4]thou [2]sign, that we may see

καὶ πιστεύσωμέν σοι; τί ἐργάζῃ; 31 οἱ
and believe thee? what workest thou? The

πατέρες ἡμῶν τὸ μάννα ἔφαγον ἐν τῇ
fathers of us the manna ate in the

ἐρήμῳ, καθώς ἐστιν γεγραμμένον· ἄρτον
desert, as it is *having been* written: Bread

bread from heaven to eat.' " ³²Jesus then said to them, "Truly, truly, I say to you, it was not Moses who gave you the bread from heaven; my Father gives you the true bread from heaven. ³³For the bread of God is that which comes down from heaven, and gives life to the world." ³⁴They said to him, "Lord, give us this bread always."

35 Jesus said to them, "I am the bread of life; he who comes to me shall not hunger, and he who believes in me shall never thirst. ³⁶But I said to you that you have seen me and yet do not believe. ³⁷All that the Father gives me will come to me; and him who comes to me I will not cast out. ³⁸For I have come down from heaven, not to do my own will, but the will of him who sent me; ³⁹and this is the will of him who sent me, that I should lose nothing of all that he has given me, but raise it up at the last day.

ἐκ τοῦ οὐρανοῦ ἔδωκεν αὐτοῖς φαγεῖν.
out of – heaven he gave them to eat.

32 Εἶπεν οὖν αὐτοῖς ὁ Ἰησοῦς· ἀμὴν
Said therefore to them – Jesus : Truly

ἀμὴν λέγω ὑμῖν, οὐ Μωϋσῆς δέδωκεν
truly I say to you, not Moses has given

ὑμῖν τὸν ἄρτον ἐκ τοῦ οὐρανοῦ, ἀλλ' ὁ
you the bread out of – heaven, but the

πατήρ μου δίδωσιν ὑμῖν τὸν ἄρτον ἐκ
Father of me gives you ¹the ³bread ⁴out of

τοῦ οὐρανοῦ τὸν ἀληθινόν· 33 ὁ γὰρ ἄρτος
– ⁵heaven the ²true; for the bread

τοῦ θεοῦ ἐστιν ὁ καταβαίνων ἐκ τοῦ
– of God is the [one] coming down out of –

οὐρανοῦ καὶ ζωὴν διδοὺς τῷ κόσμῳ.
heaven and life giving to the world.

34 εἶπον οὖν πρὸς αὐτόν· κύριε, πάντοτε
They said therefore to him : Lord, always

δὸς ἡμῖν τὸν ἄρτον τοῦτον. 35 εἶπεν
give us – bread this. Said

αὐτοῖς ὁ Ἰησοῦς· ἐγώ εἰμι ὁ ἄρτος τῆς
to them – Jesus : I am the bread –

ζωῆς· ὁ ἐρχόμενος πρὸς ἐμὲ οὐ μὴ
of life; the [one] coming to me by no means

πεινάσῃ, καὶ ὁ πιστεύων εἰς ἐμὲ οὐ μὴ
hungers, and the [one] believing in me by no means

διψήσει πώποτε. 36 Ἀλλ' εἶπον ὑμῖν ὅτι
will thirst never. But I told you that

καὶ ἑωράκατέ [με] καὶ οὐ πιστεύετε.
both ye have seen me and do not believe.

37 πᾶν ὃ δίδωσίν μοι ὁ πατὴρ πρὸς
All which gives to me the Father to

ἐμὲ ἥξει, καὶ τὸν ἐρχόμενον πρός με
me will come, and the [one] coming to me

οὐ μὴ ἐκβάλω ἔξω, 38 ὅτι καταβέβηκα
by no means I will cast out outside, because I have come down

ἀπὸ τοῦ οὐρανοῦ οὐχ ἵνα ποιῶ τὸ θέλημα
from – heaven not that I may do the ²will

τὸ ἐμὸν ἀλλὰ τὸ θέλημα τοῦ πέμψαντός
– ¹my but the will of the [one] having sent

με. 39 τοῦτο δέ ἐστιν τὸ θέλημα τοῦ
me. And this is the will of the [one]

πέμψαντός με, ἵνα πᾶν ὃ δέδωκέν μοι
having sent me, that all which he has given me

μὴ ἀπολέσω ἐξ αὐτοῦ, ἀλλὰ ἀναστήσω
I shall not lose of it, but shall raise up

αὐτὸ ἐν τῇ ἐσχάτῃ ἡμέρᾳ. 40 τοῦτο
it in the last day. this

⁴⁰For this is the will of my Father, that every one who sees the Son and believes in him should have eternal life; and I will raise him up at the last day."
41 The Jews then murmured at him, because he said, "I am the bread which came down from heaven." ⁴²They said, "Is not this Jesus, the son of Joseph, whose father and mother we know? How does he now say, 'I have come down from heaven'?" ⁴³Jesus answered them, "Do not murmur among yourselves. ⁴⁴No one can come to me unless the Father who sent me draws him; and I will raise him up at the last day. ⁴⁵It is written in the prophets, 'And they shall all be taught by God.' Every one who has heard and learned from the Father comes to me. ⁴⁶Not that any one has seen the Father except him who is from God; he has seen the Father. ⁴⁷Truly, truly, I say to you, he who believes has eternal life. ⁴⁸I am the bread of life. ⁴⁹Your

γάρ ἐστιν τὸ θέλημα τοῦ πατρός μου,
For is the will of the Father of me,

ἵνα πᾶς ὁ θεωρῶν τὸν υἱὸν καὶ πιστεύων
that everyone beholding the Son and believing

εἰς αὐτὸν ἔχῃ ζωὴν αἰώνιον, καὶ ἀναστήσω
in him may have life eternal, and will raise up

αὐτὸν ἐγὼ ἐν τῇ ἐσχάτῃ ἡμέρᾳ. 41 Ἐγόγ-
him I in the last day. Mur-

γυζον οὖν οἱ Ἰουδαῖοι περὶ αὐτοῦ ὅτι
mured therefore the Jews about him because

εἶπεν· ἐγώ εἰμι ὁ ἄρτος ὁ καταβὰς ἐκ
he said : I am the bread – having come down out

τοῦ οὐρανοῦ, 42 καὶ ἔλεγον· οὐχ οὗτός
– of heaven, and they said: Not this man

ἐστιν Ἰησοῦς ὁ υἱὸς Ἰωσήφ, οὗ ἡμεῖς
is Jesus the son of Joseph, of whom we

οἴδαμεν τὸν πατέρα καὶ τὴν μητέρα;
know the father and the mother?

πῶς νῦν λέγει ὅτι ἐκ τοῦ οὐρανοῦ
how now says he[,] – Out of – heaven

καταβέβηκα; 43 ἀπεκρίθη Ἰησοῦς καὶ εἶπεν
I have come down? Answered Jesus and said

αὐτοῖς· μὴ γογγύζετε μετ᾽ ἀλλήλων.
to them: Do not murmur with one another.

44 Οὐδεὶς δύναται ἐλθεῖν πρός με ἐὰν μὴ
No one can to come to me unless

ὁ πατὴρ ὁ πέμψας με ἐλκύσῃ αὐτόν,
the Father the [one] having sent me should draw him,

κἀγὼ ἀναστήσω αὐτὸν ἐν τῇ ἐσχάτῃ
and I will raise up him in the last

ἡμέρᾳ. 45 ἔστιν γεγραμμένον ἐν τοῖς
day. It is having been written in the

προφήταις· καὶ ἔσονται πάντες διδακτοὶ
prophets : And they shall be all taught

θεοῦ· πᾶς ὁ ἀκούσας παρὰ τοῦ πατρὸς
of God; everyone hearing from the Father

καὶ μαθὼν ἔρχεται πρὸς ἐμέ. 46 οὐχ
and learning comes to me. Not

ὅτι τὸν πατέρα ἑώρακέν τις, εἰ μὴ ὁ
that ³the ⁴Father ²has seen ¹anyone, except the [one]

ὢν παρὰ τοῦ θεοῦ, οὗτος ἑώρακεν τὸν
being with – God, this [one] has seen the

πατέρα. 47 ἀμὴν ἀμὴν λέγω ὑμῖν, ὁ
Father. Truly truly I say to you, the

πιστεύων ἔχει ζωὴν αἰώνιον. 48 Ἐγώ
[one] believing has life eternal. I

εἰμι ὁ ἄρτος τῆς ζωῆς. 49 οἱ πατέρες
am the bread – of life. The fathers

fathers ate the manna in the wilderness, and they died. ⁵⁰This is the bread which comes down from heaven, that a man may eat of it and not die. ⁵¹I am the living bread which came down from heaven; if any one eats of this bread, he will live for ever; and the bread which I shall give for the life of the world is my flesh."

52 The Jews then disputed among themselves, saying, "How can this man give us his flesh to eat?" ⁵³So Jesus said to them, "Truly, truly, I say to you, unless you eat the flesh of the Son of man and drink his blood, you have no life in you; ⁵⁴he who eats my flesh and drinks my blood has eternal life, and I will raise him up at the last day. ⁵⁵For my flesh is food indeed, and my blood is drink indeed. ⁵⁶He who eats my flesh and drinks my blood abides in me, and I in him. ⁵⁷As the living Father sent me, and I live because of the Father, so

ὑμῶν ἔφαγον ἐν τῇ ἐρήμῳ τὸ μάννα καὶ
of you ate in the desert the manna and

ἀπέθανον· 50 οὗτός ἐστιν ὁ ἄρτος ὁ ἐκ
died; this is the bread – out of

τοῦ οὐρανοῦ καταβαίνων, ἵνα τις ἐξ
– heaven coming down, that anyone of

αὐτοῦ φάγῃ καὶ μὴ ἀποθάνῃ. 51 ἐγώ
it may eat and may not die. I

εἰμι ὁ ἄρτος ὁ ζῶν ὁ ἐκ τοῦ οὐρανοῦ
am the bread – living the [one] out of – heaven

καταβάς· ἐάν τις φάγῃ ἐκ τούτου τοῦ
having come down; if anyone eats of this –

ἄρτου, ζήσει εἰς τὸν αἰῶνα· καὶ ὁ ἄρτος
bread, he will live to the age; ²indeed ³the ⁴bread

δὲ ὃν ἐγὼ δώσω ἡ σάρξ μού ἐστιν
¹and which I will give the flesh of me is

ὑπὲρ τῆς τοῦ κόσμου ζωῆς. 52 Ἐμάχοντο
for ¹the ³of the ⁴world ²life. Fought

οὖν πρὸς ἀλλήλους οἱ Ἰουδαῖοι λέγοντες·
therefore with one another the Jews saying:

πῶς δύναται οὗτος ἡμῖν δοῦναι τὴν
How can this man us to give the(his)

σάρκα φαγεῖν; 53 εἶπεν οὖν αὐτοῖς ὁ
flesh to eat? Said therefore to them –

Ἰησοῦς· ἀμὴν ἀμὴν λέγω ὑμῖν, ἐὰν μὴ
Jesus: Truly truly I say to you, unless

φάγητε τὴν σάρκα τοῦ υἱοῦ τοῦ ἀνθρώπου
ye eat the flesh of the Son – of man

καὶ πίητε αὐτοῦ τὸ αἷμα, οὐκ ἔχετε
and drink of him the blood, ye have not

ζωὴν ἐν ἑαυτοῖς. 54 ὁ τρώγων μου τὴν
life in yourselves. The [one] eating of me the

σάρκα καὶ πίνων μου τὸ αἷμα ἔχει ζωὴν
flesh and drinking of me the blood has life

αἰώνιον, κἀγὼ ἀναστήσω αὐτὸν τῇ ἐσχάτῃ
eternal, and I will raise up him in the last

ἡμέρα. 55 ἡ γὰρ σάρξ μου ἀληθής
day. For the flesh of me ²true

ἐστιν βρῶσις, καὶ τὸ αἷμά μου ἀληθής
¹is ²food, and the blood of me ²true

ἐστιν πόσις. 56 ὁ τρώγων μου τὴν
¹is ²drink. The [one] eating of me the

σάρκα καὶ πίνων μου τὸ αἷμα ἐν ἐμοὶ
flesh and drinking of me the blood in me

μένει κἀγὼ ἐν αὐτῷ. 57 καθὼς ἀπέστειλέν
remains and I in him. As sent

με ὁ ζῶν πατὴρ κἀγὼ ζῶ διὰ τὸν
me the living Father and I live because of the

he who eats me will live because of me. ⁵⁸ This is the bread which came down from heaven, not such as the fathers ate and died; he who eats this bread will live for ever." ⁵⁹ This he said in the synagogue, as he taught at Caper′na-um. 60 Many of his disciples, when they heard it, said, "This is a hard saying; who can listen to it?" ⁶¹ But Jesus, knowing in himself that his disciples murmured at it, said to them, "Do you take offense at this? ⁶² Then what if you were to see the Son of man ascending where he was before? ⁶³ It is the spirit that gives life, the flesh is of no avail; the words that I have spoken to you are spirit and life. ⁶⁴ But there are some of you that do not believe." For Jesus knew from the first who those were that did not believe, and who it was that should betray him. ⁶⁵ And he said, "This is why I told you that no one can come to me unless it is granted him by the Father."

πατέρα,   καὶ   ὁ   τρώγων   με   κἀκεῖνος
Father,   also   the [one]   eating   me   even that one

ζήσει   δι'   ἐμέ.   58 οὗτός   ἐστιν   ὁ   ἄρτος   ὁ
will live because of me.   This   is   the   bread   -

ἐξ   οὐρανοῦ   καταβάς,   οὐ   καθὼς   ἔφαγον
out of   heaven   having come down,   not   as   ate

οἱ   πατέρες   καὶ   ἀπέθανον·   ὁ   τρώγων
the   fathers   and   died;   the [one]   eating

τοῦτον   τὸν   ἄρτον   ζήσει   εἰς   τὸν   αἰῶνα.
this   -   bread   will live unto   the   age.

59 Ταῦτα   εἶπεν   ἐν   συναγωγῇ   διδάσκων   ἐν
These things   he said   in   a synagogue   teaching   in

Καφαρναούμ.   60 Πολλοὶ   οὖν   ἀκούσαντες
Capernaum.   ²Many   ¹therefore   ⁷hearing

ἐκ   τῶν   μαθητῶν   αὐτοῦ   εἶπαν·   σκληρός
³of   ⁴the   ⁵disciples   ⁶of him   said :   Hard

ἐστιν   ὁ   λόγος   οὗτος·   τίς   δύναται   αὐτοῦ
is   -   word   this;   who   can   it

ἀκούειν;   61 εἰδὼς   δὲ   ὁ   Ἰησοῦς   ἐν   ἑαυτῷ
to hear?   But knowing   -   Jesus   in   himself

ὅτι   γογγύζουσιν   περὶ   τούτου   οἱ   μαθηταὶ
that   ⁴are murmuring   ⁵about   ³this   ¹the   ²disciples

αὐτοῦ,   εἶπεν   αὐτοῖς·   τοῦτο   ὑμᾶς   σκανδαλίζει;
⁶of him,   said   to them :   This   you   offends?

62 ἐὰν   οὖν   θεωρῆτε   τὸν   υἱὸν   τοῦ   ἀνθρώπου
If   then   ye behold   the   Son   -   of man

ἀναβαίνοντα   ὅπου   ἦν   τὸ   πρότερον;   63 τὸ
ascending   where   he was   at first? †   The

πνεῦμά   ἐστιν   τὸ   ζωοποιοῦν,   ἡ   σὰρξ   οὐκ
spirit   is   the [thing]   quickening,   the   flesh   not

ὠφελεῖ   οὐδέν·   τὰ   ῥήματα   ἃ   ἐγὼ   λελάληκα
profits   no(any)thing;   the   words   which   I   have spoken

ὑμῖν   πνεῦμά   ἐστιν   καὶ   ζωή   ἐστιν.   64 ἀλλ'
to you   spirit   is(are)   and   life   is(are).   But

εἰσὶν   ἐξ   ὑμῶν   τινες   οἳ   οὐ   πιστεύουσιν.   ᾔδει
there are of   you   some   who   do not believe.   knew

γὰρ   ἐξ   ἀρχῆς   ὁ   Ἰησοῦς   τίνες   εἰσὶν
For   from [the] beginning   -   Jesus   who are(were)

οἱ   μὴ   πιστεύοντες   καὶ   τίς   ἐστιν   ὁ
the [ones]   not believing   and   who   is(was)   the

παραδώσων   αὐτόν.   65 καὶ   ἔλεγεν·
[one] betraying   him.   And   he said :

διὰ   τοῦτο   εἴρηκα   ὑμῖν   ὅτι   οὐδεὶς   δύναται
Therefore   I have told   you   that   no one   can

ἐλθεῖν   πρός   με   ἐὰν   μὴ   ᾖ   δεδομένον
to come   to   me   unless   it is *having been given*

αὐτῷ   ἐκ   τοῦ   πατρός.
to him   of   the   Father.

388

66 After this many of his disciples drew back and no longer went about with him. ⁶⁷Jesus said to the twelve, "Will you also go away?" ⁶⁸Simon Peter answered him, "Lord, to whom shall we go? You have the words of eternal life; ⁶⁹and we have believed, and have come to know, that you are the Holy One of God." ⁷⁰Jesus answered them, "Did I not choose you, the twelve, and one of you is a devil?" ⁷¹He spoke of Judas the son of Simon Iscariot, for he, one of the twelve, was to betray him.

66 Ἐκ τούτου πολλοὶ τῶν μαθητῶν
From this many of the disciples
αὐτοῦ ἀπῆλθον εἰς τὰ ὀπίσω καὶ οὐκέτι
of him went away back† and no longer
μετ᾽ αὐτοῦ περιεπάτουν. 67 εἶπεν οὖν ὁ
with him walked. Said therefore –
Ἰησοῦς τοῖς δώδεκα· μὴ καὶ ὑμεῖς
Jesus to the twelve : Not also ye
θέλετε ὑπάγειν; 68 ἀπεκρίθη αὐτῷ Σίμων
wish to go? Answered him Simon
Πέτρος· κύριε, πρὸς τίνα ἀπελευσόμεθα;
Peter : Lord, to whom shall we go away?
ῥήματα ζωῆς αἰωνίου ἔχεις· 69 καὶ ἡμεῖς
words of life eternal thou hast; and we
πεπιστεύκαμεν καὶ ἐγνώκαμεν ὅτι σὺ εἶ
have believed and have known that thou art
ὁ ἅγιος τοῦ θεοῦ. 70 ἀπεκρίθη αὐτοῖς ὁ
the holy one – of God. Answered them –
Ἰησοῦς· οὐκ ἐγὼ ὑμᾶς τοὺς δώδεκα
Jesus : ³Not ²I ⁴you ⁵the ⁶twelve
ἐξελεξάμην; καὶ ἐξ ὑμῶν εἷς διάβολός
¹chose? and of you one a devil
ἐστιν. 71 ἔλεγεν δὲ τὸν Ἰούδαν Σίμωνος
is. Now he spoke [of] – Judas [son] of Simon
Ἰσκαριώτου· οὗτος γὰρ ἔμελλεν παραδιδόναι
Iscariot; for this one was about to betray
αὐτόν, εἷς ἐκ τῶν δώδεκα.
him, one of the twelve.

CHAPTER 7

AFTER this Jesus went about in Galilee; he would not go about in Judea, because the Jews*ᵏ* sought to kill him. ²Now the Jews' feast of Tabernacles was at hand. ³So his brothers said to him, "Leave here and go to Judea, that your disciples may see the works you are doing. ⁴For no man works in

7 Καὶ μετὰ ταῦτα περιεπάτει ὁ Ἰησοῦς
And after these things walked – Jesus
ἐν τῇ Γαλιλαίᾳ· οὐ γὰρ ἤθελεν ἐν τῇ
in – Galilee; for he did not wish in –
Ἰουδαίᾳ περιπατεῖν, ὅτι ἐζήτουν αὐτὸν οἱ
Judæa to walk, because ²were seeking ⁵him ¹the
Ἰουδαῖοι ἀποκτεῖναι. 2 ἦν δὲ ἐγγὺς ἡ
²Jews ⁴to kill. Now was near the
ἑορτὴ τῶν Ἰουδαίων ἡ σκηνοπηγία. 3 εἶπον
feast of the Jews the Tabernacles. Said
οὖν πρὸς αὐτὸν οἱ ἀδελφοὶ αὐτοῦ·
therefore to him the brothers of him :
μετάβηθι ἐντεῦθεν καὶ ὕπαγε εἰς τὴν Ἰουδαίαν,
Depart hence and go into – Judæa,
ἵνα καὶ οἱ μαθηταί σου θεωρήσουσιν τὰ
that also the disciples of thee will behold the
ἔργα σου ἃ ποιεῖς· 4 οὐδεὶς γάρ τι ἐν
works of thee which thou doest; for no one anything in

ᵏ Or Judeans

secret if he seeks to be known openly. If you do these things, show yourself to the world." ⁵For even his brothers did not believe in him. ⁶Jesus said to them, "My time has not yet come, but your time is always here. ⁷The world cannot hate you, but it hates me because I testify of it that its works are evil. ⁸Go to the feast yourselves; I am not¹ going up to this feast, for my time has not yet fully come." ⁹So saying, he remained in Galilee.

10 But after his brothers had gone up to the feast, then he also went up, not publicly but in private. ¹¹The Jews were looking for him at the feast, and saying, "Where is he?" ¹²And there was much muttering about him among the people. While some said, "He is a good man," others said, "No, he is leading the people astray." ¹³Yet for fear of the Jews no one spoke openly of him.

¹ Other ancient authorities add yet

I.G.E.—14

κρυπτῷ	ποιεῖ	καὶ	ζητεῖ	αὐτὸς	ἐν	παρρησίᾳ
secret	does	and	seeks	[him]self	in	[the] open

εἶναι.	εἰ	ταῦτα	ποιεῖς,	φανέρωσον	σεαυτὸν
to be.	If	these things	thou doest,	manifest	thyself

τῷ	κόσμῳ.	5 οὐδὲ	γὰρ	οἱ	ἀδελφοὶ
to the	world.	For not		the	brothers

αὐτοῦ	ἐπίστευον	εἰς	αὐτόν.	6 λέγει	οὖν
of him	believed	in	him.	Says	therefore

αὐτοῖς	ὁ	Ἰησοῦς·	ὁ	καιρὸς	ὁ	ἐμὸς
to them	-	Jesus :	The	²time	-	¹my

οὔπω	πάρεστιν,	ὁ	δὲ	καιρὸς	ὁ	ὑμέτερος
not yet	is arrived,	but the		²time	-	¹your

πάντοτέ	ἐστιν	ἕτοιμος.	7 οὐ	δύναται	ὁ
always	is	ready.	Cannot		the

κόσμος	μισεῖν	ὑμᾶς,	ἐμὲ	δὲ	μισεῖ,	ὅτι
world	to hate	you,	but me		it hates,	because

ἐγὼ	μαρτυρῶ	περὶ	αὐτοῦ	ὅτι	τὰ	ἔργα
I	witness	about	it	that	the	works

αὐτοῦ	πονηρά	ἐστιν.	8 ὑμεῖς	ἀνάβητε	εἰς
of it	evil	is(are).	²Ye	¹go ³up	to

τὴν	ἑορτήν·	ἐγὼ	οὐκ	ἀναβαίνω	εἰς	τὴν
the	feast;	I		am not going up	to	-

ἑορτὴν	ταύτην,	ὅτι	ὁ	ἐμὸς	καιρὸς	οὔπω
feast	this,	because the		my	time	not yet

πεπλήρωται.	9 ταῦτα	δὲ	εἰπὼν	αὐτοῖς
has been fulfilled.	And these things		saying	to them

ἔμεινεν	ἐν	τῇ	Γαλιλαίᾳ.	10 Ὡς	δὲ
he remained in		-	Galilee.	But when	

ἀνέβησαν	οἱ	ἀδελφοὶ	αὐτοῦ	εἰς	τὴν	ἑορτήν,
went up	the	brothers	of him	to	the	feast,

τότε	καὶ	αὐτὸς	ἀνέβη,	οὐ	φανερῶς	ἀλλὰ
then	also	he	went up,	not	manifestly	but

ὡς	ἐν	κρυπτῷ.	11 οἱ	οὖν	Ἰουδαῖοι
as	in	secret.	Therefore the		Jews

ἐζήτουν	αὐτὸν	ἐν	τῇ	ἑορτῇ	καὶ	ἔλεγον·
sought	him	at	the	feast	and	said :

ποῦ	ἐστιν	ἐκεῖνος;	12 καὶ	γογγυσμὸς	περὶ
Where	is	that man?	And	²murmuring	⁴about

αὐτοῦ	ἦν	πολὺς	ἐν	τοῖς	ὄχλοις·	οἱ	μὲν
⁵him	¹there was	³much	in	the	crowds;	some	

ἔλεγον	ὅτι	ἀγαθός	ἐστιν·	ἄλλοι	[δὲ]
said[,]	-	A good man	he is;	but others	

ἔλεγον·	οὔ,	ἀλλὰ	πλανᾷ	τὸν	ὄχλον.
said :	No,	but	he deceives	the	crowd.

13 οὐδεὶς	μέντοι	παρρησίᾳ	ἐλάλει	περὶ
No one	however	openly	spoke	about

αὐτοῦ	διὰ	τὸν	φόβον	τῶν	Ἰουδαίων.
him	because of	the	fear	of the	Jews.

14 About the middle of the feast Jesus went up into the temple and taught. ¹⁵The Jews marveled at it, saying, "How is it that this man has learning,^m when he has never studied?" ¹⁶So Jesus answered them, "My teaching is not mine, but his who sent me; ¹⁷if any man's will is to do his will, he shall know whether the teaching is from God or whether I am speaking on my own authority. ¹⁸He who speaks on his own authority seeks his own glory; but he who seeks the glory of him who sent him is true, and in him there is no falsehood. ¹⁹Did not Moses give you the law? Yet none of you keeps the law. Why do you seek to kill me?" ²⁰The people answered, "You have a demon! Who is seeking to kill you?" ²¹Jesus answered them, "I did one deed, and you all marvel at it. ²²Moses gave you circumcision (not that it is from Moses, but from the fathers), and you circumcise a man upon the sabbath. ²³If on the

^m Or *this man knows his letters*

14 Ἤδη δὲ τῆς ἑορτῆς μεσούσης ἀνέβη
But now the feast being in [its] middle⁴ went up
= in the middle of the feast
Ἰησοῦς εἰς τὸ ἱερὸν καὶ ἐδίδασκεν.
Jesus to the temple and taught.
15 ἐθαύμαζον οὖν οἱ Ἰουδαῖοι λέγοντες·
Marvelled therefore the Jews saying :
πῶς οὗτος γράμματα οἶδεν μὴ μεμαθηκώς;
How this man letters knows not having learned?
16 ἀπεκρίθη οὖν αὐτοῖς Ἰησοῦς καὶ εἶπεν·
Answered therefore them Jesus and said :
ἡ ἐμὴ διδαχὴ οὐκ ἔστιν ἐμὴ ἀλλὰ τοῦ
The my teaching is not mine but of the
πέμψαντός με· 17 ἐάν τις θέλῃ τὸ θέλημα
[one] having sent me; if anyone wishes the will
αὐτοῦ ποιεῖν, γνώσεται περὶ τῆς διδαχῆς,
of him to do, he will know concerning the teaching,
πότερον ἐκ τοῦ θεοῦ ἐστιν ἢ ἐγὼ ἀπ'
whether of — God it is or I from
ἐμαυτοῦ λαλῶ. 18 ὁ ἀφ' ἑαυτοῦ λαλῶν
myself speak. The [one] from himself speaking
τὴν δόξαν τὴν ἰδίαν ζητεῖ· ὁ δὲ ζητῶν
his own glory seeks; but the [one] seeking
τὴν δόξαν τοῦ πέμψαντος αὐτόν, οὗτος
the glory of the [one] having sent him, this man
ἀληθής ἐστιν καὶ ἀδικία ἐν αὐτῷ οὐκ
true is and unrighteousness in him not
ἔστιν. 19 οὐ Μωϋσῆς ἔδωκεν ὑμῖν τὸν
is. Not Moses gave you the
νόμον; καὶ οὐδεὶς ἐξ ὑμῶν ποιεῖ τὸν
law? and no one of you does the
νόμον. τί με ζητεῖτε ἀποκτεῖναι;
law. Why me seek ye to kill?
20 ἀπεκρίθη ὁ ὄχλος· δαιμόνιον ἔχεις·
Answered the crowd : A demon thou hast;
τίς σε ζητεῖ ἀποκτεῖναι; 21 ἀπεκρίθη
who thee seeks to kill? Answered
Ἰησοῦς καὶ εἶπεν αὐτοῖς· ἓν ἔργον ἐποίησα
Jesus and said to them : One work I did
καὶ πάντες θαυμάζετε. 22 διὰ τοῦτο
and all ye marvel. Because of this
Μωϋσῆς δέδωκεν ὑμῖν τὴν περιτομήν, —
Moses has given you - circumcision, —
οὐχ ὅτι ἐκ τοῦ Μωϋσέως ἐστὶν ἀλλ' ἐκ
not that of — Moses it is but of
τῶν πατέρων, — καὶ ἐν σαββάτῳ
the fathers, — and on a sabbath
περιτέμνετε ἄνθρωπον. 23 εἰ περιτομὴν
ye circumcise a man. If ⁸circumcision

sabbath a man receives circumcision, so that the law of Moses may not be broken, are you angry with me because on the sabbath I made a man's whole body well? ²⁴Do not judge by appearances, but judge with right judgment."

25 Some of the people of Jerusalem therefore said, "Is not this the man whom they seek to kill? ²⁶And here he is, speaking openly, and they say nothing to him! Can it be that the authorities really know that this is the Christ? ²⁷Yet we know where this man comes from; and when the Christ appears, no one will know where he comes from." ²⁸So Jesus proclaimed, as he taught in the temple, "You know me, and you know where I come from? But I have not come of my own accord; he who sent me is true, and him you do not know. ²⁹I know him, for I come from him, and he sent me." ³⁰So they sought to arrest him; but no one laid hands on him, because his hour had not yet come. ³¹Yet many of the people believed in him; they said, "When

λαμβάνει [ὁ] ἄνθρωπος ἐν σαββάτῳ ἵνα
²receives   –   ¹a man   on   a sabbath   that

μὴ λυθῇ ὁ νόμος Μωϋσέως, ἐμοὶ χολᾶτε
is not broken the   law   of Moses,   with me are ye angry

ὅτι ὅλον ἄνθρωπον ὑγιῆ ἐποίησα ἐν
because a whole   man   healthy   I made   on

σαββάτῳ; 24 μὴ κρίνετε κατ' ὄψιν, ἀλλὰ
a sabbath?   Judge not   according to face,   but

τὴν δικαίαν κρίσιν κρίνατε. 25 Ἔλεγον
–   righteous   judgment   judge.   Said

οὖν τινες ἐκ τῶν Ἱεροσολυμιτῶν· οὐχ
therefore some   of   the   Jerusalemites :   ²Not

οὗτός ἐστιν ὃν ζητοῦσιν ἀποκτεῖναι; 26 καὶ
³this man ¹is it whom they are seeking   to kill?   and

ἴδε παρρησίᾳ λαλεῖ, καὶ οὐδὲν αὐτῷ
behold   openly   he speaks,   and   nothing   to him

λέγουσιν. μήποτε ἀληθῶς ἔγνωσαν οἱ
they say.   Perhaps   indeed   knew   the

ἄρχοντες ὅτι οὗτός ἐστιν ὁ χριστός; *
rulers   that   this   is   the   Christ? *

27 ἀλλὰ τοῦτον οἴδαμεν πόθεν ἐστίν· ὁ δὲ
But   this man   we know   whence   he is;   but ²the

χριστὸς ὅταν ἔρχηται, οὐδεὶς γινώσκει
³Christ   ¹when   comes,   no one   knows

πόθεν ἐστίν. 28 ἔκραξεν οὖν ἐν τῷ ἱερῷ
whence   he is.   ³Cried out ²therefore ⁴in ⁵the ⁶temple

διδάσκων ὁ Ἰησοῦς καὶ λέγων· κἀμὲ
⁷teaching   –   ¹Jesus   ⁸and   ⁹saying : Both me

οἴδατε καὶ οἴδατε πόθεν εἰμί· καὶ ἀπ'
ye know   and   ye know   whence   I am;   and   from

ἐμαυτοῦ οὐκ ἐλήλυθα, ἀλλ' ἔστιν ἀληθινὸς
myself   I have not come,   but   he is   true

ὁ πέμψας με, ὃν ὑμεῖς οὐκ οἴδατε·
the [one] having sent   me,   whom   ye   know not;

29 ἐγὼ οἶδα αὐτόν, ὅτι παρ' αὐτοῦ εἰμι
I   know   him,   because ²from ³him ¹I am

κἀκεῖνός με ἀπέστειλεν. 30 Ἐζήτουν οὖν
⁴and that one ⁶me   ⁵sent.   They sought therefore

αὐτὸν πιάσαι, καὶ οὐδεὶς ἐπέβαλεν ἐπ'
him   to arrest,   and   no one   laid on   on

αὐτὸν τὴν χεῖρα, ὅτι οὔπω ἐληλύθει ἡ
him   the   hand,   because not yet   had come the

ὥρα αὐτοῦ. 31 Ἐκ τοῦ ὄχλου δὲ πολλοὶ
hour   of him.   ³of ⁴the ⁵crowd ¹But ²many

ἐπίστευσαν εἰς αὐτόν, καὶ ἔλεγον· ὁ
believed   in   him,   and   said :   ²The

---

* As this question is introduced by μήποτε, a negative answer is expected; see page xiii, and note ver. 31 below.

the Christ appears, will he do more signs than this man has done?"
32 The Pharisees heard the crowd thus muttering about him, and the chief priests and Pharisees sent officers to arrest him. [33] Jesus then said, "I shall be with you a little longer, and then I go to him who sent me; [34] you will seek me and you will not find me; where I am you cannot come." [35] The Jews said to one another, "Where does this man intend to go that we shall not find him? Does he intend to go to the Dispersion among the Greeks and teach the Greeks? [36] What does he mean by saying, 'You will seek me and you will not find me,' and, 'Where I am you cannot come'?"
37 On the last day of the feast, the great day, Jesus stood up and proclaimed, "If any one thirst, let him come to me and drink. [38] He who believes in me, as[n] the scripture has said, 'Out of his heart shall flow rivers of living water.' "

[n] Or let him come to me, and let him who believes in me drink. As

χριστὸς   ὅταν   ἔλθῃ,   μὴ   πλείονα   σημεῖα
[3]Christ   [1]when   [4]comes,   not   more   signs
ποιήσει   ὧν   οὗτος   ἐποίησεν;   32 ἤκουσαν
will he do [than] which this man   did?   [3]Heard
οἱ   Φαρισαῖοι   τοῦ   ὄχλου   γογγύζοντος   περὶ
[1]the   [2]Pharisees   [4]the   [5]crowd   [6]murmuring   [8]about
αὐτοῦ   ταῦτα,   καὶ   ἀπέστειλαν   οἱ   ἀρχιερεῖς
[9]him   [7]these things,   and   [6]sent   [1]the   [2]chief priests
καὶ   οἱ   Φαρισαῖοι   ὑπηρέτας   ἵνα   πιάσωσιν
[3]and   [4]the   [5]Pharisees   [7]attendants   that they might arrest
αὐτόν.   33 εἶπεν   οὖν   ὁ   Ἰησοῦς·   ἔτι
him.   Said   therefore   –   Jesus :   Yet
χρόνον   μικρὸν   μεθ'   ὑμῶν   εἰμι   καὶ   ὑπάγω
time   a little   with   you   I am   and   I go
πρὸς   τὸν   πέμψαντά   με.   34 ζητήσετέ   με
to   the [one]   having sent   me.   Ye will seek   me
καὶ   οὐχ   εὑρήσετε,   καὶ   ὅπου   εἰμὶ   ἐγὼ
and   will not find,   and   where   am   I
ὑμεῖς   οὐ   δύνασθε   ἐλθεῖν.   35 εἶπον   οὖν
ye   cannot   to come.   Said therefore
οἱ   Ἰουδαῖοι   πρὸς   ἑαυτούς·   ποῦ   οὗτος
the   Jews   to   themselves :   Where   this man
μέλλει   πορεύεσθαι,   ὅτι   ἡμεῖς   οὐχ   εὑρήσομεν
is about   to go,   that   we   will not find
αὐτόν;   μὴ   εἰς   τὴν   διασπορὰν   τῶν   Ἑλλήνων
him?   not   to the   dispersion   of the   Greeks
μέλλει   πορεύεσθαι   καὶ   διδάσκειν   τοὺς
is he about   to go   and   to teach   the
Ἕλληνας;   36 τίς   ἐστιν   ὁ   λόγος   οὗτος
Greeks?   What   is   –   word   this
ὃν   εἶπεν·   ζητήσετέ   με   καὶ   οὐχ   εὑρήσετε,
which   he said :   Ye will seek   me   and   will not find,
καὶ   ὅπου   εἰμὶ   ἐγὼ   ὑμεῖς   οὐ   δύνασθε
and   where   am   I   ye   cannot
ἐλθεῖν;
to come?
37 Ἐν   δὲ   τῇ   ἐσχάτῃ   ἡμέρᾳ   τῇ   μεγάλῃ
Now in   the   last   day   the   great [day]
τῆς   ἑορτῆς   εἱστήκει   ὁ   Ἰησοῦς   καὶ   ἔκραξεν
of the   feast   stood   –   Jesus   and   cried out
λέγων·   ἐάν   τις   διψᾷ,   ἐρχέσθω   πρός   με
saying :   If   anyone   thirsts,   let him come   to   me
καὶ   πινέτω.   38 ὁ   πιστεύων   εἰς   ἐμέ,
and   drink.   The [one] believing   in   me,
καθὼς   εἶπεν   ἡ   γραφή,   ποταμοὶ   ἐκ   τῆς
as   said   the   scripture,   [1]rivers   [5]out of   [6]the
κοιλίας   αὐτοῦ   ῥεύσουσιν   ὕδατος   ζῶντος.
[7]belly   [8]of him   [4]will flow   [3]water   [2]of living.

³⁹ Now this he said about the Spirit, which those who believed in him were to receive; for as yet the Spirit had not been given, because Jesus was not yet glorified.

40 When they heard these words, some of the people said, "This is really the prophet." ⁴¹ Others said, "This is the Christ." But some said, "Is the Christ to come from Galilee? ⁴² Has not the scripture said that the Christ is descended from David, and comes from Bethlehem, the village where David was?" ⁴³ So there was a division among the people over him. ⁴⁴ Some of them wanted to arrest him, but no one laid hands on him.

45 The officers then went back to the chief priests and Pharisees, who said to them, "Why did you not bring him?" ⁴⁶ The officers answered, "No man ever spoke like this man!" ⁴⁷ The Pharisees answered them, "Are you led astray, you also? ⁴⁸ Have any of the authorities or of the Pharisees believed in him? ⁴⁹ But this crowd,

---

39 τοῦτο δὲ εἶπεν περὶ τοῦ πνεύματος
But this he said concerning the Spirit

οὗ ἔμελλον λαμβάνειν οἱ πιστεύσαντες
whom were about to receive the [ones] believing

εἰς αὐτόν· οὔπω γὰρ ἦν πνεῦμα, ὅτι
in him; for not yet was [?the] Spirit, because

Ἰησοῦς οὐδέπω ἐδοξάσθη. **40** Ἐκ τοῦ
Jesus not yet was glorified. [Some] of the

ὄχλου οὖν ἀκούσαντες τῶν λόγων τούτων
crowd therefore hearing – words these

ἔλεγον [ὅτι]· οὗτός ἐστιν ἀληθῶς ὁ
said : This man is truly the

προφήτης· **41** ἄλλοι ἔλεγον· οὗτός ἐστιν ὁ
prophet; Others said : This man is the

χριστός· οἱ δὲ ἔλεγον· μὴ γὰρ ἐκ τῆς
Christ; But others† said : Not then out of –

Γαλιλαίας ὁ χριστὸς ἔρχεται; **42** οὐχ ἡ
Galilee the Christ comes? not the

γραφὴ εἶπεν ὅτι ἐκ τοῦ σπέρματος Δαυίδ,
scripture said that of the seed of David,

καὶ ἀπὸ Βηθλέεμ τῆς κώμης ὅπου ἦν
and from Bethlehem the village where was

Δαυίδ, ἔρχεται ὁ χριστός; **43** σχίσμα
David, comes the Christ? A division

οὖν ἐγένετο ἐν τῷ ὄχλῳ δι' αὐτόν·
therefore became in the crowd because of him;

44 τινὲς δὲ ἤθελον ἐξ αὐτῶν πιάσαι αὐτόν,
and ¹some ⁴wished ²of ³them to arrest him,

ἀλλ' οὐδεὶς ἐπέβαλεν ἐπ' αὐτὸν τὰς χεῖρας.
but no one laid on on him the(his) hands.

45 Ἦλθον οὖν οἱ ὑπηρέται πρὸς τοὺς
Came therefore the attendants to the

ἀρχιερεῖς καὶ Φαρισαίους, καὶ εἶπον αὐτοῖς
chief priests and Pharisees, and ²said ³to them

ἐκεῖνοι· διὰ τί οὐκ ἠγάγετε αὐτόν;
¹those: Why did ye not bring him?

46 ἀπεκρίθησαν οἱ ὑπηρέται· οὐδέποτε
Answered the attendants : Never

ἐλάλησεν οὕτως ἄνθρωπος, ὡς οὗτος λαλεῖ
spoke so a man, as ¹this ²speaks

ὁ ἄνθρωπος. **47** ἀπεκρίθησαν οὖν αὐτοῖς
– ²man. Answered therefore them

οἱ Φαρισαῖοι· μὴ καὶ ὑμεῖς πεπλάνησθε;
the Pharisees : Not also ye have been deceived?

48 μή τις ἐκ τῶν ἀρχόντων ἐπίστευσεν
not anyone of the rulers believed

εἰς αὐτὸν ἢ ἐκ τῶν Φαρισαίων; **49** ἀλλὰ
in him or of the Pharisees? But

who do not know the law, are accursed." ⁵⁰Nicode′mus, who had gone to him before, and who was one of them, said to them, ⁵¹"Does our law judge a man without first giving him a hearing and learning what he does?" ⁵²They replied, "Are you from Galilee too? Search and you will see that no prophet is to rise from Galilee."°

° Other ancient authorities add 7. 53–8. 11 either here or at the end of this gospel or after Luke 21. 38, with variations of the text

8 ⁵³*They went each to his own house, ¹but Jesus went to the Mount of Olives. ²Early in the morning he came again to the temple; all the people came to him, and he sat down and taught them. ³The scribes and the Pharisees brought a woman who had been caught in adultery, and placing her in the midst ⁴they said to him, "Teacher, this woman has been caught in the act of adultery. ⁵Now in the law Moses commanded us to stone such. What do you say about her?" ⁶This they said to test him, that they might have some charge to*

ὁ ὄχλος οὗτος ὁ μὴ γινώσκων τὸν
– crowd this – not knowing the

νόμον ἐπάρατοί εἰσιν. **50** λέγει Νικόδημος
law cursed are. Says Nicodemus

πρὸς αὐτούς, ὁ ἐλθὼν πρὸς αὐτὸν πρότερον,
to them, the [one] having come to him firstly,

εἷς ὢν ἐξ αὐτῶν· **51** μὴ ὁ νόμος ἡμῶν
²one ¹being of them : *Not* the law of us

κρίνει τὸν ἄνθρωπον ἐὰν μὴ ἀκούσῃ
judges the man unless it hears

πρῶτον παρ' αὐτοῦ καὶ γνῷ τί ποιεῖ;
first from him and knows what he does?

52 ἀπεκρίθησαν καὶ εἶπαν αὐτῷ· μὴ καὶ
They answered and said to him : *Not* also

σὺ ἐκ τῆς Γαλιλαίας εἶ; ἐρεύνησον καὶ
thou of – Galilee art? search and

ἴδε ὅτι ἐκ τῆς Γαλιλαίας προφήτης οὐκ
see that out of – Galilee a prophet not

ἐγείρεται.
is raised.

53 Καὶ ἐπορεύθησαν ἕκαστος εἰς τὸν οἶκον
And they went each one to the house

αὐτοῦ, **8** Ἰησοῦς δὲ ἐπορεύθη εἰς τὸ
of him, but Jesus went to the

Ὄρος τῶν Ἐλαιῶν. **2** Ὄρθρου δὲ πάλιν
Mount of the Olives. And at dawn again

παρεγένετο εἰς τὸ ἱερόν [, καὶ πᾶς ὁ
he arrived in the temple, and all the

λαὸς ἤρχετο πρὸς αὐτόν, καὶ καθίσας
people came to him, and sitting

ἐδίδασκεν αὐτούς]. **3** Ἄγουσιν δὲ οἱ
he taught them. And lead the

γραμματεῖς καὶ οἱ Φαρισαῖοι γυναῖκα ἐπὶ
scribes and the Pharisees a woman

μοιχεία κατειλημμένην, καὶ στήσαντες αὐτὴν
adultery *having been* caught, and standing her

ἐν μέσῳ **4** λέγουσιν αὐτῷ Διδάσκαλε,
in [the] midst they say to him[,] Teacher,

αὕτη ἡ γυνὴ κατείληπται ἐπ' αὐτοφώρῳ
this – woman has been caught in the act

μοιχευομένη· **5** ἐν δὲ τῷ νόμῳ [ἡμῖν]
committing adultery; now in the law to us°

Μωυσῆς ἐνετείλατο τὰς τοιαύτας λιθάζειν·
Moses enjoined – ²such ¹to stone·

σὺ οὖν τί λέγεις; **6** [τοῦτο δὲ ἔλεγον
thou therefore what sayest thou? But this they said

πειράζοντες αὐτόν, ἵνα ἔχωσιν κατηγορεῖν
tempting him, that they might have to accuse

bring against him. Jesus bent down and wrote with his finger on the ground. ⁷And as they continued to ask him, he stood up and said to them, "Let him who is without sin among you be the first to throw a stone at her." ⁸And once more he bent down and wrote with his finger on the ground. ⁹But when they heard it, they went away, one by one, beginning with the eldest, and Jesus was left alone with the woman standing before him. ¹⁰Jesus looked up and said to her, "Woman, where are they? Has no one condemned you?" ¹¹She said, "No one, Lord." And Jesus said, "Neither do I condemn you; go, and do not sin again."

αὐτοῦ.] ὁ δὲ Ἰησοῦς κάτω κύψας τῷ
him. - But Jesus down stooping with the
δακτύλῳ κατέγραφεν εἰς τὴν γῆν. 7 ὡς δὲ
finger wrote in the earth. But as
ἐπέμενον ἐρωτῶντες [αὐτόν], ἀνέκυψεν καὶ
they remained questioning him, he stood erect and
εἶπεν [αὐτοῖς] Ὁ ἀναμάρτητος ὑμῶν
said to them[,] The [one] sinless of you
πρῶτος ἐπ᾽ αὐτὴν βαλέτω λίθον. 8 καὶ
first on her let him cast a stone. And
πάλιν κατακύψας ἔγραφεν εἰς τὴν γῆν.
again stooping down he wrote in the earth.
9 οἱ δὲ ἀκούσαντες ἐξήρχοντο εἷς καθ᾽
And they hearing went out one by
εἷς ἀρξάμενοι ἀπὸ τῶν πρεσβυτέρων, καὶ
one beginning from the older ones, and
κατελείφθη μόνος, καὶ ἡ γυνὴ ἐν μέσῳ
he was left alone, and the woman in [the] midst
οὖσα. 10 ἀνακύψας δὲ ὁ Ἰησοῦς εἶπεν
being. And standing erect - Jesus said
αὐτῇ Γύναι, ποῦ εἰσιν; οὐδείς σε κατέκρινεν;
to her[,] Woman, where are they? no one thee condemned?
11 ἡ δὲ εἶπεν Οὐδείς, κύριε. εἶπεν δὲ
And she said[,] No one, sir. So said
ὁ Ἰησοῦς Οὐδὲ ἐγώ σε κατακρίνω·
- Jesus[,] Neither I thee condemn;
πορεύου, ἀπὸ τοῦ νῦν μηκέτι ἁμάρτανε.
go, from - now no longer sin.

CHAPTER 8

¹² AGAIN Jesus spoke to them, saying, "I am the light of the world; he who follows me will not walk in darkness, but will have the light of life." ¹³The Pharisees then said to him, "You are bearing witness to yourself; your testimony is not true." ¹⁴Jesus answered, "Even if I do bear witness to myself, my testimony is true, for I know whence I have come and whither I am going, but you do

12 Πάλιν οὖν αὐτοῖς ἐλάλησεν ὁ Ἰησοῦς
Again therefore to them spoke - Jesus
λέγων· ἐγώ εἰμι τὸ φῶς τοῦ κόσμου·
saying : I am the light of the world;
ὁ ἀκολουθῶν μοι οὐ μὴ περιπατήσῃ ἐν
the [one] following me by no means will walk in
τῇ σκοτίᾳ, ἀλλ᾽ ἕξει τὸ φῶς τῆς ζωῆς.
the darkness, but will have the light - of life.
13 εἶπον οὖν αὐτῷ οἱ Φαρισαῖοι· σὺ περὶ
Said therefore to him the Pharisees; Thou concerning
σεαυτοῦ μαρτυρεῖς· ἡ μαρτυρία σου οὐκ
thyself witnessest; the witness of thee not
ἔστιν ἀληθής. 14 ἀπεκρίθη Ἰησοῦς καὶ
is true. Answered Jesus and
εἶπεν αὐτοῖς· κἂν ἐγὼ μαρτυρῶ περὶ
said to them : Even if I witness concerning
ἐμαυτοῦ, ἀληθής ἐστιν ἡ μαρτυρία μου,
myself, true is the witness of me,
ὅτι οἶδα πόθεν ἦλθον καὶ ποῦ ὑπάγω·
because I know whence I came and where I go;

not know whence I come or whither I am going. ¹⁵You judge according to the flesh, I judge no one. ¹⁶Yet even if I do judge, my judgment is true, for it is not I alone that judge, but I and he[p] who sent me. ¹⁷In your law it is written that the testimony of two men is true; ¹⁸I bear witness to myself, and the Father who sent me bears witness to me." ¹⁹They said to him therefore, "Where is your Father?" Jesus answered, "You know neither me nor my Father; if you knew me, you would know my Father also." ²⁰These words he spoke in the treasury, as he taught in the temple; but no one arrested him, because his hour had not yet come.

21 Again he said to them, "I go away, and you will seek me and die in your sin; where I am going, you cannot come." ²²Then said the Jews, "Will he kill himself, since he says, 'Where I am going, you cannot

ὑμεῖς δὲ οὐκ οἴδατε πόθεν ἔρχομαι ἢ
but ye   know not   whence   I come   or

ποῦ ὑπάγω. 15 ὑμεῖς κατὰ τὴν σάρκα
where I go.   Ye   according to the   flesh

κρίνετε, ἐγὼ οὐ κρίνω οὐδένα. 16 καὶ
judge,   I   judge not no(any)one.   ²even

ἐὰν κρίνω δὲ ἐγώ, ἡ κρίσις ἡ ἐμὴ
²if ⁵judge ¹But ⁴I, the ²judgment - ¹my

ἀληθινή ἐστιν, ὅτι μόνος οὐκ εἰμί, ἀλλ'
true   is,   because alone   I am not,   but

ἐγὼ καὶ ὁ πέμψας με. 17 καὶ ἐν τῷ
I   and the [one] having sent me.   ²even ³in   the

νόμῳ δὲ τῷ ὑμετέρῳ γέγραπται ὅτι δύο
⁵law ¹And - ⁴your   it has been written that of two

ἀνθρώπων ἡ μαρτυρία ἀληθής ἐστιν.
men   the witness   true   is.

18 ἐγώ εἰμι ὁ μαρτυρῶν περὶ ἐμαυτοῦ,
I   am the [one] witnessing concerning myself,

καὶ μαρτυρεῖ περὶ ἐμοῦ ὁ πέμψας με
and witnesses concerning me   ¹the ³having sent ⁴me

πατήρ. 19 ἔλεγον οὖν αὐτῷ· ποῦ ἐστιν ὁ
²Father. They said therefore to him : Where is   the

πατήρ σου; ἀπεκρίθη Ἰησοῦς· οὔτε ἐμὲ
Father of thee? Answered Jesus : Neither me

οἴδατε οὔτε τὸν πατέρα μου· εἰ ἐμὲ
ye know nor the Father   of me; if me

ἤδειτε, καὶ τὸν πατέρα μου ἂν ἤδειτε.
ye knew, also the Father of me ye would have known.

20 Ταῦτα τὰ ῥήματα ἐλάλησεν ἐν τῷ
These   -   words   he spoke   in   the

γαζοφυλακείῳ διδάσκων ἐν τῷ ἱερῷ· καὶ
treasury   teaching   in the temple; and

οὐδεὶς ἐπίασεν αὐτόν, ὅτι οὔπω ἐληλύθει
no one seized   him, because not yet   had come

ἡ ὥρα αὐτοῦ.
the hour of him.

21 Εἶπεν οὖν πάλιν αὐτοῖς· ἐγὼ ὑπάγω
He said therefore again to them : I   go

καὶ ζητήσετέ με, καὶ ἐν τῇ ἁμαρτίᾳ
and ye will seek me, and in the   sin

ὑμῶν ἀποθανεῖσθε· ὅπου ἐγὼ ὑπάγω ὑμεῖς
of you ye will die; where   I   go   ye

οὐ δύνασθε ἐλθεῖν. 22 ἔλεγον οὖν οἱ
cannot   to come.   Said therefore the

Ἰουδαῖοι· μήτι ἀποκτενεῖ ἑαυτόν, ὅτι
Jews :   Not   will he kill himself, because

λέγει· ὅπου ἐγὼ ὑπάγω ὑμεῖς οὐ δύνασθε
he says : Where I   go   ye   cannot

come'?" ²³He said to
them, "You are from
below, I am from above;
you are of this world, I
am not of this world. ²⁴I
told you that you would
die in your sins, for you
will die in your sins unless
you believe that I am
he." ²⁵They said to him,
"Who are you?" Jesus
said to them, "Even what
I have told you from the
beginning.ᵠ ²⁶I have much
to say about you and
much to judge; but he
who sent me is true, and
I declare to the world
what I have heard from
him." ²⁷They did not
understand that he spoke
to them of the Father.
²⁸So Jesus said, "When
you have lifted up the
Son of man, then you
will know that I am he,
and that I do nothing on
my own authority but
speak thus as the Father
taught me. ²⁹And he who
sent me is with me; he
has not left me alone, for
I always do what is
pleasing to him." ³⁰As
he spoke thus, many
believed in him.
31 Jesus then said to

ᵠ Or *Why do I talk to you at all?*

ἐλθεῖν; **23** καὶ ἔλεγεν αὐτοῖς· ὑμεῖς ἐκ
to come? And he said to them: Ye of
τῶν κάτω ἐστέ, ἐγὼ ἐκ τῶν ἄνω εἰμί·
the things below are, I of the things above am;
ὑμεῖς ἐκ τούτου τοῦ κόσμου ἐστέ, ἐγὼ
ye of this – world are, I
οὐκ εἰμὶ ἐκ τοῦ κόσμου τούτου. **24** εἶπον
am not of – world this. I said
οὖν ὑμῖν ὅτι ἀποθανεῖσθε ἐν ταῖς ἁμαρτίαις
therefore to you that ye will die in the sins
ὑμῶν· ἐὰν γὰρ μὴ πιστεύσητε ὅτι ἐγώ
of you; for if ye believe not that I
εἰμι, ἀποθανεῖσθε ἐν ταῖς ἁμαρτίαις ὑμῶν.
am, ye will die in the sins of you.
25 ἔλεγον οὖν αὐτῷ· σὺ τίς εἶ; εἶπεν
They said therefore to him: ³Thou ¹who ²art? Said
αὐτοῖς ὁ Ἰησοῦς· τὴν ἀρχὴν ὅ τι καὶ
to them – Jesus: ³at all † ¹Why ²indeed
λαλῶ ὑμῖν; **26** πολλὰ ἔχω περὶ ὑμῶν
³speak I ⁴to you? Many things I have about you
λαλεῖν καὶ κρίνειν· ἀλλ' ὁ πέμψας με
to speak and to judge; but the [one] having sent me
ἀληθής ἐστιν, κἀγὼ ἃ ἤκουσα παρ'
true is, and I what I heard from
αὐτοῦ, ταῦτα λαλῶ εἰς τὸν κόσμον.
him, these things I speak in the world.
27 οὐκ ἔγνωσαν ὅτι τὸν πατέρα αὐτοῖς
They did not know that ²the ³Father ⁴to them
ἔλεγεν. **28** εἶπεν οὖν ὁ Ἰησοῦς· ὅταν
¹he spoke [of]. Said therefore – Jesus: When
ὑψώσητε τὸν υἱὸν τοῦ ἀνθρώπου, τότε
ye lift up the Son – of man, then
γνώσεσθε ὅτι ἐγώ εἰμι, καὶ ἀπ' ἐμαυτοῦ
ye will know that I am, and from myself
ποιῶ οὐδέν, ἀλλὰ καθὼς ἐδίδαξέν με ὁ
I do nothing, but as taught me the
πατήρ, ταῦτα λαλῶ. **29** καὶ ὁ πέμψας
Father, these things I speak. And the [one] having sent
με μετ' ἐμοῦ ἐστιν· οὐκ ἀφῆκέν με
me with me is; he did not leave me
μόνον, ὅτι ἐγὼ τὰ ἀρεστὰ αὐτῷ ποιῶ
alone, because I the things pleasing to him do
πάντοτε.
always.
30 Ταῦτα αὐτοῦ λαλοῦντος πολλοὶ ἐπίσ-
These things him saying° many be-
=As he said these things
τευσαν εἰς αὐτόν. **31** ἔλεγεν οὖν ὁ Ἰησοῦς
lieved in him. Said therefore – Jesus

the Jews who had believed in him, "If you continue in my word, you are truly my disciples, ³²and you will know the truth, and the truth will make you free." ³³They answered him, "We are descendants of Abraham, and have never been in bondage to any one. How is it that you say, 'You will be made free'?"
34 Jesus answered them, "Truly, truly, I say to you, every one who commits sin is a slave to sin. ³⁵The slave does not continue in the house for ever; the son continues for ever. ³⁶So if the Son makes you free, you will be free indeed. ³⁷I know that you are descendants of Abraham; yet you seek to kill me, because my word finds no place in you. ³⁸I speak of what I have seen with my Father, and you do what you have heard from your father."
39 They answered him, "Abraham is our father." Jesus said to them, "If you were Abraham's children, you would do what Abraham did, ⁴⁰but now you seek to kill me, a man who has told you the truth which

πρὸς τοὺς πεπιστευκότας αὐτῷ Ἰουδαίους·
to   ¹the   ³having believed   ⁴him   ²Jews :

ἐὰν ὑμεῖς μείνητε ἐν τῷ λόγῳ τῷ ἐμῷ,
If   ye   continue   in   the   ²word   –   ¹my,

ἀληθῶς μαθηταί μού ἐστε, 32 καὶ γνώσεσθε
truly   disciples   of me ye are,   and ye will know

τὴν ἀλήθειαν, καὶ ἡ ἀλήθεια ἐλευθερώσει
the   truth,   and   the   truth   will free

ὑμᾶς. 33 ἀπεκρίθησαν πρὸς αὐτόν· σπέρμα
you.   They answered   to   him :   Seed

Ἀβραάμ ἐσμεν, καὶ οὐδενὶ δεδουλεύκαμεν
of Abraham   we are,   and   to no one   have we been enslaved

πώποτε· πῶς σὺ λέγεις ὅτι ἐλεύθεροι
never;   how   thou   sayest   that   free

γενήσεσθε; 34 ἀπεκρίθη αὐτοῖς ὁ Ἰησοῦς·
ye will become?   Answered   them   –   Jesus :

ἀμὴν ἀμὴν λέγω ὑμῖν ὅτι πᾶς ὁ ποιῶν
Truly   truly   I tell   you   that   everyone   doing

τὴν ἁμαρτίαν δοῦλός ἐστιν τῆς ἁμαρτίας.
–   sin   a slave   is   –   of sin.

35 ὁ δὲ δοῦλος οὐ μένει ἐν τῇ οἰκίᾳ
But the   slave   does not remain   in   the   house

εἰς τὸν αἰῶνα· ὁ υἱὸς μένει εἰς τὸν
unto the   age;   the   son   remains   unto   the

αἰῶνα. 36 ἐὰν οὖν ὁ υἱὸς ὑμᾶς ἐλευθερώσῃ,
age.   If therefore the   Son   you   frees,

ὄντως ἐλεύθεροι ἔσεσθε. 37 Οἶδα ὅτι
really   free   ye will be.   I know   that

σπέρμα Ἀβραάμ ἐστε· ἀλλὰ ζητεῖτέ με
seed   of Abraham   ye are;   but   ye seek   me

ἀποκτεῖναι, ὅτι ὁ λόγος ὁ ἐμὸς οὐ χωρεῖ
to kill,   because the   ²word   –   ¹my   finds no room

ἐν ὑμῖν. 38 ἃ ἐγὼ ἑώρακα παρὰ τῷ
in you.   What   I   have seen   with   the

πατρὶ λαλῶ· καὶ ὑμεῖς οὖν ἃ ἠκού-
Father   I speak;   and   ye   therefore what   ye

σατε παρὰ τοῦ πατρὸς ποιεῖτε. 39 ἀπεκρί-
heard   from   the   father   ye do.   They

θησαν καὶ εἶπαν αὐτῷ· ὁ πατὴρ ἡμῶν Ἀβραάμ
answered and   said   to him: The father   of us   Abraham

ἐστιν. λέγει αὐτοῖς ὁ Ἰησοῦς· εἰ τέκνα
is.   Says   to them   –   Jesus :   If   children

τοῦ Ἀβραάμ ἐστε, τὰ ἔργα τοῦ Ἀβραάμ
–   of Abraham ye are,   the   works   –   of Abraham

ποιεῖτε· 40 νῦν δὲ ζητεῖτέ με ἀποκτεῖναι,
ye do;   but now   ye seek   me   to kill,

ἄνθρωπον ὃς τὴν ἀλήθειαν ὑμῖν λελάληκα,
a man   who   the   truth   to you   has spoken,

I heard from God; this is not what Abraham did. ⁴¹You do what your father did." They said to him, "We were not born of fornication; we have one Father, even God." ⁴²Jesus said to them, "If God were your Father, you would love me, for I proceeded and came forth from God; I came not of my own accord, but he sent me. ⁴³Why do you not understand what I say? It is because you cannot bear to hear my word. ⁴⁴You are of your father the devil, and your will is to do your father's desires. He was a murderer from the beginning, and has nothing to do with the truth, because there is no truth in him. When he lies, he speaks according to his own nature, for he is a liar and the father of lies. ⁴⁵But, because I tell the truth, you do not believe me. ⁴⁶Which of you convicts me of sin? If I tell the truth, why do you not believe me? ⁴⁷He who is of God hears the words of God; the reason why you do not

ἦν ἤκουσα παρὰ τοῦ θεοῦ· τοῦτο ᾿Αβραὰμ
which I heard from – God; this Abraham

οὐκ ἐποίησεν. 41 ὑμεῖς ποιεῖτε τὰ ἔργα
did not. Ye do the works

τοῦ πατρὸς ὑμῶν. εἶπαν αὐτῷ· ἡμεῖς ἐκ
of the father of you. They said to him : We of

πορνείας οὐκ ἐγεννήθημεν, ἕνα πατέρα
fornication were not born, one father

ἔχομεν τὸν θεόν. 42 εἶπεν αὐτοῖς ὁ
we have[,] – God. Said to them –

᾿Ιησοῦς· εἰ ὁ θεὸς πατὴρ ὑμῶν ἦν,
Jesus· If – God father of you was,

ἠγαπᾶτε ἂν ἐμέ· ἐγὼ γὰρ ἐκ τοῦ θεοῦ
ye would have loved me; for I of – God

ἐξῆλθον καὶ ἥκω· οὐδὲ γὰρ ἀπ᾿ ἐμαυτοῦ
came forth and have come; for not from myself

ἐλήλυθα, ἀλλ᾿ ἐκεῖνός με ἀπέστειλεν. 43 διὰ τί
I have come, but that one me sent. Why

τὴν λαλιὰν τὴν ἐμὴν οὐ γινώσκετε;
the ²speech – ¹my know ye not?

ὅτι οὐ δύνασθε ἀκούειν τὸν λόγον τὸν
because ye cannot to hear the ²word –

ἐμόν. 44 ὑμεῖς ἐκ τοῦ πατρὸς τοῦ
¹my. Ye of the father of the

διαβόλου ἐστὲ καὶ τὰς ἐπιθυμίας τοῦ
devil are and the desires of the

πατρὸς ὑμῶν θέλετε ποιεῖν. ἐκεῖνος
father of you ye wish to do. That one

ἀνθρωποκτόνος ἦν ἀπ᾿ ἀρχῆς, καὶ ἐν
a murderer was from [the] beginning, and in

τῇ ἀληθείᾳ οὐκ ἔστηκεν, ὅτι οὐκ ἔστιν
the truth stood not, because not is

ἀλήθεια ἐν αὐτῷ. ὅταν λαλῇ τὸ ψεῦδος,
truth in him. When he speaks the lie,

ἐκ τῶν ἰδίων λαλεῖ, ὅτι ψεύστης ἐστὶν
out of his own things he speaks, because a liar he is

καὶ ὁ πατὴρ αὐτοῦ. 45 ἐγὼ δὲ ὅτι τὴν
and the father of it. But ²I ¹because ⁴the

ἀλήθειαν λέγω, οὐ πιστεύετέ μοι. 46 τίς
⁵truth ³say, ye do not believe me. Who

ἐξ ὑμῶν ἐλέγχει με περὶ ἁμαρτίας; εἰ
of you reproves me concerning sin? If

ἀλήθειαν λέγω, διὰ τί ὑμεῖς οὐ πιστεύετέ
truth I say, why ²ye ¹do not believe

μοι; 47 ὁ ὢν ἐκ τοῦ θεοῦ τὰ ῥήματα
me? The [one] being of – God the words

τοῦ θεοῦ ἀκούει· διὰ τοῦτο ὑμεῖς οὐκ
– of God hears; therefore ye not

hear them is that you are not of God."

48 The Jews answered him, "Are we not right in saying that you are a Samaritan and have a demon?" ⁴⁹Jesus answered, "I have not a demon; but I honor my Father, and you dishonor me. ⁵⁰Yet I do not seek my own glory; there is One who seeks it and he will be the judge. ⁵¹Truly, truly, I say to you, if any one keeps my word, he will never see death." ⁵²The Jews said to him, "Now we know that you have a demon. Abraham died, as did the prophets; and you say, 'If any one keeps my word, he will never taste death.' ⁵³Are you greater than our father Abraham, who died? And the prophets died! Who do you claim to be?" ⁵⁴Jesus answered, "If I glorify myself, my glory is nothing; it is my Father who glorifies me, of whom you say that he is your God. ⁵⁵But you have not known him; I know him. If I said, I do not know him, I

ἀκούετε,   ὅτι   ἐκ   τοῦ   θεοῦ   οὐκ   ἐστέ.
hear,   because   of   -   God   ye are not.

48 Ἀπεκρίθησαν   οἱ   Ἰουδαῖοι   καὶ   εἶπαν
   Answered   the   Jews   and   said

αὐτῷ·   οὐ   καλῶς   λέγομεν   ἡμεῖς   ὅτι
to him : ³Not   ⁴well   ¹say   ²we   ⁵that

Σαμαρίτης   εἶ   σὺ   καὶ   δαιμόνιον   ἔχεις;
⁶a Samaritan ⁷art ⁸thou ⁹and   ¹¹a demon   ¹⁰hast?

49 ἀπεκρίθη   Ἰησοῦς·   ἐγὼ   δαιμόνιον   οὐκ
   Answered   Jesus :   I   a demon   not

ἔχω,   ἀλλὰ   τιμῶ   τὸν   πατέρα   μου,   καὶ
have,   but   I honour the   Father   of me,   and

ὑμεῖς   ἀτιμάζετέ   με.   50 ἐγὼ   δὲ   οὐ   ζητῶ
ye   dishonour   me.   But I   seek not

τὴν   δόξαν   μου·   ἔστιν   ὁ   ζητῶν   καὶ
the   glory   of me;   there is the [one] seeking and

κρίνων.   51 ἀμὴν   ἀμὴν   λέγω   ὑμῖν,   ἐάν
judging.   Truly   truly   I tell   you,   if

τις   τὸν   ἐμὸν   λόγον   τηρήσῃ,   θάνατον
anyone   -   my   word   keeps,   death

οὐ   μὴ   θεωρήσῃ   εἰς   τὸν   αἰῶνα.   52 εἶπαν
by no means will he behold unto the   age.   Said

αὐτῷ   οἱ   Ἰουδαῖοι·   νῦν   ἐγνώκαμεν   ὅτι
to him   the   Jews :   Now   we have known   that

δαιμόνιον   ἔχεις.   Ἀβραὰμ   ἀπέθανεν   καὶ   οἱ
a demon   thou hast. Abraham   died   and   the

προφῆται,   καὶ   σὺ   λέγεις·   ἐάν   τις   τὸν
prophets,   and   thou   sayest :   If   anyone the

λόγον   μου   τηρήσῃ,   οὐ   μὴ   γεύσηται
word   of me   keeps,   by no means   will he taste

θανάτου   εἰς   τὸν   αἰῶνα.   53 μὴ   σὺ   μείζων
of death   unto   the   age.   Not   thou   greater

εἶ   τοῦ   πατρὸς   ἡμῶν   Ἀβραάμ,   ὅστις
art [than] the   father   of us   Abraham,   who

ἀπέθανεν;   καὶ   οἱ   προφῆται   ἀπέθανον·   τίνα
died?   and   the   prophets   died;.   whom

σεαυτὸν   ποιεῖς;   54 ἀπεκρίθη   Ἰησοῦς·   ἐὰν
thyself   makest thou?   Answered   Jesus :   If

ἐγὼ   δοξάσω   ἐμαυτόν,   ἡ   δόξα   μου   οὐδέν
I   glorify   myself,   the   glory   of me   nothing

ἐστιν·   ἔστιν   ὁ   πατήρ   μου   ὁ   δοξάζων   με,
is;   ⁴is   ¹the ²Father ³of me the [one] glorifying   me,

ὃν   ὑμεῖς   λέγετε   ὅτι   θεὸς   ἡμῶν   ἐστιν,
whom   ye   say[,]   -   God   of us   he is,

55 καὶ   οὐκ   ἐγνώκατε   αὐτόν,   ἐγὼ   δὲ
   and   ye have not known   him,   but I

οἶδα   αὐτόν.   κἂν   εἴπω   ὅτι   οὐκ   οἶδα
know   him.   Even if I say   that   I know not

should be a liar like you; but I do know him and I keep his word. ⁵⁶Your father Abraham rejoiced that he was to see my day; he saw it and was glad." ⁵⁷The Jews then said to him, "You are not yet fifty years old, and have you seen Abraham?"ʳ ⁵⁸Jesus said to them, "Truly, truly, I say to you, before Abraham was, I am." ⁵⁹So they took up stones to throw at him; but Jesus hid himself, and went out of the temple.

αὐτόν, ἔσομαι ὅμοιος ὑμῖν ψεύστης· ἀλλὰ
him, I shall be like you a liar; but

οἶδα αὐτὸν καὶ τὸν λόγον αὐτοῦ τηρῶ.
I know him and the word of him I keep.

56 Ἀβραὰμ ὁ πατὴρ ὑμῶν ἠγαλλιάσατο
Abraham the father of you was glad

ἵνα ἴδῃ τὴν ἡμέραν τὴν ἐμήν, καὶ εἶδεν
that he should see the ²day – ¹my, and he saw

καὶ ἐχάρη. 57 εἶπαν οὖν οἱ Ἰουδαῖοι
and rejoiced. Said therefore the Jews

πρὸς αὐτόν· πεντήκοντα ἔτη οὔπω ἔχεις
to him : Fifty years not yet thou hast

καὶ Ἀβραὰμ ἑώρακας; 58 εἶπεν αὐτοῖς
and Abraham hast thou seen? Said to them

Ἰησοῦς· ἀμὴν ἀμὴν λέγω ὑμῖν, πρὶν
Jesus: Truly truly I tell you, before

Ἀβραὰμ γενέσθαι ἐγὼ εἰμί. 59 ἦραν
Abraham to become[b] I am. They took
=became

οὖν λίθους ἵνα βάλωσιν ἐπ᾽ αὐτόν·
therefore stones that they might cast on him;

Ἰησοῦς δὲ ἐκρύβη καὶ ἐξῆλθεν ἐκ τοῦ
but Jesus was hidden and went forth out of the

ἱεροῦ.
temple.

ʳ Other ancient authorities read has Abraham seen you?

CHAPTER 9

AS he passed by, he saw a man blind from his birth. ²And his disciples asked him, "Rabbi, who sinned, this man or his parents, that he was born blind?" ³Jesus answered, "It was not that this man sinned, or his parents, but that the works of God might be made manifest in him. ⁴We must work the works of him who sent me, while it is day; night comes, when no one can work. ⁵As long as I am in the world, I am the light of the world."

9 Καὶ παράγων εἶδεν ἄνθρωπον τυφλὸν
And passing along he saw a man blind

ἐκ γενετῆς. 2 καὶ ἠρώτησαν αὐτὸν οἱ
from birth. And asked him the

μαθηταὶ αὐτοῦ λέγοντες· ῥαββί, τίς ἥμαρτεν,
disciples of him saying : Rabbi, who sinned,

οὗτος ἢ οἱ γονεῖς αὐτοῦ, ἵνα τυφλὸς
this man or the parents of him, that blind

γεννηθῇ; 3 ἀπεκρίθη Ἰησοῦς· οὔτε οὗτος
he was born? Answered Jesus : Neither this man

ἥμαρτεν οὔτε οἱ γονεῖς αὐτοῦ, ἀλλ᾽ ἵνα
sinned nor the parents of him, but that

φανερωθῇ τὰ ἔργα τοῦ θεοῦ ἐν αὐτῷ.
might be manifested the works – of God in him.

4 ἡμᾶς δεῖ ἐργάζεσθαι τὰ ἔργα τοῦ
Us it behoves to work the works of the

πέμψαντός με ἕως ἡμέρα ἐστίν· ἔρχεται
[one] having sent me while day it is; comes

νὺξ ὅτε οὐδεὶς δύναται ἐργάζεσθαι. 5 ὅταν
night when no one can to work. When

ἐν τῷ κόσμῳ ὦ, φῶς εἰμι τοῦ κόσμου.
in the world I am, light I am of the world.

⁶As he said this, he spat on the ground and made clay of the spittle and anointed the man's eyes with the clay, ⁷saying to him, "Go, wash in the pool of Silo'am" (which means Sent). So he went and washed and came back seeing. ⁸The neighbors and those who had seen him before as a beggar, said, "Is not this the man who used to sit and beg?" ⁹Some said, "It is he"; others said, "No, but he is like him." He said, "I am the man." ¹⁰They said to him, "Then how were your eyes opened?" ¹¹He answered, "The man called Jesus made clay and anointed my eyes and said to me, 'Go to Silo'am and wash'; so I went and washed and received my sight." ¹²They said to him, "Where is he?" He said, "I do not know."

13 They brought to the Pharisees the man who had formerly been blind. ¹⁴Now it was a sabbath day when Jesus made the clay and opened

6 ταῦτα εἰπὼν ἔπτυσεν χαμαὶ καὶ ἐποίησεν
These things having said he spat on the ground and made

πηλὸν ἐκ τοῦ πτύσματος, καὶ ἐπέθηκεν
clay out of the spittle, and ¹put on

αὐτοῦ τὸν πηλὸν ἐπὶ τοὺς ὀφθαλμούς,
⁷of him ²the ³clay ⁴on ⁵the ⁶eyes,

7 καὶ εἶπεν αὐτῷ· ὕπαγε νίψαι εἰς τὴν
and said to him: Go wash in the

κολυμβήθραν τοῦ Σιλωάμ (ὃ ἑρμηνεύεται
pool - of Siloam (which is translated

ἀπεσταλμένος). ἀπῆλθεν οὖν καὶ ἐνίψατο,
having been sent). He went therefore and washed,

καὶ ἦλθεν βλέπων. 8 Οἱ οὖν γείτονες
and came seeing. Therefore the neighbours

καὶ οἱ θεωροῦντες αὐτὸν τὸ πρότερον, †
and the [ones] beholding him formerly, †

ὅτι προσαίτης ἦν, ἔλεγον· οὐχ οὗτός
that a beggar he was, said: ²Not ³this man

ἐστιν ὁ καθήμενος καὶ προσαιτῶν; 9 ἄλλοι
¹is the [one] sitting and begging? Some

ἔλεγον ὅτι οὗτός ἐστιν· ἄλλοι ἔλεγον·
said[,] - This is he; others said:

οὐχί, ἀλλὰ ὅμοιος αὐτῷ ἐστιν. ἐκεῖνος
No, but like to him he is. That [one]

ἔλεγεν ὅτι ἐγώ εἰμι. 10 ἔλεγον οὖν
said[,] - I am. They said therefore

αὐτῷ· πῶς [οὖν] ἠνεῴχθησάν σου οἱ
to him: How then were opened of thee the

ὀφθαλμοί; 11 ἀπεκρίθη ἐκεῖνος· ὁ ἄνθρωπος
eyes? Answered that [one]: The man

ὁ λεγόμενος Ἰησοῦς πηλὸν ἐποίησεν καὶ
- being named Jesus clay made and

ἐπέχρισέν μου τοὺς ὀφθαλμοὺς καὶ εἶπέν
anointed of me the eyes and told

μοι ὅτι ὕπαγε εἰς τὸν Σιλωάμ καὶ
me[,] - Go to - Siloam and

νίψαι· ἀπελθὼν οὖν καὶ νιψάμενος ἀνέβλεψα.
wash; going therefore and washing I saw.

12 καὶ εἶπαν αὐτῷ· ποῦ ἐστιν ἐκεῖνος;
And they said to him: Where is that [one]?

λέγει· οὐκ οἶδα. 13 Ἄγουσιν αὐτὸν
He says: I do not know. They lead him

πρὸς τοὺς Φαρισαίους, τόν ποτε τυφλόν.
to the Pharisees, the at one time blind.

14 ἦν δὲ σάββατον ἐν ᾗ ἡμέρᾳ τὸν
Now it was a sabbath on which day ²the

πηλὸν ἐποίησεν ὁ Ἰησοῦς καὶ ἀνέῳξεν
⁴clay ⁵made - ¹Jesus and opened

his eyes. ¹⁵The Pharisees again asked him how he had received his sight. And he said to them, "He put clay on my eyes, and I washed, and I see." ¹⁶Some of the Pharisees said, "This man is not from God, for he does not keep the sabbath." But others said, "How can a man who is a sinner do such signs?" There was a division among them. ¹⁷So they again said to the blind man, "What do you say about him, since he has opened your eyes?" He said, "He is a prophet." 18 The Jews did not believe that he had been blind and had received his sight, until they called the parents of the man who had received his sight, ¹⁹and asked them, "Is this your son, who you say was born blind? How then does he now see?" ²⁰His parents answered, "We know that this is our son, and that he was born blind; ²¹but how he now sees we do not know, nor do we know who opened his

αὐτοῦ τοὺς ὀφθαλμούς. 15 πάλιν οὖν
of him the   eyes.   Again therefore

ἠρώτων αὐτὸν καὶ οἱ Φαρισαῖοι πῶς
⁴asked   ⁵him ²also ¹the ³Pharisees how

ἀνέβλεψεν. ὁ δὲ εἶπεν αὐτοῖς· πηλὸν
he saw.   And he said to them : Clay

ἐπέθηκέν μου ἐπὶ τοὺς ὀφθαλμούς, καὶ
he put on ⁴of me ¹on ²the ³eyes,   and

ἐνιψάμην, καὶ βλέπω. 16 ἔλεγον οὖν ἐκ
I washed, and I see.   Said therefore of

τῶν Φαρισαίων τινές· οὐκ ἔστιν οὖτος
the Pharisees   some : ⁴not ³is ¹This

παρὰ θεοῦ ὁ ἄνθρωπος, ὅτι τὸ σάββατον
⁵from ⁶God – ²man, because the sabbath

οὐ τηρεῖ. ἄλλοι [δὲ] ἔλεγον· πῶς δύναται
he keeps not. But others said : How can

ἄνθρωπος ἁμαρτωλὸς τοιαῦτα σημεῖα ποιεῖν;
man   a sinful   such   signs   to do?

καὶ σχίσμα ἦν ἐν αὐτοῖς. 17 λέγουσιν
And a division there was among them. They say

οὖν τῷ τυφλῷ πάλιν· τί σὺ λέγεις
therefore to the blind man again : What thou sayest

περὶ αὐτοῦ, ὅτι ἠνέῳξέν σου τοὺς
about him, because he opened of thee the

ὀφθαλμούς; ὁ δὲ εἶπεν ὅτι προφήτης ἐστίν.
eyes?   And he said[,] – A prophet he is.

18 οὐκ ἐπίστευσαν οὖν οἱ Ἰουδαῖοι περὶ
Did not believe therefore the Jews   about

αὐτοῦ ὅτι ἦν τυφλὸς καὶ ἀνέβλεψεν,
him   that he was blind and saw,

ἕως ὅτου ἐφώνησαν τοὺς γονεῖς αὐτοῦ
until   they called the parents of him

τοῦ ἀναβλέψαντος 19 καὶ ἠρώτησαν αὐτοὺς
of the [one] having seen and asked them

λέγοντες· οὖτός ἐστιν ὁ υἱὸς ὑμῶν, ὃν
saying : This is the son of you, whom

ὑμεῖς λέγετε ὅτι τυφλὸς ἐγεννήθη; πῶς
ye   say   that   blind he was born? how

οὖν βλέπει ἄρτι; 20 ἀπεκρίθησαν οὖν οἱ
then sees he now?   Answered therefore the

γονεῖς αὐτοῦ καὶ εἶπαν· οἴδαμεν ὅτι
parents of him and said : We know that

οὖτός ἐστιν ὁ υἱὸς ἡμῶν καὶ ὅτι τυφλὸς
this   is the son of us and that blind

ἐγεννήθη· 21 πῶς δὲ νῦν βλέπει οὐκ
he was born;   but how now he sees not

οἴδαμεν, ἢ τίς ἤνοιξεν αὐτοῦ τοὺς ὀφθαλμοὺς
we know, or who opened of him the eyes

eyes. Ask him; he is of age, he will speak for himself." 22 His parents said this because they feared the Jews, for the Jews had already agreed that if any one should confess him to be Christ, he was to be put out of the synagogue. 23 Therefore his parents said, "He is of age, ask him."

24 So for the second time they called the man who had been blind, and said to him, "Give God the praise; we know that this man is a sinner." 25 He answered, "Whether he is a sinner, I do not know; one thing I know, that though I was blind, now I see." 26 They said to him, "What did he do to you? How did he open your eyes?" 27 He answered them, "I have told you already, and you would not listen. Why do you want to hear it again? Do you too want to become his disciples?" 28 And they reviled him, saying, "You are his disciple, but we are disciples of Moses. 29 We know that God has spoken to Moses, but as for this man, we do not know where he comes from." 30 The man an-

ἡμεῖς οὐκ οἴδαμεν· αὐτὸν ἐρωτήσατε,
we know not; him ask ye,
ἡλικίαν ἔχει, αὐτὸς περὶ ἑαυτοῦ λαλήσει.
age he has, he about himself will speak.
22 ταῦτα εἶπαν οἱ γονεῖς αὐτοῦ ὅτι ἐφο-
These things said the parents of him because they
βοῦντο τοὺς Ἰουδαίους· ἤδη γὰρ συνετέθειντο
feared the Jews; for already had agreed
οἱ Ἰουδαῖοι ἵνα ἐάν τις αὐτὸν ὁμολογήσῃ
the Jews that if anyone him should acknowledge
χριστόν, ἀποσυνάγωγος γένηται.
[to be] Christ, put away from [the] synagogue he would be.
23 διὰ τοῦτο οἱ γονεῖς αὐτοῦ εἶπαν ὅτι
Therefore the parents of him said[,] –
ἡλικίαν ἔχει, αὐτὸν ἐπερωτήσατε. 24 Ἐφώνησαν
Age he has, him question ye. They called
οὖν τὸν ἄνθρωπον ἐκ δευτέρου ὃς ἦν
therefore the man a second time who was
τυφλός, καὶ εἶπαν αὐτῷ· δὸς δόξαν τῷ
blind, and said to him : Give glory –
θεῷ· ἡμεῖς οἴδαμεν ὅτι οὗτος ὁ ἄνθρωπος
to God; we know that this – man
ἁμαρτωλός ἐστιν. 25 ἀπεκρίθη οὖν ἐκεῖνος·
sinful is. Answered therefore that [one]:
εἰ ἁμαρτωλός ἐστιν οὐκ οἶδα· ἓν οἶδα,
If sinful he is I know not; one thing I know,
ὅτι τυφλὸς ὢν ἄρτι βλέπω. 26 εἶπαν
that blind being now I see. They said
οὖν αὐτῷ· τί ἐποίησέν σοι; πῶς ἤνοιξέν
therefore to him : What did he to thee? how opened he
σου τοὺς ὀφθαλμούς; 27 ἀπεκρίθη αὐτοῖς·
of thee the eyes? He answered them :
εἶπον ὑμῖν ἤδη καὶ οὐκ ἠκούσατε· τί
I told you already and ye heard not; why
πάλιν θέλετε ἀκούειν; μὴ καὶ ὑμεῖς
again wish ye to hear? not also ye
θέλετε αὐτοῦ μαθηταὶ γενέσθαι; 28 καὶ
wish of him disciples to become? And
ἐλοιδόρησαν αὐτὸν καὶ εἶπαν· σὺ μαθητὴς
they reviled him and said : Thou a disciple
εἶ ἐκείνου, ἡμεῖς δὲ τοῦ Μωϋσέως ἐσμὲν
art of that man, but we – of Moses are
μαθηταί· 29 ἡμεῖς οἴδαμεν ὅτι Μωϋσεῖ
disciples; we know that by Moses
λελάληκεν ὁ θεός, τοῦτον δὲ οὐκ οἴδαμεν
has spoken – God, but this man – we know not
πόθεν ἐστίν. 30 ἀπεκρίθη ὁ ἄνθρωπος
whence he is. Answered the man

swered, "Why, this is a marvel! You do not know where he comes from, and yet he opened my eyes. ³¹We know that God does not listen to sinners, but if any one is a worshiper of God and does his will, God listens to him. ³²Never since the world began has it been heard that any one opened the eyes of a man born blind. ³³If this man were not from God, he could do nothing." ³⁴They answered him, "You were born in utter sin, and would you teach us?" And they cast him out.

35 Jesus heard that they had cast him out, and having found him he said, "Do you believe in the Son of man?"ˢ ³⁶He answered, "And who is he, sir, that I may believe in him?" ³⁷Jesus said to him, "You have seen him, and it is he who speaks to you." ³⁸He said, "Lord, I be-lieve"; and he worshiped him. ³⁹Jesus said, "For judgment I came into this world, that those who do not see may see, and that those who see may become blind."

ˢ Other ancient authorities read *the Son of God*

καὶ εἶπεν αὐτοῖς· ἐν τούτῳ γὰρ τὸ
and said to them : In this then the

θαυμαστόν ἐστιν, ὅτι ὑμεῖς οὐκ οἴδατε
marvellous thing is, that ye do not know

πόθεν ἐστίν, καὶ ἤνοιξέν μου τοὺς
whence he is, and he opened of me the

ὀφθαλμούς. 31 οἴδαμεν ὅτι ὁ θεὸς
eyes. We know that - God

ἁμαρτωλῶν οὐκ ἀκούει, ἀλλ' ἐάν τις
sinful men does not hear, ◦ but if anyone

θεοσεβὴς ᾖ καὶ τὸ θέλημα αὐτοῦ ποιῇ,
godfearing is and the will of him does,

τούτου ἀκούει. 32 ἐκ τοῦ αἰῶνος οὐκ
this man he hears. From the age not

ἠκούσθη ὅτι ἠνέῳξέν τις ὀφθαλμοὺς τυφλοῦ
it was heard that ²opened ¹anyone eyes of a blind man

γεγεννημένου· 33 εἰ μὴ ἦν οὗτος παρὰ
having been born; if ³not ²was ¹this man from

θεοῦ, οὐκ ἠδύνατο ποιεῖν οὐδέν. 34 ἀπεκρίθησαν
God, he could not *to* do no(any)thing. They answered

καὶ εἶπαν αὐτῷ· ἐν ἁμαρτίαις σὺ ἐγεννήθης
and said to him : In sins thou wast born

ὅλος, καὶ σὺ διδάσκεις ἡμᾶς; καὶ ἐξέβαλον
wholly, and thou teachest us? and they cast *out*

αὐτὸν ἔξω. 35 Ἤκουσεν Ἰησοῦς ὅτι
him outside. Heard Jesus that

ἐξέβαλον αὐτὸν ἔξω, καὶ εὑρὼν αὐτὸν
they cast *out* him outside, and finding him

εἶπεν· σὺ πιστεύεις εἰς τὸν υἱὸν τοῦ
said : Thou believest in the Son -

ἀνθρώπου; 36 ἀπεκρίθη ἐκεῖνος καὶ εἶπεν·
of man? Answered that [one] and said :

καὶ τίς ἐστιν, κύριε, ἵνα πιστεύσω εἰς
And who is he, sir, that I may believe in

αὐτόν; 37 εἶπεν αὐτῷ ὁ Ἰησοῦς· καὶ
him? Said to him - Jesus : Both

ἑώρακας αὐτὸν καὶ ὁ λαλῶν μετὰ σοῦ
thou hast seen him and the [one] speaking with thee

ἐκεῖνός ἐστιν. 38 ὁ δὲ ἔφη· πιστεύω, κύριε·
that [one] is. And he said : I believe, sir;

καὶ προσεκύνησεν αὐτῷ. 39 καὶ εἶπεν ὁ
and he worshipped him. And said -

Ἰησοῦς· εἰς κρίμα ἐγὼ εἰς τὸν κόσμον
Jesus : For judgment I into - world

τοῦτον ἦλθον, ἵνα οἱ μὴ βλέποντες
this came, that the [ones] not seeing

βλέπωσιν καὶ οἱ βλέποντες τυφλοὶ γένωνται.
may see and the [ones] seeing blind may become.

⁴⁰Some of the Pharisees near him heard this, and they said to him, "Are we also blind?" ⁴¹Jesus said to them, "If you were blind, you would have no guilt; but now that you say, 'We see,' your guilt remains.

40 Ἤκουσαν ἐκ τῶν Φαρισαίων ταῦτα
⁸heard ¹[Some] ²of ³the ⁴Pharisees ⁵these things
οἱ μετ' αὐτοῦ ὄντες, καὶ εἶπαν αὐτῷ·
– ⁶with ⁷him ⁸being, and they said to him :
μὴ καὶ ἡμεῖς τυφλοί ἐσμεν; 41 εἶπεν
Not also we blind are? Said
αὐτοῖς ὁ Ἰησοῦς· εἰ τυφλοὶ ἦτε, οὐκ
to them – Jesus : If blind ye were, not
ἂν εἴχετε ἁμαρτίαν· νῦν δὲ λέγετε ὅτι
ye would have had sin; but now ye say[,] –
βλέπομεν· ἡ ἁμαρτία ὑμῶν μένει.
We see; the sin of you remains.

CHAPTER 10

"TRULY, truly, I say to you, he who does not enter the sheepfold by the door but climbs in by another way, that man is a thief and a robber; ²but he who enters by the door is the shepherd of the sheep. ³To him the gatekeeper opens; the sheep hear his voice, and he calls his own sheep by name and leads them out. ⁴When he has brought out all his own, he goes before them, and the sheep follow him, for they know his voice. ⁵A stranger they will not follow, but they will flee from him, for they do not know the voice of strangers." ⁶This figure Jesus used with them, but they did not under-

10 Ἀμὴν ἀμὴν λέγω ὑμῖν, ὁ μὴ
Truly truly I say to you, the [one] not
εἰσερχόμενος διὰ τῆς θύρας εἰς τὴν
entering through the door into the
αὐλὴν τῶν προβάτων ἀλλὰ ἀναβαίνων
fold of the sheep but going up
ἀλλαχόθεν, ἐκεῖνος κλέπτης ἐστὶν καὶ
by another way, that [one] a thief is and
λῃστής· 2 ὁ δὲ εἰσερχόμενος διὰ τῆς
a robber; but the [one] entering through the
θύρας ποιμήν ἐστιν τῶν προβάτων. 3 τούτῳ
door shepherd is of the sheep. To this [one]
ὁ θυρωρὸς ἀνοίγει, καὶ τὰ πρόβατα τῆς
the doorkeeper opens, and the sheep the
φωνῆς αὐτοῦ ἀκούει, καὶ τὰ ἴδια πρόβατα
voice of him hears, and the(his) own sheep
φωνεῖ κατ' ὄνομα καὶ ἐξάγει αὐτά.
he calls by name and leads out them.
4 ὅταν τὰ ἴδια πάντα ἐκβάλῃ, ἔμπροσθεν
When the(his) own all he puts forth, in front of
αὐτῶν πορεύεται, καὶ τὰ πρόβατα αὐτῷ
them he goes, and the sheep him
ἀκολουθεῖ, ὅτι οἴδασιν τὴν φωνὴν αὐτοῦ·
follows, because they know the voice of him;
5 ἀλλοτρίῳ δὲ οὐ μὴ ἀκολουθήσουσιν,
but a stranger by no means will they follow,
ἀλλὰ φεύξονται ἀπ' αὐτοῦ, ὅτι οὐκ
but will flee from him, because not
οἴδασιν τῶν ἀλλοτρίων τὴν φωνήν.
they know of the strangers the voice.
6 Ταύτην τὴν παροιμίαν εἶπεν αὐτοῖς ὁ
This – allegory told them the
Ἰησοῦς· ἐκεῖνοι δὲ οὐκ ἔγνωσαν τίνα
Jesus; but those men knew not what things

stand what he was saying to them.

7 So Jesus again said to them, "Truly, truly, I say to you, I am the door of the sheep. ⁸All who came before me are thieves and robbers; but the sheep did not heed them. ⁹I am the door; if any one enters by me, he will be saved, and will go in and out and find pasture. ¹⁰The thief comes only to steal and kill and destroy; I came that they may have life, and have it abundantly. ¹¹I am the good shepherd. The good shepherd lays down his life for the sheep. ¹²He who is a hireling and not a shepherd, whose own the sheep are not, sees the wolf coming and leaves the sheep and flees; and the wolf snatches them and scatters them. ¹³He flees because he is a hireling and cares nothing for the sheep. ¹⁴I am the good shepherd; I know my own and my own know me, ¹⁵as the Father knows me and I know the Father; and I lay down my life for the

ἦν   ἃ   ἐλάλει αὐτοῖς. 7 Εἶπεν οὖν πάλιν
they were which he spoke to them.   Said therefore again

ὁ   'Ιησοῦς·   ἀμὴν   ἀμὴν   λέγω   ὑμῖν   ὅτι
–   Jesus :   Truly   truly   I say   to you   that

ἐγώ   εἰμι   ἡ   θύρα   τῶν   προβάτων.   8 πάντες
I   am   the door of the sheep.   All

ὅσοι   ἦλθον   πρὸ   ἐμοῦ   κλέπται   εἰσὶν   καὶ
who   came   before   me   thieves   are   and

λησταί·   ἀλλ'   οὐκ   ἤκουσαν   αὐτῶν   τὰ
robbers;   but   did not hear   them   the

πρόβατα.   9 ἐγώ   εἰμι   ἡ   θύρα·   δι'   ἐμοῦ
sheep.   I   am   the door· through me

ἐάν   τις   εἰσέλθῃ,   σωθήσεται,   καὶ   εἰσελεύ-
if   anyone   enters,   he will be saved, and   will go

σεται   καὶ   ἐξελεύσεται   καὶ   νομὴν   εὑρήσει.
in   and   will go out   and   pasture   will find.

10 ὁ   κλέπτης   οὐκ   ἔρχεται   εἰ   μὴ   ἵνα
The   thief   comes not   except   that

κλέψῃ   καὶ   θύσῃ   καὶ   ἀπολέσῃ·   ἐγὼ   ἦλθον
he may steal and kill   and   destroy;   I   came

ἵνα   ζωὴν   ἔχωσιν   καὶ   περισσὸν   ἔχωσιν.
that   life they may have and abundantly they may have.

11 'Εγώ   εἰμι   ὁ   ποιμὴν   ὁ   καλός.   ὁ
I   am   the shepherd   –   good.   The

ποιμὴν   ὁ   καλὸς   τὴν   ψυχὴν   αὐτοῦ   τίθησιν
shepherd –   good   the   life   of him   lays down

ὑπὲρ   τῶν   προβάτων·   12 ὁ   μισθωτὸς   καὶ
for   the   sheep;   the   hireling   and

οὐκ   ὢν   ποιμήν,   οὗ   οὐκ ἔστιν τὰ πρόβατα
not being a shepherd, of whom is(are) not the sheep

ἴδια,   θεωρεῖ   τὸν   λύκον   ἐρχόμενον   καὶ
[his] own, beholds the   wolf   coming   and

ἀφίησιν   τὰ   πρόβατα   καὶ   φεύγει,   —   καὶ
leaves   the   sheep   and   flees,   —   and

ὁ   λύκος   ἁρπάζει   αὐτὰ   καὶ   σκορπίζει·   —
the wolf   seizes   them   and   scatters;   —

13 ὅτι   μισθωτός   ἐστιν   καὶ   οὐ   μέλει
because   a hireling   he is   and   it matters not

αὐτῷ   περὶ   τῶν   προβάτων.   14 ἐγώ   εἰμι
to him   about   the   sheep.   I   am

ὁ   ποιμὴν   ὁ   καλός,   καὶ   γινώσκω   τὰ
the shepherd –   good,   and   I know   –

ἐμὰ   καὶ   γινώσκουσί   με   τὰ   ἐμά,   15 καθὼς
mine and   ²know   ³me   –   ¹mine,   as

γινώσκει   με   ὁ   πατὴρ   κἀγὼ   γινώσκω   τὸν
³knows   ⁴me ¹the ²Father and I   know   the

πατέρα,   καὶ   τὴν   ψυχὴν   μου   τίθημι   ὑπὲρ
Father,   and   the   life   of me I lay down   for

sheep. ¹⁶And I have other sheep, that are not of this fold; I must bring them also, and they will heed my voice. So there shall be one flock, one shepherd. ¹⁷For this reason the Father loves me, because I lay down my life, that I may take it again. ¹⁸No one takes it from me, but I lay it down of my own accord. I have power to lay it down, and I have power to take it again; this charge I have received from my Father." 19 There was again a division among the Jews because of these words. ²⁰Many of them said, "He has a demon, and he is mad; why listen to him?" ²¹Others said, "These are not the sayings of one who has a demon. Can a demon open the eyes of the blind?" 22 It was the feast of the Dedication at Jerusalem; ²³it was winter, and Jesus was walking in the temple, in the portioo of Solomon. ²⁴So the Jews gathered round him and said to him, "How long will you keep us in suspense? If you are the

τῶν προβάτων. **16** καὶ ἄλλα πρόβατα
the　　sheep.　　　And　other　　sheep

ἔχω ἃ οὐκ ἔστιν ἐκ τῆς αὐλῆς ταύτης·
I have which is(are) not of　－　fold　　this;

κἀκεῖνα δεῖ με ἀγαγεῖν, καὶ τῆς φωνῆς
those also it behoves me to bring,　and　the　voice

μου ἀκούσουσιν, καὶ γενήσεται μία ποίμνη,
of me they will hear, and there will become one flock,

εἷς ποιμήν. **17** διὰ τοῦτό με ὁ πατὴρ
one shepherd.　　Therefore me the Father

ἀγαπᾷ ὅτι ἐγὼ τίθημι τὴν ψυχήν μου,
loves because I lay down the life of me,

ἵνα πάλιν λάβω αὐτήν. **18** οὐδεὶς ἦρεν
that again I may take it.　　　No one took

αὐτὴν ἀπ' ἐμοῦ, ἀλλ' ἐγὼ τίθημι αὐτὴν
it from me, but I lay down it

ἀπ' ἐμαυτοῦ. ἐξουσίαν ἔχω θεῖναι αὐτήν,
from myself.　Authority I have to lay down it,

καὶ ἐξουσίαν ἔχω πάλιν λαβεῖν αὐτήν·
and authority I have again to take it;

ταύτην τὴν ἐντολὴν ἔλαβον παρὰ τοῦ
this － commandment I received from the

πατρός μου. **19** Σχίσμα πάλιν ἐγένετο ἐν
Father of me.　　A division again there was among

τοῖς Ἰουδαίοις διὰ τοὺς λόγους τούτους.
the Jews because of － words these.

20 ἔλεγον δὲ πολλοὶ ἐξ αὐτῶν· δαιμόνιον
And said many of them : A demon

ἔχει καὶ μαίνεται· τί αὐτοῦ ἀκούετε;
he has and raves; why him hear ye?

21 ἄλλοι ἔλεγον· ταῦτα τὰ ῥήματα οὐκ
Others said : These － words not

ἔστιν δαιμονιζομένου· μὴ δαιμόνιον δύναται
is(are) of one demon-possessed; not a demon can

τυφλῶν ὀφθαλμοὺς ἀνοῖξαι;
of blind men eyes to open?

22 Ἐγένετο τότε τὰ ἐγκαίνια ἐν τοῖς
There was then the Dedication in －

Ἱεροσολύμοις· χειμὼν ἦν· **23** καὶ περιεπάτει
Jerusalem; winter it was; and walked

ὁ Ἰησοῦς ἐν τῷ ἱερῷ ἐν τῇ στοᾷ τοῦ
－ Jesus in the temple in the porch －

Σολομῶνος. **24** ἐκύκλωσαν οὖν αὐτὸν οἱ
of Solomon.　　Surrounded therefore him the

Ἰουδαῖοι καὶ ἔλεγον αὐτῷ· ἕως πότε
Jews and said to him: Until when

τὴν ψυχὴν ἡμῶν αἴρεις; εἰ σὺ εἶ
the life(soul) of us holdest thou * ? if thou art

* That is, in suspense.

Christ, tell us plainly."
²⁵Jesus answered them,
"I told you, and you do
not believe. The works
that I do in my Father's
name, they bear witness
to me; ²⁶but you do not
believe, because you do
not belong to my sheep.
²⁷My sheep hear my
voice, and I know them,
and they follow me;
²⁸and I give them eternal
life, and they shall never
perish, and no one shall
snatch them out of my
hand. ²⁹My Father, who
has given them to me,ᵗ
is greater than all, and
no one is able to snatch
them out of the Father's
hand. ³⁰I and the Father
are one."
31 The Jews took up
stones again to stone
him. ³²Jesus answered
them, "I have shown you
many good works from
the Father; for which of
these do you stone me?"
³³The Jews answered him,
"We stone you for no
good work but for blas-
phemy; because you,
being a man, make your-
self God." ³⁴Jesus an-

ᵗ Other ancient authorities
read *What my Father has
given to me*

ὁ χριστός, εἰπὸν ἡμῖν παρρησίᾳ. 25 ἀπεκρίθη
the Christ, tell us plainly. Answered

αὐτοῖς ὁ Ἰησοῦς· εἶπον ὑμῖν, καὶ
them – Jesus : I told you, and

οὐ πιστεύετε· τὰ ἔργα ἃ ἐγὼ ποιῶ ἐν τῷ
ye do not believe; the works which I do in the

ὀνόματι τοῦ πατρός μου, ταῦτα μαρτυρεῖ
name of the Father of me, these witnesses

περὶ ἐμοῦ· ἀλλὰ ὑμεῖς οὐ πιστεύετε,
concerning me; but ye do not believe,

26 ὅτι οὐκ ἐστὲ ἐκ τῶν προβάτων τῶν
because ye are not of the ²sheep –

ἐμῶν. 27 τὰ πρόβατα τὰ ἐμὰ τῆς φωνῆς
¹my. the sheep – My the voice

μου ἀκούουσιν, κἀγὼ γινώσκω αὐτά, καὶ
of me hear, and I know them, and

ἀκολουθοῦσίν μοι, 28 κἀγὼ δίδωμι αὐτοῖς
they follow me, and I give to them

ζωὴν αἰώνιον, καὶ οὐ μὴ ἀπόλωνται εἰς
life eternal, and by no means they perish unto

τὸν αἰῶνα, καὶ οὐχ ἁρπάσει τις αὐτὰ
the age, and ²shall not seize ¹anyone them

ἐκ τῆς χειρός μου. 29 ὁ πατήρ μου ὃ
out of the hand of me. The Father of me who

δέδωκέν μοι πάντων μεῖζόν ἐστιν, καὶ
has given to me [than] all greater is, and

οὐδεὶς δύναται ἁρπάζειν ἐκ τῆς χειρὸς
no one can to seize out of the hand

τοῦ πατρός. 30 ἐγὼ καὶ ὁ πατὴρ ἕν
of the Father. I and the Father one

ἐσμεν. 31 Ἐβάστασαν πάλιν λίθους οἱ
we are. Lifted again stones the

Ἰουδαῖοι ἵνα λιθάσωσιν αὐτόν. 32 ἀπ-
Jews that they might stone him. An-

εκρίθη αὐτοῖς ὁ Ἰησοῦς· πολλὰ ἔργα
swered them – Jesus : Many ²works

ἔδειξα ὑμῖν καλὰ ἐκ τοῦ πατρός· διὰ
³I showed ⁴you ¹good of the Father; because of

ποῖον αὐτῶν ἔργον ἐμὲ λιθάζετε;
which ²of them ¹work ⁴me ³stone ye?

33 ἀπεκρίθησαν αὐτῷ οἱ Ἰουδαῖοι· περὶ
Answered him the Jews : Concerning

καλοῦ ἔργου οὐ λιθάζομέν σε ἀλλὰ περὶ
a good work we do not stone thee but concerning

βλασφημίας, καὶ ὅτι σὺ ἄνθρωπος ὢν
blasphemy, and because thou a man being

ποιεῖς σεαυτὸν θεόν. 34 ἀπεκρίθη αὐτοῖς
makest thyself God. Answered them

swered them, "Is it not written in your law, 'I said, you are gods'? ³⁵If he called them gods to whom the word of God came (and scripture cannot be broken), ³⁶do you say of him whom the Father consecrated and sent into the world, 'You are blaspheming,' because I said, 'I am the Son of God'? ³⁷If I am not doing the works of my Father, then do not believe me; ³⁸but if I do them, even though you do not believe me, believe the works, that you may know and understand that the Father is in me and I am in the Father." ³⁹Again they tried to arrest him, but he escaped from their hands.

40 He went away again across the Jordan to the place where John at first baptized, and there he remained. ⁴¹And many came to him; and they said, "John did no sign, but everything that John said about this man was true." ⁴²And many believed in him there.

ὁ	Ἰησοῦς·	οὐκ	ἔστιν	γεγραμμένον	ἐν	τῷ
-	Jesus :	Is it not	*having been* written	in	the

νόμῳ	ὑμῶν	ὅτι	ἐγὼ	εἶπα·	θεοί	ἐστε;
law	of you[,]	-	I	said :	Gods	ye are?

35 εἰ ἐκείνους εἶπεν θεοὺς πρὸς οὓς ὁ
¹if ³those ²he called ⁴gods with whom the

λόγος τοῦ θεοῦ ἐγένετο, καὶ οὐ δύναται
word - of God was, and cannot

λυθῆναι ἡ γραφή, 36 ὃν ὁ πατὴρ
to be broken the scripture, ³[him] whom ⁴the ⁵Father

ἡγίασεν καὶ ἀπέστειλεν εἰς τὸν κόσμον
⁶sanctified ⁷and ⁸sent ⁹into ¹⁰the ¹¹world

ὑμεῖς λέγετε ὅτι βλασφημεῖς, ὅτι εἶπον·
²ye ¹tell[,] - Thou blasphemest, because I said :

υἱὸς τοῦ θεοῦ εἰμι; 37 εἰ οὐ ποιῶ τὰ ἔργα
Son - of God I am? If I do not the works

τοῦ πατρός μου, μὴ πιστεύετέ μοι· 38 εἰ δὲ
of the Father of me, do not believe me; but if

ποιῶ, κἂν ἐμοὶ μὴ πιστεύητε, τοῖς ἔργοις
I do, even if me ye do not believe, the works

πιστεύετε, ἵνα γνῶτε καὶ γινώσκητε
believe, that ye may know* and continue to know*

ὅτι ἐν ἐμοὶ ὁ πατὴρ κἀγὼ ἐν τῷ πατρί.
that in me the Father [is] and I in the Father.

39 Ἐζήτουν οὖν αὐτὸν πάλιν πιάσαι· καὶ
They sought therefore him again to arrest; and

ἐξῆλθεν ἐκ τῆς χειρὸς αὐτῶν.
he went forth out of the hand of them.

40 Καὶ ἀπῆλθεν πάλιν πέραν τοῦ
And he went away again across the

Ἰορδάνου εἰς τὸν τόπον ὅπου ἦν Ἰωάννης
Jordan to the place where was John

τὸ πρῶτον βαπτίζων, καὶ ἔμενεν ἐκεῖ.
at first baptizing, and remained there.

41 καὶ πολλοὶ ἦλθον πρὸς αὐτὸν καὶ
And many came to him and

ἔλεγον ὅτι Ἰωάννης μὲν σημεῖον ἐποίησεν
said[,] - John indeed sign did

οὐδέν, πάντα δὲ ὅσα εἶπεν Ἰωάννης περὶ
none, but all things how many said John about

τούτου ἀληθῆ ἦν. 42 καὶ πολλοὶ ἐπίστευσαν
this man true was(were). And many believed

εἰς αὐτὸν ἐκεῖ.
in him there.

CHAPTER 11

NOW a certain man was ill, Laz′arus of

11 Ἦν δέ τις ἀσθενῶν, Λάζαρος ἀπὸ
Now there was a certain [man] ailing, Lazarus from

* Different tenses (aorist and present) of the same verb.

Bethany, the village of Mary and her sister Martha. ²It was Mary who anointed the Lord with ointment and wiped his feet with her hair, whose brother Laz'arus was ill. ³So the sisters sent to him, saying, "Lord, he whom you love is ill." ⁴But when Jesus heard it he said, "This illness is not unto death; it is for the glory of God, so that the Son of God may be glorified by means of it."

5 Now Jesus loved Martha and her sister and Laz'arus. ⁶So when he heard that he was ill, he stayed two days longer in the place where he was. ⁷Then after this he said to the disciples, "Let us go into Judea again." ⁸The disciples said to him, "Rabbi, the Jews were but now seeking to stone you, and you are going there again?" ⁹Jesus answered, "Are there not twelve hours in the day? If any one walks in the day, he does not stumble, because he sees the light of this world. ¹⁰But if any one walks in the night, he stumbles,

Βηθανίας,   ἐκ   τῆς   κώμης   Μαρίας   καὶ
Bethany,   of   the   village   of Mary   and

Μάρθας   τῆς   ἀδελφῆς   αὐτῆς.   2 ἦν   δὲ
Martha   the   sister   of her.   And it was

Μαριὰμ   ἡ   ἀλείψασα   τὸν   κύριον   μύρῳ
Mary   the [one]   anointing   the   Lord   with ointment

καὶ   ἐκμάξασα   τοὺς   πόδας   αὐτοῦ   ταῖς
and   wiping off   the   feet   of him   with the

θριξὶν   αὐτῆς,   ἧς   ὁ   ἀδελφὸς   Λάζαρος
hairs   of her,   of whom   the   brother   Lazarus

ἠσθένει.   3 ἀπέστειλαν   οὖν   αἱ   ἀδελφαὶ
ailed.   Sent   therefore   the   sisters

πρὸς   αὐτὸν   λέγουσαι·   κύριε,   ἴδε   ὃν
to   him   saying :   Lord,   behold[,] [he] whom

φιλεῖς   ἀσθενεῖ.   4 ἀκούσας   δὲ   ὁ   Ἰησοῦς
thou lovest   ails.   And hearing   –   Jesus

εἶπεν·   αὕτη   ἡ   ἀσθένεια   οὐκ   ἔστιν   πρὸς
said :   This   –   ailment   is not   to

θάνατον   ἀλλ'   ὑπὲρ   τῆς   δόξης   τοῦ   θεοῦ,
death   but   for   the   glory   –   of God,

ἵνα   δοξασθῇ   ὁ   υἱὸς   τοῦ   θεοῦ   δι'   αὐτῆς.
that may be glorified the   Son   –   of God   through   it.

5 ἠγάπα   δὲ   ὁ   Ἰησοῦς   τὴν   Μάρθαν   καὶ
Now loved   –   ²Jesus   –   Martha   and

τὴν   ἀδελφὴν   αὐτῆς   καὶ   τὸν   Λάζαρον.
the   sister   of her   and   –   Lazarus.

6 ὡς   οὖν   ἤκουσεν   ὅτι   ἀσθενεῖ,   τότε   μὲν
When therefore he heard   that   he ails(ed),   then   –

ἔμεινεν   ἐν   ᾧ   ἦν   τόπῳ   δύο   ἡμέρας·
he remained ¹in   ²which ⁴he was   ³place   two   days;

7 ἔπειτα   μετὰ   τοῦτο   λέγει   τοῖς   μαθηταῖς·
then   after   this   he says   to the   disciples :

ἄγωμεν   εἰς   τὴν   Ἰουδαίαν   πάλιν.   8 λέγουσιν
Let us go into   –   Judæa   again.   Say

αὐτῷ   οἱ   μαθηταί·   ῥαββί,   νῦν   ἐζήτουν
to him   the   disciples :   Rabbi,   ⁴now ³were ⁵seeking

σε   λιθάσαι   οἱ   Ἰουδαῖοι,   καὶ   πάλιν   ὑπάγεις
⁷thee ⁶to stone ¹the   ²Jews,   and   again   goest thou

ἐκεῖ;   9 ἀπεκρίθη   Ἰησοῦς·   οὐχὶ   δώδεκα
there?   Answered   Jesus :   Not   twelve

ὧραί   εἰσιν   τῆς   ἡμέρας;   ἐάν   τις   περιπατῇ
hours are there of the   day?   if   anyone   walks

ἐν   τῇ   ἡμέρᾳ,   οὐ   προσκόπτει,   ὅτι   τὸ   φῶς
in   the   day,   he does not stumble, because the   light

τοῦ   κόσμου   τούτου   βλέπει·   10 ἐὰν   δέ
–   world   of this   he sees;   but if

τις   περιπατῇ   ἐν   τῇ   νυκτί,   προσκόπτει,
anyone   walks   in   the   night,   he stumbles,

because the light is not in him." ¹¹Thus he spoke, and then he said to them, "Our friend Laz'-arus has fallen asleep, but I go to awake him out of sleep." ¹²The disciples said to him, "Lord, if he has fallen alseep, he will recover." ¹³Now Jesus had spoken of his death, but they thought that he meant taking rest in sleep. ¹⁴Then Jesus told them plainly, "Laz'arus is dead; ¹⁵and for your sake I am glad that I was not there, so that you may believe. But let us go to him." ¹⁶Thomas, called the Twin, said to his fellow disciples, "Let us also go, that we may die with him."

17 Now when Jesus came, he found that Laz'arus had already been in the tomb four days. ¹⁸Bethany was near Jerusalem, about two miles off, ¹⁹and many of the Jews had come to Martha and Mary to console them concerning their brother. ²⁰When Martha heard that Jesus was coming, she went and met him, while Mary sat in the house. ²¹Martha

ὅτι τὸ φῶς οὐκ ἔστιν ἐν αὐτῷ. 11 ταῦτα
because the light is not in him. These things

εἶπεν, καὶ μετὰ τοῦτο λέγει αὐτοῖς·
he said, and after this he says to them :

Λάζαρος ὁ φίλος ἡμῶν κεκοίμηται· ἀλλὰ
Lazarus the friend of us has fallen asleep; but

πορεύομαι ἵνα ἐξυπνίσω αὐτόν. 12 εἶπαν
I am going that I may awaken him. Said

οὖν οἱ μαθηταὶ αὐτῷ· κύριε, εἰ κεκοίμηται,
there- the disciples to him: Lord, if he has fallen asleep,
fore

σωθήσεται. 13 εἰρήκει δὲ ὁ Ἰησοῦς περὶ
he will be healed. Now had spoken - Jesus concerning

τοῦ θανάτου αὐτοῦ· ἐκεῖνοι δὲ ἔδοξαν ὅτι
the death of him; but those men thought that

περὶ τῆς κοιμήσεως τοῦ ὕπνου λέγει.
concerning the sleep - of slumber he says.

14 τότε οὖν εἶπεν αὐτοῖς ὁ Ἰησοῦς
Then therefore told them - Jesus

παρρησίᾳ· Λάζαρος ἀπέθανεν, 15 καὶ χαίρω
plainly : Lazarus died, and I rejoice

δι᾽ ὑμᾶς, ἵνα πιστεύσητε, ὅτι οὐκ ἤμην
because of you, that ye may believe, that I was not

ἐκεῖ· ἀλλὰ ἄγωμεν πρὸς αὐτόν. 16 εἶπεν
there; but let us go to him. Said

οὖν Θωμᾶς ὁ λεγόμενος Δίδυμος τοῖς
therefore Thomas - being called Twin to the(his)

συμμαθηταῖς· ἄγωμεν καὶ ἡμεῖς ἵνα
fellow-disciples : Let go also we(us) that

ἀποθάνωμεν μετ᾽ αὐτοῦ. 17 Ἐλθὼν οὖν
we may die with him. Coming therefore

ὁ Ἰησοῦς εὗρεν αὐτὸν τέσσαρας ἤδη
- Jesus found him ²four ¹already

ἡμέρας ἔχοντα ἐν τῷ μνημείῳ. 18 ἦν δὲ
³days having(being) in the tomb. Now was

Βηθανία ἐγγὺς τῶν Ἱεροσολύμων ὡς ἀπὸ
Bethany near - Jerusalem about ²away

σταδίων δεκαπέντε. 19 πολλοὶ δὲ ἐκ τῶν
²furlongs ¹fifteen. And many of the

Ἰουδαίων ἐληλύθεισαν πρὸς τὴν Μάρθαν
Jews had come to - Martha

καὶ Μαριάμ, ἵνα παραμυθήσωνται αὐτὰς
and Mary, that they might console them

περὶ τοῦ ἀδελφοῦ. 20 ἡ οὖν Μάρθα ὡς
concerning the(ir) brother. - Therefore Martha when

ἤκουσεν ὅτι Ἰησοῦς ἔρχεται, ὑπήντησεν
she heard that Jesus is(was) coming, met

αὐτῷ· Μαριὰμ δὲ ἐν τῷ οἴκῳ ἐκαθέζετο.
him; but Mary in the house sat.

said to Jesus, "Lord, if you had been here, my brother would not have died. [22]And even now I know that whatever you ask from God, God will give you." [23]Jesus said to her, "Your brother will rise again." [24]Martha said to him, "I know that he will rise again in the resurrection at the last day." [25]Jesus said to her, "I am the resurrection and the life;[u] he who believes in me, though he die, yet shall he live, [26]and whoever lives and believes in me shall never die. Do you believe this?" [27]She said to him, "Yes, Lord; I believe that you are the Christ, the Son of God, he who is coming into the world."

28 When she had said this, she went and called her sister Mary, saying quietly, "The Teacher is here and is calling for you." [29]And when she heard it, she rose quickly and went to him. [30]Now Jesus had not yet come to the village, but was still in the place where Martha had met him. [31]When the Jews who were with her in the

[u] Other ancient authorities omit *and the life*

21 εἶπεν οὖν ἡ Μάρθα πρὸς Ἰησοῦν·
Said therefore - Martha to Jesus :
κύριε, εἰ ἦς ὧδε, οὐκ ἂν ἀπέθανεν ὁ
Lord, if thou wast here, would not have died the
ἀδελφός μου. 22 καὶ νῦν οἶδα ὅτι ὅσα ἂν
brother of me. And now I know that whatever things
αἰτήσῃ τὸν θεὸν δώσει σοι ὁ θεός.
thou askest - God ²will give ³thee - ¹God.
23 λέγει αὐτῇ ὁ Ἰησοῦς· ἀναστήσεται ὁ
Says to her - Jesus : Will rise again the
ἀδελφός σου. 24 λέγει αὐτῷ ἡ Μάρθα·
brother of thee. Says to him - Martha :
οἶδα ὅτι ἀναστήσεται ἐν τῇ ἀναστάσει
I know that he will rise again in the resurrection
ἐν τῇ ἐσχάτῃ ἡμέρᾳ. 25 εἶπεν αὐτῇ ὁ
in the last day. Said to her -
Ἰησοῦς· ἐγώ εἰμι ἡ ἀνάστασις καὶ ἡ
Jesus : I am the resurrection and the
ζωή· ὁ πιστεύων εἰς ἐμὲ κἂν ἀποθάνῃ
life; the [one] believing in me even if he should die
ζήσεται, 26 καὶ πᾶς ὁ ζῶν καὶ πιστεύων
will live, and everyone living and believing
εἰς ἐμὲ οὐ μὴ ἀποθάνῃ εἰς τὸν αἰῶνα·
in me by no means dies unto the age :
πιστεύεις τοῦτο; 27 λέγει αὐτῷ· ναί, κύριε·
believest thou this? She says to him : Yes, Lord;
ἐγὼ πεπίστευκα ὅτι σὺ εἶ ὁ χριστὸς ὁ
I have believed that thou art the Christ the
υἱὸς τοῦ θεοῦ ὁ εἰς τὸν κόσμον ἐρχόμενος.
Son - of God ¹the ²into ⁴the ⁵world ³[one] coming.
28 καὶ τοῦτο εἰποῦσα ἀπῆλθεν καὶ ἐφώνησεν
And this saying she went away and called
Μαριὰμ τὴν ἀδελφὴν αὐτῆς λάθρα εἰποῦσα·
Mary the sister of her secretly saying :
ὁ διδάσκαλος πάρεστιν καὶ φωνεῖ σε.
The Teacher is here and calls thee.
29 ἐκείνη δὲ ὡς ἤκουσεν, ἐγείρεται ταχὺ
And that [one] when she heard, rose quickly
καὶ ἤρχετο πρὸς αὐτόν· 30 οὔπω δὲ
and came to him; now not yet
ἐληλύθει ὁ Ἰησοῦς εἰς τὴν κώμην, ἀλλ'
had come - Jesus into the village, but
ἦν ἔτι ἐν τῷ τόπῳ ὅπου ὑπήντησεν
was still in the place where met
αὐτῷ ἡ Μάρθα. 31 οἱ οὖν Ἰουδαῖοι
him - Martha. Therefore the Jews
οἱ ὄντες μετ' αὐτῆς ἐν τῇ οἰκίᾳ καὶ
the [ones] being with her in the house and

house, consoling her, saw Mary rise quickly and go out, they followed her, supposing that she was going to the tomb to weep there. ³²Then Mary, when she came where Jesus was and saw him, fell at his feet, saying to him, "Lord, if you had been here, my brother would not have died." ³³When Jesus saw her weeping, and the Jews who came with her also weeping, he was deeply moved in spirit and troubled; ³⁴and he said, "Where have you laid him?" They said to him, "Lord, come and see." ³⁵Jesus wept. ³⁶So the Jews said, "See how he loved him!" ³⁷But some of them said, "Could not he who opened the eyes of the blind man have kept this man from dying?"

38 Then Jesus, deeply moved again, came to the tomb; it was a cave, and a stone lay upon it. ³⁹Jesus said, "Take away the stone." Martha, the sister of the dead man,

παραμυθούμενοι αὐτήν, ἰδόντες τὴν Μαριὰμ
consoling her, seeing - Mary

ὅτι ταχέως ἀνέστη καὶ ἐξῆλθεν,
that quickly she rose up and went out,

ἠκολούθησαν αὐτῇ, δόξαντες ὅτι ὑπάγει
followed her, thinking[,] - She is going

εἰς τὸ μνημεῖον ἵνα κλαύσῃ ἐκεῖ. 32 ἡ
to the tomb that she may weep there. -

οὖν Μαριὰμ ὡς ἦλθεν ὅπου ἦν Ἰησοῦς,
Therefore Mary when she came where was Jesus,

ἰδοῦσα αὐτὸν ἔπεσεν αὐτοῦ πρὸς τοὺς
seeing him fell of him at the

πόδας, λέγουσα αὐτῷ· κύριε, εἰ ἦς ὧδε,
feet, saying to him : Lord, if thou wast here,

οὐκ ἄν μου ἀπέθανεν ὁ ἀδελφός.
⁴would not ³of me ⁵have died ¹the ²brother.

33 Ἰησοῦς οὖν ὡς εἶδεν αὐτὴν κλαίουσαν
Jesus therefore when he saw her weeping

καὶ τοὺς συνελθόντας αὐτῇ Ἰουδαίους
and ¹the ²coming with ⁴her ²Jews

κλαίοντας, ἐνεβριμήσατο τῷ πνεύματι καὶ
weeping, groaned in the(his) spirit and

ἐτάραξεν ἑαυτόν, 34 καὶ εἶπεν· ποῦ
troubled himself, and said : Where

τεθείκατε αὐτόν; λέγουσιν αὐτῷ· κύριε,
have ye put him? They say to him : Lord,

ἔρχου καὶ ἴδε. 35 ἐδάκρυσεν ὁ Ἰησοῦς.
come and see. Shed tears - Jesus.

36 ἔλεγον οὖν οἱ Ἰουδαῖοι· ἴδε πῶς
Said therefore the Jews : See how

ἐφίλει αὐτόν. 37 τινὲς δὲ ἐξ αὐτῶν
he loved him. But some of them

εἶπαν· οὐκ ἐδύνατο οὗτος ὁ ἀνοίξας
said : Could not this man the [one] opening

τοὺς ὀφθαλμοὺς τοῦ τυφλοῦ ποιῆσαι ἵνα
the eyes of the blind man to cause that

καὶ οὗτος μὴ ἀποθάνῃ; 38 Ἰησοῦς οὖν
even this man should not die? Jesus therefore

πάλιν ἐμβριμώμενος ἐν ἑαυτῷ ἔρχεται
again groaning in himself comes

εἰς τὸ μνημεῖον· ἦν δὲ σπήλαιον, καὶ
to the tomb; now it was a cave, and

λίθος ἐπέκειτο ἐπ' αὐτῷ. 39 λέγει ὁ
a stone was lying on on it. Says -

Ἰησοῦς· ἄρατε τὸν λίθον. λέγει αὐτῷ
Jesus : Lift ye the stone. Says to him

ἡ ἀδελφὴ τοῦ τετελευτηκότος Μάρθα·
the sister of the [one] having died Martha :

said to him, "Lord, by this time there will be an odor, for he has been dead four days." ⁴⁰Jesus said to her, "Did I not tell you that if you would believe you would see the glory of God?" ⁴¹So they took away the stone. And Jesus lifted up his eyes and said, "Father, I thank thee that thou hast heard me. ⁴²I knew that thou hearest me always, but I have said this on account of the people standing by, that they may believe that thou didst send me." ⁴³When he had said this, he cried with a loud voice, "Laz′arus, come out." ⁴⁴The dead man came out, his hands and feet bound with bandages, and his face wrapped with a cloth. Jesus said to them, "Unbind him, and let him go."

45 Many of the Jews therefore, who had come with Mary and had seen what he did, believed in him; ⁴⁶but some of them went to the Pharisees and told them what Jesus had done. ⁴⁷So the chief priests and the Pharisees gathered the council, and said, "What are we to do? For this man performs many signs. ⁴⁸If

κύριε, ἤδη ὄζει· τεταρταῖος γάρ ἐστιν.
Lord, now he smells; for fourth [day] it is.

40 λέγει αὐτῇ ὁ Ἰησοῦς· οὐκ εἶπόν
Says to her — Jesus : Not I told

σοι ὅτι ἐὰν πιστεύσῃς ὄψῃ τὴν δόξαν
thee that if thou believest thou wilt see the glory

τοῦ θεοῦ; 41 ἦραν οὖν τὸν λίθον. ὁ
— of God? They lifted therefore the stone. —

δὲ Ἰησοῦς ἦρεν τοὺς ὀφθαλμοὺς ἄνω
And Jesus lifted the(his) eyes up

καὶ εἶπεν· πάτερ, εὐχαριστῶ σοι ὅτι
and said : Father, I thank thee that

ἤκουσάς μου. 42 ἐγὼ δὲ ᾔδειν ὅτι
thou didst hear me. And I knew that

πάντοτέ μου ἀκούεις· ἀλλὰ διὰ τὸν
always me thou hearest; but because of the

ὄχλον τὸν περιεστῶτα εἶπον, ἵνα
crowd — standing round I said, that

πιστεύσωσιν ὅτι σύ με ἀπέστειλας.
they may believe that thou me didst send.

43 καὶ ταῦτα εἰπὼν φωνῇ μεγάλῃ
And these things saying voice with a great

ἐκραύγασεν· Λάζαρε, δεῦρο ἔξω. 44 ἐξῆλθεν
he cried out : Lazarus, come out. Came out

ὁ τεθνηκὼς δεδεμένος τοὺς πόδας καὶ
the [one] having died having been bound the feet and

τὰς χεῖρας κειρίαις, καὶ ἡ ὄψις αὐτοῦ
the hands with bandages, and the face of him

σουδαρίῳ περιεδέδετο. λέγει αὐτοῖς ὁ
with a napkin had been bound round. Says to them —

Ἰησοῦς· λύσατε αὐτὸν καὶ ἄφετε αὐτὸν ὑπάγειν.
Jesus : Loosen him and let him to go.

45 Πολλοὶ οὖν ἐκ τῶν Ἰουδαίων, οἱ
Many therefore of the Jews, the [ones]

ἐλθόντες πρὸς τὴν Μαριὰμ καὶ θεασάμενοι
having come to — Mary and having beheld

ὁ ἐποίησεν, ἐπίστευσαν εἰς αὐτόν· 46 τινὲς δὲ
what he did, believed in him; but some

ἐξ αὐτῶν ἀπῆλθον πρὸς τοὺς Φαρισαίους
of them went away to the Pharisees

καὶ εἶπαν αὐτοῖς ἃ ἐποίησεν Ἰησοῦς.
and told them what things did Jesus.

47 συνήγαγον οὖν οἱ ἀρχιερεῖς καὶ οἱ
Assembled therefore the chief priests and the

Φαρισαῖοι συνέδριον, καὶ ἔλεγον· τί
Pharisees a council, and said : What

ποιοῦμεν, ὅτι οὗτος ὁ ἄνθρωπος πολλὰ
are we doing, because this — man ¹many

we let him go on thus, every one will believe in him, and the Romans will come and destroy both our holy place and our nation." ⁴⁹But one of them, Ca'iaphas, who was high priest that year, said to them, "You know nothing at all; ⁵⁰you do not understand that it is expedient for you that one man should die for the people, and that the whole nation should not perish." ⁵¹He did not say this of his own accord, but being high priest that year he prophesied that Jesus should die for the nation, ⁵²and not for the nation only, but to gather into one the children of God who are scattered abroad. ⁵³So from that day on they took counsel how to put him to death.

54 Jesus therefore no longer went about openly among the Jews, but went from there to the country near the wilderness, to a town called E'phraim; and there he stayed with the disciples.

55 Now the Passover of the Jews was at hand,

ποιεῖ	σημεῖα;	48	ἐὰν	ἀφῶμεν	αὐτὸν	οὕτως,
¹does	²signs?		If	we leave	him	thus,

πάντες	πιστεύσουσιν	εἰς	αὐτόν,	καὶ
all men	will believe	in	him,	and

ἐλεύσονται	οἱ	ʻΡωμαῖοι	καὶ	ἀροῦσιν	ἡμῶν
will come	the	Romans	and	will take	of us

καὶ	τὸν	τόπον	καὶ	τὸ	ἔθνος.	49	εἷς
both	the	place	and	the	nation.		²one

δέ	τις	ἐξ	αὐτῶν	Καϊαφᾶς,	ἀρχιερεὺς
¹But	²a certain	of	them[,]	Caiaphas,	high priest

ὢν	τοῦ	ἐνιαυτοῦ	ἐκείνου,	εἶπεν	αὐτοῖς·
being	-	year	of that,	said	to them :

ὑμεῖς	οὐκ	οἴδατε	οὐδέν,	50	οὐδὲ	λογίζεσθε
Ye	know not	no(any)thing,			nor	reckon

ὅτι	συμφέρει	ὑμῖν	ἵνα	εἷς	ἄνθρωπος
that	it is expedient	for us	that	one	man

ἀποθάνῃ	ὑπὲρ	τοῦ	λαοῦ	καὶ	μὴ	ὅλον
should die	for	the	people	and	not	all

τὸ	ἔθνος	ἀπόληται.	51	τοῦτο	δὲ	ἀφ'
the	nation	perish.		But this		from

ἑαυτοῦ	οὐκ	εἶπεν,	ἀλλὰ	ἀρχιερεὺς	ὢν
himself		he said not,	but	high priest	being

τοῦ	ἐνιαυτοῦ	ἐκείνου	ἐπροφήτευσεν	ὅτι
-	year	of that	he prophesied	that

ἔμελλεν	ʼΙησοῦς	ἀποθνῄσκειν	ὑπὲρ	τοῦ
was about	Jesus	to die	for	the

ἔθνους,	52	καὶ	οὐχ	ὑπὲρ	τοῦ	ἔθνους
nation,		and	not	for	the	nation

μόνον,	ἀλλ'	ἵνα	καὶ	τὰ	τέκνα	τοῦ	θεοῦ
only,	but	that	also	the	children	-	of God

τὰ	διεσκορπισμένα	συναγάγῃ	εἰς	ἕν.
-	having been scattered	he might gather	into	one.

53	ἀπ'	ἐκείνης	οὖν	τῆς	ἡμέρας	ἐβουλεύσαντο
	From	¹that	³therefore -		²day	they took counsel

ἵνα	ἀποκτείνωσιν	αὐτόν.	54	ʻΟ	οὖν
that	they might kill	him.		-	Therefore

ʼΙησοῦς	οὐκέτι	παρρησίᾳ	περιεπάτει	ἐν
Jesus	no longer	openly	walked	among

τοῖς	ʼΙουδαίοις,	ἀλλὰ	ἀπῆλθεν	ἐκεῖθεν	εἰς
the	Jews,	but	went away	thence	into

τὴν	χώραν	ἐγγὺς	τῆς	ἐρήμου,	εἰς	ʼΕφραΐμ
the	country	near	the	desert,	to	²Ephraim

λεγομένην	πόλιν,	κἀκεῖ	ἔμεινεν	μετὰ	τῶν
²being called	¹a city,	and there	remained	with	the

μαθητῶν.
disciples.

55	ʻΗν	δὲ	ἐγγὺς	τὸ	πάσχα	τῶν
	Now was		near	the	Passover	of the

and many went up from the country to Jerusalem before the Passover, to purify themselves. [56]They were looking for Jesus and saying to one another as they stood in the temple, "What do you think? That he will not come to the feast?" [57]Now the chief priests and the Pharisees had given orders that if any one knew where he was, he should let them know, so that they might arrest him.

CHAPTER 12

SIX days before the Passover, Jesus came to Bethany, where Laz'-arus was, whom Jesus had raised from the dead. [2]There they made him a supper; Martha served, and Laz'arus was one of those at table with him. [3]Mary took a pound of costly ointment of pure nard and anointed the feet of Jesus and wiped his feet with her hair; and the house was filled with the fragrance of the ointment. [4]But Judas Iscariot, one of his disciples (he who was to betray him), said, [5]"Why was this ointment not sold for three hundred denarii and given to the

Ἰουδαίων,	Jews,
καὶ	and
ἀνέβησαν	went up
πολλοὶ	many
εἰς	to
Ἰεροσόλυμα	Jerusalem
ἐκ	out of
τῆς	the
χώρας	country
πρὸ	before
τοῦ	the
πάσχα,	Passover,
ἵνα	that
ἁγνίσωσιν	they might purify
ἑαυτούς.	themselves.

56 ἐζήτουν οὖν τὸν Ἰησοῦν καὶ ἔλεγον
   They sought therefore - Jesus and said
μετ᾽ ἀλλήλων ἐν τῷ ἱερῷ ἑστηκότες·
with one another in the temple standing :
τί δοκεῖ ὑμῖν; ὅτι οὐ μὴ ἔλθῃ εἰς
What seems it to you? that by no means he comes to
τὴν ἑορτήν; 57 δεδώκεισαν δὲ οἱ ἀρχιερεῖς
the feast?   Now had given the chief priests
καὶ οἱ Φαρισαῖοι ἐντολὰς ἵνα ἐάν τις
and the Pharisees commands that if anyone
γνῷ ποῦ ἐστιν μηνύσῃ, ὅπως πιάσωσιν
knew where he is (was) he should inform, so as they might
                                            arrest
αὐτόν. 12 Ὁ οὖν Ἰησοῦς πρὸ ἐξ ἡμερῶν
him. - Therefore Jesus [3]before [1]six [2]days
τοῦ πάσχα ἦλθεν εἰς Βηθανίαν, ὅπου
the Passover came to Bethany, where
ἦν Λάζαρος, ὃν ἤγειρεν ἐκ νεκρῶν
was Lazarus, whom [2]raised [3]out of [the] [4]dead
Ἰησοῦς. 2 ἐποίησαν οὖν αὐτῷ δεῖπνον ἐκεῖ,
[1]Jesus. They made therefore for him a supper there,
καὶ ἡ Μάρθα διηκόνει, ὁ δὲ Λάζαρος εἷς
and - Martha served, - but Lazarus one
ἦν ἐκ τῶν ἀνακειμένων σὺν αὐτῷ· 3 ἡ
was of the [ones] reclining with him; -
οὖν Μαριὰμ λαβοῦσα λίτραν μύρου
therefore Mary taking a pound [2]ointment
νάρδου πιστικῆς πολυτίμου ἤλειψεν τοὺς
[4]of spikenard [1]of pure [3]costly anointed the
πόδας τοῦ Ἰησοῦ καὶ ἐξέμαξεν ταῖς
feet - of Jesus and wiped off with the
θριξὶν αὐτῆς τοὺς πόδας αὐτοῦ· ἡ δὲ
hairs of her the feet of him; and the
οἰκία ἐπληρώθη ἐκ τῆς ὀσμῆς τοῦ
house was filled of(with) the odour of the
μύρου. 4 λέγει δὲ Ἰούδας ὁ Ἰσκαριώτης
ointment. And says Judas the Iscariot
εἷς τῶν μαθητῶν αὐτοῦ, ὁ μέλλων
one of the disciples of him, the [one] being about
αὐτὸν παραδιδόναι· 5 διὰ τί τοῦτο τὸ
him to betray: Why this -
μύρον οὐκ ἐπράθη τριακοσίων δηναρίων
ointment not was sold of(for) three hundred denarii

poor?" ⁶This he said, not that he cared for the poor but because he was a thief, and as he had the money box he used to take what was put into it. ⁷Jesus said, "Let her alone, let her keep it for the day of my burial. ⁸The poor you always have with you, but you do not always have me."

9 When the great crowd of the Jews learned that he was there, they came, not only on account of Jesus but also to see Laz′arus, whom he had raised from the dead. ¹⁰So the chief priests planned to put Laz′arus also to death, ¹¹because on account of him many of the Jews were going away and believing in Jesus.

12 The next day a great crowd who had come to the feast heard that Jesus was coming to Jerusalem. ¹³So they took branches of palm trees and went out to meet him, crying, "Hosanna! Blessed is he who comes in the name of the Lord,

καὶ ἐδόθη πτωχοῖς; 6 εἶπεν δὲ τοῦτο
and given to [the] poor? But he said this
οὐχ ὅτι περὶ τῶν πτωχῶν ἔμελεν αὐτῷ,
not because about the poor it mattered to him,
ἀλλ᾽ ὅτι κλέπτης ἦν καὶ τὸ γλωσσόκομον
but because a thief he was and ²the ³bag
ἔχων τὰ βαλλόμενα ἐβάσταζεν.
¹having ⁵the things ⁶being put [in] ⁴carried. *
7 εἶπεν οὖν ὁ Ἰησοῦς· ἄφες αὐτήν,
Said therefore the Jesus : Leave her,
ἵνα εἰς τὴν ἡμέραν τοῦ ἐνταφιασμοῦ
that to the day of the burial
μου τηρήσῃ αὐτό· 8 τοὺς πτωχοὺς γὰρ
of me she may keep it; ²the ³poor ¹for
πάντοτε ἔχετε μεθ᾽ ἑαυτῶν, ἐμὲ δὲ
always ye have with yourselves, but me
οὐ πάντοτε ἔχετε. 9 Ἔγνω οὖν ὁ ὄχλος
not always ye have. Knew therefore the crowd
πολὺς ἐκ τῶν Ἰουδαίων ὅτι ἐκεῖ ἐστιν,
great of the Jews that there he is(was),
καὶ ἦλθον οὐ διὰ τὸν Ἰησοῦν μόνον,
and they came not because of - Jesus only,
ἀλλ᾽ ἵνα καὶ τὸν Λάζαρον ἴδωσιν ὃν
but that also - Lazarus they might see whom
ἤγειρεν ἐκ νεκρῶν. 10 ἐβουλεύσαντο δὲ
he raised out of [the] dead. But took counsel
οἱ ἀρχιερεῖς ἵνα καὶ τὸν Λάζαρον
the chief priests that also - Lazarus
ἀποκτείνωσιν, 11 ὅτι πολλοὶ δι᾽ αὐτὸν
they might kill, because ¹many ⁴because of ⁵him
ὑπῆγον τῶν Ἰουδαίων καὶ ἐπίστευον εἰς
⁶went ²of the ³Jews and believed in
τὸν Ἰησοῦς.
- Jesus.

12 Τῇ ἐπαύριον ὁ ὄχλος πολὺς ὁ
On the morrow the crowd much -
ἐλθὼν εἰς τὴν ἑορτήν, ἀκούσαντες ὅτι
coming to the feast, hearing that
ἔρχεται Ἰησοῦς εἰς Ἱεροσόλυμα, 13 ἔλαβον
is(was) coming Jesus to Jerusalem, took
τὰ βαΐα τῶν φοινίκων καὶ ἐξῆλθον εἰς
the branches of the palm-trees and went out to
ὑπάντησιν αὐτῷ, καὶ ἐκραύγαζον· ὡσαννά,
a meeting with him, and cried out : Hosanna,
εὐλογημένος ὁ ἐρχόμενος ἐν ὀνόματι
being blessed the [one] coming in [the] name

---

* This may mean " stole "; cf. our euphemism for " steal "—to " lift " a thing.

even the King of Israel!"
¹⁴And Jesus found a young ass and sat upon it; as it is written, ¹⁵"Fear not, daughter of Zion; behold thy king is coming, sitting on an ass's colt!" ¹⁶His disciples did not understand this at first; but when Jesus was glorified, then they remembered that this had been written of him and had been done to him. ¹⁷The crowd that had been with him when he called Laz′arus out of the tomb and raised him from the dead bore witness. ¹⁸The reason why the crowd went to meet him was that they heard he had done this sign. ¹⁹The Pharisees then said to one another, "You see that you can do nothing; look, the world has gone after him."

20 Now among those who went up to worship at the feast were some Greeks. ²¹So these came to Philip, who was from Beth-sa′ida in Galilee, and said to him, "Sir, we wish to see Jesus." ²²Philip went and told

κυρίου,　καὶ　ὁ　βασιλεὺς　τοῦ　Ἰσραήλ.
of [the] Lord,　even　the　king　-　of Israel.

14 εὑρὼν　δὲ　ὁ　Ἰησοῦς　ὀνάριον　ἐκάθισεν
And ²having found　-　¹Jesus　a young ass　sat

ἐπ᾽　αὐτό,　καθώς　ἐστιν　γεγραμμένον·
on　it,　as　it is　having been written :

15 μὴ　φοβοῦ,　θυγάτηρ　Σιών·　ἰδοὺ　ὁ
Fear not,　daughter　of Sion :　behold[,]　the

βασιλεύς　σου　ἔρχεται,　καθήμενος　ἐπὶ
king　of thee　comes,　sitting　on

πῶλον　ὄνου.　16 ταῦτα　οὐκ　ἔγνωσαν
a foal　of an ass.　These things　knew not

αὐτοῦ　οἱ　μαθηταὶ　τὸ　πρῶτον,　ἀλλ᾽　ὅτε
of him　the　disciples　at first,　but　when

ἐδοξάσθη　Ἰησοῦς,　τότε　ἐμνήσθησαν　ὅτι
was glorified　Jesus,　then　they remembered　that

ταῦτα　ἦν　ἐπ᾽　αὐτῷ　γεγραμμένα　καὶ
these things　were　on　him　having been written　and

ταῦτα　ἐποίησαν　αὐτῷ.　17 ἐμαρτύρει　οὖν
these things　they did　to him.　Witnessed therefore

ὁ　ὄχλος　ὁ　ὢν　μετ᾽　αὐτοῦ　ὅτε　τὸν
the　crowd　-　being　with　him　when　-

Λάζαρον　ἐφώνησεν　ἐκ　τοῦ　μνημείου　καὶ
Lazarus　he called　out of　the　tomb　and

ἤγειρεν　αὐτὸν　ἐκ　νεκρῶν.　18 διὰ　τοῦτο
raised　him　out of [the] dead.　Therefore

καὶ　ὑπήντησεν　αὐτῷ　ὁ　ὄχλος,　ὅτι
also　met　him　the　crowd,　because

ἤκουσαν　τοῦτο　αὐτὸν　πεποιηκέναι　τὸ
¹they heard　⁴this　³him　³to have done[b]　-

σημεῖον.　19 οἱ　οὖν　Φαρισαῖοι　εἶπαν
⁵sign.　Therefore the　Pharisees　said

πρὸς　ἑαυτούς·　θεωρεῖτε　ὅτι　οὐκ　ὠφελεῖτε
to　themselves :　Behold ye　that　ye profit not

οὐδέν·　ἴδε　ὁ　κόσμος　ὀπίσω　αὐτοῦ　ἀπῆλθεν.
no(any)thing;　see[,]　the　world　after　him　went(is gone).

20 Ἦσαν　δὲ　Ἕλληνές　τινες　ἐκ　τῶν
Now there were　²Greeks　¹some　of　the

ἀναβαινόντων　ἵνα　προσκυνήσωσιν　ἐν　τῇ
[ones] going up　that　they might worship　at　the

ἑορτῇ·　21 οὗτοι　οὖν　προσῆλθον　Φιλίππῳ
feast;　these　therefore　approached　to Philip

τῷ　ἀπὸ　Βηθσαϊδὰ　τῆς　Γαλιλαίας.　καὶ
the [one] from　Bethsaida　-　of Galilee,　and

ἠρώτων　αὐτὸν　λέγοντες·　κύριε,　θέλομεν
asked　him　saying :　Sir,　we wish

τὸν　Ἰησοῦν　ἰδεῖν.　22 ἔρχεται　ὁ　Φίλιππος
-　Jesus　to see.　Comes　-　Philip

Andrew; Andrew went with Philip and they told Jesus. ²³And Jesus answered them, "The hour has come for the Son of man to be glorified. ²⁴Truly, truly, I say to you, unless a grain of wheat falls into the earth and dies, it remains alone; but if it dies, it bears much fruit. ²⁵He who loves his life loses it, and he who hates his life in this world will keep it for eternal life. ²⁶If any one serves me, he must follow me; and where I am, there shall my servant be also; if any one serves me, the Father will honor him. 27 "Now is my soul troubled. And what shall I say? 'Father, save me from this hour'? No, for this purpose I have come to this hour. ²⁸Father, glorify thy name." Then a voice came from heaven, "I have glorified it, and I will glorify it again." ²⁹The crowd standing by heard it and said that it had thundered. Others said, "An angel had spoken to

καὶ λέγει τῷ Ἀνδρέᾳ· ἔρχεται Ἀνδρέας
and tells - Andrew; comes Andrew

καὶ Φίλιππος καὶ λέγουσιν τῷ Ἰησοῦ.
and Philip and tell - Jesus.

23 ὁ δὲ Ἰησοῦς ἀποκρίνεται αὐτοῖς λέγων·
- And Jesus answers them saying:

ἐλήλυθεν ἡ ὥρα ἵνα δοξασθῇ ὁ υἱὸς τοῦ
Has come the hour that is glorified the Son -

ἀνθρώπου. 24 ἀμὴν ἀμὴν λέγω ὑμῖν,
of man. Truly truly I say to you,

ἐὰν μὴ ὁ κόκκος τοῦ σίτου πεσὼν εἰς
unless the grain - of wheat falling into

τὴν γῆν ἀποθάνῃ, αὐτὸς μόνος μένει·
the ground dies, it alone remains;

ἐὰν δὲ ἀποθάνῃ, πολὺν καρπὸν φέρει.
but if it dies, much fruit it bears.

25 ὁ φιλῶν τὴν ψυχὴν αὐτοῦ ἀπολλύει
The [one] loving the life of him loses

αὐτήν, καὶ ὁ μισῶν τὴν ψυχὴν αὐτοῦ
it, and the [one] hating the life of him

ἐν τῷ κόσμῳ τούτῳ εἰς ζωὴν αἰώνιον
in - world this unto life eternal

φυλάξει αὐτήν. 26 ἐὰν ἐμοί τις διακονῇ,
will keep it. If me anyone serves,

ἐμοὶ ἀκολουθείτω, καὶ ὅπου εἰμὶ ἐγώ,
me let him follow, and where am I,

ἐκεῖ καὶ ὁ διάκονος ὁ ἐμὸς ἔσται·
there also the ²servant - ¹my will be;

ἐάν τις ἐμοὶ διακονῇ, τιμήσει αὐτὸν
if anyone me serves, will honour him

ὁ πατήρ. 27 νῦν ἡ ψυχή μου τετάρακται,
the Father. Now the soul of me has been troubled,

καὶ τί εἴπω; πάτερ, σῶσόν με ἐκ
and what may I say? Father, save me out of

τῆς ὥρας ταύτης. ἀλλὰ διὰ τοῦτο ἦλθον
- hour this. But therefore I came

εἰς τὴν ὥραν ταύτην. 28 πάτερ, δόξασόν
to - hour this. Father, glorify

σου τὸ ὄνομα. ἦλθεν οὖν φωνὴ ἐκ
of thee the name. Came therefore a voice out of

τοῦ οὐρανοῦ· καὶ ἐδόξασα καὶ πάλιν
- heaven : Both I glorified and again

δοξάσω. 29 ὁ οὖν ὄχλος ὁ ἑστὼς καὶ
I will glorify. Therefore the crowd - standing and

ἀκούσας ἔλεγεν βροντὴν γεγονέναι· ἄλλοι
hearing said thunder to have happened; others

ἔλεγον· ἄγγελος αὐτῷ λελάληκεν.
said : An angel to him has spoken.

him." ³⁰Jesus answered, "This voice has come for your sake, not for mine. ³¹Now is the judgment of this world, now shall the ruler of this world be cast out; ³²and I, when I am lifted up from the earth, will draw all men to myself." ³³He said this to show by what death he was to die. ³⁴The crowd answered him, "We have heard from the law that the Christ remains for ever. How can you say that the Son of man must be lifted up? Who is this Son of man?" ³⁵Jesus said to them, "The light is with you for a little longer. Walk while you have the light, lest the darkness overtake you; he who walks in the darkness does not know where he goes. ³⁶While you have the light, believe in the light, that you may become sons of light."

When Jesus had said this, he departed and hid himself from them. ³⁷Though he had done so many signs before them, yet they did not

30 ἀπεκρίθη Ἰησοῦς καὶ εἶπεν· οὐ δι' ἐμὲ
Answered Jesus and said: Not because of me

ἡ φωνὴ αὕτη γέγονεν ἀλλὰ δι' ὑμᾶς.
_ voice this has happened but because of you.

31 νῦν κρίσις ἐστὶν τοῦ κόσμου τούτου·
Now judgment is - world of this;

νῦν ὁ ἄρχων τοῦ κόσμου τούτου
now the ruler - world of this

ἐκβληθήσεται ἔξω· 32 κἀγὼ ἐὰν ὑψωθῶ
shall be cast out outside; and I if I am lifted up

ἐκ τῆς γῆς, πάντας ἑλκύσω πρὸς
out of the earth, all men will draw to

ἐμαυτόν. 33 τοῦτο δὲ ἔλεγεν σημαίνων
myself. And this he said signifying

ποίῳ θανάτῳ ἤμελλεν ἀποθνῄσκειν.
by what kind of death he was about to die.

34 ἀπεκρίθη οὖν αὐτῷ ὁ ὄχλος· ἡμεῖς
Answered therefore him the crowd : We

ἠκούσαμεν ἐκ τοῦ νόμου ὅτι ὁ χριστὸς
heard out of the law that the Christ

μένει εἰς τὸν αἰῶνα, καὶ πῶς λέγεις
remains unto the age, and how sayest

σὺ ὅτι δεῖ ὑψωθῆναι τὸν υἱὸν τοῦ
thou that it behoves to be lifted up the Son -

ἀνθρώπου; τίς ἐστιν οὗτος ὁ υἱὸς τοῦ
of man? who is this - Son -

ἀνθρώπου; 35 εἶπεν οὖν αὐτοῖς ὁ Ἰησοῦς·
of man? Said therefore to them - Jesus:

ἔτι μικρὸν χρόνον τὸ φῶς ἐν ὑμῖν
Yet a little time the light among you

ἐστιν. περιπατεῖτε ὡς τὸ φῶς ἔχετε,
is. Walk while the light ye have,

ἵνα μὴ σκοτία ὑμᾶς καταλάβῃ· καὶ
lest darkness you overtakes; and

ὁ περιπατῶν ἐν τῇ σκοτίᾳ οὐκ οἶδεν
the [one] walking in the darkness knows not

ποῦ ὑπάγει. 36 ὡς τὸ φῶς ἔχετε,
where he is going. While the light ye have,

πιστεύετε εἰς τὸ φῶς, ἵνα υἱοὶ φωτὸς
believe in the light, that sons of light

γένησθε.
ye may become.

Ταῦτα ἐλάλησεν Ἰησοῦς, καὶ ἀπελθὼν
These things spoke Jesus, and going away

ἐκρύβη ἀπ' αὐτῶν. 37 Τοσαῦτα δὲ αὐτοῦ
was hidden from them. But so many him

σημεῖα πεποιηκότος ἔμπροσθεν αὐτῶν οὐκ
signs having doneᵃ before them not
=But while he did so many signs

I.G.E.—15

believe in him; ³⁸it was that the word spoken by the prophet Isaiah might be fulfilled:
"Lord, who has believed our report, and to whom has the arm of the Lord been revealed?"
³⁹Therefore they could not believe. For Isaiah again said,
⁴⁰"He has blinded their eyes and hardened their heart,
lest they should see with their eyes and perceive with their heart,
and turn for me to heal them."
⁴¹Isaiah said this because he saw his glory and spoke of him.
⁴²Nevertheless many even of the authorities believed in him, but for fear of the Pharisees they did not confess it, lest they should be put out of the synagogue: ⁴³for they loved the praise of men more than the praise of God.
44 And Jesus cried out and said, "He who believes in me, believes not in me but in him who sent me. ⁴⁵And he who sees me sees him who sent me. ⁴⁶I have come as light into the world, that whoever believes in me

ἐπίστευον	εἰς	αὐτόν,	38 ἵνα	ὁ	λόγος
they believed	in	him,	that	the	word

Ἠσαίου	τοῦ	προφήτου	πληρωθῇ	ὃν
of Esaias	the	prophet	might be fulfilled	which

εἶπεν·	κύριε,	τίς	ἐπίστευσεν	τῇ ἀκοῇ
he said :	Lord,	who	believed	the report

ἡμῶν;	καὶ	ὁ	βραχίων	κυρίου τίνι
of us?	and	the	arm	of [the] Lord to whom

ἀπεκαλύφθη;	39 διὰ	τοῦτο	οὐκ	ἠδύναντο
was it revealed?	Therefore			they could not

πιστεύειν,	ὅτι	πάλιν	εἶπεν	Ἠσαίας·
to believe,	because	again	said	Esaias :

40 τετύφλωκεν	αὐτῶν	τοὺς	ὀφθαλμοὺς	καὶ
He has blinded	of them	the	eyes	and

ἐπώρωσεν	αὐτῶν	τὴν	καρδίαν,	ἵνα
hardened	of them	the	heart,	that

μὴ	ἴδωσιν	τοῖς ὀφθαλμοῖς	καὶ	νοήσωσιν
they might not see	with the	eyes	and	understand

τῇ	καρδίᾳ	καὶ στραφῶσιν,	καὶ	ἰάσομαι
with the heart		and might turn,	and	I will cure

αὐτούς.	41 ταῦτα	εἶπεν	Ἠσαίας	ὅτι
them.	These things	said	Esaias	because

εἶδεν	τὴν	δόξαν	αὐτοῦ,	καὶ ἐλάλησεν
he saw	the	glory	of him,	and spoke

περὶ	αὐτοῦ.	42 ὅμως	μέντοι	καὶ ἐκ
about	him.	Nevertheless	however	even of

τῶν	ἀρχόντων	πολλοὶ	ἐπίστευσαν	εἰς αὐτόν,
the	rulers	many	believed	in him,

ἀλλὰ	διὰ	τοὺς Φαρισαίους	οὐχ	ὡμολόγουν,
but	because of	the Pharisees		did not confess,

ἵνα	μὴ	ἀποσυνάγωγοι	γένωνται·
lest		put out of [the] synagogue	they should become;

43 ἠγάπησαν	γὰρ	τὴν	δόξαν	τῶν ἀνθρώπων
for they loved		the	glory	- of men

μᾶλλον	ἤπερ	τὴν	δόξαν	τοῦ θεοῦ.
more	than	the	glory	- of God.

44 Ἰησοῦς	δὲ	ἔκραξεν	καὶ	εἶπεν· ὁ
But Jesus		cried out	and	said : The

πιστεύων	εἰς	ἐμὲ	οὐ πιστεύει	εἰς ἐμὲ
[one] believing	in	me	believes not	in me

ἀλλὰ	εἰς	τὸν	πέμψαντά	με, 45 καὶ ὁ
but	in	the	[one] having sent	me, and the

θεωρῶν	ἐμὲ	θεωρεῖ	τὸν πέμψαντά με.
[one] beholding me		beholds	the [one] having sent me.

46 ἐγὼ	φῶς	εἰς	τὸν	κόσμον ἐλήλυθα,
I	a light	into	the	world have come,

ἵνα	πᾶς	ὁ	πιστεύων	εἰς ἐμὲ ἐν τῇ
that	everyone		believing	in me in the

may not remain in darkness. ⁴⁷If any one hears my sayings and does not keep them, I do not judge him; for I did not come to judge the world but to save the world. ⁴⁸He who rejects me and does not receive my sayings has a judge; the word that I have spoken will be his judge on the last day. ⁴⁹For I have not spoken on my own authority; the Father who sent me has himself given me commandment what to say and what to speak. ⁵⁰And I know that his commandment is eternal life. What I say, therefore, I say as the Father has bidden me."

σκοτίᾳ μὴ μείνῃ. **47** καὶ ἐάν τίς μου
darkness may not remain.   And if anyone of me

ἀκούσῃ τῶν ῥημάτων καὶ μὴ φυλάξῃ,
hears the words and keeps not,

ἐγὼ οὐ κρίνω αὐτόν· οὐ γὰρ ἦλθον
I do not judge him; for I came not

ἵνα κρίνω τὸν κόσμον, ἀλλ᾽ ἵνα σώσω
that I might judge the world, but that I might save

τὸν κόσμον. **48** ὁ ἀθετῶν ἐμὲ καὶ μὴ
the world.   The [one] rejecting me and not

λαμβάνων τὰ ῥήματά μου ἔχει τὸν
receiving the words of me has the

κρίνοντα αὐτόν· ὁ λόγος ὃν ἐλάλησα,
[one] judging him; the word which I spoke,

ἐκεῖνος κρινεῖ αὐτὸν ἐν τῇ ἐσχάτῃ ἡμέρᾳ.
that will judge him in the last day.

49 ὅτι ἐγὼ ἐξ ἐμαυτοῦ οὐκ ἐλάλησα,
Because I of myself did not speak,

ἀλλ᾽ ὁ πέμψας με πατὴρ αὐτός μοι
but ¹the ³having sent ⁴me ²Father ⁵he ⁷me

ἐντολὴν δέδωκεν τί εἴπω καὶ τί
⁸commandment ⁶has given what I may say and what

λαλήσω. **50** καὶ οἶδα ὅτι ἡ ἐντολὴ
I may speak.   And I know that the commandment

αὐτοῦ ζωὴ αἰώνιός ἐστιν. ἃ οὖν ἐγὼ
of him life eternal is. What things therefore I

λαλῶ, καθὼς εἴρηκέν μοι ὁ πατήρ,
speak, as has said to me the Father,

οὕτως λαλῶ.
so I speak.

CHAPTER 13

NOW before the feast of the Passover, when Jesus knew that his hour had come to depart out of this world to the Father, having loved his own who were in the world, he loved them to the end. ²And during supper, when the devil had already put it into the heart of Judas Iscariot, Simon's son, to

13 Πρὸ δὲ τῆς ἑορτῆς τοῦ πάσχα
Now before the feast of the Passover

εἰδὼς ὁ Ἰησοῦς ὅτι ἦλθεν αὐτοῦ ἡ
²knowing – ¹Jesus that came of him the

ὥρα ἵνα μεταβῇ ἐκ τοῦ κόσμου τούτου
hour that he should remove out of – world this

πρὸς τὸν πατέρα, ἀγαπήσας τοὺς ἰδίους
to the Father, loving the(his) own

τοὺς ἐν τῷ κόσμῳ, εἰς τέλος ἠγάπησεν
– in the world, to [the] end he loved

αὐτούς. **2** καὶ δείπνου γινομένου, τοῦ
them.   And supper taking place,ᵃ the
                    =during supper,

διαβόλου ἤδη βεβληκότος εἰς τὴν καρδίαν
devil now having putᵃ into the heart
=as the devil had now put

ἵνα παραδοῖ αὐτὸν Ἰούδας Σίμωνος
that ⁴should betray ⁵him ¹Judas ³[son] of Simon

betray him, ³Jesus, knowing that the Father had given all things into his hands, and that he had come from God and was going to God, ⁴rose from supper, laid aside his garments, and girded himself with a towel. ⁵Then he poured water into a basin, and began to wash the disciples' feet, and to wipe them with the towel with which he was girded. ⁶He came to Simon Peter; and Peter said to him, "Lord, do you wash my feet?" ⁷Jesus answered him, "What I am doing you do not know now, but afterward you will understand." ⁸Peter said to him, "You shall never wash my feet." Jesus answered him, "If I do not wash you, you have no part in me." ⁹Simon Peter said to him, "Lord, not my feet only but also my hands and my head!" ¹⁰Jesus said to him, "He who has bathed does not need to wash, except for his feet,ᵛ but he is clean all over; and you are clean, but not all of you."

ᵛ Other ancient authorities omit *except for his feet*

Ἰσκαριώτης,   3 εἰδὼς   ὅτι   πάντα   ἔδωκεν
²Iscariot,   knowing* that   all things gave

αὐτῷ   ὁ   πατὴρ   εἰς   τὰς   χεῖρας,   καὶ
him   the Father   into   the(his) hands,   and

ὅτι   ἀπὸ   θεοῦ   ἐξῆλθεν   καὶ   πρὸς   τὸν
that   from   God   he came forth and   to   –

θεὸν   ὑπάγει,   4 ἐγείρεται   ἐκ   τοῦ   δείπνου
God   goes,   he rises   out of(from) the   supper

καὶ   τίθησιν   τὰ   ἱμάτια,   καὶ   λαβὼν
and   places [aside] the(his) garments, and   taking

λέντιον   διέζωσεν   ἑαυτόν·   5 εἶτα   βάλλει
a towel   he girded   himself;   then   he puts

ὕδωρ   εἰς   τὸν   νιπτῆρα,   καὶ   ἤρξατο   νίπτειν
water   into   the   basin,   and   began   to wash

τοὺς   πόδας   τῶν   μαθητῶν   καὶ   ἐκμάσσειν
the   feet   of the disciples   and   to wipe off

τῷ   λεντίῳ   ᾧ   ἦν   διεζωσμένος.
with the towel   with which he was   having been girded.

6 ἔρχεται   οὖν   πρὸς   Σίμωνα   Πέτρον·
He comes   therefore to   Simon   Peter;

λέγει   αὐτῷ·   κύριε,   σύ   μου   νίπτεις   τοὺς
he says   to him :   Lord,   thou of me washest   the

πόδας;   7 ἀπεκρίθη   Ἰησοῦς   καὶ   εἶπεν   αὐτῷ·
feet?   Answered   Jesus   and   said   to him :

ὁ   ἐγὼ   ποιῶ   σὺ   οὐκ   οἶδας   ἄρτι,
What   I   am doing thou   knowest not   yet,

γνώσῃ   δὲ   μετὰ   ταῦτα.   8 λέγει   αὐτῷ
but thou wilt know after these things.   Says   to him

Πέτρος·   οὐ   μὴ   νίψῃς   μου   τοὺς   πόδας
Peter :   By no means   shalt thou wash of me the   feet

εἰς   τὸν   αἰῶνα.   ἀπεκρίθη   Ἰησοῦς   αὐτῷ·
unto   the   age.   ²Answered   ¹Jesus   ³him :

ἐὰν   μὴ   νίψω   σε,   οὐκ   ἔχεις   μέρος   μετ'
Unless   I wash   thee,   thou hast no part   with

ἐμοῦ.   9 λέγει   αὐτῷ   Σίμων   Πέτρος·
me.   Says   to him   Simon   Peter :

κύριε,   μὴ   τοὺς   πόδας   μου   μόνον   ἀλλὰ
Lord,   not   the   feet   of me   only   but

καὶ   τὰς   χεῖρας   καὶ   τὴν   κεφαλήν.   10 λέγει
also   the   hands   and   the   head.   Says

αὐτῷ   Ἰησοῦς·   ὁ   λελουμένος   οὐκ   ἔχει
to him   Jesus :   The [one] having been bathed has not

χρείαν   [εἰ   μὴ   τοὺς   πόδας]   νίψασθαι,
need   except   the   feet   to wash,

ἀλλ'   ἔστιν   καθαρὸς   ὅλος·   καὶ   ὑμεῖς
but   is   clean   wholly;   and   ye

καθαροί   ἐστε,   ἀλλ'   οὐχὶ   πάντες.   11 ᾔδει
clean   are,   but   not   all.   he knew

* Repeated from ver. 1; the subject is therefore again "Jesus".

¹¹For he knew who was to betray him; that was why he said, "You are not all clean."
12 When he had washed their feet, and taken his garments, and resumed his place, he said to them, "Do you know what I have done to you? ¹³You call me Teacher and Lord; and you are right, for so I am. ¹⁴If I then, your Lord and Teacher, have washed your feet, you also ought to wash one another's feet. ¹⁵For I have given you an example, that you also should do as I have done to you. ¹⁶Truly, truly, I say to you, a servant is not greater than his master; nor is he who is sent greater than he who sent him. ¹⁷If you know these things, blessed are you if you do them. ¹⁸I am not speaking of you all; I know whom I have chosen; it is that the scripture may be fulfilled, 'He who ate my bread has lifted his heel against me.' ¹⁹I tell you this now, before it takes place, that when it does take place you may believe that I am he. ²⁰Truly, truly, I say to you, he

γὰρ τὸν παραδιδόντα αὐτόν· διὰ τοῦτο
For the [one] betraying him; therefore
εἶπεν ὅτι οὐχὶ πάντες καθαροί ἐστε.
he said[,] – Not all clean ye are.
12 Ὅτε οὖν ἔνιψεν τοὺς πόδας αὐτῶν
When therefore he washed the feet of them
καὶ ἔλαβεν τὰ ἱμάτια αὐτοῦ καὶ ἀνέπεσεν
and took the garments of him and reclined
πάλιν, εἶπεν αὐτοῖς· γινώσκετε τί πε-
again, he said to them : Do ye know what I
ποίηκα ὑμῖν; 13 ὑμεῖς φωνεῖτέ με· ὁ
have done to you? Ye call me : The
διδάσκαλος καὶ ὁ κύριος, καὶ καλῶς
Teacher and the Lord, and well
λέγετε· εἰμὶ γάρ. 14 εἰ οὖν ἐγὼ ἔνιψα
ye say; for I am. If therefore I washed
ὑμῶν τοὺς πόδας ὁ κύριος καὶ ὁ
of you the feet the Lord and the
διδάσκαλος, καὶ ὑμεῖς ὀφείλετε ἀλλήλων
Teacher, also ye ought of one another
νίπτειν τοὺς πόδας· 15 ὑπόδειγμα γὰρ
to wash the feet; for an example
ἔδωκα ὑμῖν ἵνα καθὼς ἐγὼ ἐποίησα
I gave you that as I did
ὑμῖν καὶ ὑμεῖς ποιῆτε. 16 ἀμὴν ἀμὴν
to you also ye may do. Truly truly
λέγω ὑμῖν, οὐκ ἔστιν δοῦλος μείζων
I tell you, is not a slave greater [than]
τοῦ κυρίου αὐτοῦ, οὐδὲ ἀπόστολος μείζων
the lord of him, nor a sent one greater [than]
τοῦ πέμψαντος αὐτόν. 17 εἰ ταῦτα
the [one] sending him. If these things
οἴδατε, μακάριοί ἐστε ἐὰν ποιῆτε αὐτά.
ye know, blessed are ye if ye do them.
18 Οὐ περὶ πάντων ὑμῶν λέγω· ἐγὼ
Not concerning ²all ¹you I speak; I
οἶδα τίνας ἐξελεξάμην· ἀλλ' ἵνα ἡ
know whom I chose; but that the
γραφὴ πληρωθῇ· ὁ τρώγων μου τὸν
scripture may be fulfilled : The [one] eating of me the
ἄρτον ἐπῆρεν ἐπ' ἐμὲ τὴν πτέρναν αὐτοῦ.
bread lifted up against me the heel of him.
19 ἀπ' ἄρτι λέγω ὑμῖν πρὸ τοῦ γενέσθαι,
From now I tell you before the to happen,
=it happens,
ἵνα πιστεύητε ὅταν γένηται ὅτι ἐγώ
that ye may believe when it happens that I
εἰμι. 20 ἀμὴν ἀμὴν λέγω ὑμῖν, ὁ
am. Truly truly I say to you, the

who receives any one whom I send receives me; and he who receives me receives him who sent me."

21 When Jesus had thus spoken, he was troubled in spirit, and testified, "Truly, truly, I say to you, one of you will betray me." 22 The disciples looked at one another, uncertain of whom he spoke. 23 One of his disciples, whom Jesus loved, was lying close to the breast of Jesus; 24 so Simon Peter beckoned to him and said, "Tell us who it is of whom he speaks." 25 So lying thus, close to the breast of Jesus, he said to him, "Lord, who is it?" 26 Jesus answered, "It is he to whom I shall give this morsel when I have dipped it." So when he had dipped the morsel, he gave it to Judas, the son of Simon Iscariot. 27 Then after the morsel, Satan entered into him. Jesus said to him, "What you are going to do, do quickly." 28 Now no one at the table knew why he said this to him. 29 Some thought that, because

λαμβάνων ἄν τινα πέμψω ἐμὲ λαμβάνει,
[one] receiving whomever I may send me receives,
ὁ δὲ ἐμὲ λαμβάνων λαμβάνει τὸν
and the [one] me receiving receives the [one]
πέμψαντά με. 21 ταῦτα εἰπὼν ᾿Ιησοῦς
having sent me. These things saying Jesus
ἐταράχθη τῷ πνεύματι καὶ ἐμαρτύρησεν
was troubled in the(his) spirit and witnessed
καὶ εἶπεν· ἀμὴν ἀμὴν λέγω ὑμῖν ὅτι
and said: Truly Truly I tell you that
εἷς ἐξ ὑμῶν παραδώσει με. 22 ἔβλεπον
one of you will betray me. Looked
εἰς ἀλλήλους οἱ μαθηταὶ ἀπορούμενοι περὶ
at one another the disciples being perplexed about
τίνος λέγει. 23 ἦν ἀνακείμενος εἷς ἐκ
whom he speaks. Was reclining one of
τῶν μαθητῶν αὐτοῦ ἐν τῷ κόλπῳ τοῦ
the disciples of him in the bosom -
᾿Ιησοῦ, ὃν ἠγάπα ὁ ᾿Ιησοῦς· 24 νεύει
of Jesus, whom ²loved - ¹Jesus; nods
οὖν τούτῳ Σίμων Πέτρος καὶ λέγει
therefore to this one Simon Peter and says
αὐτῷ· εἰπὲ τίς ἐστιν περὶ οὗ λέγει.
to him : Say who it is about whom he speaks.
25 ἀναπεσὼν ἐκεῖνος οὕτως ἐπὶ τὸ
Falling back that one thus on the
στῆθος τοῦ ᾿Ιησοῦ λέγει αὐτῷ· κύριε,
breast - of Jesus he says to him : Lord,
τίς ἐστιν; 26 ἀποκρίνεται οὖν ὁ ᾿Ιησοῦς·
who is it? Answers therefore - Jesus :
ἐκεῖνός ἐστιν ᾧ ἐγὼ βάψω τὸ ψωμίον
That one it is to whom I shall dip the morsel
καὶ δώσω αὐτῷ. βάψας οὖν [τὸ]
and shall give him. Dipping therefore the
ψωμίον λαμβάνει καὶ δίδωσιν ᾿Ιούδᾳ
morsel he takes and gives to Judas
Σίμωνος ᾿Ισκαριώτου. 27 καὶ μετὰ τὸ
[son] of Simon Iscariot. And after the
ψωμίον τότε εἰσῆλθεν εἰς ἐκεῖνον ὁ
morsel then entered into that one -
σατανᾶς. λέγει οὖν αὐτῷ ᾿Ιησοῦς· ὃ
Satan. Says therefore to him Jesus : What
ποιεῖς ποίησον τάχιον. 28 τοῦτο [δὲ]
thou doest do quickly. But this
οὐδεὶς ἔγνω τῶν ἀνακειμένων πρὸς τί
no one knew of the [ones] reclining for what
εἶπεν αὐτῷ· 29 τινὲς γὰρ ἐδόκουν, ἐπεὶ
he told him; for some thought, since

Judas had the money box, Jesus was telling him, "Buy what we need for the feast"; or, that he should give something to the poor. ³⁰ So, after receiving the morsel, he immediately went out; and it was night.

31 When he had gone out, Jesus said, "Now is the Son of man glorified, and in him God is glorified; ³² if God is glorified in him, God will also glorify him in himself, and glorify him at once. ³³ Little children, yet a little while I am with you. You will seek me; and as I said to the Jews so now I say to you, 'Where I am going you cannot come.' ³⁴ A new commandment I give to you, that you love one another; even as I have loved you, that you also love one another. ³⁵ By this all men will know that you are my disciples, if you have love for one another."

36 Simon Peter said to him, "Lord, where are you going?" Jesus answered, "Where I am going you cannot follow me now; but you shall follow afterward."

τὸ γλωσσόκομον εἶχεν Ἰούδας, ὅτι λέγει
³the ⁴bag ³had ¹Judas, that tells

αὐτῷ Ἰησοῦς· ἀγόρασον ὧν χρείαν
him Jesus : Buy [the] things of which need

ἔχομεν εἰς τὴν ἑορτήν, ἢ τοῖς πτωχοῖς
we have for the feast, or to the poor

ἵνα τι δῷ. 30 λαβὼν οὖν τὸ
that something he should give. Having taken therefore the

ψωμίον ἐκεῖνος ἐξῆλθεν εὐθύς· ἦν δὲ
morsel that one went out immediately; and it was

νύξ.
night.

31 Ὅτε οὖν ἐξῆλθεν, λέγει Ἰησοῦς·
When therefore he went out, says Jesus :

νῦν ἐδοξάσθη ὁ υἱὸς τοῦ ἀνθρώπου,
Now was(is) glorified the Son - of man,

καὶ ὁ θεὸς ἐδοξάσθη ἐν αὐτῷ· 32 εἰ
and - God was(is) glorified in him; if

ὁ θεὸς ἐδοξάσθη ἐν αὐτῷ, καὶ ὁ θεὸς
- God was(is) glorified in him, both - God

δοξάσει αὐτὸν ἐν αὐτῷ, καὶ εὐθὺς
will glorify him in him, and immediately

δοξάσει αὐτόν. 33 τεκνία, ἔτι μικρὸν
will glorify him. Children, yet a little while

μεθ' ὑμῶν εἰμι· ζητήσετέ με, καὶ καθὼς
with you I am; ye will seek me, and as

εἶπον τοῖς Ἰουδαίοις ὅτι ὅπου ἐγὼ
I said to the Jews that where I

ὑπάγω ὑμεῖς οὐ δύνασθε ἐλθεῖν, καὶ
go ye cannot to come, also

ὑμῖν λέγω ἄρτι. 34 Ἐντολὴν καινὴν
to you I say now. commandment A new

δίδωμι ὑμῖν, ἵνα ἀγαπᾶτε ἀλλήλους,
I give you, that ye love one another,

καθὼς ἠγάπησα ὑμᾶς ἵνα καὶ ὑμεῖς
as I loved you that also ye

ἀγαπᾶτε ἀλλήλους. 35 ἐν τούτῳ γνώσονται
love one another. By this will know

πάντες ὅτι ἐμοὶ μαθηταί ἐστε, ἐὰν
all men that to me° disciples ye are, if

ἀγάπην ἔχητε ἐν ἀλλήλοις. 36 Λέγει
love ye have among one another. Says

αὐτῷ Σίμων Πέτρος· κύριε, ποῦ ὑπάγεις;
to him Simon Peter : Lord, where goest thou?

ἀπεκρίθη Ἰησοῦς· ὅπου ὑπάγω οὐ δύνασαί
Answered Jesus : Where I go thou canst not

μοι νῦν ἀκολουθῆσαι, ἀκολουθήσεις δὲ
me now to follow, but thou wilt follow

37 Peter said to him, "Lord, why cannot I follow you now? I will lay down my life for you." 38 Jesus answered, "Will you lay down your life for me? Truly, truly, I say to you, the cock will not crow, till you have denied me three times.

CHAPTER 14

"LET not your hearts be troubled; believe[w] in God, believe also in me. 2 In my Father's house are many rooms; if it were not so, would I have told you that I go to prepare a place for you? 3 And when I go and prepare a place for you, I will come again and will take you to myself, that where I am you may be also. 4 And you know the way where I am going."[z] 5 Thomas said to him, "Lord, we do not know where you are going; how can we know the way?" 6 Jesus said to him, "I am the way, and the truth, and the life; no one comes to the Father, but by me. 7 If you had known me, you would have known my Father also; henceforth you know him and have seen him."

8 Philip said to him,

[w] Or you believe
[z] Other ancient authorities read where I am going you know, and the way you know

ὕστερον.　37 λέγει　αὐτῷ　[ὁ]　Πέτρος·
later.　　　Says　to him　–　Peter :

κύριε，　διὰ　τί　οὐ　δύναμαί　σοι　ἀκολουθῆσαι
Lord，　why　can I not　thee　to follow

ἄρτι;　τὴν　ψυχήν　μου　ὑπὲρ　σοῦ　θήσω.
yet?　the　life　of me　for　thee I will lay down.

38 ἀποκρίνεται　Ἰησοῦς·　τὴν　ψυχήν　σου
Answers　Jesus :　The　life　of thee

ὑπὲρ　ἐμοῦ　θήσεις;　ἀμὴν　ἀμὴν　λέγω
for　me　wilt thou lay down?　truly　truly　I tell

σοι，　οὐ　μὴ　ἀλέκτωρ　φωνήσῃ　ἕως　οὗ
thee，　by no means　a cock　crows　until

ἀρνήσῃ　με　τρίς.　14 Μὴ　ταρασσέσθω
thou deniest　me　thrice.　Let not be troubled

ὑμῶν　ἡ　καρδία·　πιστεύετε　εἰς　τὸν　θεόν，　καὶ
of you　the　heart;　believe　in　–　God，　also

εἰς　ἐμὲ　πιστεύετε.　2 ἐν　τῇ　οἰκίᾳ　τοῦ
in　me　believe.　In　the　house　of the

πατρός　μου　μοναὶ　πολλαί　εἰσιν·　εἰ　δὲ　μή，
Father　of me　abodes　many　there are;　otherwise，

εἶπον　ἂν　ὑμῖν·　ὅτι　πορεύομαι　ἑτοιμάσαι
I would have told　you;　because　I go　to prepare

τόπον　ὑμῖν·　3 καὶ　ἐὰν　πορευθῶ　καὶ
a place　for you;　and　if　I go　and

ἑτοιμάσω　τόπον　ὑμῖν，　πάλιν　ἔρχομαι　καὶ
prepare　a place　for you，　again　I come　and

παραλήμψομαι　ὑμᾶς　πρὸς　ἐμαυτόν，　ἵνα
will receive　you　to　myself，　that

ὅπου　εἰμὶ　ἐγὼ　καὶ　ὑμεῖς　ἦτε.　4 Καὶ
where　am　I　also　ye　may be.　And

ὅπου　ἐγὼ　ὑπάγω　οἴδατε　τὴν　ὁδόν.
where　I　go　ye know　the　way.

5 λέγει　αὐτῷ　Θωμᾶς·　κύριε，　οὐκ　οἴδαμεν
Says　to him　Thomas :　Lord，　we know not

ποῦ　ὑπάγεις·　πῶς　οἴδαμεν　τὴν　ὁδόν;
where　thou goest·　how　do we know　the　way?

6 λέγει　αὐτῷ　Ἰησοῦς·　ἐγώ　εἰμι　ἡ　ὁδὸς
Says　to him　Jesus :　I　am　the　way

καὶ　ἡ　ἀλήθεια　καὶ　ἡ　ζωή·　οὐδεὶς　ἔρχεται
and　the　truth　and　the　life;　no one　comes

πρὸς　τὸν　πατέρα　εἰ　μὴ　δι'　ἐμοῦ.　7 εἰ
to　the　Father　except　through me.　If

ἐγνώκειτέ　με，　καὶ　τὸν　πατέρα　μου
ye had known　me，　also　the　Father　of me

ἂν　ᾔδειτε.　ἀπ'　ἄρτι　γινώσκετε　αὐτὸν
ye would have known.　From　now　ye know　him

καὶ　ἑωράκατε.　8 Λέγει　αὐτῷ　Φίλιππος·
and　have seen.　Says　to him　Philip:

"Lord, show us the Father, and we shall be satisfied." ⁹Jesus said to him, "Have I been with you so long, and yet you do not know me, Philip? He who has seen me has seen the Father; how can you say, 'Show us the Father'? ¹⁰Do you not believe that I am in the Father and the Father in me? The words that I say to you I do not speak on my own authority; but the Father who dwells in me does his works. ¹¹Believe me that I am in the Father and the Father in me; or else believe me for the sake of the works themselves.

12 "Truly, truly, I say to you, he who believes in me will also do the works that I do; and greater works than these will he do, because I go to the Father. ¹³Whatever you ask in my name, I will do it, that the Father may be glorified in the Son; ¹⁴if you ask^y anything in my name, I will do it.

15 "If you love me, you will keep my commandments. ¹⁶And I will pray the Father, and he will give you another Counselor, to be with

^y Other ancient authorities add me

κύριε,   δεῖξον   ἡμῖν   τὸν   πατέρα,   καὶ
Lord,   show   us   the   Father,   and

ἀρκεῖ   ἡμῖν.   9 λέγει   αὐτῷ   ὁ   Ἰησοῦς·
it suffices   for us.   Says   to him   –   Jesus:

τοσοῦτον   χρόνον   μεθ'   ὑμῶν   εἰμι   καὶ
So long   time   with   you   I am   and

οὐκ   ἔγνωκάς   με,   Φίλιππε;   ὁ   ἑωρακὼς
thou hast not known   me,   Philip?   The [one] having seen

ἐμὲ   ἑώρακεν   τὸν   πατέρα·   πῶς   σὺ   λέγεις·
me   has seen   the   Father;   how   thou   sayest:

δεῖξον   ἡμῖν   τὸν   πατέρα;   10 οὐ   πιστεύεις
Show   us   the   Father?   believest thou not

ὅτι   ἐγὼ   ἐν   τῷ   πατρὶ   καὶ   ὁ   πατὴρ
that   I   in   the   Father   and   the   Father

ἐν   ἐμοί   ἐστιν;   τὰ   ῥήματα   ἃ   ἐγὼ   λέγω
in   me   is?   the   words   which   I   say

ὑμῖν   ἀπ'   ἐμαυτοῦ   οὐ   λαλῶ·   ὁ   δὲ   πατὴρ
to you   from   myself   I speak not;   but the   Father

ἐν   ἐμοὶ   μένων   ποιεῖ   τὰ   ἔργα   αὐτοῦ.
in   me   remaining   does   the   works   of him.

11 πιστεύετέ   μοι   ὅτι   ἐγὼ   ἐν   τῷ   πατρὶ
Believe ye   me   that   I   in   the   Father

καὶ   ὁ   πατὴρ   ἐν   ἐμοί·   εἰ   δὲ   μή,   διὰ
and   the   Father   in   me;   otherwise,   because of

τὰ   ἔργα   αὐτὰ   πιστεύετε.   12 ἀμὴν   ἀμὴν
the   works   [them]selves   believe ye.   Truly   truly

λέγω   ὑμῖν,   ὁ   πιστεύων   εἰς   ἐμὲ   τὰ
I tell   you,   the [one]   believing   in   me   the

ἔργα   ἃ   ἐγὼ   ποιῶ   κἀκεῖνος   ποιήσει,
works   which   I   do   that one also   will do,

καὶ   μείζονα   τούτων   ποιήσει,   ὅτι   ἐγὼ
and   greater [than]   these   he will do,   because   I

πρὸς   τὸν   πατέρα   πορεύομαι·   13 καὶ   ὅ   τι
to   the   Father   am going;   and   what-

ἂν   αἰτήσητε   ἐν   τῷ   ὀνόματί   μου,   τοῦτο
ever   ye ask   in   the   name   of me,   this

ποιήσω,   ἵνα   δοξασθῇ   ὁ   πατὴρ   ἐν   τῷ
I will do,   that   may be glorified the   Father   in   the

υἱῷ.   14 ἐάν   τι   αἰτήσητέ   με   ἐν   τῷ
Son.   If   anything   ye ask   me   in   the

ὀνόματί   μου,   ἐγὼ   ποιήσω.   15 Ἐὰν
name   of me,   I   will do.   If

ἀγαπᾶτέ   με,   τὰς   ἐντολὰς   τὰς   ἐμὰς
ye love   me,   the   ²commandments   –   ²my

τηρήσετε.   16 κἀγὼ   ἐρωτήσω   τὸν   πατέρα
ye will keep.   And I   will request   the   Father

καὶ   ἄλλον   παράκλητον   δώσει   ὑμῖν,   ἵνα
and   another   Comforter   he will give   you,   that

you for ever, ¹⁷even the
Spirit of truth, whom the
world cannot receive,
because it neither sees
him nor knows him; you
know him, for he dwells
with you, and will be in
you.
18 "I will not leave
you desolate; I will come
to you. ¹⁹Yet a little
while, and the world will
see me no more, but you
will see me; because I
live, you will live also.
²⁰In that day you will
know that I am in my
Father, and you in me,
and I in you. ²¹He who
has my commandments
and keeps them, he it is
who loves me; and he
who loves me will be
loved by my Father, and
I will love him and
manifest myself to him."
²²Judas (not Iscariot)
said to him, "Lord, how
is it that you will mani-
fest yourself to us, and
not to the world?"
²³Jesus answered him,
"If a man loves me, he
will keep my word, and
my Father will love him,
and we will come to him

ᾗ   μεθ'   ὑμῶν   εἰς   τὸν   αἰῶνα,   17 τὸ
he may be with   you   unto   the   age,   the

πνεῦμα   τῆς   ἀληθείας,   ὃ   ὁ   κόσμος
Spirit   –   of truth,   which*   the   world

οὐ   δύναται   λαβεῖν,   ὅτι   οὐ   θεωρεῖ   αὐτὸ
cannot   to receive,   because   it beholds not   it*

οὐδὲ   γινώσκει·   ὑμεῖς   γινώσκετε   αὐτό,
nor   knows;   ye   know   it,*

ὅτι   παρ'   ὑμῖν   μένει   καὶ   ἐν   ὑμῖν   ἔσται.
because with   you   he remains and   in   you   will be.

18 Οὐκ   ἀφήσω   ὑμᾶς   ὀρφανούς,   ἔρχομαι
I will not leave   you   orphans,   I am coming

πρὸς   ὑμᾶς.   19 ἔτι   μικρὸν   καὶ   ὁ   κόσμος
to   you.   Yet   a little   and   the   world

με   οὐκέτι   θεωρεῖ,   ὑμεῖς   δὲ   θεωρεῖτέ
me   no longer   beholds,   but ye   behold

με,   ὅτι   ἐγὼ   ζῶ   καὶ   ὑμεῖς   ζήσετε.
me,   because   I   live   also   ye   will live.

20 ἐν   ἐκείνῃ   τῇ   ἡμέρᾳ   γνώσεσθε   ὑμεῖς
In   that   –   day   will know   ye

ὅτι   ἐγὼ   ἐν   τῷ   πατρί   μου   καὶ   ὑμεῖς
that   I   in   the   Father   of me   and   ye

ἐν   ἐμοὶ   κἀγὼ   ἐν   ὑμῖν.   21 Ὁ   ἔχων
in   me   and I   in   you.   The [one] having

τὰς   ἐντολάς   μου   καὶ   τηρῶν   αὐτάς,
the   commandments of me   and   keeping   them,

ἐκεῖνός   ἐστιν   ὁ   ἀγαπῶν   με·   ὁ   δὲ   ἀγαπῶν
that   is   the [one] loving   me;   and the [one] loving

με   ἀγαπηθήσεται   ὑπὸ   τοῦ   πατρός   μου,
me   will be loved   by   the   Father   of me,

κἀγὼ   ἀγαπήσω   αὐτὸν   καὶ   ἐμφανίσω   αὐτῷ
and I   will love   him   and   will manifest   to him

ἐμαυτόν.   22 λέγει   αὐτῷ   Ἰούδας,   οὐχ
myself.   Says   to him   Judas,   not

ὁ   Ἰσκαριώτης·   κύριε,   καὶ   τί   γέγονεν
the   Iscariot :   Lord,   and   what has happened

ὅτι   ἡμῖν   μέλλεις   ἐμφανίζειν   σεαυτὸν   καὶ
that   to us   thou art about   to manifest   thyself   and

οὐχὶ   τῷ   κόσμῳ;   23 ἀπεκρίθη   Ἰησοῦς
not   to the   world?   Answered   Jesus

καὶ   εἶπεν   αὐτῷ·   ἐάν   τις   ἀγαπᾷ   με,
and   said   to him :   If   anyone   loves   me,

τὸν   λόγον   μου   τηρήσει,   καὶ   ὁ   πατήρ
the   word   of me   he will keep,   and   the   Father

μου   ἀγαπήσει   αὐτόν,   καὶ   πρὸς   αὐτὸν
of me   will love   him,   and   to   him

* The gender of these pronouns agrees, of course, with the antecedent πνεῦμα (neuter); and this has been kept though the personal
Spirit of God is meant. Elsewhere, masculine pronouns are in
fact used.

and make our home with him. 24 He who does not love me does not keep my words; and the word which you hear is not mine but the Father's who sent me.

25 "These things I have spoken to you, while I am still with you. 26 But the Counselor, the Holy Spirit, whom the Father will send in my name, he will teach you all things, and bring to your remembrance all that I have said to you. 27 Peace I leave with you; my peace I give to you; not as the world gives do I give to you. Let not your hearts be troubled, neither let them be afraid. 28 You heard me say to you, 'I go away, and I will come to you.' If you loved me, you would have rejoiced, because I go to the Father; for the Father is greater than I. 29 And now I have told you before it takes place, so that when it does take place, you may believe. 30 I will no longer talk much with you, for the ruler of this world is coming. He has no power over me; 31 but I do as the Father has commanded

ἐλευσόμεθα καὶ μονὴν παρ' αὐτῷ
we will come and abode with him

ποιησόμεθα. 24 ὁ μὴ ἀγαπῶν με τοὺς
we will make. The [one] not loving me the

λόγους μου οὐ τηρεῖ· καὶ ὁ λόγος ὃν
words of me keeps not; and the word which

ἀκούετε οὐκ ἔστιν ἐμὸς ἀλλὰ τοῦ
ye hear is not mine but ¹of the

πέμψαντός με πατρός. 25 Ταῦτα λελάληκα
³having sent ⁴me ²Father. These things I have spoken

ὑμῖν παρ' ὑμῖν μένων· 26 ὁ δὲ παρά-
to you with you remaining; but the Com-

κλητος, τὸ πνεῦμα τὸ ἅγιον ὃ πέμψει ὁ
forter, the Spirit — Holy which will send the

πατὴρ ἐν τῷ ὀνόματί μου, ἐκεῖνος ὑμᾶς
Father in the name of me, that one you

διδάξει πάντα καὶ ὑπομνήσει ὑμᾶς πάντα
will teach all things and remind you [of] all things

ἃ εἶπον ὑμῖν ἐγώ. 27 Εἰρήνην ἀφίημι
which ²told ³you ¹I. Peace I leave

ὑμῖν, εἰρήνην τὴν ἐμὴν δίδωμι ὑμῖν·
to you, ²peace — ¹my I give you;

οὐ καθὼς ὁ κόσμος δίδωσιν ἐγὼ δίδωμι
not as the world gives I give

ὑμῖν. μὴ ταρασσέσθω ὑμῶν ἡ καρδία
you. Let not be troubled of you the heart

μηδὲ δειλιάτω. 28 ἠκούσατε ὅτι ἐγὼ
nor let it be fearful. Ye heard that I

εἶπον ὑμῖν· ὑπάγω καὶ ἔρχομαι πρὸς
told you : I go and come to

ὑμᾶς. εἰ ἠγαπᾶτέ με, ἐχάρητε ἂν ὅτι
you. If ye loved me, ye would have rejoiced that

πορεύομαι πρὸς τὸν πατέρα, ὅτι ὁ πατὴρ
I am going to the Father, because the Father

μείζων μού ἐστιν. 29 καὶ νῦν εἴρηκα
greater [than] me(I) is. And now I have told

ὑμῖν πρὶν γενέσθαι, ἵνα ὅταν γένηται
you before to happen, that when it happens
=it happens,

πιστεύσητε. 30 οὐκέτι πολλὰ λαλήσω μεθ'
ye may believe. No longer many things I will speak with

ὑμῶν, ἔρχεται γὰρ ὁ τοῦ κόσμου ἄρχων·
you, for ⁵is coming ¹the ²of the ⁴world ³ruler;

καὶ ἐν ἐμοὶ οὐκ ἔχει οὐδέν, 31 ἀλλ'
and in me he has not no(any)thing, but

ἵνα γνῷ ὁ κόσμος ὅτι ἀγαπῶ τὸν
that may know the world that I love the

πατέρα, καὶ καθὼς ἐνετείλατό μοι ὁ
Father, and as commanded me the

me, so that the world may know that I love the Father. Rise, let us go hence.

πατήρ, οὕτως ποιῶ. Ἐγείρεσθε, ἄγωμεν
Father, so I do. Rise, let us go
ἐντεῦθεν.
hence.

CHAPTER 15

"I am the true vine, and my Father is the vine-dresser. ²Every branch of mine that bears no fruit, he takes away, and every branch that does bear fruit he prunes, that it may bear more fruit. ³You are already made clean by the word which I have spoken to you. ⁴Abide in me, and I in you. As the branch cannot bear fruit by itself, unless it abides in the vine, neither can you, unless you abide in me. ⁵I am the vine, you are the branches. He who abides in me, and I in him, he it is that bears much fruit, for apart from me you can do nothing. ⁶If a man does not abide in me, he is cast forth as a branch and withers; and the branches are gathered, thrown into the fire and burned. ⁷If you abide in me, and my words abide in you, ask whatever you will, and it shall be done for you. ⁸By this my

15 Ἐγώ εἰμι ἡ ἄμπελος ἡ ἀληθινή,
I am the vine the true,
καὶ ὁ πατήρ μου ὁ γεωργός ἐστιν.
and the Father of me the husbandman is.
2 πᾶν κλῆμα ἐν ἐμοὶ μὴ φέρον καρπόν,
Every branch in me not bearing fruit,
αἴρει αὐτό, καὶ πᾶν τὸ καρπὸν φέρον,
he takes it, and every [branch] the fruit bearing,
καθαίρει αὐτὸ ἵνα καρπὸν πλείονα φέρῃ.
he prunes it that fruit more it may bear.
3 ἤδη ὑμεῖς καθαροί ἐστε διὰ τὸν λόγον
Now ye clean are because of the word
ὃν λελάληκα ὑμῖν· μείνατε ἐν ἐμοί,
which I have spoken to you; remain in me,
κἀγὼ ἐν ὑμῖν. 4 καθὼς τὸ κλῆμα
and I in you. As the branch
οὐ δύναται καρπὸν φέρειν ἀφ' ἑαυτοῦ ἐὰν μὴ
cannot fruit to bear from itself unless
μένῃ ἐν τῇ ἀμπέλῳ, οὕτως οὐδὲ ὑμεῖς
it remains in the vine, so not ye
ἐὰν μὴ ἐν ἐμοὶ μένητε. 5 ἐγώ εἰμι
unless in me ye remain. I am
ἡ ἄμπελος, ὑμεῖς τὰ κλήματα. ὁ μένων
the vine, ye the branches. The [one] remaining
ἐν ἐμοὶ κἀγὼ ἐν αὐτῷ, οὗτος φέρει
in me and I in him, this one bears
καρπὸν πολύν, ὅτι χωρὶς ἐμοῦ οὐ δύνασθε
fruit much, because apart from me ye cannot
ποιεῖν οὐδέν. 6 ἐὰν μή τις μένῃ ἐν
to do no(any)thing. Unless anyone remains in
ἐμοί, ἐβλήθη ἔξω ὡς τὸ κλῆμα καὶ
me, he was(is) cast outside as the branch and
ἐξηράνθη, καὶ συνάγουσιν αὐτὰ καὶ εἰς
was(is) dried, and they gather them and into
τὸ πῦρ βάλλουσιν, καὶ καίεται. 7 ἐὰν
the fire they cast, and they are burned. If
μείνητε ἐν ἐμοὶ καὶ τὰ ῥήματά μου
ye remain in me and the words of me
ἐν ὑμῖν μείνῃ, ὃ ἐὰν θέλητε αἰτήσασθε,
in you remains, whatever ye wish ask,
καὶ γενήσεται ὑμῖν. 8 ἐν τούτῳ ἐδοξάσθη
and it shall happen to you. By this was glorified

Father is glorified, that you bear much fruit, and so prove to be my disciples. ⁹As the Father has loved me, so have I loved you; abide in my love. ¹⁰If you keep my commandments, you will abide in my love, just as I have kept my Father's commandments and abide in his love. ¹¹These things I have spoken to you, that my joy may be in you, and that your joy may be full.

12 "This is my commandment, that you love one another as I have loved you. ¹³Greater love has no man than this, that a man lay down his life for his friends. ¹⁴You are my friends if you do what I command you. ¹⁵No longer do I call you servants, for the servant does not know what his master is doing; but I have called you friends, for all that I have heard from my Father I have made known to you. ¹⁶You did not choose me, but I chose you and appointed you that you should go and bear fruit and that your fruit should abide; so that

ὁ πατήρ μου, ἵνα καρπὸν πολὺν φέρητε
the Father of me, that fruit much ye bear
καὶ γενήσεσθε ἐμοὶ μαθηταί. 9 καθὼς
and ye will be to me° disciples. As
ἠγάπησέν με ὁ πατήρ, κἀγὼ ὑμᾶς
loved me the Father, I also you
ἠγάπησα· μείνατε ἐν τῇ ἀγάπῃ τῇ ἐμῇ.
loved; remain ye in the ²love - ¹my.
10 ἐὰν τὰς ἐντολάς μου τηρήσητε, μενεῖτε
If the commandments of me ye keep, ye will remain
ἐν τῇ ἀγάπῃ μου, καθὼς ἐγὼ τοῦ πατρός
in the love of me, as I of the Father
μου τὰς ἐντολὰς τετήρηκα καὶ μένω
of me the commandments have kept and remain
αὐτοῦ ἐν τῇ ἀγάπῃ. 11 Ταῦτα λελάληκα
of him in the love. These things I have spoken
ὑμῖν ἵνα ἡ χαρὰ ἡ ἐμὴ ἐν ὑμῖν ᾖ
to you that the ²joy - ¹my in you may be
καὶ ἡ χαρὰ ὑμῶν πληρωθῇ. 12 αὕτη
and the joy of you may be filled. This
ἐστὶν ἡ ἐντολὴ ἡ ἐμή, ἵνα ἀγαπᾶτε
is the ²commandment - ¹my, that ye love
ἀλλήλους καθὼς ἠγάπησα ὑμᾶς. 13 μείζονα
one another as I loved you. ¹Greater
ταύτης ἀγάπην οὐδεὶς ἔχει, ἵνα τις
[³than] ⁴this ²love no one has, that anyone
τὴν ψυχὴν αὐτοῦ θῇ ὑπὲρ τῶν φίλων
the life of him should lay down for the friends
αὐτοῦ. 14 ὑμεῖς φίλοι μού ἐστε, ἐὰν
of him. Ye friends of me are, if
ποιῆτε ὃ ἐγὼ ἐντέλλομαι ὑμῖν. 15 οὐκέτι
ye do what I command you. No longer
λέγω ὑμᾶς δούλους, ὅτι ὁ δοῦλος οὐκ οἶδεν
I call you slaves, because the slave knows not
τί ποιεῖ αὐτοῦ ὁ κύριος· ὑμᾶς δὲ
what does of him the lord; but you
εἴρηκα φίλους, ὅτι πάντα ἃ ἤκουσα
I have called friends, because all things which I heard
παρὰ τοῦ πατρός μου ἐγνώρισα ὑμῖν.
from the Father of me I made known to you.
16 οὐχ ὑμεῖς με ἐξελέξασθε, ἀλλ' ἐγὼ
Not ye me chose, but I
ἐξελεξάμην ὑμᾶς, καὶ ἔθηκα ὑμᾶς ἵνα
chose you, and appointed you that
ὑμεῖς ὑπάγητε καὶ καρπὸν φέρητε καὶ
ye should go and fruit should bear and
ὁ καρπὸς ὑμῶν μένῃ, ἵνα ὅ τι ἂν
the fruit of you should remain, that whatever

whatever you ask the Father in my name, he may give it to you. ¹⁷This I command you, to love one another. 18 "If the world hates you, know that it has hated me before it hated you. ¹⁹If you were of the world, the world would love its own; but because you are not of the world, but I chose you out of the world, therefore the world hates you. ²⁰Remember the word that I said to you, 'A servant is not greater than his master.' If they persecuted me, they will persecute you; if they kept my word, they will keep yours also. ²¹But all this they will do to you on my account, because they do not know him who sent me. ²²If I had not come and spoken to them, they would not have sin; but now they have no excuse for their sin. ²³He who hates me hates my Father also. ²⁴If I had not done among them the works which no one else did, they would not have sin; but now they have seen and hated both me and my Father. ²⁵It is to ful-

αἰτήσητε τὸν πατέρα ἐν τῷ ὀνόματί
ye may ask the Father in the name

μου δῷ ὑμῖν. 17 ταῦτα ἐντέλλομαι ὑμῖν,
of me he may give you. These things I command you,

ἵνα ἀγαπᾶτε ἀλλήλους. 18 Εἰ ὁ κόσμος
that ye love one another. If the world

ὑμᾶς μισεῖ, γινώσκετε ὅτι ἐμὲ πρῶτον
you hates, ye know that me before

ὑμῶν μεμίσηκεν. 19 εἰ ἐκ τοῦ κόσμου ἦτε,
you it has hated. If of the world ye were,

ὁ κόσμος ἂν τὸ ἴδιον ἐφίλει· ὅτι δὲ
the world ¹would ²the(its) ⁴own ³have loved; but because

ἐκ τοῦ κόσμου οὐκ ἐστέ, ἀλλ᾿ ἐγὼ
of the world ye are not, but I

ἐξελεξάμην ὑμᾶς ἐκ τοῦ κόσμου, διὰ τοῦτο
chose you out of the world, therefore

μισεῖ ὑμᾶς ὁ κόσμος. 20 μνημονεύετε
hates you the world. Remember ye

τοῦ λόγου οὗ ἐγὼ εἶπον ὑμῖν· οὐκ
the word which I said to you: Not

ἔστιν δοῦλος μείζων τοῦ κυρίου αὐτοῦ.
is a slave greater [than] the lord of him.

εἰ ἐμὲ ἐδίωξαν, καὶ ὑμᾶς διώξουσιν·
If me they persecuted, also you they will persecute;

εἰ τὸν λόγον μου ἐτήρησαν, καὶ τὸν
if the word of me they kept, also -

ὑμέτερον τηρήσουσιν. 21 ἀλλὰ ταῦτα πάντα
yours they will keep. But these things all

ποιήσουσιν εἰς ὑμᾶς διὰ τὸ ὄνομά μου,
they will do to you because of the name of me,

ὅτι οὐκ οἴδασιν τὸν πέμψαντά με.
because they know not the [one] having sent me.

22 εἰ μὴ ἦλθον καὶ ἐλάλησα αὐτοῖς, ἁμαρτίαν
Unless I came and spoke to them, sin

οὐκ εἴχοσαν· νῦν δὲ πρόφασιν οὐκ ἔχουσιν
they had not had; but now cloak they have not

περὶ τῆς ἁμαρτίας αὐτῶν. 23 ὁ ἐμὲ
concerning the sin of them. The [one] me

μισῶν καὶ τὸν πατέρα μου μισεῖ. 24 εἰ
hating also the Father of me hates. If

τὰ ἔργα μὴ ἐποίησα ἐν αὐτοῖς ἃ οὐδεὶς
the works I did not among them which no man

ἄλλος ἐποίησεν, ἁμαρτίαν οὐκ εἴχοσαν·
other did, sin they had not had;

νῦν δὲ καὶ ἑωράκασιν καὶ μεμισήκασιν
but now both they have seen and have hated

καὶ ἐμὲ καὶ τὸν πατέρα μου. 25 ἀλλ᾿
both me and the Father of me. But

fil the word that is written in their law, 'They hated me without a cause.' 26 But when the Counselor comes, whom I shall send to you from the Father, even the Spirit of truth, who proceeds from the Father, he will bear witness to me; 27 and you also are witnesses, because you have been with me from the beginning.

ἵνα πληρωθῇ ὁ λόγος ὁ ἐν τῷ νόμῳ
that may be fulfilled the word – in the law
αὐτῶν γεγραμμένος ὅτι ἐμίσησάν με
of them *having been* written[,] – They hated me
δωρεάν. 26 Ὅταν ἔλθῃ ὁ παράκλητος
freely. When comes the Comforter
ὃν ἐγὼ πέμψω ὑμῖν παρὰ τοῦ πατρός,
whom I will send to you from the Father,
τὸ πνεῦμα τῆς ἀληθείας ὃ παρὰ τοῦ
the Spirit – of truth which from the
πατρὸς ἐκπορεύεται, ἐκεῖνος μαρτυρήσει
Father proceeds, that one will witness
περὶ ἐμοῦ· 27 καὶ ὑμεῖς δὲ μαρτυρεῖτε,
concerning me; ³also ²ye ¹and witness,
ὅτι ἀπ' ἀρχῆς μετ' ἐμοῦ ἐστε.
because from [the] beginning with me ye are.

CHAPTER 16

"I have said all this to keep you from falling away. 2 They will put you out of the synagogues; indeed, the hour is coming when whoever kills you will think he is offering service to God. 3 And they will do this because they have not known the Father, nor me. 4 But I have said these things to you, that when their hour comes you may remember that I told you of them.

"I did not say these things to you from the beginning, because I was with you. 5 But now I am going to him who sent me; yet none of you asks me, 'Where are you going?' 6 But because I have said these things to you, sorrow has filled your hearts. 7 Nevertheless I tell you the truth:

16 Ταῦτα λελάληκα ὑμῖν ἵνα μὴ
These things I have spoken to you that not
σκανδαλισθῆτε. 2 ἀποσυναγώγους ποιή-
ye be offended. Put away from [the] synagogue they
σουσιν ὑμᾶς· ἀλλ' ἔρχεται ὥρα ἵνα πᾶς ὁ
will make you; but comes an hour that everyone
ἀποκτείνας ὑμᾶς δόξῃ λατρείαν προσφέρειν
killing you thinks service to offer
τῷ θεῷ. 3 καὶ ταῦτα ποιήσουσιν ὅτι
– to God. And these things they will do because
οὐκ ἔγνωσαν τὸν πατέρα οὐδὲ ἐμέ.
they knew not the Father nor me.
4 ἀλλὰ ταῦτα λελάληκα ὑμῖν ἵνα ὅταν
But these things I have spoken to you that when
ἔλθῃ ἡ ὥρα αὐτῶν μνημονεύητε αὐτῶν,
comes the hour of them ye may remember them,
ὅτι ἐγὼ εἶπον ὑμῖν. Ταῦτα δὲ ὑμῖν
that I told you. And these things to you
ἐξ ἀρχῆς οὐκ εἶπον, ὅτι μεθ' ὑμῶν
from [the] beginning I said not, because with you
ἤμην. 5 νῦν δὲ ὑπάγω πρὸς τὸν πέμψαντά
I was. But now I am going to the [one] having sent
με, καὶ οὐδεὶς ἐξ ὑμῶν ἐρωτᾷ με·
me, and not one of you asks me:
ποῦ ὑπάγεις; 6 ἀλλ' ὅτι ταῦτα λελάληκα
Where goest thou? but because these things I have spoken
ὑμῖν, ἡ λύπη πεπλήρωκεν ὑμῶν τὴν
to you, – grief has filled of you the
καρδίαν. 7 ἀλλ' ἐγὼ τὴν ἀλήθειαν λέγω
heart. But I the truth tell

it is to your advantage that I go away, for if I do not go away, the Counselor will not come to you; but if I go, I will send him to you. ⁸And when he comes, he will convince the world of sin and of righteousness and of judgment: ⁹of sin, because they do not believe in me; ¹⁰of righteousness, because I go to the Father, and you will see me no more; ¹¹of judgment, because the ruler of this world is judged.

12 "I have yet many things to say to you, but you cannot bear them now. ¹³When the Spirit of truth comes, he will guide you into all the truth; for he will not speak on his own authority, but whatever he hears he will speak, and he will declare to you the things that are to come. ¹⁴He will glorify me, for he will take what is mine and declare it to you. ¹⁵All that the Father has is mine; therefore I said that he will take what is mine and declare it to you.

16 "A little while, and you will see me no more; again a little while, and you will see me." ¹⁷Some

ὑμῖν,	συμφέρει	ὑμῖν	ἵνα	ἐγὼ	ἀπέλθω.
you,	it is expedient	for you	that	I	should go away.

ἐὰν γὰρ μὴ ἀπέλθω, ὁ παράκλητος
For if I go not away, the Comforter

οὐ μὴ ἔλθῃ πρὸς ὑμᾶς· ἐὰν δὲ πορευθῶ,
by no means comes to you; but if I go,

πέμψω αὐτὸν πρὸς ὑμᾶς. 8 καὶ ἐλθὼν
I will send him to you. And coming

ἐκεῖνος ἐλέγξει τὸν κόσμον περὶ ἁμαρτίας
that one will reprove the world concerning sin

καὶ περὶ δικαιοσύνης καὶ περὶ κρίσεως·
and concerning righteousness and concerning judgment;

9 περὶ ἁμαρτίας μέν, ὅτι οὐ πιστεύουσιν
concerning sin, – because they believe not

εἰς ἐμέ· 10 περὶ δικαιοσύνης δέ, ὅτι
in me; concerning righteousness, – because

πρὸς τὸν πατέρα ὑπάγω καὶ οὐκέτι
to the Father I am going and no longer

θεωρεῖτέ με· 11 περὶ δὲ κρίσεως, ὅτι
ye behold me; concerning – judgment, because

ὁ ἄρχων τοῦ κόσμου τούτου κέκριται.
the ruler – world of this has been judged.

12 Ἔτι πολλὰ ἔχω ὑμῖν λέγειν, ἀλλ᾽
Yet many things I have you to tell, but

οὐ δύνασθε βαστάζειν ἄρτι· 13 ὅταν δὲ
ye cannot to bear now; but when

ἔλθῃ ἐκεῖνος, τὸ πνεῦμα τῆς ἀληθείας,
comes that one, the Spirit – of truth,

ὁδηγήσει ὑμᾶς εἰς τὴν ἀλήθειαν πᾶσαν·
he will guide you into the truth all;

οὐ γὰρ λαλήσει ἀφ᾽ ἑαυτοῦ, ἀλλ᾽ ὅσα
for not will he speak from himself, but what things

ἀκούει λαλήσει, καὶ τὰ ἐρχόμενα
he hears he will speak, and the coming things

ἀναγγελεῖ ὑμῖν. 14 ἐκεῖνος ἐμὲ δοξάσει,
he will announce to you. That one me will glorify,

ὅτι ἐκ τοῦ ἐμοῦ λήμψεται καὶ ἀναγγελεῖ
because of the of me* he will receive and will announce

ὑμῖν. 15 πάντα ὅσα ἔχει ὁ πατὴρ ἐμά
to you. All things which has the Father mine

ἐστιν· διὰ τοῦτο εἶπον ὅτι ἐκ τοῦ ἐμοῦ
is(are); therefore I said that of the of me*

λαμβάνει καὶ ἀναγγελεῖ ὑμῖν. 16 Μικρὸν
he receives and will announce to you. A little while

καὶ οὐκέτι θεωρεῖτέ με, καὶ πάλιν
and no longer ye behold me, and again

μικρὸν καὶ ὄψεσθέ με. 17 εἶπαν οὖν
a little while and ye will see me. Said therefore

* Understand "that which is mine".

of his disciples said to one another, "What is this that he says to us, 'A little while, and you will not see me, and again a little while, and you will see me'; and, 'because I go to the Father'?" ¹⁸They said, "What does he mean by 'a little while'? We do not know what he means." ¹⁹Jesus knew that they wanted to ask him; so he said to them, "Is this what you are asking yourselves, what I meant by saying, 'A little while, and you will not see me, and again a little while, and you will see me'? ²⁰Truly, truly, I say to you, you will weep and lament, but the world will rejoice; you will be sorrowful, but your sorrow will turn into joy. ²¹When a woman is in travail she has sorrow, because her hour has come; but when she is delivered of the child, she no longer remembers the anguish, for joy that a child is born into the world. ²²So you have sorrow now, but I will see you again and your hearts will rejoice, and no one will take your joy from you. ²³In that day you will ask nothing

ἐκ   τῶν   μαθητῶν   αὐτοῦ   πρὸς   ἀλλήλους·
[some] of   the   disciples   of him   to   one another :

τί   ἐστιν   τοῦτο   ὃ   λέγει   ἡμῖν·   μικρὸν
What is   this   which he tells   us :   A little while

καὶ   οὐ   θεωρεῖτέ   με,   καὶ   πάλιν   μικρὸν
and   ye behold not   me,   and   again a little while

καὶ   ὄψεσθέ   με;   καί·   ὅτι   ὑπάγω
and   ye will see   me?   and :   Because I am going

πρὸς   τὸν   πατέρα;   **18** ἔλεγον   οὖν·   τοῦτο
to   the   Father?   They said therefore : ³This

τί   ἐστιν   ὃ   λέγει   τὸ   μικρόν;   οὐκ   οἴδαμεν
¹what ²is   which he says[,] the "little while"? We do not know

τί   λαλεῖ.   **19** ἔγνω   Ἰησοῦς   ὅτι   ἤθελον
what he speaks.   Knew   Jesus   that they wished

αὐτὸν   ἐρωτᾶν,   καὶ   εἶπεν   αὐτοῖς·   περὶ
him   to question,   and   said   to them : Concerning

τούτου   ζητεῖτε   μετ'   ἀλλήλων   ὅτι   εἶπον·
this   seek ye   with   one another because I said :

μικρὸν   καὶ   οὐ   θεωρεῖτέ   με,   καὶ   πάλιν
A little while and   ye behold not   me,   and   again

μικρὸν   καὶ   ὄψεσθέ   με;   **20** ἀμὴν   ἀμὴν
a little while and   ye will see   me?   Truly   truly

λέγω   ὑμῖν   ὅτι   κλαύσετε   καὶ   θρηνήσετε
I tell   you   that   will weep   and   will lament

ὑμεῖς,   ὁ   δὲ   κόσμος   χαρήσεται·   ὑμεῖς
ye,   and the   world   will rejoice;   ye

λυπηθήσεσθε,   ἀλλ'   ἡ   λύπη   ὑμῶν   εἰς
will be grieved,   but   the   grief   of you   into

χαρὰν   γενήσεται.   **21** ἡ   γυνὴ   ὅταν   τίκτῃ
joy   will become.   The woman   when she gives birth

λύπην   ἔχει,   ὅτι   ἦλθεν   ἡ   ὥρα   αὐτῆς·
grief   has,   because   came   the   hour   of her;

ὅταν   δὲ   γεννήσῃ   τὸ   παιδίον,   οὐκέτι
but when   she brings forth the   child,   no longer

μνημονεύει   τῆς   θλίψεως   διὰ   τὴν   χαρὰν
she remembers   the   distress   because of   the   joy

ὅτι   ἐγεννήθη   ἄνθρωπος   εἰς   τὸν   κόσμον.
that   was born   a man   into   the   world.

22 καὶ   ὑμεῖς   οὖν   νῦν   μὲν   λύπην   ἔχετε·
And   ye   therefore now   indeed   grief   have;

πάλιν   δὲ   ὄψομαι   ὑμᾶς,   καὶ   χαρήσεται
but again   I will see   you,   and   ⁴will rejoice

ὑμῶν   ἡ   καρδία,   καὶ   τὴν   χαρὰν   ὑμῶν
³of you ¹the   ²heart,   and   the   joy   of you

οὐδεὶς   αἴρει   ἀφ'   ὑμῶν.   **23** καὶ   ἐν   ἐκείνῃ   τῇ
no one   takes   from   you.   And in   that   –

ἡμέρᾳ   ἐμὲ   οὐκ   ἐρωτήσετε   οὐδέν.
day   me   ye will not question   no(any)thing.

of me. Truly, truly, I say to you, if you ask anything of the Father, he will give it to you in my name. ²⁴Hitherto you have asked nothing in my name; ask, and you will receive, that your joy may be full.

25 "I have said this to you in figures; the hour is coming when I shall no longer speak to you in figures but tell you plainly of the Father. ²⁶In that day you will ask in my name; and I do not say to you I shall pray the Father for you; ²⁷for the Father himself loves you, because you have loved me and have believed that I came from the Father. ²⁸I came from the Father and have come into the world; again, I am leaving the world and going to the Father."

29 His disciples said, "Ah, now you are speaking plainly, not in any figure! ³⁰Now we know that you know all things, and need none to question you; by this we believe that you came from God." ³¹Jesus answered them, "Do you now believe? ³²The hour

ἀμὴν	ἀμὴν	λέγω	ὑμῖν,	ἄν	τι	αἰτήσητε
Truly	truly	I tell	you,	whatever		ye ask

τὸν	πατέρα	δώσει	ὑμῖν	ἐν	τῷ	ὀνόματί
the	Father	he will give	you	in	the	name

μου.	24 ἕως	ἄρτι	οὐκ	ἠτήσατε	οὐδὲν
of me.	Until	now		ye asked not	no(any)thing

ἐν	τῷ	ὀνόματί	μου·	αἰτεῖτε,	καὶ	λήμψεσθε,
in	the	name	of me;	ask,	and	ye will receive,

ἵνα	ἡ	χαρὰ	ὑμῶν	ᾖ	πεπληρωμένη.
that	the	joy	of you	may be	*having been* filled.

25 Ταῦτα	ἐν	παροιμίαις	λελάληκα	ὑμῖν·
These things	in	allegories	I have spoken	to you;

ἔρχεται	ὥρα	ὅτε	οὐκέτι	ἐν	παροιμίαις
comes	an hour	when	no longer	in	allegories

λαλήσω	ὑμῖν,	ἀλλὰ	παρρησίᾳ	περὶ	τοῦ
I will speak	to you,	but	plainly	concerning	the

πατρὸς	ἀπαγγελῶ	ὑμῖν.	26 ἐν	ἐκείῃ	τῇ
Father	will declare	to you.	In	that	-

ἡμέρᾳ	ἐν	τῷ	ὀνόματί	μου	αἰτήσεσθε,
day	in	the	name	of me	ye will ask,

καὶ	οὐ	λέγω	ὑμῖν	ὅτι	ἐγὼ	ἐρωτήσω
and		I tell not	you	that	I	will request

τὸν	πατέρα	περὶ	ὑμῶν·	27 αὐτὸς	γὰρ
the	Father	concerning	you;		for [him]self

ὁ	πατὴρ	φιλεῖ	ὑμᾶς,	ὅτι	ὑμεῖς	ἐμὲ
the	Father	loves	you,	because	ye	me

πεφιλήκατε	καὶ	πεπιστεύκατε	ὅτι	ἐγὼ
have loved	and	have believed	that	I

παρὰ	τοῦ	θεοῦ	ἐξῆλθον.	28 ἐξῆλθον
from	-	God	came forth.	I came forth

ἐκ	τοῦ	πατρὸς	καὶ	ἐλήλυθα	εἰς	τὸν
out of	the	Father	and	have come	into	the

κόσμον·	πάλιν	ἀφίημι	τὸν	κόσμον	καὶ
world;	again	I leave	the	world	and

πορεύομαι	πρὸς	τὸν	πατέρα.	29 Λέγουσιν
go	to	the	Father.	Say

οἱ	μαθηταὶ	αὐτοῦ·	ἴδε	νῦν	ἐν	παρρησίᾳ
the	disciples	of him :	Behold[,]	now	in	plainness

λαλεῖς,	καὶ	παροιμίαν	οὐδεμίαν	λέγεις.
thou speakest, and		²allegory	¹no	thou sayest.

30 νῦν	οἴδαμεν	ὅτι	οἶδας	πάντα	καὶ
Now	we know	that	thou knowest	all things	and

οὐ	χρείαν	ἔχεις	ἵνα	τίς	σε	ἐρωτᾷ·	ἐν
no	need	hast	that	anyone	thee	should question;	by

τούτῳ	πιστεύομεν	ὅτι	ἀπὸ	θεοῦ	ἐξῆλθες.
this	we believe	that	from	God	thou camest forth.

31 ἀπεκρίθη	αὐτοῖς	Ἰησοῦς·	ἄρτι	πιστεύετε;
Answered	them	Jesus :	Now	believe ye?

is coming, indeed it has come, when you will be scattered, every man to his home, and will leave me alone; yet I am not alone, for the Father is with me. ³³I have said this to you, that in me you may have peace. In the world you have tribulation; but be of good cheer, I have overcome the world."

32 ἰδοὺ ἔρχεται ὥρα καὶ ἐλήλυθεν ἵνα
behold[,] comes an hour and has come that
σκορπισθῆτε ἕκαστος εἰς τὰ ἴδια κἀμὲ
ye are scattered each one to the(his) own and me
μόνον ἀφῆτε· καὶ οὐκ εἰμὶ μόνος, ὅτι
alone ye leave; and I am not alone, because
ὁ πατὴρ μετ᾽ ἐμοῦ ἐστιν. 33 ταῦτα
the Father with me is. These things
λελάληκα ὑμῖν ἵνα ἐν ἐμοὶ εἰρήνην
I have spoken to you that in me peace
ἔχητε. ἐν τῷ κόσμῳ θλῖψιν ἔχετε·
ye may have. In the world distress ye have;
ἀλλὰ θαρσεῖτε, ἐγὼ νενίκηκα τὸν κόσμον.
but cheer ye up, I have overcome the world.

CHAPTER 17

WHEN Jesus had spoken these words, he lifted up his eyes to heaven and said, "Father, the hour has come; glorify thy Son that the Son may glorify thee, ²since thou hast given him power over all flesh, to give eternal life to all whom thou hast given him. ³And this is eternal life, that they know thee the only true God, and Jesus Christ whom thou hast sent. ⁴I glorified thee on earth, having accomplished the work which thou gavest me to do; ⁵and now, Father, glorify thou me in thy own presence with the glory which I had with thee before the world was made. 6 "I have manifested thy name to the men whom thou gavest me

17 Ταῦτα ἐλάλησεν Ἰησοῦς, καὶ ἐπάρας
These things spoke Jesus, and lifting up
τοὺς ὀφθαλμοὺς αὐτοῦ εἰς τὸν οὐρανὸν
the eyes of him to heaven
εἶπεν· πάτερ, ἐλήλυθεν ἡ ὥρα· δόξασόν
said: Father, has come the hour; glorify
σου τὸν υἱόν, ἵνα ὁ υἱὸς δοξάσῃ σέ,
of thee the Son, that the Son may glorify thee,
2 καθὼς ἔδωκας αὐτῷ ἐξουσίαν πάσης
as thou gavest him authority of(over) all
σαρκός, ἵνα πᾶν ὃ δέδωκας αὐτῷ δώσῃ
flesh, that all which thou hast given him he may give
αὐτοῖς ζωὴν αἰώνιον. 3 αὕτη δέ ἐστιν
to them life eternal. And this is
ἡ αἰώνιος ζωή, ἵνα γινώσκωσιν σὲ τὸν
eternal life, that they may know thee the
μόνον ἀληθινὸν θεὸν καὶ ὃν ἀπέστειλας
only true God and [he] whom thou didst send
Ἰησοῦν Χριστόν. 4 ἐγώ σε ἐδόξασα
Jesus Christ. I thee glorified
ἐπὶ τῆς γῆς, τὸ ἔργον τελειώσας ὃ
on the earth, the work finishing which
δέδωκάς μοι ἵνα ποιήσω· 5 καὶ νῦν
thou hast given to me that I should do; and now
δόξασόν με σύ, πάτερ, παρὰ σεαυτῷ
glorify me thou, Father, ﹐ with thyself
τῇ δόξῃ ᾗ εἶχον πρὸ τοῦ τὸν κόσμον
with the glory which I had before *the* the world
= before the world was
εἶναι παρὰ σοί. 6 Ἐφανέρωσά σου τὸ
to beᵇ with thee. I manifested of thee the
ὄνομα τοῖς ἀνθρώποις οὓς ἔδωκάς μοι
name to the men whom thou gavest to me

out of the world; thine they were, and thou gavest them to me, and they have kept thy word. ⁷Now they know that everything that thou hast given me is from thee; ⁸for I have given them the words which thou gavest me, and they have received them and know in truth that I came from thee; and they have believed that thou didst send me. ⁹I am praying for them; I am not praying for the world but for those whom thou hast given me, for they are thine; ¹⁰all mine are thine, and thine are mine, and I am glorified in them. ¹¹And now I am no more in the world, but they are in the world, and I am coming to thee. Holy Father, keep them in thy name, which thou hast given me, that they may be one, even as we are one. ¹²While I was with them, I kept them in thy name, which thou hast given me; I have guarded them, and none of them is lost but the son of perdition, that the scripture might be fulfilled. ¹³But now I am coming to thee; and these things I speak in the world, that they may

ἐκ τοῦ κόσμου. σοὶ ἦσαν κἀμοὶ αὐτοὺς
out of the   world.   To thee° they were and to me   them
                    =Thine

ἔδωκας, καὶ τὸν λόγον σου τετήρηκαν.
thou gavest, and   the   word   of thee   they have kept.

7 νῦν ἔγνωκαν ὅτι πάντα ὅσα δέδωκάς
Now they have known that all things as many as thou hast given

μοι παρὰ σοῦ εἰσιν· 8 ὅτι τὰ ῥήματα
to me from   thee   are;   because the   words

ἃ ἔδωκάς μοι δέδωκα αὐτοῖς, καὶ αὐτοὶ
which thou gavest to me I have given to them, and   they

ἔλαβον, καὶ ἔγνωσαν ἀληθῶς ὅτι παρὰ
received,   and   knew   truly   that   from

σοῦ ἐξῆλθον, καὶ ἐπίστευσαν ὅτι σύ
thee   I came forth,   and   they believed   that thou

με ἀπέστειλας. 9 ἐγὼ περὶ αὐτῶν ἐρωτῶ·
me   didst send.   I concerning them make request;

οὐ περὶ τοῦ κόσμου ἐρωτῶ, ἀλλὰ περὶ
not concerning the   world do I make request, but concerning

ὧν δέδωκάς μοι, ὅτι σοί εἰσιν,
[those] whom thou hast given to me, because to thee° they are,
                                  =thine

10 καὶ τὰ ἐμὰ πάντα σά ἐστιν καὶ
and ²the ³my things ¹all ⁵thine ⁴is(are)   and

τὰ σὰ ἐμά, καὶ δεδόξασμαι ἐν αὐτοῖς.
the thy things mine, and I have been glorified in   them.

11 καὶ οὐκέτι εἰμὶ ἐν τῷ κόσμῳ, καὶ
And no longer am I   in   the   world,   and

αὐτοὶ ἐν τῷ κόσμῳ εἰσίν, κἀγὼ πρὸς
they   in the   world   are,   and I   to

σὲ ἔρχομαι. πάτερ ἅγιε, τήρησον αὐτοὺς
thee come.   Father   holy,   keep   them

ἐν τῷ ὀνόματί σου ᾧ δέδωκάς μοι,
in the   name   of thee which thou hast given to me,

ἵνα ὦσιν ἓν καθὼς ἡμεῖς. 12 ὅτε ἤμην
that they may be one   as   we.   When I was

μετ' αὐτῶν, ἐγὼ ἐτήρουν αὐτοὺς ἐν
with   them,   I   kept   them   in

τῷ ὀνόματί σου ᾧ δέδωκάς μοι, καὶ
the   name   of thee which thou hast given to me,   and

ἐφύλαξα, καὶ οὐδεὶς ἐξ αὐτῶν ἀπώλετο
I guarded,   and   not one   of   them   perished

εἰ μὴ ὁ υἱὸς τῆς ἀπωλείας, ἵνα ἡ
except the son   -   perdition,   that the

γραφὴ πληρωθῇ. 13 νῦν δὲ πρὸς σὲ
scripture might be fulfilled.   But now   to   thee

ἔρχομαι, καὶ ταῦτα λαλῶ ἐν τῷ κόσμῳ
I come,   and these things I speak in   the   world

ἵνα ἔχωσιν τὴν χαρὰν τὴν ἐμὴν
that   they may have the   ²joy   -   ¹my

have my joy fulfilled in themselves. ¹⁴I have given them thy word; and the world has hated them because they are not of the world, even as I am not of the world. ¹⁵I do not pray that thou shouldst take them out of the world, but that thou shouldst keep them from the evil one.ᶻ ¹⁶They are not of the world, even as I am not of the world. ¹⁷Sanctify them in the truth; thy word is truth. ¹⁸As thou didst send me into the world, so I have sent them into the world. ¹⁹And for their sake I consecrate myself, that they also may be consecrated in truth.

20 "I do not pray for these only, but also for those who believe in me through their word, ²¹that they may all be one; even as thou, Father, art in me, and I in thee, that they also may be in us, so that the world may believe that thou hast sent me. ²²The glory which thou hast given me I have given to them, that they may be one even as we are one, ²³I in them and thou in me, that they may become perfectly one, so

ᶻ Or *from evil*

πεπληρωμένην ἐν ἑαυτοῖς. 14 ἐγὼ δέδωκα
having been fulfilled in themselves.　　I　have given

αὐτοῖς τὸν λόγον σου, καὶ ὁ κόσμος
to them　the　word　of thee,　and　the　world

ἐμίσησεν αὐτούς, ὅτι οὐκ εἰσὶν ἐκ τοῦ
hated　them,　because they are not　of　the

κόσμου καθὼς ἐγὼ οὐκ εἰμὶ ἐκ τοῦ
world　as　I　am not　of　the

κόσμου. 15 οὐκ ἐρωτῶ ἵνα ἄρῃς αὐτοὺς
world.　I do not request that thou shouldest take them

ἐκ τοῦ κόσμου, ἀλλ' ἵνα τηρήσῃς αὐτοὺς
out of the　world,　but　that thou shouldest keep them

ἐκ τοῦ πονηροῦ. 16 ἐκ τοῦ κόσμου
out of the　evil [?one].　　Of　the　world

οὐκ εἰσὶν καθὼς ἐγὼ οὐκ εἰμὶ ἐκ τοῦ
they are not　as　I　am not　of　the

κόσμου. 17 ἁγίασον αὐτοὺς ἐν τῇ
world.　Sanctify　them　in(?by)　the

ἀληθείᾳ· ὁ λόγος ὁ σὸς ἀλήθειά ἐστιν.
truth;　the ²word　–　¹thy　truth　is.

18 καθὼς ἐμὲ ἀπέστειλας εἰς τὸν κόσμον,
As　me　thou didst send　into　the　world,

κἀγὼ ἀπέστειλα αὐτοὺς εἰς τὸν κόσμον·
I also　sent　them　into　the　world;

19 καὶ ὑπὲρ αὐτῶν [ἐγὼ] ἁγιάζω ἐμαυτόν,
and on behalf of　them　I　sanctify　myself,

ἵνα ὦσιν καὶ αὐτοὶ ἡγιασμένοι ἐν ἀληθείᾳ.
that ³may be ²also ¹they *having been* sanctified in　truth.

20 Οὐ περὶ τούτων δὲ ἐρωτῶ μόνον,
²Not ³concerning ⁴these ¹but I make request only,

ἀλλὰ καὶ περὶ τῶν πιστευόντων διὰ
but　also concerning　the [ones] believing　through

τοῦ λόγου αὐτῶν εἰς ἐμέ, 21 ἵνα πάντες
the　word　of them　in　me,　that　all

ἓν ὦσιν, καθὼς σύ, πατήρ, ἐν ἐμοὶ
one may be,　as　thou, Father,　in　me

κἀγὼ ἐν σοί, ἵνα καὶ αὐτοὶ ἐν ἡμῖν
and I　in　thee,　that　also　they　in　us

ὦσιν, ἵνα ὁ κόσμος πιστεύῃ ὅτι σύ
may be,　that the　world　may believe　that　thou

με ἀπέστειλας. 22 κἀγὼ τὴν δόξαν ἣν
me　didst send.　　And I　the　glory which

δέδωκάς μοι δέδωκα αὐτοῖς, ἵνα ὦσιν
thou hast given to me have given　to them,　that they may be

ἓν καθὼς ἡμεῖς ἕν· 23 ἐγὼ ἐν αὐτοῖς
one　as　we [are] one;　I　in　them

καὶ σὺ ἐν ἐμοί, ἵνα ὦσιν τετελειωμένοι
and thou in　me,　that they may be *having been* perfected

that the world may know that thou hast sent me and hast loved them even as thou hast loved me. ²¹Father, I desire that they also, whom thou hast given me, may be with me where I am, to behold my glory which thou hast given me in thy love for me before the foundation of the world. ²⁵O righteous Father, the world has not known thee, but I have known thee; and these know that thou hast sent me. ²⁶I made known to them thy name, and I will make it known, that the love with which thou hast loved me may be in them, and I in them."

εἰς ἕν, ἵνα γινώσκῃ ὁ κόσμος ὅτι σύ
in one, that may know the world that thou

με ἀπέστειλας καὶ ἠγάπησας αὐτοὺς
me didst send and didst love them

καθὼς ἐμὲ ἠγάπησας. 24 Πατήρ, ὃ
as me thou didst love. Father, what

δέδωκάς μοι, θέλω ἵνα ὅπου εἰμὶ ἐγὼ
thou hast given to me, I wish that where am I

κἀκεῖνοι ὦσιν μετ' ἐμοῦ, ἵνα θεωρῶσιν
those also may be with me, that they may behold

τὴν δόξαν τὴν ἐμήν, ἣν δέδωκάς μοι
the ²glory – ¹my, which thou hast given to me

ὅτι ἠγάπησάς. με πρὸ καταβολῆς κόσμου.
because thou didst love me before [the] foundation of [the] world.

25 πατὴρ δίκαιε, καὶ ὁ κόσμος σε
Father righteous, indeed the world thee

οὐκ ἔγνω, ἐγὼ δέ σε ἔγνων, καὶ οὗτοι
knew not, but I thee knew, and these

ἔγνωσαν ὅτι σύ με ἀπέστειλας· 26 καὶ
knew that thou me didst send; and

ἐγνώρισα αὐτοῖς τὸ ὄνομά σου καὶ
I made known to them the name of thee and

γνωρίσω, ἵνα ἡ ἀγάπη ἣν ἠγάπησάς
will make known, that the love [with] which thou lovedst

με ἐν αὐτοῖς ᾖ κἀγὼ ἐν αὐτοῖς.
me in them may be and I in them.

CHAPTER 18

WHEN Jesus had spoken these words, he went forth with his disciples across the Kidron valley, where there was a garden, which he and his disciples entered. ²Now Judas, who betrayed him, also knew the place; for Jesus often met there with his disciples. ³So Judas, procuring a band of soldiers and some officers from the chief priests and the Pharisees, went there with lanterns

18 Ταῦτα εἰπὼν Ἰησοῦς ἐξῆλθεν σὺν
These things having said Jesus went forth with

τοῖς μαθηταῖς αὐτοῦ πέραν τοῦ χειμάρρου
the disciples of him across the torrent

τοῦ Κεδρών, ὅπου ἦν κῆπος, εἰς ὃν
Kedron, where there was a garden, into which

εἰσῆλθεν αὐτὸς καὶ οἱ μαθηταὶ αὐτοῦ.
entered he and the disciples of him.

2 ᾔδει δὲ καὶ Ἰουδας ὁ παραδιδοὺς
¹Now ⁷knew ³also ²Judas ⁴the [one] ⁵betraying

αὐτὸν τὸν τόπον, ὅτι πολλάκις συνήχθη
⁶him ⁸the ⁹place, because often assembled

Ἰησοῦς ἐκεῖ μετὰ τῶν μαθητῶν αὐτου.
Jesus there with the disciples of him.

3 ὁ οὖν Ἰουδας λαβὼν τὴν σπεῖραν
– Therefore Judas taking the band

καὶ ἐκ τῶν ἀρχιερέων καὶ [ἐκ] τῶν
and ²from ³the ⁴chief priests ⁵and ⁶from ⁷the

Φαρισαίων ὑπηρέτας ἔρχεται ἐκεῖ μετὰ
⁸Pharisees ¹attendants comes there with

and torches and weapons. ⁴Then Jesus, knowing all that was to befall him, came forward and said to them, "Whom do you seek?" ⁵They answered him, "Jesus of Nazareth." Jesus said to them, "I am he." Judas, who betrayed him, was standing with them. ⁶When he said to them, "I am he," they drew back and fell to the ground. ⁷Again he asked them, "Whom do you seek?" And they said, "Jesus of Nazareth." ⁸Jesus answered, "I told you that I am he; so, if you seek me, let these men go." ⁹This was to fulfil the word which he had spoken, "Of those whom thou gavest me I lost not one." ¹⁰Then Simon Peter, having a sword, drew it and struck the high priest's slave and cut off his right ear. The slave's name was Malchus. ¹¹Jesus said to Peter, "Put your sword into its sheath; shall I not drink the cup which the Father has given me?"

12 So the band of

φανῶν καὶ λαμπάδων καὶ ὅπλων. 4 Ἰησοῦς
lanterns and lamps and weapons. Jesus

οὖν εἰδὼς πάντα τὰ ἐρχόμενα ἐπ᾽ αὐτὸν
therefore knowing all the things coming on him

ἐξῆλθεν καὶ λέγει αὐτοῖς· τίνα ζητεῖτε;
went forth and says to them; Whom seek ye?

5 ἀπεκρίθησαν αὐτῷ· Ἰησοῦν τὸν
They answered him: Jesus the

Ναζωραῖον. λέγει αὐτοῖς· ἐγώ εἰμι.
Nazarene. He tells them: I am.

εἱστήκει δὲ καὶ Ἰούδας ὁ παραδιδοὺς
Now stood also Judas the [one] betraying

αὐτὸν μετ᾽ αὐτῶν. 6 ὡς οὖν εἶπεν
him with them. When therefore he told

αὐτοῖς· ἐγώ εἰμι, ἀπῆλθαν εἰς τὰ ὀπίσω
them: I am, they went away back †

καὶ ἔπεσαν χαμαί. 7 πάλιν οὖν
and fell on the ground. Again therefore

ἐπηρώτησεν αὐτούς· τίνα ζητεῖτε; οἱ δὲ
he questioned them: Whom seek ye? And they

εἶπαν· Ἰησοῦν τὸν Ναζωραῖον. 8 ἀπεκρίθη
said: Jesus the Nazarene. Answered

Ἰησοῦς· εἶπον ὑμῖν ὅτι ἐγώ εἰμι· εἰ
Jesus: I told you that I am; if

οὖν ἐμὲ ζητεῖτε, ἄφετε τούτους ὑπάγειν·
therefore me ye seek, allow these to go;

9 ἵνα πληρωθῇ ὁ λόγος ὃν εἶπεν, ὅτι
that might be fulfilled the word which he said, —

οὓς δέδωκάς μοι, οὐκ ἀπώλεσα ἐξ
[Those] whom thou hast given to me, I lost not of

αὐτῶν οὐδένα. 10 Σίμων οὖν Πέτρος
them no(any)one. ¹Simon ³therefore ²Peter

ἔχων μάχαιραν εἵλκυσεν αὐτὴν καὶ ἔπαισεν
having a sword drew it and smote

τὸν τοῦ ἀρχιερέως δοῦλον καὶ ἀπέκοψεν
¹the ²of the ⁴high priest ³slave and cut off

αὐτοῦ τὸ ὠτάριον τὸ δεξιόν· ἦν δὲ
of him the ²ear — ¹right; and was

ὄνομα τῷ δούλῳ Μάλχος. 11 εἶπεν οὖν
name to the slave⁵ Malchus. Said therefore

ὁ Ἰησοῦς τῷ Πέτρῳ· βάλε τὴν μάχαιραν
— Jesus — to Peter: Put the sword

εἰς τὴν θήκην· τὸ ποτήριον ὃ δέδωκέν
into the sheath; the cup which has given

μοι ὁ πατήρ, οὐ μὴ πίω αὐτό;
to me the Father, by no means shall I drink it?

12 Ἡ οὖν σπεῖρα καὶ ὁ χιλίαρχος
Therefore the band and the chiliarch

soldiers and their captain and the officers of the Jews seized Jesus and bound him. ¹³First they led him to Annas; for he was the father-in-law of Ca'iaphas, who was high priest that year. ¹⁴It was Ca'iaphas who had given counsel to the Jews that it was expedient that one man should die for the people.
15 Simon Peter followed Jesus, and so did another disciple. As this disciple was known to the high priest, he entered the court of the high priest along with Jesus, ¹⁶while Peter stood outside at the door. So the other disciple, who was known to the high priest, went out and spoke to the maid who kept the door, and brought Peter in. ¹⁷The maid who kept the door said to Peter, "Are not you also one of this man's disciples?" He said, "I am not." ¹⁸Now the servants and officers had made a charcoal fire, because it was cold, and they were standing and warming themselves; Peter also was with them, standing and warming himself.
19 The high priest then questioned Jesus

καὶ οἱ ὑπηρέται τῶν Ἰουδαίων συνέλαβον
and the attendants of the Jews took

τὸν Ἰησοῦν · καὶ ἔδησαν αὐτόν, 13 καὶ
- Jesus and bound him, and

ἤγαγον πρὸς Ἄνναν πρῶτον· ἦν γὰρ
led to Annas first; for he was

πενθερὸς τοῦ Καϊαφᾶ, ὃς ἦν ἀρχιερεὺς
father-in-law - of Caiaphas, who was high priest

τοῦ ἐνιαυτοῦ ἐκείνου· 14 ἦν δὲ Καϊαφᾶς
- year of that; now it was Caiaphas

ὁ συμβουλεύσας τοῖς Ἰουδαίοις ὅτι
the [one] having advised the Jews that

συμφέρει ἕνα ἄνθρωπον ἀποθανεῖν ὑπὲρ
it is(was) expedient one man to die on behalf of

τοῦ λαοῦ. 15 Ἠκολούθει δὲ τῷ Ἰησοῦ
the people. And followed - Jesus

Σίμων Πέτρος καὶ ἄλλος μαθητής. ὁ δὲ
Simon Peter and another disciple. - And

μαθητὴς ἐκεῖνος ἦν γνωστὸς τῷ ἀρχιερεῖ,
disciple that was known to the high priest,

καὶ συνεισῆλθεν τῷ Ἰησοῦ εἰς τὴν αὐλὴν
and entered in - Jesus into the court

τοῦ ἀρχιερέως, 16 ὁ δὲ Πέτρος εἱστήκει
of the high priest, - but Peter stood

πρὸς τῇ θύρᾳ ἔξω. ἐξῆλθεν οὖν ὁ
at the door outside. Went out therefore the

μαθητὴς ὁ ἄλλος ὁ γνωστὸς τοῦ ἀρχιερέως
²disciple - ¹other - known of(to) the high priest

καὶ εἶπεν τῇ θυρωρῷ, καὶ εἰσήγαγεν
and told the portress, and brought in

τὸν Πέτρον. 17 λέγει οὖν τῷ Πέτρῳ ἡ
- Peter. Says therefore - to Peter the

παιδίσκη ἡ θυρωρός· μὴ καὶ σὺ ἐκ
maidservant the portress : Not also thou of

τῶν μαθητῶν εἶ τοῦ ἀνθρώπου τούτου;
the disciples art - man of this?

λέγει ἐκεῖνος· οὐκ εἰμί. 18 εἱστήκεισαν δὲ
Says that one : I am not. And stood

οἱ δοῦλοι καὶ οἱ ὑπηρέται ἀνθρακιὰν
the slaves and the attendants a fire

πεποιηκότες, ὅτι ψῦχος ἦν, καὶ
having made, because cold it was, and

ἐθερμαίνοντο· ἦν δὲ καὶ ὁ Πέτρος μετ᾽
were warming themselves; and was also - Peter with

αὐτῶν ἑστὼς καὶ θερμαινόμενος. 19 Ὁ
them standing and warming himself. - ¹The

οὖν ἀρχιερεὺς ἠρώτησεν τὸν Ἰησοῦν
²therefore ³high priest questioned - Jesus

about his disciples and his teaching. ²⁰Jesus answered him, "I have spoken openly to the world; I have always taught in synagogues and in the temple, where all Jews come together; I have said nothing secretly. ²¹Why do you ask me? Ask those who have heard me, what I said to them; they know what I said." ²²When he had said this, one of the officers standing by struck Jesus with his hand, saying, "Is that how you answer the high priest?" ²³Jesus answered him, "If I have spoken wrongly, bear witness to the wrong; but if I have spoken rightly, why do you strike me?" ²⁴Annas then sent him bound to Ca'iaphas the high priest.

25 Now Simon Peter was standing and warming himself. They said to him, "Are not you also one of his disciples?" He denied it and said, "I am not." ²⁶One of the servants of the high priest, a kinsman of the man whose ear Peter had cut off, asked, "Did I not see you in the garden with him?" ²⁷Peter again de-

περὶ τῶν μαθητῶν αὐτοῦ καὶ περὶ τῆς
about the disciples of him and about the
διδαχῆς αὐτοῦ. 20 ἀπεκρίθη αὐτῷ Ἰησοῦς·
teaching of him. Answered him Jesus:
ἐγὼ παρρησίᾳ λελάληκα τῷ κόσμῳ· ἐγὼ
I with plainness have spoken to the world; I
πάντοτε ἐδίδαξα ἐν συναγωγῇ καὶ ἐν
always taught in a synagogue and in
τῷ ἱερῷ, ὅπου πάντες οἱ Ἰουδαῖοι
the temple, where all the Jews
συνέρχονται, καὶ ἐν κρυπτῷ ἐλάλησα
come together, and in secret I spoke
οὐδέν. 21 τί με ἐρωτᾷς; ἐρώτησον
nothing. Why me questionest thou? question
τοὺς ἀκηκοότας τί ἐλάλησα αὐτοῖς· ἴδε
the [ones] having heard what I spoke to them; behold[,]
οὗτοι οἴδασιν ἃ εἶπον ἐγώ. 22 ταῦτα
these know what things said I. These things
δὲ αὐτοῦ εἰπόντος εἷς παρεστηκὼς τῶν
and him saying³ one standing by of the
=And as he said this
ὑπηρετῶν ἔδωκεν ῥάπισμα τῷ Ἰησοῦ
attendants gave a blow – to Jesus
εἰπών· οὕτως ἀποκρίνῃ τῷ ἀρχιερεῖ;
saying: Thus answerest thou the high priest?
23 ἀπεκρίθη αὐτῷ Ἰησοῦς· εἰ κακῶς
Answered him Jesus: If ill
ἐλάλησα, μαρτύρησον περὶ τοῦ κακοῦ·
I spoke, witness concerning the evil;
εἰ δὲ καλῶς, τί με δέρεις; 24 ἀπέστειλεν
but if well, why me beatest thou? ³Sent
οὖν αὐτὸν ὁ Ἅννας δεδεμένον πρὸς
²therefore ⁴him – ¹Annas having been bound to
Καϊάφαν τὸν ἀρχιερέα. 25 Ἦν δὲ Σίμων
Caiaphas the high priest. Now was Simon
Πέτρος ἑστὼς καὶ θερμαινόμενος. εἶπον
Peter standing and warming himself. They said
οὖν αὐτῷ· μὴ καὶ σὺ ἐκ τῶν μαθητῶν
therefore to him: Not also thou of the disciples
αὐτοῦ εἶ; ἠρνήσατο ἐκεῖνος καὶ εἶπεν·
of him art? Denied that one and said:
οὐκ εἰμί. 26 λέγει εἷς ἐκ τῶν δούλων τοῦ
I am not. Says one of the slaves of the
ἀρχιερέως, συγγενὴς ὢν οὗ ἀπέκοψεν
high priest, ³a relative ¹being ³[of him] of whom ⁵cut off
Πέτρος τὸ ὠτίον· οὐκ ἐγώ σε εἶδον
⁴Peter ⁶the ⁷ear: ²Not ¹I ⁴thee ¹saw
ἐν τῷ κήπῳ μετ᾽ αὐτοῦ; 27 πάλιν οὖν
in the garden with him? Again therefore

nied it; and at once the cock crowed.
28 Then they led Jesus from the house of Ca'iaphas to the praetorium. It was early. They themselves did not enter the praetorium, so that they might not be defiled, but might eat the passover. ²⁹So Pilate went out to them and said, "What accusation do you bring against this man?" ³⁰They answered him, "If this man were not an evildoer, we would not have handed him over." ³¹Pilate said to them, "Take him yourselves and judge him by your own law." The Jews said to him, "It is not lawful for us to put any man to death." ³²This was to fulfil the word which Jesus had spoken to show by what death he was to die.
33 Pilate entered the praetorium again and called Jesus, and said to him, "Are you the King of the Jews?" ³⁴Jesus answered, "Do you say this of your own accord, or did others say it to you about me?" ³⁵Pilate answered, "Am I a Jew?

ἠρνήσατο　　Πέτρος,　　καὶ　　εὐθέως　　ἀλέκτωρ
denied　　　　Peter,　　　and　　immediately　　a cock
ἐφώνησεν.
sounded(crew).

28 Ἄγουσιν　οὖν　τὸν　Ἰησοῦν　ἀπὸ　τοῦ
They lead　therefore　–　　Jesus　　from　　–
Καϊάφα　εἰς　τὸ　πραιτώριον·　ἦν　δὲ　πρωΐ·
Caiaphas　to　the　praetorium;　and it was　early;
καὶ　αὐτοὶ　οὐκ　εἰσῆλθον　εἰς　τὸ　πραιτώριον,
and　they　entered not　into　the　praetorium,
ἵνα　μὴ　μιανθῶσιν　ἀλλὰ　φάγωσιν　τὸ
lest　they should be defiled　but　might eat　the
πάσχα.　29 ἐξῆλθεν　οὖν　ὁ　Πιλᾶτος　ἔξω
passover.　Went forth　therefore　–　Pilate　outside
πρὸς　αὐτοὺς　καὶ　φησίν·　τίνα　κατηγορίαν
to　them　and　says :　What　accusation
φέρετε　τοῦ　ἀνθρώπου　τούτου;　30 ἀπεκρίθησαν
bring ye　–　man　of this?　They answered
καὶ　εἶπαν　αὐτῷ·　εἰ　μὴ　ἦν
and　said　to him :　Unless　was
οὗτος　κακὸν　ποιῶν,　οὐκ　ἂν　σοι
this man　evil　doing,　¹would ²not　⁷to thee
παρεδώκαμεν　αὐτόν.　31 εἶπεν　οὖν　αὐτοῖς
¹we ⁴have ⁵delivered　⁶him.　Said　therefore　to them
ὁ　Πιλᾶτος·　λάβετε　αὐτὸν　ὑμεῖς,　καὶ
–　Pilate :　Take　him　ye,　and
κατὰ　τὸν　νόμον　ὑμῶν　κρίνατε　αὐτόν.
according to　the　law　of you　judge ye　him.
εἶπον　αὐτῷ　οἱ　Ἰουδαῖοι·　ἡμῖν　οὐκ　ἔξεστιν
Said　to him　the　Jews :　For us　it is not lawful
ἀποκτεῖναι　οὐδένα·　32 ἵνα　ὁ　λόγος　τοῦ
to kill　no(any)one;　that　the　word　– ·
Ἰησοῦ　πληρωθῇ　ὃν　εἶπεν　σημαίνων　ποίῳ
of Jesus　might be fulfilled　which he said　signifying　by what
θανάτῳ　ἤμελλεν　ἀποθνήσκειν.　33 Εἰσῆλθεν
death　he was about　to die.　Entered
οὖν　πάλιν　εἰς　τὸ　πραιτώριον　ὁ　Πιλᾶτος
therefore　again　into　the　praetorium　–　Pilate
καὶ　ἐφώνησεν　τὸν　Ἰησοῦν　καὶ　εἶπεν
and　called　–　Jesus　and　said
αὐτῷ·　σὺ　εἶ　ὁ　βασιλεὺς　τῶν　Ἰουδαίων;
to him :　Thou　art　the　king　of the　Jews?
34 ἀπεκρίθη　Ἰησοῦς·　ἀφ᾽　ἑαυτοῦ　σὺ　τοῦτο
Answered　Jesus :　From　[thy]self　¹thou　³this
λέγεις,　ἢ　ἄλλοι　εἶπόν　σοι　περὶ　ἐμοῦ;
¹sayest,　or　others　told　thee　about　me?
35 ἀπεκρίθη　ὁ　Πιλᾶτος·　μήτι　ἐγὼ
Answered　–　Pilate :　not　I

Your own nation and the chief priests have handed you over to me; what have you done?" ³⁶Jesus answered, "My kingship is not of this world; if my kingship were of this world, my servants would fight, that I might not be handed over to the Jews; but my kingship is not from the world." ³⁷Pilate said to him, "So you are a king?" Jesus answered, "You say that I am a king. For this I was born, and for this I have come into the world, to bear witness to the truth. Every one who is of the truth hears my voice." ³⁸Pilate said to him, "What is truth?"

After he had said this, he went out to the Jews again, and told them, "I find no crime in him. ³⁹But you have a custom that I should release one man for you at the Passover; will you have me release for you the King of the Jews?" ⁴⁰They cried out again, "Not this man, but Barab′bas!" Now Barab′bas was a robber.

Ἰουδαῖός εἰμι; τὸ ἔθνος τὸ σὸν καὶ
a Jew am? the ²nation – ¹thy and

οἱ ἀρχιερεῖς παρέδωκάν σε ἐμοί· τί
the chief priests delivered thee to me; what

ἐποίησας; 36 ἀπεκρίθη Ἰησοῦς· ἡ βασιλεία
didst thou? Answered Jesus: The ²kingdom

ἡ ἐμὴ οὐκ ἔστιν ἐκ τοῦ κόσμου τούτου·
– ¹my is not of – world this;

εἰ ἐκ τοῦ κόσμου τούτου ἦν ἡ βασιλεία
if of – world this was the ²kingdom

ἡ ἐμή, οἱ ὑπηρέται ἂν οἱ ἐμοὶ ἠγωνίζοντο,
¹my, the ²attendants ³would – ¹my ⁴have struggled,

ἵνα μὴ παραδοθῶ τοῖς Ἰουδαίοις· νῦν
that I should not be delivered to the Jews; ²now

δὲ ἡ βασιλεία ἡ ἐμὴ οὐκ ἔστιν ἐντεῦθεν.
¹but the ²kingdom – ¹my is not hence.

37 εἶπεν οὖν αὐτῷ ὁ Πιλᾶτος· οὐκοῦν
Said therefore to him – Pilate: Not really

βασιλεὺς εἶ σύ; ἀπεκρίθη [ὁ] Ἰησοῦς·
a king art thou? Answered – Jesus:

σὺ λέγεις ὅτι βασιλεὺς εἰμι. ἐγὼ εἰς
Thou sayest that a king I am. I for

τοῦτο γεγέννημαι καὶ εἰς τοῦτο ἐλήλυθα
this have been born and for this I have come

εἰς τὸν κόσμον, ἵνα μαρτυρήσω τῇ
into the world, that I might witness to the

ἀληθείᾳ· πᾶς ὁ ὢν ἐκ τῆς ἀληθείας
truth; everyone being of the truth

ἀκούει μου τῆς φωνῆς. 38 λέγει αὐτῷ
hears of me the voice. Says to him

ὁ Πιλᾶτος· τί ἐστιν ἀλήθεια; Καὶ
– Pilate: What is truth? And

τοῦτο εἰπὼν πάλιν ἐξῆλθεν πρὸς τοὺς
this having said again he went forth to the

Ἰουδαίους, καὶ λέγει αὐτοῖς· ἐγὼ οὐδεμίαν
Jews, and tells them: ¹I ²no

εὑρίσκω ἐν αὐτῷ αἰτίαν. 39 ἔστιν δὲ
²find ⁵in ⁶him ⁴crime. But there is

συνήθεια ὑμῖν ἵνα ἕνα ἀπολύσω ὑμῖν
a custom to youᵉ that one I should release to you

ἐν τῷ πάσχα· βούλεσθε οὖν ἀπολύσω
at the Passover; will ye therefore [that] I release

ὑμῖν τὸν βασιλέα τῶν Ἰουδαίων; 40 ἐκραύ-
to you the king of the Jews? They cried

γασαν οὖν πάλιν λέγοντες· μὴ τοῦτον,
out therefore again saying: Not this man,

ἀλλὰ τὸν Βαραββᾶν. ἦν δὲ ὁ Βαραββᾶς
but – Barabbas. ¹But ²was – ²Barabbas

CHAPTER 19

THEN Pilate took
Jesus and scourged
him. ²And the soldiers
plaited a crown of thorns,
and put it on his head,
and arrayed him in a
purple robe; ³they came
up to him, saying, "Hail,
King of the Jews!" and
struck him with their
hands. ⁴Pilate went out
again, and said to them,
"Behold, I am bringing
him out to you, that you
may know that I find no
crime in him." ⁵So Jesus
came out, wearing the
crown of thorns and the
purple robe. Pilate said
to them, "Here is the
man!" ⁶When the chief
priests and the officers
saw him, they cried out,
"Crucify him, crucify
him!" Pilate said to them,
"Take him yourselves
and crucify him, for I
find no crime in him."
⁷The Jews answered him,
"We have a law, and by
that law he ought to die,
because he has made him-
self the Son of God."
⁸When Pilate heard these
words, he was the more
afraid; ⁹he entered the

ληστής.   19 Τότε οὖν ἔλαβεν ὁ Πιλᾶτος
⁴a robber.   Then therefore ²took   -   ¹Pilate

τὸν Ἰησοῦν καὶ ἐμαστίγωσεν.   2 καὶ οἱ
  -    ³Jesus and   scourged [him].   And the

στρατιῶται πλέξαντες στέφανον ἐξ ἀκανθῶν
  soldiers   having plaited a wreath out of thorns

ἐπέθηκαν αὐτοῦ τῇ κεφαλῇ, καὶ ἱμάτιον
put [it] on of him the   head,   and   ⁴garment

πορφυροῦν περιέβαλον αὐτόν, 3 καὶ ἤρχοντο
³a purple   ¹threw round ²him,   and   came

πρὸς αὐτὸν καὶ ἔλεγον· χαῖρε ὁ βασιλεὺς
  to   him   and   said :   Hail[,] -   king

τῶν Ἰουδαίων·   καὶ ἐδίδοσαν αὐτῷ
of the Jews;   and they gave   him

ῥαπίσματα.   4 Καὶ ἐξῆλθεν πάλιν ἔξω
  blows.   And   went forth again   outside

ὁ Πιλᾶτος καὶ λέγει αὐτοῖς· ἴδε ἄγω
 -   Pilate   and   says to them : Behold ¹I bring

ὑμῖν αὐτὸν ἔξω, ἵνα γνῶτε ὅτι οὐδεμίαν
⁴to you ²him ³out, that ye may know that   no

αἰτίαν εὑρίσκω ἐν αὐτῷ.   5 ἐξῆλθεν
 crime   I find   in   him.   Came forth

οὖν ὁ Ἰησοῦς ἔξω, φορῶν τὸν ἀκάνθινον
therefore - Jesus outside, wearing the   thorny

στέφανον καὶ τὸ πορφυροῦν ἱμάτιον. καὶ
  wreath   and the   purple   garment. And

λέγει αὐτοῖς· ἰδοὺ ὁ ἄνθρωπος. 6 ὅτε
he says to them : Behold[,] the   man.   When

οὖν εἶδον αὐτὸν οἱ ἀρχιερεῖς καὶ οἱ
therefore saw   him   the chief priests   and the

ὑπηρέται, ἐκραύγασαν λέγοντες· σταύρωσον
attendants,   they shouted   saying :   Crucify[,]

σταύρωσον. λέγει αὐτοῖς ὁ Πιλᾶτος·
  crucify.   Says to them -   Pilate :

λάβετε αὐτὸν ὑμεῖς καὶ σταυρώσατε·
¹Take   ³him   ²ye   and   crucify;

ἐγὼ γὰρ οὐχ εὑρίσκω ἐν αὐτῷ αἰτίαν.
for I   find not   in   him   crime.

7 ἀπεκρίθησαν αὐτῷ οἱ Ἰουδαῖοι· ἡμεῖς
  Answered   him   the   Jews :   We

νόμον ἔχομεν, καὶ κατὰ τὸν νόμον
a law   have,   and according to the   law

ὀφείλει ἀποθανεῖν, ὅτι υἱὸν θεοῦ ἑαυτὸν
he ought to die,   because Son of God himself

ἐποίησεν. 8 Ὅτε οὖν ἤκουσεν ὁ Πιλᾶτος
he made.   When therefore heard   -   Pilate

τοῦτον τὸν λόγον, μᾶλλον ἐφοβήθη, 9 καὶ
 this   -   word,   more   he was afraid,   and

praetorium again and said to Jesus, "Where are you from?" But Jesus gave no answer. ¹⁰Pilate therefore said to him, "You will not speak to me? Do you not know that I have power to release you, and power to crucify you?" ¹¹Jesus answered him, "You would have no power over me unless it had been given you from above; therefore he who delivered me to you has the greater sin."

12 Upon this Pilate sought to release him, but the Jews cried out, "If you release this man, you are not Caesar's friend; every one who makes himself a king sets himself against Caesar." ¹³When Pilate heard these words, he brought Jesus out and sat down on the judgment seat at a place called The Pavement, and in Hebrew, Gab′batha. ¹⁴Now it was the day of Preparation of the Passover; it was about the sixth hour. He said to the Jews, "Here is your King!" ¹⁵They cried out, "Away with him, away with him, crucify him!" Pilate said to them, "Shall I crucify your King?" The chief

εἰσῆλθεν   εἰς   τὸ   πραιτώριον   πάλιν   καὶ
entered   into   the   praetorium   again   and

λέγει   τῷ   'Ιησοῦ·   πόθεν   εἶ   σύ;   ὁ   δὲ
says   –   to Jesus :   Whence   art   thou?   –   But

'Ιησοῦς   ἀπόκρισιν   οὐκ   ἔδωκεν   αὐτῷ.
Jesus   answer   did not give   him.

10 λέγει   οὖν   αὐτῷ   ὁ   Πιλᾶτος·   ἐμοὶ
Says   therefore   to him   –   Pilate :   To me

οὐ   λαλεῖς;   οὐκ   οἶδας   ὅτι   ἐξουσίαν   ἔχω
speakest thou not?   knowest thou not   that   authority   I have

ἀπολῦσαί   σε   καὶ   ἐξουσίαν   ἔχω   σταυρῶσαί
to release   thee   and   authority   I have   to crucify

σε;   11 ἀπεκρίθη   'Ιησοῦς·   οὐκ   εἶχες
thee?   Answered   Jesus :   Thou hadst not

ἐξουσίαν   κατ'   ἐμοῦ   οὐδεμίαν   εἰ   μὴ   ἦν
²authority   ³against   ⁴me   ¹no(any)   unless   it was

δεδομένον   σοι   ἄνωθεν·   διὰ   τοῦτο   ὁ
having been given   thee   from above;   therefore   the [one]

παραδούς   μέ   σοι   μείζονα   ἁμαρτίαν   ἔχει.
having delivered   me   to thee   a greater   sin   has.

12 ἐκ   τούτου   ὁ   Πιλᾶτος   ἐζήτει   ἀπολῦσαι
From   this   –   Pilate   sought   to release

αὐτόν·   οἱ   δὲ   'Ιουδαῖοι   ἐκραύγασαν   λέγοντες·
him;   but the   Jews   shouted   saying :

ἐὰν   τοῦτον   ἀπολύσῃς,   οὐκ   εἶ   φίλος   τοῦ
If   this man   thou releasest,   thou art not   a friend   –

Καίσαρος·   πᾶς   ὁ   βασιλέα   ἑαυτὸν   ποιῶν
of Caesar;   everyone   a king   himself   making

ἀντιλέγει   τῷ   Καίσαρι.   13 'Ο   οὖν   Πιλᾶτος
speaks against   –   Caesar.   – Therefore   Pilate

ἀκούσας   τῶν   λόγων   τούτων   ἤγαγεν   ἔξω
hearing   –   words   these   brought   outside

τὸν   'Ιησοῦν,   καὶ   ἐκάθισεν   ἐπὶ   βήματος
–   Jesus,   and   sat   on   a tribunal

εἰς   τόπον   λεγόμενον   Λιθόστρωτον,   'Εβραϊστὶ   δὲ
in   a place   being called   Pavement,   but in Hebrew

Γαββαθά.   14 ἦν   δὲ   παρασκευὴ   τοῦ
Gabbatha.   Now it was   preparation   of the

πάσχα,   ὥρα   ἦν   ὡς   ἕκτη·   καὶ   λέγει
Passover,   hour   it was about   sixth;   and   he says

τοῖς   'Ιουδαίοις·   ἴδε   ὁ   βασιλεὺς   ὑμῶν.
to the   Jews;   Behold[,] the   king   of you.

15 ἐκραύγασαν   οὖν   ἐκεῖνοι·   ἆρον   ἆρον,
Shouted   therefore   those :   Take[,]   take,

σταύρωσον   αὐτόν.   λέγει   αὐτοῖς   ὁ   Πιλᾶτος·
crucify   him.   Says   to them   –   Pilate :

τὸν   βασιλέα   ὑμῶν   σταυρώσω;   ἀπεκρίθησαν
The   king   of you   shall I crucify?   Answered

priests answered, "We have no king but Caesar." ¹⁶Then he handed him over to them to be crucified.

17 So they took Jesus, and he went out, bearing his own cross, to the place called the place of a skull, which is called in Hebrew Gol'gotha. ¹⁸There they crucified him, and with him two others, one on either side, and Jesus between them. ¹⁹Pilate also wrote a title and put it on the cross; it read, "Jesus of Nazareth, the King of the Jews." ²⁰Many of the Jews read this title, for the place where Jesus was crucified was near the city; and it was written in Hebrew, in Latin, and in Greek. ²¹The chief priests of the Jews then said to Pilate, "Do not write, 'The King of the Jews,' but, 'This man said, I am King of the Jews.'" ²²Pilate answered, "What I have written I have written."

23 When the soldiers had crucified Jesus they

οἱ ἀρχιερεῖς· οὐκ ἔχομεν βασιλέα εἰ
the chief priests : We have not a king ex-
μὴ Καίσαρα. 16 τότε οὖν παρέδωκεν
cept Cæsar. Then therefore he delivered
αὐτὸν αὐτοῖς ἵνα σταυρωθῇ.
him to them that he should be crucified.

Παρέλαβον οὖν τὸν Ἰησοῦν· 17 καὶ
They took therefore – Jesus; and
βαστάζων ἑαυτῷ τὸν σταυρὸν ἐξῆλθεν
carrying ²to himself º ¹the ²cross he went forth
εἰς τὸν λεγόμενον κρανίου τόπον, ὃ
to ¹the ²being called ⁴of a skull ²place, which
λέγεται Ἑβραϊστὶ Γολγοθά, 18 ὅπου αὐτὸν
is called in Hebrew Golgotha, where him
ἐσταύρωσαν, καὶ μετ’ αὐτοῦ ἄλλους δύο
they crucified, and with him others two
ἐντεῦθεν καὶ ἐντεῦθεν, μέσον δὲ τὸν
on this side and on that, † and in the middle –
Ἰησοῦν. 19 ἔγραψεν δὲ καὶ τίτλον ὁ
Jesus. And wrote also a title –
Πιλᾶτος καὶ ἔθηκεν ἐπὶ τοῦ σταυροῦ·
Pilate and put [it] on the cross;
ἦν δὲ γεγραμμένον· ΙΗΣΟΥΣ Ο
and it was having been written : JESUS THE
ΝΑΖΩΡΑΙΟΣ Ο ΒΑΣΙΛΕΥΣ ΤΩΝ
NAZARENE THE KING OF THE
ΙΟΥΔΑΙΩΝ. 20 τοῦτον οὖν τὸν τίτλον
JEWS. ¹This ²therefore – ²title
πολλοὶ ἀνέγνωσαν τῶν Ἰουδαίων, ὅτι
¹many ⁴read ²of the ³Jews, because
ἐγγὺς ἦν ὁ τόπος τῆς πόλεως ὅπου
⁷near ⁶was ¹the ²place ⁸the ⁹city ³where
ἐσταυρώθη ὁ Ἰησοῦς· καὶ ἦν γεγραμμένον
⁵was crucified – ⁴Jesus; and it was having been written
Ἑβραϊστί, Ῥωμαϊστί, Ἑλληνιστί. 21 ἔλεγον
in Hebrew, in Latin, in Greek. Said
οὖν τῷ Πιλάτῳ οἱ ἀρχιερεῖς τῶν Ἰουδαίων·
therefore – to Pilate the chief priests of the Jews :
μὴ γράφε· ὁ βασιλεὺς τῶν Ἰουδαίων,
Write not : The king of the Jews,
ἀλλ’ ὅτι ἐκεῖνος εἶπεν· βασιλεύς εἰμι
but that that man said : King I am
τῶν Ἰουδαίων. 22 ἀπεκρίθη ὁ Πιλᾶτος·
of the Jews. Answered – Pilate :
ὃ γέγραφα, γέγραφα. 23 Οἱ οὖν
What I have written, I have written. Therefore the
στρατιῶται, ὅτε ἐσταύρωσαν τὸν Ἰησοῦν,
soldiers. when they crucified – Jesus,

took his garments and made four parts, one for each soldier; also his tunic. But the tunic was without seam, woven from top to bottom; 24so they said to one another, "Let us not tear it, but cast lots for it to see whose it shall be." This was to fulfil the "They parted my garments among them, and for my clothing they cast lots." 25 So the soldiers did this. But standing by the cross of Jesus were his mother, and his mother's sister, Mary the wife of Clopas, and Mary Mag'dalene. 26 When Jesus saw his mother, and the disciple whom he loved standing near, he said to his mother, "Woman, behold, your son!" 27 Then he said to the disciple, "Behold, your mother!" And from that hour the disciple took her to his own home. 28 After this Jesus, knowing that all was now finished, said (to fulfil the scripture), "I thirst." 29A bowl full of vinegar stood there; so they put a sponge full of the vinegar on hyssop and

ἔλαβον τὰ ἱμάτια αὐτοῦ καὶ ἐποίησαν
took the garments of him and made
τέσσερα μέρη, ἑκάστῳ στρατιώτῃ μέρος,
four parts, to each soldier a part,
καὶ τὸν χιτῶνα. ἦν δὲ ὁ χιτὼν ἄρραφος,
and the tunic. Now was the tunic seamless,
ἐκ τῶν ἄνωθεν ὑφαντὸς δι' ὅλου. 24 εἶπαν
from the top woven throughout. They said
οὖν πρὸς ἀλλήλους· μὴ σχίσωμεν αὐτόν,
therefore to one another : Let us not tear it,
ἀλλὰ λάχωμεν περὶ αὐτοῦ τίνος ἔσται·
but let us cast lots about it of whom it shall be;
ἵνα ἡ γραφὴ πληρωθῇ· διεμερίσαντο τὰ
that the scripture might be fulfilled : They parted the
ἱμάτιά μου ἑαυτοῖς καὶ ἐπὶ τὸν ἱματισμόν
garments of me to themselves and over the raiment
μου ἔβαλον κλῆρον. Οἱ μὲν οὖν στρατιῶται
of me they cast a lot. ³The -*²therefore ⁴soldiers
ταῦτα ἐποίησαν. 25 εἱστήκεισαν δὲ παρὰ
¹these things did. ²there stood ¹But by
τῷ σταυρῷ τοῦ Ἰησοῦ ἡ μήτηρ αὐτοῦ
the cross - of Jesus the mother of him
καὶ ἡ ἀδελφὴ τῆς μητρὸς αὐτοῦ, Μαρία
and the sister of the mother of him, Mary
ἡ τοῦ Κλωπᾶ καὶ Μαρία ἡ Μαγδαληνή.
the [?wife] - of Clopas and Mary the Magdalene.
26 Ἰησοῦς οὖν ἰδὼν τὴν μητέρα καὶ
Jesus therefore seeing the(his) mother and
τὸν μαθητὴν παρεστῶτα ὃν ἠγάπα, λέγει
the disciple standing by whom he loved, says
τῇ μητρί· γύναι, ἴδε ὁ υἱός σου.
to the(his) mother : Woman, behold[,] the son of thee.
27 εἶτα λέγει τῷ μαθητῇ· ἴδε ἡ μήτηρ
Then he says to the disciple : Behold[,] the mother
σου. καὶ ἀπ' ἐκείνης τῆς ὥρας ἔλαβεν
of thee. And from that - hour took
ὁ μαθητὴς αὐτὴν εἰς τὰ ἴδια. 28 Μετὰ
the disciple her to his own [home]. † After
τοῦτο εἰδὼς ὁ Ἰησοῦς ὅτι ἤδη πάντα
this knowing - Jesus that now all things
τετέλεσται, ἵνα τελειωθῇ ἡ γραφή, λέγει·
have been finished, that might be fulfilled the scripture, says:
διψῶ. 29 σκεῦος ἔκειτο ὄξους μεστόν·
I thirst. A vessel was set of vinegar full;
σπόγγον οὖν μεστὸν τοῦ ὄξους ὑσσώπῳ
³a sponge therefore ⁴full ⁵of the ⁶vinegar ⁸a hyssop §

* μέν is scarcely translatable. But note the δέ in ver. 25 : John contrasts two groups—the soldiers and the women.
§ It has been suggested that ὑσσώπῳ is a graphic error for ὑσσῷ (pilum), pike; but cf. Mat. 27. 48.

held it to his mouth. ³⁰When Jesus had received the vinegar, he said, "It is finished"; and he bowed his head and gave up his spirit. 31 Since it was the day of Preparation, in order to prevent the bodies from remaining on the cross on the sabbath (for that sabbath was a high day), the Jews asked Pilate that their legs might be broken, and that they might be taken away. ³²So the soldiers came and broke the legs of the first, and of the other who had been crucified with him; ³³but when they came to Jesus and saw that he was already dead, they did not break his legs. ³⁴But one of the soldiers pierced his side with a spear, and at once there came out blood and water. ³⁵He who saw it has borne witness—his testimony is true, and he knows that he tells the truth—that you also may believe. ³⁶For these things took place that the scripture might be fulfilled, "Not a bone of him shall be broken." ³⁷And again another scripture says, "They shall look on him whom

περιθέντες προσήνεγκαν αὐτοῦ τῷ · στόματι.
²putting 'round they brought [it] to of him   the   mouth.

30 ὅτε οὖν ἔλαβεν τὸ ὄξος [ὁ] Ἰησοῦς
When therefore took the vinegar – Jesus

εἶπεν· τετέλεσται, καὶ κλίνας τὴν κεφαλὴν
he said : It has been finished, and inclining the(his) head

παρέδωκεν τὸ πνεῦμα.
delivered up the(his) spirit.

31 Οἱ οὖν Ἰουδαῖοι, ἐπεὶ παρασκευὴ
The ²therefore ¹Jews, since preparation

ἦν, ἵνα μὴ μείνῃ ἐπὶ τοῦ σταυροῦ τὰ
it was, that might not remain on the cross the

σώματα ἐν τῷ σαββάτῳ, ἦν γὰρ μεγάλη
bodies on the sabbath, for was great

ἡ ἡμέρα ἐκείνου τοῦ σαββάτου, ἠρώτησαν
the day of that – sabbath, they asked

τὸν Πιλᾶτον ἵνα κατεαγῶσιν αὐτῶν τὰ
– Pilate that might be broken of them the

σκέλη καὶ ἀρθῶσιν. 32 ἦλθον οὖν οἱ
legs and they might be taken. Came therefore the

στρατιῶται, καὶ τοῦ μὲν πρώτου κατέαξαν
soldiers, and of the –* first broke

τὰ σκέλη καὶ τοῦ ἄλλου τοῦ
the legs and of the other the

συσταυρωθέντος αὐτῷ· 33 ἐπὶ δὲ τὸν
crucified with him; ²on ¹but the

Ἰησοῦν ἐλθόντες, ὡς εἶδον ἤδη αὐτὸν
⁴Jesus ²coming, when they saw already him

τεθνηκότα, οὐ κατέαξαν αὐτοῦ τὰ σκέλη,
to have died, they did not break of him the legs,

34 ἀλλ' εἷς τῶν στρατιωτῶν λόγχῃ αὐτοῦ
but one of the soldiers with a lance of him

τὴν πλευρὰν ἔνυξεν, καὶ ἐξῆλθεν εὐθὺς αἷμα
the side pricked, and there came imme- blood
         out diately

καὶ ὕδωρ. 35 καὶ ὁ ἑωρακὼς μεμαρτύρηκεν,
and water. And the [one] having seen has witnessed,

καὶ ἀληθινὴ αὐτοῦ ἐστιν ἡ μαρτυρία,
and true of him is the witness,

καὶ ἐκεῖνος οἶδεν ὅτι ἀληθῆ λέγει, ἵνα
and that one knows that truly he says, that

καὶ ὑμεῖς πιστεύητε. 36 ἐγένετο γὰρ
also ye may believe. For happened

ταῦτα ἵνα ἡ γραφὴ πληρωθῇ· ὀστοῦν
these things that the scripture might be fulfilled : A bone

οὐ συντριβήσεται αὐτοῦ. 37 καὶ πάλιν
shall not be broken of him. And again

ἑτέρα γραφὴ λέγει· ὄψονται εἰς ὃν
another scripture says : They shall look at [him] whom

* See note on 19. 24. Here see ver. 33—two actions contrasted.

they have pierced."
38 After this Joseph of Arimathe'a, who was a disciple of Jesus, but secretly, for fear of the Jews, asked Pilate that he might take away the body of Jesus, and Pilate gave him leave. So he came and took away his body. ³⁹ Nicode'mus also, who had at first come to him by night, came bringing a mixture of myrrh and aloes, about a hundred pounds' weight. ⁴⁰ They took the body of Jesus, and bound it in linen cloths with the spices, as is the burial custom of the Jews. ⁴¹ Now in the place where he was crucified there was a garden, and in the garden a new tomb where no one had ever been laid. ⁴² So because of the Jewish day of Preparation, as the tomb was close at hand, they laid Jesus there.

ἐξεκέντησαν. 38 Μετὰ δὲ ταῦτα ἠρώτησεν
they pierced.   Now after these things ¹⁴asked
τὸν   Πιλᾶτον   'Ιωσὴφ   ἀπὸ   'Αριμαθαίας,
 -      ¹⁵Pilate   ¹Joseph   ²from   ³Arimathæa,
ὢν   μαθητὴς   [τοῦ]   'Ιησοῦ   κεκρυμμένος
⁴being ⁵a disciple   -   ⁶of Jesus ⁸having been hidden
δὲ   διὰ   τὸν   φόβον   τῶν   'Ιουδαίων,   ἵνα
⁷but ⁹because ¹⁰the ¹¹fear ¹²of the ¹³Jews,   that
             of
ἄρῃ   τὸ   σῶμα   τοῦ   'Ιησοῦ·   καὶ
he might take the   body   -   of Jesus;   and
ἐπέτρεψεν   ὁ   Πιλᾶτος.   ἦλθεν   οὖν   καὶ   ἦρεν
allowed   -   Pilate.   He came   there- and   took
                                          fore
τὸ   σῶμα   αὐτοῦ.   39 ἦλθεν   δὲ   καὶ   Νικόδημος,
the   body   of him.   And came   also   Nicodemus,
ὁ   ἐλθὼν   πρὸς   αὐτὸν   νυκτὸς   τὸ   πρῶτον,
the [one] having come to   him of (by) night   at first,†
φέρων   μίγμα   σμύρνης   καὶ   ἀλόης   ὡς
bearing a mixture of myrrh   and   aloes   about
λίτρας   ἑκατόν.   40 ἔλαβον   οὖν   τὸ   σῶμα
pounds   a hundred.   They took there- the   body
                                    fore
τοῦ   'Ιησοῦ   καὶ   ἔδησαν   αὐτὸ   ὀθονίοις
 -     of Jesus   and   bound   it   in sheets
μετὰ   τῶν   ἀρωμάτων,   καθὼς   ἔθος   ἐστὶν
with   the   spices,   as   custom   is
τοῖς   'Ιουδαίοις   ἐνταφιάζειν. 41 ἦν   δὲ
with the   Jews   to bury.   Now there was
ἐν   τῷ   τόπῳ   ὅπου   ἐσταυρώθη   κῆπος,
in   the   place   where   he was crucified a garden,
καὶ   ἐν   τῷ   κήπῳ   μνημεῖον   καινόν,   ἐν
and   in   the   garden   tomb   a new,   in
ᾧ   οὐδέπω   οὐδεὶς   ἦν   τεθειμένος· 42 ἐκεῖ
which never yet no(any)   was having been put;   there
                                          one
οὖν   διὰ   τὴν   παρασκευὴν   τῶν   'Ιουδαίων,
therefore because of the preparation   of the   Jews,
ὅτι   ἐγγὺς   ἦν   τὸ   μνημεῖον,   ἔθηκαν   τὸν
because near   was   the   tomb,   they put   -
'Ιησοῦν.
Jesus.

CHAPTER 20

NOW on the first day of the week Mary Mag'dalene came to the tomb early, while it was still dark, and saw that

20 Τῇ   δὲ   μιᾷ   τῶν   σαββάτων   Μαρία
Now on the one(first) [day] of the   week   Mary
ἡ   Μαγδαληνὴ   ἔρχεται   πρωὶ   σκοτίας   ἔτι
the   Magdalene   comes   early   darkness   yet
                                        =while it was yet dark
οὔσης   εἰς   τὸ   μνημεῖον,   καὶ   βλέπει   τὸν
being*   to   the   tomb,   and   sees   the

the stone had been taken away from the tomb. ²So she ran, and went to Simon Peter and the other disciple, the one whom Jesus loved, and said to them, "They have taken the Lord out of the tomb, and we do not know where they have laid him." ³Peter then came out with the other disciple, and they went toward the tomb. ⁴They both ran, but the other disciple outran Peter and reached the tomb first; ⁵and stooping to look in, he saw the linen cloths lying there, but he did not go in. ⁶Then Simon Peter came, following him, and went into the tomb; he saw the linen cloths lying, ⁷and the napkin, which had been on his head, not lying with the linen cloths but rolled up in a place by itself. ⁸Then the other disciple, who reached the tomb first, also went in, and he saw and believed; ⁹for as yet they did not know the scripture, that he must rise from the dead. ¹⁰Then the disciples went back to their homes.

λίθον   ἠρμένον   ἐκ   τοῦ   μνημείου.
stone   having been taken out of   the   tomb.

2 τρέχει   οὖν   καὶ   ἔρχεται   πρὸς   Σίμωνα
   She runs therefore and   comes   to   Simon

Πέτρον   καὶ   πρὸς   τὸν   ἄλλον   μαθητὴν   ὃν
Peter   and   to   the   other   disciple   whom

ἐφίλει   ὁ   Ἰησοῦς,   καὶ   λέγει   αὐτοῖς·   ἦραν
²loved   —   ¹Jesus,   and   says   to them :   They
                                                        took

τὸν   κύριον   ἐκ   τοῦ   μνημείου,   καὶ   οὐκ   οἴδαμεν
the   Lord   out of the   tomb,   and   we do not know

ποῦ   ἔθηκαν   αὐτόν.   3 Ἐξῆλθεν   οὖν   ὁ
where they put   him.   Went forth therefore -

Πέτρος   καὶ   ὁ   ἄλλος   μαθητής,   καὶ   ἤρχοντο
Peter   and the   other   disciple,   and   came

εἰς   τὸ   μνημεῖον.   4 ἔτρεχον   δὲ   οἱ   δύο
to   the   tomb.   And ran   the   two

ὁμοῦ·   καὶ   ὁ   ἄλλος   μαθητὴς   προέδραμεν
together; and the   other   disciple   ran before

τάχιον   τοῦ   Πέτρου   καὶ   ἦλθεν   πρῶτος
more quickly [than] -   Peter   and   came   first

εἰς   τὸ   μνημεῖον,   5 καὶ   παρακύψας   βλέπει
to   the   tomb,   and   stooping   sees

κείμενα   τὰ   ὀθόνια,   οὐ   μέντοι   εἰσῆλθεν.
lying   the   sheets,   not   however   he entered.

6 ἔρχεται   οὖν   καὶ   Σίμων   Πέτρος   ἀκο-
   Comes   therefore also   Simon   Peter   follow-

λουθῶν   αὐτῷ,   καὶ   εἰσῆλθεν   εἰς   τὸ
ing   him,   and   entered   into   the

μνημεῖον·   καὶ   θεωρεῖ   τὰ   ὀθόνια   κείμενα,
tomb;   and   he beholds the   sheets   lying,

7 καὶ   τὸ   σουδάριον,   ὃ   ἦν   ἐπὶ   τῆς
   and   the   kerchief,   which was   on   the

κεφαλῆς   αὐτοῦ,   οὐ   μετὰ   τῶν   ὀθονίων
head   of him,   not   with   the   sheets

κείμενον   ἀλλὰ   χωρὶς   ἐντετυλιγμένον   εἰς
lying   but   apart   having been wrapped up   in

ἕνα   τόπον.   8 τότε   οὖν   εἰσῆλθεν   καὶ
one   place.   Then therefore entered   also

ὁ   ἄλλος   μαθητὴς   ὁ   ἐλθὼν   πρῶτος   εἰς
the   other   disciple   -   having come   first   to

τὸ   μνημεῖον,   καὶ   εἶδεν   καὶ   ἐπίστευσεν·
the   tomb,   and   he saw   and   believed;

9 οὐδέπω   γὰρ   ᾔδεισαν   τὴν   γραφήν,   ὅτι
   for not yet   they knew   the   scripture,   that

δεῖ   αὐτὸν   ἐκ   νεκρῶν   ἀναστῆναι.
it behoves him   from [the] dead   to rise again.

10 ἀπῆλθον   οὖν   πάλιν   πρὸς   αὐτοὺς   οἱ
    Went away therefore again   to   themselves*   the

* That is, to their own home; cf. 19. 27.

11 But Mary stood weeping outside the tomb, and as she wept she stooped to look into the tomb; ¹²and she saw two angels in white, sitting where the body of Jesus had lain, one at the head and one at the feet. ¹³They said to her, "Woman, why are you weeping?" She said to them, "Because they have taken away my Lord, and I do not know where they have laid him." ¹⁴Saying this, she turned round and saw Jesus standing, but she did not know that it was Jesus. ¹⁵Jesus said to her, "Woman, why are you weeping? Whom do you seek?" Supposing him to be the gardener, she said to him, "Sir, if you have carried him away, tell me where you have laid him, and I will take him away." ¹⁶Jesus said to her, "Mary." She turned and said to him in Hebrew, "Rab-bo'ni!" (which means Teacher). ¹⁷Jesus said to her, "Do not hold me, for I have not yet ascended to the Father; but go to my brethren and say to them, I am ascending to my Father and your Father,

μαθηταί. 11 Μαρία δὲ εἰστήκει πρὸς
disciples.   But Mary   stood   at

τῷ μνημείῳ ἔξω κλαίουσα. ὡς οὖν
the   tomb   outside   weeping.   As therefore

ἔκλαιεν, παρέκυψεν εἰς τὸ μνημεῖον,
she was weeping, she stooped   into   the   tomb,

12 καὶ θεωρεῖ δύο ἀγγέλους ἐν λευκοῖς
and beholds   two   angels   in   white

καθεζομένους, ἕνα πρὸς τῇ κεφαλῇ καὶ
sitting,   one   at   the   head   and

ἕνα πρὸς τοῖς ποσίν, ὅπου ἔκειτο τὸ
one   at   the   feet,   where   lay   the

σῶμα τοῦ Ἰησοῦ. 13 καὶ λέγουσιν αὐτῇ
body   -   of Jesus.   And   say   to her

ἐκεῖνοι· γύναι, τί κλαίεις; λέγει αὐτοῖς
those :   Woman, why weepest thou? She says to them[,]

ὅτι ἦραν τὸν κύριόν μου, καὶ οὐκ οἶδα
- They took the   Lord   of me,   and   I know not

ποῦ ἔθηκαν αὐτόν. 14 ταῦτα εἰποῦσα
where they put   him.   These things saying

ἐστράφη εἰς τὰ ὀπίσω, καὶ θεωρεῖ τὸν
she turned   back,†   and   beholds   -

Ἰησοῦν ἑστῶτα, καὶ οὐκ ᾔδει ὅτι Ἰησοῦς
Jesus   standing,   and   knew not   that   Jesus

ἐστιν. 15 λέγει αὐτῇ Ἰησοῦς· γύναι,
it is(was).   Says   to her   Jesus :   Woman,

τί κλαίεις; τίνα ζητεῖς; ἐκείνη δοκοῦσα
why weepest thou? whom seekest thou? That one thinking

ὅτι ὁ κηπουρός ἐστιν, λέγει αὐτῷ· κύριε,
that the   gardener it is(was),   says to him :   Sir,

εἰ σὺ ἐβάστασας αὐτόν, εἰπέ μοι ποῦ
if thou   didst carry   him,   tell   me where

ἔθηκας αὐτόν, κἀγὼ αὐτὸν ἀρῶ. 16 λέγει
thou didst put him,   and I   him   will take.   Says

αὐτῇ Ἰησοῦς· Μαριάμ. στραφεῖσα ἐκείνη
to her Jesus :   Mary.   Turning   that one

λέγει αὐτῷ Ἑβραϊστί· ῥαββουνί (ὃ λέγεται
says to him in Hebrew : Rabboni   (which is said

διδάσκαλε). 17 λέγει αὐτῇ Ἰησοῦς· μή
Teacher).   Says   to her   Jesus: Not

μου ἅπτου, οὔπω γὰρ ἀναβέβηκα πρὸς
me   touch,   for not yet   have I ascended   to

τὸν πατέρα· πορεύου δὲ πρὸς τοὺς
the   Father;   but go thou   to   the

ἀδελφούς μου καὶ εἰπὲ αὐτοῖς· ἀναβαίνω
brothers   of me and   tell   them :   I ascend

πρὸς τὸν πατέρα μου καὶ πατέρα ὑμῶν
to   the   Father of me and   Father   of you

to my God and your God." [18] Mary Mag'dalene went and said to the disciples, "I have seen the Lord"; and she told them that he had said these things to her. 19 On the evening of that day, the first day of the week, the doors being shut where the disciples were, for fear of the Jews, Jesus came and stood among them and said to them, "Peace be with you." [20] When he had said this, he showed them his hands and his side. Then the disciples were glad when they saw the Lord. [21] Jesus said to them again, "Peace be with you. As the Father has sent me, even so I send you." [22] And when he had said this, he breathed on them, and said to them, "Receive the Holy Spirit. [23] If you forgive the sins of any, they are forgiven; if you retain the sins of any, they are retained."
24 Now Thomas, one of the twelve, called the Twin, was not with them when Jesus came. [25] So the other disciples told him, "We have seen the

καὶ θεόν μου καὶ θεὸν ὑμῶν. 18 ἔρχεται
and God of me and God of you.   Comes

Μαριὰμ ἡ Μαγδαληνὴ ἀγγέλλουσα τοῖς
Mary the Magdalene announcing to the

μαθηταῖς ὅτι ἑώρακα τὸν κύριον, καὶ
disciples[,] – I have seen the Lord, and

ταῦτα εἶπεν αὐτῇ.
these things he said to her.

19 Οὔσης οὖν ὀψίας τῇ ἡμέρᾳ ἐκείνῃ
Being therefore early evening[a] – day on that
=Therefore when it was early evening

τῇ μιᾷ σαββάτων, καὶ τῶν θυρῶν
the one(first) of the week, and the doors

κεκλεισμένων ὅπου ἦσαν οἱ μαθηταὶ διὰ
having been shut[a] where were the disciples because of

τὸν φόβον τῶν Ἰουδαίων, ἦλθεν ὁ Ἰησοῦς
the fear of the Jews, came – Jesus

καὶ ἔστη εἰς τὸ μέσον, καὶ λέγει αὐτοῖς·
and stood in the midst, and says to them :

εἰρήνη ὑμῖν. 20 καὶ τοῦτο εἰπὼν ἔδειξεν
Peace to you. And this saying he showed

καὶ τὰς χεῖρας καὶ τὴν πλευρὰν αὐτοῖς.
both the(his) hands and the(his) side to them.

ἐχάρησαν οὖν οἱ μαθηταὶ ἰδόντες τὸν
Rejoiced therefore the disciples seeing the

κύριον. 21 εἶπεν οὖν αὐτοῖς [ὁ Ἰησοῦς]
Lord. Said therefore to them – Jesus

πάλιν· εἰρήνη ὑμῖν· καθὼς ἀπέσταλκέν
again : Peace to you; as has sent

με ὁ πατήρ, κἀγὼ πέμπω ὑμᾶς. 22 καὶ
me the Father, I also send you. And

τοῦτο εἰπὼν ἐνεφύσησεν καὶ λέγει αὐτοῖς·
this saying he breathed in and says to them :

λάβετε πνεῦμα ἅγιον. 23 ἄν τινων
Receive ye Spirit Holy. Of whomever

ἀφῆτε τὰς ἁμαρτίας, ἀφέωνται αὐτοῖς·
ye forgive the sins, they have been to them;
                                    forgiven

ἄν τινων κρατῆτε, κεκράτηνται.
of whomever ye hold, they have been held.

24 Θωμᾶς δὲ εἷς ἐκ τῶν δώδεκα,
But Thomas one of the twelve,

ὁ λεγόμενος Δίδυμος, οὐκ ἦν μετ᾽ αὐτῶν
– being called Twin, was not with them

ὅτε ἦλθεν Ἰησοῦς. 25 ἔλεγον οὖν αὐτῷ
when came Jesus. Said therefore to him

οἱ ἄλλοι μαθηταί· ἑωράκαμεν τὸν κύριον.
the other disciples : We have seen the Lord.

Lord." But he said to them, "Unless I see in his hands the print of the nails, and place my finger in the mark of the nails, and place my hand in his side, I will not believe." 26 Eight days later, his disciples were again in the house, and Thomas was with them. The doors were shut, but Jesus came and stood among them, and said, "Peace be with you." 27 Then he said to Thomas, "Put your finger here, and see my hands; and put out your hand, and place it in my side; do not be faithless, but believing." 28 Thomas answered him, "My Lord and my God!" 29 Jesus said to him, "Have you believed because you have seen me? Blessed are those who have not seen and yet believe." 30 Now Jesus did many others signs in the presence of the disciples, which are not written in this book; 31 but these are written that you may believe that Jesus is the

ὁ	δὲ	εἶπεν	αὐτοῖς·	ἐὰν	μὴ	ἴδω	ἐν
But he		said	to them :	Unless		I see	in

ταῖς	χερσὶν	αὐτοῦ	τὸν	τύπον	τῶν	ἥλων
the	hands	of him	the	mark	of the	nails

καὶ	βάλω	τὸν	δάκτυλόν	μου	εἰς	τὸν
and	put	the	finger	of me	into	the

τόπον	τῶν	ἥλων	καὶ	βάλω	μου	τὴν
place	of the	nails	and	put	of me	the

χεῖρα	εἰς	τὴν	πλευρὰν	αὐτοῦ,	οὐ	μὴ
hand	into	the	side	of him,	by no	means

πιστεύσω. 26 Καὶ μεθ᾽ ἡμέρας ὀκτὼ
will I believe. And after days eight

πάλιν ἦσαν ἔσω οἱ μαθηταὶ αὐτοῦ, καὶ
again were within the disciples of him, and

Θωμᾶς μετ᾽ αὐτῶν. ἔρχεται ὁ Ἰησοῦς
Thomas with them. Comes - Jesus

τῶν θυρῶν κεκλεισμένων, καὶ ἔστη εἰς
the doors having been shut[a], and stood in

τὸ μέσον καὶ εἶπεν· εἰρήνη ὑμῖν. 27 εἶτα
the midst and said : Peace to you. Then

λέγει τῷ Θωμᾷ· φέρε τὸν δάκτυλόν
he says - to Thomas : Bring the finger

σου ὧδε καὶ ἴδε τὰς χεῖράς μου, καὶ
of thee here and see the hands of me, and

φέρε τὴν χεῖρά σου καὶ βάλε εἰς τὴν
bring the hand of thee and put into the

πλευράν μου, καὶ μὴ γίνου ἄπιστος
side of me, and be not faithless

ἀλλὰ πιστός. 28 ἀπεκρίθη Θωμᾶς καὶ
but faithful. Answered Thomas and

εἶπεν αὐτῷ· ὁ κύριός μου καὶ ὁ θεός
said to him : The Lord of me and the God

μου. 29 λέγει αὐτῷ ὁ Ἰησοῦς· ὅτι
of me. Says to him - Jesus : Because

ἑώρακάς με, πεπίστευκας; μακάριοι οἱ
thou hast seen me, hast thou believed? blessed the [ones]

μὴ ἰδόντες καὶ πιστεύσαντες.
not seeing and§ believing.

30 Πολλὰ μὲν οὖν καὶ ἄλλα σημεῖα
Many -* therefore and other signs

ἐποίησεν ὁ Ἰησοῦς ἐνώπιον τῶν μαθητῶν,
did - Jesus before the disciples,

ἃ οὐκ ἔστιν γεγραμμένα ἐν τῷ βιβλίῳ
which is(are) not having been written in - roll

τούτῳ· 31 ταῦτα δὲ γέγραπται ἵνα
this; but these* has(ve) been written that

πιστεύ[η]τε ὅτι Ἰησοῦς ἐστιν ὁ χριστὸς ὁ
ye may believe that Jesus is the Christ the

* See note on 19. 24 and 32.
§ καί sometimes = and yet; see 5. 40; 8. 55; 9. 30; 16. 32; 17. 11.

Christ, the Son of God, and that believing you may have life in his name.

υἱὸς τοῦ θεοῦ, καὶ ἵνα πιστεύοντες ζωὴν
Son   -   of God,   and   that   believing   life
ἔχητε ἐν τῷ ὀνόματι αὐτοῦ.
ye may have in   the   name   of him.

CHAPTER 21

AFTER this Jesus revealed himself again to the disciples by the Sea of Tibe′ri-as; and he revealed himself in this way. ²Simon Peter, Thomas called the Twin, Nathan′a-el of Cana in Galilee, the sons of Zeb′edee, and two others of his disciples were together. ³Simon Peter said to them, "I am going fishing." They said to him, "We will go with you." They went out and got into the boat; but that night they caught nothing.

4 Just as day was breaking, Jesus stood on the beach; yet the disciples did not know it was Jesus. ⁵Jesus said to them, "Children, have you any fish?" They answered him, "No." ⁶He said to them, "Cast the net on the right side of the boat, and you will find some." So they cast it, and now they were not able to haul it in, for the quantity of fish. ⁷That disciple

21 Μετὰ ταῦτα ἐφανέρωσεν ἑαυτὸν πάλιν
   After   these things   manifested   himself   again
Ἰησοῦς τοῖς μαθηταῖς ἐπὶ τῆς θαλάσσης
Jesus   to the   disciples   on   the   sea
τῆς Τιβεριάδος· ἐφανέρωσεν δὲ οὕτως.
  -   of Tiberias;   and he manifested [himself]   thus.
2 ἦσαν ὁμοῦ Σίμων Πέτρος καὶ Θωμᾶς
  There were together   Simon   Peter   and   Thomas
ὁ λεγόμενος Δίδυμος καὶ Ναθαναὴλ ὁ
-   being called   Twin   and   Nathanael   -
ἀπὸ Κανὰ τῆς Γαλιλαίας καὶ οἱ τοῦ
from   Cana   -   of Galilee   and   the [sons]   -
Ζεβεδαίου καὶ ἄλλοι ἐκ τῶν μαθητῶν
of Zebedee   and   others   of   the   disciples
αὐτοῦ δύο. 3 λέγει αὐτοῖς Σίμων Πέτρος·
of him   two.   Says   to them   Simon   Peter :
ὑπάγω ἁλιεύειν. λέγουσιν αὐτῷ· ἐρχόμεθα
I am going   to fish.   They say   to him :   Are coming
καὶ ἡμεῖς σὺν σοί. ἐξῆλθον καὶ ἐνέβησαν
also   we   with thee.   They went forth and   embarked
εἰς τὸ πλοῖον, καὶ ἐν ἐκείνῃ τῇ νυκτὶ
in   the   boat,   and   in   that   -   night
ἐπίασαν οὐδέν. 4 πρωΐας δὲ ἤδη γινομένης
they caught nothing.   Early morning but now   becomingª
   =But when it became early morning
ἔστη Ἰησοῦς εἰς τὸν αἰγιαλόν· οὐ μέντοι
stood   Jesus   in(on) the   shore;   not however
ᾔδεισαν οἱ μαθηταὶ ὅτι Ἰησοῦς ἐστιν.
knew   the   disciples   that   Jesus   it is(was).
5 λέγει οὖν αὐτοῖς Ἰησοῦς· παιδία, μή
Says   therefore   to them   Jesus :   Children,   not
τι προσφάγιον ἔχετε; ἀπεκρίθησαν αὐτῷ·
any   fish   have ye?   They answered   him :
οὔ. 6 ὁ δὲ εἶπεν αὐτοῖς· βάλετε εἰς τὰ
No.   So he   said   to them :   Cast   in   the
δεξιὰ μέρη τοῦ πλοίου τὸ δίκτυον, καὶ
right   parts   of the   boat   the   net,   and
εὑρήσετε. ἔβαλον οὖν, καὶ οὐκέτι αὐτὸ
ye will find.   They cast therefore, and   ¹no longer   ⁴it
ἑλκύσαι ἴσχυον ἀπὸ τοῦ πλήθους τῶν
¹to drag   ²were they able from   the   multitude   of the
ἰχθύων. 7 λέγει οὖν ὁ μαθητὴς ἐκεῖνος
fishes.   Says   therefore   -   disciple   that

whom Jesus loved said to Peter, "It is the Lord!" When Simon Peter heard that it was the Lord, he put on his clothes, for he was stripped for work, and sprang into the sea. ⁸But the other disciples came in the boat, dragging the net full of fish, for they were not far from the land, but about a hundred yards off.

9 When they got out on land, they saw a charcoal fire there, with fish lying on it, and bread. ¹⁰Jesus said to them, "Bring some of the fish that you have just caught." ¹¹So Simon Peter went aboard and hauled the net ashore, full of large fish, a hundred and fifty-three of them; and although there were so many, the net was not torn. ¹²Jesus said to them, "Come and have breakfast." Now none of the disciples dared ask him, "Who are you?" They knew it was the Lord. ¹³Jesus came and took the bread and gave it to them, and so with the fish. ¹⁴This was now the third time that Jesus was revealed to the disciples after he was raised from the dead.

ὃν ἠγάπα ὁ Ἰησοῦς τῷ Πέτρῳ· ὁ κύριός
whom ²loved – ¹Jesus – to Peter : The Lord

ἐστιν. Σίμων οὖν Πέτρος, ἀκούσας ὅτι
it is. ²Simon ¹therefore ³Peter, hearing that

ὁ κύριός ἐστιν, τὸν ἐπενδύτην διεζώσατο,
the Lord it is(was), ²[with]the ³coat ¹girded himself,

ἦν γὰρ γυμνός, καὶ ἔβαλεν ἑαυτὸν εἰς
for he was naked, and threw himself into

τὴν θάλασσαν· 8 οἱ δὲ ἄλλοι μαθηταὶ
the sea; but the other disciples

τῷ πλοιαρίῳ ἦλθον, οὐ γὰρ ἦσαν μακρὰν
in the little boat came, for not they were far

ἀπὸ τῆς γῆς ἀλλὰ ὡς ἀπὸ πηχῶν
from the land but about from cubits

διακοσίων, σύροντες τὸ δίκτυον τῶν ἰχθύων.
two hundred dragging the net of the fishes.

9 ὡς οὖν ἀπέβησαν εἰς τὴν γῆν, βλέπουσιν
When therefore they disembarked onto the land, they see

ἀνθρακιὰν κειμένην καὶ ὀψάριον ἐπικείμενον
a coal fire lying and a fish lying on

καὶ ἄρτον. 10 λέγει αὐτοῖς ὁ Ἰησοῦς·
and bread. Says to them – Jesus :

ἐνέγκατε ἀπὸ τῶν ὀψαρίων ὧν ἐπιάσατε
Bring from the fishes which ye caught

νῦν. 11 ἀνέβη Σίμων Πέτρος καὶ εἵλκυσεν
now. Went up Simon Peter and dragged

τὸ δίκτυον εἰς τὴν γῆν μεστὸν ἰχθύων
the net to the land full fishes

μεγάλων ἑκατὸν πεντήκοντα τριῶν· καὶ
of great a hundred fifty three; and

τοσούτων ὄντων οὐκ ἐσχίσθη τὸ δίκτυον.
so many being° was not torn the net.

12 λέγει αὐτοῖς ὁ Ἰησοῦς· δεῦτε ἀριστήσατε.
Says to them – Jesus : Come breakfast ye.

οὐδεὶς ἐτόλμα τῶν μαθητῶν ἐξετάσαι
No one dared of the disciples to question

αὐτόν· σὺ τίς εἶ; εἰδότες ὅτι ὁ κύριός
him; Thou who art? knowing that the Lord

ἐστιν. 13 ἔρχεται Ἰησοῦς καὶ λαμβάνει
it is(was). Comes Jesus and takes

τὸν ἄρτον καὶ δίδωσιν αὐτοῖς, καὶ τὸ
the bread and gives to them, and the

ὀψάριον ὁμοίως. 14 τοῦτο ἤδη τρίτον
fish likewise. This [was] now [the] third [time]
[that]

ἐφανερώθη Ἰησοῦς τοῖς μαθηταῖς ἐγερθεὶς
²was manifested ¹Jesus to the disciples raised

ἐκ νεκρῶν.
from [the] dead.

15 When they had finished breakfast, Jesus said to Simon Peter, "Simon, son of John, do you love me more than these?" He said to him, "Yes, Lord; you know that I love you." He said to him, "Feed my lambs." ¹⁶A second time he said to him, "Simon, son of John, do you love me?" He said to him, "Yes, Lord; you know that I love you." He said to him, "Tend my sheep." ¹⁷He said to him the third time, "Simon, son of John, do you love me?" Peter was grieved because he said to him the third time, "Do you love me?" And he said to him, "Lord, you know everything; you know that I love you." Jesus said to him, "Feed my sheep. ¹⁸Truly, truly, I say to you, when you were young, you girded yourself and walked where you would; but when you are old, you will stretch out your hands, and another will gird you and carry you where you do not wish to go." ¹⁹(This he said to show by what death he was to glorify God.) And after this he said to him, "Follow me."

20 Peter turned and saw following them the disciple whom Jesus loved, who had lain close

15 ῞Οτε οὖν ἠρίστησαν, λέγει τῷ
When therefore they breakfasted, says –
Σίμωνι Πέτρῳ ὁ ᾿Ιησοῦς· Σίμων ᾿Ιωάννου,
to Simon Peter – Jesus : Simon [son] of John,
ἀγαπᾷς με πλέον τούτων; λέγει αὐτῷ·
lovest thou me more [than] these? He says to him :
ναί, κύριε, σὺ οἶδας ὅτι φιλῶ σε. λέγει
Yes, Lord, thou knowest that I love thee. He says
αὐτῷ· βόσκε τὰ ἀρνία μου. 16 λέγει
to him : Feed the lambs of me. He says
αὐτῷ πάλιν δεύτερον· Σίμων ᾿Ιωάννου,
to him again secondly: Simon [son] of John,
ἀγαπᾷς με; λέγει αὐτῷ· ναί, κύριε,
lovest thou me? He says to him : Yes, Lord,
σὺ οἶδας ὅτι φιλῶ σε. λέγει αὐτῷ·
thou knowest that I love thee. He says to him:
ποίμαινε τὰ προβάτιά μου. 17 λέγει
Shepherd the little sheep of me. He says
αὐτῷ τὸ τρίτον· Σίμων ᾿Ιωάννου, φιλεῖς
to him the third [time]: Simon [son] of John, lovest thou
με; ἐλυπήθη ὁ Πέτρος ὅτι εἶπεν αὐτῷ
me? Was grieved – Peter that he said to him
τὸ τρίτον· φιλεῖς με; καὶ εἶπεν αὐτῷ·
the third [time]: Lovest thou me? and said to him :
κύριε, πάντα σὺ οἶδας, σὺ γινώσκεις
Lord, all things thou knowest, thou knowest
ὅτι φιλῶ σε· λέγει αὐτῷ ᾿Ιησοῦς· βόσκε
that I love thee; says to him Jesus : Feed
τὰ προβάτιά μου. 18 ἀμὴν ἀμὴν λέγω
the little sheep of me. Truly truly I tell
σοι, ὅτε ἦς νεώτερος, ἐζώννυες σεαυτὸν
thee, when thou wast younger, thou girdedst thyself
καὶ περιεπάτεις ὅπου ἤθελες· ὅταν δὲ
and walkedst where thou wishedst; but when
γηράσῃς, ἐκτενεῖς τὰς χεῖράς σου, καὶ
thou growest thou wilt the hands of thee, and
old, stretch out
ἄλλος ζώσει σε καὶ οἴσει ὅπου οὐ θέλεις.
another will gird thee and will carry where thou wishest not.
19 τοῦτο δὲ εἶπεν σημαίνων ποίῳ θανάτῳ
And this he said signifying by what death
δοξάσει τὸν θεόν. καὶ τοῦτο εἰπὼν λέγει
he will glorify – God. And this saying he tells
αὐτῷ· ἀκολούθει μοι. 20 ἐπιστραφεὶς ὁ
him : Follow me. Turning –
Πέτρος βλέπει τὸν μαθητὴν ὃν ἠγάπα ὁ
Peter sees the disciple whom ¹loved –
᾿Ιησοῦς ἀκολουθοῦντα, ὃς καὶ ἀνέπεσεν
¹Jesus following, who also leaned

to his breast at the supper and had said, "Lord, who is it that is going to betray you?" ²¹When Peter saw him, he said to Jesus, "Lord, what about this man?" ²²Jesus said to him, "If it is my will that he remain until I come, what is that to you? Follow me!" ²³The saying spread abroad among the brethren that this disciple was not to die; yet Jesus did not say to him that he was not to die, but, "If it is my will that he remain until I come, what is that to you?"

24 This is the disciple who is bearing witness to these things, and who has written these things; and we know that his testimony is true.

25 But there are also many other things which Jesus did; were every one of them to be written, I suppose that the world itself could not contain the books that would be written.

ἐν τῷ δείπνῳ ἐπὶ τὸ στῆθος αὐτοῦ καὶ
at the supper on the breast of him and

εἶπεν· κύριε, τίς ἐστιν ὁ παραδιδοὺς σε;
said : Lord, who is the[one] betraying thee?

21 τοῦτον οὖν ἰδὼν ὁ Πέτρος λέγει τῷ
⁴This one ²therefore ³seeing - ¹Peter says -

Ἰησοῦ· κύριε, οὗτος δὲ τί; 22 λέγει
to Jesus : Lord, and this one what? Says

αὐτῷ ὁ Ἰησοῦς· ἐὰν αὐτὸν θέλω μένειν
to him - Jesus : If him I wish to remain

ἕως ἔρχομαι, τί πρὸς σέ; σύ μοι
until I come, what to thee? ²thou ³me

ἀκολούθει. 23 ἐξῆλθεν οὖν οὗτος ὁ λόγος
¹follow. Went forth therefore this - word

εἰς τοὺς ἀδελφοὺς ὅτι ὁ μαθητὴς ἐκεῖνος
to the brothers that - disciple that

οὐκ ἀποθνήσκει· οὐκ εἶπεν δὲ αὐτῷ ὁ
does not die; but said not to him -

Ἰησοῦς ὅτι οὐκ ἀποθνήσκει, ἀλλ'· ἐὰν
Jesus that he does not die, but : If

αὐτὸν θέλω μένειν ἕως ἔρχομαι, τί πρὸς
him I wish to remain until I come, what to

σέ;
thee?

24 Οὗτός ἐστιν ὁ μαθητὴς ὁ μαρτυρῶν
This is the disciple - witnessing

περὶ τούτων καὶ ὁ γράψας ταῦτα,
concerning these and - having these
things written things,

καὶ οἴδαμεν ὅτι ἀληθὴς αὐτοῦ ἡ μαρτυρία
and we know that true of him the witness

ἐστίν. 25 Ἔστιν δὲ καὶ ἄλλα πολλὰ ἃ
is. And there are also other many which
things

ἐποίησεν ὁ Ἰησοῦς, ἅτινα ἐὰν γράφηται
did - Jesus, which if they were written

καθ' ἕν, οὐδ' αὐτὸν οἶμαι τὸν κόσμον
singly,† ⁵not ⁶[it]self ¹I think ²the ³world

χωρήσειν τὰ γραφόμενα βιβλία.
⁴to contain ⁷the ⁸being written ⁹rolls.

CHAPTER 1

IN the first book, O The-oph'ilus, I have dealt with all that Jesus began to do and teach, [2] until the day when he was taken up, after he had given commandment through the Holy Spirit to the apostles whom he had chosen. [3] To them he presented himself alive after his passion by many proofs, appearing to them during forty days, and speaking of the kingdom of God. [4] And while staying[a] with them he charged them not to depart from Jerusalem, but to wait for the promise of the Father, which, he said, "you heard from me,[5] for John baptized with water, but before many days you shall be baptized with the Holy Spirit."

6 So when they had come together, they asked him, "Lord, will you at this time restore the kingdom to Israel?" [7] He said to them, "It is not for you to know times or seasons which the Father has fixed by his own authority. [8] But you shall receive power

[a] Or eating

1 Τὸν μὲν πρῶτον λόγον ἐποιησάμην
The - first account I made
περὶ πάντων, ὦ Θεόφιλε, ὧν ἤρξατο
concerning all things, O Theophilus, which began
ὁ Ἰησοῦς ποιεῖν τε καὶ διδάσκειν,
- Jesus both to do and to teach,
2 ἄχρι ἧς ἡμέρας ἐντειλάμενος τοῖς
until which day [1]having given injunctions [4]to the
=the day on which
ἀποστόλοις διὰ πνεύματος ἁγίου οὓς
[7]apostles [2]through [3]Spirit [4]Holy [5]whom
ἐξελέξατο ἀνελήμφθη· 3 οἷς καὶ παρέστησεν
[6]he chose [1]he was taken up; to whom also he presented
ἑαυτὸν ζῶντα μετὰ τὸ παθεῖν αὐτὸν ἐν
himself living after the to suffer him[b] by
=he suffered
πολλοῖς τεκμηρίοις, δι' ἡμερῶν τεσσεράκοντα
many infallible proofs, through days forty
ὀπτανόμενος αὐτοῖς καὶ λέγων τὰ περὶ
being seen by them and speaking the things concerning
τῆς βασιλείας τοῦ θεοῦ· 4 καὶ συναλιζόμενος
the kingdom - of God; and meeting with [them]
παρήγγειλεν αὐτοῖς ἀπὸ Ἱεροσολύμων μὴ
he charged them from Jerusalem not
χωρίζεσθαι, ἀλλὰ περιμένειν τὴν ἐπαγγελίαν
to depart, but to await the promise
τοῦ πατρὸς ἣν ἠκούσατέ μου· 5 ὅτι
of the Father which ye heard of me: because
Ἰωάννης μὲν ἐβάπτισεν ὕδατι, ὑμεῖς δὲ
John indeed baptized in water, but ye
ἐν πνεύματι βαπτισθήσεσθε ἁγίῳ οὐ μετὰ
in [2]Spirit [3]will be baptized [1]Holy not after
πολλὰς ταύτας ἡμέρας. 6 Οἱ μὲν οὖν
many these days. [2]the [ones] [1]So then
συνελθόντες ἠρώτων αὐτὸν λέγοντες· κύριε,
[3]coming together questioned him saying: Lord,
εἰ ἐν τῷ χρόνῳ τούτῳ ἀποκαθιστάνεις
if at this time restorest thou
τὴν βασιλείαν τῷ Ἰσραήλ; 7 εἶπεν πρὸς
the kingdom - to Israel? He said to
αὐτούς· οὐχ ὑμῶν ἐστιν γνῶναι χρόνους
them: Not of you it is to know times
ἢ καιροὺς οὓς ὁ πατὴρ ἔθετο ἐν τῇ
or seasons which the Father placed in the(his)
ἰδίᾳ ἐξουσίᾳ, 8 ἀλλὰ λήμψεσθε δύναμιν
own authority, but ye will receive power

when the Holy Spirit has come upon you; and you shall be my witnesses in Jerusalem and in all Judea and Samar'ia and to the end of the earth." [9]And when he had said this, as they were looking on, he was lifted up, and a cloud took him out of their sight. [10]And while they were gazing into heaven as he went, behold, two men stood by them in white robes, [11]and said, "Men of Galilee, why do you stand looking into heaven? This Jesus, who was taken up from you into heaven, will come in the same way as you saw him go into heaven."

12 Then they returned to Jerusalem from the mount called Olivet, which is near Jerusalem, a sabbath day's journey away; [13]and when they had entered, they went up to the upper room, where they were staying, Peter and John and James and Andrew, Philip and Thomas, Bartholomew and Matthew, James the son of Alphaeus and Simon the Zealot and Judas the

ἐπελθόντος τοῦ ἁγίου πνεύματος ἐφ' ὑμᾶς,
coming *upon* the Holy Spirit[a] upon you,
=when the Holy Spirit comes

καὶ ἔσεσθέ μου μάρτυρες ἔν τε Ἰερουσαλὴμ
and ye will be of me witnesses both in Jerusalem

καὶ ἐν πάσῃ τῇ Ἰουδαίᾳ καὶ Σαμαρείᾳ
and in all - Judæa and Samaria

καὶ ἕως ἐσχάτου τῆς γῆς. 9 καὶ ταῦτα
and unto [the] extremity of the earth. And these things

εἰπὼν βλεπόντων αὐτῶν ἐπήρθη, καὶ
saying looking them[a] he was taken up, and
=as they looked

νεφέλη ὑπέλαβεν αὐτὸν ἀπὸ τῶν ὀφθαλμῶν
a cloud received him from the eyes

αὐτῶν. 10 καὶ ὡς ἀτενίζοντες ἦσαν εἰς
of them. And as gazing they were to

τὸν οὐρανὸν πορευομένου αὐτοῦ, καὶ ἰδοὺ
- heaven going him,[a] - behold[,]
=as he went,

ἄνδρες δύο παρειστήκεισαν αὐτοῖς ἐν ἐσθήσεσι
men two stood by them in garments

λευκαῖς, 11 οἳ καὶ εἶπαν· ἄνδρες Γαλιλαῖοι,
white, who also said: *Men* Galilæans,

τί ἑστήκατε βλέποντες εἰς τὸν οὐρανόν;
why stand ye looking to - heaven?

οὗτος ὁ Ἰησοῦς ὁ ἀναλημφθεὶς
This - Jesus the [one] having been taken up

ἀφ' ὑμῶν εἰς τὸν οὐρανὸν οὕτως ἐλεύσεται
from you to - heaven thus will come

ὃν τρόπον ἐθεάσασθε αὐτὸν πορευόμενον
in the way† ye beheld him going

εἰς τὸν οὐρανόν. 12 Τότε ὑπέστρεψαν
to - heaven. Then they returned

εἰς Ἰερουσαλὴμ ἀπὸ ὄρους τοῦ καλου-
to Jerusalem from [the] mount the [one] *being*

μένου ἐλαιῶνος, ὅ ἐστιν ἐγγὺς Ἰερουσαλὴμ
called of [the] olive grove, which is near Jerusalem

σαββάτου ἔχον ὁδόν. 13 καὶ ὅτε εἰσῆλθον,
of a sabbath having a way. And when they entered,
=a sabbath's journey off.

εἰς τὸ ὑπερῷον ἀνέβησαν οὗ ἦσαν
into the upper room they went up where they were

καταμένοντες, ὅ τε Πέτρος καὶ Ἰωάννης
waiting, - both Peter and John

καὶ Ἰάκωβος καὶ Ἀνδρέας, Φίλιππος καὶ
and James and Andrew, Philip and

Θωμᾶς, Βαρθολομαῖος καὶ Μαθθαῖος,
Thomas, Bartholomew and Matthew,

Ἰάκωβος Ἀλφαίου καὶ Σίμων ὁ ζηλωτὴς
James [son] of Alphæus and Simon the zealot

son of James. ¹⁴All these with one accord devoted themselves to prayer, together with the women and Mary the mother of Jesus, and with his brothers.

15 In those days Peter stood up among the brethren (the company of persons was in all about a hundred and twenty), and said, ¹⁶"Brethren, the scripture had to be fulfilled, which the Holy Spirit spoke beforehand by the mouth of David, concerning Judas who was guide to those who arrested Jesus. ¹⁷For he was numbered among us, and was allotted his share in this ministry. ¹⁸(Now this man bought a field with the reward of his wickedness; and falling headlong⁶ he burst open in the middle and all his bowels gushed out. ¹⁹And it became known to all the inhabitants of Jerusalem, so that the field was called in their language Akel′dama, that is, Field of Blood.) ²⁰For it is written in the book of Psalms,
'Let his habitation become desolate,

⁶ Or swelling up

καὶ 'Ιούδας 'Ιακώβου. 14 οὗτοι πάντες
and Judas [brother] of James.　These all

ἦσαν προσκαρτεροῦντες ὁμοθυμαδὸν τῇ
were continuing steadfastly with one mind –

προσευχῇ σὺν γυναιξὶν καὶ Μαριὰμ τῇ
in prayer with [the] women and Mary the

μητρὶ [τοῦ] 'Ιησοῦ καὶ σὺν τοῖς ἀδελφοῖς
mother – of Jesus and with the brothers

αὐτοῦ.
of him.

15 Καὶ ἐν ταῖς ἡμέραις ταύταις ἀναστὰς
And in these days standing up

Πέτρος ἐν μέσῳ τῶν ἀδελφῶν εἶπεν·
Peter in [the] midst of the brothers said :

ἦν τε ὄχλος ὀνομάτων ἐπὶ τὸ αὐτὸ
⁶was ¹and ²[the] ³crowd ⁴of names ⁵together

ὡσεὶ ἑκατὸν εἴκοσι· 16 ἄνδρες ἀδελφοί,
about a hundred twenty : Men brothers,

ἔδει πληρωθῆναι τὴν γραφὴν ἣν
it behoved to be fulfilled the scripture which

προεῖπεν τὸ πνεῦμα τὸ ἅγιον διὰ στόματος
spoke before the Spirit – Holy through [the] mouth

Δαυὶδ περὶ 'Ιούδα τοῦ γενομένου ὁδηγοῦ
of David concerning Judas the [one] having become guide

τοῖς συλλαβοῦσιν 'Ιησοῦν, 17 ὅτι κατ-
to the [ones] taking Jesus, because having

ηριθμημένος ἦν ἐν ἡμῖν καὶ ἔλαχεν τὸν
been numbered he was among us and obtained the

κλῆρον τῆς διακονίας ταύτης. 18 οὗτος μὲν οὖν
portion of this ministry. This one therefore

ἐκτήσατο χωρίον ἐκ μισθοῦ τῆς
bought a field out of [the] reward

ἀδικίας, καὶ πρηνὴς γενόμενος ἐλάκησεν
of unrighteousness, and swollen up having become he burst asunder

μέσος, καὶ ἐξεχύθη πάντα τὰ σπλάγχνα
in the middle, and were poured out all the bowels

αὐτοῦ· 19 καὶ γνωστὸν ἐγένετο πᾶσι τοῖς
of him; and known it became to all the

κατοικοῦσιν 'Ιερουσαλήμ, ὥστε κληθῆναι
[ones] inhabiting Jerusalem, so as to be called

τὸ χωρίον ἐκεῖνο τῇ ἰδίᾳ διαλέκτῳ αὐτῶν
that field in their own language

'Ακελδαμάχ, τοῦτ' ἔστιν χωρίον
Aceldamach, this is Field

αἵματος. 20 γέγραπται γὰρ ἐν βίβλῳ
of blood. For it has been written in [the] roll

ψαλμῶν· γενηθήτω ἡ ἔπαυλις αὐτοῦ ἔρημος
of Psalms : Let become the estate of him deserted

and let there be no
one to live in it';
and
'His office let another
take.'
21 So one of the men who
have accompanied us
during all the time that
the Lord Jesus went in
and out among us,
22 beginning from the
baptism of John until
the day when he was
taken up from us—one
of these men must be-
come with us a witness to
his resurrection." 23 And
they put forward two,
Joseph called Barsabbas,
who was surnamed
Justus, and Matthi'as.
24 And they prayed and
said, "Lord, who knowest
the hearts of all men,
show which one of these
two thou hast chosen
25 to take the place in this
ministry and apostleship
from which Judas turned
aside, to go to his own
place." 26 And they cast
lots for them, and the lot
fell on Matthi'as; and he
was enrolled with the
eleven apostles.

καὶ   μὴ   ἔστω   ὁ   κατοικῶν   ἐν   αὐτῇ,   καὶ·
and   let not be   the [one] dwelling   in   it,   and :

τὴν   ἐπισκοπὴν   αὐτοῦ   λαβέτω   ἕτερος.
The   office   of him   let take   another.

21 δεῖ   οὖν   τῶν   συνελθόντων   ἡμῖν ἀνδρῶν
It behoves* therefore   [1]of the   [3]accompanying   [4]us   [2]men

ἐν   παντὶ   χρόνῳ   ᾧ   εἰσῆλθεν   καὶ
in   all   [the] time   in which   went in   and

ἐξῆλθεν   ἐφ᾽   ἡμᾶς   ὁ   κύριος   Ἰησοῦς,
went out   among   us   the   Lord   Jesus,

22 ἀρξάμενος   ἀπὸ   τοῦ   βαπτίσματος
beginning   from   the   baptism

Ἰωάννου   ἕως   τῆς   ἡμέρας   ἧς   ἀνελήμφθη
of John   until   the   day   when   he was taken up

ἀφ᾽   ἡμῶν,   μάρτυρα   τῆς   ἀναστάσεως
from   us,   [4]a witness*   [7]of the   [8]resurrection

αὐτοῦ   σὺν   ἡμῖν   γενέσθαι   ἕνα   τούτων.
[9]of him   [5]with   [6]us   [3]to become   [1]one*   [2]of these.

23 Καὶ   ἔστησαν   δύο,   Ἰωσὴφ   τὸν   καλού-
And   they set   two,   Joseph   the [one] being

μενον   Βαρσαββᾶν,   ὃς   ἐπεκλήθη   Ἰοῦστος,
called   Barsabbas,   who   was surnamed   Justus,

καὶ   Μαθθίαν.   24 καὶ   προσευξάμενοι   εἶπαν·
and   Matthias.   And   praying   they said :

σὺ   κύριε   καρδιογνῶστα   πάντων,   ἀνάδειξον
Thou Lord   Heart-knower   of all men,   show

ὃν   ἐξελέξω   ἐκ   τούτων   τῶν   δύο   ἕνα
whom thou didst choose of   these   –   two   one

25 λαβεῖν   τὸν   τόπον   τῆς   διακονίας   ταύτης
to take   the   place   of this ministry

καὶ   ἀποστολῆς,   ἀφ᾽   ἧς   παρέβη   Ἰούδας
and   apostleship,   from which   fell   Judas

πορευθῆναι   εἰς   τὸν   τόπον   τὸν   ἴδιον.
to go   to   the(his)   place   –   own.

26 καὶ   ἔδωκαν   κλήρους   αὐτοῖς,   καὶ   ἔπεσεν
And   they gave   lots   for them,   and   fell

ὁ   κλῆρος   ἐπὶ   Μαθθίαν,   καὶ   συγκατεψηφίσθη
the   lot   on   Matthias,   and   he was reckoned along with

μετὰ   τῶν   ἕνδεκα   ἀποστόλων.
with   the   eleven   apostles.

CHAPTER 2

W HEN the day of
Pentecost had
come they were all to-
gether in one place.

2 Καὶ   ἐν   τῷ   συμπληροῦσθαι   τὴν   ἡμέραν
And   in   the   to be completed   the   day
=when the day of Pentecost was completed

τῆς   πεντηκοστῆς   ἦσαν   πάντες   ὁμοῦ   ἐπὶ
–   of Pentecost[e]   they were   all   together   to-

* The object (according to the Greek construction) of the verb
δεῖ is ἕνα, with μάρτυρα as its complement after γενέσθαι.

²And suddenly a sound came from heaven like the rush of a mighty wind, and it filled all the house where they were sitting. ³And there appeared to them tongues as of fire, distributed and resting on each one of them. ⁴And they were all filled with the Holy Spirit and began to speak in other tongues, as the Spirit gave them utterance.

5 Now there were dwelling in Jerusalem Jews, devout men from every nation under heaven. ⁶And at this sound the multitude came together, and they were bewildered, because each one heard them speaking in his own language. ⁷And they were amazed and wondered, saying, "Are not all these who are speaking Galileans? ⁸And how is it that we hear, each of us in his own native language? ⁹Par'thians and Medes and E'lamites and residents of Mesopota'mia, Judea and Cappado'cia, Pontus and Asia, ¹⁰Phryg'ia and Pamphyl'ia, Egypt and the

τὸ αὐτό· 2 καὶ ἐγένετο ἄφνω ἐκ τοῦ
gether;†   and there was suddenly out of –

οὐρανοῦ ἦχος ὥσπερ φερομένης πνοῆς
heaven   a sound   as   ⁵being borne   ¹of²a ⁴wind

βιαίας καὶ ἐπλήρωσεν ὅλον τὸν οἶκον
³violent   and   it filled   all   the   house

οὗ ἦσαν καθήμενοι, 3 καὶ ὤφθησαν αὐτοῖς
where they were   sitting,   and there appeared   to them

διαμεριζόμεναι γλῶσσαι ὡσεὶ πυρός, καὶ
being distributed   tongues   as   of fire,   and

ἐκάθισεν ἐφ' ἕνα ἕκαστον αὐτῶν, 4 καὶ
it sat   on   ²one   ¹each   of them,   and

ἐπλήσθησαν πάντες πνεύματος ἁγίου, καὶ
they were filled   all   of(with) Spirit   Holy,   and

ἤρξαντο λαλεῖν ἑτέραις γλώσσαις καθὼς
began   to speak   in other   tongues   as

τὸ πνεῦμα ἐδίδου ἀποφθέγγεσθαι αὐτοῖς.
the   Spirit   gave   ²to speak out   ¹them.

5 Ἦσαν δὲ εἰς Ἰερουσαλὴμ κατοικοῦντες
Now there were   in   Jerusalem   dwelling

Ἰουδαῖοι, ἄνδρες εὐλαβεῖς ἀπὸ παντὸς ἔθνους
Jews,   men   devout   from   every   nation

τῶν ὑπὸ τὸν οὐρανόν· 6 γενομένης
of the [ones] under   –   heaven;   happening

δὲ τῆς φωνῆς ταύτης συνῆλθεν τὸ πλῆθος
and   this sound*   came together   the   multitude
=when this sound happened

καὶ συνεχύθη, ὅτι ἤκουον εἷς ἕκαστος
and   were confounded,   because   they heard   ⁴one   ³each

τῇ ἰδίᾳ διαλέκτῳ λαλούντων αὐτῶν.
⁵in his own language   ²speaking   ¹them.

7 ἐξίσταντο δὲ καὶ ἐθαύμαζον λέγοντες·
And they were amazed   and   marvelled   saying :

οὐχὶ ἰδοὺ πάντες οὗτοί εἰσιν οἱ λαλοῦντες
²not   ¹behold   ⁴all   ⁵these   ²are   ⁶the [ones] ⁷speaking

Γαλιλαῖοι; 8 καὶ πῶς ἡμεῖς ἀκούομεν
⁸Galilæans?   and   how   ²we   ¹hear

ἕκαστος τῇ ἰδίᾳ διαλέκτῳ ἡμῶν ἐν ᾗ
³each   ⁵in his own language   ⁴of us   in which

ἐγεννήθημεν, 9 Πάρθοι καὶ Μῆδοι καὶ
we were born,   Parthians   and   Medes   and

Ἐλαμῖται, καὶ οἱ κατοικοῦντες τὴν
Elamites,   and the [ones]   inhabiting   –

Μεσοποταμίαν, Ἰουδαίαν τε καὶ Καππα-
Mesopotamia,   both Judæa   and   Cappa-

δοκίαν, Πόντον καὶ τὴν Ἀσίαν, 10 Φρυγίαν
docia,   Pontus   and   –   Asia,   Phrygia

τε καὶ Παμφυλίαν, Αἴγυπτον καὶ τὰ
both   and   Pamphylia,   Egypt   and   the

parts of Libya belonging to Cyre′ne, and visitors from Rome, both Jews and proselytes, ¹¹Cretans and Arabians, we hear them telling in our own tongues the mighty works of God." ¹²And all were amazed and perplexed, saying to one another, "What does this mean?" ¹³But others mocking said, "They are filled with new wine."

14 But Peter, standing with the eleven, lifted up his voice and addressed them, "Men of Judea and all who dwell in Jerusalem, let this be known to you, and give ear to my words. ¹⁵For these men are not drunk, as you suppose, since it is only the third hour of the day; ¹⁶but this is what was spoken by the prophet Joel:
¹⁷'And in the last days it shall be, God declares,
that I will pour out my Spirit upon all flesh,
and your sons and your daughters shall prophesy,
and your young men shall see visions,

μέρη	τῆς	Λιβύης	τῆς	κατὰ	Κυρήνην,
regions	–	of Libya	–	over against	Cyrene,

καὶ	οἱ	ἐπιδημοῦντες	ʽΡωμαῖοι,	11	Ἰουδαῖοί
and	the	temporarily residing	Romans,		²Jews

τε	καὶ	προσήλυτοι,	Κρῆτες	καὶ	″Αραβες,
¹both	and	proselytes,	Cretans	and	Arabians,

ἀκούομεν	λαλούντων	αὐτῶν	ταῖς	ἡμετέραις
we hear	²speaking	¹them	in the	our

γλώσσαις	τὰ	μεγαλεῖα	τοῦ	θεοῦ;
tongues	the	great deeds	–	of God?

12	ἐξίσταντο	δὲ	πάντες	καὶ	διηπόρουντο,
	And were amazed	all		and	were troubled,

ἄλλος	πρὸς	ἄλλον	λέγοντες·	τί	θέλει
other	to	other	saying :	What	wishes

τοῦτο	εἶναι;	13	ἕτεροι	δὲ	διαχλευάζοντες
this	to be?		But others		mocking

ἔλεγον	ὅτι	γλεύκους	μεμεστωμένοι	εἰσίν.
said[,]	–	Of(with) sweet wine	having been filled	they are.

14	Σταθεὶς	δὲ	ὁ	Πέτρος	σὺν	τοῖς	ἕνδεκα
	But standing	–		Peter	with	the	eleven

ἐπῆρεν	τὴν	φωνὴν	αὐτοῦ	καὶ	ἀπεφθέγξατο
lifted up	the	voice	of him	and	spoke out

αὐτοῖς·
to them :

″Ανδρες	Ἰουδαῖοι	καὶ	οἱ	κατοικοῦντες
Men	Jews	and	the [ones]	inhabiting

Ἰερουσαλὴμ	πάντες,	τοῦτο	ὑμῖν	γνωστὸν
Jerusalem	all,	this	to you	known

ἔστω,	καὶ	ἐνωτίσασθε	τὰ	ῥήματά	μου.
let be,	and	give ear to	the	words	of me.

15	οὐ	γὰρ	ὡς	ὑμεῖς	ὑπολαμβάνετε	οὗτοι
	For not		as	ye	imagine	these men

μεθύουσιν,	ἔστιν	γὰρ	ὥρα	τρίτη	τῆς
are drunk,	for it is		hour	third	of the

ἡμέρας,	16	ἀλλὰ	τοῦτό	ἐστιν	τὸ	εἰρημένον
day,		but	this	is	the thing	having been spoken

διὰ	τοῦ	προφήτου	Ἰωήλ·	17	καὶ	ἔσται
through	the	prophet	Joel :		And it shall be

ἐν	ταῖς	ἐσχάταις	ἡμέραις,	λέγει	ὁ	θεός,
in	the	last	days,	says	–	God,

ἐκχεῶ	ἀπὸ	τοῦ	πνεύματός	μου	ἐπὶ
I will pour out	from	the	Spirit	of me	on

πᾶσαν	σάρκα,	καὶ	προφητεύσουσιν	οἱ	υἱοὶ
all	flesh,	and	will prophesy	the	sons

ὑμῶν	καὶ	αἱ	θυγατέρες	ὑμῶν,	καὶ	οἱ
of you	and	the	daughters	of you,	and	the

νεανίσκοι	ὑμῶν	ὁράσεις	ὄψονται,	καὶ	οἱ
young men	of you	visions	will see,	and	the

and your old men shall dream dreams; [18]yea, and on my menservants and my maidservants in those days I will pour out my Spirit; and they shall prophesy. [19]And I will show wonders in the heaven above and signs on the earth beneath, blood, and fire, and vapor of smoke; [20]the sun shall be turned into darkness and the moon into blood, before the day of the Lord comes, the great and manifest day. [21]And it shall be that whoever calls on the name of the Lord shall be saved.'

22 "Men of Israel, hear these words: Jesus of Nazareth, a man attested to you by God with mighty works and wonders and signs which God did through him in your midst, as you yourselves know—[23]this Jesus, delivered up according to the definite plan and foreknowledge of God, you crucified and killed by the hands of lawless men. [24]But God raised him up, having loosed the pangs of death, because it was not possible for him to be held by it. [25]For David says concerning

πρεσβύτεροι ὑμῶν ἐνυπνίοις ἐνυπνιασθήσονται·
old men   of you   dreams   will dream;

18 καὶ γε ἐπὶ τοὺς δούλους μου καὶ ἐπὶ
and –   on   the   male slaves of me   and   on

τὰς δούλας μου ἐν ταῖς ἡμέραις ἐκείναις
the female slaves of me   in   those days

ἐκχεῶ ἀπὸ τοῦ πνεύματός μου, καὶ
I will pour out from   the   Spirit   of me,   and

προφητεύσουσιν. 19 καὶ δώσω τέρατα ἐν
they will prophesy.   And   I will give   wonders   in

τῷ οὐρανῷ ἄνω καὶ σημεῖα ἐπὶ τῆς
the   heaven   above   and   signs   on   the

γῆς κάτω, αἷμα καὶ πῦρ καὶ ἀτμίδα
earth   below,   blood   and   fire   and   vapour

καπνοῦ. 20 ὁ ἥλιος μεταστραφήσεται εἰς
of smoke.   The   sun   will be turned   into

σκότος καὶ ἡ σελήνη εἰς αἷμα, πρὶν
darkness   and   the   moon   into   blood,   before

ἐλθεῖν ἡμέραν κυρίου τὴν μεγάλην καὶ
[7]to come(comes) [5]day [6]of [the] Lord [1]the [2]great [3]and

ἐπιφανῆ. 21 καὶ ἔσται πᾶς ὃς ἐὰν
[4]notable.[b]   And   it will be   everyone   whoever

ἐπικαλέσηται τὸ ὄνομα κυρίου σωθήσεται.
invokes   the   name   of [the] Lord   will be saved.

22 Ἄνδρες Ἰσραηλῖται, ἀκούσατε τοὺς
  Men   Israelites,   hear ye   –

λόγους τούτους· Ἰησοῦν τὸν Ναζωραῖον,
words   these: Jesus   the   Nazarene,

ἄνδρα ἀποδεδειγμένον ἀπὸ τοῦ θεοῦ εἰς
a man   having been approved   from   –   God   among

ὑμᾶς δυνάμεσι καὶ τέρασι καὶ σημείοις,
you   by powerful deeds   and   wonders   and   signs,

οἷς ἐποίησεν δι' αὐτοῦ ὁ θεὸς ἐν μέσῳ
which did   through   him   –   God   in [the] midst

ὑμῶν, καθὼς αὐτοὶ οἴδατε, 23 τοῦτον
of you,   as   [your]selves   ye know,   this man

τῇ ὡρισμένῃ βουλῇ καὶ προγνώσει τοῦ
[3]by the [2]having been fixed [4]counsel [5]and [6]foreknowledge –

θεοῦ ἔκδοτον διὰ χειρὸς ἀνόμων
[7]of God   [1]given up   [8]through [10][the] hand [11]of lawless men

προσπήξαντες ἀνείλατε, 24 ὃν ὁ θεὸς
[9]fastening[*]   [12]ye killed,   whom   –   God

ἀνέστησεν λύσας τὰς ὠδῖνας τοῦ θανάτου,
raised up   loosening   the   pangs   –   of death,

καθότι οὐκ ἦν δυνατὸν κρατεῖσθαι αὐτὸν
because   it was not   possible   [2]to be held   [1]him

ὑπ' αὐτοῦ. 25 Δαυὶδ γὰρ λέγει εἰς
by   it.   For David   says   [as] to

* That is, to a tree; see ch. 5. 30.

him,
'I saw the Lord always before me,
for he is at my right hand that I may not be shaken;
²⁶therefore my heart was glad, and my tongue rejoiced; moreover my flesh will dwell in hope.
²⁷For thou wilt not abandon my soul to Hades,
nor let thy Holy One see corruption.
²⁸Thou hast made known to me the ways of life; thou wilt make me full of gladness with thy presence.'
29 "Brethren, I may say to you confidently of the patriarch David that he both died and was buried, and his tomb is with us to this day.
³⁰Being therefore a prophet, and knowing that God had sworn with an oath to him that he would set one of his descendants upon his throne, ³¹he foresaw and spoke of the resurrection of the Christ, that he was not abandoned to Hades, nor did his flesh see corruption. ³²This Jesus God raised up, and of that we all are witnesses. ³³Being therefore

| αὐτόν· | προορώμην | τὸν | κύριον | ἐνώπιόν |
| him : | I foresaw | the | Lord | before |

| μου | διὰ | παντός, | ὅτι | ἐκ | δεξιῶν | μού |
| me | | always, | because | on | right | of me |

| ἔστιν, | ἵνα | μὴ | σαλευθῶ. | 26 διὰ | τοῦτο |
| he is, | | lest | I be moved. | | Therefore |

| ηὐφράνθη | μου | ἡ | καρδία | καὶ | ἠγαλλιάσατο |
| was glad | of me | the | heart | and | exulted |

| ἡ | γλῶσσά | μου, | ἔτι | δὲ | καὶ | ἡ | σάρξ |
| the | tongue | of me, | and now | | also | the | flesh |

| μου | κατασκηνώσει | ἐπ' | ἐλπίδι, | 27 ὅτι | οὐκ |
| of me | will dwell | on(in) | hope, | | because not |

| ἐγκαταλείψεις | τὴν | ψυχήν | μου | εἰς | ἅδην |
| thou wilt abandon | the | soul | of me | in | hades |

| οὐδὲ | δώσεις | τὸν | ὅσιόν | σου | ἰδεῖν |
| nor | wilt thou give | the | holy one | of thee | to see |

| διαφθοράν. | 28 ἐγνώρισάς | μοι | ὁδοὺς | ζωῆς, |
| corruption. | Thou madest known to me | | ways | of life, |

| πληρώσεις | με | εὐφροσύνης | μετὰ | τοῦ | προσώ- |
| thou wilt fill | me | of(with) gladness | with | the | pres- |

| που | σου. | 29 Ἄνδρες | ἀδελφοί, | ἐξὸν | εἰπεῖν |
| ence of thee. | | Men | brothers, | it is permitted to speak |

| μετὰ | παρρησίας | πρὸς | ὑμᾶς | περὶ | τοῦ |
| with | plainness | to | you | concerning | the |

| πατριάρχου | Δαυίδ, | ὅτι | καὶ | ἐτελεύτησεν |
| patriarch | David, | that | both | he died |

| καὶ | ἐτάφη, | καὶ | τὸ | μνῆμα | αὐτοῦ | ἔστιν |
| and | was buried, | and | the | tomb | of him | is |

| ἐν | ἡμῖν | ἄχρι | τῆς | ἡμέρας | ταύτης. |
| among | us | until | | this day. |

| 30 προφήτης | οὖν | ὑπάρχων | καὶ | εἰδὼς | ὅτι |
| A prophet | therefore | being | and | knowing | that |

| ὅρκῳ | ὤμοσεν | αὐτῷ | ὁ | θεὸς | ἐκ | καρποῦ |
| with an oath | swore | to him | - | God | of [the] | fruit |

| τῆς | ὀσφύος | αὐτοῦ | καθίσαι | ἐπὶ | τὸν | θρόνον |
| of the | loin[s] | of him | to sit | on | the | throne |

| αὐτοῦ, | 31 προϊδὼν | ἐλάλησεν | περὶ | τῆς |
| of him, | foreseeing | he spoke | concerning | the |

| ἀναστάσεως | τοῦ | Χριστοῦ, | ὅτι | οὔτε |
| resurrection | of the | Christ, | that | neither |

| ἐγκατελείφθη | εἰς | ἅδην | οὔτε | ἡ | σάρξ |
| he was abandoned | in | hades | nor | the | flesh |

| αὐτοῦ | εἶδεν | διαφθοράν. | 32 τοῦτον | τὸν |
| of him | saw | corruption. | This | - |

| Ἰησοῦν | ἀνέστησεν | ὁ | θεός, | οὗ | πάντες |
| Jesus | ²raised up | - | ¹God, | of which | all |

| ἡμεῖς | ἐσμεν | μάρτυρες· | 33 τῇ | δεξιᾷ | οὖν |
| we | are | witnesses; | | to the right [hand] | therefore |

exalted at the right hand of God, and having received from the Father the promise of the Holy Spirit, he has poured out this which you see and hear. ³⁴ For David did not ascend into the heavens; but he himself says, 'The Lord said to my Lord, Sit at my right hand, ³⁵ till I make thy enemies a stool for thy feet.' ³⁶ Let all the house of Israel therefore know assuredly that God has made him both Lord and Christ, this Jesus whom you crucified." 37 Now when they heard this they were cut to the heart, and said to Peter and the rest of the apostles, "Brethren, what shall we do?" ³⁸And Peter said to them, "Repent, and be baptized every one of you in the name of Jesus Christ for the forgiveness of your sins; and you shall receive the gift of the Holy Spirit. ³⁹ For the promise is to you and to your children and to all that are far off, every one whom the Lord our God calls to him." ⁴⁰And he testified with many other words

τοῦ θεοῦ ὑψωθεὶς τήν τε ἐπαγγελίαν
\- of God having been exalted ⁸the ¹and ⁷promise

τοῦ πνεύματος τοῦ ἁγίου λαβὼν παρὰ
⁵of the ¹⁰Spirit \- ⁹Holy ²receiving ³from

τοῦ πατρὸς ἐξέχεεν τοῦτο ὃ ὑμεῖς καὶ
⁴the ⁵Father he poured out this which ye both

βλέπετε καὶ ἀκούετε. 34 οὐ γὰρ Δαυὶδ
see and hear. For not David

ἀνέβη εἰς τοὺς οὐρανούς, λέγει δὲ αὐτός·
ascended to the heavens, but says he :

εἶπεν κύριος τῷ κυρίῳ μου· κάθου ἐκ
Said [the] LORD to the Lord of me : Sit at

δεξιῶν μου, 35 ἕως ἂν θῶ τοὺς ἐχθρούς
right of me, until I put the enemies

σου ὑποπόδιον τῶν ποδῶν σου. 36 ἀσφαλῶς
of thee a footstool of the feet of thee. Assuredly

οὖν γινωσκέτω πᾶς οἶκος Ἰσραὴλ ὅτι
therefore ¹let ⁶know ²all ³[the] ⁴house ⁵of Israel that

καὶ κύριον αὐτὸν καὶ χριστὸν ἐποίησεν
⁴both ⁵Lord ³him ⁶and ⁷Christ ²made

ὁ θεος, τοῦτον τὸν Ἰησοῦν ὃν ὑμεῖς
\- ¹God, this the Jesus whom ye

ἐσταυρώσατε. 37 Ἀκούσαντες δὲ κατενύγ-
crucified. And hearing they were

ησαν τὴν καρδίαν, εἶπόν τε πρὸς τὸν
stung [in] the heart, and said to \-

Πέτρον καὶ τοὺς λοιποὺς ἀποστόλους·
Peter and the remaining apostles :

τί ποιήσωμεν, ἄνδρες ἀδελφοί; 38 Πέτρος
What may we do, men brothers? Peter

δὲ πρὸς αὐτούς· μετανοήσατε, καὶ
And to them : Repent ye, and

βαπτισθήτω ἕκαστος ὑμῶν ἐπὶ τῷ ὀνόματι
let be baptized each of you on the name

Ἰησοῦ Χριστοῦ εἰς ἄφεσιν τῶν
of Jesus Christ [with a view] to forgiveness of the

ἁμαρτιῶν ὑμῶν, καὶ λήμψεσθε τὴν δωρεὰν
sins of you, and ye will receive the gift

τοῦ ἁγίου πνεύματος. 39 ὑμῖν γάρ ἐστιν
of the Holy Spirit. For to you is

ἡ ἐπαγγελία καὶ τοῖς τέκνοις ὑμῶν καὶ
the promise and to the children of you and

πᾶσιν τοῖς εἰς μακράν, ὅσους ἂν
to all the [ones] as far away, as many as

προσκαλέσηται κύριος ὁ θεὸς ἡμῶν.
may call to [him] [the] Lord the God of us.

40 ἑτέροις τε λόγοις πλείοσιν διεμαρτύρατο,
And with other words many he solemnly witnessed,

and exhorted them, saying, "Save yourselves from this crooked generation." ⁴¹So those who received his word were baptized, and there were added that day about three thousand souls. ⁴²And they devoted themselves to the apostles' teaching and fellowship, to the breaking of bread and the prayers.

43 And fear came upon every soul; and many wonders and signs were done through the apostles. ⁴⁴And all who believed were together and had all things in common; ⁴⁵and they sold their possessions and goods and distributed them to all, as any had need. ⁴⁶And day by day, attending the temple together and breaking bread in their homes, they partook of food with glad and generous hearts, ⁴⁷praising God and having favor with all the people. And the Lord added to their number day by day those who were being saved.

καὶ παρεκάλει αὐτοὺς λέγων· σώθητε
and exhorted them saying: Be ye saved

ἀπὸ τῆς γενεᾶς τῆς σκολιᾶς ταύτης. 41 οἱ
from - ³generation - ²perverse ¹this. The [ones]

μὲν οὖν ἀποδεξάμενοι τὸν λόγον αὐτοῦ
- therefore welcoming the word of him

ἐβαπτίσθησαν, καὶ προσετέθησαν ἐν
were baptized, and there were added in

τῇ ἡμέρᾳ ἐκείνῃ ψυχαὶ ὡσεὶ τρισχίλιαι·
that day souls about three thousand;

42 ἦσαν δὲ προσκαρτεροῦντες τῇ διδαχῇ
and they were continuing steadfastly in the teaching

τῶν ἀποστόλων καὶ τῇ κοινωνίᾳ, τῇ
of the apostles and in the fellowship, in the

κλάσει τοῦ ἄρτου καὶ ταῖς προσευχαῖς.
breaking of the loaf and in the prayers.

43 Ἐγίνετο δὲ πάσῃ ψυχῇ φόβος· πολλὰ δὲ
And came to every soul fear; and many

τέρατα καὶ σημεῖα διὰ τῶν ἀποστόλων
wonders and signs through the apostles

ἐγίνετο. 44 πάντες δὲ οἱ πιστεύσαντες
happened. And all the believing [ones]

ἐπὶ τὸ αὐτὸ εἶχον ἅπαντα κοινά, 45 καὶ
together had all things common, and

τὰ κτήματα καὶ τὰς ὑπάρξεις ἐπίπρασκον
the properties and the possessions they sold

καὶ διεμέριζον αὐτὰ πᾶσιν, καθότι ἄν
and distributed them to all, according as

τις χρείαν εἶχεν. 46 καθ' ἡμέραν τε
anyone need had. And from day to day†

προσκαρτεροῦντες ὁμοθυμαδὸν ἐν τῷ ἱερῷ,
continuing steadfastly with one mind in the temple,

κλῶντές τε κατ' οἶκον ἄρτον, μετε-
and ¹breaking ²from house to house† ³bread, they

λάμβανον τροφῆς ἐν ἀγαλλιάσει καὶ
shared food in gladness and

ἀφελότητι καρδίας, 47 αἰνοῦντες τὸν θεὸν
simplicity of heart, praising - God

καὶ ἔχοντες χάριν πρὸς ὅλον τὸν λαόν.
and having favour with all the people.

ὁ δὲ κύριος προσετίθει τοὺς σῳζομένους
And the Lord added the [ones] being saved

καθ' ἡμέραν ἐπὶ τὸ αὐτό.
from day to day† together.†

CHAPTER 3

NOW Peter and John were going up to the temple at the hour of prayer, the ninth hour. [2]And a man lame from birth was being carried, whom they laid daily at that gate of the temple which is called Beautiful to ask alms of those who entered the temple. [3]Seeing Peter and John about to go into the temple, he asked for alms. [4]And Peter directed his gaze at him, with John, and said, "Look at us." [5]And he fixed his attention upon them, expecting to receive something from them. [6]But Peter said, "I have no silver and gold, but I give you what I have; in the name of Jesus Christ of Nazareth, walk." [7]And he took him by the right hand and raised him up; and immediately his feet and ankles were made strong. [8]And leaping up he stood and walked and entered the temple with them, walking and leaping and praising God. [9]And all the people saw

3 Πέτρος δὲ καὶ Ἰωάννης ἀνέβαινον
Now Peter and John were going up
εἰς τὸ ἱερὸν ἐπὶ τὴν ὥραν τῆς προσευχῆς
to the temple at the hour of the prayer
τὴν ἐνάτην. 2 καί τις ἀνὴρ χωλὸς ἐκ
the ninth. And a certain man [1]lame [2]from
κοιλίας μητρὸς αὐτοῦ ὑπάρχων ἐβαστάζετο,
[4][the] [5]of [the] [6]of him [1]being was being carried,
   womb   mother
ὃν ἐτίθουν καθ' ἡμέραν πρὸς τὴν θύραν
whom they used from day to day† at the door
   to put
τοῦ ἱεροῦ τὴν λεγομένην ὡραίαν τοῦ
of the temple – being called Beautiful –
αἰτεῖν ἐλεημοσύνην παρὰ τῶν εἰσπορευομέ-
to ask[d] alms from the [ones] enter-
νων εἰς τὸ ἱερόν· 3 ὃς ἰδὼν Πέτρον καὶ
ing into the temple; who seeing Peter and
Ἰωάννην μέλλοντας εἰσιέναι εἰς τὸ ἱερὸν
John being about to go in into the temple
ἠρώτα ἐλεημοσύνην λαβεῖν. 4 ἀτενίσας δὲ
asked alms to receive. And [2]gazing
Πέτρος εἰς αὐτὸν σὺν τῷ Ἰωάννη εἶπεν·
[1]Peter at him with – John said:
βλέψον εἰς ἡμᾶς. 5 ὁ δὲ ἐπεῖχεν αὐτοῖς
Look at us. And he paid heed to them
προσδοκῶν τι παρ' αὐτῶν λαβεῖν. 6 εἶπεν
expecting something from them to receive. said
δὲ Πέτρος· ἀργύριον καὶ χρυσίον οὐχ
And Peter: Silver and gold not
ὑπάρχει μοι· ὃ δὲ ἔχω, τοῦτό σοι δίδωμι·
is to me[e]; but what I have, this to thee I give;
=I have not;
ἐν τῷ ὀνόματι Ἰησοῦ Χριστοῦ τοῦ
in the name of Jesus Christ the
Ναζωραίου περιπάτει. 7 καὶ πιάσας αὐτὸν τῆς
Nazarene walk. And seizing him of(by)
δεξιᾶς χειρὸς ἤγειρεν αὐτόν· παραχρῆμα
the right hand he raised him; [2]at once
δὲ ἐστερεώθησαν αἱ βάσεις αὐτοῦ καὶ τὰ
[1]and were made firm the feet of him and the
σφυδρά, 8 καὶ ἐξαλλόμενος ἔστη, καὶ
ankle-bones, and leaping up he stood, and
περιεπάτει, καὶ εἰσῆλθεν σὺν αὐτοῖς εἰς
walked, and entered with them into
τὸ ἱερὸν περιπατῶν καὶ ἀλλόμενος καὶ
the temple walking and leaping and
αἰνῶν τὸν θεόν. 9 καὶ εἶδεν πᾶς ὁ
praising – God. And [4]saw [1]all [2]the

him walking and praising God, [10] and recognized him as the one who sat for alms at the Beautiful Gate of the temple; and they were filled with wonder and amazement at what had happened to him. 11 While he clung to Peter and John, all the people ran together to them in the portico called Solomon's, astounded. [12] And when Peter saw it he addressed the people, "Men of Israel, why do you wonder at this, or why do you stare at us, as though by our own power or piety we had made him walk? [13] The God of Abraham and of Isaac and of Jacob, the God of our fathers, glorified his servant[e] Jesus, whom you delivered up and denied in the presence of Pilate, when he had decided to release him. [14] But you denied the Holy and Righteous One, and asked for a murderer to be granted to you, [15] and killed the Author of life, whom God raised from the dead. To this we are

λαὸς αὐτὸν περιπατοῦντα καὶ αἰνοῦντα
[2]people   him   walking   and   praising

τὸν θεόν· 10 ἐπεγίνωσκον δὲ αὐτόν, ὅτι
 –   God;   and they recognized   him,   that

οὗτος ἦν ὁ πρὸς τὴν ἐλεημοσύνην
this   was the [one] for   –   alms

καθήμενος ἐπὶ τῇ ὡραίᾳ πύλῃ τοῦ ἱεροῦ,
 sitting   at   the Beautiful gate of the temple,

καὶ ἐπλήσθησαν θάμβους καὶ ἐκστάσεως
and   they were filled   of(with)   and   bewilderment
                         amazement

ἐπὶ τῷ συμβεβηκότι αὐτῷ. 11 Κρατοῦντος δὲ
at the thing having happened to him.   And holding
                                              = as he held

αὐτοῦ τὸν Πέτρον καὶ τὸν Ἰωάννην
him[a]   –   Peter   and   –   John

συνέδραμεν πᾶς ὁ λαὸς πρὸς αὐτοὺς
ran together   all the people   to   them

ἐπὶ τῇ στοᾷ τῇ καλουμένῃ Σολομῶντος
at   the   porch   –   being called   of Solomon

ἔκθαμβοι. 12 ἰδὼν δὲ ὁ Πέτρος ἀπεκρίνατο
greatly amazed.   And [2]seeing – [1]Peter   answered

πρὸς τὸν λαόν· ἄνδρες Ἰσραηλῖται, τί
to   the people :   Men   Israelites,   why

θαυμάζετε ἐπὶ τούτῳ, ἢ ἡμῖν τί ἀτενίζετε
marvel ye   at   this man, or at us why   gaze ye

ὡς ἰδίᾳ δυνάμει ἢ εὐσεβείᾳ πεποιηκόσιν
as by [our] own power or   piety   having made

τοῦ περιπατεῖν αὐτόν; 13 ὁ θεὸς Ἀβραὰμ
 –   to walk[d]   him?   The God of Abraham

καὶ Ἰσαὰκ καὶ Ἰακώβ, ὁ θεὸς τῶν
and   Isaac   and   Jacob,   the God   of the

πατέρων ἡμῶν, ἐδόξασεν τὸν παῖδα αὐτοῦ
 fathers   of us,   glorified   the   servant   of him

Ἰησοῦν, ὃν ὑμεῖς μὲν παρεδώκατε καὶ
Jesus,   whom ye   –   delivered   and

ἠρνήσασθε κατὰ πρόσωπον Πιλάτου,
 denied   in   [the] presence   of Pilate,

κρίναντος ἐκείνου ἀπολύειν· 14 ὑμεῖς δὲ
having decided that one[a]   to release [him];   but ye
= when he had decided

τὸν ἅγιον καὶ δίκαιον ἠρνήσασθε, καὶ
the   holy   and just one   denied,   and

ἠτήσασθε ἄνδρα φονέα χαρισθῆναι ὑμῖν,
 asked   a man a murderer to be granted   you,

15 τὸν δὲ ἀρχηγὸν τῆς ζωῆς ἀπεκτείνατε,
and the   Author   –   of life   ye killed,

ὃν ὁ θεὸς ἤγειρεν ἐκ νεκρῶν, οὗ ἡμεῖς
whom – God raised   from [the] dead, of which we

[e] Or child

witnesses. [16]And his
name, by faith in his
name, has made this man
strong whom you see and
know; and the faith
which is through Jesus
has given the man this
perfect health in the
presence of you all.
[17] "And now, breth-
ren, I know that you
acted in ignorance, as
did also your rulers.
[18]But what God foretold
by the mouth of all the
prophets, that his Christ
should suffer, he thus
fulfilled. [19]Repent therefore, and turn again, that
your sins may be blotted
out, that times of refreshing may come from the
presence of the Lord,
[20]and that he may send
the Christ appointed for
you, Jesus, [21]whom
heaven must receive until
the time for establishing
all that God spoke by
the mouth of his holy
prophets from of old.
[22]Moses said, 'The Lord
God will raise up for you
a prophet from your
brethren as he raised me
up. You shall listen to

μάρτυρές ἐσμεν. **16** καὶ ἐπὶ τῇ πίστει
witnesses are. 　　And on the faith

τοῦ ὀνόματος αὐτοῦ τοῦτον, ὃν θεωρεῖτε
of(in) name* of him ⁵this man, ⁶whom ⁷ye behold
the

καὶ οἴδατε, ἐστερέωσεν τὸ ὄνομα αὐτοῦ,
⁸and ⁹know, ⁴made firm ¹the ²name ³of him,

καὶ ἡ πίστις ἡ δι᾽ αὐτοῦ ἔδωκεν αὐτῷ
and the faith – through him gave him

τὴν ὁλοκληρίαν ταύτην ἀπέναντι πάντων
this soundness before all

ὑμῶν. **17** καὶ νῦν, ἀδελφοί, οἶδα ὅτι
you. And now, brothers, I know that

κατὰ ἄγνοιαν ἐπράξατε, ὥσπερ καὶ οἱ
by way of ignorance ye acted, as also the

ἄρχοντες ὑμῶν· **18** ὁ δὲ θεὸς ἃ
rulers of you; – but God the things
　　　　　　　　　　　　　　　　　　which

προκατήγγειλεν διὰ στόματος πάντων
he foreannounced through [the] mouth of all

τῶν προφητῶν, παθεῖν τὸν χριστὸν αὐτοῦ,
the prophets, to suffer the Christ of him[b],
　　　　　　　=that his Christ was to suffer,

ἐπλήρωσεν οὕτως. **19** μετανοήσατε οὖν
fulfilled thus. Repent ye therefore

καὶ ἐπιστρέψατε πρὸς τὸ ἐξαλειφθῆναι
and turn for the to be wiped away
　　　　　　　=that your sins may be wiped away,

ὑμῶν τὰς ἁμαρτίας, **20** ὅπως ἂν ἔλθωσιν
of you the sins, so as may come

καιροὶ ἀναψύξεως ἀπὸ προσώπου τοῦ
times of refreshing from [the] presence of the

κυρίου καὶ ἀποστείλῃ τὸν προκεχειρισμένον
Lord and he may send ¹the ³having been foreappointed

ὑμῖν χριστὸν Ἰησοῦν, **21** ὃν δεῖ οὐρανὸν
⁴for you ²Christ ⁵Jesus, whom it behoves heaven

μὲν δέξασθαι ἄχρι χρόνων ἀποκαταστάσεως
– to receive until [the] times of restitution

πάντων ὧν ἐλάλησεν ὁ θεὸς διὰ στόματος
of all things which ²spoke – ¹God ³through ⁴[the] mouth

τῶν ἁγίων ἀπ᾽ αἰῶνος αὐτοῦ προφητῶν.
⁵of the ⁶holy ⁸from ¹⁰[the] age ⁹of him ⁷prophets.

22 Μωϋσῆς μὲν εἶπεν ὅτι προφήτην ὑμῖν
Moses indeed said[,] – ⁴A prophet ⁵for you

ἀναστήσει κύριος ὁ θεὸς ἐκ τῶν ἀδελφῶν
³will raise up ¹(the) Lord – ²God of the brothers

ὑμῶν ὡς ἐμέ· αὐτοῦ ἀκούσεσθε κατὰ
of you as me; him shall ye hear according to

---

* Objective genitive; *cf.* " the fear of God " =the fear which has
God for its object; and see Gal. 2. 20, etc.

him in whatever he tells you. ²³And it shall be that every soul that does not listen to that prophet shall be destroyed from the people.' ²⁴And all the prophets who have spoken, from Samuel and those who came afterward, also proclaimed these days. ²⁵You are the sons of the prophets and of the covenant which God gave to your fathers, saying to Abraham, 'And in your posterity shall all the families of the earth be blessed.' ²⁶God, having raised up his servant,ᵉ sent him to you first, to bless you in turning every one of you from your wickedness."

πάντα	ὅσα	ἂν	λαλήσῃ	πρὸς	ὑμᾶς.
all things	whatever		he may speak	to	you.

23 ἔσται δὲ πᾶσα ψυχὴ ἥτις ἐὰν μὴ ἀκούσῃ
And it shall be every   soul   whoever   hears not

τοῦ προφήτου ἐκείνου ἐξολεθρευθήσεται
that prophet   will be utterly destroyed

ἐκ τοῦ λαοῦ. 24 καὶ πάντες δὲ οἱ
out of the people. ²also ²all ¹And the

προφῆται ἀπὸ Σαμουὴλ καὶ τῶν καθεξῆς
prophets from   Samuel   and   the [ones] in order

ὅσοι ἐλάλησαν καὶ κατήγγειλαν τὰς ἡμέρας
as many as   spoke   also   announced   –   days

ταύτας. 25 ὑμεῖς ἐστε οἱ υἱοὶ τῶν
these.   Ye   are   the   sons   of the

προφητῶν καὶ τῆς διαθήκης ἧς ὁ θεὸς
prophets   and   of the   covenant   which   –   God

διέθετο πρὸς τοὺς πατέρας ὑμῶν, λέγων
made   with   the   fathers   of us,   saying

πρὸς Ἀβραάμ· καὶ ἐν τῷ σπέρματί
to   Abraham: And   in   the   seed

σου ἐνευλογηθήσονται πᾶσαι αἱ πατριαὶ
of thee   shall be blessed   all   the   families

τῆς γῆς. 26 ὑμῖν πρῶτον ἀναστήσας ὁ
of the earth.   To you   first   ¹having raised up   –

θεὸς τὸν παῖδα αὐτοῦ ἀπέστειλεν αὐτὸν
¹God   the   servant   of him   sent   him

εὐλογοῦντα ὑμᾶς ἐν τῷ ἀποστρέφειν
blessing   you   in   the   to turn away
                   =in turning away

ἕκαστον ἀπὸ τῶν πονηριῶν ὑμῶν.
each one   from   the   iniquities   of you.

CHAPTER 4

A ND as they were speaking to the people, the priests and the captain of the temple and the Sad'ducees came upon them, ²annoyed because they were teaching the people and proclaiming in Jesus the resurrection from the dead. ³And they arrested them and put them in custody until the morrow, for it was already evening. ⁴But many of

ᵉ Or child

4 Λαλούντων δὲ αὐτῶν πρὸς τὸν λαόν,
And speaking   themᵃ   to   the   people,
    =while they were speaking

ἐπέστησαν αὐτοῖς οἱ ἱερεῖς καὶ ὁ στρατηγὸς
came upon   them   the   priests   and   the commandant

τοῦ ἱεροῦ καὶ οἱ Σαδδουκαῖοι, 2 διαπονούμενοι
of the temple   and   the   Sadducees,   being greatly troubled

διὰ τὸ διδάσκειν αὐτοὺς τὸν λαὸν καὶ
because of the   to teach   themᵇ   the   people   and
=because they taught ... announced

καταγγέλλειν ἐν τῷ Ἰησοῦ τὴν ἀνάστασιν
to announceᵇ   by   –   Jesus   the   resurrection

τὴν ἐκ νεκρῶν, 3 καὶ ἐπέβαλον αὐτοῖς
the   from   [the] dead,   and   laid on   them

τὰς χεῖρας καὶ ἔθεντο εἰς τήρησιν εἰς
the(ir)   hands   and   put   in   guard   till

τὴν αὔριον· ἦν γὰρ ἑσπέρα ἤδη. 4 πολλοὶ
the   morrow;   for it was   evening   now.   many

those who heard the word believed; and the number of the men came to about five thousand. 5 On the morrow their rulers and elders and scribes were gathered together in Jerusalem, 6 with Annas the high priest and Ca'iaphas and John and Alexander, and all who were of the high-priestly family. 7 And when they had set them in the midst, they inquired, "By what power or by what name did you do this?" 8 Then Peter, filled with the Holy Spirit, said to them, "Rulers of the people and elders, 9 if we are being examined today concerning a good deed done to a cripple, by what means this man has been healed, 10 be it known to you all, and to all the people of Israel, that by the name of Jesus Christ of Nazareth, whom you crucified, whom God raised from the dead, by him this man is standing before you well. 11 This is the stone which was rejected by you builders, but which

δὲ τῶν ἀκουσάντων τὸν λόγον ἐπίστευσαν,
But of the [ones] hearing the word believed,
καὶ ἐγενήθη ἀριθμὸς τῶν ἀνδρῶν ὡς
and became [the] number of the men about
χιλιάδες πέντε.
thousands five.
5 Ἐγένετο δὲ ἐπὶ τὴν αὔριον
Now it came to pass on the morrow
συναχθῆναι αὐτῶν τοὺς ἄρχοντας καὶ τοὺς
to be assembled of them the rulers and the
πρεσβυτέρους καὶ τοὺς γραμματεῖς ἐν
elders and the scribes in
Ἰερουσαλήμ, 6 καὶ Ἅννας ὁ ἀρχιερεὺς
Jerusalem, and Annas* the high priest
καὶ Καϊαφᾶς καὶ Ἰωάννης καὶ Ἀλέξανδρος
and Caiaphas and John and Alexander
καὶ ὅσοι ἦσαν ἐκ γένους ἀρχιερατικοῦ,
and as many as were of [the] race high-priestly,
7 καὶ στήσαντες αὐτοὺς ἐν τῷ μέσῳ
and having stood them in the midst
ἐπυνθάνοντο· ἐν ποίᾳ δυνάμει ἢ ἐν ποίῳ
inquired: By what power or in what
ὀνόματι ἐποιήσατε τοῦτο ὑμεῖς; 8 τότε
name did this ye? Then
Πέτρος πλησθεὶς πνεύματος ἁγίου εἶπεν
Peter filled of(with) [the] Spirit Holy said
πρὸς αὐτούς· ἄρχοντες τοῦ λαοῦ καὶ
to them: Rulers of the people and
πρεσβύτεροι, 9 εἰ ἡμεῖς σήμερον ἀνα-
elders, if we to-day are be-
κρινόμεθα ἐπὶ εὐεργεσίᾳ ἀνθρώπου ἀσθενοῦς,
ing examined on a good deed man of an infirm,
=[done to] an infirm man,
ἐν τίνι οὗτος σέσωσται, 10 γνωστὸν ἔστω
by what this man has been healed, known let it be
πᾶσιν ὑμῖν καὶ παντὶ τῷ λαῷ Ἰσραήλ,
to all you and to all the people of Israel,
ὅτι ἐν τῷ ὀνόματι Ἰησοῦ Χριστοῦ τοῦ
that in the name of Jesus Christ the
Ναζωραίου, ὃν ὑμεῖς ἐσταυρώσατε, ὃν ὁ
Nazarene, whom ye crucified, whom –
θεὸς ἤγειρεν ἐκ νεκρῶν, ἐν τούτῳ οὗτος
God raised from [the] dead, in this [name] this man
παρέστηκεν ἐνώπιον ὑμῶν ὑγιής. 11 οὗτός
stands before you whole. This
ἐστιν ὁ λίθος ὁ ἐξουθενηθεὶς ὑφ' ὑμῶν
is the stone – despised by you

* The rough breathing in the Greek is ignored in the trans-
literation of some familiar proper names.

has become the head of the corner. ¹²And there is salvation in no one else, for there is no other name under heaven given among men by which we must be saved."

13 Now when they saw the boldness of Peter and John, and perceived that they were uneducated, common men, they wondered; and they recognized that they had been with Jesus. ¹⁴But seeing the man that had been healed standing beside them, they had nothing to say in opposition. ¹⁵But when they had commanded them to go aside out of the council, they conferred with one another, ¹⁶saying, "What shall we do with these men? For that a notable sign has been performed through them is manifest to all the inhabitants of Jerusalem, and we cannot deny it. ¹⁷But in order that it may spread no further among the people, let us warn them to speak no more to any one in this name." ¹⁸So they called them and charged them not to speak or teach at all in the name of Jesus. ¹⁹But

---

τῶν οἰκοδόμων, ὁ γενόμενος εἰς κεφαλὴν
the [ones] building, the [one] become *to* head

γωνίας. 12 καὶ οὐκ ἔστιν ἐν ἄλλῳ οὐδενὶ
of [the] corner. And there is not ¹in ²other ²no(any)

ἡ σωτηρία· οὐδὲ γὰρ ὄνομά ἐστιν ἕτερον
the salvation: for neither ²name ¹is there ²other

ὑπὸ τὸν οὐρανὸν τὸ δεδομένον ἐν
under – heaven – having been given among

ἀνθρώποις ἐν ᾧ δεῖ σωθῆναι ἡμᾶς.
men by which it behoves ²to be saved ¹us.

13 Θεωροῦντες δὲ τὴν τοῦ Πέτρου
And beholding the – of Peter

παρρησίαν καὶ Ἰωάννου, καὶ καταλαβόμενοι
boldness and of John, and perceiving

ὅτι ἄνθρωποι ἀγράμματοί εἰσιν καὶ
that men unlettered they are(were) and

ἰδιῶται, ἐθαύμαζον, ἐπεγίνωσκόν τε αὐτοὺς
laymen, they marvelled, and recognized them

ὅτι σὺν τῷ Ἰησοῦ ἦσαν, 14 τόν τε
that with – Jesus they were(had been), ³the ¹and

ἄνθρωπον βλέποντες σὺν αὐτοῖς ἑστῶτα τὸν
⁴man ²seeing ⁷with ⁸them ⁶standing –

τεθεραπευμένον, οὐδὲν εἶχον ἀντειπεῖν.
⁵having been healed, nothing they had to say against.

15 κελεύσαντες δὲ αὐτοὺς ἔξω τοῦ συνεδρίου
So having commanded them outside the council

ἀπελθεῖν, συνέβαλλον πρὸς ἀλλήλους
to go, they discussed *with* with one another

16 λέγοντες· τί ποιήσωμεν τοῖς ἀνθρώποις
saying : What may we do – men

τούτοις; ὅτι μὲν γὰρ γνωστὸν σημεῖον
to these? for that indeed a notable sign

γέγονεν δι' αὐτῶν, πᾶσιν τοῖς κατοικοῦσιν
has happened through t..m, to all the [ones] inhabiting

Ἰερουσαλὴμ φανερόν, καὶ οὐ δυνάμεθα
Jerusalem [is] manifest, and we cannot

ἀρνεῖσθαι· 17 ἀλλ' ἵνα μὴ ἐπὶ πλεῖον
to deny [it]; but ¹lest ²more†

διανεμηθῇ εἰς τὸν λαόν, ἀπειλησώμεθα
²it is spread abroad ⁴to the people, let us threaten

αὐτοῖς μηκέτι λαλεῖν ἐπὶ τῷ ὀνόματι
them no longer to speak on – name

τούτῳ μηδενὶ ἀνθρώπων. 18 καὶ καλέσαντες
this to no(any)one of men. And calling

αὐτοὺς παρήγγειλαν καθόλου μὴ φθέγγεσθαι
them they charged at all not to utter

μηδὲ διδάσκειν ἐπὶ τῷ ὀνόματι τοῦ
nor to teach on the name –

Peter and John answered them, "Whether it is right in the sight of God to listen to you rather than to God, you must judge; [20]for we cannot but speak of what we have seen and heard." [21]And when they had further threatened them, they let them go, finding no way to punish them, because of the people; for all men praised God for what had happened. [22]For the man on whom this sign of healing was performed was more than forty years old.

23 When they were released they went to their friends and reported what the chief priests and the elders had said to them. [24]And when they heard it, they lifted their voices together to God and said, "Sovereign Lord, who didst make the heaven and the earth and the sea and everything in them, [25]who by the mouth of our father David, thy servant,ᶜ didst say by the Holy Spirit,

'Why did the Gentiles rage,
and the peoples imagine vain things?

ᶜ Or child

Ἰησοῦ.   19 ὁ   δὲ   Πέτρος   καὶ   Ἰωάννης
of Jesus.   – But   Peter   and   John
ἀποκριθέντες   εἶπον   πρὸς   αὐτούς·   εἰ
answering   said   to   them :   If
δίκαιόν   ἐστιν   ἐνώπιον   τοῦ   θεοῦ,   ὑμῶν
right   it is   before   –   God,   you
ἀκούειν   μᾶλλον   ἢ   τοῦ   θεοῦ,   κρίνατε·
to hear   rather   than   –   God,   decide ye;
20 οὐ   δυνάμεθα   γὰρ   ἡμεῖς   ἃ   εἴδαμεν
for cannot   we   [the] things which   we saw
καὶ   ἠκούσαμεν   μὴ   λαλεῖν.   21 οἱ   δὲ
and   heard   not   to speak.   And they
προσαπειλησάμενοι   ἀπέλυσαν   αὐτούς,   μηδὲν
having added threats   released   them,   nothing
εὑρίσκοντες   τὸ   πῶς   κολάσωνται   αὐτούς,
finding   –   how   they might punish   them,
διὰ   τὸν   λαόν,   ὅτι   πάντες   ἐδόξαζον   τὸν
because of   the   people, because   all men   glorified   –
θεὸν   ἐπὶ   τῷ   γεγονότι·   22 ἐτῶν   γὰρ
God   on   the thing having happened;   for of years
ἦν   πλειόνων   τεσσεράκοντα   ὁ   ἄνθρωπος
was   more [than]   forty   the   man
ἐφ'   ὃν   γεγόνει   τὸ   σημεῖον   τοῦτο   τῆς
on   whom   had happened   this sign   of
ἰάσεως.   23 Ἀπολυθέντες   δὲ   ἦλθον   πρὸς
of cure.   And being released   they went   to
τοὺς   ἰδίους   καὶ   ἀπήγγειλαν   ὅσα   πρὸς
the(ir) own [people]   and   reported   what things   to
αὐτοὺς   οἱ   ἀρχιερεῖς   καὶ   οἱ   πρεσβύτεροι
them   the   chief priests   and   the   elders
εἶπαν.   24 οἱ   δὲ   ἀκούσαντες   ὁμοθυμαδὸν
said.   And they   having heard   with one mind
ἦραν   φωνὴν   πρὸς   τὸν   θεὸν   καὶ   εἶπαν·
lifted   voice   to   –   God   and   said :
δέσποτα,   σὺ   ὁ   ποιήσας   τὸν   οὐρανὸν   καὶ
Master,   thou the [one] having made   the   heaven   and
τὴν   γῆν   καὶ   τὴν   θάλασσαν   καὶ   πάντα
the   earth   and   the   sea   and   all things
τὰ   ἐν   αὐτοῖς,   25 ὁ   τοῦ   πατρὸς   ἡμῶν
–   in   them,   ¹the   ⁸the   ⁹father   ¹⁰of us
                                [one]
διὰ   πνεύματος   ἁγίου   στόματος   Δαυὶδ
²through   ⁵[the] Spirit   ⁴Holy   ⁶[by] mouth   ⁷of David
παιδός   σου   εἰπών·   ἱνατί   ἐφρύαξαν   ἔθνη
¹¹servant   ¹²of thee   ³saying :*   Why   raged   nations
καὶ   λαοὶ   ἐμελέτησαν   κενά;   26 παρέστησαν
and   peoples   devised   vain things?   came

* It is recognized that there is a primitive error in the text in the first half of ver. 25; it is impossible to construe it as it stands. See ch. 1. 16.

26 The kings of the earth set themselves in array, and the rulers were gathered together, against the Lord and against his Anointed'ᵈ— 27 for truly in this city there were gathered together against thy holy servantᶜ Jesus, whom thou didst anoint, both Herod and Pontius Pilate, with the Gentiles and the peoples of Israel, 28 to do whatever thy hand and thy plan had predestined to take place. 29 And now, Lord, look upon their threats, and grant to thy servants to speak thy word with all boldness, 30 while thou stretchest out thy hand to heal, and signs and wonders are performed through the name of thy holy servantᶜ Jesus." 31 And when they had prayed, the place in which they were gathered together was shaken; and they were all filled with the Holy Spirit and spoke the word of God with boldness.

32 Now the company of those who believed were of one heart and soul, and no one said that any of the things which he possessed was his own, but they had everything in common.

ᵈ Or Christ

ᶜ Or child

οἱ βασιλεῖς τῆς γῆς καὶ οἱ ἄρχοντες
the kings of the earth and the rulers
συνήχθησαν ἐπὶ τὸ αὐτὸ κατὰ τοῦ κυρίου
assembled together against the Lord
καὶ κατὰ τοῦ χριστοῦ αὐτοῦ.
and against the Christ of him.
27 συνήχθησαν γὰρ ἐπ' ἀληθείας ἐν τῇ
For assembled in truth in the
πόλει ταύτῃ ἐπὶ τὸν ἅγιον παῖδά σου
city this against the holy servant of thee
'Ἰησοῦν, ὃν ἔχρισας, 'Ἡρῴδης τε καὶ
Jesus, whom thou didst anoint, both Herod and
Πόντιος Πιλᾶτος σὺν ἔθνεσιν καὶ λαοῖς
Pontius Pilate with nations and peoples
'Ἰσραήλ, 28 ποιῆσαι ὅσα ἡ χείρ σου καὶ
of Israel, to do what the hand of thee and
things
ἡ βουλὴ προώρισεν γενέσθαι. 29 καὶ τὰ
the counsel foreordained to happen. And –
νῦν, κύριε, ἔπιδε ἐπὶ τὰς ἀπειλὰς αὐτῶν,
now, Lord, look on on the threatenings of them,
καὶ δὸς τοῖς δούλοις σου μετὰ παρρησίας
and give to the slaves of thee with ²boldness
πάσης λαλεῖν τὸν λόγον σου, 30 ἐν τῷ
¹all to speak the word of thee, by the
τὴν χεῖρα ἐκτείνειν σε εἰς ἴασιν καὶ
the hand to stretch forth theeᵇ for cure and
=by stretching forth thy hand
σημεῖα καὶ τέρατα γίνεσθαι διὰ τοῦ
signs and wonders to happen through the
ὀνόματος τοῦ ἁγίου παιδός σου 'Ἰησοῦ.
name of the holy servant of thee Jesus.
31 καὶ δεηθέντων αὐτῶν ἐσαλεύθη ὁ τόπος
And requesting themᵃ was shaken the place
=as they were making request
ἐν ᾧ ἦσαν συνηγμένοι, καὶ ἐπλήσθησαν
in which they were having been and they were filled
assembled,
ἅπαντες τοῦ ἁγίου πνεύματος, καὶ ἐλάλουν
all of(with) the Holy Spirit, and spoke
τὸν λόγον τοῦ θεοῦ μετὰ παρρησίας.
the word – of God with boldness.
32 Τοῦ δὲ πλήθους τῶν πιστευσάντων
¹Now ⁶of ⁷the ⁸multitude ⁹of the [ones] ¹⁰having believed
ἦν καρδία καὶ ψυχὴ μία, καὶ οὐδὲ
¹¹was ²[the] ³heart ⁴and ⁵soul ¹²one, and ¹not
εἷς τι τῶν ὑπαρχόντων αὐτῷ ἔλεγεν
²one ⁴any- ⁵of the ⁶possessions [belonging] ³said
thing ⁷to him⁶
ἴδιον εἶναι, ἀλλ' ἦν αὐτοῖς πάντα κοινά.
⁹[his] own ⁸to be, but were to themᶜ all things common.

³³And with great power the apostles gave their testimony to the resurrection of the Lord Jesus, and great grace was upon them all. ³⁴There was not a needy person among them, for as many as were possessors of lands or houses sold them, and brought the proceeds of what was sold ³⁵and laid it at the apostles' feet; and distribution was made to each as any had need. ³⁶Thus Joseph who was surnamed by the apostles Barnabas (which means, Son of encouragement), a Levite, a native of Cyprus, ³⁷sold a field which belonged to him, and brought the money and laid it at the apostles' feet.

33 καὶ δυνάμει μεγάλῃ ἀπεδίδουν τὸ
And ¹with ³power ²great ⁶gave ⁷the
μαρτύριον οἱ ἀπόστολοι τοῦ κυρίου Ἰησοῦ
⁵testimony ⁴the ⁵apostles ¹¹of the ¹²Lord ¹³Jesus
τῆς ἀναστάσεως, χάρις τε μεγάλη ἦν
⁹of the ¹⁰resurrection, and ²grace ¹great was
ἐπὶ πάντας αὐτούς. 34 οὐδὲ γὰρ ἐνδεής
upon all them. ¹For ²neither ⁵needy
τις ἦν ἐν αὐτοῖς· ὅσοι γὰρ κτήτορες
⁴anyone ³was among them; for as many as owners
χωρίων ἢ οἰκιῶν ὑπῆρχον, πωλοῦντες
of lands or of houses were, selling
ἔφερον τὰς τιμὰς τῶν πιπρασκομένων
brought the prices of the things being sold
35 καὶ ἐτίθουν παρὰ τοὺς πόδας τῶν
and placed at the feet of the
ἀποστόλων· διεδίδοτο δὲ ἑκάστῳ καθότι ἄν
apostles; and it was distributed to each according as
τις χρείαν εἶχεν. 36 Ἰωσὴφ δὲ ὁ
anyone need had. And Joseph the[one]
ἐπικληθεὶς Βαρναβᾶς ἀπὸ τῶν ἀποστόλων,
surnamed Barnabas from(by) the apostles,
ὅ ἐστιν μεθερμηνευόμενον υἱὸς παρακλήσεως,
which is being translated Son of consolation,
Λευίτης, Κύπριος τῷ γένει, 37 ὑπάρχοντος
a Levite, a Cypriote – by race, being
αὐτῷ ἀγροῦ, πωλήσας ἤνεγκεν τὸ χρῆμα
to him⁶ a field,ᵃ having sold [it] brought the proceeds
=as he had a field,
καὶ ἔθηκεν πρὸς τοὺς πόδας τῶν ἀποστόλων.
and placed at the feet of the apostles.

CHAPTER 5

BUT a man named Anani′as with his wife Sapphi′ra sold a piece of property, ²and with his wife's knowledge he kept back some of the proceeds, and brought only a part and laid it at the apostles' feet. ³But Peter said, "Anani′as, why has Satan filled your heart to lie to

5 Ἀνὴρ δέ τις Ἀνανίας ὀνόματι σὺν
And a certain man Ananias* by name with
Σαπφίρῃ τῇ γυναικὶ αὐτοῦ ἐπώλησεν
Sapphira the wife of him sold
κτῆμα, 2 καὶ ἐνοσφίσατο ἀπὸ τῆς τιμῆς,
a property, and appropriated from the price,
συνειδυίης καὶ τῆς γυναικός, καὶ ἐνέγκας
aware of [it] also the(his) wife,ᵃ and bringing
=his wife also being aware of it,
μέρος τι παρὰ τοὺς πόδας τῶν ἀποστόλων
a certain part at the feet of the apostles
ἔθηκεν. 3 εἶπεν δὲ ὁ Πέτρος· Ἀνανία,
placed [it]. But said – Peter : Ananias,
διὰ τί ἐπλήρωσεν ὁ σατανᾶς τὴν καρδίαν
why filled – Satan the heart

* See note to 4. 6.

the Holy Spirit and to keep back part of the proceeds of the land? ⁴While it remained unsold, did it not remain your own? And after it was sold, was it not at your disposal? How is it that you have contrived this deed in your heart? You have not lied to men but to God." ⁵When Anani′as heard these words, he fell down and died. And great fear came upon all who heard of it. ⁶The young men rose and wrapped him up and carried him out and buried him.

7 After an interval of about three hours his wife came in, not knowing what had happened. ⁸And Peter said to her, "Tell me whether you sold the land for so much." And she said, "Yes, for so much." ⁹But Peter said to her, "How is it that you have agreed together to tempt the Spirit of the Lord? Hark, the feet of those that have buried your husband are at the door, and they will carry you out." ¹⁰Immediately she fell down at his feet and died. When the young men came in they found her dead, and they carried

σου, ψεύσασθαί σε τὸ πνεῦμα τὸ ἅγιον
of thee, to deceive thee[b] the Spirit – Holy
=that thou shouldest deceive

καὶ νοσφίσασθαι ἀπὸ τῆς τιμῆς τοῦ
and to appropriate from the price of the

χωρίου; 4 οὐχὶ μένον σοὶ ἔμενεν καὶ
land? Not remaining to thee it remained and

πραθὲν ἐν τῇ σῇ ἐξουσίᾳ ὑπῆρχεν; τί ὅτι
sold in – thy authority it was? Why

ἔθου ἐν τῇ καρδίᾳ σου τὸ πρᾶγμα
was put in the heart of thee – action

τοῦτο; οὐκ ἐψεύσω ἀνθρώποις ἀλλὰ
this? thou didst not lie to men but

τῷ θεῷ. 5 ἀκούων δὲ ὁ Ἀνανίας
– to God. And hearing Ananias

τοὺς λόγους τούτους πεσὼν ἐξέψυξεν· καὶ
these words falling expired; and

ἐγένετο φόβος μέγας ἐπὶ πάντας τοὺς
came fear great on all the [ones]

ἀκούοντας. 6 ἀναστάντες δὲ οἱ νεώτεροι
hearing. And rising up the young men

συνέστειλαν αὐτὸν καὶ ἐξενέγκαντες ἔθαψαν.
wrapped him and carrying out buried [him].

7 Ἐγένετο δὲ ὡς ὡρῶν τριῶν διάστημα
¹And there was ³of about ⁵hours ⁴three ²an interval

καὶ ἡ γυνὴ αὐτοῦ μὴ εἰδυῖα τὸ γεγονὸς
and the wife of him not knowing the thing having
happened

εἰσῆλθεν. 8 ἀπεκρίθη δὲ πρὸς αὐτὴν
entered. And answered to her

Πέτρος· εἰπέ μοι, εἰ τοσούτου τὸ χωρίον
Peter : Tell me, if of(for) so much the land

ἀπέδοσθε; ἡ δὲ εἶπεν· ναί, τοσούτου.
ye sold? And she said : Yes, of(for) so much.

9 ὁ δὲ Πέτρος πρὸς αὐτήν· τί ὅτι
– And Peter to her : Why

συνεφωνήθη ὑμῖν πειράσαι τὸ πνεῦμα
was it agreed with you to tempt the Spirit

κυρίου; ἰδοὺ οἱ πόδες τῶν θαψάντων τὸν
of [the] behold[,] the feet of the [ones] having the
Lord? buried

ἄνδρα σου ἐπὶ τῇ θύρᾳ καὶ ἐξοίσουσίν
husband of thee at the door and they will
carry out

σε. 10 ἔπεσεν δὲ παραχρῆμα πρὸς τοὺς
thee. And she fell at once at the

πόδας αὐτοῦ καὶ ἐξέψυξεν· εἰσελθόντες δὲ
feet of him and expired; and entering

οἱ νεανίσκοι εὗρον αὐτὴν νεκράν, καὶ
the young men found her dead, and

her out and buried her beside her husband. [11]And great fear came upon the whole church, and upon all who heard of these things. 12 Now many signs and wonders were done among the people by the hands of the apostles. And they were all together in Solomon's Portico. [13]None of the rest dared join them, but the people held them in high honor. [14]And more than ever believers were added to the Lord, multitudes both of men and women, [15]so that they even carried out the sick into the streets, and laid them on beds and pallets, that as Peter came by at least his shadow might fall on some of them. [16]The people also gathered from the towns around Jerusalem, bringing the sick and those afflicted with unclean spirits, and they were all healed.

17 But the high priest rose up and all who were with him, that is, the party of the Sad'ducees, and filled with jealousy [18]they arrested the

ἐξενέγκαντες ἔθαψαν πρὸς τὸν ἄνδρα
carrying out buried [her] beside the husband

αὐτῆς. 11 Καὶ ἐγένετο φόβος μέγας
of her. And came fear great

ἐφ᾽ ὅλην τὴν ἐκκλησίαν καὶ ἐπὶ πάντας
on all the church and on all

τοὺς ἀκούοντας ταῦτα.
the [ones] hearing these things.

12 Διὰ δὲ τῶν χειρῶν τῶν ἀποστόλων
And through the hands of the apostles

ἐγίνετο σημεῖα καὶ τέρατα πολλὰ ἐν
[5]happened [2]signs [3]and [4]wonders [1]many among

τῷ λαῷ· καὶ ἦσαν ὁμοθυμαδὸν πάντες
the people; and were with one mind all

ἐν τῇ στοᾷ Σολομῶντος· 13 τῶν δὲ
in the porch of Solomon; and of the

λοιπῶν οὐδεὶς ἐτόλμα κολλᾶσθαι αὐτοῖς,
rest no one dared to be joined to them,

ἀλλ᾽ ἐμεγάλυνεν αὐτοὺς ὁ λαός· 14 μᾶλλον
but magnified them the people; [2]more

δὲ προσετίθεντο πιστεύοντες τῷ κυρίῳ,
[1]and were added believing [ones] to the Lord,

πλήθη ἀνδρῶν τε καὶ γυναικῶν· 15 ὥστε
multitudes both of men and of women; so as

καὶ εἰς τὰς πλατείας ἐκφέρειν τοὺς
even into the streets to bring out the
=they brought out

ἀσθενεῖς καὶ τιθέναι ἐπὶ κλιναρίων καὶ
ailing and to place on pallets and

κραβάτων, ἵνα ἐρχομένου Πέτρου κἂν ἡ σκιὰ
mattresses, that [5]coming [4]of Peter [1]if even [2]the [3]shadow

ἐπισκιάσῃ τινὶ αὐτῶν. 16 συνήρχετο δὲ
might overshadow some one of them. And came together

καὶ τὸ πλῆθος τῶν πέριξ πόλεων
also the multitude of the [2]round about [1]cities

Ἰερουσαλήμ, φέροντες ἀσθενεῖς καὶ
Jerusalem, carrying ailing [ones] and

ὀχλουμένους ὑπὸ πνευμάτων ἀκαθάρτων,
being tormented by spirits unclean,

οἵτινες ἐθεραπεύοντο ἅπαντες.
who were healed all.

17 Ἀναστὰς δὲ ὁ ἀρχιερεὺς καὶ πάντες
And rising up the high priest and all

οἱ σὺν αὐτῷ, ἡ οὖσα αἵρεσις τῶν
the[ones] with him, the existing sect of the

Σαδδουκαίων, ἐπλήσθησαν ζήλου 18 καὶ
Sadducees, were filled of(with) jealousy and

ἐπέβαλον τὰς χεῖρας ἐπὶ τοὺς ἀποστόλους
laid on the(ir) hands on the apostles

apostles and put them in the common prison. ¹⁹But at night an angel of the Lord opened the prison doors and brought them out and said, ²⁰ "Go and stand in the temple and speak to the people all the words of this Life." ²¹And when they heard this, they entered the temple at daybreak and taught.

Now the high priest came and those who were with him and called together the council and all the senate of Israel, and sent to the prison to have them brought. ²²But when the officers came, they did not find them in the prison, and they returned and reported, ²³ "We found the prison securely locked and the sentries standing at the doors, but when we opened it we found no one inside." ²⁴Now when the captain of the temple and the chief priests heard these words, they were much perplexed about them, wondering what this would come to. ²⁵And some one came and told them, "The men whom you put in prison are standing in the temple

καὶ ἔθεντο αὐτοὺς ἐν τηρήσει δημοσίᾳ.
and put them in custody publicly.

19 Ἄγγελος δὲ κυρίου διὰ νυκτὸς
But an angel of [the] Lord through(during) [the] night

ἤνοιξε τὰς θύρας τῆς φυλακῆς ἐξαγαγών τε
opened the doors of the prison and leading out

αὐτοὺς εἶπεν· 20 πορεύεσθε καὶ σταθέντες
them said: Go ye and standing

λαλεῖτε ἐν τῷ ἱερῷ τῷ λαῷ πάντα
speak in the temple to the people all

τὰ ῥήματα τῆς ζωῆς ταύτης.
the words of this life.

21 ἀκούσαντες δὲ εἰσῆλθον ὑπὸ τὸν ὄρθρον
And having heard they entered about the dawn

εἰς τὸ ἱερὸν καὶ ἐδίδασκον. Παραγενόμενος δὲ
into the temple and taught. And having come

ὁ ἀρχιερεὺς καὶ οἱ σὺν αὐτῷ
the high priest and the [ones] with him

συνεκάλεσαν τὸ συνέδριον καὶ πᾶσαν τὴν
called together the council and all the

γερουσίαν τῶν υἱῶν Ἰσραήλ, καὶ ἀπέστειλαν
senate of the sons of Israel, and sent

εἰς τὸ δεσμωτήριον ἀχθῆναι αὐτούς.ᵇ
to the jail to be brought them.

22 οἱ δὲ παραγενόμενοι ὑπηρέται οὐχ εὗρον
¹But ²the ⁴having come ³attendants found not

αὐτοὺς ἐν τῇ φυλακῇ· ἀναστρέψαντες δὲ
them in the prison; and having returned

ἀπήγγειλαν 23 λέγοντες ὅτι τὸ δεσμωτήριον
they reported saying[,] – The jail

εὕρομεν κεκλεισμένον ἐν πάσῃ ἀσφαλείᾳ
we found having been shut in all security

καὶ τοὺς φύλακας ἑστῶτας ἐπὶ τῶν
and the guards standing at the

θυρῶν, ἀνοίξαντες δὲ ἔσω οὐδένα εὕρομεν.
doors, but having opened ³inside ²no one ¹we found.

24 ὡς δὲ ἤκουσαν τοὺς λόγους τούτους
And as ⁹heard ¹⁰these ¹¹words

ὅ τε στρατηγὸς τοῦ ἱεροῦ καὶ οἱ ἀρχιερεῖς,
²the ¹both ³commandant ⁴of the ⁵temple ⁶and ⁷the ⁸chief priests,

διηπόρουν περὶ αὐτῶν τί ἂν γένοιτο
they were in doubt about them what ²might become

τοῦτο. 25 παραγενόμενος δέ τις ἀπήγγειλεν
¹this thing. And having come someone reported

αὐτοῖς ὅτι ἰδοὺ οἱ ἄνδρες, οὓς
to them[,] – Behold[,] the men, whom

ἔθεσθε ἐν τῇ φυλακῇ, εἰσὶν ἐν τῷ ἱερῷ
ye put in the prison, are in the temple

and teaching the people."
26 Then the captain with the officers went and brought them, but without violence, for they were afraid of being stoned by the people.
27 And when they had brought them, they set them before the council. And the high priest questioned them, 28 saying, "We strictly charged you not to teach in this name, yet here you have filled Jerusalem with your teaching and you intend to bring this man's blood upon us." 29 But Peter and the apostles answered, "We must obey God rather than men. 30 The God of our fathers raised Jesus whom you killed by hanging him on a tree. 31 God exalted him at his right hand as Leader and Savior, to give repentance to Israel and forgiveness of sins. 32 And we are witnesses to these things, and so is the Holy Spirit whom God has given to those who obey him."
33 When they heard

ἑστῶτες καὶ διδάσκοντες τὸν λαόν.
standing and teaching the people.

26 Τότε ἀπελθὼν ὁ στρατηγὸς σὺν τοῖς
Then going the commandant with the

ὑπηρέταις ἦγεν αὐτούς, οὐ μετὰ βίας,
attendants brought them, not with force,

ἐφοβοῦντο γὰρ τὸν λαόν, μὴ λιθασθῶσιν·
for they feared the people, lest they should be stoned;

27 ἀγαγόντες δὲ αὐτοὺς ἔστησαν ἐν τῷ
and bringing them they stood in the

συνεδρίῳ. καὶ ἐπηρώτησεν αὐτοὺς ὁ
council. And questioned them the

ἀρχιερεὺς 28 λέγων· παραγγελίᾳ παρηγ-
high priest saying : With charge we
=We strictly

γείλαμεν ὑμῖν μὴ διδάσκειν ἐπὶ
charged you not to teach on(in)

τῷ ὀνόματι τούτῳ, καὶ ἰδοὺ πεπληρώκατε
this name, and behold ye have filled

τὴν Ἰερουσαλὴμ τῆς διδαχῆς ὑμῶν, καὶ
– Jerusalem of(with) the teaching of you, and

βούλεσθε ἐπαγαγεῖν ἐφ᾽ ἡμᾶς τὸ αἷμα
intend to bring on on us the blood

τοῦ ἀνθρώπου τούτου. 29 ἀποκριθεὶς δὲ
of this man. And answering

Πέτρος καὶ οἱ ἀπόστολοι εἶπαν· πειθαρχεῖν
Peter and the apostles said : ¹to obey

δεῖ θεῷ μᾶλλον ἢ ἀνθρώποις. 30 ὁ
¹It behoves God rather than men. The

θεὸς τῶν πατέρων ἡμῶν ἤγειρεν Ἰησοῦν,
God of the fathers of us raised Jesus,

ὃν ὑμεῖς διεχειρίσασθε κρεμάσαντες ἐπὶ
whom ye killed hanging on

ξύλου· 31 τοῦτον ὁ θεὸς ἀρχηγὸν καὶ
a tree; this man – God a Ruler and

σωτῆρα ὕψωσεν τῇ δεξιᾷ αὐτοῦ τοῦ
a Saviour exalted to the right [hand] of him –

δοῦναι μετάνοιαν τῷ Ἰσραὴλ καὶ ἄφεσιν
to give[d] repentance – to Israel and forgiveness

ἁμαρτιῶν. 32 καὶ ἡμεῖς ἐσμεν μάρτυρες
of sins. And we are witnesses

τῶν ῥημάτων τούτων, καὶ τὸ πνεῦμα
of these words(things), and the Spirit

τὸ ἅγιον ὃ ἔδωκεν ὁ θεὸς τοῖς
– Holy which ²gave – ¹God to the

πειθαρχοῦσιν αὐτῷ. 33 οἱ δὲ ἀκούσαντες
[ones] obeying him. And the [ones] hearing

this they were enraged and wanted to kill them. ³⁴But a Pharisee in the council named Gama'liel, a teacher of the law, held in honor by all the people, stood up and ordered the men to be put outside for a while. ³⁵And he said to them, "Men of Israel, take care what you do with these men. ³⁶For before these days Theu'das arose, giving himself out to be somebody, and a number of men, about four hundred, joined him; but he was slain and all who followed him were dispersed and came to nothing. ³⁷After him Judas the Galilean arose in the days of the census and drew away some of the people after him; he also perished, and all who followed him were scattered. ³⁸So in the present case I tell you, keep away from these men and let them alone; for if this plan or this undertaking is of men, it will fail; ³⁹but if it is of God, you will not be able to overthrow them. You

διεπρίοντο καὶ ἐβούλοντο ἀνελεῖν αὐτούς.
were cut* and intended to kill them.

34 Ἀναστὰς δέ τις ἐν τῷ συνεδρίῳ
¹But ⁴standing up ²a certain ⁵in ⁶the ⁷council

Φαρισαῖος ὀνόματι Γαμαλιήλ, νομοδιδάσκαλος
³Pharisee by name Gamaliel, a teacher of the law

τίμιος παντὶ τῷ λαῷ, ἐκέλευσεν ἔξω
honoured by all the people, commanded ⁴outside

βραχὺ τοὺς ἀνθρώπους ποιῆσαι, 35 εἰπέν
³a little ²the ³men ¹to make(put), ²said

τε πρὸς αὐτούς· ἄνδρες Ἰσραηλῖται,
¹and to them: Men Israelites,

προσέχετε ἑαυτοῖς ἐπὶ τοῖς ἀνθρώποις τούτοις
take heed to yourselves ⁴on(to) ⁵these ⁶men

τί μέλλετε πράσσειν. 36 πρὸ γὰρ
¹what ²ye intend ³to do. For before

τούτων τῶν ἡμερῶν ἀνέστη Θευδᾶς, λέγων
these – days stood up Theudas, saying

εἶναί τινα ἑαυτόν, ᾧ προσεκλίθη ἀνδρῶν
to be someone himself, ¹to whom ⁶were attached ³of men

ἀριθμὸς ὡς τετρακοσίων· ὃς ἀνῃρέθη, καὶ
²a number ⁴about ⁵four hundreds; who was killed, and

πάντες ὅσοι ἐπείθοντο αὐτῷ διελύθησαν
all as many as obeyed him were dispersed

καὶ ἐγένοντο εἰς οὐδέν. 37 μετὰ τοῦτον
and came to nothing. After this

ἀνέστη Ἰούδας ὁ Γαλιλαῖος ἐν ταῖς
stood up Judas the Galilæan in the

ἡμέραις τῆς ἀπογραφῆς καὶ ἀπέστησεν
days of the enrolment and drew away

λαὸν ὀπίσω αὐτοῦ· κἀκεῖνος ἀπώλετο,
people after him; and that man perished,

καὶ πάντες ὅσοι ἐπείθοντο αὐτῷ
and all as many as obeyed him

διεσκορπίσθησαν. 38 καὶ τὰ νῦν λέγω
were scattered. And – now I say

ὑμῖν, ἀπόστητε ἀπὸ τῶν ἀνθρώπων τούτων
to you, stand away from these men

καὶ ἄφετε αὐτούς· ὅτι ἐὰν ᾖ ἐξ ἀνθρώπων
and leave them; because if be of men

ἡ βουλὴ αὕτη ἢ τὸ ἔργον τοῦτο,
this counsel or this work,

καταλυθήσεται· 39 εἰ δὲ ἐκ θεοῦ ἐστιν,
it will be destroyed; but if of God it is,

οὐ δυνήσεσθε καταλῦσαι αὐτούς, μήποτε
ye will not be able to destroy them, lest

* That is, to the heart; cf. 7. 54.

might even be found
opposing God!"
40 So they took his
advice, and when they
had called in the apostles,
they beat them and
charged them not to
speak in the name of
Jesus, and let them go.
⁴¹Then they left the
presence of the council,
rejoicing that they were
counted worthy to suffer
dishonor for the name.
⁴²And every day in the
temple and at home they
did not cease teaching
and preaching Jesus as
the Christ.

καὶ   θεομάχοι   εὑρεθῆτε.   ἐπείσθησαν   δὲ
even   fighters against God   ye be found.   And they obeyed
αὐτῷ,   40 καὶ   προσκαλεσάμενοι   τοὺς
him,   and   having called to [them]   the
ἀποστόλους   δείραντες   παρήγγειλαν   μὴ
apostles   beating   charged   not
λαλεῖν   ἐπὶ   τῷ   ὀνόματι   τοῦ   Ἰησοῦ   καὶ
to speak on(in) the   name   -   of Jesus   and
ἀπέλυσαν.   41 Οἱ   μὲν   οὖν   ἐπορεύοντο
released [them].   They   -   therefore   went
χαίροντες   ἀπὸ   προσώπου   τοῦ   συνεδρίου,
rejoicing   from [the]   presence   of the   council,
ὅτι   κατηξιώθησαν   ὑπὲρ   τοῦ   ὀνόματος
because   they were deemed worthy on behalf of the   name
ἀτιμασθῆναι·   42 πᾶσάν   τε   ἡμέραν   ἐν   τῷ
to be dishonoured;   and every   day   in   the
ἱερῷ   καὶ   κατ'   οἶκον   οὐκ   ἐπαύοντο
temple   and   from house to house†   they ceased not
διδάσκοντες   καὶ   εὐαγγελιζόμενοι   τὸν   χριστὸν
teaching   and   preaching   the   Christ
Ἰησοῦν.
Jesus.

CHAPTER 6

NOW in these days
when the disciples
were increasing in
number, the Hellenists
murmured against the
Hebrews because their
widows were neglected in
the daily distribution.
²And the twelve sum-
moned the body of the
disciples and said, "It is
not right that we should
give up preaching the
word of God to serve
tables. ³Therefore, brethren, pick out from among
you seven men of good
repute, full of the Spirit
and of wisdom, whom
we may appoint to this

6 Ἐν   δὲ   ταῖς   ἡμέραις   ταύταις
   Now in   these days
πληθυνόντων   τῶν   μαθητῶν   ἐγένετο
being multiplied   the   disciplesᵃ   there was
=as the disciples were multiplied
γογγυσμὸς   τῶν   Ἑλληνιστῶν   πρὸς   τοὺς
a murmuring   of the   Hellenists   against   the
Ἐβραίους,   ὅτι   παρεθεωροῦντο   ἐν   τῇ
Hebrews,   because   ⁴were overlooked   ⁵in   ⁶the
διακονίᾳ   τῇ   καθημερινῇ   αἱ   χῆραι   αὐτῶν.
⁸service   -   ⁷daily   ¹the ²widows ³of them.
2 προσκαλεσάμενοι   δὲ   οἱ   δώδεκα   τὸ
⁴having called to [them]   ¹And   ²the   ³twelve   the
πλῆθος   τῶν   μαθητῶν   εἶπαν·   οὐκ   ἀρεστόν
multitude   of the   disciples   said :   not   pleasing
ἔστιν   ἡμᾶς   καταλείψαντας   τὸν   λόγον   τοῦ
It is   us   leaving   the   word   -
θεοῦ   διακονεῖν   τραπέζαις.   3 ἐπισκέψασθε
of God   to serve   tables.   look ye out
δέ,   ἀδελφοί,   ἄνδρας   ἐξ   ὑμῶν   μαρτυρουμένους
But,   brothers,   ²men   ³of   ⁴you   ⁵being witnessed to
ἑπτὰ   πλήρεις   πνεύματος   καὶ   σοφίας,   οὓς
¹seven   [as] full   of Spirit   and   of wisdom, whom
καταστήσομεν   ἐπὶ   τῆς   χρείας   ταύτης·
we will appoint   over   this office;

duty. ⁴But we will devote ourselves to prayer and to the ministry of the word." ⁵And what they said pleased the whole multitude, and they chose Stephen, a man full of faith and of the Holy Spirit, and Philip, and Proch'orus, and Nica'nor, and Timon, and Par'menas, and Nicola'us, a proselyte of Antioch. ⁶These they set before the apostles, and they prayed and laid their hands upon them.

7 And the word of God increased; and the number of the disciples multiplied greatly in Jerusalem, and a great many of the priests were obedient to the faith.

8 And Stephen, full of grace and power, did great wonders and signs among the people. ⁹Then some of those who belonged to the synagogue of the Freedmen (as it was called), and of the Cyre'nians, and of the Alexandrians, and of those from Cili'cia and Asia, arose and disputed with Stephen. ¹⁰But they could not withstand the wisdom and the Spirit with which he spoke. ¹¹Then they secretly instigated men, who said, "We have heard him

---

4 ἡμεῖς δὲ τῇ προσευχῇ καὶ τῇ διακονίᾳ
   but we   to the   prayer   and   to the   service

τοῦ λόγου προσκαρτερήσομεν. 5 καὶ ἤρεσεν
of the   word   will keep.   And   ³pleased

ὁ λόγος ἐνώπιον παντὸς τοῦ πλήθους,
¹the   ²word   before   all   the   multitude,

καὶ ἐξελέξαντο Στέφανον, ἄνδρα πλήρη
and   they chose   Stephen,   a man   full

πίστεως καὶ πνεύματος ἁγίου, καὶ Φίλιππον
of faith   and   Spirit   of Holy,   and   Philip

καὶ Πρόχορον καὶ Νικάνορα καὶ Τίμωνα
and   Prochorus   and   Nicanor   and   Timon

καὶ Παρμενᾶν καὶ Νικόλαον προσήλυτον
and   Parmenas   and   Nicolaus   a proselyte

Ἀντιοχέα, 6 οὓς ἔστησαν ἐνώπιον τῶν
of Antioch,   whom   they set   before   the

ἀποστόλων, καὶ προσευξάμενοι ἐπέθηκαν
apostles,   and   having prayed   they placed on

αὐτοῖς τὰς χεῖρας.
them   the(ir)   hands.

7 Καὶ ὁ λόγος τοῦ θεοῦ ηὔξανεν, καὶ
  And the   word   –   of God   grew,   and

ἐπληθύνετο ὁ ἀριθμὸς τῶν μαθητῶν ἐν
was multiplied   the   number   of the   disciples   in

Ἰερουσαλὴμ σφόδρα, πολύς τε ὄχλος τῶν
Jerusalem   greatly,   and a much(great) crowd   of the

ἱερέων ὑπήκουον τῇ πίστει.
priests   obeyed   the   faith.

8 Στέφανος δὲ πλήρης χάριτος καὶ
  And Stephen   full   of grace   and

δυνάμεως ἐποίει τέρατα καὶ σημεῖα μεγάλα
of power   did   wonders   and   signs   great

ἐν τῷ λαῷ. 9 ἀνέστησαν δέ τινες τῶν
among the   people.   But rose up   some   of the

ἐκ τῆς συναγωγῆς τῆς λεγομένης
of   the   synagogue   –   being called

Λιβερτίνων καὶ Κυρηναίων καὶ Ἀλεξ-
of Freedmen   and   of Cyrenians   and   of

ανδρέων καὶ τῶν ἀπὸ Κιλικίας καὶ
Alexandrians   and   of the [ones]   from   Cilicia   and

Ἀσίας συζητοῦντες τῷ Στεφάνῳ, 10 καὶ
Asia   discussing   –   with Stephen,   and

οὐκ ἴσχυον ἀντιστῆναι τῇ σοφίᾳ καὶ
were not able   to withstand   the   wisdom   and

τῷ πνεύματι ᾧ ἐλάλει. 11 τότε ὑπέβαλον
the   spirit   with which he spoke.   Then   they suborned

ἄνδρας λέγοντας ὅτι ἀκηκόαμεν αὐτοῦ
men   saying[,]   –   We have heard   him

speak blasphemous
words against Moses and
God." ¹²And they stirred
up the people and the
elders and the scribes,
and they came upon him
and seized him and
brought him before the
council, ¹³and set up false
witnesses who said, "This
man never ceases to
speak words against this
holy place and the law;
¹⁴for we have heard him
say that this Jesus of
Nazareth will destroy
this place, and will
change the customs which
Moses delivered to us."
¹⁵And gazing at him, all
who sat in the council
saw that his face was like
the face of an angel.

λαλοῦντος   ῥήματα   βλάσφημα   εἰς   Μωϋσῆν
speaking   words   blasphemous   against   Moses
καὶ   τὸν   θεόν·   12 συνεκίνησάν   τε   τὸν
and   –   God;   and they stirred up   the
λαὸν   καὶ   τοὺς   πρεσβυτέρους   καὶ   τοὺς
people   and   the   elders   and   the
γραμματεῖς,   καὶ   ἐπιστάντες   συνήρπασαν
scribes,   and   coming on   they seized
αὐτὸν   καὶ   ἤγαγον   εἰς   τὸ   συνέδριον,
him   and   led   to   the   council,
13 ἔστησάν   τε   μάρτυρας   ψευδεῖς   λέγοντας·
and stood   witnesses   false   saying :
ὁ   ἄνθρωπος   οὗτος   οὐ   παύεται   λαλῶν
This man   ceases not   speaking
ῥήματα   κατὰ   τοῦ   τόπου   τοῦ   ἁγίου   [τούτου]
words   against   –   ²place   –   ³holy   ¹this
καὶ   τοῦ   νόμου·   14 ἀκηκόαμεν   γὰρ   αὐτοῦ
and   the   law;   for we have heard   him
λέγοντος   ὅτι   Ἰησοῦς   ὁ   Ναζωραῖος   οὗτος
saying   that   ²Jesus   ³the   ⁴Nazarene   ¹this
καταλύσει   τὸν   τόπον   τοῦτον   καὶ   ἀλλάξει
will destroy   this place   and   will change
τὰ   ἔθη   ἃ   παρέδωκεν   ἡμῖν   Μωϋσῆς.
the   customs   which   delivered   to us   Moses.
15 καὶ   ἀτενίσαντες   εἰς   αὐτὸν   πάντες   οἱ
And   gazing   at   him   all   the
καθεζόμενοι   ἐν   τῷ   συνεδρίῳ   εἶδον   τὸ
[ones] sitting   in   the   council   saw   the
πρόσωπον   αὐτοῦ   ὡσεὶ   πρόσωπον   ἀγγέλου.
face   of him   as   a face   of an angel.

CHAPTER 7

AND the high priest
said, "Is this so?"
²And Stephen said:
"Brethren and fathers,
hear me. The God of
glory appeared to our
father Abraham, when
he was in Mesopota′mia,
before he lived in Haran,
³and said to him, 'Depart
from your land and from
your kindred and go into

7 Εἶπεν   δὲ   ὁ   ἀρχιερεύς·   εἰ   ταῦτα
And said   the   high priest :   If   these things
οὕτως   ἔχει;   2 ὁ   δὲ   ἔφη·
thus   have(are)?   And he   said:
Ἄνδρες   ἀδελφοὶ   καὶ   πατέρες,   ἀκούσατε.
Men   brothers   and   fathers,   hear ye.
Ὁ   θεὸς   τῆς   δόξης   ὤφθη   τῷ   πατρὶ
The   God   –   of glory   appeared   to the   father
ἡμῶν   Ἀβραὰμ   ὄντι   ἐν   τῇ   Μεσοποταμίᾳ
of us   Abraham   being   in   –   Mesopotamia
πρὶν   ἢ   κατοικῆσαι   αὐτὸν   ἐν   Χαρράν,
before   to dwell   himᵇ   in   Charran,
                        =he dwelt
3 καὶ   εἶπεν   πρὸς   αὐτόν·   ἔξελθε   ἐκ   τῆς
and   said   to   him :   Go forth   out of   the
γῆς   σου   καὶ   τῆς   συγγενείας   σου,   καὶ
land   of thee   and   the   kindred   of thee,   and

the land which I will show you.' ⁴Then he departed from the land of the Chalde'ans, and lived in Haran. And after his father died, God removed him from there into this land in which you are now living; ⁵yet he gave him no inheritance in it, not even a foot's length, but promised to give it to him in possession and to his posterity after him, though he had no child. ⁶And God spoke to this effect, that his posterity would be aliens in a land belonging to others, who would enslave them and ill-treat them four hundred years. ⁷'But I will judge the nation which they serve,' said God, 'and after that they shall come out and worship me in this place.' ⁸And he gave him the covenant of circumcision. And so Abraham became the father of Isaac, and circumcised him on the eighth day; and Isaac became the father of Jacob, and Jacob of the twelve patriarchs.

9 "And the patriarchs, jealous of Joseph, sold

δεῦρο εἰς τὴν γῆν ἣν ἄν σοι δείξω.
come into the land whichever to thee I may show.

4 τότε ἐξελθὼν ἐκ γῆς Χαλδαίων
Then going forth out of [the] land of [the] Chaldæans

κατώκησεν ἐν Χαρράν. κἀκεῖθεν μετὰ
he dwelt in Charran. And thence after

τὸ ἀποθανεῖν τὸν πατέρα αὐτοῦ μετώκισεν
the to die the father of him[b] [God] removed
=his father died

αὐτὸν εἰς τὴν γῆν ταύτην εἰς ἣν ὑμεῖς
him into this land in which ye

νῦν κατοικεῖτε, 5 καὶ οὐκ ἔδωκεν αὐτῷ
now dwell, and gave not to him

κληρονομίαν ἐν αὐτῇ οὐδὲ βῆμα ποδός,
an inheritance in it nor a foot's space,

καὶ ἐπηγγείλατο δοῦναι αὐτῷ εἰς
and promised to give him for

κατάσχεσιν αὐτὴν καὶ τῷ σπέρματι αὐτοῦ
a possession it and to the seed of him

μετ᾽ αὐτόν, οὐκ ὄντος αὐτῷ τέκνου.
after him, not being to him[c] a child.[a]
=while he had no child.

6 ἐλάλησεν δὲ οὕτως ὁ θεός, ὅτι ἔσται
And spoke thus – God, that will be

τὸ σπέρμα αὐτοῦ πάροικον ἐν γῇ ἀλλοτρίᾳ,
the seed of him a sojourner in a land belonging to
others,

καὶ δουλώσουσιν αὐτὸ καὶ κακώσουσιν
and they will enslave it and will ill-treat

ἔτη τετρακόσια· 7 καὶ τὸ ἔθνος ᾧ ἐὰν
years four hundred; and the nation whichever

δουλεύσουσιν κρινῶ ἐγώ, ὁ θεὸς εἶπεν,
they will serve will judge I, – God said,

καὶ μετὰ ταῦτα ἐξελεύσονται καὶ
and after these things they will come forth and

λατρεύσουσίν μοι ἐν τῷ τόπῳ τούτῳ.
will worship me in this place.

8 καὶ ἔδωκεν αὐτῷ διαθήκην περιτομῆς·
And he gave him a covenant of circumcision;

καὶ οὕτως ἐγέννησεν τὸν Ἰσαὰκ καὶ
and thus he begat – Isaac and

περιέτεμεν αὐτὸν τῇ ἡμέρᾳ τῇ ὀγδόῃ,
circumcised him on the day – eighth,

καὶ Ἰσαὰκ τὸν Ἰακώβ, καὶ Ἰακὼβ
and Isaac [begat] – Jacob, and Jacob [begat]

τοὺς δώδεκα πατριάρχας. 9 Καὶ οἱ
the twelve patriarchs. And the

πατριάρχαι ζηλώσαντες τὸν Ἰωσὴφ
patriarchs becoming jealous – [a]Joseph

him into Egypt; but God was with him, ¹⁰and rescued him out of all his afflictions, and gave him favor and wisdom before Pharaoh, king of Egypt, who made him governor over Egypt and over all his household. ¹¹Now there came a famine throughout all Egypt and Canaan, and great affliction, and our fathers could find no food. ¹²But when Jacob heard that there was grain in Egypt, he sent forth our fathers the first time. ¹³And at the second visit Joseph made himself known to his brothers, and Joseph's family became known to Pharaoh. ¹⁴And Joseph sent and called to him Jacob his father and all his kindred, seventy-five souls; ¹⁵and Jacob went down into Egypt. And he died, himself and our fathers, ¹⁶and they were carried back to Shechem and laid in the tomb that Abraham had bought for a sum of silver from the sons of Hamor in Shechem.

17 "But as the time of

ἀπέδοντο   εἰς   Αἴγυπτον·   καὶ   ἦν   ὁ   θεὸς
¹sold   into   Egypt;   and   was   –   God

μετ᾽   αὐτοῦ,   10 καὶ   ἐξείλατο   αὐτὸν   ἐκ
with   him,   and   rescued   him   out of

πασῶν   τῶν   θλίψεων   αὐτοῦ,   καὶ   ἔδωκεν
all   the   afflictions   of him,   and   gave

αὐτῷ   χάριν   καὶ   σοφίαν   ἐναντίον   Φαραὼ
him   favour   and   wisdom   before   Pharaoh

βασιλέως   Αἰγύπτου,   καὶ   κατέστησεν   αὐτὸν
king   of Egypt,   and   he appointed   him

ἡγούμενον   ἐπ᾽   Αἴγυπτον   καὶ   ὅλον   τὸν
governor   over   Egypt   and   all   the

οἶκον   αὐτοῦ.   11 ἦλθεν   δὲ   λιμὸς   ἐφ᾽
household   of him.   But came   a famine   over

ὅλην   τὴν   Αἴγυπτον   καὶ   Χανάαν   καὶ
all   –   Egypt   and   Canaan   and

θλῖψις   μεγάλη,   καὶ   οὐχ   ηὕρισκον
affliction   great,   and   found not

χορτάσματα   οἱ   πατέρες   ἡμῶν.   12 ἀκούσας
sustenance   the   fathers   of us.   ³having heard

δὲ   Ἰακὼβ   ὄντα   σιτία   εἰς   Αἴγυπτον
¹But   ²Jacob   ⁵being   ⁴corn   in   Egypt

ἐξαπέστειλεν   τοὺς   πατέρας   ἡμῶν   πρῶτον·
sent forth   the   fathers   of us   first;

13 καὶ   ἐν   τῷ   δευτέρῳ   ἐγνωρίσθη   Ἰωσὴφ
and   at   the   second [time]   was made known   Joseph

τοῖς   ἀδελφοῖς   αὐτοῦ,   καὶ   φανερὸν   ἐγένετο   τῷ
to the   brothers   of him,   and   ⁵manifest   ⁴became   –

Φαραὼ   τὸ   γένος   Ἰωσήφ.   14 ἀποστείλας   δὲ
⁶to Pharaoh   ¹the   ²race   ³of Joseph.   And sending

Ἰωσὴφ   μετεκαλέσατο   Ἰακὼβ   τὸν   πατέρα
Joseph   called   Jacob   the   father

αὐτοῦ   καὶ   πᾶσαν   τὴν   συγγένειαν   ἐν
of him   and   all   the(his)   kindred   in

ψυχαῖς   ἑβδομήκοντα   πέντε.   15 καὶ   κατέβη
souls   seventy-five.   And   went down

Ἰακὼβ   εἰς   Αἴγυπτον,   καὶ   ἐτελεύτησεν
Jacob   to   ,Egypt,   and   died

αὐτὸς   καὶ   οἱ   πατέρες   ἡμῶν,   16 καὶ
he   and   the   fathers   of us,   and

μετετέθησαν   εἰς   Συχὲμ   καὶ   ἐτέθησαν   ἐν
were transferred   to   Sychem   and   were put   in

τῷ   μνήματι   ᾧ   ὠνήσατο   Ἀβραὰμ   τιμῆς
the   tomb   which   ²bought   ¹Abraham   of(for) a price

ἀργυρίου   παρὰ   τῶν   υἱῶν   Ἐμμὼρ   ἐν
of silver   from   the   sons   of Emmor   in

Συχέμ.   17 Καθὼς   δὲ   ἤγγιζεν   ὁ   χρόνος
Sychem.   And as   drew near   the   time

the promise drew near, which God had granted to Abraham, the people grew and multiplied in Egypt [18]till there arose over Egypt another king who had not known Joseph. [19]He dealt craftily with our race and forced our fathers to expose their infants, that they might not be kept alive. [20]At this time Moses was born, and was beautiful before God. And he was brought up for three months in his father's house; [21]and when he was exposed, Pharaoh's daughter adopted him and brought him up as her own son. [22]And Moses was instructed in all the wisdom of the Egyptians, and he was mighty in his words and deeds. [23]"When he was forty years old, it came into his heart to visit his brethren, the sons of Israel. [24]And seeing one of them being wronged, he defended the oppressed man and avenged him by striking the Egyptian. [25]He supposed that his brethren understood that God was

τῆς ἐπαγγελίας ἧς ὡμολόγησεν ὁ θεὸς
of the promise which [2]declared – [1]God

τῷ Ἀβραάμ, ηὔξησεν ὁ λαὸς καὶ
to Abraham, [2]grew [1]the [2]people and

ἐπληθύνθη ἐν Αἰγύπτῳ, 18 ἄχρι οὗ ἀνέστη
were multiplied in Egypt, until [2]rose up

βασιλεὺς ἕτερος ἐπ' Αἴγυπτον, ὃς οὐκ ᾔδει
[2]king [1]another over Egypt, who did not know

τὸν Ἰωσήφ. 19 οὗτος κατασοφισάμενος
– Joseph. This man dealing craftily with

τὸ γένος ἡμῶν ἐκάκωσεν τοὺς πατέρας
the race of us ill-treated the fathers

τοῦ ποιεῖν τὰ βρέφη ἔκθετα αὐτῶν
– to make[d] [1]the [2]babes [4]exposed [3]of them

εἰς τὸ μὴ ζῳογονεῖσθαι. 20 Ἐν ᾧ
to the not to be preserved alive. At which
=so that they should not be . . .

καιρῷ ἐγεννήθη Μωϋσῆς, καὶ ἦν ἀστεῖος
time was born Moses, and was fair

τῷ θεῷ· ὃς ἀνετράφη μῆνας τρεῖς ἐν
– to God; who was reared months three in

τῷ οἴκῳ τοῦ πατρός· 21 ἐκτεθέντος δὲ
the house of the(his) father; being exposed and
=and when he was exposed

αὐτοῦ ἀνείλατο αὐτὸν ἡ θυγάτηρ Φαραὼ
him[a] took up him the daughter of Pharaoh

καὶ ἀνεθρέψατο αὐτὸν ἑαυτῇ εἰς υἱόν.
and reared him to herself for a son.
=as her own son.

22 καὶ ἐπαιδεύθη Μωϋσῆς πάσῃ σοφίᾳ
And was trained Moses in all [the] wisdom

Αἰγυπτίων, ἦν δὲ δυνατὸς ἐν λόγοις
of [the] Egyptians, and was powerful in words

καὶ ἔργοις αὐτοῦ. 23 Ὡς δὲ ἐπληροῦτο
and works of him. But when [2]was fulfilled

αὐτῷ τεσσερακονταέτης χρόνος, ἀνέβη ἐπὶ
[4]to him [2]of forty years [1]a time, it came up upon

τὴν καρδίαν αὐτοῦ ἐπισκέψασθαι τοὺς
the heart of him to visit the

ἀδελφοὺς αὐτοῦ τοὺς υἱοὺς Ἰσραήλ. 24 καὶ
brothers of him the sons of Israel. And

ἰδών τινα ἀδικούμενον ἠμύνατο, καὶ
seeing one being injured he defended [him], and

ἐποίησεν ἐκδίκησιν τῷ καταπονουμένῳ
he wrought vengeance for the [one] getting the worse

πατάξας τὸν Αἰγύπτιον. 25 ἐνόμιζεν δὲ
striking the Egyptian. Now he supposed

συνιέναι τοὺς ἀδελφοὺς ὅτι ὁ θεὸς διὰ
to understand the(his) brothers[b] that – God through
=that his brothers would understand

giving them deliverance by his hand, but they did not understand. ²⁶And on the following day he appeared to them as they were quarreling and would have reconciled them, saying, 'Men, you are brethren, why do you wrong each other?' ²⁷But the man who was wronging his neighbor thrust him aside, saying, 'Who made you a ruler and a judge over us? ²⁸Do you want to kill me as you killed the Egyptian yesterday?' ²⁹At this retort Moses fled, and became an exile in the land of Mid'ian, where he became the father of two sons.

30 "Now when forty years had passed, an angel appeared to him in the wilderness of Mount Sinai, in a flame of fire in a bush. ³¹When Moses saw it he wondered at the sight; and as he drew near to look, the voice of the Lord came, ³²'I am the God of your fathers, the God of Abraham and of Isaac and of Jacob.' And Moses trembled and did not dare to look. ³³And the Lord said to him, 'Take off the shoes from your feet, for the

χειρὸς	αὐτοῦ	δίδωσιν	σωτηρίαν	αὐτοῖς·
hand	of him	would give	salvation	to them;

οἱ δὲ	οὐ συνῆκαν.	26 τῇ τε	ἐπιούσῃ
but they	understood not.	And on the	coming

ἡμέρᾳ	ὤφθη	αὐτοῖς	μαχομένοις,	καὶ
day	he appeared	to them	fighting,	and

συνήλλασσεν	αὐτοὺς	εἰς	εἰρήνην	εἰπών·
attempted to reconcile	them	in	peace	saying:

ἄνδρες,	ἀδελφοί	ἐστε·	ἱνατί	ἀδικεῖτε
Men,	brothers	ye are;	why	injure ye

ἀλλήλους;	27 ὁ δὲ	ἀδικῶν	τὸν	πλησίον
each other?	But the [one]	injuring	the(his)	neighbour

ἀπώσατο	αὐτὸν	εἰπών·	τίς	σε	κατέστησεν
thrust away	him	saying:	Who	thee	appointed

ἄρχοντα	καὶ	δικαστὴν	ἐφ'	ἡμῶν;	28 μὴ
a ruler	and	a judge	over	us?	not

ἀνελεῖν	με σὺ	θέλεις	ὃν τρόπον	ἀνεῖλες
to kill	me thou	wishest	in the same way as†	thou killedst

ἐχθὲς	τὸν	Αἰγύπτιον;	29 ἔφυγεν	δὲ
yesterday	the	Egyptian?	So fled	

Μωϋσῆς	ἐν τῷ	λόγῳ	τούτῳ,	καὶ	ἐγένετο
Moses	at	this word,		and	became

πάροικος	ἐν	γῇ	Μαδιάμ,	οὗ	ἐγέννησεν
a sojourner	in	[the] land	Midian,	where	he begat

υἱοὺς	δύο.	30 Καὶ	πληρωθέντων	ἐτῶν
sons	two.	And	being fulfilled =when forty years were fulfilled	years

τεσσεράκοντα	ὤφθη	αὐτῷ	ἐν	τῇ	ἐρήμῳ
fortyᵃ	appeared	to him	in	the	desert

τοῦ	ὄρους	Σινὰ	ἄγγελος	ἐν	φλογὶ	πυρὸς
of the	mount	Sinai	an angel	in	a flame	of fire

βάτου.	31 ὁ δὲ	Μωϋσῆς	ἰδὼν	ἐθαύμαζεν
of a thorn bush.	- And	Moses	seeing	marvelled at

τὸ	ὅραμα·	προσερχομένου	δὲ	αὐτοῦ	κατα-
the	vision;	and approaching =as he approached		himᵃ	to take

νοῆσαι	ἐγένετο	φωνὴ	κυρίου·	32 ἐγὼ ὁ
notice	there was	a voice	of [the] Lord:	I the

θεὸς	τῶν	πατέρων	σου,	ὁ θεὸς	Ἀβραὰμ
God	of the	fathers	of thee,	the God	of Abraham

καὶ	Ἰσαὰκ	καὶ	Ἰακώβ.	ἔντρομος	δὲ
and	of Isaac	and	of Jacob.	But trembling	

γενόμενος	Μωϋσῆς	οὐκ	ἐτόλμα	κατανοῆσαι.
becoming	Moses	dared not		to take notice.

33 εἶπεν	δὲ	αὐτῷ	ὁ	κύριος·	λῦσον	τὸ
And said		to him	the	Lord:	Loosen	the

ὑπόδημα	τῶν	ποδῶν	σου·	ὁ γὰρ	τόπος
sandal	of the	feet	of thee;	for the	place

place where you are
standing is holy ground.
³⁴I have surely seen the
ill-treatment of my people
that are in Egypt and
heard their groaning, and
I have come down to
deliver them. And now
come, I will send you to
Egypt.'
35 "This Moses whom
they refused, saying,
'Who made you a ruler
and a judge?' God sent
as both ruler and de-
liverer by the hand of the
angel that appeared to
him in the bush. ³⁶He led
them out, having per-
formed wonders and
signs in Egypt and at the
Red Sea, and in the
wilderness for forty years.
³⁷This is the Moses who
said to the Israelites,
'God will raise up for
you a prophet from your
brethren as he raised me
up.' ³⁸This is he who was
in the congregation in
the wilderness with the
angel who spoke to him
at Mount Sinai, and with
our fathers; and he re-
ceived living oracles to
give to us. ³⁹Our fathers
refused to obey him, but
thrust him aside, and in
their hearts they turned
to Egypt, ⁴⁰saying to

ἐφ' ᾧ ἕστηκας γῆ ἁγία ἐστίν. 34 ἰδὼν
on which thou standest ground holy is. Seeing

εἶδον τὴν κάκωσιν τοῦ λαοῦ μου τοῦ
I saw the ill-treatment of the people of me –

ἐν Αἰγύπτῳ, καὶ τοῦ στεναγμοῦ αὐτοῦ
in Egypt, and the groan of it

ἤκουσα, καὶ κατέβην ἐξελέσθαι αὐτούς·
I heard, and I came down to rescue them;

καὶ νῦν δεῦρο ἀποστείλω σε εἰς Αἴγυπτον.
and now come I will send thee to Egypt.

35 Τοῦτον τὸν Μωϋσῆν, ὃν ἠρνήσαντο
This – Moses, whom they denied

εἰπόντες· τίς σε κατέστησεν ἄρχοντα καὶ
saying: Who thee appointed a ruler and

δικαστήν; τοῦτον ὁ θεὸς καὶ ἄρχοντα
a judge? this man – God both a ruler

καὶ λυτρωτὴν ἀπέσταλκεν σὺν χειρὶ
and a redeemer has sent with [the] hand

ἀγγέλου τοῦ ὀφθέντος αὐτῷ ἐν τῇ βάτῳ.
of [the] angel – appearing to him in the bush.

36 οὗτος ἐξήγαγεν αὐτοὺς ποιήσας τέρατα
This man led forth them doing wonders

καὶ σημεῖα ἐν γῇ Αἰγύπτῳ καὶ ἐν
and signs in [the] land Egypt and in

ἐρυθρᾷ θαλάσσῃ καὶ ἐν τῇ ἐρήμῳ ἔτη
[the] Red Sea and in the desert years

τεσσεράκοντα. 37 οὗτός ἐστιν ὁ Μωϋσῆς
forty. This is the Moses

ὁ εἴπας τοῖς υἱοῖς Ἰσραήλ· προφήτην
– saying to the sons of Israel : A prophet

ὑμῖν ἀναστήσει ὁ θεὸς ἐκ τῶν ἀδελφῶν
for you will raise up – God of the brothers

ὑμῶν ὡς ἐμέ. 38 οὗτός ἐστιν ὁ γενόμενος
of you as me. This is the [one] having been

ἐν τῇ ἐκκλησίᾳ ἐν τῇ ἐρήμῳ μετὰ τοῦ
in the church in the desert with the

ἀγγέλου τοῦ λαλοῦντος αὐτῷ ἐν τῷ
angel – speaking to him in the

ὄρει Σινὰ καὶ τῶν πατέρων ἡμῶν, ὃς
mount Sinai and [with] the fathers of us, who

ἐδέξατο λόγια ζῶντα δοῦναι ὑμῖν, 39 ᾧ
received oracles living to give to you, ¹to whom

οὐκ ἠθέλησαν ὑπήκοοι γενέσθαι οἱ πατέρες
⁵wished ⁶not ⁸obedient ⁷to become ²the ³fathers

ἡμῶν, ἀλλὰ ἀπώσαντο καὶ ἐστράφησαν
⁴of us, but thrust away and turned

ἐν ταῖς καρδίαις αὐτῶν εἰς Αἴγυπτον,
in the hearts of them to Egypt,

Aaron, 'Make for us gods to go before us; as for this Moses who led us out from the land of Egypt, we do not know what has become of him.' ⁴¹And they made a calf in those days, and offered a sacrifice to the idol and rejoiced in the works of their hands. ⁴²But God turned and gave them over to worship the host of heaven, as it is written in the book of the prophets:
'Did you offer me slain beasts and sacrifices,
forty years in the wilderness, O house of Israel?
⁴³And you took up the tent of Moloch,
and the star of the god Rephan,
the figures which you made to worship;
and I will remove you beyond Babylon.'
44 "Our fathers had the tent of witness in the wilderness, even as he who spoke to Moses directed him to make it, according to the pattern that he had seen. ⁴⁵Our fathers in turn brought it in with Joshua when they dispossessed the nations which God thrust

40 εἰπόντες   τῷ   'Ααρών·   ποίησον   ἡμῖν
   saying   –   to Aaron :   Make   for us
θεοὺς   οἳ   προπορεύσονται   ἡμῶν·   ὁ   γὰρ
gods   which   will go before   us;   –   for
Μωϋσῆς   οὗτος,   ὃς   ἐξήγαγεν   ἡμᾶς   ἐκ
this Moses,   who   led forth   us   out of
γῆς   Αἰγύπτου,   οὐκ   οἴδαμεν   τί   ἐγένετο
[the] land   Egypt,   we know not   what   happened
αὐτῷ.   41 καὶ   ἐμοσχοποίησαν   ἐν
to him.   And   they made [a model of] a calf   in
ταῖς ἡμέραις ἐκείναις καὶ ἀνήγαγον θυσίαν τῷ
      those days   and brought up a sacrifice to the
εἰδώλῳ,   καὶ   εὐφραίνοντο   ἐν   τοῖς   ἔργοις
idol,   and   made merry   in   the   works
τῶν   χειρῶν   αὐτῶν.   42 ἔστρεψεν   δὲ   ὁ
of the   hands   of them.   And ²turned   –
θεὸς   καὶ   παρέδωκεν   αὐτοὺς   λατρεύειν
¹God   and   delivered   them   to worship
τῇ   στρατιᾷ   τοῦ   οὐρανοῦ, καθὼς   γέγραπται
the   host   –   of heaven, as   it has been written
ἐν   βίβλῳ   τῶν   προφητῶν·   μὴ   σφάγια
in   [the] roll   of the   prophets :   Not   victims
καὶ   θυσίας   προσηνέγκατέ   μοι   ἔτη
and   sacrifices   ye offered   to me   years
τεσσεράκοντα   ἐν   τῇ   ἐρήμῳ,   οἶκος   'Ισραήλ,
forty   in   the   desert,   [O] house   of Israel,
43 καὶ   ἀνελάβετε   τὴν   σκηνὴν   τοῦ   Μόλοχ
and   ye took up   the   tent   –   of Moloch
καὶ   τὸ   ἄστρον   τοῦ   θεοῦ   'Ρομφά,   τοὺς
and   the   star   of the   god   Rompha,   the
τύπους   οὓς   ἐποιήσατε   προσκυνεῖν   αὐτοῖς;
models   which   ye made   to worship   them?
καὶ   μετοικιῶ   ὑμᾶς   ἐπέκεινα   Βαβυλῶνος.
and   I will deport   you   beyond   Babylon.
44 'Η   σκηνὴ   τοῦ   μαρτυρίου   ἦν   τοῖς
The   tent   –   of witness   was   to the
=Our fathers had the tent of witness
πατράσιν   ἡμῶν   ἐν   τῇ   ἐρήμῳ,   καθὼς
fathers   of us⁶   in   the   desert,   as
διετάξατο   ὁ   λαλῶν   τῷ   Μωϋσῇ   ποιῆσαι
commanded the [one] speaking   –   to Moses   to make
αὐτὴν   κατὰ   τὸν   τύπον   ὃν   ἑωράκει·
it   according to   the   model   which   he had seen;
45 ἦν   καὶ   εἰσήγαγον   διαδεξάμενοι   οἱ
which   also   ³brought in   ⁴having received   ¹the
πατέρες   ἡμῶν   μετὰ   'Ιησοῦ   ἐν   τῇ   κατα-
²fathers   ³of us   with   Jesus   in   the   pos-
σχέσει   τῶν   ἐθνῶν,   ὧν   ἐξῶσεν   ὁ   θεὸς
session   of the   nations,   whom   put out   -   God

out before our fathers. So it was until the days of David, ⁴⁶who found favor in the sight of God and asked leave to find a habitation for the God of Jacob. ⁴⁷But it was Solomon who built a house for him. ⁴⁸Yet the Most High does not dwell in houses made with hands; as the prophet says, ⁴⁹'Heaven is my throne, and earth my footstool.

What house will you build for me, says the Lord, or what is the place of my rest? ⁵⁰Did not my hand make all these things?'

51 "You stiff-necked people, uncircumcised in heart and ears, you always resist the Holy Spirit. As your fathers did, so do you. ⁵²Which of the prophets did not your fathers persecute? And they killed those who announced beforehand the coming of the Righteous One, whom you have now betrayed and murdered, ⁵³you who received the law as delivered by angels and did not keep it."

54 Now when they heard these things they were enraged, and they ground their teeth against him. ⁵⁵But he, full of the

ἀπὸ προσώπου τῶν πατέρων ἡμῶν, ἕως
from [the] face of the fathers of us, until

τῶν ἡμερῶν Δαυίδ· 46 ὃς εὗρεν χάριν
the days of David; who found favour

ἐνώπιον τοῦ θεοῦ καὶ ἠτήσατο εὑρεῖν
before – God and asked to find

σκήνωμα τῷ οἴκῳ Ἰακώβ. 47 Σολομῶν δὲ
a tent for the house of Jacob. But Solomon

οἰκοδόμησεν αὐτῷ οἶκον. 48 ἀλλ'
built for him a house. But

οὐχ ὁ ὕψιστος ἐν χειροποιήτοις κατοικεῖ·
⁴not ¹the ²Most High ⁵in ⁶[places] made by hand ³dwells;

καθὼς ὁ προφήτης λέγει· 49 ὁ οὐρανός
as the prophet says : The heaven

μοι θρόνος, ἡ δὲ γῆ ὑποπόδιον τῶν
to me a throne, and the earth a footstool of the

ποδῶν μου· ποῖον οἶκον οἰκοδομήσετέ μοι,
feet of me; what house will ye build for me,

λέγει κύριος, ἢ τίς τόπος τῆς καταπαύσεώς
says [the] Lord, or what place of the rest

μου; 50 οὐχὶ ἡ χείρ μου ἐποίησεν ταῦτα
of me? not the hand of me made these things

πάντα; 51 Σκληροτράχηλοι καὶ ἀπερίτμητοι
all? Hard-necked and uncircumcised

καρδίαις καὶ τοῖς ὠσίν, ὑμεῖς ἀεὶ τῷ
in hearts and – ears, ye always the

πνεύματι τῷ ἁγίῳ ἀντιπίπτετε, ὡς οἱ
Spirit – Holy oppose, as the

πατέρες ὑμῶν καὶ ὑμεῖς. 52 τίνα τῶν
fathers of you also ye. Which of the

προφητῶν οὐκ ἐδίωξαν οἱ πατέρες ὑμῶν;
prophets persecuted not the fathers of you?

καὶ ἀπέκτειναν τοὺς προκαταγγείλαντας
and they killed the [ones] announcing beforehand

περὶ τῆς ἐλεύσεως τοῦ δικαίου, οὗ
concerning the coming of the righteous one, of whom

νῦν ὑμεῖς προδόται καὶ φονεῖς ἐγένεσθε,
now ye betrayers and murderers became,

53 οἵτινες ἐλάβετε τὸν νόμον εἰς διαταγὰς
who received the law in(by) dispositions

ἀγγέλων, καὶ οὐκ ἐφυλάξατε.
of angels, and did not keep [it].

54 Ἀκούοντες δὲ ταῦτα διεπρίοντο ταῖς
And hearing these things they were cut to the

καρδίαις αὐτῶν καὶ ἔβρυχον τοὺς ὀδόντας
hearts of them and gnashed the teeth

ἐπ' αὐτόν. 55 ὑπάρχων δὲ πλήρης
at him. But being full

Holy Spirit, gazed into
heaven and saw the
glory of God, and Jesus
standing at the right
hand of God; [56] and he
said, "Behold, I see the
heavens opened, and the
Son of man standing at
the right hand of God."
[57] But they cried out
with a loud voice and
stopped their ears and
rushed together upon
him. [58] Then they cast
him out of the city and
stoned him; and the
witnesses laid down their
garments at the feet of a
young man named Saul.
[59] And as they were stoning Stephen, he prayed,
"Lord Jesus, receive my
spirit." [60] And he knelt
down and cried with a
loud voice, "Lord, do
not hold this sin against
them." And when he had
said this, he fell asleep.

CHAPTER 8

AND Saul was con-
senting to his death.
And on that day a
great persecution arose
against the church in
Jerusalem; and they were
all scattered throughout
the region of Judea and
Samaria, except the
apostles. [2] Devout men
buried Stephen, and

πνεύματος ἁγίου ἀτενίσας εἰς τὸν οὐρανὸν
of [the] Spirit   Holy   gazing   into   -   heaven
εἶδεν δόξαν θεοῦ καὶ Ἰησοῦν ἑστῶτα ἐκ
he saw [the] glory of God and   Jesus   standing at
δεξιῶν   τοῦ θεοῦ,   56 καὶ εἶπεν· ἰδοὺ
[the] right [hand] -   of God,   and said : Behold
θεωρῶ τοὺς οὐρανοὺς διηνοιγμένους καὶ
I see   the   heavens   having been opened up and
τὸν υἱὸν τοῦ ἀνθρώπου ἐκ δεξιῶν ἑστῶτα
the Son   -   of man at [the] right [hand] standing
τοῦ θεοῦ.   57 κράξαντες δὲ φωνῇ μεγάλῃ
 -   of God.   And crying out   voice with a great
συνέσχον τὰ ὦτα αὐτῶν, καὶ ὥρμησαν
they closed the ears of them,   and   rushed
ὁμοθυμαδὸν ἐπ᾽ αὐτόν, 58 καὶ ἐκβαλόντες
with one mind on   him,   and   casting out
ἔξω τῆς πόλεως ἐλιθοβόλουν. καὶ οἱ
outside the   city   they stoned [him]. And   the
μάρτυρες ἀπέθεντο τὰ ἱμάτια αὐτῶν παρὰ
witnesses   put off   the garments of them   at
τοὺς πόδας νεανίου καλουμένου Σαύλου.
the   feet of a young man being called   Saul.
59 καὶ ἐλιθοβόλουν τὸν Στέφανον, ἐπικαλ-
And   they stoned   -   Stephen,   invok-
ούμενον καὶ λέγοντα· κύριε Ἰησοῦ, δέξαι
ing [God] and saying : Lord Jesus,   receive
τὸ πνεῦμά μου. 60 θεὶς δὲ τὰ γόνατα
the spirit of me.   And placing the   knees
                              = kneeling down
ἔκραξεν φωνῇ μεγάλῃ· κύριε, μὴ στήσῃς
he cried   voice with a great : Lord,   place not
αὐτοῖς ταύτην τὴν ἁμαρτίαν. καὶ τοῦτο
to them   this   -   sin.   And   [2] this
εἰπὼν ἐκοιμήθη. 8 Σαῦλος δὲ ἦν συνευδοκῶν
[1] saying he fell asleep.   And Saul   was   consenting
τῇ ἀναιρέσει αὐτοῦ.
to the killing   of him.
Ἐγένετο δὲ ἐν ἐκείνῃ τῇ ἡμέρᾳ
And there was in   that   -   day
διωγμὸς μέγας ἐπὶ τὴν ἐκκλησίαν τὴν
persecution a great on(against) the church   -
ἐν Ἱεροσολύμοις· πάντες [δὲ] διεσπάρησαν
in   Jerusalem;   and all   were scattered
κατὰ τὰς χώρας τῆς Ἰουδαίας καὶ
throughout the countries -   of Judæa   and
Σαμαρείας πλὴν τῶν ἀποστόλων.
Samaria   except the   apostles.
2 συνεκόμισαν δὲ τὸν Στέφανον ἄνδρες
And [3] recovered   -   [4] Stephen [2] men

made great lamentation over him. ³But Saul laid waste the church, and entering house after house, he dragged off men and women and committed them to prison.
4 Now those who were scattered went about preaching the word. ⁵Philip went down to a city of Samar'ia, and proclaimed to them the Christ. ⁶And the multitudes with one accord gave heed to what was said by Philip, when they heard him and saw the signs which he did. ⁷For unclean spirits came out of many who were possessed, crying with a loud voice; and many who were paralyzed or lame were healed. ⁸So there was much joy in that city.
9 But there was a man named Simon who had previously practiced magic in the city and amazed the nation of Samar'ia, saying that he himself was somebody great. ¹⁰They all gave heed to him, from the least to the greatest, saying, "This man is that power of God which is

εὐλαβεῖς καὶ ἐποίησαν κοπετὸν μέγαν
¹devout and made lamentation great
ἐπ' αὐτῷ. 3 Σαῦλος δὲ ἐλυμαίνετο τὴν
over him. But Saul ravaged the
ἐκκλησίαν κατὰ τοὺς οἴκους εἰσπορευόμενος,
church house by house† entering,
σύρων τε ἄνδρας καὶ γυναῖκας παρεδίδου
dragging both men and women delivered
εἰς φυλακήν.
to prison.
4 Οἱ μὲν οὖν διασπαρέντες διῆλθον
The [ones] –* therefore being scattered passed through
εὐαγγελιζόμενοι τὸν λόγον. 5 Φίλιππος δὲ
preaching the word. But Philip
κατελθὼν εἰς τὴν πόλιν τῆς
going down to the city –
Σαμαρείας ἐκήρυσσεν αὐτοῖς τὸν Χριστόν.
of Samaria proclaimed to them the Christ.
6 προσεῖχον δὲ οἱ ὄχλοι τοῖς
And gave heed the crowds to the things
λεγομένοις ὑπὸ τοῦ Φιλίππου ὁμοθυμαδὸν
being said by – Philip with one mind
ἐν τῷ ἀκούειν αὐτοὺς καὶ βλέπειν τὰ
in the to hear them and to see^be the
=as they heard and saw
σημεῖα ἃ ἐποίει. 7 πολλοὶ γὰρ τῶν
signs which he was doing. For many of the
ἐχόντων πνεύματα ἀκάθαρτα βοῶντα φωνῇ
[ones] having spirits unclean crying ²voice
μεγάλη ἐξήρχοντο· πολλοὶ δὲ παραλελυμένοι
¹with a great came out; and many having been paralysed
καὶ χωλοὶ ἐθεραπεύθησαν· 8 ἐγένετο δὲ
and lame were healed; and there was
πολλὴ χαρὰ ἐν τῇ πόλει ἐκείνῃ. 9 Ἀνὴρ δέ τις
much joy in that city. And a certain man
ὀνόματι Σίμων προϋπῆρχεν ἐν τῇ
by name Simon was previously in the
πόλει μαγεύων καὶ ἐξιστάνων τὸ
city practising sorcery and astonishing the
ἔθνος τῆς Σαμαρείας, λέγων εἶναί τινα
nation – of Samaria, saying ²to be ³someone
ἑαυτὸν μέγαν, 10 ᾧ προσεῖχον πάντες
¹himself ⁴great, to whom gave heed all
ἀπὸ μικροῦ ἕως μεγάλου λέγοντες· οὗτός
from small to great saying : This man
ἐστιν ἡ δύναμις τοῦ θεοῦ ἡ καλουμένη
is the power – of God – being called

* See note on John 19. 24.

called Great." ¹¹And they gave heed to him, because for a long time he had amazed them with his magic. ¹²But when they believed Philip as he preached good news about the kingdom of God and the name of Jesus Christ, they were baptized, both men and women. ¹³Even Simon himself believed, and after being baptized he continued with Philip. And seeing signs and great miracles performed, he was amazed.

14 Now when the apostles at Jerusalem heard that Samar′ia had received the word of God, they sent to them Peter and John, ¹⁵who came down and prayed for them that they might receive the Holy Spirit; ¹⁶for it had not yet fallen on any of them, but they had only been baptized in the name of the Lord Jesus. ¹⁷Then they laid their hands on them and they received the Holy Spirit. ¹⁸Now when Simon saw that the Spirit was given through the laying on of the apostles' hands, he offered them money,

μεγάλη. **11** προσεῖχον δὲ αὐτῷ διὰ τὸ
great.   And they gave heed to him because of the

ἱκανῷ χρόνῳ ταῖς μαγείαις ἐξεστακέναι
for a considerable time by the sorceries to have astonished
=because for a considerable time he had astonished them by his sorceries.

αὐτούς. **12** ὅτε δὲ ἐπίστευσαν τῷ Φιλίππῳ
them.   But when they believed – Philip

εὐαγγελιζομένῳ περὶ τῆς βασιλείας τοῦ
preaching about the kingdom –

θεοῦ καὶ τοῦ ὀνόματος Ἰησοῦ Χριστοῦ,
of God and the name of Jesus Christ,

ἐβαπτίζοντο ἄνδρες τε καὶ γυναῖκες.
they were baptized both men and women.

13 ὁ δὲ Σίμων καὶ αὐτὸς ἐπίστευσεν,
– And Simon also [him]self believed,

καὶ βαπτισθεὶς ἦν προσκαρτερῶν τῷ
and having been baptized was attaching himself –

Φιλίππῳ, θεωρῶν τε σημεῖα καὶ δυνάμεις
to Philip, and beholding signs and powerful deeds

μεγάλας γινομένας ἐξίστατο. **14** Ἀκούσαντες
great happening he was amazed. ⁸hearing

δὲ οἱ ἐν Ἱεροσολύμοις ἀπόστολοι ὅτι
¹And ²the ⁴in ⁵Jerusalem ³apostles that

δέδεκται ἡ Σαμάρεια τὸν λόγον τοῦ
³has received – ¹Samaria the word of the

θεοῦ, ἀπέστειλαν πρὸς αὐτοὺς Πέτρον
of God, they sent to them Peter

καὶ Ἰωάννην, **15** οἵτινες καταβάντες
and John, who going down

προσηύξαντο περὶ αὐτῶν ὅπως λάβωσιν
prayed concerning them so as they might receive

πνεῦμα ἅγιον· **16** οὐδέπω γὰρ ἦν ἐπ᾽
Spirit Holy; for ²not yet ¹he was ⁴on

οὐδενὶ αὐτῶν ἐπιπεπτωκός, μόνον δὲ
⁵no(any)one ⁶of them ³having fallen on, but only

βεβαπτισμένοι ὑπῆρχον εἰς τὸ ὄνομα τοῦ
having been baptized they were in the name of the

κυρίου Ἰησοῦ. **17** τότε ἐπετίθεσαν τὰς
Lord Jesus. Then they laid on the(ir)

χεῖρας ἐπ᾽ αὐτούς, καὶ ἐλάμβανον πνεῦμα
hands on them, and they received ²Spirit

ἅγιον. **18** ἰδὼν δὲ ὁ Σίμων ὅτι διὰ
¹Holy. And ²seeing – ¹Simon that through

τῆς ἐπιθέσεως τῶν χειρῶν τῶν ἀποστόλων
the laying on of the hands of the apostles

δίδοται τὸ πνεῦμα, προσήνεγκεν αὐτοῖς
is(was) given the Spirit, he offered them

¹⁹saying, "Give me also this power, that any one on whom I lay my hands may receive the Holy Spirit." ²⁰But Peter said to him, "Your silver perish with you, because you thought you could obtain the gift of God with money! ²¹You have neither part nor lot in this matter, for your heart is not right before God. ²²Repent therefore of this wickedness of yours, and pray to the Lord that, if possible, the intent of your heart may be forgiven you. ²³For I see that you are in the gall of bitterness and in the bond of iniquity." ²⁴And Simon answered, "Pray for me to the Lord, that nothing of what you have said may come upon me."

25 Now when they had testified and spoken the word of the Lord, they returned to Jerusalem, preaching the gospel to many villages of the Samaritans.

26 But an angel of the Lord said to Philip, "Rise and go toward the

χρήματα λέγων· 19 δότε κἀμοὶ τὴν
money   saying :   Give me also   –

ἐξουσίαν ταύτην ἵνα ᾧ ἐὰν ἐπιθῶ τὰς
authority this   that whomever I lay on the(my)

χεῖρας λαμβάνῃ πνεῦμα ἅγιον. 20 Πέτρος δὲ
hands he may receive Spirit Holy.   But Peter

εἶπεν πρὸς αὐτόν· τὸ ἀργύριόν σου
said   to   him :   The silver   of thee

σὺν σοὶ εἴη εἰς ἀπώλειαν, ὅτι τὴν δωρεὰν
with thee may it be into perdition, because the   gift

τοῦ θεοῦ ἐνόμισας διὰ χρημάτων κτᾶσθαι.
– of God thou didst suppose through money   to get.

21 οὐκ ἔστιν σοι μερὶς οὐδὲ κλῆρος
   There is not to thee° part   nor   lot
   =Thou hast no

ἐν τῷ λόγῳ τούτῳ· ἡ γὰρ καρδία σου
in this matter;   for the heart of thee

οὐκ ἔστιν εὐθεῖα ἔναντι τοῦ θεοῦ.
is not   right   before   –   God.

22 μετανόησον οὖν ἀπὸ τῆς κακίας σου
   Repent thou therefore from – ²wickedness ³of thee

ταύτης, καὶ δεήθητι τοῦ κυρίου εἰ ἄρα
¹this,   and petition the   Lord if perhaps

ἀφεθήσεταί σοι ἡ ἐπίνοια τῆς καρδίας
will be forgiven thee the   thought   of the heart

σου· 23 εἰς γὰρ χολὴν πικρίας καὶ
of thee;   for in   gall of bitterness and

σύνδεσμον ἀδικίας ὁρῶ σε ὄντα.
bond   of unrighteousness I see thee being.

24 ἀποκριθεὶς δὲ ὁ Σίμων εἶπεν· δεήθητε
   And answering – Simon said :   Petition

ὑμεῖς ὑπὲρ ἐμοῦ πρὸς τὸν κύριον, ὅπως
ye   for   me   to   the   Lord, so as

μηδὲν ἐπέλθῃ ἐπ' ἐμὲ ὧν εἰρήκατε.
¹not one ⁴may come on ⁵on ⁶me ²of the ³ye have
                         things which spoken.

25 Οἱ μὲν οὖν διαμαρτυράμενοι καὶ λαλή-
   They – therefore having solemnly witnessed and having

σαντες τὸν λόγον τοῦ κυρίου ὑπέστρεφον
spoken the   word of the Lord   returned

εἰς Ἱεροσόλυμα, πολλάς τε κώμας τῶν
to   Jerusalem,   and ²many ³villages ⁴of the

Σαμαριτῶν εὐηγγελίζοντο.
⁵Samaritans ¹evangelized.

26 Ἄγγελος δὲ κυρίου ἐλάλησεν πρὸς
   But an angel of [the] Lord spoke   to

Φίλιππον λέγων· ἀνάστηθι καὶ πορεύου
Philip   saying : Rise up   and   go

south^e to the road that goes down from Jerusalem to Gaza." This is a desert road. ²⁷And he rose and went. And behold, an Ethiopian, a eunuch, a minister of Canda'ce the queen of the Ethiopians, in charge of all her treasure, had come to Jerusalem to worship ²⁸and was returning; seated in his chariot, he was reading the prophet Isaiah. ²⁹And the Spirit said to Philip, "Go up and join this chariot." ³⁰So Philip ran to him, and heard him reading Isaiah the prophet, and asked, "Do you understand what you are reading?" ³¹And he said, "How can I, unless some one guides me?" And he invited Philip to come up and sit with him. ³²Now the passage of the scripture which he was reading was this:

"As a sheep led to the slaughter
or a lamb before its shearer is dumb,
so he opens not his mouth.
³³In his humiliation justice was denied him.

^e Or at noon

κατὰ   μεσημβρίαν   ἐπὶ   τὴν   ὁδὸν   τὴν
along   south   on   the   way   –
καταβαίνουσαν   ἀπὸ   'Ιερουσαλὴμ   εἰς   Γάζαν·
going down   from   Jerusalem   to   Gaza;
αὕτη   ἐστὶν   ἔρημος.   27 καὶ   ἀναστὰς
this   is   desert.   And   rising up
ἐπορεύθη.   καὶ   ἰδοὺ   ἀνὴρ   Αἰθίοψ   εὐνοῦχος
he went.   And   behold[,] a man Ethiopian a eunuch
δυνάστης   Κανδάκης   βασιλίσσης   Αἰθιόπων,
a courtier of Candace queen   of [the]
                                       Ethiopians,
ὃς   ἦν   ἐπὶ   πάσης   τῆς   γάζης   αὐτῆς,
who was over   all   the   treasure of her,
[ὃς]   ἐληλύθει   προσκυνήσων   εἰς   'Ιερουσαλήμ,
who   had come   worshipping   in   Jerusalem,
28 ἦν   δὲ   ὑποστρέφων   καὶ   καθήμενος   ἐπὶ
   and was   returning   and   sitting   on
τοῦ   ἅρματος   αὐτοῦ   καὶ   ἀνεγίνωσκεν   τὸν
the   chariot   of him   and   was reading   the
προφήτην   'Ησαΐαν.   29 εἶπεν   δὲ   τὸ   πνεῦμα
prophet   Esaias.   And said   the Spirit
τῷ   Φιλίππῳ·   πρόσελθε   καὶ   κολλήθητι
–   to Philip: Approach   and   keep company with
τῷ   ἅρματι   τούτῳ.   30 προσδραμὼν   δὲ
this chariot.   And running up
ὁ   Φίλιππος   ἤκουσεν   αὐτοῦ   ἀναγινώσκοντος
–   Philip   heard   him   reading
'Ησαΐαν   τὸν   προφήτην,   καὶ   εἶπεν·   ἆρά   γε
Esaias   the   prophet,   and   said: Then
γινώσκεις   ἃ   ἀναγινώσκεις;   31 ὁ   δὲ
knowest thou what things thou art reading?   And he
εἶπεν·   πῶς   γὰρ   ἂν   δυναίμην   ἐὰν   μή
said: How   indeed should I be able   unless
τις   ὁδηγήσει   με;   παρεκάλεσέν   τε   τὸν
someone shall guide   me?   And he besought
Φίλιππον   ἀναβάντα   καθίσαι   σὺν   αὐτῷ.
Philip   coming up   to sit   with   him.
32 ἡ   δὲ   περιοχὴ   τῆς   γραφῆς   ἦν   ἀνεγίνω-
Now the   passage   of the scripture which   he was
σκεν   ἦν   αὕτη·   ὡς   πρόβατον   ἐπὶ   σφαγὴν
reading was this: As   a sheep   to   slaughter
ἤχθη,   καὶ ὡς   ἀμνὸς   ἐναντίον   τοῦ   κείροντος
he was led, and as a lamb   before   the [one] shearing
αὐτὸν   ἄφωνος,   οὕτως   οὐκ   ἀνοίγει   τὸ
it   [is] dumb,   so   he opens not   the
στόμα   αὐτοῦ.   33 'Εν   τῇ   ταπεινώσει
mouth   of him.   In   the   humiliation
ἡ   κρίσις   αὐτοῦ   ἤρθη·   τὴν   γενεὰν   αὐτοῦ
the judgment of him   was taken away; the generation of him

Who can describe his generation? For his life is taken up from the earth." ³⁴And the eunuch said to Philip, "About whom, pray, does the prophet say this, about himself or about some one else?" ³⁵Then Philip opened his mouth, and beginning with this scripture he told him the good news of Jesus. ³⁶And as they went along the road they came to some water, and the eunuch said, "See, here is water! What is to prevent my being baptized?"ᶠ ³⁸And he commanded the chariot to stop, and they both went down into the water, Philip and the eunuch, and he baptized him. ³⁹And when they came up out of the water, the Spirit of the Lord caught up Philip; and the eunuch saw him no more, and went on his way rejoicing. ⁴⁰But Philip was found at Azo'tus, and passing on he preached the gospel to all the towns till he came to Caesare'a.

τίς διηγήσεται; ὅτι αἴρεται ἀπὸ τῆς
who will relate? because is taken from the
γῆς ἡ ζωὴ αὐτοῦ. 34 ἀποκριθεὶς δὲ ὁ
earth the life of him. And answering the
εὐνοῦχος τῷ Φιλίππῳ εἶπεν· δέομαί σου,
eunuch – to Philip said : I ask thee,
περὶ τίνος ὁ προφήτης λέγει τοῦτο;
about whom the prophet says this?
περὶ ἑαυτοῦ ἢ περὶ ἑτέρου τινός;
about himself or about other someone?
35 ἀνοίξας δὲ ὁ Φίλιππος τὸ στόμα
And opening – Philip the mouth
αὐτοῦ καὶ ἀρξάμενος ἀπὸ τῆς γραφῆς ταύτης
of him and beginning from this scripture
εὐηγγελίσατο αὐτῷ τὸν Ἰησοῦν.
preached to him – Jesus.
36 ὡς δὲ ἐπορεύοντο κατὰ τὴν ὁδόν,
And as they were going along the way,
ἦλθον ἐπί τι ὕδωρ, καί φησιν ὁ εὐνοῦχος·
they came upon certain water, and says the eunuch :
ἰδοὺ ὕδωρ· τί κωλύει με βαπτισθῆναι;‡
Behold[,] water; what prevents me to be baptized?
38 καὶ ἐκέλευσεν στῆναι τὸ ἅρμα, καὶ
And he commanded to stand the chariot, and
κατέβησαν ἀμφότεροι εἰς τὸ ὕδωρ, ὅ
went down both into the water, –
τε Φίλιππος καὶ ὁ εὐνοῦχος, καὶ ἐβάπτισεν
both Philip and the eunuch, and he baptized
αὐτόν. 39 ὅτε δὲ ἀνέβησαν ἐκ τοῦ ὕδατος,
him. And when they came up out of the water,
πνεῦμα κυρίου ἥρπασεν τὸν Φίλιππον,
[the] Spirit of [the] Lord seized – Philip,
καὶ οὐκ εἶδεν αὐτὸν οὐκέτι ὁ εὐνοῦχος,
and saw not him no(any) more the eunuch,
ἐπορεύετο γὰρ τὴν ὁδὸν αὐτοῦ χαίρων.
for he went the way of him rejoicing.
40 Φίλιππος δὲ εὑρέθη εἰς Ἄζωτον, καὶ
But Philip was found in Azotus, and
διερχόμενος εὐηγγελίζετο τὰς πόλεις πάσας
passing through he evangelized the cities all
ἕως τοῦ ἐλθεῖν αὐτὸν εἰς Καισάρειαν.
until the to come himᵇ to Caesarea.
=he came

ᶠ Other ancient authorities add all or most of verse 37, *And Philip said, "If you believe with all your heart, you may." And he replied, "I believe that Jesus Christ is the Son of God."*

‡ Verse 37 omitted by Nestle; *cf.* RSV footnote.

CHAPTER 9

BUT Saul, still breathing threats and murder against the disciples of the Lord, went to the high priest ²and asked him for letters to the synagogues at Damascus, so that if he found any belonging to the Way, men or women, he might bring them bound ˙ to Jerusalem. ³ Now as he journeyed he approached Damascus, and suddenly a light from heaven flashed about him. ⁴And he fell to the ground and heard a voice saying to him, "Saul, Saul, why do you persecute me?" ⁵And he said, "Who are you, Lord?" And he said, "I am Jesus, whom you are persecuting; ⁶ but rise and enter the city, and you will be told what you are to do." ⁷ The men who were traveling with him stood speechless, hearing the voice but seeing no one. ⁸ Saul arose from the ground; and when his eyes were opened, he could see nothing; so they led him by the hand and brought him into Damascus. ⁹And for three days he

9 Ὁ δὲ Σαῦλος ἔτι ἐμπνέων ἀπειλῆς
  –   But   Saul   still   breathing   threatening

καὶ φόνου εἰς τοὺς μαθητὰς τοῦ κυρίου,
and murder against the disciples of the Lord,

προσελθὼν τῷ ἀρχιερεῖ 2 ᾐτήσατο παρ᾽
approaching *to* the high priest   asked   from

αὐτοῦ ἐπιστολὰς εἰς Δαμασκὸν πρὸς τὰς
him   letters   to   Damascus   for   the

συναγωγάς, ὅπως ἐάν τινας εὕρῃ τῆς
synagogues, so as if   ²any ¹he found ⁴of the

ὁδοῦ ὄντας, ἄνδρας τε καὶ γυναῖκας, δεδεμένους
⁵way ³being, both men and women, ³having been bound

ἀγάγῃ εἰς Ἰερουσαλήμ. 3 Ἐν
¹he might bring [them] to Jerusalem.   in

δὲ τῷ πορεύεσθαι ἐγένετο αὐτὸν ἐγγίζειν
Now the   to goᵉ it came to pass him to draw nearᵇ
=as he went   =he drew near

τῇ Δαμασκῷ, ἐξαίφνης τε αὐτὸν περιήστ-
– to Damascus, and suddenly ⁵him   ⁴shone

ραψεν φῶς ἐκ τοῦ οὐρανοῦ, 4 καὶ πεσὼν
round ¹a light ²out of – ³heaven,   and   falling

ἐπὶ τὴν γῆν ἤκουσεν φωνὴν λέγουσαν
on the earth he heard a voice   saying

αὐτῷ· Σαοὺλ Σαούλ, τί με διώκεις;
to him : Saul[,] Saul, why me persecutest thou?

5 εἶπεν δέ· τίς εἶ, κύριε; ὁ δέ· ἐγώ
And he said : Who art thou, Lord? And he [said] : I

εἰμι Ἰησοῦς ὃν σὺ διώκεις· 6 ἀλλὰ
am Jesus whom thou persecutest;   but

ἀνάστηθι καὶ εἴσελθε εἰς τὴν πόλιν,
rise thou up, and enter into the city,

καὶ λαληθήσεταί σοι ὅ τί σε δεῖ ποιεῖν.
and it shall be told thee what thee it behoves to do.

7 οἱ δὲ ἄνδρες οἱ συνοδεύοντες αὐτῷ
Now the men – journeying with him

εἱστήκεισαν ἐνεοί, ἀκούοντες μὲν τῆς
stood speechless, hearing indeed the

φωνῆς, μηδένα δὲ θεωροῦντες. 8 ἠγέρθη δὲ
sound, but no man beholding.   And was raised

Σαῦλος ἀπὸ τῆς γῆς, ἀνεῳγμένων δὲ
Saul from the ground, and having been opened
              =when his eyes were opened

τῶν ὀφθαλμῶν αὐτοῦ οὐδὲν ἔβλεπεν·
the eyes of himᵃ nothing he saw;

χειραγωγοῦντες δὲ αὐτὸν εἰσήγαγον εἰς
and leading by the hand him they brought *in* into

Δαμασκόν. 9 καὶ ἦν ἡμέρας τρεῖς μὴ
Damascus.   And he was days three not

was without sight, and neither ate nor drank.

10 Now there was a disciple at Damascus named Anani′as. The Lord said to him in a vision, "Anani′as." And he said, "Here I am, Lord." ¹¹And the Lord said to him, "Rise and go to the street called Straight, and inquire in the house of Judas for a man of Tarsus named Saul; for behold, he is praying, ¹²and he has seen a man named Anani′as come in and lay his hands on him so that he might regain his sight." ¹³But Anani′as answered, "Lord, I have heard from many about this man, how much evil he has done to thy saints at Jerusalem; ¹⁴and here he has authority from the chief priests to bind all who call upon thy name." ¹⁵But the Lord said to him, "Go, for he is a chosen instrument of mine to carry my name before the Gentiles and kings and the sons of Israel; ¹⁶for I will show him how much he must suffer for the sake of my name." ¹⁷So Anani′as departed and entered the

βλέπων,   καὶ   οὐκ   ἔφαγεν   οὐδὲ   ἔπιεν.
seeing,   and   ate not   nor   drank.

10 ³Ην   δέ   τις   μαθητὴς   ἐν   Δαμασκῷ
Now there was a certain   disciple   in   Damascus
ὀνόματι   ʿΑνανίας,   καὶ   εἶπεν   πρὸς   αὐτὸν
by name   Ananias,   and   said   to   him
ἐν   ὁράματι   ὁ   κύριος·   ʿΑνανία.   ὁ   δὲ
in   a vision   the   Lord :   Ananias.   And he
εἶπεν·   ἰδοὺ   ἐγώ,   κύριε.   11 ὁ   δὲ   κύριος
said :   Behold[,]   I,   Lord.   And the   Lord
πρὸς   αὐτόν·   ἀναστὰς   πορεύθητι   ἐπὶ   τὴν
[said] to   him :   Rising up   go thou   to   the
ῥύμην   τὴν   καλουμένην   εὐθεῖαν   καὶ   ζήτησον
street   –   being called   Straight   and   seek
ἐν   οἰκίᾳ   ʾΙούδα   Σαῦλον   ὀνόματι   Ταρσέα·
in [the] house   of Judas   ²Saul   ³by name   ¹a Tarsian;
ἰδοὺ   γὰρ   προσεύχεται,   12 καὶ   εἶδεν   ἄνδρα
for behold   he is praying,   and   saw   ³a man
[ἐν   ὁράματι]   ʿΑνανίαν   ὀνόματι   εἰσελθόντα
¹in   ²a vision   Ananias   by name   coming in
καὶ   ἐπιθέντα   αὐτῷ   χεῖρας,   ὅπως   ἀναβλέψῃ.
and   putting on   him   hands,   so as   he may see again.
13 ἀπεκρίθη   δὲ   ʿΑνανίας·   κύριε,   ἤκουσα
And answered   Ananias :   Lord,   I heard
ἀπὸ   πολλῶν   περὶ   τοῦ   ἀνδρὸς   τούτου,
from   many   about   the   this man,
ὅσα   κακὰ   τοῖς   ἁγίοις   σου   ἐποίησεν
how many   evil things   to the   saints   of thee   he did
ἐν   ʾΙερουσαλήμ·   14 καὶ   ὧδε   ἔχει   ἐξουσίαν
in   Jerusalem;   and   here   he has   authority
παρὰ   τῶν   ἀρχιερέων   δῆσαι   πάντας   τοὺς
from   the   chief priests   to bind   all   the
ἐπικαλουμένους   τὸ   ὄνομά   σου.   15 εἶπεν
[ones] invoking   the   name   of thee.   said
δὲ   πρὸς   αὐτὸν   ὁ   κύριος·   πορεύου,   ὅτι
But   to   him   the   Lord :   Go thou,   because
σκεῦος   ἐκλογῆς   ἐστίν   μοι   οὗτος   τοῦ
³a vessel   ⁴of choice   ²is   ⁵to me   ¹this man   –
βαστάσαι   τὸ   ὄνομά   μου   ἐνώπιον   [τῶν]
to bearᵈ   the   name   of me   ²before   ³the
ἐθνῶν   τε   καὶ   βασιλέων   υἱῶν   τε   ʾΙσραήλ·
⁴nations   ¹both   ⁵and   ⁶kings   ⁸sons   ⁷and   ⁹of Israel;
16 ἐγὼ   γὰρ   ὑποδείξω   αὐτῷ   ὅσα   δεῖ
for I   will show   him   how many things   it behoves
αὐτὸν   ὑπὲρ   τοῦ   ὀνόματός   μου   παθεῖν.
him   on behalf of   the   name   of me   to suffer.
17 ʾΑπῆλθεν   δὲ   ʿΑνανίας   καὶ   εἰσῆλθεν
And went away   Ananias   and   entered

house. And laying his
hands on him he said,
"Brother Saul, the Lord
Jesus, who appeared to
you on the road by which
you came, has sent me
that you may regain your
sight and be filled with
the Holy Spirit." ¹⁸And
immediately something
like scales fell from his
eyes and he regained his
sight. Then he rose and
was baptized, ¹⁹and took
food and was strength-
ened.

For several days he
was with the disciples at
Damascus. ²⁰And in the
synagogues immediately
he proclaimed Jesus, say-
ing, "He is the Son of
God." ²¹And all who
heard him were amazed,
and said, "Is not this the
man who made havoc in
Jerusalem of those who
called on this name?
And he has come here
for this purpose, to bring
them bound before the
chief priests." ²²But Saul
increased all the more in
strength, and confounded
the Jews who lived in
Damascus by proving
that Jesus was the Christ.

23 When many days
had passed, the Jews
plotted to kill him, ²⁴but
their plot became known

εἰς   τὴν   οἰκίαν,   καὶ   ἐπιθεὶς   ἐπ'   αὐτὸν
into   the   house,   and   putting on   on   him

τὰς   χεῖρας   εἶπεν·   Σαοὺλ   ἀδελφέ,   ὁ
the(his)   hands   said :   Saul   brother,   the

κύριος   ἀπέσταλκέν   με,   Ἰησοῦς   ὁ   ὀφθείς   σοι
Lord   has sent   me,   Jesus   the [one] appear-   to
                                              ing   thee

ἐν   τῇ   ὁδῷ   ᾗ   ἤρχου,   ὅπως   ἀναβλέψῃς
in   the   way   which   thou camest,   so as   thou mayest see again

καὶ   πλησθῇς   πνεύματος   ἁγίου.   18 καὶ
and   be filled   of(with) Spirit   Holy.   And

εὐθέως   ἀπέπεσαν   αὐτοῦ   ἀπὸ   τῶν   ὀφθαλμῶν
immediately   fell away   of him   from   the   eyes

ὡς   λεπίδες,   ἀνέβλεψέν   τε,   καὶ   ἀναστὰς
as   scales,   and he saw again,   and   rising up

ἐβαπτίσθη,   19 καὶ   λαβὼν   τροφὴν   ἐνίσχυσεν.
was baptized,   and   taking   food   was strengthened.

Ἐγένετο   δὲ   μετὰ   τῶν   ἐν   Δαμασκῷ
Now he was   with   the   in   Damascus

μαθητῶν   ἡμέρας   τινάς,   20 καὶ   εὐθέως
disciples   days   some,   and   immediately

ἐν   ταῖς   συναγωγαῖς   ἐκήρυσσεν   τὸν   Ἰησοῦν,
in   the   synagogues   he proclaimed   –   Jesus,

ὅτι   οὗτός   ἐστιν   ὁ   υἱὸς   τοῦ   θεοῦ.
that   this one   is   the   Son   of God.

21 ἐξίσταντο   δὲ   πάντες   οἱ   ἀκούοντες   καὶ
And were amazed   all   the [ones] hearing   and

ἔλεγον·   οὐχ   οὗτός   ἐστιν   ὁ   πορθήσας
said :   Not   this man   is   the [one] having destroyed

εἰς   Ἰερουσαλὴμ   τοὺς   ἐπικαλουμένους
in   Jerusalem   the [ones]   invoking

τὸ   ὄνομα   τοῦτο,   καὶ   ὧδε   εἰς   τοῦτο   ἐληλύθει,
this name,   and   here   for   this   he had come,

ἵνα   δεδεμένους   αὐτοὺς   ἀγάγῃ   ἐπὶ   τοὺς
that   having been bound   them   he might bring   before the

ἀρχιερεῖς;   22 Σαῦλος   δὲ   μᾶλλον   ἐνε-
chief priests?   But Saul   more   was filled

δυναμοῦτο   καὶ   συνέχυννεν   Ἰουδαίους   τοὺς   κατ-
with power   and   confounded   Jews   the [ones]

οἰκοῦντας   ἐν   Δαμασκῷ,   συμβιβάζων   ὅτι   οὗτός
dwelling   in   Damascus,   proving   that this one

ἐστιν   ὁ   χριστός.   23 Ὡς   δὲ   ἐπληροῦντο
is   the   Christ.   And when   were fulfilled

ἡμέραι   ἱκαναί,   24 συνεβουλεύσαντο
days   considerable(many),   consulted together

οἱ   Ἰουδαῖοι   ἀνελεῖν   αὐτόν·   ἐγνώσθη   δὲ
the   Jews   to kill   him;   but was known

τῷ   Σαύλῳ   ἡ   ἐπιβουλὴ   αὐτῶν.   παρετη-
–   to Saul   the   plot   of them.   And they

to Saul. They were watching the gates day and night, to kill him; [25] but his disciples took him by night and let him down over the wall, lowering him in a basket.

26 And when he had come to Jerusalem he attempted to join the disciples; and they were all afraid of him, for they did not believe that he was a disciple. [27] But Barnabas took him, and brought him to the apostles, and declared to them how on the road he had seen the Lord, who spoke to him, and how at Damascus he had preached boldly in the name of Jesus. [28] So he went in and out among them at Jerusalem, [29] preaching boldly in the name of the Lord. And he spoke and disputed against the Hellenists; but they were seeking to kill him. [30] And when the brethren knew it, they brought him down to Caesare'a, and sent him off to Tarsus.

31 So the church throughout all Judea and Galilee and Samar'ia had peace and was built up;

ροῦντο δὲ καὶ τὰς πύλας ἡμέρας τε καὶ
carefully watched also the gates both by day and

νυκτὸς ὅπως αὐτὸν ἀνέλωσιν· 25 λαβόντες δὲ
by night so as him they might destroy; but [4]taking

οἱ μαθηταὶ αὐτοῦ νυκτὸς διὰ τοῦ
[1]the [3]disciples [3]of him by night through the

τείχους καθῆκαν αὐτὸν χαλάσαντες ἐν
wall let down him lowering in

σπυρίδι. 26 Παραγενόμενος δὲ εἰς
a basket. And arriving at

'Ιερουσαλὴμ ἐπείραζεν κολλᾶσθαι τοῖς
Jerusalem he tried to be joined to the

μαθηταῖς· καὶ πάντες ἐφοβοῦντο αὐτόν,
disciples; and all feared him,

μὴ πιστεύοντες ὅτι ἐστὶν μαθητής.
not believing that he is(was) a disciple.

27 Βαρναβᾶς δὲ ἐπιλαβόμενος αὐτὸν ἤγαγεν
But Barnabas taking hold of him led

πρὸς τοὺς ἀποστόλους, καὶ διηγήσατο
to the apostles, and narrated

αὐτοῖς πῶς ἐν τῇ ὁδῷ εἶδεν τὸν κύριον
to them how in the way he saw the Lord

καὶ ὅτι ἐλάλησεν αὐτῷ, καὶ πῶς ἐν
and that he spoke to him, and how in

Δαμασκῷ ἐπαρρησιάσατο ἐν τῷ ὀνόματι
Damascus he spoke boldly in the name

'Ιησοῦ. 28 καὶ ἦν μετ' αὐτῶν εἰσπορευόμενος
of Jesus. And he was with them going in

καὶ ἐκπορευόμενος εἰς 'Ιερουσαλήμ,
and going out in Jerusalem,

παρρησιαζόμενος ἐν τῷ ὀνόματι τοῦ
speaking boldly in the name of the

κυρίου, 29 ἐλάλει τε καὶ συνεζήτει πρὸς
Lord, [2]spoke [1]both [3]and [4]discussed with

τοὺς 'Ελληνιστάς· οἱ δὲ ἐπεχείρουν ἀνελεῖν
the Hellenists; and they attempted to kill

αὐτόν. 30 ἐπιγνόντες δὲ οἱ ἀδελφοὶ
him. But [3]knowing [1]the [2]brothers

κατήγαγον αὐτὸν εἰς Καισάρειαν καὶ
brought down him to Cæsarea and

ἐξαπέστειλαν αὐτὸν εἰς Ταρσόν.
sent forth him to Tarsus.

31 'Η μὲν οὖν ἐκκλησία καθ' ὅλης
[2]The - [1]therefore [3]church throughout all

τῆς 'Ιουδαίας καὶ Γαλιλαίας καὶ Σαμαρείας
- Judæa and Galilee and Samaria

εἶχεν εἰρήνην οἰκοδομουμένη καὶ πορευομένη
had peace being built and going

and walking in the fear of the Lord and in the comfort of the Holy Spirit it was multiplied. 32 Now as Peter went here and there among them all, he came down also to the saints that lived at Lydda. ³³There he found a man named Aene'as, who had been bedridden for eight years and was paralyzed. ³⁴And Peter said to him, "Aene'as, Jesus Christ heals you; rise and make your bed." And immediately he rose. ³⁵And all the residents of Lydda and Sharon saw him, and they turned to the Lord.
36 Now there was at Joppa a disciple named Tabitha, which means Dorcas or Gazelle. She was full of good works and acts of charity. ³⁷In those days she fell sick and died; and when they had washed her, they laid her in an upper room. ³⁸Since Lydda was near Joppa, the disciples, hearing that Peter was there, sent two men to him entreating him, "Please come to us without delay." ³⁹So Peter rose and

τῷ φόβῳ τοῦ κυρίου, καὶ τῇ παρακλήσει
in the fear of the Lord, and in the comfort
τοῦ ἁγίου πνεύματος ἐπληθύνετο.
of the Holy Spirit was multiplied.
32 Ἐγένετο δὲ Πέτρον διερχόμενον· διὰ
Now it came to pass Peter passing *through* through
πάντων κατελθεῖν καὶ πρὸς τοὺς ἁγίους
all [quarters] to come down[b] also to the saints
τοὺς κατοικοῦντας Λύδδα. 33 εὗρεν δὲ
- inhabiting Lydda. And he found
ἐκεῖ ἄνθρωπόν τινα ὀνόματι Αἰνέαν ἐξ
there a certain man by name Aeneas of
ἐτῶν ὀκτὼ . κατακείμενον ἐπὶ κραβάτου,
years eight lying on a mattress,
ὃς ἦν παραλελυμένος. 34 καὶ εἶπεν αὐτῷ
who was *having been* paralysed. And said to him
ὁ Πέτρος· Αἰνέα, ἰαταί σε Ἰησοῦς Χριστός·
- Peter : Aeneas, cures thee Jesus Christ;
ἀνάστηθι καὶ στρῶσον σεαυτῷ. καὶ
rise up and gird thyself. And
εὐθέως ἀνέστη. 35 καὶ εἶδαν αὐτὸν
immediately he rose up. And saw him
πάντες οἱ κατοικοῦντες Λύδδα καὶ τὸν
all the [ones] inhabiting Lydda and -
Σαρῶνα, οἵτινες ἐπέστρεψαν ἐπὶ τὸν κύριον.
Saron, who turned to the Lord.
Ἐν Ἰόππῃ δέ τις ἦν μαθήτρια ὀνόματι
²in ³Joppa ¹Now ⁵a certain ⁴was ⁶disciple by name
Ταβιθά, 36 ἡ διερμηνευομένη λέγεται
Tabitha, who being translated is called
Δορκάς· αὕτη ἦν πλήρης ἔργων ἀγαθῶν
Dorcas; this woman was full works of good
καὶ ἐλεημοσυνῶν ὧν ἐποίει. 37 ἐγένετο δὲ
and of alms which she did. And it happened
ἐν ταῖς ἡμέραις ἐκείναις ἀσθενήσασαν
in those days ailing
αὐτὴν ἀποθανεῖν· λούσαντες δὲ ἔθηκαν
she to die[b]; and having washed they put [her]
=being ill she died;
ἐν ὑπερῴῳ. 38 ἐγγὺς δὲ οὔσης Λύδδας
in an upper room. Now ³near ²being ¹Lydda[a]
τῇ Ἰόππῃ οἱ μαθηταὶ ἀκούσαντες ὅτι
- to Joppa the disciples having heard that
Πέτρος ἐστὶν ἐν αὐτῇ ἀπέστειλαν δύο
Peter is(was) in it sent two
ἄνδρας πρὸς αὐτὸν παρακαλοῦντες· μὴ
men to him beseeching: ²not
ὀκνήσῃς διελθεῖν ἕως ἡμῶν. 39 ἀναστὰς δὲ
¹hesitate to come to us. And rising up

went with them. And when he had come, they took him to the upper room. All the widows stood beside him weeping, and showing coats and garments which Dorcas made while she was with them. ⁴⁰But Peter put them all outside and knelt down and prayed; then turning to the body he said, "Tabitha, rise." And she opened her eyes, and when she saw Peter she sat up. ⁴¹And he gave her his hand and lifted her up. Then calling the saints and widows he presented her alive. ⁴²And it became known throughout all Joppa, and many believed in the Lord. ⁴³And he stayed in Joppa for many days with one Simon, a tanner.

Πέτρος συνῆλθεν αὐτοῖς· ὃν παραγενόμενον
Peter went with them; whom arriving

ἀνήγαγον εἰς τὸ ὑπερῷον, καὶ παρέστησαν
they led up into the upper room, and stood by

αὐτῷ πᾶσαι αἱ χῆραι κλαίουσαι καὶ
him all the widows weeping and

ἐπιδεικνύμεναι χιτῶνας καὶ ἱμάτια, ὅσα
showing tunics and garments, which

ἐποίει μετ' αὐτῶν οὖσα ἡ Δορκάς.
¹made ⁴with ⁵them ³being – ¹Dorcas.

40 ἐκβαλὼν δὲ ἔξω πάντας ὁ Πέτρος
And ²putting *out* ⁴outside ³all – ¹Peter

καὶ θεὶς τὰ γόνατα προσηύξατο, καὶ
and placing the knees he prayed, and
=kneeling down

ἐπιστρέψας πρὸς τὸ σῶμα εἶπεν· Ταβιθά,
turning to the body said : Tabitha,

ἀνάστηθι. ἡ δὲ ἤνοιξεν τοὺς ὀφθαλμοὺς
rise up. And she opened the eyes

αὐτῆς, καὶ ἰδοῦσα τὸν Πέτρον ἀνεκάθισεν.
of her, and seeing – Peter sat up.

41 δοὺς δὲ αὐτῇ χεῖρα ἀνέστησεν αὐτήν·
And giving her a hand he raised up her;

φωνήσας δὲ τοὺς ἁγίους καὶ τὰς χήρας
and calling the saints and the widows

παρέστησεν αὐτὴν ζῶσαν. **42** γνωστὸν δὲ
he presented her living. And known

ἐγένετο καθ' ὅλης τῆς Ἰόππης, καὶ
it became throughout all – Joppa, and

ἐπίστευσαν πολλοὶ ἐπὶ τὸν κύριον.
believed many on the Lord.

43 Ἐγένετο δὲ ἡμέρας ἱκανὰς μεῖναι ἐν
And it came to pass days several to remain in
=he remained many days

Ἰόππῃ παρά τινι Σίμωνι βυρσεῖ.
Joppa with one Simon a tanner.

CHAPTER 10

A T Caesare'a there was a man named Cornelius, a centurion of what was known as the Italian Cohort, ²a devout man who feared God with all his household, gave alms liberally

10 Ἀνὴρ δέ τις ἐν Καισαρείᾳ ὀνόματι
Now a certain man in Cæsarea by name

Κορνήλιος, ἑκατοντάρχης ἐκ σπείρης τῆς
Cornelius, a centurion of a cohort –

καλουμένης Ἰταλικῆς, **2** εὐσεβὴς καὶ
being called Italian, devout and

φοβούμενος τὸν θεὸν σὺν παντὶ τῷ οἴκῳ
fearing – God with all the household

αὐτοῦ, ποιῶν ἐλεημοσύνας πολλὰς τῷ
of him, doing alms many to the

to the people, and prayed constantly to God. ³About the ninth hour of the day he saw clearly in a vision an angel of God coming in and saying to him, "Cornelius." ⁴And he stared at him in terror, and said, "What is it, Lord?" And he said to him, "Your prayers and your alms have ascended as a memorial before God. ⁵And now send men to Joppa, and bring one Simon who is called Peter; ⁶he is lodging with Simon, a tanner, whose house is by the seaside." ⁷When the angel who spoke to him had departed, he called two of his servants and a devout soldier from among those that waited on him, ⁸and having related everything to them, he sent them to Joppa.

9 The next day, as they were on their journey and coming near the city, Peter went up on the housetop to pray, about the sixth hour. ¹⁰And he became hungry and desired something to eat; but while they

λαῷ καὶ δεόμενος τοῦ θεοῦ διὰ παντός,
people and petitioning – God continually,

3 εἶδεν ἐν ὁράματι φανερῶς, ὡσεὶ περὶ
saw in a vision clearly, as it were around

ὥραν ἐνάτην τῆς ἡμέρας, ἄγγελον τοῦ
hour ninth of the day, an angel –

θεοῦ εἰσελθόντα πρὸς αὐτὸν καὶ εἰπόντα
of God entering to him and saying

αὐτῷ· Κορνήλιε. 4 ὁ δὲ ἀτενίσας αὐτῷ
to him: Cornelius. And he gazing at him

καὶ ἔμφοβος γενόμενος εἶπεν· τί ἐστιν,
and terrified becoming said: What is it,

κύριε; εἶπεν δὲ αὐτῷ· αἱ προσευχαί
lord? And he said to him: The prayers

σου καὶ αἱ ἐλεημοσύναι σου ἀνέβησαν
of thee and the alms of thee went up

εἰς μνημόσυνον ἔμπροσθεν τοῦ θεοῦ. 5 καὶ
for a memorial before – God. And

νῦν πέμψον ἄνδρας εἰς Ἰόππην καὶ
now send men to Joppa and

μετάπεμψαι Σίμωνά τινα ὃς ἐπικαλεῖται
[summon ²Simon ¹one who is surnamed

Πέτρος· 6 οὗτος ξενίζεται παρά τινι
Peter; this man is lodged with one

Σίμωνι βυρσεῖ, ᾧ ἐστιν οἰκία παρὰ
Simon a tanner, to whom is a house° by
=who has a house

θάλασσαν. 7 ὡς δὲ ἀπῆλθεν ὁ ἄγγελος ὁ
[the] sea. And as went away the angel –

λαλῶν αὐτῷ, φωνήσας δύο τῶν οἰκετῶν
speaking to him, calling two of the household slaves

καὶ στρατιώτην εὐσεβῆ τῶν προσκαρτερούν-
and soldier a devout of the [ones] waiting

των αὐτῷ, 8 καὶ ἐξηγησάμενος ἅπαντα
on him, and explaining all things

αὐτοῖς ἀπέστειλεν αὐτοὺς εἰς τὴν Ἰόππην.
to them sent them to – Joppa.

9 Τῇ δὲ ἐπαύριον ὁδοιπορούντων ἐκείνων
And on the morrow journeying those

καὶ τῇ πόλει ἐγγιζόντων ἀνέβη Πέτρος
and to the city drawing near^a went up Peter
=as they journeyed and drew near to the city

ἐπὶ τὸ δῶμα προσεύξασθαι περὶ ὥραν
onto the roof to pray about hour

ἕκτην. 10 ἐγένετο δὲ πρόσπεινος καὶ
sixth. And he became hungry and

ἤθελεν γεύσασθαι· παρασκευαζόντων δὲ
wished to taste(eat); and preparing
=while they prepared

were preparing it, he fell into a trance [11] and saw the heaven opened, and something descending, like a great sheet, let down by four corners upon the earth. [12] In it were all kinds of animals and reptiles and birds of the air. [13] And there came a voice to him, "Rise, Peter; kill and eat." [14] But Peter said, "No, Lord; for I have never eaten anything that is common or unclean." [15] And the voice came to him again a second time, "What God has cleansed, you must not call common." [16] This happened three times, and the thing was taken up at once to heaven.

17 Now while Peter was inwardly perplexed as to what the vision which he had seen might mean, behold, the men that were sent by Cornelius, having made inquiry for Simon's house, stood before the gate [18] and called out to ask whether Simon who was called Peter was lodging there. [19] And while Peter was pondering the vision, the Spirit said to him, "Behold, three men are looking for you. [20] Rise

αὐτῶν ἐγένετο ἐπ' αὐτὸν ἔκστασις, 11 καὶ
them[a] there came on him an ecstasy, and

θεωρεῖ τὸν οὐρανὸν ἀνεῳγμένον καὶ
he beholds the heaven having been opened and

καταβαῖνον σκεῦός τι ὡς ὀθόνην μεγάλην,
coming down a certain vessel like sheet a great,

τέσσαρσιν ἀρχαῖς καθιέμενον ἐπὶ τῆς γῆς,
by four corners being let down onto the earth,

12 ἐν ᾧ ὑπῆρχεν πάντα τὰ τετράποδα
in which were all the quadrupeds

καὶ ἑρπετὰ τῆς γῆς καὶ πετεινὰ τοῦ
and reptiles of the earth and birds of the

οὐρανοῦ. 13 καὶ ἐγένετο φωνὴ πρὸς
heaven(air). And there came a voice to

αὐτόν· ἀναστάς, Πέτρε, θῦσον καὶ φάγε.
him: Rise up, Peter, slay and eat.

14 ὁ δὲ Πέτρος εἶπεν· μηδαμῶς, κύριε,
— But Peter said: Not at all, Lord,

ὅτι οὐδέποτε ἔφαγον πᾶν κοινὸν καὶ
because never did I eat every(any)thing common and

ἀκάθαρτον. 15 καὶ φωνὴ πάλιν ἐκ δευτέρου
unclean. And a voice again a second [time]

πρὸς αὐτόν· ἃ ὁ θεὸς ἐκαθάρισεν σὺ
[came] to him: What things — God cleansed [3]thou

μὴ κοίνου. 16 τοῦτο δὲ ἐγένετο ἐπὶ
[2]not [1]treat [4]as [5]unclean. And this occurred on

τρίς, καὶ εὐθὺς ἀνελήμφθη τὸ σκεῦος
three [occasions], and immediately was taken up the vessel

εἰς τὸν οὐρανόν. 17 Ὡς δὲ ἐν ἑαυτῷ
into — heaven. Now as in himself

διηπόρει ὁ Πέτρος τί ἂν εἴη τὸ ὅραμα
was doubting — Peter what might be the vision

ὃ εἶδεν, ἰδοὺ οἱ ἄνδρες οἱ ἀπεσταλμένοι
which he saw, behold[,] the men — having been sent

ὑπὸ τοῦ Κορνηλίου διερωτήσαντες τὴν
by — Cornelius asking for the

οἰκίαν τοῦ Σίμωνος ἐπέστησαν ἐπὶ τὸν
house — of Simon stood at at the

πυλῶνα, 18 καὶ · φωνήσαντες ἐπυνθάνοντο
porch, and calling inquired

εἰ Σίμων ὁ ἐπικαλούμενος Πέτρος ἐνθάδε
if Simon — being surnamed Peter here

ξενίζεται. 19 Τοῦ δὲ Πέτρου διενθυμουμένου
is lodged. — And Peter pondering[a]
=while Peter pondered

περὶ τοῦ ὁράματος εἶπεν τὸ πνεῦμα·
about the vision [3]said [1]the [2]Spirit:

ἰδοὺ ἄνδρες δύο ζητοῦντές σε· 20 ἀλλὰ
Behold[,] men two seeking thee; but

and go down, and accompany them without hesitation; for I have sent them." ²¹And Peter went down to the men and said, "I am the one you are looking for; what is the reason for your coming?" ²²And they said, "Cornelius, a centurion, an upright and God-fearing man, who is well spoken of by the whole Jewish nation, was directed by a holy angel to send for you to come to his house, and to hear what you have to say." ²³So he called them in to be his guests.
The next day he rose and went off with them, and some of the brethren from Joppa accompanied him. ²⁴And on the following day they entered Caesare′a. Cornelius was expecting them and had called together his kinsmen and close friends. ²⁵When Peter entered, Cornelius met him and fell down at his feet and worshiped him. ²⁶But Peter lifted him up, saying, "Stand up; I too am a man." ²⁷And as he

ἀναστὰς κατάβηθι, καὶ πορεύου σὺν αὐτοῖς
rising up go down, and go with them
μηδὲν διακρινόμενος, ὅτι ἐγὼ ἀπέσταλκα
nothing doubting, because I have sent
αὐτούς. 21 καταβὰς δὲ Πέτρος πρὸς
them. And going down Peter to
τοὺς ἄνδρας εἶπεν· ἰδοὺ ἐγώ εἰμι ὃν
the men said: Behold[,] I am [he] whom
ζητεῖτε· τίς ἡ αἰτία δι᾽ ἣν πάρεστε;
ye seek; what [is] the cause for which ye are here?
22 οἱ δὲ εἶπαν· Κορνήλιος ἑκατοντάρχης,
And they said: Cornelius a centurion,
ἀνὴρ δίκαιος καὶ φοβούμενος τὸν θεόν,
a man just and fearing – God,
μαρτυρούμενός τε ὑπὸ ὅλου τοῦ ἔθνους
and being witnessed to by all the nation
τῶν Ἰουδαίων, ἐχρηματίσθη ὑπὸ ἀγγέλου
of the Jews, was warned by angel
ἁγίου μεταπέμψασθαί σε εἰς τὸν οἶκον
a holy to summon thee to the house
αὐτοῦ καὶ ἀκοῦσαι ῥήματα παρὰ σοῦ.
of him and to hear words from thee.
23 εἰσκαλεσάμενος οὖν αὐτοὺς ἐξένισεν.
Calling in therefore them he lodged.
Τῇ δὲ ἐπαύριον ἀναστὰς ἐξῆλθεν σὺν
And on the morrow rising up he went forth with
αὐτοῖς, καί τινες τῶν ἀδελφῶν τῶν
them, and some of the brothers –
ἀπὸ Ἰόππης συνῆλθον αὐτῷ. 24 τῇ δὲ
from Joppa accompanied him. And on the
ἐπαύριον εἰσῆλθεν εἰς τὴν Καισάρειαν·
morrow he entered into – Cæsarea;
ὁ δὲ Κορνήλιος ἦν προσδοκῶν αὐτούς,
– and Cornelius was awaiting them,
συγκαλεσάμενος τοὺς συγγενεῖς αὐτοῦ καὶ
having called together the relatives of him and
τοὺς ἀναγκαίους φίλους. 25 Ὡς δὲ
the intimate friends. Now when
ἐγένετο τοῦ εἰσελθεῖν τὸν Πέτρον,ᵇ
it came to pass the to enter – Peter,ᵇ
= Now it came to pass when Peter entered,
συναντήσας αὐτῷ ὁ Κορνήλιος πεσὼν
²meeting ³him – ¹Cornelius falling
ἐπὶ τοὺς πόδας προσεκύνησεν. 26 ὁ δὲ
at the(his) feet worshipped. – But
Πέτρος ἤγειρεν αὐτὸν λέγων· ἀνάστηθι·
Peter raised him saying: Stand up;
καὶ ἐγὼ αὐτὸς ἄνθρωπός εἰμι. 27 καὶ
also I [my]self a man am. And

talked with him, he went in and found many persons gathered; ²⁸ and he said to them, "You yourselves know how unlawful it is for a Jew to associate with or to visit any one of another nation; but God has shown me that I should not call any man common or unclean. ²⁹ So when I was sent for, I came without objection. I ask then why you sent for me."
30 And Cornelius said, "Four days ago, about this hour, I was keeping the ninth hour of prayer in my house; and behold, a man stood before me in bright apparel, ³¹ saying, 'Cornelius, your prayer has been heard and your alms have been remembered before God. ³² Send therefore to Joppa and ask for Simon who is called Peter; he is lodging in the house of Simon, a tanner, by the seaside.' ³³ So I sent to you at once, and you have been kind enough to come. Now therefore we are all here present in the sight of God, to hear all that you have been commanded by the Lord."
34 And Peter opened

συνομιλῶν   αὐτῷ   εἰσῆλθεν,   καὶ   εὑρίσκει
talking with   him   he entered,   and   finds

συνεληλυθότας   πολλούς,   28 ἔφη   τε   πρὸς
having come together   many,   and said   to

αὐτούς·   ὑμεῖς   ἐπίστασθε   ὡς   ἀθέμιτόν   ἐστιν
them: Ye   understand   how   unlawful   it is

ἀνδρὶ   'Ιουδαίῳ   κολλᾶσθαι   ἢ   προσέρχεσθαι
for a man   a Jew   to adhere   or   to approach

ἀλλοφύλῳ·   κἀμοὶ   ὁ   θεὸς   ἔδειξεν   μηδένα
a foreigner;   and to me -   God   showed   ²not any

κοινὸν   ἢ   ἀκάθαρτον   λέγειν   ἄνθρωπον·
⁴common ⁵or   ⁶unclean   ¹to call   ³man;

29 διὸ   καὶ   ἀναντιρρήτως   ἦλθον   μετα-
wherefore indeed ²unquestioningly ²I came   ¹being

πεμφθείς.   πυνθάνομαι   οὖν,   τίνι   λόγῳ
summoned.   I inquire   therefore, for what reason

μετεπέμψασθέ   με;   30 καὶ   ὁ   Κορνήλιος
ye summoned   me?   And   -   Cornelius

ἔφη·   ἀπὸ   τετάρτης   ἡμέρας   μέχρι   ταύτης   τῆς
said: From   fourth   day   until   this   -
      = Four days ago

ὥρας   ἤμην   τὴν   ἐνάτην   προσευχόμενος
hour   I was   [at] the ninth   praying

ἐν   τῷ   οἴκῳ   μου,   καὶ   ἰδοὺ   ἀνὴρ   ἔστη
in the   house of me,   and behold[,] a man   stood

ἐνώπιόν   μου   ἐν   ἐσθῆτι   λαμπρᾷ,   31 καὶ
before   me   in clothing   bright,   and

φησίν·   Κορνήλιε,   εἰσηκούσθη   σου   ἡ
says: Cornelius,   was heard   of thee the

προσευχὴ   καὶ   αἱ   ἐλεημοσύναι σου   ἐμνήσθησαν
prayer   and the   alms   of thee were remembered

ἐνώπιον   τοῦ   θεοῦ.   32 πέμψον   οὖν   εἰς
before   -   God.   Send thou therefore to

'Ιόππην   καὶ   μετακάλεσαι   Σίμωνα   ὃς   ἐπι-
Joppa   and   send for   Simon   who   is

καλεῖται   Πέτρος·   οὗτος   ξενίζεται   ἐν   οἰκίᾳ
surnamed   Peter;   this man is lodged in [the] house

Σίμωνος   βυρσέως   παρὰ   θάλασσαν.   33 ἐξαυτῆς
of Simon   a tanner , by   [the] sea.   At once

οὖν   ἔπεμψα   πρὸς   σέ,   σύ   τε   καλῶς
therefore I sent   to   thee, and thou   well

ἐποίησας   παραγενόμενος.   νῦν   οὖν   πάντες
didst   arriving.   Now therefore all

ἡμεῖς   ἐνώπιον   τοῦ   θεοῦ   πάρεσμεν   ἀκοῦσαι
we   before   -   God   are present to hear

πάντα   τὰ   προστεταγμένα   σοι   ὑπὸ   τοῦ
all   the things having been commanded thee   by   the

κυρίου.   34 'Ανοίξας   δὲ   Πέτρος   τὸ   στόμα
Lord.   And opening   Peter   the(his) mouth

his mouth and said: "Truly I perceive that God shows no partiality, ³⁵ but in every nation any one who fears him and does what is right is acceptable to him. ³⁶ You know the word which he sent to Israel, preaching good news of peace by Jesus Christ (he is Lord of all), ³⁷ the word which was proclaimed throughout all Judea, beginning from Galilee after the baptism which John preached: ³⁸ how God anointed Jesus of Nazareth with the Holy Spirit and with power; how he went about doing good and healing all that were oppressed by the devil, for God was with him. ³⁹ And we are witnesses to all that he did both in the country of the Jews and in Jerusalem. They put him to death by hanging him on a tree; ⁴⁰ but God raised him on the third day and made him manifest; ⁴¹ not to all the people but to us who were chosen by God as witnesses, who ate and drank with him after he

εἶπεν· ἐπ' ἀληθείας καταλαμβάνομαι ὅτι
said: On(in) truth I perceive that

οὐκ ἔστιν προσωπολήμπτης ὁ θεός, 35 ἀλλ'
³not ²is ⁴a respecter of persons - ¹God, but

ἐν παντὶ ἔθνει ὁ φοβούμενος αὐτὸν καὶ
in every nation the [one] fearing him and

ἐργαζόμενος δικαιοσύνην δεκτὸς αὐτῷ ἐστιν·
working righteousness acceptable to him is;

36 τὸν λόγον ὃν ἀπέστειλεν τοῖς υἱοῖς
the word which he sent to the sons

Ἰσραὴλ εὐαγγελιζόμενος εἰρήνην διὰ Ἰησοῦ
of Israel preaching peace through Jesus

Χριστοῦ· οὗτός ἐστιν πάντων κύριος.
Christ: this one is of all Lord.

37 ὑμεῖς οἴδατε τὸ γενόμενον ῥῆμα καθ'
Ye know the having become thing throughout
= that which took place

ὅλης τῆς Ἰουδαίας, ἀρξάμενος ἀπὸ τῆς
all - Judæa, beginning from -

Γαλιλαίας μετὰ τὸ βάπτισμα ὃ ἐκήρυξεν
Galilee after the baptism which ²proclaimed

Ἰωάννης, 38 Ἰησοῦν τὸν ἀπὸ Ναζαρέθ,
¹John, Jesus the one from Nazareth,

ὡς ἔχρισεν αὐτὸν ὁ θεὸς πνεύματι ἁγίῳ
how anointed him - God with Spirit Holy

καὶ δυνάμει, ὃς διῆλθεν εὐεργετῶν καὶ
and power, who went about doing good and

ἰώμενος πάντας τοὺς καταδυναστευομένους
curing all the [ones] being oppressed

ὑπὸ τοῦ διαβόλου, ὅτι ὁ θεὸς ἦν μετ'
by the devil, because - God was with

αὐτοῦ· 39 καὶ ἡμεῖς μάρτυρες πάντων
him; and we [are] witnesses of all things

ὧν ἐποίησεν ἔν τε τῇ χώρᾳ τῶν Ἰουδαίων
which he did both in the country of the Jews

καὶ Ἰερουσαλήμ· ὃν καὶ ἀνεῖλαν
and Jerusalem; whom indeed they killed

κρεμάσαντες ἐπὶ ξύλου. 40 τοῦτον ὁ
hanging on a tree. This one -

θεὸς ἤγειρεν ἐν τῇ τρίτῃ ἡμέρᾳ καὶ
God raised on the third day and

ἔδωκεν αὐτὸν ἐμφανῆ γενέσθαι, 41 οὐ
gave him visible to become, not

παντὶ τῷ λαῷ, ἀλλὰ μάρτυσιν τοῖς
to all the people, but to witnesses -

προκεχειροτονημένοις ὑπὸ τοῦ θεοῦ, ἡμῖν,
having been previously appointed by - God, to us,

οἵτινες συνεφάγομεν καὶ συνεπίομεν αὐτῷ
who ate with and drank with him

rose from the dead. ⁴²And he commanded us to preach to the people, and to testify that he is the one ordained by God to be judge of the living and the dead. ⁴³To him all the prophets bear witness that every one who believes in him receives forgiveness of sins through his name."

44 While Peter was still saying this, the Holy Spirit fell on all who heard the word. ⁴⁵And the believers from among the circumcised who came with Peter were amazed, because the gift of the Holy Spirit had been poured out even on the Gentiles. ⁴⁶For they heard them speaking in tongues and extolling God. Then Peter declared, ⁴⁷"Can any one forbid water for baptizing these people who have received the Holy Spirit just as we have?" ⁴⁸And he commanded them to be baptized in the name of Jesus Christ. Then they asked him to remain for some days.

μετὰ   τὸ   ἀναστῆναι   αὐτὸν   ἐκ   νεκρῶν·
after   the   to rise again   him[b]   out of   [the] dead;
     =he rose again

42 καὶ   παρήγγειλεν   ἡμῖν   κηρῦξαι   τῷ   λαῷ
and   he commanded   us   to proclaim   to the people

καὶ   διαμαρτύρασθαι   ὅτι   οὗτός   ἐστιν   ὁ
and   solemnly to witness   that   this man   is   the [one]

ὡρισμένος   ὑπὸ   τοῦ   θεοῦ   κριτὴς   ζώντων
having been   by   -   God   judge   of living
designated

καὶ   νεκρῶν.   43   τούτῳ   πάντες   οἱ   προφῆται
and   of dead.   To this man   all   the   prophets

μαρτυροῦσιν,   ἄφεσιν   ἁμαρτιῶν   λαβεῖν   διὰ
witness,   ⁶forgiveness   ⁷of sins   ⁵to receive   ⁸through

τοῦ   ὀνόματος   αὐτοῦ   πάντα   τὸν   πιστεύοντα
⁹the   ¹⁰name   ¹¹of him   ¹everyone   ²believing

εἰς   αὐτόν.   44   Ἔτι   λαλοῦντος   τοῦ   Πέτρου
³in   ⁴him.   Yet   speaking   -   Peter[a]
     =While Peter was still speaking

τὰ   ῥήματα   ταῦτα   ἐπέπεσεν   τὸ   πνεῦμα
   these words   ⁴fell on   ¹the   ²Spirit

τὸ   ἅγιον   ἐπὶ   πάντας   τοὺς   ἀκούοντας
-   ³Holy   on   all   the [ones]   hearing

τὸν   λόγον.   45   καὶ   ἐξέστησαν   οἱ   ἐκ
the   discourse.   And   ⁵were amazed   ¹the   ²of [the]

περιτομῆς   πιστοὶ   ὅσοι   συνῆλθαν   τῷ   Πέτρῳ,
⁴circumcision   ³faithful   as many as   accompanied   -   Peter,

ὅτι   καὶ   ἐπὶ   τὰ   ἔθνη   ἡ   δωρεὰ   τοῦ   ἁγίου
because also   on   the nations   the   gift   of the Holy

πνεύματος   ἐκκέχυται·   46   ἤκουον   γὰρ
Spirit   has been poured out;   for they heard

αὐτῶν   λαλούντων   γλώσσαις   καὶ   μεγαλυνόν-
them   speaking   in tongues   and   magnify-

των   τὸν   θεόν.   τότε   ἀπεκρίθη   Πέτρος·
ing   -   God.   Then   answered   Peter:

47 μήτι   τὸ   ὕδωρ   δύναται   κωλῦσαί   τις
Not   ⁴the   ⁵water   ¹can   ³to forbid   ²anyone

τοῦ   μὴ   βαπτισθῆναι   τούτους,   οἵτινες   τὸ
-   ⁷not   ⁸to be baptized[d]   ⁶these,   who   the

πνεῦμα   τὸ   ἅγιον   ἔλαβον   ὡς   καὶ   ἡμεῖς;
Spirit   -   Holy   received   as   also   we?

48 προσέταξεν   δὲ   αὐτοὺς   ἐν   τῷ   ὀνόματι
And he commanded   them   in   the   name

Ἰησοῦ   Χριστοῦ   βαπτισθῆναι.   τότε   ἠρώτησαν
of Jesus   Christ   to be baptized.   Then   they asked

αὐτὸν   ἐπιμεῖναι   ἡμέρας   τινάς.
him   to remain   days   some.

CHAPTER 11

NOW the apostles and the brethren who were in Judea heard that the Gentiles also had received the word of God. ²So when Peter went up to Jerusalem, the circumcision party criticized him, ³saying, "Why did you go to uncircumcised men and eat with them?" ⁴But Peter began and explained to them in order: ⁵"I was in the city of Joppa praying; and in a trance I saw a vision, something descending, like a great sheet, let down from heaven by four corners; and it came down to me. ⁶Looking at it closely I observed animals and beasts of prey and reptiles and birds of the air. ⁷And I heard a voice saying to me, 'Rise, Peter; kill and eat.' ⁸But I said, 'No, Lord; for nothing common or unclean has ever entered my mouth.' ⁹But the voice answered a second time from heaven, 'What God has cleansed you must not call common.' ¹⁰This happened three times,

11 Ἤκουσαν δὲ οἱ ἀπόστολοι καὶ οἱ
Now heard   the   apostles   and the

ἀδελφοὶ οἱ ὄντες κατὰ τὴν Ἰουδαίαν
brothers   –   being throughout   –   Judæa

ὅτι καὶ τὰ ἔθνη ἐδέξαντο τὸν λόγον
that also the nations received   the   word

τοῦ θεοῦ. 2 Ὅτε δὲ ἀνέβη Πέτρος εἰς
– of God.   And when went up Peter   to

Ἰερουσαλήμ, διεκρίνοντο πρὸς αὐτὸν οἱ
Jerusalem,   disputed   with   him the [ones]

ἐκ περιτομῆς 3 λέγοντες ὅτι εἰσῆλθες
of [the] circumcision   saying[,] – Thou enteredst

πρὸς ἄνδρας ἀκροβυστίαν ἔχοντας καὶ
to   men   uncircumcision having and

συνέφαγες αὐτοῖς. 4 ἀρξάμενος δὲ Πέτρος
didst eat with them.   And beginning   Peter

ἐξετίθετο αὐτοῖς καθεξῆς λέγων· 5 ἐγὼ
explained to them in order saying: I

ἤμην ἐν πόλει Ἰόππῃ προσευχόμενος, καὶ
was in [the] city Joppa   praying,   and

εἶδον ἐν ἐκστάσει ὅραμα, καταβαῖνον
I saw in an ecstasy a vision, coming down

σκεῦός τι ὡς ὀθόνην μεγάλην τέσσαρσιν
a certain vessel as sheet a great by four

ἀρχαῖς καθιεμένην ἐκ τοῦ οὐρανοῦ, καὶ
corners having been let down out of – heaven, and

ἦλθεν ἄχρι ἐμοῦ· 6 εἰς ἢν ἀτενίσας
it came up to me; into which   gazing

κατενόουν, καὶ εἶδον τὰ τετράποδα τῆς
I perceived, and I saw the quadrupeds of the

γῆς καὶ τὰ θηρία καὶ τὰ ἑρπετὰ καὶ τὰ
earth and the wild beasts and the reptiles and the

πετεινὰ τοῦ οὐρανοῦ. 7 ἤκουσα δὲ καὶ
birds of the heaven(air).   And I heard also

φωνῆς λεγούσης μοι· ἀναστάς, Πέτρε,
a voice saying to me: Rise up, Peter,

θῦσον καὶ φάγε. 8 εἶπον δέ· μηδαμῶς,
slay and eat.   And I said : Not at all,

κύριε, ὅτι κοινὸν ἢ ἀκάθαρτον οὐδέποτε
Lord, because a common or unclean thing never

εἰσῆλθεν εἰς τὸ στόμα μου. 9 ἀπεκρίθη δὲ
entered into the mouth of me.   And answered

ἐκ δευτέρου φωνὴ ἐκ τοῦ οὐρανοῦ·
a second [time] a voice out of – heaven:

ἃ ὁ θεὸς ἐκαθάρισεν σὺ μὴ κοίνου.
What – God cleansed thou regard not common.
things

10 τοῦτο δὲ ἐγένετο ἐπὶ τρίς, καὶ
And this   happened on three [occasions], and

and all was drawn up again into heaven. ¹¹At that very moment three men arrived at the house in which we were, sent to me from Caesare′a. ¹²And the Spirit told me to go with them, making no distinction. These six brethren also accompanied me, and we entered the man's house. ¹³And he told us how he had seen the angel standing in his house and saying, 'Send to Joppa and bring Simon called Peter; ¹⁴he will declare to you a message by which you will be saved, you and all your household.' ¹⁵As I began to speak, the Holy Spirit fell on them just as on us at the beginning. ¹⁶And I remembered the word of the Lord, how he said, 'John baptized with water, but you shall be baptized with the Holy Spirit.' ¹⁷If then God gave the same gift to them as he gave to us when we believed in the Lord Jesus Christ, who was I that I could withstand God?" ¹⁸When they heard this they were

ἀνεσπάσθη   πάλιν   ἅπαντα   εἰς   τὸν   οὐρανόν.
was pulled up   again   all things   to   -   heaven.

11 καὶ   ἰδοὺ   ἐξαυτῆς   τρεῖς   ἄνδρες   ἐπέστησαν
And behold   at once   three   men   stood at

ἐπὶ   τὴν   οἰκίαν   ἐν   ᾗ   ἦμεν,   ἀπεσταλμένοι
at   the   house   in which   I was,   having been sent

ἀπὸ   Καισαρείας   πρός   με.   12 εἶπεν   δὲ
from   Cæsarea   to   me.   And ²told

τὸ   πνεῦμά   μοι   συνελθεῖν   αὐτοῖς   μηδὲν
¹the   ²Spirit   ⁴me   to go with   them   nothing

διακρίναντα.   ἦλθον   δὲ   σὺν   ἐμοὶ   καὶ
doubting.   And came   with   me   also

οἱ   ἐξ   ἀδελφοὶ   οὗτοι,   καὶ   εἰσήλθομεν   εἰς
-    six   brothers   these,   and   we entered   into

τὸν   οἶκον   τοῦ   ἀνδρός.   13 ἀπήγγειλεν   δὲ
the   house   of the   man.   And he reported

ἡμῖν   πῶς   εἶδεν   τὸν   ἄγγελον   ἐν   τῷ
to us   how   he saw   the   angel   in   the

οἴκῳ   αὐτοῦ   σταθέντα   καὶ   εἰπόντα·
house   of him   standing   and   saying:

ἀπόστειλον   εἰς   Ἰόππην   καὶ   μετάπεμψαι
Send   to   Joppa   and   summon

Σίμωνα   τὸν   ἐπικαλούμενον   Πέτρον,   14 ὃς
Simon   -   being surnamed   Peter,   who

λαλήσει   ῥήματα   πρὸς   σὲ   ἐν   οἷς   σωθήσῃ
will speak   words   to   thee   by   which   mayest be saved

σὺ   καὶ   πᾶς   ὁ   οἶκός   σου.   15 ἐν   δὲ
thou   and   all   the   household of thee.   And in

τῷ   ἄρξασθαί   με   λαλεῖν   ἐπέπεσεν   τὸ
the   to begin   meᵇᵉ   to speak   ⁴fell on   ²the
= as I began

πνεῦμα   τὸ   ἅγιον   ἐπ'   αὐτοὺς   ὥσπερ   καὶ
²Spirit   -   ³Holy   on   them   as   also

ἐφ'   ἡμᾶς   ἐν   ἀρχῇ.   16 ἐμνήσθην   δὲ   τοῦ
on   us   at [the] beginning.   And I remembered   the

ῥήματος   τοῦ   κυρίου,   ὡς   ἔλεγεν·   Ἰωάννης
word   of the   Lord,   how   he said: John

μὲν   ἐβάπτισεν   ὕδατι,   ὑμεῖς   δὲ   βαπτισθήσεσθε
indeed   baptized   with water,   but ye   will be baptized

ἐν   πνεύματι   ἁγίῳ.   17 εἰ   οὖν   τὴν   ἴσην
in   Spirit   Holy.   If   therefore   ⁴the   ⁵equal

δωρεὰν   ἔδωκεν   αὐτοῖς   ὁ   θεὸς   ὡς   καὶ
⁶gift   ²gave   ³them   -   ¹God   as   also

ἡμῖν,   πιστεύσασιν   ἐπὶ   τὸν   κύριον   Ἰησοῦν
to us,   having believed   on   the   Lord   Jesus

Χριστόν,   ἐγὼ   τίς   ἤμην   δυνατὸς   κωλῦσαι
Christ,   ²I   ¹who   ³was   [to be] able   to hinder

τὸν   θεόν;   18 ἀκούσαντες   δὲ   ταῦτα   ἡσύχασαν,
-    God?   And hearing   these things   they kept silence

silenced. And they glorified God, saying, "Then to the Gentiles also God has granted repentance unto life."
19 Now those who were scattered because of the persecution that arose over Stephen traveled as far as Phoeni'cia and Cyprus and Antioch, speaking the word to none except Jews. [20] But there were some of them, men of Cyprus and Cyre'ne, who on coming to Antioch spoke to the Greeks[9] also, preaching the Lord Jesus. [21] And the hand of the Lord was with them, and a great number that believed turned to the Lord. [22] News of this came to the ears of the church in Jerusalem, and they sent Barnabas to Antioch. [23] When he came and saw the grace of God, he was glad; and he exhorted them all to remain faithful to the Lord with steadfast purpose; [24] for he was a good man, full of the Holy Spirit and of faith. And a large company was added to the Lord. [25] So

[9] Other ancient authorities read *Hellenists*

καὶ   ἐδόξασαν   τὸν   θεὸν   λέγοντες·   ἄρα   καὶ
and   glorified   –   God   saying :   Then   also
τοῖς   ἔθνεσιν   ὁ   θεὸς   τὴν   μετάνοιαν   εἰς
to the   nations   –   God   –   repentance   to
ζωὴν   ἔδωκεν.
life   gave.

19 Οἱ   μὲν   οὖν   διασπαρέντες   ἀπὸ   τῆς
The [ones] –   therefore   being scattered   from   the
θλίψεως   τῆς   γενομένης   ἐπὶ   Στεφάνῳ
affliction   –   occurring   over   Stephen
διῆλθον   ἕως   Φοινίκης   καὶ   Κύπρου   καὶ
passed through   to   Phœnicia   and   Cyprus   and
'Αντιοχείας,   μηδενὶ   λαλοῦντες   τὸν   λόγον
Antioch,   to no one   speaking   the   word
εἰ   μὴ   μόνον   'Ιουδαίοις.   20 ²Ησαν   δέ
except   only   to Jews.   20 ²But ⁴were
τινες   ἐξ   αὐτῶν   ἄνδρες   Κύπριοι   καὶ
¹some   ²of   ³them   men   Cypriotes   and
Κυρηναῖοι,   οἵτινες   ἐλθόντες   εἰς   'Αντιόχειαν
Cyrenians,   who   coming   to   Antioch
ἐλάλουν   καὶ   πρὸς   τοὺς   ῾Ελληνας,
spoke   also   to   the   Greeks,
εὐαγγελιζόμενοι   τὸν   κύριον   'Ιησοῦν.   21 καὶ ἦν
preaching   the   Lord   Jesus.   And was
χεὶρ   κυρίου   μετ'   αὐτῶν,   πολύς   τε
[the] hand of [the] Lord   with   them,   and a much(great)
ἀριθμὸς   ὁ   πιστεύσας   ἐπέστρεψεν   ἐπὶ   τὸν
number   –   believing   turned   to   the
κύριον.   22 'Ηκούσθη   δὲ   ὁ   λόγος   εἰς
Lord.   And was heard   the   account   in
τὰ   ὦτα   τῆς   ἐκκλησίας   τῆς   οὔσης   ἐν
the   ears   of the   church   –   being   in
'Ιερουσαλὴμ   περὶ   αὐτῶν,   καὶ   ἐξαπέστειλαν
Jerusalem   about   them,   and   they sent out
Βαρναβᾶν   ἕως   'Αντιοχείας·   23 ὃς   παραγεν-
Barnabas   to   Antioch;   who   arriv-
όμενος   καὶ   ἰδὼν   τὴν   χάριν   τὴν   τοῦ
ing   and   seeing   the   grace   –   –
θεοῦ   ἐχάρη,   καὶ   παρεκάλει   πάντας   τῇ
of God   rejoiced,   and   exhorted   all   –
προθέσει   τῆς   καρδίας   προσμένειν   τῷ
with purpose   –   of heart   to remain with   the
κυρίῳ,   24 ὅτι   ἦν   ἀνὴρ   ἀγαθὸς   καὶ
Lord,   because   he was   man   a good   and
πλήρης   πνεύματος   ἁγίου   καὶ   πίστεως.
full   of [the] Spirit   Holy   and   of faith.
καὶ   προσετέθη   ὄχλος   ἱκανὸς   τῷ   κυρίῳ.
And   was added   a crowd   considerable   to the   Lord.

Barnabas went to Tarsus to look for Saul; ²⁶and when he had found him, he brought him to Antioch. For a whole year they met with the church, and taught a large company of people; and in Antioch the disciples were for the first time called Christians.

27 Now in these days prophets came down from Jerusalem to Antioch. ²⁸And one of them named Ag'abus stood up and foretold by the Spirit that there would be a great famine over all the world; and this took place in the days of Claudius. ²⁹And the disciples determined, every one according to his ability, to send relief to the brethren who lived in Judea; ³⁰and they did so, sending it to the elders by the hand of Barnabas and Saul.

25 ἐξῆλθεν δὲ εἰς Ταρσὸν ἀναζητῆσαι
And he went forth to Tarsus to seek
Σαῦλον, 26 καὶ εὑρὼν ἤγαγεν εἰς Ἀντιόχειαν.
Saul, and finding brought to Antioch.
ἐγένετο δὲ αὐτοῖς καὶ ἐνιαυτὸν ὅλον
And it happened to them also year a whole
συναχθῆναι ἐν τῇ ἐκκλησίᾳ καὶ διδάξαι
to be assembled in the church and to teach
ὄχλον ἱκανόν, χρηματίσαι τε πρώτως ἐν
a crowd considerable, and to call firstly in
Ἀντιοχείᾳ τοὺς μαθητὰς Χριστιανούς.
Antioch the disciples Christians.
27 Ἐν ταύταις δὲ ταῖς ἡμέραις κατῆλθον
And in these - days came down
ἀπὸ Ἱεροσολύμων προφῆται εἰς Ἀντιόχειαν·
from Jerusalem prophets to Antioch;
28 ἀναστὰς δὲ εἷς ἐξ αὐτῶν ὀνόματι
and rising up one of them by name
Ἄγαβος ἐσήμαινεν διὰ τοῦ πνεύματος
Agabus signified through the Spirit
λιμὸν μεγάλην μέλλειν ἔσεσθαι ἐφ' ὅλην τὴν
famine a great to be about to be over all the
οἰκουμένην· ἥτις ἐγένετο ἐπὶ Κλαυδίου.
inhabited earth; which happened in the time of Claudius.
29 τῶν δὲ μαθητῶν καθὼς εὐπορεῖτό
So ³of the ⁴disciples ¹as ⁵was prosperous
τις, ὥρισαν ἕκαστος αὐτῶν εἰς διακονίαν
²anyone, they determined each of them for ministration
πέμψαι τοῖς κατοικοῦσιν ἐν τῇ Ἰουδαίᾳ
to send ¹to the ³dwelling ⁴in - ⁵Judæa
ἀδελφοῖς· 30 ὃ καὶ ἐποίησαν ἀποστείλαντες
²brothers; which indeed they did sending
πρὸς τοὺς πρεσβυτέρους διὰ χειρὸς
to the elders through [the] hand
Βαρναβᾶ καὶ Σαύλου.
of Barnabas and of Saul.

CHAPTER 12

ABOUT that time Herod the king laid violent hands upon some who belonged to the church. ²He killed James the brother of John with the sword; ³and when he saw that it pleased the

12 Κατ' ἐκεῖνον δὲ τὸν καιρὸν ἐπέβαλεν
Now at that - time laid on
Ἡρώδης ὁ βασιλεὺς τὰς χεῖρας κακῶσαί
Herod the king the(his) hands to ill-treat
τινας τῶν ἀπὸ τῆς ἐκκλησίας. 2 ἀνεῖλεν δὲ
some of the [ones] from the church. And he killed
Ἰάκωβον τὸν ἀδελφὸν Ἰωάννου μαχαίρῃ.
James the brother of John with a sword.
3 ἰδὼν δὲ ὅτι ἀρεστόν ἐστιν τοῖς Ἰουδαίοις
And seeing that pleasing it is(was) to the Jews

Jews, he proceeded to arrest Peter also. This was during the days of Unleavened Bread. ⁴And when he had seized him, he put him in prison, and delivered him to four squads of soldiers to guard him, intending after the Passover to bring him out to the people. ⁵So Peter was kept in prison; but earnest prayer for him was made to God by the church.

6 The very night when Herod was about to bring him out, Peter was sleeping between two soldiers, bound with two chains, and sentries before the door were guarding the prison; ⁷and behold, an angel of the Lord appeared, and a light shone in the cell; and he struck Peter on the side and woke him, saying, "Get up quickly." And the chains fell off his hands. ⁸And the angel said to him, "Dress yourself and put on your sandals." And he did so. And he said to him, "Wrap your mantle around you and follow me." ⁹And he went out

προσέθετο συλλαβεῖν καὶ Πέτρον, ἦσαν δὲ
he added   to arrest   also Peter, and they were

ἡμέραι τῶν ἀζύμων, 4 ὃν καὶ πιάσας
days   –   of unleavened bread, whom also seizing

ἔθετο εἰς φυλακήν, παραδοὺς τέσσαρσιν
he put in   prison,   delivering to four

τετραδίοις στρατιωτῶν φυλάσσειν αὐτόν,
quaternions of soldiers   to guard   him,

βουλόμενος μετὰ τὸ πάσχα ἀναγαγεῖν
intending   after the Passover to bring up

αὐτὸν τῷ λαῷ. 5 ὁ μὲν οὖν Πέτρος
him to the people.   – –* therefore Peter

ἐτηρεῖτο ἐν τῇ φυλακῇ· προσευχὴ δὲ ἦν
was kept in the prison;   but prayer   was

ἐκτενῶς γινομένη ὑπὸ τῆς ἐκκλησίας πρὸς
earnestly being made by the church   to

τὸν θεὸν περὶ αὐτοῦ. 6 Ὅτε δὲ ἤμελλεν
–   God concerning him.   And when ²was about

προαγαγεῖν αὐτὸν ὁ Ἡρῴδης, τῇ νυκτὶ
³to bring forward ⁴him – ¹Herod, – ²night

ἐκείνῃ ἦν ὁ Πέτρος κοιμώμενος μεταξὺ
¹in that was – Peter   sleeping   between

δύο στρατιωτῶν δεδεμένος ἁλύσεσιν δυσίν,
two soldiers   having been bound with chains two,

φύλακές τε πρὸ τῆς θύρας ἐτήρουν τὴν
and guards   before the door were keeping the

φυλακήν. 7 καὶ ἰδοὺ ἄγγελος κυρίου
prison.   And behold[,] an angel of [the] Lord

ἐπέστη, καὶ φῶς ἔλαμψεν ἐν τῷ οἰκήματι·
came upon, and a light shone in the building;

πατάξας δὲ τὴν πλευρὰν τοῦ Πέτρου
and striking the side   – of Peter

ἤγειρεν αὐτὸν λέγων· ἀνάστα ἐν τάχει.
he raised him saying· Rise up in haste.

καὶ ἐξέπεσαν αὐτοῦ αἱ ἁλύσεις ἐκ τῶν
And fell off of him the chains   off the(his)

χειρῶν. 8 εἶπεν δὲ ὁ ἄγγελος πρὸς
hands.   And said   the angel to

αὐτόν· ζῶσαι καὶ ὑπόδησαι τὰ σανδάλιά
him: Gird thyself and put on the sandals

σου. ἐποίησεν δὲ οὕτως. καὶ λέγει
of thee. And he did   so.   And he tells

αὐτῷ· περιβαλοῦ τὸ ἱμάτιόν σου καὶ
him: Cast round the garment of thee and

ἀκολούθει μοι. 9 καὶ ἐξελθὼν ἠκολούθει,
follow   me.   And going forth he followed,

* μέν and δέ are in contrast : " on one hand . . ."—" on the other . . ."

and followed him; he did not know that what was done by the angel was real, but thought he was seeing a vision. ¹⁰When they had passed the first and the second guard, they came to the iron gate leading into the city. It opened to them of its own accord, and they went out and passed on through one street; and immediately the angel left him. ¹¹And Peter came to himself, and said, "Now I am sure that the Lord has sent his angel and rescued me from the hand of Herod and from all that the Jewish people were expecting."

12 When he realized this, he went to the house of Mary, the mother of John whose other name was Mark, where many were gathered together and were praying. ¹³And when he knocked at the door of the gateway, a maid named Rhoda came to answer. ¹⁴Recognizing Peter's voice, in her joy she did not open the gate but ran in and told that Peter was standing at the gate. ¹⁵They said to her, "You are mad." But she insisted that it

καὶ   οὐκ   ᾔδει   ὅτι   ἀληθές ἐστιν   τὸ
and   knew not   that   ³true ²is(was) ¹the thing
γινόμενον   διὰ   τοῦ   ἀγγέλου,   ἐδόκει   δὲ
happening   through the   angel,   but he thought
ὅραμα   βλέπειν.   10 διελθόντες   δὲ   πρώτην
a vision   to see.   And going through [the] first
φυλακὴν   καὶ   δευτέραν   ἦλθαν   ἐπὶ   τὴν
prison   and   [the] second they came   on   the
πύλην   τὴν   σιδηρᾶν   τὴν   φέρουσαν   εἰς   τὴν
gate   –   iron   –   leading   to   the
πόλιν,   ἥτις   αὐτομάτη   ἠνοίγη   αὐτοῖς,   καὶ
city,   which   of itself   was opened to them,   and
ἐξελθόντες   προῆλθον   ῥύμην   μίαν,   καὶ
going out   they went forward street   one,   and
εὐθέως   ἀπέστη   ὁ   ἄγγελος   ἀπ'   αὐτοῦ.
immediately departed   the   angel   from   him.
11 καὶ   ὁ   Πέτρος   ἐν   ἑαυτῷ   γενόμενος
And   –   Peter   in   himself   having become
εἶπεν·   νῦν   οἶδα   ἀληθῶς   ὅτι   ἐξαπέστειλεν
said: Now   I know   truly   that   sent forth
ὁ   κύριος   τὸν   ἄγγελον   αὐτοῦ   καὶ   ἐξείλατό
the   Lord   the   angel   of him   and   delivered
με   ἐκ   χειρὸς   Ἡρώδου   καὶ   πάσης   τῆς
me   out of [the] hand   of Herod and   of all   the
προσδοκίας   τοῦ   λαοῦ   τῶν   Ἰουδαίων.
expectation   of the people   of the   Jews.
12 συνιδών   τε   ἦλθεν   ἐπὶ   τὴν   οἰκίαν   τῆς
And realizing   he came   on   the   house   –
Μαρίας   τῆς   μητρὸς   Ἰωάννου   τοῦ
of Mary   the   mother   of John   –
ἐπικαλουμένου   Μάρκου,   οὗ   ἦσαν   ἱκανοὶ
being surnamed   Mark,   where   were   many
συνηθροισμένοι   καὶ   προσευχόμενοι.   13 κρού-
having been assembled and   praying.   And
σαντος   δὲ   αὐτοῦ   τὴν   θύραν   τοῦ   πυλῶνος
knocking   him ᵃ   the   door   of the   porch
=as he knocked
προσῆλθεν   παιδίσκη   ὑπακοῦσαι   ὀνόματι
approached   a maidservant   to listen   by name
Ῥόδη,   14 καὶ   ἐπιγνοῦσα   τὴν   φωνὴν   τοῦ
Rhoda,   and   recognizing   the   voice   –
Πέτρου   ἀπὸ   τῆς   χαρᾶς   οὐκ   ἤνοιξεν   τὸν
of Peter   from   –   joy   she did not open the
πυλῶνα,   εἰσδραμοῦσα   δὲ   ἀπήγγειλεν   ἑστάναι
porch,   but running in   announced   ²to stand
τὸν   Πέτρον   πρὸ   τοῦ   πυλῶνος.   15 οἱ   δὲ
–   ¹Peter   before   the   porch.   But they
πρὸς   αὐτὴν   εἶπαν·   μαίνῃ.   ἡ   δὲ   διϊσχυρίζετο
to   her   said: Thou ravest. But she emphatically asserted

was so. They said, "It is his angel!" ¹⁶But Peter continued knocking; and when they opened, they saw him and were amazed. ¹⁷But motioning to them with his hand to be silent, he described to them how the Lord had brought him out of the prison. And he said, "Tell this to James and to the brethren." Then he departed and went to another place.

18 Now when day came, there was no small stir among the soldiers over what had become of Peter. ¹⁹And when Herod had sought for him and could not find him, he examined the sentries and ordered that they should be put to death. Then he went down from Judea to Caesare′a, and remained there.

20 Now Herod was angry with the people of Tyre and Sidon; and they came to him in a body, and having persuaded Blastus, the king's chamberlain, they asked for peace, because their country depended on the king's country for food. ²¹On an appointed day Herod put on his royal robes, took his seat upon the throne, and made an oration to them. ²²And

οὕτως	ἔχειν.	οἱ	δὲ	ἔλεγον·	ὁ	ἄγγελός
so	to have(be).		So they	said:	The	angel

ἐστιν	αὐτοῦ.	16 ὁ	δὲ	Πέτρος	ἐπέμενεν
it is	of him.	– But		Peter	continued

κρούων·	ἀνοίξαντες	δὲ	εἶδαν	αὐτὸν	καὶ
knocking;	and having opened		they saw	him	and

ἐξέστησαν.	17 κατασείσας	δὲ	αὐτοῖς	τῇ
were amazed.	And beckoning		to them	with the

χειρὶ	σιγᾶν	διηγήσατο	αὐτοῖς	πῶς	ὁ
hand	to be quiet	he related	to them	how	the

κύριος	αὐτὸν	ἐξήγαγεν	ἐκ	τῆς	φυλακῆς,
Lord	him	led out	out of	the	prison,

εἶπέν	τε·	ἀπαγγείλατε	Ἰακώβῳ	καὶ	τοῖς
and said:		Report	to James	and	to the

ἀδελφοῖς	ταῦτα.	καὶ	ἐξελθὼν	ἐπορεύθη	εἰς
brothers	these things.	And	going out	he went	to

ἕτερον	τόπον.	18 Γενομένης	δὲ	ἡμέρας	ἦν
another	place.	And becoming = when it became		day* day	there was

τάραχος	οὐκ	ὀλίγος	ἐν	τοῖς	στρατιώταις,
disturbance	not	a little	among	the	soldiers,

τί	ἄρα	ὁ	Πέτρος	ἐγένετο.	19 Ἡρῴδης	δὲ
what then	–	[of]	Peter	became.	And Herod	

ἐπιζητήσας	αὐτὸν	καὶ	μὴ	εὑρών,
searching for	him	and	not	finding,

ἀνακρίνας	τοὺς	φύλακας	ἐκέλευσεν	ἀπ-
examining	the	guards	commanded	to

αχθῆναι,	καὶ	κατελθὼν	ἀπὸ	τῆς	Ἰουδαίας
be led away,*	and	going down	from	–	Judæa

εἰς	Καισάρειαν	διέτριβεν.	20 Ἦν	δὲ
to	Cæsarea	stayed.	Now he was	

θυμομαχῶν	Τυρίοις	καὶ	Σιδωνίοις·
being furiously angry with	Tyrians	and	Sidonians;

ὁμοθυμαδὸν	δὲ	παρῆσαν	πρὸς	αὐτόν,	καὶ
and with one mind		they came	to	him,	and

πείσαντες	Βλάστον	τὸν	ἐπὶ	τοῦ	κοιτῶνος
having persuaded	Blastus	the one	over	the	bedchamber

τοῦ	βασιλέως	ᾐτοῦντο	εἰρήνην,	διὰ	τὸ
of the	king	they asked	peace,	because the	

τρέφεσθαι	αὐτῶν	τὴν	χώραν	ἀπὸ	τῆς
to be fed = their country was fed	of them	the	country[b]	from	the

βασιλικῆς.	21 τακτῇ	δὲ	ἡμέρᾳ	ὁ	Ἡρῴδης
royal.	And on an appointed day			–	Herod

ἐνδυσάμενος	ἐσθῆτα βασιλικὴν	καθίσας ἐπὶ
having been arrayed with	clothing regal	sitting on

τοῦ	βήματος	ἐδημηγόρει	πρὸς	αὐτούς·
the	tribunal	made a public speech	to	them;

* That is, to execution.

the people shouted, "The voice of a god, and not of man!" ²³Immediately an angel of the Lord smote him, because he did not give God the glory; and he was eaten by worms and died. 24 But the word of God grew and multiplied. 25 And Barnabas and Saul returned from^h Jerusalem when they had fulfilled their mission, bringing with them John whose other name was Mark.

22 ὁ   δὲ   δῆμος   ἐπεφώνει·   θεοῦ   φωνὴ
   and the   mob   cried out :   Of a god   a voice

καὶ   οὐκ   ἀνθρώπου.   23 παραχρῆμα   δὲ
and   not   of a man.   And at once

ἐπάταξεν   αὐτὸν   ἄγγελος   κυρίου   ἀνθ’   ὧν
smote   him   an angel   of [the] Lord   because

οὐκ   ἔδωκεν   τὴν   δόξαν   τῷ   θεῷ,   καὶ
he gave not   the   glory   –   to God,   and

γενόμενος   σκωληκόβρωτος   ἐξέψυξεν.
becoming   eaten by worms   he expired.

24 Ὁ   δὲ   λόγος   τοῦ   κυρίου   ηὔξανεν
   But the   word   of the   Lord   grew

καὶ   ἐπληθύνετο.   25 Βαρναβᾶς   δὲ   καὶ
and   increased.   And Barnabas   and

Σαῦλος   ὑπέστρεψαν   ἐξ   Ἰερουσαλήμ,
Saul   returned   out of   Jerusalem,

πληρώσαντες   τὴν   διακονίαν,   συμπαρα-
having completed   the   ministration,   taking

λαβόντες   Ἰωάννην   τὸν   ἐπικληθέντα   Μᾶρκον.
with [them]   John   –   surnamed   Mark.

CHAPTER 13

NOW in the church at Antioch there were prophets and teachers, Barnabas, Symeon who was called Niger, Lucius of Cyre'ne, Man'a-en a member of the court of Herod the tetrarch, and Saul. ²While they were worshiping the Lord and fasting, the Holy Spirit said, "Set apart for me Barnabas and Saul for the work to which I have called them." ³Then after fasting and praying they laid their hands on them and sent them off.

4 So, being sent out

13 Ἦσαν   δὲ   ἐν   Ἀντιοχείᾳ   κατὰ   τὴν
   Now there were   in   Antioch   among   the

οὖσαν   ἐκκλησίαν   προφῆται   καὶ   διδάσκαλοι
existing   church   prophets   and   teachers

ὅ   τε   Βαρναβᾶς   καὶ   Συμεὼν   ὁ   καλούμενος
– both   Barnabas   and   Simeon   –   being called

Νίγερ,   καὶ   Λούκιος   ὁ   Κυρηναῖος,   Μαναήν   τε
Niger,   and   Lucius   the   Cyrenian,   and Manaen

Ἡρῴδου   τοῦ   τετραάρχου   σύντροφος
²of Herod   ³the   ⁴tetrarch   ¹foster brother

καὶ   Σαῦλος.   2 Λειτουργούντων   δὲ   αὐτῶν
and   Saul.   And ministering   –   them*
                              =as they ministered

τῷ   κυρίῳ   καὶ   νηστευόντων   εἶπεν   τὸ
to the   Lord   and   fasting*   said   the

πνεῦμα   τὸ   ἅγιον·   ἀφορίσατε   δή   μοι
Spirit   –   Holy·   ²Separate ye   ¹so then   ³to me

τὸν   Βαρναβᾶν   καὶ   Σαῦλον   εἰς   τὸ   ἔργον
–   Barnabas   and   Saul   for   the   work

ὅ   προσκέκλημαι   αὐτούς·   3 τότε   νηστεύ-
[to] which   I have called   them;   then   having

σαντες   καὶ   προσευξάμενοι   καὶ   ἐπιθέντες
fasted   and   having prayed   and   ¹laying ⁴on

τὰς   χεῖρας   αὐτοῖς   ἀπέλυσαν.
²the(ir)   ³hands   ⁵them   ⁶they dismissed [them].

4 Αὐτοὶ   μὲν   οὖν   ἐκπεμφθέντες   ὑπὸ   τοῦ
   They   –   therefore   sent out   by   the

^{h} Other ancient authorities read *to*

by the Holy Spirit, they went down to Seleu'cia; and from there they sailed to Cyprus. ⁵When they arrived at Sal'amis, they proclaimed the word of God in the synagogues of the Jews. And they had John to assist them. ⁶When they had gone through the whole island as far as Paphos, they came upon a certain magician, a Jewish false prophet, named Bar-Jesus. ⁷He was with the proconsul, Sergius Paulus, a man of intelligence, who summoned Barnabas and Saul and sought to hear the word of God. ⁸But El'ymas the magician (for that is the meaning of his name) withstood them, seeking to turn away the proconsul from the faith. ⁹But Saul, who is also called Paul, filled with the Holy Spirit, looked intently at him ¹⁰and said, "You son of the devil, you enemy of all righteousness, full of all deceit and villainy, will you not stop making crooked the straight paths of the Lord? ¹¹And now, behold, the hand of the Lord is upon you, and you shall be blind and unable to see the sun for a time." Immediately

ἁγίου πνεύματος κατῆλθον εἰς Σελεύκειαν,
Holy Spirit went down to Seleucia,

ἐκεῖθέν τε ἀπέπλευσαν εἰς Κύπρον, 5 καὶ
and thence sailed away to Cyprus, and

γενόμενοι ἐν Σαλαμῖνι κατήγγελλον τὸν
being in Salamis they announced the

λόγον τοῦ θεοῦ ἐν ταῖς συναγωγαῖς τῶν
word - of God in the synagogues of the

Ἰουδαίων· εἶχον δὲ καὶ Ἰωάννην ὑπηρέτην.
Jews; and they had also John [as] attendant.

6 Διελθόντες δὲ ὅλην τὴν νῆσον ἄχρι
And passing through all the island unto

Πάφου εὗρον ἄνδρα τινὰ μάγον ψευδο-
Paphos they found a certain man a sorcerer a ²false

προφήτην Ἰουδαῖον, ᾧ ὄνομα Βαριησοῦς,
²prophet ¹Jewish, to whom nameᶜ Barjesus,
=whose name was

7 ὃς ἦν σὺν τῷ ἀνθυπάτῳ Σεργίῳ
who was with the proconsul Sergius

Παύλῳ, ἀνδρὶ συνετῷ. οὗτος προσ-
Paulus, man an intelligent. This man calling

καλεσάμενος Βαρναβᾶν καὶ Σαῦλον ἐπεζήτησεν
to [him] Barnabas and Saul sought

ἀκοῦσαι τὸν λόγον τοῦ θεοῦ· 8 ἀνθίστατο δὲ
to hear the word - of God; but opposed

αὐτοῖς Ἐλύμας ὁ μάγος, οὕτως γὰρ
them Elymas the sorcerer, for so

μεθερμηνεύεται τὸ ὄνομα αὐτοῦ, ζητῶν
is translated the name of him, seeking

διαστρέψαι τὸν ἀνθύπατον ἀπὸ τῆς
to divert the proconsul from the

πίστεως. 9 Σαῦλος δέ, ὁ καὶ Παῦλος,
faith. But Saul, the [one] also Paul,

πλησθεὶς πνεύματος ἁγίου ἀτενίσας εἰς
filled of(with) Spirit Holy gazing at

αὐτὸν εἶπεν· 10 ὦ πλήρης παντὸς δόλου
him said: O full of all deceit

καὶ πάσης ῥᾳδιουργίας, υἱὲ διαβόλου,
and of all fraud, son of [the] devil,

ἐχθρὲ πάσης δικαιοσύνης, οὐ παύσῃ
enemy of all righteousness, wilt thou not cease

διαστρέφων τὰς ὁδοὺς τοῦ κυρίου τὰς
perverting the ways of the Lord -

εὐθείας; 11 καὶ νῦν ἰδοὺ χεὶρ κυρίου
right? And now behold[,] [the] hand of [the] Lord

ἐπὶ σέ, καὶ ἔσῃ τυφλὸς μὴ βλέπων
[is] on thee, and thou wilt be blind not seeing

τὸν ἥλιον ἄχρι καιροῦ. παραχρῆμα δὲ
the sun until [such] a time. And at once

mist and darkness fell upon him and he went about seeking people to lead him by the hand. ¹²Then the proconsul believed, when he saw what had occurred, for he was astonished at the teaching of the Lord. 13 Now Paul and his company set sail from Paphos, and came to Perga in Pamphyl'ia. And John left them and returned to Jerusalem; ¹⁴but they passed on from Perga and came to Antioch of Pisid'ia. And on the sabbath day they went into the synagogue and sat down. ¹⁵After the reading of the law and the prophets, the rulers of the synagogue sent to them, saying, "Brethren, if you have any word of exhortation for the people, say it." ¹⁶So Paul stood up, and motioning with his hand said:

"Men of Israel, and you that fear God, listen. ¹⁷The God of this people Israel chose our fathers and made the people great during their stay in the land of Egypt, and

ἔπεσεν ἐπ᾽ αὐτὸν ἀχλὺς καὶ σκότος, καὶ
fell   on   him   a mist and darkness, and
περιάγων ἐζήτει χειραγωγούς.   12 τότε
going about he sought leaders by the hand.   Then
ἰδὼν   ὁ   ἀνθύπατος   τὸ   γεγονὸς
³seeing ¹the   ²proconsul   the thing having occurred
ἐπίστευσεν, ἐκπλησσόμενος ἐπὶ τῇ διδαχῇ
believed,   being astounded at the teaching
τοῦ κυρίου.
of the Lord.
13 Ἀναχθέντες δὲ ἀπὸ τῆς Πάφου οἱ
And setting sail from   -   Paphos the ones
περὶ Παῦλον ἦλθον εἰς Πέργην τῆς
around(with) Paul   came   to   Perga   -
Παμφυλίας· Ἰωάννης δὲ ἀποχωρήσας ἀπ᾽
of Pamphylia; and John   departing   from
αὐτῶν ὑπέστρεψεν εἰς Ἱεροσόλυμα.
them   returned   to   Jerusalem.
14 Αὐτοὶ δὲ διελθόντες ἀπὸ τῆς Πέργης
And they   going through from   -   Perga
παρεγένοντο εἰς Ἀντιόχειαν τὴν Πισιδίαν,
arrived   in   Antioch   the   Pisidian,
καὶ ἐλθόντες εἰς τὴν συναγωγὴν τῇ
and going   into the   synagogue   on the
ἡμέρᾳ τῶν σαββάτων ἐκάθισαν.   15 μετὰ δὲ
day   of the sabbaths   sat down.   And after
τὴν ἀνάγνωσιν τοῦ νόμου καὶ τῶν
the   reading   of the law   and of the
προφητῶν ἀπέστειλαν οἱ ἀρχισυνάγωγοι
prophets   sent   the synagogue rulers
πρὸς αὐτοὺς λέγοντες· ἄνδρες ἀδελφοί,
to   them   saying: Men   brothers,
εἴ τίς ἐστιν ἐν ὑμῖν λόγος παρακλήσεως
¹if ²any ²there is ³among ⁴you ⁵word of exhortation
πρὸς τὸν λαόν, λέγετε. 16 ἀναστὰς δὲ
to   the people, say ye.   And ¹rising up
Παῦλος καὶ κατασείσας τῇ χειρὶ εἶπεν·
⁴Paul   ²and   ³beckoning ⁴with the(his) ⁵hand said:
ἄνδρες Ἰσραηλῖται καὶ οἱ φοβούμενοι τὸν
Men   Israelites   and the [ones] fearing   -
θεόν, ἀκούσατε.   17 ὁ θεὸς τοῦ λαοῦ
God,   hear ye.   The God   -   people
τούτου Ἰσραὴλ ἐξελέξατο τοὺς πατέρας
of this   Israel   chose   the   fathers
ἡμῶν, καὶ τὸν λαὸν ὕψωσεν ἐν τῇ
of us,   and ²the ²people ¹exalted in   the
παροικίᾳ ἐν γῇ Αἰγύπτου, καὶ μετὰ
sojourn   in [the] land of Egypt,   and with

with uplifted arm he led them out of it. [18]And for about forty years he bore with[i] them in the wilderness. [19]And when he had destroyed seven nations in the land of Canaan, he gave them their land as an inheritance, for about four hundred and fifty years. [20]And after that he gave them judges until Samuel the prophet. [21]Then they asked for a king; and God gave them Saul the son of Kish, a man of the tribe of Benjamin, for forty years. [22]And when he had removed him, he raised up David to be their king; of whom he testified and said, 'I have found in David the son of Jesse a man after my heart, who will do all my will.' [23]Of this man's posterity God has brought to Israel a Savior, Jesus, as he promised. [24]Before his coming John had preached a baptism of repentance to all the people of Israel. [25]And as John was finishing his course, he said, 'What do you suppose that I am? I am not he. No, but after me one is coming,

[i] Other ancient authorities read *cared for* (Deut. 1. 31)

βραχίονος   ὑψηλοῦ   ἐξήγαγεν   αὐτοὺς   ἐξ
arm   a high   he led forth them   out of
αὐτῆς,   18   καὶ   ὡς   τεσσερακονταέτη   χρόνον
it,   and   about forty years   time
ἐτροποφόρησεν   αὐτοὺς   ἐν   τῇ   ἐρήμῳ,   19   καὶ
endured   them   in   the   desert,   and
καθελὼν   ἔθνη   ἑπτὰ   ἐν   γῇ   Χανάαν
having destroyed nations seven in [the] land Canaan
κατεκληρονόμησεν   τὴν   γῆν   αὐτῶν   20   ὡς
gave as an inheritance the   land   of them   about
ἔτεσιν   τετρακοσίοις   καὶ   πεντήκοντα.   καὶ
years   four hundreds   and   fifty.   And
μετὰ   ταῦτα   ἔδωκεν   κριτὰς   ἕως   Σαμουὴλ
after these things he gave   judges   until Samuel
προφήτου.   21   κἀκεῖθεν   ᾐτήσαντο   βασιλέα,
a prophet.   And thence   they asked   a king,
καὶ   ἔδωκεν   αὐτοῖς   ὁ   θεὸς   τὸν   Σαοὺλ
and   gave   them   –   God   –   Saul
υἱὸν   Κίς,   ἄνδρα   ἐκ   φυλῆς   Βενιαμίν,
son   of Cis,   a man   of [the] tribe of Benjamin,
ἔτη   τεσσεράκοντα·   22   καὶ   μεταστήσας
years forty;   and   removing
αὐτὸν   ἤγειρεν   τὸν   Δαυὶδ   αὐτοῖς   εἰς
him   he raised   –   David   to them   for
βασιλέα,   ᾧ   καὶ   εἶπεν   μαρτυρήσας·
a king,   to whom also he said   giving witness:
εὗρον   Δαυὶδ   τὸν   τοῦ   Ἰεσσαί,   ἄνδρα
I found David   the [son] – of Jesse,   a man
κατὰ   τὴν   καρδίαν   μου,   ὃς   ποιήσει   πάντα
according to the heart   of me, who   will do   all
τὰ   θελήματά   μου.   23   τούτου   ὁ   θεὸς
the   wishes   of me.   [4]Of this man –   [5]God
ἀπὸ   τοῦ   σπέρματος   κατ'   ἐπαγγελίαν
[1]from [2]the [3]seed   according to promise
ἤγαγεν   τῷ   Ἰσραὴλ   σωτῆρα   Ἰησοῦν,
brought   –   to Israel a Saviour   Jesus,
24   προκηρύξαντος   Ἰωάννου   πρὸ   προσώπου
previously proclaiming John[a]   before face
=when John had previously proclaimed
τῆς   εἰσόδου   αὐτοῦ   βάπτισμα   μετανοίας
of the entrance of him   a baptism   of repentance
παντὶ   τῷ   λαῷ   Ἰσραήλ.   25   ὡς   δὲ
to all   the   people of Israel.   Now as
ἐπλήρου   Ἰωάννης   τὸν   δρόμον,   ἔλεγεν·
completed John   the(his) course,   he said:
τί   ἐμὲ   ὑπονοεῖτε   εἶναι;   οὐκ   εἰμὶ   ἐγώ·
What me   suppose ye   to be?   [3]Not [2]am   [1]I;
ἀλλ'   ἰδοὺ   ἔρχεται   μετ'   ἐμὲ   οὗ   οὐκ   εἰμὶ
but   behold he comes   after me of whom I am not

the sandals of whose feet
I am not worthy to
untie.'
26 "Brethren, sons of
the family of Abraham,
and those among you
that fear God, to us has
been sent the message of
this salvation. ²⁷For
those who live in Jerusa-
lem and their rulers,
because they did not
recognize him nor
understand the utter-
ances of the prophets
which are read every
sabbath, fulfilled these
by condemning him.
²⁸Though they could
charge him with nothing
deserving death, yet they
asked Pilate to have him
killed. ²⁹And when they
had fulfilled all that was
written of him, they took
him down from the tree,
and laid him in a tomb.
³⁰But God raised him
from the dead; ³¹and for
many days he appeared
to those who came up
with him from Galilee to
Jerusalem, who are now
his witnesses to the
people. ³²And we bring
you the good news that
what God promised to
the fathers, ³³this he has
fulfilled to us their children by raising Jesus; as
also it is written in the
second psalm,
'Thou art my Son,
today I have begotten
thee.'

ἄξιος   τὸ   ὑπόδημα   τῶν   ποδῶ   λῦσαι.
worthy   the   sandal   of the   feet   to loosen.
26 Ἄνδρες   ἀδελφοί,   υἱοὶ   γένους   Ἀβραὰμ
   Men   brothers,   sons of [the] race of Abraham
καὶ   οἱ   ἐν   ὑμῖν   φοβούμενοι   τὸν   θεόν,
and   the [ones] among you   fearing   -   God,
ἡμῖν   ὁ   λόγος   τῆς   σωτηρίας   ταύτης
to us   the   word   of this salvation
ἐξαπεστάλη.   27   οἱ   γὰρ   κατοικοῦντες   ἐν
was sent forth.   For the [ones] dwelling   in
Ἰερουσαλὴμ   καὶ   οἱ   ἄρχοντες   αὐτῶν   τοῦτον
Jerusalem   and   the   rulers   of them ²this man
ἀγνοήσαντες καὶ τὰς φωνὰς τῶν προφητῶν τὰς
¹not knowing   and the   voices of the   prophets   -
κατὰ   πᾶν   σάββατον   ἀναγινωσκομένας
²throughout(on) ³every ⁴sabbath   ¹being read
κρίναντες   ἐπλήρωσαν,   28 καὶ   μηδεμίαν
judging   they fulfilled,   and   no
αἰτίαν θανάτου εὑρόντες ᾐτήσαντο Πιλᾶτον
cause   of death   finding   they asked   Pilate
ἀναιρεθῆναι αὐτόν· 29 ὡς δὲ ἐτέλεσαν πάντα
to be destroyed him;   and when they finished   all
τὰ   περὶ αὐτοῦ γεγραμμένα, καθελόντες
the things concerning him having been written, taking down
ἀπὸ τοῦ ξύλου ἔθηκαν εἰς μνημεῖον.
from the   tree   they laid   in   a tomb.
30 ὁ δὲ θεὸς ἤγειρεν αὐτὸν ἐκ νεκρῶν·
   - But God   raised   him   out of [the] dead;
31 ὃς ὤφθη ἐπὶ ἡμέρας πλείους τοῖς
   who appeared over   days   many   to the [ones]
συναναβᾶσιν αὐτῷ ἀπὸ τῆς Γαλιλαίας εἰς
having come up with him   from   -   Galilee   to
Ἰερουσαλήμ, οἵτινες [νῦν] εἰσιν μάρτυρες
Jerusalem,   who   now   are   witnesses
αὐτοῦ πρὸς τὸν λαόν. 32 καὶ ἡμεῖς
of him   to   the   people.   And   we
ὑμᾶς εὐαγγελιζόμεθα τὴν πρὸς τοὺς
[to] you   preach   ¹the   ⁴to   ⁵the
πατέρας ἐπαγγελίαν γενομένην, 33 ὅτι
⁶fathers   ²promise   ³having come,   that
ταύτην ὁ θεὸς ἐκπεπλήρωκεν τοῖς τέκνοις
this [promise] - God   has fulfilled   ²to the ³children
ἡμῖν ἀναστήσας Ἰησοῦν, ὡς καὶ ἐν τῷ
¹to us raising up   Jesus,   as also in   the
ψαλμῷ γέγραπται τῷ δευτέρῳ· υἱός μου
²psalm ³it has been written -   ¹second :   Son of me
εἶ σύ, ἐγὼ σήμερον γεγέννηκά σε. 34 ὅτι δὲ
art thou, I   to-day   have begotten thee.   And that

³⁴And as for the fact that he raised him from the dead, no more to return to corruption, he spoke in this way, 'I will give you the holy and sure blessings of David.' ³⁵Therefore he says also in another psalm, ' Thou wilt not let thy Holy One see corruption.' ³⁶For David, after he had served the counsel of God in his own generation, fell asleep, and was laid with his fathers, and saw corruption; ³⁷but he whom God raised up saw no corruption. ³⁸Let it be known to you therefore, brethren, that through this man forgiveness of sins is proclaimed to you, ³⁹and by him every one that believes is freed from everything from which you could not be freed by the law of Moses. ⁴⁰Beware, therefore, lest there come upon you what is said in the prophets: ⁴¹'Behold, you scoffers, and wonder and perish; for I do a deed in your days, a deed you will never believe, if one declares it to you.' " 42 As they went out, the people begged that these things might be told them the next

ἀνέστησεν αὐτὸν ἐκ νεκρῶν μηκέτι
he raised up him out of [the] dead no more

μέλλοντα ὑποστρέφειν εἰς διαφθοράν, οὕτως
being about to return to corruption, thus

εἴρηκεν ὅτι δώσω ὑμῖν τὰ ὅσια Δαυὶδ τὰ
he has said[,] - I will give you the ²holy things ³of David the

πιστά. 35 διότι καὶ ἐν ἑτέρῳ λέγει·
¹faithful. Wherefore also in another [psalm] he says:

οὐ δώσεις τὸν ὅσιόν σου ἰδεῖν διαφθοράν.
Thou wilt not give the holy one of thee to see corruption.

36 Δαυὶδ μὲν γὰρ ἰδίᾳ γενεᾷ ὑπηρετήσας
For David indeed [his] own generation having served

τῇ τοῦ θεοῦ βουλῇ ἐκοιμήθη καὶ προσετέθη
by the - of God counsel fell asleep and was added

πρὸς τοὺς πατέρας αὐτοῦ καὶ εἶδεν
to the fathers of him and saw

διαφθοράν· 37 ὃν δὲ ὁ θεὸς ἤγειρεν,
corruption; but [he] whom - God raised,

οὐκ εἶδεν διαφθοράν. 38 γνωστὸν οὖν
did not see corruption. Known therefore

ἔστω ὑμῖν, ἄνδρες ἀδελφοί, ὅτι διὰ
let it be to you, men brothers, that through

τούτου ὑμῖν ἄφεσις ἁμαρτιῶν καταγγέλ-
this man to you forgiveness of sins is an-

λεται, καὶ ἀπὸ πάντων ὧν οὐκ ἠδυνήθητε
nounced, and from all things from which ye could not

ἐν νόμῳ Μωϋσέως δικαιωθῆναι, 39 ἐν
by [the] law of Moses to be justified, by

τούτῳ πᾶς ὁ πιστεύων δικαιοῦται. 40 βλέπετε
this man everyone believing is justified. Look ye

οὖν μὴ ἐπέλθῃ τὸ εἰρημένον
therefore lest come on [you] the thing having been said

ἐν τοῖς προφήταις· 41 ἴδετε, οἱ κατα-
in the prophets: See, the des-

φρονηταί, καὶ θαυμάσατε καὶ ἀφανίσθητε,
pisers, and marvel ye and perish,

ὅτι ἔργον ἐργάζομαι ἐγὼ ἐν ταῖς ἡμέραις
because a work work I in the days

ὑμῶν, ἔργον ὃ οὐ μὴ πιστεύσητε ἐάν
of you, a work which by no means ye believe if

τις ἐκδιηγῆται ὑμῖν. 42 Ἐξιόντων δὲ
anyone declares to you. And going out
=as they went out

αὐτῶν παρεκάλουν εἰς τὸ μεταξὺ σάββατον
themᵃ they besought in the intervening sabbath(week)

λαληθῆναι αὐτοῖς τὰ ῥήματα ταῦτα.
to be spoken to them these words.

sabbath. [43]And when the meeting of the synagogue broke up, many Jews and devout converts to Judaism followed Paul and Barnabas, who spoke to them and urged them to continue in the grace of God. [44]The next sabbath almost the whole city gathered together to hear the word of God. [45]But when the Jews saw the multitudes, they were filled with jealousy, and contradicted what was spoken by Paul, and reviled him. [46]And Paul and Barnabas spoke out boldly, saying, "It was necessary that the word of God should be spoken first to you. Since you thrust it from you, and judge yourselves unworthy of eternal life, behold, we turn to the Gentiles. [47]For so the Lord has commanded us, saying,

'I have set you to be a light for the Gentiles,
that you may bring salvation to the uttermost parts of the earth.' "

[48]And when the Gentiles heard this, they were glad and glorified the word of God; and as many as were ordained to eternal life believed. [49]And the word of the Lord spread throughout all the region. [50]But the Jews incited the devout women of high standing

---

43 λυθείσης δὲ τῆς συναγωγῆς ἠκολούθησαν
And being broken up the assembly[a] [s]followed
=when the assembly was broken up

πολλοὶ τῶν Ἰουδαίων καὶ τῶν σεβομένων
[1]many [2]of the [3]Jews [4]and [5]of the [6]worshipping

προσηλύτων τῷ Παύλῳ καὶ τῷ Βαρναβᾷ,
[7]proselytes – [9]Paul and – Barnabas,

οἵτινες προσλαλοῦντες αὐτοῖς ἔπειθον αὐτοὺς
who speaking to them persuaded them

προσμένειν τῇ χάριτι τοῦ θεοῦ. **44** Τῷ δὲ
to continue in the grace – of God. And on the

ἐρχομένῳ σαββάτῳ σχεδὸν πᾶσα ἡ
coming sabbath almost all the

πόλις συνήχθη ἀκοῦσαι τὸν λόγον τοῦ
city was assembled to hear the word –

θεοῦ. **45** ἰδόντες δὲ οἱ Ἰουδαῖοι τοὺς
of God. But [2]seeing [1]the [2]Jews the

ὄχλους ἐπλήσθησαν ζήλου, καὶ ἀντέλεγον
crowds were filled of(with) jealousy, and contradicted

τοῖς ὑπὸ Παύλου λαλουμένοις βλασφημοῦντες.
the things by Paul being spoken blaspheming.

46 παρρησιασάμενοί τε ὁ Παῦλος καὶ ὁ
And speaking boldly – Paul and –

Βαρναβᾶς εἶπαν· ὑμῖν ἦν ἀναγκαῖον πρῶτον
Barnabas said: To you it was necessary firstly

λαληθῆναι τὸν λόγον τοῦ θεοῦ· ἐπειδὴ
to be spoken the word – of God; since

ἀπωθεῖσθε αὐτὸν καὶ οὐκ ἀξίους κρίνετε
ye put away it and not worthy judge

ἑαυτοὺς τῆς αἰωνίου ζωῆς, ἰδοὺ στρεφόμεθα
yourselves of the eternal life, behold we turn

εἰς τὰ ἔθνη. **47** οὕτως γὰρ ἐντέταλται
to the nations. For thus has commanded

ἡμῖν ὁ κύριος· τέθεικά σε εἰς φῶς
us the Lord: I have set thee for a light

ἐθνῶν τοῦ εἶναί σε εἰς σωτηρίαν ἕως
of nations – to be thee[b] for salvation to

ἐσχάτου τῆς γῆς. **48** ἀκούοντα δὲ τὰ ἔθνη
[the] end of the earth. And [2]hearing [1]the [2]nations

ἔχαιρον καὶ ἐδόξαζον τὸν λόγον τοῦ κυρίου, καὶ
rejoiced and glorified the word of the Lord, and

ἐπίστευσαν ὅσοι ἦσαν τεταγμένοι εἰς
[7]believed [1]as many as [2]were [3]having been disposed [4]to

ζωὴν αἰώνιον· **49** διεφέρετο δὲ ὁ λόγος τοῦ
[5]life [5]eternal; and was carried through the word of the

κυρίου δι' ὅλης τῆς χώρας. **50** οἱ δὲ
Lord through all the country. But the

Ἰουδαῖοι παρώτρυναν τὰς σεβομένας γυναῖκας
Jews urged on the [2]worshipping [3]women

528 ACTS 13, 14

and the leading men of the city, and stirred up persecution against Paul and Barnabas, and drove them out of their district. [51] But they shook off the dust from their feet against them, and went to Ico'nium. [52] And the disciples were filled with joy and with the Holy Spirit.

τὰς εὐσχήμονας καὶ τοὺς πρώτους τῆς
\- ¹honourable and the chief men of the
πόλεως, καὶ ἐπήγειραν διωγμὸν ἐπὶ τὸν
city, and raised up persecution against \-
Παῦλον καὶ Βαρναβᾶν, καὶ ἐξέβαλον αὐτοὺς
Paul and Barnabas, and expelled them
ἀπὸ τῶν ὁρίων αὐτῶν. 51 οἱ δὲ ἐκτιναξάμενοι
from the borders of them. But they shaking off
τὸν κονιορτὸν τῶν ποδῶν ἐπ' αὐτοὺς ἦλθον
the dust of the(ir) feet on them came
εἰς Ἰκόνιον, 52 οἵ τε μαθηταὶ ἐπλη-
to Iconium, and the disciples were
ροῦντο χαρᾶς καὶ πνεύματος ἁγίου.
filled of(with) joy and of(with) Spirit Holy.

CHAPTER 14

NOW at Ico'nium they entered together into the Jewish synagogue, and so spoke that a great company believed, both of Jews and of Greeks. [2] But the unbelieving Jews stirred up the Gentiles and poisoned their minds against the brethren. [3] So they remained for a long time, speaking boldly for the Lord, who bore witness to the word of his grace, granting signs and wonders to be done by their hands. [4] But the people of the city were divided; some sided with the Jews, and some with the apostles. [5] When an attempt was made by both Gentiles and Jews, with their rulers, to

14 Ἐγένετο δὲ ἐν Ἰκονίῳ κατὰ τὸ αὐτὸ
Now it happened in Iconium ²together†
εἰσελθεῖν αὐτοὺς εἰς τὴν συναγωγὴν
¹to enter themᵇ into the synagogue
=they entered
τῶν Ἰουδαίων καὶ λαλῆσαι οὕτως ὥστε
of the Jews and to speakᵇ so as
πιστεῦσαι Ἰουδαίων τε καὶ Ἑλλήνων
to believe both of Jews and of Greeks
πολὺ πλῆθος. 2 οἱ δὲ ἀπειθήσαντες
a much(great) multitude. But the disobeying
Ἰουδαῖοι ἐπήγειραν καὶ ἐκάκωσαν τὰς
Jews excited and embittered the
ψυχὰς τῶν ἐθνῶν κατὰ τῶν ἀδελφῶν.
minds of the nations against the brothers.
3 ἱκανὸν μὲν οὖν χρόνον διέτριψαν
A considerable \- ²therefore ¹time they continued
παρρησιαζόμενοι ἐπὶ τῷ κυρίῳ τῷ μαρ-
speaking boldly on the Lord \- wit-
τυροῦντι ἐπὶ τῷ λόγῳ τῆς χάριτος αὐτοῦ,
nessing to the word of the grace of him,
διδόντι σημεῖα καὶ τέρατα γίνεσθαι διὰ
giving signs and wonders to happen through
τῶν χειρῶν αὐτῶν. 4 ἐσχίσθη δὲ τὸ
the hands of them. But was divided the
πλῆθος τῆς πόλεως, καὶ οἱ μὲν ἦσαν
multitude of the city, and some were
σὺν τοῖς Ἰουδαίοις, οἱ δὲ σὺν τοῖς
with the Jews, but others with the
ἀποστόλοις. 5 ὡς δὲ ἐγένετο ὁρμὴ τῶν
apostles. And when there was a rush ²of the
ἐθνῶν τε καὶ Ἰουδαίων σὺν τοῖς ἄρχουσιν
²nations ¹both ⁴and of Jews with the rulers

molest them and to stone them, ⁶they learned of it and fled to Lystra and Derbe, cities of Lycao'-nia, and to the surrounding country; ⁷and there they preached the gospel.

8 Now at Lystra there was a man sitting, who could not use his feet; he was a cripple from birth, who had never walked. ⁹He listened to Paul speaking; and Paul, looking intently at him and seeing that he had faith to be made well, ¹⁰said in a loud voice, "Stand upright on your feet." And he sprang up and walked. ¹¹And when the crowds saw what Paul had done, they lifted up their voices, saying in Lycao'nian, "The gods have come down to us in the likeness of men!" ¹²Barnabas they called Zeus, and Paul, because he was the chief speaker, they called Hermes. ¹³And the priest of Zeus, whose temple was in front of the city, brought oxen and garlands to the gates and wanted to offer sacrifice with the people. ¹⁴But when the apostles Barnabas and Paul heard of it, they tore their garments and rushed out

αὐτῶν	ὑβρίσαι	καὶ	λιθοβολῆσαι	αὐτούς,
of them	to insult	and	to stone	them,

6 συνιδόντες κατέφυγον εἰς τὰς πόλεις
  perceiving they escaped to the cities

τῆς Λυκαονίας Λύστραν καὶ Δέρβην καὶ
  – of Lycaonia Lystra and Derbe and

τὴν περίχωρον· 7 κἀκεῖ εὐαγγελιζόμενοι
the neighbourhood; and there evangelizing

ἦσαν. 8 Καί τις ἀνὴρ ἀδύνατος ἐν
they were. And a certain man impotent in

Λύστροις τοῖς ποσὶν ἐκάθητο, χωλὸς ἐκ
Lystra in the feet sat, lame from

κοιλίας μητρὸς αὐτοῦ ὃς οὐδέποτε
[the] womb of [the] mother of him who never

περιεπάτησεν. 9 οὗτος ἤκουεν τοῦ Παύλου
walked. This man heard – Paul

λαλοῦντος· ὃς ἀτενίσας αὐτῷ καὶ ἰδὼν
speaking; who gazing at him and seeing

ὅτι ἔχει πίστιν τοῦ σωθῆναι, 10 εἶπεν
that he has(had) faith – to be healed,ᵈ said

μεγάλῃ φωνῇ· ἀνάστηθι ἐπὶ τοὺς πόδας
with a voice: Stand up on the feet
great(loud)

σου ὀρθός. καὶ ἥλατο καὶ περιεπάτει.
of thee erect. And he leaped up and walked.

11 οἵ τε ὄχλοι ἰδόντες ὃ ἐποίησεν Παῦλος
And the crowds seeing what did Paul

ἐπῆραν τὴν φωνὴν αὐτῶν Λυκαονιστὶ
lifted up the voice of them in Lycaonian

λέγοντες· οἱ θεοὶ ὁμοιωθέντες ἀνθρώποις
saying: The gods made like men

κατέβησαν πρὸς ἡμᾶς, 12 ἐκάλουν τε τὸν
came down to us, and they called –

Βαρναβᾶν Δία, τὸν δὲ Παῦλον Ἑρμῆν,
Barnabas Zeus, – and Paul Hermes,

ἐπειδὴ αὐτὸς ἦν ὁ ἡγούμενος τοῦ λόγου.
since he was the leader of the discourse.

13 ὅ τε ἱερεὺς τοῦ Διὸς τοῦ ὄντος πρὸ
And the priest – of Zeus – being before

τῆς πόλεως, ταύρους καὶ στέμματα ἐπὶ
the city, bulls and garlands to

τοὺς πυλῶνας ἐνέγκας, σὺν τοῖς ὄχλοις
the gates bringing, with the crowds

ἤθελεν θύειν. 14 ἀκούσαντες δὲ οἱ
wished to sacrifice. But ⁶hearing ¹the

ἀπόστολοι Βαρναβᾶς καὶ Παῦλος, διαρ-
²apostles ³Barnabas ⁴and ⁵Paul, rend-

ρήξαντες τὰ ἱμάτια ἑαυτῶν ἐξεπήδησαν εἰς
ing the garments of themselves rushed out into

among the multitude, crying, [15]"Men, why are you doing this? We also are men, of like nature with you, and bring you good news, that you should turn from these vain things to a living God who made the heaven and the earth and the sea and all that is in them. [16]In past generations he allowed all the nations to walk in their own ways; [17]yet he did not leave himself without witness, for he did good and gave you from heaven rains and fruitful seasons, satisfying your hearts with food and gladness." [18]With these words they scarcely restrained the people from offering sacrifice to them. 19 But Jews came there from Antioch and Ico′nium; and having persuaded the people, they stoned Paul and dragged him out of the city, supposing that he was dead. [20]But when the disciples gathered about him, he rose up and entered the city; and on the next day he went on with Barnabas to Derbe. [21]When they had preached the gospel to

τὸν ὄχλον, κράζοντες 15 καὶ λέγοντες·
the crowd, crying out and saying:

ἄνδρες, τί ταῦτα ποιεῖτε; καὶ ἡμεῖς
Men, why these things do ye? ²also ¹we

ὁμοιοπαθεῖς ἐσμεν ὑμῖν ἄνθρωποι, εὐαγ-
⁵of like nature ³are ⁶to you ⁴men, preach-

γελιζόμενοι ὑμᾶς ἀπὸ τούτων τῶν ματαίων
ing [to] you from these – vanities

ἐπιστρέφειν ἐπὶ θεὸν ζῶντα, ὃς ἐποίησεν
to turn to God a living, who made

τὸν οὐρανὸν καὶ τὴν γῆν καὶ τὴν
the heaven and the earth and the

θάλασσαν καὶ πάντα τὰ ἐν αὐτοῖς· 16 ὃς
sea and all the things in them; who

ἐν ταῖς παρῳχημέναις γενεαῖς εἴασεν πάντα
in the having passed generations allowed all

τὰ ἔθνη πορεύεσθαι ταῖς ὁδοῖς αὐτῶν·
the nations to go in the ways of them;

17 καίτοι οὐκ ἀμάρτυρον αὐτὸν ἀφῆκεν
and yet ²not ⁴unwitnessed ³himself ¹left

ἀγαθουργῶν, οὐρανόθεν ὑμῖν ὑετοὺς διδοὺς
doing good, ⁴from heaven ³us ²rain ¹giving

καὶ καιροὺς καρποφόρους, ἐμπιπλῶν τροφῆς
and times fruit-bearing, filling of(with) food

καὶ εὐφροσύνης τὰς καρδίας ὑμῶν. 18 καὶ
and of(with) gladness the hearts of us. And

ταῦτα λέγοντες μόλις κατέπαυσαν τοὺς
these things saying scarcely they restrained the

ὄχλους τοῦ μὴ θύειν αὐτοῖς. 19 Ἐπῆλθαν
crowds – not to sacrifice to them. ⁶came upon
[the scene]

δὲ ἀπὸ Ἀντιοχείας καὶ Ἰκονίου Ἰουδαῖοι,
And ²from ³Antioch ⁴and ⁵Iconium ¹Jews,

καὶ πείσαντες τοὺς ὄχλους καὶ λιθάσαντες
and persuading the crowds and stoning

τὸν Παῦλον ἔσυρον ἔξω τῆς πόλεως,
– Paul dragged outside the city,

νομίζοντες αὐτὸν τεθνηκέναι. 20 κυκλω-
supposing him to have died. But sur-

σάντων δὲ τῶν μαθητῶν αὐτὸν ἀναστὰς
rounding the disciples him rising up
=as the disciples surrounded

εἰσῆλθεν εἰς τὴν πόλιν. Καὶ τῇ ἐπαύριον
he entered into the city. And on the morrow

ἐξῆλθεν σὺν τῷ Βαρναβᾷ εἰς Δέρβην.
he went forth with – Barnabas to Derbe.

21 εὐαγγελιζόμενοί τε τὴν πόλιν ἐκείνην
And evangelizing that city

that city and had made many disciples, they returned to Lystra and to Ico'nium and to Antioch, [22] strengthening the souls of the disciples, exhorting them to continue in the faith, and saying that through many tribulations we must enter the kingdom of God. [23] And when they had appointed elders for them in every church, with prayer and fasting, they committed them to the Lord in whom they believed. 24 Then they passed through Pisid'ia, and came to Pamphyl'ia. [25] And when they had spoken the word in Perga, they went down to Attali'a; [26] and from there they sailed to Antioch, where they had been commended to the grace of God for the work which they had fulfilled. [27] And when they arrived, they gathered the church together and declared all that God had done with them, and how he had opened a door of faith to the Gentiles. [28] And they remained no little time with the disciples.

καὶ μαθητεύσαντες ἱκανοὺς ὑπέστρεψαν εἰς
and having made disciples many they returned to

τὴν Λύστραν καὶ εἰς Ἰκόνιον καὶ [εἰς]
 –   Lystra and to Iconium and to

Ἀντιόχειαν, 22 ἐπιστηρίζοντες τὰς ψυχὰς
Antioch,   confirming the minds

τῶν μαθητῶν, παρακαλοῦντες ἐμμένειν τῇ
of the disciples, exhorting to continue in the

πίστει, καὶ ὅτι διὰ πολλῶν θλίψεων
faith, and that through many afflictions

δεῖ ἡμᾶς εἰσελθεῖν εἰς τὴν βασιλείαν τοῦ
it behoves us to enter into the kingdom –

θεοῦ. 23 χειροτονήσαντες δὲ αὐτοῖς κατ᾽
of God.   And having appointed for them in

ἐκκλησίαν πρεσβυτέρους, προσευξάμενοι
every church elders, praying

μετὰ νηστειῶν παρέθεντο αὐτοὺς τῷ κυρίῳ
with fastings they committed them to the Lord

εἰς ὃν πεπιστεύκεισαν. 24 καὶ διελθόντες
in whom they had believed.   And passing through

τὴν Πισιδίαν ἦλθον εἰς τὴν Παμφυλίαν,
 – Pisidia they came to – Pamphylia,

25 καὶ λαλήσαντες εἰς τὴν Πέργην τὸν
and speaking in – Perga the

λόγον κατέβησαν εἰς Ἀττάλειαν, κἀκεῖθεν
word they came down to Attalia, and thence

ἀπέπλευσαν εἰς Ἀντιόχειαν, 26 ὅθεν ἦσαν
sailed away to Antioch,   whence they were

παραδεδομένοι τῇ χάριτι τοῦ θεοῦ εἰς
having been commended to the grace – of God for

τὸ ἔργον ὃ ἐπλήρωσαν. 27 Παραγεν-
the work which they accomplished.   And having

όμενοι δὲ καὶ συναγαγόντες τὴν ἐκκλησίαν,
arrived and and assembling the church,

ἀνήγγελλον ὅσα ἐποίησεν ὁ θεὸς μετ᾽
they reported what things did – God with

αὐτῶν, καὶ ὅτι ἤνοιξεν τοῖς ἔθνεσιν
them, and that he opened to the nations

θύραν πίστεως. 28 διέτριβον δὲ χρόνον
a door of faith.   And they continued time

οὐκ ὀλίγον σὺν τοῖς μαθηταῖς.
not a little with the disciples.

CHAPTER 15

B UT some men came down from Judea and were teaching the

15 Καί τινες κατελθόντες ἀπὸ τῆς
And some going down from the

Ἰουδαίας ἐδίδασκον τοὺς ἀδελφοὺς ὅτι
Judæa taught the brothers[,] –

brethren, "Unless you are circumcised according to the custom of Moses, you cannot be saved." ²And when Paul and Barnabas had no small dissension and debate with them, Paul and Barnabas and some of the others were appointed to go up to Jerusalem to the apostles and the elders about this question. ³So, being sent on their way by the church, they passed through both Phoeni'cia and Samar'ia, reporting the conversion of the Gentiles, and they gave great joy to all the brethren. ⁴When they came to Jerusalem, they were welcomed by the church and the apostles and the elders, and they declared all that God had done with them. ⁵But some believers who belonged to the party of the Pharisees rose up, and said, "It is necessary to circumcise them, and to charge them to keep the law of Moses."

6 The apostles and the elders were gathered together to consider this

ἐὰν μὴ περιτμηθῆτε τῷ ἔθει τῷ Μωϋσέως,
Unless ye are circumcised by the custom - of Moses,

οὐ δύνασθε σωθῆναι. 2 γενομένης δὲ
ye cannot *to* be saved. And taking place

στάσεως καὶ ζητήσεως οὐκ ὀλίγης τῷ
discord and questioning not a littleᵃ -
=when there took place not a little . . .

Παύλῳ καὶ τῷ Βαρναβᾷ πρὸς αὐτούς,
by Paul and - Barnabas with them,

ἔταξαν ἀναβαίνειν Παῦλον καὶ Βαρναβᾶν
they assigned to go up Paul and Barnabas

καί τινας ἄλλους ἐξ αὐτῶν πρὸς τοὺς
and some others of them to the

ἀποστόλους καὶ πρεσβυτέρους εἰς Ἰερουσαλὴμ
apostles and elders in Jerusalem

περὶ τοῦ ζητήματος τούτου. 3 Οἱ μὲν
about this question. They -

οὖν προπεμφθέντες ὑπὸ τῆς ἐκκλησίας
therefore being set forward by the church

διήρχοντο τήν τε Φοινίκην καὶ Σαμάρειαν
passed through - both Phœnicia and Samaria

ἐκδιηγούμενοι τὴν ἐπιστροφὴν τῶν ἐθνῶν,
telling in detail the conversion of the nations,

καὶ ἐποίουν χαρὰν μεγάλην πᾶσιν τοῖς
and caused joy great to all the

ἀδελφοῖς. 4 παραγενόμενοι δὲ εἰς Ἰεροσόλυμα
brothers. And having arrived in Jerusalem

παρεδέχθησαν ἀπὸ τῆς ἐκκλησίας καὶ τῶν
they were welcomed from the church and the

ἀποστόλων καὶ τῶν πρεσβυτερων, ἀνήγ-
apostles and the elders, and

γειλάν τε ὅσα ὁ θεὸς ἐποίησεν μετ᾽
reported what things - God did with

αὐτῶν. 5 Ἐξανέστησαν δέ τινες τῶν
them. But stood forth some of the [ones]

ἀπὸ τῆς αἱρέσεως τῶν Φαρισαίων
from the sect of the Pharisees

πεπιστευκότες, λέγοντες ὅτι δεῖ περιτέμνειν
having believed, saying[,] - It behoves to circumcise

αὐτοὺς παραγγέλλειν τε τηρεῖν τὸν νόμον
them and to charge to keep the law

Μωϋσέως.
of Moses.

6 Συνήχθησάν τε οἱ ἀπόστολοι καὶ οἱ
And were assembled the apostles and the

πρεσβύτεροι ἰδεῖν περὶ τοῦ λόγου τούτου.
elders to see about this matter.

matter. ⁷And after there had been much debate, Peter rose and said to them, "Brethren, you know that in the early days God made choice among you, that by my mouth the Gentiles should hear the word of the gospel and believe. ⁸And God who knows the heart bore witness to them, giving them the Holy Spirit just as he did to us; ⁹and he made no distinction between us and them, but cleansed their hearts by faith. ¹⁰Now therefore why do you make trial of God by putting a yoke upon the neck of the disciples which neither our fathers nor we have been able to bear? ¹¹But we believe that we shall be saved through the grace of the Lord Jesus, just as they will."

12 And all the assembly kept silence; and they listened to Barnabas and Paul as they related what signs and wonders God had done through them among the Gentiles. ¹³After they finished speaking, James replied, "Brethren, listen to me. ¹⁴Symeon has related

7 Πολλῆς δὲ ζητήσεως γενομένης ἀναστὰς
And much   questioning having taken place[a] rising up
= When much questioning had . . .

Πέτρος εἶπεν πρὸς αὐτούς· ἄνδρες ἀδελφοί,
Peter said to them: Men brothers,

ὑμεῖς ἐπίστασθε ὅτι ἀφ' ἡμερῶν ἀρχαίων
ye understand that from days olden

ἐν ὑμῖν ἐξελέξατο ὁ θεὸς διὰ τοῦ στόματός
[a]among [4]you [2]chose – ¹God through the mouth

μου ἀκοῦσαι τὰ ἔθνη τὸν λόγον τοῦ
of me [a]to hear ¹the [a]nations the word of the

εὐαγγελίου καὶ πιστεῦσαι. 8 καὶ ὁ
gospel and to believe. And [a]the

καρδιογνώστης θεὸς ἐμαρτύρησεν αὐτοῖς
[a]Heart-knower ¹God witnessed to them

δοὺς τὸ πνεῦμα τὸ ἅγιον καθὼς καὶ
giving the Spirit – Holy as also

ἡμῖν, 9 καὶ οὐθὲν διέκρινεν μεταξὺ ἡμῶν
to us, and nothing distinguished between [a]us

τε καὶ αὐτῶν, τῇ πίστει καθαρίσας τὰς
¹both and them, – by faith cleansing the

καρδίας αὐτῶν. 10 νῦν οὖν τί πειράζετε
hearts of them. Now therefore why test ye

τὸν θεόν, ἐπιθεῖναι ζυγὸν ἐπὶ τὸν
– God, to put on a yoke on the

τράχηλον τῶν μαθητῶν, ὃν οὔτε οἱ
neck of the disciples, which neither the

πατέρες ἡμῶν οὔτε ἡμεῖς ἰσχύσαμεν
fathers of us nor we were able

βαστάσαι; 11 ἀλλὰ διὰ τῆς χάριτος τοῦ
to bear? but through the grace of the

κυρίου Ἰησοῦ πιστεύομεν σωθῆναι καθ'
Lord Jesus we believe to be saved in

ὃν τρόπον κἀκεῖνοι. 12 Ἐσίγησεν δὲ
the same way as† those also. And was silent

πᾶν τὸ πλῆθος, καὶ ἤκουον Βαρναβᾶ
all the multitude, and heard Barnabas

καὶ Παύλου ἐξηγουμένων ὅσα ἐποίησεν
and Paul relating ¹what ⁶did

ὁ θεὸς σημεῖα καὶ τέρατα ἐν τοῖς
– ⁵God ²signs ³and ⁴wonders among the

ἔθνεσιν δι' αὐτῶν. 13 Μετὰ δὲ τὸ σιγῆσαι
nations through them. And after the to keep silence
= they kept silence

αὐτοὺς ἀπεκρίθη Ἰάκωβος λέγων· 14 ἄνδρες
them[b] answered James saying: Men

ἀδελφοί, ἀκούσατέ μου. Συμεὼν ἐξηγήσατο
brothers, hear ye me. Simeon declared

how God first visited the
Gentiles, to take out of
them a people for his
name. ¹⁵And with this
the words of the prophets
agree, as it is written,
¹⁶'After this I will return,
and I will rebuild the
dwelling of David,
which has fallen;
I will rebuild its ruins,
and I will set it up,
¹⁷that the rest of men
may seek the Lord,
and all the Gentiles
who are called by
my name,
¹⁸says the Lord, who
has made these
things known from
of old.'
¹⁹Therefore my judg-
ment is that we should
not trouble those of the
Gentiles who turn to
God, ²⁰but should write
to them to abstain from
the pollutions of idols
and from unchastity and
from what is strangled ʲ
and from blood. ²¹For
from early generations
Moses had has in every
city those who preach
him, for he is read every
sabbath in the syna-
gogues."
22 Then it seemed good
to the apostles and the
elders, with the whole
church, to choose men

ʲ Other early authorities omit
and from what is strangled

καθὼς   πρῶτον   ὁ   θεὸς   ἐπεσκέψατο   λαβεῖν   ἐξ
even as   firstly   -   God   visited   to take   out of

ἐθνῶν   λαὸν   τῷ   ὀνόματι   αὐτοῦ.   15 καὶ
[the] nations a people for the   name   of him.   And

τούτῳ   συμφωνοῦσιν   οἱ   λόγοι   τῶν   προφητῶν,
to this   agree   the   words   of the   prophets,

καθὼς   γέγραπται·   16   μετὰ   ταῦτα
even as   it has been written: After   these things

ἀναστρέψω   καὶ   ἀνοικοδομήσω   τὴν   σκηνὴν
I will return   and   I will rebuild   the   tent

Δαυὶδ   τὴν   πεπτωκυῖαν,   καὶ   τὰ   κατεστραμ-
of David   -   having fallen,   and   the   having been
                                                    things

μένα   αὐτῆς   ἀνοικοδομήσω   καὶ   ἀνορθώσω
overturned   of it   I will rebuild   and   I will rear again
=its ruins

αὐτήν,   17 ὅπως   ἂν   ἐκζητήσωσιν   οἱ
it,   so as   -   ⁴may seek   ¹the

κατάλοιποι   τῶν   ἀνθρώπων   τὸν   κύριον,
²rest   -   ³of men   ⁵the   ⁶Lord,

καὶ   πάντα   τὰ   ἔθνη   ἐφ'   οὓς   ἐπικέκληται
even   all   the   nations   on   whom   has been invoked

τὸ   ὄνομά   μου   ἐπ'   αὐτούς,   λέγει   κύριος
the   name   of me   on   them,   says   [the] Lord

ποιῶν   ταῦτα   18   γνωστὰ   ἀπ'   αἰῶνος.
doing   these things   known   from   [the] age.

19 διὸ   ἐγὼ   κρίνω   μὴ   παρενοχλεῖν   τοῖς
Wherefore   I   decide   not   to trouble   the [ones]

ἀπὸ   τῶν   ἐθνῶν   ἐπιστρέφουσιν   ἐπὶ   τὸν
from   the   nations   turning   to   -

θεόν,   20 ἀλλὰ   ἐπιστεῖλαι   αὐτοῖς   τοῦ
God,   but   to write word   to them   -

ἀπέχεσθαι   τῶν   ἀλισγημάτων   τῶν   εἰδώλων
to abstain fromᵈ the   pollutions   -   of idols

καὶ   τῆς   πορνείας   καὶ   πνικτοῦ   καὶ   τοῦ
and   -   fornication   and   a thing strangled and   -

αἵματος.   21 Μωϋσῆς   γὰρ   ἐκ   γενεῶν
blood.   For ¹Moses   ²from   ⁴generations

ἀρχαίων   κατὰ   πόλιν   τοὺς   κηρύσσοντας
³ancient   ⁶in every city   ⁷the [ones]   ⁸proclaiming

αὐτὸν   ἔχει   ἐν   ταῖς   συναγωγαῖς   κατὰ
⁹him   ⁵has   ¹¹in   ¹²the   ¹³synagogues   ¹⁴on

πᾶν   σάββατον   ἀναγινωσκόμενος.   22 Τότε
¹⁵every   ¹⁶sabbath   ¹⁰being read.   Then

ἔδοξε   τοῖς   ἀποστόλοις   καὶ   τοῖς   πρεσ-
it seemed [good] to the   apostles   and   to the   el-

βυτέροις   σὺν   ὅλῃ   τῇ   ἐκκλησίᾳ   ἐκλεξαμένους
ders,   with   all   the   church   chosen

from among them and
send them to Antioch
with Paul and Barnabas.
They sent Judas called
Barsabbas, and Silas,
leading men among the
brethren, ²³with the
following letter: "The
brethren, both the
apostles and the elders,
to the brethren who are
of the Gentiles in Antioch
and Syria and Cili′cia,
greeting. ²⁴Since we have
heard that some persons
from us have troubled
you with words, un-
settling your minds,
although we gave them
no instructions, ²⁵it has
seemed good to us in
assembly to choose men
and send them to you
with our beloved Barna-
bas and Paul, ²⁶men who
have risked their lives
for the sake of our Lord
Jesus Christ. ²⁷We have
therefore sent Judas and
Silas, who themselves
will tell you the same
things by word of mouth.
²⁸For it has seemed good
to the Holy Spirit and
to us to lay upon you no
greater burden than these
necessary things: ²⁹that
you abstain from what
has been sacrificed to
idols and from blood and

ἄνδρας	ἐξ	αὐτῶν	πέμψαι	εἰς	᾿Αντιόχειαν
men	of	them	to send	to	Antioch

σὺν	τῷ	Παύλῳ	καὶ	Βαρναβᾷ,	᾿Ιούδαν
with	–	Paul	and	Barnabas,	Judas

τὸν	καλούμενον	Βαρσαββᾶν	καὶ	Σιλᾶν,
–	being called	Barsabbas	and	Silas,

ἄνδρας	ἡγουμένους	ἐν	τοῖς	ἀδελφοῖς,
men	leading	among	the	brothers,

23
γράψαντες	διὰ	χειρὸς	αὐτῶν·	Οἱ
writing	through	[the] hand	of them:	The

ἀπόστολοι	καὶ	οἱ	πρεσβύτεροι	ἀδελφοὶ
apostles	and	the	elder	brothers

τοῖς	κατὰ	τὴν	᾿Αντιόχειαν	καὶ	Συρίαν
¹to the	⁵throughout	–	⁶Antioch	⁷and	⁸Syria

καὶ	Κιλικίαν	ἀδελφοῖς	τοῖς	ἐξ	ἐθνῶν
⁹and	¹⁰Cilicia	²brothers	–	³of [the]	⁴nations

χαίρειν.	24	᾿Επειδὴ	ἠκούσαμεν	ὅτι	τινὲς
¹¹greeting.		Since	we heard	that	some

ἐξ	ἡμῶν	ἐτάραξαν	ὑμᾶς	λόγοις	ἀνασκευάζ-
of	us	troubled	you	with words	unsettl-

οντες	τὰς	ψυχὰς	ὑμῶν,	οἷς	οὐ	διεστειλάμεθα,
ing	the	minds	of you,	to whom		we did not give commission,

25
ἔδοξεν	ἡμῖν	γενομένοις	ὁμοθυμαδόν,
it seemed [good]	to us	becoming	of one mind,

ἐκλεξαμένους	ἄνδρας	πέμψαι	πρὸς	ὑμᾶς
chosen	men	to send	to	you

σὺν	τοῖς	ἀγαπητοῖς	ἡμῶν	Βαρναβᾷ	καὶ
with	the	beloved	of us	Barnabas	and

Παύλῳ,	26	ἀνθρώποις	παραδεδωκόσι	τὰς
Paul,		men	having given up	the

ψυχὰς	αὐτῶν	ὑπὲρ	τοῦ	ὀνόματος	τοῦ
lives	of them	on behalf of	the	name	of the

κυρίου	ἡμῶν	᾿Ιησοῦ	Χριστοῦ.	27	ἀπεστάλ-
Lord	of us	Jesus	Christ.		We have sent

καμεν	οὖν	᾿Ιούδαν	καὶ	Σιλᾶν,	καὶ	αὐτοὺς
	therefore	Judas	and	Silas,	and	they

διὰ	λόγου	ἀπαγγέλλοντας	τὰ	αὐτά.
through (by)	speech	announcing	the	same things.

28
ἔδοξεν	γὰρ	τῷ	πνεύματι	τῷ	ἁγίῳ
For it seemed [good]		to the	Spirit	–	Holy

καὶ	ἡμῖν	μηδὲν	πλέον	ἐπιτίθεσθαι	ὑμῖν
and	to us	³nothing	⁵more	¹to be put on	²you

βάρος	πλὴν	τούτων	τῶν	ἐπάναγκες,
⁴burden	than	these	–	necessary things,

29
ἀπέχεσθαι	εἰδωλοθύτων	καὶ	αἵματος	καὶ
to abstain from	idol sacrifices	and	blood	and

from what is strangled[j]
and from unchastity. If
you keep yourselves from
these, you will do well.
Farewell."

30 So when they were
sent off, they went down
to Antioch; and having
gathered the congrega-
tion together, they
delivered the letter. [31]And
when they read it, they
rejoiced at the exhor-
tation. [32]And Judas and
Silas, who were them-
selves prophets, exhorted
the brethren with many
words and strengthened
them. [33]And after they
had spent some time,
they were sent off in
peace by the brethren to
those who had sent
them.[k] [35]But Paul and
Barnabas remained in
Antioch, teaching and
preaching the word of
the Lord, with many
others also.

36 And after some
days Paul said to Barna-
bas, "Come, let us return
and visit the brethren in
every city where we
proclaimed the word of
the Lord, and see how
they are." [37]And Barna-
bas wanted to take with
them John called Mark.
[38]But Paul thought best
not to take with them one
who had withdrawn from

πνικτῶν   καὶ   πορνείας·   ἐξ   ὧν   διατηροῦντες
things   and   fornication; from which   keeping
strangled
ἑαυτοὺς   εὖ   πράξετε.   Ἔρρωσθε.
yourselves   well   ye will do.   Farewell.
30 Οἱ   μὲν   οὖν   ἀπολυθέντες   κατῆλθον   εἰς
They   –   therefore being dismissed   went down   to
Ἀντιόχειαν,   καὶ   συναγαγόντες   τὸ   πλῆθος
Antioch,   and   assembling   the   multitude
ἐπέδωκαν   τὴν   ἐπιστολήν.   31 ἀναγνόντες   δὲ
handed in   the   letter.   And having read
ἐχάρησαν   ἐπὶ   τῇ   παρακλήσει.   32 Ἰούδας   τε
they rejoiced   at   the   exhortation.   And Judas
καὶ   Σιλᾶς,   καὶ   αὐτοὶ   προφῆται   ὄντες,
and   Silas,   also   [them]selves prophets   being,
διὰ   λόγου   πολλοῦ   παρεκάλεσαν   τοὺς
through   speech   much   exhorted   the
(by)
ἀδελφοὺς   καὶ   ἐπεστήριξαν·   33 ποιήσαντες   δὲ
brothers   and   confirmed;   and having continued
χρόνον   ἀπελύθησαν   μετ'   εἰρήνης   ἀπὸ
a time   they were dismissed   with   peace   from
τῶν   ἀδελφῶν   πρὸς   τοὺς   ἀποστείλαντας
the   brothers   to   the [ones]   having sent
αὐτούς.   ‡ 35 Παῦλος   δὲ   καὶ   Βαρναβᾶς
them.   But Paul   and   Barnabas
διέτριβον   ἐν   Ἀντιοχείᾳ,   διδάσκοντες   καὶ
stayed   in   Antioch,   teaching   and
εὐαγγελιζόμενοι   μετὰ   καὶ   ἑτέρων   πολλῶν
preaching   [1]with   [4]also   [3]others   [2]many
τὸν   λόγον   τοῦ   κυρίου.
the   word   of the   Lord.
36 Μετὰ   δέ   τινας   ἡμέρας   εἶπεν   πρὸς
Now after   some   days   [2]said   [3]to
Βαρναβᾶν   Παῦλος·   ἐπιστρέψαντες   δὴ
[4]Barnabas   [1]Paul: Returning   then
ἐπισκεψώμεθα   τοὺς   ἀδελφοὺς   κατὰ   πόλιν
let us visit   the   brothers   throughout   [2]city
πᾶσαν   ἐν   αἷς   κατηγγείλαμεν   τὸν   λόγον
[1]every   in   which   we announced   the   word
τοῦ   κυρίου,   πῶς   ἔχουσιν.   37 Βαρναβᾶς
of the   Lord,   how   they have(are).   Barnabas
δὲ   ἐβούλετο   συμπαραλαβεῖν   καὶ   τὸν
And   wished   to take with [them]   also   –
Ἰωάννην   τὸν   καλούμενον   Μᾶρκον·   38 Παῦλος
John   –   being called   Mark;   [2]Paul
δὲ   ἠξίου,   τὸν   ἀποστάντα   ἀπ'   αὐτῶν
[1]but   [3]thought fit,   –   [7]withdrawing   [8]from   [9]them

[j] Other early authorities omit
and from what is strangled

[k] Other ancient authorities
insert verse 34, But it seemed
good to Silas to remain there

‡ Verse 34 omitted by Nestle; cf. R.V. marg.

them in Pamphyl'ia, and had not gone with them to the work. ³⁹And there arose a sharp contention, so that they separated from each other; Barnabas took Mark with him and sailed away to Cyprus, ⁴⁰but Paul chose Silas and departed, being commended by the brethren to the grace of the Lord. ⁴¹And he went through Syria and Cili'cia, strengthening the churches.

ἀπὸ Παμφυλίας καὶ μὴ συνελθόντα αὐτοῖς
¹⁰from ¹¹Pamphylia ¹²and ¹³not ¹⁴going with ¹⁵them
εἰς τὸ ἔργον, μὴ συμπαραλαμβάνειν τοῦτον.
¹⁶to ¹⁷the ¹⁸work, ⁴not ⁵to take with [them] ⁶this one.
39 ἐγένετο δὲ παροξυσμός, ὥστε ἀποχωρισ-
And there was sharp feeling, so as to separ-
θῆναι αὐτοὺς ἀπ' ἀλλήλων, τόν τε
ate them from each other, - and
Βαρναβᾶν παραλαβόντα τὸν Μᾶρκον
Barnabas taking - Mark
ἐκπλεῦσαι εἰς Κύπρον. 40 Παῦλος δὲ
to sail away to Cyprus. But Paul
ἐπιλεξάμενος Σιλᾶν ἐξῆλθεν, παραδοθεὶς
having chosen Silas went forth, being commended
τῇ χάριτι τοῦ κυρίου ὑπὸ τῶν
to the grace of the Lord by the
ἀδελφῶν· 41 διήρχετο δὲ τὴν Συρίαν
brothers; and he went through - Syria
καὶ Κιλικίαν ἐπιστηρίζων τὰς ἐκκλησίας.
and Cilicia confirming the churches.

CHAPTER 16

AND he came also to Derbe and to Lystra. A disciple was there, named Timothy, the son of a Jewish woman who was a believer; but his father was a Greek. ²He was well spoken of by the brethren at Lystra and Ico'nium. ³Paul wanted Timothy to accompany him; and he took him and circumcised him because of the Jews that were in those places, for they all knew that his father was a Greek. ⁴As they went on their way through the cities, they delivered to them for observance the

16 Κατήντησεν δὲ καὶ εἰς Δέρβην καὶ
And he came down also to Derbe and
εἰς Λύστραν. καὶ ἰδοὺ μαθητής τις ἦν
to Lystra. And behold[,] a certain disciple was
ἐκεῖ ὀνόματι Τιμόθεος, υἱὸς γυναικὸς
there by name Timothy, son ²woman
Ἰουδαίας πιστῆς πατρὸς δὲ Ἕλληνος,
²Jewish ¹of a faithful ⁴but ⁵father ⁶of a Greek,
2 ὃς ἐμαρτυρεῖτο ὑπὸ τῶν ἐν Λύστροις
who was witnessed to by ¹the ³in ⁴Lystra
καὶ Ἰκονίῳ ἀδελφῶν. 3 τοῦτον ἠθέλησεν
⁵and ⁶Iconium ²brothers. ³This one ²wished
ὁ Παῦλος σὺν αὐτῷ ἐξελθεῖν, καὶ λαβὼν
- ¹Paul with him to go forth, and taking
περιέτεμεν αὐτὸν διὰ τοὺς Ἰουδαίους τοὺς
circumcised him on account the Jews -
of
ὄντας ἐν τοῖς τόποις ἐκείνοις· ᾔδεισαν
being in those places; ²they knew
γὰρ ἅπαντες ὅτι Ἕλλην ὁ πατὴρ αὐτοῦ
¹for all that a Greek the father of him
ὑπῆρχεν. 4 Ὡς δὲ διεπορεύοντο τὰς
was. Now as they went through the
πόλεις, παρεδίδοσαν αὐτοῖς φυλάσσειν τὰ
cities, they delivered to them* to keep the

---

* Note the gender: πόλις is feminine.

decisions which had been reached by the apostles and elders who were at Jerusalem. ⁵So the churches were strengthened in the faith, and they increased in numbers daily.

6 And they went through the region of Phry'gia and Galatia, having been forbidden by the Holy Spirit to speak the word in Asia. ⁷And when they had come opposite My'sia, they attempted to go into Bithyn'ia, but the Spirit of Jesus did not allow them; ⁸so, passing by My'sia, they went down to Tro'as. ⁹And a vision appeared to Paul in the night: a man of Macedo'nia was standing beseeching him and saying, "Come over to Macedo'nia and help us." ¹⁰And when he had seen the vision, immediately we sought to go into Macedo'nia, concluding that God had called us to preach the gospel to them.

11 Setting sail therefore from Tro'as, we made a direct voyage to Sam'othrace, and the following day to Ne-ap'-olis, ¹²and from there to

δόγματα τὰ κεκριμένα ὑπὸ τῶν ἀποστόλων
decrees – having been by the apostles
     decided [on]

καὶ πρεσβυτέρων τῶν ἐν Ἱεροσολύμοις.
and elders – in Jerusalem.

5 Αἱ μὲν οὖν ἐκκλησίαι ἐστερεοῦντο
¹The ¹therefore ²churches were strengthened

τῇ πίστει καὶ ἐπερίσσευον τῷ ἀριθμῷ
in the faith and increased – in number

καθ' ἡμέραν.
daily.

6 Διῆλθον δὲ τὴν Φρυγίαν καὶ Γαλατικὴν
And they went through the Phrygian and Galatian

χώραν, κωλυθέντες ὑπὸ τοῦ ἁγίου
country, being prevented by the Holy

πνεύματος λαλῆσαι τὸν λόγον ἐν τῇ
Spirit to speak the word in –
=from speaking

Ἀσίᾳ· 7 ἐλθόντες δὲ κατὰ τὴν Μυσίαν
Asia; but coming against – Mysia

ἐπείραζον εἰς τὴν Βιθυνίαν πορευθῆναι,
they attempted into – Bithynia to go,

καὶ οὐκ εἴασεν αὐτοὺς τὸ πνεῦμα Ἰησοῦ·
and ⁴not ⁴allowed ⁵them ¹the ²Spirit ³of Jesus;

8 παρελθόντες δὲ τὴν Μυσίαν κατέβησαν
so passing by – Mysia they came down

εἰς Τρῳάδα. 9 καὶ ὅραμα διὰ νυκτὸς
to Troas. And a vision through [the]
(during) night

τῷ Παύλῳ ὤφθη, ἀνὴρ Μακεδών τις
– to Paul appeared, a man Macedonian certain

ἦν ἑστὼς καὶ παρακαλῶν αὐτὸν καὶ
was standing and beseeching him and

λέγων· διαβὰς εἰς Μακεδονίαν βοήθησον
saying: Crossing into Macedonia help

ἡμῖν. 10 ὡς δὲ τὸ ὅραμα εἶδεν, εὐθέως
us. So when the vision he saw, immediately

ἐζητήσαμεν ἐξελθεῖν εἰς Μακεδονίαν,
we sought to go forth to Macedonia,

συμβιβάζοντες ὅτι προσκέκληται ἡμᾶς ὁ
concluding that ²has(had) called ³us –

θεὸς εὐαγγελίσασθαι αὐτούς.
¹God to evangelize them.

11 Ἀναχθέντες δὲ ἀπὸ Τρῳάδος εὐθυδρο-
And setting sail from Troas we ran a

μήσαμεν εἰς Σαμοθράκην, τῇ δὲ ἐπιούσῃ
straight course to Samothracia, and on the next day

εἰς Νέαν πόλιν, 12 κἀκεῖθεν εἰς Φιλίππους,
to Neapolis, and thence to Philippi,

Philippi, which is the leading city of the district[jj] of Macedo'nia, and a Roman colony. We remained in this city some days; [13]and on the sabbath day we went outside the gate to the riverside, where we supposed there was a place of prayer; and we sat down and spoke to the women who had come together. [14]One who heard us was a woman named Lydia, from the city of Thy-ati'ra, a seller of purple goods, who was a worshiper of God. The Lord opened her heart to give heed to what was said by Paul. [15]And when she was baptized, with her household, she besought us, saying, "If you have judged me to be faithful to the Lord, come to my house and stay." And she prevailed upon us.

16 As we were going to the place of prayer, we were met by a slave girl who had a spirit of divination and brought her owners much gain by soothsaying. [17]She followed Paul and us, crying, "These men are servants of the Most High God, who proclaim

[jj] The Greek text is uncertain

ἥτις	ἐστὶν	πρώτη	τῆς	μερίδος	Μακεδονίας
which	is	¹[the] ²first	⁴of the	⁵part	⁶of Macedonia

πόλις,	κολωνία.	⁷Ἦμεν	δὲ	ἐν	ταύτῃ	τῇ
³city,	a colony.	And we were		in	this	-

πόλει	διατρίβοντες	ἡμέρας	τινάς.	13 τῇ	τε
city	staying	days	some.	And on the	

ἡμέρᾳ	τῶν	σαββάτων	ἐξήλθομεν	ἔξω	τῆς
day	of the	sabbaths	we went forth	outside	the

πύλης	παρὰ	ποταμὸν	οὗ	ἐνομίζομεν
gate	by	a river	where	we supposed

προσευχὴν	εἶναι,	καὶ	καθίσαντες	ἐλαλοῦμεν
a place of prayer to be,		and	sitting	we spoke

ταῖς	συνελθούσαις	γυναιξίν.	14 καί	τις
to the	²coming together	¹women.	And a certain	

γυνὴ	ὀνόματι	Λυδία,	πορφυρόπωλις
woman	by name	Lydia,	a dealer in purple-dyed [garments]

πόλεως	Θυατίρων,	σεβομένη	τὸν	θεόν,
of [the] city	of Thyatira,	worshipping	-	God,

ἤκουεν,	ἧς	ὁ	κύριος	διήνοιξεν	τὴν	καρδίαν
heard,	of whom	the	Lord	opened up	the	heart

προσέχειν	τοῖς	λαλουμένοις	ὑπὸ	Παύλου.
to take heed to	the things	being spoken	by	Paul.

15 ὡς	δὲ	ἐβαπτίσθη	καὶ	ὁ	οἶκος	αὐτῆς,
And when		she was baptized	and		the household	of her,

παρεκάλεσεν	λέγουσα·	εἰ	κεκρίκατέ	με
she besought	saying:	If	ye have decided	me

πιστὴν	τῷ	κυρίῳ	εἶναι,	εἰσελθόντες	εἰς
faithful	to the	Lord	to be,	entering	into

τὸν	οἶκόν	μου	μένετε·	καὶ	παρεβιάσατο
the	house	of me	remain;	and	she urged

ἡμᾶς.	16 Ἐγένετο	δὲ	πορευομένων	ἡμῶν
us.	And it happened		going = as we went	us[a]

εἰς	τὴν	προσευχήν,	παιδίσκην	τινὰ	ἔχουσαν
to	the	place of prayer,	a certain maid		having

πνεῦμα	πύθωνα	ὑπαντῆσαι	ἡμῖν,	ἥτις
a spirit	of a python	to meet	us,	who

ἐργασίαν	πολλὴν	παρεῖχεν	τοῖς	κυρίοις
²gain	³much	¹brought	to the	masters

αὐτῆς	μαντευομένη.	17 αὕτη	κατακολουθοῦσα
of her	practising soothsaying.	This one	following after

τῷ	Παύλῳ	καὶ	ἡμῖν	ἔκραζεν	λέγουσα·
-	Paul	and	us	cried out	saying:

οὗτοι	οἱ	ἄνθρωποι	δοῦλοι	τοῦ	θεοῦ	τοῦ
These		men	slaves	of the	God	-

ὑψίστου	εἰσίν,	οἵτινες	καταγγέλλουσιν	ὑμῖν
most high	are,	who	announce	to you

to you the way of salvation." ¹⁸And this she did for many days. But Paul was annoyed, and turned and said to the spirit, "I charge you in the name of Jesus Christ to come out of her." And it came out that very hour.

19 But when her owners saw that their hope of gain was gone, they seized Paul and Silas and dragged them into the market place before the rulers; ²⁰and when they had brought them to the magistrates they said, "These men are Jews and they are disturbing our city. ²¹They advocate customs which it is not lawful for us Romans to accept or practice." ²²The crowd joined in attacking them; and the magistrates tore the garments off them and gave orders to beat them with rods. ²³And when they had inflicted many blows upon them, they threw them into prison, charging the jailer to keep them safely. ²⁴Having received this charge, he put them into the inner prison and fastened their feet in the stocks.

25 But about midnight Paul and Silas were

ὁδὸν σωτηρίας. 18 τοῦτο δὲ ἐποίει ἐπὶ
a way of salvation.   And this   she did   over
πολλὰς ἡμέρας. διαπονηθεὶς δὲ Παῦλος
many   days.   But becoming greatly troubled   Paul
καὶ ἐπιστρέψας τῷ πνεύματι εἶπεν· παραγ-
and   turning   ²to the   ³spirit   ¹he said: I
γέλλω σοι ἐν ὀνόματι Ἰησοῦ Χριστοῦ
charge   thee   in   [the] name   of Jesus   Christ
ἐξελθεῖν ἀπ' αὐτῆς· καὶ ἐξῆλθεν αὐτῇ
to come out   from   her;   and   it came out   in the
τῇ ὥρᾳ. 19 Ἰδόντες δὲ οἱ κύριοι αὐτῆς
same hour.*   And ⁴seeing   ¹the   ²masters   ³of her
ὅτι ἐξῆλθεν ἡ ἐλπὶς τῆς ἐργασίας αὐτῶν,
⁵that ¹¹went out   ⁴the   ⁷hope   ⁸of the   ⁹gain   ¹⁰of them,
ἐπιλαβόμενοι τὸν Παῦλον καὶ τὸν Σιλᾶν
having seized   –   Paul   and   –   Silas
εἵλκυσαν εἰς τὴν ἀγορὰν ἐπὶ τοὺς ἄρχοντας,
dragged   to   the marketplace before the   rulers,
20 καὶ προσαγαγόντες αὐτοὺς τοῖς στρατηγοῖς
and   ¹bringing ³to   ²them   the   prætors
εἶπαν· οὗτοι οἱ ἄνθρωποι ἐκταράσσουσιν
said: These   –   men   are greatly troubling
ἡμῶν τὴν πόλιν, Ἰουδαῖοι ὑπάρχοντες,
of us   the   city,   ²Jews   ¹being,
21 καὶ καταγγέλλουσιν ἔθη ἃ οὐκ ἔξεστιν
and   they announce   customs which   it is not lawful
ἡμῖν παραδέχεσθαι οὐδὲ ποιεῖν Ῥωμαίοις
for us   to receive   nor   to do   ²Romans
οὖσιν. 22 καὶ συνεπέστη ὁ ὄχλος κατ'
¹being.   And rose up together   the   crowd   against
αὐτῶν, καὶ οἱ στρατηγοὶ περιρήξαντες
them,   and   the   prætors   tearing off
αὐτῶν τὰ ἱμάτια ἐκέλευον ῥαβδίζειν,
of them   the   garments   commanded   to flog,
23 πολλὰς δὲ ἐπιθέντες αὐτοῖς πληγὰς
and ³many   ¹laying on   ²them   ⁴stripes
ἔβαλον εἰς φυλακήν, παραγγείλαντες τῷ
threw   into   prison,   charging   the
δεσμοφύλακι ἀσφαλῶς τηρεῖν αὐτούς· 24 ὃς
jailer   securely   to keep   them;   who
παραγγελίαν τοιαύτην λαβὼν ἔβαλεν αὐτοὺς
³a charge   ²such ¹having received threw   them
εἰς τὴν ἐσωτέραν φυλακὴν καὶ τοὺς
into   the   inner   prison   and   ²the
πόδας ἠσφαλίσατο αὐτῶν εἰς τὸ ξύλον.
³feet   ¹secured   ⁴of them   in   the   stocks.
25 Κατὰ δὲ τὸ μεσονύκτιον Παῦλος καὶ
And about   –   midnight   Paul   and

* See Luke 2. 38.

praying and singing hymns to God, and the prisoners were listening to them, ²⁶ and suddenly there was a great earthquake, so that the foundations of the prison were shaken; and immediately all the doors were opened and every one's fetters were unfastened. ²⁷ When the jailer woke and saw that the prison doors were open, he drew his sword and was about to kill himself, supposing that the prisoners had escaped. ²⁸ But Paul cried with a loud voice, "Do not harm yourself, for we are all here." ²⁹ And he called for lights and rushed in, and trembling with fear he fell down before Paul and Silas, ³⁰ and brought them out and said, "Men, what must I do to be saved?" ³¹ And they said, "Believe in the Lord Jesus, and you will be saved, you and your household." ³² And they spoke the word of the Lord to him and to all that were in his house. ³³ And he took them the same hour of the night, and washed

Σιλᾶς προσευχόμενοι ὕμνουν τὸν θεόν,
Silas praying ¹praised ²in a hymn - ²God,
ἐπηκροῶντο δὲ αὐτῶν οἱ δέσμιοι· 26 ἄφνω δὲ
and ²listened to ⁴them ¹the ²prisoners; and suddenly
σεισμὸς ἐγένετο μέγας, ὥστε σαλευ-
²earthquake ¹there was ²a great, so as to be
θῆναι τὰ θεμέλια τοῦ δεσμωτηρίου·
shaken the foundations of the jail;
ἠνεῴχθησαν δὲ παραχρῆμα αἱ θύραι πᾶσαι,
and ²were opened ¹at once ²the ⁴doors ²all,
καὶ πάντων τὰ δεσμὰ ἀνέθη. 27 ἔξυπνος δὲ
and ²of all ¹the ²bonds were And ⁴awake
loosened.
γενόμενος ὁ δεσμοφύλαξ καὶ ἰδὼν
²having become ¹the ²jailer and seeing
ἀνεῳγμένας τὰς θύρας τῆς φυλακῆς,
having been opened the doors of the prison,
σπασάμενος τὴν μάχαιραν ἤμελλεν ἑαυτὸν
having drawn the sword was about himself
ἀναιρεῖν, νομίζων ἐκπεφευγέναι τοὺς
to kill, supposing to have escaped the
δεσμίους. 28 ἐφώνησεν δὲ Παῦλος μεγάλῃ
prisoners. But called Paul with a
great(loud)
φωνῇ λέγων· μηδὲν πράξῃς σεαυτῷ κακόν,
voice saying: ¹Nothing ²do ⁴thyself ²harm,
ἅπαντες γάρ ἐσμεν ἐνθάδε. 29 αἰτήσας
for ²all ¹we are ²here. asking
δὲ φῶτα εἰσεπήδησεν, καὶ ἔντρομος
And lights he rushed in, and trembling
γενόμενος προσέπεσεν τῷ Παύλῳ καὶ
becoming he fell before - Paul and
Σιλᾷ, 30 καὶ προαγαγὼν αὐτοὺς ἔξω ἔφη·
Silas, and ¹leading ²forward ²them outside said :
κύριοι, τί με δεῖ ποιεῖν ἵνα σωθῶ;
Sirs, what ²me ¹behoves it to do that I may
be saved?
31 οἱ δὲ εἶπαν· πίστευσον ἐπὶ τὸν κύριον
And they said: Believe on the Lord
Ἰησοῦν, καὶ σωθήσῃ σὺ καὶ ὁ οἶκός
Jesus, and shalt be saved thou and the household
σου. 32 καὶ ἐλάλησαν αὐτῷ τὸν λόγον
of thee. And they spoke to him the word
τοῦ θεοῦ σὺν πᾶσιν τοῖς ἐν τῇ οἰκίᾳ
- of God with all the [ones] in the house
αὐτοῦ. 33 καὶ παραλαβὼν αὐτοὺς ἐν
of him. And taking them in
ἐκείνῃ τῇ ὥρᾳ τῆς νυκτὸς ἔλουσεν ἀπὸ
that - hour of the night he washed from

their wounds, and he was baptized at once, with all his family. ³⁴Then he brought them up into his house, and set food before them; and he rejoiced with all his household that he had believed in God.

35 But when it was day, the magistrates sent the police, saying, "Let those men go." ³⁶And the jailer reported the words to Paul, saying, "The magistrates have sent to let you go; now therefore come out and go in peace." ³⁷But Paul said to them, "They have beaten us publicly, uncondemned, men who are Roman citizens, and have thrown us into prison; and do they now cast us out secretly? No! let them come themselves and take us out." ³⁸The police reported these words to the magistrates, and they were afraid when they heard that they were Roman citizens; ³⁹so they came and apologized to them. And they took them out and asked them to leave the city. ⁴⁰So they went out of the

τῶν	πληγῶν,	καὶ	ἐβαπτίσθη	αὐτὸς	καὶ
the	stripes,	and	was baptized	he	and

οἱ	αὐτοῦ	ἅπαντες	παραχρῆμα,	34	ἀναγαγών
the	of him =all his	all	at once,		²bringing up

τε	αὐτοὺς	εἰς	τὸν	οἶκον	παρέθηκεν
¹and	them	to	the	house	he set before [them]

τράπεζαν,	καὶ	ἠγαλλιάσατο	πανοικεὶ	πεπι-
a table,	and	exulted	with all the household	having

στευκὼς	τῷ	θεῷ.	35	Ἡμέρας	δὲ	γενομένης
believed	-	God.		And day		coming =when day came

ἀπέστειλαν	οἱ	στρατηγοὶ	τοὺς	ῥαβδούχους
²sent	¹the	²prætors	the	tipstaffs

λέγοντες·	ἀπόλυσον	τοὺς	ἀνθρώπους
saying:	Release	-	men

ἐκείνους.	36	ἀπήγγειλεν	δὲ	ὁ	δεσμοφύλαξ
those.		And announced	the		jailer

τοὺς	λόγους	τούτους	πρὸς	τὸν	Παῦλον,
	these words		to	-	Paul,

ὅτι	ἀπέσταλκαν	οἱ	στρατηγοὶ	ἵνα	ἀπολυθῆτε.
-	²have sent	¹The	²prætors	that	ye may be released.

νῦν	οὖν	ἐξελθόντες	πορεύεσθε	ἐν	εἰρήνῃ.
Now	therefore	going forth	proceed	in	peace.

37	ὁ	δὲ	Παῦλος	ἔφη	πρὸς	αὐτούς·
	-	But	Paul	said	to	them:

δείραντες	ἡμᾶς	δημοσίᾳ	ἀκατακρίτους,
Having beaten	us	publicly	uncondemned,

ἀνθρώπους	Ῥωμαίους	ὑπάρχοντας,	ἔβαλαν
men	²Romans	¹being,	they threw [us]

εἰς	φυλακήν·	καὶ	νῦν	λάθρα	ἡμᾶς	ἐκβάλ-
into	prison;	and	now	secretly	us	they

λουσιν;	οὐ	γάρ,	ἀλλὰ	ἐλθόντες	αὐτοὶ
expel?	No	indeed,	but	coming	[them]selves

ἡμᾶς	ἐξαγαγέτωσαν.	38	ἀπήγγειλαν	δὲ	τοῖς
us	let them bring out.		And ³reported		⁴to the

στρατηγοῖς	οἱ	ῥαβδοῦχοι	τὰ	ῥήματα	ταῦτα.
⁵prætors	¹the	²tipstaffs		these words.	

ἐφοβήθησαν	δὲ	ἀκούσαντες	ὅτι	Ῥωμαῖοι
And they were afraid		hearing	that	Romans

εἰσιν,	39	καὶ	ἐλθόντες	παρεκάλεσαν
they are(were),		and	coming	besought

αὐτούς,	καὶ	ἐξαγαγόντες	ἠρώτων	ἀπελθεῖν
them,	and	bringing out	asked	to go away

ἀπὸ	τῆς	πόλεως.	40	ἐξελθόντες	δὲ	ἀπὸ
from	the	city.		And going out		from

prison, and visited Lydia; and when they had seen the brethren, they exhorted them and departed.

τῆς φυλακῆς εἰσῆλθον πρὸς τὴν Λυδίαν,
the prison they entered to [the house of] Lydia,

καὶ ἰδόντες παρεκάλεσαν τοὺς ἀδελφοὺς
and seeing they exhorted the brothers

καὶ ἐξῆλθαν.
and went forth.

CHAPTER 17

NOW when they had passed through Amphip'olis and Apollo'-nia, they came to Thessaloni'ca, where there was a synagogue of the Jews. ²And Paul went in, as was his custom, and for three weeks he argued with them from the scriptures, ³explaining and proving that it was necessary for the Christ to suffer and to rise from the dead, and saying, "This Jesus, whom I proclaim to you, is the Christ." ⁴And some of them were persuaded, and joined Paul and Silas; as did a great many of the devout Greeks and not a few of the leading women. ⁵But the Jews were jealous, and taking some wicked fellows of the rabble, they gathered a crowd, set the city in an uproar, and attacked the house of Jason, seeking to bring them out to the people. ⁶And when they

17 Διοδεύσαντες δὲ τὴν Ἀμφίπολιν καὶ
And travelling through – Amphipolis and

τὴν Ἀπολλωνίαν ἦλθον εἰς Θεσσαλονίκην,
– Apollonia they came to Thessalonica,

ὅπου ἦν συναγωγὴ τῶν Ἰουδαίων. 2 κατὰ
where was a synagogue of the Jews. accord-ing to

δὲ τὸ εἰωθὸς τῷ Παύλῳ εἰσῆλθεν πρὸς
And the custom – with Paul⁰ he entered to

αὐτούς, καὶ ἐπὶ σάββατα τρία διελέξατο
them, and on sabbaths three lectured

αὐτοῖς ἀπὸ τῶν γραφῶν, 3 διανοίγων
to them from the scriptures, opening up

καὶ παρατιθέμενος ὅτι τὸν χριστὸν ἔδει
and setting before [them] that ²the ³Christ ¹it behoved

παθεῖν καὶ ἀναστῆναι ἐκ νεκρῶν, καὶ
to suffer and to rise again out of [the] dead, and

ὅτι οὗτός ἐστιν ὁ χριστός, ὁ Ἰησοῦς,
that this is(was) the Christ, – Jesus,

ὃν ἐγὼ καταγγέλλω ὑμῖν. 4 καί τινες
whom I announce to you. And some

ἐξ αὐτῶν ἐπείσθησαν καὶ προσεκληρώθησαν
of them were persuaded and threw in their lot

τῷ Παύλῳ καὶ τῷ Σιλᾷ, τῶν τε
– with Paul and – Silas, both of the

σεβομένων Ἑλλήνων πλῆθος πολύ, γυναικῶν τε
worshipping Greeks ²multitude ¹a much and of ³women (great),

τῶν πρώτων οὐκ ὀλίγαι. 5 Ζηλώσαντες δὲ
²the ²chief not a few. But becoming jealous

οἱ Ἰουδαῖοι καὶ προσλαβόμενοι τῶν
the Jews and taking aside of the

ἀγοραίων ἄνδρας τινὰς πονηροὺς καὶ
loungers in the marketplace men some wicked and

ὀχλοποιήσαντες ἐθορύβουν τὴν πόλιν, καὶ
having gathered a crowd disturbed the city, and

ἐπιστάντες τῇ οἰκίᾳ Ἰάσονος ἐζήτουν
coming on the house of Jason sought

αὐτοὺς προαγαγεῖν εἰς τὸν δῆμον· 6 μὴ
them to bring forward to the mob; ¹not

could not find them, they dragged Jason and some of the brethren before the city authorities, crying, "These men who have turned the world upside down have come here also, ⁷and Jason has received them; and they are all acting against the decrees of Caesar, saying that there is another king, Jesus." ⁸And the people and the city authorities were disturbed when they heard this. ⁹And when they had taken security from Jason and the rest, they let them go.

10 The brethren immediately sent Paul and Silas away by night to Beroe′a; and when they arrived they went into the Jewish synagogue. ¹¹Now these Jews were more noble than those in Thessaloni′ca, for they received the word with all eagerness, examining the scriptures daily to see if these things were so. ¹²Many of them therefore believed, with not a few Greek women of high standing as well as men. ¹³But when the Jews of Thessaloni′ca learned

εὑρόντες	δὲ	αὐτοὺς	ἔσυρον	Ἰάσονα	καί
³finding	¹but	them	they dragged	Jason	and

τινας	ἀδελφοὺς	ἐπὶ	τοὺς	πολιτάρχας,
some	brothers	to	the	politarchs,

βοῶντες	ὅτι	οἱ	τὴν	οἰκουμένην	ἀναστατώ-
crying[,]	–	²the	⁴the	⁵inhabited [ones] earth	³having turned

σαντες	οὗτοι	καὶ	ἐνθάδε	πάρεισιν,	7 οὓς
upside down	¹these men	also	here	have arrived,	whom

ὑποδέδεκται	Ἰάσων·	καὶ	οὗτοι	πάντες
²has received	¹Jason;	and	these	all

ἀπέναντι	τῶν	δογμάτων	Καίσαρος
²contrary to	³the	⁴decrees	⁵of Cæsar

πράσσουσιν,	βασιλέα	ἕτερον	λέγοντες	εἶναι
¹act,	⁴king	³another	¹saying	²to be

Ἰησοῦν.	8 ἐτάραξαν	δὲ	τὸν	ὄχλον	καὶ
⁵Jesus.	And they troubled	the	crowd	and

τοὺς	πολιτάρχας	ἀκούοντας	ταῦτα,	9 καὶ
the	politarchs	hearing	these things,	and

λαβόντες	τὸ	ἱκανὸν	παρὰ	τοῦ	Ἰάσονος
taking	the	surety	from	–	Jason

καὶ	τῶν	λοιπῶν	ἀπέλυσαν	αὐτούς.	10 Οἱ δὲ
and	the	rest	released	them.	And the

ἀδελφοὶ	εὐθέως	διὰ	νυκτὸς	ἐξεπεμψαν
brothers	immediately	through (during)	[the] night	sent forth

τόν	τε	Παῦλον	καὶ	τὸν	Σιλᾶν	εἰς	Βέροιαν,
–	both	Paul	and	–	Silas	to	Berœa,

οἵτινες	παραγενόμενοι	εἰς	τὴν	συναγωγὴν
who	having arrived	²into	³the	synagogue

τῶν	Ἰουδαίων	ἀπῄεσαν·	11 οὗτοι	δὲ	ἦσαν
⁴of the	⁵Jews	¹went;	and these	–	were

εὐγενέστεροι	τῶν	ἐν	Θεσσαλονίκῃ,	οἵτινες
more noble [than] the [ones] in			Thessalonica,	who

ἐδέξαντο	τὸν	λόγον	μετὰ	πάσης	προθυμίας,
received	the	word	with	all	eagerness,

[τὸ]	καθ᾽	ἡμέραν	ἀνακρίνοντες	τὰς	γραφὰς
–		daily	examining	the	scriptures

εἰ	ἔχοι	ταῦτα	οὕτως.	12 πολλοὶ	μὲν
if	²have(are)	¹these things	³so.	Many	–

οὖν	ἐξ	αὐτῶν	ἐπίστευσαν,	καὶ	τῶν
therefore	of	them	believed,	and	of the

Ἑλληνίδων	γυναικῶν	τῶν	εὐσχημόνων	καὶ
²Greek	³women	–	¹honourable	and

ἀνδρῶν	οὐκ	ὀλίγοι.	13 Ὡς	δὲ	ἔγνωσαν
of men	not	a few.	But when		⁵knew

οἱ	ἀπὸ	τῆς	Θεσσαλονίκης	Ἰουδαῖοι	ὅτι
¹the	²from	–	⁴Thessalonica	³Jews	that

that the word of God was proclaimed by Paul at Beroe'a also, they came there too, stirring up and inciting the crowds. ¹⁴Then the brethren immediately sent Paul off on his way to the sea, but Silas and Timothy remained there. ¹⁵Those who conducted Paul brought him as far as Athens; and receiving a command for Silas and Timothy to come to him as soon as possible, they departed.

16 Now while Paul was waiting for them at Athens, his spirit was provoked within him as he saw that the city was full of idols. ¹⁷So he argued in the synagogue with the Jews and the devout persons, and in the market place every day with those who chanced to be there. ¹⁸Some also of the Epicurean and Stoic philosophers met him. And some said, "What would this babbler say?" Others said, "He seems to be a preacher of foreign divinities"—because he preached Jesus

καὶ ἐν τῇ Βεροίᾳ κατηγγέλη ὑπὸ τοῦ
also in – Berœa was announced by –

Παύλου ὁ λόγος τοῦ θεοῦ, ἦλθον κἀκεῖ
Paul the word – of God, they came there also

σαλεύοντες καὶ ταράσσοντες τοὺς ὄχλους.
shaking and troubling the crowds.

14 εὐθέως δὲ τότε τὸν Παῦλον ἐξαπέστειλαν
So immediately then – ⁴Paul ³sent away

οἱ ἀδελφοὶ πορεύεσθαι ἕως ἐπὶ τὴν
¹the ²brothers to go as far as to the

θάλασσαν· ὑπέμεινάν τε ὅ τε Σιλᾶς καὶ
sea; ¹but ⁶remained – ²both ³Silas ⁴and

ὁ Τιμόθεος ἐκεῖ. 15 οἱ δὲ καθιστάνοντες
– ⁵Timothy ⁷there. And the [ones] conducting

τὸν Παῦλον ἤγαγον ἕως Ἀθηνῶν, καὶ
– Paul brought [him] as far as Athens, and

λαβόντες ἐντολὴν πρὸς τὸν Σιλᾶν καὶ τὸν
receiving a command to – Silas and –

Τιμόθεον ἵνα ὡς τάχιστα ἔλθωσιν πρὸς
Timothy that as quickly they should to
[as possible] come

αὐτὸν ἐξῄεσαν.
him they departed.

16 Ἐν δὲ ταῖς Ἀθήναις ἐκδεχομένου
And in – Athens awaiting
⊢while Paul awaited them,

αὐτοὺς τοῦ Παύλου, παρωξύνετο τὸ πνεῦμα
them – Paul,ᵃ ⁴was provoked ¹the ²spirit

αὐτοῦ ἐν αὐτῷ θεωροῦντος κατείδωλον
³of him in him beholding ⁴full of images

οὖσαν τὴν πόλιν. 17 διελέγετο μὲν οὖν
³being ¹the ²city. He addressed –* therefore

ἐν τῇ συναγωγῇ τοῖς Ἰουδαίοις καὶ
in the synagogue the Jews and

τοῖς σεβομένοις καὶ ἐν τῇ ἀγορᾷ κατὰ
the [ones] worshipping and in the marketplace –

πᾶσαν ἡμέραν πρὸς τοὺς παρατυγχάνοντας.
every day to the [ones] chancing to be [there].

18 τινὲς δὲ καὶ τῶν Ἐπικουρείων καὶ
But some also of the Epicurean and

Στωικῶν φιλοσόφων συνέβαλλον αὐτῷ, καί
Stoic philosophers fell in with him, and

τινες ἔλεγον· τί ἂν θέλοι ὁ σπερμολόγος
some said: What may wish – ²ignorant plagiarist

οὗτος λέγειν; οἱ δέ· ξένων δαιμονίων
¹this to say? And others [said]: Of foreign demons

δοκεῖ καταγγελεὺς εἶναι· ὅτι τὸν Ἰησοῦν
he seems an announcer to be; because – Jesus

* See note on ch. 12. 5.

and the resurrection.
¹⁹And they took hold of him and brought him to the Are-op′agus, saying, "May we know what this new teaching is which you present? ²⁰ For you bring some strange things to our ears; we wish to know therefore what these things mean." ²¹ Now all the Athenians and the foreigners who lived there spent their time in nothing except telling or hearing something new.

22 So Paul, standing in the middle of the Are-op′agus, said: "Men of Athens, I perceive that in every way you are very religious. ²³ For as I passed along, and observed the objects of your worship, I found also an altar with this inscription, 'To an unknown god.' What therefore you worship as unknown, this I proclaim to you. ²⁴ The God who made the world and everything in it, being Lord of heaven and earth, does not live in shrines made by man, ²⁵ nor is he served by human hands, as though he needed anything, since he himself gives to all men life and breath and everything. ²⁶ And he made from one every

καὶ τὴν ἀνάστασιν εὐηγγελίζετο. 19 ἐπιλα-
and the resurrection he preached. taking

βόμενοι δὲ αὐτοῦ ἐπὶ τὸν "Αρειον πάγον
hold And of him to the Areopagus

ἤγαγον, λέγοντες· δυνάμεθα γνῶναι τίς
they led [him], saying: Can we *to* know what

ἡ καινὴ αὕτη ἡ ὑπὸ σοῦ λαλουμένη
¹this ²new – ⁵by ⁶thee ⁴being spoken

διδαχή; 20 ξενίζοντα γάρ τινα εἰσφέρεις
³teaching [is]? for ²startling things ¹some thou bringest *in*

εἰς τὰς ἀκοὰς ἡμῶν· βουλόμεθα οὖν
to the ears of us; we are minded therefore

γνῶναι τίνα θέλει ταῦτα εἶναι. 21 ᾿Αθηναῖοι
to know what wishes these things to be. ²Athenians

δὲ πάντες καὶ οἱ ἐπιδημοῦντες ξένοι εἰς
Now ¹all ²and ⁴the ⁶dwelling ⁵strangers ⁸for

οὐδὲν ἕτερον ηὐκαίρουν ἢ λέγειν τι ἢ
⁹nothing ¹⁰different ⁷have leisure either to say something or

ἀκούειν τι καινότερον. 22 Σταθεὶς δὲ
to hear something newer. And standing

Παῦλος ἐν μέσῳ τοῦ ᾿Αρείου πάγου
¹Paul ¹in ²[the] midst ³of the ⁴Areopagus

ἔφη· ἄνδρες ᾿Αθηναῖοι, κατὰ πάντα ὡς
said: Men Athenians, in everything how

δεισιδαιμονεστέρους ὑμᾶς θεωρῶ. 23 διερχόμενος
very religious ²you ¹I behold. passing along

γὰρ καὶ ἀναθεωρῶν τὰ σεβάσματα ὑμῶν
For and looking up at the objects of worship of you

εὗρον καὶ βωμὸν ἐν ᾧ ἐπεγέγραπτο·
I found also an altar in which had been inscribed:

ΑΓΝΩΣΤΩ ΘΕΩ. ὃ οὖν ἀγνοοῦντες
TO AN UNKNOWN GOD. What therefore being ignorant

εὐσεβεῖτε, τοῦτο ἐγὼ καταγγέλλω ὑμῖν.
ye reverence, this I announce to you.

24 ὁ θεὸς ὁ ποιήσας τὸν κόσμον καὶ
The God the [one] having made the world and

πάντα τὰ ἐν αὐτῷ, οὗτος οὐρανοῦ καὶ
all the things in it, this one ³of heaven ⁴and

γῆς ὑπάρχων κύριος οὐκ ἐν χειροποιήτοις
⁵of earth ¹being ²lord ²not ³in ⁴hand-made

ναοῖς κατοικεῖ, 25 οὐδὲ ὑπὸ χειρῶν
⁵shrines ¹dwells, nor ²by ⁴hands

ἀνθρωπίνων θεραπεύεται προσδεόμενός
³human ¹is served having need

τινος, αὐτὸς διδοὺς πᾶσι ζωὴν καὶ πνοὴν
of anything, he giving to all life and breath

καὶ τὰ πάντα· 26 ἐποίησέν τε ἐξ ἑνὸς
and – all things; and he made of one

nation of men to live on all the face of the earth, having determined allotted periods and the boundaries of their habitation, ²⁷that they should seek God, in the hope that they might feel after him and find him. Yet he is not far from each one of us, ²⁸for 'In him we live and move and have our being'; as even some of your poets have said, 'For we are indeed his offspring.' ²⁹Being then God's offspring, we ought not to think that the Deity is like gold, or silver, or stone, a representation by the art and imagination of man. ³⁰The times of ignorance God overlooked, but now he commands all men everywhere to repent, ³¹because he has fixed a day on which he will judge the world in righteousness by a man whom he has appointed, and of this he has given assurance to all men by raising him from the dead." ³²Now when they heard of the resurrection of the dead, some mocked; but others said, "We will hear you again

πᾶν	ἔθνος	ἀνθρώπων	κατοικεῖν	ἐπὶ	παντὸς
every	nation	of men	to dwell	on	all

προσώπου	τῆς	γῆς,	ὁρίσας	προστεταγμένους
[the] face	of the	earth,	fixing	*having been* appointed

καιροὺς	καὶ	τὰς	ὁροθεσίας	τῆς	κατοικίας
seasons	and	the	boundaries	of the	dwelling

αὐτῶν,	27	ζητεῖν	τὸν	θεόν,	εἰ	ἄρα	γε
of them,		to seek	–	God,	if	perchance	

ψηλαφήσειαν	αὐτὸν	καὶ	εὕροιεν,	καὶ	γε
they might feel after	him	and	might find,		though

οὐ	μακρὰν	ἀπὸ	ἑνὸς	ἑκάστου	ἡμῶν
²not	³far	⁴from	⁶one	⁵each	⁷of us

ὑπάρχοντα.	28	ἐν	αὐτῷ	γὰρ	ζῶμεν	καὶ
¹being.		²in	³him	¹For		we live	and

κινούμεθα	καὶ	ἐσμέν,	ὡς	καί	τινες	τῶν
move	and	are,	as	indeed	some	of the

καθ᾽	ὑμᾶς	ποιητῶν	εἰρήκασιν·	τοῦ	γὰρ
²among	³you	¹poets	have said:	²of him	¹For

καὶ	γένος	ἐσμέν.	29	γένος	οὖν	ὑπάρχοντες
³also	⁵offspring	⁴we are.		Offspring	therefore	being

τοῦ	θεοῦ	οὐκ	ὀφείλομεν	νομίζειν,	χρυσῷ
–	of God	we ought not	to suppose,	⁵to gold

ἢ	ἀργύρῳ	ἢ	λίθῳ,	χαράγματι	τέχνης
⁶or	⁷*to* silver	⁸or	⁹*to* stone,	¹⁰*to* an engraved work	¹¹of art

καὶ	ἐνθυμήσεως	ἀνθρώπου,	τὸ	θεῖον	εἶναι
¹²and	¹³of meditation	¹⁴of man,	¹the	²divine nature	³to be

ὅμοιον.	30	τοὺς	μὲν	οὖν	χρόνους	τῆς
⁴like.		⁵The	¹so	²then	⁶times	–

ἀγνοίας	ὑπεριδὼν	ὁ	θεὸς	τὰ	νῦν
⁷of ignorance	⁴having overlooked	–	³God	¹the	now

ἀπαγγέλλει	τοῖς	ἀνθρώποις	πάντας	πανταχοῦ
declares	–	to men	all men	everywhere

μετανοεῖν,	31	καθότι	ἔστησεν	ἡμέραν	ἐν
to repent,		because	he set	a day	in

ᾗ	μέλλει	κρίνειν	τὴν	οἰκουμένην	ἐν
which he is about	to judge	the	inhabited earth	in

δικαιοσύνῃ,	ἐν	ἀνδρὶ	ᾧ	ὥρισεν,	πίστιν
righteousness,	by	a man	whom	he designated,	²a guarantee

παρασχὼν	πᾶσιν	ἀναστήσας	αὐτὸν	ἐκ
¹offering	to all	having raised up	him	out of

νεκρῶν.	32	ἀκούσαντες	δὲ	ἀνάστασιν
[the] dead.		And hearing [of]		a resurrection

νεκρῶν,	οἱ	μὲν	ἐχλεύαζον,	οἱ	δὲ	εἶπαν·
of dead persons,	some		scoffed,	others		said:

ἀκουσόμεθά	σου	περὶ	τούτου	καὶ	πάλιν.
We will hear	thee	concerning	this	also	again.

about this." ³³So Paul
went out from among
them. ³⁴But some men
joined him and believed,
among them Dionys'ius
the Are-op'agite and a
woman named Dam'aris
and others with them.

33 οὕτως   ὁ   Παῦλος   ἐξῆλθεν   ἐκ   μέσου
   Thus   –   Paul   went forth from [the] midst
αὐτῶν.   34 τινὲς   δὲ   ἄνδρες   κολληθέντες
of them.   But some   men   adhering
αὐτῷ   ἐπίστευσαν,   ἐν   οἷς   καὶ   Διονύσιος
to him   believed,   among whom both   Dionysius
ὁ   ’Αρεοπαγίτης   καὶ   γυνὴ   ὀνόματι   Δαμαρὶς
the   Areopagite   and a woman   by name   Damaris
καὶ   ἕτεροι   σὺν   αὐτοῖς.
and   others   with   them.

CHAPTER 18

AFTER this he left
Athens and went to
Corinth. ²And he found
a Jew named Aquila, a
native of Pontus, lately
come from Italy with his
wife Priscilla, because
Claudius had command-
ed all the Jews to leave
Rome. And he went to
see them; ³and because
he was of the same trade
he stayed with them, and
they worked, for by
trade they were tent-
makers. ⁴And he argued
in the synagogue every
sabbath, and persuaded
Jews and Greeks.
   5 When Silas and
Timothy arrived from
Macedo'nia, Paul was
occupied with preaching,
testifying to the Jews
that the Christ was Jesus.
⁶And when they opposed

18 Μετὰ   ταῦτα   χωρισθεὶς   ἐκ   τῶν
    After   these things   departing   out of
’Αθηνῶν   ἦλθεν   εἰς   Κόρινθον.   2 καὶ
 Athens   he came   to   Corinth.   And
εὑρών   τινα   ’Ιουδαῖον   ὀνόματι   ’Ακύλαν,
finding a certain   Jew   by name   Aquila,
Ποντικὸν   τῷ   γένει,   προσφάτως   ἐληλυθότα
belonging to   –   by race,   recently   having come
Pontus
ἀπὸ   τῆς   ’Ιταλίας,   καὶ   Πρίσκιλλαν   γυναῖκα
from   –   Italy,   and   Priscilla   wife
αὐτοῦ,   διὰ   τὸ   διατεταχέναι   Κλαύδιον
of him, because of the   to have commanded   Claudiusᵇ
          =because Claudius had commanded
χωρίζεσθαι   πάντας   τοὺς   ’Ιουδαίους   ἀπὸ
to depart   all   the   Jews   from
τῆς   ῾Ρώμης,   προσῆλθεν   αὐτοῖς,   3 καὶ
 –   Rome,   he came to   them,   and
διὰ   τὸ   ὁμότεχνον   εἶναι   ἔμενεν   παρ’
because of the of the same trade to beᵇ he remained with
          =because [he] was of the same trade
αὐτοῖς,   καὶ   ἠργάζοντο·   ἦσαν   γὰρ   σκηνοποιοὶ
them,   and   they wrought; for they were   tentmakers
τῇ   τέχνῃ.   4 διελέγετο   δὲ   ἐν   τῇ   συναγωγῇ
 –   by trade.   And he lectured   in   the   synagogue
κατὰ   πᾶν   σάββατον,   ἔπειθέν   τε   ’Ιουδαίους
on   every   sabbath,   he persuaded both   Jews
καὶ   ῞Ελληνας.   5 ῾Ως   δὲ   κατῆλθον   ἀπὸ
and   Greeks.   And when   came down   from
τῆς   Μακεδονίας   ὅ   τε   Σιλᾶς   καὶ   ὁ
 –   Macedonia   –   both   Silas   and   –
Τιμόθεος,   συνείχετο   τῷ   λόγῳ   ὁ   Παῦλος,
Timothy,   was pressed   by the   word   –   Paul,
διαμαρτυρόμενος   τοῖς   ’Ιουδαίοις   εἶναι   τὸν
solemnly witnessing   to the   Jews   to be   the
                                          =that Jesus was the Christ.
χριστὸν   ’Ιησοῦν.   6 ἀντιτασσομένων   δὲ   αὐτῶν
Christ   Jesus.   But resisting   them
                            =when they resisted and blasphemed

and reviled him, he shook out his garments and said to them, "Your blood be upon your heads! I am innocent. From now on I will go to the Gentiles." ⁷And he left there and went to the house of a man named Titius¹ Justus, a worshiper of God; his house was next door to the synagogue. ⁸Crispus, the ruler of the synagogue, believed in the Lord, together with all his household; and many of the Corinthians hearing Paul believed and were baptized. ⁹And the Lord said to Paul one night in a vision, "Do not be afraid, but speak and do not be silent; ¹⁰for I am with you, and no man shall attack you to harm you; for I have many people in this city." ¹¹And he stayed a year and six months, teaching the word of God among them.

12 But when Gallio was proconsul of Acha'ia, the Jews made a united attack upon Paul and brought him before the tribunal, ¹³saying, "This

καὶ βλασφημούντων ἐκτιναξάμενος τὰ ἱμάτια
and blaspheming[a] shaking off the(his) garments

εἶπεν πρὸς αὐτούς· τὸ αἷμα ὑμῶν ἐπὶ
he said to them: The blood of you on

τὴν κεφαλὴν ὑμῶν· καθαρὸς ἐγὼ ἀπὸ
the head of you; clean I from

τοῦ νῦν εἰς τὰ ἔθνη πορεύσομαι. 7 καὶ
- now to the nations will go. And

μεταβὰς ἐκεῖθεν ἦλθεν εἰς οἰκίαν τινὸς
removing thence he went into [the] house of one

ὀνόματι Τιτίου Ἰούστου σεβομένου τὸν
by name Titius Justus worshipping -

θεόν, οὗ ἡ οἰκία ἦν συνομοροῦσα τῇ
God, of whom the house was being next door to the

συναγωγῇ. 8 Κρίσπος δὲ ὁ ἀρχισυνάγωγος
synagogue. Now Crispus the synagogue ruler

ἐπίστευσεν τῷ κυρίῳ σὺν ὅλῳ τῷ οἴκῳ
believed the Lord with all the household

αὐτοῦ, καὶ πολλοὶ τῶν Κορινθίων ἀκούοντες
of him, and many of the Corinthians hearing

ἐπίστευον καὶ ἐβαπτίζοντο. 9 Εἶπεν δὲ
believed and were baptized. And said

ὁ κύριος ἐν νυκτὶ δι᾽ ὁράματος τῷ
the Lord in [the] night through a vision -

Παύλῳ· μὴ φοβοῦ, ἀλλὰ λάλει καὶ
to Paul: Do not fear, but speak and

μὴ σιωπήσῃς, 10 διότι ἐγώ εἰμι μετὰ σοῦ
keep not silence, because I am with thee

καὶ οὐδεὶς ἐπιθήσεταί σοι τοῦ κακῶσαί
and no one shall set on thee - to illtreat[d]

σε, διότι λαός ἐστί μοι πολὺς ἐν
thee, because people is to me much[e] in
=I have a great people

τῇ πόλει ταύτῃ. 11 Ἐκάθισεν δὲ ἐνιαυτὸν
this city. And he sat a year

καὶ μῆνας ἓξ διδάσκων ἐν αὐτοῖς τὸν
and months six teaching among them the

λόγον τοῦ θεοῦ. 12 Γαλλίωνος δὲ
word - of God. And Gallio
=when Gallio

ἀνθυπάτου ὄντος τῆς Ἀχαίας κατεπέστησαν
proconsul being[a] - of Achaia ⁴set on
was proconsul

ὁμοθυμαδὸν οἱ Ἰουδαῖοι τῷ Παύλῳ καὶ
³with one mind ¹the ²Jews - Paul and

ἤγαγον αὐτὸν ἐπὶ τὸ βῆμα, 13 λέγοντες
brought him to the tribunal, saying[,]

ὅτι παρὰ τὸν νόμον ἀναπείθει οὗτος
- ᵃ[differently] from ⁷the ⁸law ᵃurges ¹This man

¹ Other early authorities read Titus

Ι.G.E.—19

man is persuading men to worship God contrary to the law." ¹⁴But when Paul was about to open his mouth, Gallio said to the Jews, "If it were a matter of wrongdoing or vicious crime, I should have reason to bear with you, O Jews; ¹⁵but since it is a matter of questions about words and names and your own law, see to it yourselves; I refuse to be a judge of these things." ¹⁶And he drove them from the tribunal. ¹⁷And they all seized Sos'thenes, the ruler of the synagogue, and beat him in front of the tribunal. But Gallio paid no attention to this.

18 After this Paul stayed many days longer, and then took leave of the brethren and sailed for Syria, and with him Priscilla and Aquila. At Cen'chre-ae he cut his hair, for he had a vow. ¹⁹And they came to Ephesus, and he left them there; but he himself went into the synagogue and argued with the Jews. ²⁰When they asked him to stay for a longer period, he declined; ²¹but on taking

τοὺς ἀνθρώπους σέβεσθαι τὸν θεόν.
- ²men ⁴to worship - ⁵God.

14 μέλλοντος δὲ τοῦ Παύλου ἀνοίγειν τὸ
And being about - Paulᵃ to open the(his)
=when Paul was about

στόμα εἶπεν ὁ Γαλλίων πρὸς τοὺς
mouth said - Gallio to the

Ἰουδαίους· εἰ μὲν ἦν ἀδίκημά τι
Jews: If indeed it was crime some

ἢ ῥᾳδιούργημα πονηρόν, ὦ Ἰουδαῖοι,
or villainy evil, O Jews,

κατὰ λόγον ἂν ἀνεσχόμην ὑμῶν· 15 εἰ δὲ ζητή-
rightly I would endure you; but if ques-

ματά ἐστιν περὶ λόγου καὶ ὀνομάτων καὶ
tions it is concerning a word and names and

νόμου τοῦ καθ᾽ ὑμᾶς, ὄψεσθε αὐτοί·
law the according to you, ye will see [your]selves;
=your law,

κριτὴς ἐγὼ τούτων οὐ βούλομαι εἶναι.
a judge ¹I ⁸of these things ²do not intend ⁸to be.

16 καὶ ἀπήλασεν αὐτοὺς ἀπὸ τοῦ βήματος.
And he drove away them from the tribunal.

17 ἐπιλαβόμενοι δὲ πάντες Σωσθένην τὸν
But ²seizing ¹all Sosthenes the

ἀρχισυνάγωγον ἔτυπτον ἔμπροσθεν τοῦ
synagogue ruler they struck [him] in front of

βήματος· καὶ οὐδὲν τούτων τῷ Γαλλίωνι
tribunal; and not one of these things ²to Gallio

ἔμελεν. 18 Ὁ δὲ Παῦλος ἔτι προσμείνας
¹mattered. - But Paul yet having remained

ἡμέρας ἱκανάς, τοῖς ἀδελφοῖς ἀποταξάμενος
days many, to the brothers bidding farewell

ἐξέπλει εἰς τὴν Συρίαν, καὶ σὺν αὐτῷ
he sailed away to - Syria, and with him

Πρίσκιλλα καὶ Ἀκύλας, κειράμενος ἐν
Priscilla and Aquila, having shorn in

Κεγχρεαῖς τὴν κεφαλήν· εἶχεν γὰρ εὐχήν.
Cenchrea the(his) head; for he had a vow.

19 κατήντησαν δὲ εἰς Ἔφεσον, κἀκείνους
And they came down to Ephesus, and those

κατέλιπεν αὐτοῦ, αὐτὸς δὲ εἰσελθὼν εἰς
he left there, but he entering into

τὴν συναγωγὴν διελέξατο τοῖς Ἰουδαίοις.
the synagogue lectured to the Jews.

20 ἐρωτώντων δὲ αὐτῶν ἐπὶ πλείονα
And asking them over a more(longer)
=as they asked

χρόνον μεῖναι οὐκ ἐπένευσεν, 21 ἀλλὰ
time to remain he consented not, but

leave of them he said, "I will return to you if God wills," and he set sail from Ephesus. 22 When he had landed at Caesare'a, he went up and greeted the church, and then went down to Antioch. ²³After spending some time there he departed and went from place to place through the region of Galatia and Phryg'ia, strengthening all the disciples. 24 Now a Jew named Apol'los, a native of Alexandria, came to Ephesus. He was an eloquent man, well versed in the scriptures. ²⁵ He had been instructed in the way of the Lord; and being fervent in spirit, he spoke and taught accurately the things concerning Jesus, though he knew only the baptism of John. ²⁶ He began to speak boldly in the synagogue; but when Priscilla and Aquila heard him, they took him and expounded to him the way of God more accurately. ²⁷And when he wished to cross to Acha'ia, the brethren encouraged him, and wrote to the disciples to receive him. When he

ἀποταξάμενος καὶ εἰπών· πάλιν ἀνακάμψω
bidding farewell and saying : Again I will return

πρὸς ὑμᾶς τοῦ θεοῦ θέλοντος, ἀνήχθη
to you - God willing,ᵃ he set sail
=if God wills,

ἀπὸ τῆς Ἐφέσου, 22 καὶ κατελθὼν εἰς
from - Ephesus, and coming down to

Καισάρειαν, ἀναβὰς καὶ ἀσπασάμενος τὴν
Cæsarea, going up and greeting the

ἐκκλησίαν, κατέβη εἰς Ἀντιόχειαν, 23 καὶ
church, he went down to Antioch, and

ποιήσας χρόνον τινὰ ἐξῆλθεν, διερχόμενος
having spent time some he went forth, passing through

καθεξῆς τὴν Γαλατικὴν χώραν καὶ Φρυγίαν,
in order the Galatian country and Phrygia,

στηρίζων πάντας τοὺς μαθητάς.
confirming all the disciples.

24 Ἰουδαῖος δέ τις Ἀπολλῶς ὀνόματι,
And a certain Jew Apollos by name,

Ἀλεξανδρεὺς τῷ γένει, ἀνὴρ λόγιος,
an Alexandrian - by race, a man eloquent,

κατήντησεν εἰς Ἔφεσον, δυνατὸς ὢν ἐν
came to Ephesus, powerful being in

ταῖς γραφαῖς. 25 οὗτος ἦν κατηχημένος
the scriptures. This man was orally instructed [in]

τὴν ὁδὸν τοῦ κυρίου, καὶ ζέων τῷ
the way of the Lord, and burning -

πνεύματι ἐλάλει καὶ ἐδίδασκεν ἀκριβῶς
in spirit he spoke and taught accurately

τὰ περὶ τοῦ Ἰησοῦ, ἐπιστάμενος
the things concerning - Jesus, understanding

μόνον τὸ βάπτισμα Ἰωάννου· 26 οὗτός τε
only the baptism of John; and this man

ἤρξατο παρρησιάζεσθαι ἐν τῇ συναγωγῇ.
began to speak boldly in the synagogue.

ἀκούσαντες δὲ αὐτοῦ Πρίσκιλλα καὶ
And hearing him Priscilla and

Ἀκύλας προσελάβοντο αὐτὸν καὶ ἀκριβέστε-
Aquila took him and more accurate-

ρον αὐτῷ ἐξέθεντο τὴν ὁδὸν τοῦ θεοῦ.
ly to him explained the way - of God.

27 βουλομένου δὲ αὐτοῦ διελθεῖν εἰς τὴν
And intending himᵃ to go through into -
=when he intended

Ἀχαΐαν, προτρεψάμενοι οἱ ἀδελφοὶ ἔγραψαν
Achaia, being encouraged the brothers wrote

τοῖς μαθηταῖς ἀποδέξασθαι αὐτόν· ὃς
to the disciples to welcome him; who

arrived, he greatly helped those who through grace had believed, ²⁸for he powerfully confuted the Jews in public, showing by the scriptures that the Christ was Jesus.

παραγενόμενος   συνεβάλετο   πολὺ   τοῖς
arriving   contributed   much   to the [ones]
πεπιστευκόσιν   διὰ   τῆς   χάριτος·   28 εὐτόνως
having believed   through -   grace;   ²vehemently
γὰρ   τοῖς   Ἰουδαίοις   διακατηλέγχετο   δημοσίᾳ
¹for   ⁴the   ⁵Jews   ³he confuted   publicly
ἐπιδεικνὺς   διὰ   τῶν   γραφῶν   εἶναι   τὸν
proving   through the   scriptures   ²to be   ³the
χριστὸν   Ἰησοῦν.
⁴Christ   ¹Jesus.

CHAPTER 19

WHILE Apol'los was at Corinth, Paul passed through the upper country and came to Ephesus. There he found some disciples. ²And he said to them, "Did you receive the Holy Spirit when you believed?" And they said, "No, we have never even heard that there is a Holy Spirit." ³And he said, "Into what then were you baptized?" They said, "Into John's baptism." ⁴And Paul said, "John baptized with the baptism of repentance, telling the people to believe in the one who was to come after him, that is, Jesus." ⁵On hearing this, they were baptized in the name of the Lord Jesus. ⁶And when Paul had laid his hands upon them, the Holy Spirit came on them; and they spoke with tongues and prophesied. ⁷There were about twelve of them in all.

19 Ἐγένετο   δὲ   ἐν   τῷ   τὸν   Ἀπολλῶ
Now it came to pass   in   the   -   Apollos
                                    =while Apollos was
εἶναι ἐν   Κορίνθῳ   Παῦλον   διελθόντα   τὰ
to beᵇᵉ in   Corinth   Paul   having passed through the
ἀνωτερικὰ   μέρη   ἐλθεῖν   εἰς   Ἔφεσον   καὶ
higher   parts   to comeᵇ   to   Ephesus   and
εὑρεῖν   τινας   μαθητάς,   2 εἶπέν   τε   πρὸς
to findᵇ   some   disciples,   and said   to
αὐτούς·   εἰ   πνεῦμα   ἅγιον   ἐλάβετε   πιστεύσαν-
them: If   Spirit   Holy   ye received   believ-
τες;   οἱ   δὲ   πρὸς   αὐτόν·   ἀλλ'   οὐδ'   εἰ
ing?   And they [said]   to   him·   But   ²not   ³if
πνεῦμα   ἅγιον   ἔστιν   ἠκούσαμεν.   3 εἶπέν   τε·
⁶Spirit   ⁵Holy   ⁴there is   ¹we heard.   And he said:
εἰς   τί   οὖν   ἐβαπτίσθητε;   οἱ   δὲ   εἶπαν·
To   what therefore   were ye baptized?   And they   said:
εἰς   τὸ   Ἰωάννου   βάπτισμα.   4 εἶπεν   δὲ
To   the   of John   baptism.   And said
Παῦλος·   Ἰωάννης   ἐβάπτισεν   βάπτισμα   μετα-
Paul: John   baptized [with]   a baptism of repent-
νοίας,   τῷ   λαῷ   λέγων   εἰς   τὸν   ἐρχόμενον
ance,   ²to the   ³people   ¹saying   ⁵in   ⁷the [one]   ⁸coming
μετ'   αὐτὸν   ἵνα   πιστεύσωσιν,   τοῦτ'   ἔστιν
⁹after   ¹⁰him   ⁴that   ⁵they should believe,   this   is
εἰς   τὸν   Ἰησοῦν.   5 ἀκούσαντες   δὲ   ἐβαπτίσ-
in   -   Jesus.   And hearing   they were
θησαν   εἰς   τὸ   ὄνομα   τοῦ   κυρίου   Ἰησοῦ.
baptized   in   the   name   of the   Lord   Jesus.
6 καὶ   ἐπιθέντος   αὐτοῖς   τοῦ   Παύλου   χεῖρας
And   laying on   them   -   Paul   handsᵃ
                    =as Paul laid [his] hands on them
ἦλθε   τὸ   πνεῦμα   τὸ   ἅγιον   ἐπ'   αὐτούς,
came   the   Spirit   -   Holy   on   them,
ἐλάλουν   τε   γλώσσαις   καὶ   ἐπροφήτευον.
and they spoke   in tongues   and   prophesied.
7 ἦσαν   δὲ   οἱ   πάντες   ἄνδρες   ὡσεὶ   δώδεκα.
And ⁴were   ³the   ¹all   ²men   about   twelve.

8 And he entered the synagogue and for three months spoke boldly, arguing and pleading about the kingdom of God; ⁹but when some were stubborn and disbelieved, speaking evil of the Way before the congregation, he withdrew from them, taking the disciples with him, and argued daily in the hall of Tyran'nus.ᵐ ¹⁰This continued for two years, so that all the residents of Asia heard the word of the Lord, both Jews and Greeks.

11 And God did extraordinary miracles by the hands of Paul, ¹²so that handkerchiefs or aprons were carried away from his body to the sick, and diseases left them and the evil spirits came out of them. ¹³Then some of the itinerant Jewish exorcists undertook to pronounce the name of the Lord Jesus over those who had evil spirits, saying, "I adjure you by

8 Εἰσελθὼν δὲ εἰς τὴν συναγωγὴν
And entering into the synagogue

ἐπαρρησιάζετο ἐπὶ μῆνας τρεῖς διαλεγόμενος
he spoke boldly over months three lecturing

καὶ πείθων περὶ τῆς βασιλείας τοῦ θεοῦ.
and persuading concerning the kingdom - of God.

9 ὡς δέ τινες ἐσκληρύνοντο καὶ ἠπείθουν
But as some were hardened and disobeyed

κακολογοῦντες τὴν ὁδὸν ἐνώπιον τοῦ
speaking ill [of] the way before the

πλήθους, ἀποστὰς ἀπ᾽ αὐτῶν ἀφώρισεν
multitude, withdrawing from them he separated

τοὺς μαθητάς, καθ᾽ ἡμέραν διαλεγόμενος
the disciples, daily lecturing

ἐν τῇ σχολῇ Τυράννου. 10 τοῦτο δὲ
in the school of Tyrannus. And this

ἐγένετο ἐπὶ ἔτη δύο, ὥστε πάντας τοὺς
happened over years two, so as all the
=so that all who inhabited

κατοικοῦντας τὴν ᾽Ασίαν ἀκοῦσαι τὸν
[ones] inhabiting - Asia to hearᵇ the
Asia heard

λόγον τοῦ κυρίου, ᾽Ιουδαιους τε καὶ
word of the Lord, ²Jews ¹both and

῞Ελληνας. 11 Δυνάμεις τε οὐ τὰς τυχούσας
Greeks. And powerful deeds not the ordinary

ὁ θεὸς ἐποίει διὰ τῶν χειρῶν Παύλου,
- God did through the hands of Paul,

12 ὥστε καὶ ἐπὶ τοὺς ἀσθενοῦντας
so as even even onto the [ones] ailing
=so that there were even brought away from his skin hand-

ἀποφέρεσθαι ἀπὸ τοῦ χρωτὸς αὐτοῦ
to be brought away from the skin of him
kerchiefs or aprons onto those who ailed and the diseases were rid

σουδάρια ἢ σιμικίνθια καὶ ἀπαλλάσσεσθαι
handkerchiefs or aprons and to be rid
from them, and the evil spirits went out.

ἀπ᾽ αὐτῶν τὰς νόσους, τά τε πνεύματα
from them the diseases, and the spirits

τὰ πονηρὰ ἐκπορεύεσθαι. 13 ᾽Επεχείρησαν δέ
evil to go out. But ⁷attempted

τινες καὶ τῶν περιερχομένων ᾽Ιουδαίων
¹some ²also ³of the ⁴strolling ⁵Jews

ἐξορκιστῶν ὀνομάζειν ἐπὶ τοὺς ἔχοντας
⁶exorcists to name over the [ones] having

τὰ πνεύματα τὰ πονηρὰ τὸ ὄνομα τοῦ
the spirits - evil the name of the

κυρίου ᾽Ιησοῦ λέγοντες· ὁρκίζω ὑμᾶς τὸν
Lord Jesus saying: I exorcise you [by] -

the Jesus whom Paul preaches." ¹⁴Seven sons of a Jewish high priest named Sceva were doing this. ¹⁵But the evil spirit answered them, "Jesus I know, and Paul I know; but who are you?" ¹⁶And the man in whom the evil spirit was leaped on them, mastered all of them, and overpowered them, so that they fled out of that house naked and wounded. ¹⁷And this became known to all residents of Ephesus, both Jews and Greeks; and fear fell upon them all; and the name of the Lord Jesus was extolled. ¹⁸Many also of those who were now believers came, confessing and divulging their practices. ¹⁹And a number of those who practiced magic arts brought their books together and burned them in the sight of all; and they counted the value of them and found it came to fifty thousand pieces of silver. ²⁰So the word of the Lord grew and prevailed mightily.

Ἰησοῦν ὃν Παῦλος κηρύσσει. 14 ἦσαν δέ
Jesus whom Paul proclaims.   And there were

τινος Σκευᾶ Ἰουδαίου ἀρχιερέως ἑπτὰ
²of one ⁴Sceva ⁵a Jewish ⁶chief priest ¹seven

υἱοὶ τοῦτο ποιοῦντες. 15 ἀποκριθὲν δὲ
²sons ⁸this ⁷doing.   And answering

τὸ πνεῦμα τὸ πονηρὸν εἶπεν αὐτοῖς·
the spirit   the evil   said   to them:

τὸν [μὲν] Ἰησοῦν γινώσκω καὶ τὸν
–   ²indeed ¹Jesus I know and   –

Παῦλον ἐπίσταμαι· ὑμεῖς δὲ τίνες ἐστέ;
Paul   I understand; but ye   who   are?

16 καὶ ἐφαλόμενος ὁ ἄνθρωπος ἐπ᾽ αὐτούς,
And ⁹leaping on ¹the ²man   ¹⁰on ¹¹them,

ἐν ᾧ ἦν τὸ πνεῦμα τὸ πονηρόν,
³in ⁴whom ⁵was ⁶the ⁸spirit – ⁷evil,

κατακυριεύσας ἀμφοτέρων ἴσχυσεν κατ᾽
overmastering   both   was strong against

αὐτῶν, ὥστε γυμνοὺς καὶ τετραυματισμένους
them, so as   naked   and   having been wounded
=so that they escaped out of that house naked and

ἐκφυγεῖν ἐκ τοῦ οἴκου ἐκείνου. 17 τοῦτο
to escape out of that house.   this
wounded.

δὲ ἐγένετο γνωστὸν πᾶσιν Ἰουδαίοις τε
And became   known   to all   ²Jews   ¹both

καὶ Ἕλλησιν τοῖς κατοικοῦσιν τὴν Ἔφεσον,
and Greeks   –   inhabiting   –   Ephesus,

καὶ ἐπέπεσεν φόβος ἐπὶ πάντας αὐτούς,
and ²fell on ¹fear   ³on   ⁵all   ⁴them,

καὶ ἐμεγαλύνετο τὸ ὄνομα τοῦ κυρίου
and was magnified the name   of the Lord

Ἰησοῦ· 18 πολλοί τε τῶν πεπιστευκότων
Jesus;   and many of the [ones] having believed

ἤρχοντο ἐξομολογούμενοι καὶ ἀναγγέλλοντες
came   confessing   and   telling

τὰς πράξεις αὐτῶν. 19 ἱκανοὶ δὲ τῶν τὰ
the doings of them.   And a consider- of the the
                      able number   [ones]

περίεργα πραξάντων συνενέγκαντες τὰς βίβλους
curious things doing bringing together the   rolls

κατέκαιον ἐνώπιον πάντων· καὶ συνεψήφισαν
burnt   before   all;   and they reckoned up

τὰς τιμὰς αὐτῶν καὶ εὗρον ἀργυρίου μυριάδας
the prices of them and found [pieces] ²thousand
                                   ³of silver

πέντε. 20 Οὕτως κατὰ κράτος τοῦ κυρίου
¹five.   Thus   by   might ²of the ⁴Lord

ὁ λόγος ηὔξανεν καὶ ἴσχυεν.
¹the ²word increased and was strong.

21 Now after these events Paul resolved in the Spirit to pass through Macedo'nia and Acha'ia and go to Jerusalem, saying, "After I have been there, I must also see Rome." ²²And having sent into Macedo'nia two of his helpers, Timothy and Eras'tus, he himself stayed in Asia for a while. 23 About that time there arose no little stir concerning the Way. ²⁴For a man named Deme'trius, a silversmith, who made silver shrines of Ar'temis, brought no little business to the craftsmen. ²⁵These he gathered together, with the workmen of like occupation, and said, "Men, you know that from this business we have our wealth. ²⁶And you see and hear that not only at Ephesus but almost throughout all Asia this Paul has persuaded and turned away a considerable company of people, saying that gods made with hands are not gods. ²⁷And there is danger not only that

21 'Ως   δὲ   ἐπληρώθη   ταῦτα,   ἔθετο   ὁ
   And when   were fulfilled these things, purposed   -

Παῦλος   ἐν   τῷ   πνεύματι   διελθὼν   τὴν
Paul   in   the(his)   spirit   passing through -

Μακεδονίαν   καὶ   'Αχαΐαν   πορεύεσθαι   εἰς
Macedonia   and   Achaia   to go   to

'Ιεροσόλυμα,   εἰπὼν   ὅτι   μετὰ   τὸ   γενέσθαι
Jerusalem,   saying[,]   -   After   the   to become
                                        =After I am

με   ἐκεῖ   δεῖ   με   καὶ   'Ρώμην   ἰδεῖν.
me[b]   there   it behoves me   ²also   ¹Rome   ¹to see.

22 ἀποστείλας   δὲ   εἰς   Μακεδονίαν   δύο
   And sending   into   Macedonia   two

τῶν   διακονούντων   αὐτῷ,   Τιμόθεον   καὶ
of the [ones] ministering   to him,   Timothy   and

"Εραστον,   αὐτὸς   ἐπέσχεν   χρόνον   εἰς   τὴν
Erastus,   he   delayed   a time   in   -

'Ασίαν.   23 'Εγένετο   δὲ   κατὰ   τὸν   καιρὸν
Asia.   Now there was   about   -   time

ἐκεῖνον   τάραχος   οὐκ   ὀλίγος   περὶ   τῆς
that   ²trouble   ¹no   ³little   concerning the

ὁδοῦ.   24 Δημήτριος   γάρ   τις   ὀνόματι,
way.   For ²Demetrius   ¹one   by name,

ἀργυροκόπος,   ποιῶν   ναοὺς   ἀργυροῦς
a silversmith,   making   shrines   silver

'Αρτέμιδος   παρείχετο   τοῖς   τεχνίταις   οὐκ
of Artemis   provided   the   artisans   no

ὀλίγην   ἐργασίαν,   25 οὓς   συναθροίσας   καὶ
little   trade,   ²whom   ¹assembling   also

τοὺς   περὶ   τὰ   τοιαῦτα   ἐργάτας   εἶπεν·
¹the   ²about(in)   -   ⁴such things   ³workmen   said:

ἄνδρες,   ἐπίστασθε   ὅτι   ἐκ   ταύτης   τῆς
Men,   ye understand   that   from   this   -

ἐργασίας   ἡ   εὐπορία   ἡμῖν   ἐστιν,   26 καὶ
trade   the   gain   to us   is,°   and
           =we have [our] gain,

θεωρεῖτε   καὶ   ἀκούετε   ὅτι   οὐ   μόνον
ye behold   and   hear   that   ⁷not   ⁸only

'Εφέσου   ἀλλὰ   σχεδὸν   πάσης   τῆς   'Ασίας
⁹of Ephesus   ¹⁰but   ¹¹almost   ¹²of all   -   ¹³Asia

ὁ   Παῦλος   οὗτος   πείσας   μετέστησεν   ἱκανὸν
-   ²Paul   ¹this   ³having   ⁴perverted   ⁵a considerable
                       persuaded

ὄχλον,   λέγων   ὅτι   οὐκ   εἰσὶν   θεοὶ   οἱ   διὰ
⁶crowd,   saying   that   they are not   gods   ¹the   ²through
                                                [ones]

χειρῶν   γινόμενοι.   27 οὐ   μόνον   δὲ   τοῦτο
⁴hands   ³coming into being.   ²not   ³only   ¹Now   ⁴this

this trade of ours may come into disrepute but also that the temple of the great goddess Ar'temis may count for nothing, and that she may even be deposed from her magnificence, she whom all Asia and the world worship."

28 When they heard this they were enraged, and cried out, "Great is Ar'temis of the Ephesians!" 29 So the city was filled with the confusion; and they rushed together into the theater, dragging with them Ga'ius and Aristar'chus, Macedo'nians who were Paul's companions in travel. 30 Paul wished to go in among the crowd, but the disciples would not let him; 31 some of the A'si-archs also, who were friends of his, sent to him and begged him not to venture into the theater. 32 Now some cried one thing, some another; for the assembly was in confusion, and most of them did not know why they had come together. 33 Some of the crowd prompted Alexander, whom the Jews had put forward. And Alexander motioned with his hand, wishing to

κινδυνεύει ἡμῖν τὸ μέρος εἰς ἀπελεγμὸν
'is in danger to us the share⁶ ⁵into ⁶disrepute
=⁵our share

ἐλθεῖν, ἀλλὰ καὶ τὸ τῆς μεγάλης θεᾶς
⁷to come, but also ¹the ²of the ⁴great ⁵goddess

'Αρτέμιδος ἱερὸν εἰς οὐθὲν λογισθῆναι,
⁶Artemis ²temple ⁵for(as) ⁹nothing ⁷to be reckoned,

μέλλειν τε καὶ καθαιρεῖσθαι τῆς μεγα-
³to be about ¹and ²also ⁴to be diminished the great-

λειότητος αὐτῆς, ἣν ὅλη ἡ 'Ασία καὶ
ness of her, whom all – Asia and

ἡ οἰκουμένη σέβεται. 28 ἀκούσαντες δὲ
the inhabited earth worships. And hearing

καὶ γενόμενοι πλήρεις θυμοῦ ἔκραζον
and becoming full of anger they cried out

λέγοντες· μεγάλη ἡ "Αρτεμις 'Εφεσίων.
saying: Great [is] – Artemis of [the] Ephesians.

29 καὶ ἐπλήσθη ἡ πόλις τῆς συγχύσεως,
And was filled the city of(with) the confusion,

ὥρμησάν τε ὁμοθυμαδὸν εἰς τὸ θέατρον,
and they rushed with one mind into the theatre,

συναρπάσαντες Γάϊον καὶ 'Αρίσταρχον
keeping a firm grip on Gaius and Aristarchus[,]

Μακεδόνας, συνεκδήμους Παύλου. 30 Παύλου
Macedonians, travelling companions of Paul. Paul

δὲ βουλομένου εἰσελθεῖν εἰς τὸν δῆμον
And intending² to enter into the mob
=as Paul intended

οὐκ εἴων αὐτὸν οἱ μαθηταί· 31 τινὲς
³not ³allowed ⁴him ¹the ²disciples; some

δὲ καὶ τῶν 'Ασιαρχῶν, ὄντες αὐτῷ
and also of the Asiarchs, being to him

φίλοι, πέμψαντες πρὸς αὐτὸν παρεκάλουν
friends, sending to him besought

μὴ δοῦναι ἑαυτὸν εἰς τὸ θέατρον. 32 ἄλλοι
not to give himself in the theatre. Others

μὲν οὖν ἄλλο τι ἔκραζον· ἦν γὰρ
indeed therefore ²different ¹something cried out; for ²was

ἡ ἐκκλησία συγκεχυμένη, καὶ οἱ πλείους
¹the ²assembly *having been* confounded, and the majority

οὐκ ᾔδεισαν τίνος ἕνεκα συνεληλύθεισαν.
knew not ²of what ¹on account they had come
together.

33 ἐκ δὲ τοῦ ὄχλου συνεβίβασαν 'Αλέξανδρον,
But [some] of the crowd instructed Alexander,

προβαλόντων αὐτὸν τῶν 'Ιουδαίων· ὁ δὲ
putting forward him the Jews²; – and
=as the Jews put him forward;

'Αλέξανδρος κατασείσας τὴν χεῖρα ἤθελεν
Alexander waving the(his) hand wished

make a defense to the people. ³⁴But when they recognized that he was a Jew, for about two hours they all with one voice cried out, "Great is Ar'temis of the Ephesians!" ³⁵And when the town clerk had quieted the crowd, he said, "Men of Ephesus, what man is there who does not know that the city of the Ephesians is temple keeper of the great Ar'temis, and of the sacred stone that fell from the sky?ⁿ ³⁶Seeing then that these things cannot be contradicted, you ought to be quiet and do nothing rash. ³⁷For you have brought these men here who are neither sacrilegious nor blasphemers of our goddess. ³⁸If therefore Deme'trius and the craftsmen with him have a complaint against any one, the courts are open, and there are proconsuls; let them bring charges against one another. ³⁹But if you seek anything further,ᵒ it shall be settled in the regular assembly. ⁴⁰For we are in danger of being charged with rioting today, there being no cause that we can give to justify this commotion."

ⁿ The meaning of the Greek is uncertain
ᵒ Other ancient authorities read about other matters

ἀπολογεῖσθαι   τῷ   δήμῳ.   34 ἐπιγνόντες   δὲ
to defend himself   to the   mob.   But knowing

ὅτι   Ἰουδαῖός   ἐστιν,   φωνὴ   ἐγένετο   μία
that   a Jew   he is(was),   ³voice   ¹there was   ²one

ἐκ   πάντων,   ὡς   ἐπὶ   ὥρας   δύο   κράζοντες·
from   all,   about   over   hours   two   crying out:

μεγάλη   ἡ   "Αρτεμις   Ἐφεσίων.   35 κατα-
Great [is]   –   Artemis   of [the] Ephesians.   ⁴having

στείλας   δὲ   ὁ   γραμματεὺς   τὸν   ὄχλον
quietened   ¹And   ³the   ³town clerk   the   crowd

φησίν·   ἄνδρες   Ἐφέσιοι,   τίς   γὰρ   ἐστιν
says: Men   Ephesians,   who   indeed   is there

ἀνθρώπων   ὃς   οὐ   γινώσκει   τὴν   Ἐφεσίων
of men   who   does not know   ¹the   ²of [the] Ephesians

πόλιν   νεωκόρον   οὖσαν   τῆς   μεγάλης
²city   ⁴temple warden   ⁴being   of the   great

Ἀρτέμιδος   καὶ   τοῦ   διοπετοῦς;   36 ἀναντιρ-
Artemis   and   of the   fallen from   undeni-
                      [image]   the sky?

ρήτων   οὖν   ὄντων   τούτων   δέον   ἐστὶν
able   therefore   being   these thingsᵃ   necessary   it is
=as these things are undeniable

ὑμᾶς   κατεσταλμένους   ὑπάρχειν   καὶ   μηδὲν
you   ²having been quietened   ¹to be   and   ²nothing

προπετὲς   πράσσειν.   37 ἠγάγετε   γὰρ   τοὺς
³rash   ¹to do.   For ye brought   –

ἄνδρας   τούτους   οὔτε   ἱεροσύλους   οὔτε
men   these   neither   temple robbers   nor

βλασφημοῦντας   τὴν   θεὸν   ἡμῶν.   38 εἰ
blaspheming   the   goddess   of you.   If

μὲν   οὖν   Δημήτριος   καὶ   οἱ   σὺν   αὐτῷ
indeed therefore   Demetrius   and   ¹the   ²with   ⁴him

τεχνῖται   ἔχουσι   πρός   τινα   λόγον,   ἀγοραῖοι
²artisans   have   against   anyone   an account,   assizes

ἄγονται   καὶ   ἀνθύπατοί   εἰσιν,   ἐγκαλείτωσαν
are   and   proconsuls   there are,   let them bring a
being(held)   charge against

ἀλλήλοις.   39 εἰ   δέ   τι   περαιτέρω   ἐπιζητεῖτε,
one another.   But if   ²anything   ³further   ¹ye seek,

ἐν   τῇ   ἐννόμῳ   ἐκκλησίᾳ   ἐπιλυθήσεται.
in   the   lawful   assembly   it will be settled.

40 καὶ   γὰρ   κινδυνεύομεν   ἐγκαλεῖσθαι
For indeed   we are in danger   to be charged with

στάσεως   περὶ   τῆς   σήμερον,   μηδενὸς
insurrection   concerning   to-day,   nothing

αἰτίου   ὑπάρχοντος,   περὶ   οὗ   οὐ   δυνησόμεθα
cause   beingᵃ,   concerning which   we shall not be able
=there being no cause,

ἀποδοῦναι   λόγον   περὶ   τῆς   συστροφῆς
to give   account   concerning   –   ²crowding together

⁴¹And when he had said this, he dismissed the assembly.

ταύτης. 41 καὶ ταῦτα εἰπὼν ἀπέλυσεν τὴν
¹this.   And these things saying   he dismissed   the
ἐκκλησίαν.
assembly.

CHAPTER 20

AFTER the uproar ceased, Paul sent for the disciples and having exhorted them took leave of them and departed for Macedo'nia. ²When he had gone through these parts and had given them much encouragement, he came to Greece. ³There he spent three months, and when a plot was made against him by the Jews as he was about to set sail for Syria, he determined to return through Macedo'nia. ⁴Sop'ater of Beroe'a, the son of Pyrrhus, accompanied him; and of the Thessalo'nians, Aristar'-chus and Secun'dus; and Ga'ius of Derbe, and Timothy; and the Asians, Tych'icus and Troph'-imus. ⁵These went on and were waiting for us at Tro'as, ⁶but we sailed away from Philippi after the days of Unleavened Bread, and in five days we came to them at Tro'as, where we stayed for seven days.
7 On the first day of

20 Μετὰ δὲ τὸ παύσασθαι τὸν θόρυβον
And after   the   to cease   the   uproarᵇ
=after the uproar ceased
μεταπεμψάμενος ὁ Παῦλος τοὺς μαθητὰς
²summoning   –   ¹Paul   ⁵the   ⁶disciples
καὶ παρακαλέσας, ἀσπασάμενος ἐξῆλθεν
³and   ⁴exhorting,   taking leave   he went forth
πορεύεσθαι εἰς Μακεδονίαν. 2 διελθὼν δὲ
to go   to   Macedonia.   And having gone through
τὰ μέρη ἐκεῖνα καὶ παρακαλέσας αὐτοὺς
those parts   and   having exhorted   them
λόγῳ πολλῷ ἦλθεν εἰς τὴν Ἑλλάδα,
¹with ²speech ³much   he came   into   –   Greece,
3 ποιήσας τε μῆνας τρεῖς, γενομένης
and spending   months   three,   there being
ἐπιβουλῆς αὐτῷ ὑπὸ τῶν Ἰουδαίων
a plotᵃ   [against] him   by   the   Jews
μέλλοντι ἀνάγεσθαι εἰς τὴν Συρίαν, ἐγένετο
being about   to set sail   to(for)   –   Syria,   he was
=as he was about
γνώμης τοῦ ὑποστρέφειν διὰ Μακεδονίας.
of a mind   –   to returnᵈ   through   Macedonia.
4 συνείπετο δὲ αὐτῷ Σώπατρος Πύρρου
And there accompanied   him   Sopater [son] of Pyrrhus
Βεροιαῖος, Θεσσαλονικέων δὲ Ἀρίσταρχος
a Berœan,   and of Thessalonians   Aristarchus
καὶ Σέκουνδος, καὶ Γάϊος Δερβαῖος καὶ
and   Secundus,   and   Gaius   a Derbæan   and
Τιμόθεος, Ἀσιανοὶ δὲ Τύχικος καὶ
Timothy,   and Asians   Tychicus   and
Τρόφιμος. 5 οὗτοι δὲ προελθόντες ἔμενον
Trophimus.   And these men   going forward   awaited
ἡμᾶς ἐν Τρῳάδι· 6 ἡμεῖς δὲ ἐξεπλεύσαμεν
us   in   Troas·   and we   sailed away
μετὰ τὰς ἡμέρας τῶν ἀζύμων ἀπὸ
after   the   days   –   of unleavened bread from
Φιλίππων, καὶ ἤλθομεν πρὸς αὐτοὺς εἰς
Philippi,   and   came   to   them   in
τὴν Τρῳάδα ἄχρι ἡμερῶν πέντε, ὅπου
–   Troas   until   days   five,   where
διετρίψαμεν ἡμέρας ἑπτά. 7 Ἐν δὲ τῇ
we stayed   days   seven.   And on   the

the week, when we were gathered together to break bread, Paul talked with them, intending to depart on the morrow; and he prolonged his speech until midnight. ⁸There were many lights in the upper chamber where we were gathered. ⁹And a young man named Eu'tychus was sitting in the window. He sank into a deep sleep as Paul talked still longer; and being overcome by sleep, he fell down from the third story and was taken up dead. ¹⁰But Paul went down and bent over him, and embracing him said, "Do not be alarmed, for his life is in him." ¹¹And when Paul had gone up and had broken bread and eaten, he conversed with them a long while, until daybreak, and so departed. ¹²And they took the lad away alive, and were not a little comforted.

13 But going ahead to the ship, we set sail for Assos, intending to take

μιᾷ τῶν σαββάτων συνηγμένων ἡμῶν
one(first) of the sabbaths(week) having been us*
[day] assembled
=as we were assembled

κλάσαι ἄρτον ὁ Παῦλος διελέγετο αὐτοῖς,
to break bread - Paul lectured to them,

μέλλων ἐξιέναι τῇ ἐπαύριον, παρέτεινέν τε
being about to depart on the morrow, and continued

τὸν λόγον μέχρι μεσονυκτίου. 8 ἦσαν δὲ
the speech until midnight. Now there were

λαμπάδες ἱκαναὶ ἐν τῷ ὑπερῴῳ οὗ
lamps a considerable in the upper room where
number of

ἦμεν συνηγμένοι. 9 καθεζόμενος δέ τις
we were having been assembled. And sitting a certain

νεανίας ὀνόματι Εὔτυχος ἐπὶ τῆς θυρίδος,
young man by name Eutychus on the window sill,

καταφερόμενος ὕπνῳ βαθεῖ, διαλεγομένου
being overborne sleep by a deep, lecturing

τοῦ Παύλου ἐπὶ πλεῖον, κατενεχθεὶς ἀπὸ
- Paul* for a longer time, having been from
=while Paul lectured overborne

τοῦ ὕπνου ἔπεσεν ἀπὸ τοῦ τριστέγου
the sleep he fell from the third floor*

κάτω καὶ ἤρθη νεκρός. 10 καταβὰς δὲ
down and was taken up dead. But going down

ὁ Παῦλος ἐπέπεσεν αὐτῷ καὶ συμπεριλαβὼν
- Paul fell on him and closely embracing
[him]

εἶπεν· μὴ θορυβεῖσθε· ἡ γὰρ ψυχὴ αὐτοῦ
said: Be ye not terrified; for the life of him

ἐν αὐτῷ ἐστιν. 11 ἀναβὰς δὲ καὶ κλάσας
in him is. And going up and breaking

τὸν ἄρτον καὶ γευσάμενος, ἐφ᾽ ἱκανόν τε
the bread and tasting, and over a considerable
[time]

ὁμιλήσας ἄχρι αὐγῆς, οὕτως ἐξῆλθεν.
conversing until light [of day], thus he went forth.

12 ἤγαγον δὲ τὸν παῖδα ζῶντα, καὶ
And they brought the lad living, and

παρεκλήθησαν οὐ μετρίως. 13 Ἡμεῖς δὲ
were comforted not moderately. And we

προελθόντες ἐπὶ τὸ πλοῖον ἀνήχθημεν
going before onto the ship set sail

ἐπὶ τὴν *Ασσον, ἐκεῖθεν μέλλοντες ἀνα-
to(for) - Assos, thence intending to

* Souter remarks that it is uncertain whether the ground floor was counted or not in the enunciation; "if so, we should have to translate ' the second floor '."

Paul aboard there; for so he had arranged, intending himself to go by land. ¹⁴And when he met us at Assos, we took him on board and came to Mityle'ne. ¹⁵And sailing from there we came the following day opposite Chi os; the next day we touched at Samos; and[p] the day after that we came to Mile tus. ¹⁶For Paul had decided to sail past Ephesus, so that he might not have to spend time in Asia; for he was hastening to be at Jerusalem, if possible, on the day of Pentecost.

17 And from Mile'tus he sent to Ephesus and called to him the elders of the church. ¹⁸And when they came to him, he said to them: "You yourselves know how I lived among you all the time from the first day that I set foot in Asia, ¹⁹serving the Lord with all humility and with tears and with trials which befell me through the plots of the Jews; ²⁰how I did not shrink from declaring to you anything that was profitable, and teaching

[p] Other ancient authorities add *after remaining at Trogyllium*

λαμβάνειν   τὸν   Παῦλον·   οὕτως   γὰρ
take up   –   Paul;   for thus

διατεταγμένος   ἦν,   μέλλων   αὐτὸς   πεζεύειν.
having been arranged it was,   ²intending   ¹he   to go afoot.

14 ὡς   δὲ   συνέβαλλεν   ἡμῖν   εἰς   τὴν   Ἀσσον,
Now when   he met with   us   in   –   Assos,

ἀναλαβόντες   αὐτὸν   ἤλθομεν   εἰς   Μιτυλήνην·
taking up   him   we came   to   Mitylene;

15 κἀκεῖθεν   ἀποπλεύσαντες   τῇ   ἐπιούσῃ
and thence   sailing away   on the   next [day]

κατηντήσαμεν   ἄντικρυς   Χίου,   τῇ   δὲ   ἑτέρᾳ
we arrived   off   Chios,   and on the other(next)

παρεβάλομεν   εἰς   Σάμον,   τῇ   δὲ   ἐχομένῃ
we crossed over   to   Samos,   and on the   next

ἤλθομεν   εἰς   Μίλητον.   16 κεκρίκει   γὰρ   ὁ
we came   to   Miletus.   For had decided   –

Παῦλος   παραπλεῦσαι   τὴν   Ἔφεσον,   ὅπως
Paul   to sail past   –   Ephesus,   so as

μὴ   γένηται   αὐτῷ   χρονοτριβῆσαι   ἐν   τῇ
not   be   to him   to spend time   in   –
=so that he should not . . .

Ἀσίᾳ·   ἔσπευδεν   γάρ,   εἰ   δυνατὸν   εἴη
Asia;   for he hasted,   if   possible   it might be

αὐτῷ,   τὴν   ἡμέραν   τῆς   πεντηκοστῆς
to him,   the   day   –   of Pentecost

γενέσθαι   εἰς   Ἱεροσόλυμα.
to be   in   Jerusalem.

17 Ἀπὸ   δὲ   τῆς   Μιλήτου   πέμψας   εἰς
And from   –   Miletus   sending   to

Ἔφεσον   μετεκαλέσατο   τοὺς   πρεσβυτέρους
Ephesus   he summoned   the   elders

τῆς   ἐκκλησίας.   18 ὡς   δὲ   παρεγένοντο
of the   church.   And when   they came

πρὸς   αὐτόν,   εἶπεν   αὐτοῖς·   ὑμεῖς   ἐπίστασθε,
to   him,   he said   to them: Ye   understand,

ἀπὸ   πρώτης   ἡμέρας   ἀφ'   ἧς   ἐπέβην   εἰς
from   [the] first   day   from which I set foot *on*   in

τὴν   Ἀσίαν,   πῶς   μεθ'   ὑμῶν   τὸν   πάντα
–   Asia,   how   with   you   the   whole

χρόνον   ἐγενόμην,   19 δουλεύων   τῷ   κυρίῳ
time   I was,   serving   the   Lord

μετὰ   πάσης   ταπεινοφροσύνης   καὶ   δακρύων
with   all   humility   and   tears

καὶ   πειρασμῶν   τῶν   συμβάντων   μοι   ἐν
and   trials   –   happening   to me   by

ταῖς   ἐπιβουλαῖς   τῶν   Ἰουδαίων,   20 ὡς
the   plots   of the   Jews,   as

οὐδὲν   ὑπεστειλάμην   τῶν   συμφερόντων   τοῦ
²nothing   ¹I kept back   of the things   beneficial   –

you in public and from house to house, ²¹ testifying both to Jews and to Greeks of repentance to God and of faith in our Lord Jesus Christ. ²²And now, behold, I am going to Jerusalem, bound in the Spirit, not knowing what shall befall me there; ²³ except that the Holy Spirit testifies to me in every city that imprisonment and afflictions await me. ²⁴ But I do not account my life of any value nor as precious to myself, if only I may accomplish my course and the ministry which I received from the Lord Jesus, to testify to the gospel of the grace of God. ²⁵ And now, behold, I know that all you among whom I have gone about preaching the kingdom will see my face no more. ²⁶ Therefore I testify to you this day that I am innocent of the blood of all of you, ²⁷ for I did not shrink from declaring to you the whole counsel of God. ²⁸ Take heed to yourselves and to all the flock, in which the Holy

μὴ   ἀναγγεῖλαι   ὑμῖν   καὶ   διδάξαι   ὑμᾶς
not   to declareᵈ   to you   and   to teachᵈ   you

δημοσίᾳ   καὶ   κατ᾽   οἴκους,   21   διαμαρτυρόμενος
publicly   and   from house to house,†   solemnly witnessing

᾽Ιουδαίοις   τε   καὶ   "Ελλησιν   τὴν   εἰς   θεὸν
²to Jews   ¹both   and   to Greeks   –   toward   God

μετάνοιαν   καὶ   πίστιν   εἰς   τὸν   κύριον
repentance   and   faith   toward(?in)   the   Lord

ἡμῶν   ᾽Ιησοῦν.   22   καὶ   νῦν   ἰδοὺ   δεδεμένος
of us   Jesus.   And   now   behold   having been bound

ἐγὼ   τῷ   πνεύματι   πορεύομαι   εἰς   ᾽Ιερου-
I   by the   Spirit   am going   to   Jeru-

σαλήμ,   τὰ   ἐν   αὐτῇ   συναντήσοντα   ἐμοὶ
salem,   ³the things   ⁶in   ⁷it   ⁴going to meet   ⁵me

μὴ   εἰδώς,   23   πλὴν   ὅτι   τὸ   πνεῦμα   τὸ
¹not   ²knowing,   except   that   the   Spirit   –

ἅγιον   κατὰ   πόλιν   διαμαρτύρεταί   μοι   λέγον
Holy   in every city†   solemnly witnesses   to me   saying

ὅτι   δεσμὰ   καὶ   θλίψεις   με   μένουσιν.
that   bonds   and   afflictions   me   await.

24   ἀλλ᾽   οὐδενὸς   λόγου   ποιοῦμαι   τὴν   ψυχὴν
But   ⁴of nothing   ⁵account   ¹I make   ²the(my)   ³life

τιμίαν   ἐμαυτῷ   ὡς   τελειώσω   τὸν   δρόμον
precious   to myself   so as   I may finish   the   course

μου   καὶ   τὴν   διακονίαν   ἣν   ἔλαβον   παρὰ
of me   and   the   ministry   which   I received   from

τοῦ   κυρίου   ᾽Ιησοῦ,   διαμαρτύρασθαι   τὸ
the   Lord   Jesus,   to witness solemnly   the

εὐαγγέλιον   τῆς   χάριτος   τοῦ   θεοῦ.   25   καὶ
gospel   of the   grace   –   of God.   And

νῦν   ἰδοὺ   ἐγὼ   οἶδα   ὅτι   οὐκέτι   ὄψεσθε
now   behold   I   know   that   ⁴no more   ³will see

τὸ   πρόσωπόν   μου   ὑμεῖς   πάντες   ἐν   οἷς
⁵the   ⁶face   ⁷of me   ¹ye   ²all   among whom

διῆλθον   κηρύσσων   τὴν   βασιλείαν.   26   διότι
I went about   proclaiming   the   kingdom.   Wherefore

μαρτύρομαι   ὑμῖν   ἐν   τῇ   σήμερον   ἡμέρᾳ
I witness   to you   on   this day

ὅτι   καθαρός   εἰμι   ἀπὸ   τοῦ   αἵματος   πάντων·
that   clean   I am   from   the   blood   of all men;

27   οὐ   γὰρ   ὑπεστειλάμην   τοῦ   μὴ   ἀναγγεῖλαι
for   I kept not back   –   not   to declareᵈ

πᾶσαν   τὴν   βουλὴν   τοῦ   θεοῦ   ὑμῖν.
all   the   counsel   –   of God   to you.

28   προσέχετε   ἑαυτοῖς   καὶ   παντὶ   τῷ
Take heed   to yourselves   and   to all   the

ποιμνίῳ,   ἐν   ᾧ   ὑμᾶς   τὸ   πνεῦμα   τὸ
flock,   in   which   ⁶you   ¹the   ²Spirit   –

562   ACTS 20

Spirit has made you guardians, to feed the church of the Lord*q* which he obtained with his own blood.*r* 29 I know that after my departure fierce wolves will come in among you, not sparing the flock; 30 and from among your own selves will arise men speaking perverse things, to draw away the disciples after them. 31 Therefore be alert, remembering that for three years I did not cease night or day to admonish every one with tears. 32 And now I commend you to God and to the word of his grace, which is able to build you up and to give you the inheritance among all those who are sanctified. 33 I coveted no one's silver or gold or apparel. 34 You yourselves know that these hands ministered to my necessities, and to those who were with me. 35 In all things I have shown you that by so toiling one must help the weak, remembering the words of the Lord Jesus, how he said, 'It is more blessed

ἅγιον   ἔθετο   ἐπισκόπους,   ποιμαίνειν   τὴν
²Holy   ⁴placed   overseers,   to shepherd   the

ἐκκλησίαν   τοῦ   θεοῦ,   ἣν   περιεποιήσατο
church   –   of God,   which   he acquired

διὰ   τοῦ   αἵματος   τοῦ   ἰδίου.   29 ἐγὼ
through the   blood   of the(his)   own.*   I

οἶδα   ὅτι   εἰσελεύσονται   μετὰ   τὴν   ἄφιξίν
know   that   ⁷will come in   ¹after   ²the   ³departure

μου   λύκοι   βαρεῖς   εἰς   ὑμᾶς   μὴ   φειδόμενοι
⁴of me   ⁶wolves   ⁵grievous   ⁸into   you   not   sparing

τοῦ   ποιμνίου,   30 καὶ   ἐξ   ὑμῶν   αὐτῶν
the   flock,   and   of   you   [your]selves

ἀναστήσονται   ἄνδρες   λαλοῦντες   διεστραμμένα
will rise up   men   speaking   having been perverted things

τοῦ   ἀποσπᾶν   τοὺς   μαθητὰς   ὀπίσω   ἑαυτῶν.
–   to drag away*d*   the   disciples   after   themselves.

31 διὸ   γρηγορεῖτε,   μνημονεύοντες   ὅτι
Wherefore   watch ye,   remembering   that

τριετίαν   νύκτα   καὶ   ἡμέραν   οὐκ   ἐπαυσάμην
for three years   night   and   day   I ceased not

μετὰ   δακρύων   νουθετῶν   ἕνα   ἕκαστον.
with   tears   admonishing   ²one   ¹each.

32 καὶ   τὰ   νῦν   παρατίθεμαι   ὑμᾶς   τῷ
And   –   now   I commend   you   to the

κυρίῳ   καὶ   τῷ   λόγῳ   τῆς   χάριτος   αὐτοῦ
Lord   and   to the   word   of the   grace   of him

τῷ   δυναμένῳ   οἰκοδομῆσαι   καὶ   δοῦναι   τὴν
–   being able   to build   and   to give   the

κληρονομίαν   ἐν   τοῖς   ἡγιασμένοις   πᾶσιν.
inheritance   among ²the [ones]   ³having been   ¹all.
sanctified

33 ἀργυρίου   ἢ   χρυσίου   ἢ   ἱματισμοῦ   οὐδενὸς
Silver   or   gold   or   raiment   of no one

ἐπεθύμησα·   34 αὐτοὶ   γινώσκετε   ὅτι   ταῖς
I coveted;   [your]selves   ye know   that   ⁴to the

χρείαις   μου   καὶ   τοῖς   οὖσιν   μετ'   ἐμοῦ
⁵needs   ⁶of me   ⁷and   ⁸to the [ones]⁹being   ¹⁰with   ¹¹me

ὑπηρέτησαν   αἱ   χεῖρες   αὗται.   35 πάντα
²ministered   ¹these   ³hands.   All things

ὑπέδειξα   ὑμῖν,   ὅτι   οὕτως   κοπιῶντας   δεῖ
I showed   you,   that   thus   labouring   it behoves

ἀντιλαμβάνεσθαι   τῶν   ἀσθενούντων,   μνημονεύειν
to succour   the   ailing [ones],   ²to remember

τε   τῶν   λόγων   τοῦ   κυρίου   Ἰησοῦ,   ὅτι
¹and   the   words   of the   Lord   Jesus,   that

αὐτὸς   εἶπεν·   μακάριόν   ἐστιν   μᾶλλον   διδόναι
he   said: Blessed   it is   rather   to give

q Other ancient authorities read *of God*
r Or *with the blood of his Own*

* This = his own blood or the blood of his own [?Son].

to give than to receive.' "
36 And when he had
spoken thus, he knelt
down and prayed with
them all. ³⁷And they all
wept and embraced Paul
and kissed him,
³⁸ sorrowing most of all
because of the word he
had spoken, that they
should see his face no
more. And they brought
him to the ship.

ἤ	λαμβάνειν.	36 καὶ	ταῦτα	εἰπών,
than	to receive.	And	²these things	¹having said,

θεὶς	τὰ	γόνατα	αὐτοῦ	σὺν	πᾶσιν	αὐτοῖς
placing the		knees	of him	with	²all	¹them

= kneeling down

προσηύξατο.	37 ἱκανὸς	δὲ	κλαυθμὸς	ἐγένετο
he prayed.	And ²considerable		³weeping	¹there was

πάντων,	καὶ	ἐπιπεσόντες	ἐπὶ	τὸν	τράχηλον
of all,	and	falling on	on	the	neck

τοῦ	Παύλου	κατεφίλουν	αὐτόν,	38 ὀδυνώ-
-	of Paul	they kissed fervently	him,	suffer-

μενοι	μάλιστα	ἐπὶ	τῷ	λόγῳ	ᾧ	εἰρήκει,
ing	most	over	the	word	which	he had said,

ὅτι	οὐκέτι	μέλλουσιν	τὸ	πρόσωπον	αὐτοῦ
that	no more	they are(were)	the	face	of him

θεωρεῖν.	προέπεμπον	δὲ	αὐτὸν	εἰς	τὸ
to behold.	And they escorted		him	to	the

πλοῖον.
ship.

CHAPTER 21

AND when we had
parted from them
and set sail, we came by
a straight course to Cos,
and the next day to
Rhodes, and from there
to Pat'ara.ᵉ ²And having
found a ship crossing to
Phoeni'cia, we went
aboard, and set sail.
³When we had come in
sight of Cyprus, leaving
it on the left we sailed to
Syria, and landed at
Tyre; for there the ship
was to unload its cargo.
⁴And having sought out
the disciples, we stayed
there for seven days.
Through the Spirit they
told Paul not to go on to
Jerusalem. ⁵And when
our days there were

21 Ὡς	δὲ	ἐγένετο	ἀναχθῆναι	ἡμᾶς
Now when	it came to pass		to set sail	we

ἀποσπασθέντας	ἀπ'	αὐτῶν,	εὐθυδρομήσαντες
having been withdrawn from	them,	taking a straight course

ἤλθομεν	εἰς	τὴν	Κῶ,	τῇ	δὲ	ἐξῆς	εἰς
we came	to	-	Cos,	and on the next [day]			to

τὴν	Ῥόδον	κἀκεῖθεν	εἰς	Πάταρα·	2 καὶ
-	Rhodes	and thence	to	Patara;	and

εὑρόντες	πλοῖον	διαπερῶν	εἰς	Φοινίκην,
having found	a ship	crossing over	to	Phœnice,

ἐπιβάντες	ἀνήχθημεν.	3 ἀναφάναντες	δὲ
embarking	we set sail.	And sighting	

τὴν	Κύπρον	καὶ	καταλιπόντες	αὐτὴν
-	Cyprus	and	leaving	it

εὐώνυμον	ἐπλέομεν	εἰς	Συρίαν,	καὶ	κατήλ-
on the left	we sailed	to	Syria,	and	came

θομεν	εἰς	Τύρον·	ἐκεῖσε	γὰρ	τὸ	πλοῖον
down	to	Tyre;	for there		the	ship

ἦν	ἀποφορτιζόμενον	τὸν	γόμον.	4 ἀνευρ-
was	unloading	the	cargo.	find-

όντες	δὲ	τοὺς	μαθητὰς	ἐπεμείναμεν	αὐτοῦ
ing	And	the	disciples	we remained	there

ἡμέρας	ἑπτά·	οἵτινες	τῷ	Παύλῳ	ἔλεγον
days	seven;	who	-	²Paul	¹told

διὰ	τοῦ	πνεύματος	μὴ	ἐπιβαίνειν	εἰς
through the		Spirit	not	to go up	to

Ἱεροσόλυμα.	5 ὅτε	δὲ	ἐγένετο	ἐξαρτίσαι
Jerusalem.	But when	it came to pass		to accomplish

= we accomplished

ᵉ Other ancient authorities add
and Myra

ended, we departed and went on our journey; and they all, with wives and children, brought us on our way till we were outside the city; and kneeling down on the beach we prayed and bade one another farewell. [6]Then we went on board the ship, and they returned home.

7 When we had finished the voyage from Tyre, we arrived at Ptolema'is; and we greeted the brethren and stayed with them for one day. [8]On the morrow we departed and came to Caesare'a; and we entered the house of Philip the evangelist, who was one of the seven, and stayed with him. [9]And he had four unmarried daughters, who prophesied. [10]While we were staying for some days, a prophet named Ag'abus came down from Judea. [11]And coming to us he took Paul's girdle and bound his own feet and hands, and said, "Thus says the Holy Spirit, 'So shall the Jews at Jerusalem bind the man who owns this girdle and

ἡμᾶς   τὰς   ἡμέρας,   ἐξελθόντες   ἐπορευόμεθα
us[b]   the   days,   going forth   we journeyed

προπεμπόντων   ἡμᾶς   πάντων   σὺν   γυναιξὶ
[2]escorting   [3]us   [1]all[a]   with   women

καὶ   τέκνοις   ἕως   ἔξω   τῆς   πόλεως,   καὶ
and   children   as far as   outside   the   city,   and

θέντες   τὰ   γόνατα   ἐπὶ   τὸν   αἰγιαλὸν
placing   the   knees   on   the   shore
=kneeling

προσευξάμενοι   6 ἀπησπασάμεθα   ἀλλήλους,
praying   we gave parting greetings to   one another,

καὶ   ἐνέβημεν   εἰς   τὸ   πλοῖον,   ἐκεῖνοι   δὲ
and   embarked   in   the   ship,   and those

ὑπέστρεψαν   εἰς   τὰ   ἴδια.   7 Ἡμεῖς   δὲ
returned   to   [1]the(ir) [2]things   [2]own.   But we
            =home.

τὸν   πλοῦν   διανύσαντες   ἀπὸ   Τύρου   κατηντή-
[2]the   [3]voyage   [1]finishing   from   Tyre   ar-

σαμεν   εἰς   Πτολεμαΐδα,   καὶ   ἀσπασάμενοι
rived   at   Ptolemais,   and   greeting

τοὺς   ἀδελφοὺς   ἐμείναμεν   ἡμέραν   μίαν
the   brothers   we remained   day   one

παρ᾽   αὐτοῖς.   8 τῇ   δὲ   ἐπαύριον   ἐξελθόντες
with   them.   And on the   morrow   going forth

ἤλθομεν   εἰς   Καισάρειαν,   καὶ   εἰσελθόντες
we came   to   Cæsarea,   and   entering

εἰς   τὸν   οἶκον   Φιλίππου   τοῦ   εὐαγγελιστοῦ
into   the   house   of Philip   the   evangelist

ὄντος   ἐκ   τῶν   ἑπτά,   ἐμείναμεν   παρ᾽
being   of   the   seven,   we remained   with

αὐτῷ.   9 τούτῳ   δὲ   ἦσαν   θυγατέρες
him.   Now to this man   were   daughters
      =this man had four daughters

τέσσαρες   παρθένοι   προφητεύουσαι.   10 Ἐπιμεν-
four[c]   virgins   prophesying.   remain-

ὄντων   δὲ   ἡμέρας   πλείους   κατῆλθέν   τις
ing[a]   And   days   more(many)   [2]came down [1]a certain

ἀπὸ   τῆς   Ἰουδαίας   προφήτης   ὀνόματι
[6]from   –   [7]Judæa   [2]prophet   [3]by name

Ἄγαβος,   11 καὶ   ἐλθὼν   πρὸς   ἡμᾶς   καὶ
[4]Agabus,   and   coming   to   us   and

ἄρας   τὴν   ζώνην   τοῦ   Παύλου,   δήσας
taking   the   girdle   –   of Paul,   having bound

ἑαυτοῦ   τοὺς   πόδας   καὶ   τὰς   χεῖρας   εἶπεν·
of himself   the   feet   and   the   hands   said:

τάδε   λέγει   τὸ   πνεῦμα   τὸ   ἅγιον·   τὸν
These things says   the   Spirit   –   Holy: [7]The

ἄνδρα   οὗ   ἐστιν   ἡ   ζώνη   αὕτη   οὕτως
[8]man   [9]of whom   [10]is   [11]this [12]girdle   [1]thus

deliver him into the hands of the Gentiles.' " ¹²When we heard this, we and the people there begged him not to go up to Jerusalem. ¹³Then Paul answered, "What are you doing, weeping and breaking my heart? For I am ready not only to be imprisoned but even to die at Jerusalem for the name of the Lord Jesus." ¹⁴And when he would not be persuaded, we ceased and said, "The will of the Lord be done."

15 After these days we made ready and went up to Jerusalem. ¹⁶And some of the disciples from Caesare'a went with us, bringing us to the house of Mnason of Cyprus, an early disciple, with whom we should lodge.

17 When we had come to Jerusalem, the brethren received us gladly. ¹⁸On the following day Paul went in with us to James; and all the elders were present. ¹⁹After greeting them, he related

δήσουσιν ἐν Ἰερουσαλὴμ οἱ Ἰουδαῖοι καὶ
⁴will bind ⁵in ⁶Jerusalem ²the ³Jews and

παραδώσουσιν εἰς χεῖρας ἐθνῶν. 12 ὡς
will deliver into [the] hands of [the] nations. when

δὲ ἠκούσαμεν ταῦτα, παρεκαλοῦμεν ἡμεῖς
And we heard these things, ⁶besought ²we

τε καὶ οἱ ἐντόπιοι τοῦ μὴ ἀναβαίνειν
¹both ²and ⁴the ⁵residents - ⁸not ⁹to go up^d

αὐτὸν εἰς Ἰερουσαλήμ. 13 τότε ἀπεκρίθη
⁷him to Jerusalem. Then answered

ὁ Παῦλος τί ποιεῖτε κλαίοντες καὶ
- Paul: What are ye doing weeping and

συνθρύπτοντές μου τὴν καρδίαν; ἐγὼ γὰρ
weakening of me the heart? For I

οὐ μόνον δεθῆναι ἀλλὰ καὶ ἀποθανεῖν
not only to be bound but also to die

εἰς Ἰερουσαλὴμ ἑτοίμως ἔχω ὑπὲρ τοῦ
in Jerusalem readily have on behalf of the
= am ready

ὀνόματος τοῦ κυρίου Ἰησοῦ. 14 μὴ
name of the Lord Jesus. Not

πειθομένου δὲ αὐτοῦ ἡσυχάσαμεν εἰπόντες·
being persuaded and him² we kept silence having said:
= And when he was not persuaded

τοῦ κυρίου τὸ θέλημα γινέσθω.
⁴Of the ¹Lord ²the ³will ¹let ⁶be [done].

15 Μετὰ δὲ τὰς ἡμέρας ταύτας
And after these days

ἐπισκευασάμενοι ἀνεβαίνομεν εἰς Ἰεροσόλυμα·
having made ready we went up to Jerusalem;

16 συνῆλθον δὲ καὶ τῶν μαθητῶν ἀπὸ
and went with also [some] of the disciples from

Καισαρείας σὺν ἡμῖν, ἄγοντες παρ' ᾧ
Cæsarea with us, bringing [one] with whom

ξενισθῶμεν Μνάσωνί τινι Κυπρίῳ,
we might be lodged Mnason a certain Cypriote,

ἀρχαίῳ μαθητῇ. 17 Γενομένων δὲ ἡμῶν εἰς
an ancient disciple. And being us² in
(early) = when we were

Ἰεροσόλυμα ἀσμένως ἀπεδέξαντο ἡμᾶς οἱ
Jerusalem ⁵joyfully ²received ⁴us ¹the

ἀδελφοί. 18 τῇ δὲ ἐπιούσῃ εἰσῄει ὁ
³brothers. And on the next day went in -

Παῦλος σὺν ἡμῖν πρὸς Ἰάκωβον, πάντες
Paul with us to James, ³all

τε παρεγένοντο οἱ πρεσβύτεροι. 19 καὶ
¹and ⁶came ²the ⁴elders. And

ἀσπασάμενος αὐτοὺς ἐξηγεῖτο καθ' ἕν
having greeted them he related according to one
= singly

one by one the things that God had done among the Gentiles through his ministry. 20And when they heard it, they glorified God. And they said to him, "You see, brother, how many thousands there are among the Jews of those who have believed; they are all zealous for the law, 21and they have been told about you that you teach all the Jews who are among the Gentiles to forsake Moses, telling them not to circumcise their children or observe the customs. 22What then is to be done? They will certainly hear that you have come. 23Do therefore what we tell you. We have four men who are under a vow; 24take these men and purify yourself along with them and pay their expenses, so that they may shave their heads. Thus all will know that there is nothing in what they have been told about you but that you yourself live in observance of the law. 25But as for the Gentiles who have believed, we have sent a letter with our judgment that they should abstain from what has been sacrificed to idols and from blood and from what is strangled¹ and from unchastity." 26Then Paul

¹ Other early authorities omit *and from what is strangled*

ἕκαστον ὧν ἐποίησεν ὁ θεὸς ἐν τοῖς
each of [the did - God among the
things] which
ἔθνεσιν διὰ τῆς διακονίας αὐτοῦ. 20 οἱ
nations through the ministry of him. they
δὲ ἀκούσαντες ἐδόξαζον τὸν θεόν, εἶπάν τε
And hearing glorified - God, and said
αὐτῷ· θεωρεῖς, ἀδελφέ, πόσαι μυριάδες
to him: Thou beholdest, brother, how many *ten* thousands
εἰσὶν ἐν τοῖς Ἰουδαίοις τῶν πεπιστευκότων,
there are among the Jews - having believed,
καὶ πάντες ζηλωταὶ τοῦ νόμου ὑπάρχουσιν·
and all zealots of the law are;
21 κατηχήθησαν δὲ περὶ σοῦ ὅτι ἀποστα-
and they were informed about thee that ²apo-
σίαν διδάσκεις ἀπὸ Μωϋσέως τοὺς κατὰ
stasy ¹thou teachest ⁹from ¹⁰Moses ³the ⁵throughout
τὰ ἔθνη πάντας Ἰουδαίους, λέγων μὴ
⁶the ⁷nations ²all ⁴Jews, ¹telling ³not
περιτέμνειν αὐτοὺς τὰ τέκνα μηδὲ τοῖς
⁴to circumcise ²them the children nor in the
ἔθεσιν περιπατεῖν. 22 τί οὖν ἐστιν;
customs to walk. What therefore is it?
πάντως ἀκούσονται ὅτι ἐλήλυθας. 23 τοῦτο
At all events they will hear that thou hast come. This
οὖν ποίησον ὅ σοι λέγομεν· εἰσὶν ἡμῖν
therefore do thou which thee we tell: There are to us⁶
=We have
ἄνδρες τέσσαρες εὐχὴν ἔχοντες ἐφ᾽ ἑαυτῶν·
men four a vow having on themselves;
24 τούτους παραλαβὼν ἁγνίσθητι σὺν αὐτοῖς,
these taking be thou purified with them,
καὶ δαπάνησον ἐπ᾽ αὐτοῖς ἵνα ξυρήσονται
and spend on them that they will shave
τὴν κεφαλήν, καὶ γνώσονται πάντες ὅτι
the head, and will know all men that
ὧν κατήχηνται περὶ σοῦ οὐδέν
³[of the things] ⁴they have been ⁵about ⁶thee ²nothing
of which informed
ἐστιν, ἀλλὰ στοιχεῖς καὶ αὐτὸς φυλάσσων τὸν
¹there is, but thou walkest also [thy]self keeping the
νόμον. 25 περὶ δὲ τῶν πεπιστευκότων
law. And concerning ¹the ²having believed
ἐθνῶν ἡμεῖς ἐπεστείλαμεν κρίναντες φυλάσ-
²nations we joined in writing ¹judging ³to keep
σεσθαι αὐτοὺς τό τε εἰδωλόθυτον καὶ
themselves ²them ⁴[from] ³the ⁵both idol sacrifice and
αἷμα καὶ πνικτὸν καὶ πορνείαν. 26 τότε
blood and a thing strangled and fornication. Then

took the men, and the next day he purified himself with them and went into the temple, to give notice when the days of purification would be fulfilled and the offering presented for every one of them. 27 When the seven days were almost completed, the Jews from Asia, who had seen him in the temple, stirred up all the crowd, and laid hands on him, ²⁸crying out, "Men of Israel, help! This is the man who is teaching men everywhere against the people and the law and this place; moreover he also brought Greeks into the temple, and he has defiled this holy place." ²⁹For they had previously seen Trophimus the Ephesian with him in the city, and they supposed that Paul had brought him into the temple. ³⁰Then all the city was aroused, and the people ran together; they seized Paul and dragged him out of the temple, and at once the gates were shut. ³¹And as they

ὁ Παῦλος παραλαβὼν τοὺς ἄνδρας τῇ
– Paul taking the men on the
ἐχομένῃ ἡμέρᾳ σὺν αὐτοῖς ἀγνισθεὶς εἰσῄει
next day with them having been purified went in
εἰς τὸ ἱερόν, διαγγέλλων τὴν ἐκπλήρωσιν
to the temple, announcing the completion
τῶν ἡμερῶν τοῦ ἁγνισμοῦ, ἕως οὗ
of the days of the purification, until
προσηνέχθη ὑπὲρ ἑνὸς ἑκάστου αὐτῶν ἡ
should be offered on behalf of ²one ¹each of them the
προσφορά.
offering.

27 Ὡς δὲ ἔμελλον αἱ ἑπτὰ ἡμέραι
Now when were about the seven days
συντελεῖσθαι, οἱ ἀπὸ τῆς Ἀσίας Ἰουδαῖοι
to be fulfilled, ¹the ³from – ⁴Asia ²Jews
θεασάμενοι αὐτὸν ἐν τῷ ἱερῷ συνέχεον
seeing him in the temple stirred up
πάντα τὸν ὄχλον, καὶ ἐπέβαλαν ἐπ᾽
all the crowd, and laid on on
αὐτὸν τὰς χεῖρας, 28 κράζοντες· ἄνδρες
him the(ir) hands, crying out: Men
Ἰσραηλῖται, βοηθεῖτε· οὗτός ἐστιν ὁ
Israelites, help: this is the
ἄνθρωπος ὁ κατὰ τοῦ λαοῦ καὶ τοῦ
man ¹the [one] ⁵against ⁶the ⁷people ⁸and ⁹the
νόμου καὶ τοῦ τόπου τούτου πάντας
¹⁰law ¹¹and ¹²this ¹³place ²all men
πανταχῇ διδάσκων, ἔτι τε καὶ Ἕλληνας
⁴everywhere ³teaching, and even also Greeks
εἰσήγαγεν εἰς τὸ ἱερὸν καὶ κεκοίνωκεν
brought in into the temple and has profaned
τὸν ἅγιον τόπον τοῦτον. 29 ἦσαν γὰρ
– ²holy ³place ¹this. For they were
προεωρακότες Τρόφιμον τὸν Ἐφέσιον ἐν
having previously seen Trophimus the Ephesian in
τῇ πόλει σὺν αὐτῷ, ὃν ἐνόμιζον ὅτι
the city with him, whom they supposed that
εἰς τὸ ἱερὸν εἰσήγαγεν ὁ Παῦλος. 30 ἐκινήθη
³into ⁴the ⁵temple ²brought in – ¹Paul. ⁵was moved
τε ἡ πόλις ὅλη καὶ ἐγένετο συνδρομὴ
¹And ²the ⁴city ³whole and there was a running together
τοῦ λαοῦ, καὶ ἐπιλαβόμενοι τοῦ Παύλου
of the people, and laying hold – of Paul
εἷλκον αὐτὸν ἔξω τοῦ ἱεροῦ, καὶ εὐθέως
they dragged him outside the temple, and immediately
ἐκλείσθησαν αἱ θύραι. 31 Ζητούντων τε
were shut the doors. And [while they were]
seeking*

were trying to kill him, word came to the tribune of the cohort that all Jerusalem was in confusion. ³²He at once took soldiers and centurions, and ran down to them; and when they saw the tribune and the soldiers, they stopped beating Paul. ³³Then the tribune came up and arrested him, and ordered him to be bound with two chains. He inquired who he was and what he had done. ³⁴Some in the crowd shouted one thing, some another; and as he could not learn the facts because of the uproar, he ordered him to be brought into the barracks. ³⁵And when he came to the steps, he was actually carried by the soldiers because of the violence of the crowd; ³⁶for the mob of the people followed, crying, "Away with him!" 37 As Paul was about to be brought into the barracks, he said to the tribune, "May I say something to you?" And he said, "Do you know

αὐτὸν	ἀποκτεῖναι	ἀνέβη	φάσις	τῷ
²him	¹to kill	⁴came up	³information	to the

χιλιάρχῳ	τῆς	σπείρης	ὅτι	ὅλη	συγχύν-
chiliarch	of the	cohort	that	¹all	²is(was)in

νεται	᾿Ιερουσαλήμ·	32	ὃς	ἐξαυτῆς	παρα-
confusion	²Jerusalem;		who	at once	tak-

λαβὼν	στρατιώτας	καὶ	ἑκατοντάρχας
ing	soldiers	and	centurions

κατέδραμεν	ἐπ'	αὐτούς·	οἱ	δὲ	ἰδόντες
ran down	on	them;	and they		seeing

τὸν	χιλίαρχον	καὶ	τοὺς	στρατιώτας
the	chiliarch	and	the	soldiers

ἐπαύσαντο	τύπτοντες	τὸν	Παῦλον.	33 τότε
ceased	beating	–	Paul.	33 Then

ἐγγίσας	ὁ	χιλίαρχος	ἐπελάβετο	αὐτοῦ
drawing near	the	chiliarch	laid hold	of him

καὶ	ἐκέλευσεν	δεθῆναι	ἁλύσεσι	δυσί,	καὶ
and	commanded	to be bound	chains	with two,	and

ἐπυνθάνετο	τίς	εἴη	καὶ	τί	ἐστιν	πεποιηκώς.
inquired	who	might be	and	what	he is	having done.

34 ἄλλοι	δὲ	ἄλλο	τι	ἐπεφώνουν	ἐν	τῷ
And ¹others		⁷different	⁶some-thing	⁵called out	²among	³the

ὄχλῳ·	μὴ	δυναμένου	δὲ	αὐτοῦ	γνῶναι
⁴crowd;	and not being able =as he was not able			himᵃ	to know

τὸ	ἀσφαλὲς	διὰ	τὸν	θόρυβον,	ἐκέλευσεν
the	certain thing	because of the		uproar,	he commanded

ἄγεσθαι	αὐτὸν	εἰς	τὴν	παρεμβολήν.	35 ὅτε
to be brought	him	into	the	fort.	35 when

δὲ	ἐγένετο	ἐπὶ	τοὺς	ἀναβαθμούς,	συνέβη
And	he was	on	the	steps,	it happened

βαστάζεσθαι	αὐτὸν	ὑπὸ	τῶν	στρατιωτῶν
to be carried =he was carried	himᵇ	by	he	soldiers

διὰ	τὴν	βίαν	τοῦ	ὄχλου·	36 ἠκολούθει
because of the		violence	of the	crowd;	⁶followed

γὰρ	τὸ	πλῆθος	τοῦ	λαοῦ	κράζοντες·
¹for	²the	³multitude	⁴of the	⁵people	crying out:

αἶρε	αὐτόν.	37 Μέλλων	τε	εἰσάγεσθαι
Take away	him.	And being about		to be brought in

εἰς	τὴν	παρεμβολὴν	ὁ	Παῦλος	λέγει	τῷ
into	the	fort	–	Paul	says	to the

χιλιάρχῳ·	εἰ	ἔξεστίν	μοι	εἰπεῖν	τι	πρὸς
chiliarch:	If	it is lawful	for me	to say	something	to

σέ;	ὁ	δὲ	ἔφη·	῾Ελληνιστὶ	γινώσκεις;
thee?	And he		said:	in Greek	Knowest thou [to speak]?*

* See note on page xviii.

Greek? [38]Are you not the Egyptian, then, who recently stirred up a revolt and led the four thousand men of the Assassins out into the wilderness?" [39]Paul replied, "I am a Jew, from Tarsus in Cili'cia, a citizen of no mean city; I beg you, let me speak to the people." [40]And when he had given him leave, Paul, standing on the steps, motioned with his hand to the people; and when there was a great hush, he spoke to them in the Hebrew language, saying:

38 οὐκ ἄρα σὺ εἶ ὁ Αἰγύπτιος ὁ πρὸ
[2]Not [4]then [3]thou [1]art the Egyptian the [one] before

τούτων τῶν ἡμερῶν ἀναστατώσας καὶ
these' - days unsettling and

ἐξαγαγὼν εἰς τὴν ἔρημον τοὺς τετρα-
leading out into the desert the four

κισχιλίους ἄνδρας τῶν σικαρίων; 39 εἶπεν
thousand men of the Sicarii? said

δὲ ὁ Παῦλος· ἐγὼ ἄνθρωπος μέν εἰμι
And - Paul: I a man indeed am

Ἰουδαῖος, Ταρσεύς, τῆς Κιλικίας οὐκ
a Jew, a Tarsian, - of Cilicia not

ἀσήμου πόλεως πολίτης· δέομαι δέ σου,
of a mean city a citizen; and I beg of thee,

ἐπίτρεψόν μοι λαλῆσαι πρὸς τὸν λαόν.
permit me to speak to the people.

40 ἐπιτρέψαντος δὲ αὐτοῦ[a] ὁ Παῦλος ἑστὼς
And permitting him[a] - Paul standing
=when he gave permission

ἐπὶ τῶν ἀναβαθμῶν κατέσεισεν τῇ χειρὶ
on the steps beckoned with the(his) hand

τῷ λαῷ· πολλῆς δὲ σιγῆς γενομένης
to the people; and much silence becoming[a]
=when there was great silence

προσεφώνησεν τῇ Ἑβραΐδι διαλέκτῳ λέγων·
he addressed in the Hebrew language saying:

CHAPTER 22

"BRETHREN and fathers, hear the defense which I now make before you." 2 And when they heard that he addressed them in the Hebrew language, they were the more quiet. And he said: 3 "I am a Jew, born at Tarsus in Cili'cia, but brought up in this city at the feet of Gama'li-el, educated according to the strict manner of the law of our fathers, being zealous for God as you

22 Ἄνδρες ἀδελφοὶ καὶ πατέρες, ἀκούσατέ
Men brothers and fathers, hear ye

μου τῆς πρὸς ὑμᾶς νυνὶ ἀπολογίας.
[5]of me [1]the [3]to [4]you [2]now defence.

— 2 ἀκούσαντες δὲ ὅτι τῇ Ἑβραΐδι
(And hearing that in the Hebrew

διαλέκτῳ προσεφώνει αὐτοῖς μᾶλλον
language he addressed them more

παρέσχον ἡσυχίαν. καὶ φησίν· — 3 ἐγώ εἰμι
they showed quietness. And he says:) I am

ἀνὴρ Ἰουδαῖος, γεγεννημένος ἐν Ταρσῷ
a man a Jew, having been born in Tarsus

τῆς Κιλικίας, ἀνατεθραμμένος δὲ ἐν τῇ
- of Cilicia, and having been brought up in -

πόλει ταύτῃ, παρὰ τοὺς πόδας Γαμαλιὴλ
city this, at the feet of Gamaliel

πεπαιδευμένος κατὰ ἀκρίβειαν τοῦ πατρῴου
having been trained according exactness of the ancestral
to [the]

νόμου, ζηλωτὴς ὑπάρχων τοῦ θεοῦ καθὼς
law, a zealot being - of God even as

all are this day. ⁴I
persecuted this Way to
the death, binding and
delivering to prison both
men and women, ⁵as the
high priest and the whole
council of elders bear me
witness. From them I
received letters to the
brethren, and I journeyed
to Damascus to take
those also who were
there and bring them in
bonds to Jerusalem to be
punished.

6 "As I made my
journey and drew near to
Damascus, about noon
a great light from heaven
suddenly shone about
me. ⁷And I fell to the
ground and heard a
voice saying to me, 'Saul,
Saul, why do you per-
secute me?' ⁸And I
answered, 'Who are you,
Lord?' And he said to
me, 'I am Jesus of
Nazareth whom you are
persecuting.' ⁹Now those
who were with me saw
the light but did not hear
the voice of the one who
was speaking to me.
¹⁰And I said, 'What shall
I do, Lord?' And the
Lord said to me, 'Rise,
and go into Damascus,
and there you will be told
all that is appointed for
you to do.' ¹¹And when I
could not see because of

πάντες ὑμεῖς ἐστε σήμερον· 4 ὃς ταύτην
all   ye   are   to-day;   who   this
τὴν ὁδὸν ἐδίωξα ἄχρι θανάτου, δεσμεύων
 -   way persecuted as far as to death,   binding
καὶ παραδιδοὺς εἰς φυλακὰς ἄνδρας τε
and delivering   to prisons   both men
καὶ γυναῖκας. 5 ὡς καὶ ὁ ἀρχιερεὺς
and women.   As even the high priest
μαρτυρεῖ μοι καὶ πᾶν τὸ πρεσβυτέριον·
witnesses to me and all the   senate;
παρ' ὧν καὶ ἐπιστολὰς δεξάμενος πρὸς
from whom also   letters   having received to
τοὺς ἀδελφοὺς εἰς Δαμασκὸν ἐπορευόμην,
the brothers   in Damascus   I journeyed,
ἄξων καὶ τοὺς ἐκεῖσε ὄντας δεδεμένους
leading also the [ones] ²there ¹being having been bound
εἰς Ἰερουσαλὴμ ἵνα τιμωρηθῶσιν.
 to Jerusalem   that they might be punished.
6 Ἐγένετο δέ μοι πορευομένῳ καὶ ἐγγίζοντι
   Now it happened to me journeying and drawing near
τῇ Δαμασκῷ περὶ μεσημβρίαν ἐξαίφνης ἐκ
 - to Damascus about midday   suddenly out of
τοῦ οὐρανοῦ περιαστράψαι φῶς ἱκανὸν
 -   heaven ⁴to shine round ¹a ³light ²considerable
περὶ ἐμέ, 7 ἔπεσά τε εἰς τὸ ἔδαφος
round me,   and I fell to the ground
καὶ ἤκουσα φωνῆς λεγούσης μοι· Σαοὺλ
and heard a voice saying to me: Saul[,]
Σαούλ, τί με διώκεις; 8 ἐγὼ δὲ ἀπεκρίθην·
Saul, why me persecutest thou? And I   answered:
τίς εἶ, κύριε; εἶπέν τε πρὸς ἐμέ· ἐγώ
Who art thou, Lord? And he said to   me: I
εἰμι Ἰησοῦς ὁ Ναζωραῖος, ὃν σὺ διώκεις.
am   Jesus the Nazarene, whom thou persecutest.
9 οἱ δὲ σὺν ἐμοὶ ὄντες τὸ μὲν φῶς
Now ¹the [ones] ³with ⁴me ²being ⁷the ⁶indeed ⁸light
ἐθεάσαντο, τὴν δὲ φωνὴν οὐκ ἤκουσαν
 ⁵beheld,   but the voice   they heard not
τοῦ λαλοῦντός μοι. 10 εἶπον δέ· τί
of the [one] speaking to me.   And I said: What
ποιήσω, κύριε; ὁ δὲ κύριος εἶπεν πρός
may I do, Lord? And the Lord said   to
με· ἀναστὰς πορεύου εἰς Δαμασκόν, κἀκεῖ σοι
me: Rising up go   into Damascus, and there to thee
λαληθήσεται περὶ πάντων ὧν τέτακταί
it will be told concerning all things which has(ve) been
                                           arranged
σοι ποιῆσαι. 11 ὡς δὲ οὐκ ἐνέβλεπον
for thee to do.   And as   I saw not

the brightness of that light, I was led by the hand by those who were with me, and came into Damascus.

12 "And one Anani′as, a devout man according to the law, well spoken of by all the Jews who lived there, ¹³came to me, and standing by me said to me, 'Brother Saul, receive your sight.' And in that very hour I received my sight and saw him. ¹⁴And he said, 'The God of our fathers appointed you to know his will, to see the Just One and to hear a voice from his mouth; ¹⁵for you will be a witness for him to all men of what you have seen and heard. ¹⁶And now why do you wait? Rise and be baptized, and wash away your sins, calling on his name.'

17 "When I had returned to Jerusalem and was praying in the temple, I fell into a trance ¹⁸and saw him saying to me, 'Make haste and get quickly out of Jerusalem, because they will not accept your testimony about me.' ¹⁹And I said, 'Lord, they

ἀπὸ   τῆς   δόξης   τοῦ   φωτὸς   ἐκείνου,
from   the   glory   of that light,

χειραγωγούμενος   ὑπὸ   τῶν   συνόντων   μοι
being led by the hand   by   the [ones]   being with   me

ἦλθον   εἰς   Δαμασκόν.   12 Ἀνανίας   δέ   τις,
I went   into   Damascus.   And a certain Ananias,

ἀνὴρ   εὐλαβὴς   κατὰ   τὸν   νόμον,   μαρτυρού-
a man   devout   according to the   law,   being witnessed

μενος   ὑπὸ   πάντων   τῶν   κατοικούντων
[to]   by   all   ¹the   ³dwelling ⁴[there]

Ἰουδαίων,   13 ἐλθὼν   πρὸς   ἐμὲ   καὶ   ἐπιστὰς
²Jews,   coming   to   me   and   standing by

εἶπέν   μοι·   Σαοὺλ   ἀδελφέ,   ἀνάβλεψον.
said   to me: Saul   brother,   look up.

κἀγὼ   αὐτῇ   τῇ   ὥρᾳ   ἀνέβλεψα   εἰς   αὐτόν.
And I   in that hour*   looked up   at   him.

14 ὁ   δὲ   εἶπεν·   ὁ   θεὸς   τῶν   πατέρων
And he   said: The   God   of the   fathers

ἡμῶν   προεχειρίσατό   σε   γνῶναι   τὸ   θέλημα
of us   previously appointed   thee   to know   the   will

αὐτοῦ   καὶ   ἰδεῖν   τὸν   δίκαιον   καὶ   ἀκοῦσαι
of him   and   to see   the   Just One   and   to hear

φωνὴν   ἐκ   τοῦ   στόματος   αὐτοῦ,   15 ὅτι
a voice   out of   the   mouth   of him,   because

ἔσῃ   μάρτυς   αὐτῷ   πρὸς   πάντας   ἀνθρώπους
thou wilt be   a witness   to himᶜ   to   all   men

ὧν   ἑώρακας   καὶ   ἤκουσας.   16 καὶ   νῦν
of things which   thou hast seen   and   didst hear.   And now

τί   μέλλεις;   ἀναστὰς   βάπτισαι   καὶ   ἀπόλου-
what intendest thou?   Rising up   be baptized   and   wash

σαι   τὰς   ἁμαρτίας   σου,   ἐπικαλεσάμενος   τὸ
away   the   sins   of thee,   invoking   the

ὄνομα   αὐτοῦ.   17 Ἐγένετο   δέ   μοι   ὑποστρέ-
name   of him.   And it happened   to me   having

ψαντι   εἰς   Ἰερουσαλὴμ   καὶ   προσευχομένου
returned   to   Jerusalem   and   praying
= as I was praying

μου   ἐν   τῷ   ἱερῷ   γενέσθαι   με   ἐν   ἐκστάσει,
meᵃ   in   the   temple   to become   meᵇ   in   an ecstasy,
= I became

18 καὶ   ἰδεῖν   αὐτὸν   λέγοντά   μοι·   σπεῦσον
and   to seeᵇ   him   saying   to me;   Haste
= I saw

καὶ   ἔξελθε   ἐν   τάχει   ἐξ   Ἰερουσαλήμ,
and   go forth   quickly   out of   Jerusalem,

διότι   οὐ   παραδέξονταί   σου   μαρτυρίαν
because   they will not receive   of thee   witness

περὶ   ἐμοῦ.   19 κἀγὼ   εἶπον·   κύριε,   αὐτοὶ
concerning me.   And I   said: Lord,   they

* See Luke 2. 38.

themselves know that in every synagogue I imprisoned and beat those who believed in thee. ²⁰And when the blood of Stephen thy witness was shed, I also was standing by and approving, and keeping the garments of those who killed him.' ²¹And he said to me, 'Depart; for I will send you far away to the Gentiles.' "

22 Up to this word they listened to him; then they lifted up their voices and said, "Away with such a fellow from the earth! For he ought not to live." ²³And as they cried out and waved their garments and threw dust into the air, ²⁴the tribune commanded him to be brought into the barracks, and ordered him to be examined by scourging, to find out why they shouted thus against him. ²⁵But when they had tied him up with the thongs, Paul said to the centurion who was standing by, "Is it lawful for you to scourge a man who is a Roman citizen, and uncondemned?" ²⁶When the centurion heard that, he went to the tribune and said to

ἐπίστανται ὅτι ἐγὼ ἤμην φυλακίζων καὶ
understand that I was imprisoning and
δέρων κατὰ τὰς συναγωγὰς τοὺς πιστεύον-
beating throughout the synagogues the [ones] believ-
τας ἐπὶ σέ· 20 καὶ ὅτε ἐξεχύννετο τὸ αἷμα
ing on thee; and when was being shed the blood
Στεφάνου τοῦ μάρτυρός σου, καὶ αὐτὸς
of Stephen the witness of thee, even [my]self
ἤμην ἐφεστὼς καὶ συνευδοκῶν καὶ
I was standing by and consenting and
φυλάσσων τὰ ἱμάτια τῶν ἀναιρούντων
keeping the garments of the [ones] killing
αὐτόν. 21 καὶ εἶπεν πρός με· πορεύου,
him. And he said to me: Go,
ὅτι ἐγὼ εἰς ἔθνη μακρὰν ἐξαποστελῶ σε.
because I to nations afar will send forth thee.
22 Ἤκουον δὲ αὐτοῦ ἄχρι τούτου τοῦ
And they heard him as far as to this –
λόγου, καὶ ἐπῆραν τὴν φωνὴν αὐτῶν
word, and lifted up the voice of them
λέγοντες· αἶρε ἀπὸ τῆς γῆς τὸν τοιοῦτον·
saying: Take from the earth such a man·
οὐ γὰρ καθῆκεν αὐτὸν ζῆν. 23 κραυγαζόν-
for not it is fitting him to live. And shout-
των τε αὐτῶν καὶ ῥιπτούντων τὰ ἱμάτια
ing them and tearing* the(ir) garments
=as they shouted and tore . . .
καὶ κονιορτὸν βαλλόντων εἰς τὸν ἀέρα,
and ²dust ¹throwing* in the air,
=threw dust
24 ἐκέλευσεν ὁ χιλίαρχος εἰσάγεσθαι αὐτὸν
commanded the chiliarch to be brought in him
εἰς τὴν παρεμβολήν, εἴπας μάστιξιν
into the fort, bidding ²with scourges
ἀνετάζεσθαι αὐτόν, ἵνα ἐπιγνῷ δι᾽ ἣν
²to be examined ¹him, that he might fully know for what
αἰτίαν οὕτως ἐπεφώνουν αὐτῷ. 25 ὡς δὲ
crime thus they were calling against him. But as
προέτειναν αὐτὸν τοῖς ἱμᾶσιν, εἶπεν πρὸς
they stretched him with the thongs, ²said ³to
forward
τὸν ἑστῶτα ἑκατόνταρχον ὁ Παῦλος· εἰ
⁴the ⁶standing [by] ⁵centurion – ¹Paul: ¹If
ἄνθρωπον Ῥωμαῖον καὶ ἀκατάκριτον ἔξεστιν
a man ⁵a Roman ⁶and ⁷uncondemned ²it is lawful
ὑμῖν μαστίζειν; 26 ἀκούσας δὲ ὁ ἑκατον-
²for you ⁴to scourge? And ³hearing ¹the ²cen-
τάρχης προσελθὼν τῷ χιλιάρχῳ ἀπήγγειλεν
turion approaching to the chiliarch reported

him, "What are you about to do? For this man is a Roman citizen." ²⁷So the tribune came and said to him, "Tell me, are you a Roman citizen?" And he said, "Yes." ²⁸The tribune answered, "I bought this citizenship for a large sum." Paul said, "But I was born a citizen." ²⁹So those who were about to examine him withdrew from him instantly; and the tribune also was afraid, for he realized that Paul was a Roman citizen and that he had bound him.

30 But on the morrow, desiring to know the real reason why the Jews accused him, he unbound him, and commanded the chief priests and all the council to meet, and he brought Paul down and set him before them.

CHAPTER 23

A ND Paul, looking intently at the council, said, "Brethren, I have lived before God in all good conscience up to this day." ²And the high priest Anani'as commanded those who stood by him to strike him on the mouth. ³Then Paul

λέγων· τί μέλλεις ποιεῖν; ὁ γὰρ ἄνθρωπος
saying: What art thou about to do?   – for   ¹man

οὗτος ʻΡωμαῖός ἐστιν. 27 προσελθὼν δὲ
¹this   ⁴a Roman   ²is.   And approaching

ὁ χιλίαρχος εἶπεν αὐτῷ· λέγε μοι, σὺ
the   chiliarch   said   to him: Tell   me,   thou

ʻΡωμαῖος εἶ; ὁ δὲ ἔφη· ναί. 28 ἀπεκρίθη
a Roman   art? And he   said: Yes.   answered

δὲ ὁ χιλίαρχος· ἐγὼ πολλοῦ κεφαλαίου
And the   chiliarch: ¹I   ⁵of(for)   ⁴sum [of money]   much(great)

τὴν πολιτείαν ταύτην ἐκτησάμην. ὁ δὲ
³this ⁴citizenship   ²acquired.   –   So

Παῦλος ἔφη· ἐγὼ δὲ καὶ γεγέννημαι.
Paul   said: But I   indeed   have been born.

29 εὐθέως οὖν ἀπέστησαν ἀπ᾽ αὐτοῦ οἱ
Immediately therefore   ⁵stood away   ⁶from   ⁷him   ¹the [ones]

μέλλοντες αὐτὸν ἀνετάζειν· καὶ ὁ χιλίαρχος
²being about   ⁴him   ³to examine;   ⁴also ²the   ⁵chiliarch

δὲ ἐφοβήθη ἐπιγνοὺς ὅτι ʻΡωμαῖός ἐστιν
¹and   feared   fully knowing that   a Roman   he is(was)

καὶ ὅτι αὐτὸν ἦν δεδεκώς.
and   that   ²him   ¹he was ²having bound.

30 Τῇ δὲ ἐπαύριον βουλόμενος γνῶναι τὸ
And on the   morrow   being minded   to know the

ἀσφαλές, τὸ τί κατηγορεῖται ὑπὸ τῶν
certain thing,   –   why   he was accused   by   the

Ἰουδαίων, ἔλυσεν αὐτόν, καὶ ἐκέλευσεν
Jews,   he released   him,   and   commanded

συνελθεῖν τοὺς ἀρχιερεῖς καὶ πᾶν τὸ
to come together the   chief priests   and   all   the

συνέδριον, καὶ καταγαγὼν τὸν Παῦλον
council,   and   having brought down   –   Paul

ἔστησεν εἰς αὐτούς. 23 ἀτενίσας δὲ
set [him]   among   – them.   And ²gazing

ὁ Παῦλος τῷ συνεδρίῳ εἶπεν· ἄνδρες
–   ¹Paul   at the   council   said: Men

ἀδελφοί, ἐγὼ πάσῃ συνειδήσει ἀγαθῇ
brothers,   I   in all   conscience   good

πεπολίτευμαι τῷ θεῷ ἄχρι ταύτης τῆς
have lived   – to God   until   this

ἡμέρας. 2 ὁ δὲ ἀρχιερεὺς ʻΑνανίας
day.   And the   high priest   Ananias

ἐπέταξεν τοῖς παρεστῶσιν αὐτῷ τύπτειν
gave order to the [ones] standing by   him   to strike

αὐτοῦ τὸ στόμα. 3 τότε ὁ Παῦλος πρὸς
of him   the   mouth.   Then   –   Paul   to

said to him, "God shall strike you, you white-washed wall! Are you sitting to judge me according to the law, and yet contrary to the law you order me to be struck?" ⁴Those who stood by said, "Would you revile God's high priest?" ⁵And Paul said, "I did not know, brethren, that he was the high priest; for it is written, 'You shall not speak evil of a ruler of your people.'"

6 But when Paul perceived that one part were Sad′ducees and the other Pharisees, he cried out in the council, "Brethren, I am a Pharisee, a son of Pharisees; with respect to the hope and the resurrection of the dead I am on trial." ⁷And when he had said this, a dissension arose between the Pharisees and the Sad′ducees; and the assembly was divided. ⁸For the Sad′ducees say that there is no resurrection, nor angel, nor spirit; but the Pharisees acknowledge them all. ⁹Then a great clamor arose; and some of the scribes of the Pharisees' party stood up and contended, "We find nothing wrong in this man. What if a spirit or an angel

αὐτὸν εἶπεν· τύπτειν σε μέλλει ὁ θεός,
him said: ³To strike ⁴thee ⁵is about - ¹God,

τοῖχε κεκονιαμένε· καὶ σὺ κάθῃ κρίνων
wall *having been* whitened; and thou sittest judging

με κατὰ τὸν νόμον, καὶ παρανομῶν
me according to the law, and contravening law

κελεύεις με τύπτεσθαι; 4 οἱ δὲ παρεστῶτες
commandest me to be struck? And the [ones] standing by

εἶπαν· τὸν ἀρχιερέα τοῦ θεοῦ λοιδορεῖς;
said: The high priest - of God revilest thou?

5 ἔφη τε ὁ Παῦλος· οὐκ ᾔδειν, ἀδελφοί,
And said - Paul: I did not know, brothers,

ὅτι ἐστὶν ἀρχιερεύς· γέγραπται γὰρ ὅτι
that he is high priest; for it has been written[,] -

ἄρχοντα τοῦ λαοῦ σου οὐκ ἐρεῖς κακῶς.
A ruler of the people of thee thou shalt not speak evilly.

6 γνοὺς δὲ ὁ Παῦλος ὅτι τὸ ἓν μέρος
And knowing - Paul that the one part

ἐστὶν Σαδδουκαίων τὸ δὲ ἕτερον Φαρισαίων
is(was) of Sadducees but the other of Pharisees

ἔκραζεν ἐν τῷ συνεδρίῳ· ἄνδρες ἀδελφοί,
cried out in the council: Men brothers,

ἐγὼ Φαρισαῖός εἰμι, υἱὸς Φαρισαίων· περὶ
I a Pharisee am, a son of Pharisees; concerning

ἐλπίδος καὶ ἀναστάσεως νεκρῶν κρίνομαι.
hope and resurrection of dead ones I am being judged.

7 τοῦτο δὲ αὐτοῦ λαλοῦντος ἐγένετο
And this him saying* there was
=as he said this

στάσις τῶν Φαρισαίων καὶ Σαδδουκαίων,
a discord of the Pharisees and Sadducees,

καὶ ἐσχίσθη τὸ πλῆθος. 8 Σαδδουκαῖοι
and was divided the multitude. Sadducees

γὰρ λέγουσιν μὴ εἶναι ἀνάστασιν μήτε
For say not to be a resurrection nor

ἄγγελον μήτε πνεῦμα, Φαρισαῖοι δὲ
angel nor spirit, but Pharisees

ὁμολογοῦσιν τὰ ἀμφότερα. 9 ἐγένετο δὲ
confess - both. And there was

κραυγὴ μεγάλη, καὶ ἀναστάντες τινὲς
cry a great, and rising up some

τῶν γραμματέων τοῦ μέρους τῶν Φαρισαίων
of the scribes of the part of the Pharisees

διεμάχοντο λέγοντες· οὐδὲν κακὸν εὑρίσκομεν
strove saying: Nothing evil we find

ἐν τῷ ἀνθρώπῳ τούτῳ· εἰ δὲ πνεῦμα
in this man; and if ¹a spirit

spoke to him?" ¹⁰And when the dissension became violent, the tribune, afraid that Paul would be torn in pieces by them, commanded the soldiers to go down and take him by force from among them and bring him into the barracks.

11 The following night the Lord stood by him and said, "Take courage, for as you have testified about me at Jerusalem, so you must bear witness also at Rome."

12 When it was day, the Jews made a plot and bound themselves by an oath neither to eat nor drink till they had killed Paul. ¹³There were more than forty who made this conspiracy. ¹⁴And they went to the chief priests and elders, and said, "We have strictly bound ourselves by an oath to taste no food till we have killed Paul. ¹⁵You therefore, along with the council, give notice now to the tribune to bring him down to you, as though you were going to determine his case more exactly. And we are

---

ἐλάλησεν   αὐτῷ   ἢ   ἄγγελος —. 10 Πολλῆς δὲ
⁴spoke   ⁵to him ²or ²an angel —.   And much

γινομένης στάσεως   φοβηθεὶς   ὁ   χιλίαρχος
arising   discordᵃ   ²fearing   ¹the ²chiliarch
=when much˙ discord arose

μὴ   διασπασθῇ   ὁ   Παῦλος ὑπ᾽ αὐτῶν,
⁴lest ⁵should be   -   ²Paul   by   them,
       torn asunder

ἐκέλευσεν τὸ   στράτευμα καταβὰν   ἁρπάσαι
commanded the soldiery   coming down to seize

αὐτὸν ἐκ   μέσου   αὐτῶν   ἄγειν τε   εἰς
him   out of [the] midst of them and to bring [him] into

τὴν παρεμβολήν. 11 Τῇ   δὲ   ἐπιούσῃ
the fort.   And in the   following

νυκτὶ ἐπιστὰς   αὐτῷ   ὁ   κύριος εἶπεν·
night ²coming on ⁴to him ¹the ²Lord   said:

θάρσει·   ὡς γὰρ   διεμαρτύρω   τὰ   περὶ
Be of good for as   thou didst   the concerning
courage;   solemnly witness things

ἐμοῦ εἰς Ἰερουσαλήμ, οὕτω σε   δεῖ   καὶ
me   in   Jerusalem,   so   thee it behoves also

εἰς Ῥώμην μαρτυρῆσαι. 12 Γενομένης δὲ
in   Rome   to witness.   And becoming

ἡμέρας ποιήσαντες συστροφὴν   οἱ   Ἰουδαῖοι
dayᵃ   ²making   ⁴a conspiracy ¹the ²Jews
=when it became day

ἀνεθεμάτισαν ἑαυτούς, λέγοντες μήτε   φαγεῖν
cursed   themselves, saying   neither to eat

μήτε   πεῖν   ἕως οὗ   ἀποκτείνωσιν τὸν
nor   to drink until   they should kill -

Παῦλον. 13 ἦσαν δὲ   πλείους τεσσεράκοντα
Paul.   And there were more [than] forty

οἱ   ταύτην τὴν συνωμοσίαν   ποιησάμενοι·
the [ones] this   -   plot   making;

14 οἵτινες προσελθόντες   τοῖς   ἀρχιερεῦσιν
who   approaching   to the   chief priests

καὶ τοῖς   πρεσβυτέροις εἶπαν· ἀναθέματι
and to the elders   said: With a curse

ἀνεθεματίσαμεν ἑαυτοὺς μηδενὸς γεύσασθαι
we cursed   ourselves of nothing to taste

ἕως οὗ   ἀποκτείνωμεν τὸν Παῦλον. 15 νῦν
until   we may kill   -   Paul.   Now

οὖν   ὑμεῖς ἐμφανίσατε τῷ   χιλιάρχῳ σὺν
therefore ²ye   ¹inform   the chiliarch with

τῷ   συνεδρίῳ ὅπως   καταγάγῃ   αὐτὸι εἰς
the council   so as he may bring down him to

ὑμᾶς ὡς μέλλοντας διαγινώσκειν ἀκριβέστε-
you   as intending   to ascertain exactly more accurate-

ρον τὰ   περὶ   αὐτοῦ· ἡμεῖς δὲ   πρὸ τοῦ
ly   the things concerning him;   and we before   -

ready to kill him before he comes near."

16 Now the son of Paul's sister heard of their ambush; so he went and entered the barracks and told Paul. [17]And Paul called one of the centurions and said, "Bring this young man to the tribune; for he has something to tell him." [18]So he took him and brought him to the tribune and said, "Paul the prisoner called me and asked me to bring this young man to you, as he has something to say to you." [19]The tribune took him by the hand, and going aside asked him privately, "What is it that you have to tell me?" [20]And he said, "The Jews have agreed to ask you to bring Paul down to the council tomorrow, as though they were going to inquire somewhat more closely about him. [21]But do not yield to them; for more than forty of their men lie in ambush for him, having bound themselves by an oath neither to eat

ἐγγίσαι αὐτὸν ἔτοιμοί ἐσμεν τοῦ ἀνελεῖν
to draw near him[b] ready are – to kill[d]
=he draws near

αὐτόν. 16 Ἀκούσας δὲ ὁ υἱὸς τῆς ἀδελφῆς
him. And [6]hearing [1]the [2]son [3]of the [4]sister

Παύλου τὴν ἐνέδραν, παραγενόμενος καὶ
[5]of Paul the treachery, coming and

εἰσελθὼν εἰς τὴν παρεμβολὴν ἀπήγγειλεν
entering into the fort reported

τῷ Παύλῳ. 17 προσκαλεσάμενος δὲ ὁ
– to Paul. And [2]calling to [him] –

Παῦλος ἕνα τῶν ἑκατονταρχῶν ἔφη· τὸν
[1]Paul one of the centurions said: –

νεανίαν τοῦτον ἄπαγε πρὸς τὸν χιλίαρχον,
[3]youth [2]this [1]Bring up to the chiliarch,

ἔχει γὰρ ἀπαγγεῖλαί τι αὐτῷ. 18 ὁ
for [1]he has [3]to report [2]something [4]to him. He

μὲν οὖν παραλαβὼν αὐτὸν ἤγαγεν πρὸς
– therefore taking [2]him [1]brought to

τὸν χιλίαρχον καὶ φησίν· ὁ δέσμιος
the chiliarch and says: The prisoner

Παῦλος προσκαλεσάμενός με ἠρώτησεν
Paul calling to [him] me asked

τοῦτον τὸν νεανίσκον ἀγαγεῖν πρὸς σέ,
[2]this – [3]young man [1]to bring to thee,

ἔχοντά τι λαλῆσαί σοι. 19 ἐπιλαβόμενος
having something to tell thee. [2]laying hold

δὲ τῆς χειρὸς αὐτοῦ ὁ χιλίαρχος καὶ
And [4]of the [5]hand [6]of him [1]the [3]chiliarch and

ἀναχωρήσας κατ᾽ ἰδίαν ἐπυνθάνετο· τί
retiring [2]privately [1]inquired: What

ἐστιν ὃ ἔχεις ἀπαγγεῖλαί μοι; 20 εἶπεν
is it which thou hast to report to me? he said[,]

δὲ ὅτι οἱ Ἰουδαῖοι συνέθεντο τοῦ ἐρωτῆσαί
And – The Jews agreed – to ask[d]

σε ὅπως αὔριον τὸν Παῦλον καταγάγῃς
thee so as to-morrow – [2]Paul [1]thou shouldest bring down

εἰς τὸ συνέδριον ὡς μέλλον τι ἀκριβέστερον
to the council as intending some- more accurately thing

πυνθάνεσθαι περὶ αὐτοῦ. 21 σὺ οὖν μὴ
to inquire concerning him. Thou therefore not

πεισθῇς αὐτοῖς· ἐνεδρεύουσιν γὰρ αὐτὸν
be persuaded by them; for there lie in wait for him

ἐξ αὐτῶν ἄνδρες πλείους τεσσεράκοντα,
of them [4]men [1]more [2][than] [3]forty,

οἵτινες ἀνεθεμάτισαν ἑαυτοὺς μήτε φαγεῖν
who cursed themselves neither to eat

nor drink till they have killed him; and now they are ready, waiting for the promise from you." ²²So the tribune dismissed the young man, charging him, "Tell no one that you have informed me of this."

23 Then he called two of the centurions and said, "At the third hour of the night get ready two hundred soldiers with seventy horsemen and two hundred spearmen to go as far as Caesare'a. ²⁴Also provide mounts for Paul to ride, and bring him safely to Felix the governor." ²⁵And he wrote a letter to this effect:

26 "Claudius Lys'ias to his Excellency the governor Felix, greeting. ²⁷This man was seized by the Jews, and was about to be killed by them, when I came upon them with the soldiers and rescued him, having learned that he was a Roman citizen. ²⁸And desiring to know the charge on which they accused him, I brought him down to their council. ²⁹I found that he was accused about questions of their law,

μήτε πεῖν ἕως οὗ ἀνέλωσιν αὐτόν, καὶ νῦν
nor to drink until they kill him, and now

εἰσιν ἕτοιμοι προσδεχόμενοι τὴν ἀπὸ σοῦ
they are ' ready awaiting ¹the ²from ⁴thee

ἐπαγγελίαν. 22 ὁ μὲν οὖν χιλίαρχος
²promise. the – Therefore chiliarch

ἀπέλυσε τὸν νεανίσκον, παραγγείλας μηδενὶ
dismissed the young man, charging [him] to no one

ἐκλαλῆσαι ὅτι ταῦτα ἐνεφάνισας πρὸς ἐμέ.
to divulge that these things thou reportedst to me.

23 Καὶ προσκαλεσάμενός τινας δύο τῶν
And calling to [him] a certain two of the

ἑκατονταρχῶν εἶπεν· ἑτοιμάσατε στρατιώτας
centurions he said: Prepare ye soldiers

διακοσίους ὅπως πορευθῶσιν ἕως Καισαρείας,
two hundred so as they may go as far as Caesarea,

καὶ ἱππεῖς ἑβδομήκοντα καὶ δεξιολάβους
and horsemen seventy and spearmen

διακοσίους, ἀπὸ τρίτης ὥρας τῆς νυκτός,
two hundred, from third hour of the night,

24 κτήνη τε παραστῆσαι, ἵνα ἐπιβιβάσαντες
and beasts to stand by, that putting on

τὸν Παῦλον διασώσωσι πρὸς Φήλικα τὸν
– Paul they may bring to Felix the
[him] safely

ἡγεμόνα, 25 γράψας ἐπιστολὴν ἔχουσαν
governor, writing a letter having

τὸν τύπον τοῦτον· 26 Κλαύδιος Λυσίας τῷ
this pattern: Claudius Lysias to the

κρατίστῳ ἡγεμόνι Φήλικι χαίρειν. 27 Τὸν
most excellent governor Felix greeting. –

ἄνδρα τοῦτον συλλημφθέντα ὑπὸ τῶν
man This having been arrested by the

Ἰουδαίων καὶ μέλλοντα ἀναιρεῖσθαι ὑπ'
Jews and being about to be killed by

αὐτῶν ἐπιστὰς σὺν τῷ στρατεύματι
them coming on with the soldiery
[the scene]

ἐξειλάμην, μαθὼν ὅτι Ῥωμαῖός ἐστιν·
I rescued, having learned that a Roman he is;

28 βουλόμενός τε ἐπιγνῶναι τὴν αἰτίαν
and being minded to know fully the cause

δι' ἣν ἐνεκάλουν αὐτῷ, κατήγαγον εἰς
on ac- which they were him, I brought to
count of accusing [him] down

τὸ συνέδριον αὐτῶν· 29 ὃν εὗρον ἐγκαλούμενον
the council of them; whom I found being accused

περὶ ζητημάτων τοῦ νόμου αὐτῶν, μηδὲν
about questions of the law of them, ²nothing

but charged with nothing deserving death or imprisonment. ³⁰And when it was disclosed to me that there would be a plot against the man, I sent him to you at once, ordering his accusers also to state before you what they have against him."
31 So the soldiers, according to their instructions, took Paul and brought him by night to Antip'atris. ³²And on the morrow they returned to the barracks, leaving the horsemen to go on with him. ³³When they came to Caesare'a and delivered the letter to the governor, they presented Paul also before him. ³⁴On reading the letter, he asked to what province he belonged. When he learned that he was from Cili'cia ³⁵he said, "I will hear you when your accusers arrive." And he commanded him to be guarded in Herod's praetorium.

δὲ ἄξιον θανάτου ἢ δεσμῶν ἔχοντα
¹and ⁵worthy ⁶of death ⁷or ⁸of bonds ²having
ἔγκλημα. 30 μηνυθείσης δέ μοι ἐπιβουλῆς
⁴charge. And being revealed to me a plotᵃ
=when it was revealed to me that there was a plot
εἰς τὸν ἄνδρα ἔσεσθαι, ἐξαυτῆς ἔπεμψα
against the man to be, at once I sent
πρὸς σέ, παραγγείλας καὶ τοῖς κατηγόροις
to thee, commanding also the accusers
λέγειν πρὸς αὐτὸν ἐπὶ σοῦ. 31 Οἱ μὲν
to say to him before thee. the –
οὖν στρατιῶται κατὰ τὸ διατεταγμένον
Therefore soldiers according the having been
to thing appointed
αὐτοῖς ἀναλαβόντες τὸν Παῦλον ἤγαγον
them taking up – Paul brought
διὰ νυκτὸς εἰς τὴν Ἀντιπατρίδα· 32 τῇ δὲ
through [the] night to – Antipatris; and on the
(during)
ἐπαύριον ἐάσαντες τοὺς ἱππεῖς ἀπέρχεσθαι
morrow allowing the horsemen to depart
σὺν αὐτῷ, ὑπέστρεψαν εἰς τὴν παρεμβολήν·
with him, they returned to the fort;
33 οἵτινες εἰσελθόντες εἰς τὴν Καισάρειαν
who entering into – Cæsarea
καὶ ἀναδόντες τὴν ἐπιστολὴν τῷ ἡγεμόνι,
and handing over the letter to the governor,
παρέστησαν καὶ τὸν Παῦλον αὐτῷ.
presented also – Paul to him.
34 ἀναγνοὺς δὲ καὶ ἐπερωτήσας ἐκ ποίας
And having read and asking of what
ἐπαρχείας ἐστίν, καὶ πυθόμενος ὅτι ἀπὸ
province he is(was), and learning[,] – From
Κιλικίας, 35 διακούσομαί σου, ἔφη, ὅταν
Cilicia, I will hear thee, he said, when
καὶ οἱ κατήγοροί σου παραγένωνται·
also the accusers of thee arrive;
κελεύσας ἐν τῷ πραιτωρίῳ τοῦ Ἡρώδου
commanding in the prætorium – of Herod
=that he be kept in Herod's prætorium.
φυλάσσεσθαι αὐτόν.
to be kept him.

CHAPTER 24

AND after five days the high priest Anani'as came down with some elders and a spokesman, one Tertul'lus.

24 Μετὰ δὲ πέντε ἡμέρας κατέβη ὁ
And after five days came down the
ἀρχιερεὺς Ἀνανίας μετὰ πρεσβυτέρων τινῶν
high priest Ananias with elders some
καὶ ῥήτορος Τερτύλλου τινός, οἵτινες
and an orator Tertullus one, who

They laid before the governor their case against Paul; ²and when he was called, Tertul'lus began to accuse him, saying: "Since through you we enjoy much peace, and since by your provision, most excellent Felix, reforms are introduced on behalf of this nation, ³in every way and everywhere we accept this with all gratitude. ⁴But, to detain you no further, I beg you in your kindness to hear us briefly. ⁵For we have found this man a pestilent fellow, an agitator among all the Jews throughout the world, and a ringleader of the sect of the Nazarenes. ⁶He even tried to profane the temple, but we seized him.ᵘ ⁸By examining him yourself you will be able to learn from him about everything of which we accuse him."

9 The Jews also joined in the charge, affirming that all this was so.

10 And when the governor had motioned to him to speak, Paul replied:

"Realizing that for many years you have been judge over this

ᵘ Other ancient authorities add *and we would have judged him according to our law. ⁷But the chief captain Lysias came and with great violence took him out of our hands, ⁸commanding his accusers to come before you.*

ἐνεφάνισαν τῷ ἡγεμόνι κατὰ τοῦ Παύλου.
informed   the   governor   against   –   Paul.

2 κληθέντος δὲ [αὐτοῦ] ἤρξατο κατηγορεῖν
And being called   himᵃ   ²began   ³to accuse
=when he was called

ὁ Τέρτυλλος λέγων· πολλῆς εἰρήνης
– ¹Tertullus   saying: Much   peace

τυγχάνοντες διὰ σοῦ καὶ διορθωμάτων
obtaining   through   thee   and   reforms

γινομένων τῷ ἔθνει τούτῳ διὰ τῆς σῆς
coming   to this nation   through   –   thy

προνοίας, 3 πάντῃ τε καὶ πανταχοῦ
forethought,   both in everything   and   everywhere

ἀποδεχόμεθα, κράτιστε Φῆλιξ, μετὰ πάσης
we welcome,   most excellent   Felix,   with   all

εὐχαριστίας. 4 ἵνα δὲ μὴ ἐπὶ πλεῖόν
thankfulness.   But that   ²not   ⁴more

σε ἐγκόπτω, παρακαλῶ ἀκοῦσαί σε ἡμῶν
³thee   ¹I hinder,   I beseech   ²to hear   ¹thee   us

συντόμως τῇ σῇ ἐπιεικείᾳ. 5 εὑρόντες γὰρ
briefly   –   in thy   forbearance.   For having found

τὸν ἄνδρα τοῦτον λοιμὸν καὶ κινοῦντα
this man   pestilent   and   moving

στάσεις πᾶσιν τοῖς Ἰουδαίοις τοῖς κατὰ
seditions [among] all   the   Jews   – throughout

τὴν οἰκουμένην πρωτοστάτην τε τῆς τῶν
the   inhabited [earth]   and a ringleader   of the   ²of the

Ναζωραίων αἱρέσεως, 6 ὃς καὶ τὸ ἱερὸν
³Nazarenes   ¹sect,   who   also   ³the   ⁴temple

ἐπείρασεν βεβηλῶσαι, ὃν καὶ ἐκρατήσαμεν,
¹attempted   ²to profane,   whom also   we laid hold of,‡

8 παρ᾽ οὗ δυνήσῃ αὐτὸς ἀνακρίνας
from   whom   thou wilt be able   [thy]self   ²having examined

περὶ πάντων τούτων ἐπιγνῶναι ὧν ἡμεῖς
²concerning   ⁴all   ⁵these things   ¹to know fully   of which   we

κατηγοροῦμεν αὐτοῦ. 9 συνεπέθεντο δὲ
accuse   him.   And ²joined in

καὶ οἱ Ἰουδαῖοι · φάσκοντες ταῦτα οὕτως
²also   ¹the   ²Jews   alleging   these things   thus

ἔχειν. 10 Ἀπεκρίθη τε ὁ Παῦλος,
to have(be).   And answered   –   Paul,

νεύσαντος αὐτῷ τοῦ ἡγεμόνος λέγειν· ἐκ
³having   ⁴to him   ¹the   ²governorᵃ   to speak: ⁴of
  beckoned   (for)

πολλῶν ἐτῶν ὄντα σε κριτὴν τῷ ἔθνει τούτῳ
⁵many   ⁶years   ²being   ³thee   ⁷a judge   ⁸to ⁹this ¹⁰nation
                 (to be)

‡ Verse 7 omitted by Nestle; cf. RSV footnote.

nation, I cheerfully make my defense. [11]As you may ascertain, it is not more than twelve days since I went up to worship at Jerusalem; [12]and they did not find me disputing with any one or stirring up a crowd, either in the temple or in the synagogues, or in the city. [13]Neither can they prove to you what they now bring up against me. [14]But this I admit to you, that according to the Way, which they call a sect, I worship the God of our fathers, believing everything laid down by the law or written in the prophets, [15]having a hope in God which these themselves accept, that there will be a resurrection of both the just and the unjust. [16]So I always take pains to have a clear conscience toward God and toward men. [17]Now after some years I came to bring to my nation alms and offerings. [18]As I was

ἐπιστάμενος   εὐθύμως   τὰ   περὶ
[1]understanding [12]cheerfully [13][as to] [14]the things [16]concerning

ἐμαυτοῦ   ἀπολογοῦμαι,   11 δυναμένου   σου
[16]myself   [11]I defend myself,   being able   thee[a]
                                        =as thou art able

ἐπιγνῶναι   ὅτι   οὐ   πλείους   εἰσίν   μοι   ἡμέραι
to know fully that [2]not [4]more   [1]there [3]to [5][than] [7]days
                                        are   me

δώδεκα   ἀφ᾿   ἧς   ἀνέβην   προσκυνήσων   εἰς
[6]twelve   from   which I went up   worshipping   in
             =since

Ἰερουσαλήμ.   12 καὶ   οὔτε   ἐν   τῷ   ἱερῷ
Jerusalem.   And   neither   in   the   temple

εὑρόν   με   πρός   τινα   διαλεγόμενον   ἢ
they found me   [3]with [2]anyone [1]discoursing   or

ἐπίστασιν   ποιοῦντα   ὄχλου,   οὔτε   ἐν   ταῖς
[2]collection [1]making   of a crowd, neither in   the

συναγωγαῖς   οὔτε   κατὰ   τὴν   πόλιν,   13 οὐδὲ
synagogues   nor throughout the   city,   nor

παραστῆσαι   δύνανταί   σοι   περὶ   ὧν   νυνὶ
[2]to prove   [1]are they able to thee   con- [the] things now
                                        cerning of which

κατηγοροῦσίν   μου.   14 ὁμολογῶ   δὲ   τοῦτό
they accuse   me.   But I confess   this

σοι,   ὅτι   κατὰ   τὴν   ὁδὸν   ἣν   λέγουσιν
to thee, that according to the   way   which they say(call)

αἵρεσιν   οὕτως   λατρεύω   τῷ   πατρῴῳ   θεῷ,
a sect   thus   I worship   the   ancestral   God,

πιστεύων   πᾶσι   τοῖς   κατὰ   τὸν   νόμον   καὶ
believing   all   the   according the   law   and
                    things   to

τοῖς   ἐν   τοῖς   προφήταις   γεγραμμένοις,
the things in   the   prophets   having been written,

15 ἐλπίδα   ἔχων   εἰς   τὸν   θεόν,   ἣν   καὶ
hope   having toward   –   God,   which   [2]also

αὐτοὶ   οὗτοι   προσδέχονται,   ἀνάστασιν   μέλ-
[2][them]selves [1]these   expect,   a resurrection   to be

λειν   ἔσεσθαι   δικαίων   τε   καὶ   ἀδίκων.
about   to be   both of just   and   of unjust.

16 ἐν   τούτῳ   καὶ   αὐτὸς   ἀσκῶ   ἀπρόσκοπον
By   this   also   [2][my]self [1]I exercise [4]a blameless

συνείδησιν   ἔχειν   πρὸς   τὸν   θεὸν   καὶ   τοὺς
[5]conscience   [3]to have toward   –   God   and   –

ἀνθρώπους   διὰ   παντός.   17 δι᾿   ἐτῶν   δὲ
men   always.   And after years

πλειόνων   ἐλεημοσύνας   ποιήσων   εἰς   τὸ
many   [2]alms   [1]making(bringing) [3]to   [4]the

ἔθνος   μου   παρεγενόμην   καὶ   προσφοράς,
[5]nation   [6]of me   [9]I arrived   [7]and   [8]offerings,

doing this, they found me purified in the temple, without any crowd or tumult. But some Jews from Asia—[19] they ought to be here before you and to make an accusation, if they have anything against me. [20] Or else let these men themselves say what wrongdoing they found when I stood before the council, [21] except this one thing which I cried out while standing among them, 'With respect to the resurrection of the dead I am on trial before you this day.'"

22 But Felix, having a rather accurate knowledge of the Way, put them off, saying, "When Lys'ias the tribune comes down, I will decide your case." [23] Then he gave orders to the centurion that he should be kept in custody but should have some liberty, and that none of his friends should be prevented from attending to his needs.

24 After some days Felix came with his wife Drusil'la, who was a Jewess; and he sent for Paul and heard him speak upon faith in Christ Jesus. [25] And as he argued

18 ἐν αἷς εὗρόν με ἡγνισμένον ἐν τῷ
among which they found me having been purified in the

ἱερῷ, οὐ μετὰ ὄχλου οὐδὲ μετὰ θορύβου,
temple, not with a crowd nor with uproar,

19 τινὲς δὲ ἀπὸ τῆς Ἀσίας Ἰουδαῖοι,
but some ²from – ³Asia ¹Jews,

οὓς ἔδει ἐπὶ σοῦ παρεῖναι καὶ κατηγορεῖν
whom it be- before thee to be present and to accuse
hoved

εἴ τι ἔχοιεν πρὸς ἐμέ. 20 ἢ αὐτοὶ
if anything they have against me. Or ³[them]selves

οὗτοι εἰπάτωσαν τί εὗρον ἀδίκημα στάντος
²these ¹let ⁴say ¹what ²they found ³misdeed standing

μου ἐπὶ τοῦ συνεδρίου, 21 ἢ περὶ μιᾶς
meᵃ before the council, unless concerning ²one
=while I stood

ταύτης φωνῆς ἧς ἐκέκραξα ἐν αὐτοῖς
¹this voice which I have cried out ²among ³them

ἑστὼς ὅτι περὶ ἀναστάσεως νεκρῶν ἐγὼ
¹standing[,] – Concerning a resurrection of dead persons I

κρίνομαι σήμερον ἐφ᾽ ὑμῶν. 22 Ἀνεβάλετο
am being judged to-day before you. ²postponed

δὲ αὐτοὺς ὁ Φῆλιξ, ἀκριβέστερον εἰδὼς
And ³them – ¹Felix, more exactly knowing

τὰ περὶ τῆς ὁδοῦ, εἴπας· ὅταν Λυσίας ὁ
the con- the way, saying: When Lysias the
things cerning

χιλίαρχος καταβῇ, διαγνώσομαι τὰ καθ᾽
chiliarch comes down, I will determine the things as to

ὑμᾶς· 23 διαταξάμενος τῷ ἑκατοντάρχῃ
you; commanding the centurion

τηρεῖσθαι αὐτὸν ἔχειν τε ἄνεσιν καὶ
to keep him and to have indulgence and

μηδένα κωλύειν τῶν ἰδίων αὐτοῦ ὑπηρετεῖν
²no one ¹to forbid of his own [people] to attend

αὐτῷ. 24 Μετὰ δὲ ἡμέρας τινὰς παραγενό-
him. And after days some ²arriv-

μενος ὁ Φῆλιξ σὺν Δρουσίλλῃ τῇ ἰδίᾳ
ing – ¹Felix with Drusilla the(his) own

γυναικὶ οὔσῃ Ἰουδαίᾳ μετεπέμψατο τὸν
wife being a Jewess he sent for –

Παῦλον, καὶ ἤκουσεν αὐτοῦ περὶ τῆς
Paul, and heard him about ¹the(?his)

εἰς Χριστὸν Ἰησοῦν πίστεως. 25 διαλεγομέ-
³in ⁴Christ ⁵Jesus ²faith. discours-
=And as he discoursed

νου δὲ αὐτοῦ περὶ δικαιοσύνης καὶ
ing And himᵃ concerning righteousness and

I.G.E.—20

about justice and self-control and future judgment, Felix was alarmed and said, "Go away for the present; when I have an opportunity I will summon you." ²⁶At the same time he hoped that money would be given him by Paul. So he sent for him often and conversed with him. ²⁷But when two years had elapsed, Felix was succeeded by Porcius Festus; and desiring to do the Jews a favor, Felix left Paul in prison.

ἐγκρατείας καὶ τοῦ κρίματος τοῦ μέλλοντος
self-control and the ²judgment – ¹coming

ἔμφοβος γενόμενος ὁ Φῆλιξ ἀπεκρίθη·
afraid becoming – Felix answered:

τὸ νῦν ἔχον πορεύου, καιρὸν δὲ μεταλαβὼν
For the present† go thou, but ²time ¹taking ³later

μετακαλέσομαί σε· 26 ἅμα καὶ ἐλπίζων
I will send for thee; at the also hoping
same time

ὅτι χρήματα δοθήσεται αὐτῷ ὑπὸ τοῦ
that money will be given him by –

Παύλου· διὸ καὶ πυκνότερον αὐτὸν
Paul; wherefore also more frequently him

μεταπεμπόμενος ὡμίλει αὐτῷ. 27 Διετίας δὲ
sending for he conversed him. And two years
with

πληρωθείσης ἔλαβεν διάδοχον ὁ Φῆλιξ
being completedᵃ ²received ²a successor – ¹Felix

Πόρκιον Φῆστον· θέλων τε χάριτα κατα-
Porcius Festus; and wishing a favour to

θέσθαι τοῖς Ἰουδαίοις ὁ Φῆλιξ κατέλιπε
show to the Jews – Felix left

τὸν Παῦλον δεδεμένον.
– Paul having been bound.

CHAPTER 25

NOW when Festus had come into his province, after three days he went up to Jerusalem from Caesare′a. ²And the chief priests and the principal men of the Jews informed him against Paul; and they urged him, ³asking as a favor to have the man sent to Jerusalem, planning an ambush to kill him on the way. ⁴Festus replied that Paul was being kept at Caesare′a, and that he himself intended to go there shortly. ⁵"So," said he, "let the men of

25 Φῆστος οὖν ἐπιβὰς τῇ ἐπαρχείῳ
Festus therefore having entered the province

μετὰ τρεῖς ἡμέρας ἀνέβη εἰς Ἰεροσόλυμα
after three days went up to Jerusalem

ἀπὸ Καισαρείας, 2 ἐνεφάνισάν τε αὐτῷ
from Caesarea, and ³informed ⁹him

οἱ ἀρχιερεῖς καὶ οἱ πρῶτοι τῶν Ἰουδαίων
¹the ²chief priests ³and ⁴the ⁵chiefs ⁶of the ⁷Jews

κατὰ τοῦ Παύλου, καὶ παρεκάλουν αὐτὸν
against – Paul, and they besought him

3 αἰτούμενοι χάριν κατ᾽ αὐτοῦ, ὅπως μετα-
asking a favour against him, so as he might

πέμψηται αὐτὸν εἰς Ἰερουσαλήμ, ἐνέδραν
summon him to Jerusalem, a plot

ποιοῦντες ἀνελεῖν αὐτὸν κατὰ τὴν ὁδόν.
making to kill him by the way.

4 ὁ μὲν οὖν Φῆστος ἀπεκρίθη τηρεῖσθαι
– – Therefore Festus answered ²to be kept

τὸν Παῦλον εἰς Καισάρειαν, ἑαυτὸν δὲ
– ¹Paul in Caesarea, and ²himself

μέλλειν ἐν τάχει ἐκπορεύεσθαι· 5 οἱ οὖν
¹to intend shortly to go forth; ²the ¹therefore

authority among you go down with me, and if there is anything wrong about the man, let them accuse him."
6 When he had stayed among them not more than eight or ten days, he went down to Caesare'a; and the next day he took his seat on the tribunal and ordered Paul to be brought. ⁷And when he had come, the Jews who had gone down from Jerusalem stood about him, bringing against him many serious charges which they could not prove. ⁸Paul said in his defense, "Neither against the law of the Jews, nor against the temple, nor against Caesar have I offended at all." ⁹But Festus, wishing to do the Jews a favor, said to Paul, "Do you wish to go up to Jerusalem, and there be tried on these charges before me?" ¹⁰But Paul said, "I am standing before Caesar's tribunal, where I ought to be tried; to the Jews I have done no wrong, as you know very well. ¹¹If then I am a wrongdoer, and have committed anything for which I deserve to die, I do not seek to escape

ἐν ὑμῖν, φησίν, δυνατοὶ συγκαταβάντες,
⁴among ⁵you, ⁶he says, ³able men going down with [me],

εἴ τί ἐστιν ἐν τῷ ἀνδρὶ ἄτοπον,
if anything there is in the man amiss,

κατηγορείτωσαν αὐτοῦ. 6 Διατρίψας δὲ ἐν
let them accuse him. And having stayed among

αὐτοῖς ἡμέρας οὐ πλείους ὀκτὼ ἢ δέκα,
them days not more [than] eight or ten,

καταβὰς εἰς Καισάρειαν, τῇ ἐπαύριον
going down to Caesarea, on the morrow

καθίσας ἐπὶ τοῦ βήματος ἐκέλευσεν τὸν
sitting on the tribunal he commanded –

Παῦλον ἀχθῆναι. 7 παραγενομένου δὲ
Paul to be brought. And arriving
=when he arrived

αὐτοῦ περιέστησαν αὐτὸν οἱ ἀπὸ Ἱεροσο-
himᵃ ⁶stood round ⁷him ⁴from ⁵Jeru-

λύμων καταβεβηκότες Ἰουδαῖοι, πολλὰ καὶ
salem ⁸having come down ²Jews, many and

βαρέα αἰτιώματα καταφέροντες, ἃ οὐκ
heavy charges bringing against [him], which not

ἴσχυον ἀποδεῖξαι, 8 τοῦ Παύλου ἀπολογου-
they were able to prove, – Paul defending him-

μένου ὅτι οὔτε εἰς τὸν νόμον τῶν
self[,]ᵃ – Neither against the law of the
=while Paul defended himself,

Ἰουδαίων οὔτε εἰς τὸ ἱερὸν οὔτε εἰς
Jews nor against the temple nor against

Καίσαρά τι ἥμαρτον. 9 ὁ Φῆστος δὲ,
Cæsar anything I sinned. – But Festus,

θέλων τοῖς Ἰουδαίοις χάριν καταθέσθαι,
wishing the Jews a favour to show,

ἀποκριθεὶς τῷ Παύλῳ εἶπεν· θέλεις εἰς
answering – Paul said: Dost thou wish ²to

Ἱεροσόλυμα ἀναβὰς ἐκεῖ περὶ τούτων
³Jerusalem ¹going up ⁴there ⁵concerning ⁶these things

κριθῆναι ἐπ' ἐμοῦ; 10 εἶπεν δὲ ὁ Παῦλος·
⁵to be judged ⁶before ⁷me? And said – Paul:

ἑστὼς ἐπὶ τοῦ βήματος Καίσαρός εἰμι,
Standing before the tribunal of Cæsar I am,

οὗ με δεῖ κρίνεσθαι. Ἰουδαίους οὐδὲν
where me it behoves to be judged. Jews nothing

ἠδίκηκα, ὡς καὶ σὺ κάλλιον ἐπιγινώσκεις.
I have wronged, as indeed thou very well knowest.

11 εἰ μὲν οὖν ἀδικῶ καὶ ἄξιον θανάτου
If – therefore I do wrong and worthy of death

πέπραχά τι, οὐ παραιτοῦμαι τὸ ἀποθανεῖν·
I have done anything, I do not refuse the to die;

death; but if there is
nothing in their charges
against me, no one can
give me up to them. I
appeal to Caesar."
¹²Then Festus, when he
had conferred with his
council, answered, "You
have appealed to Caesar;
to Caesar you shall go."
13 Now when some
days had passed, Agrippa
the king and Berni'ce
arrived at Caesare'a to
welcome Festus. ¹⁴And
as they stayed there
many days, Festus laid
Paul's case before the
king, saying, "There is a
man left prisoner by
Felix; ¹⁵and when I was
at Jerusalem, the chief
priests and the elders of
the Jews gave informa-
tion about him, asking for
sentence against him.
¹⁶I answered them that it
was not the custom of the
Romans to give up any
one before the accused
met the accusers face to
face, and had oppor-
tunity to make his defense
concerning the charge
laid against him. ¹⁷When
therefore they came to-
gether here, I made no
delay, but on the next

εἰ   δὲ   οὐδέν   ἐστιν   ὧν   οὗτοι   κατηγοροῦσίν
but if   not one   there is   of [the   these   accuse
                                things] which

μου,   οὐδεὶς   με   δύναται   αὐτοῖς   χαρίσασθαι·
me,   no one   ²me   ¹can   ⁴to them   ²to grant;

Καίσαρα   ἐπικαλοῦμαι.   12 τότε   ὁ   Φῆστος
²Cæsar   ¹I appeal to.   Then   -   Festus

συλλαλήσας   μετὰ   τοῦ   συμβουλίου   ἀπεκρίθη·
having talked with   with   the   council   answered:

Καίσαρα   ἐπικέκλησαι,   ἐπὶ   Καίσαρα   πορεύσῃ.
²Cæsar   ¹thou hast appealed to,   before   Cæsar   thou shalt go.

13 Ἡμερῶν   δὲ   διαγενομένων   τινῶν
    And days   passing   someᵃ
    =when some days had passed

Ἀγρίππας   ὁ   βασιλεὺς   καὶ   Βερνίκη
Agrippa   the   king   and   Bernice

κατήντησαν   εἰς   Καισάρειαν   ἀσπασάμενοι
arrived   at   Cæsarea   greeting

τὸν   Φῆστον.   14 ὡς   δὲ   πλείους   ἡμέρας
-    Festus.   And as   more   days

διέτριβον   ἐκεῖ,   ὁ   Φῆστος   τῷ   βασιλεῖ
they stayed   there,   -   Festus   ²to the   ³king

ἀνέθετο   τὰ   κατὰ   τὸν   Παῦλον   λέγων·
¹set forth the matters regarding   -   Paul   saying:

ἀνήρ   τίς   ἐστιν   καταλελειμμένος   ὑπὸ
A certain man   there is   having been left behind   by

Φήλικος   δέσμιος,   15 περὶ   οὗ   γενομένου
Felix   prisoner,   about whom   being
                                =when I was

μου   εἰς   Ἱεροσόλυμα   ἐνεφάνισαν   οἱ   ἀρχιερεῖς
meᵃ   in   Jerusalem   ³informed   ¹the   ²chief priests

καὶ   οἱ   πρεσβύτεροι   τῶν   Ἰουδαίων,
²and   ⁴the   ⁵elders   ⁶of the   ⁷Jews,

αἰτούμενοι   κατ᾽   αὐτοῦ   καταδίκην·   16 πρὸς
asking   against   him   sentence;   to

οὓς   ἀπεκρίθην   ὅτι   οὐκ   ἔστιν   ἔθος   Ῥωμαίοις
whom   I answered   that   it is not   a custom with Romans

χαρίζεσθαί   τινα   ἄνθρωπον   πρὶν   ἢ   ὁ
to grant   any   man   before   the

κατηγορούμενος   κατὰ   πρόσωπον   ἔχοι   τοὺς
[one] being accused   face to face†   should have the

κατηγόρους   τόπον   τε   ἀπολογίας   λάβοι
accusers   ³place*   ¹and   ⁴of defence   ²receive

περὶ   τοῦ   ἐγκλήματος.   17 συνελθόντων
concerning the   charge.   Coming togetherᵃ

οὖν   ἐνθάδε   ἀναβολὴν   μηδεμίαν   ποιησάμενος
therefore thither   ³delay   ²no   ¹making

* That is, opportunity.

day took my seat on the tribunal and ordered the man to be brought in. ¹⁸When the accusers stood up, they brought no charge in his case of such evils as I supposed; ¹⁹but they had certain points of dispute with him about their own superstition and about one Jesus, who was dead, but whom Paul asserted to be alive. ²⁰Being at a loss how to investigate these questions, I asked whether he wished to go to Jerusalem and be tried there regarding them. ²¹But when Paul had appealed to be kept in custody for the decision of the emperor, I commanded him to be held until I could send him to Caesar." ²²And Agrippa said to Festus, "I should like to hear the man myself." "Tomorrow," said he, "you shall hear him."

23 So on the morrow Agrippa and Berni'ce came with great pomp, and they entered the audience hall with the military tribunes and the prominent men of the city. Then by command of Festus Paul was brought in. ²⁴And Festus said, "King Agrippa and

τῇ ἑξῆς καθίσας ἐπὶ τοῦ βήματος ἐκέλευσα
on the next [day] sitting on the tribunal I commanded

ἀχθῆναι τὸν ἄνδρα· 18 περὶ οὗ σταθέντες
to be brought the man; concerning whom standing

οἱ κατήγοροι οὐδεμίαν αἰτίαν ἔφερον ὧν
the accusers ²no ³charge ¹brought ⁴of ⁵things ⁷which

ἐγὼ ὑπενόουν πονηρῶν, 19 ζητήματα δέ
²I ³suspected ⁵evil, but ²questions

τινα περὶ τῆς ἰδίας δεισιδαιμονίας εἶχον
²certain ⁴about ⁵the(ir) own ⁶religion ¹they had

πρὸς αὐτὸν καὶ περί τινος Ἰησοῦ
with him and about one Jesus

τεθνηκότος, ὃν ἔφασκεν ὁ Παῦλος ζῆν.
having died, whom ‒ ¹Paul to live.

20 ἀπορούμενος δὲ ἐγὼ τὴν περὶ τούτων
And ²being perplexed at ¹I ³the ⁵about ⁴these things

ζήτησιν ἔλεγον εἰ βούλοιτο πορεύεσθαι εἰς
⁴debate said if he wished to go to

Ἱεροσόλυμα κἀκεῖ κρίνεσθαι περὶ τούτων.
Jerusalem and there to be judged about these things.

21 τοῦ δὲ Παύλου ἐπικαλεσαμένου τηρηθῆναι
‒ But Paul having appealed² to be kept

αὐτὸν εἰς τὴν τοῦ Σεβαστοῦ διάγνωσιν,
him to the ‒ ²of Augustus ¹decision,

ἐκέλευσα τηρεῖσθαι αὐτὸν ἕως οὗ ἀναπέμψω
I commanded to be kept him until I may send up

αὐτὸν πρὸς Καίσαρα. 22 Ἀγρίππας δὲ
him to Cæsar. And Agrippa

πρὸς τὸν Φῆστον· ἐβουλόμην καὶ αὐτὸς
[said] to ‒ Festus: I was minded also [my]self

τοῦ ἀνθρώπου ἀκοῦσαι. αὔριον, φησίν,
the man to hear. Tomorrow, he says,

ἀκούσῃ αὐτοῦ. 23 Τῇ οὖν ἐπαύριον
thou shalt hear him. ²On the ¹therefore ³morrow

ἐλθόντος τοῦ Ἀγρίππα καὶ τῆς Βερνίκης
coming ‒ Agrippa and ‒ Bernice²
=when Agrippa and Bernice came

μετὰ πολλῆς φαντασίας καὶ εἰσελθόντων
with much display and entering²

εἰς τὸ ἀκροατήριον σύν τε χιλιάρχοις
into the place of audience with both chiliarchs

καὶ ἀνδράσιν τοῖς κατ' ἐξοχὴν τῆς πόλεως,
and ²men ¹the ²chief † of the city,

καὶ κελεύσαντος τοῦ Φήστου ἤχθη ὁ
and having commanded ‒ Festus² ²was brought ‒
=when Festus commanded

Παῦλος. 24 καί φησιν ὁ Φῆστος· Ἀγρίππα
¹Paul. And says ‒ Festus: Agrippa

all who are present with
us, you see this man
about whom the whole
Jewish people petitioned
me, both at Jerusalem
and here, shouting that
he ought not to live any
longer. ²⁵But I found
that he had done nothing
deserving death; and as
he himself appealed to
the emperor, I decided
to send him. ²⁶But I have
nothing definite to write
to my lord about him.
Therefore I have brought
him before you, and,
especially before you,
King Agrippa, that, after
we have examined him, I
may have something to
write. ²⁷For it seems to
me unreasonable, in
sending a prisoner, not
to indicate the charges
against him."

βασιλεῦ καὶ πάντες οἱ συμπαρόντες ἡμῖν
king and all the ²present together with ³us
ἄνδρες, θεωρεῖτε τοῦτον περὶ οὗ ἅπαν τὸ
¹men, ye behold this man about whom all the
πλῆθος τῶν Ἰουδαίων ἐνέτυχόν μοι ἔν τε
multitude of the Jews petitioned me ²in ¹both
Ἱεροσολύμοις καὶ ἐνθάδε, βοῶντες μὴ
Jerusalem   and here, crying not
δεῖν αὐτὸν ζῆν μηκέτι. 25 ἐγὼ δὲ κατε-
ought him to live no longer. But I dis-
=that he ought not to live any longer.
λαβόμην μηδὲν ἄξιον αὐτὸν θανάτου
covered ³nothing ⁴worthy ¹him ⁵of death
πεπραχέναι, αὐτοῦ δὲ τούτου ἐπικαλεσαμένου
⁵to have done, but [him]self this man appealing to³
=when he himself appealed to
τὸν Σεβαστὸν ἔκρινα πέμπειν. 26 περὶ
– Augustus I decided to send. Concerning
οὗ ἀσφαλές τι γράψαι τῷ κυρίῳ οὐκ
whom ⁴certain ³anything ⁵to write ⁶to the ⁷lord ²not
ἔχω· διὸ προήγαγον αὐτὸν ἐφ' ὑμῶν καὶ
¹I have; where- I brought him before you and
    fore forth
μάλιστα ἐπὶ σοῦ, βασιλεῦ Ἀγρίππα, ὅπως
most of all before thee, king Agrippa, so as
=when
τῆς ἀνακρίσεως γενομένης σχῶ τί γράψω·
the examination being³ I may what I may
there has been an examination have write;
27 ἄλογον γὰρ μοι δοκεῖ πέμποντα δέσμιον
for ²unreasonable ³to me ¹it seems sending a prisoner
μὴ καὶ τὰς κατ' αὐτοῦ αἰτίας σημᾶναι.
not also ²the ⁴against ⁵him ²charges ¹to signify.

CHAPTER 26

A GRIPPA said to
Paul, "You have
permission to speak for
yourself." Then Paul
stretched out his hand
and made his defense:
2 "I think myself
fortunate that it is before
you, King Agrippa, I am
to make my defense
today against all the
accusations of the Jews,
³because you are
especially familiar with

26 Ἀγρίππας δὲ πρὸς τὸν Παῦλον ἔφη·
   And Agrippa to – Paul said:
ἐπιτρέπεταί σοι ὑπὲρ σεαυτοῦ λέγειν.
It is permitted to thee on behalf of thyself to speak.
τότε ὁ Παῦλος ἐκτείνας τὴν χεῖρα
Then – Paul stretching out the(his) hand
ἀπελογεῖτο· 2 Περὶ πάντων ὧν ἐγκαλοῦμαι
defended himself: Concerning all things of which I am being
                                              accused
ὑπὸ Ἰουδαίων, βασιλεῦ Ἀγρίππα, ἥγημαι
by Jews, king Agrippa, I consider
ἐμαυτὸν μακάριον ἐπὶ σοῦ μέλλων σήμερον
myself happy ³before ⁴thee ¹being about ²to-day
ἀπολογεῖσθαι, 3 μάλιστα γνώστην ὄντα σε
²to defend myself, most of all ³an expert ²being ¹thee

all customs and controversies of the Jews; therefore I beg you to listen to me patiently. 4 "My manner of life from my youth, spent from the beginning among my own nation and at Jerusalem, is known by all the Jews. ⁵They have known for a long time, if they are willing to testify, that according to the strictest party of our religion I have lived as a Pharisee. ⁶And now I stand here on trial for hope in the promise made by God to our fathers, ⁷to which our twelve tribes hope to attain, as they earnestly worship night and day. And for this hope I am accused by Jews, O king! ⁸Why is it thought incredible by any of you that God raises the dead?

9 "I myself was convinced that I ought to do many things in opposing the name of Jesus of Nazareth. ¹⁰And I did so in Jerusalem; I not only shut up many of the saints in prison, by authority from the chief priests, but when they were put to death I cast

πάντων τῶν κατὰ Ἰουδαίους ἐθῶν τε
⁵of all　⁶the　²among　³Jews　⁷customs ⁸both
καὶ ζητημάτων· διὸ δέομαι μακροθύμως
¹⁰and　¹¹questions;　wherefore　I beg　patiently
ἀκοῦσαί μου. 4 Τὴν μὲν οὖν βίωσίν
to hear　me.　²the　¹So ²then ⁴manner of life
μου ἐκ νεότητος τὴν ἀπ’ ἀρχῆς γενομένην
of me from　youth　－ ²from ⁴beginning ¹having been
　　　　　　　　　³[the]
ἐν τῷ ἔθνει μου ἔν τε Ἰεροσαλύμοις
in　the　nation　of me ²in ¹and　Jerusalem
ἴσασι πάντες Ἰουδαῖοι, 5 προγινώσκοντές
know　all　Jews,　previously knowing
με ἄνωθεν, ἐὰν θέλωσι μαρτυρεῖν, ὅτι
me from the first,　if　they are willing　to testify,　that
κατὰ τὴν ἀκριβεστάτην αἵρεσιν τῆς
according to the　most exact　sect　－
ἡμετέρας θρησκείας ἔζησα Φαρισαῖος. 6 καὶ
of our　religion　I lived　a Pharisee.　And
νῦν ἐπ’ ἐλπίδι τῆς εἰς τοὺς πατέρας
now　on(in)　hope　of the ⁵to　⁶the　⁷fathers
ἡμῶν ἐπαγγελίας γενομένης ὑπὸ τοῦ θεοῦ
⁸of us　¹promise　²having been [made] ³by　－ ⁴God
ἔστηκα κρινόμενος, 7 εἰς ἦν τὸ δωδεκά-
I stand　being judged,　to which　the　twelve
φυλον ἡμῶν ἐν ἐκτενείᾳ νύκτα καὶ
tribes　of us　with　earnestness　night　and
ἡμέραν λατρεῦον ἐλπίζει καταντῆσαι· περὶ
day　worshipping　hopes　to arrive;　concerning
ἧς ἐλπίδος ἐγκαλοῦμαι ὑπὸ Ἰουδαίων,
which　hope　I am accused　by　Jews,
βασιλεῦ. 8 τί ἄπιστον κρίνεται παρ’
[O] king.　Why　incredible　is it judged　by
ὑμῖν εἰ ὁ θεὸς νεκροὺς ἐγείρει; 9 ἐγὼ
you　if　－　God　²dead persons ¹raises?　³I
μὲν οὖν ἔδοξα ἐμαυτῷ πρὸς τὸ ὄνομα
¹indeed ²then ⁴thought ⁵to myself ¹⁰to ¹¹the ¹²name
Ἰησοῦ τοῦ Ναζωραίου δεῖν πολλὰ ἐναντία
¹³of Jesus ¹⁴the　¹⁵Nazarene ⁶ought ⁸many　⁹contrary
　　　　　　　　　　　things
πρᾶξαι· 10 ὃ καὶ ἐποίησα ἐν Ἰεροσαλύμοις,
⁷to do;　which indeed　I did　in　Jerusalem,
καὶ πολλούς τε τῶν ἁγίων ἐγὼ ἐν
and　many　－ of the　saints　¹I　²in
φυλακαῖς κατέκλεισα τὴν παρὰ τῶν
⁴prisons　³shut up　⁶the　⁸from　⁹the
ἀρχιερέων ἐξουσίαν λαβών, ἀναιρουμένων τε
¹⁰chief priests ⁷authority ⁵having received, being killed　and
　　　　　　　　　　= and when they were killed

my vote against them. ¹¹And I punished them often in all the synagogues and tried to make them blaspheme; and in raging fury against them, I persecuted them even to foreign cities.

12 "Thus I journeyed to Damascus with the authority and commission of the chief priests. ¹³At midday, O king, I saw on the way a light from heaven, brighter than the sun, shining round me and those who journeyed with me. ¹⁴And when we had all fallen to the ground, I heard a voice saying to me in the Hebrew language, 'Saul, Saul, why do you persecute me? It hurts you to kick against the goads.' ¹⁵And I said, 'Who are you, Lord?' And the Lord said, 'I am Jesus whom you are persecuting. ¹⁶But rise and stand upon your feet; for I have appeared to you for this purpose, to appoint you to serve and bear witness to the things in which you have seen me and to those in which I will appear to you, ¹⁷delivering you from the people and from the Gentiles—to whom I send you ¹⁸to open their eyes, that they may turn from darkness

αὐτῶν   κατήνεγκα   ψῆφον,   11 καὶ   κατὰ
themᵃ   I cast   a vote,   and throughout
πάσας   τὰς   συναγωγὰς   πολλάκις   τιμωρῶν
all   the   synagogues   often   punishing
αὐτοὺς   ἠνάγκαζον   βλασφημεῖν,   περισσῶς τε
them   I compelled [them] to blaspheme,   and excessively
ἐμμαινόμενος   αὐτοῖς   ἐδίωκον   ἕως καὶ   εἰς
raging against   them   I persecuted as far as even   to
τὰς   ἔξω   πόλεις.   12 Ἐν   οἷς   πορευόμενος
the outside cities.   In   which   journeying
εἰς   τὴν   Δαμασκὸν   μετ'   ἐξουσίας   καὶ
to   –   Damascus   with   authority   and
ἐπιτροπῆς   τῆς   τῶν   ἀρχιερέων,   13 ἡμέρας
power to decide   –   of the   chief priests,   at ²day
μέσης   κατὰ   τὴν   ὁδὸν   εἶδον,   βασιλεῦ,
¹mid   along   the   way   I saw,   [O] king,
οὐρανόθεν   ὑπὲρ   τὴν   λαμπρότητα   τοῦ   ἡλίου
²from heaven   ³above   ⁴the   ⁵brightness   ⁶of the   ⁷sun
περιλάμψαν   με   φῶς   καὶ   τοὺς   σὺν   ἐμοὶ
⁸shining round   ⁹me   ¹a light ¹⁰and ¹¹the [ones] ¹²with ¹⁴me
πορευομένους·   14 πάντων   τε   καταπεσόντων
¹²journeying;   and all   having fallen down
                                    =when we had all fallen
ἡμῶν   εἰς   τὴν   γῆν   ἤκουσα   φωνὴν   λέγουσαν
usᵃ   to   the   earth   I heard   a voice   saying
πρός   με   τῇ   Ἑβραΐδι   διαλέκτῳ·   Σαοὺλ
to   me   in the   Hebrew   language: Saul[,]
Σαούλ,   τί   με   διώκεις;   σκληρόν   σοι
Saul,   why   me   persecutest thou?   hard   for thee
πρὸς   κέντρα   λακτίζειν.   15 ἐγὼ   δὲ   εἶπα·
against   goads   to kick.   And I   said:
τίς   εἶ,   κύριε;   ὁ   δὲ   κύριος   εἶπεν·   ἐγώ
Who art thou, Lord?   And the   Lord   said: I
εἰμι   Ἰησοῦς   ὃν   σὺ   διώκεις.   16 ἀλλὰ
am   Jesus   whom   thou   persecutest.   But
ἀνάστηθι   καὶ   στῆθι   ἐπὶ   τοὺς   πόδας   σου·
rise thou up   and   stand   on   the   feet   of thee;
εἰς   τοῦτο   γὰρ   ὤφθην   σοι,   προχειρίσασθαί
²for ³this [purpose] ¹for I appeared to thee,   to appoint
σε   ὑπηρέτην   καὶ   μάρτυρα   ὧν   τε
thee   an attendant   and   a witness ²of the things ¹both
                                                   which
εἰδές   με   ὧν   τε   ὀφθήσομαί   σοι,
³thou sawest ⁴me ⁵of the things ⁶and I will appear   to thee,
                      which
17 ἐξαιρούμενός   σε   ἐκ   τοῦ   λαοῦ   καὶ   ἐκ
   delivering   thee   from   the   people   and   from
τῶν   ἐθνῶν,   εἰς   οὓς   ἐγὼ   ἀποστέλλω   σε,
the   nations,   to   whom   I   send   thee,
18 ἀνοῖξαι   ὀφθαλμοὺς   αὐτῶν,   τοῦ   ἐπιστρέψαι
   to open   eyes   of them,   –   to turnᵇ

to light and from the power of Satan to God, that they may receive forgiveness of sins and a place among those who are sanctified by faith in me.'
19 "Wherefore, O King Agrippa, I was not disobedient to the heavenly vision, ²⁰but declared first to those at Damascus, then at Jerusalem and throughout all the country of Judea, and also to the Gentiles, that they should repent and turn to God and perform deeds worthy of their repentance. ²¹For this reason the Jews seized me in the temple and tried to kill me. ²²To this day I have had the help that comes from God, and so I stand here testifying both to small and great, saying nothing but what the prophets and Moses said would come to pass: ²³that the Christ must suffer, and that, by being the first to rise from the dead, he would proclaim light both to the people and to the Gentiles."
24 And as he thus made his defense, Festus

ἀπὸ	σκότους	εἰς	φῶς	καὶ	τῆς	ἐξουσίας
from	darkness	to	light	and	[from] the	authority

τοῦ	σατανᾶ	ἐπὶ	τὸν	θεόν,	τοῦ	λαβεῖν
–	of Satan	to	–	God,	–	to receive = that they may receive

αὐτοὺς	ἄφεσιν	ἁμαρτιῶν	καὶ	κλῆρον	ἐν
them¹ᵈ	forgiveness	of sins	and	a lot	among

τοῖς	ἡγιασμένοις	πίστει	τῇ	εἰς	ἐμέ.
the [ones]	having been sanctified	by faith	–	in	me.

19 Ὅθεν, βασιλεῦ Ἀγρίππα, οὐκ ἐγενόμην
Whence, king Agrippa, I was not

ἀπειθὴς	τῇ	οὐρανίῳ	ὀπτασίᾳ,	**20**	ἀλλὰ
disobedient	to the	heavenly	vision,		but

τοῖς	ἐν	Δαμασκῷ	πρῶτόν	τε	καὶ
to the [ones] in	Damascus	firstly	and	also

Ἱεροσολύμοις,	πᾶσάν	τε	τὴν	χώραν	τῆς
[in] Jerusalem,	and all	the	country	–

Ἰουδαίας	καὶ	τοῖς	ἔθνεσιν	ἀπήγγελλον
of Judæa	and	to the	nations	I announced

μετανοεῖν	καὶ	ἐπιστρέφειν	ἐπὶ	τὸν	θεόν,
to repent	and	to turn	to	–	God,

ἄξια	τῆς	μετανοίας	ἔργα	πράσσοντας.
³worthy	⁴of the	⁵repentance	²works	¹doing.

21 ἕνεκα τούτων με Ἰουδαῖοι συλλαβόμενοι
On account of these things ³me ¹Jews ²having seized

ἐν	τῷ	ἱερῷ	ἐπειρῶντο	διαχειρίσασθαι.
in	the	temple	tried	to kill [me].

22 ἐπικουρίας οὖν τυχὼν τῆς ἀπὸ τοῦ
Succour therefore having obtained – from –

θεοῦ	ἄχρι	τῆς	ἡμέρας	ταύτης	ἔστηκα
God	until	the	day	this day	I stand

μαρτυρόμενος	μικρῷ	τε	καὶ	μεγάλῳ,	οὐδὲν
witnessing	²to small	¹both and	to great,	³nothing

ἐκτὸς	λέγων	ὧν	τε	οἱ	προφῆται
²apart from	¹saying	⁴the things which	⁵both	⁶the	⁷prophets

ἐλάλησαν	μελλόντων	γίνεσθαι	καὶ	Μωϋσῆς,
¹⁰said	¹¹being about	¹²to happen	⁸and	⁹Moses,

23 εἰ παθητὸς ὁ χριστός, εἰ πρῶτος
if subject to suffering the Christ, if first

ἐξ	ἀναστάσεως	νεκρῶν	φῶς	μέλλει
by	a resurrection	of dead persons	²a light	¹he is about

καταγγέλλειν	τῷ	τε	λαῷ	καὶ	τοῖς	ἔθνεσιν.
²to announce	⁵to the	⁴both	people	and	to the	nations.

24 Ταῦτα δὲ αὐτοῦ ἀπολογουμένου ὁ Φῆστος
And these things him defending himself³ – Festus
= as he defended himself with these things

said with a loud voice, "Paul, you are mad; your great learning is turning you mad." ²⁵ But Paul said, "I am not mad, most excellent Festus, but I am speaking the sober truth. ²⁶ For the king knows about these things, and to him I speak freely; for I am persuaded that none of these things has escaped his notice, for this was not done in a corner. ²⁷ King Agrippa, do you believe the prophets? I know that you believe." ²⁸ And Agrippa said to Paul, "In a short time you think to make me a Christian!" ²⁹ And Paul said, "Whether short or long, I would to God that not only you but also all who hear me this day might become such as I am—except for these chains."

30 Then the king rose, and the governor and Berni'ce and those who were sitting with them; ³¹ and when they had withdrawn, they said to one another, "This man is doing nothing to deserve death or imprisonment." ³² And

μεγάλη τῇ φωνῇ φησιν· μαίνῃ, Παῦλε·
²great ¹with the(his) ²voice says: Thou ravest, Paul:

τὰ πολλά σε γράμματα εἰς μανίαν
¹the ²many ⁵thee ³letters ⁶to ⁷madness

περιτρέπει. 25 ὁ δὲ Παῦλος· οὐ μαίνομαι,
⁴turn[s]. – But Paul: I do not rave,

φησίν, κράτιστε Φῆστε, ἀλλὰ ἀληθείας
he says, most excellent Festus, but ²of truth

καὶ σωφροσύνης ῥήματα ἀποφθέγγομαι.
⁴and ⁵of good sense ²words ¹speak forth.

26 ἐπίσταται γὰρ περὶ τούτων ὁ βασιλεύς,
For ²understands ⁴about ⁵these things ¹the ³king,

πρὸς ὃν καὶ παρρησιαζόμενος λαλῶ·
to whom indeed being bold of speech I speak;

λανθάνειν γὰρ αὐτὸν τούτων οὐ πείθομαι
for ⁴to be hidden [from] ⁵him ³of these things not ¹I am persuaded

οὐθέν· οὐ γάρ ἐστιν ἐν γωνίᾳ πεπραγμένον
²nothing; for ²not ²is ⁵in ⁶a corner ⁴having been done

τοῦτο. 27 πιστεύεις, βασιλεῦ Ἀγρίππα,
¹this. Believest thou, king Agrippa,

τοῖς προφήταις; οἶδα ὅτι πιστεύεις. 28 ὁ
the prophets? I know that thou believest. –

δὲ Ἀγρίππας πρὸς τὸν Παῦλον· ἐν
And Agrippa [said] to – Paul: In

ὀλίγῳ με πείθεις Χριστιανὸν ποιῆσαι.
a little ²me ¹thou persuadest ⁴a Christian ⁵to make(act).

29 ὁ δὲ Παῦλος· εὐξαίμην ἂν τῷ θεῷ
– And Paul [said]: I would pray – God

καὶ ἐν ὀλίγῳ καὶ ἐν μεγάλῳ οὐ μόνον
both in a little and in great not only

σὲ ἀλλὰ καὶ πάντας τοὺς ἀκούοντάς
thee but also all the [ones] hearing

μου σήμερον γενέσθαι τοιούτους ὁποῖος
me to-day ²to become ¹such of what kind

καὶ ἐγώ εἰμι, παρεκτὸς τῶν δεσμῶν
indeed I am, except – bonds

τούτων. 30 Ἀνέστη τε ὁ βασιλεὺς καὶ
these. Rose up both the king and

ὁ ἡγεμὼν ἥ τε Βερνίκη καὶ οἱ συγ-
the governor – and Bernice and the [ones] sit-

καθήμενοι αὐτοῖς, 31 καὶ ἀναχωρήσαντες
ting with them, and having left

ἐλάλουν πρὸς ἀλλήλους λέγοντες ὅτι οὐδὲν
spoke to one another saying [,] – ⁴nothing

θανάτου ἢ δεσμῶν ἄξιον πράσσει ὁ
⁶of death ⁷or ⁸of bonds ⁵worthy ³does –

ἄνθρωπος οὗτος. 32 Ἀγρίππας δὲ τῷ
²man ¹This. And Agrippa –

Agrippa said to Festus, "This man could have been set free if he had not appealed to Caesar."

Φήστῳ ἔφη· ἀπολελύσθαι ἐδύνατο
to Festus   said: ³to have been released   ²was able(could)
ὁ ἄνθρωπος οὗτος εἰ μὴ ἐπεκέκλητο Καίσαρα.
¹This man   if he had not appealed to   Cæsar.

CHAPTER 27

AND when it was decided that we should sail for Italy, they delivered Paul and some other prisoners to a centurion of the Augustan Cohort, named Julius. ²And embarking in a ship of Adramyttium, which was about to sail to the ports along the coast of Asia, we put to sea, accompanied by Aristarchus, a Macedonian from Thessalonica. ³The next day we put in at Sidon; and Julius treated Paul kindly, and gave him leave to go to his friends and be cared for. ⁴And putting to sea from there we sailed under the lee of Cyprus, because the winds were against us. ⁵And when we had sailed across the sea which is off Cilicia and Pamphylia, we came to Myra in Lycia. ⁶There the centurion found a ship of Alexandria sailing for Italy, and put us on board. ⁷We sailed slowly for a number of days, and

27 Ὡς δὲ ἐκρίθη τοῦ ἀποπλεῖν ἡμᾶς
And when it was decided   –   to sail   usᵇᵈ
=that we should sail
εἰς τὴν Ἰταλίαν, παρεδίδουν τόν τε
to   –   Italy,   they delivered   –   both
Παῦλον καί τινας ἑτέρους δεσμώτας
Paul   and   some   other   prisoners
ἑκατοντάρχῃ ὀνόματι Ἰουλίῳ σπείρης
to a centurion   by name   Julius   of a cohort
Σεβαστῆς. 2 ἐπιβάντες δὲ πλοίῳ Ἀδρα-
Augustan.   And embarking in   a ship   belonging to
μυττηνῷ μέλλοντι πλεῖν εἰς τοὺς κατὰ
Adramyttium being about   to sail   ¹for   ²the ⁴along[the
coast of]
τὴν Ἀσίαν τόπους ἀνήχθημεν, ὄντος σὺν
–   ⁵Asia   ³places   we set sail,   being   with
ἡμῖν Ἀριστάρχου Μακεδόνος Θεσσαλονικέως·
us   Aristarchus   a Macedonianª   of Thessalonica.
3 τῇ τε ἑτέρᾳ κατήχθημεν εἰς Σιδῶνα,
and on the   next [day] we were brought   at   Sidon,
to land
φιλανθρώπως τε ὁ Ἰούλιος τῷ Παύλῳ
and ³kindly   –   ¹Julius   –   ⁵Paul
χρησάμενος ἐπέτρεψεν πρὸς τοὺς φίλους
²treating [him]   ⁴allowed   ⁷to   ⁸the   ⁹friends
πορευθέντι ἐπιμελείας τυχεῖν. 4 κἀκεῖθεν
⁶going   ¹¹attention   ¹⁰to obtain.   And thence
ἀναχθέντες ὑπεπλεύσαμεν τὴν Κύπρον διὰ
putting to sea   we sailed close to   –   Cyprus because
of
τὸ τοὺς ἀνέμους εἶναι ἐναντίους, 5 τό τε
–   the   winds   to be(being) contrary,   and ²the
πέλαγος τὸ κατὰ τὴν Κιλικίαν καὶ
²sea   –   ⁴against   –   ⁵Cilicia   ⁶and
Παμφυλίαν διαπλεύσαντες κατήλθαμεν εἰς
⁷Pamphylia   ¹sailing over   we came down   to
Μύρα τῆς Λυκίας. 6 Κἀκεῖ εὑρὼν ὁ
Myra   –   of Lycia.   And there ³having found ¹the
ἑκατοντάρχης πλοῖον Ἀλεξανδρῖνον πλέον
²centurion   ship   an Alexandrian   sailing
εἰς τὴν Ἰταλίαν ἐνεβίβασεν ἡμᾶς εἰς
to   –   Italy   he embarked   us   in
αὐτό. 7 ἐν ἱκαναῖς δὲ ἡμέραις βραδυπλο-
it.   And in a number of   days   sailing

arrived with difficulty off Cni'dus, and as the wind did not allow us to go on, we sailed under the lee of Crete off Salmo'ne. [8] Coasting along it with difficulty, we came to a place called Fair Havens, near which was the city of Lase'a.

[9] As much time had been lost, and the voyage was already dangerous because the fast had already gone by, Paul advised them, [10] saying, "Sirs, I perceive that the voyage will be with injury and much loss, not only of the cargo and the ship, but also of our lives." [11] But the centurion paid more attention to the captain and to the owner of the ship than to what Paul said. [12] And because the harbor was not suitable to winter in, the majority advised to put to sea from there, on the chance that somehow they could reach Phoenix, a harbor of Crete, looking northeast

οὖντες καὶ μόλις γενόμενοι κατὰ τὴν
slowly and hardly coming against –
Κνίδον, μὴ προσεῶντος ἡμᾶς τοῦ ἀνέμου,
Cnidus, not allowing us the wind,[a]
= as the wind did not allow us,

ὑπεπλεύσαμεν τὴν Κρήτην κατὰ Σαλμώνην,
we sailed close to – Crete against Salmone,

8 μόλις τε παραλεγόμενοι αὐτὴν ἤλθομεν
and hardly sailing along it we came
εἰς τόπον τινὰ καλούμενον Καλοὺς λιμένας,
to place a certain being called Fair Havens,
ᾧ ἐγγὺς ἦν πόλις Λασαία. 9 Ἱκανοῦ δὲ
[2]to which [1]near was a city Lasæa. And much
= when

χρόνου διαγενομένου καὶ ὄντος ἤδη
time having passed[a] and being now
much time had passed = as the voyage

ἐπισφαλοῦς τοῦ πλοὸς διὰ τὸ καὶ τὴν
dangerous the voyage[a] on account of – also the
was now dangerous = because also the fast had now

νηστείαν ἤδη παρεληλυθέναι, παρήνει ὁ
fast now to have gone by, [2]advised –
gone by,

Παῦλος 10 λέγων αὐτοῖς· ἄνδρες, θεωρῶ
[1]Paul saying to them: Men, I see

ὅτι μετὰ ὕβρεως καὶ πολλῆς ζημίας οὐ
that with injury and much loss not
μόνον τοῦ φορτίου καὶ τοῦ πλοίου ἀλλὰ
only of the cargo and of the ship but
καὶ τῶν ψυχῶν ἡμῶν μέλλειν ἔσεσθαι
also of the lives of us [3]to be about [4]to be
= will be

τὸν πλοῦν. 11 ὁ δὲ ἑκατοντάρχης τῷ
[1]the [2]voyage. But the centurion [2]the
κυβερνήτῃ καὶ τῷ ναυκλήρῳ μᾶλλον
[3]steersman [4]and [5]the [6]shipmaster [7]rather
ἐπείθετο ἢ τοῖς ὑπὸ Παύλου λεγομένοις.
[1]was persuaded by [8]than [9]the [11]by [12]Paul [10]things said.

12 ἀνευθέτου δὲ τοῦ λιμένος ὑπάρχοντος
But unsuitable the port being[a]
= as the port was unsuitable

πρὸς παραχειμασίαν οἱ πλείονες ἔθεντο
for wintering the majority placed
= decided

βουλὴν ἀναχθῆναι ἐκεῖθεν, εἴ πως δύναιντο
counsel to set sail thence, if some- they might
how be able

καταντήσαντες εἰς Φοίνικα παραχειμάσαι,
having arrived at Phœnix to pass the winter,

λιμένα τῆς Κρήτης βλέποντα κατὰ λίβα
a port – of Crete looking toward southwest

and southeast,⁰ and winter there. 13 And when the south wind blew gently, supposing that they had obtained their purpose, they weighed anchor and sailed along Crete, close inshore. ¹⁴But soon a tempestuous wind, called the northeaster, struck down from the land; ¹⁵and when the ship was caught and could not face the wind, we gave way to it and were driven. ¹⁶And running under the lee of a small island called Cauda,ʷ we managed with difficulty to secure the boat; ¹⁷after hoisting it up, they took measures to undergird the ship; then, fearing that they should run on the Syr'tis, they lowered the gear, and so were driven. ¹⁸As we were violently storm-tossed, they began next day to throw the cargo overboard; ¹⁹and the third day they cast out with their own hands the tackle of the ship. ²⁰And when neither sun nor stars appeared for many a day, and no small tempest lay on us, all hope of our being saved was at last abandoned.

καὶ κατὰ χῶρον. 13 Ὑποπνεύσαντος δὲ
and toward north-west.   And blowing gently
= when a south wind

νότου δόξαντες τῆς προθέσεως κεκρατηκέναι,
a south wind thinking the(ir) purpose to have obtained,
blew gently

ἄραντες ἆσσον παρελέγοντο τὴν Κρήτην.
raising close in- they coasted by – Crete.
[anchor] shore

14 μετ' οὐ πολὺ δὲ ἔβαλεν κατ' αὐτῆς
And after not much there beat down it

ἄνεμος τυφωνικὸς ὁ καλούμενος εὐρακύλων·
wind a tempestuous – being called Euraquilo;

15 συναρπασθέντος δὲ τοῦ πλοίου καὶ μὴ
and being seized the ship and not

δυναμένου ἀντοφθαλμεῖν τῷ ἀνέμῳ ἐπιδόντες
being able to beat up against the wind giving way

ἐφερόμεθα. 16 νησίον δέ τι ὑποδραμόντες
we were borne. And islet a certain running under
the lee of

καλούμενον Κλαῦδα ἰσχύσαμεν μόλις
being called Clauda we were able hardly

περικρατεῖς γενέσθαι τῆς σκάφης, 17 ἦν
control to get of the boat, which

ἄραντες βοηθείαις ἐχρῶντο, ὑποζωννύντες
taking helps they used, undergirding

τὸ πλοῖον· φοβούμενοί τε μὴ εἰς τὴν
the ship; and fearing lest into –

Σύρτιν ἐκπέσωσιν, χαλάσαντες τὸ σκεῦος,
Syrtis they might fall off, lowering the tackle,

οὕτως ἐφέροντο. 18 σφοδρῶς δὲ χειμαζ-
thus they were borne. But exceedingly being in
= as we were exceedingly in . . .

ομένων ἡμῶν τῇ ἐξῆς ἐκβολὴν ἐποιοῦντο,
the grip us on the next a jettisoning they made,
of a storm [day]

19 καὶ τῇ τρίτῃ αὐτόχειρες τὴν σκευὴν
and on the third with their the tackle
[day] own hands

τοῦ πλοίου ἔρριψαν. 20 μήτε δὲ ἡλίου
of the ship they threw [out]. And neither sun
= when neither . . .

μήτε ἄστρων ἐπιφαινόντων ἐπὶ πλείονας
nor stars appearing over many
appeared

ἡμέρας, χειμῶνός τε οὐκ ὀλίγου ἐπικειμένου,
days, and stormy weather no little pressing hard,

λοιπὸν περιῃρεῖτο ἐλπὶς πᾶσα τοῦ σώζεσθαι
now was taken away hope all – to be saved
= that we might

⁰ Or southwest and northwest
ʷ Other ancient authorities read Clauda

* This is the classical Greek word for a ship being driven out of her course on to shoals, rocks, etc. (Page). See also vers 26 and 29.

21 As they had been long without food, Paul then came forward among them and said, "Men, you should have listened to me, and should not have set sail from Crete and incurred this injury and loss. ²²I now bid you take heart; for there will be no loss of life among you, but only of the ship. ²³For this very night there stood by me an angel of the God to whom I belong and whom I worship, ²⁴and he said, 'Do not be afraid, Paul; you must stand before Caesar; and lo, God has granted you all those who sail with you.' ²⁵So take heart, men, for I have faith in God that it will be exactly as I have been told. ²⁶But we shall have to run on some island."

27 When the fourteenth night had come, as we were drifting across the sea of A'dria, about midnight the sailors suspected that they were nearing land. ²⁸So they sounded and found twenty fathoms; a little farther on they

ἡμᾶς. 21 Πολλῆς τε ἀσιτίας ὑπαρχούσης
us.ᵇᵈ   And much   abstinence   being*
be saved.   = when there was long abstinence

τότε σταθεὶς ὁ Παῦλος ἐν μέσῳ αὐτῶν εἶπεν·
then ¹standing - ¹Paul in [the] midst of them said:

ἔδει μέν, ὦ ἄνδρες, πειθαρχήσαντάς
It behoved - O men, obeying
[you],

μοι μὴ ἀνάγεσθαι ἀπὸ τῆς Κρήτης
me not to set sail from - Crete

κερδῆσαί τε τὴν ὕβριν ταύτην καὶ τὴν
and to come by - injury this and -

ζημίαν. 22 καὶ τὰ νῦν παραινῶ ὑμᾶς
loss. And - now I advise you

εὐθυμεῖν· ἀποβολὴ γὰρ ψυχῆς οὐδεμία
to be of good for ²throwing away ⁴of life ²no
cheer;

ἔσται ἐξ ὑμῶν πλὴν τοῦ πλοίου.
¹there will be of you but of the ship.

23 παρέστη γάρ μοι ταύτῃ τῇ νυκτὶ
For there stood by me in this - night

τοῦ θεοῦ οὗ εἰμι, ᾧ καὶ λατρεύω,
- ²of God ³of whom ⁴I am, ⁵whom ⁶also ⁷I serve,

ἄγγελος 24 λέγων· μὴ φοβοῦ, Παῦλε·
¹an angel saying: Fear not, Paul;

Καίσαρί σε δεῖ παραστῆναι, καὶ ἰδοὺ
⁴Cæsar ³thee ¹it behoves ³to stand before, and behold

κεχάρισταί σοι ὁ θεὸς πάντας τοὺς
²has given ³thee - ¹God all the [ones]

πλέοντας μετὰ σοῦ. 25 διὸ εὐθυμεῖτε,
sailing with thee. Wherefore be ye of
good cheer,

ἄνδρες· πιστεύω γὰρ τῷ θεῷ ὅτι οὕτως
men; for I believe - God that thus

ἔσται καθ᾽ ὃν τρόπον λελάληταί μοι.
it will be in the way in which† it has been spoken to me.

26 εἰς νῆσον δέ τινα δεῖ ἡμᾶς ἐκπεσεῖν.
⁵Onto ⁷island ¹but ⁶a ²it ³us ⁴to fall off.
certain behoves

27 Ὡς δὲ τεσσαρεσκαιδεκάτη νὺξ ἐγένετο
Now when [the] fourteenth night came

διαφερομένων ἡμῶν ἐν τῷ Ἀδρίᾳ, κατ᾽
being carried about us* in the Adria, abou
= while we were being carried about

μέσον τῆς νυκτὸς ὑπενόουν οἱ ναῦται
[the] middle of the night ³supposed ¹the ²sailors

προσάγειν τινὰ αὐτοῖς χώραν. 28 καὶ
⁴to approach ⁶some ⁵to them ⁷country. And

βολίσαντες εὗρον ὀργυιὰς εἴκοσι, βραχὺ δὲ
sounding they found fathoms twenty, and ²a little

sounded again and found fifteen fathoms. ²⁹And fearing that we might run on the rocks, they let out four anchors from the stern, and prayed for day to come. ³⁰And as the sailors were seeking to escape from the ship, and had lowered the boat into the sea, under pretense of laying out anchors from the bow, ³¹Paul said to the centurion and the soldiers, "Unless these men stay in the ship, you cannot be saved." ³²Then the soldiers cut away the ropes of the boat, and let it go.

33 As day was about to dawn, Paul urged them all to take some food, saying, "Today is the fourteenth day that you have continued in suspense and without food, having taken nothing. ³⁴Therefore I urge you to take some food; it will give you strength, since not a hair is to perish from the head of any of you." ³⁵And when he had said this, he took

διαστήσαντες καὶ πάλιν βολίσαντες εὗρον
¹having moved　also　again　sounding　they found

ὀργυιὰς δεκαπέντε· 29 φοβούμενοί τε μή
fathoms　fifteen;　　and fearing　lest

που κατὰ τραχεῖς τόπους ἐκπέσωμεν,
²somewhere ³against ⁴rough ⁵places ¹we might fall off,

ἐκ πρύμνης ῥίψαντες ἀγκύρας τέσσαρας
out of [the] stern throwing anchors four

ηὔχοντο ἡμέραν γενέσθαι. 30 Τῶν δὲ
they prayed day to become. And the

ναυτῶν ζητούντων φυγεῖν ἐκ τοῦ πλοίου
sailors seeking⁵ to flee out of the ship
=when the sailors sought

καὶ χαλασάντων τὴν σκάφην εἰς τὴν
and lowering⁵ the boat into the
=lowered

θάλασσαν προφάσει ὡς ἐκ πρώρης ἀγκύρας
sea under pretence as ⁴out of ⁵[the] prow ³anchors

μελλόντων ἐκτείνειν, 31 εἶπεν ὁ Παῦλος
¹intending ²to cast out, said – Paul

τῷ ἑκατοντάρχῃ καὶ τοῖς στρατιώταις·
to the centurion and to the soldiers:

ἐὰν μὴ οὗτοι μείνωσιν ἐν τῷ πλοίῳ,
Unless these remain in the ship,

ὑμεῖς σωθῆναι οὐ δύνασθε. 32 τότε
ye ²to be saved ¹cannot. Then

ἀπέκοψαν οἱ στρατιῶται τὰ σχοινία τῆς
cut away the soldiers the ropes of the

σκάφης καὶ εἴασαν αὐτὴν ἐκπεσεῖν.
boat and let it to fall off.

33 Ἄχρι δὲ οὗ ἡμέρα ἤμελλεν γίνεσθαι,
And until day was about to come,

παρεκάλει ὁ Παῦλος ἅπαντας μεταλαβεῖν
besought – Paul all to partake

τροφῆς λέγων· τεσσαρεσκαιδεκάτην σήμερον
of food saying: ²[the] fourteenth ¹To-day [is]

ἡμέραν προσδοκῶντες ἄσιτοι διατελεῖτε,
³day ⁵waiting ⁴without food ⁴ye continued,

μηθὲν προσλαβόμενοι. 34 διὸ παρακαλῶ
nothing taking. Wherefore I beseech

ὑμᾶς μεταλαβεῖν τροφῆς· τοῦτο γὰρ πρὸς
you to partake of food; for this to

τῆς ὑμετέρας σωτηρίας ὑπάρχει· οὐδενὸς
– your salvation is; ²of no one

γὰρ ὑμῶν θρὶξ ἀπὸ τῆς κεφαλῆς ἀπολεῖται.
¹for of you a hair from the head shall perish.

35 εἴπας δὲ ταῦτα καὶ λαβὼν ἄρτον
And saying these things and taking bread

bread, and giving thanks to God in the presence of all he broke it and began to eat. [36] Then they all were encouraged and ate some food themselves. [37] (We were in all two hundred and seventy-six[z] persons in the ship.) [38] And when they had eaten enough, they lightened the ship, throwing out the wheat into the sea.

[39] Now when it was day, they did not recognize the land, but they noticed a bay with a beach, on which they planned if possible to bring the ship ashore. [40] So they cast off the anchors and left them in the sea, at the same time loosening the ropes that tied the rudders; then hoisting the foresail to the wind they made for the beach. [41] But striking a shoal they ran the vessel aground; the bow stuck and remained immovable, and the stern was broken up by the surf. [42] The soldiers' plan was to kill the prisoners, lest any should swim away and escape; [43] but the centurion, wishing to save Paul, kept them from carrying out their

εὐχαρίστησεν τῷ θεῷ ἐνώπιον πάντων
he gave thanks   –   to God   before   all

καὶ κλάσας ἤρξατο ἐσθίειν. 36 εὔθυμοι δὲ
and breaking   began   to eat.   And [4]in good spirits

γενόμενοι πάντες καὶ αὐτοὶ προσελάβοντο
[3]becoming   [1]all   [2]also   they   took

τροφῆς. 37 ἤμεθα δὲ αἱ πᾶσαι ψυχαὶ
food.   Now we were   [2]the   [1]all   souls

ἐν τῷ πλοίῳ διακόσιαι ἑβδομήκοντα ἕξ.
in   the   ship   two hundreds   [and] seventy   six.

38 κορεσθέντες δὲ τροφῆς ἐκούφιζον τὸ
And having been satisfied of(with) food they lightened the

πλοῖον ἐκβαλλόμενοι τὸν σῖτον εἰς τὴν
ship   throwing out   the   wheat   into   the

θάλασσαν. 39 Ὅτε δὲ ἡμέρα ἐγένετο,
sea.   And when   day   came,

τὴν γῆν οὐκ ἐπεγίνωσκον, κόλπον δέ
[2]the [3]land [1]they did not recognize,   but [2]bay

τινα κατενόουν ἔχοντα αἰγιαλόν, εἰς ὃν
[2]a certain [1]they noticed   having   a shore,   into which

ἐβουλεύοντο εἰ δύναιντο ἐξῶσαι τὸ πλοῖον.
they were minded if they were able to drive the ship.

40 καὶ τὰς ἀγκύρας περιελόντες εἴων
And   [2]the   [1]anchors   [1]having cast off they left [them]

εἰς τὴν θάλασσαν, ἅμα ἀνέντες τὰς
in   the   sea,   at the same time loosening   the

ζευκτηρίας τῶν πηδαλίων, καὶ ἐπάραντες
fastenings   of the   rudders,   and   raising

τὸν ἀρτέμωνα τῇ πνεούσῃ κατεῖχον εἰς
the   foresail   to the   breeze   they held [the ship] to

τὸν αἰγιαλόν. 41 περιπεσόντες δὲ εἰς
the   shore.   And coming upon   to

τόπον διθάλασσον ἐπέκειλαν τὴν ναῦν,
a place between two seas they drove the vessel,

καὶ ἡ μὲν πρῷρα ἐρείσασα ἔμεινεν
and   [2]the   [1]while   prow having run aground remained

ἀσάλευτος, ἡ δὲ πρύμνα ἐλύετο ὑπὸ
immovable,   [2]the   [1]yet   stern   was broken   by

τῆς βίας. 42 Τῶν δὲ στρατιωτῶν βουλὴ
the   force.[*]   Now [2]of the   [3]soldiers   [1][the] mind

ἐγένετο ἵνα τοὺς δεσμώτας ἀποκτείνωσιν,
was   that   [2]the   [1]prisoners   [1]they should kill,

μή τις ἐκκολυμβήσας διαφύγῃ· 43 ὁ δὲ
lest anyone   swimming out   should escape;   but the

ἑκατοντάρχης βουλόμενος διασῶσαι τὸν
centurion   being minded   to save   –

Παῦλον ἐκώλυσεν αὐτοὺς τοῦ βουλήματος,
Paul   forbade   them   the(ir)   intention,

[z] Other ancient authorities read *seventy-six* or *about seventy-six*

* That is, of the waves, as indeed some MSS have.

purpose. He ordered those who could swim to throw themselves overboard first and make for the land, **44** and the rest on planks or on pieces of the ship. And so it was that all escaped to land.

ἐκέλευσέν τε τοὺς δυναμένους κολυμβᾶν
and commanded the [ones] being able to swim

ἀπορίψαντας πρώτους ἐπὶ τὴν γῆν
casting [themselves] first onto the land
overboard

ἐξιέναι, **44** καὶ τοὺς λοιποὺς οὓς μὲν ἐπὶ
to go out, and the rest some on

σανίσιν, οὓς δὲ ἐπί τινων τῶν ἀπὸ τοῦ
planks, others on some of the things from the

πλοίου. καὶ οὕτως ἐγένετο πάντας
ship. And thus it came to pass all

διασωθῆναι ἐπὶ τὴν γῆν.
to be saved on the land.

CHAPTER 28

AFTER we had escaped, we then learned that the island was called Malta. ²And the natives showed us unusual kindness, for they kindled a fire and welcomed us all, because it had begun to rain and was cold. ³Paul had gathered a bundle of sticks and put them on the fire, when a viper came out because of the heat and fastened on his hand. ⁴When the natives saw the creature hanging from his hand, they said to one another, "No doubt this man is a murderer. Though he has escaped from the sea, justice has not allowed him to live." ⁵He, however, shook off the creature into the fire and

28 Καὶ διασωθέντες τότε ἐπέγνωμεν ὅτι
And having been saved then we found out that

Μελίτη ἡ νῆσος καλεῖται. **2** οἵ τε
Melita the island is(was) called. And the

βάρβαροι παρεῖχον οὐ τὴν τυχοῦσαν
foreigners ¹showed ³not ⁴the ⁵ordinary

φιλανθρωπίαν ἡμῖν· ἅψαντες γὰρ πυρὰν
⁶kindness ²us; for having lit a fire

προσελάβοντο πάντας ἡμᾶς διὰ τὸν ὑετὸν
they welcomed ²all ¹us because of the rain

τὸν ἐφεστῶτα καὶ διὰ τὸ ψῦχος. **3** συστρέ-
– coming on and because of the cold. col-

ψαντος δὲ τοῦ Παύλου φρυγάνων τι
lecting And – Paulᵃ ³of sticks ¹a
=when Paul collected

πλῆθος καὶ ἐπιθέντος ἐπὶ τὴν πυράν,
²quantity and putting onᵃ on the fire,
=put them

ἔχιδνα ἀπὸ τῆς θέρμης ἐξελθοῦσα καθῆψεν
a snake from the heat coming out fastened on

τῆς χειρὸς αὐτοῦ. **4** ὡς δὲ εἶδον οἱ
the hand of him. And when ³saw ¹the

βάρβαροι κρεμάμενον τὸ θηρίον ἐκ τῆς
²foreigners ⁶hanging ⁴the ⁵beast from the

χειρὸς αὐτοῦ, πρὸς ἀλλήλους ἔλεγον·
hand of him, to one another they said:

πάντως φονεύς ἐστιν ὁ ἄνθρωπος οὗτος,
To be sure ⁴a murderer ²is ¹this man,

ὃν διασωθέντα ἐκ τῆς θαλάσσης ἡ δίκη
whom having been out of the sea – justice
saved

ζῆν οὐκ εἴασεν. **5** ὁ μὲν οὖν ἀποτινάξας
²to live ¹did not allow. He – then shaking off

τὸ θηρίον εἰς τὸ πῦρ ἔπαθεν οὐδὲν
the beast into the fire suffered no

suffered no harm. ⁶They waited, expecting him to swell up or suddenly fall down dead; but when they had waited a long time and saw no misfortune come to him, they changed their minds and said that he was a god.

7 Now in the neighborhood of that place were lands belonging to the chief man of the island, named Publius, who received us and entertained us hospitably for three days. ⁸It happened that the father of Publius lay sick with fever and dysentery; and Paul visited him and prayed, and putting his hands on him healed him. ⁹And when this had taken place, the rest of the people on the island who had diseases also came and were cured. ¹⁰They presented many gifts to us;ʸ and when we sailed, they put on board whatever we needed.

11 After three months we set sail in a ship which had wintered in the island, a ship of Alexandria, with the Twin Brothers as figurehead. ¹²Putting in at Syracuse, we stayed there for three

ʸ Or honored us with many honors

κακόν· 6 οἱ δὲ προσεδόκων αὐτὸν μέλλειν
harm; but they expected him to be about

πίμπρασθαι ἢ καταπίπτειν ἄφνω νεκρόν.
to swell or to fall down suddenly dead.

ἐπὶ πολὺ δὲ αὐτῶν προσδοκώντων καὶ
But over much [time] they expecting and
= while they expected and beheld

θεωρούντων μηδὲν ἄτοπον εἰς αὐτὸν
beholding² nothing amiss ²to ³him

γινόμενον, μεταβαλόμενοι ἔλεγον αὐτὸν εἶναι
¹happening, changing their minds they said him to be

θεόν. 7 Ἐν δὲ τοῖς περὶ τὸν τόπον
a god. Now in the [parts] about – place

ἐκεῖνον ὑπῆρχεν χωρία τῷ πρώτῳ τῆς
that were lands to the chief manᶜ of the
= the chief man . . . had lands

νήσου ὀνόματι Ποπλίῳ, ὃς ἀναδεξάμενος
island by name Publius, who welcoming

ἡμᾶς ἡμέρας τρεῖς φιλοφρόνως ἐξένισεν.
us ⁴days ³three ²friendlily ¹lodged [us].

8 ἐγένετο δὲ τὸν πατέρα τοῦ Ποπλίου
Now it happened the father – of Publius

πυρετοῖς καὶ δυσεντερίῳ συνεχόμενον
²feverish attacks ⁴and ⁵dysentery ²suffering from

κατακεῖσθαι, πρὸς ὃν ὁ Παῦλος εἰσελθὼν
¹to be lying down, to whom – Paul entering

καὶ προσευξάμενος, ἐπιθεὶς τὰς χεῖρας
and praying, ¹putting ⁴on ²the(his) ³hands

αὐτῷ ἰάσατο αὐτόν. 9 τούτου δὲ γενομένου
⁵him cured him. And this happening²
= when this happened

καὶ οἱ λοιποὶ οἱ ἐν τῇ νήσῳ ἔχοντες
²also ¹the ²rest – in the island having

ἀσθενείας προσήρχοντο καὶ ἐθεραπεύοντο,
ailments came up and were healed,

10 οἳ καὶ πολλαῖς τιμαῖς ἐτίμησαν ἡμᾶς
who also with many honours honoured us

καὶ ἀναγομένοις ἐπέθεντο τὰ πρὸς τὰς
and on our putting to sea placed on [us] the things for the(our)

χρείας.
needs.

11 Μετὰ δὲ τρεῖς μῆνας ἀνήχθημεν ἐν
And after three months we embarked in

πλοίῳ παρακεχειμακότι ἐν τῇ νήσῳ,
a ship having passed the winter in the island,

Ἀλεξανδρίνῳ, παρασήμῳ Διοσκούροις. 12 καὶ
an Alexandrian, with a sign Dioscuri. And

καταχθέντες εἰς Συρακούσας ἐπεμείναμεν
being brought to land to(at) Syracuse we remained

days. ¹³And from there we made a circuit and arrived at Rhe′gium; and after one day a south wind sprang up, and on the second day we came to Pute′oli. ¹⁴There we found brethren, and were invited to stay with them for seven days. And so we came to Rome. ¹⁵And the brethren there, when they heard of us, came as far as the Forum of Ap′pius and Three Taverns to meet us. On seeing them Paul thanked God and took courage. ¹⁶And when we came into Rome, Paul was allowed to stay by himself, with the soldier that guarded him.

17 After three days he called together the local leaders of the Jews; and when they had gathered, he said to them, "Brethren, though I had done nothing against the people or the customs of our fathers, yet I was delivered prisoner from Jerusalem into the hands of the Romans. ¹⁸When they had examined me, they wished to set me at

ἡμέρας τρεῖς, 13 ὅθεν περιελθόντες κατην-
days　three,　whence　tacking　we ar-

τήσαμεν εἰς ‘Ρήγιον. καὶ μετὰ μίαν
rived　at　Rhegium.　And　after　one

ἡμέραν ἐπιγενομένου νότου δευτεραῖοι
day　coming on　a south wind*　on the
　　—as a south wind came on　second day

ἤλθομεν εἰς Ποτιόλους, 14 οὗ εὑρόντες
we came　to　Puteoli,　where having found

ἀδελφοὺς παρεκλήθημεν παρ’ αὐτοῖς ἐπιμεῖναι
brothers　we were besought　with　them　to remain

ἡμέρας ἑπτά· καὶ οὕτως εἰς τὴν ‘Ρώμην
days　seven;　and　thus　to　-　Rome

ἤλθαμεν. 15 κἀκεῖθεν οἱ ἀδελφοὶ ἀκούσαντες
we went.　And thence the　brothers　having heard

τὰ περὶ ἡμῶν ἦλθαν εἰς ἀπάντησιν ἡμῖν
the con-　us　came　to　a meeting　with us
things cerning

ἄχρι ’Αππίου φόρου καὶ Τριῶν ταβερνῶν,
as far as Appii　Forum　and　Three　Taverns,

οὓς ἰδὼν ὁ Παῦλος εὐχαριστήσας τῷ
whom seeing　-　Paul　thanking　-

θεῷ ἔλαβε θάρσος. 16 Ὅτε δὲ εἰσήλθομεν
God he took　courage.　And when　we entered

εἰς ‘Ρώμην, ἐπετράπη τῷ Παύλῳ μένειν
into　Rome,　he* permitted　-　Paul　to remain

καθ’ ἑαυτὸν σὺν τῷ φυλάσσοντι αὐτὸν
by　himself　with　¹the　³guarding　⁴him

στρατιώτῃ.
²soldier.

17 Ἐγένετο δὲ μετὰ ἡμέρας τρεῖς
And it came to pass　after　days　three

συγκαλέσασθαι αὐτὸν τοὺς ὄντας τῶν
to call together　himᵇ　the [ones]　being　of the
=he called together

’Ιουδαίων πρώτους· συνελθόντων δὲ αὐτῶν
Jews　first(chief);　and coming together　themª
　　　　　　　=and when they came together

ἔλεγεν πρὸς αὐτούς· ἐγώ, ἄνδρες ἀδελφοί,
he said　to　them:　I,　men　brothers,

οὐδὲν ἐναντίον ποιήσας τῷ λαῷ ἢ τοῖς
²nothing ³contrary ¹having done to the people or to the

ἔθεσι τοῖς πατρῴοις, δέσμιος ἐξ Ἱεροσο-
customs　-　ancestral,　a prisoner from　Jeru-

λύμων παρεδόθην εἰς τὰς χεῖρας τῶν
salem　I was delivered into the　hands　of the

‘Ρωμαίων, 18 οἵτινες ἀνακρίναντές με ἐβούλοντο
Romans,　who　having examined me were minded

* That is, the officer to whom Paul was handed over by the centurion Julius.

liberty, because there was no reason for the death penalty in my case. ¹⁹But when the Jews objected, I was compelled to appeal to Caesar—though I had no charge to bring against my nation. ²⁰For this reason therefore I have asked to see you and speak with you, since it is because of the hope of Israel that I am bound with this chain." ²¹And they said to him, "We have received no letters from Judea about you, and none of the brethren coming here has reported or spoken any evil about you. ²²But we desire to hear from you what your views are; for with regard to this sect we know that everywhere it is spoken against."

23 When they had appointed a day for him, they came to him at his lodging in great numbers. And he expounded the matter to them from morning till evening, testifying to the kingdom of God and trying to convince them about Jesus both from the law of Moses and from the prophets. ²⁴And some were convinced by what he said, while others disbelieved. ²⁵So, as they

ἀπολῦσαι διὰ τὸ μηδεμίαν αἰτίαν θανάτου
to release on account – no cause of death
of

ὑπάρχειν ἐν ἐμοί· 19 ἀντιλεγόντων δὲ
to be in me; but speaking against [this]
=when the Jews spoke

τῶν Ἰουδαίων ἠναγκάσθην ἐπικαλέσασθαι
the Jewsᵃ I was compelled to appeal to
against this

Καίσαρα, οὐχ ὡς τοῦ ἔθνους μου ἔχων
Cæsar, not as ⁴the ⁵nation ⁶of me ¹having

τι κατηγορεῖν. 20 διὰ ταύτην οὖν τὴν
²anything ³to accuse. ¹On account of ²this ⁴therefore –

αἰτίαν παρεκάλεσα ὑμᾶς ἰδεῖν καὶ προσ-
³cause I called you to see and to

λαλῆσαι· εἵνεκεν γὰρ τῆς ἐλπίδος τοῦ
speak to; for for the sake of the hope –

Ἰσραὴλ τὴν ἄλυσιν ταύτην περίκειμαι.
of Israel ²this ³chain ¹I have round [me].

21 οἱ δὲ πρὸς αὐτὸν εἶπαν· ἡμεῖς οὔτε
And they to him said: We neither

γράμματα περὶ σοῦ ἐδεξάμεθα ἀπὸ τῆς
²letters ³about ⁴thee ¹received from –

Ἰουδαίας, οὔτε παραγενόμενός τις τῶν
Judæa, nor arriving anyone of the

ἀδελφῶν ἀπήγγειλεν ἢ ἐλάλησέν τι περὶ
brothers told or spoke anything ²about

σοῦ πονηρόν. 22 ἀξιοῦμεν δὲ παρὰ σοῦ
³thee ¹evil. But we think fit from thee

ἀκοῦσαι ἃ φρονεῖς· περὶ μὲν γὰρ τῆς
to hear what thou ²concerning ³indeed ¹for –
things thinkest;

αἱρέσεως ταύτης γνωστὸν ἡμῖν ἐστιν ὅτι
⁵sect ⁴this ⁷known ⁸to us ⁶it is that

πανταχοῦ ἀντιλέγεται. 23 Ταξάμενοι δὲ
everywhere it is spoken against. And arranging

αὐτῷ ἡμέραν ἦλθον πρὸς αὐτὸν εἰς τὴν
with him a day ²came ³to ⁴him ⁵in ⁶the(his)

ξενίαν πλείονες, οἷς ἐξετίθετο διαμαρτυρ-
⁷lodging ¹more, to whom he set forth solemnly

όμενος τὴν βασιλείαν τοῦ θεοῦ, πείθων
witnessing the kingdom – of God, ²persuading

τε αὐτοὺς περὶ τοῦ Ἰησοῦ ἀπό τε τοῦ
¹and them concerning – Jesus from both the

νόμου Μωϋσέως καὶ τῶν προφητῶν, ἀπὸ
law of Moses and the prophets, from

πρωῒ ἕως ἑσπέρας. 24 καὶ οἱ μὲν
morning until evening. And some

ἐπείθοντο τοῖς λεγομένοις, 25 οἱ δὲ
were persuaded by the things being said, others

disagreed among themselves, they departed, after Paul had made one statement: "The Holy Spirit was right in saying to your fathers through Isaiah the prophet:
26 'Go to this people, and say,
You shall indeed hear but never understand,
and you shall indeed see but never perceive.
27 For this people's heart has grown dull,
and their ears are heavy of hearing,
and their eyes they have closed;
lest they should perceive with their eyes,
and hear with their ears,
and understand with their heart,
and turn for me to heal them.'
28 Let it be known to you then that this salvation of God has been sent to the Gentiles; they will listen."[z]
30 And he lived there two whole years at his own expense,[a] and welcomed all who came to him, 31 preaching the kingdom of God and teaching about the Lord Jesus Christ quite openly and unhindered.

[z] Other ancient authorities add verse 29, *And when he had said these words, the Jews departed, holding much dispute among themselves.*
[a] Or *in his own hired dwelling*

ἠπίστουν·   ἀσύμφωνοι   δὲ   ὄντες   πρὸς   ἀλλή-
disbelieved;   and ²disagreed   ¹being   with   one an-
λους   ἀπελύοντο,   εἰπόντος   τοῦ   Παύλου
other   they were dismissed,   having said   –   Paul*
=after Paul had said
ῥῆμα   ἕν,   ὅτι   καλῶς   τὸ   πνεῦμα   τὸ   ἅγιον
word   one,   Well   the   Spirit   –   Holy
ἐλάλησεν   διὰ   Ἡσαΐου   τοῦ   προφήτου   πρὸς
spoke   through   Esaias   the   prophet   to
τοὺς   πατέρας   ὑμῶν   26 λέγων·   πορεύθητι
the   fathers   of you   saying: Go thou
πρὸς   τὸν   λαὸν   τοῦτον   καὶ   εἰπόν·   ἀκοῇ
to   this people   and   say: In hearing
ἀκούσετε   καὶ   οὐ   μὴ   συνῆτε,   καὶ   βλέποντες
ye will hear   and   by no means understand, and   looking
βλέψετε   καὶ   οὐ   μὴ   ἴδητε·   27 ἐπαχύνθη
ye will look   and   by no means   see;   ²was thickened
γὰρ   ἡ   καρδία   τοῦ   λαοῦ   τούτου,   καὶ
¹for   the   heart   of this people,   and
τοῖς   ὠσὶν   βαρέως   ἤκουσαν,   καὶ   τοὺς
with the(ir) ears   heavily   they heard,   and   the
ὀφθαλμοὺς   αὐτῶν   ἐκάμμυσαν·   μήποτε   ἴδωσιν
eyes   of them   they closed;   lest at any time they see
τοῖς   ὀφθαλμοῖς   καὶ   τοῖς   ὠσὶν   ἀκούσωσιν
with the   eyes   and   with the ears   hear
καὶ   τῇ   καρδίᾳ   συνῶσιν   καὶ   ἐπιστρέψωσιν,
and with the   heart   understand   and   turn,
καὶ   ἰάσομαι   αὐτούς.   28 γνωστὸν   οὖν
and   I shall cure   them.   Known   therefore
ἔστω   ὑμῖν   ὅτι   τοῖς   ἔθνεσιν   ἀπεστάλη
let it be   to you   that   to the   nations   was sent
τοῦτο   τὸ   σωτήριον   τοῦ   θεοῦ·   αὐτοὶ   καὶ
this   –   salvation   –   of God;   and they
ἀκούσονται.‡
will hear.
30 Ἐνέμεινεν   δὲ   διετίαν   ὅλην   ἐν   ἰδίῳ
And he remained   a whole two years   in [his] own
μισθώματι,   καὶ   ἀπεδέχετο   πάντας   τοὺς
hired apartment,   and   welcomed   all   the
εἰσπορευομένους   πρὸς   αὐτόν,   31 κηρύσσων
[ones] coming in   to   him,   proclaiming
τὴν   βασιλείαν   τοῦ   θεοῦ   καὶ   διδάσκων
the   kingdom   –   of God   and   teaching
τὰ   περὶ   τοῦ   κυρίου   Ἰησοῦ   Χριστοῦ
the things   concerning   the   Lord   Jesus   Christ
μετὰ   πάσης   παρρησίας   ἀκωλύτως.
with   all   boldness   unhinderedly.

‡ Verse 29 omitted by Nestle; *cf.* RSV footnote.

CHAPTER 1

PAUL, a servant of Jesus Christ, called to be an apostle, set apart for the gospel of God ²which he promised beforehand through his prophets in the holy scriptures, ³the gospel concerning his Son, who was descended from David according to the flesh ⁴and designated Son of God in power according to the Spirit of holiness by his resurrection from the dead, Jesus Christ our Lord, ⁵through whom we have received grace and apostleship to bring about the obedience of faith for the sake of his name among all the nations, ⁶including yourselves who are called to belong to Jesus Christ; 7 To all God's beloved in Rome, who are called to be saints:

Grace to you and peace from God our Father and the Lord Jesus Christ.

8 First, I thank my God through Jesus Christ for all of you, because your faith is proclaimed in all the world. ⁹For God is my witness, whom I serve with my spirit in

1 Παῦλος   δοῦλος   Χριστοῦ   Ἰησοῦ,   κλητὸς
  Paul   a slave of Christ Jesus,   called
ἀπόστολος   ἀφωρισμένος   εἰς   εὐαγγέλιον
an apostle having been separated to   [the] gospel
θεοῦ,   2 ὃ   προεπηγγείλατο   διὰ   τῶν
of God,   which he promised beforehand through the
προφητῶν   αὐτοῦ   ἐν   γραφαῖς   ἁγίαις   3 περὶ
prophets   of him   in   writings   holy   concerning
τοῦ   υἱοῦ   αὐτοῦ   τοῦ   γενομένου   ἐκ
the   Son   of him   –   come   of
σπέρματος   Δαυὶδ   κατὰ   σάρκα,   4 τοῦ
[the] seed   of David according to [the] flesh,   –
ὁρισθέντος   υἱοῦ   θεοῦ   ἐν   δυνάμει
designated   Son   of God   in   power
κατὰ   πνεῦμα   ἁγιωσύνης   ἐξ   ἀναστάσεως
according to [the] Spirit of holiness by   a resurrection
νεκρῶν,   Ἰησοῦ   Χριστοῦ   τοῦ   κυρίου   ἡμῶν,
of dead persons, Jesus   Christ   the   Lord   of us,
5 δι'   οὗ   ἐλάβομεν   χάριν   καὶ   ἀποστολὴν
through whom we received grace   and   apostleship
εἰς   ὑπακοὴν   πίστεως   ἐν   πᾶσιν   τοῖς
for   obedience   of faith   among   all   the
ἔθνεσιν   ὑπὲρ   τοῦ   ὀνόματος   αὐτοῦ,   6 ἐν
nations on behalf of the   name   of him,   among
οἷς   ἐστε   καὶ   ὑμεῖς   κλητοὶ   Ἰησοῦ   Χριστοῦ,
whom are also   ye   called   of Jesus   Christ,
7 πᾶσιν   τοῖς   οὖσιν   ἐν   Ῥώμῃ   ἀγαπητοῖς
to all the [ones] being   in   Rome   beloved
θεοῦ,   κλητοῖς   ἁγίοις·   χάρις   ὑμῖν   καὶ
of God,   called   holy: Grace   to you   and
εἰρήνη   ἀπὸ   θεοῦ   πατρὸς   ἡμῶν   καὶ   κυρίου
peace   from   God   [the] Father of us   and   Lord
Ἰησοῦ   Χριστοῦ.
Jesus   Christ.
8 Πρῶτον   μὲν   εὐχαριστῶ   τῷ   θεῷ   μου
Firstly   –   I thank   the   God of me
διὰ   Ἰησοῦ   Χριστοῦ   περὶ   πάντων   ὑμῶν,
through Jesus   Christ   concerning all   you,
ὅτι   ἡ   πίστις   ὑμῶν   καταγγέλλεται   ἐν
because the   faith   of you   is being announced   in
ὅλῳ   τῷ   κόσμῳ.   9 μάρτυς   γάρ   μού
all   the   world.   For witness of me
ἐστιν   ὁ   θεός,   ᾧ   λατρεύω   ἐν   τῷ   πνεύματί
is   –   God, whom I serve   in   the   spirit

the gospel of his Son, that without ceasing I mention you always in my prayers, ¹⁰asking that somehow by God's will I may now at last succeed in coming to you. ¹¹For I long to see you, that I may impart to you some spiritual gift to strengthen you, ¹²that is, that we may be mutually encouraged by each other's faith, both yours and mine. ¹³I want you to know, brethren, that I have often intended to come to you (but thus far have been prevented), in order that I may reap some harvest among you as well as among the rest of the Gentiles. ¹⁴I am under obligation both to Greeks and to barbarians, both to the wise and to the foolish: ¹⁵so I am eager to preach the gospel to you also who are in Rome.

16 For I am not ashamed of the gospel: it is the power of God for salvation to every one who has faith, to the Jew first and also to the Greek. ¹⁷For in it the righteousness of God is revealed through faith for faith; as it is written,

μου	ἐν	τῷ	εὐαγγελίῳ	τοῦ	υἱοῦ	αὐτοῦ,
of me	in	the	gospel	of the	Son	of him,

ὡς	ἀδιαλείπτως	μνείαν	ὑμῶν	ποιοῦμαι
how	unceasingly	mention	of you	I make

10 πάντοτε	ἐπὶ	τῶν	προσευχῶν	μου,	
always	on(in)	the	prayers	of me,	

δεόμενος	εἴ	πως	ἤδη	ποτὲ	εὐοδω-
requesting	if	somehow	now	at some time	I shall have

θήσομαι	ἐν	τῷ	θελήματι	τοῦ	θεοῦ	ἐλθεῖν
a happy journey in	the	will	–	of God	to come	

πρὸς	ὑμᾶς.	11 ἐπιποθῶ	γὰρ	ἰδεῖν ὑμᾶς,
unto	you.	For I long		to see you,

ἵνα	τι	μεταδῶ	χάρισμα	ὑμῖν	πνευματικὸν
that	²some	¹I may impart	⁴gift	⁵to you	³spiritual

εἰς	τὸ	στηριχθῆναι	ὑμᾶς,	12 τοῦτο	δέ
for	the	to be established	you,ᵇ	and this	
	=that ye may be established,				

ἐστιν	συμπαρακληθῆναι	ἐν	ὑμῖν	διὰ	τῆς
is	to be encouraged *with*	among	you	through	¹the

ἐν	ἀλλήλοις	πίστεως	ὑμῶν	τε	καὶ	ἐμοῦ.
²in	⁴one another	³faith	⁶of you	⁵both	⁷and	⁸of me.

13 οὐ	θέλω	δὲ	ὑμᾶς	ἀγνοεῖν,	ἀδελφοί,
²not	³I wish		¹But	you	to be ignorant,	brothers,

ὅτι	πολλάκις	προεθέμην	ἐλθεῖν	πρὸς ὑμᾶς,
that	often	I purposed	to come	unto you,

καὶ	ἐκωλύθην	ἄχρι	τοῦ	δεῦρο,	ἵνα τινὰ
and	was hindered	until	the	present,	that some

καρπὸν	σχῶ	καὶ	ἐν ὑμῖν	καθὼς καὶ
fruit	I may have	also	among you	as indeed

ἐν	τοῖς	λοιποῖς	ἔθνεσιν. 14 Ἕλλησίν
among	the	remaining	nations. ²to Greeks

τε	καὶ	βαρβάροις,	σοφοῖς	τε	καὶ ἀνοήτοις
¹Both	³and	⁴to foreigners,	⁶to wise men	⁵both	⁷and ⁸to foolish

ὀφειλέτης	εἰμί·	15 οὕτως	τὸ	κατ' ἐμὲ
¹ᵇa debtor	⁹I am;	so		as far as in me liest†

πρόθυμον	καὶ	ὑμῖν	τοῖς	ἐν Ῥώμῃ
[I am] eager	²also	³to you	⁴the [ones]	⁵in ⁶Rome

εὐαγγελίσασθαι.	16 οὐ	γὰρ ἐπαισχύνομαι
¹to preach.		For I am not ashamed of

τὸ	εὐαγγέλιον·	δύναμις	γὰρ	θεοῦ ἐστιν
the	gospel;	²power	¹for	of God it is

εἰς	σωτηρίαν	παντὶ	τῷ πιστεύοντι, Ἰουδαίῳ
to	salvation	to everyone	believing, ²to Jew

τε	πρῶτον	καὶ	Ἕλληνι. 17 δικαιοσύνη
¹both	firstly	and	to Greek. a righteousness

γὰρ	θεοῦ	ἐν	αὐτῷ	ἀποκαλύπτεται	ἐκ
For	of God	in	it	is revealed	from

πίστεως	εἰς	πίστιν,	καθὼς γέγραπται·
faith	to	faith,	as it has been written:

"He who through faith is righteous shall live."[a] 18 For the wrath of God is revealed from heaven against all ungodliness and wickedness of men who by their wickedness suppress the truth. 19 For what can be known about God is plain to them, because God has shown it to them. 20 Ever since the creation of the world his invisible nature, namely, his eternal power and deity, has been clearly perceived in the things that have been made. So they are without excuse; 21 for although they knew God they did not honor him as God or give thanks to him, but they became futile in their thinking and their senseless minds were darkened. 22 Claiming to be wise, they became fools, 23 and exchanged the glory of the immortal God for images resembling mortal man or birds or animals or reptiles.

24 Therefore God gave them up in the lusts of their hearts to impurity, to the dishonoring of their bodies among themselves, 25 because they exchanged the truth about God for a lie and

[a] Or The righteous shall live by faith

ὁ δὲ δίκαιος ἐκ πίστεως ζήσεται.
Now the just man by faith will live.

18 Ἀποκαλύπτεται γὰρ ὀργὴ θεοῦ ἀπ'
For [4]is revealed [1][the] [2]wrath [3]of God from

οὐρανοῦ ἐπὶ πᾶσαν ἀσέβειαν καὶ ἀδικίαν
heaven against all impiety and unrighteousness

ἀνθρώπων τῶν τὴν ἀλήθειαν ἐν ἀδικίᾳ
of men – [2]the [3]truth [4]in [5]unrighteousness

κατεχόντων, 19 διότι τὸ γνωστὸν τοῦ θεοῦ
[1]holding fast, because the thing known – of God

φανερόν ἐστιν ἐν αὐτοῖς· ὁ θεὸς γὰρ αὐτοῖς
manifest is among them; – for God to them

ἐφανέρωσεν. 20 τὰ γὰρ ἀόρατα αὐτοῦ
manifested [it]. For the invisible things of him

ἀπὸ κτίσεως κόσμου τοῖς ποιήμασιν
[2]from [3][the] [4]creation [5]of [the] world [7]by the [8]things made

νοούμενα καθορᾶται, ἥ τε
[6]being understood [1]is(are) clearly seen, [10]the [9]both

ἀΐδιος αὐτοῦ δύναμις καὶ θειότης, εἰς
[11]everlasting [15]of him [12]power [13]and [14]divinity, for

τὸ εἶναι αὐτοὺς ἀναπολογήτους, 21 διότι
the to be them[b] without excuse, because
=so that they are

γνόντες τὸν θεὸν οὐχ ὡς θεὸν ἐδόξασαν
knowing – God [2]not [3]as [4]God [1]they glorified [him]

ἢ ηὐχαρίστησαν, ἀλλὰ ἐματαιώθησαν ἐν
[5]or [6]thanked [him], but became vain in

τοῖς διαλογισμοῖς αὐτῶν, καὶ ἐσκοτίσθη
the reasonings of them, and [5]was darkened

ἡ ἀσύνετος αὐτῶν καρδία. 22 φάσκοντες
[1]the [2]undiscerning [4]of them [3]heart. Asserting

εἶναι σοφοὶ ἐμωράνθησαν, 23 καὶ ἤλλαξαν
to be wise they became foolish, and changed

τὴν δόξαν τοῦ ἀφθάρτου θεοῦ ἐν ὁμοιώματι
the glory of the incorruptible God in[to] a likeness

εἰκόνος φθαρτοῦ ἀνθρώπου καὶ πετεινῶν
of an image of corruptible man and birds

καὶ τετραπόδων καὶ ἑρπετῶν· 24 διὸ
and quadrupeds and reptiles; wherefore

παρέδωκεν αὐτοὺς ὁ θεὸς ἐν ταῖς
[2]gave up [3]them – [1]God in the

ἐπιθυμίαις τῶν καρδιῶν αὐτῶν εἰς ἀκαθαρ-
desires of the hearts of them to unclean-

σίαν τοῦ ἀτιμάζεσθαι τὰ σώματα αὐτῶν
ness – to be dishonoured[d] the bodies of them

ἐν αὐτοῖς. 25 Οἵτινες μετήλλαξαν τὴν
among them[selves]. Who changed the

ἀλήθειαν τοῦ θεοῦ ἐν τῷ ψεύδει, καὶ
truth – of God in[to] the lie, and

worshiped and served the creature rather than the Creator, who is blessed for ever! Amen. 26 For this reason God gave them up to dishonorable passions. Their women exchanged natural relations for unnatural, 27 and the men likewise gave up natural relations with women and were consumed with passion for one another, men committing shameless acts with men and receiving in their own persons the due penalty for their error. 28 And since they did not see fit to acknowledge God, God gave them up to a base mind and to improper conduct. 29 They were filled with all all manner of wickedness, evil, covetousness, malice. Full of envy, murder, strife, deceit, malignity, they are gossips, 30 slanderers, haters of God, insolent, haughty, boastful, inventors of evil, disobedient to parents, 31 foolish, faithless, heartless, ruthless. 32 Though they know

ἐσεβάσθησαν καὶ ἐλάτρευσαν τῇ κτίσει
worshipped and served the creature
παρὰ τὸν κτίσαντα, ὅς ἐστιν εὐλογητὸς
rather the [one] having created, who is blessed
than
εἰς τοὺς αἰῶνας· ἀμήν. 26 διὰ τοῦτο
unto the ages: Amen. Therefore
παρέδωκεν αὐτοὺς ὁ θεὸς εἰς πάθη
²gave up ³them – ¹God to passions
ἀτιμίας· αἵ τε γὰρ θήλειαι αὐτῶν
of dishonour; ³the ²even ¹for females of them
μετήλλαξαν τὴν φυσικὴν χρῆσιν εἰς τὴν
changed the natural use to the [use]
παρὰ φύσιν, 27 ὁμοίως τε καὶ οἱ ἄρσενες
against nature, ²likewise ¹and also the males
ἀφέντες τὴν φυσικὴν χρῆσιν τῆς θηλείας
leaving the natural use of the female
ἐξεκαύθησαν ἐν τῇ ὀρέξει αὐτῶν εἰς
burned in the desire of them toward
ἀλλήλους, ἄρσενες ἐν ἄρσεσιν τὴν
one another, males among males ²the
ἀσχημοσύνην κατεργαζόμενοι καὶ τὴν
³unseemliness ¹working and ⁴the
ἀντιμισθίαν ἣν ἔδει τῆς πλάνης αὐτῶν
⁵requital ⁶which ¹⁰behoved ⁶of the ⁷error ⁸of them
ἐν ἑαυτοῖς ἀπολαμβάνοντες. 28 Καὶ
²in ³themselves ¹receiving back. And
καθὼς οὐκ ἐδοκίμασαν τὸν θεὸν ἔχειν
as they thought not fit – God to have
ἐν ἐπιγνώσει, παρέδωκεν αὐτοὺς ὁ θεὸς
in knowledge, ²gave up ³them – ¹God
εἰς ἀδόκιμον νοῦν, ποιεῖν τὰ μὴ καθήκοντα,
to a reprobate mind, to do the not being proper,
things
29 πεπληρωμένους πάσῃ ἀδικίᾳ πονηρίᾳ
having been filled with all unrighteousness wickedness
πλεονεξίᾳ κακίᾳ, μεστοὺς φθόνου φόνου
covetousness evil, full of envy of murder
ἔριδος δόλου κακοηθείας, ψιθυριστάς,
of strife of guile of malignity, whisperers,*
30 καταλάλους, θεοστυγεῖς, ὑβριστάς, ὑπερ-
railers, God-haters, insolent, arro-
ηφάνους, ἀλαζόνας, ἐφευρετὰς κακῶν,
gant, boasters, inventors of evil things,
γονεῦσιν ἀπειθεῖς, 31 ἀσυνέτους, ἀσυνθέτους,
to parents disobedient, undiscerning, faithless,
ἀστόργους, ἀνελεήμονας· 32 οἵτινες τὸ
without unmerciful; who ²the
natural affection,

* " In a bad sense " (Abbott-Smith).

606 — ROMANS 1, 2

God's decree that those who do such things deserve to die, they not only do them but approve those who practice them.

δικαίωμα τοῦ θεοῦ ἐπιγνόντες, ὅτι οἱ
²ordinance – ⁴of God ¹knowing, that the
τὰ τοιαῦτα πράσσοντες ἄξιοι θανάτου
the ²such things ¹[ones] practising worthy of death
εἰσίν, οὐ μόνον αὐτὰ ποιοῦσιν, ἀλλὰ
are, not only them do, but
καὶ συνευδοκοῦσιν τοῖς πράσσουσιν.
also consent to the [ones] practising.

CHAPTER 2

THEREFORE you have no excuse, O man, whoever you are, when you judge another; for in passing judgment upon him you condemn yourself, because you, the judge, are doing the very same things. ²We know that the judgment of God rightly falls upon those who do such things. ³Do you suppose, O man, that when you judge those who do such things and yet do them yourself, you will escape the judgment of God? ⁴Or do you presume upon the riches of his kindness and forbearance and patience? Do you not know that God's kindness is meant to lead you to repentance? ⁵But by your hard and impenitent heart you are storing up wrath for yourself on the day of wrath when God's righteous judgment will be revealed. ⁶For he will render to every man according to his works:

2 Διὸ ἀναπολόγητος εἶ, ὦ ἄνθρωπε
Wherefore inexcusable thou art, O man
πᾶς ὁ κρίνων· ἐν ᾧ γὰρ κρίνεις τὸν
everyone judging; ²in ³what ¹for thou judgest the
ἕτερον, σεαυτὸν κατακρίνεις· τὰ γὰρ αὐτὰ
other, thyself thou for the same
condemnest; things
πράσσεις ὁ κρίνων. 2 οἴδαμεν δὲ ὅτι τὸ
thou the judging. But we know that the
practisest [one]
κρίμα τοῦ θεοῦ ἐστιν κατὰ ἀλήθειαν ἐπὶ
judg- – of is accord- truth on
ment God ing to
τοὺς τὰ τοιαῦτα πράσσοντας. 3 λογίζῃ
the the ²such things ¹[ones] practising. reckonest thou
δὲ τοῦτο, ὦ ἄνθρωπε ὁ κρίνων τοὺς
And this, O man the judging the
[one] [ones]
τὰ τοιαῦτα πράσσοντας καὶ ποιῶν αὐτά,
the such things practising and doing them,
ὅτι σὺ ἐκφεύξῃ τὸ κρίμα τοῦ θεοῦ;
that thou wilt escape the judgment – of God?
4 ἢ τοῦ πλούτου τῆς χρηστότητος αὐτοῦ
or the riches of the kindness of him
καὶ τῆς ἀνοχῆς καὶ τῆς μακροθυμίας
and the forbearance and the longsuffering
καταφρονεῖς, ἀγνοῶν ὅτι τὸ χρηστὸν τοῦ
despisest thou, not knowing that the kindness –
θεοῦ εἰς μετάνοιάν σε ἄγει; 5 κατὰ δὲ
of God to repentance thee leads? but according to
τὴν σκληρότητά σου καὶ ἀμετανόητον
the hardness of thee and impenitent
καρδίαν θησαυρίζεις σεαυτῷ ὀργὴν ἐν
heart treasurest for thyself wrath in
ἡμέρᾳ ὀργῆς καὶ ἀποκαλύψεως δικαιοκρισίας
a day of wrath and of revelation of a righteous
judgment
τοῦ θεοῦ, 6 ὃς ἀποδώσει ἑκάστῳ κατὰ τὰ
– of God, who will requite to each man accord- the
ing to

⁷to those who by patience in well-doing seek for glory and honor and immortality, he will give eternal life; ⁸but for those who are factious and do not obey the truth, but obey wickedness, there will be wrath and fury. ⁹There will be tribulation and distress for every human being who does evil, the Jew first and also the Greek, ¹⁰but glory and honor and peace for every one who does good, the Jew first and also the Greek. ¹¹For God shóws no partiality.

12 All who have sinned without the law will also perish without the law, and all who have sinned under the law will be judged by the law. ¹³For it is not the hearers of the law who are righteous before God, but the doers of the law who will be justified. ¹⁴When Gentiles who have not the law do by nature what the law requires, they are a law to themselves, even though they do not have the law. ¹⁵They show that what the law requires is written on their hearts, while their conscience also bears witness and

ἔργα   αὐτοῦ·   7 τοῖς   μὲν   καθ'   ὑπομονὴν
works   of him :   to the   on   ²by   ²endurance
                           [ones] one hand

ἔργου   ἀγαθοῦ   δόξαν   καὶ   τιμὴν   καὶ
⁵work   ⁴of(in) good   ⁶glory   ⁷and   ⁸honour   ⁹and

ἀφθαρσίαν   ζητοῦσιν   ζωὴν   αἰώνιον·
¹⁰incorruption   ¹seeking   ¹²life   ¹¹eternal;

8 τοῖς   δὲ   ἐξ   ἐριθείας   καὶ   ἀπειθοῦσι   τῇ
to the [ones]   of   self-seeking   and   disobeying   the
on the other

ἀληθείᾳ   πειθομένοις   δὲ   τῇ   ἀδικίᾳ,   ὀργὴ
truth   ²obeying   ¹but   -   unrighteousness, wrath

καὶ   θυμός. 9 θλῖψις   καὶ   στενοχωρία   ἐπὶ
and   anger.   Affliction and   anguish   on

πᾶσαν   ψυχὴν   ἀνθρώπου   τοῦ   κατεργαζομένου
every   soul   of man   -   working

τὸ   κακόν,   Ἰουδαίου   τε   πρῶτον   καὶ
the   evil,   both of Jew   firstly   and

Ἕλληνος·   10 δόξα   δὲ   καὶ   τιμὴ   καὶ
of Greek;   but glory   and   honour   and

εἰρήνη   παντὶ   τῷ   ἐργαζομένῳ   τὸ   ἀγαθόν,
peace   to everyone   working   the   good,

Ἰουδαίῳ   τε   πρῶτον   καὶ   Ἕλληνι.   11 οὐ
both to Jew   firstly   and   to Greek.   not

γάρ   ἐστιν   προσωπολημψία   παρὰ   τῷ   θεῷ.
For   is   respect of persons   with   -   God.

12 Ὅσοι   γὰρ   ἀνόμως   ἥμαρτον,   ἀνόμως
For as many as   without law   sinned,   without law

καὶ   ἀπολοῦνται·   καὶ   ὅσοι   ἐν   νόμῳ
also   will perish;   and   as   in   law
                                   many as (under)

ἥμαρτον,   διὰ   νόμου   κριθήσονται·   13 οὐ
sinned,   through   law   will be judged;   ²not

γὰρ   οἱ   ἀκροαταὶ   νόμου   δίκαιοι   παρὰ
¹for   the   hearers   of law   [are] just   with

[τῷ]   θεῷ,   ἀλλ'   οἱ   ποιηταὶ   νόμου
-       God,   but   the   doers   of law

δικαιωθήσονται.   14 ὅταν   γὰρ   ἔθνη   τὰ
will be justified.   For whenever   nations   -

μὴ   νόμον   ἔχοντα   φύσει   τὰ   τοῦ   νόμου
¹not   ³law   ²having   by nature the things of the   law

ποιῶσιν,   οὗτοι   νόμον   μὴ   ἔχοντες   ἑαυτοῖς
do,   these   ³law   ¹not   ²having   to themselves

εἰσιν   νόμος· 15 οἵτινες   ἐνδείκνυνται   τὸ
are   a law;   who   show   the

ἔργον   τοῦ   νόμου   γραπτὸν   ἐν   ταῖς   καρδίαις
work   of the   law   written   in   the   hearts

αὐτῶν,   συμμαρτυρούσης   αὐτῶν   τῆς   συνει-
of them,   witnessing with   of them   the   con-
=while their conscience witnesses with and their

their conflicting thoughts accuse or perhaps excuse them [16] on that day when, according to my gospel, God judges the secrets of men by Christ Jesus.

17 But if you call yourself a Jew and rely upon the law and boast of your relation to God [18] and know his will and approve what is excellent, because you are instructed in the law, [19] and if you are sure that you are a guide to the blind, a light to those who are in darkness, [20] a corrector of the foolish, a teacher of children, having in the law the embodiment of knowledge and truth—[21] you then who teach others, will you not teach yourself? While you preach against stealing, do you steal? [22] You who say that one must not commit adultery, do you commit adultery? You who abhor idols, do you rob temples? [23] You who boast in the law, do you dishonor God by breaking the law? [24] For, as it is written, "The name of God is blasphemed among the Gentiles because of you."

25 Circumcision indeed is of value if you

δήσεως καὶ μεταξὺ ἀλλήλων τῶν λογισμῶν
science and between one another the thoughts
thoughts among themselves accuse or even excuse,

κατηγορούντων ἢ καὶ ἀπολογουμένων, 16 ἐν
accusing or even excusing,[a] in

ἢ ἡμέρᾳ κρίνει ὁ θεὸς τὰ κρυπτὰ τῶν
what day judges – God the hidden things –

ἀνθρώπων κατὰ τὸ εὐαγγέλιόν μου διὰ
of men according to the gospel of me through

Χριστοῦ Ἰησοῦ. 17 Εἰ δὲ σὺ Ἰουδαῖος
Christ Jesus. But if thou [2]a Jew

ἐπονομάζῃ καὶ ἐπαναπαύῃ νόμῳ καὶ
[1]art named and restest on law and

καυχᾶσαι ἐν θεῷ 18 καὶ γινώσκεις τὸ
boastest in God and knowest the

θέλημα καὶ δοκιμάζεις τὰ διαφέροντα
will and approvest the things excelling

κατηχούμενος ἐκ τοῦ νόμου, 19 πέποιθάς τε
being instructed out of the law, and having persuaded

σεαυτὸν ὁδηγὸν εἶναι τυφλῶν, φῶς
thyself a guide to be of blind a light
[persons],

τῶν ἐν σκότει, 20 παιδευτὴν ἀφρόνων,
of the in darkness, an instructor of foolish
[ones] [persons],

διδάσκαλον νηπίων, ἔχοντα τὴν μόρφωσιν
a teacher of infants, having the form

τῆς γνώσεως καὶ τῆς ἀληθείας ἐν τῷ
– of knowledge and of the truth in the

νόμῳ· 21 ὁ οὖν διδάσκων ἕτερον σεαυτὸν
law: the there- teaching another thyself
[one] fore

οὐ διδάσκεις; ὁ κηρύσσων μὴ κλέπτειν
teachest thou not? the [one] proclaiming not to steal

κλέπτεις; 22 ὁ λέγων μὴ μοιχεύειν
stealest thou? the [one] saying not to commit adultery

μοιχεύεις; ὁ βδελυσσόμενος τὰ εἴδωλα
dost thou com- the detesting the idols
mit adultery? [one]

ἱεροσυλεῖς; 23 ὃς ἐν νόμῳ καυχᾶσαι, διὰ
dost thou rob who in law boastest, through
temples?

τῆς παραβάσεως τοῦ νόμου τὸν θεὸν
– transgression of the law – [2]God

ἀτιμάζεις; 24 τὸ γὰρ ὄνομα τοῦ θεοῦ
[1]dishonourest thou? for the name – of God

δι᾽ ὑμᾶς βλασφημεῖται ἐν τοῖς ἔθνεσιν,
because you is blasphemed among the nations,
of

καθὼς γέγραπται. 25 περιτομὴ μὲν γὰρ
as it has been written. circumcision indeed For

obey the law; but if you break the law, your circumcision becomes uncircumcision. ²⁶So, if a man who is uncircumcised keeps the precepts of the law, will not his uncircumcision be regarded as circumcision? ²⁷Then those who are physically uncircumcised but keep the law will condemn you who have the written code and circumcision but break the law. ²⁸For he is not a real Jew who is one outwardly, nor is true circumcision something external and physical. ²⁹He is a Jew who is one inwardly, and real circumcision is a matter of the heart, spiritual and not literal. His praise is not from men but from God.

CHAPTER 3

THEN what advantage has the Jew? Or what is the value of circumcision? ²Much in every way. To begin with, the Jews are entrusted with the oracles of God. ³What if some were unfaithful? Does their faithlessness nullify the faithfulness of God? ⁴By no means! Let God be true though every man be false, as it is written, "That thou mayest be justified in thy words,

ὠφελεῖ ἐὰν νόμον πράσσῃς· ἐὰν δὲ
profits if law thou practisest; but if

παραβάτης νόμου ᾖς, ἡ περιτομή σου
a transgressor of law thou art, the circumcision of thee

ἀκροβυστία γέγονεν. 26 ἐὰν οὖν ἡ ἀκρο-
uncircumcision has become. If therefore the uncir-

βυστία τὰ δικαιώματα τοῦ νόμου φυλάσσῃ,
cumcision the ordinances of the law keeps,

οὐχ ἡ ἀκροβυστία αὐτοῦ εἰς περιτομὴν
not the uncircumcision of him for circumcision

λογισθήσεται; 27 καὶ κρινεῖ ἡ ἐκ φύσεως
will be reckoned? and ⁸will judge ¹the ³by ⁴nature

ἀκροβυστία τὸν νόμον τελοῦσα σὲ τὸν
²uncircumcision ⁶the ⁷law ⁵keeping ⁸thee ¹⁰the

διὰ γράμματος καὶ περιτομῆς παραβάτην
¹³through ¹⁴letter ¹⁵and ¹⁶circumcision ¹¹transgressor

νόμου. 28 οὐ γὰρ ὁ ἐν τῷ φανερῷ
¹²of law. For ²not ³the ⁵in ⁶the ⁷open

Ἰουδαῖός ἐστιν, οὐδὲ ἡ ἐν τῷ φανερῷ
⁴Jew ¹he is, nor ¹the ³in ⁴the ⁵open

ἐν σαρκὶ περιτομή· 29 ἀλλ' ὁ ἐν τῷ
⁶in ⁷flesh ²circumcision; but ¹the ³in ⁴the

κρυπτῷ Ἰουδαῖος, καὶ περιτομὴ καρδίας
⁵secret ²Jew [is], and circumcision [is] of heart

ἐν πνεύματι οὐ γράμματι, οὗ ὁ ἔπαινος
in spirit not letter, of the praise [is]
whom

οὐκ ἐξ ἀνθρώπων ἀλλ' ἐκ τοῦ θεοῦ.
not from men but from – God.

3 Τί οὖν τὸ περισσὸν τοῦ Ἰουδαίου,
What therefore the advantage of the Jew,

ἢ τίς ἡ ὠφέλεια τῆς περιτομῆς; 2 πολὺ
or what the profit – of circumcision? Much

κατὰ πάντα τρόπον. πρῶτον μὲν [γὰρ]
by every way. ³Firstly ²indeed ¹for

ὅτι ἐπιστεύθησαν τὰ λόγια τοῦ θεοῦ.
because they were the oracles – of God.
entrusted [with]

3 τί γάρ; εἰ ἠπίστησάν τινες, μὴ ἡ
For what? If ²disbelieved ¹some, not the

ἀπιστία αὐτῶν τὴν πίστιν τοῦ θεοῦ
unbelief of them the faith – of God

καταργήσει; 4 μὴ γένοιτο· γινέσθω δὲ
will destroy? May it not be; but let be

ὁ θεὸς ἀληθής, πᾶς δὲ ἄνθρωπος ψεύστης,
– God true, and every man a liar,

καθάπερ γέγραπται· ὅπως ἂν δικαιωθῇς
as it has been So as – thou mayest
written: be justified

and prevail when thou art judged."
⁵But if our wickedness serves to show the justice of God, what shall we say? That God is unjust to inflict wrath on us? (I speak in a human way.) ⁶By no means! For then how could God judge the world? ⁷But if through my falsehood God's truthfulness abounds to his glory, why am I still being condemned as a sinner? ⁸And why not do evil that good may come?—as some people slanderously charge us with saying. Their condemnation is just.
9 What then? Are we Jews any better off?[b] No, not at all; for I have already charged that all men, both Jews and Greeks, are under the power of sin, ¹⁰as it is written:
"None is righteous, no, not one;
¹¹no one understands, no one seeks for God.
¹²All have turned aside, together they have gone wrong; no one does good, not even one."
¹³"Their throat is an open grave,

[b] Or at any disadvantage?

ἐν τοῖς λόγοις σου καὶ νικήσεις ἐν
in the sayings of thee and wilt overcome in
τῷ κρίνεσθαί σε. 5 εἰ δὲ ἡ ἀδικία
the to be judged thee.[be] Now if the unright-
=when thou art judged. eousness
ἡμῶν θεοῦ δικαιοσύνην συνίστησιν, τί
of us ³of God ²a righteousness ¹commends, what
ἐροῦμεν; μὴ ἄδικος ὁ θεὸς ὁ ἐπιφέρων
shall we say? not unrighteous – God the [one] inflicting
τὴν ὀργήν; κατὰ ἄνθρωπον λέγω. 6 μὴ
– wrath? according to man I say. not
γένοιτο· ἐπεὶ πῶς κρινεῖ ὁ θεὸς τὸν
May it be; otherwise how will judge – God the
κόσμον; 7 εἰ δὲ ἡ ἀλήθεια τοῦ θεοῦ
world? But if the truth – of God
ἐν τῷ ἐμῷ ψεύσματι ἐπερίσσευσεν εἰς
by – my lie abounded to
τὴν δόξαν αὐτοῦ, τί ἔτι κἀγὼ ὡς
the glory of him, why still I also as
ἁμαρτωλὸς κρίνομαι; 8 καὶ μὴ καθὼς
a sinner am judged? and not as
βλασφημούμεθα καὶ καθώς φασίν τινες
we are blasphemed and as ²say ¹some
ἡμᾶς λέγειν ὅτι ποιήσωμεν τὰ κακὰ
us to say[,] – Let us do – evil things
=that we say,
ἵνα ἔλθῃ τὰ ἀγαθά; ὧν τὸ κρίμα
that may come – good things? of whom the judgment
ἔνδικόν ἐστιν. 9 Τί οὖν; προεχόμεθα;
just is. What therefore? Do we excel?
οὐ πάντως· προῃτιασάμεθα γὰρ Ἰουδαίους
not at all; for we previously accused ²Jews
τε καὶ Ἕλληνας πάντας ὑφ᾽ ἁμαρτίαν
¹both and Greeks all under sin
εἶναι, 10 καθὼς γέγραπται ὅτι οὐκ ἔστιν
to be, as it has been written[,] – There is not
δίκαιος οὐδὲ εἷς, οὐκ ἔστιν ὁ
a righteous man not one, there is not the [one]
συνίων, 11 οὐκ ἔστιν ὁ ἐκζητῶν τὸν θεόν·
under- there is not the seeking – God;
standing, [one]
12 πάντες ἐξέκλιναν, ἅμα ἠχρεώθησαν·
all turned away, together became unprofitable;
οὐκ ἔστιν ὁ ποιῶν χρηστότητα, οὐκ
there is not the [one] doing kindness, not
ἔστιν ἕως ἑνός. 13 τάφος ἀνεῳγμένος
there is so much as one. A grave having been opened

they use their tongues to deceive."
"The venom of asps is under their lips."
14 "Their mouth is full of curses and bitterness,"
15 "Their feet are swift to shed blood,
16 in their paths are ruin and misery,
17 and the way of peace they do not know."
18 "There is no fear of God before their eyes."
19 Now we know that whatever the law says it speaks to those who are under the law, so that every mouth may be stopped, and the whole world may be held accountable to God. 20 For no human being will be justified in his sight by works of the law, since through the law comes knowledge of sin.
21 But now the righteousness of God has been manifested apart from law, although the law and the prophets bear witness to it, 22 the righteousness of God through faith in Jesus Christ for all who believe. For there is no distinction; 23 since all have sinned and fall short of the glory of God, 24 they are justified by his grace as a gift, through the redemption which is in Christ Jesus,

ὁ	λάρυγξ	αὐτῶν,	ταῖς	γλώσσαις	αὐτῶν
the	throat	of them,	with the	tongues	of them

ἐδολιοῦσαν,	ἰὸς	ἀσπίδων	ὑπὸ	τὰ	χείλη
they acted deceitfully,	poison	of asps	under	the	lips

αὐτῶν·	14	ὧν	τὸ	στόμα	ἀρᾶς	καὶ	πικρίας
of them;		of whom the		mouth	[2]of cursing	[3]and	[4]bitterness

γέμει·	15	ὀξεῖς	οἱ	πόδες	αὐτῶν	ἐκχέαι
[1]is full;		swift	the	feet	of them	to shed

αἷμα,	16	σύντριμμα	καὶ	ταλαιπωρία	ἐν
blood,		ruin	and	misery	in

ταῖς	ὁδοῖς	αὐτῶν,	17	καὶ	ὁδὸν	εἰρήνης
the	ways	of them,		and	a way	of peace

οὐκ	ἔγνωσαν.	18	οὐκ	ἔστιν	φόβος	θεοῦ
they knew not.			There is not		fear	of God

ἀπέναντι	τῶν	ὀφθαλμῶν	αὐτῶν.	19	οἴδαμεν
before	the	eyes	of them.		we know

δὲ	ὅτι	ὅσα	ὁ	νόμος	λέγει	τοῖς	ἐν	τῷ
But	that	whatever the		law	says	to the [ones]	in	the

νόμῳ	λαλεῖ,	ἵνα	πᾶν	στόμα	φραγῇ	καὶ
law	it speaks, in order that every		mouth	may be stopped and

ὑπόδικος	γένηται	πᾶς	ὁ	κόσμος	τῷ
[5]under judgment	[4]may become	[1]all	[2]the	[3]world	−

θεῷ·	20	διότι	ἐξ	ἔργων	νόμου	οὐ
to God;		because	by	works	of law	not

δικαιωθήσεται	πᾶσα	σὰρξ	ἐνώπιον	αὐτοῦ·
will be justified	all	flesh*	before	him;

διὰ	γὰρ	νόμου	ἐπίγνωσις	ἁμαρτίας.
for through		law [is]	full knowledge	of sin.

21	Νυνὶ	δὲ	χωρὶς	νόμου	δικαιοσύνη
	But now		without	law	a righteousness

θεοῦ	πεφανέρωται,	μαρτυρουμένη	ὑπὸ	τοῦ
of God has been manifested,		being witnessed	by	the

νόμου	καὶ	τῶν	προφητῶν,	22	δικαιοσύνη
law	and	the	prophets,		[2]a righteousness

δὲ	θεοῦ	διὰ	πίστεως	['Ιησοῦ]	Χριστοῦ,
[1]and	of God	through	faith	of(in) Jesus	Christ,

εἰς	πάντας	τοὺς	πιστεύοντας·	οὐ	γὰρ
to	all	the [ones]	believing;	for not

ἔστιν	διαστολή·	23	πάντες	γὰρ	ἥμαρτον
there is	difference;		for all		sinned

καὶ	ὑστεροῦνται	τῆς	δόξης	τοῦ	θεοῦ,
and	come short	of the	glory	−	of God,

24	δικαιούμενοι	δωρεὰν	τῇ	αὐτοῦ	χάριτι
	being justified	freely	by the	of him	grace

διὰ	τῆς	ἀπολυτρώσεως	τῆς	ἐν	Χριστῷ
through the		redemption	−	in	Christ

* That is, no flesh will be justified . . .

²⁵whom God put forward as an expiation by his blood, to be received by faith. This was to show God's righteousness, because in his divine forbearance he had passed over former sins; ²⁶it was to prove at the present time that he himself is righteous and that he justifies him who has faith in Jesus.

27 Then what becomes of our boasting? It is excluded. On what principle? On the principle of works? No, but on the principle of faith. ²⁸For we hold that a man is justified by faith apart from works of law. ²⁹Or is God the God of Jews only? Is he not the God of Gentiles also? Yes, of Gentiles also, ³⁰since God is one; and he will justify the circumcised on the ground of their faith and the uncircumcised through their faith. ³¹Do we then overthrow the law by this faith? By no means! On the contrary, we uphold the law.

CHAPTER 4

WHAT then shall we say aboutᶜ Abraham, our forefather according to the flesh? ²For if Abraham was justified by works, he has something to boast about, but not before God. ³For what does the

ᶜ Other ancient authorities read *was gained by*

'Ιησοῦ· 25 ὃν προέθετο ὁ θεὸς ἱλαστήριον
Jesus; whom set forth – God a propitiation
διὰ πίστεως ἐν τῷ αὐτοῦ αἵματι, εἰς
through faith by the of him blood, for
ἔνδειξιν τῆς δικαιοσύνης αὐτοῦ διὰ τὴν
a showing of the righteousness of him because of the
forth
πάρεσιν τῶν προγεγονότων ἁμαρτημάτων
passing by of the ²having previously ¹sins
occurred
26 ἐν τῇ ἀνοχῇ τοῦ θεοῦ, πρὸς τὴν
in the forbearance – of God, for the
ἔνδειξιν τῆς δικαιοσύνης αὐτοῦ ἐν τῷ
showing of the righteousness of him in the
forth
νῦν καιρῷ, εἰς τὸ εἶναι αὐτὸν δίκαιον
present time, for the to be himᵇ just
=that he should be
καὶ δικαιοῦντα τὸν ἐκ πίστεως 'Ιησοῦ.
and justifying the [one] of faith of(in) Jesus.
27 Ποῦ οὖν ἡ καύχησις; ἐξεκλείσθη. διὰ
Where there- the boasting? It was shut out. Through
fore
ποίου νόμου; τῶν ἔργων; οὐχί, ἀλλὰ
what law? – Of works? no, but
διὰ νόμου πίστεως. 28 λογιζόμεθα γὰρ
through a law of faith. For we reckon
δικαιοῦσθαι πίστει ἄνθρωπον χωρὶς ἔργων
²to be justified ³by faith ¹a man without works
νόμου. 29 ἢ 'Ιουδαίων ὁ θεὸς μόνον;
of law. Or of Jews [is he] the God only?
οὐχὶ καὶ ἐθνῶν; ναὶ καὶ ἐθνῶν, 30 εἴπερ
not also of nations? Yes[,] also of nations, since [there is]
εἷς ὁ θεὸς ὃς δικαιώσει περιτομὴν ἐκ
one – God who will justify circumcision by
πίστεως καὶ ἀκροβυστίαν διὰ τῆς πίστεως.
faith and uncircumcision through the faith.
31 νόμον οὖν καταργοῦμεν διὰ τῆς
³Law ²therefore ¹do we destroy through the
πίστεως; μὴ γένοιτο, ἀλλὰ νόμον ἱστάνομεν.
faith? May it not be, but ²law ¹we establish.

4 Τί οὖν ἐροῦμεν εὑρηκέναι 'Αβραὰμ
What therefore shall we say to have found Abraham
τὸν προπάτορα ἡμῶν κατὰ σάρκα; 2 εἰ
the forefather of us according to flesh? if
γὰρ 'Αβραὰμ ἐξ ἔργων ἐδικαιώθη, ἔχει
For Abraham by works was justified, he has
καύχημα· ἀλλ' οὐ πρὸς θεόν. 3 τί γὰρ
a boast; but not with God. For what

scripture say? "Abraham believed God, and it was reckoned to him as righteousness." 4 Now to one who works, his wages are not reckoned as a gift but as his due. 5 And to one who does not work but trusts him who justifies the ungodly, his faith is reckoned as righteousness. 6 So also David pronounces a blessing upon the man to whom God reckons righteousness apart from works: 7 "Blessed are those whose iniquities are forgiven, and whose sins are covered; 8 blessed is the man against whom the Lord will not reckon his sin." 9 Is this blessing pronounced only upon the circumcised, or also upon the uncircumcised? We say that faith was reckoned to Abraham as righteousness. 10 How then was it reckoned to him? Was it before or after he had been circumcised? It was not after, but before he was circumcised. 11 He received circumcision as a sign or seal of the righteousness which he had by faith while he was still uncircumcised. The purpose was to make him the father of all

ἡ γραφὴ λέγει; ἐπίστευσεν δὲ Ἀβραὰμ
the scripture says? And ²believed ¹Abraham

τῷ θεῷ, καὶ ἐλογίσθη αὐτῷ εἰς
- God, and it was reckoned to him for

δικαιοσύνην. 4 τῷ δὲ ἐργαζομένῳ ὁ
righteousness. Now to the [one] working the

μισθὸς οὐ λογίζεται κατὰ χάριν ἀλλὰ
reward is not reckoned according to grace but

κατὰ ὀφείλημα· τῷ δὲ μὴ ἐργαζομένῳ,
according to debt; but to the [one] not working,

5 πιστεύοντι δὲ ἐπὶ τὸν δικαιοῦντα τὸν
but believing on the [one] justifying the

ἀσεβῆ, λογίζεται ἡ πίστις αὐτοῦ εἰς
impious man, is reckoned the faith of him for

δικαιοσύνην, 6 καθάπερ καὶ Δαυὶδ λέγει
righteousness, even as also David says

τὸν μακαρισμὸν τοῦ ἀνθρώπου ᾧ ὁ
the blessedness of the man to whom -

θεὸς λογίζεται δικαιοσύνην χωρὶς ἔργων·
God reckons righteousness without works:

7 μακάριοι ὧν ἀφέθησαν αἱ ἀνομίαι
Blessed [are they] of whom were forgiven the lawlessnesses

καὶ ὧν ἐπεκαλύφθησαν αἱ ἁμαρτίαι·
and of whom were covered over the sins;

8 μακάριος ἀνὴρ οὗ οὐ μὴ λογίσηται
blessed [is] a man of whom by no means ²may reckon

κύριος ἁμαρτίαν 9 ὁ μακαρισμὸς οὖν
¹[the] Lord sin. - ²blessedness ³then

οὗτος ἐπὶ τὴν περιτομὴν ἢ καὶ ἐπὶ
¹This on the circumcision or also on

τὴν ἀκροβυστίαν; λέγομεν γάρ· ἐλογίσθη
the uncircumcision? for we say : ³was reckoned

τῷ Ἀβραὰμ ἡ πίστις εἰς δικαιοσύνην.
- ⁴to Abraham ¹The(his) ²faith for righteousness.

10 πῶς οὖν ἐλογίσθη; ἐν περιτομῇ ὄντι
How then was it reckoned? in circumcision being

ἢ ἐν ἀκροβυστίᾳ; οὐκ ἐν περιτομῇ ἀλλ'
or in uncircumcision? not in circumcision but

ἐν ἀκροβυστίᾳ· 11 καὶ σημεῖον ἔλαβεν
in uncircumcision; and ²a sign ¹he received

περιτομῆς σφραγῖδα τῆς δικαιοσύνης τῆς
of circumcision a seal of the righteousness of the

πίστεως τῆς ἐν τῇ ἀκροβυστίᾳ, εἰς
faith - [while] in - uncircumcision, for
=so

τὸ εἶναι αὐτὸν πατέρα πάντων τῶν
the to be him a father of all the
that he should be

who believe without being circumcised and who thus have righteousness reckoned to them, [12] and likewise the father of the circumcised who are not merely circumcised but also follow the example of the faith which our father Abraham had before he was circumcised.

13 The promise to Abraham and his descendants, that they should inherit the world, did not come through the law but through the righteousness of faith. [14] If it is the adherents of the law who are to be the heirs, faith is null and the promise is void. [15] For the law bring wrath, but where there is no law there is no transgression.

16 That is why it depends on faith, in order that the promise may rest on grace and be guaranteed to all his descendants—not only to the adherents of the law but also to those who share the faith of Abraham, for he is the father of us all, [17] as it is written, "I have made you the father of many nations" —in the presence of the God in whom he believed, who gives life to

πιστευόντων δι' ἀκροβυστίας, εἰς τὸ
[ones] believing through uncircumcision, for the
=that right-

λογισθῆναι αὐτοῖς [τὴν] δικαιοσύνην, 12 καὶ
to be reckoned to them – righteousness,[b] and
eousness should be reckoned to them,

πατέρα περιτομῆς τοῖς οὐκ ἐκ περιτομῆς
a father of circumcision to the not of circumcision
[ones]

μόνον ἀλλὰ καὶ τοῖς στοιχοῦσιν τοῖς
only but also to the [ones] walking in the

ἴχνεσιν τῆς ἐν ἀκροβυστίᾳ πίστεως τοῦ
steps [1]of the [7]in [8]uncircumcision [2]faith [3]of the

πατρὸς ἡμῶν 'Αβραάμ. 13 Οὐ γὰρ διὰ
[4]father [5]of us [6]Abraham. For not through

νόμου ἡ ἐπαγγελία τῷ 'Αβραὰμ ἢ τῷ
law the promise – to Abraham or to the

σπέρματι αὐτοῦ, τὸ κληρονόμον αὐτὸν
seed of him, the heir him
=that he should be heir

εἶναι κόσμου, ἀλλὰ διὰ δικαιοσύνης πίστεως.
to be[b] of [the] world, but through a righteousness of faith.

14 εἰ γὰρ οἱ ἐκ νόμου κληρονόμοι,
For if [1]the [3][are] [4]of [5]law [2]heirs,

κεκένωται ἡ πίστις καὶ κατήργηται
[3]has been emptied – [1]faith and [3]has been destroyed

ἡ ἐπαγγελία· 15 ὁ γὰρ νόμος ὀργὴν
[1]the [2]promise; for the law [2]wrath

κατεργάζεται· οὗ δὲ οὐκ ἔστιν νόμος,
[1]works; and where there is not law,

οὐδὲ παράβασις. 16 Διὰ τοῦτο ἐκ πίστεως,
neither [is there] Therefore [it is] of faith,
transgression.

ἵνα κατὰ χάριν, εἰς τὸ εἶναι βεβαίαν
in [it may be] grace, for the to be firm
order according =so that the promise shall be firm
that to

τὴν ἐπαγγελίαν παντὶ τῷ σπέρματι, οὐ
the promise[b] to all the seed, not

τῷ ἐκ τοῦ νόμου μόνον ἀλλὰ καὶ τῷ
to the of the law only but also to the
[seed] [seed]

ἐκ πίστεως 'Αβραάμ, ὅς ἐστιν πατὴρ
of [the] faith of Abraham, who is father

πάντων ἡμῶν, 17 καθὼς γέγραπται ὅτι
of all us, as it has been written[,] –

πατέρα πολλῶν ἐθνῶν τέθεικά σε,
A father of many nations I have appointed thee,

κατέναντι οὗ ἐπίστευσεν θεοῦ τοῦ ζωο-
before [2]whom [3]he believed [1]God the [one] quick-

the dead and calls into existence the things that do not exist. ¹⁸ In hope he believed against hope, that he should become the father of many nations; as he had been told, "So shall your descendants be." ¹⁹ He did not weaken in faith when he considered his own body, which was as good as dead because he was about a hundred years old, or when he considered the barrenness of Sarah's womb. ²⁰ No distrust made him waver concerning the promise of God, but he grew strong in his faith as he gave glory to God, ²¹ fully convinced that God was able to do what he had promised. ²² That is why his faith was "reckoned to him as righteousness." ²³ But the words, "it was reckoned to him," were written not for his sake alone, ²⁴ but for ours also. It will be reckoned to us who believe in him that raised from the dead Jesus our Lord, ²⁵ who was put to death for our trespasses and raised for our justification.

ποιοῦντος	τοὺς	νεκροὺς	καὶ	καλοῦντος
ening	the	dead [ones]	and	calling

τὰ	μὴ	ὄντα	ὡς	ὄντα·	18	ὃς	παρ'	ἐλπίδα
the things	not	being	as	being;		who	beyond	hope

ἐπ'	ἐλπίδι	ἐπίστευσεν,	εἰς	τὸ	γενέσθαι
on	hope	believed,	for	the	to become
					=so that he should become

αὐτὸν	πατέρα	πολλῶν	ἐθνῶν	κατὰ	τὸ
himᵇ	a father	of many	nations	accord-ing to	the thing

εἰρημένον·	οὕτως	ἔσται	τὸ	σπέρμα	σου·
having been said :	So	shall be	the	seed	of thee;

19	καὶ	μὴ	ἀσθενήσας	τῇ	πίστει	κατενόησεν
	and	not	weakening	–	in faith	he considered

τὸ	ἑαυτοῦ	σῶμα	νενεκρωμένον,	ἑκατονταέτης
¹the	³of himself	²body	to have died,	a hundred years

που	ὑπάρχων,	καὶ	τὴν	νέκρωσιν	τῆς
about	being,	and	the	death	of the

μήτρας	Σάρρας·	20	εἰς	δὲ	τὴν	ἐπαγγελίαν
womb	of Sarah;		but ²against	³the		⁴promise

τοῦ	θεοῦ	οὐ	διεκρίθη	τῇ	ἀπιστίᾳ,	ἀλλὰ
–	⁵of God	¹he did not decide		–	⁶by unbelief,	but

ἐνεδυναμώθη	τῇ	πίστει,	δοὺς	δόξαν	τῷ
was empowered	–	by faith,	giving	glory	–

θεῷ	21	καὶ	πληροφορηθεὶς	ὅτι	ὃ	ἐπήγγελται
to God		and	being fully persuaded	that	what	he has promised

δυνατός	ἐστιν	καὶ	ποιῆσαι.	22	διὸ	[καὶ]
able	he is	also	to do.		Wherefore	also

ἐλογίσθη	αὐτῷ	εἰς	δικαιοσύνην.	23	Οὐκ
it was reckoned	to him	for	righteousness.		not

ἐγράφη	δὲ	δι'	αὐτὸν	μόνον	ὅτι	ἐλογίσθη
it was written	Now because of		him	only	that	it was reckoned

αὐτῷ,	24	ἀλλὰ	καὶ	δι'	ἡμᾶς,	οἷς	μέλλει
to him,		but	also because of		us,	to whom	it is about

λογίζεσθαι,	τοῖς	πιστεύουσιν	ἐπὶ	τὸν
to be reckoned,	to the [ones] believing		on	the [one]

ἐγείραντα	Ἰησοῦν	τὸν	κύριον	ἡμῶν	ἐκ
having raised	Jesus	the	Lord	of us	out of

νεκρῶν,	25	ὃς	παρεδόθη	διὰ	τὰ	παραπ-
[the] dead,		who	was delivered	because of	the	of-

τώματα	ἡμῶν	καὶ	ἠγέρθη	διὰ	τὴν
fences	of us	and	was raised	because of	the

δικαίωσιν	ἡμῶν.
justification	of us.

CHAPTER 5

THEREFORE, since we are justified by faith, we[d] have peace with God through our Lord Jesus Christ. [2] Through him we have obtained access[e] to this grace in which we stand, and we[f] rejoice in our hope of sharing the glory of God. [3] More than that, we[f] rejoice in our sufferings, knowing that suffering produces endurance, [4] and endurance produces character, and character produces hope, [5] and hope does not disappoint us, because God's love has been poured into our hearts through the Holy Spirit which has been given to us.

[6] While we were yet helpless, at the right time Christ died for the ungodly. [7] Why, one will hardly die for a righteous man—though perhaps for a good man one will dare even to die. [8] But God shows his love for us in that while we were yet sinners Christ died for us. [9] Since, therefore, we are now justified by his blood,

[d] Other ancient authorities read *let us*
[e] Other ancient authorities add *by faith*
[f] Or *let us*

---

5 Δικαιωθέντες οὖν ἐκ πίστεως εἰρήνην
Having been justified therefore by faith peace

ἔχομεν πρὸς τὸν θεὸν διὰ τοῦ κυρίου
we have with – God through the Lord

ἡμῶν Ἰησοῦ Χριστοῦ, 2 δι᾽ οὗ καὶ τὴν
of us Jesus Christ, through whom also the

προσαγωγὴν ἐσχήκαμεν [τῇ πίστει] εἰς
access we have had – by faith into

τὴν χάριν ταύτην ἐν ᾗ ἑστήκαμεν, καὶ
this grace in which we stand, and

καυχώμεθα ἐπ᾽ ἐλπίδι τῆς δόξης τοῦ
boast on hope of the glory –

θεοῦ. 3 οὐ μόνον δέ, ἀλλὰ καὶ καυχώμεθα
of God. And not only [so], but also we boast

ἐν ταῖς θλίψεσιν, εἰδότες ὅτι ἡ θλῖψις
in – afflictions, knowing that – affliction

ὑπομονὴν κατεργάζεται, 4 ἡ δὲ ὑπομονὴ
patience works, – and patience

δοκιμήν, ἡ δὲ δοκιμὴ ἐλπίδα· 5 ἡ δὲ
proof, – and proof hope; – and

ἐλπὶς οὐ καταισχύνει, ὅτι ἡ ἀγάπη
hope does not put to shame, because the love

τοῦ θεοῦ ἐκκέχυται ἐν ταῖς καρδίαις
– of God has been poured out in the hearts

ἡμῶν διὰ πνεύματος ἁγίου τοῦ δοθέντος
of us through Spirit Holy – given

ἡμῖν· 6 εἴ γε Χριστὸς ὄντων ἡμῶν
to us; indeed [7]Christ [2]being [1]us
      = when we were weak

ἀσθενῶν ἔτι κατὰ καιρὸν ὑπὲρ ἀσεβῶν
[4]weak[a] [3]yet [5]according [6]time [9]on [10]impious
      ing to   behalf of ones

ἀπέθανεν. 7 μόλις γὰρ ὑπὲρ δικαίου
[8]died. For hardly on behalf of a just man

τις ἀποθανεῖται· ὑπὲρ γὰρ τοῦ ἀγαθοῦ
anyone will die; for on behalf of the good man

τάχα τις καὶ τολμᾷ ἀποθανεῖν· 8 συνίστησιν
perhaps some- even dares to die; [2]commends
one

δὲ τὴν ἑαυτοῦ ἀγάπην εἰς ἡμᾶς ὁ θεὸς
but [3]the [5]of himself [4]love [6]to [7]us – [1]God

ὅτι ἔτι ἁμαρτωλῶν ὄντων ἡμῶν Χριστὸς
that yet sinners being us[a] Christ
      = while we were yet sinners

ὑπὲρ ἡμῶν ἀπέθανεν. 9 πολλῷ οὖν μᾶλλον
on be- us died. By much there- rather
half of   fore

δικαιωθέντες νῦν ἐν τῷ αἵματι αὐτοῦ
having been justified now by the blood of him

much more shall we be saved by him from the wrath of God. ¹⁰For if while we were enemies we were reconciled to God by the death of his Son, much more, now that we are reconciled, shall we be saved by his life. ¹¹Not only so, but we also rejoice in God through our Lord Jesus Christ, through whom we have now received our reconciliation.

12 Therefore as sin came into the world through one man and death through sin, and so death spread to all men because all men sinned—¹³sin indeed was in the world before the law was given, but sin is not counted where there is no law. ¹⁴Yet death reigned from Adam to Moses, even over those whose sins were not like the transgression of Adam, who was a type of the one who was to come.

15 But the free gift is not like the trespass. For if many died through one man's trespass, much more have the grace of God and the free gift in the grace of that one man

σωθησόμεθα δι' αὐτοῦ ἀπὸ τῆς ὀργῆς.
we shall be saved through him from the wrath.

10 εἰ γὰρ ἐχθροὶ ὄντες κατηλλάγημεν
For if enemies being we were reconciled

τῷ θεῷ διὰ τοῦ θανάτου τοῦ υἱοῦ αὐτοῦ,
– to God through the death of the Son of him,

πολλῷ μᾶλλον καταλλαγέντες σωθησόμεθα
by much rather having been reconciled we shall be saved

ἐν τῇ ζωῇ αὐτοῦ· 11 οὐ μόνον δὲ, ἀλλὰ
by the life of him; and not only [so], but

καὶ καυχώμενοι ἐν τῷ θεῷ διὰ τοῦ
also boasting in – God through the

κυρίου ἡμῶν Ἰησοῦ [Χριστοῦ], δι' οὗ
Lord of us Jesus Christ, through whom

νῦν τὴν καταλλαγὴν ἐλάβομεν.
now the reconciliation we received.

12 Διὰ τοῦτο ὥσπερ δι' ἑνὸς ἀνθρώπου
Therefore as through one man

ἡ ἁμαρτία εἰς τὸν κόσμον εἰσῆλθεν,
– sin into the world entered,

καὶ διὰ τῆς ἁμαρτίας ὁ θάνατος, καὶ
and through – sin – death, ²also

οὕτως εἰς πάντας ἀνθρώπους ὁ θάνατος
¹so to all men – death

διῆλθεν, ἐφ' ᾧ πάντες ἥμαρτον· 13 ἄχρι
passed, inasmuch as all sinned; until

γὰρ νόμου ἁμαρτία ἦν ἐν κόσμῳ, ἁμαρτία
for law sin was in [the] world, sin

δὲ οὐκ ἐλλογεῖται μὴ ὄντος νόμου·
but is not reckoned not being lawᵃ;
    =when there is no law;

14 ἀλλὰ ἐβασίλευσεν ὁ θάνατος ἀπὸ Ἀδὰμ
but ²reigned – ¹death from Adam

μέχρι Μωϋσέως καὶ ἐπὶ τοὺς μὴ
until Moses even over the [ones] not

ἁμαρτήσαντας ἐπὶ τῷ ὁμοιώματι τῆς
sinning on the likeness of the

παραβάσεως Ἀδάμ, ὅς ἐστιν τύπος τοῦ
transgression of Adam, who is a type of the

μέλλοντος. 15 Ἀλλ' οὐχ ὡς τὸ παράπτωμα,
[one] coming. But not as the offence,

οὕτως [καὶ] τὸ χάρισμα· εἰ γὰρ τῷ
so also the free gift; for if ¹by the

τοῦ ἑνὸς παραπτώματι οἱ πολλοὶ
²of the ⁴one [man] ³offence the many

ἀπέθανον, πολλῷ μᾶλλον ἡ χάρις τοῦ θεοῦ
died, by much rather the grace – of God

καὶ ἡ δωρεὰ ἐν χάριτι τῇ τοῦ ἑνὸς
and the gift in grace – of the one

618 ROMANS 5

Jesus Christ abounded for many. ¹⁶And the free gift is not like the effect of that one man's sin. For the judgment following one trespass brought condemnation, but the free gift following many trespasses brings justification. ¹⁷If, because of ʾone man's trespass, death reigned through that one man, much more will those who receive the abundance of grace and the free gift of righteousness reign in life through the one man Jesus Christ.

18 Then as one man's trespass led to condemnation for all men, so one man's act of righteousness leads to acquittal and life for all men. ¹⁹For as by one man's disobedience many were made sinners, so by one man's obedience many will be made righteous. ²⁰Law came in, to increase the trespass; but where sin increased, grace abounded all the more, ²¹so that, as sin reigned in death,

ἀνθρώπου ᾿Ιησοῦ Χριστοῦ εἰς τοὺς πολλοὺς
man   Jesus   Christ   to   the   many

ἐπερίσσευσεν. 16 καὶ οὐχ ὡς δι' ἑνὸς
abounded.   And not as through one
                                    [man]

ἁμαρτήσαντος τὸ δώρημα· τὸ μὲν γὰρ
sinning   the gift;   ²the ²on one hand ¹for

κρίμα ἐξ ἑνὸς εἰς κατάκριμα, τὸ δὲ
judgment [is] of one to condemna- on the other
         [offence]   tion,   the

χάρισμα ἐκ πολλῶν παραπτωμάτων εἰς
free gift [is] of many   offences   to

δικαίωμα. 17 εἰ γὰρ τῷ τοῦ ἑνὸς
justification.   For if ¹by the ²of the ⁴one [man]

παραπτώματι ὁ θάνατος ἐβασίλευσεν διὰ
²offence   –   death   reigned   through

τοῦ ἑνός, πολλῷ μᾶλλον οἱ τὴν περισσείαν
the one   by much rather ¹the ³the ⁴abundance
[man],   [ones]

τῆς χάριτος καὶ τῆς δωρεᾶς τῆς
⁵of the ⁶grace ⁷and ⁸of the ⁹gift   –

δικαιοσύνης λαμβάνοντες ἐν ζωῇ βασιλεύ-
¹⁰of righteousness ²receiving ¹²in ¹³life ¹¹will

σουσιν διὰ τοῦ ἑνὸς ᾿Ιησοῦ Χριστοῦ.
reign through the one [man] Jesus   Christ.

18 ῎Αρα οὖν ὡς δι' ἑνὸς παραπτώματος
So therefore as through one   offence

εἰς πάντας ἀνθρώπους εἰς κατάκριμα,
to   all   men   to   condemnation,

οὕτως καὶ δι' ἑνὸς δικαιώματος εἰς
so   also through one righteous act to

πάντας ἀνθρώπους εἰς δικαίωσιν ζωῆς·
all   men   to   justification of life;

19 ὥσπερ γὰρ διὰ τῆς παρακοῆς τοῦ
for as   through the disobedience of the

ἑνὸς ἀνθρώπου ἁμαρτωλοὶ κατεστάθησαν
one man   ⁴sinners   ³were constituted

οἱ πολλοί, ₍οὕτως καὶ διὰ τῆς ὑπακοῆς
¹the ²many,   so   also through the obedience

τοῦ ἑνὸς δίκαιοι κατασταθήσονται οἱ
of the one [man] ⁴righteous ³will be constituted ¹the

πολλοί. 20 νόμος δὲ παρεισῆλθεν ἵνα
²many.   But law entered   in order
                                 that

πλεονάσῃ τὸ παράπτωμα· οὗ δὲ ἐπλεόνασεν
might abound the offence;   but where abounded

ἡ ἁμαρτία, ὑπερεπερίσσευσεν ἡ χάρις,
– sin,   more abounded   – grace,

21 ἵνα ὥσπερ ἐβασίλευσεν ἡ ἁμαρτία ἐν
in order that as reigned   – sin   by

grace also might reign through righteousness to eternal life through Jesus Christ our Lord.

τῷ θανάτῳ, οὕτως καὶ ἡ χάρις βασιλεύσῃ
the death, so also - grace might reign
διὰ δικαιοσύνης εἰς ζωὴν αἰώνιον διὰ
through righteousness to life eternal through
Ἰησοῦ Χριστοῦ τοῦ κυρίου ἡμῶν.
Jesus Christ the Lord of us.

CHAPTER 6

WHAT shall we say then? Are we to continue in sin that grace may abound? [2]By no means! How can we who died to sin still live in it? [3]Do you not know that all of us who have been baptized into Christ Jesus were baptized into his death? [4]We were buried therefore with him by baptism into death, so that as Christ was raised from the dead by the glory of the Father, we too might walk in newness of life.

5 For if we have been united with him in a death like his, we shall certainly be united with him in a resurrection like his. [6]We know that our old self was crucified with him so that the sinful body might be destroyed, and we might no longer be enslaved to sin. [7]For he who has died is freed from sin. [8]But if we have died with Christ,

6 Τί οὖν ἐροῦμεν; ἐπιμένωμεν τῇ
What therefore shall we say? May we continue -
ἁμαρτίᾳ, ἵνα ἡ χάρις πλεονάσῃ; 2 μὴ
in sin, in order that - grace may abound? not
γένοιτο. οἵτινες ἀπεθάνομεν τῇ ἁμαρτίᾳ,
May it be. Who we died - to sin,
πῶς ἔτι ζήσομεν ἐν αὐτῇ; 3 ἢ ἀγνοεῖτε
how yet shall we live in it? or are ye ignorant
ὅτι ὅσοι ἐβαπτίσθημεν εἰς Χριστὸν
that as many as we were baptized into Christ
Ἰησοῦν, εἰς τὸν θάνατον αὐτοῦ ἐβαπτίσ-
Jesus, into the death of him we were
θημεν; 4 συνετάφημεν οὖν αὐτῷ διὰ τοῦ
baptized? [2]We were [1]there him through -
                  buried with fore
βαπτίσματος εἰς τὸν θάνατον, ἵνα ὥσπερ
baptism into - death, in order as
                            that
ἠγέρθη Χριστὸς ἐκ νεκρῶν διὰ τῆς
was raised Christ from [the] dead through the
δόξης τοῦ πατρός, οὕτως καὶ ἡμεῖς ἐν
glory of the Father, so also we in
καινότητι ζωῆς περιπατήσωμεν. 5 εἰ γὰρ
newness of life might walk. For if
σύμφυτοι γεγόναμεν τῷ ὁμοιώματι τοῦ
united with we have become in the likeness of the
θανάτου αὐτοῦ, ἀλλὰ καὶ τῆς ἀναστάσεως
death of him, but(so) also of the(his) resurrection
ἐσόμεθα· 6 τοῦτο γινώσκοντες, ὅτι ὁ
we shall be; this knowing, that the
παλαιὸς ἡμῶν ἄνθρωπος συνεσταυρώθη, ἵνα
[1]old [3]of us [2]man was crucified in or-
                       with [him], der that
καταργηθῇ τὸ σῶμα τῆς ἁμαρτίας, τοῦ
might be the body - of sin, -
destroyed
μηκέτι δουλεύειν ἡμᾶς τῇ ἁμαρτίᾳ· 7 ὁ
no longer to serve usbd - sin; [2]the
=that we should no longer serve (one)
γὰρ ἀποθανὼν δεδικαίωται ἀπὸ τῆς
[1]for having died has been justified from -
ἁμαρτίας. 8 εἰ δὲ ἀπεθάνομεν σὺν Χριστῷ,
sin. But if we died with Christ

we believe that we shall also live with him. ⁹For we know that Christ being raised from the dead will never die again; death no longer has dominion over him. ¹⁰The death he died he died to sin, once for all, but the life he lives he lives to God. ¹¹So you also must consider yourselves dead to sin and alive to God in Christ Jesus.

12 Let not sin therefore reign in your mortal bodies, to make you obey their passions. ¹³Do not yield your members to sin as instruments of wickedness, but yield yourselves to God as men who have been brought from death to life, and your members to God as instruments of righteousness. ¹⁴For sin will have no dominion over you, since you are not under law but under grace.

15 What then? Are we to sin because we are not under law but under grace? By no means! ¹⁶Do you not know that if you yield yourselves to any one as obedient slaves, you are slaves of the one whom you obey, either of sin, which leads to death, or of obedience,

πιστεύομεν ὅτι καὶ συζήσομεν αὐτῷ,
we believe that also we shall live with him,

9 εἰδότες ὅτι Χριστὸς ἐγερθεὶς ἐκ νεκρῶν
knowing that Christ having been raised from [the] dead

οὐκέτι ἀποθνῄσκει, θάνατος αὐτοῦ οὐκέτι
no more dies, death ²of him ¹no more

κυριεύει. 10 ὃ γὰρ ἀπέθανεν, τῇ ἁμαρτίᾳ
²lords it over. For in that† he died, to sin

ἀπέθανεν ἐφάπαξ· ὃ δὲ ζῇ, ζῇ τῷ θεῷ.
he died once; but in that† he he – to lives, lives God.

11 οὕτως καὶ ὑμεῖς λογίζεσθε ἑαυτοὺς
So also ²ye ¹reckon yourselves

εἶναι νεκροὺς μὲν τῇ ἁμαρτίᾳ ζῶντας
to be dead indeed – to sin ²living

δὲ τῷ θεῷ ἐν Χριστῷ Ἰησοῦ. 12 μὴ
¹but – to God in Christ Jesus. ³not

οὖν βασιλευέτω ἡ ἁμαρτία ἐν τῷ θνητῷ
¹There-fore ²let ⁵reign – ⁴sin ⁶in ⁷the ⁸mortal

ὑμῶν σώματι εἰς τὸ ὑπακούειν ταῖς
¹⁰of you ⁹body for the to obey the
=to obey its lusts,

ἐπιθυμίαις αὐτοῦ, 13 μηδὲ παριστάνετε τὰ
lusts of it, neither present ye the

μέλη ὑμῶν ὅπλα ἀδικίας τῇ ἁμαρτίᾳ,
members of you weapons of unright- – to sin,
eousness

ἀλλὰ παραστήσατε ἑαυτοὺς τῷ θεῷ ὡσεὶ
but present ye yourselves – to God as

ἐκ νεκρῶν ζῶντας καὶ τὰ μέλη ὑμῶν
from [the] dead living and the members of you

ὅπλα δικαιοσύνης τῷ θεῷ, 14 ἁμαρτία
weapons of righteousness – to God, ²sin

γὰρ ὑμῶν οὐ κυριεύσει· οὐ γὰρ ἐστε
¹for ⁴of you ³shall not lord it over; for ye are not

ὑπὸ νόμον ἀλλὰ ὑπὸ χάριν. 15 Τί οὖν;
under law but under grace. What therefore?

ἁμαρτήσωμεν, ὅτι οὐκ ἐσμὲν ὑπὸ νόμον
may we sin, because we are not under law

ἀλλὰ ὑπὸ χάριν; μὴ γένοιτο. 16 οὐκ
but under grace? May it not be. not

οἴδατε ὅτι ᾧ παριστάνετε ἑαυτοὺς δούλους
Know ye that to whom ye present yourselves slaves

εἰς ὑπακοήν, δοῦλοί ἐστε ᾧ ὑπακούετε,
for obedience, slaves ye are whom ye obey,

ἤτοι ἁμαρτίας εἰς θάνατον ἢ ὑπακοῆς
whether of sin to death or of obedience

which leads to righteousness? [17] But thanks be to God, that you who were once slaves of sin have become obedient from the heart to the standard of teaching to which you were committed, [18] and, having been set free from sin, have become slaves of righteousness. [19] I am speaking in human terms, because of your natural limitations. For just as you once yielded your members to impurity and to greater and greater iniquity, so now yield your members to righteousness for sanctification.
[20] When you were slaves of sin, you were free in regard to righteousness. [21] But then what return did you get from the things of which you are now ashamed? The end of those things is death. [22] But now that you have been set free from sin and have become slaves of God, the return you get is sanctification and its end, eternal life. [23] For the wages of sin is death, but the free gift of God is eternal life in Christ Jesus our Lord.

εἰς δικαιοσύνην, 17 χάρις δὲ τῷ θεῷ
to righteousness?   But thanks   –   to God

ὅτι ἦτε δοῦλοι τῆς ἁμαρτίας, ὑπηκούσατε
that ye were slaves   –   of sin,   [2]ye obeyed

δὲ ἐκ καρδίας εἰς ὃν παρεδόθητε τύπον
[1]but out of [the] heart   [3]to [4]which [5]ye were delivered [1]a form

διδαχῆς, 18 ἐλευθερωθέντες δὲ ἀπὸ τῆς
[2]of teaching,   and having been freed   from   –

ἁμαρτίας ἐδουλώθητε τῇ δικαιοσύνῃ.
sin   ye were enslaved   –   to righteousness.

19 ἀνθρώπινον λέγω διὰ τὴν ἀσθένειαν
Humanly   I say because of the   weakness

τῆς σαρκὸς ὑμῶν. ὥσπερ γὰρ παρεστήσατε
of the flesh of you.   For as   ye presented

τὰ μέλη ὑμῶν δοῦλα τῇ ἀκαθαρσίᾳ καὶ
the members of you slaves   – to uncleanness and

τῇ ἀνομίᾳ εἰς τὴν ἀνομίαν, οὕτως νῦν
– to iniquity unto   –   iniquity,   so   now

παραστήσατε τὰ μέλη ὑμῶν δοῦλα τῇ
present ye   the members of you slaves   –

δικαιοσύνῃ εἰς ἁγιασμόν. 20 ὅτε γὰρ
to righteousness unto sanctification.   For when

δοῦλοι ἦτε τῆς ἁμαρτίας, ἐλεύθεροι ἦτε
slaves ye were –   of sin,   free   ye were

τῇ δικαιοσύνῃ. 21 τίνα οὖν καρπὸν εἴχετε
– to righteousness.   What [2]therefore [1]fruit   had ye

τότε; ἐφ' οἷς νῦν ἐπαισχύνεσθε· τὸ γὰρ
then?   Over which now ye are ashamed;   for the
        things

τέλος ἐκείνων θάνατος. 22 νυνὶ δὲ ἐλευ-
end of those things [is] death.   But now   having

θερωθέντες ἀπὸ τῆς ἁμαρτίας δουλωθέντες
been freed   from   –   sin [2]having been enslaved

δὲ τῷ θεῷ, ἔχετε τὸν καρπὸν ὑμῶν εἰς
[1]and – to God, ye have   the   fruit   of you   to

ἁγιασμόν, τὸ δὲ τέλος ζωὴν αἰώνιον.
sanctification, and the   end   life   eternal.

23 τὰ γὰρ ὀψώνια τῆς ἁμαρτίας θάνατος,
    For the   wages   –   of sin   [is] death,

τὸ δὲ χάρισμα τοῦ θεοῦ ζωὴ αἰώνιος
but the   free gift   – of God life   eternal

ἐν Χριστῷ Ἰησοῦ τῷ κυρίῳ ἡμῶν.
in   Christ   Jesus   the   Lord   of us.

CHAPTER 7

DO you not know, brethren—for I am speaking to those who know the law—that the law is binding on a person only during his life? ²Thus a married woman is bound by law to her husband as long as he lives; but if her husband dies she is discharged from the law concerning the husband. ³Accordingly, she will be called an adulteress if she lives with another man while her husband is alive. But if her husband dies she is free from that law, and if she marries another man she is not an adulteress.

4 Likewise, my brethren, you have died to the law through the body of Christ, so that you may belong to another, to him who has been raised from the dead in order that we may bear fruit for God. ⁵While we were living in the flesh, our sinful passions, aroused by the law, were at work in our members to bear fruit for death. ⁶But now we are discharged from the law, dead to that which held us captive, so that we serve not under the old

7 Ἦ   ἀγνοεῖτε,   ἀδελφοί,   γινώσκουσιν   γὰρ
Or   are ye ignorant,   brothers,   for to [ones] knowing

νόμον   λαλῶ,   ὅτι   ὁ   νόμος   κυριεύει   τοῦ
law   I speak,   that   the   law   lords it over   the

ἀνθρώπου   ἐφ'   ὅσον   χρόνον   ζῇ;   2 ἢ   γὰρ
man   over   such   time [as] he lives?   For the

ὕπανδρος   γυνὴ   τῷ   ζῶντι   ἀνδρὶ   δέδεται
²married   ¹woman   to the   living   husband   has
　　　　　　　　　　　　　　　　　　　been bound

νόμῳ·   ἐὰν   δὲ   ἀποθάνῃ   ὁ   ἀνήρ,   κατήργηται
by law;   but if   dies   the husband,   she has been
　　　　　　　　　　　　　　　　　　　discharged

ἀπὸ   τοῦ   νόμου   τοῦ   ἀνδρός.   3 ἄρα   οὖν
from   the   law   of the   husband.   Therefore

ζῶντος   τοῦ   ἀνδρὸς   μοιχαλὶς   χρηματίσει
living   the   husbandª   an adulteress she will be called
= while the husband lives

ἐὰν   γένηται   ἀνδρὶ   ἑτέρῳ·   ἐὰν   δὲ   ἀποθάνῃ
if   she   ²husband   ¹to a   but if   dies
　　becomes　　　　　different;

ὁ   ἀνήρ,   ἐλευθέρα   ἐστὶν   ἀπὸ   τοῦ   νόμου,
the husband,   free   she is   from   the   law,

τοῦ   μὴ   εἶναι   αὐτὴν   μοιχαλίδα   γενομένην
–   not   to be   herᵈ   an adulteress   having become
= so that she is not

ἀνδρὶ   ἑτέρῳ.   4 ὥστε,   ἀδελφοί   μου,   καὶ
²husband   ¹to a   So,   brothers   of me,   also
　　different.

ὑμεῖς   ἐθανατώθητε   τῷ   νόμῳ   διὰ   τοῦ
ye   were put to death   to the   law   through   the

σώματος   τοῦ   Χριστοῦ,   εἰς   τὸ   γενέσθαι
body   –   of Christ,   for   the   to become
　　　　　　　　　　　　= that we might belong

ὑμᾶς   ἑτέρῳ,   τῷ   ἐκ   νεκρῶν   ἐγερθέντι,
youᵇ   to a   to the   from   dead   having been
　　different,　[one]　[the]　　　　raised,

ἵνα   καρποφορήσωμεν   τῷ   θεῷ.   5 ὅτε
in order   we may bear fruit   –   to God.   when
that

γὰρ   ἦμεν   ἐν   τῇ   σαρκί,   τὰ   παθήματα
For   we were   in   the   flesh,   the   passions

τῶν   ἁμαρτιῶν   τὰ   διὰ   τοῦ   νόμου   ἐνηργεῖτο
–   of sins   – through the   law   operated

ἐν   τοῖς   μέλεσιν   ἡμῶν   εἰς   τὸ   καρποφορῆσαι
in   the   members   of us   for   the   to bear fruit

τῷ   θανάτῳ·   6 νυνὶ   δὲ   κατηργήθημεν   ἀπὸ
–   to death;   but now   we were discharged   from

τοῦ   νόμου,   ἀποθανόντες   ἐν   ᾧ   κατειχόμεθα,
the   law,   having died [to that] in which   we were held fast,

ὥστε   δουλεύειν   [ἡμᾶς]   ἐν   καινότητι
so as   to serve   usᵇ   in   newness

written code but in the new life of the Spirit. 7 What then shall we say? That the law is sin? By no means! Yet, if it had not been for the law, I should not have known sin. I should not have known what it is to covet if the law had not said, "You shall not covet." ⁸But sin, finding opportunity in the commandment, wrought in me all kinds of covetousness. Apart from the law sin lies dead. ⁹I was once alive apart from the law, but when the commandment came, sin revived and I died; ¹⁰the very commandment which promised life proved to be death to me. ¹¹For sin, finding opportunity in the commandment, deceived me and by it killed me. ¹²So the law is holy, and the commandment is holy and just and good. 13 Did that which is good, then, bring death to me? By no means! It was sin, working death in me through what is good, in order that sin might be shown to be sin, and through the commandment might become sinful beyond

πνεύματος καὶ οὐ παλαιότητι γράμματος.
of spirit and not [in] oldness of letter.

7 Τί οὖν ἐροῦμεν; ὁ νόμος ἁμαρτία;
What therefore shall we say? the law sin?

μὴ γένοιτο· ἀλλὰ τὴν ἁμαρτίαν οὐκ
May it not be; yet – sin not

ἔγνων εἰ μὴ διὰ νόμου· τήν τε γὰρ
I knew except through law; – ²also ¹for

ἐπιθυμίαν οὐκ ᾔδειν εἰ μὴ ὁ νόμος
lust I knew not except the law

ἔλεγεν· οὐκ ἐπιθυμήσεις· 8 ἀφορμὴν δὲ
said : Thou shalt not lust; but ²occasion

λαβοῦσα ἡ ἁμαρτία διὰ τῆς ἐντολῆς
²taking – ¹sin through the commandment

κατειργάσατο ἐν ἐμοὶ πᾶσαν ἐπιθυμίαν·
wrought in me every lust;

χωρὶς γὰρ νόμου ἁμαρτία νεκρά. 9 ἐγὼ
for without law sin [is] dead. I

δὲ ἔζων χωρὶς νόμου ποτέ· ἐλθούσης δὲ
And was living without law then; but coming = when the

τῆς ἐντολῆς ἡ ἁμαρτία ἀνέζησεν, 10 ἐγὼ
the commandment² – sin revived, ²I
commandment came

δὲ ἀπέθανον, καὶ εὑρέθη μοι ἡ ἐντολὴ
¹and died, and ⁶was ⁷to me ¹the ²command-
found ment

ἡ εἰς ζωήν, αὕτη εἰς θάνατον· 11 ἡ γὰρ
– ³for ⁴life, ⁵this to death; – for

ἁμαρτία ἀφορμὴν λαβοῦσα διὰ τῆς
sin ²occasion ¹taking through the

ἐντολῆς ἐξηπάτησέν με καὶ δι' αὐτῆς
commandment deceived me and through it

ἀπέκτεινεν. 12 ὥστε ὁ μὲν νόμος ἅγιος,
killed [me]. So the – law [is] holy,

καὶ ἡ ἐντολὴ ἁγία καὶ δικαία καὶ ἀγαθή.
and the command- holy and just and good.
 ment

13 Τὸ οὖν ἀγαθὸν ἐμοὶ ἐγένετο θάνατος;
²The ¹therefore good to me became death?

μὴ γένοιτο· ἀλλὰ ἡ ἁμαρτία, ἵνα φανῇ
May it not be; yet – sin, in or- it might
der that appear

ἁμαρτία, διὰ τοῦ ἀγαθοῦ μοι κατεργα-
sin, through the good ³to me ¹work-

ζομένη θάνατον, ἵνα γένηται καθ' ὑπερβολὴν
ing ²death, in or- ⁵might ⁶excessively†
der that become

ἁμαρτωλὸς ἡ ἁμαρτία διὰ τῆς ἐντολῆς.
⁷sinful – ¹sin ²through ³the ⁴command-
ment.

measure. ¹⁴We know that the law is spiritual; but I am carnal, sold under sin. ¹⁵I do not understand my own actions. For I do not do what I want, but I do the very thing I hate. ¹⁶Now if I do what I do not want, I agree that the law is good. ¹⁷So then it is no longer I that do it, but sin which dwells within me. ¹⁸For I know that nothing good dwells within me, that is, in my flesh. I can will what is right, but I cannot do it. ¹⁹For I do not do the good I want, but the evil I do not want is what I do. ²⁰Now if I do what I do not want, it is no longer I that do it, but sin which dwells within me.

21 So I find it to be a law that when I want to do right, evil lies close at hand. ²²For I delight in the law of God, in my inmost self, ²³but I see in my members another law at war with the law of my mind and making

14 οἴδαμεν γὰρ ὅτι ὁ νόμος πνευματικός
For we know that the law spiritual

ἐστιν· ἐγὼ δὲ σάρκινός εἰμι, πεπραμένος
is; but I fleshy am, having been sold

ὑπὸ τὴν ἁμαρτίαν. 15 ὃ γὰρ κατεργάζομαι
under – sin. For what I work

οὐ γινώσκω· οὐ γὰρ ὃ θέλω τοῦτο
I know not; for not what I wish this

πράσσω, ἀλλ' ὃ μισῶ τοῦτο ποιῶ. 16 εἰ
I practise, but what I hate this I do. if

δὲ ὃ οὐ θέλω τοῦτο ποιῶ, σύμφημι
But what I wish not this I do, I agree with

τῷ νόμῳ ὅτι καλός. 17 νυνὶ δὲ οὐκέτι
the law that [it is] good. But now no longer

ἐγὼ κατεργάζομαι αὐτὸ ἀλλὰ ἡ ἐνοικοῦσα
I work it but ¹the ²indwelling

ἐν ἐμοὶ ἁμαρτία. 18 οἶδα γὰρ ὅτι οὐκ
⁴in ⁵me ²sin. For I know that not

οἰκεῖ ἐν ἐμοί, τοῦτ' ἔστιν ἐν τῇ σαρκί
dwells in me, this is in the flesh

μου, ἀγαθόν· τὸ γὰρ θέλειν παράκειταί
of me, [that which is] – for to wish is present
good;

μοι, τὸ δὲ κατεργάζεσθαι τὸ καλὸν
to me, – but ²to work ³the ⁴good

οὔ· 19 οὐ γὰρ ὃ θέλω ποιῶ ἀγαθόν,
¹not; for not what ²I wish ³I do ¹good,

ἀλλὰ ὃ οὐ θέλω κακὸν τοῦτο πράσσω.
but what ²I wish not ¹evil this I practise.

20 εἰ δὲ ὃ οὐ θέλω ἐγὼ τοῦτο ποιῶ,
But if what ²wish not ¹I this I do,

οὐκέτι ἐγὼ κατεργάζομαι αὐτὸ ἀλλὰ ἡ
no longer I work it but ¹the

οἰκοῦσα ἐν ἐμοὶ ἁμαρτία. 21 εὑρίσκω
³dwelling ⁴in ⁵me ²sin. I find

ἄρα τὸν νόμον τῷ θέλοντι ἐμοὶ ποιεῖν
then the law ²the [one] ³wishing ¹to me to do

τὸ καλόν, 22 ὅτι ἐμοὶ τὸ κακὸν παράκειται·
the good, that to me the evil is present;

συνήδομαι γὰρ τῷ νόμῳ τοῦ θεοῦ κατὰ
for I delight in the law – of God according to

τὸν ἔσω ἄνθρωπον, 23 βλέπω δὲ ἕτερον
the inner man, but I see a different

νόμον ἐν τοῖς μέλεσίν μου ἀντιστρατευόμενον
law in the members of me warring against

τῷ νόμῳ τοῦ νοός μου καὶ αἰχμαλωτίζοντά
the law of the mind of me and taking captive

me captive to the law of
sin which dwells in my
members. ²⁴Wretched
man that I am! Who will
deliver me from this
body of death? ²⁵Thanks
be to God through Jesus
Christ our Lord! So
then, I of myself serve
the law of God with my
mind, but with my flesh
I serve the law of sin.

CHAPTER 8

THERE is therefore
now no condemna-
tion for those who are in
Christ Jesus. ²For the
law of the Spirit of life in
Christ Jesus has set me
free from the law of sin
and death. ³For God has
done what the law,
weakened by the flesh,
could not do: sending his
own Son in the likeness
of sinful flesh and for sin,⁹
he condemned sin in the
flesh, ⁴in order that the
just requirement of the
law might be fulfilled in
us, who walk not accord-
ing to the flesh but
according to the Spirit.
⁵For those who live
according to the flesh set
their minds on the things
of the flesh, but those
who live according to the

μɛ	ἐν	τῷ	νόμῳ	τῆς	ἁμαρτίας	τῷ	ὄντι
me	by	the	law	–	of sin	the [one]	being

ἐν	τοῖς	μέλεσίν	μου.	24 Ταλαίπωρος
in	the	members	of me.	¹Wretched

ἐγὼ	ἄνθρωπος·	τίς	με	ῥύσεται	ἐκ	τοῦ
³I	²man;	who	me	will deliver	from	the

σώματος	τοῦ	θανάτου	τούτου;	25 χάρις
body		of this death?		Thanks

τῷ	θεῷ	διὰ	ʼΙησοῦ	Χριστοῦ	τοῦ	κυρίου
–	to God	through	Jesus	Christ	the	Lord

ἡμῶν.	ʺΑρα	οὖν	αὐτὸς	ἐγὼ	τῷ	μὲν
of us.	So then		²[my]self	¹I	⁴with	³on one the hand

νοΐ	δουλεύω	νόμῳ	θεοῦ,	τῇ	δὲ	σαρκὶ
⁵mind	serve	[the] law	of God,	on the other with the		flesh

νόμῳ	ἁμαρτίας.	8 οὐδὲν	ἄρα	νῦν	κατάκριμα
[the] law	of sin.	⁴No	¹then	³now	⁵condemnation ²[there is]

τοῖς	ἐν	Χριστῷ	ʼΙησοῦ.	2 ὁ	γὰρ	νόμος	τοῦ
to the [ones]	in	Christ	Jesus.	For the		law	of the

πνεύματος	τῆς	ζωῆς	ἐν	Χριστῷ	ʼΙησοῦ
spirit	–	of life	in	Christ	Jesus

ἠλευθέρωσέν	σε	ἀπὸ	τοῦ	νόμου	τῆς
freed	thee	from	the	law	–

ἁμαρτίας	καὶ	τοῦ	θανάτου.	3 τὸ	γὰρ
of sin	and	–	of death.		For the

ἀδύνατον	τοῦ	νόμου,	ἐν	ᾧ	ἠσθένει	διὰ
impossible thing	of the	law,	in	which	it was weak	through

τῆς	σαρκός,	ὁ	θεὸς	τὸν	ἑαυτοῦ	υἱὸν
the	flesh,	–	¹God	³the	⁵of himself	⁴Son

πέμψας	ἐν	ὁμοιώματι	σαρκὸς	ἁμαρτίας
²sending	in	likeness	of flesh	of sin

καὶ	περὶ	ἁμαρτίας	κατέκρινεν	τὴν	ἁμαρτίαν
and concerning		sin	condemned	–	sin

ἐν	τῇ	σαρκί,	4 ἵνα	τὸ	δικαίωμα	τοῦ
in	the	flesh,	in order that	the	ordinance	of the

νόμου	πληρωθῇ	ἐν	ἡμῖν	τοῖς	μὴ	κατὰ
law	may be fulfilled	in	us	the [ones]	not	according to

σάρκα	περιπατοῦσιν	ἀλλὰ	κατὰ	πνεῦμα.
flesh	walking	but	according to	spirit.

5 οἱ	γὰρ	κατὰ	σάρκα	ὄντες	τὰ	τῆς
For the [ones]		according to	flesh	being	the	of the things

σαρκὸς	φρονοῦσιν,	οἱ	δὲ	κατὰ	πνεῦμα
flesh	mind,	but the [ones]		according to	spirit

---

⁹ Or *and as a sin offering*

Spirit set their minds on the things of the Spirit. ⁶To set the mind on the flesh is death, but to set the mind on the Spirit is life and peace. ⁷For the mind that is set on the flesh is hostile to God; it does not submit to God's law, indeed it cannot; ⁸and those who are in the flesh cannot please God.

9 But you are not in the flesh, you are in the Spirit, if the Spirit of God really dwells in you. Any one who does not have the Spirit of Christ does not belong to him. ¹⁰But if Christ is in you, although your bodies are dead because of sin, your spirits are alive because of righteousness. ¹¹If the Spirit of him who raised Jesus from the dead dwells in you, he who raised Christ Jesus from the dead will give life to your mortal bodies also through his Spirit which dwells in you.

12 So then, brethren, we are debtors, not to the flesh, to live according to the flesh—¹³for if you live according to the flesh you will die, but if by the

τὰ τοῦ πνεύματος. 6 τὸ γὰρ φρόνημα
the of the Spirit. For the mind
things

τῆς σαρκὸς θάνατος, τὸ δὲ φρόνημα
of the flesh [is] death, but the mind

τοῦ πνεύματος ζωὴ καὶ εἰρήνη. 7 διότι
of the Spirit life and peace. Wherefore

τὸ φρόνημα τῆς σαρκὸς ἔχθρα εἰς θεόν·
the mind of the flesh [is] enmity against God;

τῷ γὰρ νόμῳ τοῦ θεοῦ οὐχ ὑποτάσσεται,
for to the law – of God it is not subject,

οὐδὲ γὰρ δύναται· 8 οἱ δὲ ἐν σαρκὶ
neither indeed can it; and the [ones] ²in ³flesh

ὄντες θεῷ ἀρέσαι οὐ δύνανται. 9 ὑμεῖς
¹being ⁴God ⁵to please ⁴cannot. ye

δὲ οὐκ ἐστὲ ἐν σαρκὶ ἀλλὰ ἐν πνεύματι,
But are not in flesh but in Spirit,

εἴπερ πνεῦμα θεοῦ οἰκεῖ ἐν ὑμῖν. εἰ
since [the] Spirit of God dwells in you. if

δέ τις πνεῦμα Χριστοῦ οὐκ ἔχει, οὗτος
But anyone [the] Spirit of Christ has not, this one

οὐκ ἔστιν αὐτοῦ. 10 εἰ δὲ Χριστὸς
is not of him. But if Christ

ἐν ὑμῖν, τὸ μὲν σῶμα νεκρὸν διὰ
[is] in you, ²the ¹on one ³body [is] dead because
hand of

ἁμαρτίαν, τὸ δὲ πνεῦμα ζωὴ διὰ
sin, ²the ¹on the ³spirit [is] because
other life of

δικαιοσύνην. 11 εἰ δὲ τὸ πνεῦμα τοῦ
righteousness. But if the Spirit of the
[one]

ἐγείραντος τὸν Ἰησοῦν ἐκ νεκρῶν οἰκεῖ ἐν
having raised – Jesus from [the] dead dwells in

ὑμῖν, ὁ ἐγείρας ἐκ νεκρῶν Χριστὸν
you, the having from [the] dead Christ
[one] raised

Ἰησοῦν ζωοποιήσει καὶ τὰ θνητὰ σώματα
Jesus will quicken also the mortal bodies

ὑμῶν διὰ τοῦ ἐνοικοῦντος αὐτοῦ πνεύματος
of you through the ³indwelling ²of him ¹Spirit

ἐν ὑμῖν.
⁴in ⁵you.

12 Ἄρα οὖν, ἀδελφοί, ὀφειλέται ἐσμέν,
So then, brothers, debtors we are,

οὐ τῇ σαρκὶ τοῦ κατὰ σάρκα ζῆν. 13 εἰ
not to the flesh – accord- flesh to liveᵈ. if
ing to

γὰρ κατὰ σάρκα ζῆτε, μέλλετε ἀποθνήσκειν·
For accord- flesh ye live, ye are to die:
ing to about

Spirit you put to death the deeds of the body you will live. ¹⁴For all who are led by the Spirit of God are sons of God. ¹⁵For you did not receive the spirit of slavery to fall back into fear, but you have received the spirit of sonship. When we cry, "Abba! Father!" ¹⁶it is the Spirit himself bearing witness with our spirit that we are children of God, ¹⁷and if children, then heirs, heirs of God and fellow heirs with Christ, provided we suffer with him in order that we may also be glorified with him.

18 I consider that the sufferings of this present time are not worth comparing with the glory that is to be revealed to us. ¹⁹For the creation waits with eager longing for the revealing of the sons of God; ²⁰for the creation was subjected to futility, not of its own will but by the will of him who subjected it in hope; ²¹because the creation itself will be set free from its bondage to decay and obtain the glorious liberty of the children of God. ²²We know that the whole creation has been groaning in travail

εἰ δὲ πνεύματι τὰς πράξεις τοῦ σώματος
but if by [the] Spirit the practices of the body

θανατοῦτε, ζήσεσθε. 14 ὅσοι γὰρ πνεύματι
ye put to death, ye will live. For as many as by [the] Spirit

θεοῦ ἄγονται, οὗτοι υἱοί εἰσιν θεοῦ.
of God are led, these sons are of God.

15 οὐ γὰρ ἐλάβετε πνεῦμα δουλείας πάλιν
For ye received not a spirit of slavery again

εἰς φόβον, ἀλλὰ ἐλάβετε πνεῦμα υἱοθεσίας,
for fear, but ye received a spirit of adoption,

ἐν ᾧ κράζομεν· ἀββὰ ὁ πατήρ. 16 αὐτὸ
by which we cry : Abba – Father. ²it(him)self

τὸ πνεῦμα συμμαρτυρεῖ τῷ πνεύματι ἡμῶν
¹The ²Spirit witnesses with the spirit of us

ὅτι ἐσμὲν τέκνα θεοῦ. 17 εἰ δὲ τέκνα,
that we are children of God. And if children,

καὶ κληρονόμοι· κληρονόμοι μὲν θεοῦ,
also heirs; heirs on one hand of God,

συγκληρονόμοι δὲ Χριστοῦ, εἴπερ συμπάσ-
joint heirs on the of Christ, since we suffer
other

χομεν ἵνα καὶ συνδοξασθῶμεν. 18 Λογίζομαι
with[him] in or- also we may be glorified I reckon
der that with [him].

γὰρ ὅτι οὐκ ἄξια τὰ παθήματα τοῦ
For that ⁶[are] ⁷not ⁸worthy ¹the ²sufferings ³of the

νῦν καιροῦ πρὸς τὴν μέλλουσαν δόξαν
⁴now ⁵time [to with the coming glory
(present) be compared]

ἀποκαλυφθῆναι εἰς ἡμᾶς. 19 ἡ γὰρ
to be revealed to us. For the

ἀποκαραδοκία τῆς κτίσεως τὴν ἀποκάλυψιν
anxious watching of the creation ²the ³revelation

τῶν υἱῶν τοῦ θεοῦ ἀπεκδέχεται. 20 τῇ
⁴of the ⁵sons – ⁶of God ¹is eagerly expecting. –

γὰρ ματαιότητι ἡ κτίσις ὑπετάγη, οὐχ
For to vanity the creation was subjected, not

ἑκοῦσα, ἀλλὰ διὰ τὸν ὑποτάξαντα, ἐφ'
willing[ly], but because of the [one] subjecting, in

ἐλπίδι 21 διότι καὶ αὐτὴ ἡ κτίσις
hope because even itself the creation

ἐλευθερωθήσεται ἀπὸ τῆς δουλείας τῆς
will be freed from the slavery –

φθορᾶς εἰς τὴν ἐλευθερίαν τῆς δόξης
of corruption to the freedom of the glory

τῶν τέκνων τοῦ θεοῦ. 22 οἴδαμεν γὰρ
of the children – of God. For we know

ὅτι πᾶσα ἡ κτίσις συστενάζει καὶ
that all the creation groans together and

together until now; ²³and not only the creation, but we ourselves, who have the first fruits of the Spirit, groan inwardly as we wait for adoption as sons, the redemption of our bodies. ²⁴For in this hope we were saved. Now hope that is seen is not hope. For who hopes for what he sees? ²⁵But if we hope for what we do not see, we wait for it with patience.

26 Likewise the Spirit helps us in our weakness; for we do not know how to pray as we ought, but the Spirit himself intercedes for us with sighs too deep for words. ²⁷And he who searches the hearts of men knows what is the mind of the Spirit, because[h] the Spirit intercedes for the saints according to the will of God.

28 We know that in everything God works for good[i] with those who love him, who are called according to his purpose. ²⁹For those whom he foreknew he also predestined to be conformed to the image of his Son, in order that he might be the first-born among many brethren. ³⁰And those whom he predestined he also called;

[h] Or that
[i] Other ancient authorities read in everything he works for good, or everything works for good

συνωδίνει ἄχρι τοῦ νῦν· **23** οὐ μόνον δέ,
travails together until   -   now;   and not only [so],

ἀλλὰ καὶ αὐτοὶ τὴν ἀπαρχὴν τοῦ πνεύματος
but also [our]selves ²the ³firstfruit ⁴of the ⁵Spirit

ἔχοντες [ἡμεῖς] καὶ αὐτοὶ ἐν ἑαυτοῖς
¹having   we   also [our]selves in ourselves

στενάζομεν υἱοθεσίαν ἀπεκδεχόμενοι, τὴν
groan   adoption   eagerly expecting, the

ἀπολύτρωσιν τοῦ σώματος ἡμῶν. **24** τῇ
redemption   of the body   of us.   -

γὰρ ἐλπίδι ἐσώθημεν· ἐλπὶς δὲ βλεπομένη
For by hope we were saved; but hope   being seen

οὐκ ἔστιν ἐλπίς· ὃ γὰρ βλέπει τις,
is not   hope; for what sees anyone,

τί καὶ ἐλπίζει; **25** εἰ δὲ ὃ οὐ βλέπομεν
why also he hopes?   but if what we do not see

ἐλπίζομεν, δι' ὑπομονῆς ἀπεκδεχόμεθα.
we hope [for], through patience   we eagerly expect.

26 ὡσαύτως δὲ καὶ τὸ πνεῦμα συναντιλαμ-
And similarly also the Spirit   takes

βάνεται τῇ ἀσθενείᾳ ἡμῶν· τὸ γὰρ τί
share in the weakness   of us;   - for what

προσευξώμεθα καθὸ δεῖ οὐκ οἴδαμεν, ἀλλὰ
we may pray   as it behoves we know not,   but

αὐτὸ τὸ πνεῦμα ὑπερεντυγχάνει στεναγμοῖς
it(him)self the Spirit supplicates on [our] behalf with groanings

ἀλαλήτοις· **27** ὁ δὲ ἐρευνῶν τὰς καρδίας
unutterable;   and the [one] searching the   hearts

οἶδεν τί τὸ φρόνημα τοῦ πνεύματος,
knows what [is] the mind   of the   Spirit,

ὅτι κατὰ θεὸν ἐντυγχάνει ὑπὲρ ἁγίων.
be- according God he supplicates on behalf saints.
cause to

28 οἴδαμεν δὲ ὅτι τοῖς ἀγαπῶσιν τὸν
And we know   that to the [ones] loving   -

θεὸν πάντα συνεργεῖ [ὁ θεὸς] εἰς ἀγαθόν,
God ³all things ²works together - ¹God for good,

τοῖς κατὰ πρόθεσιν κλητοῖς οὖσιν. **29** ὅτι
to the ²accord- ⁴purpose ²called ¹being.   Because
[ones] ing to

οὓς προέγνω, καὶ προώρισεν συμμόρφους
whom he foreknew, also he foreordained conformed to

τῆς εἰκόνος τοῦ υἱοῦ αὐτοῦ, εἰς τὸ
of the image of the Son   of him,   for the
                                          =that he should be

εἶναι αὐτὸν πρωτότοκον ἐν πολλοῖς
to be him[h]   firstborn   among many

ἀδελφοῖς· **30** οὓς δὲ προώρισεν, τούτους
brothers;   but whom he foreordained, these

and those whom he called he also justified; and those whom he justified he also glorified. 31 What then shall we say to this? If God is for us, who is against us? 32 He who did not spare his own Son but gave him up for us all, will he not also give us all things with him? 33 Who shall bring any charge against God's elect? It is God who justifies; 34 who is to condemn? Is it Christ Jesus, who died, yes, who was raised from the dead, who is at the right hand of God, who indeed intercedes for us?ʲ 35 Who shall separate us from the love of Christ? Shall tribulation, or distress, or persecution, or famine, or nakedness, or peril, or sword? 36 As it is written,

"For thy sake we are being killed all the day long;
we are regarded as sheep to be slaughtered."

37 No, in all these things we are more than conquerors through him who loved us. 38 For I am sure that neither death, nor life, nor angels, nor principalities, nor things present, nor things to come, nor powers, 39 nor height, nor depth, nor

ʲ Or It is Christ Jesus . . . for us

καὶ ἐκάλεσεν· καὶ οὓς ἐκάλεσεν, τούτους
also he called; and whom he called, these
καὶ ἐδικαίωσεν· οὓς δὲ ἐδικαίωσεν, τούτους
also he justified; but whom he justified, these
καὶ ἐδόξασεν. 31 Τί οὖν ἐροῦμεν πρὸς
also he glorified. What therefore shall we say to
ταῦτα; εἰ ὁ θεὸς ὑπὲρ ἡμῶν, τίς καθ᾽
these things? If – God on behalf of us, who against
ἡμῶν; ὅς γε τοῦ ἰδίου υἱοῦ οὐκ ἐφείσατο,
us? Who indeed the(his) own Son spared not,
32 ἀλλὰ ὑπὲρ ἡμῶν πάντων παρέδωκεν
but on behalf of us all delivered
αὐτόν, πῶς οὐχὶ καὶ σὺν αὐτῷ τὰ πάντα
him, how not also with him – all things
ἡμῖν χαρίσεται; 33 τίς ἐγκαλέσει κατὰ
to us will he will bring a against
freely give? charge against
ἐκλεκτῶν θεοῦ; θεὸς ὁ δικαιῶν· 34 τίς
chosen ones of God? God [is] the [one] justifying; who
ὁ κατακρινῶν; Χριστὸς Ἰησοῦς ὁ ἀποθανών,
the condemning? Christ Jesus [is] the having died,
[one] [one]
μᾶλλον δὲ ἐγερθείς, ὅς ἐστιν ἐν δεξιᾷ
but rather having who is at [the] right
been raised, [hand]
τοῦ θεοῦ, ὃς καὶ ἐντυγχάνει ὑπὲρ ἡμῶν.
– of God, who also supplicates on behalf of us.
35 τίς ἡμᾶς χωρίσει ἀπὸ τῆς ἀγάπης
Who us will separate from the love
τοῦ Χριστοῦ; θλῖψις ἢ στενοχωρία ἢ
– of Christ? affliction or distress or
διωγμὸς ἢ λιμὸς ἢ γυμνότης ἢ κίνδυνος
persecution or famine or nakedness or peril
ἢ μάχαιρα; 36 καθὼς γέγραπται ὅτι ἕνεκεν
or sword? As it has been – For the
written[,] sake
σοῦ θανατούμεθα ὅλην τὴν ἡμέραν,
of thee we are being put to death all the day,
ἐλογίσθημεν ὡς πρόβατα σφαγῆς. 37 ἀλλ᾽
we were reckoned as sheep of(for) slaughter. But
ἐν τούτοις πᾶσιν ὑπερνικῶμεν διὰ τοῦ
in these things all we overconquer through the
ἀγαπήσαντος ἡμᾶς. 38 πέπεισμαι γὰρ
[one] having loved us. For I have been persuaded
ὅτι οὔτε θάνατος οὔτε ζωὴ οὔτε ἄγγελοι
that not death nor life nor angels
οὔτε ἀρχαὶ οὔτε ἐνεστῶτα οὔτε μέλλοντα
nor rulers nor things present nor things coming
οὔτε δυνάμεις 39 οὔτε ὕψωμα οὔτε βάθος
nor powers nor height nor depth

anything else in all creation, will be able to separate us from the love of God in Christ Jesus our Lord.

οὔτε τις κτίσις ἑτέρα δυνήσεται ἡμᾶς
nor any creature other will be able us
χωρίσαι ἀπὸ τῆς ἀγάπης τοῦ θεοῦ τῆς
to separate from the love – of God –
ἐν Χριστῷ Ἰησοῦ τῷ κυρίῳ ἡμῶν.
in Christ Jesus the Lord of us.

CHAPTER 9

I am speaking the truth in Christ, I am not lying; my conscience bears me witness in the Holy Spirit, ² that I have great sorrow and unceasing anguish in my heart. ³ For I could wish that I myself were accursed and cut off from Christ for the sake of my brethren, my kinsmen by race. ⁴ They are Israelites, and to them belong the sonship, the glory, the covenants, the giving of the law, the worship, and the promises; ⁵ to them belong the patriarchs, and of their race, according to the flesh, is the Christ. God who is over all be blessed for ever.ᵏ Amen.

6 But it is not as though the word of God had failed. For not all who are descended from Israel belong to Israel, ⁷ and not all are children of Abraham because they are his descendants; but "Through Isaac shall your descendants be named." ⁸ This means that it is not the children

9 Ἀλήθειαν λέγω ἐν Χριστῷ, ου
Truth I say in Christ, not
ψεύδομαι, συμμαρτυρούσης μοι τῆς
I lie, witnessing with me the
συνειδήσεώς μου ἐν πνεύματι ἁγίῳ, 2 ὅτι
conscienceᵃ of me in [the] Spirit Holy, that
λύπη μοί ἐστιν μεγάλη καὶ ἀδιάλειπτος
grief to me is great and incessant
=I have great grief and . . .
ὀδύνη τῇ καρδίᾳ μου. 3 ηὐχόμην γὰρ
painᶜ in the heart of me. For I was praying
ἀνάθεμα εἶναι αὐτὸς ἐγὼ ἀπὸ τοῦ Χριστοῦ
ᵃa curse ᵇto be ᵇ[my]self ¹I from – Christ
ὑπὲρ τῶν ἀδελφῶν μου τῶν συγγενῶν
on behalf of the brothers of me the kinsmen
μου κατὰ σάρκα, 4 οἵτινές εἰσιν Ἰσραη-
of me according to flesh, who are Israel-
λῖται, ὧν ἡ υἱοθεσία καὶ ἡ δόξα καὶ
ites, of whom the adoption and the glory and
αἱ διαθῆκαι καὶ ἡ νομοθεσία καὶ ἡ
the covenants and the giving of [the] law and the
λατρεία καὶ αἱ ἐπαγγελίαι, 5 ὧν οἱ
service and the promises, of whom the
πατέρες, καὶ ἐξ ὧν ὁ Χριστὸς τὸ κατὰ
fathers, and from whom the Christ – according to
σάρκα· ὁ ὢν ἐπὶ πάντων θεὸς εὐλογητὸς
flesh; the [one] being over all God blessed
εἰς τοὺς αἰῶνας, ἀμήν. 6 Οὐχ οἷον δὲ
unto the ages, amen. Not of course
ὅτι ἐκπέπτωκεν ὁ λόγος τοῦ θεοῦ. οὐ
that has failed the word – of God. not
γὰρ πάντες οἱ ἐξ Ἰσραήλ, οὗτοι Ἰσραήλ·
For all the [ones] of Israel, these [are of] Israel;
7 οὐδ᾽ ὅτι εἰσὶν σπέρμα Ἀβραάμ, πάντες
neither because they are seed of [are they]
Abraham, all
τέκνα, ἀλλ᾽· ἐν Ἰσαὰκ κληθήσεταί σοι
children, but: In Isaac will be called to thee
σπέρμα. 8 τοῦτ᾽ ἔστιν, οὐ τὰ τέκνα τῆς
seed.ᶜ This is, not the children of the
=thy seed.

ᵏ Or Christ, who is God over all, blessed for ever

of the flesh who are the children of God, but the children of the promise are reckoned as descendants. ⁹For this is what the promise said, "About this time I will return and Sarah shall have a son." ¹⁰And not only so, but also when Rebecca had conceived children by one man, our forefather Isaac, ¹¹though they were not yet born and had done nothing either good or bad, in order that God's purpose of election might continue, not because of works but because of his call, ¹²she was told, "The elder will serve the younger." ¹³As it is written, "Jacob I loved, but Esau I hated."

14 What shall we say then? Is there injustice on God's part? By no means! ¹⁵For he says to Moses, "I will have mercy on whom I have mercy, and I will have compassion on whom I have compassiion." ¹⁶So it depends not upon man's will or exertion, but upon God's mercy. ¹⁷For the scripture says to Pharaoh, "I have raised you up for the very purpose of showing

σαρκὸς ταῦτα τέκνα τοῦ θεοῦ, ἀλλὰ
flesh   these   children   of   God,   but
τὰ τέκνα τῆς ἐπαγγελίας λογίζεται εἰς
the children of the   promise   is(are) reckoned for
σπέρμα. 9 ἐπαγγελίας γὰρ ὁ λόγος οὗτος·
a seed.   For ⁵of promise ³the ⁴word ¹this ²[is]:
κατὰ τὸν καιρὸν τοῦτον ἐλεύσομαι καὶ
According to   this time   I will come   and
ἔσται τῇ Σάρρᾳ υἱός. 10 οὐ μόνον δέ,
will be   to Sara   a son.°   And not only [so],
=Sarah will have a son.
ἀλλὰ καὶ Ῥεβεκκὰ ἐξ ἑνὸς κοίτην ἔχουσα,
but   also   Rebecca ²from ³one   ¹conceiving,†
Ἰσαὰκ τοῦ πατρὸς ἡμῶν· 11 μήπω γὰρ
Isaac   the   father   of us;   for not yet
γεννηθέντων μηδὲ πραξάντων τι ἀγαθὸν
being bornª   nor   practisingª anything good
ἢ φαῦλον, ἵνα ἡ κατ' ἐκλογὴν πρόθεσις
or   bad,   in order ¹the ⁴accord- ⁵choice ²purpose
          that   ing to
τοῦ θεοῦ μένῃ, 12 οὐκ ἐξ ἔργων ἀλλ'
-   ³of God   might   not   of   works   but
         remain,
ἐκ τοῦ καλοῦντος, ἐρρέθη αὐτῇ ὅτι ὁ
of the [one]   calling,   it was said to her[,]   - The
μείζων δουλεύσει τῷ ἐλάσσονι· 13 καθάπερ
greater   will serve   the   lesser;   even as
γέγραπται· τὸν Ἰακὼβ ἠγάπησα, τὸν δὲ
it has been   -   Jacob   I loved,   -   but
written:
Ἡσαῦ ἐμίσησα.
Esau   I hated.

14 Τί οὖν ἐροῦμεν; μὴ ἀδικία παρὰ
What therefore shall we say? not unrighteousness with
τῷ θεῷ; μὴ γένοιτο. 15 τῷ Μωϋσεῖ
-   God?   May it not be.   - ²to Moses
γὰρ λέγει· ἐλεήσω ὃν ἂν ἐλεῶ, καὶ
¹For   he says: I will   whomever I have   and
         have mercy on   mercy,
οἰκτιρήσω ὃν ἂν οἰκτίρω. 16 ἄρα οὖν
I will pity   whomever I pity.   So therefore
                       [it is]
οὐ τοῦ θέλοντος οὐδὲ τοῦ τρέχοντος,
not of the [one] wishing   nor   of the [one] running,
ἀλλὰ τοῦ ἐλεῶντος θεοῦ. 17 λέγει γὰρ
but of the [one] having mercy   God.   For says
ἡ γραφὴ τῷ Φαραὼ ὅτι εἰς αὐτὸ τοῦτο
the scripture   - to Pharaoh[,]   -   For   this very thing
ἐξήγειρά σε, ὅπως ἐνδείξωμαι ἐν σοὶ
I raised up   thee,   so as   I may show forth   in   thee

my power in you, so that my name may be proclaimed in all the earth." [18]So then he has mercy upon whomever he wills, and he hardens the heart of whomever he wills. 19 You will say to me then, "Why does he still find fault? For who can resist his will?" [20]But who are you, a man, to answer back to God? Will what is molded say to its molder, "Why have you made me thus?" [21]Has the potter no right over the clay, to make out of the same lump one vessel for beauty and another for menial use? [22]What if God, desiring to show his wrath and to make known his power, has endured with much patience the vessels of wrath made for destruction, [23]in order to make known the riches of his glory for the vessels of mercy, which he has prepared beforehand for glory, [24]even us whom he has called, not from the Jews only but also from the Gentiles? [25]As indeed he says in Hose'a,

"Those who were not
    my people
I will call 'my people,'
and her who was not
    beloved
I will call 'my
    beloved.' "
[26]"And in the very place

τὴν δύναμίν μου, καὶ ὅπως διαγγελῇ τὸ
the power   of me, and so as might be pub- the
                                    lished abroad
ὄνομά μου ἐν πάσῃ τῇ γῇ. 18 ἄρα οὖν
name of me in all the earth.   So therefore
ὃν θέλει ἐλεεῖ, ὃν δὲ θέλει σκληρύνει.
whom he   he has but whom he wishes he hardens.
      wishes mercy,
19 Ἐρεῖς μοι οὖν· τί ἔτι μέμφεται;
Thou wilt say to me therefore: Why still finds he fault?
τῷ γὰρ βουλήματι αὐτοῦ τίς ἀνθέστηκεν;
for ³the ⁴counsel   ⁵of him ¹who ²resisted?
20 ὦ ἄνθρωπε, μενοῦν γε σὺ τίς εἶ ὁ
O man,   nay rather ³thou ¹who ²art the
ἀνταποκρινόμενος τῷ θεῷ; μὴ ἐρεῖ τὸ
[one] replying against - God? not ³Will say ¹the
πλάσμα τῷ πλάσαντι· τί με ἐποίησας
²thing   to the having formed: Why ²me ¹madest
formed [one]   thou
οὕτως; 21 ἢ οὐκ ἔχει ἐξουσίαν ὁ κεραμεὺς
thus? or has not ²authority ¹the ²potter
τοῦ πηλοῦ ἐκ τοῦ αὐτοῦ φυράματος
of the clay out of the same lump
ποιῆσαι ὃ μὲν εἰς τιμὴν σκεῦος, ὃ δὲ
to make ¹this ²to ⁴honour ²vessel, that
εἰς ἀτιμίαν; 22 εἰ δὲ θέλων ὁ θεὸς
to dishonour? But if wishing - God
ἐνδείξασθαι τὴν ὀργὴν καὶ γνωρίσαι τὸ
to show forth the(his) wrath and to make known the
δυνατὸν αὐτοῦ ἤνεγκεν ἐν πολλῇ μακρο-
ability of him bore in much long-
θυμίᾳ σκεύη ὀργῆς κατηρτισμένα εἰς
suffering vessels of wrath having been fitted for
ἀπώλειαν, 23 καὶ ἵνα γνωρίσῃ τὸν πλοῦτον
destruction, and in or- he might the riches
              der that make known
τῆς δόξης αὐτοῦ ἐπὶ σκεύη ἐλέους, ἃ
of the glory of him on vessels of mercy, which
προητοίμασεν εἰς δόξαν, 24 οὓς καὶ
he previously prepared for glory, whom also
ἐκάλεσεν ἡμᾶς οὐ μόνον ἐξ Ἰουδαίων
he called[,] us not only of Jews
ἀλλὰ καὶ ἐξ ἐθνῶν; 25 ὡς καὶ ἐν τῷ
but also of nations? As also in -
Ὡσηὲ λέγει· καλέσω τὸν οὐ λαόν μου
Osee he says: I will call the ²not ¹people of me
λαόν μου καὶ τὴν οὐκ ἠγαπημένην
a people of me and the not having been loved
ἠγαπημένην· 26 καὶ ἔσται ἐν τῷ τόπῳ
having been loved; and it shall be in the place

where it was said to them, 'You are not my people,' they will be called 'sons of the living God.' "

27 And Isaiah cries out concerning Israel: "Though the number of the sons of Israel be as the sand of the sea, only a remnant of them will be saved; [28] for the Lord will execute his sentence upon the earth with vigor and dispatch." [29] And as Isaiah predicted, "If the Lord of hosts had not left us children, we would have fared like Sodom and been made like Gomor'rah."

30 What shall we say, then? That Gentiles who did not pursue righteousness have attained it, that is, righteousness through faith; [31] but that Israel who pursued the righteousness which is based on law did not succeed in fulfilling that law. [32] Why? Because they did not pursue it through faith, but as if it were based on works. They have stumbled over the stumbling-stone, [33] as it is written,

"Behold I am laying in Zion a stone that will make men stumble, a rock that will make them fall; and he who believes in him will not be put to shame."

οὗ ἐρρέθη [αὐτοῖς]· οὐ λαός μου ὑμεῖς,
where it was said to them: not a people of me ye [are],

ἐκεῖ κληθήσονται υἱοὶ θεοῦ ζῶντος.
there they will be called sons ²God ¹of a living.

27 Ἠσαΐας δὲ κράζει ὑπὲρ τοῦ Ἰσραήλ·
But Esaias cries on behalf of – Israel:

ἐὰν ᾖ ὁ ἀριθμὸς τῶν υἱῶν Ἰσραὴλ
If be the number of the sons of Israel

ὡς ἡ ἄμμος τῆς θαλάσσης, τὸ ὑπόλειμμα
as the sand of the sea, the remnant

σωθήσεται· 28 λόγον γὰρ συντελῶν καὶ
will be saved; for ⁶an account ¹accomplishing ²and

συντέμνων ποιήσει κύριος ἐπὶ τῆς γῆς.
³cutting short ⁵will make ⁴[the] Lord on the earth.

29 καὶ καθὼς προείρηκεν Ἠσαΐας· εἰ μὴ
And as ²has previously said ¹Esaias: Except

κύριος σαβαὼθ ἐγκατέλιπεν ἡμῖν σπέρμα,
[the] Lord of hosts left to us a seed,

ὡς Σόδομα ἂν ἐγενήθημεν καὶ ὡς Γόμορρα
as Sodom we would have become and as Gomorra

ἂν ὡμοιώθημεν.
we would have been likened.

30 Τί οὖν ἐροῦμεν; ὅτι ἔθνη τὰ μὴ
What therefore shall we say? that nations – not

διώκοντα δικαιοσύνην κατέλαβεν δικαιοσύνην,
pursuing righteousness apprehended righteousness,

δικαιοσύνην δὲ τὴν ἐκ πίστεως· 31 Ἰσραὴλ
but a righteousness – of faith; ²Israel

δὲ διώκων νόμον δικαιοσύνης εἰς νόμον
¹but pursuing a law of righteousness ⁸υ(αι) ¹a law

οὐκ ἔφθασεν. 32 διὰ τί; ὅτι οὐκ ἐκ
¹did not arrive. Why? Because not of

πίστεως ἀλλ᾽ ὡς ἐξ ἔργων· προσέκοψαν
faith but as of works; they stumbled

τῷ λίθῳ τοῦ προσκόμματος, 33 καθὼς
at the stone – of stumbling, as

γέγραπται· ἰδοὺ τίθημι ἐν Σιὼν λίθον
it has been Behold I place in Sion a stone
written:

προσκόμματος καὶ πέτραν σκανδάλου, καὶ
of stumbling and a rock of offence, and

ὁ πιστεύων ἐπ᾽ αὐτῷ οὐ καταισχυνθήσεται.
the [one] believing on him will not be put to shame.

CHAPTER 10

BRETHREN, my heart's desire and prayer to God for them is that they may be saved. ²I bear them witness that they have a zeal for God, but it is not enlightened. ³For, being ignorant of the righteousness that comes from God, and seeking to establish their own, they did not submit to God's righteousness. ⁴For Christ is the end of the law, that every one who has faith may be justified.

5 Moses writes that the man who practices the righteousness which is based on the law shall live by it. ⁶But the righteousness based on faith says, Do not say in your heart, "Who will ascend into heaven?" (that is, to bring Christ down) ⁷or "Who will descend into the abyss?" (that is, to bring Christ up from the dead). ⁸But what does it say? The word is near you, on your lips and in your heart (that is, the word of faith which we preach); ⁹because, if you confess with your lips that Jesus is Lord and believe in your heart that God raised him from the

10 Ἀδελφοί, ἡ μὲν εὐδοκία τῆς ἐμῆς
Brothers, the – good pleasure – of my
καρδίας καὶ ἡ δέησις πρὸς τὸν θεὸν
heart and the request to – God
ὑπὲρ αὐτῶν εἰς σωτηρίαν. 2 μαρτυρῶ
on behalf of them [is] for salvation. I witness
γὰρ αὐτοῖς ὅτι ζῆλον θεοῦ ἔχουσιν, ἀλλ᾽
For to them that a zeal of God they have, but
οὐ κατ᾽ ἐπίγνωσιν· 3 ἀγνοοῦντες γὰρ τὴν
not according to knowledge; for not knowing the
τοῦ θεοῦ δικαιοσύνην, καὶ τὴν ἰδίαν
– ²of God ¹righteousness, and the(ir) own
ζητοῦντες στῆσαι, τῇ δικαιοσύνῃ τοῦ θεοῦ
seeking to establish, to the righteousness – of God
οὐχ ὑπετάγησαν. 4 τέλος γὰρ νόμου
they did not submit. For end of law
Χριστὸς εἰς δικαιοσύνην παντὶ τῷ
Christ [is] for righteousness to everyone
πιστεύοντι. 5 Μωϋσῆς γὰρ γράφει ὅτι
believing. For Moses writes[,] –
τὴν δικαιοσύνην τὴν ἐκ νόμου ὁ ποιήσας
⁴the ⁵righteousness the ⁶of ⁷law ¹The ³doing
ἄνθρωπος ζήσεται ἐν αὐτῇ. 6 ἡ δὲ
²man will live by it. But the
ἐκ πίστεως δικαιοσύνη οὕτως λέγει· μὴ
²of ³faith ¹righteousness thus says: not
εἴπῃς ἐν τῇ καρδίᾳ σου· τίς ἀναβήσεται
Say in the heart of thee: Who will ascend
εἰς τὸν οὐρανόν; τοῦτ᾽ ἔστιν Χριστὸν
into – heaven? this is Christ
καταγαγεῖν· 7 ἤ· τίς καταβήσεται εἰς
to bring down; or: Who will descend into
τὴν ἄβυσσον; τοῦτ᾽ ἔστιν Χριστὸν ἐκ
the abyss? this is Christ from
νεκρῶν ἀναγαγεῖν. 8 ἀλλὰ τί λέγει;
[the] dead to bring up. But what says it?
ἐγγύς σου τὸ ῥῆμά ἐστιν, ἐν τῷ στόματί
Near thee the word is, in the mouth
σου καὶ ἐν τῇ καρδίᾳ σου· τοῦτ᾽ ἔστιν
of thee and in the heart of thee; this is
τὸ ῥῆμα τῆς πίστεως ὃ κηρύσσομεν.
the word – of faith which we proclaim.
9 ὅτι ἐὰν ὁμολογήσῃς ἐν τῷ στόματί
Because if thou confessest with the mouth
σου κύριον Ἰησοῦν, καὶ πιστεύσῃς ἐν
of thee Lord Jesus, and believest in
τῇ καρδίᾳ σου ὅτι ὁ θεὸς αὐτὸν ἤγειρεν
the heart of thee that – God him raised

dead, you will be saved. [10] For man believes with his heart and so is justified, and he confesses with his lips and so is saved. [11] The scripture says, "No one who believes in him will be put to shame." [12] For there is no distinction between Jew and Greek; the same Lord is Lord of all and bestows his riches upon all who call upon him. [13] For, "every one who calls upon the name of the Lord will be saved."

14 But how are men to call upon him in whom they have not believed? And how are they to believe in him of whom they have never heard? And how are they to hear without a preacher? [15] And how can men preach unless they are sent? As it is written, "How beautiful are the feet of those who preach good news!" [16] But they have not all heeded the gospel; for Isaiah says, "Lord, who has believed what he has heard from us?" [17] So faith comes from what is heard, and what is heard comes by the preaching of Christ.

18 But I ask, have they not heard? Indeed they have; for "Their voice has gone out to all the earth,

ἐκ   νεκρῶν,   σωθήσῃ·   10 καρδίᾳ   γὰρ
from   [the] dead,   thou wilt be saved;   for with heart

πιστεύεται   εἰς   δικαιοσύνην,   στόματι   δὲ
[one] believes   to   righteousness,   and with mouth

ὁμολογεῖται   εἰς   σωτηρίαν.   11 λέγει   γὰρ
[one] confesses   to   salvation.   For says

ἡ   γραφή·   πᾶς   ὁ   πιστεύων   ἐπ'   αὐτῷ
the   scripture: Everyone   believing   on   him

οὐ   καταισχυνθήσεται.   12 οὐ   γάρ   ἐστιν
will not be put to shame.   For there is no

διαστολὴ   Ἰουδαίου   τε   καὶ   Ἕλληνος.   ὁ
difference   ²of Jew   ¹both   ³and   ⁴of Greek.*   the

γὰρ   αὐτὸς   κύριος   πάντων,   πλουτῶν   εἰς
For   same   Lord   of all,   is rich   to

πάντας   τοὺς   ἐπικαλουμένους   αὐτόν·   13 πᾶς
all   the [ones]   calling on   him;   ²everyone

γὰρ   ὃς   ἂν   ἐπικαλέσηται   τὸ   ὄνομα   κυρίου
¹for   whoever   calls on   the   name   of [the]
Lord

σωθήσεται.   14 Πῶς   οὖν   ἐπικαλέσωνται   εἰς
will be saved.   How   therefore   may they call on   in
[one]

ὃν   οὐκ   ἐπίστευσαν;   πῶς   δὲ   πιστεύσωσιν
whom   they believed not?   And how   may they believe

οὗ   οὐκ   ἤκουσαν;   πῶς   δὲ   ἀκούσωσιν
of whom   they heard not?   And how   may they hear

χωρὶς   κηρύσσοντος;   15 πῶς   δὲ   κηρύξωσιν
without   [one] heralding?   And how   may they herald

ἐὰν   μὴ   ἀποσταλῶσιν;   καθάπερ   γέγραπται·
if   they are not sent?   As   it has been written:

ὡς   ὡραῖοι   οἱ   πόδες   τῶν   εὐαγγελιζομένων
How   beautiful   the   feet   of the [ones] announcing good

ἀγαθά.   16 ἀλλ'   οὐ   πάντες   ὑπήκουσαν   τῷ
good things.   But   not   all   obeyed   the

εὐαγγελίῳ.   Ἡσαΐας   γὰρ   λέγει·   κύριε,
gospel.   For Esaias   says: Lord,

τίς   ἐπίστευσεν   τῇ   ἀκοῇ   ἡμῶν;   17 ἄρα
who   believed   the   hearing   of us?   Then

ἡ   πίστις   ἐξ   ἀκοῆς,   ἡ   δὲ   ἀκοὴ   διὰ
-   faith [is] from   hearing,   and the   hearing through

ῥήματος   Χριστοῦ.   18 ἀλλὰ   λέγω,   μὴ
a word   of Christ.   But   I say,   not

οὐκ   ἤκουσαν;   μενοῦν   γε·   εἰς   πᾶσαν
did they not hear?   Nay   rather: To   all

τὴν   γῆν   ἐξῆλθεν   ὁ   φθόγγος   αὐτῶν,
the   earth   went out   the   utterance   of them,

* That is, between these two classes.

and their words to the ends of the world."
¹⁹Again I ask, did Israel not understand? First Moses says, "I will make you jealous of those who are not a nation; with a foolish nation I will make you angry."
²⁰Then Isaiah is so bold as to say, "I have been found by those who did not seek me; I have shown myself to those who did not ask for me."
²¹But of Israel he says, "All day long I have held out my hands to a disobedient and contrary people."

καὶ   εἰς   τὰ   πέρατα   τῆς   οἰκουμένης   τὰ
and   to   the   ends   of the   inhabited earth   the
ῥήματα   αὐτῶν.   19 ἀλλὰ   λέγω,   μὴ   Ἰσραὴλ
words   of them.   But   I say,   not   Israel
οὐκ   ἔγνω;   πρῶτος   Μωϋσῆς   λέγει·   ἐγὼ
did not know?   First   Moses   says :   I
παραζηλώσω   ὑμᾶς   ἐπ᾽   οὐκ   ἔθνει,   ἐπ᾽
will provoke to jealousy   you   on(by)   not   a nation,   on(by)
ἔθνει   ἀσυνέτῳ   παροργιῶ   ὑμᾶς.   20 Ἠσαΐας
a nation unintelligent   I will anger   you.   Esaias
δὲ   ἀποτολμᾷ   καὶ   λέγει·   εὑρέθην   τοῖς
But   is quite bold   and   says :   I was found   by the [ones]
ἐμὲ   μὴ   ζητοῦσιν,   ἐμφανὴς   ἐγενόμην   τοῖς
³me   ¹not   ²seeking,   manifest   I became   to the [ones]
ἐμὲ   μὴ   ἐπερωτῶσιν.   21 πρὸς   δὲ   τὸν
³me   ¹not   ²inquiring [for].   But to   –
Ἰσραὴλ   λέγει·   ὅλην   τὴν   ἡμέραν   ἐξεπέτασα
Israel   he says: All   the   day   I stretched out
τὰς   χεῖράς   μου   πρὸς   λαὸν   ἀπειθοῦντα
the   hands   of me   to   a people   disobeying
καὶ   ἀντιλέγοντα.
and   contradicting.

CHAPTER 11

I ask, then, has God rejected his people? By no means! I myself am an Israelite, a descendant of Abraham, a member of the tribe of Benjamin. ²God has not rejected his people whom he foreknew. Do you not know what the scripture says of Eli'jah, how he pleads with God against Israel? ³"Lord, they have killed thy prophets, they have demolished thy altars, and I alone am left, and they seek my life." ⁴But what is God's reply to him?

11 Λέγω   οὖν,   μὴ   ἀπώσατο   ὁ   θεὸς
I say   therefore,   ²did not put away   –   ¹God
τὸν   λαὸν   αὐτοῦ;   μὴ   γένοιτο·   καὶ   γὰρ
the   people   of him?   May it not be;   for even
ἐγὼ   Ἰσραηλίτης   εἰμί,   ἐκ   σπέρματος
I   an Israelite   am,   of   [the] seed
Ἀβραάμ,   φυλῆς   Βενιαμίν.   2 οὐκ   ἀπώσατο
of Abraham,   of [the] tribe   of Benjamin.   did not put away
ὁ   θεὸς   τὸν   λαὸν   αὐτοῦ   ὃν   προέγνω.
–   God   the   people   of him   whom   he foreknew.
ἢ   οὐκ   οἴδατε   ἐν   Ἠλίᾳ   τί   λέγει   ἡ
Or   know ye not   in   Elias   what   says   the
γραφή,   ὡς   ἐντυγχάνει   τῷ   θεῷ   κατὰ   τοῦ
scripture,   how   he supplicates   –   God   against
Ἰσραήλ;   3 κύριε,   τοὺς   προφήτας   σου
Israel?   Lord,   the   prophets   of thee
ἀπέκτειναν,   τὰ   θυσιαστήριά   σου   κατέσκαψαν,
they killed,   the   altars   of thee   they dug down,
κἀγὼ   ὑπελείφθην   μόνος   καὶ   ζητοῦσιν   τὴν
and I   was left behind   alone   and   they seek   the
ψυχήν   μου.   4 ἀλλὰ   τί   λέγει   αὐτῷ   ὁ
life   of me.   But   what   says   to him   the

"I have kept for myself seven thousand men who have not bowed the knee to Ba'al." ⁵So too at the present time there is a remnant, chosen by grace. ⁶But if it is by grace, it is no longer on the basis of works; otherwise grace would no longer be grace. 7 What then? Israel failed to obtain what it sought. The elect obtained it, but the rest were hardened, ⁸as it is written,
"God gave them a spirit of stupor, eyes that should not see and ears that should not hear, down to this very day."
⁹And David says, "Let their feast become a snare and a trap, a pitfall and a retribution for them; ¹⁰let their eyes be darkened so that they cannot see, and bend their backs for ever."
11 So I ask, have they stumbled so as to fall? By no means! But through their trespass salvation has come to the Gentiles, so as to make Israel jealous. ¹²Now if their trespass means riches for the world, and if their failure means

χρηματισμός; κατέλιπον ἐμαυτῷ ἑπτακισ-
[divine] response?   I reserved   to myself   seven

χιλίους ἄνδρας, οἵτινες οὐκ ἔκαμψαν γόνυ
thousands   men,   who   bowed not   knee

τῇ Βάαλ. 5 οὕτως οὖν καὶ ἐν τῷ νῦν
–   to Baal.   So therefore also   in   the present

καιρῷ λεῖμμα κατ᾽ ἐκλογὴν χάριτος
time   a remnant according to   a choice   of grace

γέγονεν· 6 εἰ δὲ χάριτι, οὐκέτι ἐξ ἔργων,
has become;   and if   by grace,   no more   of   works,

ἐπεὶ ἡ χάρις οὐκέτι γίνεται χάρις. 7 Τί
since   –   grace   no more   becomes   grace.   What

οὖν; ὃ ἐπιζητεῖ Ἰσραήλ, τοῦτο οὐκ
there-   What   ²seeks after   ¹Israel,   this   not
fore?

ἐπέτυχεν, ἡ δὲ ἐκλογὴ ἐπέτυχεν· οἱ δὲ
he obtained,   but the   choice   obtained [it];   and the

λοιποὶ ἐπωρώθησαν, 8 καθάπερ γέγραπται·
rest   were hardened,   as   it has been written:

ἔδωκεν αὐτοῖς ὁ θεὸς πνεῦμα κατανύξεως,
Gave   to them   –   God   a spirit   of torpor,

ὀφθαλμοὺς τοῦ μὴ βλέπειν καὶ ὦτα
eyes   –   not   to seeᵈ   and   ears

τοῦ μὴ ἀκούειν, ἕως τῆς σήμερον ἡμέρας
–   not   to hear,ᵈ   until   the   present†   day.

9 καὶ Δαυὶδ λέγει· γενηθήτω ἡ τράπεζα
And   David   says: Let become   the   table

αὐτῶν εἰς παγίδα καὶ εἰς θήραν καὶ
of them   for   a snare   and   for   a net   and

εἰς σκάνδαλον καὶ εἰς ἀνταπόδομα αὐτοῖς,
for   an offence   and   for   a recompence   to them,

10 σκοτισθήτωσαν οἱ ὀφθαλμοὶ αὐτῶν τοῦ
let be darkened   the   eyes   of them   –

μὴ βλέπειν, καὶ τὸν νῶτον αὐτῶν διὰ
not   to see,ᵈ   and   the   back   of them   al-

παντὸς σύγκαμψον.
ways   bending.

11 Λέγω οὖν, μὴ ἔπταισαν ἵνα πέσωσιν;
I say therefore,   did they not   in order   they might
   stumble   that   fall?

μὴ γένοιτο· ἀλλὰ τῷ αὐτῶν παραπτώματι
May it not be;   but   by the   ²of them   ¹trespass

ἡ σωτηρία τοῖς ἔθνεσιν, εἰς τὸ παραζηλῶσαι
–   salvation   to the   nations,   for   the   to provoke to
[came]   jealousy

αὐτούς. 12 εἰ δὲ τὸ παράπτωμα αὐτῶν
them.   But if   the   trespass   of them

πλοῦτος κόσμου καὶ τὸ ἥττημα αὐτῶν
[is] [the]   of [the]   and   the   defect   of them
riches   world

riches for the Gentiles, how much more will their full inclusion mean! 13 Now I am speaking to you Gentiles. Inasmuch then as I am an apostle to the Gentiles, I magnify my ministry ¹⁴in order to make my fellow Jews jealous, and thus save some of them. ¹⁵For if their rejection means the reconciliation of the world, what will their acceptance mean but life from the dead? ¹⁶If the dough offered as first fruits is holy, so is the whole lump; and if the root is holy, so are the branches.

17 But if some of the branches were broken off, and you, a wild olive shoot, were grafted in their place to share the richness¹ of the olive tree, ¹⁸do not boast over the branches. If you do boast, remember it is not you that support the root, but the root that supports you. ¹⁹You will say, "Branches were broken off so that I might be grafted in." ²⁰That is true. They were broken off because of their unbelief, but you stand fast only through faith. So do not become proud, but stand in awe. ²¹For if God did not spare the natural branches, neither will he spare you. ²²Note

¹ Other ancient authorities read *rich root*

πλοῦτος ἐθνῶν, πόσῳ μᾶλλον τὸ πλήρωμα
[is] [the] of [the] by how more the fulness
riches nations, much

αὐτῶν. 13 'Υμῖν δὲ λέγω τοῖς ἔθνεσιν.
of them. But to you ²I say[,] ¹the ²nations.

ἐφ' ὅσον μὲν οὖν εἰμι ἐγὼ ἐθνῶν ἀπόστο-
Forasmuch in- there- ²am ¹I ⁴of ³an apos-
as deed fore nations

λος, τὴν διακονίαν μου δοξάζω, 14 εἴ πως
tle, the ministry of me I glorify, if somehow

παραζηλώσω μου τὴν σάρκα καὶ σώσω
I may provoke to of me the flesh and may save
jealousy

τινὰς ἐξ αὐτῶν. 15 εἰ γὰρ ἡ ἀποβολὴ
some of them. For if the casting away

αὐτῶν καταλλαγὴ κόσμου, τίς ἡ πρόσλημψις
of them [is] [the] of [the] what the reception
reconciliation world,

εἰ μὴ ζωὴ ἐκ νεκρῶν; 16 εἰ δὲ ἡ
if not life from [the] dead? And if the

ἀπαρχὴ ἁγία, καὶ τὸ φύραμα· καὶ εἰ
firstfruit [is] holy, also the lump; and if

ἡ ῥίζα ἁγία, καὶ οἱ κλάδοι. 17 Εἰ δέ
the root [is] holy, also the branches. But if

τινες τῶν κλάδων ἐξεκλάσθησαν, σὺ δὲ
some of the branches were broken off, and thou

ἀγριέλαιος ὢν ἐνεκεντρίσθης ἐν αὐτοῖς
²a wild olive ¹being wast grafted in among them

καὶ συγκοινωνὸς τῆς ῥίζης τῆς πιότητος
and ²a partaker ³of the ⁴root* ⁵of the ⁶fatness

τῆς ἐλαίας ἐγένου, 18 μὴ κατακαυχῶ
⁷of the ⁸olive-tree ¹didst become, boast not against

τῶν κλάδων· εἰ δὲ κατακαυχᾶσαι, οὐ
of the branches; but if thou boastest, not

σὺ τὴν ῥίζαν βαστάζεις ἀλλὰ ἡ ῥίζα σέ.
thou the root bearest but the root thee.

19 ἐρεῖς οὖν· ἐξεκλάσθησαν κλάδοι ἵνα
Thou wilt therefore: ²Were broken off ¹branches in order
say that

ἐγὼ ἐγκεντρισθῶ. 20 καλῶς· τῇ ἀπιστίᾳ
I might be grafted in. Well: - for unbelief

ἐξεκλάσθησαν, σὺ δὲ τῇ πίστει ἔστηκας.
they were broken off, and thou - by faith standest.

μὴ ὑψηλὰ φρόνει, ἀλλὰ φοβοῦ· 21 εἰ
²Not ³high things ¹mind, but fear; ²if

γὰρ ὁ θεὸς τῶν κατὰ φύσιν κλάδων
¹for - ³God ⁵the ⁷according to ⁸nature ⁶branches

οὐκ ἐφείσατο, οὐδὲ σοῦ φείσεται. 22 ἴδε
⁴spared not, neither thee will he spare. See

* Some MSS insert καί (and) here; as it is, the two nouns in the genitive must be in apposition; *cf.* Col. 1. 18, 2. 2; John 8. 44.

then the kindness and the severity of God; severity toward those who have fallen, but God's kindness to you, provided you continue in his kindness; otherwise you too will be cut off. [23]And even the others, if they do not persist in their unbelief, will be grafted in, for God has the power to graft them in again. [24]For if you have been cut from what is by nature a wild olive tree, and grafted, contrary to nature, into a cultivated olive tree, how much more will these natural branches be grafted back into their own olive tree.

25 Lest you be wise in your own conceits, I want you to understand this mystery, brethren: a hardening has come upon part of Israel, until the full number of the Gentiles come in, [26]and so all Israel will be saved; as it is written, "The Deliverer will come from Zion, he will banish ungodliness from Jacob"; [27]"and this will be my covenant with them when I take away their sins."

[28]As regards the gospel they are enemies of God,

οὖν χρηστότητα καὶ ἀποτομίαν θεοῦ· ἐπὶ
therefore [the] kindness and [the] severity of God: [2]on

μὲν τοὺς πεσόντας ἀποτομία, ἐπὶ δὲ
[1]on one, the having fallen severity, [2]on [1]on the
hand [ones]   other

σὲ χρηστότης θεοῦ, ἐὰν ἐπιμένῃς τῇ
thee [the] kindness of God, if thou continuest in the
                                                              (his)

χρηστότητι, ἐπεὶ καὶ σὺ ἐκκοπήσῃ.
kindness, since also thou wilt be cut off.

23 κἀκεῖνοι δέ, ἐὰν μὴ ἐπιμένωσιν τῇ
And those also, if they continue not -

ἀπιστίᾳ, ἐγκεντρισθήσονται· δυνατὸς γάρ
in unbelief, will be grafted in; for [2]able

ἐστιν ὁ θεὸς πάλιν ἐγκεντρίσαι αὐτούς.
[2]is - [1]God [7]again [4]to graft [5]in [5]them.

24 εἰ γὰρ σὺ ἐκ τῆς κατὰ φύσιν ἐξεκόπης
For if thou [2]out [3]the [5]according [6]nature [1]wast cut
            of   to   out

ἀγριελαίου καὶ παρὰ φύσιν ἐνεκεντρίσθης
[4]wild olive and against nature wast grafted in

εἰς καλλιέλαιον, πόσῳ μᾶλλον οὗτοι οἱ
into a cultivated by how more these the
         olive,   much   [ones]

κατὰ φύσιν ἐγκεντρισθήσονται τῇ ἰδίᾳ
according to nature will be grafted in the(ir) own

ἐλαίᾳ. 25 Οὐ γὰρ θέλω ὑμᾶς ἀγνοεῖν,
olive-tree.   For I wish not you to be ignorant,

ἀδελφοί, τὸ μυστήριον τοῦτο, ἵνα μὴ
brothers, [of] this mystery, lest

ἦτε ἐν ἑαυτοῖς φρόνιμοι, ὅτι πώρωσις
ye be in yourselves wise, that hardness

ἀπὸ μέρους τῷ Ἰσραὴλ γέγονεν ἄχρι οὗ
from(in) part - to Israel has happened until

τὸ πλήρωμα τῶν ἐθνῶν εἰσέλθῃ, 26 καὶ
the fulness of the nations comes in, and

οὕτως πᾶς Ἰσραὴλ σωθήσεται, καθὼς
so all Israel will be saved, as

γέγραπται· ἥξει ἐκ Σιὼν ὁ ῥυόμενος·
it has been [3]will [4]out [5]Sion [1]The [2]delivering,
written: come of [one]

ἀποστρέψει ἀσεβείας ἀπὸ Ἰακώβ. 27 καὶ
he will turn away impiety from Jacob. And

αὕτη αὐτοῖς ἡ παρ' ἐμοῦ διαθήκη, ὅταν
this [is] [5]with them [1]the [3]from [4]me [2]covenant, when

ἀφέλωμαι τὰς ἁμαρτίας αὐτῶν. 28 κατὰ
I take away the sins of them. [2]According to

μὲν τὸ εὐαγγέλιον ἐχθροὶ δι' ὑμᾶς,
[1]on one the gospel enemies because you,
hand   of

for your sake; but as regards election they are beloved for the sake of their forefathers. [29] For the gifts and the call of God are irrevocable. [30] Just as you were once disobedient to God but now have received mercy because of their disobedience, [31] so they have now been disobedient in order that by the mercy shown to you they also may[m] receive mercy. [32] For God has consigned all men to disobedience, that he may have mercy upon all. 33 O the depth of the riches and wisdom and knowledge of God! How unsearchable are his judgments and how inscrutable his ways! [34] "For who has known the mind of the Lord, or who has been his counselor?" [35] "Or who has given a gift to him that he might be repaid?" [36] For from him and through him and to him are all things. To him be glory for ever. Amen.

CHAPTER 12

I appeal to you therefore, brethren, by the mercies of God, to present your bodies as a living sacrifice, holy and

[m] Other ancient authorities add now

κατὰ δὲ τὴν ἐκλογὴν ἀγαπητοὶ διὰ
²accord- ¹on the   the   choice   beloved   because
ing to   other   of

τοὺς πατέρας· 29 ἀμεταμέλητα γὰρ τὰ
the   fathers;   for unrepented   the

χαρίσματα καὶ ἡ κλῆσις τοῦ θεοῦ.
free gifts   and   the   calling   –   of God.

30 ὥσπερ γὰρ ὑμεῖς ποτε ἠπειθήσατε
For as   ye   then   disobeyed

τῷ θεῷ, νῦν δὲ ἠλεήθητε τῇ τούτων
–   God,   but now ye obtained mercy ¹by the ²of these

ἀπειθείᾳ, 31 οὕτως καὶ οὗτοι νῦν ἠπείθησαν
²disobedience,   so   also   these   now   disobeyed

τῷ ὑμετέρῳ ἐλέει ἵνα καὶ αὐτοὶ νῦν
–   ²by your   ³mercy ¹in order also   they   now
                      that

ἐλεηθῶσιν. 32 συνέκλεισεν γὰρ ὁ θεὸς
may obtain mercy.   For ²shut up   –   ¹God

τοὺς πάντας εἰς ἀπείθειαν ἵνα τοὺς
–   all   in   disobedience in order that   –

πάντας ἐλεήσῃ.
to all   he may show mercy.

33 Ὦ βάθος πλούτου καὶ σοφίας καὶ
O [the] depth of [the] riches and of [the] wisdom and

γνώσεως θεοῦ· ὡς ἀνεξερεύνητα τὰ κρίματα
of [the]   of God; how   inscrutable   the   judgments
knowledge

αὐτοῦ καὶ ἀνεξιχνίαστοι αἱ ὁδοὶ αὐτοῦ.
of him   and   unsearchable   the   ways   of him.

34 τίς γὰρ ἔγνω νοῦν κυρίου; ἢ τίς
For who   knew [the] mind of [the] Lord?   or   who

σύμβουλος αὐτοῦ ἐγένετο; 35 ἢ τίς
counsellor   of him   became?   or   who

προέδωκεν αὐτῷ, καὶ ἀνταποδοθήσεται
previously gave   to him,   and   it will be repaid

αὐτῷ; 36 ὅτι ἐξ αὐτοῦ καὶ δι' αὐτοῦ
to him?   Because of   him   and through   him

καὶ εἰς αὐτὸν τὰ πάντα· αὐτῷ ἡ δόξα
and   to   him   –   all things;   to him   the   glory

εἰς τοὺς αἰῶνας· ἀμήν.
unto   the   ages: Amen.

12 Παρακαλῶ οὖν ὑμᾶς, ἀδελφοί, διὰ
I beseech   therefore   you,   brothers, through

τῶν οἰκτιρμῶν τοῦ θεοῦ, παραστῆσαι τὰ
the   compassions   –   of God,   to present   the

σώματα ὑμῶν θυσίαν ζῶσαν ἁγίαν τῷ
bodies   of you   sacrifice   a living   holy   –

acceptable to God, which is your spiritual worship. [2] Do not be conformed to this world but be transformed by the renewal of your mind, that you may prove what is the will of God, what is good and acceptable and perfect.[n] 3 For by the grace given to me I bid every one among you not to think of himself more highly than he ought to think, but to think with sober judgment, each according to the measure of faith which God has assigned him. [4] For as in one body we have many members, and all the members do not have the same function, [5] so we, though many, are one body in Christ, and individually members one of another. [6] Having gifts that differ according to the grace given to us, let us use them: if prophecy, in proportion to our faith; [7] if service, in our serving; he who teaches, in his teaching; [8] he who exhorts, in his exhortation; he who contributes, in liberality; he who gives aid, with

[n] Or *what is the good and acceptable and perfect will of God*

θεῷ   εὐάρεστον,   τὴν   λογικὴν   λατρείαν
²to God   ¹well-pleasing,   the   reasonable   service

ὑμῶν·   2 καὶ   μὴ   συσχηματίζεσθε   τῷ   αἰῶνι
of you;   and   be ye not conformed   -   age

τούτῳ,   ἀλλὰ   μεταμορφοῦσθε   τῇ   ἀνακαινώσει
to this,   but   be ye transformed   by the   renewing

τοῦ   νοός,   εἰς   τὸ   δοκιμάζειν   ὑμᾶς   τί   τὸ
of the   mind,   for   the   to prove   you[b]   what   the
          =so that ye may prove

θέλημα   τοῦ   θεοῦ,   τὸ   ἀγαθὸν   καὶ   εὐάρεστον
will   -   of God,   the   good   and   well-pleasing

καὶ   τέλειον.
and   perfect.

3 Λέγω   γὰρ   διὰ   τῆς   χάριτος   τῆς
For I say   through   the   grace   -

δοθείσης   μοι   παντὶ   τῷ   ὄντι   ἐν   ὑμῖν,
given   to me   to everyone   being   among   you,

μὴ   ὑπερφρονεῖν   παρ'   ὃ   δεῖ   φρονεῖν,
not   to have high   beyond   what   it   to think,
    thoughts   behoves

ἀλλὰ   φρονεῖν   εἰς   τὸ   σωφρονεῖν,   ἑκάστῳ
but   to think   to   the   to be sober-minded,   [4]to each

ὡς   ὁ   θεὸς   ἐμέρισεν   μέτρον   πίστεως.
¹as   -   ²God   ³divided   a measure   of faith.

4 καθάπερ   γὰρ   ἐν   ἑνὶ   σώματι   πολλὰ
For as   in   one   body   many

μέλη   ἔχομεν,   τὰ   δὲ   μέλη   πάντα   οὐ   τὴν
members we have,   but ²the   ³members   ¹all   ⁵not   ⁴the

αὐτὴν   ἔχει   πρᾶξιν,   5 οὕτως   οἱ   πολλοὶ
⁷same   ⁴has(ve)   ⁸action,   so   the   many

ἓν   σῶμά   ἐσμεν   ἐν   Χριστῷ,   τὸ   δὲ   καθ'
one   body   we are   in   Christ,   -   and   each

εἷς   ἀλλήλων   μέλη.   6 ἔχοντες   δὲ   χαρίσματα
one   ²of one   ¹members.   And having   gifts
   another

κατὰ   τὴν   χάριν   τὴν   δοθεῖσαν   ἡμῖν   διάφορα,
²accord- ³the   ⁴grace   -   ⁵given   ⁶to us   ¹differing,
ing to

εἴτε   προφητείαν,   κατὰ   τὴν   ἀναλογίαν   τῆς
whether   prophecy,   according to the   proportion   of the

πίστεως·   7 εἴτε   διακονίαν,   ἐν   τῇ   διακονίᾳ·
faith;   or   ministry,   in   the   ministry;

εἴτε   ὁ   διδάσκων,   ἐν   τῇ   διδασκαλίᾳ·
or   the [one] teaching,   in   the   teaching;

8 εἴτε   ὁ   παρακαλῶν,   ἐν   τῇ   παρακλήσει·
or   the [one]   exhorting,   in   the   exhortation;

ὁ   μεταδιδοὺς   ἐν   ἁπλότητι,   ὁ   προϊστάμενος
the [one] sharing   in   simplicity,   the [one] taking the lead

zeal; he who does acts of mercy, with cheerfulness. 9 Let love be genuine; hate what is evil, hold fast to what is good; ¹⁰love one another with brotherly affection; outdo one another in showing honor. ¹¹Never flag in zeal, be aglow with the Spirit, serve the Lord. ¹²Rejoice in your hope, be patient in tribulation, be constant in prayer. ¹³Contribute to the needs of the saints, practice hospitality. 14 Bless those who persecute you; bless and do not curse them. ¹⁵Rejoice with those who rejoice, weep with those who weep. ¹⁶Live in harmony with one another; do not be haughty, but associate with the lowly;⁰ never be conceited. ¹⁷Repay no one evil for evil, but take thought for what is noble in the sight of all. ¹⁸If possible, so far as it depends upon you, live peaceably with all. ¹⁹Beloved, never avenge yourselves, but leave it to the wrath of God; for it is written, "Vengeance is mine, I will repay,

⁰ Or give yourselves to humble tasks

ἐν σπουδῇ, ὁ ἐλεῶν ἐν ἱλαρότητι. 9 ἡ
in diligence, the showing in cheerfulness. -
[one] mercy

ἀγάπη ἀνυπόκριτος. ἀποστυγοῦντες τὸ
[Let] love [be] unassumed. Shrinking from the

πονηρόν, κολλώμενοι τῷ ἀγαθῷ· 10 τῇ
evil, cleaving to the good; -

φιλαδελφίᾳ εἰς ἀλλήλους φιλόστοργοι, τῇ
in brotherly love to one another loving warmly, -

τιμῇ ἀλλήλους προηγούμενοι, 11 τῇ σπουδῇ
in one another preferring, - in zeal
honour

μὴ ὀκνηροί, τῷ πνεύματι ζέοντες, τῷ
not slothful, - in spirit burning, the

κυρίῳ δουλεύοντες, 12 τῇ ἐλπίδι χαίροντες,
Lord serving, - in hope rejoicing,

τῇ θλίψει ὑπομένοντες, τῇ προσευχῇ
- in affliction showing endurance, - in prayer

προσκαρτεροῦντες, 13 ταῖς χρείαις τῶν
steadfastly continuing, to the needs of the

ἁγίων κοινωνοῦντες, τὴν φιλοξενίαν
saints imparting, - hospitality

διώκοντες. 14 εὐλογεῖτε τοὺς διώκοντας,
pursuing. Bless ye the [ones] persecuting,

εὐλογεῖτε καὶ μὴ καταρᾶσθε. 15 χαίρειν
bless and do not curse. To rejoice

μετὰ χαιρόντων, κλαίειν μετὰ κλαιόντων.
with rejoicing [ones], to weep with weeping [ones].

16 τὸ αὐτὸ εἰς ἀλλήλους φρονοῦντες· μὴ
The same thing toward one another minding; not

τὰ ὑψηλὰ φρονοῦντες ἀλλὰ τοῖς ταπεινοῖς
²the ³high things ¹minding but to the humble

συναπαγόμενοι. μὴ γίνεσθε φρόνιμοι παρ'
condescending. Become not wise with

ἑαυτοῖς. 17 μηδενὶ κακὸν ἀντὶ κακοῦ
yourselves. To no one evil instead of evil

ἀποδιδόντες· προνοούμενοι καλὰ ἐνώπιον
returning; providing for good things before

πάντων ἀνθρώπων· 18 εἰ δυνατόν, τὸ ἐξ
all men; if possible, as far as it

ὑμῶν, μετὰ πάντων ἀνθρώπων εἰρηνεύοντες·
rests with with all men seeking peace;
you,†

19 μὴ ἑαυτοὺς ἐκδικοῦντες, ἀγαπητοί, ἀλλὰ
not ²yourselves ¹avenging, beloved, but

δότε τόπον τῇ ὀργῇ· γέγραπται γάρ·
give place - to wrath; for it has been written:

ἐμοὶ ἐκδίκησις, ἐγὼ ἀνταποδώσω, λέγει
To me vengeance,ᵉ I will repay, says
=Vengeance is mine,

says the Lord." ²⁰No, "if your enemy is hungry, feed him; if he is thirsty, give him drink; for by so doing you will heap burning coals upon his head." ²¹Do not be overcome by evil, but overcome evil with good.

CHAPTER 13

LET every person be subject to the governing authorities. For there is no authority except from God, and those that exist have been instituted by God. ²Therefore he who resists the authorities resists what God has appointed, and those who resist will incur judgment. ³For rulers are not a terror to good conduct, but to bad. Would you have no fear of him who is in authority? Then do what is good, and you will receive his approval, ⁴for he is God's servant for your good. But if you do wrong, be afraid, for he does not bear the sword in vain; he is the servant of God to execute his wrath on the wrongdoer. ⁵Therefore one must be subject, not only to avoid God's wrath but also for the sake of conscience.

κύριος. 20 ἀλλὰ ἐὰν πεινᾷ ὁ ἐχθρός
[the] Lord.   But if hungers the enemy

σου, ψώμιζε αὐτόν· ἐὰν διψᾷ, πότιζε
of thee, feed him; if he thirsts, give ²drink

αὐτόν· τοῦτο γὰρ ποιῶν ἄνθρακας πυρὸς
¹him; for this doing coals of fire

σωρεύσεις ἐπὶ τὴν κεφαλὴν αὐτοῦ. 21 μὴ
thou wilt heap on the head of him. not

νικῶ ὑπὸ τοῦ κακοῦ, ἀλλὰ νίκα
Be conquered by the evil, but conquer

ἐν τῷ ἀγαθῷ τὸ κακόν. 13 Πᾶσα
²by ⁴the ⁵good ¹the ²evil. ²Every

ψυχὴ ἐξουσίαις ὑπερεχούσαις ὑποτασσέσθω.
²soul ⁷authorities ⁶to superior ¹let ⁴be ⁵subject.

οὐ γὰρ ἔστιν ἐξουσία εἰ μὴ
For there is no authority except

ὑπὸ θεοῦ, αἱ δὲ οὖσαι ὑπὸ θεοῦ
by God, and the existing [ones] by God

τεταγμέναι εἰσίν. 2 ὥστε ὁ ἀντιτασσόμενος
having been are. So the [one] resisting
ordained

τῇ ἐξουσίᾳ τῇ τοῦ θεοῦ διαταγῇ ἀνθέστη-
the authority ²the – ⁴of God ³ordinance ¹has op-

κεν· οἱ δὲ ἀνθεστηκότες ἑαυτοῖς κρίμα
posed; and the [ones] having opposed to themselves judgment

λήμψονται. 3 οἱ γὰρ ἄρχοντες οὐκ εἰσὶν
will receive. For the rulers are not

φόβος τῷ ἀγαθῷ ἔργῳ ἀλλὰ τῷ κακῷ.
a fear to the good work but to the evil.

θέλεις δὲ μὴ φοβεῖσθαι τὴν ἐξουσίαν;
And wishest thou not to fear the authority?

τὸ ἀγαθὸν ποίει, καὶ ἕξεις ἔπαινον ἐξ
²the ³good ¹do, and thou wilt praise from
have

αὐτῆς· 4 θεοῦ γὰρ διάκονός ἐστιν σοὶ
it; for of God a minister he is to thee

εἰς τὸ ἀγαθόν. ἐὰν δὲ τὸ κακὸν ποιῇς,
for the good. But if the evil thou doest,

φοβοῦ· οὐ γὰρ εἰκῇ τὴν μάχαιραν φορεῖ·
fear; for not in vain the sword he bears;

θεοῦ γὰρ διάκονός ἐστιν ἔκδικος εἰς
for of God a minister he is an avenger for

ὀργὴν τῷ τὸ κακὸν πράσσοντι. 5 διὸ
wrath to the [one] ²the ³evil ¹practising. Wherefore

ἀνάγκη ὑποτάσσεσθαι, οὐ μόνον διὰ τὴν
it is necessary to be subject, not only because of –

ὀργὴν ἀλλὰ καὶ διὰ τὴν συνείδησιν.
wrath but also because of – conscience.

⁶For the same reason you also pay taxes, for the authorities are ministers of God, attending to this very thing. ⁷Pay all of them their dues, taxes to whom taxes are due, revenue to whom revenue is due, respect to whom respect is due, honor to whom honor is due. 8 Owe no one anything, except to love one another; for he who loves his neighbor has fulfilled the law. ⁹The commandments, "You shall not commit adultery, You shall not kill, You shall not steal, You shall not covet," and any other commandment, are summed up in this sentence, "You shall love your neighbor as yourself." ¹⁰Love does no wrong to a neighbor; therefore love is the fulfilling of the law. 11 Besides this you know what hour it is, how it is full time now for you to wake from sleep. For salvation is nearer to us now than when we first believed; ¹²the night is far gone, the day is at hand. Let us then cast off the works of darkness and put on·the

6 διὰ τοῦτο γὰρ καὶ φόρους τελεῖτε·
For therefore also taxes pay ye;
λειτουργοὶ γὰρ θεοῦ εἰσιν εἰς αὐτὸ τοῦτο
for ministers of God they are for this very thing
προσκαρτεροῦντες. 7 ἀπόδοτε πᾶσιν τὰς
attending constantly. Render to all men the
ὀφειλάς, τῷ τὸν φόρον τὸν φόρον,
dues, to the [one] the tax the tax,*
τῷ τὸ τέλος τὸ τέλος, τῷ τὸν φόβον
to the tribute the tribute, to the the fear
[one] [one]
τὸν φόβον, τῷ τὴν τιμὴν τὴν τιμήν.
the fear, to the [one] the honour the honour.
8 Μηδενὶ μηδὲν ὀφείλετε, εἰ μὴ τὸ
To no one no(any)thing owe ye, except –
ἀλλήλους ἀγαπᾶν· ὁ γὰρ ἀγαπῶν τὸν
one another to love; for the [one] loving the
ἕτερον νόμον πεπλήρωκεν. 9 τὸ γὰρ
other law has fulfilled. – For
οὐ μοιχεύσεις, οὐ φονεύσεις, οὐ κλέψεις,
Thou shalt not Thou shalt not kill, Thou shalt not
commit adultery, steal,
οὐκ ἐπιθυμήσεις, καὶ εἴ τις ἑτέρα ἐντολή,
Thou shalt not covet, and if any other command-
[there is] ment,
ἐν τῷ λόγῳ τούτῳ ἀνακεφαλαιοῦται, [ἐν
²in ³this ⁴word ¹it is summed up, in
τῷ]· ἀγαπήσεις τὸν πλησίον σου ὡς
– : Thou shalt love the neighbour of thee as
σεαυτόν. 10 ἡ ἀγάπη τῷ πλησίον κακὸν
thyself. – Love ³to the ⁴neighbour ²evil
(one's)
οὐκ ἐργάζεται· πλήρωμα οὖν νόμου ἡ
¹works not; ³[is] ⁴fulfilment ¹therefore ⁵of law –
ἀγάπη. 11 Καὶ τοῦτο εἰδότες τὸν καιρόν,
²love. And this[,] knowing the time,
ὅτι ὥρα ἤδη ὑμᾶς ἐξ ὕπνου ἐγερθῆναι·
that hour now you out of sleep to be raised;ᵇ
=it is now an hour for you to be raised out of sleep;
νῦν γὰρ ἐγγύτερον ἡμῶν ἡ σωτηρία
for now nearer [is] of us the salvation
ἢ ὅτε ἐπιστεύσαμεν. 12 ἡ νὺξ προέκοψεν,
than when we believed. The night advanced,
ἡ δὲ ἡμέρα ἤγγικεν. ἀποθώμεθα οὖν
and the day has drawn near. Let us cast off therefore
τὰ ἔργα τοῦ σκότους, ἐνδυσώμεθα δὲ
the works of the darkness, and let us put on

* The phrase between the commas is elliptical; understand—to the [one demanding] the tax [render] the tax. So of the following phrases.

armor of light; ¹³let us conduct ourselves becomingly as in the day, not in reveling and drunkenness, not in debauchery and licentiousness, not in quarreling and jealousy. ¹⁴But put on the Lord Jesus Christ, and make no provision for the flesh, to gratify its desires.

τὰ ὅπλα τοῦ φωτός.　13 ὡς ἐν ἡμέρᾳ
the weapons of the　light.　As in [the] day

εὐσχημόνως περιπατήσωμεν, μὴ κώμοις καὶ
becomingly　let us walk,　not in revellings and

μέθαις, μὴ κοίταις καὶ ἀσελγείαις, μὴ
in drunken not in beds*　and　excesses,　not
bouts,

ἔριδι καὶ ζήλῳ·　14 ἀλλὰ ἐνδύσασθε τὸν
in strife and in jealousy;　but　put ye on　the

κύριον Ἰησοῦν Χριστόν, καὶ τῆς σαρκὸς
Lord　Jesus　Christ,　and of the　flesh

πρόνοιαν μὴ ποιεῖσθε εἰς ἐπιθυμίας.
forethought　make not　for [its]　lusts.

CHAPTER 14

AS for the man who is weak in faith, welcome him, but not for disputes over opinions. ²One believes he may eat anything, while the weak man eats only vegetables. ³Let not him who eats despise him who abstains, and let not him who abstains pass judgment on him who eats; for God has welcomed him. ⁴Who are you to pass judgment on the servant of another? It is before his own master that he stands or falls. And he will be upheld, for the Master is able to make him stand.

5 One man esteems one day as better than another, while another man esteems all days alike. Let every one be fully convinced in his own mind. ⁶He who observes the day, observes

14 Τὸν δὲ ἀσθενοῦντα τῇ πίστει
Now the [one]　being weak in the faith

προσλαμβάνεσθε, μὴ εἰς διακρίσεις διαλογισ-
receive ye,　not to judgments　of

μῶν.　2 ὃς μὲν πιστεύει φαγεῖν πάντα,
thoughts.　One indeed believes to eat all things,
mant

ὁ δὲ ἀσθενῶν λάχανα ἐσθίει.　3 ὁ ἐσθίων
but the being weak herbs eats.　³The ⁴eating
[one]　[one]

τὸν μὴ ἐσθίοντα μὴ ἐξουθενείτω, ὁ δὲ
⁶the ⁷not ⁸eating ⁸not ¹let ⁵despise, and ⁸the
[one]　[one]

μὴ ἐσθίων τὸν ἐσθίοντα μὴ κρινέτω,
⁴not ⁵eating ⁷the [one] ⁸eating ⁸not ¹let ⁹judge,

ὁ θεὸς γὰρ αὐτὸν προσελάβετο.　4 σὺ
－ for God him received.　²Thou

τίς εἶ ὁ κρίνων ἀλλότριον οἰκέτην; τῷ
¹who ²art ⁴the ⁵judging ⁷belonging to ⁸a household to
[one]　another servant? the(his)

ἰδίῳ κυρίῳ στήκει ἢ πίπτει· σταθήσεται
own lord he stands or falls;　²he will stand

δέ, δυνατεῖ γὰρ ὁ κύριος στῆσαι αὐτόν.
¹but, for is able the Lord to stand him.

5 ὃς μὲν [γὰρ] κρίνει ἡμέραν παρ'
one mant indeed judges a day above

ἡμέραν, ὃς δὲ κρίνει πᾶσαν ἡμέραν·
a day,　another† judges every day;

ἕκαστος ἐν τῷ ἰδίῳ νοῖ πληροφορείσθω.
each man in the(his) own mind let him be fully
persuaded.

6 ὁ φρονῶν τὴν ἡμέραν κυρίῳ φρονεῖ.
The minding the day to [the] he minds
[one]　Lord [it].

* That is, illicit sexual intercourse.

I.G.E.—22

it in honor of the Lord He also who eats, eats in honor of the Lord, since he gives thanks to God; while he who abstains, abstains in honor of the Lord and gives thanks to God. ⁷None of us lives to himself, and none of us dies to himself. ⁸If we live, we live to the Lord, and if we die, we die to the Lord; so then, whether we live or whether we die, we are the Lord's. ⁹For to this end Christ died and lived again, that he might be Lord both of the dead and of the living.

10 Why do you pass judgment on your brother? Or you, why do you despise your brother? For we shall all stand before the judgment seat of God; ¹¹for it is written,

"As I live, says the Lord, every knee shall bow to me, and every tongue shall give praiseᵖ to God."

¹²So each of us shall give account of himself to God.

13 Then let us no more pass judgment on one another, but rather decide never to put a stumbling-block or hindrance in the way of a brother. ¹⁴I know and am persuaded in the Lord Jesus that nothing is unclean in itself; but

ᵖ Or confess

καὶ ὁ ἐσθίων κυρίῳ ἐσθίει, εὐχαριστεῖ γὰρ
And the eating to [the] he eats, for he gives thanks
[one] Lord

τῷ θεῷ· καὶ ὁ μὴ ἐσθίων κυρίῳ
– to God; and the [one] not eating to [the] Lord

οὐκ ἐσθίει, καὶ εὐχαριστεῖ τῷ θεῷ.
he eats not, and gives thanks – to God.

7 οὐδεὶς γὰρ ἡμῶν ἑαυτῷ ζῇ, καὶ οὐδεὶς
For no one of us to himself lives, and no one

ἑαυτῷ ἀποθνῄσκει· 8 ἐάν τε γὰρ ζῶμεν,
to himself dies; for whether we live,

τῷ κυρίῳ ζῶμεν, ἐάν τε ἀποθνῄσκωμεν,
to the Lord we live, or if we die,

τῷ κυρίῳ ἀποθνῄσκομεν. ἐάν τε οὖν
to the Lord we die. Whether therefore

ζῶμεν ἐάν τε ἀποθνῄσκωμεν, τοῦ κυρίου
we live or if we die, of the Lord

ἐσμέν. 9 εἰς τοῦτο γὰρ Χριστὸς ἀπέθανεν
we are. for this For Christ died

καὶ ἔζησεν, ἵνα καὶ νεκρῶν καὶ ζώντων
and lived [again], in order both of dead and of living
that [ones]

κυριεύσῃ. 10 σὺ δὲ τί κρίνεις τὸν ἀδελφόν
he might be Lord. ³thou And ¹why ²judgest the brother

σου; ἢ καὶ σὺ τί ἐξουθενεῖς τὸν ἀδελφόν
of thee? or ²indeed ⁴thou ¹why ³despisest the brother

σου; πάντες γὰρ παραστησόμεθα τῷ
of thee? for all we shall stand before the

βήματι τοῦ θεοῦ. 11 γέγραπται γάρ·
tribunal – of God. For it has been written:

ζῶ ἐγώ, λέγει κύριος, ὅτι ἐμοὶ κάμψει
Live I, says [the] Lord, that to me will bend

πᾶν γόνυ, καὶ πᾶσα γλῶσσα ἐξομολογήσεται
every knee, and every tongue will confess

τῷ θεῷ. 12 ἄρα [οὖν] ἔκαστος ἡμῶν
– to God. So therefore each one of us

περὶ ἑαυτοῦ λόγον δώσει [τῷ θεῷ].
concerning himself account will give – to God.

13 Μηκέτι οὖν ἀλλήλους κρίνωμεν· ἀλλὰ
No longer therefore one another let us judge; but

τοῦτο κρίνατε μᾶλλον, τὸ μὴ τιθέναι
this judge ye rather, – not to put

πρόσκομμα τῷ ἀδελφῷ ἢ σκάνδαλον.
a stumbling-block to the brother or an offence.

14 οἶδα καὶ πέπεισμαι ἐν κυρίῳ Ἰησοῦ
I know and have been by [the] Lord Jesus
persuaded

ὅτι οὐδὲν κοινὸν δι’ ἑαυτοῦ· εἰ μὴ
that nothing [is] common through itself; except

it is unclean for any one who thinks it unclean. ¹⁵If your brother is being injured by what you eat, you are no longer walking in love. Do not let what you eat cause the ruin of one for whom Christ died. ¹⁶So do not let what is good to you be spoken of as evil. ¹⁷For the kingdom of God does not mean food and drink but righteousness and peace and joy in the Holy Spirit; ¹⁸he who thus serves Christ is acceptable to God and approved by men. ¹⁹Let us then pursue what makes for peace and for mutual upbuilding. ²⁰Do not, for the sake of food, destroy the work of God. Everything is indeed clean, but it is wrong for any one to make others fall by what he eats; ²¹it is right not to eat meat or drink wine or do anything that makes your brother stumble.*q* ²²The faith that you have, keep between yourself and God; happy is he who has no reason to judge himself for what he approves. ²³But he

τῷ λογιζομένῳ τι κοινὸν εἶναι, ἐκείνῳ
to the reckoning anything common to be, to that man
[one] [it is]
κοινόν. 15 εἰ γὰρ διὰ βρῶμα ὁ ἀδελφός
common. For if because food the brother
of
σου λυπεῖται, οὐκέτι κατὰ ἀγάπην
of thee is grieved, no longer according to love
περιπατεῖς. μὴ τῷ βρώματί σου ἐκεῖνον
thou walkest. ²Not ³by the ⁴food ⁵of thee ⁶that man
ἀπόλλυε, ὑπὲρ οὗ Χριστὸς ἀπέθανεν.
¹destroy, on behalf of whom Christ died.
16 μὴ βλασφημείσθω οὖν ὑμῶν τὸ ἀγαθόν.
Let not be blasphemed therefore of you the good.
17 οὐ γάρ ἐστιν ἡ βασιλεία τοῦ θεοῦ
For not is the kingdom – of God
βρῶσις καὶ πόσις, ἀλλὰ δικαιοσύνη καὶ
eating and drinking, but righteousness and
εἰρήνη καὶ χαρὰ ἐν πνεύματι ἁγίῳ·
peace and joy in [the] Spirit Holy;
18 ὁ γὰρ ἐν τούτῳ δουλεύων τῷ Χριστῷ
for the [one] in this serving – Christ
εὐάρεστος τῷ θεῷ καὶ δόκιμος τοῖς
[is] well-pleasing – to God and approved –
ἀνθρώποις. 19 ἄρα οὖν τὰ τῆς εἰρήνης
by men. So there- the – of peace
fore things
διώκωμεν καὶ τὰ τῆς οἰκοδομῆς τῆς
let us pursue and the things – of building [up] –
εἰς ἀλλήλους. 20 μὴ ἕνεκεν βρώματος
for one another. Not for the sake of food
κατάλυε τὸ ἔργον τοῦ θεοῦ. πάντα
undo thou the work – of God. All things
μὲν καθαρά, ἀλλὰ κακὸν τῷ ἀνθρώπῳ
indeed [are] clean, but evil to the man
τῷ διὰ προσκόμματος ἐσθίοντι. 21 καλὸν
– ²through ³a stumbling-block ¹eating. Good [it is]
τὸ μὴ φαγεῖν κρέα μηδὲ πιεῖν οἶνον
– not to eat flesh nor to drink wine
μηδὲ ἐν ᾧ ὁ ἀδελφός σου προσκόπτει.
nor by which the brother of thee stumbles.
[anything]
22 σὺ πίστιν ἣν ἔχεις κατὰ σεαυτὸν
³Thou ¹faith ²which ⁴hast ⁶by ⁷thyself
ἔχε ἐνώπιον τοῦ θεοῦ. μακάριος ὁ
⁵have before – God. Blessed the
[one]
μὴ κρίνων ἑαυτὸν ἐν ᾧ δοκιμάζει·
not judging himself in what he approves;

q Other ancient authorities add or be upset or be weakened

who has doubts is condemned, if he eats, because he does not act from faith; for whatever does not proceed from faith is sin.[r]

CHAPTER 15

WE who are strong ought to bear with the failings of the weak, and not to please ourselves; [2] let each of us please his neighbor for his good, to edify him. [3] For Christ did not please himself; but, as it is written, "The reproaches of those who reproached thee fell on me." [4] For whatever was written in former days was written for our instruction, that by steadfastness and by the encouragement of the scriptures we might have hope. [5] May the God of steadfastness and encouragement grant you to live in such harmony with one another, in accord with Christ Jesus, [6] that together you may with one voice glorify the God and Father of our Lord Jesus Christ.

[7] Welcome one another, therefore, as Christ has welcomed you,

---

23 ὁ δὲ διακρινόμενος ἐὰν φάγῃ κατα-
but the [one] doubting if he eats has been

κέκριται, ὅτι οὐκ ἐκ πίστεως· πᾶν
condemned, because not of faith; [a]all

δὲ ὃ οὐκ ἐκ πίστεως ἁμαρτία ἐστίν.
[1]and which [is] not of faith sin is.

15 Ὀφείλομεν δὲ ἡμεῖς οἱ δυνατοὶ τὰ
[5]Ought [1]so [a]we [3]the [4]strong [7]the

ἀσθενήματα τῶν ἀδυνάτων βαστάζειν, καὶ
[8]weaknesses [9]of the [10]not strong [6]to bear, and

μὴ ἑαυτοῖς ἀρέσκειν. 2 ἕκαστος ἡμῶν
not [our]selves to please. Each one of us

τῷ πλησίον· ἀρεσκέτω εἰς τὸ ἀγαθὸν
the(his) neighbour let him please for - good

πρὸς οἰκοδομήν· 3 καὶ γὰρ ὁ Χριστὸς
to building [up]; for even - Christ

οὐχ ἑαυτῷ ἤρεσεν· ἀλλὰ καθὼς γέ-
[a]not [a]himself [1]pleased; but as it has

γραπται· οἱ ὀνειδισμοὶ τῶν ὀνειδιζόντων
been written: The reproaches of the [ones] reproaching

σε ἐπέπεσαν ἐπ᾽ ἐμέ. 4 ὅσα γὰρ
thee fell on on me. For whatever things

προεγράφη, εἰς τὴν ἡμετέραν διδασκαλίαν
were previously for - our teaching
written,

ἐγράφη, ἵνα διὰ τῆς ὑπομονῆς καὶ
were in order through - patience and
written, that

διὰ τῆς παρακλήσεως τῶν γραφῶν τὴν
through the comfort of the writings -

ἐλπίδα ἔχωμεν. 5 ὁ δὲ θεὸς τῆς ὑπομονῆς
hope we may have. And the God - of patience

καὶ τῆς παρακλήσεως δῴη ὑμῖν τὸ
and - of comfort give to you [a]the

αὐτὸ φρονεῖν ἐν ἀλλήλοις κατὰ Χριστὸν
[a]same [1]to mind among one another according to Christ
thing

Ἰησοῦν, 6 ἵνα ὁμοθυμαδὸν ἐν ἑνὶ στόματι
Jesus, in order with one accord with one mouth
that

δοξάζητε τὸν θεὸν καὶ πατέρα τοῦ
ye may glorify the God and Father of the

κυρίου ἡμῶν Ἰησοῦ Χριστοῦ.
Lord of us Jesus Christ.

7 Διὸ προσλαμβάνεσθε ἀλλήλους, καθὼς
Wherefore receive ye one another, as

καὶ ὁ Χριστὸς προσελάβετο ἡμᾶς εἰς
also - Christ received us to

---

[r] Other authorities, some ancient, insert here Ch. 16. 25–27

for the glory of God.
8 For I tell you that
Christ became a servant
to the circumcised to
show God's truthfulness,
in order to confirm the
promises given to the
patriarchs, 9 and in order
that the Gentiles might
glorify God for his
mercy. As it is written,
"Therefore I will praise
thee among the
Gentiles,
and sing to thy
name";
10 and again it is said,
"Rejoice, O Gentiles,
with his people";
11 and again,
"Praise the Lord, all
Gentiles,
and let all the peoples
praise him";
12 and further Isaiah says,
"The root of Jesse
shall come,
he who rises to rule
the Gentiles;
in him shall the
Gentiles hope."
13 May the God of hope
fill you with all joy and
peace in believing, so
that by the power of the
Holy Spirit you may
abound in hope.
14 I myself am
satisfied about you, my
brethren, that you your-
selves are full of good-
ness, filled with all
knowledge, and able to

δόξαν τοῦ θεοῦ.   8 λέγω γὰρ Χριστὸν
[the] glory - of God.   For I say   Christ

διάκονον γεγενῆσθαι περιτομῆς ὑπὲρ
a minister   to have become   of [the]   on be-
                         circumcision   half of

ἀληθείας θεοῦ, εἰς τὸ βεβαιῶσαι τὰς
[the] truth   of God,   -   -   to confirm   the

ἐπαγγελίας τῶν πατέρων, 9 τὰ δὲ ἔθνη
promises   of the   fathers,   and 1the 2nations

ὑπὲρ ἐλέους δοξάσαι τὸν θεόν, καθὼς
5on be-   4mercy   3to glorify   -   4God,   as
half of

γέγραπται· διὰ τοῦτο ἐξομολογήσομαί σοι
it has been written: Therefore   I will confess   to thee

ἐν ἔθνεσιν καὶ τῷ ὀνόματί σου ψαλῶ.
among nations   and   to the   name   of thee   I will sing
                                               praise.

10 καὶ πάλιν λέγει· εὐφράνθητε, ἔθνη,
And   again   he says: Be glad,   nations,

μετὰ τοῦ λαοῦ αὐτοῦ.   11 καὶ πάλιν·
with   the   people   of him.   And   again:

αἰνεῖτε, πάντα τὰ ἔθνη, τὸν κύριον,
Praise,   all   the   nations,   the   Lord,

καὶ ἐπαινεσάτωσαν αὐτὸν πάντες οἱ λαοί.
and   let praise   him   all   the peoples.

12 καὶ πάλιν 'Ησαΐας λέγει· ἔσται
And   again   Esaias   says: There
                                       shall be

ἡ ῥίζα τοῦ 'Ιεσσαί, καὶ ὁ ἀνιστάμενος
the root   -   of Jesse,   and   the [one] rising up

ἄρχειν ἐθνῶν· ἐπ' αὐτῷ ἔθνη ἐλπιοῦσιν.
to rule   nations;   on   him   nations   will hope.

13 'Ο δὲ θεὸς τῆς ἐλπίδος πληρώσαι
Now the   God   -   of hope   fill

ὑμᾶς πάσης χαρᾶς καὶ εἰρήνης ἐν τῷ
you   of(with) all   joy   and   peace   in   -

πιστεύειν, εἰς τὸ περισσεύειν ὑμᾶς ἐν
to believe   for   -   to abound   youb   in
(believing),

τῇ ἐλπίδι ἐν δυνάμει πνεύματος ἁγίου.
-   hope   by   [the] power   of [the] Spirit   Holy.

14 Πέπεισμαι δέ, ἀδελφοί μου, καὶ
But I have been persuaded,   brothers   of me,   even

αὐτὸς ἐγὼ περὶ ὑμῶν, ὅτι καὶ αὐτοί
2[my]self   1I   concerning   you,   that   also   [your]-
                                               selves

μεστοί ἐστε ἀγαθωσύνης, πεπληρωμένοι
full   ye are   of goodness,   having been filled

πάσης τῆς γνώσεως, δυνάμενοι καὶ
of(with) all   -   knowledge,   being able   also

instruct one another. [15] But on some points I have written to you very boldly by way of reminder, because of the grace given me by God [16] to be a minister of Christ Jesus to the Gentiles in the priestly service of the gospel of God, so that the offering of the Gentiles may be acceptable, sanctified by the Holy Spirit. [17] In Christ Jesus, then, I have reason to be proud of my work for God. [18] For I will not venture to speak of anything except what Christ has wrought through me to win obedience from the Gentiles, by word and deed, [19] by the power of signs and wonders, by the power of the Holy Spirit, so that from Jerusalem and as far round as Illyr'icum I have fully preached the gospel of Christ, [20] thus making it my ambition to preach the gospel, not where Christ has already been named, lest I build on another man's foundation, [21] but as it is written,

"They shall see who
   have never been
   told of him,

ἀλλήλους νουθετεῖν.
one another   to admonish.

15 τολμηροτέρως δὲ
    And more daringly

ἔγραψα ὑμῖν ἀπὸ μέρους, ὡς ἐπαναμιμνή-
I wrote to you in   part,   as   remind-

σκων ὑμᾶς διὰ τὴν χάριν τὴν δοθεῖσάν
ing   you   by   the   grace   -   given

μοι ἀπὸ τοῦ θεοῦ **16** εἰς τὸ εἶναί με
to me from   -   God   for   the   to be   me[b]
                       =that I should be

λειτουργὸν Χριστοῦ Ἰησοῦ εἰς τὰ ἔθνη,
a minister of Christ   Jesus   to   the   nations,

ἱερουργοῦντα τὸ εὐαγγέλιον τοῦ θεοῦ,
sacrificing   the   gospel   -   of God,

ἵνα γένηται ἡ προσφορὰ τῶν ἐθνῶν
in order [5]may be [1]the [2]offering [3]of the [4]nations
that

εὐπρόσδεκτος, ἡγιασμένη ἐν πνεύματι
acceptable,   having been sanctified   by   [the] Spirit

ἁγίῳ. **17** ἔχω οὖν τὴν καύχησιν ἐν
Holy.   I have therefore the   boasting   in

Χριστῷ Ἰησοῦ τὰ πρὸς τὸν θεόν· **18** οὐ
Christ   Jesus the things with*   -   God;   [4]not

γὰρ τολμήσω τι λαλεῖν ὧν οὐ
[1]for [3]I [5]will [6]dare [7]any- [6]to speak of [the] [8]not
                  thing   things which

κατειργάσατο Χριστὸς δι' ἐμοῦ εἰς ὑπακοὴν
[2]did [4]work [5]out   [1]Christ through me   for   obedience

ἐθνῶν, λόγῳ καὶ ἔργῳ, **19** ἐν δυνάμει
of [the] in word and   work,   by   power
nations,

σημείων καὶ τεράτων, ἐν δυνάμει πνεύματος·
of signs and   wonders, by   power   of [the] Spirit;

ὥστε με ἀπὸ Ἰερουσαλὴμ καὶ κύκλῳ
so as   me from   Jerusalem   and   around
=I should fulfil the gospel . . . from . . . Illyricum.

μέχρι τοῦ Ἰλλυρικοῦ πεπληρωκέναι τὸ
unto   -   Illyricum   to have fulfilled[b]   the

εὐαγγέλιον τοῦ Χριστοῦ. **20** οὕτως δὲ
gospel   -   of Christ.   And so

φιλοτιμούμενον εὐαγγελίζεσθαι οὐχ ὅπου
eagerly striving   to evangelize   not   where

ὠνομάσθη Χριστός, ἵνα μὴ ἐπ᾽ ἀλλότριον
[2]was named   [1]Christ, in order not   on   [3]belonging to
                 that   another

θεμέλιον οἰκοδομῶ, **21** ἀλλὰ καθὼς
[1]a foundation I should build,   but   as

γέγραπται· ὄψονται οἷς οὐκ ἀνηγγέλη
it has been They shall see to whom it was not announced
written:

* That is, the things that have to do with . . .

and they shall understand who have never heard of him."
22 This is the reason why I have so often been hindered from coming to you. ²³But now, since I no longer have any room for work in these regions, and since I have longed for many years to come to you, ²⁴I hope to see you in passing as I go to Spain, and to be sped on my journey there by you, once I have enjoyed your company for a little. ²⁵At present, however, I am going to Jerusalem with aid for the saints. ²⁶For Macedo'nia and Acha'ia have been pleased to make some contribution for the poor among the saints at Jerusalem; ²⁷they were pleased to do it, and indeed they are in debt to them, for if the Gentiles have come to share in their spiritual blessings, they ought also to be of service to them in material blessings. ²⁸When therefore I have completed this, and have delivered to them what has been raised, I shall go on by way of you to Spain; ²⁹and I know that when I come to you I shall come in the fulness of the blessing* of Christ.
30 I appeal to you,

* Other ancient authorities insert of the gospel

περὶ αὐτοῦ, καὶ οἳ οὐκ ἀκηκόασιν
concerning him, and [those] who have not heard

συνήσουσιν. 22 διὸ καὶ ἐνεκοπτόμην τὰ
will understand. Wherefore also I was hindered -

πολλὰ τοῦ ἐλθεῖν πρὸς ὑμᾶς· 23 νυνὶ
many(much) - to come^d to you; ²now

δὲ μηκέτι τόπον ἔχων ἐν τοῖς κλίμασι
¹but no longer ²place ¹having in - ²regions

τούτοις, ἐπιποθίαν δὲ ἔχων τοῦ ἐλθεῖν
¹these, and ²a desire ¹having - to come^d

πρὸς ὑμᾶς ἀπὸ ἱκανῶν ἐτῶν, 24 ὡς ἂν
to you from several years, whenever

πορεύωμαι εἰς τὴν Σπανίαν· ἐλπίζω γὰρ
I journey to - Spain; for I hope

διαπορευόμενος θεάσασθαι ὑμᾶς καὶ ὑφ᾽
journeying through to behold you and by

ὑμῶν προπεμφθῆναι ἐκεῖ, ἐὰν ὑμῶν πρῶτον
you to be set forward there, if of(with) you firstly

ἀπὸ μέρους ἐμπλησθῶ, 25 — νυνὶ δὲ
in part I may be filled, — but now

πορεύομαι εἰς Ἰερουσαλὴμ διακονῶν τοῖς
I am going to Jerusalem ministering to the

ἁγίοις. 26 ηὐδόκησαν γὰρ Μακεδονία καὶ
saints. For thought it good Macedonia and

Ἀχαΐα κοινωνίαν τινὰ ποιήσασθαι εἰς
Achaia ²contribution ²some ¹to make for

τοὺς πτωχοὺς τῶν ἁγίων τῶν ἐν Ἰερου-
the poor of the saints - in Jeru-

σαλήμ. 27 ηὐδόκησαν γάρ, καὶ ὀφειλέται
salem. For they thought it good, and debtors

εἰσὶν αὐτῶν· εἰ γὰρ τοῖς πνευματικοῖς
they are of them; for if in the spiritual things

αὐτῶν ἐκοινώνησαν τὰ ἔθνη, ὀφείλουσιν
of them ²shared ¹the ²nations, they ought

καὶ ἐν τοῖς σαρκικοῖς λειτουργῆσαι αὐτοῖς.
also in the fleshly things to minister to them.

28 τοῦτο οὖν ἐπιτελέσας, καὶ σφραγισάμενος
This therefore having completed, and having sealed

αὐτοῖς τὸν καρπὸν τοῦτον, 29 ἀπελεύσομαι
to them this fruit, I will go away

δι᾽ ὑμῶν εἰς Σπανίαν· οἶδα δὲ ὅτι
through you to Spain; and I know that

ἐρχόμενος πρὸς ὑμᾶς ἐν πληρώματι
coming to you in [the] fulness

εὐλογίας Χριστοῦ ἐλεύσομαι. 30 Παρακαλῶ
of [the] blessing of Christ I will come. I beseech

brethren, by our Lord Jesus Christ and by the love of the Spirit, to strive together with me in your prayers to God on my behalf, [31] that I may be delivered from the unbelievers in Judea, and that my service for Jerusalem may be acceptable to the saints, [32] so that by God's will I may come to you with joy and be refreshed in your company. [33] The God of peace be with you all. Amen.

δὲ ὑμᾶς, [ἀδελφοί], διὰ τοῦ κυρίου
Now you, brothers, through the Lord

ἡμῶν Ἰησοῦ Χριστοῦ καὶ διὰ τῆς ἀγάπης
of us Jesus Christ and through the love

τοῦ πνεύματος, συναγωνίσασθαί μοι ἐν
of the Spirit, to strive with me in

ταῖς προσευχαῖς ὑπὲρ ἐμοῦ πρὸς τὸν
the prayers on behalf of me to –

θεόν, 31 ἵνα ῥυσθῶ ἀπὸ τῶν ἀπειθούντων
God, in order I may be from the disobeying
that delivered [ones]

ἐν τῇ Ἰουδαίᾳ καὶ ἡ διακονία μου
in – Judæa and the ministry of me

ἡ εἰς Ἰερουσαλὴμ εὐπρόσδεκτος τοῖς
– to Jerusalem ²acceptable ³to the

ἁγίοις γένηται, 32 ἵνα ἐν χαρᾷ ἐλθὼν
⁴saints ¹may be, in order that in joy coming

πρὸς ὑμᾶς διὰ θελήματος θεοῦ συνανα-
ιο you through [the] will of God I may

παύσωμαι ὑμῖν. 33 ὁ δὲ θεὸς τῆς
rest with you. And the God –

εἰρήνης μετὰ πάντων ὑμῶν· ἀμήν.
of peace [be] with all you: Amen.

CHAPTER 16

I commend to you our sister Phoebe, a deaconess of the church at Cen'chre-ae, [2] that you may receive her in the Lord as befits the saints, and help her in whatever she may require from you, for she has been a helper of many and of myself as well.
3 Greet Prisca and Aquila, my fellow workers in Christ Jesus, [4] who risked their necks for my life, to whom not only I

16 Συνίστημι δὲ ὑμῖν Φοίβην τὴν
Now I commend to you Phœbe the

ἀδελφὴν ἡμῶν, οὖσαν [καὶ] διάκονον τῆς
sister of us, being also a minister of the

ἐκκλησίας τῆς ἐν Κεγχρεαῖς, 2 ἵνα
church – in Cenchrea, in order that

αὐτὴν προσδέξησθε ἐν κυρίῳ ἀξίως τῶν
²her ¹ye may receive in [the] Lord worthily of the

ἁγίων, καὶ παραστῆτε αὐτῇ ἐν ᾧ ἂν
saints, and may stand by her in ¹whatever

ὑμῶν χρήζῃ πράγματι· καὶ γὰρ αὐτὴ
⁴of you ²she may ²thing; for indeed she
have need

προστάτις πολλῶν ἐγενήθη καὶ ἐμοῦ αὐτοῦ.
a protectress of many became and of myself.

3 Ἀσπάσασθε Πρίσκαν καὶ Ἀκύλαν τοὺς
·Greet ye Prisca and Aquila the

συνεργούς μου ἐν Χριστῷ Ἰησοῦ, 4 οἵτινες
fellow-workers of me in Christ Jesus, who

ὑπὲρ τῆς ψυχῆς μου τὸν ἑαυτῶν τράχηλον
on be- the life of me ²the ⁴of ³neck
half of themselves

ὑπέθηκαν, οἷς οὐκ ἐγὼ μόνος εὐχαριστῶ
¹risked, to whom not I only give thanks

but also all the churches of the Gentiles give thanks; ⁵greet also the church in their house. Greet my beloved Epae'netus, who was the first convert in Asia for Christ. ⁶Greet Mary, who has worked hard among you. ⁷Greet Andron'- icus and Ju'nias, my kinsmen and my fellow prisoners; they are men of note among the apostles, and they were in Christ before me. ⁸Greet Amplia'tus, my beloved in the Lord. ⁹Greet Urba'nus, our fellow worker in Christ, and my beloved Stachys. ¹⁰Greet Apel'les, who is approved in Christ. Greet those who belong to the family of Aristob'- ulus. ¹¹Greet my kinsman Herodion. Greet those in the Lord who belong to the family of Narcis'sus. ¹²Greet those workers in the Lord, Tryphae'na and Trypho'sa. Greet the beloved Persis, who has worked hard in the Lord. ¹³Greet Rufus, eminent in the Lord, also his mother and·mine. ¹⁴Greet Asyn'critus, Phlegon, Hermes, Pat'robas, Her-

ἀλλὰ καὶ πᾶσαι αἱ ἐκκλησίαι τῶν ἐθνῶν,
but also all the churches of the nations,

5 καὶ τὴν κατ᾽ οἶκον αὐτῶν ἐκκλησίαν.
and ¹the ²in ⁴house ⁵of them ²church.

ἀσπάσασθε ᾽Επαίνετον τὸν ἀγαπητόν μου,
Greet Epænetus the beloved of me,

ὅς ἐστιν ἀπαρχὴ τῆς ᾽Ασίας εἰς Χριστόν.
who is firstfruit – of Asia for Christ.

6 ἀσπάσασθε Μαρίαν, ἥτις πολλὰ ἐκοπίασεν
Greet Mary, who many things laboured
(much)

εἰς ὑμᾶς. 7 ἀσπάσασθε ᾽Ανδρόνικον καὶ
for you. Greet Andronicus and

᾽Ιουνιᾶν τοὺς συγγενεῖς μου καὶ συναιχμα-
Junius the kinsmen of me and fellow-

λώτους μου, οἵτινές εἰσιν ἐπίσημοι ἐν
captives of me, who are notable among

τοῖς ἀποστόλοις, οἳ καὶ πρὸ ἐμοῦ γέγοναν
the apostles, who indeed before me have been

ἐν Χριστῷ. 8 ἀσπάσασθε ᾽Αμπλιᾶτον τὸν
in Christ. Greet Ampliatus the

ἀγαπητόν μου ἐν κυρίῳ. 9 ἀσπάσασθε
beloved of me in [the] Lord. Greet

Οὐρβανὸν τὸν συνεργὸν ἡμῶν ἐν Χριστῷ
Urbanus the fellow-worker of us in Christ

καὶ Στάχυν τὸν ἀγαπητόν μου. 10 ἀσπάσ-
and Stachys the beloved of me. Greet

ασθε ᾽Απελλῆν τὸν δόκιμον ἐν Χριστῷ.
Apelles the approved in Christ.

ἀσπάσασθε τοὺς ἐκ τῶν ᾽Αριστοβούλου.
Greet the [ones] of the [family] of Aristobulus.

11 ἀσπάσασθε ῾Ηρῳδίωνα τὸν συγγενῆ μου.
Greet Herodion the kinsman of me.

ἀσπάσασθε τοὺς ἐκ τῶν Ναρκίσσου τοὺς
Greet the [ones] of the [family] of Narcissus –

ὄντας ἐν κυρίῳ. 12 ἀσπάσασθε Τρύφαιναν
being in [the] Lord. Greet Tryphæna

καὶ Τρυφῶσαν τὰς κοπιώσας ἐν κυρίῳ.
and Tryphosa the [ones] labouring in [the] Lord.

ἀσπάσασθε Περσίδα τὴν ἀγαπητήν, ἥτις
Greet Persis the beloved, who

πολλὰ ἐκοπίασεν ἐν κυρίῳ. 13 ἀσπάσασθε
many things laboured in [the] Lord. Greet
(much)

῾Ροῦφον τὸν ἐκλεκτὸν ἐν κυρίῳ καὶ
Rufus the chosen in [the] Lord and

τὴν μητέρα αὐτοῦ καὶ ἐμοῦ. 14 ἀσπάσασθε
the mother of him and of me. Greet

᾽Ασύγκριτον, Φλέγοντα, ῾Ερμῆν, Πατροβᾶν,
Asyncritus, Phlegon, Hermes, Patrobas,

mas, and the brethren who are with them. [15] Greet Philol'ogus, Julia, Nereus and his sister, and Olym'pas, and all the saints who are with them. [16] Greet one another with a holy kiss. All the churches of Christ greet you.

[17] I appeal to you, brethren, to take note of those who create dissensions and difficulties, in opposition to the doctrine which you have been taught; avoid them. [18] For such persons do not serve our Lord Christ, but their own appetites, and by fair and flattering words they deceive the hearts of the simple-minded. [19] For while your obedience is known to all, so that I rejoice over you, I would have you wise as to what is good and guileless as to what is evil; [20] then the God of peace will soon crush Satan under your feet. The grace of our Lord Jesus Christ be with you.[f]

[f] Other ancient authorities omit this sentence

Ἑρμᾶν, καὶ τοὺς σὺν αὐτοῖς ἀδελφούς.
Hermas, and the ²with ³them ¹brothers.

[15] ἀσπάσασθε Φιλόλογον καὶ Ἰουλίαν,
Greet Philologus and Julia,

Νηρέα καὶ τὴν ἀδελφὴν αὐτοῦ, καὶ
Nereus and the sister of him, and

Ὀλυμπᾶν, καὶ τοὺς σὺν αὐτοῖς πάντας
Olympas, and ²the ⁴with ⁵them ¹all

ἁγίους. [16] ἀσπάσασθε ἀλλήλους ἐν φιλήματι
³saints. Greet one another with kiss

ἁγίῳ. ἀσπάζονται ὑμᾶς αἱ ἐκκλησίαι
a holy. ⁵greet ⁶you ²the ³churches

πᾶσαι τοῦ Χριστοῦ.
¹All - ⁴of Christ.

[17] Παρακαλῶ δὲ ὑμᾶς, ἀδελφοί, σκοπεῖν
Now I beseech you, brothers, to watch

τοὺς τὰς διχοστασίας καὶ τὰ σκάνδαλα
¹the ³the ⁴divisions ⁵and ⁶the ⁷offences
[ones]

παρὰ τὴν διδαχὴν ἣν ὑμεῖς ἐμάθετε
⁸beside ⁹the ¹⁰teaching ¹¹which ¹²ye ¹³learned

ποιοῦντας, καὶ ἐκκλίνετε ἀπ' αὐτῶν· [18] οἱ
¹making, and turn away from them; -

γὰρ τοιοῦτοι τῷ κυρίῳ ἡμῶν Χριστῷ
for such men ³the ⁴Lord ⁵of us ²Christ

οὐ δουλεύουσιν ἀλλὰ τῇ ἑαυτῶν κοιλίᾳ,
¹serve not but the of themselves belly,

καὶ διὰ τῆς χρηστολογίας καὶ εὐλογίας
and through - fair speech and flattering speech

ἐξαπατῶσιν τὰς καρδίας τῶν ἀκάκων.
deceive the hearts of the guileless.

[19] ἡ γὰρ ὑμῶν ὑπακοὴ εἰς πάντας
²the ¹For ⁴of you ³obedience ⁵to ⁷all men

ἀφίκετο· ἐφ' ὑμῖν οὖν χαίρω, θέλω
⁵came; over you therefore I rejoice, ⁸I wish

δὲ ὑμᾶς σοφοὺς εἶναι εἰς τὸ ἀγαθόν,
¹and you wise to be to the good,

ἀκεραίους δὲ εἰς τὸ κακόν. [20] ὁ δὲ
but simple to the evil. And the

θεὸς τῆς εἰρήνης συντρίψει τὸν σατανᾶν
God - of peace will crush - Satan

ὑπὸ τοὺς πόδας ὑμῶν ἐν τάχει.
under the feet of you soon.

Ἡ χάρις τοῦ κυρίου ἡμῶν Ἰησοῦ
The grace of the Lord of us Jesus [be]

μεθ' ὑμῶν.
with you.

21 Timothy, my fellow worker, greets you; so do Lucius and Jason and Sosip'ater, my kinsmen. 22 I Tertius, the writer of this letter, greet you in the Lord. 23 Ga'ius, who is host to me and to the whole church, greets you. Eras'tus, the city treasurer, and our brother Quartus, greet you.ᵘ

25 Now to him who is able to strengthen you according to my gospel and the preaching of Jesus Christ, according to the revelation of the mystery which was kept secret for long ages ²⁶ but is now disclosed and through the prophetic writings is made known to all nations, according to the command of the eternal God, to bring about the obedience of faith—²⁷ to the only wise God be glory for evermore through Jesus Christ! Amen.

21 ᾿Ασπάζεται ὑμᾶς Τιμόθεος ὁ συνεργός
⁵greets   ⁶you   ¹Timothy ²the ³fellow-worker
μου,   καὶ   Λούκιος   καὶ   ᾿Ιάσων   καὶ
⁴of me,   and   Lucius   and   Jason   and
Σωσίπατρος   οἱ   συγγενεῖς   μου.   22 ἀσπάζ-
Sosipater   the   kinsmen   of me.   ⁷greet
ομαι   ὑμᾶς   ἐγὼ   Τέρτιος   ὁ   γράψας   τὴν
⁸you   ¹I   ²Tertius ³the [one] ⁴writing   ⁵the
ἐπιστολὴν   ἐν   κυρίῳ.   23 ἀσπάζεται   ὑμᾶς
⁶epistle   in   [the] Lord.   ⁸greets   ¹⁰you
Γάϊος   ὁ   ξένος   μου   καὶ   ὅλης   τῆς
¹Gaius   ²the   ³host   ⁴of me   ⁵and   ⁶of all   ⁷the
ἐκκλησίας.   ἀσπάζεται   ὑμᾶς   ῎Εραστος   ὁ
⁸church.   ⁶greets   ⁷you   ¹Erastus   ²the
οἰκονόμος   τῆς   πόλεως   καὶ   Κούαρτος   ὁ
³treasurer   ⁴of the   ⁵city   and   Quartus   the
ἀδελφός.‡   (?his)
brother.

25 Τῷ   δὲ   δυναμένῳ   ὑμᾶς   στηρίξαι   κατὰ
Now to the   being able   ²you   ¹to establish accord-
[one]   ing to
τὸ   εὐαγγέλιόν   μου   καὶ   τὸ   κήρυγμα
the   gospel   of me   and   the   proclamation
᾿Ιησοῦ   Χριστοῦ,   κατὰ   ἀποκάλυψιν   μυστηρίου
of Jesus   Christ,   according [the] revelation of [the]
                        to   mystery
χρόνοις   αἰωνίοις   σεσιγημένου,   26 φανερω-
²in times   ³eternal   ¹having been kept silent,   ²mani-
θέντος   δὲ   νῦν   διά   τε   γραφῶν   προφητικῶν
fested   ¹but   now and through writings   prophetic
κατ᾿   ἐπιταγὴν   τοῦ   αἰωνίου   θεοῦ   εἰς
accord-   [the]   of the   eternal   God   ⁶for
ing to   command
ὑπακοὴν   πίστεως   εἰς   πάντα   τὰ   ἔθνη
⁷obedience   ⁸of faith   ²to   ³all   ⁴the   ⁵nations
γνωρισθέντος,   27 μόνῳ   σοφῷ   θεῷ,   διὰ
¹made known,   ²only   ³wise   ¹to God, through
᾿Ιησοῦ   Χριστοῦ,   ᾧ   ἡ   δόξα   εἰς   τοὺς
Jesus   Christ,   to whom the glory unto   the
                    (him)ᶜ
αἰῶνας   τῶν   αἰώνων·   ἀμήν.
ages   of the   ages: Amen.

ᵘ Other ancient authorities insert verse 24, *The grace of our Lord Jesus Christ be with you all. Amen.*

‡ Verse 24 omitted by Nestle; cf. RSV footnote.

CHAPTER 1

PAUL, called by the will of God to be an apostle of Christ Jesus, and our brother Sos'thenes,

2 To the church of God which is at Corinth, to those sanctified in Christ Jesus, called to be saints together with all those who in every place call on the name of our Lord Jesus Christ, both their Lord and ours:

3 Grace to you and peace from God our Father and the Lord Jesus Christ.

4 I give thanks to God[a] always for you because of the grace of God which was given you in Christ Jesus, [5]that in every way you were enriched in him with all speech—and all knowledge—[6]even as the testimony to Christ was confirmed among you—[7]so that you are not lacking in any spiritual gift, as you wait for the revealing of our Lord Jesus Christ; [8]who will sustain you to the end, guiltless in the day of our Lord Jesus Christ. [9]God is faithful, by whom you were called

[a] Other ancient authorities read *my God*

1 Παῦλος κλητὸς ἀπόστολος Χριστοῦ
Paul a called apostle of Christ

'Ιησοῦ διὰ θελήματος θεοῦ καὶ Σωσθένης
Jesus through [the] will of God and Sosthenes

ὁ ἀδελφὸς 2 τῇ ἐκκλησίᾳ τοῦ θεοῦ
the(?his) brother to the church - of God

τῇ οὔσῃ ἐν Κορίνθῳ, ἡγιασμένοις ἐν
- existing in Corinth, to [ones] in
                            having been sanctified

Χριστῷ 'Ιησοῦ, κλητοῖς ἁγίοις, σὺν πᾶσιν
Christ Jesus, called saints, with all

τοῖς ἐπικαλουμένοις τὸ ὄνομα τοῦ κυρίου
the [ones] calling on the name of the Lord

ἡμῶν 'Ιησοῦ Χριστοῦ ἐν παντὶ τόπῳ,
of us Jesus Christ in every place,

αὐτῶν καὶ ἡμῶν· 3 χάρις ὑμῖν καὶ
of them and of us: Grace to you and

εἰρήνη ἀπὸ θεοῦ πατρὸς ἡμῶν καὶ κυρίου
peace from God Father of us and Lord

'Ιησοῦ Χριστοῦ.
Jesus Christ.

4 Εὐχαριστῶ τῷ θεῷ πάντοτε περὶ
I gave thanks - to God always concerning

ὑμῶν ἐπὶ τῇ χάριτι τοῦ θεοῦ τῇ δοθείσῃ
you on the grace - of God - given

ὑμῖν ἐν Χριστῷ 'Ιησοῦ, 5 ὅτι ἐν παντὶ
to you in Christ Jesus, because in everything

ἐπλουτίσθητε ἐν αὐτῷ, ἐν παντὶ λόγῳ
ye were enriched in him, in all speech

καὶ πάσῃ γνώσει, 6 καθὼς τὸ μαρτύριον
and all knowledge, as the testimony

τοῦ Χριστοῦ ἐβεβαιώθη ἐν ὑμῖν, 7 ὥστε
- of Christ was confirmed in you, so as

ὑμᾶς μὴ ὑστερεῖσθαι ἐν μηδενὶ χαρίσματι,
you not to be wanting[b] in no(any) gift,

ἀπεκδεχομένους τὴν ἀποκάλυψιν τοῦ κυρίου
awaiting the revelation of the Lord

ἡμῶν 'Ιησοῦ Χριστοῦ· 8 ὃς καὶ βεβαιώσει
of us Jesus Christ; who also will confirm

ὑμᾶς ἕως τέλους ἀνεγκλήτους ἐν τῇ
you till [the] end blameless in the

ἡμέρᾳ τοῦ κυρίου ἡμῶν 'Ιησοῦ [Χριστοῦ].
day of the Lord of us Jesus Christ.

9 πιστὸς ὁ θεός, δι' οὗ ἐκλήθητε εἰς
Faithful [is] - God, through whom ye were called to

into the fellowship of his Son, Jesus Christ our Lord. 10 I appeal to you, brethren, by the name of our Lord Jesus Christ, that all of you agree that there be no dissensions among you, but that you be united in the same mind and the same judgment. ¹¹For it has been reported to me by Chloe's people that there is quarreling among you, my brethren. ¹²What I mean is that each one of you says, "I belong to Paul," or "I belong to Apollos," or "I belong to Cephas," or "I belong to Christ." ¹³Is Christ divided? Was Paul crucified for you? Or were you baptized in the name of Paul? ¹⁴I am thankful⁰ that I baptized none of you except Crispus and Gaius; ¹⁵lest any one should say that you were baptized in my name. ¹⁶(I did baptize also the household of Steph'anas. Beyond that, I do not know whether I baptized any one else.) ¹⁷For Christ did not send me to baptize but to preach the gospel, and not with eloquent

κοινωνίαν   τοῦ   υἱοῦ   αὐτοῦ   Ἰησοῦ   Χριστοῦ
[the] fellowship of the Son   of him   Jesus   Christ
τοῦ   κυρίου   ἡμῶν.
the   Lord   of us.

10 Παρακαλῶ   δὲ   ὑμᾶς,   ἀδελφοί,   διὰ
   Now I beseech   you,   brothers, through
τοῦ   ὀνόματος   τοῦ   κυρίου   ἡμῶν   Ἰησοῦ
the   name   of the Lord   of us   Jesus
Χριστοῦ,   ἵνα   τὸ   αὐτὸ   λέγητε   πάντες,
Christ,   in order   the   same   ye say   all,
           that   thing
καὶ   μὴ   ᾖ   ἐν   ὑμῖν   σχίσματα,   ἦτε   δὲ
and   not   be   among you   divisions,   but ye may be
κατηρτισμένοι   ἐν   τῷ   αὐτῷ   νοῒ   καὶ
having been joined in   the   same   mind   and
together
ἐν   τῇ   αὐτῇ   γνώμῃ.   11 ἐδηλώθη   γάρ   μοι
in   the   same   opinion.   For it was shown   to me
περὶ   ὑμῶν,   ἀδελφοί   μου,   ὑπὸ   τῶν
concerning you,   brothers   of me,   by   the [ones]
Χλόης,   ὅτι   ἔριδες   ἐν   ὑμῖν   εἰσιν.   12 λέγω
of Chloe, that   strifes among you   there are.   I say
δὲ   τοῦτο,   ὅτι   ἕκαστος   ὑμῶν   λέγει·   ἐγὼ
Now   this,   because each   of you   says: I
μέν   εἰμι   Παύλου,   ἐγὼ   δὲ   Ἀπολλῶ,
indeed am   of Paul,   but I   of Apollos,
ἐγὼ   δὲ   Κηφᾶ,   ἐγὼ   δὲ   Χριστοῦ.
but I   of Cephas, but I   of Christ.
13 μεμέρισται   ὁ   Χριστός;   μὴ   Παῦλος
   IIas been divided -   Christ?   Not   Paul
ἐσταυρώθη   ὑπὲρ   ὑμῶν,   ἢ   εἰς   τὸ   ὄνομα
was crucified on behalf of you,   or   in   the   name
Παύλου   ἐβαπτίσθητε;   14 εὐχαριστῶ   ὅτι
of Paul   were ye baptized?   I give thanks   that
οὐδένα   ὑμῶν   ἐβάπτισα   εἰ   μὴ   Κρίσπον
not one   of you   I baptized   except   Crispus
καὶ   Γάϊον·   15 ἵνα   μή   τις   εἴπῃ   ὅτι
and   Gaius;   lest   anyone should say that
εἰς   τὸ   ἐμὸν   ὄνομα   ἐβαπτίσθητε.   16 ἐβάπτισα   δὲ
in   -   my   name   ye were baptized.   But I baptized
καὶ   τὸν   Στεφανᾶ   οἶκον·   λοιπὸν   οὐκ   οἶδα
also   the   of Stephanas household; for the rest   I know not
εἴ   τινα   ἄλλον   ἐβάπτισα.   17 οὐ
if   any   other   I baptized.   ᵇnot
γὰρ   ἀπέστειλέν   με   Χριστὸς   βαπτίζειν
¹For   ²sent   ⁴me   ³Christ   to baptize

ἀλλὰ   εὐαγγελίζεσθαι,   οὐκ   ἐν   σοφίᾳ   λόγου,
but   to evangelize,   not   in   wisdom   of speech,

wisdom, lest the cross of Christ be emptied of its power. 18 For the word of the cross is folly to those who are perishing, but to us who are being saved it is the power of God. 19 For it is written, "I will destroy the wisdom of the wise, and the cleverness of the clever I will thwart." 20 Where is the wise man? Where is the scribe? Where is the debater of this age? Has not God made foolish the wisdom of the world? 21 For since, in the wisdom of God, the world did not know God through wisdom, it pleased God through the folly of what we preach to save those who believe. 22 For Jews demand signs and Greeks seek wisdom, 23 but we preach Christ crucified, a stumbling-block to Jews and folly to Gentiles, 24 but to those who are called, both Jews and Greeks, Christ the power of God and the wisdom of God. 25 For the foolishness of God is wiser than men, and the weakness of God is stronger than men.

ἵνα μὴ κενωθῇ ὁ σταυρὸς τοῦ Χριστοῦ.
lest ⁴be made vain ¹the ²cross – ³of Christ.

18 Ὁ λόγος γὰρ ὁ τοῦ σταυροῦ τοῖς
For the word – of the cross ²to the [ones]

μὲν ἀπολλυμένοις μωρία ἐστίν, τοῖς
¹on one ²perishing ⁵folly ⁴is, ³to the [ones]
hand

δὲ σῳζομένοις ἡμῖν δύναμις θεοῦ ἐστιν.
¹on the ⁴being saved ²to us ⁶[the] ⁷power ⁸of God ⁵it is.
other

19 γέγραπται γάρ· ἀπολῶ τὴν σοφίαν
For it has been written: I will destroy the wisdom

τῶν σοφῶν, καὶ τὴν σύνεσιν τῶν συνετῶν
of the wise ones, and the understanding of the prudent

ἀθετήσω. 20 ποῦ σοφός; ποῦ γραμματεύς;
I will set aside. Where [is the] wise man? where [is the] scribe?

ποῦ συζητητὴς τοῦ αἰῶνος τούτου; οὐχὶ
where disputant of this age? ²Not
[is the]

ἐμώρανεν ὁ θεὸς τὴν σοφίαν τοῦ κόσμου;
¹made ³foolish – ²God ⁴the ⁵wisdom ⁶of the ⁷world?

21 ἐπειδὴ γὰρ ἐν τῇ σοφίᾳ τοῦ θεοῦ
for since in the wisdom – of God

οὐκ ἔγνω ὁ κόσμος διὰ τῆς σοφίας
⁶knew ⁷not ¹the ²world ³through ⁴the(its) ⁵wisdom

τὸν θεόν, εὐδόκησεν ὁ θεὸς διὰ τῆς
– ²God, ²thought well – ¹God through the

μωρίας τοῦ κηρύγματος σῶσαι τοὺς
folly of the proclamation to save the

πιστεύοντας. 22 ἐπειδὴ καὶ Ἰουδαῖοι σημεῖα
[ones] believing. Seeing that both Jews ²signs

αἰτοῦσιν καὶ Ἕλληνες σοφίαν ζητοῦσιν,
¹ask and Greeks ²wisdom ¹seek,

23 ἡμεῖς δὲ κηρύσσομεν Χριστὸν ἐσταυρωμένον,
²we ¹yet proclaim Christ having been crucified,

Ἰουδαίοις μὲν σκάνδαλον, ἔθνεσιν δὲ
to Jews on one hand an offence, to nations on the other

μωρίαν, 24 αὐτοῖς δὲ τοῖς κλητοῖς,
folly, but to them the called ones,

Ἰουδαίοις τε καὶ Ἕλλησιν, Χριστὸν θεοῦ
²to Jews ¹both and to Greeks, Christ of God

δύναμιν καὶ θεοῦ σοφίαν. 25 ὅτι τὸ
power and of God wisdom. Because the

μωρὸν τοῦ θεοῦ σοφώτερον τῶν ἀνθρώπων
foolish thing – of God wiser [than] – men

ἐστίν, καὶ τὸ ἀσθενὲς τοῦ θεοῦ ἰσχυρότερον
is, and the weak thing – of God stronger [than]

26 For consider your call, brethren; not many of you were wise according to worldly standards, not many were powerful, not many were of noble birth; [27] but God chose what is foolish in the world to shame the wise, God chose what is weak in the world to shame the strong, [28] God chose what is low and despised in the world, even things that are not, to bring to nothing things that are, [29] so that no human being might boast in the presence of God. [30] He is the source of your life in Christ Jesus, whom God made our wisdom, our righteousness and sanctification and redemption; [31] therefore, as it is written, "Let him who boasts, boast of the Lord."

CHAPTER 2

WHEN I came to you, brethren, I did not come proclaiming to you the testimony[e] of God in lofty words or wisdom. [2] For I decided to know nothing among

[e] Other ancient authorities read *mystery* (or *secret*)

τῶν	ἀνθρώπων.	**26** Βλέπετε	γὰρ	τὴν
–	men.	For ye see		the

κλῆσιν	ὑμῶν,	ἀδελφοί,	ὅτι	οὐ	πολλοὶ
calling	of you,	brothers,	that	not	many

σοφοὶ	κατὰ	σάρκα,	οὐ	πολλοὶ	δυνατοί,
wise men	according to	flesh,	not	many	powerful,

οὐ	πολλοὶ	εὐγενεῖς·	**27** ἀλλὰ	τὰ	μωρὰ
not	many	well born;	but	the	foolish things

τοῦ	κόσμου	ἐξελέξατο	ὁ	θεὸς	ἵνα	καται-
of the	world	[2]chose	–	[1]God	in order that	he might

σχύνῃ	τοὺς	σοφούς,	καὶ	τὰ	ἀσθενῆ	τοῦ
shame	the	wise men,	and	the	weak things	of the

κόσμου	ἐξελέξατο	ὁ	θεὸς	ἵνα	καταισχύνῃ
world	[2]chose	–	[1]God	in order that	he might shame

τὰ	ἰσχυρά,	**28** καὶ	τὰ	ἀγενῆ	τοῦ	κόσμου
the	strong things,	and	the	base things	of the	world

καὶ	τὰ	ἐξουθενημένα	ἐξελέξατο	ὁ	θεός,
and	the things	being despised	[2]chose	–	[1]God,

τὰ	μὴ	ὄντα,	ἵνα	τὰ	ὄντα	καταργήσῃ,
the things	not	being,	in order that	[1]the	[2]being	[1]he might abolish,

29 ὅπως	μὴ	καυχήσηται	πᾶσα	σὰρξ
so as	not	might boast	all	flesh[*]

ἐνώπιον	τοῦ	θεοῦ.	**30** ἐξ	αὐτοῦ	δὲ	ὑμεῖς
before	–	God.	And of him		ye

ἐστε	ἐν	Χριστῷ	Ἰησοῦ,	ὃς	ἐγενήθη
are	in	Christ	Jesus,	who	became

σοφία	ἡμῖν	ἀπὸ	θεοῦ,	δικαιοσύνη	τε
wisdom	to us	from	God,	[2]righteousness	[1]both

καὶ	ἁγιασμὸς	καὶ	ἀπολύτρωσις,	**31** ἵνα	καθὼς
and	sanctification	and	redemption,	in order that	as

γέγραπται·	ὁ	καυχώμενος	ἐν	κυρίῳ	καυχάσθω.
it has been written:	The [one]	boasting	[2]in	[3][the] Lord	[1]let him boast.

2 Κἀγὼ	ἐλθὼν	πρὸς	ὑμᾶς,	ἀδελφοί,
And I	coming	to	you,	brothers,

ἦλθον	οὐ	καθ᾽	ὑπεροχὴν	λόγου	ἢ	σοφίας
came	not	according to	excellence	of speech	or	of wisdom

καταγγέλλων	ὑμῖν	τὸ	μαρτύριον	τοῦ	θεοῦ.
announcing	to you	the	testimony	–	of God.

2 οὐ	γὰρ	ἔκρινά	τι	εἰδέναι	ἐν	ὑμῖν
For I decided not			anything	to know	among	you

[*] That is, so that no flesh might boast. *Cf.* Mat. 24. 22.

you except Jesus Christ and him crucified. ³And I was with you in weakness and in much fear and trembling; ⁴and my speech and my message were not in plausible words of wisdom, but in demonstration of the Spirit and power, ⁵that your faith might not rest in the wisdom of men but in the power of God.

6 Yet among the mature we do impart wisdom, although it is not a wisdom of this age or of the rulers of this age, who are doomed to pass away. ⁷But we impart a secret and hidden wisdom of God, which God decreed before the ages for our glorification. ⁸None of the rulers of this age understood this; for if they had, they would not have crucified the Lord of glory. ⁹But, as it is written,
"What no eye has seen, nor ear heard, nor the heart of man conceived, what God has prepared for those who love him," ¹⁰God has revealed to us

εἰ   μὴ   'Ἰησοῦν   Χριστὸν   καὶ   τοῦτον
except   Jesus   Christ   and   this one

ἐσταυρωμένον.   3 κἀγὼ   ἐν   ἀσθενείᾳ   καὶ
having been crucified.   And I   in   weakness   and

ἐν   φόβῳ   καὶ   ἐν   τρόμῳ   πολλῷ   ἐγενόμην
in   fear   and   in   trembling   much   was

πρὸς   ὑμᾶς,   4 καὶ   ὁ   λόγος   μου   καὶ   τὸ
with   you,   and   the speech   of me and   the

κήρυγμά   μου   οὐκ   ἐν   πειθοῖς   σοφίας
proclamation of me   not   in   ¹persuasive ²of wisdom

λόγοις,   ἀλλ'   ἐν   ἀποδείξει   πνεύματος   καὶ
²words,   but   in   demonstration   of spirit   and

δυνάμεως,   5 ἵνα   ἡ   πίστις   ὑμῶν   μὴ   ᾖ
of power,   in order that the   faith   of you   may not be

ἐν   σοφίᾳ   ἀνθρώπων   ἀλλ'   ἐν   δυνάμει
in [the] wisdom   of men   but   in   [the] power

θεοῦ.
of God.

6 Σοφίαν   δὲ   λαλοῦμεν   ἐν   τοῖς   τελείοις,
But ²wisdom   ¹we speak   among   the   perfect ones,

σοφίαν   δὲ   οὐ   τοῦ   αἰῶνος   τούτου   οὐδὲ
yet wisdom   not   of this age   neither

τῶν   ἀρχόντων   τοῦ   αἰῶνος   τούτου   τῶν
of the   leaders   of this age   of the
                                          [ones]

καταργουμένων·   7 ἀλλὰ   λαλοῦμεν   θεοῦ
being brought to naught;   but   we speak   ²of God

σοφίαν   ἐν   μυστηρίῳ,   τὴν   ἀποκεκρυμμένην,
¹a wisdom   in   mystery,   –   having been hidden,

ἣν   προώρισεν   ὁ   θεὸς   πρὸ   τῶν   αἰώνων
which   ²foreordained   –   ¹God   before   the   ages

εἰς   δόξαν   ἡμῶν·   8 ἣν   οὐδεὶς   τῶν   ἀρχόντων
for   glory   of us;   which   not one   of the   leaders

τοῦ   αἰῶνος   τούτου   ἔγνωκεν·   εἰ   γὰρ
of this age   has known;   for if

ἔγνωσαν,   οὐκ   ἂν   τὸν   κύριον   τῆς   δόξης
they knew,   not   –   the   Lord   –   of glory

ἐσταύρωσαν·9 ἀλλὰ   καθὼς   γέγραπται·   ἃ
they would have   but   as   it has been written: Things
crucified;*   which

ὀφθαλμὸς   οὐκ   εἶδεν   καὶ   οὓς   οὐκ   ἤκουσεν
eye   saw not   and   ear   heard not

καὶ   ἐπὶ   καρδίαν   ἀνθρώπου   οὐκ   ἀνέβη,
and   on   heart   of man   came not up,

ὅσα   ἡτοίμασεν   ὁ   θεὸς   τοῖς   ἀγαπῶσιν
how many ²prepared   –   ¹God   for the [ones] loving

αὐτόν.   10 ἡμῖν   γὰρ   ἀπεκάλυψεν   ὁ   θεὸς
him.   ¹For ⁴to us   ²revealed   –   ³God

* This rendering is demanded by the preceding ἄν.

through the Spirit. For the Spirit searches everything, even the depths of God. [11]For what person knows a man's thoughts except the spirit of the man which is in him? So also no one comprehends the thoughts of God except the Spirit of God. [12]Now we have received not the spirit of the world, but the Spirit which is from God, that we might understand the gifts bestowed on us by God. [13]And we impart this in words not taught by human wisdom but taught by the Spirit, interpreting spiritual truths to those who possess the Spirit.[d]

[14] The unspiritual[e] man does not receive the gifts of the Spirit of God, for they are folly to him, and he is not able to understand them because they are spiritually discerned. [15]The spiritual man judges all things, but is himself to be judged by no one. [16]"For who has known the mind of the Lord so as to instruct him?" But we have the mind of Christ.

διὰ   τοῦ   πνεύματος·   τὸ   γὰρ   πνεῦμα   πάντα
through the   Spirit;   for the   Spirit   all things
ἐρευνᾷ,   καὶ   τὰ   βάθη   τοῦ   θεοῦ.   11 τίς
searches,   even   the   deep things   –   of God.   ²who
γὰρ   οἶδεν   ἀνθρώπων   τὰ   τοῦ   ἀνθρώπου
¹For   ⁴knows   ³of men   the things   –   of a man
εἰ   μὴ   τὸ   πνεῦμα   τοῦ   ἀνθρώπου   τὸ
except   the   spirit   –   of a man   –
ἐν   αὐτῷ;   οὕτως   καὶ   τὰ   τοῦ   θεοῦ   οὐδεὶς
in   him?   so   also the things –   of God   no one
ἔγνωκεν   εἰ   μὴ   τὸ   πνεῦμα   τοῦ   θεοῦ.
has known   except   the   Spirit   –   of God.
12 ἡμεῖς   δὲ   οὐ   τὸ   πνεῦμα   τοῦ   κόσμου
And we   not   the   spirit   of the   world
ἐλάβομεν   ἀλλὰ   τὸ   πνεῦμα   τὸ   ἐκ   τοῦ   θεοῦ,
received   but   the   Spirit   –   from   –   God,
ἵνα   εἰδῶμεν   τὰ   ὑπὸ   τοῦ   θεοῦ
in order   we may   the things   by   –   God
that   know
χαρισθέντα   ἡμῖν·   13 ἃ   καὶ   λαλοῦμεν   οὐκ
freely given   to us;   which things also   we speak   not
ἐν   διδακτοῖς   ἀνθρωπίνης   σοφίας   λόγοις,
in   ²taught   ³of human   ⁴wisdom   ¹words,
ἀλλ᾽   ἐν   διδακτοῖς   πνεύματος,   πνευματικοῖς
but   in [words] taught   of [the] Spirit,   ³with spiritual things
πνευματικὰ   συγκρίνοντες.   14 ψυχικὸς   δὲ
²spiritual things   ¹comparing.   But a natural
ἄνθρωπος   οὐ   δέχεται   τὰ   τοῦ   πνεύματος
man   receives not   the things of the   Spirit
τοῦ   θεοῦ·   μωρία   γὰρ   αὐτῷ   ἐστιν,   καὶ
–   of God;   for folly   to him   they are,   and
οὐ   δύναται   γνῶναι,   ὅτι   πνευματικῶς
he cannot   to know,   because   ²spiritually
ἀνακρίνεται.   15 ὁ   δὲ   πνευματικὸς   ἀνακρίνει
¹they are ³discerned.   But the   spiritual man   ³discerns
μὲν   πάντα,   αὐτὸς   δὲ   ὑπ᾽   οὐδενὸς
¹on one   all things,   ²he   ¹on the   ⁴by   ⁵no one
hand   other
ἀνακρίνεται.   16 τίς   γὰρ   ἔγνω   νοῦν
²is discerned.   For who   knew   [the] mind
κυρίου,   ὃς   συμβιβάσει   αὐτόν;   ἡμεῖς   δὲ
of [the]   who   will instruct   him?   But we
Lord,
νοῦν   Χριστοῦ   ἔχομεν.
[the] mind   of Christ   have.

[d] Or interpreting spiritual truths in spiritual language; or comparing spiritual things with spiritual

[e] Or natural

CHAPTER 3

BUT I, brethren, could not address you as spiritual men, but as men of the flesh, as babes in Christ. ²I fed you with milk, not solid food; for you were not ready for it; and even yet you are not ready, ³for you are still of the flesh. For while there is jealousy and strife among you, are you not of the flesh, and behaving like ordinary men? ⁴For when one says, "I belong to Paul," and another, "I belong to Apol′los," are you not merely men? 5 What then is Apol′los? What is Paul? Servants through whom you believed, as the Lord assigned to each. ⁶I planted, Apol′los watered, but God gave the growth. ⁷So neither he who plants nor he who waters is anything, but only God who gives the growth. ⁸He who plants and he who waters are equal, and each shall receive his wages according to his labor. ⁹For we are fellow workers for God; you are God's field, God's building. 10 According to the commission of God given

3 Κἀγώ, ἀδελφοί, οὐκ ἠδυνήθην λαλῆσαι
And I, brothers, was not able to speak
ὑμῖν ὡς πνευματικοῖς ἀλλ᾿ ὡς σαρκίνοις,
to you as to spiritual men but as to fleshy,
ὡς νηπίοις ἐν Χριστῷ. 2 γάλα ὑμᾶς
as to infants in Christ. ²Milk ²you
ἐπότισα, οὐ βρῶμα· οὔπω γὰρ ἐδύνασθε.
¹I gave not food; for ye were not then able.
⁴to drink,
ἀλλ᾿ οὐδὲ [ἔτι] νῦν δύνασθε, 3 ἔτι γὰρ
But neither yet now are ye able, for still
σαρκικοί ἐστε. ὅπου γὰρ ἐν ὑμῖν ζῆλος
fleshly ye are. For whereas among you [there is] jealousy
καὶ ἔρις, οὐχὶ σαρκικοί ἐστε καὶ κατὰ
and strife, ²not ²fleshly ¹are ye ⁴and ⁵according to
ἄνθρωπον περιπατεῖτε; 4 ὅταν γὰρ λέγῃ
²man ⁵walk? For whenever says
τις· ἐγὼ μέν εἰμι Παύλου, ἕτερος δέ·
anyone: I – am of Paul, and another:
ἐγὼ Ἀπολλῶ, οὐκ ἄνθρωποί ἐστε; 5 Τί
I of Apollos, ²not ²men ¹are ye? What
οὖν ἐστιν Ἀπολλῶς; τί δέ ἐστιν Παῦλος;
there- is Apollos? and what is Paul?
fore
διάκονοι δι᾿ ὧν ἐπιστεύσατε, καὶ ἑκάστῳ
Ministers through whom ye believed, even ²to each one
ὡς ὁ κύριος ἔδωκεν. 6 ἐγὼ ἐφύτευσα,
¹as the Lord gave. I planted,
Ἀπολλῶς ἐπότισεν, ἀλλὰ ὁ θεὸς ηὔξανεν·
Apollos watered, but – God made to
grow;
7 ὥστε οὔτε ὁ φυτεύων ἐστίν τι οὔτε
so as neither the [one] planting is anything nor
ὁ ποτίζων, ἀλλ᾿ ὁ αὐξάνων θεός. 8 ὁ
the watering, but ²the ³making to ¹God. ²The
[one] [one] grow [one]
φυτεύων δὲ καὶ ὁ ποτίζων ἕν εἰσιν,
³planting ¹so and the [one] watering one* are,
ἕκαστος δὲ τὸν ἴδιον μισθὸν λήμψεται
and each one the(his) own reward will receive
κατὰ τὸν ἴδιον κόπον. 9 θεοῦ γάρ ἐσμεν
accord- his own labour. For of God we are
ing to
συνεργοί· θεοῦ γεώργιον, θεοῦ οἰκοδομή
fellow-workers; ²of God ²a tillage, ⁵of God ⁴a building
ἐστε. 10 Κατὰ τὴν χάριν τοῦ θεοῦ τὴν
¹ye are. According to the grace – of God –

---

* Notice the neuter gender, though "thing" cannot very well be expressed; cf. John 10. 30.

to me, like a skilled master builder I laid a foundation, and another man is building upon it. Let each man take care how he builds upon it. ¹¹For no other foundation can any one lay than that which is laid, which is Jesus Christ. ¹²Now if any one builds on the foundation with gold, silver, precious stones, wood, hay, stubble—¹³each man's work will become manifest; for the Day will disclose it, because it will be revealed with fire, and the fire will test what sort of work each one has done. ¹⁴If the work which any man has built on the foundation survives, he will receive a reward. ¹⁵If any man's work is burned up, he will suffer loss, though he himself will be saved, but only as through fire.

16 Do you not know that you are God's temple and that God's Spirit dwells in you? ¹⁷If any one destroys God's temple, God will destroy him. For God's temple is holy, and that temple you are.

18 Let no one deceive himself. If any one among you thinks that he is wise in this age, let him become a fool that he may become wise.

δοθεῖσάν μοι ὡς σοφὸς ἀρχιτέκτων
given to me as a wise master builder
θεμέλιον ἔθηκα, ἄλλος δὲ ἐποικοδομεῖ.
a foundation I laid, but another builds on [it].
ἕκαστος δὲ βλεπέτω πῶς ἐποικοδομεῖ.
But each one let him look how he builds on [it].
11 θεμέλιον γὰρ ἄλλον οὐδεὶς δύναται θεῖναι
For foundation other no one is able to lay
παρὰ τὸν κείμενον, ὅς ἐστιν Ἰησοῦς
beside the [one] being laid, who is Jesus
Χριστός. 12 εἰ δέ τις ἐποικοδομεῖ ἐπὶ
Christ. Now if anyone builds on on
τὸν θεμέλιον χρυσίον, ἀργύριον, λίθους
the foundation gold, silver, stones
τιμίους, ξύλα, χόρτον, καλάμην, 13 ἑκάστου
precious, woods, hay, stubble, of each one
τὸ ἔργον φανερὸν γενήσεται· ἡ γὰρ ἡμέρα
the work manifest will become; for the day
δηλώσει, ὅτι ἐν πυρὶ ἀποκαλύπτεται,
will declare because by fire it is revealed,
[it],
καὶ ἑκάστου τὸ ἔργον ὁποῖόν ἐστιν
and ²of each one ¹the ²work ³of what sort ⁹it is
τὸ πῦρ αὐτὸ δοκιμάσει. 14 εἴ τινος
⁴the ⁵fire ⁷it ⁶will prove. If of anyone
τὸ ἔργον μενεῖ ὃ ἐποικοδόμησεν, μισθὸν
the work remains which he built on, a reward
λήμψεται· 15 εἴ τινος τὸ ἔργον κατακαήσ-
he will receive; if of anyone the work will be con-
εται, ζημιωθήσεται, αὐτὸς δὲ σωθήσεται,
sumed, he will suffer loss, but he will be saved,
οὕτως δὲ ὡς διὰ πυρός. 16 Οὐκ οἴδατε
yet so as through fire. Know ye not
ὅτι ναὸς θεοῦ ἐστε καὶ τὸ πνεῦμα τοῦ
that a shrine of God ye are and the Spirit -
θεοῦ ἐν ὑμῖν οἰκεῖ; 17 εἴ τις τὸν ναὸν
of God in you dwells? If anyone the shrine
τοῦ θεοῦ φθείρει, φθερεῖ τοῦτον ὁ θεός·
- of God defiles, ²will defile ³this man - ¹God;
ὁ γὰρ ναὸς τοῦ θεοῦ ἅγιός ἐστιν, οἵτινές
for the shrine - of God holy is, who(which)
ἐστε ὑμεῖς.
are ye.

18 Μηδεὶς ἑαυτὸν ἐξαπατάτω· εἴ τις
No one himself let deceive; if anyone
δοκεῖ σοφὸς εἶναι ἐν ὑμῖν ἐν τῷ αἰῶνι
thinks wise to be among you in - age
τούτῳ, μωρὸς γενέσθω, ἵνα γένηται
this, foolish let him in order he may
become, that become

¹⁹For the wisdom of this world is folly with God. For it is written, "He catches the wise in their craftiness," ²⁰and again, "The Lord knows that the thoughts of the wise are futile." ²¹So let no one boast of men. For all things are yours, ²²whether Paul or Apol'los or Cephas or the world or life or death or the present or the future, all are yours; ²³and you are Christ's; and Christ is God's.

CHAPTER 4

THIS is how one should regard us, as servants of Christ and stewards of the mysteries of God. ²Moreover it is required of stewards that they be found trustworthy. ³But with me it is a very small thing that I should be judged by you or by any human court. I do not even judge myself. ⁴I am not aware of anything against myself, but I am not thereby acquitted. It is the Lord who judges me. ⁵Therefore do not pronounce judgment before the time, before the Lord comes, who will

σοφός. wise.	**19** ἢ For the	γὰρ	σοφία wisdom	τοῦ –	κόσμοι world

τούτου   μωρία   παρὰ   τῷ   θεῷ   ἐστιν.
of this   folly   with   –   God   is.

γέγραπται   γάρ·   ὁ   δρασσόμενος   τοὺς   σοφοὺς
For it has been written: The [one] grasping   the   wise

ἐν   τῇ   πανουργίᾳ   αὐτῶν·   **20** καὶ   πάλιν·
in   the   craftiness   of them;   and   again :

κύριος   γινώσκει   τοὺς   διαλογισμοὺς   τῶν
[The] Lord   knows   the   reasonings   of the

σοφῶν,   ὅτι   εἰσὶν   μάταιοι.   **21** ὥστε   μηδεὶς
wise,   that   they are   vain.   So as   no one

καυχάσθω   ἐν   ἀνθρώποις·   πάντα   γὰρ   ὑμῶν
let boast   in   men;   for all things   of you

ἐστιν,   **22** εἴτε   Παῦλος   εἴτε   Ἀπολλῶς
is(are),   whether   Paul   or   Apollos

εἴτε   Κηφᾶς,   εἴτε   κόσμος   εἴτε   ζωὴ   εἴτε
or   Cephas,   or   [the] world   or   life   or

θάνατος,   εἴτε   ἐνεστῶτα   εἴτε   μέλλοντα,
death,   or   things present   or   things coming,

πάντα   ὑμῶν,   **23** ὑμεῖς   δὲ   Χριστοῦ,   Χριστὸς   δὲ
all things of you,   and ye   of Christ,   and Christ

θεοῦ.   **4** Οὕτως   ἡμᾶς   λογιζέσθω   ἄνθρωπος   ὡς
of God.   So   ⁴us   ¹let ³reckon   ²a man   as

ὑπηρέτας   Χριστοῦ   καὶ   οἰκονόμους   μυστηρίων
attendants   of Christ   and   stewards   of mysteries

θεοῦ.   **2** ὧδε   λοιπὸν   ζητεῖται   ἐν   τοῖς
of God.   Here   for the rest   it is sought   among   –

οἰκονόμοις   ἵνα   πιστός   τις   εὑρεθῇ.   **3** ἐμοὶ
stewards   in order ²faithful ¹anyone ²be found.   to me
        that

δὲ   εἰς   ἐλάχιστόν   ἐστιν   ἵνα   ὑφ'   ὑμῶν
And for   a very little thing   it is   in order that   by   you

ἀνακριθῶ   ἢ   ὑπὸ   ἀνθρωπίνης   ἡμέρας·   ἀλλ'
I am judged   or   by   a human   day;*   but

οὐδὲ   ἐμαυτὸν   ἀνακρίνω·   **4** οὐδὲν   γὰρ
not   myself   I judge;   for nothing

ἐμαυτῷ   σύνοιδα,   ἀλλ'   οὐκ   ἐν   τούτῳ
against myself   I know,   but   not   by   this

δεδικαίωμαι·   ὁ   δὲ   ἀνακρίνων   με   κύριός·
have I been   but the [one]   judging   me   [the] Lord
justified;

ἐστιν.   **5** ὥστε   μὴ   πρὸ   καιροῦ   τι   κρίνετε,
is.   So as   not   before   time   anything   judge ye,

ἕως   ἂν   ἔλθῃ   ὁ   κύριος,   ὃς   καὶ   φωτίσει
until   comes the   Lord,   who   both   will shed
                                               light on

* ? of judgment.

bring to light the things now hidden in darkness and will disclose the purposes of the heart. Then every man will receive his commendation from God.

6 I have applied all this to myself and Apol'los for your benefit, brethren, that you may learn by us to live according to scripture, that none of you may be puffed up in favor of one against another. ⁷For who sees anything different in you? What have you that you did not receive? If then you received it, why do you boast as if it were not a gift?

8 Already you are filled! Already you have become rich! Without us you have become kings! And would that you did reign, so that we might share the rule with you! ⁹For I think that God has exhibited us apostles as last of all, like men sentenced to death; because we have become a spectacle to the world, to angels and to men. ¹⁰We are fools for Christ's sake, but you are wise in Christ. We are weak, but you are strong. You are held in honor, but we are in disrepute. ¹¹To the present hour we hunger and thirst, we are ill-clad and buffeted and homeless,

τὰ κρυπτὰ τοῦ σκότους καὶ φανερώσει
the hidden things of the darkness and will manifest
τὰς βουλὰς τῶν καρδιῶν· καὶ τότε ὁ
the counsels of the hearts; and then the
ἔπαινος γενήσεται ἑκάστῳ ἀπὸ τοῦ θεοῦ.
praise will be to each one° from – God.
6 Ταῦτα δέ, ἀδελφοί, μετεσχημάτισα εἰς
Now these things, brothers, I adapted to
ἐμαυτὸν καὶ 'Απολλῶν δι' ὑμᾶς, ἵνα
myself and Apollos because you, in order
of that
ἐν ἡμῖν μάθητε τὸ μὴ ὑπὲρ ἃ
among us ye may learn – not [to think] above what
things
γέγραπται, ἵνα μὴ εἷς ὑπὲρ τοῦ ἑνὸς
has(ve) been written, lest ²one ³on behalf of ⁴the ⁵one
φυσιοῦσθε κατὰ τοῦ ἑτέρου. 7 τίς γάρ σε
¹ye are puffed up against the other. For who thee
διακρίνει; τί δὲ ἔχεις ὃ οὐκ ἔλαβες;
distinguishes? and what hast thou which thou didst not receive?
εἰ δὲ καὶ ἔλαβες, τί καυχᾶσαι ὡς μὴ
and if indeed thou didst why boastest thou as not
receive,
λαβών; 8 ἤδη κεκορεσμένοι ἐστέ· ἤδη
receiving? Now having been glutted ye are; now
ἐπλουτήσατε· χωρὶς ἡμῶν ἐβασιλεύσατε· καὶ
ye became rich; without us ye reigned; and
ὄφελόν γε ἐβασιλεύσατε, ἵνα
²an advantage ³really ¹[it is] [that] ye reigned, in order that
καὶ ἡμεῖς ὑμῖν συμβασιλεύσωμεν. 9 δοκῶ
also we ²you ¹might reign with. I think
γάρ, ὁ θεὸς ἡμᾶς τοὺς ἀποστόλους
For, – God us the apostles
ἐσχάτους ἀπέδειξεν ὡς ἐπιθανατίους, ὅτι
last showed forth as doomed to death, because
θέατρον ἐγενήθημεν τῷ κόσμῳ καὶ ἀγγέλοις
a spectacle we became to the world both to angels
καὶ ἀνθρώποις. 10 ἡμεῖς μωροὶ διὰ
and to men. We [are] fools because of
Χριστόν, ὑμεῖς δὲ φρόνιμοι ἐν Χριστῷ·
Christ, but ye [are] prudent in Christ;
ἡμεῖς ἀσθενεῖς, ὑμεῖς δὲ ἰσχυροί· ὑμεῖς
we [are] weak, but ye [are] strong; ye [are]
ἔνδοξοι, ἡμεῖς δὲ ἄτιμοι. 11 ἄχρι τῆς
held in honour, but we [are] unhonoured. Until the
ἄρτι ὥρας καὶ πεινῶμεν καὶ διψῶμεν
present hour ²both ¹we ³hunger and thirst
καὶ γυμνιτεύομεν καὶ κολαφιζόμεθα καὶ
and are naked and are buffeted and

¹²and we labor, working with our own hands. When reviled, we bless; when persecuted, we endure; ¹³when slandered, we try to conciliate; we have become, and are now, as the refuse of the world, the offscouring of all things.

14 I do not write this to make you ashamed, but to admonish you as my beloved children. ¹⁵For though you have countless guides in Christ, you do not have many fathers. For I became your father in Christ Jesus through the gospel. ¹⁶I urge you, then, be imitators of me. ¹⁷Therefore I sent[f] to you Timothy, my beloved and faithful child in the Lord, to remind you of my ways in Christ, as I teach them everywhere in every church. ¹⁸Some are arrogant, as though I were not coming to you. ¹⁹But I will come to you soon, if the Lord wills, and I will find out not the talk of these arrogant people but their power. ²⁰For the king-

f Or *am sending*

ἀστατοῦμεν   12 καὶ   κοπιῶμεν   ἐργαζόμενοι
are unsettled   and   labour   working

ταῖς ἰδίαις   χερσίν·   λοιδορούμενοι   εὐλο-
with the(our) own   hands;   being reviled   we

γοῦμεν, διωκόμενοι ἀνεχόμεθα,   13 δυσφημού-
bless,   being persecuted   we endure,   being de-

μενοι παρακαλοῦμεν·   ὡς περικαθάρματα τοῦ
famed   we beseech;   as   refuse   of the

κόσμου ἐγενήθημεν,   πάντων περίψημα ἕως
world   we became,   ²of all things   ¹offscouring   until

ἄρτι.
now.

14 Οὐκ ἐντρέπων ὑμᾶς γράφω ταῦτα,
  Not   shaming   you   I write   these things,

ἀλλ᾽ ὡς τέκνα μου ἀγαπητὰ νουθετῶν.
but   as   children   of me   beloved   admonishing.

15 ἐὰν γὰρ μυρίους παιδαγωγοὺς ἔχητε
For if   ten thousand   trainers   ye have

ἐν Χριστῷ, ἀλλ᾽ οὐ πολλοὺς πατέρας·
in   Christ,   yet   not   many   fathers;

ἐν γὰρ Χριστῷ Ἰησοῦ διὰ τοῦ εὐαγγελίου
for in   Christ   Jesus   through the   gospel

ἐγὼ ὑμᾶς ἐγέννησα.   16 παρακαλῶ οὖν
I   ²you   ¹begat.   I beseech   therefore

ὑμᾶς, μιμηταί μου γίνεσθε.   17 Διὰ τοῦτο
you,   imitators   of me   become ye.   Because of this

αὐτὸ ἔπεμψα ὑμῖν Τιμόθεον, ὅς ἐστίν
very thing   I sent   to you   Timothy,   who   is

μου τέκνον ἀγαπητὸν καὶ πιστὸν ἐν
of me   a child   beloved   and   faithful   in

κυρίῳ, ὃς ὑμᾶς ἀναμνήσει τὰς ὁδούς
[the] Lord,   who   ²you   ¹will remind   [of] the   ways

μου τὰς ἐν Χριστῷ [Ἰησοῦ], καθὼς
of me   –   in   Christ   Jesus,   as

πανταχοῦ ἐν πάσῃ ἐκκλησίᾳ διδάσκω.
everywhere   in   every   church   I teach.

18 ὡς μὴ ἐρχομένου δέ μου πρὸς ὑμᾶς
When   not   coming   now   meª   to   you
=Now when I did not come

ἐφυσιώθησάν τινες·   19 ἐλεύσομαι δὲ ταχέως
²were puffed up   ¹some;   but I will come   shortly

πρὸς ὑμᾶς, ἐὰν ὁ κύριος θελήσῃ, καὶ
to   you,   if   the   Lord   wills,   and

γνώσομαι οὐ τὸν λόγον τῶν πεφυσιωμένων
I will know   not   the   speech   of the   having been
  [ones]   puffed up

ἀλλὰ τὴν δύναμιν·   20 οὐ γὰρ ἐν λόγῳ
but   the   power;   for ⁴[is] ⁵not   ⁶in   ⁷speech

dom of God does not | ἡ βασιλεία τοῦ θεοῦ, ἀλλ' ἐν δυνάμει.
consist in talk but in | ¹the ²kingdom - ³of God, but in power.
power. ²¹What do you | 21 τί θέλετε; ἐν ῥάβδῳ ἔλθω πρὸς ὑμᾶς,
wish? Shall I come to | What will ye? with a rod I come to you,
you with a rod, or with | ἢ ἐν ἀγάπῃ πνεύματί τε πραΰτητος;
love in a spirit of | or in love and a spirit of meekness?
gentleness?

CHAPTER 5

5 Ὅλως ἀκούεται ἐν ὑμῖν πορνεία,
Actually is heard among you fornication,

IT is actually reported | καὶ τοιαύτη πορνεία ἥτις οὐδὲ ἐν τοῖς
that there is im- | and such fornication which [is] not among the
morality among you, and | ἔθνεσιν, ὥστε γυναῖκά τινα τοῦ πατρὸς
of a kind that is not | nations, so as ²wife ¹one ⁴of the ⁵father
found even among | ἔχειν. 2 καὶ ὑμεῖς πεφυσιωμένοι ἐστέ,
pagans; for a man is | ²to have.ᵇ And ye having been puffed up are,
living with his father's | καὶ οὐχὶ μᾶλλον ἐπενθήσατε, ἵνα ἀρθῇ
wife. ²And you are arro- | and not rather mourned, in order ²might be
gant! Ought you not | that removed
rather to mourn? Let | ἐκ μέσου ὑμῶν ὁ τὸ ἔργον τοῦτο πράξας;
him who has done this | ⁶from ⁸midst ⁹of you ¹the ³this ⁴deed ²having done?
be removed from among | ₇[the] [one]
you. | 3 ἐγὼ μὲν γάρ, ἀπὼν τῷ σώματι,
3 For though absent | For I indeed, being absent in the body,
in body I am present in | παρὼν δὲ τῷ πνεύματι, ἤδη κέκρικα
spirit, and as if present, I | but being present in the spirit, already have judged
have already pro- | ὡς παρὼν τὸν οὕτως τοῦτο κατεργα-
nounced judgment ⁴in | as being present ¹the [one] ²thus ³this thing ³having
the name of the Lord | σάμενον 4 ἐν τῷ ὀνόματι τοῦ κυρίου
Jesus on the man who | wrought in the name of the Lord
has done such a thing. | Ἰησοῦ συναχθέντων ὑμῶν καὶ τοῦ ἐμοῦ
When you are assembled, | Jesus being assembled you and - my
and my spirit is present, | =when you are assembled . . .
with the power of our | πνεύματος σὺν τῇ δυνάμει τοῦ κυρίου
Lord Jesus, ⁵you are to | spiritᵃ with the power of the Lord
deliver this man to Satan | ἡμῶν Ἰησοῦ 5 παραδοῦναι τὸν τοιοῦτον
for the destruction of the | of us Jesus to deliver such a person
flesh, that his spirit may | τῷ σατανᾷ εἰς ὄλεθρον τῆς σαρκός,
be saved in the day of | - to Satan for destruction of the flesh,
the Lord Jesus.ᵍ | ἵνα τὸ πνεῦμα σωθῇ ἐν τῇ ἡμέρᾳ τοῦ
6 Your boasting is | in order the spirit may be in the day of the
not good. Do you not | that saved
know that a little leaven | κυρίου. 6 Οὐ καλὸν τὸ καύχημα ὑμῶν.
leavens the whole lump? | Lord. Not good [is] the boast of you.
⁷Cleanse out the old | οὐκ οἴδατε ὅτι μικρὰ ζύμη ὅλον τὸ
leaven that you may be | Know ye not that a little leaven all the
a new lump, as you | φύραμα ζυμοῖ; 7 ἐκκαθάρατε τὴν παλαιὰν
| lump leavens? Purge out the old
| ζύμην, ἵνα ἦτε νέον φύραμα, καθώς
| leaven, in order ye a new lump, as
ᵍ Other ancient authorities | that may be
omit Jesus

really are unleavened. For Christ, our paschal lamb, has been sacrificed. [8]Let us, therefore, celebrate the festival, not with the old leaven, the leaven of malice and evil, but with the unleavened bread of sincerity and truth.

9 I wrote to you in my letter not to associate with immoral men; [10]not at all meaning the immoral of this world, or the greedy and robbers, or idolaters, since then you would need to go out of the world. [11]But rather I wrote[h] to you not to associate with any one who bears the name of brother if he is guilty of immorality or greed, or is an idolater, reviler, drunkard, or robber—not even to eat with such a one. [12]For what have I to do with judging outsiders? Is it not those inside the church whom you are to judge? [13]God judges those outside. "Drive out the wicked person from among you."

CHAPTER 6

WHEN one of you has a grievance against a brother, does he dare go to law before the unrighteous instead of the saints? [2]Do you not know that the saints will judge the world?

[h] Or now I write

ἐστε ἄζυμοι.	ye are unleavened.
καὶ γὰρ	For indeed
τὸ πάσχα ἡμῶν	the passover of us
ἐτύθη Χριστός.	was Christ.
8 ὥστε	So as
ἑορτάζωμεν μὴ	let us keep feast not
ἐν ζύμῃ παλαιᾷ	with leaven old
μηδὲ ἐν ζύμῃ κακίας	nor with leaven of malice
καὶ πονηρίας,	and of evil,
ἀλλ' ἐν ἀζύμοις εἰλικρινείας	but with unleavened [loaves] of sincerity
καὶ ἀληθείας.	and of truth.
9 Ἔγραψα ὑμῖν ἐν τῇ ἐπιστολῇ	9 I wrote to you in the epistle
μὴ συναναμίγνυσθαι πόρνοις,	not to associate intimately with fornicators,
10 οὐ πάντως τοῖς πόρνοις τοῦ κόσμου	10 not altogether with the fornicators – world
τούτου ἢ τοῖς πλεονέκταις	of this or with the covetous
καὶ ἅρπαξιν	and rapacious
ἢ εἰδωλολάτραις,	or idolaters,
ἐπεὶ ὠφείλετε	since ye ought
ἄρα ἐκ τοῦ κόσμου ἐξελθεῖν.	then out of the world to go out.
11 νῦν δὲ ἔγραψα ὑμῖν	But now I wrote to you
μὴ συναναμίγνυσθαι	not to associate intimately with
ἐάν τις ἀδελφὸς	if anyone a brother
ὀνομαζόμενος ἢ πόρνος	being named is a fornicator
ἢ πλεονέκτης ἢ εἰδωλολάτρης	or a covetous man or an idolater
ἢ λοίδορος ἢ μέθυσος	or a railer or a drunkard
ἢ ἅρπαξ,	or a rapacious man,
τῷ τοιούτῳ μηδὲ συνεσθίειν.	with such a man not to eat with.
12 τί γάρ μοι τοὺς ἔξω κρίνειν;	12 what For [is it] to me the ones without to judge?
οὐχὶ τοὺς ἔσω ὑμεῖς κρίνετε;	Not the ones within ye judge?
13 τοὺς δὲ ἔξω ὁ θεὸς κρινεῖ.	13 But the ones without God will judge.
ἐξάρατε τὸν πονηρὸν ἐξ ὑμῶν αὐτῶν.	Remove the evil man out of yourselves.
6 Τολμᾷ τις ὑμῶν	6 Dares anyone of you
πρᾶγμα ἔχων πρὸς τὸν ἕτερον	a matter having against the(an) other
κρίνεσθαι ἐπὶ τῶν ἀδίκων,	to be judged before the unjust,
καὶ οὐχὶ ἐπὶ τῶν ἁγίων;	and not before the saints?
2 ἢ οὐκ οἴδατε	2 or know ye not
ὅτι οἱ ἅγιοι τὸν κόσμον κρινοῦσιν;	that the saints the world will judge?
καὶ	and

And if the world is to be judged by you, are you incompetent to try trivial cases? [3]Do you not know that we are to judge angels? How much more, matters pertaining to this life! [4]If then you have such cases, why do you lay them before those who are least esteemed by the church? [5]I say this to your shame. Can it be that there is no man among you wise enough to decide between members of the brotherhood, [6]but brother goes to law against brother, and that before unbelievers?

7 To have lawsuits at all with one another is defeat for you. Why not rather suffer wrong? Why not rather be defrauded? [8]But you yourselves wrong and defraud, and that even your own brethren.

9 Do you not know that the unrighteous will not inherit the kingdom of God? Do not be deceived; neither the immoral, nor idolaters, nor adulterers, nor homosexuals,[i]　[10]nor thieves, nor the greedy, nor drunkards, nor revilers, nor robbers will inherit the kingdom of God. [11]And such were

[i] Two Greek words are rendered by this expression

εἰ ἐν ὑμῖν κρίνεται ὁ κόσμος, ἀνάξιοί
if [4]by [3]you [5]is judged [1]the [2]world, [6]unworthy
ἐστε κριτηρίων ἐλαχίστων; 3 οὐκ οἴδατε
[1]are ye [4]judgments? [3]of very little? Know ye not
ὅτι ἀγγέλους κρινοῦμεν, μήτι γε βιωτικά;
that angels we will judge, not to speak of things
of this life?
4 βιωτικὰ μὲν οὖν κριτήρια ἐὰν ἔχητε,
[3]Of this life [1]indeed [2]therefore [5]judgments [4]if [6]ye have,
τοὺς ἐξουθενημένους ἐν τῇ ἐκκλησίᾳ,
the ones being despised in the church,
τούτους καθίζετε; 5 πρὸς ἐντροπὴν ὑμῖν
these sit ye? For shame to you
λέγω. οὕτως οὐκ ἔνι ἐν ὑμῖν οὐδεὶς
I say. Thus there is no room among you [for] no one
σοφός, ὃς δυνήσεται διακρῖναι ἀνὰ μέσον
wise man, who will be able to discern in your midst
τοῦ ἀδελφοῦ αὐτοῦ; 6 ἀλλὰ ἀδελφὸς μετὰ
the brother of him? But brother with
ἀδελφοῦ κρίνεται, καὶ τοῦτο ἐπὶ ἀπίστων;
brother is judged, and this before unbelievers?
7 ἤδη μὲν οὖν ὅλως ἥττημα ὑμῖν ἐστιν
Now indeed there- [2]altogether [3]a failure [4]with [1]there is
fore you
ὅτι κρίματα ἔχετε μεθ' ἑαυτῶν. διὰ τί
[5]that [7]lawsuits [6]ye have with yourselves. Why
οὐχὶ μᾶλλον ἀδικεῖσθε; διὰ τί οὐχὶ
not rather be wronged? Why not
μᾶλλον ἀποστερεῖσθε; 8 ἀλλὰ ὑμεῖς ἀδικεῖτε
rather be deprived? But ye do wrong
καὶ ἀποστερεῖτε, καὶ τοῦτο ἀδελφούς.
and deprive, and this brothers.
9 ἢ οὐκ οἴδατε ὅτι ἄδικοι θεοῦ βασιλείαν
Or know ye not that unrighteous [3]of God [2][the]
men kingdom
οὐ κληρονομήσουσιν; μὴ πλανᾶσθε· οὔτε
[1]will not inherit? Be not led astray; not
πόρνοι οὔτε εἰδωλολάτραι οὔτε μοιχοὶ
fornicators nor idolaters nor adulterers
οὔτε μαλακοὶ οὔτε ἀρσενοκοῖται 10 οὔτε
nor voluptuous nor sodomites nor
persons
κλέπται οὔτε πλεονέκται, οὐ μέθυσοι,
thieves nor covetous persons, not drunkards,
οὐ λοίδοροι, οὐχ ἅρπαγες βασιλείαν θεοῦ
not revilers, not rapacious [2][the] kingdom [3]of
persons God
κληρονομήσουσιν. 11 καὶ ταῦτά τινες ἦτε·
[1]will inherit. And these [2]some [1]ye
things [of you] were;

some of you. But you were washed, you were sanctified, you were justified in the name of the Lord Jesus Christ and in the Spirit of our God. 12 "All things are lawful for me," but not all things are helpful. "All things are lawful for me," but I will not be enslaved by anything. ¹³ "Food is meant for the stomach and the stomach for food"—and God will destroy both one and the other. The body is not meant for immorality, but for the Lord, and the Lord for the body. ¹⁴And God raised the Lord and will also raise us up by his power. ¹⁵Do you not know that your bodies are members of Christ? Shall I therefore take the members of Christ and make them members of a prostitute? Never! ¹⁶Do you not know that he who joins himself to a prostitute becomes one body with her? For, as it is written, "The two shall become one." ¹⁷But he who is united to the Lord becomes one spirit with him. ¹⁸Shun immorality. Every other sin which a man commits is outside the body; but the immoral man sins against

ἀλλὰ ἀπελούσασθε, ἀλλὰ ἡγιάσθητε, ἀλλὰ
but ye were washed, but ye were sanctified, but

ἐδικαιώθητε ἐν τῷ ὀνόματι τοῦ κυρίου
ye were justified in the name of the Lord

Ἰησοῦ Χριστοῦ καὶ ἐν τῷ πνεύματι
Jesus Christ and by the Spirit

τοῦ θεοῦ ἡμῶν.
of the God of us.

12 Πάντα μοι ἔξεστιν, ἀλλ' οὐ πάντα
All things to me [are] lawful, but not all things

συμφέρει. πάντα μοι ἔξεστιν, ἀλλ' οὐκ
expedient. All things to me [are] lawful, but not

ἐγὼ ἐξουσιασθήσομαι ὑπό τινος. 13 τὰ
I will be ruled by anyone. 13 —

βρώματα τῇ κοιλίᾳ, καὶ ἡ κοιλία τοῖς
Foods for the belly, and the belly —

βρώμασιν· ὁ δὲ θεὸς καὶ ταύτην καὶ
for foods; — but God both this and

ταῦτα καταργήσει. τὸ δὲ σῶμα οὐ τῇ
these will destroy. But the body [is] not —

πορνείᾳ ἀλλὰ τῷ κυρίῳ, καὶ ὁ κύριος
for fornication but for the Lord, and the Lord

τῷ σώματι· 14 ὁ δὲ θεὸς καὶ τὸν κύριον
for the body; — and God both the Lord

ἤγειρεν καὶ ἡμᾶς ἐξεγερεῖ διὰ τῆς
raised and us will raise up through the

δυνάμεως αὐτοῦ. 15 οὐκ οἴδατε ὅτι τὰ
power of him. Know ye not that the

σώματα ὑμῶν μέλη Χριστοῦ ἐστιν; ἄρας
bodies of you members of Christ (is)are? Taking

οὖν τὰ μέλη τοῦ Χριστοῦ ποιήσω πόρνης
there- the members — of Christ shall I make ²of a
fore [them] harlot

μέλη; μὴ γένοιτο. 16 ἢ οὐκ οἴδατε ὅτι
¹members? May it not be. Or know ye not that

ὁ κολλώμενος τῇ πόρνῃ ἓν σῶμά ἐστιν;
the being joined — to a harlot one body is?
[one]

ἔσονται γάρ, φησίν, οἱ δύο εἰς σάρκα
For ⁴will be, ³he says, ¹the ²two ⁵into ⁷flesh

μίαν. 17 ὁ δὲ κολλώμενος τῷ κυρίῳ
⁶one. But the [one] being joined to the Lord

ἓν πνεῦμά ἐστιν. 18 φεύγετε τὴν πορνείαν.
one spirit is. Flee ye — fornication.

πᾶν ἁμάρτημα ὃ ἐὰν ποιήσῃ ἄνθρωπος
Every sin whichever ²may do ¹a man

ἐκτὸς τοῦ σώματός ἐστιν· ὁ δὲ πορνεύων
outside the body is; but the committing
[one] fornication

his own body. ¹⁹Do you not know that your body is a temple of the Holy Spirit within you, which you have from God? You are not your own; ²⁰you were bought with a price. So glorify God in your body.

εἰς τὸ ἴδιον σῶμα ἁμαρτάνει.   19
against the(his) own   body   sins.   Or
οὐκ οἴδατε ὅτι τὸ σῶμα ὑμῶν ναός
know ye not   that   the   body   of you ²a shrine
τοῦ ἐν ὑμῖν ἁγίου πνεύματός ἐστιν,
²of the ⁶in   ⁷you   ⁴Holy   ⁵Spirit   ¹is,
οὗ ἔχετε ἀπὸ θεοῦ, καὶ οὐκ ἐστὲ ἑαυτῶν;
which ye   from   God, and   ye are not   of
have   yourselves?

20 ἠγοράσθητε γὰρ τιμῆς· δοξάσατε δὴ
For ye were bought of(with) a price; glorify ye   then
τὸν θεὸν ἐν τῷ σώματι ὑμῶν.
–   God   in   the   body   of you.

CHAPTER 7

NOW concerning the matters about which you wrote. It is well for a man not to touch a woman. ²But because of the temptation to immorality, each man should have his own wife and each woman her own husband. ³The husband should give to his wife her conjugal rights, and likewise the wife to her husband. ⁴For the wife does not rule over her own body, but the husband does; likewise the husband does not rule over his own body, but the wife does. ⁵Do not refuse one another except perhaps by agreement for a season, that you may devote yourselves to prayer; but then come together again, lest Satan tempt you through lack of self-control. ⁶I say this by way of concession,

7 Περὶ δὲ ὧν ἐγράψατε, καλὸν ἀνθρώπῳ
Now about things   ye wrote, [it is] good for a man
of which
γυναικὸς μὴ ἅπτεσθαι· 2 διὰ δὲ τὰς
³a woman*   ¹not   ²to touch;   but because of   the
πορνείας ἕκαστος τὴν ἑαυτοῦ γυναῖκα
fornications   each man   ³the   ⁴of himself   ²wife
ἐχέτω, καὶ ἑκάστη τὸν ἴδιον ἄνδρα
¹let him have, and   each woman   the(her)   own   husband
ἐχέτω. 3 τῇ γυναικὶ ὁ ἀνὴρ τὴν ὀφειλὴν
let her have. To the   wife   ²the ³husband ⁴the   ⁵debt
ἀποδιδότω, ὁμοίως δὲ καὶ ἡ γυνὴ τῷ
¹let him pay,   and likewise   also   the   wife   to the
ἀνδρί. 4 ἡ γυνὴ τοῦ ἰδίου σώματος
husband.   The   wife   of the(her) own   body
οὐκ ἐξουσιάζει ἀλλὰ ὁ ἀνήρ· ὁμοίως
has not authority   but   the husband;   ²likewise
δὲ καὶ ὁ ἀνὴρ τοῦ ἰδίου σώματος οὐκ
¹and also   the   husband of the(his) own   body   not
ἐξουσιάζει ἀλλὰ ἡ γυνή. 5 μὴ ἀποστερεῖτε
has authority   but   the   wife.   Deprive not ye
ἀλλήλους, εἰ μήτι ἂν ἐκ συμφώνου πρὸς
each other,   unless   by   agreement   for
καιρὸν ἵνα σχολάσητε τῇ προσευχῇ καὶ
a time   in order ye may have   –   for prayer   and
that   leisure
πάλιν ἐπὶ τὸ αὐτὸ ἦτε, ἵνα μὴ πειράζῃ
²again   ²together   ¹ye may be, lest   ²tempt
ὑμᾶς ὁ σατανᾶς διὰ τὴν ἀκρασίαν [ὑμῶν].
²you   –   ¹Satan because the   want of   of you.
of   self-control
6 τοῦτο δὲ λέγω κατὰ συγγνώμην, οὐ
Now this   I say   by   allowance,   not

* As the same Greek word γυνή means "wife" or "(?married) woman" it is not always easy to differentiate in translating. So also the one Greek word ἀνήρ means "man" or "husband"

not of command. ⁷I wish that all were as I myself am. But each has his own special gift from God, one of one kind and one of another.

8 To the unmarried and the widows I say that it is well for them to remain single as I do. ⁹But if they cannot exercise self-control, they should marry. For it is better to marry than to be aflame with passion.

10 To the married I give charge, not I but the Lord, that the wife should not separate from her husband ¹¹(but if she does, let her remain single or else be reconciled to her husband)— and that the husband should not divorce his wife.

12 To the rest I say, not the Lord, that if any brother has a wife who is an unbeliever, and she consents to live with him, he should not divorce her. ¹³If any woman has a husband who is an unbeliever, and he consents to live with her, she should not divorce him. ¹⁴For the unbelieving husband is consecrated through his wife, and the unbelieving wife is consecrated through her husband. Otherwise, your children would be unclean, but as it is they are

κατ' ἐπιταγήν. 7 θέλω δὲ πάντας
by   command.   And I wish   all

ἀνθρώπους εἶναι ὡς καὶ ἐμαυτόν· ἀλλὰ
men   to be   as   even   myself;   but

ἔκαστος ἴδιον ἔχει χάρισμα ἐκ θεοῦ,
each man ²[his] own ¹has   gift   of   God,

ὁ μὲν οὕτως, ὁ δὲ οὕτως.
one   thus,   another   thus.

8 Λέγω δὲ τοῖς ἀγάμοις καὶ ταῖς χήραις,
Now I say   to the unmarried men and   to the   widows,

καλὸν αὐτοῖς ἐὰν μείνωσιν ὡς κἀγώ· 9 εἰ δὲ
[it is] good for them   if   they remain   as   I also;   but if

οὐκ ἐγκρατεύονται, γαμησάτωσαν· κρεῖττον
they do not exercise self-control, let them marry;   better

γάρ ἐστιν γαμεῖν ἢ πυροῦσθαι. 10 τοῖς
for   it is   to marry   than   to burn.   to the [ones]

δὲ γεγαμηκόσιν παραγγέλλω, οὐκ ἐγὼ
But   having married   I enjoin,   not   I

ἀλλὰ ὁ κύριος, γυναῖκα ἀπὸ ἀνδρὸς μὴ
but   the   Lord,   a woman   from [her] husband not

χωρισθῆναι, 11 — ἐὰν δὲ καὶ χωρισθῇ,
to be separated,ᵇ   but if   indeed   she is
                            separated,

μενέτω ἄγαμος ἢ τῷ ἀνδρὶ καταλλαγήτω,
let her   unmarried   or   to   husband   be reconciled,
remain   the(her)

— καὶ ἄνδρα γυναῖκα μὴ ἀφιέναι. 12 Τοῖς
and a husband [his] wife   not   to leave.ᵇ   to the

δὲ λοιποῖς λέγω ἐγώ, οὐχ ὁ κύριος·
And   rest   say   I,   not   the   Lord:

εἴ τις ἀδελφὸς γυναῖκα ἔχει ἄπιστον, καὶ
If any   brother   ²a wife   ¹has   unbelieving,   and

αὕτη συνευδοκεῖ οἰκεῖν μετ' αὐτοῦ, μὴ
this one   consents   to dwell   with   him,   not

ἀφιέτω αὐτήν· 13 καὶ γυνὴ ἥτις ἔχει
let him leave   her;   and   a woman   who   has

ἄνδρα ἄπιστον, καὶ οὗτος συνευδοκεῖ οἰκεῖν
a husband unbelieving, and   this one   consents   to dwell

μετ' αὐτῆς, μὴ ἀφιέτω τὸν ἄνδρα.
with   her,   let her not leave   the(her) husband.

14 ἡγίασται γὰρ ὁ ἀνὴρ ὁ ἄπιστος ἐν
For ⁴has been sanctified ¹the ²husband - ²unbelieving   by

τῇ γυναικί, καὶ ἡγίασται ἡ γυνὴ ἡ
the   wife,   and   ⁴has been   ¹the   ²wife -
                     sanctified

ἄπιστος ἐν τῷ ἀδελφῷ· ἐπεὶ ἄρα τὰ
²unbelieving by   the   brother;   since   then   the

τέκνα ὑμῶν ἀκάθαρτά ἐστιν, νῦν δὲ
children   of you   ²unclean   ¹is(are).   but now

holy. ¹⁵But if the unbelieving partner desires to separate, let it be so; in such a case the brother or sister is not bound. For God has called us^j to peace. ¹⁶Wife, how do you know whether you will save your husband? Husband, how do you know whether you will save your wife?

17 Only, let every one lead the life which the Lord has assigned to him, and in which God has called him. This is my rule in all the churches. ¹⁸Was any one at the time of his call already circumcised? Let him not seek to remove the marks of circumcision. Was any one at the time of his call uncircumcised? Let him not seek circumcision. ¹⁹For neither circumcision counts for anything nor uncircumcision, but keeping the commandments of God. ²⁰Every one should remain in the state in which he was called. ²¹Were you a slave when called? Never mind. But if you can gain your freedom, avail yourself of the opportunity^{jj}. ²²For he who was called in the Lord as a slave is a freedman of the Lord. Likewise he who was free when called is a slave of Christ. ²³You were bought with a price; do

^j Other ancient authorities read *you*
^{jj} Or *make use of your present condition instead.*

ἁγιά ἐστιν. 15 εἰ δὲ ὁ ἄπιστος χωρίζ-
²holy ¹they are. But if the unbelieving separates
one

εται, χωριζέσθω· οὐ δεδούλωται ὁ
him/herself, let him/her be ²has not been enslaved ¹the
separated;

ἀδελφὸς ἢ ἡ ἀδελφὴ ἐν τοῖς τοιούτοις·
²brother ³or ⁴the ⁵sister in such matters;

ἐν δὲ εἰρήνῃ κέκληκεν ὑμᾶς ὁ θεός.
but ⁴in ⁵peace ³has called ²you - ¹God.

16 τί γὰρ οἶδας, γύναι, εἰ τὸν ἄνδρα
For what knowest thou, wife, if the(thy) husband

σώσεις; ἢ τί οἶδας, ἄνερ, εἰ τὴν
thou wilt save? or what knowest husband, if the(thy)
thou,

γυναῖκα σώσεις; 17 Εἰ μὴ ἑκάστῳ ὡς
wife thou wilt save? Only ⁴to each , ¹as

μεμέρικεν ὁ κύριος, ἕκαστον ὡς κέκληκεν
⁴has divided ²the ³Lord, ⁴each ¹as ³has called

ὁ θεός, οὕτως περιπατείτω. καὶ οὕτως
- ¹God, so let him walk. And so

ἐν ταῖς ἐκκλησίαις πάσαις διατάσσομαι.
²in ⁴the ⁵churches ³all ¹I command.

18 περιτετμημένος τις ἐκλήθη; μὴ
⁴Having been circumcised ³anyone ¹was ²called? not

ἐπισπάσθω· ἐν ἀκροβυστίᾳ κέκληταί τις;
let him be un- in uncircumcision has been anyone?
circumcised; called

μὴ περιτεμνέσθω. 19 ἡ περιτομὴ οὐδέν
let him not be circumcised. - Circumcision nothing

ἐστιν, καὶ ἡ ἀκροβυστία οὐδέν ἐστιν,
is, and - uncircumcision nothing is,

ἀλλὰ τήρησις ἐντολῶν θεοῦ. 20 ἕκαστος
but [the] of command- of Each one
keeping ments God.

ἐν τῇ κλήσει ᾗ ἐκλήθη, ἐν ταύτῃ
in the calling in which he was called, in this

μενέτω. 21 δοῦλος ἐκλήθης; μή σοι
let him remain. A slave wast thou called? not to thee

μελέτω· ἀλλ' εἰ καὶ δύνασαι ἐλεύθερος
let it matter; but if indeed thou art able ²free

γενέσθαι, μᾶλλον χρῆσαι. 22 ὁ γὰρ ἐν
¹to become, ²rather ³use [it]. For ¹the [one] ⁴in

κυρίῳ κληθεὶς δοῦλος ἀπελεύθερος κυρίου
⁵[the] ²called ³a slave ⁷a freed man ⁸of [the]
Lord Lord

ἐστίν· ὁμοίως ὁ ἐλεύθερος κληθεὶς δοῦλός
⁶is; likewise ¹the ²a free man ²called ³a slave
[one]

ἐστιν Χριστοῦ. 23 τιμῆς ἠγοράσθητε· μὴ
⁴is ⁵of Christ. Of(with) a price ye were bought; not

not become slaves of men. ²⁴So, brethren, in whatever state each was called, there let him remain with God.

25 Now concerning the unmarried, I have no command of the Lord, but I give my opinion as one who by the Lord's mercy is trustworthy. ²⁶I think that in view of the impending[k] distress it is well for a person to remain as he is. ²⁷Are you bound to a wife? Do not seek to be free. Are you free from a wife? Do not seek marriage. ²⁸But if you marry, you do not sin, and if a girl marries she does not sin. Yet those who marry will have worldly troubles, and I would spare you that. ²⁹I mean, brethren, the appointed time has grown very short; from now on, let those who have wives live as though they had none, ³⁰and those who mourn as though they were not mourning, and those who rejoice as though they were not rejoicing, and those who buy as though they had no goods, ³¹and those who deal with the world as though they

γίνεσθε   δοῦλοι   ἀνθρώπων.   24 ἕκαστος   ἐν
become ye   slaves   of men.   Each one   in

ᾧ   ἐκλήθη,   ἀδελφοί,   ἐν   τούτῳ   μενέτω
what   he was   brothers,   in   this   let him
[state]   called,   remain

παρὰ   θεῷ.
with   God.

25 Περὶ   δὲ   τῶν   παρθένων   ἐπιταγὴν
    Now about   the   virgins   a command

κυρίου   οὐκ   ἔχω,   γνώμην   δὲ   δίδωμι   ὡς
of [the] Lord   I have not,   but an opinion   I give   as

ἠλεημένος   ὑπὸ   κυρίου   πιστὸς   εἶναι.
having had mercy   by   [the] Lord   faithful   to be.

26 Νομίζω   οὖν   τοῦτο   καλὸν   ὑπάρχειν
    I suppose   therefore   this   good   to be

διὰ   τὴν   ἐνεστῶσαν   ἀνάγκην,   ὅτι   καλὸν
because the   present   necessity,   that [it is]   good
of

ἀνθρώπῳ   τὸ   οὕτως   εἶναι.   27 δέδεσαι
for a man   –   so   to be.   Hast thou
                            been bound

γυναικί;   μὴ   ζήτει   λύσιν·   λέλυσαι   ἀπὸ
to a woman?   do not seek   release;   hast thou been   from
                            released

γυναικός;   μὴ   ζήτει   γυναῖκα.   28 ἐὰν
a woman?   do not seek   a woman.   if

δὲ   καὶ   γαμήσῃς,   οὐχ   ἥμαρτες,   καὶ   ἐὰν
But indeed   thou marriest,   thou sinnedst not,   and   if

γήμῃ   ἡ   παρθένος,   οὐχ   ἥμαρτεν·   θλῖψιν
³marries   ¹the   ²virgin,   she sinned not;   ³affliction

δὲ   τῇ   σαρκὶ   ἕξουσιν   οἱ   τοιοῦτοι,   ἐγὼ
but   ⁴in the   ⁵flesh   ²will have   –   ¹such,   ²I

δὲ   ὑμῶν   φείδομαι.   29 Τοῦτο   δέ   φημι,
¹and   ⁴you   ³am sparing.   But this   I say,

ἀδελφοί,   ὁ   καιρὸς   συνεσταλμένος   ἐστίν·
brothers,   the   time   having been shortened   is;

τὸ   λοιπὸν   ἵνα   καὶ   οἱ   ἔχοντες   γυναῖκας
for the rest   in order   both   the [ones] having   wives
          that

ὡς   μὴ   ἔχοντες   ὦσιν,   30 καὶ   οἱ   κλαίοντες
as   not   having   may be,   and the [ones] weeping

ὡς   μὴ   κλαίοντες,   καὶ   οἱ   χαίροντες   ὡς
as   not   weeping,   and the [ones] rejoicing   as

μὴ   χαίροντες,   καὶ   οἱ   ἀγοράζοντες   ὡς
not   rejoicing,   and the [ones]   buying   as

μὴ   κατέχοντες,   31 καὶ   οἱ   χρώμενοι   τὸν
not   holding,   and the [ones]   using   the

κόσμον   ὡς   μὴ   καταχρώμενοι·   παράγει
world   as   not   abusing [it];   ⁴is passing
                             away

ᵏ Or present

had no dealings with it. For the form of this world is passing away. 32 I want you to be free from anxieties. The unmarried man is anxious about the affairs of the Lord, how to please the Lord; 33 but the married man is anxious about worldly affairs, how to please his wife, 34 and his interests are divided. And the unmarried woman or girl is anxious about the affairs of the Lord, how to be holy in body and spirit; but the married woman is anxious about worldly affairs, how to please her husband. 35 I say this for your own benefit, not to lay any restraint upon you, but to promote good order and to secure your undivided devotion to the Lord.

36 If any one thinks that he is not behaving properly toward his betrothed, if his passions are strong, and it has to be, let him do as he wishes: let them marry— it is no sin. 37 But whoever is firmly established in his heart, being under no necessity but having his desire under control, and has determined this

γὰρ τὸ σχῆμα τοῦ κόσμου τούτου.
for ¹the ²fashion ³of this world.

32 Θέλω δὲ ὑμᾶς ἀμερίμνους εἶναι. ὁ
But I wish you without care to be. The

ἄγαμος μεριμνᾷ τὰ τοῦ κυρίου, 33 πῶς
unmarried cares for the of the Lord, how
man things

ἀρέσῃ τῷ κυρίῳ· ὁ δὲ γαμήσας μεριμνᾷ
he may the Lord; but the having married cares for
please [one]

τὰ τοῦ κόσμου, πῶς ἀρέσῃ τῇ γυναικί,
the of the world, how he may the(his) wife,
things please

34 καὶ μεμέρισται. καὶ ἡ γυνὴ ἡ ἄγαμος
and has been divided. And the ²woman – ¹unmarried

καὶ ἡ παρθένος μεριμνᾷ τὰ τοῦ κυρίου,
and the virgin cares for the things of the Lord,

ἵνα ᾖ ἁγία καὶ τῷ σώματι καὶ τῷ
in she holy both in the body and in
order may the
that be

πνεύματι· ἡ δὲ γαμήσασα μεριμνᾷ τὰ
spirit; but the [one] having married cares for the
things

τοῦ κόσμου, πῶς ἀρέσῃ τῷ ἀνδρί.
of the world, how she may please the(her) husband.

35 τοῦτο δὲ πρὸς τὸ ὑμῶν αὐτῶν σύμφορον
And ²this ³for ⁴the ⁵of yourselves ⁶advantage

λέγω, οὐχ ἵνα βρόχον ὑμῖν ἐπιβάλω,
¹I say, not in order ²a restraint ³you ¹I may put on,
that

ἀλλὰ πρὸς τὸ εὔσχημον καὶ εὐπάρεδρον
but for the thing comely and waiting on

τῷ κυρίῳ ἀπερισπάστως. 36 Εἰ δέ τις
the Lord undistractedly. But if anyone

ἀσχημονεῖν ἐπὶ τὴν παρθένον αὐτοῦ
²to behave ³toward ⁴the ⁵virgin ⁶of him
dishonourably

νομίζει, ἐὰν ᾖ ὑπέρακμος, καὶ οὕτως
¹thinks, if he/she is past the bloom and so
of youth,

ὀφείλει γίνεσθαι, ὃ θέλει ποιείτω· οὐχ
ought to be, what he wishes let him do; not

ἁμαρτάνει· γαμείτωσαν. 37 ὃς δὲ ἕστηκεν
he sins; let them marry. But [he] who stands

ἐν τῇ καρδίᾳ αὐτοῦ ἑδραῖος, μὴ
in the heart of him firm, not

ἔχων ἀνάγκην, ἐξουσίαν δὲ ἔχει περὶ
having necessity, but authority has concerning

τοῦ ἰδίου θελήματος, καὶ τοῦτο κέκρικεν
the(his) own will, and this has decided

I. CORINTHIANS 7, 8

in his heart, to keep her as his betrothed, he will do well. ³⁸So that he who marries his betrothed does well; and he who refrains from marriage will do better.
39 A wife is bound to her husband as long as he lives. If the husband dies, she is free to be married to whom she wishes, only in the Lord. ⁴⁰But in my judgment she is happier if she remains as she is. And I think that I have the Spirit of God.

ἐν   τῇ   ἰδίᾳ   καρδίᾳ,   τηρεῖν   τὴν   ἑαυτοῦ
in the(his) own   heart,   to keep   the   of himself

παρθένον,   καλῶς   ποιήσει.   38 ὥστε   καὶ
virgin,   ²well   ¹he will do.   So as   both

ὁ   γαμίζων   τὴν   ἑαυτοῦ   παρθένον   καλῶς
the marrying   the   of himself   virgin   ²well
[one]

ποιεῖ,   καὶ   ὁ   μὴ   γαμίζων   κρεῖσσον   ποιήσει.
¹does,   and   the   not   marrying   ²better   ¹will do.
            [one]

39 Γυνὴ   δέδεται   ἐφ'   ὅσον   χρόνον   ζῇ
A wife   has been bound for   so long a time as   lives

ὁ   ἀνὴρ   αὐτῆς·   ἐὰν   δὲ   κοιμηθῇ   ὁ   ἀνήρ,
the husband of her;   but if   sleeps   the husband,

ἐλευθέρα   ἐστὶν   ᾧ   θέλει   γαμηθῆναι,   μόνον
²free   ¹she is   ⁴to   ⁵she   ³to be married,   only
                    whom wishes

ἐν   κυρίῳ.   40 μακαριωτέρα   δέ   ἐστιν
in [the] Lord.   But happier   she is

ἐὰν   οὕτως   μείνῃ,   κατὰ   τὴν   ἐμὴν   γνώμην·
if   so   she   according -   my   opinion;
              remains,   to

δοκῶ   δὲ   κἀγὼ   πνεῦμα   θεοῦ   ἔχειν.
and I think   I also   [the] Spirit of God   to have.

CHAPTER 8

NOW concerning food offered to idols: we know that "all of us possess knowledge." "Knowledge" puffs up, but love builds up. ²If any one imagines that he knows something, he does not yet know as he ought to know. ³But if one loves God, one is known by him.
4 Hence, as to the eating of food offered to idols, we know that "an idol has no real existence," and that "there is no God but one." ⁵For although there may be so-called gods in heaven or on earth—as indeed there are many "gods"

8 Περὶ   δὲ   τῶν   εἰδωλοθύτων,   οἴδαμεν
Now about the   idolatrous sacrifices,   we know

ὅτι   πάντες   γνῶσιν   ἔχομεν.   ἡ   γνῶσις
that   ²all   ⁴knowledge   ¹we ³have.   -   Knowledge

φυσιοῖ,   ἡ   δὲ   ἀγάπη   οἰκοδομεῖ·   εἴ   τις
puffs up,   -   but   love   builds up;   if anyone

δοκεῖ   ἐγνωκέναι   τι,   2 οὔπω   ἔγνω   καθὼς
thinks to have known anything, not yet he knew   as

δεῖ   γνῶναι·   3 εἰ   δέ   τις   ἀγαπᾷ   τὸν
it be- to know;   but if   anyone   loves   -
hoves [him]

θεόν,   οὗτος   ἔγνωσται   ὑπ'   αὐτοῦ.   4 Περὶ
God,   this one has been known by   him.   About

τῆς   βρώσεως   οὖν   τῶν   εἰδωλοθύτων
the   eating   therefore   - of idolatrous sacrifices

οἴδαμεν   ὅτι   οὐδὲν   εἴδωλον   ἐν   κόσμῳ,
we know   that   [there is] no   idol   in [the] world,

καὶ   ὅτι   οὐδεὶς   θεὸς   εἰ   μὴ   εἷς.   5 καὶ
and   that [there is] no God   except   one.   even

γὰρ   εἴπερ   εἰσὶν   λεγόμενοι   θεοὶ   εἴτε   ἐν
For   if   there are   being called   gods   either   in

οὐρανῷ   εἴτε   ἐπὶ   γῆς,   ὥσπερ   εἰσὶν   θεοὶ
heaven   or   on   earth,   even as   there are   gods

and many "lords"—⁶yet for us there is one God, the Father, from whom are all things and for whom we exist, and one Lord, Jesus Christ, through whom are all things and through whom we exist. 7 However, not all possess this knowledge. But some, through being hitherto accustomed to idols, eat food as really offered to an idol; and their conscience, being weak, is defiled. ⁸Food will not commend us to God. We are no worse off if we do not eat, and no better off if we do. ⁹Only take care lest this liberty of yours somehow become a stumblingblock to the weak. ¹⁰For if any one sees you, a man of knowledge, at table in an idol's temple, might he not be encouraged, if his conscience is weak, to eat food offered to idols? ¹¹And so by your knowledge this weak man is destroyed, the brother for whom Christ died. ¹²Thus, sinning against your brethren and wounding their conscience when it is weak, you sin against Christ. ¹³Therefore, if food is a cause of my brother's falling, I will never eat

πολλοὶ   καὶ   κύριοι   πολλοί,   6 ἀλλ'   ἡμῖν
many   and   lords   many,   yet   to us

εἷς θεὸς ὁ πατήρ,   ἐξ οὗ   τὰ πάντα καὶ
[there God the Father,   of whom – [are] all   and
is] one   things

ἡμεῖς εἰς αὐτόν,   καὶ εἷς κύριος Ἰησοῦς
we   in   him,   and   one Lord   Jesus

Χριστός,   δι' οὗ   τὰ πάντα καὶ ἡμεῖς
Christ,   through whom – [are] all   and   we
                             things

δι' αὐτοῦ.   7 Ἀλλ'   οὐκ ἐν πᾶσιν ἡ
through him.   But [there is] not   in   all men   the
                                    (this)

γνῶσις·   τινὲς δὲ τῇ συνηθείᾳ ἕως ἄρτι
knowledge;   and some by the habit   until   now

τοῦ εἰδώλου ὡς εἰδωλόθυτον ἐσθίουσιν,
²of the ²idol   ⁴as   ⁵an idolatrous sacrifice   ¹eat,

καὶ ἡ συνείδησις αὐτῶν ἀσθενὴς οὖσα
and the conscience of them   ²weak   ¹being

μολύνεται.   8 βρῶμα δὲ ἡμᾶς οὐ παραστήσει
is defiled.   But food   ²us   ¹will not commend

τῷ θεῷ·   οὔτε ἐὰν μὴ φάγωμεν ὑστερούμεθα,
– to God; neither if   we eat not   are we behind,

οὔτε ἐὰν φάγωμεν περισσεύομεν.   9 βλέπετε
nor   if   we eat   do we excel.   look ye

δὲ μή πως ἡ ἐξουσία ὑμῶν αὕτη
But lest somehow the   ²authority   ⁸of you   ¹this

πρόσκομμα γένηται τοῖς ἀσθενέσιν.   10 ἐὰν
a stumbling-block becomes to the   weak ones.   if

γάρ τις ἴδῃ σὲ τὸν ἔχοντα γνῶσιν ἐν
For anyone sees thee the [one] having   knowledge   ⁵in

εἰδωλείῳ κατακείμενον, οὐχὶ ἡ συνείδησις
²an idol's temple ¹sitting,   ²not ³the   ⁴conscience

αὐτοῦ ἀσθενοῦς ὄντος οἰκοδομηθήσεται εἰς
⁵of him   ⁷weak   ⁶[he]being⁸   ¹will ⁸be emboldened   –

τὸ τὰ εἰδωλόθυτα ἐσθίειν;   11 ἀπόλλυται
– ¹⁰the ¹¹idolatrous sacrifices ⁹to eat?   ²is destroyed

γὰρ ὁ ἀσθενῶν ἐν τῇ σῇ γνώσει, ὁ
For ¹the [one] ²being weak by   – thy knowledge, the

ἀδελφὸς δι' ὃν Χριστὸς ἀπέθανεν.   12 οὕτως
brother because whom Christ died.   so
           of

δὲ ἁμαρτάνοντες εἰς τοὺς ἀδελφοὺς καὶ
And sinning   against the   brothers   and

τύπτοντες αὐτῶν τὴν συνείδησιν ἀσθενοῦσαν
wounding of them the conscience   being weak

εἰς Χριστὸν ἁμαρτάνετε.   13 διόπερ εἰ
²against ³Christ   ¹ye sin.   Wherefore if

βρῶμα σκανδαλίζει τὸν ἀδελφόν μου, οὐ
food offends the   brother   of me, by no

meat, lest I cause my brother to fall.

μὴ   φάγω   κρέα   εἰς   τὸν   αἰῶνα,   ἵνα   μὴ
means I eat   flesh   unto   the   age,   lest

τὸν   ἀδελφόν   μου   σκανδαλίσω.
²the   ³brother   ⁴of me   ¹I offend.

CHAPTER 9

A M I not free? Am I not an apostle? Have I not seen Jesus our Lord? Are not you my workmanship in the Lord? ²If to others I am not an apostle, at least I am to you; for you are the seal of my apostleship in the Lord. 3 This is my defense to those who would examine me. ⁴Do we not have the right to our food and drink? ⁵Do we not have the right to be accompanied by a wife,¹ as the other apostles and the brothers of the Lord and Cephas? ⁶Or is it only Barnabas and I who have no right to refrain from working for a living? ⁷Who serves as a soldier at his own expense? Who plants a vineyard without eating any of its fruit? Who tends a flock without getting some of the milk? 8 Do I say this on human authority? Does not the law say the same? ⁹For it is written in the law of Moses, "You shall not muzzle

9 Οὐκ   εἰμὶ   ἐλεύθερος;   οὐκ   εἰμὶ   ἀπόστολος;
   Am I not   free?   am I not   an apostle?

οὐχὶ   ᾽Ιησοῦν   τὸν   κύριον   ἡμῶν   ἑόρακα;
not   Jesus   the   Lord   of us   I have seen?

οὐ   τὸ   ἔργον   μου   ὑμεῖς   ἐστε   ἐν   κυρίῳ;
not   the   work   of me   ye   are   in   [the] Lord?

2 εἰ   ἄλλοις   οὐκ   εἰμὶ   ἀπόστολος,   ἀλλά
  If   to others   I am not   an apostle,   yet

γε   ὑμῖν   εἰμι·   ἡ   γὰρ   σφραγίς   μου   τῆς
indeed to you I am;   for the   seal   ²of me ¹of the

ἀποστολῆς   ὑμεῖς   ἐστε   ἐν   κυρίῳ.   3 ῾Η
²apostleship   ye   are   in   [the] Lord.   -

ἐμὴ   ἀπολογία   τοῖς   ἐμὲ   ἀνακρίνουσίν   ἐστιν
My   defence   to the   ²me   ¹examining   is
                  [ones]

αὕτη.   4 μὴ   οὐκ   ἔχομεν   ἐξουσίαν   φαγεῖν
this.   not   Have we not   authority   to eat

καὶ   πεῖν;   5 μὴ   οὐκ   ἔχομεν   ἐξουσίαν
and   to drink?   not   have we not   authority

ἀδελφὴν   γυναῖκα   περιάγειν,   ὡς   καὶ   οἱ
a sister   a wife   to lead about,   as   also   the

λοιποὶ   ἀπόστολοι   καὶ   οἱ   ἀδελφοὶ   τοῦ
remaining   apostles   and   the   brothers   of the

κυρίου   καὶ   Κηφᾶς;   6 ἢ   μόνος   ἐγὼ   καὶ
Lord   and   Cephas?   or   only   I   and

Βαρναβᾶς   οὐκ   ἔχομεν   ἐξουσίαν   μὴ
Barnabas   have we not   authority   not

ἐργάζεσθαι;   7 Τίς   στρατεύεται   ἰδίοις
to work?   Who   soldiers   at [his] own

ὀψωνίοις   ποτέ;   τίς   φυτεύει   ἀμπελῶνα   καὶ
wages   at any time? who   plants   a vineyard   and

τὸν   καρπὸν   αὐτοῦ   οὐκ   ἐσθίει;   ἢ   τίς
the   fruit   of it   eats not?   or   who

ποιμαίνει   ποίμνην   καὶ   ἐκ   τοῦ   γάλακτος
shepherds   a flock   and   of   the   milk

τῆς   ποίμνης   οὐκ   ἐσθίει;   8 μὴ   κατὰ
of the   flock   eats not?   Not according to

ἄνθρωπον   ταῦτα   λαλῶ,   ἢ   καὶ   ὁ   νόμος
man   these things   I speak,   or   also   the   law

ταῦτα   οὐ   λέγει;   9 ἐν   γὰρ   τῷ   Μωϋσέως
these things   says not?   for in   the   of Moses

¹ Greek a sister as wife

νόμῳ   γέγραπται·   οὐ   κημώσεις   βοῦν
law   it has been written: Thou shalt not muzzle   an ox

an ox when it is treading out the grain." Is it for oxen that God is concerned? [10]Does he not speak entirely for our sake? It was written for our sake, because the plowman should plow in hope and the thresher thresh in hope of a share in the crop. [11]If we have sown spiritual good among you, is it too much if we reap your material benefits? [12]If others share this rightful claim upon you, do not we still more?

Nevertheless, we have not made use of this right, but we endure anything rather than put an obstacle in the way of the gospel of Christ. [13]Do you not know that those who are employed in the temple service get their food from the temple, and those who serve at the altar share in the sacrificial offerings? [14]In the same way, the Lord commanded that those who proclaim the gospel should get their living by the gospel.

15 But I have made no use of any of these rights, nor am I writing this to secure any such provision. For I would rather die than have any one deprive me of my ground for boasting. [16]For if I preach the gospel, that gives me no

ἀλοῶντα.	μὴ	τῶν	βοῶν	μέλει	τῷ	θεῷ;
threshing.	not	–	of oxen	matters it	–	to God?

10 ἢ   δι'   ἡμᾶς   πάντως   λέγει;   δι'   ἡμᾶς
or because of   us   altogether   he says? because of   us

γὰρ   ἐγράφη,   ὅτι   ὀφείλει   ἐπ'   ἐλπίδι
for   it was written, because   ⁵ought   ⁶on(in)   ⁶hope

ὁ   ἀροτριῶν   ἀροτριᾶν,   καὶ   ὁ   ἀλοῶν   ἐπ'
¹the   ²ploughing   ⁴to plough,   and   the   threshing on(in)
[one]   [one]

ἐλπίδι   τοῦ   μετέχειν.   11 εἰ   ἡμεῖς   ὑμῖν
hope   of the   to partake.   If   we   to you
      =of partaking.

τὰ   πνευματικὰ   ἐσπείραμεν,   μέγα   εἰ   ἡμεῖς
–   spiritual things   sowed, [is it] a great thing if   we

ὑμῶν   τὰ   σαρκικὰ   θερίσομεν;   12 εἰ   ἄλλοι
of you   –   fleshly things   shall reap?   If   others

τῆς   ὑμῶν   ἐξουσίας   μετέχουσιν,   οὐ
²of the   ⁶of you   ³authority   ¹have a share of,   not

μᾶλλον   ἡμεῖς;   ἀλλ'   οὐκ   ἐχρησάμεθα
rather   we?   But   we did not use

τῇ   ἐξουσίᾳ   ταύτῃ,   ἀλλὰ   πάντα   στέγομεν
   this authority,   but   ²all things ¹we put up with

ἵνα   μή   τινα   ἐγκοπὴν   δῶμεν   τῷ   εὐαγγελίῳ
lest   ²anyone   ³an obstacle   ¹we should to the   gospel
                  give

τοῦ   Χριστοῦ.   13 Οὐκ   οἴδατε   ὅτι   οἱ
–   of Christ.   Know ye not   that   the
                           [ones]

τὰ   ἱερὰ   ἐργαζόμενοι   τὰ   ἐκ   τοῦ   ἱεροῦ
– ²sacred things ¹working [at]   ⁴the things ⁵of   ⁶the   ⁷temple

ἐσθίουσιν,   οἱ   τῷ   θυσιαστηρίῳ   παρεδρεύοντες
²eat,   the   ²the   ³altar   ¹attending [on]
      [ones]

τῷ   θυσιαστηρίῳ   συμμερίζονται;   14 οὕτως
⁴the   ⁵altar   ⁶partake with?   So

καὶ   ὁ   κύριος   διέταξεν   τοῖς   τὸ   εὐαγγέλιον
also the   Lord   ordained   the [ones] ²the   ³gospel

καταγγέλλουσιν   ἐκ   τοῦ   εὐαγγελίου   ζῆν.
¹announcing   ⁵of   ⁶the   ⁷gospel   ⁴to live.

15 ἐγὼ   δὲ   οὐ   κέχρημαι   οὐδενὶ   τούτων.
But I   have not used   not one   of these
                           things.

Οὐκ   ἔγραψα   δὲ   ταῦτα   ἵνα   οὕτως   γένηται
And I did not write   these   in order   so   it might be
              things   that

ἐν   ἐμοί·   καλὸν   γάρ   μοι   μᾶλλον   ἀποθανεῖν
in   me;   for good [it is] to me   rather   to die

ἢ   —   τὸ   καύχημά   μου   οὐδεὶς   κενώσει.
than —   the   boast   of me   no man   shall empty.

16 ἐὰν   γάρ   εὐαγγελίζωμαι,   οὐκ   ἔστιν
For if   I preach good news,   there is not
                      =I have no boast;

ground for boasting. For necessity is laid upon me. Woe to me if I do not preach the gospel! ¹⁷For if I do this of my own will, I have a reward; but if not of my own will, I am entrusted with a commission. ¹⁸What then is my reward? Just this: that in my preaching I may make the gospel free of charge, not making full use of my right in the gospel.

19 For though I am free from all men, I have made myself a slave to all, that I might win the more. ²⁰To the Jews I became as a Jew, in order to win Jews; to those under the law I became as one under the law—though not being myself under the law— that I might win those under the law. ²¹To those outside the law I became as one outside the law— not being without law toward God but under the law of Christ—that I might win those outside the law. ²²To the weak I became weak, that I might win the weak. I have become all things to all men, that I might by all means save some. ²³I do it all for the sake of the gospel, that I may share in its blessings.

μοι   καύχημα·   ἀνάγκη   γάρ   μοι   ἐπίκειται·
to me   boast;°   for necessity   ²me   ¹is laid on;

οὐαὶ   γάρ   μοί   ἐστιν   ἐὰν   μὴ   εὐαγγελίσωμαι.
for woe   ²to me   ¹is   if   I do not preach good tidings.

17 εἰ   γὰρ   ἑκὼν   τοῦτο   πράσσω,   μισθὸν
For if   willingly   ²this   ¹I do,   ²a reward

ἔχω·   εἰ   δὲ   ἄκων,   οἰκονομίαν   πεπίστευμαι.
¹I have;   but if   unwillingly,   ²a stewardship   ¹I have been
                                                    entrusted [with].

18 τίς   οὖν   μού   ἐστιν   ὁ   μισθός;   ἵνα
What therefore   ⁴of me   ¹is   ²the   ³reward?   in order
                                                            that

εὐαγγελιζόμενος   ἀδάπανον   θήσω   τὸ
preaching good tidings   ⁴without charge   ¹I may place   ²the

εὐαγγέλιον,   εἰς   τὸ   μὴ   καταχρήσασθαι
³good tidings,   so as†   not   to use to the full

τῇ   ἐξουσίᾳ   μου   ἐν   τῷ   εὐαγγελίῳ.
the   authority   of me   in   the   good tidings.

19 Ἐλεύθερος   γὰρ   ὢν   ἐκ   πάντων   πᾶσιν
For ²free   ¹being   of   all men   ³to all men

ἐμαυτὸν   ἐδούλωσα,   ἵνα   τοὺς   πλείονας
²myself   ¹I enslaved,   in order that   the   more

κερδήσω·   20 καὶ   ἐγενόμην   τοῖς   Ἰουδαίοις
I might gain;   and   I became   to the   Jews

ὡς   Ἰουδαῖος,   ἵνα   Ἰουδαίους   κερδήσω·
as   a Jew,   in order that   Jews   I might gain;

τοῖς   ὑπὸ   νόμον   ὡς   ὑπὸ   νόμον,   μὴ   ὢν
to the   under   law   as   under   law,   not being
ones

αὐτὸς   ὑπὸ   νόμον,   ἵνα   τοὺς   ὑπὸ   νόμον
[my]self   under   law,   in order   the   under   law
                            that   ones

κερδήσω·   21 τοῖς   ἀνόμοις   ὡς   ἄνομος,
I might gain;   to the ones   without law   as   without law,

μὴ   ὢν   ἄνομος   θεοῦ   ἀλλ'   ἔννομος   Χριστοῦ,
not being   without   of God   but   under   of Christ,
            [the] law   [the] law

ἵνα   κερδάνω   τοὺς   ἀνόμους·   22 ἐγενόμην
in order   I may gain   the ones   without law;   I became
that

τοῖς   ἀσθενέσιν   ἀσθενής,   ἵνα   τοὺς   ἀσθενεῖς
²to the   ³weak   ¹weak,   in order   the   weak
                                        that

κερδήσω·   τοῖς   πᾶσιν   γέγονα   πάντα,   ἵνα
I might gain;   –   to all men   I have   all   in order
                                become   things,   that

πάντως   τινὰς   σώσω.   23 πάντα   δὲ   ποιῶ
in any case   ²some   ¹I might save.   But all things   I do

διὰ   τὸ   εὐαγγέλιον,   ἵνα   συγκοινωνὸς   αὐτοῦ
because the   good tidings,   in order   ²a joint partaker   ³of it
of   that

24 Do you not know that in a race all the runners compete, but only one receives the prize? So run that you may obtain it. ²⁵ Every athlete exercises self-control in all things. They do it to receive a perishable wreath, but we an imperishable. ²⁶ Well, I do not run aimlessly, I do not box as one beating the air; ²⁷ but I pommel my body and subdue it, lest after preaching to others I myself should be disqualified.

γένωμαι.   24 Οὐκ οἴδατε ὅτι οἱ ἐν
¹I may become.   Know ye not   that the [ones] ²in

σταδίῳ τρέχοντες πάντες μὲν τρέχουσιν,
²a racecourse ¹running   all   indeed   run,

εἶς δὲ λαμβάνει τὸ βραβεῖον; οὕτως
but one   receives   the   prize?   So

τρέχετε ἵνα καταλάβητε.   25 πᾶς δὲ ὁ
run   in order that ye may obtain.   And everyone

ἀγωνιζόμενος πάντα ἐγκρατεύεται, ἐκεῖνοι
struggling   [in] all things exercises self-control, those

μὲν οὖν ἵνα φθαρτὸν στέφανον λάβωσιν,
indeed there- in order ²a corruptible ⁰crown ¹they may
fore   that   receive,

ἡμεῖς δὲ ἄφθαρτον.   26 ἐγὼ τοίνυν οὕτως
but we   an incorruptible.   I accordingly so

τρέχω ὡς οὐκ ἀδήλως, οὕτως πυκτεύω
run   as   not   unclearly,   so   I box

ὡς οὐκ ἀέρα δέρων· 27 ἀλλὰ ὑπωπιάζω
as   not   ²air   ¹beating;   but   I treat severely

μου τὸ σῶμα καὶ δουλαγωγῶ, μή πως
of me the   body   and lead [it] as a slave,   lest

ἄλλοις κηρύξας αὐτὸς ἀδόκιμος γένωμαι.
to others having pro- ²[my]self ⁵disapproved ¹I ³may
      claimed   ⁴become.

CHAPTER 10

I want you to know, brethren, that our fathers were all under the cloud, and all passed through the sea, ² and all were baptized into Moses in the cloud and in the sea, ³ and all ate the same supernatural food ⁴ and all drank the same supernatural drink. For they drank from the supernatural Rock which followed them, and the Rock was Christ. ⁵ Nevertheless with most of them God was not pleased; for they were overthrown in the wilderness.

10 Οὐ θέλω γὰρ ὑμᾶς ἀγνοεῖν, ἀδελφοί,
  For I wish not   you   to be ignorant, brothers,

ὅτι οἱ πατέρες ἡμῶν πάντες ὑπὸ τὴν
that the   fathers   of us   all   under the

νεφέλην ἦσαν καὶ πάντες διὰ τῆς θαλάσσης
cloud   were and   all   through the   sea

διῆλθον, 2 καὶ πάντες εἰς τὸν Μωϋσῆν
passed through, and   all   ²to   -   ³Moses

ἐβαπτίσαντο ἐν τῇ νεφέλῃ καὶ ἐν τῇ
¹were baptized   in   the   cloud   and   in   the

θαλάσσῃ, 3 καὶ πάντες τὸ αὐτὸ πνευματικὸν
sea,   and   all   ²the ³same   ⁴spiritual

βρῶμα ἔφαγον, 4 καὶ πάντες τὸ αὐτὸ
⁵food   ¹ate,   and   all   ²the   ³same

πνευματικὸν ἔπιον πόμα· ἔπινον γὰρ ἐκ
⁴spiritual   ¹drank   ⁵drink;   for they drank   of

πνευματικῆς ἀκολουθούσης πέτρας, ἡ πέτρα
a spiritual   ²following   ¹rock,   ²the   ³rock

δὲ ἦν ὁ Χριστός. 5 Ἀλλ’ οὐκ ἐν τοῖς
¹and was the   Christ.   But   ⁷not ¹in(with) ²the

πλείοσιν αὐτῶν εὐδόκησεν ὁ θεός·
³majority   ⁴of them   ⁶was ⁸well ⁹pleased   -   ⁵God;

κατεστρώθησαν γὰρ ἐν τῇ ἐρήμῳ.
for they were scattered   in   the   desert.

6 Now these things are warnings for us, not to desire evil as they did. [7] Do not be idolaters as some of them were; as it is written, "The people sat down to eat and drink and rose up to dance." [8] We must not indulge in immorality as some of them did and twenty-three thousand fell in a single day. [9] We must not put the Lord[m] to the test, as some of them did and were destroyed by serpents; [10] nor grumble, as some of them did and were destroyed by the Destroyer. [11] Now these things happened to them as a warning, but they were written down for our instruction, upon whom the end of the ages has come. [12] Therefore let any one who thinks that he stands take heed lest he fall. [13] No temptation has overtaken you that is not common to man. God is faithful, and he will not let you be tempted beyond your strength, but with the temptation will also provide the way of escape, that you may be able to endure it.

[m] Other ancient authorities read Christ

6 ταῦτα δὲ τύποι ἡμῶν ἐγενήθησαν, εἰς
Now these things types of us were, for

τὸ μὴ εἶναι ἡμᾶς ἐπιθυμητὰς κακῶν,
the not to be us[b] longers after evil things,
=so that we should not be . . .

καθὼς κἀκεῖνοι ἐπεθύμησαν. 7 μηδὲ
as those indeed longed. Neither

εἰδωλολάτραι γίνεσθε, καθώς τινες αὐτῶν·
idolaters be ye, as some of them;

ὥσπερ γέγραπται· ἐκάθισεν ὁ λαὸς φαγεῖν
as it has been written: Sat the people to eat

καὶ πεῖν, καὶ ἀνέστησαν παίζειν. 8 μηδὲ
and to drink, and stood up to play. Neither

πορνεύωμεν, καθώς τινες αὐτῶν ἐπόρνευσαν
let us commit as some of them committed
fornication, fornication

καὶ ἔπεσαν μιᾷ ἡμέρᾳ εἴκοσι τρεῖς
and fell in one day twenty-three

χιλιάδες. 9 μηδὲ ἐκπειράζωμεν τὸν κύριον,
thousands. Neither let us overtempt the Lord,

καθώς τινες αὐτῶν ἐπείρασαν καὶ ὑπὸ
as some of them tempted and by

τῶν ὄφεων ἀπώλλυντο. 10 μηδὲ γογγύζετε,
the serpents were destroyed. Neither murmur ye,

καθάπερ τινὲς αὐτῶν ἐγόγγυσαν, καὶ
even as some of them murmured, and

ἀπώλοντο ὑπὸ τοῦ ὀλεθρευτοῦ. 11 ταῦτα δὲ
were destroyed by the destroyer. Now these things

τυπικῶς συνέβαινεν ἐκείνοις, ἐγράφη δὲ
[2]typically [1]happened [3]to those men, and was(were)
written

πρὸς νουθεσίαν ἡμῶν, εἰς οὓς τὰ
for admonition of us, to whom the

τέλη τῶν αἰώνων κατήντηκεν. 12 Ὥστε
ends of the ages has(ve) arrived. So as

ὁ δοκῶν ἑστάναι βλεπέτω μὴ πέσῃ.
the thinking to stand let him look lest he falls.
[one]

13 πειρασμὸς ὑμᾶς οὐκ εἴληφεν εἰ μὴ
Temptation you has not taken except

ἀνθρώπινος· πιστὸς δὲ ὁ θεός, ὃς οὐκ
[what is] human; but faithful [is] – God, who not

ἐάσει ὑμᾶς πειρασθῆναι ὑπὲρ ὃ δύνασθε,
will allow you to be tempted beyond what you are able
[to bear],

ἀλλὰ ποιήσει σὺν τῷ πειρασμῷ καὶ τὴν
but will make with the temptation also the

ἔκβασιν τοῦ δύνασθαι ὑπενεγκεῖν.
way out – to be able to endure.[d]
=so that ye may be able . . .

14 Therefore, my be-
loved, shun the worship
of idols. [15] I speak as to
sensible men; judge for
yourselves what I say.
[16] The cup of blessing
which we bless, is it not a
participation in the blood
of Christ? The bread
which we break, is it not
a participation in the
body of Christ? [17] Be-
cause there is one bread,
we who are many are one
body, for we all partake
of the same loaf.
[18] Consider the practice
of Israel; are not those
who eat the sacrifices
partners in the altar?
[19] What do I imply then?
That food offered to
idols is anything, or
that an idol is anything?
[20] No, I imply that what
pagans sacrifice they offer
to demons and not to
God. I do not want you
to be partners with
demons. [21] You cannot
drink the cup of the Lord
and the cup of demons.
You cannot partake of
the table of the Lord
and the table of demons.
[22] Shall we provoke the
Lord to jealousy? Are
we stronger than he?
23 "All things are
lawful," but not all
things are helpful. "All
things are lawful," but
not all things build up.

14 Διόπερ,   ἀγαπητοί   μου,   φεύγετε   ἀπό
Wherefore,   beloved   of me,   flee ye   from
τῆς   εἰδωλολατρίας.   15 ὡς   φρονίμοις   λέγω·
–   idolatry.   [2]As [3]to prudent men   [1]I say;
κρίνατε   ὑμεῖς   ὅ   φημι.   16 Τὸ   ποτήριον
judge   ye   what   I say.   The   cup
τῆς   εὐλογίας   ὃ   εὐλογοῦμεν,   οὐχὶ   κοινωνία
–   of blessing   which   we bless,   [2]not [3]a communion
ἐστὶν   τοῦ   αἵματος   τοῦ   Χριστοῦ;   τὸν
[1]is it   of the   blood   –   of Christ?   the
ἄρτον   ὃν   κλῶμεν,   οὐχὶ   κοινωνία   τοῦ
bread   which   we break,   [2]not   [3]a communion [4]of the
σώματος   τοῦ   Χριστοῦ   ἐστιν;   17 ὅτι   εἶς
[5]body   –   [6]of Christ   [1]is it?   Because [4]one
ἄρτος,   ἓν   σῶμα   οἱ   πολλοί   ἐσμεν·   οἱ   γὰρ
[5]bread,   [6]one   [7]body   [2]the   [3]many   [1]we are;   –   for
πάντες   ἐκ   τοῦ   ἑνὸς   ἄρτου   μετέχομεν.
all   of   the   one   bread   we partake.
18 βλέπετε   τὸν   Ἰσραὴλ   κατὰ   σάρκα·
See ye   –   Israel   according to [the] flesh;
οὐχ   οἱ   ἐσθίοντες   τὰς   θυσίας   κοινωνοὶ
[2]not [3]the [ones]   [4]eating   [5]the   [6]sacrifices   [7]sharers
τοῦ   θυσιαστηρίου   εἰσίν;   19 τί   οὖν   φημι;
[8]of the   [9]altar   [1]are?   What there-   do I say?
                                                fore
ὅτι   εἰδωλόθυτόν   τί   ἐστιν;   ἢ   ὅτι   εἰδωλόν
that   an idolatrous [2]anything   [1]is?   or   that   an idol
                      sacrifice
τί   ἐστιν;   20 ἀλλ'   ὅτι   ἃ   θύουσιν,
[2]anything   [1]is?   but   that [the] things   they
                                        which   sacrifice,
δαιμονίοις   και   οὐ   θεῷ   θύουσιν·   οὐ   θέλω
to demons   and   not   to God   they sacrifice;   [2]not   [2]I wish
δὲ   ὑμᾶς   κοινωνοὺς   τῶν   δαιμονίων   γίνεσθαι.
[1]and   you   sharers   of the   demons   to become.
21 οὐ   δύνασθε   ποτήριον   κυρίου   πίνειν
Ye cannot   [2]a cup   [3]of [the] Lord   [1]to drink
καὶ   ποτήριον   δαιμονίων·   οὐ   δύνασθε
and   a cup   of demons;   ye cannot
τραπέζης   κυρίου   μετέχειν   καὶ   τραπέζης
[2]of a table   [3]of [the] Lord   [1]to partake   and   of a table
δαιμονίων.   22 ἢ   παραζηλοῦμεν   τὸν   κύριον;
of demons.   Or   do we make jealous   the   Lord?
μὴ   ἰσχυρότεροι   αὐτοῦ   ἐσμεν;
Not   [2]stronger [than]   [3]he   [1]are we?
23 Πάντα   ἔξεστιν,   ἀλλ'   οὐ   πάντα
All things   [are] lawful,   but   not   all things
συμφέρει·   πάντα   ἔξεστιν,   ἀλλ'   οὐ   πάντα
[are] expedient; all things   lawful,   but   not   all things
                                [are]

²⁴Let no one seek his own good, but the good of his neighbor. ²⁵Eat whatever is sold in the meat market without raising any question on the ground of conscience. ²⁶For "the earth is the Lord's, and everything in it." ²⁷If one of the unbelievers invites you to dinner and you are disposed to go, eat whatever is set before you without raising any question on the ground of conscience. ²⁸(But if some one says to you, "This has been offered in sacrifice," then out of consideration for the man who informed you, and for conscience' sake—²⁹I mean his conscience, not yours—do not eat it.) For why should my liberty be determined by another man's scruples? ³⁰If I partake with thankfulness, why am I denounced because of that for which I give thanks?

31 So, whether you eat or drink, or whatever you do, do all to the glory of God. ³²Give no offense to Jews or to Greeks or to the church of God, ³³just as I try to please all men in everything I do, not seeking my own advantage, but that of many, that they may be saved.

οἰκοδομεῖ.
edifies(fy).

24 μηδεὶς τὸ ἑαυτοῦ ζητείτω
No one the thing of himself let him seek

ἀλλὰ τὸ τοῦ ἑτέρου.
but the thing of the other.

25 Πᾶν τὸ ἐν
Everything ²in

μακέλλῳ πωλούμενον ἐσθίετε μηδὲν
²a meat market ¹being sold eat ye ²nothing

ἀνακρίνοντες διὰ τὴν συνείδησιν·
¹examining because of - conscience;

26 τοῦ
²of the

κυρίου γὰρ ἡ γῆ καὶ τὸ πλήρωμα
³Lord ¹for the earth and the fulness

αὐτῆς. 27 εἴ τις καλεῖ ὑμᾶς τῶν ἀπίστων
of it. If anyone invites you of the unbelievers

καὶ θέλετε πορεύεσθαι, πᾶν τὸ παρατι-
and ye wish to go, ²everything ³being set

θέμενον ὑμῖν ἐσθίετε μηδὲν ἀνακρίνοντες
before ⁴you ¹eat ⁶nothing ⁵examining

διὰ τὴν συνείδησιν. 28 ἐὰν δέ τις ὑμῖν
because - conscience. But if anyone ²to you
of

εἴπῃ· τοῦτο ἱερόθυτόν ἐστιν, μὴ ἐσθίετε
¹says· This ²slain in sacrifice ¹is, do not eat

δι' ἐκεῖνον τὸν μηνύσαντα καὶ τὴν
because that the pointing out and -
of man [one]

συνείδησιν· 29 συνείδησιν δὲ λέγω οὐχὶ
conscience: ²conscience ¹but ²I say not

τὴν ἑαυτοῦ ἀλλὰ τὴν τοῦ ἑτέρου.* ἱνατί
the one of himself but the one of the other.* why

γὰρ ἡ ἐλευθερία μου κρίνεται ὑπὸ ἄλλης
For the freedom of me is judged by ²of another

συνειδήσεως; 30 εἰ ἐγὼ χάριτι μετέχω,
¹conscience? If I by grace partake,

τί βλασφημοῦμαι ὑπὲρ οὗ ἐγὼ εὐχαριστῶ;
why am I evil because what I give thanks
spoken of of [for]?

31 Εἴτε οὖν ἐσθίετε εἴτε πίνετε εἴτε
Whether therefore ye eat or ye drink or

τι ποιεῖτε, πάντα εἰς δόξαν θεοῦ ποιεῖτε.
what ye do, all things to [the] glory of God do ye.
[ever]

32 ἀπρόσκοποι καὶ Ἰουδαίοις γίνεσθε καὶ
²Without offence ³both ⁴to Jews ¹be ye ⁵and

Ἕλλησιν καὶ τῇ ἐκκλησίᾳ τοῦ θεοῦ,
⁶to Greeks and to the church - of God,

33 καθὼς κἀγὼ πάντα πᾶσιν ἀρέσκω,
as I also [in] all things all men please,

μὴ ζητῶν τὸ ἐμαυτοῦ σύμφορον ἀλλὰ
not seeking the of myself advantage but

* That is, not the conscience of the person invited, to whom the apostle's words are addressed, but the conscience of the person " pointing out."

CHAPTER 11

BE imitators of me, as I am of Christ. 2 I commend you because you remember me in everything and maintain the traditions even as I have delivered them to you. ³ But I want you to understand that the head of every man is Christ, the head of a woman is her husband, and the head of Christ is God. ⁴ Any man who prays or prophesies with his head covered dishonors his head, ⁵ but any woman who prays or prophesies with her head unveiled dishonors her head—it is the same as if her head were shaven. ⁶ For if a woman will not veil herself, then she should cut off her hair; but if it is disgraceful for a woman to be shorn or shaven, let her wear a veil. ⁷ For a man ought not to cover his head, since he is the image and glory of God; but woman is the glory of man. ⁸ (For man was not made from woman, but woman from man. ⁹ Neither was man created

τὸ τῶν πολλῶν, ἵνα σωθῶσιν. 11 μιμηταί
the of the many, in order they may   Imitators
(that)   that be saved.

μου γίνεσθε, καθὼς κἀγὼ Χριστοῦ.
of me be ye,   as   I also [am] of Christ.

2 Ἐπαινῶ δὲ ὑμᾶς ὅτι πάντα μου
But I praise   you   because ²all things ³of me

μέμνησθε καὶ καθὼς παρέδωκα ὑμῖν τὰς
¹ye have   and   ⁴as   ⁵I delivered ⁶to you ²the
remembered

παραδόσεις κατέχετε. 3 Θέλω δὲ ὑμᾶς
³traditions ¹ye hold fast.   But I wish   you

εἰδέναι ὅτι παντὸς ἀνδρὸς ἡ κεφαλὴ ὁ
to know that ⁵of every ⁶man ³the ⁴head   –

Χριστός ἐστιν, κεφαλὴ δὲ γυναικὸς ὁ
¹Christ ²is,   and [the] head of a woman the

ἀνήρ, κεφαλὴ δὲ τοῦ Χριστοῦ ὁ θεός.
man, and [the] head – of Christ – God.

4 πᾶς ἀνὴρ προσευχόμενος ἢ προφητεύων
Every man   praying   or   prophesying

κατὰ κεφαλῆς ἔχων καταισχύνει τὴν
³down over ⁴[his] head ¹having   shames   the
                    ²[anything]

κεφαλὴν αὐτοῦ. 5 πᾶσα δὲ γυνὴ προσ-
head   of him.   But every   woman pray-

ευχομένη ἢ προφητεύουσα ἀκατακαλύπτῳ
ing   or   prophesying   ³unveiled

τῇ κεφαλῇ καταισχύνει τὴν κεφαλὴν αὐτῆς·
¹with ²head   shames   the   head   of her;
the(her)

ἓν γάρ ἐστιν καὶ τὸ αὐτὸ τῇ ἐξυρημένῃ.
for ²one ¹it is and the same with the having been
                     thing woman shaved.

6 εἰ γὰρ οὐ κατακαλύπτεται γυνή, καὶ
For if   ²is not veiled   ¹a woman, also

κειράσθω· εἰ δὲ αἰσχρὸν γυναικὶ τὸ
let her be shorn; but if shameful for a woman –

κείρασθαι ἢ ξυρᾶσθαι, κατακαλυπτέσθω.
to be shorn or to be shaved,   let her be veiled.

7 ἀνὴρ μὲν γὰρ οὐκ ὀφείλει κατα-
For a man indeed   ought not   to be

καλύπτεσθαι τὴν κεφαλήν, εἰκὼν καὶ δόξα
veiled   the   head,ᵇ ²[the] image ³and ⁴glory

θεοῦ ὑπάρχων· ἡ γυνὴ δὲ δόξα ἀνδρός
⁵of God ¹being;   but the woman ²[the] glory ³of a man

ἐστιν. 8 οὐ γάρ ἐστιν ἀνὴρ ἐκ γυναικός,
¹is.   For ²not ²is ¹man of woman,

ἀλλὰ γυνὴ ἐξ ἀνδρός· 9 καὶ γὰρ οὐκ
but woman of man;   for indeed ³not

for woman, but woman for man.) [10]That is why a woman ought to have a veil[n] on her head, because of the angels. [11](Nevertheless, in the Lord woman is not independent of man nor man of woman; [12]for as woman was made from man, so man is now born of woman. And all things are from God.) [13]Judge for yourselves; is it proper for a woman to pray to God with her head uncovered? [14]Does not nature itself teach you that for a man to wear long hair is degrading to him, [15]but if a woman has long hair, is it her pride? For her hair is given to her for a covering. [16]If any one is disposed to be contentious, we recognize no other practice, nor do the churches of God.

17 But in the following instructions I do not commend you, because when you come together it is not for the better but for the worse. [18]For, in the first place, when you assemble as a church, I hear that there are divisions among you;·

[n] Greek authority (the veil being a symbol of this)

ἐκτίσθη	ἀνὴρ	διὰ	τὴν	γυναῖκα,	ἀλλὰ
²was ⁴created	¹man	because of	the	woman,	but

γυνὴ	διὰ	τὸν	ἄνδρα.	10 διὰ	τοῦτο
woman	because of	the	man.		Therefore

ὀφείλει	ἡ	γυνὴ	ἐξουσίαν	ἔχειν	ἐπὶ	τῆς
ought	the	woman	authority	to have	on	the

κεφαλῆς	διὰ	τοὺς	ἀγγέλους.	11 πλὴν
head	because of	the	angels.	Nevertheless

οὔτε	γυνὴ	χωρὶς	ἀνδρὸς	οὔτε	ἀνὴρ	χωρὶς
neither	woman	without	man	nor	man	without

γυναικὸς	ἐν	κυρίῳ·	12 ὥσπερ	γὰρ	ἡ
woman	in	[the] Lord;	for as		the

γυνὴ	ἐκ	τοῦ	ἀνδρός,	οὕτως	καὶ	ὁ	ἀνὴρ
woman	of	the	man,	so	also	the	man

διὰ	τῆς	γυναικός·	τὰ	δὲ	πάντα	ἐκ	τοῦ
through the		woman;	-	but	all things	of	-

θεοῦ.	13 Ἐν	ὑμῖν	αὐτοῖς	κρίνατε·	πρέπον
God.	Among	you	[your]selves	judge:	²fitting

ἐστὶν	γυναῖκα	ἀκατακάλυπτον	τῷ	θεῷ
¹is it	²[for] ⁴a woman	⁷unveiled	-	⁶to God

προσεύχεσθαι;	14 οὐδὲ	ἡ	φύσις	αὐτὴ
⁵to pray?	Not	-	nature	[her]self

διδάσκει	ὑμᾶς	ὅτι	ἀνὴρ	μὲν	ἐὰν	κομᾷ,
teaches	you	that	a man	indeed	if	he wears his hair long,

ἀτιμία	αὐτῷ	ἐστιν,	15 γυνὴ	δὲ	ἐὰν
²a dishonour	³to him	¹it is,	but a woman		if

κομᾷ,	δόξα	αὐτῇ	ἐστιν;	ὅτι	ἡ	κόμη
she wears her hair long,	²a glory	³to her	¹it is?	because	the	long hair

ἀντὶ	περιβολαίου	δέδοται	αὐτῇ.	16 Εἰ
instead of	a veil	has been given	to her.	if

δέ	τις	δοκεῖ	φιλόνεικος	εἶναι,	ἡμεῖς
But	anyone	thinks	²contentious	¹to be,	we

τοιαύτην	συνήθειαν	οὐκ	ἔχομεν,	οὐδὲ	αἱ
²such	³a custom	¹have not,		neither	the

ἐκκλησίαι	τοῦ	θεοῦ.
churches	-	of God.

17 Τοῦτο	δὲ	παραγγέλλων	οὐκ	ἐπαινῶ
But this		charging		I do not praise

ὅτι	οὐκ	εἰς	τὸ	κρεῖσσον	ἀλλὰ	εἰς	τὸ
because not		for	the	better	but	for	the

ἧσσον	συνέρχεσθε.	18 πρῶτον	μὲν	γὰρ
worse	ye come together.		For firstly	indeed

συνερχομένων	ὑμῶν	ἐν	ἐκκλησίᾳ	ἀκούω
coming together	you*	in	church	I hear

*=when ye come together

σχίσματα	ἐν	ὑμῖν	ὑπάρχειν,	καὶ	μέρος
divisions	among	you	to be,	and	²part

and I partly believe it, [19]for there must be factions among you in order that those who are genuine among you may be recognized. [20]When you meet together, it is not the Lord's supper that you eat. [21]For in eating, each one goes ahead with his own meal, and one is hungry and another is drunk. [22]What! Do you not have houses to eat and drink in? Or do you despise the church of God and humiliate those who have nothing? What shall I say to you? Shall I commend you in this? No, I will not. 23 For I received from the Lord what I also delivered to you, that the Lord Jesus on the night when he was betrayed took bread, [24]and when he had given thanks, he broke it, and said, "This is my body which is for[o] you. Do this in remembrance of me." [25]In the same way also the cup, after supper, saying, "This cup is the new covenant in my blood. Do this, as often

τι πιστεύω.   **19** δεῖ γὰρ καὶ αἱρέσεις
[1]some I believe.   For it behoves indeed   sects

ἐν ὑμῖν εἶναι, ἵνα [καὶ] οἱ δόκιμοι
among you to be, in order also the approved
        that   ones

φανεροὶ γένωνται ἐν ὑμῖν.   **20** Συν-
manifest may become among you.   Coming

ἐρχομένων οὖν ὑμῶν ἐπὶ τὸ αὐτὸ οὐκ
together therefore you[a]   together   not
=When therefore ye come

ἔστιν κυριακὸν δεῖπνον φαγεῖν· **21** ἕκαστος
it is of the Lord* a supper to eat;   [2]each one

γὰρ τὸ ἴδιον δεῖπνον προλαμβάνει ἐν
[1]for the(his) own supper takes before in

τῷ φαγεῖν, καὶ ὃς μὲν πεινᾷ, ὃς δὲ
- to eat(eating), and one† hungers, another†

μεθύει.   **22** μὴ γὰρ οἰκίας οὐκ ἔχετε
is drunken.   Not indeed [2]houses [1]have ye not

εἰς τὸ ἐσθίειν καὶ πίνειν; ἢ τῆς ἐκκλησίας
- - to eat and to drink? or the church

τοῦ θεοῦ καταφρονεῖτε, καὶ καταισχύνετε
- of God despise ye, and shame

τοὺς μὴ ἔχοντας; τί εἴπω ὑμῖν; ἐπαινέσω
the not having? What may I say to you? shall I praise
[ones]

ὑμᾶς; ἐν τούτῳ οὐκ ἐπαινῶ.   **23** Ἐγὼ
you? In this I praise not.   I

γὰρ παρέλαβον ἀπὸ τοῦ κυρίου, ὃ καὶ
For received from the Lord, what also

παρέδωκα ὑμῖν, ὅτι ὁ κύριος Ἰησοῦς
I delivered to you, that the Lord Jesus

ἐν τῇ νυκτὶ ᾗ παρεδίδοτο ἔλαβεν ἄρτον
in the night in which he was took bread
                    betrayed

24 καὶ εὐχαριστήσας ἔκλασεν καὶ εἶπεν·
and having given thanks broke and said:

τοῦτό μού ἐστιν τὸ σῶμα τὸ ὑπὲρ
This of me is the body - on be-
                          half of

ὑμῶν· τοῦτο ποιεῖτε εἰς τὴν ἐμὴν
you; this do ye for - my

ἀνάμνησιν. **25** ὡσαύτως καὶ τὸ ποτήριον
remembrance. Similarly also the cup

μετὰ τὸ δειπνῆσαι, λέγων· τοῦτο τὸ
after the to sup, saying: This -

ποτήριον ἡ καινὴ διαθήκη ἐστὶν ἐν τῷ
cup [2]the [3]new [4]covenant [1]is in -

ἐμῷ αἵματι· τοῦτο ποιεῖτε, ὁσάκις ἐὰν
my blood; this do ye, as often as

[o] Other ancient authorities read *broken for*

* Note that κυριακός is an adjective, for which no exact English equivalent is available. Only other occurrence in N.T., Rev. 1. 10.

as you drink it, in remembrance of me." [26] For as often as you eat this bread and drink the cup, you proclaim the Lord's death until he comes.

27 Whoever, therefore, eats the bread or drinks the cup of the Lord in an unworthy manner will be guilty of profaning the body and blood of the Lord. [28] Let a man examine himself, and so eat of the bread and drink of the cup. [29] For any one who eats and drinks without discerning the body eats and drinks judgment upon himself. [30] That is why many of you are weak and ill, and some have died. [31] But if we judged ourselves truly, we should not be judged. [32] But when we are judged by the Lord, we are chastened[p] so that we may not be condemned along with the world.

33 So then, my brethren, when you come together to eat, wait for one another—[34] if any one is hungry, let him eat at home—lest you come together to be condemned. About the other things I will give directions when I come.

[p] Or when we are judged we are being chastened by the Lord

πίνητε, εἰς τὴν ἐμὴν ἀνάμνησιν.   26 ὁσάκις
ye drink,   for   -   my   remembrance.   as often

γὰρ ἐὰν ἐσθίητε τὸν ἄρτον τοῦτον καὶ
For   as   ye eat   this bread   and

τὸ ποτήριον πίνητε, τὸν θάνατον τοῦ
²the   ³cup   ¹drink,   the   death   of the

κυρίου καταγγέλλετε, ἄχρι οὗ ἔλθῃ.
Lord   ye declare,   until   he comes.

27 Ὥστε ὃς ἂν ἐσθίῃ τὸν ἄρτον ἢ
So as   whoever   eats   the   bread   or

πίνῃ τὸ ποτήριον τοῦ κυρίου ἀναξίως,
drinks   the   cup   of the   Lord   unworthily,

ἔνοχος ἔσται τοῦ σώματος καὶ τοῦ
guilty   will be   of the   body   and   of the

αἵματος τοῦ κυρίου.   28 δοκιμαζέτω δὲ
blood   of the   Lord.   But ¹let ³prove

ἄνθρωπος ἑαυτόν, καὶ οὕτως ἐκ τοῦ
²a man   ⁴himself,   and   so   of   the

ἄρτου ἐσθιέτω καὶ ἐκ τοῦ ποτηρίου
bread   let him eat   and   of   the   cup

πινέτω·   29 ὁ γὰρ ἐσθίων καὶ πίνων
let him drink;   for the [one]   eating   and   drinking

κρίμα ἑαυτῷ ἐσθίει καὶ πίνει μὴ διακρίνων
⁴judgment ⁵to   ¹eats   ²and ³drinks   not   discerning
      himself

τὸ σῶμα.   30 διὰ τοῦτο ἐν ὑμῖν πολλοὶ
the   body.   Therefore   among   you   many

ἀσθενεῖς καὶ ἄρρωστοι καὶ κοιμῶνται
[are] weak   and   feeble   and   ²sleep

ἱκανοί.   31 εἰ δὲ ἑαυτοὺς διεκρίνομεν,
¹a number.   But if   ourselves   we discerned,

οὐκ ἂν ἐκρινόμεθα·   32 κρινόμενοι δὲ ὑπὸ
we should not be judged;   but being judged   by

τοῦ κυρίου παιδευόμεθα, ἵνα μὴ σὺν
the   Lord   we are chastened,   lest   with

τῷ κόσμῳ κατακριθῶμεν.   33 Ὥστε,
the   world   we are condemned.   So as,

ἀδελφοί μου, συνερχόμενοι εἰς τὸ φαγεῖν
brothers   of me,   coming together   for   the   to eat

ἀλλήλους ἐκδέχεσθε.   34 εἴ τις πεινᾷ,
one another   await ye.   If   anyone   hungers,

ἐν οἴκῳ ἐσθιέτω, ἵνα μὴ εἰς κρίμα
at home   let him eat,   lest   to   judgment

συνέρχησθε. τὰ δὲ λοιπὰ ὡς ἂν ἔλθω
ye come together. And the remaining matters whenever   I come

διατάξομαι.
I will arrange.

CHAPTER 12

NOW concerning spiritual gifts, brethren, I do not want you to be uninformed. ²You know that when you were heathen, you were led astray to dumb idols, however you may have been moved. ³Therefore I want you to understand that no one speaking by the Spirit of God ever says "Jesus be cursed!" and no one can say "Jesus is Lord" except by the Holy Spirit.

4 Now there are varieties of gifts, but the same Spirit;⁵ and there are varieties of service, but the same Lord; ⁶and there are varieties of working, but it is the same God who inspires them all in every one. ⁷To each is given the manifestation of the Spirit for the common good. ⁸To one is given through the Spirit the utterance of wisdom, and to another the utterance of knowledge according to the same Spirit, ⁹to another faith by the same Spirit, to another gifts of healing by the one Spirit, ¹⁰to another the working of miracles, to another prophecy, to another the ability to distinguish between spirits, to another various kinds of tongues,

12 Περὶ δὲ τῶν πνευματικῶν, ἀδελφοί,
Now about the spiritual matters, brothers,
οὐ θέλω ὑμᾶς ἀγνοεῖν. 2 Οἴδατε ὅτι
I do not wish you to be ignorant. Ye know that
ὅτε ἔθνη ἦτε πρὸς τὰ εἴδωλα τὰ ἄφωνα
when ⁸nations ¹ye were ⁴to ⁵the ⁷idols – ⁶voiceless
ὡς ἂν ἤγεσθε ἀπαγόμενοι. 3 διὸ γνωρίζω
⁸however ⁹ye were led ⁹[ye were] Where- I make
¹⁰being led away.* fore known
ὑμῖν ὅτι οὐδεὶς ἐν πνεύματι θεοῦ λαλῶν
to you that no one ²by ³[the] Spirit ⁴of God ¹speaking
λέγει· ΑΝΑΘΕΜΑ ΙΗΣΟΥΣ, καὶ οὐδεὶς
says: A CURSE [IS] JESUS, and no one
δύναται εἰπεῖν· ΚΥΡΙΟΣ ΙΗΣΟΥΣ, εἰ μὴ
can to say: LORD JESUS, except
ἐν πνεύματι ἁγίῳ.
by [the] ²Spirit ¹Holy.

4 Διαιρέσεις δὲ χαρισμάτων εἰσίν, τὸ δὲ αὐτὸ
Now differences of gifts there are, but the same
πνεῦμα· 5 καὶ διαιρέσεις διακονιῶν εἰσιν, καὶ
Spirit; and differences of ministries there are, and
ὁ αὐτὸς κύριος· 6 καὶ διαιρέσεις ἐνεργημάτων
the same Lord; and differences of operations
εἰσίν, ὁ δὲ αὐτὸς θεὸς ὁ ἐνεργῶν τὰ
there are, but the same God – operating –
πάντα ἐν πᾶσιν. 7 ἑκάστῳ δὲ δίδοται
all things in all. But to each one is given
ἡ φανέρωσις τοῦ πνεύματος πρὸς τὸ
the manifestation of the Spirit to the
συμφέρον. 8 ᾧ μὲν γὰρ διὰ τοῦ πνεύματος
profiting. For to one through the Spirit
δίδοται λόγος σοφίας, ἄλλῳ δὲ λόγος
is given a word of wisdom, and to another a word
γνώσεως κατὰ τὸ αὐτὸ πνεῦμα, 9 ἑτέρῳ
of accord- the same Spirit, to
knowledge ing to another
πίστις ἐν τῷ αὐτῷ πνεύματι, ἄλλῳ δὲ
faith by the same Spirit, and to another
χαρίσματα ἰαμάτων ἐν τῷ ἑνὶ πνεύματι,
gifts of cures by the one Spirit,
10 ἄλλῳ δὲ ἐνεργήματα δυνάμεων, ἄλλῳ
and to another operations of powers, to another
[δὲ] προφητεία, ἄλλῳ δὲ διακρίσεις πνευ-
and prophecy, and to another discernings of
μάτων, ἑτέρῳ γένη γλωσσῶν, ἄλλῳ δὲ
spirits, to another kinds of tongues, and to another

* It is thought that there is a scribal error in this verse; see commentaries on the Greek text. We have been guided by G. G. Findlay, *The Expositor's Greek Testament*.

to another the interpretation of tongues. [11]All these are inspired by one and the same Spirit, who apportions to each one individually as he wills.

[12] For just as the body is one and has many members, and all the members of the body, though many, are one body, so it is with Christ. [13]For by one Spirit we were all baptized into one body—Jews or Greeks, slaves or free—and all were made to drink of one Spirit.

[14] For the body does not consist of one member but of many. [15]If the foot should say, "Because I am not a hand, I do not belong to the body," that would not make it any less a part of the body. [16]And if the ear should say, "Because I am not an eye, I do not belong to the body," that would not make it any less a part of the body. [17]If the whole body were an eye, where would be the hearing? If the whole body were an ear, where would be the sense of smell? [18]But as it is, God arranged the organs in the body, each one of them, as he chose. [19]If all were a single organ, where would the body be? [20]As it is, there are

ἑρμηνεία   γλωσσῶν·   11 πάντα   δὲ   ταῦτα
interpretation   of tongues: and [8]all   [9]these things

ἐνεργεῖ   τὸ   ἓν   καὶ   τὸ   αὐτὸ   πνεῦμα,
[7]operates   [1]the   [2]one   [3]and   [4]the   [5]same   [6]Spirit,

διαιροῦν   ἰδίᾳ   ἑκάστῳ   καθὼς   βούλεται.
distributing [2]separately† [1]to each one   as   he purposes.

12 Καθάπερ   γὰρ   τὸ   σῶμα   ἕν   ἐστιν
   For as   the   body   [3]one   [1]is

καὶ   μέλη   πολλὰ   ἔχει,   πάντα   δὲ   τὰ
and   [3]members   [2]many   [1]has,   but all   the

μέλη   τοῦ   σώματος   πολλὰ   ὄντα   ἕν   ἐστιν
members of the   body   [2]many   [1]being   [4]one   [3]is(are)

σῶμα,   οὕτως   καὶ   ὁ   Χριστός·   13 καὶ   γὰρ
body,   so   also   the   Christ;   for indeed

ἐν   ἑνὶ   πνεύματι   ἡμεῖς   πάντες   εἰς   ἓν
[4]by   [5]one   [6]Spirit   [1]we   [2]all   [7]into   [8]one

σῶμα   ἐβαπτίσθημεν,   εἴτε   Ἰουδαῖοι   εἴτε
[9]body   [3]were baptized,   whether   Jews   or

Ἕλληνες,   εἴτε   δοῦλοι   εἴτε   ἐλεύθεροι,   καὶ
Greeks,   whether   slaves   or   free,   and

πάντες   ἓν   πνεῦμα   ἐποτίσθημεν.   14 καὶ
all   one   Spirit   we were given to drink.   indeed

γὰρ   τὸ   σῶμα   οὐκ   ἔστιν   ἓν   μέλος   ἀλλὰ
For   the   body   is not   one member   but

πολλά.   15 ἐὰν   εἴπῃ   ὁ   πούς·   ὅτι   οὐκ
many.   If   [2]says   [1]the   [2]foot: Because   not

εἰμὶ   χείρ,   οὐκ   εἰμὶ   ἐκ   τοῦ   σώματος,
I am   a hand,   I am not   of   the   body,

οὐ   παρὰ   τοῦτο   οὐκ   ἔστιν   ἐκ   τοῦ   σώματος.
not   for   this   it is not   of   the   body.

16 καὶ   ἐὰν   εἴπῃ   τὸ   οὖς·   ὅτι   οὐκ   εἰμὶ
  And   if   says   the   ear: Because   not   I am not

ὀφθαλμός,   οὐκ   εἰμὶ   ἐκ   τοῦ   σώματος,
an eye,   I am not   of   the   body,

οὐ   παρὰ   τοῦτο   οὐκ   ἔστιν   ἐκ   τοῦ   σώματος.
not   for   this   it is not   of   the   body.

17 εἰ   ὅλον   τὸ   σῶμα   ὀφθαλμός,   ποῦ
  If   all   the   body   [was] an eye,   where

ἡ   ἀκοή;   εἰ   ὅλον   ἀκοή,   ποῦ   ἡ   ὄσφρησις;
[would be]   if   all   hearing,   where the   smelling?
the hearing?

18 νῦν   δὲ   ὁ   θεὸς   ἔθετο   τὰ   μέλη,   ἓν
  But now   –   God   set   the   members,   [2]one

ἕκαστον   αὐτῶν   ἐν   τῷ   σώματι   καθὼς
[1]each   of them   in   the   body   as

ἠθέλησεν.   19 εἰ   δὲ   ἦν   τὰ   πάντα   ἓν
he wished.   And if   [2]was   –   [1]all   one

μέλος,   ποῦ   τὸ   σῶμα;   20 νῦν   δὲ   πολλὰ
member,   where   the   body?   But now   many

many parts, yet one body. 21 The eye cannot say to the hand, "I have no need of you," nor again the head to the feet, "I have no need of you." 22 On the contrary, the parts of the body which seem to be weaker are indispensable, 23 and those parts of the body which we think less honorable we invest with the greater honor, and our unpresentable parts are treated with greater modesty, 24 which our more presentable parts do not require. But God has so adjusted the body, giving the greater honor to the inferior part, 25 that there may be no discord in the body, but that the members may have the same care for one another. 26 If one member suffers, all suffer together; if one member is honored, all rejoice together.

27 Now you are the body of Christ and individually members of it. 28 And God has appointed in the church first apostles, second prophets, third teachers, then workers of miracles, then healers, helpers,

μὲν μέλη, ἐν δὲ σῶμα. 21 οὐ δύναται
²indeed ¹members, but one body. ²cannot

δὲ ὁ ὀφθαλμὸς εἰπεῖν τῇ χειρί· χρείαν
And ¹the ²eye to say to the hand: Need

σου οὐκ ἔχω, ἢ πάλιν ἡ κεφαλὴ τοῖς
of thee I have not, or again the head to the

ποσίν· χρείαν ὑμῶν οὐκ ἔχω· 22 ἀλλὰ
feet: Need of you I have not; but

πολλῷ μᾶλλον τὰ δοκοῦντα μέλη τοῦ
by much more ¹the ²seeming ³members ⁴of the

σώματος ἀσθενέστερα ὑπάρχειν ἀναγκαῖά ἐστιν,
⁴body ⁷weaker ⁶to be ⁹necessary ⁸is(are),

23 καὶ ἃ δοκοῦμεν ἀτιμότερα εἶναι
and ¹[members] ⁵we think ⁷less honourable ⁶to be
⁴which

τοῦ σώματος, τούτοις τιμὴν περισσοτέραν
²of the ³body, to these honour more abundant

περιτίθεμεν, καὶ τὰ ἀσχήμονα ἡμῶν
we put round, and the uncomely [members] of us

εὐσχημοσύνην περισσοτέραν ἔχει, 24 τὰ δὲ
²comeliness ³more abundant ¹has(ve), but th⌐

εὐσχήμονα ἡμῶν οὐ χρείαν ἔχει. ἀλλὰ ὁ
comely [members] of us ²no ³need ¹has(ve). But —

θεὸς συνεκέρασεν τὸ σῶμα, τῷ ὑστερουμένῳ
God blended together the body, ⁴to the [member] ⁵lacking

περισσοτέραν δοὺς τιμήν, 25 ἵνα μὴ ᾖ
²more abundant ¹giving ³honour, lest there be

σχίσμα ἐν τῷ σώματι, ἀλλὰ τὸ αὐτὸ
division in the body, but ⁴the ⁵same

ὑπὲρ ἀλλήλων μεριμνῶσιν τὰ μέλη.
⁶on behalf of ⁷one another ³should care ¹the ²members.

26 καὶ εἴτε πάσχει ἐν μέλος, συμπάσχει
And whether ³suffers ¹one ²member, ⁷suffers with [it]

πάντα τὰ μέλη· εἴτε δοξάζεται μέλος,
⁴all ⁵the ⁶members; or ²is glorified ¹a member,

συγχαίρει πάντα τὰ μέλη. 27 ὑμεῖς
⁶rejoices with [it] ³all ⁴the ⁵members. ye

δέ ἐστε σῶμα Χριστοῦ καὶ μέλη ἐκ
And are a body of Christ and members in

μέρους. 28 Καὶ οὓς μὲν ἔθετο ὁ θεὸς
part. And ³some† ²placed — ¹God

ἐν τῇ ἐκκλησίᾳ πρῶτον ἀποστόλους, δεύτε-
in the church firstly apostles, second-

ρον προφήτας, τρίτον διδασκάλους, ἔπειτα
ly prophets, thirdly teachers, then

δυνάμεις, ἔπειτα χαρίσματα ἰαμάτων,
powers, then gifts of cures,

administrators, speakers in various kinds of tongues. 29 Are all apostles? Are all prophets? Are all teachers? Do all work miracles? 30 Do all possess gifts of healing? Do all speak with tongues? Do all interpret? 31 But earnestly desire the higher gifts.

And I will show you a still more excellent way.

CHAPTER 13

IF I speak in the tongues of men and of angels, but have not love, I am a noisy gong or a clanging cymbal. 2 And if I have prophetic powers, and understand all mysteries and all knowledge, and if I have all faith, so as to remove mountains, but have not love, I am nothing. 3 If I give away all I have, and if I deliver my body to be burned,[q] but have not love, I gain nothing.

4 Love is patient and kind; love is not jealous or boastful; 5 it is not arrogant or rude. Love does not insist on its own way; it is not irritable or resentful; 6 it does not rejoice at wrong, but

[q] Other ancient authorities read *body that I may glory*

ἀντιλήμψεις, κυβερνήσεις, γένη γλωσσῶν,
helps, governings, kinds of tongues.

29 μὴ πάντες ἀπόστολοι; μὴ πάντες
Not all [are] apostles? not all

προφῆται; μὴ πάντες διδάσκαλοι; μὴ
prophets; not all teachers? not

πάντες δυνάμεις; 30 μὴ πάντες χαρίσματα
all powers? not all [2]gifts

ἔχουσιν ἰαμάτων; μὴ πάντες γλώσσαις
[1]have of cures? not all [2]with tongues

λαλοῦσιν; μὴ πάντες διερμηνεύουσιν;
[1]speak? not all interpret?

31 ζηλοῦτε δὲ τὰ χαρίσματα τὰ μείζονα.
but desire ye eagerly the [2]gifts – [1]greater.

Καὶ ἔτι καθ' ὑπερβολὴν ὁδὸν ὑμῖν
And yet [4]according to [5]excellence [3]a way [2]to you

δείκνυμι. 13 Ἐὰν ταῖς γλώσσαις τῶν ἀνθρώπων
[1]I show. If in the tongues – of men

λαλῶ καὶ τῶν ἀγγέλων, ἀγάπην δὲ
I speak and – of angels, but love

μὴ ἔχω, γέγονα χαλκὸς ἠχῶν ἢ
I have not, I have become [2]brass [1]sounding or

κύμβαλον ἀλαλάζον. 2 καὶ ἐὰν ἔχω
cymbal a tinkling. And if I have

προφητείαν καὶ εἰδῶ τὰ μυστήρια πάντα
prophecy and know [2]the [3]mysteries [1]all

καὶ πᾶσαν τὴν γνῶσιν, κἂν ἔχω πᾶσαν
and all – knowledge, and if I have all

τὴν πίστιν ὥστε ὄρη μεθιστάναι, ἀγάπην
– faith so as mountains to remove, [2]love

δὲ μὴ ἔχω, οὐθέν εἰμι. 3 κἂν ψωμίσω
[1]but I have not, nothing I am. And if I dole out

πάντα τὰ ὑπάρχοντά μου, καὶ ἐὰν παραδῶ
all the goods of me, and if I deliver

τὸ σῶμά μου ἵνα καυθήσομαι, ἀγάπην
the body of me in order that I shall be burned, [2]love

δὲ μὴ ἔχω, οὐδὲν ὠφελοῦμαι. 4 Ἡ
[1]but I have not, nothing I am profited. –

ἀγάπη μακροθυμεῖ, χρηστεύεται ἡ ἀγάπη,
Love suffers long, is kind – love,

οὐ ζηλοῖ, ἡ ἀγάπη οὐ περπερεύεται,
is not jealous, – love does not vaunt itself,

οὐ φυσιοῦται, 5 οὐκ ἀσχημονεῖ, οὐ ζητεῖ
is not puffed up, does not act unbecomingly, does not seek

τὰ ἑαυτῆς, οὐ παροξύνεται, οὐ λογίζεται
the things of her(it)self, is not provoked, does not reckon

τὸ κακόν, 6 οὐ χαίρει ἐπὶ τῇ ἀδικίᾳ,
the evil, rejoices not over the wrong,

rejoices in the right. ⁷Love bears all things, believes all things, hopes all things, endures all things.

8 Love never ends; as for prophecies, they will pass away; as for tongues, they will cease; as for knowledge, it will pass away. ⁹For our knowledge is imperfect and our prophecy is imperfect; ¹⁰but when the perfect comes, the imperfect will pass away. ¹¹When I was a child, I spoke like a child, I thought like a child, I reasoned like a child; when I became a man, I gave up childish ways. ¹²For now we see in a mirror dimly, but then face to face. Now I know in part; then I shall understand fully, even as I have been fully understood. ¹³So faith, hope, love abide, these three; but the greatest of these is love.

συγχαίρει δὲ τῇ ἀληθείᾳ· 7 πάντα στέγει,
but rejoices with the truth; all things covers,

πάντα πιστεύει, πάντα ἐλπίζει, πάντα
all things believes, all things hopes, all things

ὑπομένει. 8 Ἡ ἀγάπη οὐδέποτε πίπτει·
endures. – Love never falls;

εἴτε δὲ προφητεῖαι, καταργηθήσονται· εἴτε
but whether prophecies, they will be abolished; or

γλῶσσαι, παύσονται· εἴτε γνῶσις, κατ-
tongues, they will cease; or knowledge, it will

αργηθήσεται. 9 ἐκ μέρους γὰρ γινώσκομεν
be abolished. For in part we know

καὶ ἐκ μέρους προφητεύομεν· 10 ὅταν
and in part we prophesy; ²when

δὲ ἔλθῃ τὸ τέλειον, τὸ ἐκ μέρους
¹but ⁵comes ³the ⁴perfect thing, the thing in part

καταργηθήσεται. 11 ὅτε ἤμην νήπιος,
will be abolished. When I was an infant,

ἐλάλουν ὡς νήπιος, ἐφρόνουν ὡς νήπιος,
I spoke as an infant, I thought as an infant,

ἐλογιζόμην ὡς νήπιος· ὅτε γέγονα ἀνήρ,
I reckoned as an infant; when I have become a man,

κατήργηκα τὰ τοῦ νηπίου. 12 βλέπομεν
I have the of the infant. we see
abolished things

γὰρ ἄρτι δι' ἐσόπτρου ἐν αἰνίγματι,
For yet through a mirror in a riddle,

τότε δὲ πρόσωπον πρὸς πρόσωπον· ἄρτι
but then face to face; yet

γινώσκω ἐκ μέρους, τότε δὲ ἐπιγνώσομαι
I know in part, but then I shall fully know

καθὼς καὶ ἐπεγνώσθην. 13 νυνὶ δὲ μένει
as also I was fully known. But now remains

πίστις, ἐλπίς, ἀγάπη, τὰ τρία ταῦτα·
faith, hope, love, these three;

μείζων δὲ τούτων ἡ ἀγάπη.
and [the] greater of these [is] – love.

CHAPTER 14

MAKE love your aim, and earnestly desire the spiritual gifts, especially that you may prophesy. ²For one who speaks in a tongue speaks not to men but to God; for no one understands him, but he utters mysteries in the Spirit.

14 Διώκετε τὴν ἀγάπην, ζηλοῦτε δὲ
Pursue ye – love, but desire eagerly

τὰ πνευματικά, μᾶλλον δὲ ἵνα προφητεύητε.
the spiritual [gifts], and rather in order ye may prophesy.
that

2 ὁ γὰρ λαλῶν γλώσσῃ οὐκ ἀνθρώποις
For the [one] speaking in a tongue ²not ·to men

λαλεῖ ἀλλὰ θεῷ· οὐδεὶς γὰρ ἀκούει,
¹speaks but to God; for no one hears,

πνεύματι δὲ λαλεῖ μυστήρια· 3 ὁ δὲ
but in spirit he speaks mysteries; but the [one]

³On the other hand, he who prophesies speaks to men for their upbuilding and encouragement and consolation. ⁴He who speaks in a tongue edifies himself, but he who prophesies edifies the church. ⁵Now I want you all to speak in tongues, but even more to prophesy. He who prophesies is greater than he who speaks in tongues unless some one interprets, so that the church may be edified.

6 Now, brethren, if I come to you speaking in tongues, how shall I benefit you unless I bring you some revelation or knowledge or prophecy or teaching? ⁷If even lifeless instruments, such as the flute or the harp, do not give distinct notes, how will any one know what is played? ⁸And if the bugle gives an indistinct sound, who will get ready for battle? ⁹So with yourselves; if you in a tongue utter speech that is not intelligible, how will any one know what is said? For you will be speaking into the air. ¹⁰There are doubtless many different languages in the world,

---

προφητεύων ἀνθρώποις λαλεῖ οἰκοδομὴν καὶ
prophesying to men speaks edification and

παράκλησιν καὶ παραμυθίαν. 4 ὁ λαλῶν
encouragement and consolation. The [one] speaking

γλώσσῃ ἑαυτὸν οἰκοδομεῖ· ὁ δὲ προφητεύων
in a tongue himself edifies; but the [one] prophesying

ἐκκλησίαν οἰκοδομεῖ. 5 θέλω δὲ πάντας
a church edifies. Now I wish all

ὑμᾶς λαλεῖν γλώσσαις, μᾶλλον δὲ ἵνα
you to speak in tongues, but rather in order that

προφητεύητε· μείζων δὲ ὁ προφητεύων ἢ
ye may prophesy; and greater the [one] prophesying than

ὁ λαλῶν γλώσσαις, ἐκτὸς εἰ μὴ διερμηνεύῃ,
the speaking in tongues, except unless he interprets,
[one]

ἵνα ἡ ἐκκλησία οἰκοδομὴν λάβη. 6 νῦν δέ,
in or- the church edification may receive. But now,
der that

ἀδελφοί, ἐὰν ἔλθω πρὸς ὑμᾶς γλώσσαις
brothers, if I come to you in tongues

λαλῶν, τί ὑμᾶς ὠφελήσω, ἐὰν μὴ ὑμῖν
speaking, what ²you ¹shall I profit, except ²to you

λαλήσω ἢ ἐν ἀποκαλύψει ἢ ἐν γνώσει
¹I speak either in a revelation or in knowledge

ἢ ἐν προφητείᾳ ἢ διδαχῇ; 7 ὅμως τὰ
or in prophecy or in teaching? Yet -

ἄψυχα φωνὴν διδόντα, εἴτε αὐλὸς εἴτε
lifeless things ²a sound ¹giving, whether pipe or

κιθάρα, ἐὰν διαστολὴν τοῖς φθόγγοις μὴ
harp, if ²a distinction ⁴in the ³sounds ¹not

δῷ, πῶς γνωσθήσεται τὸ αὐλούμενον ἢ
¹they how will it be known the being piped or
give,
thing

τὸ κιθαριζόμενον; 8 καὶ γὰρ ἐὰν ἄδηλον
the being harped? For indeed if ²an
thing uncertain

σάλπιγξ φωνὴν δῷ, τίς παρασκευάσεται
¹a trumpet ⁴sound ³gives, who will prepare himself

εἰς πόλεμον; 9 οὕτως καὶ ὑμεῖς διὰ
for war? so also ¹ye ⁴through

τῆς γλώσσης ἐὰν μὴ εὔσημον λόγον
⁷the ⁸tongue ¹unless ⁴a clear ⁵word

δῶτε, πῶς γνωσθήσεται τὸ λαλούμενον;
²give, how will it be known the thing being said?

ἔσεσθε γὰρ εἰς ἀέρα λαλοῦντες. 10 τοσαῦτα
for ¹ye will be ²into ⁴air ³speaking. ²So many

εἰ τύχοι γένη φωνῶν εἰσιν ἐν κόσμῳ,
²it may be† ⁴kinds ⁵of sounds ¹there are in [the] world,

and none is without meaning; ¹¹but if I do not know the meaning of the language, I shall be a foreigner to the speaker and the speaker a foreigner to me. ¹²So with yourselves; since you are eager for manifestations of the Spirit, strive to excel in building up the church.

13 Therefore, he who speaks in a tongue should pray for the power to interpret. ¹⁴For if I pray in a tongue, my spirit prays but my mind is unfruitful. ¹⁵What am I to do? I will pray with the spirit and I will pray with the mind also; I will sing with the spirit and I will sing with the mind also. ¹⁶Otherwise, if you bless^r with the spirit, how can any one in the position of an outsider^s say the "Amen" to your thanksgiving when he does not know what you are saying? ¹⁷For you may give thanks well enough, but the other man is not edified. ¹⁸I thank God that I speak in tongues more than you all; ¹⁹nevertheless, in church I would rather speak five words with my mind, in order to instruct others, than ten thousand

^r That is, *give thanks to God*
^s Or *him that is without gifts*

καὶ   οὐδὲν   ἄφωνον·   11 ἐὰν   οὖν   μὴ   εἰδῶ
and   not one [is]   voiceless;   if   therefore   I know not
τὴν   δύναμιν   τῆς   φωνῆς,   ἔσομαι   τῷ
the   power   of the   sound,   I shall be   to the
λαλοῦντι   βάρβαρος   καὶ   ὁ   λαλῶν   ἐν   ἐμοὶ
[one] speaking   a foreigner   and   the   speaking   in(to)   me
                                        [one]
βάρβαρος.   12 οὕτως   καὶ   ὑμεῖς,   ἐπεὶ
a foreigner.   So   also   ye,   since
ζηλωταί   ἐστε   πνευμάτων,   πρὸς   τὴν
zealots   ye are   of spirit[ual thing]s,   ²to   ³the
οἰκοδομὴν   τῆς   ἐκκλησίας   ζητεῖτε   ἵνα   περισ-
⁴edification   ⁵of the   ⁶church   ¹seek ye   in order   ye may
                                        that
σεύητε.   13 Διὸ   ὁ   λαλῶν   γλώσσῃ   προσευχ-
abound.   Wherefore   the   speaking   in a tongue   let him
                        [one]
έσθω   ἵνα   διερμηνεύῃ.   14 ἐὰν   γὰρ   προσεύχωμαι
pray   in order   he may   For if   I pray
        that   interpret.
γλώσσῃ,   τὸ   πνεῦμά   μου   προσεύχεται,
in a tongue,   the   spirit   of me   prays,
ὁ   δὲ   νοῦς   μου   ἄκαρπός   ἐστιν.   15 τί
but the   mind   of me   unfruitful   is.   What
οὖν   ἐστιν;   προσεύξομαι   τῷ   πνεύματι,
therefore   is it?   I will pray   with the   spirit,
προσεύξομαι   δὲ   καὶ   τῷ   νοΐ·   ψαλῶ   τῷ
²I will pray   ¹and   ³also   with   mind;   I will   with
                        the   sing   the
πνεύματι,   ψαλῶ   δὲ   καὶ   τῷ   νοΐ.   16 ἐπεὶ
spirit,   ²I will sing   ¹and   ³also   with the mind.   Otherwise
ἐὰν   εὐλογῇς   [ἐν]   πνεύματι,   ὁ   ἀναπληρῶν
if   thou blessest   in   spirit,   the [one]   occupying
τὸν   τόπον   τοῦ   ἰδιώτου   πῶς   ἐρεῖ   τὸ
the   place   of the   uninstructed   how   will he say   the
ἀμὴν   ἐπὶ   τῇ   σῇ   εὐχαριστίᾳ;   ἐπειδὴ   τί
"amen"   at   -   thy   giving thanks?   Since   what
λέγεις   οὐκ   οἶδεν·   17 σὺ   μὲν   γὰρ   καλῶς
thou sayest   he knows not;   ²thou   ³indeed   ¹for   ⁴well
εὐχαριστεῖς,   ἀλλ'   ὁ   ἕτερος   οὐκ   οἰκοδομεῖται.
⁴givest thanks,   but   the   other   is not edified.
18 εὐχαριστῶ   τῷ   θεῷ,   πάντων   ὑμῶν   μᾶλ-
I give thanks   -   to God,   ²all   ⁴you   ⁵more
λον   γλώσσαις   λαλῶ·   19 ἀλλὰ   ἐν   ἐκκλησίᾳ
than   ³in tongues   ¹I speak;   but   in   a church
θέλω   πέντε   λόγους   τῷ   νοΐ   μου   λαλῆσαι,
¹I wish   ²five   ⁴words   ⁵with the   ⁶mind   ⁷of me   ³to speak,
ἵνα   καὶ   ἄλλους   κατηχήσω,   ἢ   μυρίους
in or-   also   others   I may instruct,   than   ten
der that   thousands

words in a tongue.
20 Brethren, do not be children in your thinking; be babes in evil, but in thinking be mature. 21 In the law it is written, "By men of strange tongues and by the lips of foreigners will I speak to this people, and even then they will not listen to me, says the Lord." 22 Thus, tongues are a sign not for believers but for unbelievers, while prophecy is not for unbelievers but for believers. 23 If, therefore, the whole church assembles and all speak in tongues, and outsiders or unbelievers enter, will they not say that you are mad? 24 But if all prophesy, and an unbeliever or outsider enters, he is convicted by all, he is called to account by all, 25 the secrets of his heart are disclosed; and so, falling on his face, he will worship God and declare that God is really among you.
26 What then, brethren? When you come together, each one has a hymn, a lesson, a revelation, a tongue, or an interpretation. Let all

λόγους ἐν γλώσσῃ. 20 Ἀδελφοί, μὴ
words in a tongue. Brothers, ²not

παιδία γίνεσθε ταῖς φρεσίν, ἀλλὰ τῇ
³children ¹be ye in the(your) minds, but –

κακίᾳ νηπιάζετε, ταῖς δὲ φρεσὶν τέλειοι
in malice be ye infantlike, and in the(your) minds mature

γίνεσθε. 21 ἐν τῷ νόμῳ γέγραπται ὅτι
be ye. In the law it has been written that

ἐν ἑτερογλώσσοις καὶ ἐν χείλεσιν ἑτέρων
in other tongues and in lips of others

λαλήσω τῷ λαῷ τούτῳ, καὶ οὐδ' οὕτως
I will speak to this people, and not so

εἰσακούσονταί μου, λέγει κύριος. 22 ὥστε
will they hear me, says [the] Lord. So as

αἱ γλῶσσαι εἰς σημεῖόν εἰσιν οὐ τοῖς
the tongues ²for ²a sign ¹are not to the

πιστεύουσιν ἀλλὰ τοῖς ἀπίστοις, ἡ δὲ
[ones] believing but to the unbelievers, and the

προφητεία οὐ τοῖς ἀπίστοις ἀλλὰ τοῖς
prophecy [is] not to the unbelievers but to the

πιστεύουσιν. 23 Ἐὰν οὖν συνέλθῃ ἡ
[ones] believing. If therefore ⁴comes ¹the together

ἐκκλησία ὅλη ἐπὶ τὸ αὐτὸ καὶ πάντες
³church ²whole together and all

λαλῶσιν γλώσσαις, εἰσέλθωσιν δὲ ἰδιῶται
speak in tongues, and ⁴enter ¹uninstructed

ἢ ἄπιστοι, οὐκ ἐροῦσιν ὅτι μαίνεσθε;
²or ³unbelievers, will they not say that ye rave?

24 ἐὰν δὲ πάντες προφητεύωσιν, εἰσέλθῃ δέ
but if all prophesy, and ⁵enters

τις ἄπιστος ἢ ἰδιώτης, ἐλέγχεται ὑπὸ
¹some ²unbeliever ³or ⁴uninstructed, he is convicted by

πάντων, ἀνακρίνεται ὑπὸ πάντων, 25 τὰ
all, he is judged by all, the

κρυπτὰ τῆς καρδίας αὐτοῦ φανερὰ γίνεται,
hidden of the heart of him ²manifest ¹becomes, things

καὶ οὕτως πεσὼν ἐπὶ πρόσωπον προσκυνή-
and so falling on [his] face he will wor-

σει τῷ θεῷ, ἀπαγγέλλων ὅτι ὄντως
ship – God, declaring that really

ὁ θεὸς ἐν ὑμῖν ἐστιν. 26 Τί οὖν ἐστιν,
– God ²among ³you ¹is. What therefore is it,

ἀδελφοί; ὅταν συνέρχησθε, ἕκαστος ψαλμὸν
brothers? whenever ye come together, each one a psalm

ἔχει, διδαχὴν ἔχει, ἀποκάλυψιν ἔχει, γλῶσ-
has, a teaching he has, a revelation he has, a

σαν ἔχει, ἑρμηνείαν ἔχει· πάντα πρὸς
tongue he has, an interpretation he has; ²all things ⁴for

things be done for edification. ²⁷If any speak in a tongue, let there be only two or at most three, and each in turn; and let one interpret. ²⁸But if there is no one to interpret, let each of them keep silence in church and speak to himself and to God. ²⁹Let two or three prophets speak, and let the others weigh what is said. ³⁰If a revelation is made to another sitting by, let the first be silent. ³¹For you can all prophesy one by one, so that all may learn and all be encouraged; ³²and the spirits of prophets are subject to prophets. ³³For God is not a God of confusion but of peace.

As in all the churches of the saints, ³⁴the women should keep silence in the churches. For they are not permitted to speak, but should be subordinate, as even the law says. ³⁵If there is anything they desire to know, let them ask their husbands at home. For it is shameful for a woman to speak in church. ³⁶What! Did the word of God originate with you, or are you the only ones it has reached?

37 If any one thinks that he is a prophet, or spiritual, he should

οἰκοδομὴν γινέσθω.   27 εἴτε γλώσσῃ τις
ᵇedification   ¹let ᵃbe.   If in a tongue anyone

λαλεῖ, κατὰ δύο ἢ τὸ πλεῖστον τρεῖς,
speaks, by two or the most three,

καὶ ἀνὰ μέρος,   28 καὶ εἷς διερμηνευέτω·
and in turn,†   and ᵃone ¹let ³interpret;

ἐὰν δὲ μὴ ᾖ διερμηνευτής, σιγάτω ἐν
but if there is not an interpreter, let him be silent in

ἐκκλησίᾳ, ἑαυτῷ δὲ λαλείτω καὶ τῷ
church, and to himself let him speak and -

θεῷ.   29 προφῆται δὲ δύο ἢ τρεῖς λαλεί-
to God.   And prophets two or three let them

τωσαν,   30 καὶ οἱ ἄλλοι διακρινέτωσαν·
speak, and the others let discern;

ἐὰν δὲ ἄλλῳ ἀποκαλυφθῇ καθημένῳ, ὁ
but if ¹to another ³[something] ²sitting, the
⁴is revealed

πρῶτος σιγάτω.   31 δύνασθε γὰρ καθ'
first let be silent.   For ye can ²sin-

ἕνα πάντες προφητεύειν, ἵνα πάντες
gly†   ¹all   ²to prophesy, in order that all

μανθάνωσιν καὶ πάντες παρακαλῶνται.
may learn and all may be encouraged.

32 καὶ πνεύματα προφητῶν προφήταις
And [the] spirits of prophets to prophets

ὑποτάσσεται·   33 οὐ γάρ ἐστιν ἀκαταστασίας
is(are) subject;   for ³not ²is ⁴of tumult

ὁ θεὸς ἀλλὰ εἰρήνης.   Ὡς ἐν πάσαις
- ¹God but of peace.   As in all

ταῖς ἐκκλησίαις τῶν ἁγίων, 34 αἱ γυναῖκες
the churches of the saints, ¹the ³women

ἐν ταῖς ἐκκλησίαις σιγάτωσαν· οὐ γὰρ
ᵃin ⁶the ⁷churches ¹let ⁴be silent; ³not ¹for

ἐπιτρέπεται αὐταῖς λαλεῖν, ἀλλὰ ὑποτασ-
²it is ⁴permitted to them to speak, but let them

σέσθωσαν, καθὼς καὶ ὁ νόμος λέγει.
be subject, as also the law says.

35 εἰ δέ τι μαθεῖν θέλουσιν, ἐν οἴκῳ
But if ³anything ²to learn ¹they wish, ⁵at home

τοὺς ἰδίους ἄνδρας ἐπερωτάτωσαν· αἰσχρὸν
³the(ir) ⁴own ⁵husbands ¹let them question; ²a shame

γάρ ἐστιν γυναικὶ λαλεῖν ἐν ἐκκλησίᾳ.
¹for ²it is for a woman to speak in a church.

36 ἢ ἀφ' ὑμῶν ὁ λόγος τοῦ θεοῦ ἐξῆλθεν,
Or from you ²the ³word - ⁴of God ¹went forth,

ἢ εἰς ὑμᾶς μόνους κατήντησεν;   37 Εἴ
or to you only did it reach?   If

τις δοκεῖ προφήτης εἶναι ἢ πνευματικός,
anyone thinks ²a prophet ¹to be or a spiritual man,

acknowledge that what I am writing to you is a command of the Lord. ³⁸If any one does not recognize this, he is not recognized. ³⁹So, my brethren, earnestly desire to prophesy, and do not forbid speaking in tongues; ⁴⁰but all things should be done decently and in order.

ἐπιγινωσκέτω   ἃ   γράφω   ὑμῖν   ὅτι
let him clearly   [the] things   I write   to you   that
know   which

κυρίου   ἐστὶν   ἐντολή·   38 εἰ   δέ   τις
of [the] Lord they are   a commandment;   but if   anyone

ἀγνοεῖ,   ἀγνοεῖται.   39 Ὥστε,   ἀδελφοί
is ignorant, let him be ignorant.   So as,   brothers

μου,   ζηλοῦτε   τὸ   προφητεύειν,   καὶ   τὸ
of me, be ye eager   –   to prophesy,   and   –

λαλεῖν   μὴ   κωλύετε   γλώσσαις·   40 πάντα
²to speak   ¹forbid not   in tongues;   ²all things

δὲ   εὐσχημόνως   καὶ   κατὰ   τάξιν   γινέσθω.
and   ⁴becomingly   ⁵and ⁶according to ⁷order   ¹let ³be done.

CHAPTER 15

NOW I would remind you, brethren, in what terms I preached to you the gospel, which you received, in which you stand, ²by which you are saved, if you hold it fast—unless you believed in vain.

3 For I delivered to you as of first importance what I also received, that Christ died for our sins in accordance with the scriptures, ⁴that he was buried, that he was raised on the third day in accordance with the scriptures, ⁵and that he appeared to Cephas, then to the twelve. ⁶Then he appeared to more than five hundred brethren at one time, most of whom are still alive, though some have fallen asleep. ⁷Then he appeared to James, then to all the apostles. ⁸Last of all, as

15 Γνωρίζω   δὲ   ὑμῖν,   ἀδελφοί,   τὸ
Now I make known   to you,   brothers,   the

εὐαγγέλιον   ὃ   εὐηγγελισάμην   ὑμῖν,   ὃ   καὶ
good tidings   which   I preached   to you, which also

παρελάβετε,   ἐν   ᾧ   καὶ   ἑστήκατε,   2 δι᾽
ye received,   in which also   ye stand,   through

οὗ   καὶ   σώζεσθε,   τίνι   λόγῳ   εὐηγγελισάμην
which also   ye are saved,   ³to what ⁴word   ⁵I preached

ὑμῖν   εἰ   κατέχετε,   ἐκτὸς   εἰ   μὴ   εἰκῇ
⁶to you   ¹if   ²ye hold fast,   except   unless   in vain

ἐπιστεύσατε.   3 παρέδωκα   γὰρ   ὑμῖν   ἐν
ye believed.   For I delivered   to you among

πρώτοις,   ὃ   καὶ   παρέλαβον,   ὅτι   Χριστὸς
[the] first   what also   I received,   that   Christ
things,

ἀπέθανεν   ὑπὲρ   τῶν   ἁμαρτιῶν   ἡμῶν   κατὰ
died   on be-   the   sins   of us   accord-
half of   ing to

τὰς   γραφάς,   4 καὶ   ὅτι   ἐτάφη,   καὶ   ὅτι
the   scriptures,   and   that he was buried, and   that

ἐγήγερται   τῇ   ἡμέρᾳ   τῇ   τρίτῃ   κατὰ
he has   on the   ³day   –   ¹third   accord-
been raised   ing to

τὰς   γραφάς,   5 καὶ   ὅτι   ὤφθη   Κηφᾷ,
the   scriptures,   and   that   he was seen by Cephas,

εἶτα   τοῖς   δώδεκα·   6 ἔπειτα   ὤφθη   ἐπάνω
then   by the   twelve;   afterward he was seen   ²over

πεντακοσίοις   ἀδελφοῖς   ἐφάπαξ,   ἐξ   ὧν   οἱ
¹by ²five hundreds   brothers   at one time,   of whom the

πλείονες   μένουσιν   ἕως   ἄρτι,   τινὲς   δὲ
majority   remain   until   now,   though some

ἐκοιμήθησαν·   7 ἔπειτα   ὤφθη   Ἰακώβῳ,   εἶτα
fell asleep;   afterward he was seen by James,   then

τοῖς   ἀποστόλοις   πᾶσιν·   8 ἔσχατον   δὲ
by the   apostles   all;   and lastly

to one untimely born, he appeared also to me. ⁹For I am the least of the apostles, unfit to be called an apostle, because I persecuted the church of God. ¹⁰But by the grace of God I am what I am, and his grace toward me was not in vain. On the contrary, I worked harder than any of them, though it was not I, but the grace of God which is with me. ¹¹Whether then it was I or they, so we preach and so you believed.

12 Now if Christ is preached as raised from the dead, how can some of you say that there is no resurrection of the dead? ¹³But if there is no resurrection of the dead, then Christ has not been raised; ¹⁴if Christ has not been raised, then our preaching is in vain and your faith is in vain. ¹⁵We are even found to be misrepresenting God, because we testified of God that he raised Christ, whom he did not raise if it is true that the dead are not raised. ¹⁶For if the dead are not raised, then Christ has not been raised. ¹⁷If Christ has not been raised, your faith is

πάντων ὡσπερεὶ τῷ ἐκτρώματι ὤφθη
of all   even as if to the(an) abortion   he was seen
κἀμοί. 9 Ἐγὼ γάρ εἰμι ὁ ἐλάχιστος
by me also.   For I   am the   least
τῶν ἀποστόλων, ὃς οὐκ εἰμὶ ἱκανὸς
of the apostles,   who am not   sufficient
καλεῖσθαι ἀπόστολος, διότι ἐδίωξα τὴν
to be called   an apostle,   because I persecuted the
ἐκκλησίαν τοῦ θεοῦ· 10 χάριτι δὲ θεοῦ
church   -   of God;   but by [the] grace of God
εἰμι ὅ εἰμι, καὶ ἡ χάρις αὐτοῦ ἡ εἰς
I am what I am, and the grace of him - to
ἐμὲ οὐ κενὴ ἐγενήθη, ἀλλὰ περισσότερον
me not empty was, but ²more abundantly [than]
αὐτῶν πάντων ἐκοπίασα, οὐκ ἐγὼ δὲ
³them ⁴all   ¹I laboured, ²not ³I ¹yet
ἀλλὰ ἡ χάρις τοῦ θεοῦ σὺν ἐμοί. 11 εἴτε
but the grace - of God with me.   Whether
οὖν ἐγὼ εἴτε ἐκεῖνοι, οὕτως κηρύσσομεν
therefore I or those,   so   we proclaim
καὶ οὕτως ἐπιστεύσατε.
and   so   ye believed.

12 Εἰ δὲ Χριστὸς κηρύσσεται ὅτι ἐκ
But if   Christ   is proclaimed that from
νεκρῶν ἐγήγερται, πῶς λέγουσιν ἐν ὑμῖν
[the] dead he has been raised, how say ²among ¹you
τινες ὅτι ἀνάστασις νεκρῶν οὐκ ἔστιν;
¹some that a resurrection of dead persons there is not?
13 εἰ δὲ ἀνάστασις νεκρῶν οὐκ ἔστιν,
Now if   a resurrection of dead persons there is not,
οὐδὲ Χριστὸς ἐγήγερται· 14 εἰ δὲ Χριστὸς
neither Christ has been raised;   and if   Christ
οὐκ ἐγήγερται, κενὸν ἄρα τὸ κήρυγμα
has not been raised, empty then the proclamation
ἡμῶν, κενὴ καὶ ἡ πίστις ὑμῶν· 15 εὑρισκ-
of us, empty also the faith of you;   ²we are
όμεθα δὲ καὶ ψευδομάρτυρες τοῦ θεοῦ,
found ¹and also false witnesses - of God,
ὅτι ἐμαρτυρήσαμεν κατὰ τοῦ θεοῦ ὅτι
because we witnessed as to - God that
ἤγειρεν τὸν Χριστόν, ὃν οὐκ ἤγειρεν
he raised - Christ, whom he raised not
εἴπερ ἄρα νεκροὶ οὐκ ἐγείρονται. 16 εἰ
if then dead persons are not raised.   if
γὰρ νεκροὶ οὐκ ἐγείρονται, οὐδὲ Χριστὸς
For dead persons are not raised, neither Christ
ἐγήγερται· 17 εἰ δὲ Χριστὸς οὐκ ἐγήγερται,
has been raised; and if   Christ has not been raised,

futile and you are still in your sins. [18]Then those also who have fallen asleep in Christ have perished. [19]If for this life only we have hoped in Christ, we are of all men most to be pitied.

20 But in fact Christ has been raised from the dead, the first fruits of those who have fallen asleep. [21]For as by a man came death, by a man has come also the resurrection of the dead. [22]For as in Adam all die, so also in Christ shall all be made alive. [23]But each in his own order: Christ the first fruits, then at his coming those who belong to Christ. [24]Then comes the end, when he delivers the kingdom to God the Father after destroying every rule and every authority and power. [25]For he must reign until he has put all his enemies under his feet. [26]The last enemy to be destroyed is death. [27]"For God has put all things in subjection under his feet." But when it says, "All things are put in subjection under him," it is

ματαία ἡ πίστις ὑμῶν [ἐστιν], ἔτι ἐστὲ
¹useless ¹the ²faith ³of you ⁴is, ²still ¹ye are
ἐν ταῖς ἁμαρτίαις ὑμῶν. 18 ἄρα καὶ οἱ
in the sins of you. Then also the [ones]
κοιμηθέντες ἐν Χριστῷ ἀπώλοντο. 19 εἰ
having fallen asleep in Christ perished. If
ἐν τῇ ζωῇ ταύτῃ ἐν Χριστῷ ἠλπικότες
in this life ³in ⁴Christ ²having hoped
ἐσμὲν μόνον, ἐλεεινότεροι πάντων ἀνθρώπων
¹we are ⁵only, more pitiful [than] all men
ἐσμέν. 20 Νυνὶ δὲ Χριστὸς ἐγήγερται
we are. But now Christ has been raised
ἐκ νεκρῶν, ἀπαρχὴ τῶν κεκοιμημένων.
from [the] dead, firstfruit of the [ones] having fallen asleep.
21 ἐπειδὴ γὰρ δι' ἀνθρώπου θάνατος, καὶ
For since through a man death [came], also
δι' ἀνθρώπου ἀνάστασις νεκρῶν. 22 ὥσπερ
through a man a resurrection of dead persons as
[came].
γὰρ ἐν τῷ Ἀδὰμ πάντες ἀποθνῄσκουσιν,
For in - Adam all die,
οὕτως καὶ ἐν τῷ Χριστῷ πάντες ζωοποιη-
so also in - Christ all will be
θήσονται. 23 Ἕκαστος δὲ ἐν τῷ ἰδίῳ
made alive. But each one in the(his) own
τάγματι· ἀπαρχὴ Χριστός, ἔπειτα οἱ τοῦ
order: [the] Christ, afterward the -
firstfruit [ones]
Χριστοῦ ἐν τῇ παρουσίᾳ αὐτοῦ, 24 εἶτα
of Christ in the presence of him, then
τὸ τέλος, ὅταν παραδιδοῖ τὴν βασιλείαν
the end, whenever he delivers the kingdom
τῷ θεῷ καὶ πατρί, ὅταν καταργήσῃ
- to God even [the] Father, whenever he abolishes
πᾶσαν ἀρχὴν καὶ πᾶσαν ἐξουσίαν καὶ
all rule and all authority and
δύναμιν. 25 δεῖ γὰρ αὐτὸν βασιλεύειν
power. For it behoves him to reign
ἄχρι οὗ θῇ πάντας τοὺς ἐχθροὺς ὑπὸ
until he puts all the(his) enemies under
τοὺς πόδας αὐτοῦ. 26 ἔσχατος ἐχθρὸς
the feet of him. [The] last enemy
καταργεῖται ὁ θάνατος· πάντα γὰρ ὑπέταξεν
is abolished - death; for all things he subjected
ὑπὸ τοὺς πόδας αὐτοῦ. 27 ὅταν δὲ
under the feet of him. But whenever
εἴπῃ ὅτι πάντα ὑποτέτακται, δῆλον ὅτι
he says that all things have been subjected, [it is] clear that

plain that he is excepted who put all things under him. ²⁸ When all things are subjected to him, then the Son himself will also be subjected to him who put all things under him, that God may be everything to every one. 29 Otherwise, what do people mean by being baptized on behalf of the dead? If the dead are not raised at all, why are people baptized on their behalf? ³⁰ Why am I in peril every hour? ³¹ I protest, brethren, by my pride in you which I have in Christ Jesus our Lord, I die every day! ³² What do I gain if, humanly speaking, I fought with beasts at Ephesus? If the dead are not raised, "Let us eat and drink, for to-morrow we die." ³³ Do not be deceived: "Bad company ruins good morals." ³⁴ Come to your right mind, and sin no more. For some have no knowledge of God. I say this to your shame.

35 But some one will ask, "How are the dead raised? With what kind of body do they come?" ³⁶ You foolish man! What you sow does not come to life unless it dies.

ἐκτὸς τοῦ ὑποτάξαντος αὐτῷ τὰ πάντα.
[it is] the having to him - all
apart from [one] subjected things.

28 ὅταν δὲ ὑποταγῇ αὐτῷ τὰ πάντα,
But whenever is(are) subjected to him - all things,

τότε καὶ αὐτὸς ὁ υἱὸς ὑποταγήσεται
then also ³[him]self ¹the ²Son will be subjected

τῷ ὑποτάξαντι αὐτῷ τὰ πάντα, ἵνα
to the having to him - all in order
[one] subjected things, that

ᾖ ὁ θεὸς πάντα ἐν πᾶσιν. 29 Ἐπεὶ
²may - ¹God all in all. Other-
be things wise

τί ποιήσουσιν οἱ βαπτιζόμενοι ὑπὲρ τῶν
what will they do the [ones] being baptized on behalf of the

νεκρῶν; εἰ ὅλως νεκροὶ οὐκ ἐγείρονται,
dead? if actually dead persons are not raised,

τί καὶ βαπτίζονται ὑπὲρ αὐτῶν; 30 τί
why indeed are they baptized on behalf of them? why

καὶ ἡμεῖς κινδυνεύομεν πᾶσαν ὥραν;
also ²we ¹are ³in danger every hour?

31 καθ' ἡμέραν ἀποθνήσκω, νὴ τὴν
Daily I die, by -

ὑμετέραν καύχησιν, ἀδελφοί, ἣν ἔχω ἐν
your boasting, brothers, which I have in

Χριστῷ Ἰησοῦ τῷ κυρίῳ ἡμῶν. 32 εἰ
Christ Jesus the Lord of us. If

κατὰ ἄνθρωπον ἐθηριομάχησα ἐν Ἐφέσῳ,
according man I fought with wild in Ephesus,
to beasts

τί μοι τὸ ὄφελος; εἰ νεκροὶ οὐκ ἐγείρονται,
what to me the profit?⁰ If dead persons are not raised,
=what profit have I?

φάγωμεν καὶ πίωμεν, αὔριον γὰρ ἀποθνή-
let us eat and let us drink, for to-morrow we

σκομεν. 33 μὴ πλανᾶσθε· φθείρουσιν ἤθη
die. Be ye not led astray: ²Corrupt ⁵customs

χρηστὰ ὁμιλίαι κακαί. 34 ἐκνήψατε δικαίως
⁴good ²associations ¹bad. Become ye sober righteously

καὶ μὴ ἁμαρτάνετε· ἀγνωσίαν γὰρ θεοῦ
and do not sin; for ³ignorance ⁴of God

τινες ἔχουσιν· πρὸς ἐντροπὴν ὑμῖν λαλῶ.
¹some ²have: ³for ⁴shame ²to you ¹I speak.

35 Ἀλλὰ ἐρεῖ τις· πῶς ἐγείρονται οἱ
But ²will say ¹someone: How are raised the

νεκροί; ποίῳ δὲ σώματι ἔρχονται; 36 ἄφρων,
dead? and with what body do they Foolish
sort [of] come? man,

σὺ ὃ σπείρεις, οὐ ζωοποιεῖται ἐὰν μὴ
²thou ¹what sowest, is not made alive unless

³⁷And what you sow is not the body which is to be, but a bare kernel, perhaps of wheat or of some other grain. ³⁸But God gives it a body as he has chosen, and to each kind of seed its own body. ³⁹For not all flesh is alike, but there is one kind for men, another for animals, another for birds, and another for fish. ⁴⁰There are celestial bodies and there are terrestrial bodies; but the glory of the celestial is one, and the glory of the terrestrial is another. ⁴¹There is one glory of the sun, and another glory of the moon, and another glory of the stars; for star differs from star in glory.
42 So is it with the resurrection of the dead. What is sown is perishable, what is raised is imperishable. ⁴³It is sown in dishonor, it is raised in glory. It is sown in weakness, it is raised in power. ⁴⁴It is sown a physical body, it is raised a spiritual body. If there is a physical body, there is also a spiritual body. ⁴⁵Thus it is written, "The first man Adam became a living being"; the last

ἀποθάνῃ·³⁷ καὶ ὃ σπείρεις, οὐ τὸ σῶμα	it dies; and what thou sowest, not the body
τὸ γενησόμενον σπείρεις, ἀλλὰ γυμνὸν	– going to become thou sowest, but a naked
κόκκον εἰ τύχοι σίτου ἤ τινος τῶν	grain it may be† of wheat or some one of the
λοιπῶν· 38 ὁ δὲ θεὸς δίδωσιν αὐτῷ	rest; – but God gives to it
σῶμα καθὼς ἠθέλησεν, καὶ ἑκάστῳ τῶν	a body as he wished, and to each of the
σπερμάτων ἴδιον σῶμα. 39 οὐ πᾶσα	seeds [its] own body. ²[is] not ¹All
σὰρξ ἡ αὐτὴ σάρξ, ἀλλὰ ἄλλη μὲν	²flesh the same flesh, but other(one) indeed
ἀνθρώπων, ἄλλη δὲ σὰρξ κτηνῶν, ἄλλη δὲ	of men, and another flesh of animals, and another
σὰρξ πτηνῶν, ἄλλη δὲ ἰχθύων. 40 καὶ	flesh of birds, and another of fishes. And [there
σώματα ἐπουράνια, καὶ σώματα ἐπίγεια·	are] bodies heavenly, and bodies earthly;
ἀλλὰ ἑτέρα μὲν ἡ τῶν ἐπουρανίων δόξα,	but ⁷other ⁵[is] ¹the ⁸of the ⁴heavenly ²glory, (one) ⁶indeed [bodies]
ἑτέρα δὲ ἡ τῶν ἐπιγείων. 41 ἄλλη	and other the [glory] of the earthly [bodies]. Other(one)
δόξα ἡλίου, καὶ ἄλλη δόξα σελήνης,	glory of [the] sun, and another glory of [the] moon,
καὶ ἄλλη δόξα ἀστέρων· ἀστὴρ γὰρ	and another glory of [the] stars; for star
ἀστέρος διαφέρει ἐν δόξῃ. 42 οὕτως καὶ	from star differs in glory. So also
ἡ ἀνάστασις τῶν νεκρῶν. σπείρεται ἐν	the resurrection of the dead. It is sown in
φθορᾷ, ἐγείρεται ἐν ἀφθαρσίᾳ· 43 σπείρεται	corruption, it is raised in incorruption; it is sown
ἐν ἀτιμίᾳ, ἐγείρεται ἐν δόξῃ· σπείρεται	in dishonour, it is raised in glory; it is sown
ἐν ἀσθενείᾳ, ἐγείρεται ἐν δυνάμει· 44 σπείρ-	in weakness, it is raised in power; it is
εται σῶμα ψυχικόν, ἐγείρεται σῶμα	sown body a natural, it is raised body
πνευματικόν Εἰ ἔστιν σῶμα ψυχικόν,	a spiritual. If there is body a natural,
ἔστιν καὶ πνευματικόν. 45 οὕτως καὶ	there is also a spiritual [body]. So also
γέγραπται· ἐγένετο ὁ πρῶτος ἄνθρωπος	it has been written: ⁵became ¹The ²first ³man
Ἀδὰμ εἰς ψυχὴν ζῶσαν· ὁ ἔσχατος	⁴Adam – soul a living; the last

Adam became a life-giving spirit. ⁴⁶But it is not the spiritual which is first but the physical, and then the spiritual. ⁴⁷The first man was from the earth, a man of dust; the second man is from heaven. ⁴⁸As was the man of dust, so are those who are of the dust; and as is the man of heaven, so are those who are of heaven. ⁴⁹Just as we have borne the image of the man of dust, we shall[u] also bear the image of the man of heaven. ⁵⁰I tell you this, brethren: flesh and blood cannot inherit the kingdom of God, nor does the perishable inherit the imperishable.

⁵¹Lo! I tell you a mystery. We shall not all sleep, but we shall all be changed, ⁵²in a moment, in the twinkling of an eye, at the last trumpet. For the trumpet will sound, and the dead will be raised imperishable, and we shall be changed. ⁵³For this perishable nature must put on the imperishable, and this mortal nature must put on immortality. ⁵⁴When the perishable puts on the imperishable, and the mortal puts on immortality, then shall come to pass the saying that is written:

"Death is swallowed

[u] Other ancient authorities read *let us*

'Αδὰμ   εἰς   πνεῦμα   ζωοποιοῦν.   **46** ἀλλ'
Adam   –   spirit   a life-giving.   But

οὐ   πρῶτον   τὸ   πνευματικὸν   ἀλλὰ   τὸ
not   firstly   the   spiritual [body]   but   the

ψυχικόν,   ἔπειτα   τὸ   πνευματικόν.   **47** ὁ
natural,   afterward   the   spiritual.   The

πρῶτος   ἄνθρωπος   ἐκ   γῆς   χοϊκός,   ὁ
first   man   [was] out of earth   earthy,   the

δεύτερος   ἄνθρωπος   ἐξ   οὐρανοῦ.   **48** οἷος ὁ
second   man [is]   out of   heaven.   Such the

χοϊκός,   τοιοῦτοι   καὶ   οἱ   χοϊκοί,   καὶ   οἷος
earthy man,   such   also   the   earthy ones,   and   such

ὁ   ἐπουράνιος,   τοιοῦτοι   καὶ   οἱ   ἐπουράνιοι·
the heavenly man,   such   also   the   heavenly ones;

49 καὶ   καθὼς   ἐφορέσαμεν   τὴν   εἰκόνα   τοῦ
and   as   we bore   the   image   of the

χοϊκοῦ,   φορέσομεν   καὶ   τὴν   εἰκόνα   τοῦ
earthy man,   we shall bear   also   the   image   of the

ἐπουρανίου.   **50** Τοῦτο   δὲ   φημι,   ἀδελφοί,
heavenly man.   And this   I say,   brothers,

ὅτι   σὰρξ   καὶ   αἷμα   βασιλείαν   θεοῦ   κληρο-
that   flesh   and   blood   ³[the] kingdom   ⁴of God   ¹to

νομῆσαι   οὐ   δύναται,   οὐδὲ   ἡ   φθορὰ   τὴν
inherit   ¹cannot,   neither   –   ¹corruption   –

ἀφθαρσίαν   κληρονομεῖ.   **51** ἰδοὺ   μυστήριον
²incorruption   ²inherits.   Behold[,]   a mystery

ὑμῖν   λέγω·   πάντες   οὐ   κοιμηθησόμεθα,
to you   I tell: all   not   We shall not fall asleep,

πάντες   δὲ   ἀλλαγησόμεθα,   **52** ἐν   ἀτόμῳ,
but all   we shall be changed,   in   a moment,

ἐν   ῥιπῇ   ὀφθαλμοῦ,   ἐν   τῇ   ἐσχάτῃ   σάλπιγγι·
in a glance   of an eye,   at   the   last   trumpet;

σαλπίσει   γάρ,   καὶ   οἱ   νεκροὶ   ἐγερθήσονται
for a trumpet will   and   the   dead   will be raised
sound,

ἄφθαρτοι,   καὶ   ἡμεῖς   ἀλλαγησόμεθα.   **53** Δεῖ
incorruptible,   and   we   shall be changed.   it behoves

γὰρ   τὸ   φθαρτὸν   τοῦτο   ἐνδύσασθαι
For   –   corruptible   this   to put on

ἀφθαρσίαν   καὶ   τὸ   θνητὸν   τοῦτο   ἐνδύσασθαι
incorruption   and   –   mortal   this   to put on

ἀθανασίαν.   **54** ὅταν   δὲ   τὸ   φθαρτὸν   τοῦτο
immortality.   And whenever   this [that is] corruptible

ἐνδύσηται   ἀφθαρσίαν   καὶ   τὸ   θνητὸν   τοῦτο
shall put on   incorruption   and   this [that is] mortal

ἐνδύσηται   ἀθανασίαν,   τότε   γενήσεται   ὁ
shall put on   immortality,   then   will be   the

λόγος   ὁ   γεγραμμένος·   κατεπόθη   ὁ   θάνατος
word   –   having been   ²was   –   ¹Death
        written: swallowed up

up in victory."
⁵⁵"O death, where is thy victory?
O death, where is thy sting?"
⁵⁶The sting of death is sin, and the power of sin is the law. ⁵⁷But thanks be to God, who gives us the victory through our Lord Jesus Christ.
58 Therefore, my beloved brethren, be steadfast, immovable, always abounding in the work of the Lord, knowing that in the Lord your labor is not in vain.

εἰς νῖκος. 55 ποῦ σου, θάνατε, τὸ νῖκος;
in victory.   Where of thee, [O] death, the victory?

ποῦ σου, θάνατε, τὸ κέντρον; 56 τὸ δὲ
where of thee, [O] death, the sting?   Now the

κέντρον τοῦ θανάτου ἡ ἁμαρτία, ἡ δὲ
sting   -   of death   -   [is] sin,   and the

δύναμις τῆς ἁμαρτίας ὁ νόμος· 57 τῷ
power   -   of sin [is] the   law;   -

δὲ θεῷ χάρις τῷ διδόντι ἡμῖν τὸ νῖκος
but to God thanks the [one] giving   to us   the victory

διὰ τοῦ κυρίου ἡμῶν Ἰησοῦ Χριστοῦ.
through the   Lord   of us   Jesus   Christ.

58 Ὥστε, ἀδελφοί μου ἀγαπητοί, ἑδραῖοι
So as,   brothers   of me   beloved,   firm

γίνεσθε, ἀμετακίνητοι, περισσεύοντες ἐν τῷ
be ye,   unmovable,   abounding   in   the

ἔργῳ τοῦ κυρίου πάντοτε, εἰδότες ὅτι
work   of the   Lord   always,   knowing   that

ὁ κόπος ὑμῶν οὐκ ἔστιν κενὸς ἐν κυρίῳ.
the labour   of you   is not   empty   in [the] Lord.

CHAPTER 16

NOW concerning the contribution for the saints: as I directed the churches of Galatia, so you also are to do. ²On the first day of every week, each of you is to put something aside and store it up, as he may prosper, so that contributions need not be made when I come. ³And when I arrive, I will send those whom you accredit by letter to carry your gift to Jerusalem. ⁴If it seems advisable that I should go also, they will accompany me.
5 I will visit you after passing through Mace-

16 Περὶ δὲ τῆς λογείας τῆς εἰς τοὺς
Now about   the collection   -   for the

ἁγίους, ὥσπερ διέταξα ταῖς ἐκκλησίαις
saints,   as   I charged   the   churches

τῆς Γαλατίας, οὕτως καὶ ὑμεῖς ποιήσατε.
-    of Galatia,   so   also   ²ye   ¹do.

2 κατὰ μίαν σαββάτου ἕκαστος ὑμῶν
Every   one   of a week   each   of you
=On the first day of every week

παρ' ἑαυτῷ τιθέτω θησαυρίζων ὅ τι ἐὰν
by   himself   let him put   storing up   whatever

εὐοδῶται, ἵνα μὴ ὅταν ἔλθω τότε λογεῖαι
he is prospered,   lest   whenever I come   then   ²collections

γίνωνται. 3 ὅταν δὲ παραγένωμαι, οὓς
¹there are.   And whenever   I arrive,   whom-

ἐὰν δοκιμάσητε, δι' ἐπιστολῶν τούτους
ever   ye approve,   through   epistles   these

πέμψω ἀπενεγκεῖν τὴν χάριν ὑμῶν εἰς
I will send   to carry   the   grace(gift)   of you   to

Ἰερουσαλήμ· 4 ἐὰν δὲ ἄξιον ᾖ τοῦ κἀμὲ
Jerusalem;   and if   ²fitting ¹it is   -   me also

πορεύεσθαι, σὺν ἐμοὶ πορεύσονται.
to go,ᵈ   with   me   they shall go.

5 Ἐλεύσομαι δὲ πρὸς ὑμᾶς ὅταν Μακε-
And I will come   to   you   whenever   ²Mace-

do'nia, for I intend to pass through Macedo'nia, ⁶and perhaps I will stay with you or even spend the winter, so that you may speed me on my journey, wherever I go. ⁷For I do not want to see you now just in passing; I hope to spend some time with you, if the Lord permits. ⁸But I will stay in Ephesus until Pentecost, ⁹for a wide door for effective work has opened to me, and there are many adversaries.

10 When Timothy comes, see that you put him at ease among you, for he is doing the work of the Lord, as I am. ¹¹So let no one despise him. Speed him on his way in peace, that he may return to me; for I am expecting him with the brethren.

12 As for our brother Apol'los, I strongly urged him to visit you with the other brethren, but it was not at all his willʳ to come now. He will come when he has opportunity.

13 Be watchful, stand

δονίαν διέλθω· Μακεδονίαν γὰρ διέρχομαι,
donia ¹I pass for ²Macedonia ¹I am passing
through; through,*

6 πρὸς ὑμᾶς δὲ τυχὸν καταμενῶ ἢ
⁷with ⁸you ¹and ²possibly ³I will remain ⁴or

καὶ παραχειμάσω, ἵνα ὑμεῖς με προπέμ-
⁵even ⁶spend the winter, in order ¹ye ¹me may set
that

ψητε οὗ ἐὰν πορεύωμαι. 7 οὐ θέλω γὰρ
forward wherever I may go. For I do not wish

ὑμᾶς ἄρτι ἐν παρόδῳ ἰδεῖν· ἐλπίζω γὰρ
²you ³yet ⁴in ⁵passage ¹to see; for I am hoping

χρόνον τινὰ ἐπιμεῖναι πρὸς ὑμᾶς, ἐὰν
³time ²some ¹to remain with you, if

ὁ κύριος ἐπιτρέψῃ. 8 ἐπιμενῶ δὲ ἐν
the Lord permits. But I will remain in

Ἐφέσῳ ἕως τῆς πεντηκοστῆς· 9 θύρα
Ephesus until - Pentecost; ⁵door

γάρ μοι ἀνέῳγεν μεγάλη καὶ ἐνεργής,
¹for ⁷to me ⁶opened ²a great ³and ⁴effective,

καὶ ἀντικείμενοι πολλοί. 10 Ἐὰν δὲ
and ²opposing ¹many. Now if

ἔλθῃ Τιμόθεος, βλέπετε ἵνα ἀφόβως
²comes ¹Timothy, see in order that fearlessly

γένηται πρὸς ὑμᾶς· τὸ γὰρ ἔργον κυρίου
he is with you; for the work of [the] Lord

ἐργάζεται ὡς κἀγώ· 11 μή τις οὖν αὐτὸν
he works as I also; ³not ⁵any- ⁴there- ²him
one fore

ἐξουθενήσῃ. προπέμψατε δὲ αὐτὸν ἐν
¹despise. But set ye forward him in

εἰρήνῃ, ἵνα ἔλθῃ πρός με· ἐκδέχομαι γὰρ
peace, in order he may to me; for I am awaiting
that come

αὐτὸν μετὰ τῶν ἀδελφῶν. 12 Περὶ δὲ
him with the brothers. Now about

Ἀπολλῶ τοῦ ἀδελφοῦ, πολλὰ παρεκάλεσα
²Apollos the ¹brother, ³much ¹I besought

αὐτὸν ἵνα ἔλθῃ πρὸς ὑμᾶς μετὰ τῶν
²him in order he would to you with the
that come

ἀδελφῶν· καὶ πάντως οὐκ ἦν θέλημα
brothers; and altogether it was not [his] will

ἵνα νῦν ἔλθῃ, ἐλεύσεται δὲ ὅταν εὐκαιρήσῃ.
in ²now ¹he but he will come whenever he has
order should opportunity.
that come,

13 Γρηγορεῖτε, στήκετε ἐν τῇ πίστει,
Watch ye, stand in the faith,

ʳ Or God's will for him

* " Futuristic present "; cf. John 14. 3 and ch. 15. 32.

firm in your faith, be courageous, be strong. ¹⁴Let all that you do be done in love.

15 Now, brethren, you know that the household of Steph'anas were the first converts in Acha'ia, and they have devoted themselves to the service of the saints; ¹⁶I urge you to be subject to such men and to every fellow worker and laborer. ¹⁷I rejoice at the coming of Steph'anas and Fortuna'tus and Acha'icus, because they have made up for your absence; ¹⁸for they refreshed my spirit as well as yours. Give recognition to such men. 19 The churches of Asia send greetings. Aquila and Prisca, together with the church in their house, send you hearty greetings in the Lord. ²⁰All the brethren send greetings. Greet one another with a holy kiss. 21 I, Paul, write this greeting with my own hand. ²²If any one has no love for the Lord, let him be accursed. Our Lord, come! ²³The grace of the Lord Jesus be with you. ²⁴My love be with you all in Christ Jesus. Amen.

ἀνδρίζεσθε, κραταιοῦσθε. 14 πάντα ὑμῶν
play the man,   be strong.   ²All things ²of you
ἐν ἀγάπῃ γινέσθω.
⁴in ⁵love   ¹let be.

15 Παρακαλῶ δὲ ὑμᾶς, ἀδελφοί· οἴδατε
Now I beseech   you,   brothers: Know ye
τὴν οἰκίαν Στεφανᾶ, ὅτι ἐστὶν ἀπαρχὴ
the household of Stephanas, that   it is   firstfruit
τῆς Ἀχαΐας καὶ εἰς διακονίαν τοῖς
-   of Achaia   and   to   ministry   to the
ἁγίοις ἔταξαν ἑαυτούς· 16 ἵνα καὶ ὑμεῖς
saints   they   themselves;   in order also   ye
   appointed   that
ὑποτάσσησθε τοῖς τοιούτοις καὶ παντὶ τῷ
may submit   -   to such ones   and   to everyone
συνεργοῦντι καὶ κοπιῶντι. 17 χαίρω δὲ
working with [?me] and   labouring.   Now I rejoice
ἐπὶ τῇ παρουσίᾳ Στεφανᾶ καὶ Φορτουνάτου
at   the   presence   of Stephanas and   of Fortunatus
καὶ Ἀχαϊκοῦ, ὅτι τὸ ὑμέτερον ὑστέρημα
and   of Achaicus,   that   -   ²your   ⁴lack
οὗτοι ἀνεπλήρωσαν· 18 ἀνέπαυσαν γὰρ τὸ
¹these   ²supplied;   for they refreshed   -
ἐμὸν πνεῦμα καὶ τὸ ὑμῶν. ἐπιγινώσκετε
my   spirit   and   - of you(yours).   Recognize ye
οὖν τοὺς τοιούτους.
therefore -   such ones.

19 Ἀσπάζονται ὑμᾶς αἱ ἐκκλησίαι τῆς
   ⁴Greet   ⁵you   ¹the   ²churches
Ἀσίας. ἀσπάζεται ὑμᾶς ἐν κυρίῳ πολλὰ
²of Asia.   ⁴Greets   ⁵you   ⁷in   ⁸[the] Lord   ⁶much
Ἀκύλας καὶ Πρῖσκα σὺν τῇ κατ᾽ οἶκον
¹Aquila   ²and   ³Prisca   ⁹with   ¹⁰the   ¹¹in [the] house
αὐτῶν ἐκκλησίᾳ. 20 ἀσπάζονται ὑμᾶς οἱ
¹²of them   ¹¹church.   ⁴Greet   ⁵you   ²the
ἀδελφοὶ πάντες. Ἀσπάσασθε ἀλλήλους ἐν
³brothers   ¹all.   Greet ye   one another with
φιλήματι ἁγίῳ. 21 Ὁ ἀσπασμὸς τῇ
kiss   a holy.   ¹The   ²greeting
ἐμῇ χειρὶ Παύλου. 22 εἴ τις οὐ φιλεῖ
⁴with my ⁵hand   ³of Paul.   If anyone   loves not
τὸν κύριον, ἤτω ἀνάθεμα. μαράνα θά.
the   Lord,   let him be   a curse.   Marana   tha.
23 ἡ χάρις τοῦ κυρίου Ἰησοῦ μεθ᾽ ὑμῶν.
The   grace   of the   Lord   Jesus [be] with   you.
24 ἡ ἀγάπη μου μετὰ πάντων ὑμῶν ἐν
The   love   of me [be] with   ²all   ¹you   in
Χριστῷ Ἰησοῦ.
Christ   Jesus.

CHAPTER 1

PAUL, an apostle of Christ Jesus by the will of God, and Timothy our brother.

To the church of God which is at Corinth, with all the saints who are in the whole of Acha'ia:

2 Grace to you and peace from God our Father and the Lord Jesus Christ.

3 Blessed be the God and Father of our Lord Jesus Christ, the Father of mercies and God of all comfort, [4] who comforts us in all our affliction, so that we may be able to comfort those who are in any affliction, with the comfort with which we ourselves are comforted by God. [5] For as we share abundantly in Christ's sufferings, so through Christ we share abundantly in comfort too.[a]

[6] If we are afflicted, it is for your comfort and salvation; and if we are comforted, it is for your comfort, which you experience when you patiently endure the

[a] Or, For as the suffering of Christ abound for us, so also our comfort abounds through Christ.

---

1 Παῦλος   ἀπόστολος   Χριστοῦ   Ἰησοῦ
  Paul   an apostle   of Christ   Jesus

διὰ   θελήματος   θεοῦ   καὶ   Τιμόθεος   ὁ
through [the] will   of God   and   Timothy   the

ἀδελφὸς   τῇ   ἐκκλησίᾳ   τοῦ   θεοῦ   τῇ   οὔσῃ
brother   to the church   -   of God   -   being

ἐν   Κορίνθῳ   σὺν   τοῖς   ἁγίοις   πᾶσιν   τοῖς
in   Corinth   with   [2]the   [3]saints   [1]all   -

οὖσιν   ἐν   ὅλῃ   τῇ   Ἀχαΐᾳ·   2 χάρις   ὑμῖν   καὶ
being   in   all   -   Achaia: Grace   to you   and

εἰρήνη   ἀπὸ   θεοῦ   πατρὸς   ἡμῶν   καὶ   κυρίου
peace   from   God   [the] Father of us   and   [the] Lord

Ἰησοῦ   Χριστοῦ.
Jesus   Christ.

3 Εὐλογητὸς   ὁ   θεὸς   καὶ   πατὴρ   τοῦ
  Blessed [be]   the   God   and   Father   of the

κυρίου   ἡμῶν   Ἰησοῦ   Χριστοῦ,   ὁ   πατὴρ
Lord   of us   Jesus   Christ,   the   Father

τῶν   οἰκτιρμῶν   καὶ   θεὸς   πάσης   παρακλήσ-
 -     of compassions and   God   of all   com-

εως,   4 ὁ   παρακαλῶν   ἡμᾶς   ἐπὶ   πάσῃ
fort,   the [one] comforting   us   on(in)   all

τῇ   θλίψει   ἡμῶν,   εἰς   τὸ   δύνασθαι   ἡμᾶς
the   affliction   of us,   [with a -   to be able   us[b]
                            view] to   =our being able

παρακαλεῖν   τοὺς   ἐν   πάσῃ   θλίψει   διὰ
to comfort   the ones   in   every   affliction through

τῆς   παρακλήσεως   ἧς   παρακαλούμεθα   αὐτοὶ
the   comfort   of(with) we are comforted   [our-]
                        which   selves

ὑπὸ   τοῦ   θεοῦ.   5 ὅτι   καθὼς   περισσεύει   τὰ
by   -   God.   Because   as   abounds   the

παθήματα   τοῦ   Χριστοῦ   εἰς   ἡμᾶς,   οὕτως
sufferings   -   of Christ   in   us,   so

διὰ   τοῦ   Χριστοῦ   περισσεύει   καὶ   ἡ   παρά-
through -   Christ   abounds   also   the   com-

κλησις   ἡμῶν.   6 εἴτε   δὲ   θλιβόμεθα,   ὑπὲρ
fort   of us.   Now whether   we are   on be-
                                   afflicted,   half of

τῆς   ὑμῶν   παρακλήσεως   καὶ   σωτηρίας·   εἴτε
the   [4]of you   [1]comfort   [2]and   [3]salvation;   or

παρακαλούμεθα,   ὑπὲρ   τῆς   ὑμῶν   παρακλή-
we are comforted,   on behalf of the   [2]of you   [1]com-

σεως   τῆς   ἐνεργουμένης   ἐν   ὑπομονῇ   τῶν
fort   -   operating   in   endurance   of the

708   II. CORINTHIANS 1

same sufferings that we
suffer. ⁷Our hope for you
is unshaken; for we
know that as you share
in our sufferings, you will
also share in our comfort.
8 For we do not want
you to be ignorant,
brethren, of the affliction
we experienced in Asia;
for we were so utterly,
unbearably crushed that
we despaired of life
itself. ⁹Why, we felt that
we had received the
sentence of death; but
that was to make us rely
not on ourselves but on
God who raises the dead;
¹⁰he delivered us from so
deadly a peril, and he will
deliver us; on him we
have set our hope that he
will deliver us again.
¹¹You also must help
us by prayer, so that
many will give thanks on
our behalf for the
blessing granted us in
answer to many prayers.
12 For our boast is
this, the testimony of our
conscience that we have

αὐτῶν παθημάτων ὧν καὶ ἡμεῖς πάσχομεν,
same   sufferings   which also   we   suffer,

7 καὶ ἡ ἐλπὶς ἡμῶν βεβαία ὑπὲρ ὑμῶν
and   the hope of us [is] firm on behalf of you

εἰδότες ὅτι ὡς κοινωνοί ἐστε τῶν παθημά-
knowing that as partakers ye are of the   suffer-

των, οὕτως καὶ τῆς παρακλήσεως. 8 Οὐ
ings,   so   also of the   comfort.   not

γὰρ θέλομεν ὑμᾶς ἀγνοεῖν, ἀδελφοί, ὑπὲρ
For we wish you to be ignorant, brothers, as to

τῆς θλίψεως ἡμῶν τῆς γενομένης ἐν
the affliction of us   –   having been   in

τῇ Ἀσίᾳ, ὅτι καθ᾽ ὑπερβολὴν ὑπὲρ
–   Asia, that   excessively†   beyond

δύναμιν ἐβαρήθημεν, ὥστε ἐξαπορηθῆναι
power   we were burdened, so as   to despair
                              =so that we despaired even

ἡμᾶς καὶ τοῦ ζῆν· 9 ἀλλὰ αὐτοὶ ἐν
usᵇ   even –   to live; but [our]selves in
of life;

ἑαυτοῖς τὸ ἀπόκριμα τοῦ θανάτου ἐσχήκα-
ourselves the sentence   –   of death   we have

μεν, ἵνα μὴ πεποιθότες ὦμεν ἐφ᾽ ἑαυτοῖς
had, in order ²not ³having ¹we on ourselves
       that   trusted   might be

ἀλλ᾽ ἐπὶ τῷ θεῷ τῷ ἐγείροντι τοὺς
but   on   –   God the [one] raising   the

νεκρούς· 10 ὃς ἐκ τηλικούτου θανάτου
dead;   who out of so great   a death

ἐρρύσατο ἡμᾶς καὶ ῥύσεται, εἰς ὃν
delivered   us   and will deliver, in whom

ἠλπίκαμεν [ὅτι] καὶ ἔτι ῥύσεται, 11 συν-
we have hoped that indeed yet he will deliver, co-

υπουργούντων καὶ ὑμῶν ὑπὲρ ἡμῶν τῇ
operating   also   youᵃ on behalf of us   –
=while ye also coöperate

δεήσει, ἵνα ἐκ πολλῶν προσώπων τὸ
in petition, in order ⁴by ⁵many   ⁶persons   ⁷[for]
         that   ⁸the

εἰς ἡμᾶς χάρισμα διὰ πολλῶν εὐχαριστηθῇ
¹⁰to ¹¹us ⁹gift ¹²through ¹³many   ¹thanks may
                                        be given

ὑπὲρ ἡμῶν.
²on behalf of ³us.

12 Ἡ γὰρ καύχησις ἡμῶν αὕτη ἐστίν,
   For the boasting   of us ²this ¹is,

τὸ μαρτύριον τῆς συνειδήσεως ἡμῶν, ὅτι
the testimony of the   conscience   of us, because

ἐν ἁγιότητι καὶ εἰλικρινείᾳ τοῦ θεοῦ,
in sanctity   and   sincerity   – of God,

behaved in the world, and still more toward you, with holiness and godly sincerity, not by earthly wisdom but by the grace of God. [13]For we write you nothing but what you can read and understand; I hope you will understand fully, [14]as you have understood in part, that you can be proud of us as we can be of you, on the day of the Lord Jesus.

15 Because I was sure of this, I wanted to come to you first, so that you might have a double pleasure;[b] [16]I wanted to visit you on my way to Macedo'nia, and to come back to you from Macedo'nia and have you send me on my way to Judea. [17]Was I vacillating when I wanted to do this? Do I make my plans like a worldly man, ready to say Yes and No at once? [18]As surely as God is faithful, our word to you has not been Yes and No. [19]For the Son of God, Jesus Christ, whom we preached among you,

οὐκ ἐν σοφίᾳ σαρκικῇ ἀλλ᾽ ἐν χάριτι
not in wisdom fleshly but in [the] grace

θεοῦ, ἀνεστράφημεν ἐν τῷ κόσμῳ, περισ-
of God, we behaved in the world, ²more

σοτέρως δὲ πρὸς ὑμᾶς. 13 οὐ γὰρ ἄλλα
²especially ¹and with you. ³Not ¹for ⁴other
                                                things

γράφομεν ὑμῖν ἀλλ᾽ ἢ ἃ ἀναγινώσκετε
²we write to you other than what ye read

ἢ καὶ ἐπιγινώσκετε, ἐλπίζω δὲ ὅτι
or even perceive, and I hope that

ἕως τέλους ἐπιγνώσεσθε, 14 καθὼς καὶ
to [the] end ye will perceive, as also

ἐπέγνωτε ἡμᾶς ἀπὸ μέρους, ὅτι καύχημα
ye perceived us from(in) part, because ²boast

ὑμῶν ἐσμεν καθάπερ καὶ ὑμεῖς ἡμῶν
³of you ¹we are even as also ye of us

ἐν τῇ ἡμέρᾳ τοῦ κυρίου ἡμῶν Ἰησοῦ.
in the day of the Lord of us Jesus.

15 Καὶ ταύτῃ τῇ πεποιθήσει ἐβουλόμην
And in this - persuasion I determined

πρότερον πρὸς ὑμᾶς ἐλθεῖν ἵνα δευτέραν
formerly to you to come in order a second
                                        that

χάριν σχῆτε, 16 καὶ δι᾽ ὑμῶν διελθεῖν
grace ye might have, and through you to pass through

εἰς Μακεδονίαν, καὶ πάλιν ἀπὸ Μακεδονίας
into Macedonia, and again from Macedonia

ἐλθεῖν πρὸς ὑμᾶς καὶ ὑφ᾽ ὑμῶν
to come to you and by you

προπεμφθῆναι εἰς τὴν Ἰουδαίαν. 17 τοῦτο
to be set forward to - Judæa. This

οὖν βουλόμενος μήτι ἄρα τῇ ἐλαφρίᾳ
therefore determining not ³then - ²fickleness

ἐχρησάμην; ἢ ἃ βουλεύομαι κατὰ σάρκα
¹did I use? or [the] I determine according [the]
            things which to flesh

βουλεύομαι, ἵνα ᾖ παρ᾽ ἐμοὶ τὸ ναὶ
do I determine, in order there with me the Yes
            that may be

ναὶ καὶ τὸ οὖ οὔ; 18 πιστὸς δὲ ὁ
yes and the No no? But faithful [is] -

θεὸς ὅτι ὁ λόγος ἡμῶν ὁ πρὸς ὑμᾶς
God that the word of us - to you

οὐκ ἔστιν ναὶ καὶ οὔ. 19 ὁ τοῦ θεοῦ
is not yes and no. ³the - ⁴of God

γὰρ υἱὸς Χριστὸς Ἰησοῦς ὁ ἐν ὑμῖν
¹For ²Son Christ Jesus ¹the ³among ⁴you
                                        [one]

[b] Other ancient authorities read *favor*

I.G.E.—24

Silva'nus and Timothy and I, was not Yes and No; but in him it is always Yes. ²⁰ For all the promises of God find their Yes in him. That is why we utter the Amen through him, to the glory of God. ²¹ But it is God who establishes us with you in Christ, and has commissioned us; ²²he has put his seal upon us and given us his Spirit in our hearts as a guarantee.

23 But I call God to witness against me—it was to spare you that I refrained from coming to Corinth. ²⁴ Not that we lord it over your faith; we work with you for your joy, for you stand firm in your faith.

CHAPTER 2

FOR I made up my mind not to make you another painful visit. ²For if I cause you pain, who is there to make me glad but the one whom I have pained? ³And I wrote as I did, so that when I came I might not be pained by those who should have made me rejoice, for I felt sure of all of you, that my joy would be the joy of you

---

δι' ἡμῶν κηρυχθείς, δι' ἐμοῦ καὶ Σιλουανοῦ
²through ⁴us ³proclaimed, through me and Silvanus

καὶ Τιμοθέου, οὐκ ἐγένετο ναὶ καὶ οὔ,
and Timothy, was not yes and no,

ἀλλὰ ναὶ ἐν αὐτῷ γέγονεν. 20 ὅσαι γὰρ
but ²Yes ³in ⁴him ¹has been.   For as many

ἐπαγγελίαι θεοῦ, ἐν αὐτῷ τὸ ναί· διὸ
[as are] of God, in him [is] the Yes; where-
promises   fore

καὶ δι' αὐτοῦ τὸ ἀμὴν τῷ θεῷ πρὸς
also through him the Amen – ²to God ¹unto

δόξαν δι' ἡμῶν. 21 ὁ δὲ βεβαιῶν ἡμᾶς
²glory through us.   But the [one] making firm us

σὺν ὑμῖν εἰς Χριστὸν καὶ χρίσας ἡμᾶς
with you in Christ and having anointed us [is]

θεός, 22 ὁ καὶ σφραγισάμενος ἡμᾶς καὶ
God,   the [one] both having sealed us and

δοὺς τὸν ἀρραβῶνα τοῦ πνεύματος ἐν
having the earnest of the Spirit in
given

ταῖς καρδίαις ἡμῶν.
the hearts of us.

23 Ἐγὼ δὲ μάρτυρα τὸν θεὸν ἐπικαλοῦμαι
Now ⁴I ⁷[as] witness – ⁶God ⁵invoke

ἐπὶ τὴν ἐμὴν ψυχήν, ὅτι φειδόμενος
¹on – ²my ³life, that sparing

ὑμῶν οὐκέτι ἦλθον εἰς Κόρινθον. 24 οὐχ ὅτι
you ²no more ¹I came to Corinth.   Not that

κυριεύομεν ὑμῶν τῆς πίστεως, ἀλλὰ συνεργοί
we rule over ³of you ¹the ²faith, but ²fellow-
workers

ἐσμεν τῆς χαρᾶς ὑμῶν· τῇ γὰρ πίστει
¹we are of the joy of you; – for by faith

ἐστήκατε. 2 ἔκρινα δὲ ἐμαυτῷ τοῦτο, τὸ μὴ
ye stand.   But I decided in myself this, – not

πάλιν ἐν λύπῃ πρὸς ὑμᾶς ἐλθεῖν. 2 εἰ
again ⁴in ⁵grief ²to ³you ¹to come.   if

γὰρ ἐγὼ λυπῶ ὑμᾶς, καὶ τίς ὁ εὐφραίνων
For I grieve you, then who the making glad
[one]

με εἰ μὴ ὁ λυπούμενος ἐξ ἐμοῦ; 3 καὶ
me except the [one] being grieved by me?   And

ἔγραψα τοῦτο αὐτὸ ἵνα μὴ ἐλθὼν λύπην
I wrote this very thing lest coming grief

σχῶ ἀφ' ὧν ἔδει με χαίρειν, πεποιθὼς
I should from [those] it me to rejoice, having
have whom behoved confidence

ἐπὶ πάντας ὑμᾶς ὅτι ἡ ἐμὴ χαρὰ πάντων
in ²all ¹you that – my joy ²all

all. ⁴For I wrote you out of much affliction and anguish of heart and with many tears, not to cause you pain but to let you know the abundant love that I have for you. 5 But if any one has caused pain, he has caused it not to me, but in some measure—not to put it too severely—to you all. ⁶For such a one this punishment by the majority is enough; ⁷so you should rather turn to forgive and comfort him, or he may be overwhelmed by excessive sorrow. ⁸So I beg you to reaffirm your love for him. ⁹For this is why I wrote, that I might test you and know whether you are obedient in everything. ¹⁰Any one whom you forgive, I also forgive. What I have forgiven, if I have forgiven anything, has been for your sake in the presence of Christ, ¹¹to keep Satan from gaining the advantage over us; for we are not ignorant of his designs.

12 When I came to Tro′as to preach the gospel of Christ, a door was opened for me in the Lord; ¹³but my mind

---

ὑμῶν ἐστιν.
²of you　¹is.

4 ἐκ γὰρ πολλῆς θλίψεως
For out of　much　affliction

καὶ συνοχῆς καρδίας ἔγραψα ὑμῖν διὰ
and anxiety of heart I wrote to you through

πολλῶν δακρύων, οὐχ ἵνα λυπηθῆτε, ἀλλὰ
many tears, not in order ye should be but
　　　　　　　　　that grieved,

τὴν ἀγάπην ἵνα γνῶτε ἣν ἔχω περισ-
⁴the ⁴love ¹in order ²ye should ⁵which I have more
　　　　that know

σοτέρως εἰς ὑμᾶς. 5 Εἰ δέ τις λελύπηκεν,
abundantly to you. But if anyone has grieved,

οὐκ ἐμὲ λελύπηκεν, ἀλλὰ ἀπὸ μέρους,
not me he has grieved, but from(in) part,

ἵνα μὴ ἐπιβαρῶ, πάντας ὑμᾶς. 6 ἱκανὸν
lest I am burdensome, ²all ¹you. Enough

τῷ τοιούτῳ ἡ ἐπιτιμία αὕτη ἡ ὑπὸ
for such a one this punishment - by

τῶν πλειόνων, 7 ὥστε τοὐναντίον μᾶλλον
the majority, so as on the contrary rather

ὑμᾶς χαρίσασθαι καὶ παρακαλέσαι, μή πως
you to forgive and to comfort,ᵇ lest
=ye should rather forgive and comfort,

τῇ περισσοτέρᾳ λύπῃ καταποθῇ ὁ τοιοῦτος.
³by ⁴more abundant ⁵grief ²should be ¹such a one.
the swallowed up

8 διὸ παρακαλῶ ὑμᾶς κυρῶσαι εἰς αὐτὸν
Wherefore I beseech you to confirm to him

ἀγάπην· 9 εἰς τοῦτο γὰρ καὶ ἔγραψα,
[your] love; ²to ³this [end] ¹for indeed I wrote,

ἵνα γνῶ τὴν δοκιμὴν ὑμῶν, εἰ εἰς πάντα
in or- I might the proof of you, if in all things
der that know

ὑπήκοοί ἐστε. 10 ᾧ δέ τι χαρίζεσθε,
obedient ye are. Now to whom anything ye forgive,

κἀγώ· καὶ γὰρ ἐγὼ ὃ κεχάρισμαι, εἴ
I also; for indeed ²I ¹what ³have forgiven, if

τι κεχάρισμαι, δι' ὑμᾶς ἐν προσώπῳ
²any- ¹I have [it is] on you in [the] person
thing forgiven, account of

Χριστοῦ, 11 ἵνα μὴ πλεονεκτηθῶμεν ὑπὸ
of Christ, lest we are taken advantage of by

τοῦ σατανᾶ· οὐ γὰρ αὐτοῦ τὰ νοήματα
-　Satan; for ²not ⁷of him ⁸the ⁶designs

ἀγνοοῦμεν. 12 Ἐλθὼν δὲ εἰς τὴν Τρῳάδα εἰς
¹we ²are ⁴ignorant [of]. But coming to - Troas in

τὸ εὐαγγέλιον τοῦ Χριστοῦ, καὶ θύρας
the gospel - of Christ, and a door

μοι ἀνεῳγμένης ἐν κυρίῳ, 13 οὐκ ἔσχηκα
to me having been by [the] Lord, I have had no
opened*

could not rest because I did not find my brother Titus there. So I took leave of them and went on to Macedo'nia.

14 But thanks be to God, who in Christ always leads us in triumph, and through us spreads the fragrance of the knowledge of him everywhere. ¹⁵ For we are the aroma of Christ to God among those who are being saved and among those who are perishing, ¹⁶ to one a fragrance from death to death, to the other a fragrance from life to life. Who is sufficient for these things? ¹⁷ For we are not, like so many, peddlers of God's word; but as men of sincerity, as commissioned by God, in the sight of God we speak in Christ.

ἄνεσιν τῷ πνεύματί μου τῷ μὴ εὑρεῖν
rest   to the   spirit   of me in the not to find
= when I did not find ...

με Τίτον τὸν ἀδελφόν μου, ἀλλὰ ἀποτα-
me⁶ᵉ Titus the brother of me, but   saying

ξάμενος αὐτοῖς ἐξῆλθον εἰς Μακεδονίαν.
farewell to them I went forth into Macedonia.

14 Τῷ δὲ θεῷ χάρις τῷ πάντοτε
-   But ²to God ¹thanks the [one] always

θριαμβεύοντι ἡμᾶς ἐν τῷ Χριστῷ καὶ
leading in triumph us in   - Christ and

τὴν ὀσμὴν τῆς γνώσεως αὐτοῦ φανεροῦντι
⁴the ⁵odour ⁶of the ⁷knowledge ⁸of him ¹manifesting

δι’ ἡμῶν ἐν παντὶ τόπῳ· 15 ὅτι Χριστοῦ
²through ³us in every place; because of Christ

εὐωδία ἐσμὲν τῷ θεῷ ἐν τοῖς σωζομένοις
a sweet we are - to God in the [ones] being saved
smell

καὶ ἐν τοῖς ἀπολλυμένοις, 16 οἷς μὲν
and in the [ones] perishing,   to the [latter]†

ὀσμὴ ἐκ θανάτου εἰς θάνατον, οἷς δὲ
an odour out of death unto death, to the [former]†

ὀσμὴ ἐκ ζωῆς εἰς ζωήν. καὶ πρὸς
an odour out of life unto life.   And for

ταῦτα τίς ' ἱκανός; 17 οὐ γάρ ἐσμεν
these things who [is] competent? For we are not

ὡς οἱ πολλοὶ καπηλεύοντες τὸν λόγον
as the many hawking the word

τοῦ θεοῦ, ἀλλ’ ὡς ἐξ εἰλικρινείας, ἀλλ’
- of God, but as of sincerity, but

ὡς ἐκ θεοῦ κατέναντι θεοῦ ἐν Χριστῷ
as of God before God in Christ

λαλοῦμεν.
we speak.

CHAPTER 3

ARE we beginning to commend ourselves again? Or do we need, as some do, letters of recommendation to you, or from you? ² You yourselves are our letter of recommendation, written on your ᶜ hearts, to be known and read by all men; ³ and you show that you are a letter

ᶜ Other ancient authorities read *our*

3 Ἀρχόμεθα πάλιν ἑαυτοὺς συνιστάνειν;
Do we begin again ourselves to commend?

ἢ μὴ χρῄζομεν ὥς τινες συστατικῶν
or not need we as some commendatory

ἐπιστολῶν πρὸς ὑμᾶς ἢ ἐξ ὑμῶν; 2 ἡ
epistles to you or from you? The

ἐπιστολὴ ἡμῶν ὑμεῖς ἐστε, ἐγγεγραμμένη
epistle of us ye are, having been inscribed

ἐν ταῖς καρδίαις ἡμῶν, γινωσκομένη καὶ
in the hearts of us, being known and

ἀναγινωσκομένη ὑπὸ πάντων ἀνθρώπων,
being read by all men,

3 φανερούμενοι ὅτι ἐστὲ ἐπιστολὴ Χριστοῦ
being manifested that ye are an epistle of Christ

from Christ delivered by us, written not with ink but with the Spirit of the living God, not on tablets of stone but on tablets of human hearts. 4 Such is the confidence that we have through Christ toward God. 5 Not that we are sufficient of ourselves to claim anything as coming from us; our sufficiency is from God, 6 who has qualified us to be ministers of a new covenant, not in a written code but in the Spirit; for the written code kills, but the Spirit gives life.

7 Now if the dispensation of death, carved in letters on stone, came with such splendor that the Israelites could not look at Moses' face because of its brightness, fading as this was, 8 will not the dispensation of the Spirit be attended with greater splendor? 9 For if there was splendor in the dispensation of condemnation, the dispensation of righteousness must far exceed it in splendor. 10 Indeed, in this case, what once had splendor has come to have no splendor at all, because of the splen-

διακονηθεῖσα	ministered
ὑφ'	by
ἡμῶν,	us,
ἐγγεγραμμένη	having been inscribed
οὐ	not
μέλανι	by ink
ἀλλὰ	but
πνεύματι	by [the] Spirit
θεοῦ	of ²God
ζῶντος,	¹a living,
οὐκ	not
ἐν	in
πλαξὶν	²tablets
λιθίναις	¹stony
ἀλλ'	but
ἐν	in
πλαξὶν	tablets
καρδίαις	[which are] ²hearts
σαρκίναις.	¹fleshy.

4 Πεποίθησιν   ²confidence
δὲ   ¹And
τοιαύτην   ²such
ἔχομεν   we have
διὰ   through
τοῦ   -
Χριστοῦ   Christ
πρὸς   toward
τὸν   -
θεόν.   God.
5 οὐχ   Not
ὅτι   that
ἀφ'   ²from
ἑαυτῶν   ⁴ourselves
ἱκανοί   ²competent
ἐσμεν   ¹we are
λογίσασθαί   to reckon
τι   any-thing
ὡς   as
ἐξ   of
ἑαυτῶν,   ourselves,
ἀλλ'   but
ἡ   the
ἱκανότης   competence
ἡμῶν   of us [is]
ἐκ   of
τοῦ   -
θεοῦ,   God,
6 ὃς   who
καὶ   also
ἱκάνωσεν   made competent
ἡμᾶς   us
διακόνους   [as] ministers
καινῆς   of a new
διαθήκης,   covenant,
οὐ   not
γράμματος   of letter
ἀλλὰ   but
πνεύματος·   of spirit;
τὸ   for the
γὰρ
γράμμα   letter
ἀποκτείνει,   kills,
τὸ   but the
δὲ
πνεῦμα   spirit
ζωοποιεῖ.   makes alive.
7 Εἰ   if
δὲ
ἡ   the
διακονία   ministry
τοῦ   -
θανάτου   of death
ἐν   in
γράμμασιν   letters
ἐντετυπωμένη   having been engraved
λίθοις   in stones
ἐγενήθη   was
ἐν   in
δόξῃ,   glory,
ὥστε   so as
μὴ   not
δύνασθαι   to be able
ἀτενίσαι   to gaze
τοὺς   the
υἱοὺς   sons
= so that the sons of Israel were not able to gaze
Ἰσραὴλ   of Israel[b]
εἰς   at
τὸ   the
πρόσωπον   face
Μωϋσέως   of Moses
διὰ   on account of
τὴν   the
δόξαν   glory
τοῦ   of the
προσώπου   face
αὐτοῦ   of him
τὴν   -
καταργουμένην,   being done away,
8 πῶς   how
οὐχὶ   ²not
μᾶλλον   ²rather
ἡ   ⁴the
διακονία   ⁵ministry
τοῦ   ⁶of the
πνεύματος   ⁷Spirit
ἔσται   ¹will ⁸be
ἐν   in
δόξῃ;   glory?
9 εἰ   For if
γὰρ
ἡ   the
διακονία   ministry
τῆς   -
κατακρίσεως   of condemnation
δόξα,   [was] glory,
πολλῷ   by much
μᾶλλον   rather
περισσεύει   ⁶abounds
ἡ   ¹the
διακονία   ²ministry
τῆς   -
δικαιοσύνης   ³of righteousness
δόξῃ.   in glory.
10 καὶ   For indeed
γὰρ
οὐ   ²not
δεδόξασται   ⁴has been glorified
τὸ   ¹the
δεδοξασμένον   ²having been glorified
ἐν   in
τούτῳ   this
[thing]

dor that surpasses it. ¹¹For if what faded away came with splendor, what is permanent must have much more splendor.

12 Since we have such a hope, we are very bold, ¹³not like Moses, who put a veil over his face so that the Israelites might not see the end of the fading splendor. ¹⁴But their minds were hardened; for to this day, when they read the old covenant, that same veil remains unlifted, because only through Christ is it taken away. ¹⁵Yes, to this day whenever Moses is read a veil lies over their minds; ¹⁶but when a man turns to the Lord the veil is removed. ¹⁷Now the Lord is the Spirit, and where the Spirit of the Lord is, there is freedom. ¹⁸And we all, with unveiled face, beholdingᵈ the glory of the Lord, are being changed into his likeness from one degree of glory to another; for this comes from the Lord who is the Spirit.

ᵈ Or reflecting

τῷ μέρει εἵνεκεν τῆς ὑπερβαλλούσης δόξης.
\- respect for the the excelling glory.
sake of

11 εἰ γὰρ τὸ καταργούμενον διὰ δόξης,
For if the being done away [was] glory,
[thing] through

πολλῷ μᾶλλον τὸ μένον ἐν δόξῃ.
by much more the [thing] remaining [is] in glory.

12 Ἔχοντες οὖν τοιαύτην ἐλπίδα πολλῇ
Having therefore such hope ²much

παρρησίᾳ χρώμεθα, 13 καὶ οὐ καθάπερ
³boldness ¹we use, and not as

Μωϋσῆς ἐτίθει κάλυμμα ἐπὶ τὸ πρόσωπον
Moses put a veil on the face

αὐτοῦ, πρὸς τὸ μὴ ἀτενίσαι τοὺς υἱοὺς
of him, for the ⁴not ⁵to gaze ¹the ²sons

Ἰσραὴλᵇ εἰς τὸ τέλος τοῦ καταργουμένου.
³of Israel at the end of the [thing] being done away.

14 ἀλλὰ ἐπωρώθη τὰ νοήματα αὐτῶν.
But were hardened the thoughts of them.

ἄχρι γὰρ τῆς σήμερον ἡμέρας τὸ αὐτὸ
For until the present day the same

κάλυμμα ἐπὶ τῇ ἀναγνώσει τῆς παλαιᾶς
veil ²on(at) ³the ⁴reading ⁵of the ⁶old

διαθήκης μένει, μὴ ἀνακαλυπτόμενον ὅτι
⁷covenant ¹remains, not being unveiled* that

ἐν Χριστῷ καταργεῖται. 15 ἀλλ' ἕως
in Christ it is being done away. But until

σήμερον ἡνίκα ἂν ἀναγινώσκηται Μωϋσῆς
to-day whenever ²is being read ¹Moses

κάλυμμα ἐπὶ τὴν καρδίαν αὐτῶν κεῖται·
a veil ²on ³the ⁴heart ⁵of them ¹lies;

16 ἡνίκα δὲ ἐὰν ἐπιστρέψῃ πρὸς κύριον,
but whenever it§ turns to [the] Lord,

περιαιρεῖται τὸ κάλυμμα. 17 ὁ δὲ κύριος
³is taken away ¹the ²veil. Now the Lord

τὸ πνεῦμά ἐστιν· οὗ δὲ τὸ πνεῦμα
²the ³Spirit ¹is; and where the Spirit

κυρίου, ἐλευθερία. 18 ἡμεῖς δὲ πάντες
of [the] [there is] freedom. But we all
Lord [is],

ἀνακεκαλυμμένῳ προσώπῳ τὴν δόξαν
²having been unveiled ¹with face ²the ³glory

κυρίου κατοπτριζόμενοι τὴν αὐτὴν εἰκόνα
⁴of [the] ¹beholding in ⁶the ⁷same ⁸image
Lord a mirror

μεταμορφούμεθα ἀπὸ δόξης εἰς δόξαν,
⁵are being changed [into] from glory to glory,

καθάπερ ἀπὸ κυρίου πνεύματος.
even as from [the] Lord Spirit.

* That is, revealed (Conybeare and Howson). § ? their heart.

CHAPTER 4

THEREFORE, having this ministry by the mercy of God, we do not lose heart. ²We have renounced disgraceful, underhanded ways; we refuse to practice cunning or to tamper with God's word, but by the open statement of the truth we would commend ourselves to every man's conscience in the sight of God. ³And even if our gospel is veiled, it is veiled only to those who are perishing. ⁴In their case the god of this world has blinded the minds of the unbelievers, to keep them from seeing the light of the gospel of the glory of Christ, who is the likeness of God. ⁵For what we preach is not ourselves, but Jesus Christ as Lord, with ourselves as your servants for Jesus' sake. ⁶For it is the God who said, "Let light shine out of darkness," who has shone in our hearts to give the light of the knowledge of the glory of God in the face of Christ.

7 But we have this treasure in earthen vessels, to show that the

---

4 Διὰ τοῦτο, ἔχοντες τὴν διακονίαν
Therefore, having - ministry
ταύτην, καθὼς ἠλεήθημεν, οὐκ ἐγκακοῦμεν,
this, as we obtained mercy, we faint not,
2 ἀλλὰ ἀπειπάμεθα τὰ κρυπτὰ τῆς αἰσχύνης,
but we have renounced the hidden things - of shame,
μὴ περιπατοῦντες ἐν πανουργίᾳ μηδὲ
not walking in craftiness nor
δολοῦντες τὸν λόγον τοῦ θεοῦ, ἀλλὰ
adulterating the word - of God, but
τῇ φανερώσει τῆς ἀληθείας συνιστάνοντες
by the manifestation of the truth commending
ἑαυτοὺς πρὸς πᾶσαν συνείδησιν ἀνθρώπων
ourselves to every conscience of men
ἐνώπιον τοῦ θεοῦ. **3** εἰ δὲ καὶ ἔστιν
before - God. But if indeed ⁴is
κεκαλυμμένον τὸ εὐαγγέλιον ἡμῶν, ἐν
⁵having been hidden ¹the ²gospel ³of us, in
τοῖς ἀπολλυμένοις ἐστὶν κεκαλυμμένον, **4** ἐν
the [ones] perishing it is having been hidden, in
οἷς ὁ θεὸς τοῦ αἰῶνος τούτου ἐτύφλωσεν
whom the god of this age blinded
τὰ νοήματα τῶν ἀπίστων εἰς τὸ μὴ
the thoughts of the unbelieving [with a the not
[ones] view] to
=so that the enlightenment . . . should not shine forth,
αὐγάσαι τὸν φωτισμὸν τοῦ εὐαγγελίου
to shine forth the enlightenment of the gospel
τῆς δόξης τοῦ Χριστοῦ, ὅς ἐστιν εἰκὼν
of the glory - of Christ, who is [the] image
τοῦ θεοῦ. **5** οὐ γὰρ ἑαυτοὺς κηρύσσομεν
- of God. For ²not ³ourselves ¹we proclaim
ἀλλὰ Χριστὸν Ἰησοῦν κύριον, ἑαυτοὺς δὲ
but Christ Jesus [as] Lord, and ourselves
δούλους ὑμῶν διὰ Ἰησοῦν. **6** ὅτι ὁ
slaves of you on account of Jesus. Because -
θεὸς ὁ εἰπών· ἐκ σκότους φῶς λάμψει,
God the [one] saying: Out of darkness light shall shine,
ὃς ἔλαμψεν ἐν ταῖς καρδίαις ἡμῶν πρὸς
[is] [he] shone in the hearts of us for
who
φωτισμὸν τῆς γνώσεως τῆς δόξης τοῦ
enlightenment of the knowledge of the glory -
θεοῦ ἐν προσώπῳ Χριστοῦ.
of God in [the] face of Christ.

7 Ἔχομεν δὲ τὸν θησαυρὸν τοῦτον ἐν
And we have this treasure in
ὀστρακίνοις σκεύεσιν, ἵνα ἡ ὑπερβολὴ
earthenware vessels, in order that the excellence

transcendent power belongs to God and not to us. ⁸We are afflicted in every way, but not crushed; perplexed, but not driven to despair; ⁹persecuted, but not forsaken; struck down, but not destroyed; ¹⁰always carrying in the body the death of Jesus, so that the life of Jesus may also be manifested in our bodies. ¹¹For while we live we are always being given up to death for Jesus' sake, so that the life of Jesus may be manifested in our mortal flesh. ¹²So death is at work in us, but life in you.

13 Since we have the same spirit of faith as he had who wrote, "I believed, and so I spoke," we too believe, and so we speak, ¹⁴knowing that he who raised the Lord Jesus will raise us also with Jesus and bring us with you into his presence. ¹⁵For it is all for your sake, so that as grace extends to more

τῆς	δυνάμεως	ἦ	τοῦ	θεοῦ	καὶ	μὴ	ἐξ
of the	power	may be	-	of God	and	not	of

ἡμῶν·	8 ἐν	παντὶ	θλιβόμενοι	ἀλλ'	οὐ
us;	in	every [way]	being afflicted	but	not

στενοχωρούμενοι,	ἀπορούμενοι	ἀλλ'	οὐκ
being restrained,	being in difficulties	but	not

ἐξαπορούμενοι,	9 διωκόμενοι	ἀλλ'	οὐκ
despairing,	being persecuted	but	not

ἐγκαταλειπόμενοι,	καταβαλλόμενοι	ἀλλ'	οὐκ
being deserted,	being cast down	but	not

ἀπολλύμενοι,	10 πάντοτε	τὴν	νέκρωσιν	τοῦ
perishing,	always	⁵the	⁶dying	-

Ἰησοῦ	ἐν	τῷ	σώματι	περιφέροντες,	ἵνα
⁷of Jesus	²in	³the	⁴body	¹bearing about,	in order that

καὶ	ἡ	ζωὴ	τοῦ	Ἰησοῦ	ἐν	τῷ	σώματι
also	the	life	-	of Jesus	in	the	body

ἡμῶν	φανερωθῇ.	11 ἀεὶ	γὰρ	ἡμεῖς	οἱ
of us	might be manifested.	For always		we	the

ζῶντες	εἰς	θάνατον	παραδιδόμεθα	διὰ
[ones] living	to	death	are being delivered	on account of

Ἰησοῦν,	ἵνα	καὶ	ἡ	ζωὴ	τοῦ	Ἰησοῦ
Jesus,	in order that	also	the	life	-	of Jesus

φανερωθῇ	ἐν	τῇ	θνητῇ	σαρκὶ	ἡμῶν.
might be manifested	in	the	mortal	flesh	of us.

12 ὥστε	ὁ	θάνατος	ἐν	ἡμῖν	ἐνεργεῖται,
So as	-	death	in	us	operates,

ἡ	δὲ	ζωὴ	ἐν	ὑμῖν.	13 ἔχοντες	δὲ	τὸ
-	but	life	in	you.	And having		the

αὐτὸ	πνεῦμα	τῆς	πίστεως,	κατὰ	τὸ
same	spirit	-	of faith,	according to	the thing

γεγραμμένον·	ἐπίστευσα,	διὸ	ἐλάλησα,	καὶ
having been written:	I believed,	therefore	I spoke,	both

ἡμεῖς	πιστεύομεν,	διὸ	καὶ	λαλοῦμεν,	14 εἰδότες
we	believe,	and therefore		we speak,	knowing

ὅτι	ὁ	ἐγείρας	τὸν	κύριον	Ἰησοῦν	καὶ
that	the [one]	having raised	the	Lord	Jesus	²also

ἡμᾶς	σὺν	Ἰησοῦ	ἐγερεῖ	καὶ	παραστήσει
²us	⁴with	⁵Jesus	¹will raise	and	will present [us]

σὺν	ὑμῖν.	15 τὰ	γὰρ	πάντα	δι'	ὑμᾶς,
with	you.	-	For	all things [are]	on account of	you,

ἵνα	ἡ	χάρις	πλεονάσασα	διὰ	τῶν	πλειόνων
in order that	-	grace	increased	through	the	majority

and more people it may increase thanksgiving, to the glory of God. 16 So we do not lose heart. Though our outer nature is wasting away, our inner nature is being renewed every day. [17] For this slight momentary affliction is preparing for us an eternal weight of glory beyond all comparison, [18] because we look not to the things that are seen but to the things that are unseen; for the things that are seen are transient, but the things that are unseen are eternal.

τὴν εὐχαριστίαν περισσεύσῃ εἰς τὴν δόξαν
*the *thanksgiving ¹may cause to abound to the glory

τοῦ θεοῦ. 16 Διὸ οὐκ ἐγκακοῦμεν, ἀλλ᾽
- of God. Wherefore we faint not, but

εἰ καὶ ὁ ἔξω ἡμῶν ἄνθρωπος διαφθείρεται,
if indeed the outward ²of us ¹man is being disabled,

ἀλλ᾽ ὁ ἔσω ἡμῶν ἀνακαινοῦται ἡμέρᾳ
yet the inward [man] of us is being renewed day

καὶ ἡμέρᾳ. 17 τὸ γὰρ παραυτίκα ἐλαφρὸν
and(by) day. For the present lightness

τῆς θλίψεως καθ᾽ ὑπερβολὴν εἰς ὑπερβολὴν
of the affliction ²excessively ⁴to ⁵excess

αἰώνιον βάρος δόξης κατεργάζεται ἡμῖν,
⁶an eternal ⁷weight ⁸of glory ¹works ²for us,

18 μὴ σκοπούντων ἡμῶν τὰ βλεπόμενα
not considering us⁸ the things being seen
=while we do not consider

ἀλλὰ τὰ μὴ βλεπόμενα· τὰ γὰρ βλεπόμενα
but the not being seen; for the things being seen
things

πρόσκαιρα, τὰ δὲ μὴ βλεπόμενα αἰώνια.
[are] temporary, but the things not being seen [are] eternal.

CHAPTER 5

FOR we know that if the earthly tent we live in is destroyed, we have a building from God, a house not made with hands, eternal in the heavens. ²Here indeed we groan, and long to put on our heavenly dwelling, ³so that by putting it on we may not be found naked. ⁴For while we are still in this tent, we sigh with anxiety; not that we would be unclothed, but that we would be further clothed, so that what is mortal may be swallowed up by life. ⁵He who has

5 Οἴδαμεν γὰρ ὅτι ἐὰν ἡ ἐπίγειος
For we know that if the earthly

ἡμῶν οἰκία τοῦ σκήνους καταλυθῇ,
⁶of us ¹house ²of the ³tabernacle is destroyed,

οἰκοδομὴν ἐκ θεοῦ ἔχομεν, οἰκίαν ἀχειρο-
a building of God we have, a house not made

ποίητον αἰώνιον ἐν τοῖς οὐρανοῖς. 2 καὶ
by hands eternal in the heavens. indeed

γὰρ ἐν τούτῳ στενάζομεν, τὸ οἰκητήριον
For in this* we groan, ³the ⁴dwelling-place

ἡμῶν τὸ ἐξ οὐρανοῦ ἐπενδύσασθαι ἐπιπο-
⁵of us - ⁶out of ⁷heaven ⁸to put on ¹greatly

θοῦντες, 3 εἴ γε καὶ ἐνδυσάμενοι οὐ
desiring, if indeed being clothed not

γυμνοὶ εὑρεθησόμεθα. 4 καὶ γὰρ οἱ
naked we shall be found. For indeed ²the
[ones]

ὄντες ἐν τῷ σκήνει στενάζομεν βαρούμενοι,
³being ⁴in ⁵the ⁶tabernacle ¹we groan being burdened,

ἐφ᾽ ᾧ οὐ θέλομεν ἐκδύσασθαι ἀλλ᾽
inasmuch as we do not wish to put off but

ἐπενδύσασθαι, ἵνα καταποθῇ τὸ θνητὸν
to put on, in order ³may be ¹the ²mortal
that swallowed up

ὑπὸ τῆς ζωῆς. 5 ὁ δὲ κατεργασάμενος
by the life. Now the [one] having wrought

* Neuter, going back to σκῆνος in the preceding verse.

prepared us for this very thing is God, who has given us the Spirit as a guarantee. 6 So we are always of good courage; we know that while we are at home in the body we are away from the Lord, ⁷for we walk by faith, not by sight. ⁸We are of good courage, and we would rather be away from the body and at home with the Lord. ⁹So whether we are at home or away, we make it our aim to please him. ¹⁰For we must all appear before the judgment seat of Christ, so that each one may receive good or evil, according to what he has done in the body. 11 Therefore, knowing the fear of the Lord, we persuade men; but what we are is known to God, and I hope it is known also to your conscience. ¹²We are not commending ourselves to you again but giving you cause to be proud of us, so that you may be able

ἡμᾶς εἰς αὐτὸ τοῦτο θεός, ὁ δοὺς
us for this very thing [is] the having
God, [one] given

ἡμῖν τὸν ἀρραβῶνα τοῦ πνεύματος. 6 Θαρ-
to us the earnest of the Spirit. Being

ροῦντες οὖν πάντοτε καὶ εἰδότες ὅτι
of good therefore always and knowing that
cheer

ἐνδημοῦντες ἐν τῷ σώματι ἐκδημοῦμεν
being at home in the body we are away
from home

ἀπὸ τοῦ κυρίου· 7 διὰ πίστεως γὰρ
from the Lord; ²through ³faith ¹for

περιπατοῦμεν, οὐ διὰ εἴδους· 8 θαρροῦμεν
we walk, not through appearance; we are of
good cheer

δὲ καὶ εὐδοκοῦμεν μᾶλλον ἐκδημῆσαι ἐκ
then and think it good rather to go away out
from home of

τοῦ σώματος καὶ ἐνδημῆσαι πρὸς τὸν
the body and to come home to the

κύριον. 9 διὸ καὶ φιλοτιμούμεθα, εἴτε
Lord. Wherefore also we are ambitious, whether

ἐνδημοῦντες εἴτε ἐκδημοῦντες, εὐάρεστοι
being at home or being away from home, wellpleasing

αὐτῷ εἶναι. 10 τοὺς γὰρ πάντας ἡμᾶς
to him to be. - For ³all ²us

φανερωθῆναι δεῖ ἔμπροσθεν τοῦ βήματος
⁴to be manifested ¹it behoves before the tribunal

τοῦ Χριστοῦ, ἵνα κομίσηται ἕκαστος τὰ
- of Christ, in order ²may receive ¹each one the
that things

διὰ τοῦ σώματος πρὸς ἃ ἔπραξεν, εἴτε
through the body accord- what he either
ing to things practised,

ἀγαθὸν εἴτε φαῦλον.
good or worthless.

11 Εἰδότες οὖν τὸν φόβον τοῦ κυρίου
Knowing therefore the fear of the Lord

ἀνθρώπους πείθομεν, θεῷ δὲ πεφανερώμεθα·
²men ¹we persuade, and to God we have been made
manifest;

ἐλπίζω δὲ καὶ ἐν ταῖς συνειδήσεσιν
and I hope also in the consciences

ὑμῶν πεφανερῶσθαι. 12 οὐ πάλιν ἑαυτοὺς
of you to have been made Not again ²ourselves
manifest.

συνιστάνομεν ὑμῖν, ἀλλὰ ἀφορμὴν διδόντες
¹we commend to you, but ²an occasion ¹giving

ὑμῖν καυχήματος ὑπὲρ ἡμῶν, ἵνα ἔχητε
²to you of a boast on be- us, in order ye may
half of that have [it]

to answer those who pride themselves on a man's position and not on his heart. [13]For if we are beside ourselves, it is for God; if we are in our right mind, it is for you. [14]For the love of Christ controls us, because we are convinced that one has died for all; therefore all have died. [15]And he died for all, that those who live might live no longer for themselves but for him who for their sake died and was raised.

16 From now on, therefore, we regard no one from a human point of view; even though we once regarded Christ from a human point of view, we regard him thus no longer. [17]Therefore, if any one is in Christ, he is a new creation;[e] the old has passed away, behold, the new has come. [18]All this is from God, who through Christ reconciled us to himself and gave us the ministry of reconciliation; [19]that is, God was in Christ reconciling[f] the world to himself, not counting their trespasses against them, and entrusting to us the message of reconciliation. [20]So we are ambassadors for Christ,

[e] Or creature
[f] Or in Christ God was reconciling

πρὸς τοὺς ἐν προσώπῳ καυχωμένους καὶ
in refer- the   ²in   ³face   ¹boasting   and
ence to [ones]

μὴ ἐν καρδίᾳ.   13 εἴτε γὰρ ἐξέστημεν,
not in heart.   For whether we are mad,

θεῷ· εἴτε σωφρονοῦμεν. ὑμῖν. 14 ἡ γὰρ
[it is]   or   we are in our senses, [it is]   For the
to God;   for you.

ἀγάπη τοῦ Χριστοῦ συνέχει ἡμᾶς, κρίναντας
love   –   of Christ constrains us,   judging

τοῦτο, ὅτι εἷς ὑπὲρ πάντων ἀπέθανεν·
this,   that one on behalf of all men   died;

ἄρα οἱ πάντες ἀπέθανον· 15 καὶ ὑπὲρ
then the   all   died;   and   ²on be-
                                half of

πάντων ἀπέθανεν ἵνα οἱ ζῶντες μηκέτι
³all   ¹he died in order the living   no more
                that [ones]

ἑαυτοῖς ζῶσιν ἀλλὰ τῷ ὑπὲρ αὐτῶν
to themselves may live   but to the on behalf them
                       [one]   of

ἀποθανόντι καὶ ἐγερθέντι. 16 Ὥστε ἡμεῖς
having died   and having been raised. So as ³we

ἀπὸ τοῦ νῦν οὐδένα οἴδαμεν κατὰ σάρκα·
¹from – ²now ⁵no man ⁴know according to flesh;

εἰ καὶ ἐγνώκαμεν κατὰ σάρκα Χριστόν,
if indeed ¹we have known ³according to ⁴flesh   ²Christ,

ἀλλὰ νῦν οὐκέτι γινώσκομεν. 17 ὥστε
yet   now   no more   we know [him].   So as

εἴ τις ἐν Χριστῷ, καινὴ κτίσις· τὰ
if anyone [is] in Christ, [he is] a new creation; the

ἀρχαῖα παρῆλθεν, ἰδοὺ γέγονεν καινά.
old things passed away, behold they have become new.

18 τὰ δὲ πάντα ἐκ τοῦ θεοῦ τοῦ καταλ-
– And all things [are] of –   God the [one] having

λάξαντος ἡμᾶς ἑαυτῷ διὰ Χριστοῦ καὶ
reconciled   us   to himself through Christ   and

δόντος ἡμῖν τὴν διακονίαν τῆς καταλλαγῆς,
having given to us the   ministry   – of reconciliation,

19 ὡς ὅτι θεὸς ἦν ἐν Χριστῷ κόσμον
as that God was in   Christ ²[the] world

καταλλάσσων ἑαυτῷ, μὴ λογιζόμενος αὐτοῖς
¹reconciling to himself, not reckoning   to them

τὰ παραπτώματα αὐτῶν, καὶ θέμενος
the   trespasses   of them, and placing

ἐν ἡμῖν τὸν λόγον τῆς καταλλαγῆς.
in us   the word   – of reconciliation.

20 Ὑπὲρ Χριστοῦ οὖν πρεσβεύομεν ὡς
On behalf of Christ therefore we are ambassadors as

God making his appeal through us. We beseech you on behalf of Christ, be reconciled to God. ²¹For our sake he made him to be sin who knew no sin, so that in him we might become the righteousness of God.

τοῦ θεοῦ παρακαλοῦντος δι' ἡμῶν· δεόμεθα
\- God beseeching⁸ through us; we beg
ὑπὲρ Χριστοῦ, καταλλάγητε τῷ θεῷ.
on behalf of Christ, Be ye reconciled \- to God.
21 τὸν μὴ γνόντα ἁμαρτίαν ὑπὲρ ἡμῶν
²The [one] ²not ⁴knowing ⁵sin ⁷on behalf of ⁸us
ἁμαρτίαν ἐποίησεν, ἵνα ἡμεῖς γενώμεθα
⁸sin ¹he made, in order that we might become
δικαιοσύνη θεοῦ ἐν αὐτῷ.
[the] righteousness of God in him.

CHAPTER 6

WORKING together with him, then, we entreat you not to accept the grace of God in vain. ²For he says,
"At the acceptable time I have listened to you,
and helped you on the day of salvation."
Behold, now is the acceptable time; behold, now is the day of salvation. ³We put no obstacle in anyone's way, so that no fault may be found with our ministry, ⁴but as servants of God we commend ourselves in every way: through great endurance, in afflictions, hardships, calamities, ⁵beatings, imprisonments, tumults, labors, watching, hunger; ⁶by purity, knowledge, forbearance, kindness, the Holy Spirit, genuine love, ⁷truthful speech, and the power of God; with the weapons of righteousness for the right hand and for the left; ⁸in honor and dis-

6 Συνεργοῦντες δὲ καὶ παρακαλοῦμεν μὴ
And working together also we beseech ²not
εἰς κενὸν τὴν χάριν τοῦ θεοῦ δέξασθαι
⁷to no purpose ⁴the ⁵grace \- ⁶of God ⁸to receive
ὑμᾶς· 2 λέγει γάρ· καιρῷ δεκτῷ ἐπήκουσά
¹you; for he says: In a time acceptable I heard
σου καὶ ἐν ἡμέρα σωτηρίας ἐβοήθησά
thee and in a day of salvation I helped
σοι· ἰδοὺ νῦν καιρὸς εὐπρόσδεκτος, ἰδοὺ
thee; behold now a time acceptable, behold
νῦν ἡμέρα σωτηρίας· 3 — μηδεμίαν ἐν
now a day of salvation; ²no ⁴in
μηδενὶ διδόντες προσκοπήν, ἵνα μὴ
²no(any)thing ¹giving ³cause of stumbling, lest
μωμηθῇ ἡ διακονία, 4 ἀλλ' ἐν παντὶ
²be blamed ¹the ²ministry, but in everything
συνιστάνοντες ἑαυτοὺς ὡς θεοῦ διάκονοι,
commending ourselves as ²of God ¹ministers,
ἐν ὑπομονῇ πολλῇ, ἐν θλίψεσιν, ἐν
in ²endurance ¹much, in afflictions, in
ἀνάγκαις, ἐν στενοχωρίαις, ἐν πληγαῖς,
necessities, in straits, in stripes,
5 ἐν φυλακαῖς, ἐν ἀκαταστασίαις, ἐν κόποις,
in prisons, in commotions, in labours,
ἐν ἀγρυπνίαις, ἐν νηστείαις, 6 ἐν ἁγνότητι,
in watchings, in fastings, in purity,
ἐν γνώσει, ἐν μακροθυμίᾳ, ἐν χρηστότητι,
in knowledge, in long-suffering, in kindness,
ἐν πνεύματι ἁγίῳ, ἐν ἀγάπῃ ἀνυποκρίτῳ,
in spirit a holy, in love unfeigned,
7 ἐν λόγῳ ἀληθείας, ἐν δυνάμει θεοῦ·
in a word of truth, in power of God;
διὰ τῶν ὅπλων τῆς δικαιοσύνης τῶν
through the weapons \- of righteousness of the
δεξιῶν καὶ ἀριστερῶν, 8 διὰ δόξης καὶ
right [hand] and of left, through glory and

honor, in ill repute and good repute. We are treated as impostors, and yet are true; [9] as unknown, and yet well known; as dying, and behold we live; as punished, and yet not killed; [10] as sorrowful, yet always rejoicing; as poor, yet making many rich; as having nothing, and yet possessing everything. [11] Our mouth is open to you, Corinthians; our heart is wide. [12] You are not restricted by us, but you are restricted in your own affections. [13] In return—I speak as to children—widen your hearts also. [14] Do not be mismated with unbelievers. For what partnership have righteousness and iniquity? Or what fellowship has light with darkness? [15] What accord has Christ with Be'lial? Or what has a believer in common with an unbeliever? [16] What agreement has the temple of God with idols? For we are the temple of the living God; as God said, "I will live in them and move among

ἀτιμίας,   διὰ   δυσφημίας   καὶ   εὐφημίας·
dishonour,   through   ill report   and   good report;

ὡς   πλάνοι   καὶ   ἀληθεῖς,   9 ὡς   ἀγνοούμενοι
as   deceivers   and*   true men,   as   being unknown

καὶ   ἐπιγινωσκόμενοι,   ὡς   ἀποθνῄσκοντες   καὶ
and*   being well known,   as   dying   and

ἰδοὺ   ζῶμεν,   ὡς   παιδευόμενοι   καὶ   μὴ
behold   we live,   as   being chastened   and   not

θανατούμενοι,   10 ὡς   λυπούμενοι   ἀεὶ   δὲ
being put to death,   as   being grieved   ²always   ¹but

χαίροντες,   ὡς   πτωχοὶ   πολλοὺς   δὲ   πλουτίζ-
rejoicing,   as   poor   ³many   ¹but   ²en-

οντες,   ὡς   μηδὲν   ἔχοντες   καὶ   πάντα
riching,   as   ²nothing   ¹having   ³and*   ⁵all things

κατέχοντες.
⁴possessing.

11 Τὸ   στόμα   ἡμῶν   ἀνέῳγεν   πρὸς   ὑμᾶς,
The   mouth   of us   has opened   to   you,

Κορίνθιοι,   ἡ   καρδία   ἡμῶν   πεπλάτυνται·
Corinthians,   the   heart   of us   has been enlarged;

12 οὐ   στενοχωρεῖσθε   ἐν   ἡμῖν,   στενοχωρεῖσθε
ye are not restrained   in   us,   ²ye are restrained

δὲ   ἐν   τοῖς   σπλάγχνοις   ὑμῶν·   13 τὴν   δὲ
¹but   in   the   bowels   of you;   but [for] the

αὐτὴν   ἀντιμισθίαν,   ὡς   τέκνοις   λέγω,
same   recompence,   as   to children   I say,

πλατύνθητε   καὶ   ὑμεῖς.
be enlarged   also   ye.

14 Μὴ   γίνεσθε   ἑτεροζυγοῦντες   ἀπίστοις·
Do not ye become   unequally yoked [with] unbelievers;

τίς   γὰρ   μετοχὴ   δικαιοσύνῃ   καὶ   ἀνομίᾳ,
for what   share   righteousness°   and   lawlessness,°
                =have righteousness and lawlessness,

ἢ   τίς   κοινωνία   φωτὶ   πρὸς   σκότος;   15 τίς
or   what   fellowship   light°   with   darkness?   what
             =has light

δὲ   συμφώνησις   Χριστοῦ   πρὸς   Βελιάρ,
and   agreement   of Christ   with   Beliar,

ἢ   τίς   μερὶς   πιστῷ   μετὰ   ἀπίστου;   16 τίς
or   what   part   a believer°   with   an unbeliever?   what
           =has a believer

δὲ   συγκατάθεσις   ναῷ   θεοῦ   μετὰ   εἰδώλων;
and   union   a shrine° of God   with   idols?
         =has a shrine

ἡμεῖς   γὰρ   ναὸς   θεοῦ   ἐσμεν   ζῶντος·
For ¹we   ³a shrine   ⁵God   ²are   ⁴of a living;

καθὼς   εἶπεν   ὁ   θεὸς   ὅτι   ἐνοικήσω   ἐν
as   said   –   God[,]   –   I will dwell among

* Evidently = and yet, as in some other places; cf. John 20. 29.

them,
and I will be their God,
and they shall be my people.
¹⁷ Therefore come out from them,
and be separate from them, says the Lord,
and touch nothing unclean;
then I will welcome you,
¹⁸ and I will be a father to you,
and you shall be my sons and daughters,
says the Lord Almighty."

CHAPTER 7

SINCE we have these promises, beloved, let us cleanse ourselves from every defilement of body and spirit, and make holiness perfect in the fear of God.
2 Open your hearts to us; we have wronged no one, we have corrupted no one, we have taken advantage of no one. ³ I do not say this to condemn you, for I said before that you are in our hearts, to die together and to live together. ⁴ I have great confidence in you; I have great pride in you; I am filled with comfort. With all our affliction, I am overjoyed.
5 For even when we came into Macedo′nia, our bodies had no rest but we were afflicted at every turn—fighting without and fear within.

αὐτοῖς καὶ ἐμπεριπατήσω, καὶ ἔσομαι
them and *I* will walk among [them], and I will be

αὐτῶν θεός, καὶ αὐτοὶ ἔσονταί μου λαός.
of them God, and they shall be of me a people.

17 διὸ ἐξέλθατε ἐκ μέσου αὐτῶν καὶ
Wherefore come ye out from [the] midst of them and

ἀφορίσθητε, λέγει κύριος, καὶ ἀκαθάρτου
be ye separated, says [the] Lord, and an unclean thing

μὴ ἅπτεσθε· 18 κἀγὼ εἰσδέξομαι ὑμᾶς, καὶ
do not touch; and I will welcome in you, and

ἔσομαι ὑμῖν εἰς πατέρα, καὶ ὑμεῖς ἔσεσθέ
I will be to you for a father, and ye shall be

μοι εἰς υἱοὺς καὶ θυγατέρας, λέγει κύριος
to me for sons and daughters, says [the] Lord

παντοκράτωρ. 7 ταύτας οὖν ἔχοντες τὰς ἐπ-
[the] Almighty. ²These ²therefore ¹having - ⁴pro·

αγγελίας, ἀγαπητοί, καθαρίσωμεν ἑαυτοὺς ἀπὸ
mises, beloved, let us cleanse ourselves from

παντὸς μολυσμοῦ σαρκὸς καὶ πνεύματος,
all pollution of flesh and of spirit,

ἐπιτελοῦντες ἁγιωσύνην ἐν φόβῳ θεοῦ.
perfecting holiness in [the] fear of God.

2 Χωρήσατε ἡμᾶς· οὐδένα ἠδικήσαμεν,
Make room for us; no one we wronged,

οὐδένα ἐφθείραμεν, οὐδένα ἐπλεονεκτήσαμεν.
no one we injured, no one we defrauded.

3 πρὸς κατάκρισιν οὐ λέγω· προείρηκα
For condemnation I say not; ²I have previously said

γὰρ ὅτι ἐν ταῖς καρδίαις ἡμῶν ἐστε
¹for that in the hearts of us ye are

εἰς τὸ συναποθανεῖν καὶ συζῆν. 4 πολλή
for - to die with [you] and to live with [you]. Much

μοι παρρησία πρὸς ὑμᾶς, πολλή μοι
to me° boldness toward you, much to me°
=I have much =I have much

καύχησις ὑπὲρ ὑμῶν· πεπλήρωμαι τῇ
boasting on behalf of you; I have been filled

παρακλήσει, ὑπερπερισσεύομαι τῇ χαρᾷ ἐπὶ
with comfort, I overflow - with joy on(in)

πάσῃ τῇ θλίψει ἡμῶν. 5 Καὶ γὰρ
all the affliction of us. For indeed

ἐλθόντων ἡμῶν εἰς Μακεδονίαν οὐδεμίαν
coming us⁴ into Macedonia ⁵no
=when we came

ἔσχηκεν ἄνεσιν ἡ σὰρξ ἡμῶν, ἀλλ᾽ ἐν
⁴has had ⁶rest ¹the ²flesh ³of us, but in

παντὶ θλιβόμενοι· ἔξωθεν μάχαι, ἔσωθεν
every way being afflicted; without [were] fightings, within

⁶But God, who comforts the downcast, comforted us by the coming of Titus, ⁷and not only by his coming but also by the comfort with which he was comforted in you, as he told us of your longing, your mourning, your zeal for me, so that I rejoiced still more. ⁸For even if I made you sorry with my letter, I do not regret it (though I did regret it), for I see that that letter grieved you, though only for a while. ⁹As it is, I rejoice, not because you were grieved, but because you were grieved into repenting; for you felt a godly grief, so that you suffered no loss through us. ¹⁰For godly grief produces a repentance that leads to salvation and brings no regret, but worldly grief produces death. ¹¹For see what earnestness this godly grief has produced in you, what eagerness to clear yourselves, what indignation, what alarm, what longing, what zeal, what punishment! At every point you have proved yourselves guiltless in the matter. ¹²So

φόβοι.　6 ἀλλ' ὁ παρακαλῶν τοὺς ταπεινοὺς
[were] fears.　But ²the [one] ³comforting ⁴the ⁵humble

παρεκάλεσεν ἡμᾶς ὁ θεὸς ἐν τῇ παρουσίᾳ
⁶comforted ⁷us － ¹God by the presence

Τίτου·　7 οὐ μόνον δὲ ἐν τῇ παρουσίᾳ
of Titus;　and not only by the presence

αὐτοῦ, ἀλλὰ καὶ ἐν τῇ παρακλήσει ᾗ
of him,　but also by the comfort with which

παρεκλήθη ἐφ' ὑμῖν, ἀναγγέλλων ἡμῖν
he was comforted over you, reporting to us

τὴν ὑμῶν ἐπιπόθησιν, τὸν ὑμῶν ὀδυρμόν,
¹the ²of you ³eager longing, ¹the ²of you ³mourning,

τὸν ὑμῶν ζῆλον ὑπὲρ ἐμοῦ, ὥστε με
¹the ²of you ³zeal on behalf of me, so as me

μᾶλλον χαρῆναι.　8 Ὅτι εἰ καὶ ἐλύπησα
more to rejoice.ᵇ Because if indeed I grieved
＝so that I rejoiced more.

ὑμᾶς ἐν τῇ ἐπιστολῇ, οὐ μεταμέλομαι·
you by the epistle, I do not regret;

εἰ καὶ μετεμελόμην, βλέπω ὅτι ἡ ἐπιστολὴ
if indeed I regretted, I see that － epistle

ἐκείνη εἰ καὶ πρὸς ὥραν ἐλύπησεν ὑμᾶς,
that if indeed for an hour it grieved you,

9 νῦν χαίρω, οὐχ ὅτι ἐλυπήθητε, ἀλλ'
now I rejoice, not that ye were grieved, but

ὅτι ἐλυπήθητε εἰς μετάνοιαν· ἐλυπήθητε
that ye were grieved to repentance; ²ye were grieved

γὰρ κατὰ θεόν, ἵνα ἐν μηδενὶ ζημιωθῆτε
¹for according God, in order in nothing ye might suffer
to that loss

ἐξ ἡμῶν.　10 ἡ γὰρ κατὰ θεὸν λύπη
by us. For ¹the ²according to ⁴God ²grief

μετάνοιαν εἰς σωτηρίαν ἀμεταμέλητον
⁷repentance ⁸to ⁹salvation ⁶unregrettable

ἐργάζεται· ἡ δὲ τοῦ κόσμου λύπη θάνατον
⁵works; but ¹the ²of the ⁴world ³grief ⁵death

κατεργάζεται.　11 ἰδοὺ γὰρ αὐτὸ τοῦτο
⁶works out. For behold this very thing[,]

τὸ κατὰ θεὸν λυπηθῆναι πόσην κατειργά-
－ ²according to ³God ¹to be grieved[,] ¹what ²it worked

σατο ὑμῖν σπουδήν, ἀλλὰ ἀπολογίαν, ἀλλὰ
out ⁴in you ²earnestness, but [what] defence, but

ἀγανάκτησιν, ἀλλὰ φόβον, ἀλλὰ ἐπιπόθησιν,
vexation, but fear, but eager desire,

ἀλλὰ ζῆλον, ἀλλὰ ἐκδίκησιν.　ἐν παντὶ
but zeal, but vengeance. In everything

συνεστήσατε ἑαυτοὺς ἁγνοὺς εἶναι τῷ
ye commended yourselves pure to be in the

although I wrote to you, it was not on account of the one who did the wrong, nor on account of the one who suffered the wrong, but in order that your zeal for us might be revealed to you in the sight of God. ¹³Therefore we are comforted.

And besides our own comfort we rejoiced still more at the joy of Titus, because his mind has been set at rest by you all. ¹⁴For if I have expressed to him some pride in you, I was not put to shame; but just as everything we said to you was true, so our boasting before Titus has proved true. ¹⁵And his heart goes out all the more to you, as he remembers the obedience of you all, and the fear and trembling with which you received him. ¹⁶I rejoice, because I have perfect confidence in you.

πράγματι.   12 ἄρα   εἰ   καὶ   ἔγραψα   ὑμῖν,
affair.   Then   if   indeed   I wrote   to you,

οὐχ   ἕνεκεν   τοῦ   ἀδικήσαντος   οὐδὲ   ἕνεκεν
not   for the   the [one]   having done   nor   for the
    sake of   wrong   sake of

τοῦ   ἀδικηθέντος,   ἀλλ'   ἕνεκεν   τοῦ   φανερω-
the   having been   but   for the   -   to be mani-
[one]   wronged,   sake of

θῆναι   τὴν   σπουδὴν   ὑμῶν   τὴν   ὑπὲρ   ἡμῶν
fested   the   earnestnessᵇᵈ   of you   -   on behalf of   us

πρὸς   ὑμᾶς   ἐνώπιον   τοῦ   θεοῦ.   13 διὰ
toward   you   before   -   God.   There-

τοῦτο   παρακεκλήμεθα.   Ἐπὶ   δὲ   τῇ
fore   we have been comforted.   But as to   the

παρακλήσει   ἡμῶν   περισσοτέρως   μᾶλλον
comfort   of us   abundantly   more

ἐχάρημεν   ἐπὶ   τῇ   χαρᾷ   Τίτου,   ὅτι   ἀναπέ-
we rejoiced   over   the   joy   of Titus,   because   has been

παυται   τὸ   πνεῦμα   αὐτοῦ   ἀπὸ   πάντων
rested   the   spirit   of him   from(by)   all

ὑμῶν·   14 ὅτι   εἴ   τι   αὐτῷ   ὑπὲρ   ὑμῶν
you;   because   if   ³anything   ³to him   ⁴on behalf of   ⁵you

κεκαύχημαι,   οὐ   κατῃσχύνθην,   ἀλλ'   ὡς
¹I have boasted,   I was not shamed,   but   as

πάντα   ἐν   ἀληθείᾳ   ἐλαλήσαμεν   ὑμῖν,   οὕτως
³all things   ²in   ⁴truth   ¹we spoke   ⁵to you,   so

καὶ   ἡ   καύχησις   ἡμῶν   ἐπὶ   Τίτου   ἀλήθεια
also   the   boasting   of us   over   Titus   ³truth

ἐγενήθη.   15 καὶ   τὰ   σπλάγχνα   αὐτοῦ
¹became.   And   the   bowels   of him

περισσοτέρως   εἰς   ὑμᾶς   ἐστιν   ἀναμιμνησκομέ-
²abundantly   ³toward   ⁴you   ¹is(are)   [he]   remember-

νου   τὴν   πάντων   ὑμῶν   ὑπακοήν,   ὡς   μετὰ
ingᵃ   ¹the   ³of all   ⁴you   ²obedience,   as   with

φόβου   καὶ   τρόμου   ἐδέξασθε   αὐτόν.
fear   and   trembling   ye received   him.

16 χαίρω   ὅτι   ἐν   παντὶ   θαρρῶ   ἐν   ὑμῖν.
I rejoice   that   in everything   I am confident in   you.

CHAPTER 8

WE want you to know, brethren, about the grace of God which has been shown in the churches of Macedo'-nia, ²for in a severe test of affliction, their abundance of joy and their extreme poverty

8 Γνωρίζομεν   δὲ   ὑμῖν,   ἀδελφοί,   τὴν
Now we make known   to you,   brothers,   the

χάριν   τοῦ   θεοῦ   τὴν   δεδομένην   ἐν   ταῖς
grace   -   of God   -   having been given among   the

ἐκκλησίαις   τῆς   Μακεδονίας,   2 ὅτι   ἐν   πολλῇ
churches   -   of Macedonia,   that   in   much

δοκιμῇ   θλίψεως   ἡ   περισσεία   τῆς   χαρᾶς
proving   of affliction   the   abundance   of the   joy

αὐτῶν   καὶ   ἡ   κατὰ   βάθους   πτωχεία
of them   and   ¹the   ²according to   ⁴depth   ²poverty
                   =their extreme poverty

have overflowed in a wealth of liberality on their part. ³For they gave according to their means, as I can testify, and beyond their means, of their own free will, ⁴begging us earnestly for the favor of taking part in the relief of the saints —⁵and this, not as we expected, but first they gave themselves to the Lord and to us by the will of God. ⁶Accordingly we have urged Titus that as he had already made a beginning, he should also complete among you this gracious work. ⁷Now as you excel in everything— in faith, in utterance, in knowledge, in all earnestness, and in your love for us—see that you excel in this gracious work also.

8 I say this not as a command, but to prove by the earnestness of others that your love also is genuine. ⁹For you know the grace of our Lord Jesus Christ, that though he was rich, yet for your sake he became poor, so that by his poverty you might become rich. ¹⁰And in this matter I give my advice:

αὐτῶν ἐπερίσσευσεν εἰς τὸ πλοῦτος τῆς
of them abounded   to the riches of the

ἁπλότητος αὐτῶν· 3 ὅτι κατὰ δύναμιν,
liberality of them;   that according [their]
                                   to power,

μαρτυρῶ, καὶ παρὰ δύναμιν, αὐθαίρετοι
I witness, and beyond [their] power, of their own
                                       accord

4 μετὰ πολλῆς παρακλήσεως δεόμενοι ἡμῶν
  with much beseeching requesting of us

τὴν χάριν καὶ τὴν κοινωνίαν τῆς διακονίας
the grace and the fellowship of the ministry

τῆς εἰς τοὺς ἁγίους, 5 καὶ οὐ καθὼς
– to the saints, and not as

ἠλπίσαμεν, ἀλλὰ ἑαυτοὺς ἔδωκαν πρῶτον
we hoped, but themselves gave firstly

τῷ κυρίῳ καὶ ἡμῖν διὰ θελήματος θεοῦ,
to the Lord and to us through [the] will of God,

6 εἰς τὸ παρακαλέσαι ἡμᾶς Τίτον, ἵνα
  for – to beseech usᵇ Titus, in order
=that we should beseech   that

καθὼς προενήρξατο οὕτως καὶ ἐπιτελέσῃ
as previously he began so also he should
                                  complete

εἰς ὑμᾶς καὶ τὴν χάριν ταύτην. 7 ἀλλ'
in you also this grace. But

ὥσπερ ἐν παντὶ περισσεύετε, πίστει καὶ
as in everything ye abound, in faith and

λόγῳ καὶ γνώσει καὶ πάσῃ σπουδῇ
in word and in knowledge and in all diligence

καὶ τῇ ἐξ ἡμῶν ἐν ὑμῖν ἀγάπῃ, ἵνα
and – ²from ³us ⁴in(to) ⁵you ¹in love, [see] that

καὶ ἐν ταύτῃ τῇ χάριτι περισσεύητε.
²also ³in ⁴this τῇ – ⁵grace ¹ye may abound.

8 Οὐ κατ' ἐπιταγὴν λέγω, ἀλλὰ διὰ
²Not ³by way of ⁴command ¹I say,* but through

τῆς ἑτέρων σπουδῆς καὶ τὸ τῆς ὑμετέρας
¹the ²of others ³diligence also ²the – ⁴of your

ἀγάπης γνήσιον δοκιμάζων· 9 γινώσκετε
⁵love ³reality ¹proving; ²ye know

γὰρ τὴν χάριν τοῦ κυρίου ἡμῶν Ἰησοῦ
¹for the grace of the Lord of us Jesus

[Χριστοῦ], ὅτι δι' ὑμᾶς ἐπτώχευσεν
Christ, that on account you ³he impoverished
                  of   [himself]

πλούσιος ὤν, ἵνα ὑμεῖς τῇ ἐκείνου πτωχείᾳ
²rich ¹being, in or- ye ¹by ²of that ²poverty
           der that   the one

πλουτήσητε. 10 καὶ γνώμην ἐν τούτῳ
might become rich. And ⁴an opinion ¹in ²this

* That is, Paul is not issuing a command. Cf. I. Cor. 7. 6.

it is best for you now to complete what a year ago you began not only to do but to desire, [11] so that your readiness in desiring it may be matched by your completing it out of what you have. [12] For if the readiness is there, it is acceptable according to what a man has, not according to what he has not. [13] I do not mean that others should be eased and you burdened, [14] but that as a matter of equality your abundance at the present time should supply their want, so that their abundance may supply your want, that there may be equality. [15] As it is written, "He who gathered much had nothing over, and he who gathered little had no lack."

16 But thanks be to God who puts the same earnest care for you into the heart of Titus. [17] For he not only accepted our appeal, but being himself very earnest he is going to you of his own accord. [18] With him we are sending the brother

δίδωμι· τοῦτο γὰρ ὑμῖν συμφέρει, οἵτινες
[3]I give: for this   [2]for you   [1]is expedient,   who

οὐ μόνον τὸ ποιῆσαι ἀλλὰ καὶ τὸ θέλειν
not   only   the   to do   but   also   the   to will

προενήρξασθε ἀπὸ πέρυσι· 11 νυνὶ δὲ καὶ
previously ye began   from   last year;   but now   also
                    = a year ago;

τὸ ποιῆσαι ἐπιτελέσατε, ὅπως καθάπερ ἡ
[2]the   [3]to do   [1]complete ye,   so as   as   the

προθυμία τοῦ θέλειν, οὕτως καὶ τὸ
eagerness   of the   to will,   so   also   the

ἐπιτελέσαι ἐκ τοῦ ἔχειν. 12 εἰ γὰρ ἡ
to complete   out of   the   to have.   For if   the
              = what ye have.

προθυμία πρόκειται, καθὸ ἐὰν ἔχῃ
eagerness   is already there,   according to   whatever   one has

εὐπρόσδεκτος, οὐ καθὸ οὐκ ἔχει. 13 οὐ
it is acceptable,   not   according   [what] one   not
               to   has not.

γὰρ ἵνα ἄλλοις ἄνεσις, ὑμῖν θλῖψις,
For   in order   to others   relief,   to you   distress,
    that   [there may be]

ἀλλ' ἐξ ἰσότητος 14 ἐν τῷ νῦν καιρῷ
but   by   equality   at   the   present   time

τὸ ὑμῶν περίσσευμα εἰς τὸ ἐκείνων
the   [2]of you   [1]abundance [may be] for   the   [2]of those

ὑστέρημα, ἵνα καὶ τὸ ἐκείνων περίσσευμα
[1]lack,   in order   also   the   [2]of those   [1]abundance
      that

γένηται εἰς τὸ ὑμῶν ὑστέρημα, ὅπως
may be   for   the   [2]of you   [1]lack,   so as

γένηται ἰσότης, 15 καθὼς γέγραπται· ὁ
there may be   equality,   as   it has been   He
                    written:

τὸ πολὺ οὐκ ἐπλεόνασεν, καὶ ὁ τὸ
the   much   did not abound,   and   he   the

ὀλίγον οὐκ ἠλαττόνησεν. 16 Χάρις δὲ
little   had not less.   But thanks [be]

τῷ θεῷ τῷ διδόντι τὴν αὐτὴν σπουδὴν
–   to God   –   giving   the   same   diligence

ὑπὲρ ὑμῶν ἐν τῇ καρδίᾳ Τίτου, 17 ὅτι
on be-   you   in   the   heart   of Titus,   because
half of

τὴν μὲν παράκλησιν ἐδέξατο, σπουδαιότερος
[2]the   [1]indeed   [4]beseeching   [3]he received,   [5]more diligent

δὲ ὑπάρχων αὐθαίρετος ἐξῆλθεν πρὸς ὑμᾶς.
[1]and   [2]being   of his own   he went   to   you.
            accord   forth

18 συνεπέμψαμεν δὲ μετ' αὐτοῦ τὸν
   And we sent with   with   him   the

who is famous among all the churches for his preaching of the gospel; ¹⁹and not only that, but he has been appointed by the churches to travel with us in this gracious work which we are carrying on, for the glory of the Lord and to show our good will. ²⁰We intend that no one should blame us about this liberal gift which we are administering, ²¹for we aim at what is honorable not only in the Lord's sight but also in the sight of men. ²²And with them we are sending our brother whom we have often tested and found earnest in many matters, but who is now more earnest than ever because of his great confidence in you. ²³As for Titus, he is my partner and fellow worker in your service; and as for our brethren, they are messengers of the churches, the glory of Christ. ²⁴So give proof, before the churches, of your love and of our boasting about you to these men.

ἀδελφὸν οὗ ὁ ἔπαινος ἐν τῷ εὐαγγελίῳ
brother of whom the praise in the gospel

διὰ πασῶν τῶν ἐκκλησιῶν, 19 οὐ μόνον δὲ
[is] all the churches, and not only [this]
through[out]

ἀλλὰ καὶ χειροτονηθεὶς ὑπὸ τῶν ἐκκλησιῶν
but also ²having been elected ⁴by ³the ⁵churches

συνέκδημος ἡμῶν ἐν τῇ χάριτι ταύτῃ
¹a travelling ²of us in this grace
companion

τῇ διακονουμένῃ ὑφ' ἡμῶν πρὸς τὴν
–   being ministered by us to ¹the

αὐτοῦ τοῦ κυρίου δόξαν καὶ προθυμίαν
³[him]self ²of the ⁴Lord ²glory and eagerness

ἡμῶν, 20 στελλόμενοι τοῦτο, μή τις ἡμᾶς
of us, avoiding this, lest anyone ²us

μωμήσηται ἐν τῇ ἁδρότητι ταύτῃ τῇ
¹should blame in this bounty

διακονουμένῃ ὑφ' ἡμῶν· 21 προνοοῦμεν γὰρ
being ministered by us; for we provide

καλὰ οὐ μόνον ἐνώπιον κυρίου ἀλλὰ καὶ
good not only before [the] Lord but also
things

ἐνώπιον ἀνθρώπων. 22 συνεπέμψαμεν δὲ
before men. And we sent with

αὐτοῖς τὸν ἀδελφὸν ἡμῶν, ὃν ἐδοκιμάσαμεν
them the brother of us, whom ¹we proved

ἐν πολλοῖς πολλάκις σπουδαῖον ὄντα, νυνὶ
⁵in ⁶many things ⁴many times ³diligent ²being, ²now

δὲ πολὺ σπουδαιότερον πεποιθήσει πολλῇ
¹and much more diligent ¹in ²confidence ³much

τῇ εἰς ὑμᾶς. 23 εἴτε ὑπὲρ Τίτου, κοινωνὸς
– toward you. Whether as to Titus, ²partner

ἐμὸς καὶ εἰς ὑμᾶς συνεργός· εἴτε ἀδελφοὶ
¹my ²and ⁵for ⁶you ⁴fellow-worker; or brothers

ἡμῶν, ἀπόστολοι ἐκκλησιῶν, δόξα Χριστοῦ.
of us, apostles of churches, [the] of Christ.
glory

24 τὴν οὖν ἔνδειξιν τῆς ἀγάπης ὑμῶν
⁷The ¹therefore ⁸demon- ⁹of the ¹⁰love ¹¹of you
stration

καὶ ἡμῶν καυχήσεως ὑπὲρ ὑμῶν εἰς
¹²and ¹⁴of us ¹³boasting ¹⁵on behalf of ¹⁶you ¹⁷to

αὐτοὺς ἐνδεικνύμενοι εἰς πρόσωπον τῶν
¹⁸them ²showing forth ³in ⁴[the] presence ⁵of the

ἐκκλησιῶν.
⁶churches.

CHAPTER 9

NOW it is superfluous for me to write to you about the offering for the saints, ²for I know your readiness, of which I boast about you to the people of Macedo'-nia, saying that Acha'ia has been ready since last year; and your zeal has stirred up most of them. ³But I am sending the brethren so that our boasting about you may not prove vain in this case, so that you may be ready, as I said you would be; ⁴lest if some Macedo'nians come with me and find that you are not ready, we be humiliated—to say nothing of you—for being so confident. ⁵So I thought it necessary to urge the brethren to go on to you before me, and arrange in advance for this gift you have promised, so that it may be ready not as an exaction but as a willing gift.

6 The point is this: he who sows sparingly will also reap sparingly, and he who sows bountifully will also reap bountifully. ⁷Each one must do

9 Περὶ   μὲν   γὰρ   τῆς   διακονίας   τῆς
²Concerning ²indeed   ¹for   the   ministry   –

εἰς   τοὺς   ἁγίους   περισσόν   μοί   ἐστιν   τὸ
to   the   saints   ²superfluous   ³for me   ¹it is   –

γράφειν   ὑμῖν·   2 οἶδα   γὰρ   τὴν   προθυμίαν
to write   to you;   for I know   the   eagerness

ὑμῶν   ἣν   ὑπὲρ   ὑμῶν   καυχῶμαι   Μακε-
of you   which on behalf of   you   I boast   to Mace-

δόσιν   ὅτι   Ἀχαΐα   παρεσκεύασται   ἀπὸ
donians   that   Achaia   has made preparations   from

πέρυσι,   καὶ   τὸ   ὑμῶν   ζῆλος   ἠρέθισεν
last year,   and   the   ²of you   ¹zeal   stirred up
=a year ago,

τοὺς   πλείονας.   3 ἔπεμψα   δὲ   τοὺς   ἀδελφούς,
the   greater number.   And I sent   the   brothers,

ἵνα   μὴ   τὸ   καύχημα   ἡμῶν   τὸ   ὑπὲρ
lest   the   boast   of us   – on behalf

ὑμῶν   κενωθῇ   ἐν   τῷ   μέρει   τούτῳ,   ἵνα
of you   should be   in   this respect,   in order
    emptied   that

καθὼς   ἔλεγον   παρεσκευασμένοι   ἦτε,   4 μή
as   I said   having been prepared   ye were,

πως   ἐὰν   ἔλθωσιν   σὺν   ἐμοὶ   Μακεδόνες
lest   if   ²come   ³with   ⁴me   ¹Macedonians

καὶ   εὕρωσιν   ὑμᾶς   ἀπαρασκευάστους
and   find   you   unprepared

καταισχυνθῶμεν   ἡμεῖς,   ἵνα   μὴ   λέγωμεν
²should be shamed   ¹we,   in order   we say not
    that

ὑμεῖς,   ἐν   τῇ   ὑποστάσει   ταύτῃ.   5 ἀναγκαῖον
ye,   in   this confidence.   ²Necessary

οὖν   ἡγησάμην   παρακαλέσαι   τοὺς   ἀδελφοὺς
²there-   ¹I thought [it]   to beseech   the   brothers
fore

ἵνα   προέλθωσιν   εἰς   ὑμᾶς   καὶ   προκαταρτί-
in order   they go   to   you   and   arrange before-
that   forward

σωσιν   τὴν   προεπηγγελμένην   εὐλογίαν   ὑμῶν,
hand   ¹the   ⁴having been promised   ²blessing   ³of you,

ταύτην   ἑτοίμην   εἶναι   οὕτως   ὡς   εὐλογίαν
this   ready   to be   thus   as   a blessing

καὶ   μὴ   ὡς   πλεονεξίαν.   6 Τοῦτο   δέ,
and   not   as   greediness.   And this,

ὁ   σπείρων   φειδομένως   φειδομένως   καὶ
the [one] sowing   sparingly   ²sparingly   ²also

θερίσει,   καὶ   ὁ   σπείρων   ἐπ᾽   εὐλογίαις   ἐπ᾽
¹will reap,   and the [one] sowing   on(for)   blessings   ²on(for)

εὐλογίαις   καὶ   θερίσει.   7 ἕκαστος   καθὼς
⁴blessings   ²also   ¹will reap.   Each one   as

as he has made up his mind, not reluctantly or under compulsion, for God loves a cheerful giver. ⁸And God is able to provide you with every blessing in abundance, so that you may always have enough of everything and may provide in abundance for every good work. ⁹As it is written,

"He scatters abroad,
  he gives to the poor;
his righteousness⁹
  endures for ever."

¹⁰He who supplies seed to the sower and bread for food will supply and multiply your resources and increase the harvest of your righteousness.⁹ ¹¹You will be enriched in every way for great generosity, which through us will produce thanksgiving to God; ¹²for the rendering of this service not only supplies the wants of the saints but also overflows in many thanksgivings to God. ¹³Under the test of this service, youʰ will glorify God by your obedience in acknowledging the gospel of Christ, and by the generosity of your contribution for them and for all others; ¹⁴while they long for you and pray

⁹ Or benevolence
ʰ Or they

προῄρηται τῇ καρδίᾳ, μὴ ἐκ λύπης ἢ
he chose in the(his) heart, not of grief or
ἐξ ἀνάγκης· ἱλαρὸν γὰρ δότην ἀγαπᾷ ὁ
of necessity; for ²a cheerful ⁴giver ³loves –
θεός. 8 δυνατεῖ δὲ ὁ θεὸς πᾶσαν χάριν
¹God. And ²is able – ¹God ⁴all ⁵grace
περισσεῦσαι εἰς ὑμᾶς, ἵνα ἐν παντὶ
³to cause to abound toward you, in order that ⁵in ⁶everything
πάντοτε πᾶσαν αὐτάρκειαν ἔχοντες περισ-
¹always ²all ⁴self-sufficiency ³having ye may
σεύητε εἰς πᾶν ἔργον ἀγαθόν, 9 καθὼς
abound to every work good, as
γέγραπται· ἐσκόρπισεν, ἔδωκεν τοῖς πένησιν,
it has been written: He scattered, he gave to the poor,
ἡ δικαιοσύνη αὐτοῦ μένει εἰς τὸν αἰῶνα.
the righteousness of him remains unto the age.
10 ὁ δὲ ἐπιχορηγῶν σπέρμα τῷ σπείροντι
Now the [one] providing seed for the [one] sowing
καὶ ἄρτον εἰς βρῶσιν χορηγήσει καὶ
¹both ³bread ⁴for ⁵food ²will supply and
πληθυνεῖ τὸν σπόρον ὑμῶν καὶ αὐξήσει
will multiply the seed of you and will increase
τὰ γενήματα τῆς δικαιοσύνης ὑμῶν· 11 ἐν
the fruits of the righteousness of you; in
παντὶ πλουτιζόμενοι εἰς πᾶσαν ἁπλότητα,
everything being enriched to all liberality,
ἥτις κατεργάζεται δι' ἡμῶν εὐχαριστίαν
which works out through us thanksgiving
τῷ θεῷ· 12 ὅτι ἡ διακονία τῆς λειτουργίας
– to God; because the ministry of the service
ταύτης οὐ μόνον ἐστὶν προσαναπληροῦσα
of this not only is making up
τὰ ὑστερήματα τῶν ἁγίων, ἀλλὰ καὶ
the things lacking of the saints, but [is] also
περισσεύουσα διὰ πολλῶν εὐχαριστιῶν τῷ
abounding through many thanksgivings –
θεῷ· 13 διὰ τῆς δοκιμῆς τῆς διακονίας
to God; through the proof – ministry
ταύτης δοξάζοντες τὸν θεὸν ἐπὶ τῇ
of this glorifying – God on the
ὑποταγῇ τῆς ὁμολογίας ὑμῶν εἰς τὸ
submission of the confession of you to the
εὐαγγέλιον τοῦ Χριστοῦ καὶ ἁπλότητι
gospel – of Christ and [on the] liberality
τῆς κοινωνίας εἰς αὐτοὺς καὶ εἰς πάντας,
of the fellowship toward them and toward all men,
14 καὶ αὐτῶν δεήσει ὑπὲρ ὑμῶν ἐπιποθούν-
and ¹them ⁴with ⁵on be- ⁶you ²longing
             request half of

for you, because of the surpassing grace of God in you. ¹⁵Thanks be to God for his inexpressible gift!

των	ὑμᾶς	διὰ	τὴν	ὑπερβάλλουσαν	χάριν
afterª	³you	on account of	the	excelling	grace

τοῦ	θεοῦ	ἐφ'	ὑμῖν.	15 Χάρις	τῷ	θεῷ
-	of God	upon	you.	Thanks	-	to God

ἐπὶ	τῇ	ἀνεκδιηγήτῳ	αὐτοῦ	δωρεᾷ.
for	the	indescribable	of him	gift.

CHAPTER 10

I, Paul, myself entreat you, by the meekness and gentleness of Christ —I who am humble when face to face with you, but bold to you when I am away!—²I beg of you that when I am present I may not have to show boldness with such confidence as I count on showing against some who suspect us of acting in worldly fashion. ³For though we live in the world we are not carrying on a worldly war, ⁴for the weapons of our warfare are not worldly but have divine power to destroy strongholds. ⁵We destroy arguments and every proud obstacle to the knowledge of God, and take every thought captive to obey Christ, ⁶being ready to punish every disobedience, when your obedience is complete.

7 Look at what is before your eyes. If any one is confident that he is Christ's, let him re-

10 Αὐτὸς	δὲ	ἐγὼ	Παῦλος	παρακαλῶ
[my]self	Now	I	Paul	beseech

ὑμᾶς	διὰ	τῆς	πραΰτητος	καὶ	ἐπιεικείας
you	through	the	meekness	and	forbearance

τοῦ	Χριστοῦ,	ὃς	κατὰ	πρόσωπον	μὲν
-	of Christ,	who	according to	face	indeed

ταπεινὸς	ἐν	ὑμῖν,	ἀπὼν	δὲ	θαρρῶ	εἰς
[am] humble among	you,		but	being absent	am bold toward

ὑμᾶς·	2 δέομαι	δὲ	τὸ	μὴ	παρὼν	θαρρῆσαι
you:	now I request		-	not	being present	to be bold

τῇ	πεποιθήσει	ᾗ	λογίζομαι	τολμῆσαι	ἐπί
in the	confidence	which	I reckon	to be daring	toward

τινας	τοὺς	λογιζομένους	ἡμᾶς	ὡς	κατὰ
some	the [ones]	reckoning	us	as	²accord-ing to

σάρκα	περιπατοῦντας.	3 Ἐν	σαρκὶ	γὰρ
³flesh	¹walking.	in	flesh	For

περιπατοῦντες	οὐ	κατὰ	σάρκα	στρατευόμεθα,
walking	not	accord-ing to	flesh	we war,

4 τὰ	γὰρ	ὅπλα	τῆς	στρατείας	ἡμῶν
for the		weapons	of the	warfare	of us [are]

οὐ	σαρκικὰ	ἀλλὰ	δυνατὰ	τῷ	θεῷ	πρὸς
not	fleshly	but	powerful	-	to God	to

καθαίρεσιν	ὀχυρωμάτων,	λογισμοὺς	καθαιροῦν-
overthrow	of strongholds,	²reasonings	¹overthrow-

τες	5 καὶ	πᾶν	ὕψωμα	ἐπαιρόμενον	κατὰ
ing	and	every	high thing	rising up	against

τῆς	γνώσεως	τοῦ	θεοῦ,	καὶ	αἰχμαλωτίζοντες
the	knowledge	-	of God,	and	taking captive

πᾶν	νόημα	εἰς	τὴν	ὑπακοὴν	τοῦ	Χριστοῦ,
every	design	to	the	obedience	-	of Christ,

6 καὶ	ἐν	ἑτοίμῳ	ἔχοντες	ἐκδικῆσαι	πᾶσαν
and	in	readiness =being ready	having	to avenge	all

παρακοήν,	ὅταν	πληρωθῇ	ὑμῶν	ἡ	ὑπακοή.
disobedience,	whenever	⁴is fulfilled	³of you	¹the	²obedience.

7 Τὰ	κατὰ	πρόσωπον	βλέπετε.	εἴ	τις
²The things	³according to	⁴face (appearance)	¹ye look [at].	If	any-one

πέποιθεν	ἑαυτῷ	Χριστοῦ	εἶναι,	τοῦτο
has persuaded	himself	²of Christ	¹to be,	this

II. CORINTHIANS 10

731

mind himself that as he is Christ's, so are we. ⁸For even if I boast a little too much of our authority, which the Lord gave for building you up and not for destroying you, I shall not be put to shame. ⁹I would not seem to be frightening you with letters. ¹⁰For they say, "His letters are weighty and strong, but his bodily presence is weak, and his speech of no account." ¹¹Let such people understand that what we say by letter when absent, we do when present. ¹²Not that we venture to class or compare ourselves with some of those who commend themselves. But when they measure themselves by one another, and compare themselves with one another, they are without understanding. 13 But we will not boast beyond limit, but will keep to the limits God has apportioned us, to reach even to you. ¹⁴For we are not over-extending ourselves, as though we did not reach you; we were the first to come all the way to you

λογιζέσθω πάλιν ἐφ' ἑαυτοῦ, ὅτι καθὼς
let him reckon again as to himself, that as

αὐτὸς Χριστοῦ, οὕτως καὶ ἡμεῖς. 8 ἐάν
he [is] of Christ, so also [are] we. ⁸if

τε γὰρ περισσότερόν τι καυχήσωμαι περὶ
²even ¹For ³more abundantly ⁵some- ⁴I should boast concern-
what ing

τῆς ἐξουσίας ἡμῶν, ἧς ἔδωκεν ὁ κύριος
the authority of us, which ³gave ¹the ²Lord

εἰς οἰκοδομὴν καὶ οὐκ εἰς καθαίρεσιν
for edification and not for overthrow

ὑμῶν, οὐκ αἰσχυνθήσομαι, 9 ἵνα μὴ δόξω
of you, I shall not be shamed, in order that I may not seem

ὡσὰν ἐκφοβεῖν ὑμᾶς διὰ τῶν ἐπιστολῶν.
as though to frighten you through the epistles.

10 ὅτι αἱ ἐπιστολαὶ μέν, φησίν, βαρεῖαι
Because the(his) epistles indeed, he says, [are] weighty

καὶ ἰσχυραί, ἡ δὲ παρουσία τοῦ σώματος
and strong, but the presence of the(his) body [is]

ἀσθενὴς καὶ ὁ λόγος ἐξουθενημένος.
weak, and the(his) speech being despised.

11 τοῦτο λογιζέσθω ὁ τοιοῦτος, ὅτι οἷοί
This let reckon such a one, that such as

ἐσμεν τῷ λόγῳ δι' ἐπιστολῶν ἀπόντες,
we are – in word through epistles being absent,

τοιοῦτοι καὶ παρόντες τῷ ἔργῳ. 12 Οὐ
such also being present – in work. ²not

γὰρ τολμῶμεν ἐγκρῖναι ἢ συγκρῖναι
¹For ²we dare to class with or to compare

ἑαυτούς τισιν τῶν ἑαυτοὺς συνιστανόντων·
ourselves with some of the ²themselves ¹commending;
[ones]

ἀλλὰ αὐτοὶ ἐν ἑαυτοῖς ἑαυτοὺς μετροῦντες
but they ³among ⁴them- ²them- ¹measuring
selves selves

καὶ συγκρίνοντες ἑαυτοὺς ἑαυτοῖς οὐ
and comparing themselves with themselves not

συνιᾶσιν. 13 ἡμεῖς δὲ οὐκ εἰς τὰ ἄμετρα
do understand. But we ²not ⁴immeasurably†

καυχησόμεθα, ἀλλὰ κατὰ τὸ μέτρον τοῦ
¹will ²boast, but according to the measure of the

κανόνος οὗ ἐμέρισεν ἡμῖν ὁ θεὸς μέτρου,
rule which ²divided ³to us – ¹God of(in) measure,

ἐφικέσθαι ἄχρι καὶ ὑμῶν. 14 οὐ γὰρ
to reach as far as even you. For not

ὡς μὴ ἐφικνούμενοι εἰς ὑμᾶς ὑπερεκτείνομεν
as not reaching to you do we overstretch

ἑαυτούς, ἄχρι γὰρ καὶ ὑμῶν ἐφθάσαμεν
ourselves, for as far as even you we came

with the gospel of Christ.
¹⁵We do not boast be-
yond limit, in other men's
labors; but our hope is
that as your faith in-
creases, our field among
you may be greatly
enlarged, ¹⁶so that we
may preach the gospel
in lands beyond you,
without boasting of work
already done in another's
field. ¹⁷"Let him who
boasts, boast of the
Lord." ¹⁸For it is not the
man who commends
himself that is accepted,
but the man whom the
Lord commends.

ἐν   τῷ   εὐαγγελίῳ   τοῦ   Χριστοῦ,   15 οὐκ
in   the   gospel   -   of Christ,   not

εἰς   τὰ   ἄμετρα   καυχώμενοι   ἐν   ἀλλοτρίοις
immeasurably†   boasting   in   others'†

κόποις,   ἐλπίδα   δὲ   ἔχοντες   αὐξανομένης
labours,   but ²hope   ¹having   growing
                                      =as your faith grows

τῆς   πίστεως   ὑμῶν   ἐν   ὑμῖν   μεγαλυνθῆναι
the   faith   of you⁵ ²among ³you   ¹to be magnified

κατὰ   τὸν   κανόνα   ἡμῶν   εἰς   περισσείαν,
according the   rule   of us   in   abundance,
to

16 εἰς   τὰ   ὑπερέκεινα   ὑμῶν   εὐαγγελίσασθαι,
in   the [parts] beyond   you   to preach good tidings,

οὐκ   ἐν   ἀλλοτρίῳ   κανόνι   εἰς   τὰ   ἕτοιμα
not   ²in   ³another's†   ⁴rule   ⁵in   - ⁶things ready

καυχήσασθαι.   17 Ὁ   δὲ   καυχώμενος   ἐν
¹to boast.   But the [one]   boasting   ²in

κυρίῳ   καυχάσθω·   18 οὐ   γὰρ   ὁ   ἑαυτὸν
³[the] Lord ¹let him boast;   for not   the [one] himself

συνιστάνων,   ἐκεῖνός   ἐστιν   δόκιμος,   ἀλλὰ
commending,   that one   is   approved,   but

ὃν   ὁ   κύριος   συνίστησιν.
whom the   Lord   commends.

CHAPTER 11

I wish you would bear
  with me in a little
foolishness. Do bear with
me! ²I feel a divine
jealousy for you, for I
betrothed you to Christ
to present you as a
pure bride to her one
husband. ³But I am
afraid that as the serpent
deceived Eve by his
cunning, your thoughts
will be led astray from a
sincere and pure
devotion to Christ. ⁴For
if some one comes and
preaches another Jesus
than the one we
preached, or if you re-
ceive a different spirit

11 Ὄφελον   ἀνείχεσθέ   μου   μικρόν   τι
   I would that   ye endured   me   a little [bit]

ἀφροσύνης·   ἀλλὰ   καὶ   ἀνέχεσθέ   μου.
of foolishness;   but   indeed   ye do endure   me.

2 ζηλῶ   γὰρ   ὑμᾶς   θεοῦ   ζήλῳ,   ἡρμοσάμην
For I am jealous [of] you   ²of God ¹with a   ²I betrothed
                                              jealousy,

γὰρ   ὑμᾶς   ἑνὶ   ἀνδρὶ   παρθένον   ἁγνὴν
¹for   you   to one   husband   ²virgin   ³a pure

παραστῆσαι   τῷ   Χριστῷ·   3 φοβοῦμαι   δὲ
¹to present   -   to Christ;   and I fear

μή   πως,   ὡς   ὁ   ὄφις   ἐξηπάτησεν   Εὔαν
lest somehow,   as   the   serpent   deceived   Eve

ἐν   τῇ   πανουργίᾳ   αὐτοῦ,   φθαρῇ   τὰ   νοήματα
by   the   cleverness   of him,   ⁴should ¹the ²thoughts
                                       be seduced

ὑμῶν   ἀπὸ   τῆς   ἁπλότητος   [καὶ   τῆς
³of you   from   the   simplicity   and   the

ἁγνότητος]   τῆς   εἰς   Χριστόν.   4 εἰ   μὲν
purity]   -   in   Christ.   ²if ³indeed

γὰρ   ὁ   ἐρχόμενος   ἄλλον   Ἰησοῦν   κηρύσσει
¹For the [one]   coming   ²another   ³Jesus   ¹proclaims

ὃν   οὐκ   ἐκηρύξαμεν,   ἢ   πνεῦμα   ἕτερον
whom   we did not proclaim,   or   ³spirit   ²a different

from the one you received, or if you accept a different gospel from the one you accepted, you submit to it readily enough. ⁵I think that I am not in the least inferior to these superlative apostles. ⁶Even if I am unskilled in speaking, I am not in knowledge; in every way we have made this plain to you in all things.

7 Did I commit a sin in abasing myself so that you might be exalted, because I preached God's gospel without cost to you? ⁸I robbed other churches by accepting support from them in order to serve you. ⁹And when I was with you and was in want, I did not burden any one, for my needs were supplied by the brethren who came from Macedo'nia. So I refrained and will refrain from burdening you in any way. ¹⁰As the truth of Christ is in me, this boast of mine shall not be silenced in the regions of Acha'ia. ¹¹And why? Because I do not love you? God knows I do!

12 And what I do I will continue to do, in order to undermine the claim of those who would like to claim that in their

λαμβάνετε ὃ οὐκ ἐλάβετε, ἢ εὐαγγέλιον
¹ye receive which ye did not receive, or ²gospel

ἕτερον ὃ οὐκ ἐδέξασθε, καλῶς ἀνέχεσθε.
¹a different which ye did not receive, ²[him] ²well ¹ye endure.

5 λογίζομαι γὰρ μηδὲν ὑστερηκέναι τῶν
For I reckon nothing to have come behind of the

ὑπερλίαν ἀποστόλων. 6 εἰ δὲ καὶ ἰδιώτης
super- apostles. But if indeed unskilled
[I am]

τῷ λόγῳ, ἀλλ' οὐ τῇ γνώσει, ἀλλ' ἐν
- in speech, yet not - in knowledge, but in

παντὶ φανερώσαντες ἐν πᾶσιν εἰς ὑμᾶς.
every having manifested in all things to you.
[way] [ourselves]

7 Ἢ ἁμαρτίαν ἐποίησα ἐμαυτὸν ταπεινῶν
Or ²sin ¹did I commit ⁴myself ³humbling

ἵνα ὑμεῖς ὑψωθῆτε, ὅτι δωρεὰν τὸ τοῦ
in order ye might be because ⁵freely ²the -
that exalted,

θεοῦ εὐαγγέλιον εὐηγγελισάμην ὑμῖν;
⁴of God ³gospel ¹I preached good tidings to you?

8 ἄλλας ἐκκλησίας ἐσύλησα λαβὼν ὀψώνιον
Other churches I robbed taking wages

πρὸς τὴν ὑμῶν διακονίαν, 9 καὶ παρὼν
for ¹the ²of you ³ministry, and being present

πρὸς ὑμᾶς καὶ ὑστερηθεὶς οὐ κατενάρκησα
with you and lacking I was not an encumbrance

οὐθενός· τὸ γὰρ ὑστέρημά μου προσανε-
of no man; for the lack of me ⁶made

πλήρωσαν οἱ ἀδελφοὶ ἐλθόντες ἀπὸ Μικε-
up ¹the ²brothers ³coming ⁴from ⁵Mace-

δονίας· καὶ ἐν παντὶ ἀβαρῆ ἐμαυτὸν
donia; and in every [way] ³unburdensome ²myself

ὑμῖν ἐτήρησα καὶ τηρήσω. 10 ἔστιν
⁴to you ¹I kept and I will keep. ²is

ἀλήθεια Χριστοῦ ἐν ἐμοί, ὅτι ἡ καύχησις
¹[The] truth ²of Christ in me, that - boasting

αὕτη οὐ φραγήσεται εἰς ἐμὲ ἐν τοῖς
this shall not be stopped in me in the

κλίμασιν τῆς Ἀχαίας. 11 διὰ τί; ὅτι
regions - of Achaia. Why? because

οὐκ ἀγαπῶ ὑμᾶς; ὁ θεὸς οἶδεν. 12 Ὃ
I love not you? - God knows. what

δὲ ποιῶ, καὶ ποιήσω, ἵνα ἐκκόψω τὴν
But I do, also I will do, in order I may cut the
that off

ἀφορμὴν τῶν θελόντων ἀφορμήν, ἵνα ἐν
occasion of the desiring an occasion, in or- where-
[ones] der that

boasted mission they work on the same terms as we do. ¹³For such men are false apostles, deceitful workmen, disguising themselves as apostles of Christ. ¹⁴And no wonder, for even Satan disguises himself as an angel of light. ¹⁵So it is not strange if his servants also disguise themselves as servants of righteousness. Their end will correspond to their deeds.

16 I repeat, let no one think me foolish; but even if you do, accept me as a fool, so that I too may boast a little. ¹⁷(What I am saying I say not with the Lord's authority but as a fool, in this boastful confidence; ¹⁸since many boast of worldly things, I too will boast.) ¹⁹For you gladly bear with fools, being wise yourselves! ²⁰For you bear it if a man makes slaves of you, or preys upon you, or takes advantage of you, or puts on airs, or strikes you in the face. ²¹To my shame, I must say, we were too weak for that!

But whatever any one dares to boast of—I am speaking as a fool—I also

---

ᾧ καυχῶνται εὑρεθῶσιν καθὼς καὶ ἡμεῖς.
in   they boast   they may be found   as   also   we.

13 οἱ γὰρ τοιοῦτοι ψευδαπόστολοι, ἐργάται
 -   For   such [are]   false apostles,   ²workmen

δόλιοι, μετασχηματιζόμενοι εἰς ἀποστόλους
¹deceitful,   transforming themselves   into   apostles

Χριστοῦ. 14 καὶ οὐ θαῦμα· αὐτὸς γὰρ
of Christ.   And   no   wonder;   ²[him]self   ¹for

ὁ σατανᾶς μετασχηματίζεται εἰς ἄγγελον
 -   ²Satan   transforms himself   into   an angel

φωτός. 15 οὐ μέγα οὖν εἰ καὶ οἱ
of light.   No   great thing therefore   if   also   the

διάκονοι αὐτοῦ μετασχηματίζονται ὡς
ministers   of him   transform themselves   as

διάκονοι δικαιοσύνης· ὧν τὸ τέλος ἔσται
ministers   of righteousness;   of whom the   end   will be

κατὰ τὰ ἔργα αὐτῶν.
according to the   works   of them.

16 Πάλιν λέγω, μή τίς με δόξῃ ἄφρονα
Again   I say,   ²not   ³anyone   ⁴me   ¹think   ⁵foolish

εἶναι· εἰ δὲ μή γε, κἂν ὡς ἄφρονα
⁵to be;   otherwise,   even if   as   foolish

δέξασθέ με, ἵνα κἀγὼ μικρόν τι καυχήσ-
receive ye   me, in order   I also   a little [bit]   may
         that

ωμαι. 17 ὃ λαλῶ, οὐ κατὰ κύριον λαλῶ,
boast.   What I speak,   not according [the] Lord   I speak,
        to

ἀλλ' ὡς ἐν ἀφροσύνῃ, ἐν ταύτῃ τῇ
but   as   in   folly,   in   this   -

ὑποστάσει τῆς καυχήσεως. 18 ἐπεὶ πολλοὶ
confidence   -   of boasting.   Since   many

καυχῶνται κατὰ [τὴν] σάρκα, κἀγὼ
boast   according to   the   flesh,   I also

καυχήσομαι. 19 ἡδέως γὰρ ἀνέχεσθε τῶν
will boast.   For gladly   ye endure   -

ἀφρόνων φρόνιμοι ὄντες· 20 ἀνέχεσθε γὰρ
fools   ²prudent   ¹being;   for ye endure

εἴ τις ὑμᾶς καταδουλοῖ, εἴ τις κατεσθίει,
if anyone   ²you   ¹enslaves,   if anyone devours [you],

εἴ τις λαμβάνει, εἴ τις ἐπαίρεται, εἴ
if   anyone receives [you],*   if anyone lifts himself up,   if

τις εἰς πρόσωπον ὑμᾶς δέρει. 21 κατὰ
anyone ³in   ⁴[the] face   ²you   ¹beats(hits).   According to

ἀτιμίαν λέγω, ὡς ὅτι ἡμεῖς ἠσθενήκαμεν·
dishonour   I say,   as   that   we   have been weak;

ἐν ᾧ δ' ἄν τις τολμᾷ, ἐν ἀφροσύνῃ
but in whatever [respect]   anyone   dares,   in   folly

* ? takes [you in].

dare to boast of that. ²²Are they Hebrews? So am I. Are they Israelites? So am I. Are they descendants of Abraham? So am I. ²³Are they servants of Christ? I am a better one—I am talking like a madman— with far greater labors, far more imprisonments, with countless beatings, and often near death. ²⁴Five times I have received at the hands of the Jews the forty lashes less one. ²⁵Three times I have been beaten with rods; once I was stoned. Three times I have been shipwrecked; a night and a day I have been adrift at sea; ²⁶on frequent journeys, in danger from rivers, danger from robbers, danger from my own people, danger from Gentiles, danger in the city, danger in the wilderness, danger at sea, danger from false brethren; ²⁷in toil and hardship, through many a sleepless night, in hunger and thirst, often without food, in cold and exposure. ²⁸And, apart from other things, there is the daily pressure upon me of my anxiety for all the churches. ²⁹Who is weak, and I am not weak? Who is made to fall, and I am not indignant?

30 If I must boast, I will boast of the things that show my weakness.

λέγω, τολμῶ κἀγώ. 22 Ἑβραῖοί εἰσιν;
I say, ²dare ¹I ²also. Hebrews are they?

κἀγώ. Ἰσραηλῖταί εἰσιν; κἀγώ. σπέρμα
I also. Israelites are they? I also. Seed

Ἀβραάμ εἰσιν; κἀγώ. 23 διάκονοι Χριστοῦ
of Abraham are they? I also. Ministers of Christ

εἰσιν; παραφρονῶν λαλῶ, ὑπὲρ ἐγώ· ἐν
are they? being out of I speak, ²beyond ¹I: in
         my mind   (more)

κόποις περισσοτέρως, ἐν φυλακαῖς περισ-
labours more abundantly, in prisons more

σοτέρως, ἐν πληγαῖς ὑπερβαλλόντως, ἐν
abundantly, in stripes excessively, in

θανάτοις πολλάκις. 24 ὑπὸ Ἰουδαίων
deaths many times. By Jews

πεντάκις τεσσεράκοντα παρὰ μίαν ἔλαβον,
five times forty [stripes] less one I received,

25 τρὶς ἐρραβδίσθην, ἅπαξ ἐλιθάσθην, τρὶς
thrice I was beaten with rods, once I was stoned, thrice

ἐναυάγησα, 26 νυχθήμερον ἐν τῷ βυθῷ
I was shipwrecked, a night and a day in the deep

πεποίηκα· ὁδοιπορίαις πολλάκις, κινδύνοις
I have done(been); in travels many times, in perils

ποταμῶν, κινδύνοις λῃστῶν, κινδύνοις ἐκ
of rivers, in perils of robbers, in perils of

γένους, κινδύνοις ἐξ ἐθνῶν, κινδύνοις ἐν
[my] kind, in perils of nations, in perils in

πόλει, κινδύνοις ἐν ἐρημίᾳ, κινδύνοις ἐν
a city, in perils in a desert, in perils in(at)

θαλάσσῃ, κινδύνοις ἐν ψευδαδέλφοις, 27 κόπῳ
sea, in perils among false brothers, in labour

καὶ μόχθῳ, ἐν ἀγρυπνίαις πολλάκις, ἐν
and hardship, in watchings many times, in

λιμῷ καὶ δίψει, ἐν νηστείαις πολλάκις,
famine and thirst, in fastings many times,

ἐν ψύχει καὶ γυμνότητι· 28 χωρὶς τῶν
in cold and nakedness; apart from the things

παρεκτὸς ἡ ἐπίστασίς μοι ἡ καθ’ ἡμέραν,
without[.] the conspiring me - daily,
         against

ἡ μέριμνα πασῶν τῶν ἐκκλησιῶν. 29 τίς
the care of all the churches. Who

ἀσθενεῖ, καὶ οὐκ ἀσθενῶ; τίς σκανδαλίζεται,
is weak, and I am not weak? who is offended,

καὶ οὐκ ἐγὼ πυροῦμαι; 30 εἰ καυχᾶσθαι
and ²not ¹I ²burn? If to boast

δεῖ, τὰ τῆς ἀσθενείας μου καυχήσομαι.
it be- the of the weakness of me I will boast.
hoves things
[me],

³¹The God and Father of the Lord Jesus, he who is blessed for ever, knows that I do not lie. ³²At Damascus, the governor under King Ar'etas guarded the city of Damascus in order to seize me, ³³but I was let down in a basket through a window in the wall, and escaped his hands.

CHAPTER 12

I must boast; there is nothing to be gained by it, but I will go on to visions and revelations of the Lord. ²I know a man in Christ who fourteen years ago was caught up to the third heaven—whether in the body or out of the body I do not know, God knows. ³And I know that this man was caught up into Paradise—whether in the body or out of the body I do not know, God knows—⁴and he heard things that cannot be told, which man may not utter. ⁵On behalf of this man I will boast, but on my own behalf I will not boast, except of my weaknesses. ⁶Though if I wish to boast, I shall not be a fool, for I shall

31 ὁ θεὸς καὶ πατὴρ τοῦ κυρίου Ἰησοῦ
The God and Father of the Lord Jesus
οἶδεν, ὁ ὢν εὐλογητὸς εἰς τοὺς αἰῶνας,
knows, the being blessed unto the ages,
[one]
ὅτι οὐ ψεύδομαι. 32 ἐν Δαμασκῷ ὁ
that I am not lying. In Damascus the
ἐθνάρχης Ἁρέτα τοῦ βασιλέως ἐφρούρει
ethnarch of Aretas of the king guarded
τὴν πόλιν Δαμασκηνῶν πιάσαι με, 33 καὶ
the city of [the] Damascenes to seize me, and
διὰ θυρίδος ἐν σαργάνῃ ἐχαλάσθην διὰ
through a window in a basket I was lowered through
τοῦ τείχους καὶ ἐξέφυγον τὰς χεῖρας αὐτοῦ.
the wall and escaped the hands of him.

12 Καυχᾶσθαι δεῖ, οὐ συμφέρον μέν,
To boast it behoves not expedient indeed,
[me],
ἐλεύσομαι δὲ εἰς ὀπτασίας καὶ ἀποκαλύψεις
so I will come to visions and revelations
κυρίου. 2 οἶδα ἄνθρωπον ἐν Χριστῷ
of [the] Lord. I know a man in Christ
πρὸ ἐτῶν δεκατεσσάρων, — εἴτε ἐν
before years fourteen, (whether in
σώματι οὐκ οἶδα, εἴτε ἐκτὸς τοῦ σώματος
[the] body I know not, or outside the body
οὐκ οἶδα, ὁ θεὸς οἶδεν, — ἁρπαγέντα
I know not, - God knows,) ²caught
τὸν τοιοῦτον ἕως τρίτου οὐρανοῦ. 3 καὶ
- ¹such a one to [the] third heaven. And
οἶδα τὸν τοιοῦτον ἄνθρωπον — εἴτε
I know - such a man (whether
ἐν [τῷ] σώματι εἴτε χωρὶς τοῦ σώματος
in [the] body or apart from the body
[οὐκ οἶδα], ὁ θεὸς οἶδεν, — 4 ὅτι
I know not, - God knows,) that
ἡρπάγη εἰς τὸν παράδεισον καὶ ἤκουσεν
he was caught into the paradise and heard
ἄρρητα ῥήματα, ἃ οὐκ ἐξὸν ἀνθρώπῳ
unspeakable words, which it is not for a man
permissible
λαλῆσαι. 5 ὑπὲρ τοῦ τοιούτου καυχήσομαι,
to speak. On behalf of - such a one I will boast,
ὑπὲρ δὲ ἐμαυτοῦ οὐ καυχήσομαι εἰ
but on behalf of myself I will not boast ex-
μὴ ἐν ταῖς ἀσθενείαις. 6 ἐὰν γὰρ θελήσω
cept in the(my) weaknesses. For if I shall wish
καυχήσασθαι, οὐκ ἔσομαι ἄφρων, ἀλήθειαν
to boast, I shall not be foolish, ²truth

be speaking the truth. But I refrain from it, so that no one may think more of me than he sees in me or hears from me. ⁷And to keep me from being too elated by the abundance of revelations, a thorn was given me in the flesh, a messenger of Satan, to harass me, to keep me from being too elated. ⁸Three times I besought the Lord about this, that it should leave me; ⁹but he said to me, "My grace is sufficient for you, for my power is made perfect in weakness." I will boast of the more gladly boast of my weaknesses, that the power of Christ may rest upon me. ¹⁰For the sake of Christ, then, I am content with weaknesses, insults, hardships, persecutions, and calamities; for when I am weak, then I am strong. 11 I have been a fool! You forced me to it, for I ought to have been commended by you. For I am not at all inferior to these superlative apostles, even though I am nothing. ¹²The signs of a true apostle were performed among you in all patience, with signs and wonders and mighty works. ¹³For in what were

γὰρ ἐρῶ· φείδομαι δέ, μή τις εἰς ἐμὲ
¹for ²I will speak; but I spare, lest anyone to me
λογίσηται ὑπὲρ ὃ βλέπει με ἢ ἀκούει
reckons beyond what he sees me or hears
ἐξ ἐμοῦ 7 καὶ τῇ ὑπερβολῇ τῶν ἀποκα-
of me and by the excess of the revela-
λύψεων. διὸ ἵνα μὴ ὑπεραίρωμαι, ἐδόθη
tions. Where- lest I should be there was
fore exceedingly uplifted, given
μοι σκόλοψ τῇ σαρκί, ἄγγελος σατανᾶ,
to me a thorn in the flesh, a messenger of Satan,
ἵνα με κολαφίζῃ, ἵνα μὴ ὑπεραίρωμαι.
in order ²me ¹he might buffet, lest I should be
that exceedingly uplifted.
8 ὑπὲρ τούτου τρὶς τὸν κύριον παρεκάλεσα,
As to this thrice the Lord I besought,
ἵνα ἀποστῇ ἀπ' ἐμοῦ. 9 καὶ εἴρηκέν
in or- it might from me. And he has said
der that depart
μοι· ἀρκεῖ σοι ἡ χάρις μου· ἡ γὰρ
to me: ⁴Suffices ⁵thee ¹the ²grace ³of me; for the(my)
δύναμις ἐν ἀσθενείᾳ τελεῖται. Ἥδιστα
power in weakness is perfected. Most gladly
οὖν μᾶλλον καυχήσομαι ἐν ταῖς ἀσθενείαις,
therefore rather I will boast in the(my) weaknesses,
ἵνα ἐπισκηνώσῃ ἐπ' ἐμὲ ἡ δύναμις τοῦ
in order ⁴might over ⁵me ¹the ²power –
that overshadow
Χριστοῦ. 10 διὸ εὐδοκῶ ἐν ἀσθενείαις,
³of Christ. Wherefore I am well in weaknesses,
pleased
ἐν ὕβρεσιν, ἐν ἀνάγκαις, ἐν διωγμοῖς
in insults, in necessities, in persecutions
καὶ στενοχωρίαις, ὑπὲρ Χριστοῦ· ὅταν
and difficulties, on behalf of Christ; ²whenever
γὰρ ἀσθενῶ, τότε δυνατός εἰμι.
¹for I am weak, then ²powerful ¹I am.
11 Γέγονα ἄφρων· ὑμεῖς με ἠναγκάσατε.
I have become foolish; ye me compelled.
ἐγὼ γὰρ ὤφειλον ὑφ' ὑμῶν συνίστασθαι.
For I ought by you to be commended.
οὐδὲν γὰρ ὑστέρησα τῶν ὑπερλίαν
For nothing I lacked of the super-
ἀποστόλων, εἰ καὶ οὐδέν εἰμι. 12 τὰ
apostles, ²if ¹even ⁴nothing ³I am. ²The
μὲν σημεῖα τοῦ ἀποστόλου κατειργάσθη
¹indeed signs of the apostle were wrought
ἐν ὑμῖν ἐν πάσῃ ὑπομονῇ, σημείοις τε
among you in all endurance, ³by signs ¹both
καὶ τέρασιν καὶ δυνάμεσιν. 13 τί γὰρ
and by wonders and by powerful deeds. For what

you less favored than the rest of the churches, except that I myself did not burden you? Forgive me this wrong! 14 Here for the third time I am ready to come to you. And I will not be a burden, for I seek not what is yours but you; for children ought not to lay up for their parents, but parents for their children. ¹⁵ I will most gladly spend and be spent for your souls. If I love you the more, am I to be loved the less? ¹⁶ But granting that I myself did not burden you, I was crafty, you say, and got the better of you by guile. ¹⁷ Did I take advantage of you through any of those whom I sent to you? ¹⁸ I urged Titus to go, and sent the brother with him. Did Titus take advantage of you? Did we not act in the same spirit? Did we not take the same steps?

19 Have you been thinking all along that we have been defending ourselves before you? It is in the sight of God that we have been speaking in Christ, and all for your upbuilding, be-

ἐστιν	ὃ	ἡσσώθητε	ὑπὲρ	τὰς	λοιπὰς
is it	which	ye were less	than	the	remaining

ἐκκλησίας,	εἰ	μὴ	ὅτι	αὐτὸς	ἐγὼ	οὐ
churches,		except	that	²[my]self	¹I	⁵not

κατενάρκησα	ὑμῶν;	χαρίσασθέ	μοι	τὴν
³encumbered	⁴of you?	Forgive ye	me	–

ἀδικίαν	ταύτην.	14 Ἰδοὺ	τρίτον	τοῦτο
wrong	this.	Behold	²[the] third [time]	¹this [is]

ἑτοίμως	ἔχω	ἐλθεῖν	πρὸς	ὑμᾶς,	καὶ
I am ready†		to come	to	you,	and

οὐ	καταναρκήσω·	οὐ	γὰρ	ζητῶ	τὰ	ὑμῶν
I will not encumber [you];		²not	¹for	²I seek	the things	of you

ἀλλὰ	ὑμᾶς.	οὐ	γὰρ	ὀφείλει	τὰ	τέκνα
but	you.	For ⁴not		³ought	¹the	²children

τοῖς	γονεῦσιν	θησαυρίζειν,	ἀλλὰ	οἱ	γονεῖς
for the	parents	to lay up treasure,	but	the	parents

τοῖς	τέκνοις.	15 ἐγὼ	δὲ	ἥδιστα	δαπανήσω
for the	children.	But I		most gladly	will spend

καὶ	ἐκδαπανηθήσομαι	ὑπὲρ	τῶν	ψυχῶν
and	will be spent out	on behalf of	the	souls

ὑμῶν.	εἰ	περισσοτέρως	ὑμᾶς	ἀγαπῶ,
of you.	If	more abundantly	²you	¹I love,

ἧσσον	ἀγαπῶμαι;	16 Ἔστω	δέ,	ἐγὼ	οὐ
[the] less	am I loved?	But let it be,		I	not

κατεβάρησα	ὑμᾶς·	ἀλλὰ	ὑπάρχων	πανοῦργος
burdened	you;	but	being	crafty

δόλῳ	ὑμᾶς	ἔλαβον.	17 μή	τινα	ὧν
²with guile	²you	¹I took.	Not	anyone	of whom

ἀπέσταλκα	πρὸς	ὑμᾶς,	18 δι'	αὐτοῦ
I have sent	to	you,	through	him

ἐπλεονέκτησα	ὑμᾶς;	παρεκάλεσα	Τίτον	καὶ
did I defraud	you?	I besought	Titus	and

συναπέστειλα	τὸν	ἀδελφόν·	μήτι	ἐπλεο-
sent with [him]	the	brother;	not	²de-

νέκτησεν	ὑμᾶς	Τίτος;	οὐ	τῷ	αὐτῷ
frauded	²you	¹Titus?	²not	³by the	⁴same

πνεύματι	περιεπατήσαμεν;	οὐ	τοῖς	αὐτοῖς
⁵spirit	¹walked we?	not	in the	same

ἴχνεσιν;
steps?

19 Πάλαι	δοκεῖτε	ὅτι	ὑμῖν	ἀπολογούμεθα.
Already	ye think	that	to you	we are making a defence.

κατέναντι	θεοῦ	ἐν	Χριστῷ	λαλοῦμεν·	τὰ
Before	God	in	Christ	we speak;	–

δὲ	πάντα,	ἀγαπητοί,	ὑπὲρ	τῆς	ὑμῶν
but	all things,	beloved,	[are] on behalf of	¹the	²of you

loved. [20] For I fear that perhaps I may come and find you not what I wish, and that you may find me not what you wish; that perhaps there may be quarreling, jealousy, anger, selfishness, slander, gossip, conceit, and disorder. [21] I fear that when I come again my God may humble me before you, and I may have to mourn over many of those who sinned before and have not repented of the impurity, immorality, and licentiousness which they have practiced.

οἰκοδομῆς.   20 φοβοῦμαι γὰρ μή πως ἐλθὼν
[2]edification.   For I fear   lest   coming

οὐχ οἵους θέλω εὕρω ὑμᾶς, κἀγὼ εὑρεθῶ
[3]not [4]such as [5]I wish [1]I may find [2]you, and I am found

ὑμῖν οἷον οὐ θέλετε, μή πως ἔρις,
by you such as ye wish not, lest   strife,

ζῆλος, θυμοί, ἐριθεῖαι, καταλαλιαί, ψιθυρισ-
jealousy, angers, rivalries, detractions, whisper-

μοί, φυσιώσεις, ἀκαταστασίαι· 21 μὴ πάλιν
ings, puffings up, disturbances;   lest again

ἐλθόντος μου ταπεινώσῃ με ὁ θεός μου
coming me[a] [4]may humble [5]me [1]the [2]God [3]of me
=when I come

πρὸς ὑμᾶς, καὶ πενθήσω πολλοὺς τῶν
with you, and I shall mourn many of the
                                                          [ones]

προημαρτηκότων καὶ μὴ μετανοησάντων
having previously sinned and not repenting

ἐπὶ τῇ ἀκαθαρσίᾳ καὶ πορνείᾳ καὶ
over the uncleanness and fornication and

ἀσελγείᾳ ᾗ ἔπραξαν.   13 Τρίτον τοῦτο
lewdness which they practised.   [2][The] third [1]this
                                                  [time] [is]

CHAPTER 13

THIS is the third time I am coming to you. Any charge must be sustained by the evidence of two or three witnesses. [2] I warned those who sinned before and all the others, and I warn them now while absent, as I did when present on my second visit, that if I come again I will not spare them—[3] since you desire proof that Christ is speaking in me. He is not weak in dealing with you, but is powerful in you. [4] For he was crucified in weakness, but lives by the power of God. For we are weak in him, but in dealing with you we shall live

ἔρχομαι πρὸς ὑμᾶς· ἐπὶ στόματος
I am coming to you; at [the] mouth

δύο μαρτύρων καὶ τριῶν σταθήσεται
of two witnesses and of three shall be established

πᾶν ῥῆμα.   2 προείρηκα καὶ προλέγω,
every word.   I have previously and I say
                      said   beforehand,

ὡς παρὼν τὸ δεύτερον καὶ ἀπὼν
as being present the second [time] and being absent

νῦν, τοῖς προημαρτηκόσιν καὶ τοῖς
now, to the [ones] having previously sinned and [1]to [3]the

λοιποῖς πᾶσιν, ὅτι ἐὰν ἔλθω εἰς τὸ
[4]remaining [2]all, that if I come in the
[ones]

πάλιν οὐ φείσομαι, 3 ἐπεὶ δοκιμὴν ζητεῖτε
again I will not spare, since [2]a proof [1]ye seek

τοῦ ἐν ἐμοὶ λαλοῦντος Χριστοῦ, ὃς εἰς
- [5]in [6]me [4]speaking [3]of Christ, who toward

ὑμᾶς οὐκ ἀσθενεῖ ἀλλὰ δυνατεῖ ἐν ὑμῖν.
you is not weak but is powerful in you.

4 καὶ γὰρ ἐσταυρώθη ἐξ ἀσθενείας, ἀλλὰ
For indeed he was crucified out of weakness, but

ζῇ ἐκ δυνάμεως θεοῦ. καὶ γὰρ ἡμεῖς
he lives by [the] power of God. For indeed we

ἀσθενοῦμεν ἐν αὐτῷ, ἀλλὰ ζήσομεν σὺν
are weak in him, but we shall live with

with him by the power of God.
5 Examine yourselves, to see whether you are holding to your faith. Test yourselves. Do you not realize that Jesus Christ is in you?—unless indeed you fail to meet the test! ⁶I hope you will find out that we have not failed. ⁷But we pray God that you may not do wrong—not that we may appear to have met the test, but that you may do what is right, though we may seem to have failed. ⁸For we cannot do anything against the truth, but only for the truth. ⁹For we are glad when we are weak and you are strong. What we pray for is your improvement. ¹⁰I write this while I am away from you, in order that when I come I may not have to be severe in my use of the authority which the Lord has given me for building up and not for tearing down. 11 Finally, brethren, farewell. Mend your ways, heed my appeal, agree with one another, live in peace, and the God of love and peace will be with you. ¹²Greet one

αὐτῷ   ἐκ   δυνάμεως   θεοῦ   εἰς   ὑμᾶς.
him   by   [the] power   of God   toward   you.

5 ʽΕαυτοὺς   πειράζετε   εἰ   ἐστὲ   ἐν   τῇ
²Yourselves   ¹test   if   ye are   in   the

πίστει,   ἑαυτοὺς   δοκιμάζετε·   ἢ   οὐκ
faith,   ²yourselves   ¹prove;   or   not

ἐπιγινώσκετε   ἑαυτοὺς   ὅτι   ᾽Ιησοῦς   Χριστὸς
perceive ye   yourselves   that   Jesus   Christ [is]

ἐν   ὑμῖν,   εἰ   μήτι   ἀδόκιμοί   ἐστε.   6 ἐλπίζω
in   you,   unless   ²counterfeits   ¹ye are.   I hope

δὲ   ὅτι   γνώσεσθε   ὅτι   ἡμεῖς   οὐκ   ἐσμὲν
But   that   ye will know   that   we   are not

ἀδόκιμοι.   7 εὐχόμεθα   δὲ   πρὸς   τὸν   θεὸν
counterfeits.   Now we pray   to   -   God

μὴ   ποιῆσαι   ὑμᾶς   κακὸν   μηδέν,   οὐχ
not   to do   youᵖ   evil   none,   not
=that ye do no . . .

ἵνα   ἡμεῖς   δόκιμοι   φανῶμεν,   ἀλλ᾽   ἵνα
in order   we   ²approved   ¹may appear,   but   in order
that   that

ὑμεῖς   τὸ   καλὸν   ποιῆτε,   ἡμεῖς   δὲ   ὡς
ye   ²the   ²good   ¹may do,   and we   ²as

ἀδόκιμοι   ὦμεν.   8 οὐ   γὰρ   δυνάμεθά
²counterfeits   ¹may be.   For we cannot [do]

τι   κατὰ   τῆς   ἀληθείας,   ἀλλὰ   ὑπὲρ   τῆς
any-   against   the   truth,   but   on behalf of   the
thing

ἀληθείας.   9 χαίρομεν   γὰρ   ὅταν   ἡμεῖς
truth.   For we rejoice   whenever   we

ἀσθενῶμεν,   ὑμεῖς   δὲ   δυνατοὶ   ἦτε·   τοῦτο
are weak,   and ye   powerful   are;   this

καὶ   εὐχόμεθα,   τὴν   ὑμῶν   κατάρτισιν.   10 Διὰ
also   we pray,   the   ²of you   ¹restoration.   There-

τοῦτο   ταῦτα   ἀπὼν   γράφω,   ἵνα   παρὼν
fore   ²these things   ³being   ¹I write,   in order   being
        absent   that   present

μὴ   ἀποτόμως   χρήσωμαι   κατὰ   τὴν   ἐξουσίαν
²not   ³sharply   ¹I may deal   according to the   authority

ἣν   ὁ   κύριος   ἔδωκέν   μοι   εἰς   οἰκοδομὴν
which the   Lord   gave   me   for   edification

καὶ   οὐκ   εἰς   καθαίρεσιν.
and   not   for   overthrow.

11 Λοιπόν,   ἀδελφοί,   χαίρετε,   καταρτίζεσθε,
For the rest,†   brothers,   rejoice,   restore yourselves,

παρακαλεῖσθε,   τὸ   αὐτὸ   φρονεῖτε,   εἰρηνεύετε,
admonish yourselves,   the same thing   think,   be at peace,

καὶ   ὁ   θεὸς   τῆς   ἀγάπης   καὶ   εἰρήνης
and   the   God   -   of love   and   of peace

ἔσται   μεθ᾽   ὑμῶν.   12 ᾽Ασπάσασθε   ἀλλήλους
will be   with   you.   Greet ye   one another

another with a holy kiss. ¹³All the saints greet you.

14 The grace of the Lord Jesus Christ and the love of God and the fellowship of⁴ the Holy Spirit be with you all.

ἐν ἁγίῳ φιλήματι.
with a holy kiss.

ἅγιοι πάντες.
²saints ¹All.

'Ασπάζονται ὑμᾶς οἱ
⁴greet ⁵you ³the

13 Ἡ χάρις τοῦ κυρίου Ἰησοῦ Χριστοῦ
The grace of the Lord Jesus Christ

καὶ ἡ ἀγάπη τοῦ θεοῦ καὶ ἡ κοινωνία
and the love – of God and the fellowship

τοῦ ἁγίου πνεύματος μετὰ πάντων ὑμῶν.
of the Holy Spirit [be] with ²all ¹you.

GALATIANS 1

CHAPTER 1

PAUL an apostle— not from men nor through man, but through Jesus Christ and God the Father, who raised him from the dead—²and all the brethren who are with me,

To the churches of Galatia:

3 Grace to you and peace from God the Father and our Lord Jesus Christ, ⁴who gave himself for our sins to deliver us from the present evil age, according to the will of our God and Father; ⁵to whom be the glory for ever and ever. Amen.

---

⁴ Or *and participation in*

ΠΡΟΣ ΓΑΛΑΤΑΣ
To Galatians

1 Παῦλος ἀπόστολος, οὐκ ἀπ᾿ ἀνθρώπων
Paul an apostle, not from men

οὐδὲ δι᾿ ἀνθρώπου ἀλλὰ διὰ Ἰησοῦ
nor through man but through Jesus

Χριστοῦ καὶ θεοῦ πατρὸς τοῦ ἐγείραντος
Christ and God [the] Father the [one] having raised

αὐτὸν ἐκ νεκρῶν, 2 καὶ οἱ σὺν ἐμοὶ
him out of [the] dead, and ²the ⁴with ⁵me

πάντες ἀδελφοί, ταῖς ἐκκλησίαις τῆς
¹all ³brothers, to the churches –

Γαλατίας· 3 χάρις ὑμῖν καὶ εἰρήνη ἀπὸ
of Galatia: Grace to you and peace from

θεοῦ πατρὸς ἡμῶν καὶ κυρίου Ἰησοῦ
God Father of us and Lord Jesus

Χριστοῦ, 4 τοῦ δόντος ἑαυτὸν ὑπὲρ τῶν
Christ, the [one] having given himself on behalf of the

ἁμαρτιῶν ἡμῶν, ὅπως ἐξέληται ἡμᾶς ἐκ
sins of us, so as he might deliver us out of

τοῦ αἰῶνος τοῦ ἐνεστῶτος πονηροῦ κατὰ
the ²age – ¹present ²evil according to

τὸ θέλημα τοῦ θεοῦ καὶ πατρὸς ἡμῶν,
the will of the God and Father of us,

5 ᾧ ἡ δόξα εἰς τοὺς αἰῶνας τῶν
to whom the glory unto the ages of the
[be]

αἰώνων· ἀμήν.
ages: Amen.

6 I am astonished that you are so quickly deserting him who called you in the grace of Christ and turning to a different gospel—⁷not that there is another gospel, but there are some who trouble you and want to pervert the gospel of Christ. ⁸But even if we, or an angel from heaven, should preach to you a gospel contrary to that which we preached to you, let him be accursed. ⁹As we have said before, so now I say again, If any one is preaching to you a gospel contrary to that which you received, let him be accursed.

10 Am I now seeking the favor of men, or of God? Or am I trying to please men? If I were still pleasing men, I should not be a servant of Christ. 11 For I would have you know, brethren, that the gospel which was preached by me is not man's gospel. ¹²For I did not receive it from man, nor was I taught it, but it came through a revelation of Jesus Christ. ¹³For you have heard of my former life in Judaism, how I persecuted the church of

6 Θαυμάζω ὅτι οὕτως ταχέως μετατίθεσθε
I wonder that thus quickly ye are removing

ἀπὸ τοῦ καλέσαντος ὑμᾶς ἐν χάριτι
from the [one] having called you by [the] grace

Χριστοῦ εἰς ἕτερον εὐαγγέλιον, 7 ὃ οὐκ
of Christ to another gospel, which not

ἔστιν ἄλλο· εἰ μή τινές εἰσιν οἱ ταράσ-
is another; only ²some ¹there are - troubl-

σοντες ὑμᾶς καὶ θέλοντες μεταστρέψαι
ing you and wishing to pervert

τὸ εὐαγγέλιον τοῦ Χριστοῦ. 8 ἀλλὰ
the gospel - of Christ. But

καὶ ἐὰν ἡμεῖς ἢ ἄγγελος ἐξ οὐρανοῦ
even if we or an angel out of heaven

εὐαγγελίσηται [ὑμῖν] παρ᾽ ὃ εὐηγγελισάμεθα
should preach to you beside what we preached
a gospel

ὑμῖν, ἀνάθεμα ἔστω. 9 ὡς προειρήκαμεν,
to you, ²a curse ¹let him be. As we have previously said,

καὶ ἄρτι πάλιν λέγω, εἴ τις ὑμᾶς εὐαγ-
also now again I say, if anyone ²you ¹preaches

γελίζεται παρ᾽ ὃ παρελάβετε, ἀνάθεμα
²a gospel beside what ye received, ²a curse

ἔστω.
¹let him be.

10 Ἄρτι γὰρ ἀνθρώπους πείθω ἢ τὸν
For now men do I persuade or -

θεόν; ἢ ζητῶ ἀνθρώποις ἀρέσκειν; εἰ
God? or do I seek men to please? If

ἔτι ἀνθρώποις ἤρεσκον, Χριστοῦ δοῦλος
still men I pleased, ²of Christ ²a slave

οὐκ ἂν ἤμην. 11 γνωρίζω γὰρ ὑμῖν,
¹I would not have been. For I make known to you,

ἀδελφοί, τὸ εὐαγγέλιον τὸ εὐαγγελισθὲν
brothers, the gospel - preached

ὑπ᾽ ἐμοῦ ὅτι οὐκ ἔστιν κατὰ ἄνθρωπον
by me that it is not according to man;

12 οὐδὲ γὰρ ἐγὼ παρὰ ἀνθρώπου παρέλαβον
for ¹not ¹I ⁵from ⁶man ²received

αὐτὸ οὔτε ἐδιδάχθην, ἀλλὰ δι᾽ ἀποκαλύψεως
²it nor was I taught but through a revelation
[by man],

Ἰησοῦ Χριστοῦ. 13 Ἠκούσατε γὰρ τὴν
of Jesus Christ. For ye heard -

ἐμὴν ἀναστροφήν ποτε ἐν τῷ Ἰουδαϊσμῷ,
my conduct then in - Judaism,

ὅτι καθ᾽ ὑπερβολὴν ἐδίωκον τὴν ἐκκλησίαν
that excessively† I persecuted the church

God violently and tried to destroy it; [14]and I advanced in Judaism beyond many of my own age among my people, so extremely zealous was I for the traditions of my fathers. [15]But when he who had set me apart before I was born, and had through his grace, [16]was pleased to reveal his Son to me, in order that I might preach him among the Gentiles, I did not confer with flesh and blood, [17]nor did I go up to Jerusalem to those who were apostles before me, but I went away into Arabia; and again I returned to Damascus.

18 Then after three years I went up to Jerusalem to visit Cephas, and remained with him fifteen days. [19]But I saw none of the other apostles except James the Lord's brother. [20](In what I am writing to you, before God, I do not lie!) [21]Then I went into the regions of Syria and Cili'cia. [22]And I was still not known by sight to the churches of Christ

τοῦ θεοῦ καὶ ἐπόρθουν αὐτήν, 14 καὶ
– of God and wasted it, and

προέκοπτον ἐν τῷ Ἰουδαϊσμῷ ὑπὲρ πολλοὺς
progressed in – Judaism beyond many

συνηλικιώτας ἐν τῷ γένει μου, περισ-
contemporaries in the race of me, ²abun-

σοτέρως ζηλωτὴς ὑπάρχων τῶν πατρικῶν
dantly ³a zealot ¹being ⁴of the ⁵ancestral

μου παραδόσεων. 15 Ὅτε δὲ εὐδόκησεν
⁷of me ⁶traditions. But when ¹⁴was pleased

ὁ ἀφορίσας με ἐκ κοιλίας μητρός μου
¹the ²having ³me ⁴from ⁵[the] womb ⁶of mother ⁷of me
[one] separated

καὶ καλέσας διὰ τῆς χάριτος αὐτοῦ
⁸and ⁹having called ¹⁰through ¹¹the ¹²grace ¹³of him

16 ἀποκαλύψαι τὸν υἱὸν αὐτοῦ ἐν ἐμοί,
to reveal the Son of him in me,

ἵνα εὐαγγελίζωμαι αὐτὸν ἐν τοῖς ἔθνεσιν,
in order I might preach him among the nations,
that

εὐθέως οὐ προσανεθέμην σαρκὶ καὶ αἵματι,
immediately I conferred not with flesh and blood,

17 οὐδὲ ἀνῆλθον εἰς Ἱεροσόλυμα πρὸς
neither did I go up to Jerusalem to

τοὺς πρὸ ἐμοῦ ἀποστόλους, ἀλλὰ ἀπῆλθον
¹the ³before ⁴me ²apostles, but I went away

εἰς Ἀραβίαν, καὶ πάλιν ὑπέστρεψα εἰς
into Arabia, and again returned to

Δαμασκόν. 18 Ἔπειτα μετὰ τρία ἔτη
Damascus. Then after three years

ἀνῆλθον εἰς Ἱεροσόλυμα ἱστορῆσαι Κηφᾶν,
I went up to Jerusalem to visit Cephas,

καὶ ἐπέμεινα πρὸς αὐτὸν ἡμέρας δεκαπέντε·
and remained with him days fifteen;

19 ἕτερον δὲ τῶν ἀποστόλων οὐκ εἶδον,
but other of the apostles I saw not,

εἰ μὴ Ἰάκωβον τὸν ἀδελφὸν τοῦ κυρίου.
except James the brother of the Lord.

20 ἃ δὲ γράφω ὑμῖν, ἰδοὺ ἐνώπιον τοῦ
Now what I write to you, behold before –
things

θεοῦ ὅτι οὐ ψεύδομαι. 21 ἔπειτα ἦλθον
God – I lie not. Then I went

εἰς τὰ κλίματα τῆς Συρίας καὶ τῆς
into the regions – of Syria and –

Κιλικίας. 22 ἤμην δὲ ἀγνοούμενος τῷ
of Cilicia. And I was being unknown –

προσώπῳ ταῖς ἐκκλησίαις τῆς Ἰουδαίας
by face to the churches – of Judæa

in Judea; ²³they only heard it said, "He who once persecuted us is now preaching the faith he once tried to destroy." ²⁴And they glorified God because of me.

CHAPTER 2

THEN after fourteen years I went up again to Jerusalem with Barnabas, taking Titus along with me. ²I went up by revelation; and I laid before them (but privately before those who were of repute) the gospel which I preach among the Gentiles, lest somehow I should be running or had run in vain. ³But even Titus, who was with me, was not compelled to be circumcised, though he was a Greek. ⁴But because of false brethren secretly brought in, who slipped in to spy out our freedom which we have in Christ Jesus, that they might bring us into bondage—⁵to them we did not yield submission even for a moment, that the truth of the gospel might be preserved for you. ⁶And from those who were reputed to be something (what they were makes no difference to me; God shows no partiality)—those, I say, who were of repute added nothing to me;

ταῖς ἐν Χριστῷ. 23 μόνον δὲ ἀκούοντες
\-   in   Christ.   But only   hearing

ἦσαν ὅτι ὁ διώκων ἡμᾶς ποτε νῦν
they were that the [one] ²persecuting ³us ¹then now

εὐαγγελίζεται τὴν πίστιν ἥν ποτε ἐπόρθει,
preaches   the   faith   which then   he was
                                                 destroying,

24 καὶ ἐδόξαζον ἐν ἐμοὶ τὸν θεόν.
    and   they glorified ²in ³me   -   ¹God.

2 Ἔπειτα διὰ δεκατεσσάρων ἐτῶν πάλιν
   Then through   fourteen   years   again

ἀνέβην εἰς Ἱεροσόλυμα μετὰ Βαρναβᾶ,
I went up to   Jerusalem   with   Barnabas,

συμπαραλαβὼν καὶ Τίτον· 2 ἀνέβην δὲ
taking with [me]   also   Titus;   and I went up

κατὰ ἀποκάλυψιν· καὶ ἀνεθέμην αὐτοῖς
according to a revelation;   and   I put before   them

τὸ εὐαγγέλιον ὃ κηρύσσω ἐν τοῖς ἔθνεσιν,
the gospel   which I proclaim among the   nations,

κατ' ἰδίαν δὲ τοῖς δοκοῦσιν, μή πως
²privately ¹but to the [ones] seeming,*   lest

εἰς κενὸν τρέχω ἢ ἔδραμον. 3 ἀλλ'
in   vain   I run or   I ran.   But

οὐδὲ Τίτος ὁ σὺν ἐμοί, Ἕλλην ὤν,
not   Titus the [one] with   me,   a Greek   being,

ἠναγκάσθη περιτμηθῆναι· 4 διὰ δὲ τοὺς
was compelled   to be circumcised;   but on account of ¹the

παρεισάκτους ψευδαδέλφους, οἵτινες παρεισ-
²brought in secretly   ²false brothers,   who   stole

ἦλθον κατασκοπῆσαι τὴν ἐλευθερίαν ἡμῶν
in   to spy on   the   freedom   of us

ἣν ἔχομεν ἐν Χριστῷ Ἰησοῦ, ἵνα ἡμᾶς
which we have in   Christ   Jesus, in order that ²us

καταδουλώσουσιν· 5 οἷς οὐδὲ πρὸς ὥραν
¹they will(might) enslave; to whom not   for   an hour

εἴξαμεν τῇ ὑποταγῇ, ἵνα ἡ ἀλήθεια
yielded we   -   in subjection, in order that   the   truth

τοῦ εὐαγγελίου διαμείνῃ πρὸς ὑμᾶς. 6 ἀπὸ
of the gospel   might continue with   you.   from

δὲ τῶν δοκούντων εἶναί τι, — ὁποῖοί
But the [ones]   seeming   to be something, (of what kind

ποτε ἦσαν οὐδέν μοι διαφέρει· πρόσωπον
²then ¹they were ⁴nothing ⁵to me   ³matters: ³[the] face

[ὁ] θεὸς ἀνθρώπου οὐ λαμβάνει — ἐμοὶ
\-   ⁴God ⁵of a man   ⁷receives not,)   ⁸to me

γὰρ οἱ δοκοῦντες οὐδὲν προσανέθεντο,
¹for the [ones] seeming*   nothing   added,

* Cf. the full expressions in vers. 6 (earlier) and 9.

7but on the contrary, when they saw that I had been entrusted with the gospel to the uncircumcised, just as Peter had been entrusted with the gospel to the circumcised 8(for he who worked through Peter for the mission to the circumcised worked through me also for the Gentiles), 9and when they perceived the grace that was given to me, James and Cephas and John, who were reputed to be pillars, gave to me and Barnabas the right hand of fellowship, that we should go to the Gentiles and they to the circumcised; 10only they would have us remember the poor, which very thing I was eager to do.

11 But when Cephas came to Antioch I opposed him to his face, because he stood condemned. 12For before certain men came from James, he ate with the Gentiles; but when they came he drew back and separated himself, fearing the circumcision party. 13And with him the rest of the Jews acted insincerely, so that even Barnabas was carried away by their insincerity. 14But when I saw that they were not straightforward about the truth of the gospel, I said to

7 ἀλλὰ	τοὐναντίον	ἰδόντες	ὅτι	πεπίστευμαι
but	on the contrary	seeing	that	I have been entrusted [with]

τὸ	εὐαγγέλιον	τῆς	ἀκροβυστίας	καθὼς
the	gospel	of the	uncircumcision	as

Πέτρος	τῆς	περιτομῆς,	8 ὁ	γὰρ	ἐνεργήσας
Peter	[that] of the	circumcision,	for the [one]		operating

Πέτρῳ	εἰς	ἀποστολὴν	τῆς	περιτομῆς
in Peter	to	an apostleship	of the	circumcision

ἐνήργησεν	καὶ	ἐμοὶ	εἰς	τὰ	ἔθνη,	9 καὶ
operated	also	in me	to	the	nations,	and

γνόντες	τὴν	χάριν	τὴν	δοθεῖσάν	μοι,
knowing	the	grace	–	given	to me,

Ἰάκωβος	καὶ	Κηφᾶς	καὶ	Ἰωάννης,	οἱ
James	and	Cephas	and	John,	the

δοκοῦντες	στῦλοι	εἶναι,	δεξιὰς	ἔδωκαν
[ones] seeming	²pillars	¹to be,	⁸right [hands]	¹gave

ἐμοὶ	καὶ	Βαρναβᾷ	κοινωνίας,	ἵνα	ἡμεῖς
²to me	³and	⁴to Barnabas	⁶of fellowship,	in order	we that [should

εἰς	τὰ	ἔθνη,	αὐτοὶ	δὲ	εἰς	τὴν	περιτομήν·
go] to	the	nations,	but they		to	the	circumcision;

10 μόνον	τῶν	πτωχῶν	ἵνα	μνημονεύωμεν,
only	³the	⁴poor	in order ¹that ²we might remember,

ὃ	καὶ	ἐσπούδασα	αὐτὸ	τοῦτο	ποιῆσαι.
which indeed	²I was eager	¹this very thing			to do.

11 Ὅτε	δὲ	ἦλθεν	Κηφᾶς	εἰς	Ἀντιόχειαν,
But when	²came	¹Cephas	to	Antioch,

κατὰ	πρόσωπον	αὐτῷ	ἀντέστην,	ὅτι
against	[his] face	to him	I opposed,	because

κατεγνωσμένος	ἦν.	12 πρὸ	τοῦ	γὰρ
²having been condemned	¹he was.	Before	the	for
			=For before some came ...	

ἐλθεῖν	τινας	ἀπὸ	Ἰακώβου	μετὰ	τῶν
to come	someᵇ	from	James	²with	⁸the

ἐθνῶν	συνήσθιεν·	ὅτε	δὲ	ἦλθον,	ὑπέστελλεν
⁴nations	¹he ate with;	but when	they came,		he withdrew

καὶ	ἀφώριζεν	ἑαυτόν,	φοβούμενος	τοὺς
and	separated	himself,	fearing	the [ones]

ἐκ	περιτομῆς·	13 καὶ	συνυπεκρίθησαν	αὐτῷ
of [the] circumcision;	and	dissembled along with	him

[καὶ]	οἱ	λοιποὶ	Ἰουδαῖοι,	ὥστε	καὶ
also	the	remaining	Jews,	so as	even

Βαρναβᾶς	συναπήχθη	αὐτῶν	τῇ	ὑποκρίσει.
Barnabas	was led away with	⁸of them	¹the	²dissembling.

14 ἀλλ'	ὅτε	εἶδον	ὅτι	οὐκ	ὀρθοποδοῦσιν
But	when	I saw	that	they walk[ed] not straight

πρὸς	τὴν	ἀλήθειαν	τοῦ	εὐαγγελίου,	εἶπον
with	the	truth	of the	gospel,	I said

Cephas before them all, "If you, though a Jew, live like a Gentile and not like a Jew, how can you compel the Gentiles to live like Jews?" [15] We ourselves, who are Jews by birth and not Gentile sinners, [16] yet who know that a man is not justified[a] by works of the law but through faith in Jesus Christ, even we have believed in Christ Jesus, in order to be justified by faith in Christ, and not by works of the law, because by works of the law shall no one be justified. [17] But if, in our endeavor to be justified in Christ, we ourselves were found to be sinners, is Christ then an agent of sin? Certainly not! [18] But if I build up again those things which I tore down, then I prove myself a transgressor. [19] For I through the law died to the law, that I might live to God. [20] I have been crucified with Christ; it is no longer I who live, but Christ who lives in me; and the life I now live in the flesh I live by faith in the Son of God, who loved me and gave himself for me.

[a] Or reckoned righteous; and so elsewhere

τῷ   Κηφᾷ   ἔμπροσθεν   πάντων·   εἰ   σὺ
-   to Cephas   in front of   all: If   thou

Ἰουδαῖος   ὑπάρχων   ἐθνικῶς   καὶ   οὐκ
[2]a Jew   [1]being   as a Gentile   and   not

Ἰουδαϊκῶς   ζῇς,   πῶς   τὰ   ἔθνη   ἀναγκάζεις
as a Jew   livest,   how   [2]the [3]nations [1]compellest thou

ἰουδαΐζειν;   15 Ἡμεῖς   φύσει   Ἰουδαῖοι   καὶ
to judaize?   We   by nature   Jews   and

οὐκ   ἐξ   ἐθνῶν   ἁμαρτωλοί,   16 εἰδότες   δὲ
not   [2]of [3]nations   [1]sinners,   and knowing

ὅτι   οὐ   δικαιοῦται   ἄνθρωπος   ἐξ   ἔργων
that   [2]is not justified   [1]a man   by   works

νόμου   ἐὰν   μὴ   διὰ   πίστεως   Χριστοῦ
of law   except(but)   through   faith   of(in) Christ

Ἰησοῦ,   καὶ   ἡμεῖς   εἰς   Χριστὸν   Ἰησοῦν
Jesus,*   even   we   [2]in   [3]Christ   [4]Jesus

ἐπιστεύσαμεν,   ἵνα   δικαιωθῶμεν   ἐκ   πίστεως
[1]believed,   in order that we might be   by   faith
                                justified

Χριστοῦ   καὶ   οὐκ   ἐξ   ἔργων   νόμου,   ὅτι
of(in) Christ*   and   not   by   works   of law, because

ἐξ   ἔργων   νόμου   οὐ   δικαιωθήσεται   πᾶσα
by   works   of law   not   will be justified   all
                        =no flesh will be justified.

σάρξ.   17 εἰ   δὲ   ζητοῦντες   δικαιωθῆναι
flesh.   But if   seeking   to be justified

ἐν   Χριστῷ   εὑρέθημεν   καὶ   αὐτοὶ   ἁμαρτωλοί,
in   Christ   we were found   also   [our]selves   sinners,

ἆρα   Χριστὸς   ἁμαρτίας   διάκονος;   μὴ
then   [is] Christ   [2]of sin   [1]a minister?   not

γένοιτο.   18 εἰ   γὰρ   ἃ   κατέλυσα   ταῦτα
May it be.   For if   what things I destroyed these things

πάλιν   οἰκοδομῶ,   παραβάτην   ἐμαυτὸν   συνισ-
again   I build,   [3]a transgressor   [2]myself   [1]I con-

τάνω.   19 ἐγὼ   γὰρ   διὰ   νόμου   νόμῳ
stitute.   For I   through   law   [2]to law

ἀπέθανον   ἵνα   θεῷ   ζήσω.   Χριστῷ   συνεσ-
[1]died   in order to God I might live. With Christ   I have
            that

ταύρωμαι·   20 ζῶ   δὲ   οὐκέτι   ἐγώ,   ζῇ   δὲ
been co-crucified;   and [2]live [3]no more   [1]I,   but [2]lives

ἐν   ἐμοὶ   Χριστός·   ὃ   δὲ   νῦν   ζῶ   ἐν   σαρκί,
[3]in [4]me   [1]Christ;   and what now I live in [the] flesh,

ἐν   πίστει   ζῶ   τῇ   τοῦ   υἱοῦ   τοῦ   θεοῦ
[2]by   [3]faith   [1]I live   -   of(in) the Son   -   of God

τοῦ   ἀγαπήσαντός   με   καὶ   παραδόντος   ἑαυτὸν
-   loving   me   and   giving up   himself

* Objective genitive, as is shown by the intervening sentence see also 3. 22, 26). Cf. " fear of God".

²¹I do not nullify the grace of God; for if justification[b] were through the law, then Christ died to no purpose.

ὑπὲρ ἐμοῦ.   **21** Οὐκ ἀθετῶ τὴ,ν χάριν
on behalf of me.   I do not set aside   the   grace
τοῦ θεοῦ· εἰ γὰρ διὰ νόμου δικαιοσύνη,
– of God;   for if   through   law   righteousness [comes],
ἄρα Χριστὸς δωρεὰν ἀπέθανεν.
then   Christ   without cause   died.

CHAPTER 3

O foolish Galatians! Who has bewitched you, before whose eyes Jesus Christ was publicly portrayed as crucified? ²Let me ask you only this: Did you receive the Spirit by works of the law, or by hearing with faith? ³Are you so foolish? Having begun with the Spirit, are you now ending with the flesh? ⁴Did you experience so many things in vain?—if it really is in vain. ⁵Does he who supplies the Spirit to you and works miracles among you do so by works of the law, or by hearing with faith? 6 Thus Abraham "believed God, and it was reckoned to him as righteousness." ⁷So you see that it is men of faith who are the sons of Abraham. ⁸And the scripture, foreseeing that God would justify the Gentiles by faith, preached the gospel beforehand to Abraham, saying, "In you shall all the nations be blessed." ⁹So then, those who are men of faith are blessed

3 Ὦ ἀνόητοι Γαλάται, τίς ὑμᾶς
O   foolish   Galatians,   who   you
ἐβάσκανεν, οἷς κατ' ὀφθαλμοὺς Ἰησοῦς
bewitched,   to whom   before [the] eyes   Jesus
Χριστὸς προεγράφη ἐσταυρωμένος; **2** τοῦτο
Christ   was portrayed   having been crucified?   This
μόνον θέλω μαθεῖν ἀφ' ὑμῶν, ἐξ ἔργων
only   I wish   to learn   from   you,   by   works
νόμου τὸ πνεῦμα ἐλάβετε ἢ ἐξ ἀκοῆς
of law   the   Spirit   received ye   or   by   hearing
πίστεως; **3** οὕτως ἀνόητοί ἐστε; ἐναρξάμενοι
of faith?   thus   foolish   are ye?   having begun
πνεύματι νῦν σαρκὶ ἐπιτελεῖσθε; **4** τοσαῦτα
in [the] Spirit   now   in [the] flesh   are ye being perfected?   so many things
ἐπάθετε εἰκῆ; **5** εἴ γε καὶ εἰκῆ. ὁ
suffered ye   in vain?   if   indeed   in vain.   The [one]
οὖν ἐπιχορηγῶν ὑμῖν τὸ πνεῦμα καὶ
therefore   supplying   to you   the   Spirit   and
ἐνεργῶν δυνάμεις ἐν ὑμῖν ἐξ ἔργων
working   powerful deeds   among   you [is it] by   works
νόμου ἢ ἐξ ἀκοῆς πίστεως; **6** Καθὼς
of law   or   by   hearing   of faith?   As
Ἀβραὰμ ἐπίστευσεν τῷ θεῷ, καὶ ἐλογίσθη
Abraham   believed   –   God,   and it was reckoned
αὐτῷ εἰς δικαιοσύνην. **7** γινώσκετε ἄρα
to him   for   righteousness.   Know ye   then
ὅτι οἱ ἐκ πίστεως, οὗτοι υἱοί εἰσιν
that the [ones]   by   faith,   ¹these   ³sons   ²are
Ἀβραάμ. **8** προϊδοῦσα δὲ ἡ γραφὴ ὅτι
⁴of Abraham.   And ³foreseeing   ¹the   ²scripture   ⁴that
ἐκ πίστεως δικαιοῖ τὰ ἔθνη ὁ θεός,
⁸by   ¹⁰faith   ⁶would justify   ⁷the   ⁹nations   –   ⁵God,
προευηγγελίσατο τῷ Ἀβραὰμ ὅτι ἐνευλογη-
preached good tidings   –   to Abraham   that   ⁶will be
before
θήσονται ἐν σοὶ πάντα τὰ ἔθνη. **9** ὥστε
blessed   ¹in   ²thee   ³all   ⁴the ⁵nations.   So as
οἱ ἐκ πίστεως εὐλογοῦνται σὺν τῷ πιστῷ
the[ones]of   faith   are blessed   with   the   believing

[b] Or *righteousness*

with Abraham who had faith.

10 For all who rely on works of the law are under a curse; for it is written, "Cursed be every one who does not abide by all things written in the book of the law, and do them." [11] Now it is evident that no man is justified before God by the law; for "He who through faith is righteous shall live";[c] [12] but the law does not rest on faith, for "He who does them shall live by them." [13] Christ redeemed us from the curse of the law, having become a curse for us—for it is written, "Cursed be every one who hangs on a tree"—[14] that in Christ Jesus the blessing of Abraham might come upon the Gentiles, that we might receive the promise of the Spirit through faith.

15 To give a human example, brethren: no man annuls even a man's will[d] or adds to it, once it has been ratified. [16] Now the promises were made to Abraham and to his offspring. It does not say, "And to off-springs," referring to many; but, referring to one, "And to your off-spring," which is Christ. [17] This is what I mean:

[c] Or the righteous shall live by faith
[d] Or covenant (as in verse 17)

'Αβραάμ.   **10** Ὅσοι γὰρ ἐξ ἔργων νόμου
Abraham.   For as many as ³of ³works ⁴of law
εἰσίν, ὑπὸ κατάραν εἰσίν· γέγραπται γὰρ
¹are, ⁴under ⁷a curse ⁵are; for it has been written[,]
ὅτι ἐπικατάρατος πᾶς ὃς οὐκ ἐμμένει
–   Accursed   everyone who   continues not
πᾶσιν τοῖς γεγραμμένοις ἐν τῷ βιβλίῳ
in all the things having been written in the roll
τοῦ νόμου τοῦ ποιῆσαι αὐτά.   **11** ὅτι
of the law – to do[d] them.   that
δὲ ἐν νόμῳ οὐδεὶς δικαιοῦται παρὰ τῷ
Now by law no man is justified before –
θεῷ δῆλον, ὅτι ὁ δίκαιος ἐκ πίστεως
God [is] clear, because the just man by faith
ζήσεται·   **12** ὁ δὲ νόμος οὐκ ἔστιν ἐκ
will live; and the law is not of
πίστεως, ἀλλ' ὁ ποιήσας αὐτὰ ζήσεται
faith, but the [one] doing them will live
ἐν αὐτοῖς.   **13** Χριστὸς ἡμᾶς ἐξηγόρασεν
by them.   Christ ²us ¹redeemed
ἐκ τῆς κατάρας τοῦ νόμου γενόμενος
out of the curse of the law becoming
ὑπὲρ ἡμῶν κατάρα, ὅτι γέγραπται·
²on behalf of ³us ¹a curse, because it has been written:
ἐπικατάρατος πᾶς ὁ κρεμάμενος ἐπὶ
Accursed everyone hanging on
ξύλου,   **14** ἵνα εἰς τὰ ἔθνη ἡ εὐλογία
a tree, in order that ⁵to ⁶the ⁷nations ¹the ²blessing
τοῦ 'Αβραὰμ γένηται ἐν 'Ιησοῦ Χριστῷ,
– ³of Abraham ⁴might be in Jesus Christ,
ἵνα τὴν ἐπαγγελίαν τοῦ πνεύματος λάβωμεν
in order ²the ³promise ⁴of the ⁵Spirit ¹we might
that   receive
διὰ τῆς πίστεως.   **15** 'Αδελφοί, κατὰ
through the faith.   Brothers, according to
ἄνθρωπον λέγω. ὅμως ἀνθρώπου κεκυρω-
man I say. Nevertheless ⁶of man ⁷having been
μένην διαθήκην οὐδεὶς ἀθετεῖ ἢ ἐπιδια-
ratified ⁵a covenant ¹no one ²sets aside ³or ⁴makes
τάσσεται.   **16** τῷ δὲ 'Αβραὰμ ἐρρέθησαν
additions [to].   –   Now to Abraham were said
αἱ ἐπαγγελίαι καὶ τῷ σπέρματι αὐτοῦ.
the promises and to the seed of him.
οὐ λέγει· καὶ τοῖς σπέρμασιν, ὡς ἐπὶ
It says not: And to the seeds, as concerning
πολλῶν, ἀλλ' ὡς ἐφ' ἑνός· καὶ τῷ
many, but as concerning one: And to the
σπέρματί σου, ὅς ἐστιν Χριστός. **17** τοῦτο δὲ
seed of thee, who is Christ.   And this

the law, which came four hundred and thirty years afterward, does not annul a covenant previously ratified by God, so as to make the promise void. ¹⁸ For if the inheritance is by the law, it is no longer by promise; but God gave it to Abraham by a promise. 19 Why then the law? It was added because of transgressions, till the offspring should come to whom the promise had been made; and it was ordained by angels through an intermediary. ²⁰ Now an intermediary implies more than one; but God is one. 21 Is the law then against the promises of God? Certainly not; for if a law had been given which could make alive, then righteousness would indeed be by the law. ²² But the scripture consigned all things to sin, that what was promised to faith in Jesus Christ might be given to those who believe. 23 Now before faith came, we were confined under the law, kept under restraint until faith should be revealed. ²⁴ So that the law was our custodian until Christ

λέγω·   διαθήκην   προκεκυρωμένην   ὑπὸ
I say: ¹⁰A covenant   ¹¹having been previously ratified   ¹²by

τοῦ   θεοῦ   ὁ   μετὰ   τετρακόσια   καὶ   τριάκοντα
–   ¹³God   ¹the   ⁴after   ⁵four hundred   ⁶and   ⁷thirty

ἔτη   γεγονὼς   νόμος   οὐκ   ἀκυροῖ,   εἰς   τὸ
⁸years   ⁹having come   ¹law   ⁸does not annul,   so as†
into being

καταργῆσαι   τὴν   ἐπαγγελίαν.   18 εἰ   γὰρ
to abolish   the   promise.   18 For if

ἐκ   νόμου   ἡ   κληρονομία,   οὐκέτι   ἐξ
⁴of   ⁵law   ¹the   ²inheritance ³[is],   no more [is it]   of

ἐπαγγελίας·   τῷ   δὲ   Ἀβραὰμ   δι'   ἐπαγγελίας
promise;   –   but   ⁴to Abraham   ⁵through   ⁶promise

κεχάρισται   ὁ   θεός.   19 Τί   οὖν   ὁ   νόμος;
²has given ³[it]   –   ¹God.   Why therefore the   law?

τῶν   παραβάσεων   χάριν   προσετέθη,   ἄχρις
³the   ⁴transgressions ²by reason of   ¹it was added,   until

ἂν   ἔλθῃ   τὸ   σπέρμα   ᾧ   ἐπήγγελται,
³should come   ¹the   ²seed   to whom   it has been
promised,

διαταγεὶς   δι'   ἀγγέλων,   ἐν   χειρὶ   μεσίτου.
being ordained through   angels,   by [the]   hand of a mediator.

20 ὁ   δὲ   μεσίτης   ἑνὸς   οὐκ   ἔστιν,   ὁ
Now the   mediator   ²of one   ¹is not,   –

δὲ   θεὸς   εἷς   ἐστιν.   21 ὁ   οὖν   νόμος   κατὰ
but   God   ²one   ¹is.   [Is] the   ²therefore ¹law   against

τῶν   ἐπαγγελιῶν   [τοῦ   θεοῦ];   μὴ   γένοιτο.
the   promises   – of God?   May it not be.

εἰ   γὰρ   ἐδόθη   νόμος   ὁ   δυνάμενος   ζωοποι-
For if   ²was given   ¹a law   –   being able   to make

ῆσαι,   ὄντως   ἐκ   νόμου   ἂν   ἦν   ἡ   δικαιοσύνη·
alive,   really   ³by   ⁴law   ²would   –   ¹righteousness;
have been

22 ἀλλὰ   συνέκλεισεν   ἡ   γραφὴ   τὰ   πάντα
but   ³shut up   ¹the   ²scripture   all mankind†

ὑπὸ   ἁμαρτίαν   ἵνα   ἡ   ἐπαγγελία   ἐκ   πίστεως
under   sin   in or- the   promise   by   faith
der that

Ἰησοῦ   Χριστοῦ   δοθῇ   τοῖς   πιστεύουσιν.
of(in) Jesus   Christ   might be given to the [ones]   believing.

23 Πρὸ   τοῦ   δὲ   ἐλθεῖν   τὴν   πίστιν   ὑπὸ
before   the   But   to come   the   faithᵇ   under
=But before faith came

νόμον   ἐφρουρούμεθα   συγκλειόμενοι   εἰς   τὴν
law   we were guarded   being shut up   to   the

μέλλουσαν   πίστιν   ἀποκαλυφθῆναι.   24 ὥστε
²being about   ¹faith   to be revealed.   So as

ὁ   νόμος   παιδαγωγὸς   ἡμῶν   γέγονεν   εἰς
the   law   ²a trainer   ³of us   ¹has become   [up] to

came, that we might be justified by faith. ²⁵ But now that faith has come, we are no longer under a custodian; ²⁶ for in Christ Jesus you are all sons of God, through faith. ²⁷ For as many of you as were baptized into Christ have put on Christ. ²⁸ There is neither Jew not Greek, there is neither slave nor free, there is neither male nor female; for you are all one in Christ Jesus. ²⁹ And if you are Christ's, then you are Abraham's offspring, heirs according to promise.

Χριστόν,　ἵνα　ἐκ　πίστεως　δικαιωθῶμεν·
Christ,　in order that　by　faith　we might be justified;
25 ἐλθούσης　δὲ　τῆς　πίστεως　οὐκέτι　ὑπὸ
but ³having come　¹the　²faith⁴　³no more　⁵under
παιδαγωγόν　ἐσμεν.　26 Πάντες　γὰρ　υἱοὶ
⁷a trainer　⁴we are.　For all　sons
θεοῦ　ἐστε　διὰ　τῆς　πίστεως　ἐν　Χριστῷ
of God　ye are　through　the　faith　in　Christ
Ἰησοῦ·　27 ὅσοι　γὰρ　εἰς　Χριστὸν　ἐβαπτίσ-
Jesus;　for as many as　²into　³Christ　¹ye were
θητε,　Χριστὸν　ἐνεδύσασθε.　28 οὐκ　ἔνι
baptized,　²Christ　¹ye put on.　There cannot be
Ἰουδαῖος　οὐδὲ　Ἕλλην,　οὐκ　ἔνι　δοῦλος
Jew　nor　Greek,　there cannot be　slave
οὐδὲ　ἐλεύθερος,　οὐκ　ἔνι　ἄρσεν　καὶ　θῆλυ·
nor　freeman,　there cannot be　male　and　female;
πάντες　γὰρ　ὑμεῖς　εἷς　ἐστε　ἐν　Χριστῷ
for ²all　¹ye　⁴one　³are　in　Christ
Ἰησοῦ.　29 εἰ　δὲ　ὑμεῖς　Χριστοῦ,　ἄρα
Jesus.　But if　ye [are]　of Christ,　then
τοῦ　Ἀβραὰμ　σπέρμα　ἐστέ,　κατ'　ἐπαγγελίαν
–　²of Abraham　²a seed　¹are ye, according to　promise
κληρονόμοι.　4 Λέγω　δέ,　ἐφ'　ὅσον　χρόνον　ὁ
heirs.　But I say,　over　so long a time as　the

CHAPTER 4

I mean that the heir, as long as he is a child, is no better than a slave, though he is the owner of all the estate; ² but he is under guardians and trustees until the date set by the father. ³ So with us; when we were children, we were slaves to the elemental spirits of the universe. ⁴ But when the time had fully come, God sent forth his Son, born of woman, born under the law, ⁵ to redeem those who were under the law, so that we might receive adoption as sons. ⁶ And because you are sons,

κληρονόμος　νήπιός　ἐστιν,　οὐδὲν　διαφέρει
heir　²an infant　¹is,　²nothing　¹he differs
δούλου　κύριος　πάντων　ὤν,　2 ἀλλὰ　ὑπὸ
³[from]
⁴a slave　⁶lord　⁷of all　⁵being,　but　²under
ἐπιτρόπους　ἐστὶν　καὶ　οἰκονόμους　ἄχρι　τῆς
²guardians　¹is　and　stewards　until　the
προθεσμίας　τοῦ　πατρός.　3 οὕτως　καὶ
term previously　of the　father.　So　also
appointed
ἡμεῖς,　ὅτε　ἦμεν　νήπιοι,　ὑπὸ　τὰ　στοιχεῖα
we,　when　we were　infants,　under　the　elements
τοῦ　κόσμου　ἤμεθα　δεδουλωμένοι·　4 ὅτε
of the　world　we were　having been enslaved;　when
δὲ　ἦλθεν　τὸ　πλήρωμα　τοῦ　χρόνου,
but　came　the　fulness　of the　time,
ἐξαπέστειλεν　ὁ　θεὸς　τὸν　υἱὸν　αὐτοῦ,
sent forth　–　God　the　Son　of him,
γενόμενον　ἐκ　γυναικός,　γενόμενον　ὑπὸ
becoming　of　a woman,　becoming　under
νόμον,　5 ἵνα　τοὺς　ὑπὸ　νόμον　ἐξαγοράσῃ,
law,　in order that ²the ones　²under　⁴law　¹he might redeem,
ἵνα　τὴν　υἱοθεσίαν　ἀπολάβωμεν.　6 Ὅτι　δέ
in order ²the ³adoption of sons ¹we might receive.　And because
that

God has sent the Spirit of his Son into our hearts, crying, "Abba! Father!" ⁷So through God you are no longer a slave but a son, and if a son then an heir.

8 Formerly, when you did not know God, you were in bondage to beings that by nature are no gods; ⁹but now that you have come to know God, or rather to be known by God, how can you turn back again to the weak and beggarly elemental spirits, whose slaves you want to be once more? ¹⁰You observe days, and months, and seasons, and years! ¹¹I am afraid I have labored over you in vain.

12 Brethren, I beseech you, become as I am, for I also have become as you are. You did me no wrong; ¹³you know it was because of a bodily ailment that I preached the gospel to you at first; ¹⁴and though my condition was a trial to you, you did not scorn or despise me, but received me as an angel of God, as Christ Jesus. ¹⁵What has become of the satisfaction you felt? For I bear you witness that, if possible, you would have plucked out your

ἐστε	υἱοί,	ἐξαπέστειλεν	ὁ	θεὸς τὸ
ye are	sons,	²sent forth	-	¹God the

πνεῦμα τοῦ υἱοῦ αὐτοῦ εἰς τὰς καρδίας
Spirit of the Son of him into the hearts

ἡμῶν, κρᾶζον· ἀββὰ ὁ πατήρ. 7 ὥστε
of us, crying: Abba - Father. So as

οὐκέτι εἶ δοῦλος ἀλλὰ υἱός· εἰ δὲ υἱός,
no more art thou a slave but a son; and if a son,

καὶ κληρονόμος διὰ θεοῦ.
also an heir through God.

8 Ἀλλὰ τότε μὲν οὐκ εἰδότες θεὸν
But then indeed not knowing God

ἐδουλεύσατε τοῖς φύσει μὴ οὖσιν θεοῖς·
ye served as slaves ¹the ³by nature ⁴not ⁵being ²gods;

9 νῦν δὲ γνόντες θεόν, μᾶλλον δὲ
but now knowing God, but rather

γνωσθέντες ὑπὸ θεοῦ, πῶς ἐπιστρέφετε
being known by God, how turn ye

πάλιν ἐπὶ τὰ ἀσθενῆ καὶ πτωχὰ στοιχεῖα,
again to the weak and poor elements,

οἷς πάλιν ἄνωθεν δουλεῦσαι θέλετε;
to which again ³anew ²to serve ¹ye wish?

10 ἡμέρας παρατηρεῖσθε καὶ μῆνας καὶ
²days ¹Ye observe and months and

καιροὺς καὶ ἐνιαυτούς. 11 φοβοῦμαι ὑμᾶς
seasons and years. I fear [for] you

μή πως εἰκῆ κεκοπίακα εἰς ὑμᾶς.
lest in vain I have laboured among you.

12 Γίνεσθε ὡς ἐγώ, ὅτι κἀγὼ ὡς
Be ye as I [am], because I also [am] as

ὑμεῖς, ἀδελφοί, δέομαι ὑμῶν. οὐδέν με
ye [are], brothers, I beg of you. Nothing me

ἠδικήσατε· 13 οἴδατε δὲ ὅτι δι᾽ ἀσθένειαν
ye wronged; and ye know that an account of weakness

τῆς σαρκὸς εὐηγγελισάμην ὑμῖν τὸ
of the flesh I preached good tidings to you -

πρότερον, 14 καὶ τὸν πειρασμὸν ὑμῶν
formerly, and the trial of you

ἐν τῇ σαρκί μου οὐκ ἐξουθενήσατε οὐδὲ
in the flesh of me ye despised not nor

ἐξεπτύσατε, ἀλλὰ ὡς ἄγγελον θεοῦ ἐδέξασθέ
disdained ye, but as a messenger of God ye received

με, ὡς Χριστὸν Ἰησοῦν. 15 ποῦ οὖν
me, as Christ Jesus. Where therefore

ὁ μακαρισμὸς ὑμῶν; μαρτυρῶ γὰρ ὑμῖν
the felicitation of you?* for I witness to you

ὅτι εἰ δυνατὸν τοὺς ὀφθαλμοὺς ὑμῶν
that if possible ²the ³eyes ⁴of you

* That is, "your felicitation [of me]".

eyes and given them to me. ¹⁶ Have I then become your enemy by telling you the truth?ᵉ ¹⁷ They make much of you, but for no good purpose; they want to shut you out, that you may make much of them. ¹⁸ For a good purpose it is always good to be made much of, and not only when I am present with you. ¹⁹ My little children, with whom I am again in travail until Christ be formed in you! ²⁰ I could wish to be present with you now and to change my tone, for I am perplexed about you.

21 Tell me, you who desire to be under law, do you not hear the law? ²² For it is written that Abraham had two sons, one by a slave and one by a free woman. ²³ But the son of the slave was born according to the flesh, the son of the free woman through promise. ²⁴ Now this is an allegory: these women are two covenants. One is from Mount Sinai, bearing children for slavery; she is Hagar. ²⁵ Now Hagar is Mount Sinai in Arabia;ᶠ she corresponds to the present Jerusalem, for she is in slavery with

ᵉ Or by dealing truly with you
ᶠ Other ancient authorities read For Sinai is a mountain in Arabia

---

ἐξορύξαντες ἐδώκατέ μοι. 16 ὥστε ἐχθρὸς
¹gouging out   ye gave [them] to me.   So that ²an enemy

ὑμῶν γέγονα ἀληθεύων ὑμῖν; 17 ζηλοῦσιν
³of you ¹have I become speaking truth to you?   They are zealous of

ὑμᾶς οὐ καλῶς, ἀλλὰ ἐκκλεῖσαι ὑμᾶς
you   not   well,   but   ²to exclude   ³you

θέλουσιν, 18 ἵνα αὐτοὺς ζηλοῦτε. καλὸν δὲ
¹wish,   in order them   ye may be   But [it is] good
            that   zealous of.

ζηλοῦσθαι ἐν καλῷ πάντοτε, καὶ μὴ
to be zealous   in a good thing   always,   and   not

μόνον ἐν τῷ παρεῖναί με πρὸς ὑμᾶς,
only   in the   to be present   meᵇᵉ   with   you,
        =when I am present

19 τέκνα μου, οὓς πάλιν ὠδίνω μέχρις οὗ
children of me,[for] whom again   I travail   until
                            in birth

μορφωθῇ Χριστὸς ἐν ὑμῖν· 20 ἤθελον δὲ
²is formed ¹Christ   in   you;   and I wished

παρεῖναι πρὸς ὑμᾶς ἄρτι καὶ ἀλλάξαι
to be present   with   you   just now and   to change

τὴν φωνήν μου, ὅτι ἀποροῦμαι ἐν ὑμῖν.
the   voice   of me, because I am perplexed in(about) you.

21 Λέγετέ μοι, οἱ ὑπὸ νόμον θέλοντες
Tell   me, the [ones] ³under   ⁴law   ¹wishing

εἶναι, τὸν νόμον οὐκ ἀκούετε; 22 γέγραπται
²to be,   ²the ³law   ¹hear ye not?   ²it has been written

γὰρ ὅτι Ἀβραὰμ δύο υἱοὺς ἔσχεν, ἕνα
¹for   that   Abraham   two   sons   had,   one

ἐκ τῆς παιδίσκης καὶ ἕνα ἐκ τῆς ἐλευ-
of   the   maidservant   and   one   of   the   free

θέρας. 23 ἀλλ' ὁ [μὲν] ἐκ τῆς παιδίσκης
woman.   But the [one] indeed of   the   maidservant

κατὰ σάρκα γεγέννηται, ὁ δὲ ἐκ τῆς
according to flesh   has been born,   and the [one] of   the

ἐλευθέρας διὰ τῆς ἐπαγγελίας. 24 ἅτινά
free woman through the   promise.   Which things

ἐστιν ἀλληγορούμενα· αὗται γάρ εἰσιν
is(are)   being allegorized;   for these   are

δύο διαθῆκαι, μία μὲν ἀπὸ ὄρους Σινά,
two   covenants,   one indeed from   mount   Sina,

εἰς δουλείαν γεννῶσα, ἥτις ἐστὶν Ἀγάρ.
to   slavery   bringing forth, which   is   Hagar.

25 τὸ δὲ Ἀγὰρ Σινὰ ὄρος ἐστὶν ἐν
ᶜThe ¹now ²Hagar ³Sina ⁴mount   ⁵is   in

τῇ Ἀραβίᾳ· συστοιχεῖ δὲ τῇ νῦν
–   Arabia;   and corresponds   to the   now

Ἰερουσαλήμ, δουλεύει γὰρ μετὰ τῶν
Jerusalem,   for she serves as a slave   with   the

her children. ²⁶But the Jerusalem above is free, and she is our mother. ²⁷For it is written,

"Rejoice, O barren one that dost not bear; break forth and shout, thou who art not in travail; for the desolate hath more children than she who hath a husband."

²⁸Now we,ᵍ brethren, like Isaac, are children of promise. ²⁹But as at that time he who was born according to the flesh persecuted him who was born according to the Spirit, so it is now. ³⁰But what does the scripture say? "Cast out the slave and her son; for the son of the slave shall not inherit with the son of the free woman." ³¹So, brethren, we are not children of the slave but of the free woman.

τέκνων αὐτῆς. 26 ἡ δὲ ἄνω Ἰερουσαλὴμ
children of her. But the above Jerusalem

ἐλευθέρα ἐστίν, ἥτις ἐστὶν μήτηρ ἡμῶν·
free is, who is mother of us;

27 γέγραπται γάρ· εὐφράνθητι, στεῖρα ἡ
for it has been written: Be thou glad, barren[,] the
[one]

οὐ τίκτουσα, ῥῆξον καὶ βόησον, ἡ οὐκ
not bearing, break forth and shout, the [one] not

ὠδίνουσα· ὅτι πολλὰ τὰ τέκνα τῆς ἐρήμου
travailing; because many [are] the children of the desolate

μᾶλλον ἢ τῆς ἐχούσης τὸν ἄνδρα. 28 ὑμεῖς
rather than of the having the husband. ye
[one]

δέ, ἀδελφοί, κατὰ Ἰσαὰκ ἐπαγγελίας τέκνα
But, brothers, ⁴according to ⁵Isaac ³of promise ²children

ἐστέ. 29 ἀλλ' ὥσπερ τότε ὁ κατὰ σάρκα
¹are. But even as then the [one] according to flesh

γεννηθεὶς ἐδίωκεν τὸν κατὰ πνεῦμα, οὕτως
born persecuted the [one] according spirit, so
[born] to

καὶ νῦν. 30 ἀλλὰ τί λέγει ἡ γραφή;
also now. But what says the scripture?

ἔκβαλε τὴν παιδίσκην καὶ τὸν υἱὸν αὐτῆς·
Cast out the maidservant and the son of her;

οὐ γὰρ μὴ κληρονομήσει ὁ υἱὸς τῆς
for by no means ⁵shall inherit ¹the ²son ³of the

παιδίσκης μετὰ τοῦ υἱοῦ τῆς ἐλευθέρας.
⁴maidservant with the son of the free woman.

31 διό, ἀδελφοί, οὐκ ἐσμὲν παιδίσκης
Wherefore, brothers, we are not ²of a maidservant

τέκνα ἀλλὰ τῆς ἐλευθέρας.
¹children but of the free woman.

CHAPTER 5

FOR freedom Christ has set us free; stand fast therefore, and do not submit again to a yoke of slavery.

2 Now I, Paul, say to you that if you receive circumcision, Christ will be of no advantage to you. ³I testify again to every man who receives circumcision that he is

5 Τῇ ἐλευθερίᾳ ἡμᾶς Χριστὸς ἠλευθέρωσεν·
For the freedom ³us ¹Christ ²freed;

στήκετε οὖν καὶ μὴ πάλιν ζυγῷ δουλείας
stand firm therefore and not again with a yoke of slavery

ἐνέχεσθε.
be entangled.

2 Ἴδε ἐγὼ Παῦλος λέγω ὑμῖν ὅτι
Behold[,] I Paul tell you that

ἐὰν περιτέμνησθε Χριστὸς ὑμᾶς οὐδὲν
if ye are circumcised Christ ²you ¹nothing

ὠφελήσει. 3 μαρτύρομαι δὲ πάλιν παντὶ
¹will profit. And I testify again to every

ἀνθρώπῳ περιτεμνομένῳ ὅτι ὀφειλέτης ἐστὶν
man being circumcised that ²a debtor ¹he is

ᵍ Other ancient authorities read you

bound to keep the whole law. ⁴You are severed from Christ, you who would be justified by the law; you have fallen away from grace. ⁵For through the Spirit, by faith, we wait for the hope of righteousness. ⁶For in Christ Jesus neither circumcision nor uncircumcision is of any avail, but faith working through love. ⁷You were running well; who hindered you from obeying the truth? ⁸This persuasion is not from him who called you. ⁹A little leaven leavens the whole lump. ¹⁰I have confidence in the Lord that you will take no other view than mine; and he who is troubling you will bear his judgment, whoever he is. ¹¹But if I, brethren, still preach circumcision, why am I still persecuted? In that case the stumbling-block of the cross has been removed. ¹²I wish those who unsettle you would mutilate themselves! 13 For you were called to freedom, brethren; only do not use your freedom as an opportunity for the flesh, but through love be servants of one another. ¹⁴For the whole law is fulfilled in one word, "You shall love your neighbor as

ὅλον   τὸν   νόμον   ποιῆσαι.   4 κατηργήθητε
⁴all   ⁵the   ⁶law   ³to do.   Ye were discharged

ἀπὸ   Χριστοῦ   οἵτινες   ἐν   νόμῳ   δικαιοῦσθε,
from   Christ   who   by   law   are justified,

τῆς   χάριτος   ἐξεπέσατε.   5 ἡμεῖς   γὰρ
the   ²grace   ¹ye fell from.   For we

πνεύματι   ἐκ   πίστεως   ἐλπίδα   δικαιοσύνης
in spirit   by   faith   [the] hope   of righteousness

ἀπεκδεχόμεθα.   6 ἐν   γὰρ   Χριστῷ   Ἰησοῦ
eagerly expect.   For in   Christ   Jesus

οὔτε   περιτομή   τι   ἰσχύει   οὔτε   ἀκροβυστία,
neither   circumcision   ²anything   ¹avails   nor   uncircumcision,

ἀλλὰ   πίστις   δι'   ἀγάπης   ἐνεργουμένη.
but   faith   ²through   ³love   ¹operating.

7 Ἐτρέχετε   καλῶς·   τίς   ὑμᾶς   ἐνέκοψεν
Ye were running   well: who   ²you   ¹hindered

ἀληθείᾳ   μὴ   πείθεσθαι;   8 ἡ   πεισμονὴ   οὐκ
¹by truth   ²not   ⁴to be persuaded?   the(this) persuasion   not

ἐκ   τοῦ   καλοῦντος   ὑμᾶς.   9 μικρὰ   ζύμη
of   the [one]   calling   you.   A little   leaven

ὅλον   τὸ   φύραμα   ζυμοῖ.   10 ἐγὼ   πέποιθα
all   the   lump   leavens.   I   trust

εἰς   ὑμᾶς   ἐν   κυρίῳ   ὅτι   οὐδὲν   ἄλλο   φρο-
as to†   you   in [the] Lord   that   ²nothing   ³other   ¹ye

νήσετε·   ὁ   δὲ   ταράσσων   ὑμᾶς   βαστάσει
will think;   but the [one]   troubling   you   shall bear

τὸ   κρίμα,   ὅστις   ἐὰν   ᾖ.   11 Ἐγὼ   δέ,
the   judgment,   whoever   he may be.   ²But ⁴I,

ἀδελφοί,   εἰ   περιτομὴν   ἔτι   κηρύσσω,   τί
²brothers,   ³if   ⁷circumcision   ⁵still   ⁶proclaim,   why

ἔτι   διώκομαι;   ἄρα   κατήργηται   τὸ
still   am I being persecuted?   then   has been annulled   the

σκάνδαλον   τοῦ   σταυροῦ.   12 Ὄφελον   καὶ
offence   of the   cross.   I would that indeed

ἀποκόψονται   οἱ   ἀναστατοῦντες   ὑμᾶς.
⁴will(might) cut   ¹the [ones]   ²unsettling   ³you.
themselves off

13 Ὑμεῖς   γὰρ   ἐπ'   ἐλευθερίᾳ   ἐκλήθητε,
For ye   for   freedom   were called,

ἀδελφοί·   μόνον   μὴ   τὴν   ἐλευθερίαν   εἰς
brothers;   only [use]   not   the   freedom   for

ἀφορμὴν   τῇ   σαρκί,   ἀλλὰ   διὰ   τῆς   ἀγάπης
advantage   to the   flesh,   but   through   –   love

δουλεύετε   ἀλλήλοις.   14 ὁ   γὰρ   πᾶς   νόμος
serve ye as slaves one another.   For the   whole   law

ἐν   ἑνὶ   λόγῳ   πεπλήρωται,   ἐν   τῷ·   ἀγα-
in   one   word   has been summed up,   in the [word]: Thou

πήσεις   τὸν   πλησίον   σου   ὡς   σεαυτόν.
shalt love   the   neighbour   of thee   as   thyself.

yourself." ¹⁵But if you bite and devour one another take heed that you are not consumed by one another.

16 But I say, walk by the Spirit, and do not gratify the desires of the flesh. ¹⁷For the desires of the flesh are against the Spirit, and the desires of the Spirit are against the flesh; for these are opposed to each other, to prevent you from doing what you would. ¹⁸But if you are led by the Spirit you are not under the law. ¹⁹Now the works of the flesh are plain: immorality, impurity, licentiousness, ²⁰idolatry, sorcery, enmity, strife, jealousy, anger, selfishness, dissension, party spirit,²¹ envy,ʰ drunkenness, carousing, and the like. I warn you, as I warned you before, that those who do such things shall not inherit the kingdom of God. ²²But the fruit of the Spirit is love, joy, peace, patience, kindness, goodness, faithfulness, ²³gentleness, self-control; against such there is no law. ²⁴And those who belong to Christ Jesus have crucified the flesh with its passions and desires.

25 If we live by the Spirit, let us also walk by the Spirit. ²⁶Let us

ʰ Other ancient authorities add murder

15 εἰ δὲ ἀλλήλους δάκνετε καὶ κατεσθίετε,
But if ⁴one another ¹ye bite ²and ³ye devour,
βλέπετε μὴ ὑπ' ἀλλήλων ἀναλωθῆτε.
see lest by one another ye are destroyed.
16 Λέγω δέ, πνεύματι περιπατεῖτε καὶ
Now I say, in spirit walk ye and
ἐπιθυμίαν σαρκὸς οὐ μὴ τελέσητε. 17 ἡ
[the] lust of [the] flesh by no means ye will perform. the
γὰρ σὰρξ ἐπιθυμεῖ κατὰ τοῦ πνεύματος,
For flesh lusts against the spirit,
τὸ δὲ πνεῦμα κατὰ τῆς σαρκός, ταῦτα
and the spirit against the flesh, ²these
γὰρ ἀλλήλοις ἀντίκειται, ἵνα μὴ ἃ ἐὰν
¹for ⁴each other ³opposes, lest whatever things
θέλητε ταῦτα ποιῆτε. 18 εἰ δὲ πνεύματι
ye wish these ye do. But if by [the] Spirit
ἄγεσθε, οὐκ ἐστὲ ὑπὸ νόμον. 19 φανερὰ δέ
ye are led, ye are not under law. Now ⁶manifest
ἐστιν τὰ ἔργα τῆς σαρκός, ἅτινά ἐστιν
⁵is(are) ¹the ²works ³of the ⁴flesh, which is(are)
πορνεία, ἀκαθαρσία, ἀσέλγεια, 20 εἰδωλο-
fornication, uncleanness, lewdness, idola-
λατρία, φαρμακεία, ἔχθραι, ἔρις, ζῆλος,
try, sorcery, enmities, strife, jealousy,
θυμοί, ἐριθεῖαι, διχοστασίαι, αἱρέσεις,
angers, rivalries, divisions, sects,
21 φθόνοι, μέθαι, κῶμοι, καὶ τὰ ὅμοια
envyings, drunken- revellings, and - like
nesses, things
τούτοις, ἃ προλέγω ὑμῖν καθὼς προεῖπον,
to these, which I tell ²beforehand ¹you as I previously
said,
ὅτι οἱ τὰ τοιαῦτα πράσσοντες βασιλείαν
that the [ones] - ²such things ¹practising ⁴[the] kingdom
θεοῦ οὐ κληρονομήσουσιν. 22 ὁ δὲ καρπὸς
⁵of God ³will not inherit. But the fruit
τοῦ πνεύματός ἐστιν ἀγάπη, χαρά, εἰρήνη,
of the Spirit is love, joy, peace,
μακροθυμία, χρηστότης, ἀγαθωσύνη, πίστις,
longsuffering, kindness, goodness, faithfulness,
23 πραΰτης, ἐγκράτεια· κατὰ τῶν τοιούτων
meekness, self-control; against - such things
οὐκ ἔστιν νόμος. 24 οἱ δὲ τοῦ Χριστοῦ
there is no law. Now the ones - of Christ
Ἰησοῦ τὴν σάρκα ἐσταύρωσαν σὺν τοῖς
Jesus ²the ³flesh ¹crucified with the(its)
παθήμασιν καὶ ταῖς ἐπιθυμίαις. 25 Εἰ
passions and the(its) lusts. If
ζῶμεν πνεύματι, πνεύματι καὶ στοιχῶμεν.
we live in [the] Spirit, in [the] Spirit also let us walk.

have no self-conceit, no provoking of one another, no envy of one another.

CHAPTER 6

BRETHREN, if a man is overtaken in any trespass, you who are spiritual should restore him in a spirit of gentleness. Look to yourself, lest you too be tempted. ²Bear one another's burdens, and so fulfil the law of Christ. ³For if any one thinks he is something, when he is nothing, he deceives himself. ⁴But let each one test his own work, and then his reason to boast will be in himself alone and not in his neighbor. ⁵For each man will have to bear his own load.

6 Let him who is taught the word share all good things with him who teaches.

7 Do not be deceived; God is not mocked, for whatever a man sows, that he will also reap. ⁸For he who sows to his own flesh will from the flesh reap corruption; but he who sows to the Spirit will from the Spirit reap eternal life. ⁹And let us not grow weary in well-doing, for

26 μὴ γινώμεθα κενόδοξοι, ἀλλήλους
Let us not become   vainglorious,   one another

προκαλούμενοι, ἀλλήλοις φθονοῦντες.
provoking,   one another   envying.

6 Ἀδελφοί, ἐὰν καὶ προλημφθῇ ἄνθρω-
Brothers, if indeed ²is overtaken   ¹a

πος ἐν τινι παραπτώματι, ὑμεῖς οἱ
man in some   trespass,   ye   the

πνευματικοὶ καταρτίζετε τὸν τοιοῦτον ἐν
spiritual [ones] restore   –   such a one in

πνεύματι πραΰτητος, σκοπῶν σεαυτόν, μὴ
a spirit of meekness, considering thyself, lest

καὶ σὺ πειρασθῇς. 2 Ἀλλήλων τὰ βάρη
also thou art tempted. Of one another the loads

βαστάζετε, καὶ οὕτως ἀναπληρώσετε τὸν
bear ye, and   so   ye will fulfil   the

νόμον τοῦ Χριστοῦ. 3 εἰ γὰρ δοκεῖ
law   – of Christ.   For if ²thinks

τις εἶναί τι μηδὲν ὤν, φρεναπατᾷ ἑαυτόν.
¹anyone ²to be ³some- ⁴no- ⁵being, he deceives himself.
          thing thing

4 τὸ δὲ ἔργον ἑαυτοῦ δοκιμαζέτω ἕκαστος,
But the work of himself ¹let ²prove ²each man,

καὶ τότε εἰς ἑαυτὸν μόνον τὸ καύχημα
and then in himself alone the boast

ἕξει καὶ οὐκ εἰς τὸν ἕτερον· 5 ἕκαστος
he will and not in the other man; ²each man
have

γὰρ τὸ ἴδιον φορτίον βαστάσει. 6 Κοινωνείτω δὲ
¹for the(his) own burden   will bear.   And ⁵let him share

ὁ κατηχούμενος τὸν λόγον τῷ κατη-
¹the ³being instructed [in] ²the ⁴word ⁶with the [one] in-
[one]

χοῦντι ἐν πᾶσιν ἀγαθοῖς. 7 Μὴ πλανᾶσθε,
structing in all good things. Be ye not led astray,

θεὸς οὐ μυκτηρίζεται. ὃ γὰρ ἐὰν σπείρῃ
God is not mocked.   For whatever ²may sow

ἄνθρωπος, τοῦτο καὶ θερίσει· 8 ὅτι ὁ
¹a man,   this   also he will reap; because the

σπείρων εἰς τὴν σάρκα ἑαυτοῦ ἐκ τῆς
[one] sowing to the flesh of himself of the

σαρκὸς θερίσει φθοράν, ὁ δὲ σπείρων
flesh   will reap corruption, but the [one] sowing

εἰς τὸ πνεῦμα ἐκ τοῦ πνεύματος θερίσει
to the spirit of the Spirit   will reap

ζωὴν αἰώνιον. 9 τὸ δὲ καλὸν ποιοῦντες
life eternal. And ²the ²good   ¹doing

μὴ ἐγκακῶμεν· καιρῷ γὰρ ἰδίῳ
let us not lose heart;   for in its own time

in due season we shall reap, if we do not lose heart. [10] So then, as we have opportunity, let us do good to all men, and especially to those who are of the household of faith. [11] See with what large letters I am writing to you with my own hand. [12] It is those who want to make a good showing in the flesh that would compel you to be circumcised, and only in order that they may not be persecuted for the cross of Christ. [13] For even those who receive circumcision do not themselves keep the law, but they desire to have you circumcised that they may glory in your flesh. [14] But far be it from me to glory except in the cross of our Lord Jesus Christ, by which[i] the world has been crucified to me, and I to the world. [15] For neither circumcision counts for anything, nor uncircumcision, but a new creation. [16] Peace and mercy be upon all who walk by this rule, upon the Israel of God.

[17] Henceforth let no man trouble me; for I bear on my body the marks of Jesus.

[i] Or *through whom*

θερίσομεν μὴ ἐκλυόμενοι. 10 "Αρα οὖν
we shall reap   not   failing.   Then therefore

ὡς καιρὸν ἔχομεν, ἐργαζώμεθα τὸ ἀγαθὸν
as ²time ¹we have,   let us do   the   good

πρὸς πάντας, μάλιστα δὲ πρὸς τοὺς
to   all men,   and most of all   to   the

οἰκείους τῆς πίστεως.
members of of the   faith.
the family

11 "Ιδετε πηλίκοις ὑμῖν γράμμασιν
Ye see   in how large ²to you ¹letters

ἔγραψα τῇ ἐμῇ χειρί. 12 "Οσοι θέλουσιν
²I wrote – with my hand.   As many as   wish

εὐπροσωπῆσαι ἐν σαρκί, οὗτοι ἀναγκάζουσιν
to look well   in [the] flesh, these compel

ὑμᾶς περιτέμνεσθαι, μόνον ἵνα τῷ
you   to be circumcised,   only in order that ²for the

σταυρῷ τοῦ Χριστοῦ ['Ιησοῦ] μὴ
³cross   –   ⁵of Christ   ⁴Jesus   ¹not

διώκωνται. 13 οὐδὲ γὰρ οἱ περιτεμνόμενοι
²they are persecuted. For ⁵not ¹the [ones] ²being circumcised

αὐτοὶ νόμον φυλάσσουσιν, ἀλλὰ θέλουσιν
³themselves ⁴law   ⁴keep,   but   they wish

ὑμᾶς περιτέμνεσθαι ἵνα ἐν τῇ ὑμετέρᾳ
you   to be circumcised in order that ²in – ³your

σαρκὶ καυχήσωνται. 14 ἐμοὶ δὲ μὴ γένοιτο
⁴flesh ¹they may boast. But to me may it not be

καυχᾶσθαι εἰ μὴ ἐν τῷ σταυρῷ τοῦ
to boast   except   in   the   cross   of the

κυρίου ἡμῶν 'Ιησοῦ Χριστοῦ, δι' οὗ
Lord   of us   Jesus   Christ, through whom

ἐμοὶ κόσμος ἐσταύρωται κἀγὼ κόσμῳ.
to me [the] world has been crucified and I to [the] world.

15 οὔτε γὰρ περιτομή τί ἐστιν οὔτε
For neither   circumcision ²anything ¹is   nor

ἀκροβυστία, ἀλλὰ καινὴ κτίσις. 16 καὶ
uncircumcision, but a new creation.

ὅσοι τῷ κανόνι τούτῳ στοιχήσουσιν,
as many as by this rule   will walk,

εἰρήνη ἐπ' αὐτοὺς καὶ ἔλεος, καὶ ἐπὶ τὸν
peace   on them   and mercy, and on the

'Ισραὴλ τοῦ θεοῦ.
Israel   – of God.

17 Τοῦ λοιποῦ κόπους μοι μηδεὶς
For the rest ²troubles ⁴me ³no one

παρεχέτω· ἐγὼ γὰρ τὰ στίγματα τοῦ
¹let ²cause; for ¹I   ⁴the ⁵brands   –

'Ιησοῦ ἐν τῷ σώματί μου βαστάζω.
⁵of Jesus ⁶in ⁷the ⁸body ⁹of me ²bear.

18 The grace of our Lord Jesus Christ be with your spirit, brethren. Amen.

18 Ἡ χάρις τοῦ κυρίου ἡμῶν Ἰησοῦ
The grace of the Lord of us Jesus
Χριστοῦ μετὰ τοῦ πνεύματος ὑμῶν,
Christ with the spirit of you,
ἀδελφοί· ἀμήν.
brothers : Amen.

EPHESIANS 1

ΠΡΟΣ ΕΦΕΣΙΟΥΣ
To Ephesians

CHAPTER 1

PAUL, an apostle of Christ Jesus by the will of God,
To the saints who are also faithful[a] in Christ Jesus:
2 Grace to you and peace from God our Father and the Lord Jesus Christ.
3 Blessed be the God and Father of our Lord Jesus Christ, who has blessed us in Christ with every spiritual blessing in the heavenly places, [4]even as he chose us in him before the foundation of the world, that we should be holy and blameless before him. [5]He destined us in love[b] to be his sons through Jesus Christ, according to the purpose of his will, [6]to the praise of his

1 Παῦλος ἀπόστολος Χριστοῦ Ἰησοῦ διὰ
Paul an apostle of Christ Jesus through
θελήματος θεοῦ τοῖς ἁγίοις τοῖς οὖσιν
[the] will of God to the saints – being
[ἐν Ἐφέσῳ] καὶ πιστοῖς ἐν Χριστῷ
in Ephesus and faithful in Christ
Ἰησοῦ· 2 χάρις ὑμῖν καὶ εἰρήνη ἀπὸ
Jesus: Grace to you and peace from
θεοῦ πατρὸς ἡμῶν καὶ κυρίου Ἰησοῦ
God Father of us and Lord Jesus
Χριστοῦ.
Christ.

3 Εὐλογητὸς ὁ θεὸς καὶ πατὴρ τοῦ
Blessed the God and Father of the
κυρίου ἡμῶν Ἰησοῦ Χριστοῦ, ὁ εὐλογήσας
Lord of us Jesus Christ, the [one] having blessed
ἡμᾶς ἐν πάσῃ εὐλογίᾳ πνευματικῇ ἐν
us with every blessing spiritual in
τοῖς ἐπουρανίοις ἐν Χριστῷ, 4 καθὼς
the heavenlies in Christ, as
ἐξελέξατο ἡμᾶς ἐν αὐτῷ πρὸ καταβολῆς
he chose us in him before [the] foundation
κόσμου, εἶναι ἡμᾶς ἁγίους καὶ ἀμώμους
of [the] world, to be us holy and unblemished[b]
= that we should be . . .
κατενώπιον αὐτοῦ, ἐν ἀγάπῃ 5 προορίσας
before him, in love predestinating
ἡμᾶς εἰς υἱοθεσίαν διὰ Ἰησοῦ Χριστοῦ
us to adoption of sons through Jesus Christ
εἰς αὐτόν, κατὰ τὴν εὐδοκίαν τοῦ
to him[self], according to the good pleasure of the
θελήματος αὐτοῦ, 6 εἰς ἔπαινον δόξης
will of him, to [the] praise of [the] glory

[a] Other ancient authorities read who are at Ephesus and faithful
[b] Or before him in love, having destined us

glorious grace which he freely bestowed on us in the Beloved. [7] In him we have redemption through his blood, the forgiveness of our trespasses, according to the riches of his grace [8] which he lavished upon us. [9] For he has made known to us in all wisdom and insight the mystery of his will, according to his purpose which he set forth in Christ [10] as a plan for the fulness of time, to unite all things in him, things in heaven and things on earth.

11 In him, according to the purpose of him who accomplishes all things according to the counsel of his will, [12] we who first hoped in Christ have been destined and appointed to live for the praise of his glory. [13] In him you also, who have heard the word of truth, the gospel of your salvation, and have believed in him, were sealed with the promised Holy

τῆς χάριτος αὐτοῦ, ἧς ἐχαρίτωσεν ἡμᾶς
of the grace of him, of(with) he favoured us
                          which

ἐν τῷ ἠγαπημένῳ, 7 ἐν ᾧ ἔχομεν τὴν
in the [one] *having been* loved, in whom we have the

ἀπολύτρωσιν διὰ τοῦ αἵματος αὐτοῦ, τὴν
redemption through the blood of him, the

ἄφεσιν τῶν παραπτωμάτων, κατὰ τὸ
forgiveness – of trespasses, according to the

πλοῦτος τῆς χάριτος αὐτοῦ, 8 ἧς ἐπερίσ-
riches of the grace of him, which he made to

σευσεν εἰς ἡμᾶς ἐν πάσῃ σοφίᾳ καὶ
abound to us in all wisdom and

φρονήσει 9 γνωρίσας ἡμῖν τὸ μυστήριον
intelligence making known to us the mystery

τοῦ θελήματος αὐτοῦ, κατὰ τὴν εὐδοκίαν
of the will of him, according to the good pleasure

αὐτοῦ, ἣν προέθετο ἐν αὐτῷ 10 εἰς
of him, which he purposed in him[self] for

οἰκονομίαν τοῦ πληρώματος τῶν καιρῶν,
a stewardship of the fulness of the times,

ἀνακεφαλαιώσασθαι τὰ πάντα ἐν τῷ
to head up – all things in the

Χριστῷ, τὰ ἐπὶ τοῖς οὐρανοῖς καὶ τὰ
Christ, the things on(in) *the* heavens and the
                                                        things

ἐπὶ τῆς γῆς· ἐν αὐτῷ, 11 ἐν ᾧ καὶ
on the earth; in him, in whom also

ἐκληρώθημεν προορισθέντες κατὰ πρόθεσιν
we were chosen as being predestinated according to [the] purpose
[his] inheritance

τοῦ τὰ πάντα ἐνεργοῦντος κατὰ τὴν
of the – ²all things ¹operating according to the
[one]

βουλὴν τοῦ θελήματος αὐτοῦ, 12 εἰς τὸ
counsel of the will of him, for *the*

εἶναι ἡμᾶς εἰς ἔπαινον δόξης αὐτοῦ
to be usᵇ to [the] praise of [the] glory of him
=that we should be

τοὺς προηλπικότας ἐν τῷ Χριστῷ· 13 ἐν
the having previously in – Christ; in
[ones] hoped

ᾧ καὶ ὑμεῖς, ἀκούσαντες τὸν λόγον
whom also ye, hearing the word

τῆς ἀληθείας, τὸ εὐαγγέλιον τῆς σωτηρίας
– of truth, the gospel of the salvation

ὑμῶν, ἐν ᾧ καὶ πιστεύσαντες ἐσφραγίσθητε
of you, in whom also believing ye were sealed

τῷ πνεύματι τῆς ἐπαγγελίας τῷ ἁγίῳ,
with ¹the ³Spirit – ⁴of promise – ²holy,

Spirit, ¹⁴which is the guarantee of our inheritance until we acquire possession of it, to the praise of his glory.

15 For this reason, because I have heard of your faith in the Lord Jesus and your love[c] toward all the saints, ¹⁶I do not cease to give thanks for you, remembering you in my prayers, ¹⁷that the God of our Lord Jesus Christ, the Father of glory, may give you a spirit of wisdom and of revelation in the knowledge of him, ¹⁸having the eyes of your hearts enlightened, that you may know what is the hope to which he has called you, what are the riches of his glorious inheritance in the saints, ¹⁹and what is the immeasurable greatness of his power in us who believe, according to the working of his great might ²⁰which he accomplished in Christ when he raised him from the dead and made him sit at his right hand in the heavenly places, ²¹far above all rule and authority and power and dominion, and above

[c] Other ancient authorities omit *your love*

14 ὅς ἐστιν ἀρραβὼν τῆς κληρονομίας
who is an earnest of the inheritance
ἡμῶν, εἰς ἀπολύτρωσιν τῆς περιποιήσεως,
of us, till [the] redemption of the possession.
εἰς ἔπαινον τῆς δόξης αὐτοῦ.
to [the] praise of the glory of him.

15 Διὰ τοῦτο κἀγώ, ἀκούσας τὴν καθ᾽
Therefore I also, hearing the ²among
ὑμᾶς πίστιν ἐν τῷ κυρίῳ Ἰησοῦ καὶ
²you ¹faith in the Lord Jesus and
τὴν ἀγάπην τὴν εἰς πάντας τοὺς ἁγίους,
the love – to all the saints,

16 οὐ παύομαι εὐχαριστῶν ὑπὲρ ὑμῶν
do not cease giving thanks on behalf of you
μνείαν ποιούμενος ἐπὶ τῶν προσευχῶν
mention making on(in) the prayers
μου, 17 ἵνα ὁ θεὸς τοῦ κυρίου ἡμῶν
of me, in order that the God of the Lord of us
Ἰησοῦ Χριστοῦ, ὁ πατὴρ τῆς δόξης,
Jesus Christ, the Father – of glory,
δῴη ὑμῖν πνεῦμα σοφίας καὶ ἀποκαλύψεως
may give to you a spirit of wisdom and of revelation
ἐν ἐπιγνώσει αὐτοῦ, 18 πεφωτισμένους τοὺς
in a full knowledge of him, having been enlightened the
ὀφθαλμοὺς τῆς καρδίας [ὑμῶν,] εἰς τὸ
eyes of the heart of you, for the
εἰδέναι ὑμᾶς τίς ἐστιν ἡ ἐλπὶς τῆς
to know you[b] what is the hope of the
=that ye should know
κλήσεως αὐτοῦ, τίς ὁ πλοῦτος τῆς δόξης
calling of him, what the riches of the glory
τῆς κληρονομίας αὐτοῦ ἐν τοῖς ἁγίοις,
of the inheritance of him in the saints,
19 καὶ τί τὸ ὑπερβάλλον μέγεθος τῆς
and what the excelling greatness of the
δυνάμεως αὐτοῦ εἰς ἡμᾶς τοὺς πιστεύοντας
power of him toward us the [ones] believing
κατὰ τὴν ἐνέργειαν τοῦ κράτους τῆς
according to the operation of the might of the
ἰσχύος αὐτοῦ, 20 ἣν ἐνήργηκεν ἐν τῷ
strength of him, which he has operated in –
Χριστῷ ἐγείρας αὐτὸν ἐκ νεκρῶν, καὶ
Christ raising him from [the] dead, and
καθίσας ἐν δεξιᾷ αὐτοῦ ἐν τοῖς ἐπου-
seating [him] at [the] right [hand] of him in the heaven-
ρανίοις 21 ὑπεράνω πάσης ἀρχῆς καὶ
lies far above all rule and
ἐξουσίας καὶ δυνάμεως καὶ κυριότητος
authority and power and lordship

every name that is
named, not only in this
age but also in that
which is to come; ²²and
he has put all things
under his feet and has
made him the head over
all things for the church,
²³which is his body, the
fulness of him who fills
all in all.

καὶ   παντὸς   ὀνόματος   ὀνομαζομένου   οὐ
and   every   name   being named   not

μόνον ἐν   τῷ   αἰῶνι   τούτῳ   ἀλλὰ   καὶ
only   in   the age   this   but   also

ἐν   τῷ   μέλλοντι· 22 καὶ πάντα   ὑπέταξεν
in   the coming;   and all things subjected

ὑπὸ   τοὺς   πόδας   αὐτοῦ,   καὶ   αὐτὸν   ἔδωκεν
under the   feet   of him, and   ²him   ¹gave

κεφαλὴν   ὑπὲρ   πάντα   τῇ   ἐκκλησίᾳ,   23 ἥτις
[to be] head over all things to the church,   which

ἐστὶν   τὸ   σῶμα   αὐτοῦ,   τὸ   πλήρωμα
is   the body   of him, the fulness

τοῦ   τὰ   πάντα   ἐν   πᾶσιν   πληρουμένου.
of the   -   ²all things ³with ⁴all things ¹filling.
[one]

CHAPTER 2

AND you he made
alive, when you
were dead through the
trespasses and sins ²in
which you once walked,
following the course of
this world, following the
prince of the power of the
air, the spirit that is now
at work in the sons of
disobedience. ³Among
these we all once lived
in the passions of our
flesh, following the de-
sires of body and mind,
and so we were by nature
children of wrath, like
the rest of mankind.
⁴But God, who is rich in
mercy, out of the great
love with which he loved
us, ⁵even when we were
dead through our tres-
passes, made us alive
together with Christ (by
grace you have been

2 Καὶ   ὑμᾶς   ὄντας   νεκροὺς   τοῖς   παραπτώ-
  And   you   being   dead   in the   tres-

μασιν   καὶ   ταῖς   ἁμαρτίαις   ὑμῶν,   2 ἐν
passes   and   in the sins   of you,   in

αἷς   ποτε   περιεπατήσατε   κατὰ   τὸν   αἰῶνα
which then   ye walked   according to the   age

τοῦ   κόσμου   τούτου,   κατὰ   τὸν   ἄρχοντα
of this world,   according to the   ruler

τῆς   ἐξουσίας   τοῦ   ἀέρος,   τοῦ   πνεύματος
of the authority of the air,   of the spirit

τοῦ   νῦν   ἐνεργοῦντος   ἐν   τοῖς   υἱοῖς   τῆς
-     now   operating   in   the   sons   -

ἀπειθείας· 3 ἐν   οἷς   καὶ   ἡμεῖς   πάντες
of disobedience; among whom also   we   all

ἀνεστράφημέν   ποτε   ἐν   ταῖς   ἐπιθυμίαις
conducted ourselves then   in   the   lusts

τῆς   σαρκὸς   ἡμῶν,   ποιοῦντες   τὰ   θελήματα
of the flesh   of us,   doing   the   wishes

τῆς   σαρκὸς   καὶ   τῶν   διανοιῶν,   καὶ
of the flesh   and   of the understandings, and

ἤμεθα   τέκνα   φύσει   ὀργῆς   ὡς   καὶ   οἱ
were   ²children ¹by nature of wrath as   also the

λοιποί· 4 ὁ   δὲ   θεὸς   πλούσιος   ὢν   ἐν
rest;   -   but   God   ²rich   ¹being in

ἐλέει,   διὰ   τὴν   πολλὴν   ἀγάπην   αὐτοῦ
mercy, because of the   much   love   of his

ἣν   ἠγάπησεν   ἡμᾶς,   5 καὶ   ὄντας   ἡμᾶς
[with] he loved   us,   even   being   us
which   =when we were

νεκροὺς   τοῖς   παραπτώμασιν   συνεζωοποίησεν
dead   -   in trespasses   quickened [us] with

τῷ   Χριστῷ,   —   χάριτί   ἐστε   σεσωσμένοι,
-    Christ,   (by grace ye are having been saved,)

saved), ⁶ and raised us up with him, and made us sit with him in the heavenly places in Christ Jesus, ⁷ that in the coming ages he might show the immeasurable riches of his grace in kindness toward us in Christ Jesus. ⁸ For by grace you have been saved through faith; and this is not your own doing, it is the gift of God—⁹ not because of works, lest any man should boast. ¹⁰ For we are his workmanship, created in Christ Jesus for good works, which God prepared beforehand, that we should walk in them.

11 Therefore remember that at one time you Gentiles in the flesh, called the uncircumcision by what is called the circumcision, which is made in the flesh by hands—¹² remember that you were at that time separated from Christ, alienated from the commonwealth of Israel, and strangers to the covenants of promise, having no hope and without God in the world. ¹³ But now in Christ Jesus you who once were far off have been brought near in the blood of Christ. ¹⁴ For

— 6 καὶ συνήγειρεν καὶ συνεκάθισεν ἐν
and raised [us] with and seated [us] with in

τοῖς ἐπουρανίοις ἐν Χριστῷ Ἰησοῦ, 7 ἵνα
the heavenlies in Christ Jesus, in order that

ἐνδείξηται ἐν τοῖς αἰῶσιν τοῖς ἐπερχομένοις
he might show in the ages – coming on
forth

τὸ ὑπερβάλλον πλοῦτος τῆς χάριτος αὐτοῦ
the excelling riches of the grace of him

ἐν χρηστότητι ἐφ' ἡμᾶς ἐν Χριστῷ
in kindness toward us in Christ

Ἰησοῦ. 8 τῇ γὰρ χάριτί ἐστε σεσωσμένοι
Jesus. – For by grace ye are *having been* saved

διὰ πίστεως· καὶ τοῦτο οὐκ ἐξ ὑμῶν,
through faith; and this not of you,

θεοῦ τὸ δῶρον· 9 οὐκ ἐξ ἔργων, ἵνα μή
of [is] the gift; not of works, lest
God

τις καυχήσηται. 10 αὐτοῦ γάρ ἐσμεν
anyone should boast. For of him we are

ποίημα, κτισθέντες ἐν Χριστῷ Ἰησοῦ
a product, created in Christ Jesus

ἐπὶ ἔργοις ἀγαθοῖς, οἷς προητοίμασεν
unto works good, which ²previously prepared

ὁ θεὸς ἵνα ἐν αὐτοῖς περιπατήσωμεν.
– ¹God in order that in them we might walk.

11 Διὸ μνημονεύετε ὅτι ποτὲ ὑμεῖς τὰ
Wherefore remember ye that when ye the

ἔθνη ἐν σαρκί, οἱ λεγόμενοι ἀκροβυστία
nations in [the] flesh, the [ones] *being* called uncircumcision

ὑπὸ τῆς λεγομένης περιτομῆς ἐν σαρκὶ
by the *being* called circumcision in [the] flesh

χειροποιήτου, 12 ὅτι ἦτε τῷ καιρῷ ἐκείνῳ
made by hand, that ye were at that time

χωρὶς Χριστοῦ, ἀπηλλοτριωμένοι τῆς
without Christ, having been alienated from the

πολιτείας τοῦ Ἰσραὴλ καὶ ξένοι τῶν
commonwealth – of Israel and strangers of(from)
the

διαθηκῶν τῆς ἐπαγγελίας, ἐλπίδα μὴ
covenants – of promise, hope not

ἔχοντες καὶ ἄθεοι ἐν τῷ κόσμῳ. 13 νυνὶ
having and godless in the world. now

δὲ ἐν Χριστῷ Ἰησοῦ ὑμεῖς οἵ ποτε
But in Christ Jesus ye the [ones] then

ὄντες μακρὰν ἐγενήθητε ἐγγὺς ἐν τῷ
being afar became near by the

αἵματι τοῦ Χριστοῦ. 14 Αὐτὸς γάρ
blood – of Christ. For he

he is our peace, who has made us both one, and has broken down the dividing wall of hostility, [15]by abolishing in his flesh the law of commandments and ordinances, that he might create in himself one new man in place of the two, so making peace, [16]and might reconcile us both to God in one body through the cross, thereby bringing the hostility to an end. [17]And he came and preached peace to you who were far off and peace to those who were near; [18]for through him we both have access in one Spirit to the Father. [19]So then you are no longer strangers and sojourners, but you are fellow citizens with the saints and members of the household of God, [20]built upon the foundation of the apostles and prophets, Christ Jesus himself being the chief cornerstone, [21]in whom the whole structure is joined together and grows into a holy temple in the Lord; [22]in whom you also are built into it for a dwelling place of God in the Spirit.

ἐστιν ἡ εἰρήνη ἡμῶν, ὁ ποιήσας τὰ
is   the peace of us, the [one] having made -

ἀμφότερα ἐν καὶ τὸ μεσότοιχον τοῦ
both   one and [2]the [3]middle wall   -

φραγμοῦ λύσας, τὴν ἔχθραν, ἐν τῇ σαρκὶ
[4]of partition [1]having the enmity, [2]in [3]the [4]flesh
           broken,

αὐτοῦ 15 τὸν νόμον τῶν ἐντολῶν ἐν
[5]of him [6]the [7]law [8]of the [9]commandments [10]in

δόγμασιν καταργήσας, ἵνα τοὺς δύο κτίσῃ
[11]decrees [1]having abolished, in order [4]the [5]two [3]he might
                       that   create

ἐν αὐτῷ εἰς ἕνα καινὸν ἄνθρωπον ποιῶν
[6]in [7]him[self] [8]into [9]one [10]new [11]man [1]making

εἰρήνην, 16 καὶ ἀποκαταλλάξῃ τοὺς
[2]peace,   and   might reconcile   the

ἀμφοτέρους ἐν ἑνὶ σώματι τῷ θεῷ διὰ
both   in one body   -   to God through

τοῦ σταυροῦ, ἀποκτείνας τὴν ἔχθραν ἐν
the cross,   killing   the enmity in

αὐτῷ· 17 καὶ ἐλθὼν εὐηγγελίσατο εἰρήνην
him[self];   and coming   preached   peace

ὑμῖν τοῖς μακρὰν καὶ εἰρήνην τοῖς ἐγγύς·
to you the ones afar   and peace to the ones near;

18 ὅτι δι' αὐτοῦ ἔχομεν τὴν προσαγωγὴν
because through him [1]we [3]have   -   [4]access

οἱ ἀμφότεροι ἐν ἑνὶ πνεύματι πρὸς τὸν
-   [2]both   in one Spirit   unto the

πατέρα. 19 ἄρα οὖν οὐκέτι ἐστὲ ξένοι
Father.   Then therefore no more are ye strangers

καὶ πάροικοι, ἀλλὰ ἐστὲ συμπολῖται τῶν
and sojourners, but ye are fellow-citizens of the

ἁγίων καὶ οἰκεῖοι τοῦ θεοῦ, 20 ἐποικοδομη-
saints and members of   - of God,   having been
            the family

θέντες ἐπὶ τῷ θεμελίῳ τῶν ἀποστόλων
built on on the foundation of the apostles

καὶ προφητῶν, ὄντος ἀκρογωνιαίου αὐτοῦ
and prophets,   [4]being [5]cornerstone [3][him]self

Χριστοῦ Ἰησοῦ, 21 ἐν ᾧ πᾶσα οἰκοδομὴ
[1]Christ [2]Jesus,[a]   in whom all [the] building

συναρμολογουμένη αὔξει εἰς ναὸν ἅγιον
being fitted together grows into shrine a holy

ἐν κυρίῳ, 22 ἐν ᾧ καὶ ὑμεῖς συνοικοδομεῖσθε
in [the] Lord,   in whom also ye are being built together

εἰς κατοικητήριον τοῦ θεοῦ ἐν πνεύματι.
into a dwelling-place   - of God in spirit.

CHAPTER 3

FOR this reason I, Paul, a prisoner for Christ Jesus on behalf of you Gentiles—²assuming that you have heard of the stewardship of God's grace that was given to me for you, ³how the mystery was made known to me by revelation, as I have written briefly. ⁴When you read this you can perceive my insight into the mystery of Christ, ⁵which was not made known to the sons of men in other generations as it has now been revealed to his holy apostles and prophets by the Spirit; ⁶that is, how the Gentiles are fellow heirs, members of the same body, and partakers of the promise in Christ Jesus through the gospel.

7 Of this gospel I was made a minister according to the gift of God's grace which was given me by the working of his power. ⁸To me, though I am the very least of all the saints, this grace was given, to preach to the Gentiles the unsearchable riches of Christ, ⁹and to make all men see what is the plan of the mystery hidden for

3 Τούτου χάριν ἐγὼ Παῦλος ὁ δέσμιος
*of this ¹By reason of I   Paul   the   prisoner

τοῦ Χριστοῦ Ἰησοῦ ὑπὲρ ὑμῶν τῶν
-   of Christ   Jesus   on behalf of   you   the

ἐθνῶν 2 — εἴ γε ἠκούσατε τὴν οἰκονομίαν
nations   — if indeed ye heard the   stewardship

τῆς χάριτος τοῦ θεοῦ τῆς δοθείσης μοι
of the   grace   -   of God   -   given   to me

εἰς ὑμᾶς, 3 ὅτι κατὰ ἀποκάλυψιν ἐγνωρίσθη
for   you,   that by way of revelation   was made known

μοι τὸ μυστήριον, καθὼς προέγραψα ἐν
to me the   mystery,   as   I previously wrote in

ὀλίγῳ, 4 πρὸς ὃ δύνασθε ἀναγινώσκοντες
brief,   as to which ²ye can   ¹reading

νοῆσαι τὴν σύνεσίν μου ἐν τῷ μυστηρίῳ
*to realize the understanding of me in   the   mystery

τοῦ Χριστοῦ, 5 ὃ ἑτέραις γενεαῖς οὐκ
-   of Christ,   which in other generations not

ἐγνωρίσθη τοῖς υἱοῖς τῶν ἀνθρώπων ὡς
was made known to the   sons   -   of men   as

νῦν ἀπεκαλύφθη τοῖς ἁγίοις ἀποστόλοις
now it was revealed to the   holy   apostles

αὐτοῦ καὶ προφήταις ἐν πνεύματι, 6 εἶναι
of him   and   prophets   in   spirit,   ³to be

τὰ ἔθνη συγκληρονόμα καὶ σύσσωμα καὶ
¹the ²nations   joint-heirs   and   a joint-body   and

συμμέτοχα τῆς ἐπαγγελίας ἐν Χριστῷ
joint-sharers of the   promise   in   Christ

Ἰησοῦ διὰ τοῦ εὐαγγελίου, 7 οὗ ἐγενήθην
Jesus through the   gospel,   of which I became

διάκονος κατὰ τὴν δωρεὰν τῆς χάριτος
a minister according to the   gift   of the   grace

τοῦ θεοῦ τῆς δοθείσης μοι κατὰ τὴν
-   of God   -   given   to me according to the

ἐνέργειαν τῆς δυνάμεως αὐτοῦ. 8 ἐμοὶ
operation of the   power   of him.   To me

τῷ ἐλαχιστοτέρῳ πάντων ἁγίων ἐδόθη
the   leaster*   of all   saints   was given

ἡ χάρις αὕτη, τοῖς ἔθνεσιν εὐαγγελίσασθαι
this grace,   to the   nations   to preach

τὸ ἀνεξιχνίαστον πλοῦτος τοῦ Χριστοῦ,
the   unsearchable   riches   of Christ,

9 καὶ φωτίσαι τίς ἡ οἰκονομία τοῦ
and to bring to light what [is] the stewardship   of the

μυστηρίου τοῦ ἀποκεκρυμμένου ἀπὸ τῶν
mystery   -   having been hidden   from   the

* This is quite literal!—the apostle coins a word.

ages in[d] God who created all things; [10]that through the church the manifold wisdom of God might now be made known to the principalities and powers in the heavenly places. [11]This was according to the eternal purpose which he has realized in Christ Jesus our Lord, [12]in whom we have boldness and confidence of access through our faith in him. [13]So I ask you not to[e] lose heart over what I am suffering for you, which is your glory.

14 For this reason I bow my knees before the Father, [15]from whom every family in heaven and on earth is named, [16]that according to the riches of his glory he may grant you to be strengthened with might through his Spirit in the inner man, [17]and that Christ may dwell in your hearts through faith; that you, being rooted and grounded in love, [18]may have power to comprehend with all the saints what is the breadth and

αἰώνων ἐν τῷ θεῷ τῷ τὰ πάντα κτίσαντι,
ages in - God [1]the - [3]all things [2]having
[one] created,

10 ἵνα γνωρισθῇ νῦν ταῖς ἀρχαῖς καὶ
in order might be made now to the rulers and
that known

ταῖς ἐξουσίαις ἐν τοῖς ἐπουρανίοις διὰ
to the authorities in the heavenlies through

τῆς ἐκκλησίας ἡ .πολυποίκιλος σοφία τοῦ
the church the manifold wisdom -

θεοῦ, 11 κατὰ πρόθεσιν τῶν αἰώνων ἣν
of God, according to [the] purpose of the ages which

ἐποίησεν ἐν τῷ Χριστῷ Ἰησοῦ τῷ κυρίῳ
he made in - Christ Jesus the Lord

ἡμῶν, 12 ἐν ᾧ ἔχομεν τὴν παρρησίαν
of us, in whom we have - boldness

καὶ προσαγωγὴν ἐν πεποιθήσει διὰ τῆς
and access in confidence through the

πίστεως αὐτοῦ. 13 διὸ αἰτοῦμαι μὴ
faith of(in) him.* Wherefore I ask [you] not

ἐγκακεῖν ἐν ταῖς θλίψεσίν μου ὑπὲρ
to faint in the afflictions of me on behalf

ὑμῶν, ἥτις ἐστὶν δόξα ὑμῶν. 14 Τούτου
of you, which is glory of you. [2]of this

χάριν κάμπτω τὰ γόνατά μου πρὸς
[1]By reason of I bend the knees of me unto

τὸν πατέρα, 15 ἐξ οὗ πᾶσα πατριὰ
the Father, of whom every fatherhood

ἐν οὐρανοῖς καὶ ἐπὶ γῆς ὀνομάζεται,
in heavens and on earth is named,

16 ἵνα δῷ ὑμῖν κατὰ τὸ πλοῦτος τῆς
in order he may you according to the riches of the
that give

δόξης αὐτοῦ δυνάμει κραταιωθῆναι διὰ
glory of him by power to become mighty through

τοῦ πνεύματος αὐτοῦ εἰς τὸν ἔσω ἄνθρω-
the Spirit of him in the inward man,

πον, 17 κατοικῆσαι τὸν Χριστὸν διὰ τῆς
to dwell - Christ[b] through -
=that Christ may dwell

πίστεως ἐν ταῖς καρδίαις ὑμῶν, ἐν
faith in the hearts of you, in

ἀγάπῃ ἐρριζωμένοι καὶ τεθεμελιωμένοι,
love having been rooted and having been founded,

18 ἵνα ἐξισχύσητε καταλαβέσθαι σὺν πᾶσιν
in order ye may have strength to apprehend with all
that

τοῖς ἁγίοις τί τὸ πλάτος καὶ μῆκος
the saints what [is] the breadth and length

[d] Or by

[e] Or I ask that I may not

* See Gal. 2. 16.

length and height and
depth, ¹⁹and to know the
love of Christ which
surpasses knowledge,
that you may be filled
with all the fulness of
God.
20 Now to him who
by the power at work
within us is able to do far
more abundantly than all
that we ask or think, ²¹to
him be glory in the
church and in Christ
Jesus to all generations,
for ever and ever. Amen.

καὶ   ὕψος   καὶ   βάθος,   19   γνῶναί   τε   τὴν
and   height   and   depth,   and to know   ¹the
ὑπερβάλλουσαν   τῆς   γνώσεως   ἀγάπην   τοῦ
⁴excelling   -   ⁵knowledge   ²love   -
Χριστοῦ,   ἵνα   πληρωθῆτε   εἰς   πᾶν   τὸ
²of Christ,   in order that ye may be filled   to   all   the
πλήρωμα   τοῦ   θεοῦ.
fulness   -   of God.
20 Τῷ   δὲ   δυναμένῳ   ὑπὲρ   πάντα   ποιῆσαι
Now to the [one]   being able   beyond   all things   to do
ὑπερεκπερισσοῦ   ὧν   αἰτούμεθα   ἢ   νοοῦμεν
superabundantly   of which   we ask   or   we think
κατὰ   τὴν   δύναμιν   τὴν   ἐνεργουμένην   ἐν
according to the   power   -   operating   in
ἡμῖν,   21 αὐτῷ   ἡ   δόξα   ἐν   τῇ   ἐκκλησίᾳ
us,   to him [be] the   glory   in   the   church
καὶ   ἐν   Χριστῷ   Ἰησοῦ   εἰς   πάσας   τὰς
and   in   Christ   Jesus   unto   all   the
γενεὰς   τοῦ   αἰῶνος   τῶν   αἰώνων·   ἀμήν.
generations of the   age   of the   ages: Amen.

CHAPTER 4

I therefore, a prisoner
for the Lord, beg you
to lead a life worthy of
the calling to which you
have been called, ²with
all lowliness and meek-
ness, with patience, for-
bearing one another in
love, ³eager to maintain
the unity of the Spirit in
the bond of peace. ⁴There
is one body and one
Spirit, just as you were
called to the one hope
that belongs to your call,
⁵one Lord, one faith,
one baptism, ⁶one God
and Father of us all, who
is above all and through
all and in all. ⁷But grace
was given to each of us
according to the measure

4 Παρακαλῶ   οὖν   ὑμᾶς   ἐγὼ   ὁ   δέσμιος
⁷beseech   ⁶therefore   ⁵you   ¹I   ²the   ³prisoner
ἐν   κυρίῳ   ἀξίως   περιπατῆσαι   τῆς   κλήσεως
⁴in   ⁵[the] Lord   ¹⁰worthily   ⁹to walk   of the   calling
ἧς   ἐκλήθητε,   2 μετὰ   πάσης   ταπεινοφροσύνης
of(with) ye were   with   all   humility
which   called,
καὶ   πραΰτητος,   μετὰ   μακροθυμίας,
and   meekness,   with   longsuffering,
ἀνεχόμενοι   ἀλλήλων   ἐν   ἀγάπῃ,   3 σπου-
forbearing   one another   in   love,   being
δάζοντες   τηρεῖν   τὴν   ἑνότητα   τοῦ   πνεύματος
eager   to keep   the   unity   of the   Spirit
ἐν   τῷ   συνδέσμῳ   τῆς   εἰρήνης·   ἐν   σῶμα
in   the   bond   -   of peace; [there is] one body
καὶ   ἓν   πνεῦμα,   4 καθὼς   καὶ   ἐκλήθητε
and   one   Spirit,   as   also   ye were called
ἐν   μιᾷ   ἐλπίδι   τῆς   κλήσεως   ὑμῶν·   5 εἷς
in   one   hope   of the   calling   of you;   one
κύριος,   μία   πίστις,   ἓν   βάπτισμα·   6 εἷς
Lord,   one   faith,   one   baptism;   one
θεὸς   καὶ   πατὴρ   πάντων,   ὁ   ἐπὶ   πάντων
God   and   Father   of all,   the [one] over   all
καὶ   διὰ   πάντων   καὶ   ἐν   πᾶσιν.   7 Ἑνὶ
and   through   all   and   in   all.   ²to ⁴one
δὲ   ἑκάστῳ   ἡμῶν   ἐδόθη   ἡ   χάρις   κατὰ
¹But   ³each   of us   was given   -   grace according to

of Christ's gift. ⁸Therefore it is said,
"When he ascended on high he led a host of captives,
and he gave gifts to men."
⁹(In saying, "He ascended," what does it mean but that he had also descended into the lower parts of the earth? ¹⁰He who descended is he who also ascended far above all the heavens, that he might fill all things.) ¹¹And his gifts were that some should be apostles, some prophets, some evangelists, some pastors and teachers, ¹²for the equipment of the saints, for the work of ministry, for building up the body of Christ, ¹³until we all attain to the unity of the faith and of the knowledge of the Son of God, to mature manhood, to the measure of the stature of the fulness of Christ; ¹⁴so that we may no longer be children, tossed to and fro and carried about with every wind of doctrine, by the cunning of men, by their craftiness in deceitful wiles. ¹⁵Rather, speaking the truth in love, we are to grow up in every way into him who is the head,

τὸ μέτρον τῆς δωρεᾶς τοῦ Χριστοῦ.
the measure of the gift - of Christ.

8 διὸ λέγει· ἀναβὰς εἰς ὕψος ᾐχμαλώτευσεν
Wherefore he says: Having to height he led captive
ascended

αἰχμαλωσίαν, ἔδωκεν δόματα τοῖς ἀνθρώποις.
captivity, he gave gifts - to men.

9 τὸ δὲ ἀνέβη τί ἐστιν εἰ μὴ ὅτι καὶ
Now the "he what is it except that also
ascended"

κατέβη εἰς τὰ κατώτερα μέρη τῆς γῆς;
he descended into the lower parts of the earth?

10 ὁ καταβὰς αὐτός ἐστιν καὶ ὁ ἀναβὰς
The descending himself is also the ascending
[one] [one]

ὑπεράνω πάντων τῶν οὐρανῶν, ἵνα
far above all the heavens, in order that

πληρώσῃ τὰ πάντα. 11 καὶ αὐτὸς ἔδωκεν
he might fill - all things. And he gave

τοὺς μὲν ἀποστόλους, τοὺς δὲ προφήτας,
some† apostles, some† prophets,

τοὺς δὲ εὐαγγελιστάς, τοὺς δὲ ποιμένας
some† evangelists, some† shepherds

καὶ διδασκάλους, 12 πρὸς τὸν καταρτισμὸν
and teachers, for the perfecting

τῶν ἁγίων εἰς ἔργον διακονίας, εἰς
of the saints to [the] work of ministry, to

οἰκοδομὴν τοῦ σώματος τοῦ Χριστοῦ,
building of the body - of Christ,

13 μέχρι καταντήσωμεν οἱ πάντες εἰς
until ¹we ³arrive - ²all at

τὴν ἑνότητα τῆς πίστεως καὶ τῆς ἐπιγνώ-
the unity of the faith and of the full know-

σεως τοῦ υἱοῦ τοῦ θεοῦ, εἰς ἄνδρα τέλειον,
ledge of the Son - of God, at ²man ¹a complete,

εἰς μέτρον ἡλικίας τοῦ πληρώματος τοῦ
at [the] measure of [the] of the fulness -
stature

Χριστοῦ, 14 ἵνα μηκέτι ὦμεν νήπιοι,
of Christ, in order that no more we may be infants,

κλυδωνιζόμενοι καὶ περιφερόμενοι παντὶ ἀνέμῳ
being blown and being carried round by every wind

τῆς διδασκαλίας ἐν τῇ κυβείᾳ τῶν ἀνθρώ-
- of teaching in the sleight - of

πων, ἐν πανουργίᾳ πρὸς τὴν μεθοδείαν
men, in cleverness unto the craftiness

τῆς πλάνης, 15 ἀληθεύοντες δὲ ἐν ἀγάπῃ
- of error, but speaking truth in love

αὐξήσωμεν εἰς αὐτὸν τὰ πάντα, ὅς ἐστιν
we may grow into him in all respects,† who is

into Christ, ¹⁶from whom the whole body, joined and knit together by every joint with which it is supplied, when each part is working properly, makes bodily growth and upbuilds itself in love.

17 Now this I affirm and testify in the Lord, that you must no longer live as the Gentiles do, in the futility of their minds; ¹⁸they are darkened in their understanding, alienated from the life of God because of the ignorance that is in them, due to their hardness of heart; ¹⁹they have become callous and have given themselves up to licentiousness, greedy to practice every kind of uncleanness. ²⁰You did not so learn Christ!—²¹assuming that you have heard about him and were taught in him, as the truth is in Jesus. ²²Put off your old nature which belongs to your former manner of life and is corrupt through deceitful lusts, ²³and be renewed in the

ἡ κεφαλή, Χριστός, 16 ἐξ οὗ πᾶν τὸ
the head, Christ, of whom all the

σῶμα συναρμολογούμενον καὶ συμβιβαζόμενον
body being fitted together and being brought together

διὰ πάσης ἁφῆς τῆς ἐπιχορηγίας κατ'
through every band - of supply according to

ἐνέργειαν ἐν μέτρῳ ἑνὸς ἑκάστου μέρους
[the] operation in measure of ²one ¹each part

τὴν αὔξησιν τοῦ σώματος ποιεῖται εἰς
²the ²growth ⁴of the ⁵body ¹makes for

οἰκοδομὴν ἑαυτοῦ ἐν ἀγάπῃ.
building of itself in love.

17 Τοῦτο οὖν λέγω καὶ μαρτύρομαι ἐν
This therefore I say and witness in

κυρίῳ, μηκέτι ὑμᾶς περιπατεῖν καθὼς
[the] Lord, no more you to walk as

καὶ τὰ ἔθνη περιπατεῖ ἐν ματαιότητι
also the nations walks in vanity

τοῦ νοὸς αὐτῶν, 18 ἐσκοτωμένοι τῇ
of the mind of them, ²having been darkened ²in the (their)

διανοίᾳ ὄντες, ἀπηλλοτριωμένοι τῆς ζωῆς
⁴intellect ¹being, having been alienated [from] the life

τοῦ θεοῦ, διὰ τὴν ἄγνοιαν τὴν οὖσαν
of God, through the ignorance - being

ἐν αὐτοῖς, διὰ τὴν πώρωσιν τῆς καρδίας
in them, on account of the hardness of the heart

αὐτῶν, 19 οἵτινες ἀπηλγηκότες ἑαυτοὺς
of them, who having ceased to care ²themselves

παρέδωκαν τῇ ἀσελγείᾳ εἰς ἐργασίαν
¹gave up - to lewdness for work

ἀκαθαρσίας πάσης ἐν πλεονεξίᾳ. 20 ὑμεῖς
²uncleanness ¹of all in greediness. ye

δὲ οὐχ οὕτως ἐμάθετε τὸν Χριστόν,
But not so learned - Christ,

21 εἴ γε αὐτὸν ἠκούσατε καὶ ἐν αὐτῷ
if indeed ²him ¹ye heard and ²by ³him

ἐδιδάχθητε καθώς ἐστιν ἀλήθεια ἐν τῷ
¹were taught as ²is ¹truth in -

Ἰησοῦ, 22 ἀποθέσθαι ὑμᾶς κατὰ τὴν
Jesus, to put off youᵇ as regards the(your)
=that ye put off

προτέραν ἀναστροφὴν τὸν παλαιὸν ἄνθρωπον
former conduct the old man

τὸν φθειρόμενον κατὰ τὰς ἐπιθυμίας τῆς
- being corrupted according to the lusts

ἀπάτης, 23 ἀνανεοῦσθαι δὲ τῷ πνεύματι
of deceit, and to be renewed in the spirit

spirit of your minds, ²⁴and put on the new nature, created after the likeness of God in true righteousness and holiness.

25 Therefore, putting away falsehood, let every one speak the truth with his neighbor, for we are members one of another. ²⁶Be angry but do not sin; do not let the sun go down on your anger, ²⁷and give no opportunity to the devil. ²⁸Let the thief no longer steal, but rather let him labor, doing honest work with his hands, so that he may be able to give to those in need. ²⁹Let no evil talk come out of your mouths, but only such as is good for edifying, as fits the occasion, that it may impart grace to those who hear. ³⁰And do not grieve the Holy Spirit of God, in whom you were sealed for the day of redemption. ³¹Let all bitterness and wrath and anger and clamor and slander be put away from you, with all malice, ³²and be kind to one another, tenderhearted,

---

τοῦ νοὸς ὑμῶν 24 καὶ ἐνδύσασθαι τὸν
of the mind of you and to put on the

καινὸν ἄνθρωπον τὸν κατὰ θεὸν κτισθέντα
new man – ²according to ²God ¹created

ἐν δικαιοσύνῃ καὶ ὁσιότητι τῆς ἀληθείας.
in righteousness and holiness – of truth.

25 Διὸ ἀποθέμενοι τὸ ψεῦδος λαλεῖτε
Wherefore putting off the lie speak ye

ἀλήθειαν ἕκαστος μετὰ τοῦ πλησίον αὐτοῦ,
truth each man with the neighbour of him,

ὅτι ἐσμὲν ἀλλήλων μέλη. 26 ὀργίζεσθε
because we are of one another members. Be ye wrathful

καὶ μὴ ἁμαρτάνετε· ὁ ἥλιος μὴ
and do not sin; ²the ⁴sun ²not

ἐπιδυέτω ἐπὶ παροργισμῷ ὑμῶν, 27 μηδὲ
¹let ⁵set on on provocation of you, nor

δίδοτε τόπον τῷ διαβόλῳ. 28 ὁ κλέπτων
give ye place to the devil. The [one] stealing

μηκέτι κλεπτέτω, μᾶλλον δὲ κοπιάτω
no more let him steal, but rather let him labour

ἐργαζόμενος ταῖς ἰδίαις χερσὶν τὸ ἀγαθόν,
working with the(his) own hands the good thing,

ἵνα ἔχῃ μεταδιδόναι τῷ χρείαν ἔχοντι.
in order he may to share [with] the [one] ²need ¹having
that have

29 πᾶς λόγος σαπρὸς ἐκ τοῦ στόματος
Every ²word ¹corrupt out of the mouth

ὑμῶν μὴ ἐκπορευέσθω·, ἀλλὰ εἴ τις
of you let not proceed•, but if any

ἀγαθὸς πρὸς οἰκοδομὴν τῆς χρείας, ἵνα
[is] good to improvement of the need, in order
that

δῷ χάριν τοῖς ἀκούουσιν. 30 καὶ μὴ λυπεῖτε
it may grace to the [ones] hearing. And do not grieve
give

τὸ πνεῦμα τὸ ἅγιον τοῦ θεοῦ, ἐν ᾧ
the Spirit – Holy – of God, by whom

ἐσφραγίσθητε εἰς ἡμέραν ἀπολυτρώσεως.
ye were sealed for a day of redemption.

31 πᾶσα πικρία καὶ θυμὸς καὶ
All bitterness and anger and

ὀργὴ καὶ κραυγὴ καὶ βλασφημία ἀρθήτω
wrath and clamour and blasphemy let it be
removed

ἀφ' ὑμῶν σὺν πάσῃ κακίᾳ. 32 γίνεσθε
from you with all evil. be ye

δὲ εἰς ἀλλήλους χρηστοί, εὐσπλαγχνοι,
And to one another kind, tenderhearted,

• That is, "let no corrupt word proceed ..."

forgiving one another, as God in Christ forgave you.

CHAPTER 5

THEREFORE be imitators of God, as beloved children. ²And walk in love, as Christ loved us and gave himself up for us, a fragrant offering and sacrifice to God.
3 But immorality and all impurity or covetousness must not even be named among you, as is fitting among saints. ⁴Let there be no filthiness, nor silly talk, nor levity, which are not fitting; but instead let there be thanksgiving. ⁵Be sure of this, that no immoral or impure man, or one who is covetous (that is, an idolator), has any inheritance in the kingdom of Christ and of God. ⁶Let no one deceive you with empty words, for it is because of these things that the wrath of God comes upon the sons of disobedience. ⁷Therefore do not associate with them, ⁸for once you were darkness, but now you are light in the Lord; walk as children of light ⁹(for the fruit of light is found in all that is good and right and true), ¹⁰and try to learn what is

χαριζόμενοι   ἑαυτοῖς   καθὼς   καὶ   ὁ   θεὸς
forgiving   yourselves   as   also   -   God
ἐν   Χριστῷ   ἐχαρίσατο   ὑμῖν.   5 Γίνεσθε
in   Christ   forgave   you.   Be ye
οὖν   μιμηταὶ   τοῦ   θεοῦ,   ὡς   τέκνα
therefore imitators   -   of God,   as   children
ἀγαπητά,   2 καὶ   περιπατεῖτε   ἐν   ἀγάπῃ,
beloved,   and   walk ye   in   love,
καθὼς   καὶ   ὁ   Χριστὸς   ἠγάπησεν   ὑμᾶς
as   also   -   Christ   loved   you
καὶ   παρέδωκεν   ἑαυτὸν   ὑπὲρ   ἡμῶν
and   gave up   himself   on behalf of us
προσφορὰν   καὶ   θυσίαν   τῷ   θεῷ   εἰς   ὀσμὴν
an offering   and   a sacrifice -   to God for   an odour
εὐωδίας.   3 Πορνεία   δὲ   καὶ   ἀκαθαρσία
of sweet smell. But fornication and   ²uncleanness
πᾶσα   ἢ   πλεονεξία   μηδὲ   ὀνομαζέσθω   ἐν
¹all   or   greediness   not   let it be named among
ὑμῖν,   καθὼς   πρέπει   ἁγίοις,   4 καὶ   αἰσχρότης
you,   as   is fitting for saints, and   baseness
καὶ   μωρολογία   ἢ   εὐτραπελία,   ἃ   οὐκ
and   foolish talking or   raillery,   which things not
ἀνῆκεν,   ἀλλὰ   μᾶλλον   εὐχαριστία.   5 τοῦτο
are becoming, but   rather   thanksgiving.   this
γὰρ   ἴστε   γινώσκοντες,   ὅτι   πᾶς   πόρνος
For   be ye   knowing,   that   every fornicator
ἢ   ἀκάθαρτος   ἢ   πλεονέκτης,   ὃ   ἐστιν
or   unclean man   or   greedy,   who   is
εἰδωλολάτρης,   οὐκ   ἔχει   κληρονομίαν   ἐν   τῇ
an idolater,   not   has   inheritance   in   the
βασιλείᾳ   τοῦ   Χριστοῦ   καὶ   θεοῦ.   6 Μηδεὶς
kingdom   -   of Christ   and   of God.   ²No man
ὑμᾶς   ἀπατάτω   κενοῖς   λόγοις·   διὰ   ταῦτα
⁴you   ¹let ²deceive with empty words;   because these
                                                of
γὰρ   ἔρχεται   ἡ   ὀργὴ   τοῦ   θεοῦ   ἐπὶ   τοὺς
for   is coming   the   wrath   -   of God   on   the
υἱοὺς   τῆς   ἀπειθείας.   7 μὴ   οὖν   γίνεσθε
sons   -   of disobedience. Not therefore be ye
συμμέτοχοι   αὐτῶν·   8 ἦτε   γὰρ   ποτε   σκότος,
partakers   of them;   for ye were then   darkness,
νῦν   δὲ   φῶς   ἐν   κυρίῳ·   ὡς   τέκνα   φωτὸς
but now   light   in   [the] Lord;   as   children of light
περιπατεῖτε,   9 —   ὁ   γὰρ   καρπὸς   τοῦ
walk ye,   (for the   fruit   of the
φωτὸς   ἐν   πάσῃ   ἀγαθωσύνῃ   καὶ   δικαιοσύνῃ
light [is] in   all   goodness   and   righteousness
καὶ   ἀληθείᾳ,   —   10 δοκιμάζοντες   τί   ἐστιν
and   truth,)   proving   what   is

pleasing to the Lord. [11] Take no part in the unfruitful works of darkness, but instead expose them. [12] For it is a shame even to speak of the things that they do in secret; [13] but when anything is exposed by the light it becomes visible, for anything that becomes visible is light. [14] Therefore it is said,
"Awake, O sleeper,
and arise from the dead,
and Christ shall give you light."
15 Look carefully then how you walk, not as unwise men but as wise, [16] making the most of the time, because the days are evil. [17] Therefore do not be foolish, but understand what the will of the Lord is. [18] And do not get drunk with wine, for that is debauchery; but be filled with the Spirit, [19] addressing one another in psalms and hymns and spiritual songs, singing and making melody to the Lord with all your heart, [20] always and for everything giving thanks in the name of our Lord Jesus Christ to God the Father.
21 Be subject to one another out of reverence for Christ. [22] Wives, be subject to your husbands,

εὐάρεστον τῷ κυρίῳ, 11 καὶ μὴ συγκοι-
well-pleasing to the Lord,   and do not have fellow-

νωνεῖτε τοῖς ἔργοις τοῖς ἀκάρποις τοῦ
ship with the ²works - ¹unfruitful -

σκότους, μᾶλλον δὲ καὶ ἐλέγχετε, 12 τὰ
of darkness, but rather even reprove [them], ⁵the

γὰρ κρυφῇ γινόμενα ὑπ' αὐτῶν αἰσχρόν
for ⁶hidden things ⁷being done ⁸by ⁹them ²shameful

ἐστιν καὶ λέγειν· 13 τὰ δὲ πάντα ἐλεγχόμενα
¹it is ³even ⁴to speak [of]; - but all things being reproved

ὑπὸ τοῦ φωτὸς φανεροῦται· 14 πᾶν γὰρ
by the light is(are) manifested; for everything

τὸ φανερούμενον φῶς ἐστιν. διὸ λέγει·
- being manifested ²light ¹is. Wherefore he says:

ἔγειρε, ὁ καθεύδων, καὶ ἀνάστα ἐκ τῶν
Rise, the sleeping [one], and stand up out of the

νεκρῶν, καὶ ἐπιφαύσει σοι ὁ Χριστός.
dead [ones], and will shine on thee - Christ.

15 Βλέπετε οὖν ἀκριβῶς πῶς περιπατεῖτε,
See ye therefore carefully how ye walk,

μὴ ὡς ἄσοφοι ἀλλ' ὡς σοφοί, 16 ἐξαγοραζ-
not as unwise but as wise, redeem-

όμενοι τὸν καιρόν, ὅτι αἱ ἡμέραι πονηραί
ing the time, because the days evil

εἰσιν. 17 διὰ τοῦτο μὴ γίνεσθε ἄφρονες,
are. Therefore be ye not foolish,

ἀλλὰ συνίετε τί τὸ θέλημα τοῦ κυρίου.
but understand what the will of the Lord [is].

18 καὶ μὴ μεθύσκευθε οἴνῳ, ἐν ᾧ ἐστιν
And be ye not drunk with wine, in which is

ἀσωτία, ἀλλὰ πληροῦσθε ἐν πνεύματι,
wantonness, but be filled by [the] Spirit,

19 λαλοῦντες ἑαυτοῖς ψαλμοῖς καὶ ὕμνοις
speaking to yourselves in psalms and hymns

καὶ ᾠδαῖς πνευματικαῖς, ᾄδοντες καὶ
and songs spiritual, singing and

ψάλλοντες τῇ καρδίᾳ ὑμῶν τῷ κυρίῳ,
psalming with the heart of you to the Lord,

20 εὐχαριστοῦντες πάντοτε ὑπὲρ πάντων
giving thanks always for all things

ἐν ὀνόματι τοῦ κυρίου ἡμῶν Ἰησοῦ
in [the] name of the Lord of us Jesus

Χριστοῦ τῷ θεῷ καὶ πατρί, 21 ὑποτασ-
Christ - to God even [the] Father, being

σόμενοι ἀλλήλοις ἐν φόβῳ Χριστοῦ. 22 Αἱ
subject to one another in [the] fear of Christ. The

γυναῖκες τοῖς ἰδίοις ἀνδράσιν ὡς τῷ
wives to the(ir) own husbands as to the

as to the Lord. [23] For the husband is the head of the wife as Christ is the head of the church, his body, and is himself its Savior. [24] As the church is subject to Christ, so let wives also be subject in everything to their husbands. [25] Husbands, love your wives, as Christ loved the church and gave himself up for her, [26] that he might sanctify her, having cleansed her by the washing of water with the word, [27] that he might present the church to himself in splendor, without spot or wrinkle or any such thing, that she might be holy and without blemish. [28] Even so husbands should love their wives as their own bodies. He who loves his wife loves himself. [29] For no man ever hates his own flesh, but nourishes and cherishes it, as Christ does the church, [30] because we are members of his body. [31] "For this reason a man shall leave his father and mother and

κυρίῳ, 23 ὅτι ἀνήρ ἐστιν κεφαλὴ τῆς
Lord, because a man is head of the

γυναικὸς ὡς καὶ ὁ Χριστὸς κεφαλὴ
woman as also – Christ [is] head

τῆς ἐκκλησίας, αὐτὸς σωτὴρ τοῦ σώματος.
of the church, [him]self Saviour of the body.

24 ἀλλὰ ὡς ἡ ἐκκλησία ὑποτάσσεται τῷ
But as the church is subject –

Χριστῷ, οὕτως καὶ αἱ γυναῖκες τοῖς
to Christ, so also the wives to the(ir)

ἀνδράσιν ἐν παντί. 25 Οἱ ἄνδρες, ἀγαπᾶτε
husbands in everything. The husbands, love ye

τὰς γυναῖκας, καθὼς καὶ ὁ Χριστὸς
the(your) wives, as also – Christ

ἠγάπησεν τὴν ἐκκλησίαν καὶ ἑαυτὸν
loved the church and himself

παρέδωκεν ὑπὲρ αὐτῆς, 26 ἵνα αὐτὴν
gave up on behalf of it, in order that it

ἁγιάσῃ καθαρίσας τῷ λουτρῷ τοῦ
he might sanctify cleansing by the washing of the

ὕδατος ἐν ῥήματι, 27 ἵνα παραστήσῃ αὐτὸς
water by word, in order that [2]might present [1]he

ἑαυτῷ ἔνδοξον τὴν ἐκκλησίαν, μὴ ἔχουσαν
[1]to himself [3]glorious [2]the [4]church, not having

σπίλον ἢ ῥυτίδα ἤ τι τῶν τοιούτων,
spot or wrinkle or any of the such things,

ἀλλ᾽ ἵνα ᾖ ἁγία καὶ ἄμωμος. 28 οὕτως
but in order it might holy and unblemished. So
that be

ὀφείλουσιν [καὶ] οἱ ἄνδρες ἀγαπᾶν τὰς
ought also the husbands to love the

ἑαυτῶν γυναῖκας ὡς τὰ ἑαυτῶν σώματα.
of themselves wives as the of themselves bodies.

ὁ ἀγαπῶν τὴν ἑαυτοῦ γυναῖκα ἑαυτὸν
The [one] loving the of himself wife himself

ἀγαπᾷ· 29 οὐδεὶς γάρ ποτε τὴν ἑαυτοῦ
loves; for no man ever the of himself

σάρκα ἐμίσησεν, ἀλλὰ ἐκτρέφει καὶ θάλπει
flesh hated, but nourishes and cherishes

αὐτήν, καθὼς καὶ ὁ Χριστὸς τὴν ἐκ-
it, as also – Christ the

κλησίαν, 30 ὅτι μέλη ἐσμὲν τοῦ σώματος
church, because members we are of the body

αὐτοῦ. 31 ἀντὶ τούτου καταλείψει ἄνθρωπος
of him. For this [2]shall leave [1]a man

[τὸν] πατέρα καὶ [τὴν] μητέρα καὶ
the(his) father and the(his) mother and

be joined to his wife, and the two shall become one." ³²This is a great mystery, and I take it to mean Christ and the church; ³³however, let each one of you love his wife as himself, and let the wife see that she respects her husband.

προσκολληθήσεται πρὸς τὴν γυναῖκα αὐτοῦ,
shall cleave   to   the   wife   of him,

καὶ ἔσονται οἱ δύο εἰς σάρκα μίαν·
and ²shall be ¹the ²two ⁴for ⁶flesh ⁵one.

32 τὸ μυστήριον τοῦτο μέγα ἐστίν, ἐγὼ
    This mystery   great   is,   ²I

δὲ λέγω εἰς Χριστὸν καὶ [εἰς] τὴν
¹but say as to   Christ   and   as to   the

ἐκκλησίαν. 33 πλὴν καὶ ὑμεῖς οἱ
church.   Nevertheless also   ye   the

καθ᾽ ἕνα ἕκαστος τὴν ἑαυτοῦ γυναῖκα
one by one†   each   ¹the ²of himself ²wife

οὕτως ἀγαπάτω ὡς ἑαυτόν, ἡ δὲ
so   let him love   as   himself,   and the

CHAPTER 6

γυνὴ ἵνα φοβῆται τὸν ἄνδρα. 6 Τὰ
wife in order that she fears the(her) husband.   The

CHILDREN, obey your parents in the Lord, for this is right. ²"Honor your father and mother" (this is the first commandment with a promise), ³"that it may be well with you and that you may live long on the earth." ⁴Fathers, do not provoke your children to anger, but bring them up in the discipline and instruction of the Lord.

5 Slaves, be obedient to those who are your earthly masters, with fear and trembling, in singleness of heart, as to Christ; ⁶not in the way of eye-service, as men-pleasers, but as servants of Christ, doing the will of God from the heart, ⁷rendering service with a good will as to the Lord and not to men, ⁸knowing that whatever good

τέκνα, ὑπακούετε τοῖς γονεῦσιν ὑμῶν
children,   obey ye   the   parents   of you

ἐν κυρίῳ· τοῦτο γάρ ἐστιν δικαίον.
in [the] Lord;   for this   is   right.

2 τίμα τὸν πατέρα σου καὶ τὴν μητέρα,
Honour the   father   of thee and the   mother,

ἥτις ἐστὶν ἐντολὴ πρώτη ἐν ἐπαγγελίᾳ,
which   is   ²commandment ¹[the] ²first with a promise,

3 ἵνα εὖ σοι γένηται καὶ ἔσῃ μακρο-
in order well with thee it may be and thou may- long-
that   est be

χρόνιος ἐπὶ τῆς γῆς. 4 Καὶ οἱ πατέρες,
timed(lived) on   the   earth.   And   the   fathers,

μὴ παροργίζετε τὰ τέκνα ὑμῶν, ἀλλὰ
do not ye provoke to wrath the children of you,   but

ἐκτρέφετε αὐτὰ ἐν παιδείᾳ καὶ νουθεσίᾳ
nurture   them in [the] discipline and   admonition

κυρίου. 5 Οἱ δοῦλοι, ὑπακούετε τοῖς
of [the] Lord. The   slaves,   obey ye   ¹the(your)

κατὰ σάρκα κυρίοις μετὰ φόβου καὶ
²according to ⁴flesh ²lords   with   fear   and

τρόμου ἐν ἁπλότητι τῆς καρδίας ὑμῶν
trembling in   singleness of the   heart   of you

ὡς τῷ Χριστῷ, 6 μὴ κατ᾽ ὀφθαλμοδουλίαν
as   -   to Christ,   not by way of   eye-service

ὡς ἀνθρωπάρεσκοι, ἀλλ᾽ ὡς δοῦλοι Χριστοῦ
as   men-pleasers,   but   as   slaves   of Christ

ποιοῦντες τὸ θέλημα τοῦ θεοῦ ἐκ ψυχῆς,
doing   the   will   of God from [the] soul,

7 μετ᾽ εὐνοίας δουλεύοντες ὡς τῷ κυρίῳ
with   goodwill serving as slaves as   to the Lord

καὶ οὐκ ἀνθρώποις, 8 εἰδότες ὅτι ἕκαστος
and   not   to men,   knowing   that each man

any one does, he will receive the same again from the Lord, whether he is a slave or free. ⁹ Masters, do the same to them, and forbear threatening, knowing that he who is both their Master and yours is in heaven, and that there is no partiality with him. 10 Finally, be strong in the Lord and in the strength of his might. ¹¹ Put on the whole armor of God, that you may be able to stand against the wiles of the devil. ¹² For we are not contending against flesh and blood, but against the principalities, against the powers, against the world rulers of this present darkness, against the spiritual hosts of wickedness in the heavenly places. ¹³ Therefore take the whole armor of God, that you may be able to withstand in the evil day, and having done all, to stand. ¹⁴ Stand therefore, having girded your loins with truth, and having put on the breastplate of righteousness, ¹⁵ and having

ἐάν τι ποιήσῃ ἀγαθόν, τοῦτο κομίσεται
whatever ²he does ¹good thing, this he will get

παρὰ κυρίου, εἴτε δοῦλος εἴτε ἐλεύθερος.
from [the] Lord, whether a slave or a freeman.

9 Καὶ οἱ κύριοι, τὰ αὐτὰ ποιεῖτε πρὸς
And the lords, the same things do ye toward

αὐτούς, ἀνιέντες τὴν ἀπειλήν, εἰδότες ὅτι
them, forbearing the threatening, knowing that

καὶ αὐτῶν καὶ ὑμῶν ὁ κύριός ἐστιν
both of them and of you the Lord is

ἐν οὐρανοῖς, καὶ προσωπολημψία οὐκ
in heavens, and respect of persons not

ἔστιν παρ' αὐτῷ.
is with him.

10 Τοῦ λοιποῦ, ἐνδυναμοῦσθε ἐν κυρίῳ
For the rest,† be ye empowered in [the] Lord

καὶ ἐν τῷ κράτει τῆς ἰσχύος αὐτοῦ.
and in the might of the strength of him.

11 ἐνδύσασθε τὴν πανοπλίαν τοῦ θεοῦ
Put ye on the whole armour - of God

πρὸς τὸ δύνασθαι ὑμᾶς στῆναι πρὸς
for the to be able youᵇ to stand against
=so that ye are able . . .

τὰς μεθοδείας τοῦ διαβόλου· 12 ὅτι οὐκ
the craftinesses of the devil; because not

ἔστιν ἡμῖν ἡ πάλη πρὸς αἷμα καὶ σάρκα,
is to us the conflictᶜ against blood and flesh,
=our conflict is not

ἀλλὰ πρὸς τὰς ἀρχάς, πρὸς τὰς ἐξουσίας,
but against the rulers, against the authorities,

πρὸς τοὺς κοσμοκράτορας τοῦ σκότους
against the world rulers - darkness

τούτου, πρὸς τὰ πνευματικὰ τῆς πονηρίας
of this, against the spiritual [hosts] - of evil

ἐν τοῖς ἐπουρανίοις. 13 διὰ τοῦτο
in the heavenlies. Therefore

ἀναλάβετε τὴν πανοπλίαν τοῦ θεοῦ, ἵνα
take ye up the whole armour - of God, in order
that

δυνηθῆτε ἀντιστῆναι ἐν τῇ ἡμέρᾳ τῇ
ye may be able to resist in the day -

πονηρᾷ καὶ ἅπαντα κατεργασάμενοι στῆναι.
evil and all things having wrought to stand.

14 στῆτε οὖν περιζωσάμενοι τὴν ὀσφὺν
Stand ye therefore girding round the loin[s]

ὑμῶν ἐν ἀληθείᾳ, καὶ ἐνδυσάμενοι τὸν
of you with truth, and putting on the

θώρακα τῆς δικαιοσύνης, 15 καὶ ὑπο-
breastplate - of righteousness, and shoe-

shod your feet with the equipment of the gospel of peace; ¹⁶above all taking the shield of faith, with which you can quench all the flaming darts of the evil one. ¹⁷And take the helmet of salvation, and the sword of the Spirit, which is the word of God. ¹⁸Pray at all times in the Spirit, with all prayer and supplication. To that end keep alert with all perseverance, making supplication for all the saints, ¹⁹and also for me, that utterance may be given me in opening my mouth boldly to proclaim the mystery of the gospel, ²⁰for which I am an ambassador in chains; that I may declare it boldly, as I ought to speak.

21 Now that you also may know how I am and what I am doing, Tych'icus the beloved brother and faithful minister in the Lord will tell you everything. ²²I have sent him to you for

δησάμενοι τοὺς πόδας ἐν ἑτοιμασίᾳ τοῦ
ing the feet with readiness of the

εὐαγγελίου τῆς εἰρήνης, 16 ἐν πᾶσιν
gospel - of peace, in all

ἀναλαβόντες τὸν θυρεὸν τῆς πίστεως, ἐν
taking up the shield - of faith, by

ᾧ δυνήσεσθε πάντα τὰ βέλη τοῦ πονηροῦ
which ye will be able ²all ³the ⁴darts ⁶of the ⁷evil one

τὰ πεπυρωμένα σβέσαι· 17 καὶ τὴν
- ⁵having been equipped ¹to quench; and the
with fire

περικεφαλαίαν τοῦ σωτηρίου δέξασθε, καὶ
helmet - of salvation take ye, and

τὴν μάχαιραν τοῦ πνεύματος, ὅ ἐστιν
the sword of the Spirit, which* is

ῥῆμα θεοῦ, 18 διὰ πάσης προσευχῆς καὶ
[the] word of God, by means of all prayer and

δεήσεως, προσευχόμενοι ἐν παντὶ καιρῷ
petition, praying at every time

ἐν πνεύματι, καὶ εἰς αὐτὸ ἀγρυπνοῦντες
in spirit, and ²to ³it ¹watching

ἐν πάσῃ προσκαρτερήσει καὶ δεήσει περὶ
in all perseverance and petition concerning

πάντων τῶν ἁγίων, 19 καὶ ὑπὲρ ἐμοῦ,
all the saints, and on behalf of me,

ἵνα μοι δοθῇ λόγος ἐν ἀνοίξει τοῦ
in order to me may be given speech in opening of the
that

στόματός μου, ἐν παρρησίᾳ γνωρίσαι τὸ
mouth of me, in boldness to make known the

μυστήριον τοῦ εὐαγγελίου, 20 ὑπὲρ οὗ
mystery of the gospel, on behalf of which

πρεσβεύω ἐν ἁλύσει, ἵνα ἐν αὐτῷ παρ-
I am an in a chain, in order in it I may
ambassador that

ρησιάσωμαι ὡς δεῖ με λαλῆσαι.
speak boldly as it behoves me to speak.

21 Ἵνα δὲ εἰδῆτε καὶ ὑμεῖς τὰ κατ'
Now in order that ²may know ²also ¹ye the things about

ἐμέ, τί πράσσω, πάντα γνωρίσει ὑμῖν
me, what I am doing, all things ¹⁰will make ¹¹to you
known

Τύχικος ὁ ἀγαπητὸς ἀδελφὸς καὶ πιστὸς
¹Tychicus ²the ³beloved ⁴brother ⁵and ⁶faithful

διάκονος ἐν κυρίῳ, 22 ὃν ἔπεμψα πρὸς
⁷minister ⁸in ⁹[the] Lord, whom I sent to

* Neuter, agreeing with πνεῦμα, not feminine to agree with μάχαιρα.

this very purpose, that you may know how we are, and that he may encourage your hearts. 23 Peace be to the brethren, and love with faith, from God the Father and the Lord Jesus Christ. ²⁴Grace be with all who love our Lord Jesus Christ with love undying.

ὑμᾶς εἰς αὐτὸ τοῦτο, ἵνα γνῶτε τὰ
you for this very thing, in order ye may the
that know things

περὶ ἡμῶν καὶ παρακαλέσῃ τὰς καρδίας
concerning us and may comfort the hearts

ὑμῶν.
of you.

23 Εἰρήνη τοῖς ἀδελφοῖς καὶ ἀγάπη
Peace to the brothers and love

μετὰ πίστεως ἀπὸ θεοῦ πατρὸς καὶ
with faith from God [the] Father and

κυρίου Ἰησοῦ Χριστοῦ. 24 ἡ χάρις μετὰ
[the] Lord Jesus Christ. - Grace [be] with

πάντων τῶν ἀγαπώντων τὸν κύριον ἡμῶν
all the [ones] loving the Lord of us

Ἰησοῦν Χριστὸν ἐν ἀφθαρσίᾳ.
Jesus Christ in incorruptibility.

PHILIPPIANS 1

ΠΡΟΣ ΦΙΛΙΠΠΗΣΙΟΥΣ
To Philippians

CHAPTER 1

PAUL and Timothy, servants of Christ Jesus,
To all the saints in Christ Jesus who are at Philippi, with the bishopsᵃ and deacons:
2 Grace to you and peace from God our Father and the Lord Jesus Christ.
3 I thank my God in all my remembrance of you, ⁴always in every prayer of mine for you all making my prayer with joy, ⁵thankful for your partnership in the gospel

ᵃ Or overseers

1 Παῦλος καὶ Τιμόθεος δοῦλοι Χριστοῦ
Paul and Timothy slaves of Christ

Ἰησοῦ πᾶσιν τοῖς ἁγίοις ἐν Χριστῷ
Jesus to all the saints in Christ

Ἰησοῦ τοῖς οὖσιν ἐν Φιλίπποις σὺν
Jesus - being in Philippi with

ἐπισκόποις καὶ διακόνοις· 2 χάρις ὑμῖν
bishops and ministers: Grace to you

καὶ εἰρήνη ἀπὸ θεοῦ πατρὸς ἡμῶν καὶ
and peace from God Father of us and

κυρίου Ἰησοῦ Χριστοῦ.
[the] Lord Jesus Christ.

3 Εὐχαριστῶ τῷ θεῷ μου ἐπὶ πάσῃ
I thank the God of me at all

τῇ μνείᾳ ὑμῶν, 4 πάντοτε ἐν πάσῃ
the remembrance of you, always in every

δεήσει μου ὑπὲρ πάντων ὑμῶν μετὰ
petition of me on behalf of all you with

χαρᾶς τὴν δέησιν ποιούμενος, 5 ἐπὶ τῇ
joy the petition making, over the

κοινωνίᾳ ὑμῶν εἰς τὸ εὐαγγέλιον ἀπὸ
fellowship of you in the gospel from

from the first day until now. ⁶And I am sure that he who began a good work in you will bring it to completion at the day of Jesus Christ. ⁷It is right for me to feel thus about you all, because I hold you in my heart, for you are all partakers with me of grace, both in my imprisonment and in the defense and confirmation of the gospel. ⁸For God is my witness, how I yearn for you all with the affection of Christ Jesus. ⁹And it is my prayer that your love may abound more and more, with knowledge and all discernment, ¹⁰so that you may approve what is excellent, and may be pure and blameless for the day of Christ, ¹¹filled with the fruits of righteousness which come through Jesus Christ, to the glory and praise of God.

12 I want you to know, brethren, that what has happened to me has really served to

τῆς πρώτης ἡμέρας ἄχρι τοῦ νῦν,
the first day until the now,

6 πεποιθὼς αὐτὸ τοῦτο, ὅτι ὁ ἐναρξάμενος
being confident this very thing, that the having begun
[of] [one]

ἐν ὑμῖν ἔργον ἀγαθὸν ἐπιτελέσει ἄχρι
in you work a good will complete [it] until

ἡμέρας Χριστοῦ Ἰησοῦ· 7 καθώς ἐστιν
[the] day of Christ Jesus; as it is

δίκαιον ἐμοὶ τοῦτο φρονεῖν ὑπὲρ πάντων,
right for me this to think on behalf of all

ὑμῶν, διὰ τὸ ἔχειν με ἐν τῇ καρδίᾳ
you, because of the to have meᵇ in the heart,
= because I have you in the(my) heart,

ὑμᾶς, ἔν τε τοῖς δεσμοῖς μου καὶ ἐν
you, both in the bonds of me and in

τῇ ἀπολογίᾳ καὶ βεβαιώσει τοῦ εὐαγγελίου
the defence and confirmation of the gospel

συγκοινωνούς μου τῆς χάριτος πάντας
⁴partakers ⁷of me ⁵of the ⁶grace ²all

ὑμᾶς ὄντας. 8 μάρτυς γάρ μου ὁ θεός,
¹you ³being. ⁴witness ¹For ⁵of me - ²God
³[is],

ὡς ἐπιποθῶ πάντας ὑμᾶς ἐν σπλάγχνοις
how I long after all you in [the] bowels

Χριστοῦ Ἰησοῦ. 9 Καὶ τοῦτο προσεύχομαι,
of Christ Jesus. And this I pray,

ἵνα ἡ ἀγάπη ὑμῶν ἔτι μᾶλλον καὶ
in order the love of you yet more and
that

μᾶλλον περισσεύῃ ἐν ἐπιγνώσει καὶ πάσῃ
more may abound in full knowledge and all

αἰσθήσει, 10 εἰς τὸ δοκιμάζειν ὑμᾶς τὰ
perception, for the to prove youᵇ the
= that ye may prove things

διαφέροντα, ἵνα ἦτε εἰλικρινεῖς καὶ
differing, in order ye may sincere and
that be

ἀπρόσκοποι εἰς ἡμέραν Χριστοῦ, 11 πεπληρω-
unoffending in [the] day of Christ, having been

μένοι καρπὸν δικαιοσύνης τὸν διὰ Ἰησοῦ
filled [with] [the] fruit of righteousness - through Jesus

Χριστοῦ, εἰς δόξαν καὶ ἔπαινον θεοῦ.
Christ, to [the] glory and praise of God.

12 Γινώσκειν δὲ ὑμᾶς βούλομαι, ἀδελφοί,
Now ²to know ³you ¹I wish, brothers,

ὅτι τὰ κατ᾽ ἐμὲ μᾶλλον εἰς προκοπὴν
that the about me* ²rather ³to ⁴[the] advance
things
= my affairs

• Cf. ver. 27; ch. 2. 19, 20, 23; Eph. 6. 21, 22; Col. 4. 7, 8.

advance the gospel, [13] so that it has become known throughout the whole praetorian guard and to all the rest that my imprisonment is for Christ; [14] and most of the brethren have been made confident in the Lord because of my imprisonment, and are much more bold to speak the word of God without fear.

15 Some indeed preach Christ from envy and rivalry, but others from good will. [16] The latter do it out of love, knowing that I am put here for the defense of the gospel; [17] the former proclaim Christ out of partisanship, not sincerely but thinking to afflict me in my imprisonment. [18] What then? Only that in every way, whether in pretense or in truth, Christ is proclaimed; and in that I rejoice.

19 Yes, and I shall rejoice. For I know that through your prayers and the help of the Spirit of Jesus Christ this will turn out for my deliverance, [20] as it is my eager expectation and hope that I shall not be at all ashamed, but that with full courage now as always Christ will be

τοῦ   εὐαγγελίου   ἐλήλυθεν,   13 ὥστε   τοὺς
[5]of the   [6]gospel   [1]has(ve) come,   so as   the
δεσμούς   μου   φανερούς   ἐν   Χριστῷ   γενέσθαι
bonds   of me   [2]manifest   [3]in   [4]Christ   [1]to become
ἐν   ὅλῳ   τῷ   πραιτωρίῳ   καὶ   τοῖς   λοιποῖς
in   all   the   praetorium   and   to [2]the   [3]rest
πᾶσιν,   14 καὶ   τοὺς   πλείονας   τῶν   ἀδελφῶν
[1]all,   and   the   majority   of the   brothers
ἐν   κυρίῳ   πεποιθότας   τοῖς   δεσμοῖς   μου
in   [the] Lord   being confident   in the   bonds   of me
περισσοτέρως   τολμᾶν   ἀφόβως   τὸν   λόγον
[2]more exceedingly   [1]to dare   [3]fearlessly   [5]the   [6]word
τοῦ   θεοῦ   λαλεῖν.   15 τινὲς   μὲν   καὶ   διὰ
-      [7]of God   [4]to speak.   Some   indeed   even   because of
φθόνον   καὶ   ἔριν,   τινὲς   δὲ   καὶ   δι'   εὐδοκίαν
envy   and   strife,   but some   also   because   of   good-will
τὸν   Χριστὸν   κηρύσσουσιν·   16 οἱ   μὲν   ἐξ
-      Christ   proclaim;   these†   from
ἀγάπης,   εἰδότες   ὅτι   εἰς   ἀπολογίαν   τοῦ
love,   knowing   that   for   defence   of the
εὐαγγελίου   κεῖμαι,   17 οἱ   δὲ   ἐξ   ἐριθείας
gospel   I am set,   those†   from   rivalry
τὸν   Χριστὸν   καταγγέλλουσιν,   οὐχ   ἁγνῶς,
-      [2]Christ   [1]announce,   not   purely,
οἰόμενοι   θλῖψιν   ἐγείρειν   τοῖς   δεσμοῖς   μου.
thinking   [2]affliction   [1]to raise   to the   bonds   of me.
18 Τί   γάρ;   πλὴν   ὅτι   παντὶ   τρόπῳ,
What   then?   nevertheless   that   in every   way,
εἴτε   προφάσει   εἴτε   ἀληθείᾳ,   Χριστὸς
whether   in pretence   or   in truth,   Christ
καταγγέλλεται,   καὶ   ἐν   τούτῳ   χαίρω·   ἀλλὰ
is announced,   and   in   this   I rejoice;   yet
καὶ   χαρήσομαι·   19 οἶδα   γὰρ   ὅτι   τοῦτό
also   I will rejoice;   for I know   that   this
μοι   ἀποβήσεται   εἰς   σωτηρίαν   διὰ   τῆς
to me   will result   in   salvation   through   the
ὑμῶν   δεήσεως   καὶ   ἐπιχορηγίας   τοῦ
[2]of you   [1]petition   and   supply   of the
πνεύματος   Ἰησοῦ   Χριστοῦ,   20 κατὰ   τὴν
spirit   of Jesus   Christ,   according to   the
ἀποκαραδοκίαν   καὶ   ἐλπίδα   μου   ὅτι   ἐν
eager expectation   and   hope   of me   that   in
οὐδενὶ   αἰσχυνθήσομαι,   ἀλλ'   ἐν   πάσῃ   παρ-
nothing   I shall be shamed,   but   with   all   bold-
ρησίᾳ   ὡς   πάντοτε   καὶ   νῦν   μεγαλυνθήσεται
ness   as   always   also   now   shall be magnified

honored in my body, whether by life or by death. ²¹For to me to live is Christ, and to die is gain. ²²If it is to be life in the flesh, that means fruitful labor for me. Yet which I shall choose I cannot tell. ²³I am hard pressed between the two. My desire is to depart and be with Christ, for that is far better. ²⁴But to remain in the flesh is more necessary on your account. ²⁵Convinced of this, I know that I shall remain and continue with you all, for your progress and joy in the faith, ²⁶so that in me you may have ample cause to glory in Christ Jesus, because of my coming to you again.

27 Only let your manner of life be worthy of the gospel of Christ, so that whether I come and see you or am absent, I may hear of you that you stand firm in one spirit, with one mind striving side by side for the faith of the gospel, ²⁸and not frightened in

Χριστὸς	ἐν	τῷ	σώματί	μου,	εἴτε	διὰ
Christ	in	the	body	of me,	whether	through

ζωῆς	εἴτε	διὰ	θανάτου.	21 ἐμοὶ	γὰρ
life	or	through	death.	For to me	

τὸ	ζῆν	Χριστὸς	καὶ	τὸ	ἀποθανεῖν	κέρδος.
–	to live	[is] Christ	and	–	to die	[is] gain.

22 εἰ	δὲ	τὸ	ζῆν	ἐν	σαρκί,	τοῦτό	μοι
But if	–	to live	in	[the] flesh,	this	to me	

καρπὸς	ἔργου,	καὶ	τί	αἱρήσομαι	οὐ
[is] fruit	of [?my] work,	and	what	I shall choose	not

γνωρίζω.	23 συνέχομαι	δὲ	ἐκ	τῶν	δύο,
I perceive.	But I am constrained	by	the	two,	

τὴν	ἐπιθυμίαν	ἔχων	εἰς	τὸ	ἀναλῦσαι	καὶ
³the	²desire	¹having	for	the	to depart	and

σὺν	Χριστῷ	εἶναι,	πολλῷ	γὰρ	μᾶλλον
⁴with	⁵Christ	¹to be,	for by much	[this is] rather	

κρεῖσσον·	24 τὸ	δὲ	ἐπιμένειν	τῇ	σαρκὶ
better;	–	but	to remain	in the	flesh [is]

ἀναγκαιότερον	δι'	ὑμᾶς.	25 καὶ	τοῦτο
more necessary	on account of you.		And	this

πεποιθὼς	οἶδα,	ὅτι	μενῶ	καὶ	παραμενῶ
being confident	I know,	that	I shall remain	and	continue

πᾶσιν	ὑμῖν	εἰς	τὴν	ὑμῶν	προκοπὴν	καὶ
with all	you	for	the	⁶of you	¹advance	²and

χαρὰν	τῆς	πίστεως,	26 ἵνα	τὸ	καύχημα
³joy	⁴of the	⁵faith,	in order that	the	boast

ὑμῶν	περισσεύῃ	ἐν	Χριστῷ	Ἰησοῦ	ἐν
of you	may abound	in	Christ	Jesus	in

ἐμοὶ	διὰ	τῆς	ἐμῆς	παρουσίας	πάλιν
me	through	–	my	presence	again

πρὸς	ὑμᾶς.
with	you.

27 Μόνον	ἀξίως	τοῦ	εὐαγγελίου	τοῦ
Only	²worthily	³of the	⁴gospel	–

Χριστοῦ	πολιτεύεσθε,	ἵνα	εἴτε	ἐλθὼν	καὶ
⁵of Christ	¹conduct yourselves,	in order that	whether	coming	and

ἰδὼν	ὑμᾶς	εἴτε	ἀπὼν	ἀκούω	τὰ	περὶ
seeing	you	or	being absent	I hear	the	con-things cerning

ὑμῶν,	ὅτι	στήκετε	ἐν	ἑνὶ	πνεύματι,
you,	that	ye stand	in	one	spirit,

μιᾷ	ψυχῇ	συναθλοῦντες	τῇ	πίστει	τοῦ
with one soul		striving together	in the	faith	of the

εὐαγγελίου,	28 καὶ	μὴ	πτυρόμενοι	ἐν
gospel,	and	not	being terrified	in

anything by your opponents. This is a clear omen to them of their destruction, but of your salvation, and that from God. [29] For it has been granted to you that for the sake of Christ you should not only believe in him but also suffer for his sake, [30] engaged in the same conflict which you saw and now hear to be mine.

CHAPTER 2

SO if there is any encouragement in Christ, any incentive of love, any participation in the Spirit, any affection and sympathy, [2] complete my joy by being of the same mind, having the same love, being in full accord and of one mind. [3] Do nothing from selfishness or conceit, but in humility count others better than yourselves. [4] Let each of you look not only to his own interests, but also to the interests of others. [5] Have this mind among yourselves, which you have in Christ Jesus, [6] who, though he was in the form of God, did not count equality with God a thing to be grasped, [7] but emptied himself,

μηδενὶ ὑπὸ τῶν ἀντικειμένων, ἥτις ἐστὶν
no(any) by the [ones] opposing, which is
thing

αὐτοῖς ἔνδειξις ἀπωλείας, ὑμῶν δὲ
to them a proof of destruction, but of you

σωτηρίας, καὶ τοῦτο ἀπὸ θεοῦ· 29 ὅτι
of salvation, and this from God; because

ὑμῖν ἐχαρίσθη τὸ ὑπὲρ Χριστοῦ, οὐ
to you it was given – on behalf of Christ, not

μόνον τὸ εἰς αὐτὸν πιστεύειν ἀλλὰ καὶ
only – in him to believe but also

τὸ ὑπὲρ αὐτοῦ πάσχειν, 30 τὸν αὐτὸν
– on behalf of him to suffer, the same

ἀγῶνα ἔχοντες οἷον εἴδετε ἐν ἐμοὶ
struggle having which ye saw in me

καὶ νῦν ἀκούετε ἐν ἐμοί. 2 Εἴ τις
and now hear in me. [1]If [there [2]any
is]

οὖν παράκλησις ἐν Χριστῷ, εἴ τι
[1]therefore comfort in Christ, if any

παραμύθιον ἀγάπης, εἴ τις κοινωνία
consolation of love, if any fellowship

πνεύματος, εἴ τις σπλάγχνα καὶ οἰκτιρμοί,
of spirit, if any compassions and pities,

2 πληρώσατέ μου τὴν χαρὰν ἵνα τὸ
fulfil ye of me the joy in order that the

αὐτὸ φρονῆτε, τὴν αὐτὴν ἀγάπην ἔχοντες,
same thing ye think, the same love having,

σύμψυχοι, τὸ ἓν φρονοῦντες, 3 μηδὲν κατ᾽
one in soul, the one thinking, [doing] by
thing nothing way of

ἐριθείαν μηδὲ κατὰ κενοδοξίαν, ἀλλὰ τῇ
rivalry nor by way of vainglory, but –

ταπεινοφροσύνῃ ἀλλήλους ἡγούμενοι ὑπερ-
in humility [2]one another [1]deeming sur-

έχοντας ἑαυτῶν, 4 μὴ τὰ ἑαυτῶν ἕκαστοι
passing themselves, not [3]the [4]of them- [1]each ones
things selves

σκοποῦντες, ἀλλὰ καὶ τὰ ἑτέρων ἕκαστοι.
[2]looking at, but [2]also [3]the [4]of [1]each ones.
things others

5 τοῦτο φρονεῖτε ἐν ὑμῖν ὃ καὶ ἐν
This think ye among you which also [was] in

Χριστῷ Ἰησοῦ, 6 ὃς ἐν μορφῇ θεοῦ
Christ Jesus, who in [the] form of God

ὑπάρχων οὐχ ἁρπαγμὸν ἡγήσατο τὸ εἶναι
subsisting [2]not [3]robbery [1]deemed [it] the to be

ἴσα θεῷ, 7 ἀλλὰ ἑαυτὸν ἐκένωσεν μορφὴν
equal with God, but himself emptied [2][the] form
things

taking the form of a servant, being born in the likeness of men. ⁸And being found in human form he humbled himself and became obedient unto death, even death on a cross. ⁹Therefore God has highly exalted him and bestowed on him the name which is above every name, ¹⁰that at the name of Jesus every knee should bow, in heaven and on earth and under the earth, ¹¹and every tongue confess that Jesus Christ is Lord, to the glory of God the Father.

12 Therefore, my beloved, as you have always obeyed, so now, not only as in my presence but much more in my absence, work out your own salvation with fear and trembling; ¹³for God is at work in you, both to will and to work for his good pleasure.

14 Do all things without grumbling or questioning, ¹⁵that you may be blameless and innocent, children of God without blemish in the midst of a crooked and perverse generation, among whom you shine as lights in the world,

δούλου λαβών, ἐν ὁμοιώματι ἀνθρώπων
²of a slave ¹taking, ²in ³likeness ⁴of men
γενόμενος· καὶ σχήματι εὑρεθεὶς ὡς
¹becoming; and ²in fashion ¹being found as
ἄνθρωπος 8 ἐταπείνωσεν ἑαυτὸν γενόμενος
a man   he humbled himself becoming
ὑπήκοος μέχρι θανάτου, θανάτου δὲ σταυροῦ.
obedient until death, and death of a cross.
9 διὸ καὶ ὁ θεὸς αὐτὸν ὑπερύψωσεν
Wherefore also – God ²him ¹highly exalted
καὶ ἐχαρίσατο αὐτῷ τὸ ὄνομα τὸ ὑπὲρ
and gave to him the name – above
πᾶν ὄνομα, 10 ἵνα ἐν τῷ ὀνόματι Ἰησοῦ
every name, in order in the name of Jesus
          that
πᾶν γόνυ κάμψῃ ἐπουρανίων καὶ ἐπιγείων
every knee should of heavenly and earthly
          bend [beings] [beings]
καὶ καταχθονίων, 11 καὶ πᾶσα γλῶσσα
and [beings] under the earth, and every tongue
ἐξομολογήσηται ὅτι κυρίος Ἰησοῦς
should acknowledge that ²Lord ¹Jesus
Χριστὸς εἰς δόξαν θεοῦ πατρός.
²Christ [is] to [the] glory of God [the] Father.
12 Ὥστε, ἀγαπητοί μου, καθὼς πάντοτε
So as, beloved of me, as always
ὑπηκούσατε, μὴ ὡς ἐν τῇ παρουσίᾳ
ye obeyed, not as in the presence
μου μόνον ἀλλὰ νῦν πολλῷ μᾶλλον ἐν
of me only but now by more rather in
τῇ ἀπουσίᾳ μου, μετὰ φόβου καὶ τρόμου
the absence of me, with fear and trembling
τὴν ἑαυτῶν σωτηρίαν κατεργάζεσθε· 13 θεὸς
¹the ²of yourselves ²salvation work out; ²God
γάρ ἐστιν ὁ ἐνεργῶν ἐν ὑμῖν καὶ τὸ
¹for is the [one] operating in you both the
θέλειν καὶ τὸ ἐνεργεῖν ὑπὲρ τῆς εὐδοκίας.
to will and the to operate on behalf of the(his) goodwill.
14 πάντα ποιεῖτε χωρὶς γογγυσμῶν καὶ
All things do ye without murmurings and
διαλογισμῶν, 15 ἵνα γένησθε ἄμεμπτοι καὶ
disputings, in order that ye may be blameless and
ἀκέραιοι, τέκνα θεοῦ ἄμωμα μέσον
harmless, children of God faultless in the
                                        midst of
γενεᾶς σκολιᾶς καὶ διεστραμμένης, ἐν
a generation crooked and having been perverted, among
οἷς φαίνεσθε ὡς φωστῆρες ἐν κόσμῳ,
whom ye shine as luminaries in [the] world,

16 holding fast the word of life, so that in the day of Christ I may be proud that I did not run in vain or labor in vain. 17 Even if I am to be poured as a libation upon the sacrificial offering of your faith, I am glad and rejoice with you all. 18 Likewise you also should be glad and rejoice with me.

19 I hope in the Lord Jesus to send Timothy to you soon, so that I may be cheered by news of you. 20 I have no one like him, who will be genuinely anxious for your welfare. 21 They all look after their own interests, not those of Jesus Christ. 22 But Timothy's worth you know, how as a son with a father he has served with me in the gospel. 23 I hope therefore to send him just as soon as I see how it will go with me; 24 and I trust in the Lord that shortly I myself shall come also.

25 I have thought it necessary to send to you Epaphrodi'tus my brother and fellow worker and fellow soldier, and your messenger and minister to

16 λόγον ζωῆς ἐπέχοντες, εἰς καύχημα
a word of life holding up, for a boast
ἐμοὶ εἰς ἡμέραν Χριστοῦ, ὅτι οὐκ εἰς
to me⁰ in [the] day of Christ, that not in
κενὸν ἔδραμον οὐδὲ εἰς κενὸν ἐκοπίασα.
vain I ran nor in vain laboured.

17 Ἀλλὰ εἰ καὶ σπένδομαι ἐπὶ τῇ θυσίᾳ
But if indeed I am poured out on the sacrifice
καὶ λειτουργίᾳ τῆς πίστεως ὑμῶν, χαίρω
and service of the faith of you, I rejoice
καὶ συγχαίρω πᾶσιν ὑμῖν· 18 τὸ δὲ αὐτὸ
and rejoice with ²all ¹you; and the same
καὶ ὑμεῖς χαίρετε καὶ συγχαίρετέ μοι.
also ye rejoice and rejoice with me.

19 Ἐλπίζω δὲ ἐν κυρίῳ Ἰησοῦ Τιμόθεον
But I hope in [the] Lord Jesus ²Timothy
ταχέως πέμψαι ὑμῖν, ἵνα κἀγὼ εὐψυχῶ
⁴shortly ¹to send ²to you, in order I also may be of
that good cheer
γνοὺς τὰ περὶ ὑμῶν. 20 οὐδένα γὰρ
knowing the con- you. For no one
things cerning
ἔχω ἰσόψυχον, ὅστις γνησίως τὰ περὶ
I have likeminded, who genuinely ²the ³con-
things cerning
ὑμῶν μεριμνήσει· 21 οἱ πάντες γὰρ τὰ
⁴you ¹will care for; the for all ²the
things
ἑαυτῶν ζητοῦσιν, οὐ τὰ Χριστοῦ Ἰησοῦ.
³of them- ¹seek, not the of Christ Jesus.
selves things
22 τὴν δὲ δοκιμὴν αὐτοῦ γινώσκετε, ὅτι
But the character of him ye know, that
ὡς πατρὶ τέκνον σὺν ἐμοὶ ἐδούλευσεν
as ²a father ¹a child²[serves] ⁴with ⁵me ⁴he served
εἰς τὸ εὐαγγέλιον. 23 τοῦτον μὲν οὖν
in the gospel. This one – therefore
ἐλπίζω πέμψαι ὡς ἂν ἀφίδω τὰ περὶ
I hope to send ²whenever ³I see ⁴the ⁵con-
things cerning
ἐμὲ ἐξαυτῆς· 24 πέποιθα δὲ ἐν κυρίῳ
⁶me ¹immediately; but I trust in [the] Lord
ὅτι καὶ αὐτὸς ταχέως ἐλεύσομαι. 25 Ἀναγ-
that ²also ³[my]self ⁴shortly ¹I will come. ²neces-
καῖον δὲ ἡγησάμην Ἐπαφρόδιτον τὸν
sary But ¹I deemed [it] ⁶Epaphroditus ³the
ἀδελφὸν καὶ συνεργὸν καὶ συστρατιώτην
⁸brother ⁹and ¹⁰fellow-worker ¹¹and ¹²fellow-soldier
μου, ὑμῶν δὲ ἀπόστολον καὶ λειτουργὸν
¹³of me, ¹⁴and ¹⁵of you ¹⁵apostle ¹⁷and ¹⁸minister

my need, ²⁶for he has been longing for you all, and has been distressed because you heard that he was ill. ²⁷Indeed he was ill, near to death. But God had mercy on him, and not only on him but on me also, lest I should have sorrow upon sorrow. ²⁸I am the more eager to send him, therefore, that you may rejoice at seeing him again, and that I may be less anxious. ²⁹So receive him in the Lord with all joy; and honor such men, ³⁰for he nearly died for the work of Christ, risking his life to complete your service to me.

τῆς χρείας μου, πέμψαι πρὸς ὑμᾶς,
¹⁹of the ²⁰need ²¹of me, ²to send ⁴to ⁵you,

26 ἐπειδὴ ἐπιποθῶν ἦν πάντας ὑμᾶς, καὶ
since ²longing after ¹he was ⁴all ³you, and

ἀδημονῶν, διότι ἠκούσατε ὅτι ἠσθένησεν.
[was] being because ye heard that he ailed.
troubled,

27 καὶ γὰρ ἠσθένησεν παραπλήσιον θανάτῳ·
For indeed he ailed coming near to death;

ἀλλὰ ὁ θεὸς ἠλέησεν αὐτόν, οὐκ αὐτὸν
but - God had mercy on him, ²not ³him

δὲ μόνον ἀλλὰ καὶ ἐμέ, ἵνα μὴ λύπην
¹and only but also me, lest grief

ἐπὶ λύπην σχῶ. 28 σπουδαιοτέρως οὖν
on grief I should have. More eagerly therefore

ἔπεμψα αὐτόν, ἵνα ἰδόντες αὐτὸν πάλιν
I sent him, in order that seeing him again

χαρῆτε κἀγὼ ἀλυπότερος ὦ. 29 προσδέχεσθε
ye may and ¹I ²less grieved ²may be. Receive ye
rejoice

οὖν αὐτὸν ἐν κυρίῳ μετὰ πάσης χαρᾶς,
therefore him in [the] Lord with all joy,

καὶ τοὺς τοιούτους ἐντίμους ἔχετε, 30 ὅτι
and - ²such ones ³honoured ¹hold ye, because

διὰ τὸ ἔργον Χριστοῦ μέχρι θανάτου
on ac- the work of Christ ²as far as ³death
count of

ἤγγισεν παραβολευσάμενος τῇ ψυχῇ, ἵνα
¹he drew exposing the(his) life, in or-
near der that

ἀναπληρώσῃ τὸ ὑμῶν ὑστέρημα τῆς πρός
he might fill up ¹the ²of you ³lack - ⁴toward

με λειτουργίας.
⁴me ⁵of service.

CHAPTER 3

FINALLY, my brethren, rejoice in the Lord. To write the same things to you is not irksome to me, and is safe for you.

2 Look out for the dogs, look out for the evil-workers, look out for those who mutilate

3 Τὸ λοιπόν, ἀδελφοί μου, χαίρετε ἐν
For the rest, brothers of me, rejoice ye in

κυρίῳ. τὰ αὐτὰ γράφειν ὑμῖν ἐμοὶ μὲν
[the] Lord. The ²same things ¹to write to you for me indeed

οὐκ ὀκνηρόν, ὑμῖν δὲ ἀσφαλές.
[is] not irksome, but for you safe.

2 Βλέπετε τοὺς κύνας, βλέπετε τοὺς
Look [to] the dogs, look [to] the

κακοὺς ἐργάτας, βλέπετε τὴν κατατομήν.*
evil workmen, look [to] the concision.*

* The apostle uses a " studiously contemptuous paronomasia " (Ellicott). He does not use περιτομή, the proper word for " circumcision ", " as this, though now abrogated in Christ, had still its spiritual aspects."

the flesh. [3] For we are the true circumcision, who worship God in spirit,[b] and glory in Christ Jesus, and put no confidence in the flesh. [4] Though I myself have reason for confidence in the flesh also. If any other man thinks he has reason for confidence in the flesh, I have more: [5] circumcised on the eighth day, of the people of Israel, of the tribe of Benjamin, a Hebrew born of Hebrews; as to the law a Pharisee, [6] as to zeal a persecutor of the church, as to righteousness under the law blameless. [7] But whatever gain I had, I counted as loss for the sake of Christ. [8] Indeed I count everything as loss because of the surpassing worth of knowing Christ Jesus my Lord. For his sake I have suffered the loss of all things, and count them as refuse, in order that I may gain Christ [9] and be found in him, not having a righteousness of my own, based on law, but that which is through faith in Christ, the righteousness from God that depends

3 ἡμεῖς γάρ ἐσμεν ἡ περιτομή, οἱ
For we are the circumcision, the [ones]

πνεύματι θεοῦ λατρεύοντες καὶ καυχώμενοι
[3]by [the] Spirit [3]of God [1]worshipping and boasting

ἐν Χριστῷ Ἰησοῦ καὶ οὐκ ἐν σαρκὶ
in Christ Jesus and [2]not [3]in [the] [4]flesh

πεποιθότες, 4 καίπερ ἐγὼ ἔχων πεποίθησιν
[1]trusting, even though I having trust

καὶ ἐν σαρκί. Εἴ τις δοκεῖ ἄλλος
also in [the] flesh. If any [2]thinks [1]other man

πεποιθέναι ἐν σαρκί, ἐγὼ μᾶλλον·
to trust in [the] flesh, I more:

5 περιτομῇ ὀκταήμερος, ἐκ γένους Ἰσραήλ,
in circumcision eighth day, of [the] race of Israel,

φυλῆς Βενιαμίν, Ἑβραῖος ἐξ Ἑβραίων,
[the] tribe of Benjamin, a Hebrew of Hebrew [parents],

κατὰ νόμον Φαρισαῖος, 6 κατὰ ζῆλος
according [the] law a Pharisee, by way of zeal
to

διώκων τὴν ἐκκλησίαν, κατὰ δικαιοσύνην
persecuting the church, according [the]
to righteousness

τὴν ἐν νόμῳ γενόμενος ἄμεμπτος. 7 ἀλλὰ
– in [the] law being blameless. But

ἅτινα ἦν μοι κέρδη, ταῦτα ἥγημαι διὰ
what were to me gain, these I have [2]on ac-
things deemed count of

τὸν Χριστὸν ζημίαν. 8 ἀλλὰ μενοῦν γε
– [3]Christ [1]loss. But nay rather

καὶ ἡγοῦμαι πάντα ζημίαν εἶναι διὰ
[2]also [1]I deem [3]all things [5]loss [4]to be on account of

τὸ ὑπερέχον τῆς γνώσεως Χριστοῦ Ἰησοῦ
the excellency of the knowledge of Christ Jesus

τοῦ κυρίου μου, δι᾽ ὃν τὰ πάντα
the Lord of me, on ac- whom – all things
count of

ἐζημιώθην, καὶ ἡγοῦμαι σκύβαλα ἵνα
I suffered loss, and deem [them] refuse in order
that

Χριστὸν κερδήσω 9 καὶ εὑρεθῶ ἐν αὐτῷ,
Christ I might gain and be found in him,

μὴ ἔχων ἐμὴν δικαιοσύνην τὴν ἐκ νόμου,
not having my righteousness the [one] of law,

ἀλλὰ τὴν διὰ πίστεως Χριστοῦ, τὴν
but the [one] through faith of(in) Christ,* [1]the

ἐκ θεοῦ δικαιοσύνην ἐπὶ τῇ πίστει,
[3]of [4]God [2]righteousness [based] on – faith,

[b] Other ancient authorities read *worship by the Spirit of God*

* See Gal. 2. 20.

on faith; ¹⁰that I may know him and the power of his resurrection, and may share his sufferings, becoming like him in his death, ¹¹that if possible I may attain the resurrection from the dead.

12 Not that I have already obtained this or am already perfect; but I press on to make it my own, because Christ Jesus has made me his own. ¹³Brethren, I do not consider that I have made it my own; but one thing I do, forgetting what lies behind and straining forward to what lies ahead, ¹⁴I press on toward the goal for the prize of the upward call of God in Christ Jesus. ¹⁵Let those of us who are mature be thus minded; and if in anything you are otherwise minded, God will reveal that also to you. ¹⁶Only let us hold true to what we have attained.

17 Brethren, join in imitating me, and mark those who so live as you have an example in us. ¹⁸For many, of whom I have often told you and now tell you even with tears, live as enemies of the cross of Christ.

10 τοῦ γνῶναι αὐτὸν καὶ τὴν δύναμιν
— to know[d] him and the power

τῆς ἀναστάσεως αὐτοῦ καὶ κοινωνίαν
of the resurrection of him and [the] fellowship

παθημάτων αὐτοῦ, συμμορφιζόμενος τῷ
of sufferings of him, being conformed to the

θανάτῳ αὐτοῦ, 11 εἴ πως καταντήσω εἰς
death of him, if [some]how I may attain to to

τὴν ἐξανάστασιν τὴν ἐκ νεκρῶν. 12 Οὐχ
the out-resurrection — from [the] dead. Not

ὅτι ἤδη ἔλαβον ἢ ἤδη τετελείωμαι,
that already I received or already have been perfected,

διώκω δὲ εἰ καὶ καταλάβω, ἐφ' ᾧ
but I follow if indeed I may lay hold, inasmuch as

καὶ κατελήμφθην ὑπὸ Χριστοῦ Ἰησοῦ.
also I was laid hold of by Christ Jesus.

13 ἀδελφοί, ἐγὼ ἐμαυτὸν οὔπω λογίζομαι
Brothers, ²I ⁴myself ¹not yet ³reckon

κατειληφέναι· ἓν δέ, τὰ μὲν ὀπίσω
to have but one thing ³the ²on one ⁴behind
laid hold; [I do], things hand

ἐπιλανθανόμενος τοῖς δὲ ἔμπροσθεν ἐπεκ-
¹forgetting ³the ¹on the ⁴before ²stretching
things other

τεινόμενος, 14 κατὰ σκοπὸν διώκω εἰς
forward to, according to a mark I follow for

τὸ βραβεῖον τῆς ἄνω κλήσεως τοῦ θεοῦ
the prize of the above calling — of God

ἐν Χριστῷ Ἰησοῦ. 15 Ὅσοι οὖν τέλειοι,
in Christ Jesus. ²As many ¹there- [are]
as fore perfect,

τοῦτο φρονῶμεν· καὶ εἴ τι ἑτέρως
²this ¹let us think; and if anything otherwise

φρονεῖτε, καὶ τοῦτο ὁ θεὸς ὑμῖν ἀποκα-
ye think, even this — God to you will

λύψει· 16 πλὴν εἰς ὃ ἐφθάσαμεν, τῷ
reveal; nevertheless to what we arrived, by the

αὐτῷ στοιχεῖν. 17 Συμμιμηταί μου
same to walk. Fellow-imitators of me

γίνεσθε, ἀδελφοί, καὶ σκοπεῖτε τοὺς οὕτω
be ye, brothers, and mark the [ones] thus

περιπατοῦντας καθὼς ἔχετε τύπον ἡμᾶς.
walking as ye have ²an example ¹us.

18 πολλοὶ γὰρ περιπατοῦσιν οὓς πολλάκις
For many walk [of] whom often

ἔλεγον ὑμῖν, νῦν δὲ καὶ κλαίων λέγω,
I said to you, and now also weeping I say,

τοὺς ἐχθροὺς τοῦ σταυροῦ τοῦ Χριστοῦ,
the enemies of the cross — of Christ,

¹⁹Their end is destruction, their god is the belly, and they glory in their shame, with minds set on earthly things. ²⁰But our commonwealth is in heaven, and from it we await a Savior, the Lord Jesus Christ, ²¹who will change our lowly body to be like his glorious body, by the power which enables him even to subject all things to himself.

19 ὧν τὸ τέλος ἀπώλεια, ὧν ὁ θεὸς
of whom the end [is] destruction, of whom the god [is]

ἡ κοιλία καὶ ἡ δόξα ἐν τῇ αἰσχύνῃ
the belly and the glory in the shame

αὐτῶν, οἱ τὰ ἐπίγεια φρονοῦντες. 20 ἡμῶν
of them, the the earthly things thinking. of us
[ones]

γὰρ τὸ πολίτευμα ἐν οὐρανοῖς ὑπάρχει,
For the citizenship in heavens is,

ἐξ οὗ καὶ σωτῆρα ἀπεκδεχόμεθα κύριον
from where also ²a Saviour ¹we await Lord

Ἰησοῦν Χριστόν, 21 ὃς μετασχηματίσει τὸ
Jesus Christ, who will change the

σῶμα τῆς ταπεινώσεως ἡμῶν σύμμορφον
body of the humiliation of us [making it]
conformed

τῷ σώματι τῆς δόξης αὐτοῦ, κατὰ τὴν
to the body of the glory of him, according to the

ἐνέργειαν τοῦ δύνασθαι αὐτὸν καὶ ὑποτάξαι
operation of the to be able himᵇ even to subject
=of his ability

αὐτῷ τὰ πάντα. 4 Ὥστε, ἀδελφοί μου
to him[self] – all things. So as, brothers of me

CHAPTER 4

THEREFORE, my brethren, whom I love and long for, my joy and crown, stand firm thus in the Lord, my beloved.
2 I entreat Eu-o'dia and I entreat Syn'tyche to agree in the Lord. ³And I ask you also, true yokefellow, help these women, for they have labored side by side with me in the gospel together with Clement and the rest of my fellow workers, whose names are in the book of life.
4 Rejoice in the Lord always; again I will say, Rejoice. ⁵Let all men know your forbearance. The Lord is at hand. ⁶Have no anxiety about anything, but in everything by prayer and

ἀγαπητοὶ καὶ ἐπιπόθητοι, χαρὰ καὶ
beloved and longed for, joy and

στέφανός μου, οὕτως στήκετε ἐν κυρίῳ, ἀγαπητοί.
crown of me, so stand in [the] Lord, beloved.

2 Εὐοδίαν παρακαλῶ καὶ Συντύχην
²Euodia ¹I beseech and ²Syntyche

παρακαλῶ τὸ αὐτὸ φρονεῖν ἐν κυρίῳ.
¹I beseech ⁴the ⁵same thing ³to think in [the] Lord.

3 ναὶ ἐρωτῶ καὶ σέ, γνήσιε σύζυγε,
Yes[,] I ask also thee, genuine yoke-fellow,

συλλαμβάνου αὐταῖς, αἵτινες ἐν τῷ εὐαγ-
help them, who ²in ⁴the ⁵gos-

γελίῳ συνήθλησάν μοι μετὰ καὶ Κλήμεντος
pel ¹struggled with ²me with both Clement

καὶ τῶν λοιπῶν συνεργῶν μου, ὧν
and the remaining fellow-workers of me, of
whom

τὰ ὀνόματα ἐν βίβλῳ ζωῆς. 4 Χαίρετε
the names [are] in [the] book of life. Rejoice ye

ἐν κυρίῳ πάντοτε· πάλιν ἐρῶ, χαίρετε.
in [the] Lord always; again I will say, rejoice.

5 τὸ ἐπιεικὲς ὑμῶν γνωσθήτω πᾶσιν
The forbearance of you let it be known to all

ἀνθρώποις. ὁ κύριος ἐγγύς. 6 μηδὲν
men. The Lord [is] near. ²Nothing

μεριμνᾶτε, ἀλλ᾽ ἐν παντὶ τῇ προσευχῇ
¹be ye anxious but in everything – by prayer
about,

supplication with thanksgiving let your requests be made known to God. [7]And the peace of God, which passes all understanding, will keep your hearts and your minds in Christ Jesus.

8 Finally, brethren, whatever is true, whatever is honorable, whatever is just, whatever is pure, whatever is lovely, whatever is gracious, if there is any excellence, if there is anything worthy of praise, think about these things. [9]What you have learned and received and heard and seen in me, do; and the God of peace will be with you.

10 I rejoice in the Lord greatly that now at length you have revived your concern for me; you were indeed concerned for me, but you had no opportunity. [11]Not that I complain of want; for I have learned, in whatever state I am, to be content. [12]I know how to be abased, and I know how to abound; in any and all circumstances I have learned the secret of facing plenty and hunger,

καὶ   τῇ   δεήσει   μετὰ   εὐχαριστίας   τὰ
and   –   by petition   with   thanksgivings   the

αἰτήματα   ὑμῶν   γνωριζέσθω   πρὸς   τὸν
requests   of you   let be made known   to   –

θεόν.   7 καὶ   ἡ   εἰρήνη   τοῦ   θεοῦ   ἡ
God.   And   the   peace   –   of God   –

ὑπερέχουσα   πάντα   νοῦν   φρουρήσει   τὰς
surpassing   all   understanding   will guard   the

καρδίας   ὑμῶν   καὶ   τὰ   νοήματα   ὑμῶν
hearts   of you   and   the   thoughts   of you

ἐν   Χριστῷ   Ἰησοῦ.   8 Τὸ   λοιπόν,   ἀδελφοί,
in   Christ   Jesus.   For the rest,   brothers,

ὅσα   ἐστὶν   ἀληθῆ,   ὅσα   σεμνά,   ὅσα   δίκαια,
whatever are   true,   whatever grave, whatever just,
things   things   things

ὅσα   ἀγνά,   ὅσα   προσφιλῆ,   ὅσα   εὔφημα,
whatever pure, whatever   lovable,   whatever well-spoken
things   things   things   of,

εἴ   τις   ἀρετὴ   καὶ   εἴ   τις   ἔπαινος,   9 ταῦτα
if   any   virtue   and   if   any   praise,   these things

λογίζεσθε·   ἃ   καὶ   ἐμάθετε   καὶ   παρελάβετε
consider ye; which [2]both [1]ye [3]learned and   ye received
              things

καὶ   ἠκούσατε   καὶ   εἴδετε   ἐν   ἐμοί,   ταῦτα
and   ye heard   and   ye saw   in   me,   these

πράσσετε·   καὶ   ὁ   θεὸς   τῆς   εἰρήνης   ἔσται
practise;   and   the   God   –   of peace   will be

μεθ’   ὑμῶν.
with   you.

10 Ἐχάρην   δὲ   ἐν   κυρίῳ   μεγάλως   ὅτι
Now I rejoiced   in   [the] Lord   greatly   that

ἤδη   ποτὲ   ἀνεθάλετε   τὸ   ὑπὲρ   ἐμοῦ   φρονεῖν·
al-   at one   ye revived   the   on behalf   me   to think;
ready time   of
= now at length   = your thought for me;

ἐφ’   ᾧ   καὶ   ἐφρονεῖτε,   ἠκαιρεῖσθε   δέ.
as to   which indeed ye thought,   but ye had no opportunity.

11 οὐχ   ὅτι   καθ’   ὑστέρησιν   λέγω·   ἐγὼ
Not   that   [2]by way of   [3]lack   [1]I say;   [2]I

γὰρ   ἔμαθον   ἐν   οἷς   εἰμι   αὐτάρκης   εἶναι.
[1]for   learned   in   what   I am   [2]self-   [1]to be.
                        conditions   sufficient

12 οἶδα   καὶ   ταπεινοῦσθαι,   οἶδα   καὶ   περισ-
I know   both   to be humbled,   and I know   to

σεύειν·   ἐν   παντὶ   καὶ   ἐν   πᾶσιν   μεμύημαι,
abound;   in   everything   and   in   all things   I have been
                                                         initiated,

καὶ   χορτάζεσθαι   καὶ   πεινᾶν,   καὶ   περισ-
both   to be filled   and   to hunger,   both   to

abundance and want. [13]I can do all things in him who strengthens me.
14 Yet it was kind of you to share my trouble. [15]And you Philippians yourselves know that in the beginning of the gospel, when I left Macedo'nia, no church entered into partnership with me in giving and receiving except you only; [16]for even in Thessaloni'ca you sent me help[c] once and again. [17]Not that I seek the gift; but I seek the fruit which increases to your credit. [18]I have received full payment, and more; I am filled, having received from Epaphrodi'tus the gifts you sent, a fragrant offering, a sacrifice acceptable and pleasing to God. [19]And my God will supply every need of yours according to his riches in glory in Christ Jesus. [20]To our God and Father be glory for ever and ever. Amen.
21 Greet every saint in Christ Jesus. The brethren who are with me greet you. [22]All the

[c] Other ancient authorities read *money for my needs*

σεύειν καὶ ὑστερεῖσθαι.
abound and to lack.

13 πάντα ἰσχύω
²All things ¹I can do

ἐν τῷ ἐνδυναμοῦντί με.
in the [one] empowering me.

14 πλὴν καλῶς
Nevertheless ²well

ἐποιήσατε συγκοινωνήσαντές μου τῇ θλίψει.
¹ye did having partnership in ²of me ¹the ²affliction.

15 οἴδατε δὲ καὶ ὑμεῖς, Φιλιππήσιοι, ὅτι
And ²know ²also ¹ye, Philippians, that

ἐν ἀρχῇ τοῦ εὐαγγελίου, ὅτε ἐξῆλθον
in [the] of the gospel, when I went out
beginning

ἀπὸ Μακεδονίας, οὐδεμία μοι ἐκκλησία
from Macedonia, not one ²me ¹church

ἐκοινώνησεν εἰς λόγον δόσεως καὶ λήμψεως
²shared with in matter of giving and receiving

εἰ μὴ ὑμεῖς μόνοι, 16 ὅτι καὶ ἐν
except ye only, because indeed in

Θεσσαλονίκῃ καὶ ἅπαξ καὶ δὶς εἰς τὴν
Thessalonica both once and twice to the
=to my need

χρείαν μοι ἐπέμψατε. 17 οὐχ ὅτι ἐπιζητῶ
need to me[c] ye sent. Not that I seek

τὸ δόμα, ἀλλὰ ἐπιζητῶ τὸν καρπὸν
the gift, but I seek the fruit

τὸν πλεονάζοντα εἰς λόγον ὑμῶν. 18 ἀπέχω
– increasing to account of you. I have

δὲ πάντα καὶ περισσεύω· πεπλήρωμαι
But all things and abound; I have been filled

δεξάμενος παρὰ Ἐπαφροδίτου τὰ παρ'
receiving from Epaphroditus the things from

ὑμῶν, ὀσμὴν εὐωδίας, θυσίαν δεκτήν,
you, an odour of sweet smell, a sacrifice acceptable,

εὐάρεστον τῷ θεῷ. 19 ὁ δὲ θεός μου
well-pleasing – to God. And the God of me

πληρώσει πᾶσαν χρείαν ὑμῶν κατὰ τὸ
will fill every need of you according to the

πλοῦτος αὐτοῦ ἐν δόξῃ ἐν Χριστῷ Ἰησοῦ.
riches of him in glory in Christ Jesus.

20 τῷ δὲ θεῷ καὶ πατρὶ ἡμῶν ἡ δόξα
to the Now God and Father of us [be] the glory

εἰς τοὺς αἰῶνας τῶν αἰώνων· ἀμήν.
unto the ages of the ages: Amen.

21 Ἀσπάσασθε πάντα ἅγιον ἐν Χριστῷ
Greet ye every saint in Christ

Ἰησοῦ. ἀσπάζονται ὑμᾶς οἱ σὺν ἐμοὶ
Jesus. ⁵greet ⁶you ¹The ²with ⁴me

ἀδελφοί. 22 ἀσπάζονται ὑμᾶς πάντες οἱ
²brothers. ⁴greet ⁵you ¹All ²the

saints greet you, especially those of Caesar's household.
23 The grace of the Lord Jesus Christ be with your spirit.

ἄγιοι, μάλιστα δὲ οἱ ἐκ τῆς Καίσαρος
²saints, but most of all the ones of ¹the ²of Cæsar
οἰκίας.
²household.

23 ʽΗ χάρις τοῦ κυρίου ᾽Ιησοῦ Χριστοῦ
The grace of the Lord Jesus Christ
μετὰ τοῦ πνεύματος ὑμῶν.
[be] with the spirit of you.

COLOSSIANS 1

ΠΡΟΣ ΚΟΛΟΣΣΑΕΙΣ
To Colossians

CHAPTER 1

PAUL, an apostle of Christ Jesus by the will of God, and Timothy our brother,
2 To the saints and faithful brethren in Christ at Colos'sae:
Grace to you and peace from God our Father.
3 We always thank God, the Father of our Lord Jesus Christ, when we pray for you, ⁴because we have heard of your faith in Christ Jesus and of the love which you have for all the saints, ⁵because of the hope laid up for you in heaven. Of this you have heard before in the word of the truth, the gospel ⁶which has come to you, as indeed in the whole world it is bearing fruit and growing—so

1 Παῦλος ἀπόστολος Χριστοῦ ᾽Ιησοῦ διὰ
Paul an apostle of Christ Jesus through
θελήματος θεοῦ καὶ Τιμόθεος ὁ ἀδελφὸς
[the] will of God and Timothy the brother
2 τοῖς ἐν Κολοσσαῖς ἁγίοις καὶ πιστοῖς
to the in Colossae saints and faithful
ἀδελφοῖς ἐν Χριστῷ· χάρις ὑμῖν καὶ
brothers in Christ: Grace to you and
εἰρήνη ἀπὸ θεοῦ πατρὸς ἡμῶν.
peace from God Father of us.
3 Εὐχαριστοῦμεν τῷ θεῷ πατρὶ τοῦ
We give thanks – to God Father of the
κυρίου ἡμῶν ᾽Ιησοῦ [Χριστοῦ] πάντοτε
Lord of us Jesus Christ always
περὶ ὑμῶν προσευχόμενοι, 4 ἀκούσαντες
²concerning ³you ¹praying, having heard
τὴν πίστιν ὑμῶν ἐν Χριστῷ ᾽Ιησοῦ
the faith of you in Christ Jesus
καὶ τὴν ἀγάπην ἣν ἔχετε εἰς πάντας
and the love which ye have toward all
τοὺς ἁγίους 5 διὰ τὴν ἐλπίδα τὴν
the saints because of the hope –
ἀποκειμένην ὑμῖν ἐν τοῖς οὐρανοῖς, ἣν
being laid up for you in the heavens, which
προηκούσατε ἐν τῷ λόγῳ τῆς ἀληθείας
ye previously in the word of the truth
heard
τοῦ εὐαγγελίου 6 τοῦ παρόντος εἰς ὑμᾶς,
of the gospel – coming to you,
καθὼς καὶ ἐν παντὶ τῷ κόσμῳ ἐστὶν
as also in all the world it is
καρποφορούμενον καὶ αὐξανόμενον καθὼς
bearing fruit and growing as

among yourselves, from the day you heard and understood the grace of God in truth, [7] as you learned it from Ep'aphras our beloved fellow servant. He is a faithful minister of Christ on our[a] behalf [8] and has made known to us your love in the Spirit.

[9] And so, from the day we heard of it, we have not ceased to pray for you, asking that you may be filled with the knowledge of his will in all spiritual wisdom and understanding, [10] to lead a life worthy of the Lord, fully pleasing to him, bearing fruit in every good work and increasing in the knowledge of God. [11] May you be strengthened with all power, according to his glorious might, for all endurance and patience with joy, [12] giving thanks to the Father, who has qualified us[b] to share in the inheritance of the saints in light. [13] He has delivered us from the dominion of darkness

καὶ	ἐν	ὑμῖν,	ἀφ'	ἧς	ἡμέρας	ἠκούσατε
also	in	you,	from	which	day	ye heard
					= the day on which	

καὶ	ἐπέγνωτε	τὴν	χάριν	τοῦ	θεοῦ	ἐν
and	fully knew	the	grace	–	of God	in

ἀληθείᾳ·	7 καθὼς	ἐμάθετε	ἀπὸ	'Επαφρᾶ
truth;	as	ye learned	from	Epaphras

τοῦ	ἀγαπητοῦ	συνδούλου	ἡμῶν,	ὅς	ἐστιν
the	beloved	fellow-slave	of us,	who	is

πιστὸς	ὑπὲρ	ὑμῶν	διάκονος	τοῦ	Χριστοῦ,
[1]a faithful	[4]on behalf of	[5]you	[2]minister	–	[3]of Christ,

8 ὁ	καὶ	δηλώσας	ἡμῖν	τὴν	ὑμῶν	ἀγάπην
the [one]	also	having shown	to us	[1]the	[3]of you	[2]love

ἐν	πνεύματι.
in	spirit.

9 Διὰ	τοῦτο	καὶ	ἡμεῖς,	ἀφ'	ἧς	ἡμέρας
Therefore		also	we,	from	which	day
						= the day on which

ἠκούσαμεν,	οὐ	παυόμεθα	ὑπὲρ	ὑμῶν
we heard,	do not cease		on behalf of	you

προσευχόμενοι	καὶ	αἰτούμενοι	ἵνα	πληρω-
praying	and	asking	in order that	ye may be

θῆτε	τὴν	ἐπίγνωσιν	τοῦ	θελήματος	αὐτοῦ
filled [with]	the	full knowledge	of the	will	of him

ἐν	πάσῃ	σοφίᾳ	·καὶ	συνέσει	πνευματικῇ,
in	all	wisdom	and	understanding	spiritual,

10 περιπατῆσαι	ἀξίως	τοῦ	κυρίου	εἰς
to walk	worthily	of the	Lord	to

πᾶσαν	ἀρεσκείαν,	ἐν	παντὶ	ἔργῳ	ἀγαθῷ
all	pleasing,	in	every	work	good

καρποφοροῦντες	καὶ	αὐξανόμενοι	τῇ
bearing fruit	and	growing	in the

ἐπιγνώσει	τοῦ	θεοῦ,	11 ἐν	πάσῃ	δυνάμει
full knowledge	–	of God,	with	all	power

δυναμούμενοι	κατὰ	τὸ	κράτος	τῆς	δόξης
being empowered	according to the		might	of the	glory

αὐτοῦ	εἰς	πᾶσαν	ὑπομονὴν	καὶ	μακρο-
of him	to	all	endurance	and	long-

θυμίαν,	μετὰ	χαρᾶς	12 εὐχαριστοῦντες	τῷ
suffering,	with	joy	giving thanks	to the

πατρὶ	τῷ	ἱκανώσαντι	ὑμᾶς	εἰς	τὴν	μερίδα
Father	–	having made [2]fit	[1]you	for	the	part

τοῦ	κλήρου	τῶν	ἁγίων	ἐν	τῷ	φωτί·
of the	lot	of the	saints	in	the	light;

13 ὃς	ἐρρύσατο	ἡμᾶς	ἐκ	τῆς	ἐξουσίας
who	delivered	us	out of	the	authority

[a] Other ancient authorities read *your*
[b] Other ancient authorities read *you*

and transferred us to the
kingdom of his beloved
Son, [14]in whom we have
redemption, the forgive-
ness of sins.
15 He is the image of
the invisible God, the
first-born of all creation;
[16]for in him all things
were created, in heaven
and on earth, visible and
invisible, whether thrones
or dominions or princi-
palities or authorities—
all things were created
through him and for him.
[17]He is before all things,
and in him all things hold
together. [18]He is the
head of the body, the
church; he is the be-
ginning, the first-born
from the dead, that in
everything he might be
preëminent. [19]For in him
all the fulness of God
was pleased to dwell,
[20]and through him to
reconcile to himself all
things, whether on earth
or in heaven, making
peace by the blood of his
cross.
21 And you, who
once were estranged and

τοῦ   σκότους   καὶ   μετέστησεν   εἰς   τὴν
of the   darkness   and   transferred   into   the

βασιλείαν   τοῦ   υἱοῦ   τῆς   ἀγάπης   αὐτοῦ,
kingdom   of the   Son   of the   love   of him,

14 ἐν   ᾧ   ἔχομεν   τὴν   ἀπολύτρωσιν,   τὴν
in   whom   we have   the   redemption,   the

ἄφεσιν   τῶν   ἁμαρτιῶν·   15 ὅς   ἐστιν   εἰκὼν
forgiveness of the   sins;   who   is   an image
(our)

τοῦ   θεοῦ   τοῦ   ἀοράτου,   πρωτότοκος   πάσης
of the   God   –   invisible,   firstborn   of all

κτίσεως,   16 ὅτι   ἐν   αὐτῷ   ἐκτίσθη   τὰ
creation,   because   in   him   were created   –

πάντα   ἐν   τοῖς   οὐρανοῖς   καὶ   ἐπὶ   τῆς
all things   in   the   heavens   and   on   the

γῆς,   τὰ   ὁρατὰ   καὶ   τὰ   ἀόρατα,   εἴτε
earth,   the   visible   and   the   invisible,   whether

θρόνοι   εἴτε   κυριότητες   εἴτε   ἀρχαὶ   εἴτε
thrones   or   lordships   or   rulers   or

ἐξουσίαι·   τὰ   πάντα   δι’   αὐτοῦ   καὶ   εἰς
authorities;   –   all things   through   him   and   for

αὐτὸν   ἔκτισται·   17 καὶ   αὐτός   ἐστιν   πρὸ
him   have been created;   and   he   is   before

πάντων   καὶ   τὰ   πάντα   ἐν   αὐτῷ   συνέστηκεν,
all things   and   –   all things   in   him   consisted,

18 καὶ   αὐτός   ἐστιν   ἡ   κεφαλὴ   τοῦ   σώματος,
and   he   is   the   head   of the   body,

τῆς   ἐκκλησίας·   ὅς   ἐστιν   ἀρχή,   πρωτότοκος
of the   church;   who   is   [the]   firstborn
beginning,

ἐκ   τῶν   νεκρῶν,   ἵνα   γένηται   ἐν   πᾶσιν
from   the   dead,   in order   [4]may be   [2]in   [3]all
that   things

αὐτὸς   πρωτεύων,   19 ὅτι   ἐν   αὐτῷ   εὐδόκησεν
[1]he   [5]holding the   because   in   him   [4]was well
first place,   pleased

πᾶν   τὸ   πλήρωμα   κατοικῆσαι   20 καὶ   δι’
[1]all   [2]the   [3]fulness   to dwell   and through

αὐτοῦ   ἀποκαταλλάξαι   τὰ   πάντα   εἰς   αὐτόν,
him   to reconcile   –   all things   to   him[?self],

εἰρηνοποιήσας   διὰ   τοῦ   αἵματος   τοῦ   σταυροῦ
making peace   through   the   blood   of the   cross

αὐτοῦ,   δι’   αὐτοῦ   εἴτε   τὰ   ἐπὶ   τῆς   γῆς
of him,   through   him   whether   the   on   the   earth
things

εἴτε   τὰ   ἐν   τοῖς   οὐρανοῖς.   21 Καὶ   ὑμᾶς
or   the things in   the   heavens.   And   you

ποτε   ὄντας   ἀπηλλοτριωμένους   καὶ   ἐχθροὺς
then   being   having been alienated   and   enemies

hostile in mind, doing evil deeds, [22] he has now reconciled in his body of flesh by his death, in order to present you holy and blameless and irreproachable before him, [23] provided that you continue in the faith, stable and steadfast, not shifting from the hope of the gospel which you heard, which has been preached to every creature under heaven, and of which I, Paul, became a minister.

24 Now I rejoice in my sufferings for your sake, and in my flesh I complete what is lacking in Christ's afflictions for the sake of his body, that is, the church, [25] of which I became a minister according to the divine office which was given to me for you, to make the word of God fully known, [26] the mystery hidden for ages and generations[c] but now made manifest to his saints. [27] To them God chose to make known how great among the Gentiles are the riches of

[c] Or *from angels and men*

τῇ διανοίᾳ ἐν τοῖς ἔργοις τοῖς πονηροῖς,
in the mind   by the(your) works   evil,

22 νυνὶ δὲ ἀποκατήλλαξεν ἐν τῷ σώματι
but now   he reconciled   in the   body

τῆς σαρκὸς αὐτοῦ διὰ τοῦ θανάτου,
of the flesh   of him through the(his) death,

παραστῆσαι ὑμᾶς ἁγίους καὶ ἀμώμους
to present   you   holy   and blameless

καὶ ἀνεγκλήτους κατενώπιον αὐτοῦ, 23 εἴ
and irreproachable before   him,   23 if

γε ἐπιμένετε τῇ πίστει τεθεμελιωμένοι
indeed ye continue in the faith having been founded

καὶ ἑδραῖοι καὶ μὴ μετακινούμενοι ἀπὸ
and steadfast and not being moved away from

τῆς ἐλπίδος τοῦ εὐαγγελίου οὗ ἠκούσατε,
the   hope   of the gospel   which ye heard,

τοῦ κηρυχθέντος ἐν πάσῃ κτίσει τῇ
 -   proclaimed in all creation -

ὑπὸ τὸν οὐρανόν, οὗ ἐγενόμην ἐγὼ
under the heaven, of which [1]became [1]I

Παῦλος διάκονος.
[1]Paul a minister.

24 Νῦν χαίρω ἐν τοῖς παθήμασιν ὑπὲρ
Now I rejoice in the(my) sufferings on be-
                                            half of

ὑμῶν, καὶ ἀνταναπληρῶ τὰ ὑστερήματα
you,   and   fill up   the things lacking

τῶν θλίψεων τοῦ Χριστοῦ ἐν τῇ σαρκί
of the afflictions - of Christ in the flesh

μου ὑπὲρ τοῦ σώματος αὐτοῦ, ὅ ἐστιν
of me on behalf of the body   of him, which is

ἡ ἐκκλησία, 25 ἧς ἐγενόμην ἐγὼ διάκονος
the church, of which became   I   a minister

κατὰ τὴν οἰκονομίαν τοῦ θεοῦ τὴν
accord- the stewardship   - of God -
ing to

δοθεῖσάν μοι εἰς ὑμᾶς πληρῶσαι τὸν
given   to me for you to fulfil the

λόγον τοῦ θεοῦ, 26 τὸ μυστήριον τὸ
word   - of God, the mystery   -

ἀποκεκρυμμένον ἀπὸ τῶν αἰώνων καὶ
having been hidden from the ages   and

ἀπὸ τῶν γενεῶν — νῦν δὲ ἐφανερώθη
from the generations — but now was manifested

τοῖς ἁγίοις αὐτοῦ, 27 οἷς ἠθέλησεν ὁ
to the saints of him, to whom [2]wished -

θεὸς γνωρίσαι τί τὸ πλοῦτος τῆς δόξης
[1]God to make known what [is] the riches of the glory

the glory of this mystery, which is Christ in you, the hope of glory. ²⁸Him we proclaim, warning every man and teaching every man in all wisdom, that we may present every man mature in Christ. ²⁹For this I toil, striving with all the energy which he mightily inspires within me.

τοῦ   μυστηρίου   τούτου   ἐν   τοῖς   ἔθνεσιν,
-     mystery   of this   among the   nations,

ὅς   ἐστιν   Χριστὸς   ἐν   ὑμῖν,   ἡ   ἐλπὶς   τῆς
who is   Christ   in   you,   the hope   of the

δόξης·   28 ὃν   ἡμεῖς   καταγγέλλομεν   νου-
glory;   whom we   announce   warn-

θετοῦντες   πάντα   ἄνθρωπον   καὶ   διδάσκοντες
ing   every   man   and   teaching

πάντα   ἄνθρωπον   ἐν   πάσῃ   σοφίᾳ,
every   man   in   all   wisdom,

ἵνα   παραστήσωμεν   πάντα   ἄνθρωπον
in or-   we may present   every   man
der that

τέλειον   ἐν   Χριστῷ·   29 εἰς   ὃ   καὶ   κοπιῶ
mature   in   Christ;   for which also I labour

ἀγωνιζόμενος   κατὰ   τὴν   ἐνέργειαν   αὐτοῦ
struggling   accord- the   operation   of him
               ing to

τὴν   ἐνεργουμένην   ἐν   ἐμοὶ   ἐν   δυνάμει.
-     operating   in   me   in   power.

CHAPTER 2

F OR I want you to know how greatly I strive for you, and for those at La-odice′a, and for all who have not seen my face, ²that their hearts may be encouraged as they are knit together in love, to have all the riches of assured understanding and the knowledge of God's mystery, of Christ, ³in whom are hid all the treasures of wisdom and knowledge. ⁴I say this in order that no one may delude you with beguiling speech. ⁵For though I am absent in body, yet I am with you in spirit, rejoicing to see your good

2 Θέλω   γὰρ   ὑμᾶς   εἰδέναι   ἡλίκον   ἀγῶνα
For I wish   you   to know   how great a struggle

ἔχω   ὑπὲρ   ὑμῶν   καὶ   τῶν   ἐν   Λαοδικείᾳ
I have on behalf of you   and   the [ones] in   Laodicea

καὶ   ὅσοι   οὐχ   ἑόρακαν   τὸ   πρόσωπόν   μου
and as many as have not seen the   face   of me

ἐν   σαρκί,   2 ἵνα   παρακληθῶσιν   αἱ   καρδίαι
in   flesh,   in order ⁴may be   ¹the ²hearts
             that   comforted

αὐτῶν,   συμβιβασθέντες   ἐν   ἀγάπῃ   καὶ   εἰς
³of them, being joined together in   love   and   for

πᾶν   πλοῦτος   τῆς   πληροφορίας   τῆς
all   riches   of the full assurance   -

συνέσεως,   εἰς   ἐπίγνωσιν   τοῦ   μυστηρίου
of under-   for   full knowledge of the mystery
standing,

τοῦ   θεοῦ,   Χριστοῦ,   3 ἐν   ᾧ   εἰσιν   πάντες
-     of God, of Christ,   in whom ¹are   ³all

οἱ   θησαυροὶ   τῆς   σοφίας   καὶ   γνώσεως
⁴the ⁵treasures   -   ⁶of wisdom ⁷and ⁸of knowledge

ἀπόκρυφοι.   4 Τοῦτο   λέγω   ἵνα   μηδεὶς
²hidden.   This   I say   in order no one
                                 that

ὑμᾶς   παραλογίζηται   ἐν   πιθανολογίᾳ.   5 εἰ
²you   ¹may beguile   with persuasive speech.   if

γὰρ   καὶ   τῇ   σαρκὶ   ἄπειμι,   ἀλλὰ   τῷ
For   indeed in the flesh   I am absent, yet   in the

πνεύματι   σὺν   ὑμῖν   εἰμι,   χαίρων   καὶ
spirit   ²with ³you   ¹I am,   rejoicing   and

order and the firmness of your faith in Christ.

6 As therefore you received Christ Jesus the Lord, so live in him, [7] rooted and built up in him and established in the faith, just as you were taught, abounding in thanksgiving.

8 See to it that no one makes a prey of you by philosophy and empty deceit, according to human tradition, according to the elemental spirits of the universe, and not according to Christ. [9] For in him the whole fulness of deity dwells bodily, [10] and you have come to fulness of life in him, who is the head of all rule and authority. [11] In him also you were circumcised with a circumcision made without hands, by putting off the body of flesh in the circumcision of Christ; [12] and you were buried with him in baptism, in which you were also raised with him through faith in the working of God, who raised him from the dead. [13] And you, who

βλέπων ὑμῶν τὴν τάξιν καὶ τὸ στερέωμα
seeing ²of you ¹the ²order and the firmness
τῆς εἰς Χριστὸν πίστεως ὑμῶν.
of the ²in ⁴Christ ¹faith ²of you.

6 Ὡς οὖν παρελάβετε τὸν Χριστὸν
As therefore ye received – Christ
Ἰησοῦν τὸν κύριον, ἐν αὐτῷ περιπατεῖτε,
Jesus the Lord, in him walk ye,
7 ἐρριζωμένοι καὶ ἐποικοδομούμενοι ἐν αὐτῷ
having been rooted and being built up in him
καὶ βεβαιούμενοι τῇ πίστει καθὼς ἐδιδάχ-
and being confirmed in the faith as ye were
θητε, περισσεύοντες ἐν εὐχαριστίᾳ.
taught, abounding in thanksgiving.

8 Βλέπετε μή τις ὑμᾶς ἔσται ὁ συλαγωγῶν
Look ye lest ²anyone ⁴you ¹there – ²robbing
shall be
διὰ τῆς φιλοσοφίας καὶ κενῆς ἀπάτης
through – philosophy and empty deceit
κατὰ τὴν παράδοσιν τῶν ἀνθρώπων, κατὰ
accord- the tradition – of men, according to ing to
τὰ στοιχεῖα τοῦ κόσμου καὶ οὐ κατὰ
the elements of the world and not according to
Χριστόν· 9 ὅτι ἐν αὐτῷ κατοικεῖ πᾶν
Christ; because in him dwells all
τὸ πλήρωμα τῆς θεότητος σωματικῶς,
the fulness of the Godhead bodily,
10 καὶ ἐστὲ ἐν αὐτῷ πεπληρωμένοι, ὅς
and ye are in him having been filled, who
ἐστιν ἡ κεφαλὴ πάσης ἀρχῆς καὶ ἐξουσίας,
is the head of all rule and authority,
11 ἐν ᾧ καὶ περιετμήθητε περιτομῇ
in whom also ye were with a
circumcised circumcision
ἀχειροποιήτῳ ἐν τῇ ἀπεκδύσει τοῦ σώματος
not handwrought by the putting off of the body
τῆς σαρκός, ἐν τῇ περιτομῇ τοῦ Χριστοῦ,
of the flesh, by the circumcision – of Christ,
12 συνταφέντες αὐτῷ ἐν τῷ βαπτίσματι,
co-buried with him in the baptism,
ἐν ᾧ καὶ συνηγέρθητε διὰ τῆς πίστεως
in whom also ye were co-raised through the faith
τῆς ἐνεργείας τοῦ θεοῦ τοῦ ἐγείραντος
of(in) the operation – of God – raising
αὐτὸν ἐκ νεκρῶν· 13 καὶ ὑμᾶς νεκροὺς
him from [the] dead; and you dead

were dead in trespasses and the uncircumcision of your flesh, God made alive together with him, having forgiven us all our trespasses, [14]having canceled the bond which stood against us with its legal demands; this he set aside, nailing it to the cross. [15]He disarmed the principalities and powers and made a public example of them, triumphing over them in him.[d]

[16]Therefore let no one pass judgment on you in questions of food and drink or with regard to a festival or a new moon or a sabbath. [17]These are only a shadow of what is to come; but the substance belongs to Christ. [18]Let no one disqualify you, insisting on self-abasement and worship of angels, taking his stand on visions, puffed up without reason by his sensuous mind, [19]and not holding fast to the Head, from whom the whole body, nourished and knit together through its joints and ligaments, grows with a growth that is from God.

[d] Or *in it* (that is, the cross)

ὄντας τοῖς παραπτώμασιν καὶ τῇ ἀκρο-
being in the trespasses and in the uncir-

βυστίᾳ τῆς σαρκὸς ὑμῶν, συνεζωοποίησεν
cumcision of the flesh of you, he co-quickened

ὑμᾶς σὺν αὐτῷ, χαρισάμενος ἡμῖν πάντα
you with him, forgiving you all

τὰ παραπτώματα· 14 ἐξαλείψας τὸ καθ'
the trespasses; wiping out [1]the [2]against

ἡμῶν χειρόγραφον τοῖς δόγμασιν ὃ ἦν
[1]us [2]handwriting in ordinances which was

ὑπεναντίον ἡμῖν, καὶ αὐτὸ ἦρκεν ἐκ
contrary to us, and [2]it [1]has taken out of

τοῦ μέσου, προσηλώσας αὐτὸ τῷ σταυρῷ·
the midst(way), nailing it to the cross;

15 ἀπεκδυσάμενος τὰς ἀρχὰς καὶ τὰς
putting off the rulers and the

ἐξουσίας ἐδειγμάτισεν ἐν παρρησίᾳ,
authorities he exposed [them] with openness,

θριαμβεύσας αὐτοὺς ἐν αὐτῷ.
triumphing [over] them in it.

16 Μὴ οὖν τις ὑμᾶς κρινέτω ἐν βρώσει
[2]Not [3]there-[4]any-[5]you [1]let [5]judge in eating
      fore one

καὶ ἐν πόσει ἢ ἐν μέρει ἑορτῆς ἢ
and in drinking or in respect of a feast or

νεομηνίας ἢ σαββάτων, 17 ἅ ἐστιν σκιὰ
of a new moon or of sabbaths, which is(are) a
                                  things   shadow

τῶν μελλόντων, τὸ δὲ σῶμα τοῦ Χριστοῦ.
of things coming, but the body [is] – of Christ.

18 μηδεὶς ὑμᾶς καταβραβευέτω θέλων ἐν
[2]No one [4]you [1]let [3]give judgment wishing in
                        against   [to do so]

ταπεινοφροσύνῃ καὶ θρησκείᾳ τῶν ἀγγέλων,
humility* and worship of the angels,

ἃ ἑόρακεν ἐμβατεύων, εἰκῇ φυσιούμενος
[2]things [3]he has [1]intruding into, in vain being puffed up
which   seen

ὑπὸ τοῦ νοὸς τῆς σαρκὸς αὐτοῦ, 19 καὶ
by the mind of the flesh of him, and

οὐ κρατῶν τὴν κεφαλήν, ἐξ οὗ πᾶν
not holding the head, from whom all

τὸ σῶμα διὰ τῶν ἁφῶν καὶ συνδέσμων
the body [4]by means [5]the [6]joints [7]and [8]bands
              of   (its)

ἐπιχορηγούμενον καὶ συμβιβαζόμενον αὔξει
[1]being supplied [2]and [3]being joined together will grow

τὴν αὔξησιν τοῦ θεοῦ.
[with] the growth – of God.

* Ellicott supplies " false ". Cf. ver. 23.

20 If with Christ you died to the elemental spirits of the universe, why do you live as if you still belonged to the world? Why do you submit to regulations, 21 "Do not handle, Do not taste, Do not touch" 22 (referring to things which all perish as they are used), according to human precepts and doctrines? 23 These have indeed an appearance of wisdom in promoting rigor of devotion and self-abasement and severity to the body, but they are of no value in checking the indulgence of the flesh.[e]

CHAPTER 3

IF then you have been raised with Christ, seek the things that are above, where Christ is, seated at the right hand of God. 2 Set your minds on things that are above, not on things that are on earth. 3 For you have died, and your life is hid with Christ in God. 4 When Christ who is our life appears, then you also will appear with him in glory.

5 Put to death therefore what is earthly in you: immorality, impurity, passion, evil desire, and covetousness, which is idolatry. 6 On account of these the

---

20 Εἰ ἀπεθάνετε σὺν Χριστῷ ἀπὸ τῶν στοι-
If ye died with Christ from the ele-
χείων τοῦ κόσμου, τί ὡς ζῶντες ἐν κόσμῳ
ments of the world, why as living in [the] world
δογματίζεσθε· 21 μὴ ἅψῃ μηδὲ γεύσῃ μηδὲ
are ye subject to Do not touch nor taste nor
[its] decrees:
θίγῃς, 22 ἅ ἐστιν πάντα εἰς φθορὰν
handle, which is(are) all for corruption
things
τῇ ἀποχρήσει, κατὰ τὰ ἐντάλματα καὶ
in the using, according to the injunctions and
διδασκαλίας τῶν ἀνθρώπων; 23 ἅτινά ἐστιν
teachings - of men? ¹which ²is(are)
things
λόγον μὲν ἔχοντα σοφίας ἐν ἐθελοθρησκίᾳ
²a repute ²indeed ⁴having of wisdom in self-imposed
worship
καὶ ταπεινοφροσύνῃ καὶ ἀφειδίᾳ σώματος, οὐκ
and humility and severity of [the] body, not
ἐν τιμῇ τινι πρὸς πλησμονὴν τῆς σαρκός.
in ²honour ¹any for satisfaction of the flesh.

3 Εἰ οὖν συνηγέρθητε τῷ Χριστῷ, τὰ
If therefore ye were co-raised - with Christ, the
things
ἄνω ζητεῖτε, οὗ ὁ Χριστός ἐστιν ἐν
above seek, where - Christ ¹is ²at
δεξιᾷ τοῦ θεοῦ καθήμενος· 2 τὰ ἄνω
⁴[the] right - ⁵of God ³sitting; the above
[hand] things
φρονεῖτε, μὴ τὰ ἐπὶ τῆς γῆς. 3 ἀπεθάνετε
mind ye, not the on the earth. ye died
things
γάρ, καὶ ἡ ζωὴ ὑμῶν κέκρυπται σὺν
For, and the life of you has been hidden with
τῷ Χριστῷ ἐν τῷ θεῷ· 4 ὅταν ὁ Χριστὸς
- Christ in - God; whenever - Christ
φανερωθῇ, ἡ ζωὴ ἡμῶν, τότε καὶ ὑμεῖς
is manifested, the life of us, then also ye
σὺν αὐτῷ φανερωθήσεσθε ἐν δόξῃ.
with him will be manifested in glory.

5 Νεκρώσατε οὖν τὰ μέλη τὰ ἐπὶ
Put ye to death therefore the members - on
(your)
τῆς γῆς, πορνείαν, ἀκαθαρσίαν, πάθος,
the earth, fornication, uncleanness, passion,
ἐπιθυμίαν κακήν, καὶ τὴν πλεονεξίαν ἥτις
desire bad, and - covetousness which
ἐστὶν εἰδωλολατρία, 6 δι᾽ ἃ ἔρχεται ἡ
is idolatry, because which is coming the
of things

---

[e] Or are of no value, serving only to indulge the flesh

wrath of God is coming.*f* *7* In these you once walked, when you lived in them. *8* But now put them all away; anger, wrath, malice, slander, and foul talk from your mouth. *9* Do not lie to one another, seeing that you have put off the old nature with its practices *10* and have put on the new nature, which is being renewed in knowledge after the image of its creator. *11* Here there cannot be Greek and Jew, circumcised and uncircumcised, barbarian, Scyth'ian, slave, free man, but Christ is all, and in all.

12 Put on then, as God's chosen ones, holy and beloved, compassion, kindness, lowliness, meekness, and patience, *13* forbearing one another and, if one has a complaint against another, forgiving each other; as the Lord has forgiven you, so you also must forgive. *14* And above all these put on love, which binds everything together in perfect harmony. *15* And let the peace of Christ rule in your

f Other ancient authorities add *upon the sons of disobedience*

ὀργὴ τοῦ θεοῦ· **7** ἐν οἷς καὶ ὑμεῖς
wrath — of God; in which indeed ye

περιεπατήσατέ ποτε, ὅτε ἐζῆτε ἐν τούτοις·
walked then, when ye lived in these things;

8 νυνὶ δὲ ἀπόθεσθε καὶ ὑμεῖς τὰ πάντα,
but now ¹put ²away ⁴also ³ye – all things,

ὀργήν, θυμόν, κακίαν, βλασφημίαν, αἰσχρο-
wrath, anger, malice, blasphemy, a-

λογίαν ἐκ τοῦ στόματος ὑμῶν· **9** μὴ
buse out of the mouth of you; not

ψεύδεσθε εἰς ἀλλήλους, ἀπεκδυσάμενοι τὸν
lie ye to one another, having put off the

παλαιὸν ἄνθρωπον σὺν ταῖς πράξεσιν
old man with the practices

αὐτοῦ, **10** καὶ ἐνδυσάμενοι τὸν νέον τὸν
of him, and having put on the new man –

ἀνακαινούμενον εἰς ἐπίγνωσιν κατ' εἰκόνα
being renewed in full knowledge according [the]
to image

τοῦ κτίσαντος αὐτόν, **11** ὅπου οὐκ ἔνι
of the [one] creating him, where ⁴have no place

Ἕλλην καὶ Ἰουδαῖος, περιτομὴ καὶ
¹Greek ²and ³Jew, circumcision and

ἀκροβυστία, βάρβαρος, Σκύθης, δοῦλος,
uncircumcision, barbarian, Scythian, slave,

ἐλεύθερος, ἀλλὰ πάντα καὶ ἐν πᾶσιν
freeman, but ²all things ⁴and ⁵in ⁶all

Χριστός. **12** Ἐνδύσασθε οὖν, ὡς ἐκλεκτοὶ
¹Christ ²[is]. Put ye on therefore, as chosen ones

τοῦ θεοῦ ἅγιοι καὶ ἠγαπημένοι, σπλάγχνα
– of God holy and having been loved, bowels

οἰκτιρμοῦ, χρηστότητα, ταπεινοφροσύνην,
of compassion, kindness, humility,

πραΰτητα, μακροθυμίαν, **13** ἀνεχόμενοι ἀλ-
meekness, long-suffering, forbearing one

λήλων καὶ χαριζόμενοι ἑαυτοῖς, ἐάν τις
another and forgiving yourselves, if anyone

πρός τινα ἔχῃ μομφήν· καθὼς καὶ ὁ
²against ⁴anyone ¹has ²a complaint; as indeed the

κύριος ἐχαρίσατο ὑμῖν οὕτως καὶ ὑμεῖς·
Lord forgave you so also ye;

14 ἐπὶ πᾶσιν δὲ τούτοις τὴν ἀγάπην,
²over ³all ¹and these things – love,

ὅ ἐστιν σύνδεσμος τῆς τελειότητος. **15** καὶ
which is [the] bond – of completeness. And

ἡ εἰρήνη τοῦ Χριστοῦ βραβευέτω ἐν ταῖς
²the ³peace – ⁴of Christ ¹let ⁵rule in the

hearts, to which indeed you were called in the one body. And be thankful. ¹⁶ Let the word of Christ dwell in you richly, as you teach and admonish one another in all wisdom, and as you sing psalms and hymns and spiritual songs with thankfulness in your hearts to God. ¹⁷ And whatever you do, in word or deed, do everything in the name of the Lord Jesus, giving thanks to God the Father through him.
18 Wives, be subject to your husbands, as is fitting in the Lord. ¹⁹ Husbands, love your wives, and do not be harsh with them. ²⁰ Children, obey your parents in everything, for this pleases the Lord. ²¹ Fathers, do not provoke your children, lest they become discouraged. ²² Slaves, obey in everything those who are your earthly masters, not with eyeservice, as menpleasers, but in singleness of heart, fearing the Lord. ²³ Whatever

καρδίαις ὑμῶν, εἰς ἣν καὶ ἐκλήθητε
hearts of you, to which indeed ye were called
ἐν ἑνὶ σώματι· καὶ εὐχάριστοι γίνεσθε.
in one body; and thankful be ye.
16 ὁ λόγος τοῦ Χριστοῦ ἐνοικείτω ἐν
²The ³word - ⁴of Christ ¹let ⁵indwell in
ὑμῖν πλουσίως, ἐν πάσῃ σοφίᾳ διδάσκοντες
you richly, in all wisdom teaching
καὶ νουθετοῦντες ἑαυτούς, ψαλμοῖς ὕμνοις
and admonishing yourselves, in psalms[,] hymns[,]
ᾠδαῖς πνευματικαῖς ἐν τῇ χάριτι ᾄδοντες
[and] ²songs ¹spiritual with - grace singing
ἐν ταῖς καρδίαις ὑμῶν τῷ θεῷ· 17 καὶ
in the hearts of you - to God; and
πᾶν ὅ τι ἐὰν ποιῆτε ἐν λόγῳ ἢ ἐν
every-thing whatever ye do in word or in
ἔργῳ, πάντα ἐν ὀνόματι κυρίου Ἰησοῦ,
work, all things [do] in [the] name of [the] Lord Jesus,
εὐχαριστοῦντες τῷ θεῷ πατρὶ δι᾿ αὐτοῦ.
giving thanks - to God [the] through him.
Father

18 Αἱ γυναῖκες, ὑποτάσσεσθε τοῖς
The wives, be ye subject to the(your)
ἀνδράσιν, ὡς ἀνῆκεν ἐν κυρίῳ. 19 Οἱ
husbands, as is befitting in [the] Lord. The
ἄνδρες, ἀγαπᾶτε τὰς γυναῖκας καὶ μὴ
husbands, love ye the(your) wives and not
πικραίνεσθε πρὸς αὐτάς. 20 Τὰ τέκνα,
be bitter toward them. The children,
ὑπακούετε τοῖς γονεῦσιν κατὰ πάντα,
obey ye the(your) parents in all respects,
τοῦτο γὰρ εὐάρεστόν ἐστιν ἐν κυρίῳ.
for this well-pleasing is in [the] Lord.
21 Οἱ πατέρες, μὴ ἐρεθίζετε τὰ τέκνα
The fathers, do not ye provoke the children
ὑμῶν, ἵνα μὴ ἀθυμῶσιν. 22 Οἱ δοῦλοι,
of you, lest they be disheartened. The slaves,
ὑπακούετε κατὰ πάντα τοῖς κατὰ σάρκα
obey ye in all respects ¹the ²accord- ⁴[the]
(your) ing to flesh
κυρίοις, μὴ ἐν ὀφθαλμοδουλίαις ὡς
²lords, not with eyeservice as
ἀνθρωπάρεσκοι, ἀλλ᾿ ἐν ἁπλότητι καρδίας
men-pleasers, but in singleness of heart
φοβούμενοι τὸν κύριον. 23 ὃ ἐὰν ποιῆτε,
fearing the Lord. Whatever ye do,

your task, work heartily, as serving the Lord and not men, [24]knowing that from the Lord you will receive the inheritance as your reward; you are serving the Lord Christ. [25]For the wrongdoer will be paid back for the wrong he has done, and there is no partiality.

CHAPTER 4

MASTERS, treat your slaves justly and fairly, knowing that you also have a Master in heaven.

2 Continue steadfastly in prayer, being watchful in it with thanksgiving; [3]and pray for us also, that God may open to us a door for the word, to declare the mystery of Christ, on account of which I am in prison, [4]that I may make it clear, as I ought to speak.

5 Conduct yourselves wisely toward outsiders, making the most of the time. [6]Let your speech always be gracious, seasoned with salt, so that you may know how you ought to answer every one.

7 Tych'icus will tell you all about my affairs;

ἐκ   ψυχῆς   ἐργάζεσθε   ὡς   τῷ   κυρίῳ   καὶ
from [the] soul   work ye   as   to the   Lord   and

οὐκ   ἀνθρώποις,   24 εἰδότες   ὅτι   ἀπὸ   κυρίου
not   to men,   knowing   that   from [the] Lord

ἀπολήμψεσθε   τὴν   ἀνταπόδοσιν   τῆς   κλη-
ye will receive   the   reward   of the   in-

ρονομίας.   τῷ   κυρίῳ   Χριστῷ   δουλεύετε·
heritance.   The   Lord   Christ   ye serve;

25 ὁ   γὰρ   ἀδικῶν   κομίσεται   ὃ   ἠδίκησεν,
for the [one]   doing wrong   will receive   what he did wrong,

καὶ   οὐκ   ἔστιν   προσωπολημψία.   4 Οἱ   κύριοι,
and   there is no   respect of persons.   The   lords,

τὸ   δίκαιον   καὶ   τὴν   ἰσότητα   τοῖς   δούλοις
²the   ³just thing   ⁴and   ⁵the   ⁶equality   ⁷to the(your)   ⁸slaves

παρέχεσθε,   εἰδότες   ὅτι   καὶ   ὑμεῖς   ἔχετε
¹supply ye,   knowing   that   also   ye   have

κύριον   ἐν   οὐρανῷ.
a Lord   in   heaven.

2 Τῇ   προσευχῇ   προσκαρτερεῖτε,   γρηγο-
In the   prayer   continue ye,   watch-

ροῦντες   ἐν   αὐτῇ   ἐν   εὐχαριστίᾳ,   3 προσευ-
ing   in   it   with   thanksgiving,   pray-

χόμενοι   ἅμα   καὶ   περὶ   ἡμῶν,   ἵνα   ὁ
ing   together   also   concerning   us,   in order   that

θεὸς   ἀνοίξῃ   ἡμῖν   θύραν   τοῦ   λόγου,
God   may open   to us   a door   of the   word,

λαλῆσαι   τὸ   μυστήριον   τοῦ   Χριστοῦ,   δι'
to speak   the   mystery   –   of Christ,   because of

ὃ   καὶ   δέδεμαι,   4 ἵνα   φανερώσω   αὐτὸ
which indeed I have been   in order   I may manifest   it
bound,   that

ὡς   δεῖ   με   λαλῆσαι.   5 Ἐν   σοφίᾳ
as   it behoves   me   to speak.   In   wisdom

περιπατεῖτε   πρὸς   τοὺς   ἔξω,   τὸν   καιρὸν
walk ye   toward   the ones   outside,   ²the   ³time

ἐξαγοραζόμενοι.   6 ὁ   λόγος   ὑμῶν   πάντοτε
¹redeeming.   The   speech   of you   always
   [let it be]

ἐν   χάριτι,   ἅλατι   ἠρτυμένος,   εἰδέναι   πῶς
in   grace,   with salt   having been   to know   how
   seasoned,

δεῖ   ὑμᾶς   ἑνὶ   ἑκάστῳ   ἀποκρίνεσθαι.
it be-   you   ³one   ²each   ¹to answer.
hoves

7 Τὰ   κατ'   ἐμὲ   πάντα   γνωρίσει   ὑμῖν   Τύχικος
¹The   ³about   ⁴me   ¹all   ⁶will make   ⁷to you   ⁵Tychicus
things   known

he is a beloved brother and faithful minister and fellow servant in the Lord. [8]I have sent him to you for this very purpose, that you may know how we are and that he may encourage your hearts, [9]and with him Ones'imus, the faithful and beloved brother, who is one of yourselves. They will tell you of everything that has taken place here.

10 Aristar'chus my fellow prisoner greets you, and Mark the cousin of Barnabas (concerning whom you have received instructions—if he comes to you, receive him), [11]and Jesus who is called Justus. These are the only men of the circumcision among my fellow workers for the kingdom of God, and they have been a comfort to me. [12]Ep'aphras, who is one of yourselves, a servant of Christ Jesus, greets you, always remembering you earnestly in his prayers, that you may stand mature and fully assured in all the will of God. [13]For I bear him witness that he has worked hard for you and for those in La-odice'a and in

ὁ	ἀγαπητὸς	ἀδελφὸς	καὶ	πιστὸς	διάκονος
the	beloved	brother	and	faithful	minister

καὶ	σύνδουλος	ἐν	κυρίῳ,	8 ὃν	ἔπεμψα
and	fellow-slave	in	[the] Lord,	whom	I sent

πρὸς	ὑμᾶς	εἰς	αὐτὸ	τοῦτο,	ἵνα	γνῶτε
to	you	for	this very thing,		in order that	ye might know

τὰ	περὶ	ἡμῶν	καὶ	παρακαλέσῃ	τὰς
the things	concerning	us	and	he might comfort	the

καρδίας	ὑμῶν,	9 σὺν	Ὀνησίμῳ	τῷ	πιστῷ
hearts	of you,	with	Onesimus	the	faithful

καὶ	ἀγαπητῷ	ἀδελφῷ,	ὅς	ἐστιν	ἐξ	ὑμῶν·
and	beloved	brother,	who	is	of	you;

πάντα	ὑμῖν	γνωρίσουσιν	τὰ	ὧδε.
[1]all	[5]to you	[4]they will make known	[2]the	[3]here.

10 Ἀσπάζεται	ὑμᾶς	Ἀρίσταρχος	ὁ
[3]greets	[4]you	[1]Aristarchus	[2]the

συναιχμάλωτός	μου,	καὶ	Μάρκος	ὁ	ἀνεψιὸς
[3]fellow-captive	[4]of me,	and	Mark	the	cousin

Βαρναβᾶ,	(περὶ	οὗ	ἐλάβετε	ἐντολάς,	ἐὰν
of Barnabas,	(concerning	whom	ye received	commandments,	if

ἔλθη	πρὸς	ὑμᾶς,	δέξασθε	αὐτόν,)	11 καὶ
he comes	to	you,	receive ye	him,)	and

Ἰησοῦς	ὁ	λεγόμενος	Ἰοῦστος,	οἱ	ὄντες
Jesus	the [one]	being named	Justus,	the [ones]	being

ἐκ	περιτομῆς	οὗτοι	μόνοι	συνεργοὶ	εἰς
of	[the] circumcision	these	only	fellow-workers	for

τὴν	βασιλείαν	τοῦ	θεοῦ,	οἵτινες	ἐγενή-
the	kingdom	–	of God,	who	be-

θησάν	μοι	παρηγορία.	12 ἀσπάζεται	ὑμᾶς
came	to me	a comfort.	[2]greets	[3]you

Ἐπαφρᾶς	ὁ	ἐξ	ὑμῶν,	δοῦλος	Χριστοῦ
[1]Epaphras	the [one]	of	you,	a slave	of Christ

Ἰησοῦ,	πάντοτε	ἀγωνιζόμενος	ὑπὲρ	ὑμῶν
Jesus,	always	struggling	on behalf of	you

ἐν	ταῖς	προσευχαῖς,	ἵνα	σταθῆτε	τέλειοι
in	the	prayers,	in order that	ye may stand	complete

καὶ	πεπληροφορημένοι	ἐν	παντὶ	θελήματι
and	having been fully assured	in	all	[the] will

τοῦ	Θεοῦ.	13 μαρτυρῶ	γὰρ	αὐτῷ	ὅτι
–	of God.	For I bear witness		to him	that

ἔχει	πολὺν	πόνον	ὑπὲρ	ὑμῶν	καὶ	τῶν
he has	much	distress	on behalf of	you	and	the ones

ἐν	Λαοδικείᾳ	καὶ	τῶν	ἐν	Ἱεραπόλει.
in	Laodicea	and	the ones	in	Hierapolis.

Hi-erap'olis. ¹⁴Luke the beloved physician and Demas greet you. ¹⁵Give my greetings to the brethren at La-odice'a, and to Nympha and the church in her house. ¹⁶And when this letter has been read among you, have it read also in the church of the La-odice'ans; and see that you read also the letter from La-odice'a. ¹⁷And say to Archip'pus, "See that you fulfil the ministry which you have received in the Lord." 18 I, Paul, write this greeting with my own hand. Remember my fetters. Grace be with you.

14 ἀσπάζεται ὑμᾶς Λουκᾶς ὁ ἰατρὸς ὁ
   ˀgreets   ⁿyou   ¹Luke   ²the ⁴physician -

ἀγαπητὸς καὶ Δημᾶς.   15 Ἀσπάσασθε
  ³beloved   ⁿand   ⁶Demas.   Greet ye

τοὺς ἐν Λαοδικείᾳ ἀδελφοὺς καὶ Νύμφαν
 ¹the ²in ⁴Laodicea   ²brothers and   Nymphas

καὶ τὴν κατ᾽ οἶκον αὐτῆς ἐκκλησίαν.
and ¹the ²at ⁴[the] house ⁵of her   ²church.

16 καὶ ὅταν ἀναγνωσθῇ παρ᾽ ὑμῖν ἡ
   And whenever   is read   before   you the(this)

ἐπιστολή, ποιήσατε ἵνα καὶ ἐν τῇ
  epistle,   cause   in order that ⁸also   ²in ⁴the

Λαοδικέων ἐκκλησίᾳ ἀναγνωσθῇ, καὶ τὴν
 ⁶of [the]   ⁵church   ¹it is read,   and   ⁵the
Laodiceans   [one]

ἐκ Λαοδικείας ἵνα καὶ ὑμεῖς ἀναγνῶτε.
 ⁶of   ˀLaodicea ¹in order ²also ²ye   ⁴read.
                that

17 καὶ εἴπατε Ἀρχίππῳ· βλέπε τὴν
   And   tell   Archippus : Look [to]   the

διακονίαν ἣν παρέλαβες ἐν κυρίῳ, ἵνα
  ministry   which thou receivedst in [the] Lord, in order that

αὐτὴν πληροῖς.
  ²it   ¹thou mayest fulfil.

18 Ὁ ἀσπασμὸς τῇ ἐμῇ χειρὶ Παύλου.
   The   greeting - by my hand[,] of Paul.

μνημονεύετέ μου τῶν δεσμῶν. ἡ χάρις
Remember ye of me the   bonds. - Grace [be]

μεθ᾽ ὑμῶν.
with   you.

I.
THESSALONIANS
1

CHAPTER 1

PAUL, Silva'nus, and Timothy,
To the church of the Thessalo'nians in God the Father and the Lord Jesus Christ:
Grace to you and peace.
2 We give thanks to God always for you all,

ΠΡΟΣ ΘΕΣΣΑΛΟΝΙΚΕΙΣ Α
To Thessalonians 1

1 Παῦλος καὶ Σιλουανὸς καὶ Τιμόθεος
   Paul   and   Silvanus   and   Timothy

τῇ ἐκκλησίᾳ Θεσσαλονικέων ἐν θεῷ πατρὶ
to the church of [the] Thessalonians in God [the] Father

καὶ κυρίῳ Ἰησοῦ Χριστῷ· χάρις ὑμῖν
and [the] Lord Jesus Christ: Grace [be] to you

καὶ εἰρήνη.
and   peace.

2 Εὐχαριστοῦμεν τῷ θεῷ πάντοτε περὶ
  We give thanks - to God always con-
                            cerning

constantly mentioning you in our prayers, [3]remembering before our God and Father your work of faith and labor of love and steadfastness of hope in our Lord Jesus Christ. [4]For we know, brethren beloved by God, that he has chosen you; [5]for our gospel came to you not only in word, but also in power and in the Holy Spirit and with full conviction. You know what kind of men we proved to be among you for your sake. [6]And you became imitators of us and of the Lord, for you received the word in much affliction, with joy inspired by the Holy Spirit; [7]so that you became an example to all the believers in Macedo'nia and in Acha'ia. [8]For not only has the word of the Lord sounded forth from you in Macedo'nia and Acha'ia, but your faith in God has gone forth everywhere, so that we need not say anything. [9]For they them-

πάντων   ὑμῶν,   μνείαν   ποιούμενοι   ἐπὶ   τῶν
[2]all   [1]you,   mention   making   on(in)   the

προσευχῶν   ἡμῶν,   ἀδιαλείπτως   3 μνημο-
prayers,   of us,   unceasingly   remember-

νεύοντες   ὑμῶν   τοῦ   ἔργου   τῆς   πίστεως
ing   of you   the   work   –   of faith

καὶ   τοῦ   κόπου   τῆς   ἀγάπης   καὶ   τῆς
and   the   labour   –   of love   and   the

ὑπομονῆς   τῆς   ἐλπίδος   τοῦ   κυρίου   ἡμῶν
endurance   –   of hope   of(in) the Lord   of us

Ἰησοῦ   Χριστοῦ   ἔμπροσθεν   τοῦ   θεοῦ   καὶ
Jesus   Christ   before   the   God   and

πατρὸς   ἡμῶν,   4 εἰδότες,   ἀδελφοὶ   ἠγαπημένοι
Father   of us,   knowing,   brothers   having been loved

ὑπὸ   [τοῦ]   θεοῦ,   τὴν   ἐκλογὴν   ὑμῶν,
by   –   God,   the   choice   of you,

5 ὅτι   τὸ   εὐαγγέλιον   ἡμῶν   οὐκ   ἐγενήθη
because   the   gospel   of us   became not

εἰς   ὑμᾶς   ἐν   λόγῳ   μόνον,   ἀλλὰ   καὶ   ἐν
to   you   in   word   only,   but   also   in

δυνάμει   καὶ   ἐν   πνεύματι   ἁγίῳ   καὶ
power   and   in   Spirit   Holy   and

πληροφορίᾳ   πολλῇ,   καθὼς   οἴδατε   οἷοι
[2]assurance   [1]much,   as   ye know   what sort

ἐγενήθημεν   ἐν   ὑμῖν   δι᾽   ὑμᾶς.   6 καὶ
we were   among you   because of you.   And

ὑμεῖς   μιμηταὶ   ἡμῶν   ἐγενήθητε   καὶ   τοῦ
[1]ye   [2]imitators [4]of us   [3]became   and   of the

κυρίου,   δεξάμενοι   τὸν   λόγον   ἐν   θλίψει
Lord,   welcoming   the   word   in   [2]affliction

πολλῇ   μετὰ   χαρᾶς   πνεύματος   ἁγίου,   7 ὥστε
[1]much   with   joy   of [2]Spirit   [1][the] Holy,   so as

γενέσθαι   ὑμᾶς   τύπον   πᾶσιν   τοῖς   πιστεύουσιν
to become   you[b]   a pattern   to all   the [ones] believing
=so that ye became

ἐν   τῇ   Μακεδονίᾳ   καὶ   ἐν   τῇ   Ἀχαΐᾳ.
in   –   Macedonia   and   in   –   Achaia.

8 ἀφ᾽   ὑμῶν   γὰρ   ἐξήχηται   ὁ   λόγος   τοῦ
[2]from   [3]you   [1]For   sounded   the   word   of the

κυρίου   οὐ   μόνον   ἐν   τῇ   Μακεδονίᾳ   καὶ
Lord   not   only   in   –   Macedonia   and

Ἀχαΐᾳ,   ἀλλ᾽   ἐν   παντὶ   τόπῳ   ἡ   πίστις
Achaia,   but   in   every   place   the   faith

ὑμῶν   ἡ   πρὸς   τὸν   θεὸν   ἐξελήλυθεν,   ὥστε
of you   –   toward   –   God   has gone out,   so as

μὴ   χρείαν   ἔχειν   ἡμᾶς   λαλεῖν   τι·   9 αὐτοὶ
not   need   to have   us[b]   to speak anything;   [2][them]-
=so that we have no need   selves

selves report concerning us what a welcome we had among you, and how you turned to God from idols, to serve a living and true God, [10] and to wait for his Son from heaven, whom he raised from the dead, Jesus who delivers us from the wrath to come.

γὰρ περὶ ἡμῶν ἀπαγγέλλουσιν ὁποίαν
¹for ⁴concerning ⁵us ³they relate what sort of

εἴσοδον ἔσχομεν πρὸς ὑμᾶς, καὶ πῶς
entrance we had to you, and how

ἐπεστρέψατε πρὸς τὸν θεὸν ἀπὸ τῶν
ye turned to - God from the

εἰδώλων δουλεύειν θεῷ ζῶντι καὶ ἀληθινῷ,
idols to serve a God living and true,

10 καὶ ἀναμένειν τὸν υἱὸν αὐτοῦ ἐκ
and to await the Son of him from

τῶν οὐρανῶν, ὃν ἤγειρεν ἐκ τῶν νεκρῶν,
the heavens, whom he raised from the dead,

Ἰησοῦν τὸν ῥυόμενον ἡμᾶς ἐκ τῆς ὀργῆς
Jesus the [one] delivering us from the wrath

τῆς ἐρχομένης.
- coming.

CHAPTER 2

FOR you yourselves know, brethren, that our visit to you was not in vain; ²but though we had already suffered and been shamefully treated at Philippi, as you know, we had courage in our God to declare to you the gospel of God in the face of great opposition. ³For our appeal does not spring from error or uncleanness, nor is it made with guile; ⁴but just as we have been approved by God to be entrusted with the gospel, so we speak, not to please men, but to please God who tests our hearts. ⁵For we never used either words of flattery, as you know, or a cloak

2 Αὐτοὶ γὰρ οἴδατε, ἀδελφοί, τὴν
For [your]selves ye know, brothers, the

εἴσοδον ἡμῶν τὴν πρὸς ὑμᾶς, ὅτι οὐ
entrance of us - to you, that not

κενὴ γέγονεν, 2 ἀλλὰ προπαθόντες καὶ
in vain it has been, but having previously and
suffered

ὑβρισθέντες καθὼς οἴδατε ἐν Φιλίπποις
having been as ye know in Philippi
insulted

ἐπαρρησιασάμεθα ἐν τῷ θεῷ ἡμῶν λαλῆσαι
we were bold in the God of us to speak

πρὸς ὑμᾶς τὸ εὐαγγέλιον τοῦ θεοῦ ἐν
to you the gospel - of God in

πολλῷ ἀγῶνι. 3 ἡ γὰρ παράκλησις
much struggle. For the exhortation

ἡμῶν οὐκ ἐκ πλάνης οὐδὲ ἐξ ἀκαθαρσίας
of us not of error nor of uncleanness

οὐδὲ ἐν δόλῳ, 4 ἀλλὰ καθὼς δεδοκιμάσμεθα
nor in guile, but as we have been
approved

ὑπὸ τοῦ θεοῦ πιστευθῆναι τὸ εὐαγγέλιον
by - God to be entrusted [with] the gospel

οὕτως λαλοῦμεν, οὐχ ὡς ἀνθρώποις ἀρέ-
so we speak, not as ¹men ¹pleas-

σκοντες, ἀλλὰ θεῷ τῷ δοκιμάζοντι τὰς
ing, but God the [one] proving the

καρδίας ἡμῶν. 5 οὔτε γὰρ ποτε ἐν
hearts of us. For neither then with

λόγῳ κολακείας ἐγενήθημεν, καθὼς οἴδατε,
word of flattery were we, as ye know.

for greed, as God is witness; [6] nor did we seek glory from men, whether from you or from others, though we might have made demands as apostles of Christ. [7] But we were gentle[a] among you, like a nurse taking care of her children. [8] So, being affectionately desirous of you, we were ready to share with you not only the gospel of God but also our own selves, because you had become very dear to us.

[9] For you remember our labor and toil, brethren; we worked night and day, that we might not burden any of you, while we preached to you the gospel of God. [10] You are witnesses, and God also, how holy and righteous and blameless was our behavior to you believers; [11] for you know how, like a father with his children, we exhorted each one of you and encouraged you and charged you [12] to lead a life worthy of God, who

οὔτε   ἐν   προφάσει   πλεονεξίας,   θεὸς   μάρτυς,
nor   with   pretext   of covetousness,   God [is] witness,

6 οὔτε   ζητοῦντες   ἐξ   ἀνθρώπων   δόξαν,
  nor   seeking   from   men   glory,

οὔτε   ἀφ'   ὑμῶν   οὔτε   ἀπ'   ἄλλων,   7 δυνάμε-
neither   from   you   nor   from   others,   being

νοι   ἐν   βάρει   εἶναι   ὡς   Χριστοῦ   ἀπόστολοι·
able   [3]with   [2]weight*   [1]to be   as   [2]of Christ   [1]apostles;

ἀλλὰ   ἐγενήθημεν   ἤπιοι   ἐν   μέσῳ   ὑμῶν,
but   we were   gentle   in [the]   midst   of you,

ὡς   ἐὰν   τροφὸς   θάλπῃ   τὰ   ἑαυτῆς   τέκνα·
as   if   a nurse   should   [1]the   [2]of herself   [3]children;
                    cherish

8 οὕτως   ὁμειρόμενοι   ὑμῶν   ηὐδοκοῦμεν
  so   longing for   you   we were well
                        pleased

μεταδοῦναι   ὑμῖν   οὐ   μόνον   τὸ   εὐαγγέλιον
to impart   to you   not   only   the   gospel

τοῦ   θεοῦ   ἀλλὰ   καὶ   τὰς   ἑαυτῶν   ψυχάς,
-    of God   but   also   [1]the   [2]of ourselves   [3]souls,

διότι   ἀγαπητοὶ   ἡμῖν   ἐγενήθητε.   9 μνημο-
because   [3]beloved   [2]to us   [1]ye became.   ye re-

νεύετε   γάρ,   ἀδελφοί,   τὸν   κόπον   ἡμῶν
member   For,   brothers,   the   labour   of us

καὶ   τὸν   μόχθον·   νυκτὸς   καὶ   ἡμέρας
and   the   toil;   night   and   day

ἐργαζόμενοι   πρὸς   τὸ   μὴ   ἐπιβαρῆσαί   τινα
working   for   the   not   to put a burden   any-
                        on   one

ὑμῶν   ἐκηρύξαμεν   εἰς   ὑμᾶς   τὸ   εὐαγγέλιον
of you   we proclaimed   to   you   the   gospel

τοῦ   θεοῦ.   10 ὑμεῖς   μάρτυρες   καὶ   ὁ
-    of God.   Ye [are]   witnesses   and   -

θεός,   ὡς   ὁσίως   καὶ   δικαίως   καὶ   ἀμέμπτως
God,   how   holily   and   righteously   and   blamelessly

ὑμῖν   τοῖς   πιστεύουσιν   ἐγενήθημεν,   11 καθά-
[1]to you   [3]the [ones]   [4]believing   [1]we were,   even

περ   οἴδατε   ὡς   ἕνα   ἕκαστον   ὑμῶν   ὡς
as   ye know   how   [2]one   [1]each   of you   as

πατὴρ   τέκνα   ἑαυτοῦ   παρακαλοῦντες   ὑμᾶς
a father   children   of himself   exhorting   you

καὶ   παραμυθούμενοι 12 καὶ   μαρτυρόμενοι   εἰς
and   consoling   and   witnessing   for

τὸ   περιπατεῖν   ὑμᾶς   ἀξίως   τοῦ   θεοῦ
the   to walk   you[b]   worthily   -   of God
=that ye should walk

---

[a] Other ancient authorities read babes

* ? dignity, authority.

calls you into his own kingdom and glory. 13 And we also thank God constantly for this, that when you received the word of God which you heard from us, you accepted it not as the word of men but as what it really is, the word of God, which is at work in you believers. ¹⁴For you, brethren, became imitators of the churches of God in Christ Jesus which are in Judea; for you suffered the same things from your own countrymen as they did from the Jews, ¹⁵who killed both the Lord Jesus and the prophets, and drove us out, and displease God and oppose all men ¹⁶by hindering us from speaking to the Gentiles that they may be saved—so as always to fill up the measure of their sins. But God's wrath has come upon them at last!ᵇ 17 But since we were bereft of you, brethren,

τοῦ καλοῦντος ὑμᾶς εἰς τὴν ἑαυτοῦ
the [one] calling you to ¹the ⁵of himself
βασιλείαν καὶ δόξαν.
²kingdom ³and ⁴glory.

13 Καὶ διὰ τοῦτο καὶ ἡμεῖς εὐχαρισ-
And therefore also we give
τοῦμεν τῷ θεῷ ἀδιαλείπτως, ὅτι παρα-
thanks – to God unceasingly, that having
λαβόντες λόγον ἀκοῆς παρ' ἡμῶν τοῦ
received ¹[the] word ³of hearing ⁴from ⁵us –
θεοῦ ἐδέξασθε οὐ λόγον ἀνθρώπων ἀλλὰ
²of God ye welcomed not [as] a word of men but
[it]
καθὼς ἀληθῶς ἐστιν λόγον θεοῦ, ὃς
as truly it is a word of God, which
καὶ ἐνεργεῖται ἐν ὑμῖν τοῖς πιστεύουσιν.
also operates in you the [ones] believing.

14 ὑμεῖς γὰρ μιμηταὶ ἐγενήθητε, ἀδελφοί,
For ye ²imitators ¹became, brothers,
τῶν ἐκκλησιῶν τοῦ θεοῦ τῶν οὐσῶν ἐν
of the churches – of God the – being in
τῇ Ἰουδαίᾳ ἐν Χριστῷ Ἰησοῦ, ὅτι τὰ
– Judæa in Christ Jesus, because ⁴the
αὐτὰ ἐπάθετε καὶ ὑμεῖς ὑπὸ τῶν ἰδίων
⁵same ³suffered ²also ¹ye by the(your) own
things
συμφυλετῶν, καθὼς καὶ αὐτοὶ ὑπὸ τῶν
fellow-tribesmen, as also they by the
Ἰουδαίων, 15 τῶν καὶ τὸν κύριον
Jews, the [ones] ¹both ²the ⁴Lord
ἀποκτεινάντων Ἰησοῦν καὶ τοὺς προφήτας,
³killing ⁵Jesus and the prophets,
καὶ ἡμᾶς ἐκδιωξάντων, καὶ θεῷ μὴ
and ²us ¹chasing ³out, and ²God ¹not
ἀρεσκόντων, καὶ πᾶσιν ἀνθρώποις ἐναντίων,
²pleasing, and to all men contrary,
16 κωλυόντων ἡμᾶς τοῖς ἔθνεσιν λαλῆσαι
hindering us ²to the ³nations ¹to speak
=from speaking...
ἵνα σωθῶσιν, εἰς τὸ ἀναπληρῶσαι αὐτῶν
in order they may for the to fill up ³of them
that be saved,
τὰς ἁμαρτίας πάντοτε. ἔφθασεν δὲ ἐπ'
¹the ²sins always. But ³came ⁴on
αὐτοὺς ἡ ὀργὴ εἰς τέλος.
⁵them ¹the ²wrath to [the] end.

17 Ἡμεῖς δέ, ἀδελφοί, ἀπορφανισθέντες
But we brothers, being bereaved

ᵇ Or completely, or for ever
I.G.E.—27

for a short time, in person not in heart, we endeavored the more eagerly and with great desire to see you face to face; [18] because we wanted to come to you— I, Paul, again and again —but Satan hindered us. [19] For what is our hope or joy or crown of boasting before our Lord Jesus at his coming? Is it not you? [20] For you are our glory and joy.

ἀφ᾽ ὑμῶν πρὸς καιρὸν ὥρας προσώπῳ
from you   for   time of an hour in face
                                   (presence)

οὐ καρδίᾳ, περισσοτέρως ἐσπουδάσαμεν τὸ
not in heart, more abundantly were eager ²the

πρόσωπον ὑμῶν ἰδεῖν ἐν πολλῇ ἐπιθυμίᾳ.
³face   ⁴of you ¹to see with much   desire.

18 διότι ἠθελήσαμεν ἐλθεῖν πρὸς ὑμᾶς,
Wherefore we wished to come to   you,

ἐγὼ μὲν Παῦλος καὶ ἅπαξ καὶ δίς,
I ²indeed ¹Paul both once and twice
                                  (again),

καὶ ἐνέκοψεν ἡμᾶς ὁ σατανᾶς.   19 τίς
and ²hindered ³us - ¹Satan.   what

γὰρ ἡμῶν ἐλπὶς ἢ χαρὰ ἢ στέφανος
For [is] ²of us ¹hope or joy or crown

καυχήσεως — ἢ οὐχὶ καὶ ὑμεῖς —
of boasting - - not even ye —

ἔμπροσθεν τοῦ κυρίου ἡμῶν Ἰησοῦ
before   the Lord of us Jesus

ἐν τῇ αὐτοῦ παρουσίᾳ; 20 ὑμεῖς γάρ
in(at) the ²of him ¹presence?   for ye

ἐστε ἡ δόξα ἡμῶν καὶ ἡ χαρά.
are ¹the ²glory ⁶of us ²and ⁴the ⁵joy.

CHAPTER 3

THEREFORE when we could bear it no longer, we were willing to be left behind at Athens alone, [2] and we sent Timothy, our brother and God's servant in the gospel of Christ, to establish you in your faith and to exhort you, [3] that no one be moved by these afflictions. You yourselves know that this is to be our lot. [4] For when we were with you, we told you beforehand that we were to suffer affliction; just as it has come to pass, and as you know.

3 Διὸ μηκέτι στέγοντες ηὐδοκήσαμεν
Wherefore no longer bearing up we were well pleased

καταλειφθῆναι ἐν Ἀθήναις μόνοι, 2 καὶ
to be left   in Athens   alone,   and

ἐπέμψαμεν Τιμόθεον, τὸν ἀδελφὸν ἡμῶν
we sent   Timothy, the brother of us

καὶ συνεργὸν τοῦ θεοῦ ἐν τῷ εὐαγγελίῳ
and fellow-worker - of God in the gospel

τοῦ Χριστοῦ, εἰς τὸ στηρίξαι ὑμᾶς καὶ
- of Christ, for the to establish you and

παρακαλέσαι ὑπὲρ τῆς πίστεως ὑμῶν 3 τὸ
to exhort on behalf of the faith of you -

μηδένα σαίνεσθαι ἐν ταῖς θλίψεσιν ταύταις.
no one to be drawn by   these afflictions.
       aside[b]

αὐτοὶ γὰρ οἴδατε ὅτι εἰς τοῦτο κείμεθα·
For [your]selves ye know that to this we are
                                     appointed;

4 καὶ γὰρ ὅτε πρὸς ὑμᾶς ἦμεν,
  for even when with you we were,

προελέγομεν ὑμῖν ὅτι μέλλομεν θλίβεσθαι,
we said before to you that we are about to be afflicted,

καθὼς καὶ ἐγένετο καὶ οἴδατε. 5 διὰ
as indeed it happened and ye know.   There-

⁵For this reason, when I could bear it no longer, I sent that I might know your faith, for fear that somehow the tempter had tempted you and that our labor would be in vain.

6 But now that Timothy has come to us from you, and has brought us the good news of your faith and love and reported that you always remember us kindly and long to see us, as we long to see you— ⁷for this reason, brethren, in all our distress and affliction we have been comforted about you through your faith; ⁸for now we live, if you stand fast in the Lord. ⁹For what thanksgiving can we render to God for you, for all the joy which we feel for your sake before our God, ¹⁰praying earnestly night and day that we may see you face to face and supply what is lacking in your faith?

11 Now may our God and Father himself, and our Lord Jesus, direct our way to you; ¹²and

τοῦτο κἀγὼ μηκέτι στέγων ἔπεμψα εἰς
fore I also no longer bearing up sent for

τὸ γνῶναι τὴν πίστιν ὑμῶν, μή πως
the to know the faith of you, lest [some]how

ἐπείρασεν ὑμᾶς ὁ πειράζων καὶ εἰς
²tempted ⁸you ¹the [one] ²tempting and in
= the tempter

κενὸν γένηται ὁ κόπος ἡμῶν. 6 Ἄρτι
vain became the labour of us.   now

δὲ ἐλθόντος Τιμοθέου πρὸς ἡμᾶς ἀφ'
But coming Timothyᵃ to us from
= when Timothy came

ὑμῶν καὶ εὐαγγελισαμένου ἡμῖν τὴν πίστιν
you and announcing good newsᵃ to us [of] the faith

καὶ τὴν ἀγάπην ὑμῶν, καὶ ὅτι ἔχετε
and the love of you, and that ye have

μνείαν ἡμῶν ἀγαθὴν πάντοτε, ἐπιποθοῦντες
²remem- ³of us ¹good always, longing
brance

ἡμᾶς ἰδεῖν καθάπερ καὶ ἡμεῖς ὑμᾶς,
²us ¹to see even as also we you,

7 διὰ τοῦτο παρεκλήθημεν, ἀδελφοί, ἐφ'
therefore we were comforted, brothers, over

ὑμῖν ἐπὶ πάσῃ τῇ ἀνάγκῃ καὶ θλίψει
you on all the distress and affliction

ἡμῶν διὰ τῆς ὑμῶν πίστεως, 8 ὅτι
of us through the ²of you ¹faith, because

νῦν ζῶμεν ἐὰν ὑμεῖς στήκετε ἐν κυρίῳ.
now we live if ye stand in [the] Lord.

9 τίνα γὰρ εὐχαριστίαν δυνάμεθα τῷ θεῷ
For what thanks are we able - to God

ἀνταποδοῦναι περὶ ὑμῶν ἐπὶ πάσῃ τῇ
to return concerning you over all the

χαρᾷ ᾗ χαίρομεν δι' ὑμᾶς ἔμπροσθεν
joy [with] we rejoice because you before
which of

τοῦ θεοῦ ἡμῶν, 10 νυκτὸς καὶ ἡμέρας
the God of us, night and day

ὑπερεκπερισσοῦ δεόμενοι εἰς τὸ ἰδεῖν ὑμῶν
exceedingly petitioning for the to see of you

τὸ πρόσωπον καὶ καταρτίσαι τὰ ὑστερήματα
the face and to adjust the shortcomings

τῆς πίστεως ὑμῶν; 11 Αὐτὸς δὲ ὁ θεὸς
of the faith of you? Now [him]self the God

καὶ πατὴρ ἡμῶν καὶ ὁ κύριος ἡμῶν
and Father of us and the Lord of us

Ἰησοῦς κατευθύναι τὴν ὁδὸν ἡμῶν πρὸς
Jesus may he direct the way of us to

may the Lord make you increase and abound in love to one another and to all men, as we do to you, [13] so that he may establish your hearts unblamable in holiness before our God and Father, at the coming of our Lord Jesus with all his saints.

ὑμᾶς·	12	ὑμᾶς	δὲ	ὁ	κύριος	πλεονάσαι
you;		and	[4]you	[1]the	[2]Lord	[3]make [5]to abound

καὶ	περισσεῦσαι	τῇ	ἀγάπῃ	εἰς	ἀλλήλους
and	to exceed	–	in love	to	one another

καὶ	εἰς	πάντας,	καθάπερ	καὶ	ἡμεῖς
and	to	all men,	even as	also	we

εἰς	ὑμᾶς,	13	εἰς	τὸ	στηρίξαι	ὑμῶν	τὰς
to	you,		for	the	to establish	of you	the

καρδίας	ἀμέμπτους	ἐν	ἁγιωσύνῃ	ἔμπροσθεν
hearts	blameless	in	holiness	before

τοῦ	θεοῦ	καὶ	πατρὸς	ἡμῶν	ἐν	τῇ	παρουσίᾳ
the	God	and	Father	of us	in(at)	the	presence

τοῦ	κυρίου	ἡμῶν	Ἰησοῦ	μετὰ	πάντων
of the	Lord	of us	Jesus	with	all

τῶν	ἁγίων	αὐτοῦ.
the	saints	of him.

CHAPTER 4

FINALLY, brethren, we beseech and exhort you in the Lord Jesus, that as you learned from us how you ought to live and to please God, just as you are doing, you do so more and more. [2] For you know what instructions we gave you through the Lord Jesus. [3] For this is the will of God, your sanctification: that you abstain from immorality; [4] that each one of you know how to take a wife for himself in holiness and honor, [5] not in the passion of lust like heathen who do not know God; [6] that no man transgress, and

4	Λοιπὸν	οὖν,	ἀδελφοί,	ἐρωτῶμεν	ὑμᾶς
	For the rest	therefore,	brothers,	we ask	you

καὶ	παρακαλοῦμεν	ἐν	κυρίῳ	Ἰησοῦ,	ἵνα
and	we beseech	in	[the] Lord	Jesus,	in order that

καθὼς	παρελάβετε	παρ'	ἡμῶν	τὸ	πῶς
as	ye received	from	us	the	how

δεῖ	ὑμᾶς	περιπατεῖν	καὶ	ἀρέσκειν	θεῷ,
it behoves	you	to walk	and	to please	God,

καθὼς	καὶ	περιπατεῖτε,	ἵνα	περισσεύητε
as	indeed	ye do walk,	in order that	ye abound

μᾶλλον.	2	οἴδατε	γὰρ	τίνας	παραγγελίας
more.		For ye know		what	injunctions

ἐδώκαμεν	ὑμῖν	διὰ	τοῦ	κυρίου	Ἰησοῦ.
we gave	you	through	the	Lord	Jesus.

3	Τοῦτο	γάρ	ἐστιν	θέλημα	τοῦ	θεοῦ,
	For this		is	[the] will	–	of God,

ὁ	ἁγιασμὸς	ὑμῶν,	ἀπέχεσθαι	ὑμᾶς	ἀπὸ
the	sanctification	of you,	to abstain	you[b]	from

τῆς	πορνείας,	4	εἰδέναι	ἕκαστον	ὑμῶν
–	fornication,		[3]to know*	[1]each one[b]	[2]of you

τὸ	ἑαυτοῦ	σκεῦος	κτᾶσθαι	ἐν	ἁγιασμῷ
[5]the	[7]of himself	[6]vessel	[4]to possess	in	sanctification

καὶ	τιμῇ,	5	μὴ	ἐν	πάθει	ἐπιθυμίας
and	honour,		not	in	passion	of lust

καθάπερ	καὶ	τὰ	ἔθνη	τὰ	μὴ	εἰδότα
even as	indeed	the	nations	–	not	knowing

τὸν	θεόν,	6	τὸ	μὴ	ὑπερβαίνειν	καὶ
–	God,		–	not	to go beyond	and

* That is, " to be able "; see note on page xviii.

wrong his brother in this matter,ᶜ because the Lord is an avenger in all these things, as we solemnly forewarned you. ⁷For God has not called us for uncleanness, but in holiness. ⁸Therefore whoever disregards this, disregards not man but God, who gives his Holy Spirit to you.

9 But concerning love of the brethren you have no need to have any one write to you, for you yourselves have been taught by God to love one another; ¹⁰and indeed you do love all the brethren throughout Macedo′nia. But we exhort you, brethren, to do so more and more, ¹¹to aspire to live quietly, to mind your own affairs, and to work with your hands, as we charged you; ¹²so that you may command the respect of outsiders, and be dependent on nobody.

13 But we would not have you ignorant,

πλεονεκτεῖν   ἐν   τῷ   πράγματι   τὸν   ἀδελφὸν
to defraud   in   the   matter   the   brother

αὐτοῦ,   διότι   ἔκδικος   κύριος   περὶ   πάντων
of him,   be-   ²[the]   ¹[the] Lord   con-   all
          cause   avenger   [is]   cerning

τούτων,   καθὼς   καὶ   προείπαμεν   ὑμῖν   καὶ
these,   as   in-   we previously   you   and
               deed   told

διεμαρτυράμεθα.   7 οὐ   γὰρ   ἐκάλεσεν   ἡμᾶς
solemnly witnessed.   For ⁴not   ²called   ³us

ὁ   θεὸς   ἐπὶ   ἀκαθαρσίᾳ   ἀλλ᾽   ἐν   ἁγιασμῷ.
–   ¹God   to   uncleanness   but   in   sanctification.

8 τοιγαροῦν   ὁ   ἀθετῶν   οὐκ   ἄνθρωπον
Wherefore   the [one] rejecting   ²not   ³man

ἀθετεῖ   ἀλλὰ   τὸν   θεὸν   τὸν   καὶ   διδόντα
¹rejects   but   –   God   the   in-   giving
                        [one]   deed

τὸ   πνεῦμα   αὐτοῦ   τὸ   ἅγιον   εἰς   ὑμᾶς.
the   ²Spirit   ³of him   –   ¹Holy   to   you.

9 Περὶ   δὲ   τῆς   φιλαδελφίας   οὐ   χρείαν
Now concerning   –   brotherly love   not   need

ἔχετε   γράφειν   ὑμῖν·   αὐτοὶ   γὰρ   ὑμεῖς
ye have   to write   to you;   for ²[your]selves   ¹ye
[for me]

θεοδίδακτοί   ἐστε   εἰς   τὸ   ἀγαπᾶν   ἀλλήλους·
⁴taught by God   ³are   for   the   to love   one another;

10 καὶ   γὰρ   ποιεῖτε   αὐτὸ   εἰς   πάντας
for indeed   ye do   it   toward   all

τοὺς   ἀδελφοὺς   [τοὺς]   ἐν   ὅλῃ   τῇ   Μακεδο-
the   brothers   –   in   all   the   Macedo-

νίᾳ.   Παρακαλοῦμεν   δὲ   ὑμᾶς,   ἀδελφοί,
nia.   But we exhort   you,   brothers,

περισσεύειν   μᾶλλον,   11 καὶ   φιλοτιμεῖσθαι
to abound   more,   and   to strive eagerly

ἡσυχάζειν   καὶ   πράσσειν   τὰ   ἴδια   καὶ
to be quiet   and   to practise   the   own   and
                              (your)   things

ἐργάζεσθαι   ταῖς   χερσὶν   ὑμῶν,   καθὼς   ὑμῖν
to work   with the   hands   of you,   as   ²you

παρηγγείλαμεν,   12 ἵνα   περιπατῆτε   εὐσχη-
¹we enjoined,   in or-   ye may walk   becom-
              der that

μόνως   πρὸς   τοὺς   ἔξω   καὶ   μηδενὸς
ingly   toward   the [ones]   outside   and   ³of nothing

χρείαν   ἔχητε.
²need   ¹ye may have.

13 Οὐ   θέλομεν   δὲ   ὑμᾶς   ἀγνοεῖν,   ἀδελφοί,
Now we do not wish   you   to be   brothers,
                        ignorant,

ᶜ Or defraud his brother in business

brethren, concerning those who are asleep, that you may not grieve as others do who have no hope. [14] For since we believe that Jesus died and rose again, even so, through Jesus, God will bring with him those who have fallen asleep. [15] For this we declare to you by the word of the Lord, that we who are alive, who are left until the coming of the Lord, shall not precede those who have fallen asleep. [16] For the Lord himself will descend from heaven with a cry of command, with the archangel's call, and with the sound of the trumpet of God. And the dead in Christ will rise first; [17] then we who are alive, who are left, shall be caught up together with them in the clouds to meet the Lord in the air; and so we shall always be with the Lord. [18] Therefore comfort one another with these words.

περὶ   τῶν   κοιμωμένων,   ἵνα   μὴ   λυπῆσθε
con-   the   sleeping,   lest   not   ye grieve
cerning [ones]

καθὼς   καὶ   οἱ   λοιποὶ   οἱ   μὴ   ἔχοντες
as   indeed   the   rest   -   not   having

ἐλπίδα.   14 εἰ   γὰρ   πιστεύομεν   ὅτι   Ἰησοῦς
hope.   For if   we believe   that   Jesus

ἀπέθανεν   καὶ   ἀνέστη,   οὕτως   καὶ   ὁ   θεὸς
died   and   rose again,   so   also   -   ⁵God

τοὺς   κοιμηθέντας   διὰ   τοῦ   Ἰησοῦ   ἄξει
¹the   ²having slept   ³through   -   ⁴Jesus   will
[ones]   bring

σὺν   αὐτῷ.   15 Τοῦτο   γὰρ   ὑμῖν   λέγομεν
with   him.   For this   to you   we say

ἐν   λόγῳ   κυρίου,   ὅτι   ἡμεῖς   οἱ   ζῶντες
by   a word   of [the]   that   we   the   living
                 Lord,   [ones]

οἱ   περιλειπόμενοι   εἰς   τὴν   παρουσίαν   τοῦ
-      remaining   to   the   presence   of the

κυρίου   οὐ   μὴ   φθάσωμεν   τοὺς   κοιμηθέντας·
Lord   by no   may precede   the   having slept;
           means   [ones]

16 ὅτι   αὐτὸς   ὁ   κύριος   ἐν   κελεύσματι,
be-   ³[him]-   ¹the   ²Lord   with   a word of
cause   self   command,

ἐν   φωνῇ   ἀρχαγγέλου   καὶ   ἐν   σάλπιγγι
with   a voice   of an archangel   and   with   a trumpet

θεοῦ,   καταβήσεται   ἀπ'   οὐρανοῦ,   καὶ   οἱ
of God,   will descend   from   heaven,   and   the

νεκροὶ   ἐν   Χριστῷ   ἀναστήσονται   πρῶτον,
dead   in   Christ   will rise again   firstly,

17 ἔπειτα   ἡμεῖς   οἱ   ζῶντες   οἱ   περιλειπόμενοι
   then   we   the   living   -   remaining
                         [ones]

ἅμα   σὺν   αὐτοῖς   ἁρπαγησόμεθα   ἐν   νεφέλαις
to-   with   them   shall be seized   in   clouds
gether

εἰς   ἀπάντησιν   τοῦ   κυρίου   εἰς   ἀέρα·
to   a meeting   of the   Lord   in   air;

καὶ   οὕτως   πάντοτε   σὺν   κυρίῳ   ἐσόμεθα.
and   so   always   with   [the] Lord   we shall be.

18 Ὥστε   παρακαλεῖτε   ἀλλήλους   ἐν   τοῖς   λόγοις
   Therefore   comfort ye   one   with   -   words
                                 another

τούτοις.
these.

CHAPTER 5

BUT as to the times and the seasons, brethren, you have no need to have anything written to you. ²For you yourselves know well that the day of the Lord will come like a thief in the night. ³When people say, "There is peace and security," then sudden destruction will come upon them as travail comes upon a woman with child, and there will be no escape. ⁴But you are not in darkness, brethren, for that day to surprise you like a thief. ⁵For you are all sons of light and sons of the day; we are not of the night or of darkness. ⁶So then let us not sleep, as others do, but let us keep awake and be sober. ⁷For those who sleep sleep at night, and those who get drunk are drunk at night. ⁸But, since we belong to the day, let us be sober, and put on the breastplate of faith and love, and for a helmet the hope of salvation. ⁹For God has not destined us for wrath, but to obtain salvation through our Lord Jesus Christ, ¹⁰who died for us so that whether we wake or

5 Περὶ	δὲ	τῶν χρόνων	καὶ	τῶν καιρῶν,
But concerning	the	times	and	the seasons,

ἀδελφοί,	οὐ	χρείαν ἔχετε	ὑμῖν	γράφεσθαι·
brothers,	²not	³need ¹ye have	⁴to you	⁴to be written;

2 αὐτοὶ	γὰρ	ἀκριβῶς	οἴδατε	ὅτι ἡμέρα
for ²[your]selves	³accurately	¹ye know	that	[the] day

κυρίου	ὡς	κλέπτης	ἐν νυκτὶ	οὕτως
of [the] Lord	as	a thief	at night	so

ἔρχεται.	3 ὅταν λέγωσιν·	εἰρήνη	καὶ
it comes.	Whenever they say :	Peace	and

ἀσφάλεια,	τότε αἰφνίδιος	αὐτοῖς	ἐφίσταται
safety,	then ¹sudden	⁴them	²comes on

ὄλεθρος	ὥσπερ ἡ	ὠδὶν τῇ	ἐν γαστρὶ
²destruction	as	the birth pang to the	pregnant

ἐχούσῃ,	καὶ	οὐ μὴ	ἐκφύγωσιν. 4 ὑμεῖς
woman,†	and	by no means	may they escape. ye

δέ,	ἀδελφοί,	οὐκ ἐστὲ	ἐν σκότει, ἵνα
But,	brothers,	are not	in dark-ness, in or-der that

ἡ ἡμέρα	ὑμᾶς ὡς	κλέπτης	καταλάβῃ·
the day	you as	a thief	should overtake;

5 πάντες	γὰρ ὑμεῖς	υἱοὶ	φωτός ἐστε
for all	ye	²sons	³of light ¹are

καὶ υἱοὶ	ἡμέρας.	Οὐκ ἐσμὲν	νυκτὸς
and sons	of [the] day.	We are not	of [the] night

οὐδὲ σκότους·	6 ἄρα οὖν	μὴ	καθεύδωμεν
nor of darkness;	therefore	let us not sleep	

ὡς οἱ λοιποί,	ἀλλὰ	γρηγορῶμεν	καὶ
as the rest,	but	let us watch	and

νήφωμεν.	7 οἱ γὰρ	καθεύδοντες	νυκτὸς
be sober.	For the [ones]	sleeping	by night

καθεύδουσιν,	καὶ οἱ	μεθυσκόμενοι	νυκτὸς
sleep,	and the [ones] being drunk		by night

μεθύουσιν·	8 ἡμεῖς	δὲ ἡμέρας	ὄντες
are drunk;	but we	of [the] day	being

νήφωμεν,	ἐνδυσάμενοι	θώρακα πίστεως	καὶ
let us be sober,	putting on	a breastplate of faith	and

ἀγάπης	καὶ περικεφαλαίαν	ἐλπίδα	σωτηρίας·
of love	and a helmet	hope	of salvation;

9 ὅτι	οὐκ ἔθετο	ἡμᾶς ὁ θεὸς	εἰς ὀργὴν
because	²did not appoint	³us – ¹God	to wrath

ἀλλὰ	εἰς περιποίησιν	σωτηρίας	διὰ τοῦ
but	to obtainment	of salvation	through the

κυρίου	ἡμῶν Ἰησοῦ	Χριστοῦ,	10 τοῦ
Lord	of us Jesus	Christ,	the

ἀποθανόντος	περὶ ἡμῶν,	ἵνα εἴτε	γρηγορ-
[one] having died	concern-ing us,	in or-der that whether	we

sleep we might live with him. [11] Therefore encourage one another and build one another up, just as you are doing. 12 But we beseech you, brethren, to respect those who labor among you and are over you in the Lord and admonish you, [13] and to esteem them very highly in love because of their work. Be at peace among yourselves. [14] And we exhort you, brethren, admonish the idle, encourage the fainthearted, help the weak, be patient with them all. [15] See that none of you repays evil for evil, but always seek to do good to one another and to all. [16] Rejoice always, [17] pray constantly, [18] give thanks in all circumstances; for this is the will of God in Christ Jesus for you. [19] Do not quench the Spirit, [20] do not despise prophesying, [21] but test everything; hold fast what is good, [22] abstain from every form of evil.

ὦμεν   εἴτε   καθεύδωμεν   ἅμα   σὺν   αὐτῷ
watch   or   we sleep   [2]together   [3]with   [4]him

ζήσωμεν.   11 Διὸ   παρακαλεῖτε   ἀλλήλους
[1]we may live.   There-   comfort ye   one another
                   fore

καὶ   οἰκοδομεῖτε   εἰς   τὸν   ἕνα,   καθὼς   καὶ
and   edify ye   one   the one(other),   as   indeed

ποιεῖτε.
ye do.

12 Ἐρωτῶμεν   δὲ   ὑμᾶς,   ἀδελφοί,   εἰδέναι
     Now we ask   you,   brothers,   to know

τοὺς   κοπιῶντας   ἐν   ὑμῖν   καὶ   προϊσταμένους
the [ones] labouring   among   you   and   taking the lead

ὑμῶν   ἐν   κυρίῳ   καὶ   νουθετοῦντας   ὑμᾶς,
of you   in   [the] Lord   and   admonishing   you,

13 καὶ   ἡγεῖσθαι   αὐτοὺς   ὑπερεκπερισσῶς
     and   consider   them   most exceedingly

ἐν   ἀγάπῃ   διὰ   τὸ   ἔργον   αὐτῶν.   εἰρηνεύετε
in   love   be-   the   work   of them.   Be at peace
              cause of

ἐν   ἑαυτοῖς.   14 Παρακαλοῦμεν   δὲ   ὑμᾶς,
among yourselves.   And we exhort   you,

ἀδελφοί,   νουθετεῖτε   τοὺς   ἀτάκτους,   παρα-
brothers,   admonish   the   idle,   con-

μυθεῖσθε   τοὺς   ὀλιγοψύχους,   ἀντέχεσθε   τῶν
sole   the   faint-hearted,   hold on to   the
                                              [ones]

ἀσθενῶν,   μακροθυμεῖτε   πρὸς   πάντας.
being weak,   be longsuffering   with   all men.

15 ὁρᾶτε   μή   τις   κακὸν   ἀντὶ   κακοῦ   τινι
See   lest   anyone   [2]evil   [4]instead   [5]evil   [2]to
                                   of   anyone

ἀποδῷ,   ἀλλὰ   πάντοτε   τὸ   ἀγαθὸν   διώκετε
[1]returns,   but   always   [2]the   [2]good   [1]follow ye

εἰς   ἀλλήλους   καὶ   εἰς   πάντας.   16 Πάντοτε
in re-   one another   and   in re-   all men.   Always
gard to   gard to

χαίρετε,   17 ἀδιαλείπτως   προσεύχεσθε,   18 ἐν
rejoice ye,   unceasingly   pray,   in

παντὶ   εὐχαριστεῖτε·   τοῦτο   γὰρ   θέλημα
everything   give thanks;   for this [is]   [the] will

θεοῦ   ἐν   Χριστῷ   Ἰησοῦ   εἰς   ὑμᾶς.   19 τὸ
of God   in   Christ   Jesus   in regard to you.   The

πνεῦμα   μὴ   σβέννυτε,   20 προφητείας   μὴ
Spirit   do not quench,   . prophecies   not

ἐξουθενεῖτε·   21 πάντα   δὲ   δοκιμάζετε,   τὸ
despise;   and [2]all things   [1]prove,   the

καλὸν   κατέχετε·   22 ἀπὸ   παντὸς   εἴδους
good   hold fast;   from   every   form

23 May the God of peace himself sanctify you wholly; and may your spirit and soul and body be kept sound and blameless at the coming of our Lord Jesus Christ. ²⁴ He who calls you is faithful, and he will do it.

25 Brethren, pray for us.

26 Greet all the brethren with a holy kiss.

27 I adjure you by the Lord that this letter be read to all the brethren.

28 The grace of our Lord Jesus Christ be with you.

πονηροῦ   ἀπέχεσθε.
of evil   abstain.

23 Αὐτὸς   δὲ   ὁ   θεὸς
And ⁴[him]self ¹the ²God

τῆς   εἰρήνης   ἁγιάσαι   ὑμᾶς   ὁλοτελεῖς,   καὶ
–   ³of peace   may he sanctify   you   complete,   and

ὁλόκληρον   ὑμῶν   τὸ   πνεῦμα   καὶ   ἡ   ψυχὴ
entire   of you   the   spirit   and   the   soul

καὶ   τὸ   σῶμα   ἀμέμπτως   ἐν   τῇ   παρουσίᾳ
and   the   body   blamelessly   in(at) the   presence

τοῦ   κυρίου   ἡμῶν   Ἰησοῦ   Χριστοῦ   τηρηθείη.
of the   Lord   of us   Jesus   Christ   may be kept.

24 πιστὸς   ὁ   καλῶν   ὑμᾶς,   ὃς   καὶ   ποιήσει.
Faithful [is]   the [one] calling   you,   who indeed   will do [it].

25 Ἀδελφοί,   προσεύχεσθε   [καὶ]   περὶ
Brothers,   pray ye   also   concerning

ἡμῶν.
us.

26 Ἀσπάσασθε   τοὺς   ἀδελφοὺς   πάντας
Greet ye   ²the   ³brothers   ¹all

ἐν   φιλήματι   ἁγίῳ.   **27** Ἐνορκίζω   ὑμᾶς   τὸν
with   kiss   a holy.   I adjure   you [by] the

κύριον   ἀναγνωσθῆναι   τὴν   ἐπιστολὴν   πᾶσιν
Lord   ³to be read   ¹the(this)   ²epistle   to all

τοῖς   ἀδελφοῖς.
the   brothers.

28 Ἡ   χάρις   τοῦ   κυρίου   ἡμῶν   Ἰησοῦ
The   grace   of the   Lord   of us   Jesus

Χριστοῦ   μεθ'   ὑμῶν.
Christ   [be] with   you.

II. THESSALONIANS 1

CHAPTER 1

PAUL, Silva′nus, and Timothy.

To the church of the Thessalo′nians in God our Father and the Lord Jesus Christ:

2 Grace to you and peace from God the Father and the Lord Jesus Christ.

3 We are bound to give thanks to God

ΠΡΟΣ ΘΕΣΣΑΛΟΝΙΚΕΙΣ Β

To Thessalonians 2

1 Παῦλος   καὶ   Σιλουανὸς   καὶ   Τιμόθεος
Paul   and   Silvanus   and   Timothy

τῇ   ἐκκλησίᾳ   Θεσσαλονικέων   ἐν   θεῷ   πατρὶ
to the   church   of [the] Thessalonians   in   God   Father

ἡμῶν   καὶ   κυρίῳ   Ἰησοῦ   Χριστῷ·   **2** χάρις
of us   and   [the] Lord   Jesus   Christ: Grace [be]

ὑμῖν   καὶ   εἰρήνη   ἀπὸ   θεοῦ   πατρὸς   καὶ
to you   and   peace   from   God   [the] Father   and

κυρίου   Ἰησοῦ   Χριστοῦ.
[the] Lord   Jesus   Christ.

3 Εὐχαριστεῖν   ὀφείλομεν   τῷ   θεῷ   πάντοτε
To give thanks   we ought   –   to God   always

always for you, brethren, as is fitting, because your faith is growing abundantly, and the love of every one of you for one another is increasing. ⁴Therefore we ourselves boast of you in the churches of God for your steadfastness and faith in all your persecutions and in the afflictions which you are enduring.

5 This is evidence of the righteous judgment of God, that you may be made worthy of the kingdom of God, for which you are suffering —⁶since indeed God deems it just to repay with affliction those who afflict you, ⁷and to grant rest with us to you who are afflicted, when the Lord Jesus is revealed from heaven with his mighty angels in flaming fire, ⁸inflicting vengeance upon those who do not know God and upon those who do not obey the gospel of our Lord Jesus. ⁹They shall suffer the punishment of eternal destruction and

περὶ ὑμῶν, ἀδελφοί, καθὼς ἄξιόν ἐστιν,
con-　you,　brothers,　as　²meet　¹it is,
cerning

ὅτι ὑπεραυξάνει ἡ πίστις ὑμῶν καὶ
because ⁴grows ¹the ²faith ³of you and
　　　exceedingly

πλεονάζει ἡ ἀγάπη ἑνὸς ἑκάστου πάντων
²increases ¹the ²love ⁴one ³of each ⁴all

ὑμῶν εἰς ἀλλήλους, 4 ὥστε αὐτοὺς ἡμᾶς
⁵of you ⁷to ⁸one another,　so as [our]selves us
　　　　　=so that we ourselves boast

ἐν ὑμῖν ἐγκαυχᾶσθαι ἐν ταῖς ἐκκλησίαις
in you to boastᵇ in the churches

τοῦ θεοῦ ὑπὲρ τῆς ὑπομονῆς ὑμῶν καὶ
– of God for the ¹endurance ⁴of you ²and

πίστεως ἐν πᾶσιν τοῖς διωγμοῖς ὑμῶν
³faith in all the persecutions of you

καὶ ταῖς θλίψεσιν αἷς ἀνέχεσθε, 5 ἔνδειγμα
and the afflictions which ye endure, a plain token

τῆς δικαίας κρίσεως τοῦ θεοῦ, εἰς τὸ
of the just judgment – of God, for the

καταξιωθῆναι ὑμᾶς τῆς βασιλείας τοῦ
to be accounted youᵇ of the kingdom –
worthy
=so that ye may be accounted worthy

θεοῦ, ὑπὲρ ἧς καὶ πάσχετε, 6 εἴπερ
of God, on behalf which indeed ye suffer, since
　　　of

δίκαιον παρὰ θεῷ ἀνταποδοῦναι τοῖς
[it is] a just with God to repay ²to the
thing　　　　　　　　　[ones]

θλίβουσιν ὑμᾶς θλῖψιν 7 καὶ ὑμῖν τοῖς
³afflicting ⁴you ¹affliction and ⁴to you ⁵the
　　　　　　　　　　　　　　　[ones]

θλιβομένοις ἄνεσιν μεθ' ἡμῶν, ἐν τῇ
⁶being afflicted ¹rest ²with ³us, at the

ἀποκαλύψει τοῦ κυρίου Ἰησοῦ ἀπ'
revelation of the Lord Jesus from

οὐρανοῦ μετ' ἀγγέλων δυνάμεως αὐτοῦ
heaven with angels of power of him

8 ἐν πυρὶ φλογός, διδόντος ἐκδίκησιν τοῖς
in fire of flame, giving full vengeance to the
　　　　　　　　　　　　　　　　[ones]

μὴ εἰδόσιν θεὸν καὶ τοῖς μὴ ὑπακούουσιν
not knowing God and to the not obeying
　　　　　　　　[ones]

τῷ εὐαγγελίῳ τοῦ κυρίου ἡμῶν Ἰησοῦ,
the gospel of the Lord of us Jesus,

9 οἵτινες δίκην τίσουσιν ὄλεθρον αἰώνιον
who ²[the] penalty ¹will pay ⁴destruction ³eternal

exclusion from the presence of the Lord and from the glory of his might, ¹⁰when he comes on that day to be glorified in his saints, and to be marveled at in all who have believed, because our testimony to you was believed. ¹¹To this end we always pray for you, that our God may make you worthy of his call, and may fulfil every good resolve and work of faith by his power, ¹²so that the name of our Lord Jesus may be glorified in you, and you in him, according to the grace of our God and the Lord Jesus Christ.

ἀπὸ προσώπου τοῦ κυρίου καὶ ἀπὸ
from [the] face of the Lord and from
τῆς δόξης τῆς ἰσχύος αὐτοῦ, 10 ὅταν
the glory of the strength of him, whenever
ἔλθῃ ἐνδοξασθῆναι ἐν τοῖς ἁγίοις αὐτοῦ
he comes to be glorified in the saints of him
καὶ θαυμασθῆναι ἐν πᾶσιν τοῖς πιστεύσασιν,
and to be admired in all the [ones] having believed,
ὅτι ἐπιστεύθη τὸ μαρτύριον ἡμῶν ἐφ᾽
be- ⁵was believed ¹the ²testimony ³of us ⁴to
cause
ὑμᾶς, ἐν τῇ ἡμέρα ἐκείνῃ. 11 Εἰς ὃ
⁵you, in that day. For which
καὶ προσευχόμεθα πάντοτε περὶ ὑμῶν,
indeed we pray always concerning you,
ἵνα ὑμᾶς ἀξιώσῃ τῆς κλήσεως ὁ θεὸς
in or- ⁶you ⁴may ⁵deem ³of the ⁸calling ¹the ²God
der that ⁷worthy
ἡμῶν καὶ πληρώσῃ πᾶσαν εὐδοκίαν
³of us and may fulfil every good pleasure
ἀγαθωσύνης καὶ ἔργον πίστεως ἐν δυνάμει,
of goodness and work of faith in power,
12 ὅπως ἐνδοξασθῇ τὸ ὄνομα τοῦ κυρίου
so as ⁷may be glorified ¹the ²name ³of the ⁴Lord
ἡμῶν Ἰησοῦ ἐν ὑμῖν, καὶ ὑμεῖς ἐν
⁵of us ⁶Jesus in you, and ye in
αὐτῷ, κατὰ τὴν χάριν τοῦ θεοῦ ἡμῶν
him, according to the grace of the ¹God ⁴of us
καὶ κυρίου Ἰησοῦ Χριστοῦ.
²and ³Lord Jesus Christ.

CHAPTER 2

NOW concerning the coming of our Lord Jesus Christ and our assembling to meet him, we beg you, brethren, ²not to be quickly shaken in mind or excited, either by spirit or by word, or by letter purporting to be from us, to the effect that the day of the Lord has

2 Ἐρωτῶμεν δὲ ὑμᾶς, ἀδελφοί, ὑπὲρ
Now we request you, brothers, by
τῆς παρουσίας τοῦ κυρίου [ἡμῶν] Ἰησοῦ
the presence of the Lord of us Jesus
Χριστοῦ καὶ ἡμῶν ἐπισυναγωγῆς ἐπ᾽ αὐτόν,
Christ and ²of us ¹gathering together to him,
2 εἰς τὸ μὴ ταχέως σαλευθῆναι ὑμᾶς
– – not quickly to be shaken youᵇ
ἀπὸ τοῦ νοὸς μηδὲ θροεῖσθαι, μήτε
from the(your) mind nor to be disturbed, neither
διὰ πνεύματος μήτε διὰ λόγου μήτε
through a spirit nor through speech nor
δι᾽ ἐπιστολῆς ὡς δι᾽ ἡμῶν, ὡς ὅτι
through an epistle as through us, as that
ἐνέστηκεν ἡ ἡμέρα τοῦ κυρίου. 3 μή
⁵is come ¹the ²day ³of the ⁴Lord. Not

come. ³Let no one deceive you in any way; for that day will not come, unless the rebellion comes first, and the man of lawlessness* is revealed, the son of perdition, ⁴who opposes and exalts himself against every so-called god or object of worship, so that he takes his seat in the temple of God, proclaiming himself to be God. ⁵Do you not remember that when I was still with you I told you this? ⁶And you know what is restraining him now so that he may be revealed in his time. ⁷For the mystery of lawlessness is already at work; only he who now restrains it will do so until he is out of the way. ⁸And then the lawless one will be revealed, and the Lord Jesus will slay him with the breath of his mouth and destroy him by his appearing and his coming. ⁹The coming of the lawless one by the activity of Satan will be with all power and with pretended signs and wonders, ¹⁰and with all wicked deception for those who are to perish, because they refused to

*Other ancient authorities read *sin*

τις   ὑμᾶς   ἐξαπατήσῃ   κατὰ   μηδένα   τρόπον·
anyone   ²you   ¹may deceive by(in)   no(any)   way;

ὅτι   ἐὰν   μὴ   ἔλθῃ   ἡ   ἀποστασία   πρῶτον
because   unless   ²comes ¹the   ²apostasy   ⁴firstly

καὶ   ἀποκαλυφθῇ   ὁ   ἄνθρωπος τῆς   ἀνομίας,
and   ⁴is revealed ¹the ²man   -   ³of lawlessness,

ὁ   υἱὸς   τῆς   ἀπωλείας,   4 ὁ   ἀντικείμενος
the   son   -   of perdition, the [one] setting against

καὶ   ὑπεραιρόμενος   ἐπὶ   πάντα   λεγόμενον
and   exalting himself over   everything *being* called

θεὸν   ἢ   σέβασμα,   ὥστε   αὐτὸν   εἰς   τὸν
God   or object of worship, so as   him   in   the

ναὸν   τοῦ   θεοῦ   καθίσαι,   ἀποδεικνύντα   ἑαυ-
shrine   -   of God   to sit,ᵇ   showing   him-

τὸν   ὅτι   ἐστὶν   θεός.   5 Οὐ   μνημονεύετε
self   that   he is   a god.   Do ye not remember

ὅτι   ἔτι   ὢν   πρὸς   ὑμᾶς   ταῦτα   ἔλεγον
that   yet   being   with   you   ²these   ¹I used
                                          things   to tell

ὑμῖν;   6 καὶ   νῦν   τὸ   κατέχον   οἴδατε,
²you?   and   now   the   restraining ye know,
                                [thing]

εἰς   τὸ   ἀποκαλυφθῆναι   αὐτὸν   ἐν   τῷ
for   the   ²to be revealed   ¹himᵇ   in   the

αὐτοῦ   καιρῷ.   7 τὸ   γὰρ   μυστήριον   ἤδη
²of him   ¹time.   For the   mystery   ²already

ἐνεργεῖται   τῆς   ἀνομίας·   μόνον   ὁ   κατέχων
²operates   -   ¹of lawless-   only   the   restraining
                              ness;   [there is] [one]

ἄρτι   ἕως   ἐκ   μέσου   γένηται.   8 καὶ   τότε
just now until   ²out of ³[the] midst ¹it comes.   And   then

ἀποκαλυφθήσεται   ὁ   ἄνομος,   ὃν   ὁ   κύριος
    will be revealed   the   lawless   whom the   Lord
                                  one,

[Ἰησοῦς]   ἀνελεῖ   τῷ   πνεύματι   τοῦ   στό-
Jesus   will destroy by the   spirit   of the   mouth

ματος   αὐτοῦ   καὶ   καταργήσει   τῇ   ἐπιφανείᾳ
of him   and   bring to nothing by the   outshining

τῆς   παρουσίας   αὐτοῦ,   9 οὗ   ἐστιν   ἡ
of the   presence   of him,   of whom   ²is   ¹the

παρουσία   κατ'   ἐνέργειαν   τοῦ   σατανᾶ   ἐν
²presence   according operation   -   of Satan   with
              to [the]

πάσῃ   δυνάμει   καὶ   σημείοις   καὶ   τέρασιν
all   power   and   signs   and   wonders

ψεύδους   10 καὶ   ἐν   πάσῃ   ἀπάτῃ   ἀδικίας
of a lie   and   with   all   deceit   of unright-
                                                   eousness

τοῖς   ἀπολλυμένοις,   ἀνθ'   ὧν   τὴν   ἀγάπην
in the [ones] perishing,   because   the   love

love the truth and so be saved. ¹¹Therefore God sends upon them a strong delusion, to make them believe what is false, ¹²so that all may be condemned who did not believe the truth but had pleasure in unrighteousness.

13 But we are bound to give thanks to God always for you, brethren beloved by the Lord, because God chose you from the beginning[b] to be saved, through sanctification by the Spirit[c] and belief in the truth. ¹⁴To this he called you through our gospel, so that you may obtain the glory of our Lord Jesus Christ. ¹⁵So then, brethren, stand firm and hold to the traditions which you were taught by us, either by word of mouth or by letter.

16 Now may our Lord Jesus Christ himself, and God our Father, who loved us and gave us eternal comfort and good hope through grace, ¹⁷comfort your hearts and establish them in every good work and word.

τῆς ἀληθείας οὐκ ἐδέξαντο εἰς τὸ σωθῆναι
of the truth they received not for *the* ²to be saved

αὐτούς. 11 καὶ διὰ τοῦτο πέμπει αὐτοῖς
¹them.[b] And therefore ²sends ³to them

ὁ θεὸς ἐνέργειαν πλάνης εἰς τὸ πιστεῦσαι
– ¹God an operation of error for *the* ²to believe

αὐτοὺς τῷ ψεύδει, 12 ἵνα κριθῶσιν πάντες
¹them[b] the lie, in or- ¹⁰may be ¹all
der that judged

οἱ μὴ πιστεύσαντες τῇ ἀληθείᾳ ἀλλὰ
²the ³not ⁴having believed ⁵the ⁶truth ⁷but
[ones]

εὐδοκήσαντες τῇ ἀδικίᾳ.
⁸having had pleasure – ⁹in unrighteousness.

13 Ἡμεῖς δὲ ὀφείλομεν εὐχαριστεῖν τῷ
But we ought to thank –

θεῷ πάντοτε περὶ ὑμῶν, ἀδελφοὶ ἠγαπη-
God always concerning you, brothers having been

μένοι ὑπὸ κυρίου, ὅτι εἵλατο ὑμᾶς ὁ
loved by [the] Lord, because ²chose ³you –

θεὸς ἀπαρχὴν εἰς σωτηρίαν ἐν ἁγιασμῷ
¹God firstfruit to salvation by sanctification

πνεύματος καὶ πίστει ἀληθείας, 14 εἰς
of spirit and faith of(in) [the] truth, to

ὁ καὶ ἐκάλεσεν ὑμᾶς διὰ τοῦ εὐαγγελίου
which also he called you through the gospel

ἡμῶν, εἰς περιποίησιν δόξης τοῦ κυρίου
of us, to obtainment of [the] glory of the Lord

ἡμῶν Ἰησοῦ Χριστοῦ. 15 Ἄρα οὖν,
of us Jesus Christ. So then,

ἀδελφοί, στήκετε, καὶ κρατεῖτε τὰς
brothers, stand, and hold the

παραδόσεις ἃς ἐδιδάχθητε εἴτε διὰ λόγου
traditions which ye were taught either through speech

εἴτε δι' ἐπιστολῆς ἡμῶν. 16 Αὐτὸς δὲ
or through an epistle of us. And ⁶[him]self

ὁ κύριος ἡμῶν Ἰησοῦς Χριστὸς καὶ
¹the ²Lord ³of us ⁴Jesus ⁵Christ and

ὁ θεὸς ὁ πατὴρ ἡμῶν, ὁ ἀγαπήσας
the God the Father of us, the [one] having loved

ἡμᾶς καὶ δοὺς παράκλησιν αἰωνίαν καὶ
us and having given ²comfort ¹eternal ³and

ἐλπίδα ἀγαθὴν ἐν χάριτι, 17 παρακαλέσαι
³hope ⁴a good by grace, may he comfort

ὑμῶν τὰς καρδίας καὶ στηρίξαι ἐν παντὶ
of you the hearts and *may he confirm* in every

ἔργῳ καὶ λόγῳ ἀγαθῷ.
²work ³and ⁴word ¹good.

CHAPTER 3

FINALLY, brethren, pray for us, that the word of the Lord may speed on and triumph, as it did among you, [2] and that we may be delivered from wicked and evil men; for not all have faith. [3] But the Lord is faithful; he will strengthen you and guard you from evil.[d] [4] And we have confidence in the Lord about you, that you are doing and will do the things which we command. [5] May the Lord direct your hearts to the love of God and to the steadfastness of Christ.

6 Now we command you, brethren, in the name of our Lord Jesus Christ, that you keep away from any brother who is living in idleness and not in accord with the tradition that you received from us. [7] For you yourselves know how you ought to imitate us; we were not idle when we were with you, [8] we did not eat any one's bread without paying, but with toil and labor we worked night and day, that we

[d] Or the evil one

3 Τὸ λοιπὸν προσεύχεσθε, ἀδελφοί, περὶ
For the rest   pray ye,   brothers, concerning
ἡμῶν, ἵνα ὁ λόγος τοῦ κυρίου τρέχῃ
us,   in or- the word of the Lord may run
       der that
καὶ δοξάζηται καθὼς καὶ πρὸς ὑμᾶς,
and be glorified as indeed with you,
2 καὶ ἵνα ῥυσθῶμεν ἀπὸ τῶν ἀτόπων
and in or- we may be from – perverse
     der that delivered
καὶ πονηρῶν ἀνθρώπων· οὐ γὰρ πάντων
and evil   men;   for [is] not [of all] men
ἡ πίστις. 3 Πιστὸς δέ ἐστιν ὁ κύριος,
[the] [faith]. But faithful is the Lord,
ὃς στηρίξει ὑμᾶς καὶ φυλάξει ἀπὸ τοῦ
who will confirm you and will guard from the
πονηροῦ. 4 πεποίθαμεν δὲ ἐν κυρίῳ
evil [?one]. And we are persuaded in [the] Lord
ἐφ' ὑμᾶς, ὅτι ἃ παραγγέλλομεν [καὶ]
as to you, that what we charge both
       things
ποιεῖτε καὶ ποιήσετε. 5 Ὁ δὲ κύριος
ye do and will do.   And [the] [Lord]
κατευθύναι ὑμῶν τὰς καρδίας εἰς τὴν
[may] [direct] [of] you [the] [hearts] into the
ἀγάπην τοῦ θεοῦ καὶ εἰς τὴν ὑπομονὴν
love – of God and into the patience
τοῦ Χριστοῦ.
– of Christ.

6 Παραγγέλλομεν δὲ ὑμῖν, ἀδελφοί, ἐν
Now we charge   you, brothers, in
ὀνόματι τοῦ κυρίου Ἰησοῦ Χριστοῦ,
[the] name of the Lord Jesus Christ,
στέλλεσθαι ὑμᾶς ἀπὸ παντὸς ἀδελφοῦ
to draw back you[b] from every brother
ἀτάκτως περιπατοῦντος καὶ μὴ κατὰ τὴν
[idly]   [walking]   and not accord- the
                                    ing to
παράδοσιν ἣν παρελάβετε παρ' ἡμῶν.
tradition which ye received from us.
7 αὐτοὶ γὰρ οἴδατε πῶς δεῖ μιμεῖσθαι
For [your]selves ye know how it be- to imitate
                                hoves
ἡμᾶς, ὅτι οὐκ ἠτακτήσαμεν ἐν ὑμῖν,
us, because we were not idle among you,
8 οὐδὲ δωρεὰν ἄρτον ἐφάγομεν παρά τινος,
nor [as] a gift [bread] [ate] [from] [anyone],
ἀλλ' ἐν κόπῳ καὶ μόχθῳ νυκτὸς καὶ
but by labour and struggle by night and

might not burden any of you. ⁹It was not because we have not that right, but to give you in our conduct an example to imitate. ¹⁰For even when we were with you, we gave you this command: If any one will not work, let him not eat. ¹¹For we hear that some of you are living in idleness, mere busybodies, not doing any work. ¹²Now such persons we command and exhort in the Lord Jesus Christ to do their work in quietness and to earn their own living. ¹³Brethren, do not be weary in well-doing.

14 If any one refuses to obey what we say in this letter, note that man, and have nothing to do with him, that he may be ashamed. ¹⁵Do not look on him as an enemy, but warn him as a brother.

16 Now may the Lord of peace himself give you peace at all times in all ways. The Lord be with you all.

ἡμέρας	ἐργαζόμενοι	πρὸς	τὸ	μὴ	ἐπιβαρῆσαί
by day	working	for	the	not	to emburden

τινα	ὑμῶν·	9 οὐχ	ὅτι	οὐκ	ἔχομεν
anyone	of you;	not	that		we have not

ἐξουσίαν,	ἀλλ'	ἵνα	ἑαυτοὺς	τύπον	δῶμεν
authority,	but	in or-der that	²our-selves	³an example	¹we might give

ὑμῖν	εἰς	τὸ	μιμεῖσθαι	ἡμᾶς.	10 καὶ
to you	for	the	to imitate	us.	even

γὰρ	ὅτε	ἦμεν	πρὸς	ὑμᾶς,	τοῦτο	παρηγ-
For	when	we were	with	you,	this	we

γέλλομεν	ὑμῖν,	ὅτι	εἴ	τις	οὐ	θέλει
charged	you,	that	if	anyone		does not wish

ἐργάζεσθαι,	μηδὲ	ἐσθιέτω.	11 ἀκούομεν
to work,	neither	let him eat.	we hear [of]

γάρ	τινας	περιπατοῦντας	ἐν	ὑμῖν	ἀτάκτως,
For	some	walking	among	you	idly,

μηδὲν	ἐργαζομένους	ἀλλὰ	περιεργαζομένους·
nothing	working	but	working round;

12 τοῖς	δὲ	τοιούτοις	παραγγέλλομεν	καὶ
–	and	to such	we charge	and

παρακαλοῦμεν	ἐν	κυρίῳ	Ἰησοῦ	Χριστῷ
exhort	in	[the] Lord	Jesus	Christ

ἵνα	μετὰ	ἡσυχίας	ἐργαζόμενοι	τὸν
in or-der that	²with	³quietness	¹working	⁵the

ἑαυτῶν	ἄρτον	ἐσθίωσιν.	13 Ὑμεῖς	δέ,
⁷of them-selves	⁶bread	⁴they may eat.		And ye,

ἀδελφοί,	μὴ	ἐγκακήσητε	καλοποιοῦντες
brothers,		do not lose heart	doing good.

14 εἰ	δέ	τις	οὐχ	ὑπακούει	τῷ	λόγῳ
And if		anyone		obeys not	the	word

ἡμῶν	διὰ	τῆς	ἐπιστολῆς,	τοῦτον	σημειοῦσθε,
of us	through	the	epistle,	this man	mark,

μὴ	συναναμίγνυσθαι	αὐτῷ,	ἵνα	ἐντραπῇ·
not to mix with*		him,	in or-der that	he may be put to shame;

15 καὶ	μὴ	ὡς	ἐχθρὸν	ἡγεῖσθε,	ἀλλὰ
and yet	not	as	an enemy	deem ye [him],	but

ˉουθετεῖτε	ὡς	ἀδελφόν.	16 Αὐτὸς	δὲ
admonish	as	a brother.		And ⁴[him]self

ὁ	κύριος	τῆς	εἰρήνης	δῴη	ὑμῖν	τὴν
¹the	²Lord	–	³of peace	may he give	to you	the (?his)

εἰρήνην	διὰ	παντὸς	ἐν	παντὶ	τρόπῳ.
peace	always		in	every	way.

ὁ	κύριος	μετὰ	πάντων	ὑμῶν.
The	Lord [be]	with	²all	¹you.

* Imperatival infinitive, as elsewhere (Phil. 3. 16, etc.).

17 I, Paul, write this greeting with my own hand. This is the mark in every letter of mine; it is the way I write. [18]The grace of our Lord Jesus Christ be with you all.

17 Ὁ ἀσπασμὸς τῇ ἐμῇ χειρὶ Παύλου,
The greeting - by my hand[,] of Paul,
ὃ ἐστιν σημεῖον ἐν πάσῃ ἐπιστολῇ·
which is a sign in every epistle:
οὕτως γράφω. 18 ἡ χάρις τοῦ κυρίου
thus I write. The grace of the Lord
ἡμῶν Ἰησοῦ Χριστοῦ μετὰ πάντων ὑμῶν.
of us Jesus Christ [be] with ²all ¹you.

I. TIMOTHY
1

ΠΡΟΣ ΤΙΜΟΘΕΟΝ Α
To Timothy 1

CHAPTER 1

PAUL, an apostle of Christ Jesus by command of God our Savior and of Christ Jesus our hope,
2 To Timothy, my true child in the faith:
Grace, mercy, and peace from God the Father and Christ Jesus our Lord.
3 As I urged you when I was going to Macedo'-nia, remain at Ephesus that you may charge certain persons not to teach any different doctrine, [4]nor to occupy themselves with myths and endless genealogies which promote speculations rather than the divine training[a] that is in faith; [5]whereas the aim of our charge is love that issues from a pure heart and a good conscience and sincere faith.

1 Παῦλος ἀπόστολος Χριστοῦ Ἰησοῦ κατ'
Paul an apostle of Christ Jesus according to
ἐπιταγὴν θεοῦ σωτῆρος ἡμῶν καὶ Χριστοῦ
a command of God Saviour of us and of Christ
Ἰησοῦ τῆς ἐλπίδος ἡμῶν 2 Τιμοθέῳ
Jesus the hope of us to Timothy
γνησίῳ τέκνῳ ἐν πίστει· χάρις, ἔλεος,
a true child in [the] faith: Grace, mercy,
εἰρήνη ἀπὸ θεοῦ πατρὸς καὶ Χριστοῦ
peace from God [the] Father and Christ
Ἰησοῦ τοῦ κυρίου ἡμῶν.
Jesus the Lord of us.
3 Καθὼς παρεκάλεσά σε προσμεῖναι ἐν
As I besought thee to remain in
Ἐφέσῳ, πορευόμενος εἰς Μακεδονίαν, ἵνα
Ephesus, [I] going into Macedonia, in order that
παραγγείλῃς τισὶν μὴ ἑτεροδιδασκαλεῖν
thou mightest certain not to teach differently
charge persons
4 μηδὲ προσέχειν μύθοις καὶ γενεαλογίαις
nor to pay attention to tales and to ²genealogies
ἀπεράντοις, αἵτινες ἐκζητήσεις παρέχουσιν
¹unending, which ²questionings ¹provide
μᾶλλον ἢ οἰκονομίαν θεοῦ τὴν ἐν πίστει·
rather than a stewardship of God - in faith:
5 τὸ δὲ τέλος τῆς παραγγελίας ἐστὶν
now the end of the charge is
ἀγάπη ἐκ καθαρᾶς καρδίας καὶ συνειδήσεως
love out of a clean heart and conscience
ἀγαθῆς καὶ πίστεως ἀνυποκρίτου, 6 ὧν
a good and faith unfeigned, from which
things

---

[a] Or stewardship, or order

⁶Certain persons by swerving from these have wandered away into vain discussion, ⁷desiring to be teachers of the law, without understanding either what they arc saying or the things about which they make assertions.
8 Now we know that the law is good, if any one uses it lawfully, ⁹understanding this, that the law is not laid down for the just but for the lawless and disobedient, for the ungodly and sinners, for the unholy and profane, for murderers of fathers and murderers of mothers, for manslayers, ¹⁰immoral persons, sodomites, kidnapers, liars, perjurers, and whatever else is contrary to sound doctrine, ¹¹in accordance with the glorious gospel of the blessed God with which I have been entrusted.
12 I thank him who has given me strength for this, Christ Jesus our Lord, because he judged me faithful by appointing me to his service, ¹³though I formerly blasphemed and persecuted and insulted him; but I received mercy because I had acted ignorantly in unbelief, ¹⁴and the grace of our Lord overflowed for me with the faith and love that are in Christ Jesus. ¹⁵The saying is sure and

τινες ἀστοχήσαντες ἐξετράπησαν εἰς
some missing aim turned aside to
ματαιολογίαν, 7 θέλοντες εἶναι νομοδιδάσ-
vain talking, wishing to be law-
καλοι, μὴ νοοῦντες μήτε ἃ λέγουσιν
teachers, not understanding either what things they say
μήτε περὶ τίνων διαβεβαιοῦνται. 8 οἴδαμεν
nor concerning what things they emphatically assert. we know
δὲ ὅτι καλὸς ὁ νόμος, ἐάν τις αὐτῷ
Now that ³[is] ⁴good ¹the ²law, if anyone ²it
νομίμως χρῆται, 9 εἰδὼς τοῦτο, ὅτι
³lawfully ¹uses, knowing this, that
δικαίῳ νόμος οὐ κεῖται, ἀνόμοις δὲ
²for a just ¹law ²is not laid down, but for lawless men
man
καὶ ἀνυποτάκτοις, ἀσεβέσι καὶ ἁμαρτωλοῖς,
and for unruly, for impious and for sinners,
ἀνοσίοις καὶ βεβήλοις, πατρολῴαις καὶ
for unholy and for profane, for parricides and
μητρολῴαις, ἀνδροφόνοις, 10 πόρνοις, ἀρ-
for matricides, for menkillers, for fornicators, for
σενοκοίταις, ἀνδραποδισταῖς, ψεύσταις, ἐπιόρ-
paederasts, for menstealers, for liars, for per-
κοις, καὶ εἴ τι ἕτερον τῇ ὑγιαινούσῃ
jurers, and if any other thing ²to the ³being healthful
διδασκαλίᾳ ἀντίκειται, 11 κατὰ τὸ εὐαγ-
⁴teaching ¹opposes, according to the gos-
γέλιον τῆς δόξης τοῦ μακαρίου θεοῦ,
pel of the glory of the blessed God,
ὃ ἐπιστεύθην ἐγώ. 12 Χάριν ἔχω τῷ
which ²was entrusted ¹I. Thanks I have to the
[with]
ἐνδυναμώσαντί με Χριστῷ Ἰησοῦ τῷ κυρίῳ
[one] empowering me Christ Jesus the Lord
ἡμῶν, ὅτι πιστόν με ἡγήσατο θέμενος
of us, because ³faithful ²me ¹he deemed putting [me]
εἰς διακονίαν, 13 τὸ πρότερον ὄντα
into [the] ministry, formerly being
βλάσφημον καὶ διώκτην καὶ ὑβριστήν·
a blasphemer and a persecutor and insolent;
ἀλλὰ ἠλεήθην, ὅτι ἀγνοῶν ἐποίησα ἐν
but I obtained mercy, because being ignorant I acted in
ἀπιστίᾳ, 14 ὑπερεπλεόνασεν δὲ ἡ χάρις
unbelief, and superabounded the grace
τοῦ κυρίου ἡμῶν μετὰ πίστεως καὶ
of the Lord of us with faith and
ἀγάπης τῆς ἐν Χριστῷ Ἰησοῦ. 15 πιστὸς
love – in Christ Jesus. Faithful [is]

worthy of full accept-
ance, that Christ Jesus
came into the world to
save sinners. And I am
the foremost of sinners;
¹⁶ but I received mercy
for this reason, that in
me, as the foremost,
Jesus Christ might dis-
play his perfect patience
for an example to those
who were to believe in
him for eternal life. ¹⁷ To
the King of ages,
immortal, invisible, the
only God, be honor and
glory for ever and ever.
Amen.

18 This charge I com-
mit to you, Timothy,
my son, in accordance
with the prophetic
utterances which pointed
to you, that inspired by
them you may wage the
good warfare, ¹⁹ holding
faith and a good con-
science. By rejecting
conscience, certain per-
sons have made ship-
wreck of their faith,
²⁰ among them Hymen-
ae'us and Alexander,
whom I have delivered
to Satan that they may
learn not to blaspheme.

ὁ   λόγος   καὶ   πάσης   ἀποδοχῆς   ἄξιος·
the   word   and   ²of all   ³acceptance   ¹worthy,

ὅτι   Χριστὸς   Ἰησοῦς   ἦλθεν   εἰς   τὸν   κόσμον
that   Christ   Jesus   came   into   the   world

ἁμαρτωλοὺς   σῶσαι·   ὧν   πρῶτός   εἰμι   ἐγώ·
sinners   to save;   of whom first(chief) am   I;

16 ἀλλὰ   διὰ   τοῦτο   ἠλεήθην,   ἵνα   ἐν
but   because of   this   I obtained   in or-   in
                                mercy,   der that

ἐμοὶ   πρώτῳ   ἐνδείξηται   Ἰησοῦς   Χριστὸς
me   first   might show forth   Jesus   Christ

τὴν   ἅπασαν   μακροθυμίαν,   πρὸς   ὑποτύπωσιν
 -      all   longsuffering,   for   a pattern

τῶν   μελλόντων   πιστεύειν   ἐπ'   αὐτῷ   εἰς
of the [ones] coming   to believe   on   him   to

ζωὴν   αἰώνιον.   17 Τῷ   δὲ   βασιλεῖ   τῶν
life   eternal.   Now to the King   of the

αἰώνων,   ἀφθάρτῳ   ἀοράτῳ   μόνῳ   θεῷ,   τιμὴ
ages,   incorruptible invisible   only   God,   [be]
                                                   honour

καὶ   δόξα   εἰς   τοὺς   αἰῶνας   τῶν   αἰώνων·
and   glory   unto   the   ages   of the   ages:

ἀμήν.   18 Ταύτην   τὴν   παραγγελίαν   παρα-
Amen.   This   -   charge   I com-

τίθεμαί   σοι,   τέκνον   Τιμόθεε,   κατὰ   τὰς
mit   to thee,   child   Timothy,   according to the

προαγούσας   ἐπὶ   σὲ   προφητείας,   ἵνα
preceding   ²respecting ³thee ¹prophecies,   in order
                                                  that

στρατεύῃ   ἐν   αὐταῖς   τὴν   καλὴν   στρατείαν,
thou   by   them   the   good   warfare,
mightest war

19 ἔχων   πίστιν   καὶ   ἀγαθὴν   συνείδησιν,
having   faith   and   a good   conscience,

ἣν   τινες   ἀπωσάμενοι   περὶ   τὴν   πίστιν
which some   thrusting away   ²concerning ³the   ⁴faith

ἐναυάγησαν·   20 ὧν   ἐστιν   Ὑμέναιος   καὶ
¹made ship-   of whom   is   Hymenæus   and
wreck;

Ἀλέξανδρος,   οὓς   παρέδωκα   τῷ   σατανᾷ,
Alexander,   whom   I delivered   -   to Satan,

ἵνα   παιδευθῶσιν   μὴ   βλασφημεῖν.
in or- they may be taught not   to blaspheme.
der that

CHAPTER 2

FIRST of all, then, I
urge that supplica-
tions, prayers, interces-

2 Παρακαλῶ   οὖν   πρῶτον   πάντων
  I exhort   therefore   firstly   of all

ποιεῖσθαι   δεήσεις,   προσευχάς,   ἐντεύξεις,
to be made   petitions,   prayers,   intercessions,

sions, and thanksgivings be made for all men, ²for kings and all who are in high positions, that we may lead a quiet and peaceable life, godly and respectful in every way. ³This is good, and it is acceptable in the sight of God our Savior, ⁴who desires all men to be saved and to come to the knowledge of the truth. ⁵For there is one God, and there is one mediator between God and men, the man Christ Jesus, ⁶who gave himself as a ransom for all, the testimony to which was borne at the proper time. ⁷For this I was appointed a preacher and apostle (I am telling the truth, I am not lying), a teacher of the Gentiles in faith and truth.

8 I desire then that in every place the men should pray, lifting holy hands without anger or quarreling; ⁹also that women should adorn themselves modestly and sensibly in seemly apparel, not with braided hair or gold or pearls or costly attire ¹⁰but by good deeds, as befits women who profess

εὐχαριστίας, ὑπὲρ πάντων ἀνθρώπων,
thanksgivings, on behalf of all men,

2 ὑπὲρ βασιλέων καὶ πάντων τῶν ἐν
on behalf of kings and all the [ones] ²in

ὑπεροχῇ ὄντων, ἵνα ἤρεμον καὶ ἡσύχιον
³eminence ¹being, in or- ²a tranquil ³and ⁴quiet
der that

βίον διάγωμεν ἐν πάσῃ εὐσεβείᾳ καὶ
⁵life ¹we may lead in all piety and

σεμνότητι. 3 τοῦτο καλὸν καὶ ἀπόδεκτον
gravity. This [is] good and acceptable

ἐνώπιον τοῦ σωτῆρος ἡμῶν θεοῦ, 4 ὅς
before the Saviour of us God, who

πάντας ἀνθρώπους θέλει σωθῆναι καὶ εἰς
²all ³men ¹wishes to be saved and ²to

ἐπίγνωσιν ἀληθείας ἐλθεῖν. 5 εἷς γὰρ
³a full ⁴of truth ¹to come. For ²one
knowledge

θεός, εἷς καὶ μεσίτης θεοῦ καὶ ἀνθρώπων,
¹[there one also mediator of God and of men,
is] ³God,

ἄνθρωπος Χριστὸς Ἰησοῦς, 6 ὁ δοὺς
a man Christ Jesus, the [one] having
given

ἑαυτὸν ἀντίλυτρον ὑπὲρ πάντων, τὸ
himself a ransom on behalf of all, the

μαρτύριον καιροῖς ἰδίοις· 7 εἰς ὃ ἐτέθην
testimony in its own times; for which ¹was
appointed

ἐγὼ κῆρυξ καὶ ἀπόστολος, ἀλήθειαν λέγω,
¹I a herald and an apostle, ²truth ¹I say,

οὐ ψεύδομαι, διδάσκαλος ἐθνῶν ἐν πίστει
I do not lie, a teacher of nations in faith

καὶ ἀληθείᾳ. 8 Βούλομαι οὖν προσεύχεσθαι
and truth. I desire therefore ²to pray

τοὺς ἄνδρας ἐν παντὶ τόπῳ ἐπαίροντας
¹the ²men in every place lifting up

ὁσίους χεῖρας χωρὶς ὀργῆς καὶ διαλογισμοῦ.
holy hands without wrath and doubting.

9 Ὡσαύτως γυναῖκας ἐν καταστολῇ κοσμίῳ,
Similarly women in clothing orderly,

μετὰ αἰδοῦς καὶ σωφροσύνης κοσμεῖν
³with ⁴modesty ⁵and ⁶sobriety ¹to adorn

ἑαυτάς, μὴ ἐν πλέγμασιν καὶ χρυσίῳ
²themselves, not with plaiting and gold

ἢ μαργαρίταις ἢ ἱματισμῷ πολυτελεῖ,
or pearls or raiment costly,

10 ἀλλ' ὃ πρέπει γυναιξὶν ἐπαγγελλομέναις
but what suits women professing

religion. ¹¹Let a woman learn in silence with all submissiveness. ¹²I permit no woman to teach or to have authority over men; she is to keep silent. ¹³For Adam was formed first, then Eve; ¹⁴and Adam was not deceived, but the woman was deceived and became a transgressor. ¹⁵Yet woman will be saved through bearing children,*b* if she continues in faith and love and holiness, with modesty.

θεοσέβειαν,   δι'   ἔργων   ἀγαθῶν.   11 γυνὴ
reverence,   by   ²works   ¹good.   A woman
       means of

ἐν   ἡσυχίᾳ   μανθανέτω   ἐν   πάσῃ   ὑποταγῇ·
in   silence   let learn   in   all   subjection;

12 διδάσκειν   δὲ   γυναικὶ   οὐκ   ἐπιτρέπω,
     but ³to teach   ²a woman   ¹I do not permit,

οὐδὲ   αὐθεντεῖν   ἀνδρός,   ἀλλ'   εἶναι   ἐν
nor   to exercise   of(over) a man,   but   to be   in
     authority

ἡσυχίᾳ.   13 Ἀδὰμ   γὰρ   πρῶτος   ἐπλάσθη,
silence.   For Adam   first   was formed,

εἶτα   Εὔα.   14 καὶ   Ἀδὰμ   οὐκ   ἠπατήθη,
then   Eve.   And   Adam   was not deceived,

ἡ   δὲ   γυνὴ   ἐξαπατηθεῖσα   ἐν   παραβάσει
but the   woman   being deceived   ²in   ³transgression

γέγονεν·   15 σωθήσεται   δὲ   διὰ   τῆς
¹has become;   but she will be saved   through the(her)

τεκνογονίας,   ἐὰν   μείνωσιν   ἐν   πίστει   καὶ
childbearing,   if   they remain   in   faith   and

ἀγάπῃ   καὶ   ἁγιασμῷ   μετὰ   σωφροσύνης.
love   and   sanctification   with   sobriety.

CHAPTER 3

THE saying is sure: If any one aspires to the office of bishop, he desires a noble task. ²Now a bishop must be above reproach, the husband of one wife, temperate, sensible, dignified hospitable, an apt teacher, ³no drunkard, not violent but gentle, not quarrelsome, and no lover of money. ⁴He must manage his own household well, keeping his children submissive and respectful in every way; ⁵for if a man does not know how to manage his own household, how can he care for God's church? ⁶He

3 Πιστὸς   ὁ   λόγος·   εἴ   τις   ἐπισκοπῆς
Faithful [is]   the   word: If   anyone   ²oversight

ὀρέγεται,   καλοῦ   ἔργου   ἐπιθυμεῖ.   2 δεῖ
¹aspires to,   ²a good   ³work   ¹he desires.   It behoves

οὖν   τὸν   ἐπίσκοπον   ἀνεπίλημπτον   εἶναι,
there-   the   bishop   without reproach   to be,
fore

μιᾶς   γυναικὸς   ἄνδρα,   νηφάλιον,   σώφρονα,
of one   wife   husband,   temperate,   sensible,

κόσμιον,   φιλόξενον,   διδακτικόν,   3 μὴ
orderly,   hospitable,   apt at teaching,   not

πάροινον,   μὴ   πλήκτην,   ἀλλὰ   ἐπιεικῆ,
an excessive   not   a striker,   but   forbearing,
drinker,

ἄμαχον,   ἀφιλάργυρον,   4 τοῦ   ἰδίου   οἴκου
uncontentious, not avaricious,   ³the(his)   ⁴own   ⁵household

καλῶς   προϊστάμενον,   τέκνα   ἔχοντα   ἐν
²well   ¹ruling,   children   having   in

ὑποταγῇ   μετὰ   πάσης   σεμνότητος,   5 (εἰ
subjection   with   all   gravity,   ³(if

δέ   τις   τοῦ   ἰδίου   οἴκου   προστῆναι   οὐκ
¹but ²anyone ⁷the(his) ⁸own   ⁹household   ⁶to rule   ⁵not*

οἶδεν,   πῶς   ἐκκλησίας   θεοῦ   ἐπιμελήσεται;)
⁴knows,   how   ²a church   ³of God   ¹will he care for ?)

b Or *by the birth of the child*

* That is, " cannot "; see note on page xviii.

must not be a recent convert, or he may be puffed up with conceit and fall into the condemnation of the devil;[d] [7] moreover he must be well thought of by outsiders, or he may fall into reproach and the snare of the devil.[d] [8] Deacons likewise must be serious, not double-tongued, not addicted to much wine, not greedy for gain; [9] they must hold the mystery of the faith with a clear conscience. [10] And let them also be tested first; then if they prove themselves blameless let them serve as deacons. [11] The women likewise must be serious, no slanderers, but temperate, faithful in all things. [12] Let deacons be the husband of one wife, and let them manage their children and their households well; [13] for those who serve well as deacons gain a good standing for themselves and also great confidence in the faith which is in Christ Jesus.

[14] I hope to come to you soon, but I am writing these instructions to you so that, [15] if I am delayed, you may know how one ought to behave in the household of God, which is the church of the living God, the pillar

---

[6] μὴ   νεόφυτον,   ἵνα   μὴ   τυφωθεὶς   εἰς
not a neophyte(recent   lest   being puffed up [2] into
convert),

κρίμα   ἐμπέσῃ   τοῦ   διαβόλου.   [7] δεῖ   δὲ
[3] judgment [1] he fall in of the   devil.   And it behoves

καὶ   μαρτυρίαν   καλὴν   ἔχειν   ἀπὸ   τῶν
also   [3] witness   [2] a good [1] to have from the [ones]

ἔξωθεν,   [7] ἵνα   μὴ   εἰς   ὀνειδισμὸν   ἐμπέσῃ
outside,   lest   [2] into [3] reproach [1] he fall in

καὶ   παγίδα   τοῦ   διαβόλου.   [8] Διακόνους
and   a snare   of the   devil.   [It behoves] deacons

ὡσαύτως   σεμνούς,   μὴ   διλόγους,   μὴ   οἴνῳ
similarly [to be] grave,   not double-tongued, not [3] wine

πολλῷ   προσέχοντας,   μὴ   αἰσχροκερδεῖς,
[2] to much [1] being addicted,   not   fond of base gain,

[9] ἔχοντας   τὸ   μυστήριον   τῆς   πίστεως   ἐν
having   the   mystery   of the   faith   with

καθαρᾷ   συνειδήσει.   [10] καὶ   οὗτοι   δὲ
a clean   conscience.   [4] Also   [3] these [1] and

δοκιμαζέσθωσαν   πρῶτον,   εἶτα   διακονείτωσαν
[2] let [5] be proved   firstly,   then   let them minister

ἀνέγκλητοι   ὄντες.   [11] γυναῖκας   ὡσαύτως
[2] irreproachable [1] being.   [It behoves]* wives   similarly

σεμνάς,   μὴ   διαβόλους,   νηφαλίους,   πιστὰς
[to be] grave, not   slanderers,   sober,   faithful

ἐν   πᾶσιν.   [12] διάκονοι   ἔστωσαν   μιᾶς
in   all things.   [2] Deacons   [1] let [3] be [5] of one

γυναικὸς   ἄνδρες,   τέκνων   καλῶς   προϊστάμενοι
[6] wife   [4] husbands, [2] children [6] well   [1] ruling

καὶ   τῶν   ἰδίων   οἴκων.   [13] οἱ   γὰρ   καλῶς
[3] and [4] the(ir) own   [5] households.   For the [ones] [2] well

διακονήσαντες   βαθμὸν   ἑαυτοῖς   καλὸν
[1] having ministered [6] position [4] for themselves [5] a good

περιποιοῦνται   καὶ   πολλὴν   παρρησίαν   ἐν
[3] acquire   and   much   boldness   in

πίστει   τῇ   ἐν   Χριστῷ   Ἰησοῦ.   [14] Ταῦτά
faith   the [one] in   Christ   Jesus.   These things

σοι   γράφω   ἐλπίζων   ἐλθεῖν   πρὸς   σὲ
to thee   I write   hoping   to come   to   thee

τάχιον·   [15] ἐὰν   δὲ   βραδύνω,   ἵνα   εἰδῇς
shortly;   but if   I delay,   in order   thou
that   mayest
know

πῶς   δεῖ   ἐν   οἴκῳ   θεοῦ   ἀναστρέφεσθαι,
how   it behoves in   [the]   of God   to behave,
household

ἥτις   ἐστὶν   ἐκκλησία   θεοῦ   ζῶντος,   στῦλος
which   is   [the] church [2] God [1] of [the] living, pillar

---

[d] Or slanderer

* See verses 7 and 8.

and bulwark of the truth.
¹⁶Great indeed, we con-
fess, is the mystery of
our religion:
He^e was manifested in
the flesh,
vindicated^f in the
Spirit,
seen by angels,
preached among the
nations,
believed on in the
world,
taken up in glory.

καὶ   ἑδραίωμα   τῆς   ἀληθείας.   **16** καὶ
and   bulwark   of the   truth.   And

ὁμολογουμένως   μέγα   ἐστὶν   τὸ   τῆς   εὐσεβείας
confessedly   great   is   the   –   ²of piety

μυστήριον·   ὃς   ἐφανερώθη   ἐν   σαρκί,
¹mystery: Who   was manifested   in   flesh,

ἐδικαιώθη   ἐν   πνεύματι,   ὤφθη   ἀγγέλοις,
was justified   in   spirit,   was seen   by angels,

ἐκηρύχθη   ἐν   ἔθνεσιν,   ἐπιστεύθη   ἐν   κόσμῳ,
was pro-   among   nations,   was believed   in [the] world,
claimed

ἀνελήμφθη   ἐν   δόξῃ.
was taken up   in   glory.

CHAPTER 4

NOW the Spirit
expressly says that
in later times some will
depart from the faith by
giving heed to deceitful
spirits and doctrines of
demons, ²through the
pretensions of liars whose
consciences are seared,
³who forbid marriage
and enjoin abstinence
from foods which God
created to be received
with thanksgiving by
those who believe and
know the truth. ⁴For
everything created by
God is good, and nothing
is to be rejected if it is
received with thanks-
giving; ⁵for then it is
consecrated by the word
of God and prayer.
6 If you put these
instructions before the
brethren, you will be a
good minister of Christ
Jesus, nourished on the
words of the faith and of

4 Τὸ   δὲ   πνεῦμα   ῥητῶς   λέγει   ὅτι
     Now the   Spirit   ²in words† ¹says   that

ἐν   ὑστέροις   καιροῖς   ἀποστήσονταί   τινες
in   later   times   ²will depart from   ¹some

τῆς   πίστεως,   προσέχοντες   πνεύμασιν
the   faith,   attending to   ²spirits

πλάνοις   καὶ   διδασκαλίαις   δαιμονίων,   **2** ἐν
¹misleading and   teachings   of demons,   ²in

ὑποκρίσει   ψευδολόγων,   κεκαυστηριασμένων
³hypocrisy   ¹of men who speak lies,   having been branded on

τὴν   ἰδίαν   συνείδησιν,   **3** κωλυόντων   γαμεῖν,
the(ir) own   conscience,   forbidding   to marry,

ἀπέχεσθαι   βρωμάτων,   ἃ   ὁ   θεὸς   ἔκτισεν
[bidding] to   foods,   which –   God   created
abstain from

εἰς   μετάλημψιν   μετὰ   εὐχαριστίας   τοῖς
for   partaking   with   thanksgiving   by the

πιστοῖς   καὶ   ἐπεγνωκόσι   τὴν   ἀλήθειαν.
believers   and [those] having fully the   truth.
                              known

4 ὅτι   πᾶν   κτίσμα   θεοῦ   καλόν,   καὶ
    Because every   creature   of God [is] good,   and

οὐδὲν   ἀπόβλητον   μετὰ   εὐχαριστίας   λαμβαν-
nothing   to be put away   ²with   ³thanksgiving   ¹being
[is]

όμενον·   **5** ἁγιάζεται   γὰρ   διὰ   λόγου   θεοῦ
received;   for it is being sanctified through   a word   of God

καὶ   ἐντεύξεως.   **6** Ταῦτα   ὑποτιθέμενος
and   petition.   ²These things   ¹suggesting

τοῖς   ἀδελφοῖς   καλὸς   ἔσῃ   διάκονος   Χριστοῦ
³to the ⁴brothers   ⁶a good   ⁵thou   ⁷minister   of Christ
                                 wilt be

Ἰησοῦ,   ἐντρεφόμενος   τοῖς   λόγοις   τῆς
Jesus,   being nourished   by the   words   of the

---

^e Greek *Who;* other ancient
authorities read *God;* others,
Which
^f Or *justified*

the good doctrine which you have followed. [7] Have nothing to do with godless and silly myths. Train yourself in godliness; [8] for while bodily training is of some value, godliness is of value in every way, as it holds promise for the present life and also for the life to come. [9] The saying is sure and worthy of full acceptance. [10] For to this end we toil and strive,[f] because we have our hope set on the living God, who is the Savior of all men, especially of those who believe.

11 Command and teach these things. [12] Let no one despise your youth, but set the believers an example in speech and conduct, in love, in faith, in purity. [13] Till I come, attend to the public reading of scripture, to preaching, to teaching. [14] Do not neglect the gift you have, which was given you by prophetic utterance when the elders laid their hands upon you.

πίστεως καὶ τῆς καλῆς διδασκαλίας ᾗ
faith and of the good teaching which

παρηκολούθηκας· 7 τοὺς δὲ βεβήλους καὶ
thou hast followed; but the profane and

γραώδεις μύθους παραιτοῦ. γύμναζε δὲ
old-womanish tales refuse. And exercise

σεαυτὸν πρὸς εὐσέβειαν. 8 ἡ γὰρ σωματικὴ
thyself to piety. – For bodily

γυμνασία πρὸς ὀλίγον ἐστὶν ὠφέλιμος·
exercise ³for ⁴a little ¹is ²profitable;

ἡ δὲ εὐσέβεια πρὸς πάντα ὠφέλιμός
– but piety ³for ⁴all things ²profitable

ἐστιν, ἐπαγγελίαν ἔχουσα ζωῆς τῆς νῦν
¹is, promise having ³life ¹of the ²now
(present)

καὶ τῆς μελλούσης. 9 πιστὸς ὁ λόγος
and of the coming. Faithful [is] the word

καὶ πάσης ἀποδοχῆς ἄξιος· 10 εἰς τοῦτο
and ²of all ³acceptance ¹worthy; ²to ³this

γὰρ κοπιῶμεν καὶ ἀγωνιζόμεθα, ὅτι
¹for we labour and struggle, because

ἠλπίκαμεν ἐπὶ θεῷ ζῶντι, ὅς ἐστιν
we have set on ²God ¹a living, who is
[our] hope

σωτὴρ πάντων ἀνθρώπων, μάλιστα πιστῶν.
[the] of all men, especially of believers.
Saviour

11 Παράγγελλε ταῦτα καὶ δίδασκε.
Charge thou these things and teach.

12 μηδείς σου τῆς νεότητος καταφρονείτω,
²No one ⁵of thee ³the ⁴youth ¹let despise,

ἀλλὰ τύπος γίνου τῶν πιστῶν ἐν λόγῳ,
but ²a pattern ¹become of the believers in speech,
thou

ἐν ἀναστροφῇ, ἐν ἀγάπῃ, ἐν πίστει,
in behaviour, in love, in faith,

ἐν ἁγνείᾳ. 13 ἕως ἔρχομαι πρόσεχε
in purity. Until I come attend

τῇ ἀναγνώσει, τῇ παρακλήσει, τῇ διδασ-
to the reading,* to the exhortation, to the teach-

καλίᾳ. 14 μὴ ἀμέλει τοῦ ἐν σοὶ
ing. Do not be neglectful ¹of the ³in ⁴thee

χαρίσματος, ὃ ἐδόθη σοι διὰ προφητείας
²gift, which was to thee by prophecy
given means of

μετὰ ἐπιθέσεως τῶν χειρῶν τοῦ πρε-
with laying on of the hands of the body

[f] Other ancient authorities read *suffer reproach*

* That is, the reading aloud in public worship of the Scriptures (as nearly always in the N.T.).

¹⁵Practice these duties, devote yourself to them, so that all may see your progress. ¹⁶Take heed to yourself and to your teaching; hold to that, for by so doing you will save both yourself and your hearers.

σβυτερίου. **15** ταῦτα μελέτα, ἐν τούτοις
of elders.   ²These things ¹attend to,   ²in ³these things

ἴσθι,   ἵνα   σου   ἡ   προκοπὴ   φανερὰ   ᾖ
¹be   in order   of thee   the   advance   clear   may
thou,   that   be

πᾶσιν. **16** ἔπεχε σεαυτῷ καὶ τῇ διδασκαλίᾳ,
to all men.   Take heed to thyself   and   to the   teaching,

ἐπίμενε   αὐτοῖς·   τοῦτο   γὰρ   ποιῶν   καὶ
continue   in them;   for this   doing   both

σεαυτὸν σώσεις καὶ τοὺς ἀκούοντάς σου.
thyself   thou wilt save   and   the [ones] hearing   thee.

CHAPTER 5

DO not rebuke an older man but exhort him as you would a father; treat younger men like brothers, ²older women like mothers, younger women like sisters, in all purity.
3 Honor widows who are real widows. ⁴If a widow has children or grandchildren, let them first learn their religious duty to their own family and make some return to their parents; for this is acceptable in the sight of God. ⁵She who is a real widow, and is left all alone, has set her hope on God and continues in supplications and prayers night and day; ⁶whereas she who is self-indulgent is dead even while she lives. ⁷Command this, so that they may be without reproach. ⁸If any one does not provide for his relatives, and especially

5 Πρεσβυτέρῳ   μὴ   ἐπιπλήξῃς,   ἀλλὰ
An older man   do not rebuke,   but

παρακάλει   ὡς   πατέρα,   νεωτέρους   ὡς
exhort   as   a father,   younger men   as

ἀδελφούς,   **2** πρεσβυτέρας   ὡς   μητέρας,
brothers,   older women   as   mothers,

νεωτέρας   ὡς   ἀδελφὰς   ἐν   πάσῃ   ἁγνείᾳ.
younger women as   sisters   with   all   purity.

3 Χήρας   τίμα   τὰς   ὄντως   χήρας.   **4** εἰ δέ
²Widows   ¹honour   ³the   ⁴really   ⁵widows.   But if

τις   χήρα   τέκνα   ἢ   ἔκγονα   ἔχει,   μαν-
any   widow   ²children   ³or ⁴grandchildren ¹has,   let

θανέτωσαν πρῶτον τὸν ἴδιον οἶκον εὐσεβεῖν
them learn   firstly   ²the(ir)   ³own ⁴household ¹to show
                                           piety to

καὶ   ἀμοιβὰς   ἀποδιδόναι   τοῖς   προγόνοις·
and   ²requitals   ¹to return   to the(ir)   forebears;

τοῦτο   γάρ   ἐστιν   ἀπόδεκτον   ἐνώπιον   τοῦ
for this   is   acceptable   before   --

θεοῦ. **5** ἡ δὲ ὄντως χήρα καὶ μεμονωμένη
God.   But the   really   widow   and   having been left
                                           alone

ἤλπικεν   ἐπὶ   θεὸν   καὶ   προσμένει   ταῖς
has set   on   God   and   continues   in the
[her] hope

δεήσεσιν   καὶ   ταῖς   προσευχαῖς   νυκτὸς   καὶ
petitions   and   the   prayers   night   and

ἡμέρας·   **6** ἡ   δὲ   σπαταλῶσα   ζῶσα   τέθνηκεν.
day;   but the   living wantonly   ²living   ¹has died.
            [one]

7 καὶ   ταῦτα   παράγγελλε,   ἵνα   ἀνεπίλημπτοι
And   these   charge thou,   in order   ²without reproach
      things   that

ὦσιν. **8** εἰ δέ τις τῶν ἰδίων καὶ μάλιστα
¹they   But if anyone ²the(his) ³own   ⁴and   ⁵especially
may be.   [people]

for his own family, he has disowned the faith and is worse than an unbeliever. 9 Let a widow be enrolled if she is not less than sixty years of age, having been the wife of one husband; 10 and she must be well attested for her good deeds, as one who has brought up children, shown hospitality, washed the feet of the saints, relieved the afflicted, and devoted herself to doing good in every way. 11 But refuse to enrol younger widows; for when they grow wanton against Christ they desire to marry, 12 and so they incur condemnation for having violated their first pledge. 13 Besides that, they learn to be idlers, gadding about from house to house, and not only idlers but gossips and busybodies, saying what they should not. 14 So I would have younger widows marry, bear children, rule their households, and give the enemy no occasion to revile us. 15 For some have already strayed after Satan. 16 If any believing woman[i] has relatives who are widows, let her assist them; let the church not be burdened,

οἰκείων   οὐ   προνοεῖ,   τὴν   πίστιν   ἤρνηται
[his]   ¹provides not [for],   ²the   ³faith   ¹he has
⁶family   denied

καὶ   ἔστιν   ἀπίστου   χείρων.   9 χήρα
and   is   ²an unbeliever   ¹worse [than].   A widow

καταλεγέσθω   μὴ   ἔλαττον   ἐτῶν   ἑξήκοντα
let be enrolled   ²not   ³less [than]   ⁵of years   ⁴sixty

γεγονυῖα,   ἑνὸς   ἀνδρὸς   γυνή,   10 ἐν   ἔργοις
¹having   of one   man   wife,   ²by   ⁴works
become,

καλοῖς   μαρτυρουμένη,   εἰ   ἐτεκνοτρόφησεν,
³good   ¹being witnessed,   if   she brought up children,

εἰ   ἐξενοδόχησεν,   εἰ   ἁγίων   πόδας   ἔνιψεν,
if   she entertained   if   ³of saints   ²feet   ¹she
strangers,   washed,

εἰ   θλιβομένοις   ἐπήρκεσεν,   εἰ   παντὶ   ἔργῳ
if   ²being afflicted   ¹she relieved,   if   ²every   ⁴work
[ones],

ἀγαθῷ   ἐπηκολούθησεν.   11 νεωτέρας   δὲ
³good   ¹she followed after.   But younger

χήρας   παραιτοῦ·   ὅταν   γὰρ   καταστρηνιάσωσιν
widows   refuse;   for whenever   they grow wanton against

τοῦ   Χριστοῦ,   γαμεῖν   θέλουσιν,   12 ἔχουσαι
-    Christ,   ²to marry   ¹they wish,   having

κρίμα   ὅτι   τὴν   πρώτην   πίστιν   ἠθέτησαν·
judgment because ²the(ir)   ³first   ⁴faith   ¹they set aside;

13 ἅμα   δὲ   καὶ   ἀργαὶ   μανθάνουσιν
and at the same time   also   ²idle   ¹they learn [to be]

περιερχόμεναι   τὰς   οἰκίας,   οὐ   μόνον   δὲ
going round   the   houses,   ²not   ³only   ¹and

ἀργαὶ   ἀλλὰ   καὶ   φλύαροι   καὶ   περίεργοι,
idle   but   also   gossips   and   busybodies,

λαλοῦσαι   τὰ   μὴ   δέοντα.   14 βούλομαι
speaking   the things   not   proper.   I will

οὖν   νεωτέρας   γαμεῖν,   τεκνογονεῖν,
there-   younger women   to marry,   to bear children,
fore

οἰκοδεσποτεῖν,   μηδεμίαν   ἀφορμὴν   διδόναι
to be mistress of   ²no   ³occasion   ¹to give
a house,

τῷ   ἀντικειμένῳ   λοιδορίας   χάριν·   15 ἤδη
to the [one] opposing   ²reproach   ¹on account of;   ²already

γάρ   τινες   ἐξετράπησαν   ὀπίσω   τοῦ   σατανᾶ.
¹for   some   turned aside   behind   -   Satan.

16 εἴ   τις   πιστὴ   ἔχει   χήρας,   ἐπαρκείτω
If   any   believing   has   widows,   let her relieve
woman

αὐταῖς,   καὶ   μὴ   βαρείσθω   ἡ   ἐκκλησία,
them,   and   not   let be burdened   the   church,

---

[i] Other ancient authorities read man or woman; others, simply man

so that it may assist those who are real widows.

17 Let the elders who rule well be considered worthy of double honor, especially those who labor in preaching and teaching; 18 for the scripture says, "You shall not muzzle an ox when it is treading out the grain," and, "The laborer deserves his wages." 19 Never admit any charge against an elder except on the evidence of two or three witnesses. 20 As for those who persist in sin, rebuke them in the presence of all, so that the rest may stand in fear. 21 In the presence of God and of Christ Jesus and of the elect angels I charge you to keep these rules without favor, doing nothing from partiality. 22 Do not be hasty in the laying on of hands, nor participate in another man's sins; keep yourself pure.

23 No longer drink only water, but use a little wine for the sake of your stomach and your frequent ailments.

24 The sins of some men are conspicuous, pointing to judgment, but the sins of others appear later. 25 So also

ἵνα	ταῖς	ὄντως	χήραις	ἐπαρκέσῃ.	17 Οἱ
in order that	²the	³really	⁴widows	¹it may relieve.	²The

καλῶς	προεστῶτες	πρεσβύτεροι	διπλῆς
⁵well	⁴ruling	³elders	⁵of double

τιμῆς	ἀξιούσθωσαν,	μάλιστα	οἱ	κοπιῶντες
¹⁰honour	¹let ⁶be ⁷deemed ⁸worthy,	especially	the	labouring [ones]

ἐν	λόγῳ	καὶ	διδασκαλίᾳ.	18 λέγει	γὰρ
in	speech	and	teaching.	For says	

ἡ	γραφή·	βοῦν	ἀλοῶντα	οὐ	φιμώσεις,
the	scripture:	An ox	threshing	thou shalt not muzzle,	

καί·	ἄξιος	ὁ	ἐργάτης	τοῦ	μισθοῦ	αὐτοῦ.
and:	Worthy [is]	the	workman	of the	pay	of him.

19 κατὰ	πρεσβυτέρου	κατηγορίαν	μὴ	παρα-
Against	an elder	accusation	do not re-	

δέχου,	ἐκτὸς	εἰ	μὴ	ἐπὶ	δύο	ἢ	τριῶν
ceive,	except	unless		on [the word of]	two	or	three

μαρτύρων.	20 Τοὺς	ἁμαρτάνοντας	ἐνώπιον
witnesses.	The [ones]	sinning	²before

πάντων	ἔλεγχε,	ἵνα	καὶ	οἱ	λοιποὶ	φόβον
²all	¹reprove thou,	in order that	³also	¹the	²rest	⁵fear

ἔχωσιν.	21 Διαμαρτύρομαι	ἐνώπιον	τοῦ
⁴may have.	I solemnly witness	before	–

θεοῦ	καὶ	Χριστοῦ	Ἰησοῦ	καὶ	τῶν
God	and	Christ	Jesus	and	the

ἐκλεκτῶν	ἀγγέλων	ἵνα	ταῦτα	φυλάξῃς
chosen	angels	in order that	these things	thou guard

χωρὶς	προκρίματος,	μηδὲν	ποιῶν	κατὰ
without	prejudgment,	²nothing	¹doing	by way of

πρόσκλισιν.	22 χεῖρας	ταχέως	μηδενὶ
inclination.	²Hands	³quickly	⁴no man

ἐπιτίθει,	μηδὲ	κοινώνει	ἁμαρτίαις	ἀλ-
¹lay ³on,	nor	share	²sins	¹in

λοτρίαις·	σεαυτὸν	ἁγνὸν	τήρει.	23 Μηκέτι
others'†;	³thyself	³pure	¹keep.	No longer

ὑδροπότει,	ἀλλὰ	οἴνῳ	ὀλίγῳ	χρῶ	διὰ
drink water,	but	³wine	²a little	¹use	on account of

τὸν	στόμαχον	καὶ	τὰς	πυκνάς	σου
the(thy)	stomach	and	the	frequent	²of thee

ἀσθενείας.	24 Τινῶν	ἀνθρώπων	αἱ	ἁμαρτίαι
¹weaknesses.	³of some	⁴men	¹The	²sins

πρόδηλοί	εἰσιν	προάγουσαι	εἰς	κρίσιν,
⁶clear beforehand	⁵are	going before	to	judgment,

τισὶν	δὲ	καὶ	ἐπακολουθοῦσιν·	25 ὡσαύτως
but some	indeed		they follow on;	similarly

good deeds are conspicuous; and even when they are not, they cannot remain hidden.

καὶ τὰ ἔργα τὰ καλὰ πρόδηλα, καὶ
also the ²works – ¹good [are] clear and
                                    beforehand,
τὰ ἄλλως ἔχοντα κρυβῆναι οὐ δύνανται.
the ²otherwise ¹having ⁴to be hidden ³cannot.
[ones] (being)

CHAPTER 6

6 Ὅσοι εἰσὶν ὑπὸ ζυγὸν δοῦλοι, τοὺς
As many as are under a yoke slaves, ²the(ir)
                 [being]

LET all who are under the yoke of slavery regard their masters as worthy of all honor, so that the name of God and the teaching may not be defamed. ²Those who have believing masters must not be disrespectful on the ground that they are brethren; rather they must serve all the better since those who benefit by their service are believers and beloved. Teach and urge these duties. ³If any one teaches otherwise and does not agree with the sound words of our Lord Jesus Christ and the teaching which accords with godliness, ⁴he is puffed up with conceit, he knows nothing; he has a morbid craving for controversy and for disputes about words, which produce envy, dissension, slander, base suspicions, ⁵and wrangling among men who are depraved in mind and bereft of the truth, imagining that godliness is a means of

ἰδίους δεσπότας πάσης τιμῆς ἀξίους ἡγείσ-
³own ⁴masters ⁶of all ⁷honour ⁵worthy ¹let them
θωσαν, ἵνα μὴ τὸ ὄνομα τοῦ θεοῦ καὶ
deem, lest the name – of God and
ἡ διδασκαλία βλασφημῆται. 2 οἱ δὲ
the teaching be blasphemed. And ¹the [ones]
πιστοὺς ἔχοντες δεσπότας μὴ καταφρο-
³believing ²having ⁴masters not let them
νείτωσαν, ὅτι ἀδελφοί εἰσιν, ἀλλὰ μᾶλλον
despise [them], because brothers they are, but rather
δουλευέτωσαν, ὅτι πιστοί εἰσιν καὶ
let them serve as slaves, because ⁶believing ⁵are ⁷and
ἀγαπητοὶ οἱ τῆς εὐεργεσίας ἀντιλαμ-
³beloved ¹the [ones] ²of the ⁴good service ²receiving in
βανόμενοι.
return.
Ταῦτα δίδασκε καὶ παρακάλει. 3 εἴ
These things teach thou and exhort. If
τις ἑτεροδιδασκαλεῖ καὶ μὴ προσέρχεται
anyone teaches differently and consents not
ὑγιαίνουσιν λόγοις τοῖς τοῦ κυρίου ἡμῶν
to being healthy words the of the Lord of us
               [words]
Ἰησοῦ Χριστοῦ, καὶ τῇ κατ᾽ εὐσέβειαν
Jesus Christ, and ¹to the ³accord- ⁴piety
                     ing to
διδασκαλίᾳ, 4 τετύφωται, μηδὲν ἐπιστά-
²teaching, he has been puffed up, ²nothing ¹under-
μενος, ἀλλὰ νοσῶν περὶ ζητήσεις καὶ
standing, but being diseased about questionings and
λογομαχίας, ἐξ ὧν γίνεται φθόνος, ἔρις,
battles of words, out of which comes envy, strife,
βλασφημίαι, ὑπόνοιαι πονηραί, 5 διαπαρα-
blasphemies, ²suspicions ¹evil, perpetual
τριβαὶ διεφθαρμένων ἀνθρώπων τὸν νοῦν
wranglings ²having been corrupted ¹of men the mind
        =of men with corrupted mind
καὶ ἀπεστερημένων τῆς ἀληθείας, νομιζ-
and having been deprived of the truth, sup-
όντων πορισμὸν εἶναι τὴν εὐσέβειαν.
posing ³gain ²to be the ¹piety.*

* For order of words see note on John 1. 1.

gain. ⁶There is great gain in godliness with contentment; ⁷for we brought nothing into the world, andʲ we cannot take anything out of the world; ⁸but if we have food and clothing, with these we shall be content. ⁹But those who desire to be rich fall into temptation, into a snare, into many senseless and hurtful desires that plunge men into ruin and destruction. ¹⁰For the love of money is the root of all evils; it is through this craving that some have wandered away from the faith and pierced their hearts with many pangs.

11 But as for you, man of God, shun all this; aim at righteousness, godliness, faith, love, steadfastness, gentleness. ¹²Fight the good fight of the faith; take hold of the eternal life to which you were called when you made the good confession in the presence of many witnesses. ¹³In the presence of God who gives life to all things, and of Christ Jesus who in his testimony before

6 ἔστιν δὲ πορισμὸς μέγας ἡ εὐσέβεια
But ⁴is   ⁵gain   ⁶great   the   ¹piety

μετὰ αὐταρκείας· 7 οὐδὲν γὰρ εἰσηνέγκαμεν
⁴with   ⁵self-sufficiency;*   for nothing   we have brought in

εἰς τὸν κόσμον, ὅτι οὐδὲ ἐξενεγκεῖν
into   the   world,   because   neither   ²to carry out

τι δυνάμεθα· 8 ἔχοντες δὲ διατροφὰς καὶ
³any- ¹can we;   but having   foods   and
thing

σκεπάσματα, τούτοις ἀρκεσθησόμεθα. 9 οἱ
clothings,   with these things   we will be satisfied.   the

δὲ βουλόμενοι πλουτεῖν ἐμπίπτουσιν εἰς
But [ones] resolving   to be rich   fall in   into

πειρασμὸν καὶ παγίδα καὶ ἐπιθυμίας πολλὰς
temptation   and   a snare   and   ²lusts   ¹many

ἀνοήτους καὶ βλαβεράς, αἵτινες βυθίζουσιν
²foolish   ³and   ⁴injurious,   which   ¹cause ²to sink

τοὺς ἀνθρώπους εἰς ὄλεθρον καὶ ἀπώλειαν.
-   ²men   into   ruin   and   destruction.

10 ῥίζα γὰρ πάντων τῶν κακῶν ἐστιν
For ⁴a root   ⁵of all   -   ⁶evils   ³is

ἡ φιλαργυρία, ἧς τινες ὀρεγόμενοι
¹the   ²love of money,*   of which   some   hankering after

ἀπεπλανήθησαν ἀπὸ τῆς πίστεως καὶ
wandered away   from   the   faith   and

ἑαυτοὺς περιέπειραν ὀδύναις πολλαῖς. 11 Σὺ
themselves   pierced round   ²pains   ¹by many.   thou

δέ, ὦ ἄνθρωπε θεοῦ, ταῦτα φεῦγε· δίωκε
But, O   man   of God,   these things   flee;   ²pursue

δὲ δικαιοσύνην, εὐσέβειαν, πίστιν, ἀγάπην,
¹and righteousness,   piety,   faith,   love,

ὑπομονήν, πραϋπαθίαν. 12 ἀγωνίζου τὸν
endurance,   meekness.   Struggle   the

καλὸν ἀγῶνα τῆς πίστεως, ἐπιλαβοῦ τῆς
good   struggle   of the   faith,   lay hold on   the

αἰωνίου ζωῆς, εἰς ἣν ἐκλήθης καὶ ὡμολό-
eternal   life,   to which   thou wast   and   didst con-
                called

γησας τὴν καλὴν ὁμολογίαν ἐνώπιον
fess   the   good   confession   before

πολλῶν μαρτύρων. 13 παραγγέλλω ἐνώπιον
many   witnesses.   I charge   before

τοῦ θεοῦ τοῦ ζῳογονοῦντος τὰ πάντα
-   God   the [one]   quickening   -   all things

καὶ Χριστοῦ Ἰησοῦ τοῦ μαρτυρήσαντος
and   Christ   Jesus   the [one] having witnessed

ʲ Other ancient authorities insert it is certain that

* For order of words see note on John 1. 1.

Pontius Pilate made the good confession, ¹⁴ I charge you to keep the commandment unstained and free from reproach until the appearing of our Lord Jesus Christ; ¹⁵ and this will be made manifest at the proper time by the blessed and only Sovereign, the King of kings and Lord of lords, ¹⁶ who alone has immortality and dwells in unapproachable light, whom no man has ever seen or can see. To him be honor and eternal dominion. Amen.

17 As for the rich in this world, charge them not to be haughty, nor to set their hopes on uncertain riches but on God who richly furnishes us with everything to enjoy. ¹⁸ They are to do good, to be rich in good deeds, liberal and generous, ¹⁹ thus laying up for themselves a good foundation for the future, so that they may take hold of the life which is life indeed.

20 O Timothy, guard what has been entrusted to you. Avoid the godless

ἐπὶ Ποντίου Πιλάτου τὴν καλὴν ὁμολογίαν,
in the Pontius Pilate the good confession,
time of

14 τηρῆσαί σε τὴν ἐντολὴν ἄσπιλον
²to keep ¹thee* the(this) commandment unspotted

ἀνεπίλημπτον μέχρι τῆς ἐπιφανείας τοῦ
without reproach until the appearance of the

κυρίου ἡμῶν Ἰησοῦ Χριστοῦ, 15 ἦν
Lord of us Jesus Christ, which§

καιροῖς ἰδίοις δείξει ὁ μακάριος καὶ
⁷in its/his own times ⁶will show ¹the ²blessed ³and

μόνος δυνάστης, ὁ βασιλεὺς τῶν βασιλευ-
⁴only ⁵Potentate, the King of the [ones] reign-

όντων καὶ κύριος τῶν κυριευόντων, 16 ὁ
ing and Lord of the [ones] ruling, the

μόνος ἔχων ἀθανασίαν, φῶς οἰκῶν
only [one] having immortality, ²light ¹inhabiting

ἀπρόσιτον, ὃν εἶδεν οὐδεὶς ἀνθρώπων οὐδὲ
unapproach- whom ²saw ¹no one ²of men nor
able,

ἰδεῖν δύναται· ᾧ τιμὴ καὶ κράτος αἰώνιον·
²to see ¹can; to [be] and might eternal:
whom honour

ἀμήν. 17 Τοῖς πλουσίοις ἐν τῷ νῦν
Amen. ²the ³rich ⁴in ⁵the ⁶now
(present)

αἰῶνι παράγγελλε μὴ ὑψηλοφρονεῖν, μηδὲ
⁷age ¹Charge thou not to be highminded, nor

ἠλπικέναι ἐπὶ πλούτου ἀδηλότητι, ἀλλ᾽
to have set on ²of riches ¹[the] uncertainty, but
[their] hope

ἐπὶ θεῷ τῷ παρέχοντι ἡμῖν πάντα
on God the [one] offering to us all things

πλουσίως εἰς ἀπόλαυσιν, 18 ἀγαθοεργεῖν,
richly for enjoyment, to work good,

πλουτεῖν ἐν ἔργοις καλοῖς, εὐμεταδότους
to be rich in ²works ¹good, ¹ready to impart

εἶναι, κοινωνικούς, 19 ἀποθησαυρίζοντας
¹to be, generous, treasuring away

ἑαυτοῖς θεμέλιον καλὸν εἰς τὸ μέλλον,
for ²foundation ¹a good for the future,
themselves

ἵνα ἐπιλάβωνται τῆς ὄντως ζωῆς. 20 Ὦ
in or- they may lay the really life. O
der that hold on

Τιμόθεε, τὴν παραθήκην φύλαξον, ἐκτρεπ-
Timothy, ²the ³deposit ¹guard, turning

* " thee " is the direct object of the verb " charge " in ver. 13:
"I charge . . . thee to keep . . ."
§ The antecedent to this relative pronoun is " appearing ",
not " Jesus Christ ".

chatter and contradictions of what is falsely called knowledge, 21 for by professing it some have missed the mark as regards the faith. Grace be with you.

ὄμενος τὰς βεβήλους κενοφωνίας καὶ
aside from the profane empty utterances and
ἀντιθέσεις τῆς ψευδωνύμου γνώσεως, 21 ἥν
opposing of the falsely named knowledge, which
tenets
τινες ἐπαγγελλόμενοι περὶ τὴν πίστιν
some promising concerning the faith
ἠστόχησαν.
missed aim.
Ἡ χάρις μεθ' ὑμῶν.
- Grace [be] with you.

II. TIMOTHY 1

ΠΡΟΣ ΤΙΜΟΘΕΟΝ Β
To Timothy 2

CHAPTER 1

PAUL, an apostle of Christ Jesus by the will of God according to the promise of the life which is in Christ Jesus,
2 To Timothy, my beloved child:
Grace, mercy, and peace from God the Father and Christ Jesus our Lord.
3 I thank God whom I serve with a clear conscience, as did my fathers, when I remember you constantly in my prayers. 4As I remember your tears, I long night and day to see you, that I may be filled with joy. 5I am reminded of your sincere faith, a faith that

1 Παῦλος ἀπόστολος Χριστοῦ Ἰησοῦ διὰ
Paul an apostle of Christ Jesus through
θελήματος θεοῦ κατ' ἐπαγγελίαν ζωῆς
[the] will of God by way of a promise of life
τῆς ἐν Χριστῷ Ἰησοῦ 2 Τιμοθέῳ ἀγαπητῷ
- in Christ Jesus to Timothy beloved
τέκνῳ· χάρις, ἔλεος, εἰρήνη ἀπὸ θεοῦ
child: Grace, mercy, peace from God
πατρὸς καὶ Χριστοῦ Ἰησοῦ τοῦ κυρίου
[our] Father and Christ Jesus the Lord
ἡμῶν.
of us.
3 Χάριν ἔχω τῷ θεῷ, ᾧ λατρεύω
Thanks I have - to God, whom I worship
ἀπὸ προγόνων ἐν καθαρᾷ συνειδήσει, ὡς
from [my] forebears in a clean conscience, as
ἀδιάλειπτον ἔχω τὴν περὶ σοῦ μνείαν
unceasingly I have 1the 2concerning 4thee 3remem-
brance
ἐν ταῖς δεήσεσίν μου νυκτὸς καὶ ἡμέρας,
in the petitions of me night and day,
4 ἐπιποθῶν σε ἰδεῖν, μεμνημένος σου
longing 2thee 1to see, having been 2of thee
reminded
τῶν δακρύων, ἵνα χαρᾶς πληρωθῶ,
1of the 2tears, in order of(with) joy I may be filled,
that
5 ὑπόμνησιν λαβὼν τῆς ἐν σοὶ ἀνυποκρίτου
2recollection 1taking 3of the 5in 7thee 4unfeigned

dwelt first in your grandmother Lo'is and your mother Eunice and now, I am sure, dwells in you. ⁶Hence I remind you to rekindle the gift of God that is within you through the laying on of my hands; ⁷for God did not give us a spirit of timidity but a spirit of power and love and self-control.

8 Do not be ashamed then of testifying to our Lord, nor of me his prisoner, but take your share of suffering for the gospel in the power of God, ⁹who saved us and called us with a holy calling, not in virtue of our works but in virtue of his own purpose and the grace which he gave us in Christ Jesus ages ago, ¹⁰and now has manifested through the appearing of our Savior Christ Jesus, who abolished death and brought life and immortality to light through the gospel. ¹¹For this gospel I was appointed a preacher and apostle

πίστεως, ἥτις ἐνῴκησεν πρῶτον ἐν τῇ
⁵faith, which indwelt firstly in the

μάμμῃ σου Λωΐδι καὶ τῇ μητρί σου
grand- of thee Lois and [in] the mother of thee
mother

Εὐνίκῃ, πέπεισμαι δὲ ὅτι καὶ ἐν σοί.
Eunice, and I have been that [it dwells] in thee.
persuaded also

6 Δι' ἣν αἰτίαν ἀναμιμνήσκω σε ἀνα-
For which cause I remind thee to fan

ζωπυρεῖν τὸ χάρισμα τοῦ θεοῦ, ὅ ἐστιν
the flame [of] the gift of God, which is

ἐν σοὶ διὰ τῆς ἐπιθέσεως τῶν χειρῶν
in thee through the laying on of the hands

μου. 7 οὐ γὰρ ἔδωκεν ἡμῖν ὁ θεὸς
of me. ²not For ³gave ⁴to us - ¹God

πνεῦμα δειλίας, ἀλλὰ δυνάμεως καὶ ἀγάπης
a spirit of cowardice, but of power and of love

καὶ σωφρονισμοῦ. 8 μὴ οὖν ἐπαισχυνθῇς
and of self-control. ²not ¹Therefore ³be ⁴thou
ashamed [of]

τὸ μαρτύριον τοῦ κυρίου ἡμῶν μηδὲ
the testimony of the Lord of us nor

ἐμὲ τὸν δέσμιον αὐτοῦ, ἀλλὰ συγ-
[of] me the prisoner of him, but suffer

κακοπάθησον τῷ εὐαγγελίῳ κατὰ δύναμιν
ill with the gospel according to [the] power

θεοῦ, 9 τοῦ σώσαντος ἡμᾶς καὶ καλέσαντος
of God, of the having saved us and having called
[one]

κλήσει ἁγίᾳ, οὐ κατὰ τὰ ἔργα ἡμῶν
²calling ¹with a holy, not according to the works of us

ἀλλὰ κατὰ ἰδίαν πρόθεσιν καὶ χάριν,
but according to [his] own purpose and grace,

τὴν δοθεῖσαν ἡμῖν ἐν Χριστῷ Ἰησοῦ
- given to us in Christ Jesus

πρὸ χρόνων αἰωνίων, 10 φανερωθεῖσαν δὲ
before times eternal, but manifested

νῦν διὰ τῆς ἐπιφανείας τοῦ σωτῆρος
now through the appearance of the Saviour

ἡμῶν Χριστοῦ Ἰησοῦ, καταργήσαντος μὲν
of us Christ Jesus, ²abrogating ¹on one
hand

τὸν θάνατον φωτίσαντος δὲ ζωὴν καὶ
- death ³bringing to ¹on the life and
light other

ἀφθαρσίαν διὰ τοῦ εὐαγγελίου, 11 εἰς ὃ
incorruption through the gospel, for which

ἐτέθην ἐγὼ κῆρυξ καὶ ἀπόστολος καὶ
²was ¹I a herald and an apostle and
appointed

and teacher, [12]and therefore I suffer as I do. But I am not ashamed, for I know whom I have believed, and I am sure that he is able to guard until that Day what has been entrusted to me.[a] [13]Follow the pattern of the sound words which you have heard from me, in the faith and love which are in Christ Jesus; [14]guard the truth that has been entrusted to you by the Holy Spirit who dwells within us.

15 You are aware that all who are in Asia turned away from me, and among them Phy'gelus and Hermog'-enes. [16]May the Lord grant mercy to the household of Onesiph'-orus, for he often re-freshed me; he was not ashamed of my chains, [17]but when he arrived in Rome he searched for me eagerly and found me—[18]may the Lord grant him to find mercy from the Lord on that Day—and you well know all the service he rendered at Ephesus.

CHAPTER 2

YOU then, my son, be strong in the grace that is in Christ

a Or what I have entrusted to him

διδάσκαλος· **12** δι' ἦν αἰτίαν καὶ ταῦτα
a teacher;   for which cause also these things

πάσχω, ἀλλ' οὐκ ἐπαισχύνομαι, οἶδα γὰρ
I suffer, but   I am not ashamed,   for I know

ᾧ πεπίστευκα, καὶ πέπεισμαι ὅτι δυνατός
whom I have   and I have been that ²able
       believed,   persuaded

ἐστιν τὴν παραθήκην μου φυλάξαι εἰς
¹he is ⁴the ⁵deposit ⁶of me ³to guard to

ἐκείνην τὴν ἡμέραν. **13** ὑποτύπωσιν ἔχε
that   –   day.   ²a pattern ¹Have
                                              thou

ὑγιαινόντων λόγων ὧν παρ' ἐμοῦ ἤκουσας
of being healthy words which ²from ³me ¹thou
                                              heardest

ἐν πίστει καὶ ἀγάπῃ τῇ ἐν Χριστῷ
in faith and love   – in Christ

Ἰησοῦ· **14** τὴν καλὴν παραθήκην φύλαξον
Jesus;   the good   deposit   guard

διὰ πνεύματος ἁγίου τοῦ ἐνοικοῦντος ἐν
through Spirit [the] Holy – indwelling in

ἡμῖν. **15** Οἶδας τοῦτο, ὅτι ἀπεστράφησάν
us.   Thou knowest this, that turned away from

με πάντες οἱ ἐν τῇ Ἀσίᾳ, ὧν ἐστιν
me all the ones in – Asia, of whom is

Φύγελος καὶ Ἑρμογένης. **16** δῴη ἔλεος
Phygelus and Hermogenes.   ¹May ⁴give ⁵mercy

ὁ κύριος τῷ Ὀνησιφόρου οἴκῳ, ὅτι
²the ³Lord ⁶to the ⁸of Onesiphorus ⁷house- because
                                           hold,

πολλάκις με ἀνέψυξεν καὶ τὴν ἅλυσίν
often   me he refreshed and the chain

μου οὐκ ἐπαισχύνθη, **17** ἀλλὰ γενόμενος
of me was not ashamed [of], but coming to be

ἐν Ῥώμῃ σπουδαίως ἐζήτησέν με καὶ
in Rome ²diligently ¹he ³sought ⁶me ⁴and

εὗρεν· — **18** δῴη αὐτῷ ὁ κύριος εὑρεῖν
⁵found; (¹May ⁴give ⁵to him ²the ³Lord to find

ἔλεος παρὰ κυρίου ἐν ἐκείνῃ τῇ ἡμέρᾳ·
mercy from [the] Lord in that   –   day;)

— καὶ ὅσα ἐν Ἐφέσῳ διηκόνησεν,
and what things in Ephesus he served,

βέλτιον σὺ γινώσκεις.
very well thou knowest.

2 Σὺ οὖν, τέκνον μου, ἐνδυναμοῦ ἐν
Thou therefore, child of me, be empowered by

τῇ χάριτι τῇ ἐν Χριστῷ Ἰησοῦ, **2** καὶ
the grace – in Christ Jesus.   and

Jesus, ²and what you have heard from me before many witnesses entrust to faithful men who will be able to teach others also. ³Take your share of suffering as a good soldier of Christ Jesus. ⁴No soldier on service gets entangled in civilian pursuits, since his aim is to satisfy the one who enlisted him. ⁵An athlete is not crowned unless he competes according to the rules. ⁶It is the hardworking farmer who ought to have the first share of the crops. ⁷Think over what I say, for the Lord will grant you understanding in everything.

8 Remember Jesus Christ, risen from the dead, descended from David, as preached in my gospel, ⁹the gospel for which I am suffering and wearing fetters like a criminal. But the word of God is not fettered. ¹⁰Therefore I endure everything for the sake of the elect, that they also may obtain the salvation which in Christ Jesus goes with eternal glory. ¹¹The saying is sure:

ἃ ἤκουσας παρ' ἐμοῦ διὰ πολλῶν
what thou from me through many
things heardest

μαρτύρων, ταῦτα παράθου πιστοῖς ἀνθρώ-
witnesses, these commit to faithful men,

ποις, οἵτινες ἱκανοὶ ἔσονται καὶ ἑτέρους
who ²competent ¹will be ⁵also ⁴others

διδάξαι. 3 Συγκακοπάθησον ὡς καλὸς
³to teach. Suffer ill with* as a good

στρατιώτης Χριστοῦ Ἰησοῦ. 4 οὐδεὶς
soldier of Christ Jesus. No one

στρατευόμενος ἐμπλέκεται ταῖς τοῦ βίου
soldiering is involved ¹with the – ²of life

πραγματείαις, ἵνα τῷ στρατολογήσαντι
²affairs, in order ²the ³having enlisted
that [one] [him]

ἀρέσῃ. 5 ἐὰν δὲ καὶ ἀθλῇ τις, οὐ
¹he may And if also ²wrestles ¹any- not
please. one,

στεφανοῦται ἐὰν μὴ νομίμως ἀθλήσῃ.
he is crowned unless ²lawfully ¹he wrestles.

6 τὸν κοπιῶντα γεωργὸν δεῖ πρῶτον τῶν
²the ³labouring ⁴husbandman ¹It be- ⁶firstly ⁷of the
hoves

καρπῶν μεταλαμβάνειν. 7 νόει ὃ λέγω·
⁸fruits ⁵to partake. Consider what I say;

δώσει γάρ σοι ὁ κύριος σύνεσιν ἐν
for ³will give ⁴thee ¹the ²Lord understanding in

πᾶσιν. 8 μνημόνευε Ἰησοῦν Χριστὸν
all things. Remember Jesus Christ

ἐγηγερμένον ἐκ νεκρῶν, ἐκ σπέρματος
having been raised from [the] dead, of [the] seed

Δαυίδ, κατὰ τὸ εὐαγγέλιόν μου· 9 ἐν
of David, according to the gospel of me; in

ᾧ κακοπαθῶ μέχρι δεσμῶν ὡς κακοῦργος,
which I suffer ill unto bonds as an evildoer,

ἀλλὰ ὁ λόγος τοῦ θεοῦ οὐ δέδεται.
but the word – of God has not been bound.

10 διὰ τοῦτο πάντα ὑπομένω διὰ τοὺς
Therefore all things I endure on ac- the
count of

ἐκλεκτούς, ἵνα καὶ αὐτοὶ σωτηρίας τύχωσιν
chosen ones, in or- ²also ¹they ⁴salvation ³may obtain
der that

τῆς ἐν Χριστῷ Ἰησοῦ μετὰ δόξης
– in Christ Jesus with glory

αἰωνίου. 11 πιστὸς ὁ λόγος· εἰ γὰρ
eternal. Faithful [is] the word: for if

* See 1. 8.

838   II. TIMOTHY 2

If we have died with him, we shall also live with him; [12]if we endure, we shall also reign with him; if we deny him, he also will deny us; [13]if we are faithless, he remains faithful—for he cannot deny himself.

14 Remind them of this, and charge them before the Lord[b] to avoid disputing about words, which does no good, but only ruins the hearers. [15]Do your best to present yourself to God as one approved, a workman who has no need to be ashamed, rightly handling the word of truth. [16]Avoid such godless chatter, for it will lead people into more and more ungodliness, [17]and their talk will eat its way like gangrene. Among them are Hymenae′us and Phile′tus, [18]who have swerved from the truth by holding that the resurrection is past already. They are upsetting the faith of some. [19]But God's firm foundation stands, bearing this seal: "The Lord knows those who are his," and "Let every one who names the name of the Lord depart from iniquity."

[b] Other ancient authorities read God

συναπεθάνομεν,   καὶ   συζήσομεν·   12 εἰ
we died with [him],   also   we shall live with [him];   if

ὑπομένομεν,   καὶ   συμβασιλεύσομεν·   εἰ
we endure,   also   we shall reign with [him];   if

ἀρνησόμεθα,   κἀκεῖνος   ἀρνήσεται   ἡμᾶς·   13 εἰ
we shall deny,   that one also   will deny   us;   if

ἀπιστοῦμεν,   ἐκεῖνος   πιστὸς   μένει,   ἀρνή-
we disbelieve,   that one   [2]faithful   [1]remains,   [2]to

σασθαι   γὰρ   ἑαυτὸν   οὐ   δύναται.   14 Ταῦτα
deny   [1]for   [4]himself   [3]he cannot.   These things

ὑπομίμνῃσκε,   διαμαρτυρόμενος   ἐνώπιον   τοῦ
remind thou   solemnly witnessing   before
[them] [of],

θεοῦ   μὴ   λογομαχεῖν,   ἐπ'   οὐδὲν   χρήσιμον,
God   not to fight with words,   [2]for   [3]nothing   [1]useful,

ἐπὶ   καταστροφῇ   τῶν   ἀκουόντων.   15 σπού-
for   overthrowing   of the (ones) hearing.   [1]Be

δασον   σεαυτὸν   δόκιμον   παραστῆσαι   τῷ
eager   [3]thyself   [4]approved   [2]to present   –

θεῷ,   ἐργάτην   ἀνεπαίσχυντον,   ὀρθοτομοῦντα
to God,   a workman   unashamed,   cutting straight

τὸν   λόγον   τῆς   ἀληθείας.   16 τὰς   δὲ
the   word   –   of truth.   –   But

βεβήλους   κενοφωνίας   περιίστασο·   ἐπὶ   πλεῖον
profane   empty   shun;   [2]to   [4]more
   utterances

γὰρ   προκόψουσιν   ἀσεβείας,   17 καὶ   ὁ   λόγος
[1]for   [3]they will advance   of impiety,   and   the   word

αὐτῶν   ὡς   γάγγραινα   νομὴν   ἕξει·   ὧν
of them   as   a canker   feeding   will have;   of
   whom

ἐστιν   Ὑμέναιος   καὶ   Φίλητος,   18 οἵτινες
is(are)   Hymenæus   and   Philetus,   who

περὶ   τὴν   ἀλήθειαν   ἠστόχησαν,   λέγοντες
con-   the   truth   missed aim,   saying
cerning

ἀνάστασιν   ἤδη   γεγονέναι,   καὶ   ἀνατρέπουσιν
[the]   already   to have   and   overturn
resurrection   become,

τήν   τινων   πίστιν.   19 ὁ   μέντοι   στερεὸς
the   [2]of some   [1]faith.   [2]the   [1]However   firm

θεμέλιος   τοῦ   θεοῦ   ἕστηκεν,   ἔχων   τὴν
foundation   –   of God   stands,   having   –

σφραγῖδα   ταύτην·   ἔγνω   κύριος   τοὺς   ὄντας
seal   this: [2]knew   [1][The]   the   being
   Lord   [ones]

αὐτοῦ,   καί·   ἀποστήτω   ἀπὸ   ἀδικίας   πᾶς
of him,   and: Let stand away   from   iniquity   every-

ὁ   ὀνομάζων   τὸ   ὄνομα   κυρίου.   20 ἐν
one   naming   the   name   of [the] Lord.   [2]in

20 In a great house there are not only vessels of gold and silver but also of wood and earthenware, and some for noble use, some for ignoble. ²¹ If any one purifies himself from what is ignoble, then he will be a vessel for noble use, consecrated and useful to the master of the house, ready for any good work. ²² So shun youthful passions and aim at righteousness, faith, love, and peace, along with those who call upon the Lord from a pure heart. ²³ Have nothing to do with stupid, senseless controversies; you know that they breed quarrels. ²⁴ And the Lord's servant must not be quarrelsome but kindly to every one, an apt teacher, forbearing, ²⁵ correcting his opponents with gentleness. God may perhaps grant that they will repent and come to know the truth, ²⁶ and they may escape from the snare of the devil, after being captured by him to do his will.ᶜ

μεγάλη	δὲ	οἰκίᾳ	οὐκ	ἔστιν	μόνον	σκεύη
²a great	¹Now	⁴house	there is(are) not		only	vessels

χρυσᾶ	καὶ	ἀργυρᾶ,	ἀλλὰ	καὶ	ξύλινα
golden	and	silvern,	but	also	wooden

καὶ	ὀστράκινα,	καὶ	ἃ	μὲν	εἰς	τιμὴν	ἃ	δὲ
and	earthen,	and	some		to	honour	others	

εἰς	ἀτιμίαν·	21 ἐὰν	οὖν	τις	ἐκκαθάρῃ
to	dishonour;	if	therefore	anyone	cleanses

ἑαυτὸν	ἀπὸ	τούτων,	ἔσται	σκεῦος	εἰς
himself	from	these [latter],	he will be	a vessel	to

τιμήν,	ἡγιασμένον,	εὔχρηστον	τῷ	δεσπότῃ,
honour,	having been sanctified;	suitable	for the	master,

εἰς	πᾶν	ἔργον	ἀγαθὸν	ἡτοιμασμένον.
to	every	work	good	having been prepared.

22 τὰς	δὲ	νεωτερικὰς	ἐπιθυμίας	φεῦγε,
Now the		²youthful	²lusts	¹flee,

δίωκε	δὲ	δικαιοσύνην,	πίστιν,	ἀγάπην,
but pursue		righteousness,	faith,	love,

εἰρήνην	μετὰ	τῶν	ἐπικαλουμένων	τὸν
peace	with	the [ones]	calling on	the

κύριον	ἐκ	καθαρᾶς	καρδίας.	23 τὰς	δὲ
Lord	out of	a clean	heart.	–	But

μωρὰς	καὶ	ἀπαιδεύτους	ζητήσεις	παραιτοῦ,
foolish	and	uninstructed	questionings	refuse,

εἰδὼς	ὅτι	γεννῶσιν	μάχας·	24 δοῦλον	δὲ
knowing	that	they beget	fights;	and ²a slave	

κυρίου	οὐ	δεῖ	μάχεσθαι	ἀλλὰ	ἤπιον
³of [the] Lord	¹it behoves not		to fight	but	gentle

εἶναι	πρὸς	πάντας,	διδακτικόν,	ἀνεξίκακον,
to be	toward	all men,	apt to teach,	forbearing,

25 ἐν	πραΰτητι	παιδεύοντα	τοὺς	ἀντιδιατι-
in	meekness	instructing	the [ones]	oppos-

θεμένους,	μήποτε	δῴη	αὐτοῖς	ὁ	θεὸς
ing,	[if] perhaps	²may give	³them	–	¹God

μετάνοιαν	εἰς	ἐπίγνωσιν	ἀληθείας,	26 καὶ
repentance	for	a full knowledge	of truth,	and

ἀνανήψωσιν	ἐκ	τῆς	τοῦ	διαβόλου	παγίδος,
they may return to soberness	out of	¹the	²of the	⁴devil	²snare,

ἐζωγρημένοι	ὑπ'	αὐτοῦ	εἰς	τὸ	ἐκείνου	θέλημα.
having been caught	by	him[,]	to	¹the	²of that one*	²will.

ᶜ Or by him, to do his (that is, God's) will

* That is, of God (the remoter antecedent).

CHAPTER 3

BUT understand this, that in the last days there will come times of stress. [2] For men will be lovers of self, lovers of money, proud, arrogant, abusive, disobedient to their parents, ungrateful, unholy, [3] inhuman, implacable, slanderers, profligates, fierce, haters of good, [4] treacherous, reckless, swollen with conceit, lovers of pleasure rather than lovers of God, [5] holding the form of religion but denying the power of it. Avoid such people. [6] For among them are those who make their way into households and capture weak women, burdened with sins and swayed by various impulses, [7] who will listen to anybody and can never arrive at a knowledge of the truth. [8] As Jannes and Jambres opposed Moses, so these men also oppose the truth, men of corrupt mind and counterfeit faith; [9] but they will not get very far, for their

3 Τοῦτο δὲ γίνωσκε, ὅτι ἐν ἐσχάταις
And this　　 know thou,　that　in　[the] last

ἡμέραις ἐνστήσονται καιροὶ χαλεποί·
days　 [3]will be at hand　[2]times　 [1]grievous;

2 ἔσονται γὰρ οἱ ἄνθρωποι φίλαυτοι,
for [2]will be　 － 　[1]men　 self-lovers,

φιλάργυροι, ἀλαζόνες, ὑπερήφανοι, βλάσφημοι,
money-lovers,　 boasters,　 arrogant,　 blasphemers,

γονεῦσιν ἀπειθεῖς, ἀχάριστοι, ἀνόσιοι,
[2]to parents [1]disobedient,　 unthankful,　 unholy,

3 ἄστοργοι, ἄσπονδοι, διάβολοι, ἀκρατεῖς,
without natural　implacable,　 slanderers,　 incontinent,
affection,

ἀνήμεροι, ἀφιλάγαθοι, 4 προδόται, προπετεῖς,
untamed,　 haters of good　 betrayers,　 reckless,
　　　　　 [things/men],

τετυφωμένοι, φιλήδονοι μᾶλλον ἢ φιλόθεοι,
having been　 pleasure-lovers　rather　than　God-lovers,
puffed up,

5 ἔχοντες μόρφωσιν εὐσεβείας τὴν δὲ
having　 a form　 of piety　　 but the

δύναμιν αὐτῆς ἠρνημένοι· καὶ τούτους
power　　 of it　having denied:　and　[2]these

ἀποτρέπου. 6 ἐκ τούτων γάρ εἰσιν οἱ
[3]turn away [1]from.　 [2]of　[3]these　[1]For　 are　the

ἐνδύνοντες εἰς τὰς οἰκίας καὶ αἰχμαλωτίζ-
[ones] creeping into　 －　 houses　and　 captur-

οντες γυναικάρια σεσωρευμένα ἁμαρτίαις,
ing　　 silly women　 having been heaped*　 with sins,

ἀγόμενα ἐπιθυμίαις ποικίλαις, 7 πάντοτε
being led*　 lusts　　 by various,　　 always

μανθάνοντα καὶ μηδέποτε εἰς ἐπίγνωσιν
learning*　 and　　 never　 [3]to [4]a full knowledge

ἀληθείας ἐλθεῖν δυνάμενα. 8 ὃν τρόπον
[5]of truth　 [2]to come　[1]being able.*　 by what way

δὲ Ἰάννης καὶ Ἰαμβρῆς ἀντέστησαν
Now　Jannes　 and　 Jambres　 opposed

Μωϋσεῖ, οὕτως καὶ οὗτοι ἀνθίστανται τῇ
Moses,　 so　 also　 these　 oppose　 the

ἀληθείᾳ, ἄνθρωποι κατεφθαρμένοι τὸν νοῦν,
truth,　　 men　 having been corrupted the　 mind,
　　　　　　 ＝with corrupted mind,

ἀδόκιμοι περὶ τὴν πίστιν. 9 ἀλλ' οὐ
reprobate　 as to　 the　 faith.　　 But　 not

προκόψουσιν ἐπὶ πλεῖον· ἡ γὰρ ἄνοια
they will advance　 to　 more;　 for the　 folly
＝farther;

* Agreeing with "silly women" (neut. pl.).

folly will be plain to all, as was that of those two men.

10 Now you have observed my teaching, my conduct, my aim in life, my faith, my patience, my love, my steadfastness, [11] my persecutions, my sufferings, what befell me at Antioch, at Ico'nium, and at Lystra, what persecutions I endured; yet from them all the Lord rescued me. [12] Indeed all who desire to live a godly life in Christ Jesus will be persecuted, [13] while evil men and impostors will go on from bad to worse, deceivers and deceived. [14] But as for you, continue in what you have learned and have firmly believed, knowing from whom you learned it [15] and how from childhood you have been acquainted with the sacred writings which are able to instruct you for salvation through faith in Christ Jesus. [16] All scripture is inspired by God and[d] profitable for teaching, for reproof, for correction, and for training in righteousness, [17] that the man of God may be complete,

αὐτῶν ἔκδηλος ἔσται πᾶσιν, ὡς καὶ
of them very clear will be to all men, as also

ἡ ἐκείνων ἐγένετο. 10 Σὺ δὲ παρηκολού-
the of those became. But thou hast closely

θησάς μου τῇ διδασκαλίᾳ, τῇ ἀγωγῇ,
[folly] followed of me the teaching, the conduct,

τῇ προθέσει, τῇ πίστει, τῇ μακροθυμίᾳ,
the purpose, the faith, the longsuffering,

τῇ ἀγάπῃ, τῇ ὑπομονῇ, 11 τοῖς διωγμοῖς,
the love, the endurance, the persecutions,

τοῖς παθήμασιν, οἷά μοι ἐγένετο ἐν
the sufferings, which [2]to me [1]happened in

Ἀντιοχείᾳ, ἐν Ἰκονίῳ, ἐν Λύστροις· οἵους
Antioch, in Iconium, in Lystra: what

διωγμοὺς ὑπήνεγκα, καὶ ἐκ πάντων με
persecutions I bore, and out of all [4]me

ἐρρύσατο ὁ κύριος. 12 καὶ πάντες δὲ
[3]delivered [1]the [2]Lord. [2]indeed [3]all [1]And

οἱ θέλοντες ζῆν εὐσεβῶς ἐν Χριστῷ
the [ones] wishing to live piously in Christ

Ἰησοῦ διωχθήσονται. 13 πονηροὶ δὲ ἄν-
Jesus will be persecuted. But evil men

θρωποι καὶ γόητες προκόψουσιν ἐπὶ τὸ
and impostors will advance to the

χεῖρον, πλανῶντες καὶ πλανώμενοι. 14 σὺ
worse, deceiving and being deceived. [2]thou

δὲ μένε ἐν οἷς ἔμαθες καὶ ἐπιστώθης,
But [1]continue in what thou didst and wast assured of,
things learn

εἰδὼς παρὰ τίνων ἔμαθες, 15 καὶ ὅτι
knowing from whom* thou didst learn, and that

ἀπὸ βρέφους ἱερὰ γράμματα οἶδας, τὰ
from a babe [2]sacred [3]letters [1]thou know- the
est, [ones]

δυνάμενά σε σοφίσαι εἰς σωτηρίαν διὰ
being able thee to make wise to salvation through

πίστεως τῆς ἐν Χριστῷ Ἰησοῦ. 16 πᾶσα
faith – in Christ Jesus. Every

γραφὴ θεόπνευστος καὶ ὠφέλιμος πρὸς
scripture [is] God-breathed and profitable for

διδασκαλίαν, πρὸς ἐλεγμόν, πρὸς ἐπανόρ-
teaching, for reproof, for cor-

θωσιν, πρὸς παιδείαν τὴν ἐν δικαιοσύνῃ,
rection, for instruction – in righteousness,

17 ἵνα ἄρτιος ᾖ ὁ τοῦ θεοῦ ἄνθρωπος,
in order [5]fitted [4]may [1]the – [2]of God [3]man,
that be

[d] Or Every scripture inspired by God

* Plural.

equipped for every good work.

CHAPTER 4

I charge you in the presence of God and of Christ Jesus who is to judge the living and the dead, and by his appearing and his kingdom: ²preach the word, be urgent in season and out of season, convince, rebuke, and exhort, be unfailing in patience and in teaching. ³For the time is coming when people will not endure sound teaching, but having itching ears they will accumulate for themselves teachers to suit their own likings, ⁴and will turn away from listening to the truth and wander into myths. ⁵As for you, always be steady, endure suffering, do the work of an evangelist, fulfil your ministry.

6 For I am already on the point of being sacrificed; the time of my departure has come. ⁷I have fought the good fight, I have finished the race, I have kept the faith. ⁸Henceforth there is laid up for me the crown of righteousness, which the Lord, the righteous judge, will

πρὸς πᾶν ἔργον ἀγαθὸν ἐξηρτισμένος.
for every work good having been furnished.

4 Διαμαρτύρομαι ἐνώπιον τοῦ θεοῦ καὶ
I solemnly witness before - God and

Χριστοῦ Ἰησοῦ, τοῦ μέλλοντος κρίνειν
Christ Jesus, the [one] being about to judge

ζῶντας καὶ νεκρούς, καὶ τὴν ἐπιφάνειαν
living [ones] and dead, both [by] the appearance

αὐτοῦ καὶ τὴν βασιλείαν αὐτοῦ· 2 κήρυξον
of him and [by] the kingdom of him: proclaim

τὸν λόγον, ἐπίστηθι εὐκαίρως ἀκαίρως,
the word, be attentive seasonably[,] unseasonably,

ἔλεγξον, ἐπιτίμησον, παρακάλεσον, ἐν πάσῃ
reprove, admonish, exhort, with all

μακροθυμίᾳ καὶ διδαχῇ. 3 ἔσται γὰρ
longsuffering and teaching. For there will be

καιρὸς ὅτε τῆς ὑγιαινούσης διδασκαλίας
a time when ²the ³being healthy ⁴teaching

οὐκ ἀνέξονται, ἀλλὰ κατὰ τὰς ἰδίας
¹they will not bear with, but according to the(ir) own

ἐπιθυμίας ἑαυτοῖς ἐπισωρεύσουσιν διδασ-
lusts ³to themselves ¹they will heap up ²teach-

κάλους κνηθόμενοι τὴν ἀκοήν, 4 καὶ ἀπὸ
ers tickling the ear, and ⁵from

μὲν τῆς ἀληθείας τὴν ἀκοὴν ἀποστρέψουσιν,
¹on ⁶the ⁷truth ³the ⁴ear ²will turn away,
one hand

ἐπὶ δὲ τοὺς μύθους ἐκτραπήσονται. 5 σὺ
³to ¹on the the ⁴tales ²will be turned aside. ³thou
other

δὲ νῆφε ἐν πᾶσιν, κακοπάθησον, ἔργον
But ¹be in all things, suffer evil, ²[the] work
sober

ποίησον εὐαγγελιστοῦ, τὴν διακονίαν σου
¹do of an evangelist, ²the ³ministry ⁴of thee

πληροφόρησον. 6 Ἐγὼ γὰρ ἤδη σπένδομαι,
¹fulfil. For I already am being
poured out,

καὶ ὁ καιρὸς τῆς ἀναλύσεώς μου ἐφέστη-
and the time of the departure of me has

κεν. 7 τὸν καλὸν ἀγῶνα ἠγώνισμαι,
arrived. The good struggle I have struggled,

τὸν δρόμον τετέλεκα, τὴν πίστιν τετήρηκα·
the course I have finished, the faith I have kept:

8 λοιπὸν ἀπόκειταί μοι ὁ τῆς δικαιοσύνης
for the rest there is laid up for me ¹the - ²of righteousness

στέφανος, ὃν ἀποδώσει μοι ὁ κύριος
²crown, which ⁶will render ⁷to me ¹the ²Lord

ἐν ἐκείνῃ τῇ ἡμέρᾳ, ὁ δίκαιος κριτής,
⁸in ⁹that - ¹⁰day, ²the ⁴righteous ⁵judge,

award to me on that Day, and not only to me but also to all who have loved his appearing. 9 Do your best to come to me soon. ¹⁰For Demas, in love with this present world, has deserted me and gone to Thessaloni′ca; Crescens has gone to Galatia,ᵉ Titus to Dalmatia. ¹¹Luke alone is with me. Get Mark and bring him with you; for he is very useful in serving me. ¹²Tych′icus I have sent to Ephesus. ¹³When you come, bring the cloak that I left with Carpus at Tro′as, also the books, and above all the parchments. ¹⁴Alexander the coppersmith did me great harm; the Lord will requite him for his deeds. ¹⁵Beware of him yourself, for he strongly opposed our message. ¹⁶At my first defense no one took my part; all deserted me. May it not be charged against them! ¹⁷But the Lord stood by me and gave me strength to proclaim the word fully, that all the Gentiles might hear it. So I was

ᵉ Other ancient authorities read *Gaul*

οὐ μόνον δὲ ἐμοὶ ἀλλὰ καὶ πᾶσι τοῖς
²not ³only ¹and to me but also to all the [ones]
ἠγαπηκόσι τὴν ἐπιφάνειαν αὐτοῦ.
having loved the appearance of him.
9 Σπούδασον ἐλθεῖν πρός με ταχέως·
Hasten to come to me shortly;
10 Δημᾶς γάρ με ἐγκατέλιπεν ἀγαπήσας
²Demas ¹For ⁴me ³forsook loving
τὸν νῦν αἰῶνα, καὶ ἐπορεύθη εἰς Θεσσαλο-
the now age, and went to Thessalo-
(present)
νίκην, Κρήσκης εἰς Γαλατίαν, Τίτος εἰς
nica, Crescens to Galatia, Titus to
Δαλματίαν· 11 Λουκᾶς ἐστιν μόνος μετ'
Dalmatia; Luke is alone with
ἐμοῦ. Μᾶρκον ἀναλαβὼν ἄγε μετὰ σεαυτοῦ·
me. Mark taking bring with thyself;
ἔστιν γάρ μοι εὔχρηστος εἰς διακονίαν.
²he is ¹for ⁴to me ³useful for ministry.
12 Τύχικον δὲ ἀπέστειλα εἰς Ἔφεσον.
And Tychicus I sent to Ephesus.
13 τὸν φαιλόνην, ὃν ἀπέλιπον ἐν Τρῳάδι
The cloak, which I left in Troas
παρὰ Κάρπῳ, ἐρχόμενος φέρε, καὶ τὰ
with Carpus, coming bring thou, and the
βιβλία, μάλιστα τὰς μεμβράνας. 14 Ἀλέξ-
scrolls, especially the parchments. Alex-
ανδρος ὁ χαλκεὺς πολλά μοι κακὰ
ander the coppersmith ³many ²to me ⁴evils
ἐνεδείξατο· ἀποδώσει αὐτῷ ὁ κύριος κατὰ
¹showed; ⁵will render ⁴to him ¹the ²Lord according to
τὰ ἔργα αὐτοῦ· 15 ὃν καὶ σὺ φυλάσσου·
the works of him; whom also ²thou ¹guard
³[against];
λίαν γὰρ ἀντέστη τοῖς ἡμετέροις λόγοις.
for greatly he opposed – our words.
16 Ἐν τῇ πρώτῃ μου ἀπολογίᾳ οὐδείς
At the first ²of me ¹defence no one
μοι παρεγένετο, ἀλλὰ πάντες με ἐγκατέ-
²me ¹was beside, but all men ²me ¹for-
λιπον· μὴ αὐτοῖς λογισθείη· 17 ὁ δὲ
sook; not to them may it be reckoned; but the
κύριός μοι παρέστη καὶ ἐνεδυνάμωσέν με,
Lord ²me ¹stood with and empowered me,
ἵνα δι' ἐμοῦ τὸ κήρυγμα πληροφορηθῇ
in or- through me the proclamation might be
der that accomplished
καὶ ἀκούσωσιν πάντα τὰ ἔθνη, καὶ
and ⁴might hear ¹all ²the ³nations, and

rescued from the lion's mouth. [18]The Lord will rescue me from every evil and save me for his heavenly kingdom. To him be the glory for ever and ever. Amen.

19 Greet Prisca and Aquila, and the household of Onesiph'orus. [20]Eras'tus remained at Corinth; Troph'imus I left ill at Mile'tus. [21]Do your best to come before winter. Eubu'lus sends greetings to you, as do Pudens and Linus and Claudia and all the brethren.

22 The Lord be with your spirit. Grace be with you.

ἐρρύσθην ἐκ στόματος λέοντος. 18 ῥύσεταί
I was   out of [the] mouth of [the] lion.   [2]will deliver
delivered

με ὁ κύριος ἀπὸ παντὸς ἔργου πονηροῦ
[4]me [1]The [2]Lord from   every   work   wicked

καὶ σώσει εἰς τὴν βασιλείαν αὐτοῦ τὴν
and will save to   the [2]kingdom [3]of him —

ἐπουράνιον· ᾧ ἡ δόξα εἰς τοὺς αἰῶνας
[1]heavenly: to [be] glory unto the   ages
            whom the

τῶν αἰώνων, ἀμήν.
of the ages,   Amen.

19 Ἄσπασαι Πρίσκαν καὶ Ἀκύλαν καὶ
   Greet   Prisca   and Aquila   and

τὸν Ὀνησιφόρου οἶκον.   20 Ἔραστος
the [2]of Onesiphorus [1]household.   Erastus

ἔμεινεν ἐν Κορίνθῳ, Τρόφιμον δὲ ἀπέλιπον
remained in Corinth,   but Trophimus   I left

ἐν Μιλήτῳ ἀσθενοῦντα.   21 Σπούδασον
in Miletus   ailing.   Hasten

πρὸ χειμῶνος ἐλθεῖν. Ἀσπάζεταί σε
before winter   to come.   Greets   thee

Εὔβουλος καὶ Πούδης καὶ Λίνος καὶ
Eubulus   and Pudens and Linus and

Κλαυδία καὶ οἱ ἀδελφοὶ πάντες.
Claudia and [2]the [3]brothers [1]all.

22 Ὁ κύριος μετὰ τοῦ πνεύματός σου.
   The Lord [be] with the   spirit   of thee.

ἡ χάρις μεθ' ὑμῶν.
— Grace [be] with you.

TITUS 1

ΠΡΟΣ ΤΙΤΟΝ
To Titus

CHAPTER 1

PAUL, a servant of God and an apostle of Jesus Christ, to further the faith of God's elect and their knowledge of the truth which accords with godliness, [2]in hope of eternal life which God,

1 Παῦλος δοῦλος θεοῦ, ἀπόστολος δὲ
  Paul   a slave of God,   and an apostle

Ἰησοῦ Χριστοῦ κατὰ πίστιν ἐκλεκτῶν
of Jesus Christ according to [the] faith of chosen ones

θεοῦ καὶ ἐπίγνωσιν ἀληθείας τῆς κατ'
of God and   full know-   of [the]   — accord-
            ledge   truth   ing to

εὐσέβειαν 2 ἐπ' ἐλπίδι ζωῆς αἰωνίον,
  piety   on(in) hope   life of eternal,

ἣν ἐπηγγείλατο ὁ ἀψευδὴς θεὸς πρὸ
which [4]promised [1]the [2]unlying [3]God before

who never lies, promised ages ago [3]and at the proper time manifested in his word through the preaching with which I have been entrusted by command of God our Savior; 4 To Titus, my true child in a common faith: Grace and peace from God the Father and Christ Jesus our Savior. 5 This is why I left you in Crete, that you might amend what was defective, and appoint elders in every town as I directed you, [6]if any man is blameless, the husband of one wife, and his children are believers and not open to the charge of being profligate or insubordinate. [7]For a bishop, as God's steward, must be blameless; he must not be arrogant or quick-tempered or a drunkard or violent or greedy for gain, [8]but hospitable, a lover of goodness, master of himself, upright, holy, and self-controlled; [9]he must hold firm to the sure word as taught, so that he may be able to give instruction in sound doctrine and also to confute those who contradict it. [10]For there

χρόνων	αἰωνίων,	3 ἐφανέρωσεν	δὲ	καιροῖς
times	eternal,	but [3]manifested		[2]times

ἰδίοις	τὸν	λόγον	αὐτοῦ	ἐν	κηρύγματι
[1]in [its] own	the	word	of him	in	a proclamation

ὃ	ἐπιστεύθην	ἐγὼ	κατ'	ἐπιταγὴν	τοῦ
which [2]was entrusted [with]		[1]I	according to	command	of the

σωτῆρος	ἡμῶν	θεοῦ,	4 Τίτῳ	γνησίῳ	τέκνῳ
Saviour	of us	God,	to Titus	a true	child

κατὰ	κοινὴν	πίστιν·	χάρις	καὶ	εἰρήνη
according to	a common	faith:	Grace	and	peace

ἀπὸ	θεοῦ	πατρὸς	καὶ	Χριστοῦ	Ἰησοῦ
from	God	[the] Father	and	Christ	Jesus

τοῦ	σωτῆρος	ἡμῶν.
the	Saviour	of us.

5 Τούτου χάριν ἀπέλιπόν σε ἐν Κρήτῃ,
For this reason† I left thee in Crete,

ἵνα	τὰ	λείποντα	ἐπιδιορθώσῃ,	καὶ
in order that	the things	wanting	thou shouldest set in order,	and

καταστήσῃς	κατὰ	πόλιν	πρεσβυτέρους,	ὡς	ἐγώ
shouldest appoint	in each city		elders,	as	I

σοι	διεταξάμην,	6 εἴ	τίς	ἐστιν	ἀνέγκλητος,
[2]thee	[1]charged,	if	anyone	is	unreprovable,

μιᾶς	γυναικὸς	ἀνήρ,	τέκνα	ἔχων	πιστά,
[2]of one	[3]wife	[1]husband,	children	[1]having	[2]believing,

μὴ	ἐν	κατηγορίᾳ	ἀσωτίας	ἢ	ἀνυπότακτα.
not	in	accusation	of profligacy	or	unruly.*

7 δεῖ γὰρ τὸν ἐπίσκοπον ἀνέγκλητον εἶναι
For it behoves the bishop [2]unreprovable [1]to be

ὡς	θεοῦ	οἰκονόμον,	μὴ	αὐθάδη,	μὴ
as	of God	a steward,	not	self-pleasing,	not

ὀργίλον,	μὴ	πάροινον,	μὴ	πλήκτην,	μὴ
passionate,	not	given to wine,	not	a striker,	not

αἰσχροκερδῆ,	8 ἀλλὰ	φιλόξενον,	φιλάγαθον,
greedy of base gain,	but	hospitable,	a lover of good [men/things],

σώφρονα,	δίκαιον,	ὅσιον,	ἐγκρατῆ,	9 ἀντεχ-
sensible,	just,	holy,	self-controlled,	holding

όμενον	τοῦ	κατὰ	τὴν	διδαχὴν	πιστοῦ
to	[1]the	[4]according to	[5]the	[6]teaching	[2]faithful

λόγου,	ἵνα	δυνατὸς	ᾖ	καὶ	παρακαλεῖν
[2]word,	in order that	[2]able	[1]he may be	both	to exhort

ἐν	τῇ	διδασκαλίᾳ	τῇ	ὑγιαινούσῃ	καὶ
by	the	[2]teaching	–	[1]being healthy	and

τοὺς	ἀντιλέγοντας	ἐλέγχειν.	10 Εἰσὶν	γὰρ
[2]the [ones]	[3]contradicting	[1]to convince.	For there are	

* In agreement with " children " (neut. pl.).

are many insubordinate men, empty talkers and deceivers, especially the circumcision party; [11]they must be silenced, since they are upsetting whole families by teaching for base gain what they have no right to teach. [12]One of themselves, a prophet of their own, said, "Cretans are always liars, evil beasts, lazy gluttons." [13]This testimony is true. Therefore rebuke them sharply, that they may be sound in the faith, [14]instead of giving heed to Jewish myths or to commands of men who reject the truth. [15]To the pure all things are pure, but to the corrupt and unbelieving nothing is pure; their very minds and consciences are corrupted. [16]They profess to know God, but they deny him by their deeds; they are detestable, disobedient, unfit for any good deed.

πολλοὶ ἀνυπότακτοι, ματαιολόγοι καὶ
many   unruly men,   vain talkers   and

φρεναπάται, μάλιστα οἱ ἐκ τῆς περιτομῆς,
deceivers,   specially   the ones of   the   circumcision,

11 οὓς δεῖ ἐπιστομίζειν, οἵτινες ὅλους
whom   it   to stop the   who   ²whole
     behoves   mouth,

οἴκους ἀνατρέπουσιν διδάσκοντες ἃ μὴ
²households ¹overturn   teaching   things ²not
                         which

δεῖ αἰσχροῦ κέρδους χάριν. 12 εἶπέν
¹it be- ⁴base   ⁵gain   ³for the   ⁷Said
hoves   sake of.

τις ἐξ αὐτῶν ἴδιος αὐτῶν προφήτης·
¹a cer- ²of   ³them   ⁴an own   ⁵of them   ⁶prophet:
tain one

Κρῆτες ἀεὶ ψεῦσται, κακὰ θηρία, γαστέρες
Cretans   always   liars,   evil   beasts,   ²gluttons
[are]

ἀργαί. 13 ἡ μαρτυρία αὕτη ἐστὶν ἀληθής.
¹idle.   This witness   is   true.

δι᾽ ἣν αἰτίαν ἔλεγχε αὐτοὺς ἀποτόμως,
For which   cause   reprove   them   severely,

ἵνα ὑγιαίνωσιν ἐν τῇ πίστει, 14 μὴ
in or-   they may   in   the   faith,   not
der that   be healthy

προσέχοντες Ἰουδαϊκοῖς μύθοις καὶ
giving heed   to Jewish   tales   and

ἐντολαῖς ἀνθρώπων ἀποστρεφομένων τὴν
commandments   of men   perverting   the

ἀλήθειαν. 15 πάντα καθαρὰ τοῖς καθαροῖς·
truth.   All things [are] clean   to the   clean;

τοῖς δὲ μεμιαμμένοις καὶ ἀπίστοις οὐδὲν
but to   having been   and   unfaithful   nothing
the [ones]   defiled

καθαρόν, ἀλλὰ μεμίανται αὐτῶν καὶ ὁ
[is] clean,   but ⁵has(ve) been defiled ⁷of them   ¹both ²the

νοῦς καὶ ἡ συνείδησις. 16 θεὸν ὁμολο-
³mind ⁴and ⁵the   ⁶conscience.   ³God   ¹they pro-

γοῦσιν εἰδέναι, τοῖς δὲ ἔργοις ἀρνοῦνται,
fess   ²to know,   but by the(ir)   works they deny [him],

βδελυκτοὶ ὄντες καὶ ἀπειθεῖς καὶ πρὸς
²abominable ¹being   and   disobedient   and   to

πᾶν ἔργον ἀγαθὸν ἀδόκιμοι.
every ²work ¹good   reprobate.

CHAPTER 2

BUT as for you, teach what befits sound doctrine. ²Bid the older

2 Σὺ δὲ λάλει ἃ πρέπει τῇ ὑγιαινούσῃ
But ²thou ¹speak things becomes the   being
            which   healthy

διδασκαλίᾳ. 2 Πρεσβύτας νηφαλίους εἶναι,
teaching.   Aged men   ²sober   ¹to be,

men be temperate, serious, sensible, sound in faith, in love, and in steadfastness. ³Bid the older women likewise to be reverent in behavior, not to be slanderers or slaves to drink; they are to teach what is good, ⁴and so train the young women to love their husbands and children, ⁵to be sensible, chaste, domestic, kind, and submissive to their husbands, that the word of God may not be discredited. ⁶Likewise urge the younger men to control themselves. ⁷Show yourself in all respects a model of good deeds, and in your teaching show integrity, gravity, ⁸and sound speech that cannot be censured, so that an opponent may be put to shame, having nothing evil to say of us. ⁹Bid slaves to be submissive to their masters and to give satisfaction in every respect; they are not to be refractory, ¹⁰nor to pilfer, but to show entire and true fidelity, so that in everything they may adorn the doctrine of God our Savior. 11 For the grace of God has appeared for the salvation of all men,

σεμνούς,   σώφρονας,   ὑγιαίνοντας   τῇ   πίστει,
grave,   sensible,   being healthy   in the   faith,

τῇ   ἀγάπῃ,   τῇ   ὑπομονῇ·   3 πρεσβύτιδας
–   in love,   –   in endurance;   aged women

ὡσαύτως   ἐν   καταστήματι   ἱεροπρεπεῖς,   μὴ
similarly   in   demeanour   reverent,   not

διαβόλους,   μηδὲ   οἴνῳ   πολλῷ   δεδουλωμένας,
slanderers,   nor   ³wine   ²by much   ¹having been
                                                    enslaved,

καλοδιδασκάλους,   4 ἵνα   σωφρονίζωσιν   τὰς
teachers of what is good,   in or-   they may train   the
                                    der that

νέας   φιλάνδρους   εἶναι,   φιλοτέκνους,
young   ²lovers of   ¹to be,   child-lovers,
women   [their] husbands

5 σώφρονας,   ἁγνάς,   οἰκουργούς,   ἀγαθάς,
sensible,   pure,   home-workers,   good,

ὑποτασσομένας   τοῖς   ἰδίοις   ἀνδράσιν,
being subject   to the(ir)   own   husbands,

ἵνα   μὴ   ὁ   λόγος   τοῦ   θεοῦ   βλασφημῆται.
lest   the   word   –   of God   be blasphemed.

6 Τοὺς   νεωτέρους   ὡσαύτως   παρακάλει
The   younger men   similarly   exhort

σωφρονεῖν   7 περὶ   πάντα,   σεαυτὸν   παρ-
to be sensible   about   all things,   ²thyself   ¹show-

εχόμενος   τύπον   καλῶν   ἔργων,   ἐν   τῇ
ing   a pattern   of good   works,   in   the

διδασκαλίᾳ   ἀφθορίαν,   σεμνότητα,   8 λόγον
teaching   uncorruptness,   gravity,   ³speech

ὑγιῆ   ἀκατάγνωστον,   ἵνα   ὁ   ἐξ   ἐναντίας
¹healthy   ²irreprehensible,   in or-   the   of   contrary
                                    der that man   [the]   [side]

ἐντραπῇ   μηδὲν   ἔχων   λέγειν   περὶ   ἡμῶν
may be put   ²nothing   ¹having   ⁴to say   ³about   ⁵us
to shame

φαῦλον.   9 Δούλους   ἰδίοις   δεσπόταις
³bad.   Slaves   to [their] own   masters

ὑποτάσσεσθαι   ἐν   πᾶσιν,   εὐαρέστους   εἶναι,
to be subject   in   all things,   well-pleasing   to be,

μὴ   ἀντιλέγοντας,   10 μὴ   νοσφιζομένους,   ἀλλὰ
not   contradicting,   not   peculating,   but

πᾶσαν   πίστιν   ἐνδεικνυμένους   ἀγαθήν,   ἵνα
²all   ⁴faith   ¹showing   ³good,   in or-
                                    der that

τὴν   διδασκαλίαν   τὴν   τοῦ   σωτῆρος   ἡμῶν
²the   ³teaching   the   –   ⁵Saviour   ⁶of us
                            ⁴of the

θεοῦ   κοσμῶσιν   ἐν   πᾶσιν.   11 Ἐπεφάνη
⁷God   ¹they may adorn   in   all things.   ⁵appeared

γὰρ   ἡ   χάρις   τοῦ   θεοῦ   σωτήριος   πᾶσιν
For   ¹the   ²grace   –   ³of God   ⁴saving   to all

¹²training us to renounce irreligion and worldly passions, and to live sober, upright, and godly lives in this world, ¹³awaiting our blessed hope, the appearing of the glory of our great God and Savior[a] Jesus Christ, ¹⁴who gave himself for us to redeem us from all iniquity and to purify for himself a people of his own who are zealous for good deeds.

15 Declare these things; exhort and reprove with all authority. Let no one disregard you.

CHAPTER 3

REMIND them to be submissive to rulers and authorities, to be obedient, to be ready for any honest work, ²to speak evil of no one, to avoid quarreling, to be gentle, and to show perfect courtesy toward all men. ³For we ourselves were once foolish, disobedient, led astray, slaves to various passions and pleasures, passing our days in malice and envy, hated by men and hating one another; ⁴but when the goodness and loving kindness of God our Savior appeared, ⁵he

[a] Or of the great God and our Savior

ἀνθρώποις,   12 παιδεύουσα   ἡμᾶς,   ἵνα
men,   instructing   us,   in order
                                          that

ἀρνησάμενοι τὴν ἀσέβειαν καὶ τὰς κοσμικὰς
denying   -   impiety and   worldly

ἐπιθυμίας   σωφρόνως   καὶ   δικαίως   καὶ
lusts   ²sensibly   ³and ⁴righteously ⁵and

εὐσεβῶς   ζήσωμεν   ἐν   τῷ   νῦν   αἰῶνι,
⁶piously ¹we might live in   the now(present) age,

13 προσδεχόμενοι τὴν μακαρίαν ἐλπίδα καὶ
   expecting   the blessed   hope and

ἐπιφάνειαν τῆς δόξης τοῦ μεγάλου θεοῦ
appearance of the glory of the   great   God

καὶ σωτῆρος ἡμῶν Χριστοῦ Ἰησοῦ, 14 ὃς
and Saviour of us   Christ   Jesus,   who

ἔδωκεν ἑαυτὸν ὑπὲρ ἡμῶν ἵνα λυτρώσηται
gave   himself on behalf us in or-   he might
                of   der that   ransom

ἡμᾶς ἀπὸ πάσης ἀνομίας καὶ καθαρίσῃ
us   from all   iniquity and might cleanse

ἑαυτῷ λαὸν περιούσιον, ζηλωτὴν καλῶν ἔργων.
for   a people [his] own zealous of good works.
himself   possession,

15 Ταῦτα λάλει καὶ παρακάλει καὶ ἔλεγχε
These things speak thou and exhort   and reprove

μετὰ πάσης ἐπιταγῆς· μηδείς σου περιφρονείτω.
with   all   command; ²no one ⁴of thee ¹let ³despise.

3 Ὑπομίμνησκε αὐτοὺς ἀρχαῖς ἐξουσίαις
Remind thou   them ²to rulers ³[and] ⁴authorities

ὑποτάσσεσθαι, πειθαρχεῖν, πρὸς πᾶν ἔργον
¹to be subject, to be obedient, ²to ⁴every ⁵work

ἀγαθὸν ἑτοίμους εἶναι, 2 μηδένα βλασ-
⁵good   ²ready ¹to be,   no one   to

φημεῖν, ἀμάχους εἶναι, ἐπιεικεῖς, πᾶσαν
rail at, uncontentious to be, forbearing, ²all

ἐνδεικνυμένους πραΰτητα πρὸς πάντας
¹showing forth   meekness   to   all

ἀνθρώπους. 3 Ἦμεν γάρ ποτε καὶ ἡμεῖς
men.   For ³were ⁴then ²also ¹we

ἀνόητοι, ἀπειθεῖς, πλανώμενοι, δουλεύοντες
senseless, disobedient, being deceived, serving [as slaves]

ἐπιθυμίαις καὶ ἡδοναῖς ποικίλαις, ἐν κακίᾳ
²lusts   ³and ⁴pleasures ¹various, ²in ³evil

καὶ φθόνῳ διάγοντες, στυγητοί, μισοῦντες
⁴and ⁵envy ¹living,   hateful,   hating

ἀλλήλους. 4 ὅτε δὲ ἡ χρηστότης καὶ
one another. But when the kindness   and

ἡ φιλανθρωπία ἐπεφάνη τοῦ σωτῆρος ἡμῶν
the love to man   ⁵appeared ¹of the ²Saviour ³of us

saved us, not because of deeds done by us in righteousness, but in virtue of his own mercy, by the washing of regeneration and renewal in the Holy Spirit, ⁶ which he poured out upon us richly through Jesus Christ our Savior, ⁷ so that we might be justified by his grace and become heirs in hope of eternal life. ⁸ The saying is sure. I desire you to insist on these things, so that those who have believed in God may be careful to apply themselves to good deeds;ᵇ these are excellent and profitable to men. ⁹ But avoid stupid controversies, genealogies, dissensions, and quarrels over the law, for they are unprofitable and futile. ¹⁰ As for a man who is factious, after admonishing him once or twice, have nothing more to do with him, ¹¹ knowing that such a person is perverted and sinful; he is self-condemned.

12 When I send Artemas or Tych'icus to you, do your best to

ᵇ Or enter honorable occupations

θεοῦ,	5	οὐκ	ἐξ	ἔργων	τῶν	ἐν	δικαιοσύνῃ
⁴God,		not	by	works	–	⁴in	⁵righteousness

ἃ	ἐποιήσαμεν	ἡμεῖς,	ἀλλὰ	κατὰ	τὸ
¹which	³did	²we,	but	according to	the

αὐτοῦ	ἔλεος	ἔσωσεν	ἡμᾶς	διὰ	λουτροῦ
of him	mercy	he saved	us	through [the]	washing

παλιγγενεσίας	καὶ	ἀνακαινώσεως	πνεύματος
of regeneration	and	renewal	⁵Spirit

ἁγίου,	6	οὗ	ἐξέχεεν	ἐφ'	ἡμᾶς	πλουσίως
¹of [the] Holy,		which	he shed	on	us	richly

διὰ	Ἰησοῦ	Χριστοῦ	τοῦ	σωτῆρος	ἡμῶν,
through	Jesus	Christ	the	Saviour	of us,

7	ἵνα	δικαιωθέντες	τῇ	ἐκείνου	χάριτι
	in order that	being justified	¹by the	²of that one	²grace

κληρονόμοι	γενηθῶμεν	κατ'	ἐλπίδα	ζωῆς
heirs	we might become	according to	a hope	of life

αἰωνίου.	8	Πιστὸς	ὁ	λόγος,	καὶ	περὶ
eternal.		Faithful [is] the		word,	and	as to

τούτων	βούλομαί	σε	διαβεβαιοῦσθαι,	ἵνα
these things	I wish	thee	to affirm confidently,	in order that

φροντίζωσιν	καλῶν	ἔργων	προΐστασθαι	οἱ
⁴may take thought	⁶of good	⁷works	⁵to maintain	¹the [ones]

πεπιστευκότες	θεῷ.	ταῦτά	ἐστιν	καλὰ
³having believed	²God.	These things	is(are)	good

καὶ	ὠφέλιμα	τοῖς	ἀνθρώποις·	9	μωρὰς
and	profitable	–	to men;		²foolish

δὲ	ζητήσεις	καὶ	γενεαλογίας	καὶ	ἔριν
¹but	questionings	and	genealogies	and	strife

καὶ	μάχας	νομικὰς	περιΐστασο·	εἰσὶν	γὰρ
and	²fights	¹legal	shun thou;	for they are

ἀνωφελεῖς	καὶ	μάταιοι.	10	αἱρετικὸν
unprofitable	and	vain.		A factious

ἄνθρωπον	μετὰ	μίαν	καὶ	δευτέραν
man	after	one	and	a second

νουθεσίαν	παραιτοῦ,	11	εἰδὼς	ὅτι	ἐξέστραπ-
admonition	avoid,		knowing	that	³has been per-

ται	ὁ	τοιοῦτος	καὶ	ἁμαρτάνει	ὢν	αὐτο-
verted		¹such a man	and	sins	being	self-

κατάκριτος.
condemned.

12	Ὅταν	πέμψω	Ἀρτεμᾶν	πρὸς	σὲ
	Whenever	I send	Artemas	to	thee

ἢ	Τύχικον,	σπούδασον	ἐλθεῖν	πρός	με
or	Tychicus,	hasten	to come	to	me

come to me at Nicop'-olis, for I have decided to spend the winter there. [13]Do your best to speed Zenas the lawyer and Apol'los on their way; see that they lack nothing. [14]And let our people learn to apply themselves to good deeds,[c] so as to help cases of urgent need, and not to be unfruitful.
15 All who are with me send greetings to you. Greet those who love us in the faith.
Grace be with you all.

εἰς Νικόπολιν· ἐκεῖ γὰρ κέκρικα παραχειμά-
in Nicopolis; for there I have decided to spend [the]
σαι. 13 Ζηνᾶν τὸν νομικὸν καὶ ᾿Απολλῶν
winter. Zenas the lawyer and Apollos
σπουδαίως πρόπεμψον, ἵνα μηδὲν αὐτοῖς
urgently send forward, in or- nothing to them
der that
λείπῃ. 14 μανθανέτωσαν δὲ καὶ οἱ ἡμέτεροι
may be lacking. And [1]let [4]learn [2]also – [3]our [people]
καλῶν ἔργων προΐστασθαι εἰς τὰς ἀναγ-
[6]of good [7]works [5]to maintain for – neces-
καίας χρείας, ἵνα μὴ ὦσιν ἄκαρποι.
sary wants, lest they be unfruitful.
15 ᾿Ασπάζονταί σε οἱ μετ᾿ ἐμοῦ πάντες.
[2]greet [6]thee [3]the [5]with [4]me [1]All.
[ones]
ἄσπασαι τοὺς φιλοῦντας ἡμᾶς ἐν πίστει.
Greet thou the [ones] loving us in [the] faith.
῾Η χάρις μετὰ πάντων ὑμῶν.
– Grace [be] with [2]all [1]you.

[c] Or enter honorable occupations

PHILEMON

ΠΡΟΣ ΦΙΛΗΜΟΝΑ
To Philemon

PAUL, a prisoner for Christ Jesus, and Timothy our brother,
To Phile'mon our beloved fellow worker [2]and Ap'phia our sister and Archip'pus our fellow soldier, and the church in your house:
3 Grace to you and peace from God our Father and the Lord Jesus Christ.
4 I thank my God always when I remember you in my prayers, [5]because I hear of your love and of the faith

1 Παῦλος δέσμιος Χριστοῦ ᾿Ιησοῦ καὶ
Paul a prisoner of Christ Jesus and
Τιμόθεος ὁ ἀδελφὸς Φιλήμονι τῷ ἀγαπητῷ
Timothy the brother to Philemon the beloved
καὶ συνεργῷ ἡμῶν 2 καὶ ᾿Απφίᾳ τῇ
and a fellow-worker of us and to Apphia the
ἀδελφῇ καὶ ᾿Αρχίππῳ τῷ συστρατιώτῃ
sister and to Archippus the fellow-soldier
ἡμῶν καὶ τῇ κατ᾿ οἶκόν σου ἐκκλησίᾳ·
of us and [1]to the [2]at [4]house [5]of thee [3]church:
3 χάρις ὑμῖν καὶ εἰρήνη ἀπὸ θεοῦ πατρὸς
Grace to you and peace from God Father
ἡμῶν καὶ κυρίου ᾿Ιησοῦ Χριστοῦ.
of us and Lord Jesus Christ.
4 Εὐχαριστῶ τῷ θεῷ μου πάντοτε μνείαν
I give thanks to the God of me always [2]mention
σου ποιούμενος ἐπὶ τῶν προσευχῶν μου,
[5]of thee [1]making at the prayers of me,
5 ἀκούων σου τὴν ἀγάπην καὶ τὴν
hearing of thee the love and the

which you have toward the Lord Jesus and all the saints, [6]and I pray that the sharing of your faith may promote the knowledge of all the good that is ours in Christ. [7]For I have derived much joy and comfort from your love, my brother, because the hearts of the saints have been refreshed through you.

8 Accordingly, though I am bold enough in Christ to command you to do what is required, [9]yet for love's sake I prefer to appeal to you— I, Paul, an ambassador[a] and now a prisoner also for Christ Jesus—[10]I appeal to you for my child, Ones'imus, whose father I have become in my imprisonment. [11](Formerly he was useless to you, but now he is indeed useful[b] to you and to me.) [12]I am sending him back to you, sending my very heart. [13]I would have been glad to keep him with me, in order that he might serve me on your behalf during my imprisonment for the gospel; [14]but I preferred to do nothing

[a] Or an old man
[b] The name Onesimus means useful or (compare verse 20) beneficial

πίστιν	ἣν	ἔχεις	πρὸς	τὸν	κύριον	Ἰησοῦν
faith	which	thou hast	toward	the	Lord	Jesus

καὶ	εἰς	πάντας	τοὺς	ἁγίους,	6 ὅπως
and	to	all	the	saints,	so as

ἡ	κοινωνία	τῆς	πίστεώς	σου	ἐνεργὴς
the	fellowship	of the	faith	of thee	[1]operative

γένηται	ἐν	ἐπιγνώσει	παντὸς	ἀγαθοῦ	τοῦ
[1]may become	in	a full knowledge	of every	good thing	-

ἐν	ἡμῖν	εἰς	Χριστόν.	7 χαρὰν	γὰρ
in	us	for	Christ.	[4]joy	[1]For

πολλὴν	ἔσχον	καὶ	παράκλησιν	ἐπὶ	τῇ
[3]much	[2]I had	and	consolation	over	the

ἀγάπῃ	σου,	ὅτι	τὰ	σπλάγχνα	τῶν	ἁγίων
love	of thee,	because	the	bowels	of the	saints

ἀναπέπαυται	διὰ	σοῦ,	ἀδελφέ.	8 Διό,
has(ve) been refreshed	through	thee,	brother.	Wherefore,

πολλὴν	ἐν	Χριστῷ	παρρησίαν	ἔχων	ἐπιτάσ-
[2]much	[4]in	[5]Christ	[3]boldness	[1]having	to

σειν	σοι	τὸ	ἀνῆκον,	9 διὰ	τὴν	ἀγάπην
charge	thee	the	befitting, thing	because of	-	love

μᾶλλον	παρακαλῶ·	τοιοῦτος	ὢν	ὡς	Παῦλος
rather	I beseech;	such a one	being	as	Paul

πρεσβύτης,	νυνὶ	δὲ	καὶ	δέσμιος	Χριστοῦ
an old man,	and now		also	a prisoner	of Christ

Ἰησοῦ,	10 παρακαλῶ	σε	περὶ	τοῦ	ἐμοῦ
Jesus,	I beseech	thee	con-cerning	-	my

τέκνου,	ὃν	ἐγέννησα	ἐν	τοῖς	δεσμοῖς,
child,	whom	I begat	in	the(my)	bonds,

Ὀνήσιμον,	11 τόν	ποτέ	σοι	ἄχρηστον
Onesimus,	the [one]	then (formerly)	[2]to thee	[1]useless

νυνὶ	δὲ	καὶ	σοὶ	καὶ	ἐμοὶ	εὔχρηστον,
but now		[2]both	[3]to thee	[4]and	[5]to me	[1]useful,

12 ὃν	ἀνέπεμψά	σοι,	αὐτόν,	τοῦτ'	ἔστιν
whom	I sent back	to thee,	him,	this	is

τὰ	ἐμὰ	σπλάγχνα·	13 ὃν	ἐγὼ	ἐβουλόμην
-	my	bowels;	whom	I	resolved

πρὸς	ἐμαυτὸν	κατέχειν,	ἵνα	ὑπὲρ	σοῦ
with	myself	to retain,	in order that	on behalf of	thee

μοι	διακονῇ	ἐν	τοῖς	δεσμοῖς	τοῦ	εὐαγ-
to me	he might minister	in	the	bonds	of the	gos-

γελίου,	14 χωρὶς	δὲ	τῆς	σῆς	γνώμης
pel,	but without	-		thy	opinion

without your consent in order that your goodness might not be by compulsion but of your own free will.

15 Perhaps this is why he was parted from you for a while, that you might have him back for ever, [16] no longer as a slave but more than a slave, as a beloved brother, especially to me but how much more to you, both in the flesh and in the Lord. [17] So if you consider me your partner, receive him as you would receive me. [18] If he has wronged you at all, or owes you anything, charge that to my account. [19] I, Paul, write this with my own hand, I will repay it—to say nothing of your owing me even your own self. [20] Yes, brother, I want some benefit from you in the Lord. Refresh my heart in Christ.

21 Confident of your obedience, I write to you, knowing that you will do even more than I say. [22] At the same time, prepare a guest room for me, for I am hoping through your prayers to be granted to you.

23 Ep'aphras, my

οὐδὲν ἠθέλησα ποιῆσαι, ἵνα μὴ ὡς κατὰ
[3]nothing [1]I was [2]to do, lest [5]as [6]by way
willing of

ἀνάγκην τὸ ἀγαθόν σου ᾖ ἀλλὰ κατὰ
[7]necessity [1]the [2]good [3]of [4]might but by way
thee be of

ἑκούσιον. 15 τάχα γὰρ διὰ τοῦτο ἐχωρίσθη
[being] For perhaps therefore he departed
voluntary.

πρὸς ὥραν, ἵνα αἰώνιον αὐτὸν ἀπέχῃς,
for an hour, in order [3]eternally [2]him [1]thou mightest
that receive,

16 οὐκέτι ὡς δοῦλον ἀλλὰ ὑπὲρ δοῦλον,
no longer as a slave but beyond a slave,

ἀδελφὸν ἀγαπητόν, μάλιστα ἐμοί, πόσῳ
a brother beloved, specially to me, [2]by how
much

δὲ μᾶλλον σοὶ καὶ ἐν σαρκὶ καὶ ἐν
[1]and more to thee both in [the] flesh and in

κυρίῳ. 17 εἰ οὖν με ἔχεις κοινωνόν,
[the] Lord. If therefore me thou hast [as] a partner,

προσλαβοῦ αὐτὸν ὡς ἐμέ. 18 εἰ δέ
receive him as me. And if

τι ἠδίκησέν σε ἢ ὀφείλει, τοῦτο ἐμοὶ
any- he wronged thee or owes, [2]this [3]to me
thing

ἐλλόγα· 19 ἐγὼ Παῦλος ἔγραψα τῇ ἐμῇ
[1]reckon: I Paul wrote – with my

χειρί, ἐγὼ ἀποτίσω· ἵνα μὴ λέγω σοι
hand, I will repay; lest I say to thee

ὅτι καὶ σεαυτόν μοι προσοφείλεις. 20 ναί,
that indeed [2]thyself [3]to me [1]thou owest besides. Yes,

ἀδελφέ, ἐγώ σου ὀναίμην ἐν κυρίῳ·
brother, [2]I [5]of thee [1]may [3]have [4]help in [the] Lord;

ἀνάπαυσόν μου τὰ σπλάγχνα ἐν Χριστῷ.
refresh of me the bowels in Christ.

21 Πεποιθὼς τῇ ὑπακοῇ σου ἔγραψά
Having trusted to the obedience of thee I wrote

σοι, εἰδὼς ὅτι καὶ ὑπὲρ ἃ λέγω ποιήσεις.
to knowing that indeed beyond what I say thou wilt
thee, things do.

22 ἅμα δὲ καὶ ἑτοίμαζέ μοι ξενίαν·
And at the also prepare for me lodging;
same time

ἐλπίζω γὰρ ὅτι διὰ τῶν προσευχῶν
for I hope that through the prayers

ὑμῶν χαρισθήσομαι ὑμῖν.
of you I shall be given to you.

23 Ἀσπάζεταί σε Ἐπαφρᾶς ὁ συναιχμά-
[2]greets [3]thee [1]Epaphras [3]the [3]fellow-

HEBREWS 1

fellow prisoner in Christ Jesus, sends greetings to you, 24 and so do Mark, Aristar'chus, Demas, and Luke, my fellow workers. 25 The grace of the Lord Jesus Christ be with your spirit.

λωτός μου ἐν Χριστῷ Ἰησοῦ, 24 Μᾶρκος,
captive *of me *in *Christ *Jesus, [also] Mark,

Ἀρίσταρχος, Δημᾶς, Λουκᾶς, οἱ συνεργοί
Aristarchus, Demas, Luke, the fellow-workers

μου.
of me.

25 Ἡ χάρις τοῦ κυρίου Ἰησοῦ Χριστοῦ
The grace of the Lord Jesus Christ

μετὰ τοῦ πνεύματος ὑμῶν.
[be] with the spirit of you.

HEBREWS 1

ΠΡΟΣ ΕΒΡΑΙΟΥΣ
To Hebrews

CHAPTER 1

IN many and various ways God spoke of old to our fathers by the prophets; 2 but in these last days he has spoken to us by a Son, whom he appointed the heir of all things, through whom also he created the world. 3 He reflects the glory of God and bears the very stamp of his nature, upholding the universe by his word of power. When he had made purification for sins, he sat down at the right hand of the Majesty on high, 4 having become as much superior to angels as the name he has obtained is more excellent than theirs.

1 Πολυμερῶς καὶ πολυτρόπως πάλαι ὁ
*In many *and ʼin many ways *of old –
portions

θεὸς λαλήσας τοῖς πατράσιν ἐν τοῖς
¹God ²having spoken ³to the ⁴fathers by the

προφήταις 2 ἐπ' ἐσχάτου τῶν ἡμερῶν
prophets in [the] last – days

τούτων ἐλάλησεν ἡμῖν ἐν υἱῷ, ὃν ἔθηκεν
of these spoke to us in a Son, whom he appointed

κληρονόμον πάντων, δι' οὗ καὶ ἐποίησεν
heir of all through whom indeed he made
things,

τοὺς αἰῶνας· 3 ὃς ὢν ἀπαύγασμα τῆς
the ages; who being [the] radiance of the (his)

δόξης καὶ χαρακτὴρ τῆς ὑποστάσεως αὐτοῦ,
glory and [the] of the reality of him,
representation

φέρων τε τὰ πάντα τῷ ῥήματι τῆς
and bearing – all things by the word of the

δυνάμεως αὐτοῦ, καθαρισμὸν τῶν ἁμαρτιῶν
power of him, ²cleansing – ³of sins

ποιησάμενος ἐκάθισεν ἐν δεξιᾷ τῆς
¹having made sat on [the] right [hand] of the

μεγαλωσύνης ἐν ὑψηλοῖς, 4 τοσούτῳ
greatness in high places, ²by so much

κρείττων γενόμενος τῶν ἀγγέλων ὅσῳ
²better ¹becoming ⁴[than] the angels as

διαφορώτερον παρ' αὐτοὺς κεκληρονόμηκεν
²a more excellent ⁴than ⁵them ¹he has inherited

5 For to what angel did God ever say,
"Thou art my Son, today I have begotten thee"?
Or again,
"I will be to him a father, and he shall be to me a son"?
⁶And again, when he brings the first-born into the world, he says, "Let all God's angels worship him."
⁷Of the angels he says, "Who makes his angels winds, and his servants flames of fire."
⁸But of the Son he says, "Thy throne, O God,ᵃ is for ever and ever, the righteous scepter is the scepter of thyᵇ kingdom.
⁹Thou hast loved righteousness and hated lawlessness; therefore God, thy God, has anointed thee with the oil of gladness beyond thy comrades."
¹⁰And, "Thou, Lord, didst found the earth in the beginning, and the heavens are the work of thy hands;
¹¹they will perish, but thou remainest; they will all grow old like a garment,
¹²like a mantle thou wilt roll them up,

ᵃ Or God is thy throne
ᵇ Other ancient authorities read his

ὄνομα.
²name.

5 Τίνι γὰρ εἶπέν ποτε τῶν
For to which ³said he ⁴ever ¹of the

ἀγγέλων· υἱός μου εἶ σύ, ἐγὼ σήμερον
²angels: Son of me art thou, I to-day

γεγέννηκά σε; καὶ πάλιν· ἐγὼ ἔσομαι
have begotten thee? and again: I will be

αὐτῷ εἰς πατέρα, καὶ αὐτὸς ἔσται μοι
to him for a father, and he shall be to me

εἰς υἱόν; 6 ὅταν δὲ πάλιν εἰσαγάγῃ
for a son? and whenever again he brings in

τὸν πρωτότοκον εἰς τὴν οἰκουμένην, λέγει·
the firstborn into the inhabited [earth], he says:

καὶ προσκυνησάτωσαν αὐτῷ πάντες ἄγγελοι
And let worship him all angels

θεοῦ. 7 καὶ πρὸς μὲν τοὺς ἀγγέλους
of God. And with re- – the angels
gard to

λέγει· ὁ ποιῶν τοὺς ἀγγέλους αὐτοῦ
he says: The making the angels of him
[one]

πνεύματα, καὶ τοὺς λειτουργοὺς αὐτοῦ
spirits, and the ministers of him

πυρὸς φλόγα· 8 πρὸς δὲ τὸν υἱόν· ὁ
²of fire ¹a flame; but with regard to the Son: The

θρόνος σου ὁ θεὸς εἰς τὸν αἰῶνα τοῦ
throne of thee[,] – God[,]*[is] unto the age of the

αἰῶνος, καὶ ἡ ῥάβδος τῆς εὐθύτητος
age, and the rod – of uprightness [is]

ῥάβδος τῆς βασιλείας αὐτοῦ. 9 ἠγάπησας
[the] rod of the kingdom of him. Thou lovedst

δικαιοσύνην καὶ ἐμίσησας ἀνομίαν· διὰ
righteousness and hatedst lawlessness; there-

τοῦτο ἔχρισέν σε, ὁ θεός, ὁ θεός σου
fore ⁴anointed ⁵thee, – ⁶God,* ¹the ²God ³of thee

ἔλαιον ἀγαλλιάσεως παρὰ τοὺς μετόχους
[with] oil of gladness above the partners

σου. 10 καὶ· σὺ κατ' ἀρχάς, κύριε,
of thee. And: Thou at [the] beginnings, Lord,

τὴν γῆν ἐθεμελίωσας, καὶ ἔργα τῶν
¹the ²earth ¹didst found, and ²works ⁴works ⁵of the

χειρῶν σού εἰσιν οἱ οὐρανοί· 11 αὐτοὶ
⁶hands ⁷of thee ³are ¹the ²heavens; they

ἀπολοῦνται, σὺ δὲ διαμένεις· καὶ πάντες
will perish, but thou remainest; and all

ὡς ἱμάτιον παλαιωθήσονται, 12 καὶ ὡσεὶ
as a garment will become old, and as

περιβόλαιον ἑλίξεις αὐτούς, ὡς ἱμάτιον
a mantle thou wilt roll up them, as a garment

* Articular vocative; see ver. 10.

and they will be changed.[c]
But thou art the same,
and thy years will never end."
13 But to what angel has he ever said,
"Sit at my right hand,
till I make thy enemies
a stool for thy feet"?
14 Are they not all ministering spirits sent forth to serve, for the sake of those who are to obtain salvation?

CHAPTER 2

THEREFORE we must pay the closer attention to what we have heard, lest we drift away from it. 2 For if the message declared by angels was valid and every transgression or disobedience received a just retribution, 3 how shall we escape if we neglect such a great salvation? It was declared at first by the Lord, and it was attested to us by those who heard him, 4 while God also bore witness by signs and wonders and various miracles and by gifts of the Holy Spirit distributed according to his own will.
5 For it was not to angels that God subjected the world to come,

καὶ ἀλλαγήσονται· σὺ δὲ ὁ αὐτὸς εἶ
also they will be changed; but thou the same art

καὶ τὰ ἔτη σου οὐκ ἐκλείψουσιν. 13 πρὸς
and the years of thee will not fail. [2]to

τίνα δὲ τῶν ἀγγέλων εἴρηκέν ποτε·
[3]which [1]But of the angels has he said at any time:

κάθου ἐκ δεξιῶν μου ἕως ἂν θῶ τοὺς
Sit at [the] right of me until I put the

ἐχθρούς σου ὑποπόδιον τῶν ποδῶν σου;
enemies of thee a footstool of the feet of thee?

14 οὐχὶ πάντες εἰσὶν λειτουργικὰ πνεύματα
[2]not [3]all [1]are they [4]ministering [5]spirits

εἰς διακονίαν ἀποστελλόμενα διὰ τοὺς
[7]for [8]service [6]being sent forth because of the [ones]

μέλλοντας κληρονομεῖν σωτηρίαν; . 2 Διὰ
being about to inherit salvation? There-

τοῦτο δεῖ περισσοτέρως προσέχειν ἡμᾶς
fore [1]it behoves [4]more abundantly [3]to give heed [2]us

τοῖς ἀκουσθεῖσιν, μήποτε παραρυῶμεν.
to the things heard, lest we drift away.

2 εἰ γὰρ ὁ δι᾽ ἀγγέλων λαληθεὶς λόγος
For if [1]the [4]through [5]angels [3]spoken [2]word

ἐγένετο βέβαιος, καὶ πᾶσα παράβασις
was firm, and every transgression

καὶ παρακοὴ ἔλαβεν ἔνδικον μισθαποδοσίαν,
and disobedience received a just recompence,

3 πῶς ἡμεῖς ἐκφευξόμεθα τηλικαύτης
how [2]we [1]shall [2]escape [4]so great

ἀμελήσαντες σωτηρίας; ἥτις ἀρχὴν λαβοῦσα
[4]neglecting [5]a salvation? which [2]a beginning [1]having received

λαλεῖσθαι διὰ τοῦ κυρίου, ὑπὸ τῶν
to be spoken through the Lord, by the

ἀκουσάντων εἰς ἡμᾶς ἐβεβαιώθη, 4 συνεπι-
[ones] hearing to us was confirmed, [2]bearing

μαρτυροῦντος τοῦ θεοῦ σημείοις τε καὶ
witness with – [1]God[a] [4]by signs [3]both and

τέρασιν καὶ ποικίλαις δυνάμεσιν καὶ
by wonders and by various powerful deeds and

πνεύματος ἁγίου μερισμοῖς κατὰ τὴν αὐτοῦ
[3]Spirit [2]of [the] [1]by distribu- according the [2]of him
Holy tions to

θέλησιν.
[1]will.

5 Οὐ γὰρ ἀγγέλοις ὑπέταξεν τὴν
For not to angels subjected he the

οἰκουμένην τὴν μέλλουσαν, περὶ ἧς
[2]inhabited [earth] – [1]coming, about which

of which we are speaking. [6] It has been testified somewhere,
"What is man that thou art mindful of him,
or the son of man, that thou carest for him?
[7] Thou didst make him for a little while lower than the angels,
thou hast crowned him with glory and honor,[d]
[8] putting everything in subjection under his feet."
Now in putting everything in subjection to him, he left nothing outside his control. As it is, we do not yet see everything in subjection to him. [9] But we see Jesus, who for a little while was made lower than the angels, crowned with glory and honor because of the suffering of death, so that by the grace of God he might taste death for every one.
10 For it was fitting that he, for whom and by whom all things exist, in bringing many sons to glory, should make the pioneer of their salvation perfect through suffering. [11] For he who sanctifies and those who are sanctified have all one origin. That is why he is not ashamed to call

[d] Other ancient authorities insert *and didst set him over the works of thy hands*

λαλοῦμεν. **6** διεμαρτύρατο δέ πού τις
we speak. But [2]solemnly witnessed [3]some- [1]one
where

λέγων· τί ἐστιν ἄνθρωπος ὅτι μιμνῄσκῃ
saying: What is man that thou rememberest

αὐτοῦ; ἤ υἱὸς ἀνθρώπου ὅτι ἐπισκέπτῃ
him? or a son of man that thou observest

αὐτόν; **7** ἠλάττωσας αὐτὸν βραχύ τι παρ᾽
him? Thou madest [3]less [1]him [2]a little than

ἀγγέλους, δόξῃ καὶ τιμῇ ἐστεφάνωσας
angels, with glory and *with* honour thou crownedst

αὐτόν, **8** πάντα ὑπέταξας ὑποκάτω τῶν
him, all things thou subjectedst underneath the

ποδῶν αὐτοῦ. ἐν τῷ γὰρ ὑποτάξαι
feet of him. [1]in the For [3]to subject[ing]

[αὐτῷ] τὰ πάντα οὐδὲν ἀφῆκεν αὐτῷ
[4]to him – [3]all things [6]nothing [5]he left [8]to him

ἀνυπότακτον. Νῦν δὲ οὔπω ὁρῶμεν
[7]unsubjected. But now not yet we see

αὐτῷ τὰ πάντα ὑποτεταγμένα· **9** τὸν δὲ
[3]to him – [1]all things [2]having been [3]the [1]but
subjected; [one]

βραχύ τι παρ᾽ ἀγγέλους ἠλαττωμένον
[5]a little [6]than [7]angels [4]having been
made less

βλέπομεν Ἰησοῦν διὰ τὸ πάθημα τοῦ
[2]we see [3]Jesus because of the suffering –

θανάτου δόξῃ καὶ τιμῇ ἐστεφανωμένον,
of death with glory and *with* honour having been
crowned,

ὅπως χάριτι θεοῦ ὑπὲρ παντὸς γεύσηται
so as by [the] of God [3]on [4]every man [1]he might
grace behalf of taste

θανάτου. **10** ἔπρεπεν γὰρ αὐτῷ, δι᾽
of [2]death. For it was fitting for him, because
of

ὃν τὰ πάντα καὶ δι᾽ οὗ τὰ πάντα,
whom – all things and through whom – all things,

πολλοὺς υἱοὺς εἰς δόξαν ἀγαγόντα τὸν
[10]many [11]sons [12]to [13]glory [9]leading [4]the

ἀρχηγὸν τῆς σωτηρίας αὐτῶν διὰ
[6]author [5]of the [7]salvation [8]of them [2]through

παθημάτων τελειῶσαι. **11** ὅ τε γὰρ
[3]sufferings [1]to perfect. [3]the [one] [2]both [1]For

ἀγιάζων καὶ οἱ ἀγιαζόμενοι ἐξ ἑνὸς
sanctifying and the [ones] being sanctified [are] [2]of [3]one

πάντες· δι᾽ ἥν αἰτίαν οὐκ ἐπαισχύνεται
[1]all; for which cause he is not ashamed

them brethren, [12]saying, "I will proclaim thy name to my brethren, in the midst of the congregation I will praise thee." [13]And again, "I will put my trust in him." And again, "Here am I, and the children God has given me." 14 Since therefore the children share in flesh and blood, he himself likewise partook of the same nature, that through death he might destroy him who has the power of death, that is, the devil, [15]and deliver all those who through fear of death were subject to lifelong bondage. [16]For surely it is not with angels that he is concerned but with the descendants of Abraham. [17]Therefore he had to be made like his brethren in every respect, so that he might become a merciful and faithful high priest in the service of God, to make expiation for the sins of the people. [18]For because he himself has suffered and been tempted, he is able to help those who are tempted.

ἀδελφοὺς αὐτοὺς καλεῖν, 12 λέγων· ἀπαγ-
[3]brothers [2]them [1]to call, saying: I will

γελῶ τὸ ὄνομά σου τοῖς ἀδελφοῖς μου,
announce the name of thee to the brothers of me,

ἐν μέσῳ ἐκκλησίας ὑμνήσω σε· 13 καὶ
in [the] midst of [the] church I will hymn thee; and

πάλιν· ἐγὼ ἔσομαι πεποιθὼς ἐπ' αὐτῷ·
again: I will be having trusted on(in) him;

καὶ πάλιν· ἰδοὺ ἐγὼ καὶ τὰ παιδία
and again: Behold[,] I and the children

ἃ μοι ἔδωκεν ὁ θεός. 14 Ἐπεὶ οὖν
whom [3]to me [2]gave - [1]God. Since therefore

τὰ παιδία κεκοινώνηκεν αἵματος καὶ
the children has(ve) partaken of blood and

σαρκός, καὶ αὐτὸς παραπλησίως μετέσχεν
of flesh, [2]also [3][him]self [4]in like manner [1]he shared

τῶν αὐτῶν, ἵνα διὰ τοῦ θανάτου
the same things, in order that through the(?his) death

καταργήσῃ τὸν τὸ κράτος ἔχοντα τοῦ
he might destroy [1]the [one] [3]the [4]might [2]having -

θανάτου, τοῦτ' ἔστιν τὸν διάβολον, 15 καὶ
of death, this is the devil, and

ἀπαλλάξῃ τούτους, ὅσοι φόβῳ θανάτου
release these, as many as by fear of death

διὰ παντὸς τοῦ ζῆν ἔνοχοι ἦσαν δουλείας.
through all the(ir) to [time] live [2]involved [1]were slavery.

16 οὐ γὰρ δήπου ἀγγέλων ἐπιλαμβάνεται,
[4]not [1]For [2]of course [5]of angels [3]he takes hold,

ἀλλὰ σπέρματος Ἀβραὰμ ἐπιλαμβάνεται.
but of [the] seed of Abraham he takes hold.

17 ὅθεν ὤφειλεν κατὰ πάντα τοῖς ἀδελφοῖς
Whence he owed (ought) by all means† [2]to the (his) [3]brothers

ὁμοιωθῆναι, ἵνα ἐλεήμων γένηται καὶ
[1]to become like, in order that [2]a merciful [1]he might become and

πιστὸς ἀρχιερεὺς τὰ πρὸς τὸν θεόν,
faithful high priest [in] the things in regard to - God,

εἰς τὸ ἱλάσκεσθαι τὰς ἁμαρτίας τοῦ
for the to make propitiation for the sins of the

λαοῦ. 18 ἐν ᾧ γὰρ πέπονθεν αὐτὸς
people. [2]in [3]what [way] [1]For [5]has suffered [4]he

πειρασθείς, δύναται τοῖς πειραζομένοις
being tempted, he is able [2]the [ones] [3]being tempted

βοηθῆσαι.
[1]to help.

858

HEBREWS 3

CHAPTER 3

THEREFORE, holy brethren, who share in a heavenly call, consider Jesus, the apostle and high priest of our confession. ²He was faithful to him who appointed him, just as Moses also was faithful in*e* God's house. ³Yet Jesus has been counted worthy of as much more glory than Moses as the builder of a house has more honor than the house. ⁴(For every house is built by some one, but the builder of all things is God.) ⁵Now Moses was faithful in all God's house as a servant, to testify to the things that were to be spoken later, ⁶but Christ was faithful over God's house as a son. And we are his house if we hold fast our confidence and pride in our hope*f*.

7 Therefore, as the Holy Spirit says,
"Today, when you hear his voice,
⁸do not harden your hearts as in the rebellion,
on the day of testing in the wilderness,
⁹where your fathers

e Other ancient authorities insert *all*
f Other ancient authorities insert *firm to the end*

3 Ὅθεν, ἀδελφοὶ ἅγιοι, κλήσεως
Whence, brothers holy, ²calling
ἐπουρανίου μέτοχοι, κατανοήσατε τὸν
²of a heavenly ¹sharers, consider the
ἀπόστολον καὶ ἀρχιερέα τῆς ὁμολογίας
apostle and high priest of the confession
ἡμῶν Ἰησοῦν, 2 πιστὸν ὄντα τῷ ποιήσαντι
of us[,] Jesus, faithful being to the [one] making
αὐτόν, ὡς καὶ Μωϋσῆς ἐν [ὅλῳ] τῷ
him, as also Moses in all the
οἴκῳ αὐτοῦ. 3 πλείονος γὰρ οὗτος δόξης
household of him. For ³of more ¹this one ⁴glory
παρὰ Μωϋσῆν ἠξίωται καθ᾽ ὅσον πλείονα
⁵than ⁶Moses ²has been by so much as ⁸more
counted worthy
τιμὴν ἔχει τοῦ οἴκου ὁ κατασκευάσας
⁶honour ⁴has ⁸the ⁹house ¹the ²having prepared
⁷[than] [one]
αὐτόν. 4 πᾶς γὰρ οἶκος κατασκευάζεται
³it. For every house is prepared
ὑπό τινος, ὁ δὲ πάντα κατασκευάσας
by someone, but ¹the [one] ³all things ²having prepared
θεός. 5 καὶ Μωϋσῆς μὲν πιστὸς ἐν
[is] God. And Moses on one hand faithful in
[was]
ὅλῳ τῷ οἴκῳ αὐτοῦ ὡς θεράπων εἰς
all the household of him as a servant for
μαρτύριον τῶν λαληθησομένων, 6 Χριστὸς
a testimony of the things being spoken Christ
[in the future],
δὲ ὡς υἱὸς ἐπὶ τὸν οἶκον αὐτοῦ· οὗ
on the as a Son over the household of him; of
other whom
οἶκός ἐσμεν ἡμεῖς, ἐὰν τὴν παρρησίαν
a household are we, if ²the ³confidence
καὶ τὸ καύχημα τῆς ἐλπίδος [μέχρι
⁴and ⁵the ⁶boast ⁷of the ⁸hope ¹⁰until
τέλους βεβαίαν] κατάσχωμεν. 7 Διό,
¹¹[the] end ⁹firm ¹we hold fast. Wherefore,
καθὼς λέγει τὸ πνεῦμα τὸ ἅγιον· σήμερον
as says the Spirit - Holy: To-day
ἐὰν τῆς φωνῆς αὐτοῦ ἀκούσητε, 8 μὴ
if the voice of him ye hear, not
σκληρύνητε τὰς καρδίας ὑμῶν ὡς ἐν
harden ye the hearts of you as in
τῷ παραπικρασμῷ κατὰ τὴν ἡμέραν τοῦ
the provocation in the day of the
πειρασμοῦ ἐν τῇ ἐρήμῳ, 9 οὗ ἐπείρασαν
temptation in the desert, when ⁴tempted

put me to the test and saw my works for forty years. [10]Therefore I was provoked with that generation, and said, 'They always go astray in their hearts; they have not known my ways.' [11]As I swore in my wrath, 'They shall never enter my rest.' " [12]Take care, brethren, lest there be in any of you an evil, unbelieving heart, leading you to fall away from the living God. [13]But exhort one another every day, as long as it is called "today," that none of you may be hardened by the deceitfulness of sin. [14]For we share in Christ, if only we hold our first confidence firm to the end, [15]while it is said, "Today, when you hear his voice do not harden your hearts as in the rebellion." [16]Who were they that heard and yet were rebellious? Was it not all those who left Egypt under the leadership of Moses? [17]And with whom was he provoked

οἱ	πατέρες	ὑμῶν	ἐν	δοκιμασίᾳ	καὶ	εἶδον
[1]the	[2]fathers	[3]of you	in	proving	and	saw

τὰ	ἔργα	μου	τεσσεράκοντα	ἔτη·	[10]διὸ
the	works	of me	forty	years;	wherefore

προσώχθισα	τῇ	γενεᾷ	ταύτῃ	καὶ	εἶπον·
I was angry		with this generation		and	I said:

ἀεὶ	πλανῶνται	τῇ	καρδίᾳ·	αὐτοὶ	δὲ
Always	they err	in the	heart;		and they

οὐκ	ἔγνωσαν	τὰς	ὁδούς	μου,	[11]ὡς
knew not		the	ways	of me,	as

ὤμοσα	ἐν	τῇ	ὀργῇ	μου·	εἰ	εἰσελεύσονται
I swore	in	the	wrath	of me:	If	they shall enter

εἰς	τὴν	κατάπαυσίν	μου.	[12]Βλέπετε,
into	the	rest	of me.	Look ye,

ἀδελφοί,	μήποτε	ἔσται	ἔν	τινι	ὑμῶν
brothers,	lest	there shall be in		anyone	of you

καρδία	πονηρὰ	ἀπιστίας	ἐν	τῷ	ἀποστῆναι
[a]heart	[1]an evil	of unbelief	in	the	to depart[ing]

ἀπὸ	θεοῦ	ζῶντος,	[13]ἀλλὰ	παρακαλεῖτε
from	God	a living,	but	exhort

ἑαυτοὺς	καθ'	ἑκάστην	ἡμέραν,	ἄχρις	οὗ
yourselves	–	each	day,		while

τὸ	σήμερον	καλεῖται,	ἵνα	μὴ	σκληρυνθῇ
the	to-day	it is being called,	lest		[4]be hardened

τις	ἐξ	ὑμῶν	ἀπάτῃ	τῆς	ἁμαρτίας·	[14]μέτ-
[1]any-one	[2]of	[3]you	by [the] deceit		of sin;	[3]shar-

οχοι	γὰρ	τοῦ	Χριστοῦ	γεγόναμεν,	ἐάνπερ
ers	[1]for	[4]of the	[5]Christ	[2]we have become,	if indeed

τὴν	ἀρχὴν	τῆς	ὑποστάσεως	μέχρι	τέλους
[2]the	[3]beginning	[4]of the	[5]assurance	[7]until	[8][the] end

βεβαίαν	κατάσχωμεν.	[15]ἐν	τῷ	λέγεσθαι·
[6]firm	[1]we hold fast.	In	the	to be said[6]:
				=While it is said:

σήμερον	ἐὰν	τῆς	φωνῆς	αὐτοῦ	ἀκούσητε,
To-day	if	the	voice	of him	ye hear,

μὴ	σκληρύνητε	τὰς	καρδίας	ὑμῶν	ὡς
do not harden		the	hearts	of you	as

ἐν	τῷ	παραπικρασμῷ.	[16]τίνες	γὰρ
in	the	provocation.	For some	

ἀκούσαντες	παρεπίκραναν;	ἀλλ'	οὐ	πάντες
hearing	provoked?	yet	not	all

οἱ	ἐξελθόντες	ἐξ	Αἰγύπτου	διὰ
the [ones] coming out		out of	Egypt	through

Μωϋσέως;	[17]τίσιν	δὲ	προσώχθισεν	τεσ-
Moses?	but with whom		was he angry	for-

forty years? Was it not with those who sinned, whose bodies fell in the wilderness? [18]And to whom did he swear that they should never enter his rest, but to those who were disobedient? [19]So we see that they were unable to enter because of unbelief.

CHAPTER 4

THEREFORE, while the promise of entering his rest remains, let us fear lest any of you be judged to have failed to reach it. [2]For good news came to us just as to them; but the message which they heard did not benefit them, because it did not meet with faith in the hearers.[g] [3]For we who have believed enter that rest, as he has said,
"As I swore in my wrath,
They shall never enter my rest,' "
although his works were finished from the foundation of the world. [4]For he has somewhere spoken of the seventh day in this way, "And God rested on the seventh day from all his works." [5]And again in this place he said,
"They shall never enter my rest."

[g] Other manuscripts read *they were not united in faith with the hearers*

σεράκοντα ἔτη; οὐχὶ τοῖς ἁμαρτήσασιν,
ty years? [was it] with the [ones] sinning,
not

ὧν τὰ κῶλα ἔπεσεν ἐν τῇ ἐρήμῳ;
of the corpses fell in the desert?
whom

18 τίσιν δὲ ὤμοσεν μὴ εἰσελεύσεσθαι εἰς
and to whom swore he not to enter into

τὴν κατάπαυσιν αὐτοῦ εἰ μὴ τοῖς
the rest of him except to the

ἀπειθήσασιν; 19 καὶ βλέπομεν ὅτι οὐκ
[ones] disobeying? and we see that not

ἠδυνήθησαν εἰσελθεῖν δι' ἀπιστίαν.
they were able to enter because of disbelief.

4 Φοβηθῶμεν οὖν μήποτε καταλειπομένης
Let us fear therefore lest [2]being left

ἐπαγγελίας εἰσελθεῖν εἰς τὴν κατάπαυσιν
[1]a promise[a] to enter into the rest

αὐτοῦ δοκῇ τις ἐξ ὑμῶν ὑστερηκέναι.
of him [4]seems [1]anyone [2]of [3]you to have come short.

2 καὶ γάρ ἐσμεν εὐηγγελισμένοι καθάπερ
For indeed we are having had good news even as
preached [to us]

κἀκεῖνοι· ἀλλ' οὐκ ὠφέλησεν ὁ λόγος
those also; but [4]did not profit [1]the [2]word

τῆς ἀκοῆς ἐκείνους μὴ συγκεκερασμένος
- [3]of hearing those not having been mixed
together

τῇ πίστει τοῖς ἀκούσασιν. 3 Εἰσερχόμεθα
- with faith in the [ones] hearing. we enter

γὰρ εἰς [τὴν] κατάπαυσιν οἱ πιστεύσαντες,
For into the rest the [ones] believing,

καθὼς εἴρηκεν· ὡς ὤμοσα ἐν τῇ ὀργῇ
as he has said: As I swore in the wrath

μου· εἰ εἰσελεύσονται εἰς τὴν κατάπαυσίν
of me: If they shall enter into the rest

μου, καίτοι τῶν ἔργων ἀπὸ καταβολῆς
of me, though the works [2]from [3][the] foundation

κόσμου γενηθέντων. 4 εἴρηκεν γάρ που
[4]of [the] [1]having come into For he has said some-
world being.[a] where

περὶ τῆς ἑβδόμης οὕτως· καὶ κατέπαυσεν
con- the seventh [day] thus: And [2]rested
cerning

ὁ θεὸς ἐν τῇ ἡμέρᾳ τῇ ἑβδόμῃ ἀπὸ
- [1]God in the [2]day - [1]seventh from

πάντων τῶν ἔργων αὐτοῦ· 5 καὶ ἐν
all the works of him; and in

τούτῳ πάλιν· εἰ εἰσελεύσονται εἰς τὴν
this [place] again: If they shall enter into the

⁶Since therefore it remains for some to enter it, and those who formerly received the good news failed to enter because of disobedience, ⁷again he sets a certain day, "Today," saying through David so long afterward, in the words already quoted, "Today, when you hear his voice, do not harden your hearts." ⁸For if Joshua had given them rest, God would not speak later of another day. ⁹So then, there remains a sabbath rest for the people of God; ¹⁰for whoever enters God's rest also ceases from his labors as God did from his. 11 Let us therefore strive to enter that rest, that no one fall by the same sort of disobedience. ¹²For the word of God is living and active, sharper than any two-edged sword, piercing to the division of soul and spirit, of joints and

κατάπαυσίν μου. 6 ἐπεὶ οὖν ἀπολείπεται
rest of me. Since therefore it remains

τινὰς εἰσελθεῖν εἰς αὐτήν, καὶ οἱ πρότερον
[for] to enter into it, and the formerly
some [ones]

εὐαγγελισθέντες οὐκ εἰσῆλθον δι᾽ ἀπείθειαν,
having good news did not enter because of disobedience,
preached [to them] of

7 πάλιν τινὰ ὁρίζει ἡμέραν, σήμερον, ἐν
again ²a certain ¹he de- day, to-day, ²in
fines

Δαυὶδ λέγων μετὰ τοσοῦτον χρόνον, καθὼς
³David ¹saying after such a time, as

προείρηται· σήμερον ἐὰν τῆς φωνῆς αὐτοῦ
he has To-day if the voice of him
previously said:

ἀκούσητε, μὴ σκληρύνητε τὰς καρδίας
ye hear, do not harden the hearts

ὑμῶν. 8 εἰ γὰρ αὐτοὺς Ἰησοῦς κατέπαυσεν,
of you. For if ³them ¹Jesus(Joshua) ²rested,

οὐκ ἂν περὶ ἄλλης ἐλάλει μετὰ ταῦτα
²not - ⁵concerning ⁶another ¹he ²would ³after ⁹these
⁴have spoken things

ἡμέρας. 9 ἄρα ἀπολείπεται σαββατισμὸς
⁷day. Then ²remains ¹a sabbath rest

τῷ λαῷ τοῦ θεοῦ. 10 ὁ γὰρ εἰσελθὼν
to the people - of God. For the [one] having
entered

εἰς τὴν κατάπαυσιν αὐτοῦ καὶ αὐτὸς
into the rest of him also [him]self

κατέπαυσεν ἀπὸ τῶν ἔργων αὐτοῦ,
rested from the works of him,

ὥσπερ ἀπὸ τῶν ἰδίων ὁ θεός. 11 Σπου-
as from the(his) own - God [did]. Let us

δάσωμεν οὖν εἰσελθεῖν εἰς ἐκείνην τὴν
be eager therefore to enter into that

κατάπαυσιν, ἵνα μὴ ἐν τῷ αὐτῷ τις
rest, lest ³in ⁴the ⁵same ¹anyone

ὑποδείγματι πέσῃ τῆς ἀπειθείας. 12 Ζῶν
⁶example ²falls - of dis- [⁴is] ⁵living
obedience.

γὰρ ὁ λόγος τοῦ θεοῦ καὶ ἐνεργὴς
For ¹the ²word - ³of God and operative

καὶ τομώτερος ὑπὲρ πᾶσαν μάχαιραν
and sharper beyond every ²sword

δίστομον καὶ διϊκνούμενος ἄχρι μερισμοῦ
¹two-mouthed and passing through as far as division
(edged)

ψυχῆς καὶ πνεύματος, ἁρμῶν τε καὶ
of soul and of spirit, ²of joints ¹both and

marrow, and discerning the thoughts and intentions of the heart. [13]And before him no creature is hidden, but all are open and laid bare to the eyes of him with whom we have to do. 14 Since then we have a great high priest who has passed through the heavens, Jesus, the Son of God, let us hold fast our confession. [15]For we have not a high priest who is unable to sympathize with our weaknesses, but one who in every respect has been tempted as we are, yet without sinning. [16]Let us then with confidence draw near to the throne of grace, that we may receive mercy and find grace to help in time of need.

μυελῶν,   καὶ   κριτικὸς   ἐνθυμήσεων   καὶ
of marrows,   and   able to judge   of thoughts   and

ἐννοιῶν   καρδίας·   13 καὶ   οὐκ   ἔστιν   κτίσις
intentions   of a heart;   and   there is no   creature

ἀφανὴς   ἐνώπιον   αὐτοῦ,   πάντα   δὲ   γυμνὰ
unmanifest   before   him,   but all things [are] naked

καὶ   τετραχηλισμένα   τοῖς   ὀφθαλμοῖς   αὐτοῦ,
and   having been laid open   to the   eyes   of him,

πρὸς   ὃν   ἡμῖν   ὁ   λόγος.
with   whom   to us [is]   the   word(account).ᶜ
            =is our account.

14 Ἔχοντες   οὖν   ἀρχιερέα   μέγαν   διεληλυ-
Having   there-fore   high priest   a great   having gone

θότα   τοὺς   οὐρανούς,   Ἰησοῦν   τὸν   υἱὸν
through   the   heavens,   Jesus   the   Son

τοῦ   θεοῦ,   κρατῶμεν   τῆς   ὁμολογίας.   15 οὐ
–   of God,   let us hold   the   confession.   ²not

γὰρ   ἔχομεν   ἀρχιερέα   μὴ   δυνάμενον
¹For   ²we have   a high priest   not   being able

συμπαθῆσαι   ταῖς   ἀσθενείαις   ἡμῶν,   πεπει-
to suffer with   the   weaknesses   of us,   ²having

ρασμένον   δὲ   κατὰ   πάντα   καθ'   ὁμοιότητα
been tempted ¹but   in all respects†   accord-ing to   [our] likeness

χωρὶς   ἁμαρτίας.   16 προσερχώμεθα   οὖν
apart from   sin.   Let us approach   there-fore

μετὰ   παρρησίας   τῷ   θρόνῳ   τῆς   χάριτος,
with   confidence   to the   throne   –   of grace,

ἵνα   λάβωμεν   ἔλεος   καὶ   χάριν   εὕρωμεν
in or-der that   we may receive   mercy   and   ²grace   we ¹may find

εἰς   εὔκαιρον   βοήθειαν.
for   timely   help.

CHAPTER 5

FOR every high priest chosen from among men is appointed to act on behalf of men in relation to God, to offer gifts and sacrifices for sins. ²He can deal gently with the ignorant and wayward, since he him-

5 Πᾶς   γὰρ   ἀρχιερεὺς   ἐξ   ἀνθρώπων
For every   high priest   ²out of   ³men

λαμβανόμενος   ὑπὲρ   ἀνθρώπων   καθίσταται
¹being taken   on behalf of   men   is appointed [in]

τὰ   πρὸς   τὸν   θεόν,   ἵνα   προσφέρῃ   δῶρά
the   in re-gard to   –   God,   in order that   he may offer   ²gifts

τε   καὶ   θυσίας   ὑπὲρ   ἁμαρτιῶν,   2 μετριο-
¹both and   sacrifices   on behalf of   sins,   ²to feel in

παθεῖν   δυνάμενος   τοῖς   ἀγνοοῦσιν   καὶ
due measure   ¹being able   for the [ones] not knowing   and

πλανωμένοις,   ἐπεὶ   καὶ   αὐτὸς   περίκειται
being led astray,   since   also   he   is set round [with]

self is beset with weakness. ³Because of this he is bound to offer sacrifice for his own sins as well as for those of the people. ⁴And one does not take the honor upon himself, but he is called by God, just as Aaron was.

5 So also Christ did not exalt himself to be made a high priest, but was appointed by him who said to him,
"Thou art my Son, today I have begotten thee";
⁶as he says also in another place,
"Thou art a priest for ever,
after the order of Melchiz'edek."

7 In the days of his flesh, Jesus offered up prayers and supplications, with loud cries and tears, to him who was able to save him from death, and he was heard for his godly fear. ⁸Although he was a Son, he learned obedience through what he suffered; ⁹and being made perfect he became the source of eternal salvation to all who obey him, ¹⁰being designated by God a high priest after the order of Melchiz'edek.

ἀσθένειαν, 3 καὶ δι᾽ αὐτὴν ὀφείλει, καθὼς
weakness, and because it he ought, as
of

περὶ τοῦ λαοῦ, οὕτως καὶ περὶ ἑαυτοῦ
concern- the people, so also concerning himself
ing

προσφέρειν περὶ ἁμαρτιῶν. 4 καὶ οὐχ
to offer concerning sins. And ²not

ἑαυτῷ τις λαμβάνει τὴν τιμήν, ἀλλὰ
⁴to him- ¹anyone ²takes the honour, but
self

καλούμενος ὑπὸ τοῦ θεοῦ, καθώσπερ καὶ
being called by God, even as indeed

Ἀαρών. 5 Οὕτως καὶ ὁ Χριστὸς οὐχ
Aaron. So also – Christ ²not

ἑαυτὸν ἐδόξασεν γενηθῆναι ἀρχιερέα, ἀλλ᾽
³himself ¹glorified to become a high priest, but

ὁ λαλήσας πρὸς αὐτόν· υἱός μου εἶ
the [one] speaking to him: Son of me art

σύ, ἐγὼ σήμερον γεγέννηκά σε· 6 καθὼς
thou, I to-day have begotten thee; as

καὶ ἐν ἑτέρῳ λέγει· σὺ ἱερεὺς εἰς τὸν
also in another he says: Thou a priest unto the
[psalm] [art]

αἰῶνα κατὰ τὴν τάξιν Μελχισέδεκ. 7 ὃς
age according the order of Melchisedec. Who
to

ἐν ταῖς ἡμέραις τῆς σαρκὸς αὐτοῦ δεήσεις
in the days of the flesh of him ⁸petitions

τε καὶ ἱκετηρίας πρὸς τὸν δυνάμενον
²both ⁴and ⁵entreaties ¹¹to ¹²the [one] ¹³being able

σῴζειν αὐτὸν ἐκ θανάτου μετὰ κραυγῆς
¹⁴to save ¹⁵him ¹⁶out of ¹⁷death ⁶with ⁸crying

ἰσχυρᾶς καὶ δακρύων προσενέγκας καὶ
⁷strong ⁹and ¹⁰tears ¹offering and

εἰσακουσθεὶς ἀπὸ τῆς εὐλαβείας, 8 καίπερ
being heard from(for) the(his) devoutness, though

ὢν υἱός, ἔμαθεν ἀφ᾽ ὧν ἔπαθεν τὴν
being a Son, he ²from ³[the] ⁴he suffered –
learned things which

ὑπακοήν, 9 καὶ τελειωθεὶς ἐγένετο πᾶσιν
¹obedience, and being perfected he became to all

τοῖς ὑπακούουσιν αὐτῷ αἴτιος σωτηρίας
the [ones] obeying him [the] cause ²salvation

αἰωνίου, 10 προσαγορευθεὶς ὑπὸ τοῦ θεοῦ
¹of eternal, being designated by – God

ἀρχιερεὺς κατὰ τὴν τάξιν Μελχισέδεκ.
a high priest accord- the order of Melchisedec.
ing to

11 About this we have much to say which is hard to explain, since you have become dull of hearing. ¹²For though by this time you ought to be teachers, you need some one to teach you again the first principles of God's word. You need milk, not solid food; ¹³for every one who lives on milk is unskilled in the word of righteousness, for he is a child. ¹⁴But solid food is for the mature, for those who have their faculties trained by practice to distinguish good from evil.

CHAPTER 6

THEREFORE let us leave the elementary doctrines of Christ and go on to maturity, not laying again a foundation of repentance from dead works and of faith toward God, ²with instruction[h] about ablutions, the laying on of hands, the resurrection of the dead, and eternal judgment. ³And this we will do if God permits.[i] ⁴For it is impossible to

[h] Other ancient manuscripts read *of instruction*
[i] Other ancient manuscripts read *let us do this if God permits*

11 Περὶ οὗ πολὺς ἡμῖν ὁ λόγος καὶ
Concern- whom much to us the ¹word° ²and
ing   =we have much to say and hard . . .

δυσερμήνευτος λέγειν, ἐπεὶ νωθροὶ γεγόνατε
⁴hard to interpret ²to say, since dull ye have become

ταῖς ἀκοαῖς. 12 καὶ γὰρ ὀφείλοντες
in the hearings. For indeed owing*

εἶναι διδάσκαλοι διὰ τὸν χρόνον, πάλιν
to be teachers because of the time, ²again

χρείαν ἔχετε τοῦ διδάσκειν ὑμᾶς τινα
²need ¹ye have - ⁵to teach[d] ⁶you ⁴someone

τὰ στοιχεῖα τῆς ἀρχῆς τῶν λογίων
the rudiments of the beginning of the oracles

τοῦ θεοῦ, καὶ γεγόνατε χρείαν ἔχοντες
- of God, and ye have become ²need ¹having

γάλακτος, οὐ στερεᾶς τροφῆς. 13 πᾶς
of milk, not of solid food. every

γὰρ ὁ μετέχων γάλακτος ἄπειρος λόγου
For one partaking of milk [is] without experience of [the] word

δικαιοσύνης, νήπιος γάρ ἐστιν· 14 τελείων δέ
of righteousness, for ²an infant ¹he is; but ⁴of mature men

ἐστιν ἡ στερεὰ τροφή, τῶν διὰ τὴν
³is the ¹solid ²food, of the [ones] because the(ir) of

ἕξιν τὰ αἰσθητήρια γεγυμνασμένα ἐχόντων
con- ²the(ir) ³faculties having been ⁴exercised ¹having
dition

πρὸς διάκρισιν καλοῦ τε καὶ κακοῦ.
for distinction ²of good ¹both and of bad.

6 Διὸ ἀφέντες τὸν τῆς ἀρχῆς τοῦ Χριστοῦ
Wherefore leaving ¹the ³of the ⁴beginning - ⁵of Christ

λόγον ἐπὶ τὴν τελειότητα φερώμεθα, μὴ
²word ⁷on to - ⁶maturity ⁶let us be borne, not

πάλιν θεμέλιον καταβαλλόμενοι μετανοίας
again ²a foundation ¹laying down of repentance

ἀπὸ νεκρῶν ἔργων, καὶ πίστεως ἐπὶ
from dead works, and of faith toward

θεόν, 2 βαπτισμῶν διδαχῆς, ἐπιθέσεώς τε
God, ²of baptisms ¹of teaching, and of laying on

χειρῶν, ἀναστάσεως νεκρῶν, καὶ κρίματος
of hands, of resurrection of dead persons, and ²judgment

αἰωνίου. 3 καὶ τοῦτο ποιήσομεν, ἐάνπερ
¹of eternal. And this will we do, if indeed

ἐπιτρέπῃ ὁ θεός. 4 Ἀδύνατον γὰρ τοὺς
²permits - ¹God. For [it is] impossible [for] the [ones]

* That is, " ye ought . . . "

restore again to repentance those who have once been enlightened, who have tasted the heavenly gift, and have become partakers of the Holy Spirit, ⁵and have tasted the goodness of the word of God and the powers of the age to come, ⁶if they then commit apostasy, since they crucify the Son of God on their own account and hold him up to contempt. ⁷For land which has drunk the rain that often falls upon it, and brings forth vegetation useful to those for whose sake it is cultivated, receives a blessing from God. ⁸But if it bears thorns and thistles, it is worthless and near to being cursed; its end is to be burned.

9 Though we speak thus, yet in your case, beloved, we feel sure of better things that belong to salvation. ¹⁰For God is not so unjust as to overlook your work and the love which you showed for his sake in serving the saints, as you still do. ¹¹And we desire each one of you to show the same earnestness in realizing the full assurance of hope until the

---

ἅπαξ   φωτισθέντας   γευσαμένους   τε   τῆς
once   being enlightened   and tasting   of the

δωρεᾶς   τῆς   ἐπουρανίου   καὶ   μετόχους
²gift   -   ¹heavenly   and   sharers

γενηθέντας   πνεύματος   ἁγίου   5 καὶ   καλὸν
becoming   Spirit   of [the] Holy   and ²[the] good

γευσαμένους   θεοῦ   ῥῆμα   δυνάμεις   τε
¹tasting   ⁴of God   ³word   and powerful deeds

μέλλοντος   αἰῶνος,   6 καὶ   παραπεσόντας,   πάλιν
of a coming   age,   and   falling away,   again

ἀνακαινίζειν   εἰς   μετάνοιαν,   ἀνασταυροῦντας
to renew   to   repentance,   crucifying again

ἑαυτοῖς   τὸν   υἱὸν   τοῦ   θεοῦ   καὶ   παρα-
for them-   the   Son   -   of God   and   putting
selves

δειγματίζοντας.   7 γῆ   γὰρ   ἡ   πιοῦσα
[him] to open shame.   For earth   -   drinking

τὸν   ἐπ᾽   αὐτῆς   ἐρχόμενον   πολλάκις   ὑετὸν
¹the   ⁵upon   ⁶it   ³coming   ⁴often   ²rain

καὶ   τίκτουσα   βοτάνην   εὔθετον   ἐκείνοις
and   bearing   fodder   suitable   for those

δι᾽   οὓς   καὶ   γεωργεῖται,   μεταλαμβάνει
on ac-   whom   indeed   it is farmed,   receives
count of

εὐλογίας   ἀπὸ   τοῦ   θεοῦ·   8 ἐκφέρουσα   δὲ
blessing   from   -   God;   but bringing forth

ἀκάνθας   καὶ   τριβόλους   ἀδόκιμος   καὶ
thorns   and   thistles [it is]   disapproved   and

κατάρας   ἐγγύς,   ἧς   τὸ   τέλος   εἰς   καῦσιν.
²a curse   ¹near,   of which the   end [is] for   burning.

9 Πεπείσμεθα   δὲ   περὶ   ὑμῶν,   ἀγαπητοί,
But we have been   concerning   you,   beloved,
persuaded

τὰ   κρείσσονα   καὶ   ἐχόμενα   σωτηρίας,   εἰ
the   better things   and   having   salvation,   if

καὶ   οὕτως   λαλοῦμεν.   10 οὐ   γὰρ   ἄδικος
indeed   ²so   ¹we speak.   For ²not   ³unjust

ὁ   θεὸς   ἐπιλαθέσθαι   τοῦ   ἔργου   ὑμῶν
-    ¹God [is]   to be forgetful   of the   work   of you

καὶ   τῆς   ἀγάπης   ἧς   ἐνεδείξασθε   εἰς   τὸ
and   of the   love   which   ye showed   to   the

ὄνομα   αὐτοῦ,   διακονήσαντες   τοῖς   ἁγίοις
name   of him,   having ministered   to the   saints

καὶ   διακονοῦντες.   11 ἐπιθυμοῦμεν   δὲ
and   ministering.   But we desire

ἕκαστον   ὑμῶν   τὴν   αὐτὴν   ἐνδείκνυσθαι
each one   of you   ²the   ³same   ¹to show

σπουδὴν   πρὸς   τὴν   πληροφορίαν   τῆς   ἐλπίδος
eagerness   to   the   full assurance   of the   hope

end, ¹²so that you may not be sluggish, but imitators of those who through faith and patience inherit the promises.

13 For when God made a promise to Abraham, since he had no one greater by whom to swear, he swore by himself, ¹⁴saying, "Surely I will bless you and multiply you." ¹⁵And thus Abraham, having patiently endured, obtained the promise. ¹⁶Men indeed swear by a greater than themselves, and in all their disputes an oath is final for confirmation. ¹⁷So when God desired to show more convincingly to the heirs of the promise the unchangeable character of his purpose, he interposed with an oath, ¹⁸so that through two unchangeable things, in which it is impossible that God should prove false, we who have fled for refuge might have strong encouragement to seize the hope set before us. ¹⁹We have this as a sure and steadfast anchor of the soul, a hope that enters into the inner shrine behind the curtain, ²⁰where Jesus has gone as a forerunner on our

ἄχρι τέλους, 12 ἵνα μὴ νωθροὶ γένησθε,
unto [the] end, lest dull ye become,

μιμηταὶ δὲ τῶν διὰ πίστεως καὶ μακρο-
but imitators of the through faith and long-
[ones]

θυμίας κληρονομούντων τὰς ἐπαγγελίας.
suffering inheriting the promises.

13 Τῷ γὰρ Ἀβραὰμ ἐπαγγειλάμενος ὁ
- For ³to Abraham ²making promise -

θεός, ἐπεὶ κατ᾽ οὐδενὸς εἶχεν μείζονος
¹God, since ²by ³no one ¹he had ⁴greater

ὀμόσαι, ὤμοσεν καθ᾽ ἑαυτοῦ, 14 λέγων·
to swear, swore by himself, saying:

εἰ μὴν εὐλογῶν εὐλογήσω σε καὶ πληθύνων
If surely blessing I will bless thee and multiplying

πληθυνῶ σε· 15 καὶ οὕτως μακροθυμήσας
I will multiply thee; and so being longsuffering

ἐπέτυχεν τῆς ἐπαγγελίας. 16 ἄνθρωποι γὰρ
he obtained the promise. For men

κατὰ τοῦ μείζονος ὀμνύουσιν, καὶ πάσης
by the greater swear, and ⁶of all

αὐτοῖς ἀντιλογίας πέρας εἰς βεβαίωσιν ὁ
²[is] ⁴to ⁷contradiction ⁵an end ⁸for ⁹confirmation ¹the
them

ὅρκος· 17 ἐν ᾧ περισσότερον βουλόμενος
²oath; wherein ³more abundantly ²resolving

ὁ θεὸς ἐπιδεῖξαι τοῖς κληρονόμοις τῆς
- ¹God to show to the heirs of the

ἐπαγγελίας τὸ ἀμετάθετον τῆς βουλῆς
promise the unchangeableness of the resolve

αὐτοῦ ἐμεσίτευσεν ὅρκῳ, 18 ἵνα διὰ
of him interposed by an in or- through
oath, der that

δύο πραγμάτων ἀμεταθέτων, ἐν οἷς ἀδύνατον
two ²things ¹unchangeable, in which impossible
[it was]

ψεύσασθαι θεόν, ἰσχυρὰν παράκλησιν ἔχωμεν
²to lie ¹God,ᵇ ²a strong ³consolation ¹we may
have[,]

οἱ καταφυγόντες κρατῆσαι τῆς προκειμένης
the [ones] having fled to lay hold of the ²set before [us]

ἐλπίδος· 19 ἣν ὡς ἄγκυραν ἔχομεν τῆς
¹hope; which as an anchor we have of the

ψυχῆς ἀσφαλῆ τε καὶ βεβαίαν καὶ
soul ²safe ¹both and firm and

εἰσερχομένην εἰς τὸ ἐσώτερον τοῦ κατα-
entering into the inner [side] of the veil,

πετάσματος, 20 ὅπου πρόδρομος ὑπὲρ ἡμῶν
where a forerunner on us
behalf of

behalf, having become a high priest for ever after the order of Melchiz'edek.

εἰσῆλθεν　'Ιησοῦς,　κατὰ　τὴν　τάξιν　Μελχισέ-
entered[,]　Jesus,　ᵉaccording ⁷the　ᵉorder　⁹of Melchise-
　　　　　　　　　to

δεκ　ἀρχιερεὺς　γενόμενος　εἰς　τὸν　αἰῶνα.
dec　ᵉa high priest　¹becoming　²unto　³the　⁴age.

CHAPTER 7

FOR this Melchiz'-edek, king of Salem, priest of the most high God, met Abraham returning from the slaughter of the kings and blessed him; ²and to him Abraham apportioned a tenth part of everything. He is first, by translation of his name, king of righteousness, and then he is also king of Salem, that is, king of peace. ³He is without father or mother or genealogy, and has neither beginning of days nor end of life, but resembling the Son of God he continues a priest for ever.

4 See how great he is! Abraham the patriarch gave him a tithe of the spoils. ⁵And those descendants of Levi who· receive the priestly office have a commandment in the law to take tithes from the people, that is, from their brethren, though these also are descended from Abraham.

7 Οὗτος　γὰρ　ὁ　Μελχισέδεκ,　βασιλεὺς
For this　-　　Melchisedec,　king

Σαλήμ,　ἱερεὺς　τοῦ　θεοῦ　τοῦ　ὑψίστου,
of Salem,　priest　-　³God　¹of the　²most high,

ὁ　συναντήσας　'Αβραὰμ　ὑποστρέφοντι　ἀπὸ
the [one] meeting　Abraham　returning　from

τῆς　κοπῆς　τῶν　βασιλέων　καὶ　εὐλογήσας
the　slaughter　of the　kings　and　blessing

αὐτόν,　2 ᾧ　καὶ　δεκάτην　ἀπὸ　πάντων
him,　to whom indeed　ᵃa tenth　⁴from　⁸all

ἐμέρισεν　'Αβραάμ,　πρῶτον　μὲν　ἑρμηνευ-
³divided　¹Abraham,　firstly　on one　being inter-
　　　　　　　　　hand

όμενος　βασιλεὺς　δικαιοσύνης,　ἔπειτα　δὲ　καὶ
preted　King　of righteousness,　then　on the also
　　　　　　　　　other

βασιλεὺς　Σαλήμ,　ὅ　ἐστιν　βασιλεὺς　εἰρήνης,
King　of Salem,　which　is　King　of peace,

3 ἀπάτωρ,　ἀμήτωρ,　ἀγενεαλόγητος,　μήτε
without father,　without mother,　without pedigree,　²neither

ἀρχὴν　ἡμερῶν　μήτε　ζωῆς　τέλος　ἔχων,
³beginning　⁴of days　⁵nor　⁷of life　ᵉend　¹having,

ἀφωμοιωμένος　δὲ　τῷ　υἱῷ　τοῦ　θεοῦ,　μένει
but having been made　to the　Son　-　of God,　remains
like

ἱερεὺς　εἰς　τὸ　διηνεκές.　4 Θεωρεῖτε　δὲ
a priest　in　the　perpetuity.　Now behold ye

πηλίκος　οὗτος,　ᾧ　δεκάτην　'Αβραὰμ
how great　this man　to　ᵃa tenth　ᵃAbraham
　　　　[was],　whom

ἔδωκεν　ἐκ　τῶν　ἀκροθινίων　ὁ　πατριάρχης.
⁴gave　ᵉof　⁷the　ᵉspoils　¹the　²patriarch.

5 καὶ　οἱ　μὲν　ἐκ　τῶν　υἱῶν　Λευὶ　τὴν
And　²the ¹on one　³of　⁴the　⁵sons　ᵉof Levi　⁸the
　　[ones] hand

ἱερατείαν　λαμβάνοντες　ἐντολὴν　ἔχουσιν
⁹priesthood　⁷receiving　¹¹a commandment　¹⁰have

ἀποδεκατοῦν　τὸν　λαὸν　κατὰ　τὸν　νόμον,
to take tithes　the　people　according to　the　law,
from

τοῦτ'　ἔστιν　τοὺς　ἀδελφοὺς　αὐτῶν,　καίπερ
this　is　the　brothers　of them,　though

ἐξεληλυθότας　ἐκ　τῆς　ὀσφύος　'Αβραάμ·
having come forth　out of　the　loin[s]　of Abraham;

⁶But this man who has not their genealogy received tithes from Abraham and blessed him who had the promises. ⁷It is beyond dispute that the inferior is blessed by the superior. ⁸Here tithes are received by mortal men; there, by one of whom it is testified that he lives. ⁹One might even say that Levi himself, who receives tithes, paid tithes through Abraham, ¹⁰for he was still in the loins of his ancestor when Melchiz′edek met him. 11 Now if perfection had been attainable through the Levit′ical priesthood (for under it the people received the law), what further need would there have been for another priest to arise after the order of Melchiz′edek, rather than one named after the order of Aaron? ¹²For when there is a change in the priesthood, there is necessarily a change in the law as well. ¹³For the one of whom these things are spoken belonged to another tribe, from which no one has ever served at the altar. ¹⁴For

6 ὁ   δὲ   μὴ   γενεαλογούμενος   ἐξ   αὐτῶν
²the   ¹on the not   counting [his] pedigree from   them
[one]   other

δεδεκάτωκεν   ᾿Αβραάμ,   καὶ   τὸν   ἔχοντα
has tithed   Abraham,   and   ²the [one] ³having

τὰς   ἐπαγγελίας   εὐλόγηκεν.   7 χωρὶς   δὲ
⁴the   ⁵promises   ¹has blessed.   And without

πάσης   ἀντιλογίας   τὸ   ἔλαττον   ὑπὸ   τοῦ
all(any) contradiction the   less   ²by   ³the

κρείττονος   εὐλογεῖται.   8 καὶ   ὧδε   μὲν
⁴better   ¹is blessed.   And   here   on one
                                              hand

δεκάτας   ἀποθνήσκοντες   ἄνθρωποι   λαμβά-
⁴tithes   ¹dying   ²men   ³re-

νουσιν,   ἐκεῖ   δὲ   μαρτυρούμενος   ὅτι   ζῇ.
ceive,   there   on the being witnessed   that   he
                    other   lives.

9 καὶ   ὡς   ἔπος   εἰπεῖν,   δι᾽   ᾿Αβραὰμ
And   as   a word   to say,   through Abraham
              =so to speak,

καὶ   Λευὶς   ὁ   δεκάτας   λαμβάνων   δεδε-
indeed Levi   ¹the [one] ³tithes ²receiving   has

κάτωται·   10 ἔτι   γὰρ   ἐν   τῇ   ὀσφύϊ   τοῦ
been tithed;   for ²yet ³in   ⁴the ⁵loin[s]   ⁶of
                                                  the(his)

πατρὸς   ἦν   ὅτε   συνήντησεν   αὐτῷ   Μελχισέ-
⁷father   ¹he was ⁸when   ¹⁰met   ¹¹him   ⁹Melchise-

δεκ.   11 Εἰ   μὲν   οὖν   τελείωσις   διὰ   τῆς
dec.   If   - therefore perfection   ²through ³the

Λευιτικῆς   ἱερωσύνης   ἦν,   ὁ   λαὸς   γὰρ
⁴Levitical   ⁵priestly office ¹was, ⁴the ⁵people ¹for

ἐπ᾽   αὐτῆς   νενομοθέτηται,   τίς   ἔτι   χρεία
²under* ³it   has been furnished   why   yet   need
              with law,

κατὰ   τὴν   τάξιν   Μελχισέδεκ   ἔτερον
[was there ⁵the ⁶order   ⁷of Melchisedec ¹another
for] ⁴accord-
ing to

ἀνίστασθαι   ἱερέα   καὶ   οὐ   κατὰ   τὴν   τάξιν
³to arise   ²priest   and   not   ²accord- ³the   ⁴order
                                      ing to

᾿Ααρὼν   λέγεσθαι;   12 μετατιθεμένης   γὰρ
⁵of Aaron ¹to be said(named)?   for ³being changed

τῆς   ἱερωσύνης   ἐξ   ἀνάγκης   καὶ   νόμου
¹the   ²priestly office³ ⁴of ⁷necessity ⁵also   ⁹of law

μετάθεσις   γίνεται.   13 ἐφ᾽   ὃν   γὰρ   λέγεται
⁸a change   ⁴there   ²[he] ³with ⁴whom ¹For ⁵is(are) said
             occurs.   respect to

ταῦτα,   φυλῆς   ἐτέρας   μετέσχηκεν,   ἀφ᾽
⁴these things, ²tribe ³of another ¹has partaken,   from

ἧς   οὐδεὶς   προσέσχηκεν   τῷ   θυσιαστηρίῳ·
which no one   has devoted himself to the   altar;

* See note on ch. 9. 15.

it is evident that our Lord was descended from Judah, and in connection with that tribe Moses said nothing about priests.

15 This becomes even more evident when another priest arises in the likeness of Melchiz'-edek, ¹⁶who has become a priest, not according to a legal requirement concerning bodily descent but by the power of an indestructible life. ¹⁷For it is witnessed of him, "Thou art a priest for ever,
after the order of Melchiz'edek."

¹⁸On the one hand, a former commandment is set aside because of its weakness and uselessness ¹⁹(for the law made nothing perfect); on the other hand, a better hope is introduced through which we draw near to God.
20 And it was not without an oath. ²¹Those who formerly became priests took their office without an oath, but this one was addressed with an oath.
"The Lord has sworn and will not change his mind,
'Thou art a priest for ever.' "
²²This makes Jesus the

14 πρόδηλον γὰρ ὅτι ἐξ Ἰούδα ἀνατέταλκεν
for it is perfectly clear that out of Juda has risen

ὁ κύριος ἡμῶν, εἰς ἣν φυλὴν περὶ ἱερέων
the Lord of us, as to which tribe concerning priests

οὐδὲν Μωϋσῆς ἐλάλησεν. 15 καὶ περισ-
²nothing ¹Moses ²spoke. And more

σότερον ἔτι κατάδηλόν ἐστιν, εἰ κατὰ
abundantly still quite clear is it, if according to

τὴν ὁμοιότητα Μελχισέδεκ ἀνίσταται ἱερεὺς
the likeness of Melchisedec arises priest

ἕτερος, 16 ὃς οὐ κατὰ νόμον ἐντολῆς
another, who not accord-ing to [the] law ²command-ment

σαρκίνης γέγονεν ἀλλὰ κατὰ δύναμιν ζωῆς
¹of a fleshy has become but accord-ing to [the] power life

ἀκαταλύτου. 17 μαρτυρεῖται γὰρ ὅτι σὺ
of an indissoluble. For it is witnessed that Thou

ἱερεὺς εἰς τὸν αἰῶνα κατὰ τὴν τάξιν
a priest unto the age according to the order

Μελχισέδεκ. 18 ἀθέτησις μὲν γὰρ γίνεται
of Melchisedec. ⁴an annul-ment ²on one ¹For ³there comes about

προαγούσης ἐντολῆς διὰ τὸ αὐτῆς ἀσθενὲς
of [the] preceding command-ment because ¹the ⁵of it ²weak[ness] of

καὶ ἀνωφελές, 19 οὐδὲν γὰρ ἐτελείωσεν
³and ⁴unprofitable[ness], for ⁴nothing ³perfected

ὁ νόμος, ἐπεισαγωγὴ δὲ κρείττονος ἐλπίδος,
¹the ²law, ²a bringing in ¹on the of a better other hope,

δι᾽ ἧς ἐγγίζομεν τῷ θεῷ. 20 καὶ καθ᾽
through which we draw near – to God. And in pro-

ὅσον οὐ χωρὶς ὀρκωμοσίας, — οἱ μὲν
portion not without oath-taking, ²the ²on one as (they) hand

γὰρ χωρὶς ὀρκωμοσίας εἰσὶν ἱερεῖς
¹for ⁷without ⁶oath-taking ⁴are ⁵priests

γεγονότες, 21 ὁ δὲ μετὰ ὀρκωμοσίας διὰ
⁵having become, the on the with (he) other oath-taking through

τοῦ λέγοντος πρὸς αὐτόν· ὤμοσεν κύριος,
the [one] saying to him: swore [The] Lord,

καὶ οὐ μεταμεληθήσεται· σὺ ἱερεὺς εἰς
and will not change [his] mind: Thou [art] a priest unto

τὸν αἰῶνα· — 22 κατὰ τοσοῦτο καὶ
the age;) by so much indeed

I.G.E.—29

surety of a better covenant.

23 The former priests were many in number, because they were prevented by death from continuing in office; [24] but he holds his priesthood permanently, because he continues for ever. [25] Consequently he is able for all time to save those who draw near to God through him, since he always lives to make intercession for them.

26 For it was fitting that we should have such a high priest, holy, blameless, unstained, separated from sinners, exalted above the heavens. [27] He has no need, like those high priests, to offer sacrifices daily, first for his own sins and then for those of the people; he did this once for all when he offered up himself. [28] Indeed, the law appoints men in their weakness as high priests, but the word of the oath, which came later than the law, appoints a Son who has been made perfect for ever.

κρείττονος διαθήκης γέγονεν ἔγγυος Ἰησοῦς.
[4]of a better [5]covenant [2]has become [3]surety [1]Jesus.

23 καὶ οἱ μὲν πλείονές εἰσιν γεγονότες
And the on one [3]many [1]are [2]having become
(they) hand

ἱερεῖς διὰ τὸ θανάτῳ κωλύεσθαι παραμέ-
[4]priests because the [2]by death [1]to be prevented [3]to con-
of =being prevented by death from continuing;

νειν· 24 ὁ δὲ διὰ τὸ μένειν αὐτὸν εἰς
tinue; the on the because the to remain him[b] unto
(he) other of
=because he remains

τὸν αἰῶνα ἀπαράβατον ἔχει τὴν ἱερωσύνην·
the age [3]intransmissible [1]has [2]the [3]priestly office;

25 ὅθεν καὶ σῴζειν εἰς τὸ παντελὲς
whence indeed [2]to save [3]to [4]the [5]entire
= entirely

δύναται τοὺς προσερχομένους δι' αὐτοῦ
[1]he is able the [ones] [1]approaching [2]through [4]him

τῷ θεῷ, πάντοτε ζῶν εἰς τὸ ἐντυγχάνειν
- [2]to God, always living for the to intercede

ὑπὲρ αὐτῶν. 26 τοιοῦτος γὰρ ἡμῖν καὶ
on be- them. For [1]such [2]to us [3]indeed
half of

ἔπρεπεν ἀρχιερεύς, ὅσιος, ἄκακος, ἀμίαντος,
[4]was [3]a high priest. holy, harmless, undefiled,
suitable

κεχωρισμένος ἀπὸ τῶν ἁμαρτωλῶν, καὶ
having been from - sinners, and
separated

ὑψηλότερος τῶν οὐρανῶν γενόμενος· 27 ὃς
higher [than] the heavens becoming; who

οὐκ ἔχει καθ' ἡμέραν ἀνάγκην, ὥσπερ
has not [2]daily [1]necessity, as

οἱ ἀρχιερεῖς, πρότερον ὑπὲρ τῶν ἰδίων
the high priests, firstly on behalf of the(his) own

ἁμαρτιῶν θυσίας ἀναφέρειν, ἔπειτα τῶν
sins sacrifices to offer up, then the [sins]

τοῦ λαοῦ· τοῦτο γὰρ ἐποίησεν ἐφάπαξ
of the people; for this he did once for all

ἑαυτὸν ἀνενέγκας. 28 ὁ νόμος γὰρ
himself offering up. For the law

ἀνθρώπους καθίστησιν ἀρχιερεῖς ἔχοντας
[2]men [1]appoints [5]high priests [3]having

ἀσθένειαν, ὁ λόγος δὲ τῆς ὁρκωμοσίας
[4]weakness, but the word of the oath-taking

τῆς μετὰ τὸν νόμον υἱὸν εἰς τὸν αἰῶνα
- after the law a Son [2]unto [3]the [4]age
[appoints]

τετελειωμένον.
[1]having been perfected.

CHAPTER 8

NOW the point in what we are saying is this: we have such a high priest, one who is seated at the right hand of the throne of the Majesty in heaven, ²a minister in the sanctuary and the true tentʲ which is set up not by man but by the Lord. ³For every high priest is appointed to offer gifts and sacrifices; hence it is necessary for this priest also to have something to offer. ⁴Now if he were on earth, he would not be a priest at all, since there are priests who offer gifts according to the law. ⁵They serve a copy and shadow of the heavenly sanctuary; for when Moses was about to erect the tent,ʲ he was instructed by God, saying, "See that you make everything according to the pattern which was shown you on the mountain." ⁶But as it is, Christ has obtained a ministry which is as much more excellent than the old as the covenant he mediates is better, since it is enacted on better promises. ⁷For if that first covenant had been faultless, there would

ʲ Or tabernacle

8 Κεφάλαιον δὲ ἐπὶ τοῖς λεγομένοις,
Now a summary   over(of) the things   being said,

τοιοῦτον ἔχομεν ἀρχιερέα, ὃς ἐκάθισεν
²such   ¹we have   a high priest,   who   sat

ἐν δεξιᾷ τοῦ θρόνου τῆς μεγαλωσύνης
at [the] right of the   throne   of the   greatness

ἐν τοῖς οὐρανοῖς, 2 τῶν ἁγίων λειτουργὸς
in   the   heavens,   ²of the ³holy things ¹a minister

καὶ ͺῆς σκηνῆς τῆς ἀληθινῆς, ἣν ἔπηξεν
and   of the ²tabernacle   –   ¹true,   which ³erected

ὁ κύριος, οὐκ ἄνθρωπος. 3 Πᾶς γὰρ
¹the ¹Lord,   not   man.   For every

ἀρχιερεὺς εἰς τὸ προσφέρειν δῶρά τε
high priest   for   the   ²to offer   ⁴gifts ³both

καὶ θυσίας καθίσταται· ὅθεν ἀναγκαῖον
⁵and   ⁶sacrifices   ¹is appointed;   whence   [it is] necessary

ἔχειν τι καὶ τοῦτον ὃ προσενέγκῃ. 4 εἰ
³to have ⁴some- ²also   ¹this   which   he may offer.   If
thing   [priest]

μὲν οὖν ἦν ἐπὶ γῆς, οὐδ' ἂν ἦν ἱερεύς,
–   there-   he   on   earth,   he would not be   a priest,
fore   were

ὄντων τῶν προσφερόντων κατὰ νόμον
[there]   the [ones]   offering ͣ   ²according to   ⁴law
being

τὰ δῶρα· 5 οἵτινες ὑποδείγματι καὶ σκιᾷ
¹the ²gifts;   who   ²an example   ³and   ⁴a
shadow

λατρεύουσιν τῶν ἐπουρανίων, καθὼς
¹serve   of the   heavenly things,   as

κεχρημάτισται Μωϋσῆς μέλλων ἐπιτελεῖν
²has been warned   ¹Moses   being about   to complete

τὴν σκηνήν· ὅρα γάρ φησιν, ποιήσεις
the   tabernacle;   for See[,]   he says,   thou shalt
make

πάντα κατὰ τὸν τύπον τὸν δειχθέντα
all   according to   the   pattern   –   shown
things

σοι ἐν τῷ ὄρει· 6 νῦν δὲ διαφορωτέρας
to thee in   the   mount;   but now   ²a more excellent

τέτυχεν λειτουργίας, ὅσῳ καὶ κρείττονός
¹he has   ministry,   by so   indeed   ⁴of a better
obtained   much

ἐστιν διαθήκης μεσίτης, ἥτις ἐπὶ κρείττοσιν
¹[as]   ⁵covenant ²mediator,   which   ³on   ³better
²he is

ἐπαγγελίαις νενομοθέτηται. 7 εἰ γὰρ ἡ
⁴promises   ¹has been enacted.   For if   –

πρώτη ἐκείνη ἦν ἄμεμπτος, οὐκ ἂν
²first [covenant] ¹that   was   faultless,   ²would not

have been no occasion for a second.
8 For he finds fault with them when he says: "The days will come, says the Lord, when I will establish a new covenant with the house of Israel and with the house of Judah; 9 not like the covenant that I made with their fathers on the day when I took them by the hand to lead them out of the land of Egypt; for they did not continue in my covenant, and so I paid no heed to them, says the Lord. 10 This is the covenant that I will make with the house of Israel after those days, says the Lord: I will put my laws into their minds, and write them on their hearts, and I will be their God, and they shall be my people. 11 And they shall not teach every one his fellow or every one his brother, saying, 'Know the Lord,' for all shall know me, from the least of them to the greatest. 12 For I will be merciful toward their iniquities,

δευτέρας ἐζητεῖτο τόπος. 8 μεμφόμενος
⁴of(for) a ³have been ¹place.   finding fault [with]
 second   sought

γὰρ αὐτοὺς λέγει· ἰδοὺ ἡμέραι ἔρχονται,
For them he says: Behold[,] days are coming,

λέγει κύριος, καὶ συντελέσω ἐπὶ τὸν
says [the] Lord, and I will effect over the

οἶκον Ἰσραὴλ καὶ ἐπὶ τὸν οἶκον Ἰούδα
household of Israel and over the household of Juda

διαθήκην καινήν, 9 οὐ κατὰ τὴν διαθήκην
covenant a new, not accord- the covenant
                      ing to

ἦν ἐποίησα τοῖς πατράσιν αὐτῶν ἐν
which I made with the fathers of them in

ἡμέρᾳ ἐπιλαβομένου μου τῆς χειρὸς αὐτῶν
[the] day taking me* the hand of them
       =when I took

ἐξαγαγεῖν αὐτοὺς ἐκ γῆς Αἰγύπτου, ὅτι
to lead forth them out [the] of Egypt, because
                  of land

αὐτοὶ οὐκ ἐνέμειναν ἐν τῇ διαθήκῃ μου,
they continued not in in the covenant of me,

κἀγὼ ἠμέλησα αὐτῶν, λέγει κύριος. 10 ὅτι
and I disregarded them, says [the] Lord. Because

αὕτη ἡ διαθήκη ἣν διαθήσομαι τῷ οἴκῳ
this [is] the covenant which I will with house-
              covenant the hold

Ἰσραὴλ μετὰ τὰς ἡμέρας ἐκείνας, λέγει
of Israel after those days, says

κύριος, διδοὺς νόμους μου εἰς τὴν διάνοιαν
[the] Lord, giving laws of me into the mind

αὐτῶν, καὶ ἐπὶ καρδίας αὐτῶν ἐπιγράψω
of them, and on hearts of them I will inscribe

αὐτούς, καὶ ἔσομαι αὐτοῖς εἰς θεὸν
them, and I will be to them for God

καὶ αὐτοὶ ἔσονταί μοι εἰς λαόν. 11 καὶ
and they shall be to me for a people. And

οὐ μὴ διδάξωσιν ἕκαστος τὸν πολίτην
by no means may they teach each man the citizen

αὐτοῦ καὶ ἕκαστος τὸν ἀδελφὸν αὐτοῦ,
of him and each man the brother of him,

λέγων· γνῶθι τὸν κύριον, ὅτι πάντες
saying: Know thou the Lord, because all

εἰδήσουσίν με ἀπὸ μικροῦ ἕως μεγάλου
will know me from little to great

αὐτῶν. 12 ὅτι ἵλεως ἔσομαι ταῖς ἀδικίαις
of them. Because merciful I will be to the unrighteous-
                                        nesses

αὐτῶν, καὶ τῶν ἁμαρτιῶν αὐτῶν οὐ μὴ
of them, and the sins of them by no means

and I will remember their sins no more." [13] In speaking of a new covenant he treats the first as obsolete. And what is becoming obsolete and growing old is ready to vanish away.

μνησθῶ ἔτι.
I may remember more.

13 ἐν τῷ λέγειν καινὴν
In the to say[e] 'new'
=When he says

πεπαλαίωκεν τὴν πρώτην· τὸ δὲ παλαι-
he has made old the first; and the thing being

ούμενον καὶ γηράσκον ἐγγὺς ἀφανισμοῦ.
made old and growing aged [is] near vanishing.

CHAPTER 9

NOW even the first covenant had regulations for worship and an earthly sanctuary. [2] For a tent[k] was prepared, the outer one, in which were the lampstand and the table and the bread of the Presence;[l] it is called the Holy Place. [3] Behind the second curtain stood a tent[k] called the Holy of Holies, [4] having the golden altar of incense and the ark of the covenant covered on all sides with gold, which contained a golden urn holding the manna, and Aaron's rod that budded, and the tables of the covenant; [5] above it were the cherubim of glory overshadowing the mercy seat. Of these things we cannot now speak in detail.

6 These preparations having thus been made, the priests go continually into the outer tent,[k]

9 Εἶχε μὲν οὖν καὶ ἡ πρώτη δικαι-
[5]had [1]So then [6]both [3]the [2]first ordin-
[4][covenant]

ώματα λατρείας τό τε ἅγιον κοσμικόν.
ances of service [3]the [1]and [4]holy place [2]worldly.

2 σκηνὴ γὰρ κατεσκευάσθη ἡ πρώτη,
For a tabernacle was prepared[,] the first,

ἐν ᾗ ἥ τε λυχνία καὶ ἡ τράπεζα καὶ
in which [3]the [1]both lampstand and the table and
[were]

ἡ πρόθεσις τῶν ἄρτων, ἥτις λέγεται
the setting forth of the loaves, which is called

"Αγια· **3** μετὰ δὲ τὸ δεύτερον καταπέτασμα
Holy; and after the second veil

σκηνὴ ἡ λεγομένη "Αγια 'Αγίων, **4** χρυσοῦν
a taber- the being called Holy of Holies, [2]a golden
nacle [one]

ἔχουσα θυμιατήριον καὶ τὴν κιβωτὸν τῆς
[1]having altar and the ark of the

διαθήκης περικεκαλυμμένην πάντοθεν χρυσίῳ,
covenant having been covered round on all sides with gold,

ἐν ᾗ στάμνος χρυσῆ ἔχουσα τὸ μάννα
in which pot a golden having the manna
[were]

καὶ ἡ ῥάβδος 'Ααρὼν ἡ βλαστήσασα
and the rod of Aaron – budded

καὶ αἱ πλάκες τῆς διαθήκης, **5** ὑπεράνω
and the tablets of the covenant, [2]above

δὲ αὐτῆς Χερουβὶν δόξης κατασκιάζοντα
[1]and it cherubim of glory overshadowing

τὸ ἱλαστήριον· περὶ ὧν οὐκ ἔστιν νῦν
the mercy-seat; concern- which there is not now
ing things [?time]

λέγειν κατὰ μέρος. **6** τούτων δὲ οὕτως
to speak in detail. These things now thus
=Now when these things had

κατεσκευασμένων εἰς μὲν τὴν πρώτην
having been prepared[a] [6]into [1]on one [7]the [2]first
been thus prepared hand

σκηνὴν διὰ παντὸς εἰσίασιν οἱ ἱερεῖς
[3]tabernacle [4]at all times [5]go in [8]the [9]priests

[k] Or tabernacle
[l] Greek the presentation of the loaves

performing their ritual duties; [7] but into the second only the high priest goes, and he but once a year, and not without taking blood which he offers for himself and for the errors of the people. [8] By this the Holy Spirit indicates that the way into the sanctuary is not yet opened as long as the outer tent[k] is still standing [9] (which is symbolic for the present age). According to this arrangement, gifts and sacrifices are offered which cannot perfect the conscience of the worshiper, [10] but deal only with food and drink and various ablutions, regulations for the body imposed until the time of reformation.

[11] But when Christ appeared as a high priest of the good things that have come,[m] then through the greater and more perfect tent[k] (not made with hands, that is, not of this creation) [12] he entered once for all into the Holy Place, taking not the blood of goats and calves but his own blood, thus securing an eternal redemption.

[k] Or tabernacle
[m] Other manuscripts read good things to come

τὰς λατρείας ἐπιτελοῦντες, 7 εἰς δὲ τὴν
[11] the [12] services [10] accomplishing, [2] into [1] on the [8] the
                                                        other

δευτέραν ἅπαξ τοῦ ἐνιαυτοῦ μόνος ὁ
[4] second [8] once [9] of(in) the [10] year [goes] [5] the
                                                    [7] alone

ἀρχιερεύς, οὐ χωρὶς αἵματος ὃ προσφέρει
[6] high priest, not without blood which he offers

ὑπὲρ ἑαυτοῦ καὶ τῶν τοῦ λαοῦ ἀγνοημά-
on be- himself and [1] the [3] of the [4] people [2] ignor-
half of

των, 8 τοῦτο δηλοῦντος τοῦ πνεύματος
ances, [5] this [4] showing [1] the [3] Spirit

τοῦ ἁγίου, μήπω πεφανερῶσθαι τὴν τῶν
-   [2] Holy,[a] [5] not yet [6] to have been [1] the [3] of the
                              manifested

ἁγίων ὁδὸν ἔτι τῆς πρώτης σκηνῆς
[4] holies [3] way [10] still [7] the [8] first [9] tabernacle

ἐχούσης στάσιν, 9 ἥτις παραβολὴ εἰς τὸν
[11] having[a] [12] standing, which [was] a parable for the

καιρὸν τὸν ἐνεστηκότα, καθ' ἣν δῶρά
time - present, accord- which [2] gifts
                              ing to

τε καὶ θυσίαι προσφέρονται μὴ δυνάμεναι
[1] both and sacrifices are being offered not being able

κατὰ συνείδησιν τελειῶσαι τὸν λατρεύοντα,
in respect conscience to perfect the [one] serving,
of

10 μόνον ἐπὶ βρώμασιν καὶ πόμασιν καὶ
only on foods and drinks and

διαφόροις βαπτισμοῖς, δικαιώματα σαρκὸς
various washings, ordinances of flesh

μέχρι καιροῦ διορθώσεως ἐπικείμενα.
[2] until [3] a time [4] of amendment [1] being imposed.

11 Χριστὸς δὲ παραγενόμενος ἀρχιερεὺς
But Christ having appeared a high priest

τῶν γενομένων ἀγαθῶν, διὰ τῆς μείζονος
[1] of the [3] having come [2] good things, through the greater
about

καὶ τελειοτέρας σκηνῆς οὐ χειροποιήτου,
and more perfect tabernacle not made by hand,

τοῦτ' ἔστιν οὐ ταύτης τῆς κτίσεως,
this is not of this - creation,

12 οὐδὲ δι' αἵματος τράγων καὶ μόσχων,
nor through blood of goats and of calves,

διὰ δὲ τοῦ ἰδίου αἵματος εἰσῆλθεν ἐφάπαξ
but the own blood entered once for
through (his)   all

εἰς τὰ ἅγια, αἰωνίαν λύτρωσιν εὑράμενος.
into the holies, eternal redemption having found.

[13] For if the sprinkling of defiled persons with the blood of goats and bulls and with the ashes of a heifer sanctifies for the purification of the flesh, [14] how much more shall the blood of Christ, who through the eternal Spirit offered himself without blemish to God, purify your[n] conscience from dead works to serve the living God.

[15] Therefore he is the mediator of a new covenant, so that those who are called may receive the promised eternal inheritance, since a death has occurred which redeems them from the transgressions under the first covenant.[o] [16] For where a will[o] is involved, the death of the one who made it must be established. [17] For a will[o] takes effect only at death, since it is not in force as long as the one who made it is alive. [18] Hence even the first covenant was not ratified without blood. [19] For when every commandment of the law had been declared by Moses to all the people, he took the blood of calves and

13 εἰ γὰρ τὸ αἷμα τράγων καὶ ταύρων
For if the blood of goats and of bulls

καὶ σποδὸς δαμάλεως ῥαντίζουσα τοὺς
and ashes of a heifer sprinkling the [ones]

κεκοινωμένους ἁγιάζει πρὸς τὴν τῆς
having been polluted sanctifies to ¹the ²of the

σαρκὸς καθαρότητα, 14 πόσῳ μᾶλλον τὸ
⁴flesh ²cleanness, by how much more the

αἷμα τοῦ Χριστοῦ, ὃς διὰ πνεύματος
blood - of Christ, who through ²Spirit

αἰωνίου ἑαυτὸν προσήνεγκεν ἄμωμον τῷ
¹[the] eternal himself ²offered unblemished -

θεῷ, καθαριεῖ τὴν συνείδησιν ἡμῶν ἀπὸ
to God, will cleanse the conscience of us from

νεκρῶν ἔργων εἰς τὸ λατρεύειν θεῷ
dead works for the to serve ²God

ζῶντι. 15 καὶ διὰ τοῦτο διαθήκης καινῆς
¹[the] living. And therefore ⁴covenant ⁵of a new

μεσίτης ἐστίν, ὅπως θανάτου γενομένου
¹mediator ¹he is, so as death having occurred²

εἰς ἀπολύτρωσιν τῶν ἐπὶ τῇ πρώτῃ
for redemption ¹of the ²under * ⁴the ⁵first

διαθήκῃ παραβάσεων τὴν ἐπαγγελίαν
⁶covenant ⁷transgressions ¹⁰the ¹¹promise

λάβωσιν οἱ κεκλημένοι τῆς αἰωνίου
⁹may receive ⁷the ⁸having been ¹²of the ¹³eternal
[ones] called

κληρονομίας. 16 Ὅπου γὰρ διαθήκη,
¹⁴inheritance. For where [there is] a
covenant,

θάνατον ἀνάγκη φέρεσθαι τοῦ διαθεμένου·
³[the] death ¹[there is] ²to be offered ⁴of the ⁵making
necessity [one] covenant;

17 διαθήκη γὰρ ἐπὶ νεκροῖς βεβαία, ἐπεὶ
for a covenant over dead [? bodies] [is] firm, since

μήποτε ἰσχύει ὅτε ζῇ ὁ διαθέμενος.
never has it when ³lives ¹the ²making
strength [one] covenant.

18 ὅθεν οὐδὲ ἡ πρώτη χωρὶς αἵματος
Whence neither the first [covenant] ²without ³blood

ἐγκεκαίνισται. 19 λαληθείσης γὰρ πάσης
¹has been dedicated. For ³having been spoken ¹every

ἐντολῆς κατὰ τὸν νόμον ὑπὸ Μωϋσέως
²command- ⁹accord- ¹⁰the ¹¹law ⁴by ⁵Moses
ment⁸ ing to

παντὶ τῷ λαῷ, λαβὼν τὸ αἷμα τῶν
⁶to all ⁷the ⁸people, taking the blood of the

---

[n] Other manuscripts read *our*
[o] The Greek word here used means *covenant* and *will*

* It may seem strange to translate a preposition which means "on" or "over" by "under"; but *ἐπί* has the meaning of "during the time of" (see Mark 2. 26; I. Tim. 6. 13).

goats, with water and scarlet wool and hyssop, and sprinkled both the book itself and all the people, ²⁰saying, "This is the blood of the covenant which God commanded you." ²¹And in the same way he sprinkled with the blood both the tent^k and all the vessels used in worship. ²²Indeed, under the law almost everything is purified with blood, and without the shedding of blood there is no forgiveness of sins.

23 Thus it was necessary for the copies of the heavenly things to be purified with these rites, but the heavenly things themselves with better sacrifices than these. ²⁴For Christ has entered, not into a sanctuary made with hands, a copy of the true one, but into heaven itself, now to appear in the presence of God on our behalf. ²⁵Nor was it to offer himself repeatedly, as the high priest enters the Holy Place yearly with blood not his own; ²⁶for then he would have had to suffer repeatedly since the foundation of the

---

μόσχων   καὶ   τῶν   τράγων   μετὰ   ὕδατος
calves   and   of the goats   with   water

καὶ   ἐρίου   κοκκίνου   καὶ   ὑσσώπου,   αὐτό
and   ²wool   ¹scarlet   and   hyssop,   ³it[self]

τε   τὸ   βιβλίον   καὶ   πάντα   τὸν   λαὸν
²both ³the ⁴scroll   ⁵and   ⁷all   ⁸the ⁹people

ἐρράντισεν,   20 λέγων·   τοῦτο   τὸ   αἷμα   τῆς
¹he sprinkled,   saying: This [is] the   blood of the

διαθήκης   ἧς   ἐνετείλατο   πρὸς   ὑμᾶς   ὁ
covenant   which ²enjoined   ³to   ⁴you   –

θεός.   21 καὶ   τὴν   σκηνὴν   δὲ   καὶ   πάντα
¹God.   ²both   ³the   ⁴tabernacle ¹And and   all

τὰ   σκεύη   τῆς   λειτουργίας   τῷ   αἵματι
the   vessels of the service   with the blood

ὁμοίως   ἐρράντισεν.   22 καὶ   σχεδὸν   ἐν
likewise he sprinkled.   And ⁴almost ⁷by

αἵματι   πάντα   καθαρίζεται   κατὰ   τὸν   νόμον,
³blood   ⁵all things ⁶is(are) cleansed ¹accord- ²the ³law,
                                      ing to

καὶ   χωρὶς   αἱματεκχυσίας   οὐ   γίνεται
and   without bloodshedding   there becomes no

ἄφεσις.   23 ἀνάγκη   οὖν   τὰ   μὲν   ὑπο-
remission.   [There was] therefore ²[for] ¹on one ⁴ex-
             necessity   ³the   hand

δείγματα   τῶν   ἐν   τοῖς   οὐρανοῖς   τούτοις
amples   of the   in   the   heavens   ²by these
things

καθαρίζεσθαι,   αὐτὰ   δὲ   τὰ   ἐπουράνια
¹to be cleansed, ⁵[them]-   ¹on the ²[for] ⁴heavenly
                 selves   other ³the   things

κρείττοσιν   θυσίαις   παρὰ   ταύτας.   24 οὐ
by better   sacrifices than   these.   not

γὰρ   εἰς   χειροποίητα   εἰσῆλθεν   ἅγια   Χριστός,
For   into ²made by hand ⁴entered   ¹holies ³Christ,

ἀντίτυπα   τῶν   ἀληθινῶν,   ἀλλ'   εἰς   αὐτὸν
figures   of the true things, but   into ³[it]self

τὸν   οὐρανόν,   νῦν   ἐμφανισθῆναι   τῷ   προσώπῳ
¹the ²heaven,   now   to appear in   the   presence

τοῦ   θεοῦ   ὑπὲρ   ἡμῶν·   25 οὐδ'   ἵνα   πολ-
–   of God on behalf of us;   nor in order that often

λάκις   προσφέρῃ   ἑαυτόν,   ὥσπερ   ὁ   ἀρχιερεὺς
        he should offer himself, even as the   high priest

εἰσέρχεται   εἰς   τὰ   ἅγια   κατ'   ἐνιαυτὸν
enters   into   the   holies year by year†

ἐν   αἵματι   ἀλλοτρίῳ,   26 ἐπεὶ   ἔδει   αὐτὸν
with   blood   belonging to others,   since it behoved him

πολλάκις   παθεῖν   ἀπὸ   καταβολῆς   κόσμου·
often   to suffer from [the] foundation of [the]
                                          world;

---

^k Or *tabernacle*

world. But as it is, he has appeared once for all at the end of the age to put away sin by the sacrifice of himself. ²⁷And just as it is appointed for men to die once, and after that comes judgment, ²⁸so Christ, having been offered once to bear the sins of many, will appear a second time, not to deal with sin but to save those who are eagerly waiting for him.

νυνὶ δὲ ἅπαξ ἐπὶ συντελείᾳ τῶν αἰώνων
but now once at [the] completion of the ages
εἰς ἀθέτησιν τῆς ἁμαρτίας διὰ τῆς θυσίας
for annulment – of sin through the sacrifice
αὐτοῦ πεφανέρωται.   27 καὶ καθ' ὅσον
of him he has been manifested.   And   as
ἀπόκειται τοῖς ἀνθρώποις ἅπαξ ἀποθανεῖν,
it is reserved – to men   once to die,
μετὰ δὲ τοῦτο κρίσις,   28 οὕτως καὶ
and after this judgment,   so   also
ὁ Χριστός, ἅπαξ προσενεχθεὶς εἰς τὸ
– Christ,   once having been offered for the
πολλῶν ἀνενεγκεῖν ἁμαρτίας, ἐκ δευτέρου
²of many ¹to bear ²sins, ²a second [time]
χωρὶς ἁμαρτίας ὀφθήσεται τοῖς αὐτὸν
³without ⁴sin ¹will appear ⁵to the [ones] ⁷him
ἀπεκδεχομένοις εἰς σωτηρίαν.
⁶expecting for salvation.

CHAPTER 10

FOR since the law has but a shadow of the good things to come instead of the true form of these realities, it can never, by the same sacrifices which are continually offered year after year, make perfect those who draw near. ²Otherwise, would they not have ceased to be offered? If the worshipers had once been cleansed, they would no longer have any consciousness of sin. ³But in these sacrifices there is a reminder of sin year after year. ⁴For it is impossible that the blood of bulls and goats should take away sins.

5 Consequently, when Christ came into the world, he said,
"Sacrifices and offerings thou hast not desired,
but a body hast thou prepared for me;

10 Σκιὰν γὰρ ἔχων ὁ νόμος τῶν
For ⁴a shadow ³having ¹the ²law of the
μελλόντων ἀγαθῶν, οὐκ αὐτὴν τὴν εἰκόνα
coming good things, not ³[it]self ¹the ²image
τῶν πραγμάτων, κατ' ἐνιαυτὸν ταῖς αὐταῖς
of the matters, ⁵every ⁶year† ³by the ⁴same
θυσίαις ἃς προσφέρουσιν εἰς τὸ διηνεκὲς
⁵sacrifices ⁶which ⁷they offer ¹⁰continually†
οὐδέποτε δύναται τοὺς προσερχομένους
⁹never ¹can ¹²the [ones] ¹³approaching
τελειῶσαι·   2 ἐπεὶ οὐκ ἂν ἐπαύσαντο
¹¹to perfect;   since would not they have ceased
προσφερόμεναι, διὰ τὸ μηδεμίαν ἔχειν
being offered, because of the ⁷no ⁸to have
ἔτι συνείδησιν ἁμαρτιῶν τοὺς λατρεύοντας
⁶still ⁸conscience ⁹of sins ¹the [ones] ²serving
ἅπαξ κεκαθαρισμένους; 3 ἀλλ' ἐν αὐταῖς
³once ⁴having been cleansed ? But in them [there
ἀνάμνησις ἁμαρτιῶν κατ' ἐνιαυτόν·
is] a remembrance of sins yearly†;
4 ἀδύνατον γὰρ αἷμα ταύρων καὶ τράγων
for [it is] impossible blood of bulls and of goats
ἀφαιρεῖν ἁμαρτίας. 5 Διὸ εἰσερχόμενος εἰς
to take away sins. Wherefore entering into
τὸν κόσμον λέγει· θυσίαν καὶ προσφορὰν
the world he says: Sacrifice and offering
οὐκ ἠθέλησας, σῶμα δὲ κατηρτίσω μοι·
thou didst not wish, but a body thou didst prepare for me;

⁶in burnt offerings and sin offerings thou hast taken no pleasure.
⁷Then I said, 'Lo, I have come to do thy will, O God,' as it is written of me in the roll of the book."
⁸When he said above, "Thou hast neither desired nor taken pleasure in sacrifices and offerings and burnt offerings and sin offerings" (these are offered according to the law), ⁹then he added, "Lo, I have come to do thy will." He abolishes the first in order to establish the second. ¹⁰And by that will we have been sanctified through the offering of the body of Jesus Christ once for all.
11 And every priest stands daily at his service, offering repeatedly the same sacrifices, which can never take away sins. ¹²But when Christ had offered for all time a single sacrifice for sins, he sat down at the right hand of God, ¹³then

6 ὁλοκαυτώματα   καὶ   περὶ   ἁμαρτίας   οὐκ
  burnt offerings   and concerning   sins   not
                 [sacrifices]

εὐδόκησας.   7 τότε   εἶπον·   ἰδοὺ   ἥκω,
thou wast well   Then   I said: Behold   I have
pleased [with].   come,

ἐν   κεφαλίδι   βιβλίου   γέγραπται   περὶ   ἐμοῦ,
in   a heading   of a scroll   it has been   concerning me,
                           written

τοῦ   ποιῆσαι   ὁ   θεὸς   τὸ   θέλημά   σου.
–   to do[,]ᵈ   –   God[,]*   the   will   of thee.

8 ἀνώτερον   λέγων   ὅτι   θυσίας   καὶ   προσ-
   Above   saying   that   sacrifices   and   offer-

φορὰς   καὶ   ὁλοκαυτώματα   καὶ   περὶ   ἁμαρτίας
ings   and   burnt offerings   and   [sacrifices]   sins
                                 concerning

οὐκ   ἠθέλησας   οὐδὲ   εὐδόκησας,   αἵτινες
thou didst not wish   nor   *thou* wast well   which
                    pleased [with],

κατὰ   νόμον   προσφέρονται,   9 τότε   εἴρηκεν·
accord-   law   are offered,   then   he *has* said:
ing to

ἰδοὺ   ἥκω   τοῦ   ποιῆσαι   τὸ   θέλημά   σου.
Behold   I have   –   to doᵈ   the   will   of thee.
      come

ἀναιρεῖ   τὸ   πρῶτον   ἵνα   τὸ   δεύτερον
He takes   the   first   in order   the   second
away   that

στήσῃ·   10 ἐν   ᾧ   θελήματι   ἡγιασμένοι   ἐσμὲν
he may   by   which   will   ²having been   ¹we are
set up;   sanctified

διὰ   τῆς   προσφορᾶς   τοῦ   σώματος   Ἰησοῦ
through   the   offering   of the   body   of Jesus

Χριστοῦ   ἐφάπαξ.   11 Καὶ   πᾶς   μὲν   ἱερεὺς
Christ   once for all.   And   ²every ¹on one   ²priest
                              hand

ἕστηκεν   καθ'   ἡμέραν   λειτουργῶν   καὶ   τὰς
stands   daily†   ministering   and   ³the

αὐτὰς   πολλάκις   προσφέρων   θυσίας,   αἵτινες
⁴same   ¹often   ²offering   ⁵sacrifices,   which

οὐδέποτε   δύνανται   περιελεῖν   ἁμαρτίας·   12 οὗτος
never   can   *to* take away   sins;   ²this
                           [priest]

δὲ   μίαν   ὑπὲρ   ἁμαρτιῶν   προσενέγκας
¹on the   ⁴one   ⁶on behalf of   ⁷sins   ³having offered
other

θυσίαν   εἰς   τὸ   διηνεκὲς   ἐκάθισεν   ἐν   δεξιᾷ
²sacrifice   ⁹in   –   ¹⁰perpetuity   ⁸sat   at [the] right
                               [hand]

τοῦ   θεοῦ,   13 τὸ   λοιπὸν   ἐκδεχόμενος   ἕως
–   of God,   henceforth   expecting   till

* The "articular vocative"; cf. 1. 8, 9.

to wait until his enemies should be made a stool for his feet. ¹⁴For by a single offering he has perfected for all time those who are sanctified. ¹⁵And the Holy Spirit also bears witness to us; for after saying,

¹⁶ "This is the covenant that I will make with them after those days, says the Lord:
I will put my laws on their hearts,
and write them on their minds,"
¹⁷ then he adds,
"I will remember their sins and their misdeeds no more."
¹⁸Where there is forgiveness of these, there is no longer any offering for sin.

19 Therefore, brethren, since we have confidence to enter the sanctuary by the blood of Jesus, ²⁰by the new and living way which he opened for us through the curtain, that is, through his flesh, ²¹and since we have a great priest over the house of God, ²²let us draw near with a true heart in full assurance of faith, with our hearts sprinkled clean from an evil conscience and our bodies

---

τεθῶσιν οἱ ἐχθροὶ αὐτοῦ ὑποπόδιον τῶν
⁴are put ¹the ²enemies ³of him a footstool of the

ποδῶν αὐτοῦ. 14 μιᾷ γὰρ προσφορᾷ
feet of him. For by one offering

τετελείωκεν εἰς τὸ διηνεκὲς τοὺς ἁγιαζ-
he has perfected in - perpetuity the [ones] being

ομένους. 15 Μαρτυρεῖ δὲ ἡμῖν καὶ
sanctified. And ⁵witnesses ⁶to us ⁴indeed

τὸ πνεῦμα τὸ ἅγιον· μετὰ γὰρ τὸ
¹the ²Spirit - ²Holy; for after the

εἰρηκέναι· 16 αὕτη ἡ διαθήκη ἣν δια-
to have said: This [is] the covenant which I will
=having said:

θήσομαι πρὸς αὐτοὺς μετὰ τὰς ἡμέρας
covenant to them after - days

ἐκείνας, λέγει κύριος· διδοὺς νόμους μου
those, says [the] Lord: Giving laws of me

ἐπὶ καρδίας αὐτῶν, καὶ ἐπὶ τὴν διάνοιαν
on hearts of them, also on the mind

αὐτῶν ἐπιγράψω αὐτούς, 17 καὶ τῶν
of them I will inscribe them, and the

ἁμαρτιῶν αὐτῶν καὶ τῶν ἀνομιῶν αὐτῶν
sins of them and the iniquities of them

οὐ μὴ μνησθήσομαι ἔτι. 18 ὅπου δὲ
by no means I will remember still. Now where

ἄφεσις τούτων, οὐκέτι προσφορὰ περὶ
forgiveness of these [is], no longer offering concerning
[there is]

ἁμαρτίας.
sins.

19 Ἔχοντες οὖν, ἀδελφοί, παρρησίαν εἰς
Having therefore, brothers, confidence for

τὴν εἴσοδον τῶν ἁγίων ἐν τῷ αἵματι
the entering of the holies by the blood

Ἰησοῦ, 20 ἣν ἐνεκαίνισεν ἡμῖν ὁδὸν
of Jesus, which he dedicated for us[,] a way

πρόσφατον καὶ ζῶσαν διὰ τοῦ κατα-
fresh and living through the veil,

πετάσματος, τοῦτ' ἔστιν τῆς σαρκὸς αὐτοῦ,
this is the flesh of him,

21 καὶ ἱερέα μέγαν ἐπὶ τὸν οἶκον τοῦ
and priest a great over the household -

θεοῦ, 22 προσερχώμεθα μετὰ ἀληθινῆς
of God, let us approach with a true

καρδίας ἐν πληροφορίᾳ πίστεως, ῥεραν-
heart in full assurance of faith, having been

τισμένοι τὰς καρδίας ἀπὸ συνειδήσεως
sprinkled [as to] the hearts from ³conscience

washed with pure water.
²³Let us hold fast the
confession of our hope
without wavering, for he
who promised is faithful;
²⁴and let us consider how
to stir up one another to
love and good works,
²⁵not neglecting to meet
together, as is the habit
of some, but encouraging
one another, and all the
more as you see the Day
drawing near.

26 For if we sin
deliberately after receiving the knowledge of the
truth, there no longer
remains a sacrifice for
sins, ²⁷but a fearful
prospect of judgment,
and a fury of fire which
will consume the adver-
saries. ²⁸A man who has
violated the law of Moses
dies without mercy at
the testimony of two or
three witnesses. ²⁹How
much worse punishment
do you think will be
deserved by the man who
has spurned the Son of
God, and profaned the
blood of the covenant by
which he was sanctified,
and outraged the Spirit

πονηρᾶς   καὶ   λελουσμένοι   τὸ   σῶμα   ὕδατι
¹an evil   and   having been [as to] body   ²water
                  bathed   the

καθαρῷ·   23 κατέχωμεν   τὴν   ὁμολογίαν   τῆς
¹in clean;   let us hold fast the   confession   of the
                                                    (our)

ἐλπίδος   ἀκλινῆ,   πιστὸς   γὰρ   ὁ   ἐπαγ-
hope   unyieldingly, for faithful [is] the [one] pro-

γειλάμενος,   24 καὶ   κατανοῶμεν   ἀλλήλους
mising,   and   let us consider   one another

εἰς   παροξυσμὸν   ἀγάπης   καὶ   καλῶν   ἔργων,
to   incitement   of love   and   of good   works,

25 μὴ   ἐγκαταλείποντες   τὴν   ἐπισυναγωγὴν
not   forsaking   the   coming together

ἑαυτῶν,   καθὼς   ἔθος   τισίν,   ἀλλὰ   παρα-
of [our]selves,   as   custom with some [is], but   ex-

καλοῦντες,   καὶ   τοσούτῳ   μᾶλλον   ὅσῳ
horting,   and   by so much   more   as

βλέπετε   ἐγγίζουσαν   τὴν   ἡμέραν.   26 Ἑκουσίως
ye see   ²drawing near   ¹the   ²day.   wilfully

γὰρ   ἁμαρτανόντων   ἡμῶν   μετὰ   τὸ   λαβεῖν
For   sinning   us²   after   the   to receive
=when we sin wilfully   =receiving

τὴν   ἐπίγνωσιν   τῆς   ἀληθείας,   οὐκέτι   περὶ
the   full knowledge of the   truth,   ⁵no more   ²con-
                                                        cerning

ἁμαρτιῶν   ἀπολείπεται   θυσία,   27 φοβερὰ
²sins   ⁴remains   ¹a sacrifice,   ³fearful

δέ   τις   ἐκδοχὴ   κρίσεως   καὶ   πυρὸς   ζῆλος
¹but ²some expectation of judgment and   ²of fire   ¹zeal

ἐσθίειν   μέλλοντος   τοὺς   ὑπεναντίους.
⁴to consume ³being about   the   adversaries.

28 ἀθετήσας   τις   νόμον   Μωϋσέως   χωρὶς
²Disregarding ¹anyone   ³law   ⁴of Moses   ⁵without

οἰκτιρμῶν   ἐπὶ   δυσὶν   ἢ   τρισὶν   μάρτυσιν
⁷compassions ⁸on [the   ⁹two   ¹⁰or   ¹¹three   ¹²witnesses
              word of]

ἀποθνῄσκει·   29 πόσῳ   δοκεῖτε   χείρονος
⁶dies;   by how much   think ye   ²of worse

ἀξιωθήσεται   τιμωρίας   ὁ   τὸν   υἱὸν   τοῦ
¹will be thought ³punishment ⁴the   ⁶the   ⁷Son   -
worthy   [one]

θεοῦ   καταπατήσας   καὶ   τὸ   αἷμα   τῆς
⁸of God ⁵having trampled and   ⁹the   ⁶blood   ⁵of the
         [on]

διαθήκης   κοινὸν   ἡγησάμενος,   ἐν   ᾧ   ἡγιάσθη,
⁶covenant   ²common   ¹having   by which   he was
                      deemed,   sanctified,

καὶ   τὸ   πνεῦμα   τῆς   χάριτος   ἐνυβρίσας.
and   ²the   ³Spirit   -   ⁴of grace   ¹having insulted.

of grace? [30] For we know him who said, "Vengeance is mine, I will repay." And again, "The Lord will judge his people." [31] It is a fearful thing to fall into the hands of the living God. [32] But recall the former days when, after you were enlightened, you endured a hard struggle with sufferings, [33] sometimes being publicly exposed to abuse and affliction, and sometimes being partners with those so treated. [34] For you had compassion on the prisoners, and you joyfully accepted the plundering of your property, since you knew that you yourselves had a better possession and an abiding one. [35] Therefore do not throw away your confidence, which has a great reward. [36] For you have need of endurance, so that you may do the will of God and receive what is promised. [37] "For yet a little while, and the coming one shall come and shall not tarry; [38] but my righteous one shall live by faith, and if he shrinks back,

30 οἴδαμεν γὰρ τὸν εἰπόντα· ἐμοὶ
For we know   the [one]   having said: To me
                            =Vengeance

ἐκδίκησις, ἐγὼ ἀνταποδώσω· καὶ πάλιν·
vengeance,*   I   will repay;   and   again:
is mine,

κρινεῖ κύριος τὸν λαὸν αὐτοῦ. 31 φοβερὸν
¹will judge [¹The]   the   people   of him.   A fearful
Lord   thing [it is]

τὸ ἐμπεσεῖν εἰς χεῖρας θεοῦ ζῶντος.
the   to fall in   into   [the] hands   ²God   ¹of a living.

32 Ἀναμιμνῄσκεσθε δὲ τὰς πρότερον ἡμέρας,
But remember ye   the   ²formerly   ¹days,

ἐν αἷς φωτισθέντες πολλὴν ἄθλησιν
in   which   being enlightened   ²a much(great)   ³struggle

ὑπεμείνατε παθημάτων, 33 τοῦτο μὲν
¹ye endured   ⁴of sufferings,   this on one hand

ὀνειδισμοῖς τε καὶ θλίψεσιν θεατριζόμενοι,
²to reproaches   ³both   ⁴and   ⁵to afflictions   ¹being exposed,

τοῦτο δὲ κοινωνοὶ τῶν οὕτως ἀναστρεφ-
this   on the   ²sharers   ³of the   ⁴thus   ⁴liv-
      other   [ones]

ομένων γενηθέντες. 34 καὶ γὰρ τοῖς
ing   ¹having become.   For indeed   in the

δεσμίοις συνεπαθήσατε, καὶ τὴν ἁρπαγὴν
bonds   ye suffered together,   and   ⁴the   ⁵seizure

τῶν ὑπαρχόντων ὑμῶν μετὰ χαρᾶς
⁶of the   ⁷possessions   ⁸of you   ¹with   ²joy

προσεδέξασθε, γινώσκοντες ἔχειν ἑαυτοὺς
¹ye accepted,   knowing   ²to have   ¹[your]selves

κρείσσονα ὕπαρξιν καὶ μένουσαν. 35 Μὴ
²a better   ³possession   ⁴and   ⁵remaining.   not

ἀποβάλητε οὖν τὴν παρρησίαν ὑμῶν, ἥτις
Cast ye away   therefore   the   confidence   of you,   which

ἔχει μεγάλην μισθαποδοσίαν. 36 ὑπομονῆς
has   a great   recompence.   ²of endurance

γὰρ ἔχετε χρείαν ἵνα τὸ θέλημα τοῦ
For   ¹ye have   ²need   in order   ³the   ³will   –
                  that

θεοῦ ποιήσαντες κομίσησθε τὴν ἐπαγγελίαν.
⁴of God   ¹having   ye may obtain   the   promise.
       done

37 ἔτι γὰρ μικρὸν ὅσον ὅσον, ὁ ἐρχόμενος
   For yet   ²little   ¹a very,*   the coming [one]

ἥξει καὶ οὐ χρονίσει· 38 ὁ δὲ δίκαιός
will come and   will not delay;   but the   just man

μου ἐκ πίστεως ζήσεται, καὶ ἐὰν ὑπο-
of me   by   faith   will live,   and   if   he

* Cf. our "so so".

my soul has no pleasure in him."
39 But we are not of those who shrink back and are destroyed, but of those who have faith and keep their souls.

στείληται, οὐκ εὐδοκεῖ ἡ ψυχή μου
withdraws, ⁴is not well pleased ¹the ²soul ³of me
ἐν αὐτῷ. 39 ἡμεῖς δὲ οὐκ ἐσμὲν ὑποστολῆς
in him. But we are not of withdrawal
εἰς ἀπώλειαν, ἀλλὰ πίστεως εἰς περιποίησιν
to destruction, but of faith to possession
ψυχῆς.
of soul.

CHAPTER 11

NOW faith is the assurance of things hoped for, the conviction of things not seen. ²For by it the men of old received divine approval. ³By faith we understand that the world was created by the word of God, so that what is seen was made out of things which do not appear.

4 By faith Abel offered to God a more acceptable sacrifice than Cain, through which he received approval as righteous, God bearing witness by accepting his gifts; he died, but through his faith he is still speaking. ⁵By faith Enoch was taken up so that he should not see death; and he was not found, because God had taken him. Now before he was taken he was attested as having pleased God. ⁶And without faith it is impossible to please him. For whoever would draw near to God must

11 Ἔστιν δὲ πίστις ἐλπιζομένων ὑπό-
Now ²is ¹faith ⁴of things being hoped ³[the]
στασις, πραγμάτων ἔλεγχος οὐ βλεπομένων.
reality, ²of things ¹[the] proof not being seen.
2 ἐν ταύτῃ γὰρ ἐμαρτυρήθησαν οἱ
by this For ²obtained witness ¹the
πρεσβύτεροι. 3 Πίστει νοοῦμεν κατηρτίσθαι
²elders. By faith we understand ²to have been
adjusted
τοὺς αἰῶνας ῥήματι θεοῦ, εἰς τὸ μὴ
¹the ³ages by a word of God, so as† ²not
ἐκ φαινομένων τὸ βλεπόμενον γεγονέναι.
²out ⁴things ¹the ³being seen ⁵to have
of appearing thing become.
4 Πίστει πλείονα θυσίαν Ἄβελ παρὰ
By faith ⁴a greater(? better) ⁵sacrifice ¹Abel ⁶than
Κάϊν προσήνεγκεν τῷ θεῷ, δι' ἧς
⁷Cain ²offered - ²to God, through which
ἐμαρτυρήθη εἶναι δίκαιος, μαρτυροῦντος ἐπὶ
he obtained to be just, ²witnessing ³over
witness
τοῖς δώροις αὐτοῦ τοῦ θεοῦ, καὶ δι'
⁴the ⁵gifts ⁶of him - ¹God,² and through
αὐτῆς ἀποθανὼν ἔτι λαλεῖ. 5 Πίστει
it having died still he speaks. By faith
Ἐνὼχ μετετέθη τοῦ μὴ ἰδεῖν θάνατον,
Enoch was removed - not to seeᵈ death,
καὶ οὐχ ηὑρίσκετο διότι μετέθηκεν αὐτὸν
and was not found because ²removed ³him
ὁ θεός. 6 πρὸ γὰρ τῆς μεταθέσεως
- ¹God. For before the(his) removal
μεμαρτύρηται εὐαρεστηκέναι τῷ θεῷ· χωρὶς
he has obtained to have been well- - to God; ²without
witness pleasing
δὲ πίστεως ἀδύνατον εὐαρεστῆσαι· πιστεῦσαι
¹but faith [it is] impossible to be well-pleasing [to God]; ⁴to believe
γὰρ δεῖ τὸν προσερχόμενον [τῷ] θεῷ,
¹for ³it ²the [one] ⁴approaching - ⁵to God,
behoves

believe that he exists and that he rewards those who seek him. ⁷By faith Noah, being warned by God concerning events as yet unseen, took heed and constructed an ark for the saving of his household; by this he condemned the world and became an heir of the righteousness which comes by faith.

8 By faith Abraham obeyed when he was called to go out to a place which he was to receive as an inheritance; and he went out, not knowing where he was to go. ⁹By faith he sojourned in the land of promise, as in a foreign land, living in tents with Isaac and Jacob, heirs with him of the same promise. ¹⁰For he looked forward to the city which has foundations, whose builder and maker is God. ¹¹"By faith Sarah herself received power to conceive, even when she was past the age, since she considered him faithful who had promised. ¹²Therefore from one man, and him as good as dead, were born descendants as many as the stars

ὅτι	ἔστιν	καὶ	τοῖς	ἐκζητοῦσιν	αὐτὸν
that	he is	and	²to the [ones]	⁴seeking ⁵out	³him

μισθαποδότης	γίνεται.	7 Πίστει	χρηματισ-	
¹a rewarder	¹becomes.	By faith	²having been warned [by	

θεὶς	Νῶε	περὶ	τῶν	μηδέπω	βλεπομένων,
God*]	¹Noah	concerning	the things	not yet	being seen,

εὐλαβηθεὶς	κατεσκεύασεν	κιβωτὸν	εἰς
being devout	prepared	an ark	for

σωτηρίαν	τοῦ	οἴκου	αὐτοῦ,	δι' ἧς
[the] salvation	of the	household	of him,	through which

κατέκρινεν	τὸν	κόσμον,	καὶ	τῆς κατὰ
he condemned	the	world,	and	²of the ³according to

πίστιν	δικαιοσύνης	ἐγένετο	κληρονόμος.
⁴faith	⁴righteousness	¹became	²heir.

8 Πίστει	καλούμενος	Ἀβραὰμ	ὑπήκουσεν	
By faith	¹being called	¹Abraham	¹⁰obeyed	

ἐξελθεῖν	εἰς	τόπον	ὃν ἤμελλεν	λαμβάνειν
³to go forth	⁴to	⁵a place	⁶which ⁷he was about	⁸to receive

εἰς	κληρονομίαν,	καὶ	ἐξῆλθεν μὴ	ἐπιστάμε-
⁹for	¹⁰an inheritance,	and	went forth not	understand-

νος	ποῦ	ἔρχεται.	9 Πίστει	παρῴκησεν
ing	where	he goes(went).	By faith	he sojourned

εἰς	γῆν	τῆς ἐπαγγελίας	ὡς	ἀλλοτρίαν,
in	a land	- of promise	as	a foreigner,

ἐν	σκηναῖς	κατοικήσας,	μετὰ	Ἰσαὰκ καὶ
in	tents	dwelling,	with	Isaac and

Ἰακὼβ	τῶν	συγκληρονόμων	τῆς	ἐπαγ-
Jacob	the	co-heirs	of the	³pro-

γελίας	τῆς	αὐτῆς·	10 ἐξεδέχετο	γὰρ	τὴν
mise	-	¹same;	for he expected		the

τοὺς	θεμελίους	ἔχουσαν	πόλιν,	ἧς τεχνίτης	
²the	⁴foundations	³having	¹city,	of which ²artificer	

καὶ	δημιουργὸς	ὁ θεός.	11 Πίστει	καὶ
⁴and	⁵maker	- ¹God ²[is].	By faith	also

αὐτὴ	Σάρρα	δύναμιν	εἰς	καταβολὴν
²[her]self	¹Sara	⁴power	⁵for	⁶conception

σπέρματος	ἔλαβεν	καὶ	παρὰ	καιρὸν ἡλικίας,
⁷of seed	³received	even	beyond	time of age,

ἐπεὶ	πιστὸν	ἡγήσατο	τὸν ἐπαγγειλάμενον.
since	²faithful	¹she deemed	the [one] having promised.

12 διὸ	καὶ	ἀφ' ἑνὸς	ἐγενήθησαν,	καὶ
Wherefore	indeed	from one	there became,	and

ταῦτα	νενεκρωμένου,	καθὼς	τὰ	ἄστρα
that too†	[he] having died,ᵃ	as	the	stars

* This must be understood, as the word always (or at least generally) has reference to a divine communication.

of heaven and as the innumerable grains of sand by the seashore.
13 These all died in faith, not having received what was promised, but having seen it and greeted it from afar, and having acknowledged that they were strangers and exiles on the earth. ¹⁴ For people who speak thus make it clear that they are seeking a homeland. ¹⁵ If they had been thinking of that land from which they had gone out, they would have had opportunity to return. ¹⁶ But as it is, they desire a better country, that is, a heavenly one. Therefore God is not ashamed to be called their God, for he has prepared for them a city.
17 By faith Abraham, when he was tested, offered up Isaac, and he who had received the promises was ready to offer up his only son, ¹⁸ of whom it was said, "Through Isaac shall your descendants be named." ¹⁹ He considered that God was able to raise men even from the dead; hence, figuratively speaking, he did receive him back. ²⁰ By faith

τοῦ οὐρανοῦ τῷ πλήθει καὶ ὡς ἡ ἄμμος
of the heaven – in multitude and as the ²sand
ἡ παρὰ τὸ χεῖλος τῆς θαλάσσης ἡ
– ³by ⁴the ⁵lip ⁶of the ⁷sea –
ἀναρίθμητος. 13 Κατὰ πίστιν ἀπέθανον
¹innumerable. ⁴By way of ⁵faith ²died
οὗτοι πάντες, μὴ κομισάμενοι τὰς ἐπαγ-
¹these ²all, not having obtained the pro-
γελίας, ἀλλὰ πόρρωθεν αὐτὰς ἰδόντες καὶ
mises, but ⁵from afar ⁴them ¹seeing ²and
ἀσπασάμενοι, καὶ ὁμολογήσαντες ὅτι · ξένοι
²greeting, and confessing that ²strangers
καὶ παρεπίδημοί εἰσιν ἐπὶ τῆς γῆς.
²and ⁴sojourners ¹they are on the earth
(? land).
14 οἱ γὰρ τοιαῦτα λέγοντες ἐμφανίζουσιν
For the [ones] ²such things ¹saying make manifest
ὅτι πατρίδα ἐπιζητοῦσιν. 15 καὶ εἰ μὲν
that ²a fatherland ¹they seek. And if on one
hand
ἐκείνης ἐμνημόνευον ἀφ' ἧς ἐξέβησαν,
²that ¹they remembered from which they came out,
εἶχον ἂν καιρὸν ἀνακάμψαι· 16 νῦν
they might time(opportunity) to return; now
have had
δὲ κρείττονος ὀρέγονται, τοῦτ' ἔστιν
on the ²a better ¹they aspire to, this is
other
ἐπουρανίου. διὸ οὐκ ἐπαισχύνεται αὐτοὺς
a heavenly. Wherefore ²is not ashamed [of] ³them
ὁ θεὸς θεὸς ἐπικαλεῖσθαι αὐτῶν· ἡτοίμασεν
– ¹God ⁵God ⁴to be called ⁶of them; ¹he prepared
γὰρ αὐτοῖς πόλιν. 17 Πίστει προσενήνοχεν
⁷for for them a city. By faith ³has offered up
'Αβραὰμ τὸν 'Ισαὰκ πειραζόμενος, καὶ
¹Abraham – ⁴Isaac ²being tested, and
τὸν μονογενῆ προσέφερεν ὁ τὰς ἐπαγγελίας
⁵the ⁷only begotten ⁶was ¹the ²the ⁴promises
(his) offering up [one]
ἀναδεξάμενος, 18 πρὸς ὃν ἐλαλήθη ὅτι
³having undertaken, as to whom it was spoken[,] –
ἐν 'Ισαὰκ κληθήσεταί σοι σπέρμα,
In Isaac shall be called to thee a seed,
=thy seed,
19 λογισάμενος ὅτι καὶ ἐκ νεκρῶν ἐγείρειν
reckoning that ⁴even ⁶from ⁷dead ⁵to raise
δυνατὸς ὁ θεός· ὅθεν αὐτὸν καὶ ἐν
²[was] ³able – ¹God; whence ⁵him ¹indeed ²in
παραβολῇ ἐκομίσατο. 20 Πίστει καὶ περὶ
³a parable ⁴he obtained. By faith also ⁶con-
cerning

Isaac invoked future blessings on Jacob and Esau. 21 By faith Jacob, when dying, blessed each of the sons of Joseph, bowing in worship over the head of his staff. 22 By faith Joseph, at the end of his life, made mention of the exodus of the Israelites and gave directions concerning his burial.

23 By faith Moses, when he was born, was hid for three months by his parents, because they saw that the child was beautiful; and they were not afraid of the king's edict. 24 By faith Moses, when he was grown up, refused to be called the son of Pharaoh's daughter, 25 choosing rather to share ill-treatment with the people of God than to enjoy the fleeting pleasures of sin. 26 He considered abuse suffered for the Christ greater wealth than the treasures of Egypt, for he looked to the reward. 27 By faith he left Egypt, not being afraid of the anger of the king; for he endured as seeing him who is invisible. 28 By faith he kept the Passover and sprinkled the blood, so that the

μελλόντων	εὐλόγησεν	Ἰσαὰκ	τὸν	Ἰακὼβ
¹coming things	²blessed	¹Isaac	-	²Jacob

καὶ	τὸν	Ἠσαῦ.	21	Πίστει	Ἰακὼβ
⁴and	-	⁵Esau.		By faith	Jacob

ἀποθνήσκων	ἕκαστον	τῶν	υἱῶν	Ἰωσὴφ
dying	²each	³of the	⁴sons	⁵of Joseph

εὐλόγησεν,	καὶ	προσεκύνησεν	ἐπὶ	τὸ	ἄκρον
¹blessed,	and	worshipped	on	the	tip

τῆς	ῥάβδου	αὐτοῦ.	22	Πίστει	Ἰωσὴφ
of the	rod	of him.		By faith	Joseph

τελευτῶν	περὶ	τῆς	ἐξόδου	τῶν	υἱῶν
dying	²concerning	³the	⁴exodus	⁵of the	⁶sons

Ἰσραὴλ	ἐμνημόνευσεν	καὶ	περὶ	τῶν
⁷of Israel	¹remembered	and	²concerning	³the

ὀστέων	αὐτοῦ	ἐνετείλατο.	23	Πίστει
⁴bones	⁵of him	¹gave orders.		By faith

Μωϋσῆς	γεννηθεὶς	ἐκρύβη	τρίμηνον	ὑπὸ
Moses	having been born	was hidden	three months	by

τῶν	πατέρων	αὐτοῦ,	διότι	εἶδον	ἀστεῖον
the	parents	of him,	because	they saw	²[to be] fine

τὸ	παιδίον,	καὶ	οὐκ	ἐφοβήθησαν	τὸ
¹the	²child,	and	not	they did not fear	the

διάταγμα	τοῦ	βασιλέως.	24	Πίστει	Μωϋσῆς
decree	of the	king.		By faith	Moses

μέγας	γενόμενος	ἠρνήσατο	λέγεσθαι	υἱὸς
³great	¹having become	denied	to be said(called)	son

θυγατρὸς	Φαραώ,	25	μᾶλλον	ἑλόμενος
of [the] daughter of Pharaoh,			rather	choosing

συγκακουχεῖσθαι	τῷ	λαῷ	τοῦ	θεοῦ	ἢ
to be ill treated with	the	people	-	of God than

πρόσκαιρον	ἔχειν	ἁμαρτίας	ἀπόλαυσιν,
for a time	to have	²of sin	¹enjoyment,

26	μείζονα	πλοῦτον	ἡγησάμενος	τῶν
	⁵greater	⁶riches	¹deeming	⁷[than] ⁸the

Αἰγύπτου	θησαυρῶν	τὸν	ὀνειδισμὸν	τοῦ
¹⁰of Egypt	⁹treasures	²the	³reproach	-

Χριστοῦ·	ἀπέβλεπεν	γὰρ	εἰς	τὴν	μισθ-
⁴of Christ;	for he was looking away	to	the	recom-

αποδοσίαν.	27	Πίστει	κατέλιπεν	Αἴγυπτον,
pence.		By faith	he left	Egypt,

μὴ	φοβηθεὶς	τὸν	θυμὸν	τοῦ	βασιλέως·
not	fearing	the	anger	of the	king;

τὸν	γὰρ	ἀόρατον	ὡς	ὁρῶν	ἐκαρτέρησεν.
⁴the	⁵for	⁵unseen [one]	²as	³seeing	¹he endured.

28	Πίστει	πεποίηκεν	τὸ	πάσχα	καὶ	τὴν
	By faith	he has made	the	passover	and	the

πρόσχυσιν	τοῦ	αἵματος,	ἵνα	μὴ	ὁ
affusion	of the	blood,	lest		the

Destroyer of the first-born might not touch them.
29 By faith the people crossed the Red Sea as if on dry land; but the Egyptians, when they attempted to do the same, were drowned.
30 By faith the walls of Jericho fell down after they had been encircled for seven days.
31 By faith Rahab the harlot did not perish with those who were disobedient, because she had given friendly welcome to the spies.
32 And what more shall I say? For time would fail me to tell of Gideon, Barak, Samson, Jephthah, of David and Samuel and the prophets
—33 who through faith conquered kingdoms, enforced justice, received promises, stopped the mouths of lions,
34 quenched raging fire, escaped the edge of the sword, won strength out of weakness, became mighty in war, put foreign armies to flight.
35 Women received their dead by resurrection. Some were tortured, refusing to accept release, that they might rise again to a better life.

ὀλεθρεύων τὰ πρωτότοκα θίγῃ αὐτῶν.
[one] destroying ²the ³firstborns ¹should ⁴of them.
                         touch

29 Πίστει διέβησαν τὴν ἐρυθρὰν θάλασσαν
By faith they went the Red Sea
        through

ὡς διὰ ξηρᾶς γῆς, ἧς πεῖραν λαβόντες
as through dry land, which ⁴trial ³taking

οἱ Αἰγύπτιοι κατεπόθησαν. 30 Πίστει
¹the ²Egyptians were swallowed up.   By faith

τὰ τείχη Ἰεριχὼ ἔπεσαν κυκλωθέντα ἐπὶ
the walls of Jericho fell having been during
                      encircled

ἑπτὰ ἡμέρας. 31 Πίστει Ῥαὰβ ἡ πόρνη
seven days.   By faith Rahab the prostitute

οὐ συναπώλετο τοῖς ἀπειθήσασιν, δεξαμένη
did not perish with the [ones] disobeying, having received

τοὺς κατασκόπους μετ᾽ εἰρήνης. 32 Καὶ
the spies with peace.   And

τί ἔτι λέγω; ἐπιλείψει με γὰρ διηγούμενον
what more may ⁴will fail ⁵me ¹for °recounting
I say?

ὁ χρόνος περὶ Γεδεών, Βαράκ, Σαμψών,
²the ³time concerning Gedeon, Barak, Sampson,

Ἰεφθάε, Δαυίδ τε καὶ Σαμουὴλ καὶ
Jephthae, ²David ¹both and Samuel and

τῶν προφητῶν, 33 οἳ διὰ πίστεως
the prophets,   who through faith

κατηγωνίσαντο βασιλείας, ἠργάσαντο δι-
overcame kingdoms, wrought right-

καιοσύνην, ἐπέτυχον ἐπαγγελιῶν, ἔφραξαν
eousness, obtained promises, stopped

στόματα λεόντων, 34 ἔσβεσαν δύναμιν
mouths of lions,   quenched [the] power

πυρός, ἔφυγον στόματα μαχαίρης, ἐδυναμώ-
of fire, escaped mouths(edges) of [the] sword, were em-

θησαν ἀπὸ ἀσθενείας, ἐγενήθησαν ἰσχυροὶ
powered from weakness, became strong

ἐν πολέμῳ, παρεμβολὰς ἔκλιναν ἀλλοτρίων.
in war, ¹armies ³made to yield ²of foreigners.

35 ἔλαβον γυναῖκες ἐξ ἀναστάσεως τοὺς
²received ¹women ⁶by ⁷resurrection ³the

νεκροὺς αὐτῶν· ἄλλοι δὲ ἐτυμπανίσθησαν,
⁴dead ⁵of them; but others were beaten to death,

οὐ προσδεξάμενοι τὴν ἀπολύτρωσιν, ἵνα
not accepting – deliverance, in or-
                         der that

κρείττονος ἀναστάσεως τύχωσιν· 36 ἕτεροι
²a better ³resurrection ¹they might others
               obtain;

36 Others suffered mocking and scourging, and even chains and imprisonment. 37 They were stoned, they were sawn in two,p they were killed with the sword; they went about in skins of sheep and goats, destitute, afflicted, ill-treated —38 of whom the world was not worthy— wandering over deserts and mountains, and in dens and caves of the earth.

39 And all these, though well attested by their faith, did not receive what was promised, 40 since God had foreseen something better for us, that apart from us they should not be made perfect.

δὲ ἐμπαιγμῶν καὶ μαστίγων πεῖραν ἔλαβον,
and ³of mockings ⁴and ⁵of scourgings ²trial ¹took,

ἔτι δὲ δεσμῶν καὶ φυλακῆς· 37 ἐλιθάσ-
and more of bonds and of prison; they were

θησαν, ἐπειράσθησαν, ἐπρίσθησαν, ἐν φόνῳ
stoned, they were tried, they were ²by ³murder
                                    sawn asunder,

μαχαίρης ἀπέθανον, περιῆλθον ἐν μηλωταῖς,
⁴of sword ¹they died, they went about in sheepskins,

ἐν αἰγείοις δέρμασιν, ὑστερούμενοι,
in goatskins, being in want,

θλιβόμενοι, κακουχούμενοι, 38 ὧν οὐκ ἦν
being afflicted, being ill treated, of whom was not

ἄξιος ὁ κόσμος, ἐπὶ ἐρημίαις πλανώμενοι
worthy the world, ²over ³deserts ¹wandering

καὶ ὄρεσιν καὶ σπηλαίοις καὶ ταῖς ὀπαῖς
and mountains and caves and the holes

τῆς γῆς. 39 Καὶ οὗτοι πάντες μαρτυρη-
of the earth. And these all having obtained

θέντες διὰ τῆς πίστεως οὐκ ἐκομίσαντο
witness through the(ir) faith obtained not

τὴν ἐπαγγελίαν, 40 τοῦ θεοῦ περὶ ἡμῶν
the promise, – God ⁴concerning ⁵us

κρεῖττόν τι προβλεψαμένου, ἵνα μὴ χωρὶς
²better ³some- ¹having foreseen,² in or- not without
        thing   der that

ἡμῶν τελειωθῶσιν.
us they should be perfected.

CHAPTER 12

THEREFORE, since we are surrounded by so great a cloud of witnesses, let us also lay aside every weight, and sin which clings so closely, and let us run with perseverance the race that is set before us, 2 looking to Jesus the pioneer and perfecter of our faith, who for the joy that was set before him endured the cross, despising the shame, and is seated at the right hand of the throne of God.

p Other manuscripts add they were tempted

12 Τοιγαροῦν καὶ ἡμεῖς, τοσοῦτον ἔχοντες
So therefore ²also ¹we, ²such ¹having

περικείμενον ἡμῖν νέφος μαρτύρων, ὄγκον
⁵lying around ⁶us ²a cloud ⁴of witnesses, ²encum-
                                        brance

ἀποθέμενοι πάντα καὶ τὴν εὐπερίστατον
¹putting away ²every ⁴and ⁵the ⁷most besetting

ἁμαρτίαν, δι᾽ ὑπομονῆς τρέχωμεν τὸν
⁶sin, through endurance let us run ¹the

προκείμενον ἡμῖν ἀγῶνα, 2 ἀφορῶντες εἰς
³set before ⁴us ²contest(race), looking away to

τὸν τῆς πίστεως ἀρχηγὸν καὶ τελειωτὴν
¹the ⁵of the ⁶faith ²author ³and ⁴finisher

Ἰησοῦν, ὃς ἀντὶ τῆς προκειμένης αὐτῷ
Jesus, who against ¹the ²set before ⁴him

χαρᾶς ὑπέμεινεν σταυρὸν αἰσχύνης κατα-
²joy endured a cross ²shame ¹de-

φρονήσας, ἐν δεξιᾷ τε τοῦ θρόνου τοῦ
spising, ²at ⁴[the] ¹and ⁵of the ³throne –
          right [hand]

3 Consider him who endured from sinners such hostility against himself, so that you may not grow weary or faint-hearted. ⁴In your struggle against sin you have not yet resisted to the point of shedding your blood. ⁵And have you forgotten the exhortation which addresses you as sons?—
"My son, do not regard lightly the discipline of the Lord, nor lose courage when you are punished by him. ⁶For the Lord disciplines him whom he loves, and chastises every son whom he receives." ⁷It is for discipline that you have to endure. God is treating you as sons; for what son is there whom his father does not discipline? ⁸If you are left without discipline, in which all have participated, then you are illegitimate children and not sons. ⁹Besides this, we have had earthly fathers to discipline us and we respected them. Shall we not much more be subject to the Father of spirits and live? ¹⁰For they disciplined us for a short time at their pleasure, but he disciplines us for our good,

θεοῦ κεκάθικεν.
'of ²has taken
God [his] seat.

3 ἀναλογίσασθε γὰρ τὸν
For consider ye ¹the
[one]

τοιαύτην ὑπομεμενηκότα ὑπὸ τῶν ἁμαρτω-
²such ³having endured ⁵by - ⁶of sin-

λῶν εἰς ἑαυτὸν ἀντιλογίαν, ἵνα μὴ κάμητε
ners ⁷against ⁸himself ⁴contradiction, lest ye grow weary

ταῖς ψυχαῖς ὑμῶν ἐκλυόμενοι. 4 Οὔπω
²in the ³souls ⁴of you ¹fainting. Not yet

μέχρις αἵματος ἀντικατέστητε πρὸς τὴν
³until ²blood ¹ye resisted ⁵against

ἁμαρτίαν ἀνταγωνιζόμενοι, 5 καὶ ἐκλέλησθε
⁶sin ⁴struggling against, and ye have forgotten

τῆς παρακλήσεως, ἥτις ὑμῖν ὡς ⁶υἱοῖς
the exhortation, which ²with you ³as ⁴with sons

διαλέγεται· υἱέ μου, μὴ ὀλιγώρει παιδείας
¹discourses: Son of me, do not make light of [the] discipline

κυρίου, μηδὲ ἐκλύου ὑπ' αὐτοῦ ἐλεγχόμενος·
of [the] nor faint ²by ³him ¹being reproved;
Lord,

6 ὃν γὰρ ἀγαπᾷ κύριος παιδεύει, μαστιγοῖ
for whom ²loves ¹[the] Lord he disciplines, ²scourges

δὲ πάντα υἱὸν ὃν παραδέχεται. 7 εἰς
¹and every son whom he receives. For

παιδείαν ὑπομένετε· ὡς υἱοῖς ὑμῖν
discipline endure ye; ⁴as ⁵with sons ³with you

προσφέρεται ὁ θεός· τίς γὰρ υἱὸς ὃν
²is dealing - ¹God; for what son whom
[is there]

οὐ παιδεύει πατήρ; 8 εἰ δὲ χωρίς ἐστε
²disciplines not ¹a father? But if ²without ¹ye are

παιδείας, ἧς μέτοχοι γεγόνασιν πάντες,
discipline, of which ³sharers ²have become ¹all,

ἄρα νόθοι καὶ οὐχ υἱοί ἐστε. 9 εἶτα
then bastards and not sons ye are. Furthermore

τοὺς μὲν τῆς σαρκὸς ἡμῶν πατέρας
the - ²of the ⁴flesh ⁵of us ²fathers

εἴχομεν παιδευτὰς καὶ ἐνετρεπόμεθα· οὐ
¹we had ⁶correctors and we respected [them]: ³not

πολὺ μᾶλλον ὑποταγησόμεθα τῷ πατρὶ
⁶much ⁷more ¹shall ²we ³be ⁵subject to the Father

τῶν πνευμάτων καὶ ζήσομεν; 10 οἱ μὲν
- of spirits and we shall live? ²they³indeed

γὰρ πρὸς ὀλίγας ἡμέρας κατὰ τὸ δοκοῦν
¹for for a few days accord- the seeming
ing to thing [good]

αὐτοῖς ἐπαίδευον, ὁ δὲ ἐπὶ τὸ συμφέρον
to them disciplined [us], but he for the(our) profit

that we may share his holiness. [11] For the moment all discipline seems painful rather than pleasant; later it yields the peaceful fruit of righteousness to those who have been trained by it.

[12] Therefore lift your drooping hands and strengthen your weak knees, [13] and make straight paths for your feet, so that what is lame may not be put out of joint but rather be healed. [14] Strive for peace with all men, and for the holiness without which no one will see the Lord. [15] See to it that no one fail to obtain the grace of God; that no "root of bitterness" spring up and cause trouble, and by it the many become defiled; [16] that no one be immoral or irreligious like Esau, who sold his birthright for a single meal. [17] For you know that afterward, when he desired to inherit the blessing, he was rejected, for he found no chance to repent, though he sought it with tears.

[18] For you have not

εἰς τὸ μεταλαβεῖν τῆς ἁγιότητος αὐτοῦ.
for the to partake of the sanctity of him.

[11] πᾶσα μὲν παιδεία πρὸς μὲν τὸ παρὸν
²All ¹on ³discipline ⁴for ⁷in- ⁵the ⁶present
one hand deed

οὐ δοκεῖ χαρᾶς εἶναι ἀλλὰ λύπης, ὕστερον
seems not ²of joy ¹to be but of grief, ²later

δὲ καρπὸν εἰρηνικὸν τοῖς δι' αὐτῆς
¹on the ⁵fruit ⁴peaceable ⁷to the ⁸through ¹⁰it
other [ones]

γεγυμνασμένοις ἀποδίδωσιν δικαιοσύνης.
⁸having been exercised ²it gives back ⁶of righteousness.

[12] Διὸ τὰς παρειμένας χεῖρας καὶ τὰ
Where- ²the ³having been ⁴hands ⁵and ⁶the
fore wearied

παραλελυμένα γόνατα ἀνορθώσατε, [13] καὶ
⁷having been paralysed ⁸knees ¹straighten ye, and

τροχιὰς ὀρθὰς ποιεῖτε τοῖς ποσὶν ὑμῶν,
tracks straight make for the feet of you,

ἵνα μὴ τὸ χωλὸν ἐκτραπῇ, ἰαθῇ δὲ
lest the lame be turned ³may ¹but
aside, be cured

μᾶλλον. [14] Εἰρήνην διώκετε μετὰ πάντων,
²rather. Peace follow with all men,

καὶ τὸν ἁγιασμόν, οὗ χωρὶς οὐδεὶς
and – sanctification, ²which ¹without no one

ὄψεται τὸν κύριον, [15] ἐπισκοποῦντες μή
will see the Lord, observing not(lest)

τις ὑστερῶν ἀπὸ τῆς χάριτος τοῦ θεοῦ,
anyone failing from the grace – of God,

μή τις ῥίζα πικρίας ἄνω φύουσα ἐνοχλῇ
not any root of bitterness ²up ¹growing disturb
(lest)

καὶ διὰ ταύτης μιανθῶσιν οἱ πολλοί,
and through this ²be defiled the ¹many,

[16] μή τις πόρνος ἢ βέβηλος ὡς Ἠσαῦ,
not(lest) any fornicator or profane man as Esau,

ὃς ἀντὶ βρώσεως μιᾶς ἀπέδοτο τὰ
who against ²eating ¹one gave up the

πρωτοτόκια ἑαυτοῦ. [17] ἴστε γὰρ ὅτι
rights of of himself. For ye know that
the firstborn

καὶ μετέπειτα θέλων κληρονομῆσαι τὴν
indeed afterwards wishing to inherit the

εὐλογίαν ἀπεδοκιμάσθη, μετανοίας γὰρ
blessing he was rejected, for ⁴of repentance

τόπον οὐχ εὗρεν, καίπερ μετὰ δακρύων
²place ²not ¹he found, though with tears

ἐκζητήσας αὐτήν. [18] Οὐ γὰρ προσεληλύθατε
seeking out it. For ²not ¹ye ³have ⁴approached

come to what may be touched, a blazing fire, and darkness, and gloom, and a tempest, [19] and the sound of a trumpet, and a voice whose words made the hearers entreat that no further messages be spoken to them. [20] For they could not endure the order that was given, "If even a beast touches the mountain, it shall be stoned." [21] Indeed, so terrifying was the sight that Moses said, "I tremble with fear." [22] But you have come to Mount Zion and to the city of the living God, the heavenly Jerusalem, and to innumerable angels in festal gathering, [23] and to the assembly[q] of the first-born who are enrolled in heaven, and to a judge who is God of all, and to the spirits of just men made perfect, [24] and to Jesus, the mediator of a new covenant, and to the sprinkled blood that speaks more graciously than the blood of Abel.

25 See that you do not refuse him who is speaking. For if they did not escape when they refused him who warned them on earth, much less shall we escape if we reject him who warns from

ψηλαφωμένῳ καὶ κεκαυμένῳ πυρὶ καὶ
to [a mountain] and having been with and
being felt ignited fire

γνόφῳ καὶ ζόφῳ καὶ θυέλλῃ 19 καὶ
to darkness and *to* deep gloom and *to* whirlwind and

σάλπιγγος ἤχῳ καὶ φωνῇ ῥημάτων, ἧς
*of trumpet [to a sound and *to a voice of words, which

οἱ ἀκούσαντες παρῃτήσαντο μὴ προστεθῆναι
the [ones] hearing entreated not to be added

αὐτοῖς λόγον· 20 οὐκ ἔφερον γὰρ τὸ
to them a word; *not *they bore ¹for the
thing

διαστελλόμενον· κἂν θηρίον θίγῃ τοῦ ὄρους,
being charged: If even a beast touches the mountain,

λιθοβοληθήσεται· 21 καί, οὕτω φοβερὸν ἦν
it shall be stoned; and, so fearful was

τὸ φανταζόμενον, Μωϋσῆς εἶπεν· ἔκφοβός
the thing appearing, Moses said: ²Terrified

εἰμι καὶ ἔντρομος· 22 ἀλλὰ προσεληλύθατε
¹I am and trembling; but ye have approached

Σιὼν ὄρει καὶ πόλει θεοῦ ζῶντος,
²Zion ¹to mount and to a city ²God ¹of [the] living,

Ἰερουσαλὴμ ἐπουρανίῳ, καὶ μυριάσιν
²Jerusalem ¹to a heavenly, and to myriads

ἀγγέλων, 23 πανηγύρει καὶ ἐκκλησίᾳ
of angels, to an assembly and a church

πρωτοτόκων ἀπογεγραμμένων ἐν οὐρανοῖς,
of firstborn [ones] having been enrolled in heavens,

καὶ κριτῇ θεῷ πάντων, καὶ πνεύμασι
and ²judge ¹to God of all men, and to spirits

δικαίων τετελειωμένων, 24 καὶ διαθήκης
of just men having been made and ⁴covenant
perfect,

νέας μεσίτῃ Ἰησοῦ, καὶ αἵματι ῥαντισμοῦ
³of a ²mediator ¹to Jesus, and to blood of sprinkling
new

κρεῖττον λαλοῦντι παρὰ τὸν Ἄβελ.
²a better thing ¹speaking than – Abel.

25 Βλέπετε μὴ παραιτήσησθε τὸν λαλοῦντα·
Look ye [that] ²not ¹ye refuse the [one] speaking;

εἰ γὰρ ἐκεῖνοι οὐκ ἐξέφυγον ἐπὶ γῆς
for if those escaped not ⁴on ⁵earth

παραιτησάμενοι τὸν χρηματίζοντα, πολὺ
¹refusing ²the [one] ³warning, much

μᾶλλον ἡμεῖς οἱ τὸν ἀπ' οὐρανῶν
more we* ¹the ²the [one] ⁵from ⁶heavens
[ones] ⁴[warning]

[q] Or angels, and to the festal gathering and assembly

* That is, "much more [shall] we [not escape]"; or, putting it in another way, "much less shall we escape."

heaven. ²⁶His voice then shook the earth; but now he has promised, "Yet once more I will shake not only the earth but also the heaven." ²⁷This phrase, "Yet once more," indicates the removal of what is shaken, as of what has been made, in order that what cannot be shaken may remain. ²⁸Therefore let us be grateful for receiving a kingdom that cannot be shaken, and thus let us offer to God acceptable worship, with reverence and awe; ²⁹for our God is a consuming fire.

ἀποστρεφόμενοι·	26 οὗ	ἡ	φωνὴ	τὴν	γῆν
¹turning from;	of whom	the	voice	²the	⁴earth

ἐσάλευσεν	τότε,	νῦν	δὲ	ἐπήγγελται	λέγων·
²shook	¹then,	but now		he has promised	saying:

ἔτι	ἅπαξ	ἐγὼ	σείσω	οὐ	μόνον	τὴν
Yet	once	I	will shake	not	only	the

γῆν	ἀλλὰ	καὶ	τὸν	οὐρανόν.	27 τὸ	δὲ
earth	but	also	*the*	heaven.		Now the
						[phrase]

ἔτι	ἅπαξ	δηλοῖ	τὴν	τῶν	σαλευομένων
'Yet	once'	declares	¹the	³of the things	⁴being shaken

μετάθεσιν	ὡς	πεποιημένων,	ἵνα	μείνῃ	τὰ
²removal	as	of things having	in or-	⁴may	¹the
		been made,	der that	remain	things

μὴ	σαλευόμενα.	28 Διὸ	βασιλείαν	ἀσάλευτος
¹not	³being shaken.	Wherefore	³kingdom	²an unshakable

παραλαμβάνοντες	ἔχωμεν	χάριν,	δι᾽	ἧς
¹receiving	let us have	grace,	through which

λατρεύωμεν	εὐαρέστως	τῷ	θεῷ,	μετὰ
we may serve	²well-pleasingly	–	¹God,	with

εὐλαβείας	καὶ	δέους·	29 καὶ	γὰρ	ὁ	θεὸς
devoutness	and	awe;	for indeed		the	God

ἡμῶν	πῦρ	καταναλίσκον.
of us [is]	fire	a consuming.

CHAPTER 13

LET brotherly love continue. ²Do not neglect to show hospitality to strangers, for thereby some have entertained angels unawares. ³Remember those who are in prison, as though in prison with them; and those who are ill-treated, since you also are in the body. ⁴Let marriage be held in honor among all, and let the marriage bed be undefiled; for God will judge the immoral and adulterous. ⁵Keep your life free from love of money, and be content with what you have; for

13 Ἡ	φιλαδελφία	μενέτω.	2 τῆς
–	³brotherly love	¹Let it ²remain.	–

φιλοξενίας	μὴ	ἐπιλανθάνεσθε·	διὰ	ταύτης
of hospitality	Be ye not forgetful;		¹through	³this

γὰρ	ἔλαθόν	τινες	ξενίσαντες	ἀγγέλους.
²for	⁵unconsciously†	⁴some	⁶entertaining(ed)	⁷angels.

3 μιμνήσκεσθε	τῶν	δεσμίων	ὡς	συνδεδεμένοι,
Be ye mindful	of the	prisoners	as	*having been* bound
				with [them],

τῶν	κακουχουμένων	ὡς	καὶ	αὐτοὶ	ὄντες
of the	*being* ill treated	as	also	[your]selves	being
[ones]					

ἐν	σώματι.	4 Τίμιος	ὁ	γάμος	ἐν	πᾶσιν
in [the] body.		⁴honourable	–	²marriage	in	all
		¹[Let]		³[be]		

καὶ	ἡ	κοίτη	ἀμίαντος·	πόρνους	γὰρ
and	the	bed	undefiled;	for fornicators

καὶ	μοιχοὺς	κρινεῖ	ὁ	θεός.	5 Ἀφιλάργυρος
and	adulterers	²will judge	–	¹God.	²without love of
					money

ὁ	τρόπος,	ἀρκούμενοι	τοῖς	παροῦσιν·
¹[Let]	³way of	being satisfied	the things	present;
²the	life ⁴[be],	with		
(your)				

he has said, "I will never fail you nor forsake you." ⁶Hence we can confidently say,

"The Lord is my helper,
I will not be afraid;
what can man do to me?"

7 Remember your leaders, those who spoke to you the word of God; consider the outcome of their life, and imitate their faith. ⁸Jesus Christ is the same yesterday and today and for ever. ⁹Do not be led away by diverse and strange teachings; for it is well that the heart be strengthened by grace, not by foods, which have not benefited their adherents. ¹⁰We have an altar from which those who serve the tent[r] have no right to eat. ¹¹For the bodies of those animals whose blood is brought into the sanctuary by the high priest as a sacrifice for sin are burned outside the camp. ¹²So Jesus also suffered outside the gate in order to sanctify the people through his own blood. ¹³Therefore let us go

[r] Or tabernacle

αὐτὸς γὰρ εἴρηκεν· οὐ μή σε ἀνῶ οὐδ'
for he has said: By no means thee will I nor leave

οὐ μή σε ἐγκαταλίπω· 6 ὥστε θαρροῦντας
by no(any) thee I forsake; so as being of good
means cheer

ἡμᾶς λέγειν· κύριος ἐμοὶ βοηθός, οὐ
us to say[b]: [The] Lord to me[c] [is] a helper, not

φοβηθήσομαι· τί ποιήσει μοι ἄνθρωπος;
I will fear; what ¹will ³do ⁴to me ²man?

7 Μνημονεύετε τῶν ἡγουμένων ὑμῶν,
Remember the [ones] leading of you,

οἵτινες ἐλάλησαν ὑμῖν τὸν λόγον τοῦ
who spoke to you the word –

θεοῦ, ὧν ἀναθεωροῦντες τὴν ἔκβασιν τῆς
of God, ⁶of ¹looking at ²the ³result ⁴of
whom the

ἀναστροφῆς μιμεῖσθε τὴν πίστιν. 8 Ἰησοῦς
⁶conduct imitate ye the(ir) faith. Jesus

Χριστὸς ἐχθὲς καὶ σήμερον ὁ αὐτὸς
Christ ⁴yesterday ⁵and ⁶to-day ¹[is] ²the ³same

καὶ εἰς τοὺς αἰῶνας. 9 Διδαχαῖς ποικίλαις
and unto the ages. ⁵teachings ²by various

καὶ ξέναις μὴ παραφέρεσθε· καλὸν γὰρ
²and ⁴strange ¹Do not be carried away; for [it is] good

χάριτι βεβαιοῦσθαι τὴν καρδίαν, οὐ
⁴by grace ³to be confirmed ¹the ²heart,[b] not

βρώμασιν, ἐν οἷς οὐκ ὠφελήθησαν οἱ
by foods, by which ²were not profited ¹the

περιπατοῦντες. 10 ἔχομεν θυσιαστήριον ἐξ
²[ones] walking. We have an altar of

οὗ φαγεῖν οὐκ ἔχουσιν ἐξουσίαν οἱ τῇ
which ⁷to eat ⁵have not ⁶authority ¹the ³the
[ones]

σκηνῇ λατρεύοντες. 11 ὧν γὰρ εἰσφέρεται
⁴tabernacle ²serving. For ³of what ⁷is brought in

ζῴων τὸ αἷμα περὶ ἁμαρτίας εἰς τὰ
⁴animals ¹the ²blood ⁵concerning ⁶sins into the

ἅγια διὰ τοῦ ἀρχιερέως, τούτων τὰ
holies through the high priest, of these the

σώματα κατακαίεται ἔξω τῆς παρεμβολῆς.
bodies is(are) burned outside the camp.

12 διὸ καὶ Ἰησοῦς, ἵνα ἁγιάσῃ διὰ
Where- in- Jesus, in order he might ³through
fore deed that sanctify

τοῦ ἰδίου αἵματος τὸν λαόν, ἔξω τῆς
⁴the(his) ⁵own ⁶blood ¹the ²people, outside the

πύλης ἔπαθεν. 13 τοίνυν ἐξερχώμεθα πρὸς
gate suffered. So let us go forth to

forth to him outside the camp, bearing abuse for him. [14] For here we have no lasting city, but we seek the city which is to come. [15] Through him then let us continually offer up a sacrifice of praise to God, that is, the fruit of lips that acknowledge his name. [16] Do not neglect to do good and to share what you have, for such sacrifices are pleasing to God.

17 Obey your leaders and submit to them; for they are keeping watch over your souls, as men who will have to give account. Let them do this joyfully, and not sadly, for that would be of no advantage to you.

18 Pray for us, for we are sure that we have a clear conscience, desiring to act honorably in all things. [19] I urge you the more earnestly to do this in order that I may be restored to you the sooner.

20 Now may the God of peace who brought again from the dead our Lord Jesus, the great shepherd of the sheep,

αὐτὸν ἔξω τῆς παρεμβολῆς τὸν ὀνειδισμὸν
him outside the camp the reproach

αὐτοῦ φέροντες· 14 οὐ γὰρ ἔχομεν ὧδε
of him bearing; for ²not ¹we have here

μένουσαν πόλιν, ἀλλὰ τὴν μέλλουσαν
a continuing city, but the [one] coming

ἐπιζητοῦμεν. 15 Δι᾽ αὐτοῦ οὖν ἀναφέρωμεν
we seek. Through him therefore let us offer up

θυσίαν αἰνέσεως διὰ παντὸς τῷ θεῷ,
a sacrifice of praise always – to God,

τοῦτ᾽ ἔστιν καρπὸν χειλέων ὁμολογούντων
this is fruit of lips confessing

τῷ ὀνόματι αὐτοῦ. 16 τῆς δὲ εὐποιΐας
to the name of him. But of the doing good

καὶ κοινωνίας μὴ ἐπιλανθάνεσθε· τοιαύταις
and sharing be ye not forgetful; ²with such

γὰρ θυσίαις εὐαρεστεῖται ὁ θεός. 17 Πεί-
¹for sacrifices ²is well pleased – ¹God. Obey

θεσθε τοῖς ἡγουμένοις ὑμῶν καὶ ὑπείκετε·
ye the [ones] leading of you and submit to
[them];

αὐτοὶ γὰρ ἀγρυπνοῦσιν ὑπὲρ τῶν ψυχῶν
for they watch on behalf of the souls

ὑμῶν ὡς λόγον ἀποδώσοντες· ἵνα μετὰ
of you as ²account ¹rendering*; in or- with
der that

χαρᾶς τοῦτο ποιῶσιν καὶ μὴ στενάζ-
joy ²this ¹they may do and not groan-

οντες· ἀλυσιτελὲς γὰρ ὑμῖν τοῦτο.
ing; for profitless to you this
[would be].

18 Προσεύχεσθε περὶ ἡμῶν· πειθόμεθα
Pray ye concerning us; ²we are persuaded

γὰρ ὅτι καλὴν συνείδησιν ἔχομεν, ἐν
¹for that a good conscience we have, ⁴in

πᾶσιν καλῶς θέλοντες ἀναστρέφεσθαι.
³all [respects] ³well ¹wishing ²to behave.

19 περισσοτέρως δὲ παρακαλῶ τοῦτο
And more abundantly I beseech [you] this

ποιῆσαι, ἵνα τάχιον ἀποκατασταθῶ ὑμῖν.
to do, in or- sooner I may be restored to you.
der that

20 Ὁ δὲ θεὸς τῆς εἰρήνης, ὁ ἀναγαγὼν
Now the God – of peace, the having led up
[one]

ἐκ νεκρῶν τὸν ποιμένα τῶν προβάτων
out [the] dead the ²shepherd ³of the ⁴sheep
of

* In the future.

894　　　　　　JAMES 1

by the blood of the eternal covenant, ²¹equip you with everything good that you may do his will, working in you* that which is pleasing in his sight, through Jesus Christ; to whom be glory for ever and ever. Amen.
22 I appeal to you, brethren, bear with my word of exhortation, for I have written to you briefly. ²³You should understand that our brother Timothy has been released, with whom I shall see you if he comes soon. ²⁴Greet all your leaders and all the saints. Those who come from Italy send you greetings. ²⁵Grace be with all of you. Amen.

τὸν μέγαν ἐν αἵματι διαθήκης αἰωνίου,
the ¹great in(? with) blood ²covenant ¹of an eternal,
τὸν κύριον ἡμῶν Ἰησοῦν, 21 καταρτίσαι
the Lord of us Jesus, may he adjust
ὑμᾶς ἐν παντὶ ἀγαθῷ εἰς τὸ ποιῆσαι
you in every good thing for the to do
τὸ θέλημα αὐτοῦ, ποιῶν ἐν ἡμῖν τὸ
the will of him, doing in us the [thing]
εὐάρεστον ἐνώπιον αὐτοῦ διὰ Ἰησοῦ
wellpleasing before him through Jesus
Χριστοῦ, ᾧ ἡ δόξα εἰς τοὺς αἰῶνας
Christ, to [be] glory unto the ages
whom the
τῶν αἰώνων· ἀμήν. 22 Παρακαλῶ δὲ
of the ages: Amen. And I beseech
ὑμᾶς, ἀδελφοί, ἀνέχεσθε τοῦ λόγου τῆς
you. brothers, endure the word –
παρακλήσεως· καὶ γὰρ διὰ βραχέων
of beseeching; for indeed through few [words]
ἐπέστειλα ὑμῖν. 23 Γινώσκετε τὸν ἀδελφὸν
I wrote to you. Know ye the brother
ἡμῶν Τιμόθεον ἀπολελυμένον, μεθ’ οὗ
of us Timothy having been released, with whom
ἐὰν τάχιον ἔρχηται ὄψομαι ὑμᾶς.
if sooner I come I will see you.
24 Ἀσπάσασθε πάντας τοὺς ἡγουμένους
Greet ye all the [ones] leading
ὑμῶν καὶ πάντας τοὺς ἁγίους. Ἀσπάζονται
of you and all the saints. ⁴greet
ὑμᾶς οἱ ἀπὸ τῆς Ἰταλίας.
⁵you ¹The [ones] ²from – ³Italy.
25 Ἡ χάρις μετὰ πάντων ὑμῶν.
– Grace [be] with all you.

JAMES 1
CHAPTER 1

JAMES, a servant of God and of the Lord Jesus Christ, To the twelve tribes in the Dispersion: Greeting.

* Other ancient authorities read us

ΙΑΚΩΒΟΥ ΕΠΙΣΤΟΛΗ
²Of James ¹Epistle

1 Ἰάκωβος θεοῦ καὶ κυρίου Ἰησοῦ
James ²of God ³and ⁴of [the] Lord ⁵Jesus
Χριστοῦ δοῦλος ταῖς δώδεκα φυλαῖς ταῖς
⁶Christ ¹a slave to the twelve tribes –
ἐν τῇ διασπορᾷ χαίρειν.
in the dispersion greeting.*

* See note on Phil. 3.16 in Introduction.

2 Count it all joy, my brethren, when you meet various trials, ³for you know that the testing of your faith produces steadfastness. ⁴And let steadfastness have its full effect, that you may be perfect and complete, lacking in nothing.

5 If any of you lacks wisdom, let him ask God, who gives to all men generously and without reproaching, and it will be given him. ⁶But let him ask in faith, with no doubting, for he who doubts is like a wave of the sea that is driven and tossed by the wind. ⁷,⁸For that person must not suppose that a double-minded man, unstable in all his ways, will receive anything from the Lord.

9 Let the lowly brother boast in his exaltation, ¹⁰and the rich in his humiliation, because like the flower of the grass he will pass away. ¹¹For the sun rises with its scorching heat and withers the grass; its flower falls, and its beauty perishes.

2 Πᾶσαν χαρὰν ἡγήσασθε, ἀδελφοί μου,
All joy deem [it], brothers of me,

ὅταν πειρασμοῖς περιπέσητε ποικίλοις,
whenever ³trials ¹ye fall ²into various,

3 γινώσκοντες ὅτι τὸ δοκίμιον ὑμῶν τῆς
knowing that the approved part ³of you ¹of the
=that which is approved in your faith

πίστεως κατεργάζεται ὑπομονήν. 4 ἡ δὲ
²faith works endurance. – And

ὑπομονὴ ἔργον τέλειον ἐχέτω, ἵνα ἦτε
endurance ³work ²perfect ¹let it in or- ye may
have, der that be

τέλειοι καὶ ὁλόκληροι, ἐν μηδενὶ λειπόμενοι.
perfect and entire, in nothing wanting.

5 Εἰ δέ τις ὑμῶν λείπεται σοφίας, αἰτείτω
if But any- of you wants wisdom, let him
one ask

παρὰ τοῦ διδόντος θεοῦ πᾶσιν ἁπλῶς
from ²the ³giving ¹God to all unre-
[one] servedly

καὶ μὴ ὀνειδίζοντος, καὶ δοθήσεται αὐτῷ.
and not reproaching, and it will be given to him.

6 αἰτείτω δὲ ἐν πίστει, μηδὲν διακριν-
But let him ask in faith, nothing doubt-

όμενος· ὁ γὰρ διακρινόμενος ἔοικεν κλύδωνι
ing; for the [one] doubting is like a wave

θαλάσσης ἀνεμιζομένῳ καὶ ῥιπιζομένῳ.
of [the] sea being driven by wind and being tossed.

7 μὴ γὰρ οἰέσθω ὁ ἄνθρωπος ἐκεῖνος
For let not ³suppose ¹that ²man

ὅτι λήμψεταί τι παρὰ τοῦ κυρίου, 8 ἀνὴρ
that he will any- from the Lord, a man
receive thing

δίψυχος, ἀκατάστατος ἐν πάσαις ταῖς
two-souled, unsettled in all the

ὁδοῖς αὐτοῦ. 9 Καυχάσθω δὲ ὁ ἀδελφὸς
ways of him. But let ⁴boast ¹the ³brother

ὁ ταπεινὸς ἐν τῷ ὕψει αὐτοῦ, 10 ὁ δὲ
– ²humble in the height of him, and the

πλούσιος ἐν τῇ ταπεινώσει αὐτοῦ, ὅτι
rich one in the humiliation of him, because

ὡς ἄνθος χόρτου παρελεύσεται. 11 ἀνέτειλεν
as a flower of grass he will pass away. ⁴rose

γὰρ ὁ ἥλιος σὺν τῷ καύσωνι καὶ ἐξήρανεν
¹For ²the ³sun with the hot wind and dried

τὸν χόρτον, καὶ τὸ ἄνθος αὐτοῦ ἐξέπεσεν
the grass, and the flower of it fell out

καὶ ἡ εὐπρέπεια τοῦ προσώπου αὐτοῦ
and the comeliness of the appearance of it

So will the rich man fade away in the midst of his pursuits. 12 Blessed is the man who endures trial, for when he has stood the test he will receive the crown of life which God has promised to those who love him. ¹³ Let no one say when he is tempted, "I am tempted by God"; for God cannot be tempted with evil and he himself tempts no one; ¹⁴ but each person is tempted when he is lured and enticed by his own desire. ¹⁵ Then desire when it has conceived gives birth to sin; and sin when it is full-grown brings forth death. 16 Do not be deceived, my beloved brethren. ¹⁷ Every good endowment and every perfect gift is from above, coming down from the Father of lights with whom there is no variation or shadow due to change.ᵃ ¹⁸ Of his own will he brought us forth by the word of truth that we should be a kind of first fruits of his creatures.

19 Know this, my beloved brethren. Let

ἀπώλετο·   οὕτως   καὶ   ὁ   πλούσιος   ἐν   ταῖς
perished;   thus   also   the   rich man   in   the

πορείαις   αὐτοῦ   μαρανθήσεται.   12 Μακάριος
goings   of him   will fade away.   Blessed

ἀνὴρ   ὃς   ὑπομένει   πειρασμόν,   ὅτι   δόκιμος
[the]   who   endures   trial,   because   ²approved
man

γενόμενος   λήμψεται   τὸν   στέφανον   τῆς
¹having become   he will receive   the   crown   –

ζωῆς,   ὃν   ἐπηγγείλατο   τοῖς   ἀγαπῶσιν   αὐτόν.
of life,   which   he promised   to the [ones] loving   him.

13 Μηδεὶς   πειραζόμενος   λεγέτω   ὅτι   ἀπὸ
²no man   ³being tempted   ¹Let ⁴say[,]   –   From

θεοῦ   πειράζομαι·   ὁ   γὰρ   θεὸς   ἀπείραστός
God   I am tempted;   –   for   God   ²untempted

ἐστιν   κακῶν,   πειράζει   δὲ   αὐτὸς   οὐδένα.
¹is   of(with)   and ²tempts   ¹he   no man.
evil things,

14 ἕκαστος   δὲ   πειράζεται   ὑπὸ   τῆς   ἰδίας
But each man   is tempted   by   the(his)   own

ἐπιθυμίας   ἐξελκόμενος   καὶ   δελεαζόμενος·
lusts   being drawn out   and   being enticed;

15 εἶτα   ἡ   ἐπιθυμία   συλλαβοῦσα   τίκτει
then   –   lust   having conceived   bears

ἁμαρτίαν,   ἡ   δὲ   ἁμαρτία   ἀποτελεσθεῖσα
sin,   –   and   sin   having been
                                         fully formed

ἀποκύει   θάνατον.   16 Μὴ   πλανᾶσθε,   ἀδελφοί
brings forth   death.   Do not err,   ²brothers

μου   ἀγαπητοί.
²of me   ¹beloved.

17 Πᾶσα   δόσις   ἀγαθὴ   καὶ   πᾶν   δώρημα
Every   ²giving   ¹good   and   every   ²gift

τέλειον   ἄνωθέν   ἐστιν   καταβαῖνον   ἀπὸ   τοῦ
¹perfect   ⁴from above   ²is   coming down   from   the

πατρὸς   τῶν   φώτων,   παρ'   ᾧ   οὐκ   ἔνι
Father   of the   lights,   with   whom   ⁵has no place

παραλλαγὴ   ἢ   τροπῆς   ἀποσκίασμα.   18 βου-
¹change   ²or   ⁴of turning   ³shadow.   Having

ληθεὶς   ἀπεκύησεν   ἡμᾶς   λόγῳ   ἀληθείας,
purposed   he brought forth   us   by a word   of truth,

εἰς   τὸ   εἶναι   ἡμᾶς   ἀπαρχήν   τινα   τῶν
for   the   to be   usᵇ   ²firstfruit   ¹a certain   ²of
=that we should be   the

αὐτοῦ   κτισμάτων.
ᵇof him   ⁴creatures.

19 Ἴστε,   ἀδελφοί   μου   ἀγαπητοί.   ἔστω
Know ye,   ²brothers   ³of me   ¹beloved.   ²let be

every man be quick to hear, slow to speak, slow to anger, [20] for the anger of man does not work the righteousness of God. [21] Therefore put away all filthiness and rank growth of wickedness and receive with meekness the implanted word, which is able to save your souls.

22 But be doers of the word, and not hearers only, deceiving yourselves. [23] For if any one is a hearer of the word and not a doer, he is like a man who observes his natural face in a mirror; [24] for he observes himself and goes away and at once forgets what he was like. [25] But he who looks into the perfect law, the law of liberty, and perseveres, being no hearer that forgets but a doer that acts, he shall be blessed in his doing.

26 If any one thinks he is religious, and does not bridle his tongue but deceives his heart, this man's religion is vain. [27] Religion that is pure and undefiled before God

δὲ πᾶς ἄνθρωπος ταχὺς εἰς τὸ ἀκοῦσαι,
[1]But every man swift for the to hear,

βραδὺς εἰς τὸ λαλῆσαι, βραδὺς εἰς ὀργήν·
slow for the to speak, slow to wrath;

20 ὀργὴ γὰρ ἀνδρὸς δικαιοσύνην θεοῦ
for [the] wrath of a man [5][the] righteousness [5]of God

οὐκ ἐργάζεται. 21 διὸ ἀποθέμενοι πᾶσαν
[1]works not. Wherefore putting away all

ῥυπαρίαν καὶ περισσείαν κακίας ἐν πραΰ-
filthiness and superfluity of evil in meek-

τητι δέξασθε τὸν ἔμφυτον λόγον τὸν
ness receive ye the implanted word –

δυνάμενον σῶσαι τὰς ψυχὰς ὑμῶν. 22 γίν-
being able to save the souls of you. be-

εσθε δὲ ποιηταὶ λόγου, καὶ μὴ ἀκροαταὶ
come ye And doers of [the] word, and not hearers

μόνον παραλογιζόμενοι ἑαυτούς. 23 ὅτι
only misleading yourselves. Because

εἴ τις ἀκροατὴς λόγου ἐστὶν καὶ οὐ
if anyone [2]a hearer [3]of [the] word [1]is and not

ποιητής, οὗτος ἔοικεν ἀνδρὶ κατανοοῦντι
a doer, this one is like a man perceiving

τὸ πρόσωπον τῆς γενέσεως αὐτοῦ ἐν
the face of the birth of him in

ἐσόπτρῳ· 24 κατενόησεν γὰρ ἑαυτὸν καὶ
a mirror; for he perceived himself and

ἀπελήλυθεν, καὶ εὐθέως ἐπελάθετο ὁποῖος
has gone away, and straightway forgot what sort

ἦν. 25 ὁ δὲ παρακύψας εἰς νόμον
he was. But the [one] having looked into into [3]law

τέλειον τὸν τῆς ἐλευθερίας καὶ παραμείνας,
[2]perfect [1]the – of freedom and remaining,

οὐκ ἀκροατὴς ἐπιλησμονῆς γενόμενος ἀλλὰ
not [2]a hearer [3]of forgetfulness* [1]becoming but

ποιητὴς ἔργου, οὗτος μακάριος ἐν τῇ
a doer of [the] work, this one [2]blessed [3]in [4]the

ποιήσει αὐτοῦ ἔσται. 26 Εἴ τις δοκεῖ
[5]doing [6]of him [1]will be. If anyone thinks

θρησκὸς εἶναι, μὴ χαλιναγωγῶν γλῶσσαν
[2]religious [1]to be, not bridling tongue

ἑαυτοῦ ἀλλὰ ἀπατῶν καρδίαν ἑαυτοῦ,
of himself but deceiving heart of himself,

τούτου μάταιος ἡ θρησκεία. 27 θρησκεία
of this one vain the religion. Religion

καθαρὰ καὶ ἀμίαντος παρὰ τῷ θεῷ
clean and undefiled before the God

* Genitive of quality: " a forgetful hearer."

and the Father is this: to visit orphans and widows in their affliction, and to keep oneself unstained from the world.

καὶ   πατρὶ   αὕτη   ἐστίν,   ἐπισκέπτεσθαι
and   Father   ²this   ¹is,   to visit

ὀρφανοὺς   καὶ   χήρας   ἐν   τῇ   θλίψει   αὐτῶν,
orphans   and   widows   in   the   affliction   of them,

ἄσπιλον   ἑαυτὸν   τηρεῖν   ἀπὸ   τοῦ   κόσμου.
unspotted   himself   to keep   from   the   world.

CHAPTER 2

MY brethren, show no partiality as you hold the faith of our Lord Jesus Christ, the Lord of glory. ²For if a man with gold rings and in fine clothing comes into your assembly, and a poor man in shabby clothing also comes in, ³and you pay attention to the one who wears the fine clothing and say, "Have a seat here, please," while you say to the poor man, "Stand there," or, "Sit at my feet," ⁴have you not made distinctions among yourselves, and become judges with evil thoughts? ⁵Listen, my beloved brethren. Has not God chosen those who are poor in the world to be rich in faith and heirs of the kingdom which he has promised to those who love him? ⁶But you have dishonored the poor man. Is it not the rich who oppress you, is it not they who drag you into court? ⁷Is it not

2 Ἀδελφοί   μου,   μὴ   ἐν   προσωπολημψίαις
   Brothers   of me,   not   in   respects of persons

ἔχετε   τὴν   πίστιν   τοῦ   κυρίου   ἡμῶν   Ἰησοῦ
have ye   the   faith   of the   Lord   of us   Jesus

Χριστοῦ   τῆς   δόξης.   2 ἐὰν   γὰρ   εἰσέλθῃ
Christ[,]   of the   glory.*   For if   [there] enters

εἰς   συναγωγὴν   ὑμῶν   ἀνὴρ   χρυσοδακτύλιος
into   a synagogue   of you   a man   gold-fingered

ἐν   ἐσθῆτι   λαμπρᾷ,   εἰσέλθῃ   δὲ   καὶ   πτωχὸς
in   ²clothing   ¹splendid,   and [there] enters   also a poor man

ἐν   ῥυπαρᾷ   ἐσθῆτι,   3 ἐπιβλέψητε   δὲ   ἐπὶ
in   shabby   clothing,   and ye look on   on

τὸν   φοροῦντα   τὴν   ἐσθῆτα   τὴν   λαμπρὰν
the [one] wearing   the   clothing   -   splendid

καὶ   εἴπητε·   σὺ   κάθου   ὧδε   καλῶς,   καὶ
and   say: ²thou   ¹Sit   here   well,   and

τῷ   πτωχῷ   εἴπητε·   σὺ   στῆθι   ἐκεῖ   ἢ
to the   poor man   ye say: ²thou   ¹Stand   there   or

κάθου   ὑπὸ   τὸ   ὑποπόδιόν   μου,   4 οὐ
sit   under   the   footstool   of me,   not

διεκρίθητε   ἐν   ἑαυτοῖς   καὶ   ἐγένεσθε   κριταὶ
did ye dis-   among yourselves   and   became   judges
criminate

διαλογισμῶν   πονηρῶν;   5 Ἀκούσατε,   ἀδελφοί
²thoughts   ¹of evil ?§   Hear ye,   brothers

μου   ἀγαπητοί.   οὐχ   ὁ   θεὸς   ἐξελέξατο
of me   beloved.   ²not   -   ³God   ¹Chose

τοὺς   πτωχοὺς   τῷ   κόσμῳ   πλουσίους   ἐν
the   poor   in the   world   rich   in

πίστει   καὶ   κληρονόμους   τῆς   βασιλείας
faith   and   heirs   of the   kingdom

ἧς   ἐπηγγείλατο   τοῖς   ἀγαπῶσιν   αὐτόν;
which   he promised   to the [ones]   loving   him?

6 ὑμεῖς   δὲ   ἠτιμάσατε   τὸν   πτωχόν.   οὐχ
But ye   dishonoured   the   poor man. [Do] not

οἱ   πλούσιοι   καταδυναστεύουσιν   ὑμῶν,   καὶ
the   rich men   oppress   you,   and

αὐτοὶ   ἕλκουσιν   ὑμᾶς   εἰς   κριτήρια;   7 οὐκ
they   drag   you   to   tribunals ?   [Do] not

* That is, taking "the glory" as in apposition to "Jesus Christ"; see Luke 2. 32b.

§ Genitive of quality: "evil-thinking judges."

they who blaspheme that honorable name by which you are called? 8 If you really fulfil the royal law, according to the scripture, "You shall love your neighbor as yourself," you do well. 9 But if you show partiality, you commit sin, and are convicted by the law as transgressors. 10 For whoever keeps the whole law but fails in one point has become guilty of all of it. 11 For he who said, "Do not commit adultery," said also, "Do not kill." If you do not commit adultery but do kill, you have become a transgressor of the law. 12 So speak and so act as those who are to be judged under the law of liberty. 13 For judgment is without mercy to one who has shown no mercy; yet mercy triumphs over judgment.

14 What does it profit, my brethren, if a man says he has faith but has not works? Can his faith save him? 15 If a brother or sister is ill-clad and in lack of daily food, 16 and one of you says to them, "Go in

αὐτοὶ βλασφημοῦσιν τὸ καλὸν ὄνομα τὸ
they blaspheme the good name –

ἐπικληθὲν ἐφ᾽ ὑμᾶς; 8 εἰ μέντοι νόμον
called on on you? If indeed ³law

τελεῖτε βασιλικὸν κατὰ τὴν γραφήν·
¹ye fulfil ²a royal according to the scripture:

ἀγαπήσεις τὸν πλησίον σου ὡς σεαυτόν,
Thou shalt love the neighbour of thee as thyself,

καλῶς ποιεῖτε· 9 εἰ δὲ προσωπολημπτεῖτε,
²well ¹ye do; but if ye respect persons,

ἁμαρτίαν ἐργάζεσθε, ἐλεγχόμενοι ὑπὸ τοῦ
²sin ¹ye work, being reproved by the

νόμου ὡς παραβάται. 10 ὅστις γὰρ
law as transgressors. For ¹[he] who

ὅλον τὸν νόμον τηρήσῃ, πταίσῃ δὲ ἐν
³all ⁴the ⁵law ²keeps, yet stumbles in

ἑνί, γέγονεν πάντων ἔνοχος. 11 ὁ γὰρ
one thing, he has ²of all ¹guilty. For the
become [one]

εἰπών· μὴ μοιχεύσῃς, εἶπεν καὶ· μὴ
saying: Do not commit adultery, said also: not

φονεύσῃς· εἰ δὲ οὐ μοιχεύεις, φονεύεις
Do murder; now if thou dost not ¹murderest
commit adultery,

δέ, γέγονας παραβάτης νόμου. 12 οὕτως
¹but, thou hast a transgressor of [the] So
become law.

λαλεῖτε καὶ οὕτως ποιεῖτε ὡς διὰ νόμου
speak ye and so do ye as ³through ⁴a law

ἐλευθερίας μέλλοντες κρίνεσθαι. 13 ἡ γὰρ
⁵of freedom ¹being about ²to be judged. For the

κρίσις ἀνέλεος τῷ μὴ ποιήσαντι ἔλεος·
judg- [will unmerci- to the not do(show)ing mercy;
ment be] ful [one]

κατακαυχᾶται ἔλεος κρίσεως. 14 Τί τὸ
²exults over ¹mercy of judgment. What [is] the

ὄφελος, ἀδελφοί μου, ἐὰν πίστιν λέγῃ
profit, brothers of me, if ⁴faith ²says

τις ἔχειν ἔργα δὲ μὴ ἔχῃ; μὴ δύναται
¹any- ³to have ⁸works ⁵but ⁷not ⁶has? not can
one

ἡ πίστις σῶσαι αὐτόν; 15 ἐὰν ἀδελφὸς
the faith to save him? If a brother

ἢ ἀδελφὴ γυμνοὶ ὑπάρχωσιν καὶ λειπόμενοι
or a sister ²naked ¹are and lacking

τῆς ἐφημέρου τροφῆς, 16 εἴπῃ δέ τις
of the daily food, and ⁴says ¹anyone

αὐτοῖς ἐξ ὑμῶν· ὑπάγετε ἐν εἰρήνῃ,
⁵to them ²of ³you: Go ye in peace,

peace, be warmed and filled," without giving them the things needed for the body, what does it profit? ¹⁷So faith by itself, if it has no works, is dead.

18 But some one will say, "You have faith and I have works." Show me your faith apart from your works, and I by my works will show you my faith. ¹⁹You believe that God is one; you do well. Even the demons believe —and shudder. ²⁰Do you want to be shown, you foolish fellow, that faith apart from works is barren? ²¹Was not Abraham our father justified by works, when he offered his son Isaac upon the altar? ²²You see that faith was active along with his works, and faith was completed by works, ²³and the scripture was fulfilled which says, "Abraham believed God, and it was reckoned to him as righteousness"; and he was called the friend of God. ²⁴You see that a man is justified by works and not by faith alone. ²⁵And in the same way

θερμαίνεσθε καὶ χορτάζεσθε, μὴ δῶτε
be warmed   and   filled,   ⁴not   ³ye give

δὲ αὐτοῖς τὰ ἐπιτήδεια τοῦ σώματος,
¹but ²them   the   necessaries   of the   body,

τί τὸ ὄφελος; 17 οὕτως καὶ ἡ πίστις,
what [is] the profit?   17   So   indeed - faith.

ἐὰν μὴ ἔχῃ ἔργα, νεκρά ἐστιν καθ᾽
if it has not works, ²dead ¹is   by

ἑαυτήν. 18 ἀλλ᾽ ἐρεῖ τις· σὺ πίστιν
itself.   18   But ²will say ¹someone: Thou ²faith

ἔχεις, κἀγὼ ἔργα ἔχω· δεῖξόν μοι τὴν
¹hast, and I ²works ¹have;   show   me   the

πίστιν σου χωρὶς τῶν ἔργων, κἀγώ
faith of thee without the   works,   and I

σοι δείξω ἐκ τῶν ἔργων μου τὴν πίστιν.
thee will show ⁴by ⁵the ⁶works ³of me ¹the ²faith.

19 σὺ πιστεύεις ὅτι εἷς ἐστιν ὁ θεός;
Thou believest that ³one ²is - ¹God?

καλῶς ποιεῖς· καὶ τὰ δαιμόνια πιστεύουσιν
²well ¹thou doest; also the demons believe

καὶ φρίσσουσιν. 20 θέλεις δὲ γνῶναι,
and shudder.   20 But art thou willing to know,

ὦ ἄνθρωπε κενέ, ὅτι ἡ πίστις χωρὶς
O ²man ¹vain, that - faith without

τῶν ἔργων ἀργή ἐστιν; 21 Ἀβραὰμ ὁ
- works barren is?   21   Abraham the

πατὴρ ἡμῶν οὐκ ἐξ ἔργων ἐδικαιώθη,
father of us not by works was justified,

ἀνενέγκας Ἰσαὰκ τὸν υἱὸν αὐτοῦ ἐπὶ
offering up Isaac the son of him on

τὸ θυσιαστήριον; 22 βλέπεις ὅτι ἡ πίστις
the altar?   22 Thou seest that - faith

συνήργει τοῖς ἔργοις αὐτοῦ, καὶ ἐκ
worked with the works of him, and by

τῶν ἔργων ἡ πίστις ἐτελειώθη, 23 καὶ
the works the faith was perfected, 23 and

ἐπληρώθη ἡ γραφὴ ἡ λέγουσα· ἐπίστευσεν
was fulfilled the scripture - saying: believed

δὲ Ἀβραὰμ τῷ θεῷ, καὶ ἐλογίσθη αὐτῷ
And Abraham - God, and it was reckoned to him

εἰς δικαιοσύνην, καὶ φίλος θεοῦ ἐκλήθη.
for righteousness, and ²friend ³of God ¹he was
called.

24 ὁρᾶτε ὅτι ἐξ ἔργων δικαιοῦται ἄνθρωπος
Ye see that by works ²is justified ¹a man

καὶ οὐκ ἐκ πίστεως μόνον. 25 ὁμοίως
and not by faith only.   25 likewise

was not also Rahab the harlot justified by works when she received the messengers and sent them out another way? [26] For as the body apart from the spirit is dead, so faith apart from works is dead.

δὲ καὶ 'Ραὰβ ἡ πόρνη οὐκ ἐξ ἔργων
And also Rahab the prostitute not by works

ἐδικαιώθη, ὑποδεξαμένη τοὺς ἀγγέλους καὶ
was justified, entertaining the messengers and

ἑτέρᾳ ὁδῷ ἐκβαλοῦσα; 26 ὥσπερ γὰρ τὸ
by a way sending [them] For as the
different forth?

σῶμα χωρὶς πνεύματος νεκρόν ἐστιν, οὕτως
body without spirit ²dead ¹is, so

καὶ ἡ πίστις χωρὶς ἔργων νεκρά ἐστιν.
also – faith without works ²dead ¹is.

CHAPTER 3

L ET not many of you become teachers, my brethren, for you know that we who teach shall be judged with greater strictness. ²For we all make many mistakes, and if any one makes no mistakes in what he says he is a perfect man, able to bridle the whole body also. ³If we put bits into the mouths of horses that they may obey us, we guide their whole bodies. ⁴Look at the ships also; though they are so great and are driven by strong winds, they are guided by a very small rudder wherever the will of the pilot directs. ⁵So the tongue is a little member and boasts of great things. How great a forest is set ablaze by a small fire!

6 And the tongue is a fire. The tongue is an unrighteous world among our members, staining

3 Μὴ πολλοὶ διδάσκαλοι γίνεσθε, ἀδελφοί
²not ³many ⁴teachers ¹Become ye, brothers

μου, εἰδότες ὅτι μεῖζον κρίμα λημψόμεθα.
of me, knowing that greater judgment we shall receive.

2 πολλὰ γὰρ πταίομεν ἅπαντες· εἴ τις
For [in] many [respects] we stumble all; if anyone

ἐν λόγῳ οὐ πταίει, οὗτος τέλειος ἀνήρ,
²in ³word ¹stumbles not, this [is] a perfect man,

δυνατὸς χαλιναγωγῆσαι καὶ ὅλον τὸ σῶμα.
able ²to bridle ¹indeed all the body.

3 εἰ δὲ τῶν ἵππων τοὺς χαλινοὺς εἰς
Now if – ⁶of horses – ²bridles ³into

τὰ στόματα βάλλομεν εἰς τὸ πείθεσθαι
⁴the ⁵mouths ¹we put for the to obey
=to make them obey us,

αὐτοὺς ἡμῖν, καὶ ὅλον τὸ σῶμα αὐτῶν
them⁵ to us, and ²all ¹the ³body ⁴of them

μετάγομεν. 4 ἰδοὺ καὶ τὰ πλοῖα, τηλικαῦτα
¹we direct. Behold also the ships, ²so great

ὄντα καὶ ὑπὸ ἀνέμων σκληρῶν ἐλαυνόμενα,
¹being ²and ⁵by ⁷winds ⁶hard(strong) ⁴being driven,

μετάγεται ὑπὸ ἐλαχίστου πηδαλίου ὅπου
is(are) directed by a very little helm where

ἡ ὁρμὴ τοῦ εὐθύνοντος βούλεται· 5 οὕτως
the impulse of the [one] steering resolves; so

καὶ ἡ γλῶσσα μικρὸν μέλος ἐστὶν καὶ
also the tongue ²a little ³member ¹is and

μεγάλα αὐχεῖ. ἰδοὺ ἡλίκον πῦρ ἡλίκον
great things boasts. Behold how little a fire ²how great

ὕλην ἀνάπτει· 6 καὶ ἡ γλῶσσα πῦρ,
³wood ¹kindles; and the tongue [is] a fire,

ὁ κόσμος τῆς ἀδικίας, ἡ γλῶσσα καθίστα-
the world – of iniquity, the tongue is

ται ἐν τοῖς μέλεσιν ἡμῶν, ἡ σπιλοῦσα
set among the members of us, – spotting

the whole body, setting on fire the cycle of nature,[b] and set on fire by hell. [7]For every kind of beast and bird, of reptile and sea creature, can be tamed and has been tamed by humankind, [8]but no human being can tame the tongue—a restless evil, full of deadly poison. [9]With it we bless the Lord and Father, and with it we curse men, who are made in the likeness of God. [10]From the same mouth come blessing and cursing. My brethren, this ought not to be so. [11]Does a spring pour forth from the same opening fresh water and brackish? [12]Can a fig tree, my brethren, yield olives, or a grapevine figs? No more can salt water yield fresh.

13 Who is wise and understanding among you? By his good life let him show his works in the meekness of wisdom. [14]But if you have bitter jealousy and selfish ambition in your hearts, do

ὅλον　τὸ　σῶμα　καὶ　φλογίζουσα　τὸν
all　the　body　and　inflaming　the

τροχὸν　τῆς　γενέσεως　καὶ　φλογιζομένη
course　-　of nature　and　being inflamed

ὑπὸ　τῆς　γεέννης.　7 πᾶσα　γὰρ　φύσις
by　-　gehenna.　For every　nature

θηρίων　τε　καὶ　πετεινῶν,　ἑρπετῶν　τε
²of beasts　¹both　and　of birds,　²of reptiles　¹both

καὶ　ἐναλίων　δαμάζεται　καὶ　δεδάμασται
and　of marine creatures　is tamed　and　has been tamed

τῇ　φύσει　τῇ　ἀνθρωπίνῃ,　8 τὴν　δὲ
by the　²nature　-　¹human,　　but the

γλῶσσαν　οὐδεὶς　δαμάσαι　δύναται　ἀνθρώπων·
tongue　¹no one　⁴to tame　³is able　²of men;

ἀκατάστατον　κακόν,　μεστὴ　ἰοῦ　θανατηφόρου.
an unruly　evil,　full　²poison　¹of death-dealing.

9 ἐν　αὐτῇ　εὐλογοῦμεν　τὸν　κύριον　καὶ
By　this　we bless　the　Lord　and

πατέρα,　καὶ　ἐν　αὐτῇ　καταρώμεθα　τοὺς
Father,　and　by　this　we curse　-

ἀνθρώπους　τοὺς　καθ᾽　ὁμοίωσιν　θεοῦ
men　-　²according to　³likeness　⁴of God

γεγονότας·　10 ἐκ　τοῦ　αὐτοῦ　στόματος　ἐξέρχεται
¹having become;　out of the　same　mouth　comes forth

εὐλογία　καὶ　κατάρα.　οὐ　χρή,　ἀδελφοί
blessing　and　cursing.　It is not fitting,　brothers

μου,　ταῦτα　οὕτως　γίνεσθαι.　11 μήτι
of me,　these things　so　to be.　　Not

ἡ　πηγὴ　ἐκ　τῆς　αὐτῆς　ὀπῆς　βρύει　τὸ
the fountain　out of the　same　hole　sends forth the

γλυκὺ　καὶ　τὸ　πικρόν;　12 μὴ　δύναται,
sweet　and　the　bitter ?　　Not　can,

ἀδελφοί　μου,　συκῆ　ἐλαίας　ποιῆσαι　ἢ
brothers　of me,　a fig-tree　²olives　¹to produce　or

ἄμπελος　σῦκα;　οὔτε　ἁλυκὸν　γλυκὺ
a vine　figs ?　neither　¹salt　⁴sweet

ποιῆσαι　ὕδωρ.　13 Τίς　σοφὸς　καὶ　ἐπιστήμων
³to make　¹water.　Who [is] wise　and　knowing

ἐν　ὑμῖν;　δειξάτω　ἐκ　τῆς　καλῆς　ἀναστροφῆς
among you ?　let him show　by the(his) good　conduct

τὰ　ἔργα　αὐτοῦ　ἐν　πραΰτητι　σοφίας.*
the　works　of him　in　meekness　of wisdom.*

14 εἰ　δὲ　ζῆλον　πικρὸν　ἔχετε　καὶ　ἐριθείαν
But if　³jealousy　²bitter　¹ye have　and　rivalry

ἐν　τῇ　καρδίᾳ　ὑμῶν,　μὴ　κατακαυχᾶσθε
in　the　heart　of you,　do not exult over

[b] Or wheel of birth

* Genitive of quality : " a wise meekness."

not boast and be false to the truth. ¹⁵ This wisdom is not such as comes down from above, but is earthly, unspiritual, devilish. ¹⁶ For where jealousy and selfish ambition exist, there will be disorder and every vile practice. ¹⁷ But the wisdom from above is first pure, then peaceable, gentle, open to reason, full of mercy and good fruits, without uncertainty or insincerity. ¹⁸ And the harvest of righteousness is sown in peace by those who make peace.

καὶ ψεύδεσθε κατὰ τῆς ἀληθείας.   15 οὐκ
and   lie   against the   truth.   ⁴not

ἔστιν αὕτη ἡ σοφία ἄνωθεν κατερχομένη,
³is   ¹This – ²wisdom ⁶from above ⁵coming down,

ἀλλὰ ἐπίγειος, ψυχική, δαιμονιώδης· 16 ὅπου
but [is] earthly, natural, demon-like;   ²where

γὰρ ζῆλος καὶ ἐριθεία, ἐκεῖ ἀκαταστασία
¹for jealousy and rivalry [are], there [is] tumult

καὶ πᾶν φαῦλον πρᾶγμα.   17 ἡ δὲ ἄνωθεν
and every worthless practice.   But ¹the   ²from
                                                        above

σοφία πρῶτον μὲν ἁγνή ἐστιν, ἔπειτα
²wisdom ⁵firstly   –   ⁶pure   ⁴is.   then

εἰρηνική, ἐπιεικής, εὐπειθής, μεστὴ ἐλέους
peaceable, forbearing, compliant,   full   of mercy

καὶ καρπῶν ἀγαθῶν, ἀδιάκριτος, ἀνυπό-
and   ²fruits ¹of good, without uncertainty,   un-

κριτος.   18 καρπὸς δὲ δικαιοσύνης ἐν
feigned.   And [the] fruit of righteousness   ²in

εἰρήνῃ σπείρεται τοῖς ποιοῦσιν εἰρήνην.
³peace   ¹is sown for the [ones] making   peace.

CHAPTER 4

WHAT causes wars, and what causes fightings among you? Is it not your passions that are at war in your members? ² You desire and do not have; so you kill. And you covet[c] and cannot obtain; so you fight and wage war. You do not have, because you do not ask. ³ You ask and do not receive, because you ask wrongly, to spend it on your passions. ⁴ Unfaithful creatures! Do you not know that friendship with the world is enmity with God? Therefore who-

4 Πόθεν πόλεμοι καὶ πόθεν μάχαι ἐν
  Whence   wars   and whence fights among

ὑμῖν; οὐκ ἐντεῦθεν, ἐκ τῶν ἡδονῶν
you?   not   thence,   out of the   pleasures

ἡμῶν τῶν στρατευομένων ἐν τοῖς μέλεσιν
of you –   soldiering   in   the   members

ὑμῶν; 2 ἐπιθυμεῖτε, καὶ οὐκ ἔχετε·
of you?   Ye desire,   and have not;

φονεύετε καὶ ζηλοῦτε, καὶ οὐ δύνασθε
ye murder and are jealous, and are not able

ἐπιτυχεῖν· μάχεσθε καὶ πολεμεῖτε. οὐκ
to obtain;   ye fight   and   ye war.   not

ἔχετε διὰ τὸ μὴ αἰτεῖσθαι ὑμᾶς· 3 αἰτεῖτε
Ye have be- the not   to ask   you[b];   ye ask
       cause of
       = because ye ask not;

καὶ οὐ λαμβάνετε, διότι κακῶς αἰτεῖσθε,
and   receive not,   because ²ill   ¹ye ask,

ἵνα ἐν ταῖς ἡδοναῖς ὑμῶν δαπανήσητε.
in or- in the   pleasures of you ye may spend.
der that

4 μοιχαλίδες, οὐκ οἴδατε ὅτι ἡ φιλία
  Adulteresses, know ye not that the friendship

τοῦ κόσμου ἔχθρα τοῦ θεοῦ ἐστιν; ὃς
of the world   ²enmity   –   ²of God   ¹is? Who-

---

[c] Or you kill and you covet

ever wishes to be a friend of the world makes himself an enemy of God. [5]Or do you suppose it is in vain that the scripture says, "He yearns jealously over the spirit which he has made to dwell in us"? [6]But he gives more grace; therefore it says, "God opposes the proud, but gives grace to the humble." [7]Submit yourselves therefore to God. Resist the devil and he will flee from you. [8]Draw near to God and he will draw near to you. Cleanse your hands, you sinners, and purify your hearts, you men of double mind. [9]Be wretched and mourn and weep. Let your laughter be turned to mourning and your joy to dejection. [10]Humble yourselves before the Lord and he will exalt you.
[11] Do not speak evil against one another, brethren. He that speaks evil against a brother or judges his brother, speaks evil against the law and judges the law. But if you judge the law, you are not a doer of the law but a judge. [12]There is one lawgiver and judge, he who is able to save

ἐὰν οὖν βουληθῇ φίλος εἶναι τοῦ κόσμου,
ever therefore ¹resolves ³a friend ²to be of the world,

ἐχθρὸς τοῦ θεοῦ καθίσταται. 5 ἢ δοκεῖτε
²an enemy – ³of God ¹is constituted. Or think ye

ὅτι κενῶς ἡ γραφὴ λέγει· πρὸς φθόνον
that vainly the scripture says: ³to ⁴envy

ἐπιποθεῖ τὸ πνεῦμα ὃ κατῴκισεν ἐν
⁷yearns ¹The ²Spirit ³which ⁴dwelt ⁵in

ἡμῖν; 6 μείζονα δὲ δίδωσιν χάριν· διὸ
⁶you? But ²greater ¹he gives ²grace; wherefore

λέγει· ὁ θεὸς ὑπερηφάνοις ἀντιτάσσεται,
it* says: – God ²arrogant men ¹resists,

ταπεινοῖς δὲ δίδωσιν χάριν. 7 ὑποτάγητε
but to humble men he gives grace. Be ye subject

οὖν τῷ θεῷ· ἀντίστητε δὲ τῷ διαβόλῳ,
there- – to God; but oppose the devil,
fore

καὶ φεύξεται ἀφ᾽ ὑμῶν· 8 ἐγγίσατε τῷ
and he will flee from you; draw near –

θεῷ, καὶ ἐγγίσει ὑμῖν. καθαρίσατε
to God, and he will draw near to you. Cleanse ye

χεῖρας, ἁμαρτωλοί, καὶ ἁγνίσατε καρδίας,
hands, sinners, and purify hearts,

δίψυχοι. 9 ταλαιπωρήσατε καὶ πενθήσατε
two-souled Be ye distressed and mourn
(double-minded).

καὶ κλαύσατε· ὁ γέλως ὑμῶν εἰς πένθος
and weep; the laughter of you to mourning

μετατραπήτω καὶ ἡ χαρὰ εἰς κατήφειαν.
let it be turned and the joy to dejection.

10 ταπεινώθητε ἐνώπιον κυρίου, καὶ ὑψώσει
Be ye humbled before [the] Lord, and he will exalt

ὑμᾶς. 11 Μὴ καταλαλεῖτε ἀλλήλων, ἀδελφοί.
you. Speak not against one another, brothers.

ὁ καταλαλῶν ἀδελφοῦ ἢ κρίνων τὸν
The speaking a brother or judging the
[one] against

ἀδελφὸν αὐτοῦ καταλαλεῖ νόμου καὶ κρίνει
brother of him speaks against law and judges

νόμον· εἰ δὲ νόμον κρίνεις, οὐκ εἶ
law; and if law thou judgest, thou art not

ποιητὴς νόμου ἀλλὰ κριτής. 12 εἷς ἐστιν
a doer of law but a judge. One is

νομοθέτης καὶ κριτής, ὁ δυνάμενος
lawgiver and judge, the [one] being able

* That is, " the scripture " (as ver. 5).

and to destroy. But who are you that you judge your neighbor?

13 Come now, you who say, "Today or tomorrow we will go into such and such a town and spend a year there and trade and get gain"; 14 whereas you do not know about tomorrow. What is your life? For you are a mist that appears for a little time and then vanishes. 15 Instead you ought to say, "If the Lord wills, we shall live and we shall do this or that." 16 As it is, you boast in your arrogance. All such boasting is evil. 17 Whoever knows what is right to do and fails to do it, for him it is sin.

CHAPTER 5

COME now, you rich, weep and howl for the miseries that are coming upon you. 2 Your riches have rotted and your garments are motheaten. 3 Your gold and silver have rusted, and their rust will be evidence against you and will eat

σῶσαι καὶ ἀπολέσαι· σὺ δὲ τίς εἶ, ὁ
to save and to destroy; 'thou 'and 'who 'art, the
κρίνων τὸν πλησίον;
[one] judging the(thy) neighbour?

13 Ἄγε νῦν οἱ λέγοντες· σήμερον ἢ
Come now the [ones] saying: To-day or
αὔριον πορευσόμεθα εἰς τήνδε τὴν πόλιν
to-morrow we will go into this - city
καὶ ποιήσομεν ἐκεῖ ἐνιαυτὸν καὶ ἐμπορευ-
and we will do there a year and we will
σόμεθα καὶ κερδήσομεν· 14 οἵτινες οὐκ
trade and we will make a profit; who not
ἐπίστασθε τῆς αὔριον ποία ἡ ζωὴ ὑμῶν.
ye know 'of the 'morrow 'what 'the 'life 'of you
[will be].
ἀτμὶς γάρ ἐστε ἡ πρὸς ὀλίγον φαινομένη,
For 'a vapour 'ye are - 'for 'a little while 'appearing,
ἔπειτα καὶ ἀφανιζομένη· 15 ἀντὶ τοῦ
thereafter indeed disappearing; instead of the
λέγειν ὑμᾶς· ἐὰν ὁ κύριος θελήσῃ, καὶ
to say you[b]: If the Lord wills, both
=your saying:
ζήσομεν καὶ ποιήσομεν τοῦτο ἢ ἐκεῖνο.
we will live and we will do this or that.
16 νῦν δὲ καυχᾶσθε ἐν ταῖς ἀλαζονείαις
But now ye boast in the vauntings
ὑμῶν· πᾶσα καύχησις τοιαύτη πονηρά
of you; all 'boasting 'such 'evil
ἐστιν. 17 εἰδότι οὖν καλὸν ποιεῖν καὶ
'is. 'to [one] 'There-'good 'to do and
knowing' fore
μὴ ποιοῦντι, ἁμαρτία αὐτῷ ἐστιν.
not doing, 'sin 'to him 'it is.

5 Ἄγε νῦν οἱ πλούσιοι, κλαύσατε
Come now the rich men, weep ye
ὀλολύζοντες ἐπὶ ταῖς ταλαιπωρίαις ὑμῶν
crying aloud over the hardships of you
ταῖς ἐπερχομέναις. 2 ὁ πλοῦτος ὑμῶν
coming upon. The riches of you
σέσηπεν, καὶ τὰ ἱμάτια ὑμῶν σητόβρωτα
have become and the garments of you moth-eaten
corrupted,
γέγονεν, 3 ὁ χρυσὸς ὑμῶν καὶ ὁ ἄργυρος
have become, the gold of you and the silver
κατίωται, καὶ ὁ ἰὸς αὐτῶν εἰς μαρτύριον
has become and the poison of them for a testimony
rusted over,
ὑμῖν ἔσται καὶ φάγεται τὰς σάρκας
to(against) will and will eat the fleshes
you be

* See note on page xviii.

your flesh like fire. You have laid up treasure[d] for the last days. 4 Behold, the wages of the laborers who mowed your fields, which you kept back by fraud, cry out; and the cries of the harvesters have reached the ears of the Lord of hosts. 5 You have lived on the earth in luxury and in pleasure; you have fattened your hearts in a day of slaughter. 6 You have condemned, you have killed the righteous man; he does not resist you.

7 Be patient, therefore, brethren, until the coming of the Lord. Behold, the farmer waits for the precious fruit of the earth, being patient over it until it receives the early and the late rain. 8 You also be patient. Establish your hearts, for the coming of the Lord is at hand. 9 Do not grumble, brethren, against one another, that you may not be judged; behold, the Judge is standing at the doors. 10 As an example of suffering and patience, brethren, take the prophets who spoke in the name of the Lord. 11 Behold, we call those

---

ὑμῶν ὡς πῦρ. ἐθησαυρίσατε ἐν ἐσχάταις
of you as fire. Ye treasured in [the] last

ἡμέραις. 4 ἰδοὺ ὁ μισθὸς τῶν ἐργατῶν
days. Behold[,] the wages of the workmen

τῶν ἀμησάντων τὰς χώρας ὑμῶν ὁ
– having reaped the lands of you –

ἀφυστερημένος ἀφ᾽ ὑμῶν κράζει, καὶ αἱ
being kept back from(by) you cries, and the

βοαὶ τῶν θερισάντων εἰς τὰ ὦτα κυρίου
cries of the having reaped ²into ³the ⁴ears ⁵of [the]
[ones] Lord

σαβαὼθ εἰσελήλυθαν. 5 ἐτρυφήσατε ἐπὶ
⁶of hosts ¹have entered. Ye lived daintily on

τῆς γῆς καὶ ἐσπαταλήσατε, ἐθρέψατε τὰς
the earth and lived riotously, ye nourished the

καρδίας ὑμῶν ἐν ἡμέρᾳ σφαγῆς. 6 κατε-
hearts of you in a day of slaughter. Ye

δικάσατε, ἐφονεύσατε τὸν δίκαιον· οὐκ
condemned, ye murdered the righteous man; not

ἀντιτάσσεται ὑμῖν.
he resists you.

7 Μακροθυμήσατε οὖν, ἀδελφοί, ἕως τῆς
Be ye longsuffering therefore, brothers, until the

παρουσίας τοῦ κυρίου. ἰδοὺ ὁ γεωργὸς
presence of the Lord. Behold[,] the farmer

ἐκδέχεται τὸν τίμιον καρπὸν τῆς γῆς,
awaits the precious fruit of the earth,

μακροθυμῶν ἐπ᾽ αὐτῷ ἕως λάβῃ πρόϊμον
being over it until he receives early
longsuffering

καὶ ὄψιμον. 8 μακροθυμήσατε καὶ ὑμεῖς,
and latter [rain]. Be ³longsuffering ²also ¹ye,

στηρίξατε τὰς καρδίας ὑμῶν, ὅτι ἡ
establish the hearts of you, because the

παρουσία τοῦ κυρίου ἤγγικεν. 9 μὴ
presence of the Lord has drawn near. not

στενάζετε, ἀδελφοί, κατ᾽ ἀλλήλων ἵνα μὴ
Murmur ye, brothers, against one another lest

κριθῆτε· ἰδοὺ ὁ κριτὴς πρὸ τῶν θυρῶν
ye be behold[,] the judge ²before ³the ⁴doors
judged;

ἕστηκεν. 10 ὑπόδειγμα λάβετε, ἀδελφοί,
¹stands. ⁵an example ¹Take ye, ²brothers,

τῆς κακοπαθίας καὶ τῆς μακροθυμίας
– ⁶of suffering ill ⁷and – ⁸of longsuffering

τοὺς προφήτας, οἳ ἐλάλησαν ἐν τῷ
³the ⁴prophets, who spoke in the

ὀνόματι κυρίου. 11 ἰδοὺ μακαρίζομεν τοὺς
name of [the] Lord. Behold we count blessed the

---

[d] Or will eat your flesh, since you have stored up fire

happy who were steadfast. You have heard of the steadfastness of Job, and you have seen the purpose of the Lord, how the Lord is compassionate and merciful. 12 But above all, my brethren, do not swear, either by heaven or by earth or with any other oath, but let your yes be yes and your no be no, that you may not fall under condemnation. 13 Is any one among you suffering? Let him pray. Is any cheerful? Let him sing praise. ¹⁴Is any among you sick? Let him call for the elders of the church, and let them pray over him, anointing him with oil in the name of the Lord; ¹⁵and the prayer of faith will save the sick man, and the Lord will raise him up; and if he has committed sins, he will be forgiven. ¹⁶Therefore confess your sins to one another, and pray for one another, that you may be healed. The prayer of a righteous man has great power in its effects. ¹⁷Eli′jah was a man of like nature with ourselves and he prayed fervently that it might not rain, and for three

ὑπομείναντας· τὴν ὑπομονὴν Ἰὼβ ἠκούσατε,
[ones] enduring; ²the ²endurance ⁴of Job ¹ye heard [of],

καὶ τὸ τέλος κυρίου εἴδετε, ὅτι πολύand ²the ³end ⁴of [the] Lord ¹ye saw, that ⁴very

σπλαγχνός ἐστιν ὁ κύριος καὶ οἰκτίρμων.
compassionate ³is ¹the ²Lord and pitiful.

12 Πρὸ πάντων δέ, ἀδελφοί μου, μὴ
²before ³all things ¹But, brothers of me, not

ὀμνύετε, μήτε τὸν οὐρανὸν μήτε τὴν
swear ye, neither the by the heaven nor by the

γῆν μήτε ἄλλον τινὰ ὅρκον· ἤτω δὲ
earth nor ²other ¹any oath; but let be

ὑμῶν τὸ ναὶ ναί, καὶ τὸ οὒ οὔ, ἵνα μὴ
of you the Yes yes, and the No no, lest

ὑπὸ κρίσιν πέσητε. 13 Κακοπαθεῖ τις
²under ³judgment ¹ye fall. Suffers ill anyone

ἐν ὑμῖν; προσευχέσθω· εὐθυμεῖ τις;
among you? let him pray; is cheerful anyone?

ψαλλέτω. 14 ἀσθενεῖ τις ἐν ὑμῖν;
let him sing a psalm. Is weak anyone among you?

προσκαλεσάσθω τοὺς πρεσβυτέρους τῆς
let him summon the elders of the

ἐκκλησίας, καὶ προσευξάσθωσαν ἐπ' αὐτὸν
church, and let them pray over him

ἀλείψαντες ἐλαίῳ ἐν τῷ ὀνόματι τοῦ
having anointed with oil ιn the name of the
[him]

κυρίου. 15 καὶ ἡ εὐχὴ τῆς πίστεως
Lord. And the prayer – of faith

σώσει τὸν κάμνοντα, καὶ ἐγερεῖ αὐτὸν
will heal the [one] being sick, and ²will raise ⁴him

ὁ κύριος· κἂν ἁμαρτίας ᾖ πεποιηκώς,
¹the ²Lord; and if ²sins ¹he ²having done,
may be

ἀφεθήσεται αὐτῷ. 16 ἐξομολογεῖσθε οὖν
it will be forgiven him. Confess ye therefore

ἀλλήλοις τὰς ἁμαρτίας, καὶ προσεύχεσθε
to one the(your) sins, and pray ye
another

ὑπὲρ ἀλλήλων, ὅπως ἰαθῆτε. πολὺ
on be- one another, so as ye may ⁵much(very)
half of be cured.

ἰσχύει δέησις δικαίου ἐνεργουμένη.
⁴is ⁶strong ¹a petition ²of a ³being made effective.
righteous man

17 Ἡλίας ἄνθρωπος ἦν ὁμοιοπαθὴς ἡμῖν,
Elias ²a man ¹was of like feeling to us,

καὶ προσευχῇ προσηύξατο τοῦ μὴ βρέξαι,
and ²in prayer ¹he prayed – not to rain,ᵈ
=that it should not rain,

years and six months it
did not rain on the earth.
18 Then he prayed again
and the heaven gave rain,
and the earth brought
forth its fruit.

19 My brethren, if any
one among you wanders
from the truth and some
one brings him back,
20 let him know that
whoever brings back a
sinner from the error of
his way will save his
soul from death and will
cover a multitude of sins.

καὶ οὐκ ἔβρεξεν ἐπὶ τῆς γῆς ἐνιαυτοὺς
and it rained not on the earth ²years
τρεῖς καὶ μῆνας ἕξ· 18 καὶ πάλιν προσ-
¹three and ²months ¹six; and again he
ηύξατο, καὶ ὁ οὐρανὸς ὑετὸν ἔδωκεν καὶ
prayed, and the heaven ²rain ¹gave and
ἡ γῆ ἐβλάστησεν τὸν καρπὸν αὐτῆς.
the earth brought forth the fruit of it.
19 Ἀδελφοί μου, ἐάν τις ἐν ὑμῖν πλανηθῇ
Brothers of me, if anyone among you errs
ἀπὸ τῆς ἀληθείας καὶ ἐπιστρέψῃ τις
from the truth and ²turns ¹anyone
αὐτόν, 20 γινώσκετε ὅτι ὁ ἐπιστρέψας
him, know ye that the [one] turning
ἁμαρτωλὸν ἐκ πλάνης ὁδοῦ αὐτοῦ σώσει
a sinner out of [the] error of way of him will save
ψυχὴν αὐτοῦ ἐκ θανάτου καὶ καλύψει
soul of him out of death and will hide
πλῆθος ἁμαρτιῶν.
a multitude of sins.

I. PETER 1

ΠΕΤΡΟΥ Α
Of Peter 1

CHAPTER 1

PETER, an apostle of
Jesus Christ,
To the exiles of the
Dispersion in Pontus,
Galatia, Cappado'cia,
Asia, and Bithyn'ia,
² chosen and destined by
God the Father and
sanctified by the Spirit
for obedience to Jesus
Christ and for sprinkling
with his blood:
May grace and peace
be multiplied to you.
3 Blessed be the God
and Father of our Lord
Jesus Christ! By his

1 Πέτρος ἀπόστολος Ἰησοῦ Χριστοῦ
Peter an apostle of Jesus Christ
ἐκλεκτοῖς παρεπιδήμοις διασπορᾶς Πόντου,
to [the] chosen sojourners of [the] dispersion of Pontus,
Γαλατίας, Καππαδοκίας, Ἀσίας καὶ
of Galatia, of Cappadocia, of Asia and
Βιθυνίας, 2 κατὰ πρόγνωσιν θεοῦ πατρός,
of Bithynia, according [the] of God Father,
to foreknowledge
ἐν ἁγιασμῷ πνεύματος, εἰς ὑπακοὴν καὶ
in sanctification of spirit, to obedience and
ῥαντισμὸν αἵματος Ἰησοῦ Χριστοῦ· χάρις
sprinkling of [the] blood of Jesus Christ: Grace
ὑμῖν καὶ εἰρήνη πληθυνθείη.
to you and peace may it be multiplied.
3 Εὐλογητὸς ὁ θεὸς καὶ πατὴρ τοῦ
Blessed [be] the God and Father of the
κυρίου ἡμῶν Ἰησοῦ Χριστοῦ, ὁ κατὰ τὸ
Lord of us Jesus Christ, the accord- the
[one] ing to

great mercy we have been born anew to a living hope through the resurrection of Jesus Christ from the dead, 4and to an inheritance which is imperishable, undefiled, and unfading, kept in heaven for you, 5who by God's power are guarded through faith for a salvation ready to be revealed in the last time. 6In this you rejoice,ᵃ though now for a little while you may have to suffer various trials, 7so that the genuineness of your faith, more precious than gold which though perishable is tested by fire, may redound to praise and glory and honor at the revelation of Jesus Christ. 8Without having seenᵇ him youᶜ love him; though you do not now see him youᶜ believe in him and rejoice with unutterable and exalted joy. 9As the outcome of your faith you obtain the salvation of your souls.

10 The prophets who prophesied of the grace that was to be yours searched and inquired about this salvation; 11they inquired what person or time was indicated by the Spirit of Christ

ᵃ Or Rejoice in this
ᵇ Other ancient authorities read known
ᶜ Or omit you

πολὺ   αὐτοῦ   ἔλεος   ἀναγεννήσας   ἡμᾶς   εἰς
much   of him   mercy   having regenerated   us   to
(great)

ἐλπίδα   ζῶσαν   δι'   ἀναστάσεως   'Ιησοῦ
²hope   ¹a living   through   [the] resurrection   of Jesus

Χριστοῦ   ἐκ   νεκρῶν,   4 εἰς   κληρονομίαν
Christ   from   [the] dead,   to   an inheritance

ἄφθαρτον   καὶ   ἀμίαντον   καὶ   ἀμάραντον,
incorruptible   and   undefiled   and   unfading,

τετηρημένην   ἐν   οὐρανοῖς   εἰς   ὑμᾶς   5 τοὺς
having been kept   in   heavens   for   you   the [ones]

ἐν   δυνάμει   θεοῦ   φρουρουμένους   διὰ   πίστεως
²by   ³[the] power   ⁴of God   ¹being guarded   through   faith

εἰς   σωτηρίαν   ἑτοίμην   ἀποκαλυφθῆναι   ἐν
to   a salvation   ready   to be revealed   at

καιρῷ   ἐσχάτῳ.   6 ἐν   ᾧ   ἀγαλλιᾶσθε,
²time   ¹[the] last.   In   which   ye exult,

ὀλίγον   ἄρτι   εἰ   δέον   λυπηθέντες   ἐν
a little [while]   yet   if   necessary   grieving   by

ποικίλοις   πειρασμοῖς,   7 ἵνα   τὸ   δοκίμιον
manifold   trials,   in order that the   proving

ὑμῶν   τῆς   πίστεως   πολυτιμότερον   χρυσίου
²of you   ¹of the   ²faith[,]   much more precious   [than] ²gold

τοῦ   ἀπολλυμένου,   διὰ   πυρὸς   δὲ   δοκιμαζ-
-       ¹of perishing,   ²through   ⁴fire   ¹yet   ²being

ομένου,   εὑρεθῇ   εἰς   ἔπαινον   καὶ   δόξαν
proved,   may be found to   praise   and   glory

καὶ   τιμὴν   ἐν   ἀποκαλύψει   'Ιησοῦ   Χριστοῦ·
and   honour   at   [the] revelation   of Jesus   Christ;

8 ὃν   οὐκ   ἰδόντες   ἀγαπᾶτε,   εἰς   ὃν   ἄρτι
whom   not   having seen   ye love,   in   whom   yet

μὴ   ὁρῶντες   πιστεύοντες   δὲ   ἀγαλλιᾶσθε
not   seeing   ²believing   ¹but   ye exult

χαρᾷ   ἀνεκλαλήτῳ   καὶ   δεδοξασμένη,
with joy   unspeakable   and   having been glorified,

9 κομιζόμενοι   τὸ   τέλος   τῆς   πίστεως
obtaining   the   end   of the(your)   faith

σωτηρίαν   ψυχῶν.   10 περὶ   ἧς   σωτηρίας
[the] salvation of [your] souls.   Concerning which   salvation

ἐξεζήτησαν   καὶ   ἐξηρεύνησαν   προφῆται   οἱ
²sought out   ¹⁰and   ¹¹searched out   ¹prophets   ²the

περὶ   τῆς   εἰς   ὑμᾶς   χάριτος   προφητεύσαντες,
⁴con-   ⁶the   ⁷for   ⁸you   ⁶grace   ³[ones] prophesying,
cerning

11 ἐρευνῶντες   εἰς   τίνα   ἢ   ποῖον   καιρὸν
searching   for   what   or what sort of   time

ἐδήλου   τὸ   ἐν   αὐτοῖς   πνεῦμα   Χριστοῦ
⁴made clear   ¹the   ³in   ⁵them   ²Spirit   ²of Christ

within them when predicting the sufferings of Christ and the subsequent glory. [12]It was revealed to them that they were serving not themselves but you, in the things which have now been announced to you by those who preached the good news to you through the Holy Spirit sent from heaven, things into which angels long to look. [13]Therefore gird up your minds, be sober, set your hope fully upon the grace that is coming to you at the revelation of Jesus Christ. [14]As obedient children, do not be conformed to the passions of your former ignorance, [15]but as he who called you is holy, be holy yourselves in all your conduct; [16]since it is written, "You shall be holy, for I am holy." [17]And if you invoke as Father him who judges each one impartially according to his deeds, conduct yourselves with fear throughout the time of your exile. [18]You know that you were ransomed from the futile

προμαρτυρόμενον τὰ εἰς Χριστὸν παθήματα
[7]forewitnessing [8]the [10]for [11]Christ [9]sufferings
καὶ τὰς μετὰ ταῦτα δόξας. 12 οἷς
[12]and [13]the [15]after [16]these [14]glories. To whom
ἀπεκαλύφθη ὅτι οὐχ ἑαυτοῖς ὑμῖν δὲ
it was revealed that not to themselves [2]to you [1]but
διηκόνουν αὐτά, ἃ νῦν ἀνηγγέλη ὑμῖν
they the same which now were to you
ministered things, announced
διὰ τῶν εὐαγγελισαμένων ὑμᾶς ἐν
through the [ones] having evangelized you by
πνεύματι ἁγίῳ ἀποσταλέντι ἀπ' οὐρανοῦ,
[2]Spirit [1][the] Holy sent forth from heaven,
εἰς ἃ ἐπιθυμοῦσιν ἄγγελοι παρακῦψαι.
into [1]which [3]long [2]angels [4]to look into.
things
13 Διὸ ἀναζωσάμενοι τὰς ὀσφύας τῆς
Wherefore girding up the loins of the
διανοίας ὑμῶν, νήφοντες, τελείως ἐλπίσατε
mind of you, being sober, perfectly hope
ἐπὶ τὴν φερομένην ὑμῖν χάριν ἐν
on [1]the [3]being brought [4]to you [2]grace at
ἀποκαλύψει Ἰησοῦ Χριστοῦ. 14 ὡς τέκνα
[the] revelation of Jesus Christ. As children
ὑπακοῆς, μὴ συσχηματιζόμενοι ταῖς πρότε-
of obedience,* not fashioning yourselves to the [6]form-
ρον ἐν τῇ ἀγνοίᾳ ὑμῶν ἐπιθυμίαις, 15 ἀλλὰ
erly [2]in [3]the [4]ignorance [5]of you [1]longings, but
κατὰ τὸν καλέσαντα ὑμᾶς ἅγιον καὶ
according to [1]the [3]having called [4]you [2]holy [one] [5]also
αὐτοὶ ἅγιοι ἐν πάσῃ ἀναστροφῇ γενήθητε,
[5][your]- [3]holy [6]in [10]all [11]conduct [8]become ye,
selves
16 διότι γέγραπται· [ὅτι] ἅγιοι ἔσεσθε,
because it has been written: - Holy ye shall be,
ὅτι ἐγὼ ἅγιος. 17 καὶ εἰ πατέρα
because I [am] holy. And if [1]Father
ἐπικαλεῖσθε τὸν ἀπροσωπολήμπτως κρίνοντα
[1]ye invoke [as] [3]the [one] [5]without respect to persons [4]judging
κατὰ τὸ ἑκάστου ἔργον, ἐν φόβῳ τὸν
accord- the [2]of each man [1]work, [2]in [3]fear [4]the
ing to
τῆς παροικίας ὑμῶν χρόνον ἀναστράφητε,
[6]of the [7]sojourning [8]of you [5]time [1]pass,
18 εἰδότες ὅτι οὐ φθαρτοῖς, ἀργυρίῳ ἢ
knowing that not with corruptible silver or
things,

* Genitive of quality: " obedient children."

ways inherited from your fathers, not with perishable things such as silver or gold, [19]but with the precious blood of Christ, like that of a lamb without blemish or spot. [20]He was destined before the foundation of the world but was made manifest at the end of the times for your sake. [21]Through him you have confidence in God, who raised him from the dead and gave him glory, so that your faith and hope are in God.[d]

[22] Having purified your souls by your obedience to the truth for a sincere love of the brethren, love one another earnestly from the heart. [23]You have been born anew, not of perishable seed but of imperishable, through the living and abiding word of God; [24]for

"All flesh is like grass and all its glory like the flower of grass. The grass withers, and the flower falls, [25]but the word of the Lord abides for ever."

That word is the good news which was preached to you.

CHAPTER 2

So put away all malice and all guile and insincerity and envy and all slander. [2]Like new-

[d] Or so that your faith is hope in God

χρυσίῳ, ἐλυτρώθητε ἐκ τῆς ματαίας ὑμῶν
gold,   ye were redeemed from the   vain   [2]of you

ἀναστροφῆς πατροπαραδότου, 19 ἀλλὰ τιμίῳ
[1]conduct   delivered from   but   with
    [your] fathers,   precious

αἵματι ὡς ἀμνοῦ ἀμώμου καὶ ἀσπίλου
blood[,]   as   of a lamb   unblemished   and   unspotted[,]

Χριστοῦ, 20 προεγνωσμένου μὲν πρὸ κατα-
of Christ,   having been foreknown   on one   from   [the]
              hand

βολῆς κόσμου, φανερωθέντος δὲ ἐπ’ ἐσχάτου
founda-   of [the]   manifested   on the in   [the] last
tion   world,   other

τῶν χρόνων δι’ ὑμᾶς 21 τοὺς δι’ αὐτοῦ
of the   times   because of you   the ones through   him

πιστοὺς εἰς θεὸν τὸν ἐγείραντα αὐτὸν
believing   in   God   the [one]   having raised   him

ἐκ νεκρῶν καὶ δόξαν αὐτῷ δόντα, ὥστε
from [the] dead   and   [2]glory   [3]to him   [1]having given.   so as

τὴν πίστιν ὑμῶν καὶ ἐλπίδα εἶναι εἰς
the   [1]faith   [2]of you   [2]and   [3]hope   to be   in

θεόν. 22 Τὰς ψυχὰς ὑμῶν ἡγνικότες
God.   [2]The   [3]souls   [4]of you   [1]having purified

ἐν τῇ ὑπακοῇ τῆς ἀληθείας εἰς φιλαδελφίαν
by   —   obedience of(to) the   truth   to   [2]brotherly love

ἀνυπόκριτον, ἐκ καρδίας ἀλλήλους ἀγαπήσατε
[1]unfeigned,   [4]from [5][the] heart [2]one another   [1]love ye

ἐκτενῶς, 23 ἀναγεγεννημένοι οὐκ ἐκ σπορᾶς
[2]earnestly,   having been regenerated   not   by   [2]seed

φθαρτῆς ἀλλὰ ἀφθάρτου, διὰ λόγου ζῶντος
[1]corruptible   but   incorruptible, through   [4]word   [1][the] living

θεοῦ καὶ μένοντος. 24 διότι πᾶσα σὰρξ
[5]of God [2]and   [3]remaining.   Because   all   flesh [is]

ὡς χόρτος, καὶ πᾶσα δόξα αὐτῆς ὡς
as   grass,   and   all   [the] glory   of it   as

ἄνθος χόρτου· ἐξηράνθη ὁ χόρτος, καὶ
a flower   of grass;   was dried   the   grass,   and

τὸ ἄνθος ἐξέπεσεν· 25 τὸ δὲ ῥῆμα κυρίου
the   flower   fell out;   but the   word of [the] Lord

μένει εἰς τὸν αἰῶνα. τοῦτο δέ ἐστιν
remains   unto   the   age.   And this   is

τὸ ῥῆμα τὸ εὐαγγελισθὲν εἰς ὑμᾶς.
the   word   —   preached [as good news] to   you.

2 Ἀποθέμενοι οὖν πᾶσαν κακίαν καὶ
  Putting away   therefore   all   malice   and

πάντα δόλον καὶ ὑποκρίσεις καὶ φθόνους
all   guile   and   hypocrisies   and   envies

καὶ πάσας καταλαλιάς, 2 ὡς ἀρτιγέννητα
and   all   detractions,   as   newborn

born babes, long for the pure spiritual milk, that by it you may grow up to salvation; [3]for you have tasted the kindness of the Lord.

4 Come to him, to that living stone, rejected by men but in God's sight chosen and precious; [5]and like living stones be yourselves built into a spiritual house, to be a holy priesthood, to offer spiritual sacrifices acceptable to God through Jesus Christ. [6]For it stands in scripture:
"Behold, I am laying in Zion a stone, a cornerstone chosen and precious,
and he who believes in him will not be put to shame."
[7]To you therefore who believe, he is precious, but for those who do not believe,
"The very stone which the builders rejected
has become the head of the corner,"
[8]and
"A stone that will make men stumble, a rock that will make them fall";
for they stumble because they disobey the word, as they were destined to do.

9 But you are a chosen race, a royal priesthood, a holy nation, God's own people, that you may declare the wonderful

βρέφη   τὸ   λογικὸν   ἄδολον   γάλα   ἐπιποθήσατε,
babes   [2]the   [2]spiritual   [4]pure   [5]milk   [1]desire ye,

ἵνα   ἐν   αὐτῷ   αὐξηθῆτε   εἰς   σωτηρίαν,
in or-   by   it   ye may grow   to   salvation,
der that

3 εἰ   ἐγεύσασθε   ὅτι   χρηστὸς   ὁ   κύριος.
if   ye tasted   that   [2]good   [1]the   [2]Lord [is].

4 πρὸς   ὃν   προσερχόμενοι,   λίθον   ζῶντα,
to   whom   approaching,   [2]stone   [1]a living,

ὑπὸ   ἀνθρώπων   μὲν   ἀποδεδοκιμασμένον   παρὰ
by   men   on one   having been rejected   [3]by
       hand

δὲ   θεῷ   ἐκλεκτὸν   ἔντιμον,   5 καὶ
[1]on the   [4]God   [2]chosen[,]   precious,   [2]also
other

αὐτοὶ   ὡς   λίθοι   ζῶντες   οἰκοδομεῖσθε   οἶκος
[1][your]-   [2]as   [3]stones   [4]living   are being built   [2]house
selves

πνευματικὸς   εἰς   ἱεράτευμα   ἅγιον,   ἀνενέγκαι
[1]a spiritual   for   [2]priesthood   [1]a holy,   to offer

πνευματικὰς   θυσίας   εὐπροσδέκτους   θεῷ   διὰ
spiritual   sacrifices   acceptable   to   through
       God

Ἰησοῦ   Χριστοῦ·   6 διότι   περιέχει   ἐν   γραφῇ·
Jesus   Christ;   because   it is   in   scripture:
       contained

ἰδοὺ   τίθημι   ἐν   Σιὼν   λίθον   ἐκλεκτὸν
Behold   I lay   in   Sion   [4]stone   [1]a chosen

ἀκρογωνιαῖον   ἔντιμον,   καὶ   ὁ   πιστεύων
[2]corner foundation   [3]precious,   and   the [one]   believing

ἐπ'   αὐτῷ   οὐ   μὴ   καταισχυνθῇ.   7 ὑμῖν
on   it(him)   by no means   will be shamed.   To you
       =Yours

οὖν   ἡ   τιμὴ   τοῖς   πιστεύουσιν·   ἀπιστοῦσιν
there-   [3][is]   [1]honour   [1]the [ones]   [2]believing[c];   [2]to unbelieving
fore   [4]the   [ones]
therefore who believe is the honour;

δὲ   λίθος   ὃν   ἀπεδοκίμασαν   οἱ   οἰκοδομοῦντες,
[1]but a stone which   [2]rejected   [1]the [ones]   [2]building,

οὗτος   ἐγενήθη   εἰς   κεφαλὴν   γωνίας   8 καὶ
this   came to be   for   head   of [the] corner   and

λίθος   προσκόμματος   καὶ   πέτρα   σκανδάλου·
a stone   of stumbling   and   a rock   of offence;

οἳ   προσκόπτουσιν   τῷ   λόγῳ   ἀπειθοῦντες,
who   stumble   at the   word   disobeying,

9 εἰς   ὃ   καὶ   ἐτέθησαν·   ὑμεῖς   δὲ   γένος
to   which indeed   they were   but ye   [are] [2]race
       appointed;

ἐκλεκτόν,   βασίλειον   ἱεράτευμα,   ἔθνος   ἅγιον,
[1]a chosen,   a royal   priesthood,   nation   a holy,

λαὸς   εἰς   περιποίησιν,   ὅπως   τὰς   ἀρετὰς
a people   for   possession,   so as   [2]the   [1]virtues

deeds of him who called you out of darkness into his marvelous light. ¹⁰Once you were no people but now you are God's people; once you had not received mercy but now you have received mercy. 11 Beloved, I beseech you as aliens and exiles to abstain from the passions of the flesh that wage war against your soul. ¹²Maintain good conduct among the Gentiles, so that in case they speak against you as wrongdoers, they may see your good deeds and glorify God on the day of visitation.

13 Be subject for the Lord's sake to every human institution,* whether it be to the emperor as supreme, ¹⁴or to governors as sent by him to punish those who do wrong and to praise those who do right. ¹⁵For it is God's will that by doing right you should put to silence the ignorance of foolish men. ¹⁶Live as free men, yet without using your freedom as a pretext for evil; but live as servants of God. ¹⁷Honor all

* Or every institution ordained for men

ἐξαγγείλητε τοῦ ἐκ σκότους ὑμᾶς καλέ-
¹ye may tell out ⁴of the ⁷out ⁸darkness ⁶you ⁵having
[one] of

σαντος εἰς τὸ θαυμαστὸν αὐτοῦ φῶς·
called into the marvellous ²of him ¹light;

10 οἵ ποτε οὐ λαός, νῦν δὲ λαὸς θεοῦ,
who then not a but [are] a of
[were] people, now people God,

οἱ οὐκ ἠλεημένοι, νῦν δὲ ἐλεηθέντες.
the not having been pitied, but now pitied.
[ones]

11 Ἀγαπητοί, παρακαλῶ ὡς παροίκους
Beloved, I exhort [you] as sojourners

καὶ παρεπιδήμους ἀπέχεσθαι τῶν σαρκικῶν
and aliens to abstain from – fleshly

ἐπιθυμιῶν, αἵτινες στρατεύονται κατὰ τῆς
lusts, which war against the

ψυχῆς· 12 τὴν ἀναστροφὴν ὑμῶν ἐν τοῖς
soul; ²the ³conduct ⁴of you ⁵among ⁶the

ἔθνεσιν ἔχοντες καλήν, ἵνα ἐν ᾧ κατα-
⁷nations ¹having ⁸good, in order while they
that

λαλοῦσιν ὑμῶν ὡς κακοποιῶν, ἐκ τῶν
speak against you as evildoers, by the
(your)

καλῶν ἔργων ἐποπτεύοντες δοξάσωσιν τὸν
good works observing they may glorify –

θεὸν ἐν ἡμέρᾳ ἐπισκοπῆς.
God in a day of visitation.

13 Ὑποτάγητε πάσῃ ἀνθρωπίνῃ κτίσει
Submit to every human ordinance

διὰ τὸν κύριον· εἴτε βασιλεῖ ὡς ὑπερέχοντι,
be- the Lord: whether to a king as being supreme,
cause of

14 εἴτε ἡγεμόσιν ὡς δι' αὐτοῦ πεμπομένοις
or to governors as through him being sent

εἰς ἐκδίκησιν κακοποιῶν ἔπαινον δὲ
for vengeance of(on) evildoers ²praise ¹but

ἀγαθοποιῶν· 15 ὅτι οὕτως ἐστὶν τὸ
of welldoers; because so is the

θέλημα τοῦ θεοῦ, ἀγαθοποιοῦντας φιμοῦν
will – of God, doing good to silence

τὴν τῶν ἀφρόνων ἀνθρώπων ἀγνωσίαν·
¹the – ²of foolish ⁴men ³ignorance;

16 ὡς ἐλεύθεροι, καὶ μὴ ὡς ἐπικάλυμμα
as free, and not ³as ⁴a cloak

ἔχοντες τῆς κακίας τὴν ἐλευθερίαν, ἀλλ'
¹having the ⁵of evil the ²freedom, but

ὡς θεοῦ δοῦλοι. 17 πάντας τιμήσατε,
as of God slaves. ¹All men ¹honour ye,

men. Love the brotherhood. Fear God. Honor the emperor.
18 Servants, be submissive to your masters with all respect, not only to the kind and gentle but also to the overbearing. ¹⁹ For one is approved if, mindful of God, he endures pain while suffering unjustly. ²⁰ For what credit is it, if when you do wrong and are beaten for it you take it patiently? But if when you do right and suffer for it you take it patiently, you have God's approval. ²¹ For to this you have been called, because Christ also suffered for you, leaving you an example, that you should follow in his steps. ²² He committed no sin; no guile was found on his lips. ²³ When he was reviled, he did not revile in return; when he suffered, he did not threaten; but he trusted to him who judges justly. ²⁴ He himself bore our sins in his body on the tree,ᶠ that we might die to sin and live to righteousness. By his wounds you have been healed. ²⁵ For you

ᶠ Or *carried up . . . to the tree*

τὴν   ἀδελφότητα   ἀγαπᾶτε,   τὸν   θεὸν
²the   ³brotherhood   ¹love,   –   ²God

φοβεῖσθε,   τὸν   βασιλέα   τιμᾶτε.   18 Οἱ
¹fear,   ²the   ³king   ¹honour.   –

οἰκέται,   ὑποτασσόμενοι   ἐν   παντὶ   φόβῳ
House servants,   submitting yourselves   in   all   fear

τοῖς   δεσπόταις,   οὐ   μόνον   τοῖς   ἀγαθοῖς
to the(your) masters,   not   only   to the   good

καὶ   ἐπιεικέσιν   ἀλλὰ   καὶ   τοῖς   σκολιοῖς.
and   forbearing   but   also   to the   perverse.

19 τοῦτο   γὰρ   χάρις   εἰ   διὰ   συνείδησιν
For this   [is] a favour   if   because of   conscience

θεοῦ   ὑποφέρει   τις   λύπας   πάσχων   ἀδίκως.
of God   ²bears   ¹anyone   griefs   suffering   unjustly.

20 ποῖον   γὰρ   κλέος   εἰ   ἁμαρτάνοντες   καὶ
For what   glory [is it] if   sinning   and

κολαφιζόμενοι   ὑπομενεῖτε;   ἀλλ᾽   εἰ   ἀγαθο-
being buffeted   ye endure?   but   if   doing

ποιοῦντες   καὶ   πάσχοντες   ὑπομενεῖτε,   τοῦτο
good   and   suffering   ye endure,   this [is]

χάρις   παρὰ   θεῷ.   21 εἰς   τοῦτο   γὰρ
a favour   with   God.   ²to   ³this   ¹For

ἐκλήθητε,   ὅτι   καὶ   Χριστὸς   ἔπαθεν   ὑπὲρ
ye were called,   because   indeed   Christ   suffered   on behalf of

ὑμῶν,   ὑμῖν   ὑπολιμπάνων   ὑπογραμμὸν   ἵνα
you,   ²to you   ¹leaving behind   an example   in order that

ἐπακολουθήσητε   τοῖς   ἴχνεσιν   αὐτοῦ·   22 ὃς
ye should follow   the   steps   of him;   who

ἁμαρτίαν   οὐκ   ἐποίησεν   οὐδὲ   εὑρέθη   δόλος
³sin   ²not   ¹did   nor   was ²found   ¹guile

ἐν   τῷ   στόματι   αὐτοῦ·   23 ὃς   λοιδορούμενος
in   the   mouth   of him;   who   being reviled

οὐκ   ἀντελοιδόρει,   πάσχων   οὐκ   ἠπείλει,
reviled not in return,   suffering   he threatened not,

παρεδίδου   δὲ   τῷ   κρίνοντι   δικαίως·   24 ὃς
but delivered [himself]   to the [one]   judging   righteously;   who

τὰς   ἁμαρτίας   ἡμῶν   αὐτὸς   ἀνήνεγκεν   ἐν
³the   ⁴sins   ⁵of us   ¹[him]self   ²carried up   in

τῷ   σώματι   αὐτοῦ   ἐπὶ   τὸ   ξύλον,   ἵνα
the   body   of him   onto   the   tree,   in order that

ταῖς   ἁμαρτίαις   ἀπογενόμενοι   τῇ   δικαιοσύνῃ
–   ²to sins   ¹dying   – ⁴to righteousness

ζήσωμεν·   οὗ   τῷ   μώλωπι   ἰάθητε.
³we might live;   ³of whom   ¹by the   ²bruise   ye were cured.

were straying like sheep, but have now returned to the Shepherd and Guardian of your souls.

CHAPTER 3

LIKEWISE you wives, be submissive to your husbands, so that some, though they do not obey the word, may be won without a word by the behavior of their wives, ²when they see your reverent and chaste behavior. ³Let not yours be the outward adorning with braiding of hair, decoration of gold, and wearing of robes, ⁴but let it be the hidden person of the heart with the imperishable jewel of a gentle and quiet spirit, which in God's sight is very precious. ⁵So once the holy women who hoped in God used to adorn themselves and were submissive to their husbands, ⁶as Sarah obeyed Abraham, calling him lord. And you are now her children if you do right and let nothing terrify you.

7 Likewise you husbands, live considerately with your wives, bestowing honor on the woman as the weaker

25 ἦτε	γὰρ	ὡς	πρόβατα πλανώμενοι,
²ye were	¹For	⁴as	⁵sheep ³wandering,

ἀλλὰ	ἐπεστράφητε	νῦν ἐπὶ	τὸν ποιμένα
but	ye turned	now to	the shepherd

καὶ	ἐπίσκοπον	τῶν	ψυχῶν ὑμῶν.
and	bishop	of the	souls of you.

3 Ὁμοίως γυναῖκες, ὑποτασσόμεναι τοῖς
  Likewise   wives,   submitting yourselves   to the (your)

ἰδίοις ἀνδράσιν, ἵνα καὶ εἴ τινες ἀπειθοῦσιν
own   husbands,   in or- even if any   disobey
      der that

τῷ λόγῳ, διὰ τῆς τῶν γυναικῶν ἀναστροφῆς
the   word, through ¹the ³of ⁴wives ²conduct
          the(ir)

ἄνευ λόγου κερδηθήσονται, 2 ἐποπτεύσαντες
without a word they will(may) be gained,   observing

τὴν ἐν φόβῳ ἁγνὴν ἀναστροφὴν ὑμῶν.
¹the ⁵in ⁶fear ²pure ³conduct ⁴of you.

3 ὧν ἔστω οὐχ ὁ ἔξωθεν ἐμπλοκῆς
Of whom let it be not ¹the ²outward ⁴of plaiting

τριχῶν καὶ περιθέσεως χρυσίων ἢ ἐνδύσεως
⁵of hairs ⁶and ⁷of putting ⁸of gold ⁹or ¹⁰of clothing
        round(on) [ornaments]

ἱματίων κόσμος, 4 ἀλλ' ὁ κρυπτὸς τῆς
¹¹of(with) ²adorning,   but ¹the ²hidden ⁴of the
garments

καρδίας ἄνθρωπος ἐν τῷ ἀφθάρτῳ τοῦ
³heart ³man in(?by) the   incorruptible of the
                      [adorning]

πραέος καὶ ἡσυχίου πνεύματος, ὅ ἐστιν
meek and   quiet   spirit, which is

ἐνώπιον τοῦ θεοῦ πολυτελές. 5 οὕτως
before   –   God of great value.   so

γάρ ποτε καὶ αἱ ἅγιαι γυναῖκες αἱ
For then indeed the   holy   women   –

ἐλπίζουσαι εἰς θεὸν ἐκόσμουν ἑαυτάς,
hoping   in God   adorned   themselves,

ὑποτασσόμεναι τοῖς ἰδίοις ἀνδράσιν, 6 ὡς
submitting themselves to the(ir) own   husbands,   as

Σάρρα ὑπήκουσεν τῷ Ἀβραάμ, κύριον
Sara   obeyed   – Abraham,   ³lord

αὐτὸν καλοῦσα· ἧς ἐγενήθητε τέκνα
²him ¹calling; of whom ye became children

ἀγαθοποιοῦσαι καὶ μὴ φοβούμεναι μηδεμίαν
doing good   and not   fearing   no(any)

πτόησιν. 7 Οἱ ἄνδρες ὁμοίως, συνοικοῦντες
terror.   – Husbands likewise, dwelling together

κατὰ γνῶσιν ὡς ἀσθενεστέρῳ σκεύει τῷ
accord- knowledge as   with a weaker   vessel the
ing to

sex, since you are joint heirs of the grace of life, in order that your prayers may not be hindered. 8 Finally, all of you, have unity of spirit, sympathy, love of the brethren, a tender heart and a humble mind. 9 Do not return evil for evil or reviling for reviling; but on the contrary bless, for to this you have been called, that you may obtain a blessing. 10 For "He that would love life
and see good days,
let him keep his tongue from evil
and his lips from speaking guile;
11 let him turn away from evil and do right;
let him seek peace and pursue it.
12 For the eyes of the Lord are upon the righteous,
and his ears are open to their prayer.
But the face of the Lord is against those that do evil."
13 Now who is there to harm you if you are zealous for what is right? 14 But even if you do suffer for righteousness' sake, you will be blessed. Have no fear of them, nor be troubled, 15 but in your hearts

γυναικείῳ, ἀπονέμοντες τιμὴν ὡς καὶ
female, assigning honour as indeed

συγκληρονόμοις χάριτος ζωῆς, εἰς τὸ μὴ
co-heirs of [the] grace of life, for the not

ἐγκόπτεσθαι τὰς προσευχὰς ὑμῶν. 8 Τὸ δὲ
to be hindered the prayers of you.[b] Now the

τέλος πάντες ὁμόφρονες, συμπαθεῖς,
end[,] [be ye] all of one mind, sympathetic,

φιλάδελφοι, εὔσπλαγχνοι, ταπεινόφρονες,
loving [the] brothers, compassionate, humble-minded,

9 μὴ ἀποδιδόντες κακὸν ἀντὶ κακοῦ ἢ
not giving back evil instead of evil or

λοιδορίαν ἀντὶ λοιδορίας, τοὐναντίον δὲ
reviling instead of reviling, but on the contrary

εὐλογοῦντες, ὅτι εἰς τοῦτο ἐκλήθητε ἵνα
blessing, because to this ye were called in order that

εὐλογίαν κληρονομήσητε. 10 ὁ γὰρ θέλων
blessing ye might inherit. For the [one] wishing

ζωὴν ἀγαπᾶν καὶ ἰδεῖν ἡμέρας ἀγαθάς,
²life ¹to love and to see ²days ¹good,

παυσάτω τὴν γλῶσσαν ἀπὸ κακοῦ καὶ
let him the(his) tongue from evil and
restrain

χείλη τοῦ μὴ λαλῆσαι δόλον, 11 ἐκκλινάτω
[his] lips - not to speak[d] guile, ²let him turn aside

δὲ ἀπὸ κακοῦ καὶ ποιησάτω ἀγαθόν,
¹and from evil and let him do good,

ζητησάτω εἰρήνην καὶ διωξάτω αὐτήν·
let him seek peace and pursue it;

12 ὅτι ὀφθαλμοὶ κυρίου ἐπὶ δικαίους καὶ
because [the] eyes of [the] [are] on [the] and
Lord righteous

ὦτα αὐτοῦ εἰς δέησιν αὐτῶν, πρόσωπον
[the] of him [open] to [the] of them, ²[the] face
ears petition

δὲ κυρίου ἐπὶ ποιοῦντας κακά.
¹but of [the] [is] [ones] doing evil things.
Lord against

13 Καὶ τίς ὁ κακώσων ὑμᾶς ἐὰν τοῦ
And who the harming you if ³of the
[is] [one]

ἀγαθοῦ ζηλωταὶ γένησθε; 14 ἀλλ' εἰ καὶ
⁴good ²zealots ¹ye become ? but if indeed

πάσχοιτε διὰ δικαιοσύνην, μακάριοι. τὸν
ye suffer because of righteousness, blessed [are ye]. ²the

δὲ φόβον αὐτῶν μὴ φοβηθῆτε μηδὲ
¹But ⁴fear ⁵of them ²fear ye not nor

ταραχθῆτε, 15 κύριον δὲ τὸν Χριστὸν
be ye troubled, ¹but ⁴[as] ⁵Lord - ²Christ

reverence Christ as Lord. Always be prepared to make a defense to any one who calls you to account for the hope that is in you, yet do it with gentleness and reverence; [16]and keep your conscience clear. so that, when you are abused, those who revile your good behavior in Christ may be put to shame. [17]For it is better to suffer for doing right, if that should be God's will, than for doing wrong. [18]For Christ also died[f] for sins once for all, the righteous for the unrighteous, that he might bring us to God, being put to death in the flesh but made alive in the spirit; [19]in which he went and preached to the spirits in prison, [20]who formerly did not obey, when God's patience waited in the days of Noah, during the building of the ark, in which a few, that is, eight persons, were saved through water. [21]Baptism, which corresponds to this, now saves you, not as a removal of dirt from the body but as an appeal to God for a clear conscience, through the

ἁγιάσατε ἐν ταῖς καρδίαις ὑμῶν, ἕτοιμοι
[s]sanctify in the hearts of you, ready

ἀεὶ πρὸς ἀπολογίαν παντὶ τῷ αἰτοῦντι
always for defence to every one asking

ὑμᾶς λόγον περὶ τῆς ἐν ὑμῖν ἐλπίδος,
you a word concerning [1]the [3]in [4]you [2]hope,

16 ἀλλὰ μετὰ πραΰτητος καὶ φόβου,
but with meekness and fear,

συνείδησιν ἔχοντες ἀγαθήν, ἵνα ἐν ᾧ
[3]conscience [1]having [2]a good, in order that while

καταλαλεῖσθε καταισχυνθῶσιν οἱ ἐπηρεάζον-
ye are spoken against [3]may be shamed [by] [1]the [ones] [2]abusing

τες ὑμῶν τὴν ἀγαθὴν ἐν Χριστῷ
[you] [7]of you [4]the [5]good [8]in [9]Christ

ἀναστροφήν. 17 κρεῖττον γὰρ ἀγαθοποι-
[6]conduct. For [it is] better doing

οῦντας, εἰ θέλοι τὸ θέλημα τοῦ θεοῦ,
good, if [4]wills [1]the [2]will - [3]of God,

πάσχειν ἢ κακοποιοῦντας. 18 ὅτι καὶ
to suffer than doing evil. Because indeed

Χριστὸς ἅπαξ περὶ ἁμαρτιῶν ἀπέθανεν,
Christ once [2]concerning [3]sins [1]died,

δίκαιος ὑπὲρ ἀδίκων, ἵνα ὑμᾶς προσαγάγῃ
a righteous on be- unrighteous in or- [2]you [1]he might
man half of ones, der that bring

τῷ θεῷ, θανατωθεὶς μὲν σαρκὶ ζωοποιηθεὶς
- to being put to on one in [the] quickened
God, death hand flesh[,]

δὲ πνεύματι· 19 ἐν ᾧ καὶ τοῖς ἐν
on the in [the] in which indeed [3]to the [4]in
other spirit;

φυλακῇ πνεύμασιν πορευθεὶς ἐκήρυξεν,
[3]prison [3]spirits [1]going he proclaimed,

20 ἀπειθήσασίν ποτε ὅτε ἀπεξεδέχετο ἡ
to disobeying ones then when [4]waited [1]the

τοῦ θεοῦ μακροθυμία ἐν ἡμέραις Νῶε
- [3]of God [2]longsuffering in [the] days of Noe

κατασκευαζομένης κιβωτοῦ, εἰς ἣν ὀλίγοι,
[2]being prepared [1]an ark,[a] in which a few,

τοῦτ' ἔστιν ὀκτὼ ψυχαί, διεσώθησαν δι'
this is eight souls, were through
quite saved

ὕδατος. 21 ὃ καὶ ὑμᾶς ἀντίτυπον νῦν
water. [1]Which [3]also [5]us [2]figure [4]now

σώζει βάπτισμα, οὐ σαρκὸς ἀπόθεσις
[5]saves [even] baptism, not [3]of [the] [1]a putting
flesh away

ῥύπου ἀλλὰ συνειδήσεως ἀγαθῆς ἐπερώτημα
[2]of [the] but [3]conscience [2]of a good [1]an answer
filth

resurrection of Jesus Christ, [22]who has gone into heaven and is at the right hand of God, with angels, authorities, and powers subject to him.

CHAPTER 4

SINCE therefore Christ suffered in the flesh,[h] arm yourselves with the same thought, for whoever has suffered in the flesh has ceased from sin, [2]so as to live for the rest of the time in the flesh no longer by human passions but by the will of God. [3]Let the time that is past suffice for doing what the Gentiles like to do, living in licentiousness, passions, drunkenness, revels, carousing, and lawless idolatry. [4]They are surprised that you do not now join them in the same wild profligacy, and they abuse you; [5]but they will give account to him who is ready to judge the living and the dead. [6]For this is why the gospel was preached even to the dead, that though judged in the flesh like men, they might live in the spirit like God.

[h] Other ancient authorities add *for us;* some *for you*

εἰς θεόν, δι' ἀναστάσεως Ἰησοῦ Χριστοῦ,
toward God, through [the] resurrection of Jesus Christ,

22 ὅς ἐστιν ἐν δεξιᾷ θεοῦ, πορευθεὶς
who is at [the] right of God, having gone
            [hand]

εἰς οὐρανόν, ὑποταγέντων αὐτῷ ἀγγέλων
into heaven, [6]being subjected [7]to him [1]angels

καὶ ἐξουσιῶν καὶ δυνάμεων.
[2]and [3]authorities [4]and [5]powers[a].

4 Χριστοῦ οὖν παθόντος σαρκὶ καὶ ὑμεῖς
[2]Christ [1]there- having in [the] [2]also [1]ye
       fore suffered[a] flesh

τὴν αὐτὴν ἔννοιαν ὁπλίσασθε, ὅτι ὁ
[4]the [5]same [6]mind [3]arm your- because the
            selves [with],   [one]

παθὼν σαρκὶ πέπαυται ἁμαρτίας, 2 εἰς
having in [the] flesh has ceased from sin, for
suffered

τὸ μηκέτι ἀνθρώπων ἐπιθυμίαις ἀλλὰ
the [1]no longer [9]of men [8]in [the] lusts [10]but

θελήματι θεοῦ τὸν ἐπίλοιπον ἐν σαρκὶ
[11]in [the] will [12]of God [3]the [4]remaining [6]in [7][the] flesh

βιῶσαι χρόνον. 3 ἀρκετὸς γὰρ ὁ παρεληλυ-
[5]to live [5]time. For [5]sufficient [1]the [3]having passed

θὼς χρόνος τὸ βούλημα τῶν ἐθνῶν
away [2]time [4][is] [7]the [8]purpose [9]of the [10]nations

κατειργάσθαι, πεπορευμένους ἐν ἀσελγείαις,
[6]to have worked out, having gone [on] in licentiousnes*es*,

ἐπιθυμίαις, οἰνοφλυγίαις, κώμοις, πότοις
lusts, debaucheries, carousals, drinking
                            bouts

καὶ ἀθεμίτοις εἰδωλολατρίαις. 4 ἐν ᾧ
and unlawful idolatries. While

ξενίζονται μὴ συντρεχόντων ὑμῶν εἰς
they are surprised [2]not [3]running with [1]you[a] to

τὴν αὐτὴν τῆς ἀσωτίας ἀνάχυσιν, βλασ-
the same – [2]of profligacy [1]excess, blas-

φημοῦντες· 5 οἳ ἀποδώσουσιν λόγον τῷ
pheming; who will render account to the
                             [one]

ἑτοίμως ἔχοντι κρῖναι ζῶντας καὶ νεκρούς.
readily having to judge living and dead.
= who is ready

6 εἰς τοῦτο γὰρ καὶ νεκροῖς εὐηγγελίσθη,
[2]for [3]this [1]For indeed [2]to [1]good news
                  dead men was preached,

ἵνα κριθῶσι μὲν κατὰ ἀνθρώπους
in order [3]they might [1]on one according to men
that be judged hand

σαρκί, ζῶσι δὲ κατὰ θεὸν πνεύματι.
in [the] [2]might [1]on the according God in [the] spirit.
flesh, live other to

7 The end of all things is at hand; therefore keep sane and sober for your prayers. ⁸Above all hold unfailing your love for one another, since love covers a multitude of sins. ⁹Practice hospitality ungrudgingly to one another. ¹⁰As each has received a gift, employ it for one another, as good stewards of God's varied grace: ¹¹whoever speaks, as one who utters oracles of God; whoever renders service, as one who renders it by the strength which God supplies; in order that in everything God may be glorified through Jesus Christ. To him belong glory and dominion for ever and ever. Amen. 12 Beloved, do not be surprised at the fiery ordeal which comes upon you to prove you, as though something strange were happening to you. ¹³But rejoice in so far as you share Christ's sufferings, that you may also rejoice and be glad when his glory is revealed. ¹⁴If you are reproached for the name of Christ, you are blessed, because the spirit of glory[i] and of

---

7 Πάντων δὲ τὸ τέλος ἤγγικεν.
Now of all things the end has drawn near.

σωφρονήσατε οὖν καὶ νήψατε εἰς
Be ye soberminded therefore and be ye sober unto

προσευχάς· 8 πρὸ πάντων τὴν εἰς ἑαυτοὺς
prayers; before all things – ⁴to ⁵yourselves

ἀγάπην ἐκτενῆ ἔχοντες, ὅτι ἀγάπη
³love ²fervent ¹having, because love

καλύπτει πλῆθος ἁμαρτιῶν· 9 φιλόξενοι εἰς
covers a multitude of sins; [be] hospitable to

ἀλλήλους ἄνευ γογγυσμοῦ· 10 ἕκαστος καθὼς
one another without murmuring; each one as

ἔλαβεν χάρισμα, εἰς ἑαυτοὺς αὐτὸ διακον-
he received a gift, ³to ⁴yourselves ²it ¹minister-

οῦντες ὡς καλοὶ οἰκονόμοι ποικίλης χάριτος
ing as good stewards of [the] manifold grace

θεοῦ· 11 εἴ τις λαλεῖ, ὡς λόγια θεοῦ·
of God; if anyone speaks, as [the] oracles of God;

εἴ τις διακονεῖ, ὡς ἐξ ἰσχύος ἧς χορηγεῖ
if anyone ministers, as by strength which ²supplies

ὁ θεός· ἵνα ἐν πᾶσιν δοξάζηται ὁ θεὸς
– ¹God; in or- in all things ²may be glorified – ¹God
der that

διὰ Ἰησοῦ Χριστοῦ, ᾧ ἐστιν ἡ δόξα
through Jesus Christ, to whom is° the glory
=whose is

καὶ τὸ κράτος εἰς τοὺς αἰῶνας τῶν
and the might unto the ages of the

αἰώνων· ἀμήν.
ages : Amen.

12 Ἀγαπητοί, μὴ ξενίζεσθε τῇ ἐν ὑμῖν
Beloved, be not surprised [at] ¹the ⁴among ⁵you

πυρώσει πρὸς πειρασμὸν ὑμῖν γινομένῃ,
²fiery trial ⁶for ⁷trial ⁸to you ³happening,

ὡς ξένου ὑμῖν συμβαίνοντος, 13 ἀλλὰ
as a surprising ²to you ¹occurringª, but
thing

καθὸ κοινωνεῖτε τοῖς τοῦ Χριστοῦ
²as ³ye share ⁴the – ¹of Christ

παθήμασιν χαίρετε, ἵνα καὶ ἐν τῇ ἀπο-
⁵sufferings ⁷rejoice, in order also at the reve-
that

καλύψει τῆς δόξης αὐτοῦ χαρῆτε ἀγαλ-
lation of the glory of him ye may exult-
rejoice

λιώμενοι. 14 εἰ ὀνειδίζεσθε ἐν ὀνόματι
ing. If ye are reproached in [the] name

Χριστοῦ, μακάριοι, ὅτι τὸ τῆς δόξης
of Christ, blessed [are ye], because ¹the – ²of glory

God rests upon you. [15]But let none of you suffer as a murderer, or a thief, or a wrongdoer, or a mischief-maker; [16]yet if one suffers as a Christian, let him not be ashamed, but under that name let him glorify God. [17]For the time has come for judgment to begin with the household of God; and if it begins with us, what will be the end of those who do not obey the gospel of God? [18]And

"If the righteous man
    is scarcely saved,
where   will   the
    impious and sinner
    appear?"

[19]Therefore let those who suffer according to God's will do right and entrust their souls to a faithful Creator.

καὶ   τὸ   τοῦ   θεοῦ   πνεῦμα   ἐφ’   ὑμᾶς
[4]and [5]the(?that) –   [6]of God [2]spirit [8]on [9]you

ἀναπαύεται.   15 μὴ γάρ τις ὑμῶν πασχέτω
[7]rests.   [3]Not [1]for [4]anyone [5]of you [2]let [6]suffer

ὡς   φονεὺς   ἢ   κλέπτης   ἢ   κακοποιὸς   ἢ
as a murderer or a thief or an evildoer or

ὡς   ἀλλοτριεπίσκοπος·   16 εἰ   δὲ   ὡς
as a pryer into other men's affairs;   but if   as

Χριστιανός,   μὴ   αἰσχυνέσθω,   δοξαζέτω   δὲ
a Christian, let him not be shamed, but let him glorify

τὸν   θεὸν   ἐν   τῷ   ὀνόματι   τούτῳ.   17 ὅτι
–   God by   this name.   Because

[ὁ]   καιρὸς   τοῦ   ἄρξασθαι   τὸ   κρίμα   ἀπὸ
the   time   –   to begin[d]   the judgment from
    [?has come]

τοῦ   οἴκου   τοῦ   θεοῦ·   εἰ   δὲ   πρῶτον   ἀφ’
the household   –   of God; and if   firstly   from

ἡμῶν,   τί   τὸ   τέλος   τῶν   ἀπειθούντων
us, what [will be] the   end   of the [ones]   disobeying

τῷ   τοῦ   θεοῦ   εὐαγγελίῳ;   18 καὶ   εἰ   ὁ
the   –   [2]of God   [1]gospel?   and   if   the

δίκαιος   μόλις   σώζεται,   ὁ   [δὲ]   ἀσεβὴς
righteous man scarcely is saved, [3]the   –   [4]impious

καὶ   ἁμαρτωλὸς   ποῦ   φανεῖται;   19 ὥστε
[5]and [6]sinner [1]where [2]will [7]appear ?   so as

καὶ   οἱ   πάσχοντες   κατὰ   τὸ   θέλημα   τοῦ
indeed the   suffering   accord- the will   –
[ones]   ing to

θεοῦ   πιστῷ   κτίστῃ   παρατιθέσθωσαν   τὰς
of God [5]to a [6]Creator [1]let them commit   [2]the
    faithful

ψυχὰς   αὐτῶν   ἐν   ἀγαθοποιΐᾳ.
[3]souls [4]of them in   welldoing.

CHAPTER 5

SO I exhort the elders among you, as a fellow elder and a witness of the sufferings of Christ as well as a partaker in the glory that is to be revealed. [2]Tend the flock of God that is your charge,[j] not by constraint but willingly,[k]

[j] Other ancient authorities add exercising the oversight
[k] Other ancient authorities add as God would have you

5 Πρεσβυτέρους   οὖν   ἐν   ὑμῖν   παρακαλῶ
Elders   there- among you   I exhort
    fore

ὁ   συμπρεσβύτερος   καὶ   μάρτυς   τῶν   τοῦ
the   co-elder   and   witness   [1]of the   –

Χριστοῦ   παθημάτων,   ὁ   καὶ   τῆς   μελλούσης
[3]of Christ [2]sufferings. [1]the [3]also [4]of the [5]being about

ἀποκαλύπτεσθαι   δόξης   κοινωνός·   2 ποιμάνατε
[7]to be revealed [5]glory [2]sharer :   shepherd

τὸ   ἐν   ὑμῖν   ποίμνιον   τοῦ   θεοῦ,   μὴ
[1]the [4]among [5]you   [2]flock   –   [3]of God, not

ἀναγκαστῶς   ἀλλὰ   ἑκουσίως   κατὰ   θεόν,
by way of   but   willingly   accord-   God,
compulsion   ing to

not for shameful gain but eagerly, ³not as domineering over those in your charge but being examples to the flock. ⁴And when the chief Shepherd is manifested you will obtain the unfading crown of glory. ⁵Likewise you that are younger be subject to the elders. Clothe yourselves, all of you, with humility toward one another, for "God opposes the proud, but gives grace to the humble."

6 Humble yourselves therefore under the mighty hand of God, that in due time he may exalt you. ⁷Cast all your anxieties on him, for he cares about you. ⁸Be sober, be watchful. Your adversary the devil prowls around like a roaring lion, seeking some one to devour. ⁹Resist him, firm in your faith, knowing that the same experience of suffering is required of your brotherhood throughout the world. ¹⁰And after you have suffered a little while, the God of all grace, who has called you to his eternal glory in Christ, will himself restore, establish, and strengthen¹ you. ¹¹To

μηδὲ αἰσχροκερδῶς ἀλλὰ προθύμως, 3 μηδ'
nor   from eagerness for   but   eagerly,   nor
       base gain

ὡς κατακυριεύοντες τῶν κλήρων ἀλλὰ
as   exercising lordship over   the   lots*   but

τύποι γινόμενοι τοῦ ποιμνίου· 4 καὶ
²examples ¹becoming   of the   flock;   and

φανερωθέντος τοῦ ἀρχιποίμενος κομιεῖσθε
appearing   the   chief shepherdª   ye will receive
=when the chief shepherd appears

τὸν ἀμαράντινον τῆς δόξης στέφανον.
the   unfading   -   ²of glory   ¹crown.

5 Ὁμοίως, νεώτεροι, ὑποτάγητε πρεσβυτέ-
Likewise,   younger men,   submit yourselves   to older

ροις· πάντες δὲ ἀλλήλοις τὴν ταπεινοφρο-
men;   and all   ²to one another   -   ²humil-

σύνην ἐγκομβώσασθε, ὅτι ὁ θεὸς ὑπερηφάνοις
ity   ¹gird ye on,   because - God   ²arrogant men

ἀντιτάσσεται, ταπεινοῖς δὲ δίδωσιν χάριν.
¹resists,   but to humble men   he gives   grace.

6 Ταπεινώθητε οὖν ὑπὸ τὴν κραταιὰν
Be ye humbled   therefore under   the   mighty

χεῖρα τοῦ θεοῦ, ἵνα ὑμᾶς ὑψώσῃ ἐν
hand   -   of God, in order   ²you   ¹he may exalt   in
                     that

καιρῷ, 7 πᾶσαν τὴν μέριμναν ὑμῶν
time,   ²all   ³the   ⁴anxiety   ⁵of you

ἐπιρίψαντες ἐπ' αὐτόν, ὅτι αὐτῷ μέλει
¹casting   on   him,   because ²to him ¹it matters

περὶ ὑμῶν. 8 Νήψατε, γρηγορήσατε. ὁ
concerning you.   Be ye sober,   watch ye.   The

ἀντίδικος ὑμῶν διάβολος ὡς λέων ὠρυόμενος
adversary   of you   [the] devil   as   a lion   roaring

περιπατεῖ ζητῶν τινα καταπιεῖν· 9 ᾧ
walks about   seeking   whom   to devour;   whom

ἀντίστητε στερεοὶ τῇ πίστει, εἰδότες τὰ
oppose   firm   in the   faith,   knowing   the

αὐτὰ τῶν παθημάτων τῇ ἐν τῷ κόσμῳ
same   of the   sufferings   ²in   ⁵in   ⁴the   ⁷world
things   the

ὑμῶν ἀδελφότητι ἐπιτελεῖσθαι. 10 Ὁ δὲ
⁴of you   ³brotherhood   ¹to be accomplished.   ²the ¹Now

θεὸς πάσης χάριτος, ὁ καλέσας ὑμᾶς
God   of all   grace,   the [one] having called   you

εἰς τὴν αἰώνιον αὐτοῦ δόξαν ἐν Χριστῷ,
to   the   ¹eternal   ³of him   ²glory   in   Christ,

ὀλίγον παθόντας αὐτὸς καταρτίσει, στηρίξει,
¹[you]   ²having   [him]self   will adjust,   confirm,
ⁱa little   suffered

¹ Other ancient authorities read restore, establish, strengthen and settle

* That is, the various spheres assigned to the elders.

him be the dominion for ever and ever. Amen.

12 By Silva'nus, a faithful brother as I regard him, I have written briefly to you, exhorting and declaring that this is the true grace of God; stand fast in it. [13] She who is at Babylon, who is likewise chosen, sends you greetings; and so does my son Mark. [14] Greet one another with the kiss of love.

Peace to all of you that are in Christ.

σθενώσει,   θεμελιώσει.   11 αὐτῷ   τὸ   κράτος
strengthen,   found.   To him [is]ᶜ the   might
=His is*

εἰς   τοὺς   αἰῶνας   τῶν   αἰώνων·   ἀμήν.
unto   the   ages   of the   ages: Amen.

12 Διὰ   Σιλουανοῦ   ὑμῖν   τοῦ   πιστοῦ
Through   Silvanus   to you   the   faithful

ἀδελφοῦ,   ὡς   λογίζομαι,   δι' ὀλίγων   ἔγραψα,
brother,   as   I reckon,   by   a few   I wrote,
means of [words]

παρακαλῶν   καὶ   ἐπιμαρτυρῶν   ταύτην   εἶναι
exhorting   and   witnessing   this   to be

ἀληθῆ   χάριν   τοῦ   θεοῦ,   εἰς   ἣν   στῆτε.
[the] true   grace   -   of God,   in   which   ye stand.

13 Ἀσπάζεται   ὑμᾶς   ἡ   ἐν   Βαβυλῶνι
¹⁰greets   ¹¹you   ¹The   ²in   ⁴Babylon

συνεκλεκτὴ   καὶ   Μᾶρκος   ὁ   υἱός   μου.
²co-chosen   ⁵and   ⁶Mark   ⁷the   ⁸son   ⁹of me.
[? church]

14 ἀσπάσασθε   ἀλλήλους   ἐν   φιλήματι   ἀγάπης.
Greet ye   one another   with   a kiss   of love.

Εἰρήνη   ὑμῖν   πᾶσιν   τοῖς   ἐν   Χριστῷ.
Peace   to you   all   the ones   in   Christ.

II. PETER 1

ΠΕΤΡΟΥ Β
Of Peter 2

CHAPTER 1

SIMON Peter, a servant and apostle of Jesus Christ,

To those who have obtained a faith of equal standing with ours in the righteousness of our God and Savior Jesus Christ:[a]

2 May grace and peace be multiplied to you in the knowledge of God and of Jesus our Lord.

3 His divine power has granted to us all things

1 Συμεὼν   Πέτρος   δοῦλος   καὶ   ἀπόστολος
Symeon   Peter   a slave   and   an apostle

Ἰησοῦ   Χριστοῦ   τοῖς   ἰσότιμον   ἡμῖν
of Jesus   Christ   ¹to the   ²equally   ⁵with
[ones]   precious   us

λαχοῦσιν   πίστιν   ἐν   δικαιοσύνῃ   τοῦ   θεοῦ
²having   ⁴faith   in   righteousness   of the   God
obtained   [the]

ἡμῶν   καὶ   σωτῆρος   Ἰησοῦ   Χριστοῦ·
of us   and   Saviour   Jesus   Christ :

2 χάρις   ὑμῖν   καὶ   εἰρήνη   πληθυνθείη   ἐν
Grace   to you   anu   peace   may it be multiplied by

ἐπιγνώσει   τοῦ   θεοῦ   καὶ   Ἰησοῦ   τοῦ
a full knowledge   -   of God   and   of Jesus   the

κυρίου   ἡμῶν.
Lord   of us.

3 Ὡς   τὰ   πάντα   ἡμῖν   τῆς   θείας   δυνάμεως
As   -   all things   to us   the   divine   power
=his divine power has given us all things . . .

ᵃ Or *of our God and the Savior Jesus Christ*

* Cf. 4. 11 (a statement of fact, not a wish).

that pertain to life and godliness, through the knowledge of him who called us to[b] his own glory and excellence, [4]by which he has granted to us his precious and very great promises, that through these you may escape from the corruption that is in the world because of passion, and become partakers of the divine nature. [5]For this very reason make every effort to supplement your faith with virtue, and virtue with knowledge, [6]and knowledge with self-control, and self-control with steadfastness, and steadfastness with godliness, [7]and godliness with brotherly affection, and brotherly affection with love. [8]For if these things are yours and abound, they keep you from being ineffective or unfruitful in the knowledge of our Lord Jesus Christ. [9]For whoever lacks these things is blind and shortsighted and has forgotten that he was cleansed from his old sins. [10]Therefore, brethren, be the more zealous

[b] Or by

αὐτοῦ τὰ πρὸς ζωὴν καὶ εὐσέβειαν δεδωρημένης
of him – [belong- life and piety having given[a]
ing] to

διὰ τῆς ἐπιγνώσεως τοῦ καλέσαντος ἡμᾶς
through the full knowledge of the [one] having called us

ἰδίᾳ δόξῃ καὶ ἀρετῇ, 4 δι᾽ ὧν τὰ τίμια
to [his] glory and virtue, through which the [2]precious
own things

καὶ μέγιστα ἡμῖν ἐπαγγέλματα δεδώρηται,
[4]and [5]very great [2]to us [6]promises [1]he has given,

ἵνα διὰ τούτων γένησθε θείας κοινωνοὶ
in or- through these ye might [2]of a divine [1]sharers
der that become

φύσεως, ἀποφυγόντες τῆς ἐν τῷ κόσμῳ
[3]nature, escaping from [1]the [3]in [4]the [5]world

ἐν ἐπιθυμίᾳ φθορᾶς. 5 καὶ αὐτὸ τοῦτο
[6]by [7]lust [2]corruption. [2]also [3]for this very thing
(reason)

δὲ σπουδὴν πᾶσαν παρεισενέγκαντες
[1]But [4]diligence [5]all [4]bringing in

ἐπιχορηγήσατε ἐν τῇ πίστει ὑμῶν τὴν
supply in the faith of you –

ἀρετήν, ἐν δὲ τῇ ἀρετῇ τὴν γνῶσιν,
virtue, and in – virtue – knowledge,

6 ἐν δὲ τῇ γνώσει τὴν ἐγκράτειαν,
and in – knowledge – self-control,

ἐν δὲ τῇ ἐγκρατείᾳ τὴν ὑπομονήν, ἐν
and in – self-control – endurance, [2]in

δὲ τῇ ὑπομονῇ τὴν εὐσέβειαν, 7 ἐν δὲ
[1]and – endurance – piety, and in

τῇ εὐσεβείᾳ τὴν φιλαδελφίαν, ἐν δὲ
– piety – brotherly friendship, and in

τῇ φιλαδελφίᾳ τὴν ἀγάπην. 8 ταῦτα
– brotherly friendship – love. these things

γὰρ ὑμῖν ὑπάρχοντα καὶ πλεονάζοντα
For [2]in you [1]being and abounding

οὐκ ἀργοὺς οὐδὲ ἀκάρπους καθίστησιν
[3]not [4]barren [5]nor [6]unfruitful [1]makes [2][you]

εἰς τὴν τοῦ κυρίου ἡμῶν Ἰησοῦ Χριστοῦ
in [1]the [3]of the [4]Lord [5]of us [6]Jesus [7]Christ

ἐπίγνωσιν· 9 ᾧ γὰρ μὴ πάρεστιν ταῦτα,
[2]full knowledge; for [he] [3]not [2]is(are) [1]these
in whom [4]present things,

τυφλός ἐστιν μυωπάζων, λήθην λαβὼν
[2]blind [1]is being short-sighted, forgetfulness taking
= being forgetful

τοῦ καθαρισμοῦ τῶν πάλαι αὐτοῦ ἁμαρτιῶν.
of the cleansing of the [2]in time [3]of him [1]sins.
past

10 διὸ μᾶλλον, ἀδελφοί, σπουδάσατε
Wherefore rather, brothers, be ye diligent

to confirm your call and election, for if you do this you will never fall; ¹¹so there will be richly provided for you an entrance into the eternal kingdom of our Lord and Savior Jesus Christ. 12 Therefore I intend always to remind you of these things, though you know them and are established in the truth that you have. ¹³I think it right, as long as I am in this body,ᶜ to arouse you by way of reminder, ¹⁴since I know that the putting off of my bodyᶜ will be soon, as our Lord Jesus Christ showed me. ¹⁵And I will see to it that after my departure you may be able at any time to recall these things.
16 For we did not follow cleverly devised myths when we made known to you the power and coming of our Lord Jesus Christ, but we were eyewitnesses of his majesty. ¹⁷For when he received honor and glory from God the Father and the voice was borne to him by the Majestic

ᶜ Greek tent

βεβαίαν ὑμῶν τὴν κλῆσιν καὶ ἐκλογὴν
²firm ⁷of you ⁸the ⁴calling ⁵and ⁶choice

ποιεῖσθαι· ταῦτα γὰρ ποιοῦντες οὐ μὴ
¹to make; for these things doing by no means

πταίσητέ ποτε. 11 οὕτως γὰρ πλουσίως
ye will fail ever. For so ²richly

ἐπιχορηγηθήσεται ὑμῖν ἡ εἴσοδος εἰς τὴν
¹will be supplied ²to you the entrance into the

αἰώνιον βασιλείαν τοῦ κυρίου ἡμῶν καὶ
eternal kingdom of the Lord of us and

σωτῆρος Ἰησοῦ Χριστοῦ.
Saviour Jesus Christ.

12 Διὸ μελλήσω ἀεὶ ὑμᾶς ὑπομιμνήσκειν
Wherefore I will intend always you to remind

περὶ τούτων, καίπερ εἰδότας καὶ
concerning these things, though knowing and

ἐστηριγμένους ἐν τῇ παρούσῃ ἀληθείᾳ.
having been confirmed in the present truth.

13 δίκαιον δὲ ἡγοῦμαι, ἐφ᾽ ὅσον εἰμὶ
And ²right ¹I deem [it], so long as† I am

ἐν τούτῳ τῷ σκηνώματι, διεγείρειν ὑμᾶς
in this – tabernacle, to rouse you

ἐν ὑπομνήσει, 14 εἰδὼς ὅτι ταχινή ἐστιν
by a reminder, knowing that soon is

ἡ ἀπόθεσις τοῦ σκηνώματός μου, καθὼς
the putting off of the tabernacle of me, as

καὶ ὁ κύριος ἡμῶν Ἰησοῦς Χριστὸς
indeed the Lord of us Jesus Christ

ἐδήλωσέν μοι· 15 σπουδάσω δὲ καὶ
made clear to me; and I will be diligent also

ἑκάστοτε ἔχειν ὑμᾶς μετὰ τὴν ἐμὴν
⁶always ⁷to have ¹you ²after – ⁴my

ἔξοδον τὴν τούτων μνήμην ποιεῖσθαι.
⁵exodus ⁸the ¹⁰of these things ⁹memory ¹to cause.

16 οὐ γὰρ σεσοφισμένοις μύθοις ἐξακολου-
For not ³having been ²fables ¹follow-
cleverly devised

θήσαντες ἐγνωρίσαμεν ὑμῖν τὴν τοῦ κυρίου
ing we made known to you ¹the ⁵of the ⁶Lord

ἡμῶν Ἰησοῦ Χριστοῦ δύναμιν καὶ
⁷of us ⁸Jesus ⁹Christ ²power ³and

παρουσίαν, ἀλλ᾽ ἐπόπται γενηθέντες τῆς
⁴presence, but ²eyewitnesses ¹having become ³of the

ἐκείνου μεγαλειότητος. 17 λαβὼν γὰρ
⁵of that one ⁴majesty. For receiving

παρὰ θεοῦ πατρὸς τιμὴν καὶ δόξαν
from God [the] Father honour and glory

φωνῆς ἐνεχθείσης αὐτῷ τοιᾶσδε ὑπὸ τῆς
²a voice ³being borne⁴ ¹to him ⁵such by the

Glory, "This is my beloved Son,[d] with whom I am well pleased," [18]we heard this voice borne from heaven, for we were with him on the holy mountain. [19]And we have the prophetic word made more sure. You will do well to pay attention to this as to a lamp shining in a dark place, until the day dawns and the morning star rises in your hearts. [20]First of all you must understand this, that no prophecy of scripture is a matter of one's own interpretation, [21]because no prophecy ever came by the impulse of man, but men moved by the Holy Spirit spoke from God.[e]

| μεγαλοπρεποῦς | δόξης· | ὁ | υἱός | μου | ὁ |
| magnificent | glory : | The | Son | of me | the |

| ἀγαπητός | μου | οὗτός | ἐστιν, | εἰς | ὃν | ἐγὼ |
| beloved | of me | this | is, | in | whom | I |

| εὐδόκησα, | — 18 | καὶ | ταύτην | τὴν | φωνὴν |
| was wellpleased,— | | and | this | – | voice |

| ἡμεῖς | ἠκούσαμεν | ἐξ | οὐρανοῦ | ἐνεχθεῖσαν |
| we | heard | ²out of | ³heaven | ¹being borne |

| σὺν | αὐτῷ | ὄντες | ἐν | τῷ | ἁγίῳ | ὄρει. | 19 καὶ |
| ⁵with | ⁶him | ⁴being | in | the | holy | mountain. | And |

| ἔχομεν | βεβαιότερον | τὸν | προφητικὸν | λόγον, |
| we have | more firm | the | prophetic | word, |

| ᾧ | καλῶς | ποιεῖτε | προσέχοντες | ὡς | λύχνῳ |
| to which | ²well | ¹ye do | taking heed | as | to a lamp |

| φαίνοντι | ἐν | αὐχμηρῷ | τόπῳ, | ἕως | οὗ |
| shining | in | a murky | place, | until |

| ἡμέρα | διαυγάσῃ | καὶ | φωσφόρος | ἀνατείλῃ |
| day | dawns | and | [the] daystar | rises |

| ἐν | ταῖς | καρδίαις | ὑμῶν· | 20 τοῦτο | πρῶτον |
| in | the | hearts | of you; | ²this | ³firstly |

γινώσκοντες,	ὅτι	πᾶσα	προφητεία	γραφῆς
¹knowing,	that	every	prophecy	of scripture
		=no . . . is . . .		

| ἰδίας | ἐπιλύσεως | οὐ | γίνεται· | 21 οὐ | γὰρ |
| of [its] own | solution | not | becomes; | for not |

| θελήματι | ἀνθρώπου | ἠνέχθη | προφητεία |
| by will | of man | ²was borne | ¹prophecy |

| ποτέ, | ἀλλὰ | ὑπὸ | πνεύματος | ἁγίου | φερόμενοι |
| at any time, | but | ⁶by | ⁸Spirit | ⁷[the] Holy | ⁴being borne |

| ἐλάλησαν | ἀπὸ | θεοῦ | ἄνθρωποι. |
| ²spoke | ³from | ⁴God | ¹men. |

CHAPTER 2

BUT false prophets also arose among the people, just as there will be false teachers among you, who will secretly bring in destructive heresies, even denying the Master who bought them, bringing upon themselves swift destruction. [2]And many

| 2 Ἐγένοντο | δὲ | καὶ | ψευδοπροφῆται | ἐν |
| But there were | | also | false prophets | among |

| τῷ | λαῷ, | ὡς | καὶ | ἐν | ὑμῖν | ἔσονται |
| the | people, | as | indeed | among | you | there will be |

| ψευδοδιδάσκαλοι, | οἵτινες | παρεισάξουσιν |
| false teachers, | who | will secretly bring in |

| αἱρέσεις | ἀπωλείας, | καὶ | τὸν | ἀγοράσαντα |
| opinions | of destruction,* | and | ²the | ⁴having bought |

| αὐτοὺς | δεσπότην | ἀρνούμενοι, | ἐπάγοντες |
| ⁵them | ³Master | ¹denying, | bringing on |

| ἑαυτοῖς | ταχινὴν | ἀπώλειαν· | 2 καὶ | πολλοὶ |
| themselves | swift | destruction; | and | many |

[d] Or my Son, my (or the) Beloved

[e] Other authorities read moved by the Holy Spirit holy men of God spoke

* Genitive of quality : " destructive opinions."

will follow their licentiousness, and because of them the way of truth will be reviled. ³And in their greed they will exploit you with false words; from of old their condemnation has not been idle, and their destruction has not been asleep.

4 For if God did not spare the angels when they sinned, but cast them into hell and committed them to pits of nether gloom to be kept until the judgment; ⁵if he did not spare the ancient world, but preserved Noah, a herald of righteousness, with seven other persons, when he brought a flood upon the world of the ungodly; ⁶if by turning the cities of Sodom and Gomor'rah to ashes he condemned them to extinction and made them an example to those who were to be ungodly; ⁷and if he rescued righteous Lot, greatly distressed by the licentiousness of the wicked ⁸(for by what that righteous man saw and heard as he lived among them, he was vexed in his righteous soul day after day with their lawless deeds), ⁹then the Lord knows how to rescue the godly from

ἐξακολουθήσουσιν   αὐτῶν   ταῖς   ἀσελγείαις,
will follow   ³of them ¹the   ²licentiousnesses,

δι'   οὓς   ἡ   ὁδὸς   τῆς   ἀληθείας   βλασφημη-
be-   whom the way   of the truth   will be
cause of

θήσεται·   3 καὶ   ἐν   πλεονεξίᾳ   πλαστοῖς
blasphemed;   and   by   covetousness with fabricated

λόγοις   ὑμᾶς   ἐμπορεύσονται·   οἷς   τὸ   κρίμα
words   ²you   ¹they will make   for   the   judg-
                 merchandise of;   whom   ment

ἔκπαλαι   οὐκ   ἀργεῖ,   καὶ   ἡ   ἀπώλεια
of old   lingers not,   and   the   destruction

αὐτῶν   οὐ   νυστάζει.   4 εἰ   γὰρ   ὁ   θεὸς
of them   slumbers not.   For if   -   God

ἀγγέλων   ἁμαρτησάντων   οὐκ   ἐφείσατο,   ἀλλὰ
²angels   ³sinning   ¹spared not,   but

σιροῖς   ζόφου   ταρταρώσας   παρέδωκεν
²in pits ³of gloom ¹consigning to Tartarus ⁴delivered [them]

εἰς   κρίσιν   τηρουμένους,   5 καὶ   ἀρχαίου
⁶to   ⁷judgment ⁵being kept,   and   ²[the] ancient

κόσμου   οὐκ   ἐφείσατο,   ἀλλὰ   ὄγδοον   Νῶε
³world   ¹spared not,   but   ²[the]   ³Noe
                                  eighth man

δικαιοσύνης   κήρυκα   ἐφύλαξεν,   κατακλυσμὸν
⁵of righteousness ⁴a herald ¹guarded,   ²a flood

κόσμῳ   ἀσεβῶν   ἐπάξας,   6 καὶ   πόλεις
⁴a world ⁵of impious men ¹bringing ³on,   and   ³[the] cities

Σοδόμων   καὶ   Γομόρρας   τεφρώσας
⁴of Sodom   ⁵and   ⁶Gomorra   ¹covering [them]
                                    with ashes

καταστροφῇ   κατέκρινεν,   ὑπόδειγμα   μελ-
⁷by an overthrow ²condemned,   ³an example ³of men

λόντων   ἀσεβεῖν   τεθεικώς,   7 καὶ   δίκαιον
intending ⁴to live ¹having set(made), and   ²righteous
           impiously

Λῶτ   καταπονούμενον   ὑπὸ   τῆς   τῶν   ἀθέσμων
³Lot   ⁴being oppressed   ⁵by   ⁶the   ¹⁰of the   ¹¹lawless

ἐν   ἀσελγείᾳ   ἀναστροφῆς   ἐρρύσατο·   8 βλέμ-
⁸in   ⁹licentiousness ⁷conduct   ¹delivered;   ²in

ματι   γὰρ   καὶ   ἀκοῇ   ὁ   δίκαιος   ἐγκατοικῶν
seeing ¹for   and   in hear- the   righteous   dwelling
                     ing (that)   man

ἐν   αὐτοῖς   ἡμέραν   ἐξ   ἡμέρας   ψυχὴν
among them   day   after†   day   ²[his] ⁴soul

δικαίαν   ἀνόμοις   ἔργοις   ἐβασάνιζεν·
³righteous ⁵with [their] lawless ⁴works   ¹tormented;

9 οἶδεν   κύριος   εὐσεβεῖς   ἐκ   πειρασμοῦ
³knows*   ¹[the] Lord ⁴pious men ⁵out of   ⁶trial

* That is, " the Lord can deliver "; see note on page xviii.

trial, and to keep the unrighteous under punishment until the day of judgment, [10] and especially those who indulge in the lust of defiling passion and despise authority.

Bold and wilful, they are not afraid to revile the glorious ones, [11] whereas angels, though greater in might and power, do not pronounce a reviling judgment upon them before the Lord. [12] But these, like irrational animals, creatures of instinct, born to be caught and killed, reviling in matters of which they are ignorant, will be destroyed in the same destruction with them, [13] suffering wrong for their wrongdoing. They count it pleasure to revel in the daytime. They are blots and blemishes, reveling in their dissipation,[f] carousing with you. [14] They have eyes full of adultery, insatiable for sin. They entice unsteady souls. They have hearts trained in greed. Accursed children! [15] Forsaking the right way they have gone astray; they have followed the way of Balaam, the son of Be'or, who loved gain

[f] Other ancient authorities read love feasts

ῥύεσθαι,   ἀδίκους   δὲ   εἰς   ἡμέραν   κρίσεως
[3]to deliver,   [2]unjust men   [1]but   [5]for   [6]a day   [7]of judgment
κολαζομένους   τηρεῖν,   10 μάλιστα   δὲ   τοὺς
[4]being punished   [2]to keep,   and most of all   [1]the
ὀπίσω   σαρκὸς   ἐν   ἐπιθυμίᾳ   μιασμοῦ
[3]after   [4]flesh   [5]in   [6]lust   [7]of defilement*
πορευομένους   καὶ   κυριότητος   καταφρονοῦντας.
[2][ones] going   [8]and   [10]dominion   [9]despising.
τολμηταὶ   αὐθάδεις,   δόξας   οὐ   τρέμουσιν
[2]darers   [1]Self-satisfied,   glories   they do not tremble [at]
βλασφημοῦντες,   11 ὅπου   ἄγγελοι   ἰσχύϊ   καὶ
blaspheming,   where   angels   [2]in strength   [4]and
δυνάμει   μείζονες   ὄντες   οὐ   φέρουσιν   κατ᾽
[3]in power   [2]greater   [1]being   do not bring   against
αὐτῶν   παρὰ   κυρίῳ   βλάσφημον   κρίσιν.
them   before   [the] Lord   railing   judgment.
12 οὗτοι   δέ,   ὡς   ἄλογα   ζῷα   γεγεννημένα
But these   [1]as   [4]without   [3]animals   [5]having been
men,   reason   born
φυσικὰ   εἰς   ἅλωσιν   καὶ   φθοράν,   ἐν   οἷς
[2]natural   for   capture   and   corruption,   [3]in [3]things
                                                which
ἀγνοοῦσιν   βλασφημοῦντες,   ἐν   τῇ   φθορᾷ
[4]they are   [1]railing,   in   the   corruption
ignorant [of]
αὐτῶν   καὶ   φθαρήσονται,   13 ἀδικούμενοι
of them   indeed   they will be corrupted,   suffering wrong
μισθὸν   ἀδικίας·   ἡδονὴν   ἡγούμενοι   τὴν
[as] wages   of wrong;   [5][to be] pleasure   [1]deeming   –
ἐν   ἡμέρᾳ   τρυφήν,   ὑπίλοι   καὶ   μῶμοι
[3]in   [4][the] day   [2]luxury,   spots   and   blemishes
ἐντρυφῶντες   ἐν   ταῖς   ἀπάταις   αὐτῶν
revelling   in   the   deceits   of them
συνευωχούμενοι   ὑμῖν,   14 ὀφθαλμοὺς   ἔχοντες
feasting along with   you,   [2]eyes   [1]having
μεστοὺς   μοιχαλίδος   καὶ   ἀκαταπαύστους
full   of an adulteress   and   not ceasing from
ἁμαρτίας,   δελεάζοντες   ψυχὰς   ἀστηρίκτους,
sin,   alluring   [2]souls   [1]unsteady,
καρδίαν   γεγυμνασμένην   πλεονεξίας   ἔχοντες,
[2]a heart   [3]having been exercised   [4]of(in) covetousness   [1]having,
κατάρας   τέκνα·   15 καταλείποντες   εὐθεῖαν
[2]of curse   [1]children;   forsaking   a straight
ὁδὸν   ἐπλανήθησαν,   ἐξακολουθήσαντες   τῇ
way   they erred,   following   the
ὁδῷ   τοῦ   Βαλαὰμ   τοῦ   Βεώρ,   ὃς   μισθὸν
way   –   of Balaam   the [son] of   who   [2][the]
                              Beor,   wages

* Genitive of quality: " defiling lust."

from wrongdoing, ¹⁶but was rebuked for his own transgression; a dumb ass spoke with human voice and restrained the prophet's madness. 17 These are waterless springs and mists driven by a storm; for them the nether gloom of darkness has been reserved. ¹⁸For, uttering loud boasts of folly, they entice with licentious passions of the flesh men who have barely escaped from those who live in error. ¹⁹They promise them freedom, but they themselves are slaves of corruption; for whatever overcomes a man, to that he is enslaved. ²⁰For if, after they have escaped the defilements of the world through the knowledge of our Lord and Savior Jesus Christ, they are again entangled in them and overpowered, the last state has become worse for them than the first. ²¹For it would have been better for them never to have known the way of righteousness than after knowing it to turn back from the holy commandment delivered to them. ²²It has happened to them according to the true proverb, The dog

ἀδικίας   ἠγάπησεν,   16 ἔλεγξιν   δὲ   ἔσχεν
²of wrong   ¹loved,   and ²reproof   ¹had
ἰδίας   παρανομίας·   ὑποζύγιον   ἄφωνον   ἐν
of [his] own transgression;   ²ass   ¹a dumb   ⁴with
ἀνθρώπου   φωνῇ   φθεγξάμενον   ἐκώλυσεν
⁶of a man   ⁵voice   ²speaking   restrained
τὴν   τοῦ   προφήτου   παραφρονίαν.   17 οὗτοί
¹the   ³of the   ⁴prophet   ²madness.   These men
εἰσιν   πηγαὶ   ἄνυδροι   καὶ   ὁμίχλαι   ὑπὸ
are   ²springs   ¹waterless   and   ³mists   ²by
λαίλαπος   ἐλαυνόμεναι,   οἷς   ὁ   ζόφος   τοῦ
²storm   ¹being driven,   for whom the   gloom   of the
σκότους   τετήρηται.   18 ὑπέρογκα   γὰρ
darkness   has been kept.   For ²immoderate [words]
ματαιότητος   φθεγγόμενοι   δελεάζουσιν   ἐν
²of vanity   ¹speaking   they allure   by
ἐπιθυμίαις   σαρκὸς   ἀσελγείαις   τοὺς   ὀλίγως
[the] lusts   of [the] flesh   in excesses   the [ones]   almost
ἀποφεύγοντας   τοὺς   ἐν   πλάνῃ   ἀναστρε-
escaping   ¹the [ones]   ²in   ⁴error   ²liv-
φομένους,   19 ἐλευθερίαν   αὐτοῖς   ἐπαγγελ-
ing,   ²freedom   ²to them   ¹promis-
λόμενοι,   αὐτοὶ   δοῦλοι   ὑπάρχοντες   τῆς
ing,   [them]selves   ²slaves   ¹being   -
φθορᾶς·   ᾧ   γάρ   τις   ἥττηται,   τούτῳ
of corrup-   for by whom   anyone   has been   to this
tion;   defeated,   man
δεδούλωται.   20 εἰ   γὰρ   ἀποφυγόντες   τὰ
he has been enslaved.   For if   having escaped   the
μιάσματα   τοῦ   κόσμου   ἐν   ἐπιγνώσει   τοῦ
defilements   of the   world   by a full knowledge of the
κυρίου   καὶ   σωτῆρος   Ἰησοῦ   Χριστοῦ,
Lord   and   Saviour   Jesus   Christ,
τούτοις   δὲ   πάλιν   ἐμπλακέντες   ἡττῶνται,
yet by these   again   having been   have been
                          entangled   defeated,
γέγονεν   αὐτοῖς   τὰ   ἔσχατα   χείρονα   τῶν
²have become ⁴to them   ¹the   ²last things   worse   [than] the
πρώτων.   21 κρεῖττον   γὰρ   ἦν   αὐτοῖς
first.   For better   it was   for them
μὴ   ἐπεγνωκέναι   τὴν   ὁδὸν   τῆς   δικαιοσύνης,
not to have fully known   the   way   –   of righteousness,
ἢ   ἐπιγνοῦσιν   ὑποστρέψαι   ἐκ   τῆς   παρα-
than fully knowing   to turn   from   ¹the   ⁴de-
δοθείσης   αὐτοῖς   ἁγίας   ἐντολῆς.   22 συμβέ-
livered   ⁵to them   ²holy   ³commandment.   ⁵has
βηκεν   αὐτοῖς   τὸ   τῆς   ἀληθοῦς   παροιμίας·
happened   ⁴to them   ¹The   ²of the   ³true   ⁴proverb:
          thing

turns back to his own vomit, and the sow is washed only to wallow in the mire.

κύων ἐπιστρέψας ἐπὶ τὸ ἴδιον ἐξέραμα,
[The] dog turning upon the(its) own vomit,
καὶ· ὗς λουσαμένη εἰς κυλισμὸν βορβόρου.
and: [The] washed to wallowing of mud.
    sow

CHAPTER 3

THIS is now the second letter that I have written to you, beloved, and in both of them I have aroused your sincere mind by way of reminder; ²that you should remember the predictions of the holy prophets and the commandment of the Lord and Savior through your apostles. ³First of all you must understand this, that scoffers will come in the last days with scoffing, following their own passions ⁴and saying, "Where is the promise of his coming? For ever since the fathers fell asleep, all things have continued as they were from the beginning of creation." ⁵They deliberately ignore this fact, that by the word of God heavens existed long ago, and an earth formed out of water and by means of water, ⁶through which the world that then existed was deluged with water

3 Ταύτην ἤδη, ἀγαπητοί, δευτέραν ὑμῖν
¹This ⁶now, ⁴beloved, ²second ⁷to you
γράφω ἐπιστολήν, ἐν αἷς διεγείρω ὑμῶν
⁵I write ³epistle, in [both] which I rouse ⁴of you
ἐν ὑπομνήσει τὴν εἰλικρινῆ διάνοιαν,
⁵by ⁶reminder ¹the ²sincere ³mind,
2 μνησθῆναι τῶν προειρημένων ῥημάτων
to remember the ²having been ¹words
       previously spoken
ὑπὸ τῶν ἁγίων προφητῶν καὶ τῆς τῶν
by the holy prophets and ¹the ²of the
ἀποστόλων ὑμῶν ἐντολῆς τοῦ κυρίου καὶ
⁴apostles ⁵of you ²commandment of the Lord and
σωτῆρος, 3 τοῦτο πρῶτον γινώσκοντες, ὅτι
Saviour, ¹this ³firstly ¹knowing, that
ἐλεύσονται ἐπ᾽ ἐσχάτων τῶν ἡμερῶν ἐν
there will come during [the] last of the days ²in
ἐμπαιγμονῇ ἐμπαῖκται κατὰ τὰς ἰδίας
⁴mocking ¹mockers ²according to ⁶the(ir) ⁷own
ἐπιθυμίας αὐτῶν πορευόμενοι 4 καὶ λέγοντες·
⁸lusts of them ²going and saying:
ποῦ ἐστιν ἡ ἐπαγγελία τῆς παρουσίας
Where is the promise of the presence
αὐτοῦ; ἀφ᾽ ἧς γὰρ οἱ πατέρες ἐκοι-
of him? ²from ³which [day] ¹for the fathers fell
       =for from the day when . . .
μήθησαν, πάντα οὕτως διαμένει ἀπ᾽
asleep, all things so remains from
ἀρχῆς κτίσεως. 5 λανθάνει γὰρ αὐτοὺς
[the] of creation. For ²is concealed ²them
beginning   [from]
τοῦτο θέλοντας ὅτι οὐρανοὶ ἦσαν ἔκπαλαι
¹this wishing* that heavens were of old
καὶ γῆ ἐξ ὕδατος καὶ δι᾽ ὕδατος
and earth by water and through water
συνεστῶσα τῷ τοῦ θεοῦ λόγῳ, 6 δι᾽
¹having been ²by – ⁴of God ³word, through
held together the
ὧν ὁ τότε κόσμος ὕδατι κατακλυσθεὶς
which the then§ world ²by water ¹being inundated
things

* That is, they wish it to be so.
§ This is allowable English : cf. " the then Prime Minister."

and perished. ⁷But by the same word the heavens and earth that now exist have been stored up for fire, being kept until the day of judgment and destruction of ungodly men.

8 But do not ignore this one fact, beloved, that with the Lord one day is as a thousand years, and a thousand years as one day. ⁹The Lord is not slow about his promise as some count slowness, but is forbearing toward you,ᵍ not wishing that any should perish, but that all should reach repentance. ¹⁰But the day of the Lord will come like a thief, and then the heavens will pass away with a loud noise, and the elements will be dissolved with fire, and the earth and the works that are upon it will be burned up.

11 Since all these things are thus to be dissolved, what sort of persons ought you to be in lives of holiness and godliness, ¹²waiting for and hasteningʰ the coming of the day of God, because of which the heavens will be kindled and dissolved, and the elements will melt with

ᵍ Other ancient authorities read *on your account*
ʰ Or *earnestly desiring*

ἀπώλετο· **7** οἱ δὲ νῦν οὐρανοὶ καὶ ἡ
perished;   but the now   heavens and the

γῆ τῷ αὐτῷ λόγῳ τεθησαυρισμένοι εἰσὶν
earth by the same word ²having been stored up ¹are

πυρὶ τηρούμενοι εἰς ἡμέραν κρίσεως καὶ
²for fire ¹being kept in a day of judgment and

ἀπωλείας τῶν ἀσεβῶν ἀνθρώπων. **8** ⁰Ἐν
destruction of ʰhe impious men.   ²one

δὲ τοῦτο μὴ λανθανέτω ὑμᾶς, ἀγαπητοί,
But ¹this let not be concealed you, beloved,
   ²thing   [from]

ὅτι μία ἡμέρα παρὰ κυρίῳ ὡς χίλια
that one day with [the] Lord [is] as a thousand

ἔτη καὶ χίλια ἔτη ὡς ἡμέρα μία. **9** οὐ
years and a thousand years as ²day ¹one.   ³not

βραδύνει κύριος τῆς ἐπαγγελίας, ὥς τινες
²is ⁴slow ¹[The] of the promise, as some
       Lord (his)

βραδύτητα ἡγοῦνται, ἀλλὰ μακροθυμεῖ εἰς
²slowness ¹deem, but is longsuffering toward

ὑμᾶς, μὴ βουλόμενός τινας ἀπολέσθαι
you, not purposing any to perish

ἀλλὰ πάντας εἰς μετάνοιαν χωρῆσαι.
but all men ²to ³repentance ¹to come.

10 Ἥξει δὲ ἡμέρα κυρίου ὡς κλέπτης,
But will come [the] day of [the] Lord as a thief,

ἐν ᾗ οἱ οὐρανοὶ ῥοιζηδὸν παρελεύσονται,
in which the heavens ²with rushing ¹will pass away,
                     sound

στοιχεῖα δὲ καυσούμενα λυθήσεται, καὶ
and [the] elements burning will be dissolved, and

γῆ καὶ τὰ ἐν αὐτῇ ἔργα εὑρεθήσεται.
[the] and ¹the ³in ⁴it ²works will be
earth   discovered.

11 Τούτων οὕτως πάντων λυομένων
²these things ³thus ¹All ⁴being dissolvedᵃ

ποταποὺς δεῖ ὑπάρχειν [ὑμᾶς] ἐν ἁγίαις
what sort it be- ²to be ¹you in holy
of men hoves

ἀναστροφαῖς καὶ εὐσεβείαις, **12** προσδοκῶντας
conduct* and piety,* awaiting

καὶ σπεύδοντας τὴν παρουσίαν τῆς τοῦ
and hastening the presence ¹of the –

θεοῦ ἡμέρας, δι᾽ ἣν οὐρανοὶ πυρούμενοι
²of God ¹day, on ac- which [the] being set on fire
              count of heavens

λυθήσονται καὶ στοιχεῖα καυσούμενα
will be dissolved and [the] elements burning

* The Greek plurals cannot be literally reproduced in English.

fire! ¹³But according to his promise we wait for new heavens and a new earth in which righteousness dwells.

14 Therefore, beloved, since you wait for these, be zealous to be found by him without spot or blemish, and at peace. ¹⁵And count the forbearance of our Lord as salvation. So also our beloved brother Paul wrote to you according to the wisdom given him, ¹⁶speaking of this as he does in all his letters. There are some things in them hard to understand, which the ignorant and unstable twist to their own destruction, as they do the other scriptures. ¹⁷You therefore, beloved, knowing this beforehand, beware lest you be carried away with the error of lawless men and lose your own stability. ¹⁸But grow in the grace and knowledge of our Lord and Savior Jesus Christ. To him be the glory both now and to the day of eternity. Amen.

τήκεται.   13 καινοὺς   δὲ   οὐρανοὺς   καὶ
melts.   But new   heavens   and

γῆν   καινὴν   κατὰ   τὸ   ἐπάγγελμα   αὐτοῦ
²earth ¹a new   accord- the   promise   of him
                  ing to

προσδοκῶμεν,   ἐν   οἷς   δικαιοσύνη   κατοικεῖ.
we await,   in   which righteousness dwells.

14 Διό,   ἀγαπητοί,   ταῦτα   προσδοκῶντες
Wherefore, beloved,   ²these things ¹awaiting

σπουδάσατε   ἄσπιλοι   καὶ   ἀμώμητοι   αὐτῷ
be diligent   ⁵spotless   ⁶and   ⁷unblemished ²by him

εὑρεθῆναι   ἐν   εἰρήνῃ,   15 καὶ   τὴν   τοῦ
¹to be found ³in   ⁴peace,   and   ²the   ⁴of the

κυρίου   ἡμῶν   μακροθυμίαν   σωτηρίαν   ἡγεῖσθε,
⁵Lord   ⁶of us   ³longsuffering ⁷salvation   ¹deem,

καθὼς   καὶ   ὁ   ἀγαπητὸς   ἡμῶν   ἀδελφὸς
as   indeed the beloved   ²of us   ¹brother

Παῦλος   κατὰ   τὴν   δοθεῖσαν   αὐτῷ   σοφίαν
Paul   accord- ¹the   ²given   ⁴to him ²wisdom
           ing to

ἔγραψεν   ὑμῖν,   16 ὡς   καὶ   ἐν   πάσαις
wrote   to you,   as   also   in   all [his]

ἐπιστολαῖς   λαλῶν   ἐν   αὐταῖς   περὶ   τούτων,
epistles   speaking in   them   concerning these
                                                    things,

ἐν   αἷς   ἐστιν   δυσνόητά   τινα,   ἃ   οἱ
in   which is(are)   ³hard to   τινα,   ¹some which the
                      understand   things,

ἀμαθεῖς   καὶ   ἀστήρικτοι   στρεβλοῦσιν   ὡς
unlearned   and   unsteady   twist   as

καὶ   τὰς   λοιπὰς   γραφὰς   πρὸς   τὴν   ἰδίαν
also   the   remaining scriptures to   the(ir) own

αὐτῶν   ἀπώλειαν.   17 Ὑμεῖς   οὖν,   ἀγαπητοί,
of them   destruction.   Ye   therefore, beloved,

προγινώσκοντες   φυλάσσεσθε   ἵνα   μὴ   τῇ
knowing before   guard   lest   μὴ   ²by the

τῶν   ἀθέσμων   πλάνῃ   συναπαχθέντες   ἐκπέ-
⁴of the ⁵lawless   ³error   ¹being led away with ye fall

σητε   τοῦ   ἰδίου   στηριγμοῦ,   18 αὐξάνετε
from   the(your) own   stability,   ²grow ye

δὲ   ἐν   χάριτι   καὶ   γνώσει   τοῦ   κυρίου
¹but   in   grace   and   knowledge of the   Lord

ἡμῶν   καὶ   σωτῆρος   Ἰησοῦ   Χριστοῦ.
of us   and   Saviour   Jesus   Christ.

αὐτῷ   ἡ   δόξα   καὶ   νῦν   καὶ   εἰς
To himᶜ [is] the glory   both   now   and   unto
=His is*   =for ever.

ἡμέραν   αἰῶνος.
a day   of age. §

* See note on I. Pet. 5. 11.   § ? "An age-lasting (i.e. eternal) day."

CHAPTER 1

THAT which was from the beginning, which we have heard, which we have seen with our eyes, which we have looked upon and touched with our hands, concerning the word of life—²the life was made manifest, and we saw it, and testify to it, and proclaim to you the eternal life which was with the Father and was made manifest to us—³that which we have seen and heard we proclaim also to you, so that you may have fellowship with us; and our fellowship is with the Father and with his Son Jesus Christ. ⁴And we are writing this that our*ᵃ* joy may be complete.

5 This is the message we have heard from him and proclaim to you, that God is light and in him is no darkness at all. ⁶If we say we have fellowship with him while we walk in darkness, we lie and do not

---

1 ῞Ο ἦν ἀπ᾽ ἀρχῆς, ὃ ἀκηκόαμεν,
What was from [the] what we have heard,
beginning,
ὃ ἑωράκαμεν τοῖς ὀφθαλμοῖς ἡμῶν, ὃ
what we have seen with the eyes of us, what
ἐθεασάμεθα καὶ αἱ χεῖρες ἡμῶν ἐψηλάφησαν,
we beheld and the hands of us touched,
περὶ τοῦ λόγου τῆς ζωῆς, — 2 καὶ
concern- the word - of life, — and
ing
ἡ ζωὴ ἐφανερώθη, καὶ ἑωράκαμεν καὶ
the life was manifested, and we have seen and
μαρτυροῦμεν καὶ ἀπαγγέλλομεν ὑμῖν τὴν
we bear witness and we announce to you the
ζωὴν τὴν αἰώνιον, ἥτις ἦν πρὸς τὸν
life - eternal, which was with the
πατέρα καὶ ἐφανερώθη ἡμῖν, — 3 ὃ
Father and was manifested to us, — what
ἑωράκαμεν καὶ ἀκηκόαμεν, ἀπαγγέλλομεν
we have seen and we have heard, we announce
καὶ ὑμῖν, ἵνα καὶ ὑμεῖς κοινωνίαν ἔχητε
also to you, in order ²also ¹ye ⁴fellowship ³may
that have
μεθ᾽ ἡμῶν. καὶ ἡ κοινωνία δὲ ἡ ἡμετέρα
with us. ²indeed the ⁴fellowship ¹And - ³our
μετὰ τοῦ πατρὸς καὶ μετὰ τοῦ υἱοῦ
[is] with the Father and with the Son
αὐτοῦ Ἰησοῦ Χριστοῦ. 4 καὶ ταῦτα
of him Jesus Christ. And these things
γράφομεν ἡμεῖς ἵνα ἡ χαρὰ ἡμῶν ᾖ
write we in order the joy of us may
that be
πεπληρωμένη.
having been fulfilled.

5 Καὶ ἔστιν αὕτη ἡ ἀγγελία ἣν
And ²is ¹this the message which
ἀκηκόαμεν ἀπ᾽ αὐτοῦ καὶ ἀναγγέλλομεν
we have heard from him and we announce
ὑμῖν, ὅτι ὁ θεὸς φῶς ἐστιν καὶ σκοτία
to you, that - God ²light ¹is and ⁵darkness
ἐν αὐτῷ οὐκ ἔστιν οὐδεμία. 6 Ἐὰν
¹in ²him ⁴not ³is none. If
εἴπωμεν ὅτι κοινωνίαν ἔχομεν μετ᾽ αὐτοῦ
we say that ²fellowship ¹we have with him
καὶ ἐν τῷ σκότει περιπατῶμεν, ψευδόμεθα
and ²in ³the ⁴darkness ¹we walk, we lie

ᵃ Other ancient authorities read *your*

live according to the truth; [7] but if we walk in the light, as he is in the light, we have fellowship with one another, and the blood of Jesus his Son cleanses us from all sin. [8] If we say we have no sin, we deceive ourselves, and the truth is not in us. [9] If we confess our sins, he is faithful and just, and will forgive our sins and cleanse us from all unrighteousness. [10] If we say we have not sinned, we make him a liar, and his word is not in us.

καὶ	οὐ	ποιοῦμεν	τὴν	ἀλήθειαν·	[7] ἐὰν
and	are not doing		the	truth;	[2]if

δὲ	ἐν	τῷ	φωτὶ	περιπατῶμεν	ὡς	αὐτός
[1]but	[4]in	[5]the	[6]light	[3]we walk	as	he

ἐστιν	ἐν	τῷ	φωτί,	κοινωνίαν	ἔχομεν
is	in	the	light,	[2]fellowship	[1]we have

μετ᾽	ἀλλήλων	καὶ	τὸ	αἷμα	Ἰησοῦ	τοῦ
with	each other	and	the	blood	of Jesus	the

υἱοῦ	αὐτοῦ	καθαρίζει	ἡμᾶς	ἀπὸ	πάσης
Son	of him	cleanses	us	from	all

ἁμαρτίας.	[8] ἐὰν	εἴπωμεν	ὅτι	ἁμαρτίαν
sin.	If	we say	that	sin

οὐκ	ἔχομεν,	ἑαυτοὺς	πλανῶμεν	καὶ	ἡ
	we have not,	[2]ourselves	[1]we deceive	and	the

ἀλήθεια	οὐκ	ἔστιν	ἐν	ἡμῖν.	[9] ἐὰν
truth	is not		in	us.	If

ὁμολογῶμεν	τὰς	ἁμαρτίας	ἡμῶν,	πιστός
we confess	the	sins	of us,	faithful

ἐστιν	καὶ	δίκαιος,	ἵνα	ἀφῇ	ἡμῖν	τὰς
he is	and	righteous,	in order that	he may forgive	us	the

ἁμαρτίας	καὶ	καθαρίσῃ	ἡμᾶς	ἀπὸ	πάσης
sins	and	he may cleanse	us	from	all

ἀδικίας.	[10] ἐὰν	εἴπωμεν	ὅτι	οὐχ
iniquity.	If	we say	that	not

ἡμαρτήκαμεν,	ψεύστην	ποιοῦμεν	αὐτὸν
we have sinned,	a liar	we make	him

καὶ	ὁ	λόγος	αὐτοῦ	οὐκ	ἔστιν	ἐν	ἡμῖν.
and	the	word	of him	is not		in	us.

CHAPTER 2

MY little children, I am writing this to you so that you may not sin; but if any one does sin, we have an advocate with the Father, Jesus Christ the righteous; [2] and he is the expiation for our sins, and not for ours only but also for the sins of the whole world. [3] And by this we may be ·sure that we know him, if we keep his commandments. [4] He

[2] Τεκνία	μου,	ταῦτα	γράφω	ὑμῖν	ἵνα
Little children	of me,	these things	I write	to you	in order that

μὴ	ἁμάρτητε.	καὶ	ἐὰν	τις	ἁμάρτῃ,
	ye sin not.	And	if	anyone	sins,

παράκλητον	ἔχομεν	πρὸς	τὸν	πατέρα,
an advocate	we have	with	the	Father,

Ἰησοῦν	Χριστὸν	δίκαιον·	[2] καὶ	αὐτός
Jesus	Christ	[the] righteous;	and	he

ἱλασμός	ἐστιν	περὶ	τῶν	ἁμαρτιῶν	ἡμῶν,
[2]a propitiation	[1]is	concerning	the	sins	of us,

οὐ	περὶ	τῶν	ἡμετέρων	δὲ	μόνον	ἀλλὰ
[2]not	[3]concerning	–	[4]ours	[1]but	only	but

καὶ	περὶ	ὅλου	τοῦ	κόσμου.	[3] καὶ	ἐν
also	concerning	all	the	world.	And	by

τούτῳ	γινώσκομεν	ὅτι	ἐγνώκαμεν	αὐτόν,
this	we know	that	we have known	him,

ἐὰν	τὰς	ἐντολὰς	αὐτοῦ	τηρῶμεν.	[4] ὁ
if	[2]the	[3]command-ments	[4]of him	[1]we keep.	The [one]

who says "I know him" but disobeys his commandments is a liar, and the truth is not in him; [5] but whoever keeps his word, in him truly love for God is perfected. By this we may be sure that we are in him: [6] he who says he abides in him ought to walk in the same way in which he walked.

[7] Beloved, I am writing you no new commandment, but an old commandment which you had from the beginning; the old commandment is the word which you have heard. [8] Yet I am writing you a new commandment, which is true in him and in you, because[b] the darkness is passing away and the true light is already shining. [9] He who says he is in the light and hates his brother is in the darkness still. [10] He who loves his brother abides in the light, and in it[c] there is no cause for stumbling. [11] But he who hates his brother is in the

λέγων ὅτι ἔγνωκα αὐτόν, καὶ τὰς ἐντολὰς
saying[,] – I have known him, and [2]the [4]command-
ments

αὐτοῦ μὴ τηρῶν, ψεύστης ἐστίν, καὶ
[5]of him [1]not [2]keeping, [3]a liar [1]is, and

ἐν τούτῳ ἡ ἀλήθεια οὐκ ἔστιν· 5 ὃς δ'
in this man the truth is not; but who-

ἂν τηρῇ αὐτοῦ τὸν λόγον, ἀληθῶς ἐν
ever keeps [3]of him [1]the [2]word, truly in

τούτῳ ἡ ἀγάπη τοῦ θεοῦ τετελείωται.
this man the love – of God has been perfected.

ἐν τούτῳ γινώσκομεν ὅτι ἐν αὐτῷ ἐσμεν.
By this we know that [2]in [3]him [1]we are.

6 ὁ λέγων ἐν αὐτῷ μένειν ὀφείλει καθὼς
The [one] saying in him to remain ought as

ἐκεῖνος περιεπάτησεν καὶ αὐτὸς οὕτως
that [one]* walked also [him]self so

περιπατεῖν.
to walk.

7 Ἀγαπητοί, οὐκ ἐντολὴν καινὴν γράφω
Beloved, [2]not [4]commandment [3]a new [1]I write

ὑμῖν, ἀλλ' ἐντολὴν παλαιὰν ἣν εἴχετε
to you, but [2]commandment [1]an old which ye had

ἀπ' ἀρχῆς· ἡ ἐντολὴ ἡ παλαιά ἐστιν
from [the] the [2]command- – [1]old is
beginning; ment

ὁ λόγος ὃν ἠκούσατε. 8 πάλιν ἐντολὴν
the word which ye heard. Again [2]command-
ment

καινὴν γράφω ὑμῖν, ὃ ἐστιν ἀληθὲς
[1]a new I write to you, what is true

ἐν αὐτῷ καὶ ἐν ὑμῖν, ὅτι ἡ σκοτία
in him and in you, because the darkness

παράγεται καὶ τὸ φῶς τὸ ἀληθινὸν
is passing and the [2]light – [1]true

ἤδη φαίνει. 9 ὁ λέγων ἐν τῷ φωτὶ
already shines. The [one] saying in the light

εἶναι καὶ τὸν ἀδελφὸν αὐτοῦ μισῶν
to be and the brother of him hating

ἐν τῇ σκοτίᾳ ἐστὶν ἕως ἄρτι. 10 ὁ
in the darkness is until now. The

ἀγαπῶν τὸν ἀδελφὸν αὐτοῦ ἐν τῷ φωτὶ
[one] loving the brother of him in the light

μένει, καὶ σκάνδαλον ἐν αὐτῷ οὐκ ἔστιν·
remains, and offence in him is not;

11 ὁ δὲ μισῶν τὸν ἀδελφὸν αὐτοῦ ἐν
but the [one] hating the brother of him in

[b] Or that
[c] Or him

* In a number of places John uses this demonstrative adjective as a substitute for " Christ " : " the remoter antecedent." See also John 2. 21.

darkness and walks in the darkness, and does not know where he is going, because the darkness has blinded his eyes. 12 I am writing to you, little children, because your sins are forgiven for his sake. ¹³ I am writing to you, fathers, because you know him who is from the beginning. I am writing to you, young men, because you have overcome the evil one. I write to you, children, because you know the Father. ¹⁴ I write to you, fathers, because you know him who is from the beginning. I write to you, young men, because you are strong, and the word of God abides in you, and you have overcome the evil one.
15 Do not love the world or the things in the world. If any one loves the world, love for the Father is not in him. ¹⁶ For all that is in the world, the lust of the flesh and the lust of the eyes and the pride of life, is not of the Father but is of the world. ¹⁷ And

τῇ	σκοτίᾳ	ἐστὶν	καὶ	ἐν	τῇ	σκοτίᾳ
the	darkness	is	and	in	the	darkness

περιπατεῖ,	καὶ	οὐκ	οἶδεν	ποῦ	ὑπάγει,
walks,	and	knows not		where	he is going,

ὅτι	ἡ	σκοτία	ἐτύφλωσεν	τοὺς	ὀφθαλμοὺς
be- cause	the	darkness	blinded	the	eyes

αὐτοῦ.	12 Γράφω	ὑμῖν,	τεκνία,	ὅτι
of him.	I write	to you,	little children,	because

ἀφέωνται	ὑμῖν	αἱ	ἁμαρτίαι	διὰ	τὸ	ὄνομα
have been forgiven	to you	the	sins	on ac- count of	the	name
(your)						

αὐτοῦ.	13 γράφω	ὑμῖν,	πατέρες,	ὅτι
of him.	I write	to you,	fathers,	because

ἐγνώκατε	τὸν	ἀπ᾽	ἀρχῆς.	γράφω	ὑμῖν,
ye have known	the [one]	from	[the] beginning.	I write	to you,

νεανίσκοι,	ὅτι	νενικήκατε	τὸν	πονηρόν.
young men,	because	ye have overcome	the	evil one.

14 ἔγραψα	ὑμῖν,	παιδία,	ὅτι	ἐγνώκατε
I wrote	to you,	young children,	because	ye have known

τὸν	πατέρα.	ἔγραψα	ὑμῖν,	πατέρες,
the	Father.	I wrote	to you,	fathers,

ὅτι	ἐγνώκατε	τὸν	ἀπ᾽	ἀρχῆς.	ἔγραψα
be- cause	ye have known	the [one]	from	[the] beginning.	I wrote

ὑμῖν,	νεανίσκοι,	ὅτι	ἰσχυροί	ἐστε	καὶ
to you,	young men,	because	strong	ye are	and

ὁ	λόγος	τοῦ	θεοῦ	ἐν	ὑμῖν	μένει	καὶ
the	word	–	of God	in	you	remains	and

νενικήκατε	τὸν	πονηρόν.	15 Μὴ	ἀγαπᾶτε
ye have overcome the		evil one.		Love ye not

τὸν	κόσμον	μηδὲ	τὰ	ἐν	τῷ	κόσμῳ.
the	world	nor	the things	in	the	world.

ἐάν	τις	ἀγαπᾷ	τὸν	κόσμον,	οὐκ	ἔστιν
If	anyone	loves	the	world,	⁶not	⁵is

ἡ	ἀγάπη	τοῦ	πατρὸς	ἐν	αὐτῷ·	16 ὅτι
¹the	²love	³of the	⁴Father	in	him;	because

πᾶν	τὸ	ἐν	τῷ	κόσμῳ,	ἡ	ἐπιθυμία	τῆς
all that which†	[is]	in	the	world,	the	lust	of the

σαρκὸς	καὶ	ἡ	ἐπιθυμία	τῶν	ὀφθαλμῶν
flesh	and	the	lust	of the	eyes

καὶ	ἡ	ἀλαζονεία	τοῦ	βίου,	οὐκ	ἔστιν
and	the	vainglory	–	of life,		is not

ἐκ	τοῦ	πατρός,	ἀλλὰ	ἐκ	τοῦ	κόσμου
of	the	Father,	but	of	the	world

the world passes away, and the lust of it; but he who does the will of God abides for ever.

18 Children, it is the last hour; and as you have heard that antichrist is coming, so now many antichrists have come; therefore we know that it is the last hour. [19]They went out from us, but they were not of us; for if they had been of us, they would have continued with us; but they went out, that it might be plain that they all are not of us. [20]But you have been anointed by the Holy One, and you all know.[d] [21]I write to you, not because you do not know the truth, but because you know it, and know that no lie is of the truth. [22]Who is the liar but he who denies that Jesus is the Christ? This is the antichrist, he who denies the Father and the Son. [23]No one who denies the Son has the Father. He who confesses the Son has the Father also. [24]Let what you heard from the beginning abide in you.

[d] Other ancient authorities read *you know everything*

ἐστίν.   17 καὶ   ὁ   κόσμος   παράγεται   καὶ
is.   And   the   world   is passing away   and

ἡ   ἐπιθυμία   αὐτοῦ·   ὁ   δὲ   ποιῶν   τὸ   θέλημα
the   lust   of it;   but the [one] doing   the   will

τοῦ   θεοῦ   μένει   εἰς   τὸν   αἰῶνα.
– of God   remains   unto   the   age.

18 Παιδία,   ἐσχάτη   ὥρα   ἐστίν,   καὶ
Young children,   a last   hour   it is,   and

καθὼς   ἠκούσατε   ὅτι   ἀντίχριστος   ἔρχεται,
as   ye heard   that   antichrist   is coming,

καὶ   νῦν   ἀντίχριστοι   πολλοὶ   γεγόνασιν·
even   now   [2]antichrists   [1]many   have arisen;

ὅθεν   γινώσκομεν   ὅτι   ἐσχάτη   ὥρα   ἐστίν.
whence   we know   that   a last   hour   it is.

19 ἐξ   ἡμῶν   ἐξῆλθαν,   ἀλλ᾽   οὐκ   ἦσαν
From   us   they went out,   but   they were not

ἐξ   ἡμῶν·   εἰ   γὰρ   ἐξ   ἡμῶν   ἦσαν,   μεμενή-
of   us;   for if   of   us   they were,   they would

κεισαν   ἂν   μεθ᾽   ἡμῶν·   ἀλλ᾽   ἵνα   φανερω-
have remained   with   us;   but   in order   it might be
                                             that

θῶσιν   ὅτι   οὐκ   εἰσὶν   πάντες   ἐξ   ἡμῶν.
manifested   that   they are not   all   of   us.

20 καὶ   ὑμεῖς   χρῖσμα   ἔχετε   ἀπὸ   τοῦ
And   ye   an anointing   have   from   the

ἁγίου,   καὶ   οἴδατε   πάντες.   21 οὐκ   ἔγραψα
Holy One, and   [1]ye [3]know   [2]all.   I wrote not

ὑμῖν   ὅτι   οὐκ   οἴδατε   τὴν   ἀλήθειαν,   ἀλλ᾽
to you because   ye know not   the   truth,   but

ὅτι   οἴδατε   αὐτήν,   καὶ   ὅτι   πᾶν   ψεῦδος
because ye know   it,   and because   every   lie
                                         =no lie is . . .

ἐκ   τῆς   ἀληθείας   οὐκ   ἔστιν.   22 Τίς
of   the   truth   is not.   Who

ἐστιν   ὁ   ψεύστης   εἰ   μὴ   ὁ   ἀρνούμενος
is   the   liar   except   the [one]   denying

ὅτι   Ἰησοῦς   οὐκ   ἔστιν   ὁ   χριστός;   οὗτός
that   Jesus   not   is   the   Christ?   this

ἐστιν   ὁ   ἀντίχριστος,   ὁ   ἀρνούμενος   τὸν
is   the   antichrist,   the [one]   denying   the

πατέρα   καὶ   τὸν   υἱόν.   23 πᾶς   ὁ   ἀρνούμενος
Father   and   the   Son.   Everyone   denying

τὸν   υἱὸν   οὐδὲ   τὸν   πατέρα   ἔχει·   ὁ
the   Son   [2]neither   [3]the   [4]Father   [1]has;   the

ὁμολογῶν   τὸν   υἱὸν   καὶ   τὸν   πατέρα   ἔχει.
[one] confessing the   Son   [2]also   [3]the   [4]Father   [1]has.

24 ὑμεῖς   ὃ   ἠκούσατε   ἀπ᾽   ἀρχῆς,   ἐν
[2]Ye   [1]what   heard   from [the] beginning,   in

If what you heard from
the beginning abides in
you, then you will abide
in the Son and in the
Father. ²⁵And this is
what he has promised us,ᵉ
eternal life.

26 I write this to you
about those who would
deceive you; ²⁷but the
anointing which you re-
ceived from him abides in
you, and you have no
need that any one
should teach you; as his
anointing teaches you
about everything, and is
true, and is no lie, just
as it has taught you,
abide in him.

28 And now, little
children, abide in him,
so that when he appears
we may have confidence
and not shrink from him
in shame at his coming.
²⁹If you know that he is
righteous, you may be
sure that every one who
does right is born of him.

CHAPTER 3

SEE what love the
Father has given us,
that we should be called
children of God; and so
we are. The reason why
the world does not know

ᵉ Other ancient authorities
read you

ὑμῖν μενέτω. ἐὰν ἐν ὑμῖν μείνῃ ὃ ἀπ'
you   let it remain. If ⁶in ⁷you ⁵remains ¹what ²from

ἀρχῆς ἠκούσατε, καὶ ὑμεῖς ἐν τῷ υἱῷ
⁴[the]   ²ye heard, ³both ¹ye ⁴in ⁵the ⁶Son
beginning

καὶ [ἐν] τῷ πατρὶ μενεῖτε.   25 καὶ
⁷and ⁸in ⁹the ¹⁰Father ⁵will remain.   And

αὕτη ἐστὶν ἡ ἐπαγγελία ἣν αὐτὸς ἐπηγ-
this   is the promise   which he   pro-

γείλατο ἡμῖν, τὴν ζωὴν τὴν αἰώνιον.
mised   us,   the life   –   eternal.

26 Ταῦτα ἔγραψα ὑμῖν περὶ τῶν πλανών-
   These   I wrote to you concern- the leading
   things   ing [ones]

των ὑμᾶς.   27 καὶ ὑμεῖς τὸ χρῖσμα
²astray ¹you.   And ⁴ye ¹the ²anointing

ὃ ἐλάβετε ἀπ' αὐτοῦ μένει ἐν ὑμῖν,
³which received from   him remains in you,

καὶ οὐ χρείαν ἔχετε ἵνα τις διδάσκῃ
and ²no ³need ¹ye have in order anyone should
                        that   teach

ὑμᾶς· ἀλλ' ὡς τὸ αὐτοῦ χρῖσμα διδάσκει
you; but as the ²of him ¹anointing teaches

ὑμᾶς περὶ πάντων, καὶ ἀληθές ἐστιν
you concerning all things, and ²true ¹is

καὶ οὐκ ἔστιν ψεῦδος, καὶ καθὼς ἐδίδαξεν
and is not a lie, and as   he/it taught

ὑμᾶς, μένετε ἐν αὐτῷ.
you, remain ye in him.

28 Καὶ νῦν, τεκνία, μένετε ἐν αὐτῷ,
   And now, little children, remain ye in him,

ἵνα ἐὰν φανερωθῇ σχῶμεν παρρησίαν καὶ
in or- if he is manifested we may confidence and
der that   have

μὴ αἰσχυνθῶμεν ἀπ' αὐτοῦ ἐν τῇ παρουσίᾳ
not be shamed from him in the presence

αὐτοῦ.   29 ἐὰν εἰδῆτε ὅτι δίκαιός ἐστιν,
of him.   If ye know that ²righteous ¹he is,

γινώσκετε ὅτι καὶ πᾶς ὁ ποιῶν τὴν
know ye   that also every one doing –

δικαιοσύνην ἐξ αὐτοῦ γεγέννηται.
righteousness ²of ³him ¹has been born.

3 Ἴδετε ποταπὴν ἀγάπην δέδωκεν ἡμῖν
  See ye what manner of love ²has given ⁴to us

ὁ πατὴρ ἵνα τέκνα θεοῦ κληθῶμεν,
¹the ²Father in order ³children ⁵of God ¹we may be
            that   called,

καὶ ἐσμέν. διὰ τοῦτο ὁ κόσμος οὐ
and we are. Therefore the world ²not

us is that it did not know him. ²Beloved, we are God's children now; it does not yet appear what we shall be, but we know that when he appears we shall be like him, for we shall see him as he is. ³And every one who thus hopes in him purifies himself as he is pure.

4 Every one who commits sin is guilty of lawlessness; sin is lawlessness. ⁵You know that he appeared to take away sins, and in him there is no sin. ⁶No one who abides in him sins; no one who sins has either seen him or known him. ⁷Little children, let no one deceive you. He who does right is righteous, as he is righteous. ⁸He who commits sin is of the devil; for the devil has sinned from the beginning. The reason the Son of God appeared was to destroy the works of the devil. ⁹No one born of God commits sin;

γινώσκει ἡμᾶς, ὅτι οὐκ ἔγνω αὐτόν.
¹knows ²us, because it knew not him.

2 ἀγαπητοί, νῦν τέκνα θεοῦ ἐσμεν, καὶ
Beloved, ²now ³children ⁴of God ¹we are, and

οὔπω ἐφανερώθη τί ἐσόμεθα. οἴδαμεν
not yet was it manifested what we shall be. We know

ὅτι ἐὰν φανερωθῇ ὅμοιοι αὐτῷ ἐσόμεθα,
that if he(?it) is manifested like him we shall be,

ὅτι ὀψόμεθα αὐτὸν καθώς ἐστιν. 3 καὶ
be- we shall see him as he is. And
cause

πᾶς ὁ ἔχων τὴν ἐλπίδα ταύτην ἐπ᾽
everyone having this hope on

αὐτῷ ἁγνίζει ἑαυτὸν καθὼς ἐκεῖνος ἁγνός
him purifies himself as that one* ²pure

ἐστιν. 4 πᾶς ὁ ποιῶν τὴν ἁμαρτίαν
¹is. Everyone doing - sin

καὶ τὴν ἀνομίαν ποιεῖ, καὶ ἡ ἁμαρτία
²also - ³lawlessness ¹does, and - sin

ἐστὶν ἡ ἀνομία. 5 καὶ οἴδατε ὅτι ἐκεῖνος
is - lawlessness. And ye know that that one*

ἐφανερώθη ἵνα τὰς ἁμαρτίας ἄρῃ, καὶ
was manifested in order - sins he might and
that bear,

ἁμαρτία ἐν αὐτῷ οὐκ ἔστιν. 6 πᾶς ὁ
sin ²in ³him ¹is not. Everyone

ἐν αὐτῷ μένων οὐχ ἁμαρτάνει· πᾶς ὁ
²in ³him ¹remaining sins not; everyone

ἁμαρτάνων οὐχ ἑώρακεν αὐτὸν οὐδὲ
sinning has not seen him nor

ἔγνωκεν αὐτόν. 7 Τεκνία, μηδεὶς πλανάτω
has known him. Little ²no man ¹let ³lead
children, ²astray

ὑμᾶς· ὁ ποιῶν τὴν δικαιοσύνην δίκαιός
⁴you; the [one] doing - righteousness ²righteous

ἐστιν, καθὼς ἐκεῖνος δίκαιός ἐστιν· 8 ὁ
¹is, as that one* ²righteous ¹is; the

ποιῶν τὴν ἁμαρτίαν ἐκ τοῦ διαβόλου
[one] doing - sin ²of ³the ⁴devil

ἐστίν, ὅτι ἀπ᾽ ἀρχῆς ὁ διάβολος ἁμαρτάνει.
¹is, because ⁴from ⁵[the] ¹the ²devil ³sins.
beginning

εἰς τοῦτο ἐφανερώθη ὁ υἱὸς τοῦ θεοῦ,
For this was manifested the Son - of God,

ἵνα λύσῃ τὰ ἔργα τοῦ διαβόλου.
in or- he might the works of the devil.
der that undo

9 Πᾶς ὁ γεγεννημένος ἐκ τοῦ θεοῦ
Everyone having been begotten of - God

* See ch. 2. 6.

for God's nature abides in him, and he cannot sin because he is[f] born of God. [10]By this it may be seen who are the children of God, and who are the children of the devil: whoever does not do right is not of God, nor he who does not love his brother. [11]For this is the message which you have heard from the beginning, that we should love one another, [12]and not be like Cain who was of the evil one and murdered his brother. And why did he murder him? Because his own deeds were evil and his brother's righteous. [13]Do not wonder, brethren, that the world hates you. [14]We know that we have passed out of death into life, because we love the brethren. He who does not love remains in death. [15]Any one who hates his brother is a murderer, and you know that no murderer has eternal life abiding in

ἁμαρτίαν	οὐ	ποιεῖ,	ὅτι	σπέρμα	αὐτοῦ
[2]sin	[2]not	[1]does,	because	seed	of him

ἐν	αὐτῷ	μένει·	καὶ	οὐ	δύναται	ἁμαρτάνειν,
in	him	remains;	and	he cannot	to sin,

ὅτι	ἐκ	τοῦ	θεοῦ	γεγέννηται.	10	ἐν
because of		-	God	he has been begotten.		By

τούτῳ	φανερά	ἐστιν	τὰ	τέκνα	τοῦ	θεοῦ
this	[2]manifest	[1]is(are)	the	children	-	of God

καὶ	τὰ	τέκνα	τοῦ	διαβόλου·	πᾶς	ὁ
and	the	children	of the	devil;	everyone	

μὴ	ποιῶν	δικαιοσύνην	οὐκ	ἔστιν	ἐκ
not	doing	righteousness	is not		of

τοῦ	θεοῦ,	καὶ	ὁ	μὴ	ἀγαπῶν	τὸν	ἀδελφὸν
-	God,	and	the [one]	not	loving	the	brother

αὐτοῦ.	11	ὅτι	αὕτη	ἐστὶν	ἡ	ἀγγελία
of him.		Because	this	is	the	message

ἣν	ἠκούσατε	ἀπ'	ἀρχῆς,	ἵνα	ἀγαπῶμεν
which	ye heard	from	[the] beginning,	in order that	we should love

ἀλλήλους·	12	οὐ	καθὼς	Κάϊν	ἐκ	τοῦ
one another;		not	as	Cain	[2]of	[1]the

πονηροῦ	ἦν	καὶ	ἔσφαξεν	τὸν	ἀδελφὸν
[2]evil one	[1]was	and	slew	the	brother

αὐτοῦ·	καὶ	χάριν	τίνος	ἔσφαξεν	αὐτόν;
of him;	and	for the sake of	what	slew he	him?

ὅτι	τὰ	ἔργα	αὐτοῦ	πονηρὰ	ἦν,	τὰ	δὲ
because	the	works	of him	[2]evil	[1]was(were),	but the	[works]

τοῦ	ἀδελφοῦ	αὐτοῦ	δίκαια.	13	μὴ
of the	brother	of him	righteous.		not

θαυμάζετε,	ἀδελφοί,	εἰ	μισεῖ	ὑμᾶς	ὁ
Marvel ye,	brothers,	if	[3]hates	[4]you	[1]the

κόσμος.	14	ἡμεῖς	οἴδαμεν	ὅτι	μεταβεβή-
[2]world.		We	know	that	we have re-

καμεν	ἐκ	τοῦ	θανάτου	εἰς	τὴν	ζωήν,
moved	out of	the	death	into	the	life,

ὅτι	ἀγαπῶμεν	τοὺς	ἀδελφούς·	ὁ	μὴ
because	we love	the	brothers;	the [one]	not

ἀγαπῶν	μένει	ἐν	τῷ	θανάτῳ.	15	πᾶς
loving	remains	in	-	death.		Every-

ὁ	μισῶν	τὸν	ἀδελφὸν	αὐτοῦ	ἀνθρωποκτόνος
one hating	the	brother	of him	[2]a murderer

ἐστίν,	καὶ	οἴδατε	ὅτι	πᾶς	ἀνθρωποκτόνος
[1]is,	and	ye know	that	every	murderer
					=no murderer has ...

[f] Or for the offspring of God abide in him, and they cannot sin because they are

οὐκ	ἔχει	ζωὴν	αἰώνιον	ἐν	αὐτῷ	μένουσαν.
has not	life	eternal	in	him	remaining.

him. ¹⁶By this we know love, that he laid down his life for us; and we ought to lay down our lives for the brethren. ¹⁷But if any one has the world's goods and sees his brother in need, yet closes his heart against him, how does God's love abide in him? ¹⁸Little children let us not love in word or speech but in deed and in truth. 19 By this we shall know that we are of the truth, and reassure our hearts before him ²⁰whenever our hearts condemn us; for God is greater than our hearts, and he knows everything. ²¹Beloved, if our hearts do not condemn us, we have confidence before God; ²²and we receive from him whatever we ask, because we keep his commandments and do what pleases him. ²³And this is his commandment, that we should believe in the name of his Son Jesus

16 ἐν τούτῳ ἐγνώκαμεν τὴν ἀγάπην, ὅτι
By this we have known - love, because
ἐκεῖνος ὑπὲρ ἡμῶν τὴν ψυχὴν αὐτοῦ
that one* on behalf of us the life of him
ἔθηκεν· καὶ ἡμεῖς ὀφείλομεν ὑπὲρ τῶν
laid down; and we ought on behalf of the
ἀδελφῶν τὰς ψυχὰς θεῖναι. 17 ὃς δ'
brothers the(our) lives to lay down. Who-
ἂν ἔχῃ τὸν βίον τοῦ κόσμου καὶ θεωρῇ
ever has the means of the world and beholds
of life
τὸν ἀδελφὸν αὐτοῦ χρείαν ἔχοντα καὶ
the brother of him ²need ¹having and
κλείσῃ τὰ σπλάγχνα αὐτοῦ ἀπ' αὐτοῦ,
shuts the bowels of him from him,
πῶς ἡ ἀγάπη τοῦ θεοῦ μένει ἐν αὐτῷ;
how ²the ³love - ⁴of God ¹remains in him?
18 Τεκνία, μὴ ἀγαπῶμεν λόγῳ μηδὲ τῇ
Little children, let us not love in word nor in the
γλώσσῃ, ἀλλὰ ἐν ἔργῳ καὶ ἀληθείᾳ.
tongue, but in work and truth.
19 ἐν τούτῳ γνωσόμεθα ὅτι ἐκ τῆς ἀληθείας
By this we shall know that ³of ²the ⁴truth
ἐσμέν, καὶ ἔμπροσθεν αὐτοῦ πείσομεν
¹we are, and before him shall persuade
τὴν καρδίαν ἡμῶν 20 ὅτι ἐὰν καταγινώσκῃ
the heart of us that if ⁴blames [us]
ἡμῶν ἡ καρδία, ὅτι μείζων ἐστὶν ὁ
³of us ¹the ²heart, that greater is -
θεὸς τῆς καρδίας ἡμῶν καὶ γινώσκει
God [than] the heart of us and knows
πάντα. 21 Ἀγαπητοί, ἐὰν ἡ καρδία
all things. Beloved, if the(our) heart
μὴ καταγινώσκῃ, παρρησίαν ἔχομεν πρὸς
does not blame [us], confidence we have with
τὸν θεόν, 22 καὶ ὃ ἐὰν αἰτῶμεν λαμβάν-
- God, and whatever we ask we re-
ομεν ἀπ' αὐτοῦ, ὅτι τὰς ἐντολὰς αὐτοῦ
ceive from him, because ²the ³command- ⁴of him
ments
τηροῦμεν καὶ τὰ ἀρεστὰ ἐνώπιον αὐτοῦ
¹we keep and ²the ³pleasing ⁴before ⁵him
things
ποιοῦμεν. 23 καὶ αὕτη ἐστὶν ἡ ἐντολὴ
¹we do. And this is the commandment
αὐτοῦ, ἵνα πιστεύσωμεν τῷ ὀνόματι τοῦ
of him, in order we should believe the name of the
that

* See ch. 2. 6, 3. 3, 5, 7.

Christ and love one another, just as he has commanded us. ²⁴All who keep his commandments abide in him, and he in them. And by this we know that he abides in us, by the Spirit which he has given us.

υἱοῦ αὐτοῦ Ἰησοῦ Χριστοῦ καὶ ἀγαπῶμεν
Son of him Jesus Christ and love

ἀλλήλους καθὼς ἔδωκεν ἐντολὴν ἡμῖν.
one another as he gave commandment to us.

24 καὶ ὁ τηρῶν τὰς ἐντολὰς αὐτοῦ ἐν
And the keeping the command- of him in
[one] ments

αὐτῷ μένει καὶ αὐτὸς ἐν αὐτῷ· καὶ
him remains and he in him; and

ἐν τούτῳ γινώσκομεν ὅτι μένει ἐν ἡμῖν,
by this we know that he remains in us,

ἐκ τοῦ πνεύματος οὗ ἡμῖν ἔδωκεν.
by the Spirit whom to us he gave.

CHAPTER 4

BELOVED, do not believe every spirit, but test the spirits to see whether they are of God; for many false prophets have gone out into the world. ²By this you know the Spirit of God: every spirit which confesses that Jesus Christ has come in the flesh is of God, ³and every spirit which does not confess Jesus is not of God. This is the spirit of antichrist, of which you heard that it was coming, and now it is in the world already. ⁴Little children, you are of God, and have overcome them; for he who is in you is greater than he who is in the world. ⁵They are of the world, therefore

4 Ἀγαπητοί, μὴ παντὶ πνεύματι
Beloved, ²not ³every ⁴spirit

πιστεύετε, ἀλλὰ δοκιμάζετε τὰ πνεύματα
¹believe ye, but prove the spirits

εἰ ἐκ τοῦ θεοῦ ἐστιν, ὅτι πολλοὶ
if of – God they are, because many

ψευδοπροφῆται ἐξεληλύθασιν εἰς τὸν
false prophets have gone forth into the

κόσμον. 2 ἐν τούτῳ γινώσκετε τὸ πνεῦμα
world. By this know ye the Spirit

τοῦ θεοῦ· πᾶν πνεῦμα ὃ ὁμολογεῖ Ἰησοῦν
– of God: every spirit which confesses Jesus

Χριστὸν ἐν σαρκὶ ἐληλυθότα ἐκ τοῦ
Christ ²in ³[the] flesh ¹having come ⁵of –

θεοῦ ἐστιν, 3 καὶ πᾶν πνεῦμα ὃ μὴ
⁶God ⁴is, and every spirit which not

ὁμολογεῖ τὸν Ἰησοῦν ἐκ τοῦ θεοῦ οὐκ
confesses – Jesus ²of – ⁴God ¹not

ἔστιν· καὶ τοῦτό ἐστιν τὸ τοῦ ἀντιχρίστου,
¹is; and this is the of antichrist,
[spirit] the

ὃ ἀκηκόατε ὅτι ἔρχεται, καὶ νῦν ἐν
which ye have that it is coming, and ²now ⁴in
heard

τῷ κόσμῳ ἐστὶν ἤδη. 4 ὑμεῖς ἐκ τοῦ
⁵the ⁶world ¹is ³already. Ye of –

θεοῦ ἐστε, τεκνία, καὶ νενικήκατε αὐτούς,
God are, little and have overcome them,
children,

ὅτι μείζων ἐστὶν ὁ ἐν ὑμῖν ἢ ὁ ἐν
because greater is the in you than the in
[one] [one]

τῷ κόσμῳ. 5 αὐτοὶ ἐκ τοῦ κόσμου
the world. ¹They ³of ⁴the ⁵world

what they say is of the world, and the world listens to them. ⁶We are of God. Whoever knows God listens to us, and he who is not of God does not listen to us. By this we know the spirit of truth and the spirit of error.

7 Beloved, let us love one another; for love is of God, and he who loves is born of God and knows God. ⁸He who does not love does not know God; for God is love. ⁹In this the love of God was made manifest among us, that God sent his only Son into the world, so that we might live through him. ¹⁰In this is love, not that we loved God but that he loved us and sent his Son to be the expiation for our sins. ¹¹Beloved, if God so loved us, we also ought to love one another. ¹²No man has ever seen God; if we love one another, God

εἰσίν· διὰ τοῦτο ἐκ τοῦ κόσμου λαλοῦσιν
²are; therefore ³of ³the ⁴world ¹they speak
καὶ ὁ κόσμος αὐτῶν ἀκούει. 6 ἡμεῖς
and the world them hears. ¹We
ἐκ τοῦ θεοῦ ἐσμεν· ὁ γινώσκων τὸν
²of - ⁴God ²are; the [one] knowing -
θεὸν ἀκούει ἡμῶν, ὃς οὐκ ἔστιν ἐκ
God hears us, [he] who is not of
τοῦ θεοῦ οὐκ ἀκούει ἡμῶν. ἐκ τούτου
- God hears not us. From this
γινώσκομεν τὸ πνεῦμα τῆς ἀληθείας καὶ
we know the spirit - of truth and
τὸ πνεῦμα τῆς πλάνης.
the spirit - of error.

7 Ἀγαπητοί, ἀγαπῶμεν ἀλλήλους, ὅτι
   Beloved, let us love one another, because
ἡ ἀγάπη ἐκ τοῦ θεοῦ ἐστιν, καὶ πᾶς ὁ
- love ²of - ³God ¹is, and everyone
ἀγαπῶν ἐκ τοῦ θεοῦ γεγέννηται καὶ
loving ²of - ³God ¹has been begotten and
γινώσκει τὸν θεόν. 8 ὁ μὴ ἀγαπῶν
knows - God. The [one] not loving
οὐκ ἔγνω τὸν θεόν, ὅτι ὁ θεὸς ἀγάπη
knew not - God, because - God ²love
ἐστίν. 9 ἐν τούτῳ ἐφανερώθη ἡ ἀγάπη
¹is. By this was manifested the love
τοῦ θεοῦ ἐν ἡμῖν, ὅτι τὸν υἱὸν αὐτοῦ
- of God in(to) us, because ³the ⁵Son ⁶of him
τὸν μονογενῆ ἀπέσταλκεν ὁ θεὸς εἰς
- ⁴only begotten ²has sent - ¹God into
τὸν κόσμον ἵνα ζήσωμεν δι' αὐτοῦ.
the world in order we might live through him.
                that

10 ἐν τούτῳ ἐστὶν ἡ ἀγάπη, οὐχ ὅτι
In this is - love, not that
ἡμεῖς ἠγαπήκαμεν τὸν θεόν, ἀλλ' ὅτι
we have loved - God, but that
αὐτὸς ἠγάπησεν ἡμᾶς καὶ ἀπέστειλεν τὸν
he loved us and sent the
υἱὸν αὐτοῦ ἱλασμὸν περὶ τῶν ἁμαρτιῶν
Son of him a propitiation concerning the sins
ἡμῶν. 11 ἀγαπητοί, εἰ οὕτως ὁ θεὸς
of us. Beloved, if so - God
ἠγάπησεν ἡμᾶς, καὶ ἡμεῖς ὀφείλομεν
loved us, ²also ¹we ²ought
ἀλλήλους ἀγαπᾶν. 12 θεὸν οὐδεὶς πώποτε
³one another ⁴to love. ⁴God ¹no man ²ever
τεθέαται· ἐὰν ἀγαπῶμεν ἀλλήλους, ὁ θεὸς
³has beheld; if we love one another, - God

abides in us and his love is perfected in us. 13 By this we know that we abide in him and he in us, because he has given us of his own Spirit. ¹⁴And we have seen and testify that the Father has sent his Son as the Savior of the world. ¹⁵Whoever confesses that Jesus is the Son of God, God abides in him, and he in God. ¹⁶So we know and believe the love God has for us. God is love, and he who abides in love abides in God, and God abides in him. ¹⁷In this is love perfected with us, that we may have confidence for the day of judgment, because as he is so are we in this world. ¹⁸There is no fear in love, but perfect love casts out fear. For fear has to do with punishment, and he who fears is not perfected in love. ¹⁹We love, because he first

ἐν	ἡμῖν	μένει	καὶ	ἡ	ἀγάπη	αὐτοῦ
in	us	remains	and	the	love	of him

τετελειωμένη	ἐν	ἡμῖν	ἐστιν.	13	'Εν
²having been perfected	³in	⁴us	¹is.		By

τούτῳ	γινώσκομεν	ὅτι	ἐν	αὐτῷ	μένομεν
this	we know	that	in	him	we remain

καὶ	αὐτὸς	ἐν	ἡμῖν,	ὅτι	ἐκ	τοῦ	πνεύματος
and	he	in	us,	because	²of	⁴the	⁵Spirit

αὐτοῦ	δέδωκεν	ἡμῖν.	14	καὶ	ἡμεῖς
⁶of him	¹he has given	²us.		And	we

τεθεάμεθα	καὶ	μαρτυροῦμεν	ὅτι	ὁ	πατὴρ
have beheld	and	bear witness	that the		Father

ἀπέσταλκεν	τὸν	υἱὸν	σωτῆρα	τοῦ	κόσμου.
has sent	the	Son [as] Saviour		of the	world.

15	ὃς	ἐὰν	ὁμολογήσῃ	ὅτι	'Ιησοῦς	ἐστιν
	Whoever		confesses	that	Jesus	is

ὁ	υἱὸς	τοῦ	θεοῦ,	ὁ	θεὸς	ἐν	αὐτῷ	μένει
the	Son	-	of God,	-	God	in	him	remains

καὶ	αὐτὸς	ἐν	τῷ	θεῷ.	16	καὶ	ἡμεῖς
and	he	in	-	God.		And	we

ἐγνώκαμεν	καὶ	πεπιστεύκαμεν	τὴν	ἀγάπην
have known	and	have believed	the	love

ἣν	ἔχει	ὁ	θεὸς	ἐν	ἡμῖν.	'Ο	θεὸς	ἀγάπη
which	²has	-	¹God	in(to)	us.	-	God	²love

ἐστίν,	καὶ	ὁ	μένων	ἐν	τῇ	ἀγάπῃ	ἐν
¹is,	and	the remaining [one]		in	-	love	²in

τῷ	θεῷ	μένει	καὶ	ὁ	θεὸς	ἐν	αὐτῷ
-	²God	¹remains	and	-	God	²in	³him

μένει.	17	'Εν	τούτῳ	τετελείωται	ἡ	ἀγάπη
¹remains.		By	this	²has been perfected -		¹love

μεθ'	ἡμῶν,	ἵνα	παρρησίαν	ἔχωμεν	ἐν
with	us,	in order that	²confidence	¹we may have	in

τῇ	ἡμέρᾳ	τῆς	κρίσεως,	ὅτι	καθὼς	ἐκεῖνός
the	day	-	of judgment,	because	as	that one*

ἐστιν	καὶ	ἡμεῖς	ἐσμεν	ἐν	τῷ	κόσμῳ
is	²also	¹we	²are	in	-	world

τούτῳ.	18	φόβος	οὐκ	ἔστιν	ἐν	τῇ	ἀγάπῃ,
this.		Fear	is not		in	-	love,

ἀλλ'	ἡ	τελεία	ἀγάπη	ἔξω	βάλλει	τὸν
but	-	perfect	love	²out	¹casts	the

φόβον,	ὅτι	ὁ	φόβος	κόλασιν	ἔχει,	ὁ	δὲ
fear,	because	-	fear	²punishment	¹has,		and the

φοβούμενος	οὐ	τετελείωται	ἐν	τῇ	ἀγάπῃ.
[one] fearing	has not been perfected		in	-	love.

19	ἡμεῖς	ἀγαπῶμεν,	ὅτι	αὐτὸς	πρῶτος
	We	love,	because	he	first

* See ch. 2. 6, 3. 3, 5, 7, 16.

loved us. ²⁰If any one says, "I love God," and hates his brother, he is a liar; for he who does not love his brother whom he has seen, can-not⁹ love God whom he has not seen. ²¹And this commandment we have from him, that he who loves God should love his brother also.

ἠγάπησεν   ἡμᾶς.   20 ἐάν   τις   εἴπῃ   ὅτι
loved   us.   If   anyone says[,]   -

ἀγαπῶ   τὸν   θεόν,   καὶ   τὸν   ἀδελφὸν   αὐτοῦ
I love   -   God,   and   ²the   ³brother   ⁴of him

μισῇ,   ψεύστης   ἐστίν·   ὁ   γὰρ   μὴ   ἀγαπῶν
¹hates,   ²a liar   ¹he is;   for the [one] not   loving

τὸν   ἀδελφὸν   αὐτοῦ   ὃν   ἑώρακεν,   τὸν
the   brother   of him   whom he has seen,   -

θεὸν   ὃν   οὐχ   ἑώρακεν   οὐ   δύναται   ἀγαπᾶν.
³God   ⁴whom ⁵he has not seen   ¹he cannot   ²to love.

21 καὶ   ταύτην   τὴν   ἐντολὴν   ἔχομεν   ἀπ’
And   this   -   commandment we have   from

αὐτοῦ,   ἵνα   ὁ   ἀγαπῶν   τὸν   θεὸν   ἀγαπᾷ
him,   in order the   loving   -   God   loves
        that [one]

καὶ   τὸν   ἀδελφὸν   αὐτοῦ.
also   the   brother   of him.

CHAPTER 5

EVERY one who believes that Jesus is the Christ is a child of God, and every one who loves the parent loves the child. ²By this we know that we love the children of God, when we love God and obey his commandments. ³For this is the love of God, that we keep his commandments. And his commandments are not burdensome. ⁴For what-ever is born of God overcomes the world; and this is the victory that overcomes the world, our faith. ⁵Who

5 Πᾶς   ὁ   πιστεύων   ὅτι   Ἰησοῦς   ἐστιν
Everyone   believing   that   Jesus   is

ὁ   χριστὸς   ἐκ   τοῦ   θεοῦ   γεγέννηται,   καὶ
the Christ   ²of   -   ³God ¹has been begotten, and

πᾶς   ὁ   ἀγαπῶν   τὸν   γεννήσαντα   ἀγαπᾷ
everyone   loving   the [one]   begetting   loves

τὸν   γεγεννημένον   ἐξ   αὐτοῦ.   2 ἐν   τούτῳ
the   having been begotten of   him.   By   this
[one]

γινώσκομεν   ὅτι   ἀγαπῶμεν   τὰ   τέκνα   τοῦ
we know   that   we love   the   children   -

θεοῦ,   ὅταν   τὸν   θεὸν   ἀγαπῶμεν   καὶ   τὰς
of God, whenever   -   ²God ¹we love   and   ²the

ἐντολὰς   αὐτοῦ   ποιῶμεν.   3 αὕτη   γάρ
³command-   ⁴of him   ¹we do.   For this
ments

ἐστιν   ἡ   ἀγάπη   τοῦ   θεοῦ,   ἵνα   τὰς   ἐντολὰς
is   the   love   -   of   in order ²the ³command-
                    God,   that   ments

αὐτοῦ   τηρῶμεν·   καὶ   αἱ   ἐντολαὶ   αὐτοῦ
⁴of him   ¹we keep;   and   the   commandments of him

βαρεῖαι   οὐκ   εἰσίν,   4 ὅτι   πᾶν   τὸ   γεγεν-
heavy   are not,   because everything   having

νημένον   ἐκ   τοῦ   θεοῦ   νικᾷ   τὸν   κόσμον·
been begotten of   -   God   overcomes the   world;

καὶ   αὕτη   ἐστὶν   ἡ   νίκη   ἡ   νικήσασα   τὸν
and   this   is   the   victory   -   overcoming   the

κόσμον,   ἡ   πίστις   ἡμῶν.   5 Τίς   ἐστιν
world,   the   faith   of us.   ²Who   ³is

⁹ Other ancient authorities read how can he

is it that overcomes the world but he who believes that Jesus is the Son of God? 6 This is he who came by water and blood, Jesus Christ, not with the water only but with the water and the blood. 7And the Spirit is the witness, because the Spirit is the truth. 8There are three witnesses, the Spirit, the water, and the blood; and these three agree. 9If we receive the testimony of men, the testimony of God is greater; for this is the testimony of God that he has borne witness to his Son. 10He who believes in the Son of God has the testimony in himself. He who does not believe God, has made him a liar, because he has not believed in the testimony that God has borne to his Son. 11And this is the testimony, that God gave us eternal life, and this life is in his Son. 12He

[δὲ] ὁ νικῶν τὸν κόσμον εἰ μὴ ὁ
1and the overcoming the world except the
　　　　[one]

πιστεύων ὅτι Ἰησοῦς ἐστιν ὁ υἱὸς τοῦ
[one] believing that Jesus is the Son -

θεοῦ; 6 οὗτός ἐστιν ὁ ἐλθὼν δι' ὕδατος
of God? This is the coming through water
　　　　　　　　　　　　　　　　[one]

καὶ αἵματος, Ἰησοῦς Χριστός· οὐκ ἐν
and blood, Jesus Christ; not by

τῷ ὕδατι μόνον, ἀλλ' ἐν τῷ ὕδατι καὶ
the water only, but by the water and

ἐν τῷ αἵματι· καὶ τὸ πνεῦμά ἐστιν τὸ
by the blood; and the Spirit is the

μαρτυροῦν, ὅτι τὸ πνεῦμά ἐστιν ἡ ἀλήθεια.
[one] bearing be- the Spirit is the truth.
witness, cause

7 ὅτι τρεῖς εἰσιν οἱ μαρτυροῦντες, 8 τὸ
Because three there are the bearing witness, the
　　　　　　　　　[ones]

πνεῦμα καὶ τὸ ὕδωρ καὶ τὸ αἷμα, καὶ
Spirit and the water and the blood, and

οἱ τρεῖς εἰς τὸ ἕν εἰσιν. 9 εἰ τὴν
the three ²in the ³one ¹are. If ²the

μαρτυρίαν τῶν ἀνθρώπων λαμβάνομεν, ἡ
³witness - ⁶of men ⁵we receive, the

μαρτυρία τοῦ θεοῦ μείζων ἐστίν, ὅτι
witness - of God ²greater ¹is, because

αὕτη ἐστὶν ἡ μαρτυρία τοῦ θεοῦ, ὅτι
this is the witness - of God, because

μεμαρτύρηκεν περὶ τοῦ υἱοῦ αὐτοῦ. 10 ὁ
he has borne concern- the Son of him. The
witness ing

πιστεύων εἰς τὸν υἱὸν τοῦ θεοῦ ἔχει
[one] believing in the Son - of God has

τὴν μαρτυρίαν ἐν αὐτῷ. ὁ μὴ πιστεύων
the witness in him. The not believing
　　　　　　　　　　　　　　[one]

τῷ θεῷ ψεύστην πεποίηκεν αὐτόν, ὅτι
- God ³a liar ¹has made ²him, because

οὐ πεπίστευκεν εἰς τὴν μαρτυρίαν ἣν
he has not believed in the witness which

μεμαρτύρηκεν ὁ θεὸς περὶ τοῦ υἱοῦ
²has borne witness - ¹God concerning the Son

αὐτοῦ. 11 καὶ αὕτη ἐστὶν ἡ μαρτυρία,
of him. And this is the witness,

ὅτι ζωὴν αἰώνιον ἔδωκεν ὁ θεὸς ἡμῖν,
that ⁵life ⁴eternal ²gave - ¹God ³to us,

καὶ αὕτη ἡ ζωὴ ἐν τῷ υἱῷ αὐτοῦ
and this - life ²in ³the ⁴Son ⁵of him

who has the Son has life; he who has not the Son of God has not life. 13 I write this to you who believe in the name of the Son of God, that you may know that you have eternal life. ¹⁴And this is the confidence which we have in him, that if we ask anything according to his will he hears us. ¹⁵And if we know that he hears us in whatever we ask, we know that we have obtained the requests made of him. ¹⁶If any one sees his brother committing what is not a mortal sin, he will ask, and God will give him life for those whose sin is not mortal. There is sin which is mortal; I do not say that one is to pray for that. ¹⁷All wrongdoing is sin, but there is sin which is not mortal. 18 We know that any one born of God does not sin, but He who was born of God keeps him, and the evil one does not touch him. 19 We know that we

ἐστιν.   12 ὁ   ἔχων   τὸν   υἱὸν   ἔχει   τὴν
¹is.   The [one] having   the   Son   has   the
ζωήν·   ὁ   μὴ   ἔχων   τὸν   υἱὸν   τοῦ   θεοῦ
life;   the   not   having   the   Son   -   of God
[one]
τὴν   ζωὴν   οὐκ   ἔχει.
the   life   has not.

13 Ταῦτα   ἔγραψα   ὑμῖν   ἵνα   εἰδῆτε   ὅτι
These   I wrote   to you   in order   ye may   that
things   that   know
ζωὴν   ἔχετε   αἰώνιον,   τοῖς   πιστεύουσιν
²life   ¹ye have   ²eternal,   to the [ones] believing
εἰς   τὸ   ὄνομα   τοῦ   υἱοῦ   τοῦ   θεοῦ.   14 Καὶ
in   the   name   of the   Son   -   of God.   And
αὕτη   ἐστὶν   ἡ   παρρησία   ἣν   ἔχομεν   πρὸς
this   is   the   confidence   which   we have   toward
αὐτόν,   ὅτι   ἐάν   τι   αἰτώμεθα   κατὰ   τὸ
him,   that   if   ²anything   ¹we ask   according to the
θέλημα   αὐτοῦ   ἀκούει   ἡμῶν.   15 καὶ
will   of him   he hears   us.   And
ἐὰν   οἴδαμεν   ὅτι   ἀκούει   ἡμῶν   ὃ   ἐὰν
if   we know   that   he hears   us   whatever
αἰτώμεθα,   οἴδαμεν   ὅτι   ἔχομεν   τὰ   αἰτήματα
we ask,   we know   that   we have   the   requests
ἃ   ἠτήκαμεν   ἀπ᾽   αὐτοῦ.   16 Ἐάν   τις
which   we have   from   him.   If   anyone
asked
ἴδῃ   τὸν   ἀδελφὸν   αὐτοῦ   ἁμαρτάνοντα
sees   the   brother   of him   sinning
ἁμαρτίαν   μὴ   πρὸς   θάνατον,   αἰτήσει,   καὶ
a sin   not   unto   death,   he shall ask,   and
δώσει   αὐτῷ   ζωήν,   τοῖς   ἁμαρτάνουσιν
he will give to him   life,   to the [ones] sinning
μὴ   πρὸς   θάνατον.   ἔστιν   ἁμαρτία   πρὸς
not   unto   death.   There is   a sin   unto
θάνατον·   οὐ   περὶ   ἐκείνης   λέγω   ἵνα
death;   not   concerning that   do I say in order
that
ἐρωτήσῃ.   17 πᾶσα   ἀδικία   ἁμαρτία   ἐστίν,
he should inquire.   All   iniquity   ²sin   ¹is,
καὶ   ἔστιν   ἁμαρτία   οὐ   πρὸς   θάνατον.
and   there is   a sin   not   unto   death.
18 Οἴδαμεν   ὅτι   πᾶς   ὁ   γεγεννημένος   ἐκ
We know   that   everyone   having been begotten   of
τοῦ   θεοῦ   οὐχ   ἁμαρτάνει,   ἀλλ᾽   ὁ   γεννηθεὶς
-         God   sins not,   but   the [one] begotten
ἐκ   τοῦ   θεοῦ   τηρεῖ   αὐτόν,   καὶ   ὁ   πονηρὸς
of   -   God   keeps   him,   and   the   evil one
οὐχ   ἅπτεται   αὐτοῦ.   19 οἴδαμεν   ὅτι   ἐκ
does not touch   him.   We know   that   of

are of God, and the whole world is in the power of the evil one. 20 And we know that the Son of God has come and has given us understanding, to know him who is true; and we are in him who is true, in his Son Jesus Christ. This is the true God and eternal life. 21 Little children, keep yourselves from idols.

τοῦ θεοῦ ἐσμεν, καὶ ὁ κόσμος ὅλος ἐν
 – God we are, and the ²world ¹whole in

τῷ πονηρῷ κεῖται. 20 οἴδαμεν δὲ ὅτι
the evil one lies.   ²we know ¹And that

ὁ υἱὸς τοῦ θεοῦ ἥκει, καὶ δέδωκεν
the Son – of God is come, and has given

ἡμῖν διάνοιαν ἵνα γινώσκωμεν τὸν
to us an understanding in order we might know the
               that

ἀληθινόν· καὶ ἐσμὲν ἐν τῷ ἀληθινῷ,
true [one]; and we are in the true [one],

ἐν τῷ υἱῷ αὐτοῦ Ἰησοῦ Χριστῷ. οὗτός
in the Son of him Jesus Christ. This

ἐστιν ὁ ἀληθινὸς θεὸς καὶ ζωὴ αἰώνιος.
is the true God and life eternal.

21 Τεκνία, φυλάξατε ἑαυτὰ ἀπὸ τῶν
Little children, guard yourselves from the

εἰδώλων.
idols.

II. JOHN

THE elder to the elect lady and her children, whom I love in the truth, and not only I but also all who know the truth, 2 because of the truth which abides in us and will be with us for ever:
3 Grace, mercy, and peace will be with us, from God the Father and from Jesus Christ the Father's Son, in truth and love.

1 Ὁ πρεσβύτερος ἐκλεκτῇ κυρίᾳ καὶ
The elder to [the] chosen lady and

τοῖς τέκνοις αὐτῆς, οὓς ἐγὼ ἀγαπῶ ἐν
to the children of her, whom I love in

ἀληθείᾳ, καὶ οὐκ ἐγὼ μόνος ἀλλὰ καὶ
truth, and not I alone but also

πάντες οἱ ἐγνωκότες τὴν ἀλήθειαν, 2 διὰ
all the having known the truth, because of
  [ones]

τὴν ἀλήθειαν τὴν μένουσαν ἐν ἡμῖν,
the truth – remaining among us,

καὶ μεθ’ ἡμῶν ἔσται εἰς τὸν αἰῶνα.
and with us will be unto the age.

3 ἔσται μεθ’ ἡμῶν χάρις ἔλεος εἰρήνη
 ⁴will be ⁵with ⁶us ¹Grace[,] ²mercy[,] ³peace

παρὰ θεοῦ πατρός, καὶ παρὰ Ἰησοῦ
from God [the] Father, and from Jesus

Χριστοῦ τοῦ υἱοῦ τοῦ πατρός, ἐν ἀληθείᾳ
Christ the Son of the Father, in truth

καὶ ἀγάπῃ.
and love.

4 I rejoiced greatly to find some of your children following the truth, just as we have been commanded by the Father. ⁵And now I beg you, lady, not as though I were writing you a new commandment, but the one we have had from the beginning, that we love one another. ⁶And this is love, that we follow his commandments; this is the commandment, as you have heard from the beginning, that you follow love. ⁷For many deceivers have gone out into the world, men who will not acknowledge the coming of Jesus Christ in the flesh; such a one is the deceiver and the antichrist. ⁸Look to yourselves, that you may not lose what you*a* have worked for, but may win a full reward. ⁹Any one who goes ahead and does not abide in the doctrine of Christ does not have God; he who abides in the doctrine has both the Father and the Son. ¹⁰If any one comes to you and does not bring this

---

4 Ἐχάρην   λίαν   ὅτι   εὕρηκα   ἐκ   τῶν
I rejoiced greatly because I have   of   the
                              found [some]

τέκνων   σου   περιπατοῦντας   ἐν   ἀληθείᾳ,
children of thee walking   in   truth,

καθὼς   ἐντολὴν   ἐλάβομεν   παρὰ   τοῦ   πατρός.
as   command-   we received from   the   Father.
         ment

5 καὶ   νῦν   ἐρωτῶ   σε,   κυρία,   οὐχ   ὡς
And   now   I request thee,   lady,   not   as

ἐντολὴν   γράφων   σοι   καινήν,   ἀλλὰ   ἣν
²command- ¹writing ⁴to thee ²a new,   but   which
ment

εἴχομεν   ἀπ'   ἀρχῆς,   ἵνα   ἀγαπῶμεν
we had   from   [the]   in order we should
                  beginning, that   love

ἀλλήλους.   **6** καὶ   αὕτη   ἐστὶν   ἡ   ἀγάπη,
one another.   And   this   is   -   love,

ἵνα   περιπατῶμεν   κατὰ   τὰς   ἐντολὰς
in order we should walk   accord-   the   command-
that   ing to   ments

αὐτοῦ·   αὕτη   ἡ   ἐντολή   ἐστιν,   καθὼς
of him;   this   ²the ²commandment ¹is,   as

ἠκούσατε   ἀπ'   ἀρχῆς,   ἵνα   ἐν   αὐτῇ
ye heard   from   [the]   in order ²in   ³it
                   beginning, that

περιπατῆτε.   **7** ὅτι   πολλοὶ   πλάνοι   ἐξῆλθον
¹ye should walk.   Because many   deceivers went forth

εἰς   τὸν   κόσμον,   οἱ   μὴ   ὁμολογοῦντες
into   the   world,   the   not   confessing
                        [ones]

Ἰησοῦν   Χριστὸν   ἐρχόμενον   ἐν   σαρκί·
Jesus   Christ   coming   in   [the] flesh;

οὗτός   ἐστιν   ὁ   πλάνος   καὶ   ὁ   ἀντίχριστος.
this   is   the   deceiver and   the   antichrist.

8 βλέπετε   ἑαυτούς,   ἵνα   μὴ   ἀπολέσητε
See   yourselves,   lest   ye lose

ἃ   ἠργασάμεθα,   ἀλλὰ   μισθὸν   πλήρη
[the] we wrought,   but   ²reward   ¹a full
things which

ἀπολάβητε.   **9** πᾶς   ὁ   προάγων   καὶ   μὴ
¹ye may receive.   Everyone   going forward and   not

μένων   ἐν   τῇ   διδαχῇ   τοῦ   Χριστοῦ   θεὸν
remaining in   the   teaching   -   of Christ   ²God

οὐκ   ἔχει·   ὁ   μένων   ἐν   τῇ   διδαχῇ,   οὗτος
²not   ¹has;   the   remaining in   the   teaching,   this one

καὶ   τὸν   πατέρα   καὶ   τὸν   υἱὸν   ἔχει.
²both   ³the   ⁴Father   ⁵and   ⁶the   ⁷Son   ¹has.

10 εἴ   τις   ἔρχεται   πρὸς   ὑμᾶς   καὶ   ταύτην
If   anyone comes   to   you   and   this

---

a Other ancient authorities read *we*

doctrine, do not receive him into the house or give him any greeting; [11]for he who greets him shares his wicked work.

12 Though I have much to write to you, I would rather not use paper and ink, but I hope to come to see you and talk with you face to face, so that our joy may be complete.

13 The children of your elect sister greet you.

τὴν διδαχὴν οὐ φέρει, μὴ λαμβάνετε
teaching brings not, do not ye receive

αὐτὸν εἰς οἰκίαν, καὶ χαίρειν αὐτῷ μὴ
him into [your] and ⁴to rejoice ³him ²not
house,

λέγετε· 11 ὁ λέγων γὰρ αὐτῷ χαίρειν
¹tell ye*; ²the ²telling ¹for him to rejoice
[one]

κοινωνεῖ τοῖς ἔργοις αὐτοῦ τοῖς πονηροῖς.
shares in the ²works ³of him - ¹evil.

12 Πολλὰ ἔχων ὑμῖν γράφειν οὐκ
²Many things ¹having ⁴to you ³to write ⁵not

ἐβουλήθην διὰ χάρτου καὶ μέλανος, ἀλλὰ
⁵I purpose by means paper and ink, but
of

ἐλπίζω γενέσθαι πρὸς ὑμᾶς καὶ στόμα
I am hoping to be with you and ²mouth

πρὸς στόμα λαλῆσαι, ἵνα ἡ χαρὰ ἡμῶν
³to ⁴mouth ¹to speak, in or- the joy of us
der that

πεπληρωμένη ᾖ. 13 Ἀσπάζεταί σε τὰ
having been may be. ⁷greets ⁸thee ¹The
fulfilled

τέκνα τῆς ἀδελφῆς σου τῆς ἐκλεκτῆς.
²children ³of the ⁵sister ⁶of thee - ⁴chosen.

III. JOHN

THE elder to the beloved Ga'ius, whom I love in the truth.

2 Beloved, I pray that all may go well with you and that you may be in health; I know that it is well with your soul. [3]For I greatly rejoiced when some of the brethren arrived and testified to the truth of your life, as

1 Ὁ πρεσβύτερος Γαΐῳ τῷ ἀγαπητῷ,
The elder to Gaius the beloved,

ὃν ἐγὼ ἀγαπῶ ἐν ἀληθείᾳ.
whom I love in truth.

2 Ἀγαπητέ, περὶ πάντων εὔχομαί σε
Beloved, concerning all things I pray thee
= that

εὐοδοῦσθαι καὶ ὑγιαίνειν, καθὼς εὐοδοῦταί
to prosper and to be in health, as ⁴prospers
thou mayest prosper ...

σου ἡ ψυχή. 3 ἐχάρην γὰρ λίαν ἐρχομένων
²of ¹the ³soul. For I rejoiced greatly coming
thee = when [some]

ἀδελφῶν καὶ μαρτυρούντων σου τῇ
brothers and bearing witness* of thee in the
brothers came and bore witness

* That is, "do not greet him."

indeed you do follow the truth. ⁴No greater joy can I have than this, to hear that my children follow the truth.

5 Beloved, it is a loyal thing you do when you render any service to the brethren, especially to strangers, ⁶who have testified to your love before the church. You will do well to send them on their journey as befits God's service. ⁷For they have set out for his sake and have accepted nothing from the heathen. ⁸So we ought to support such men, that we may be fellow workers in the truth.

9 I have written something to the church; but Diot'rephes, who likes to put himself first, does not acknowledge my authority. ¹⁰So if I come, I will bring up what he is doing, prating against me with evil words. And not content with that, he refuses himself to welcome the brethren, and also stops those who want to welcome them and puts them out of the church.

11 Beloved, do not imitate evil but imitate

ἀληθείᾳ,   καθὼς   σὺ   ἐν   ἀληθείᾳ   περιπατεῖς.
truth,   as   thou   in   truth   walkest.

4 μειζοτέραν   τούτων   οὐκ   ἔχω   χαράν,   ἵνα
³greater ⁴[than]   ⁵these   ¹I have no   ²joy,   in order
    things   that

ἀκούω   τὰ   ἐμὰ   τέκνα   ἐν   τῇ   ἀληθείᾳ
I hear   –   my   children   ²in   ³the   ⁴truth

περιπατοῦντα.   5 Ἀγαπητέ,   πιστὸν   ποιεῖς
¹walking.   Beloved,   faithfully   thou
                                   doest

ὃ   ἐὰν   ἐργάσῃ   εἰς   τοὺς   ἀδελφοὺς   καὶ
whatever   thou workest   for   the   brothers   and

τοῦτο   ξένους,   6 οἳ   ἐμαρτύρησάν   σου   τῇ
this   strangers,   who   bore witness   of thee   –

ἀγάπῃ   ἐνώπιον   ἐκκλησίας,   οὓς   καλῶς
in love   before   [the] church,   whom   well

ποιήσεις   προπέμψας   ἀξίως   τοῦ   θεοῦ·
thou wilt do   sending forward   worthily   –   of God;

7 ὑπὲρ   γὰρ   τοῦ   ὀνόματος   ἐξῆλθαν   μηδὲν
for   on behalf of   the   name   they went forth   ²nothing

λαμβάνοντες   ἀπὸ   τῶν   ἐθνικῶν.   8 ἡμεῖς
¹taking   from   the   Gentiles.   We

οὖν   ὀφείλομεν   ὑπολαμβάνειν   τοὺς   τοιούτους,
there-   ought   to entertain   –   such men,
fore

ἵνα   συνεργοὶ   γινώμεθα   τῇ   ἀληθείᾳ.
in or-   ²co-workers   ¹we may become   in the   truth.
der that

9 Ἔγραψά   τι   τῇ   ἐκκλησίᾳ·   ἀλλ'   ὁ
I wrote   some-   to the   church;   but   the
         thing   [one]

φιλοπρωτεύων   αὐτῶν   Διοτρέφης   οὐκ
loving to be first   of them   Diotrephes   not

ἐπιδέχεται   ἡμᾶς.   10 διὰ   τοῦτο,   ἐὰν
receives   us.   Therefore,   if

ἔλθω,   ὑπομνήσω   αὐτοῦ   τὰ   ἔργα   ἃ   ποιεῖ
I come,   I will remember   ²of him   ¹the   ²works   which he does

λόγοις   πονηροῖς   φλυαρῶν   ἡμᾶς,   καὶ   μὴ
⁴words   ³with evil   ¹prating against   ²us,   and   not

ἀρκούμενος   ἐπὶ   τούτοις   οὔτε   αὐτὸς
being satisfied   on(with)   these   ²neither   ¹he

ἐπιδέχεται   τοὺς   ἀδελφοὺς   καὶ   τοὺς
²receives   the   brothers   and   the

βουλομένους   κωλύει   καὶ   ἐκ   τῆς   ἐκκλησίας
[ones] purposing   he prevents   and   ³out of   ³the   ⁴church

ἐκβάλλει.
¹puts out.

11 Ἀγαπητέ,   μὴ   μιμοῦ   τὸ   κακὸν   ἀλλὰ
Beloved,   imitate not   the   bad   but

good. He who does good is of God; he who does evil has not seen God. ¹²Deme'trius has testimony from every one, and from the truth itself; I testify to him too, and you know my testimony is true.

13 I had much to write to you, but I would rather not write with pen and ink; ¹⁴I hope to see you soon, and we will talk together face to face. 15 Peace be to you. The friends greet you. Greet the friends, every one of them.

τὸ	ἀγαθόν.	ὁ	ἀγαθοποιῶν	ἐκ	τοῦ	θεοῦ
the	good.	The [one]	doing good	²of	–	¹God

ἐστιν·	ὁ	κακοποιῶν	οὐχ	ἐώρακεν	τὸν
¹is;	the [one]	doing ill		has not seen	–

θεόν.	12 Δημητρίῳ	μεμαρτύρηται	ὑπὸ
God.	To Demetrius	witness has been borne	by

πάντων	καὶ	ὑπὸ	αὐτῆς	τῆς	ἀληθείας·
all	and	by	²[it]self	¹the	²truth;

καὶ	ἡμεῖς	δὲ	μαρτυροῦμεν,	καὶ	οἶδας
²also	²we	¹and	bear witness,	and	thou knowest

ὅτι	ἡ	μαρτυρία	ἡμῶν	ἀληθής	ἐστιν.
that	the	witness	of us	²true	¹is.

13 Πολλὰ	εἶχον	γράψαι	σοι,	ἀλλ'	οὐ
²Many things	¹I had	to write	to thee,	but	not

θέλω	διὰ	μέλανος	καὶ	καλάμου	σοι
I wish	²by means of	⁴ink	³and	⁵pen	¹to thee

γράφειν·	14 ἐλπίζω	δὲ	εὐθέως	σε	ἰδεῖν,
¹to write;	but I am hoping		²immediately	³thee	¹to see,

καὶ	στόμα	πρὸς	στόμα	λαλήσομεν.
and	²mouth	³to	⁴mouth	¹we will speak.

15 Εἰρήνη	σοι.	ἀσπάζονταί	σε	οἱ	φίλοι.
Peace	to thee.	²greet	⁴thee	¹The	²friends.

ἀσπάζου	τοὺς	φίλους	κατ'	ὄνομα.
Greet thou	the	friends	by	name.

JUDE

ΙΟΥΔΑ
Of Jude

JUDE, a servant of Jesus Christ and brother of James,
To those who are called, beloved in God the Father and kept for Jesus Christ:
2 May mercy, peace, and love be multiplied to you.
3 Beloved, being very

1 Ἰούδας	Ἰησοῦ	Χριστοῦ	δοῦλος,	ἀδελφὸς
Jude	of Jesus	Christ	a slave,	²brother

δὲ	Ἰακώβου,	τοῖς	ἐν	θεῷ	πατρὶ
¹and	of James,	¹to the [ones]	⁴by	⁵God	⁶[the] Father

ἠγαπημένοις	καὶ	Ἰησοῦ	Χριστῷ
³having been loved	⁷and	⁸for Jesus	¹⁰Christ

τετηρημένοις	κλητοῖς.	2 ἔλεος	ὑμῖν	καὶ
⁹having been kept	²called.	Mercy	to you	and

εἰρήνη	καὶ	ἀγάπη	πληθυνθείη.
peace	and	love	may it be multiplied.

3 Ἀγαπητοί,	πᾶσαν	σπουδὴν	ποιούμενος
Beloved,	²all	³haste	¹making

eager to write to you of our common salvation, I found it necessary to write appealing to you to contend for the faith which was once for all delivered to the saints. 4 For admission has been secretly gained by some who long ago were designated for this condemnation, ungodly persons who pervert the grace of our God into licentiousness and deny our only Master and Lord, Jesus Christ.[a] 5 Now I desire to remind you, though you were once for all fully informed, that he[b] who saved a people out of the land of Egypt, afterward destroyed those who did not believe. 6 And the angels that did not keep their own position but left their proper dwelling have been kept by him in eternal chains in the nether gloom until the judgment of the great day; 7 just as Sodom and Gomor'rah and the surrounding cities, which likewise acted immorally and indulged in unnatural lust, serve as an example by undergoing a punishment of eternal fire.
8 Yet in like manner

[a] Or *the only Master and our Lord Jesus Christ*
[b] Ancient authorities read *Jesus* or *the Lord* or *God*

γράφειν ὑμῖν περὶ τῆς κοινῆς ἡμῶν
to write to you concerning the common [1]of us

σωτηρίας, ἀνάγκην ἔσχον γράψαι ὑμῖν
[1]salvation, necessity I had to write to you

παρακαλῶν ἐπαγωνίζεσθαι τῇ ἅπαξ
exhorting to contend for [1]the [2]once

παραδοθείσῃ τοῖς ἁγίοις πίστει. 4 παρεισε-
[4]delivered [5]to the [6]saints [2]faith. [2]crept

δύησαν γάρ τινες ἄνθρωποι, οἱ πάλαι
in For [1]certain [2]men, the [ones] of old

προγεγραμμένοι εἰς τοῦτο τὸ κρίμα,
having been for this - judgment,
previously written

ἀσεβεῖς, τὴν· τοῦ θεοῦ ἡμῶν χάριτα
impious men, [3]the [4]of the [5]God [6]of us [3]grace

μετατιθέντες εἰς ἀσέλγειαν καὶ τὸν μόνον
[1]making [7]a pretext for wantonness and [8]the [9]only

δεσπότην καὶ κύριον ἡμῶν Ἰησοῦν Χριστὸν
[4]Master [6]and [5]Lord [7]of us [2]Jesus [3]Christ

ἀρνούμενοι. 5 Ὑπομνῆσαι δὲ ὑμᾶς βούλομαι,
[1]denying. But [2]to remind [3]you [1]I purpose,

εἰδότας ἅπαξ πάντα, ὅτι κύριος λαὸν
[2]knowing [1]once all that [the] [2][the]
things, Lord people

ἐκ γῆς Αἰγύπτου σώσας τὸ δεύτερον
[3]out [4][the] [5]of Egypt [1]having in the second place
of land saved

τοὺς μὴ πιστεύσαντας ἀπώλεσεν, 6 ἀγγέλους
[2]the [3]not [4]believing [1]destroyed, [2]angels
[ones]

τε τοὺς μὴ τηρήσαντας τὴν ἑαυτῶν
[1]and - not having kept the [2]of themselves

ἀρχὴν ἀλλὰ ἀπολιπόντας τὸ ἴδιον
[1]rule but having deserted the(ir) own

οἰκητήριον εἰς κρίσιν μεγάλης ἡμέρας
habitation [6]for [7][the] judgment [8]of [the] great [9]day

δεσμοῖς ἀϊδίοις ὑπὸ ζόφον τετήρηκεν·
[3]bonds [2]in everlasting [4]under [5]gloom [1]he has kept;

7 ὡς Σόδομα καὶ Γόμορρα καὶ αἱ περὶ
as Sodom and Gomorra and [1]the [2]round

αὐτὰς πόλεις, τὸν ὅμοιον τρόπον τούτοις
[4]them [3]cities, in the like manner to these

ἐκπορνεύσασαι καὶ ἀπελθοῦσαι ὀπίσω σαρκὸς
committing and going away after [2]flesh
fornication

ἑτέρας, πρόκεινται δεῖγμα πυρὸς αἰωνίου
[1]different, are set forth an example [4]fire [3]of eternal

δίκην ὑπέχουσαι. 8 Ὁμοίως μέντοι καὶ
[2]ven- [1]undergoing. Likewise indeed also
geance

these men in their dreamings defile the flesh, reject authority, and revile the glorious ones. ⁹But when the archangel Michael, contending with the devil, disputed about the body of Moses, he did not presume to pronounce a reviling judgment upon him, but said, "The Lord rebuke you." ¹⁰But these men revile whatever they do not understand, and by those things that they know by instinct as irrational animals do, they are destroyed. ¹¹Woe to them! For they walk in the way of Cain, and abandon themselves for the sake of gain to Balaam's error, and perish in Korah's rebellion. ¹²These are blemishes^c on your love feasts, as they boldly carouse together, looking after themselves; waterless clouds, carried along by winds; fruitless trees in late autumn, twice dead, uprooted; ¹³wild waves of the sea, casting up the foam of their own shame; wandering stars for whom the nether gloom of darkness has been reserved for ever.

^c Or reefs

οὗτοι ἐνυπνιαζόμενοι σάρκα μὲν μιαίνουσιν,
these dreaming [ones] ³flesh ¹on one ²defile,
hand

κυριότητα δὲ ἀθετοῦσιν, δόξας δὲ
²lordship ¹on the other ²despise, and ²glories

βλασφημοῦσιν. 9 Ὁ δὲ Μιχαὴλ ὁ ἀρχάγ-
¹rail at. - But Michael the arch-

γελος, ὅτε τῷ διαβόλῳ διακρινόμενος
angel, when ²with the ³devil ¹contending

διελέγετο περὶ τοῦ Μωϋσέως σώματος,
he argued about ¹the ²of Moses ³body,

οὐκ ἐτόλμησεν κρίσιν ἐπενεγκεῖν βλασφημίας,
durst not ²a judgment ¹to bring on of railing,

ἀλλὰ εἶπεν· ἐπιτιμήσαι σοι κύριος. 10 οὗτοι
but said: ²rebuke ³thee ¹[The] Lord. these men

δὲ ὅσα μὲν οὐκ οἴδασιν βλασφημοῦσιν,
But what on one they know not they rail at,
things hand

ὅσα δὲ φυσικῶς ὡς τὰ ἄλογα ζῷα
what on the ²naturally ²as ⁴the ⁶without ⁵animals
things other reason

ἐπίστανται, ἐν τούτοις φθείρονται. 11 οὐαὶ
¹they understand, by these they are corrupted. Woe

αὐτοῖς, ὅτι τῇ ὁδῷ τοῦ Κάϊν ἐπορεύθησαν,
to them, because in the way - of Cain they went,

καὶ τῇ πλάνῃ τοῦ Βαλαὰμ μισθοῦ
and ²to the ²error - ⁴of Balaam ⁵of(for)
reward

ἐξεχύθησαν, καὶ τῇ ἀντιλογίᾳ τοῦ Κόρε
¹gave themselves and ²in the ²dispute - ⁴of
up, Korah

ἀπώλοντο. 12 Οὗτοί εἰσιν οἱ ἐν ταῖς
¹perished. These men are ¹the ²in ⁴the

ἀγάπαις ὑμῶν σπιλάδες συνευωχούμενοι
²love feasts ⁸of you ²rocks feasting together

ἀφόβως, ἑαυτοὺς ποιμαίνοντες, νεφέλαι
without fear, ²themselves ¹feeding, ²clouds

ἄνυδροι ὑπὸ ἀνέμων παραφερόμεναι, δένδρα
¹waterless ⁴by ⁵winds ²being carried away, ³trees

φθινοπωρινὰ ἄκαρπα δὶς ἀποθανόντα
¹autumn without fruit twice dying

ἐκριζωθέντα, 13 κύματα ἄγρια θαλάσσης
having been uprooted, ³waves ¹fierce ²of [the] sea

ἐπαφρίζοντα τὰς ἑαυτῶν αἰσχύνας, ἀστέρες
⁴foaming up ⁵the ⁷of themselves ⁶shames, ²stars

πλανῆται, οἷς ὁ ζόφος τοῦ σκότους
¹wandering, for whom the gloom - of darkness

εἰς αἰῶνα τετήρηται. 14 Ἐπροφήτευσεν
unto [the] age has been kept. ⁷prophesied

14 It was of these also that Enoch in the seventh generation from Adam prophesied, saying, "Behold, the Lord came with his holy myriads, ¹⁵to execute judgment on all, and to convict all the ungodly of all their deeds of ungodliness which they have committed in such an ungodly way, and of all the harsh things which ungodly sinners have spoken against him." ¹⁶These are grumblers, malcontents, following their own passions, loud-mouthed boasters, flattering people to gain advantage.

17 But you must remember, beloved, the predictions of the apostles of our Lord Jesus Christ; ¹⁸they said to you, "In the last time there will be scoffers, following their own ungodly passions." ¹⁹It is these who set up divisions, worldly people, devoid of the Spirit. ²⁰But you, beloved, build yourselves up on your most holy faith; pray in the Holy Spirit; ²¹keep yourselves in the love of

δὲ	καὶ	τούτοις	ἔβδομος	ἀπὸ	Ἀδὰμ
¹And	²also	³to these men	⁴[the] seventh	⁵from	⁶Adam

Ἐνὼχ	λέγων·	ἰδοὺ	ἦλθεν	κύριος	ἐν
²Enoch	saying :	Behold	came	[the] Lord	with

ἁγίαις	μυριάσιν	αὐτοῦ,	15 ποιῆσαι	κρίσιν
saints	ten thousands	of him,	to do	judgment

κατὰ	πάντων	καὶ	ἐλέγξαι	πάντας	τοὺς
against	all men	and	to rebuke	all	the

ἀσεβεῖς	περὶ	πάντων	τῶν	ἔργων	ἀσεβείας
impious	concerning	all	the	works	of impiety

αὐτῶν	ὧν	ἠσέβησαν	καὶ	περὶ	πάντων
of them	which they impiously did	and	concerning	all

τῶν	σκληρῶν	ὧν	ἐλάλησαν	κατ'	αὐτοῦ
the	hard things	which	³spoke	⁴against	⁵him

ἁμαρτωλοὶ	ἀσεβεῖς.	16 Οὗτοί	εἰσιν	γογ-
²sinners	¹impious.	These men	are	¹mur-

γυσταὶ	μεμψίμοιροι,	κατὰ	τὰς	ἐπιθυμίας
murers	²querulous,	²according to	³the	⁴lusts

αὐτῶν	πορευόμενοι,	καὶ	τὸ	στόμα	αὐτῶν
⁵of them	¹going,	and	the	mouth	of them

λαλεῖ	ὑπέρογκα,	θαυμάζοντες	πρόσωπα
speaks	arrogant things,	admiring	faces

ὠφελείας	χάριν.
²advantage	¹for the sake of.

17 Ὑμεῖς	δέ,	ἀγαπητοί,	μνήσθητε	τῶν
But ye,		beloved,	be mindful of	the

ῥημάτων	τῶν	προειρημένων	ὑπὸ	τῶν
words	–	previously spoken	by	the

ἀποστόλων	τοῦ	κυρίου	ἡμῶν	Ἰησοῦ
apostles	of the	Lord	of us	Jesus

Χριστοῦ,	18 ὅτι	ἔλεγον	ὑμῖν·	ἐπ'	ἐσχάτου
Christ,	because	they told	you:	At	[the] last

τοῦ	χρόνου	ἔσονται	ἐμπαῖκται	κατὰ	τὰς
of the	time	will be	mockers	²according to	³the

ἑαυτῶν	ἐπιθυμίας	πορευόμενοι	τῶν	ἀσεβειῶν.
⁶of them-selves	⁴lusts	¹going	–	⁵of impious things.

19 Οὗτοί	εἰσιν	οἱ	ἀποδιορίζοντες,	ψυχικοί,
These men	are	the [ones]	making separations,	natural,

πνεῦμα	μὴ	ἔχοντες.	20 ὑμεῖς	δέ,	ἀγαπητοί,
²spirit	¹not	³having.	But ye,		beloved,

ἐποικοδομοῦντες	ἑαυτοὺς	τῇ	ἁγιωτάτῃ	ὑμῶν
building up	yourselves	in the	most holy	²of you

πίστει,	ἐν	πνεύματι	ἁγίῳ	προσευχόμενοι,
¹faith,	²in	⁴Spirit	³[the] Holy	¹praying,

21 ἑαυτοὺς	ἐν	ἀγάπῃ	θεοῦ	τηρήσατε,
²yourselves	³in	⁴[the] love	⁵of God	¹keep,

God; wait for the mercy of our Lord Jesus Christ unto eternal life. ²²And convince some, who doubt; ²³save some, by snatching them out of the fire; on some have mercy with fear, hating even the garment spotted by the flesh.ᵈ

24 Now to him who is able to keep you from falling and to present you without blemish before the presence of his glory with rejoicing, ²⁵to the only God, our Savior through Jesus Christ our Lord, be glory, majesty, dominion, and authority, before all time and now and for ever. Amen.

προσδεχόμενοι τὸ ἔλεος τοῦ κυρίου ἡμῶν
awaiting the mercy of the Lord of us

'Ιησοῦ Χριστοῦ εἰς ζωὴν αἰώνιον. 22 καὶ
Jesus Christ to life eternal. And

οὓς μὲν ἐλεᾶτε διακρινομένους 23 σώζετε
some ²pity ye ¹[who are] wavering ²save

ἐκ πυρὸς ἁρπάζοντες, οὓς δὲ ἐλεᾶτε
³out of ⁴fire ¹seizing, · others pity

ἐν φόβῳ, μισοῦντες καὶ τὸν ἀπὸ τῆς
with fear, hating even ¹the ⁴from ⁵the

σαρκὸς ἐσπιλωμένον χιτῶνα.
⁶flesh ³having been spotted ²tunic.

24 Τῷ δὲ δυναμένῳ φυλάξαι ὑμᾶς
Now to the [one] being able to guard you

ἀπταίστους καὶ στῆσαι κατενώπιον τῆς
without stumbling and to set [you] before the

δόξης αὐτοῦ ἀμώμους ἐν ἀγαλλιάσει,
glory of him unblemished with exultation,

25 μόνῳ θεῷ σωτῆρι ἡμῶν διὰ 'Ιησοῦ
to [the] only God Saviour of us through Jesus

Χριστοῦ τοῦ κυρίου ἡμῶν δόξα μεγαλωσύνη
Christ the Lord of us [be] glory[,] greatness[,]

κράτος καὶ ἐξουσία πρὸ παντὸς τοῦ
might[,] and authority before all the

αἰῶνος καὶ νῦν καὶ εἰς πάντας τοὺς
age and now and unto all the

αἰῶνας· ἀμήν.
ages: Amen.

ᵈ The Greek text in this sentence is uncertain at several points

CHAPTER 1

THE revelation of Jesus Christ, which God gave him to show to his servants what must soon take place; and he made it known by sending his angel to his servant John, [2]who bore witness to the word of God and to the testimony of Jesus Christ, even to all that he saw. [3]Blessed is he who reads aloud the words of the prophecy, and blessed are those who hear, and who keep what is written therein; for the time is near.

[4] John to the seven churches that are in Asia:

Grace to you and peace from him who is and who was and who is to come, and from the seven spirits who are before his throne, [5]and from Jesus Christ the faithful witness, the firstborn of the dead, and the ruler of kings on earth.

To him who loves us and has freed us from our sins by his blood

---

1 Ἀποκάλυψις   Ἰησοῦ   Χριστοῦ,   ἦν
A revelation   of Jesus   Christ,   which

ἔδωκεν   αὐτῷ   ὁ   θεός,   δεῖξαι   τοῖς   δούλοις
[2]gave   [3]to him   –   [1]God,   to show   to the   slaves

αὐτοῦ   ἃ   δεῖ   γενέσθαι   ἐν   τάχει,   καὶ
of him   things   it be-   to occur   with   speed,   and
      which hoves

ἐσήμανεν   ἀποστείλας   διὰ   τοῦ   ἀγγέλου
he signified   sending   through   the   angel

αὐτοῦ   τῷ   δούλῳ   αὐτοῦ   Ἰωάννῃ,   **2** ὃς
of him   to the   slave   of him   John,   who

ἐμαρτύρησεν   τὸν   λόγον   τοῦ   θεοῦ   καὶ
bore witness [of]   the   word   –   of God   and

τὴν   μαρτυρίαν   Ἰησοῦ   Χριστοῦ,   ὅσα   εἶδεν.
the   witness   of Jesus   Christ,   as many   he saw.
      things as

3 Μακάριος   ὁ   ἀναγινώσκων   καὶ   οἱ
Blessed [is]   the [one]   reading   and   the

ἀκούοντες   τοὺς   λόγους   τῆς   προφητείας
[ones] hearing   the   words   of the   prophecy

καὶ   τηροῦντες   τὰ   ἐν   αὐτῇ   γεγραμμένα·
and   keeping   the things   [2]in   [3]it   [1]having been written;

ὁ   γὰρ   καιρὸς   ἐγγύς.
[2]the   [1]for   time [is]   near.

4 Ἰωάννης   ταῖς   ἑπτὰ   ἐκκλησίαις   ταῖς
John   to the   seven   churches   –

ἐν   τῇ   Ἀσίᾳ·   χάρις   ὑμῖν   καὶ   εἰρήνη
in   –   Asia: Grace   to you   and   peace

ἀπὸ   ὁ   ὢν   καὶ   ὁ   ἦν   καὶ   ὁ   ἐρχόμενος,
from   the   being   and   the   was   and   the [one] coming,
      [one]   [one who]
      =the one who is

καὶ   ἀπὸ   τῶν   ἑπτὰ   πνευμάτων   ἃ   ἐνώπιον
and   from   the   seven   spirits   which   before
      [are]

τοῦ   θρόνου   αὐτοῦ,   **5** καὶ   ἀπὸ   Ἰησοῦ
the   throne   of him,   and   from   Jesus

Χριστοῦ,   ὁ   μάρτυς   ὁ   πιστός,   ὁ   πρωτότοκος
Christ,   the   [2]witness   –   [1]faithful,   the   firstborn

τῶν   νεκρῶν   καὶ   ὁ   ἄρχων   τῶν   βασιλέων
of the   dead   and   the   ruler   of the   kings

τῆς   γῆς.   Τῷ   ἀγαπῶντι   ἡμᾶς   καὶ   λύσαντι
of the earth.   To   loving   us   and   having
      the [one]   loosed

ἡμᾶς   ἐκ   τῶν   ἁμαρτιῶν   ἡμῶν   ἐν   τῷ
us   out of   the   sins   of us   by   the

⁶and made us a kingdom, priests to his God and Father, to him be glory and dominion for ever and ever. Amen. ⁷Behold, he is coming with the clouds, and every eye will see him, every one who pierced him; and all tribes of the earth will wail on account of him. Even so. Amen.

8 "I am the Alpha and the Omega," says the Lord God, who is and who was and who is to come, the Almighty.

9 I John, your brother, who share with you in Jesus the tribulation and the kingdom and the patient endurance, was on the island called Patmos on account of the word of God and the testimony of Jesus. ¹⁰I was in the Spirit on the Lord's day, and I heard behind me a loud voice like a trumpet ¹¹saying, "Write what you see in a book and send it to the seven churches, to

αἵματι	αὐτοῦ,	6 καὶ	ἐποίησεν	ἡμᾶς
blood	of him,	and	made	us

βασιλείαν,	ἱερεῖς	τῷ	θεῷ	καὶ	πατρὶ
a kingdom,	priests	to the	God	and	Father

αὐτοῦ,	αὐτῷ	ἡ	δόξα	καὶ	τὸ	κράτος
of him,	to him⁰ [is] the		glory	and	the	might
	= his is					

εἰς	τοὺς	αἰῶνας	τῶν	αἰώνων·	ἀμήν.
unto	the	ages	of the	ages:	Amen.

7 | Ἰδοὺ | ἔρχεται | μετὰ | τῶν | νεφελῶν, |
|---|---|---|---|---|
| Behold | he comes | with | the | clouds, |

καὶ	ὄψεται	αὐτὸν	πᾶς	ὀφθαλμὸς	καὶ
and	²will see	⁴him	¹every	³eye	and

οἵτινες	αὐτὸν	ἐξεκέντησαν,	καὶ	κόψονται
[those] who	²him	¹pierced,	and	⁶will wail

ἐπ'	αὐτὸν	πᾶσαι	αἱ	φυλαὶ	τῆς	γῆς.
⁷over	⁵him	¹all	²the	³tribes	⁴of the	⁵land.

ναί,	ἀμήν.
Yes,	amen.

8 | Ἐγώ | εἰμι | τὸ | ἄλφα | καὶ | τὸ | ὦ, | λέγει |
|---|---|---|---|---|---|---|---|
| I | am | the | alpha | and | the omega, | | says |

κύριος	ὁ	θεός,	ὁ	ὢν	καὶ	ὁ	ἦν
[the] Lord	–	God,	the [one] being =the one who is	and	the [one who]	was

καὶ	ὁ	ἐρχόμενος,	ὁ	παντοκράτωρ.
and	the [one] coming,		the	Almighty.

9 | Ἐγὼ | Ἰωάννης, | ὁ | ἀδελφὸς | ὑμῶν | καὶ |
|---|---|---|---|---|---|
| I | John, | the | brother | of you | and |

συγκοινωνὸς	ἐν	τῇ	θλίψει	καὶ	βασιλείᾳ
co-sharer	in	the	affliction	and	kingdom

καὶ	ὑπομονῇ	ἐν	Ἰησοῦ,	ἐγενόμην	ἐν
and	endurance	in	Jesus,	came to be	in

τῇ	νήσῳ	τῇ	καλουμένῃ	Πάτμῳ	διὰ
the	island	–	being called	Patmos	on account of

τὸν	λόγον	τοῦ	θεοῦ	καὶ	τὴν	μαρτυρίαν
the	word	–	of God	and	the	witness

Ἰησοῦ.	10 ἐγενόμην	ἐν	πνεύματι	ἐν
of Jesus.	I came to be	in	[the] spirit	on

τῇ	κυριακῇ	ἡμέρᾳ,	καὶ	ἤκουσα	ὀπίσω
the	imperial*	day,	and	heard	behind

μου	φωνὴν	μεγάλην	ὡς	σάλπιγγος
me	²voice	¹a great(loud)	as	of a trumpet

11 | λεγούσης· | ὃ | βλέπεις | γράψον | εἰς | βιβλίον |
|---|---|---|---|---|---|
| | saying: | What | thou seest | write | in | a scroll |

καὶ	πέμψον	ταῖς	ἑπτὰ	ἐκκλησίαις,	εἰς
and	send	to the	seven	churches,	to

* See I. Cor. 11. 20.

Ephesus and to Smyrna and to Per'gamum and to Thyati'ra and to Sardis and to Philadelphia and to Laodice'a."

12 Then I turned to see the voice that was speaking to me, and on turning I saw seven golden lampstands, 13 and in the midst of the lampstands one like a son of man, clothed with a long robe and with a golden girdle round his breast; 14 his head and his hair were white as white wool, white as snow; his eyes were like a flame of fire, 15 his feet were like burnished bronze, refined as in a furnace, and his voice was like the sound of many waters; 16 in his right hand he held seven stars, from his mouth issued a sharp two-edged sword, and his face was like the sun shining in full strength.

17 When I saw him, I fell at his feet as though dead. But he laid his right hand upon me, saying, "Fear not, I am the first and the last,

"Εφεσον καὶ εἰς Σμύρναν καὶ εἰς Πέργαμον
Ephesus and to Smyrna and to Pergamum
καὶ εἰς Θυάτιρα καὶ εἰς Σάρδεις καὶ
and to Thyatira and to Sardis and
εἰς Φιλαδέλφειαν καὶ εἰς Λαοδίκειαν.
to Philadelphia and to Laodicea.
12 Καὶ ἐπέστρεψα βλέπειν τὴν φωνὴν
And I turned to see the voice
ἥτις ἐλάλει μετ' ἐμοῦ· καὶ ἐπιστρέψας
which spoke with me; and having turned
εἶδον ἑπτὰ λυχνίας χρυσᾶς, 13 καὶ ἐν
I saw seven ²lampstands ¹golden, and in
μέσῳ τῶν λυχνιῶν ὅμοιον υἱὸν ἀνθρώπου,
[the] of the lampstands [one] like a son of man,*
midst
ἐνδεδυμένον ποδήρη καὶ περιεζωσμένον
having been clothed to the feet and having been girdled round
πρὸς τοῖς μαστοῖς ζώνην χρυσᾶν· 14 ἡ
at the breasts ²girdle ¹[with] a golden; ²the
δὲ κεφαλὴ αὐτοῦ καὶ αἱ τρίχες λευκαὶ
¹and head of him and the hairs white
ὡς ἔριον λευκὸν ὡς χιών, καὶ οἱ ὀφθαλμοὶ
as wool white as snow, and the eyes
αὐτοῦ ὡς φλὸξ πυρός, 15 καὶ οἱ πόδες
of him as a flame of fire, and the feet
αὐτοῦ ὅμοιοι χαλκολιβάνῳ ὡς ἐν καμίνῳ
of him like to burnished brass as ²in ¹a furnace
πεπυρωμένης, καὶ ἡ φωνὴ αὐτοῦ ὡς
¹having been fired, and the voice of him as
φωνὴ ὑδάτων πολλῶν, 16 καὶ ἔχων ἐν
a sound waters of many, and having in
τῇ δεξιᾷ χειρὶ αὐτοῦ ἀστέρας ἑπτά,
the right hand of him ²stars ¹seven;
καὶ ἐκ τοῦ στόματος αὐτοῦ ῥομφαία
and out of the mouth of him ⁴sword
δίστομος ὀξεῖα ἐκπορευομένη, καὶ ἡ ὄψις
³two- ²a sharp ¹proceeding, and the face
mouthed(edged)
αὐτοῦ ὡς ὁ ἥλιος φαίνει ἐν τῇ δυνάμει
of him as the sun shines in the power
αὐτοῦ. 17 Καὶ ὅτε εἶδον αὐτόν, ἔπεσα
of it. And when I saw him, I fell
πρὸς τοὺς πόδας αὐτοῦ ὡς νεκρός· καὶ
at the feet of him as dead; and
ἔθηκεν τὴν δεξιὰν αὐτοῦ ἐπ' ἐμὲ λέγων·
he placed the right [hand] of him on me saying:
μὴ φοβοῦ· ἐγώ εἰμι ὁ πρῶτος καὶ
Fear not: I am the first and

* Anarthrous; see also ch. 14. 14 and John 5. 27, and cf. Heb. 2. 6.

¹⁸and the living one; I died, and behold I am alive for evermore, and I have the keys of Death and Hades. ¹⁹Now write what you see, what is and what is to take place hereafter. ²⁰As for the mystery of the seven stars which you saw in my right hand, and the seven golden lampstands, the seven stars are the angels of the seven churches and the seven lampstands are the seven churches.

ὁ	ἔσχατος	18 καὶ	ὁ	ζῶν,	καὶ	ἐγενόμην
the	last	and		the living [one], and		I became

νεκρὸς	καὶ	ἰδοὺ	ζῶν	εἰμι	εἰς	τοὺς
dead	and	behold	²living	¹I am	unto	the

αἰῶνας	τῶν	αἰώνων,	καὶ	ἔχω	τὰς	κλεῖς
ages	of the	ages,	and	I have	the	keys

τοῦ	θανάτου	καὶ	τοῦ	ᾅδου.	19 γράψον
–	of death	and	–	of hades.	Write thou

οὖν	ἃ	εἶδες	καὶ	ἃ	εἰσὶν	καὶ	ἃ
there-fore	[the] things which	thou sawest	and	[the] things which	are	and	[the] things which

μέλλει	γενέσθαι	μετὰ	ταῦτα.	20 τὸ
(is)are about	to occur	after	these things.	The

μυστήριον	τῶν	ἑπτὰ	ἀστέρων	οὓς	εἶδες
mystery	of the	seven	stars	which	thou sawest

ἐπὶ	τῆς	δεξιᾶς	μου,	καὶ	τὰς	ἑπτὰ
on	the	right [hand]	of me,	and	the	seven

λυχνίας	τὰς	χρυσᾶς·	οἱ	ἑπτὰ	ἀστέρες
²lampstands	–	¹golden:	the	seven	stars

ἄγγελοι	τῶν	ἑπτὰ	ἐκκλησιῶν	εἰσιν,	καὶ
messengers*	of the	seven	churches	are,	and

αἱ	λυχνίαι	αἱ	ἑπτὰ	ἑπτὰ	ἐκκλησίαι	εἰσίν.
the	²lampstands	–	¹seven	⁴seven	⁵churches	³are.

CHAPTER 2

"TO the angel of the church in Ephesus write: 'The words of him who holds the seven stars in his right hand, who walks among the seven golden lampstands.

2 "'I know your works, your toil and your patient endurance, and how you cannot bear evil men but have tested those who call themselves apostles but are not, and found them to be false;

2 Τῷ	ἀγγέλῳ	τῆς	ἐν	Ἐφέσῳ	ἐκκλησίας
To the	messenger	¹of the	²in	⁴Ephesus	²church

γράψον·
write thou:

Τάδε	λέγει	ὁ	κρατῶν	τοὺς	ἑπτὰ
These things	says	the [one]	holding	the	seven

ἀστέρας	ἐν	τῇ	δεξιᾷ	αὐτοῦ,	ὁ	περιπατῶν
stars	in	the	right [hand]	of him,	the [one]	walking

ἐν	μέσῳ	τῶν	ἑπτὰ	λυχνιῶν	τῶν
in	[the] midst	of the	seven	²lampstands	–

χρυσῶν·	2 οἶδα	τὰ	ἔργα	σου	καὶ	τὸν
¹golden:	I know	the	works	of thee	and	the

κόπον	καὶ	τὴν	ὑπομονήν	σου,	καὶ	ὅτι
labour	and	the	endurance	of thee,	and	that

οὐ	δύνῃ	βαστάσαι	κακούς,	καὶ	ἐπείρασας
thou canst not	to bear	bad men,		and	didst try

τοὺς	λέγοντας	ἑαυτοὺς	ἀποστόλους	καὶ
the [ones]	say(call)ing	themselves	apostles	and

οὐκ	εἰσίν,	καὶ	εὗρες	αὐτοὺς	ψευδεῖς·
are not,		and	didst find	them	liars;

---

* This, of course, is the prime meaning of the word: whether these beings were " messengers " from the churches, or supernatural beings, " angels " as usually understood, is a matter of exegesis.

³I know you are enduring patiently and bearing up for my name's sake, and you have not grown weary. ⁴But I have this against you, that you have abandoned the love you had at first. ⁵Remember then from what you have fallen, repent and do the works you did at first. If not, I will come to you and remove your lampstand from its place, unless you repent. ⁶Yet this you have, you hate the works of the Nicola'itans, which I also hate. ⁷He who has an ear, let him hear what the Spirit says to the churches. To him who conquers I will grant to eat of the tree of life, which is in the paradise of God.'

8 "And to the angel of the church in Smyrna write: 'The words of the first and the last, who died and came to life. 9 " 'I know your tribulation and your poverty (but you are rich) and the slander of those who say that they are Jews and are not, but are a synagogue of Satan.

3 καὶ   ὑπομονὴν   ἔχεις,   καὶ   ἐβάστασας
and   ²endurance   ¹thou hast,   and   didst bear

διὰ   τὸ   ὄνομά   μου,   καὶ   οὐ   κεκοπίακας.
be-   the   name   of me,   and   hast not grown weary.
cause of

4 ἀλλὰ   ἔχω   κατὰ   σοῦ   ὅτι   τὴν   ἀγάπην
But   I have   against   thee   that   ²the   ⁴love

σου   τὴν   πρώτην   ἀφῆκας.   5 μνημόνευε
⁵of thee   -   ³first   ¹thou didst leave.   Remember

οὖν   πόθεν   πέπτωκας,   καὶ   μετανόησον
therefore   whence   thou hast fallen,   and   repent

καὶ   τὰ   πρῶτα   ἔργα   ποίησον·   εἰ   δὲ
and   ²the   ³first   ⁴works   ¹do;   and if

μή,   ἔρχομαί   σοι   καὶ   κινήσω   τὴν   λυχνίαν
not,   I am coming to thee   and   will move   the   lampstand

σου   ἐκ   τοῦ   τόπου   αὐτῆς,   ἐὰν   μὴ
of thee out of   the   place   of it,   unless

μετανοήσῃς.   6 ἀλλὰ   τοῦτο   ἔχεις,   ὅτι
thou repentest.   But   this   thou hast,   that

μισεῖς   τὰ   ἔργα   τῶν   Νικολαϊτῶν,   ἃ
thou hatest   the   works   of the   Nicolaitans,   which

κἀγὼ   μισῶ.   7 Ὁ   ἔχων   οὓς   ἀκουσάτω
I also   hate.   The [one] having   an ear   let him hear

τί   τὸ   πνεῦμα   λέγει   ταῖς   ἐκκλησίαις.
what   the   Spirit   says   to the   churches.

Τῷ   νικῶντι   δώσω   αὐτῷ   φαγεῖν   ἐκ
To   overcoming   I will give   to him   to eat   of
the [one]

τοῦ   ξύλου   τῆς   ζωῆς,   ὅ   ἐστιν   ἐν   τῷ
the   tree   -   of life,   which   is   in   the

παραδείσῳ   τοῦ   θεοῦ.
paradise   -   of God.

8 Καὶ   τῷ   ἀγγέλῳ   τῆς   ἐν   Σμύρνῃ
And   to the   messenger   ¹of the   ²in   ⁴Smyrna

ἐκκλησίας   γράψον·
²church   write thou:

Τάδε   λέγει   ὁ   πρῶτος   καὶ   ὁ   ἔσχατος,
These things says   the   first   and the   last,

ὃς   ἐγένετο   νεκρὸς   καὶ   ἔζησεν·   9 οἶδά
who   became   dead   and   lived [again]·   I know

σου   τὴν   θλῖψιν   καὶ   τὴν   πτωχείαν,   ἀλλὰ
⁶of thee ¹the   ²affliction   ³and   ⁴the   ⁵poverty,   but

πλούσιος   εἶ,   καὶ   τὴν   βλασφημίαν   ἐκ
rich   thou art,   and   the   railing   of

τῶν   λεγόντων   Ἰουδαίους   εἶναι   ἑαυτούς,
the [ones]   say(call)ing   ²Jews   ²to be   ¹themselves,

καὶ   οὐκ   εἰσὶν   ἀλλὰ   συναγωγὴ   τοῦ   σατανᾶ,
and   they are not   but   a synagogue   -   of Satan.

¹⁰Do not fear what you are about to suffer. Behold, the devil is about to throw some of you into prison, that you may be tested, and for ten days you will have tribulation. Be faithful unto death, and I will give you the crown of life. ¹¹He who has an ear, let him hear what the Spirit says to the churches. He who conquers shall not be hurt by the second death.'

12 "And to the angel of the church in Per'gamum write: 'The words of him who has the sharp two-edged sword.

13 "'I know where you dwell, where Satan's throne is; you hold fast my name and you did not deny my faith even in the days of An'tipas my witness, my faithful one, who was killed among you, where Satan dwells. ¹⁴But I have a few things against you: you have some there who hold the teaching of Balaam, who taught Balak to put a stumbling block before the sons of

---

10 μὴ   φοβοῦ   ἃ   μέλλεις   πάσχειν.   ἰδοὺ
   Do not fear   [the]   thou art   to suffer.   Behold[.]
        things which   about

μέλλει   βάλλειν   ὁ   διάβολος   ἐξ   ὑμῶν
²is about   ⁴to cast   ¹the   ²devil   [some] of   you

εἰς   φυλακὴν   ἵνα   πειρασθῆτε,   καὶ   ἕξετε
into   prison   in order that ye may be tried,   and ye will have

θλῖψιν   ἡμερῶν   δέκα.   γίνου   πιστὸς   ἄχρι
affliction   ²days   ¹ten.   Be thou   faithful   until

θανάτου,   καὶ   δώσω   σοι   τὸν   στέφανον
death,   and   I will give   thee   the   crown

τῆς   ζωῆς.   11 Ὁ   ἔχων   οὖς   ἀκουσάτω
   -   of life.   The [one] having   an ear   let him hear

τί   τὸ   πνεῦμα   λέγει   ταῖς   ἐκκλησίαις.
what   the   Spirit   says   to the   churches.

Ὁ   νικῶν   οὐ μὴ   ἀδικηθῇ   ἐκ   τοῦ   θανάτου
The   over-   by no   will be   by   the   ²death
[one]   coming   means   hurt

τοῦ   δευτέρου.
   -   ¹second.

12 Καὶ   τῷ   ἀγγέλῳ   τῆς   ἐν   Περγάμῳ
   And   to the   messenger   ¹of the   ³in   ⁴Pergamum

ἐκκλησίας   γράψον·
²church   write thou:

Τάδε   λέγει   ὁ   ἔχων   τὴν   ρομφαίαν   τὴν
These things   says   the   having   the   ³sword   -
      [one]

δίστομον   τὴν   ὀξεῖαν·   13 οἶδα   ποῦ   κατοικεῖς·
¹two-mouthed   -   ²sharp: I know   where   thou
(edged)   dwellest;

ὅπου   ὁ   θρόνος   τοῦ   σατανᾶ·   καὶ   κρατεῖς
where   the   throne   -   of Satan [is];   and thou holdest

τὸ   ὄνομά   μου,   καὶ   οὐκ   ἠρνήσω   τὴν
the   name   of me,   and   didst not deny   the

πίστιν   μου   καὶ   ἐν   ταῖς   ἡμέραις   Ἀντιπᾶς
faith   of me   even   in   the   days   of Antipas

ὁ   μάρτυς   μου   ὁ   πιστός   μου,   ὃς
¹the   ³witness   ⁴of me   the   ²faithful   of me,   who

ἀπεκτάνθη   παρ'   ὑμῖν,   ὅπου   ὁ   σατανᾶς
was killed   among   you,   where   -   Satan

κατοικεῖ.   14 ἀλλ'   ἔχω   κατὰ   σοῦ   ὀλίγα,
dwells.   But   I have   against   thee   a few
                  things,

ὅτι   ἔχεις   ἐκεῖ   κρατοῦντας   τὴν   διδαχὴν
be-   thou   there   [ones] holding   the   teaching
cause   hast

Βαλαάμ,   ὃς   ἐδίδασκεν   τῷ   Βαλὰκ   βαλεῖν
of Balaam,   who   taught   -   Balak   to cast

σκάνδαλον   ἐνώπιον   τῶν   υἱῶν   Ἰσραήλ,
a stumbling-block   before   the   sons   of Israel,

Israel, that they might eat food sacrificed to idols and practice immorality. ¹⁵So you also have some who hold the teaching of the Nicola'-itans. ¹⁶ Repent then. If not, I will come to you soon and war against them with the sword of my mouth. ¹⁷ He who has an ear, let him hear what the Spirit says to the churches. To him who conquers I will give some of the hidden manna, and I will give him a white stone, with a new name written on the stone which no one knows except him who receives it.'

18 "And to the angel of the church in Thyati'ra write: 'The words of the Son of God, who has eyes like a flame of fire, and whose feet are like burnished bronze. 19 " 'I know your works, your love and faith and service and patient endurance, and that your latter works exceed the first. ²⁰But I have this against you, that you tolerate the woman Jez'ebel, who calls herself a prophetess and is teaching and beguiling my servants to

φαγεῖν   εἰδωλόθυτα   καὶ   πορνεῦσαι.   15 οὕτως
to eat   idol sacrifices   and   to commit fornication.   So

ἔχεις   καὶ   σὺ   κρατοῦντας   τὴν   διδαχὴν
²hast   ²also   ¹thou   [ones] holding   the   teaching

τῶν   Νικολαϊτῶν   ὁμοίως.   16 μετανόησον
of the   Nicolaitans   likewise.   Repent thou

οὖν·   εἰ   δὲ   μή,   ἔρχομαί   σοι   ταχὺ   καὶ
therefore;   otherwise,   I am coming to thee   quickly   and

πολεμήσω   μετ'   αὐτῶν   ἐν   τῇ   ῥομφαίᾳ
will fight   with   them   with   the   sword

τοῦ   στόματός   μου.   17 Ὁ   ἔχων   οὖς
of the   mouth   of me.   The [one] having   an ear

ἀκουσάτω   τί   τὸ   πνεῦμα   λέγει   ταῖς
let him hear   what   the   Spirit   says   to the

ἐκκλησίαις.   Τῷ   νικῶντι   δώσω   αὐτῷ
churches.   To the [one] overcoming   I will give   to him

τοῦ   μάννα   τοῦ   κεκρυμμένου,   καὶ   δώσω
of the   ²manna   -   ¹having been hidden,   and   I will give

αὐτῷ   ψῆφον   λευκήν,   καὶ   ἐπὶ   τὴν   ψῆφον
him   ²stone   ¹a white,   and   on   the   stone

ὄνομα   καινὸν   γεγραμμένον,   ὃ   οὐδεὶς   οἶδεν
²name   ¹a new   having been written, which   no man   knows

εἰ   μὴ   ὁ   λαμβάνων.
except   the [one] receiving [it].

18 Καὶ   τῷ   ἀγγέλῳ   τῆς   ἐν   Θυατίροις
And   to the   messenger   ¹of the   ²in   ⁴Thyatira

ἐκκλησίας   γράψον·
³church   write thou:

Τάδε   λέγει   ὁ   υἱὸς   τοῦ   θεοῦ,   ὁ   ἔχων
These things says   the   Son   -   of God,   the   having
[one]

τοὺς   ὀφθαλμοὺς   [αὐτοῦ]   ὡς   φλόγα   πυρός,
the   eyes   of him   as   a flame   of fire,

καὶ   οἱ   πόδες   αὐτοῦ   ὅμοιοι   χαλκολιβάνῳ·
and   the   feet   of him   like   to burnished brass·

19 οἶδά   σου   τὰ   ἔργα   καὶ   τὴν   ἀγάπην
I know   of thee   the   works   and   the   love

καὶ   τὴν   πίστιν   καὶ   τὴν   διακονίαν   καὶ
and   the   faith   and   the   ministry   and

τὴν   ὑπομονήν   σου,   καὶ   τὰ   ἔργα   σου
the   endurance   of thee,   and   the   ²works   ³of thee

τὰ   ἔσχατα   πλείονα   τῶν   πρώτων.   20 ἀλλὰ
the   ¹last   more [than]   the   first.   But

ἔχω   κατὰ   σοῦ   ὅτι   ἀφεῖς   τὴν   γυναῖκα
I have   against   thee   that thou permittest the   woman

Ἰεζάβελ,   ἡ   λέγουσα   ἑαυτὴν   προφῆτιν,
Jezabel,   the [one]   say(call)ing   herself   a prophetess,

καὶ   διδάσκει   καὶ   πλανᾷ   τοὺς   ἐμοὺς
and   she teaches   and   deceives   -   my

practice immorality and to eat food sacrificed to idols. ²¹I gave her time to repent, but she refuses to repent of her immorality. ²²Behold, I will throw her on a sickbed, and those who commit adultery with her I will throw into great tribulation, unless they repent of her doings; ²³and I will strike her children dead. And all the churches shall know that I am he who searches mind and heart, and I will give to each of you as your works deserve. ²⁴But to the rest of you in Thyati'ra, who do not hold this teaching, who have not learned what some call the deep things of Satan, to you I say, I do not lay upon you any other burden; ²⁵only hold fast what you have, until I come. ²⁶He who conquers and who keeps my works until the end, I will give him power over the nations, ²⁷and he shall rule them with a rod of iron, as when earthen pots are broken in pieces, even as I myself have received power from my Father; ²⁸and I will give him the

δούλους   πορνεῦσαι   καὶ   φαγεῖν   εἰδωλόθυτα·
slaves   to commit fornication and   to eat   idol sacrifices;

21 καὶ   ἔδωκα   αὐτῇ   χρόνον   ἵνα   μετανοήσῃ,
and   I gave   her   time   in order   she might
                                              that   repent,

καὶ   οὐ   θέλει   μετανοῆσαι   ἐκ   τῆς   πορνείας
and   she wishes not   to repent   of   the   fornication

αὐτῆς.   22 ἰδοὺ   βάλλω   αὐτὴν   εἰς   κλίνην,
of her.   Behold[,] I am casting her   into   a bed,

καὶ   τοὺς   μοιχεύοντας   μετ᾽   αὐτῆς   εἰς
and   the [ones] committing adultery   with   her   into

θλῖψιν   μεγάλην,   ἐὰν   μὴ   μετανοήσουσιν
²affliction   ¹great,   unless   they shall repent

ἐκ   τῶν   ἔργων   αὐτῆς·   23 καὶ   τὰ   τέκνα
of   the   works   of her;   and   the   children

αὐτῆς   ἀποκτενῶ   ἐν   θανάτῳ·   καὶ   γνώσονται
of her   I will kill   with   death;   and   ⁴will know

πᾶσαι   αἱ   ἐκκλησίαι   ὅτι   ἐγώ   εἰμι   ὁ
¹all   ²the   ³churches   that   I   am   the
                                                 [one]

ἐρευνῶν   νεφροὺς   καὶ   καρδίας,   καὶ   δώσω
searching   kidneys   and   hearts,   and   I will give

ὑμῖν   ἑκάστῳ   κατὰ   τὰ   ἔργα   ὑμῶν.
to you   each one   according to the   works   of you.

24 ὑμῖν   δὲ   λέγω   τοῖς   λοιποῖς   τοῖς   ἐν
But to you   I say   to the   rest   -   in

Θυατίροις,   ὅσοι   οὐκ   ἔχουσιν   τὴν   διδαχὴν
Thyatira,   as many as   have not   -   teaching

ταύτην,   οἵτινες   οὐκ   ἔγνωσαν   τὰ   βαθέα
this,   who   knew not   the deep things

τοῦ   σατανᾶ,   ὡς   λέγουσιν·   οὐ   βάλλω
-    of Satan,   as   they say: I am not casting

ἐφ᾽   ὑμᾶς   ἄλλο   βάρος·   25 πλὴν   ὃ   ἔχετε
on   you   another   burden;   nevertheless what ye have

κρατήσατε   ἄχρι   οὗ   ἂν   ἥξω.   26 Καὶ
hold   until   ὃ   ἂν   I shall come.   And

ὁ   νικῶν   καὶ   ὁ   τηρῶν   ἄχρι   τέλους   τὰ
the   over-   and   the   keeping   until   [the]   the
[one] coming   [one]   end

ἔργα   μου,   δώσω   αὐτῷ   ἐξουσίαν   ἐπὶ
works   of me,   I will give   him   authority   over

τῶν   ἐθνῶν,   27 καὶ   ποιμανεῖ   αὐτοὺς   ἐν
the   nations,   and he will shepherd   them   with

ῥάβδῳ   σιδηρᾷ,   ὡς   τὰ   σκεύη   τὰ   κεραμικὰ
¹staff   ¹an iron,   as   the   ²vessels   -   ¹clay

συντρίβεται,   ὡς   κἀγὼ   εἴληφα   παρὰ
is(are) broken,   as   I also   have received   from

τοῦ   πατρός   μου,28 καὶ   δώσω   αὐτῷ   τὸν
the   Father   of me,   and   I will give   him   the

964

REVELATION 2, 3

morning star. ²⁹He who has an ear, let him hear what the Spirit says to the churches.'

ἀστέρα τὸν πρωϊνόν. 29 Ὁ ἔχων οὖς
²star - ¹morning. The [one] having an ear
ἀκουσάτω τί τὸ πνεῦμα λέγει ταῖς
let him hear what the Spirit says to the
ἐκκλησίαις
churches.

CHAPTER 3

"AND to the angel of the church in Sardis write: 'The words of him who has the seven spirits of God and the seven stars. "'I know your works; you have the name of being alive, and you are dead. ²Awake, and strengthen what remains and is on the point of death, for I have not found your works perfect in the sight of my God. ³Remember then what you received and heard; keep that, and repent. If you will not awake, I will come like a thief, and you will not know at what hour I will come upon you. ⁴Yet you have still a few names in Sardis, people who have not soiled their garments; and they shall walk with me in white, for they are worthy. ⁵He who conquers shall be clad thus in white garments, and I will not blot his

3 Καὶ τῷ ἀγγέλῳ τῆς ἐν Σάρδεσιν
And to the messenger ¹of the ²in ⁴Sardis
ἐκκλησίας γράψον·
²church write thou:
Τάδε λέγει ὁ ἔχων τὰ ἑπτὰ πνεύματα
These things says the having the seven Spirits
[one]
τοῦ θεοῦ καὶ τοὺς ἑπτὰ ἀστέρας· οἶδά
- of God and the seven stars: I know
σου τὰ ἔργα, ὅτι ὄνομα ἔχεις ὅτι ζῆς,
³of ¹the ²works, that a name thou that thou
thee hast livest,
καὶ νεκρὸς εἶ. 2 γίνου γρηγορῶν, καὶ
and [yet] ²dead ¹thou art. Be thou watching, and
στήρισον τὰ λοιπὰ ἃ ἔμελλον ἀποθανεῖν·
establish the remain- which were to die;
things ing about
οὐ γὰρ εὕρηκά σου ἔργα πεπληρωμένα
for I have not found of thee works having been fulfilled
ἐνώπιον τοῦ θεοῦ μου· 3 μνημόνευε οὖν
before the God of me; remember therefore
πῶς εἴληφας καὶ ἤκουσας, καὶ τήρει
how thou hast received and didst hear, and keep
καὶ μετανόησον. ἐὰν οὖν μὴ γρηγορήσῃς,
and repent. If therefore thou dost not watch,
ἥξω ὡς κλέπτης, καὶ οὐ μὴ γνῷς ποίαν
I will as a thief, and by no thou at what
come means knowest
ὥραν ἥξω ἐπὶ σέ. 4 ἀλλὰ ἔχεις ὀλίγα
hour I will come on thee. But thou hast a few
ὀνόματα ἐν Σάρδεσιν ἃ οὐκ ἐμόλυναν τὰ
names in Sardis which did not defile the
ἱμάτια αὐτῶν, καὶ περιπατήσουσιν μετ'
garments of them, and they shall walk with
ἐμοῦ ἐν λευκοῖς, ὅτι ἄξιοί εἰσιν. 5 Ὁ
me in white because ²worthy ¹they are. The
[garments], [one]
νικῶν οὕτως περιβαλεῖται ἐν ἱματίοις
overcoming ²thus ¹shall be clothed in ²garments
λευκοῖς, καὶ οὐ μὴ ἐξαλείψω τὸ ὄνομα
¹white, and by no means will I blot out the name

name out of the book of
life; I will confess his
name before my Father
and before his angels.
⁶He who has an ear, let
him hear what the Spirit
says to the churches.'
7 "And to the angel of
the church in Philadel-
phia write: 'The words of
the holy one, the true
one, who has the key of
David, who opens and
no one shall shut, who
shuts and no one opens.
8 " 'I know your
works. Behold, I have
set before you an open
door, which no one is
able to shut; I know
that you have but little
power, and yet you have
kept my word and have
not denied my name.
⁹Behold, I will make
those of the synagogue of
Satan who say that they
are Jews and are not, but
lie—behold, I will make
them come and bow
down before your feet,
and learn that I have
loved you. ¹⁰Because you
have kept my word of

αὐτοῦ ἐκ τῆς βίβλου τῆς ζωῆς, καὶ
of him out of the scroll – of life, and

ὁμολογήσω τὸ ὄνομα αὐτοῦ ἐνώπιον τοῦ
I will confess the name of him before the

πατρός μου καὶ ἐνώπιον τῶν ἀγγέλων
Father of me and before the angels

αὐτοῦ. 6 Ὁ ἔχων οὖς ἀκουσάτω τί τὸ
of him. The [one] having an ear let him hear what the

πνεῦμα λέγει ταῖς ἐκκλησίαις.
Spirit says to the churches.

7 Καὶ τῷ ἀγγέλῳ τῆς ἐν Φιλαδελφείᾳ
And to the messenger ¹of the ²in ⁴Philadelphia

ἐκκλησίας γράψον·
²church write thou:

Τάδε λέγει ὁ ἅγιος, ὁ ἀληθινός, ὁ
These says the holy the true the
things [one], [one], [one]

ἔχων τὴν κλεῖν Δαυίδ, ὁ ἀνοίγων καὶ
having the key of David, the [one] opening and

οὐδεὶς κλείσει, καὶ κλείων καὶ οὐδεὶς
no one shall shut, and shutting and no one

ἀνοίγει· 8 οἶδά σου τὰ ἔργα· ἰδοὺ
opens: I know of thee the works; behold[,]

δέδωκα ἐνώπιόν σου θύραν ἠνεῳγμένην,
I have given before thee a door having been opened,

ἣν οὐδεὶς δύναται κλεῖσαι αὐτήν· ὅτι
which no one can to shut it; because

μικρὰν ἔχεις δύναμιν, καὶ ἐτήρησάς μου
³a little ¹thou hast power, and didst keep of me

τὸν λόγον καὶ οὐκ ἠρνήσω τὸ ὄνομά
the word and didst not deny the name

μου. 9 ἰδοὺ διδῶ ἐκ τῆς συναγωγῆς
of me. Behold[,] I may [some] the synagogue
(will) give of

τοῦ σατανᾶ, τῶν λεγόντων ἑαυτοὺς
– of Satan, the [ones] say(call)ing themselves

Ἰουδαίους εἶναι, καὶ οὐκ εἰσὶν ἀλλὰ
Jews to be, and they are not but

ψεύδονται· ἰδοὺ ποιήσω αὐτοὺς ἵνα
they lie; behold[,] I will make them in order
that

ἥξουσιν καὶ προσκυνήσουσιν ἐνώπιον τῶν
they shall and they shall worship before the
come

ποδῶν σου, καὶ γνῶσιν ὅτι ἐγὼ ἠγάπησά
feet of thee, and they that I loved
shall know

σε. 10 ὅτι ἐτήρησας τὸν λόγον τῆς
thee. Because thou didst keep the word of the

I.G.E.—32

patient endurance, I will keep you from the hour of trial which is coming on the whole world, to try those who dwell upon the earth. [11]I am coming soon; hold fast what you have, so that no one may seize your crown. [12]He who conquers, I will make him a pillar in the temple of my God; never shall he go out of it, and I will write on him the name of my God, and the name of the city of my God, the New Jerusalem which comes down from my God out of heaven, and my own new name. [13]He who has an ear, let him hear what the Spirit says to the churches.'

14 "And to the angel of the church in La-odice′a write: 'The words of the Amen, the faithful and true witness, the beginning of God's creation.

15 "'I know your works: you are neither cold nor hot. Would that you were cold or hot!

[16]So, because you are lukewarm, and neither cold nor hot, I will spew

---

ὑπομονῆς μου, κἀγώ σε τηρήσω ἐκ
endurance of me, I also ²thee ¹will keep out of

τῆς ὥρας τοῦ πειρασμοῦ τῆς μελλούσης
the hour – of trial – being about

ἔρχεσθαι ἐπὶ τῆς οἰκουμένης ὅλης, πειράσαι
to come on ²the ³inhabited [earth] ¹all, to try

τοὺς κατοικοῦντας ἐπὶ τῆς γῆς. 11 ἔρχομαι
the [ones] dwelling on the earth. I am coming

ταχύ· κράτει ὃ ἔχεις, ἵνα μηδεὶς λάβῃ
quickly; hold what thou in order no one takes
hast, that

τὸν στέφανόν σου. 12 Ὁ νικῶν, ποιήσω
the crown of thee. The [one] overcoming, I will make

αὐτὸν στῦλον ἐν τῷ ναῷ τοῦ θεοῦ
him a pillar in the shrine of the God

μου, καὶ ἔξω οὐ μὴ ἐξέλθῃ ἔτι, καὶ
of me, and out by no he will [any] and
means go forth longer,

γράψω ἐπ᾽ αὐτὸν τὸ ὄνομα τοῦ θεοῦ
I will write on him the name of the God

μου καὶ τὸ ὄνομα τῆς πόλεως τοῦ
of me and the name of the city of the

θεοῦ μου, τῆς καινῆς Ἰερουσαλήμ ἡ
God of me, of the new Jerusalem –

καταβαίνουσα ἐκ τοῦ οὐρανοῦ ἀπὸ τοῦ
descending out of – heaven from the

θεοῦ μου, καὶ τὸ ὄνομά μου τὸ καινόν.
God of me, and ¹the ³name ⁴of me – ²new.

13 Ὁ ἔχων οὖς ἀκουσάτω τί τὸ πνεῦμα
The [one] having an ear let him hear what the Spirit

λέγει ταῖς ἐκκλησίαις.
says to the churches.

14 Καὶ τῷ ἀγγέλῳ τῆς ἐν Λαοδικείᾳ
And to the messenger ¹of the ³in ⁴Laodicea

ἐκκλησίας γράψον·
²church write thou:

Τάδε λέγει ὁ ἀμήν, ὁ μάρτυς ὁ
These things says the Amen, the ⁴witness –

πιστὸς καὶ ἀληθινός, ἡ ἀρχὴ τῆς κτίσεως
¹faithful ²and ³true, the chief of the creation

τοῦ θεοῦ· 15 οἶδά σου τὰ ἔργα, ὅτι
– of God: I know of thee the works, that

οὔτε ψυχρὸς εἶ οὔτε ζεστός. ὄφελον
neither cold art thou nor hot. I would that†

ψυχρὸς ἦς ἢ ζεστός. 16 οὕτως ὅτι
cold thou wast or hot. So because

χλιαρὸς εἶ, καὶ οὔτε ζεστὸς οὔτε ψυχρός,
lukewarm thou art, and neither hot nor cold,

you out of my mouth. ¹⁷For you say, I am rich, I have prospered, and I need nothing; not knowing that you are wretched, pitiable, poor, blind, and naked. ¹⁸Therefore I counsel you to buy from me gold refined by fire, that you may be rich, and white garments to clothe you and to keep the shame of your nakedness from being seen, and salve to anoint your eyes, that you may see. ¹⁹Those whom I love, I reprove and chasten; so be zealous and repent. ²⁰Behold, I stand at the door and knock; if any one hears my voice and opens the door, I will come in to him and eat with him, and he with me. ²¹He who conquers, I will grant him to sit with me on my throne, as I myself conquered and sat down with my Father on his throne.

μέλλω	σε	ἐμέσαι	ἐκ	τοῦ	στόματός	μου.
I am about*	²thee	¹to vomit	out of	the	mouth	of me.

17 ὅτι λέγεις ὅτι πλούσιός εἰμι καὶ
Because thou sayest[,] – ²rich ¹I am and

πεπλούτηκα καὶ οὐδὲν χρείαν ἔχω, καὶ
I have become rich and ²no ³need ¹I have, and

οὐκ οἶδας ὅτι σὺ εἶ ὁ ταλαίπωρος
knowest not that thou art the [one] wretched

καὶ ἐλεεινὸς καὶ πτωχὸς καὶ τυφλὸς
and pitiable and poor and blind

καὶ γυμνός, **18** συμβουλεύω σοι ἀγοράσαι
and naked, I counsel thee to buy

παρ' ἐμοῦ χρυσίον πεπυρωμένον ἐκ πυρὸς
from me gold having been refined by fire
by fire

ἵνα πλουτήσῃς, καὶ ἱμάτια λευκὰ ἵνα
in or- thou mayest and ²garments ¹white in order
der that be rich, that

περιβάλῃ καὶ μὴ φανερωθῇ ἡ αἰσχύνη
thou mayest and ⁶may not be ¹the ²shame
be clothed manifested

τῆς γυμνότητός σου, καὶ κολλύριον
³of the ⁴nakedness ⁵of thee, and eyesalve

ἐγχρῖσαι τοὺς ὀφθαλμούς σου ἵνα βλέπῃς.
to anoint the eyes of in order thou
thee that mayest see.

19 ἐγὼ ὅσους ἐὰν φιλῶ ἐλέγχω καὶ
²I ¹as many as love I rebuke and

παιδεύω· ζήλευε οὖν καὶ μετανόησον.
I chasten; be hot therefore and repent thou.

20 Ἰδοὺ ἔστηκα ἐπὶ τὴν θύραν καὶ
Behold[,] I stand at the door and

κρούω· ἐάν τις ἀκούσῃ τῆς φωνῆς μου
I knock; if anyone hears the voice of me

καὶ ἀνοίξῃ τὴν θύραν, εἰσελεύσομαι πρὸς
and opens the door, I will enter to

αὐτὸν καὶ δειπνήσω μετ' αὐτοῦ καὶ
him and I will dine with him and

αὐτὸς μετ' ἐμοῦ. **21** Ὁ νικῶν, δώσω
he with me. The overcoming, I will
[one] give

αὐτῷ καθίσαι μετ' ἐμοῦ ἐν τῷ θρόνῳ
him to sit with me in the throne

μου, ὡς κἀγὼ ἐνίκησα καὶ ἐκάθισα
of me, as I also overcame and sat

μετὰ τοῦ πατρός μου ἐν τῷ θρόνῳ
with the Father of me in the throne

* As so often (see also ch. 1. 19, 2. 10), this verb does not necessarily connote imminence, but only simple futurity.

²²He who has an ear, let him hear what the Spirit says to the churches.' "

αὐτοῦ.   **22** Ὁ ἔχων οὓς ἀκουσάτω τί
of him.   The [one] having an ear let him hear what

τὸ πνεῦμα λέγει ταῖς ἐκκλησίαις.
the Spirit   says to the churches.

CHAPTER 4

AFTER this I looked, and lo, in heaven an open door! And the first voice, which I had heard speaking to me like a trumpet, said, "Come up hither, and I will show what must take place after this." ²At once I was in the Spirit, and lo, a throne stood in heaven, with one seated on the throne! ³And he who sat there appeared like jasper and carnelian, and round the throne was a rainbow that looked like an emerald. ⁴Round the throne were twenty-four thrones, and seated on the thrones were twenty-four elders, clad in white garments, with golden crowns upon their heads. ⁵From the throne issue flashes of lightning, and voices and peals of thunder, and before the throne burn seven torches of fire, which are the seven spirits of God; ⁶and

4 Μετὰ ταῦτα εἶδον, καὶ ἰδοὺ θύρα
After these things I saw, and behold[,] a door

ἠνεῳγμένη ἐν τῷ οὐρανῷ, καὶ ἡ φωνὴ
having been in –   heaven, and the ¹voice
opened

ἡ πρώτη ἦν ἤκουσα ὡς σάλπιγγος
– ¹first which I heard as of a trumpet

λαλούσης μετ᾽ ἐμοῦ, λέγων· ἀνάβα ὧδε,
speaking with me, saying: Come up here,

καὶ δείξω σοι ἃ δεῖ γενέσθαι μετὰ
and I will thee things it be- to occur after
show which hoves

ταῦτα. εὐθέως ἐγενόμην ἐν πνεύματι·
these things. Immediately I became in spirit;

2 καὶ ἰδοὺ θρόνος ἔκειτο ἐν τῷ οὐρανῷ,
and behold[,] a throne was set in – heaven,

καὶ ἐπὶ τὸν θρόνον καθήμενος, **3** καὶ
and on the throne a sitting [one], and

ὁ καθήμενος ὅμοιος ὁράσει λίθῳ ἰάσπιδι
the [one] sitting [was] like in appearance ⁴to a jasper ¹to a jasper
                                         stone

καὶ σαρδίῳ, καὶ ἶρις κυκλόθεν τοῦ
²and ²a sardius, and a rain- round the
              [there was] bow

θρόνου ὅμοιος ὁράσει σμαραγδίνῳ. **4** καὶ
throne like in appearance to an emerald. And

κυκλόθεν τοῦ θρόνου θρόνους εἴκοσι
round the throne [I saw] ²thrones ¹twenty-

τέσσαρας, καὶ ἐπὶ τοὺς θρόνους εἴκοσι
four, and on the thrones twenty-

τέσσαρας πρεσβυτέρους καθημένους περι-
four elders sitting having been

βεβλημένους ἐν ἱματίοις λευκοῖς, καὶ ἐπὶ
clothed in garments white, and on

τὰς κεφαλὰς αὐτῶν στεφάνους χρυσοῦς
the heads of them ²crowns ¹golden.

5 καὶ ἐκ τοῦ θρόνου ἐκπορεύονται ἀστραπαὶ
And out of the throne come forth lightnings

καὶ φωναὶ καὶ βρονταί· καὶ ἑπτὰ λαμπάδες
and voices* and thunders; and seven lamps

πυρὸς καιόμεναι ἐνώπιον τοῦ θρόνου, ἃ
of fire [are] burning before the throne, which

εἰσιν τὰ ἑπτὰ πνεύματα τοῦ θεοῦ· **6** καὶ
are the seven Spirits – of God; and

* Or "sounds"; and so elsewhere.

before the throne there is as it were a sea of glass, like crystal.

And round the throne, on each side of the throne, are four living creatures, full of eyes in front and behind: [7]the first living creature like a lion, the second living creature like an ox, the third living creature with the face of a man, and the fourth living creature like a flying eagle. [8]And the four living creatures, each of them with six wings, are full of eyes all round and within, and day and night they never cease to sing,

"Holy, holy, holy, is the Lord God Almighty,
who was and is and is to come!"

[9]And whenever the living creatures give glory and honor and thanks to him who is seated on the throne, who lives for ever and ever, [10]the twenty-four elders fall down before him who is seated on the throne and

ἐνώπιον	τοῦ	θρόνου	ὡς	θάλασσα	ὑαλίνη
before	the	throne	as	[2]sea	[1]a glassy

ὁμοία	κρυστάλλῳ·	καὶ	ἐν	μέσῳ	τοῦ
like	to crystal;	and	in	[the] midst	of the

θρόνου	καὶ	κύκλῳ	τοῦ	θρόνου	τέσσερα
throne	and	round	the	throne	four

ζῷα	γέμοντα	ὀφθαλμῶν	ἔμπροσθεν	καὶ
living creatures	filling(full)	of eyes	before	and

ὄπισθεν.	7 καὶ	τὸ	ζῷον	τὸ	πρῶτον
behind.	And	the	[2]living creature	τὸ	[1]first

ὅμοιον	λέοντι,	καὶ	τὸ	δεύτερον	ζῷον
[was] like	to a lion,	and	the	second	living creature

ὅμοιον	μόσχῳ,	καὶ	τὸ	τρίτον	ζῷον	ἔχων
like	to a calf,	and	the	third	living creature	having

τὸ	πρόσωπον	ὡς	ἀνθρώπου,	καὶ	τὸ
the(its)	face	as	of a man,	and	the

τέταρτον	ζῷον	ὅμοιον	ἀετῷ	πετομένῳ.
fourth	living creature	like	eagle	to a flying.

8 καὶ	τὰ	τέσσερα	ζῷα,	ἓν	καθ'	ἓν
And	the	four	living creatures,	one	by	one

αὐτῶν	ἔχων	ἀνὰ	πτέρυγας	ἕξ,	κυκλόθεν
of them	having	each	[2]wings	[1]six,	around

καὶ	ἔσωθεν	γέμουσιν	ὀφθαλμῶν·	καὶ
and	within	are full	of eyes;	and

ἀνάπαυσιν	οὐκ	ἔχουσιν	ἡμέρας	καὶ	νυκτὸς
respite	they have not	day	and	night

λέγοντες·	ἅγιος	ἅγιος	ἅγιος	κύριος	ὁ
saying·	Holy[,]	holy[,]	holy[,]	Lord	–

θεὸς	ὁ	παντοκράτωρ,	ὁ	ἦν	καὶ	ὁ	ὢν
God	the	Almighty,	[one who]	the was	and	the [one]	being

= the one who is

καὶ	ὁ	ἐρχόμενος.	9 Καὶ	ὅταν	δώσουσιν
and	the	coming [one].	And	whenever	[3]shall give

τὰ	ζῷα	δόξαν	καὶ	τιμὴν	καὶ	εὐχαριστίαν
[1]the	[2]living creatures	glory	and	honour	and	thanks

τῷ	καθημένῳ	ἐπὶ	τῷ	θρόνῳ	τῷ	ζῶντι
to the [one]	sitting	on	the	throne[,]	to the [one]	living

εἰς	τοὺς	αἰῶνας	τῶν	αἰώνων,	10 πεσοῦνται
unto	the	ages	of the	ages,	[4]will fall

οἱ	εἴκοσι	τέσσαρες	πρεσβύτεροι	ἐνώπιον
[1]the	[2]twenty-four		[3]elders	before

τοῦ	καθημένου	ἐπὶ	τοῦ	θρόνου,	καὶ
the [one]	sitting	on	the	throne,	and

worship him who lives for ever and ever; they cast their crowns before the throne, singing, 11"Worthy art thou, our Lord and God, to receive glory and honor and power, for thou didst create all things, and by thy will they existed and were created."

προσκυνήσουσιν τῷ ζῶντι εἰς τοὺς αἰῶνας
they will worship the [one] living unto the ages

τῶν αἰώνων, καὶ βαλοῦσιν τοὺς στεφάνους
of the ages, and will cast the crowns

αὐτῶν ἐνώπιον τοῦ θρόνου, λέγοντες·
of them before the throne, saying:

11 ἄξιος εἶ, ὁ κύριος καὶ ὁ θεὸς ἡμῶν,
Worthy art thou, the Lord and the God of us,

λαβεῖν τὴν δόξαν καὶ τὴν τιμὴν καὶ
to receive the glory and the honour and

τὴν δύναμιν, ὅτι σὺ ἔκτισας τὰ πάντα,
the power, because thou createdst - all things,*

καὶ διὰ τὸ θέλημά σου ἦσαν καὶ
and on ac- the will of thee they were and
count of

ἐκτίσθησαν.
they were created.

CHAPTER 5

AND I saw in the right hand of him who was seated on the throne a scroll written within and on the back, sealed with seven seals; ²and I saw a strong angel proclaiming with a loud voice, "Who is worthy to open the scroll and break its seals?" ³And no one in heaven or on earth or under the earth was able to open the scroll or to look into it, ⁴and I wept much that no one was found worthy to open the scroll or to look into it. ⁵Then one of the elders said to me, "Weep

5 Καὶ εἶδον ἐπὶ τὴν δεξιὰν τοῦ
And I saw on the right of the
[hand] [one]

καθημένου ἐπὶ τοῦ θρόνου βιβλίον
sitting on the throne a scroll

γεγραμμένον ἔσωθεν καὶ ὄπισθεν,
having been written within and on the reverse side,

κατεσφραγισμένον σφραγῖσιν ἑπτά. 2 καὶ
having been sealed with ²seals ¹seven. And

εἶδον ἄγγελον ἰσχυρὸν κηρύσσοντα ἐν
I saw angel a strong proclaiming in

φωνῇ μεγάλῃ· τίς ἄξιος ἀνοῖξαι τὸ
²voice ¹a great(loud): Who [is] worthy to open the

βιβλίον καὶ λῦσαι τὰς σφραγῖδας αὐτοῦ;
scroll and to loosen the seals of it?

3 καὶ οὐδεὶς ἐδύνατο ἐν τῷ οὐρανῷ
And no one was able in heaven

οὐδὲ ἐπὶ τῆς γῆς οὐδὲ ὑποκάτω τῆς
nor on the earth nor underneath the

γῆς ἀνοῖξαι τὸ βιβλίον οὔτε βλέπειν
earth to open the scroll nor to see(look at)

αὐτό. 4 καὶ ἔκλαιον πολύ, ὅτι οὐδεὶς
it. And I wept much, because no one

ἄξιος εὑρέθη ἀνοῖξαι τὸ βιβλίον οὔτε
worthy was found to open the scroll nor

βλέπειν αὐτό. 5 καὶ εἷς ἐκ τῶν πρεσ-
to look at it. And one of the el-

βυτέρων λέγει μοι· μὴ κλαῖε· ἰδοὺ
ders says to me: Weep not; behold[,]

* τὰ πάντα = the universe.

not; lo, the Lion of the tribe of Judah, the Root of David, has conquered, so that he can open the scroll and its seven seals."

6 And between the throne and the four living creatures and among the elders, I saw a Lamb standing, as though it had been slain, with seven horns and with seven eyes, which are the seven spirits of God sent out into all the earth; [7]and he went and took the scroll from the right hand of him who was seated on the throne. [8]And when he had taken the scroll, the four living creatures and the twenty-four elders fell down before the Lamb, each holding a harp, and with golden bowls full of incense, which are the prayers of the saints; [9]and they sang a new song, saying,
  "Worthy art thou to take the scroll and to open its seals, for thou wast slain and by thy blood didst ransom men for God from every tribe and tongue and people and nation,
[10]and hast made them a kingdom and priests to our God,

ἐνίκησεν	ὁ	λέων	ὁ	ἐκ	τῆς	φυλῆς	Ἰούδα,
[10]overcame	[1]the	[2]Lion	–	[3]of	[4]the	[5]tribe	[6]Juda,

ἡ	ῥίζα	Δαυίδ,	ἀνοῖξαι	τὸ	βιβλίον	καὶ
[7]the	[8]root	[9]of David,	to open	the	scroll	and

τὰς	ἑπτὰ	σφραγῖδας	αὐτοῦ.	6 Καὶ	εἶδον
the	seven	seals	of it.	And	I saw

ἐν	μέσῳ	τοῦ	θρόνου	καὶ	τῶν	τεσσάρων
in [the] midst	of the	throne	and	of the	four

ζώων	καὶ	ἐν	μέσῳ	τῶν	πρεσβυτέρων
living creatures	and	in	[the] midst	of the	elders

ἀρνίον	ἑστηκὸς	ὡς	ἐσφαγμένον,	ἔχων
a Lamb	standing	as	having been slain,	having

κέρατα	ἑπτὰ	καὶ	ὀφθαλμοὺς	ἑπτά,	οἱ
[3]horns	[1]seven	and	[2]eyes	[1]seven,	which

εἰσιν	τὰ	ἑπτὰ	πνεύματα	τοῦ	θεοῦ
are	the	seven	Spirits	–	of God

ἀπεσταλμένοι	εἰς	πᾶσαν	τὴν	γῆν.	7 καὶ
having been sent forth into	all	the	earth.	And

ἦλθεν	καὶ	εἴληφεν	ἐκ	τῆς	δεξιᾶς	τοῦ
he came	and	has taken	out of	the	right [hand]	of the

καθημένου	ἐπὶ	τοῦ	θρόνου.	8 Καὶ	ὅτε
[one] sitting	on	the	throne.	And	when

ἔλαβεν	τὸ	βιβλίον,	τὰ	τέσσερα	ζῷα
he took	the	scroll,	the	four	living creatures

καὶ	οἱ	εἴκοσι	τέσσαρες	πρεσβύτεροι	ἔπεσαν
and	the	twenty-four		elders	fell

ἐνώπιον	τοῦ	ἀρνίου,	ἔχοντες	ἕκαστος
before	the	Lamb,	having	each one

κιθάραν	καὶ	φιάλας	χρυσᾶς	γεμούσας
a harp	and	[2]bowls	[1]golden	being full

θυμιαμάτων,	αἵ	εἰσιν	αἱ	προσευχαὶ	τῶν
of incenses,	which	are	the	prayers	of the

ἁγίων.	9 καὶ	ᾄδουσιν	ᾠδὴν	καινὴν
saints.	And	they sing	[2]song	[1]a new

λέγοντες·	ἄξιος	εἶ	λαβεῖν	τὸ	βιβλίον
saying:	Worthy	art thou	to receive	the	scroll

καὶ	ἀνοῖξαι	τὰς	σφραγῖδας	αὐτοῦ,	ὅτι
and	to open	the	seals	of it,	because

ἐσφάγης	καὶ	ἠγόρασας	τῷ	θεῷ	ἐν	τῷ
thou wast slain	and	didst purchase	–	to God	by	the

αἵματί	σου	ἐκ	πάσης	φυλῆς	καὶ	γλώσσης
blood	of thee	out of	every	tribe	and	tongue

καὶ	λαοῦ	καὶ	ἔθνους,	10 καὶ	ἐποίησας
and	people	and	nation,	and	didst make

αὐτοὺς	τῷ	θεῷ	ἡμῶν	βασιλείαν·	καὶ
them	to the	God	of us	a kingdom	and

and they shall reign on earth."

[11]Then I looked, and I heard around the throne and the living creatures and the elders the voice of many angels, numbering myriads of myriads and thousands of thousands, [12]saying with a loud voice, "Worthy is the Lamb who was slain, to receive power and wealth and wisdom and might and honor and glory and blessing!" [13]And I heard every creature in heaven and on earth and under the earth and in the sea, and all therein, saying, "To him who sits upon the throne and to the Lamb be blessing and honor and glory and might for ever and ever!" [14]And the four living creatures said, "Amen!" and the elders fell down and worshiped.

ἱερεῖς,   καὶ   βασιλεύσουσιν   ἐπὶ   τῆς   γῆς.
priests,   and   they will reign   on(? over) the   earth.
11 καὶ   εἶδον,   καὶ   ἤκουσα   φωνὴν   ἀγγέλων
And   I saw,   and   I heard   a sound   ²angels
πολλῶν   κύκλῳ   τοῦ   θρόνου   καὶ   τῶν
¹of many   round   the   throne   and   the
ζῴων   καὶ   τῶν   πρεσβυτέρων,   καὶ   ἦν
living   and   the   elders,   and   ⁴was
creatures
ὁ   ἀριθμὸς   αὐτῶν   μυριάδες   μυριάδων   καὶ
¹the   ²number   ³of them   myriads   of myriads   and
χιλιάδες   χιλιάδων,   12 λέγοντες   φωνῇ
thousands   of thousands,   saying   ²voice
μεγάλῃ·   ἄξιός   ἐστιν   τὸ   ἀρνίον   τὸ
¹with a great   Worthy   is   the   Lamb   –
(loud):
ἐσφαγμένον   λαβεῖν   τὴν   δύναμιν   καὶ   πλοῦτον
having been slain to receive   the   power   and   riches
καὶ   σοφίαν   καὶ   ἰσχὺν   καὶ   τιμὴν   καὶ
and   wisdom   and   strength   and   honour   and
δόξαν   καὶ   εὐλογίαν.   13 καὶ   πᾶν   κτίσμα
glory   and   blessing.   And   every   creature
ὃ   ἐν   τῷ   οὐρανῷ   καὶ   ἐπὶ   τῆς   γῆς   καὶ
which ²in   –   ³heaven   ⁴and   ⁵on   ⁶the   ⁷earth   ⁸and
ὑποκάτω   τῆς   γῆς   καὶ   ἐπὶ   τῆς   θαλάσσης
⁹underneath   ¹⁰the   ¹¹earth   ¹²and   ¹³on   ¹⁴the   ¹⁵sea
[ἐστίν],   καὶ   τὰ   ἐν   αὐτοῖς   πάντα,   ἤκουσα
¹is,   and   –   ²in   ³them   ¹all things,   I heard
λέγοντας·   τῷ   καθημένῳ   ἐπὶ   τῷ   θρόνῳ
saying: To the [one] sitting   on   the   throne
καὶ   τῷ   ἀρνίῳ   ἡ   εὐλογία   καὶ   ἡ   τιμὴ
and   to the   Lamb   the   blessing   and   the   honour
καὶ   ἡ   δόξα   καὶ   τὸ   κράτος   εἰς   τοὺς
and   the   glory   and   the   might   unto   the
αἰῶνας   τῶν   αἰώνων.   14 καὶ   τὰ   τέσσερα
ages   of the   ages.   And   the   four
ζῷα   ἔλεγον·   ἀμήν,   καὶ   οἱ   πρεσβύτεροι
living   said: Amen,   and   the   elders
creatures
ἔπεσαν   καὶ   προσεκύνησαν.
fell   and   worshipped.

CHAPTER 6

NOW I saw when the Lamb opened one of the seven seals, and I heard one of the four living creatures say, as

6 Καὶ   εἶδον   ὅτε   ἤνοιξεν   τὸ   ἀρνίον
And   I saw   when   ³opened   ¹the   ²Lamb
μίαν   ἐκ   τῶν   ἑπτὰ   σφραγίδων,   καὶ   ἤκουσα
one   of   the   seven   seals,   and   I heard
ἑνὸς   ἐκ   τῶν   τεσσάρων   ζῴων   λέγοντος
one   of   the   four   living creatures   saying

with a voice of thunder, "Come!" ²And I saw, and behold, a white horse, and its rider had a bow; and a crown was given to him, and he went out conquering and to conquer.

3 When he opened the second seal, I heard the second living creature say, "Come!" ⁴And out came another horse, bright red; its rider was permitted to take peace from the earth, so that men should slay one another; and he was given a great sword.

5 When he opened the third seal, I heard the third living creature say, "Come!" And I saw, and behold, a black horse, and its rider had a balance in his hand; ⁶and I heard what seemed to be a voice in the midst of the four living creatures saying, "A quart of wheat for a denarius, and three quarts of barley for a denarius; but do not harm oil and wine!"

7 When he opened the fourth seal, I heard the

ὡς   φωνῇ   βροντῆς·   ἔρχου.   2 καὶ   εἶδον,
as with a sound of thunder: Come.   And   I saw,

καὶ   ἰδοὺ   ἵππος   λευκός,   καὶ   ὁ   καθήμενος
and behold[,]   ²horse   ¹a white,   and the [one] sitting

ἐπ'   αὐτὸν   ἔχων   τόξον,   καὶ   ἐδόθη   αὐτῷ
on   it   having   a bow,   and   ²was given   ³to him

στέφανος,   καὶ   ἐξῆλθεν   νικῶν   καὶ   ἵνα
¹a crown,   and   he went forth   overcoming   and   in order that

νικήσῃ.   3 Καὶ   ὅτε   ἤνοιξεν   τὴν   σφραγῖδα
he might   And   when   he opened   the   ²seal
overcome.

τὴν   δευτέραν,   ἤκουσα   τοῦ   δευτέρου   ζῴου
-   ¹second,   I heard   the   second   living
                                                        creature

λέγοντος·   ἔρχου.   4 καὶ   ἐξῆλθεν   ἄλλος
saying: Come.   And   ⁴went forth   ¹another

ἵππος   πυρρός,   καὶ   τῷ   καθημένῳ   ἐπ'
²horse[,]   ³red,   and   to the [one]   sitting   on

αὐτὸν   ἐδόθη   αὐτῷ   λαβεῖν   τὴν   εἰρήνην
it   was given   to him   to take   -   peace

ἐκ   τῆς   γῆς   καὶ   ἵνα   ἀλλήλους   σφάξουσιν,
out   the   earth   and   in order   ²one   ¹they
of   that   another   shall slay,

καὶ   ἐδόθη   αὐτῷ   μάχαιρα   μεγάλη.   5 Καὶ
and   ³was given   ⁴to him   ²sword   ¹a great.   And

ὅτε   ἤνοιξεν   τὴν   σφραγῖδα   τὴν   τρίτην,
when   he opened   the   ²seal   -   ¹third,

ἤκουσα   τοῦ   τρίτου   ζῴου   λέγοντος·   ἔρχου.
I heard   the   third   living   saying: Come.
                            creature

καὶ   εἶδον,   καὶ   ἰδοὺ   ἵππος   μέλας,   καὶ
And   I saw,   and   behold[,]   ²horse   ¹a black,   and

ὁ   καθήμενος   ἐπ'   αὐτὸν   ἔχων   ζυγὸν
the [one] sitting   on   it   having   a balance

ἐν   τῇ   χειρὶ   αὐτοῦ.   6 καὶ   ἤκουσα   ὡς
in   the   hand   of him.   And   I heard   as

φωνὴν   ἐν   μέσῳ   τῶν   τεσσάρων   ζῴων
a voice   in   [the]   of the   four   living
               midst   creatures

λέγουσαν·   χοῖνιξ   σίτου   δηναρίου,   καὶ   τρεῖς
saying: A   of   of(for)   and   three
          choenix   wheat   a denarius,

χοίνικες   κριθῶν   δηναρίου·   καὶ   τὸ   ἔλαιον
choenixes   of barley   of(for)   and   ²the   ²oil
                          a denarius;

καὶ   τὸν   οἶνον   μὴ   ἀδικήσῃς.   7 Καὶ
⁴and   ⁵the   ⁶wine   ¹do not harm.   And

ὅτε   ἤνοιξεν   τὴν   σφραγῖδα   τὴν   τετάρτην,
when   he opened   the   ²seal   -   ¹fourth,

voice of the fourth living creature say, "Come!" ⁸And I saw, and behold, a pale horse, and its rider's name was Death, and Hades followed him; and they were given power over a fourth of the earth, to kill with sword and with famine and with pestilence and by wild beasts of the earth.

9 When he opened the fifth seal, I saw under the altar the souls of those who had been slain for the word of God and for the witness they had borne; ¹⁰they cried out with a loud voice, "O Sovereign Lord, holy and true, how long before thou wilt judge and avenge our blood on those who dwell upon the earth?" ¹¹Then they were each given a white robe and told to rest a little longer, until the number of their fellow servants and their brethren should be complete, who were to be killed as they themselves had been.

12When he opened the

ἤκουσα φωνὴν τοῦ τετάρτου ζῴου λέγοντος·
I heard [the] voice of the fourth living creature saying:

ἔρχου. 8 καὶ εἶδον, καὶ ἰδοὺ ἵππος
Come. And I saw, and behold[,] ²horse

χλωρός, καὶ ὁ καθήμενος ἐπάνω αὐτοῦ,
¹a pale green, and the [one] sitting upon it,

ὄνομα αὐτῷ [ὁ] θάνατος, καὶ ὁ ᾅδης
name to himᶜ – death, and – hades

ἠκολούθει μετ᾽ αὐτοῦ, καὶ ἐδόθη αὐτοῖς
followed with him, and ²was ³to them
given

ἐξουσία ἐπὶ τὸ τέταρτον τῆς γῆς,
¹authority over the fourth [part] of the earth,

ἀποκτεῖναι ἐν ῥομφαίᾳ καὶ ἐν λιμῷ
to kill with sword and with famine

καὶ ἐν θανάτῳ καὶ ὑπὸ τῶν θηρίων
and with death and by the wild beasts

τῆς γῆς. 9 Καὶ ὅτε ἤνοιξεν τὴν πέμπτην
of the earth. And when he opened the fifth

σφραγῖδα, εἶδον ὑποκάτω τοῦ θυσιαστηρίου
seal, I saw underneath the altar

τὰς ψυχὰς τῶν ἐσφαγμένων διὰ τὸν
the souls of the having been on account the
[ones] slain of

λόγον τοῦ θεοῦ καὶ διὰ τὴν μαρτυρίαν
word – of God and on the witness
account of

ἣν εἶχον. 10 καὶ ἔκραξαν φωνῇ μεγάλῃ
which they had. And they cried ²voice ¹with a
great(loud)

λέγοντες· ἕως πότε, ὁ δεσπότης ὁ ἅγιος
saying: Until when, the Master – holy

καὶ ἀληθινός, οὐ κρίνεις καὶ ἐκδικεῖς
and true, judgest thou not and avengest

τὸ αἷμα ἡμῶν ἐκ τῶν κατοικούντων
the blood of us of the [ones] dwelling

ἐπὶ τῆς γῆς; 11 καὶ ἐδόθη αὐτοῖς ἑκάστῳ
on the earth? And ³was ⁴to them ⁵each one
given

στολὴ λευκή, καὶ ἐρρέθη αὐτοῖς ἵνα
²robe ¹a white, and it was said to them in order
that

ἀναπαύσωνται ἔτι χρόνον μικρόν, ἕως
they should rest yet ²time ¹a little, until

πληρωθῶσιν καὶ οἱ σύνδουλοι αὐτῶν καὶ
should be fulfilled also the fellow-slaves of them and

οἱ ἀδελφοὶ αὐτῶν οἱ μέλλοντες ἀποκτέν-
the brothers of them the [ones] being about to be

νεσθαι ὡς καὶ αὐτοί. 12 Καὶ εἶδον
killed as also they. And I saw

sixth seal, I looked, and behold, there was a great earthquake; and the sun became black as sackcloth, the full moon became like blood, 13 and the stars of the sky fell to the earth as the fig tree sheds its winter fruit when shaken by a gale; 14 the sky vanished like a scroll that is rolled up, and every mountain and island was removed from its place. 15 Then the kings of the earth and the great men and the generals and the rich and the strong, and every one, slave and free, hid in the caves and among the rocks of the mountains, 16 calling to the mountains and rocks, "Fall on us and hide us from the face of him who is seated on the throne, and from the wrath of the Lamb; 17 for the great day of their wrath has come, and who can stand before it?"

ὅτε   ἤνοιξεν   τὴν   σφραγῖδα   τὴν   ἕκτην,
when   he opened   the   ²seal   –   ¹sixth,

καὶ   σεισμὸς   μέγας   ἐγένετο,   καὶ   ὁ   ἥλιος
and   ²earthquake   ¹a great   occurred,   and   the   sun

ἐγένετο   μέλας   ὡς   σάκκος   τρίχινος,   καὶ
became   black   as   sackcloth   made of hair,   and

ἡ   σελήνη   ὅλη   ἐγένετο   ὡς   αἷμα,   13 καὶ
the   ²moon   ¹whole   became   as   blood,   and

οἱ   ἀστέρες   τοῦ   οὐρανοῦ   ἔπεσαν   εἰς   τὴν
the   stars   –   of heaven   fell   to   the

γῆν,   ὡς   συκῆ   βάλλει   τοὺς   ὀλύνθους
earth,   as   a fig-tree   casts   the   unripe figs

αὐτῆς   ὑπὸ   ἀνέμου   μεγάλου   σειομένη,
of it   ²by   ⁴wind   ³a great(strong)   ¹being shaken,

14 καὶ   ὁ   οὐρανὸς   ἀπεχωρίσθη   ὡς   βιβλίον
and   the   heaven   departed   as   a scroll

ἐλισσόμενον,   καὶ   πᾶν   ὄρος   καὶ   νῆσος
being rolled up,   and   every   mountain   and   island

ἐκ   τῶν   τόπων   αὐτῶν   ἐκινήθησαν.   15 καὶ
out of the   places   of them   were moved.   And

οἱ   βασιλεῖς   τῆς   γῆς   καὶ   οἱ   μεγιστᾶνες
the   kings   of the   earth   and   the   great men

καὶ   οἱ   χιλίαρχοι   καὶ   οἱ   πλούσιοι   καὶ
and   the   chiliarchs   and   the   rich men   and

οἱ   ἰσχυροὶ   καὶ   πᾶς   δοῦλος   καὶ   ἐλεύθερος
the   strong men   and   every   slave   and   free man

ἔκρυψαν   ἑαυτοὺς   εἰς   τὰ   σπήλαια   καὶ
hid   themselves   in   the   caves   and

εἰς   τὰς   πέτρας   τῶν   ὀρέων,   16 καὶ
in   the   rocks   of the   mountains,   and

λέγουσιν   τοῖς   ὄρεσιν   καὶ   ταῖς   πέτραις·
they say   to the   mountains   and   to the   rocks:

πέσετε   ἐφ'   ἡμᾶς   καὶ   κρύψατε   ἡμᾶς
Fall ye   on   us   and   hide   us

ἀπὸ   προσώπου   τοῦ   καθημένου   ἐπὶ   τοῦ
from   [the] face   of the [one]   sitting   on   the

θρόνου   καὶ   ἀπὸ   τῆς   ὀργῆς   τοῦ   ἀρνίου,
throne   and   from   the   wrath   of the   Lamb,

17 ὅτι   ἦλθεν   ἡ   ἡμέρα   ἡ   μεγάλη   τῆς
because   ⁷came   ¹the   ³day   –   ²great   ⁴of the

ὀργῆς   αὐτῶν,   καὶ   τίς   δύναται   σταθῆναι;
⁵wrath   ⁶of them,   and   who   can   to stand?

CHAPTER 7

AFTER this I saw four angels standing at the four corners of the

7 Μετὰ   τοῦτο   εἶδον   τέσσαρας   ἀγγέλους
After   this   I saw   four   angels

ἑστῶτας   ἐπὶ   τὰς   τέσσαρας   γωνίας   τῆς
standing   on   the   four   corners   of the

earth, holding back the four winds of the earth, that no wind might blow on earth or sea or against any tree. ²Then I saw another angel ascend from the rising of the sun, with the seal of the living God, and he called with a loud voice to the four angels who had been given power to harm earth and sea, ³saying, "Do not harm the earth or the sea or the trees, till we have sealed the servants of our God upon their foreheads." ⁴And I heard the number of the sealed, a hundred and forty-four thousand sealed, out of every tribe of the sons of Israel, ⁵twelve thousand sealed out of the tribe of Judah, twelve thousand of the tribe of Reuben, twelve thousand of the tribe of Gad, ⁶twelve thousand of the tribe of Asher, twelve thousand of the tribe of Naph'tali, twelve thousand of the tribe of Manas'seh, ⁷twelve thousand of the tribe of Simeon, twelve thousand of the tribe of Levi, twelve thousand of

γῆς,	κρατοῦντας	τοὺς	τέσσαρας	ἀνέμους
earth,	holding	the	four	winds

τῆς	γῆς,	ἵνα	μὴ	πνέῃ	ἄνεμος	ἐπὶ	τῆς
of the	earth,	in order that	³not	²should ⁴blow	¹wind	on	the

γῆς	μήτε	ἐπὶ	τῆς	θαλάσσης	μήτε	ἐπὶ
earth	nor	on	the	sea	nor	on

πᾶν	δένδρον.	2 καὶ	εἶδον	ἄλλον	ἄγγελον
every(any)	tree.	And	I saw	another	angel

ἀναβαίνοντα	ἀπὸ	ἀνατολῆς	ἡλίου,	ἔχοντα
coming up	from	[the] rising	of [the] sun,	having

σφραγῖδα	θεοῦ	ζῶντος,	καὶ	ἔκραξεν	φωνῇ
a seal	God	of [the] living,	and	he cried	²voice

μεγάλῃ	τοῖς	τέσσαρσιν	ἀγγέλοις	οἷς
¹with a great(loud)	to the	four	angels	to whom

ἐδόθη	αὐτοῖς	ἀδικῆσαι	τὴν	γῆν	καὶ
it was given	to them	to harm	the	earth	and

τὴν	θάλασσαν,	3 λέγων·	μὴ	ἀδικήσητε
the	sea,	saying:	Do not harm

τὴν	γῆν	μήτε	τὴν	θάλασσαν	μήτε	τὰ
the	earth	nor	the	sea	nor	the

δένδρα,	ἄχρι	σφραγίσωμεν	τοὺς	δούλους
trees,	until	we may seal	the	slaves

τοῦ	θεοῦ	ἡμῶν	ἐπὶ	τῶν	μετώπων	αὐτῶν.
of the	God	of us	on	the	foreheads	of them.

4 Καὶ	ἤκουσα	τὸν	ἀριθμὸν	τῶν	ἐσφραγισ-
And	I heard	the	number	of the [ones]	having been

μένων,	ἑκατὸν	τεσσεράκοντα	τέσσαρες
sealed,	a hundred [and]	forty-four

χιλιάδες	ἐσφραγισμένοι	ἐκ	πάσης	φυλῆς
thousands	having been sealed	out of	every	tribe

υἱῶν	Ἰσραήλ·	5 ἐκ	φυλῆς	Ἰούδα	δώδεκα
of sons	of Israel:	of [the]	tribe	Juda	twelve

χιλιάδες	ἐσφραγισμένοι,	ἐκ	φυλῆς	Ῥουβὴν
thousands	having been sealed,	of [the]	tribe	Reuben

δώδεκα	χιλιάδες,	ἐκ	φυλῆς	Γὰδ	δώδεκα
twelve	thousands,	of [the]	tribe	Gad	twelve

χιλιάδες,	6 ἐκ	φυλῆς	Ἀσὴρ	δώδεκα
thousands,	of [the]	tribe	Aser	twelve

χιλιάδες,	ἐκ	φυλῆς	Νεφθαλὶμ	δώδεκα
thousands,	of [the]	tribe	Nephthalim	twelve

χιλιάδες,	ἐκ	φυλῆς	Μανασσῆ	δώδεκα
thousands,	of [the]	tribe	Manasse	twelve

χιλιάδες,	7 ἐκ	φυλῆς	Συμεὼν	δώδεκα
thousands,	of [the]	tribe	Symeon	twelve

χιλιάδες,	ἐκ	φυλῆς	Λευὶ	δώδεκα	χιλιάδες,
thousands,	of [the] tribe	Levi	twelve	thousands,

the tribe of Is'sachar, **8**twelve thousand of the tribe of Zeb'ulun, twelve thousand of the tribe of Joseph, twelve thousand sealed out of the tribe of Benjamin.

9 After this I looked, and behold, a great multitude which no man could number, from every nation, from all tribes and peoples and tongues, standing before the throne and before the Lamb, clothed in white robes, with palm branches in their hands, **10**and crying out with a loud voice, "Salvation belongs to our God who sits upon the throne, and to the Lamb!" **11**And all the angels stood round the throne and round the elders and the four living creatures, and they fell on their faces before the throne and worshiped God, **12**saying, "Amen! Blessing and glory and wisdom and thanksgiving and honor and power and might be to our God for ever and ever! Amen."

13 Then one of the

ἐκ φυλῆς Ἰσσαχὰρ δώδεκα χιλιάδες,
of [the] tribe Issachar twelve thousands,

8 ἐκ φυλῆς Ζαβουλὼν δώδεκα χιλιάδες,
of [the] tribe Zabulon twelve thousands,

ἐκ φυλῆς Ἰωσὴφ δώδεκα χιλιάδες, ἐκ
of [the] tribe Joseph twelve thousands, of

φυλῆς Βενιαμίν δώδεκα χιλιάδες ἐσφραγισ-
[the] tribe Benjamin twelve thousands having been

μένοι. 9 Μετὰ ταῦτα εἶδον, καὶ ἰδοὺ ὄχλος
sealed. After these things I saw, and behold[,] [2]crowd

πολύς, ὃν ἀριθμῆσαι αὐτὸν οὐδεὶς ἐδύνατο,
[1]a much which [2]to number it [1]no one [3]was able,
(great),

ἐκ παντὸς ἔθνους καὶ φυλῶν καὶ λαῶν
out of every nation and tribes and peoples

καὶ γλωσσῶν, ἐστῶτες ἐνώπιον τοῦ θρόνου
and tongues, standing before the throne

καὶ ἐνώπιον τοῦ ἀρνίου, περιβεβλημένους
and before the Lamb, having been clothed [with]

στολὰς λευκάς, καὶ φοίνικες ἐν ταῖς
[2]robes [1]white, and palms in the

χερσὶν αὐτῶν· 10 καὶ κράζουσιν φωνῇ
hands of them; and they cry [2]voice

μεγάλῃ λέγοντες· ἡ σωτηρία τῷ θεῷ
[1]with a great(loud) saying: – Salvation to the God[c]

ἡμῶν τῷ καθημένῳ ἐπὶ τῷ θρόνῳ καὶ
of us – sitting on the throne and

τῷ ἀρνίῳ. 11 καὶ πάντες οἱ ἄγγελοι
to the Lamb.[c] And all the angels

εἱστήκεισαν κύκλῳ τοῦ θρόνου καὶ τῶν
stood round the throne and the

πρεσβυτέρων καὶ τῶν τεσσάρων ζῴων,
elders and the four living
creatures,

καὶ ἔπεσαν ἐνώπιον τοῦ θρόνου ἐπὶ
and fell before the throne on

τὰ πρόσωπα αὐτῶν καὶ προσεκύνησαν
the faces of them and worshipped

τῷ θεῷ, 12 λέγοντες· ἀμήν, ἡ εὐλογία
– God, saying: Amen, – blessing

καὶ ἡ δόξα καὶ ἡ σοφία καὶ ἡ εὐχαριστία
and – glory and – wisdom and – thanks

καὶ ἡ τιμὴ καὶ ἡ δύναμις καὶ ἡ ἰσχὺς
and – honour and – power and – strength

τῷ θεῷ ἡμῶν εἰς τοὺς αἰῶνας τῶν
to the God[c] of us unto the ages of the

αἰώνων· ἀμήν. 13 Καὶ ἀπεκρίθη εἷς
ages: Amen. And [2]answered [1]one

elders addressed me, saying, "Who are these, clothed in white robes, and whence have they come?" ¹⁴I said to him, "Sir, you know." And he said to me, "These are they who have come out of the great tribulation; they have washed their robes and made them white in the blood of the Lamb.
¹⁵Therefore are they before the throne of God,
and serve him day and night within his temple;
and he who sits upon the throne will shelter them with his presence.
¹⁶They shall hunger no more, neither thirst any more;
the sun shall not strike them, nor any scorching heat.
¹⁷For the Lamb in the midst of the throne will be their shepherd,
and he will guide them to springs of living water;
and God will wipe away every tear from their eyes."

ἐκ	τῶν	πρεσβυτέρων	λέγων	μοι·	οὗτοι
²of	³the	⁴elders	saying	to me:	These

οἱ	περιβεβλημένοι	τὰς	στολὰς	τὰς
the [ones]	having been clothed [with]	the	²robes	–

λευκὰς	τίνες	εἰσὶν	καὶ	πόθεν	ἦλθον;
¹white	who	are they	and	whence	came they?

14 καὶ	εἴρηκα	αὐτῷ·	κύριέ	μου,	σὺ
And	I have said	to him:	Lord	of me,	thou

οἶδας.	καὶ	εἶπέν	μοι·	οὗτοί	εἰσιν	οἱ
knowest.	And	he told	me:	These	are	the

ἐρχόμενοι	ἐκ	τῆς	θλίψεως	τῆς	μεγάλης
[ones] coming	out of	the	²affliction	–	¹great

καὶ	ἔπλυναν	τὰς	στολὰς	αὐτῶν	καὶ
and	washed	the	robes	of them	and

ἐλεύκαναν	αὐτὰς	ἐν	τῷ	αἵματι	τοῦ
whitened	them	in	the	blood	of the

ἀρνίου.	15 διὰ	τοῦτό	εἰσιν	ἐνώπιον	τοῦ
Lamb.	Therefore		are they	before	the

θρόνου	τοῦ	θεοῦ,	καὶ	λατρεύουσιν	αὐτῷ
throne	–	of God,	and	serve	him

ἡμέρας	καὶ	νυκτὸς	ἐν	τῷ	ναῷ	αὐτοῦ,
day	and	night	in	the	shrine	of him,

καὶ	ὁ	καθήμενος	ἐπὶ	τοῦ	θρόνου	σκηνώσει
and the [one]		sitting	on	the	throne	will spread [his] tent

ἐπ᾽	αὐτούς.	16 οὐ	πεινάσουσιν	ἔτι	οὐδὲ
over	them.		They will not hunger	longer	nor

διψήσουσιν	ἔτι,	οὐδὲ	μὴ	πέσῃ	ἐπ᾽	αὐτοὺς
will they thirst	longer,	neither	not	fall	on	them

ὁ	ἥλιος	οὐδὲ	πᾶν	καῦμα,	17 ὅτι	τὸ
the	sun	nor	every(any)	heat,		because the

ἀρνίον	τὸ	ἀνὰ	μέσον	τοῦ	θρόνου	ποιμανεῖ
Lamb	–	in the midst		of the	throne	will shepherd

αὐτοὺς	καὶ	ὁδηγήσει	αὐτοὺς	ἐπὶ	ζωῆς
them	and	will lead	them	upon	²of life

πηγὰς	ὑδάτων·	καὶ	ἐξαλείψει	ὁ	θεὸς
¹fountains	²of waters;	and	³will wipe off	–	¹God

πᾶν	δάκρυον	ἐκ	τῶν	ὀφθαλμῶν	αὐτῶν.
every	tear	out of	the	eyes	of them.

CHAPTER 8

WHEN the Lamb opened the seventh seal, there was silence in heaven for about half an hour. ²Then I saw the

8 Καὶ	ὅταν	ἤνοιξεν	τὴν	σφραγῖδα	τὴν
And	whenever	he opened	the	²seal	–

ἑβδόμην,	ἐγένετο	σιγὴ	ἐν	τῷ	οὐρανῷ
¹seventh,	occurred	a silence	in	–	heaven

ὡς	ἡμίωρον.	2 Καὶ	εἶδον	τοὺς	ἑπτα
about	a half-hour.	And	I saw	the	seven

seven angels who stand before God, and seven trumpets were given to them. ³And another angel came and stood at the altar with a golden censer; and he was given much incense to mingle with the prayers of all the saints upon the golden altar before the throne; ⁴and the smoke of the incense rose with the prayers of the saints from the hand of the angel before God. ⁵Then the angel took the censer and filled it with fire from the altar and threw it on the earth; and there were peals of thunder, loud noises, flashes of lightning, and an earthquake.

6 Now the seven angels who had the seven trumpets made ready to blow them.

7 The first angel blew his trumpet, and there followed hail and fire, mixed with blood, which fell on the earth; and a third of the earth was burnt up, and a third of

ἀγγέλους	οἳ	ἐνώπιον	τοῦ	θεοῦ	ἐστήκασιν,
angels	who	before	–	God	stood,

καὶ	ἐδόθησαν	αὐτοῖς	ἑπτὰ	σάλπιγγες.
and	there were given	to them	seven	trumpets.

3 Καὶ ἄλλος ἄγγελος ἦλθεν καὶ ἐστάθη
And another angel came and stood

ἐπὶ τοῦ θυσιαστηρίου ἔχων λιβανωτὸν
on the altar having ²censer

χρυσοῦν, καὶ ἐδόθη αὐτῷ θυμιάματα πολλά,
¹a golden, and there was to him incenses many
given (much),

ἵνα δώσει ταῖς προσευχαῖς τῶν ἁγίων
in order he will with the prayers of ²the ³saints
that give [it]

πάντων ἐπὶ τὸ θυσιαστήριον τὸ χρυσοῦν
¹all on the ²altar – ¹golden

τὸ ἐνώπιον τοῦ θρόνου. **4** καὶ ἀνέβη
– before the throne. And went up

ὁ καπνὸς τῶν θυμιαμάτων ταῖς προσευχαῖς
the smoke of the incenses with the prayers

τῶν ἁγίων ἐκ χειρὸς τοῦ ἀγγέλου ἐνώπιον
of the saints out of [the] hand of the angel before

τοῦ θεοῦ. **5** καὶ εἴληφεν ὁ ἄγγελος
– God. And ³has taken ¹the ²angel

τὸν λιβανωτόν, καὶ ἐγέμισεν αὐτὸν ἐκ
the censer, and filled it from

τοῦ πυρὸς τοῦ θυσιαστηρίου καὶ ἔβαλεν
the fire of the altar and cast

εἰς τὴν γῆν· καὶ ἐγένοντο βρονταὶ καὶ
into the earth; and there occurred thunders and

φωναὶ καὶ ἀστραπαὶ καὶ σεισμός.
sounds and lightnings and an earthquake.

6 Καὶ οἱ ἑπτὰ ἄγγελοι οἱ ἔχοντες
And the seven angels – having

τὰς ἑπτὰ σάλπιγγας ἡτοίμασαν αὐτοὺς
the seven trumpets prepared themselves

ἵνα σαλπίσωσιν. **7** Καὶ ὁ πρῶτος
in order they might And the first
that trumpet.

ἐσάλπισεν· καὶ ἐγένετο χάλαζα καὶ πῦρ
trumpeted; and there occurred hail and fire

μεμιγμένα ἐν αἵματι καὶ ἐβλήθη εἰς
having been in blood and it was cast to
mixed (with)

τὴν γῆν· καὶ τὸ τρίτον τῆς γῆς
the earth; and the third [part] of the earth

κατεκάη, καὶ τὸ τρίτον τῶν δένδρων
was burnt and the third [part] of the trees
down(up),

the trees were burnt up, and all green grass was burnt up.

8 The second angel blew his trumpet, and something like a great mountain, burning with fire, was thrown into the sea; ⁹and a third of the sea became blood, a third of the living creatures in the sea died, and a third of the ships were destroyed.

10 The third angel blew his trumpet, and a great star fell from heaven, blazing like a torch, and it fell on a third of the rivers and on the fountains of water. ¹¹The name of the star is Wormwood. A third of the waters became wormwood, and many men died of the water, because it was made bitter.

12 The fourth angel blew his trumpet, and a third of the sun was struck, and a third of the moon, and a third of the stars, so that a third of their light was darkened; a third of the day was kept from shining, and likewise a third of the night.

κατεκάη, καὶ πᾶς χόρτος χλωρὸς κατεκάη.
was burnt and all ²grass ¹green was burnt
down(up), down(up).

8 Καὶ ὁ δεύτερος ἄγγελος ἐσάλπισεν·
And the second angel trumpeted;

καὶ ὡς ὄρος μέγα πυρὶ καιόμενον ἐβλήθη
and as ²mountain ¹a great ⁴with fire ³burning was cast

εἰς τὴν θάλασσαν· καὶ ἐγένετο τὸ τρίτον
into the sea; and ⁵became ¹the ²third
[part]

τῆς θαλάσσης αἷμα, 9 καὶ ἀπέθανεν τὸ
²of the ⁴sea ⁶blood, and ¹⁰died ¹the

τρίτον τῶν κτισμάτων τῶν ἐν τῇ θαλάσσῃ,
²third ³of the ⁴creatures – ⁵in ⁶the ⁷sea,
[part]

τὰ ἔχοντα ψυχάς, καὶ τὸ τρίτον τῶν
– ⁸having ⁹souls, and the third [part] of the

πλοίων διεφθάρησαν. 10 Καὶ ὁ τρίτος
ships were destroyed. And the third

ἄγγελος ἐσάλπισεν· καὶ ἔπεσεν ἐκ τοῦ
angel trumpeted; and fell out of –

οὐρανοῦ ἀστὴρ μέγας καιόμενος ὡς
heaven star a great burning as

λαμπάς, καὶ ἔπεσεν ἐπὶ τὸ τρίτον τῶν
a lamp, and it fell onto the third [part] of the

ποταμῶν καὶ ἐπὶ τὰς πηγὰς τῶν ὑδάτων.
rivers and onto the fountains of the waters.

11 καὶ τὸ ὄνομα τοῦ ἀστέρος λέγεται
And the name of the star is said(called)

ὁ Ἄψινθος. καὶ ἐγένετο τὸ τρίτον τῶν
– Wormwood. And ⁵became ¹the ²third ³of
[part] the

ὑδάτων εἰς ἄψινθον, καὶ πολλοὶ τῶν
⁴waters into wormwood, and many of the

ἀνθρώπων ἀπέθανον ἐκ τῶν ὑδάτων ὅτι
men died from the waters because

ἐπικράνθησαν. 12 Καὶ ὁ τέταρτος ἄγγελος
they were made bitter. And the fourth angel

ἐσάλπισεν· καὶ ἐπλήγη τὸ τρίτον τοῦ
trumpeted; and ⁵was struck ¹the ²third [part] ³of the

ἡλίου καὶ τὸ τρίτον τῆς σελήνης καὶ
⁴sun and the third [part] of the moon and

τὸ τρίτον τῶν ἀστέρων, ἵνα σκοτισθῇ
the third of the stars, in order ⁴might be
[part] that darkened

τὸ τρίτον αὐτῶν καὶ ἡ ἡμέρα μὴ φάνῃ
¹the ²third [part] ³of them and the day might not appear

τὸ τρίτον αὐτῆς, καὶ ἡ νὺξ ὁμοίως.
the third [part] of it, and the night likewise.

13 Then I looked, and I heard an eagle crying with a loud voice, as it flew in midheaven, "Woe, woe, woe to those who dwell on the earth, at the blasts of the other trumpets which the three angels are about to blow!"

13 Καὶ εἶδον, καὶ ἤκουσα ἑνὸς ἀετοῦ
   And   I saw,   and   I heard   one   eagle

πετομένου ἐν μεσουρανήματι λέγοντος φωνῇ
flying   in   mid-heaven   saying   ²voice

μεγάλη· οὐαὶ οὐαὶ οὐαὶ τοὺς κατοικοῦν-
¹with a   Woe[,]   woe[,]   woe   to the [ones]   dwell-
great(loud):

τας ἐπὶ τῆς γῆς ἐκ τῶν λοιπῶν φωνῶν
ing   on   the   earth   from   the   remaining   voices

τῆς σάλπιγγος τῶν τριῶν ἀγγέλων τῶν
of the   trumpet   of the   three   angels   -

μελλόντων σαλπίζειν.
being about   to trumpet.

CHAPTER 9

AND the fifth angel blew his trumpet, and I saw a star fallen from heaven to earth, and he was given the key of the shaft of the bottomless pit; ²he opened the shaft of the bottomless pit, and from the shaft rose smoke like the smoke of a great furnace, and the sun and the air were darkened with the smoke from the shaft. ³Then from the smoke came locusts on the earth, and they were given power like the power of scorpions of the earth; ⁴they were told not to harm the grass of the earth or any green growth or any tree, but only those of mankind who have not the seal of God upon their fore-

9 Καὶ ὁ πέμπτος ἄγγελος ἐσάλπισεν·
  And   the   fifth   angel   trumpeted;

καὶ εἶδον ἀστέρα ἐκ τοῦ οὐρανοῦ πεπτω-
and   I saw   a star   out of   -   heaven   having

κότα εἰς τὴν γῆν, καὶ ἐδόθη αὐτῷ
fallen   onto   the   earth,   and   was given   to it

ἡ κλεὶς τοῦ φρέατος τῆς ἀβύσσου. 2 καὶ
the   key   of the   shaft   of the   abyss.   And

ἤνοιξεν τὸ φρέαρ τῆς ἀβύσσου· καὶ
he opened   the   shaft   of the   abyss;   and

ἀνέβη καπνὸς ἐκ τοῦ φρέατος ὡς
went up   a smoke   out of   the   shaft   as

καπνὸς καμίνου μεγάλης, καὶ ἐσκοτώθη
smoke   ²furnace   ¹of a great,   and   ⁶was darkened

ὁ ἥλιος καὶ ὁ ἀὴρ ἐκ τοῦ καπνοῦ
¹the   ²sun   ³and   ⁴the   ⁵air   by   the   smoke

τοῦ φρέατος. 3 καὶ ἐκ τοῦ καπνοῦ
of the   shaft.   And   out of   the   smoke

ἐξῆλθον ἀκρίδες εἰς τὴν γῆν, καὶ ἐδόθη
came forth   locusts   to   the   earth,   and'   ²was given

αὐτοῖς ἐξουσία ὡς ἔχουσιν ἐξουσίαν οἱ
³to them   ¹authority   as   ⁵have   ⁶authority   ¹the

σκορπίοι τῆς γῆς. 4 καὶ ἐρρέθη αὐτοῖς
²scorpions   ³of the   ⁴earth.   And   it was said   to them

ἵνα μὴ ἀδικήσουσιν τὸν χόρτον τῆς
in order   they shall not harm   the   grass   of the
that

γῆς οὐδὲ πᾶν χλωρὸν οὐδὲ πᾶν δένδρον,
earth   nor   every   greenstuff   nor   every   tree,
               (any)   (any)

εἰ μὴ τοὺς ἀνθρώπους οἵτινες οὐκ ἔχουσιν
except   the   men   who   have not

τὴν σφραγῖδα τοῦ θεοῦ ἐπὶ τῶν μετώπων.
the   seal   - of God   on   the(ir)   foreheads.

heads; ⁵they were
allowed to torture them
for five months, but not
to kill them, and their
torture was like the
torture of a scorpion,
when it stings a man.
⁶And in those days men
will seek death and will
not find it; they will long
to die, and death will fly
from them.

7 In appearance the
locusts were like horses
arrayed for battle; on
their heads were what
looked like crowns of
gold; their faces were
like human faces, ⁸their
hair like women's hair,
and their teeth like lions'
teeth; ⁹they had scales
like iron breastplates,
and the noise of their
wings was like the noise
of many chariots with
horses rushing into
battle. ¹⁰They have tails
like scorpions, and stings,
and their power of hurt-
ing men for five months
lies in their tails. ¹¹They
have as king over them
the angel of the bottom-

5 καὶ   ἐδόθη   αὐτοῖς   ἵνα   μὴ   ἀποκτείνωσιν
And   it was   to them   in order   they should not kill
        given   that

αὐτούς,   ἀλλ'   ἵνα   βασανισθήσονται   μῆνας
them,   but   in order   they shall be tormented   ¹months
                that

πέντε·   καὶ   ὁ   βασανισμὸς   αὐτῶν   ὡς
¹five;   and   the   torment   of them   [is] as

βασανισμὸς   σκορπίου,   ὅταν   παίσῃ   ἄνθρωπον.
[the] torment   of a scorpion,   whenever it stings   a man.

6 καὶ   ἐν   ταῖς   ἡμέραις   ἐκείναις   ζητήσουσιν
And   in   those days   ²will seek

οἱ   ἄνθρωποι   τὸν   θάνατον   καὶ   οὐ   μὴ
-    ¹men   -   death   and   by no means

εὑρήσουσιν   αὐτόν,   καὶ   ἐπιθυμήσουσιν
will they find   it,   and   they will long

ἀποθανεῖν   καὶ   φεύγει   ὁ   θάνατος   ἀπ'
to die   and   ²flees   -   ¹death   from

αὐτῶν.   7 καὶ   τὰ   ὁμοιώματα   τῶν   ἀκρίδων
them.   And   the   likenesses   of the   locusts

ὅμοιοι   ἵπποις   ἡτοιμασμένοις   εἰς   πόλεμον,
like   to horses   having been prepared   for   war,

καὶ   ἐπὶ   τὰς   κεφαλὰς   αὐτῶν   ὡς   στέφανοι
and   on   the   heads   of them   as   crowns

ὅμοιοι   χρυσῷ,   καὶ   τὰ   πρόσωπα   αὐτῶν
like   to gold,   and   the   faces   of them

ὡς   πρόσωπα   ἀνθρώπων,   8 καὶ   εἶχον
as   faces   of men,   and   they had

τρίχας   ὡς   τρίχας   γυναικῶν,   καὶ   οἱ
hairs   as   hairs   of women,   and   the

ὀδόντες   αὐτῶν   ὡς   λεόντων   ἦσαν,   9 καὶ
teeth   of them   ²as   ³of lions   ¹were,   and

εἶχον   θώρακας   ὡς   θώρακας   σιδηροῦς,
they had   breastplates   as   ²breastplates   ¹iron,

καὶ   ἡ   φωνὴ   τῶν   πτερύγων   αὐτῶν   ὡς
and   the   sound   of the   wings   of them   as

φωνὴ   ἁρμάτων   ἵππων   πολλῶν   τρεχόντων
sound   ²chariots   ³of horses   ¹of many   running

εἰς   πόλεμον.   10 καὶ   ἔχουσιν   οὐρὰς   ὁμοίας
to   war.   And   they have   tails   like

σκορπίοις   καὶ   κέντρα,   καὶ   ἐν   ταῖς   οὐραῖς
to scorpions   and   stings,   and   ⁶with   ⁷the   ⁸tails

αὐτῶν   ἡ   ἐξουσία   αὐτῶν   ἀδικῆσαι   τοὺς
⁹of them   ¹the   ²authority   ³of them   ⁴[is] to harm   -

ἀνθρώπους   μῆνας   πέντε.   11 ἔχουσιν   ἐπ'
⁵men   ¹¹months   ¹⁰five.   They have   over

αὐτῶν   βασιλέα   τὸν   ἄγγελον   τῆς   ἀβύσσου,
them   a king   the   angel   of the   abyss,

less pit; his name in Hebrew is Abad'don, and in Greek he is called Apol'lyon.[a] 12 The first woe has passed; behold, two woes are still to come. 13 Then the sixth angel blew his trumpet, and I heard a voice from the four horns of the golden altar before God, 14 saying to the sixth angel who had the trumpet, "Release the four angels who are bound at the great river Eu-phra'tes." 15 So the four angels were released, who had been held ready for the hour, the day, the month, and the year, to kill a third of mankind. 16 The number of the troops of cavalry was twice ten thousand times ten thousand; I heard their number. 17 And this was how I saw the horses in my vision: the riders wore breastplates the color of fire and of sapphire[b] and of sulphur, and the heads of the horses were like lions' heads, and fire and smoke and sulphur issued from

ὄνομα   αὐτῷ   ʽΕβραϊστὶ   ʼΑβαδδών,   καὶ
name   to him⁹   in Hebrew   Abaddon,   and

ἐν   τῇ   ʽΕλληνικῇ   ὄνομα   ἔχει   ʼΑπολλύων.
in   the   Greek   ²[the] name ¹he has   Apollyon.

12 ʽΗ   οὐαὶ   ἡ   μία   ἀπῆλθεν·   ἰδοὺ   ἔρχεται
The   ²woe   – ¹one(first) passed away; behold   ⁴comes

ἔτι   δύο   οὐαὶ   μετὰ   ταῦτα.
¹yet   ²two   ³woes   after   these things.

13 Καὶ   ὁ   ἕκτος   ἄγγελος   ἐσάλπισεν·
And   the   sixth   angel   trumpeted;

καὶ   ἤκουσα   φωνὴν   μίαν   ἐκ   τῶν   τεσσάρων
and   I heard   ²voice   ¹one   out of the   four

κεράτων   τοῦ   θυσιαστηρίου   τοῦ   χρυσοῦ
horns   of the   ²altar   –   ¹golden

τοῦ   ἐνώπιον   τοῦ   θεοῦ,   14 λέγοντα   τῷ
–   before   –   God,   saying   to the

ἕκτῳ   ἀγγέλῳ,   ὁ   ἔχων   τὴν   σάλπιγγα·
sixth   angel,   –   having   the   trumpet:

λῦσον   τοὺς   τέσσαρας   ἀγγέλους   τοὺς
Loose   the   four   angels   –

δεδεμένους   ἐπὶ   τῷ   ποταμῷ   τῷ   μεγάλῳ
having been bound at   the   ²river   –   ¹great

Εὐφράτῃ.   15 καὶ   ἐλύθησαν   οἱ   τέσσαρες
Euphrates.   And   were loosed   the   four

ἄγγελοι   οἱ   ἡτοιμασμένοι   εἰς   τὴν   ὥραν
angels   –   having been prepared for the   hour

καὶ   ἡμέραν   καὶ   μῆνα   καὶ   ἐνιαυτόν,
and   day   and   month   and   year,

ἵνα   ἀποκτείνωσιν   τὸ   τρίτον   τῶν   ἀνθρώπων.
in or- they should kill   the   third   of men.
der that   [part]

16 καὶ   ὁ   ἀριθμὸς   τῶν   στρατευμάτων   τοῦ
And   the   number   of the   bodies of soldiers   of the

ἱππικοῦ   δισμυριάδες   μυριάδων·   ἤκουσα   τὸν
cavalry   [was] two myriads   of myriads;   I heard   the

ἀριθμὸν   αὐτῶν.   17 καὶ   οὕτως   εἶδον
number   of them.   And   thus   I saw

τοὺς   ἵππους   ἐν   τῇ   ὁράσει   καὶ   τοὺς
the   horses   in   the   vision   and   the

καθημένους   ἐπʼ   αὐτῶν,   ἔχοντας   θώρακας
[ones] sitting   on   them,   having   breastplates

πυρίνους   καὶ   ὑακινθίνους   καὶ   θειώδεις·
fire-coloured   and   dusky red   and   sulphurous;

καὶ   αἱ   κεφαλαὶ   τῶν   ἵππων   ὡς   κεφαλαὶ
and   the   heads   of the   horses   as   heads

λεόντων,   καὶ   ἐκ   τῶν   στομάτων   αὐτῶν
of lions,   and   out of the   mouths   of them

ἐκπορεύεται   πῦρ   καὶ   καπνὸς   καὶ   θεῖον.
proceeds   fire   and   smoke   and   sulphur.

[a] Or Destroyer
[b] Greek hyacinth

their mouths. ¹⁸ By these three plagues a third of mankind was killed, by the fire and smoke and sulphur issuing from their mouths. ¹⁹ For the power of the horses is in their mouths and in their tails; their tails are like serpents, with heads, and by means of them they wound.

20 The rest of mankind, who were not killed by these plagues, did not repent of the works of their hands nor give up worshiping demons and idols of gold and silver and bronze and stone and wood, which cannot either see or hear or walk; ²¹ nor did they repent of their murders or their sorceries or their immorality or their thefts.

18 ἀπὸ	τῶν	τριῶν	πληγῶν	τούτων	ἀπεκτάν-
From	the	²three	³plagues	¹these	were

θησαν	τὸ	τρίτον	τῶν	ἀνθρώπων,	ἐκ
killed	the	third [part]	–	of men,	by

τοῦ	πυρὸς	καὶ	τοῦ	καπνοῦ	καὶ	τοῦ
the	fire	and	the	smoke	and	the

θείου	τοῦ	ἐκπορευομένου	ἐκ	τῶν	στομάτων
sulphur	–	proceeding	out of	the	mouths

αὐτῶν.	19 ἡ	γὰρ	ἐξουσία	τῶν	ἵππων
of them.	For the	authority	of the	horses

ἐν	τῷ	στόματι	αὐτῶν	ἐστιν	καὶ	ἐν
²in	³the	⁴mouth	⁵of them	¹is	and	in

ταῖς	οὐραῖς	αὐτῶν·	αἱ	γὰρ	οὐραὶ	αὐτῶν
the	tails	of them;	for the	tails	of them

ὅμοιαι	ὄφεσιν,	ἔχουσαι	κεφαλάς,	καὶ	ἐν
[are] like	to serpents,	having	heads,	and with

αὐταῖς	ἀδικοῦσιν.	20 καὶ	οἱ	λοιποὶ	τῶν
them	they do harm.	And	the	rest	–

ἀνθρώπων,	οἳ	οὐκ	ἀπεκτάνθησαν	ἐν	ταῖς
of men,	who	were not killed	by	–

πληγαῖς	ταύταις,	οὐδὲ	μετενόησαν	ἐκ
plagues	these,	not even	repented	of

τῶν	ἔργων	τῶν	χειρῶν	αὐτῶν,	ἵνα	μὴ
the	works	of the	hands	of them,	in order not	that

προσκυνήσουσιν	τὰ	δαιμόνια	καὶ	τὰ	εἴδωλα
they will worship	–	demons	and	–	idols

τὰ	χρυσᾶ	καὶ	τὰ	ἀργυρᾶ	καὶ	τὰ	χαλκᾶ
–	golden	and	–	silver	and	–	bronze

καὶ	τὰ	λίθινα	καὶ	τὰ	ξύλινα,	ἃ	οὔτε
and	–	stone	and	–	wooden,	which	²neither

βλέπειν	δύνανται	οὔτε	ἀκούειν	οὔτε
³to see	¹can	nor	to hear	nor

περιπατεῖν,	21 καὶ	οὐ	μετενόησαν	ἐκ	τῶν
to walk,	and	they repented not	of	the

φόνων	αὐτῶν	οὔτε	ἐκ	τῶν	φαρμακειῶν
murders	of them	nor	of	the	sorceries

αὐτῶν	οὔτε	ἐκ	τῆς	πορνείας	αὐτῶν
of them	nor	of	the	fornication	of them

οὔτε	ἐκ	τῶν	κλεμμάτων	αὐτῶν.
nor	of	the	thefts	of them.

CHAPTER 10

THEN I saw another mighty angel coming down from heaven, wrapped in a cloud, with a rainbow over his head,

10 Καὶ	εἶδον	ἄλλον	ἄγγελον	ἰσχυρὸν
And	I saw	another	²angel	¹strong

καταβαίνοντα	ἐκ	τοῦ	οὐρανοῦ,	περιβεβλημέ-
coming down	out of	–	heaven,	having been clothed

νον	νεφέλην,	καὶ	ἡ	ἶρις	ἐπὶ	τὴν	κεφαλὴν
[with]	a cloud,	and	the rainbow	on	the	head

and his face was like the sun, and his legs like pillars of fire. ²He had a little scroll open in his hand. And he set his right foot on the sea, and his left foot on the land, ³and called out with a loud voice, like a lion roaring; when he called out, the seven thunders sounded. ⁴And when the seven thunders had sounded, I was about to write, but I heard a voice from heaven saying, "Seal up what the seven thunders have said, and do not write it down." ⁵And the angel whom I saw standing on sea and land lifted up his right hand to heaven ⁶and swore by him who lives for ever and ever, who created heaven and what is in it, the earth and what is in it, and the sea and what is in it, that there should be no more delay, ⁷but that in the days of the trumpet call to be sounded by the seventh angel, the

αὐτοῦ, καὶ τὸ πρόσωπον αὐτοῦ ὡς ὁ
of him,   and   the   face   of him   as   the

ἥλιος, καὶ οἱ πόδες αὐτοῦ ὡς στῦλοι
sun,   and the feet   of him   as   pillars

πυρός, 2 καὶ ἔχων ἐν τῇ χειρὶ αὐτοῦ
of fire,   and having in the hand   of him

βιβλαρίδιον ἠνεῳγμένον.   καὶ ἔθηκεν τὸν
a little scroll having been opened.   And he placed ¹the

πόδα αὐτοῦ τὸν δεξιὸν ἐπὶ τῆς θαλάσσης,
²foot ⁴of him   -   ³right   on the   sea,

τὸν δὲ εὐώνυμον ἐπὶ τῆς γῆς, 3 καὶ
and the   left   on the land,   and

ἔκραξεν φωνῇ μεγάλῃ ὥσπερ λέων μυκᾶται.
cried   ²voice ¹with a   as   a lion roars.
              great(loud)

καὶ ὅτε ἔκραξεν, ἐλάλησαν αἱ ἑπτὰ
And when he cried, ⁴spoke(uttered) ¹the ²seven

βρονταὶ τὰς ἑαυτῶν φωνάς. 4 Καὶ ὅτε
³thunders ⁵the ⁷of themselves ⁶voices.   And when

ἐλάλησαν αἱ ἑπτὰ βρονταί, ἤμελλον
spoke   the seven thunders,   I was about

γράφειν· καὶ ἤκουσα φωνὴν ἐκ τοῦ
to write; and I heard a voice out of   -

οὐρανοῦ λέγουσαν· σφράγισον ἃ ἐλάλησαν
heaven   saying: Seal thou [the] ⁴spoke
                                things which

αἱ ἑπτὰ βρονταί, καὶ μὴ αὐτὰ γράψῃς.
¹the ²seven ³thunders,   and ³not ²them thou mayest
                                              ¹write.

5 Καὶ ὁ ἄγγελος, ὃν εἶδον ἑστῶτα
And the angel,   whom I saw standing

ἐπὶ τῆς θαλάσσης καὶ ἐπὶ τῆς γῆς,
on the   sea   and on the land,

ἦρεν τὴν χεῖρα αὐτοῦ τὴν δεξιὰν εἰς
lifted ¹the ³hand ⁴of him   -   ²right   to

τὸν οὐρανόν, 6 καὶ ὤμοσεν ἐν τῷ ζῶντι
-   heaven,   and swore   by the [one] living

εἰς τοὺς αἰῶνας τῶν αἰώνων, ὃς ἔκτισεν
unto the   ages   of the ages,   who created

τὸν οὐρανὸν καὶ τὰ ἐν αὐτῷ καὶ τὴν
the heaven   and the things in it   and the

γῆν καὶ τὰ ἐν αὐτῇ καὶ τὴν θάλασσαν
earth and the in it   and the   sea
        things

καὶ τὰ ἐν αὐτῇ, ὅτι χρόνος οὐκέτι
and the things in it,   that time   ²no longer

ἔσται, 7 ἀλλ’ ἐν ταῖς ἡμέραις τῆς
¹shall be,   but in the   days   of the

φωνῆς τοῦ ἑβδόμου ἀγγέλου, ὅταν μέλλῃ
voice of the seventh   angel, whenever he is about

mystery of God, as he announced to his servants the prophets, should be fulfilled.

8 Then the voice which I had heard from heaven spoke to me again, saying, "Go, take the scroll which is open in the hand of the angel who is standing on the sea and on the land." ⁹ So I went to the angel and told him to give me the little scroll; and he said to me, "Take it and eat; it will be bitter to your stomach, but sweet as honey in your mouth." ¹⁰And I took the little scroll from the hand of the angel and ate it; it was sweet as honey in my mouth, but when I had eaten it my stomach was made bitter. ¹¹And I was told, "You must again prophesy about many peoples and nations and tongues and kings."

σαλπίζειν, καὶ ἐτελέσθη τὸ μυστήριον
to trumpet, even was finished the mystery

τοῦ θεοῦ, ὡς εὐηγγέλισεν τοὺς ἑαυτοῦ
- of God, as he preached [to] the ²of himse*lf*

δούλους τοὺς προφήτας. 8 Καὶ ἡ φωνὴ
¹slaves the prophets. And the voice

ἣν ἤκουσα ἐκ τοῦ οὐρανοῦ, πάλιν
which I heard out of - heaven, again

λαλοῦσαν μετ' ἐμοῦ καὶ λέγουσαν· ὕπαγε
speaking with me and saying: Go thou

λάβε τὸ βιβλίον τὸ ἠνεῳγμένον ἐν τῇ
take the scroll - having been opened in the

χειρὶ τοῦ ἀγγέλου τοῦ ἑστῶτος ἐπὶ
hand of the angel - standing on

τῆς θαλάσσης καὶ ἐπὶ τῆς γῆς. 9 καὶ
the sea and on the land. And

ἀπῆλθα πρὸς τὸν ἄγγελον, λέγων αὐτῷ
I went away toward the angel, telling him

δοῦναί μοι τὸ βιβλαρίδιον. καὶ λέγει
to give me the little scroll. And he says

μοι· λάβε καὶ κατάφαγε αὐτό, καὶ
to me: Take and devour it, and

πικρανεῖ σου τὴν κοιλίαν, ἀλλ' ἐν τῷ
it will embitter ²of thee ¹the ²stomach, but in the

στόματί σου ἔσται γλυκὺ ὡς μέλι.
mouth of thee it will be sweet as honey.

10 καὶ ἔλαβον τὸ βιβλαρίδιον ἐκ τῆς
And I took the little scroll out of the

χειρὸς τοῦ ἀγγέλου καὶ κατέφαγον αὐτό,
hand of the angel and devoured it,

καὶ ἦν ἐν τῷ στόματί μου ὡς μέλι
and it was in the mouth of me as ²honey

γλυκύ· καὶ ὅτε ἔφαγον αὐτό, ἐπικράνθη
¹sweet; and when I ate it, ⁴was made bitter

ἡ κοιλία μου. 11 καὶ λέγουσίν μοι·
¹the ²stomach ³of me. And they say to me:

δεῖ σε πάλιν προφητεῦσαι ἐπὶ λαοῖς
It behoves thee again to prophesy before peoples

καὶ ἔθνεσιν καὶ γλώσσαις καὶ βασιλεῦσιν
and nations and tongues and ²kings

CHAPTER 11

THEN I was given a measuring rod like a staff, and I was told: "Rise and measure the temple of God and the altar and those who worship there, ²but do

πολλοῖς. 11 Καὶ ἐδόθη μοι κάλαμος ὅμοιος
¹many. And was given to me a reed like

ῥάβδῳ, λέγων· ἔγειρε καὶ μέτρησον τὸν ναὸν
to a staff, saying: Rise and measure the shrine

τοῦ θεοῦ καὶ τὸ θυσιαστήριον καὶ τοὺς
- of God and the altar and the

προσκυνοῦντας ἐν αὐτῷ. 2 καὶ τὴν
[ones] worshipping in it. And the

not measure the court outside the temple; leave that out, for it is given over to the nations, and they will trample over the holy city for forty-two months. ³And I will grant my two witnesses power to prophesy for one thousand two hundred and sixty days, clothed in sackcloth."

4 These are the two olive trees and the two lampstands which stand before the Lord of the earth. ⁵And if any one would harm them, fire pours from their mouth and consumes their foes; if any one would harm them, thus he is doomed to be killed. ⁶They have power to shut the sky, that no rain may fall during the days of their prophesying, and they have power over the waters to turn them into blood, and to smite the earth with every plague, as often as they desire. ⁷And when they have finished their testimony, the beast that ascends from the bottomless pit will make war upon them

αὐλὴν τὴν ἔξωθεν τοῦ ναοῦ ἔκβαλε
²court – ¹outside of the shrine cast out

ἔξωθεν καὶ μὴ αὐτὴν μετρήσῃς, ὅτι
outside and ³not ²it thou mayest because
¹measure,

ἐδόθη τοῖς ἔθνεσιν, καὶ τὴν πόλιν τὴν
it was given to the nations, and the ²city –

ἁγίαν πατήσουσιν μῆνας τεσσεράκοντα
¹holy they will trample ³months ¹forty-

[καὶ] δύο. 3 καὶ δώσω τοῖς δυσὶν
and ²two.   And I will give to the two

μάρτυσίν μου, καὶ προφητεύσουσιν ἡμέρας
witnesses of me, and they will prophesy ⁵days

χιλίας διακοσίας ἑξήκοντα περιβεβλημένοι
¹a thousand ²two hundred ³[and] ⁴sixty having been clothed

σάκκους. 4 οὗτοί εἰσιν αἱ δύο ἐλαῖαι
[in] sackclothes. These are the two olive-trees

καὶ αἱ δύο λυχνίαι αἱ ἐνώπιον τοῦ
and the two lampstands – ²before ⁴the

κυρίου τῆς γῆς ἑστῶτες. 5 καὶ εἴ τις
⁴Lord ⁶of the ⁵earth ¹standing. And if anyone

αὐτοὺς θέλει ἀδικῆσαι, πῦρ ἐκπορεύεται·
³them ¹wishes ²to harm, fire proceeds

ἐκ τοῦ στόματος αὐτῶν καὶ κατεσθίει
out of the mouth of them and devours

τοὺς ἐχθροὺς αὐτῶν· καὶ εἴ τις θελήσῃ
the enemies of them; and if anyone should wish

αὐτοὺς ἀδικῆσαι, οὕτως δεῖ αὐτὸν
²them ¹to harm, thus it behoves him

ἀποκτανθῆναι. 6 οὗτοι ἔχουσιν τὴν ἐξουσίαν
to be killed. These have the authority

κλεῖσαι τὸν οὐρανόν, ἵνα μὴ ὑετὸς
to shut – heaven, in order that ²not ¹rain

βρέχῃ τὰς ἡμέρας τῆς προφητείας αὐτῶν,
²may the days of the prophecy of them,
⁴rain(fall)

καὶ ἐξουσίαν ἔχουσιν ἐπὶ τῶν ὑδάτων
and authority they have over the waters

στρέφειν αὐτὰ εἰς αἷμα καὶ πατάξαι
to turn them into blood and to strike

τὴν γῆν ἐν πάσῃ πληγῇ ὁσάκις ἐὰν
the earth with every [kind of] plague as often as

θελήσωσιν. 7 Καὶ ὅταν τελέσωσιν τὴν
they may wish. And whenever they finish the

μαρτυρίαν αὐτῶν, τὸ θηρίον τὸ ἀναβαῖνον
witness of them, the beast – coming up

ἐκ τῆς ἀβύσσου ποιήσει μετ᾽ αὐτῶν
out of the abyss ¹will make ³with ⁴them

and conquer them and kill them, ⁸and their dead bodies will lie in the street of the great city which is allegorically called Sodom and Egypt, where their Lord was crucified. ⁹For three days and a half men from the people and tribes and tongues and nations gaze at their dead bodies and refuse to let them be placed in a tomb, ¹⁰and those who dwell on the earth will rejoice over them and make merry and exchange presents, because these two prophets had been a torment to those who dwell on the earth. ¹¹But after the three and a half days a breath of life from God entered them, and they stood up on their feet, and great fear fell on those who saw them. ¹²Then they heard a loud voice from heaven saying to them, "Come up hither!" And in the sight of their foes they went up to heaven in a cloud. ¹³And at that

πόλεμον   καὶ   νικήσει   αὐτοὺς   καὶ   ἀποκτενεῖ
²war   and will overcome   them   and   will kill

αὐτούς.   8 καὶ   τὸ   πτῶμα   αὐτῶν   ἐπὶ
them.   And   the   corpse   of them   on

τῆς   πλατείας   τῆς   πόλεως   τῆς   μεγάλης,
the   open street   of the   ²city   –   ¹great,

ἥτις   καλεῖται   πνευματικῶς   Σόδομα   καὶ
which   is called   spiritually   Sodom   and

Αἴγυπτος,   ὅπου   καὶ   ὁ   κύριος   αὐτῶν
Egypt,   where   indeed   the   Lord   of them

ἐσταυρώθη.   9 καὶ   βλέπουσιν   ἐκ   τῶν.
was crucified.   And   ¹⁰see   ¹[some] of   ²the

λαῶν   καὶ   φυλῶν   καὶ   γλωσσῶν   καὶ
²peoples   ⁴and   ⁵tribes   ⁶and   ⁷tongues   ⁸and

ἐθνῶν   τὸ   πτῶμα   αὐτῶν   ἡμέρας   τρεῖς
⁹nations   the   corpse   of them   ⁴days   ¹three

καὶ   ἥμισυ,   καὶ   τὰ   πτώματα   αὐτῶν
²and   ³a half,   and   ²the   ³corpses   ⁴of them

οὐκ   ἀφίουσιν   τεθῆναι   εἰς   μνῆμα.   10 καὶ
¹they do not allow   to be placed   in   a tomb.   And

οἱ   κατοικοῦντες   ἐπὶ   τῆς   γῆς   χαίρουσιν
the [ones]   dwelling   on   the   earth   rejoice

ἐπ'   αὐτοῖς   καὶ   εὐφραίνονται,   καὶ   δῶρα
over   them   and   are glad,   and   ²gifts

πέμψουσιν   ἀλλήλοις,   ὅτι   οὗτοι   οἱ   δύο
¹they will send   to one another,   because   these   –   two

προφῆται   ἐβασάνισαν   τοὺς   κατοικοῦντας
prophets   tormented   the [ones]   dwelling

ἐπὶ   τῆς   γῆς.   11 Καὶ   μετὰ   [τὰς]   τρεῖς
on   the   earth.   And   after   the   ¹three

ἡμέρας   καὶ   ἥμισυ   πνεῦμα   ζωῆς   ἐκ   τοῦ
⁴days   ²and   ³a half   a spirit   of life   out of   –

θεοῦ   εἰσῆλθεν   ἐν   αὐτοῖς,   καὶ   ἔστησαν
God   entered   in[to]   them,   and   they stood

ἐπὶ   τοὺς   πόδας   αὐτῶν,   καὶ   φόβος   μέγας
on   the   feet   of them,   and   ²fear   ¹great

ἐπέπεσεν   ἐπὶ   τοὺς   θεωροῦντας   αὐτούς.
fell on   on   the [ones]   beholding   them.

12 καὶ   ἤκουσαν   φωνῆς   μεγάλης   ἐκ   τοῦ
And   they heard   ²voice   ¹a great(loud)   out of   –

οὐρανοῦ   λεγούσης   αὐτοῖς·   ἀνάβατε   ὧδε·
heaven   saying   to them: Come ye up   here;

καὶ   ἀνέβησαν   εἰς   τὸν   οὐρανὸν   ἐν   τῇ
and   they went up   to   –   heaven   in   the

νεφέλῃ,   καὶ   ἐθεώρησαν   αὐτοὺς   οἱ   ἐχθροὶ
cloud,   and   ⁴beheld   ⁵them   ¹the   ²enemies

αὐτῶν.   13 Καὶ   ἐν   ἐκείνῃ   τῇ   ὥρᾳ   ἐγένετο
³of them.   And   in   that   –   hour   ³occurred

hour there was a great earthquake, and a tenth of the city fell; seven thousand people were killed in the earthquake, and the rest were terrified and gave glory to the God of heaven.

14 The second woe has passed; behold, the third woe is soon to come.

15 Then the seventh angel blew his trumpet, and there were loud voices in heaven, saying, "The kingdom of the world has become the kingdom of our Lord and of his Christ, and he shall reign for ever and ever." 16And the twenty-four elders who sit on their thrones before God fell on their faces and worshiped God, 17saying,

"We give thanks to thee, Lord God almighty, who art and who wast, that thou hast taken thy great power and begun to reign. 18The nations raged, but thy wrath came, and the time for the dead to be judged,

σεισμὸς μέγας, καὶ τὸ δέκατον τῆς
²earthquake ¹a great, and the tenth [part] of the

πόλεως ἔπεσεν, καὶ ἀπεκτάνθησαν ἐν τῷ
city fell, and ⁵were killed ⁶in ⁷the

σεισμῷ ὀνόματα ἀνθρώπων χιλιάδες ἑπτά,
⁸earthquake ³names ⁴of men ²thousands ¹seven,

καὶ οἱ λοιποὶ ἔμφοβοι ἐγένοντο καὶ
and the rest ²terrified ¹became and

ἔδωκαν δόξαν τῷ θεῷ τοῦ οὐρανοῦ.
gave glory to the God – of heaven.

14 Ἡ οὐαὶ ἡ δευτέρα ἀπῆλθεν· ἰδοὺ
The ²woe – ¹second passed away; behold[,]

ἡ οὐαὶ ἡ τρίτη ἔρχεται ταχύ.
the ²woe – ¹third is coming quickly.

15 Καὶ ὁ ἕβδομος ἄγγελος ἐσάλπισεν·
And the seventh angel trumpeted;

καὶ ἐγένοντο φωναὶ μεγάλαι ἐν τῷ
and there were voices great(loud) in –

οὐρανῷ, λέγοντες· ἐγένετο ἡ βασιλεία
heaven, saying: ⁵became ¹The ²kingdom

τοῦ κόσμου τοῦ κυρίου ἡμῶν καὶ τοῦ
³of the ⁴world of the Lord of us and of the

χριστοῦ αὐτοῦ, καὶ βασιλεύσει εἰς τοὺς
Christ of him, and he shall reign unto the

αἰῶνας τῶν αἰώνων. 16 καὶ οἱ εἴκοσι
ages of the ages. And the twenty-

τέσσαρες πρεσβύτεροι, οἱ ἐνώπιον τοῦ
four elders, – ²before –

θεοῦ καθήμενοι ἐπὶ τοὺς θρόνους αὐτῶν,
³God ¹sitting on the thrones of them,

ἔπεσαν ἐπὶ τὰ πρόσωπα αὐτῶν καὶ
fell on the faces of them and

προσεκύνησαν τῷ θεῷ, 17 λέγοντες·
worshipped – God, saying:

εὐχαριστοῦμέν σοι, κύριε ὁ θεὸς ὁ
We thank thee, [O] Lord – God the

παντοκράτωρ, ὁ ὢν καὶ ὁ ἦν, ὅτι
Almighty, the [one] being and the was, because
=the one who is [one who]

εἴληφας τὴν δύναμίν σου τὴν μεγάλην
thou hast taken ¹the ³power ⁴of thee – ²great

καὶ ἐβασίλευσας· 18 καὶ τὰ ἔθνη ὠργίσ-
and didst reign; and the nations were

θησαν, καὶ ἦλθεν ἡ ὀργή σου καὶ ὁ
wrathful, and ⁴came ¹the ²wrath ³of thee and the

καιρὸς τῶν νεκρῶν κριθῆναι καὶ δοῦναι
time of the dead to be judged and to give

for rewarding thy servants, the prophets and saints, and those who fear thy name, both small and great, and for destroying the destroyers of the earth." 19 Then God's temple in heaven was opened, and the ark of his covenant was seen within his temple; and there were flashes of lightning, loud noises, peals of thunder, an earthquake, and heavy hail.

τὸν μισθὸν τοῖς δούλοις σου τοῖς προφήταις
the reward to the slaves of thee *to* the prophets
καὶ τοῖς ἁγίοις καὶ τοῖς φοβουμένοις
and to the saints and to the [ones] fearing
τὸ ὄνομά σου, τοῖς μικροῖς καὶ τοῖς
the name of thee, to the small and to the
μεγάλοις, καὶ διαφθεῖραι τοὺς διαφθείροντας
great, and to destroy the [ones] destroying
τὴν γῆν. 19 καὶ ἠνοίγη ὁ ναὸς τοῦ
the earth. And was opened the shrine –
θεοῦ ὁ ἐν τῷ οὐρανῷ, καὶ ὤφθη ἡ
of God – in – heaven, and was seen the
κιβωτὸς τῆς διαθήκης αὐτοῦ ἐν τῷ
ark of the covenant of him in the
ναῷ αὐτοῦ, καὶ ἐγένοντο ἀστραπαὶ καὶ
shrine of him, and occurred lightnings and
φωναὶ καὶ βρονταὶ καὶ σεισμὸς καὶ
voices and thunders and an earthquake and
χάλαζα μεγάλη.
²hail ¹a great.

CHAPTER 12

AND a great portent appeared in heaven, a woman clothed with the sun, with the moon under her feet, and on her head a crown of twelve stars; ²she was with child and she cried out in her pangs of birth, in anguish for delivery. ³And another portent appeared in heaven; behold a great red dragon, with seven heads and ten horns, and seven diadems upon his heads. ⁴His tail swept down a third of the stars of heaven, and cast them to the earth. And the

12 Καὶ σημεῖον μέγα ὤφθη ἐν τῷ
And ²sign ¹a great was seen in –
οὐρανῷ, γυνὴ περιβεβλημένη τὸν ἥλιον,
heaven, a woman *having been* clothed [with] the sun,
καὶ ἡ σελήνη ὑποκάτω τῶν ποδῶν αὐτῆς,
and the moon underneath the feet of her,
καὶ ἐπὶ τῆς κεφαλῆς αὐτῆς στέφανος
and on the head of her a crown
ἀστέρων δώδεκα, 2 καὶ ἐν γαστρὶ ἔχουσα,
²stars ¹of twelve, and in womb having,
= being pregnant,
καὶ κράζει ὠδίνουσα καὶ βασανιζομένη
and she cries suffering birth-pains and being distressed
τεκεῖν. 3 καὶ ὤφθη ἄλλο σημεῖον
to bear. And was seen another sign
ἐν τῷ οὐρανῷ, καὶ ἰδοὺ δράκων μέγας
in – heaven, and behold[,] ³dragon ¹a great
πυρρός, ἔχων κεφαλὰς ἑπτὰ καὶ κέρατα
²red, having ²heads ¹seven and ²horns
δέκα καὶ ἐπὶ τὰς κεφαλὰς αὐτοῦ ἑπτὰ
¹ten and on the heads of him seven
διαδήματα, 4 καὶ ἡ οὐρὰ αὐτοῦ σύρει
diadems, and the tail of him draws
τὸ τρίτον τῶν ἀστέρων τοῦ οὐρανοῦ,
the third [part] of the stars – of heaven,
καὶ ἔβαλεν αὐτοὺς εἰς τὴν γῆν. Καὶ
and cast them to the earth. And

dragon stood before the woman who was about to bear a child, that he might devour her child when she brought it forth; [5]she brought forth a male child, one who is to rule all the nations with a rod of iron, but her child was caught up to God and to his throne, [6]and the woman fled into the wilderness, where she has a place prepared by God, in which to be nourished for one thousand two hundred and sixty days.

[7]Now war arose in heaven, Michael and his angels fighting against the dragon; and the dragon and his angels fought, [8]but they were defeated and there was no longer any place for them in heaven. [9]And the great dragon was thrown down, that ancient serpent, who is called the Devil and Satan, the deceiver of the whole world—he was thrown down to the earth, and his angels were thrown down with him. [10]And I heard a loud voice in heaven,

ὁ	δράκων	ἔστηκεν	ἐνώπιον	τῆς	γυναικὸς
the	dragon	stood	before	the	woman

τῆς	μελλούσης	τεκεῖν,	ἵνα	ὅταν	τέκῃ
-	being about	to bear,	in order that	whenever	she bears

τὸ	τέκνον	αὐτῆς	καταφάγῃ.	5 καὶ
[2]the	[3]child	[4]of her	[1]he might devour.	And

ἔτεκεν	υἱὸν	ἄρσεν,	ὃς	μέλλει	ποιμαίνειν
she bore	a son[,]	a male,	who	is about	to shepherd

πάντα	τὰ	ἔθνη	ἐν	ῥάβδῳ	σιδηρᾷ·	καὶ
all	the	nations	with	[2]staff	[1]an iron;	and

ἡρπάσθη	τὸ	τέκνον	αὐτῆς	πρὸς	τὸν
[4]was seized	[1]the	[2]child	[3]of her	to	-

θεὸν	καὶ	πρὸς	τὸν	θρόνον	αὐτοῦ.	6 καὶ
God	and	to	the	throne	of him.	And

ἡ	γυνὴ	ἔφυγεν	εἰς	τὴν	ἔρημον,	ὅπου
the	woman	fled	into	the	desert,	where

ἔχει	ἐκεῖ	τόπον	ἡτοιμασμένον	ἀπὸ
she has	there	a place	having been prepared	from

τοῦ	θεοῦ,	ἵνα	ἐκεῖ	τρέφωσιν	αὐτὴν
-	God,	in order that there	they might nourish	her

ἡμέρας	χιλίας	διακοσίας	ἑξήκοντα.
[5]days	[1]a thousand	[2]two hundred	[3][and] [4]sixty.

7 Καὶ	ἐγένετο	πόλεμος	ἐν	τῷ	οὐρανῷ,
And	occurred	war	in	-	heaven,

ὁ	Μιχαὴλ	καὶ	οἱ	ἄγγελοι	αὐτοῦ	τοῦ
-	Michael	and	the	angels	of him	-

πολεμῆσαι	μετὰ	τοῦ	δράκοντος.	καὶ ὁ
to make war[d]	with	the	dragon.	And the

δράκων	ἐπολέμησεν	καὶ	οἱ	ἄγγελοι	αὐτοῦ,
dragon	warred	and	the	angels	of him.

8 καὶ	οὐκ	ἴσχυσεν,	οὐδὲ	τόπος	εὑρέθη
and	prevailed not,		not even	place	was found

αὐτῶν	ἔτι	ἐν	τῷ	οὐρανῷ.	9 καὶ	ἐβλήθη
of them	still	in	-	heaven.	And	was cast

ὁ	δράκων	ὁ	μέγας,	ὁ	ὄφις	ὁ	ἀρχαῖος,
[1]the	[2]dragon	-	[2]great,	[4]the	[5]serpent	-	[5]old,

ὁ	καλούμενος	Διάβολος	καὶ	ὁ	Σατανᾶς,
-	being called	Devil	and	the	Satan,

ὁ	πλανῶν	τὴν	οἰκουμένην	ὅλην,	ἐβλήθη
the deceiving [one]		the	[2]inhabited [earth]	[1]whole,	was cast

εἰς	τὴν	γῆν,	καὶ	οἱ	ἄγγελοι	αὐτοῦ	μετ᾽
to	the	earth,	and	the	angels	of him	with

αὐτοῦ	ἐβλήθησαν.	10 καὶ	ἤκουσα	φωνὴν
him	were cast.	And	I heard	[2]voice

μεγάλην	ἐν	τῷ	οὐρανῷ	λέγουσαν	ἄρτι
[1]a great(loud)	in	-	heaven	saying:	Now

saying, "Now the salvation and the power and the kingdom of our God and the authority of his Christ have come, for the accuser of our brethren has been thrown down, who accuses them day and night before our God. ¹¹And they have conquered him by the blood of the Lamb and by the word of their testimony, for they loved not their lives even unto death. ¹²Rejoice then, O heaven and you that dwell therein! But woe to you, O earth and sea, for the devil has come down to you in great wrath, because he knows that his time is short!

13 And when the dragon saw that he had been thrown down to the earth, he pursued the woman who had borne the male child. ¹⁴But the woman was given the two wings of the great eagle that she might fly from the serpent into the wilderness, to the place where she is to be nourished for a time, and times, and half a time. ¹⁵The serpent poured water like a river out of his mouth after the

ἐγένετο ἡ σωτηρία καὶ ἡ δύναμις καὶ
became the salvation and the power and

ἡ βασιλεία τοῦ θεοῦ ἡμῶν καὶ ἡ ἐξουσία
the kingdom of the God of us and the authority

τοῦ χριστοῦ αὐτοῦ, ὅτι ἐβλήθη ὁ κατήγωρ
of the Christ of him, because ⁶was cast ¹the ²accuser

τῶν ἀδελφῶν ἡμῶν, ὁ κατηγορῶν αὐτοὺς
²of the ⁴brothers ⁵of us, the [one] accusing them

ἐνώπιον τοῦ θεοῦ ἡμῶν ἡμέρας καὶ
before the God of us day and

νυκτός. 11 καὶ αὐτοὶ ἐνίκησαν αὐτὸν
night.   And they overcame him

διὰ τὸ αἷμα τοῦ ἀρνίου καὶ διὰ τὸν
be- the blood of the Lamb and because the
cause of   of

λόγον τῆς μαρτυρίας αὐτῶν, καὶ οὐκ
word of the witness of them, and not

ἠγάπησαν τὴν ψυχὴν αὐτῶν ἄχρι θανάτου.
they loved the life of them until death.

12 διὰ τοῦτο εὐφραίνεσθε, οὐρανοὶ καὶ
Therefore be ye glad, heavens and

οἱ ἐν αὐτοῖς σκηνοῦντες· οὐαὶ τὴν
the ²in ³them ¹tabernacling; woe [to] the
[ones]

γῆν καὶ τὴν θάλασσαν, ὅτι κατέβη ὁ
earth and the sea, because ²came down ¹the

διάβολος πρὸς ὑμᾶς ἔχων θυμὸν μέγαν,
²devil to you having ²anger ¹great.

εἰδὼς ὅτι ὀλίγον καιρὸν ἔχει. 13 Καὶ
knowing that ²few(short) ³time ¹he has. And

ὅτε εἶδεν ὁ δράκων ὅτι ἐβλήθη εἰς
when ²saw ¹the ²dragon that he was cast to

τὴν γῆν, ἐδίωξεν τὴν γυναῖκα ἥτις
the earth, he pursued the woman who

ἔτεκεν τὸν ἄρσενα. 14 καὶ ἐδόθησαν
bore the male. And were given

τῇ γυναικὶ αἱ δύο πτέρυγες τοῦ ἀετοῦ
to the woman the two wings of the ²eagle

τοῦ μεγάλου, ἵνα πέτηται εἰς τὴν ἔρημον
 - ¹great, in order she might to the desert
that fly

εἰς τὸν τόπον αὐτῆς, ὅπου τρέφεται
to the place of her, where she is nourished

ἐκεῖ καιρὸν καὶ καιροὺς καὶ ἥμισυ καιροῦ
there a time and times and half of a time

ἀπὸ προσώπου τοῦ ὄφεως. 15 καὶ ἔβαλεν
from [the] face of the serpent. And ²cast

ὁ ὄφις ἐκ τοῦ στόματος αὐτοῦ ὀπίσω
¹the ²serpent out of the mouth of him behind

woman, to sweep her away with the flood. ¹⁶But the earth came to the help of the woman, and the earth opened its mouth and swallowed the river which the dragon had poured from his mouth. ¹⁷Then the dragon was angry with the woman, and went off to make war on the rest of her offspring, on those who keep the commandments of God and bear testimony to Jesus. And he stood^c on the sand of the sea.

τῆς	γυναικὸς	ὕδωρ	ὡς	ποταμόν,	ἵνα
the	woman	water	as	a river,	in order that

αὐτὴν	ποταμοφόρητον	ποιήσῃ.		16 καὶ
²her	³carried off by [the] river	¹he might make.		And

ἐβοήθησεν	ἡ	γῆ	τῇ	γυναικί,	καὶ	ἤνοιξεν
³helped	¹the	²earth	the	woman,	and	³opened

ἡ	γῆ	τὸ	στόμα	αὐτῆς	καὶ	κατέπιεν
¹the	²earth	the	mouth	of it	and	swallowed

τὸν	ποταμὸν	ὃν	ἔβαλεν	ὁ	δράκων	ἐκ
the	river	which	³cast	¹the	²dragon	out of

τοῦ	στόματος	αὐτοῦ.		17 καὶ	ὠργίσθη
the	mouth	of him.		And	³was enraged

ὁ	δράκων	ἐπὶ	τῇ	γυναικί,	καὶ	ἀπῆλθεν
¹the	²dragon	over	the	woman,	and	went away

ποιῆσαι	πόλεμον	μετὰ	τῶν	λοιπῶν	τοῦ
to make	war	with	the	rest	of the

σπέρματος	αὐτῆς,	τῶν	τηρούντων	τὰς
seed	of her,	the [ones]	keeping	the

ἐντολὰς	τοῦ	θεοῦ	καὶ	ἐχόντων	τὴν
commandments	–	of God	and	having	the

μαρτυρίαν	Ἰησοῦ·	(18)	καὶ	ἐστάθη	ἐπὶ	τὴν
witness	of Jesus;		and	he stood	on	the

ἄμμον	τῆς	θαλάσσης.
sand	of the	sea.

CHAPTER 13

AND I saw a beast rising out of the sea, with ten horns and seven heads, with ten diadems upon its horns and a blasphemous name upon its heads. ²And the beast that I saw was like a leopard, its feet were like a bear's, and its mouth was like a lion's mouth. And to it the

13 Καὶ	εἶδον	ἐκ	τῆς	θαλάσσης	θηρίον
And	I saw	³out of	⁴the	⁵sea	¹a beast

ἀναβαῖνον,	ἔχον	κέρατα	δέκα	καὶ	κεφαλὰς
²coming up,	having	²horns	¹ten	and	²heads

ἑπτά,	καὶ	ἐπὶ	τῶν	κεράτων	αὐτοῦ	δέκα
¹seven,	and	on	the	horns	of it*	ten

διαδήματα,	καὶ	ἐπὶ	τὰς	κεφαλὰς	αὐτοῦ
diadems,	and	on	the	heads	of it

ὀνόματα	βλασφημίας.		2 καὶ	τὸ	θηρίον
names	of blasphemy.		And	the	beast

ὃ	εἶδον	ἦν	ὅμοιον	παρδάλει,	καὶ	οἱ
which I saw	was	like	to a leopard,	and	the

πόδες	αὐτοῦ	ὡς	ἄρκου,	καὶ	τὸ	στόμα
feet	of it	as	of a bear,	and	the	mouth

αὐτοῦ	ὡς	στόμα	λέοντος.	καὶ	ἔδωκεν
of it	as	[the] mouth	of a lion.	And	³gave

* αὐτοῦ, of course, may be neuter or masculine—" of it " or " of him". δράκων being masculine (=Satan), we have kept to the masculine. But θηρίον is neuter. Yet if it stands for a person, as θηρίον certainly does, it too should be treated, as to the pronoun, as a masculine. However, not to enter the province of interpretation, we have rendered αὐτοῦ by " of it ", though it will be seen that αὐτόν (him) is used in ver. 8. τίς (who?) in ver. 4, and ὅς (who) in ver. 14. See also ch. 17. 11.

^c Other ancient authorities read *And I stood*, connecting the sentence with 13. 1

dragon gave his power and his throne and great authority. ³One of its heads seemed to have a mortal wound, but its mortal wound was healed, and the whole earth followed the beast with wonder. ⁴Men worshiped the dragon, for he had given his authority to the beast, and they worshiped the beast, saying, "Who is like the beast, and who can fight against it?"
5 And the beast was given a mouth uttering haughty and blasphemous words, and it was allowed to exercise authority for forty-two months; ⁶it opened its mouth to utter blasphemies against God, blaspheming his name and his dwelling, that is, those who dwell in heaven ⁷Also it was allowed to make war on the saints and to conquer them.ᵈ And authority was given it over every tribe and people and tongue and nation, ⁸and all who dwell on earth will worship it, every one whose name has not been

αὐτῷ ὁ δράκων τὴν δύναμιν αὐτοῦ καὶ
⁴to it ¹the ²dragon the power of it and
τὸν θρόνον αὐτοῦ καὶ ἐξουσίαν μεγάλην.
the throne of it and ²authority ¹great.
3 καὶ μίαν ἐκ τῶν κεφαλῶν αὐτοῦ ὡς
And one of the heads of it as
ἐσφαγμένην εἰς θάνατον, καὶ ἡ πληγὴ
having been slain to death, and the stroke
τοῦ θανάτου αὐτοῦ ἐθεραπεύθη. καὶ
of the death of it was healed. And
ἐθαυμάσθη ὅλη ἡ γῆ ὀπίσω τοῦ θηρίου,
⁴wondered ¹all ²the ³earth after the beast,
4 καὶ προσεκύνησαν τῷ δράκοντι, ὅτι
and they worshipped the dragon, because
ἔδωκεν τὴν ἐξουσίαν τῷ θηρίῳ, καὶ
he gave the authority to the beast, and
προσεκύνησαν τῷ θηρίῳ λέγοντες· τίς
they worshipped the beast saying: Who
ὅμοιος τῷ θηρίῳ, καὶ τίς δύναται
[is] like to the beast, and who can
πολεμῆσαι μετ᾽ αὐτοῦ; 5 καὶ ἐδόθη αὐτῷ
to make war with it? And was given to it
στόμα λαλοῦν μεγάλα καὶ βλασφημίας,
a mouth speaking great things and blasphemies,
καὶ ἐδόθη αὐτῷ ἐξουσία ποιῆσαι μῆνας
and was given to it authority to act ²months
τεσσεράκοντα [καὶ] δύο. 6 καὶ ἤνοιξεν
¹forty-two. And it opened
τὸ στόμα αὐτοῦ εἰς βλασφημίας πρὸς
the mouth of it in blasphemies against
τὸν θεόν, βλασφημῆσαι τὸ ὄνομα αὐτοῦ
－ God, to blaspheme the name of him
καὶ τὴν σκηνὴν αὐτοῦ, τοὺς ἐν τῷ
and the tabernacle of him, ¹the [ones] ²in －
οὐρανῷ σκηνοῦντας. 7 καὶ ἐδόθη αὐτῷ
⁴heaven ²tabernacling. And it was given to it
ποιῆσαι πόλεμον μετὰ τῶν ἁγίων καὶ
to make war with the saints and
νικῆσαι αὐτούς, καὶ ἐδόθη αὐτῷ ἐξουσία
to overcome them, and ²was given ³to it ¹authority
ἐπὶ πᾶσαν φυλὴν καὶ λαὸν καὶ γλῶσσαν
over every tribe and people and tongue
καὶ ἔθνος. 8 καὶ προσκυνήσουσιν αὐτὸν
and nation. And ⁷will worship ⁸him
πάντες οἱ κατοικοῦντες ἐπὶ τῆς γῆς,
¹all ²the [ones] ³dwelling ⁴on ⁵the ⁶earth,
οὗ οὐ γέγραπται τὸ ὄνομα αὐτοῦ ἐν
⁸of ⁴has not been written ¹the ²name of him in
whom

ᵈ Other ancient authorities omit this sentence

written before the foundation of the world in the book of life of the Lamb that was slain. ⁹ If any one has an ear, let him hear:
¹⁰ If any one is to be taken captive, to captivity he goes; if any one slays with the sword, with the sword must he be slain. Here is a call for the endurance and faith of the saints.

11 Then I saw another beast which rose out of the earth; it had two horns like a lamb and it spoke like a dragon. ¹² It exercises all the authority of the first beast in its presence, and makes the earth and its inhabitants worship the first beast, whose mortal wound was healed. ¹³ It works great signs, even making fire come down from heaven to earth in the sight of men; ¹⁴ and by the signs which it is allowed to work in the presence of the beast, it deceives those who dwell

τῷ βιβλίῳ τῆς ζωῆς τοῦ ἀρνίου τοῦ
the scroll – of life of the Lamb –
ἐσφαγμένου ἀπὸ καταβολῆς κόσμου.
having been slain from [the] foundation of [the] world.
9 Εἴ τις ἔχει οὖς ἀκουσάτω. 10 εἴ
If anyone has an ear let him hear. If
τις εἰς αἰχμαλωσίαν, εἰς αἰχμαλωσίαν
anyone [is] for captivity, to captivity
ὑπάγει· εἴ τις ἐν μαχαίρῃ ἀποκτενεῖ,
he goes; if anyone by a sword will kill,
δεῖ αὐτὸν ἐν μαχαίρῃ ἀποκτανθῆναι.
it behoves him by a sword to be killed.
Ὧδέ ἐστιν ἡ ὑπομονὴ καὶ ἡ πίστις
Here is the endurance and the faith
τῶν ἁγίων.
of the saints.

11 Καὶ εἶδον ἄλλο θηρίον ἀναβαῖνον
And I saw another beast coming up
ἐκ τῆς γῆς, καὶ εἶχεν κέρατα δύο
out of the earth, and it had ²horns ¹two
ὅμοια ἀρνίῳ, καὶ ἐλάλει ὡς δράκων.
like to a lamb, and spoke as a dragon.
12 καὶ τὴν ἐξουσίαν τοῦ πρώτου θηρίου
And ³the ⁴authority ⁵of the ⁶first ⁷beast
πᾶσαν ποιεῖ ἐνώπιον αὐτοῦ. καὶ ποιεῖ
²all ¹it does(exercises) before it. And it makes
τὴν γῆν καὶ τοὺς ἐν αὐτῇ κατοικοῦντας
the earth and ¹the [ones] ²in ⁴it ³dwelling
ἵνα προσκυνήσουσιν τὸ θηρίον τὸ πρῶτον,
in or- they shall worship the ²beast – ¹first,
der that
οὗ ἐθεραπεύθη ἡ πληγὴ τοῦ θανάτου
of which ⁴was healed ¹the ⁵stroke – ²of death
αὐτοῦ. 13 καὶ ποιεῖ σημεῖα μεγάλα,
of it. And it does ²signs ¹great,
ἵνα καὶ πῦρ ποιῇ ἐκ τοῦ οὐρανοῦ
in or- ²even ⁴fire ¹it ³makes ⁶out of – ⁷heaven
der that
καταβαίνειν εἰς τὴν γῆν ἐνώπιον τῶν
⁵to come down onto the earth before the
ἀνθρώπων. 14 καὶ πλανᾷ τοὺς κατοι-
men. And it deceives the [ones] dwell-
κοῦντας ἐπὶ τῆς γῆς διὰ τὰ σημεῖα
ing on the earth because of the signs
ἃ ἐδόθη αὐτῷ ποιῆσαι ἐνώπιον τοῦ
which it was given to it to do before the
θηρίου, λέγων τοῖς κατοικοῦσιν ἐπὶ τῆς
beast, telling to the [ones] dwelling on the

on earth, bidding them make an image for the beast which was wounded by the sword and yet lived; [15] and it was allowed to give breath to the image of the beast so that the image of the beast should even speak, and to cause those who would not worship the image of the beast to be slain. [16] Also it causes all, both small and great, both rich and poor, both free and slave, to be marked on the right hand or the forehead, [17] so that no one can buy or sell unless he has the mark, that is, the name of the beast or the number of its name. [18] This calls for wisdom: let him who has understanding reckon the number of the beast, for it is a human number, its number is six hundred and sixty-six.[ᵉ]

γῆς   ποιῆσαι   εἰκόνα   τῷ   θηρίῳ,   ὃς   ἔχει
earth   to make   an image   to the   beast,   who   has

τὴν   πληγὴν   τῆς   μαχαίρης   καὶ   ἔζησεν.
the   stroke   of the   sword   and lived [again].

15 καὶ   ἐδόθη   αὐτῷ   δοῦναι   πνεῦμα   τῇ
And   it was given   to it   to give   spirit   to the

εἰκόνι   τοῦ   θηρίου,   ἵνα   καὶ   λαλήσῃ   ἡ
image   of the   beast,   in order   ᵉeven   ⁶might   ¹the
that   ⁷speak

εἰκὼν   τοῦ   θηρίου,   καὶ   ποιήσῃ   [ἵνα]
²image   ³of the   ⁴beast,   and   might make   in order
that

ὅσοι   ἐὰν   μὴ   προσκυνήσωσιν   τῇ   εἰκόνι
as many as   might not worship   the   image

τοῦ   θηρίου   ἀποκτανθῶσιν.   16 καὶ   ποιεῖ
of the   beast   should be killed.   And   it makes

πάντας,   τοὺς   μικροὺς   καὶ   τοὺς   μεγάλους,
all men,   the   small   and   the   great,

καὶ   τοὺς   πλουσίους   καὶ   τοὺς   πτωχούς,
both   the   rich   and   the   poor,

καὶ   τοὺς   ἐλευθέρους   καὶ   τοὺς   δούλους,
both   the   free men   and   the   slaves,

ἵνα   δῶσιν   αὐτοῖς   χάραγμα   ἐπὶ   τῆς
in order   they   to them   a mark   on   the
that   should give

χειρὸς   αὐτῶν   τῆς   δεξιᾶς   ἢ   ἐπὶ   τὸ
²hand   ³of them   –   ¹right   or   on   the

μέτωπον   αὐτῶν,   17 [καὶ]   ἵνα   μή   τις
forehead   of them,   and   lest   anyone

δύνηται   ἀγοράσαι   ἢ   πωλῆσαι   εἰ   μὴ
could   to buy   or   to sell   except

ὁ   ἔχων   τὸ   χάραγμα   τὸ   ὄνομα   τοῦ
the   having   the   mark[,]   the   name   of the
[one]

θηρίου   ἢ   τὸν   ἀριθμὸν   τοῦ   ὀνόματος
beast   or   the   number   of the   name

αὐτοῦ.   18 ᵗὨδε   ἡ   σοφία   ἐστίν.   ὁ   ἔχων
of it.   Here   –   ²wisdom   ¹is.   The   having
[one]

νοῦν   ψηφισάτω   τὸν   ἀριθμὸν   τοῦ   θηρίου·
reason   let him count   the   number   of the   beast;

ἀριθμὸς   γὰρ   ἀνθρώπου   ἐστίν.   καὶ   ὁ
for   ²[the] ³number   ⁴of a man   ¹it is.   And   the

ἀριθμὸς   αὐτοῦ   ἑξακόσιοι   ἑξήκοντα   ἕξ.
number   of it   [is]   six hundreds   [and] sixty-six.

CHAPTER 14

THEN I looked, and lo, on Mount Zion stood the Lamb, and with him a hundred and

14 Καὶ   εἶδον,   καὶ   ἰδοὺ   τὸ   ἀρνίον
And   I saw,   and   behold[,]   the   Lamb

ἑστὸς   ἐπὶ   τὸ   ὄρος   Σιών,   καὶ   μετ᾽   αὐτοῦ
standing   on   the   mount   Sion,   and   with   him

forty-four thousand who had his name and his Father's name written on their foreheads. ²And I heard a voice from heaven like the sound of many waters and like the sound of loud thunder; the voice I heard was like the sound of harpers playing on their harps, ³and they sing a new song before the throne and before the four living creatures and before the elders. No one could learn that song except the hundred and forty-four thousand who had been redeemed from the earth. ⁴It is these who have not defiled themselves with women, for they are chaste;ᶠ it is these who follow the Lamb wherever he goes; these have been redeemed from mankind as first fruits for God and the Lamb, ⁵and in their mouth no lie was found, for they are spotless.

6 Then I saw another angel flying in mid-heaven, with an eternal gospel to proclaim to those who dwell on

ᶠ Greek virgins

I.G.E.—33

ἑκατὸν τεσσεράκοντα τέσσαρες χιλιάδες
a hundred [and] forty-four thousands

ἔχουσαι τὸ ὄνομα αὐτοῦ καὶ τὸ ὄνομα
having the name of him and the name

τοῦ πατρὸς αὐτοῦ γεγραμμένον ἐπὶ τῶν
of the Father of him having been written on the

μετώπων αὐτῶν. 2 καὶ ἤκουσα φωνὴν
foreheads of them. And I heard a sound

ἐκ τοῦ οὐρανοῦ ὡς φωνὴν ὑδάτων πολλῶν
out of – heaven as a sound ²waters ¹of many

καὶ ὡς φωνὴν βροντῆς μεγάλης, καὶ
and as a sound ²thunder ¹of great(loud), and

ἡ φωνὴ ἣν ἤκουσα ὡς κιθαρῳδῶν
the sound which I heard [was] as of harpers

κιθαριζόντων ἐν ταῖς κιθάραις αὐτῶν.
harping with the harps of them.

3 καὶ ᾄδουσιν ᾠδὴν καινὴν ἐνώπιον τοῦ
And they sing ²song ¹a new before the

θρόνου καὶ ἐνώπιον τῶν τεσσάρων ζῴων
throne and before the four living creatures

καὶ τῶν πρεσβυτέρων· καὶ οὐδεὶς ἐδύνατο
and the elders; and no man could

μαθεῖν τὴν ᾠδὴν εἰ μὴ αἱ ἑκατὸν
to learn the song except the hundred

τεσσεράκοντα τέσσαρες χιλιάδες, οἱ
[and] forty-four thousands, the

ἠγορασμένοι ἀπὸ τῆς γῆς. 4 οὗτοί εἰσιν
[ones] having been purchased from the earth. These are

οἱ μετὰ γυναικῶν οὐκ ἐμολύνθησαν·
[those] ²with ²women ¹were not defiled;
who

παρθένοι γάρ εἰσιν. οὗτοι οἱ ἀκολουθοῦντες
for ²celibates ¹they are. These the [ones] following
[are]

τῷ ἀρνίῳ ὅπου ἂν ὑπάγῃ. οὗτοι ἠγοράσ-
the Lamb wherever he may go. These were

θησαν ἀπὸ τῶν ἀνθρώπων ἀπαρχὴ τῷ
purchased from – men firstfruit –

θεῷ καὶ τῷ ἀρνίῳ, 5 καὶ ἐν τῷ στόματι
to God and to the Lamb, and in the mouth

αὐτῶν οὐχ εὑρέθη ψεῦδος· ἄμωμοί εἰσιν.
of them was not found a lie; ²unblemished ¹they are.

6 Καὶ εἶδον ἄλλον ἄγγελον πετόμενον
And I saw another angel flying

ἐν μεσουρανήματι, ἔχοντα εὐαγγέλιον
in mid-heaven, having ²gospel

αἰώνιον εὐαγγελίσαι ἐπὶ τοὺς καθημένους
¹an eternal to preach over the [ones] sitting

earth, to every nation and tribe and tongue and people; [7]and he said with a loud voice, "Fear God and give him glory, for the hour of his judgment has come; and worship him who made heaven and earth, the sea and the fountains of water."

8 Another angel, a second, followed, saying, "Fallen, fallen is Babylon the great, she who made all nations drink the wine of her impure passion."

9 And another angel, a third, followed them, saying with a loud voice, "If any one worships the beast and its image, and receives a mark on his forehead or on his hand, [10]he also shall drink the wine of God's wrath, poured unmixed into the cup of his anger, and he shall be tormented with fire and brimstone in the presence of the holy angels and in the presence of the Lamb. [11]And the smoke of their torment goes up for ever and ever; and they have no rest, day or night, these

ἐπὶ	τῆς	γῆς	καὶ	ἐπὶ	πᾶν	ἔθνος	καὶ
on	the	earth	and	over	every	nation	and

φυλὴν	καὶ	γλῶσσαν	καὶ	λαόν,	7	λέγων
tribe	and	tongue	and	people,		saying

ἐν	φωνῇ	μεγάλῃ·	φοβήθητε	τὸν	θεὸν
in	²voice	¹a great(loud):	Fear ye	-	God

καὶ	δότε	αὐτῷ	δόξαν,	ὅτι	ἦλθεν	ἡ	ὥρα
and	give	²to him	¹glory,	because	came	the	hour

τῆς	κρίσεως	αὐτοῦ,	καὶ	προσκυνήσατε
of the	judgment	of him,	and	worship

τῷ	ποιήσαντι	τὸν	οὐρανὸν	καὶ	τὴν	γῆν
the [one] having made	the	heaven	and	the	earth

καὶ	θάλασσαν	καὶ	πηγὰς	ὑδάτων.	8 Καὶ
and	sea	and	fountains	of waters.	And

ἄλλος	ἄγγελος	δεύτερος	ἠκολούθησεν	λέγων·
another	angel	a second	followed	saying:

ἔπεσεν	ἔπεσεν	Βαβυλὼν	ἡ	μεγάλη,	ἡ
Fell[,]	fell	Babylon	the	great,	which

ἐκ	τοῦ	οἴνου	τοῦ	θυμοῦ	τῆς	πορνείας
of	the	wine	of the	anger	of the	fornication

αὐτῆς	πεπότικεν	πάντα	τὰ	ἔθνη.	9 Καὶ
of her	has made to drink	all	the	nations.	And

ἄλλος	ἄγγελος	τρίτος	ἠκολούθησεν	αὐτοῖς
another	angel	a third	followed	them

λέγων	ἐν	φωνῇ	μεγάλῃ·	εἴ	τις	προσκυνεῖ
saying	in	²voice	¹a great(loud):	If	anyone	worships

τὸ	θηρίον	καὶ	τὴν	εἰκόνα	αὐτοῦ,	καὶ
the	beast	and	the	image	of it,	and

λαμβάνει	χάραγμα	ἐπὶ	τοῦ	μετώπου	αὐτοῦ
receives	a mark	on	the	forehead	of him

ἢ	ἐπὶ	τὴν	χεῖρα	αὐτοῦ,	10 καὶ	αὐτὸς
or	on	the	hand	of him,	even	he

πίεται	ἐκ	τοῦ	οἴνου	τοῦ	θυμοῦ	τοῦ
shall drink	of	the	wine	of the	anger	-

θεοῦ	τοῦ	κεκερασμένου	ἀκράτου	ἐν	τῷ
of God	-	having been mixed	undiluted	in	the

ποτηρίῳ	τῆς	ὀργῆς	αὐτοῦ,	καὶ	βασανισθήσε-
cup	of the	wrath	of him,	and	will be torment-

ται	ἐν	πυρὶ	καὶ	θείῳ	ἐνώπιον	ἀγγέλων
ed	by	fire	and	sulphur	before	²angels

ἁγίων	καὶ	ἐνώπιον	τοῦ	ἀρνίου.	11 καὶ
¹holy	and	before	the	Lamb.	And

ὁ	καπνὸς	τοῦ	βασανισμοῦ	αὐτῶν	εἰς
the	smoke	of the	torment	of them	unto

αἰῶνας	αἰώνων	ἀναβαίνει,	καὶ	οὐκ	ἔχουσιν
ages	of ages	goes up,	and	they have not

ἀνάπαυσιν	ἡμέρας	καὶ	νυκτὸς	οἱ	προσκυ-
rest	day	and	night	the [ones]	wor-

worshipers of the beast and its image, and whoever receives the mark of its name."

12 Here is a call for the endurance of the saints, those who keep the commandments of God and the faith of Jesus.

13 And I heard a voice from heaven saying, "Write this: Blessed are the dead who die in the Lord henceforth." "Blessed indeed," says the Spirit, "that they may rest from their labors, for their deeds follow them!"

14 Then I looked, and lo, a white cloud, and seated on the cloud one like a son of man, with a golden crown on his head, and a sharp sickle in his hand. [15]And another angel came out of the temple, calling with a loud voice to him who sat upon the cloud, "Put in your sickle, and reap, for the hour to reap has come, for the harvest of the earth is fully ripe." [16]So he who sat upon the cloud swung his sickle

| νοῦντες | τὸ | θηρίον | καὶ | τὴν | εἰκόνα | αὐτοῦ, |
| shipping | the | beast | and | the | image | of it, |

| καὶ | εἴ | τις | λαμβάνει | τὸ | χάραγμα | τοῦ |
| and | if | anyone | receives | the | mark | of the |

| ὀνόματος | αὐτοῦ. | 12 | ῀Ωδε | ἡ | ὑπομονὴ |
| name | of it. | | [1]Here | [3]the | [4]endurance |

| τῶν | ἁγίων | ἐστίν, | οἱ | τηροῦντες | τὰς |
| [5]of the | [6]saints | [2]is, | the [ones] | keeping | the |

| ἐντολὰς | τοῦ | θεοῦ | καὶ | τὴν | πίστιν | ᾿Ιησοῦ. |
| command-ments | - | of God | and | the | faith | of Jesus. |

13 | Καὶ | ἤκουσα | φωνῆς | ἐκ | τοῦ | οὐρανοῦ
| And | I heard | a voice | out of | - | heaven

| λεγούσης· | γράψον· | μακάριοι | οἱ | νεκροὶ |
| saying: | Write thou: | Blessed [are] | the | dead |

| οἱ | ἐν | κυρίῳ | ἀποθνῄσκοντες | ἀπ᾿ | ἄρτι. |
| [1]the [ones] | [2]in | [4][the] Lord | [3]dying | from | now. |

| ναί, | λέγει | τὸ | πνεῦμα, | ἵνα | ἀναπαήσονται |
| Yes, | says | the | Spirit, | in order that | they shall rest |

| ἐκ | τῶν | κόπων | αὐτῶν· | τὰ | γὰρ | ἔργα |
| from | the | labours | of them; | for the | | work- |

| αὐτῶν | ἀκολουθεῖ | μετ᾿ | αὐτῶν. |
| of them | follows | with | them. |

14 | Καὶ | εἶδον, | καὶ | ἰδοὺ | νεφέλη | λευκή, |
| And | I saw, | and | behold[,] | [2]cloud | [1]a white, |

| καὶ | ἐπὶ | τὴν | νεφέλην | καθήμενον | ὅμοιον |
| and | on | the | cloud | [one] sitting | like |

| υἱὸν | ἀνθρώπου, | ἔχων | ἐπὶ | τῆς | κεφαλῆς |
| a son | of man,[*] | having | on | the | head |

| αὐτοῦ | στέφανον | χρυσοῦν | καὶ | ἐν | τῇ | χειρὶ |
| of him | crown | a golden | and | in | the | hand |

| αὐτοῦ | δρέπανον | ὀξύ. | 15 | καὶ | ἄλλος | ἄγγελος |
| of him | sickle | a sharp. | | And | another | angel |

| ἐξῆλθεν | ἐκ | τοῦ | ναοῦ, | κράζων | ἐν | φωνῇ |
| went forth | out of | the | shrine, | crying | in | [2]voice |

| μεγάλη | τῷ | καθημένῳ | ἐπὶ | τῆς | νεφέλης· |
| [1]a great (loud) | to the [one] | sitting | on | the | cloud: |

| πέμψον | τὸ | δρέπανόν | σου | καὶ | θέρισον, |
| Send(Thrust) | the | sickle | of thee | and | reap thou, |

| ὅτι | ἦλθεν | ἡ | ὥρα | θερίσαι, | ὅτι | ἐξηράνθη |
| because | came | the | hour | to reap, | because | was dried |

| ὁ | θερισμὸς | τῆς | γῆς. | 16 | καὶ | ἔβαλεν |
| the | harvest | of the | earth. | | And | [4]thrust |

| ὁ | καθήμενος | ἐπὶ | τῆς | νεφέλης | τὸ | δρέπανον |
| [1]the [one] | [2]sitting | [3]on | [4]the | [5]cloud | the | sickle |

* See also ch. 1. 13 and John 5. 27.

on the earth, and the earth was reaped.

17 And another angel came out of the temple in heaven, and he too had a sharp sickle. [18]Then another angel came out from the altar, the angel who has power over fire, and he called with a loud voice to him who had the sharp sickle, "Put in your sickle, and gather the clusters of the vine of the earth, for its grapes are ripe." [19]So the angel swung his sickle on the earth and gathered the vintage of the earth, and threw it into the great wine press of the wrath of God; [20]and the wine press was trodden outside the city, and blood flowed from the wine press, as high as a horse's bridle, for one thousand six hundred stadia.[g]

CHAPTER 15

THEN I saw another portent in heaven, great and wonderful, seven angels with seven plagues, which are the last, for with them the wrath of God is ended.

2 And I saw what appeared to be a sea of glass mingled with fire.

[g] About two hundred miles

αὐτοῦ ἐπὶ τὴν γῆν, καὶ ἐθερίσθη ἡ
of him over the earth, and [3]was reaped [1]the

γῆ. 17 Καὶ ἄλλος ἄγγελος ἐξῆλθεν ἐκ
[2]earth. And another angel went forth out of

τοῦ ναοῦ τοῦ ἐν τῷ οὐρανῷ, ἔχων καὶ
the shrine – in – heaven, [3]having [2]also

αὐτὸς δρέπανον ὀξύ. 18 καὶ ἄλλος ἄγγελος
[1]he [5]sickle [4]a sharp. And another angel

ἐξῆλθεν ἐκ τοῦ θυσιαστηρίου, [ὁ] ἔχων
went forth out of the altar, the [one] having

ἐξουσίαν ἐπὶ τοῦ πυρός, καὶ ἐφώνησεν
authority over the fire, and he spoke

φωνῇ μεγάλῃ τῷ ἔχοντι τὸ δρέπανον
[2]voice [1]in a great to the having the [2]sickle
(loud) [one]

τὸ ὀξὺ λέγων· πέμψον σου τὸ δρέπανον
– [1]sharp saying: Send(Thrust) [4]of thee [1]the [3]sickle

τὸ ὀξὺ καὶ τρύγησον τοὺς βότρυας τῆς
– [2]sharp and gather the clusters of the

ἀμπέλου τῆς γῆς, ὅτι ἤκμασαν αἱ
vine of the earth, because [4]ripened [1]the

σταφυλαὶ αὐτῆς. 19 καὶ ἔβαλεν ὁ ἄγγελος
[2]grapes [3]of it. And [3]thrust [1]the [2]angel

τὸ δρέπανον αὐτοῦ εἰς τὴν γῆν, καὶ
the sickle of him into the earth, and

ἐτρύγησεν τὴν ἄμπελον τῆς γῆς καὶ
gathered the vine of the earth and

ἔβαλεν εἰς τὴν ληνὸν τοῦ θυμοῦ τοῦ
cast into the [2]winepress [3]of the [4]anger –

θεοῦ τὸν μέγαν. 20 καὶ ἐπατήθη ἡ
[5]of God – [1]great. And [3]was trodden [1]the

ληνὸς ἔξωθεν τῆς πόλεως, καὶ ἐξῆλθεν
[2]winepress outside the city, and [2]went out

αἷμα ἐκ τῆς ληνοῦ ἄχρι τῶν χαλινῶν
[1]blood out of the winepress as far as the bridles

τῶν ἵππων, ἀπὸ σταδίων χιλίων ἑξακοσίων.
of the horses, from [3]furlongs [1]a thousand [2]six hundred.

15 Καὶ εἶδον ἄλλο σημεῖον ἐν τῷ
And I saw another sign in –

οὐρανῷ μέγα καὶ θαυμαστόν, ἀγγέλους
heaven[,] great and wonderful, [2]angels

ἑπτὰ ἔχοντας πληγὰς ἑπτὰ τὰς ἐσχάτας,
[1]seven having [2]plagues [1]seven the last,

ὅτι ἐν αὐταῖς ἐτελέσθη ὁ θυμὸς τοῦ
because in them [4]was finished [1]the [2]anger –

θεοῦ. 2 Καὶ εἶδον ὡς θάλασσαν ὑαλίνην
[3]of God. And I saw as [2]sea [1]a glassy

and those who had conquered the beast and its image and the number of its name, standing beside the sea of glass with harps of God in their hands. ³And they sing the song of Moses, the servant of God, and the song of the Lamb, saying,
"Great and wonderful are thy deeds,
O Lord God the Almighty!
Just and true are thy ways,
O King of the ages!ʰ
⁴Who shall not fear and glorify thy name, O Lord?
For thou alone art holy.
All nations shall come and worship thee,
for thy judgments have been revealed."
5 After this I looked, and the temple of the tent of witness in heaven was opened, ⁶and out of the temple came the seven angels with the seven plagues, robed in pure bright linen, and their breasts girded with golden girdles. ⁷And one of the four living creatures gave the seven angels seven golden

μεμιγμένην   πυρί,   καὶ   τοὺς   νικῶντας
having been mixed with fire,   and   the [ones]   overcoming

ἐκ   τοῦ   θηρίου   καὶ   ἐκ   τῆς   εἰκόνος   αὐτοῦ
of   the   beast   and   of   the   image   of it

καὶ   ἐκ   τοῦ   ἀριθμοῦ   τοῦ   ὀνόματος   αὐτοῦ
and   of   the   number   of the   name   of it

ἐστῶτας   ἐπὶ   τὴν   θάλασσαν   τὴν   ὑαλίνην,
standing   on   the   ²sea   -   ¹glassy,

ἔχοντας   κιθάρας   τοῦ   θεοῦ.   3 καὶ   ᾄδουσιν
having   harps   -   of God.   And   they sing

τὴν   ᾠδὴν   Μωϋσέως   τοῦ   δούλου   τοῦ
the   song   of Moses   the   slave   -

θεοῦ   καὶ   τὴν   ᾠδὴν   τοῦ   ἀρνίου,   λέγοντες·
of God   and   the   song   of the   Lamb,   saying:

μεγάλα   καὶ   θαυμαστὰ   τὰ   ἔργα   σου,
Great   and   wonderful   the   works   of thee,

κύριε   ὁ   θεὸς   ὁ   παντοκράτωρ·   δίκαιαι
[O] Lord   -   God   the   Almighty;   righteous

καὶ   ἀληθιναὶ   αἱ   ὁδοί   σου,   ὁ   βασιλεὺς
and   true   the   ways   of thee,   the   king

τῶν   ἐθνῶν·   4 τίς   οὐ   μὴ   φοβηθῇ,   κύριε,
of the   nations;   who   will not fear,   [O] Lord,

καὶ   δοξάσει   τὸ   ὄνομά   σου;   ὅτι   μόνος
and   will glorify   the   name   of thee? because   [thou] only

ὅσιος,   ὅτι   πάντα   τὰ   ἔθνη   ἥξουσιν   καὶ
[art] holy, because   all   the   nations   will come   and

προσκυνήσουσιν   ἐνώπιόν   σου,   ὅτι   τὰ
will worship   before   thee,   because   the

δικαιώματά   σου   ἐφανερώθησαν.   5 Καὶ
ordinances   of thee   were made manifest.   And

μετὰ   ταῦτα   εἶδον,   καὶ   ἠνοίγη   ὁ   ναὸς
after   these things   I saw,   and   was opened the   shrine

τῆς   σκηνῆς   τοῦ   μαρτυρίου   ἐν   τῷ   οὐρανῷ,
of the tabernacle   of the   testimony   in   -   heaven,

6 καὶ   ἐξῆλθον   οἱ   ἑπτὰ   ἄγγελοι   οἱ   ἔχοντες
and   ⁹came forth   ¹the   ²seven   ³angels   -   ⁴having

τὰς   ἑπτὰ   πληγὰς   ἐκ   τοῦ   ναοῦ,   ἐνδεδυμένοι
⁵the   ⁶seven   ⁷plagues out of the   shrine,   having been clothed [in]

λίνον   καθαρὸν   λαμπρὸν   καὶ   περιεζωσμένοι
³linen   ¹clean   ²bright   and   having been girdled

περὶ   τὰ   στήθη   ζώνας   χρυσᾶς.   7 καὶ
round   the   breasts [with]   ²girdles   ¹golden.   And

ἓν   ἐκ   τῶν   τεσσάρων   ζώων   ἔδωκεν   τοῖς
one   of   the   four   living creatures   gave   to the

ἑπτὰ   ἀγγέλοις   ἑπτὰ   φιάλας   χρυσᾶς
seven   angels   seven   ⁹bowls   ¹golden

ʰ Other ancient authorities read the nations

bowls full of the wrath of God who lives for ever and ever; ⁸and the temple was filled with smoke from the glory of God and from his power, and no one could enter the temple until the seven plagues of the seven angels were ended.

CHAPTER 16

THEN I heard a loud voice from the temple telling the seven angels, "Go and pour out on the earth the seven bowls of the wrath of God."

2 So the first angel went and poured his bowl on the earth, and foul and evil sores came upon the men who bore the mark of the beast and worshiped its image.

3 The second angel poured his bowl into the sea, and it became like the blood of a dead man, and every living thing died that was in the sea.

4 The third angel poured his bowl into the rivers and the fountains of water, and they became blood. ⁵And I heard the angel of water say,

---

γεμούσας τοῦ θυμοῦ τοῦ θεοῦ τοῦ ζῶντος
being filled of(with) anger   of   living
    the   God

εἰς τοὺς αἰῶνας τῶν αἰώνων. 8 καὶ
unto the ages of the ages.   And

ἐγεμίσθη ὁ ναὸς καπνοῦ ἐκ τῆς δόξης
was filled the shrine of(with) smoke of(with) the glory

τοῦ θεοῦ καὶ ἐκ τῆς δυνάμεως αὐτοῦ,
— of God and of the power of him,

καὶ οὐδεὶς ἐδύνατο εἰσελθεῖν εἰς τὸν
and no one could to enter into the

ναὸν ἄχρι τελεσθῶσιν αἱ ἑπτὰ πληγαὶ
shrine until should be finished the seven plagues

τῶν ἑπτὰ ἀγγέλων. 16 Καὶ ἤκουσα
of the seven angels. And I heard

μεγάλης φωνῆς ἐκ τοῦ ναοῦ λεγούσης τοῖς
a great(loud) voice out of the shrine saying to the

ἑπτὰ ἀγγέλοις· ὑπάγετε καὶ ἐκχέετε τὰς ἑπτὰ
seven angels: Go ye and pour out the seven

φιάλας τοῦ θυμοῦ τοῦ θεοῦ εἰς τὴν γῆν.
bowls of the anger — of God onto the earth.

2 Καὶ ἀπῆλθεν ὁ πρῶτος καὶ ἐξέχεεν τὴν
And ²went away ¹the ²first and poured out the

φιάλην αὐτοῦ εἰς τὴν γῆν· καὶ ἐγένετο
bowl of him onto the earth; and ⁵came

ἕλκος κακὸν καὶ πονηρὸν ἐπὶ τοὺς ἀνθρώπους
⁴sore ¹a bad ²and ³evil on the men

τοὺς ἔχοντας τὸ χάραγμα τοῦ θηρίου καὶ
- having the mark of the beast and

τοὺς προσκυνοῦντας τῇ εἰκόνι αὐτοῦ. 3 Καὶ
- worshipping the image of it. And

ὁ δεύτερος ἐξέχεεν τὴν φιάλην αὐτοῦ
the second poured out the bowl of him

εἰς τὴν θάλασσαν· καὶ ἐγένετο αἷμα
onto the sea; and it became blood

ὡς νεκροῦ, καὶ πᾶσα ψυχὴ ζωῆς ἀπέθανεν,
as of a dead and every soul of life died,
man,

τὰ ἐν τῇ θαλάσσῃ. 4 Καὶ ὁ τρίτος
the in the sea. And the third
things

ἐξέχεεν τὴν φιάλην αὐτοῦ εἰς τοὺς
poured out the bowl of him onto the

ποταμοὺς καὶ τὰς πηγὰς τῶν ὑδάτων·
rivers and the fountains of the waters;

καὶ ἐγένετο αἷμα. 5 Καὶ ἤκουσα τοῦ
and it became blood. And I heard the

ἀγγέλου τῶν ὑδάτων λέγοντος· δίκαιος
angel of the waters saying: Righteous

"Just art thou in these thy judgments, thou who art and wast, O Holy One.
⁶ For men have shed the blood of saints and prophets, and thou hast given them blood to drink. It is their due!"
⁷And I heard the altar cry,
"Yea, Lord God the Almighty, true and just are thy judgments!"
8 The fourth angel poured his bowl on the sun, and it was allowed to scorch men with fire; ⁹men were scorched by the fierce heat, and they cursed the name of God who had power over these plagues, and they did not repent and give him glory.
10 The fifth angel poured his bowl on the throne of the beast, and its kingdom was in darkness; men gnawed their tongues in anguish ¹¹and cursed the God of heaven for their pain and sores, and did not repent of their deeds.
12 The sixth angel poured his bowl on the great river Euphra'tes,

εἶ, ὁ ὢν καὶ ὁ ἦν, ὁ ὅσιος, ὅτι
art the being and the was, the holy because
thou, [one]   [one who]   [one],
=the one who is

ταῦτα ἔκρινας, 6 ὅτι αἷμα ἁγίων
²these ¹thou judgedst, because ²[the] blood ³of saints
things

καὶ προφητῶν ἐξέχεαν, καὶ αἷμα αὐτοῖς
⁴and ⁵of prophets ¹they shed, and blood to them

δέδωκας πεῖν· ἄξιοί εἰσιν. 7 Καὶ ἤκουσα
thou hast to drink; ²worthy ¹they are. And I heard
given

τοῦ θυσιαστηρίου λέγοντος· ναί, κύριε
the altar saying: Yes, [O] Lord

ὁ θεὸς ὁ παντοκράτωρ, ἀληθιναὶ καὶ
- God the Almighty, true and

δίκαιαι αἱ κρίσεις σου. 8 Καὶ ὁ τέταρτος
righteous the judgments of thee. And the fourth

ἐξέχεεν τὴν φιάλην αὐτοῦ ἐπὶ τὸν ἥλιον·
poured out the bowl of him onto the sun;

καὶ ἐδόθη αὐτῷ καυματίσαι τοὺς
and it was given to him to burn -

ἀνθρώπους ἐν πυρί. 9 καὶ ἐκαυματίσθησαν
men with fire. And ²were burnt [with]

οἱ ἄνθρωποι καῦμα μέγα, καὶ ἐβλασ-
- ¹men ⁴heat ³great, and they blas-

φήμησαν τὸ ὄνομα τοῦ θεοῦ τοῦ ἔχοντος
phemed the name - of God the [one] having

τὴν ἐξουσίαν ἐπὶ τὰς πληγὰς ταύτας,
the authority over these plagues,

καὶ οὐ μετενόησαν δοῦναι αὐτῷ δόξαν.
and they repented not to give ²to him ¹glory.

10 Καὶ ὁ πέμπτος ἐξέχεεν τὴν φιάλην
And the fifth poured out the bowl

αὐτοῦ ἐπὶ τὸν θρόνον τοῦ θηρίου· καὶ
of him onto the throne of the beast; and

ἐγένετο ἡ βασιλεία αὐτοῦ ἐσκοτωμένη,
⁴became ¹the ²kingdom ³of it having been darkened,

καὶ ἐμασῶντο τὰς γλώσσας αὐτῶν ἐκ
and they(men) gnawed the tongues of them from

τοῦ πόνου, 11 καὶ ἐβλασφήμησαν τὸν θεὸν
the pain, and they blasphemed the God

τοῦ οὐρανοῦ ἐκ τῶν πόνων αὐτῶν καὶ
- of heaven from the pains of them and

ἐκ τῶν ἑλκῶν αὐτῶν, καὶ οὐ μετενόησαν
from the sores of them, and they repented not

ἐκ τῶν ἔργων αὐτῶν. 12 Καὶ ὁ ἕκτος
of the works of them. And the sixth

ἐξέχεεν τὴν φιάλην αὐτοῦ ἐπὶ τὸν ποταμὸν
poured out the bowl of him onto the ²river

and its water was dried up, to prepare the way for the kings from the east. [13]And I saw, issuing from the mouth of the dragon and from the mouth of the beast and from the mouth of the false prophet, three foul spirits like frogs; [14]for they are demonic spirits, performing signs, who go abroad to the kings of the whole world, to assemble them for battle on the great day of God the Almighty. [15]("Lo, I am coming like a thief! Blessed is he who is awake, keeping his garments that he may not go naked and be seen exposed!") [16]And they assembled them at the place which is called in Hebrew Armaged'don.

17 The seventh angel poured his bowl into the air, and a great voice came out of the temple, from the throne, saying, "It is done!" [18]And there were flashes of lightning, loud noises, peals of thunder, and a great earthquake such as had

τὸν	μέγαν	Εὐφράτην·	καὶ	ἐξηράνθη	τὸ
-	[1]great	Euphrates;	and	[4]was dried	[1]the

ὕδωρ	αὐτοῦ,	ἵνα	ἑτοιμασθῇ	ἡ	ὁδὸς	τῶν
[2]water	[3]of it,	in order that	[5]might be prepared	[1]the	[2]way	[3]of the

βασιλέων	τῶν	ἀπὸ	ἀνατολῆς	ἡλίου.	13 Καὶ
[4]kings	-	[5]from	[6][the] rising	[7]of [the] sun.	And

εἶδον	ἐκ	τοῦ	στόματος	τοῦ	δράκοντος
I saw	out of	the	mouth	of the	dragon

καὶ	ἐκ	τοῦ	στόματος	τοῦ	θηρίου	καὶ
and	out of	the	mouth	of the	beast	and

ἐκ	τοῦ	στόματος	τοῦ	ψευδοπροφήτου
out of	the	mouth	of the	false prophet

πνεύματα	τρία	ἀκάθαρτα	ὡς	βάτραχοι·
[2]spirits	[1]three	[3]unclean [coming] as		frogs;

14 εἰσὶν	γὰρ	πνεύματα	δαιμονίων	ποιοῦντα
for they are		spirits	of demons	doing

σημεῖα,	ἃ	ἐκπορεύεται	ἐπὶ	τοὺς	βασιλεῖς
signs,	which	goes forth	unto	the	kings

τῆς	οἰκουμένης	ὅλης,	συναγαγεῖν	αὐτοὺς
of the	[2]inhabited [earth]	[1]whole,	to assemble	them

εἰς	τὸν	πόλεμον	τῆς	ἡμέρας	τῆς	μεγάλης
to	the	war	of the	[2]day	-	[1]great

τοῦ	θεοῦ	τοῦ	παντοκράτορος.	15 Ἰδοὺ
-	of God	of the	Almighty.	Behold

ἔρχομαι	ὡς	κλέπτης·	μακάριος	ὁ	γρηγορῶν
I am coming as		a thief:	blessed [is]	the [one] watching

καὶ	τηρῶν	τὰ	ἱμάτια	αὐτοῦ,	ἵνα	μὴ
and	keeping	the	garments	of him,		lest

γυμνὸς	περιπατῇ	καὶ	βλέπωσιν	τὴν
naked	he walk	and	they(men) see	the

ἀσχημοσύνην	αὐτοῦ.	16 Καὶ	συνήγαγεν
shame	of him.	And [t]he[y] assembled

αὐτοὺς	εἰς	τὸν	τόπον	τὸν	καλούμενον
them	in	the	place	-	being called

Ἑβραϊστὶ	Ἁρμαγεδών.	17 Καὶ	ὁ	ἕβδομος
in Hebrew	Harmagedon.	And	the	seventh

ἐξέχεεν	τὴν	φιάλην	αὐτοῦ	ἐπὶ	τὸν	ἀέρα·
poured out	the	bowl	of him	on	the	air;

καὶ	ἐξῆλθεν	φωνὴ	μεγάλη	ἐκ	τοῦ	ναοῦ
and	[2]came out	[3]voice	[1]a great(loud)	out of	the	shrine

ἀπὸ	τοῦ	θρόνου	λέγουσα·	γέγονεν.	18 καὶ
from	the	throne	saying:	It has occurred.	And

ἐγένοντο	ἀστραπαὶ	καὶ	φωναὶ	καὶ	βρονταί,
there were	lightnings	and	voices	and	thunders,

καὶ	σεισμὸς	ἐγένετο	μέγας,	οἷος	οὐκ
and	[2]earthquake	[3]occurred	[1]a great,	such as	not

never been since men
were on the earth, so
great was that earth-
quake. ¹⁹The great city
was split into three parts,
and the cities of the
nations fell, and God
remembered great Baby-
lon, to make her drain
the cup of the fury of his
wrath. ²⁰And every island
fled away, and no
mountains were to be
found; ²¹and great hail-
stones, heavy as a
hundredweight, dropped
on men from heaven, till
men cursed God for the
plague of the hail, so
fearful was that plague.

ἐγένετο   ἀφ'   οὗ   ἄνθρωπος   ἐγένετο   ἐπὶ
did occur   from   when†   man   was   on

τῆς   γῆς,   τηλικοῦτος   σεισμὸς   οὕτω   μέγας.
the   earth,   such   an earthquake   so   great.

19 καὶ   ἐγένετο   ἡ   πόλις   ἡ   μεγάλη   εἰς
And   ⁴became   ¹the   ³city   –   ²great   into

τρία   μέρη,   καὶ   αἱ   πόλεις   τῶν   ἐθνῶν
three   parts,   and   the   cities   of the   nations

ἔπεσαν.   καὶ   Βαβυλὼν   ἡ   μεγάλη   ἐμνήσθη
fell.   And   Babylon   the   great   was
    remembered

ἐνώπιον   τοῦ   θεοῦ   δοῦναι   αὐτῇ   τὸ   ποτήριον
before   –   God   to give   to her/it*   the   cup

τοῦ   οἴνου   τοῦ   θυμοῦ   τῆς   ὀργῆς   αὐτοῦ.
of the   wine   of the   anger   of the   wrath   of him.

20 καὶ   πᾶσα   νῆσος   ἔφυγεν,   καὶ   ὄρη
And   every   island   fled,   and mountains

οὐχ   εὑρέθησαν.   21 καὶ   χάλαζα   μεγάλη
were not found.   And   ²hail   ¹a great

ὡς   ταλαντιαία   καταβαίνει   ἐκ   τοῦ   οὐρανοῦ
as   a talent in size   comes down   out of   –   heaven

ἐπὶ   τοὺς   ἀνθρώπους·   καὶ   ἐβλασφήμησαν
on   –   men;   and   ²blasphemed

οἱ   ἄνθρωποι   τὸν   θεὸν   ἐκ   τῆς   πληγῆς
–   ¹men   –   God   from   the   plague

τῆς   χαλάζης,   ὅτι   μεγάλη   ἐστὶν   ἡ   πληγὴ
of the   hail,   because   ⁶great   ⁴is   ¹the   ²plague

αὐτῆς   σφόδρα.
³of it   ⁵exceeding.

CHAPTER 17

THEN one of the
seven angels who
had the seven bowls came
and said to me, "Come,
I will show you the
judgment of the great
harlot who is seated upon
many waters, ²with
whom the kings of the
earth have committed
fornication, and with the
wine of whose fornica-
tion the dwellers on
earth have become
drunk." ³And he carried

17 Καὶ   ἦλθεν   εἷς   ἐκ   τῶν   ἑπτὰ   ἀγγέλων
And   came   one   of   the   seven   angels

τῶν   ἐχόντων   τὰς   ἑπτὰ   φιάλας,   καὶ
–   having   the   seven   bowls,   and

ἐλάλησεν   μετ'   ἐμοῦ   λέγων·   δεῦρο,   δείξω
spoke   with   me   saying: Come,   I will show

σοι   τὸ   κρίμα   τῆς   πόρνης   τῆς   μεγάλης
thee   the   judgment   of the   ²harlot   –   ¹great

τῆς   καθημένης   ἐπὶ   ὑδάτων   πολλῶν,   2 μεθ'
–   sitting   on   ²waters   ¹many,   with

ἧς   ἐπόρνευσαν   οἱ   βασιλεῖς   τῆς   γῆς,
whom   ⁵practised   ¹the   ²kings   ³of the   ⁴earth,
  fornication

καὶ   ἐμεθύσθησαν   οἱ   κατοικοῦντες   τὴν   γῆν
and   ⁵became drunk   ¹the   ²dwelling [on]   ³the   ⁴earth
  [ones]

ἐκ   τοῦ   οἴνου   τῆς   πορνείας   αὐτῆς.   3 καὶ
from   the   wine   of the   fornication   of her.   And

* Even in English a city is often personified as feminine.

me away in the Spirit into a wilderness, and I saw a woman sitting on a scarlet beast which was full of blasphemous names, and it had seven heads and ten horns. ⁴The woman was arrayed in purple and scarlet, and bedecked with gold and jewels and pearls, holding in her hand a golden cup full of abominations and the impurities of her fornication; ⁵and on her forehead was written a name of mystery: "Babylon the great, mother of harlots and of earth's abominations." ⁶And I saw the woman, drunk with the blood of the saints and the blood of the martyrs of Jesus. When I saw her I marveled greatly. ⁷But the angel said to me, "Why marvel? I will tell you the mystery of the woman, and of the beast with seven heads and ten horns that carries her. ⁸The beast that you saw was, and is not, and is to

ἀπήνεγκέν με εἰς ἔρημον ἐν πνεύματι.
he carried away me into a desert in spirit.

καὶ εἶδον γυναῖκα καθημένην ἐπὶ θηρίον
And I saw a woman sitting on ²beast

κόκκινον, γέμοντα ὀνόματα βλασφημίας,
¹a scarlet, being filled [with] names of blasphemy,

ἔχοντα κεφαλὰς ἑπτὰ καὶ κέρατα δέκα.
having ²heads ¹seven and ²horns ¹ten.

4 καὶ ἡ γυνὴ ἦν περιβεβλημένη πορφυροῦν
And the woman was having been clothed [in] purple

καὶ κόκκινον, καὶ κεχρυσωμένη χρυσίῳ
and scarlet, and having been gilded with gold

καὶ λίθῳ τιμίῳ καὶ μαργαρίταις, ἔχουσα
and ²stone ¹precious and pearls, having

ποτήριον χρυσοῦν ἐν τῇ χειρὶ αὐτῆς
²cup ¹a golden in the hand of her

γέμον βδελυγμάτων καὶ τὰ ἀκάθαρτα
being filled of (with) and the unclean things
abominations

τῆς πορνείας αὐτῆς, 5 καὶ ἐπὶ τὸ
of the fornication of her, and on the

μέτωπον αὐτῆς ὄνομα γεγραμμένον,
forehead of her a name having been written,

μυστήριον, ΒΑΒΥΛΩΝ Η ΜΕΓΑΛΗ,
a mystery, BABYLON THE GREAT,

Η ΜΗΤΗΡ ΤΩΝ ΠΟΡΝΩΝ ΚΑΙ
The Mother of the Harlots and

ΤΩΝ ΒΔΕΛΥΓΜΑΤΩΝ ΤΗΣ ΓΗΣ.
of the Abominations of the Earth.

6 καὶ εἶδον τὴν γυναῖκα μεθύουσαν ἐκ
And I saw the woman being drunk from

τοῦ αἵματος τῶν ἁγίων καὶ ἐκ τοῦ
the blood of the saints and from the

αἵματος τῶν μαρτύρων Ἰησοῦ. Καὶ
blood of the witnesses of Jesus. And

ἐθαύμασα ἰδὼν αὐτὴν θαῦμα μέγα. 7 καὶ
²I wondered ¹seeing ³her ⁴[with] ⁶wonder ⁵a great. And

εἶπέν μοι ὁ ἄγγελος· διὰ τί ἐθαύμασας;
²said ⁴to me ¹the ³angel: Why didst thou wonder?

ἐγὼ ἐρῶ σοι τὸ μυστήριον τῆς γυναικὸς
I will tell thee the mystery of the woman

καὶ τοῦ θηρίου τοῦ βαστάζοντος αὐτὴν
and of the beast – carrying her

τοῦ ἔχοντος τὰς ἑπτὰ κεφαλὰς καὶ τὰ
– having the seven heads and the

δέκα κέρατα. 8 Τὸ θηρίον ὃ εἶδες ἦν
ten horns. The beast which thou wa⁰
sawest

ascend from the bottomless pit and go to perdition; and the dwellers on earth whose names have not been written in the book of life from the foundation of the world, will marvel to behold the beast, because it was and is not and is to come. ⁹This calls for a mind with wisdom: the seven heads are seven hills on which the woman is seated; ¹⁰they are also seven kings, five of whom have fallen, one is, the other has not yet come, and when he comes he must remain only a little while. ¹¹As for the beast that was and is not, it is an eighth but it belongs to the seven, and it goes to perdition. ¹²And the ten horns that you saw are ten kings who have not yet received royal power, but they are to receive authority as kings for one hour, together with the beast. ¹³These are of one mind and give over their power and authority to the beast; ¹⁴they will make war on the Lamb, and the Lamb

καὶ   οὐκ   ἔστιν,   καὶ   μέλλει   ἀναβαίνειν
and   is not,   and   is about   to come up

ἐκ   τῆς   ἀβύσσου   καὶ   εἰς   ἀπώλειαν   ὑπάγει·
out of the   abyss   and   ²to   ³destruction   ¹goes;

καὶ   θαυμασθήσονται   οἱ   κατοικοῦντες   ἐπὶ
and   ⁶will wonder   ¹the [ones]   ²dwelling   ⁵on

τῆς   γῆς,   ὧν   οὐ   γέγραπται   τὸ   ὄνομα
⁴the   ⁵earth,   of whom   ³has not been written   ¹the   ²name

ἐπὶ   τὸ   βιβλίον   τῆς   ζωῆς   ἀπὸ   καταβολῆς
on   the   scroll   –   of life   from [the] foundation

κόσμου,   βλεπόντων   τὸ   θηρίον   ὅτι   ἦν
of [the] world,   seeing   the   beast   that it was

καὶ   οὐκ   ἔστιν   καὶ   παρέσται.   9 ὧδε
and   is not   and   is present.   Here [is]

ὁ   νοῦς   ὁ   ἔχων   σοφίαν.   αἱ   ἑπτὰ
the   mind   –   having   wisdom.   The   seven

κεφαλαὶ   ἑπτὰ   ὄρη   εἰσίν,   ὅπου   ἡ   γυνὴ
heads   ²seven   ³mountains   ¹are,   where   the   woman

κάθηται   ἐπ'   αὐτῶν,   καὶ   βασιλεῖς   ἑπτά
sits   on   them,   and   ²kings   ¹seven

εἰσιν·   10 οἱ   πέντε   ἔπεσαν,   ὁ   εἷς   ἔστιν,
¹are: the   five   fell,   the   one   is,

ὁ   ἄλλος   οὔπω   ἦλθεν,   καὶ   ὅταν   ἔλθῃ
the   other   not yet   came,   and   whenever he comes

ὀλίγον   αὐτὸν   δεῖ   μεῖναι.   11 καὶ   τὸ
²a little   ³him   ¹it behoves   ²to   And   the
[while]   remain.

θηρίον   ὃ   ἦν   καὶ   οὐκ   ἔστιν,   καὶ   αὐτὸς
beast   which was   and   is not,   even   he

ὄγδοός   ἐστιν,   καὶ   ἐκ   τῶν   ἑπτά   ἐστιν,
²an eighth   ¹is,   and   ²of   ³the   ⁴seven   ¹is,

καὶ   εἰς   ἀπώλειαν   ὑπάγει.   12 καὶ   τὰ
and   to   destruction   goes.   And   the

δέκα   κέρατα   ἃ   εἶδες   δέκα   βασιλεῖς
ten   horns   which   thou   ²ten   ³kings
sawest

εἰσιν,   οἵτινες   βασιλείαν   οὔπω   ἔλαβον,
¹are,   who   a kingdom   not yet   received,

ἀλλὰ   ἐξουσίαν   ὡς   βασιλεῖς   μίαν   ὥραν
but   ²authority   ³as   ⁴kings   ⁵one   ⁶hour

λαμβάνουσιν   μετὰ   τοῦ   θηρίου.   13 οὗτοι
¹receive   with   the   beast.   These

μίαν   γνώμην   ἔχουσιν,   καὶ   τὴν   δύναμιν
one   mind   have,   and   the   power

καὶ   ἐξουσίαν   αὐτῶν   τῷ   θηρίῳ   διδόασιν.
and   authority   of them   to the   beast   they give.

14 οὗτοι   μετὰ   τοῦ   ἀρνίου   πολεμήσουσιν
These   ²with   ³the   ⁴Lamb   ¹will make war

willconquerthem,forheis Lord of lords and King of kings, and those with him are called and chosen and faithful."

15 And he said to me, "The waters that you saw, where the harlot is seated, are people and multitudes and nations and tongues. ¹⁶And the ten horns that you saw, they and the beast will hate the harlot; they will make her desolate and naked, and devour her flesh and burn her up with fire, ¹⁷for God has put it into their hearts to carry out his purpose by being of one mind and giving over their royal power to the beast, until the words of God shall be fulfilled. ¹⁸And the woman that you saw is the great city which has dominion over the kings of the earth."

καὶ τὸ ἀρνίον νικήσει αὐτούς, ὅτι κύριος
and the Lamb will overcome them, because ²Lord

κυρίων ἐστὶν καὶ βασιλεὺς βασιλέων, καὶ
²of lords ¹he is and King of kings, and

οἱ μετ' αὐτοῦ κλητοὶ καὶ ἐκλεκτοὶ καὶ
the with him [are] called and chosen and
[ones]

πιστοί. 15 Καὶ λέγει μοι· τὰ ὕδατα
faithful. And he says to me: The waters

ἃ εἶδες, οὗ ἡ πόρνη κάθηται, λαοὶ
which thou where the harlot sits, peoples
sawest,

καὶ ὄχλοι εἰσὶν καὶ ἔθνη καὶ γλῶσσαι.
and crowds are and nations and tongues.

16 καὶ τὰ δέκα κέρατα ἃ εἶδες καὶ
And the ten horns which thou sawest and

τὸ θηρίον, οὗτοι μισήσουσιν τὴν πόρνην,
the beast, these will hate the harlot,

καὶ ἠρημωμένην ποιήσουσιν αὐτὴν καὶ
and ²having been desolated ¹will make ²her and

γυμνήν, καὶ τὰς σάρκας αὐτῆς φάγονται,
naked, and ²the ³fleshes ⁴of her ¹will eat,

καὶ αὐτὴν κατακαύσουσιν [ἐν] πυρί· 17 ὁ
and ²her ¹will consume with fire; –

γὰρ θεὸς ἔδωκεν εἰς τὰς καρδίας αὐτῶν
for God gave into the hearts of them

ποιῆσαι τὴν γνώμην αὐτοῦ, καὶ ποιῆσαι
to do the mind of him, and to make

μίαν γνώμην καὶ δοῦναι τὴν βασιλείαν
one mind and to give the kingdom

αὐτῶν τῷ θηρίῳ, ἄχρι τελεσθήσονται οἱ
of them to the beast, until ⁴shall be accomplished ¹the

λόγοι τοῦ θεοῦ. 18 καὶ ἡ γυνὴ ἦν
²words – ³of God. And the woman whom

εἶδες ἔστιν ἡ πόλις ἡ μεγάλη ἡ ἔχουσα
thou is the ²city – ¹great – having
sawest

βασιλείαν ἐπὶ τῶν βασιλέων τῆς γῆς.
a kingdom over the kings of the earth.

CHAPTER 18

AFTER this I saw another angel coming down from heaven, having great authority; and the earth was made bright with his splendor. ²And he called out with a mighty voice,

18 Μετὰ ταῦτα εἶδον ἄλλον ἄγγελον
After these things I saw another angel

καταβαίνοντα ἐκ τοῦ οὐρανοῦ, ἔχοντα
coming down out of – heaven, having

ἐξουσίαν μεγάλην, καὶ ἡ γῆ ἐφωτίσθη
²authority ¹great, and the earth was enlightened

ἐκ τῆς δόξης αὐτοῦ. 2 καὶ ἔκραξεν
from the glory of him. And he cried

"Fallen, fallen is Babylon the great! It has become a dwelling place of demons, a haunt of every foul spirit, a haunt of every foul and hateful bird;
[3] for all nations have drunk[i] the wine of her impure passion, and the kings of the earth have committed fornication with her, and the merchants of the earth have grown rich with the wealth of her wantonness."
[4] Then I heard another voice from heaven saying,
"Come out of her, my people, lest you take part in her sins, lest you share in her plagues;
[5] for her sins are heaped high as heaven, and God has remembered her iniquities.
[6] Render to her as she herself has rendered, and repay her double for her deeds; mix a double draught for her in the cup she mixed.
[7] As she glorified herself and played the wanton, so give her a like measure of torment and mourning.

[i] Other ancient authorities read *fallen by*

ἐν ἰσχυρᾷ φωνῇ λέγων· ἔπεσεν ἔπεσεν
in a strong voice saying: Fell[,] fell

Βαβυλὼν ἡ μεγάλη, καὶ ἐγένετο κατοικητή-
Babylon the great, and became a dwelling-

ριον δαιμονίων καὶ φυλακὴ παντὸς
place of demons and a prison of every

πνεύματος ἀκαθάρτου καὶ φυλακὴ παντὸς
²spirit ¹unclean and a prison of every

ὀρνέου ἀκαθάρτου καὶ μεμισημένου, 3 ὅτι
⁴bird ¹unclean ²and ³having been hated, because

ἐκ τοῦ οἴνου τοῦ θυμοῦ τῆς πορνείας
⁵of ⁶the ⁷wine ⁸of the ⁹anger ¹⁰of the ¹¹fornication

αὐτῆς πέπωκαν πάντα τὰ ἔθνη, καὶ
¹²of her ⁴have drunk ¹all ²the ³nations, and

οἱ βασιλεῖς τῆς γῆς μετ' αὐτῆς ἐπόρνευσαν,
the kings of the earth with her practised fornication,

καὶ οἱ ἔμποροι τῆς γῆς ἐκ τῆς δυνάμεως
and the merchants of the earth ²from ³the ⁴power

τοῦ στρήνους αὐτῆς ἐπλούτησαν. 4 Καὶ
⁵of the ⁶luxury ⁷of her ¹became rich. And

ἤκουσα ἄλλην φωνὴν ἐκ τοῦ οὐρανοῦ
I heard another voice out of - heaven

λέγουσαν· ἐξέλθατε ὁ λαός μου ἐξ αὐτῆς,
saying: Come ye out[,] the people of me[,] out of her,

ἵνα μὴ συγκοινωνήσητε ταῖς ἁμαρτίαις
lest ye share in the sins

αὐτῆς, καὶ ἐκ τῶν πληγῶν αὐτῆς ἵνα
of her, and ²of ⁴the ⁵plagues ⁶of her ¹lest

μὴ λάβητε· 5 ὅτι ἐκολλήθησαν αὐτῆς αἱ
²ye receive; because ³joined together ¹of her ¹the

ἁμαρτίαι ἄχρι τοῦ οὐρανοῦ, καὶ ἐμνημό-
²sins up to - heaven, and ²remem-

νευσεν ὁ θεὸς τὰ ἀδικήματα αὐτῆς.
bered - ¹God the misdeeds of her.

6 ἀπόδοτε αὐτῇ ὡς καὶ αὐτὴ ἀπέδωκεν,
Give ye back to her as indeed she gave back,

καὶ διπλώσατε τὰ διπλᾶ κατὰ τὰ ἔργα
and double ye the double according to the works

αὐτῆς· ἐν τῷ ποτηρίῳ ᾧ ἐκέρασεν
of her; in the cup in which she mixed

κεράσατε αὐτῇ διπλοῦν· 7 ὅσα ἐδόξασεν
mix ye to her double; ' by what she glorified
                                              things

αὐτὴν καὶ ἐστρηνίασεν, τοσοῦτον δότε
her[self] and luxuriated, by so much give ye

αὐτῇ βασανισμὸν καὶ πένθος. ὅτι ἐν
to her torment and ⟨rro v.⟩. Because in

Since in her heart she says, 'A queen I sit, I am no widow, mourning I shall never see,' ⁸so shall her plagues come in a single day, pestilence and mourning and famine, and she shall be burned with fire; for mighty is the Lord God who judges her."
9 And the kings of the earth, who committed fornication and were wanton with her, will weep and wail over her when they see the smoke of her burning; ¹⁰they will stand far off, in fear of her torment, and say, "Alas! alas! thou great city, thou mighty city, Babylon! In one hour has thy judgment come."
11 And the merchants of the earth weep and mourn for her, since no one buys their cargo any more, ¹²cargo of gold, silver, jewels and pearls, fine linen, purple, silk and scarlet, all kinds of scented wood, all articles of ivory, all articles of costly wood,

| τῇ | καρδίᾳ | αὐτῆς | λέγει | ὅτι | κάθημαι |
|the|heart|of her|she says[,]|–|I sit|

βασίλισσα καὶ χήρα οὐκ εἰμὶ καὶ πένθος
a queen and a widow I am not and sorrow

οὐ μὴ ἴδω· 8 διὰ τοῦτο ἐν μιᾷ ἡμέρᾳ
by no means I see; therefore in one day

ἥξουσιν αἱ πληγαὶ αὐτῆς, θάνατος καὶ
will come the plagues of her, death and

πένθος καὶ λιμός, καὶ ἐν πυρὶ κατακαυ-
sorrow and famine, and with fire she will be

θήσεται· ὅτι ἰσχυρὸς κύριος ὁ θεὸς ὁ
consumed; because strong [is] [the] Lord – God the

κρίνας αὐτήν. 9 καὶ κλαύσουσιν καὶ
[one] judging her. And ¹will weep ²and

κόψονται ἐπ' αὐτὴν οἱ βασιλεῖς τῆς
⁷wail ⁸over ⁹her ¹the ²kings ³of the

γῆς οἱ μετ' αὐτῆς πορνεύσαντες καὶ
⁴earth ¹⁰the ¹¹with ¹²her ¹³having practised and
[ones] fornication

στρηνιάσαντες, ὅταν βλέπωσιν τὸν καπνὸν
having luxuriated, whenever they see the smoke

τῆς πυρώσεως αὐτῆς, 10 ἀπὸ μακρόθεν
of the burning of her, ²from ³afar

ἑστηκότες διὰ τὸν φόβον τοῦ βασανισμοῦ
¹standing because of the fear of the torment

αὐτῆς, λέγοντες· οὐαὶ οὐαί, ἡ πόλις
of her, saying: Woe[,] woe, the ²city

ἡ μεγάλη, Βαβυλὼν ἡ πόλις ἡ ἰσχυρά,
– ¹great, Babylon the ²city – ¹strong,

ὅτι μιᾷ ὥρᾳ ἦλθεν ἡ κρίσις σου. 11 καὶ
be- in hour came the judgment of thee. And
cause one

οἱ ἔμποροι τῆς γῆς κλαίουσιν καὶ
the merchants of the earth weep and

πενθοῦσιν ἐπ' αὐτήν, ὅτι τὸν γόμον
sorrow over her, because ⁴the ⁵cargo

αὐτῶν οὐδεὶς ἀγοράζει οὐκέτι, 12 γόμον
⁶of them ¹no one ²buys ³any more, cargo

χρυσοῦ καὶ ἀργύρου καὶ λίθου τιμίου
of gold and of silver and ²stone ¹of valuable

καὶ μαργαριτῶν καὶ βυσσίνου καὶ πορφύρας
and of pearls and of fine linen and of purple

καὶ σηρικοῦ καὶ κοκκίνου, καὶ πᾶν
and of silk and of scarlet, and all

ξύλον θύϊνον καὶ πᾶν σκεῦος ἐλεφάντινον
²wood ¹thyine and every ²vessel ¹ivory

καὶ πᾶν σκεῦος ἐκ ξύλου τιμιωτάτου
and every vessel of ²wood ¹very valuable

bronze, iron and marble, [13]cinnamon, spice, incense, myrrh, frankincense, wine, oil, fine flour and wheat, cattle and sheep, horses and chariots, and slaves, that is, human souls. [14]"The fruit for which thy soul longed has gone from thee, and all thy dainties and thy splendor are lost to thee, never to be found again!" [15]The merchants of these wares, who gained wealth from her, will stand far off, in fear of her torment, weeping and mourning aloud, [16]"Alas, alas, for the great city that was clothed in fine linen, in purple and scarlet, bedecked with gold, with jewels, and with pearls! [17]In one hour all this wealth has been laid waste." And all shipmasters and seafaring men, sailors and all whose trade is on the sea, stood

καὶ　χαλκοῦ　καὶ　σιδήρου　καὶ　μαρμάρου,
and　of bronze　and　of iron　and　of marble,

13 καὶ　κιννάμωμον　καὶ　ἄμωμον　καὶ
and　cinnamon　and　spice　and

θυμιάματα　καὶ　μύρον　καὶ　λίβανον　καὶ
incenses　and　ointment　and　frankincense　and

οἶνον　καὶ　ἔλαιον　καὶ　σεμίδαλιν　καὶ　σῖτον
wine　and　oil　and　fine meal　and　corn

καὶ　κτήνη　καὶ　πρόβατα,　καὶ　ἵππων
and beasts of burden and　sheep,　and　of horses

καὶ　ῥεδῶν　καὶ　σωμάτων,　καὶ　ψυχὰς
and　of carriages　and　of bodies,　and　souls

ἀνθρώπων.　14 καὶ　ἡ　ὀπώρα　σου　τῆς
of men.　And　the　fruit　¹of thee ²of the

ἐπιθυμίας　τῆς　ψυχῆς　ἀπῆλθεν　ἀπὸ　σοῦ,
²lust　³of the　⁴soul　went away　from　thee,

καὶ　πάντα　τὰ　λιπαρὰ　καὶ　τὰ　λαμπρὰ
and　all　the　sumptuous　and　the　bright
　　　　　　　things　　　　　things

ἀπώλετο　ἀπὸ　σοῦ,　καὶ　οὐκέτι　οὐ　μὴ
perished　from　thee,　and　no more　by no(any)
　　　　　　　　　　　　　　means

αὐτὰ　εὑρήσουσιν.　15 οἱ　ἔμποροι　τούτων,
²them　¹shall they find.　The　merchants　of these
　　　　　　　　　　　　　　　　things,

οἱ　πλουτήσαντες　ἀπ᾽　αὐτῆς,　ἀπὸ　μακρόθεν
the　having been rich　from　her,　²from　³afar
[ones]

στήσονται　διὰ　τὸν　φόβον　τοῦ　βασανισμοῦ
¹will stand because of the　fear　of the　torment

αὐτῆς　κλαίοντες　καὶ　πενθοῦντες,　16 λέγοντες·
of her　weeping　and　sorrowing,　saying:

οὐαὶ　οὐαί,　ἡ　πόλις　ἡ　μεγάλη,　ἡ　περι-
Woe[,]　woe,　the　²city　–　¹great,　–　having

βεβλημένη　βύσσινον　καὶ　πορφυροῦν　καὶ
been clothed [with] fine linen　and　purple　and

κόκκινον,　καὶ　κεχρυσωμένη　ἐν　χρυσίῳ
scarlet,　and　having been gilded　with　gold

καὶ　λίθῳ　τιμίῳ　καὶ　μαργαρίτῃ,　17 ὅτι
and　²stone　¹valuable　and　pearl,　because

μιᾷ　ὥρᾳ　ἠρημώθη　ὁ　τοσοῦτος　πλοῦτος.
in one　hour　³was made　such great　²wealth.
　　　　　desolate

καὶ　πᾶς　κυβερνήτης　καὶ　πᾶς　ὁ　ἐπὶ
And　every　steersman　and　¹every　²one　⁴to

τόπον　πλέων　καὶ　ναῦται　καὶ　ὅσοι　τὴν
²a place　³sailing　and　sailors　and as many as ³the

θάλασσαν　ἐργάζονται,　ἀπὸ　μακρόθεν　ἔστησαν
²sea　¹work,　²from　³afar　¹stood

far off ¹⁸and cried out as they saw the smoke of her burning,
"What city was like the great city?"
¹⁹And they threw dust on their heads, as they wept and mourned, crying out, "Alas, alas, for the great city where all who had ships at sea grew rich by her wealth! In one hour she has been laid waste.
²⁰Rejoice over her, O heaven,
O saints and apostles and prophets,
for God has given judgment for you against her!"
21 Then a mighty angel took up a stone like a great millstone and threw it into the sea, saying,
"So shall Babylon the great city be thrown down with violence, and shall be found no more;
²²and the sound of harpers and minstrels, of flute players and trumpeters, shall be heard in thee no more; and a craftsman of any craft shall be found in thee no more; and the sound of the millstone shall be heard in thee no more;
²³and the light of a lamp shall shine in thee no more;

---

18 καὶ   ἔκραζον   βλέποντες   τὸν   καπνὸν
and   cried out   seeing   the   smoke

τῆς   πυρώσεως   αὐτῆς   λέγοντες·   τίς   ὁμοία
of the   burning   of her   saying: Who(What) [is] like

τῇ   πόλει   τῇ   μεγάλῃ;   19 καὶ   ἔβαλον
to the   ²city   –   ¹great?   And   they cast

χοῦν   ἐπὶ   τὰς   κεφαλὰς   αὐτῶν   καὶ   ἔκραζον
dust   on   the   heads   of them   and   cried out

κλαίοντες   καὶ   πενθοῦντες,   λέγοντες·   οὐαὶ
weeping   and   sorrowing,   saying: Woe[,]

οὐαί,   ἡ   πόλις   ἡ   μεγάλη,   ἐν   ᾗ   ἐπλούτησαν
woe, the   ²city   –   ¹great,   by which   ⁵were rich

πάντες   οἱ   ἔχοντες   τὰ   πλοῖα   ἐν   τῇ
¹all   ²the [ones]   ³having   ⁴the   ⁵ships   ⁶in   ⁷the

θαλάσσῃ   ἐκ   τῆς   τιμιότητος   αὐτῆς,   ὅτι
⁸sea   from   the   worth   of her, because

μιᾷ   ὥρᾳ   ἠρημώθη.   20 Εὐφραίνου   ἐπ'
in one   hour   she was made desolate.   Be thou glad   over

αὐτῇ,   οὐρανὲ   καὶ   οἱ   ἅγιοι   καὶ   οἱ   ἀπό-
her,   heaven   and   the   saints   and   the   apost-

στολοι   καὶ   οἱ   προφῆται,   ὅτι   ἔκρινεν   ὁ
les   and   the   prophets,   because   ²judged   –

θεὸς   τὸ   κρίμα   ὑμῶν   ἐξ   αὐτῆς.   21 Καὶ
¹God   the   judgment   of you   by   her.   And

ἦρεν   εἷς   ἄγγελος   ἰσχυρὸς   λίθον   ὡς
⁴lifted   ¹one   ²angel   ³strong   a stone   as

μύλινον   μέγαν,   καὶ   ἔβαλεν   εἰς   τὴν   θά-
²millstone   ¹a great,   and   threw   into   the   sea

λασσαν   λέγων·   οὕτως   ὁρμήματι   βληθήσεται
  saying: Thus   with a rush   ⁵shall be thrown

Βαβυλὼν   ἡ   μεγάλη   πόλις,   καὶ   οὐ   μὴ
¹Babylon   ²the   ³great   ⁴city,   and   by no means

εὑρεθῇ   ἔτι.   22 καὶ   φωνὴ   κιθαρῳδῶν
[shall] be   longer.   And   sound   of harpers
found

καὶ   μουσικῶν   καὶ   αὐλητῶν   καὶ   σαλπιστῶν
and   of musicians   and   of flutists   and   of trumpeters

οὐ   μὴ   ἀκουσθῇ   ἐν   σοὶ   ἔτι,   καὶ   πᾶς
by no means [shall] be heard in   thee   longer,   and   every

τεχνίτης   πάσης   τέχνης   οὐ   μὴ   εὑρεθῇ
craftsman   of every   craft   by no means   [shall]
be found

ἐν   σοὶ   ἔτι,   καὶ   φωνὴ   μύλου   οὐ   μὴ
in   thee   longer,   and   sound   of a mill by no means

ἀκουσθῇ   ἐν   σοὶ   ἔτι,   23 καὶ   φῶς
[shall] be heard in   thee   longer,   and   light

λύχνου   οὐ   μὴ   φάνῃ   ἐν   σοὶ   ἔτι,   καὶ
of a   by no means   [shall]   in   thee   longer,   and
lamp   shine

and the voice of bridegroom and bride shall be heard in thee no more; for thy merchants were the great men of the earth, and all nations were deceived by thy sorcery.

²⁴And in her was found the blood of prophets and of saints, and of all who have been slain on earth."

φωνὴ νυμφίου καὶ νύμφης οὐ μὴ
voice of bridegroom and of bride by no means
ἀκουσθῇ ἐν σοὶ ἔτι· ὅτι [οἱ] ἔμποροί
[shall] be heard in thee longer; because the merchants
σου ἦσαν οἱ μεγιστᾶνες τῆς γῆς, ὅτι
of thee were the great ones of the earth, because
ἐν τῇ φαρμακείᾳ σου ἐπλανήθησαν πάντα
by the sorcery of thee ⁴were deceived ¹all
τὰ ἔθνη, 24 καὶ ἐν αὐτῇ αἷμα προφητῶν
²the ³nations, and in her ³blood ²of prophets
καὶ ἁγίων εὑρέθη καὶ πάντων τῶν
⁴and ⁵of saints ¹was found and of all the [ones]
ἐσφαγμένων ἐπὶ τῆς γῆς.
having been slain on the earth.

CHAPTER 19

AFTER this I heard what seemed to be the mighty voice of a great multitude in heaven, crying, "Hallelujah! Salvation and glory and power belong to our God,

²for his judgments are true and just; he has judged the great harlot who corrupted the earth with her fornication, and he has avenged on her the blood of his servants."

³Once more they cried, "Hallelujah! The smoke from her goes up for ever and ever."

⁴And the twenty-four elders and the four living creatures fell down and worshiped God who is seated on the throne,

19 Μετὰ ταῦτα ἤκουσα ὡς φωνὴν
After these things I heard as ²voice
μεγάλην ὄχλου πολλοῦ ἐν τῷ οὐρανῷ
¹a great ⁴crowd ³of a much in – heaven
(loud) (great)
λεγόντων· ἀλληλουϊά· ἡ σωτηρία καὶ ἡ
saying: Halleluia: The salvation and the
δόξα καὶ ἡ δύναμις τοῦ θεοῦ ἡμῶν,
glory and the power of the God of us,
2 ὅτι ἀληθιναὶ καὶ δίκαιαι αἱ κρίσεις
because true and righteous the judgments
αὐτοῦ· ὅτι ἔκρινεν τὴν πόρνην τὴν
of him; because he judged the ²harlot –
μεγάλην ἥτις ἔφθειρεν τὴν γῆν ἐν τῇ
¹great who defiled the earth with the
πορνείᾳ αὐτῆς, καὶ ἐξεδίκησεν τὸ αἷμα
fornication of her, and he avenged the blood
τῶν δούλων αὐτοῦ ἐκ χειρὸς αὐτῆς.
of the slaves of him out of [the] hand of her.
3 καὶ δεύτερον εἴρηκαν· ἀλληλουϊά· καὶ
And secondly they have said: Halleluia; and
ὁ καπνὸς αὐτῆς ἀναβαίνει εἰς τοὺς
the smoke of her goes up unto the
αἰῶνας τῶν αἰώνων. 4 καὶ ἔπεσαν οἱ
ages of the ages. And ²fell ¹the
πρεσβύτεροι οἱ εἴκοσι τέσσαρες καὶ τὰ
²elders – ³twenty-four ⁴and ⁵the
τέσσερα ζῷα, καὶ προσεκύνησαν τῷ θεῷ
⁶four ⁷living and worshipped – God
creatures,
τῷ καθημένῳ ἐπὶ τῷ θρόνῳ λέγοντες·
– sitting on the throne saying:

saying, "Amen. Hallelujah!" ⁵And from the throne came a voice crying, "Praise our God, all you his servants, you who fear him, small and great." ⁶Then I heard what seemed to be the voice of a great multitude, like the sound of many waters and like the sound of mighty thunderpeals, crying, "Hallelujah! For the Lord our God the Almighty reigns. ⁷Let us rejoice and exult and give him the glory, for the marriage of the Lamb has come, and his Bride has made herself ready; ⁸it was granted her to be clothed with fine linen, bright and pure"— for the fine linen is the righteous deeds of the saints.

9 And the angel said to me, "Write this: Blessed are those who are invited to the marriage supper of the Lamb." And he said to me, "These are true words of God." ¹⁰Then I fell down at his feet to worship him, but he said to me, "You must not do that! I am a fellow servant with you and your brethren who hold

---

ἀμὴν ἀλληλουϊά.   5 καὶ φωνὴ ἀπὸ τοῦ
Amen[,] halleluia.   And a voice ²from ¹the

θρόνου ἐξῆλθεν λέγουσα· αἰνεῖτε τῷ θεῷ
⁴throne ¹came out saying: Praise ye the God

ἡμῶν, πάντες οἱ δοῦλοι αὐτοῦ, οἱ
of us, all the slaves of him, the

φοβούμενοι αὐτόν, οἱ μικροὶ καὶ οἱ
[ones] fearing him, the small and the

μεγάλοι.   6 Καὶ ἤκουσα ὡς φωνὴν ὄχλου
great.   And I heard as a sound ²crowd

πολλοῦ καὶ ὡς φωνὴν ὑδάτων πολλῶν
¹of a and as a sound ²waters ¹of many
much(great)

καὶ ὡς φωνὴν βροντῶν ἰσχυρῶν, λεγόντων·
and as a sound ²thunders ¹of strong saying:
                   (loud),

ἀλληλουϊά, ὅτι ἐβασίλευσεν κύριος ὁ θεὸς
Halleluia, because ⁷reigned ¹[the] Lord ²the ³God

ἡμῶν ὁ παντοκράτωρ.   7 χαίρωμεν καὶ
⁴of us ⁵the ⁶Almighty.   Let us rejoice and

ἀγαλλιῶμεν, καὶ δώσομεν τὴν δόξαν αὐτῷ,
let us exult, and we will give the glory to him,

ὅτι ἦλθεν ὁ γάμος τοῦ ἀρνίου, καὶ
because ²came ¹the ³marriage ²of the ⁴Lamb, and

ἡ γυνὴ αὐτοῦ ἡτοίμασεν ἑαυτήν, 8 καὶ
the wife of him prepared herself, and

ἐδόθη αὐτῇ ἵνα περιβάληται βύσσινον
it was to her in order she might be ²fine linen
given that clothed [with]

λαμπρὸν καθαρόν· τὸ γὰρ βύσσινον τὰ
¹bright ⁴clean; for the fine linen ³the

δικαιώματα τῶν ἁγίων ἐστίν.   9 Καὶ
²righteous deeds ⁴of the ⁵saints ¹is.   And

λέγει μοι· γράψον· μακάριοι οἱ εἰς τὸ
he tells me: Write thou; blessed ¹the [ones] ²to ⁴the

δεῖπνον τοῦ γάμου τοῦ ἀρνίου κεκλημένοι.
³supper ⁵of ⁷marriage ⁶of ⁸Lamb ³having been
          the   called.

καὶ λέγει μοι· οὗτοι οἱ λόγοι ἀληθινοὶ
And he says to me: ¹These - ²words ³true

τοῦ θεοῦ εἰσιν.   10 καὶ ἔπεσα ἔμπροσθεν
- ³of God ⁴are.   And I fell before

τῶν ποδῶν αὐτοῦ προσκυνῆσαι αὐτῷ.
the feet of him to worship him.

καὶ λέγει μοι· ὅρα μή· σύνδουλός σού
And he says to me: See thou not; ²a fellow- ²of
                   [do it]   slave   thee

εἰμι καὶ τῶν ἀδελφῶν σου τῶν ἐχόντων
¹I am and of the brothers of thee - having

the testimony of Jesus.
Worship God." For the
testimony of Jesus is the
spirit of prophecy.
11 Then I saw heaven
opened, and behold, a
white horse! He who sat
upon it is called Faithful
and True, and in right-
eousness he judges and
makes war. [12] His eyes
are like a flame of fire,
and on his head are many
diadems; and he has a
name inscribed which no
one knows but himself.
[13] He is clad in a robe
dipped in[j] blood, and the
name by which he is
called is The Word of
God. [14] And the armies
of heaven, arrayed in
fine linen, white and
pure, followed him on
white horses. [15] From his
mouth issues a sharp
sword with which to
smite the nations, and
he will rule them with a
rod of iron; he will
tread the wine press of
the fury of the wrath of
God the Almighty. [16] On
his robe and on his

τὴν μαρτυρίαν Ἰησοῦ· τῷ θεῷ προσκύνησον.
the witness of Jesus; – ²God ¹worship thou.

ἡ γὰρ μαρτυρία Ἰησοῦ ἐστιν τὸ πνεῦμα
For the witness of Jesus is the spirit

τῆς προφητείας.
– of prophecy.

11 Καὶ εἶδον τὸν οὐρανὸν ἠνεῳγμένον,
And I saw – heaven having been opened,

καὶ ἰδοὺ ἵππος λευκός, καὶ ὁ καθήμενος
and behold[,] ²horse ¹a white, and the [one] sitting

ἐπ᾽ αὐτὸν πιστὸς καλούμενος καὶ ἀληθινός,
on it ²faithful ¹being called and true,

καὶ ἐν δικαιοσύνῃ κρίνει καὶ πολεμεῖ.
and in righteousness he judges and makes war.

12 οἱ δὲ ὀφθαλμοὶ αὐτοῦ φλὸξ πυρός,
And the eyes of him [are as] a flame of fire,

καὶ ἐπὶ τὴν κεφαλὴν αὐτοῦ διαδήματα
and on the head of him ²diadems

πολλά, ἔχων ὄνομα γεγραμμένον ὃ οὐδεὶς
¹many, having a name having been written which no one

οἶδεν εἰ μὴ αὐτός, 13 καὶ περιβεβλημένος
knows except [him]self, and having been clothed [with]

ἱμάτιον βεβαμμένον αἵματι, καὶ κέκληται
a garment having been dipped in blood, and ⁴has been called

τὸ ὄνομα αὐτοῦ ὁ λόγος τοῦ θεοῦ.
¹the ²name ³of him The Word – of God.

14 καὶ τὰ στρατεύματα τὰ ἐν τῷ οὐρανῷ
And the armies – in – heaven

ἠκολούθει αὐτῷ ἐφ᾽ ἵπποις λευκοῖς, ἐνδεδυμένοι
followed him on ²horses ¹white, having been dressed [in]

βύσσινον λευκὸν καθαρόν. 15 καὶ ἐκ
²fine linen ¹white ²clean. And out of

τοῦ στόματος αὐτοῦ ἐκπορεύεται ῥομφαία
the mouth of him proceeds ²sword

ὀξεῖα, ἵνα ἐν αὐτῇ πατάξῃ τὰ ἔθνη·
¹a sharp, in order that with it he may smite the nations;

καὶ αὐτὸς ποιμανεῖ αὐτοὺς ἐν ῥάβδῳ
and he will shepherd them with ²staff

σιδηρᾷ· καὶ αὐτὸς πατεῖ τὴν ληνὸν
¹an iron; and he treads the winepress

τοῦ οἴνου τοῦ θυμοῦ τῆς ὀργῆς τοῦ
of the wine of the anger[,] of the wrath –

θεοῦ τοῦ παντοκράτορος. 16 καὶ ἔχει
of God of the Almighty. And he has

ἐπὶ τὸ ἱμάτιον καὶ ἐπὶ τὸν μηρὸν
on the garment and on the thigh

[j] Other ancient authorities
read *sprinkled with*

thigh he has a name inscribed, King of kings and Lord of lords. 17 Then I saw an angel standing in the sun, and with a loud voice he called to all the birds that fly in midheaven, "Come, gather for the great supper of God, 18 to eat the flesh of kings, the flesh of captains, the flesh of mighty men, the flesh of horses and their riders, and the flesh of all men, both free and slave, both small and great." 19And I saw the beast and the kings of the earth with their armies gathered to make war against him who sits upon the horse and against his army. 20And the beast was captured, and with it the false prophet who in its presence had worked the signs by which he deceived those who had received the mark of the beast and those who worshiped its image. These two were thrown

αὐτοῦ	ὄνομα	γεγραμμένον·	ΒΑΣΙΛΕΥΣ
of him	a name	having been written:	KING

ΒΑΣΙΛΕΩΝ	ΚΑΙ	ΚΥΡΙΟΣ	ΚΥΡΙΩΝ.
OF KINGS	AND	LORD	OF LORDS.

17 Καὶ	εἶδον	ἕνα	ἄγγελον	ἑστῶτα	ἐν
And	I saw	one	angel	standing	in

τῷ	ἡλίῳ,	καὶ	ἔκραξεν	ἐν	φωνῇ	μεγάλῃ
the	sun,	and	he cried out	in	²voice	¹a great (loud)

λέγων	πᾶσιν	τοῖς	ὀρνέοις	τοῖς	πετομένοις
saying	to all	the	birds	–	flying

ἐν	μεσουρανήματι·	δεῦτε	συνάχθητε	εἰς
in	mid-heaven:	Come ye[,]	assemble ye	to

τὸ	δεῖπνον	τὸ	μέγα	τοῦ	θεοῦ,	18 ἵνα
the	²supper	–	¹great	–	of God,	in order that

φάγητε	σάρκας	βασιλέων	καὶ	σάρκας
ye may eat	fleshes	of kings	and	fleshes

χιλιάρχων	καὶ	σάρκας	ἰσχυρῶν	καὶ	σάρκας
of chiliarchs	and	fleshes	of strong men	and	fleshes

ἵππων	καὶ	τῶν	καθημένων	ἐπ᾽	αὐτῶν,
of horses	and	of the [ones]	sitting	on	them,

καὶ	σάρκας	πάντων	ἐλευθέρων	τε	καὶ
and	fleshes	of all	²free men	¹both	and

δούλων	καὶ	μικρῶν	καὶ	μεγάλων.	19 Καὶ
slaves	both	small	and	great.	And

εἶδον	τὸ	θηρίον	καὶ	τοὺς	βασιλεῖς	τῆς
I saw	the	beast	and	the	kings	of the

γῆς	καὶ	τὰ	στρατεύματα	αὐτῶν	συνηγμένα
earth	and	the	armies	of them	having been assembled

ποιῆσαι	τὸν	πόλεμον	μετὰ	τοῦ	καθημένου
to make	the	war	with	the [one]	sitting

ἐπὶ	τοῦ	ἵππου	καὶ	μετὰ	τοῦ	στρατεύματος
on	the	horse	and	with	the	army

αὐτοῦ.	20 καὶ	ἐπιάσθη	τὸ	θηρίον	καὶ
of him.	And	²was seized	¹the	²beast	and

μετ᾽	αὐτοῦ	ὁ	ψευδοπροφήτης	ὁ	ποιήσας
with	it	the	false prophet	the [one]	having done

τὰ	σημεῖα	ἐνώπιον	αὐτοῦ,	ἐν	οἷς	ἐπλάνη-
the	signs	before	it,	by which		he de-

σεν	τοὺς	λαβόντας	τὸ	χάραγμα	τοῦ
ceived	the [ones]	having received	the	mark	of the

θηρίου	καὶ	τοὺς	προσκυνοῦντας	τῇ	εἰκόνι
beast	and	the [ones]	worshipping	the	image

αὐτοῦ·	ζῶντες	ἐβλήθησαν	οἱ	δύο	εἰς
of it;	⁴living	³were cast	¹the	²two	into

alive into the lake of fire that burns with brimstone. ²¹And the rest were slain by the sword of him who sits upon the horse, the sword that issues from his mouth; and all the birds were gorged with their flesh.

τὴν λίμνην τοῦ πυρὸς τῆς καιομένης
the   lake   –   of fire   –   burning*

ἐν θείῳ.   21 καὶ οἱ λοιποὶ ἀπεκτάνθησαν
with sulphur.   And the rest   were killed

ἐν τῇ ῥομφαίᾳ τοῦ καθημένου ἐπὶ τοῦ
with the   sword   of the [one] sitting   on   the

ἵππου τῇ ἐξελθούσῃ ἐκ τοῦ στόματος
horse   –   proceeding§   out of the   mouth

αὐτοῦ, καὶ πάντα τὰ ὄρνεα ἐχορτάσθησαν
of him,   and   all   the   birds   were filled

ἐκ τῶν σαρκῶν αὐτῶν.
by   the   fleshes   of them.

CHAPTER 20

THEN I saw an angel coming down from heaven, holding in his hand the key of the bottomless pit and a great chain. ²And he seized the dragon, that ancient serpent, who is the Devil and Satan, and bound him for a thousand years, ³and threw him into the pit, and shut it and sealed it over him, that he should deceive the nations no more, till the thousand years were ended. After that he must be loosed for a little while.

4 Then I saw thrones, and seated on them were those to whom judgment was committed. Also I saw the souls of those who had been beheaded for their testimony to Jesus and for the word of

20 Καὶ εἶδον ἄγγελον καταβαίνοντα ἐκ
    And   I saw   an angel   coming down out of

τοῦ οὐρανοῦ, ἔχοντα τὴν κλεῖν τῆς
–   heaven,   having   the   key   of the

ἀβύσσου καὶ ἅλυσιν μεγάλην ἐπὶ τὴν χεῖρα
abyss   and   ²chain   ¹a great   on   the   hand

αὐτοῦ.   2 καὶ ἐκράτησεν τὸν δράκοντα,
of him.   And   he laid hold [of] the   dragon,

ὁ ὄφις ὁ ἀρχαῖος, ὅς ἐστιν Διάβολος
the ²serpent   –   ¹old,   who   is   Devil

καὶ ὁ Σατανᾶς, καὶ ἔδησεν αὐτὸν χίλια
and   –   Satan,   and   bound   him   a thousand

ἔτη, 3 καὶ ἔβαλεν αὐτὸν εἰς τὴν ἄβυσσον,
years,   and   cast   him   into the   abyss,

καὶ ἔκλεισεν καὶ ἐσφράγισεν ἐπάνω αὐτοῦ,
and   shut   and   sealed   over   him,

ἵνα μὴ πλανήσῃ ἔτι τὰ ἔθνη, ἄχρι
in or-   he should not deceive longer the   nations,   until
der that

τελεσθῇ τὰ χίλια ἔτη· μετὰ ταῦτα
⁴are finished ¹the   ²thousand ³years;   after these things

δεῖ λυθῆναι αὐτὸν μικρὸν χρόνον.
it be-   ²to be   ¹him   a little   time.
hoves   loosed

4 Καὶ εἶδον θρόνους, καὶ ἐκάθισαν ἐπ'
  And   I saw   thrones,   and   they sat   on

αὐτούς, καὶ κρίμα ἐδόθη αὐτοῖς, καὶ
them,   and   judgment was given   to them,   and

τὰς ψυχὰς τῶν πεπελεκισμένων διὰ τὴν
the   souls   of the   having been   because the
         [ones]   beheaded   of

μαρτυρίαν Ἰησοῦ καὶ διὰ τὸν λόγον
witness   of Jesus   and because of the   word

---

* Feminine, agreeing with λίμνη, not with the neuter πῦρ.

§ Agreeing, of course, with ῥομφαίᾳ.

God, and who had not worshiped the beast or its image and had not received its mark on their foreheads or their hands. They came to life and reigned with Christ a thousand years. ⁵The rest of the dead did not come to life until the thousand years were ended. This is the first resurrection. ⁶Blessed and holy is he who shares in the first resurrection! Over such the second death has no power, but they shall be priests of God and of Christ, and they shall reign with him a thousand years.

7 And when the thousand years are ended, Satan will be loosed from his prison ⁸and will come out to deceive the nations which are at the four corners of the earth, that is, Gog and Magog, to gather them for battle; their number is like the sand of the sea. ⁹And they marched up over the broad earth and surrounded the camp of the saints and the beloved

τοῦ	θεοῦ,	καὶ	οἵτινες	οὐ	προσεκύνησαν
–	of God,	and	who		did not worship

τὸ	θηρίον	οὐδὲ	τὴν	εἰκόνα	αὐτοῦ	καὶ
the	beast	nor	the	image	of it	and

οὐκ	ἔλαβον	τὸ	χάραγμα	ἐπὶ	τὸ	μέτωπον
did not receive		the	mark	on	the	forehead

καὶ	ἐπὶ	τὴν	χεῖρα	αὐτῶν·	καὶ	ἔζησαν
and	on	the	hand	of them;	and	they lived [again]

καὶ	ἐβασίλευσαν	μετὰ	τοῦ	Χριστοῦ	χίλια
and	reigned	with	–	Christ	a thousand

ἔτη.	5 οἱ	λοιποὶ	τῶν	νεκρῶν	οὐκ	ἔζησαν
years.	The	rest	of the	dead	did not live [again]

ἄχρι	τελεσθῇ	τὰ	χίλια	ἔτη.	Αὕτη	ἡ
until	were finished	the	thousand	years.	This [is]	the

ἀνάστασις	ἡ	πρώτη.	6 μακάριος	καὶ
¹resurrection	–	¹first.	Blessed	and

ἅγιος	ὁ	ἔχων	μέρος	ἐν	τῇ	ἀναστάσει
holy [is]	the [one]	having	part	in	the	²resurrection

τῇ	πρώτῃ·	ἐπὶ	τούτων	ὁ	δεύτερος	θάνατος
–	¹first;	over	these	the	second	death

οὐκ	ἔχει	ἐξουσίαν,	ἀλλ'	ἔσονται	ἱερεῖς
has not	authority,	but	they will be	priests

τοῦ	θεοῦ	καὶ	τοῦ	Χριστοῦ,	καὶ	βασιλεύ-
–	of God	and	–	of Christ,	and	will

σουσιν	μετ'	αὐτοῦ	[τὰ]	χίλια	ἔτη.
reign	with	him	the	thousand	years.

7 Καὶ	ὅταν	τελεσθῇ	τὰ	χίλια	ἔτη,
And	whenever	are finished	the	thousand	years,

λυθήσεται	ὁ	σατανᾶς	ἐκ	τῆς	φυλακῆς
²will be loosed	–	¹Satan	out of	the	prison

αὐτοῦ,	8 καὶ	ἐξελεύσεται	πλανῆσαι	τὰ
of him,	and	will go forth	to deceive	the

ἔθνη	τὰ	ἐν	ταῖς	τέσσαρσιν	γωνίαις	τῆς
nations	–	in	the	four	corners	of the

γῆς,	τὸν	Γὼγ	καὶ	Μαγώγ,	συναγαγεῖν
earth,	–	Gog	and	Magog,	to assemble

αὐτοὺς	εἰς	τὸν	πόλεμον,	ὧν	ὁ	ἀριθμὸς
them	to	the	war,	of whom	the	number

αὐτῶν	ὡς	ἡ	ἄμμος	τῆς	θαλάσσης.	9 καὶ
of them [is]	as	the	sand	of the	sea.	And

ἀνέβησαν	ἐπὶ	τὸ	πλάτος	τῆς	γῆς,	καὶ
they went up	over	the	breadth	of the	land,	and

ἐκύκλευσαν	τὴν	παρεμβολὴν	τῶν	ἁγίων
encircled	the	camp	of the	saints

καὶ	τὴν	πόλιν	τὴν	ἠγαπημένην·	καὶ
and	the	²city	–	having been ¹loved;	and

city; but fire came down from heaven[k] and consumed them, [10]and the devil who had deceived them was thrown into the lake of fire and brimstone where the beast and the false prophet were, and they will be tormented day and night for ever and ever.

[11] Then I saw a great white throne and him who sat upon it; from his presence earth and sky fled away, and no place was found for them. [12]And I saw the dead, great and small, standing before the throne, and books were opened. Also another book was opened, which is the book of life. And the dead were judged by what was written in the books, by what they had done. [13]And the sea gave up the dead in it, Death and Hades gave up the dead in them, and all were judged by what they had done. [14]Then Death and Hades were thrown into the lake of fire. This

κατέβη πῦρ ἐκ τοῦ οὐρανοῦ καὶ κατέφαγεν
²came ¹fire out – heaven and devoured
down of

αὐτούς· 10 καὶ ὁ διάβολος ὁ πλανῶν αὐτοὺς
them; and the Devil – deceiving them

ἐβλήθη εἰς τὴν λίμνην τοῦ πυρὸς καὶ
was cast into the lake – of fire and

θείου, ὅπου καὶ τὸ θηρίον καὶ ὁ
sulphur, where [were] also the beast and the

ψευδοπροφήτης, καὶ βασανισθήσονται ἡμέρας
false prophet, and they will be tormented day

καὶ νυκτὸς εἰς τοὺς αἰῶνας τῶν αἰώνων.
and night unto the ages of the ages.

11 Καὶ εἶδον θρόνον μέγαν λευκὸν καὶ
And I saw ²throne ¹a great ³white and

τὸν καθήμενον ἐπ' αὐτὸν οὗ ἀπὸ τοῦ
the sitting on it ⁴of ¹from ²the
[one] whom

προσώπου ἔφυγεν ἡ γῆ καὶ ὁ οὐρανός,
⁶face ⁵fled ¹the ²earth ³and ⁴the ⁵heaven,

καὶ τόπος οὐχ εὑρέθη αὐτοῖς. 12 καὶ
and a place was not found for them. And

εἶδον τοὺς νεκρούς, τοὺς μεγάλους καὶ
I saw the dead, the great and

τοὺς μικρούς, ἑστῶτας ἐνώπιον τοῦ θρόνου,
the small, standing before the throne,

καὶ βιβλία ἠνοίχθησαν· καὶ ἄλλο βιβλίον
and scrolls were opened; and another scroll

ἠνοίχθη, ὃ ἐστιν τῆς ζωῆς· καὶ ἐκρίθησαν
was which is [the – of life; and ²were judged
opened, scroll]

οἱ νεκροὶ ἐκ τῶν γεγραμμένων ἐν τοῖς
¹the ²dead by the having been in the
things written

βιβλίοις κατὰ τὰ ἔργα αὐτῶν. 13 καὶ
scrolls accord- the works of them. And
ing to

ἔδωκεν ἡ θάλασσα τοὺς νεκροὺς τοὺς
²gave ¹the ²sea the dead –

ἐν αὐτῇ, καὶ ὁ θάνατος καὶ ὁ ᾅδης
in it, and – death and – hades

ἔδωκαν τοὺς νεκροὺς τοὺς ἐν αὐτοῖς,
gave the dead – in them,

καὶ ἐκρίθησαν ἕκαστος κατὰ τὰ ἔργα
and they were judged each one according to the works

αὐτῶν. 14 καὶ ὁ θάνατος καὶ ὁ ᾅδης
of them. And – death and – hades

ἐβλήθησαν εἰς τὴν λίμνην τοῦ πυρός.
were cast into the lake – of fire.

[k] Other ancient authorities read *from God, out of heaven,* or *out of heaven from God*

is the second death, the lake of fire; [15]and if any one's name was not found written in the book of life, he was thrown into the lake of fire.

οὗτος   ὁ   θάνατος   ὁ   δεύτερός   ἐστιν,   ἡ
This   [2]the   [4]death   -   [3]second   [1]is,   the

λίμνη   τοῦ   πυρός.   15 καὶ   εἴ   τις   οὐχ
lake   -   of fire.   And   if   anyone   not

εὑρέθη   ἐν   τῇ   βίβλῳ   τῆς   ζωῆς   γεγραμ-
was found   [2]in   [3]the   [4]scroll   -   [5]of life   [1]having been

μένος,   ἐβλήθη   εἰς   τὴν   λίμνην   τοῦ   πυρός.
written,   he was cast   into   the   lake   -   of fire.

CHAPTER 21

THEN I saw a new heaven and a new earth; for the first heaven and the first earth had passed away, and the sea was no more. [2]And I saw the holy city, new Jerusalem, coming down out of heaven from God, prepared as a bride adorned for her husband; [3]and I heard a great voice from the throne saying, "Behold, the dwelling of God is with men. He will dwell with them, and they shall be his people,[l] and God himself will be with them;[m] [4]he will wipe away every tear from their eyes, and death shall be no more, neither shall there be mourning nor crying nor pain any more, for the former things have passed away."

5 And he who sat upon the throne said, "Behold, I make all things new." Also he said, "Write this, for

21 Καὶ   εἶδον   οὐρανὸν   καινὸν   καὶ   γῆν
And   I saw   [1]heaven   [2]a new   and   [3]earth

καινήν·   ὁ   γὰρ   πρῶτος   οὐρανὸς   καὶ   ἡ
[4]a new;   for the   first   heaven   and   the

πρώτη   γῆ   ἀπῆλθαν,   καὶ   ἡ   θάλασσα
first   earth   passed away,   and   the   sea

οὐκ   ἔστιν   ἔτι.   2 καὶ   τὴν   πόλιν   τὴν
is not   longer.   And   [3]the   [4]city   -

ἁγίαν   Ἰερουσαλὴμ   καινὴν   εἶδον   κατα-
[3]holy   [4]Jerusalem   [5]new   [1]I saw   coming

βαίνουσαν   ἐκ   τοῦ   οὐρανοῦ   ἀπὸ   τοῦ   θεοῦ,
down   out of   -   heaven   from   -   God,

ἡτοιμασμένην   ὡς   νύμφην   κεκοσμημένην
having been prepared   as   a bride   having been adorned

τῷ   ἀνδρὶ   αὐτῆς.   3 καὶ   ἤκουσα   φωνῆς
for the husband   of her.   And   I heard   [2]voice

μεγάλης   ἐκ   τοῦ   θρόνου   λεγούσης·   ἰδοὺ
[1]a great(loud)   out of   the   throne   saying: Behold[,]

ἡ   σκηνὴ   τοῦ   θεοῦ   μετὰ   τῶν   ἀνθρώπων,
the tabernacle   -   of God [is] with   -   men,

καὶ   σκηνώσει   μετ᾽   αὐτῶν,   καὶ   αὐτοὶ
and   he will tabernacle   with   them,   and   they

λαοὶ   αὐτοῦ   ἔσονται,   καὶ   αὐτὸς   ὁ   θεὸς
[3]peoples   [2]of him   [1]will be,   and   [2][him]self   -   [1]God

μετ᾽   αὐτῶν   ἔσται,   4 καὶ   ἐξαλείψει   πᾶν
with   them   will be,   and   will wipe off   every

δάκρυον   ἐκ   τῶν   ὀφθαλμῶν   αὐτῶν,   καὶ
tear   out of   the   eyes   of them,   and

ὁ   θάνατος   οὐκ   ἔσται   ἔτι,   οὔτε   πένθος
-    death   will not be   longer,   nor   sorrow

οὔτε   κραυγὴ   οὔτε   πόνος   οὐκ   ἔσται   ἔτι·
nor   clamour   nor   pain   will not be   longer;

ὅτι   τὰ   πρῶτα   ἀπῆλθαν.   5 καὶ   εἶπεν
because the   first things   passed away.   And   [2]said

ὁ   καθήμενος   ἐπὶ   τῷ   θρόνῳ·   ἰδοὺ   καινὰ
[1]the [one]   [3]sitting   [4]on   [5]the   [6]throne: Behold   [2]new

ποιῶ   πάντα.   καὶ   λέγει·   γράψον,   ὅτι
[1]I make   [3]all things.   And   he says: Write thou,   because

---

[l] Other ancient authorities read *peoples*

[m] Other ancient authorities add *and be*

these words are trustworthy and true." ⁶And he said to me, "It is done! I am the Alpha and the Omega, the beginning and the end. To the thirsty I will give water without price from the fountain of the water of life. ⁷He who conquers shall have this heritage, and I will be his God and he shall be my son. ⁸But as for the cowardly, the faithless, the polluted, as for murderers, fornicators, sorcerers, idolaters, and all liars, their lot shall be in the lake that burns with fire and brimstone, which is the second death."

9 Then came one of the seven angels who had the seven bowls full of the seven last plagues, and spoke to me, saying, "Come, I will show you the Bride, the wife of the Lamb." ¹⁰And in the Spirit he carried me away to a great, high mountain, and showed me the holy city Jerusalem coming down out of heaven from God, ¹¹having the glory of

οὗτοι οἱ λόγοι πιστοὶ καὶ ἀληθινοί εἰσιν.
these － words faithful and true are.

6 καὶ εἶπέν μοι· γέγοναν. ἐγὼ τὸ ἄλφα
And he said to me: It has occurred.* I [am] the alpha

καὶ τὸ ὦ, ἡ ἀρχὴ καὶ τὸ τέλος. ἐγὼ
and the omega, the beginning and the end. ¹I

τῷ διψῶντι δώσω ἐκ τῆς πηγῆς
¹to the [one] ²thirsting ⁴will give out of the fountain

τοῦ ὕδατος τῆς ζωῆς δωρεάν. 7 ὁ νικῶν
of the water － of life freely. The over-[one] coming

κληρονομήσει ταῦτα, καὶ ἔσομαι αὐτῷ
shall inherit these things, and I will be to him

θεὸς καὶ αὐτὸς ἔσται μοι υἱός. 8 τοῖς δὲ
God and he shall be to me a son. But for the

δειλοῖς καὶ ἀπίστοις καὶ ἐβδελυγμένοις
cowardly and unbelieving and having become foul

καὶ φονεῦσιν καὶ πόρνοις καὶ φαρμακοῖς
and murderers and fornicators and drugers

καὶ εἰδωλολάτραις καὶ πᾶσιν τοῖς ψευδέσιν
and idolaters and all the false [ones]

τὸ μέρος αὐτῶν ἐν τῇ λίμνῃ τῇ καιομένῃ
the part of them in the lake － burning

πυρὶ καὶ θείῳ, ὅ ἐστιν ὁ θάνατος ὁ
with fire and with which is the ²death －

δεύτερος.
¹second [, shall be].

9 Καὶ ἦλθεν εἷς ἐκ τῶν ἑπτὰ ἀγγέλων
And came one of the seven angels

τῶν ἐχόντων τὰς ἑπτὰ φιάλας, τῶν
－ having the seven bowls, －

γεμόντων τῶν ἑπτὰ πληγῶν τῶν ἐσχάτων,
being filled of(with) seven ²plagues － ¹last,
the

καὶ ἐλάλησεν μετ᾽ ἐμοῦ λέγων· δεῦρο,
and spoke with me saying: Come,

δείξω σοι τὴν νύμφην τὴν γυναῖκα
I will show thee the bride[,] the wife

τοῦ ἀρνίου. 10 καὶ ἀπήνεγκέν με ἐν
of the Lamb. And he bore away me in

πνεύματι ἐπὶ ὄρος μέγα καὶ ὑψηλόν,
spirit onto ⁴mountain ¹a great ²and ³high,

καὶ ἔδειξέν μοι τὴν πόλιν τὴν ἁγίαν
and showed me the ²city － ¹holy

Ἰερουσαλὴμ καταβαίνουσαν ἐκ τοῦ οὐρανοῦ
Jerusalem coming down out of － heaven

ἀπὸ τοῦ θεοῦ, 11 ἔχουσαν τὴν δόξαν
from － God, having the glory

* Collective neuter plural; cf. ch. 16. 17.

God, its radiance like a most rare jewel, like a jasper, clear as crystal. [12]It had a great, high wall, with twelve gates, and at the gates twelve angels, and on the gates the names of the twelve tribes of the sons of Israel were inscribed; [13]on the east three gates, on the north three gates, on the south three gates, and on the west three gates. [14]And the wall of the city had twelve foundations, and on them the twelve names of the twelve apostles of the Lamb.

15 And he who talked to me had a measuring rod of gold to measure the city and its gates and walls. [16]The city lies foursquare, its length the same as its breadth; and he measured the city with his rod, twelve thousand stadia;[n] its length and breadth and height are equal. [17]He also measured its wall, a hundred and forty-four cubits by a man's

τοῦ θεοῦ· ὁ φωστὴρ αὐτῆς ὅμοιος λίθῳ
- of God; the   light   of it [was] like to a stone

τιμιωτάτῳ, ὡς λίθῳ ἰάσπιδι κρυσταλλίζοντι·
very valuable, as ²stone ¹to a jasper being clear as crystal;

12 ἔχουσα τεῖχος μέγα καὶ ὑψηλόν,
   having ⁴wall ¹a great ²and ³high,

ἔχουσα πυλῶνας δώδεκα, καὶ ἐπὶ τοῖς
having ²gates   ¹twelve, and at the

πυλῶσιν ἀγγέλους δώδεκα, καὶ ὀνόματα
gates   ²angels   ¹twelve, and names

ἐπιγεγραμμένα, ἃ ἐστιν τῶν δώδεκα
having been inscribed, which is(are) of the twelve

φυλῶν υἱῶν Ἰσραήλ. 13 ἀπὸ ἀνατολῆς
tribes of sons of Israel.   From   east

πυλῶνες τρεῖς, καὶ ἀπὸ βορρᾶ πυλῶνες
²gates   ¹three, and from north ²gates

τρεῖς, καὶ ἀπὸ νότου πυλῶνες τρεῖς,
¹three, and from south ²gates   ¹three,

καὶ ἀπὸ δυσμῶν πυλῶνες τρεῖς. 14 καὶ
and from west ²gates   ¹three.   And

τὸ τεῖχος τῆς πόλεως ἔχων θεμελίους
the wall of the city having ²foundations

δώδεκα, καὶ ἐπ᾽ αὐτῶν δώδεκα ὀνόματα
¹twelve, and on them twelve names

τῶν δώδεκα ἀποστόλων τοῦ ἀρνίου. 15 Καὶ
of the twelve apostles of the Lamb.   And

ὁ λαλῶν μετ᾽ ἐμοῦ εἶχεν μέτρον κάλαμον
the speak- with me had ²measure ²reed
[one] ing

χρυσοῦν, ἵνα μετρήσῃ τὴν πόλιν καὶ
¹a golden, in order he might the city and
         that   measure

τοὺς πυλῶνας αὐτῆς καὶ τὸ τεῖχος αὐτῆς.
the gates of it and the wall of it.

16 καὶ ἡ πόλις τετράγωνος κεῖται, καὶ
   And the city ²square   ¹lies, and

τὸ μῆκος αὐτῆς ὅσον τὸ πλάτος. καὶ
the length of it [is] as much as the breadth. And

ἐμέτρησεν τὴν πόλιν τῷ καλάμῳ ἐπὶ
he measured the city with the reed at

σταδίων δώδεκα χιλιάδων· τὸ μῆκος καὶ
²furlongs ¹twelve ²thousands; the length and

τὸ πλάτος καὶ τὸ ὕψος αὐτῆς ἴσα ἐστίν.
the breadth and the height of it ²equal ¹is(are).

17 καὶ ἐμέτρησεν τὸ τεῖχος αὐτῆς ἑκατὸν
   And he measured the wall of it of a hundred

τεσσεράκοντα τεσσάρων πηχῶν, μέτρον
[and]   forty-four   cubits, a measure

[n] About fifteen hundred miles

measure, that is, an angel's. ¹⁸The wall was built of jasper, while the city was pure gold, clear as glass. ¹⁹The foundations of the wall of the city were adorned with every jewel; the first was jasper, the second sapphire, the third agate, the fourth emerald, ²⁰the fifth onyx, the sixth carnelian, the seventh chrysolite, the eighth beryl, the ninth topaz, the tenth chrysoprase, the eleventh jacinth, the twelfth amethyst. ²¹And the twelve gates were twelve pearls, each of the gates made of a single pearl, and the street of the city was pure gold, transparent as glass. 22 And I saw no temple in the city, for its temple is the Lord God the Almighty and the Lamb. ²³And the city has no need of sun or moon to shine upon it, for the glory of God is its light, and its lamp is the Lamb. ²⁴By its light shall

ἀνθρώπου, ὅ ἐστιν ἀγγέλου. 18 καὶ
of a man, which is of an angel. And

ἡ ἐνδώμησις τοῦ τείχους αὐτῆς ἴασπις,
the coping of the wall of it [was] jasper,

καὶ ἡ πόλις χρυσίον καθαρὸν ὅμοιον
and the city [was] ²gold ¹clean(pure) like

ὑάλῳ καθαρῷ. 19 οἱ θεμέλιοι τοῦ τείχους
²glass ¹to clean(pure). The foundations of the wall

τῆς πόλεως παντὶ λίθῳ τιμίῳ κεκοσμημένοι·
of the city ²with ⁴stone ³precious ¹having been adorned;
 every

ὁ θεμέλιος ὁ πρῶτος ἴασπις, ὁ δεύτερος
the foundation - first jasper, the second

σάπφιρος, ὁ τρίτος χαλκηδών, ὁ τέταρτος
sapphire, the third chalcedony, the fourth

σμάραγδος, 20 ὁ πέμπτος σαρδόνυξ, ὁ
emerald, the fifth sardonyx, the

ἕκτος σάρδιον, ὁ ἕβδομος χρυσόλιθος,
sixth sardius, the seventh chrysolite,

ὁ ὄγδοος βήρυλλος, ὁ ἔνατος τοπάζιον,
the eighth beryl, the ninth topaz,

ὁ δέκατος χρυσόπρασος, ὁ ἑνδέκατος
the tenth chrysoprasus, the eleventh

ὑάκινθος, ὁ δωδέκατος ἀμέθυστος. 21 καὶ
hyacinth, the twelfth amethyst. And

οἱ δώδεκα πυλῶνες δώδεκα μαργαρῖται·
the twelve gates [were] twelve pearls;

ἀνὰ εἷς ἕκαστος τῶν πυλώνων ἦν ἐξ
respec- ²one ¹each of the gates was of
tively†

ἑνὸς μαργαρίτου. καὶ ἡ πλατεία τῆς
one pearl. And the street of the

πόλεως χρυσίον καθαρὸν ὡς ὕαλος διαυγής.
city [was] ²gold ¹clean(pure) as ²glass ¹transparent.

22 Καὶ ναὸν οὐκ εἶδον ἐν αὐτῇ· ὁ γὰρ
And a shrine I saw not in it; for the

κύριος ὁ θεὸς ὁ παντοκράτωρ ναὸς αὐτῆς
Lord - God the Almighty shrine of it

ἐστιν, καὶ τὸ ἀρνίον. 23 καὶ ἡ πόλις
is, and the Lamb. And the city

οὐ χρείαν ἔχει τοῦ ἡλίου οὐδὲ τῆς
not need has of the sun nor of the

σελήνης, ἵνα φαίνωσιν αὐτῇ· ἡ γὰρ
moon, in order they might in it; for the
  that shine

δόξα τοῦ θεοῦ ἐφώτισεν αὐτήν, καὶ
glory - of God enlightened it, and

ὁ λύχνος αὐτῆς τὸ ἀρνίον. 24 καὶ
the lamp of it [is] the Lamb. And

the nations walk; and
the kings of the earth
shall bring their glory
into it, ²⁵and its gates
shall never be shut by
day—and there shall be
no night there; ²⁶they
shall bring into it the
glory and the honor of
the nations. ²⁷But noth-
ing unclean shall enter
it, nor any one who
practices abomination or
falsehood, but only those
who are written in the
Lamb's book of life.

περιπατήσουσιν τὰ ἔθνη διὰ τοῦ φωτὸς
²shall walk about ¹the ²nations through the light

αὐτῆς, καὶ οἱ βασιλεῖς τῆς γῆς φέρουσιν
of it, and the kings of the earth bring

τὴν δόξαν αὐτῶν εἰς αὐτήν· 25 καὶ οἱ
the glory of them into it; and the

πυλῶνες αὐτῆς οὐ μὴ κλεισθῶσιν ἡμέρας,
gates of it by no means may be shut by day,

νὺξ γὰρ οὐκ ἔσται ἐκεῖ· 26 καὶ οἴσουσιν
for night shall not be there; and they will
bring

τὴν δόξαν καὶ τὴν τιμὴν τῶν ἐθνῶν
the glory and the honour of the nations

εἰς αὐτήν. 27 καὶ οὐ μὴ εἰσέλθῃ εἰς
into it. And by no means may enter into

αὐτὴν πᾶν κοινὸν καὶ [ὁ] ποιῶν
it every(any) profane thing and the [one] making

βδέλυγμα καὶ ψεῦδος, εἰ μὴ οἱ γεγραμ-
an and a lie, except the having been
abomination [ones]

μένοι ἐν τῷ βιβλίῳ τῆς ζωῆς τοῦ ἀρνίου.
written in the scroll – of life of the Lamb.

CHAPTER 22

THEN he showed me
the river of the
water of life, bright as
crystal, flowing from the
throne of God and of the
Lamb ²through the
middle of‧ the street of
the city; also, on either
side of the river, the tree
of life° with its twelve
kinds of fruit, yielding
its fruit each month; and
the leaves of the tree
were for the healing of
the nations. ³There shall
no more be anything
accursed, but the throne
of God and of the Lamb
shall be in it, and his
servants shall worship

22 Καὶ ἔδειξέν μοι ποταμὸν ὕδατος
And he showed me a river of water

ζωῆς λαμπρὸν ὡς κρύσταλλον, ἐκπορευόμε-
of life bright as crystal, proceed-

νον ἐκ τοῦ θρόνου τοῦ θεοῦ καὶ τοῦ
ing out of the throne – of God and of the

ἀρνίου. 2 ἐν μέσῳ τῆς πλατείας αὐτῆς
Lamb. In [the] midst of the street of it

καὶ τοῦ ποταμοῦ ἐντεῦθεν καὶ ἐκεῖθεν
and of the river hence and thence

ξύλον ζωῆς ποιοῦν καρποὺς δώδεκα,
a tree of life producing fruits twelve,

κατὰ μῆνα ἕκαστον ἀποδιδοῦν τὸν καρπὸν
accord- ²month ¹each rendering the fruit
ing to

αὐτοῦ, καὶ τὰ φύλλα τοῦ ξύλου εἰς
of it, and the leaves of the tree [will be] for

θεραπείαν τῶν ἐθνῶν. 3 καὶ πᾶν κατάθεμα
healing of the nations. And every curse
=no curse will be any

οὐκ ἔσται ἔτι. καὶ ὁ θρόνος τοῦ θεοῦ
will not be longer. And the throne – of God
longer.

καὶ τοῦ ἀρνίου ἐν αὐτῇ ἔσται, καὶ οἱ
and of the Lamb ²in ³it ¹will be, and the

δοῦλοι αὐτοῦ λατρεύσουσιν αὐτῷ, 4 καὶ
slaves of him will do service to him, and

° Or the Lamb. In the midst of
the street of the city, and on
either side of the river, was the
tree of life, etc.

him; ⁴they shall see his face, and his name shall be on their foreheads. ⁵And night shall be no more; they need no light of lamp or sun, for the Lord God will be their light, and they shall reign for ever and ever.

6 And he said to me, "These words are trustworthy and true. And the Lord, the God of the spirits of the prophets, has sent his angel to show his servants what must soon take place. ⁷And behold, I am coming soon." Blessed is he who keeps the words of the prophecy of this book.

8 I John am he who heard and saw these things. And when I heard and saw them, I fell down to worship at the feet of the angel who showed them to me; ⁹but he said to me, "You must not do that! I am a fellow servant with you and your brethren the prophets, and with those who keep the words of this book. Worship God."

10 And he said to me, "Do not seal up the words of the prophecy

ὄψονται   τὸ   πρόσωπον   αὐτοῦ,   καὶ   τὸ
they will see   the   face   of him,   and   the

ὄνομα   αὐτοῦ   ἐπὶ   τῶν   μετώπων   αὐτῶν.
name   of him [will be] on   the   foreheads   of them.

5 καὶ   νὺξ   οὐκ   ἔσται   ἔτι,   καὶ   οὐκ
And   night   will not be   longer,   and   not

ἔχουσιν   χρείαν   φωτὸς   λύχνου   καὶ   φωτὸς
they have   need   of light   of lamp   and   of light

ἡλίου,   ὅτι   κύριος   ὁ   θεὸς   φωτίσει   ἐπ᾽
of sun,   because [the] Lord   –   God   will shed light   on

αὐτούς,   καὶ   βασιλεύσουσιν   εἰς   τοὺς
them,   and   they will reign   unto   the

αἰῶνας   τῶν   αἰώνων.
ages   of the   ages.

6 Καὶ   εἶπέν   μοι·   οὗτοι   οἱ   λόγοι   πιστοὶ
And   he said   to me: These   –   words [are]   faithful

καὶ   ἀληθινοί,   καὶ   ὁ   κύριος   ὁ   θεὸς   τῶν
and   true,   and   the   Lord   the   God   of the

πνευμάτων   τῶν   προφητῶν   ἀπέστειλεν   τὸν
spirits   of the   prophets   sent   the

ἄγγελον   αὐτοῦ   δεῖξαι   τοῖς   δούλοις   αὐτοῦ
angel   of him   to show   to the   slaves   of him

ἃ   δεῖ   γενέσθαι   ἐν   τάχει.   7 καὶ   ἰδοὺ
things it be-   to occur   quickly.   And   behold
which hoves

ἔρχομαι   ταχύ.   μακάριος   ὁ   τηρῶν   τοὺς
I am coming quickly.   Blessed [is] the [one] keeping   –   the

λόγους   τῆς   προφητείας   τοῦ   βιβλίου   τούτου.
words   of the   prophecy   of this scroll.

8 Κἀγὼ   Ἰωάννης   ὁ   ἀκούων   καὶ   βλέπων
And I   John [am] the [one] hearing   and   seeing

ταῦτα.   καὶ   ὅτε   ἤκουσα   καὶ   ἔβλεψα,
these things.   And   when   I heard   and   I saw,

ἔπεσα   προσκυνῆσαι   ἔμπροσθεν   τῶν   ποδῶν
I fell   to worship   before   the   feet

τοῦ   ἀγγέλου   τοῦ   δεικνύοντός   μοι   ταῦτα.
of the   angel   of the   showing   me these things.

9 καὶ   λέγει   μοι·   ὅρα   μή·   σύνδουλός
And   he tells   me: See thou [do] not;   ²a fellow-slave

σού   εἰμι   καὶ   τῶν   ἀδελφῶν   σου   τῶν
²of thee   ¹I am   and   of the   brothers   of thee   the

προφητῶν   καὶ   τῶν   τηρούντων   τοὺς   λόγους
prophets   and of the [ones] keeping   the   words

τοῦ   βιβλίου   τούτου·   τῷ   θεῷ   προσκύνησον.
of this scroll: –   ²God   ¹worship thou.

10 Καὶ   λέγει   μοι·   μὴ   σφραγίσῃς   τοὺς
And   he tells   me: Seal not   the

λόγους   τῆς   προφητείας   τοῦ   βιβλίου   τούτου·
words   of the   prophecy   of this scroll;

of this book, for the time is near. [11]Let the evildoer still do evil, and the filthy still be filthy, and the righteous still do right, and the holy still be holy."

[12] "Behold, I am coming soon, bringing my recompense, to repay every one for what he has done. [13]I am the Alpha and the Omega, the first and the last, the beginning and the end."

[14] Blessed are those who wash their robes,[p] that they may have the right to the tree of life and that they may enter the city by the gates. [15]Outside are the dogs and sorcerers and fornicators and murderers and idolaters, and every one who loves and practices falsehood.

[16] "I Jesus have sent my angel to you with this testimony for the churches. I am the root and the offspring of David, the bright morning star."

[17] The Spirit and the Bride say, "Come." And

[p] Other ancient authorities read *do his commandments*

ὁ καιρὸς γὰρ ἐγγύς ἐστιν
ⁱthe ²time ¹for ⁴near

11 ὁ ἀδικῶν
⁴is. The acting
[one] unjustly

ἀδικησάτω ἔτι, καὶ ὁ ῥυπαρὸς ῥυπανθήτω
let him act still, and the filthy [one] let him act
unjustly filthily

ἔτι, καὶ ὁ δίκαιος δικαιοσύνην ποιησάτω
still, and the righteous [one] ²righteousness ¹let him do

ἔτι, καὶ ὁ ἅγιος ἁγιασθήτω ἔτι.
still, and the holy [one] let him be hallowed still.

12 Ἰδοὺ ἔρχομαι ταχύ, καὶ ὁ μισθός
Behold I am coming quickly, and the reward

μου μετ᾽ ἐμοῦ, ἀποδοῦναι ἑκάστῳ ὡς
of me [is] with me, to render to each man as

τὸ ἔργον ἐστὶν αὐτοῦ. **13** ἐγὼ τὸ ἄλφα
the work ²is ¹of him. I [am] the alpha

καὶ τὸ ὦ, ὁ πρῶτος καὶ ὁ ἔσχατος,
and the omega, the first and the last,

ἡ ἀρχὴ καὶ τὸ τέλος. **14** μακάριοι οἱ
the begin- and the end. Blessed the
ning [are] [ones]

πλύνοντες τὰς στολὰς αὐτῶν, ἵνα ἔσται
washing the robes of them, in or- ⁴will be
der that

ἡ ἐξουσία αὐτῶν ἐπὶ τὸ ξύλον τῆς
¹the ²authority ³of them over the tree -

ζωῆς καὶ τοῖς πυλῶσιν εἰσέλθωσιν εἰς
of life and ³by the ²gates ¹they may enter into

τὴν πόλιν. **15** ἔξω οἱ κύνες καὶ οἱ φαρμακοὶ
the city. Outside the dogs and the sorcerers
[are]

καὶ οἱ πόρνοι καὶ οἱ φονεῖς καὶ οἱ
and the fornicators and the murderers and the

εἰδωλολάτραι καὶ πᾶς φιλῶν καὶ ποιῶν
idolaters and everyone loving and making

ψεῦδος.
a lie.

16 Ἐγὼ Ἰησοῦς ἔπεμψα τὸν ἄγγελόν
I Jesus sent the angel

μου μαρτυρῆσαι ὑμῖν ταῦτα ἐπὶ ταῖς
of me to witness to you these things over(in) the

ἐκκλησίαις. ἐγὼ εἰμι ἡ ῥίζα καὶ τὸ
churches. I am the root and the

γένος Δαυίδ, ὁ ἀστὴρ ὁ λαμπρὸς ὁ
offspring of David, the ²star - ¹bright -

πρωϊνός.
²morning.

17 Καὶ τὸ πνεῦμα καὶ ἡ νύμφη λέγουσιν·
And the Spirit and the bride say:

let him who hears say' "Come." And let him who is thirsty come, let him who desires take the water of life without price.

18 1 warn every one who hears the words of the prophecy of this book: if any one adds to them, God will add to him the plagues described in this book, 19 and if any one takes away from the words of the book of this prophecy, God will take away his share in the tree of life and in the holy city, which are described in this book.

20 He who testifies to these things says, "Surely I am coming soon." Amen. Come, Lord Jesus!

21 The grace of the Lord Jesus be with all the saints.[q] Amen.

ἔρχου.   καὶ   ὁ   ἀκούων   εἰπάτω·   ἔρχου.
Come.   And the [one] hearing   let him say: Come.

καὶ   ὁ   διψῶν   ἐρχέσθω,   ὁ   θέλων   λαβέτω
And   the thirsting   let him   the   wishing   let him
      [one]   come,   [one]   take

ὕδωρ   ζωῆς   δωρεάν.
[the]   of life   freely.
water

18 Μαρτυρῶ   ἐγὼ   παντὶ   τῷ   ἀκούοντι
   ²witness   ¹I   to everyone   hearing

τοὺς   λόγους   τῆς   προφητείας   τοῦ   βιβλίου
the   words   of the   prophecy   –   ²scroll

τούτου· ἐάν   τις   ἐπιθῇ   ἐπ'   αὐτά,   ἐπιθήσει
¹of this: If   anyone adds   upon(to) them,* ²will add

ὁ   θεὸς   ἐπ'   αὐτὸν   τὰς   πληγὰς   τὰς
–   ¹God   upon   him   the   plagues   –

γεγραμμένας   ἐν   τῷ   βιβλίῳ   τούτῳ· 19 καὶ
having been written in   this scroll;   and

ἐάν   τις   ἀφέλῃ   ἀπὸ   τῶν   λόγων   τοῦ
if   anyone takes away from   the   words   of the

βιβλίου   τῆς   προφητείας   ταύτης,   ἀφελεῖ
scroll   of this prophecy,   ²will take
                                        away

ὁ   θεὸς   τὸ   μέρος   αὐτοῦ   ἀπὸ   τοῦ   ξύλου
–   ¹God   the   part   of him   from   the   tree

τῆς   ζωῆς   καὶ   ἐκ   τῆς   πόλεως   τῆς   ἁγίας,
–   of life and out of the   ²city   –   ¹holy,

τῶν   γεγραμμένων   ἐν   τῷ   βιβλίῳ   τούτῳ.
of the   having been   in   this scroll.
things   written

20 Λέγει   ὁ   μαρτυρῶν   ταῦτα· ναί,   ἔρχομαι
   Says   the   witnessing   these   Yes,   I am
          [one]   things: coming

ταχύ.   'Αμήν,   ἔρχου   κύριε   'Ιησοῦ.
quickly.   Amen,   come[,]   Lord   Jesus.

21 'Η   χάρις   τοῦ   κυρίου   'Ιησοῦ   μετὰ
   The   grace   of the   Lord   Jesus [be] with

πάντων.
all.

* Neuter plural; see last clause of ver. 19.